PETERSON'S GUIDE TO
MBA
PROGRAMS

PETERSON'S GUIDE TO

MBA

PROGRAMS

*A Comprehensive Directory
of Graduate Business Education
U.S., Canadian, and Select
International Business Schools*

Peterson's
Princeton, New Jersey

Visit Peterson's Education Center on the Internet (World Wide Web) at
http://www.petersons.com

Editorial inquiries concerning this book should be addressed to the editor at: Peterson's
Guides, P.O. Box 2123, Princeton, New Jersey 08543-2123.

ISSN 1080-2533
ISBN 1-56079-366-X

Printed in the United States of America

10   9   8   7   6   5   4   3   2   1

Contents

How to Use This Book

---

*P*eterson's *Guide to MBA Programs* provides detailed information on over 700 schools offering over 1,200 programs of study leading to a Master of Business Administration (M.B.A.) degree or an equivalent graduate-level degree. These programs are offered by accredited colleges and universities in the United States and its territories and by institutions in Canada, Europe, Mexico, Asia, and Africa that offer equivalent or comparable programs of study. Some U.S. programs included in the guide are also accredited by the American Assembly of Collegiate Schools of Business (AACSB). Programs accredited by the AACSB are indicated by a dot in the quick reference chart that precedes the Program Profiles section.

Data Collection Procedures

Information contained in the Program Profiles, At-A-Glance Chart, and Index sections of the guide was collected between fall 1994 and spring 1995 through Peterson's Survey of MBA Programs. Questionnaires were sent to more than 700 U.S. and international institutions offering M.B.A. and equivalent programs. Information was requested from M.B.A. program department contacts, admissions officers, or other appropriate personnel within these institutions in order to ensure its accuracy and currency. In some cases, this information was also supplemented with data available from school catalogs and brochures in order to provide as much detail as possible on a particular school's M.B.A. offerings.

The omission of any particular item from a profile, chart, or index entry indicates that the item was either not applicable, not available at the time of publication, or not provided by the institution. Users of this guide should check with specific colleges and universities at the time of application to verify figures such as tuition and fees that may have changed since the publication of this guide.

MBA Programs At-A-Glance

This quick reference chart provides an overview of the programs offered at all the colleges and universities included in this guide. Entries in the chart are arranged geographically under the state, territory, province, or country in which they are located. Use this section to compare key facts about schools and the programs they offer as you begin your search for the right M.B.A. program. For additional details on particular programs, refer to the Program Profiles section and the Full Descriptions that many schools have chosen to provide.

Entries in the chart include the following information:

Name of institution

Page reference to Program Profile

Degree options offered

Areas of concentration or specialization

AACSB accreditation

Matriculation calendar (fall, winter, spring, summer, deferred)

Admission requirements (minimum GMAT score, minimum GPA, minimum TOEFL)

Full-time tuition

Part-time tuition

Financial aid availability

Minimum months to obtain degree

Credit hours required

Time offered (day, evening, weekend, summer)

Program Profiles

Overview

This section provides general information about the college or university and its M.B.A. offerings, including institutional control (i.e., public vs. private, religious affiliation, etc.), joint program offerings with other colleges and universities, the year the institution was founded, campus setting, total enrollment, the year in which the institution's M.B.A. program was first offered, and whether the institution is accredited by the American Assembly of Collegiate Schools of Business (AACSB).

Institutions may also be described as one or more of the following:

Coed: coeducational, enrolling both men and women

Comprehensive: awards baccalaureate degrees, and offers graduate degree programs primarily at the master's, specialist, or professional level, although some doctoral programs may be offered

Independent: nonprofit

Independent-religious: sponsored by or affiliated with a certain religious group or having a nondenominational or interdenominational religious orientation

Proprietary: profit making

Province-supported: for Canadian institutions

Specialized: offers degrees in one field only

State-supported: supported by state funding

State and locally supported: supported by state and local funding

University: offers four years of undergraduate work plus graduate degrees through the doctorate in more than two academic or professional fields

Program Highlights

This portion of each profile features the following key information for quick reference and comparison: Cost (on a 5-point scale with $ denoting least expensive and $$$$$ denoting most expensive); minimum tuition and fees for full-time study, for both resident and nonresident students; room and board; entrance difficulty (on a 5-point scale with * denoting noncompetitive and ***** denoting most difficult);[1] average GMAT score of entering students; average GPA of entering students; M.B.A. enrollment figures for the most recent academic year, including average age of M.B.A. students upon entrance, percentage of M.B.A. enrollees with work experience, and percentage of women, international, and minority students enrolled; and average class size for M.B.A. courses.

Academics

This section provides information pertaining to the "core" or basic M.B.A. program offered by the institution and business school described. This basic program typically includes courses of study that are required of all M.B.A. students, regardless of the area of specialization or concentration that is chosen. Information on other graduate management and master's-level degrees such as a Master of Science in Management that are considered comparable or equivalent to an M.B.A. is also provided here.

Keep in mind that basic programs at different schools may vary considerably in academic focus, philosophy, and degree requirements although each is offering an M.B.A. degree or equivalent graduate-level program. Always contact schools directly for details on their programs, curricula, and individual approaches.

Details in this section include minimum and maximum length of the program in months or years; academic calendar (semesters, trimesters, quarters, etc.); number of credits required, including elective credits, required courses; curricular focus (approach of course work, such as teamwork, entrepreneurship, international business, etc.); areas of concentration or specialization offered (accounting/finance, economics, marketing, operations, etc.); number of full-time and part-time faculty, and the number holding doctoral-level degrees; teaching methodology (lecture, team projects, case studies, etc.); language(s) in which courses are taught (for non–U.S. schools); and special opportunities, such as international exchange or internship programs.

Student Statistics

Statistics pertaining to students enrolled in the M.B.A. program during the most recent academic year are provided here. Based on the total number of students enrolled, the percentage of students from different U.S. regions is reported along with the total percentage of students from countries other than the U.S. For European schools and schools located in countries other than the U.S. and Canada, student statistics are reported by country of origin when this information was provided.

In addition, approximate percentage breakdowns for undergraduate fields of study are reported (engineering, business, social sciences, etc.) when schools provided this information.

Facilities

This section contains details on computer and communications equipment, library and information resources, other technical facilities available for use by M.B.A. students, and housing available on campus. Details include name of the library that houses the school's business reference resources, total number of bound volumes in the school's business collection, number of periodical subscriptions, number of reference sources available on CD-ROM, number of resources available on videocassette, other business-related bibliographic and reference resources, and available on-line services, including Internet access and gateways and services such as CompuServe, Dialog, LEXIS/NEXIS, news and information services offered by Dow Jones, and others.[2]

When reported by schools, details are also included on the following: whether M.B.A. students must have their own personal computer and, if so, what type; how many computer terminals are provided on campus for use by M.B.A. students and where they are located; whether facilities are available for videoconferencing, telecommunications, and multimedia presentations; type of campuswide network in use (if applicable); whether campuswide e-mail is available; how frequently computers are used in M.B.A. course work; business software utilized in course work; and the dollar amount budgeted per M.B.A. student for academic computer support.

Admission

The percentage of M.B.A. applicants accepted, specific entrance requirements, specific application requirements, application deadlines and fees, and acceptance of transfer credit are described here.

Application requirements may include letters of recommendation, a written essay, an interview, copies of transcripts for previous college study, a resume/curriculum vitae, a

---

[1] Most Difficult (*****): average GMAT score over 600, minimum GPA 3.0, about 30% or fewer of all applicants accepted
  Very Difficult (****): average GMAT score over 550, minimum GPA 3.0, about 60% or fewer of all applicants accepted
  Moderately Difficult (***): average GMAT score over 500, minimum GPA 2.75, about 85% or fewer of all applicants accepted
  Minimally Difficult (**): average GMAT score over 475, minimum GPA 2.5, up to 90% of all applicants accepted
  Noncompetitive (*): most applicants accepted regardless of GMAT score or GPA.

[2] CompuServe is a service of CompuServe, Inc.; Dialog is a service of Dialog/Knight-Ridder, Inc.; LEXIS/NEXIS is a service of LEXIS/NEXIS.

personal statement, computer experience, or other specific requirements. Application deadlines for spring, fall, or other admission are provided by most schools. Some may process applications on a continuous or rolling basis or offer a deferred entrance plan. Electronic application procedures are indicated by some schools currently offering students the option of submitting applications on computer disk.

Entrance requirements may include a specific bachelor's degree, submission of GMAT (Graduate Management Admission Test) scores, minimum GPA (grade point average), minimum acceptable TOEFL (Test of English as a Foreign Language) score, minimum acceptable IELT (International English Language Test) score, proof of adequate funds, proof of health immunizations (for non–U.S. applicants), and previous work experience.

Financials

Information on tuition, fees, room and board, and financial aid is provided in this section. Tuition expenses may be indicated separately for full-time, part-time day, part-time evening, summer, and weekend sessions. Tuition and fees are expressed as dollar amounts or ranges per course, credit hour, hour, quarter hour, semester hour, unit, quarter, semester, trimester, term, academic year, and degree program as specified by the institution. Fees include only charges that apply to all students—not charges for optional services or specific courses. Figures for tuition and fees are designated as official 1994–95, estimated 1995–96, or official 1995–96. For public institutions where tuition differs according to residence, separate figures are given for area or state residents and for nonresidents. Some non–U.S. institutions have chosen to report figures in currencies other than U.S. dollars. In these instances, readers should refer to current exchange rates in determining equivalents in U.S. dollars.

Average room and board expenses are indicated in either U.S. dollars or non–U.S. currencies. Both on-campus and off-campus costs may be indicated, depending upon the types of housing provided and whether institutions provided this data.

Financial aid information includes the percentage of M.B.A. students who received college-administered financial aid in 1994–95; what types of aid were granted (grants, scholarships, work-study, loans, etc.); the dollar amount or dollar range of aid awards to M.B.A. students for the 1994–95 academic year; whether aid is awarded to part-time students; deadlines for submission of financial aid applications (fall, spring, or continuous); and contact information, including name, address, phone, fax, and e-mail address.

International Students

An international student is defined, in this guide, as a person who is not a citizen of the country in which a particular college, university, or other institution is located but is in that country on a visa or temporary basis and does not have the right to remain indefinitely.

This section provides information regarding entrance and application requirements for international students, international student enrollment, country of origin, special services or facilities available to international students, international graduate student housing, deadlines for submission of international student applications (fall, spring, continuous), application fees for international students, and financial aid available to international students.

Entrance requirements for international students may include a specific bachelor's degree, submission of GMAT (Graduate Management Admission Test) scores, minimum GPA (grade point average), minimum acceptable TOEFL (Test of English as a Foreign Language) score, minimum acceptable IELT (International English Language Test) score, proof of adequate funds, proof of health immunizations (for non–U.S. applicants), and previous work experience.

Application requirements for international students may include letters of recommendation, written essay, an interview, copies of transcripts for previous college study, a resume/ curriculum vitae, a personal statement, computer experience, or other specific requirements. International student application deadlines for spring, fall, or other admission may be provided. Some may process applications on a continuous or rolling basis or offer a deferred entrance plan. Electronic application procedures are indicated by some schools currently offering students the option of submitting applications on computer disk.

Where applicable, the name, address, phone, fax, and e-mail address for the on-campus adviser or other person responsible for working with international students or exchange students is provided.

Alternate MBA Programs

Program options such as joint degrees (M.B.A./J.D., M.B.A./M.A., etc.), executive M.B.A.'s, accelerated programs, and other special options are described in this section. Refer to "Abbreviations Used in This Guide" for a complete list of degree combinations referred to in this guide.

Executive M.B.A.: These programs are designed primarily for the mature, experienced business professional. Evening and/or weekend course work is usually required and program length may be shorter than some basic M.B.A. programs.

M.B.A./J.D. (M.B.A./Juris Doctor): Combines an M.B.A. program with a law degree; programs normally take three to four years to complete on a full-time basis.

M.B.A./M.S.N. (M.B.A./Master of Science in Nursing): Combines an M.B.A. with an M.S. in Nursing degree.

M.B.A./M.A. (M.B.A./Master of Arts): Combines an M.B.A. with a master's degree in one or more specific areas of concentration.

One-Year M.B.A.: Designed for both recent undergraduates and experienced professionals, these new programs require twelve months or less of full-time study. Basic course work is compressed into a shorter time period and is usually very intensive.

Details in this section may include minimum and maximum length of the program in months or years; academic calendar (semesters, trimesters, quarters, etc.); number of credits required, including elective credits, required courses; other special requirements related to completing the program;

average class size; language(s) in which courses are taught (for non–U.S. schools); campus locations where classes are taught; times when classes are offered (day, evening, weekend, summer); and whether distance learning options are offered.

Placement

This section provides information on job placement services available to M.B.A. students, the number of organizations that have participated in on-campus recruiting, how many on-campus job interviews were conducted with M.B.A. students during the previous academic year who gained employment within three months of graduation, average starting salaries for recent M.B.A. graduates, starting salary range for recent M.B.A. graduates, and the percentage of recent graduates who obtained employment according to type of employer (such as manufacturing, service, nonprofit, etc.) and type of job function (such as marketing/sales, operations, etc.).

Placement services available on campus may include an alumni network, career placement, career counseling/planning, career fairs, career library, an electronic job bank, arrangement of job interviews, resume preparation, job search courses, and referral of resumes to employers.

Program Contact

The name, title, mailing address, telephone number, fax number, and e-mail address of the person who should receive applications for admission are provided at the end of the profile. Toll-free telephone numbers may also be included.

Additional Information

A special Announcement may follow the profile for some schools that have chosen to provide additional details on their M.B.A. program offerings. In addition, other schools have provided Full Descriptions that appear in the Descriptions of M.B.A. Programs section immediately following the Program Profiles. In these two-page descriptions, schools have chosen to provide even more information about their institution and M.B.A. programs.

Abbreviations Used in This Guide

AACSB	American Assembly of Collegiate Schools of Business
BA/MBA	Bachelor of Arts/Master of Business Administration
EMBA	Executive Master of Business Administration
EMIB	Executive Master of International Business
EMIM	Executive Master of International Management
EMOD	Executive Master of Organization Development
ESL	English as a Second Language
FEMBA	fully employed MBA
GMAT	Graduate Management Admission Test
GPA	Grade Point Average
IELT	International English Language Test
IMBA	International Master of Business Administration
MA	Master of Arts
MAAE	Master of Arts in Applied Economics
MAB	Master of Arts in Business
MAc	Master of Accountancy
MAcc	Master of Accountancy or Master of Accounting
MAE	Master of Arts in Applied Economics
MArch/MBA	Master of Architecture/Master of Business Administration
MAS	Master of Accounting Science, Master of Applied Science, Master of Actuarial Science, or Master of Administrative Science
MBA	Master of Business Administration
MBA/HCM	Master of Business Administration/ Health Care Management
MBA/JD	Master of Business Administration/Juris Doctor
MBA/LLB	Master of Business Administration/ Bachelor of Laws (Canadian)
MBA/MA	Master of Business Administration/ Master of Arts
MBA/MAIS	Master of Business Administration/ Master of Arts in International Studies

MBA/MArch	Master of Business Administration/ Master of Architecture
MBA/MBI	Master of Business Administration/ Master of Business Informatics
MBA/MCRP	Master of Business Administration/ Master of City and Regional Planning
MBA/MDIV or MDiv	Master of Business Administration/ Master of Divinity
MBA/ME	Master of Business Administration/ Master of Engineering
MBA/MEng	Master of Business Administration/ Master of Engineering
MBA/MH	Master of Business Administration/ Master of Humanities
MBA/MHA	Master of Business Administration/ Master of Health Administration
MBA/ MHMS	Master of Business Administration/ Master of Health Management Science
MBA/MILR	Master of Business Administration/ Master of Industrial Labor Relations
MBA/MIM	Master of Business Administration/ Master of International Management
MBA/MLS	Master of Business Administration/ Master of Library Science
MBA/MPH	Master of Business Administration/ Master of Public Health
MBA/ MRED	Master of Business Administration/ Master of Real Estate Development
MBA/MRM	Master of Business Administration/ Master of Resources Management
MBA/MRP	Master of Business Administration/ Master of Resource Planning
MBA/MSFS	Master of Business Administration/ Master of Science in Foreign Service
MBA/MSN	Master of Business Administration/ Master of Science in Nursing
MBA/MSW	Master of Business Administration/ Master of Social Work
MBA/ PharmD	Master of Business Administration/ Doctor of Pharmacy
MBA/PhD	Master of Business Administration/ Doctor of Philosophy
MBC	Master of Business Communication

MBE	Master of Business Economics or Master of Business Education
MBIS	Master of Business Information Systems
MBS	Master of Business Studies
MBT	Master of Business Taxation
MCSM	Master of Computer Systems Management
MD/MBA	Doctor of Medicine/Master of Business Administration
MHA	Master of Health Administration
MIB	Master of International Business
MIBA	Master of International Business Administration
MIBS	Master of International Business Studies
MIHM	Master of International Health Management
MIM	Master of International Management
MIS	Management Information Systems or Management Information Science
MLS	Master of Library Science
MM	Master of Management
MM/JD	Master of Management/Juris Doctor
MMA	Master of Management and Administration
MMIS	Master of Management Information Systems
MMM	Master of Management in Manufacturing
MMS	Master of Management Studies
MOB	Master of Organizational Behavior
MPA	Master of Professional Accountancy, or Master of Professional Accounting, or Master of Public Administration
MPAcc	Master of Professional Accounting
MPER	Master of Personnel and Employee Relations
MPH	Master of Public Health
MPhil	Master of Philosophy in Management Studies
MPM	Master of Public Management or Master of Project Management
MPP	Master of Public Policy
MPPHA	Master of Public and Private Health Administration
MPPM	Master of Public and Private Management
MS	Master of Science
MSA	Master of Science in Accountancy or Accounting or Master of Science in Administration

MSAc	Master of Science in Accounting
MS/Accy	Master of Science in Accountancy
MSAE	Master of Science in Applied Economics
MSB	Master of Science in Business
MSBA	Master of Science in Business Administration
MSBM	Master of Science in Business Management
MSc	Master of Science
MSC	Master of Science in Commerce
MSCIS	Master of Science in Computer Information Systems
MSF	Master of Science in Finance
MSHROD	Master of Science in Human Resource and Organizational Development
MSIA	Master of Science in Industrial Administration
MSIA/MSE	Master of Science in Industrial Administration/Master of Software Engineering
MSIM	Master of Science in Industrial Management
MSIS	Master of Science in Information Systems
MSJBS	Master of Science in Japanese Business Studies
MSM	Master of Science in Management
MS/MIS	Master of Science/Management Information Systems
MSMS	Master of Science in Management Systems
MSOB	Master of Science in Organizational Behavior
MSOD	Master of Science in Organizational Development
MSSM	Master of Science in Strategic Management
MST	Master of Science in Taxation
MSTax	Master of Science in Taxation
MT	Master of Taxation
MTA	Master of Tax Accounting
MTM	Master of Transport Management
N/R	Not reported
PC	Personal Computer
PhD	Doctor of Philosophy
TOEFL	Test of English as a Foreign Language
TQM	Total Quality Management

Why an MBA? Future Trends and Opportunities in the Twenty-first Century

by John C. Hallenborg

If you have purchased this book and are beginning the process of deciding whether and where to pursue an M.B.A. degree, you are no doubt aware of the value that an M.B.A. degree offers to both prospective students and employers. Some 100,000 students will obtain an M.B.A. degree in the U.S. in 1995, according to the National Center for Education Statistics. This is more than double the number of M.B.A. degrees granted by business schools approximately twenty years ago. Obviously, the M.B.A. still holds strong appeal to both recent college graduates and experienced professionals as a stepping-stone to a more lucrative and challenging career path. The plentiful supply of M.B.A.'s, however, has allowed employers to be quite discriminating in hiring in recent years, requiring many M.B.A.'s to arrive equipped with specialized training and hands-on experience suited to their particular business niche. In addition, business is playing a key role in shaping the evolution of many M.B.A. programs both in the U.S. and abroad, some even expressing interest in in-house M.B.A. programs. This evolution of the M.B.A. and its role in the job market will no doubt continue to change as the twentieth century comes to a close.

The multitude of new M.B.A. programs, their costs, and the demands of a competitive, global economy have made the process of selecting the right business school and the right M.B.A. graduate quite rigorous for both students and employers. Both are trying to anticipate long-term needs in preparation for the marketplace of the twenty-first century.

Closing the Loop: Business Schools and Corporations

Ambitious M.B.A. candidates in the late 1990s, looking forward to their careers or perhaps to the exciting prospect of entrepreneurship, cannot afford to presume that every M.B.A. program will meet the educational requirements specific to an industry or profession. In today's job market and that of the near future, just as no one would consider applying for a secretarial job without having both well-honed computer and administrative skills, the M.B.A. graduate, class of 2000, will be expected to deliver both technical and nontechnical skills in every business and industrial sector. As in other areas of graduate study and related employment, the focus is, and will continue to be, on specialized expertise in business management. For business,

opportunities abound to work with universities to create new M.B.A. programs that will prepare candidates to fulfill an array of specialized leadership roles. For schools, this phenomenon continues to spur revamping of curricula almost annually to keep pace with the real-world demands that will be placed upon future M.B.A. graduates.

Is it safe to presume that the recruitment managers at most major companies are aware of the changing makeup of the leading business school programs? The answer is most definitely yes, and apparent in the variety of degree options, concentrations, and alternative courses of study available to today's M.B.A. student.

How the degree can be attained today also closely mirrors current business trends—the expectation of an early return on investment, preferably within one to two years. Future M.B.A. programs will likely continue to reflect the two basic choices seen today: the one-year degree, which often dispenses with core programs in favor of specialized courses tailored to specific career paths; and the more traditional two-year and extended M.B.A. programs, which have been the basis of graduate business degrees for decades.

Certainly for the last twenty years or so, benchmark companies and top graduate schools have worked intensively to match academic programs to corporate needs. These relationships are likely to strengthen, as more corporations and prospective students, hesitant to invest in two-year courses, are more willing to commit to emerging one-year programs.

Two-Year MBA vs. One-Year MBA

By all accounts, the composition of the M.B.A. degree, and how it is acquired, will change significantly over the next five to ten years. The perceived value of the M.B.A. degree has changed considerably in the student community and within the corporations that hire M.B.A. graduates by the thousands every year. After a period of flat growth several years ago, the degree now appears dynamic and evolving. Affordable, highly focused, and time-efficient versions of the degree have replaced some multiyear courses of study.

The upsurge seen recently in one-year degrees has been driven, for the most part, by corporate demand, serving mostly experienced professionals and recent undergraduates with some work experience. Although two-year programs are still the norm in most business schools, accelerated and specialized one-year programs are seeing slight increases in enrollment. Business schools have been adversely impacted by this trend, in fact, and are offering degree options that combine an undergraduate business degree with an M.B.A. in a five-year program.

The primary difference between one-year and traditional two-year programs is that with the shorter version, there is little if any overlap with undergraduate business curricula. Thus, it is highly recommended that students who decide on a one-year program should enroll soon after receiving their undergraduate degree and be able to satisfy all core business course requirements. However, some one-year programs require from two to five years' work experience in lieu of the traditional first-year M.B.A. core study courses. In most cases, one-year elective courses are all but tailored to the applicant's career, so that the graduate can reenter the workforce as quickly as possible. Classic two-year programs most often focus on elective and specialized course work in the second year after completion of core requirements in the first year.

A number of emerging realities will highlight the one-year M.B.A. degree: technology-based information media will replace class time in many cases, as students gain access to CD-ROM and on-line services; fewer faculty may be required, as schools combine resources to teach fewer classes to more students; and distance learning from remote locations will replace some on-campus classes. For most schools and students of the future, technology will certainly dictate the learning medium.

In the relatively brief period that one-year M.B.A. graduates have been working, corporations have been neutral about recruiting one-year program versus two-year program graduates, as there is no published evidence that graduates of two-year programs outperform their one-year counterparts.

Albert W. Niemi Jr., dean of the University of Georgia's Terry College of Business, explains that "I don't see, in the data that we have collected—in terms of starting salaries—that there is any difference in the way one-year people are treated by industry. One-year grads do as well as two-year grads in terms of earning power in the marketplace."

Despite Niemi's findings, to date there has not been significant movement toward the one-year degree, as at present there are relatively few such programs compared to the total number of M.B.A. programs offered nationwide.

Traditional Course Work Vs. In-House Training

Rather than sending employees off company premises for continuing education, in the future, many companies may choose to hire competent teachers as staff members to provide in-house training. This trend is not yet fully under way, but it is seen as a cost-effective alternative to traditional M.B.A. programs. The one-year M.B.A. and in-house training represent new models for graduate education. "Our dynamic economy is forcing change on all of us, if we are to be competitive and meet new challenges," offers Wil-

Melvin Goodes, CEO, Warner-Lambert

When we hire any new M.B.A. graduate, we place a hefty bet on the table. Between recruitment, training, compensation, and 'learning curve' costs, the first-year investment in an entry-level college graduate can exceed $100,000. Add to that the reality that most graduates joining us work with multimillion-dollar customers or on complex project development.

Specifically, we want people with well-defined visions. People who can work in a global arena. People with a bias for action.

Vision. Global perspective. Resilience... Companies now recognize that only so much can be done to mold people. What does this mean [for the fresh M.B.A. graduate]? It means that [job candidates] need to define how they want to contribute to an enterprise before they approach it for a position: Understand and be able to demonstrate that you are able to drive your own career.

Understand that you will have an international career... We've even banished the word 'domestic' from our corporate lexicon. You may never receive an overseas posting, but you will have an international career.

Speed of action has emerged as one of the surest routes to competitive success. Be ready to prove your bias for action in your resume and your job interview.

Resilience [as defined within W-L] is the ability to cope with change that is coming almost absurdly quickly. One good gauge of resilience is seeing how people cope with failure. We're intrigued by people who can envision and reach for the big ideas—even at the risk of failure. And we are impressed by those with the inner will—the resilience—to shake off failure, learn from these experiences, and move on to greater successes.

liam K. Laidlaw Jr., executive vice president of the American Assembly of Collegiate Schools of Business (AACSB).

Among the upstart in-house programs on the horizon are those directed at problem solving within a limited number of companies or even a single company. These programs are tailored to very specific company issues. Typically, collaborative tutoring teams are composed of university professors and corporate upper management.

Changes in the Financial Sector

In the top tiers of the financial markets, there have been many changes following the scandals and management excesses of the 1980s. By close association with these events, the reputation of the M.B.A. degree was somewhat tainted, directly or by implication. Today's graduates are under scrutiny to improve the standing of the degree in the academic and corporate worlds. Clearly, teamwork has

Rebecca Baybrook-Heckenbach, Assistant VP, Human Resources, Knight-Ridder

We think of the M.B.A. in two different ways: 1) the schools where traditionally we have recruited M.B.A.'s are very selective in their admittance procedures, so they provide us with prescreening of candidates. They attract high caliber individuals with leadership potential. Then, once they have completed a rigorous academic program, we come along and say that we would like to see those individuals who are interested in our industry; and 2) we look at the marketing challenges faced by the newspaper industry today, and we look for individuals who understand the transition a company like ours is undergoing. We are leaving the newspaper industry and entering this growing electronically based information domain. This emerging industry is generating new challenges in electronic media. We are looking at M.B.A. holders who are strong in understanding the marketing concepts that relate to these new media.

In the past, we've relied on only two schools, but recently, given Knight-Ridder's current spread throughout the country, we now look at graduates from five schools. We need to recruit in a way that more closely mirrors the company's geography.

Knight-Ridder also considers management candidates from the pool of people who bring relevant experience in lieu of an M.B.A. This type of candidate generally has a set of experiences that may be unusual but are interesting to us. This is especially true when we are looking to fill a particular niche in the company. We value internships and volunteer work, as well.

superseded personal glory in most corporate environments, and the financial community is no exception.

There has been a considerable shakeout in the better sectors of the financial job market, and many large financial organizations are as vigilant in maintaining a positive public image as they are about profit levels. Any M.B.A. candidate seeking a spot at one of the top investment banks, for example, will have to be aware of issues of public relations in addition to more predictable questions about money markets. Expect this sensitivity to public opinion to remain high for many years. In fact, a reputation for aboveboard dealings is nearly as important as bottom-line performance in today's financial sphere.

At present, the M.B.A. degree is still key in the world of investment banking, as recruitment specialists at banks large and small report that about 90 percent of new hires have the degree.

The New MBA Attitude

How does this job market realignment affect the M.B.A. holder's chances for a lucrative career in finance? The answer is oftentimes more in the attitude of the prospect than in the present and future states of the job market. These behavioral issues resound throughout not only the financial sector but also the finance departments of major corporations. The message is: bring us good grades from a good school, but please also bring along maturity and a problem-solving attitude.

Despite the fact that compensation at the higher levels in banking is very bonus-oriented, the fresh M.B.A. graduate should avoid being a self-serving maverick. The M.B.A. of tomorrow, more than ever before, will have to display strengths in leadership, teamwork, problem solving, and dealing with people. Upper management will be looking for well-rounded individuals who offer a balanced perspective and are ready and able to apply their education in a real-life setting.

Working for Smaller Companies

And what about the option of employment by the thousands of small and mid-sized firms that populate the American business landscape? The ideal of a "secure job forever" has been replaced by the reality that most Americans will have two or three careers in their lifetimes and may even change jobs every five years or so. Small and middle-market corporations have become the most fertile ground for M.B.A. recruitment in the 1990s and will likely continue to hire more M.B.A.'s into the next century. In many instances, it is easier for a talented M.B.A. holder to make a significant contribution to a mid-sized firm in a high-growth mode. The key, of course, may be to identify likely high-growth companies that have the potential for continued growth over a three- to five-year period.

Once again, preparation for a specific industry niche, or better yet a specific company or companies, is key to landing those choice spots that feature a daunting 50:1, or 500:1, applicant/position ratio. Most competing M.B.A.'s are aware that the key to landing the desired job is to positively differentiate oneself from other equally qualified candidates. Some M.B.A. students have gone so far as to research potential employers at the beginning of their course work, studying the details of annual reports, product brochures, etc., for the duration of the typical two-year M.B.A. program.

Skills learned in M.B.A. core and specialized courses can be especially valuable in helping to transform technical ideas and concepts into tangible, marketable products. In both large and small businesses in the future, managers will certainly be expected to bring not only technical expertise to the table but also the ability to translate new ideas into profit-sustaining products and services.

The small and mid-sized firm is often the perfect venue for such creative expression coupled with pragmatic implementation. Smaller firms are already actively recruiting from the ranks of new M.B.A. degree holders to discover the talented individuals whose skills and judgment will drive future growth and product improvement.

Nick Deane, senior vice president at Faulkner & Gray, a subsidiary of the Canadian publishing giant Thompson group, feels that "the in-depth study of sophisticated financial concepts is the key attribute that sets the M.B.A. degree apart. I like to see well-placed employees armed with this advanced knowledge of finance." Deane agrees, however, that all sharp-minded candidates deserve a fair shot, as "there are experienced people who perform well without an M.B.A. degree." Faulkner & Gray, a publisher of professional journals, magazines, and reference materials, is typical of the high end of the publishing sector that is using technology to migrate from paper-based products to on-line and other electronically based formats.

M.B.A. candidates should be very selective in targeting small and mid-sized companies, however, as many smaller firms are adopting a lean corporate structure by not instituting a middle layer of management until they reach the 1,000 employee mark. For the M.B.A. holder this may mean more responsibility within a flat organizational structure and the need to "wear many hats." High-tech, high-growth, small-to mid-sized firms such as Dallas Semiconductor (Dallas, TX) with 1,000 employees, software maker Wonderware (Irvine, CA), with 220 employees, and California Micro Devices (Milpitas, CA) with 240 employees are all focused on hiring individuals with variations of the master's degree.

Richard Helfrich, a vice president at California Micro, a semiconductor maker, considers the M.B.A. to be "a strong plus in our hiring considerations. I weigh the degree as the equivalent of three years of solid work experience. But because our products are so technology-based, the master's degree is still our primary qualifier."

Tomorrow's MBA Entrepreneur

There will also be a place for the ambitious M.B.A. holder who cannot wait for others to bring his ideas to the marketplace. Given the possibility for relatively static growth in available jobs in the next ten years, for many fearless graduates, starting or buying a business may be a quicker and more lucrative route to success. Those with the best chance of making it this way will most likely combine prior technical training with the marketing and financial knowledge acquired with an M.B.A. degree, for example, the electrical engineering whiz who starts a small, niche-focused circuit design firm.

Still, the appeal of running a small business does not get as much media coverage as it should, if the Harvard M.B.A. Class of 1970 is any indication. In a recent survey of the 723 alumni who are now as a group generally in the peak phases of their careers, only 13 percent worked for Business Week 1000 companies. By contrast, 36 percent were self-employed and the majority worked in small businesses (less than 500 employees) in one capacity or another.

Opportunities for MBA's in the Year 2000

Because management and finance are functions common to every conceivable type of business or industry, it is difficult to make predictions about job growth for M.B.A.'s in particular markets. However, although it may sound simplistic, it is still true that career opportunities will most likely continue to exist for talented M.B.A.'s in nearly all areas

Kathleen Kennedy, Vice President, Recruitment, Merrill Lynch

The summer internship is important in that M.B.A. graduates can put their teamwork training to use in a real work setting. Five years ago, I do not think that business schools were stressing the team building element. Teamwork is a critical component for working at today's Merrill Lynch.

In the past three years, we have developed a relationship with nine core business schools, which provide us with about 70 percent of our yearly number of some 130 M.B.A. hires. However, through other schools and through referrals and student solicitations, we currently have in our summer internship program thirty-three schools represented by some 100 students. These nine schools admit students with proven leadership skills, who can then hone their native abilities within the M.B.A. programs.

The nine major schools we consider as our main sources of M.B.A. candidates deliver individuals with solid core skills backed by particular major interests in finance, where quantitative issues and in-depth analytical skills are developed. The exception is MIT, where we find candidates for the trading area to work in derivatives and financial modeling, for example. It is not unusual for us to hire people with strong undergraduate backgrounds in engineering and mathematics.

of the marketplace into the next century. Although manufacturing and investment firms have experienced somewhat of a downswing in top management positions in the last few years, a tremendous variety of positions still attract M.B.A.'s to accounting, commercial banking, management consulting, consumer products, health care, insurance, services, and chemical companies in functions including marketing, finance, operations, information systems, and long-term planning. Even many nonprofits are recruiting M.B.A.'s to help them redefine and reshape their organizations both economically and socially.

So, what are some of the growth areas for the M.B.A. graduates to consider? As in the 1980s and early 1990s, there appears to be no limit to the growth potential in the software and telecommunications industries, particularly in the convergence of data and voice technologies. The number of professional jobs in computer software and hardware development and marketing will also likely only increase over the next ten years, although many companies may start up and then fold or be bought out in these volatile fields.

Telecommunications giants such as AT&T, MCI, and the Regional Bell Companies are already driving much of the development in this sector and will certainly require M.B.A. graduates with a broad range of business and technical skills. M.B.A.'s with well-honed analytical and marketing skills

Jim Shunk, Manager of Corporate College Recruiting, Hewlett-Packard

Insofar as Hewlett-Packard presently interviews M.B.A. students and graduates from thirty-eight schools, I can report that almost all of these schools offer a traditional two-year program. The number of schools we look at has been cut in the last seven years by at least a factor of two, however. One-year programs have not had much impact.

We are now entering a phase of increased hiring. M.B.A.'s will comprise the bulk, by far, of new hires. We will undoubtedly hire people with other advanced degrees, but to fill most spots in marketing and finance, M.B.A.'s will be sought.

The schools we look at are predominantly near our manufacturing locations on the East and West coasts, but we plan to look more at schools in the Midwest and South. We do include a number of Big Ten schools now, which are in the Midwest.

Regarding curricula, we like to see heavy exposure to finance and marketing courses, which fits naturally into our corporate plans for the future. Familiarity with technology also plays an important role for us.

Our new M.B.A. hires represent a variety of undergraduate degrees, including liberal arts, engineering, and science. For field staff, we clearly prefer that M.B.A.'s have technical undergraduate degrees.

---

will certainly be needed as telecommunications companies continue making forays into the information and entertainment services markets.

Another area for consideration by the eager M.B.A. is publishing and information services. Innumerable products in CD-ROM, CD-I, and on-line formats are displacing paper equivalents most notably in the professional and academic domains. Books, newspapers, and other information products are certain to follow this trend toward electronic versus paper distribution. Publishing professionals armed with M.B.A. degrees will certainly supply much of the marketing, financial, and strategic expertise needed to help such companies enter these new markets.

Still another high growth area that may lure many M.B.A.'s is the world of entertainment. The creative entrepreneur seeking entree into the television, film, or music industries could be well positioned with an M.B.A., since bottom line business issues usually determine if projects are produced. Consulting opportunities for the freelance M.B.A. holder are already numerous in the entertainment industry. This should continue as a promising area of activity for the creative M.B.A.

For U.S.–based firms in other industry sectors, a significant amount of future growth may come from overseas operations. In the chemicals and polymers sector, for example, many of the management jobs will be in maintaining investments

on the Pacific Rim and Eastern Europe, where most of the largest petrochemical conglomerates have joint ventures in place. M.B.A. graduates should be willing to travel abroad to land these types of positions.

Most sources indicate that U.S. industries overall will experience moderate, 3 to 7 percent annual growth in the next ten years. Hiring of M.B.A.'s in industries such as construction and real estate, general manufacturing, foods and beverages, and electronics is predicted to be moderate by comparison.

Which sectors will be the toughest to enter, based on a flat industry growth forecast for the next ten years? Aerospace, oil and gas, health care, retail, and apparel are some of the major industries that are likely to experience fluctuating growth at best.

Recent data indicates that the rate of increase in the number of M.B.A. degrees awarded in the near future will about double overall growth in the U.S. economy, at about 8 percent versus 4 percent. Some 100,000 students will earn an M.B.A. degree in the U.S. in 1995. This is out of some 377,000 total master's degrees awarded in all disciplines, according to the National Center for Education Statistics. Thus, employers can afford to be very selective in choosing from future pools of M.B.A. holders.

Year	Master's Graduates in all Disciplines	Master's Graduates in Business & Management		
		Male	Female	Total
1990-91	337,168	50,883	27,372	78,255
1991-92*	352,838	54,705	29,937	84,542
1992-93	364,000			
1993-94	370,000			
1994-95	377,000			

*Latest year for which figures are available on number of business school graduates

Source: National Center for Education Statistics, U.S. Department of Education

Go Global

By the year 2000, with the continued advance of telecommunications as the primary medium for data transfer, banks and corporations will have permanently erased many commercial barriers between nations. This borderless, global market should be an exciting prospect for the ambitious M.B.A.

An in-depth review of international trade regulations will serve tomorrow's M.B.A. well since American firms already derive some 50 percent of gross revenues from overseas operations. Given the prodigious growth rate of economies in the developing nations, particularly in Asia and South America, virtually any M.B.A. with skills to lend to those market explosions should find much success.

There will be more exciting opportunities in the former Eastern Bloc nations as these countries struggle to establish free-market economies. But the challenges are as enormous as the potential rewards. Still, the fearless M.B.A., armed with street smarts, a good command of the host country's language, and a firm grasp of the cultural keys to market entry, will find plenty of qualified European partners ready to forge ahead.

Similarly, at home, most large companies will be importing and exporting huge quantities of commodities, consumer goods, and financial services. For Amercan M.B.A.'s seeking careers at home, the importance of global awareness cannot be overstressed. Ten years from now, there will be impressive opportunities for international licensing of technologies, trademarks, and copyrighted products and processes that most Americans take for granted. Clearly, the cosmopolitan M.B.A. will be the first to reap the rewards from emerging international markets in the twenty-first century.

John C. Hallenborg is a writer and business consultant based in New York City.

The New MBA: What to Look for in Today's Reinvented Programs

by Carter A. Prescott

Your team's assignment: Climb through different size openings in a massive rope web without touching anything—and do it faster than competing teams. Another assignment: Tell a fellow student about an experience in which you felt odd or left out. Sound like typical M.B.A. fare? If you answered yes, you pass.

Today's graduate business programs are undergoing what some experts tout as nothing less than revolutionary change. In response to new competitive demands on corporations and increasing globalization—both of which require tomorrow's business leaders to be flexible and manage workforces and internal structures that cross cultural and political lines—M.B.A. programs are diversifying and redefining themselves. You'll still graduate with a firm grounding in the staples of business education—finance, strategy, operations management, marketing, and the like—but you'll also learn how to work in teams, how to motivate others, and how to see the "big picture" when solving problems. Strong communication and interpersonal skills are just as important in today's new M.B.A. programs as technical knowledge and the ability to "crunch numbers."

"There's more churning going on right now in management education than at any time in 35 years," says Charles W. Freeman, director of projects and services at the American Assembly of Collegiate Schools of Business (AACSB), which accredits M.B.A. programs in the United States. "The emphasis today is changing from teaching to learning," Freeman notes. "The front-end-load module, where you dump two years of education into a student's head and then sew it up, is over. The world is moving too fast. Companies want M.B.A. graduates to know how to learn, because lifelong learning is the key to success for practicing managers and executives. The M.B.A. is not an end in itself. It positions the degree-holder for a variety of general management positions."

What, you may ask, can you expect to learn from the rope exercise? How to plan, pay attention to detail, and work in teams, according to the Lubin School of Business at New York's Pace University, which puts all new students through such challenging physical experiences. And the lesson behind baring your soul to a colleague? How to become sensitive to gender and ethnic diversity in order to manage it effectively.

The days when M.B.A. graduates could dazzle their bosses with only a few mentions of decision trees, regression analysis, net present value, and gap planning are gone. You'll still learn these concepts, but you'll be synthesizing them into a broader skill set. Dennis J. Weidenaar, dean of the Krannert Graduate School of Management at Purdue University, calls it the "new management environment." He says it is characterized by "teamwork and alliances, continuous changes in technologies, globalization, and networks that are in instantaneous communication with each other."

How specifically do today's M.B.A. programs prepare you to succeed in this environment? Here are 10 primary ways:

1. Cross-Functional, Interdisciplinary Curricula

You'll hear these phrases so often they'll sound like a mantra. Even the venerable Harvard Business School voted to overhaul its M.B.A. curriculum, effective in January 1996, to offer students more interdisciplinary courses and more freedom in choosing electives. Across the country, M.B.A. schools are reshaping curricula to teach students the importance of solving problems by synthesizing a variety of subjects. Faculty members from different disciplines coordinate their syllabi and teach in teams to students who work in teams. When Stanford added a new course in human resource management, for example, it was designed by professors of organizational behavior and of economics. A cross-functional approach also has proved resoundingly popular with students. After Wharton tested a dramatically revised curriculum, surveys showed that a full 94 percent of its 1993 graduates who participated in the pilot would do so again, while 60 percent of those who studied under the traditional program would have preferred the new one.

2. New Programs

Whether they are specific sequences or subjects woven into the fabric of an M.B.A. curriculum, you'll find strong mentions of entrepreneurship, ethics, Total Quality Management (TQM), information technology management, and leadership development in nearly all basic M.B.A. programs. Purdue's PL+S Program (Preparing Leaders and Stewards) provides additional course work, community service opportunities, self-assessment, and self-directed team consulting projects with companies, all as avenues for developing leadership skills. Harvard's new "foundations" program will place heavy emphasis on career planning, self-assessment, working in groups, and business ethics. Ethical challenges are constantly reinforced in the Pepperdine University curriculum, says Stanley K. Mann, professor of law. "We are training managers to take on responsibilities and obligations, not to put the dollar ahead of everything else."

A new emphasis on entrepreneurship reflects the reality that "the majority of M.B.A. graduates will not work in Fortune 500 companies, because they have been downsizing the most," notes Charles Freeman of the AACSB. Accordingly, many universities—notably Indiana, the University of California at Berkeley, and Vanderbilt—help students develop better job-hunting and career development skills.

3. Global Perspectives

Because U.S. corporations increasingly compete around the world, globalization is serious business in the nation's M.B.A. programs. Stanford offers four times as many internationally focused electives as it did ten years ago. Even though Pace University has featured an international business major for twenty years, "we now view it as a jumping-off point to integrate international issues throughout the curriculum," says Dean Arthur L. Centonze. Pepperdine University in Malibu, California, designed a specific Master of International Business program that Stanley Mann, its director, describes as "very much a 'throw 'em to the wolves' approach." The six-year-old program features eight months of study and internships in France or Germany. Students are required to find their own internships and to be proficient in French or German. Although 6 percent routinely drop out, another third stay abroad for at least a year, postponing their graduation to gain valuable work experience.

4. Increased Student and Faculty Diversity

Business schools have realized that the best way to teach tomorrow's managers to tap the talents of an increasingly diverse workforce is to surround students with a widely diverse student body. They're also recruiting more faculty members who reflect diverse viewpoints and philosophies as well as national origin. While more and more schools are quick to point to their rising numbers of international students, they also refer to the diverse backgrounds and experiences among their M.B.A. students—like the Olympic cyclist at the University of Texas at Austin or the professional stand-up comedian at Stanford. Female students—including more than 40 percent at Pace and Pepperdine—are swelling the ranks of M.B.A. graduates as well. "We view students from diverse countries and backgrounds to be a resource that complements what faculty members know and what other students bring to the program," says Shari Holmer Lewis, director of M.B.A. programs at the University of Illinois at Chicago.

5. Teamwork, Teamwork, and More Teamwork

Schools are working hard to encourage the same environment of teamwork that graduates will experience in the working world. "Cohort structures," for example, have gained in popularity. Cohorts means that you are placed with a specified number of fellow students—deliberately chosen for their diversity—either for the first few weeks of class or for the entire first year. Together with other members of your cohort, you'll solve problems as a team, resolve conflicts, sustain morale, achieve accountability, and, it is hoped, learn to reach your goals by becoming interdependent with others, just as you would in a corporate setting.

Reinvented M.B.A. programs are learning to "pit students against the curriculum and not against one another," says Sam Lundquist, Wharton's director of admissions. Stanford says its cooperative learning environment is a significant factor in the program's "joy coefficient," as George Parker, associate dean for academic affairs, describes it.

6. Richer Learning Environment

Hand in hand with curriculum improvements, business schools are finding new ways to strengthen teaching and foster improved student-faculty relationships. Indeed, the "most exciting part" of Wharton's new cross-functional curriculum, Lundquist says, is that teams of faculty now teach the same students for the entire first year, which "drastically improves the quality of relationships between students and faculty members."

As M.B.A. programs bolster the quality of the learning experience, they are focusing a laser beam on how well professors help students learn. Pace University views faculty members as "the managers of the student learning process," says Centonze. As a result, all programs and courses have objectives that are measured by student exit surveys, faculty questionnaires, and yearly performance evaluations for faculty members. Any underperforming teachers are coached at the school's Center for Faculty Development and Teaching Effectiveness, where their syllabi are reviewed and their classes videotaped.

Increasingly, a variety of teaching methods are employed, including lectures, case studies, computer simulations, and consulting projects. Harvard's curriculum reform was notable for adopting alternative teaching methods in addition to its reliance on the traditional case-study approach and for developing ways to have faculty members spend less time teaching basics.

7. Greater Use of Learning Technologies

M.B.A. programs are making increasing use of such state-of-the-art technologies as distance learning, which uses interactive cable television and computers to take courses directly to students' homes. Both the University of Maryland and the University of Arizona, for instance, use distance learning and team teaching to bundle their assets and hire big-name teachers. Distance learning also is "favored heavily" in Europe, where virtually all programs are part-time, according to Roger McCormick, director general of the Association of M.B.A.'s in the United Kingdom. Distance learning allows students to learn at their own pace, which is especially helpful for remedial courses and quantitative work, he says.

Business schools are avidly employing other technologies as well, such as interactive cases on CD-ROMs and real-time data feeds from Wall Street. The University of Texas at Austin is building a $1.5-million trading room so that its students can experience trading in real time with real dollars from a $2-million investment fund. Purdue is even investigating how to bring virtual reality experiences into the classroom. Meanwhile, videoconferencing is used for classroom presentations or off-site interviews with corporations.

8. More Applied Learning

There's nothing like real-world experience to realize that "disciplines don't work in a vacuum," says Holmer Lewis of the University of Illinois at Chicago. Student and faculty teams there tackle corporate projects by interviewing corporate executives, writing reports, and presenting recommendations to the company and to their fellow students. They're not alone. Students at the University of Texas at Austin helped Ford Motor Company better segment its Hispanic marketing efforts. The University of Michigan adopted a medical school model, requiring students to get considerable practical experience working at corporations. At Stanford, corporate leaders such as Andrew S. Grove of Intel team with professors to teach classes on strategy in the high-technology industry.

9. Strategic Alliances

To better leverage their resources, schools are joining forces to teach students and to conduct postgraduate training for corporate executives. The Thunderbird School reserves seats at its learning centers around the world for its partner schools in the United States. Business schools at the University of Florida and Fordham University in New York team up with AT&T and MCI, respectively, to offer customized programs for their executives. Corporate advisory boards, long a staple of most M.B.A. programs, are increasingly relied on to provide advice on curricula as well as hiring opportunities. Corporate partners also contribute other sorely needed resources. Purdue has one of the most extensive computing labs of any business school, thanks to the generosity of such high-tech partners as AT&T, Hewlett Packard, IBM, Microsoft, and PictureTel. "The business

environment is moving fast, and even elite schools don't have all the money they need to access new markets, technology, and faculty expertise," says the AACSB's Freeman.

10. A Customer Focus

It's not uncommon to hear business school professors routinely refer to students and companies as customers—and to treat their needs with the same respect. The University of Maryland, University of Wisconsin, and Oregon State are applying Total Quality Management (TQM) principles to operating the business schools themselves. They're becoming more customer-focused, reducing the cycle time for admissions processing and curriculum development, and becoming more efficient to lower tuition or keep it from rising quickly. Seattle University takes classes to the customers, dispatching faculty members to teach evening and breakfast courses near Seattle's biggest employers. "Business schools are developing niches and more focus now, because not every school can do everything," says Holmer Lewis. "Schools will need to re-tool with increasing rapidity in the next five years."

With such evolution occurring day by day at business schools, more than ever before, today's reinvented M.B.A. programs aim to prepare you for the real world of work, where you will work in teams, take a global view, and analyze problems from a multitude of perspectives. To accomplish these goals, M.B.A. programs intend to equip you with the ability to embrace change, accept ambiguity, and lead others with the vision and confidence gained from continuous learning.

With a newly minted M.B.A. degree, you are better qualified to enter new fields, better able to leverage your prior work experience, and more likely to sustain higher earnings over the course of your career. Equally important, you'll have the opportunity to make a significant difference on as broad a scale as you wish. As Stanley Mann at Pepperdine University points out, "With finely honed analytical skills, the ability to work well with people, and the desire to keep learning, today's M.B.A. graduates can succeed in a broad range of general management positions and add more value than ever before."

Carter A. Prescott is a management communications consultant in New York City.

Choosing the Right Program for Your Career Needs

by Richard L. White, Director of Career Services, Rutgers University

In recent senior surveys, more than 80 percent of Rutgers University students have indicated that they intend to pursue graduate study at some point in the future. Many are thinking about an M.B.A. The intentions of Rutgers students reflect a national trend: More and more students want additional education, and, in fact, many feel they will need it to achieve their fullest career potential.

From your first thoughts about graduate school to your actual admission and decision to attend a school, you are engaged in an extensive, complex, competitive process. The emphasis of the program you select will greatly impact the direction of your career. In selecting an M.B.A. program, it's critical to match your strengths, interests, and goals with the specific offerings of the school and program.

To organize and manage the process, develop a strategy for evaluating your choices and developing an action plan. At the heart of your action plan are four basic questions that are simple to ask but require self-exploration and research:

- Why do I want to pursue an M.B.A.?
- When and how do I want to pursue an M.B.A.?
- Where do I want to pursue an M.B.A.?
- What schools and programs are right for me?

1. Why Pursue an MBA?

Typically, you are probably thinking about pursuing an M.B.A. for four basic reasons:

- Your chosen profession demands further study.
- You want to enhance your marketability and salary.
- You want to change careers.
- You are committed to further study in your current discipline or a new discipline.

Most applicants fit one or more of these profiles:

- You're currently working with an employer that you would like to stay with long term. You've talked to your boss and some other colleagues, and they feel that getting an M.B.A. will improve your business and technical knowledge and thus increase your performance and promotional opportunities with the employer. You understand that there probably won't be a big jump in salary when you complete your degree, but in the long term it will pay off. And besides, your employer will pick up the tab through its tuition reimbursement program.

- You're currently working with an employer who doesn't fit into your longer term plans. You're planning to leave in the near future. You plan to gain your M.B.A. to open up new opportunities in the same field or brand-new fields and also to increase salary prospects. You realize that you're on your own with regard to costs (no employer assistance), but you see the short-term investment paying off in the long run.

- You're a senior in college. You've looked at the job market, but you're really leaning toward an M.B.A. program. You're very interested in pursuing your business education, especially because your bachelor's degree is not in business. You understand that the best business schools accept only a small percentage of applicants directly from undergraduate programs, but you have a strong academic record and some good internship and part-time work experience.

Whatever your profile may be, make sure you can articulate your reasons for pursuing an M.B.A. clearly, succinctly, and persuasively both orally and in writing. Review the evolution of your thinking from first thoughts about an M.B.A. to major influences (people, courses, positions) and research.

To understand your motivation for pursuing an M.B.A., follow these action steps:

1. Takes notes on yourself.
2. Write or revise your resume.
3. Develop a generic personal statement (2 to 3 typed pages), indicating what makes you special and why you want an M.B.A. degree.
4. Request a sampling of M.B.A. applications and begin crafting sample answers to the questions, using parts of your generic personal statement.
5. Read *How to Write a Winning Personal Statement for Graduate and Professional School* by Richard Stelzer (Peterson's Guides). Check your college's career services library, your campus bookstore, or a well-stocked local bookstore in the Education/Reference section.
6. Determine job prospects for M.B.A.'s in your intended field—both short-term and long-term. The best resources for short-term job prospects are individual placement reports from business schools, which you can request from the schools of your choice. For long-term prospects,

talk to relatives, family friends, or professors. Another great source is alumni, if your school has an alumni career network.

2. When and How Do You Want to Pursue Your MBA?

There are four fairly clear-cut options about when and how to pursue your M.B.A.:

- Full-time beginning in the fall after your graduation from college. Keep in mind that, typically, M.B.A. programs look for candidates with at least one to two years of full-time work experience. If you are a student early in your undergraduate career, one option to explore is a five-year dual degree (B.S./M.B.A.) program.
- Full-time after a year or more of work. M.B.A. programs value the diversity and quality of candidates' work experiences, which bring "real-world" perspectives and new ideas into the classroom. Moreover, many M.B.A. students indicate that their M.B.A. course work has even more significance after they continue their professional and career development.
- Part-time beginning anytime while working. In most cases, you will take evening classes. As part of your preliminary research, find out if your employer provides full or partial tuition remission. Also explore whether or not your employer values an M.B.A. and whether it will really contribute to your long-term promotability. Finally, try to determine how flexible your employer may be if, for example, you need to take a 4:30 class or need one or two days off to complete a school project.
- Part-time beginning anytime while not working. If you're not working, you can take either day or evening classes. But if you're looking for a daytime job, bear in mind that you might want to remain flexible during the day and therefore take your classes at night. The reverse is true if you have a part-time evening job.

To sort out the different possibilities, take these action steps:

Research the schools of your choice, using this guide. Compare these five key elements: percentage of full-time vs. part-time enrollees; percentage of incoming M.B.A.'s who came directly from undergraduate programs; average age; average work experience; and costs.

Research the profession and prospective employers, utilizing corporate recruiters, friends in the corporate world, career services and admissions professionals, professional associations, alumni networks, professors, and publications. Consider these elements: availability of tuition remission programs; value of the M.B.A. within the profession or company; balance between company B.A./B.S. recruiting and M.B.A. recruiting.

Balance all of the above elements with your personal life and lifestyle and those of the people closest to you.

3. Where Do You Want to Pursue Your MBA?

This is the most complex step in the process, because there are many variables. However, by taking these action steps, you can gain firm control of the process and manage it to your advantage.

Note that these steps are in no order of preference. It would be helpful to put them in rank order in terms of importance for you—or at least group them by "very important," "important," and "less important."

Determine the availability of degree programs in your specific field. For example, if you are thinking about an M.B.A. in international business, this guide will tell you which schools offer that program.

Determine the quality and reputation of the programs of your choice. This is a crucial element. Employers often base their recruiting decisions on quality and reputation, and you will be associated with the name of your M.B.A. school for the remainder of your career. Three key factors in assessing quality and reputation are faculty, facilities, and student body. In addition to utilizing this guide and perhaps other resources, talk to professors and professionals and "read between the lines" of the admissions literature and placement reports. Feel free to consult various national rankings, but don't take them too seriously. These are often based on journalistic endeavors rather than hard research and often overlook the special offerings of individual programs.

Determine the costs of graduate programs—the simple part—and your ability to pay through loans, income, savings, financial aid, and parental support—the not so simple part. Pursue those programs that are affordable. Consult the "Paying for Your M.B.A." section in this guide for an overview of the financing process.

Determine the locations of your preferred graduate programs. Do you prefer urban, suburban, or rural locations? Do you have any personal geographical restrictions or preferences? Think about spouses, family, and friends. Think about the time and cost of commuting and travel.

Determine the size of the programs and the institutions. Most M.B.A. programs are relatively small, but the size of institutions varies considerably. Size is critical to the overall environment, character, academic resources, and student-faculty ratios and relationships.

4. What Schools and Programs Are Right for You?

Here, you are putting it all together and generating a list of 5 to 10 schools where you intend to apply. Typically, you will want one or two "stretch" schools, a handful of "good bets," and one or two "safety" schools. Feel free to rank your preferences at the outset of the admissions process, but remain flexible. As you receive admissions decisions, your preferences will probably change and need to change.

Once your admissions acceptances are in hand, how do you make the final important decision? Consider these steps:

Rank the five most important features of the M.B.A. experience for you. You might also want a second-tier group of five additional features. Focus on these ten features (feel free to add others to the list):

1. Career and placement services (placement report, number of employers recruiting on campus, quality of operation)
2. Class offerings (day, evening, summer, weekend)
3. Cost (tuition, room, board, travel, living expenses)
4. Curricular focus (ethics, diversity, international, etc.)
5. Facilities (dorms, classrooms, libraries)
6. Faculty (general quality, individual faculty members)
7. Location (geographic, urban, rural)
8. Personal considerations (spouse, family, friends)
9. Quality and reputation (rankings, general comments)
10. Teaching methodology (lectures, case studies, team projects)

Systematically compare each school with regard to each feature. Rank schools within each feature, assigning a score if you wish.

Once you have done all the analyses, make sure your heart agrees with your head. If it's a toss-up, go with your instincts. They're probably right.

Using This Guide to Compare Programs

This guide provides answers to many of the key questions you will have about the numerous M.B.A. programs that are available. Consult the individual program profiles as you research and gather information about schools and their specific M.B.A. offerings. You will find the following topics addressed in each profile:

Overview

1. What are the overall characteristics of the college or university (public, private, coed, etc.)?
2. What is the entrance difficulty (mean GMAT and mean GPA)?
3. What is the cost of tuition and room and board?
4. What is the enrollment profile (full-time vs. part-time, total MBA enrollment, average age, work experience, international, women, minorities)?
5. Where and when are classes offered (day, evening, location, average class size)?
6. What are the distinguishing features of the M.B.A. program?
7. Where is the business school's M.B.A. program offered (urban, suburban, distance from your home or place of work)?
8. What notable alumni are graduates of the program?

Academics

9. What are the academic requirements for graduation (credits, required courses)?
10. What is the curricular focus (teams, business issues, ethics, diversity, etc.)?

11. What is the faculty profile (total number, full-time vs. part-time, doctorates)?
12. What is the teaching methodology (percentage of lectures, case studies, team projects, etc.)?
13. What special international and other opportunities are available?

Students

14. What is the geographic distribution of students?
15. What is the undergraduate distribution of majors?

Facilities

16. What information and library resources are available?
17. What housing opportunities are available?
18. What technology and computers are available to M.B.A. students?

Admission

19. What are the acceptance rates?
20. What are the entrance requirements?
21. What are the application requirements, including deadlines?

Financial

22. What is the cost for state and out-of-state residents (tuition, room, board)?
23. How many students receive financial aid and what is the range of aid packages?

International Students

24. What is the distribution of international students by country?
25. Are there special facilities, such as international housing or centers, on campus?
26. How and when do international students apply?

Alternate M.B.A. Programs

27. What alternate programs are available in addition to the basic M.B.A. degree, such as Executive M.B.A.'s, joint degrees, accelerated programs, and international options?

Placement

28. How many companies recruited on campus during the past year?
29. What was the placement rate and average starting salary?
30. What was the distribution of employer types and job functions?

Once you complete your research and request applications from the schools of your choice, you are ready for the next step: getting accepted.

Getting Admitted to MBA Programs

by Samuel T. Lundquist, Director of MBA Admissions, The Wharton School of Business, University of Pennsylvania

Applicants to M.B.A. programs often spend more time trying to figure out how to get into business school than actual time spent researching the program itself. Hence, the prospective student has made the first critical error of the admissions process—seeking the elusive "admissions formula" versus making a quality presentation that demonstrates knowledge of self and graduate business education.

There really is not any formula that can predict admission to an M.B.A. program. Business school applicants must enter the selection process understanding the difference between being admissible and being admitted. The distinction between the two varies considerably among business schools, depending on the level of selectivity in the admissions process. While some M.B.A. programs admit all qualified students, others may deny admission to four of every five applicants who are qualified to be admitted. Understanding this difference is the first step to a successful application.

The Evaluative Process

Applicants to M.B.A. programs should understand how they will be evaluated during the admissions process. In general, presentation, academic profile, professional work experience, and personal qualities will be the four areas in which each applicant will be evaluated. Admissions officers generally evaluate the factors influencing applicants' educational and professional decisions and the corresponding outcomes. Admissions committees do not spend a lot of time evaluating the labels that tend to categorize applicants into special groups. For instance, candidates for admission often assume that the quality of the undergraduate institution that they attended will affect the outcome of their application. A common misconception is that applicants with undergraduate degrees from Ivy League schools are always more desirable candidates for business schools. In fact, candidates are generally judged, whether they attended a public or private college, on a combination of factors— academic background, work experience, personal characteristics, and post-M.B.A. goals.

Applicants are evaluated as individuals. The environment in which they have studied or worked is relevant only when it is given meaning in the context of their life experiences. How the culture of a campus or workplace has influenced one's success is interesting and important to the admissions committee's ability to fully evaluate an application. Therefore, applicants who provide only factual information about their academic and professional profile miss the most important opportunity to present the compelling and distinguishing characteristics of their candidacy.

The M.B.A. degree is not a professional license that is required to practice management. Therefore, people of all ages are known to pursue the degree at different stages of their careers. Older applicants (32 years old and up) often fear that because they are atypical to the traditional graduate school student profile they will likewise be less desirable to business schools. On the contrary, older students offer professional experience, maturity, and perspective that are highly valued in the classroom. The admissions committee does expect older applicants to have highly developed reasons for pursuing the M.B.A. at this stage of their life. Post-M.B.A. goals are expected to be clearer and more defined than those of their younger counterparts.

Applicants have much more control of the admissions process than they realize. Prospective students determine all of the information that is presented in the application forms, essays, and interview. They even get to select the people who will serve as references to support their candidacy. The only aspect of the process that an applicant does not control is the competition; that is, who else applies for admission. It is the competition that will determine the threshold between admissibility and acceptance.

Presentation is obviously one of the most important factors in admission. Three other areas are evaluated during the evaluative process. They include academic profile, professional work experience, and personal qualities.

Academic Profile

Business schools seek students who can survive the demands of a rigorous and demanding program, and the best way to show your intellectual strength is to demonstrate strong classroom achievement and high aptitude. Your ability to excel as an undergraduate student is directly related to your ability to succeed in a graduate program as well.

Your undergraduate specialization will have little effect on admission to business school. It is not necessary to take undergraduate courses in business administration because most M.B.A. programs offer or require a core curriculum of basic business courses as part of the graduate degree. However, it is advisable to have basic skills in economics, calculus, and statistics in preparation for graduate study in business.

The Graduate Management Admission Test (GMAT)

Most business schools require applicants to submit the results of their Graduate Management Admission Test (GMAT). The importance of the GMAT in admissions will vary depending on the school. Minimum score requirements do not exist at some business schools. Test scores are certainly not the sole criteria for admission to an M.B.A. program, but to one degree or another, all business schools use them as part of the admissions process.

The GMAT uses a standardized set of criteria to evaluate the basic skills of college graduates, which allows graduate schools to compare and judge applicants. The test measures general verbal and math skills so that schools can assess an applicant's ability to succeed in a graduate-level environment.

• Quantitative section—this section measures mathematical skills and the ability to solve quantitative problems.
• Qualitative section—this section focuses on verbal skills, the ability to understand and interpret written materials, and basic English writing skills.
• Scoring—total scores range from 200 to 800. Most business schools accept scores between 500 and 600.
• Taking the test—you can take the GMAT at a testing center in your area. Testing takes place on four days each year—generally in January, March, June, and October. Contact the graduate admissions office at your local college or university for specific dates and times and details on how to register.

Professional Work Experience

Admission to selective, international business programs often requires full-time, professional work experience prior to enrollment. While professional work experience is needed to provide a context for the interpretation and use of classroom material, students must also be able to contribute to class discussions and group projects in meaningful ways. Career success is the most effective way to prove your potential for leadership in a managerial capacity.

Personal Qualities

M.B.A. programs want to enroll students who can lead people. The admissions committee seeks men and women who will eventually be responsible for the management of entire organizations. Leadership is one of the basic ingredients for success. Communication skills, initiative, and motivation can become the most important aspects of the admis-

sions process. Personal qualities set the tone for the entire review of an application. It is the one part of an application that is most likely to distinguish a candidacy in a compelling way.

The Interview

The interview is the one aspect of the admissions process that varies the most among schools. Some schools, like the Kellogg School at Northwestern, require all applicants to interview prior to admission. Others, such as Stanford's Graduate School of Business, do not interview any of their applicants. Most schools, like Wharton at the University of Pennsylvania, leave the decision to interview up to the applicant. It is one more part of the admissions process that the applicant can control. For those prospective students who do have the interview available to them, it is a highly recommended experience. It is also a great opportunity to take initiative in the admissions process.

If an interview is part of the admissions process, it can be an invaluable opportunity for the applicant to show the strengths and leadership qualities that most business schools are seeking in M.B.A. candidates. The most effective and interesting interviews are those discussions that go beyond the information provided in the written application. Too often interviews remain focused solely on the candidate's resume. The meeting becomes nothing more than a redundancy in the evaluation of a candidacy. It is up to both the interviewer and the applicant to create an exchange of information that solicits useful information that will help the admissions committee understand the context of the choices that the applicant has made throughout life.

Categories and labels do not play as significant a role in the process as most applicants assume. Prospective M.B.A. students should take a high level of initiative during the admission process, while exercising discretion when determining what information is most important for a school to properly evaluate their candidacy.

These guidelines are the first step in understanding the nature of the admissions process from the perspective of an admissions officer. It is vital to recognize that each school has its own policies and procedures in admissions that will alter the way in which an applicant can interact with the admissions committee. Careful research and communication will, fundamentally, have the greatest impact on the success of an M.B.A. application.

Paying for Your MBA

by Bart Astor

Now that you've made a commitment to getting your M.B.A., the next question is likely to be "How will I pay for it?"

The first thing you will have to decide is whether you will go to school part-time and continue working full-time, or go to school full-time while working part-time. About two thirds of M.B.A. students get their degree while they continue working at a full-time job. And though it will take you longer to get your M.B.A. this way, the costs are more manageable and the amount of money you'll need to borrow is kept to a minimum. Furthermore, if you work for one of the many companies that offer either full or partial tuition reimbursement to their employees, this will further reduce your expenses.

Some M.B.A. programs, on the other hand, are only available to full-time students. If you go to one of these schools, it will be impossible for you to work full-time. Therefore, you will have to make some other arrangement to pay the expenses of your schooling and to find the necessary resources to maintain your living expenses.

But it is not only possible to find the resources you will need; it is also quite likely. Unfortunately, though, for most full-time M.B.A. students, most of the money is available through student loans. And the amount of debt an M.B.A. student takes on can be quite sizable.

Nevertheless, most M.B.A. students feel it is worthwhile to take on some debt to pay for this degree that they believe will offer them considerable career advancement. In that sense, then, they view these costs as an investment in their earnings potential. And the numbers have consistently supported this claim. A quick look at Table 1: Average Starting Salaries for Non-MBA and MBA Graduates shows that the salary for holders of an M.B.A. is 25 to 40 percent higher than for non-M.B.A. graduates. Looking only at earnings potential, getting an M.B.A. has certainly proved to be an excellent financial investment. And, of course, this does not even consider career opportunities or quality of life issues.

The Costs

Now let's look at the cost of getting your M.B.A. degree. All students are required to pay some sort of tuition or fee to go to school (in some state-supported business schools, this may be called a "fee"). This can be a total amount for the year, regardless of the number of credits you take, or a per-credit amount. The annual tuition for a full-time student can range from $2000 or $3000 at some of the state-supported schools to over $20,000 at some of the higher-priced business schools. In addition, some business schools require all students to pay fees for such things as student activities, health services, etc., much like you may have paid as an undergraduate.

Most business school students pay a little more for books and supplies than they did as an undergraduate. While the amount will differ at each school, the annual amount for a full-time student ranges from $500 to $800. If you will need a computer, that will naturally add a considerable amount to the total cost. Many business schools make computers available to their students, so be sure to check with the school before you purchase a computer. These are the two obvious additional expense categories you will face when you go to business school, and they are generally referred to as "direct costs."

In addition, however, there are other, "indirect costs" you face that you may not think of as business school expenses. Rent and living expenses are certainly the largest two. But indirect costs also include transportation to and from school, travel from your home town to the city in which the school is located, personal expenses, and other expenses if appropriate (such as car loan payments and insurance, child care, disabled student expenses, summer tuition, medical expenses, etc.). If you are going to business school straight out of college, you may not have had to personally pay for these expenses before (although your parents certainly did). If you have been paying them already, then you know you may need to cut back on the amount you spend on some discretionary items, such as clothing and entertainment. As a student, you will have to budget your expenses as carefully as you budget your time. Most business schools can tell you what the average cost of living will be in the

---

TABLE 1: AVERAGE STARTING SALARIES FOR NON-MBA AND MBA GRADUATES

Degree (field of study)	Starting Salary
B.A. (Arts & Letters)	$22,068
B.A. (Business)	24,791
B.A. (Engineering)	33,660
M.B.A. (nontechnical undergraduate degree)	$35,734
M.B.A. (technical undergraduate degree)	41,313

(Sources: College Placement Council and Michigan State University Salary Report)

---

area and may offer subsidized housing or, at the very least, a housing office to help you find a place to live.

Financial Aid

Once you've calculated the total amount it will cost you to go to business school, you may find that the amount of income you receive won't be enough. That's where financial aid comes in. If you received financial aid as an undergraduate, then you have a head start: at least you understand some of the basics.

But financial aid is quite different for graduate students. For one, all graduate students are considered independent for federal financial aid. That means your parents are not required to assist you financially (although if they are willing and able, that would certainly help). Secondly, there is very little grant and scholarship money available to graduate students. The bulk of your expenses will be paid either from money you've already saved, money you will earn while you are attending school, or money you will borrow and pay back out of future earnings.

Most business school students take on considerable debt to pay their expenses since there are very few alternatives. If you're going to school part-time and working full-time, your salary in combination with your savings may be enough to avoid having to borrow very much. However, you may still decide it is better to borrow through a government-subsidized loan program than take the necessary funds out of your savings or current income.

If you've decided to go to school full-time, you will probably need to borrow, although many business schools offer fellowships and teaching and research assistantships to some students. Some of these positions and awards may be awarded based on your previous academic and employment record (merit-based) and some based on how much you need it. While everyone will say they need assistance, the definition of need for financial aid is up to the school, not you.

Applying for Financial Aid

When you apply for financial aid, you are generally applying for both need-based and merit-based aid. The application process will be changing significantly for students applying for the 1996–97 academic year. To qualify for federal aid, most of which will be in the form of loans, every student will be required to complete the Free Application for Federal Student Aid (FAFSA). This form is available in both business school and undergraduate school financial aid offices (your local community college or even your local high school guidance office will have them available as well). Soon after January 1, 1996 (for students entering in the fall of 1996), you should complete this application, which asks about your 1995 income and current assets.

Some business schools will require that you complete a different application, new for the 1996–97 year, and may require you to complete it earlier than the FAFSA (as early as October of 1995). This new form is called the Financial Aid PROFILE, which will also be available from the same places as the FAFSA. You may have to complete both

Types of Financial Aid

Gift Aid (money you do not have to pay back)
Individual grants, scholarships, and fellowships (may be merit-based or need-based)
Sources: business schools, foundations, private companies, community groups

Tuition waivers (awarded by individual business schools)

Company employee educational benefits (a personnel benefit for employees of many large and some small companies. Generally covers only a portion of tuition)

Federal grants (very limited and based on need)

State grants (also very limited)

Self-Help Aid (money you must earn or pay back later)

Work Programs
Federal Work Study (need-based and awarded by business school)—Source: federal government

Teaching Assistantships—Source: business school

Resident Assistantships—Source: business school

Research Assistantships—Source: business school

Loans
Federal Perkins Loan (need-based, lender is business school)

Federal Subsidized Stafford Loan (need-based, lender is a bank, savings & loan, etc.)

Federal Unsubsidized Stafford Loan (non-need-based)

Federal Direct Loan (similar to Stafford Loans; lender is the federal government)

Private loan programs (e.g., M.B.A. Loans; Business Access Loans, etc.)

Tuition payment plans (private or school-based)

financial aid applications, and the only ways you'll know to do so are by reading the business school literature or asking someone in the business school financial aid office. The instructions for the PROFILE will list those schools that have said they will require this application, but since it is so new, more schools will have signed up before those instructions went to print. If you will be attending business school prior to the 1996–97 academic year, check with the financial aid office at the school you will be attending to see what application to use.

The business schools you have designated on either financial aid application you filed will receive an output showing an amount you can afford to contribute to your education, calculated based on your income and assets. This number is called the "Family Contribution" or FC. The FC from the federal form is the official amount that determines whether you will qualify for federal aid. If this amount is less than the total cost of attendance of the M.B.A. program, you have demonstrated need and will qualify for aid, again, usually low-cost, government-subsidized loans. The output from the PROFILE will give the school an estimate of your federal eligibility and will also give an expected contribution based on additional criteria you provided. This contribution will be used by those schools using the PROFILE to award their own funds. And, like the federal FC, if your contribution is less than the total cost of the school, you qualify for need-based aid.

But even if your family contribution is higher than the cost of the school, you may still qualify for aid. For one, this FC is based on your previous year's income, which will likely change significantly when you go to school full-time. You can appeal to the business school financial aid office and ask them to recalculate your need based on the amount you will have when you go to school, rather than on your previous year's income. Secondly, there are government, institutional, and private loans available to students regardless of whether they have demonstrated need (such as the Federal Unsubsidized Stafford Loan, M.B.A. Loans, and Business Access Loans). Although these loans ultimately cost borrowers more since they are not subsidized, they are still sources of income for you to pay your business school costs.

Your Credit History

Since most M.B.A. students have to borrow to pay for their education, making sure you qualify for a loan is critical.

For the most part that means your credit record must be free of default or delinquency. You can check your credit history with one or more of the following three major credit bureaus and clean up any adverse credit that appears. You can look up the local numbers in your phone book or call the numbers below:

Equifax Credit Information Services (CBI)
P.O. Box 105873
Atlanta, GA 30348
(800) 685-1111
Fax (404) 612-3150

Trans Union Corporation
P.O. Box 390
Springfield, PA 19064-0390
(601) 933-1200

TRW
P.O. Box 2350
Chatsworth, CA 91313-2350
(800) 520-1221

Debt Management

Although the limits M.B.A. students can borrow from federal and private programs are quite high, you will want to make sure you are not borrowing more than you will later be able to repay. Use Table 2 below to estimate your M.B.A. school loan monthly payments. Then by estimating your income and the total amount you'll need to borrow for your M.B.A. education, you can use Table 3 to determine whether your loan payments will be affordable.

Table 2: Estimated Loan Repayment Schedule
Monthly Payments for Every $1000 Borrowed

Rate	5 years	10 years	15 years	20 years	25 years
5%	$18.87	$10.61	$ 7.91	$ 6.60	$ 5.85
8%	20.28	12.13	9.56	8.36	7.72
9%	20.76	12.67	10.14	9.00	8.39
10%	21.74	13.77	10.75	9.65	9.09
12%	22.24	14.35	12.00	11.01	10.53
14%	23.27	15.53	13.32	12.44	12.04

You can use this table to estimate your monthly payments on a loan for any of the five repayment periods (5, 10, 15, 20, and 25 years). The amounts listed are the monthly payments for a $1000 loan for each of the interest rates. To estimate your monthly payment, choose the closest interest rate and multiply the amount of the payment listed by the total amount of your loan and then divide by 1,000. For example, for a total loan of $15,000 at 9% to be paid back over 10 years, multiply $12.67 times 15,000 (190,050) divided by 1,000. This yields $190.05 per month.

TABLE 3: DEBT MANAGEMENT GUIDE

Total Outstanding Loan	Years in Repayment	Monthly Payment	Suggested Minimum Monthly Income
$10,000	10	$126	$ 840
20,000	10	253	1,687
30,000	10	380	2,533
40,000	10	506	3,373
50,000	10	633	4,220
20,000	20	179	1,193
30,000	20	270	1,800
40,000	20	360	2,400
50,000	20	450	3,000

International Students

Costs of U.S. business schools for international students are the same as or slightly higher than for U.S. residents. Your Certificate of Eligibility for a student visa will require that you prove that you have sufficient funds for the entire M.B.A. program. United States government aid for international students is virtually nonexistent, and very few business schools make any resources available. You should make sure you have obtained the necessary funds from your own resources, including from your own government.

Additional Information

For more information about financing your education, refer to the personnel office at the company for whom you work and the business school financial aid office. You can also obtain additional information on possible sources of aid from the following Peterson's publications, some of which are available on-line via the Internet.

- Peterson's Paying Less for College
- Grants for Graduate and Postdoctoral Study
- Financing Graduate School
- M.B.A.'s Guide to Career Planning
- USA TODAY Financial Aid for College

For information about loan options, you can contact the following organizations:

Academic Management Services (AMS)
50 Vision Boulevard
East Providence, RI 02914
(800) 635-0120

The Access Group
P.O. Box 7400
Wilmington, DE 19803-0400
(800) 292-1330

Business and Professional Women's Foundation
Loan Programs
2012 Massachusetts Avenue, NW
Washington, DC 20036
(202) 293-1200

Consern Loans for Education
205 Van Buren Street, Suite 200
Herndon, VA 22070
(800) SOS-LOAN

The Education Resource Institute (TERI)
330 Stuart Street, Suite 500
Boston, MA 02116
(800) 255-TERI

Knight College Resource Group
855 Boylston Street
Boston, MA 02116-2611
(617) 267-1500, (800) 225-6783

MBA Loans
2400 Broadway, Suite 230
Santa Monica, CA 90404
(800) 366-6227

New England Education Loan Marketing Corporation
(Nellie Mae)
50 Braintree Hill Park, Suite 300
Braintree, MA 02184
(800) 634-9308

Option 4 Loan Program
(800) 635-3785

PLATO
205 Van Buren Street, Suite 200
Herndon, VA 22070
(800) SOS-LOAN

Smart Loan Consolidation
P.O. Box 1304
Merrifield, VA 22116-1304
(800) 524-9100

U.S. Department of Education
Office of Student Financial Assistance
400 Maryland Avenue
Washington, DC 20202
(800) 433-3243 (Federal Student Aid Information Center)

Going Abroad for Your MBA

by Richard Edelstein, American Assembly of Collegiate Schools of Business

Students are increasingly going abroad to obtain their M.B.A. education. Why? Individuals seeking a management career must prepare themselves to function in international contexts on a global scale. Studying abroad is one of the most effective ways of obtaining knowledge and developing skills that respond to these new demands. In large measure, this reflects the changing nature of business where the globalization of markets and companies is forcing a rethinking of the types of education and experience necessary to pursue a successful career as a manager.

International mobility, cross-cultural skills, and foreign language proficiency have all increased in value to employers. Technical skills remain critical, but international experience and knowledge are increasingly appreciated by companies. Choosing to pursue your M.B.A. education abroad is an excellent way to acquire knowledge and skills that are necessary for the global economy.

This trend of attaching increased value to international experience is most noteworthy in transnational companies that have operations and management responsibility distributed in numerous countries. Hewlett-Packard, for example, recently reorganized its personal computer division and made Grenoble, France, the location of its top management team. This reflects the reality that most of H-P's personal computer sales are outside the U.S. It also may be related to the rapid growth of communications technologies that allow companies to communicate easily with management teams irrespective of geographic location.

Another indication of increased demand for managers with specialized international experience and skills is the growth in importance of the so-called "transitional economies" like China, India, Russia, Brazil, and Indonesia. Many firms want to develop joint ventures or start-up operations in these countries but are constrained by lack of personnel who can manage in such different cultural and linguistic contexts. Demand for M.B.A.'s who have experience in these countries and have language skills is very high.

Career Paths in Different Countries

The M.B.A. degree is not recognized as the ideal qualification for a business career in all countries. Its acceptance in the U.S. and by many multinational firms as a primary qualification for future managers sometimes leaves the impression of a universal acceptance worldwide. In fact, the majority of countries outside the U.S. have significantly different educational and career paths for their managers. For example, the most common educational qualification for future managers in many countries is an engineering degree. This is the case in Germany, Switzerland, the Scandinavian countries, and many countries in the developing world, such as India and China. Even in France, Belgium, Italy, and Spain, engineering training is a major source of recruitment of managers. Another educational qualification for a business career quite common in other nations is a law degree.

The lack of universal acceptance of the M.B.A. does not imply that it may not be an excellent way to launch your own career. In a world full of different educational philosophies, cultural values, and economic systems, there cannot be a single form of preparation for becoming a manager. The M.B.A. is still the most common qualification for business managers. Nevertheless, it is important to keep in mind that it may not be seen with the same degree of acceptance in all countries. This is important to consider if you have particular aspirations to work in countries where it may not have the same recognition that it does in the U.S. It also is useful information for anyone who plans to work in a multinational enterprise where professional colleagues may come from any country. The M.B.A. is only one way to acquire the knowledge and skills necessary to manage a company.

Markets, Hierarchies, and Prestige

Not all M.B.A.'s are created equal! Given the choice between going to Harvard or a correspondence course from an unknown institution for your M.B.A., the answer is obvious. In reality the choice is never that clear, and many individuals must make compromises between where they would like to pursue their degree and where they have a serious chance of being accepted. This is true whether you are applying to institutions in your home country or abroad.

If you want to pursue an M.B.A. abroad, it is important to do some research about the schools you are considering. Learn about their status in the prestige hierarchy and the types of companies that are likely to employ their graduates. Going to a school of high prestige is not always the best choice, depending upon your own abilities and professional goals.

Students applying to American schools from abroad frequently assume that the only schools worth attending are the most elite and prestigious schools with international reputations. In fact, the range of schools offering high-quality M.B.A. programs is much larger in number than the top 20 institutions that make it on the *Business Week* survey.

Reputation and prestige are important factors to consider in planning your M.B.A. education, but keep in mind that prestige alone does not assure you of an education that is best suited to your individual needs. This is true abroad as well as at home.

Making the Decision to Study Abroad

Why go abroad for your M.B.A. when you can just as easily enter an American program that has an international dimension built into the program? The answer for many people is that they want and need a more intensive experience abroad that allows them to acquire foreign language and cultural skills and to build professional networks that cannot be obtained through an American program. Traveling and becoming a "citizen of the world" are also appealing, although more romantic, reasons for some students. Before you decide to pursue your M.B.A. in another country, however, it is important to consider a few key points.

Personal Goals and Foreign Language Ability

Personal attributes will define whether or not study abroad for an M.B.A. is the right choice for you. Have you already had extensive experiences abroad? Previous experience may make the added value of doing your graduate business studies abroad less significant. But, what about building on the skills you acquired in your previous experience and developing high levels of language competence and specialized knowledge in the country or region where you would like to study?

Studying abroad is clearly a more intensive international experience than anything you could pursue in the U.S. In the end, it is this intensity that distinguishes the option of doing the M.B.A. abroad from staying at home. If you are doubtful about the need for this intensity of international experience, then you may want to consider staying in the U.S. and entering a program that includes an international emphasis of less intensive character.

Foreign language proficiency can be a defining criterion in deciding whether or not to consider studying abroad. Although there are an increasing number of M.B.A. programs abroad that are taught in English, many of them require some level of proficiency in foreign languages. The United Kingdom, Australia, New Zealand, Hong Kong, and Singapore have M.B.A. programs in English, but most of them are oriented toward a national employment market. Many of the European English-language M.B.A. programs outside these countries are targeted to foreign nationals and actually include few students from the home country where the school is located. The "flagship" management studies program of the school is often taught in the local language and limits admission to students who can demonstrate language proficiency.

A distinction should be made between international M.B.A. programs taught in English and national M.B.A. programs taught in the local language. Each has its market niche and serves different needs. A good example of an institution offering both types of programs is SDA Bocconi in Italy.

Bocconi created an English-language international M.B.A. that responds to the needs of students who seek to develop an international career. The traditional Bocconi degree program is more prestigious and has an international reputation for training managers, especially for the Italian market. In considering which program to apply to, an American needs to consider both foreign language proficiency and personal needs and goals.

Structure and Cost of MBA Programs Abroad

M.B.A. programs outside the U.S. are frequently structured differently. In Europe, for example, some M.B.A.'s are only one year long. Typically this involves 12 months of intensive study with no summer break. In the U.K., the M.B.A. is most often two years in length, following a more American model. Whatever the length of the program, it may have somewhat different course requirements and curricula. Frequently, teaching approaches are also different. Sometimes they are closely tied to the patterns of university education in the host country. Increasing attention is being paid to teaching skills related to teamwork and working in cross-national groups.

Another point to consider is the tendency of off-shore M.B.A. programs to be more application-oriented and less tied to the research faculty. M.B.A. programs in other countries vary significantly in the emphasis placed on teaching versus research as a major focus of faculty reward systems.

The cost of M.B.A. programs outside the U.S. is generally quite competitive, even when you consider the added cost of airfare. Tuition costs for graduate education in the U.S., especially at elite private universities, are among the highest in the world. All in all, you may find the cost of an M.B.A. abroad surprisingly reasonable by comparison. Keep in mind that there is significant variation among schools, so the generalization that programs are less costly has its exceptions.

Cultural Adjustment

Cultural adjustment is a factor that should be considered in applying to an overseas program. Unless you have spent an extended period of time in the country you plan to study in, you are likely to be affected by this change. Reactions to living in another culture vary considerably depending on the person and on the culture. Although it is true that adapting to British culture may appear to be easier than Mexico or Italy, there is always more difference in lifestyle, values, and professional life than expected, no matter which country. As noted earlier, acquiring the skill to work and learn in more than one culture is a primary reason for wanting to study abroad in the first place. Still, do not assume this is an easy adjustment or task. It takes a serious commitment to self-improvement and a willingness to be open to entirely new situations to succeed in cross-cultural settings.

Building Professional Networks

One of the keys to a career as a successful manager is the capacity to develop networks of individuals whom you can work with and learn from. These professional networks may be within your present employer, with colleagues in other firms, and, increasingly, in other nations. By choosing to pursue an M.B.A. abroad, you should recognize that you will build different professional networks than you would in the U.S. Alumni associations that are a fixture in American universities and business schools. They tend to be less well developed in other countries, but where you went to school is often a critical factor in what job opportunities you may have on graduation as well as in the future.

In some cases, Americans have some advantages when it comes to applying to M.B.A. programs abroad. Since the M.B.A. is essentially an American invention, one of the most significant ways of gaining credibility for an M.B.A. program outside the U.S. is to begin attracting American students who might otherwise attend an American institution. Although poorly qualified candidates will not be admitted no matter what their national origin, all things being equal, Americans sometimes have an advantage in the selection process at some schools. This may not continue to be true for very long as more Americans begin enrolling in foreign programs. But for the time being, many M.B.A. programs abroad are interested in recruiting Americans.

Finding the Right Program
Where Do You Want to Work?

One obvious reason for choosing to study for an M.B.A. abroad is to increase your chances of obtaining employment outside the U.S. If you have your heart set on living and working in France or Indonesia, then it makes sense to seriously consider attending an institution in that country. This is especially true if you select a school and program linked to the national employment market. While global markets are certainly a long-term trend, national employment markets are still the norm for most firms, and doing your studies in a particular country will generally enhance your chances of obtaining employment in that country.

This is accomplished in two ways. First, your degree and school/university will be more easily recognized in that national employment market. Second, the school may have placement services, alumni relations, and other ways of connecting graduates into the labor market for management positions. Even if you elect to work for a transnational firm, there are significant benefits to being able to access this national network of business professionals.

Which Country and What Language?

M.B.A.-type degrees are more prevalent in countries like England, France, Belgium, and the Netherlands than in other European countries. In these countries there may be numerous institutions from which to choose. In the remaining European countries, choices are much more limited and may require significant foreign language skill. One way to increase your options is to consider enrolling in a university program in business and economics. In France, for example, there are many degree programs in universities that offer business degrees that are targeted to the national and European

job market, often based in an Institut d'Administration des Enterprises or IAE. University-based options are also available in other European countries but in virtually all cases require host country language fluency and a willingness to be one of few foreigners in a program.

In Latin America, the options are numerous if one includes university-based programs in business and economics. Pure M.B.A.-type options are much more limited and often involve only one or two institutions in the country. Still, Latin American countries have created a number of good business schools that offer M.B.A. programs that have international standing. Gatulio Vargas in São Paulo, ESAN in Peru, IESE in Venezuela, and INCAE in Costa Rica/ Nicaragua are examples of institutions that offer programs that may interest prospective American students.

In Asia and the Pacific Rim, options are more limited. This is partly due to distinctly different educational systems that reflect different recruitment practices for managers. Japan is well-known for a manager recruitment structure that relies on in-company training rather than professional education in the university. This pattern can also be found in other Asian countries, though to a somewhat lesser degree. In Japan, the language barrier can be significant since very few Japanese universities have programs targeted to foreigners taught in English. Combined with the cultural tendency toward in-company education, this makes Japan especially difficult for foreigners to penetrate. One noteworthy exception is the IUJ, the International University of Japan, which does offer an M.B.A. program in English.

Hong Kong, Australia, and New Zealand have M.B.A. programs that are open to Americans taught in English. Most are university-based business schools that follow either the American or British models of university education. The Hong Kong programs tend to be focused on special needs of Hong Kong and China. The Australian programs are frequently oriented toward doing business in Asia, especially Southeast Asia. Schools in the Philippines, Indonesia, Malaysia, Singapore, and Thailand may also be of interest to those interested in working in one of the countries that are developing dynamic economies in the midst of transition and rapid growth. The English-based M.B.A. courses are very limited, however, and careful research needs to be done to ensure that the program is up to international standards. The Asian Institute of Management in Manila and Singapore National University are two programs that have gained international credibility in the last decade.

Foreign language requirements are often significant, even at schools that teach in English. Since the study of foreign languages is more commonplace outside the U.S., you should be prepared to study a foreign language even if you are entering an English language–based program. Be sure to inform yourself about foreign language requirements prior to entering a program as this may be an important consideration in preparing for your experience.

Evaluating Quality

In evaluating the quality of a school you need to go deeper than the promotional piece typically sent to prospective students. Are the school and degree accredited by the Ministry of Education in the country where the degree is offered? Too often the school may be licensed by the department of commerce or industry as a business, but its degrees are not recognized by the country's university-level education authorities, usually in the Ministry of Education. If a program is not recognized as academically legitimate in the country where it operates, it is doubtful that its graduates have credibility in the international employment market. The embassy or consulate of the country in which an institution is located can also provide useful information.

A close, common-sense look at faculty qualifications is also important. Are faculty members qualified to teach at the advanced level of an M.B.A.-type program by virtue of their education and experience? How many are full-time permanent faculty? How many are part-time or "contact only" faculty? How many faculty members hold a doctoral degree in the field in which they teach? Be cautious of schools that say they have no full-time faculty because they prefer part-time instructors. This can be a ploy to avoid paying qualified people who require higher levels of salary. Is their doctorate in the field in which they are teaching? Have they done any research or published any articles? Do they have corporate or professional experience related to the course work?

It is always useful to speak with some graduates of the school prior to making a commitment to enroll. Schools will usually provide you with the names of several graduates whom you can contact about their experiences with the school. You can usually get a sense of the quality of the experience they had by asking questions about what the classes were like, how good were the faculty, and what kind of placement services the school provided. If it is possible to make a visit to the school and meet with current students, this is even better.

Financing Your International MBA

As noted earlier, tuition costs abroad are rarely more than those found among leading M.B.A. programs in the U.S. That is not saying much since costs in the U.S. can be as high as $25,000 annually for tuition alone! Still, you are likely to find that M.B.A. programs abroad compare favorably to most cost/benefit analyses. This is especially true for some of the less well-known programs that may be outside major capital cities. In instances where the program is less than two years in length, this may also be a factor in considering costs.

Where you may run into problems is in obtaining federally subsidized loans such as are commonly available through many American university financial aid offices. Most of these loans have some restrictions regarding the status of institutions and programs that you can attend and still be eligible for the loan program. Although some loan programs have been more flexible than others in allowing foreign study, you should check with your bank or lender regarding the regulations that apply.

Some institutions have their own loan programs and scholarships to help defray the costs of tuition. Less common are work opportunities, since M.B.A. programs generally require a full-time commitment. Still, it is worth asking the school about the potential for working on campus or assisting in research or consulting activity.

Other major costs to consider are round-trip air travel and the costs of living abroad. In some countries, especially in Europe and Asia, the cost of housing and food will be significantly higher than in the U.S., depending on the specific location.

Studying and Living Abroad

Living abroad requires adaptability, an adventuresome spirit, and a willingness to adjust to living in another culture. You will acquire a set of skills and experiences that will contribute to your preparation as a manager and a deeper understanding of your strengths, weaknesses, and values, even if you already have some cross-cultural experience.

Cross-cultural experience is always a challenge and an opportunity. It is always useful to do a lot of reading on the country and region you will live in prior to your departure. Knowing something about the history, geography, and culture is critical to learning how to adapt in your new culture. There are many good reference books available at bookstores and libraries that can help prepare you for your experience abroad. You might also explore the Internet for "chat" groups sharing information on studying and working abroad.

There are often support networks that you can take advantage of when you are abroad. Although you may have a desire to "go native" and avoid anything that is American while abroad, you may want to consider joining groups such as churches, university clubs, and alumni groups abroad as a means to enlarge your support system while living abroad.

The important thing is to remember that you will not just be adapting to the rigors of pursuing an M.B.A. program, but that it will also require energy and effort to deal with the adaptation required of the foreign visitor. But, again, this is precisely the reason for pursuing this path in the first place.

International Programs at U.S. Schools

If you are still having doubts as to whether or not studying for an M.B.A. abroad is the right choice for you, you can consider attending one of many M.B.A. programs in the U.S. that incorporate some international experience into the curriculum. This is clearly a less intensive option and cannot compare with living abroad but may be preferable depending upon your needs and goals.

This guide includes information on a range of M.B.A. programs that have international dimensions built into their programs. Several schools that offer a master's degree in international business (requiring significant language and cultural knowledge) rather than a classic M.B.A. are the

Lauder Program at the University of Pennsylvania (a joint program of the Wharton School and the College of Arts and Science), the M.I.B.S. program at the University of South Carolina, Columbia University, and the American Graduate School of International Management–Thunderbird in Glendale, Arizona.

An increasing number of M.B.A. programs include an international track or international fellows program that requires advanced foreign language competence and an internship abroad. These programs are usually highly selective and limited to 10–20 students per class. Programs offering this type of option include UCLA, University of Washington, University of Michigan, University of Chicago, University of Pittsburgh, University of Memphis, Indiana University, San Diego State University, University of Hawaii, and the University of Southern California.

A few M.B.A. programs include joint-degree or double-degree options in conjunction with a business school in another country. The University of Texas at Austin has several double-degree programs that allow a student to pursue a Texas M.B.A. and with a year abroad also acquire a French, German, or Mexican degree at the same time. NYU's Stern School has one of the most extensive exchange programs with foreign business schools of any U.S. university, and a significant percentage of M.B.A. students take advantage of this option. Also available are joint-degree programs that combine an M.B.A. with a master's or doctoral degree in an area specialty like Asian studies or Eastern European studies. The University of Pittsburgh, the University of Michigan, and the University of California at Berkeley are among the business schools offering this type of option.

Many other M.B.A. programs are including international internships and group projects outside the U.S. as a major component of their programs. The University of Pennsylvania's Wharton School has integrated a project abroad into the M.B.A. program for a portion of its students. The same is true for the University of California at Berkeley and the University of Michigan.

Does the trend in American M.B.A. programs to integrate international experience for some students make the case for going abroad for the M.B.A. any less compelling? Probably not. An M.B.A. program in the U.S. can never match the intense learning experience of spending a year or two in another country studying business. Moreover, the personal and professional contacts you make while abroad allow you to create an international network that cannot be easily duplicated when studying in most American M.B.A. programs. In the end, you need to weigh the benefits of gaining an intense international experience along with other factors, such as the quality and prestige of the institutions you are considering.

International Students Considering U.S. Programs

According to Open Doors[1] there were 87,000 students from abroad studying business in the U.S. in 1993–94. This represents 19 percent of all foreign students studying in American colleges and universities. Recent years have seen significant increases in the percentages of foreign student enrollments in M.B.A. programs. It is clear that obtaining an M.B.A. in the U.S. is very attractive for many students. Why?

American higher education continues to have a level of quality that places it among the best places to obtain a postgraduate-level degree in the world. It is also attractive because the M.B.A. was invented in the U.S., and obtaining the "original and genuine article" still has some prestige, especially as viewed from abroad. Perhaps an even more important, but less recognized, factor is that studying in the U.S. gives foreign students many of the same international skills and networks that are described above. This can be a tremendous advantage for students who aspire to work for companies with global markets and international management teams.

Will M.B.A. study in the U.S. continue to be as attractive in the future and will it be for the same reasons? The answer to these questions is less clear for several reasons. As business education becomes more of a global commodity and schools outside the U.S. improve the quality of their programs, it may be less appealing to pay the high cost of studying in the U.S. Second, distance learning capabilities may result in greater possibilities for undertaking M.B.A. education without coming to the U.S. Questions of quality and intensity of interaction with other students and faculty make this option less attractive for now, but this is already changing at some U.S. institutions. Finally, M.B.A. education may increasingly be offered by joint ventures or partnerships among and between institutions in several countries, using faculty and facilities in numerous locations. This internationalization of the postgraduate education market will, if it actually happens, alter many of the structures and processes that are currently considered "normal" for most universities and management education centers.

---

[1] Open Doors 1993-1994: Report on International Educational Exchange, 1994. Todd M. Davies ed. New York Institute of International Education.

Returning to School for Your MBA

by Barbara B. Reinhold, Ed.D., Director, Career Development, Smith College

Some decisions can be made and implemented quickly—you can often choose a new car, a new place to live, or even a new relationship rather impetuously and have it work out just fine. For the returning student, however, the process of deciding, applying to school, and then earning an M.B.A. is seldom simple. It has to be done with a great deal of forethought and awareness of the considerable sacrifice required.

The good news about being a more mature student is that you'll probably get much more out of it, because there is more of you to take to the classroom—more experience, better judgment, clearer goals, and more appreciation for learning. The bad news is that your life will be more "squeezed" than it would have been before you took on all of life's responsibilities, particularly balancing work and family. In general, however, later is often better than sooner when it comes to getting an M.B.A.

For mature women and men alike, there are many things to consider before upending your life to pursue an M.B.A. First, be sure you really need one. It is silly to waste your time and resources being "retooled" in an M.B.A. program if your career goals could be accomplished just as easily by taking targeted courses, getting more training and supervision through your employer, or using your connections to enter a different field or organization and move up. If you are trying to determine if an M.B.A. is really the key to where you want to go, find ways to network with people whose lives and career goals are similar to yours. You might discover that a variety of routes could lead you to your desired goal.

It's essential that you make your own decision about whether and where to apply, using a blend of logic and intuition. Though an M.B.A. requires strong quantitative skills, you'll also need good organizational, decision-making, and communication skills. For returning students, success in an M.B.A. program is often due more to life and work experience than technical knowledge alone. You have more information, more common sense, and more self-awareness at your disposal than you did as an undergraduate student. Use these assets along with your intuition in deciding whether this is really right for you now.

TEN TIPS FOR RETURNING STUDENTS

DECIDING

1. Be sure an M.B.A. is the best route to where you're going—don't embark on a trip until your destination is clear.
2. Make your own decision, using a blend of logic and intuition.
3. Be a discerning customer; ask hard questions about which programs best meet your own specific needs.

ARRIVING

4. Learn to market yourself; don't launch the campaign until you're ready.
5. Be sure your support system is in order—at home and at work.
6. Review your skills—technical, quantitative, written, and oral. If you're not really ready to do well yet, take an extra year to polish those skills.
7. Measure your confidence level—if it's weak, consider counseling to learn how to manage your anxieties and self-doubts.
8. Get your life in good shape before you begin—paying attention to nutrition, exercise, relationships, and all the other things you'll need to sustain you.

THRIVING

9. Ascertain your own most effective learning style (from your own self-assessment or more formalized measurements, such as the Learning Styles Inventory or the Myers-Briggs Type Inventory) and design routines and study regimens that best fit your style.
10. Find a group of friends/colleagues right away; collaboration is the key to succeeding and staying healthy through one of the most demanding experiences you'll ever have.

It's important also to be an informed and demanding customer on the front end of the process. Be sure to ask hard questions about how well a school is prepared to respond to the particular concerns you might have, such as being a minority candidate, having children, needing special accommodations of some type, or being in your forties or fifties. The ball will be in their court later; in the first half of the game, however, be aggressive about getting the information you need. For more mature students, the philosophy, resources, and services of the school can be much more important than ranking or reputation.

The application stage is also a great time to practice your marketing skills. Given today's roller coaster economy, an M.B.A. can be an expensive gamble, not a guarantee of employment. This may be the first of many times when you'll have to convince someone of your worth. For returning students this is often frightening. Some have been out of the job market for awhile, while others either want to change careers or are feeling stuck at a career plateau. Any of these situations is likely to leave you feeling less than competitive. This is a good time to figure out what you really have to offer to a particular school and to adjust to the notion of lifelong self-advocacy.

As you begin the difficult task of self-assessment, be honest about your strengths and weaknesses. If your technical, quantitative, or communication competencies are not what they should be in order for you to begin course work in a confident frame of mind, spend a year or so coming up to speed in these areas. Although you'll be taking accounting, statistics, and computer courses as part of the core requirements, it's best to be comfortable with these basic disciplines before you enroll.

Once enrolled, you can do two things to make your life easier. First, take an honest look at your own learning style. Try to determine which methods work best for you; use methods that fit your personality—outlines, memorizing, listening to tapes, discussing concepts with other people, etc.—be proactive, and establish a routine. As a returning student with many other life responsibilities, you'll need to take a different approach to studying than you did in undergraduate school.

You'll also find that connecting with classmates, whether you live on or off campus, is a critical part of doing well. You may be assigned to project teams, but it's a good idea to seek out your own support group as well. Join study groups and relevant student organizations, even though it may seem you can't spare the time. In business school, as in business itself, collaboration and networking are everything!

Becoming a student again is a great adventure—earning an M.B.A. will tax you, test you, stretch you, and reward you. But only you can know if it's right for you. When you applied to college as a high school student you had all the answers. What's different now is that, although you still don't have all the answers, you probably know much more than you think.

This table includes the names and locations of colleges, universities, and other institutions offering MBA programs. Schools appear in geographical sequence by U.S. state or territory or by country, and then alphabetically by school name. Specific degree information is detailed within the profile for each school. Refer to the page number in the table for the school's profile. If a school submitted incomplete data, one or more columns opposite the school name may be blank.

School	Page Number	Executive MBA	MBA/JD	MBA/MA	MBA/MSN	One-Year	Other	Management	Accounting/Finance	Arts Administration	Economics	Entrepreneurial	Health Care	Hotel Management	Human Resources	Information Systems/Technology	International Business	Manufacturing	Marketing	Operations Management	Org. Behavior/Development	Public Administration	Public Policy	Quality Management	Quantitative Analysis	Real Estate	Strategic Analysis	Transportation	Other	AACSB Accredited
ALABAMA																														
Alabama Agricultural and Mechanical University, Department of Business Administration	116							•	•			•				•	•		•										•	
Auburn University, College of Business	116							•	•			•				•	•		•	•	•		•					•	•	•
Auburn University at Montgomery, School of Business	117								•							•	•												•	•
Jacksonville State University, College of Commerce and Business Administration	118							•	•																				•	
Samford University, School of Business	119	•	•					•	•																					
Spring Hill College, Division of Business and Management	119								•																					
Troy State University, Sorrell College of Business	120					•			•																					
Troy State University at Dothan, School of Business	121	•						•	•							•	•													
Troy State University in Montgomery, School of Business	121							•	•							•	•								•					
University of Alabama, Manderson Graduate School of Business	122	•	•					•	•								•		•	•			•				•			•
University of Alabama at Birmingham, Graduate School of Management	123				•			•	•																					•
University of Alabama in Huntsville, College of Administrative Science	124								•																				•	
University of Mobile, School of Business	124								•																					
University of North Alabama, School of Business	125							•	•										•											
University of South Alabama, College of Business and Management Studies	126							•	•																					•
ALASKA																														
Alaska Pacific University, Management Department	127								•																				•	
University of Alaska Anchorage, School of Business	127								•										•											
University of Alaska Fairbanks, School of Management	128							•	•			•					•				•	•	•			•		•		•
University of Alaska Southeast, School of Business and Public Administration	129							•																						

MATRICULATION	ADMISSION REQUIREMENTS			FULL-TIME TUITION	PART-TIME TUITION				TIME OFFERED
Fall Winter Spring Summer Deferred	GMAT Score	Undergraduate GPA	TOEFL Score	(R) State Resident (NR) Non-Resident	(R) State Resident (NR) Non-Resident	Financial Aid	Minimum Months to Obtain Degree	Credit Hours Required	Day Evening Weekend Summer
F,SP			550	$103/semester hour (R) $206/semester hour (NR)		•	18	36	E,S
F,W,SP,SU,D			550	$700/quarter (R) $2,100/quarter (NR)	$58/credit hour (R) $174/credit hour (NR)	•	18	87	D,S
	400		500	$635/quarter (R) $1,905/quarter (NR)		•	12	50	D,E,S
			550	$895/semester (R) $1,343/semester (NR)	$90/hour (R) $135/hour (NR)	•	18	36	E,S
D			550	$858/course		•	12	36	E,S
F,SP,D			550		$255/credit hour	•	24	36	E,S
	450	2.5	525			•			
				$58/quarter hour (R) $104/quarter hour (NR)		•	18	60	E,S
D	450	2.5		$46/quarter hour (R) $92/quarter hour (NR)		•		96	E,W,S
F,D			580	$1,130/semester (R) $2,821/semester (NR)		•	20	49	D
F,W,SP,SU,D			550	$830/quarter (R) $1,660/quarter (NR)		•	24	30	E
D			500	$110-$132/credit hour (R) $220-$264/credit hour (NR)	$135-$166/credit hour (R) $269-$332/credit hour (NR)	•	12	33	E
F,SP	400	2.5	550	$250/hour		•	24	40	D,E,W,S
F,SP,D	450	2.5	500	$79/semester hour (R) $79/semester hour (NR)		•	12	33	D,E,W,S
F,W,SP,SU		3.0	525	$62/quarter hour (R) $62/quarter hour (NR)		•	12	48	E,S
F,SP,D		3.0	550	$315/semester hour			12	36	E,S
			550	$1,206/semester (R) $2,412/semester (NR)		•	18	36	E,W,S
D	400			$1,152/semester (R) $2,304/semester (NR)	$150/credit hour (R) $300/credit hour (NR)	•	9	30-57	E
		3.0						36	

This table includes the names and locations of colleges, universities, and other institutions offering MBA programs. Schools appear in geographical sequence by U.S. state or territory or by country, and then alphabetically by school name. Specific degree information is detailed within the profile for each school. Refer to the page number in the table for the school's profile. If a school submitted incomplete data, one or more columns opposite the school name may be blank.

	Page Number	Executive MBA	MBA/JD	MBA/MA	MBA/MSN	OneYear	Other	Management	Accounting/Finance	Arts Administration	Economics	Entrepreneurial	Health Care	Hotel Management	Human Resources	Information Systems/Technology	International Business	Manufacturing	Marketing	Operations Management	Org. Behavior/Development	Public Administration	Public Policy	Quality Management	Quantitative Analysis	Real Estate	Strategic Analysis	Transportation	Other	AACSB Accredited
ARIZONA																															
American Graduate School of International Management	129							•	•	•				•			•	•		•		•		•				•			
Arizona State University, College of Business	130	•						•	•	•		•	•	•	•		•		•		•						•		•	•	•
Arizona State University West, School of Management	131							•	•	•			•			•	•	•		•		•									
Grand Canyon University, College of Business	132							•	•		•		•			•			•									•		•	
Northern Arizona University, College of Business Administration	132							•								•													•	•
University of Arizona, Karl Eller Graduate School of Management	133	•						•	•	•	•	•	•		•	•	•	•	•	•	•	•	•				•	•	•	•
University of Phoenix	134							•		•										•					•	•	•			
Western International University	134							•	•						•	•	•		•				•							
ARKANSAS																															
Arkansas State University, College of Business	135							•																						•
Henderson State University, School of Business	136							•																						
University of Arkansas, College of Business Administration	136	•			•			•	•		•				•	•	•		•		•							•		•
University of Arkansas at Little Rock, College of Business Administration	137	•						•	•									•												•
University of Central Arkansas, College of Business Administration	138							•																						
CALIFORNIA																															
Armstrong University, Graduate School of Business Administration	138							•	•							•			•											
Azusa Pacific University, School of Business and Management	139							•								•		•		•		•						•		
California Institute of Integral Studies, School for Transformative Learning	139							•																					•	
California Lutheran University, School of Business	140							•	•		•	•		•	•		•		•											
California Polytechnic State University, San Luis Obispo, College of Business	141	•						•	•																				•	•

MATRICULATION (Fall, Winter, Spring, Summer, Deferred)	ADMISSION REQUIREMENTS			FULL-TIME TUITION (R) State Resident (NR) Non-Resident	PART-TIME TUITION (R) State Resident (NR) Non-Resident	Financial Aid	Minimum Months to Obtain Degree	Credit Hours Required	TIME OFFERED (Day, Evening, Weekend, Summer)
	GMAT Score	Undergraduate GPA	TOEFL Score						
F,SP,SU,D	500	3.0	500	$700-$9,200/term		•	12	42	
F,D		3.0	580	$1,828 (R) $7,434 (NR)		•	18	48	D,E,S
F,SP,SU,D			500	$914/semester (R) $3,717/semester (NR)		•	18	45	E,W,S
F,SP	500	3.0	550		$229/credit hour	•	24	36	E
F,SP	450	3.0		$76-$131/hour (R) $278/hour (NR)	$96/hour (R)	•	11	33	
F		3.0	600	$947/semester (R) $3,250/semester (NR)	$605/semester (R) $1,899/semester (NR)	•	21	60	D,E
		2.5	580	$198/credit hour				37	
		2.75	550		$6,600-$10,050/degree program	•	15	39	E,S
	400	2.5	550	$78-$80/hour (R) $142-$144/hour (NR)	$82-$91/hour (R) $146-$155/hour (NR)	•	12	33	D,E,S
F,SP	350	2.5							
F,SP,D	550	3.2	550			•			
F,SP,D	450	2.75	525	$1,176/semester (R) $2,544/semester (NR)	$110/hour (R) $236/hour (NR)	•	12	30	E,S
F,SP,SU	400	2.7	550	$109/hour (R) $202/hour (NR)		•	12	30	E
		2.5		$4,920	$205/unit		24	56	D,E,S
F	450	3.0	550	$355/unit			12	36	E,W,S
F,W		3.0	550	$8,500	$270/unit	•	24	72	D,E,W
D	400		550	$350/credit			30	42	E,W,S
F	530	3.0	550	$454-$676/quarter (R) $164/unit (NR)		•	24	96	D

This table includes the names and locations of colleges, universities, and other institutions offering MBA programs. Schools appear in geographical sequence by U.S. state or territory or by country, and then alphabetically by school name. Specific degree information is detailed within the profile for each school. Refer to the page number in the table for the school's profile. If a school submitted incomplete data, one or more columns opposite the school name may be blank.

School	Page Number	Executive MBA	MBA/JD	MBA/MA	MBA/MSN	One-Year	Other	Management	Accounting/Finance	Arts Administration	Economics	Entrepreneurial	Health Care	Hotel Management	Human Resources	Information Systems/Technology	International Business	Manufacturing	Marketing	Operations Management	Org. Behavior/Development	Public Administration	Public Policy	Quality Management	Quantitative Analysis	Real Estate	Strategic Analysis	Transportation	Other	AACSB Accredited
California State Polytechnic University, Pomona, College of Business Administration	141								•	•			•		•	•	•	•			•	•	•				•			
California State University, Bakersfield, School of Business and Public Administration	142								•																					•
California State University, Chico, College of Business	143									•							•		•	•	•									•
California State University, Dominguez Hills, School of Management	143	•							•								•													
California State University, Fresno, Sid Craig School of Business	144								•	•							•		•		•									•
California State University, Fullerton, School of Business Administration and Economics	145								•	•		•							•		•						•			•
California State University, Hayward, School of Business and Economics	146						•		•	•		•	•			•	•		•			•					•		•	•
California State University, Long Beach, College of Business Administration	146								•	•							•		•										•	•
California State University, Los Angeles, School of Business and Economics	147								•	•		•					•		•	•										
California State University, Northridge, School of Business Administration and Economics	148								•	•		•				•	•		•	•		•					•	•		
California State University, Sacramento, School of Business Administration	149									•							•										•			•
California State University, San Bernardino, School of Business and Public Administration	149								•	•						•	•		•	•			•							
California State University, Stanislaus, School of Business Administration	150								•	•							•			•	•									
Chapman University, School of Business and Economics	151								•	•		•	•			•	•		•		•	•					•		•	
Claremont Graduate School, The Peter F. Drucker Graduate Management Center	152	•							•	•					•	•	•		•						•				•	•
College of Notre Dame, Business Division	152									•						•	•		•		•		•							
Dominican College of San Rafael, Graduate Division	153																•													
Golden Gate University, School of Management	153	•	•						•	•	•				•	•	•	•	•		•	•								
Holy Names College, Department of Business	154								•	•										•										
Humboldt State University, School of Business and Economics	155								•																					
John F. Kennedy University, School of Management	155								•								•												•	

Matriculation (Fall, Winter, Spring, Summer, Deferred)	GMAT Score	Undergraduate GPA	TOEFL Score	Full-Time Tuition (R) State Resident (NR) Non-Resident	Part-Time Tuition (R) State Resident (NR) Non-Resident	Financial Aid	Minimum Months to Obtain Degree	Credit Hours Required	Time Offered (Day, Evening, Weekend, Summer)
	450	3.0	580	$1,440 (R) $164/unit (NR)	$834 (R) $164/unit (NR)		18	48	E,W
F,W,SP,SU,D	500	2.75	550	$480/quarter (R) $164/unit (NR)	$278/quarter (R) $164/unit (NR)	•	9	45	E,S
F,SP,D	500	2.75	550	$1,200/semester (R) $246/unit (NR)		•	15	30	E,W
F,SP	450	2.75	550	$898/semester (R) $246/unit (NR)		•	18	30	E,W,S
F,SP,D		2.75	550	$901/semester (R) $246/unit (NR)		•	16	33	E,S
D	450	2.5	570	$900/semester (R) $246/unit (NR)	$567/semester (R) $246/unit (NR)	•	30	31	E
F,W,SP,SU,D		2.75	550						
F,SP,D			550	$1,019/semester (R) $246/unit (NR)		•	24	33	E,S
F,W,SP,SU	400	2.5	550	$575/quarter (R) $164/unit (NR)		•	24	52	E,S
F,SP		3.0	550	$958/semester (R) $246/unit (NR)			24	30	E,S
F,SP	400	2.7	550	$930/semester (R) $246/unit (NR)		•	24	31	E,S
F,W,SP,D	400	2.5	550	$1,896 (R) $164/unit (NR)		•	18	48	D,E,S
F,SP	450	2.5	550	$851/semester (R) $246/unit (NR)			24	33	E,S
D	400	2.5	550	$400/credit		•	18	33	D,E,S
F,SP,D			550	$16,800	$755/unit	•	20	48	D,E
F,SP,SU		2.5	550		$1,140-$3,420		24	30-54	E,S
		3.0	600	$5,175/semester	$432/unit			51	
D			550	$348/unit		•	24	36	D,E,W,S
F,SP,D		2.8	550			•	12	33	W
F,SP,D		2.5	550	$1,678 (R) $246/unit (NR)			12	30	E,S
F,W,SP,SU,D		2.0	550	$237/unit		•	30	52	E,W,S

This table includes the names and locations of colleges, universities, and other institutions offering MBA programs. Schools appear in geographical sequence by U.S. state or territory or by country, and then alphabetically by school name. Specific degree information is detailed within the profile for each school. Refer to the page number in the table for the school's profile. If a school submitted incomplete data, one or more columns opposite the school name may be blank.

DEGREE OPTIONS / **AREAS OF CONCENTRATION**

School	Page Number	Executive MBA	MBA/JD	MBA/MA	MBA/MSN	One-Year	Other	Management	Accounting/Finance	Arts Administration	Economics	Entrepreneurial	Health Care	Hotel Management	Human Resources	Information Systems/Technology	International Business	Manufacturing	Marketing	Operations Management	Org. Behavior/Development	Public Administration	Public Policy	Quality Management	Quantitative Analysis	Real Estate	Strategic Analysis	Transportation	Other	AACSB Accredited
La Sierra University, School of Business and Management	156							•	•						•		•		•											
Lincoln University	157								•								•	•											•	
Loyola Marymount University, College of Business Administration	157	•						•	•						•		•		•	•	•	•				•				•
Monterey Institute of International Studies, Graduate School of International Management	158					•			•		•	•				•	•												•	
National University, School of Management and Technology	159							•	•							•	•							•						
Pepperdine University, School of Business and Management	160	•		•		•	•		•								•				•									
Saint Mary's College of California, School of Economics and Business Administration	161	•							•								•		•											
San Diego State University, College of Business Administration	161								•	•					•	•	•	•	•	•	•	•				•	•	•	•	•
San Francisco State University, College of Business	162								•	•					•	•	•		•	•	•					•	•			•
San Jose State University, College of Business	163	•															•												•	•
Santa Clara University, Thomas and Dorothy Leavey School of Business and Administration	163		•						•	•		•	•			•	•		•	•						•	•			•
Sonoma State University, School of Business and Economics	164								•																					
Stanford University, Stanford Graduate School of Business	165		•					•	•		•	•			•	•	•	•	•	•	•	•	•				•	•		•
United States International University, College of Business Administration	166							•	•								•		•		•						•			
University of California, Berkeley, Haas School of Business	167		•	•				•	•		•	•	•			•	•		•	•	•					•	•	•	•	•
University of California, Davis, Graduate School of Management	168			•				•	•		•						•				•									•
University of California, Irvine, Graduate School of Management	169	•							•		•					•	•		•		•				•	•	•	•		
University of California, Los Angeles, The John E. Anderson Graduate School of Management	169	•	•	•	•				•	•	•	•	•	•		•	•		•	•	•					•	•	•		•
University of California, Riverside, The A. Gary Anderson Graduate School of Management	170								•	•							•	•	•							•				
University of Judaism, David Leiber School of Graduate Studies	171																				•								•	
University of La Verne, School of Business and Economics	172							•	•	•						•	•					•	•							

MATRICULATION (Fall, Winter, Spring, Summer, Deferred)	ADMISSION REQUIREMENTS			FULL-TIME TUITION (R) State Resident (NR) Non-Resident	PART-TIME TUITION (R) State Resident (NR) Non-Resident	Financial Aid	Minimum Months to Obtain Degree	Credit Hours Required	TIME OFFERED (Day, Evening, Weekend, Summer)
	GMAT Score	Undergraduate GPA	TOEFL Score						
	500		550	$346/credit		•	12	48	E,S
F,SP,SU		2.7		$220/unit			24	36	D,E,S
D	400		600	$495/unit		•	11	30-60	E,S
F,SP,SU,D		3.0	550	$7,600/semester		•	21	64	D,W
D		2.5	550	$730/course		•	15	75	E
F,D			550	$9,100/trimester	$570/unit	•	12	48	D,E,W
D	500	3.0	550		$1,146/course	•		72	D,E,S
F,SP			570	$1,902 (R) $256/unit (NR)	$1,236 (R) $256/unit (NR)		12	30	D,E,S
F,W,SP,SU	470	2.7	550	$896/semester (R) $246/unit (NR)	$598/semester (R) $246/unit (NR)		12	54	D,E,S
F,SP	500	3.0	550		$657/semester (R) $2,133/semester (NR)	•	18	30	E,S
F,W,SP,SU,D			580	$1,071/course		•	15	45	E
		2.5	550	$1,045/semester (R) $346/unit (NR)	$712/semester (R) $346/unit (NR)		24	30	E
F,D				$7,063/quarter		•	18	100	D
F,W,SP,SU,D	350	2.75	550	$2,400/quarter		•	12	60	E,W,S
F		3.0	570	$6,662 (R) $7,700 (NR)		•	21	52	D,E
F,D			600	$2,206/quarter (R) $2,566/quarter (NR)		•	24	72	D,E
F		3.0	600	$6,807 (R) $7,699 (NR)		•	21	92	D,E,S
F		3.5	600	$6,486 (R) $14,185 (NR)		•	24	96	D
F,W,SP			550	$1,936/quarter (R) $2,566/quarter (NR)		•	18	92	D,E,S
F,SP		3.0	550	$10,560			20	52	E,S
F,SP		3.0	550	$305/semester hour		•	24	36	E,W,S

This table includes the names and locations of colleges, universities, and other institutions offering MBA programs. Schools appear in geographical sequence by U.S. state or territory or by country, and then alphabetically by school name. Specific degree information is detailed within the profile for each school. Refer to the page number in the table for the school's profile. If a school submitted incomplete data, one or more columns opposite the school name may be blank.

School	Page Number	Executive MBA	MBA/JD	MBA/MA	MBA/MSN	One-Year	Other	Management	Accounting/Finance	Arts Administration	Economics	Entrepreneurial	Health Care	Hotel Management	Human Resources	Information Systems/Technology	International Business	Manufacturing	Marketing	Operations Management	Org. Behavior/Development	Public Administration	Public Policy	Quality Management	Quantitative Analysis	Real Estate	Strategic Analysis	Transportation	Other	AACSB Accredited
University of Redlands	173														•		•													
University of San Diego, School of Business Administration	173		•			•	•	•	•				•				•	•	•										•		•
University of San Francisco, McLaren School of Business, Graduate School of Management	174	•	•					•	•								•				•									•	•
University of Southern California, Graduate School of Business Administration	175	•		•		•	•	•	•			•	•	•		•	•	•	•	•	•				•		•	•	•	•
University of the Pacific, School of Business and Public Administration	176					•	•	•	•				•																		•
West Coast University, College of Business and Management	177							•	•								•	•	•											•	
Woodbury University, School of Business and Management	177							•	•								•	•	•												
COLORADO																														
Colorado State University, College of Business	178							•	•								•		•	•	•									•	•
Regis University, School for Professional Studies	179								•								•	•		•	•										
University of Colorado at Boulder, Graduate School of Business Administration	179		•					•	•			•							•	•										•	•
University of Colorado at Colorado Springs, Graduate School of Business Administration	180							•	•								•	•	•	•										•	•
University of Colorado at Denver, Graduate School of Business Administration	181	•					•	•	•	•	•	•	•				•	•	•	•	•					•		•		•
University of Denver, Daniels College of Business	181	•	•					•	•		•	•			•				•							•	•			•
University of Southern Colorado, School of Business	182							•	•																					
CONNECTICUT																														
Central Connecticut State University, School of Business	183																	•												•
Fairfield University, School of Business	184								•								•		•											•
The Hartford Graduate Center, School of Management	185							•	•							•	•		•				•	•						
Quinnipiac College, School of Business	185							•	•				•						•										•	
Sacred Heart University, Faculty of Business Administration	185				•			•	•				•				•	•	•		•									

MATRICULATION: Fall / Winter / Spring / Summer / Deferred	GMAT Score	Undergraduate GPA	TOEFL Score	FULL-TIME TUITION (R) State Resident / (NR) Non-Resident	PART-TIME TUITION (R) State Resident / (NR) Non-Resident	Financial Aid	Minimum Months to Obtain Degree	Credit Hours Required	TIME OFFERED: Day / Evening / Weekend / Summer
F		3.0			$357/unit		24	45	E
F,SP,SU,D	500	2.75	600	$505/unit		•		30	D,E,S
F,SP,SU,D			600	$552/unit		•	21	48	D,E,W,S
F,D			600	$17,230	$11,258-$15,851	•	20	63	D,E,S
F,SP,SU,D	500	3.0	550	$510/credit	$510/credit	•	24	30-48	E,S
		2.5	450	$370/unit		•	12	39	E,W,S
F,W,SP,SU,D		2.0	550	$325/unit		•	24	48	D,E,W,S
F,SP,SU,D	480	3.0		$1,223/semester (R) $4,388/semester (NR)	$102/semester credit hour (R) $366/semester credit hour (NR)	•	10	33	D
				$275/credit hour			18	45	E
F	590	3.2		$1,745/semester (R) $6,507/semester (NR)	$582/course (R) $2,169/course (NR)	•	24	52	D
F,SP,SU,D			550	$1,328/semester (R) $4,403/semester (NR)	$111/credit hour (R) $361/credit hour (NR)		12	30-48	E,S
F,SP,SU,D	400		500	$1,254-$1,743/semester (R) $4,008-$5,567/semester (NR)		•	12	30	D,E,W,S
F,SP,D			550	$5,064/quarter			18	72	D,E,S
F,SP,SU,D		2.5	500	$79/semester hour (R) $323/semester hour (NR)		•	12	36	E,W,S
F,SP		2.7	550	$1,146/semester (R) $3,196/semester (NR)		•	30	33	E,S
F,SP,SU			550	$400/credit		•	24	45	E,W,S
					$425/credit hour			46	D,W,S
	400	2.5	600	$330/credit hour			18	36	D,E,W,S
F,SP		2.5	550	$420/credit	$320/credit	•	24	48	D,E,W,S

This table includes the names and locations of colleges, universities, and other institutions offering MBA programs. Schools appear in geographical sequence by U.S. state or territory or by country, and then alphabetically by school name. Specific degree information is detailed within the profile for each school. Refer to the page number in the table for the school's profile. If a school submitted incomplete data, one or more columns opposite the school name may be blank.

School	Page Number	Executive MBA	MBA/JD	MBA/MA	MBA/MSN	One-Year	Other	Management	Accounting/Finance	Arts Administration	Economics	Entrepreneurial	Health Care	Hotel Management	Human Resources	Information Systems/Technology	International Business	Manufacturing	Marketing	Operations Management	Org. Behavior/Development	Public Administration	Public Policy	Quality Management	Quantitative Analysis	Real Estate	Strategic Analysis	Transportation	Other	AACSB Accredited
University of Bridgeport, School of Business	186							•	•			•				•	•	•		•										•
University of Connecticut, School of Business Administration	187	•	•	•				•	•	•				•		•	•	•		•	•	•					•			•
University of Hartford, Barney School of Business and Public Administration	188							•	•						•	•	•				•	•	•							
University of New Haven, School of Business	189							•	•			•			•	•	•		•	•	•		•				•	•	•	
Western Connecticut State University, Ancell School of Business	189							•	•																					
Yale University, Yale School of Management	190							•																						•
DELAWARE																														
Delaware State University, School of Business and Economics	191							•																						
University of Delaware, College of Business and Economics	192	•		•				•	•		•						•		•	•								•	•	
Wilmington College, Division of Business	192							•																						
DISTRICT OF COLUMBIA																														
American University, Kogod College of Business Administration	193		•	•				•	•	•	•	•			•	•	•		•	•	•	•			•		•	•	•		•
Georgetown University, School of Business	194	•	•			•	•																							•
The George Washington University, School of Business and Public Management	195	•	•	•				•	•					•	•	•	•	•	•	•	•	•	•		•	•	•	•	•		•
Howard University, School of Business	196		•						•			•																		•
Southeastern University, Graduate School	196							•	•		•				•	•	•						•							
University of the District of Columbia, College of Professional Studies	197							•																						
FLORIDA																														
Barry University, Andreas School of Business	197	•			•			•	•	•		•		•		•	•				•									
Embry-Riddle Aeronautical University, Department of Aviation Business Administration	198					•																								
Florida Atlantic University, Graduate School of Business	199	•						•	•		•				•	•	•	•	•						•					•

MATRICULATION	ADMISSION REQUIREMENTS			FULL-TIME TUITION	PART-TIME TUITION	Financial Aid	Minimum Months to Obtain Degree	Credit Hours Required	TIME OFFERED
Fall / Winter / Spring / Summer / Deferred	GMAT Score	Undergraduate GPA	TOEFL Score	(R) State Resident / (NR) Non-Resident	(R) State Resident / (NR) Non-Resident				Day / Evening / Weekend / Summer
F,SP,D		2.5	575	$310/credit		•	12	30	E,W,S
F,D	500	3.0	550	$2,353/semester (R) $6,115/semester (NR)		•	16	57	D,E,S
F			550	$320/credit hour		•	12	48	D,E
D		3.0	500	$320/credit		•	18	57	E,S
F,SP	500	3.0		$145/credit hour (R)			48	57	E,W,S
D			600	$20,990		•	24	18	D
F,SP,SU,D		2.75	550	$120/credit hour (R) $242/credit hour (NR)		•	12	30	E
F,SP,D	500		585	$2,321/semester (R) $5,110/semester (NR)		•	12	36	E,S
			500		$660/course		24	36	E,S
F,SP,SU,D			550	$9,000/semester		•	17	54	D,E,S
F			600	$19,584		•	22	60	D
F,SP,D		3.0	550	$575/credit hour		•	18	33	D,E,S
F,SP,D			500	$8,705		•	21	39	E,S
		3.0	550	$228/credit hour		•	12	45	D,E,W,S
F,SP,SU		2.5		$312/credit (R) $624/credit (NR)			12	36	E,S
	450	2.8	550	$365/credit hour		•	15	36	E,W,S
F,SP	500	2.5	550			•			
F,SP,D	500	3.0	600	$112/credit hour (R) $365/credit hour (NR)		•	18	36	E,S

This table includes the names and locations of colleges, universities, and other institutions offering MBA programs. Schools appear in geographical sequence by U.S. state or territory or by country, and then alphabetically by school name. Specific degree information is detailed within the profile for each school. Refer to the page number in the table for the school's profile. If a school submitted incomplete data, one or more columns opposite the school name may be blank.

	Page Number	DEGREE OPTIONS						AREAS OF CONCENTRATION																							
		Executive MBA	MBA/JD	MBA/MA	MBA/MSN	One-Year	Other	Management	Accounting/Finance	Arts Administration	Economics	Entrepreneurial	Health Care	Hotel Management	Human Resources	Information Systems/Technology	International Business	Manufacturing	Marketing	Operations Management	Org. Behavior/Development	Public Administration	Public Policy	Quality Management	Quantitative Analysis	Real Estate	Strategic Analysis	Transportation	Other	AACSB Accredited
Florida Institute of Technology, School of Business	200								•						•		•												•	
Florida International University, Department of Management and International Business	200							•	•							•	•		•									•		•
Florida Southern College	201							•	•																					
Florida State University, College of Business	202	•				•		•																						•
Jacksonville University, College of Business	203	•						•	•								•		•										•	
Nova Southeastern University, School of Business and Entrepreneurship	203	•			•	•	•	•	•					•		•	•		•											
Orlando College, Division of Business Administration	204							•	•							•	•		•					•				•		
Palm Beach Atlantic College, Rinker School of Business	205							•																						
Rollins College, Roy E. Crummer Graduate School of Business	205	•						•	•								•		•	•	•									•
St. Thomas University, School of Business Administration	206							•	•					•		•	•	•	•		•		•			•		•	•	
Stetson University, School of Business Administration	207		•					•																						
Tampa College, Department of Business Administration	208							•							•		•													
University of Central Florida, College of Business Administration	208	•						•	•		•	•			•	•		•						•	•				•
University of Florida, College of Business Administration	209	•	•			•	•	•	•	•	•	•	•	•	•	•		•	•	•			•		•		•		•
University of Miami, School of Business Administration	210	•						•	•				•		•	•	•	•	•	•	•		•			•			
University of North Florida, College of Business Administration	211							•	•		•				•	•		•											•
University of Sarasota, College of Management and Business	212							•	•		•			•		•	•	•	•		•		•				•		
University of South Florida, College of Business Administration	212	•				•		•	•		•	•			•	•		•											•
The University of Tampa, College of Business	213			•				•	•						•		•	•		•								•	
University of West Florida, College of Business	214							•	•		•								•									•	

MATRICULATION (Fall, Winter, Spring, Summer, Deferred)	GMAT Score	Undergraduate GPA	TOEFL Score	FULL-TIME TUITION (R) State Resident (NR) Non-Resident	PART-TIME TUITION (R) State Resident (NR) Non-Resident	Financial Aid	Minimum Months to Obtain Degree	Credit Hours Required	TIME OFFERED (Day, Evening, Weekend, Summer)
F,SP,D		2.6	550	$515/credit hour				36	
	460	3.0	500	$108/credit hour (R) $361/credit hour (NR)		•	24	41	D,E,S
F,SP,SU	450	2.5	550	$260/credit hour			18	36	E,S
F,SP,SU,D	470	3.0	600	$112/hour (R) $365/hour (NR)		•	24	60	D,E,S
F,SP,SU	450		550	$335/semester hour		•	24	30	E,W,S
F,SP	450	2.5	550	$3,000-$3,500/quarter	$350/credit hour	•	12	41	D,W,S
F,W,SP,SU		2.75	550	$10,250/degree program		•	18	56	D,E,W,S
F,SP	450	3.0	500	$240/credit hour		•	24	39	E,S
F				$16,500	$27,000/degree program	•	20	53	D,E,S
F,SP,D		3.0	550	$330/credit		•	18	42	E,W,S
F,D		2.5	550	$275/credit hour		•	12	36	E,S
D	450	2.75	550	$56/credit		•	24	56	E,W,S
F,SP,SU	500	3.0	575	$109/hour (R) $362/hour (NR)		•	24	33	D,E,S
F,D	500	3.0	550	$105/hour (R) $358/hour (NR)		•	16	48	D
F,SP,D			550	$672/credit		•	12	36	D,E,S
F,SP,SU,D	500		500	$110/credit hour (R) $363/credit hour (NR)		•	18	39	E,W,S
D		2.8	470	$275/semester hour		•	18	45	E,W,S
F,SP,D	500	3.0	550	$114/credit hour (R) $367/credit hour (NR)		•	21	60	D,E,W,S
F,SP,D	450	2.75	550	$275/hour		•	16	39-58	E,S
F,SP,SU	450		500	$88/semester hour (R) $329/semester hour (NR)			12	36	D,E,S

This table includes the names and locations of colleges, universities, and other institutions offering MBA programs. Schools appear in geographical sequence by U.S. state or territory or by country, and then alphabetically by school name. Specific degree information is detailed within the profile for each school. Refer to the page number in the table for the school's profile. If a school submitted incomplete data, one or more columns opposite the school name may be blank.

School	Page Number	Executive MBA	MBA/JD	MBA/MA	MBA/MSN	One-Year	Other	Management	Accounting/Finance	Arts Administration	Economics	Entrepreneurial	Health Care	Hotel Management	Human Resources	Information Systems/Technology	International Business	Manufacturing	Marketing	Operations Management	Org. Behavior/Development	Public Administration	Public Policy	Quality Management	Quantitative Analysis	Real Estate	Strategic Analysis	Transportation	Other	AACSB Accredited
GEORGIA																															
Albany State College, School of Business	215								•	•										•										
Augusta College, School of Business Administration	215								•																					
Berry College, School of Business	216								•																					
Brenau University, Department of Business	217								•	•										•										
Clark Atlanta University, School of Business Administration	217									•							•													•
Columbus College, Abbott Turner School of Business	218								•																					
Emory University, Roberto C. Goizueta Business School	218	•	•				•	•	•	•			•			•	•	•	•	•	•					•	•		•	•
Georgia College, J. Whitney Bunting School of Business	219				•				•	•									•											
Georgia Institute of Technology, School of Management	220								•	•		•	•			•	•		•	•	•			•		•	•	•	•	•
Georgia Southern University, College of Business Administration	221								•	•	•								•											•
Georgia State University, College of Business Administration	222	•	•				•	•	•			•			•	•		•	•	•						•	•		•	•
Kennesaw State College, Michael J. Coles School of Business	223	•						•	•			•				•		•	•				•							
LaGrange College, Division of Business and Economics	224								•																					
Mercer University, Stetson School of Business and Economics	224	•	•					•	•			•			•			•		•										
Mercer University, Cecil B. Day Campus, Stetson School of Business and Economics	225	•						•	•			•			•	•		•				•								
Southern College of Technology, School of Management	226																												•	
University of Georgia, Terry College of Business	226		•			•		•	•		•	•			•	•	•	•	•	•			•		•	•	•	•	•	•
Valdosta State University, College of Business Administration	227								•																					•
West Georgia College, School of Business	228								•	•		•							•											•

MATRICULATION (Fall, Winter, Spring, Summer, Deferred)	ADMISSION REQUIREMENTS			FULL-TIME TUITION (R) State Resident (NR) Non-Resident	PART-TIME TUITION (R) State Resident (NR) Non-Resident	Financial Aid	Minimum Months to Obtain Degree	Credit Hours Required	TIME OFFERED (Day, Evening, Weekend, Summer)
	GMAT Score	Undergraduate GPA	TOEFL Score						
F,W,SP,SU		2.5	550	$532/quarter (R) $1,332/quarter (NR)	$200/course (R) $600/course (NR)		24	60	E
F,W,SP,SU,D	450		550	$40/quarter hour (R) $120/quarter hour (NR)		•	18	60	E,S
			550	$287/semester hour $287/semester hour (NR)			12	36	E,S
	325			$110/credit hour			15	50	E,W,S
F,D			600	$328/semester hour		•	21	60	D,S
F,W,SP,D			500	$551/quarter (R) $1,422/quarter (NR)	$40/hour (R) $120/hour (NR)	•	24	60	E,W
F,D			600	$18,850	$12,570	•	24	58	D,E,S
F,W,SP			500	$600/quarter		•	12	60	E,S
F,D			600	$781/quarter (R) $2,311/quarter (NR)		•	21	81	D
D		2.0		$370-$626/quarter (R) $1,010-$1,574/quarter (NR)	$185/quarter (R) $505/quarter (NR)	•	18	48	E
F,W,SP,SU			550	$42/quarter hour (R) $144/quarter hour (NR)		•	12	60	D,E,W,S
F,W,SP,SU	450	2.75	550	$474/quarter (R) $1,422/quarter (NR)		•	12	60	D,E,W,S
F,W,SP			500	$170/quarter hour		•	24	60	E
			550	$130/quarter hour			18	65	E,W,S
D	400	2.75	550	$825/course		•	18	65	E,W,S
F,SP						•	24	82	E,W,S
F,SU,D		2.6	585	$1,899 (R) $5,197 (NR)		•	21	99	D
F	450	3.0	550	$521/quarter (R) $1,321/quarter (NR)		•	18	60	E
F,SP,D	450	2.5	550	$474/quarter (R) $1,422/quarter (NR)	$40/quarter hour (R) $120/quarter hour (NR)	•	12	50	E,S

This table includes the names and locations of colleges, universities, and other institutions offering MBA programs. Schools appear in geographical sequence by U.S. state or territory or by country, and then alphabetically by school name. Specific degree information is detailed within the profile for each school. Refer to the page number in the table for the school's profile. If a school submitted incomplete data, one or more columns opposite the school name may be blank.

School	Page Number	Executive MBA	MBA/JD	MBA/MA	MBA/MSN	One-Year	Other	Management	Accounting/Finance	Arts Administration	Economics	Entrepreneurial	Health Care	Hotel Management	Human Resources	Information Systems/Technology	International Business	Manufacturing	Marketing	Operations Management	Org. Behavior/Development	Public Administration	Public Policy	Quality Management	Quantitative Analysis	Real Estate	Strategic Analysis	Transportation	Other	AACSB Accredited
HAWAII																														
Chaminade University of Honolulu, School of Business	229								•	•			•		•	•	•			•							•		•	
Hawaii Pacific University, Center for Graduate Studies	229						•		•	•					•	•	•			•									•	
University of Hawaii at Manoa, College of Business Administration	230								•	•					•	•	•								•		•			•
IDAHO																														
Boise State University, College of Business	231								•																					•
Idaho State University, College of Business	232								•	•																				•
ILLINOIS																														
Aurora University, School of Business and Professional Studies	233								•																					
Bradley University, Foster College of Business Administration	233								•	•		•							•	•	•									•
College of St. Francis	234								•																					
DePaul University, Kellstadt Graduate School of Business	235									•		•	•				•	•	•		•	•								•
Eastern Illinois University, Lumpkin College of Business and Applied Sciences	235								•																					
Governors State University, College of Business and Public Administration	236								•	•					•	•	•			•					•				•	
Illinois Benedictine College	237						•	•	•	•				•					•	•	•	•	•							
Illinois Institute of Technology, Stuart School of Business	238	•						•	•	•						•	•		•	•									•	
Illinois State University, College of Business, Graduate Programs and Research	239								•	•									•		•			•						•
Keller Graduate School of Management, School of General Management	239								•	•					•	•			•										•	
Lake Forest Graduate School of Management	240									•							•	•		•								•	•	
Lewis University, Graduate School of Management	240									•					•	•			•	•									•	
Loyola University Chicago, Graduate School of Business	241	•		•					•	•		•	•			•	•		•	•										•

MATRICULATION Fall Winter Spring Summer Deferred	ADMISSION REQUIREMENTS			FULL-TIME TUITION (R) State Resident (NR) Non-Resident	PART-TIME TUITION (R) State Resident (NR) Non-Resident	Financial Aid	Minimum Months to Obtain Degree	Credit Hours Required	TIME OFFERED Day Evening Weekend Summer
	GMAT Score	Undergraduate GPA	TOEFL Score						
F,W,SP,SU,D		3.0	550	$240/credit hour		•	12	36	E,W,S
D				$6,300		•	15	45	D,E,W,S
F,SP		2.7	500	$83/credit hour (R) $254/ credit hour (NR)		•	24	36	D,E,S
F,SP,SU	475	2.9	550	$1,155/semester (R) $3,248/ semester (NR)		•	30	33	F
F,SP,SU	440	2.75	550	$1,015/semester (R) $2,822/ semester (NR)		•	21	30	E,S
F,SP		2.75	550	$1,025/course		•	24	50	E,W,S
	500	2.5	525	$295/hour		•	12	36	E,W,S
F,SP,SU		2.75			$285/semester hour		36	36	E,W,S
F,W,SP,SU,D					$1,540/course	•	24	60	
F,SP,SU			550	$2,004 (R) $6,012 (NR)		•	12	33	E,S
F,SP,D			550	$1,038/trimester (R) $3,114/ trimester (NR)		•	12	33	D,E,W,S
	400	2.0	600	$245/credit hour		•	24	64	E,W
F,W,SP,D			500	$1,260/course		•	24	72	E,W,S
F,SP,D		2.75	600	$1,113-$1,459/semester (R) $2,690-$3,563/semester (NR)	$346-$693/semester (R) $872-$1,744/semester (NR)		15	39	D,E,W,S
								64	
					$1,400/course			16	
D				$348/hour		•	24	36	E,W,S
F,W,SP			550	$1,505/course		•	12	54	E

This table includes the names and locations of colleges, universities, and other institutions offering MBA programs. Schools appear in geographical sequence by U.S. state or territory or by country, and then alphabetically by school name. Specific degree information is detailed within the profile for each school. Refer to the page number in the table for the school's profile. If a school submitted incomplete data, one or more columns opposite the school name may be blank.

School	Page Number	Executive MBA	MBA/JD	MBA/MA	MBA/MSN	One-Year	Other	Management	Accounting/Finance	Arts Administration	Economics	Entrepreneurial	Health Care	Hotel Management	Human Resources	Information Systems/Technology	International Business	Manufacturing	Marketing	Operations Management	Org. Behavior/Development	Public Administration	Public Policy	Quality Management	Quantitative Analysis	Real Estate	Strategic Analysis	Transportation	Other	AACSB Accredited
North Central College, Department of Business Administration	241							•		•							•	•		•										•	
Northeastern Illinois University, College of Business and Management	242							•		•									•												
Northern Illinois University, College of Business	243							•																							•
Northwestern University, J. L. Kellogg Graduate School of Management	243							•	•	•	•	•	•	•	•	•	•	•	•	•	•						•	•	•	•	•
Olivet Nazarene University, Division of Business	244							•																							
Quincy University, Division of Business and Computer Science	245							•																							
Rockford College, Department of Economics, Business and Accounting	245									•																				•	
Roosevelt University, Walter E. Heller College of Business Administration	246							•	•	•		•			•	•			•		•		•				•				
Saint Xavier University, Graham School of Management	247					•	•	•		•						•	•		•											•	
Sangamon State University, Department of Business Administration	248									•						•				•	•	•	•		•		•				
Southern Illinois University at Carbondale, College of Business and Administration	249	•						•		•						•			•	•								•			•
Southern Illinois University at Edwardsville, School of Business	249							•	•	•	•		•			•	•	•	•	•							•				•
University of Chicago, Graduate School of Business	250	•	•	•				•		•		•					•		•	•	•						•				•
University of Illinois at Chicago, College of Business Administration	251		•	•		•	•	•		•	•	•	•			•	•		•		•							•		•	•
University of Illinois at Urbana-Champaign	252	•	•				•	•	•		•				•	•	•	•	•	•								•			•
Western Illinois University, College of Business and Technology	253							•		•			•		•		•	•		•							•				•
INDIANA																															
Ball State University, College of Business	254							•		•	•				•	•			•												•
Butler University, College of Business Administration	255							•																							
Indiana State University, School of Business	255							•		•	•				•	•	•		•	•							•			•	•
Indiana University Bloomington, Graduate School of Business	256							•			•				•	•	•		•	•											•

MATRICULATION (Fall, Winter, Spring, Summer, Deferred)	ADMISSION REQUIREMENTS			FULL-TIME TUITION (R) State Resident (NR) Non-Resident	PART-TIME TUITION (R) State Resident (NR) Non-Resident	Financial Aid	Minimum Months to Obtain Degree	Credit Hours Required	TIME OFFERED (Day, Evening, Weekend, Summer)
	GMAT Score	Undergraduate GPA	TOEFL Score						
F,W,SP,D		2.75		$1,189/course		•	18	16	E,W,S
F,SP,D	450	2.75	550	$1,002/semester (R) $3,006/semester (NR)	$84/credit hour (R) $251/credit hour (NR)	•	24	36	E,W,S
F,SP,SU	450	2.75	550		$113-$225/credit hour		12	30	E,S
F,D				$20,634-$27,200	$1,994/course	•	21	23	D,E,W
		2.5	550		$295/credit		24	35	E
			600		$915/course		24	30	E,S
F,SP			550	$6,200/semester	$320/credit hour	•	24	36	E,S
	460	2.7		$350/credit hour		•	9	36	E,W,S
D			550	$393/credit hour		•	12	36	E,W,S
	400	2.5	550	$80/semester hour (R) $240/semester hour (NR)		•	18	48	E,W,S
F,SP,SU,D	500	2.7	550	$77/semester hour (R) $232/semester hour (NR)		•	16	30	D,E,W,S
	400		550	$1,112-$1,368/semester (R) $2,267-$2,964/semester (NR)	$498-$824/semester (R) $812-$1,518/semester (NR)	•	18	33	E,W,S
F,D			550	$21,350		•	18	105	D,E,W,S
F,SP			570	$3,300 (R) $9,900 (NR)		•	24	54	D,E,S
F		3.0	550	$2,400/semester (R) $6,314/semester (NR)		•	22	20	D
F,SP,SU,D	450	2.5	550	$972/semester (R) $2,916/semester (NR)		•	12	33	D,E,S
F,SP,D	400	2.5	550	$1,504/semester (R) $3,764/semester (NR)		•	12	36	D,E,W,S
F,SP,SU			550		$185-$250/credit hour		36	39	E,W
D	470	2.7	550	$120/semester hour (R) $271/semester hour (NR)		•	24	36	E,S644864
F,D	580		580	$3,420/semester (R) $6,840/semester (NR)		•	20	54	D,E,S

This table includes the names and locations of colleges, universities, and other institutions offering MBA programs. Schools appear in geographical sequence by U.S. state or territory or by country, and then alphabetically by school name. Specific degree information is detailed within the profile for each school. Refer to the page number in the table for the school's profile. If a school submitted incomplete data, one or more columns opposite the school name may be blank.

	Page Number	**DEGREE OPTIONS**						**AREAS OF CONCENTRATION**																						
		Executive MBA	MBA/JD	MBA/MA	MBA/MSN	One-Year	Other	Management	Accounting/Finance	Arts Administration	Economics	Entrepreneurial	Health Care	Hotel Management	Human Resources	Information Systems/Technology	International Business	Manufacturing	Marketing	Operations Management	Org. Behavior/Development	Public Administration	Public Policy	Quality Management	Quantitative Analysis	Real Estate	Strategic Analysis	Transportation	Other	AACSB Accredited
Indiana University Kokomo, Division of Business and Economics	257							•	•				•				•		•		•	•	•			•		•			
Indiana University Northwest, Division of Business and Economics	258							•	•								•				•		•							•
Indiana University–Purdue University Fort Wayne, School of Business and Management Science	259							•																						•
Indiana University–Purdue University Indianapolis, Indiana University School of Business at Indianapolis	259	•						•																						
Indiana University South Bend, Division of Business and Economics	260							•																						•
Indiana Wesleyan University, Division of Adult and Professional Studies	261							•																						
Purdue University, Krannert Graduate School of Management	261	•						•	•		•						•		•	•	•				•		•		•	•
Saint Francis College, Department of Business Administration	262							•	•											•		•								
University of Indianapolis, School of Business	263	•						•																						
University of Notre Dame, College of Business Administration	263		•			•		•	•							•	•	•		•										•
University of Southern Indiana, School of Business	264																													
IOWA																														
Drake University, College of Business and Public Administration	265		•			•	•																							•
Iowa State University of Science and Technology, College of Business	265							•	•							•	•		•	•								•	•	
Maharishi International University, School of Management	266							•	•						•	•	•	•	•		•			•	•					
St. Ambrose University, College of Business	267								•							•	•		•											
University of Dubuque, School of Business	268							•																						
The University of Iowa, School of Management	268	•	•	•	•	•		•	•				•				•	•		•	•	•								•
University of Northern Iowa, College of Business Administration	269							•																						
KANSAS																														
Emporia State University, School of Business	270								•																					

MATRICULATION (Fall, Winter, Spring, Summer, Deferred)	ADMISSION REQUIREMENTS GMAT Score	Undergraduate GPA	TOEFL Score	FULL-TIME TUITION (R) State Resident (NR) Non-Resident	PART-TIME TUITION (R) State Resident (NR) Non-Resident	Financial Aid	Minimum Months to Obtain Degree	Credit Hours Required	TIME OFFERED (Day, Evening, Weekend, Summer)
F,SP,SU	480		550	$127/credit hour (R) $286/credit hour (NR)		•	12	36	E,S
F,SP,SU,D		2.0	550	$116/credit hour (R) $265/credit hour (NR)		•	24	42-54	E,S
F,SP,SU,D	430	2.5	550	$105/credit (R) $236/credit (NR)		•	36	33	E,W,S
F,SP,D			550		$200/credit hour (R) $400/credit hour (NR)		32	50	E,S
F,SP,SU,D	450	2.5	550	$121/credit hour (R) $290/credit hour (NR)		•	24	45	E,S
		2.5	550	$225/credit hour		•	26	41	E
F,D	550	3.0	575	$2,025/semester (R) $5,520/semester (NR)		•	20	60	D,W
D	400	2.5		$279/hour		•	24	33	E,W,S
F,SP,SU			550	$198/semester hour		•		42	E
F,SU			600	$17,400		•	24	62	D
	450	2.5	550	$106/credit hour (R) $212/credit hour (NR)			20	36	E,S
F,SP,D			550	$7,015/semester		•	16	36	E,W,S
F,D			570	$2,721 (R) $7,873 (NR)	$152/credit (R) $438/credit (NR)	•	24	48	D,W
	400		580	$375/credit		•	23	72	D
D	400		550	$325/credit hour			24	45	E,W,S
D	400		500	$310/semester hour		•	18	36	E,W,S
F,SP,D		2.5	600	$1,775/semester (R) $4,681/semester (NR)		•	21	60	D,E,S
F,SP,D	500		500	$1,328/semester (R) $3,296/semester (NR)		•	18	33	E
F			550	$1,009/semester (R) $2,561/semester (NR)	$86/credit hour (R) $215/credit hour (NR)	•	12	36	D,E,S

This table includes the names and locations of colleges, universities, and other institutions offering MBA programs. Schools appear in geographical sequence by U.S. state or territory or by country, and then alphabetically by school name. Specific degree information is detailed within the profile for each school. Refer to the page number in the table for the school's profile. If a school submitted incomplete data, one or more columns opposite the school name may be blank.

DEGREE OPTIONS

AREAS OF CONCENTRATION

School	Page Number	Executive MBA	MBA/JD	MBA/MA	MBA/MSN	One-Year	Other	Management	Accounting/Finance	Arts Administration	Economics	Entrepreneurial	Health Care	Hotel Management	Human Resources	Information Systems/Technology	International Business	Manufacturing	Marketing	Operations Management	Org. Behavior/Development	Public Administration	Public Policy	Quality Management	Quantitative Analysis	Real Estate	Strategic Analysis	Transportation	Other	AACSB Accredited
Fort Hays State University, College of Business	271							•	•												•									
Kansas State University, College of Business Administration	271							•	•								•				•								•	•
MidAmerica Nazarene College	272							•	•		•	•			•		•		•	•	•	•					•	•		
Pittsburg State University, Gladys A. Kelce School of Business	273							•	•																					
University of Kansas, School of Business	273	•				•		•	•								•		•	•	•	•						•		•
Washburn University of Topeka, School of Business	274								•																					
Wichita State University, W. Frank Barton School of Business	275							•	•		•	•					•	•	•		•			•		•	•			•
KENTUCKY																														
Bellarmine College, W. Fielding Rubel School of Business	276							•																						
Eastern Kentucky University, College of Business	276							•																						
Morehead State University, College of Business	277	•						•																						
Murray State University, College of Business and Public Affairs	278							•	•			•					•	•	•	•	•	•								•
Northern Kentucky University, College of Business	279							•	•								•				•									
University of Kentucky, College of Business and Economics	279		•					•	•						•		•	•	•	•	•							•	•	•
University of Louisville, College of Business and Public Administration	280		•					•																						•
LOUISIANA																														
Centenary College of Louisiana, Frost School of Business	281	•						•																						
Grambling State University, College of Business	282							•									•	•												
Louisiana State University and Agricultural and Mechanical College, College of Business Administration	282							•	•			•					•	•	•	•	•	•	•	•	•	•	•	•	•	•
Louisiana State University in Shreveport, College of Business Administration	283							•																						•
Louisiana Tech University, College of Administration and Business	284							•	•			•					•				•				•					•

MATRICULATION (Fall, Winter, Spring, Summer, Deferred)	GMAT Score	Undergraduate GPA	TOEFL Score	FULL-TIME TUITION (R) State Resident (NR) Non-Resident	PART-TIME TUITION (R) State Resident (NR) Non-Resident	Financial Aid	Minimum Months to Obtain Degree	Credit Hours Required	TIME OFFERED (Day, Evening, Weekend, Summer)
F,SP			550	$83/credit hour (R) $212/credit hour (NR)			18	30	D,E,S
F,SP,SU,D		3.0	590	$990/semester (R) $3,269/semester (NR)		•	24	51	D,E,S
F,SP		3.0	600	$2,684/semester			22	43	E,W,S
F,SP,SU,D			550	$1,021/semester (R) $2,573/semester (NR)	$86/credit hour (R) $215/credit hour (NR)	•	12	33	D,E,S
F,D			600	$111/credit hour (R) $300/credit hour (NR)		•	24	56	D,E,S
F,SP			550	$114/semester hour (R) $197/semester hour (NR)			12	30	E,S
F,SP,D		2.75	550	$1,174/semester (R) $3,442/semester (NR)		•	24	30	E,S
	500	3.0	500	$286/credit hour			24	36	E,W,S
F,SP,SU	350	2.5	550	$870/semester (R) $2,610/semester (NR)	$109/hour (R) $302/hour (NR)	•	15	33	E,W,S
F,SP	400	2.5	540	$1,850/semester (R) $5,170/semester (NR)	$103/credit hour (R) $287/credit hour (NR)	•	12	30	D,E,S
F,SP			510	$1,010/semester (R) $2,750/semester (NR)	$103/hour (R) $295/hour (NR)	•	12	30	D,E,S
F,SP,SU	450	2.3	550	$900/semester (R) $2,720/semester (NR)	$107/credit hour (R) $300/credit hour (NR)	•	24	39	E
F	500	2.5	550	$1,200/semester (R) $3,600/semester (NR)		•	15	36	D,E
F,SP,SU		2.75	550	$1,305/semester (R) $3,705/semester (NR)		•	18	36	E,S
			550		$600/course	•	18	45	E,S
F,SP,D	350	2.5	450	$919/semester (R) $1,894/semester (NR)		•	24	36	D,E
F	500	3.0	550	$1,314/semester (R) $2,964/semester (NR)	$495/semester (R) $1,195/semester (NR)	•	21	54	D,E,S
F,SP,D	400	2.75	550	$95/credit hour (R) $285/credit hour (NR)		•	18	33	E,S
F,W,SP,SU		2.25	550	$754/quarter (R) $1,319/quarter (NR)		•	12	33	D,E,S

This table includes the names and locations of colleges, universities, and other institutions offering MBA programs. Schools appear in geographical sequence by U.S. state or territory or by country, and then alphabetically by school name. Specific degree information is detailed within the profile for each school. Refer to the page number in the table for the school's profile. If a school submitted incomplete data, one or more columns opposite the school name may be blank.

School	Page Number	Executive MBA	MBA/JD	MBA/MA	MBA/MSN	One-Year	Other	Management	Accounting/Finance	Arts Administration	Economics	Entrepreneurial	Health Care	Hotel Management	Human Resources	Information Systems/Technology	International Business	Manufacturing	Marketing	Operations Management	Org. Behavior/Development	Public Administration	Public Policy	Quality Management	Quantitative Analysis	Real Estate	Strategic Analysis	Transportation	Other	AACSB Accredited
Loyola University, New Orleans, The Joseph A Butt, S.J. College of Business Administration	285																	•												•
McNeese State University, College of Business	285							•																						•
Nicholls State University, College of Business Administration	286							•		•		•																	•	•
Northeast Louisiana University, College of Business Administration	287																												•	•
Northwestern State University of Louisiana	287							•																						
Southeastern Louisiana University, College of Business	288							•		•		•	•								•	•						•		•
Tulane University, A. B. Freeman School of Business	288	•	•	•	•			•		•		•	•				•	•	•		•	•	•				•	•		•
University of New Orleans, College of Business Administration	289									•		•						•									•			•
University of Southwestern Louisiana, College of Business Administration	290							•																						
MAINE																														
Thomas College, Graduate School	290							•							•		•													
University of Maine, College of Business Administration	291							•																						•
University of Southern Maine, School of Business, Economics and Management	292							•																						
MARYLAND																														
Frostburg State University, School of Business	292							•																						
Hood College, Department of Economics and Management	293							•		•							•				•								•	
Loyola College, Joseph A. Sellinger, S. J. School of Business and Management	294	•						•		•	•		•				•	•			•								•	•
Morgan State University, School of Business and Management	294							•	•																					
Mount Saint Mary's College	296							•		•		•					•	•			•									
Salisbury State University, Franklin P. Perdue School of Business	296							•		•		•				•	•	•	•	•	•	•	•	•	•			•		
University of Baltimore, Robert G. Merrick School of Business	297		•		•			•				•	•			•		•											•	•

MATRICULATION	ADMISSION REQUIREMENTS			FULL-TIME TUITION	PART-TIME TUITION	Financial Aid	Minimum Months to Obtain Degree	Credit Hours Required	TIME OFFERED
Fall Winter Spring Summer Deferred	GMAT Score	Undergraduate GPA	TOEFL Score	(R) State Resident (NR) Non-Resident	(R) State Resident (NR) Non-Resident				Day Evening Weekend Summer
F,SP,SU,D			550	$424/credit hour		•	12	30	E,S
F,SP		2.5	525	$980/semester (R)	$530/semester (R)	•	24	33	E
		2.0	550	$993/semester (R) $2,289/semester (NR)		•	16	33	D,E,S
F,SP,D	400	2.5	600	$825/semester (R) $1,905/semester (NR)	$276-$736/semester (R) $276-$1,696/semester (NR)	•	12	33	D,E,S
F,SP			550					36	
F,SP,SU			500	$950/semester (R) $950/semester (NR)		•	18	33	D,E,W,S
F,D				$9,020-$18,040		•	21	63	D,E,S
F,SP,SU	400	2.5	550		$373-$928/semester (R) $903-$1,888/semester (NR)	•	12	33	D,E,S
		2.75	550						
					$140/credit		18	36	E,W
F,SP,SU,D	470		550	$1,368/semester (R) $3,861/semester (NR)		•	12	30	D,E,S
	500		550	$146/credit hour (R) $412/credit hour (NR)		•	24	45	E,S
F,SP		2.5	560		$146/credit hour (R) $161/credit hour (NR)	•	16	45	E,S
		2.5	530	$235/credit hour			12	36	E,W,S
F,SP,SU	500	3.0	550		$315/credit	•	12	30	D,E,W,S
F,SP				$125/credit hour (R) $190/credit hour (NR)		•	24	33	E,W,S
F,SP,D	400		500	$210/credit hour		•	24	37	E,S
F,SP,D		3.0	550	$123/credit hour (R) $152/credit hour (NR)		•	12	30	E
F,SP,SU,D	400		550	$179/credit hour (R) $210/credit hour (NR)		•	30	30	E,W,S

	DEGREE OPTIONS						AREAS OF CONCENTRATION																							
This table includes the names and locations of colleges, universities, and other institutions offering MBA programs. Schools appear in geographical sequence by U.S. state or territory or by country, and then alphabetically by school name. Specific degree information is detailed within the profile for each school. Refer to the page number in the table for the school's profile. If a school submitted incomplete data, one or more columns opposite the school name may be blank.	Page Number	Executive MBA	MBA/JD	MBA/MA	MBA/MSN	One-Year	Other	Management	Accounting/Finance	Arts Administration	Economics	Entrepreneurial	Health Care	Hotel Management	Human Resources	Information Systems/Technology	International Business	Manufacturing	Marketing	Operations Management	Org. Behavior/Development	Public Administration	Public Policy	Quality Management	Quantitative Analysis	Real Estate	Strategic Analysis	Transportation	Other	AACSB Accredited
University of Maryland College Park, The Maryland Business School	297							•	•				•		•	•	•		•	•					•		•		•	•
MASSACHUSETTS																														
American International College, School of Business Administration	298							•	•												•									
Anna Maria College	299							•						•																
Arthur D. Little Management Education Institute	300																												•	
Assumption College, Department of Business Studies	300							•	•												•									
Babson College, Babson Graduate School of Business	300					•			•			•						•		•									•
Bentley College, Graduate School of Business	301							•	•		•					•	•		•	•									•	•
Boston College, Wallace E. Carroll Graduate School of Management	302	•		•		•	•	•									•		•	•							•			•
Boston University, School of Management	303	•	•	•			•	•	•		•		•	•	•	•		•	•	•	•	•	•				•			•
Clark University, Graduate School of Management	304			•										•		•		•			•									•
Harvard University, Graduate School of Business	305	•						•																						•
Massachusetts Institute of Technology, Sloan School of Management	306			•		•	•		•		•		•	•	•		•	•							•	•		•	•	•
Nichols College	307							•	•								•		•	•										
Northeastern University, Graduate School of Business Administration	307	•						•											•											•
Salem State College, Graduate School	308			•				•																						
Simmons College, Graduate School of Management	309							•																						
Suffolk University, School of Management	310	•	•					•	•			•			•	•	•			•	•	•	•				•		•	
University of Massachusetts Amherst, School of Management	310							•	•										•	•	•									•
University of Massachusetts Boston, College of Management	311							•	•						•			•	•											
University of Massachusetts Dartmouth, College of Business and Industry	312							•																						

MATRICULATION — Fall, Winter, Spring, Summer, Deferred	ADMISSION REQUIREMENTS — GMAT Score	Undergraduate GPA	TOEFL Score	FULL-TIME TUITION — (R) State Resident (NR) Non-Resident	PART-TIME TUITION — (R) State Resident (NR) Non-Resident	Financial Aid	Minimum Months to Obtain Degree	Credit Hours Required	TIME OFFERED — Day, Evening, Weekend, Summer
F,D			580	$5,040-$6,300 (R) $8,760-$10,950 (NR)		•	19	54	D,E,S
D	475	2.6	500		$595/course	•	15	12	E,W,S
			550	$27,525			11	53.5	D,S
D				$267/credit hour	$001/course		30	36	E,S
F,SP,SU,D			580	$20,000	$1,810/course	•	21	62	D,E,S
F,SP,D			580	$1,650/course	$1,650/course	•	12	30	D,E,W,S
F,SP,D	500		600	$17,794	$612/credit hour	•	21	55	E,S
F,D			580	$18,420	$576/credit	•	24	64	D,E,S
F,SP			550	$1,600/course		•	18	57	D,E,S
				$21,000		•	18		D,S
F,D			580	$21,690		•	18	204	D
D			550		$770/course		30	30	E,S
D				$400/credit $400/credit (NR)		•	21	84	D,E,W,S
F,SP,D		2.5	500	$140/credit hour (R) $230/credit hour (NR)		•	24	54	E,W,S
D			550	$25,380	$564/credit	•	11	45	D,E,S
F,SP,SU,D	450	2.7	550	$14,124	$1,413/course		12	57	D,E,S
F,D		2.75	575	$2,780 (R) $8,570 (NR)		•	21	55	D,E,S
F		3.0	550		$116/credit hour (R) $357/credit hour (NR)		36	57	E
F,SP,D			500	$3,552 (R) $7,613 (NR)			24	39	E

This table includes the names and locations of colleges, universities, and other institutions offering MBA programs. Schools appear in geographical sequence by U.S. state or territory or by country, and then alphabetically by school name. Specific degree information is detailed within the profile for each school. Refer to the page number in the table for the school's profile. If a school submitted incomplete data, one or more columns opposite the school name may be blank.

School	Page Number	Executive MBA	MBA/JD	MBA/MA	MBA/MSN	One-Year	Other	Management	Accounting/Finance	Arts Administration	Economics	Entrepreneurial	Health Care	Hotel Management	Human Resources	Information Systems/Technology	International Business	Manufacturing	Marketing	Operations Management	Org. Behavior/Development	Public Administration	Public Policy	Quality Management	Quantitative Analysis	Real Estate	Strategic Analysis	Transportation	Other	AACSB Accredited
University of Massachusetts Lowell, College of Management	312								•																					•
Western New England College, School of Business	313	•							•	•					•				•		•									
Worcester Polytechnic Institute	314								•									•		•									•	
MICHIGAN																														
Andrews University, School of Business	315								•	•		•			•		•	•	•		•									
Aquinas College	316																•		•											
Central Michigan University, College of Business Administration	316								•																					•
Eastern Michigan University, College of Business	317								•	•							•	•	•		•	•					•		•	•
Grand Valley State University, F. E. Seidman School of Business	318								•	•											•									
Lake Superior State University, School of Business	318	•							•																					
Lawrence Technological University, College of Management	319																•				•						•			
Madonna University, School of Business	319						•											•			•									
Michigan State University, Eli Broad Graduate School of Management	320	•							•	•							•				•	•						•	•	•
Northwood University, Richard DeVos Graduate School of Management	321	•							•																					
Oakland University, School of Business Administration	321								•	•		•			•		•	•	•		•	•								•
University of Detroit Mercy, College of Business Administration	322		•						•	•	•	•	•			•	•	•		•	•			•			•			•
University of Michigan, Michigan Business School	323		•	•				•	•	•	•	•	•		•		•	•	•		•	•			•		•	•	•	•	•
University of Michigan–Dearborn, School of Management	324								•																					
University of Michigan–Flint, School of Management	325								•																					•
Wayne State University, School of Business Administration	325		•						•	•							•	•	•		•				•				•	•
Western Michigan University, Haworth College of Business	326								•	•		•									•								•	•

MATRICULATION — Fall, Winter, Spring, Summer, Deferred	ADMISSION REQUIREMENTS — GMAT Score	Undergraduate GPA	TOEFL Score	FULL-TIME TUITION — (R) State Resident (NR) Non-Resident	PART-TIME TUITION — (R) State Resident (NR) Non-Resident	Financial Aid	Minimum Months to Obtain Degree	Credit Hours Required	TIME OFFERED — Day, Evening, Weekend, Summer
F,SP,D			500	$1,130/semester (R) $1,695-$3,514/semester (NR)	$94/credit hour (R) $141-$293/credit hour (NR)	•	24	33	E,S
D					$286/credit hour		36	48	E,S
F,SP,D			550	$532/credit		•	24	45	E
D	400		550	$233/credit		•	12	48	E
		2.75		$281/credit hour		•	48	32	E,W,S
D	400	2.5	550		$122/credit hour (R) $243/credit hour (NR)	•	15	36	E,S
F,W,SP,D	450	2.5	500	$130/credit hour (R) $300/credit hour (NR)		•	12	33	E,W,S
F,SP,SU,D	450	2.8	550	$130/credit (R) $275/credit (NR)		•	12	33	E,S
F,SP,SU,D			550			•			
					$300/credit hour		36	36	E,W,S
		3.0			$220/semester hour		24	36	E,W,S
F,D				$226/credit (R) $517/credit (NR)		•	21	54	D
D		3.0	550						
F,SP	450	2.5	500	$188/credit hour (R) $395/credit hour (NR)		•	24	36	E,W,S
F,SP,SU,D	450	3.0		$408/credit hour		•	24	36	E,W,S
F			600	$14,100 (R) $20,800 (NR)		•	16	60	D,E,S
F,W,SP,D			560	$216/credit hour (R) $694/credit hour (NR)		•	24	60	E,S
F,SP			550		$269-$309/credit		36	48	E
F,W,SP	450	2.5	550	$142/credit hour (R) $307/credit hour (NR)			12	36	E,W,S
F,SP									

This table includes the names and locations of colleges, universities, and other institutions offering MBA programs. Schools appear in geographical sequence by U.S. state or territory or by country, and then alphabetically by school name. Specific degree information is detailed within the profile for each school. Refer to the page number in the table for the school's profile. If a school submitted incomplete data, one or more columns opposite the school name may be blank.

DEGREE OPTIONS · **AREAS OF CONCENTRATION**

School	Page Number	Executive MBA	MBA/JD	MBA/MA	MBA/MSN	One-Year	Other	Management	Accounting/Finance	Arts Administration	Economics	Entrepreneurial	Health Care	Hotel Management	Human Resources	Information Systems/Technology	International Business	Manufacturing	Marketing	Operations Management	Org. Behavior/Development	Public Administration	Public Policy	Quality Management	Quantitative Analysis	Real Estate	Strategic Analysis	Transportation	Other	AACSB Accredited
MINNESOTA																														
Mankato State University, College of Business	326							•																						
Moorhead State University, Department of Business Administration	327							•																						
St. Cloud State University, College of Business	328							•	•								•	•	•	•	•									•
University of Minnesota, Duluth, School of Business and Economics	329							•	•			•					•		•	•										
University of Minnesota, Twin Cities Campus, Carlson School of Management	329	•					•	•	•					•			•		•	•	•						•			•
University of St. Thomas, Graduate School of Business	330	•						•	•							•	•	•	•	•	•					•			•	
Winona State University, Department of Management and Marketing	331							•																						
MISSISSIPPI																														
Delta State University, School of Business	332	•						•	•												•									
Jackson State University, College of Commerce and Business Administration	332							•																						
Millsaps College, Else School of Management	333							•	•												•									•
Mississippi College, School of Business	334							•																						
Mississippi State University, Graduate Studies in Business	334							•	•		•						•				•					•				•
University of Mississippi, School of Business Administration	335							•	•		•						•	•	•	•	•					•	•		•	•
University of Southern Mississippi, College of Business Administration	336					•		•																						•
William Carey College, School of Business	337											•		•	•						•			•						
MISSOURI																														
Avila College, Department of Business and Economics	337							•	•						•	•	•	•	•	•										
Central Missouri State University, College of Business and Economics	338							•	•																					
Drury College, Breech School of Business Administration	339							•																						

MATRICULATION (Fall/Winter/Spring/Summer/Deferred)	GMAT Score	Undergraduate GPA	TOEFL Score	FULL-TIME TUITION (R) State Resident (NR) Non-Resident	PART-TIME TUITION (R) State Resident (NR) Non-Resident	Financial Aid	Minimum Months to Obtain Degree	Credit Hours Required	TIME OFFERED (Day/Evening/Weekend/Summer)
F,SP,D	450	2.75	550	$79/quarter hour (R) $119/quarter hour (NR)		•	12	52	D,E,S
			550	$69/credit (R) $110/credit (NR)		•	9	48	E
D	470	2.75	550	$77/credit (R) $110/credit (NR)		•	15	48	D,E
F,W,SP,D		2.5	550	$1,836/quarter (R)		•	24	39	E
F,W,D			580	$8,260 (R) $12,610 (NR)		•	10	90	D,E,S
F,SP,D	500	2.5	500	$996/course		•	24	36	D,E,W,S
F,W,SP		2.5	575	$72/credit (R) $103/credit (NR)		•	24	45	E,W
F,SP,D	400	2.75	550	$1,147/semester (R) $2,264/semester (NR)	$110/hour (R) $234/hour (NR)	•	24	36	D,E,S
		2.5		$1,115/semester	$124/hour		18	36	E
F,SP,D	450	2.5	560	$449/hour		•	12	30	D,E,S
F,SP,D	400	2.5	500	$615/course		•	30	30	E
F,SP,D	500	3.0	575	$111/credit hour (R) $216/credit hour (NR)	$142/credit hour (R)	•	12	30	D,E,S
F,SP,SU,D	450	3.0	550	$998/semester (R) $2,228/semester (NR)		•	12	36	D
F,D			550	$1,214/semester (R) $2,444/semester (NR)		•	24	61.5	E
			550	$160/hour			12	30	E,S
D	450	3.0	550	$9,000	$230/credit hour	•	24	30	E,S
D	400	2.5	550	$95/hour (R) $187/hour (NR)		•	24	33	D,E,S
F,SP	500	3.0	550	$205/semester hour		•	12	29	E,S

This table includes the names and locations of colleges, universities, and other institutions offering MBA programs. Schools appear in geographical sequence by U.S. state or territory or by country, and then alphabetically by school name. Specific degree information is detailed within the profile for each school. Refer to the page number in the table for the school's profile. If a school submitted incomplete data, one or more columns opposite the school name may be blank.

	Page Number	Executive MBA	MBA/JD	MBA/MA	MBA/MSN	One-Year	Other	Management	Accounting/Finance	Arts Administration	Economics	Entrepreneurial	Health Care	Hotel Management	Human Resources	Information Systems/Technology	International Business	Manufacturing	Marketing	Operations Management	Org. Behavior/Development	Public Administration	Public Policy	Quality Management	Quantitative Analysis	Real Estate	Strategic Analysis	Transportation	Other	AACSB Accredited
Fontbonne College	340															•	•		•	•	•						•		•	
Lincoln University, College of Business	340							•																						
Lindenwood College, Division of Management and Lindenwood College for Individualized Education	340							•	•	•		•	•		•	•	•		•								•	•		
Maryville University of Saint Louis, John E. Simon School of Business	341							•																						
Northwest Missouri State University, College of Business, Government, and Computer Science	341							•	•																					
Rockhurst College, School of Management	342	•						•	•						•				•											
Saint Louis University, School of Business and Administration	343		•		•		•	•	•		•				•	•	•		•							•				•
Southwest Missouri State University, College of Business Administration	344							•	•						•	•												•	•	
University of Missouri–Columbia, College of Business and Public Administration	345		•					•	•		•		•			•			•											
University of Missouri–Kansas City, Henry W. Bloch School of Business and Public Administration	345	•	•					•	•		•		•		•	•		•	•	•	•					•			•	•
University of Missouri–St. Louis, School of Business Administration	346		•					•	•		•			•		•	•		•	•	•		•			•		•		
Washington University, John M. Olin School of Business	347	•	•	•			•	•	•		•		•		•	•		•	•	•	•					•			•
Webster University, School of Business and Management	348							•	•					•		•		•								•		•	
William Woods University, College of Graduate and Adult Studies	349																												
MONTANA																														
The University of Montana–Missoula, School of Business Management	349	•			•		•																						•
NEBRASKA																														
Creighton University, College of Business Administration	350		•					•	•	•		•			•	•		•	•	•	•				•				•
University of Nebraska at Kearney, College of Business and Technology	351							•																					
University of Nebraska at Omaha, College of Business Administration	352							•																					
University of Nebraska–Lincoln, College of Business Administration	352							•				•	•	•	•		•	•	•							•		•

MATRICULATION (Fall, Winter, Spring, Summer, Deferred)	ADMISSION REQUIREMENTS			FULL-TIME TUITION (R) State Resident (NR) Non-Resident	PART-TIME TUITION (R) State Resident (NR) Non-Resident	Financial Aid	Minimum Months to Obtain Degree	Credit Hours Required	TIME OFFERED (Day, Evening, Weekend, Summer)
	GMAT Score	Undergraduate GPA	TOEFL Score						
		3.0	525	$270/semester hour			22	43	E,W,S
		2.5	500		$102/hour (R) $204/hour (NR)		24	36	E
F,SP		3.0	550	$215-$220/semester hour		•	18	36	
F,SP		3.6	550	$4,325	$275/credit				
F,SP,SU,D		2.5	550	$1,068/semester (R) $1,896/ semester (NR)	$89/credit hour (R) $158/ credit hour (NR)	•	12	33	D,E,S
F,SP,SU,D	450	2.75	550	$280/credit hour		•	48	36	E,W,S
D			550	$10,500		•	12	39	D,E,W,S
F,SP,SU,D	400	2.75	550	$89/credit hour (R) $178/ credit hour (NR)		•	18	33	D,E,S
F,SP,D	500	3.0	575	$128/credit hour (R) $373/ credit hour (NR)		•	15	39	D,S
F,SP,SU,D	500	2.75	550	$128/credit hour (R) $373/ credit hour (NR)		•	12	30	E,S
F,SP,SU,D	500	3.0	550	$1,534/semester (R) $4,476/ semester (NR)		•	24	39	E,S
F			550	$18,350	$555/credit	•	22	67	D,E,S
F,D			550	$220-$280/credit hour		•	24	48	E,W,S
		2.5	550	$240/credit			20	36	E,S
D		2.5	525			•			
F,SP,D	450	2.5	550	$332/credit hour		•	12	33	E,S
F,SP	450	2.75	550	$69/hour (R) $130/hour (NR)		•	24	36	E,S
F,SP,D	450	2.7	550	$78/credit hour (R) $188/ credit hour (NR)		•	12	36	E,S
F,SP	450	2.5	550	$91/hour (R) $224/hour (NR)		•	24	48	E

DEGREE OPTIONS | **AREAS OF CONCENTRATION**

This table includes the names and locations of colleges, universities, and other institutions offering MBA programs. Schools appear in geographical sequence by U.S. state or territory or by country, and then alphabetically by school name. Specific degree information is detailed within the profile for each school. Refer to the page number in the table for the school's profile. If a school submitted incomplete data, one or more columns opposite the school name may be blank.

School	Page	Exec. MBA	MBA/JD	MBA/MA	MBA/MSN	One-Year	Other	Management	Accounting/Finance	Arts Administration	Economics	Entrepreneurial	Health Care	Hotel Management	Human Resources	Information Systems/Technology	International Business	Manufacturing	Marketing	Operations Management	Org. Behavior/Development	Public Administration	Public Policy	Quality Management	Quantitative Analysis	Real Estate	Strategic Analysis	Transportation	Other	AACSB Accredited
Wayne State College, Division of Business	353								•	•																				
NEVADA																														
University of Nevada, Las Vegas, College of Business and Economics	354								•	•		•					•	•	•			•	•	•	•	•	•	•		•
University of Nevada, Reno, College of Business Administration	355								•	•	•	•	•		•		•				•								•	•
NEW HAMPSHIRE																														
Dartmouth College, Amos Tuck School of Business	355								•	•							•				•						•		•	•
New Hampshire College, Graduate School of Business	356							•	•	•					•	•	•	•			•									
Plymouth State College of the University System of New Hampshire, Business Department	357								•	•		•					•				•								•	
Rivier College, Graduate Business Department	358							•	•								•				•								•	
University of New Hampshire, The Whittemore School of Business and Economics	358	•								•						•	•				•	•	•							
NEW JERSEY																														
Fairleigh Dickinson University, Teaneck-Hackensack Campus, Samuel J. Silberman College of Business Administration	359	•							•	•		•			•	•	•	•	•		•					•				
Monmouth University, School of Business	360								•	•		•									•									
Montclair State University, School of Business Administration	361									•		•									•						•	•		
Rider University, College of Business Administration	361								•	•		•					•	•	•		•				•		•			•
Rowan College of New Jersey, School of Business Administration	362								•	•																			•	
Rutgers, The State University of New Jersey, Camden, School of Business	363								•	•					•		•	•	•		•									
Rutgers, The State University of New Jersey, Newark, Graduate School of Management	363	•	•						•	•	•	•		•		•	•	•	•		•					•	•	•	•	•
Saint Peter's College	364								•							•	•													
Seton Hall University, W. Paul Stillman School of Business	365							•	•	•		•					•		•								•			•
William Paterson College of New Jersey, School of Humanities, Management and Social Sciences	366								•	•											•									

MATRICULATION (Fall / Winter / Spring / Summer / Deferred)	GMAT Score	Undergraduate GPA	TOEFL Score	FULL-TIME TUITION (R) State Resident (NR) Non-Resident	PART-TIME TUITION (R) State Resident (NR) Non-Resident	Financial Aid	Minimum Months to Obtain Degree	Credit Hours Required	TIME OFFERED (Day / Evening / Weekend / Summer)
D				$188/course (R) $337/course (NR)		•	24	36	E,S
F,SP,D	450	2.75	550	$87/credit hour (R) $87/credit hour (NR)		•	24	30	D,E,S
F,SP	450	2.75	550		$81/credit hour (R) $81/credit hour (NR)		42	51	E,W,S
SP	500			$21,225		•	18	54	D,E
D		2.5	550	$13,436/degree program	$750/course	•	18	36	D,E,W,S
D		2.5	550	$595/course (R) $655/course (NR)		•	9	36	E,S
F,SP,SU,D			600	$762/course		•	24	36	D,E,W
F,D			550	$3,970 (R) $12,290 (NR)		•	21	60	D
F,SP,D				$423/credit		•	24	36	D,E,W,S
F,SP	450	3.0	525	$379/credit		•	18	30	E,S
F,SP	500	3.0		$164/credit hour (R) $204/credit hour (NR)			24	33	E,W,S
F,SP,SU				$1,044/course		•	12	57	E
		2.5	550	$1,752/semester (R) $2,772/semester (NR)	$146/semester hour (R) $231/semester hour (NR)		12	36	E,W,S
F,SP,D	500	2.5	550	$3,591/semester (R) $5,353/semester (NR)	$297/credit (R) $444/credit (NR)	•	24	42	E,S
F,SP,D		2.8	600	$3,592/term (R) $5,354/term (NR)	$297/credit (R) $444/credit (NR)	•	15	60	D,E,S
F,W,SP,D			500	$376/credit		•	36	48	E,S
F,SP,D	500		600	$431/credit		•	24	60	E,S
F,SP,D			550	$148/credit (R) $210/credit (NR)			24	42	E,S

This table includes the names and locations of colleges, universities, and other institutions offering MBA programs. Schools appear in geographical sequence by U.S. state or territory or by country, and then alphabetically by school name. Specific degree information is detailed within the profile for each school. Refer to the page number in the table for the school's profile. If a school submitted incomplete data, one or more columns opposite the school name may be blank.

	DEGREE OPTIONS						AREAS OF CONCENTRATION																						
Page Number	Executive MBA	MBA/JD	MBA/MA	MBA/MSN	One-Year	Other	Management	Accounting/Finance	Arts Administration	Economics	Entrepreneurial	Health Care	Hotel Management	Human Resources	Information Systems/Technology	International Business	Manufacturing	Marketing	Operations Management	Org. Behavior/Development	Public Administration	Public Policy	Quality Management	Quantitative Analysis	Real Estate	Strategic Analysis	Transportation	Other	AACSB Accredited
NEW MEXICO																													
College of Santa Fe, Business Department	367							•	•						•		•													
Eastern New Mexico University, College of Business	367								•																					
New Mexico Highlands University, School of Business	368							•	•																					
New Mexico State University, College of Business Administration and Economics	369							•	•		•	•	•		•	•	•		•	•								•		•
University of New Mexico, Robert O. Anderson Graduate School of Management	369	•	•	•				•							•	•	•		•	•			•						•	•
Western New Mexico University, Department of Business Administration	370							•																							
NEW YORK																														
Adelphi University, School of Management and Business	371							•	•						•		•		•										•	
Baruch College of the City University of New York, School of Business	372	•	•					•	•			•	•		•	•	•		•	•	•	•	•			•				•
Canisius College, Richard J. Wehle School of Business	372							•	•				•				•	•	•										•	•
Clarkson University, School of Business	373							•	•			•					•	•	•	•							•			•
College of Insurance	374								•																					
College of Saint Rose, School of Business	375		•			•		•	•		•	•			•												•			
Columbia University, Columbia Business School	375							•	•			•					•	•	•	•	•				•	•	•			•
Cornell University, Johnson Graduate School of Management	376		•	•	•	•	•	•																						•
Dowling College, School of Business	377	•						•	•																	•	•	•	•	
Fordham University, Graduate School of Business Administration	378		•				•																							•
Hofstra University, Frank G. Zarb School of Business	379		•					•	•							•	•		•											•
Iona College, Graduate School of Business	380							•	•		•	•			•		•		•							•	•		•	
Long Island University, Brooklyn Campus, School of Business, Public Administration and Information Science	381							•	•								•	•	•	•			•							

MATRICULATION (Fall, Winter, Spring, Summer, Deferred)	ADMISSION REQUIREMENTS			FULL-TIME TUITION	PART-TIME TUITION	Financial Aid	Minimum Months to Obtain Degree	Credit Hours Required	TIME OFFERED (Day, Evening, Weekend, Summer)
	GMAT Score	Undergraduate GPA	TOEFL Score	(R) State Resident / (NR) Non-Resident	(R) State Resident / (NR) Non-Resident				
	450	3.0	500	$204/credit hour		•	12	36	E,W,S
	450	3.0	550	$591/semester (R) $2,622/semester (NR)		•	15	33	D,E,S
		3.0		$696/semester (R) $2,600/semester (NR)	$58/semester hour (R) $58/semester hour (NR)		18	36	D,E,S
F,SP,D	500	3.0	550	$1,050/semester (R) $3,276/semester (NR)	$88/credit (R) $88-$273/credit (NR)	•	24	36	D,E,W,S
F,SP,SU,D	500		550	$86/credit hour (R) $305/credit hour (NR)		•	24	60	D,E,S
D			550	$787/semester (R) $2,714/semester (NR)	$312-$740/semester (R) $312-$2,506/semester (NR)	•	12	36	E,W,S
F,SP,SU	450	2.5	550	$6,750/semester	$400/credit	•	30	45	E,S
D	510		570	$1,675/semester (R) $2,925/semester (NR)	$145/credit (R) $250/credit (NR)	•	24	54	E,S
F,SP,SU	490	2.85	550	$400/credit hour		•	36	48	E,S
D	500	2.75	600	$17,200	$532/credit hour	•	9	32	D,E
F,SP,D	500	3.0	550	$427/credit		•	20	51	E,W,S
F,SP,SU		3.0		$292/semester hour			24	36	E,W,S
F,SP			610	$2,140/course		•	16	60	D,S
F,D			600	$20,400		•	21	60	D
	500	3.0		$380/credit		•	16	36	E,W,S
F,W,SP,D			600			•	12	60	D,E,W,S
F,SP,D			580	$382/credit	$382/credit	•	12	36	D,E,S
	425	3.0		$390/credit		•	18	61	E,W,S
	380			$382/credit		•	24	36	E,W

This table includes the names and locations of colleges, universities, and other institutions offering MBA programs. Schools appear in geographical sequence by U.S. state or territory or by country, and then alphabetically by school name. Specific degree information is detailed within the profile for each school. Refer to the page number in the table for the school's profile. If a school submitted incomplete data, one or more columns opposite the school name may be blank.

School	Page Number	Executive MBA	MBA/JD	MBA/MA	MBA/MSN	One-Year	Other	Management	Accounting/Finance	Arts Administration	Economics	Entrepreneurial	Health Care	Hotel Management	Human Resources	Information Systems/Technology	International Business	Manufacturing	Marketing	Operations Management	Org. Behavior/Development	Public Administration	Public Policy	Quality Management	Quantitative Analysis	Real Estate	Strategic Analysis	Transportation	Other	AACSB Accredited
Long Island University, C.W. Post Campus, College of Management	381							•	•	•							•	•		•											
Manhattan College, School of Business	382								•	•																				•	
Marist College, Division of Management Studies	383								•	•						•	•	•													
Mount Saint Mary College, Division of Business	383								•																						
New York Institute of Technology, School of Management	384								•	•						•	•	•		•							•			•	
New York University, Leonard N. Stern School of Business, Graduate Division	385	•	•	•					•	•	•	•		•	•	•	•		•		•	•		•	•	•	•	•		•
Niagara University, Graduate Division of Business Administration	386								•	•					•															
Pace University, Lubin School of Business	387	•	•						•	•		•			•	•	•	•		•						•		•		•
Rensselaer Polytechnic Institute, School of Management	388	•	•				•		•			•																	•	•
Rochester Institute of Technology, College of Business	389	•							•	•					•	•	•	•	•		•			•	•				•	•
Russell Sage College, Sage Graduate School	389					•			•	•											•									
St. Bonaventure University, School of Business	390	•							•	•								•		•										•
St. John Fisher College, Graduate School of Management	391								•	•						•	•	•												
St. John's University, College of Business Administration	392		•						•	•		•					•		•						•				•	•
St. Thomas Aquinas College, Business Administration Division	393								•	•										•										
State University of New York at Binghamton, School of Management	393								•	•						•	•	•		•	•									•
State University of New York at Buffalo, School of Management	394	•	•	•			•		•						•	•	•	•		•	•					•			•	•
State University of New York at Oswego, School of Business	395								•	•							•													
Syracuse University, School of Management	396	•	•			•			•	•								•	•	•						•				•
Union College, Graduate Management Institute	397		•						•	•					•					•						•	•			
University at Albany, State University of New York, School of Business	397									•						•			•										•	•

MATRICULATION (Fall, Winter, Spring, Summer, Deferred)	ADMISSION REQUIREMENTS GMAT Score	Undergraduate GPA	TOEFL Score	FULL-TIME TUITION (R) State Resident (NR) Non-Resident	PART-TIME TUITION (R) State Resident (NR) Non-Resident	Financial Aid	Minimum Months to Obtain Degree	Credit Hours Required	TIME OFFERED (Day, Evening, Weekend, Summer)
F,SP,D			500	$365/credit		•	18	36-60	D,E,W,S
F,SP,SU		3.0	550	$390/credit			18	39	E,W,S
F,SP,SU,D	450	2.7	550	$349/semester credit hour		•	16	30	E,W,S
		2.5		$286/credit hour		•	30	34	E,S
D	400	2.5	500	$320/credit		•	12	36-54	E,W,S
F			600	$19,500	$2,294	•	21	60	D,E,W,S
D			500	$337/credit hour		•	23	48	E,S
F,SP,SU,D	500		550	$425/credit		•	24	36	D,E,S
F,SP,D			550	$16,200		•	18	60	D,E,S
F,W,SP,SU,D	500	2.75	550	$15,384-$20,516	$1,725-$3,450/quarter	•	15	72	D,E,S
	500	2.75	560	$825/course		•	36	51	E,W,S
D	400	2.0	600	$1,020/course		•	12	30	E,S
F,SP,D			500	$13,050	$1,305/course	•	24	60	E,S
			500	$450/credit		•	15	39	E
		2.8					12	36	E,W,S
F,SP,D	500	3.0	550	$4,000 (R) $7,316 (NR)	$168/hour (R) $308/hour (NR)	•	24	32	D,E
F,D				$2,000/semester (R) $3,658/semester (NR)		•	16	60	D,E,S
D	350		550	$2,000/semester (R) $3,658/semester (NR)	$168/credit hour (R) $308/credit hour (NR)	•	12	36	D,E
F,D	550		580	$456/credit		•	21	39	D,E
F,W,SP,D		3.0	550	$10,620		•	18	60	D,E,S
F,D			580	$2,000/semester (R) $3,658/semester (NR)		•	24	47	D,E,S

This table includes the names and locations of colleges, universities, and other institutions offering MBA programs. Schools appear in geographical sequence by U.S. state or territory or by country, and then alphabetically by school name. Specific degree information is detailed within the profile for each school. Refer to the page number in the table for the school's profile. If a school submitted incomplete data, one or more columns opposite the school name may be blank.

School	Page Number	Executive MBA	MBA/JD	MBA/MA	MBA/MSN	One-Year	Other	Management	Accounting/Finance	Arts Administration	Economics	Entrepreneurial	Health Care	Hotel Management	Human Resources	Information Systems/Technology	International Business	Manufacturing	Marketing	Operations Management	Org. Behavior/Development	Public Administration	Public Policy	Quality Management	Quantitative Analysis	Real Estate	Strategic Analysis	Transportation	Other	AACSB Accredited
University of Rochester, William E. Simon Graduate School of Business Administration	398	•		•				•	•	•		•	•				•	•			•	•				•					•
Wagner College, Department of Economics and Business Administration	399	•						•	•										•		•									
NORTH CAROLINA																														
Appalachian State University, John A. Walker College of Business	400							•	•								•	•		•	•									•
Campbell University, Lundy-Fetterman School of Business	400		•					•	•																					
Duke University, Fuqua School of Business	401	•	•					•	•		•	•	•			•	•		•	•	•		•		•		•			•
East Carolina University, School of Business	402							•	•		•	•	•	•		•	•	•	•	•	•	•				•	•	•	•	•	•
Elon College, The Martha and Spencer Love School of Business	403								•																					
Fayetteville State University, School of Business and Economics	404							•	•										•		•									
Gardner-Webb University, School of Business	404							•	•		•	•				•	•	•	•		•	•	•			•				
Meredith College, John W. Weems Graduate School	405							•																						
North Carolina Central University, School of Business	406							•	•												•							•		
North Carolina State University, College of Management	407																•				•								•	
Pfeiffer College	408								•						•															
Queens College, Division of Business and Economics	408	•							•																					
University of North Carolina at Chapel Hill, The Kenan-Flagler Business School	408	•	•					•	•	•					•	•			•		•	•	•	•				•	•		•
University of North Carolina at Charlotte, Belk College of Business Administration	409							•	•		•								•										•	•	•
University of North Carolina at Greensboro, Joseph M. Bryan School of Business and Economics	410								•						•	•	•	•	•									•		•
University of North Carolina at Wilmington, Cameron School of Business Administration	411								•																					•
Wake Forest University, Babcock Graduate School of Management	412	•	•					•	•																					•
Western Carolina University, College of Business	412								•																					•

MATRICULATION (Fall, Winter, Spring, Summer, Deferred)	ADMISSION REQUIREMENTS			FULL-TIME TUITION (R) State Resident (NR) Non-Resident	PART-TIME TUITION (R) State Resident (NR) Non-Resident	Financial Aid	Minimum Months to Obtain Degree	Credit Hours Required	TIME OFFERED (Day, Evening, Weekend, Summer)
	GMAT Score	Undergraduate GPA	TOEFL Score						
F,SP,D				$19,080		•	18	67	D,E
F,SP,D	550	2.7	550	$455/hour		•	18	42	E
F	450	2.5	550	$382/semester (R) $3,624/semester (NR)	$203/semester (R) $1,013/semester (NR)	•	24	36	D,E,S
F,SP,SU	450	2.7			$150/semester hour		24	30	E
F,D				$20,800		•	20	85	D
F,SP,SU,D			550	$382/semester (R) $3,624/semester (NR)		•	20	60	D,E,S
F,SP,D	400	2.0	500	$195/hour		•	18	36	E,S
F,SP,D			550		$70/credit hour (R) $425/credit hour (NR)	•	12	36	E,W,S
F	450	2.5	500	$165/semester hour		•	24	36	E,S
F,SP,SU	350	2.5	500		$190/semester hour	•	24	36	E,S
F,SP				$1,338 (R) $7,821 (NR)		•	24	33	E
F,SP,D			550	$749/semester (R) $4,270/semester (NR)	$215-$535/semester (R) $1,095-$3,176/semester (NR)	•	18	45	D,E,S
F,D	450	2.7	550	$215/credit hour			24	36	E,S
	450	2.5	550		$230/credit hour		24	30	E,S
F			600	$874 (R) $8,400 (NR)		•	24	30	D
F,SP,D	450	2.5	550	$61-$81/hour (R) $331-$441/hour (NR)		•	30	42	D,S
F,SP,D			550	$859/semester (R) $4,379/semester (NR)		•	20	48	E
F,D	480			$746/semester (R) $3,779/semester (NR)			24	48	E,W,S
F,D	500	2.0	500	$17,000	$1,700/course	•	20	66	D,E,S
D	400		550	$382/semester (R) $3,624-$3,624/semester (NR)		•	16	36	D,E,S

This table includes the names and locations of colleges, universities, and other institutions offering MBA programs. Schools appear in geographical sequence by U.S. state or territory or by country, and then alphabetically by school name. Specific degree information is detailed within the profile for each school. Refer to the page number in the table for the school's profile. If a school submitted incomplete data, one or more columns opposite the school name may be blank.

DEGREE OPTIONS / AREAS OF CONCENTRATION

School	Page Number	Executive MBA	MBA/JD	MBA/MA	MBA/MSN	One-Year	Other	Management	Accounting/Finance	Arts Administration	Economics	Entrepreneurial	Health Care	Hotel Management	Human Resources	Information Systems/Technology	International Business	Manufacturing	Marketing	Operations Management	Org. Behavior/Development	Public Administration	Public Policy	Quality Management	Quantitative Analysis	Real Estate	Strategic Analysis	Transportation	Other	AACSB Accredited
Wingate College, School of Business and Economics	413							•																						
NORTH DAKOTA																														
North Dakota State University, College of Business Administration	414								•												•									
University of North Dakota, College of Business and Public Administration	415								•																					•
OHIO																														
Ashland University, School of Business Administration and Economics	416								•																					
Baldwin-Wallace College, Division of Business Administration	417	•				•											•													
Bowling Green State University, College of Business Administration	417	•							•	•										•	•								•	•
Capital University, Graduate School of Administration	418		•			•		•																						
Case Western Reserve University, Weatherhead School of Management	418	•	•			•	•	•		•			•	•	•		•	•	•	•	•	•				•	•		•	•
Cleveland State University, James J. Nance College of Business Administration	419		•			•	•	•	•		•				•		•	•	•		•	•	•			•	•	•		•
Franciscan University of Steubenville, Department of Business Administration	420							•	•																					
Franklin University, Graduate School of Business	421							•																						
John Carroll University, School of Business	422							•	•		•	•	•	•	•		•			•	•	•					•	•	•	•
Kent State University, Graduate School of Management	422	•		•	•		•		•							•	•	•		•									•	•
Lake Erie College, Department of Business Administration	423							•																					•	
Miami University, Richard T. Farmer School of Business Administration	424							•	•								•			•						•				•
Ohio State University, Max M. Fisher College of Business	425							•							•		•	•	•	•	•	•					•		•	•
Ohio University, College of Business Administration	426	•						•	•		•				•	•	•			•	•								•	•
Tiffin University	426							•																						
University of Akron, College of Business Administration	427		•					•	•										•		•									

Matriculation	GMAT Score	Undergraduate GPA	TOEFL Score	Full-Time Tuition (R) State Resident (NR) Non-Resident	Part-Time Tuition (R) State Resident (NR) Non-Resident	Financial Aid	Minimum Months to Obtain Degree	Credit Hours Required	Time Offered
F,SP,D			550		$200/credit hour	•	24	33	E,S
F,SP,D	420	2.6	550	$1,260/semester (R) $1,550-$3,197/semester (NR)	$105/credit hour (R) $129-$266/credit hour (NR)	•	12	30	D,E,S
F,SP,D	450	2.75	550	$1,319/semester (R) $1,609-$3,256/semester (NR)		•	12	32	E,S
F,SP,SU,D		2.75	550	$275/credit hour		•	24	36	E,W,S
D			500	$1,330/course	$266/quarter hour		24	60	E,W,S
F,SP		2.7	570	$2,257/semester (R) $4,759/semester (NR)			11	34	D,E,S
	450	2.7	550		$235/semester hour		30	40	E,W,S
F,SP,D	470	2.5	570	$8,808/semester	$2,202/course	•	21	60	D,E,S
F,W,SP,D	350	2.0	525	$1,457/quarter (R) $2,914/quarter (NR)		•	18	48	D,E,S
F,SP,D	460	2.5	550		$275/credit hour	•	15	40	E,W,S
F,W,SP,D		2.75	550		$240/hour	•	24	42	E,S
D			550		$475/credit hour	•	24	36	E,W,S
F,D		2.75	550	$2,091/semester (R) $4,055/semester (NR)	$190/hour (R) $369/hour (NR)	•	12	39	D,E,S
D			590	$352/semester hour		•	24	36	E,S
F,D	475	2.75	550	$2,412/semester (R) $4,970/semester (NR)	$165/credit (R) $378/credit (NR)	•	22	76	D,E,S
F			600	$1,614/quarter (R) $4,000/quarter (NR)	$1,316/quarter (R) $3,225-$4,000/quarter (NR)	•	21	104	D,E,S
F	500	3.0	600	$1,430/quarter (R) $2,789/quarter (NR)	$178/hour (R) $347/hour (NR)	•	13	72	E,W,S
F,SP,D			550	$1,000/course		•	24	36	E,W,S
F,SP,SU	450		550	$145/credit (R) $271/credit (NR)		•	16	34	E,S

This table includes the names and locations of colleges, universities, and other institutions offering MBA programs. Schools appear in geographical sequence by U.S. state or territory or by country, and then alphabetically by school name. Specific degree information is detailed within the profile for each school. Refer to the page number in the table for the school's profile. If a school submitted incomplete data, one or more columns opposite the school name may be blank.

School	Page Number	Executive MBA	MBA/JD	MBA/MA	MBA/MSN	One-Year	Other	Management	Accounting/Finance	Arts Administration	Economics	Entrepreneurial	Health Care	Hotel Management	Human Resources	Information Systems/Technology	International Business	Manufacturing	Marketing	Operations Management	Org. Behavior/Development	Public Administration	Public Policy	Quality Management	Quantitative Analysis	Real Estate	Strategic Analysis	Transportation	Other	AACSB Accredited
University of Cincinnati, College of Business Administration	428		•	•				•	•	•							•	•		•	•					•	•		•	•
University of Dayton, School of Business Administration	429							•									•												•	•
University of Toledo, College of Business Administration	430	•	•					•	•								•		•											•
Walsh University, Graduate Studies	431							•																						
Wright State University, College of Business and Administration	431							•			•	•				•	•		•	•									•	•
Xavier University, College of Business Administration	432	•						•	•		•				•	•	•		•										•	
Youngstown State University, Williamson College of Business Administration	433	•						•	•										•											
OKLAHOMA																														
Cameron University, School of Business	434							•																						
Northeastern State University, College of Business and Industry	434							•																						
Oklahoma City University, Meinders School of Business	435	•						•	•		•				•	•		•												
Oklahoma State University, College of Business Administration	435		•	•	•		•			•	•	•			•	•	•	•									•	•
Oral Roberts University, School of Business	436							•	•						•	•		•												
Phillips University, School of Business	437							•																						
Southern Nazarene University, MSM Department	438							•																						
Southwestern Oklahoma State University, School of Business	438							•	•		•							•												
University of Central Oklahoma, College of Business Administration	439							•	•		•				•	•		•									•			
University of Oklahoma, College of Business Administration	440		•	•		•	•	•		•		•		•	•	•	•		•	•	•								•
University of Tulsa, College of Business Administration	440							•	•																					•
OREGON																														
George Fox College, Department of Business and Economics	441							•																						

MATRICULATION	ADMISSION REQUIREMENTS			FULL-TIME TUITION	PART-TIME TUITION	Minimum Months to Obtain Degree		TIME OFFERED
Fall Winter Spring Summer Deferred	GMAT Score	Undergraduate GPA	TOEFL Score	(R) State Resident (NR) Non-Resident	(R) State Resident (NR) Non-Resident	Financial Aid	Credit Hours Required	Day Evening Weekend Summer
SU,D	550	3.0	600	$7,500 (R) $15,400 (NR)		•	12	66	E,W
F,SP,SU,D	400		550	$329/semester hour		•	12	33	D,E,W,S
F,W,SP,SU,D	450	2.7	550	$1,362/quarter (R) $1,362/quarter (NR)		•	12	48	D,E,S
		2.6		$289/semester hour			20	42	E,S
D			550	$1,363/quarter hour (R) $2,441/quarter hour (NR)		•	12	48	D,E,S
			550	$325/credit hour		•	24	33	E,W,S
F,W,SP,D	450	2.7	525	$72/credit (R) $1,536-$1,992/quarter (NR)		•	12	54	E,S
F,SP			550	$68/credit (R) $156/credit (NR)		•	18	33	D,E,S
F,SP,SU	430	2.5	550	$63/hour (R) $153/hour (NR)			12	32	E,S
		2.5	550	$270/credit			24	36-39	D,E
F,SP,D			550	$78/credit (R) $227/credit (NR)		•	21	45	D,E,S
F,SP,D	400	3.0	600	$215/hour		•	18	39.5	D,E,S
F,SP	500	2.75	550	$237/credit hour (NR)	$97/credit hour	•	24	36	E,S
D		2.5	550			•	15	32	E
		2.5	500	$47-$60/credit hour (R) $123-$148/credit hour (NR)			12	33	D,E,S
F,SP,SU,D	375	2.75	550	$54/semester hour (R) $54/semester hour (NR)		•	15	36	D,E,S
F,SP,D			550	$76/credit hour (R) $225/credit hour (NR)			24	55	D,E,S
D			575	$440/credit hour		•	12	30	D,E,S
F,D		3.0	550	$17,900/degree program		•	24	39	E,W,S

This table includes the names and locations of colleges, universities, and other institutions offering MBA programs. Schools appear in geographical sequence by U.S. state or territory or by country, and then alphabetically by school name. Specific degree information is detailed within the profile for each school. Refer to the page number in the table for the school's profile. If a school submitted incomplete data, one or more columns opposite the school name may be blank.

School	Page Number	Executive MBA	MBA/JD	MBA/MA	MBA/MSN	One-Year	Other	Management	Accounting/Finance	Arts Administration	Economics	Entrepreneurial	Health Care	Hotel Management	Human Resources	Information Systems/Technology	International Business	Manufacturing	Operations Management	Marketing	Org. Behavior/Development	Public Administration	Public Policy	Quality Management	Quantitative Analysis	Real Estate	Strategic Analysis	Transportation	Other	AACSB Accredited
Marylhurst College, Department of Business and Management	442									•						•	•				•		•								
Oregon State University, College of Business	443							•																							•
Portland State University, School of Business Administration	443							•	•				•			•	•	•			•		•						•		•
Southern Oregon State College, School of Business	444					•		•	•					•	•					•	•										
University of Oregon, Charles H. Lundquist College of Business	445	•	•	•		•		•	•		•				•		•		•		•	•	•				•		•		•
University of Portland, School of Business Administration	446							•																							•
Willamette University, George H. Atkinson Graduate School of Management	446					•	•	•							•		•			•			•						•		

PENNSYLVANIA

School	Page Number	Executive MBA	MBA/JD	MBA/MA	MBA/MSN	One-Year	Other	Management	Accounting/Finance	Arts Administration	Economics	Entrepreneurial	Health Care	Hotel Management	Human Resources	Information Systems/Technology	International Business	Manufacturing	Operations Management	Marketing	Org. Behavior/Development	Public Administration	Public Policy	Quality Management	Quantitative Analysis	Real Estate	Strategic Analysis	Transportation	Other	AACSB Accredited
Allentown College of St. Francis de Sales, Graduate Division	447							•	•				•									•									
Bloomsburg University of Pennsylvania, College of Business	448							•																							
Bucknell University, Department of Management	448							•																							
California University of Pennsylvania	449							•																							
Carnegie Mellon University, Graduate School of Industrial Administration	449							•	•		•	•				•	•	•		•	•	•				•		•			•
Clarion University of Pennsylvania, College of Business Administration	450							•	•		•								•	•	•					•					
Drexel University, College of Business and Administration	451							•	•		•				•	•		•	•	•	•				•				•	•
Duquesne University, Graduate School of Business	452		•		•		•	•	•		•				•	•	•		•						•				•	•
Eastern College	453							•	•		•	•			•		•		•		•		•		•		•	•	•	
Gannon University, Dahlkemper School of Business	453			•				•	•		•	•			•			•	•	•	•	•		•			•			
Indiana University of Pennsylvania, College of Business	454	•						•	•						•	•														
Kutztown University of Pennsylvania, College of Business	455							•																							
La Salle University, School of Business Administration	455							•	•						•	•	•			•										

MATRICULATION (Fall, Winter, Spring, Summer, Deferred)	ADMISSION REQUIREMENTS			FULL-TIME TUITION (R) State Resident (NR) Non-Resident	PART-TIME TUITION (R) State Resident (NR) Non-Resident	Financial Aid	Minimum Months to Obtain Degree	Credit Hours Required	TIME OFFERED (Day, Evening, Weekend, Summer)
	GMAT Score	Undergraduate GPA	TOEFL Score						
F,SP,D		3.0	550	$212/credit hour $212/credit hour (NR)		•	24	60	E,W
F	500	3.0	600	$1,575/quarter (R) $2,530/quarter (NR)		•	12	59	D,E,W,S
F,W	450	2.75	550	$1,389/quarter (R) $2,344/quarter (NR)	$1,224/quarter (R) $2,088/quarter (NR)	•	18	60	D,E,S
D	450		540			•			
F,D	550	3.0	600	$1,645/quarter (R) $2,620/quarter (NR)	$1,150/quarter (R) $1,804/quarter (NR)	•	18	73	D
F,SP,D	450	2.75	570	$405/credit hour		•	12	30-51	F,S
F,D		2.0	550	$440/credit		•	18	63	D,E,S
		3.0		$350/credit hour			24	36	E,W,S
	450	2.5	550	$1,477/semester (R) $2,598/semester (NR)	$164/semester hour (R) $289/semester hour (NR)			36	
F,SP		2.8							
			550	$171/credit hour (R) $308/credit hour (NR)			24	39	D,E,S
F,D				$15,480-$20,500		•	15	68	D,E
F,SP,D		2.75	550	$1,477/semester (R) $2,598/semester (NR)		•	24	33	E,S
F,D	500	3.0		$414/credit			12	48	D,E,W,S
F,SP,D		2.5	550	$391/credit		•	24	56	E,W,S
D	450	2.5		$340/credit		•	24	33	D,E,S
F,SP	450	2.5		$350/credit		•	12	30	E,W,S
F,SP,D		2.75	520	$1,543/semester (R) $2,772/semester (NR)		•	12	33	D,E,S
F,SP									
F,SP,D			550		$407/credit	•	24	36	E,W,S

This table includes the names and locations of colleges, universities, and other institutions offering MBA programs. Schools appear in geographical sequence by U.S. state or territory or by country, and then alphabetically by school name. Specific degree information is detailed within the profile for each school. Refer to the page number in the table for the school's profile. If a school submitted incomplete data, one or more columns opposite the school name may be blank.

	Page Number	DEGREE OPTIONS						AREAS OF CONCENTRATION																						
		Executive MBA	MBA/JD	MBA/MA	MBA/MSN	One-Year	Other	Management	Accounting/Finance	Arts Administration	Economics	Entrepreneurial	Health Care	Hotel Management	Human Resources	Information Systems/Technology	International Business	Manufacturing	Marketing	Operations Management	Org. Behavior/Development	Public Administration	Public Policy	Quality Management	Quantitative Analysis	Real Estate	Strategic Analysis	Transportation	Other	AACSB Accredited
Lehigh University, College of Business and Economics	456							•																						•
Marywood College, Business and Managerial Science Department	457								•						•				•	•									•	
Moravian College	458								•																					
Pennsylvania State University at Erie, The Behrend College, School of Business	458								•	•		•	•				•	•	•								•	•		
Pennsylvania State University at Harrisburg—The Capital College, School of Business Administration	459								•	•		•					•	•	•		•	•	•					•		
Pennsylvania State University University Park Campus, The Smeal College of Business Administration	460								•	•			•		•	•	•		•	•	•	•				•	•	•	•	•
Philadelphia College of Textiles and Science, School of Business Administration	460							•	•	•					•				•		•								•	
Point Park College, Department of Business, Accounting, and Computer Sciences	461														•															
Robert Morris College, School of Graduate Studies	462								•	•						•			•										•	
Saint Francis College	463									•						•													•	
Saint Joseph's University, College of Business and Administration	463								•	•					•	•	•		•											
Temple University, School of Business and Management	464	•	•						•	•		•			•	•	•		•	•						•	•	•		•	•
University of Pennsylvania, The Wharton School	465		•						•	•	•	•			•	•	•		•	•	•	•	•			•	•	•	•	•
University of Pittsburgh, Joseph M. Katz, Graduate School of Business	466	•	•	•	•				•	•			•		•	•	•		•	•						•		•		•
University of Scranton, The Graduate School	467									•									•	•										
Villanova University, College of Commerce and Finance	468							•																						•
Waynesburg College	468								•	•		•			•	•	•		•	•	•							•	•	
West Chester University of Pennsylvania, School of Business and Public Affairs	469	•							•	•		•																		
Widener University, School of Management	470		•					•	•	•		•			•	•	•		•	•	•									
Wilkes University, School of Business, Society, and Public Policy	471								•	•					•	•	•		•	•						•	•			
York College of Pennsylvania, Department of Business Administration	471								•	•					•	•			•											

MATRICULATION (Fall, Winter, Spring, Summer, Deferred)	ADMISSION REQUIREMENTS			FULL-TIME TUITION (R) State Resident (NR) Non-Resident	PART-TIME TUITION (R) State Resident (NR) Non-Resident	Financial Aid	Minimum Months to Obtain Degree	Credit Hours Required	TIME OFFERED (Day, Evening, Weekend, Summer)
	GMAT Score	Undergraduate GPA	TOEFL Score						
F,SP,SU,D			580	$525/credit hour		•	12	30-48	E,S
D			500	$6,300		•	24	36	E,W,S
D			480		$1,100/course		24	30	E,S
F,SP,D			550	$267/credit (R) $515/credit (NR)		•	15	48	E,W,S
F,SP,SU,D			550	$267/credit (R) $515/credit (NR)		•	18	48	E,S
F,D	500	2.2	550	$2,777/semester (R) $5,663/semester (NR)	$234/credit (R) $473/credit (NR)	•	18	48	D
D			550	$359/credit hour		•	24	37	E
F,SP,SU,D		2.75	500	$313/credit		•	16	39	E,W,S
	450	2.5	550	$270/credit		•	24	36	E,W,S
F,SP,D		2.5	550	$345/credit		•	18	36-60	E,W
F,SP,SU,D	450	2.8	550	$6,930	$385/credit	•	18	33	E,W,S
F,SP,SU,D			575	$258/credit (R) $366/credit (NR)		•	12	36	D,E,S
F				$19,604		•	18	20	D
D			600	$13,476 (R) $22,734 (NR)		•	11	52.5	D,E,W,S
D			500	$375/credit		•	18	36	E,S
F,SP,D			600	$410/credit		•		60	E,S
D				$270/credit		•	12	36	E,S
D	450	2.75	575	$1,543/semester (R) $2,772/semester (NR)	$171/credit (R) $308/credit (NR)	•	36	36	E
F,SP,SU	450	2.5	550	$375/credit		•	18	36	E
	350	2.75		$390/credit hour		•	12	33	E,W,S
F,SP,D	450			$243/credit		•	12	33	D,E,W

This table includes the names and locations of colleges, universities, and other institutions offering MBA programs. Schools appear in geographical sequence by U.S. state or territory or by country, and then alphabetically by school name. Specific degree information is detailed within the profile for each school. Refer to the page number in the table for the school's profile. If a school submitted incomplete data, one or more columns opposite the school name may be blank.

DEGREE OPTIONS / AREAS OF CONCENTRATION

School	Page Number	Executive MBA	MBA/JD	MBA/MA	MBA/MSN	One-Year	Other	Management	Accounting/Finance	Arts Administration	Economics	Entrepreneurial	Health Care	Hotel Management	Human Resources	Information Systems/Technology	International Business	Manufacturing	Marketing	Operations Management	Org. Behavior/Development	Public Administration	Public Policy	Quality Management	Quantitative Analysis	Real Estate	Strategic Analysis	Transportation	Other	AACSB Accredited
RHODE ISLAND																														
Bryant College, The Graduate School	472					•		•	•		•		•			•	•		•	•										
Johnson & Wales University, Graduate School	473							•									•		•											
Providence College, Department of Business Administration	474							•	•			•					•		•						•		•			
Salve Regina University, The Business Division of the Graduate School	475							•	•								•	•												
University of Rhode Island, College of Business Administration	475							•	•																					•
SOUTH CAROLINA																														
Charleston Southern University, School of Business	476								•												•								•	
The Citadel, The Military College of South Carolina, Department of Business Administration	476							•																						
Clemson University, College of Commerce and Industry	477							•	•	•	•					•	•		•	•	•									•
Francis Marion University, School of Business	477							•																						
University of South Carolina, College of Business Administration	478	•						•	•	•				•		•	•	•	•	•	•					•	•			•
SOUTH DAKOTA																														
University of South Dakota, School of Business	479	•						•							•		•													•
TENNESSEE																														
Belmont University, Jack C. Massey Graduate School of Business	480							•	•																					
Christian Brothers University, School of Business	481							•	•						•												•		•	
East Tennessee State University, College of Business	481							•																						•
Middle Tennessee State University, College of Business	482							•	•		•																			•
Tennessee State University, School of Business	482						•	•	•												•									
Tennessee Technological University, College of Business Administration, Division of MBA Studies	483								•								•													•

MATRICULATION (Fall, Winter, Spring, Summer, Deferred)	ADMISSION REQUIREMENTS			FULL-TIME TUITION (R) State Resident (NR) Non-Resident	PART-TIME TUITION (R) State Resident (NR) Non-Resident	Financial Aid	Minimum Months to Obtain Degree	Credit Hours Required	TIME OFFERED (Day, Evening, Weekend, Summer)
	GMAT Score	Undergraduate GPA	TOEFL Score						
F,SP,D		2.75	550	$12,000	$750/course	•	24	60	D,E,S
D		2.75	550	$214/quarter hour	$154/quarter hour	•	12	54	D,E
D				$210/credit		•	12	36	E,W,S
D				$250/credit		•	24	36	E,S
F,SP			575					36-59	
D			550	$164/semester hour		•	24	30	E,W
F,SP,SU			550	$120/credit hour				30	E
F,D			550	$116/credit hour (R) $232/credit hour (NR)		•	24	60	D,E,S
F,SP			550		$450/course		30	36	E,S
F	550	3.0	600	$1,670/semester (R) $6,650-$12,600/semester (NR)	$163/hour (R) $138-$494/hour (NR)	•	21	60	D,E,W,S
F,SP,SU	400	2.7	550	$71/credit hour (R) $164/credit hour (NR)		•	12	33	D,E
F,SP,SU	450		550	$420-$470/credit hour		•	24	42	E
D	450		600	$275/credit hour		•	12	30	E,W
F,SP	450	2.5	550	$1,096/semester (R) $3,063/semester (NR)			24	39	E,S
F,SP	450	2.5	525	$1,063/semester (R) $3,030/semester (NR)	$107/hour (R) $299/hour (NR)	•	24	36	E,S
D			500			•			
F,SP,SU	350	2.5	550	$114/hour (R) $286/hour (NR)		•	12	36	D,E,S

This table includes the names and locations of colleges, universities, and other institutions offering MBA programs. Schools appear in geographical sequence by U.S. state or territory or by country, and then alphabetically by school name. Specific degree information is detailed within the profile for each school. Refer to the page number in the table for the school's profile. If a school submitted incomplete data, one or more columns opposite the school name may be blank.

	Page Number	Executive MBA	MBA/JD	MBA/MA	MBA/MSN	One-Year	Other	Management	Accounting/Finance	Arts Administration	Economics	Entrepreneurial	Health Care	Hotel Management	Human Resources	Information Systems/Technology	International Business	Manufacturing	Marketing	Operations Management	Org. Behavior/Development	Public Administration	Public Policy	Quality Management	Quantitative Analysis	Real Estate	Strategic Analysis	Transportation	Other	AACSB Accredited
Union University, School of Business Administration	484								•	•		•									•									
The University of Memphis, Fogelman College of Business and Economics	485	•						•	•	•		•					•	•	•		•	•				•	•	•	•	•
University of Tennessee at Chattanooga, School of Business Administration	486							•	•			•			•				•	•	•									•
University of Tennessee at Martin, School of Business Administration	486								•	•																				
University of Tennessee, Knoxville, College of Business Administration	487	•	•					•	•	•		•	•				•		•		•	•					•	•	•	•
Vanderbilt University, Owen Graduate School of Management	488	•	•			•				•							•	•			•		•							•
TEXAS																														
Abilene Christian University, College of Business Administration	489								•																					
Amber University, Department of Business Administration	489								•	•							•													
Angelo State University, Department of Business Administration	490								•	•																			•	
Baylor University, Hankamer School of Business	491	•	•					•	•	•	•	•					•	•			•									•
Dallas Baptist University, College of Business	491								•	•							•	•	•											
East Texas State University, College of Business and Technology	492					•			•	•		•					•		•		•									•
East Texas State University at Texarkana, Division of Business Administration	493								•																					
Hardin-Simmons University, School of Business	494								•	•		•									•									
Incarnate Word College, Department of Professional Studies	494				•				•	•		•					•	•	•		•					•				
Lamar University–Beaumont, College of Business	495								•	•																				•
LeTourneau University, Business Division	496								•																					
Midwestern State University, Division of Business Administration	496								•																					
Our Lady of the Lake University of San Antonio, School of Business and Public Administration	497								•	•												•							•	
Prairie View A&M University, College of Business	498								•																					

MATRICULATION	ADMISSION REQUIREMENTS			FULL-TIME TUITION	PART-TIME TUITION	Financial Aid	Minimum Months to Obtain Degree	Credit Hours Required	TIME OFFERED
Fall Winter Spring Summer Deferred	GMAT Score	Undergraduate GPA	TOEFL Score	(R) State Resident (NR) Non-Resident	(R) State Resident (NR) Non-Resident				Day Evening Weekend Summer
F,SP			500	$250/hour			18	33	E,S
F,SP,SU,D	430	2.0	550	$1,233/semester (R) $1,967/ semester (NR)	$118/hour (R) $172/hour (NR)	•	12	33	D,E,S
F,SP,D		2.5	500	$1,026-$1,087/semester (R) $2,619-$3,053/semester (NR)	$114/hour (R) $177/hour (NR)	•	24	36	E
	400	2.5	525	$1,192/semester (R) $3,158/ semester (NR)		•	12	30	E,S
F			550	$1,139/semester (R) $3,106/ semester (NR)		•	21	54	D,E
F				$19,650		•	20	63	D
D			550	$248/hour		•	12	33	E,S
F,SP,D		3.0		$400/course			24	36	E,W,S
F,SP		2.5	550	$55-$67/semester credit hour (R) $196-$208/semester credit hour (NR)		•	27	39	E,S
F,SP,SU,D	500	2.7	550	$232/hour		•	12	36	D,S
	400	3.0	550	$235/credit hour		•	24	36	D,E,W,S
F,SP,D	375	2.75	500			•			
	375		550	$70-$144/hour (R) $213-$215/hour (NR)		•	12	36	E,S
D	450			$220/hour		•	18	36	E
		2.5	560	$290/hour			30	36	E
F,SP,SU,D		2.75	525	$336/semester (R) $1,944/ semester (NR)		•	12	36	E,S
D		2.8	600	$267/credit		•	20	39	E,S
F	400	3.0	550	$793/semester (R) $2,938/ semester (NR)	$55-$164/credit hour (R) $198-$235/credit hour (NR)	•	12	33	D,E,S
F,W,SP	550	2.5	550			•	24	36	W
	350	2.75	550	$568-$1,231/semester (R) $1,819-$4,289/semester (NR)	$173-$510/semester (R) $244-$1,622/semester (NR)	•	24	36-57	E

This table includes the names and locations of colleges, universities, and other institutions offering MBA programs. Schools appear in geographical sequence by U.S. state or territory or by country, and then alphabetically by school name. Specific degree information is detailed within the profile for each school. Refer to the page number in the table for the school's profile. If a school submitted incomplete data, one or more columns opposite the school name may be blank.

School	Page Number	Executive MBA	MBA/JD	MBA/MA	MBA/MSN	One-Year	Other	Management	Accounting/Finance	Arts Administration	Economics	Entrepreneurial	Health Care	Hotel Management	Human Resources	Information Systems/Technology	International Business	Manufacturing	Marketing	Operations Management	Org. Behavior/Development	Public Administration	Public Policy	Quality Management	Quantitative Analysis	Real Estate	Strategic Analysis	Transportation	Other	AACSB Accredited
Rice University, Jesse H. Jones Graduate School of Administration	499								•	•			•				•	•	•		•	•			•			•			
St. Edward's University, School of Business and Public Administration	499								•	•	•	•					•	•	•	•	•	•	•	•	•	•	•	•	•	•	
St. Mary's University of San Antonio, School of Business and Administration	500		•						•	•								•													
Sam Houston State University, College of Business Administration	501								•	•	•							•													
Southern Methodist University, The Edwin L. Cox School of Business	502	•	•	•					•	•	•		•				•		•	•	•	•				•	•			•
Southwest Texas State University, School of Business	502								•	•																					
Stephen F. Austin State University, College of Business	503								•																					•
Sul Ross State University, Department of Business Administration	504								•										•												
Tarleton State University, College of Business Administration	505								•	•								•		•										
Texas A&M International University, Graduate School of International Trade and Business Administration	505		•				•	•	•								•	•										•		
Texas A&M University, College of Business Administration and Graduate School of Business	506								•	•	•	•				•	•	•	•	•	•	•	•	•	•	•	•	•		•
Texas A&M University–Corpus Christi, College of Business Administration	507								•	•								•	•									•		
Texas A&M University–Kingsville, College of Business Administration	507								•																					
Texas Christian University, M. J. Neeley School of Business	508								•	•							•	•	•	•	•	•			•	•		•		•
Texas Southern University, Jesse H. Jones School of Business	509								•																					
Texas Tech University, College of Business Administration	510		•		•				•	•			•		•		•	•	•	•	•				•					•
Texas Woman's University, Department of Business and Economics	510								•																					
University of Dallas, Graduate School of Management	511								•	•			•				•	•	•									•		
University of Houston, College of Business Administration	512	•	•	•				•	•	•							•	•		•	•							•	•	
University of Houston–Clear Lake, College of Business and Public Administration	513								•																				•	
University of Houston–Victoria, Division of Business Administration	513								•																					

MATRICULATION (Fall, Winter, Spring, Summer, Deferred)	ADMISSION REQUIREMENTS			FULL-TIME TUITION (R) State Resident (NR) Non-Resident	PART-TIME TUITION (R) State Resident (NR) Non-Resident	Financial Aid	Minimum Months to Obtain Degree	Credit Hours Required	TIME OFFERED (Day, Evening, Weekend, Summer)
	GMAT Score	Undergraduate GPA	TOEFL Score						
F,D				$12,300		•	18	64	D
F,SP,SU,D	500	2.75	500		$333/credit hour	•	12	36	E,W,S
D			550	$303/hour		•	24	33-39	E,S
F,SP,SU	450		550	$28/semester hour (R) $162/semester hour (NR)		•	24	36	E
				$547/hour		•	21	60	D,E,W,S
F,SP,SU	450	2.75	550	$336/semester (R) $2,052/semester (NR)	$168/semester (R) $1,026/semester (NR)	•	12	36	E,S
			550	$26/hour (R) $162/hour (NR)		•	18	36-57	E,S
D	400		520	$28-$100/semester hour (R) $171/semester hour (NR)		•	12	36	D,E,W,S
		2.5	550	$168/semester (R) $1,026/semester (NR)			12	36	E,W
			550	$539/semester (R) $2,255/semester (NR)	$159-$275/course (R) $572-$1,133/semester (NR)	•	18	36	D,E,S
F,D				$944/semester (R) $2,768/semester (NR)		•	21	53	D
F,SP,SU,D	400		550	$473-$1,028/semester (R) $1,679-$2,119/semester (NR)	$129-$421/semester (R) $191-$1,493/semester (NR)	•	12	36	E,S
		2.5	550	$501-$963/semester (R) $1,689-$3,603/semester (NR)	$131-$446/semester (R)		18	36	D,E,W,S
F,D			550	$288/semester hour		•	24	48	D,E
F,SP,SU		2.5	550	$432/semester (R) $2,100/semester (NR)		•	12	30	E,S
F,SP	500	3.0	550	$56/credit (R) $162/credit (NR)		•	12	36	D,E,S
D	400		550	$50/semester hour (R) $191/semester hour (NR)		•	18	30-36	D,E,S
F,W,SP,D	400	3.0		$316/credit hour		•	12	37	D,E,W,S
F,SP,D				$812-$1,696/semester (R) $1,847-$4,226/semester (NR)	$192-$739/semester (R) $263-$1,659/semester (NR)	•	24	54	D,E,S
F,SP,D	450	2.5		$456-$836/semester (R) $2,052-$3,762/semester (NR)		•	12	36	D,E,S

This table includes the names and locations of colleges, universities, and other institutions offering MBA programs. Schools appear in geographical sequence by U.S. state or territory or by country, and then alphabetically by school name. Specific degree information is detailed within the profile for each school. Refer to the page number in the table for the school's profile. If a school submitted incomplete data, one or more columns opposite the school name may be blank.

School	Page Number	Executive MBA	MBA/JD	MBA/MA	MBA/MSN	One-Year	Other	Management	Accounting/Finance	Arts Administration	Economics	Entrepreneurial	Health Care	Hotel Management	Human Resources	Information Systems/Technology	International Business	Manufacturing	Marketing	Operations Management	Org. Behavior/Development	Public Administration	Public Policy	Quality Management	Quantitative Analysis	Real Estate	Strategic Analysis	Transportation	Other	AACSB Accredited
University of Mary Hardin-Baylor, School of Business	514							•																						
University of North Texas, College of Business Administration	515							•																						•
University of St. Thomas, Cameron School of Business	515								•										•		•									
University of Texas at Arlington, College of Business Administration	516								•	•		•	•				•	•	•		•	•	•			•	•			•
University of Texas at Austin, Graduate School of Business	516								•					•			•	•	•		•	•	•	•					•	•
University of Texas at Dallas, School of Management	517	•							•		•		•	•	•		•		•		•	•	•	•	•		•	•	•	
University of Texas at El Paso, College of Business Administration	518							•																						•
University of Texas at San Antonio	519								•		•																		•	•
University of Texas at Tyler, School of Business Administration	519			•					•	•					•		•		•		•		•							
University of Texas of the Permian Basin, Division of Business	520								•	•											•									
University of Texas–Pan American, School of Business Administration	520							•																						•
Wayland Baptist University, Division of Business	521								•	•					•														•	
West Texas A&M University, T. Boone Pickens College of Business	522								•	•		•							•		•									
UTAH																														
Brigham Young University, Marriott School of Management	522	•							•										•		•	•	•							•
University of Utah, David Eccles School of Business	523	•	•			•	•	•	•					•	•				•		•	•				•	•			•
Utah State University, College of Business	524								•	•			•				•	•			•		•							•
Westminster College of Salt Lake City, Gore School of Business	525								•				•	•			•	•		•									•	
VERMONT																														
University of Vermont, School of Business Administration	525							•																						•

Matriculation (Fall, Winter, Spring, Summer, Deferred)	GMAT Score	Undergraduate GPA	TOEFL Score	Full-Time Tuition (R) State Resident (NR) Non-Resident	Part-Time Tuition (R) State Resident (NR) Non-Resident	Financial Aid	Minimum Months to Obtain Degree	Credit Hours Required	Time Offered (Day, Evening, Weekend, Summer)
		2.5		$217/semester hour			12	36	E,S
F,SP,SU,D	400	2.5	550	$315/semester hour		•	24	36	E,S
F,SP,SU,D	480	3.0	550	$73-$78/semester hour (R) $217-$220/semester hour (NR)		•	12	30	D,E,S
F,D			550	$56/credit (R) $221/credit (NR)		•	24	60	D,S
F,SP,D	450	3.0	550	$82-$91/semester hour (R) $227-$236/semester hour (NR)	$92-$236/semester hour (R) $237-$317/semester hour (NR)	•	24	48	D,E,S
F,SP,SU	500	2.75	600		$56/credit hour (R) $191/credit hour (NR)		27	36	E,W,S
F,SP,SU	500	3.0	550		$144/course (R) $516/course (NR)		15	33	E,S
F,SP			550		$30/credit hour (R) $171/credit hour (NR)	•	24	36	E
				$336/semester (R) $2,052/semester (NR)				30	E,S
F,SP		2.5	600	$465/semester (R) $1,671/semester (NR)		•	24	33	E,W,S
	500	2.7	500	$180/semester hour		•	12	36	D,E,W
			500	$342/semester (R) $1,629/semester (NR)			24	36	D,E,W,S
F,D	520	3.0	570	$2,300-$3,450/semester		•	16	60	D
F,SU		3.0	560	$748/quarter (R) $2,638/quarter (NR)			11	64	D,E
F,SP,D		3.0	550	$622/quarter (R) $1,869/quarter (NR)		•	9	45	D,E,S
	500	3.0	550	$2,526/semester	$358/credit hour		24	43	E,W,S
F,SP,D			550	$3,105/semester (R) $7,758/semester (NR)		•	24	48	E,S

This table includes the names and locations of colleges, universities, and other institutions offering MBA programs. Schools appear in geographical sequence by U.S. state or territory or by country, and then alphabetically by school name. Specific degree information is detailed within the profile for each school. Refer to the page number in the table for the school's profile. If a school submitted incomplete data, one or more columns opposite the school name may be blank.

School	Page Number	Executive MBA	MBA/JD	MBA/MA	MBA/MSN	OneYear	Other	Management	Accounting/Finance	Arts Administration	Economics	Entrepreneurial	Health Care	Hotel Management	Human Resources	Information Systems/Technology	International Business	Manufacturing	Marketing	Operations Management	Org. Behavior/Development	Public Administration	Public Policy	Quality Management	Quantitative Analysis	Real Estate	Strategic Analysis	Transportation	Other	AACSB Accredited
VIRGINIA																														
Averett College	526							•																						
College of William and Mary, Graduate School of Business	527	•						•	•				•			•	•	•	•	•	•				•	•	•			•
George Mason University, School of Business Administration	528	•						•	•						•	•		•												•
Hampton University, School of Business	529							•																						
James Madison University, College of Business	529											•																•		•
Lynchburg College, School of Business	530							•	•					•				•												
Marymount University, School of Business Administration	531							•	•			•			•	•		•	•	•			•		•					
Old Dominion University, Graduate School of Business and Public Administration	531							•	•		•	•	•			•	•		•			•					•	•		•
Radford University, College of Business and Economics	532							•	•		•						•		•											•
Regent University, School of Business	533							•	•			•					•		•											
Shenandoah University, Byrd School of Business	534							•	•						•	•		•												
University of Richmond, E. Claiborne Robins School of Business	534		•					•																						•
University of Virginia, Darden Graduate School of Business Administration	535		•	•	•		•	•																						•
Virginia Commonwealth University, School of Business	536							•	•		•				•	•	•		•	•	•				•	•	•			•
Virginia Polytechnic Institute and State University, Pamplin College of Business	537							•	•						•	•		•												•
WASHINGTON																														
City University, Graduate School of Business and Management Professions	538						•	•	•			•			•			•		•									•	
Eastern Washington University, College of Business Administration	538						•	•						•															•
Gonzaga University, School of Business Administration	539		•					•	•																					•
Pacific Lutheran University, School of Business	540						•	•			•				•			•											•

MATRICULATION	ADMISSION REQUIREMENTS			FULL-TIME TUITION	PART-TIME TUITION	Financial Aid	Minimum Months to Obtain Degree	Credit Hours Required	TIME OFFERED
Fall / Winter / Spring / Summer / Deferred	GMAT Score	Undergraduate GPA	TOEFL Score	(R) State Resident / (NR) Non-Resident	(R) State Resident / (NR) Non-Resident				Day / Evening / Weekend / Summer
		3.0		$9,000/degree program			21	36	E,S
F,D	570	3.0	590	$175/hour (R) $456/hour (NR)		•	24	65	D,E,S
F,SP,D	500		575	$1,515-$2,020/semester (R) $4,050-$5,400/semester (NR)		•	21	57	D,E
F,SP,D		2.6			$185/credit hour	•	24	36	E,S
D	500	2.7	500	$126/credit hour (R) $351/credit hour (NR)			18	33	E,S
F	450	2.7	550	$210/credit hour		•	12	31	E
D	400	2.0	600	$340/credit hour		•	18	36	E,W,S
F,SP,SU			550	$154-$166/hour (R) $221-$434/hour (NR)		•	20	49	D,E,S
F,SP	450	2.75	550	$1,593/semester (R) $3,030/semester (NR)	$133/credit hour (R) $253/credit hour (NR)	•	24	36	E,S
D				$295/semester credit hour		•	24	57	D,E,S
			450	$350/semester credit hour			15	36	E,W,S
F,SP,SU	500		550	$7,300/semester		•	20	30	E,S
F				$9,385 (R) $17,839 (NR)		•	24	78	D
F,SP,D	550	2.7	550	$1,796/semester (R) $5,109/semester (NR)		•	24	30	E,S
F,SP,D			550	$2,278/semester (R) $3,363/semester (NR)		•	24	48	D,E
				$232/credit		•	18	45	D,E,W,S
	500	3.0	580	$1,200/quarter (R) $3,645/quarter (NR)		•	12	48	E
	500			$340/credit hour		•	12	33	E,S
F,SP,D	470	2.75	550	$416/semester hour $416/semester hour (NR)		•	16	48	E,S

This table includes the names and locations of colleges, universities, and other institutions offering MBA programs. Schools appear in geographical sequence by U.S. state or territory or by country, and then alphabetically by school name. Specific degree information is detailed within the profile for each school. Refer to the page number in the table for the school's profile. If a school submitted incomplete data, one or more columns opposite the school name may be blank.

School	Page Number	Executive MBA	MBA/JD	MBA/MA	MBA/MSN	One-Year	Other	Management	Accounting/Finance	Arts Administration	Economics	Entrepreneurial	Health Care	Hotel Management	Human Resources	Information Systems/Technology	International Business	Manufacturing	Marketing	Operations Management	Org. Behavior/Development	Public Administration	Public Policy	Quality Management	Quantitative Analysis	Real Estate	Strategic Analysis	Transportation	Other	AACSB Accredited
Saint Martin's College, Department of Economics and Business Administration	541							•																						
Seattle Pacific University, School of Business and Economics	541							•	•				•				•	•											•	
Seattle University, Albers School of Business and Economics	542					•		•	•			•	•				•	•	•		•	•				•	•	•		•
University of Washington, Graduate School of Business Administration	543	•	•	•		•	•	•	•		•	•	•	•			•	•	•	•	•	•	•	•	•	•	•	•	•	•
Washington State University, College of Business and Economics	544							•	•						•	•	•	•	•										•	•
Western Washington University, College of Business and Economics	545							•																						•
WEST VIRGINIA																														
Marshall University, College of Business	545							•	•			•					•				•	•					•	•	•	
University of Charleston, Jones-Benedum Division of Business	546	•						•																						
West Virginia Graduate College, School of Business	547							•																						
West Virginia University, College of Business and Economics	547							•																						•
West Virginia Wesleyan College, Faculty of Business	548							•	•			•										•								
Wheeling Jesuit College	548							•																						
WISCONSIN																														
Cardinal Stritch College, Business and Management Division	549																		•								•			
Marquette University, College of Business Administration	549							•	•			•					•	•	•										•	•
University of Wisconsin–Eau Claire, School of Business	550							•																						•
University of Wisconsin–La Crosse, College of Business Administration	551							•																						•
University of Wisconsin–Madison, School of Business	552	•						•	•								•	•	•	•						•	•			•
University of Wisconsin–Milwaukee, School of Business Administration	553							•																			•			•
University of Wisconsin–Oshkosh, College of Business Administration	553							•																						•

MATRICULATION	ADMISSION REQUIREMENTS			FULL-TIME TUITION	PART-TIME TUITION	Financial Aid	Minimum Months to Obtain Degree	Credit Hours Required	TIME OFFERED
Fall Winter Spring Summer Deferred	GMAT Score	Undergraduate GPA	TOEFL Score	(R) State Resident (NR) Non-Resident	(R) State Resident (NR) Non-Resident	Financial Aid	Minimum Months to Obtain Degree	Credit Hours Required	Day Evening Weekend Summer
D			525		$385/semester hour	•	18	33	E,S
F,W,SP,SU,D	450	3.0	560	$355/credit		•	24	45	E,S
F,W,SP,SU,D	500	3.0	560	$4,440/quarter	$2,220/quarter	•	12	48	D,E,W,S
F			580	$4,566 (R) $11,436 (NR)		•	18	96	D
	500	3.0	580	$2,283/semester (R) $5,718/semester (NR)		•	12	32	D,E,S
SU	460	3.0	565	$1,200/quarter (R) $3,645/quarter (NR)		•	18	60	E
F,SP,SU	450	2.5	525	$130/credit hour (R) $351/credit hour (NR)		•	12	36	E,W,S
		2.75	500			•			
F,SP								36	
F,D			580	$1,068/semester (R) $3,078/semester (NR)		•		48	D,W
F,SP					$275/credit hour			36	E,W
F,SP,SU	470	2.75	550	$300/credit hour		•	15	36	E,S
D		2.5	600	$4,200/term		•		36	E,S
F,SP,SU,D				$434/credit hour		•	12	33	E,W,S
SP,D		2.75	550	$117-$156/credit (R) $356-$475/credit (NR)		•	18	30	E
F,SP,D	450	2.85	550	$186/credit (R) $467/credit (NR)		•	18	30	E
F,SP		3.0	600	$2,329/semester (R) $6,252/semester (NR)		•	24	54	D,W,S
F,SP			550						
F,SP,SU,D	450	2.75	550	$170/credit (R) $480/credit (NR)		•	18	30	E,W

This table includes the names and locations of colleges, universities, and other institutions offering MBA programs. Schools appear in geographical sequence by U.S. state or territory or by country, and then alphabetically by school name. Specific degree information is detailed within the profile for each school. Refer to the page number in the table for the school's profile. If a school submitted incomplete data, one or more columns opposite the school name may be blank.

School	Page Number	Executive MBA	MBA/JD	MBA/MA	MBA/MSN	One-Year	Other	Management	Accounting/Finance	Arts Administration	Economics	Entrepreneurial	Health Care	Hotel Management	Human Resources	Information Systems/Technology	International Business	Manufacturing	Marketing	Operations Management	Org. Behavior/Development	Public Administration	Public Policy	Quality Management	Quantitative Analysis	Real Estate	Strategic Analysis	Transportation	Other	AACSB Accredited
University of Wisconsin–Parkside, School of Business and Administrative Science	554							•																						
University of Wisconsin–Whitewater, College of Business and Economics	554							•	•						•	•				•	•									•
WYOMING																														
University of Wyoming, College of Business	555							•																						•
GUAM																														
University of Guam, College of Business and Public Administration	555																													
PUERTO RICO																														
Inter American University of Puerto Rico, San Germán Campus, Department of Business Administration	556								•								•				•								•	
Pontifical Catholic University of Puerto Rico	556		•					•	•								•													
Universidad del Turabo	557							•	•								•				•								•	
University of Puerto Rico, Río Piedras, Graduate School of Business	558							•	•			•								•	•									
University of the Sacred Heart, Business School	558							•									•													
VIRGIN ISLANDS																														
University of the Virgin Islands, Division of Business Administration	559							•																						
AUSTRALIA																														
Australian National University	560							•																						
Bond University, School of Business	560	•						•	•				•			•	•	•		•		•	•				•	•		
Curtin University of Technology	561					ƒ		•	•			•	•			•	•	•		•		•	•	•			•	•	•	
Deakin University, Faculty of Management	562							•	•																					
Edith Cowan University, Faculty of Business	562							•	•		•	•				•	•		•	•										
Monash University, Faculty of Economics and Politics, MBA Division	563							•	•		•			•	•	•	•		•	•	•	•	•		•			•		

MATRICULATION (Fall, Winter, Spring, Summer, Deferred)	GMAT Score	Undergraduate GPA	TOEFL Score	FULL-TIME TUITION (R) State Resident (NR) Non-Resident	PART-TIME TUITION (R) State Resident (NR) Non-Resident	Financial Aid	Minimum Months to Obtain Degree	Credit Hours Required	TIME OFFERED (Day, Evening, Weekend, Summer)
F,SP,SU			550	$333-$486/course (R) $970-$1,442/course (NR)			30	33	E,S
F,SP,SU,D	450	2.75	550	$1,588/semester (R) $4,457/semester (NR)	$176/credit (R) $495/credit (NR)	•	18	36	D,E,S
D	500	3.0	550	$1,008/semester (R) $3,042/semester (NR)	$112/credit hour (R) $338/credit hour (NR)		12	30	D,E,W,S
	400	3.0	550	$63/credit (R) $140/credit (NR)				36	
F,SP,D		2.5		$130/credit		•	30	42	E,W
F,SP,SU,D		2.5		$120/credit	$120/credit	•	30	43	E,W
F		2.75		$720-$1,440/semester			30	39	E,W,S
F		3.0		$75/credit (R) $75/credit (NR)			30	36	D,E,S
F,SP,D	500	2.8				•		48	E
F,SP		2.5	550	$138/credit (R) $276/credit (NR)		•	36	36	E,S
D			570	25,000 Australian $/degree program (NR)		•	14	24	D
D			600	1,980 Australian $/unit		•	12		D,E,W
F,SP	520		550	4,817 Australian $ (R) 24,400 Australian $ (NR)			18	400	D,E,W,S
W,SU,D					650 Australian $/unit (R) 1,300 Australian $/unit (NR)		24	16	
F,D							24	16	D,E
			580	6,800 Australian $ 13,500 Australian $ (NR)	850 Australian dollars/course		21	16	D,S

This table includes the names and locations of colleges, universities, and other institutions offering MBA programs. Schools appear in geographical sequence by U.S. state or territory or by country, and then alphabetically by school name. Specific degree information is detailed within the profile for each school. Refer to the page number in the table for the school's profile. If a school submitted incomplete data, one or more columns opposite the school name may be blank.

DEGREE OPTIONS / **AREAS OF CONCENTRATION**

School	Page Number	Executive MBA	MBA/JD	MBA/MA	MBA/MSN	One-Year	Other	Management	Accounting/Finance	Arts Administration	Economics	Entrepreneurial	Health Care	Hotel Management	Human Resources	Information Systems/Technology	International Business	Manufacturing	Marketing	Operations Management	Org. Behavior/Development	Public Administration	Public Policy	Quality Management	Quantitative Analysis	Real Estate	Strategic Analysis	Transportation	Other	AACSB Accredited
Murdoch University, School of Economics and Commerce	564						•	•										•													
The University of Adelaide, Graduate School of Management	564							•	•								•			•		•		•				•			
University of Melbourne, Melbourne Business School	565							•	•			•	•				•		•		•	•	•	•				•	•		
University of Newcastle, Faculty of Economics	566																														
University of New South Wales, Australian Graduate School of Management	566							•	•			•				•			•		•	•				•		•			
The University of Sydney, Graduate School of Business	567							•	•		•				•		•		•		•		•	•	•			•	•	•	
The University of Western Australia, The Graduate School of Management	568							•	•							•			•	•		•		•							•
University of Western Sydney, Macarthur, Faculty of Business and Technology	569							•	•			•	•				•			•		•		•					•		
BANGLADESH																															
International University of Business Agriculture and Technology (IUBAT), College of Business Administration	570							•	•							•			•	•	•	•						•	•		
BELGIUM																															
European University, International Business School	570						•	•								•				•									•	•	
Katholieke Universiteit Leuven, Department of Applied Economic Sciences	571							•	•		•				•	•	•		•	•	•							•	•		
St. Ignatius University Faculty of Antwerp (UFSIA), Center for Business Administration	572							•	•			•	•			•			•	•		•						•	•		
CANADA																															
ALBERTA																															
University of Alberta, Faculty of Business	572		•	•		•							•			•			•		•		•	•						•	•
University of Calgary, Faculty of Management	573		•					•			•				•	•	•		•	•	•	•						•		•	•
BRITISH COLUMBIA																															
Simon Fraser University, Faculty of Business Administration	574					•	•	•			•					•	•	•		•	•	•				•		•	•		
University of British Columbia, Faculty of Commerce and Business Administration	574					•			•			•				•			•		•							•	•	•	

96 · *Peterson's Guide to MBA Programs*

MATRICULATION (Fall, Winter, Spring, Summer, Deferred)	GMAT Score	Undergraduate GPA	TOEFL Score	FULL-TIME TUITION (R) State Resident (NR) Non-Resident	PART-TIME TUITION (R) State Resident (NR) Non-Resident	Financial Aid	Minimum Months to Obtain Degree	Credit Hours Required	TIME OFFERED (Day, Evening, Weekend, Summer)
F,D	500		550			•			
F,SP			550	350 Australian $/credit (R) / 650 Australian $/credit (NR)			17	48	D,E,W
F,SP,D			620	$7,000 $12,600 (NR)	$700/course	•	20	20	D,E
			550	10,600 Australian $			26	160	E
D	500			10,000 Australian $ (R) / 19,500 Australian $ (NR)		•	24	21	D
F,SP,D			580	756 Australian $/course (R) / 1,512 Australian $/course (NR)		•	18	40	D,E,W,S
F,SP,D		2.75	550	600 Australian $/unit		•	16	16	D,E,W,S
F,SP,D				16,000 Australian $			12	16	D,E
F,SP,SU,D	450		550	$125/trimester (R) $125/trimester (NR)	$48-$50/credit hour (R) / $56-$66/credit hour (NR)	•	20	74	D,E,W,S
F,SP,D	450	3.0	550						
F,D	550			17,600 Belgian francs			9	12	D,E,W
F,D				17,600 Belgian francs			9	60	D
F	500	3.0	600	315 Canadian $/course (R) / 630 Canadian $/course (NR)	315 Canadian $/course (R) / 630 Canadian $/course (NR)	•	18	57	D,E,S
F	500	3.0	550						
F,SP,SU	550	3.0	670	823 Canadian $/semester			20	36	D
F	550	3.0	600	7,350 Canadian $/degree program (R)		•	15	51	D,E,W,S

This table includes the names and locations of colleges, universities, and other institutions offering MBA programs. Schools appear in geographical sequence by U.S. state or territory or by country, and then alphabetically by school name. Specific degree information is detailed within the profile for each school. Refer to the page number in the table for the school's profile. If a school submitted incomplete data, one or more columns opposite the school name may be blank.

School	Page Number	Executive MBA	MBA/JD	MBA/MA	MBA/MSN	One-Year	Other	Management	Accounting/Finance	Arts Administration	Economics	Entrepreneurial	Health Care	Hotel Management	Human Resources	Information Systems/Technology	International Business	Manufacturing	Marketing	Operations Management	Org. Behavior/Development	Public Administration	Public Policy	Quality Management	Quantitative Analysis	Real Estate	Strategic Analysis	Transportation	Other	AACSB Accredited
University of Victoria, School of Business	575												•				•												•	
MANITOBA																														
University of Manitoba, Faculty of Management	576					•			•																					
NEW BRUNSWICK																														
Université de Moncton, Faculté d'Administration	577								•																					
University of New Brunswick, School of Graduate Studies	577								•																					
NEWFOUNDLAND																														
Memorial University of Newfoundland, Faculty of Business Administration	577								•		•						•		•	•										
NOVA SCOTIA																														
Dalhousie University, School of Business Administration	578								•		•						•		•	•										
Saint Mary's University, Frank H. Sobey Faculty of Commerce	578	•							•		•																			
ONTARIO																														
Carleton University, School of Business	579								•		•						•		•										•	
Laurentian University, School of Commerce and Administration	580								•		•				•				•			•					•			
McMaster University, Michael G. DeGroote School of Business	580										•				•		•	•		•	•					•			•	
Queen's University at Kingston, School of Business	581					•					•						•			•	•									
University of Ottawa, Faculty of Administration	582	•						•					•		•		•			•				•			•			
University of Toronto, Faculty of Management	583										•																			
The University of Western Ontario, Western Business School	583	•							•		•										•									
University of Windsor, Faculty of Business Administration	584								•		•		•				•	•	•	•	•	•				•		•		
Wilfrid Laurier University, School of Business and Economics	584								•		•		•				•	•	•	•								•		

MATRICULATION (Fall / Winter / Spring / Summer / Deferred)	ADMISSION REQUIREMENTS GMAT Score	Undergraduate GPA	TOEFL Score	FULL-TIME TUITION (R) State Resident / (NR) Non-Resident	PART-TIME TUITION (R) State Resident / (NR) Non-Resident	Financial Aid	Minimum Months to Obtain Degree	Credit Hours Required	TIME OFFERED (Day / Evening / Weekend / Summer)
D		5	575	908 Canadian $/term		•	17	26	D,E
F,D	450	3.0	550	16,000 Canadian $ (R) 16,000 Canadian $ (NR)		•		66	E,W,S
F,SP		3.0		$2,200 (R) $4,400 (NR)			24	48	D,E
F		3.0						60	
F,D	520	2.75	590	697 Canadian $/semester	462 Canadian $/semester	•	24	22	D,E,S
F	500	3.0	580	3,435 Canadian $			16	23	D,E
F,D				2,850 Canadian $ (R) 5,100 Canadian $ (NR)	530 Canadian dollars/course (R) 870 Canadian $/course (NR)	•	16	11	D,E,S
F,W	550	3.0	550	1,325 Canadian $/term (R) 5,344 Canadian $/term (NR)			14	5	D
F,D	500	3.5	500	3,174 Canadian $ (R) 15,408 Canadian $ (NR)		•	24	60	E,S
F	500	3.0		3,354 Canadian $ (R) 15,408 Canadian $ (NR)	1,029 Canadian dollars (R) 280 Canadian $/course (NR)	•	20		D,E,S
SP,D	550	3.0	600			•			
F,SP		3.1		1,200-1,400 Canadian $/semester (R) 2,700-3,500 Canadian dollars/semester (NR)		•	24	60	D,E,S
F,D	560	2.8	600	3,300 Canadian $ (R) 11,200 Canadian $ (NR)		•	20	18	D
F,D	500	2.7	600	990-1,485 Canadian $/semester (R) 4,190-4,201 Canadian $/semester (NR)		•	18	70	D,E,S
F,D	550	3.0	550	605-1,119 Canadian $/term (R) 3,790 Canadian $/term (NR)		•	12		D,E,S

This table includes the names and locations of colleges, universities, and other institutions offering MBA programs. Schools appear in geographical sequence by U.S. state or territory or by country, and then alphabetically by school name. Specific degree information is detailed within the profile for each school. Refer to the page number in the table for the school's profile. If a school submitted incomplete data, one or more columns opposite the school name may be blank.

School	Page Number	Executive MBA	MBA/JD	MBA/MA	MBA/MSN	One-Year	Other	Management	Accounting/Finance	Arts Administration	Economics	Entrepreneurial	Health Care	Hotel Management	Human Resources	Information Systems/Technology	International Business	Manufacturing	Marketing	Operations Management	Org. Behavior/Development	Public Administration	Public Policy	Quality Management	Quantitative Analysis	Real Estate	Strategic Analysis	Transportation	Other	AACSB Accredited
York University, Faculty of Administrative Studies	585							•	•	•	•	•	•		•	•	•		•	•	•	•	•		•		•	•	•	•	
QUEBEC																															
Concordia University, Faculty of Commerce and Administration	586								•																						
École des Hautes Études Commerciales, School of Business Administration	586									•							•	•	•		•	•								•
McGill University, Faculty of Management	587							•	•	•						•	•	•		•	•						•			
Université de Sherbrooke, Faculty of Administration	588								•																					
Université du Québec à Montréal, École des Sciences de la Gestion	588	•							•	•						•	•	•		•	•	•							•	•
Université Laval, Faculté des Sciences de l'Administration	589								•	•	•		•			•		•	•							•				
SASKATCHEWAN																															
University of Saskatchewan, College of Commerce	589								•																					
CAYMAN ISLANDS																															
International College of the Cayman Islands	590																													
COSTA RICA																															
Instituto Centroamericano de Administración de Empresas	591	•						•			•																		•	
CZECH REPUBLIC																															
Czechoslovak Management Center, Business School	591					•			•		•					•	•	•		•	•								•	
EGYPT																															
American University in Cairo	592																													
FINLAND																															
Helsinki School of Economics and Business Administration, International Center	593							•	•		•	•				•	•	•		•	•	•					•		•	

| MATRICULATION (Fall, Winter, Spring, Summer, Deferred) | ADMISSION REQUIREMENTS | | | FULL-TIME TUITION | PART-TIME TUITION | Financial Aid | Minimum Months to Obtain Degree | Credit Hours Required | TIME OFFERED (Day, Evening, Weekend, Summer) |
	GMAT Score	Undergraduate GPA	TOEFL Score	(R) State Resident / (NR) Non-Resident	(R) State Resident / (NR) Non-Resident				
F,W,D	550	3.0	600	1,349 Canadian $/semester (R) 5,241 Canadian $/semester (NR)			16	60	D,E,S
								63	
F,W,D	550	2.8		62 Canadian $/credit (R) 255 Canadian $/credit (NR)		•	16	60	D,E,W,S
F	550	3.0	600	1,900-2,000 Canadian $ (R) 8,250-8,500 Canadian $ (NR)	69-150 Canadian $/credit (R) 260-343 Canadian $/credit (NR)	•	24	60	D,E
F		3.2		1,800 Canadian $ (R) 8,000 Canadian $ (NR)			24	60	D,E,W
F,SP,D		3.2		667 Canadian $/semester (R) 3,728 Canadian $/semester (NR)			16	45	D,E
F,SP,D			550	3,038 Canadian $ (R) 3,038 Canadian $ (NR)		•	16	51-60	D,E,S
F,W,SP,SU,D				$88/quarter hour		•	18	60	E,W,S
F,D				$8,450		•	18		D
W	500			$40,000/term (R) $55,000/term (NR)		•	36	51	W
F			550					42	
F,D				38,000 Finnish markkas/degree program		•	20	98	D

This table includes the names and locations of colleges, universities, and other institutions offering MBA programs. Schools appear in geographical sequence by U.S. state or territory or by country, and then alphabetically by school name. Specific degree information is detailed within the profile for each school. Refer to the page number in the table for the school's profile. If a school submitted incomplete data, one or more columns opposite the school name may be blank.

	Page Number	Executive MBA	MBA/JD	MBA/MA	MBA/MSN	One-Year	Other	Management	Accounting/Finance	Arts Administration	Economics	Entrepreneurial	Health Care	Hotel Management	Human Resources	Information Systems/Technology	International Business	Manufacturing	Marketing	Operations Management	Org. Behavior/Development	Public Administration	Public Policy	Quality Management	Quantitative Analysis	Real Estate	Strategic Analysis	Transportation	Other	AACSB Accredited
FRANCE																														
EAP-European School of Management	593	•						•	•			•				•	•	•		•	•	•	•		•				•		•
L'École Nationale des Ponts et Chaussées	594							•	•			•					•											•			
École Superieur de Commerce de Rouen	595	•						•	•		•					•	•	•		•	•	•			•		•	•		•	•
École Supérieure des Sciences Économiques et Commerciales, International Management Development	595	•						•									•													
The European Institute of Business Administration (INSEAD)	596							•	•		•	•				•	•	•		•	•	•					•			
Groupe CERAM	597	•						•	•		•	•				•	•		•	•	•	•					•			
Groupe ESC Clermont, Clermont Graduate School of Management	597							•	•			•															•			
Groupe ESC Lyon	597					•		•																						
Groupe ESC Nantes Atlantique	598						•		•	•		•				•	•	•								•	•		•	
HEC Graduate School of Management, Institute Supérieur des Affaires	599				•	•	•		•			•			•		•		•	•	•						•			
Institut Superieur de Gestion	600							•																						
Reims Graduate Business School, Reims Business School	600			•				•	•	•					•	•		•	•	•	•				•				•	•
Schiller International University	601			•								•				•													
Schiller International University	602			•								•																	
Theseus Institute	602			•				•	•		•	•			•	•	•		•	•	•		•				•		•	
GERMANY																														
Koblenz School of Corporate Management (WHU), Otto Beisheim Graduate School	603							•		•	•				•	•		•											•	
Schiller International University	604			•												•													
Schiller International University	604			•								•				•													

MATRICULATION (Fall / Winter / Spring / Summer / Deferred)	ADMISSION REQUIREMENTS			FULL-TIME TUITION (R) State Resident (NR) Non-Resident	PART-TIME TUITION (R) State Resident (NR) Non-Resident	Financial Aid	Minimum Months to Obtain Degree	Credit Hours Required	TIME OFFERED (Day / Evening / Weekend / Summer)
	GMAT Score	Undergraduate GPA	TOEFL Score						
D	550					•			
F,SP,SU,D	500		500	100,000 French francs/ degree program			13	19	D,E,W
D		3.0	550						
F,D			450			•			
F,SP			600	145,000 French francs		•		21	D,W,S
F,D									
F				29,000 French francs			21	60	D
F,D	580		580			•			
F,D									
F,D	450	2.5	600	12,000 French francs/degree program		•	16	1,100	
F		2.5	550	$15,000			14	60	D,W,S
F,D									
		2.8	550			•			
		2.8	550			•			
SP	550		600			•			
F	520		560	5,500 German marks/ semester		•	18	610	D
		2.8	550			•			
		2.8	550			•			

This table includes the names and locations of colleges, universities, and other institutions offering MBA programs. Schools appear in geographical sequence by U.S. state or territory or by country, and then alphabetically by school name. Specific degree information is detailed within the profile for each school. Refer to the page number in the table for the school's profile. If a school submitted incomplete data, one or more columns opposite the school name may be blank.

	Page Number	Executive MBA	MBA/JD	MBA/MA	MBA/MSN	One-Year	Other	Management	Accounting/Finance	Arts Administration	Economics	Entrepreneurial	Health Care	Hotel Management	Human Resources	Information Systems/Technology	International Business	Manufacturing	Marketing	Operations Management	Org. Behavior/Development	Public Administration	Public Policy	Quality Management	Quantitative Analysis	Real Estate	Strategic Analysis	Transportation	Other	AACSB Accredited
HONG KONG																														
The Chinese University of Hong Kong, Faculty of Business Administration	605	•							•		•		•				•		•		•	•					•			
Hong Kong Baptist College, School of Business	606								•	•		•	•			•			•	•	•	•						•		•	
The Hong Kong University of Science and Technology, The School of Business and Management	606								•	•		•	•	•		•		•	•	•	•	•	•	•				•		•	
University of Hong Kong, University of Hong Kong Business School	607								•	•		•	•			•	•		•	•	•	•						•		•	
INDONESIA																														
Institut Pengembangan Manajemen Indonesia	608					•											•														
IRELAND																														
University College Cork, Faculty of Commerce	608								•																						
University College Dublin, Graduate School of Business	609	•							•	•			•				•	•	•		•	•	•	•	•	•		•			
University College, Galway, School of Economics and Business Studies	610	•							•	•		•	•			•	•		•	•	•						•		•	
University of Limerick, College of Business	610	•										•					•												•	
ISRAEL																														
Tel Aviv University, The Leon Recamaty Graduate School of Administration	611	•							•	•			•			•	•		•	•	•								•	
ITALY																														
Bocconi University	611																•												•	
JAPAN																														
The International University of Japan, Graduate School of International Management	612								•	•							•		•									•		
MEXICO																														
Instituto Tecnológico y de Estudios Superiores de Monterrey, México City Campus	613								•																					

MATRICULATION	ADMISSION REQUIREMENTS			FULL-TIME TUITION	PART-TIME TUITION				TIME OFFERED
Fall Winter Spring Summer Deferred	GMAT Score	Undergraduate GPA	TOEFL Score	(R) State Resident (NR) Non-Resident	(R) State Resident (NR) Non-Resident	Financial Aid	Minimum Months to Obtain Degree	Credit Hours Required	Day Evening Weekend Summer
F	550	3.0		12,000 Hong Kong dollars/term		•	24	54	D,E
F	500				42,000 Hong Kong dollars		24	36	E
F,D		2.75		$4,401 (R)	$5,795 (R)	•	24	64	D,E,W,S
F	500		550		40,000 Hong Kong dollars		27		E,W
SP,D	500		500						
F							24	18	
F,D	480		600	5,750 Irish pounds (R)			12	21	D,E,W,S
F	450								
F	500		550						
F,SP				$2,400			24	32	D,E,S
F,D			600			•	16	30	
F,SP,D	530		530			•	18	51	D

This table includes the names and locations of colleges, universities, and other institutions offering MBA programs. Schools appear in geographical sequence by U.S. state or territory or by country, and then alphabetically by school name. Specific degree information is detailed within the profile for each school. Refer to the page number in the table for the school's profile. If a school submitted incomplete data, one or more columns opposite the school name may be blank.

DEGREE OPTIONS   **AREAS OF CONCENTRATION**

School	Page Number	Executive MBA	MBA/JD	MBA/MA	MBA/MSN	One-Year	Other	Management	Accounting/Finance	Arts Administration	Economics	Entrepreneurial	Health Care	Hotel Management	Human Resources	Information Systems/Technology	International Business	Manufacturing	Marketing	Operations Management	Org. Behavior/Development	Public Administration	Public Policy	Quality Management	Quantitative Analysis	Real Estate	Strategic Analysis	Transportation	Other	AACSB Accredited
MONACO																														
University of Southern Europe, Monaco Graduate School of Finance and Marketing	613						•		•																					•	
NETHERLANDS																														
Erasmus University Rotterdam, Rotterdam School of Management	614							•											•											•	
Nijenrode University, The Netherlands Business School	614						•												•												
University of Twente, TSM Business School	615	•							•	•		•	•			•	•	•			•	•	•					•		•	
NEW ZEALAND																														
University of Auckland, The Graduate School of Business	616								•																						
University of Otago	617	•							•																						
Victoria University of Wellington, Graduate School of Business and Government Management	617								•						•					•	•									
NORWAY																														
Norwegian School of Management, Graduate School	618						•		•																				•		
PAKISTAN																														
Lahore University of Management Sciences, Graduate School of Business Administration	619								•	•									•												
PORTUGAL																														
Instituto Empresarial Portuense	619	•							•	•							•	•		•	•									
Universidade do Porto	620								•																						
Universidade Nova de Lisboa, Faculdade de Economia-Gestaño	620						•		•	•									•												
REPUBLIC OF SINGAPORE																														
Nanyang Technological University, School of Accountancy and Business	621								•							•	•	•											•	
National University of Singapore, School of Postgraduate Management Studies	621																														

| MATRICULATION | ADMISSION REQUIREMENTS | | | FULL-TIME TUITION | PART-TIME TUITION | | | TIME OFFERED |
Fall Winter Spring Summer Deferred	GMAT Score	Undergraduate GPA	TOEFL Score	(R) State Resident (NR) Non-Resident	(R) State Resident (NR) Non-Resident	Minimum Months to Obtain Degree	Financial Aid	Credit Hours Required	Day Evening Weekend Summer
F,D	500						•		
F,D				39,000 Dutch guilders/ degree program				18	25	D
F,D	550		600				•		
F				79,500 Dutch guilders/ degree program	60,000 Dutch guilders/ degree program			18	17	D,E
	400						•		
D	550								
SP			580	17,000 New Zealand dollars/degree program 25,000 New Zealand dollars/degree program (NR)			•	36	D,E,W,S
F									
F,D	450						•	21	23	D
F							•		
F	400								
D			550	$2,000/trimester (R) $2,000/ trimester (NR)	$1,333/trimester (R) $1,333/ trimester (NR)		•	16	54	D,E,W

This table includes the names and locations of colleges, universities, and other institutions offering MBA programs. Schools appear in geographical sequence by U.S. state or territory or by country, and then alphabetically by school name. Specific degree information is detailed within the profile for each school. Refer to the page number in the table for the school's profile. If a school submitted incomplete data, one or more columns opposite the school name may be blank.

School	Page Number	Executive MBA	MBA/JD	MBA/MA	MBA/MSN	One-Year	Other	Management	Accounting/Finance	Arts Administration	Economics	Entrepreneurial	Health Care	Hotel Management	Human Resources	Information Systems/Technology	International Business	Manufacturing	Marketing	Operations Management	Org. Behavior/Development	Public Administration	Public Policy	Quality Management	Quantitative Analysis	Real Estate	Strategic Analysis	Transportation	Other	AACSB Accredited
SLOVENIA																														
International Executive Development Centre	622	•							•	•		•	•																	
SOUTH AFRICA																														
University of Cape Town, Graduate School of Business	622				•				•			•				•	•		•	•	•						•			
University of the Witwatersrand, Graduate School of Business Administration	623					•	•		•		•				•	•	•		•	•	•	•	•		•		•			
SPAIN																														
EAP-European School of Management, Business School	624	•				•	•		•		•	•			•	•	•		•	•	•					•		•		
Escola d'Alta Direcció i Administració (EADA)	624	•				•																								
Escuela Superior de Administracion y Direccion de Empresas	625					•		•			•			•		•	•		•	•		•	•				•			
Instituto de Empresa	626				•	•		•	•			•			•	•	•		•	•	•	•			•	•				
Schiller International University	626			•							•					•														
University of Navarra, International Graduate School of Management	626				•																									
SWITZERLAND																														
American Graduate School of Business	627																•													
International Institute for Management Development	628					•																								
Oekreal Graduate School of Business	629	•				•	•		•		•	•			•	•	•		•	•	•					•		•		
Schiller International University, American College of Switzerland, Schiller International University	629				•										•			•												
Université de Lausanne, École des Hautes Etudes Commerciales	630				•		•	•		•					•	•	•		•	•	•					•		•		
THAILAND																														
Bangkok University, Graduate School	630					•	•			•					•	•	•		•	•	•					•				
Chulalongkorn University, Sasin Graduate Institute of Business Administration	631	•				•	•								•		•													

MATRICULATION	ADMISSION REQUIREMENTS			FULL-TIME TUITION	PART-TIME TUITION				TIME OFFERED
Fall Winter Spring Summer Deferred	GMAT Score	Undergraduate GPA	TOEFL Score	(R) State Resident (NR) Non-Resident	(R) State Resident (NR) Non-Resident	Financial Aid	Minimum Months to Obtain Degree	Credit Hours Required	Day Evening Weekend Summer
F						•			
F,D	500		600			•			
F,D				21,000 South African rand/degree program		•	18		D,E
F									
F,D							9	62	D
F			580				21		D,E
D	550			$18,800/degree program		•	15		D,E
		2.8	550			•			
F,D			600				21	30	D
D						•	11	39	D,E,S
	500			38,000 Swiss francs/degree program			12	950	D,E,W,S
D	500		500						
		2.8	550			•			
F,SP,D									
F	450	2.5	550	$8,000/degree program			24	48	E,W
SP,D				$8,580			22	75	D

This table includes the names and locations of colleges, universities, and other institutions offering MBA programs. Schools appear in geographical sequence by U.S. state or territory or by country, and then alphabetically by school name. Specific degree information is detailed within the profile for each school. Refer to the page number in the table for the school's profile. If a school submitted incomplete data, one or more columns opposite the school name may be blank.

School	Page Number	Executive MBA	MBA/JD	MBA/MA	MBA/MSN	One Year	Other	Management	Accounting/Finance	Arts Administration	Economics	Entrepreneurial	Health Care	Hotel Management	Human Resources	Information Systems/Technology	International Business	Manufacturing	Marketing	Operations Management	Org. Behavior/Development	Public Administration	Public Policy	Quality Management	Quantitative Analysis	Real Estate	Strategic Analysis	Transportation	Other	AACSB Accredited
TURKEY																														
Bilkent University, Faculty of Business	632								•	•											•		•					•			
UNITED KINGDOM																														
Ashridge Management College	632								•	•		•				•	•	•		•	•	•					•		•	•	
Aston University, Aston Business School	633								•	•		•			•	•	•	•	•	•	•	•	•		•		•		•		•
City University	634									•					•			•													•
Cranfield University, Cranfield School of Management	634	•						•																							
De Montfort University, Leicester Business School	635					•		•	•			•			•			•			•						•				
Henley Management College	636							•	•		•				•	•	•		•	•	•			•			•				
Heriot-Watt University, Business School Edinburgh	636							•	•	•	•	•			•	•			•			•				•		•			
Huron University, London Campus	637					•		•																							
Imperial College, Management School	638					•																									
Kingston University, Kingston Business School	638							•																							
Lancaster University, The Management School	638							•	•		•	•			•	•	•		•	•	•						•		•		•
Manchester Metropolitan University, Faculty of Management and Business	639							•	•							•			•	•	•										
Middlesex University, Business School	639					•		•	•							•			•	•											
Richmond College, The American International University in London	639							•								•															•
Schiller International University	640					•		•						•		•															
Sheffield Hallam University, Business School	641					•		•	•		•	•			•	•	•		•	•	•	•		•		•					
University of Bath, School of Management	641								•			•			•			•	•	•	•						•				
University of Bradford, Bradford Management Center	642					•			•		•	•			•	•	•		•	•	•						•			•

110

MATRICULATION (Fall / Winter / Spring / Summer / Deferred)	ADMISSION REQUIREMENTS			FULL-TIME TUITION (R) State Resident / (NR) Non-Resident	PART-TIME TUITION (R) State Resident / (NR) Non-Resident	Financial Aid	Minimum Months to Obtain Degree	Credit Hours Required	TIME OFFERED (Day / Evening / Weekend / Summer)
	GMAT Score	Undergraduate GPA	TOEFL Score						
F	450		550			•	21	60	D
F,SP,D	550		570	6,000-14,000 British pounds/degree program		•	12	650	
D	550		600	7,000 British pounds/degree program 8,500 British pounds/degree program (NR)			12		D,E,W
F	550			9,000 British pounds (R) 9,750 British pounds (NR)		•	12		D,S
D	550		650	11,000 British pounds/degree program		•	12	43	D,S
D									
D			550	9,790 British pounds (R) 12,100 British pounds (NR)	6,175 British pounds (R) 7,888 British pounds (NR)	•	12	10	D,W
F	550		600				12		D
D	450	2.75	550			•			
F						•			
					3,750 British pounds			30	E,W
D	580		580	7,450 British pounds (R) 7,950 British pounds (NR)		•	12		D
								30	E
F	500		600						
		3.0		4,385 British pounds/semester (R) 4,385 British pounds/semester (NR)	885 British pounds/course (R) 885 British pounds/course (NR)	•	9	30	D,E,S
		2.8	550			•			
			550			•			
				8,000 British pounds		•		24	D,W,S
D	550		550			•			

This table includes the names and locations of colleges, universities, and other institutions offering MBA programs. Schools appear in geographical sequence by U.S. state or territory or by country, and then alphabetically by school name. Specific degree information is detailed within the profile for each school. Refer to the page number in the table for the school's profile. If a school submitted incomplete data, one or more columns opposite the school name may be blank.

School	Page Number	Executive MBA	MBA/JD	MBA/MA	MBA/MSN	One-Year	Other	Management	Accounting/Finance	Arts Administration	Economics	Entrepreneurial	Health Care	Hotel Management	Human Resources	Information Systems/Technology	International Business	Manufacturing	Marketing	Operations Management	Org. Behavior/Development	Public Administration	Public Policy	Quality Management	Quantitative Analysis	Real Estate	Strategic Analysis	Transportation	Other	AACSB Accredited
University of Brighton, Business School	643	•							•	•		•			•	•	•		•	•	•								•	•	•
University of Bristol, Graduate School of International Business	644							•	•		•	•		•		•		•		•		•						•		•	•
University of Durham	644							•																							
University of Edinburgh, Edinburgh University Management School	645							•	•		•	•			•	•		•		•	•	•						•		•	
University of Glasgow	645							•																							
University of Hull, School of Management	645							•							•															•	
University of London, London Business School	646							•	•		•	•			•	•	•		•	•	•						•		•		
University of Newcastle upon Tyne, School of Business Management	647					•		•	•			•						•	•	•							•		•		
University of Nottingham, School of Management and Finance	647	•						•	•		•	•	•		•	•	•		•	•	•		•			•		•		•	•
University of Oxford, School of Management	648							•																							
University of Sheffield, Management School	648							•						•		•															
University of Stirling, School of Management	649					•		•	•		•					•	•		•		•						•				
University of Strathclyde, Graduate Business School	649					•									•			•													
University of the West of England, Bristol, Bristol Business School	650							•	•		•				•	•		•	•	•							•		•		
University of Ulster at Jordanstown, Ulster Business School	650							•	•		•	•					•													•	
University of Warwick, Warwick Business School	651					•		•	•		•	•			•	•	•		•	•	•						•		•		
University of Westminster	652							•																							
The Victoria University of Manchester, Manchester Business School	652							•	•		•	•	•		•	•	•		•	•	•	•	•					•			

MATRICULATION (Fall, Winter, Spring, Summer, Deferred)	ADMISSION REQUIREMENTS			FULL-TIME TUITION (R) State Resident (NR) Non-Resident	PART-TIME TUITION (R) State Resident (NR) Non-Resident	Financial Aid	Minimum Months to Obtain Degree	Credit Hours Required	TIME OFFERED (Day, Evening, Weekend, Summer)
	GMAT Score	Undergraduate GPA	TOEFL Score						
D	500			$8,000/degree program (R) $9,500/degree program (NR)		•	12	120	D,E
F,D	500			11,600 British pounds/degree program	4,000 British pounds	•	15		D
				$7,000-$9,000			12		
D			550	5,950 British pounds (R) 7,450 British pounds (NR)		•	12	13	D,E
F	500	3.0	550	6,500 British pounds			12	12	D,E,W
F				15,500 British pounds	13,200 British pounds	•	21	25	D,E,W,S
D	500								
D			600	7,100 British pounds/degree program		•	12	14	D,E
F				3,750-4,050 British pounds 7,120-7,420 British pounds (NR)			24		
D	550	3.5	575	6,500 British pounds (R) 7,700 British pounds (NR)		•	18	15	D
D		2.7	550						
F,SP	550		600			•			
F,D					2,200 British pounds		30		E,S
	450		550	2,450 British pounds (R) 7,000 British pounds (NR)			12		D,E,S
D			600	9,300 British pounds (R) 11,000 British pounds (NR)		•	42	12	S
F,D	530		580	15,000 British pounds (R) 18,000 British pounds (NR)			16	1,200	D,E

Profiles of Business Schools and M.B.A. Programs

This section contains factual profiles of colleges, with a focus on their M.B.A. programs. Each profile will cover such items as enrollment figures, tuition, entrance and admission requirements, financial aid, programs of study, placement, and whom to contact for program information.

The information in each profile was collected via Peterson's International Guide to M.B.A. Programs survey, which was sent to the dean or director of the business school or M.B.A. program at each institution.

The index is arranged geographically then alphabetically within the state or country.

ALABAMA

Alabama Agricultural and Mechanical University

Department of Business Administration

Normal, Alabama

OVERVIEW
Alabama Agricultural and Mechanical University is a state-supported coed institution. Founded 1875. Setting: 2,001-acre suburban campus. Total institutional enrollment: 5,500. Program was first offered in 1970.

MBA HIGHLIGHTS

Entrance Difficulty**
Mean GMAT: 400
Mean GPA: 2.8

Cost $
Tuition: $103/semester hour
(Nonresident: $206/semester hour)
Room & Board: $12,000 (off-campus)

Enrollment Profile
Full-time: 45	Work Exp: 80%
Part-time: 85	International: 20%
Total: 130	Women: 35%
Average Age: 25	Minorities: 60%

Average Class Size: 25

ACADEMICS
Length of Program Minimum: 18 months. Maximum: 7 years.
Calendar Semesters.
Full-time Classes Main campus; evening, summer.
Part-time Classes Main campus; evening, summer.
Degree Requirements 36 semester hours including 12 elective semester hours.
Required Courses Accounting analysis for management, business policy and interpretation, financial management and policy, legal environment and ethics, management information systems, management of marketing activities, managerial economics, organizational behavior, production and operations management, quantitative business analysis. Courses may be waived through: previous course work.
Curricular Focus Business issues and problems, general management, problem solving and decision making.
Concentrations Accounting, economics, finance, human resources management, logistics, contract and acquisition management, total quality management, management, management information systems, marketing.
Faculty Full-time: 10, 90% with doctorates.
Teaching Methodology Case study: 5%, lecture: 60%, research: 15%, student presentations: 5%, team projects: 15%.
Special Opportunities Internship program available.

STUDENT STATISTICS
Geographic Representation State residents 70%. By region: South 60%; Northeast 10%; Midwest 10%. International 20%.
Undergraduate Majors Business 80%; engineering/technology 10%; humanities 5%; social sciences 5%.
Other Background Graduate degrees in other disciplines: 5%.

FACILITIES
Information Resources Main library with 349,134 bound volumes, 528,867 titles on microform, 1,683 periodical subscriptions, 3,145 records/tapes/CDs, 113 CD-ROMs. Business collection includes 200 bound volumes, 187 periodical subscriptions, 2 CD-ROMs, 66 videos.
Housing College housing not available.
Technology Computers are used moderately in course work. 40 computer terminals/PCs are available for use by students in program; they are located in computer labs. Students in the program are not required to have their own PC.

Computer Resources/On-line Services
Training	Yes	Dialog	Yes $
E-Mail	No		

ADMISSION
Acceptance 1994-95 Of those applying, 75% were accepted.
Entrance Requirements Bachelor's degree, GMAT score. Core courses waived through: previous course work.
Application Requirements Application form, copies of transcript.
Application Deadlines 6/1 for fall, 10/1 for spring.

FINANCIALS
Costs for 1994-95 Tuition: Full-time: $103/semester hour for state residents, $206/semester hour for nonresidents. Average room and board costs are $12,000 per academic year (off-campus).
Financial Aid In 1994-95, 18% of candidates received some institutionally administered aid in the form of assistantships, work-study, tuition assistance waivers. Total awards ranged from $267-$6,700. Financial aid is available to part-time students. Application deadlines: 4/1 for fall, 11/15 for spring. Contact: Mr. Percy Lanier, Director of Financial Aid, PO Box 907, Normal, AL 35762. (205) 851-5400.

INTERNATIONAL STUDENTS
Demographics 20% of students enrolled in the program are international; Asia 60%, Africa 30%, South America 1%, other 9%.
Services and Facilities ESL courses, counseling/support services.
Applying TOEFL required, minimum score of 550; proof of adequate funds; health insurance. Financial aid is available to international students. Financial aid application deadlines: 6/1 for fall, 10/1 for spring. Admission application deadlines: 6/1 for fall, 10/1 for spring.

PLACEMENT
In 1993-94, 6 organizations participated in on-campus recruiting; 6 on-campus interviews were conducted. Placement services include career counseling/planning, career fairs, career library, career placement, electronic job bank, job interviews, resume preparation, and resume referral to employers. Of 1994 graduates, the average starting salary was $29,250, the range was $14,000-$56,000.
Jobs by Employer Type Manufacturing 9%; service 27%; government 64%.
Jobs by Functional Area Marketing/sales 18%; finance 18%; operations 18%; management 18%; strategic planning 18%; technical management 10%.

Program Contact: Dr. Marsha Griffin, Director, MBA Program, Alabama Agricultural and Mechanical University, PO Box 1357, Normal, AL 35762-1357. (205) 851-5496; Fax: (205) 851-5492.

Auburn University

College of Business

Auburn, Alabama

OVERVIEW
Auburn University is a state-supported coed institution. Founded 1856. Setting: 1,875-acre small-town campus. Total institutional enrollment: 21,226. Program was first offered in 1969. AACSB-accredited.

MBA HIGHLIGHTS

Entrance Difficulty**
Mean GMAT: 560
Mean GPA: 3.3

Cost $
Tuition: $700/quarter
(Nonresident: $2,100/quarter)
Room & Board: $5,040

Enrollment Profile
Full-time: 112	Work Exp: 57%
Part-time: 111	International: 10%
Total: 223	Women: 30%
Average Age: 27	Minorities: 11%

Average Class Size: 32

ACADEMICS
Length of Program Minimum: 18 months. Maximum. 5 years.
Calendar Quarters.
Full-time Classes Main campus; day, early morning, summer.
Part-time Classes Main campus; day, early morning, summer.
Degree Requirements 87 credits including 20 elective credits.
Required Courses Financial management, information systems, management science, managerial accounting, managerial economics, marketing management, operations and quality management, organizational behavior, professional development, statistics, strategic management. Courses may be waived through: previous course work.
Curricular Focus Economic and financial theory, teamwork, technology management.
Concentrations Economics, finance, human resources management, international business, management information systems, marketing, operations management, public administration, technology management, agribusiness, transportation.
Faculty Full-time: 77, 100% with doctorates.
Teaching Methodology Case study: 15%, lecture: 60%, seminars by members of the business community: 3%, student presentations: 7%, team projects: 15%.
Special Opportunities Internship program available.

STUDENT STATISTICS
Geographic Representation State residents 60%. By region: South 75%; Northeast 8%; Midwest 5%; West 2%. International 10%.
Undergraduate Majors Business 44%; engineering/technology 25%; humanities 11%; science/mathematics 5%; social sciences 14%; other 1%.
Other Background Graduate degrees in other disciplines: 10%. Work experience: On average, students have 4 years of work experience on entrance to the program.

FACILITIES
Information Resources Main library with 2.2 million bound volumes, 2.9 million titles on microform, 19,636 periodical subscriptions, 13,634 records/tapes/CDs, 280 CD-ROMs.
Housing 5% of students in program live in college-owned or -operated housing.
Technology Computers are used moderately in course work. 600 computer terminals/PCs, linked by a campus-wide computer network, are available for use by students in program; they are located in the student center, classrooms, learning resource center, the library, the computer center, computer labs. Students in the program are not required to have their own PC.
Computer Resources/On-line Services

Training	Yes	Dun's	No
Internet	Yes	Dow Jones	No
E-Mail	Yes	Dialog	No
LEXIS/NEXIS	Yes	Bloomberg	No
CompuServe	No		

ADMISSION
Acceptance 1994-95 Of those applying, 75% were accepted.
Entrance Requirements Bachelor's degree, one course each in calculus and statistics, GMAT score. Core courses waived through: previous course work.
Application Requirements Application form, copies of transcript, 3 letters of recommendation.
Application Deadlines 9/1 for fall, 12/1 for winter, 3/1 for spring, 6/1 for summer.

FINANCIALS
Costs for 1994-95 Tuition: Full-time: $700/quarter for state residents, $2,100/quarter for nonresidents; Part-time day: $58/credit hour for state residents, $174/credit hour for nonresidents. Average room and board costs are $5,040 per academic year (on-campus) and $7,100 per academic year (off-campus).
Financial Aid In 1994-95, 65% of candidates received some institutionally administered aid in the form of loans, assistantships. Financial aid is available to part-time students. Application deadline: 4/15 for fall. Contact: Mr. Clark Aldridge, Director, Mary Martin Hall, Auburn, AL 36849. (334) 844-4723.

INTERNATIONAL STUDENTS
Demographics 10% of students enrolled in the program are international; Asia 60%, Europe 20%, Central America 10%, Africa 5%, other 5%.

Services and Facilities International student office, visa services, ESL courses, special assistance for nonnative speakers of English, counseling/support services.
Applying TOEFL required, minimum score of 550; proof of health; proof of adequate funds. Financial aid is available to international students. Assistantships are open to these students. Admission application deadlines: 9/1 for fall, 12/1 for winter, 3/1 for spring, 6/1 for summer. Contact: Ms. Mary Jo Wear, Assistant Director of International Programs, Suite 146, Lowder Business Building, 6 Box P, Auburn, AL 36849-0001. (334) 844-4505.

PLACEMENT
In 1993-94, 65 organizations participated in on-campus recruiting; 520 on-campus interviews were conducted. Placement services include alumni network, career counseling/planning, career fairs, career library, career placement, electronic job bank, job interviews, job search course, resume preparation, and resume referral to employers. Of 1994 graduates, 60% were employed within three months of graduation, the average starting salary was $34,550, the range was $20,400-$50,000.
Jobs by Employer Type Manufacturing 47%; service 34%; government 1%; consulting 18%.
Jobs by Functional Area Marketing/sales 11%; finance 20%; operations 12%; management 18%; technical management 6%; consulting 18%; other 15%.

Program Contact: Dr. Charlotte Sutton, Assistant Dean, Auburn University, Auburn, AL 36849-0001. (334) 844-4060; Fax: (334) 844-4861.

Auburn University at Montgomery

School of Business

Montgomery, Alabama

OVERVIEW
Auburn University at Montgomery is a state-supported comprehensive coed institution. Part of Auburn University. Founded 1967. Setting: 500-acre urban campus. Total institutional enrollment: 6,200. Program was first offered in 1977. AACSB-accredited.

MBA HIGHLIGHTS

Entrance Difficulty***
Mean GMAT: 550
Mean GPA: 2.93

Cost $
Tuition: $635/quarter
(Nonresident: $1,905/quarter)
Room & Board: N/R

Enrollment Profile

Full-time: 232	Work Exp: 100%
Part-time: 35	International: 13%
Total: 267	Women: 47%
Average Age: 31	Minorities: 20%

Average Class Size: 30

ACADEMICS
Length of Program Minimum: 12 months. Maximum: 5 years.
Calendar Quarters.
Full-time Classes Main campus; day, evening, summer.
Part-time Classes Main campus; day, evening, summer.
Degree Requirements 50 quarter hours including 10 elective quarter hours.
Required Courses Advanced corporate finance, business statistics, legal and social environment of business, managerial accounting, strategic management and business policy. Courses may be waived through: previous course work, work experience.
Curricular Focus Business issues and problems, leadership, problem solving and decision making.
Concentrations Accounting, finance, human resources management, management information systems, nursing.
Teaching Methodology Case study: 25%, faculty seminars: 5%, lecture: 30%, research: 10%, seminars by members of the business community: 5%, student presentations: 10%, team projects: 15%.

STUDENT STATISTICS

Geographic Representation State residents 27%. By region: South 100%. International 13%.

Undergraduate Majors Business 50%; education 2%; engineering/technology 30%; humanities 5%; nursing 2%; science/mathematics 5%; social sciences 5%; other 1%.

Other Background Graduate degrees in other disciplines: 1%.

FACILITIES

Information Resources Main library with 235,258 bound volumes, 790,000 titles on microform, 1,537 periodical subscriptions, 4,364 records/tapes/CDs, 161 CD-ROMs. Business collection includes 27,701 bound volumes, 244 periodical subscriptions, 13 CD-ROMs, 77 videos.

Housing College housing not available.

Technology Computers are used moderately in course work. 40 computer terminals/PCs, linked by a campus-wide computer network, are available for use by students in program; they are located in computer labs. Students in the program are not required to have their own PC.

Computer Resources/On-line Services

Training	No	Dun's	No
Internet	Yes	Dow Jones	No
E-Mail	No	Dialog	No
LEXIS/NEXIS	No	Bloomberg	No
CompuServe	No		

ADMISSION

Acceptance 1994-95 51 applied for admission; 100% were accepted.

Entrance Requirements Bachelor's degree, GMAT score of 400. Core courses waived through: previous course work, work experience.

Application Requirements Application form, copies of transcript.

Application Deadline Applications are processed on a rolling basis.

FINANCIALS

Costs for 1994-95 Tuition: Full-time: $635/quarter for state residents, $1,905/quarter for nonresidents.

Financial Aid In 1994-95, 10% of candidates received some institutionally administered aid in the form of loans. Financial aid is available to part-time students. Applications are processed on a rolling basis. Contact: Mr. James Berry, Director of Financial Aid, 7300 University Drive, Montgomery, AL 36117-3596. (205) 244-3368.

INTERNATIONAL STUDENTS

Demographics 13% of students enrolled in the program are international.

Services and Facilities ESL courses, counseling/support services.

Applying TOEFL required, minimum score of 500; proof of adequate funds; I-20 form. Financial aid is not available to international students. Admission applications are processed on a rolling basis. Contact: Dr. Neville Duarte, Adviser for International Student Association, 7300 University Drive, Montgomery, AL 36117-3596. (205) 244-3308.

PLACEMENT

In 1993-94, 25 organizations participated in on-campus recruiting. Placement services include career counseling/planning, career fairs, career placement, job interviews, resume preparation, and resume referral to employers. Of 1994 graduates, 99% were employed within three months of graduation, the average starting salary was $35,000, the range was $25,000-$65,000.

Jobs by Employer Type Manufacturing 25%; service 35%; government 30%; nonprofit 10%.

Jobs by Functional Area Marketing/sales 15%; finance 25%; operations 10%; management 20%; strategic planning 10%; technical management 20%.

Program Contact: Dr. Jane R. Goodson, MBA Director, Auburn University at Montgomery, 7300 University Drive, Montgomery, AL 36117-3596. (205) 244-3450; Fax: (205) 244-3792.

Jacksonville State University

College of Commerce and Business Administration

Jacksonville, Alabama

OVERVIEW

Jacksonville State University is a state-supported comprehensive coed institution. Founded 1883. Setting: 345-acre small-town campus with easy access to Birmingham. Total institutional enrollment: 7,500. Program was first offered in 1968.

MBA HIGHLIGHTS

Entrance Difficulty**
Mean GMAT: 475
Mean GPA: 2.75

Cost $
Tuition: $895/semester
(Nonresident: $1,343/semester)
Room & Board: N/R

Enrollment Profile

Full-time: 20	Work Exp: 50%
Part-time: 65	International: 10%
Total: 85	Women: 40%
Average Age: 28	Minorities: 10%

Average Class Size: 15

ACADEMICS

Length of Program Minimum: 18 months.

Calendar Semesters.

Full-time Classes Main campus; evening, summer.

Part-time Classes Main campus, Gadsden; evening, summer.

Degree Requirements 36 credits including 9 elective credits.

Required Courses Accounting information analysis, business forecasting, business policy and strategy, financial planning and policy, international course, leadership, managerial economics, marketing administration, technology and total quality.

Curricular Focus Organizational development and change management, problem solving and decision making, teamwork.

Concentrations Accounting, computer information systems, finance, management.

Faculty Full-time: 18, 100% with doctorates.

Teaching Methodology Case study: 30%, lecture: 20%, research: 10%, student presentations: 10%, team projects: 30%.

Special Opportunities Internship program available.

STUDENT STATISTICS

Geographic Representation State residents 75%. By region: South 90%; Northeast 5%; West 5%. International 10%.

Undergraduate Majors Business 90%; education 1%; engineering/technology 8%; nursing 1%.

Other Background Graduate degrees in other disciplines: 3%. Work experience: On average, students have 4-5 years of work experience on entrance to the program.

FACILITIES

Information Resources Main library with 593,034 bound volumes, 203,676 titles on microform, 2,697 periodical subscriptions, 11,456 records/tapes/CDs, 36 CD-ROMs.

Housing 1% of students in program live in college-owned or -operated housing.

Technology Computers are used moderately in course work. 150 computer terminals/PCs, linked by a campus-wide computer network, are available for use by students in program; they are located in learning resource center, the library, the computer center, computer labs. Students in the program are not required to have their own PC.

Computer Resources/On-line Services

Training	Yes	CompuServe	No
Internet	Yes	Dun's	No
E-Mail	Yes	Dow Jones	No
Multimedia Center	Yes	Dialog	No
LEXIS/NEXIS	No	Bloomberg	No

ADMISSION

Acceptance 1994-95 30 applied for admission; 100% were accepted.

Entrance Requirements GMAT score. Core courses waived through: previous course work.

Application Requirements Interview, application form, copies of transcript.

Application Deadline Applications are processed on a rolling basis.

FINANCIALS

Costs for 1994-95 Tuition: Full-time: $895/semester for state residents, $1,343/semester for nonresidents; Part-time day: $90/hour for state residents, $135/hour for nonresidents.

Financial Aid In 1994-95, 40% of candidates received some institutionally administered aid in the form of loans. Financial aid is not available to part-time students. Application deadline: 4/1 for fall. Contact: Mr. Larry Smith, Director of Financial Aid, 700 Pelham Road, Jacksonville, AL 36265-9982. (205) 782-5781.

INTERNATIONAL STUDENTS
Demographics 10% of students enrolled in the program are international; Africa 34%, Asia 33%, Europe 33%.

Services and Facilities International student office, international student center, visa services.

Applying TOEFL required, minimum score of 550; proof of adequate funds. Financial aid is not available to international students. Admission applications are processed on a rolling basis.

PLACEMENT
In 1993-94, 10 organizations participated in on-campus recruiting; 15 on-campus interviews were conducted. Placement services include career counseling/planning and career placement. Of 1994 graduates, 75% were employed within three months of graduation, the average starting salary was $30,000.

Program Contact: Dr. Louise Clark, Associate Dean, MBA Director, Jacksonville State University, 700 Pelham Road, Jacksonville, AL 36265-9982. (205) 782-5780; Fax: (205) 782-5312.

Samford University

School of Business

Birmingham, Alabama

OVERVIEW
Samford University is an independent Baptist comprehensive coed institution. Founded 1841. Setting: 280-acre suburban campus. Total institutional enrollment: 4,400. Program was first offered in 1965.

MBA HIGHLIGHTS

Entrance Difficulty***
Mean GMAT: 510
Mean GPA: 3.1

Cost $$
Tuition: $858/course
Room & Board: N/R

Enrollment Profile

Full-time: 12	Work Exp: 100%
Part-time: 138	International: 6%
Total: 150	Women: 38%
Average Age: 31	Minorities: 10%

Average Class Size: 24

ACADEMICS
Length of Program Minimum: 12 months. Maximum: 7 years.
Calendar Semesters.
Full-time Classes Main campus; evening, summer.
Part-time Classes Main campus; evening, summer.
Degree Requirements 36 credits including 6 elective credits.
Required Courses Accounting: measuring and reporting economic performance, environmental analysis, management of organizational systems, managerial decision making, managerial economics, managerial finance, managing the dynamics of marketing, operations management, organizational behavior, practicum in strategic management, the legal and social environment of business, the management control process, the post-industrial organization, the strategic management process.
Curricular Focus General management, problem solving and decision making.
Concentration Management.
Faculty Full-time: 13, 77% with doctorates; part-time: 2.
Teaching Methodology Case study: 75%, lecture: 15%, student presentations: 10%.

STUDENT STATISTICS
Geographic Representation State residents 94%. By region: South 94%. International 6%.

Undergraduate Majors Business 46%; education 6%; engineering/technology 24%; humanities 3%; nursing 2%; science/mathematics 5%; social sciences 7%; other 7%.

Other Background Graduate degrees in other disciplines: 4%. Work experience: On average, students have 9 years of work experience on entrance to the program.

FACILITIES
Information Resources Main library with 512,051 bound volumes, 288,559 titles on microform, 1,644 periodical subscriptions, 7 CD-ROMs. Business collection includes 16,500 bound volumes, 160 periodical subscriptions, 1 CD-ROM, 50 videos.

Housing College housing not available.

Technology Computer terminals/PCs, linked by a campus-wide computer network, are available for use by students in program; they are located in computer labs. Students in the program are not required to have their own PC.

Computer Resources/On-line Services

Training	Yes	E-Mail	Yes
Internet	Yes	Dialog	Yes

ADMISSION
Acceptance 1994-95 80 applied for admission; 88% were accepted.
Entrance Requirements Bachelor's degree, GMAT score, minimum 3 years of work experience. Core courses waived through: previous course work, work experience.
Application Requirements Application form, copies of transcript, resume/curriculum vitae, 2 letters of recommendation.
Application Deadline Applications are processed on a rolling basis.

FINANCIALS
Costs for 1994-95 Tuition: Full-time: $858/course.
Financial Aid In 1994-95, 3% of candidates received some institutionally administered aid in the form of loans. Total awards ranged from $4,000-$14,750. Financial aid is available to part-time students. Application deadline: 3/1 for fall. Contact: Mr. Clyde Walker, Director of Financial Aid, 800 Lakeshore Drive, Birmingham, AL 35229-0002. (205) 870-2905.

INTERNATIONAL STUDENTS
Demographics 6% of students enrolled in the program are international; Africa 45%, Asia 11%, Europe 11%, other 33%.

Services and Facilities International student office, visa services, counseling/support services.

Applying TOEFL required, minimum score of 550; proof of health; proof of adequate funds. Financial aid is not available to international students. Admission applications are processed on a rolling basis. Contact: Ms. Paulette Glasscock, Foreign Student Adviser, 800 Lakeshore Drive, Birmingham, AL 35229-0002. (205) 870-2871.

ALTERNATE MBA PROGRAMS
Executive MBA (EMBA) Length of program: Minimum: 21 months. Maximum: 7 years. Degree requirements: 45 credits.
MBA/JD Length of program: Minimum: 36 months. Maximum: 7 years. Degree requirements: 138 credits.
MBA/M Div Length of program: May range up to 7 years. Degree requirements: 118 credits.

PLACEMENT
Placement services include alumni network, career counseling/planning, career fairs, career library, career placement, electronic job bank, job interviews, job search course, resume preparation, and resume referral to employers. Of 1994 graduates, 100% were employed within three months of graduation.

Program Contact: Mr. Scott Battle, Director of Graduate Programs, Samford University, 800 Lakeshore Drive, Birmingham, AL 35229-0002. (205) 870-2931; Fax: (205) 870-2464.

Spring Hill College

Division of Business and Management

Mobile, Alabama

OVERVIEW
Spring Hill College is an independent Roman Catholic (Jesuit) comprehensive coed institution. Founded 1830. Setting: 500-acre suburban campus. Total

institutional enrollment: 1,349. Program was first offered in 1986.

MBA HIGHLIGHTS

Entrance Difficulty**
Mean GMAT: 490
Mean GPA: N/R

Cost $
Tuition: $255/credit hour
Room & Board: N/R

Enrollment Profile
Full-time: 2	Work Exp: 90%
Part-time: 61	International: 0%
Total: 63	Women: 35%
Average Age: 34	Minorities: 8%

Average Class Size: 14

ACADEMICS
Length of Program Minimum: 24 months. Maximum: 6 years.
Calendar Semesters.
Part-time Classes Main campus; evening, summer.
Degree Requirements 36 credit hours including 12 elective credit hours.
Required Courses Accounting for management control, business ethics, management of financial resources, management strategy and policy, managerial economics, marketing management, organizational behavior, quantitative business analysis.
Curricular Focus Business ethics and social responsibility, general management, strategic analysis and planning.
Concentration Management.
Faculty Full-time: 6, 100% with doctorates; part-time: 3, 66% with doctorates.
Teaching Methodology Case study: 25%, lecture: 25%, student presentations: 25%, team projects: 25%.

FACILITIES
Information Resources Main library with 148,293 bound volumes, 35,535 titles on microform, 766 periodical subscriptions, 21 CD-ROMs.
Housing College housing not available.
Technology Computers are used moderately in course work.
Computer Resources/On-line Services
Multimedia Center	Yes

ADMISSION
Entrance Requirements Bachelor's degree, GMAT score. Core courses waived through: previous course work.
Application Requirements Application form, copies of transcript.
Application Deadlines 8/1 for fall, 12/1 for spring. Applications are processed on a rolling basis.

FINANCIALS
Costs for 1994-95 Tuition: Part-time day: $255/credit hour.
Financial Aid In 1994-95, 10% of candidates received some institutionally administered aid in the form of loans. Total awards ranged from $1,000-$5,000. Financial aid is available to part-time students. Application deadlines: 6/15 for fall, 10/30 for spring. Applications are on a rolling basis. Contact: Ms. Betty Harlan, Director of Financial Aid, 4000 Dauphin Street, Mobile, AL 36608-1791. (334) 380-3460.

INTERNATIONAL STUDENTS
Applying TOEFL required, minimum score of 550; proof of health; proof of adequate funds. Financial aid is not available to international students. Admission application deadlines: 8/1 for fall, 12/1 for spring. Applications are processed on a rolling basis.

PLACEMENT
Placement services include career placement.

Program Contact: Ms. Joyce Genz, Director of Graduate Studies, Spring Hill College, 4000 Dauphin Street, Mobile, AL 36608-1791. (334) 380-3094; Fax: (334) 460-2190.

Troy State University

Sorrell College of Business

Troy, Alabama

OVERVIEW
Troy State University is a state-supported comprehensive coed institution. Part of Troy State University System. Founded 1887. Setting: 500-acre small-town campus. Total institutional enrollment: 5,800.

MBA HIGHLIGHTS
Entrance Difficulty**
Mean GMAT: 470
Mean GPA: 3.4

Cost
Tuition: N/R
(Nonresident: N/R)
Room & Board: $2,600

Enrollment Profile
Full-time: 30	Work Exp: 20%
Part-time: 7	International: 4%
Total: 37	Women: 40%
Average Age: 26	Minorities: 5%

Average Class Size: 24

ACADEMICS
Calendar Quarters.
Curricular Focus Business issues and problems, general management, problem solving and decision making.
Concentration Accounting.
Teaching Methodology Case study: 20%, lecture: 70%, team projects: 10%.

STUDENT STATISTICS
Geographic Representation State residents 84%. International 4%.
Undergraduate Majors Engineering/technology 96%; humanities 2%; social sciences 2%.

FACILITIES
Information Resources Main library with 275,962 bound volumes, 23,205 titles on microform, 3,762 periodical subscriptions, 8,594 records/tapes/CDs.
Housing 1% of students in program live in college-owned or -operated housing.
Technology Computers are used moderately in course work. 40 computer terminals/PCs are available for use by students in program; they are located in computer labs. Students in the program are not required to have their own PC.
Computer Resources/On-line Services
Training	No	E-Mail	No

ADMISSION
Entrance Requirements Bachelor's degree, prerequisite courses required for applicants with non-business degree, GMAT score of 450, minimum 2.5 GPA, if GMAT and/or GPA are less than required, admission is conditional. Core courses waived through: previous course work.
Application Requirements Application form, copies of transcript.

FINANCIALS
Financial Aid In 1994-95, candidates received some institutionally administered aid in the form of fellowships, assistantships. Financial aid is not available to part-time students. Application deadline: 6/30 for fall. Contact: Dr. Wilfred Bibbins, MBA Coordinator, Bibb Graves Hall, Room 03, Troy, AL 36082. (334) 670-3509.

INTERNATIONAL STUDENTS
Demographics 4% of students enrolled in the program are international.
Applying TOEFL required, minimum score of 525; proof of health; proof of adequate funds. Financial aid is available to international students. Financial aid application deadline: 6/31 for fall. Admission applications are processed on a rolling basis.

PROGRAM
One-Year MBA Length of program: Minimum: 12 months. Maximum: 8 years. Full-time classes: Main campus; evening, summer. Part-time classes: Main campus; evening, summer. Degree requirements: 50 hours including 1 elective hour.

Program Contact: Dr. Wilfred J. Bibbins, MBA Coordinator, Troy State University, Bibb Graves Hall, Room 03, Troy, AL 36082. (334) 670-3509.

Troy State University at Dothan

School of Business

Dothan, Alabama

OVERVIEW

Troy State University at Dothan is a state-supported comprehensive coed institution. Part of Troy State University System. Founded 1961. Setting: 250-acre small-town campus. Total institutional enrollment: 2,606. Program was first offered in 1985.

MBA HIGHLIGHTS

Entrance Difficulty*
Mean GMAT: 500
Mean GPA: 3.0

Cost $
Tuition: $58/quarter hour
(Nonresident: $104/quarter hour)
Room & Board: N/R

Enrollment Profile

Full-time: 49	Work Exp: N/R
Part-time: 12	International: 5%
Total: 61	Women: 33%
Average Age: 30	Minorities: 13%

Average Class Size: 40

ACADEMICS

Length of Program Minimum: 18 months. Maximum: 6 years.
Calendar Quarters.
Full-time Classes Main campus, Fort Rucker; evening, summer.
Part-time Classes Main campus, Fort Rucker; evening, summer.
Degree Requirements 60 quarter hours including 15 elective quarter hours.
Required Courses Business research, business strategy, management information systems concepts, managerial accounting, managerial economics, managerial finance, marketing management, operations management, organization theory.
Curricular Focus Economic and financial theory, problem solving and decision making, strategic analysis and planning.
Concentrations Accounting, human resources management, management, management information systems.
Faculty Full-time: 15, 100% with doctorates.
Teaching Methodology Case study: 10%, lecture: 60%, research: 10%, student presentations: 10%, team projects: 10%.

STUDENT STATISTICS

Geographic Representation State residents 72%. By region: South 95%. International 5%.
Undergraduate Majors Business 80%; engineering/technology 5%; other 15%.
Other Background Graduate degrees in other disciplines: 5%. Work experience: On average, students have 6 years of work experience on entrance to the program.

FACILITIES

Information Resources Main library with 80,825 bound volumes, 178,794 titles on microform, 697 periodical subscriptions, 4,761 records/tapes/CDs, 17 CD-ROMs.
Housing College housing not available.
Technology Computers are used moderately in course work. 90 computer terminals/PCs are available for use by students in program; they are located in learning resource center, the computer center, computer labs. Students in the program are not required to have their own PC.

Computer Resources/On-line Services

Training	Yes	Multimedia Center	Yes
Internet	Yes	Dialog	Yes
E-Mail	Yes		

ADMISSION

Entrance Requirements Bachelor's degree, GMAT score.
Application Requirements Application form, copies of transcript.
Application Deadline Applications are processed on a rolling basis.

FINANCIALS

Costs for 1994-95 Tuition: Full-time: $58/quarter hour for state residents, $104/quarter hour for nonresidents.
Financial Aid In 1994-95, candidates received some institutionally administered aid in the form of loans. Total awards ranged from $1,825-$8,500. Financial aid is available to part-time students. Application deadline: 5/1 for fall. Contact: Ms. Jonua Byrd, Director of Financial Aid and Veteran's Affairs, PO Box 8368, Dothan, AL 36304-0368. (205) 983-6556 Ext. 255.

INTERNATIONAL STUDENTS

Demographics 5% of students enrolled in the program are international.
Applying TOEFL required; proof of health; proof of adequate funds. Financial aid is not available to international students.

ALTERNATE MBA PROGRAM

Executive MBA (EMBA) Length of program: Minimum: 24 months. Maximum: 8 years. Degree requirements: 85 quarter hours. Bachelor's degree in a non-business field. Average class size: 15.

PLACEMENT

Placement services include alumni network, career counseling/planning, career fairs, resume preparation, and resume referral to employers. Of 1994 graduates, 90% were employed within three months of graduation.

Program Contact: Dr. Steven Cross, Dean of the School of Business, Troy State University at Dothan, PO Box 8368, Dothan, AL 36304-0368. (205) 983-6556 Ext. 265; Fax: (205) 983-6322.

Troy State University in Montgomery

School of Business

Montgomery, Alabama

OVERVIEW

Troy State University in Montgomery is a state-supported comprehensive coed institution. Part of Troy State University System. Founded 1957. Setting: urban campus. Total institutional enrollment: 3,600.

MBA HIGHLIGHTS

Entrance Difficulty**

Cost $
Tuition: $46/quarter hour
(Nonresident: $92/quarter hour)
Room & Board: N/R

Enrollment Profile

Full-time: N/R	Work Exp: 95%
Part-time: N/R	International: 2%
Total: 120	Women: 56%
Average Age: N/R	Minorities: 40%

Average Class Size: 20

ACADEMICS

Length of Program May range up to 8 years.
Calendar Quarters.
Full-time Classes Main campus, distance learning option; evening, weekends, summer.
Part-time Classes Main campus, distance learning option; evening, weekends, summer.
Degree Requirements 96 quarter hours including 55 elective quarter hours.
Required Courses Business strategy, decision theory, managerial accounting, managerial economics, managerial finance, marketing management, organizational behavior, research methods.

Curricular Focus Managing diversity, problem solving and decision making, teamwork.

Concentrations Accounting, human resources management, management, management information systems, quantitative analysis.

Teaching Methodology Case study: 20%, faculty seminars: 10%, lecture: 10%, research: 20%, student presentations: 20%, team projects: 20%.

Special Opportunities International exchange program available.

STUDENT STATISTICS

Geographic Representation State residents 75%. International 2%.

Other Background Work experience: On average, students have 10 years of work experience on entrance to the program.

FACILITIES

Information Resources Main library with 22,410 bound volumes, 1,473 titles on microform, 337 periodical subscriptions, 2,217 records/tapes/CDs.

Housing College housing not available.

Technology Computers are used moderately in course work. Computer terminals/PCs are available for use by students in program; they are located in learning resource center, the library, the computer center, computer labs. Students in the program are not required to have their own PC.

Computer Resources/On-line Services

| E-Mail | No | Multimedia Center | Yes |

ADMISSION

Entrance Requirements Bachelor's degree, prerequisite courses required for applicants with non-business degree, GMAT score of 450, minimum 2.5 GPA. Core courses waived through: previous course work.

Application Requirements Interview, application form, copies of transcript.

Application Deadline Applications are processed on a rolling basis. Application discs available.

FINANCIALS

Costs for 1994-95 Tuition: Full-time: $46/quarter hour for state residents, $92/quarter hour for nonresidents.

Financial Aid In 1994-95, candidates received some institutionally administered aid in the form of loans. Total awards ranged from $1,800-$8,500. Financial aid is available to part-time students. Applications are processed on a rolling basis. Contact: Ms. Evelyn McKeithen, Director of Financial Aid, PO Drawer 4419, Montgomery, AL 36103-4419. (334) 241-9510.

INTERNATIONAL STUDENTS

Demographics 2% of students enrolled in the program are international.

Applying Undergraduate degree must be reviewed by World Education Services in New York. Financial aid is not available to international students. Admission applications are processed on a rolling basis.

PLACEMENT

Placement services include alumni network, career counseling/planning, career placement, job interviews, resume preparation, and resume referral to employers. Of 1994 graduates, 90% were employed within three months of graduation.

Program Contact: Dr. H. R. Russell, Assistant Professor of Management, Troy State University in Montgomery, PO Drawer 4419, Montgomery, AL 36103-4419. (334) 241-9600; Fax: (334) 241-9696.

University of Alabama

Manderson Graduate School of Business

Tuscaloosa, Alabama

OVERVIEW

The University of Alabama is a state-supported coed institution. Part of University of Alabama System. Founded 1831. Setting: 1,000-acre small-town campus with easy access to Birmingham. Total institutional enrollment: 19,000. Program was first offered in 1945. AACSB-accredited.

Entrance Difficulty**
Mean GMAT: 580
Mean GPA: 3.25

Cost $
Tuition: $1,130/semester
(Nonresident: $2,821/semester)
Room & Board: N/R

Enrollment Profile

Full-time: 135	Work Exp: N/R
Part-time: 0	International: 15%
Total: 135	Women: 35%
Average Age: 26	Minorities: 10%

Class Size: 60 - 65

ACADEMICS

Length of Program Minimum: 20 months. Maximum: 2 years.

Calendar Semesters.

Full-time Classes Main campus; day.

Degree Requirements 49 hours including 15 elective hours.

Required Courses Business law, financial and managerial accounting, human resources management, managerial communications, managerial economics, marketing, statistics, strategic management. Courses may be waived through: previous course work.

Curricular Focus Business issues and problems, professional development, teamwork.

Concentrations Accounting, finance, human resources management, international business, management, marketing, operations management, strategic management.

Teaching Methodology Case study: 33%, lecture: 33%, student presentations: 1%, team projects: 33%.

Special Opportunities Internship program available.

STUDENT STATISTICS

Geographic Representation State residents 55%. International 15%.

Undergraduate Majors Business 75%; other 25%.

Other Background Graduate degrees in other disciplines: 2%.

FACILITIES

Information Resources Main library with 2 million bound volumes, 3 million titles on microform, 16,692 periodical subscriptions, 19,266 records/tapes/CDs, 426 CD-ROMs. Business collection in Angelo Bruno Business Library includes 150,000 bound volumes, 1,200 periodical subscriptions.

Housing 2% of students in program live in college-owned or -operated housing.

Technology Computers are used moderately in course work. Computer terminals/PCs, linked by a campus-wide computer network, are available for use by students in program; they are located in the computer center. Students in the program are not required to have their own PC.

Computer Resources/On-line Services

Training	Yes	Dun's	Yes
Internet	Yes	Dow Jones	Yes
E-Mail	Yes	Dialog	No
LEXIS/NEXIS	Yes	Bloomberg	Yes
CompuServe	No		

ADMISSION

Acceptance 1994-95 Of those applying, 70% were accepted.

Entrance Requirements Bachelor's degree, statistics, pre-calculus, GMAT score. Core courses waived through: previous course work.

Application Requirements Written essay, application form, copies of transcript, resume/curriculum vitae, personal statement, 3 letters of recommendation.

Application Deadline 7/1 for fall.

FINANCIALS

Costs for 1994-95 Tuition: Full-time: $1,130/semester for state residents, $2,821/semester for nonresidents.

Financial Aid In 1994-95, candidates received some institutionally administered aid in the form of scholarships, loans, fellowships, assistantships. Application deadline: 7/1 for fall. Contact: Ms. Molly Lawrence, Director of Student Financial Services, Box 870166, Tuscaloosa, AL 35487-0166. (205) 348-6816.

INTERNATIONAL STUDENTS

Demographics 15% of students enrolled in the program are international; Asia 98%, Other 2%.

Services and Facilities International student center, visa services, language tutoring, ESL courses, counseling/support services.

Applying TOEFL required, minimum score of 580. Financial aid is available to international students. Financial aid application deadline: 4/30 for fall. Admission application deadline: 5/15 for fall. Contact: Mr. Greg Leonard, Director of International Student and Scholar Services, Box 870304, Tuscaloosa, AL 35487-0223. (205) 348-5402.

ALTERNATE MBA PROGRAMS

Executive MBA (EMBA) Length of program: Minimum: 17 months. Maximum: 2 years. Degree requirements: 48 hours. Minimum 3 years work experience. Average class size: 30.

MBA/JD Length of program: Minimum: 48 months. Degree requirements: Separate applications must be submitted to both business and law.

PLACEMENT

Placement services include alumni network, career counseling/planning, career fairs, career library, career placement, electronic job bank, job interviews, resume preparation, and southeastern MBA consortium. Of 1994 graduates, 95% were employed within three months of graduation, the average starting salary was $35,600, the range was $24,000-$55,000.

Jobs by Functional Area Finance 58%; operations 20%; consulting 15%; other 7%.

Program Contact: Mr. Jim Johnson, Coordinator, Graduate Recruiting, University of Alabama, Box 870166, Tuscaloosa, AL 35487-0166. (205) 348-6517, or (800) 365-8583; Fax: (205) 348-2951.
See full description on page 848.

University of Alabama at Birmingham

Graduate School of Management

Birmingham, Alabama

OVERVIEW

The University of Alabama at Birmingham is a state-supported coed institution. Part of University of Alabama System. Founded 1969. Setting: 265-acre urban campus. Total institutional enrollment: 16,000. Program was first offered in 1971. AACSB-accredited.

MBA HIGHLIGHTS

Entrance Difficulty**
Mean GMAT: 490
Mean GPA: 2.8

Cost $
Tuition: $830/quarter
(Nonresident: $1,660/quarter)
Room & Board: N/R

Enrollment Profile

Full-time: 40	Work Exp: 80%
Part-time: 360	International: 5%
Total: 400	Women: 40%
Average Age: 26	Minorities: 5%

Average Class Size: 35

ACADEMICS

Length of Program Minimum: 24 months. Maximum: 7 years.

Calendar Semesters.

Full-time Classes Main campus; evening.

Part-time Classes Main campus; evening.

Degree Requirements 30 semester hours including 3-12 elective semester hours.

Required Courses Business policy, cost and control, financial management, international business, macroeconomics, organizational behavior, production management or social, ethical and legal environment or management information services, quantitative methods, seminar marketing.

Curricular Focus Economic and financial theory, general management, problem solving and decision making.

Concentration Management.

Faculty Full-time: 40, 100% with doctorates; part-time: 4.

Teaching Methodology Case study: 35%, lecture: 35%, student presentations: 10%, team projects: 20%.

STUDENT STATISTICS

Geographic Representation State residents 90%. By region: South 95%. International 5%.

Undergraduate Majors Business 50%; education 1%; engineering/technology 43%; humanities 1%; nursing 2%; science/mathematics 1%; social sciences 1%; other 1%.

Other Background Work experience: On average, students have 2 years of work experience on entrance to the program.

FACILITIES

Information Resources Main library with 1.5 million bound volumes, 416,175 titles on microform, 5,390 periodical subscriptions, 50,361 records/tapes/CDs, 20 CD-ROMs.

Housing College housing available.

Technology Computers are used moderately in course work. 80 computer terminals/PCs are available for use by students in program; they are located in learning resource center, the library, computer labs. Students in the program are not required to have their own PC.

Computer Resources/On-line Services

Training	No	E-Mail	Yes
Internet	Yes		

ADMISSION

Acceptance 1994-95 334 applied for admission; 90% were accepted.

Entrance Requirements Bachelor's degree, undergraduate calculus course, GMAT score. Core courses waived through: previous course work.

Application Requirements Application form, copies of transcript, resume/curriculum vitae, personal statement.

Application Deadlines 7/1 for fall, 11/1 for winter, 2/1 for spring, 4/1 for summer. Applications are processed on a rolling basis.

FINANCIALS

Costs for 1994-95 Tuition: Full-time: $830/quarter for state residents, $1,660/quarter for nonresidents. Fees: Full-time: $73-$103/quarter for state residents, $73-$103/quarter for nonresidents.

Financial Aid In 1994-95, candidates received some institutionally administered aid in the form of grants, loans, assistantships, work-study. Financial aid is available to part-time students. Application deadline: 5/1 for fall. Contact: Mr. Claude McCann, Director of Financial Aid, HUC 317, Birmingham, AL 35294-1150. (205) 934-8223.

INTERNATIONAL STUDENTS

Demographics 5% of students enrolled in the program are international.

Services and Facilities International student office, international student center, counseling/support services.

Applying TOEFL required, minimum score of 550; proof of health; proof of adequate funds. Financial aid is available to international students. Financial aid application deadline: 5/1 for fall. Admission application deadlines: 7/1 for fall, 2/1 for spring. Applications are processed on a rolling basis. Contact: Ms. Carol Argo, Associate Director, Center for International Programs, HUC 318, Birmingham, AL 35294-1150. (205) 934-3328.

ALTERNATE MBA PROGRAMS

MBA/MSN Length of program: Minimum: 24 months. Full-time classes: Main campus; day, evening, weekends, summer. Part-time classes: Main campus; day, evening, weekends, summer. Degree requirements: 66 semester hours.

MBA/MPH Length of program: Minimum: 24 months. Full-time classes: Main campus; day, evening, weekends, summer. Part-time classes: Main campus; day, evening, weekends, summer. Degree requirements: 66 semester hours.

MBA/MSHA Length of program: Minimum: 24 months. Full-time classes: Main campus; day, evening, weekends, summer. Part-time classes: Main campus; day, evening, weekends, summer. Degree requirements: 66 semester hours.

PLACEMENT

Placement services include alumni network, career counseling/planning, career fairs, career library, career placement, electronic job bank, job interviews, resume preparation, and resume referral to employers.

Program Contact: Ms. Susan Williams, Graduate Adviser, University of Alabama at Birmingham, UAB Station, Birmingham, AL 35294-1150. (205) 934-8817; Fax: (205) 975-6234.

University of Alabama in Huntsville

College of Administrative Science

Huntsville, Alabama

OVERVIEW
The University of Alabama in Huntsville is a state-supported coed institution. Part of University of Alabama System. Founded 1950. Setting: 337-acre suburban campus. Total institutional enrollment: 8,500. Program was first offered in 1965.

PROGRAM HIGHLIGHTS

Entrance Difficulty**
Mean GMAT: 486
Mean GPA: 3.1

Cost $
Tuition: $110 - $132/credit hour
(Nonresident: $220 - $264/credit hour)
Room & Board: $4,360

Enrollment Profile
Full-time: 35
Part-time: 90
Total: 125
Average Age: 32

Work Exp: 90%
International: 6%
Women: 43%
Minorities: 6%

Average Class Size: 20

ACADEMICS
Calendar Semesters.

Curricular Focus Technology management.

Concentrations Management, technology management.

Faculty Full-time: 30, 100% with doctorates; part-time: 5, 100% with doctorates.

Teaching Methodology Case study: 20%, lecture: 30%, seminars by members of the business community: 10%, student presentations: 20%, team projects: 20%.

Special Opportunities International exchange and internship programs available.

STUDENT STATISTICS
Geographic Representation State residents 90%. International 6%.

Undergraduate Majors Business 68%; engineering/technology 15%; humanities 5%; science/mathematics 6%; social sciences 5%; other 1%.

Other Background Graduate degrees in other disciplines: 5%. Work experience: On average, students have 5 years of work experience on entrance to the program.

FACILITIES
Information Resources Main library with 426,344 bound volumes, 413,909 titles on microform, 3,105 periodical subscriptions, 1,835 records/tapes/CDs. Business collection includes 33,000 bound volumes, 1,300 periodical subscriptions, 15 CD-ROMs, 50 videos.

Housing 5% of students in program live in college-owned or -operated housing.

Technology Computers are used heavily in course work. 40 computer terminals/PCs, linked by a campus-wide computer network, are available for use by students in program; they are located in computer labs. Students in the program are not required to have their own PC.

Computer Resources/On-line Services

Training	Yes	Videoconference Center	Yes
Internet	Yes	Dialog	Yes
E-Mail	Yes		

Other on-line services: OCLC.

ADMISSION
Acceptance 1994-95 80 applied for admission; 88% were accepted.

Entrance Requirements Bachelor's degree, GMAT score. Core courses waived through: previous course work.

Application Requirements Application form, copies of transcript.

Application Deadline Applications are processed on a rolling basis.

FINANCIALS
Costs for 1994-95 Tuition: Full-time: $110-$132/credit hour for state residents, $220-$264/credit hour for nonresidents; Part-time day: $135-$166/credit hour for state residents, $269-$332/credit hour for nonresidents. Fees: Full-time: $55/semester for state residents, $55/semester for nonresidents; Part-time day: $35/semester for state residents, $35/semester for nonresidents. Average room and board costs are $4,360 per academic year (on-campus) and $4,920 per academic year (off-campus).

Financial Aid In 1994-95, 20% of candidates received some institutionally administered aid in the form of loans, assistantships. Total awards ranged from $4,400-$8,800. Financial aid is available to part-time students. Application deadlines: 3/1 for fall, 10/1 for spring. Contact: Mr. James Gibson, Director of Financial Aid, University Center 124-D, Huntsville, AL 35899. (205) 895-6241.

INTERNATIONAL STUDENTS
Demographics 6% of students enrolled in the program are international; Asia 90%, Europe 5%, South America 5%.

Services and Facilities Visa services, ESL courses.

Applying TOEFL required, minimum score of 500; proof of health; proof of adequate funds. Financial aid is not available to international students. Admission application deadlines: 5/1 for fall, 9/20 for spring. Applications are processed on a rolling basis. Contact: Ms. Reva Bailey, Registrar, University Center 119, Huntsville, AL 35899. (205) 895-6753.

PROGRAM
MSM Length of program: Minimum: 12 months. Maximum: 6 years. Full-time classes: Main campus; evening. Part-time classes: Main campus, distance learning option; evening. Degree requirements: 33 credit hours including 6 elective credit hours.

PLACEMENT
Placement services include career counseling/planning, career fairs, career library, career placement, job interviews, job search course, resume preparation, and resume referral to employers. Of 1994 graduates, the average starting salary was $36,000, the range was $30,000-$50,000.

Jobs by Functional Area Finance 14%; management 14%; technical management 23%; other 49%.

Program Contact: Dr. Dorla Evans, Assistant Dean, University of Alabama in Huntsville, ASB 102, Huntsville, AL 35899. (205) 895-6025, or (800) 824-2255; Fax: (205) 895-6328; Internet Address: evansd@email.uah.edu.

University of Mobile

School of Business

Mobile, Alabama

OVERVIEW
The University of Mobile is an independent Baptist comprehensive coed institution. Founded 1961. Setting: 765-acre suburban campus. Total institutional enrollment: 2,251. Program was first offered in 1986.

MBA HIGHLIGHTS

Entrance Difficulty*
Mean GMAT: 423
Mean GPA: 2.9

Cost $
Tuition: $250/hour
Room & Board: N/R

Enrollment Profile
Full-time: 3
Part-time: 57
Total: 60
Average Age: 34

Work Exp: 95%
International: 15%
Women: 46%
Minorities: 29%

Average Class Size: 12

The University of Mobile's M.B.A. program provides advanced study for men and women currently in managerial or administrative positions or who aspire to such positions. The primary objective of the program is to provide students with realistic business knowledge and skills essential for successful functioning as administrators in business, industry, churches, government, and other types of organizations. Specific objectives of the program include assisting advanced students to develop an ethical approach to making and applying managerial decisions; improve team-building, communication, analytical, problem-solving, and decision-making skills; integrate organizational experience with current theories of leadership and management in order to develop new managerial concepts; analyze alternative solutions to managerial problems involving technological, social, economic, functional, political, and ethical factors; develop strategies for coping with the challenges of new organizational systems and changing technology, including modern application of computers, word processors, robotics, telecommunications, and other technological developments; view opportunities and challenges from a global perspective; and think and act like an executive. The program emphasizes group activities and in-depth original research. Students work in small voluntary groups in most of their courses. Nearly all courses have a global dimension, with at least one elective course in global business recommended, and realistic involvement in actual business activities is encouraged.

ACADEMICS
Length of Program Minimum: 24 months. Maximum: 6 years.
Calendar Semesters.
Full-time Classes Main campus; day, evening, weekends, summer.
Part-time Classes Main campus; day, evening, weekends, summer.
Degree Requirements 40 hours including 6 elective hours.
Required Courses Accounting, business law, communications, economics, finance, management, management information systems, marketing, policy. Courses may be waived through: previous course work, work experience.
Curricular Focus General management, human relations approach to management, qualitative approach.
Concentration Management.
Faculty Full-time: 8, 87% with doctorates; part-time: 2, 100% with doctorates.
Teaching Methodology Case study: 10%, faculty seminars: 5%, lecture: 40%, research: 20%, seminars by members of the business community: 5%, student presentations: 10%, team projects: 10%.

STUDENT STATISTICS
Geographic Representation State residents 83%. By region: South 83%; Midwest 2%. International 15%.
Other Background Graduate degrees in other disciplines: 2%. Work experience: On average, students have 5 years of work experience on entrance to the program.

FACILITIES
Information Resources Main library with 125,344 bound volumes, 581 titles on microform, 81,820 periodical subscriptions, 87,417 records/tapes/CDs, 8 CD-ROMs. Business collection includes 5,100 bound volumes, 49 periodical subscriptions, 11 CD-ROMs, 1,077 videos.
Housing 2% of students in program live in college-owned or -operated housing.
Technology Computers are used moderately in course work. 40 computer terminals/PCs are available for use by students in program; they are located in learning resource center, the computer center. Students in the program are not required to have their own PC.

Computer Resources/On-line Services

Training	No	CompuServe	No
Internet	No	Dun's	No
E-Mail	No	Dow Jones	No
Multimedia Center	Yes	Dialog	Yes $
LEXIS/NEXIS	No	Bloomberg	No

ADMISSION
Acceptance 1994-95 Of those applying, 95% were accepted.
Entrance Requirements Bachelor's degree, GMAT score of 400, minimum 2.5 GPA. Core courses waived through: previous course work.
Application Requirements Application form, copies of transcript.
Application Deadlines 7/1 for fall, 12/1 for spring.

FINANCIALS
Costs for 1994-95 Tuition: Full-time: $250/hour.
Financial Aid In 1994-95, 80% of candidates received some institutionally administered aid in the form of scholarships, assistantships. Total awards ranged from $500-$12,000. Financial aid is available to part-time students. Application deadline: 3/31 for fall. Contact: Ms. Lydia Herrington, Director of Financial Aid, PO Box 13220, Mobile, AL 36663-0220. (334) 675-5990.

INTERNATIONAL STUDENTS
Demographics 15% of students enrolled in the program are international.

Applying TOEFL required, minimum score of 550; proof of adequate funds. Financial aid is available to international students. Financial aid application deadline: 7/1 for fall. Admission application deadlines: 7/1 for fall, 12/1 for spring.

PLACEMENT
Placement services include career counseling/planning, career fairs, career placement, job interviews, resume preparation, and resume referral to employers. Of 1994 graduates, 90% were employed within three months of graduation, the average starting salary range was $30,000-$37,000.

Program Contact: Dr. Anne B. Lowery, MBA Director, University of Mobile, PO Box 13220, Mobile, AL 36663-0220. (334) 675-5990, or (800) 946-7267 (AL only); Fax: (334) 675-3404.

University of North Alabama

School of Business

Florence, Alabama

OVERVIEW
The University of North Alabama is a state-supported comprehensive coed institution. Founded 1872. Setting: 100-acre suburban campus. Total institutional enrollment: 5,400.

MBA HIGHLIGHTS

Entrance Difficulty**
Mean GMAT: 475
Mean GPA: 3.0

Cost $
Tuition: $79/semester hour
(Nonresident: $79/semester hour)
Room & Board: $2,600

Enrollment Profile

Full-time: 10	Work Exp: 95%
Part-time: 140	International: 10%
Total: 150	Women: 35%
Average Age: 30	Minorities: 10%

Average Class Size: 18

ACADEMICS
Length of Program Minimum: 12 months. Maximum: 7 years.
Calendar Semesters.
Full-time Classes Main campus, Corinith; day, evening, weekends, early morning, summer.
Part-time Classes Main campus; day, evening, weekends, early morning, summer.
Degree Requirements 33 semester hours including 9 elective semester hours.
Required Courses Cost for management decision analysis, decision theory, management policy, managerial economics or economic analysis, managerial finance, marketing strategy, quantitative techniques in business, research and report writing.
Curricular Focus Business issues and problems, general management, problem solving and decision making.
Concentrations Accounting, finance, management, marketing.
Faculty Full-time: 15, 100% with doctorates.
Teaching Methodology Case study: 20%, lecture: 50%, research: 10%, student presentations: 10%, team projects: 10%.
Special Opportunities International exchange in Netherlands, Turkey.

STUDENT STATISTICS
Geographic Representation International 10%.
Undergraduate Majors Business 60%; engineering/technology 10%; humanities 10%; science/mathematics 10%; social sciences 10%.
Other Background Graduate degrees in other disciplines: 4%. Work experience: On average, students have 6 years of work experience on entrance to the program.

FACILITIES
Information Resources Main library with 294,359 bound volumes, 202,003 titles on microform, 2,046 periodical subscriptions, 4,693 records/tapes/CDs.

Housing 10% of students in program live in college-owned or -operated housing.

Technology Computers are used moderately in course work. 260 computer terminals/PCs, linked by a campus-wide computer network, are available for use by students in program; they are located in dormitories, the student center, classrooms, learning resource center, the library, the computer center, computer labs, School of Business resource lab. Students in the program are not required to have their own PC.

Computer Resources/On-line Services

Training	Yes	E-Mail	No

ADMISSION

Entrance Requirements Bachelor's degree, GMAT score of 450, minimum 2.5 GPA. Core courses waived through: previous course work.

Application Requirements Application form, copies of transcript.

Application Deadlines 8/1 for fall, 12/1 for spring. Applications are processed on a rolling basis.

FINANCIALS

Costs for 1994-95 Tuition: Full-time: $79/semester hour for state residents, $79/semester hour for nonresidents. Fees: Full-time: $633/semester for nonresidents. Average room and board costs are $2,600 per academic year (on-campus) and $3,820 per academic year (off-campus).

Financial Aid In 1994-95, 10% of candidates received some institutionally administered aid in the form of loans. Financial aid is not available to part-time students. Applications are processed on a rolling basis. Contact: Dr. Jo Ann Weaver, Director of Financial Aid and Student Financial Services, Box 5014, Florence, AL 35631. (205) 760-4278.

INTERNATIONAL STUDENTS

Demographics 10% of students enrolled in the program are international.

Services and Facilities International student center, language tutoring, ESL courses.

Applying TOEFL required, minimum score of 500; proof of health; proof of adequate funds. Financial aid is not available to international students. Admission application deadlines: 8/1 for fall, 12/1 for spring. Applications are processed on a rolling basis. Contact: Mrs. Alice Dill, Director of International Studies, Box 5312, Florence, AL 35631. (205) 760-3136.

PLACEMENT

Placement services include alumni network, career placement, job interviews, resume preparation, and resume referral to employers. Of 1994 graduates, 95% were employed within three months of graduation.

Program Contact: Dr. Rick Lester, Professor of Management and MBA Adviser, University of North Alabama, Box 5159, Florence, AL 35631. (205) 760-4405, or (800) TALK-UNA; Fax: (205) 760-4811.

University of South Alabama

College of Business and Management Studies

Mobile, Alabama

OVERVIEW

The University of South Alabama is a state-supported coed institution. Founded 1963. Setting: 1,215-acre urban campus. Total institutional enrollment: 12,500. Program was first offered in 1972. AACSB-accredited.

MBA HIGHLIGHTS

Entrance Difficulty**
Mean GMAT: 495
Mean GPA: 3.0

Cost $
Tuition: $62/quarter hour
(Nonresident: $62/quarter hour)
Room & Board: N/R

Enrollment Profile

Full-time: 20	Work Exp: 80%
Part-time: 180	International: 30%
Total: 200	Women: 40%
Average Age: 30	Minorities: N/R

Average Class Size: 20

ACADEMICS

Length of Program Minimum: 12 months. Maximum: 5 years.

Calendar Quarters.

Full-time Classes Main campus; evening, summer.

Part-time Classes Main campus; evening, summer.

Degree Requirements 48 quarter hours including 12 elective quarter hours.

Required Courses Basic computing principles and applications, business policy and administrative action in global economy, cost analysis and controls, economic theory, financial accounting, financial management, international business: environment and enterprise, management information systems, managerial economics, marketing management, organizational behavior in contemporary organizations, statistical analysis, survey of marketing, survey of quantitative methods, theory and practice of financial management. Courses may be waived through: previous course work.

Curricular Focus Business issues and problems, general management, leadership.

Concentrations Accounting, management.

Faculty Full-time: 42, 100% with doctorates.

Teaching Methodology Case study: 20%, lecture: 50%, student presentations: 10%, team projects: 20%.

Special Opportunities International exchange in France, Germany.

STUDENT STATISTICS

Geographic Representation By region: South 70%. International 30%.

Other Background Graduate degrees in other disciplines: 5%. Work experience: On average, students have 8 years of work experience on entrance to the program.

FACILITIES

Information Resources Main library with 430,015 bound volumes, 767,830 titles on microform, 3,695 periodical subscriptions, 5,254 records/tapes/CDs, 312 CD-ROMs.

Housing 5% of students in program live in college-owned or -operated housing.

Technology Computers are used moderately in course work. Computer terminals/PCs are available for use by students in program; they are located in the computer center, computer labs. Students in the program are not required to have their own PC.

Computer Resources/On-line Services

Training	Yes	Dun's	No
Internet	No	Dow Jones	No
E-Mail	No	Dialog	No
LEXIS/NEXIS	No	Bloomberg	No
CompuServe	No		

ADMISSION

Acceptance 1994-95 Of those applying, 80% were accepted.

Entrance Requirements Bachelor's degree, prerequisite courses required for applicants with non-business degree, GMAT score, minimum 3.0 GPA. Core courses waived through: previous course work.

Application Requirements Copies of transcript.

Application Deadlines 9/1 for fall, 12/10 for winter, 3/10 for spring, 6/1 for summer.

FINANCIALS

Costs for 1994-95 Tuition: Full-time: $62/quarter hour for state residents, $62/quarter hour for nonresidents. Fees: Full-time: $63/quarter for state residents, $350/quarter for nonresidents.

Financial Aid In 1994-95, 4% of candidates received some institutionally administered aid in the form of assistantships. Financial aid is not available to part-time students. Application deadline: 7/10 for fall. Contact: Dr. W. Randolph Flynn, Associate Dean, Mobile, AL 36688. (205) 460-6418.

INTERNATIONAL STUDENTS

Demographics 30% of students enrolled in the program are international.

Services and Facilities International student housing; international student center, language tutoring, ESL courses, counseling/support services.

Applying TOEFL required, minimum score of 525; proof of adequate funds; 2 letters of recommendation, 2 passport size photographs. Financial aid is not available to international students. Admission application deadlines:

6/15 for fall, 10/1 for winter, 1/1 for spring, 4/1 for summer. Contact: Mr. Joseph Sheehan, Office of International Services, Administration Building, Mobile, AL 36688. (205) 460-6050.

PLACEMENT
Placement services include career counseling/planning, career fairs, career library, career placement, and resume referral to employers.

Program Contact: Dr. W. Randolph Flynn, Associate Dean, University of South Alabama, Mobile, AL 36688. (205) 460-6418; Fax: (205) 460-6529.

ALASKA

Alaska Pacific University

Management Department

Anchorage, Alaska

OVERVIEW
Alaska Pacific University is an independent United Methodist comprehensive coed institution. Founded 1959. Setting: 270-acre urban campus. Total institutional enrollment: 525. Program was first offered in 1982.

MBA HIGHLIGHTS
Entrance Difficulty***

Cost $
Tuition: $315/semester hour
Room & Board: $4,360

Enrollment Profile

Full-time: 18	Work Exp: N/R
Part-time: 51	International: 3%
Total: 69	Women: 36%
Average Age: 37	Minorities: 10%

Class Size: 12 - 15

ACADEMICS
Length of Program Minimum: 12 months. Maximum: 7 years.
Calendar Semesters.
Full-time Classes Main campus; evening, summer.
Part-time Classes Main campus; evening, summer.
Degree Requirements 36 credits including 12-15 elective credits.
Required Courses Accounting for executive action, administration: theory and practice, decision models, information systems, and computers, entrepreneurship, international trade and finance, managerial finance and economics, marketing research and strategy, organizational behavior.
Curricular Focus Business issues and problems, organizational development and change management, problem solving and decision making.
Concentrations Management, telecommunications management.
Faculty Full-time: 5, 100% with doctorates; part-time: 10, 20% with doctorates.
Teaching Methodology Case study: 20%, faculty seminars: 5%, lecture: 40%, research: 10%, seminars by members of the business community: 5%, student presentations: 10%, team projects: 10%.
Special Opportunities Internship program available.

STUDENT STATISTICS
Geographic Representation State residents 97%. By region: West 97%. International 3%.

FACILITIES
Information Resources Main library with 425,801 bound volumes, 419,314 titles on microform, 3,871 periodical subscriptions, 3,086 records/tapes/CDs, 96 CD-ROMs.
Housing College housing available.
Technology Computers are used moderately in course work. 25 computer terminals/PCs are available for use by students in program; they are located in the student center, the computer center, computer labs, graduate assistant office. Students in the program are not required to have their own PC.

Computer Resources/On-line Services

Training	Yes	E Mail	No

ADMISSION
Entrance Requirements Bachelor's degree, prerequisite courses required for applicants with non-business degree, minimum 3.0 GPA. Core courses waived through: previous course work.
Application Requirements Interview, application form, copies of transcript.
Application Deadlines 8/15 for fall, 12/15 for spring. Applications are processed on a rolling basis.

FINANCIALS
Costs for 1995-96 Tuition: Full-time: $315/semester hour. Fees: Full-time: $15-$65/semester. Average room and board costs are $4,360 per academic year (on-campus).
Financial Aid Application deadlines: 3/15 for fall, 8/15 for spring. Applications are processed on a rolling basis. Contact: Ms. Joye Freeman, Director of Financial Aid, 4101 University Drive, Anchorage, AK 99508-4672. (907) 564-8248.

INTERNATIONAL STUDENTS
Demographics 3% of students enrolled in the program are international; Asia 50%, Europe 50%.
Services and Facilities Counseling/support services.
Applying TOEFL required, minimum score of 550; proof of adequate funds. Financial aid is available to international students. Financial aid application deadlines: 3/15 for fall, 3/15 for spring. Applications are processed on a rolling basis. Admission application deadlines: 7/1 for fall, 11/1 for spring. Applications are processed on a rolling basis. Contact: Ms. Hazel Blackmore, Director, Multicultural Programs, 4101 University Drive, Anchorage, AK 99508-4672. (907) 561-1266.

PLACEMENT
Placement services include career counseling/planning.

Program Contact: Ms. Kristy Gladkoff, Assistant Director of Admissions for Graduate Studies, Alaska Pacific University, 4101 University Drive, Anchorage, AK 99508-4672. (907) 561-1266, or (800) 252-7528; Fax: (907) 562-4276.

University of Alaska Anchorage

School of Business

Anchorage, Alaska

OVERVIEW
The University of Alaska Anchorage is a state-supported comprehensive coed institution. Part of University of Alaska System. Founded 1954. Setting: 428-acre urban campus. Total institutional enrollment: 14,694. Program was first offered in 1972.

MBA HIGHLIGHTS
Entrance Difficulty***
Mean GMAT: 534
Mean GPA: 3.13

Cost $
Tuition: $1,206/semester
(Nonresident: $2,412/semester)
Room & Board: $4,000

Enrollment Profile

Full-time: 14	Work Exp: 95%
Part-time: 85	International: 10%
Total: 99	Women: 43%
Average Age: 33	Minorities: 15%

Average Class Size: 18

ACADEMICS
Length of Program Minimum: 18 months. Maximum: 7 years.
Calendar Semesters.
Full-time Classes Main campus; evening, weekends, summer.
Part-time Classes Main campus; evening, weekends, summer.
Degree Requirements 36 credits including 9 elective credits.
Required Courses Business environment analysis, creating the successful organization, current marketing issues seminar, financial decision making,

management project, organization behavior and human resources management, problem formulation and decision analysis, seminar in executive uses of accounting, strategic management seminar. Courses may be waived through: previous course work.

Curricular Focus Business issues and problems, general management, problem solving and decision making.

Concentrations International business, management.

Faculty Full-time: 15, 100% with doctorates.

Teaching Methodology Case study: 20%, lecture: 50%, student presentations: 20%, team projects: 10%.

Special Opportunities International exchange in Republic of Korea. Internships include government.

STUDENT STATISTICS

Geographic Representation State residents 85%. International 10%.

Undergraduate Majors Business 30%; engineering/technology 20%; science/mathematics 5%; other 45%.

Other Background Graduate degrees in other disciplines: 5%. Work experience: On average, students have 8 years of work experience on entrance to the program.

FACILITIES

Information Resources Main library with 522,495 bound volumes, 419,314 titles on microform, 3,479 periodical subscriptions.

Housing 1% of students in program live in college-owned or -operated housing.

Technology Computers are used heavily in course work. 100 computer terminals/PCs are available for use by students in program; they are located in the library, the computer center, computer labs. Students in the program are not required to have their own PC.

Computer Resources/On-line Services

Training	No	E-Mail	Yes
Internet	Yes		

ADMISSION

Acceptance 1994-95 Of those applying, 90% were accepted.

Entrance Requirements Bachelor's degree, GMAT score. Core courses waived through: previous course work.

Application Requirements Application form.

Application Deadline Applications are processed on a rolling basis.

FINANCIALS

Costs for 1994-95 Tuition: Full-time: $1,206/semester for state residents, $2,412/semester for nonresidents. Fees: Full-time: $57/semester for state residents, $57/semester for nonresidents. Average room and board costs are $4,000 per academic year (on-campus) and $4,500 per academic year (off-campus).

Financial Aid In 1994-95, 20% of candidates received some institutionally administered aid in the form of scholarships, loans, assistantships. Application deadline: 4/1 for fall. Applications are processed on a rolling basis. Contact: Mr. Jim Upchurch, Student Financial Aid Director, 3211 Providence Drive, Anchorage, AK 99508-8060. (907) 786-1586.

INTERNATIONAL STUDENTS

Demographics 10% of students enrolled in the program are international.

Services and Facilities Visa services, language tutoring, ESL courses, counseling/support services.

Applying TOEFL required, minimum score of 550; proof of adequate funds. Financial aid is available to international students. Applications are processed on a rolling basis. Admission applications are processed on a rolling basis. Contact: Ms. Leslie Tuovinen, International Student Adviser, Enrollment Services, 3211 Providence Drive, Anchorage, AK 99508-8060. (907) 786-1480.

PLACEMENT

Placement services include alumni network, career counseling/planning, career placement, job interviews, resume preparation, and resume referral to employers.

Program Contact: Ms. Shellie Huffman, MBA Program Assistant, University of Alaska Anchorage, 3211 Providence Drive, Anchorage, AK 99508-8060. (907) 786-4129; Fax: (907) 786-4119.

University of Alaska Fairbanks

School of Management

Fairbanks, Alaska

OVERVIEW

The University of Alaska Fairbanks is a state-supported coed institution. Part of University of Alaska System. Founded 1917. Setting: 2,250-acre small-town campus. Total institutional enrollment: 5,072. Program was first offered in 1975. AACSB-accredited.

MBA HIGHLIGHTS

Entrance Difficulty*
Mean GMAT: 550
Mean GPA: 3.2

Cost $
Tuition: $1,152/semester
(Nonresident: $2,304/semester)
Room & Board: $3,000

Enrollment Profile

Full-time: 40	Work Exp: N/R
Part-time: 5	International: 10%
Total: 45	Women: 55%
Average Age: 28	Minorities: N/R

Average Class Size: 15

ACADEMICS

Length of Program Minimum: 9 months.

Calendar Semesters.

Full-time Classes Main campus; evening.

Part-time Classes Main campus; evening.

Degree Requirements 30-57 credit hours including 6-12 elective credit hours.

Required Courses Corporate strategy, human resources, management accounting seminar, quantitative methods, seminar in finance, seminar in marketing, seminar in production management, sources of business information. Courses may be waived through: previous course work, work experience.

Curricular Focus General management, problem solving and decision making, strategic analysis and planning.

Concentrations Accounting, economics, finance, human resources management, management, marketing, operations management, organizational behavior, quantitative analysis, strategic management.

Faculty Full-time: 20, 100% with doctorates.

Teaching Methodology Case study: 20%, lecture: 20%, research: 20%, student presentations: 20%, team projects: 20%.

Special Opportunities Internships include finance, accounting, and marketing.

STUDENT STATISTICS

Geographic Representation By region: West 90%. International 10%.

FACILITIES

Information Resources Main library with 809,890 bound volumes, 882,765 titles on microform, 6,699 periodical subscriptions, 17,506 records/tapes/CDs.

Housing 10% of students in program live in college-owned or -operated housing.

Technology Computers are used moderately in course work. 50 computer terminals/PCs, linked by a campus-wide computer network, are available for use by students in program; they are located in computer labs. Students in the program are not required to have their own PC.

Computer Resources/On-line Services

Training	Yes	E-Mail	Yes
Internet	Yes $	CompuServe	Yes $

ADMISSION

Acceptance 1994-95 Of those applying, 90% were accepted.

Entrance Requirements Bachelor's degree, GMAT score of 400. Core courses waived through: previous course work, work experience.

Application Requirements Application form, copies of transcript, resume/curriculum vitae, personal statement, 3 letters of recommendation.

Application Deadline Applications are processed on a rolling basis.

FINANCIALS

Costs for 1995-96 Tuition: Full-time: $1,152/semester for state residents, $2,304/semester for nonresidents; Part-time day: $150/credit hour for state residents, $300/credit hour for nonresidents. Fees: Full-time: $165/semester for state residents, $165/semester for nonresidents. Average room and board costs are $3,000 per academic year (on-campus) and $3,750 per academic year (off-campus).

Financial Aid In 1994-95, 15% of candidates received some institutionally administered aid in the form of scholarships, assistantships. Financial aid is not available to part-time students. Contact: Mr. Donald Schaeffer, Director, PO Box 756080, Fairbanks, AK 99775-6080. (907) 474-7256.

INTERNATIONAL STUDENTS

Demographics 10% of students enrolled in the program are international; Asia 80%, Other 20%.

Applying TOEFL required; proof of adequate funds.

PLACEMENT

Placement services include career counseling/planning, career fairs, career placement, electronic job bank, job interviews, resume preparation, and resume referral to employers.

Program Contact: Dr. Mary Lindahl, MBA Program Director, University of Alaska Fairbanks, PO Box 756080, Fairbanks, AK 99775-6080. (907) 474-6656; Fax: (907) 474-5219; Internet Address: famba@fortune.uafsom.alaska.edu.

University of Alaska Southeast

School of Business and Public Administration

Juneau, Alaska

OVERVIEW

The University of Alaska Southeast is a state-supported comprehensive coed institution. Part of University of Alaska System. Founded 1972. Setting: 198-acre small-town campus. Total institutional enrollment: 3,606.

ACADEMICS

Calendar Semesters.

Degree Requirements 36 credits.

Concentration Management.

FACILITIES

Information Resources Main library with 102,171 bound volumes, 250,000 titles on microform, 1,500 periodical subscriptions, 1,976 records/tapes/CDs, 25 CD-ROMs.

ADMISSION

Entrance Requirements Bachelor's degree, GMAT score, minimum 3.0 GPA.

Application Requirements Written essay, application form, copies of transcript, personal statement, 3 letters of recommendation.

Program Contact: Mr. Bruce Gifford, Director of Admissions, University of Alaska Southeast, 11120 Glacier Highway, Juneau, AK 99801-8625. (907) 465-6461; Fax: (907) 465-6365.

ARIZONA

American Graduate School of International Management

Glendale, Arizona

OVERVIEW

American Graduate School of International Management is an independent nonprofit graduate-only specialized coed institution. Programs offered jointly with Univeristy of Arizona, Arizona. Founded 1946. Setting: suburban campus. Total institutional enrollment: 1,421. Program was first offered in 1946. Accredited by AACSB, NCA.

PROGRAM HIGHLIGHTS

Entrance Difficulty****
Mean GMAT: 580
Mean GPA: 3.39

Cost $$$$
Tuition: $700 - $9,200/term
Room & Board: $4,570

Enrollment Profile

Full-time: 1,421	Work Exp: 87%
Part-time: 0	International: 31%
Total: 1,421	Women: 36%
Average Age: 27	Minorities: 8%

Average Class Size: 40

ACADEMICS

Curricular Focus International business, managing diversity, teamwork.

Concentrations Accounting, entrepreneurship, finance, international business, management, management information systems, marketing, organizational behavior, public policy, strategic management.

Faculty Full-time: 93, 77% with doctorates; part-time: 27, 37% with doctorates.

Special Opportunities International exchange in Costa Rica, Finland, France, Germany, Japan, Mexico, Norway, People's Republic of China, Spain. Internships include marketing research in consumer products, international trade in import/export, treasury analysis in industrial manufacturing, auditing in CPA firms, and brand management in industrial marketing.

STUDENT STATISTICS

Geographic Representation State residents 5%. By region: Northeast 20%, West 20%; Midwest 18%; South 11%. International 31%.

Undergraduate Majors Business 38%; engineering/technology 6%; humanities 17%; science/mathematics 5%; social sciences 34%.

Other Background Graduate degrees in other disciplines: 11%. Work experience: On average, students have 3 years of work experience on entrance to the program.

FACILITIES

Information Resources Main library with 60,000 bound volumes, 1,200 periodical subscriptions. Business collection includes 70,000 bound volumes, 1,200 periodical subscriptions, 11 CD-ROMs, 600 videos.

Housing 32% of students in program live in college-owned or -operated housing. Assistance with housing search provided.

Technology Computers are used moderately in course work. 120 computer terminals/PCs, linked by a campus-wide computer network, are available for use by students in program; they are located in the student center, classrooms, the library, the computer center, computer labs, the research center. Students in the program are required to have their own PC. $300 are budgeted per student for computer support.

Computer Resources/On-line Services

Training	Yes	LEXIS/NEXIS	Yes
Internet	Yes	CompuServe	Yes
E-Mail	Yes	Dialog	Yes $
Multimedia Center	Yes		

Other on-line services: Datastar.

ADMISSION

Acceptance 1994-95 3,584 applied for admission; 40% were accepted.

Entrance Requirements Bachelor's degree, GMAT score of 500, minimum 3.0 GPA. Core courses waived through: previous course work.

Application Requirements Application form, copies of transcript, resume/curriculum vitae, personal statement, 3 letters of recommendation.

Application Deadlines 1/31 for fall, 6/30 for spring, 1/31 for summer.

FINANCIALS

Estimated Costs for 1995-96 Tuition: Full-time: $700-$9,200/term. Average room and board costs are $4,570 per academic year (on-campus) and $5,560 per academic year (off-campus).

Financial Aid In 1994-95, candidates received some institutionally administered aid in the form of grants, scholarships, loans, fellowships, assistantships, work-study. Total awards ranged from $200-$27,734. Application deadlines: 4/1 for fall, 10/1 for spring, 3/1 for summer. Applications are processed on a rolling basis. Contact: Ms. Catherine King-Todd, Director of Financial Aid, 15249 North 59th Avenue, Glendale, AZ 85306-3236. (602) 978-7130.

INTERNATIONAL STUDENTS

Demographics 31% of students enrolled in the program are international; Asia 39%, Europe 36%, Central America 16%, South America 3%, Africa 1%, Australia 1%, other 5%.

Services and Facilities International student office, visa services, ESL courses, counseling/support services, predeparture orientation, career development services.

Applying TOEFL required, minimum score of 500; proof of adequate funds. Financial aid is available to international students. Financial aid application deadlines: 3/1 for fall, 10/1 for spring, 3/1 for summer. Admission application deadlines: 1/31 for fall, 6/30 for spring, 1/31 for summer. Contact: Ms. Mary Lee Carter, Foreign Student Adviser, 15249 North 59th Avenue, Glendale, AZ 85306-3236. (602) 978-7599.

PROGRAMS

International MBA Length of program: Minimum: 12 months. Maximum: 5 years. Degree requirements: 42 credit hours including 24 elective credit hours. Second language proficiency.

MBA/MIM Length of program: Minimum: 18 months. Degree requirements: Attendance and separate applications to both degree granting institution and American Graduate School of International Management; 30 credits required for MIM; number of credits required for MBA determined by cooperating institution.

PLACEMENT

In 1993-94, 252 organizations participated in on-campus recruiting; 2,769 on-campus interviews were conducted. Placement services include alumni network, career counseling/planning, career fairs, career library, career placement, electronic job bank, job interviews, job search course, resume preparation, and resume referral to employers. Of 1994 graduates, 87% were employed within three months of graduation, the average starting salary was $43,000, the range was $10,000-$120,000.

Jobs by Employer Type Manufacturing 40%; service 42%; government 6%; consulting 5%; nonprofit 1%; communications 5%; other 1%.

Jobs by Functional Area Marketing/sales 42%; finance 28%; operations 3%; management 7%; strategic planning 5%; technical management 2%; human resources 1%; consulting 6%; other 6%.

Program Contact: Ms. Stephen R. Beaver, Associate Dean of Admissions, American Graduate School of International Management, 15249 North 59th Avenue, Glendale, AZ 85306-3236. (602) 978-7133, or (800) 848-9084; Fax: (602) 439-5432; Internet Address: beavers@ mhs.t-bird.edu.

See full description on page 660.

Arizona State University

College of Business

Tempe, Arizona

OVERVIEW

Arizona State University is a state-supported coed institution. Founded 1885. Setting: 700-acre suburban campus with easy access to Phoenix. Total institutional enrollment: 42,189. Program was first offered in 1961. AACSB-accredited.

MBA HIGHLIGHTS

Entrance Difficulty**
Mean GMAT: 605
Mean GPA: 3.3

Cost $
Tuition: $1,828
(Nonresident: $7,434)
Room & Board: $3,586

Enrollment Profile

Full-time: N/R	Work Exp: 97%
Part-time: N/R	International: 11%
Total: 273	Women: 36%
Average Age: 27	Minorities: 24%

Average Class Size: 30

ACADEMICS

Length of Program Minimum: 18 months. Maximum: 2 years.

Calendar Semesters.

Full-time Classes Main campus; day, evening, summer.

Part-time Classes Main campus; evening.

Degree Requirements 48 credit hours including 12 elective credit hours.

Required Courses Financial accounting, legal and ethical studies, management accounting, management finance, management information and decision support systems, managerial communication, managerial decision analysis, managerial economics, marketing management, operations and logistics management, organizational theory and behavior, strategic management.

Concentrations Accounting, economics, entrepreneurship, finance, health services, international business, management, management information systems, marketing, operations management, quantitative analysis, strategic management, transportation.

Faculty Full-time: 165, 100% with doctorates.

Teaching Methodology Case study: 20%, faculty seminars: 5%, lecture: 40%, research: 5%, seminars by members of the business community: 5%, student presentations: 5%, team projects: 20%.

Special Opportunities International exchange in Belgium, France, Norway. Internships include finance in banking, operations in high technology, and marketing in telecommunications manufacturing.

STUDENT STATISTICS

Geographic Representation International 11%.

Other Background Work experience: On average, students have 4 years of work experience on entrance to the program.

FACILITIES

Information Resources Main library with 3 million bound volumes, 6 million titles on microform, 32,241 periodical subscriptions, 38,230 records/tapes/CDs, 50 CD-ROMs.

Housing 1% of students in program live in college-owned or -operated housing.

Technology Computers are used heavily in course work. Computer terminals/PCs, linked by a campus-wide computer network, are available for use by students in program; they are located in learning resource center, the computer center, computer labs, the research center, MBA Project Room. Students in the program are not required to have their own PC.

Computer Resources/On-line Services

Training	Yes	E-Mail	Yes
Internet	Yes	Multimedia Center	Yes

ADMISSION

Entrance Requirements Bachelor's degree, GMAT score, minimum 3.0 GPA, minimum 2 years of work experience, calculus or 65% in the quantitative section of the GMAT.

Application Requirements Application form, copies of transcript, resume/curriculum vitae, personal statement, interview recommended.

Application Deadlines 5/1 for fall. Applications are processed on a rolling basis.

FINANCIALS

Costs for 1994-95 Fees: Full-time: $1,828 for state residents, $7,434 for nonresidents. Average room and board costs are $3,586 per academic year (on-campus) and $4,000 per academic year (off-campus).

Financial Aid In 1994-95, candidates received some institutionally administered aid in the form of scholarships, assistantships. Total awards ranged from $3,550-$5,606. Financial aid is available to part-time students. Contact: Ms. Joanne Severson, MBA Counselor, Student Financial Assistance Office, Box 870412, Tempe, AZ 85287. (602) 965-1160.

INTERNATIONAL STUDENTS

Demographics 11% of students enrolled in the program are international.

Services and Facilities International student office, international student center, ESL courses.

Applying TOEFL required, minimum score of 580; proof of health; proof of adequate funds; minimum score of 230 or waiver of Test of Standard Written English. Financial aid is available to international students. Financial aid application deadline: 5/1 for fall. Applications are processed on a rolling basis. Admission application deadline: 5/1 for fall. Applications are processed on a rolling basis. Contact: Ms. Suzanne Steadman, Coordinator, International Student Office, Student Life, Tempe, AZ 85287. (602) 965-7451.

ALTERNATE MBA PROGRAMS

MBA/JD Length of program: Minimum: 36 months. Maximum: 4 years. Full-time classes: Main campus; day, weekends, summer. Part-time classes:

Main campus; evening. Degree requirements: 117 credits including 41 elective credits. Separate applications must be submitted to both business and law.

MBA/MIM Length of program: Minimum: 18 months. Degree requirements: 66 credits including 12 elective credits. Separate applications must be submitted to the Arizona State University College of Business and The American Graduate School of International Management.

PLACEMENT
In 1993-94, 55 organizations participated in on-campus recruiting. Placement services include alumni network, career counseling/planning, career fairs, career library, career placement, job interviews, job search course, resume preparation, and resume referral to employers. Of 1994 graduates, 89% were employed within three months of graduation, the average starting salary was $42,521, the range was $25,000-$70,000.

Jobs by Employer Type Manufacturing 63%; service 27%; government 1%; consulting 10%.

Jobs by Functional Area Marketing/sales 22%; finance 15%; operations 6%; management 25%; strategic planning 13%; technical management 5%; other 15%.

Program Contact: College of Business, Arizona State University, MBA Program Office, Tempe, AZ 85287. (602) 965-3332; Fax: (602) 965-8569.
See full description on page 664.

Arizona State University West

School of Management

Phoenix, Arizona

OVERVIEW
Arizona State University West is a state-supported upper-level coed institution. Part of Arizona State University. Founded 1984. Setting: 300-acre suburban campus. Total institutional enrollment: 5,000. Program was first offered in 1986.

MBA HIGHLIGHTS

Entrance Difficulty**
Mean GMAT: 583
Mean GPA: 3.2

Cost $
Tuition: $914/semester
(Nonresident: $3,717/semester)
Room & Board: $5,035 (off-campus)

Enrollment Profile
Full-time: 25	Work Exp: 98%
Part-time: 225	International: 5%
Total: 250	Women: 34%
Average Age: 33	Minorities: 12%

Average Class Size: 22

ACADEMICS
Length of Program Minimum: 18 months. Maximum: 6 years.
Calendar Semesters.
Full-time Classes Main campus, Downtown Center; evening, weekends, summer.
Part-time Classes Main campus, Downtown Center; evening, weekends, summer.
Degree Requirements 45 credits including 12 elective credits.
Required Courses Financial accounting, legal and ethical issues, management information systems, managerial accounting, managerial economics, managerial finance, marketing management, operations and logistics management, organization theory and behavior, quantitative business analysis, strategic management. Courses may be waived through: previous course work.
Curricular Focus General management, problem solving and decision making, teamwork.
Concentrations Entrepreneurship, finance, human resources management, international business, management, management information systems, marketing, organizational behavior.
Faculty Full-time: 38, 100% with doctorates.

Teaching Methodology Case study: 20%, experiential learning: 10%, lecture: 50%, student presentations: 10%, team projects: 10%.
Special Opportunities International exchange in Canada, Germany, Italy, Mexico. Internship program available. Other: independent study.

STUDENT STATISTICS
Geographic Representation State residents 95%. International 5%.
Undergraduate Majors Business 38%; engineering/technology 30%; science/mathematics 5%; social sciences 27%.
Other Background Graduate degrees in other disciplines: 10%. Work experience: On average, students have 8 years of work experience on entrance to the program.

FACILITIES
Information Resources Main library with 235,022 bound volumes, 16,410 titles on microform, 2,177 periodical subscriptions, 2,828 records/tapes/CDs, 40 CD-ROMs. Business collection includes 37,000 bound volumes, 621 periodical subscriptions, 9 CD-ROMs, 147 videos.
Housing College housing not available.
Technology Computers are used moderately in course work. 100 computer terminals/PCs, linked by a campus-wide computer network, are available for use by students in program; they are located in the library. Students in the program are not required to have their own PC.

Computer Resources/On-line Services
Training	Yes	Dun's	Yes
Internet	Yes	Dow Jones	Yes
E-Mail	Yes	Dialog	Yes
LEXIS/NEXIS	Yes	Bloomberg	Yes
CompuServe	No		

Other on-line services: SEC.

ADMISSION
Acceptance 1994-95 Of those applying, 50% were accepted.
Entrance Requirements Bachelor's degree, GMAT score. Core courses waived through: previous course work.
Application Requirements Application form, copies of transcript, resume/curriculum vitae, personal statement, 2 letters of recommendation.
Application Deadlines 7/15 for fall, 11/15 for spring, 4/15 for summer.

FINANCIALS
Costs for 1994-95 Tuition: Full-time: $914/semester for state residents, $3,717/semester for nonresidents. Average room and board costs are $5,035 per academic year (off-campus).
Financial Aid In 1994-95, 5% of candidates received some institutionally administered aid in the form of scholarships, loans, assistantships. Total awards ranged from $576-$2,568. Financial aid is available to part-time students. Application deadlines: 7/15 for fall, 11/15 for spring. Contact: Ms. Cecile Babicsh Morrow, Program Coordinator, 4701 West Thunderbird Road, Phoenix, AZ 85069-7100. (602) 543-8178.

INTERNATIONAL STUDENTS
Demographics 5% of students enrolled in the program are international.
Services and Facilities International student center, language tutoring, ESL courses, special assistance for nonnative speakers of English.
Applying TOEFL required, minimum score of 500; proof of adequate funds. Financial aid is available to international students. Financial aid application deadlines: 7/15 for fall, 11/15 for spring. Admission application deadlines: 4/15 for fall, 7/15 for spring, 11/15 for summer.

ALTERNATE MBA PROGRAM
MBA/MIM Length of program: Minimum: 24 months. Maximum: 6 years. Degree requirements: 69 credits including 15 elective credits. MIM degree requirements are completed at the American Graduate School of International Management. Separate applications must be submitted to both schools.

PLACEMENT
Placement services include career counseling/planning, career fairs, career library, career placement, community career network, job interviews, resume preparation, and resume referral to employers.

Program Contact: Ms. Renata Geurtz, Admissions Representative, Arizona State University West, 4701 West Thunderbird Road, Phoenix, AZ 85069-7100. (602) 543-6239; Fax: (602) 543-6221.

Grand Canyon University

College of Business

Phoenix, Arizona

OVERVIEW

Grand Canyon University is an independent Southern Baptist comprehensive coed institution. Founded 1949. Setting: 70-acre urban campus. Total institutional enrollment: 2,035. Program was first offered in 1986.

MBA HIGHLIGHTS

Entrance Difficulty***
Mean GMAT: 500
Mean GPA: 3.0

Cost $
Tuition: $229/credit hour
Room & Board: N/R

Enrollment Profile

Full-time: 0	Work Exp: 97%
Part-time: 60	International: 90%
Total: 60	Women: 41%
Average Age: 30	Minorities: 25%

Average Class Size: 15

ACADEMICS

Length of Program Minimum: 24 months. Maximum: 5 years.
Calendar Trimesters.
Part-time Classes Main campus; evening.
Degree Requirements 36 credits including 9 elective credits.
Required Courses Business ethics and society, management information and support systems, management of the total enterprise, managerial accounting, managerial economics, managerial finance, marketing management, organizational theory and behavior, quantitative methods in business. Courses may be waived through: previous course work.
Curricular Focus Business issues and problems, general management, problem solving and decision making.
Concentrations Accounting, business ethics, economics, entrepreneurship, finance, international business, management, management information systems, marketing, organizational behavior, quantitative analysis, strategic management.
Faculty Full-time: 7, 86% with doctorates; part-time: 3, 33% with doctorates.
Teaching Methodology Case study: 20%, lecture: 65%, student presentations: 5%, team projects: 10%.

STUDENT STATISTICS

Geographic Representation State residents 10%. By region: West 90%. International 90%.
Undergraduate Majors Business 60%; education 5%; engineering/technology 8%; humanities 3%; nursing 2%; science/mathematics 10%; social sciences 10%; other 2%.
Other Background Graduate degrees in other disciplines: 1%. Work experience: On average, students have 3 years of work experience on entrance to the program.

FACILITIES

Information Resources Main library with 134,452 bound volumes, 41,412 titles on microform, 642 periodical subscriptions, 4,113 records/tapes/CDs, 14 CD-ROMs. Business collection includes 3,337 bound volumes, 95 periodical subscriptions, 7 CD-ROMs.
Housing College housing available.
Technology Computers are used moderately in course work. 150 computer terminals/PCs, linked by a campus-wide computer network, are available for use by students in program; they are located in the computer center, computer labs. Students in the program are not required to have their own PC.

Computer Resources/On-line Services

Training	No	Dun's	No
Internet	No	Dow Jones	No
E-Mail	No	Dialog	No
LEXIS/NEXIS	No	Bloomberg	No
CompuServe	No		

ADMISSION

Acceptance 1994-95 Of those applying, 90% were accepted.
Entrance Requirements Bachelor's degree, GMAT score of 500, minimum 3.0 GPA, minimum 2 years of work experience. Core courses waived through: previous course work.
Application Requirements Interview, application form, copies of transcript, personal statement.
Application Deadlines 8/15 for fall, 12/1 for spring.

FINANCIALS

Costs for 1994-95 Tuition: Part-time evening: $229/credit hour. Fees: Part-time evening: $136/semester.
Financial Aid In 1994-95, 14% of candidates received some institutionally administered aid in the form of scholarships, loans. Total awards ranged from $200-$10,000. Financial aid is available to part-time students. Application deadlines: 3/15 for fall, 10/15 for spring. Contact: Ms. Pat Peppin, Interim Director of Financial Aid, 3300 West Camelback Road, Phoenix, AZ 85017. (602) 589-2885.

INTERNATIONAL STUDENTS

Demographics 90% of students enrolled in the program are international.
Services and Facilities Language tutoring, ESL courses, special assistance for nonnative speakers of English, counseling/support services.
Applying TOEFL required, minimum score of 550; proof of health; proof of adequate funds. Financial aid is not available to international students. Admission application deadlines: 8/15 for fall, 12/1 for spring. Contact: Ms. Treva Gibson, Director, International Programs, 3300 West Camelback Road, Phoenix, AZ 85017. (602) 589-2808.

PLACEMENT

Placement services include alumni network and career counseling/planning. Of 1994 graduates, 97% were employed within three months of graduation.
Jobs by Employer Type Manufacturing 6%; service 55%; government 7%; consulting 3%; nonprofit 3%; engineering 26%.
Jobs by Functional Area Marketing/sales 15%; finance 21%; operations 6%; management 50%; strategic planning 3%; technical management 5%.

Program Contact: Dr. Michael S. Nichols, Director, MBA Program, Grand Canyon University, 3300 West Camelback Road, Phoenix, AZ 85017. (602) 589-2824, or (800) 800-9776; Fax: (602) 589-2532.

Northern Arizona University

College of Business Administration

Flagstaff, Arizona

OVERVIEW

Northern Arizona University is a state-supported coed institution. Founded 1899. Setting: 730-acre small-town campus. Total institutional enrollment: 19,242. Program was first offered in 1971. AACSB-accredited.

MBA HIGHLIGHTS

Entrance Difficulty**
Mean GMAT: 470
Mean GPA: 3.1

Cost $
Tuition: $76 - $131/hour
(Nonresident: $278/hour)
Room & Board: $3,132

Enrollment Profile

Full-time: 60	Work Exp: 58%
Part-time: 34	International: 19%
Total: 94	Women: 34%
Average Age: 32	Minorities: 13%

Average Class Size: 18

ACADEMICS

Length of Program Minimum: 11 months. Maximum: 6 years.

Calendar Semesters.

Degree Requirements 33 credits including 6 elective credits.

Required Courses Advanced managerial accounting, data base management systems, financial analysis for business decisions, integrating seminar, management information systems, management theory and analysis, managerial economics, quantitative analysis, strategic marketing management. Courses may be waived through: previous course work.

Curricular Focus General management, problem solving and decision making, teamwork.

Concentrations Management, management information systems, wood products industry.

Faculty Full-time: 12, 100% with doctorates.

Teaching Methodology Case study: 25%, lecture: 30%, research: 10%, seminars by members of the business community: 5%, student presentations: 10%, team projects: 20%.

STUDENT STATISTICS

Geographic Representation State residents 73%. By region: West 74%; Northeast 3%; Midwest 3%; South 1%. International 19%.

Undergraduate Majors Business 73%; education 2%; engineering/technology 8%; science/mathematics 6%; social sciences 2%; other 9%.

Other Background Graduate degrees in other disciplines: 5%. Work experience: On average, students have 13 years of work experience on entrance to the program.

FACILITIES

Information Resources Main library with 1.4 million bound volumes, 581,470 titles on microform, 5,831 periodical subscriptions, 18,749 records/tapes/CDs.

Housing College housing available.

Technology Computers are used moderately in course work. Computer terminals/PCs, linked by a campus-wide computer network, are available for use by students in program; they are located in classrooms, learning resource center, the library, the computer center, computer labs, the research center, MBA student study area. Students in the program are not required to have their own PC.

Computer Resources/On-line Services

Training	Yes	Dow Jones	Yes
Internet	Yes	Dialog	Yes $
E-Mail	Yes		

ADMISSION

Acceptance 1994-95 Of those applying, 72% were accepted.

Entrance Requirements Bachelor's degree, prerequisite courses required for applicants with non-business degree, GMAT score of 450, minimum 3.0 GPA. Core courses waived through: previous course work.

Application Requirements Written essay, application form, copies of transcript, 3 letters of recommendation.

Application Deadlines 3/1 for fall, 10/15 for spring.

FINANCIALS

Costs for 1994-95 Tuition: Full-time: $76-$131/hour for state residents, $278/hour for nonresidents; Part-time day: $96/hour for state residents. Fees: Full-time: $8/semester for state residents, $8/semester for nonresidents; Part-time day: $4/semester for state residents. Average room and board costs are $3,132 per academic year (on-campus).

Financial Aid In 1994-95, candidates received some institutionally administered aid in the form of scholarships, assistantships. Total awards ranged from $500-$14,000. Financial aid is not available to part-time students. Application deadlines: 3/1 for fall, 10/15 for spring. Contact: Mr. James Pritchard, Director of Financial Aid, Box 4108, Flagstaff, AZ 86011. (602) 523-4951.

INTERNATIONAL STUDENTS

Demographics 19% of students enrolled in the program are international; Asia 75%, Africa 8%, Europe 8%, South America 4%, other 4%.

Services and Facilities Program in intensive English.

Applying TOEFL required; proof of health; proof of adequate funds. Financial aid is available to international students. Financial aid application deadlines: 3/1 for fall, 10/15 for spring. Admission application

deadlines: 3/1 for fall, 10/15 for spring. Contact: Dr. Joan Fagerburg, International Student Adviser, Box 6015, Flagstaff, AZ 86011. (602) 523-6772.

PLACEMENT

Placement services include alumni network, career counseling/planning, career fairs, career library, career placement, electronic job bank, job interviews, resume preparation, and resume referral to employers.

Program Contact: Dr. Chris A. Lockwood, Director, MBA Program, Northern Arizona University, Box 4132, Flagstaff, AZ 86011. (602) 523-7342; Fax: (602) 523-7331.

University of Arizona

Karl Eller Graduate School of Management

Tucson, Arizona

OVERVIEW

The University of Arizona is a state-supported coed institution. Founded 1885. Setting: 325-acre suburban campus. Total institutional enrollment: 35,000. Program was first offered in 1953. AACSB-accredited.

MBA HIGHLIGHTS

Entrance Difficulty***
Mean GMAT: 599
Mean GPA: 3.2

Cost $
Tuition: $947/semester
(Nonresident: $3,250/semester)
Room & Board: $5,550

Enrollment Profile

Full-time: 155	Work Exp: 80%
Part-time: 50	International: 10%
Total: 205	Women: 30%
Average Age: 29	Minorities: 20%

Average Class Size: 40

ACADEMICS

Length of Program Minimum: 21 months. Maximum: 3 years.

Calendar Semesters.

Full-time Classes Main campus; day.

Part-time Classes Main campus; evening.

Degree Requirements 60 units including 27 elective units.

Required Courses Design and control of production systems, environmental scanning and business policy, financial accounting, management and evaluation of information systems, managerial accounting, managerial economics, managerial finance, marketing management, statistical decision making.

Curricular Focus Leadership, problem solving and decision making, teamwork.

Concentrations Accounting, economics, entrepreneurship, finance, health services, human resources management, international business, management, management information systems, marketing, operations management, organizational behavior, public administration, quality management, quality control, legal studies, quantitative analysis, strategic management.

Faculty Full-time: 65, 100% with doctorates.

Teaching Methodology Case study: 20%, lecture: 25%, research: 10%, seminars by members of the business community: 5%, simulations: 15%, student presentations: 10%, team projects: 15%.

Special Opportunities International exchange program available. Internships include business and government.

STUDENT STATISTICS

Geographic Representation State residents 30%. By region: West 45%; Midwest 30%; Northeast 10%; South 5%. International 10%.

Undergraduate Majors Business 29%; engineering/technology 21%; humanities 10%; science/mathematics 18%; social sciences 10%; other 12%.

Other Background Graduate degrees in other disciplines: 10%. Work experience: On average, students have 4 years of work experience on entrance to the program.

FACILITIES

Information Resources Main library with 4.1 million bound volumes, 4.6 million titles on microform, 24,052 periodical subscriptions, 33,900 records/tapes/CDs.

Housing 5% of students in program live in college-owned or -operated housing.

Technology Computers are used heavily in course work. 400 computer terminals/PCs, linked by a campus-wide computer network, are available for use by students in program; they are located in the student center, classrooms, learning resource center, the library, the computer center, computer labs. Students in the program are not required to have their own PC.

Computer Resources/On-line Services

Training	Yes	Dun's	Yes $
Internet	Yes	Dow Jones	Yes
E-Mail	Yes	Dialog	Yes $
LEXIS/NEXIS	No	Bloomberg	No
CompuServe	No		

Other on-line services: OCLC, First Search.

ADMISSION

Acceptance 1994-95 542 applied for admission; 43% were accepted.

Entrance Requirements Bachelor's degree, GMAT score, minimum 3.0 GPA.

Application Requirements Written essay, interview, application form, copies of transcript, resume/curriculum vitae, personal statement, 2 letters of recommendation.

Application Deadline 4/1 for fall. Application discs available.

FINANCIALS

Costs for 1994-95 Tuition: Full-time: $947/semester for state residents, $3,250/semester for nonresidents; Part-time evening: $605/semester for state residents, $1,899/semester for nonresidents; Summer: $93/unit for state residents, $93/unit for nonresidents. Average room and board costs are $5,550 per academic year (on-campus) and $5,550 per academic year (off-campus).

Financial Aid In 1994-95, 85% of candidates received some institutionally administered aid in the form of scholarships, loans, fellowships, assistantships, work-study. Total awards ranged from $2,500-$22,500. Financial aid is available to part-time students. Application deadline: 2/1 for fall. Contact: Ms. Diana B. Vidal, Director of MBA Admissions, Karl Eller Graduate School of Management McClelland Hall 210, Tuscon, AZ 85721. (602) 621-2855.

INTERNATIONAL STUDENTS

Demographics 10% of students enrolled in the program are international.

Services and Facilities International student center, visa services, language tutoring, ESL courses, special assistance for nonnative speakers of English, counseling/support services.

Applying TOEFL required, minimum score of 600; proof of health; proof of adequate funds. Financial aid is available to international students. Financial aid application deadline: 2/1 for fall. Admission application deadline: 2/1 for fall. Contact: Ms. Nura Dualeh, International Student Adviser, Center for International Students and Scholars, 915 North Tyndall Avenue, Tucson, AZ 85721. (602) 621-4627.

ALTERNATE MBA PROGRAMS

MBA/JD Length of program: Minimum: 48 months. Maximum: 4 years. Degree requirements: 145 credits.

MBA/MIM Length of program: Minimum: 30 months. Maximum: 3 years. Degree requirements: 90 credits including 45 elective credits. Offered in conjunction with the American Graduate School of International Management.

PLACEMENT

In 1993-94, 60 organizations participated in on-campus recruiting; 500 on-campus interviews were conducted. Placement services include alumni network, career counseling/planning, career fairs, career library, career placement, electronic job bank, job interviews, resume preparation, and resume referral to employers. Of 1994 graduates, 90% were employed within three months of graduation, the average starting salary was $42,500, the range was $25,000-$60,000.

Jobs by Employer Type Manufacturing 37%; service 37%; government 9%; consulting 17%.

Jobs by Functional Area Marketing/sales 23%; finance 26%; operations 14%; management 6%; strategic planning 14%; technical management 14%; human resources 3%.

Program Contact: MBA Admissions Office, University of Arizona, Karl Eller Graduate School of Management, Tuscon, AZ 85721. (602) 621-2169; Fax: (602) 621-2606.
See full description on page 850.

University of Phoenix

Phoenix, Arizona

OVERVIEW

The University of Phoenix is an independent proprietary comprehensive coed institution. Founded 1976. Setting: urban campus. Total institutional enrollment: 13,800.

ACADEMICS

Calendar Modular.

Degree Requirements 37 credits.

Concentrations Economics, finance, human relations, organizational behavior, quantitative analysis, strategic management.

FACILITIES

Information Resources Main library with 3,500 titles on microform, 840 periodical subscriptions.

ADMISSION

Entrance Requirements Bachelor's degree, minimum 2.5 GPA, minimum 3 years of work experience, ALOA Test.

Application Requirements Written essay, application form, copies of transcript, resume/curriculum vitae.

FINANCIALS

Costs for 1994-95 Tuition: Full-time: $198/credit hour.

INTERNATIONAL STUDENTS

Applying TOEFL required, minimum score of 580.

Program Contact: Ms. Nina Omelchenko, Vice President of University Services, University of Phoenix, 4615 East Elwood Street, PO Box 52076, Phoenix, AZ 85072-9382. (602) 966-9577 Ext. 1712; Fax: (602) 829-9030.

Western International University

Phoenix, Arizona

OVERVIEW

Western International University is an independent nonprofit comprehensive coed institution. Founded 1978. Setting: 4-acre urban campus. Total institutional enrollment: 1,514.

MBA HIGHLIGHTS

Entrance Difficulty**
Mean GMAT: 550
Mean GPA: N/R

Cost $$
Tuition: $6,600 - $10,050/degree program
Room & Board: $5,000 (off-campus)

Enrollment Profile

Full-time: N/R	Work Exp: N/R
Part-time: N/R	International: 11%
Total: 625	Women: 45%
Average Age: N/R	Minorities: 15%

Average Class Size: 15

ACADEMICS

Length of Program Minimum: 15 months.

Calendar Semesters.

Part-time Classes Main campus, Fort Huachuca; evening, summer.

Degree Requirements 39 credits.

Curricular Focus International business, leadership, problem solving and decision making.

Concentrations Accounting, finance, health services, international business, management, management information systems, marketing, public administration.

Teaching Methodology Case study: 10%, lecture: 50%, research: 10%, student presentations: 10%, team projects: 20%.

STUDENT STATISTICS
Geographic Representation International 11%.

FACILITIES
Information Resources Main library with 7,500 bound volumes, 50 titles on microform, 200 periodical subscriptions, 63 records/tapes/CDs, 150 CD-ROMs.

Housing College housing not available.

ADMISSION
Entrance Requirements Bachelor's degree, minimum 2.75 GPA. Core courses waived through: previous course work, work experience.

Application Requirements Written essay, application form, copies of transcript, personal statement.

Application Deadline Applications are processed on a rolling basis.

FINANCIALS
Costs for 1994-95 Tuition: Part-time evening: $6,600-$10,050/degree program. Average room and board costs are $5,000 per academic year (off-campus).

Financial Aid In 1994-95, 30% of candidates received some institutionally administered aid in the form of loans. Applications are processed on a rolling basis. Contact: Mr. John Medley, Director of Financial Aid, 9215 North Black Canyon Highway, Phoenix, AZ 85021-2718. (602) 943-2311 Ext. 141.

INTERNATIONAL STUDENTS
Demographics 11% of students enrolled in the program are international; Asia 65%, Africa 10%, Europe 10%, Central America 5%, South America 5%, North America 5%.

Services and Facilities Language tutoring, ESL courses, special assistance for nonnative speakers of English, counseling/support services.

Applying TOEFL required, minimum score of 550; proof of health; proof of adequate funds. Financial aid is not available to international students. Admission applications are processed on a rolling basis.

Program Contact: Ms. Kelly Walters, Director of Admissions, Western International University, 9215 North Black Canyon Highway, Phoenix, AZ 85021-2718. (602) 943-2311; Fax: (602) 371-8637.
See full description on page 932.

ARKANSAS

Arkansas State University

College of Business

Jonesboro, Arkansas

OVERVIEW
Arkansas State University is a state-supported comprehensive coed institution. Founded 1909. Setting: 800-acre small-town campus with easy access to Memphis. Total institutional enrollment: 12,300. Program was first offered in 1970. AACSB-accredited.

MBA HIGHLIGHTS

Entrance Difficulty**
Mean GMAT: 460
Mean GPA: 3.1

Cost $
Tuition: $78 - $80/hour
(Nonresident: $142 - $144/hour)
Room & Board: N/R

Enrollment Profile
Full-time: 61
Part-time: 31
Total: 92
Average Age: N/R

Work Exp: 40%
International: 36%
Women: 34%
Minorities: 5%

Average Class Size: N/R

ACADEMICS
Length of Program Minimum: 12 months. Maximum: 6 years.

Calendar Semesters.

Full-time Classes Main campus; day, evening, summer.

Degree Requirements 33 hours including 12 elective hours.

Required Courses Advanced management of finance, management information systems, management science, managerial economics, managerial policies, marketing policies.

Curricular Focus General management, leadership, problem solving and decision making.

Concentration Management.

Faculty Full-time: 24, 100% with doctorates.

Teaching Methodology Case study: 10%, lecture: 75%, student presentations: 5%, team projects: 10%.

Special Opportunities Internships include manufacturing, wholesale, banking, and service.

STUDENT STATISTICS
Geographic Representation State residents 60%. By region: South 55%; Midwest 10%; Northeast 2%; West 2%. International 36%.

Undergraduate Majors Business 80%; engineering/technology 5%; science/mathematics 5%; social sciences 10%.

Other Background Graduate degrees in other disciplines: 1%.

FACILITIES
Information Resources Main library with 496,367 bound volumes, 424,064 titles on microform, 2,458 periodical subscriptions, 7,814 records/tapes/CDs.

Housing 15% of students in program live in college-owned or -operated housing.

Technology Computers are used moderately in course work. 250 computer terminals/PCs, linked by a campus-wide computer network, are available for use by students in program; they are located in classrooms, the library, the computer center, computer labs. Students in the program are not required to have their own PC.

Computer Resources/On-line Services

Training	Yes	E-Mail		Yes
Internet	Yes	Dialog		Yes $

Other on-line services: OCLC.

ADMISSION
Acceptance 1994-95 Of those applying, 90% were accepted.

Entrance Requirements Bachelor's degree, GMAT score of 400, minimum 2.5 GPA.

Application Requirements Application form, copies of transcript.

Application Deadline Applications are processed on a rolling basis.

FINANCIALS
Costs for 1994-95 Tuition: Full-time: $78-$80/hour for state residents, $142-$144/hour for nonresidents; Part-time day: $82-$91/hour for state residents, $146-$155/hour for nonresidents. Fees: Full-time: $48-$52 for state residents, $48-$52 for nonresidents; Part-time day: $4-$44 for state residents, $4-$44 for nonresidents.

Financial Aid In 1994-95, 13% of candidates received some institutionally administered aid in the form of assistantships. Financial aid is not available to part-time students. Application deadlines: 7/1 for fall, 12/1 for spring. Contact: Mr. Terry Roach, Director of Graduate Programs, PO Box 2220, State University, AR 72467-1630. (501) 972-3430.

INTERNATIONAL STUDENTS
Demographics 36% of students enrolled in the program are international; Asia 88%, Other 12%.

Services and Facilities International student center, language tutoring, ESL courses.

Applying TOEFL required, minimum score of 550; proof of health; proof of adequate funds. Financial aid is available to international students. Financial aid application deadlines: 7/1 for fall, 12/1 for spring. Admission applications are processed on a rolling basis.

PLACEMENT

In 1993-94, 21 organizations participated in on-campus recruiting; 68 on-campus interviews were conducted. Placement services include career counseling/planning, career fairs, career placement, electronic job bank, job interviews, resume preparation, and resume referral to employers. Of 1994 graduates, 80% were employed within three months of graduation, the average starting salary was $29,500, the range was $25,000-$45,000.

Program Contact: Mr. Terry Roach, Director of Graduate Programs, Arkansas State University, PO Box 2220, State University, AR 72467-1630. (501) 972-3430; Fax: (501) 972-3868; Internet Address: t.d. roach@cherokee.astate.edu.

Henderson State University

School of Business

Arkadelphia, Arkansas

OVERVIEW

Henderson State University is a state-supported comprehensive coed institution. Founded 1890. Setting: 132-acre small-town campus. Total institutional enrollment: 4,460.

ACADEMICS

Calendar Semesters.

Concentration Management.

FACILITIES

Information Resources Main library with 200,000 bound volumes, 192,780 titles on microform, 1,564 periodical subscriptions, 4,548 records/tapes/CDs.

ADMISSION

Entrance Requirements Bachelor's degree, GMAT score of 350, minimum 2.5 GPA.

Application Requirements Application form, copies of transcript.

Application Deadlines 8/23 for fall, 1/10 for spring.

INTERNATIONAL STUDENTS

Applying Admission application deadlines: 8/23 for fall, 1/10 for spring.

Program Contact: Mr. Tom Gattin, Registrar, Henderson State University, 1100 Henderson Street, Arkadelphia, AR 71999-0001. (501) 230-5000 Ext. 3293.

University of Arkansas

College of Business Administration

Fayetteville, Arkansas

OVERVIEW

The University of Arkansas is a state-supported coed institution. Part of University of Arkansas System. Founded 1871. Setting: 420-acre small-town campus. Total institutional enrollment: 14,500. Program was first offered in 1946. AACSB-accredited.

MBA HIGHLIGHTS

Entrance Difficulty**
Mean GMAT: 588
Mean GPA: 3.43

Cost
Tuition: N/R
(Nonresident: N/R)
Room & Board: $3,610

Enrollment Profile
Full-time: 95
Part-time: 67
Total: 162
Average Age: 26

Work Exp: 60%
International: 25%
Women: 32%
Minorities: 4%

Average Class Size: 27

ACADEMICS

Calendar Semesters.

Curricular Focus Organizational development and change management, problem solving and decision making, strategic analysis and planning.

Concentrations Accounting, economics, finance, human resources management, international business, management, management information systems, marketing, organizational behavior, transportation.

Faculty Full-time: 10, 100% with doctorates.

Teaching Methodology Case study: 30%, lecture: 30%, seminars by members of the business community: 10%, student presentations: 15%, team projects: 15%.

STUDENT STATISTICS

Geographic Representation State residents 31%. By region: South 50%; West 15%; Midwest 10%. International 25%.

Undergraduate Majors Business 65%; engineering/technology 15%; humanities 15%; social sciences 5%.

Other Background Graduate degrees in other disciplines: 5%. Work experience: On average, students have 2 years of work experience on entrance to the program.

FACILITIES

Information Resources Main library with 1.4 million bound volumes, 810,288 titles on microform, 16,540 periodical subscriptions, 16,220 records/tapes/CDs, 142 CD-ROMs.

Housing 25% of students in program live in college-owned or -operated housing. Assistance with housing search provided.

Technology Computers are used moderately in course work. 600 computer terminals/PCs, linked by a campus-wide computer network, are available for use by students in program; they are located in dormitories, learning resource center, the computer center, computer labs. Students in the program are not required to have their own PC.

Computer Resources/On-line Services

Training	Yes	Dun's	Yes
Internet	Yes	Dow Jones	Yes
E-Mail	Yes	Dialog	No
LEXIS/NEXIS	Yes	Bloomberg	No
CompuServe	Yes		

ADMISSION

Acceptance 1994-95 283 applied for admission; 29% were accepted.

Entrance Requirements Bachelor's degree, prerequisite courses required for applicants with non-business degree, GMAT score of 550, minimum 3.2 GPA. Core courses waived through: previous course work, work experience.

Application Requirements Application form, copies of transcript, personal statement, 3 letters of recommendation.

Application Deadlines 3/15 for fall, 10/15 for spring.

FINANCIALS

Financial Aid In 1994-95, 45% of candidates received some institutionally administered aid in the form of scholarships, assistantships. Total awards ranged from $4,500-$10,000. Financial aid is not available to part-time students. Application deadlines: 3/15 for fall, 10/15 for spring. Applications are processed on a rolling basis. Contact: Ms. Rebecca Dunn, Graduate Secretary, CBA Suite 475, Fayetteville, AR 72701. (501) 575-2851.

INTERNATIONAL STUDENTS

Demographics 25% of students enrolled in the program are international; Asia 60%, Central America 5%, Europe 5%, South America 5%, other 25%.

Services and Facilities International student office, international student center, visa services, language tutoring, ESL courses, special assistance for nonnative speakers of English, counseling/support services.

Applying TOEFL required, minimum score of 550; proof of health; proof of adequate funds. Financial aid is available to international students. Financial aid application deadlines: 3/15 for fall, 10/15 for spring. Applications are processed on a rolling basis. Admission application deadlines: 3/15 for fall, 10/15 for spring. Contact: Ms. Lynn Mosseso, International Admissions Adviser, 215 Hunt Hall, Fayetteville, AR 23701. (501) 575-6245.

PROGRAMS

One-Year MBA Length of program: Minimum: 11 months. Maximum: 6 years. Full-time classes: Main campus; day, evening, summer. Part-time classes: Main campus, Fort Smith; evening, summer. Degree requirements: 30 hours including 9 elective hours. Average class size: 25.

MBA/JD .

PLACEMENT

In 1993-94, 25 organizations participated in on-campus recruiting. Placement services include career counseling/planning, career placement, job interviews, and resume referral to employers. Of 1994 graduates, 90% were employed within three months of graduation, the average starting salary was $33,900, the range was $19,500-$51,000.

Jobs by Employer Type Manufacturing 55%; service 45%.

Jobs by Functional Area Marketing/sales 60%; finance 25%; management 5%; consulting 10%.

Program Contact: Dr. Dub Ashton, Associate Dean, University of Arkansas, CBA Suite 975, Fayetteville, AR 72701. (501) 575-2851; Fax: (501) 575-8721.

See full description on page 852.

University of Arkansas at Little Rock

College of Business Administration

Little Rock, Arkansas

OVERVIEW

The University of Arkansas at Little Rock is a state-supported coed institution. Part of University of Arkansas System. Founded 1927. Setting: 150-acre urban campus. Total institutional enrollment: 12,500. Program was first offered in 1970. AACSB-accredited.

MBA HIGHLIGHTS

Entrance Difficulty**
Mean GMAT: 540
Mean GPA: 3.34

Cost $
Tuition: $1,176/semester
(Nonresident: $2,544/semester)
Room & Board: N/R

Enrollment Profile

Full-time: 25	Work Exp: 75%
Part-time: 150	International: 7%
Total: 175	Women: 40%
Average Age: 29	Minorities: 4%

Average Class Size: 25

ACADEMICS

Length of Program Minimum: 12 months. Maximum: 6 years.

Calendar Semesters.

Full-time Classes Main campus; evening, summer.

Part-time Classes Main campus; evening, summer.

Degree Requirements 30 credits including 12 elective credits.

Required Courses Accounting, applied organizational behavior, concepts in management, corporate strategy, financial planning, issues in manufacturing and operations management, legal environment of business, managerial economics, marketing strategy, principles of marketing, statistics.

Curricular Focus Economic and financial theory, problem solving and decision making, strategic analysis and planning.

Concentrations Accounting, finance, management, marketing.

Faculty Full-time: 45, 98% with doctorates.

Teaching Methodology Case study: 25%, faculty seminars: 5%, lecture: 25%, research: 10%, seminars by members of the business community: 5%, student presentations: 10%, team projects: 20%.

STUDENT STATISTICS

Geographic Representation State residents 77%. By region: South 93%. International 7%.

Undergraduate Majors Business 40%; engineering/technology 10%; humanities 10%; social sciences 20%; other 20%.

Other Background Graduate degrees in other disciplines: 5%. Work experience: On average, students have 2-4 years of work experience on entrance to the program.

FACILITIES

Information Resources Main library with 397,529 bound volumes, 691,612 titles on microform, 2,626 periodical subscriptions, 6,426 records/tapes/CDs, 266 CD-ROMs.

Housing 3% of students in program live in college-owned or -operated housing.

Technology Computers are used moderately in course work. 120 computer terminals/PCs, linked by a campus-wide computer network, are available for use by students in program; they are located in the student center, the library, the computer center, computer labs, College of Business building. Students in the program are not required to have their own PC.

Computer Resources/On-line Services

Training	Yes	E-Mail	Yes
Internet	Yes	Multimedia Center	Yes

ADMISSION

Acceptance 1994-95 80 applied for admission; 90% were accepted.

Entrance Requirements Bachelor's degree, GMAT score of 450, minimum 2.75 GPA. Core courses waived through: previous course work.

Application Requirements Application form, copies of transcript.

Application Deadlines 6/1 for fall, 10/1 for spring.

FINANCIALS

Costs for 1994-95 Tuition: Full-time: $1,176/semester for state residents, $2,544/semester for nonresidents, $2,544/semester for international students; Part-time day: $110/hour for state residents, $236/hour for nonresidents, $236/hour for international students. Fees: Full-time: $61/semester for state residents, $61/semester for nonresidents, $91/semester for international students; Part-time day: $45-$56/semester for state residents, $45-$56/semester for nonresidents, $75-$86/semester for international students.

Financial Aid In 1994-95, 65% of candidates received some institutionally administered aid in the form of loans, assistantships, work-study. Total awards ranged from $5,000-$8,000. Financial aid is available to part-time students. Application deadlines: 7/1 for fall, 9/1 for spring. Contact: Office of Financial Aid, 2801 South University Avenue, Little Rock, AR 72204. (501) 569-3130.

INTERNATIONAL STUDENTS

Demographics 7% of students enrolled in the program are international; Asia 75%, Africa 5%, Europe 5%, South America 5%, other 10%.

Services and Facilities International student office, visa services, language tutoring, ESL courses, counseling/support services.

Applying TOEFL required, minimum score of 525; proof of health; proof of adequate funds. Financial aid is available to international students. Admission application deadlines: 5/1 for fall, 9/1 for spring. Contact: Ms. Robin Fullmore, International and Immigration Adviser, 2801 South University Avenue, Little Rock, AR 72204. (501) 569-3582.

ALTERNATE MBA PROGRAM

MBA/JD Length of program: Minimum: 54 months. Full-time classes: Main campus; day, evening, weekends, summer. Part-time classes: Main campus; evening, summer. Degree requirements: 84 credits.

PLACEMENT

In 1993-94, 16 organizations participated in on-campus recruiting. Placement services include alumni network, career counseling/planning, career fairs, career placement, resume preparation, and resume referral to employers. Of 1994 graduates, 80% were employed within three months of graduation, the average starting salary range was $25,000-$34,000.

Jobs by Employer Type Government 4%; consulting 26%; corporate management 70%.

Jobs by Functional Area Marketing/sales 20%; finance 60%; management 20%.

Program Contact: Ms. Tammy Lawrence, MBA Program Adviser, University of Arkansas at Little Rock, 2801 South University Avenue, Little Rock, AR 72204. (501) 569-3356; Fax: (501) 569-8898; Internet Address: talawrence@ualr.edu.

University of Central Arkansas

College of Business Administration

Conway, Arkansas

OVERVIEW

The University of Central Arkansas is a state-supported comprehensive coed institution. Founded 1907. Setting: 256-acre urban campus. Total institutional enrollment: 9,200. Program was first offered in 1968. AACSB-accredited.

MBA HIGHLIGHTS

Entrance Difficulty***
Mean GMAT: 435
Mean GPA: 3.14

Cost $
Tuition: $109/hour
(Nonresident: $202/hour)
Room & Board: $3,000

Enrollment Profile

Full-time: 32	Work Exp: 75%
Part-time: 45	International: 32%
Total: 77	Women: 34%
Average Age: 28	Minorities: 4%

Average Class Size: 25

ACADEMICS

Length of Program Minimum: 12 months. Maximum: 7 years.

Calendar Semesters.

Full-time Classes Main campus; evening.

Part-time Classes Main campus; evening.

Degree Requirements 30 credits including 6 elective credits.

Required Courses Accounting for planning and control, applied economic theory, business and economic research, business information systems, financial decision making, management, marketing. Courses may be waived through: previous course work.

Curricular Focus Business issues and problems, problem solving and decision making, teamwork.

Concentration Management.

Faculty Part-time: 20, 100% with doctorates.

Teaching Methodology Case study: 10%, lecture: 40%, student presentations: 25%, team projects: 25%.

STUDENT STATISTICS

Geographic Representation International 32%.

Undergraduate Majors Business 98%; engineering/technology 2%.

FACILITIES

Information Resources Main library with 493,179 bound volumes, 62,710 titles on microform, 2,652 periodical subscriptions, 4,115 records/tapes/CDs, 16 CD-ROMs.

Housing 2% of students in program live in college-owned or -operated housing.

Technology Computers are used moderately in course work. 130 computer terminals/PCs, linked by a campus-wide computer network, are available for use by students in program; they are located in the library, the computer center, computer labs. Students in the program are not required to have their own PC.

Computer Resources/On-line Services

Training	Yes	E-Mail	Yes
Internet	Yes		

ADMISSION

Acceptance 1994-95 50 applied for admission; 60% were accepted.

Entrance Requirements Bachelor's degree, GMAT score of 400, minimum 2.7 GPA. Core courses waived through: previous course work.

Application Requirements Interview, application form, copies of transcript.

Application Deadlines 6/1 for fall, 10/1 for spring, 3/1 for summer. Application discs available.

FINANCIALS

Costs for 1994-95 Tuition: Full-time: $109/hour for state residents, $202/hour for nonresidents. Average room and board costs are $3,000 per academic year (on-campus).

Financial Aid In 1994-95, 17% of candidates received some institutionally administered aid in the form of assistantships. Financial aid is not available to part-time students. Contact: Ms. Sherry Byrd, Financial Aid Director, Bernard Hall 201, Conway, AR 72035-0001. (501) 450-3140.

INTERNATIONAL STUDENTS

Demographics 32% of students enrolled in the program are international; Asia 98%, Europe 2%.

Services and Facilities Language tutoring, ESL courses, special assistance for nonnative speakers of English.

Applying TOEFL required, minimum score of 550; proof of health; proof of adequate funds. Financial aid is available to international students. Financial aid application deadlines: 6/1 for fall, 10/1 for spring, 3/1 for summer. Admission application deadlines: 6/1 for fall, 10/1 for spring, 3/1 for summer. Contact: Dr. Doug Podoll, Director of International Programs, Center for International Programs, 201 Donaghey, 109 South Minton, Conway, AR 72035-0001. (501) 450-3445.

PLACEMENT

Placement services include alumni network, career counseling/planning, career fairs, career placement, job interviews, resume preparation, and resume referral to employers. Of 1994 graduates, 100% were employed within three months of graduation.

Program Contact: Mr. James Barr, MBA Director, University of Central Arkansas, Conway, AR 72035-0001. (501) 450-5303; Fax: (501) 450-5302.

CALIFORNIA

Armstrong University

Graduate School of Business Administration

Berkeley, California

OVERVIEW

Armstrong University is an independent proprietary comprehensive coed institution. Founded 1918. Setting: urban campus with easy access to San Francisco. Total institutional enrollment: 125.

MBA HIGHLIGHTS

Entrance Difficulty**

Cost $
Tuition: $4,920
Room & Board: $5,500 (off-campus)

Enrollment Profile

Full-time: N/R	Work Exp: N/R
Part-time: N/R	International: 94%
Total: 80	Women: 44%
Average Age: N/R	Minorities: 2%

Average Class Size: 15

ACADEMICS

Length of Program Minimum: 24 months.

Calendar Quarters.

Full-time Classes Main campus; day, evening, summer.

Part-time Classes Main campus; day, evening, summer.

Degree Requirements 56 credits.

Curricular Focus Economic and financial theory, international business, teamwork.

Concentrations Accounting, finance, international business, management, marketing.

STUDENT STATISTICS

Geographic Representation State residents 4%. International 94%.

FACILITIES

Information Resources Main library with 12,000 bound volumes, 1 title on microform, 100 periodical subscriptions, 10 records/tapes/CDs, 7 CD-ROMs.

Housing College housing not available.

ADMISSION
Entrance Requirements Bachelor's degree, minimum 2.5 GPA.

Application Requirements Application form, copies of transcript, 3 letters of recommendation.

Application Deadline Applications are processed on a rolling basis.

FINANCIALS
Costs for 1994-95 Tuition: Full-time: $4,920; Part-time day: $205/unit. Fees: Full-time: $40/quarter. Average room and board costs are $5,500 per academic year (off-campus).

INTERNATIONAL STUDENTS
Demographics 94% of students enrolled in the program are international.

Applying Proof of adequate funds. Admission applications are processed on a rolling basis.

Program Contact: Ms. Ziba Mahdavi, Director of Admissions, Armstrong University, 2222 Harold Way, Berkeley, CA 94704-1489. (510) 848-2500; Fax: (510) 848-9438.

Azusa Pacific University

School of Business and Management

Azusa, California

OVERVIEW
Azusa Pacific University is an independent nondenominational comprehensive coed institution. Founded 1899. Setting: 60-acre suburban campus with easy access to Los Angeles. Total institutional enrollment: 4,000. Program was first offered in 1977.

MBA HIGHLIGHTS
Entrance Difficulty**
Mean GMAT: 500
Mean GPA: 3.2

Cost $$$
Tuition: $355/unit
Room & Board: N/R

Enrollment Profile
Full-time: 75	Work Exp: 60%
Part-time: 25	International: 50%
Total: 100	Women: 30%
Average Age: 28	Minorities: 10%

Average Class Size: 20

ACADEMICS
Length of Program Minimum: 12 months. Maximum: 5 years.

Calendar Trimesters.

Full-time Classes Main campus; evening, weekends, summer.

Part-time Classes Main campus; evening, weekends, summer.

Degree Requirements 36 credits including 3 elective credits.

Required Courses Financial analysis, information systems for managers, international business management, managerial economics, managerial ethics, managing behavior in organizations, market planning, planning and strategy, research methodology. Courses may be waived through: previous course work, work experience.

Curricular Focus Leadership, problem solving and decision making, teamwork.

Concentrations International business, management, marketing, organizational behavior, strategic management.

Faculty Full-time: 10, 50% with doctorates; part-time: 2.

Teaching Methodology Lecture: 30%, team and case study: 70%.

STUDENT STATISTICS
Geographic Representation State residents 40%. By region: West 40%; Midwest 10%. International 50%.

Undergraduate Majors Business 70%; science/mathematics 10%; social sciences 10%; other 10%.

Other Background Graduate degrees in other disciplines: 10%. Work experience: On average, students have 5 years of work experience on entrance to the program.

FACILITIES
Information Resources Main library with 110,000 bound volumes, 237 titles on microform, 850 periodical subscriptions, 8,000 records/tapes/CDs, 6 CD-ROMs.

Housing College housing not available.

Technology Computers are used moderately in course work. 60 computer terminals/PCs are available for use by students in program; they are located in learning resource center, computer labs. Students in the program are not required to have their own PC.

Computer Resources/On-line Services
Training	Yes	Multimedia Center	Yes
Internet	Yes $	LEXIS/NEXIS	Yes
E-Mail	No	Dialog	Yes

ADMISSION
Acceptance 1994-95 Of those applying, 60% were accepted.

Entrance Requirements Bachelor's degree, GMAT score of 450, minimum 3.0 GPA. Core courses waived through: previous course work.

Application Requirements Application form, copies of transcript, resume/curriculum vitae, personal statement.

Application Deadlines 8/15 for fall. Applications are processed on a rolling basis.

FINANCIALS
Costs for 1994-95 Tuition: Full-time: $355/unit. Fees: Full-time: $50/trimester.

Financial Aid Financial aid is not available to part-time students. Application deadlines: 7/15 for fall, 11/30 for spring, 3/15 for summer. Contact: Ms. Beverly Jordan, Director of Student Financial Services, 901 East Alosta Avenue, Azusa, CA 91702-2701. (818) 812-3009.

INTERNATIONAL STUDENTS
Demographics 50% of students enrolled in the program are international.

Services and Facilities International student center, visa services, language tutoring, ESL courses.

Applying TOEFL required, minimum score of 550; proof of health; proof of adequate funds. Financial aid is not available to international students. Admission application deadlines: 7/15 for fall, 11/15 for spring. Contact: International Student Services, 901 East Alosta Avenue, Azusa, CA 91702-2701. (818) 812-3055.

PLACEMENT
Placement services include alumni network, career counseling/planning, career fairs, career library, and resume preparation.

Program Contact: Ms. Debi Cade, Administrative Assistant to Dean, Azusa Pacific University, 901 East Alosta Avenue, Azusa, CA 91702-2701. (818) 812-3090; Fax: (818) 815-3802.

California Institute of Integral Studies

School for Transformative Learning

San Francisco, California

OVERVIEW
California Institute of Integral Studies is graduate-only institution. Founded 1968. Setting: urban campus. Total institutional enrollment: 920.

PROGRAM HIGHLIGHTS
Entrance Difficulty**

Cost $$
Tuition: $8,500
Room & Board: N/R

Enrollment Profile
Full-time: N/R	Work Exp: N/R
Part-time: N/R	International: 10%
Total: 75	Women: 50%
Average Age: N/R	Minorities: 10%

Average Class Size: 16

ACADEMICS
Calendar Quarters.

Curricular Focus Organizational development and change management, social responsibility, teamwork.

Concentrations Management, organizational development.
Teaching Methodology Case study: 10%, faculty seminars: 20%, on-line communications: 30%, seminars by members of the business community: 10%, student presentations: 10%, team projects: 20%.
Special Opportunities Internship program available.

STUDENT STATISTICS
Geographic Representation State residents 50%. International 10%.

FACILITIES
Information Resources Main library with 40,000 bound volumes.

ADMISSION
Acceptance 1994-95 35 applied for admission; 68% were accepted.
Entrance Requirements Bachelor's in business, minimum 3.0 GPA.
Application Requirements Interview, application form, copies of transcript, personal statement.
Application Deadlines 8/1 for fall, 12/1 for winter. Applications are processed on a rolling basis.

FINANCIALS
Costs for 1994-95 Tuition: Full-time: $8,500; Part-time day: $270/unit. Fees: Full-time: $220; Part-time day: $220.
Financial Aid In 1994-95, 30% of candidates received some institutionally administered aid in the form of grants, scholarships, loans, work-study. Application deadline: 8/1 for fall. Applications are processed on a rolling basis. Contact: Mr. Michael Szkotak, Director, 765 Ashbury, San Francisco, CA 94117-4013. (415) 753-6100.

INTERNATIONAL STUDENTS
Demographics 10% of students enrolled in the program are international.
Services and Facilities International student office, counseling/support services.
Applying TOEFL required, minimum score of 550; proof of health; proof of adequate funds. Financial aid is available to international students. Applications are processed on a rolling basis. Admission application deadlines: 8/1 for fall, 12/1 for winter. Applications are processed on a rolling basis. Contact: Ms. Kathleen Wydler, Foreign Student Adviser, 765 Ashbury, San Francisco, CA 94117-4013. (415) 753-6100.

PROGRAM
MAB Length of program: Minimum: 24 months. Full-time classes: Main campus; day, evening, weekends. Part-time classes: Main campus; day, evening, weekends. Degree requirements: 72 credits.

PLACEMENT
Placement services include alumni network, career counseling/planning, career library, career placement, and job search course.

Program Contact: Inquiry Office, California Institute of Integral Studies, 765 Ashbury, San Francisco, CA 94117-4013. (415) 753-6100 Ext. 459.
See full description on page 686.

California Lutheran University

School of Business

Thousand Oaks, California

OVERVIEW
California Lutheran University is an independent Lutheran comprehensive coed institution. Founded 1959. Setting: 290-acre suburban campus with easy access to Los Angeles. Total institutional enrollment: 2,400. Program was first offered in 1978.

MBA HIGHLIGHTS

Entrance Difficulty*
Mean GMAT: 600
Mean GPA: 3.0

Cost $
Tuition: $350/credit
Room & Board: N/R

Enrollment Profile

Full-time: 18	Work Exp: 95%
Part-time: 351	International: 2%
Total: 369	Women: 42%
Average Age: 35	Minorities: 20%

Average Class Size: 11

ACADEMICS
Length of Program Minimum: 30 months. Maximum: 7 years.
Calendar Semesters.
Full-time Classes Main campus, Warner Center, Oxnard Extension; evening, weekends, summer.
Part-time Classes Main campus, Warner Center, Oxnard Extension; evening, weekends, summer.
Degree Requirements 42 credits including 12 elective credits.
Required Courses Business ethics, computer use in management, financial principles, management, managerial accounting, managerial economics, marketing theory, organizational theory, statistics.
Curricular Focus Business issues and problems, organizational development and change management, strategic analysis and planning.
Concentrations Entrepreneurship, finance, health services, international business, management, management information systems, marketing.
Faculty Full-time: 9, 60% with doctorates; part-time: 20, 50% with doctorates.
Teaching Methodology Case study: 10%, discussion: 10%, lecture: 45%, research: 5%, seminars by members of the business community: 5%, student presentations: 5%, team projects: 20%.

STUDENT STATISTICS
Geographic Representation State residents 98%. By region: West 98%. International 2%.
Undergraduate Majors Business 50%; engineering/technology 20%; nursing 10%; science/mathematics 2%; social sciences 10%; other 8%.
Other Background Graduate degrees in other disciplines: 5%. Work experience: On average, students have 10 years of work experience on entrance to the program.

FACILITIES
Information Resources Main library with 113,214 bound volumes, 368 titles on microform, 627 periodical subscriptions, 2,475 records/tapes/CDs, 11 CD-ROMs.
Housing College housing not available.
Technology Computers are used heavily in course work. Computer terminals/PCs, linked by a campus-wide computer network, are available for use by students in program; they are located in classrooms, the library, computer labs. Students in the program are not required to have their own PC.
Computer Resources/On-line Services

Training	No	E-Mail	Yes
Internet	Yes		

ADMISSION
Acceptance 1994-95 93 applied for admission; 83% were accepted.
Entrance Requirements Bachelor's degree, GMAT score of 400. Core courses waived through: previous course work.
Application Requirements Written essay, interview, application form, copies of transcript, personal statement, 3 letters of recommendation.
Application Deadline Applications are processed on a rolling basis.

FINANCIALS
Costs for 1994-95 Tuition: Full-time: $350/credit.
Financial Aid Application deadlines: 7/1 for fall, 9/1 for spring. Applications are processed on a rolling basis. Contact: Ms. Betsy Kocher, Director, 60 West Olsen Road, Thousand Oaks, CA 91360. (805) 493-3115.

INTERNATIONAL STUDENTS
Demographics 2% of students enrolled in the program are international.
Applying TOEFL required, minimum score of 550. Financial aid is available to international students. Applications are processed on a rolling basis. Admission applications are processed on a rolling basis.

PLACEMENT

Placement services include alumni network, career counseling/planning, career fairs, career placement, resume preparation, and resume referral to employers.

Program Contact: Ms. Cathy Kalvelage, Graduate Admissions Counselor, California Lutheran University, 60 West Olsen Road, Thousand Oaks, CA 91360. (805) 493-3125; Fax: (805) 493-3542; Internet Address: kalvilage@robles.callutheran.edu.

California Polytechnic State University, San Luis Obispo

College of Business

San Luis Obispo, California

OVERVIEW

California Polytechnic State University, San Luis Obispo is a state-supported comprehensive coed institution. Part of California State University System. Founded 1901. Setting: 5,000-acre small-town campus. Total institutional enrollment: 15,500. Program was first offered in 1971. AACSB-accredited.

MBA HIGHLIGHTS

Entrance Difficulty***
Mean GMAT: 551
Mean GPA: 3.14

Cost $
Tuition: $454 - $676/quarter
(Nonresident: $164/unit)
Room & Board: N/R

Enrollment Profile

Full-time: 150	Work Exp: 90%
Part-time: 8	International: N/R
Total: 158	Women: 40%
Average Age: 28	Minorities: N/R

Average Class Size: 35

ACADEMICS

Length of Program Minimum: 24 months. Maximum: 7 years.

Calendar Quarters.

Full-time Classes Main campus; day.

Degree Requirements 96 units including 42 elective units.

Required Courses Aggregate economics, business strategy and policy, business, government, and society, financial accounting, information systems, management science, managerial accounting, managerial economics, marketing management, organizational behavior, production and operations management, quantitative analysis.

Curricular Focus Business issues and problems, problem solving and decision making, teamwork.

Concentrations Engineering management, agribusiness, architectural management, management.

Faculty Full-time: 30, 100% with doctorates.

Teaching Methodology Case study: 20%, lecture: 50%, research: 5%, seminars by members of the business community: 5%, student presentations: 10%, team projects: 10%.

Special Opportunities Internships include forecasting, marketing, and management consulting.

STUDENT STATISTICS

Geographic Representation By region: West 95%; Northeast 5%.

Undergraduate Majors Business 44%; engineering/technology 28%; humanities 10%; science/mathematics 3%; social sciences 15%.

Other Background Graduate degrees in other disciplines: 3%.

FACILITIES

Information Resources Main library with 864,000 bound volumes, 2.4 million titles on microform, 3,500 periodical subscriptions, 62,000 records/tapes/CDs, 1 CD-ROM.

Housing 5% of students in program live in college-owned or -operated housing.

Technology Computers are used heavily in course work. 1,000 computer terminals/PCs, linked by a campus-wide computer network, are available for use by students in program; they are located in classrooms, the library, the computer center, computer labs. Students in the program are not required to have their own PC.

Computer Resources/On-line Services

Training	Yes	LEXIS/NEXIS	Yes
Internet	Yes	CompuServe	Yes
E-Mail	Yes	Dun's	Yes
Videoconference Center	Yes	Dow Jones	Yes
Multimedia Center	Yes	Bloomberg	Yes

ADMISSION

Acceptance 1994-95 141 applied for admission; 74% were accepted.

Entrance Requirements Bachelor's degree, GMAT score of 530, minimum 3.0 GPA. Core courses waived through: previous course work.

Application Requirements Written essay, application form, copies of transcript, resume/curriculum vitae, personal statement, 2 letters of recommendation.

Application Deadlines 7/1 for fall. Applications are processed on a rolling basis. Application discs available.

FINANCIALS

Costs for 1994-95 Tuition: Full-time: $164/unit for nonresidents. Fees: Full-time: $454-$676/quarter for state residents, $454-$676/quarter for nonresidents.

Financial Aid In 1994-95, 25% of candidates received some institutionally administered aid in the form of loans. Total awards ranged from $8,500-$16,826. Financial aid is not available to part-time students. Application deadline: 3/2 for fall. Applications are processed on a rolling basis. Contact: Financial Aid Office, San Luis Obispo, CA 93407. (805) 756-2927.

INTERNATIONAL STUDENTS

Services and Facilities International student office, language tutoring, ESL courses, counseling/support services.

Applying TOEFL required, minimum score of 550; proof of health; proof of adequate funds. Financial aid is not available to international students. Admission application deadline: 6/1 for fall. Contact: Ms. Marilyn York, Coordinator, International Programs, San Luis Obispo, CA 93407. (805) 756-1477.

ALTERNATE MBA PROGRAMS

Executive MBA (EMBA) Length of program: Minimum: 24 months. Full-time classes: Main campus; evening, weekends. Degree requirements: 96 credits. Minimum 5 years work experience.

MBA/MS Length of program: Minimum: 24 months. Full-time classes: Main campus; day, summer. Degree requirements: 111 credits. MS is in engineering.

PLACEMENT

In 1993-94, 50 organizations participated in on-campus recruiting; 200 on-campus interviews were conducted. Placement services include career counseling/planning, career placement, job interviews, and resume referral to employers. Of 1994 graduates, 90% were employed within three months of graduation, the average starting salary was $33,400, the range was $31,000-$35,800.

Jobs by Employer Type Manufacturing 10%; service 60%; government 5%; consulting 10%; nonprofit 10%; other 5%.

Jobs by Functional Area Marketing/sales 50%; finance 10%; management 15%; technical management 25%.

Program Contact: Dr. Walter Rice, Director of Graduate Management Program, California Polytechnic State University, San Luis Obispo, San Luis Obispo, CA 93407. (805) 756-2285 Ext. 2637; Fax: (805) 756-0110; Internet Address: di687@academic.calpoly.edu.

California State Polytechnic University, Pomona

College of Business Administration

Pomona, California

OVERVIEW

California State Polytechnic University, Pomona is a state-supported comprehensive coed institution. Part of California State University System.

Founded 1938. Setting: 1,400-acre urban campus with easy access to Los Angeles. Total institutional enrollment: 16,304.

MBA HIGHLIGHTS

Entrance Difficulty*
Mean GMAT: 500
Mean GPA: N/R

Cost $
Tuition: $1,440
(Nonresident: $164/unit)
Room & Board: $15,000 (off-campus)

Enrollment Profile
Full-time: N/R	Work Exp: N/R
Part-time: N/R	International: 16%
Total: 500	Women: 42%
Average Age: N/R	Minorities: 35%

Average Class Size: 24

ACADEMICS
Length of Program Minimum: 18 months.
Calendar Quarters.
Full-time Classes Main campus, distance learning option; evening, weekends.
Part-time Classes Main campus, Pasadena, Rosemead, Ontario, distance learning option; evening, weekends.
Degree Requirements 48 credits including 8 elective credits.
Required Courses Advanced financial management, business research methods, information systems seminar, management policy and strategies, management science seminar, management seminar, marketing seminar, seminar in organizational behavior.
Curricular Focus General management, problem solving and decision making, teamwork.
Concentrations Accounting, entrepreneurship, finance, hotel management, human resources management, international business, management, management information systems, marketing, operations management, organizational behavior, real estate.
Teaching Methodology Case study: 30%, lecture: 10%, research: 20%, seminars by members of the business community: 10%, student presentations: 10%, team projects: 20%.

STUDENT STATISTICS
Geographic Representation State residents 79%. International 16%.

FACILITIES
Information Resources Main library with 592,433 bound volumes, 2 million titles on microform, 2,964 periodical subscriptions, 4,349 records/tapes/CDs, 19 CD-ROMs.
Housing College housing not available.

ADMISSION
Entrance Requirements Bachelor's degree, GMAT score of 450, minimum 3.0 GPA, minimum 3 years of work experience.
Application Requirements Application form, copies of transcript, resume/curriculum vitae, personal statement.
Application Deadline Applications are processed on a rolling basis.

FINANCIALS
Costs for 1994-95 Tuition: Full-time: $164/unit for nonresidents; Part-time day: $164/unit for nonresidents. Fees: Full-time: $1,440 for state residents, $1,440 for nonresidents; Part-time day: $834 for state residents, $834 for nonresidents. Average room and board costs are $15,000 per academic year (off-campus).
Financial Aid Applications are processed on a rolling basis. Contact: Mr. Arthur Covarrubias, Director, 3801 West Temple Avenue, Pomona, CA 91768-2557. (909) 869-4672.

INTERNATIONAL STUDENTS
Demographics 16% of students enrolled in the program are international.
Applying TOEFL required, minimum score of 580; proof of health; proof of adequate funds. Financial aid is not available to international students. Admission applications are processed on a rolling basis.

Program Contact: Dr. Rhonda Rhodes, Director, Graduate Business Programs, California State Polytechnic University, Pomona, 3801 West Temple Avenue, Pomona, CA 91768-2557. (909) 869-2363; Fax: (909) 869-4353; Internet Address: rrhodes@csupomona.edu.

California State University, Bakersfield

School of Business and Public Administration

Bakersfield, California

OVERVIEW
California State University, Bakersfield is a state-supported comprehensive coed institution. Part of California State University System. Founded 1970. Setting: 575-acre urban campus. Total institutional enrollment: 5,243. AACSB-accredited.

MBA HIGHLIGHTS

Entrance Difficulty*
Mean GMAT: 490
Mean GPA: 3.0

Cost $
Tuition: $480/quarter
(Nonresident: $164/unit)
Room & Board: $3,570

Enrollment Profile
Full-time: 0	Work Exp: 45%
Part-time: 172	International: N/R
Total: 172	Women: N/R
Average Age: 30	Minorities: N/R

Average Class Size: 25

ACADEMICS
Length of Program Minimum: 9 months. Maximum: 7 years.
Calendar Quarters.
Part-time Classes Main campus; evening, summer.
Degree Requirements 45 credits including 15 elective credits.
Required Courses Accounting for management decision makers, seminar in business policy, seminar in financial policy, seminar in management and organizational behavior, seminar in marketing management, seminar in operations management.
Curricular Focus General management, international business, strategic analysis and planning.
Concentration Management.
Faculty Full-time: 17, 100% with doctorates.
Teaching Methodology Case study: 25%, faculty seminars: 25%, lecture: 50%.

FACILITIES
Information Resources Main library with 337,800 bound volumes, 545,110 titles on microform, 2,500 periodical subscriptions, 3,700 records/tapes/CDs.
Housing College housing available.
Technology 52 computer terminals/PCs, linked by a campus-wide computer network, are available for use by students in program; they are located in the library, computer labs. Students in the program are not required to have their own PC.

Computer Resources/On-line Services
Training	Yes	CompuServe	No
Internet	Yes	Dun's	No
E-Mail	Yes	Dow Jones	No
Multimedia Center	Yes	Dialog	No
LEXIS/NEXIS	Yes	Bloomberg	No

Other on-line services: Carl.

ADMISSION
Acceptance 1994-95 Of those applying, 99% were accepted.
Entrance Requirements Bachelor's degree, prerequisite courses required for applicants with non business degree, GMAT score of 500, minimum 2.75 GPA, upper division writing competency.
Application Requirements Application form, copies of transcript.
Application Deadlines 11/1 for fall, 6/1 for winter, 8/1 for spring, 2/1 for summer.

FINANCIALS
Costs for 1994-95 Tuition: Full-time: $164/unit for nonresidents; Part-time day: $164/unit for nonresidents. Fees: Full-time: $480/quarter for state residents, $480/quarter for nonresidents; Part-time day: $278/quarter

for state residents, $278/quarter for nonresidents. Average room and board costs are $3,570 per academic year (on-campus) and $4,080 per academic year (off-campus).

Financial Aid In 1994-95, candidates received some institutionally administered aid in the form of grants, scholarships, loans. Application deadline: 3/2 for fall. Contact: Financial Aid Office, 9001 Stockdale Highway, Bakersfield, CA 93311-1022. (805) 664-3016.

INTERNATIONAL STUDENTS
Applying TOEFL required, minimum score of 550; proof of health; proof of adequate funds. Financial aid is available to international students. Financial aid application deadline: 3/2 for fall. Admission applications are processed on a rolling basis.

PLACEMENT
Placement services include career fairs and career placement.

Program Contact: Coordinator, MBA Program, California State University, Bakersfield, 9001 Stockdale Highway, Bakersfield, CA 93311-1022. (805) 664-2157, or (800) 788-2782; Fax: (805) 664-2438.

California State University, Chico

College of Business

Chico, California

OVERVIEW
California State University, Chico is a state-supported comprehensive coed institution. Part of California State University System. Founded 1887. Setting: 119-acre suburban campus. Total institutional enrollment: 14,500. Program was first offered in 1972. AACSB-accredited.

MBA HIGHLIGHTS

Entrance Difficulty***
Mean GMAT: 530
Mean GPA: 3.2

Cost $
Tuition: $1,200/semester
(Nonresident: $246/unit)
Room & Board: $5,000

Enrollment Profile

Full-time: 37	Work Exp: 88%
Part-time: 21	International: 20%
Total: 58	Women: 38%
Average Age: 30	Minorities: N/R

Average Class Size: 25

ACADEMICS
Length of Program Minimum: 15 months. Maximum: 5 years.
Calendar Semesters.
Full-time Classes Main campus; evening.
Part-time Classes Main campus, Redding; weekends.
Degree Requirements 30 credits including 9 elective credits.
Required Courses Business communication skills, financial management, management control systems, management information systems, management of people and organizations, strategic management, strategic marketing. Courses may be waived through: previous course work.
Curricular Focus Problem solving and decision making, strategic analysis and planning, teamwork.
Concentrations Accounting, finance, management information systems, marketing, operations management.
Faculty Full-time: 15, 100% with doctorates.
Teaching Methodology Case study: 33%, lecture: 34%, team projects: 33%.
Special Opportunities Internship program available.

STUDENT STATISTICS
Geographic Representation State residents 80%. By region: West 79%; South 1%. International 20%.
Undergraduate Majors Business 52%; engineering/technology 2%; humanities 2%; nursing 2%; science/mathematics 5%; social sciences 2%; other 35%.

Other Background Graduate degrees in other disciplines: 1%. Work experience: On average, students have 4 years of work experience on entrance to the program.

FACILITIES
Information Resources Main library with 1.4 million bound volumes, 927,111 titles on microform, 3,380 periodical subscriptions, 13,997 records/tapes/CDs.
Housing College housing available.
Technology Computers are used heavily in course work. 50 computer terminals/PCs, linked by a campus-wide computer network, are available for use by students in program; they are located in computer labs. Students in the program are not required to have their own PC.

Computer Resources/On-line Services

Training	No	LEXIS/NEXIS	Yes
Internet	Yes	Dow Jones	Yes
E-Mail	Yes		

ADMISSION
Acceptance 1994-95 Of those applying, 50% were accepted.
Entrance Requirements Bachelor's degree, GMAT score of 500, minimum 2.75 GPA. Core courses waived through: previous course work.
Application Requirements Application form, copies of transcript, resume/curriculum vitae, personal statement, 3 letters of recommendation.
Application Deadlines 4/1 for fall, 10/15 for spring.

FINANCIALS
Estimated Costs for 1995-96 Tuition: Full-time: $246/unit for nonresidents. Fees: Full-time: $1,200/semester for state residents, $1,200/semester for nonresidents. Average room and board costs are $5,000 per academic year (on-campus) and $5,000 per academic year (off-campus).
Financial Aid In 1994-95, 50% of candidates received some institutionally administered aid in the form of grants, loans, assistantships. Financial aid is not available to part-time students. Application deadline: 3/1 for fall. Contact: Financial Aid Office, Chico, CA 95929-0150. (916) 898-6451.

INTERNATIONAL STUDENTS
Demographics 20% of students enrolled in the program are international; Asia 90%, South America 1%, other 9%.
Services and Facilities ESL courses.
Applying TOEFL required, minimum score of 550; proof of health; proof of adequate funds. Financial aid is not available to international students. Admission application deadlines: 3/1 for fall, 10/1 for spring. Contact: Mr. James Sewagudde, International Student Adviser, Chico, CA 95929-0150. (916) 898-5712.

PLACEMENT
In 1993-94, 100 organizations participated in on-campus recruiting. Placement services include alumni network, career counseling/planning, career fairs, career placement, resume preparation, and resume referral to employers. Of 1994 graduates, 95% were employed within three months of graduation, the average starting salary was $38,000, the range was $28,000-$43,000.
Jobs by Employer Type Manufacturing 40%; service 10%; government 10%; consulting 20%; accounting 20%.
Jobs by Functional Area Marketing/sales 10%; finance 30%; operations 20%; management 10%; technical management 10%; consulting 20%.

Program Contact: Dr. Steven J. Adams, Coordinator, California State University, Chico, Chico, CA 95929-0150. (916) 898-4425; Fax: (916) 898-4584.

California State University, Dominguez Hills

School of Management

Carson, California

OVERVIEW
California State University, Dominguez Hills is a state-supported comprehensive coed institution. Part of California State University System. Founded 1960. Setting: 350-acre urban campus with easy access to Los Angeles. Total institutional enrollment: 13,000. Program was first offered in 1970.

MBA HIGHLIGHTS

Entrance Difficulty***
Mean GMAT: 520
Mean GPA: 3.1

Cost $
Tuition: $898/semester
(Nonresident: $246/unit)
Room & Board: $3,800

Enrollment Profile
Full-time: 40	Work Exp: 90%
Part-time: 105	International: 20%
Total: 145	Women: 40%
Average Age: 32	Minorities: 40%

Average Class Size: 20

ACADEMICS
Length of Program Minimum: 18 months. Maximum: 5 years.
Calendar Semesters.
Full-time Classes Main campus; evening, weekends, summer.
Part-time Classes Main campus, distance learning option; evening, weekends, summer.
Degree Requirements 30 units including 9 elective units.
Required Courses Organizational behavior, seminar in finance, seminar in marketing, seminar in strategic management. Courses may be waived through: previous course work, work experience.
Curricular Focus Entrepreneurship, international business, problem solving and decision making.
Concentrations International business, management.
Faculty Full-time: 55, 98% with doctorates.
Teaching Methodology Case study: 20%, faculty seminars: 10%, lecture: 20%, research: 10%, student presentations: 20%, team projects: 20%.
Special Opportunities International exchange in Mexico.

STUDENT STATISTICS
Geographic Representation State residents 80%. By region: West 80%. International 20%.
Undergraduate Majors Business 50%; engineering/technology 20%; social sciences 20%; other 10%.
Other Background Graduate degrees in other disciplines: 5%. Work experience: On average, students have 7 years of work experience on entrance to the program.

FACILITIES
Information Resources Main library with 411,000 bound volumes, 602,004 titles on microform, 2,222 periodical subscriptions, 7,424 records/tapes/CDs, 73 CD-ROMs. Business collection includes 40,000 bound volumes, 100 periodical subscriptions, 3 CD-ROMs.
Housing 15% of students in program live in college-owned or -operated housing.
Technology Computers are used moderately in course work. 40 computer terminals/PCs, linked by a campus-wide computer network, are available for use by students in program; they are located in computer labs, the research center. Students in the program are not required to have their own PC.

Computer Resources/On-line Services
Training	Yes	CompuServe	Yes
Internet	Yes	Dun's	No
E-Mail	Yes	Dow Jones	No
Multimedia Center	Yes	Dialog	No
LEXIS/NEXIS	Yes $	Bloomberg	No

Other on-line services: Carl, OCLC.

ADMISSION
Acceptance 1994-95 Of those applying, 50% were accepted.
Entrance Requirements Bachelor's degree, GMAT score of 450, minimum 2.75 GPA. Core courses waived through: previous course work, work experience.
Application Requirements Application form, copies of transcript, personal statement.
Application Deadlines 6/1 for fall, 12/1 for spring.

FINANCIALS
Costs for 1994-95 Tuition: Full-time: $246/unit for nonresidents. Fees: Full-time: $898/semester for state residents, $106/semester for nonresidents. Average room and board costs are $3,800 per academic year (on-campus).

Financial Aid In 1994-95, 5% of candidates received some institutionally administered aid in the form of grants, loans. Financial aid is available to part-time students. Application deadlines: 11/1 for fall, 4/1 for spring. Contact: Mr. James Wood, Director of Financial Aid, Financial Aid Office, Carson, CA 90747-0001. (310) 516-3691.

INTERNATIONAL STUDENTS
Demographics 20% of students enrolled in the program are international; Asia 95%, Europe 2%, Africa 1%, Central America 1%, South America 1%.
Services and Facilities International student center, visa services, language tutoring, ESL courses, special assistance for nonnative speakers of English, counseling/support services.
Applying TOEFL required, minimum score of 550; proof of health; proof of adequate funds. Financial aid is not available to international students. Admission application deadlines: 4/1 for fall, 10/1 for spring. Contact: Mr. Dan A. Joseffini, Coordinator, International Student Services, 1000 East Victoria Street, Carson, CA 90747-0001. (310) 516-4215.

ALTERNATE MBA PROGRAM
Executive MBA (EMBA) Length of program: Minimum: 24 months. Maximum: 5 years. Degree requirements: 45 credits including 9 elective credits. Limited to employees of sponsoring company. Average class size: 15.

PLACEMENT
In 1993-94, 45 organizations participated in on-campus recruiting. Placement services include alumni network, career counseling/planning, career fairs, career library, career placement, job interviews, resume preparation, and resume referral to employers. Of 1994 graduates, 95% were employed within three months of graduation.

Program Contact: MBA Director, California State University, Dominguez Hills, 1000 East Victoria Street, Carson, CA 90747-0001. (310) 516-3465; Fax: (310) 516-4178; Internet Address: tvmba@dhvx20.csudh. edu.

California State University, Fresno

Sid Craig School of Business

Fresno, California

OVERVIEW
California State University, Fresno is a state-supported comprehensive coed institution. Part of California State University System. Founded 1911. Setting: 1,410-acre urban campus. Total institutional enrollment: 18,000. Program was first offered in 1965. AACSB-accredited.

MBA HIGHLIGHTS

Entrance Difficulty***
Mean GMAT: 540
Mean GPA: 3.3

Cost $
Tuition: $901/semester
(Nonresident: $246/unit)
Room & Board: N/R

Enrollment Profile
Full-time: 31	Work Exp: 70%
Part-time: 137	International: 21%
Total: 168	Women: 31%
Average Age: 29	Minorities: 5%

Average Class Size: 18

ACADEMICS
Length of Program Minimum: 16 months. Maximum: 5 years.
Calendar Semesters.
Full-time Classes Main campus; evening, summer.
Part-time Classes Main campus; evening, summer.
Degree Requirements 33 units including 9-12 elective units.
Required Courses Business policy and strategy, financial management, management information systems, managerial accounting, marketing management, organization theory and development, regulatory and ethical environment of business.

Curricular Focus Entrepreneurship, international business, strategic analysis and planning.

Concentrations Accounting, finance, international business, management, management information systems, marketing.

Faculty Full-time: 30, 90% with doctorates.

Teaching Methodology Case study: 20%, lecture: 50%, seminars by members of the business community: 5%, student presentations: 10%, team projects: 15%.

STUDENT STATISTICS

Geographic Representation State residents 78%. International 21%.

Undergraduate Majors Business 62%; engineering/technology 22%; science/mathematics 9%; other 7%.

Other Background Graduate degrees in other disciplines: 1%. Work experience: On average, students have 4 years of work experience on entrance to the program.

FACILITIES

Information Resources Main library with 866,211 bound volumes, 1.2 million titles on microform, 2,928 periodical subscriptions, 55,940 records/tapes/CDs, 8 CD-ROMs.

Housing 3% of students in program live in college-owned or -operated housing.

Technology Computers are used heavily in course work. 50 computer terminals/PCs, linked by a campus-wide computer network, are available for use by students in program; they are located in student rooms, the library, the computer center, computer labs. Students in the program are not required to have their own PC.

Computer Resources/On-line Services

Training	Yes	Multimedia Center	Yes
E-Mail	Yes		

ADMISSION

Acceptance 1994-95 Of those applying, 40% were accepted.

Entrance Requirements Bachelor's degree, GMAT score, minimum 2.75 GPA.

Application Requirements Written essay, application form, copies of transcript, 2 letters of recommendation.

Application Deadlines 6/1 for fall, 10/1 for spring.

FINANCIALS

Costs for 1994-95 Tuition: Full-time: $246/unit for nonresidents. Fees: Full-time: $901/semester for state residents, $901/semester for nonresidents.

Financial Aid In 1994-95, candidates received some institutionally administered aid in the form of loans, assistantships. Financial aid is available to part-time students. Application deadlines: 2/1 for fall, 5/1 for spring. Contact: Mr. Joseph W. Heuston, Director, Financial Aid Office, Joyal Administration Building, Room 296, Fresno, CA 93740. (209) 278-2182.

INTERNATIONAL STUDENTS

Demographics 21% of students enrolled in the program are international; Asia 19%, Europe 2%, Africa 1%, South America 1%, other 76%.

Services and Facilities International student center, ESL courses, counseling/support services.

Applying TOEFL required, minimum score of 550; proof of adequate funds. Financial aid is not available to international students. Admission application deadlines: 4/1 for fall, 9/1 for spring. Contact: Ms. Carol Munshower, Director, International Programs, Joyal Administration, Building Room 211, Fresno, CA 93740-0056. (209) 278-2782.

PLACEMENT

Placement services include career counseling/planning and career placement.

Program Contact: Dr. Donald Stengel, Director of Graduate Business Program, California State University, Fresno, 5241 North Maple Avenue, Fresno, CA 93740. (209) 278-2107; Fax: (209) 278-4911.

California State University, Fullerton

School of Business Administration and Economics

Fullerton, California

OVERVIEW

California State University, Fullerton is a state-supported comprehensive coed institution. Part of California State University System. Founded 1957. Setting: 225-acre urban campus with easy access to Los Angeles. Total institutional enrollment: 22,097. Program was first offered in 1964. AACSB-accredited.

MBA HIGHLIGHTS

Entrance Difficulty***
Mean GMAT: 529
Mean GPA: 3.19

Cost $
Tuition: $900/semester
(Nonresident: $246/unit)
Room & Board: $5,500

Enrollment Profile

Full-time: 36	Work Exp: 90%
Part-time: 326	International: 33%
Total: 362	Women: 45%
Average Age: 28	Minorities: 24%

Average Class Size: 26

ACADEMICS

Length of Program Minimum: 30 months. Maximum: 5 years.

Calendar Semesters.

Full-time Classes Main campus; evening.

Part-time Classes Main campus; evening.

Degree Requirements 31 credits including 3-12 elective credits.

Required Courses Comprehensive business management, decision models, macroeconomic theory and policy, seminar in corporate financial management, seminar in managerial accounting, seminar in marketing problems, seminar in organizational behavior and administration. Courses may be waived through: previous course work.

Curricular Focus Oral and written communications, problem solving and decision making, teamwork.

Concentrations Accounting, economics, finance, international business, management, marketing, quantitative analysis.

Faculty Full-time: 45, 100% with doctorates.

Teaching Methodology Case study: 20%, faculty seminars: 5%, lecture: 25%, research: 5%, seminars by members of the business community: 5%, student presentations: 20%, team projects: 20%.

STUDENT STATISTICS

Geographic Representation State residents 68%. By region: West 67%; Midwest 1%. International 33%.

Undergraduate Majors Business 65%; engineering/technology 10%; science/mathematics 11%; social sciences 14%.

Other Background Work experience: On average, students have 4-6 years of work experience on entrance to the program.

FACILITIES

Information Resources Main library with 654,790 bound volumes, 964,344 titles on microform, 2,455 periodical subscriptions, 15,786 records/tapes/CDs.

Housing College housing available.

Technology Computers are used moderately in course work. 200 computer terminals/PCs, linked by a campus-wide computer network, are available for use by students in program; they are located in classrooms, the library, the computer center, computer labs. Students in the program are not required to have their own PC.

Computer Resources/On-line Services

Training	Yes	LEXIS/NEXIS	Yes3
Internet	Yes	Dow Jones	Yes
E-Mail	Yes		

Other on-line services: First Search, Carl, RLIN.

ADMISSION

Acceptance 1994-95 Of those applying, 45% were accepted.

Entrance Requirements Bachelor's degree, GMAT score of 450, minimum 2.5 GPA. Core courses waived through: previous course work.

Application Requirements Written essay, application form, copies of transcript, personal statement.

Application Deadline Applications are processed on a rolling basis.

FINANCIALS

Costs for 1994-95 Tuition: Full-time: $246/unit for nonresidents; Part-time day: $246/unit for nonresidents. Fees: Full-time: $900/semester for state residents, $900/semester for nonresidents; Part-time day: $567/semester for state residents, $567/semester for nonresidents. Average room and board costs are $5,500 per academic year (on-campus) and $7,000 per academic year (off-campus).

Financial Aid In 1994-95, 4% of candidates received some institutionally administered aid in the form of grants, scholarships, loans, assistantships. Financial aid is available to part-time students. Applications are processed on a rolling basis. Contact: Ms. Deborah S. Gordon, Director of Financial Aid, University Hall 146, Fullerton, CA 92634. (714) 773-3128.

INTERNATIONAL STUDENTS

Demographics 33% of students enrolled in the program are international; Asia 49%, Europe 18%, Africa 1%, Central America 1%, South America 1%, other 30%.

Services and Facilities International student center, language tutoring, ESL courses, special assistance for nonnative speakers of English.

Applying TOEFL required, minimum score of 570. Financial aid is available to international students. Applications are processed on a rolling basis. Admission applications are processed on a rolling basis. Contact: Ms. Paulette Hunter, Foreign Student Adviser, University Hall 244, Fullerton, CA 92634. (714) 773-2787.

PLACEMENT

Placement services include alumni network, career library, and career placement.

Program Contact: Dr. Richard W. Stolz, Associate Dean of Graduate Studies, California State University, Fullerton, PO Box 34080, Fullerton, CA 92634. (714) 773-2101, or (800) 900-4MBA (CA only); Fax: (714) 449-7101.

California State University, Hayward

School of Business and Economics

Hayward, California

OVERVIEW

California State University, Hayward is a state-supported comprehensive coed institution. Part of California State University System. Founded 1957. Setting: 343-acre suburban campus with easy access to San Francisco and San Jose. Total institutional enrollment: 12,000. AACSB-accredited.

MBA HIGHLIGHTS

Entrance Difficulty***
Mean GMAT: 510
Mean GPA: N/R

Cost
Tuition: N/R
(Nonresident: N/R)
Room & Board: $4,000

Enrollment Profile

Full-time: 0		Work Exp: N/R
Part-time: 700		International: N/R
Total: 700		Women: 45%
Average Age: N/R		Minorities: 40%

Average Class Size: 24

ACADEMICS

Calendar Quarters.

Curricular Focus Economic and financial theory, international business.

Concentrations Accounting, computer information systems, taxation, economics, entrepreneurship, finance, human resources management, international business, management, management information systems, marketing, organizational behavior, quantitative analysis.

Teaching Methodology Case study: 30%, lecture: 50%, student presentations: 20%.

FACILITIES

Information Resources Main library with 736,035 bound volumes, 693,548 titles on microform, 2,137 periodical subscriptions, 19,161 records/tapes/CDs, 58 CD-ROMs.

Housing College housing available.

Computer Resources/On-line Services

Training	Yes	Multimedia Center	Yes

ADMISSION

Entrance Requirements Bachelor's degree, GMAT score, minimum 2.75 GPA. Core courses waived through: previous course work.

Application Requirements Written essay, application form, copies of transcript, personal statement, 2 letters of recommendation.

Application Deadlines 6/1 for fall, 9/1 for winter, 1/1 for spring, 3/1 for summer.

FINANCIALS

Financial Aid Application deadline: 3/1 for fall. Contact: Ms. Betty Harris, Director of Financial Aid, 25800 Carlos Bee Boulevard, Hayward, CA 94542. (510) 881-3616.

INTERNATIONAL STUDENTS

Demographics 25% of students on campus are international.

Services and Facilities ESL courses, counseling/support services.

Applying TOEFL required, minimum score of 550; proof of health. Financial aid is not available to international students. Admission application deadline: 3/1 for fall.

PROGRAM

One-Year MBA Length of program: Minimum: 24 months. Part-time classes: Main campus; evening, summer. Degree requirements: 45 units.

PLACEMENT

Placement services include alumni network, career counseling/planning, career fairs, career library, career placement, job interviews, and resume preparation.

Program Contact: Student Services Center, California State University, Hayward, School of Business and Economics, Hayward, CA 94542. (510) 881-3323; Fax: (510) 727-2039.

California State University, Long Beach

College of Business Administration

Long Beach, California

OVERVIEW

California State University, Long Beach is a state-supported comprehensive coed institution. Part of California State University System. Founded 1949. Setting: 320-acre urban campus with easy access to Los Angeles. Total institutional enrollment: 19,422. Program was first offered in 1965. AACSB-accredited.

MBA HIGHLIGHTS

Entrance Difficulty****
Mean GMAT: 543
Mean GPA: 3.09

Cost $
Tuition: $1,019/semester
(Nonresident: $246/unit)
Room & Board: $12,000 (off-campus)

Enrollment Profile
Full-time: 65	Work Exp: 82%
Part-time: 358	International: 18%
Total: 423	Women: 40%
Average Age: 31	Minorities: 9%

Average Class Size: 25

ACADEMICS
Length of Program Minimum: 24 months. Maximum: 7 years.
Calendar Semesters.
Full-time Classes Main campus; evening, summer.
Part-time Classes Main campus; evening, summer.
Degree Requirements 33 units including 12 elective units.
Curricular Focus Problem solving and decision making, strategic analysis and planning.
Concentrations Engineering systems, finance, human resources management, management, management information systems, marketing.
Faculty Full-time: 57, 95% with doctorates; part-time: 10, 70% with doctorates.
Teaching Methodology Case study: 45%, lecture: 20%, research: 10%, student presentations: 10%, team projects: 15%.

STUDENT STATISTICS
Geographic Representation State residents 92%. By region: West 60%; Midwest 15%; Northeast 7%; South 3%. International 18%.
Undergraduate Majors Business 39%; engineering/technology 21%; humanities 3%; science/mathematics 9%; social sciences 8%; other 19%.
Other Background Graduate degrees in other disciplines: 10%. Work experience: On average, students have 6 years of work experience on entrance to the program.

FACILITIES
Information Resources Main library with 1 million bound volumes, 1.5 million titles on microform, 5,854 periodical subscriptions, 36,688 records/tapes/CDs.
Housing 8% of students in program live in college-owned or -operated housing.
Technology Computers are used moderately in course work. 1,450 computer terminals/PCs, linked by a campus-wide computer network, are available for use by students in program; they are located in classrooms, learning resource center, the library, the computer center, computer labs. Students in the program are not required to have their own PC.

Computer Resources/On-line Services
Training	Yes	LEXIS/NEXIS	Yes
Internet	Yes	CompuServe	No
E-Mail	No	Dow Jones	Yes
Multimedia Center	Yes	Dialog	Yes

ADMISSION
Acceptance 1994-95 Of those applying, 60% were accepted.
Entrance Requirements GMAT score. Core courses waived through: previous course work.
Application Requirements Written essay, application form, copies of transcript, resume/curriculum vitae, personal statement, 2 letters of recommendation.
Application Deadlines 4/30 for fall, 10/31 for spring.

FINANCIALS
Costs for 1994-95 Tuition: Full-time: $246/unit for nonresidents. Fees: Full-time: $1,019/semester for state residents, $1,019/semester for nonresidents. Average room and board costs are $12,000 per academic year (off-campus).
Financial Aid In 1994-95, candidates received some institutionally administered aid in the form of scholarships, loans, fellowships, assistantships, work-study. Financial aid is available to part-time students. Application deadline: 4/1 for fall. Contact: Ms. Gloria Kapp, Director, 1250 Bellflower Boulevard, Long Beach, CA 90840. (310) 985-4641.

INTERNATIONAL STUDENTS
Demographics 18% of students enrolled in the program are international; Asia 66%, Europe 27%, Central America 7%.
Services and Facilities International student housing; international student center, ESL courses, counseling/support services.
Applying TOEFL required, minimum score of 550; proof of adequate funds. Financial aid is not available to international students. Admission application deadlines: 11/30 for fall, 8/30 for spring. Contact: Mr. Paul Lewis, Director, Center for International Education, 1250 Bellflower Boulevard, Long Beach, CA 90840. (310) 985-4106.

PLACEMENT
Placement services include career counseling/planning, career library, career placement, job interviews, and resume preparation.

Program Contact: Dr. David Horne, MBA Director, California State University, Long Beach, 1250 Bellflower Boulevard, Long Beach, CA 90840. (310) 985-1797; Fax: (310) 985-5742.

California State University, Los Angeles

School of Business and Economics

Los Angeles, California

OVERVIEW
California State University, Los Angeles is a state-supported comprehensive coed institution. Part of California State University System. Founded 1947. Setting: 173-acre urban campus. Total institutional enrollment: 18,200. Program was first offered in 1963. AACSB-accredited.

MBA HIGHLIGHTS

Entrance Difficulty****
Mean GMAT: 590
Mean GPA: 3.3

Cost $
Tuition: $575/quarter
(Nonresident: $164/unit)
Room & Board: $2,750

Enrollment Profile
Full-time: 45	Work Exp: 100%
Part-time: 153	International: 20%
Total: 198	Women: 46%
Average Age: N/R	Minorities: 53%

Class Size: 20 - 25

ACADEMICS
Length of Program Minimum: 24 months. Maximum: 7 years.
Calendar Quarters.
Full-time Classes Main campus; evening, summer.
Part-time Classes Main campus; evening, summer.
Degree Requirements 52 quarter hours including 20 elective quarter hours. Other: Writing proficiency exam; minimum 3.0 GPA; comprehensive exam.
Required Courses Accounting graduate directed study, administrative behavior and systems management, business finance, economic analysis and business operation, finance graduate directed study, management accounting theory, management graduate directed study, management information systems, marketing graduate directed study, marketing management, policy integration and strategy, quantitative approach to managerial decisions. Courses may be waived through: previous course work.
Curricular Focus Business issues and problems, problem solving and decision making, strategic analysis and planning.
Concentrations Accounting, economics, finance, international business, management, management information systems, marketing.
Faculty Full-time: 53, 100% with doctorates.
Teaching Methodology Case study: 25%, lecture: 25%, research: 25%, student presentations: 25%.
Special Opportunities International exchange program available.

STUDENT STATISTICS
Geographic Representation International 20%.

FACILITIES

Information Resources Main library with 1.4 million bound volumes, 588,859 titles on microform, 4,277 periodical subscriptions. Business collection includes 100,000 bound volumes, 450 periodical subscriptions.

Housing 5% of students in program live in college-owned or -operated housing.

Technology Computers are used heavily in course work. 600 computer terminals/PCs, linked by a campus-wide computer network, are available for use by students in program; they are located in classrooms, the library, computer labs. Students in the program are not required to have their own PC.

Computer Resources/On-line Services

Training	Yes	CompuServe	No
Internet	Yes	Dun's	Yes
E-Mail	Yes	Dow Jones	Yes
LEXIS/NEXIS	Yes	Dialog	Yes

Other on-line services: OCLC, Carl.

ADMISSION

Acceptance 1994-95 153 applied for admission; 51% were accepted.

Entrance Requirements Bachelor's degree, prerequisite courses required for applicants with non-business degree, GMAT score of 400, minimum 2.5 GPA, minimum 2 years of work experience. Core courses waived through: previous course work.

Application Requirements Written essay, application form, copies of transcript, resume/curriculum vitae, personal statement, 3 letters of recommendation.

Application Deadlines 7/1 for fall, 10/1 for winter, 12/1 for spring, 3/1 for summer. Application discs available.

FINANCIALS

Costs for 1994-95 Tuition: Full-time: $164/unit for nonresidents. Fees: Full-time: $575/quarter for state residents, $575/quarter for nonresidents. Average room and board costs are $2,750 per academic year (on-campus).

Financial Aid In 1994-95, 6% of candidates received some institutionally administered aid in the form of grants, scholarships, loans. Total awards ranged from $976-$10,472. Financial aid is available to part-time students. Application deadlines: 3/2 for fall, 3/2 for spring. Contact: Mr. Vincent DeAnda, Director of Student Financial Services, 5151 State University Drive, Los Angeles, CA 90032-8402. (213) 343-3247.

INTERNATIONAL STUDENTS

Demographics 20% of students enrolled in the program are international; Asia 92%, Africa 2%, Central America 2%, Europe 2%, South America 2%.

Services and Facilities International student center, visa services, language tutoring, ESL courses, special assistance for nonnative speakers of English, counseling/support services.

Applying TOEFL required, minimum score of 550; proof of health; proof of adequate funds. Financial aid is available to international students. Applications are processed on a rolling basis. Admission application deadlines: 3/1 for fall, 9/1 for winter, 10/1 for spring. Contact: Mr. Harold Martin, International Student Adviser, 5151 State University Drive, Los Angeles, CA 90032-8365. (213) 343-3170.

PLACEMENT

Placement services include alumni network, career counseling/planning, career fairs, career library, career placement, electronic job bank, job interviews, resume preparation, and resume referral to employers.

Program Contact: Dr. George N. Engler, Associate Dean for Academic Affairs and Resources, California State University, Los Angeles, 5151 State University Drive, Los Angeles, CA 90032-4221. (213) 343-2800; Fax: (213) 343-2813.

California State University, Northridge

School of Business Administration and Economics

Northridge, California

OVERVIEW

California State University, Northridge is a state-supported comprehensive coed institution. Part of California State University System. Founded 1958. Setting: 353-acre suburban campus with easy access to Los Angeles. Total institutional enrollment: 27,282. AACSB-accredited.

MBA HIGHLIGHTS

Entrance Difficulty**
Mean GMAT: 570
Mean GPA: N/R

Cost $
Tuition: $958/semester
(Nonresident: $246/unit)
Room & Board: N/R

Enrollment Profile

Full-time: 24	Work Exp: N/R
Part-time: 286	International: 10%
Total: 310	Women: 48%
Average Age: N/R	Minorities: N/R

Average Class Size: 20

ACADEMICS

Length of Program Minimum: 24 months. Maximum: 5 years.

Calendar Semesters.

Full-time Classes Main campus; evening, summer.

Part-time Classes Main campus; evening, summer.

Degree Requirements 30 credits including 12 elective credits.

Required Courses Computer based management information systems, directed comprehensive studies, marketing seminar, seminar in applied econometrics, seminar in financial theory and policy, seminar in production and management systems analysis, seminar in strategic management. Courses may be waived through: previous course work.

Curricular Focus International business, problem solving and decision making, strategic analysis and planning.

Concentrations Economics, finance, human resources management, international business, management, management information systems, marketing, operations management, organizational behavior, quantitative analysis, strategic management.

Teaching Methodology Case study: 30%, lecture: 10%, team projects: 60%.

STUDENT STATISTICS

Geographic Representation State residents 90%. International 10%.

FACILITIES

Information Resources Main library with 1 million bound volumes, 2.5 million titles on microform, 3,700 periodical subscriptions, 20,000 records/tapes/CDs.

Housing College housing available.

Technology Computer terminals/PCs are available for use by students in program; they are located in computer labs. Students in the program are not required to have their own PC.

ADMISSION

Acceptance 1994-95 Of those applying, 50% were accepted.

Entrance Requirements Bachelor's degree, GMAT score, minimum 3.0 GPA. Core courses waived through: previous course work.

Application Requirements Application form, copies of transcript.

Application Deadlines 4/30 for fall, 9/30 for spring.

FINANCIALS

Costs for 1994-95 Tuition: Full-time: $246/unit for nonresidents. Fees: Full-time: $958/semester for state residents, $958/semester for nonresidents.

Financial Aid Application deadline: 3/2 for fall. Applications are processed on a rolling basis. Contact: Dr. Diane Ryan, Director of Financial Aid, California State University, Northridge, Northridge, CA 91330-0001. (818) 885-2374.

INTERNATIONAL STUDENTS

Demographics 10% of students enrolled in the program are international.

Applying TOEFL required, minimum score of 550; proof of health; proof of adequate funds. Financial aid is not available to international students. Admission application deadlines: 11/30 for fall, 8/31 for spring.

PLACEMENT

Placement services include resume referral to employers.

Program Contact: Graduate Office, California State University, Northridge, 18111 Nordhoff Street, Northridge, CA 91330-0001. (818) 885-2467.

California State University, Sacramento

School of Business Administration

Sacramento, California

OVERVIEW
California State University, Sacramento is a state-supported comprehensive coed institution. Part of California State University System. Founded 1947. Setting: 288-acre suburban campus. Total institutional enrollment: 22,788. Program was first offered in 1964. AACSB-accredited.

MBA HIGHLIGHTS

Entrance Difficulty*
Mean GMAT: 490
Mean GPA: 3.0

Cost $
Tuition: $930/semester
(Nonresident: $246)
Room & Board: $5,300

Enrollment Profile

Full-time: 140	Work Exp: 98%
Part-time: 293	International: 7%
Total: 433	Women: 43%
Average Age: 30	Minorities: 4%

Average Class Size: 20

ACADEMICS
Length of Program Minimum: 24 months. Maximum: 7 years.
Calendar Semesters.
Full-time Classes Main campus; evening, summer.
Part-time Classes Main campus, distance learning option; evening, summer.
Degree Requirements 31 credits including 9 elective credits. Other: Comprehensive exam or thesis/project.
Required Courses Behavioral science applications in management, financial management, issues in productivity management, management accounting, management information systems, management of international operations, marketing management. Courses may be waived through: previous course work.
Curricular Focus Business issues and problems, general management, problem solving and decision making.
Concentrations Accounting, management information systems, real estate.
Faculty Full-time: 8, 100% with doctorates.
Teaching Methodology Case study: 50%, lecture: 20%, student presentations: 10%, team projects: 20%.
Special Opportunities International exchange in Germany, United Kingdom. Internship program available.

STUDENT STATISTICS
Geographic Representation State residents 92%. By region: West 88%; Midwest 3%; Northeast 1%; South 1%. International 7%.
Undergraduate Majors Business 60%; engineering/technology 20%; social sciences 20%.
Other Background Graduate degrees in other disciplines: 2%. Work experience: On average, students have 4 years of work experience on entrance to the program.

FACILITIES
Information Resources Main library with 962,516 bound volumes, 32,596 titles on microform, 5,419 periodical subscriptions, 8,252 records/tapes/CDs. Business collection includes 102,000 bound volumes, 418 periodical subscriptions, 167 videos.
Housing 2% of students in program live in college-owned or -operated housing.
Technology Computers are used moderately in course work. 300 computer terminals/PCs, linked by a campus-wide computer network, are available for use by students in program; they are located in classrooms, the library, the computer center, computer labs. Students in the program are not required to have their own PC.

Computer Resources/On-line Services

Training	Yes	CompuServe	No
Internet	Yes	Dun's	No
E-Mail	Yes	Dow Jones	No
Multimedia Center	Yes	Dialog	No
LEXIS/NEXIS	Yes	Bloomberg	No

ADMISSION
Acceptance 1994-95 497 applied for admission; 70% were accepted.
Entrance Requirements Bachelor's degree, GMAT score of 400, minimum 2.7 GPA. Core courses waived through: previous course work.
Application Requirements Application form, copies of transcript, personal statement.
Application Deadlines 4/1 for fall, 10/1 for spring.

FINANCIALS
Costs for 1994-95 Tuition: Full-time: $246 for nonresidents. Fees: Full-time: $930/semester for state residents, $930/semester for nonresidents. Average room and board costs are $5,300 per academic year (on-campus) and $5,300 per academic year (off-campus).
Financial Aid In 1994-95, candidates received some institutionally administered aid in the form of grants, scholarships, loans, assistantships. Total awards ranged from $100-$8,000. Financial aid is available to part-time students. Application deadlines: 3/2 for fall, 3/2 for spring. Contact: Ms. Linda Clemons, Director of Financial Aid, 6000 J Street, Sacramento, CA 95819-6044. (916) 278-6554.

INTERNATIONAL STUDENTS
Demographics 7% of students enrolled in the program are international.
Services and Facilities International student center, visa services, ESL courses, counseling/support services.
Applying TOEFL required, minimum score of 550; proof of health; proof of adequate funds. Financial aid is available to international students. Assistantships are available f. Admission application deadlines: 4/1 for fall, 10/1 for spring. Contact: Mr. Eric Merchant, Coordinator, International Students Programs, 6000 J Street, Sacramento, CA 95819-6012. (916) 278-6686.

PLACEMENT
Placement services include career counseling/planning, career fairs, career placement, and resume preparation.

Program Contact: Dr. Herbert Blake Jr., Director, Graduate Programs, California State University, Sacramento, 6000 J Street, Sacramento, CA 95819-6048. (916) 278-6772; Fax: (916) 278-4979.

California State University, San Bernardino

School of Business and Public Administration

San Bernardino, California

OVERVIEW
California State University, San Bernardino is a state-supported comprehensive coed institution. Part of California State University System. Founded 1965. Setting: 430-acre urban campus with easy access to Los Angeles. Total institutional enrollment: 12,500. Program was first offered in 1965.

MBA HIGHLIGHTS

Entrance Difficulty**
Mean GMAT: 490
Mean GPA: 3.1

Cost $
Tuition: $1,896
(Nonresident: $164/unit)
Room & Board: N/R

Enrollment Profile

Full-time: 380	Work Exp: 20%
Part-time: 30	International: 30%
Total: 410	Women: 55%
Average Age: 28	Minorities: 10%

Average Class Size: 15

ACADEMICS

Length of Program Minimum: 18 months. Maximum: 7 years.

Calendar Quarters.

Full-time Classes Main campus; day, evening, summer.

Part-time Classes Main campus; day, evening, summer.

Degree Requirements 48 quarter hours including 20 elective quarter hours. Other: Comprehensive exams in concentrations.

Required Courses Accounting for managerial decision making, advanced financial accounting, corporate policy analysis, financial planning and control, information management systems, marketing management, operations management, organization theory and behavior.

Curricular Focus Entrepreneurship, international business, managing diversity, strategic analysis and planning.

Concentrations Accounting, finance, human resources management, management, management information systems, marketing, operations management, public administration.

Faculty Full-time: 30, 100% with doctorates.

Teaching Methodology Case study: 10%, faculty seminars: 5%, lecture: 50%, research: 10%, student presentations: 2%, team projects: 23%.

Special Opportunities Internships include accounting in CPA firms, marketing in marketing/advertising, management in government, manufacturing in manufacturing firms, and finance in financial institutions.

STUDENT STATISTICS

Geographic Representation State residents 60%. International 30%.

Undergraduate Majors Business 50%; education 10%; engineering/technology 10%; humanities 10%; social sciences 20%.

Other Background Graduate degrees in other disciplines: 5%. Work experience: On average, students have 2 years of work experience on entrance to the program.

FACILITIES

Information Resources Main library with 466,000 bound volumes, 585,000 titles on microform, 2,350 periodical subscriptions, 12,716 records/tapes/CDs.

Housing 2% of students in program live in college-owned or -operated housing.

Technology Computers are used moderately in course work. 300 computer terminals/PCs, linked by a campus-wide computer network, are available for use by students in program; they are located in classrooms, the computer center, computer labs, the research center. Students in the program are not required to have their own PC.

Computer Resources/On-line Services

Training	Yes	Multimedia Center	Yes
Internet	Yes	LEXIS/NEXIS	Yes
E-Mail	Yes		

ADMISSION

Acceptance 1994-95 300 applied for admission; 70% were accepted.

Entrance Requirements Bachelor's degree, GMAT score of 400, minimum 2.5 GPA. Core courses waived through: previous course work.

Application Requirements Written essay, application form, copies of transcript, 2 letters of recommendation.

Application Deadlines 7/1 for fall, 10/1 for winter, 2/10 for spring. Applications are processed on a rolling basis.

FINANCIALS

Costs for 1994-95 Tuition: Full-time: $164/unit for nonresidents. Fees: Full-time: $1,896 for state residents, $1,896 for nonresidents.

Financial Aid In 1994-95, candidates received some institutionally administered aid in the form of scholarships, loans, fellowships, assistantships, work-study. Total awards ranged from $1,000-$5,000. Financial aid is available to part-time students. Application deadlines: 7/1 for fall, 10/1 for winter, 2/1 for spring. Applications are processed on a rolling basis. Contact: Financial Aid Officer, 5500 University Parkway, San Bernardino, CA 92407. (909) 880-5000.

INTERNATIONAL STUDENTS

Demographics 30% of students enrolled in the program are international.

Services and Facilities International student housing.

Applying TOEFL required, minimum score of 550; proof of adequate funds. Financial aid is available to international students. Financial aid application deadlines: 7/1 for fall, 10/1 for winter, 2/1 for spring. Admission application deadlines: 7/1 for fall, 10/1 for winter, 2/10 for spring. Contact: Ms. Elsa Fernandez, International Student Adviser, 5500 University Parkway, San Bernardino, CA 92407. (909) 880-5000.

PLACEMENT

In 1993-94, 200 organizations participated in on-campus recruiting; 250 on-campus interviews were conducted. Placement services include alumni network, career counseling/planning, career fairs, career placement, job interviews, resume preparation, and resume referral to employers. Of 1994 graduates, 95% were employed within three months of graduation, the average starting salary was $39,000.

Jobs by Employer Type Manufacturing 15%; service 40%; government 30%; consulting 15%.

Program Contact: Admissions Office, California State University, San Bernardino, 5500 University Parkway, San Bernardino, CA 92407. (909) 880-5000.

California State University, Stanislaus

School of Business Administration

Turlock, California

OVERVIEW

California State University, Stanislaus is a state-supported comprehensive coed institution. Part of California State University System. Founded 1957. Setting: 220-acre small-town campus. Total institutional enrollment: 5,877.

MBA HIGHLIGHTS

Entrance Difficulty**
Mean GMAT: 500
Mean GPA: N/R

Cost $
Tuition: $851/semester
(Nonresident: $246/unit)
Room & Board: $5,300

Enrollment Profile

Full-time: N/R	Work Exp: N/R
Part-time: N/R	International: N/R
Total: 126	Women: 30%
Average Age: N/R	Minorities: 1%

Average Class Size: 20

ACADEMICS

Length of Program Minimum: 24 months.

Calendar 4-1-4.

Full-time Classes Main campus, Stockton Center, distance learning option; evening, summer.

Part-time Classes Main campus, Stockton Center, distance learning option; evening, summer.

Degree Requirements 33 credits including 12 elective credits.

Required Courses Accounting, finance, management, management information systems, marketing, operations management.

Curricular Focus Business issues and problems, general management, problem solving and decision making.

Concentrations Accounting, finance, management, management information systems, marketing, operations management.

Teaching Methodology Case study: 20%, lecture: 50%, research: 5%, student presentations: 15%, team projects: 10%.

STUDENT STATISTICS

Geographic Representation State residents 66%.

FACILITIES

Information Resources Main library with 268,829 bound volumes, 179,876 titles on microform, 3,882 periodical subscriptions, 978 records/tapes/CDs.

Housing College housing available.

ADMISSION

Entrance Requirements Bachelor's degree, GMAT score of 450, minimum 2.5 GPA.

Application Requirements Application form, copies of transcript, personal statement, 3 letters of recommendation.

Application Deadlines 7/31 for fall, 1/2 for spring. Applications are processed on a rolling basis.

FINANCIALS
Costs for 1994-95 Tuition: Full-time: $246/unit for nonresidents. Fees: Full-time: $851/semester for state residents, $851/semester for nonresidents. Average room and board costs are $5,300 per academic year (on-campus) and $5,778 per academic year (off-campus).
Financial Aid Application deadlines: 3/2 for fall, 3/2 for spring. Applications are processed on a rolling basis. Contact: Ms. Joan Hillary, Director, 801 West Monte Vista Avenue, Turlock, CA 95382. (209) 667-3336.

INTERNATIONAL STUDENTS
Applying TOEFL required, minimum score of 550; proof of health; proof of adequate funds. Financial aid is not available to international students. Admission application deadlines: 7/31 for fall, 1/2 for spring. Applications are processed on a rolling basis.

Program Contact: Ms. Mary Coker, Director, Graduate Studies, California State University, Stanislaus, 801 West Monte Vista Avenue, Turlock, CA 95382. (209) 667-3129; Fax: (209) 667-3333.

Chapman University

School of Business and Economics

Orange, California

OVERVIEW
Chapman University is an independent comprehensive coed institution, affiliated with Christian Church (Disciples of Christ). Founded 1861. Setting: 40-acre suburban campus with easy access to Los Angeles. Total institutional enrollment: 3,780. Program was first offered in 1975.

MBA HIGHLIGHTS

Entrance Difficulty**
Mean GMAT: 513
Mean GPA: 3.2

Cost $$
Tuition: $400/credit
Room & Board: $5,780

Enrollment Profile

Full-time: 53	Work Exp: 85%
Part-time: 122	International: 20%
Total: 175	Women: 36%
Average Age: 27	Minorities: 31%

Average Class Size: 20

ACADEMICS
Length of Program Minimum: 18 months. Maximum: 7 years.
Calendar Semesters.
Full-time Classes Main campus; day, evening, summer.
Part-time Classes Main campus; evening, summer.
Degree Requirements 33 credits including 9 elective credits.
Required Courses Accounting, business forecasting, finance, international business, marketing, organizational theory and behavior, quantitative decision models, strategy. Courses may be waived through: previous course work.
Curricular Focus Economic and financial theory, problem solving and decision making.
Concentrations Accounting, economics, entrepreneurship, finance, human resources management, international business, management, management information systems, marketing, operations management, organizational behavior, quantitative analysis, strategic management.
Faculty Full-time: 10, 90% with doctorates; part-time: 7, 71% with doctorates.
Teaching Methodology Case study: 25%, faculty seminars: 5%, lecture: 30%, research: 10%, seminars by members of the business community: 10%, student presentations: 10%, team projects: 10%.
Special Opportunities Internship program available.

STUDENT STATISTICS
Geographic Representation State residents 88%. By region: West 91%; Midwest 2%. International 20%.

Undergraduate Majors Business 48%; engineering/technology 20%; humanities 10%; science/mathematics 6%; social sciences 14%; other 2%.
Other Background Work experience: On average, students have 4 years of work experience on entrance to the program.

FACILITIES
Information Resources Main library with 189,028 bound volumes, 300 titles on microform, 1,806 periodical subscriptions, 5,492 records/tapes/CDs, 15 CD-ROMs. Business collection includes 8,581 bound volumes, 257 periodical subscriptions, 3 CD-ROMs, 81 videos.
Housing 5% of students in program live in college-owned or -operated housing.
Technology Computers are used moderately in course work. 60 computer terminals/PCs, linked by a campus-wide computer network, are available for use by students in program; they are located in the library, computer labs. Students in the program are not required to have their own PC.

Computer Resources/On-line Services

Training	Yes	Dun's	No
Internet	Yes	Dow Jones	Yes $
E-Mail	Yes	Dialog	Yes $
LEXIS/NEXIS	No	Bloomberg	No
CompuServe	No		

Other on-line services: OCLC, First Search.

ADMISSION
Acceptance 1994-95 Of those applying, 69% were accepted.
Entrance Requirements Bachelor's degree, GMAT score of 400, minimum 2.5 GPA. Core courses waived through: previous course work.
Application Requirements Written essay, application form, copies of transcript, personal statement.
Application Deadline Applications are processed on a rolling basis.

FINANCIALS
Costs for 1994-95 Tuition: Full-time: $400/credit. Average room and board costs are $5,780 per academic year (on-campus).
Financial Aid In 1994-95, 35% of candidates received some institutionally administered aid in the form of grants, scholarships, fellowships, assistantships. Financial aid is available to part-time students. Application deadline: 3/2 for fall. Contact: Ms. Phyllis Coldiron, Director of Financial Aid, 333 North Glassell Street, Orange, CA 92666-1011. (714) 997-6740.

INTERNATIONAL STUDENTS
Demographics 20% of students enrolled in the program are international; Asia 63%, Europe 30%, South America 5%, Australia 1%, other 1%.
Services and Facilities Visa services, language tutoring, ESL courses, special assistance for nonnative speakers of English, counseling/support services.
Applying TOEFL required, minimum score of 550; proof of adequate funds. Financial aid is available to international students. Assistantships are available for these students after one semester. Admission application deadlines: 6/15 for fall, 11/15 for spring, 4/15 for summer. Contact: Ms. Vicky Koerner, Director, International Student Services and Study Abroad, 333 North Glassell Street, Orange, CA 92666-1011. (714) 997-6829.

PLACEMENT
In 1993-94, 48 organizations participated in on-campus recruiting; 20 on-campus interviews were conducted. Placement services include alumni network, career counseling/planning, career fairs, career library, career placement, electronic job bank, and resume preparation.

Program Contact: Dr. Homa Shabahang, Associate Dean, Chapman University, 333 North Glassell Street, Orange, CA 92666-1011. (714) 997-6684, or (800) 723-7330; Fax: (714) 532-6081; Internet Address: shabahan@nexus.chapman.edu.
See full description on page 692.

Claremont Graduate School

The Peter F. Drucker Graduate Management Center

Claremont, California

OVERVIEW
Claremont Graduate School is graduate-only institution. Founded 1925. Setting: suburban campus. Total institutional enrollment: 6,000. Program was first offered in 1971. AACSB-accredited.

MBA HIGHLIGHTS

Entrance Difficulty**
Mean GMAT: 562
Mean GPA: 3.2

Cost $$$
Tuition: $16,800
Room & Board: N/R

Enrollment Profile

Full-time: 85	Work Exp: 95%
Part-time: 120	International: 24%
Total: 205	Women: 42%
Average Age: 28	Minorities: 20%

Average Class Size: 26

ACADEMICS
Length of Program Minimum: 20 months. Maximum: 6 years.
Calendar Semesters.
Full-time Classes Main campus; day, evening.
Part-time Classes Main campus; evening.
Degree Requirements 48 credits including 16 elective credits.
Required Courses Accounting, economics, finance, human component in organizations, managerial economics, marketing, statistics, strategy. Courses may be waived through: previous course work.
Curricular Focus General management, leadership, organizational development and change management.
Concentrations Cost management and control systems, finance, human resources management, international business, management, management information systems, marketing, public policy, strategic management.
Faculty Full-time: 16, 100% with doctorates; part-time: 18, 94% with doctorates.
Teaching Methodology Case study: 30%, consulting/field study: 10%, lecture: 30%, seminars by members of the business community: 10%, student presentations: 10%, team projects: 10%.
Special Opportunities International exchange in Canada, France, Japan, Mexico. Internship program available. Other: intensive consulting engagements.

STUDENT STATISTICS
Geographic Representation State residents 76%. By region: West 70%; Northeast 4%; Midwest 2%. International 24%.
Undergraduate Majors Business 34%; engineering/technology 10%; humanities 15%; science/mathematics 8%; social sciences 33%.
Other Background Graduate degrees in other disciplines: 5%. Work experience: On average, students have 5 years of work experience on entrance to the program.

FACILITIES
Information Resources Main library with 2 million bound volumes, 1.2 million titles on microform, 5,922 periodical subscriptions. Business collection includes 100,000 bound volumes, 150 periodical subscriptions.
Housing 25% of students in program live in college-owned or -operated housing.
Technology Computers are used moderately in course work. Computer terminals/PCs, linked by a campus-wide computer network, are available for use by students in program; they are located in the library, the computer center, computer labs, office of career services. Students in the program are not required to have their own PC.

Computer Resources/On-line Services

Training	Yes	Dun's	Yes $
Internet	Yes	Dow Jones	Yes $
E-Mail	Yes	Dialog	Yes
LEXIS/NEXIS	Yes	Bloomberg	No
CompuServe	Yes		

Other on-line services: First Search.

ADMISSION
Acceptance 1994-95 246 applied for admission; 55% were accepted.
Entrance Requirements Bachelor's degree, GMAT score. Core courses waived through: previous course work.
Application Requirements Written essay, application form, copies of transcript, resume/curriculum vitae, personal statement, 3 letters of recommendation.
Application Deadlines 6/1 for fall, 11/1 for spring.

FINANCIALS
Costs for 1994-95 Tuition: Full-time: $16,800; Part-time day: $755/unit. Fees: Full-time: $110; Part-time day: $110.
Financial Aid In 1994-95, candidates received some institutionally administered aid in the form of loans, fellowships, assistantships, work-study. Total awards ranged from $800-$10,000. Financial aid is available to part-time students. Application deadlines: 7/15 for fall, 11/1 for spring. Contact: Ms. Germaine Graham, Assistant Director, Financial Aid, McManus 131, Claremont, CA 91711-6163. (909) 621-8337.

INTERNATIONAL STUDENTS
Demographics 24% of students enrolled in the program are international; Asia 60%, South America 12%, Central America 8%, Europe 8%, Africa 4%, other 8%.
Services and Facilities International student center, visa services, language tutoring, ESL courses, counseling/support services.
Applying TOEFL required, minimum score of 550; proof of adequate funds. Financial aid is available to international students. Financial aid application deadlines: 2/15 for fall, 11/1 for spring. Admission application deadlines: 6/1 for fall, 11/1 for spring. Contact: Ms. Leslie Rusch, International Student Adviser, 170 East Tenth Street, Claremont, CA 91711-6163. (909) 621-8069.

ALTERNATE MBA PROGRAM
Executive MBA (EMBA) Length of program: Minimum: 24 months. Maximum: 6 years. Degree requirements: 48 credits. Participants select 24 courses out of a 70 course curriculum. Average class size: 22.

PLACEMENT
Placement services include alumni network, career counseling/planning, career fairs, career library, career placement, job interviews, resume preparation, and resume referral to employers. Of 1994 graduates, 90% were employed within three months of graduation, the average starting salary was $50,700, the range was $35,000-$85,000.
Jobs by Employer Type Manufacturing 45%; service 41%; government 3%; consulting 9%; nonprofit 2%.
Jobs by Functional Area Marketing/sales 13%; finance 29%; operations 11%; management 32%; strategic planning 9%; technical management 6%.

Program Contact: Mr. Michael Kraft, Director, MBA Programs, Claremont Graduate School, 170 East Tenth Street, Claremont, CA 91711-6163. (909) 621-8073; Fax: (909) 621-8543; Internet Address: kraftm@cgs.edu.
See full description on page 698.

College of Notre Dame

Business Division

Belmont, California

OVERVIEW
College of Notre Dame is an independent Roman Catholic comprehensive coed institution. Founded 1851. Setting: 80-acre suburban campus with easy access to San Francisco. Total institutional enrollment: 1,707.

MBA HIGHLIGHTS

Entrance Difficulty**
Mean GMAT: 450
Mean GPA: N/R

Cost $
Tuition: $1,140 - $3,420
Room & Board: $7,200

Enrollment Profile

Full-time: N/R	Work Exp: N/R
Part-time: N/R	International: 26%
Total: 138	Women: 53%
Average Age: N/R	Minorities: 17%

Average Class Size: 20

ACADEMICS
Length of Program Minimum: 24 months.
Calendar Semesters.
Part-time Classes Main campus; evening, summer.
Degree Requirements 30-54 credits.
Curricular Focus General management, international business, problem solving and decision making.
Concentrations Finance, international business, management information systems, marketing, organizational behavior.
Teaching Methodology Case study: 25%, lecture: 25%, research: 10%, seminars by members of the business community: 5%, student presentations: 10%, team projects: 25%.

STUDENT STATISTICS
Geographic Representation International 26%.

FACILITIES
Information Resources Main library with 95,710 bound volumes, 16,487 titles on microform, 670 periodical subscriptions, 7,500 records/tapes/CDs, 1 CD-ROM.
Housing College housing available.

ADMISSION
Entrance Requirements Bachelor's degree, GMAT score, minimum 2.5 GPA, minimum 1 year of work experience.
Application Requirements Application form, copies of transcript.
Application Deadlines 8/1 for fall, 12/1 for spring, 4/1 for summer. Applications are processed on a rolling basis.

FINANCIALS
Costs for 1994-95 Tuition: Part-time day: $1,140-$3,420. Average room and board costs are $7,200 per academic year (on-campus) and $7,000 per academic year (off-campus).
Financial Aid Application deadlines: 8/1 for fall, 12/1 for spring, 4/1 for summer. Contact: Ms. Sun Hoong Ow, Director of Financial Aid, 1500 Ralston Avenue, Belmont, CA 94002. (415) 508-3580.

INTERNATIONAL STUDENTS
Demographics 26% of students enrolled in the program are international.
Applying TOEFL required, minimum score of 550; proof of adequate funds. Financial aid is not available to international students. Admission application deadlines: 8/1 for fall, 12/1 for spring, 4/1 for summer. Applications are processed on a rolling basis.

Program Contact: Ms. Barbara Sterner, Assistant to the Graduate Dean for Admissions, College of Notre Dame, Graduate School, 1500 Ralston Avenue, Belmont, CA 94002. (415) 508-3527; Fax: (415) 508-3736.

Dominican College of San Rafael

Graduate Division

San Rafael, California

OVERVIEW
Dominican College of San Rafael is an independent Roman Catholic comprehensive coed institution. Founded 1890. Setting: 80-acre suburban campus with easy access to San Francisco. Total institutional enrollment: 1,048.

ACADEMICS
Calendar Semesters.
Degree Requirements 51 credits.
Concentration International business.

FACILITIES
Information Resources Main library with 93,115 bound volumes, 2,361 titles on microform, 297 periodical subscriptions, 1,475 records/tapes/CDs.
Housing College housing available.

ADMISSION
Entrance Requirements GMAT score, minimum 3.0 GPA.
Application Requirements Application form, copies of transcript.

FINANCIALS
Costs for 1994-95 Tuition: Full-time: $5,175/semester; Part-time day: $432/unit. Fees: Full-time: $125/semester. Average room and board costs are $5,680 per academic year (on-campus).
Financial Aid Contact: Ms. Jean LaVane, Financial Aid Officer, 50 Acacia Avenue, San Rafael, CA 94901-8008. (415) 485-3294.

INTERNATIONAL STUDENTS
Applying TOEFL required, minimum score of 600.

Program Contact: Ms. Lydia Hull, Director of Admissions, Dominican College of San Rafael, 50 Acacia Avenue, San Rafael, CA 94901-8008. (415) 485-3247, or (800) 788-3522 (CA only).

Golden Gate University

School of Management

San Francisco, California

OVERVIEW
Golden Gate University is an independent nonprofit coed institution. Founded 1853. Setting: urban campus. Total institutional enrollment: 6,613.

MBA HIGHLIGHTS

Entrance Difficulty***

Cost $$
Tuition: $348/unit
Room & Board: N/R

Enrollment Profile

Full-time: 330	Work Exp: N/R
Part-time: 1,226	International: 13%
Total: 1,556	Women: 35%
Average Age: N/R	Minorities: 31%

Average Class Size: 13

ACADEMICS
Length of Program Minimum: 24 months.
Calendar Trimesters.
Full-time Classes Main campus, San Francisco, Sacramento, Los Altos; day, evening, weekends, summer.
Part-time Classes Main campus, San Francisco, Sacramento, Los Altos; day, evening, weekends, summer.
Degree Requirements 36 units.
Curricular Focus Business issues and problems, general management, problem solving and decision making.
Concentrations Accounting, arts administration, finance, health services, hotel management, human resources management, international business, management, management information systems, marketing, operations management.
Special Opportunities Internship program available.

STUDENT STATISTICS
Geographic Representation State residents 86%. International 13%.

FACILITIES
Information Resources Main library with 126,486 bound volumes, 709,319 titles on microform, 1,500 periodical subscriptions, 437 records/tapes/CDs, 19 CD-ROMs.
Housing College housing not available.

ADMISSION

Acceptance 1994-95 454 applied for admission; 84% were accepted.

Entrance Requirements Bachelor's degree, GMAT score. Core courses waived through: previous course work.

Application Requirements Written essay, application form, copies of transcript.

Application Deadline Applications are processed on a rolling basis. Application discs available.

FINANCIALS

Costs for 1994-95 Tuition: Full-time: $348/unit.

Financial Aid In 1994-95, 14% of candidates received some institutionally administered aid in the form of grants, scholarships, loans, work-study. Total awards ranged from $100-$20,000. Financial aid is available to part-time students. Application deadlines: 3/2 for fall, 10/1 for spring. Applications are processed on a rolling basis. Contact: Financial Aid Office, 536 Mission Street, San Francisco, CA 94105. (415) 442-7270.

INTERNATIONAL STUDENTS

Demographics 13% of students enrolled in the program are international.

Services and Facilities International student office.

Applying TOEFL required, minimum score of 550; proof of adequate funds. Admission application deadlines: 7/1 for fall, 11/1 for spring. Applications are processed on a rolling basis. Contact: Mr. Arthur Levine, International Program Director, 536 Mission Street, San Francisco, CA 94105. (415) 442-7291.

ALTERNATE MBA PROGRAMS

Executive MBA (EMBA) Length of program: Minimum: 20 months.

MBA/JD

PLACEMENT

Placement services include alumni network, career counseling/planning, career fairs, and career placement.

Program Contact: Mr. Archie Porter, Executive Director, Enrollment and Student Services, Golden Gate University, 536 Mission Street, San Francisco, CA 94105-2968. (415) 442-7209, or (800) 448-4968 (CA only); Fax: (415) 495-2671.
See full description on page 748.

Holy Names College

Department of Business

Oakland, California

OVERVIEW

Holy Names College is an independent Roman Catholic comprehensive coed institution. Founded 1868. Setting: 60-acre urban campus with easy access to San Francisco. Total institutional enrollment: 950. Program was first offered in 1980.

MBA HIGHLIGHTS

Entrance Difficulty**
Mean GMAT: 450
Mean GPA: 3.2

Cost $$
Tuition: $405/unit
Room & Board: N/R

Enrollment Profile
Full-time: 5	Work Exp: 80%
Part-time: 15	International: 20%
Total: 20	Women: 60%
Average Age: 27	Minorities: 35%

Average Class Size: 15

ACADEMICS

Length of Program Minimum: 12 months. Maximum: 7 years.

Calendar Trimesters.

Part-time Classes Main campus; weekends.

Degree Requirements 33 credits including 6 elective credits.

Required Courses Advertising management, business ethics, business policy, financial management, international business management, managerial accounting, managerial economics, marketing management, operations management.

Curricular Focus Economic and financial theory, entrepreneurship, general management, international business, leadership, managing diversity, organizational development and change management, problem solving and decision making, teamwork.

Concentrations Finance, management, marketing.

Faculty Full-time: 5, 100% with doctorates; part-time: 2, 50% with doctorates.

Teaching Methodology Case study: 20%, lecture: 35%, research: 10%, student presentations: 15%, team projects: 20%.

Special Opportunities Internships include financial analysis.

STUDENT STATISTICS

Geographic Representation State residents 80%. By region: West 80%. International 20%.

Undergraduate Majors Business 60%; engineering/technology 20%; humanities 10%; nursing 10%.

Other Background Graduate degrees in other disciplines: 10%. Work experience: On average, students have 5 years of work experience on entrance to the program.

FACILITIES

Information Resources Main library with 109,067 bound volumes, 144 titles on microform, 448 periodical subscriptions, 4,299 records/tapes/CDs.

Housing 5% of students in program live in college-owned or -operated housing.

Technology Computers are used moderately in course work. 30 computer terminals/PCs are available for use by students in program; they are located in learning resource center, the computer center, computer labs. Students in the program are not required to have their own PC.

Computer Resources/On-line Services
Training	No	Dun's	No
Internet	No	Dow Jones	No
E-Mail	No	Dialog	No
LEXIS/NEXIS	No	Bloomberg	No
CompuServe	No		

ADMISSION

Acceptance 1994-95 15 applied for admission; 80% were accepted.

Entrance Requirements Bachelor's degree, minimum 2.8 GPA. Core courses waived through: previous course work.

Application Requirements Application form, copies of transcript, 2 letters of recommendation.

Application Deadlines 8/1 for fall, 12/1 for spring. Application discs available.

FINANCIALS

Costs for 1994-95 Tuition: Weekends: $405/unit.

Financial Aid In 1994-95, 60% of candidates received some institutionally administered aid in the form of grants. Total awards ranged from $1,200-$1,600. Financial aid is available to part-time students. Application deadlines: 10/15 for fall, 2/15 for winter, 5/1 for spring. Contact: Ms. Paula Lehrberger, Director of Financial Aid, 3500 Mountain Boulevard, Oakland, CA 94619. (510) 436-1328.

INTERNATIONAL STUDENTS

Demographics 20% of students enrolled in the program are international; Asia 80%, Africa 20%.

Services and Facilities International student office, ESL courses.

Applying TOEFL required, minimum score of 550; proof of health; proof of adequate funds. Financial aid is not available to international students. Admission application deadlines: 8/10 for fall, 12/1 for spring. Applications are processed on a rolling basis. Contact: Dr. David Angrisani, Director, MBA Program, 3500 Mountain Boulevard, Oakland, CA 94619. (510) 436-1465.

PLACEMENT

Placement services include career placement and resume referral to employers. Of 1994 graduates, 80% were employed within three months of graduation.

Program Contact: Ms. Caryl Mutti, Graduate Admissions Director, Holy Names College, 3520 Mountain Boulevard, Oakland, CA 94619. (510) 436-1361; Fax: (510) 436-1199.

Humboldt State University

School of Business and Economics

Arcata, California

OVERVIEW

Humboldt State University is a state-supported comprehensive coed institution. Part of California State University System. Founded 1913. Setting: 161-acre small-town campus. Total institutional enrollment: 7,122.

MBA HIGHLIGHTS

Entrance Difficulty***
Mean GMAT: 521
Mean GPA: 3.2

Cost $
Tuition: $1,678
(Nonresident: $246/unit)
Room & Board: $4,500

Enrollment Profile

Full-time: 12		Work Exp: 95%	
Part-time: 11		International: 4%	
Total: 23		Women: 22%	
Average Age: 33		Minorities: 26%	

Average Class Size: 10

ACADEMICS

Length of Program Minimum: 12 months. Maximum: 7 years.
Calendar Semesters.
Full-time Classes Main campus; evening, summer.
Part-time Classes Main campus; evening, summer.
Degree Requirements 30 credits. Other: Thesis, practicum or project.
Required Courses Advanced international business, data acquisition/analysis/presentation, management accounting, management theory, managerial economics, managerial finance, managerial marketing, policy and strategy, social environment and ethics.
Curricular Focus General management.
Concentration Management.
Faculty Full-time: 11, 100% with doctorates; part-time: 8, 12% with doctorates.
Teaching Methodology Faculty seminars: 100%.

STUDENT STATISTICS

Geographic Representation State residents 96%. International 4%.
Other Background Graduate degrees in other disciplines: 9%.

FACILITIES

Information Resources Main library with 470,536 bound volumes, 58,809 titles on microform, 2,291 periodical subscriptions, 12,006 records/tapes/CDs, 27 CD-ROMs.
Housing College housing available.
Technology Computer terminals/PCs are available for use by students in program; they are located in computer labs. Students in the program are not required to have their own PC.
Computer Resources/On-line Services
Other on-line services: SEC.

ADMISSION

Entrance Requirements Bachelor's degree, GMAT score, minimum 2.5 GPA. Core courses waived through: previous course work.
Application Requirements Application form.
Application Deadlines 5/1 for fall, 11/1 for spring.

FINANCIALS

Costs for 1994-95 Tuition: Full-time: $246/unit for nonresidents. Fees: Full-time: $1,678 for state residents, $1,678 for nonresidents. Average room and board costs are $4,500 per academic year (on-campus).
Financial Aid In 1994-95, 50% of candidates received some form of institutionally administered aid. Application deadline: 3/2 for fall. Contact: Ms. Kay Burgess, Director of Financial Aid, Arcata, CA 95521-8299. (707) 826-4321.

INTERNATIONAL STUDENTS

Demographics 4% of students enrolled in the program are international.

Applying TOEFL required, minimum score of 550; proof of adequate funds. Financial aid is not available to international students. Admission application deadline: 2/1 for fall.

PLACEMENT

Placement services include career counseling/planning. Of 1994 graduates, 75% were employed within three months of graduation, the average starting salary was $24,000, the range was $21,000-$27,000.

Program Contact: Dr. Robert L. Hines, Chair, Humboldt State University, Arcata, CA 95521-8299. (707) 826-6026.

John F. Kennedy University

School of Management

Orinda, California

OVERVIEW

John F. Kennedy University is an independent nonprofit comprehensive coed institution. Founded 1964. Setting: 14-acre suburban campus with easy access to San Francisco. Total institutional enrollment: 1,800. Program was first offered in 1965.

MBA HIGHLIGHTS

Entrance Difficulty*

Cost $
Tuition: $237/unit
Room & Board: N/R

Enrollment Profile

Full-time: 20		Work Exp: 99%	
Part-time: 98		International: 17%	
Total: 118		Women: 50%	
Average Age: 37		Minorities: N/R	

Average Class Size: 15

ACADEMICS

Length of Program Minimum: 30 months.
Calendar Quarters.
Full-time Classes Main campus, Walnut Creek; evening, weekends, summer.
Part-time Classes Main campus, Walnut Creek; evening, weekends, summer.
Degree Requirements 52 units including 15 elective units. Other: Math and writing competency.
Required Courses Applied managerial accounting, computers and information, ethical issues in management, financial management, human resources management, management communications, marketing management, personal power and leadership, quantitative methods, systems in organizations, the global economy, visionary leadership.
Curricular Focus General management, leadership, organizational development and change management.
Concentrations International business, management, organizational leadership, financial management.
Faculty Full-time: 1; part-time: 20.
Teaching Methodology Case study: 30%, faculty seminars: 15%, lecture: 10%, research: 5%, seminars by members of the business community: 10%, student presentations: 10%, team projects: 20%.

STUDENT STATISTICS

Geographic Representation State residents 83%. International 17%.
Other Background Graduate degrees in other disciplines: 3%.

FACILITIES

Information Resources Main library with 56,643 bound volumes, 29 titles on microform, 433 periodical subscriptions, 1,003 records/tapes/CDs. Business collection in Business Library includes 4,000 bound volumes, 120 periodical subscriptions, 3 CD-ROMs, 50 videos.
Housing College housing not available.
Technology 10 computer terminals/PCs are available for use by students in program; they are located in the computer center. Students in the program are not required to have their own PC.

Computer Resources/On-line Services

Training	No	Dun's	No
Internet	No	Dow Jones	No
E-Mail	No	Dialog	Yes
LEXIS/NEXIS	No	Bloomberg	No
CompuServe	No		

ADMISSION
Acceptance 1994-95 62 applied for admission; 85% were accepted.

Entrance Requirements Bachelor's degree, minimum 2.0 GPA. Core courses waived through: previous course work.

Application Requirements Interview, application form, copies of transcript, resume/curriculum vitae, personal statement.

Application Deadlines 9/1 for fall, 12/1 for winter, 3/1 for spring, 6/1 for summer. Applications are processed on a rolling basis. Application discs available.

FINANCIALS
Costs for 1994-95 Tuition: Full-time: $237/unit. Fees: Full-time: $8/quarter.

Financial Aid In 1994-95, candidates received some institutionally administered aid in the form of grants, scholarships, loans, fellowships. Financial aid is available to part-time students. Application deadline: 3/2 for fall. Applications are processed on a rolling basis. Contact: Ms. Cathy Larnach, Director of Financial Aid, 12 Altarinda Road, Orinda, CA 94563-2689. (510) 254-0200 Ext. 385.

INTERNATIONAL STUDENTS
Demographics 17% of students enrolled in the program are international; Asia 50%, Europe 50%.

Applying TOEFL required, minimum score of 550; proof of health; proof of adequate funds. Financial aid is available to international students. Financial aid application deadline: 3/2 for fall. Applications are processed on a rolling basis. Admission application deadlines: 8/1 for fall, 11/1 for winter, 2/1 for spring, 5/1 for summer. Applications are processed on a rolling basis. Contact: Ms. Sherri Hedman, International Student Adviser, 12 Altarinda Road, Orinda, CA 94563-2689. (510) 253-4339.

PLACEMENT
Placement services include career counseling/planning, career library, job search course, and resume preparation.

Program Contact: Ms. Ellena Bloedorn, Director of Admissions and Records, John F. Kennedy University, 12 Altarinda Road, Orinda, CA 94563-2689. (510) 254-0200; Fax: (510) 254-6964.

La Sierra University

School of Business and Management

Riverside, California

OVERVIEW
La Sierra University is an independent Seventh-day Adventist comprehensive coed institution. Founded 1922. Setting: 630-acre suburban campus with easy access to Los Angeles. Total institutional enrollment: 1,500. Program was first offered in 1982.

MBA HIGHLIGHTS

Entrance Difficulty***
Mean GMAT: 500
Mean GPA: N/R

Cost $$$
Tuition: $346/credit
Room & Board: $2,190

Enrollment Profile

Full-time: 29	Work Exp: N/R
Part-time: 11	International: 25%
Total: 40	Women: 45%
Average Age: 27	Minorities: 40%

Average Class Size: 12

ACADEMICS
Length of Program Minimum: 12 months. Maximum: 5 years.
Calendar Quarters.

Full-time Classes Main campus; evening, summer.
Part-time Classes Main campus; evening, summer.
Degree Requirements 48 credits.
Required Courses Business research methods, cost determination and analysis, financial management, marketing management, organizational theory and behavior, quality management and theory analysis, strategic management and policy analysis.
Curricular Focus General management, problem solving and decision making, strategic analysis and planning.
Concentrations Accounting, finance, health services, human resources management, management, marketing.
Faculty Full-time: 4, 75% with doctorates; part-time: 7, 42% with doctorates.
Teaching Methodology Case study: 15%, lecture: 50%, research: 15%, student presentations: 10%, team projects: 10%.

STUDENT STATISTICS
Geographic Representation By region: West 40%; Northeast 18%; Midwest 17%. International 25%.
Undergraduate Majors Business 42%; engineering/technology 1%; nursing 1%; science/mathematics 1%; social sciences 1%; other 54%.

FACILITIES
Information Resources Main library with 223,791 bound volumes, 285,572 titles on microform, 1,331 periodical subscriptions, 3,655 records/tapes/CDs.
Housing 2% of students in program live in college-owned or -operated housing.
Technology Computers are used moderately in course work. 55 computer terminals/PCs, linked by a campus-wide computer network, are available for use by students in program; they are located in the computer center. Students in the program are not required to have their own PC. $500 are budgeted per student for computer support.

Computer Resources/On-line Services

Training	Yes	E-Mail	Yes
Internet	Yes	Multimedia Center	Yes

Other on-line services: First Search.

ADMISSION
Acceptance 1994-95 60 applied for admission; 85% were accepted.

Entrance Requirements Bachelor's degree, GMAT score of 500. Core courses waived through: previous course work.

Application Requirements Application form, copies of transcript, 3 letters of recommendation.

Application Deadline Applications are processed on a rolling basis.

FINANCIALS
Costs for 1994-95 Tuition: Full-time: $346/credit. Average room and board costs are $2,190 per academic year (on-campus).

Financial Aid In 1994-95, 37% of candidates received some institutionally administered aid in the form of scholarships. Total awards ranged from $1,500-$3,600. Financial aid is available to part-time students. Application deadlines: 5/15 for fall, 12/15 for spring. Contact: Dr. Ignatius Yacoub, Dean, School of Business and Management, 4700 Pierce Street, Riverside, CA 92515. (909) 785-2464.

INTERNATIONAL STUDENTS
Demographics 25% of students enrolled in the program are international; Asia 46%, Central America 8%, Europe 4%, South America 4%, other 38%.

Services and Facilities Visa services, language tutoring, ESL courses, counseling/support services.

Applying TOEFL required, minimum score of 550. Financial aid is available to international students. Financial aid application deadlines: 5/15 for fall, 12/15 for spring. Admission applications are processed on a rolling basis. Contact: Mr. David Pendleton, International Student Adviser, 4700 Pierce Street, Riverside, CA 92515. (909) 785-2237.

PLACEMENT
In 1993-94, 40 organizations participated in on-campus recruiting; 5 on-campus interviews were conducted. Placement services include career fairs and job interviews. Of 1994 graduates, 100% were employed within three months of graduation, the average starting salary was $33,000, the range was $30,000-$36,000.

Jobs by Employer Type Manufacturing 10%; service 40%; nonprofit 50%.
Jobs by Functional Area Marketing/sales 30%; finance 40%; operations 10%; management 20%.

Program Contact: Dr. Ignatius Yacoub, Dean, La Sierra University, 4700 Pierce Street, Riverside, CA 92515. (909) 785-2064, or (800) 874-5587 (CA only).

Lincoln University

San Francisco, California

OVERVIEW
Lincoln University is an independent nonprofit comprehensive coed institution. Founded 1919. Setting: urban campus. Total institutional enrollment: 363. Program was first offered in 1972.

MBA HIGHLIGHTS

Entrance Difficulty N/R
Mean GMAT: N/R
Mean GPA: 2.7

Cost $
Tuition: $220/unit
Room & Board: $8,400 (off-campus)

Enrollment Profile

Full-time: 261	Work Exp: N/R
Part-time: 0	International: 92%
Total: 261	Women: 42%
Average Age: 28	Minorities: 8%

Average Class Size: 25

ACADEMICS
Length of Program Minimum: 24 months. Maximum: 2 years.
Calendar Semesters.
Full-time Classes Main campus; day, evening, summer.
Part-time Classes Main campus; day, evening, summer.
Degree Requirements 36 units.
Required Courses Advanced accounting and financial control, business policies and managerial decision making, business research methodology, managerial economics, marketing management, organizational behavior and administration, political and social environment of business, research project. Courses may be waived through: previous course work.
Curricular Focus General management, international business.
Concentrations Asian business, international business, management, management information systems.
Faculty Full-time: 5, 80% with doctorates; part-time: 7, 71% with doctorates.
Teaching Methodology Case study: 20%, lecture: 40%, research: 10%, student presentations: 20%, team projects: 10%.

STUDENT STATISTICS
Geographic Representation State residents 8%. By region: West 8%. International 92%.
Other Background Graduate degrees in other disciplines: 5%.

FACILITIES
Information Resources Main library with 16,000 bound volumes, 5,270 titles on microform, 88 periodical subscriptions.
Housing College housing not available.
Technology Computers are used moderately in course work. 16 computer terminals/PCs are available for use by students in program; they are located in the computer center. Students in the program are not required to have their own PC.

Computer Resources/On-line Services

Training	Yes	E-Mail	No
Internet	Yes	Dialog	Yes

ADMISSION
Acceptance 1994-95 150 applied for admission; 65% were accepted.
Entrance Requirements Bachelor's degree, minimum 2.7 GPA. Core courses waived through: previous course work.
Application Requirements Application form.
Application Deadlines 8/1 for fall, 12/1 for spring, 5/1 for summer.

FINANCIALS
Costs for 1994-95 Tuition: Full-time: $220/unit. Fees: Full-time: $150/semester. Average room and board costs are $8,400 per academic year (off-campus).

INTERNATIONAL STUDENTS
Demographics 92% of students enrolled in the program are international.
Services and Facilities Language tutoring, ESL courses, special assistance for nonnative speakers of English, counseling/support services.
Applying Proof of adequate funds. Financial aid is not available to international students. Admission application deadlines: 8/1 for fall, 12/1 for spring, 5/1 for summer. Contact: Ms. Stephanie Griffin, Director of Student Service, 281 Masonic Avenue, San Francisco, CA 94118-4498. (415) 221-1212.

PLACEMENT
Placement services include career counseling/planning, career fairs, job search course, resume preparation, and workshops.

Program Contact: Dr. Pete Bogue, Registrar, Director of Admissions, Lincoln University, 281 Masonic Avenue, San Francisco, CA 94118-4498. (415) 221-1212 Ext. 116; Fax: (415) 387-9730.

Loyola Marymount University

College of Business Administration

Los Angeles, California

OVERVIEW
Loyola Marymount University is an independent Roman Catholic comprehensive coed institution. Founded 1911. Setting: 100-acre urban campus. Total institutional enrollment: 4,000. Program was first offered in 1974. AACSB-accredited.

MBA HIGHLIGHTS

Entrance Difficulty*
Mean GMAT: 522
Mean GPA: 3.2

Cost $$
Tuition: $495/unit
Room & Board: N/R

Enrollment Profile

Full-time: 288	Work Exp: 85%
Part-time: 72	International: N/R
Total: 360	Women: 42%
Average Age: 27	Minorities: N/R

Average Class Size: 25

The flexibility of Loyola Marymount University's M.B.A. program attracts both fully employed professionals who attend on a part-time basis and full-time students. Classes are offered year-round, with all classes scheduled in the late afternoon and evening. The M.B.A. program is accredited by the American Assembly of Collegiate Schools of Business. Well over 90 percent of all classes are taught by faculty members with doctorates from prestigious universities.

Beginning in August 1995, M.B.A. classes will be held in a variety of state-of-the-art student-centered classrooms in the magnificent Conrad N. Hilton Center for Business. The facility will offer M.B.A. students access to many advanced technological features.

M.B.A. students participate in panel discussions during the annual Business Ethics Week. Loyola Marymount's commitment to business ethics has been enhanced by the recent appointment of Dr. Thomas White to the Hilton Chair in Business Ethics.

The international program has been enhanced by the addition of a semester-long foreign experience available through an exchange program with the EDHEC Graduate School of Business in Lille, France. In addition, students find the comparative-management-systems sequence, featuring visits to a number of foreign companies over a three-week period, to be very valuable.

ACADEMICS
Length of Program Minimum: 11 months. Maximum: 5 years.
Calendar Semesters.
Full-time Classes Main campus; evening, summer.
Part-time Classes Main campus; evening, summer.
Degree Requirements 30-60 units including 27-33 elective units. Other: Thesis; 2 international classes or 3 strategy classes.

Required Courses Business economics, business statistics, finance and managerial accounting, financial management, legal and ethical environments of business, management and organization behavior, management information sciences, marketing management, operations analysis and decision support systems. Courses may be waived through: previous course work.

Curricular Focus General management, international business, problem solving and decision making.

Concentrations Entrepreneurship, finance, international business, management, management information systems, marketing, operations management, organizational behavior, quantitative analysis.

Faculty Full-time: 37, 97% with doctorates; part-time: 4, 75% with doctorates.

Special Opportunities Internship program available.

STUDENT STATISTICS
Other Background Graduate degrees in other disciplines: 5%. Work experience: On average, students have 7 years of work experience on entrance to the program.

FACILITIES
Information Resources Main library with 447,045 bound volumes, 124,158 titles on microform, 8,670 periodical subscriptions, 10,558 records/tapes/CDs.

Housing College housing not available.

Technology Computers are used moderately in course work. 100 computer terminals/PCs, linked by a campus-wide computer network, are available for use by students in program; they are located in the computer center, computer labs. Students in the program are required to have their own PC.

Computer Resources/On-line Services

Training	Yes	CompuServe	No
Internet	Yes	Dun's	No
E-Mail	No	Dow Jones	No
Multimedia Center	Yes	Dialog	No
LEXIS/NEXIS	No	Bloomberg	No

ADMISSION
Entrance Requirements Bachelor's degree, GMAT score of 400. Core courses waived through: previous course work.

Application Requirements Application form, copies of transcript, personal statement, 2 letters of recommendation.

Application Deadline Applications are processed on a rolling basis.

FINANCIALS
Costs for 1994-95 Tuition: Full-time: $495/unit. Fees: Full-time: $126/semester.

Financial Aid In 1994-95, candidates received some institutionally administered aid in the form of grants, loans, assistantships. Financial aid is available to part-time students. Application deadlines: 8/15 for fall, 1/3 for spring. Contact: Ms. Darlene Wilson, Counselor, Financial Aid Office, 7101 West 80th Street, Los Angeles, CA 90045-2699. (310) 338-1852.

INTERNATIONAL STUDENTS
Services and Facilities International student center, visa services, ESL courses, counseling/support services.

Applying TOEFL required, minimum score of 600. Financial aid is not available to international students. Admission applications are processed on a rolling basis. Contact: Mr. Les Santos, Coordinator, Office of International Services, 7101 West 80th Street, Los Angeles, CA 90045-2699. (310) 338-2937.

ALTERNATE MBA PROGRAM
MBA/JD Length of program: Minimum: 48 months. Maximum: 5 years. Degree requirements: 117 units.

PLACEMENT
Placement services include alumni network, career counseling/planning, career fairs, career library, career placement, electronic job bank, resume preparation, and resume referral to employers. Of 1994 graduates, 85% were employed within three months of graduation.

Program Contact: Ms. Karen Stevens, MBA Coordinator, Loyola Marymount University, 7101 West 80th Street, Los Angeles, CA 90045-2699. (310) 338-2848; Fax: (310) 338-2899.
See full description on page 776.

Monterey Institute of International Studies

Monterey, California

OVERVIEW
Monterey Institute of International Studies is an independent nonprofit upper-level coed institution. Founded 1955. Setting: 5-acre small-town campus. Total institutional enrollment: 750. Program was first offered in 1978.

MBA HIGHLIGHTS
Entrance Difficulty***
Mean GMAT: 525
Mean GPA: 3.2

Cost $$$
Tuition: $7,600/semester
Room & Board: N/R

Enrollment Profile

Full-time: 190	Work Exp: 95%
Part-time: 0	International: 50%
Total: 190	Women: 45%
Average Age: 26	Minorities: 10%

Average Class Size: 25

ACADEMICS
Length of Program Minimum: 21 months.

Calendar Semesters.

Full-time Classes Main campus; day, weekends, early morning.

Degree Requirements 64 credits including 12 elective credits.

Required Courses Decision sciences and information systems, economics for managers, finance and accounting, global business strategy, international business plan, marketing management, organizational behavior, statistics and information systems.

Curricular Focus Entrepreneurship, international business, teamwork.

Concentrations Economics, entrepreneurship, finance, human resources management, international business, international trade management, global business, regional business environments, marketing.

Faculty Full-time: 12, 75% with doctorates; part-time: 10, 80% with doctorates.

Teaching Methodology Case study: 30%, lecture: 40%, student presentations: 10%, team projects: 20%.

Special Opportunities International exchange in France, Mexico, People's Republic of China.

STUDENT STATISTICS
Geographic Representation State residents 50%. By region: West 30%; Midwest 12%; Northeast 8%. International 50%.

Undergraduate Majors Business 27%; humanities 53%; other 20%.

Other Background Graduate degrees in other disciplines: 5%. Work experience: On average, students have 2 years of work experience on entrance to the program.

FACILITIES
Information Resources Main library with 64,200 bound volumes, 500 periodical subscriptions, 5,000 records/tapes/CDs. Business collection includes 8,800 bound volumes, 70 periodical subscriptions.

Housing College housing not available.

Technology Computers are used moderately in course work. 50 computer terminals/PCs, linked by a campus-wide computer network, are available for use by students in program; they are located in classrooms, the computer center, computer labs, the research center. Students in the program are not required to have their own PC.

Computer Resources/On-line Services

Training	Yes	CompuServe	No
Internet	Yes	Dun's	No
E-Mail	Yes	Dow Jones	No
Multimedia Center	Yes	Dialog	Yes
LEXIS/NEXIS	No	Bloomberg	No

Other on-line services: RLIN.

ADMISSION
Acceptance 1994-95 Of those applying, 85% were accepted.

Entrance Requirements Bachelor's degree, GMAT score, minimum 3.0 GPA, foreign language proficiency. Core courses waived through: previous course work.

Application Requirements Application form, copies of transcript, personal statement, 2 letters of recommendation.

Application Deadlines 8/1 for fall, 12/1 for spring, 6/1 for summer. Applications are processed on a rolling basis.

FINANCIALS
Costs for 1995-96 Tuition: Full-time: $7,600/semester; Summer: $6,400/semester. Fees: Full-time: $45/semester.

Financial Aid In 1994-95, candidates received some institutionally administered aid in the form of grants, scholarships, loans, work-study. Total awards ranged from $4,000-$21,000. Application deadlines: 3/15 for fall, 11/1 for spring, 3/15 for summer. Applications are processed on a rolling basis. Contact: Mr. Michael Benson, Director of Financial Aid, 425 Van Buren Street, Monterey, CA 93940-2691. (408) 647-4119.

INTERNATIONAL STUDENTS
Demographics 50% of students enrolled in the program are international; Europe 57%, Asia 33%, other 10%.

Services and Facilities International student office, visa services, ESL courses.

Applying TOEFL required, minimum score of 550; proof of adequate funds. Financial aid is available to international students. Financial aid application deadline: 2/1 for fall. Admission application deadlines: 6/1 for fall, 10/1 for spring, 4/1 for summer. Applications are processed on a rolling basis. Contact: Mrs. Jane Roberts, International Admissions Officer, 425 Van Buren Street, Monterey, CA 93940-2691. (408) 647-4123.

ALTERNATE MBA PROGRAM
One-Year MBA Length of program: Minimum: 10 months. Full-time classes: Main campus; day, weekends, early morning, summer. Degree requirements: 42 credits including 12 elective credits.

PLACEMENT
In 1993-94, 27 organizations participated in on-campus recruiting. Placement services include alumni network, career counseling/planning, career fairs, career library, job interviews, resume preparation, and resume referral to employers. Of 1994 graduates, 50% were employed within three months of graduation, the average starting salary was $37,300, the range was $25,000-$65,000.

Jobs by Employer Type Manufacturing 18%; service 12%; government 7%; consulting 6%; nonprofit 3%; accounting/banking/finance 17%; high technology 15%; trade and transportation 10%; other 12%.

Jobs by Functional Area Marketing/sales 42%; finance 17%; operations 13%; management 19%; strategic planning 6%; other 3%.

Program Contact: Ms. Whitney Gravel, Dean of Admissions and Student Affairs, Monterey Institute of International Studies, 425 Van Buren Street, Monterey, CA 93940-2691. (408) 647-4123; Fax: (408) 647-6405.
See full description on page 784.

National University

School of Management and Technology

San Diego, California

OVERVIEW
National University is an independent nonprofit comprehensive coed institution. Founded 1971. Setting: 15-acre urban campus. Total institutional enrollment: 14,000. Program was first offered in 1972.

MBA HIGHLIGHTS

Entrance Difficulty**

Cost $$
Tuition: $730/course
Room & Board: N/R

Enrollment Profile

Full-time: 700	Work Exp: 95%
Part-time: 500	International: 5%
Total: 1,200	Women: 56%
Average Age: N/R	Minorities: 23%

Average Class Size: 15

ACADEMICS
Length of Program Minimum: 15 months.

Calendar Quarters.

Full-time Classes Main campus; evening.

Part-time Classes Main campus; evening.

Degree Requirements 75 units including 25 elective units. Other: Research project.

Required Courses Applied business statistics, global business environment, information systems management, management accounting, managerial economics, managing human resources, seminar in financial management, seminar in general management, seminar in marketing.

Curricular Focus Business issues and problems, problem solving and decision making, teamwork.

Concentrations Accounting, finance, health services, human resources management, management, marketing, public administration, technology management.

Faculty Full-time: 20, 60% with doctorates; part-time: 250, 40% with doctorates.

Teaching Methodology Case study: 15%, lecture: 50%, research: 10%, seminars by members of the business community: 5%, student presentations: 10%, team projects: 10%.

Special Opportunities Internships include healthcare, accountancy/taxation, international business, and marketing.

STUDENT STATISTICS
Geographic Representation State residents 72%. By region: West 100%. International 5%.

Other Background Work experience: On average, students have 5 years of work experience on entrance to the program.

FACILITIES
Information Resources Main library with 134,766 bound volumes, 1,050 titles on microform, 2,737 periodical subscriptions, 2,622 records/tapes/CDs, 4 CD-ROMs.

Housing College housing not available.

Technology Computers are used moderately in course work. 400 computer terminals/PCs, linked by a campus-wide computer network, are available for use by students in program; they are located in classrooms, the library, the computer center, computer labs. Students in the program are not required to have their own PC.

Computer Resources/On-line Services

Training	Yes	CompuServe	Yes
Internet	Yes	Dun's	Yes $
E-Mail	Yes	Dow Jones	Yes $
Videoconference Center	Yes	Dialog	Yes $
Multimedia Center	Yes	Bloomberg	No
LEXIS/NEXIS	Yes $		

ADMISSION
Acceptance 1994-95 632 applied for admission; 79% were accepted.

Entrance Requirements Bachelor's degree, prerequisite courses required for applicants with non-business degree, minimum 2.5 GPA, minimum 5 years of work experience. Core courses waived through: previous course work.

Application Requirements Interview, application form, copies of transcript, resume/curriculum vitae.

Application Deadline Applications are processed on a rolling basis.

FINANCIALS
Costs for 1994-95 Tuition: Full-time: $730/course.

Financial Aid In 1994-95, candidates received some institutionally administered aid in the form of scholarships, loans, work-study. Total awards ranged from $1,000-$15,000. Financial aid is available to part-time students. Applications are processed on a rolling basis. Contact: Mr. Michael Batimca, Director of Financial Aid, 4025 Camino Del Rio South, San Diego, CA 92108-4107. (619) 563-2526.

INTERNATIONAL STUDENTS

Demographics 5% of students enrolled in the program are international.

Services and Facilities International student office, visa services, ESL courses, counseling/support services, orientation.

Applying TOEFL required, minimum score of 550; proof of adequate funds. Financial aid is not available to international students. Admission applications are processed on a rolling basis. Contact: Mr. Clyde Bover, International Admissions Adviser, 4007 Camino Del Rio South, San Diego, CA 92108-4107. (619) 563-7414.

PLACEMENT

Placement services include career counseling/planning, career library, electronic job bank, job search course, and resume preparation.

Program Contact: Ms. Nancy Rohland, Director, Enrollment Management, National University, 4025 Camino Del Rio South, San Diego, CA 92108-4107. (619) 563-7349, or (800) NAT-UNIV (CA only); Fax: (619) 563-7496; Internet Address: crich@somt.nu.edu.

Pepperdine University

School of Business and Management

Malibu, California

OVERVIEW

Pepperdine University is an independent upper-level coed institution, affiliated with Church of Christ. Founded 1937. Setting: 1-acre suburban campus with easy access to Los Angeles. Total institutional enrollment: 7,800. Program was first offered in 1969.

MBA HIGHLIGHTS

Entrance Difficulty**
Mean GMAT: 540
Mean GPA: 3.0

Cost $$$$$
Tuition: $9,100/trimester
Room & Board: $4,330

Enrollment Profile

Full-time: 240	Work Exp: 75%
Part-time: 1,600	International: 30%
Total: 1,840	Women: 40%
Average Age: 26	Minorities: 1%

Average Class Size: 25

Founded in 1937, Pepperdine University is a private university located in Malibu, California. The University comprises four schools that enroll approximately 7,800 students: the School of Business and Management, the School of Law, the Graduate School of Education and Psychology, and Seaver College, the undergraduate school.

The School of Business and Management, one of the largest in the United States, focuses primarily on the development of managers. Management in this context is identifying and setting objectives and motivating people to increase the effectiveness of the organization's operations. The fundamental teaching philosophy is to help students grow in their learning ability. In summary, the School's objective is to provide the student with advanced abilities in many areas. Students gain knowledge of research theory and method; management functions; legal, social, political, economic, and other environmental systems; ethics in business and organizations, information, behavior, and other subordinate systems. One improves attitudes toward oneself as a person and a manager and towards subordinates, associates, and superiors; towards research and problem solving; and towards change. Students acquire skills in problem solving and research, planning, decision making, and other management functions; learn to initiate, implement, and adapt to change; communicate both orally and in writing; improve interpersonal relations; and achieve results.

ACADEMICS

Length of Program Minimum: 12 months. Maximum: 7 years.

Calendar Trimesters.

Full-time Classes Main campus; day.

Part-time Classes Main campus, Culver City, Long Beach, Orange County, Encino, Ventura City; evening, weekends.

Degree Requirements 48 units including 16-28 elective units.

Required Courses Business strategy, financial markets and institutions, human behavior in organizations, legal/political/regulatory issues of management, national income policy and corporate response, organization and management, price theory and industrial policy, quantitative analysis and information systems. Courses may be waived through: previous course work.

Curricular Focus International business, problem solving and decision making, teamwork.

Concentrations Finance, international business, marketing.

Faculty Full-time: 57, 93% with doctorates; part-time: 61.

Teaching Methodology Case study: 15%, faculty seminars: 5%, lecture: 35%, research: 10%, seminars by members of the business community: 5%, student presentations: 10%, team projects: 20%.

Special Opportunities International exchange in France, Germany. Internship program available.

STUDENT STATISTICS

Geographic Representation State residents 35%. By region: West 61%; Northeast 16%; Midwest 14%; South 9%. International 30%.

Undergraduate Majors Business 45%; engineering/technology 6%; humanities 8%; science/mathematics 3%; social sciences 29%; other 9%.

Other Background Work experience: On average, students have 2 years of work experience on entrance to the program.

FACILITIES

Information Resources Main library with 110,937 bound volumes, 280,892 titles on microform, 555 periodical subscriptions.

Housing 1% of students in program live in college-owned or -operated housing.

Technology Computers are used heavily in course work. 40 computer terminals/PCs, linked by a campus-wide computer network, are available for use by students in program; they are located in computer labs. Students in the program are not required to have their own PC.

Computer Resources/On-line Services

Training	Yes	CompuServe	No
Internet	Yes	Dun's	No
E-Mail	Yes	Dow Jones	Yes
Multimedia Center	Yes	Dialog	No
LEXIS/NEXIS	Yes	Bloomberg	No

ADMISSION

Acceptance 1994-95 Of those applying, 70% were accepted.

Entrance Requirements Bachelor's degree, GMAT score, minimum 0-2 years work experience depending upon program years of work experience. Core courses waived through: previous course work.

Application Requirements Written essay, application form, copies of transcript, personal statement, 2 letters of recommendation.

Application Deadline 5/1 for fall.

FINANCIALS

Costs for 1994-95 Tuition: Full-time: $9,100/trimester; Part-time evening: $570/unit. Fees: Full-time: $30/trimester. Average room and board costs are $4,330 per academic year (on-campus) and $5,600 per academic year (off-campus).

Financial Aid In 1994-95, 45% of candidates received some institutionally administered aid in the form of scholarships, assistantships. Total awards ranged from $1,000-$6,000. Financial aid is available to part-time students. Application deadline: 6/1 for fall. Contact: Ms. Sandi Ford, Financial Aid Analyst, 400 Corporate Pointe, Culver City, CA 90230. (310) 568-5530.

INTERNATIONAL STUDENTS

Demographics 30% of students enrolled in the program are international; Asia 41%, Europe 30%, South America 6%, Africa 1%, other 22%.

Services and Facilities International student center, visa services, language tutoring, ESL courses, special assistance for nonnative speakers of English, counseling/support services.

Applying TOEFL required, minimum score of 550; proof of adequate funds. Financial aid is not available to international students. Admission application deadline: 5/1 for fall. Contact: Mr. Richard Dawson, Director, International Student Services, 24255 Pacific Coast Highway, Malibu, CA 90263-4246. (310) 456-4246.

ALTERNATE MBA PROGRAMS

Executive MBA (EMBA) Length of program: Minimum: 20 months. Degree requirements: 50 credits including 10 elective credits.

One-Year MBA Length of program: Minimum: 11 months. Maximum: 7 years. Degree requirements: 48 credits including 16 elective credits.

MBA/JD Length of program: Minimum: 45 months. Degree requirements: 130 credits including 18-20 elective credits.

Masters of International Business Length of program: Minimum: 20 months. Full-time classes: Main campus, Paris (France), Frankfurt (Germany); day, evening, summer. Degree requirements: 58 credits. Second year overseas; internship.

PLACEMENT

In 1993-94, 5 organizations participated in on-campus recruiting; 40 on-campus interviews were conducted. Placement services include alumni network, career counseling/planning, career fairs, career library, career placement, electronic job bank, job interviews, resume preparation, and resume referral to employers. Of 1994 graduates, 63% were employed within three months of graduation, the average starting salary was $44,500.

Jobs by Employer Type Manufacturing 18%; service 46%; consulting 18%; nonprofit 2%; banking/finance 16%.

Jobs by Functional Area Marketing/sales 36%; finance 33%; management 13%; consulting 18%.

Program Contact: Ms. Nan Papenhausen, Associate Director of Marketing, Pepperdine University, 24255 Pacific Coast Highway, Malibu, CA 90263-4100. (310) 456-4858, or (800) 726-9283 (CA only); Fax: (310) 456-4126; Internet Address: npapen@pepperdine.edu.
See full description on page 800.

Saint Mary's College of California

School of Economics and Business Administration

Moraga, California

OVERVIEW

Saint Mary's College of California is an independent Roman Catholic comprehensive coed institution. Founded 1863. Setting: 440-acre small-town campus with easy access to San Francisco. Total institutional enrollment: 3,500. Program was first offered in 1975.

MBA HIGHLIGHTS

Entrance Difficulty*
Mean GMAT: 513
Mean GPA: 3.05

Cost $$
Tuition: $1,146/course
Room & Board: $11,000 (off-campus)

Enrollment Profile

Full-time: 17	Work Exp: 80%
Part-time: 350	International: 7%
Total: 367	Women: 33%
Average Age: 32	Minorities: 16%

Average Class Size: 24

ACADEMICS

Length of Program Minimum: 13 months. Maximum: 6 years.
Calendar Quarters.
Full-time Classes Main campus; day, evening, summer.
Part-time Classes Main campus; evening, summer.
Degree Requirements 72 credits including 12 elective credits.
Required Courses Business strategy, entrepreneurship and business development, financial accounting, industry analysis, legal and ethical aspects of business, management communications, management science, managerial accounting, managerial economics, managerial finance, managerial forecasting, marketing management, organizational behavior and management, political and social environment of business, quantitative methods. Courses may be waived through: previous course work.
Curricular Focus General management, problem solving and decision making, teamwork.
Concentrations International business, management, marketing.
Faculty Full-time: 7, 100% with doctorates; part-time: 19, 42% with doctorates.
Special Opportunities International exchange in Czech Republic, France, United Kingdom.

STUDENT STATISTICS

Geographic Representation State residents 93%. By region: West 93%. International 7%.
Other Background Graduate degrees in other disciplines: 14%. Work experience: On average, students have 6 years of work experience on entrance to the program.

FACILITIES

Information Resources Main library with 179,485 bound volumes, 177,756 titles on microform, 1,097 periodical subscriptions, 3,380 records/tapes/CDs.
Housing College housing not available.
Technology Computers are used moderately in course work. Computer terminals/PCs, linked by a campus-wide computer network, are available for use by students in program; they are located in the library, computer labs. Students in the program are not required to have their own PC.

Computer Resources/On-line Services

Training	Yes	E-Mail	Yes
Internet	Yes $	Dialog	Yes $

ADMISSION

Acceptance 1994-95 Of those applying, 71% were accepted.
Entrance Requirements Bachelor's degree, GMAT score of 500, minimum 3.0 GPA, for EMBA, must be employed as manager or supervisor. Core courses waived through: previous course work.
Application Requirements Interview, application form, copies of transcript, personal statement, 2 letters of recommendation.
Application Deadline Applications are processed on a rolling basis.

FINANCIALS

Costs for 1994-95 Tuition: Part-time day: $1,146/course. Average room and board costs are $11,000 per academic year (off-campus).
Financial Aid In 1994-95, 80% of candidates received some institutionally administered aid in the form of loans. Total awards ranged from $4,000-$8,700. Financial aid is available to part-time students. Application deadline: 3/2. Contact: Ms. Billie Jones, Director of Financial Aid, Box 4530, Moraga, CA 94575-4530. (510) 631-4370.

INTERNATIONAL STUDENTS

Demographics 7% of students enrolled in the program are international.
Services and Facilities International student office, visa services, language tutoring, ESL courses, special assistance for nonnative speakers of English, counseling/support services.
Applying TOEFL required, minimum score of 550; proof of adequate funds. Financial aid is not available to international students. Admission applications are processed on a rolling basis. Contact: Mr. Louis Gecenok, Director, International Student Programs, PO Box 3091, Moraga, CA 94575-3091. (510) 631-4352.

ALTERNATE MBA PROGRAM

Executive MBA (EMBA) Length of program: Minimum: 21 months. Degree requirements: 56 credits including 12 elective credits.

PLACEMENT

Placement services include alumni network, career counseling/planning, career library, resume preparation, and resume referral to employers. Of 1994 graduates, 100% were employed within three months of graduation.

Program Contact: Ms. Maria N. Garvey-Tara, Director of Admissions, Saint Mary's College of California, 1928 St. Mary's Road, Moraga, CA 94575. (510) 631-4500, or (800) 332-4622 (CA only); Fax: (510) 376-6521.
See full description on page 824.

San Diego State University

College of Business Administration

San Diego, California

OVERVIEW

San Diego State University is a state-supported coed institution. Part of California State University System. Founded 1897. Setting: 300-acre urban campus. Total institutional enrollment: 30,369. AACSB-accredited.

MBA HIGHLIGHTS

Entrance Difficulty**
Mean GMAT: 555
Mean GPA: N/R

Cost $
Tuition: $1,902
(Nonresident: $256/unit)
Room & Board: $8,600 (off-campus)

Enrollment Profile

Full-time: N/R	Work Exp: N/R
Part-time: N/R	International: 13%
Total: 790	Women: 46%
Average Age: N/R	Minorities: N/R

Average Class Size: 35

ACADEMICS

Length of Program Minimum: 12 months.

Calendar Semesters.

Full-time Classes Main campus; day, summer.

Part-time Classes Main campus; evening, summer.

Degree Requirements 30 credits. Other: Computer language; thesis or comprehensive exam.

Curricular Focus Entrepreneurship, international business, problem solving and decision making.

Concentrations Accounting, entrepreneurship, finance, financial and tax planning, human resources management, international business, management, management information systems, marketing, operations management, organizational behavior, quantitative analysis, real estate, strategic management, transportation.

Teaching Methodology Case study: 15%, faculty seminars: 10%, lecture: 30%, research: 10%, seminars by members of the business community: 10%, student presentations: 10%, team projects: 15%.

STUDENT STATISTICS

Geographic Representation State residents 71%. International 13%.

FACILITIES

Information Resources Main library with 1.1 million bound volumes, 3.4 million titles on microform, 5,979 periodical subscriptions, 8,477 records/tapes/CDs, 1 CD-ROM.

Housing College housing not available.

ADMISSION

Entrance Requirements Bachelor's degree, GMAT score.

Application Requirements Application form, copies of transcript.

Application Deadlines 7/1 for fall, 12/1 for spring. Applications are processed on a rolling basis.

FINANCIALS

Estimated Costs for 1995-96 Tuition: Full-time: $256/unit for nonresidents, $256/unit for international students; Part-time day: $256/unit for nonresidents. Fees: Full-time: $1,902 for state residents, $1,902 for nonresidents, $1,902 for international students; Part-time day: $1,236 for state residents, $1,236 for nonresidents. Average room and board costs are $8,600 per academic year (off-campus).

Financial Aid Application deadline: 3/2 for fall. Applications are processed on a rolling basis. Contact: Director of Financial Aid, 5500 Campanile Drive, San Diego, CA 92182. (619) 594-6323.

INTERNATIONAL STUDENTS

Demographics 13% of students enrolled in the program are international.

Applying TOEFL required, minimum score of 570; proof of health; proof of adequate funds. Financial aid is not available to international students. Admission application deadlines: 5/21 for fall, 8/31 for spring. Applications are processed on a rolling basis.

Program Contact: Ms. Patricia Martin, Graduate Admission Coordinator, San Diego State University, 5500 Campanile Drive, San Diego, CA 92182. (619) 594-5217; Fax: (619) 594-1573.

San Francisco State University

College of Business

San Francisco, California

OVERVIEW

San Francisco State University is a state-supported comprehensive coed institution. Part of California State University System. Founded 1899. Setting: 90-acre urban campus. Total institutional enrollment: 25,716. AACSB-accredited.

MBA HIGHLIGHTS

Entrance Difficulty*

Cost $
Tuition: $896/semester
(Nonresident: $246/unit)
Room & Board: $9,600 (off-campus)

Enrollment Profile

Full-time: N/R	Work Exp: N/R
Part-time: N/R	International: 24%
Total: 845	Women: 45%
Average Age: N/R	Minorities: 35%

Average Class Size: 22

ACADEMICS

Length of Program Minimum: 12 months.

Calendar Semesters.

Full-time Classes Main campus; day, evening, early morning, summer.

Part-time Classes Main campus; day, evening, early morning, summer.

Degree Requirements 54 credits.

Curricular Focus General management, international business.

Concentrations Accounting, entrepreneurship, finance, human resources management, international business, management, management information systems, marketing, operations management, organizational behavior, quantitative analysis, strategic management.

Teaching Methodology Case study: 15%, faculty seminars: 10%, lecture: 50%, research: 5%, seminars by members of the business community: 5%, student presentations: 5%, team projects: 10%.

STUDENT STATISTICS

Geographic Representation State residents 76%. International 24%.

FACILITIES

Information Resources Main library with 770,000 bound volumes, 880,000 titles on microform, 4,000 periodical subscriptions.

Housing College housing not available.

ADMISSION

Entrance Requirements Bachelor's degree, GMAT score of 470, minimum 2.7 GPA.

Application Requirements Application form, copies of transcript, personal statement.

Application Deadlines 11/1 for fall, 6/1 for winter, 8/1 for spring, 2/1 for summer.

FINANCIALS

Costs for 1994-95 Tuition: Full-time: $246/unit for nonresidents; Part-time day: $246/unit for nonresidents. Fees: Full-time: $896/semester for state residents, $896/semester for nonresidents; Part-time day: $598/semester for state residents, $598/semester for nonresidents; Summer: $107/unit for state residents, $107/unit for nonresidents. Average room and board costs are $9,600 per academic year (off-campus).

Financial Aid Application deadline: 1/2 for fall. Contact: Student Financial Aid Office, 354 Administration, 1600 Holloway Avenue, San Francisco, CA 94132. (415) 338-1581.

INTERNATIONAL STUDENTS

Demographics 24% of students enrolled in the program are international.

Applying TOEFL required, minimum score of 550. Financial aid is not available to international students. Admission application deadlines: 3/1 for fall, 8/31 for spring. Applications are processed on a rolling basis.

Program Contact: Ms. Cija Briegleb, Admissions Coordinator, San Francisco State University, Business 325, 1600 Holloway Avenue, San Francisco, CA 94132. (415) 338-1935; Fax: (415) 338-6237.

San Jose State University

College of Business

San Jose, California

OVERVIEW

San Jose State University is a state-supported comprehensive coed institution. Part of California State University System. Founded 1857. Setting: 104-acre urban campus. Total institutional enrollment: 26,000. Program was first offered in 1973. AACSB-accredited.

MBA HIGHLIGHTS

Entrance Difficulty**
Mean GMAT: 570
Mean GPA: 3.51

Cost $
Tuition: $657/semester
(Nonresident: $2,133/semester)
Room & Board: $6,000

Enrollment Profile

Full-time: 0	Work Exp: 95%
Part-time: 584	International: 10%
Total: 584	Women: 36%
Average Age: 31	Minorities: 28%

Average Class Size: 35

ACADEMICS

Length of Program Minimum: 18 months. Maximum: 7 years.
Calendar Semesters.
Part-time Classes Main campus; evening, summer.
Degree Requirements 30 units including 12 elective units.
Required Courses Business strategy and policy, managerial corporate finance, managerial decision analysis, managing organizational behavior, marketing management and strategy, productions and operations management. Courses may be waived through: previous course work.
Curricular Focus International business, taxation, technology and innovation.
Concentrations International business, taxation, manufacturing management, global business practices, technology and innovation, leadership and organizational change.
Faculty Full-time: 38, 100% with doctorates; part-time: 5, 80% with doctorates.
Teaching Methodology Case study: 30%, lecture: 30%, seminars by members of the business community: 5%, student presentations: 10%, team projects: 25%.
Special Opportunities International exchange in France, Italy, Netherlands. Internship program available.

STUDENT STATISTICS

Geographic Representation State residents 90%. By region: West 87%; Northeast 1%; South 1%; Midwest 1%. International 10%.
Undergraduate Majors Business 45%; education 1%; engineering/technology 25%; humanities 1%; nursing 2%; science/mathematics 5%; social sciences 20%; other 1%.
Other Background Graduate degrees in other disciplines: 10%. Work experience: On average, students have 5 years of work experience on entrance to the program.

FACILITIES

Information Resources Main library with 877,609 bound volumes, 650,000 titles on microform, 3,127 periodical subscriptions, 36,909 records/tapes/CDs, 36 CD-ROMs. Business collection includes 55,000 bound volumes, 300 periodical subscriptions, 15 CD-ROMs.
Housing 5% of students in program live in college-owned or -operated housing.
Technology Computers are used moderately in course work. 100 computer terminals/PCs, linked by a campus-wide computer network, are available for use by students in program; they are located in the library, the computer center, computer labs. Students in the program are not required to have their own PC.

Computer Resources/On-line Services

Training	No	LEXIS/NEXIS	Yes
Internet	Yes	CompuServe	Yes
E-Mail	Yes	Dow Jones	Yes
Videoconference Center	Yes	Dialog	Yes

Other on-line services: Carl.

ADMISSION

Acceptance 1994-95 Of those applying, 55% were accepted.
Entrance Requirements Bachelor's degree, GMAT score of 500, minimum 3.0 GPA. Core courses waived through: previous course work.
Application Requirements Application form, copies of transcript, personal statement.
Application Deadlines 6/1 for fall, 12/1 for spring.

FINANCIALS

Estimated Costs for 1995-96 Tuition: Part-time evening: $657/semester for state residents, $2,133/semester for nonresidents; Summer: $150/unit for state residents, $150/unit for nonresidents. Fees: Summer: $450/course for state residents, $450/course for nonresidents. Average room and board costs are $6,000 per academic year (on-campus) and $5,000 per academic year (off-campus).
Financial Aid In 1994-95, 5% of candidates received some institutionally administered aid in the form of grants, loans. Financial aid is available to part-time students. Application deadline: 3/2 for fall. Contact: Financial Aid Office, One Washington Square, San Jose, CA 95192-0001. (408) 924-6100.

INTERNATIONAL STUDENTS

Demographics 10% of students enrolled in the program are international; Asia 69%, Europe 17%, South America 4%, Africa 3%, Central America 3%, other 3%.
Services and Facilities International student housing; international student center, visa services, ESL courses, counseling/support services.
Applying TOEFL required, minimum score of 550; proof of adequate funds. Financial aid is not available to international students. Admission application deadlines: 3/1 for fall, 9/1 for spring. Contact: Mr. Louie Barrozi, Director, Foreign Student Advisement Center, San Jose, CA 95192-0221. (408) 924-5920.

ALTERNATE MBA PROGRAM

Executive MBA (EMBA) Length of program: Minimum: 22 months. Maximum: 7 years. Degree requirements: 30 units including 12 elective units.

PLACEMENT

In 1993-94, 30 organizations participated in on-campus recruiting. Placement services include alumni network, career counseling/planning, career fairs, career library, career placement, cooperative programs, electronic job bank, job interviews, resume preparation, and resume referral to employers. Of 1994 graduates, 95% were employed within three months of graduation, the average starting salary was $40,000, the range was $36,000-$54,000.

Program Contact: Ms. Reena Kishen, Graduate Adviser, San Jose State University, One Washington Square, San Jose, CA 95192-0001. (408) 924-3422; Fax: (408) 924-3426.

Santa Clara University

Thomas and Dorothy Leavey School of Business and Admin.

Santa Clara, California

OVERVIEW

Santa Clara University is an independent Roman Catholic (Jesuit) comprehensive coed institution. Founded 1851. Setting: 104-acre suburban campus with easy access to San Francisco and San Jose. Total institutional enrollment: 7,514. Program was first offered in 1961. AACSB-accredited.

MBA HIGHLIGHTS

Entrance Difficulty**
Mean GMAT: 580
Mean GPA: 3.2

Cost $$
Tuition: $1,071/course
Room & Board: $8,370 (off-campus)

Enrollment Profile

Full-time: 205	Work Exp: 98%
Part-time: 870	International: 9%
Total: 1,075	Women: 37%
Average Age: 28	Minorities: 18%

Average Class Size: 35

ACADEMICS

Length of Program Minimum: 15 months. Maximum: 6 years.

Calendar Quarters.

Full-time Classes Main campus, San Ramon; evening.

Part-time Classes Main campus; evening.

Degree Requirements 45 credits including 24 elective credits.

Required Courses Business decisions, business policy, computer decision models, finance elective, financial management, macroeconomics, managerial competencies, marketing, math analysis, microeconomics, operations management, organizational analysis, social environment of business, statistics.

Curricular Focus General management, teamwork, technology management.

Concentrations Economics, entrepreneurship, finance, innovation and technology management, agribusiness, international business, management, management information systems, marketing, operations management, organizational behavior, quantitative analysis.

Faculty Full-time: 62, 98% with doctorates; part-time: 20, 25% with doctorates.

Teaching Methodology Case study: 25%, faculty seminars: 5%, lecture: 20%, research: 5%, seminars by members of the business community: 5%, student presentations: 15%, team projects: 25%.

STUDENT STATISTICS

Geographic Representation International 9%.

Undergraduate Majors Business 30%; engineering/technology 28%; humanities 20%; science/mathematics 5%; social sciences 10%; other 7%.

Other Background Graduate degrees in other disciplines: 20%. Work experience: On average, students have 5 years of work experience on entrance to the program.

FACILITIES

Information Resources Main library with 593,593 bound volumes, 36,939 titles on microform, 5,763 periodical subscriptions. Business collection includes 58,000 bound volumes, 600 periodical subscriptions, 5 CD-ROMs.

Housing College housing not available.

Technology Computers are used heavily in course work. 100 computer terminals/PCs, linked by a campus-wide computer network, are available for use by students in program; they are located in classrooms, the library, computer labs. Students in the program are not required to have their own PC.

Computer Resources/On-line Services

Training	No	CompuServe	No
Internet	Yes	Dun's	No
E-Mail	Yes	Dow Jones	Yes
Videoconference Center	Yes	Dialog	No
LEXIS/NEXIS	No	Bloomberg	No

ADMISSION

Acceptance 1994-95 800 applied for admission; 63% were accepted.

Entrance Requirements Bachelor's degree, GMAT score. Core courses waived through: previous course work.

Application Requirements Written essay, application form, copies of transcript, 2 letters of recommendation.

Application Deadlines 6/15 for fall, 9/15 for winter, 12/15 for spring, 3/15 for summer. Applications are processed on a rolling basis.

FINANCIALS

Costs for 1994-95 Tuition: Full-time: $1,071/course. Fees: Full-time: $19/quarter. Average room and board costs are $8,370 per academic year (off-campus).

Financial Aid In 1994-95, 10% of candidates received some institutionally administered aid in the form of grants, scholarships, assistantships. Financial aid is available to part-time students. Application deadlines: 7/1 for fall, 10/1 for winter, 1/1 for spring. Applications are processed on a rolling basis. Contact: Ms. Donna Hunting, Financial Aid Coordinator, Santa Clara, CA 95053-0001. (408) 554-4500.

INTERNATIONAL STUDENTS

Demographics 9% of students enrolled in the program are international; Asia 77%, Europe 15%, South America 3%, North America 2%, Africa 1%, Central America 1%.

Services and Facilities International student center, counseling/support services.

Applying TOEFL required, minimum score of 580; proof of adequate funds; minimum score of 4.0 on Test of Standard Written English. Financial aid is not available to international students. Admission application deadlines: 5/1 for fall, 5/1 for winter, 10/1 for spring, 10/1 for summer. Applications are processed on a rolling basis. Contact: Ms. Barbara Colyar, International Student Adviser, Benson 203, Santa Clara, CA 95053-0001. (408) 554-4109.

ALTERNATE MBA PROGRAM

MBA/JD Length of program: Minimum: 42 months. Maximum: 6 years.

PLACEMENT

In 1993-94, 101 organizations participated in on-campus recruiting. Placement services include alumni network, career counseling/planning, career library, career placement, resume preparation, and resume referral to employers. Of 1994 graduates, 95% were employed within three months of graduation, the average starting salary was $57,515, the range was $28,500-$170,000.

Jobs by Employer Type Manufacturing 69%; service 24%; government 1%; consulting 5%; nonprofit 1%.

Jobs by Functional Area Marketing/sales 20%; finance 25%; operations 10%; management 10%; strategic planning 5%; technical management 25%; human resources 5%.

Program Contact: Ms. Elizabeth Ford, Director, MBA Admissions, Santa Clara University, Santa Clara, CA 95053-0001. (408) 554-4500; Fax: (408) 554-4571; Internet Address: eford@scuacc.scu.edu.

See full description on page 826.

Sonoma State University

School of Business and Economics

Rohnert Park, California

OVERVIEW

Sonoma State University is a state-supported comprehensive coed institution. Part of California State University System. Founded 1960. Setting: 220-acre small-town campus with easy access to San Francisco. Total institutional enrollment: 7,400. Program was first offered in 1986.

MBA HIGHLIGHTS

Entrance Difficulty*
Mean GMAT: 496
Mean GPA: N/R

Cost $
Tuition: $1,045/semester
(Nonresident: $346/unit)
Room & Board: $5,430

Enrollment Profile

Full-time: 5	Work Exp: 95%
Part-time: 50	International: 5%
Total: 55	Women: 50%
Average Age: N/R	Minorities: 4%

Average Class Size: 20

ACADEMICS

Length of Program Minimum: 24 months. Maximum: 7 years.

Calendar Semesters.

Part-time Classes Main campus; evening.

Degree Requirements 30 units including 16-18 elective units. Other: Thesis, project or exam.

Required Courses Policy analysis, seminar in managerial finance, seminar in organization and management theory, seminar in strategic marketing management.

Curricular Focus General management, organizational development and change management, problem solving and decision making.

Concentration Management.

Faculty Full-time: 15, 100% with doctorates; part-time: 1, 100% with doctorates.

STUDENT STATISTICS

Geographic Representation State residents 95%. By region: West 95%. International 5%.

FACILITIES

Information Resources Main library with 468,307 bound volumes, 1.3 million titles on microform, 2,071 periodical subscriptions, 24,000 records/ tapes/CDs.

Housing College housing available.

ADMISSION

Acceptance 1994-95 Of those applying, 60% were accepted.

Entrance Requirements Bachelor's degree, GMAT score, minimum 2.5 GPA. Core courses waived through: previous course work.

Application Requirements Application form, copies of transcript, personal statement, 3 letters of recommendation.

Application Deadline 11/1 for opening date for fall applications, 08/01 for opening date for spring applications. Applications prior to these dates will not be accepted.

FINANCIALS

Estimated Costs for 1995-96 Tuition: Full-time: $346/unit for nonresidents; Part-time evening: $346/unit for nonresidents. Fees: Full-time: $1,045/ semester for state residents, $1,045/semester for nonresidents; Part-time evening: $712/semester for state residents, $712/semester for nonresidents. Average room and board costs are $5,430 per academic year (on-campus).

Financial Aid In 1994-95, 10% of candidates received some form of institutionally administered aid. Total awards ranged from $200-$2,000. Financial aid is available to part-time students. Application deadline: 3/2 for fall. Contact: Financial Aid Office, 1801 East Cotati Avenue, Rohnert Park, CA 94928-3609. (707) 664-2359.

INTERNATIONAL STUDENTS

Demographics 5% of students enrolled in the program are international.

Applying TOEFL required, minimum score of 550; proof of health; proof of adequate funds. Financial aid is not available to international students. Admission application deadline: 11/1 for opening date for fall applications, 08/01 for opening date for spring applications. Applications prior to these dates will not be accepted.

PLACEMENT

Placement services include alumni network, career fairs, and career placement.

Program Contact: MBA Coordinator, Sonoma State University, 1801 East Cotati Avenue, Rohnert Park, CA 94928-3609. (707) 664-2377; Fax: (707) 664-4009.

Stanford University

Stanford Graduate School of Business

Stanford, California

OVERVIEW

Stanford University is an independent nonprofit coed institution. Founded 1891. Setting: 8,180-acre suburban campus with easy access to San Francisco. Total institutional enrollment: 14,002. Program was first offered in 1925. AACSB-accredited.

MBA HIGHLIGHTS

Entrance Difficulty*****

Cost $$$$
Tuition: $7,063/quarter
Room & Board: $8,604

Enrollment Profile

Full-time: 717	Work Exp: 100%
Part-time: 0	International: 22%
Total: 717	Women: 27%
Average Age: 27	Minorities: 21%

Class Size: 40 - 60

ACADEMICS

Length of Program Minimum: 18 months.

Calendar Quarters.

Full-time Classes Main campus; day.

Degree Requirements 100 credits.

Required Courses Cost accounting, data and decisions, economic analysis and policy, finance, financial accounting, human resources management, management in non-market environments, marketing management, operations, organizational behavior, strategic management, systems. Courses may be waived through examination.

Curricular Focus General management, teamwork.

Concentrations Accounting, economics, entrepreneurship, finance, health services, human resources management, international business, management, management information systems, marketing, operations management, organizational behavior, public administration, public policy, quantitative analysis, real estate, strategic management.

Faculty Full-time: 82, 99% with doctorates; part-time: 5, 50% with doctorates.

Teaching Methodology Case study: 30%, lecture: 30%, research: 5%, seminars by members of the business community: 15%, student presentations: 10%, team projects: 10%.

Special Opportunities Internship program available.

STUDENT STATISTICS

Geographic Representation International 22%.

Undergraduate Majors Business 13%; engineering/technology 27%; humanities 12%; science/mathematics 10%; social sciences 12%; other 26%.

Other Background Graduate degrees in other disciplines: 14%. Work experience: On average, students have 3 years of work experience on entrance to the program.

FACILITIES

Information Resources Main library with 6.4 million bound volumes, 4.2 million titles on microform, 65,600 periodical subscriptions, 245,620 records/tapes/CDs. Business collection in Jackson Library includes 400,000 bound volumes, 2,000 periodical subscriptions, 20 CD-ROMs.

Housing College housing available.

Technology Computers are used heavily in course work. 105 computer terminals/PCs, linked by a campus-wide computer network, are available for use by students in program; they are located in the student center, the library, the computer center. Students in the program are not required to have their own PC.

Computer Resources/On-line Services

Internet	Yes	LEXIS/NEXIS	Yes
E-Mail	Yes	Dow Jones	Yes
Multimedia Center	Yes	Dialog	Yes

ADMISSION

Entrance Requirements Bachelor's degree, GMAT score.

Application Requirements Written essay, application form, copies of transcript, 3 letters of recommendation.

Application Deadline 3/15 for fall.

FINANCIALS

Costs for 1994-95 Tuition: Full-time: $7,063/quarter. Average room and board costs are $8,604 per academic year (on-campus) and $11,052 per academic year (off-campus).

Financial Aid In 1994-95, 65% of candidates received some institutionally administered aid in the form of grants, loans, fellowships. Application deadline: 3/1 for fall. Contact: Financial Aid Office, Graduate School of Business, Stanford, CA 94305-5015. (415) 723-3282.

INTERNATIONAL STUDENTS

Demographics 22% of students enrolled in the program are international.

Services and Facilities International student center, visa services, special assistance for nonnative speakers of English, counseling/support services.

Applying TOEFL required; proof of adequate funds. Financial aid is not available to international students. Admission application deadline: 3/15 for fall.

ALTERNATE MBA PROGRAMS

MBA/JD Length of program: Minimum: 48 months. Degree requirements: 185 credits. Separate applications must be submitted to both business and law.

MBA/MS Length of program: Minimum: 28 months. Degree requirements: 131 credits including 57 elective credits. Separate applications must be submitted to business and engineering. MS is in manufacturing systems engineering.

PLACEMENT

In 1993-94, 200 organizations participated in on-campus recruiting; 8,000 on-campus interviews were conducted. Placement services include alumni network, career counseling/planning, career fairs, career library, career placement, electronic job bank, job interviews, off-site recruiting, resume preparation, and resume referral to employers. Of 1994 graduates, 96% were employed within three months of graduation, the average starting salary was $83,688, the range was $40,000-$165,000.

Jobs by Employer Type Manufacturing 20%; service 62%; nonprofit 1%; other 17%.

Jobs by Functional Area Marketing/sales 16%; finance 24%; operations 3%; management 5%; strategic planning 3%; consulting 30%; other 19%.

Program Contact: MBA Admissions, Stanford University, Graduate School of Business, Stanford, CA 94305-9991. (415) 723-2766; Fax: (415) 725-7831.

United States International University

College of Business Administration

San Diego, California

OVERVIEW

United States International University is an independent nonprofit coed institution. Part of International University (other campuses in Nairobi and Mexico City). Founded 1952. Setting: 200-acre suburban campus. Total institutional enrollment: 2,520. Program was first offered in 1972.

MBA HIGHLIGHTS

Entrance Difficulty*
Mean GMAT: 490
Mean GPA: 3.2

Cost $$
Tuition: $2,400/quarter
Room & Board: $4,225

Enrollment Profile
Full-time: 165
Part-time: 37
Total: 202
Average Age: 30

Work Exp: 80%
International: 42%
Women: 45%
Minorities: 15%

Average Class Size: 19

ACADEMICS

Length of Program Minimum: 12 months. Maximum: 4 years.

Calendar Quarters.

Full-time Classes Main campus, Mexico City, Mexico, Nairobi, Kenya; evening, weekends, summer.

Part-time Classes Main campus, Mexico City, Mexico, Nairobi, Kenya; evening, weekends, summer.

Degree Requirements 60 credits including 4-12 elective credits.

Required Courses Business values/ethics/social strategy, corporate strategy, cross cultural management, human resources management, introduction to competitive management, introduction to strategic management, leadership and management of change, managerial economics, total quality management. Courses may be waived through: previous course work.

Curricular Focus International business, organizational development and change management, strategic analysis and planning.

Concentrations Finance, international business, management, marketing, organizational behavior, strategic management.

Faculty Full-time: 16, 100% with doctorates; part-time: 6, 90% with doctorates.

Teaching Methodology Case study: 5%, faculty seminars: 5%, lecture: 60%, research: 5%, seminars by members of the business community: 5%, student presentations: 5%, team projects: 15%.

Special Opportunities International exchange in Kenya, Mexico. Internships include financial services, manufacturing, import/export, hospitality/tourism, and government.

STUDENT STATISTICS

Geographic Representation State residents 35%. By region: West 30%; Midwest 12%; Northeast 8%; South 8%. International 42%.

Undergraduate Majors Business 50%; education 5%; engineering/technology 5%; humanities 10%; nursing 5%; science/mathematics 5%; social sciences 15%; other 5%.

Other Background Graduate degrees in other disciplines: 10%. Work experience: On average, students have 5 years of work experience on entrance to the program.

FACILITIES

Information Resources Main library with 202,701 bound volumes, 28,733 titles on microform, 1,207 periodical subscriptions, 1,220 records/tapes/CDs, 10 CD-ROMs.

Housing 25% of students in program live in college-owned or -operated housing.

Technology Computers are used moderately in course work. 50 computer terminals/PCs are available for use by students in program; they are located in computer labs. Students in the program are not required to have their own PC. $200 are budgeted per student for computer support.

Computer Resources/On-line Services

Training	Yes	CompuServe	No
Internet	Yes	Dun's	Yes $
E-Mail	Yes	Dow Jones	Yes $
Multimedia Center	Yes	Dialog	Yes $
LEXIS/NEXIS	No	Bloomberg	No

ADMISSION

Acceptance 1994-95 Of those applying, 65% were accepted.

Entrance Requirements Bachelor's degree, GMAT score of 350, minimum 2.75 GPA. Core courses waived through: previous course work.

Application Requirements Written essay, application form, copies of transcript, personal statement, 2 letters of recommendation.

Application Deadlines 8/1 for fall, 11/1 for winter, 3/1 for spring, 5/1 for summer.

FINANCIALS

Costs for 1994-95 Tuition: Full-time: $2,400/quarter. Fees: Full-time: $85/quarter. Average room and board costs are $4,225 per academic year (on-campus) and $6,000 per academic year (off-campus).

Financial Aid In 1994-95, 30% of candidates received some institutionally administered aid in the form of grants, loans, assistantships, work-study. Total awards ranged from $700-$6,000. Financial aid is available to part-time students. Application deadlines: 3/1 for fall, 11/1 for winter, 2/1 for spring. Contact: Ms. Tina Muncada, Financial Aid Administrator, 10455 Pomerado Road, San Diego, CA 92131-1799. (619) 635-4700.

INTERNATIONAL STUDENTS

Demographics 42% of students enrolled in the program are international; Asia 25%, Europe 25%, Africa 20%, Central America 10%, South America 10%, Australia 5%, other 5%.

Services and Facilities International student center, visa services, language tutoring, ESL courses, special assistance for nonnative speakers of English, counseling/support services.

Applying TOEFL required, minimum score of 550; proof of health; proof of adequate funds. Financial aid is available to international students. Applications are processed on a rolling basis. Admission application deadlines: 8/1 for fall, 11/1 for winter, 3/1 for spring, 5/1 for summer. Contact: Dr. Bijan Massrour, Director, International Students Office, 10455 Pomerado Road, San Diego, CA 92131-1799. (619) 635-4672.

ALTERNATE MBA PROGRAM

International MBA Length of program: Minimum: 12 months. Maximum: 4 years. Degree requirements: 60 credits including 4-12 elective credits.

PLACEMENT

In 1993-94, 15 organizations participated in on-campus recruiting; 40 on-campus interviews were conducted. Placement services include alumni network, career counseling/planning, career library, career placement, job interviews, resume preparation, and resume referral to employers. Of 1994 graduates, 85% were employed within three months of graduation, the average starting salary was $30,000, the range was $16,000-$48,000.

Jobs by Employer Type Manufacturing 20%; service 30%; government 20%; consulting 10%; nonprofit 20%.

Jobs by Functional Area Marketing/sales 20%; finance 20%; operations 10%; management 20%; strategic planning 20%; technical management 10%.

Program Contact: Dr. Mink Stavenga, Dean, United States International University, 10455 Pomerado Road, San Diego, CA 92131-1799. (619) 635-4615; Fax: (619) 635-4528.

University of California, Berkeley

Haas School of Business

Berkeley, California

OVERVIEW
The University of California, Berkeley is a state-supported coed institution. Part of University of California System. Founded 1868. Setting: 1,232-acre urban campus with easy access to San Francisco. Total institutional enrollment: 30,000. Program was first offered in 1944. AACSB-accredited.

MBA HIGHLIGHTS

Entrance Difficulty*****

Cost $$
Tuition: $6,662
(Nonresident: $7,700)
Room & Board: $8,100

Enrollment Profile
Full-time: 480
Part-time: 250
Total: 730
Average Age: 27

Work Exp: 99%
International: 29%
Women: 26%
Minorities: 19%

Average Class Size: 40

ACADEMICS
Length of Program Minimum: 21 months. Maximum: 7 years.
Calendar Semesters.
Full-time Classes Main campus; day.
Part-time Classes Main campus; evening.
Degree Requirements 52 credits including 24 elective credits.
Required Courses Business and public policy, communications, finance, financial accounting, information technology management, macroeconomics, managerial accounting, marketing, microeconomics, operations, organizational behavior, quantitative methods, statistics. Courses may be waived through examination.
Curricular Focus Entrepreneurship, international business, technology management.
Concentrations Accounting, economics, entrepreneurship, finance, human resources management, international business, management information systems, marketing, operations management, organizational behavior, public policy, quantitative analysis, real estate, strategic management, technology management, nonprofit management.
Faculty Full-time: 80, 100% with doctorates; part-time: 40, 80% with doctorates.
Teaching Methodology Case study: 50%, lecture: 25%, seminars by members of the business community: 5%, student presentations: 10%, team projects: 10%.
Special Opportunities International exchange in Austria, Belgium, Brazil, France, Germany, Hong Kong, Italy, Japan, Mexico, Netherlands, Spain, Sweden, Switzerland. Internship program available.

STUDENT STATISTICS
Geographic Representation By region: West 36%; Northeast 26%; South 5%; Midwest 4%. International 29%.

Undergraduate Majors Business 36%; engineering/technology 28%; humanities 11%; science/mathematics 7%; social sciences 13%; other 5%.
Other Background Graduate degrees in other disciplines: 19%. Work experience: On average, students have 4 years of work experience on entrance to the program.

FACILITIES
Information Resources Main library with 8 million bound volumes, 3 million titles on microform, 89,750 periodical subscriptions, 61,900 records/tapes/CDs. Business collection in Business and Economics Library includes 125,000 bound volumes, 2,700 periodical subscriptions, 10 CD-ROMs.
Housing 5% of students in program live in college-owned or -operated housing.
Technology Computers are used heavily in course work. 80 computer terminals/PCs, linked by a campus-wide computer network, are available for use by students in program; they are located in student rooms, the student center, classrooms, learning resource center, the library, the computer center, computer labs, the research center. Students in the program are required to have their own PC. $600 are budgeted per student for computer support.

Computer Resources/On-line Services

Training	Yes	CompuServe	No
Internet	Yes	Dun's	No
E-Mail	Yes	Dow Jones	Yes
Videoconference Center	Yes	Dialog	Yes $
Multimedia Center	Yes	Bloomberg	No
LEXIS/NEXIS	Yes		

Other on-line services: OCLC, RLIN.

ADMISSION
Acceptance 1994-95 2,069 applied for admission; 20% were accepted.
Entrance Requirements Bachelor's degree, entry level calculus course, GMAT score, minimum 3.0 GPA. Core courses waived through: exams.
Application Requirements Written essay, application form, copies of transcript, personal statement, 2 letters of recommendation.
Application Deadline 3/28 for fall.

FINANCIALS
Costs for 1994-95 Tuition: Full-time: $7,700 for nonresidents. Fees: Full-time: $6,662 for state residents, $6,662 for nonresidents. Average room and board costs are $8,100 per academic year (on-campus) and $9,000 per academic year (off-campus).
Financial Aid In 1994-95, candidates received some institutionally administered aid in the form of grants, scholarships, loans, fellowships, assistantships, work-study. Total awards ranged from $500-$20,000. Financial aid is available to part-time students. Application deadlines: 3/2 for fall, 9/1 for spring. Contact: Graduate Financial Aid Office, 201 Sproul Hall, Berkeley, CA 94720. (510) 642-0485.

INTERNATIONAL STUDENTS
Demographics 29% of students enrolled in the program are international; Asia 44%, Europe 34%, South America 7%, Australia 2%, Central America 2%, Africa 1%, other 10%.
Services and Facilities International student housing; international student center, visa services, language tutoring, ESL courses, special assistance for nonnative speakers of English, counseling/support services.
Applying TOEFL required, minimum score of 570; proof of adequate funds. Financial aid is not available to international students. Admission application deadline: 2/15 for fall. Contact: Services for International Students and Scholars, 2299 Piedmont Avenue, Berkeley, CA 91720. (510) 642-2818.

ALTERNATE MBA PROGRAMS
MBA/JD Length of program: Minimum: 45 months. Maximum: 7 years. Degree requirements: 120 credits including 16 elective credits. Separate applications must be submitted to both law and business.
MBA/MA Length of program: Minimum: 33 months. Degree requirements: 78 credits including 24 elective credits. Must be admitted to both the Group in Asian Studies as well as the Haas School of Business and have 2 years of an Asian language.
MBA/MPH Length of program: Minimum: 33 months. Maximum: 7 years. Degree requirements: 84 credits including 25 elective credits. Must be admitted to the concurrent degree program.

PLACEMENT
In 1993-94, 150 organizations participated in on-campus recruiting; 3,000 on-campus interviews were conducted. Placement services include

alumni network, career counseling/planning, career fairs, career library, career placement, electronic job bank, job interviews, resume preparation, and resume referral to employers. Of 1994 graduates, 95% were employed within three months of graduation, the average starting salary was $62,608, the range was $40,000-$140,000.

Jobs by Employer Type Manufacturing 8%; service 63%; consulting 16%; nonprofit 7%; real estate 6%.

Jobs by Functional Area Marketing/sales 18%; finance 34%; management 14%; strategic planning 5%; consulting 24%; real estate 5%.

Program Contact: Ms. Fran Hill, Director of MBA Admissions, University of California, Berkeley, MBA Program #1902, Berkeley, CA 94720. (510) 642-0915; Fax: (510) 643-6659; Internet Address: mbaadms@ haas.berkeley.edu.

University of California, Davis

Graduate School of Management

Davis, California

OVERVIEW
The University of California, Davis is a state-supported coed institution. Part of University of California System. Founded 1905. Setting: 5,974-acre small-town campus with easy access to San Francisco. Total institutional enrollment: 23,000. Program was first offered in 1981. AACSB-accredited.

MBA HIGHLIGHTS

Entrance Difficulty***
Mean GMAT: 640
Mean GPA: 3.2

Cost $$
Tuition: $2,206/quarter
(Nonresident: $2,566/quarter)
Room & Board: N/R

Enrollment Profile
Full-time: 121
Part-time: 4
Total: 125
Average Age: 27

Work Exp: 86%
International: 6%
Women: 28%
Minorities: 10%

Class Size: 20 - 55

ACADEMICS
Length of Program Minimum: 24 months. Maximum: 3 years.
Calendar Quarters.
Full-time Classes Main campus; day, evening, early morning.
Degree Requirements 72 credits including 33 elective credits. Other: Minimum 3.0 GPA.
Required Courses Business, government, and the international economy, data analysis for managers, decision making and management science, financial accounting, financial theory and policy, forecasting and managerial research methods, management information services, management policy and strategy, managerial accounting, marketing management, markets and the firm, organizational structure and strategy, the individual and group dynamics.
Curricular Focus Problem solving and decision making, strategic analysis and planning.
Concentrations Accounting, finance, management, management information systems, marketing.
Faculty Full-time: 24, 96% with doctorates; part-time: 9, 22% with doctorates.
Teaching Methodology Case study: 20%, directed team projects: 15%, lecture: 65%.
Special Opportunities International exchange in Finland, Netherlands. Other: education abroad program.

STUDENT STATISTICS
Geographic Representation State residents 88%. By region: West 91%; Northeast 1%; Midwest 1%. International 6%.
Undergraduate Majors Business 12%; engineering/technology 12%; humanities 22%; science/mathematics 8%; social sciences 19%; other 27%.

Other Background Graduate degrees in other disciplines: 7%. Work experience: On average, students have 4 years of work experience on entrance to the program.

FACILITIES
Information Resources Main library with 2.7 million bound volumes, 3.3 million titles on microform, 49,098 periodical subscriptions, 13,882 records/tapes/CDs. Business collection includes 141,500 bound volumes, 3,020 periodical subscriptions.
Housing College housing available.
Technology Computers are used heavily in course work. 379 computer terminals/PCs, linked by a campus-wide computer network, are available for use by students in program; they are located in the library, computer labs. Students in the program are not required to have their own PC.

Computer Resources/On-line Services

Training	No	Dun's	Yes
E-Mail	Yes	Dow Jones	No
Multimedia Center	Yes	Dialog	No
LEXIS/NEXIS	No	Bloomberg	Yes
CompuServe	No		

Other on-line services: First Search.

ADMISSION
Acceptance 1994-95 252 applied for admission; 46% were accepted.
Entrance Requirements Bachelor's degree, GMAT score. Core courses waived through: previous course work.
Application Requirements Written essay, application form, copies of transcript, resume/curriculum vitae.
Application Deadlines 4/1 for fall. Applications are processed on a rolling basis.

FINANCIALS
Costs for 1994-95 Tuition: Full-time: $2,566/quarter for nonresidents. Fees: Full-time: $2,206/quarter for state residents, $2,206/quarter for nonresidents.
Financial Aid In 1994-95, 56% of candidates received some institutionally administered aid in the form of grants, loans, fellowships, assistantships. Financial aid is available to part-time students. Application deadlines: 2/28 for fall, 2/28 for spring. Applications are processed on a rolling basis. Contact: Ms. Cathy Penn, Financial Aid Counselor, Graduate and Professional Students, Graduate Financial Aid Office, 207 Voorhies, Davis, CA 95616. (916) 752-9296.

INTERNATIONAL STUDENTS
Demographics 6% of students enrolled in the program are international; Asia 50%, Europe 25%, South America 25%.
Services and Facilities International student office.
Applying TOEFL required, minimum score of 600; proof of health; proof of adequate funds. Financial aid is not available to international students. Admission application deadline: 4/1 for fall. Contact: Ms. Kath-Ann Gerhardt, Associate Director, Services for International Students and Scholars, 300 South Hall, Davis, CA 95616. (916) 752-1011.

ALTERNATE MBA PROGRAMS
MBA/JD Length of program: Minimum: 48 months. Maximum: 5 years. Degree requirements: 142.5 credits including 70.5 elective credits. Minimum 3.0 GPA.
MBA/MS Length of program: Minimum: 24 months. Maximum: 3 years. Degree requirements: 59 credits.
MBA/M Eng

PLACEMENT
In 1993-94, 33 organizations participated in on-campus recruiting; 274 on-campus interviews were conducted. Placement services include alumni network, career counseling/planning, career fairs, career library, job interviews, job search course, resume preparation, and resume referral to employers. Of 1994 graduates, 76% were employed within three months of graduation, the average starting salary was $46,000, the range was $28,000-$100,000.
Jobs by Employer Type Manufacturing 28%; service 10%; consulting 33%; nonprofit 8%; accounting/finance 21%.
Jobs by Functional Area Marketing/sales 14%; finance 17%; operations 17%; management 17%; strategic planning 11%; technical management 24%.

Program Contact: Mr. Donald Blodger, Director of Student Services, University of California, Davis, Davis, CA 95616. (916) 752-7661; Fax: (916) 752-2924; Internet Address: dablodger@ucdavis.edu.
See full description on page 860.

University of California, Irvine

Graduate School of Management

Irvine, California

OVERVIEW
The University of California, Irvine is a state-supported coed institution. Part of University of California System. Founded 1965. Setting: 1,489-acre suburban campus with easy access to Los Angeles. Total institutional enrollment: 16,000. Program was first offered in 1981. AACSB-accredited.

MBA HIGHLIGHTS

Entrance Difficulty**
Mean GMAT: 590
Mean GPA: 3.2

Cost $$
Tuition: $6,807
(Nonresident: $7,699)
Room & Board: $6,723

Enrollment Profile
Full-time: 185	Work Exp: 91%
Part-time: 280	International: 75%
Total: 465	Women: 36%
Average Age: 28	Minorities: 10%

Average Class Size: 18

ACADEMICS
Length of Program Minimum: 21 months. Maximum: 3 years.

Calendar Quarters.

Full-time Classes Main campus; day, evening, summer.

Degree Requirements 92 credits including 36 elective credits. Other: International case study.

Required Courses Accounting, decision sciences, finance, government and public policy, macroeconomics, management information systems, marketing, microeconomics, operation management, organizational behavior, strategy. Courses may be waived through: previous course work, work experience.

Curricular Focus General management, teamwork.

Concentrations Accounting, finance, health services, international business, management, management information systems, marketing, operations management, organizational behavior, public policy, quantitative analysis, real estate, strategic management.

Faculty Full-time: 38, 100% with doctorates; part-time: 35.

Teaching Methodology Case study: 35%, field studies case study: 2%, lecture: 10%, practicum: 4%, research: 4%, seminars by members of the business community: 5%, student presentations: 5%, team projects: 35%.

Special Opportunities International exchange in Austria, Belgium, Finland, France, Hong Kong, Hungary, Italy, Mexico, People's Republic of China. Internship program available.

STUDENT STATISTICS
Geographic Representation State residents 20%. By region: West 75%; Northeast 5%. International 75%.

Undergraduate Majors Business 27%; engineering/technology 18%; humanities 5%; nursing 4%; science/mathematics 15%; social sciences 9%; other 20%.

Other Background Graduate degrees in other disciplines: 5%. Work experience: On average, students have 4 years of work experience on entrance to the program.

FACILITIES
Information Resources Main library with 1.5 million bound volumes, 1.8 million titles on microform, 19,500 periodical subscriptions, 11,800 records/tapes/CDs.

Housing 30% of students in program live in college-owned or -operated housing.

Technology Computers are used heavily in course work. 40 computer terminals/PCs, linked by a campus-wide computer network, are available for use by students in program; they are located in computer labs. Students in the program are not required to have their own PC. $1,222 are budgeted per student for computer support.

Computer Resources/On-line Services
Training	Yes	Dun's	No
Internet	Yes	Dow Jones	No
E-Mail	Yes	Dialog	No
LEXIS/NEXIS	Yes	Bloomberg	No
CompuServe	No		

ADMISSION
Acceptance 1994-95 Of those applying, 35% were accepted.

Entrance Requirements Bachelor's degree, GMAT score, minimum 3.0 GPA, minimum 2 years of work experience. Core courses waived through: previous course work, work experience.

Application Requirements Written essay, application form, copies of transcript, personal statement, 3 letters of recommendation.

Application Deadline 5/1 for fall. Application discs available.

FINANCIALS
Costs for 1994-95 Tuition: Full-time: $7,699 for nonresidents. Fees: Full-time: $6,807 for state residents, $6,807 for nonresidents. Average room and board costs are $6,723 per academic year (on-campus) and $8,037 per academic year (off-campus).

Financial Aid In 1994-95, 45% of candidates received some institutionally administered aid in the form of grants, scholarships, loans, fellowships. Total awards ranged from $250-$6,000. Financial aid is available to part-time students. Application deadline: 5/1 for fall. Contact: Mr. Marty Bell, Assistant Director, Graduate School of Management, Irvine, CA 92717-3125. (714) 824-7967.

INTERNATIONAL STUDENTS
Demographics 75% of students enrolled in the program are international; Asia 97%, Europe 2%, Africa 1%.

Services and Facilities International student office, international student center, visa services, language tutoring, ESL courses, special assistance for nonnative speakers of English, counseling/support services.

Applying TOEFL required, minimum score of 600; proof of health; proof of adequate funds. Financial aid is not available to international students. Admission application deadline: 5/1 for fall. Contact: Ms. Julie Sully, Graduate School of Management, Irvine, CA 92717-3125. (714) 824-6437.

PLACEMENT
In 1993-94, 32 organizations participated in on-campus recruiting; 336 on-campus interviews were conducted. Placement services include alumni network, career counseling/planning, career fairs, career library, career placement, electronic job bank, job interviews, resume preparation, and resume referral to employers. Of 1994 graduates, 70% were employed within three months of graduation, the average starting salary was $44,531, the range was $30,000-$77,000.

Jobs by Employer Type Manufacturing 47%; service 31%; government 2%; consulting 6%; other 13%.

Jobs by Functional Area Marketing/sales 16%; finance 23%; operations 4%; management 21%; strategic planning 2%; technical management 4%; other 30%.

Program Contact: Ms. Victoria Lester, Administrative Assistant, University of California, Irvine, Graduate School of Management, Irvine, CA 92717-1425. (714) 824-4949; Fax: (714) 824-2235.
See full description on page 862.

University of California, Los Angeles

The John E. Anderson Graduate School of Management

Los Angeles, California

OVERVIEW
The University of California, Los Angeles is a state-supported coed institution. Part of University of California System. Founded 1919. Setting: 419-acre suburban campus. Total institutional enrollment: 34,447. Program was first offered in 1935. AACSB-accredited.

MBA HIGHLIGHTS

Entrance Difficulty***
Mean GMAT: 640
Mean GPA: 3.5

Cost $$
Tuition: $6,486
(Nonresident: $14,185)
Room & Board: $13,700 (off-campus)

Enrollment Profile
Full-time: 612   Work Exp: 99%
Part-time: 305   International: 21%
Total: 917   Women: 27%
Average Age: 27   Minorities: 19%

Average Class Size: 60

ACADEMICS
Length of Program Minimum: 24 months.
Calendar Quarters.
Full-time Classes Main campus; day.
Part-time Classes Main campus.
Degree Requirements 96 units including 44 elective units.
Required Courses Data analysis, statistics, and decision making, elements of marketing, financial accounting, information systems, management of organizations, management policy, managerial economics, managerial finance, managerial model building, managing human resources in organization, operations and technology management, the global economy. Courses may be waived through: previous course work, examination.
Curricular Focus General management, leadership, teamwork.
Concentrations Accounting, arts administration, economics, entrepreneurship, finance, human resources management, international business, management, management information systems, marketing, operations management, organizational behavior, quantitative analysis, real estate, strategic management.
Faculty Full-time: 99, 78% with doctorates; part-time: 52.
Special Opportunities International exchange in Japan, Mexico. Internship program available.

STUDENT STATISTICS
Geographic Representation By region: West 56%; Northeast 16%; Midwest 7%; South 2%. International 21%.
Undergraduate Majors Business 18%; engineering/technology 23%; humanities 11%; science/mathematics 6%; social sciences 37%; other 5%.
Other Background Graduate degrees in other disciplines: 13%. Work experience: On average, students have 4 years of work experience on entrance to the program.

FACILITIES
Information Resources Main library with 6.3 million bound volumes, 5.8 million titles on microform, 96,003 periodical subscriptions, 155,087 records/tapes/CDs, 299 CD-ROMs. Business collection in Anderson Management Library includes 146,670 bound volumes, 2,822 periodical subscriptions, 5 CD-ROMs.
Housing 1% of students in program live in college-owned or -operated housing.
Technology Computers are used moderately in course work. 100 computer terminals/PCs, linked by a campus-wide computer network, are available for use by students in program; they are located in computer labs. Students in the program are not required to have their own PC. $800 are budgeted per student for computer support.

Computer Resources/On-line Services

Training	Yes	Dun's	No
Internet	Yes	Dow Jones	Yes
E-Mail	Yes	Dialog	Yes
LEXIS/NEXIS	Yes	Bloomberg	No
CompuServe	No		

ADMISSION
Acceptance 1994-95 2,776 applied for admission; 23% were accepted.
Entrance Requirements Bachelor's degree, GMAT score, minimum 3.5 GPA, minimum 4 years of work experience. Core courses waived through: previous course work, exams.
Application Requirements Written essay, application form, copies of transcript, 2 letters of recommendation.
Application Deadline 3/1 for fall.

FINANCIALS
Costs for 1994-95 Tuition: Full-time: $6,486 for state residents, $14,185 for nonresidents. Fees: Full-time: $425 for state residents, $425 for nonresidents. Average room and board costs are $13,700 per academic year (off-campus).
Financial Aid In 1994-95, candidates received some institutionally administered aid in the form of loans, fellowships. Total awards ranged from $500-$15,000. Application deadline: 3/2 for fall. Applications are processed on a rolling basis. Contact: Ms. Marta Peterson-Klock, Director of Fellowships and Financial Aid, 405 Hilgard Avenue, Los Angeles, CA 90024. (310) 825-6944.

INTERNATIONAL STUDENTS
Demographics 21% of students enrolled in the program are international; Asia 50%, Europe 18%, South America 13%, Central America 2%, Australia 1%, Other 15%.
Services and Facilities International student center, language tutoring, counseling/support services.
Applying TOEFL required, minimum score of 600; proof of adequate funds. Financial aid is not available to international students. Admission application deadline: 2/27 for fall. Contact: Mr. Randy Rutledge, International Student Adviser, 405 Hilgard Avenue, Los Angeles, CA 90024. (310) 825-6944.

ALTERNATE MBA PROGRAMS
Executive MBA (EMBA) Length of program: Minimum: 24 months. Degree requirements: 68 units including 2 elective units.
MBA/JD Length of program: Minimum: 48 months. Degree requirements: 76 semester units in business, 73 semester units in law; 120 weeks of residence credit.
MBA/MA Length of program: Minimum: 36 months. Degree requirements: 36 courses. MA is in Latin American studies or urban planning.
MBA/MLS Length of program: Minimum: 36 months. Degree requirements: 132 units.
MBA/MPH Length of program: Minimum: 36 months. Degree requirements: 132 units.
MBA/MS Length of program: Minimum: 36 months. Degree requirements: 18 courses in business; 10 courses in computer science; 2 quarter field study. MS is in computer science.
MBA/MN Length of program: Minimum: 36 months. Degree requirements: 20 courses in business, 10 courses in nursing; School of Nursing comprehensive exam.

PLACEMENT
In 1993-94, 125 organizations participated in on-campus recruiting. Placement services include alumni network, career counseling/planning, career fairs, career library, career placement, electronic job bank, job interviews, resume preparation, and resume referral to employers. Of 1994 graduates, 85% were employed within three months of graduation, the average starting salary was $60,500.

Program Contact: Ms. Linda Baldwin, Director of Admissions, University of California, Los Angeles, 405 Hilgard Avenue, Los Angeles, CA 90024. (310) 825-6944; Fax: (310) 825-8582.
See full description on page 864.

University of California, Riverside

The A. Gary Anderson Graduate School of Management

Riverside, California

OVERVIEW
The University of California, Riverside is a state-supported coed institution. Part of University of California System. Founded 1954. Setting: 1,200-acre urban campus with easy access to Los Angeles. Total institutional enrollment: 8,591. Program was first offered in 1983.

MBA HIGHLIGHTS

Entrance Difficulty**
Mean GMAT: 560
Mean GPA: 3.38

Cost $
Tuition: $1,936/quarter
(Nonresident: $2,566/quarter)
Room & Board: $9,000

Enrollment Profile

Full-time: 90	Work Exp: 60%
Part-time: 18	International: 35%
Total: 108	Women: 33%
Average Age: 26	Minorities: 27%

Average Class Size: 17

ACADEMICS

Length of Program Minimum: 18 months. Maximum: 5 years.

Calendar Quarters.

Full-time Classes Main campus; day, evening, summer.

Part-time Classes Main campus; day, evening, summer.

Degree Requirements 92 credits including 36 elective credits. Other: Workshop in management communications; case analysis or thesis.

Required Courses Business policy and strategy, business, government, and society, computer systems for management, cost and management accounting, financial management, human resources management, introduction to management science, management synthesis, managerial economics, managing behavior in organizations, marketing management, production and operations management, statistics for management.

Curricular Focus Managing through information, problem solving and decision making, teamwork.

Concentrations Accounting, finance, human resources management, international business, management, management information systems, marketing, operations management, organizational behavior, quantitative analysis.

Faculty Full-time: 21, 100% with doctorates; part-time: 6, 67% with doctorates.

Teaching Methodology Case study: 15%, lecture: 40%, research: 15%, seminars by members of the business community: 5%, student presentations: 10%, team projects: 15%.

Special Opportunities International exchange program available. Internships include finance in investment/banking, accounting in consulting, marketing and advertising in healthcare public relations, human resources, and management information systems.

STUDENT STATISTICS

Geographic Representation State residents 50%. By region: West 47%; Northeast 8%; Midwest 6%; South 4%. International 35%.

Undergraduate Majors Business 40%; engineering/technology 13%; humanities 6%; science/mathematics 15%; social sciences 26%.

Other Background Graduate degrees in other disciplines: 10%. Work experience: On average, students have 3 years of work experience on entrance to the program.

FACILITIES

Information Resources Main library with 1.7 million bound volumes, 1.4 million titles on microform, 13,621 periodical subscriptions, 13,040 records/tapes/CDs. Business collection includes 108,000 bound volumes, 900 periodical subscriptions, 2 CD-ROMs.

Housing 40% of students in program live in college-owned or -operated housing.

Technology Computers are used heavily in course work. 162 computer terminals/PCs, linked by a campus-wide computer network, are available for use by students in program; they are located in dormitories, classrooms, learning resource center, the library, the computer center, computer labs. Students in the program are not required to have their own PC. $1,700 are budgeted per student for computer support.

Computer Resources/On-line Services

Training	Yes	CompuServe	No
Internet	Yes	Dun's	No
E-Mail	Yes	Dow Jones	No
Videoconference Center	Yes	Dialog	Yes
Multimedia Center	Yes	Bloomberg	No
LEXIS/NEXIS	No		

ADMISSION

Acceptance 1994-95 312 applied for admission; 48% were accepted.

Entrance Requirements Bachelor's degree, GMAT score. Core courses waived through: previous course work.

Application Requirements Application form, copies of transcript, personal statement, 2 letters of recommendation.

Application Deadlines 5/1 for fall, 9/1 for winter, 12/1 for spring. Applications are processed on a rolling basis.

FINANCIALS

Costs for 1994-95 Tuition: Full-time: $2,566/quarter for nonresidents. Fees: Full-time: $1,936/quarter for state residents, $1,936/quarter for nonresidents. Average room and board costs are $9,000 per academic year (on-campus) and $9,000 per academic year (off-campus).

Financial Aid In 1994-95, candidates received some institutionally administered aid in the form of grants, loans, fellowships, assistantships. Total awards ranged from $1,000-$15,000. Financial aid is available to part-time students. Application deadlines: 7/1 for fall, 6/1 for spring. Applications are processed on a rolling basis. Contact: Dr. Charlotte Weber, Associate Dean, A. Gary Anderson Graduate School of Management, 900 University Avenue, Riverside, CA 92521-0102. (909) 787-4551.

INTERNATIONAL STUDENTS

Demographics 35% of students enrolled in the program are international.

Services and Facilities International student office, international student center, visa services, language tutoring, ESL courses, special assistance for nonnative speakers of English, counseling/support services.

Applying TOEFL required, minimum score of 550; proof of adequate funds. Financial aid is available to international students. Financial aid application deadlines: 2/1 for fall, 7/1 for winter, 10/1 for spring. Applications are processed on a rolling basis. Admission application deadlines: 2/1 for fall, 7/1 for winter, 10/1 for spring. Applications are processed on a rolling basis. Contact: Ms. Judy Mitchell, International Student Adviser, 900 University Avenue, Riverside, CA 92521-0102. (909) 787-4113.

PLACEMENT

In 1993-94, 32 organizations participated in on-campus recruiting; 128 on-campus interviews were conducted. Placement services include alumni network, career counseling/planning, career fairs, career library, career placement, electronic job bank, job interviews, job search course, resume preparation, and resume referral to employers. Of 1994 graduates, 80% were employed within three months of graduation, the average starting salary was $42,200, the range was $31,000-$56,000.

Jobs by Employer Type Government 5%; consulting 5%; nonprofit 5%; educational institutions 5%; business and industry 80%.

Jobs by Functional Area Marketing/sales 33%; finance 14%; operations 5%; management 33%; technical management 10%; human resources 5%.

Program Contact: Dr. Charlotte Weber, Associate Dean, A. Gary Anderson Graduate School of Management, University of California, Riverside, 900 University Avenue, Riverside, CA 92521-0102. (909) 787-4551; Fax: (909) 787-3970; Internet Address: agsmmba@ucrac1.ucr.edu.

See full description on page 866.

University of Judaism

David Leiber School of Graduate Studies

Los Angeles, California

OVERVIEW

The University of Judaism is an independent Jewish comprehensive coed institution. Founded 1947. Setting: 28-acre suburban campus. Total institutional enrollment: 202.

MBA HIGHLIGHTS

Entrance Difficulty**

Cost $$
Tuition: $10,560
Room & Board: N/R

Enrollment Profile
Full-time: N/R
Part-time: N/R
Total: 30
Average Age: N/R

Work Exp. N/R
International: 4%
Women: 60%
Minorities: 10%

Average Class Size: 10

ACADEMICS
Length of Program Minimum: 20 months.
Calendar Semesters.
Full-time Classes Main campus; evening, summer.
Part-time Classes Main campus; evening, summer.
Degree Requirements 52 units.
Curricular Focus Nonprofit management, problem solving and decision making, teamwork.
Concentrations Financial resources and planning, marketing.
Teaching Methodology Case study: 30%, lecture: 30%, research: 10%, student presentations: 10%, team projects: 20%.

STUDENT STATISTICS
Geographic Representation State residents 70%. International 4%.

FACILITIES
Information Resources Main library with 105,000 bound volumes, 2,000 titles on microform, 400 periodical subscriptions.

ADMISSION
Entrance Requirements Bachelor's degree, prerequisite courses required for applicants with non-business degree, minimum 3.0 GPA.
Application Requirements Written essay, interview, application form, copies of transcript, personal statement, 2 letters of recommendation.
Application Deadlines 3/31 for fall, 11/1 for spring. Applications are processed on a rolling basis.

FINANCIALS
Costs for 1994-95 Tuition: Full-time: $10,560. Fees: Full-time: $400.
Financial Aid Application deadline: 3/2 for fall. Applications are processed on a rolling basis. Contact: Ms. Robin Bailey-Chen, Director, 15600 Mulholland Drive, Los Angeles, CA 90077-1599. (310) 476-9777 Ext. 252.

INTERNATIONAL STUDENTS
Demographics 4% of students enrolled in the program are international.
Applying TOEFL required, minimum score of 550; proof of health. Financial aid is available to international students. Financial aid application deadlines: 3/31 for fall, 11/1 for spring. Applications are processed on a rolling basis. Admission application deadlines: 3/31 for fall, 11/1 for spring. Applications are processed on a rolling basis.

Program Contact: Ms. Tamara Greenebaum, Dean of Admissions and Enrollment Management, University of Judaism, 15600 Mulholland Drive, Los Angeles, CA 90077-1599. (310) 476-9777 Ext. 261; Fax: (310) 471-1278.

University of La Verne

School of Business and Economics

La Verne, California

OVERVIEW
The University of La Verne is an independent nonprofit coed institution. Founded 1891. Setting: 26-acre suburban campus with easy access to Los Angeles. Total institutional enrollment: 1,113. Program was first offered in 1973.

MBA HIGHLIGHTS
Entrance Difficulty*
Mean GMAT: 520
Mean GPA: N/R

Cost $
Tuition: $305/semester hour
Room & Board: N/R

Enrollment Profile
Full-time: N/R
Part-time: N/R
Total: 400
Average Age: N/R

Work Exp: N/R
International: 19%
Women: 53%
Minorities: 32%

Average Class Size: 17

ACADEMICS
Length of Program Minimum: 24 months.
Calendar 4-1-4.
Part-time Classes Main campus; evening, weekends, summer.
Degree Requirements 36 credits including 9 elective credits.
Required Courses Applied statistics, economics of the firm, financial management, management accounting, management information systems, managing in a global economy, seminar in marketing management, seminar in organization theory.
Curricular Focus Economic and financial theory, general management, problem solving and decision making.
Concentrations Finance, health services, international business, management, operations management, organizational behavior.
Faculty Full-time: 8, 90% with doctorates; part-time: 11, 82% with doctorates.
Teaching Methodology Case study: 15%, lecture: 55%, research: 10%, student presentations: 10%, team projects: 10%.

STUDENT STATISTICS
Geographic Representation International 19%.

FACILITIES
Information Resources Main library with 180,000 bound volumes, 1,987 periodical subscriptions, 10 CD-ROMs.

ADMISSION
Acceptance 1994-95 120 applied for admission; 73% were accepted.
Entrance Requirements Bachelor's degree, minimum 3.0 GPA. Core courses waived through: previous course work.
Application Requirements Application form, copies of transcript, personal statement, 3 letters of recommendation.
Application Deadlines 5/1 for fall, 10/1 for spring. Applications are processed on a rolling basis.

FINANCIALS
Estimated Costs for 1995-96 Tuition: Full-time: $305/semester hour. Fees: Full-time: $30/semester.
Financial Aid In 1994-95, 50% of candidates received some institutionally administered aid in the form of loans. Application deadlines: 5/1 for fall, 10/1 for spring. Contact: Mrs. Donna Kent, Assistant Director, Financial Aid, 1950 Third Street, La Verne, CA 91750-4443. (909) 593-3511.

INTERNATIONAL STUDENTS
Demographics 19% of students enrolled in the program are international; Asia 65%, Europe 15%, Africa 5%, Central America 5%, South America 5%, other 5%.
Applying TOEFL required, minimum score of 550; proof of adequate funds. Financial aid is not available to international students. Admission application deadlines: 5/1 for fall, 10/1 for spring. Applications are processed on a rolling basis.

ALTERNATE MBA PROGRAM
MBA/MS Length of program: Minimum: 36 months. Part-time classes: Main campus; evening, weekends, summer. Degree requirements: 45 credits.

Program Contact: Mr. Kenneth Poertner, Chairman, Graduate Business Programs, University of La Verne, 1950 Third Street, La Verne, CA 91750-4443. (909) 593-3511; Fax: (909) 596-2537.

University of Redlands

Redlands, California

OVERVIEW

The University of Redlands is an independent nonprofit comprehensive coed institution. Founded 1907. Setting: 130-acre small-town campus with easy access to Los Angeles. Total institutional enrollment: 3,844.

MBA HIGHLIGHTS

Entrance Difficulty**

Cost $$
Tuition: $357/unit
Room & Board: N/R

Enrollment Profile

Full-time: N/R	Work Exp: N/R
Part-time: N/R	International: 0%
Total: 500	Women: 35%
Average Age: N/R	Minorities: N/R

Average Class Size: 15

ACADEMICS

Length of Program Minimum: 24 months.

Calendar 4-1-4.

Full-time Classes Main campus, Irvine, Woodland Hills, Torrance, distance learning option; evening.

Degree Requirements 45 units. Other: Research project practicum.

Curricular Focus Organizational development and change management, problem solving and decision making, teamwork.

Concentrations Human resources management, international business.

Teaching Methodology Case study: 20%, lecture: 20%, research: 20%, student presentations: 20%, team projects: 20%.

FACILITIES

Information Resources Main library with 225,000 bound volumes, 45,000 titles on microform, 1,623 periodical subscriptions, 7,779 records/tapes/CDs, 14 CD-ROMs.

Housing College housing not available.

ADMISSION

Entrance Requirements Bachelor's degree, minimum 3.0 GPA, minimum 5 years of work experience.

Application Requirements Written essay, application form, copies of transcript, personal statement.

Application Deadlines 9/1 for fall. Applications are processed on a rolling basis.

FINANCIALS

Costs for 1994-95 Tuition: Part-time evening: $357/unit. Fees: Part-time evening: $140.

Financial Aid Application deadline: 5/1 for fall. Applications are processed on a rolling basis. Contact: Ms. Sue Jarvis, Director, PO Box 3080, Redlands, CA 92373-0999. (909) 335-4047.

INTERNATIONAL STUDENTS

Applying Financial aid is not available to international students.

Program Contact: Alfred North Whitehead Center for Lifelong Learning Admissions Office, University of Redlands, PO Box 3080, Redlands, CA 92373-0999. (909) 335-4060.

University of San Diego

School of Business Administration

San Diego, California

OVERVIEW

The University of San Diego is an independent Roman Catholic coed institution. Founded 1949. Setting: 180-acre urban campus. Total institutional enrollment: 6,000. Program was first offered in 1975. AACSB-accredited.

MBA HIGHLIGHTS

Entrance Difficulty***
Mean GMAT: 547
Mean GPA: 3.21

Cost $$$
Tuition: $505/unit
Room & Board: N/R

Enrollment Profile

Full-time: N/R	Work Exp: N/R
Part-time: N/R	International: 30%
Total: 392	Women: 40%
Average Age: 26	Minorities: 10%

Average Class Size: 22

ACADEMICS

Length of Program May range up to 7 years.

Calendar Semesters.

Full-time Classes Main campus; day, evening, summer.

Part-time Classes Main campus; evening, summer.

Degree Requirements 30 credits. Other: Minimum of 30 units must be earned at University of San Diego; capstone course.

Required Courses Managerial accounting, managerial economics, managerial finance, managerial marketing, operations management, social and legal environment of business. Courses may be waived through: previous course work.

Curricular Focus Entrepreneurship, general management, international business

Concentrations Entrepreneurship, international business, management, management information systems, operations management, strategic management.

Teaching Methodology Case study: 40%, lecture: 50%, student presentations: 10%.

Special Opportunities International exchange in France, United Kingdom. Internship program available.

STUDENT STATISTICS

Geographic Representation State residents 45%. International 30%.

FACILITIES

Information Resources Main library with 488,079 bound volumes, 95,581 titles on microform, 7,749 periodical subscriptions, 3,800 records/tapes/CDs, 137 CD-ROMs.

Housing College housing available.

Technology Computer terminals/PCs, linked by a campus-wide computer network, are available for use by students in program; they are located in computer labs.

Computer Resources/On-line Services

Internet	Yes	E-Mail	Yes

ADMISSION

Entrance Requirements Bachelor's degree, GMAT score of 500, minimum 2.75 GPA. Core courses waived through: previous course work.

Application Requirements Application form, copies of transcript, personal statement, 3 letters of recommendation.

Application Deadlines 6/15 for fall, 11/15 for spring, 3/15 for summer.

FINANCIALS

Estimated Costs for 1995-96 Tuition: Full-time: $505/unit. Fees: Full-time: $15-$25/semester.

Financial Aid In 1994-95, candidates received some institutionally administered aid in the form of grants, scholarships, loans, fellowships. Application deadline: 5/1 for fall. Contact: Ms. Judith L. Logue, Director of Financial Aid, Office of Financial Aid, San Diego, CA 92110-2492. (619) 260-4514.

INTERNATIONAL STUDENTS

Demographics 30% of students enrolled in the program are international.

Services and Facilities International student center, counseling/support services.

Applying TOEFL required, minimum score of 600; proof of health; proof of adequate funds. Financial aid is not available to international students. Admission application deadlines: 6/15 for fall, 11/15 for spring. Contact: Ms. Yvette Fontain, Director, International Resources, 5998 Alcala Park, San Diego, CA 92110-2492. (619) 260-4678.

ALTERNATE MBA PROGRAMS

International MBA Length of program: Minimum: 15 months. Degree requirements: 60 credits including 12 elective credits. Capstone course, oral competency in a foreign language.
MBA/JD Length of program: Minimum: 60 months. Maximum: 7 years. Degree requirements: 115 credits.
MBA/MSN Length of program: Minimum: 15 months. Maximum: 6 years. Degree requirements: 78 credits.

PLACEMENT

In 1993-94, 3 organizations participated in on-campus recruiting. Placement services include alumni network, career counseling/planning, career fairs, career library, career placement, job interviews, and resume preparation.

Program Contact: Ms. Mary J. Tiernan, Director, Graduate Admissions, University of San Diego, 104 Founders Hall, 5998 Alcala Park, San Diego, CA 92110-2492. (619) 260-4524; Fax: (619) 260-2393.

University of San Francisco

McLaren School of Business, Graduate School of Management

San Francisco, California

OVERVIEW

The University of San Francisco is an independent Roman Catholic (Jesuit) coed institution. Founded 1855. Setting: 55-acre urban campus. Total institutional enrollment: 6,000. Program was first offered in 1968. AACSB-accredited.

MBA HIGHLIGHTS

Entrance Difficulty****
Mean GMAT: 540
Mean GPA: 3.25

Cost $$
Tuition: $552/unit
Room & Board: N/R

Enrollment Profile

Full-time: 325	Work Exp: 60%
Part-time: 235	International: 36%
Total: 560	Women: 39%
Average Age: 28	Minorities: 18%

Average Class Size: 18

ACADEMICS

Length of Program Minimum: 21 months. Maximum: 5 years.
Calendar Semesters.
Full-time Classes Main campus; day, evening, weekends, summer.
Part-time Classes Main campus; day, evening, weekends, summer.
Degree Requirements 48 units including 12 elective units.
Required Courses Communication strategy, data analysis, decision modeling, financial accounting, global management, information telecommunications technology, leadership dynamics, macroeconomics, managerial economics, managerial environment, managerial finance, marketing management, strategy and competitive advantage.
Curricular Focus Business issues and problems, international business, problem solving and decision making.
Concentrations Finance, international business, management, marketing, telecommunications management.
Faculty Full-time: 43, 95% with doctorates; part-time: 35, 40% with doctorates.
Teaching Methodology Case study: 10%, lecture: 65%, seminars by members of the business community: 5%, student presentations: 10%, team projects: 10%.
Special Opportunities International exchange in France, Spain, United Kingdom. Other: International study tours, student-initiated internship projects, Experiential learning community service projects.

STUDENT STATISTICS

Geographic Representation State residents 64%. By region: West 45%; Northeast 5%; South 5%; Midwest 5%. International 36%.

Undergraduate Majors Business 50%; education 2%; engineering/technology 10%; humanities 6%; nursing 2%; science/mathematics 10%; social sciences 10%; other 10%.
Other Background Graduate degrees in other disciplines: 1%. Work experience: On average, students have 5 years of work experience on entrance to the program.

FACILITIES

Information Resources Main library with 695,312 bound volumes, 725,716 titles on microform, 2,689 periodical subscriptions, 383 CD-ROMs.
Housing 10% of students in program live in college-owned or -operated housing. Assistance with housing search provided.
Technology Computers are used heavily in course work. 60 computer terminals/PCs, linked by a campus-wide computer network, are available for use by students in program; they are located in the student center, classrooms, learning resource center, the library, the computer center, computer labs. Students in the program are not required to have their own PC. $200 are budgeted per student for computer support.

Computer Resources/On-line Services

Training	Yes	CompuServe	Yes
Internet	Yes	Dun's	No
E-Mail	Yes	Dow Jones	Yes
Videoconference Center	Yes	Dialog	No
Multimedia Center	Yes	Bloomberg	No
LEXIS/NEXIS	Yes		

ADMISSION

Acceptance 1994-95 700 applied for admission; 80% were accepted.
Entrance Requirements Bachelor's degree, GMAT score. Core courses waived through: previous course work.
Application Requirements Written essay, application form, copies of transcript, personal statement.
Application Deadlines 7/1 for fall, 11/30 for spring, 4/15 for summer. Applications are processed on a rolling basis.

FINANCIALS

Estimated Costs for 1995-96 Tuition: Full-time: $552/unit. Fees: Full-time: $45/unit.
Financial Aid In 1994-95, 21% of candidates received some institutionally administered aid in the form of grants, scholarships, loans, fellowships. Total awards ranged from $250-$30,000. Financial aid is available to part-time students. Application deadline: 2/15 for fall. Applications are processed on a rolling basis. Contact: Ms. Susan Murphy, Associate Dean, 2130 Fulton Street, Cam, 81, San Francisco, CA 94117-1080. (415) 666-6303.

INTERNATIONAL STUDENTS

Demographics 36% of students enrolled in the program are international; Asia 55%, Europe 14%, Central America 12%, South America 10%, Africa 5%, Australia 2%, North America 2%.
Services and Facilities International student office, international student center, visa services, language tutoring, ESL courses, special assistance for nonnative speakers of English, counseling/support services.
Applying TOEFL required, minimum score of 600; proof of health; proof of adequate funds. Financial aid is not available to international students. Admission application deadlines: 7/1 for fall, 11/30 for spring, 4/15 for summer. Applications are processed on a rolling basis. Contact: Ms. Carole Shaffer, International Student Adviser, 2130 Fulton Street, San Francisco, CA 94117-1080. (415) 666-2654.

ALTERNATE MBA PROGRAM

Executive MBA (EMBA) Length of program: Minimum: 21 months. Maximum: 2 years. Full-time classes: Main campus; day, weekends. Degree requirements: 56 units.

PLACEMENT

In 1993-94, 97 organizations participated in on-campus recruiting; 201 on-campus interviews were conducted. Placement services include alumni network, career counseling/planning, career fairs, career library, career placement, electronic job bank, job interviews, job search course, resume preparation, and resume referral to employers. Of 1994 graduates, 86% were employed within three months of graduation, the average starting salary was $47,500, the range was $35,000-$62,000.

Program Contact: Ms. Cathy Fusco, Director, MBA Program, University of San Francisco, 2130 Fulton Street, San Francisco, CA 94117-1080. (415) 666-6314; Fax: (415) 666-2502; Internet Address: mbausf@usfca.edu.

See full description on page 914.

University of Southern California

Graduate School of Business Administration

Los Angeles, California

OVERVIEW
The University of Southern California is an independent nonprofit coed institution. Founded 1880. Setting: 150-acre urban campus. Total institutional enrollment: 27,000. Program was first offered in 1960. AACSB-accredited.

MBA HIGHLIGHTS

Entrance Difficulty***
Mean GMAT: 610
Mean GPA: 3.1

Cost $$$
Tuition: $17,530
Room & Board: $10,000

Enrollment Profile
Full-time: 395
Part-time: 850
Total: 1,245
Average Age: 27

Work Exp: 96%
International: 16%
Women: 30%
Minorities: 14%

Average Class Size: 40

The University of Southern California School of Business Administration's one-year International Executive M.B.A. program is unique in North America. It is an AACSB-accredited M.B.A. program for midcareer managers who are pursuing international and Pacific Rim–related careers. The International Business and Education Center (IBEAR) M.B.A. Program, which begins in mid-August each year, includes a three-week preparatory program and nineteen M.B.A. courses in four 11-week terms. It also includes special features such as international consulting projects for major U.S. firms, a team-building retreat, optional language courses, attendance at off-campus international business events, and an extensive international guest executive speaker series. Participants have access to the extensive resources of the School of Business Administration, which has 170 full-time faculty members and was ranked in the top twenty by U.S. News & World Report (1994).

IBEAR M.B.A. participants average 34 years of age and 10 years of work experience. They come from thirteen or more countries each year. Approximately 60 percent are corporate-sponsored, while the remainder are self-sponsored. Enrollment is limited to 48 participants. Graduates join a network of more than 650 well-placed IBEAR alumni working in forty-one countries as well as 42,000 USC business school alumni.

ACADEMICS
Length of Program Minimum: 20 months.
Calendar Semesters.
Full-time Classes Main campus; day, evening, summer.
Part-time Classes Main campus, Orange County; evening, summer.
Degree Requirements 63 credits including 24 elective credits.
Required Courses Accounting and financial reporting, accounting control, behavior and organization, business field project, business, government, and society, communications, corporate finances, information systems, managerial economics, marketing, national and international economy, operations management, strategy.
Curricular Focus Economic and financial theory, problem solving and decision making.
Concentrations Accounting, economics, entertainment management, consulting services, technology management, venture management, entrepreneurship, finance, health services, human resources management, international business, management, management information systems, marketing, operations management, organizational behavior, public policy, real estate, strategic management.
Faculty Full-time: 90, 95% with doctorates; part-time: 15, 5% with doctorates.
Teaching Methodology Case study: 25%, faculty seminars: 10%, lecture: 25%, research: 10%, student presentations: 10%, team projects: 20%.
Special Opportunities International exchange in Australia, Austria, Brazil, Chile, Costa Rica, Egypt, Germany, Hong Kong, Mexico, Philippines, Republic of Korea, Singapore, Spain, Switzerland.

STUDENT STATISTICS
Geographic Representation State residents 57%. By region: West 74%; Northeast 9%; Midwest 2%; South 1%. International 16%.
Undergraduate Majors Business 23%; engineering/technology 16%; humanities 10%; science/mathematics 15%; social sciences 23%; other 13%.
Other Background Work experience: On average, students have 5 years of work experience on entrance to the program.

FACILITIES
Information Resources Main library with 3.2 million bound volumes, 1.5 million titles on microform, 18,000 periodical subscriptions.
Housing College housing available.
Technology Computers are used heavily in course work. 700 computer terminals/PCs, linked by a campus-wide computer network, are available for use by students in program; they are located in classrooms, learning resource center, the library, the computer center, computer labs. Students in the program are not required to have their own PC.
Computer Resources/On-line Services

Training	Yes	Videoconference Center	Yes
Internet	Yes	Multimedia Center	Yes
E-Mail	Yes	LEXIS/NEXIS	Yes

ADMISSION
Acceptance 1994-95 1,266 applied for admission; 35% were accepted.
Entrance Requirements Bachelor's degree, GMAT score, minimum 2-4 years of work experience.
Application Requirements Written essay, interview, application form, copies of transcript, resume/curriculum vitae, personal statement, 2 letters of recommendation.
Application Deadlines 3/15 for fall. Applications are processed on a rolling basis.

FINANCIALS
Costs for 1994-95 Tuition: Full-time: $17,230; Part-time evening: $10,858-$15,051; Summer: $1,700/course. Fees: Full-time: $300; Part-time evening: $400-$800. Average room and board costs are $10,000 per academic year (on-campus) and $10,000 per academic year (off-campus).
Financial Aid In 1994-95, candidates received some institutionally administered aid in the form of grants, scholarships, fellowships, work-study. Total awards ranged from $1,292-$29,638. Financial aid is available to part-time students. Application deadline: 2/15 for fall. Applications are processed on a rolling basis. Contact: Ms. Edith Trimble, Fellowship Coordinator, University Park Campus, Los Angeles, CA 90089-1421. (213) 740-0668.

INTERNATIONAL STUDENTS
Demographics 16% of students enrolled in the program are international; Asia 90%, Europe 3%, North America 3%, Central America 2%, other 2%.
Services and Facilities Visa services, language tutoring, ESL courses, counseling/support services.
Applying TOEFL required, minimum score of 600; proof of health; proof of adequate funds. Financial aid is not available to international students. Admission application deadline: 3/15 for fall. Applications are processed on a rolling basis. Contact: Ms. Mary Randall, Associate Dean, Director, Graduate and International Admissions, STU-311, Los Angeles, CA 90089-1421. (213) 740-5679.

ALTERNATE MBA PROGRAMS
Executive MBA (EMBA) Length of program: Minimum: 21 months. Maximum: 2 years. Full-time classes: Main campus; day, weekends. Degree requirements: 60 credits. 6 day residential at start of program; international trip in second year. Average class size: 60.
International MBA Length of program: 12 months. Full-time classes: Main campus; day. Degree requirements: 56 credits including 3 elective credits. Average class size: 48.
One-Year MBA Length of program: 12 months. Degree requirements: 54 credits including 6 elective credits. International and Pacific Rim applicants for management with significant work experience may apply. Average class size: 65.
MBA/JD Length of program: Minimum: 45 months. Maximum: 5 years. Degree requirements: 138 credits including 15 elective credits.
MBA/MRP Length of program: Minimum: 32 months. Maximum: 5 years. Degree requirements: 84 credits including 9 elective credits.
MBA/MSN Length of program: Minimum: 36 months. Degree requirements: 75 credits including 12 elective credits.
MBA/DDS Length of program: Minimum: 60 months. Maximum: 5 years. Degree requirements: 183 credits including 12 elective credits.

MBA/MRED Length of program: Minimum: 32 months. Maximum: 5 years. Degree requirements: 80 credits including 6 elective credits. Comprehensive exam.

MBA/MSG Length of program: Minimum: 32 months. Maximum: 5 years. Degree requirements: 78 credits including 3 elective credits.

MBA/Pharm D Length of program: Minimum: 60 months. Maximum: 5 years. Degree requirements: 192 credits including 12 elective credits.

PLACEMENT

In 1993-94, 174 organizations participated in on-campus recruiting; 1,755 on-campus interviews were conducted. Placement services include alumni network, career counseling/planning, career library, career placement, electronic job bank, job interviews, resume preparation, and resume referral to employers. Of 1994 graduates, 95% were employed within three months of graduation, the average starting salary was $51,000, the range was $36,000-$110,000.

Jobs by Employer Type Manufacturing 26%; service 48%; consulting 19%; nonprofit 4%; human resources 3%.

Jobs by Functional Area Marketing/sales 16%; finance 41%; operations 5%; management 3%; strategic planning 2%; other 33%.

Program Contact: Ms. Annette Loschert, Assistant Dean, University of Southern California, MBA Program Admissions, Los Angeles, CA 90089-1421. (213) 740-6422; Fax: (213) 749-8520; Internet Address: uscmba@sba.usc.edu.

See full description on page 918.

University of the Pacific

School of Business and Public Administration

Stockton, California

OVERVIEW

The University of the Pacific is an independent nonprofit coed institution. Founded 1851. Setting: 175-acre suburban campus with easy access to Sacramento. Total institutional enrollment: 4,000. Program was first offered in 1993. AACSB-accredited.

MBA HIGHLIGHTS

Entrance Difficulty***
Mean GMAT: 498
Mean GPA: 2.96

Cost $$
Tuition: $510/credit
Room & Board: $5,330

Enrollment Profile

Full-time: 26	Work Exp: 65%
Part-time: 61	International: 5%
Total: 87	Women: 40%
Average Age: 27	Minorities: 30%

Average Class Size: 25

ACADEMICS

Length of Program Minimum: 24 months. Maximum: 5 years.

Calendar Semesters.

Part-time Classes Main campus; evening, summer.

Degree Requirements 30-48 credits including 6-12 elective credits. Other: Summer internship.

Required Courses Business and public policy, corporate finance, global business competition, leadership and change, managing quality and productivity, strategic management, strategic marketing, technology and innovation.

Curricular Focus Entrepreneurship, general management, leadership.

Concentrations Entrepreneurship, finance, management.

Faculty Full-time: 22, 100% with doctorates.

Teaching Methodology Case study: 20%, faculty seminars: 10%, lecture: 30%, research: 5%, seminars by members of the business community: 10%, student presentations: 5%, team projects: 20%.

Special Opportunities Internships include consulting in management consulting, marketing in consumer products, marketing in cable television, finance and accounting in retail, and consulting in nonprofit.

STUDENT STATISTICS

Geographic Representation State residents 95%. By region: West 70%; Northeast 10%; Midwest 10%; South 5%. International 5%.

Undergraduate Majors Business 55%; engineering/technology 20%; humanities 10%; science/mathematics 5%; social sciences 10%.

Other Background Graduate degrees in other disciplines: 5%. Work experience: On average, students have 6 years of work experience on entrance to the program.

FACILITIES

Information Resources Main library with 437,742 bound volumes, 531,129 titles on microform, 2,652 periodical subscriptions, 18,166 records/tapes/CDs, 10 CD-ROMs.

Housing 5% of students in program live in college-owned or -operated housing.

Technology Computers are used moderately in course work. 150 computer terminals/PCs, linked by a campus-wide computer network, are available for use by students in program; they are located in computer labs. Students in the program are not required to have their own PC. $400 are budgeted per student for computer support.

Computer Resources/On-line Services

Training	Yes	Dun's	Yes
Internet	Yes	Dow Jones	No
E-Mail	Yes	Dialog	Yes
LEXIS/NEXIS	No	Bloomberg	No
CompuServe	No		

Other on-line services: First Search, OCLC.

ADMISSION

Acceptance 1994-95 80 applied for admission; 100% were accepted.

Entrance Requirements Bachelor's degree, GMAT score of 500, minimum 3.0 GPA. Core courses waived through: previous course work.

Application Requirements Written essay, application form, copies of transcript, 3 letters of recommendation.

Application Deadlines 7/31 for fall, 12/31 for spring, 4/30 for summer. Applications are processed on a rolling basis.

FINANCIALS

Costs for 1994-95 Tuition: Full-time: $510/credit; Part-time day: $510/credit; Part-time evening: $510/credit; Summer: $510/credit. Fees: Full-time: $225. Average room and board costs are $5,330 per academic year (on-campus) and $5,500 per academic year (off-campus).

Financial Aid In 1994-95, 65% of candidates received some institutionally administered aid in the form of scholarships, loans, assistantships. Financial aid is available to part-time students. Applications are processed on a rolling basis. Contact: Office of Financial Aid, 3601 Pacific Avenue, Stockton, CA 95211-0197. (209) 946-2421.

INTERNATIONAL STUDENTS

Demographics 5% of students enrolled in the program are international; Asia 73%, Europe 12%, South America 10%, other 5%.

Services and Facilities International student housing; international student office, visa services, language tutoring, ESL courses, special assistance for nonnative speakers of English, counseling/support services.

Applying TOEFL required, minimum score of 550; proof of adequate funds. Financial aid is available to international students. Financial aid application deadlines: 3/1 for fall, 12/1 for spring. Applications are processed on a rolling basis. Admission application deadlines: 7/31 for fall, 12/31 for spring, 4/30 for summer. Applications are processed on a rolling basis. Contact: Ms. Barbara St. Urbain, Director of International Services, 3601 Pacific Avenue, Stockton, CA 95211-0197. (209) 946-2246.

ALTERNATE MBA PROGRAM

One-Year MBA Length of program: Minimum: 10 months. Maximum: 1 year. Full-time classes: Main campus; day, summer. Degree requirements: 30 credits including 6 elective credits. Average class size: 25.

PLACEMENT

Placement services include alumni network, career counseling/planning, career fairs, resume preparation, and resume referral to employers.

Program Contact: Ms. Paula Tatsch, Director, MBA Recruiting, University of the Pacific, 3601 Pacific Avenue, Stockton, CA 95211-0197. (209) 946-2629; Fax: (209) 946-2586.

See full description on page 920.

West Coast University

College of Business and Management

Los Angeles, California

OVERVIEW
West Coast University is an independent nonprofit comprehensive coed institution. Founded 1909. Setting: 2-acre urban campus. Total institutional enrollment: 1,000. Program was first offered in 1976.

MBA HIGHLIGHTS

Entrance Difficulty*
Mean GMAT: N/R
Mean GPA: 2.75

Cost $$
Tuition: $370/unit
Room & Board: N/R

Enrollment Profile
Full-time: 165
Part-time: 0
Total: 165
Average Age: 26

Work Exp: 75%
International: N/R
Women: N/R
Minorities: N/R

Average Class Size: 10

ACADEMICS
Length of Program Minimum: 12 months.
Calendar 6 terms.
Full-time Classes Main campus; evening, weekends, summer.
Degree Requirements 39 units including 12 elective units.
Required Courses Business development and entrepreneurship, comparative management, financial analysis, global economics, marketing analysis and strategies, organizational development and research, strategic management 1: management challenge, strategic management 2: leadership challenge.
Curricular Focus International business, management information systems and environmental management, strategic analysis and planning.
Concentrations Accounting, acquisition and contract management, environmental operations administration, technology management, finance, international business, management, management information systems, marketing.
Faculty Full-time: 5, 55% with doctorates; part-time: 150, 55% with doctorates.
Teaching Methodology Case study: 5%, faculty seminars: 5%, lecture: 40%, research: 20%, student presentations: 10%, team projects: 20%.
Special Opportunities Internships include international trade.

STUDENT STATISTICS
Undergraduate Majors Business 65%; engineering/technology 25%; humanities 3%; social sciences 3%; other 4%.
Other Background Graduate degrees in other disciplines: 10%. Work experience: On average, students have 5 years of work experience on entrance to the program.

FACILITIES
Information Resources Main library with 15,000 bound volumes, 84,000 titles on microform, 250 periodical subscriptions, 50 records/tapes/CDs.
Housing College housing not available.
Technology Computers are used moderately in course work. 20 computer terminals/PCs are available for use by students in program; they are located in computer labs, MBA computer lab. Students in the program are not required to have their own PC.

Computer Resources/On-line Services

Training	Yes	Videoconference Center	Yes
E-Mail	No	Multimedia Center	Yes

ADMISSION
Acceptance 1994-95 100 applied for admission; 75% were accepted.
Entrance Requirements Bachelor's degree, minimum 2.5 GPA. Core courses waived through: previous course work.
Application Requirements Application form, copies of transcript, personal statement.
Application Deadline Applications are processed on a rolling basis.

FINANCIALS
Costs for 1994-95 Tuition: Full-time: $370/unit. Fees: Full-time: $20-$120.
Financial Aid In 1994-95, 3% of candidates received some institutionally administered aid in the form of loans. Financial aid is available to part-time students. Applications are processed on a rolling basis. Contact: Mr. Ray Dominguez, Dean of Financial Aid, 440 Shatto Place, Los Angeles, CA 90020-1765. (213) 427-4400.

INTERNATIONAL STUDENTS
Demographics 45% of students on campus are international.
Services and Facilities International student office, international student center, visa services, language tutoring, ESL courses, special assistance for nonnative speakers of English, counseling/support services.
Applying TOEFL required, minimum score of 450; proof of health; proof of adequate funds; overseas transcripts mailed directly to school, health insurance. Financial aid is not available to international students. Admission applications are processed on a rolling basis.

Program Contact: Mr. Roger Miller, Dean of Admissions and Registrar, West Coast University, 440 Shatto Place, Los Angeles, CA 90020-1765. (213) 427-4400, or (800) 248-4WCU; Fax: (213) 380-4362.

Woodbury University

School of Business and Management

Burbank, California

OVERVIEW
Woodbury University is an independent nonprofit comprehensive coed institution. Founded 1884. Setting: 23-acre suburban campus with easy access to Los Angeles. Total institutional enrollment: 1,049. Program was first offered in 1979.

MBA HIGHLIGHTS

Entrance Difficulty**
Mean GMAT: 500
Mean GPA: 3.4

Cost $$
Tuition: $325/unit
Room & Board: $6,000

Enrollment Profile
Full-time: 24
Part-time: 89
Total: 113
Average Age: 29

Work Exp: 92%
International: 46%
Women: 47%
Minorities: 35%

Average Class Size: 18

ACADEMICS
Length of Program Minimum: 24 months. Maximum: 6 years.
Calendar Quarters.
Full-time Classes Main campus; evening, weekends, summer.
Part-time Classes Main campus; day, weekends, summer.
Degree Requirements 48 credits including 15 elective credits.
Required Courses Accounting for managers, business computing applications, business economics, business finance, financial accounting, information systems for managers, management and organizational behavior, management communications, marketing concepts and strategies, quantitative methods for business decisions, the legal environment of business.
Curricular Focus Entrepreneurship, general management, problem solving and decision making, teamwork.
Concentrations Accounting, finance, international business, management, management information systems, marketing.
Faculty Full-time: 7, 60% with doctorates; part-time: 13, 50% with doctorates.
Teaching Methodology Case study: 20%, lecture: 35%, student presentations: 20%, team projects: 25%.
Special Opportunities Internships include management in financial services, marketing in entertainment, accounting in manufacturing, and real estate.

STUDENT STATISTICS
Geographic Representation By region: West 51%; Northeast 2%; Midwest 1%. International 46%.

Undergraduate Majors Business 40%; engineering/technology 7%; humanities 15%; science/mathematics 3%; social sciences 15%; other 20%.

Other Background Graduate degrees in other disciplines: 4%. Work experience: On average, students have 8 years of work experience on entrance to the program.

FACILITIES

Information Resources Main library with 68,738 bound volumes, 82,502 titles on microform, 641 periodical subscriptions, 703 records/tapes/CDs, 4 CD-ROMs. Business collection includes 13,047 bound volumes, 297 periodical subscriptions, 1 CD-ROM, 37 videos.

Housing 3% of students in program live in college-owned or -operated housing. Assistance with housing search provided.

Technology Computers are used moderately in course work. Computer terminals/PCs, linked by a campus-wide computer network, are available for use by students in program; they are located in learning resource center, the library, the computer center, computer labs. Students in the program are not required to have their own PC. $300 are budgeted per student for computer support.

Computer Resources/On-line Services

Training	Yes	Dun's	No
Internet	Yes	Dow Jones	No
E-Mail	Yes	Dialog	Yes
LEXIS/NEXIS	No	Bloomberg	No
CompuServe	No		

Other on-line services: First Search.

ADMISSION

Acceptance 1994-95 160 applied for admission; 90% were accepted.

Entrance Requirements Bachelor's degree, GMAT score, minimum 2.0 GPA. Core courses waived through: previous course work.

Application Requirements Written essay, application form, copies of transcript, 2 letters of recommendation.

Application Deadlines 8/1 for fall, 12/11 for winter, 3/1 for spring, 5/1 for summer. Applications are processed on a rolling basis.

FINANCIALS

Costs for 1995-96 Tuition: Full-time: $325/unit. Fees: Full-time: $100/quarter. Average room and board costs are $6,000 per academic year (on-campus) and $6,500 per academic year (off-campus).

Financial Aid In 1994-95, candidates received some institutionally administered aid in the form of loans. Total awards ranged from $2,500-$16,800. Financial aid is available to part-time students. Application deadlines: 8/1 for fall, 11/1 for winter, 2/1 for spring. Applications are processed on a rolling basis. Contact: Mr. William Wagoner, Director of Financial Aid, 7500 Glenoaks Boulevard, Burbank, CA 91510-7846. (818) 767-0888.

INTERNATIONAL STUDENTS

Demographics 46% of students enrolled in the program are international; Asia 88%, Europe 12%.

Services and Facilities Visa services, ESL courses, counseling/support services.

Applying TOEFL required, minimum score of 550; proof of adequate funds. Financial aid is not available to international students. Admission application deadlines: 8/1 for fall, 12/1 for winter, 3/1 for spring, 5/1 for summer. Applications are processed on a rolling basis. Contact: Ms. Donna Huchel, Director, International Student Services, 7500 Glenoaks Boulevard, Burbank, CA 91510-7846. (818) 767-0888.

PLACEMENT

In 1993-94, 33 organizations participated in on-campus recruiting; 10 on-campus interviews were conducted. Placement services include alumni network, career counseling/planning, career fairs, career library, career placement, job interviews, job search course, resume preparation, and resume referral to employers. Of 1994 graduates, 90% were employed within three months of graduation, the average starting salary was $34,000, the range was $32,400-$44,500.

Jobs by Employer Type Manufacturing 10%; government 5%; corporate management 85%.

Jobs by Functional Area Marketing/sales 13%; finance 30%; operations 14%; management 30%; strategic planning 13%.

Program Contact: Ms. Linda Parks, Graduate Admissions Assistant, Woodbury University, 7500 Glenoaks Boulevard, Burbank, CA 91510-7846. (818) 767-0888 Ext. 264.

See full description on page 938.

COLORADO

Colorado State University

College of Business

Fort Collins, Colorado

OVERVIEW

Colorado State University is a state-supported coed institution. Part of Colorado State University System. Founded 1870. Setting: 666-acre urban campus with easy access to Denver. Total institutional enrollment: 21,461. Program was first offered in 1973. AACSB-accredited.

MBA HIGHLIGHTS

Entrance Difficulty***
Mean GMAT: 530
Mean GPA: 3.52

Cost $
Tuition: $1,223/semester
(Nonresident: $4,388/semester)
Room & Board: N/R

Enrollment Profile

Full-time: 79	Work Exp: 72%
Part-time: 65	International: 20%
Total: 144	Women: 40%
Average Age: 31	Minorities: 5%

Average Class Size: 26

ACADEMICS

Length of Program Minimum: 10 months. Maximum: 10 years.

Calendar Semesters.

Full-time Classes Main campus, distance learning option; day.

Part-time Classes Main campus, distance learning option; day.

Degree Requirements 33 credits including 3 elective credits.

Required Courses Business policy, business research, computer applications in decision making, financial management, management, managerial accounting, managerial economics, marketing strategy, production administration, statistical decision making.

Curricular Focus Business issues and problems, problem solving and decision making, teamwork.

Concentrations Accounting, agriculture, quality improvement, technology management, finance, human resources management, management, management information systems, marketing, operations management, organizational behavior.

Faculty Full-time: 58, 99% with doctorates; part-time: 2.

Teaching Methodology Case study: 35%, lecture: 45%, student presentations: 10%, team projects: 10%.

STUDENT STATISTICS

Geographic Representation By region: Midwest 55%; West 16%; South 5%; Northeast 4%. International 20%.

Undergraduate Majors Business 55%; engineering/technology 8%; science/mathematics 10%; social sciences 10%; other 17%.

FACILITIES

Information Resources Main library with 1.8 million bound volumes, 1.6 million titles on microform, 20,000 periodical subscriptions, 8,300 records/tapes/CDs.

Housing College housing available.

Technology Computers are used heavily in course work. 150 computer terminals/PCs, linked by a campus-wide computer network, are available for use by students in program; they are located in computer labs. Students in the program are not required to have their own PC.

Computer Resources/On-line Services

Training	Yes	CompuServe	No
Internet	Yes	Dun's	No
E-Mail	Yes	Dow Jones	No
Multimedia Center	Yes	Dialog	Yes
LEXIS/NEXIS	Yes	Bloomberg	No

ADMISSION

Acceptance 1994-95 462 applied for admission; 23% were accepted.

Entrance Requirements Bachelor's degree, GMAT score of 480, minimum 3.0 GPA. Core courses waived through: previous course work.

Application Requirements Application form, copies of transcript, personal statement, 3 letters of recommendation.

Application Deadlines 2/1 for fall, 4/1 for spring, 11/1 for summer.

FINANCIALS

Costs for 1994-95 Tuition: Full-time: $1,223/semester for state residents, $4,388/semester for nonresidents; Part-time day: $102/semester credit hour for state residents, $366/semester credit hour for nonresidents. Fees: Full-time: $292/semester for state residents, $292/semester for nonresidents; Part-time day: $26-$292/semester for state residents, $26-$292/semester for nonresidents.

Financial Aid In 1994-95, candidates received some institutionally administered aid in the form of loans, fellowships, assistantships. Application deadline: 3/1 for fall. Applications are processed on a rolling basis. Contact: Ms. Kay Jacks, Director of Enrollment Services, 108 Student Services Building, Fort Collins, CO 80523. (970) 491-6321.

INTERNATIONAL STUDENTS

Demographics 20% of students enrolled in the program are international.

Services and Facilities International student office, ESL courses.

Applying TOEFL required; proof of health; proof of adequate funds. Financial aid is not available to international students. Admission application deadlines: 2/1 for fall, 4/1 for spring, 11/1 for summer. Applications are processed on a rolling basis. Contact: Ms. Betty Shoemaker, Foreign Student Adviser, International Student Office, 315 Aylesworth, Fort Collins, CO 80523. (970) 491-5919.

PLACEMENT

Placement services include alumni network, career counseling/planning, career fairs, career library, resume preparation, and resume referral to employers.

Program Contact: Dr. Jon Clark, Associate Dean, Colorado State University, Fort Collins, CO 80523. (970) 491-6471; Fax: (970) 491-0596; Internet Address: jclark@vines.colostate.edu.
See full description on page 710.

Regis University

School for Professional Studies

Denver, Colorado

OVERVIEW

Regis University is an independent Roman Catholic (Jesuit) comprehensive coed institution. Founded 1877. Setting: 90-acre suburban campus. Total institutional enrollment: 7,517.

MBA HIGHLIGHTS

Entrance Difficulty N/R

Cost $$
Tuition: $275/credit hour
Room & Board: N/R

Total Enrollment: 750

Average Class Size: 15

ACADEMICS

Length of Program Minimum: 18 months.

Calendar Semesters.

Full-time Classes Main campus; evening.

Part-time Classes Main campus; evening.

Degree Requirements 45 credit hours including 5 elective credit hours.

Curricular Focus International business, problem solving and decision making, strategic analysis and planning.

Concentrations Accounting, international business, management information systems, marketing, operations management.

Teaching Methodology Case study: 20%, lecture: 20%, research: 20%, student presentations: 20%, team projects: 20%.

FACILITIES

Information Resources Main library with 246,839 bound volumes, 86,273 titles on microform, 2,232 periodical subscriptions.

FINANCIALS

Costs for 1994-95 Tuition: Full-time: $275/credit hour.

Program Contact: Ms. B. Jennings, Director of Graduate Admissions, Regis University, 3333 Regis Boulevard, Denver, CO 80211-1099. (303) 458-4100.

University of Colorado at Boulder

Graduate School of Business Administration

Boulder, Colorado

OVERVIEW

The University of Colorado at Boulder is a state-supported coed institution. Part of University of Colorado System. Founded 1876. Setting: 600-acre suburban campus with easy access to Denver. Total institutional enrollment: 25,013. Program was first offered in 1992. AACSB-accredited.

MBA HIGHLIGHTS

Entrance Difficulty**
Mean GMAT: 580
Mean GPA: 3.1

Cost $
Tuition: $1,745/semester
(Nonresident: $6,507/semester)
Room & Board: $4,000

Enrollment Profile

Full-time: 128	Work Exp: 98%
Part-time: 9	International: 15%
Total: 137	Women: 30%
Average Age: 27	Minorities: 15%

Average Class Size: 30

ACADEMICS

Length of Program Minimum: 24 months. Maximum: 5 years.

Calendar Semesters.

Full-time Classes Main campus; day.

Part-time Classes Main campus, distance learning option; day.

Degree Requirements 52 credit hours including 15 elective credit hours.

Required Courses Business policy, corporate finance, decision analysis, financial accounting, managerial economics, managing behavior in organizations, marketing management, quantitative methods.

Curricular Focus Integrative skills, teamwork.

Concentrations Entrepreneurship, finance, management, marketing, organizational behavior, technology and innovation management.

Special Opportunities Internship program available.

STUDENT STATISTICS

Geographic Representation State residents 50%. By region: Midwest 45%; West 30%; Northeast 5%; South 5%. International 15%.

Undergraduate Majors Business 50%; engineering/technology 30%; humanities 5%; science/mathematics 10%; social sciences 5%.

Other Background Graduate degrees in other disciplines: 5%. Work experience: On average, students have 5 years of work experience on entrance to the program.

FACILITIES

Information Resources Main library with 2.5 million bound volumes, 4.9 million titles on microform, 28,440 periodical subscriptions, 50,000 records/tapes/CDs, 170 CD-ROMs. Business collection in William M. White Business Library includes 75,779 bound volumes, 650 periodical subscriptions, 433 CD-ROMs, 76 videos.

Housing 2% of students in program live in college-owned or -operated housing.

Technology Computers are used heavily in course work. 650 computer terminals/PCs, linked by a campus-wide computer network, are available for use by students in program; they are located in the library, the computer center, computer labs. Students in the program are not required to have their own PC.

Computer Resources/On-line Services

Training	Yes	LEXIS/NEXIS	Yes
Internet	Yes	Dialog	Yes
E-Mail	Yes		

ADMISSION

Acceptance 1994-95 Of those applying, 30% were accepted.

Entrance Requirements Bachelor's degree, one semester of college calculus, GMAT score of 590, minimum 3.2 GPA, minimum 2 years of work experience.

Application Requirements Interview, application form, copies of transcript, resume/curriculum vitae, personal statement, 3 letters of recommendation.

Application Deadline 4/1 for fall.

FINANCIALS

Costs for 1994-95 Tuition: Full-time: $1,745/semester for state residents, $6,507/semester for nonresidents; Part-time day: $582/course for state residents, $2,169/course for nonresidents. Fees: Full-time: $400/semester for state residents, $400/semester for nonresidents. Average room and board costs are $4,000 per academic year (on-campus) and $3,600 per academic year (off-campus).

Financial Aid In 1994-95, 50% of candidates received some institutionally administered aid in the form of grants, scholarships, loans, fellowships, work-study. Financial aid is available to part-time students. Application deadline: 4/1 for fall. Contact: Ms. Karon Johnson, Financial Aid Counselor, Office of Financial Aid, Campus Box 106, Boulder, CO 80309. (303) 492-5091.

INTERNATIONAL STUDENTS

Demographics 15% of students enrolled in the program are international.

Services and Facilities International student center, ESL courses.

Applying TOEFL required; proof of adequate funds. Financial aid is not available to international students. Admission application deadline: 4/1 for fall.

ALTERNATE MBA PROGRAM

MBA/JD Length of program: Minimum: 48 months. Maximum: 4 years. Degree requirements: 141 credit hours including 60 elective credit hours. Separate applications must be submitted to both business and law.

PLACEMENT

Placement services include alumni network, career counseling/planning, career fairs, career placement, job interviews, resume preparation, and resume referral to employers.

Program Contact: Ms. Bernadette Langbein, Director, University of Colorado at Boulder, Boulder, CO 80309. (303) 492-1831; Fax: (303) 492-1727.

University of Colorado at Colorado Springs

Graduate School of Business Administration

Colorado Springs, Colorado

OVERVIEW

The University of Colorado at Colorado Springs is a state-supported comprehensive coed institution. Part of University of Colorado System. Founded 1965. Setting: 400-acre urban campus with easy access to Denver. Total institutional enrollment: 6,000. Program was first offered in 1965. AACSB-accredited.

MBA HIGHLIGHTS

Entrance Difficulty*
Mean GMAT: 530
Mean GPA: 3.1

Cost $
Tuition: $1,328/semester
(Nonresident: $4,403/semester)
Room & Board: N/R

Enrollment Profile

Full-time: N/R		Work Exp: 90%
Part-time: N/R		International: N/R
Total: 337		Women: 40%
Average Age: 30		Minorities: 15%

Class Size: 20 - 22

ACADEMICS

Length of Program Minimum: 12 months. Maximum: 5 years.

Calendar Semesters.

Full-time Classes Main campus; evening, summer.

Part-time Classes Main campus; evening, summer.

Degree Requirements 30-48 credits including 15 elective credits.

Required Courses Accounting for the modern manager, business, government, and society, information technology in business, leading and managing in changing times, marketing strategy, maximizing company value through financial management, strategic management, world class manufacturing.

Curricular Focus Business issues and problems, strategic analysis and planning, teamwork.

Concentrations Accounting, finance, human resources management, international business, management, management information systems, marketing, operations management, organizational behavior, technology management, services management.

Faculty Full-time: 29, 100% with doctorates.

Teaching Methodology Case study: 10%, lecture: 50%, research: 10%, student presentations: 10%, team projects: 20%.

Special Opportunities Internship program available.

STUDENT STATISTICS

Geographic Representation State residents 95%.

Undergraduate Majors Business 50%; engineering/technology 25%; other 25%.

Other Background Graduate degrees in other disciplines: 10%. Work experience: On average, students have 10 years of work experience on entrance to the program.

FACILITIES

Information Resources Main library with 301,616 bound volumes, 431,382 titles on microform, 2,417 periodical subscriptions, 3,996 records/tapes/CDs, 302 CD-ROMs.

Housing College housing available.

Technology Computers are used heavily in course work. Computer terminals/PCs, linked by a campus-wide computer network, are available for use by students in program; they are located in computer labs. Students in the program are not required to have their own PC.

Computer Resources/On-line Services

Training	Yes	E-Mail	Yes

ADMISSION

Acceptance 1994-95 1,213 applied for admission; 14% were accepted.

Entrance Requirements Bachelor's degree, prerequisite courses required for applicants with non-business degree, GMAT score.

Application Requirements Application form, copies of transcript.

Application Deadlines 5/1 for fall, 11/1 for spring, 4/1 for summer. Applications are processed on a rolling basis.

FINANCIALS

Costs for 1994-95 Tuition: Full-time: $1,328/semester for state residents, $4,403/semester for nonresidents; Part-time day: $111/credit hour for state residents, $361/credit hour for nonresidents. Fees: Full-time: $151/semester for state residents, $151/semester for nonresidents; Part-time day: $83-$128/semester for state residents, $83-$128/semester for nonresidents.

Financial Aid Application deadline: 4/1 for fall. Contact: Ms. Lee Ingalls, Director of Financial Aid, PO Box 7150, Colorado Springs, CO 80933-7150. (719) 593-3466.

INTERNATIONAL STUDENTS

Applying TOEFL required, minimum score of 550; proof of adequate funds. Financial aid is not available to international students. Admission application deadlines: 4/1 for fall, 10/1 for spring. Contact: Ms. Carolyn Curry, Program Specialist, PO Box 7150, Colorado Springs, CO 80933-7150. (719) 593-3408.

Program Contact: Ms. Carolyn Curry, Program Specialist, University of Colorado at Colorado Springs, PO Box 7150, Colorado Springs, CO 80933-7150. (719) 593-3408; Fax: (719) 593-3494; Internet Address: ctcurry@uccs.edu.

University of Colorado at Denver

Graduate School of Business Administration

Denver, Colorado

OVERVIEW

The University of Colorado at Denver is a state-supported coed institution. Part of University of Colorado System. Founded 1912. Setting: 171-acre urban campus. Total institutional enrollment: 10,538. Program was first offered in 1982. AACSB-accredited.

MBA HIGHLIGHTS

Entrance Difficulty***
Mean GMAT: 510
Mean GPA: 3.2

Cost $
Tuition: $1,254 - $1,743/semester
(Nonresident: $4,008 - $5,567/semester)
Room & Board: $6,500 (off-campus)

Enrollment Profile

Full-time: 412	Work Exp: 92%
Part-time: 825	International: 11%
Total: 1,237	Women: 44%
Average Age: 29	Minorities: 8%

Average Class Size: 45

ACADEMICS

Length of Program Minimum: 12 months.

Calendar Semesters.

Full-time Classes Main campus; evening, summer.

Part-time Classes Main campus; day, evening, weekends, summer.

Degree Requirements 30 semester hours including 15 elective semester hours.

Required Courses Analyzing and interpreting accounting information, applied economics for managers, business systems and design, data analysis for managers, financial management, legal and ethical environment of business, managerial communications, managing individuals and teams, marketing management, operations management, strategic management.

Curricular Focus Economic and financial theory, international business, teamwork.

Concentrations Accounting, communication, economics, entrepreneurship, finance, health services, human resources management, international business, management, management information systems, marketing, operations management, organizational behavior, quantitative analysis, strategic management.

Faculty Full-time: 70, 100% with doctorates; part-time: 20, 80% with doctorates.

Teaching Methodology Case study: 10%, faculty seminars: 5%, lecture: 60%, research: 5%, student presentations: 10%, team projects: 10%.

Special Opportunities International exchange in France, Japan. Internships include accounting, financial, health care administration, information systems, and management.

STUDENT STATISTICS

Geographic Representation International 11%.

Other Background Graduate degrees in other disciplines: 12%. Work experience: On average, students have 5 years of work experience on entrance to the program.

FACILITIES

Information Resources Main library with 522,303 bound volumes, 644,956 titles on microform, 3,581 periodical subscriptions, 14,512 records/tapes/CDs, 64 CD-ROMs. Other resources: Infotrac, ABI/Inform, CARL.

Housing College housing not available.

Technology Computers are used heavily in course work. 40 computer terminals/PCs, linked by a campus-wide computer network, are available for use by students in program; they are located in computer labs. Students in the program are not required to have their own PC.

Computer Resources/On-line Services

Training	Yes	LEXIS/NEXIS	Yes
Internet	Yes	CompuServe	Yes
E-Mail	Yes	Dow Jones	Yes

Other on-line services: Carl.

ADMISSION

Acceptance 1994-95 615 applied for admission; 72% were accepted.

Entrance Requirements Bachelor's degree, GMAT score of 400, minimum 3 years of work experience. Core courses waived through: previous course work.

Application Requirements Written essay, application form, copies of transcript.

Application Deadlines 7/1 for fall, 11/1 for spring, 4/1 for summer. Applications are processed on a rolling basis.

FINANCIALS

Costs for 1994-95 Tuition: Full-time: $1,254-$1,743/semester for state residents, $4,008-$5,567/semester for nonresidents. Fees: Full-time: $119/semester for state residents, $119/semester for nonresidents. Average room and board costs are $6,500 per academic year (off-campus).

Financial Aid In 1994-95, 30% of candidates received some institutionally administered aid in the form of scholarships, loans, assistantships. Total awards ranged from $600-$8,000. Financial aid is available to part-time students. Application deadline: 4/1 for fall. Applications are processed on a rolling basis. Contact: Ms. Ellie Miller, Director, Campus Box 125, PO Box 173364, Denver, CO 80217-3364. (303) 556-2886.

INTERNATIONAL STUDENTS

Demographics 11% of students enrolled in the program are international.

Services and Facilities International student office, international student center, language tutoring, counseling/support services.

Applying TOEFL required, minimum score of 500; proof of adequate funds; 2 letters of recommendation. Financial aid is not available to international students. Admission application deadlines: 4/1 for fall, 7/1 for spring, 1/1 for summer. Applications are processed on a rolling basis. Contact: Office of International Education, Campus Box 185, PO Box 173364, Denver, CO 80217-3364. (303) 556-3489.

ALTERNATE MBA PROGRAMS

Executive MBA (EMBA) Length of program: Minimum: 22 months. Degree requirements: 48 semester hours. 8 years of business experience including at least 3 years in a managerial position.

MBA/MS Length of program: Minimum: 32 months. Maximum: 7 years. Degree requirements: 66 semester hours.

PLACEMENT

Placement services include career counseling/planning, career fairs, career library, career placement, electronic job bank, resume preparation, and resume referral to employers. Of 1994 graduates, 98% were employed within three months of graduation.

Program Contact: Ms. Heather A. Bowdy, Graduate Programs Coordinator, University of Colorado at Denver, PO Box 173364, Denver, CO 80217-3364. (303) 556-5875.

University of Denver

Daniels College of Business

Denver, Colorado

OVERVIEW

The University of Denver is an independent nonprofit coed institution. Founded 1864. Setting: 125-acre suburban campus. Total institutional enrollment: 8,500. Program was first offered in 1949. AACSB-accredited.

MBA HIGHLIGHTS

Entrance Difficulty***
Mean GMAT: 530
Mean GPA: 3.2

Cost $$$
Tuition: $5,064/quarter
Room & Board: $8,000

Enrollment Profile

Full-time: 193	Work Exp: 80%
Part-time: 231	International: 20%
Total: 424	Women: 43%
Average Age: 27	Minorities: 10%

Average Class Size: 25

ACADEMICS

Length of Program Minimum: 18 months. Maximum: 5 years.
Calendar Quarters.
Full-time Classes Main campus, Summit County Vail; day, evening, early morning, summer.
Part-time Classes Main campus; day, evening, early morning, summer.
Degree Requirements 72 quarter hours including 12 elective quarter hours.
Required Courses Accounting, communication, economics, ethics, finance, law, leadership, management information systems, marketing, negotiations communication, public policy, statistics, strategy.
Curricular Focus Business issues and problems, problem solving and decision making, teamwork.
Concentrations Accounting, economics, entrepreneurship, finance, hotel management, international business, management, management information systems, marketing, organizational behavior, quantitative analysis, real estate.
Faculty Full-time: 35, 95% with doctorates; part-time: 5, 95% with doctorates.
Teaching Methodology Case study: 20%, experiential learning: 10%, faculty seminars: 5%, lecture: 20%, research: 10%, seminars by members of the business community: 5%, student presentations: 10%, team projects: 20%.
Special Opportunities International exchange in Denmark, Sweden. Internship program available. Other: international travel courses.

STUDENT STATISTICS

Geographic Representation State residents 55%. By region: West 60%; Northeast 8%; Midwest 8%; South 4%. International 20%.
Undergraduate Majors Business 50%; engineering/technology 10%; humanities 20%; science/mathematics 8%; social sciences 12%.
Other Background Graduate degrees in other disciplines: 5%. Work experience: On average, students have 2 years of work experience on entrance to the program.

FACILITIES

Information Resources Main library with 1.8 million bound volumes, 879,528 titles on microform, 5,102 periodical subscriptions. Business collection includes 125,000 bound volumes, 500 periodical subscriptions, 150 CD-ROMs.
Housing 10% of students in program live in college-owned or -operated housing.
Technology Computers are used moderately in course work. 130 computer terminals/PCs are available for use by students in program; they are located in the library, computer labs. Students in the program are not required to have their own PC.

Computer Resources/On-line Services

Training	Yes	CompuServe	No
Internet	Yes	Dun's	No
E-Mail	Yes	Dow Jones	No
Multimedia Center	Yes	Dialog	Yes
LEXIS/NEXIS	Yes	Bloomberg	No

Other on-line services: First Search, SEC.

ADMISSION

Acceptance 1994-95 670 applied for admission; 84% were accepted.
Entrance Requirements Bachelor's degree, GMAT score.
Application Requirements Written essay, application form, copies of transcript, 2 letters of recommendation.
Application Deadlines 6/2 for fall, 12/30 for spring.

FINANCIALS

Costs for 1994-95 Tuition: Full-time: $5,064/quarter. Fees: Full-time: $600. Average room and board costs are $8,000 per academic year (on-campus) and $8,000 per academic year (off-campus).
Financial Aid In 1994-95, candidates received some institutionally administered aid in the form of grants, scholarships, loans, assistantships, work-study. Total awards ranged from $500-$25,000. Financial aid is available to part-time students. Application deadlines: 2/28 for fall, 2/28 for spring. Contact: Ms. Darlene Mornes, Admissions and Academic Coordinator, University Park, Denver, CO 80208. (303) 871-2161.

INTERNATIONAL STUDENTS

Demographics 20% of students enrolled in the program are international; Asia 40%, Europe 30%, Central America 5%, South America 5%, other 20%.
Services and Facilities Language tutoring, ESL courses, counseling/support services.
Applying TOEFL required, minimum score of 550; proof of adequate funds. Financial aid is not available to international students. Admission application deadlines: 6/2 for fall, 12/30 for spring. Contact: Ms. Connie Busch, Provost, International Student Adviser, Driscoll Center South 076, 2050 East Evans Avenue, Denver, CO 80208. (303) 871-3863.

ALTERNATE MBA PROGRAMS

Executive MBA (EMBA) Length of program: Minimum: 18 months. Maximum: 5 years. Degree requirements: 52 quarter hours.
MBA/JD Length of program: Minimum: 36 months. Maximum: 7 years. Degree requirements: 150 credits including 22 elective credits.

PLACEMENT

In 1993-94, 70 organizations participated in on-campus recruiting. Placement services include alumni network, career counseling/planning, career fairs, career library, career placement, electronic job bank, job interviews, job search course, resume preparation, and resume referral to employers. Of 1994 graduates, 85% were employed within three months of graduation, the average starting salary was $43,050, the range was $25,000-$86,000.
Jobs by Employer Type Manufacturing 20%; service 46%; government 12%; consulting 7%; nonprofit 3%; real estate 12%.
Jobs by Functional Area Marketing/sales 15%; finance 30%; operations 10%; management 25%; strategic planning 6%; technical management 2%; real estate 12%.

Program Contact: Ms. Kathy Decker Frueh, Director of Admissions, University of Denver, University Park, Denver, CO 80208. (303) 877-3416, or (800) 622-4723; Fax: (303) 871-4466.

University of Southern Colorado

School of Business

Pueblo, Colorado

OVERVIEW

The University of Southern Colorado is a state-supported comprehensive coed institution. Part of Colorado State University System. Founded 1933. Setting: 275-acre suburban campus. Total institutional enrollment: 4,500. Program was first offered in 1984.

MBA HIGHLIGHTS

Entrance Difficulty***
Mean GMAT: 490
Mean GPA: 3.02

Cost $
Tuition: $79/semester hour
(Nonresident: $323/semester hour)
Room & Board: N/R

Enrollment Profile

Full-time: 38
Part-time: 78
Total: 116
Average Age: 33

Work Exp: 90%
International: 36%
Women: 40%
Minorities: 9%

Average Class Size: 20

ACADEMICS

Length of Program Minimum: 12 months. Maximum: 6 years.

Calendar Semesters.

Full-time Classes Main campus, Mesa State College; evening, weekends, summer.

Part-time Classes Main campus, Mesa State College; evening, weekends, summer.

Degree Requirements 36 credits including 6 elective credits. Other: International business and choice of two listed electives, or six hours of a directed research and a choice of one listed elective.

Required Courses Business ethics and environment, financial management, management information systems, management of organizational behavior, management policy and strategy, managerial accounting, managerial economics, marketing management, production and operations management. Courses may be waived through: previous course work.

Curricular Focus General management, international business, problem solving and decision making.

Concentrations Accounting, management.

Faculty Full-time: 15, 80% with doctorates.

Teaching Methodology Case study: 25%, lecture: 30%, research: 10%, student presentations: 10%, team projects: 25%.

Special Opportunities International exchange program available.

STUDENT STATISTICS

Geographic Representation State residents 30%. By region: West 50%; Midwest 8%; Northeast 4%; South 2%. International 36%.

Undergraduate Majors Business 51%; engineering/technology 15%; science/mathematics 6%; social sciences 12%; other 13%.

Other Background Graduate degrees in other disciplines: 2%. Work experience: On average, students have 10 years of work experience on entrance to the program.

FACILITIES

Information Resources Main library with 190,000 bound volumes, 6,440 titles on microform, 1,300 periodical subscriptions, 16,000 records/tapes/CDs, 20 CD-ROMs. Business collection includes 15,400 bound volumes, 132 periodical subscriptions, 30 CD-ROMs, 75 videos.

Housing 2% of students in program live in college-owned or -operated housing.

Technology Computers are used heavily in course work. 104 computer terminals/PCs, linked by a campus-wide computer network, are available for use by students in program; they are located in the library, the computer center, computer labs. Students in the program are not required to have their own PC. $400 are budgeted per student for computer support.

Computer Resources/On-line Services

Training	Yes	CompuServe	No
Internet	Yes	Dun's	No
E-Mail	Yes	Dow Jones	No
Videoconference Center	Yes	Dialog	No
Multimedia Center	Yes	Bloomberg	No
LEXIS/NEXIS	No		

Other on-line services: OCLC.

ADMISSION

Acceptance 1994-95 80 applied for admission; 60% were accepted.

Entrance Requirements Bachelor's degree, prerequisite courses required for applicants with non-business degree, GMAT score, minimum 2.5 GPA. Core courses waived through: previous course work.

Application Requirements Application form, copies of transcript.

Application Deadlines 8/20 for fall, 1/8 for spring, 5/1 for summer.

FINANCIALS

Costs for 1994-95 Tuition: Full-time: $79/semester hour for state residents, $323/semester hour for nonresidents. Fees: Full-time: $16 for state residents, $16 for nonresidents.

Financial Aid In 1994-95, 5% of candidates received some institutionally administered aid in the form of scholarships, loans, assistantships. Total awards ranged from $3,000-$7,500. Financial aid is available to part-time students. Application deadlines: 4/15 for fall, 11/1 for spring, 4/15 for summer. Contact: Ms. Linda DiPrince, Associate Director, 2200 Bonforte Boulevard, Pueblo, CO 81001-4990. (719) 549-2789.

INTERNATIONAL STUDENTS

Demographics 36% of students enrolled in the program are international; Asia 50%, Europe 25%, Central America 15%, South America 5%, other 5%.

Services and Facilities International student center, visa services, language tutoring, special assistance for nonnative speakers of English, counseling/support services.

Applying TOEFL required, minimum score of 500; proof of health; proof of adequate funds. Financial aid is available to international students. Assistantships are available for these students. Admission application deadlines: 7/1 for fall, 11/1 for spring, 4/1 for summer. Contact: Dr. Abhay Shah, MBA Director, 2200 Bonforte Boulevard, Pueblo, CO 81001-4900. (719) 549-2128.

PLACEMENT

In 1993-94, 4 organizations participated in on-campus recruiting; 2 on-campus interviews were conducted. Placement services include alumni network, career counseling/planning, career fairs, career library, job interviews, resume preparation, and resume referral to employers. Of 1994 graduates, 75% were employed within three months of graduation, the average starting salary was $21,900, the range was $13,000-$43,000.

Program Contact: Dr. Abhay Shah, MBA Program Director, University of Southern Colorado, 2200 Bonforte Boulevard, Pueblo, CO 81001-4990. (719) 549-2128; Fax: (719) 549-2909.

CONNECTICUT

Central Connecticut State University

School of Business

New Britain, Connecticut

OVERVIEW

Central Connecticut State University is a state-supported comprehensive coed institution. Part of Connecticut State University System. Founded 1849. Setting: 176-acre urban campus. Total institutional enrollment: 11,959. Program was first offered in 1994.

MBA HIGHLIGHTS

Entrance Difficulty*
Mean GMAT: 480
Mean GPA: 3.2

Cost $
Tuition: $1,146/semester
(Nonresident: $3,196/semester)
Room & Board: $4,370

Enrollment Profile

Full-time: 0
Part-time: 8
Total: 8
Average Age: N/R

Work Exp: 100%
International: N/R
Women: N/R
Minorities: N/R

Average Class Size: N/R

ACADEMICS

Length of Program Minimum: 30 months. Maximum: 6 years.

Calendar Semesters.

Full-time Classes Main campus; evening.

Part-time Classes Main campus; evening, summer.

Degree Requirements 33 credits including 12 elective credits.

Required Courses Contemporary issues in international business, global strategy, international accounting, international financial management, international management, international management information systems, international marketing. Courses may be waived through: previous course work.

Curricular Focus Business issues and problems, international business, leadership.

Concentrations International and area studies, international business.

Faculty Full-time: 8, 100% with doctorates.

Teaching Methodology Case study: 20%, lecture: 40%, research: 10%, student presentations: 20%, team projects: 10%.

Special Opportunities International exchange program available.

STUDENT STATISTICS

Geographic Representation By region: Northeast 75%.

Undergraduate Majors Business 75%; engineering/technology 25%.

Other Background Graduate degrees in other disciplines: 25%.

FACILITIES

Information Resources Main library with 534,224 bound volumes, 430,657 titles on microform, 3,027 periodical subscriptions, 6,537 records/tapes/CDs, 15 CD-ROMs. Business collection includes 15,602 bound volumes, 306 periodical subscriptions, 3 CD-ROMs, 6 videos.

Housing College housing available.

Technology Computers are used moderately in course work. 125 computer terminals/PCs are available for use by students in program; they are located in computer labs. Students in the program are not required to have their own PC.

Computer Resources/On-line Services

Training	Yes	Multimedia Center	Yes
Internet	Yes	Dialog	Yes
E-Mail	Yes		

Other on-line services: OCLC, First Search.

ADMISSION

Entrance Requirements Bachelor's degree, GMAT score, minimum 2.7 GPA.

Application Requirements Application form, copies of transcript.

Application Deadlines 3/1 for fall, 12/1 for spring. Applications are processed on a rolling basis.

FINANCIALS

Costs for 1994-95 Tuition: Full-time: $1,146/semester for state residents, $3,196/semester for nonresidents. Fees: Full-time: $632/semester for state residents, $1,036/semester for nonresidents. Average room and board costs are $4,370 per academic year (on-campus).

Financial Aid In 1994-95, 10% of candidates received some institutionally administered aid in the form of scholarships, loans, assistantships, work-study. Financial aid is available to part-time students. Application deadlines: 3/15 for fall, 11/15 for spring. Contact: Director of Financial Aid, 1615 Stanley Street, New Britain, CT 06050-4010. (203) 832-2200.

INTERNATIONAL STUDENTS

Demographics 1% of students on campus are international; Asia 40%, Europe 17%, South America 5%, Africa 3%, other 35%.

Services and Facilities Visa services, ESL courses, special assistance for nonnative speakers of English, counseling/support services.

Applying TOEFL required, minimum score of 550; proof of health; proof of adequate funds. Financial aid is not available to international students. Admission application deadlines: 6/1 for fall, 12/1 for spring. Applications are processed on a rolling basis. Contact: Ms. Susan Lesser, Assistant Director, International Affairs Center, 1615 Stanley Street, New Britain, CT 06050-4010. (203) 832-2050.

PLACEMENT

Placement services include career counseling/planning, career fairs, career placement, resume preparation, and resume referral to employers.

Program Contact: Mr. George F. Claffey, Director, Graduate Business Programs, Central Connecticut State University, 1615 Stanley Street, New Britain, CT 06050-4010. (203) 832-3210; Fax: (203) 832-3219.
See full description on page 690.

Fairfield University

School of Business

Fairfield, Connecticut

OVERVIEW

Fairfield University is an independent Roman Catholic (Jesuit) comprehensive coed institution. Founded 1942. Setting: 200-acre suburban campus with easy access to New York City. Total institutional enrollment: 4,777.

PROGRAM HIGHLIGHTS

Entrance Difficulty***
Mean GMAT: 550
Mean GPA: N/R

Cost $$
Tuition: $400/credit
Room & Board: $6,200

Enrollment Profile

Full-time: N/R	Work Exp: N/R
Part-time: N/R	International: 5%
Total: 175	Women: 47%
Average Age: N/R	Minorities: 10%

Average Class Size: 25

ACADEMICS

Calendar Semesters.

Curricular Focus International business, organizational development and change management, problem solving and decision making.

Concentrations Finance, financial management, human resources management, international business, marketing.

Teaching Methodology Case study: 15%, faculty seminars: 5%, lecture: 30%, research: 15%, seminars by members of the business community: 5%, student presentations: 15%, team projects: 15%.

STUDENT STATISTICS

Geographic Representation State residents 90%. International 5%.

FACILITIES

Information Resources Main library with 310,000 bound volumes, 433,800 titles on microform, 1,797 periodical subscriptions, 6,278 records/tapes/CDs, 16 CD-ROMs.

Housing College housing available.

ADMISSION

Acceptance 1994-95 112 applied for admission; 91% were accepted.

Entrance Requirements Bachelor's degree, prerequisite courses required for applicants with non-business degree.

Application Requirements Copies of transcript, personal statement, 2 letters of recommendation.

Application Deadlines 9/1 for fall, 12/1 for spring, 5/1 for summer. Applications are processed on a rolling basis.

FINANCIALS

Estimated Costs for 1995-96 Tuition: Full-time: $400/credit. Fees: Full-time: $20/semester. Average room and board costs are $6,200 per academic year (on-campus) and $6,200 per academic year (off-campus).

Financial Aid In 1994-95, 2% of candidates received some institutionally administered aid in the form of research assistantships. Applications are processed on a rolling basis. Contact: Office of Graduate Admissions, Fairfield, CT 06430-5195. (203) 254-4180.

INTERNATIONAL STUDENTS

Demographics 5% of students enrolled in the program are international.

Services and Facilities International student housing; international student office, visa services, language tutoring, special assistance for nonnative speakers of English, counseling/support services.

Applying TOEFL required, minimum score of 550; proof of health; proof of adequate funds. Financial aid is not available to international students. Admission applications are processed on a rolling basis. Contact: Fr. Laurence O'Neil, Director of Student Support Services, Fairfield, CT 06430-5195. (203) 254-2445.

PROGRAM

MSFM Length of program: Minimum: 24 months. Full-time classes: Main campus; evening, weekends, summer. Part-time classes: Main campus; evening, weekends, summer. Degree requirements: 45 credits.

PLACEMENT

Placement services include alumni network, career counseling/planning, career fairs, career library, career placement, electronic job bank, job interviews, job search course, resume preparation, and resume referral to employers.

Program Contact: Office of Graduate Admissions, Fairfield University, Fairfield, CT 06430-5195. (203) 254-4180.
See full description on page 736.

The Hartford Graduate Center

School of Management

Hartford, Connecticut

OVERVIEW

The Hartford Graduate Center is graduate-only institution. Total institutional enrollment: 1,961.

ACADEMICS

Full-time Classes Main campus; day, summer.

Part-time Classes Main campus; weekends.

Degree Requirements 46 credits.

Curricular Focus Interface between technology and people, problem solving and decision making, strategic analysis and planning.

Concentrations Finance, health services, human resources management, international business, management, marketing, operations management.

FACILITIES

Information Resources Main library with 30,000 bound volumes, 43,141 titles on microform, 460 periodical subscriptions.

ADMISSION

Entrance Requirements Bachelor's degree.

Application Requirements Copies of transcript, 2 letters of recommendation.

Application Deadline Applications are processed on a rolling basis.

FINANCIALS

Costs for 1994-95 Tuition: Part-time day: $425/credit hour.

Financial Aid Contact: Ms. Linda Gilbert, Admissions Administrator and Financial Aid Officer, 275 Windsor Street, Hartford, CT 06120. (203) 548-2422 Ext. 422.

Program Contact: Ms. Rebecca Denchak, Director of Student Affairs, The Hartford Graduate Center, 275 Windsor Street, Hartford, CT 06120. (203) 548-2421, or (800) 433-4723 (CT only).

Quinnipiac College

School of Business

Hamden, Connecticut

OVERVIEW

Quinnipiac College is an independent nonprofit comprehensive coed institution. Founded 1929. Setting: 180-acre suburban campus with easy access to Hartford. Total institutional enrollment: 4,660.

MBA HIGHLIGHTS

Entrance Difficulty*
Mean GMAT: 470
Mean GPA: N/R

Cost $
Tuition: $330/credit hour
Room & Board: $9,100

Enrollment Profile
Full-time: N/R
Part-time: N/R
Total: 180
Average Age: N/R
Work Exp: N/R
International: 2%
Women: 40%
Minorities: 5%

Average Class Size: 15

ACADEMICS

Length of Program Minimum: 18 months.

Calendar Semesters.

Full-time Classes Main campus; day, evening, weekends, summer.

Part-time Classes Main campus; day, evening, weekends, summer.

Degree Requirements 36 credit hours.

Curricular Focus Leadership, problem solving and decision making, teamwork.

Concentrations Accounting, computer science, economics, finance, management, marketing.

Teaching Methodology Case study: 40%, faculty seminars: 20%, lecture: 20%, research: 15%, seminars by members of the business community: 5%.

STUDENT STATISTICS

Geographic Representation State residents 92%. International 2%.

FACILITIES

Information Resources Main library with 292,000 bound volumes, 155,850 titles on microform, 4,291 periodical subscriptions, 2,350 records/tapes/CDs, 30 CD-ROMs.

Housing College housing available.

ADMISSION

Entrance Requirements Bachelor's degree, prerequisite courses required for applicants with non-business degree, GMAT score of 400, minimum 2.5 GPA.

Application Requirements Application form, copies of transcript, resume/curriculum vitae, 2 letters of recommendation.

Application Deadline Applications are processed on a rolling basis.

FINANCIALS

Costs for 1994-95 Tuition: Full-time: $330/credit hour. Average room and board costs are $9,100 per academic year (on-campus) and $9,100 per academic year (off-campus).

Financial Aid Financial aid is available to part-time students. Contact: Director of Financial Aid, Financial Aid Office, Mount Carmel Avenue, Hamden, CT 06518-1904. (203) 281-8750.

INTERNATIONAL STUDENTS

Demographics 2% of students enrolled in the program are international.

Applying TOEFL required, minimum score of 600; proof of health; proof of adequate funds. Financial aid is available to international students. Assistantships are available for these students. Admission applications are processed on a rolling basis.

Program Contact: Ms. Elizabeth Truebert, Director of Graduate Admissions, Quinnipiac College, Mount Carmel Avenue, Hamden, CT 06518-1904. (203) 281-8795; Fax: (203) 281-8749.

Sacred Heart University

Faculty of Business Administration

Fairfield, Connecticut

OVERVIEW

Sacred Heart University is an independent Roman Catholic comprehensive coed institution. Founded 1963. Setting: 56-acre suburban campus with easy access to New York City. Total institutional enrollment: 5,450. Program was first offered in 1979.

MBA HIGHLIGHTS

Entrance Difficulty**
Mean GMAT: 450
Mean GPA: 2.9

Cost $
Tuition: $420/credit
Room & Board: $5,500

Enrollment Profile
Full-time: 21
Part-time: 714
Total: 735
Average Age: 26

Work Exp: 90%
International: 1%
Women: 54%
Minorities: 10%

Average Class Size: 25

ACADEMICS
Length of Program Minimum: 24 months. Maximum: 6 years.
Calendar Trimesters.
Full-time Classes Main campus, Stamford; day, evening, weekends, summer.
Part-time Classes Main campus, Stamford, Danbury; day, evening, weekends, summer.
Degree Requirements 48 credits including 12 elective credits. Other: Research paper.
Required Courses Administrative policy, ethics, financial management, international business, legal environment of business, management information systems, management of organization, managerial accounting, managerial economics, marketing management, organizational behavior, production and operations management. Courses may be waived through: previous course work.
Curricular Focus International business, problem solving and decision making, teamwork.
Concentrations Accounting, finance, health services, human resources management, international business, management, management information systems, marketing.
Teaching Methodology Case study: 25%, lecture: 30%, research: 10%, seminars by members of the business community: 5%, student presentations: 10%, team projects: 20%.
Special Opportunities International exchange in Belgium. Internships include management of nonprofit organizations.

STUDENT STATISTICS
Geographic Representation By region: Northeast 95%. International 1%.
Undergraduate Majors Business 45%; engineering/technology 25%; humanities 15%; nursing 5%; science/mathematics 5%; social sciences 5%.
Other Background Graduate degrees in other disciplines: 5%. Work experience: On average, students have 5 years of work experience on entrance to the program.

FACILITIES
Information Resources Main library with 160,507 bound volumes, 64,665 titles on microform, 1,311 periodical subscriptions, 11,073 records/tapes/CDs, 16 CD-ROMs. Business collection includes 30,000 bound volumes, 250 periodical subscriptions, 400 CD-ROMs.
Housing 5% of students in program live in college-owned or -operated housing.
Technology Computers are used moderately in course work. 150 computer terminals/PCs, linked by a campus-wide computer network, are available for use by students in program; they are located in classrooms, learning resource center, computer labs. Students in the program are not required to have their own PC.
Computer Resources/On-line Services

| Training | Yes | E-Mail | No |
| Internet | Yes | LEXIS/NEXIS | Yes $ |

ADMISSION
Acceptance 1994-95 Of those applying, 90% were accepted.
Entrance Requirements Bachelor's degree, minimum 2.5 GPA, minimum 3 years of work experience. Core courses waived through: previous course work.
Application Requirements Interview, application form, copies of transcript, resume/curriculum vitae, 2 letters of recommendation.
Application Deadlines 8/1 for fall, 11/1 for spring.

FINANCIALS
Costs for 1994-95 Tuition: Full-time: $420/credit; Part-time day: $320/credit. Fees: Full-time: $63/semester; Part-time day: $63/semester. Average room and board costs are $5,500 per academic year (on-campus).
Financial Aid In 1994-95, 10% of candidates received some institutionally administered aid in the form of loans, assistantships. Financial aid is available to part-time students. Application deadlines: 3/1 for fall, 9/1 for spring. Contact: Ms. Julie Savino, Director of Financial Assistance, 5151 Park Avenue, Fairfield, CT 06432-1000. (203) 371-7980.

INTERNATIONAL STUDENTS
Demographics 1% of students enrolled in the program are international.
Services and Facilities Language tutoring, ESL courses, counseling/support services.
Applying TOEFL required, minimum score of 550; proof of adequate funds. Financial aid is not available to international students. Admission application deadlines: 7/1 for fall, 10/1 for spring.

ALTERNATE MBA PROGRAM
MBA/MSN Length of program: Minimum: 24 months. Maximum: 6 years. Degree requirements: 48 credits including 15 elective credits.

PLACEMENT
In 1993-94, 15 organizations participated in on-campus recruiting. Placement services include alumni network, career counseling/planning, career fairs, career placement, and resume preparation.

Program Contact: Ms. Kathy Murphy, Graduate Admissions Counselor, Sacred Heart University, 5151 Park Avenue, Fairfield, CT 06432-1000. (203) 371-7833; Fax: (203) 365-7538.

University of Bridgeport

School of Business

Bridgeport, Connecticut

OVERVIEW
The University of Bridgeport is an independent nonprofit comprehensive coed institution. Founded 1927. Setting: 86-acre urban campus with easy access to New York City. Total institutional enrollment: 1,939. Program was first offered in 1950. AACSB-accredited.

MBA HIGHLIGHTS

Entrance Difficulty***
Mean GMAT: 400
Mean GPA: N/R

Cost $$$
Tuition: $310/credit
Room & Board: $6,810

Enrollment Profile
Full-time: 74
Part-time: 71
Total: 145
Average Age: 31

Work Exp: 75%
International: 53%
Women: 32%
Minorities: 19%

Average Class Size: 15

ACADEMICS
Length of Program Minimum: 12 months. Maximum: 7 years.
Calendar Semesters.
Full-time Classes Main campus, Stamford; evening, weekends, summer.
Part-time Classes Main campus, Stamford; evening, weekends, summer.
Degree Requirements 30 credits.
Required Courses Accounting concepts, business and society, business policy, economic analysis, financial management, management science and management information systems, marketing concepts, operations management, organizational behavior, statistical decision theory.
Curricular Focus Entrepreneurship, international business, strategic analysis and planning.
Concentrations Accounting, economics, finance, human resources management, international business, management, management information systems, marketing.
Faculty Full-time: 13, 85% with doctorates; part-time: 15, 75% with doctorates.

Teaching Methodology Case study: 20%, lecture: 20%, research: 15%, seminars by members of the business community: 10%, student presentations: 15%, team projects: 20%.

Special Opportunities International exchange and internship programs available.

STUDENT STATISTICS
Geographic Representation State residents 37%. By region: Northeast 47%. International 53%.

Undergraduate Majors Business 70%; engineering/technology 10%; humanities 5%; science/mathematics 5%; social sciences 5%; other 5%.

Other Background Graduate degrees in other disciplines: 15%.

FACILITIES
Information Resources Main library with 263,788 bound volumes, 970,703 titles on microform, 1,682 periodical subscriptions, 5,944 records/tapes/CDs, 20 CD-ROMs.

Housing 10% of students in program live in college-owned or -operated housing.

Technology Computers are used moderately in course work. 200 computer terminals/PCs are available for use by students in program; they are located in classrooms, learning resource center, the library, computer labs. Students in the program are not required to have their own PC.

Computer Resources/On-line Services

Training	Yes	Videoconference Center	Yes
Internet	Yes	LEXIS/NEXIS	Yes
E-Mail	Yes		

Other on-line services: OCLC.

ADMISSION
Acceptance 1994-95 230 applied for admission; 90% were accepted.

Entrance Requirements Bachelor's degree, GMAT score, minimum 2.5 GPA. Core courses waived through: previous course work.

Application Requirements Written essay, application form, copies of transcript, personal statement, 3 letters of recommendation.

Application Deadlines 4/1 for fall, 10/1 for spring. Applications are processed on a rolling basis.

FINANCIALS
Costs for 1994-95 Tuition: Full-time: $310/credit. Fees: Full-time: $624. Average room and board costs are $6,810 per academic year (on-campus) and $6,810 per academic year (off-campus).

Financial Aid In 1994-95, 20% of candidates received some institutionally administered aid in the form of scholarships, loans, assistantships, work-study. Total awards ranged from $500-$5,580. Financial aid is available to part-time students. Application deadlines: 4/1 for fall, 10/1 for spring. Applications are processed on a rolling basis. Contact: Mr. Harry White, Director of Admissions and Financial Aid, 380 University Avenue, Bridgeport, CT 06601. (203) 576-4552.

INTERNATIONAL STUDENTS
Demographics 53% of students enrolled in the program are international; Asia 67%, Africa 13%, Europe 13%, South America 7%.

Applying TOEFL required, minimum score of 575; proof of health; proof of adequate funds. Financial aid is available to international students. Financial aid application deadlines: 4/1 for fall, 10/1 for spring. Applications are processed on a rolling basis. Admission application deadlines: 4/1 for fall, 10/1 for spring. Applications are processed on a rolling basis. Contact: Ms. Dawn Valenti, Director of International Affairs, 380 University Avenue, Bridgeport, CT 06601. (203) 576-4395.

PLACEMENT
Placement services include alumni network, career counseling/planning, career fairs, career library, career placement, electronic job bank, job interviews, resume preparation, and resume referral to employers.

Program Contact: Mr. Andrew G. Nelson, Dean of Admissions and Financial Aid, University of Bridgeport, 380 University Avenue, Bridgeport, CT 06601. (203) 576-4552, or (800) 972-9488 (CT only), or (800) 243-9496 (out-of-state); Fax: (203) 576-4941.
See full description on page 856.

University of Connecticut

School of Business Administration

Storrs, Connecticut

OVERVIEW
The University of Connecticut is a state-supported coed institution. Founded 1881. Setting: 4,000-acre small-town campus. Total institutional enrollment: 21,000. Program was first offered in 1959. AACSB-accredited.

MBA HIGHLIGHTS
Entrance Difficulty**
Mean GMAT: 550
Mean GPA: 3.2

Cost $
Tuition: $2,353/semester
(Nonresident: $6,115/semester)
Room & Board: $6,000

Enrollment Profile

Full-time: 230	Work Exp: 90%
Part-time: 1,060	International: 35%
Total: 1,290	Women: 39%
Average Age: 26	Minorities: 14%

Average Class Size: 30

ACADEMICS
Length of Program Minimum: 16 months. Maximum: 5 years.

Calendar Semesters.

Full-time Classes Main campus; day.

Part-time Classes Main campus, Hartford, Stamford; evening, summer.

Degree Requirements 57 credits including 18 elective credits.

Required Courses Business, law and ethics in modern society, cost analysis and control, economic analysis for business, financial accounting and reporting, financial management, leadership and interpersonal dynamics, management information systems, management statistics, managerial communication, managing organizational dynamics, market-driven management, operation management, strategy, policy, and planning.

Curricular Focus Business issues and problems, general management, international business.

Concentrations Accounting, finance, health services, human resources management, international business, management, management information systems, marketing, operations management, real estate.

Faculty Full-time: 31, 100% with doctorates; part-time: 3.

Teaching Methodology Case study: 10%, lecture: 45%, simulations: 15%, student presentations: 10%, team projects: 20%.

Special Opportunities International exchange in Canada, France, Germany. Internship program available.

STUDENT STATISTICS
Geographic Representation State residents 60%. By region: Northeast 65%. International 35%.

Undergraduate Majors Business 40%; education 5%; engineering/technology 12%; humanities 5%; nursing 5%; science/mathematics 5%; social sciences 23%; other 5%.

Other Background Graduate degrees in other disciplines: 2%. Work experience: On average, students have 3 years of work experience on entrance to the program.

FACILITIES
Information Resources Main library with 1.9 million bound volumes, 2.8 million titles on microform, 9,589 periodical subscriptions, 21,985 records/tapes/CDs. Business collection includes 66,893 bound volumes, 155 periodical subscriptions, 13 CD-ROMs, 25 videos.

Housing 35% of students in program live in college-owned or -operated housing.

Technology Computers are used heavily in course work. 250 computer terminals/PCs, linked by a campus-wide computer network, are available for use by students in program; they are located in classrooms, the library, the computer center, computer labs. Students in the program are not required to have their own PC.

187

Computer Resources/On-line Services

Training	Yes	LEXIS/NEXIS	Yes
Internet	Yes	CompuServe	Yes
E-Mail	Yes	Dow Jones	Yes
Videoconference Center	Yes	Dialog	Yes

ADMISSION

Acceptance 1994-95 466 applied for admission; 60% were accepted.

Entrance Requirements Bachelor's degree, GMAT score of 500, minimum 3.0 GPA. Core courses waived through: previous course work.

Application Requirements Written essay, application form, copies of transcript, 2 letters of recommendation.

Application Deadlines 4/1 for fall. Applications are processed on a rolling basis.

FINANCIALS

Costs for 1994-95 Tuition: Full-time: $2,353/semester for state residents, $6,115/semester for nonresidents. Fees: Full-time: $350/semester for state residents, $350/semester for nonresidents. Average room and board costs are $6,000 per academic year (on-campus) and $6,000 per academic year (off-campus).

Financial Aid In 1994-95, candidates received some institutionally administered aid in the form of grants, scholarships, loans, assistantships, work-study. Financial aid is not available to part-time students. Applications are processed on a rolling basis. Contact: Mr. Robert Packard, Director of MBA Program, 368 Fairfield Road, U-41 MBA, Storrs, CT 06269-2041. (203) 486-2872.

INTERNATIONAL STUDENTS

Demographics 35% of students enrolled in the program are international; Asia 60%, Europe 25%, Africa 5%, North America 5%, other 5%.

Services and Facilities International student office, international student center, visa services, language tutoring, ESL courses, counseling/support services.

Applying TOEFL required, minimum score of 550; proof of health; proof of adequate funds. Financial aid is available to international students. Financial aid is available to second year students. Financial aid application deadline: 4/1 for spring. Admission application deadline: 4/1 for fall. Applications are processed on a rolling basis. Contact: Mr. Robert Chudy, Program Director, International Affairs, 843 Bolton Road, Human Development Center, Room 0006, Storrs, CT 06269-1182. (203) 486-3855.

ALTERNATE MBA PROGRAMS

Executive MBA (EMBA) Length of program: Minimum: 21 months. Full-time classes: Main campus, Hartford, Stamford; weekends. Degree requirements: 48 credits.

MBA/JD Length of program: Minimum: 46 months. Full-time classes: Main campus; day, evening, summer. Degree requirements: 114 credits.

MBA/MA Length of program: Minimum: 29 months. Full-time classes: Main campus; day, summer. Degree requirements: 72 credits. MA is in international studies.

MBA/MIM Length of program: Minimum: 23 months. Full-time classes: Main campus, Lyons, France, Hartford; day. Degree requirements: 60 credits.

MBA/MSW Length of program: Minimum: 46 months. Full-time classes: Main campus, Hartford; day, summer. Degree requirements: 109 credits.

PLACEMENT

In 1993-94, 45 organizations participated in on-campus recruiting; 300 on-campus interviews were conducted. Placement services include alumni network, career counseling/planning, career fairs, career library, career placement, job interviews, resume preparation, and resume referral to employers. Of 1994 graduates, 77% were employed within three months of graduation, the average starting salary was $41,300, the range was $28,000-$80,000.

Jobs by Employer Type Manufacturing 20%; service 17%; consulting 9%; real estate 4%; healthcare 9%; accounting 17%; banking/finance 24%.

Jobs by Functional Area Marketing/sales 13%; finance 45%; operations 5%; management 5%; technical management 2%; real estate 13%; consulting and human resources 17%.

Program Contact: Mr. Robert Packard, Director, Storrs MBA Program, University of Connecticut, 368 Fairfield Road, U-41 MBA, Storrs, CT 06269-2041. (203) 486-2872; Fax: (203) 486-5222.
See full description on page 868.

University of Hartford

Barney School of Business and Public Administration

West Hartford, Connecticut

OVERVIEW

The University of Hartford is an independent nonprofit comprehensive coed institution. Founded 1877. Setting: suburban campus with easy access to Hartford. Total institutional enrollment: 6,000.

MBA HIGHLIGHTS

Entrance Difficulty*
Mean GMAT: 475
Mean GPA: N/R

Cost $$$
Tuition: $320/credit hour
Room & Board: $9,600

Enrollment Profile

Full-time: 200	Work Exp: N/R
Part-time: 411	International: 26%
Total: 611	Women: 40%
Average Age: 25	Minorities: 2%

Class Size: 25 - 30

ACADEMICS

Length of Program Minimum: 12 months.

Calendar Semesters.

Full-time Classes Main campus, Paris, France; day, evening.

Part-time Classes Main campus; day, evening.

Degree Requirements 48 credits.

Curricular Focus International business, problem solving and decision making, strategic analysis and planning.

Concentrations Accounting, finance, human resources management, international business, management, marketing, organizational behavior, public administration.

Faculty Full-time: 50.

Teaching Methodology Case study: 40%, lecture: 30%, research: 5%, seminars by members of the business community: 10%, student presentations: 5%, team projects: 10%.

STUDENT STATISTICS

Geographic Representation International 26%.

FACILITIES

Information Resources Main library with 408,000 bound volumes, 231,318 titles on microform, 3,620 periodical subscriptions, 25,697 records/tapes/CDs, 15 CD-ROMs.

ADMISSION

Entrance Requirements Bachelor's degree, GMAT score. Core courses waived through: previous course work.

Application Requirements Written essay, application form, copies of transcript, resume/curriculum vitae, personal statement, 2 letters of recommendation.

Application Deadlines 7/1 for fall. Applications are processed on a rolling basis.

FINANCIALS

Costs for 1994-95 Tuition: Full-time: $320/credit hour. Average room and board costs are $9,600 per academic year (on-campus).

Financial Aid In 1994-95, candidates received some institutionally administered aid in the form of fellowships, assistantships. Financial aid is available to part-time students. Application deadline: 5/1 for fall. Applications are processed on a rolling basis. Contact: Mr. Joseph Martinkovic, Director, 200 Bloomfield Avenue, West Hartford, CT 06117-1500. (203) 768-4904.

INTERNATIONAL STUDENTS

Demographics 26% of students enrolled in the program are international.

Applying TOEFL required, minimum score of 550; proof of adequate funds. Financial aid is available to international students. Applications are processed on a rolling basis. Admission applications are processed on a rolling basis. Contact: Mr. Richard Lazzerini, Associate Director for the International Center, 200 Bloomfield Avenue, West Hartford, CT 06117-1500. (203) 768-5100.

Program Contact: Office of Academic Services, University of Hartford, 200 Bloomfield Avenue, West Hartford, CT 06117-1500. (203) 768-4444; Fax: (203) 768-4198.

University of New Haven

School of Business

West Haven, Connecticut

OVERVIEW

The University of New Haven is an independent nonprofit comprehensive coed institution. Founded 1920. Setting: 73-acre suburban campus with easy access to Hartford. Total institutional enrollment: 5,365. Program was first offered in 1969.

MBA HIGHLIGHTS

Entrance Difficulty**
Mean GMAT: N/R
Mean GPA: 3.55

Cost $
Tuition: $320/credit
Room & Board: $12,000 (off-campus)

Enrollment Profile

Full-time: 149	Work Exp: 80%
Part-time: 608	International: N/R
Total: 757	Women: 44%
Average Age: 29	Minorities: N/R

Average Class Size: 22

ACADEMICS

Length of Program Minimum: 18 months. Maximum: 5 years.

Calendar Trimesters.

Full-time Classes Main campus.

Part-time Classes Main campus, Groton, Waterbury evening, Trumbull evening; evening, summer.

Degree Requirements 57 credits including 15 elective credits.

Required Courses Business and society, finance, integrated marketing topics, international business, macroglobal economics, managerial accounting, managerial economics, managerial theory, managing technology, marketing, operations management, organizational behavior, policy and strategy, statistics.

Curricular Focus General management, problem solving and decision making, strategic analysis and planning.

Concentrations Accounting, finance, health services, human resources management, international business, management, marketing, operations management, policy and strategy, computer and information science, operations research, technology management, public administration, strategic management.

Faculty Full-time: 50, 85% with doctorates; part-time: 20, 50% with doctorates.

Teaching Methodology Case study: 20%, faculty seminars: 5%, lecture: 50%, research: 10%, student presentations: 5%, team projects: 10%.

Special Opportunities International exchange in Cyprus, Israel. Internships include public relations, advertising, health care management, international business, and marketing, telecommunications.

STUDENT STATISTICS

Undergraduate Majors Business 55%; education 5%; engineering/technology 10%; humanities 15%; nursing 10%; social sciences 5%.

Other Background Graduate degrees in other disciplines: 10%. Work experience: On average, students have 3 years of work experience on entrance to the program.

FACILITIES

Information Resources Main library with 343,681 bound volumes, 414,812 titles on microform, 1,079 periodical subscriptions, 484 records/tapes/CDs, 93 CD-ROMs.

Housing College housing not available.

Technology Computers are used moderately in course work. 59 computer terminals/PCs are available for use by students in program; they are located in learning resource center, the computer center, computer labs. Students in the program are not required to have their own PC.

Computer Resources/On-line Services

Training	No	Dun's	Yes
Internet	Yes	Dow Jones	Yes
E-Mail	Yes	Dialog	Yes $
LEXIS/NEXIS	Yes	Bloomberg	No
CompuServe	No		

Other on-line services: First Search.

ADMISSION

Acceptance 1994-95 Of those applying, 69% were accepted.

Entrance Requirements Bachelor's degree, minimum 3.0 GPA. Core courses waived through: previous course work.

Application Requirements Application form, copies of transcript, 2 letters of recommendation.

Application Deadline Applications are processed on a rolling basis.

FINANCIALS

Costs for 1994-95 Tuition: Full-time: $320/credit. Fees: Full-time: $10/trimester. Average room and board costs are $12,000 per academic year (off-campus).

Financial Aid In 1994-95, candidates received some institutionally administered aid in the form of grants, loans, fellowships, assistantships, work-study. Financial aid is available to part-time students. Application deadlines: 5/1 for fall, 10/15 for winter, 1/15 for spring. Applications are processed on a rolling basis. Contact: Ms. Jane Sangeloty, Director of Financial Aid, 300 Orange Avenue, West Haven, CT 06516-1916. (203) 932-7312.

INTERNATIONAL STUDENTS

Demographics 10% of students on campus are international; Asia 85%, Africa 5%, Europe 5%, South America 5%.

Services and Facilities International student office, language tutoring, ESL courses, special assistance for nonnative speakers of English, counseling/support services.

Applying TOEFL required, minimum score of 500; proof of health; proof of adequate funds. Financial aid is not available to international students. Admission application deadlines: 6/1 for fall, 10/15 for winter, 1/15 for spring. Applications are processed on a rolling basis. Contact: Ms. Lisa Carraretto, Director, International Services, 300 Orange Avenue, West Haven, CT 06516-1916. (203) 932-7338.

PLACEMENT

Placement services include career counseling/planning, career fairs, job interviews, and resume preparation.

Program Contact: Mr. Joe Spellman, Director, Graduate Admissions and Operations, University of New Haven, 300 Orange Avenue, West Haven, CT 06516-1916. (203) 932-7138, or (800) DIAL-UNH; Fax: (203) 932-7137.

See full description on page 900.

Western Connecticut State University

Ancell School of Business

Danbury, Connecticut

OVERVIEW

Western Connecticut State University is a state-supported comprehensive coed institution. Part of Connecticut State University System. Founded 1903. Setting: 340-acre small-town campus with easy access to New York City. Total institutional enrollment: 7,000. Program was first offered in 1988.

MBA HIGHLIGHTS

Entrance Difficulty***
Mean GMAT: 550
Mean GPA: 3.0

Cost $
Tuition: $145/credit hour
Room & Board: N/R

Enrollment Profile
Full-time: 7	Work Exp: 80%
Part-time: 102	International: 0%
Total: 109	Women: 25%
Average Age: 29	Minorities: 10%

Class Size: 15 - 20

ACADEMICS
Length of Program Minimum: 48 months. Maximum: 8 years.
Calendar Semesters.
Part-time Classes Main campus; evening, weekends, summer.
Degree Requirements 57 semester hours including 15 elective semester hours.
Required Courses Accounting, economics, finance, law, management, management information systems, marketing, statistics.
Curricular Focus General management, leadership, problem solving and decision making.
Concentrations Accounting, management.

STUDENT STATISTICS
Geographic Representation State residents 70%. By region: Northeast 100%.
Undergraduate Majors Business 20%; education 20%; engineering/technology 30%; humanities 20%; science/mathematics 10%.

FACILITIES
Information Resources Main library with 154,503 bound volumes, 50,268 titles on microform, 1,669 periodical subscriptions, 3,575 records/tapes/CDs.
Technology Computers are used moderately in course work.
Computer Resources/On-line Services
E-Mail   Yes

ADMISSION
Entrance Requirements Bachelor's degree, GMAT score of 500, minimum 3.0 GPA. Core courses waived through: previous course work.
Application Requirements Application form, copies of transcript, resume/curriculum vitae, personal statement, 2 letters of recommendation.
Application Deadlines 8/5 for fall, 1/5 for spring.

FINANCIALS
Estimated Costs for 1995-96 Tuition: Full-time: $145/credit hour for state residents. Fees: Full-time: $10/semester for state residents.
Financial Aid Application deadline: 4/15 for fall. Contact: Mr. William Hawkins, Director of Financial Aid and Veteran's Affairs, 181 White Street, Danbury, CT 06810-6885. (203) 837-8581.

INTERNATIONAL STUDENTS
Demographics 10% of students on campus are international.
Applying TOEFL required; proof of health. Financial aid is available to international students. Financial aid application deadline: 4/15 for fall. Admission application deadlines: 8/1 for fall, 1/1 for spring.

Program Contact: Ms. Sally Connolly, Administrative Assistant, Graduate Programs, Western Connecticut State University, 181 White Street, Danbury, CT 06810-6885. (203) 837-8245; Fax: (203) 837-8527.

Yale University

Yale School of Management

New Haven, Connecticut

OVERVIEW
Yale University is an independent nonprofit coed institution. Founded 1701. Setting: 170-acre urban campus with easy access to New York City. Total institutional enrollment: 10,844. Program was first offered in 1976. AACSB-accredited.

PROGRAM HIGHLIGHTS

Entrance Difficulty***
Mean GMAT: 656
Mean GPA: 3.4

Cost $$$$
Tuition: $20,990
Room & Board: $7,560

Enrollment Profile
Full-time: 431	Work Exp: 100%
Part-time: 0	International: 33%
Total: 431	Women: 33%
Average Age: 27	Minorities: 18%

Average Class Size: 49

ACADEMICS
Calendar Semesters.
Curricular Focus Economic and financial theory, problem solving and decision making, teamwork.
Concentration Management.
Faculty Full-time: 40, 100% with doctorates; part-time: 9, 80% with doctorates.
Teaching Methodology Case study: 30%, faculty seminars: 5%, lecture: 50%, student presentations: 5%, team projects: 10%.

STUDENT STATISTICS
Geographic Representation State residents 67%. By region: Northeast 45%; West 10%; South 7%; Midwest 6%. International 33%.
Undergraduate Majors Business 16%; engineering/technology 12%; humanities 24%; science/mathematics 13%; social sciences 35%.
Other Background Graduate degrees in other disciplines: 18%. Work experience: On average, students have 5 years of work experience on entrance to the program.

FACILITIES
Information Resources Main library with 10.2 million bound volumes, 4 million titles on microform, 54,601 periodical subscriptions. Business collection in Social Science Library includes 137,589 bound volumes, 7,199 periodical subscriptions, 13 CD-ROMs.
Housing 10% of students in program live in college-owned or -operated housing. Assistance with housing search provided.
Technology Computers are used heavily in course work. 100 computer terminals/PCs, linked by a campus-wide computer network, are available for use by students in program; they are located in dormitories, classrooms, the library, the computer center, computer labs. Students in the program are not required to have their own PC. $475 are budgeted per student for computer support.
Computer Resources/On-line Services

Training	Yes	Dun's	No
Internet	Yes	Dow Jones	Yes
E-Mail	Yes	Dialog	No
LEXIS/NEXIS	Yes	Bloomberg	No
CompuServe	No		

ADMISSION
Acceptance 1994-95 2,392 applied for admission; 39% were accepted.
Entrance Requirements Bachelor's degree, GMAT score. Core courses waived through: exams.
Application Requirements Written essay, application form, copies of transcript, resume/curriculum vitae, personal statement, 3 letters of recommendation.
Application Deadline Applications are processed on a rolling basis. Application discs available.

FINANCIALS
Costs for 1994-95 Tuition: Full-time: $20,990. Fees: Full-time: $565. Average room and board costs are $7,560 per academic year (on-campus) and $7,560 per academic year (off-campus).
Financial Aid In 1994-95, 51% of candidates received some institutionally administered aid in the form of grants, scholarships, loans, fellowships, assistantships, work-study. Total awards ranged from $2,400-$28,000. Financial aid is not available to part-time students. Application deadline: 3/1 for fall. Applications are processed on a rolling basis. Contact: Ms. Karen Wellman, Financial Aid Administrator, New Haven, CT 06520. (203) 432-5173.

INTERNATIONAL STUDENTS

Demographics 33% of students enrolled in the program are international; Asia 42%, Europe 27%, Central America 10%, North America 8%, Africa 4%, Australia 3%, South America 2%, other 4%.

Services and Facilities International student office, visa services, ESL courses.

Applying TOEFL required, minimum score of 600; proof of health; proof of adequate funds. Financial aid is available to international students. Financial aid application deadline: 3/1 for fall. Applications are processed on a rolling basis. Admission applications are processed on a rolling basis. Contact: Ms. Roberta Grossman, Director, Office of Foreign Students and Scholars, 442 Temple Street, New Haven, CT 06520. (203) 432-2305.

PROGRAM

MPPM Length of program: Minimum: 24 months. Maximum: 2 years. Full-time classes: Main campus; day. Degree requirements: 18 courses including 7 elective courses.

PLACEMENT

In 1993-94, 91 organizations participated in on-campus recruiting; 1,360 on-campus interviews were conducted. Placement services include alumni network, career counseling/planning, career fairs, career library, career placement, electronic job bank, job interviews, job search course, resume preparation, and resume referral to employers. Of 1994 graduates, 91% were employed within three months of graduation, the average starting salary was $58,464, the range was $29,000-$98,000.

Jobs by Employer Type Manufacturing 12%; service 47%; government 3%; consulting 30%; nonprofit 8%.

Jobs by Functional Area Marketing/sales 7%; finance 39%; operations 1%; management 11%; strategic planning 4%; technical management 1%; consulting 31%; other 6%.

Program Contact: Mr. Richard Silverman, Executive Director, Admissions, Yale University, Box 208200/135 Prospect Street, New Haven, CT 06520. (203) 432-5932; Fax: (203) 432-9991; Internet Address: silvermn@admin.som.yale.edu.

DELAWARE

Delaware State University

School of Business and Economics

Dover, Delaware

OVERVIEW

Delaware State University is a state-supported comprehensive coed institution. Founded 1891. Setting: 400-acre small-town campus. Total institutional enrollment: 3,300. Program was first offered in 1985.

MBA HIGHLIGHTS

Entrance Difficulty**
Mean GMAT: 425
Mean GPA: 3.5

Cost $
Tuition: $120/credit hour
(Nonresident: $242/credit hour)
Room & Board: N/R

Enrollment Profile

Full-time: 2	Work Exp: 95%
Part-time: 33	International: 10%
Total: 35	Women: 45%
Average Age: 30	Minorities: 45%

Average Class Size: 15

ACADEMICS

Length of Program Minimum: 12 months. Maximum: 7 years.
Calendar Semesters.
Full-time Classes Main campus; evening.
Part-time Classes Main campus; evening.

Degree Requirements 30 credit hours including 9 elective credit hours.

Required Courses Business policy, financial management, managerial accounting, managerial economics, marketing management, organizational behavior, quantitative methods in business.

Curricular Focus General management, problem solving and decision making.

Concentration Management.

Faculty Full-time: 2, 100% with doctorates; part-time: 3, 100% with doctorates.

Teaching Methodology Case study: 25%, faculty seminars: 25%, lecture: 25%, student presentations: 10%, team projects: 15%.

STUDENT STATISTICS

Geographic Representation State residents 75%. By region: Northeast 90%. International 10%.

Undergraduate Majors Business 70%; engineering/technology 15%; humanities 5%; social sciences 5%; other 5%.

Other Background Graduate degrees in other disciplines: 2%. Work experience: On average, students have 4 years of work experience on entrance to the program.

FACILITIES

Information Resources Main library with 173,996 bound volumes, 73,266 titles on microform, 2,850 periodical subscriptions, 5,641 records/tapes/CDs, 30 CD-ROMs.

Housing College housing available.

Technology Computers are used moderately in course work. Computer terminals/PCs are available for use by students in program; they are located in the library, computer labs. Students in the program are not required to have their own PC.

Computer Resources/On-line Services

Training	Yes	Dun's	Yes
Internet	No	Dow Jones	No
E-Mail	No	Dialog	Yes
LEXIS/NEXIS	No	Bloomberg	No

ADMISSION

Acceptance 1994-95 50 applied for admission; 70% were accepted.

Entrance Requirements Bachelor's degree, GMAT score, minimum 2.75 GPA. Core courses waived through: previous course work.

Application Requirements Application form, copies of transcript, 3 letters of recommendation.

Application Deadlines 6/30 for fall, 11/30 for spring, 4/30 for summer. Applications are processed on a rolling basis.

FINANCIALS

Costs for 1994-95 Tuition: Full-time: $120/credit hour for state residents, $242/credit hour for nonresidents. Fees: Full-time: $65/semester for state residents, $65/semester for nonresidents.

Financial Aid In 1994-95, candidates received some institutionally administered aid in the form of loans, assistantships, tuition waivers. Total awards ranged from $3,000-$3,200. Application deadline: 4/1 for fall. Contact: Mr. Richard K. Bieker, Director of MBA Program, 1200 North DuPont Highway, Dover, DE 19901-2277. (302) 739-3525.

INTERNATIONAL STUDENTS

Demographics 10% of students enrolled in the program are international; Africa 50%, Asia 25%, Europe 25%.

Services and Facilities International student office, ESL courses.

Applying TOEFL required, minimum score of 550; proof of health; proof of adequate funds. Financial aid is not available to international students. Admission application deadlines: 6/30 for fall, 11/30 for spring. Applications are processed on a rolling basis. Contact: Mrs. Janet Johnson, Director of Student Activities, 1200 North DuPont Highway, Dover, DE 19901-2277. (302) 739-5730.

PLACEMENT

Placement services include alumni network, career counseling/planning, career fairs, career placement, and job interviews. Of 1994 graduates, 100% were employed within three months of graduation.

Program Contact: Dr. Richard K. Bieker, Director, MBA Program, Delaware State University, 1200 North DuPont Highway, Dover, DE 19901-2277. (302) 739-3525; Fax: (302) 739-3517.

University of Delaware

College of Business and Economics

Newark, Delaware

OVERVIEW

The University of Delaware is a state-related coed institution. Founded 1743. Setting: 1,000-acre small-town campus with easy access to Philadelphia and Baltimore. Total institutional enrollment: 18,000. Program was first offered in 1953. AACSB-accredited.

MBA HIGHLIGHTS

Entrance Difficulty*
Mean GMAT: 580
Mean GPA: 3.1

Cost $
Tuition: $2,321/semester
(Nonresident: $5,110/semester)
Room & Board: $8,000

Enrollment Profile
Full-time: N/R
Part-time: N/R
Total: 385
Average Age: 29

Work Exp: 90%
International: 6%
Women: 32%
Minorities: 10%

Average Class Size: 27

ACADEMICS

Length of Program Minimum: 12 months. Maximum: 5 years.
Calendar Semesters.
Full-time Classes Main campus; evening, summer.
Part-time Classes Main campus; evening, summer.
Degree Requirements 36 credits including 12 elective credits. Other: One international course.
Required Courses Competitive marketing strategy, corporate strategy, data analysis and quality management, design and management of operations, financial management, financial reporting and analysis, macroeconomics for managers, management control systems, managerial economics, organizational behavior and administration, social, ethical, legal, and political environment firm.
Curricular Focus Electronic communications, general management, teamwork.
Concentrations Accounting, economics, finance, international business, management, marketing, operations management, technology and innovation management.
Faculty Full-time: 60, 100% with doctorates; part-time: 1, 100% with doctorates.
Teaching Methodology Case study: 40%, lecture: 40%, research: 5%, seminars by members of the business community: 5%, student presentations: 5%, team projects: 5%.
Special Opportunities International exchange program available.

STUDENT STATISTICS

Geographic Representation State residents 94%. International 6%.
Undergraduate Majors Business 43%; engineering/technology 40%; humanities 7%; social sciences 7%; other 3%.
Other Background Graduate degrees in other disciplines: 9%. Work experience: On average, students have 5 years of work experience on entrance to the program.

FACILITIES

Information Resources Main library with 2.1 million bound volumes, 2.4 million titles on microform, 20,000 periodical subscriptions, 4,800 records/tapes/CDs, 64 CD-ROMs.
Housing College housing available.
Technology Computers are used heavily in course work. 100 computer terminals/PCs, linked by a campus-wide computer network, are available for use by students in program; they are located in the library, computer labs. Students in the program are not required to have their own PC.

Computer Resources/On-line Services

Training	Yes	E-Mail	Yes
Internet	Yes	Dialog	Yes $

ADMISSION

Acceptance 1994-95 355 applied for admission; 55% were accepted.
Entrance Requirements Bachelor's degree, GMAT score of 500. Core courses waived through: previous course work.
Application Requirements Written essay, application form, copies of transcript, personal statement, 2 letters of recommendation.
Application Deadlines 5/1 for fall, 11/1 for spring.

FINANCIALS

Costs for 1994-95 Tuition: Full-time: $2,321/semester for state residents, $5,110/semester for nonresidents. Fees: Full-time: $167/semester for state residents, $167/semester for nonresidents. Average room and board costs are $8,000 per academic year (on-campus) and $9,000 per academic year (off-campus).
Financial Aid In 1994-95, 30% of candidates received some institutionally administered aid in the form of fellowships, assistantships. Total awards ranged from $6,300-$13,000. Financial aid is not available to part-time students. Application deadlines: 2/15 for fall, 11/1 for spring. Contact: Mr. Robert Barker, Director of MBA Programs, Newark, DE 19716. (302) 831-2221.

INTERNATIONAL STUDENTS

Demographics 6% of students enrolled in the program are international; Asia 50%, Europe 45%, South America 5%.
Services and Facilities International student center, English language institute.
Applying TOEFL required, minimum score of 585; proof of health; proof of adequate funds. Financial aid is available to international students. Financial aid application deadlines: 2/15 for fall, 11/1 for spring. Admission application deadlines: 5/1 for fall, 11/1 for spring. Applications are processed on a rolling basis.

ALTERNATE MBA PROGRAMS

Executive MBA (EMBA) Length of program: Minimum: 19 months. Full-time classes: Main campus; weekends. Degree requirements: 48 credits.
MBA/MA

PLACEMENT

In 1993-94, 20 organizations participated in on-campus recruiting. Placement services include alumni network, career counseling/planning, career fairs, career placement, job interviews, and resume referral to employers. Of 1994 graduates, 95% were employed within three months of graduation, the average starting salary was $35,000.
Jobs by Functional Area Marketing/sales 15%; finance 37%; operations 10%; management 17%; strategic planning 11%; technical management 10%.

Program Contact: Mr. Robert Barker, Director, MBA Programs, University of Delaware, Newark, DE 19716. (302) 831-2221.
See full description on page 872.

Wilmington College

Division of Business

New Castle, Delaware

OVERVIEW

Wilmington College is an independent nonprofit comprehensive coed institution. Founded 1967. Setting: 13-acre suburban campus with easy access to Philadelphia. Total institutional enrollment: 2,898.

MBA HIGHLIGHTS

Entrance Difficulty**

Cost $
Tuition: $660/course
Room & Board: N/R

Enrollment Profile
Full-time: N/R
Part-time: N/R
Total: 283
Average Age: N/R

Work Exp: N/R
International: N/R
Women: 46%
Minorities: 25%

Average Class Size: 20

ACADEMICS
Length of Program Minimum: 24 months. Maximum: 5 years.
Calendar Semesters.
Part-time Classes Main campus, Georgetown; evening, summer.
Degree Requirements 36 credits.
Curricular Focus General management, leadership, problem solving and decision making.
Concentration Management.
Teaching Methodology Case study: 20%, lecture: 40%, student presentations: 20%, team projects: 20%.

FACILITIES
Information Resources Main library with 75,199 bound volumes, 6,350 titles on microform, 500 periodical subscriptions, 6,200 records/tapes/CDs.
Housing College housing not available.

ADMISSION
Entrance Requirements Bachelor's degree, prerequisite courses required for applicants with non-business degree, GMAT score, minimum 3 years of work experience.
Application Requirements Interview, application form, copies of transcript, 2 letters of recommendation.
Application Deadline Applications are processed on a rolling basis.

FINANCIALS
Costs for 1994-95 Tuition: Part-time evening: $660/course. Fees: Part-time evening: $25/semester.
Financial Aid Application deadlines: 4/15 for fall, 11/15 for spring. Contact: Ms. J.Lynn Iocono, Financial Aid Officer, 518 North King Street, Wilmington, DE 19801. (302) 328-9401 Ext. 106.

INTERNATIONAL STUDENTS
Applying TOEFL required, minimum score of 500; proof of health; proof of adequate funds. Financial aid is available to international students. Financial aid application deadlines: 4/15 for fall, 11/15 for spring. Applications are processed on a rolling basis. Admission application deadlines: 4/15 for fall, 11/15 for spring. Applications are processed on a rolling basis.

Program Contact: Mr. Clint Robertson, Program Director, Wilmington College, 518 North King Street, Wilmington, DE 19801. (302) 655-5400.

DISTRICT OF COLUMBIA

American University

Kogod College of Business Administration

Washington, District of Columbia

OVERVIEW
American University is an independent Methodist coed institution. Founded 1893. Setting: 77-acre urban campus. Total institutional enrollment: 12,000. Program was first offered in 1949. AACSB-accredited.

MBA HIGHLIGHTS

Entrance Difficulty**
Mean GMAT: 555
Mean GPA: 3.1

Cost $$$$
Tuition: $9,000/semester
Room & Board: $10,000

Enrollment Profile
Full-time: 332
Part-time: 233
Total: 565
Average Age: 27

Work Exp: 90%
International: 38%
Women: 43%
Minorities: 15%

Average Class Size: 30

ACADEMICS
Length of Program Minimum: 17 months. Maximum: 5 years.
Calendar Semesters.
Full-time Classes Main campus; day, evening, summer.
Part-time Classes Main campus; evening.
Degree Requirements 54 credits including 6 elective credits.
Required Courses Business and society, financial accounting, financial management, legal environment of global business, management in a global economy, management information systems, manager in the international economy, managerial accounting, managerial economics, marketing management, organizational behavior, quality management, quantitative methods.
Curricular Focus International business, leadership, teamwork.
Concentrations Accounting, arts administration, economics, entrepreneurship, finance, human resources management, international business, management, management information systems, marketing, operations management, organizational behavior, public administration, quantitative analysis, real estate, strategic management.
Faculty Full-time: 60, 95% with doctorates.
Teaching Methodology Case study: 25%, lecture: 35%, research: 10%, student presentations: 15%, team projects: 15%.
Special Opportunities International exchange and internship programs available.

STUDENT STATISTICS
Geographic Representation By region: Northeast 40%; South 10%; Midwest 7%; West 7%. International 38%.
Undergraduate Majors Business 35%; engineering/technology 20%; humanities 10%; science/mathematics 15%; social sciences 10%; other 10%.
Other Background Graduate degrees in other disciplines: 20%. Work experience: On average, students have 4-7 years of work experience on entrance to the program.

FACILITIES
Information Resources Main library with 580,000 bound volumes, 1.5 million titles on microform, 2,900 periodical subscriptions, 10,093 records/tapes/CDs.
Housing 25% of students in program live in college-owned or -operated housing.
Technology Computers are used heavily in course work. Computer terminals/PCs, linked by a campus-wide computer network, are available for use by students in program; they are located in learning resource center, the library, the computer center, computer labs, the research center. Students in the program are not required to have their own PC.

Computer Resources/On-line Services

Training	Yes	Multimedia Center	Yes
Internet	Yes	LEXIS/NEXIS	Yes
E-Mail	Yes	Dow Jones	Yes

ADMISSION
Acceptance 1994-95 Of those applying, 61% were accepted.
Entrance Requirements Bachelor's degree, GMAT score.
Application Requirements Written essay, application form, copies of transcript, personal statement, 2 letters of recommendation.
Application Deadlines 6/1 for fall, 11/1 for spring, 3/15 for summer.

FINANCIALS
Costs for 1994-95 Tuition: Full-time: $9,000/semester. Fees: Full-time: $75/semester. Average room and board costs are $10,000 per academic year (on-campus) and $10,000 per academic year (off-campus).

Financial Aid In 1994-95, 35% of candidates received some institutionally administered aid in the form of loans, fellowships, assistantships. Total awards ranged from $1,000-$12,000. Financial aid is not available to part-time students. Application deadlines: 2/1 for fall, 10/1 for spring. Contact: Financial Aid Counselor, Office of Financial Aid 4400 Massachusetts Avenue, NW, Washington, DC 20016-8001. (202) 885-6000.

INTERNATIONAL STUDENTS
Demographics 38% of students enrolled in the program are international; Asia 48%, Europe 39%, Central America 7%, South America 6%.

Services and Facilities International student center, language tutoring, ESL courses, special assistance for nonnative speakers of English, counseling/support services.

Applying TOEFL required, minimum score of 550; proof of adequate funds. Financial aid is available to international students. Financial aid application deadlines: 2/1 for fall, 10/1 for spring. Admission application deadlines: 5/1 for fall, 10/1 for spring. Contact: Mr. John Hart, Foreign Student Services Manager, Butler Pavilion, 4th Floor, Washington, DC 20016-8001. (202) 885-3357.

ALTERNATE MBA PROGRAMS
MBA/JD Length of program: Minimum: 48 months. Degree requirements: 121 credits including 64 elective credits.

MBA/MA Full-time classes: Main campus; day, evening, summer. Part-time classes: Main campus; evening. Degree requirements: 62 credits including 12 elective credits. Field study/thesis project. MA is in international service.

PLACEMENT
In 1993-94, 50 organizations participated in on-campus recruiting; 100 on-campus interviews were conducted. Placement services include alumni network, career counseling/planning, career fairs, career library, career placement, electronic job bank, job interviews, resume preparation, and resume referral to employers. Of 1994 graduates, 85% were employed within three months of graduation, the average starting salary was $40,310, the range was $23,000-$76,000.

Jobs by Employer Type Manufacturing 22%; government 10%; consulting 25%; computer services 9%; accounting 12%; financial services 18%; other 4%.

Program Contact: Ms. Judith Sugarman, Director of Admissions and Placement, American University, 4400 Massachusetts Avenue, NW, Washington, DC 20016-8001. (202) 885-1913, or (800) AN AU MBA (out-of-state); Fax: (202) 885-1992; Internet Address: j.sugar@american. edu.
See full description on page 662.

Georgetown University

School of Business

Washington, District of Columbia

OVERVIEW
Georgetown University is an independent Roman Catholic (Jesuit) coed institution. Founded 1789. Setting: 110-acre urban campus. Total institutional enrollment: 12,617. Program was first offered in 1981. AACSB-accredited.

MBA HIGHLIGHTS

Entrance Difficulty**
Mean GMAT: 618
Mean GPA: 3.2

Cost $$$$
Tuition: $19,584
Room & Board: $8,800 (off-campus)

Enrollment Profile
Full-time: 400	Work Exp: 90%
Part-time: 0	International: 29%
Total: 400	Women: 35%
Average Age: 27	Minorities: 12%

Class Size: 30 - 43

ACADEMICS
Length of Program Minimum: 22 months.

Calendar Semesters.

Full-time Classes Main campus; day.

Degree Requirements 60 credits including 18 elective credits.

Required Courses Business and public policy, business ethics, business policy and strategic planning, financial accounting, financial management, global environment of business, information technology and business strategy, management communication, management science, managerial economics, marketing, organizational behavior, production and operations management, statistics.

Curricular Focus General management, international business, teamwork.

Concentration Management.

Faculty Full-time: 64, 94% with doctorates; part-time: 31.

Teaching Methodology Case study: 45%, faculty seminars: 5%, lecture: 20%, research: 5%, seminars by members of the business community: 5%, student presentations: 10%, team projects: 10%.

Special Opportunities International exchange in Australia, Belgium, Czech Republic, Finland, France, Germany, Japan, Mexico, Spain, United Kingdom. Internship program available. Other: MBA Enterprise Corps.

STUDENT STATISTICS
Geographic Representation By region: Northeast 36%; South 15%; West 13%; Midwest 7%. International 29%.

Undergraduate Majors Business 19%; engineering/technology 15%; humanities 16%; social sciences 50%.

Other Background Graduate degrees in other disciplines: 5%. Work experience: On average, students have 4 years of work experience on entrance to the program.

FACILITIES
Information Resources Main library with 2 million bound volumes, 170,000 titles on microform, 24,763 periodical subscriptions, 48,007 records/tapes/CDs, 35 CD-ROMs.

Housing College housing not available.

Technology Computers are used heavily in course work. 110 computer terminals/PCs, linked by a campus-wide computer network, are available for use by students in program; they are located in classrooms, the library, the computer center, computer labs, MBA student lounge. Students in the program are not required to have their own PC. $250 are budgeted per student for computer support.

Computer Resources/On-line Services
Training	Yes	Dun's	No
Internet	Yes	Dow Jones	Yes
E-Mail	Yes	Dialog	No
LEXIS/NEXIS	Yes	Bloomberg	No
CompuServe	No		

ADMISSION
Acceptance 1994-95 1,231 applied for admission; 48% were accepted.

Entrance Requirements Bachelor's degree, GMAT score. Core courses waived through: previous course work.

Application Requirements Written essay, application form, copies of transcript, resume/curriculum vitae.

Application Deadline 4/15 for fall. Application discs available.

FINANCIALS
Costs for 1994-95 Tuition: Full-time: $19,584. Average room and board costs are $8,800 per academic year (off-campus).

Financial Aid In 1994-95, 76% of candidates received some institutionally administered aid in the form of scholarships, loans, fellowships. Total awards ranged from $4,662-$18,650. Contact: Ms. Greta Kendrick, Counselor, Office of Financial Aid, 37th and O Street, NW, Washington, DC 20057. (202) 687-4547.

INTERNATIONAL STUDENTS
Demographics 29% of students enrolled in the program are international; South America 31%, Asia 27%, Europe 27%, Africa 4%, other 11%.

Services and Facilities Visa services, language tutoring, ESL courses, special assistance for nonnative speakers of English, counseling/support services, international student orientation.

Applying TOEFL required, minimum score of 600. Admission application deadline: 4/15 for fall. Contact: Ms. Karla Stillwell, Coordinator, International Programs and Student Services, 37th and O Street, NW, Washington, DC 20057-1008. (202) 687-4200.

ALTERNATE MBA PROGRAMS

Executive MBA (EMBA) Length of program: Minimum: 18 months. Degree requirements: 60 credits. 1 week-long overseas residency program. Average class size: 40.

MBA/JD Length of program: Minimum: 48 months. Degree requirements: 122 credits including 27-30 elective credits. Separate applications must be submitted to both the law and business administration programs.

MBA/MSFS Length of program: Minimum: 36 months. Degree requirements: 90 credits including 24 elective credits. Must apply to each program separately by February 1 and complete evaluative interview with admissions staff of each program. Program includes overseas summer internship.

PLACEMENT

In 1993-94, 51 organizations participated in on-campus recruiting; 496 on-campus interviews were conducted. Placement services include alumni network, career counseling/planning, career fairs, career library, career placement, consortia, job interviews, resume preparation, and resume referral to employers. Of 1994 graduates, 93% were employed within three months of graduation, the average starting salary was $52,917, the range was $12,360-$90,000.

Jobs by Employer Type Government 3%; consulting 28%; finance 18%; telecommunications 43%; other 8%.

Jobs by Functional Area Marketing/sales 21%; finance 21%; management 3%; strategic planning 9%; consulting 30%; law 7%; other 9%.

Program Contact: Ms. Nancy D. Moncrief, Director, Graduate Business Admissions and Services, Georgetown University, 37th and O Street, NW, Washington, DC 20057. (202) 687-4200; Fax: (202) 687-7809. See full description on page 744.

The George Washington University

School of Business and Public Management

Washington, District of Columbia

OVERVIEW

The George Washington University is an independent nonprofit coed institution. Founded 1821. Setting: 45-acre urban campus. Total institutional enrollment: 15,242. Program was first offered in 1948. AACSB-accredited.

MBA HIGHLIGHTS

Entrance Difficulty***
Mean GMAT: 540
Mean GPA: 3.11

Cost $$$
Tuition: $575/credit hour
Room & Board: $8,300 (off-campus)

Enrollment Profile

Full-time: 676	Work Exp: 75%
Part-time: 630	International: 49%
Total: 1,306	Women: 41%
Average Age: 28	Minorities: 11%

Average Class Size: 33

ACADEMICS

Length of Program Minimum: 18 months. Maximum: 5 years.

Calendar Semesters.

Full-time Classes Main campus; day, evening, summer.

Degree Requirements 33 credit hours including 15 elective credit hours.

Required Courses Business and public policy, economics, finance, financial and managerial accounting, information systems, marketing, operations, organization, management, and leadership, statistics, strategy formulation and implementation, world economy. Courses may be waived through: previous course work.

Curricular Focus Business and public policy, international business, problem solving and decision making.

Concentrations Accounting, finance, health services, human resources management, international business, management, management information systems, marketing, operations management, organizational behavior, public administration, public policy, quantitative analysis, real estate, strategic management, tourism administration; sciencce, technology, and innovation management.

Faculty Full-time: 78, 93% with doctorates.

Teaching Methodology Case study: 20%, lecture: 40%, student presentations: 20%, team projects: 20%.

Special Opportunities International exchange in Chile, Denmark, France, Germany, Hungary, Portugal, Republic of Korea, Spain, Sweden, Thailand. Internship program available. Other: cooperative education program.

STUDENT STATISTICS

Geographic Representation District residents 51%. By region: South 31%; Northeast 28%; Midwest 2%; West 1%. International 49%.

Undergraduate Majors Business 45%; engineering/technology 7%; science/mathematics 6%; other 42%.

Other Background Graduate degrees in other disciplines: 12%. Work experience: On average, students have 3 years of work experience on entrance to the program.

FACILITIES

Information Resources Main library with 1.7 million bound volumes, 2 million titles on microform, 14,129 periodical subscriptions, 102 CD-ROMs.

Housing College housing not available.

Technology Computers are used moderately in course work. 250 computer terminals/PCs, linked by a campus-wide computer network, are available for use by students in program; they are located in classrooms, computer labs. Students in the program are not required to have their own PC.

Computer Resources/On-line Services

Training	Yes	CompuServe	No
Internet	Yes	Dun's	Yes
E-Mail	Yes	Dow Jones	Yes
Videoconference Center	Yes	Dialog	Yes
LEXIS/NEXIS	Yes	Bloomberg	Yes

ADMISSION

Acceptance 1994-95 1,724 applied for admission; 67% were accepted.

Entrance Requirements Bachelor's degree, GMAT score, minimum 3.0 GPA, minimum 2 years of work experience. Core courses waived through: previous course work.

Application Requirements Written essay, application form, copies of transcript, resume/curriculum vitae, 3 letters of recommendation.

Application Deadlines 4/1 for fall, 10/1 for spring.

FINANCIALS

Costs for 1994-95 Tuition: Full-time: $575/credit hour. Fees: Full-time: $30/credit hour. Average room and board costs are $8,300 per academic year (off-campus).

Financial Aid In 1994-95, candidates received some institutionally administered aid in the form of scholarships, loans, fellowships, assistantships, work-study. Financial aid is not available to part-time students. Application deadlines: 4/1 for fall, 10/1 for spring. Contact: Office of Student Financial Assistance, Washington, DC 20052. (202) 994-6620.

INTERNATIONAL STUDENTS

Demographics 49% of students enrolled in the program are international; Asia 87%, Europe 7%, Africa 2%, South America 2%, Central America 1%, other 1%.

Services and Facilities International student center, visa services, language tutoring, ESL courses, special assistance for nonnative speakers of English, counseling/support services.

Applying TOEFL required, minimum score of 550; proof of health; proof of adequate funds. Financial aid is not available to international students. Admission application deadlines: 4/1 for fall, 10/1 for spring. Contact: Mr. Donald Driver, Director, International Services, 2129 G Street, NW, Washington, DC 20052. (202) 994-6860.

ALTERNATE MBA PROGRAMS

Executive MBA (EMBA) Length of program: Minimum: 18 months. Maximum: 5 years. Degree requirements: 60 credit hours. Class size: 35-40.

MBA/JD Length of program: Minimum: 36 months. Maximum: 5 years. Degree requirements: 118 credit hours. Class size: 10-15.

MBA/MA Length of program: Minimum: 24 months. Maximum: 5 years. Degree requirements: 66 credit hours including 18 elective credit hours. Foreign language proficiency. MA is in international affairs. Class size: 35-40.

PLACEMENT

In 1993-94, 75 organizations participated in on-campus recruiting. Placement services include alumni network, career counseling/planning, career fairs, career library, career placement, electronic job bank, resume preparation, and resume referral to employers. Of 1994 graduates, the average starting salary was $42,100, the range was $28,000-$68,000.

Jobs by Functional Area Marketing/sales 15%; finance 36%; operations 4%; management 17%; technical management 28%.

Program Contact: Mr. George B. LeNoir, Director of Enrollment Services, The George Washington University, Washington, DC 20052. (202) 994-6584; Fax: (202) 994-6382.
See full description on page 746.

Howard University

School of Business

Washington, District of Columbia

OVERVIEW

Howard University is an independent nonprofit coed institution. Founded 1867. Setting: 242-acre urban campus. Total institutional enrollment: 10,500. Program was first offered in 1970. AACSB-accredited.

MBA HIGHLIGHTS

Entrance Difficulty*
Mean GMAT: 470
Mean GPA: 2.9

Cost $$
Tuition: $8,705
Room & Board: $7,830

Enrollment Profile

Full-time: 120	Work Exp: 78%
Part-time: 81	International: 23%
Total: 201	Women: 55%
Average Age: 26	Minorities: 99%

Average Class Size: 25

ACADEMICS

Length of Program Minimum: 21 months. Maximum: 5 years.
Calendar Semesters.
Full-time Classes Main campus; evening, summer.
Part-time Classes Main campus; evening.
Degree Requirements 39 credit hours including 3 elective credit hours.
Required Courses Business and society, economics, finance, management, managerial accounting, marketing, policy, production operations management, report preparation, seminar in management, statistics.
Curricular Focus General management, leadership, minorities in business.
Concentrations Finance, health services.
Faculty Full-time: 21, 90% with doctorates; part-time: 3, 67% with doctorates.
Teaching Methodology Case study: 30%, faculty seminars: 3%, lecture: 40%, research: 4%, seminars by members of the business community: 3%, student presentations: 10%, team projects: 10%.

STUDENT STATISTICS

Geographic Representation District residents 77%. International 23%.
Undergraduate Majors Business 63%; engineering/technology 14%; humanities 4%; nursing 2%; social sciences 17%.
Other Background Graduate degrees in other disciplines: 2%. Work experience: On average, students have 3 years of work experience on entrance to the program.

FACILITIES

Information Resources Main library with 1.9 million bound volumes, 3.5 million titles on microform, 25,564 periodical subscriptions, 27 records/tapes/CDs, 27 CD-ROMs.
Housing College housing available.
Technology Computers are used moderately in course work. 50 computer terminals/PCs are available for use by students in program; they are located in the computer center, computer labs. Students in the program are not required to have their own PC.

Computer Resources/On-line Services

Training	Yes	E-Mail	Yes

ADMISSION

Acceptance 1994-95 400 applied for admission; 60% were accepted.
Entrance Requirements Bachelor's degree, GMAT score. Core courses waived through: previous course work.
Application Requirements Written essay, application form, copies of transcript, resume/curriculum vitae, 2 letters of recommendation.
Application Deadlines 2/1 for fall, 11/1 for spring.

FINANCIALS

Costs for 1994-95 Tuition: Full-time: $8,705. Average room and board costs are $7,830 per academic year (on-campus) and $9,890 per academic year (off-campus).
Financial Aid In 1994-95, 50% of candidates received some institutionally administered aid in the form of grants, scholarships, loans, assistantships. Total awards ranged from $2,250-$16,000. Financial aid is not available to part-time students. Application deadline: 4/1 for fall. Contact: Dr. Charles M. Ermer, Director of Graduate Studies, 2400 Sixth Street, NW, Washington, DC 20059-0002. (202) 806-1500.

INTERNATIONAL STUDENTS

Demographics 23% of students enrolled in the program are international; North America 70%, Africa 30%.
Services and Facilities International student office, international student center, counseling/support services.
Applying TOEFL required, minimum score of 500; proof of health. Financial aid is available to international students. Financial aid application deadline: 4/1 for fall. Admission application deadlines: 2/1 for fall, 11/1 for spring. Applications are processed on a rolling basis.

ALTERNATE MBA PROGRAM

MBA/JD Length of program: Minimum: 48 months. Full-time classes: Main campus; day, evening, summer. Degree requirements: 127 credits.

PLACEMENT

In 1993-94, 140 organizations participated in on-campus recruiting; 60 on-campus interviews were conducted. Placement services include career fairs, career placement, job interviews, and resume referral to employers. Of 1994 graduates, 95% were employed within three months of graduation, the average starting salary was $47,250, the range was $42,500-$52,000.

Program Contact: Dr. Charles M. Ermer, Director of Graduate Studies, Howard University, 2400 Sixth Street, NW, Washington, DC 20059-0002. (202) 806-1500; Fax: (202) 797-6393.
See full description on page 756.

Southeastern University

Graduate School

Washington, District of Columbia

OVERVIEW

Southeastern University is an independent nonprofit comprehensive coed institution. Founded 1879. Setting: 1-acre urban campus. Total institutional enrollment: 670.

MBA HIGHLIGHTS

Entrance Difficulty**

Cost $
Tuition: $228/credit hour
Room & Board: N/R

Enrollment Profile

Full-time: N/R	Work Exp: N/R
Part-time: N/R	International: 30%
Total: 250	Women: 40%
Average Age: N/R	Minorities: 70%

Class Size: 15 - 25

ACADEMICS

Length of Program Minimum: 12 months.
Calendar 4 quad-semesters.

Full-time Classes Main campus, Abu Dhabi, United Arab Emirates, Dubai, United Arab Emirates, London, United Kingdom, Karachi, Pakistan, Cyprus, distance learning option; day, evening, weekends, summer.

Part-time Classes Main campus, Abu Dhabi, United Arab Emirates, Dubai, United Arab Emirates, London, United Kingdom, Karachi, Pakistan, Cyprus, distance learning option; day, evening, weekends, summer.

Degree Requirements 45 credit hours.

Curricular Focus Entrepreneurship, general management, international business.

Concentrations Accounting, economics, finance, health services, international business, management, management information systems, marketing, public administration.

Teaching Methodology Case study: 10%, faculty seminars: 5%, lecture: 55%, research: 20%, student presentations: 5%, team projects: 5%.

STUDENT STATISTICS
Geographic Representation District residents 70%. International 30%.

FACILITIES
Information Resources Main library with 37,000 bound volumes, 300 titles on microform, 700 periodical subscriptions, 368 records/tapes/CDs.

ADMISSION
Acceptance 1994-95 Of those applying, 80% were accepted.

Entrance Requirements Bachelor's degree, minimum 3.0 GPA.

Application Requirements Interview, application form, copies of transcript, personal statement, 2 letters of recommendation.

Application Deadline Applications are processed on a rolling basis.

FINANCIALS
Estimated Costs for 1995-96 Tuition: Full-time: $228/credit hour.

Financial Aid In 1994-95, 60% of candidates received some institutionally administered aid in the form of scholarships, loans, work-study. Total awards ranged from $5,000-$15,000. Financial aid is available to part-time students. Application deadlines: 7/1 for fall, 12/1 for spring. Applications are processed on a rolling basis. Contact: Mr. Willis Parker, Financial Aid Administrator, 501 Eye Street, SW, Washington, DC 20074. (202) 488-8163.

INTERNATIONAL STUDENTS
Demographics 30% of students enrolled in the program are international.

Applying TOEFL required, minimum score of 550; proof of health; proof of adequate funds. Financial aid is not available to international students. Admission applications are processed on a rolling basis.

PLACEMENT
Placement services include career counseling/planning and career placement.

Program Contact: Mr. Jack Flinter Jr., Assistant Director of Admissions, Southeastern University, 501 Eye Street, SW, Washington, DC 20024. (202) 265-5343.

University of the District of Columbia

College of Professional Studies

Washington, District of Columbia

OVERVIEW
The University of the District of Columbia is a district-supported comprehensive coed institution. Founded 1976. Setting: 28-acre urban campus. Total institutional enrollment: 10,608.

MBA HIGHLIGHTS

Entrance Difficulty**
Mean GMAT: 350
Mean GPA: N/R

Cost $
Tuition: $312/credit
(Nonresident: $624/credit)
Room & Board: N/R

Enrollment Profile

Full-time: 113	Work Exp: N/R
Part-time: 37	International: N/R
Total: 150	Women: 55%
Average Age: N/R	Minorities: N/R

Average Class Size: 30

ACADEMICS
Length of Program Minimum: 12 months.

Calendar Semesters.

Full-time Classes Main campus; evening, summer.

Degree Requirements 36 hours.

Curricular Focus Entrepreneurship, international business, minorities in business.

Concentration Management.

Teaching Methodology Case study: 10%, lecture: 75%, research: 5%, student presentations: 10%.

FACILITIES
Information Resources Main library with 522,123 bound volumes, 605,281 titles on microform, 1,983 periodical subscriptions, 19,030 records/tapes/CDs.

ADMISSION
Acceptance 1994-95 200 applied for admission; 60% were accepted.

Entrance Requirements Bachelor's degree, minimum 2.5 GPA.

Application Requirements Application form, copies of transcript, resume/curriculum vitae, personal statement.

Application Deadlines 6/1 for fall, 11/15 for spring, 4/1 for summer.

FINANCIALS
Costs for 1994-95 Tuition: Full-time: $312/credit for district residents, $624/credit for nonresidents. Fees: Full-time: $55/term for district residents, $55/term for nonresidents.

Financial Aid Application deadline: 3/15 for fall. Contact: Mr. Kenneth Howard, Financial Aid Director, 4200 Connecticut Avenue, Washington, DC 20008-1175. (202) 274-5060.

INTERNATIONAL STUDENTS
Services and Facilities International student housing.

Applying TOEFL required; proof of health; proof of adequate funds. Financial aid is available to international students. Financial aid application deadline: 3/15 for fall. Admission application deadlines: 5/1 for fall, 9/15 for spring.

Program Contact: Dr. Arakal Joseph, Coordinator, MBA Program, University of the District of Columbia, 4200 Connecticut Avenue, NW, Washington, DC 20008-1175. (202) 282-3737.

FLORIDA

Barry University

Andreas School of Business

Miami Shores, Florida

OVERVIEW
Barry University is an independent Roman Catholic comprehensive coed institution. Founded 1940. Setting: 90-acre urban campus with easy access to Miami. Total institutional enrollment: 5,500. Program was first offered in 1984.

MBA HIGHLIGHTS

Entrance Difficulty**
Mean GMAT: 470
Mean GPA: 2.9

Cost $
Tuition: $365/credit hour
Room & Board: N/R

Enrollment Profile

Full-time: 25	Work Exp: 80%
Part-time: 200	International: 30%
Total: 225	Women: 60%
Average Age: 29	Minorities: 65%

Average Class Size: 20

ACADEMICS

Length of Program Minimum: 15 months. Maximum: 5 years.

Calendar Semesters.

Part-time Classes Main campus; evening, weekends, summer.

Degree Requirements 36 credit hours including 9 elective credit hours.

Curricular Focus International business.

Concentrations Accounting, economics, finance, health services, international business, management, management information systems, marketing, public administration.

Faculty Full-time: 21, 100% with doctorates; part-time: 6, 100% with doctorates.

Teaching Methodology Case study: 10%, lecture: 60%, student presentations: 10%, team projects: 20%.

Special Opportunities International exchange in Jamaica, Venezuela. Internship program available.

STUDENT STATISTICS

Geographic Representation State residents 70%. By region: South 70%. International 30%.

Undergraduate Majors Business 85%; humanities 5%; nursing 10%.

Other Background Graduate degrees in other disciplines: 5%. Work experience: On average, students have 2 years of work experience on entrance to the program.

FACILITIES

Information Resources Main library with 200,000 bound volumes, 450,000 titles on microform, 2,300 periodical subscriptions, 4,200 records/tapes/CDs, 30 CD-ROMs. Business collection includes 11,828 bound volumes, 205 periodical subscriptions, 5 CD-ROMs, 100 videos.

Housing 2% of students in program live in college-owned or -operated housing.

Technology Computers are used moderately in course work. 60 computer terminals/PCs, linked by a campus-wide computer network, are available for use by students in program; they are located in the computer center, computer labs. Students in the program are not required to have their own PC.

Computer Resources/On-line Services

Training	Yes	E-Mail	Yes
Internet	Yes	Multimedia Center	Yes

ADMISSION

Acceptance 1994-95 Of those applying, 85% were accepted.

Entrance Requirements Bachelor's degree, GMAT score of 450, minimum 2.8 GPA.

Application Requirements Written essay, application form, copies of transcript, personal statement, 2 letters of recommendation.

Application Deadline Applications are processed on a rolling basis.

FINANCIALS

Costs for 1994-95 Tuition: Full-time: $365/credit hour. Fees: Full-time: $10.

Financial Aid In 1994-95, 3% of candidates received some institutionally administered aid in the form of scholarships, assistantships. Total awards ranged from $3,000-$20,000. Financial aid is not available to part-time students. Application deadline: 3/1 for fall. Contact: Mr. Juan Rivas, Director of Financial Aid, 11300 Northeast Second Avenue, Miami Shores, FL 33161-6695. (305) 899-3117.

INTERNATIONAL STUDENTS

Demographics 30% of students enrolled in the program are international; Central America 10%, Europe 3%, other 87%.

Services and Facilities International student center.

Applying TOEFL required, minimum score of 550; proof of health; proof of adequate funds. Financial aid is not available to international students. Admission applications are processed on a rolling basis. Contact: Ms. Joy DeMarchis, Director, Student Services, Box ADM, 11300 Northeast Second Avenue, Miami Shores, FL 33161-6695. (305) 899-3116.

ALTERNATE MBA PROGRAMS

Executive MBA (EMBA) Length of program: May range up to 5 years. Degree requirements: 36 credits including 9 elective credits.

MBA/MSN Degree requirements: 63 credits.

MBA/MSSM Degree requirements: 57 credits including 6 elective credits. Must be accepted into both curriculums.

PLACEMENT

In 1993-94, 55 organizations participated in on-campus recruiting. Placement services include alumni network, career counseling/planning, career fairs, career library, career placement, job interviews, and resume preparation.

Program Contact: Graduate Admissions, Barry University, 11300 Northeast Second Avenue, Miami Shores, FL 33161-6695. (305) 899-3125, or (800) 289-1111; Fax: (305) 892-6412.

Embry-Riddle Aeronautical University

Department of Aviation Business Administration

Daytona Beach, Florida

OVERVIEW

Embry-Riddle Aeronautical University is an independent nonprofit comprehensive specialized coed institution. Part of Embry-Riddle Aeronautical University. Founded 1926. Setting: 152-acre small-town campus with easy access to Orlando. Total institutional enrollment: 4,036. Program was first offered in 1986.

MBA HIGHLIGHTS

Entrance Difficulty***
Mean GMAT: 513
Mean GPA: 2.9

Cost
Tuition: N/R
Room & Board: $4,000 (off-campus)

Enrollment Profile

Full-time: 34	Work Exp: N/R
Part-time: 18	International: N/R
Total: 52	Women: 33%
Average Age: 28	Minorities: 30%

Average Class Size: 15

ACADEMICS

Calendar Semesters.

Curricular Focus Entrepreneurship, strategic analysis and planning, teamwork.

Faculty Full-time: 10, 80% with doctorates.

Teaching Methodology Case study: 15%, faculty seminars: 10%, lecture: 20%, research: 15%, student presentations: 10%, team projects: 30%.

Special Opportunities International exchange program available. Internships include airlines, airports, and aerospace industry. Other: Cooperative Programs.

STUDENT STATISTICS

Geographic Representation By region: South 25%; Northeast 20%; Midwest 20%; West 20%.

FACILITIES

Information Resources Main library with 72,444 bound volumes, 44,949 titles on microform, 690 periodical subscriptions, 13 CD-ROMs.

Housing College housing not available.

Technology Computers are used moderately in course work. 100 computer terminals/PCs, linked by a campus-wide computer network, are available for use by students in program; they are located in classrooms, computer labs. Students in the program are not required to have their own PC.

Computer Resources/On-line Services

Training	Yes	E-Mail	Yes
Internet	Yes	Dialog	Yes

ADMISSION

Acceptance 1994-95 180 applied for admission; 55% were accepted.

Entrance Requirements Bachelor's degree, GMAT score of 500, minimum 2.5 GPA. Core courses waived through: previous course work.

Application Requirements Application form.

Application Deadlines 8/7 for fall, 12/7 for spring.

FINANCIALS

Financial Aid In 1994-95, 21% of candidates received some institutionally administered aid in the form of scholarships, fellowships, assistantships, work-study. Financial aid is available to part-time students. Application deadlines: 4/15 for fall, 10/15 for spring. Contact: Ms. Marline Downs, Senior Evaluator, 600 South Clyde Morris Boulevard, Daytona Beach, FL 32114-3900. (904) 226-6300.

INTERNATIONAL STUDENTS

Demographics 15% of students on campus are international; Asia 28%, Europe 19%, Africa 10%, South America 6%, Central America 2%, other 35%.

Services and Facilities International student center, visa services, language tutoring, ESL courses, counseling/support services.

Applying TOEFL required, minimum score of 550; proof of adequate funds. Financial aid is not available to international students. Admission application deadlines: 3/1 for fall, 6/1 for spring. Contact: Ms. Judith Assad, Director, International Student Services, 600 South Clyde Morris Boulevard, Daytona Beach, FL 32114-3900. (904) 226-6579.

PROGRAM

Master of Business Administration in Aviation Length of program: Minimum: 18 months. Maximum: 7 years. Full-time classes: Main campus; day, evening, early morning. Part-time classes: Main campus; day, evening, weekends, early morning. Degree requirements: 36 credits including 9 elective credits.

PLACEMENT

Placement services include alumni network, career counseling/planning, career fairs, career library, career placement, electronic job bank, job interviews, resume preparation, and resume referral to employers.

Program Contact: Ms. Janet LaRossa, Administrative Assistant to the Director, Embry-Riddle Aeronautical University, 600 South Clyde Morris Boulevard, Daytona Beach, FL 32114-3900. (904) 226-6100, or (800) 222-ERAU (out-of-state); Fax: (904) 226-7070.

Florida Atlantic University

Graduate School of Business

Boca Raton, Florida

OVERVIEW

Florida Atlantic University is a state-supported coed institution. Part of State University System of Florida. Founded 1961. Setting: 850-acre urban campus with easy access to Miami. Total institutional enrollment: 17,364. Program was first offered in 1967. AACSB-accredited.

MBA HIGHLIGHTS

Entrance Difficulty***
Mean GMAT: 523
Mean GPA: 3.23

Cost $
Tuition: $112/credit hour
(Nonresident: $365/credit hour)
Room & Board: $1,854

Enrollment Profile

Full-time: 150		Work Exp: 80%
Part-time: 535		International: N/R
Total: 685		Women: 45%
Average Age: 28		Minorities: 5%

Average Class Size: 24

ACADEMICS

Length of Program Minimum: 18 months. Maximum: 7 years.

Calendar Semesters.

Full-time Classes Main campus, Broward, North Palm Beach; evening, summer.

Degree Requirements 36 credit hours including 6 elective credit hours.

Required Courses Accounting, business organizations and environments, data for managers analysis, finance, graduate business communications, information systems, international business, marketing, operations management, organizational behavior. Courses may be waived through: previous course work.

Curricular Focus Business communications, business issues and problems, problem solving and decision making.

Concentrations Accounting, entrepreneurship, finance, human resources management, international business, management, management information systems, marketing, operations management, organizational behavior, quantitative analysis, real estate, strategic management.

Faculty Full-time: 100, 98% with doctorates; part-time: 45, 98% with doctorates.

Teaching Methodology Case study: 30%, lecture: 30%, student presentations: 30%, team projects: 10%.

Special Opportunities International exchange in Finland, Germany, Norway, Russia, Spain. Internship program available. Other: cooperative education.

STUDENT STATISTICS

Geographic Representation By region: South 90%; Northeast 5%; Midwest 2%; West 1%.

Undergraduate Majors Business 80%; engineering/technology 10%; humanities 1%; science/mathematics 2%; social sciences 5%; other 2%.

Other Background Graduate degrees in other disciplines: 5%. Work experience: On average, students have 3 years of work experience on entrance to the program.

FACILITIES

Information Resources Main library with 611,462 bound volumes, 19,152 titles on microform, 3,997 periodical subscriptions, 23,213 records/tapes/CDs, 152 CD-ROMs.

Housing 5% of students in program live in college-owned or -operated housing.

Technology Computers are used heavily in course work. Computer terminals/PCs, linked by a campus-wide computer network, are available for use by students in program; they are located in the computer center, computer labs, the research center. Students in the program are not required to have their own PC.

Computer Resources/On-line Services

Training	Yes	E-Mail	Yes
Internet	Yes	CompuServe	Yes

ADMISSION

Acceptance 1994-95 Of those applying, 67% were accepted.

Entrance Requirements Bachelor's degree, GMAT score of 500, minimum 3.0 GPA. Core courses waived through: previous course work.

Application Requirements Application form, copies of transcript.

Application Deadlines 6/15 for fall, 10/15 for spring.

FINANCIALS

Costs for 1994-95 Tuition: Full-time: $112/credit hour for state residents, $365/credit hour for nonresidents. Fees: Full-time: $5/semester for state residents, $5/semester for nonresidents. Average room and board costs are $1,854 per academic year (on-campus).

Financial Aid In 1994-95, 5% of candidates received some institutionally administered aid in the form of loans, fellowships, assistantships, work-study. Financial aid is available to part-time students. Application deadlines: 6/1 for fall, 10/1 for spring. Contact: Ms. Olga Moas, Director of Financial Aid, SSB225, Boca Raton, FL 33431. (407) 367-3526.

INTERNATIONAL STUDENTS

Demographics 1% of students on campus are international; Asia 40%, Europe 25%, Central America 14%, South America 12%, Africa 2%, other 7%.

Services and Facilities Visa services, language tutoring, ESL courses.

Applying TOEFL required, minimum score of 600; proof of health; proof of adequate funds; proof of insurance. Financial aid is not available to international students. Admission application deadlines: 6/1 for fall, 10/1 for spring. Contact: Ms. Susan D'Amico, Director, International Students and Scholars Services, BUW 100-A, Boca Raton, FL 33431. (407) 367-3049.

ALTERNATE MBA PROGRAM

Executive MBA (EMBA) Length of program: Minimum: 20 months. Maximum: 7 years. Degree requirements: 39 credits including 6 elective credits. 5 years managerial experience. Average class size: 30.

PLACEMENT

In 1993-94, 87 organizations participated in on-campus recruiting. Placement services include alumni network, career counseling/planning, career fairs, career library, career placement, job interviews, resume preparation, and resume referral to employers.

Jobs by Employer Type Manufacturing 30%; service 30%; government 10%; consulting 15%; nonprofit 5%; self-employed 10%.

Jobs by Functional Area Marketing/sales 30%; finance 10%; operations 10%; management 20%; strategic planning 10%; technical management 2%; other 18%.

Program Contact: Ms. Ella Smith, Graduate Adviser, Florida Atlantic University, 777 Glades Road, Boca Raton, FL 33431. (407) 367-3650; Fax: (407) 367-3978; Internet Address: smith@acc.fau.edu.

Florida Institute of Technology

School of Business

Melbourne, Florida

OVERVIEW

Florida Institute of Technology is an independent nonprofit coed institution. Founded 1958. Setting: 175-acre small-town campus with easy access to Orlando. Total institutional enrollment: 4,600. Program was first offered in 1975.

MBA HIGHLIGHTS

Entrance Difficulty***
Mean GMAT: 480
Mean GPA: N/R

Cost $$
Tuition: $515/credit hour
Room & Board: $4,000

Enrollment Profile

Full-time: 154	Work Exp: 70%
Part-time: 46	International: 21%
Total: 200	Women: 43%
Average Age: N/R	Minorities: 7%

Average Class Size: 13

ACADEMICS

Length of Program May range up to 5 years.

Calendar Semesters.

Degree Requirements 36 credit hours including 9 elective credit hours.

Required Courses Advanced analytical methods for management, corporate finance, economics for business, information systems, intermediate managerial statistics, managerial accounting, marketing, organizational behavior, policy and strategy for business.

Curricular Focus Business issues and problems, general management, international business, problem solving and decision making.

Concentrations Health services, human resources management, management, technology management, contract and acquisition.

Faculty Full-time: 12, 100% with doctorates; part-time: 15, 85% with doctorates.

Teaching Methodology Case study: 15%, faculty seminars: 2%, lecture: 45%, research: 3%, seminars by members of the business community: 5%, student presentations: 10%, team projects: 20%.

Special Opportunities International exchange in Belgium, France. Internships include information systems in manufacturing high technology, management of technology in manufacturing high technology, healthcare administration in hospitals, and contract and acquisition in high technology.

STUDENT STATISTICS

Geographic Representation State residents 73%. By region: South 75%; Midwest 3%; Northeast 1%. International 21%.

Other Background Graduate degrees in other disciplines: 10%. Work experience: On average, students have 5 years of work experience on entrance to the program.

FACILITIES

Information Resources Main library with 264,626 bound volumes, 184,285 titles on microform, 1,700 periodical subscriptions, 64 records/tapes/CDs, 578 CD-ROMs.

Housing 25% of students in program live in college-owned or -operated housing. Assistance with housing search provided.

Technology Computers are used heavily in course work. 50 computer terminals/PCs, linked by a campus-wide computer network, are available for use by students in program; they are located in classrooms, the library, the computer center, computer labs, the research center. Students in the program are not required to have their own PC.

Computer Resources/On-line Services

Training	Yes	Multimedia Center	Yes
E-Mail	Yes		

ADMISSION

Entrance Requirements Bachelor's degree, GMAT score, minimum 2.6 GPA. Core courses waived through: previous course work.

Application Requirements Application form, copies of transcript.

Application Deadlines 5/1 for fall, 9/1 for spring. Applications are processed on a rolling basis.

FINANCIALS

Costs for 1994-95 Tuition: Full-time: $515/credit hour. Average room and board costs are $4,000 per academic year (on-campus) and $7,000 per academic year (off-campus).

Financial Aid Application deadlines: 5/1 for fall, 9/1 for spring. Applications are processed on a rolling basis. Contact: Student Financial Aid, 150 West University Boulevard, Melbourne, FL 32901-6988. (407) 768-8000 Ext. 8070.

INTERNATIONAL STUDENTS

Demographics 21% of students enrolled in the program are international; North America 75%, Europe 6%, other 19%.

Services and Facilities International student housing; international student office, international student center, visa services, language tutoring, ESL courses, special assistance for nonnative speakers of English.

Applying TOEFL required, minimum score of 550; proof of health; proof of adequate funds. Financial aid is available to international students. Financial aid application deadlines: 5/1 for fall, 9/1 for spring. Admission application deadlines: 5/1 for fall, 9/1 for spring. Applications are processed on a rolling basis. Contact: Ms. Gail Knowlton, Director, International Student Affairs, 150 West University Boulevard, Melbourne, FL 32901-6988. (407) 768-8000 Ext. 8053.

PLACEMENT

In 1993-94, 10 organizations participated in on-campus recruiting. Placement services include alumni network, career counseling/planning, career placement, job interviews, and resume referral to employers. Of 1994 graduates, 60% were employed within three months of graduation.

Program Contact: Ms. Carolyn Farior, Associate Dean, Graduate Admissions, Florida Institute of Technology, 150 West University Boulevard, Melbourne, FL 32901-6988. (407) 768-8000 Ext. 8027, or (800) 944-4348; Fax: (407) 768-8000 Ext. 8897; Internet Address: farrior@roo.fit.edu.

Florida International University

Department of Management and International Business

Miami, Florida

OVERVIEW

Florida International University is a state-supported coed institution. Part of State University System of Florida. Founded 1965. Setting: 544-acre urban campus. Total institutional enrollment: 25,500. Program was first offered in 1972. AACSB-accredited.

MBA HIGHLIGHTS

Entrance Difficulty***
Mean GMAT: 530
Mean GPA: 3.5

Cost $
Tuition: $108/credit hour
(Nonresident: $361/credit hour)
Room & Board: N/R

Enrollment Profile
Full-time: 84	Work Exp: 50%
Part-time: 266	International: 8%
Total: 350	Women: 38%
Average Age: 34	Minorities: 50%

Average Class Size: 30

ACADEMICS

Length of Program Minimum: 24 months. Maximum: 6 years.

Calendar Semesters.

Full-time Classes Main campus; day, evening, summer.

Part-time Classes Main campus; day, evening, summer.

Degree Requirements 41 credits including 12 elective credits.

Required Courses Advanced marketing management, financial management, financial reporting and analysis, operations management, organization and management theory, organization information systems, organization information systems lab, organizational behavior, policy analysis, quantitative methods in financial analysis. Courses may be waived through: previous course work.

Curricular Focus General management, international business, strategic analysis and planning.

Concentrations Accounting, finance, international business, management, management information systems, marketing, strategic management.

Faculty Full-time: 45, 95% with doctorates.

Teaching Methodology Case study: 15%, lecture: 50%, research: 5%, student presentations: 15%, team projects: 15%.

Special Opportunities International exchange program available.

STUDENT STATISTICS

Geographic Representation State residents 80%. By region: South 87%; Northeast 2%; West 2%; Midwest 1%. International 8%.

Undergraduate Majors Business 75%; engineering/technology 18%; nursing 2%; science/mathematics 2%; social sciences 2%; other 1%.

Other Background Graduate degrees in other disciplines: 3%. Work experience: On average, students have 2 years of work experience on entrance to the program.

FACILITIES

Information Resources Main library with 1 million bound volumes, 2.7 million titles on microform, 11,931 periodical subscriptions, 10,705 records/tapes/CDs.

Housing 5% of students in program live in college-owned or -operated housing.

Technology Computers are used moderately in course work. 100 computer terminals/PCs, linked by a campus-wide computer network, are available for use by students in program; they are located in classrooms, the library, the computer center, computer labs. Students in the program are not required to have their own PC.

Computer Resources/On-line Services
Training	Yes	Multimedia Center	Yes
Internet	Yes	LEXIS/NEXIS	Yes
E-Mail	Yes	Dialog	Yes $

ADMISSION

Acceptance 1994-95 750 applied for admission; 35% were accepted.

Entrance Requirements Bachelor's degree, GMAT score of 460, minimum 3.0 GPA, minimum 2 years of work experience.

Application Requirements Application form, copies of transcript, personal statement, 3 letters of recommendation.

Application Deadline Applications are processed on a rolling basis.

FINANCIALS

Costs for 1994-95 Tuition: Full-time: $108/credit hour for state residents, $361/credit hour for nonresidents. Fees: Full-time: $80 for state residents, $80 for nonresidents.

Financial Aid In 1994-95, 1% of candidates received some institutionally administered aid in the form of loans, partial tuition waivers. Financial aid is not available to part-time students. Application deadline: 4/1 for fall. Contact: Ms. Ana R. Sarasti, Director of Financial Aid, PC 125, Miami, FL 33199. (305) 348-2347.

INTERNATIONAL STUDENTS

Demographics 8% of students enrolled in the program are international.

Services and Facilities International student center, language tutoring, ESL courses, special assistance for nonnative speakers of English, counseling/support services.

Applying TOEFL required, minimum score of 500; proof of health; proof of adequate funds. Financial aid is not available to international students. Admission applications are processed on a rolling basis. Contact: Ms. Ana Sippin, Director of International Student Services, GC-217, Miami, FL 33199. (305) 348-2421.

PLACEMENT

In 1993-94, 67 organizations participated in on-campus recruiting; 603 on-campus interviews were conducted. Placement services include alumni network, career counseling/planning, career fairs, career placement, electronic job bank, job interviews, resume preparation, and resume referral to employers. Of 1994 graduates, 77% were employed within three months of graduation, the average starting salary was $38,401, the range was $35,000-$39,000.

Jobs by Employer Type Manufacturing 13%; service 58%; government 6%; consulting 14%; nonprofit 2%; self-employed 7%.

Jobs by Functional Area Marketing/sales 38%; finance 27%; operations 12%; management 11%; strategic planning 7%; technical management 5%.

Program Contact: Mr. Lee Sevald, MBA Coordinator, Florida International University, University Park, Miami, FL 33199. (305) 348-4239; Fax: (305) 348-4245.

Florida Southern College

Lakeland, Florida

OVERVIEW

Florida Southern College is an independent comprehensive coed institution, affiliated with United Methodist Church. Founded 1885. Setting: 100-acre suburban campus with easy access to Tampa and Orlando. Total institutional enrollment: 1,800.

MBA HIGHLIGHTS

Entrance Difficulty***

Cost $
Tuition: $260/credit hour
Room & Board: N/R

Total Enrollment: 100

Average Class Size: 12

ACADEMICS

Length of Program Minimum: 18 months.

Calendar Semesters.

Full-time Classes Main campus; evening, summer.

Part-time Classes Main campus; evening, summer.

Degree Requirements 36 credit hours.

Curricular Focus Business issues and problems, economic and financial theory, entrepreneurship, general management, international business, leadership, managing diversity, organizational development and change management, problem solving and decision making, strategic analysis and planning, teamwork.

Concentrations Accounting, management.

STUDENT STATISTICS

Geographic Representation State residents 100%.

FACILITIES

Information Resources Main library with 158,143 bound volumes, 335,062 titles on microform, 746 periodical subscriptions, 7,000 records/tapes/CDs, 87 CD-ROMs.

ADMISSION

Entrance Requirements Bachelor's degree, GMAT score of 450, minimum 2.5 GPA.

Application Requirements Application form, copies of transcript, resume/curriculum vitae, 3 letters of recommendation.

Application Deadlines 8/1 for fall, 12/1 for spring, 4/1 for summer.

FINANCIALS
Costs for 1994-95 Tuition: Full-time: $260/credit hour.

Financial Aid Applications are processed on a rolling basis. Contact: Mr. Robert Sterling, Financial Aid Director, 111 Lake Hollingsworth Drive, Lakeland, FL 33801-5698. (813) 680-4140.

INTERNATIONAL STUDENTS
Applying TOEFL required, minimum score of 550; proof of health; proof of adequate funds. Financial aid is not available to international students. Admission application deadlines: 8/1 for fall, 12/1 for spring, 4/1 for summer.

Program Contact: Ms. Kim Pickering, Evening and Graduate Admissions Counselor, Florida Southern College, 111 Lake Hollingsworth Drive, Lakeland, FL 33801-5698. (813) 680-4203.

Florida State University

College of Business

Tallahassee, Florida

OVERVIEW
Florida State University is a state-supported coed institution. Part of State University System of Florida. Founded 1857. Setting: 422-acre urban campus. Total institutional enrollment: 29,000. Program was first offered in 1960. AACSB-accredited.

MBA HIGHLIGHTS

Entrance Difficulty*
Mean GMAT: 575
Mean GPA: 3.2

Cost $
Tuition: $112/hour
(Nonresident: $365/hour)
Room & Board: $5,000

Enrollment Profile

Full-time: 102	Work Exp: 95%
Part-time: 77	International: 5%
Total: 179	Women: 15%
Average Age: 27	Minorities: 10%

Average Class Size: 15

ACADEMICS
Length of Program Minimum: 24 months. Maximum: 2 years.

Calendar Semesters.

Full-time Classes Main campus, Panama City; day, summer.

Part-time Classes Main campus, Panama City; day, evening, summer.

Degree Requirements 60 credits including 3 elective credits.

Required Courses Business conditions analysis, communication and decision processes, individual and group work behavior, information and technology management, investments and financial services, legal environment, managerial accounting, managerial economics, marketing strategy, problems in financial management, production and operations management, quantitative methods, strategy and business policy. Courses may be waived through: previous course work.

Curricular Focus Business issues and problems, general management, problem solving and decision making.

Concentration Management.

Faculty Full-time: 15, 100% with doctorates; part-time: 1, 100% with doctorates.

Teaching Methodology Case study: 20%, lecture: 50%, research: 10%, student presentations: 10%, team projects: 10%.

Special Opportunities International exchange in France. Internship program available.

STUDENT STATISTICS
Geographic Representation State residents 80%. By region: South 91%; Northeast 2%; West 2%; Midwest 1%. International 5%.

Undergraduate Majors Business 65%; education 1%; engineering/technology 24%; humanities 1%; science/mathematics 5%; social sciences 3%; other 1%.

Other Background Graduate degrees in other disciplines: 3%. Work experience: On average, students have 5 years of work experience on entrance to the program.

FACILITIES
Information Resources Main library with 2 million bound volumes, 4.2 million titles on microform, 18,498 periodical subscriptions, 35,277 records/tapes/CDs, 15 CD-ROMs.

Housing 15% of students in program live in college-owned or -operated housing.

Technology Computers are used moderately in course work. 18 computer terminals/PCs, linked by a campus-wide computer network, are available for use by students in program; they are located in computer labs. Students in the program are not required to have their own PC.

Computer Resources/On-line Services

Training	Yes	E-Mail	Yes
Internet	Yes		

ADMISSION
Acceptance 1994-95 400 applied for admission; 41% were accepted.

Entrance Requirements Bachelor's degree, GMAT score of 470, minimum 3.0 GPA, minimum 2 years of work experience. Core courses waived through: previous course work.

Application Requirements Written essay, application form, copies of transcript, resume/curriculum vitae, personal statement, 3 letters of recommendation.

Application Deadlines 6/1 for fall, 10/1 for spring, 3/1 for summer.

FINANCIALS
Costs for 1994-95 Tuition: Full-time: $112/hour for state residents, $365/hour for nonresidents. Average room and board costs are $5,000 per academic year (on-campus) and $6,600 per academic year (off-campus).

Financial Aid In 1994-95, 65% of candidates received some institutionally administered aid in the form of grants, scholarships, loans, fellowships. Total awards ranged from $1,000-$20,000. Financial aid is available to part-time students. Application deadlines: 3/1 for fall, 11/1 for summer. Contact: Mr. Robert McCloud, Director, Office of Financial Aid, Tallahassee, FL 32306. (904) 644-0539.

INTERNATIONAL STUDENTS
Demographics 5% of students enrolled in the program are international; North America 50%, South America 20%, Africa 15%, Central America 15%.

Services and Facilities International student center, visa services, language tutoring, special assistance for nonnative speakers of English, counseling/support services.

Applying TOEFL required, minimum score of 600; proof of health; proof of adequate funds; proof of insurance and immunizations. Financial aid is available to international students. Financial aid application deadlines: 3/1 for fall, 11/1 for summer. Admission application deadlines: 3/1 for fall, 11/1 for summer. Contact: Ms. Kristen Hagen, Assistant Director, International Student Center, 107 South Wildwood, Tallahassee, FL 32306. (904) 644-1702.

ALTERNATE MBA PROGRAMS
One-Year MBA Length of program: 12 months. Degree requirements: 42 credits including 3 elective credits. Minimum 3 years work experience. Average class size: 15.

MBA/JD Length of program: Minimum: 48 months. Degree requirements: 125 credits.

PLACEMENT
Placement services include alumni network, career counseling/planning, career fairs, career library, career placement, job interviews, resume preparation, and resume referral to employers. Of 1994 graduates, the average starting salary was $34,000, the range was $22,000-$43,000.

Jobs by Employer Type Manufacturing 6%; government 16%; consulting 10%; banking 20%; healthcare 20%; other 28%.

Jobs by Functional Area Marketing/sales 14%; finance 27%; management 14%; technical management 9%; other 36%.

Program Contact: Mr. Ron Motter, Graduate Program Assistant, Florida State University, College of Business, Graduate Office, Tallahassee, FL 32306. (904) 644-6455; Fax: (904) 644-0915.

Jacksonville University

College of Business

Jacksonville, Florida

OVERVIEW
Jacksonville University is an independent nonprofit comprehensive coed institution. Founded 1934. Setting: 260-acre suburban campus. Total institutional enrollment: 2,480. Program was first offered in 1984.

MBA HIGHLIGHTS

Entrance Difficulty**
Mean GMAT: 481
Mean GPA: 3.02

Cost $
Tuition: $335/semester hour
Room & Board: $4,400 (off-campus)

Enrollment Profile

Full-time: 31	Work Exp: 85%
Part-time: 76	International: 13%
Total: 107	Women: 38%
Average Age: 30	Minorities: 11%

Average Class Size: 14

ACADEMICS
Length of Program Minimum: 24 months. Maximum: 5 years.
Calendar Semesters.
Full-time Classes Main campus; evening, weekends, summer.
Part-time Classes Main campus; evening, weekends, summer.
Degree Requirements 30 semester hours including 9 elective semester hours.
Required Courses Advanced organizational behavior, advanced strategy and policy, business and society, managerial economics, managerial finance, quantitative methods, strategic marketing planning.
Curricular Focus Economic and financial theory, international business, strategic analysis and planning.
Concentrations Finance, healthcare administration, international business, management, marketing.
Faculty Full-time: 11, 100% with doctorates; part-time: 8, 100% with doctorates.
Teaching Methodology Case study: 12%, lecture: 70%, student presentations: 8%, team projects: 10%.
Special Opportunities International exchange in United Kingdom.

STUDENT STATISTICS
Geographic Representation State residents 72%. International 13%.
Other Background Graduate degrees in other disciplines: 2%. Work experience: On average, students have 3 years of work experience on entrance to the program.

FACILITIES
Information Resources Main library with 351,963 bound volumes, 112,550 titles on microform, 833 periodical subscriptions, 9,532 records/tapes/CDs. Business collection includes 17,000 bound volumes, 150 periodical subscriptions, 500 CD-ROMs.
Housing 2% of students in program live in college-owned or -operated housing.
Technology Computers are used heavily in course work. 25 computer terminals/PCs are available for use by students in program; they are located in computer labs. Students in the program are not required to have their own PC.

Computer Resources/On-line Services

Training	Yes	E-Mail	Yes
Internet	Yes	Dialog	Yes

Other on-line services: OCLC.

ADMISSION
Acceptance 1994-95 Of those applying, 88% were accepted.
Entrance Requirements Bachelor's degree, GMAT score of 450.
Application Requirements Interview, application form, copies of transcript, personal statement, 2 letters of recommendation.
Application Deadlines 7/15 for fall, 11/15 for spring, 3/1 for summer.

FINANCIALS
Costs for 1994-95 Tuition: Full-time: $335/semester hour. Fees: Full-time: $80/semester. Average room and board costs are $4,400 per academic year (off-campus).
Financial Aid In 1994-95, 6% of candidates received some institutionally administered aid in the form of scholarships, loans. Financial aid is available to part-time students. Application deadlines: 9/1 for fall, 1/5 for spring, 5/1 for summer. Contact: Mr. William Spiers, Director, Student Financial Assistance, 2800 University Boulevard North, Jacksonville, FL 32211-3394. (904) 745-7060.

INTERNATIONAL STUDENTS
Demographics 13% of students enrolled in the program are international; Asia 50%, Europe 20%, South America 20%, Africa 5%, Central America 5%.
Services and Facilities Language tutoring, ESL courses, special assistance for nonnative speakers of English.
Applying TOEFL required, minimum score of 550. Admission application deadlines: 7/1 for fall, 1/1 for spring, 3/1 for summer. Contact: Ms. Sara Myers, Assistant Dean of Students, 2800 University Boulevard North, Jacksonville, FL 32211-3394. (904) 745-7066.

ALTERNATE MBA PROGRAM
Executive MBA (EMBA) Length of program: Minimum: 16 months. Maximum: 5 years. Degree requirements: 43 credits.

PLACEMENT
Placement services include alumni network, career counseling/planning, career fairs, career placement, and resume preparation.

Program Contact: Dr. Thomas O. McConnell, Director, Graduate Business Programs, Jacksonville University, 2800 University Boulevard North, Jacksonville, FL 32211-3394. (904) 745-7437; Fax: (904) 745-7463.

Nova Southeastern University

School of Business and Entrepreneurship

Fort Lauderdale, Florida

OVERVIEW
Nova Southeastern University is an independent nonprofit coed institution. Founded 1964. Setting: 200-acre urban campus with easy access to Miami. Total institutional enrollment: 14,000.

MBA HIGHLIGHTS

Entrance Difficulty**
Mean GMAT: 440
Mean GPA: N/R

Cost $$
Tuition: $3,000 - $3,500/quarter
Room & Board: $3,000

Enrollment Profile

Full-time: 90	Work Exp: 90%
Part-time: 900	International: 5%
Total: 990	Women: 45%
Average Age: 29	Minorities: 18%

Average Class Size: 28

ACADEMICS
Length of Program Minimum: 12 months.
Calendar Quarters.
Full-time Classes Main campus; day, summer.
Part-time Classes Main campus; weekends, summer.
Degree Requirements 41 credit hours.
Required Courses Business policy, entrepreneurship, ethics, finance, human resources management, management, managerial accounting, managerial economics, marketing, organizational behavior, quantitative methods, total quality management, values based leadership.
Curricular Focus General management, leadership, teamwork.
Concentrations Entrepreneurship, finance, human resources management, management, management information systems, marketing.

Teaching Methodology Case study: 10%, lecture: 40%, research: 10%, student presentations: 20%, team projects: 20%.

Special Opportunities Internship program available.

STUDENT STATISTICS

Geographic Representation State residents 85%. International 5%.

Other Background Graduate degrees in other disciplines: 2%. Work experience: On average, students have 6 years of work experience on entrance to the program.

FACILITIES

Information Resources Main library with 220,000 bound volumes, 250 titles on microform, 6,538 periodical subscriptions, 695 records/tapes/CDs, 94 CD-ROMs.

Housing College housing available.

Technology Computers are used moderately in course work. 60 computer terminals/PCs, linked by a campus-wide computer network, are available for use by students in program; they are located in computer labs. Students in the program are required to have their own PC.

Computer Resources/On-line Services

Training	No	CompuServe	No
Internet	Yes	Dun's	No
E-Mail	Yes	Dow Jones	No
Videoconference Center	Yes	Dialog	No
LEXIS/NEXIS	No	Bloomberg	No

ADMISSION

Acceptance 1994-95 1,000 applied for admission; 90% were accepted.

Entrance Requirements Bachelor's degree, GMAT score of 450, minimum 2.5 GPA. Core courses waived through: previous course work.

Application Requirements Written essay, application form, copies of transcript, 3 letters of recommendation.

Application Deadlines 8/1 for fall, 2/1 for spring. Applications are processed on a rolling basis.

FINANCIALS

Costs for 1994-95 Tuition: Full-time: $3,000-$3,500/quarter; Part-time day: $350/credit hour; Weekends: $2,000-$2,500/quarter. Average room and board costs are $3,000 per academic year (on-campus) and $2,000 per academic year (off-campus).

Financial Aid In 1994-95, 30% of candidates received some institutionally administered aid in the form of scholarships, fellowships, assistantships, work-study. Application deadlines: 4/1 for fall, 10/1 for spring. Applications are processed on a rolling basis. Contact: Mr. Juan Ramirez, Graduate Financial Aid Counselor, 3301 College Avenue, Fort Lauderdale, FL 33314. (305) 476-8995.

INTERNATIONAL STUDENTS

Demographics 5% of students enrolled in the program are international.

Applying TOEFL required, minimum score of 550. Financial aid is available to international students. Financial aid application deadlines: 4/1 for fall, 10/1 for spring. Admission application deadlines: 8/1 for fall, 12/1 for spring. Applications are processed on a rolling basis.

ALTERNATE MBA PROGRAMS

International MBA/JD

MBA/JD

PLACEMENT

Placement services include alumni network and resume referral to employers.

Program Contact: Mr. Greg Stiber, Director of Marketing, Nova Southeastern University, 3301 College Avenue, Fort Lauderdale, FL 33314. (305) 475-7533, or (800) 672-7223; Fax: (305) 476-4865. See full description on page 794.

Orlando College

Division of Business Administration

Orlando, Florida

OVERVIEW

Orlando College is an independent proprietary comprehensive coed institution. Part of Phillips Colleges, Inc. Founded 1918. Setting: 1-acre urban campus. Total institutional enrollment: 700. Program was first offered in 1986.

MBA HIGHLIGHTS

Entrance Difficulty*
Mean GMAT: 460
Mean GPA: 3.1

Cost $$
Tuition: $10,250/degree program
Room & Board: $9,600 (off-campus)

Enrollment Profile

Full-time: 140	Work Exp: 98%
Part-time: 0	International: 41%
Total: 140	Women: 68%
Average Age: 36	Minorities: 59%

Average Class Size: 15

ACADEMICS

Length of Program Minimum: 18 months.

Calendar Quarters.

Full-time Classes Main campus; day, evening, weekends, summer.

Part-time Classes Main campus; day, evening, weekends, summer.

Degree Requirements 56 quarter hours.

Curricular Focus Economic and financial theory, entrepreneurship, problem solving and decision making, strategic analysis and planning, teamwork, women in business.

Concentrations Accounting, international business, management, management information systems, marketing, public administration, strategic management.

Faculty Full-time: 3, 50% with doctorates; part-time: 2, 50% with doctorates.

Teaching Methodology Case study: 30%, lecture: 20%, research: 10%, student presentations: 10%, team projects: 30%.

STUDENT STATISTICS

Geographic Representation State residents 28%. By region: South 51%; Northeast 8%. International 41%.

Undergraduate Majors Business 55%; education 15%; humanities 15%; social sciences 15%.

Other Background Graduate degrees in other disciplines: 12%. Work experience: On average, students have 3 years of work experience on entrance to the program.

FACILITIES

Information Resources Main library with 10,000 bound volumes, 105 periodical subscriptions, 97 records/tapes/CDs.

Housing College housing not available.

Technology Computers are used moderately in course work. 30 computer terminals/PCs are available for use by students in program; they are located in learning resource center, the library, computer labs. Students in the program are required to have their own PC.

Computer Resources/On-line Services

Training	Yes	Dun's	No
Internet	No	Dow Jones	No
E-Mail	No	Dialog	No
LEXIS/NEXIS	Yes	Bloomberg	No
CompuServe	No		

ADMISSION

Acceptance 1994-95 80 applied for admission; 95% were accepted.

Entrance Requirements Bachelor's degree, minimum 2.75 GPA.

Application Requirements Written essay, interview, application form, copies of transcript, personal statement.

Application Deadlines 9/15 for fall, 12/15 for winter, 3/15 for spring, 6/15 for summer. Applications are processed on a rolling basis.

FINANCIALS

Costs for 1994-95 Tuition: Full-time: $10,250/degree program. Average room and board costs are $9,600 per academic year (off-campus).

Financial Aid In 1994-95, 90% of candidates received some institutionally administered aid in the form of scholarships, loans, work-study. Financial aid is available to part-time students. Application deadlines: 9/15 for fall, 12/15 for winter, 3/15 for spring, 6/15 for summer. Applications are processed on a rolling basis. Contact: Ms. Linda Kaisrlik, Finance Director, 5421 Diplomat Circle, Orlando, FL 32810-5674. (407) 628-5870.

INTERNATIONAL STUDENTS

Demographics 41% of students enrolled in the program are international.

Applying TOEFL required, minimum score of 550; proof of health; proof of adequate funds; English equivalency examination. Financial aid is not available to international students. Admission application deadlines: 9/15 for fall, 12/15 for winter, 3/15 for spring. Applications are processed on a rolling basis.

PLACEMENT
In 1993-94, 18 organizations participated in on-campus recruiting. Placement services include alumni network, career counseling/planning, career fairs, career placement, job interviews, resume preparation, and resume referral to employers. Of 1994 graduates, 98% were employed within three months of graduation.

Program Contact: Mr. Robert Chapman, Chair, Graduate Business and Accounting, Orlando College, 5421 Diplomat Circle, Orlando, FL 32810-5674. (407) 628-5870, or (800) 628-5870; Fax: (407) 628-1344.

Palm Beach Atlantic College

Rinker School of Business

West Palm Beach, Florida

OVERVIEW
Palm Beach Atlantic College is an independent Southern Baptist comprehensive coed institution. Founded 1968. Setting: 25-acre urban campus with easy access to Miami. Total institutional enrollment: 1,894.

MBA HIGHLIGHTS
Entrance Difficulty***
Mean GMAT: 460
Mean GPA: N/R

Cost $
Tuition: $240/credit hour
Room & Board: $4,500

Enrollment Profile

Full-time: 20	Work Exp: N/R
Part-time: 80	International: 3%
Total: 100	Women: 49%
Average Age: N/R	Minorities: 8%

Average Class Size: 23

ACADEMICS
Length of Program Minimum: 24 months. Maximum: 6 years.
Calendar Semesters.
Full-time Classes Main campus; evening, summer.
Part-time Classes Main campus; evening, summer.
Degree Requirements 39 credit hours including 9 elective credit hours.
Required Courses Business policy, financial and managerial accounting, human resources management, humanities for executives, independent study, international business, international marketing, investments, legal environment of business, macroeconomics, managerial finance, marketing management, organizational behavior, organizational development, organizational theory, physical distribution systems, promotion strategy, quantitative methods, real estate management, small business management.
Curricular Focus General management.
Concentration Management.
Teaching Methodology Case study: 20%, faculty seminars: 5%, lecture: 60%, research: 5%, student presentations: 5%, team projects: 5%.

STUDENT STATISTICS
Geographic Representation State residents 98%. International 3%.

FACILITIES
Information Resources Main library with 68,250 bound volumes, 551 titles on microform, 856 periodical subscriptions, 2,495 records/tapes/CDs, 16 CD-ROMs.
Housing College housing available.
Technology Computer terminals/PCs are available for use by students in program; they are located in computer labs.

ADMISSION
Acceptance 1994-95 53 applied for admission; 81% were accepted.
Entrance Requirements Bachelor's degree, GMAT score of 450, minimum 3.0 GPA. Core courses waived through: previous course work.

Application Requirements Written essay, interview, application form, copies of transcript, resume/curriculum vitae, 2 letters of recommendation.
Application Deadlines 6/1 for fall, 10/1 for spring. Applications are processed on a rolling basis.

FINANCIALS
Costs for 1994-95 Tuition: Full-time: $240/credit hour. Average room and board costs are $4,500 per academic year (on-campus) and $4,500 per academic year (off-campus).
Financial Aid In 1994-95, candidates received some institutionally administered aid in the form of loans. Applications are processed on a rolling basis. Contact: Ms. Carolanne Brown, Graduate Admissions Counselor, 901 South Flagler Drive, PO Box 24708, West Palm Beach, FL 33416-4708. (407) 650-7700.

INTERNATIONAL STUDENTS
Demographics 3% of students enrolled in the program are international.
Applying TOEFL required, minimum score of 500; proof of health; proof of adequate funds. Admission application deadlines: 6/1 for fall, 10/1 for spring.

Program Contact: Ms. Carolanne Brown, Graduate Studies Admissions Counselor, Palm Beach Atlantic College, 901 South Flagler Drive, PO Box 24708, West Palm Beach, FL 33416-4708. (407) 835-4477, or (800) 238-3998 (FL only); Fax: (407) 835-4374; Internet Address: cbrown@goliath.pbac.edu.

Rollins College

Roy E. Crummer Graduate School of Business

Winter Park, Florida

OVERVIEW
Rollins College is an independent nonprofit comprehensive coed institution. Founded 1885. Setting: 67-acre suburban campus with easy access to Orlando. Total institutional enrollment: 3,284. Program was first offered in 1957. AACSB-accredited.

MBA HIGHLIGHTS
Entrance Difficulty****
Mean GMAT: 590
Mean GPA: 3.1

Cost $$$
Tuition: $16,500
Room & Board: $11,860 (off-campus)

Enrollment Profile

Full-time: 182	Work Exp: 80%
Part-time: 117	International: 13%
Total: 299	Women: 28%
Average Age: 26	Minorities: 14%

Average Class Size: 22

ACADEMICS
Length of Program Minimum: 20 months. Maximum: 6 years.
Calendar Semesters.
Full-time Classes Main campus; day, early morning.
Part-time Classes Main campus; evening, summer.
Degree Requirements 53 credits including 18 elective credits.
Required Courses Economics for managers, financial accounting, financial management, international business concepts, management policy, managerial accounting, marketing management, operation management, organizational behavior, quantitative methods.
Curricular Focus Computer applications, leadership, problem solving and decision making.
Concentrations Accounting, finance, international business, management, marketing, operations management.
Faculty Full-time: 17, 94% with doctorates; part-time: 6, 83% with doctorates.
Teaching Methodology Case study: 50%, computer applications: 10%, lecture: 5%, seminars by members of the business community: 5%, student presentations: 10%, team projects: 20%.
Special Opportunities International exchange in Bulgaria, France, Ireland, Mexico, Spain. Internship program available.

STUDENT STATISTICS

Geographic Representation State residents 70%. International 13%.

Undergraduate Majors Business 37%; education 4%; engineering/technology 25%; humanities 7%; nursing 2%; science/mathematics 10%; social sciences 15%.

Other Background Graduate degrees in other disciplines: 5%. Work experience: On average, students have 3 years of work experience on entrance to the program.

FACILITIES

Information Resources Main library with 263,658 bound volumes, 37,758 titles on microform, 1,554 periodical subscriptions, 3,640 records/tapes/CDs. Business collection includes 22,300 bound volumes, 251 periodical subscriptions, 3 CD-ROMs, 25 videos.

Housing College housing not available.

Technology Computers are used heavily in course work. 30 computer terminals/PCs, linked by a campus-wide computer network, are available for use by students in program; they are located in student rooms, computer labs, MBA Career Services Center. Students in the program are required to have their own PC. $2,300 are budgeted per student for computer support.

Computer Resources/On-line Services

Training	Yes	Dun's	No
Internet	Yes	Dow Jones	No
E-Mail	Yes	Dialog	Yes
LEXIS/NEXIS	Yes	Bloomberg	No
CompuServe	No		

Other on-line services: First Search.

ADMISSION

Acceptance 1994-95 537 applied for admission; 48% were accepted.

Entrance Requirements Bachelor's degree, GMAT score.

Application Requirements Written essay, interview, application form, copies of transcript, resume/curriculum vitae, personal statement.

Application Deadline 4/1 for fall.

FINANCIALS

Costs for 1994-95 Tuition: Full-time: $16,500; Part-time evening: $27,000/degree program. Average room and board costs are $11,860 per academic year (off-campus).

Financial Aid In 1994-95, 50% of candidates received some institutionally administered aid in the form of scholarships, assistantships. Total awards ranged from $3,000-$20,000. Financial aid is not available to part-time students. Application deadlines: 8/1 for fall, 12/1 for spring. Contact: Ms. Susan Darling, Assistant Director, Student Financial Planning, 1000 Holt Avenue-2704, Winter Park, FL 32789-4499. (407) 646-2395.

INTERNATIONAL STUDENTS

Demographics 13% of students enrolled in the program are international; Asia 33%, Europe 12%, Africa 8%, Central America 8%, South America 5%, Australia 4%, other 30%.

Services and Facilities Visa services, counseling/support services.

Applying TOEFL required; proof of adequate funds. Financial aid is available to international students. Admission application deadline: 4/1 for fall. Contact: Ms. Marisol Colon, Coordinator, Records and Registration, 1000 Holt Avenue-2722, Winter Park, FL 32789-4499. (407) 646-2415.

ALTERNATE MBA PROGRAM

Executive MBA (EMBA) Length of program: Minimum: 20 months. Maximum: 6 years. Degree requirements: 49 credits including 12 elective credits. International travel component.

PLACEMENT

In 1993-94, 15 organizations participated in on-campus recruiting; 95 on-campus interviews were conducted. Placement services include alumni network, career counseling/planning, career library, career placement, job interviews, resume preparation, and resume referral to employers. Of 1994 graduates, 85% were employed within three months of graduation, the average starting salary was $36,094, the range was $18,000-$52,000.

Jobs by Employer Type Manufacturing 22%; service 69%; consulting 9%.

Jobs by Functional Area Marketing/sales 24%; finance 37%; operations 7%; management 15%; technical management 2%; consulting 15%.

Program Contact: Mr. Stephen Gauthier, Assistant Dean, Rollins College, 1000 Holt Avenue, Winter Park, FL 32789-4499. (407) 866-2405, or (800) 866-2405; Fax: (407) 866-1550; Internet Address: stephengauthier@rollins.edu.

St. Thomas University

School of Business Administration

Miami, Florida

OVERVIEW

St. Thomas University is an independent Roman Catholic comprehensive coed institution. Founded 1961. Setting: 140-acre suburban campus. Total institutional enrollment: 2,600.

MBA HIGHLIGHTS

Entrance Difficulty**

Cost $
Tuition: $330/credit
Room & Board: $4,600

Enrollment Profile

Full-time: 40	Work Exp: N/R
Part-time: 30	International: N/R
Total: 70	Women: 50%
Average Age: N/R	Minorities: N/R

Average Class Size: 15

The M.B.A. curriculum is designed to provide students from diverse academic backgrounds with a basic knowledge in the primary core areas of business and intensive preparation in one of five specializations: accounting, health management, international business, management, and sports administration. The accounting specialization is only available to students with an undergraduate degree in accounting or its equivalent. Depending upon the student's academic background, 42 to 51 hours of course work may be required for the degree. A series of three preparatory courses provides the needed base skills—accounting, economics, statistics—for students with no prior education in business.

The program's objective is to develop managers who not only have the knowledge necessary for today's rapidly changing business environment but also have the skills to apply and utilize this knowledge appropriately.

The M.B.A. program provides a balance between the quantitative and qualitative aspects of management and focuses on the needs of part-time students who may have special concerns because of their employment responsibilities. The M.B.A. also provides an opportunity for full-time students to complete the program in four semesters. The program has full-time and adjunct faculty representing a broad background in management, international business, sports administration, and accounting.

ACADEMICS

Length of Program Minimum: 18 months. Maximum: 7 years.

Calendar Semesters.

Full-time Classes Main campus; evening, weekends, summer.

Part-time Classes Main campus; evening, weekends, summer.

Degree Requirements 42 credits.

Required Courses Advanced information systems, advanced operations management, financial management, management writing and reporting, managerial accounting, managerial ethics, organizational behavior, policy planning and strategy systems. Courses may be waived through: previous course work.

Curricular Focus International business, leadership, strategic analysis and planning.

Concentrations Accounting, finance, health services, human resources management, international business, management, management information systems, marketing, organizational behavior, quantitative analysis, sports administration, strategic management.

Faculty Full-time: 8, 90% with doctorates; part-time: 15, 90% with doctorates.

Teaching Methodology Case study: 20%, experiential learning: 20%, lecture: 20%, student presentations: 20%, team projects: 20%.

Special Opportunities Internship program available.

FACILITIES

Information Resources Main library with 135,000 bound volumes, 16,500 titles on microform, 900 periodical subscriptions, 700 records/tapes/CDs. Business collection includes 14,000 bound volumes, 315 periodical subscriptions, 6 CD-ROMs, 73 videos.

Housing College housing available.

Technology Computers are used moderately in course work. 75 computer terminals/PCs are available for use by students in program; they are located in learning resource center, computer labs, law school library. Students in the program are not required to have their own PC.

Computer Resources/On-line Services

Training	Yes	CompuServe	No
Internet	Yes	Dun's	Yes $
E-Mail	No	Dialog	Yes $
Multimedia Center	Yes		

ADMISSION

Acceptance 1994-95 Of those applying, 39% were accepted.

Entrance Requirements Bachelor's degree, prerequisite courses required for applicants with non-business degree, GMAT score, minimum 3.0 GPA, writing assessment test. Core courses waived through: previous course work.

Application Requirements Application form, copies of transcript, resume/curriculum vitae, personal statement, 2 letters of recommendation, 3 letters of recommendation for MBA/sports administration specialization.

Application Deadlines 6/15 for fall, 11/15 for spring.

FINANCIALS

Costs for 1994-95 Tuition: Full-time: $330/credit. Fees: Full-time: $27/semester. Average room and board costs are $4,600 per academic year (on-campus).

Financial Aid In 1994-95, candidates received some institutionally administered aid in the form of scholarships, loans, assistantships, work-study. Financial aid is available to part-time students. Application deadlines: 4/1 for fall, 11/1 for spring, 3/1 for summer. Contact: Ms. Marie Kaplan, Financial Aid Counselor, 16400 Northwest 32nd Street, Miami, FL 33054-6459. (305) 628-6725.

INTERNATIONAL STUDENTS

Demographics 11% of students on campus are international.

Services and Facilities ESL courses, counseling/support services.

Applying TOEFL required, minimum score of 550; proof of adequate funds. Financial aid is not available to international students. Admission application deadlines: 5/1 for fall, 11/1 for spring, 3/1 for summer.

PLACEMENT

Placement services include alumni network, career counseling/planning, career fairs, career library, career placement, job interviews, resume preparation, and resume referral to employers.

Program Contact: Ms. Mary Conway, Director of Graduate Admissions, St. Thomas University, 16400 Northwest 32nd Avenue, Miami, FL 33054-6459. (305) 628-6710, or (800) 367-9006 (FL only), or (800) 367-9010 (out-of-state); Fax: (305) 628-6510.

Stetson University

School of Business Administration

DeLand, Florida

OVERVIEW

Stetson University is an independent nonprofit comprehensive coed institution. Founded 1883. Setting: 150-acre suburban campus with easy access to Orlando. Total institutional enrollment: 2,700. Program was first offered in 1968.

MBA HIGHLIGHTS

Entrance Difficulty**
Mean GMAT: 530
Mean GPA: 3.2

Cost $$
Tuition: $275/credit hour
Room & Board: N/R

Enrollment Profile

Full-time: 60		Work Exp: 40%
Part-time: 50		International: 10%
Total: 110		Women: 40%
Average Age: 27		Minorities: 1%

Average Class Size: 16

ACADEMICS

Length of Program Minimum: 12 months. Maximum: 8 years.

Calendar Semesters.

Full-time Classes Main campus; evening, summer.

Part-time Classes Main campus; evening, summer.

Degree Requirements 36 credits including 6 elective credits.

Required Courses Advanced financial accounting, advanced managerial accounting, business and its environment, financial management, international business and finance, managing information technology, marketing decision making, operations research, organizational theory and behavior, strategic management.

Curricular Focus Business issues and problems, leadership, managing diversity.

Concentration Management.

Faculty Full-time: 15, 100% with doctorates.

Teaching Methodology Case study: 40%, faculty seminars: 10%, lecture: 30%, team projects: 20%.

Special Opportunities Roland George investment program.

STUDENT STATISTICS

Geographic Representation State residents 70%. By region: South 70%; Northeast 10%. International 10%.

Undergraduate Majors Business 60%; engineering/technology 10%; social sciences 30%.

Other Background Graduate degrees in other disciplines: 1%.

FACILITIES

Information Resources Main library with 336,486 bound volumes, 6,532 titles on microform, 1,339 periodical subscriptions, 15,000 records/tapes/CDs, 191 CD-ROMs. Business collection includes 28,000 bound volumes, 425 periodical subscriptions, 15 CD-ROMs, 45 videos.

Housing 15% of students in program live in college-owned or -operated housing. Assistance with housing search provided.

Technology Computers are used moderately in course work. 50 computer terminals/PCs, linked by a campus-wide computer network, are available for use by students in program; they are located in the student center, the library, the computer center, computer labs. Students in the program are not required to have their own PC.

Computer Resources/On-line Services

E-Mail	Yes	Dun's	Yes
Videoconference Center	Yes	Dow Jones	Yes
LEXIS/NEXIS	Yes	Dialog	Yes $
CompuServe	Yes		

ADMISSION

Acceptance 1994-95 300 applied for admission; 60% were accepted.

Entrance Requirements Bachelor's degree, minimum 2.5 GPA. Core courses waived through: previous course work.

Application Requirements Written essay, application form, copies of transcript, 3 letters of recommendation.

Application Deadline 7/15 for fall.

FINANCIALS

Costs for 1994-95 Tuition: Full-time: $275/credit hour.

Financial Aid In 1994-95, candidates received some institutionally administered aid in the form of loans, assistantships. Total awards ranged from $1,000-$2,000. Financial aid is not available to part-time students. Application deadlines: 7/15 for fall, 11/15 for spring. Applications are processed on a rolling basis. Contact: Ms. Sharon Ellis, Loan Officer and Supervisor, PO Box 8318, DeLand, FL 32720. (904) 822-7040.

INTERNATIONAL STUDENTS

Demographics 10% of students enrolled in the program are international; North America 93%, South America 5%, Asia 2%.

Services and Facilities International student office, international student center, visa services, language tutoring, special assistance for nonnative speakers of English.

Applying TOEFL required, minimum score of 550; proof of health; proof of adequate funds. Financial aid is available to international students. Financial aid application deadlines: 7/15 for fall, 11/15 for spring. Admission application deadlines: 7/15 for fall, 11/15 for spring. Applications are processed on a rolling basis. Contact: Mrs. Jeanne Bosco, Administrative Assistant, School of Business, DeLand, FL 32720. (904) 822-7411.

ALTERNATE MBA PROGRAM

MBA/JD Length of program: Minimum: 42 months. Degree requirements: 112 credits.

PLACEMENT

In 1993-94, 75 organizations participated in on-campus recruiting. Placement services include career counseling/planning, career placement, and job interviews. Of 1994 graduates, 95% were employed within three months of graduation, the average starting salary was $32,000, the range was $22,000-$38,000.

Jobs by Employer Type Manufacturing 2%; service 80%; government 10%; consulting 8%.

Program Contact: Dr. Frank DeZoort, Director, Graduate Business Programs, Stetson University, Campus Box 8398, DeLand, FL 32720. (904) 822-7410; Fax: (904) 822-7430; Internet Address: dezoort@ suvax1.stetson.edu.

Tampa College

Department of Business Administration

Tampa, Florida

OVERVIEW

Tampa College is an independent proprietary comprehensive coed institution. Part of Phillips Colleges, Inc. Founded 1890. Setting: 4-acre suburban campus. Total institutional enrollment: 1,150. Program was first offered in 1985.

MBA HIGHLIGHTS

Entrance Difficulty**

Cost $
Tuition: $56/credit
Room & Board: N/R

Enrollment Profile

Full-time: 105	Work Exp: 95%
Part-time: 10	International: 10%
Total: 115	Women: 51%
Average Age: 30	Minorities: 25%

Average Class Size: 25

ACADEMICS

Length of Program Minimum: 24 months.

Calendar Quarters.

Full-time Classes Main campus; evening, weekends, summer.

Part-time Classes Main campus; evening, weekends, summer.

Degree Requirements 56 credits including 16 elective credits. Other: Minimum 3.0 GPA.

Required Courses Advanced business policy and administration, financial management, management accounting, management communication, management of human resources, managerial economics, managerial ethics, marketing management, organizational behavior, quantitative methods.

Curricular Focus General management, international business, problem solving and decision making.

Concentrations Accounting, human resources management, international business.

Faculty Full-time: 2, 50% with doctorates; part-time: 8, 75% with doctorates.

Teaching Methodology Case study: 15%, lecture: 25%, research: 10%, student presentations: 25%, team projects: 25%.

STUDENT STATISTICS

Geographic Representation State residents 90%. International 10%.

FACILITIES

Information Resources Main library with 5,000 bound volumes, 20 titles on microform, 80 periodical subscriptions, 200 records/tapes/CDs, 2 CD-ROMs.

Housing College housing not available.

Technology Computers are used moderately in course work. 50 computer terminals/PCs, linked by a campus-wide computer network, are avail-

able for use by students in program; they are located in the library, computer labs. Students in the program are not required to have their own PC.

Computer Resources/On-line Services

Training	No	E-Mail	No
Internet	Yes	Dialog	Yes

Other on-line services: Westlaw.

ADMISSION

Acceptance 1994-95 38 applied for admission; 92% were accepted.

Entrance Requirements Bachelor's degree, GMAT score of 450, minimum 2.75 GPA.

Application Requirements Interview, application form, copies of transcript.

Application Deadline Applications are processed on a rolling basis.

FINANCIALS

Costs for 1994-95 Tuition: Full-time: $56/credit.

Financial Aid In 1994-95, 80% of candidates received some institutionally administered aid in the form of loans. Financial aid is available to part-time students. Applications are processed on a rolling basis. Contact: Ms. Dawn Gunn, Director of Student Finance, 3319 West Hillsborough Avenue, Tampa, FL 33614-5899. (813) 879-6000.

INTERNATIONAL STUDENTS

Demographics 10% of students enrolled in the program are international.

Services and Facilities International student office, counseling/support services.

Applying TOEFL required, minimum score of 550; proof of adequate funds. Financial aid is not available to international students. Admission applications are processed on a rolling basis. Contact: Mr. Christopher Karras, International Student Adviser, 3319 West Hillsborough Avenue, Tampa, FL 33614-5899. (813) 879-6000.

PLACEMENT

In 1993-94, 50 organizations participated in on-campus recruiting. Placement services include alumni network, career counseling/planning, career fairs, career library, career placement, and resume referral to employers. Of 1994 graduates, 90% were employed within three months of graduation, the average starting salary range was $18,000-$40,000.

Program Contact: Mr. Foster Thomas, Associate Director of Admissions, Tampa College, 3319 West Hillsborough Avenue, Tampa, FL 33614-5899. (813) 879-6000; Fax: (813) 871-2483.

University of Central Florida

College of Business Administration

Orlando, Florida

OVERVIEW

The University of Central Florida is a state-supported coed institution. Part of State University System of Florida. Founded 1963. Setting: 1,227-acre suburban campus. Total institutional enrollment: 25,000. Program was first offered in 1969. AACSB-accredited.

MBA HIGHLIGHTS

Entrance Difficulty****
Mean GMAT: 548
Mean GPA: 3.3

Cost $
Tuition: $109/hour
(Nonresident: $362/hour)
Room & Board: $1,800

Enrollment Profile

Full-time: 149	Work Exp: 99%
Part-time: 456	International: 5%
Total: 605	Women: 49%
Average Age: 29	Minorities: 10%

Average Class Size: 30

ACADEMICS

Length of Program Minimum: 24 months. Maximum: 7 years.

Calendar Semesters.

Full-time Classes Main campus, Brevard, Daytona Beach; day, evening, summer.

Part-time Classes Main campus, Brevard, Daytona Beach; evening, summer.

Degree Requirements 33 hours including 9 elective hours.

Required Courses Business policy and responsibility, economic analysis of the firm, financial analysis and management, managerial accounting analysis, marketing policy, organizational behavior and development, quantitative models for business decisions, statistical methods for business. Courses may be waived through: previous course work.

Curricular Focus Communications, managing diversity, organizational development and change management, teamwork.

Concentrations Accounting, economics, entrepreneurship, finance, international business, management, management information systems, marketing, quantitative analysis, real estate.

Faculty Full-time: 63, 100% with doctorates.

Teaching Methodology Case study: 10%, lecture: 50%, student presentations: 20%, team projects: 20%.

Special Opportunities International exchange in Portugal, Sweden. Internship program available.

STUDENT STATISTICS

Geographic Representation State residents 80%. By region: South 87%; Northeast 5%; Midwest 1%; West 1%. International 5%.

Undergraduate Majors Business 45%; engineering/technology 25%; humanities 10%; science/mathematics 10%; social sciences 5%; other 5%.

Other Background Graduate degrees in other disciplines: 5%. Work experience: On average, students have 4 years of work experience on entrance to the program.

FACILITIES

Information Resources Main library with 955,903 bound volumes, 1.2 million titles on microform, 4,838 periodical subscriptions, 5,820 records/tapes/CDs.

Housing College housing available.

Technology Computers are used heavily in course work. 800 computer terminals/PCs are available for use by students in program; they are located in the student center, learning resource center, the computer center, computer labs. Students in the program are not required to have their own PC.

Computer Resources/On-line Services

Training	Yes	LEXIS/NEXIS	Yes
Internet	Yes $	CompuServe	No
E-Mail	Yes	Dialog	No
Multimedia Center	Yes		

Other on-line services: Carl.

ADMISSION

Acceptance 1994-95 257 applied for admission; 58% were accepted.

Entrance Requirements Bachelor's degree, GMAT score of 500, minimum 3.0 GPA. Core courses waived through: previous course work.

Application Requirements Written essay, application form, resume/curriculum vitae, 3 letters of recommendation.

Application Deadlines 6/15 for fall, 11/1 for spring, 3/15 for summer.

FINANCIALS

Costs for 1994-95 Tuition: Full-time: $109/hour for state residents, $362/hour for nonresidents. Fees: Full-time: $47/semester for state residents, $47/semester for nonresidents. Average room and board costs are $1,800 per academic year (on-campus).

Financial Aid In 1994-95, 37% of candidates received some institutionally administered aid in the form of loans, assistantships. Total awards ranged from $2,700-$3,400. Financial aid is available to part-time students. Application deadlines: 3/1 for fall, 8/1 for spring. Contact: Ms. Mary McKinney, Director, AMD 129, Orlando, FL 32816. (407) 823-2827.

INTERNATIONAL STUDENTS

Demographics 5% of students enrolled in the program are international; Asia 34%, Europe 22%, Africa 11%, Central America 11%, South America 11%, Other 11%.

Services and Facilities International student center, ESL courses, special assistance for nonnative speakers of English.

Applying TOEFL required, minimum score of 575; proof of health; proof of adequate funds. Financial aid is not available to international students.

Admission application deadlines: 6/15 for fall, 11/1 for spring, 3/15 for summer. Contact: Mr. Douglas Mowry, Director, AMD 123, Orlando, FL 32816. (407) 823-5491.

ALTERNATE MBA PROGRAM

Executive MBA (EMBA) Length of program: Minimum: 18 months. Degree requirements: 33 credits. Average class size: 30.

PLACEMENT

Placement services include career counseling/planning, career fairs, career library, career placement, electronic job bank, job interviews, resume preparation, and resume referral to employers. Of 1994 graduates, the average starting salary was $32,817, the range was $22,000-$42,000.

Program Contact: Graduate Admissions, University of Central Florida, PO Box 25000, Orlando, FL 32816-1400. (407) 823-2766; Fax: (407) 823-6446.

University of Florida

College of Business Administration

Gainesville, Florida

OVERVIEW

The University of Florida is a state-supported coed institution. Part of State University System of Florida. Founded 1853. Setting: 2,000-acre small-town campus with easy access to Jacksonville. Total institutional enrollment: 38,000. Program was first offered in 1946. AACSB-accredited.

MBA HIGHLIGHTS

Entrance Difficulty***
Mean GMAT: 612
Mean GPA: 3.28

Cost $
Tuition: $105/hour
(Nonresident: $358/hour)
Room & Board: $6,000

Enrollment Profile

Full-time: 280	Work Exp: 95%
Part-time: 0	International: 23%
Total: 280	Women: 31%
Average Age: 25	Minorities: 13%

Average Class Size: 60

ACADEMICS

Length of Program Minimum: 16 months. Maximum: 2 years.

Calendar Semesters.

Full-time Classes Main campus; day.

Degree Requirements 48 hours including 18 elective hours.

Required Courses Business policy, corporate finance, economics of business decisions, financial and managerial accounting, financial management, information systems in organizations, managerial statistics, marketing management, organizational behavior, production management.

Curricular Focus Entrepreneurship, international business, teamwork.

Concentrations Arts administration, economics, entrepreneurship, finance, health services, human resources management, international business, management, management information systems, marketing, operations management, organizational behavior, public policy, real estate.

Faculty Full-time: 53, 100% with doctorates.

Teaching Methodology Case study: 15%, lecture: 40%, research: 5%, student presentations: 10%, team projects: 30%.

Special Opportunities International exchange in Austria, France, Germany, Hong Kong, Italy, Netherlands, Norway, Spain, United Kingdom. Internship program available.

STUDENT STATISTICS

Geographic Representation By region: South 41%; Northeast 23%; Midwest 9%; West 5%. International 23%.

Undergraduate Majors Business 40%; engineering/technology 15%; humanities 7%; science/mathematics 6%; social sciences 17%; other 15%.

Other Background Work experience: On average, students have 4 years of work experience on entrance to the program.

FACILITIES

Information Resources Main library with 3 million bound volumes, 4.2 million titles on microform, 24,191 periodical subscriptions, 25,126 records/tapes/CDs.

Housing 10% of students in program live in college-owned or -operated housing.

Technology Computers are used heavily in course work. 277 computer terminals/PCs, linked by a campus-wide computer network, are available for use by students in program; they are located in computer labs. Students in the program are not required to have their own PC.

Computer Resources/On-line Services

Training	Yes	CompuServe	No
Internet	Yes	Dun's	No
E-Mail	Yes	Dow Jones	Yes
Multimedia Center	Yes	Dialog	Yes
LEXIS/NEXIS	Yes	Bloomberg	No

Other on-line services: OCLC.

ADMISSION

Acceptance 1994-95 1,000 applied for admission; 23% were accepted.

Entrance Requirements Bachelor's degree, undergraduate degree in business for three-term students, GMAT score of 500, minimum 3.0 GPA.

Application Requirements Written essay, interview, application form, copies of transcript, resume/curriculum vitae, 2 letters of recommendation.

Application Deadlines 3/31 for fall, 2/15 for three-term program.

FINANCIALS

Costs for 1994-95 Tuition: Full-time: $105/hour for state residents, $358/hour for nonresidents. Fees: Full-time: $1,300/semester for state residents, $4,300/semester for nonresidents. Average room and board costs are $6,000 per academic year (on-campus) and $8,500 per academic year (off-campus).

Financial Aid In 1994-95, 90% of candidates received some institutionally administered aid in the form of scholarships, loans, fellowships, assistantships. Financial aid is not available to part-time students. Application deadline: 4/1 for fall. Contact: Office for Student Financial Affairs, PO Box 118140, Gainesville, FL 32611-8140. (904) 392-1275.

INTERNATIONAL STUDENTS

Demographics 23% of students enrolled in the program are international.

Services and Facilities International student center, visa services, counseling/support services, orientation.

Applying TOEFL required, minimum score of 550; proof of adequate funds; health insurance. Financial aid is not available to international students. Admission application deadline: 3/1 for fall. Contact: Ms. Margaritha Micha, Assistant Director of International Studies, 123 Tigert Hall, Gainesville, FL 32611-8140. (904) 392-5323.

ALTERNATE MBA PROGRAMS

Executive MBA (EMBA) Length of program: Minimum: 24 months. Maximum: 2 years. Degree requirements: 48 hours. 5 years full-time work experience. Average class size: 30.

One-Year MBA Length of program: Minimum: 11 months. Maximum: 1 year. Degree requirements: 32 hours including 18 elective hours. Undergraduate degree in business within last 5 years; 2-5 years work experience.

MBA/JD Length of program: Minimum: 48 months. Degree requirements: 36 credits including 9 elective credits. Average class size: 4.

MBA/MIM Length of program: Minimum: 24 months. Full-time classes: Main campus. Degree requirements: 66 hours. Completion of second year at American Graduate School of International Management, Glendale, AZ.

MBA/MHS Length of program: Minimum: 30 months. Maximum: 3 years. Degree requirements: 66 hours including 3 elective hours. 6 credits of administrative residency; 5 continuous semesters of academic study. Average class size: 20.

PLACEMENT

In 1993-94, 78 organizations participated in on-campus recruiting; 960 on-campus interviews were conducted. Placement services include alumni network, career counseling/planning, career fairs, career library, career placement, consortia, electronic job bank, job interviews, resume preparation, and resume referral to employers. Of 1994 graduates, 86% were employed within three months of graduation, the average starting salary was $44,826, the range was $29,000-$65,000.

Jobs by Employer Type Manufacturing 27%; service 34%; consulting 25%; transportation 11%; other 3%.

Jobs by Functional Area Marketing/sales 11%; finance 53%; management 17%; technical management 19%.

Program Contact: Ms. Laura Baker, Director of Admissions, University of Florida, PO Box 118140, Gainesville, FL 32611-8140. (904) 392-7992 Ext. 200; Fax: (904) 392-8791.

University of Miami

School of Business Administration

Coral Gables, Florida

OVERVIEW

The University of Miami is an independent nonprofit coed institution. Founded 1925. Setting: 260-acre suburban campus with easy access to Miami. Total institutional enrollment: 14,000. Program was first offered in 1929. AACSB-accredited.

MBA HIGHLIGHTS

Entrance Difficulty***
Mean GMAT: 504
Mean GPA: 2.93

Cost $$$$$
Tuition: $672/credit
Room & Board: $3,263

Enrollment Profile

Full-time: 358	Work Exp: 40%
Part-time: 153	International: 29%
Total: 511	Women: 39%
Average Age: 26	Minorities: N/R

Average Class Size: 30

ACADEMICS

Length of Program Minimum: 12 months. Maximum: 5 years.

Calendar Semesters.

Full-time Classes Main campus; day, evening, summer.

Part-time Classes Main campus; day, evening, summer.

Degree Requirements 36 credits including 24 elective credits.

Curricular Focus International business, managing diversity, strategic analysis and planning.

Concentrations Accounting, economics, finance, health services, human resources management, international business, management, management information systems, marketing, operations management, organizational behavior, public policy, strategic management.

Faculty Full-time: 102, 100% with doctorates.

Teaching Methodology Case study: 25%, lecture: 50%, seminars by members of the business community: 5%, student presentations: 10%, team projects: 10%.

Special Opportunities International exchange and internship programs available.

STUDENT STATISTICS

Geographic Representation State residents 60%. By region: South 40%; Northeast 20%; Midwest 9%; West 5%. International 29%.

Undergraduate Majors Business 57%; engineering/technology 13%; humanities 18%; social sciences 4%; other 8%.

Other Background Work experience: On average, students have 4 years of work experience on entrance to the program.

FACILITIES

Information Resources Main library with 2 million bound volumes, 3 million titles on microform, 19,025 periodical subscriptions, 35,754 records/tapes/CDs.

Housing 10% of students in program live in college-owned or -operated housing.

Technology Computers are used moderately in course work. 50 computer terminals/PCs, linked by a campus-wide computer network, are available for use by students in program; they are located in dormitories, the library, the computer center, computer labs. Students in the program are not required to have their own PC.

Computer Resources/On-line Services

Training	Yes	LEXIS/NEXIS	Yes
Internet	Yes	Dialog	Yes
E-Mail	Yes		

ADMISSION

Entrance Requirements Bachelor's degree, GMAT score. Core courses waived through: previous course work.

Application Requirements Written essay, application form, copies of transcript, resume/curriculum vitae, 2 letters of recommendation.

Application Deadlines 11/30 for fall, 6/30 for spring.

FINANCIALS

Costs for 1994-95 Tuition: Full-time: $672/credit. Fees: Full-time: $87/semester. Average room and board costs are $3,263 per academic year (on-campus) and $3,500 per academic year (off-campus).

Financial Aid In 1994-95, candidates received some institutionally administered aid in the form of grants, scholarships, loans, fellowships, assistantships. Total awards ranged from $500-$14,000. Financial aid is not available to part-time students. Application deadlines: 7/31 for fall, 11/30 for spring. Contact: Ms. Monica Foo, Fiscal Director, University of Miami Branch, Coral Gables, FL 33124. (305) 284-2510.

INTERNATIONAL STUDENTS

Demographics 29% of students enrolled in the program are international.

Services and Facilities International student center, visa services, language tutoring, ESL courses, special assistance for nonnative speakers of English, counseling/support services.

Applying TOEFL required, minimum score of 550; proof of adequate funds. Financial aid is not available to international students. Admission application deadlines: 11/30 for fall, 6/30 for spring. Contact: Ms. Teresa de la Guardia, Director, International Student Services, Building 21-F, Coral Gables, FL 33124. (305) 284-2928.

ALTERNATE MBA PROGRAM

Executive MBA (EMBA) Length of program: Minimum: 24 months. Maximum: 2 years. Degree requirements: 51 credits.

PLACEMENT

In 1993-94, 45 organizations participated in on-campus recruiting. Placement services include alumni network, career counseling/planning, career fairs, career library, career placement, electronic job bank, job interviews, resume preparation, and resume referral to employers. Of 1994 graduates, 89% were employed within three months of graduation.

Program Contact: Ms. Jennifer del Pino, Director, Graduate Business Recruiting and Admissions, University of Miami, University of Miami Branch, Coral Gables, FL 33124. (305) 284-4607, or (800) 531-7137; Fax: (305) 284-5905.

University of North Florida

College of Business Administration

Jacksonville, Florida

OVERVIEW

The University of North Florida is a state-supported comprehensive coed institution. Part of State University System of Florida. Founded 1965. Setting: 1,000-acre suburban campus. Total institutional enrollment: 10,000. Program was first offered in 1972. AACSB-accredited.

MBA HIGHLIGHTS

Entrance Difficulty*
Mean GMAT: 510
Mean GPA: 3.4

Cost $
Tuition: $110/credit hour
(Nonresident: $363/credit hour)
Room & Board: N/R

Enrollment Profile

Full-time: 120		Work Exp: 95%
Part-time: 380		International: 15%
Total: 500		Women: 45%
Average Age: N/R		Minorities: 15%

Average Class Size: 25

ACADEMICS

Length of Program Minimum: 18 months.

Calendar Semesters.

Full-time Classes Main campus; evening, weekends, summer.

Part-time Classes Main campus; evening, weekends, summer.

Degree Requirements 39 credit hours.

Curricular Focus Business issues and problems, general management, problem solving and decision making.

Concentrations Accounting, economics, finance, health services, human resources management, management, management information systems, marketing, organizational behavior.

Faculty Full-time: 22, 100% with doctorates; part-time: 6, 75% with doctorates.

Teaching Methodology Case study: 30%, faculty seminars: 5%, lecture: 40%, research: 5%, seminars by members of the business community: 5%, student presentations: 5%, team projects: 10%.

Special Opportunities International exchange in France.

STUDENT STATISTICS

Geographic Representation State residents 80%. International 15%.

Undergraduate Majors Business 60%; education 5%; engineering/technology 12%; humanities 5%; nursing 2%; science/mathematics 9%; social sciences 3%; other 4%.

Other Background Graduate degrees in other disciplines: 10%. Work experience: On average, students have 12 years of work experience on entrance to the program.

FACILITIES

Information Resources Main library with 466,801 bound volumes, 702,221 titles on microform, 3,200 periodical subscriptions, 10,500 records/tapes/CDs, 500 CD-ROMs.

Housing 10% of students in program live in college-owned or -operated housing.

Technology 25 computer terminals/PCs are available for use by students in program; they are located in learning resource center, computer labs. Students in the program are not required to have their own PC.

Computer Resources/On-line Services

Training	Yes	E-Mail	No

ADMISSION

Acceptance 1994-95 375 applied for admission; 80% were accepted.

Entrance Requirements Bachelor's degree, GMAT score of 500. Core courses waived through: previous course work.

Application Requirements Application form, copies of transcript.

Application Deadlines 7/7 for fall, 11/4 for spring, 3/13 for summer. Applications are processed on a rolling basis.

FINANCIALS

Costs for 1994-95 Tuition: Full-time: $110/credit hour for state residents, $363/credit hour for nonresidents.

Financial Aid In 1994-95, candidates received some institutionally administered aid in the form of scholarships, assistantships. Financial aid is available to part-time students. Application deadline: 4/1 for fall. Contact: Ms. Janice Nowak, Director of Financial Aid, 4567 St. John's Bluff Road South, Jacksonville, FL 32224-2645. (904) 646-2604.

INTERNATIONAL STUDENTS

Demographics 15% of students enrolled in the program are international.

Applying TOEFL required, minimum score of 500; proof of health; proof of adequate funds. Financial aid is available to international students. Financial aid application deadlines: 5/2 for fall, 10/3 for spring, 2/1 for summer. Admission application deadlines: 5/2 for fall, 10/3 for spring, 2/1 for summer. Applications are processed on a rolling basis. Contact: Ms. Victoria LaPlaca, International Student Affairs Coordinator, 4567 St. John's Bluff Road South, Jacksonville, FL 32224-2645. (904) 646-2768.

PLACEMENT

Placement services include alumni network, career counseling/planning, career fairs, career library, career placement, electronic job bank, resume preparation, and resume referral to employers.

Program Contact: Dr. Donald K. Graham, Director of Graduate Studies, University of North Florida, 4567 St. John's Bluff Road South, Jacksonville, FL 32224-2645. (904) 646-2575; Fax: (904) 646-2590; Internet Address: dgraham@unf1vm.cis.unf.edu.

University of Sarasota

College of Management and Business

Sarasota, Florida

OVERVIEW
The University of Sarasota is an independent nonprofit graduate-only coed institution. Founded 1974. Setting: suburban campus. Total institutional enrollment: 603. Program was first offered in 1986.

MBA HIGHLIGHTS

Entrance Difficulty*
Mean GMAT: N/R
Mean GPA: 3.4

Cost $$
Tuition: $275/semester hour
Room & Board: $4,500 (off-campus)

Enrollment Profile

Full-time: 26	Work Exp: 80%
Part-time: 56	International: 15%
Total: 82	Women: 48%
Average Age: 34	Minorities: 7%

Average Class Size: 14

ACADEMICS
Length of Program Minimum: 18 months. Maximum: 5 years.
Calendar 6 eight-week terms plus intensive two-week terms.
Full-time Classes Main campus; evening, weekends, summer.
Part-time Classes Main campus; evening, weekends, summer.
Degree Requirements 45 credits including 18 elective credits.
Required Courses Economics analysis, effective communications, financial accounting for management, management information systems, managerial finance, marketing management, organization behavior, quantitative business analysis. Courses may be waived through: previous course work.
Curricular Focus Leadership, problem solving and decision making, teamwork.
Concentrations Accounting, economics, finance, health services, human resources management, international business, management, management information systems, marketing, organizational behavior, quantitative analysis.
Faculty Full-time: 6, 84% with doctorates; part-time: 5, 75% with doctorates.
Teaching Methodology Case study: 20%, lecture: 30%, research: 10%, seminars by members of the business community: 10%, student presentations: 10%, team projects: 20%.
Special Opportunities Internship program available.

STUDENT STATISTICS
Geographic Representation State residents 80%. By region: South 80%; Northeast 5%. International 15%.
Undergraduate Majors Business 60%; education 10%; engineering/technology 5%; humanities 5%; nursing 10%; social sciences 5%; other 5%.
Other Background Graduate degrees in other disciplines: 20%. Work experience: On average, students have 8 years of work experience on entrance to the program.

FACILITIES
Information Resources Main library with 5,000 bound volumes, 100 periodical subscriptions. Business collection includes 2,000 bound volumes, 35 periodical subscriptions, 40 CD-ROMs.
Housing College housing not available.
Technology Computers are used heavily in course work. 18 computer terminals/PCs are available for use by students in program; they are located in the library, computer labs. Students in the program are not required to have their own PC. $1,000 are budgeted per student for computer support.

Computer Resources/On-line Services

Training	Yes	E-Mail	Yes
Internet	Yes	CompuServe	Yes

ADMISSION
Acceptance 1994-95 Of those applying, 70% were accepted.
Entrance Requirements Bachelor's degree, minimum 2.8 GPA. Core courses waived through: previous course work.
Application Requirements Written essay, interview, application form, copies of transcript, resume/curriculum vitae, personal statement, 3 letters of recommendation.
Application Deadline Applications are processed on a rolling basis.

FINANCIALS
Estimated Costs for 1995-96 Tuition: Full-time: $275/semester hour. Average room and board costs are $4,500 per academic year (off-campus).
Financial Aid In 1994-95, candidates received some institutionally administered aid in the form of scholarships, work-study. Total awards ranged from $1,000-$10,000. Financial aid is available to part-time students. Applications are processed on a rolling basis. Contact: Ms. Linda Volz, Director of Enrollment Management, 5250 17th Street, Sarasota, FL 34235-8242. (813) 379-0404.

INTERNATIONAL STUDENTS
Demographics 15% of students enrolled in the program are international; Asia 40%, Europe 30%, South America 30%.
Services and Facilities Visa services, language tutoring, ESL courses, special assistance for nonnative speakers of English.
Applying TOEFL required, minimum score of 470; proof of health; proof of adequate funds. Financial aid is not available to international students. Admission applications are processed on a rolling basis. Contact: Mr. Dan Hass, Enrollment Management Staff, 5250 17th Street, Sarasota, FL 34235-8242. (813) 379-0404.

PLACEMENT
Placement services include alumni network, career counseling/planning, career library, and resume referral to employers. Of 1994 graduates, 90% were employed within three months of graduation.

Program Contact: Ms. Linda Volz, Director of Enrollment Management, University of Sarasota, 5250 17th Street, Sarasota, FL 34235-8242. (813) 379-0404, or (800) 331-5995; Fax: (813) 379-9464.

University of South Florida

College of Business Administration

Tampa, Florida

OVERVIEW
The University of South Florida is a state-supported coed institution. Part of State University System of Florida. Founded 1956. Setting: 1,695-acre urban campus. Total institutional enrollment: 36,000. Program was first offered in 1965. AACSB-accredited.

MBA HIGHLIGHTS

Entrance Difficulty*
Mean GMAT: 540
Mean GPA: 3.15

Cost $
Tuition: $114/credit hour
(Nonresident: $367/credit hour)
Room & Board: $3,600

Enrollment Profile

Full-time: 178	Work Exp: 60%
Part-time: 379	International: 5%
Total: 557	Women: 38%
Average Age: 27	Minorities: 15%

Average Class Size: 25

ACADEMICS
Length of Program Minimum: 21 months. Maximum: 5 years.
Calendar Semesters.
Full-time Classes Main campus, Saint Petersburg, Sarasota, Fort Myers; day, evening, weekends, early morning, summer.

Part-time Classes Main campus, Saint Petersburg, Sarasota, Fort Myers; day, evening, weekends, early morning, summer.

Degree Requirements 60 credits including 24 elective credits. Other: International course; 1 course in each functional area.

Required Courses Business policy and strategy, environment of business, financial accounting for managers, financial management, information systems for management, management process, marketing management, microeconomic analysis, quantitative methods, statistical methods for management. Courses may be waived through: previous course work.

Curricular Focus Business issues and problems, problem solving and decision making, strategic analysis and planning.

Concentrations Accounting, economics, entrepreneurship, finance, international business, management, management information systems, marketing.

Faculty Full-time: 32, 97% with doctorates.

Teaching Methodology Case study: 30%, lecture: 35%, seminars by members of the business community: 5%, student presentations: 12%, team projects: 18%.

Special Opportunities International exchange in Costa Rica, France.

STUDENT STATISTICS

Geographic Representation State residents 88%. By region: South 90%; Midwest 3%; Northeast 2%. International 5%.

Undergraduate Majors Business 62%; education 2%; engineering/technology 7%; humanities 8%; nursing 1%; science/mathematics 11%; social sciences 7%; other 2%.

Other Background Graduate degrees in other disciplines: 5%. Work experience: On average, students have 3 years of work experience on entrance to the program.

FACILITIES

Information Resources Main library with 1 million bound volumes, 2,704 titles on microform, 5,460 periodical subscriptions, 29,744 records/tapes/CDs.

Housing 5% of students in program live in college-owned or -operated housing.

Technology 100 computer terminals/PCs, linked by a campus-wide computer network, are available for use by students in program; they are located in computer labs. Students in the program are not required to have their own PC.

Computer Resources/On-line Services

Training	Yes	E-Mail	Yes
Internet	Yes	LEXIS/NEXIS	Yes

ADMISSION

Acceptance 1994-95 Of those applying, 68% were accepted.

Entrance Requirements Bachelor's degree, GMAT score of 500, minimum 3.0 GPA, minimum GRE score of 1050. Core courses waived through: previous course work.

Application Requirements Application form, copies of transcript.

Application Deadlines 5/15 for fall, 10/15 for spring.

FINANCIALS

Costs for 1994-95 Tuition: Full-time: $114/credit hour for state residents, $367/credit hour for nonresidents. Average room and board costs are $3,600 per academic year (on-campus) and $3,600 per academic year (off-campus).

Financial Aid In 1994-95, candidates received some institutionally administered aid in the form of scholarships, loans, fellowships, assistantships. Contact: Financial Aid Office, 4202 East Fowler Avenue, Tampa, FL 33620-9951. (813) 974-4700.

INTERNATIONAL STUDENTS

Demographics 5% of students enrolled in the program are international.

Services and Facilities International student center, language tutoring, ESL courses, counseling/support services.

Applying TOEFL required, minimum score of 550; proof of health; proof of adequate funds. Financial aid is not available to international students. Admission application deadlines: 2/1 for fall, 7/1 for spring. Contact: Dr. David Austell, Director, International Student and Scholar Services, Tampa, FL 33620-9951. (813) 974-5102.

ALTERNATE MBA PROGRAMS

Executive MBA (EMBA) Length of program: Minimum: 20 months. Degree requirements: 60 credits including 27 elective credits. 6 years of managerial experience. Average class size: 30.

MBA for Physicians Length of program: Minimum: 21 months. Degree requirements: 40 credits. MD or DO degree. Average class size: 35.

PLACEMENT

Placement services include alumni network, career counseling/planning, career fairs, career library, career placement, electronic job bank, job interviews, resume preparation, and resume referral to employers. Of 1994 graduates, the average starting salary was $30,000, the range was $24,000-$65,000.

Program Contact: Ms. Ewana Hinson, Administrative Assistant, University of South Florida, 4202 East Fowler Avenue, Tampa, FL 33620-9951. (813) 974-3335; Fax: (813) 974-4518.

The University of Tampa

College of Business

Tampa, Florida

OVERVIEW

The University of Tampa is an independent nonprofit comprehensive coed institution. Founded 1931. Setting: 69-acre urban campus. Total institutional enrollment: 2,357. Program was first offered in 1973.

MBA HIGHLIGHTS

Entrance Difficulty***
Mean GMAT: 507
Mean GPA: 3.35

Cost $
Tuition: $275/hour
Room & Board: $2,400

Enrollment Profile

Full-time: 63	Work Exp: 90%
Part-time: 321	International: 13%
Total: 384	Women: 43%
Average Age: 31	Minorities: 10%

Average Class Size: 20

ACADEMICS

Length of Program Minimum: 16 months. Maximum: 7 years.

Calendar Semesters.

Full-time Classes Main campus; evening, summer.

Part-time Classes Main campus; evening, summer.

Degree Requirements 39-58 credits including 9-15 elective credits.

Required Courses Accounting and control, dynamic process management, financial management, leadership laboratory, macroeconomics and global issues, management information systems, managerial economics, marketing management, organizational behavior, quantitative methods, seminar in business policy. Courses may be waived through: previous course work.

Curricular Focus International business, leadership, teamwork.

Concentrations Accounting, finance, health services, international business, management, management information systems, marketing, quality leadership.

Faculty Full-time: 37, 78% with doctorates.

Special Opportunities International exchange in France, Mexico, Netherlands, Spain. Internship program available.

STUDENT STATISTICS

Geographic Representation State residents 85%. By region: South 80%; Northeast 7%. International 13%.

Undergraduate Majors Business 30%; engineering/technology 10%; humanities 18%; nursing 2%; social sciences 30%; other 10%.

Other Background Graduate degrees in other disciplines: 10%. Work experience: On average, students have 4 years of work experience on entrance to the program.

FACILITIES

Information Resources Main library with 238,355 bound volumes, 50,000 titles on microform, 1,883 periodical subscriptions, 2,312 records/tapes/CDs, 65 CD-ROMs.

Housing 2% of students in program live in college-owned or -operated housing.

Technology Computers are used moderately in course work. 30 computer terminals/PCs are available for use by students in program; they are located in the student center, the library, the computer center, computer labs. Students in the program are not required to have their own PC.

Computer Resources/On-line Services

Training	Yes	E-Mail	Yes

ADMISSION
Acceptance 1994-95 152 applied for admission; 63% were accepted.

Entrance Requirements Bachelor's degree, GMAT score of 450, minimum 2.75 GPA.

Application Requirements Application form, copies of transcript, 2 letters of recommendation.

Application Deadlines 8/15 for fall, 1/15 for spring.

FINANCIALS
Estimated Costs for 1995-96 Tuition: Full-time: $275/hour. Average room and board costs are $2,400 per academic year (on-campus).

Financial Aid In 1994-95, 4% of candidates received some institutionally administered aid in the form of assistantships. Total awards ranged from $4,000-$8,000. Financial aid is not available to part-time students. Applications are processed on a rolling basis. Contact: Ms. Catherine N. Huntress, Assistant Director, 401 West Kennedy Boulevard, Tampa, FL 33606-1490. (813) 253-6219.

INTERNATIONAL STUDENTS
Demographics 13% of students enrolled in the program are international; Europe 29%, Asia 27%, South America 25%, Africa 4%, Central America 2%, Other 13%.

Services and Facilities International student center, ESL courses, counseling/support services.

Applying TOEFL required, minimum score of 550; proof of adequate funds. Financial aid is not available to international students. Admission application deadlines: 7/30 for fall, 11/30 for spring. Contact: Ms. Sally Moorehead, Coordinator, International Student Affairs, 401 West Kennedy Boulevard, Box 2736, Tampa, FL 33606. (813) 253-3333 Ext. 3659.

ALTERNATE MBA PROGRAM
MBA/MSN Length of program: Minimum: 30 months. Maximum: 7 years. Degree requirements: 69 hours including 9-15 elective hours.

PLACEMENT
Placement services include alumni network, career counseling/planning, career placement, job interviews, resume preparation, and resume referral to employers.

Program Contact: Mr. Fernando A. Nolasco, Director, MBA Admissions, The University of Tampa, 401 West Kennedy Boulevard, Tampa, FL 33606-1490. (813) 258-7409, or (800) 733-4773; Fax: (813) 258-7408.

University of West Florida

College of Business

Pensacola, Florida

OVERVIEW
The University of West Florida is a state-supported comprehensive coed institution. Part of State University System of Florida. Founded 1963. Setting: 1,000-acre suburban campus. Total institutional enrollment: 8,000. Program was first offered in 1969.

MBA HIGHLIGHTS

Entrance Difficulty*
Mean GMAT: 530
Mean GPA: 3.08

Cost $
Tuition: $88/semester hour
(Nonresident: $329/semester hour)
Room & Board: $4,478

Enrollment Profile

Full-time: 50	Work Exp: 95%
Part-time: 183	International: 6%
Total: 233	Women: 34%
Average Age: 30	Minorities: 10%

Class Size: 30 - 35

ACADEMICS
Length of Program Minimum: 12 months. Maximum: 4 years.

Calendar Semesters.

Full-time Classes Main campus, Eglin Air Force Base; day, evening, summer.

Part-time Classes Main campus, Eglin Air Force Base.

Degree Requirements 36 semester hours including 9 elective semester hours. Other: Minimum 3.0 GPA.

Required Courses Accounting aspects business policy, advanced managerial economics, business and economic environment, financial management, management and organizational behavior, marketing management, operations management problems, quantitative decision making, strategic management and policy formula.

Curricular Focus Economic and financial theory, problem solving and decision making, strategic analysis and planning.

Concentrations Accounting, economics, finance, management, marketing, organization development leadership.

Faculty Full-time: 24, 100% with doctorates.

Teaching Methodology Case study: 30%, lecture: 40%, research: 10%, simulations: 10%, student presentations: 10%.

Special Opportunities Internships include government.

STUDENT STATISTICS
Geographic Representation State residents 87%. By region: South 89%; Northeast 1%. International 6%.

Undergraduate Majors Business 48%; engineering/technology 25%; humanities 5%; science/mathematics 9%; social sciences 6%; other 4%.

Other Background Graduate degrees in other disciplines: 1%. Work experience: On average, students have 2 years of work experience on entrance to the program.

FACILITIES
Information Resources Main library with 627,000 bound volumes, 980,000 titles on microform, 6,338 periodical subscriptions, 4,000 records/tapes/CDs. Business collection includes 56,150 bound volumes, 427 periodical subscriptions, 11 CD-ROMs.

Housing 5% of students in program live in college-owned or -operated housing.

Technology Computers are used heavily in course work. 125 computer terminals/PCs, linked by a campus-wide computer network, are available for use by students in program; they are located in the library, the computer center, computer labs. Students in the program are not required to have their own PC.

Computer Resources/On-line Services

Training	Yes	E-Mail	Yes
Internet	Yes	Dialog	Yes $

Other on-line services: Datastar, Westlaw.

ADMISSION
Acceptance 1994-95 250 applied for admission; 93% were accepted.

Entrance Requirements Bachelor's degree, GMAT score of 450, minimum 2 years of work experience.

Application Requirements Written essay, interview, application form, copies of transcript, resume/curriculum vitae, 2 letters of recommendation.

Application Deadlines 7/1 for fall, 11/1 for spring, 4/1 for summer.

FINANCIALS
Costs for 1994-95 Tuition: Full-time: $88/semester hour for state residents, $329/semester hour for nonresidents. Fees: Full-time: $20/semester hour for state residents, $20/semester hour for nonresidents. Average room and board costs are $4,478 per academic year (on-campus) and $4,478 per academic year (off-campus).

Financial Aid Financial aid is available to part-time students. Contact: Dr. Ray Bennett, Director of Financial Aid, 11000 University Parkway, Building 21, Pensacola, FL 32514-5750. (904) 474-2400.

INTERNATIONAL STUDENTS
Demographics 6% of students enrolled in the program are international; Asia 77%, Europe 22%.

Services and Facilities ESL courses.

Applying TOEFL required, minimum score of 500; proof of health; proof of adequate funds. Financial aid is not available to international students. Admission application deadlines: 5/15 for fall, 10/15 for spring, 2/15 for summer. Contact: Ms. Jill Cappadona, International Student Adviser, 11000 University Parkway, Pensacola, FL 32514-5750. (904) 474-2384.

PLACEMENT
In 1993-94, 20 organizations participated in on-campus recruiting; 19 on-campus interviews were conducted. Placement services include career counseling/planning, career fairs, career library, job interviews, and resume preparation.

Program Contact: Ms. Mary F. Dowhal, Admission and Registration Officer, University of West Florida, 11000 University Parkway, Pensacola, FL 32514-5750. (904) 474-3125; Fax: (904) 474-2716; Internet Address: fdowhal@uwf.cc.uwf.edu.

GEORGIA

Albany State College

School of Business

Albany, Georgia

OVERVIEW
Albany State College is a state-supported comprehensive coed institution. Part of University System of Georgia. Founded 1903. Setting: 131-acre urban campus. Total institutional enrollment: 3,300. Program was first offered in 1980.

MBA HIGHLIGHTS

Entrance Difficulty**
Mean GMAT: 450
Mean GPA: 2.5

Cost $
Tuition: $532/quarter
(Nonresident: $1,332/quarter)
Room & Board: N/R

Enrollment Profile
Full-time: 10	Work Exp: 80%
Part-time: 40	International: 2%
Total: 50	Women: 50%
Average Age: N/R	Minorities: 60%

Average Class Size: 15

ACADEMICS
Length of Program Minimum: 24 months. Maximum: 6 years.
Calendar Quarters.
Full-time Classes Main campus, distance learning option; evening.
Part-time Classes Main campus, Tifton, Thomasville, distance learning option; evening.
Degree Requirements 60 credits including 20 elective credits. Other: Comprehensive exam.
Required Courses Accounting analysis, decision science, financial management, macroeconomics, marketing management, microeconomics, organizational behavior, strategic management.
Curricular Focus Business issues and problems, leadership, problem solving and decision making, teamwork.
Concentrations Accounting, management, marketing.
Faculty Full-time: 8, 100% with doctorates.
Teaching Methodology Case study: 20%, lecture: 20%, research: 20%, student presentations: 20%, team projects: 20%.

STUDENT STATISTICS
Geographic Representation State residents 98%. By region: South 98%. International 2%.
Undergraduate Majors Business 50%; engineering/technology 10%; nursing 10%; social sciences 10%; other 20%.

FACILITIES
Information Resources Main library with 181,664 bound volumes, 13,584 titles on microform, 1,066 periodical subscriptions, 500 records/tapes/CDs, 3 CD-ROMs.
Housing College housing not available.
Technology Computers are used moderately in course work. Computer terminals/PCs are available for use by students in program; they are located in the library, computer labs. Students in the program are not required to have their own PC.

Computer Resources/On-line Services
Training	No	Dun's	No
Internet	Yes	Dow Jones	No
E-Mail	No	Dialog	No
LEXIS/NEXIS	No	Bloomberg	No
CompuServe	No		

ADMISSION
Entrance Requirements Bachelor's degree, prerequisite courses required for applicants with non-business degree, GMAT score, minimum 2.5 GPA. Core courses waived through: previous course work.
Application Requirements Application form, copies of transcript.
Application Deadlines 9/1 for fall, 12/1 for winter, 3/1 for spring, 5/15 for summer.

FINANCIALS
Costs for 1994-95 Tuition: Full-time: $532/quarter for state residents, $1,332/quarter for nonresidents; Part-time day: $200/course for state residents, $600/course for nonresidents.
Financial Aid Financial aid is not available to part-time students. Contact: Financial Aid Office, 504 College Drive, Albany, GA 31705-2717. (912) 430-4650.

INTERNATIONAL STUDENTS
Demographics 2% of students enrolled in the program are international.
Applying TOEFL required, minimum score of 550; proof of health; proof of adequate funds. Financial aid is not available to international students. Admission application deadline: 7/1 for fall. Applications are processed on a rolling basis.

PLACEMENT
Placement services include career placement. Of 1994 graduates, 100% were employed within three months of graduation.

Program Contact: Ms. Diane Frink, Graduate Admissions Counselor, Albany State College, 504 College Drive, Albany, GA 31705-2717. (912) 430-5118; Fax: (912) 430-3936.

Augusta College

School of Business Administration

Augusta, Georgia

OVERVIEW
Augusta College is a state-supported comprehensive coed institution. Part of University System of Georgia. Founded 1925. Setting: 72-acre small-town campus. Total institutional enrollment: 5,670. Program was first offered in 1972.

MBA HIGHLIGHTS

Entrance Difficulty***
Mean GMAT: 506
Mean GPA: 3.0

Cost $
Tuition: $40/quarter hour
(Nonresident: $120/quarter hour)
Room & Board: N/R

Enrollment Profile

Full-time: 49	Work Exp: 90%
Part-time: 97	International: 6%
Total: 146	Women: 39%
Average Age: 30	Minorities: 14%

Class Size: 18 - 20

ACADEMICS
Length of Program Minimum: 18 months. Maximum: 6 years.
Calendar Quarters.
Full-time Classes Main campus; evening, summer.
Part-time Classes Main campus; evening, summer.
Degree Requirements 60 quarter hours including 10 elective quarter hours.
Required Courses Accounting systems for planning and control, applied business research, communication for managers, economics topics and issues for management, ethics in business decision making, information systems management and application, managerial finance, marketing management, operational planning and data analysis, organizational behavior, strategic management and organizational policy.
Curricular Focus Problem solving and decision making, strategic analysis and planning, teamwork.
Concentration Management.
Faculty Full-time: 15, 100% with doctorates.
Teaching Methodology Case study: 10%, faculty seminars: 5%, lecture: 10%, research: 10%, seminars by members of the business community: 5%, student presentations: 10%, team projects: 50%.
Special Opportunities Internship program available.

STUDENT STATISTICS
Geographic Representation By region: South 75%; Northeast 9%; West 8%; Midwest 6%. International 6%.
Undergraduate Majors Business 48%; engineering/technology 18%; humanities 6%; nursing 10%; science/mathematics 10%; social sciences 6%; other 2%.
Other Background Graduate degrees in other disciplines: 1%. Work experience: On average, students have 7-8 years of work experience on entrance to the program.

FACILITIES
Information Resources Main library with 458,503 bound volumes, 896,141 titles on microform, 2,014 periodical subscriptions, 3,673 records/tapes/CDs, 395 CD-ROMs.
Housing 1% of students in program live in college-owned or -operated housing.
Technology Computers are used moderately in course work. 150 computer terminals/PCs, linked by a campus-wide computer network, are available for use by students in program; they are located in the library, computer labs. Students in the program are not required to have their own PC.

Computer Resources/On-line Services

Training	No	Multimedia Center	Yes
E-Mail	Yes		

ADMISSION
Acceptance 1994-95 110 applied for admission; 79% were accepted.
Entrance Requirements Prerequisite courses required for applicants with non-business degree, GMAT score of 450. Core courses waived through: previous course work.
Application Requirements Application form, copies of transcript.
Application Deadlines 8/19 for fall, 12/5 for winter, 2/28 for spring, 5/20 for summer.

FINANCIALS
Costs for 1994-95 Tuition: Full-time: $40/quarter hour for state residents, $120/quarter hour for nonresidents. Fees: Full-time: $80/quarter hour for state residents, $80/quarter hour for nonresidents.
Financial Aid In 1994-95, 12% of candidates received some institutionally administered aid in the form of loans, assistantships. Financial aid is available to part-time students. Applications are processed on a rolling basis. Contact: Mr. Kevin G. Wellwood, Director of Financial Aid, 2500 Walton Way, Augusta, GA 30904-2200. (706) 737-1431.

INTERNATIONAL STUDENTS
Demographics 6% of students enrolled in the program are international; Europe 67%, Central America 33%.
Services and Facilities ESL courses.
Applying TOEFL required, minimum score of 550; proof of health; proof of adequate funds. Financial aid is not available to international students.

Admission application deadlines: 7/15 for fall, 11/1 for winter, 2/1 for spring, 4/15 for summer. Applications are processed on a rolling basis. Contact: Dr. Frank H. Chou, 2500 Walton Way, Augusta, GA 30904-2200. (706) 737-1496.

PLACEMENT
In 1993-94, 20 on-campus interviews were conducted. Placement services include career counseling/planning, career fairs, career library, career placement, job interviews, resume preparation, and resume referral to employers. Of 1994 graduates, 88% were employed within three months of graduation, the average starting salary was $28,000, the range was $25,000-$32,000.

Program Contact: Dr. Richard M. Bramblett, Director of Graduate Studies, Augusta College, 2500 Walton Way, Augusta, GA 30904-2200. (706) 737-1565; Fax: (706) 667-4064.

Berry College

School of Business

Mount Berry, Georgia

OVERVIEW
Berry College is an independent nonprofit comprehensive coed institution. Founded 1902. Setting: 28,000-acre small-town campus with easy access to Atlanta. Total institutional enrollment: 1,876.

MBA HIGHLIGHTS

Entrance Difficulty*
Mean GMAT: 500
Mean GPA: N/R

Cost $
Tuition: $287/semester hour
(Nonresident: $287/semester hour)
Room & Board: $4,800 (off-campus)

Enrollment Profile

Full-time: N/R	Work Exp: N/R
Part-time: N/R	International: 5%
Total: 58	Women: 40%
Average Age: N/R	Minorities: 8%

Average Class Size: 12

ACADEMICS
Length of Program Minimum: 12 months.
Calendar Semesters.
Full-time Classes Main campus, Calhoun, distance learning option; evening, summer.
Part-time Classes Main campus, Calhoun, distance learning option; evening, summer.
Degree Requirements 36 credits.
Curricular Focus Business issues and problems, problem solving and decision making, strategic analysis and planning.
Concentration Management.
Teaching Methodology Case study: 20%, lecture: 40%, student presentations: 20%, team projects: 20%.

STUDENT STATISTICS
Geographic Representation International 5%.

FACILITIES
Information Resources Main library with 150,755 bound volumes, 389,454 titles on microform, 1,280 periodical subscriptions, 1,788 records/tapes/CDs.
Housing College housing not available.

ADMISSION
Entrance Requirements Bachelor's degree, GMAT score.
Application Requirements Application form, copies of transcript, 2 letters of recommendation.
Application Deadline Applications are processed on a rolling basis.

FINANCIALS
Costs for 1995-96 Tuition: Full-time: $287/semester hour, $287/semester hour for international students. Average room and board costs are $4,800 per academic year (off-campus).

Financial Aid Applications are processed on a rolling basis. Contact: Mr. William Fron, Director of Financial Aid, 5007 Mount Berry Station, Mount Berry, GA 30149-0159. (706) 236-2276.

INTERNATIONAL STUDENTS
Demographics 5% of students enrolled in the program are international.

Applying TOEFL required, minimum score of 550. Financial aid is available to international students. Applications are processed on a rolling basis. Admission applications are processed on a rolling basis.

Program Contact: Ms. Madalyn McLead, Secretary of Graduate Studies, Berry College, Berry College School of Business, Mount Berry, GA 30149-5024. (706) 236-1751; Fax: (706) 295-2921.

Brenau University

Department of Business

Gainesville, Georgia

OVERVIEW
Brenau University is an independent nonprofit comprehensive primarily women institution. Founded 1878. Setting: 50-acre small-town campus with easy access to Atlanta. Total institutional enrollment: 2,241.

MBA HIGHLIGHTS
Entrance Difficulty***
Mean GMAT: 485
Mean GPA: N/R

Cost $
Tuition: $110/credit hour
Room & Board: N/R

Enrollment Profile

Full-time: N/R	Work Exp: N/R
Part-time: N/R	International: 5%
Total: 500	Women: 55%
Average Age: N/R	Minorities: 10%

Average Class Size: 18

ACADEMICS
Length of Program Minimum: 15 months.
Calendar Semesters.
Full-time Classes Main campus, Atlanta, Augusta, Athens; evening, weekends, summer.
Part-time Classes Main campus, Atlanta, Augusta, Athens; evening, weekends, summer.
Degree Requirements 50 quarter hours.
Curricular Focus General management.
Concentrations Accounting, finance, management, marketing.
Teaching Methodology Case study: 30%, lecture: 30%, student presentations: 30%, team projects: 10%.

STUDENT STATISTICS
Geographic Representation State residents 90%. International 5%.

FACILITIES
Information Resources Main library with 86,217 bound volumes, 190,457 titles on microform, 1,190 periodical subscriptions, 12,324 records/tapes/CDs, 43 CD-ROMs.

ADMISSION
Entrance Requirements Bachelor's degree, GMAT score of 325.
Application Requirements Application form, copies of transcript, 3 letters of recommendation, can schedule interview instead of letters of recommendation.
Application Deadline Applications are processed on a rolling basis.

FINANCIALS
Costs for 1994-95 Tuition: Full-time: $110/credit hour.
Financial Aid Application deadline: 5/1 for fall. Applications are processed on a rolling basis. Contact: Financial Aid Officer, Office of Financial Aid, Gainesville, GA 30501-3697. (404) 534-6152.

INTERNATIONAL STUDENTS
Demographics 5% of students enrolled in the program are international.

Applying TOEFL required. Financial aid is not available to international students. Admission applications are processed on a rolling basis.

Program Contact: Dr. John Blair, Chairman of Department of Business Administration, Brenau University, One Centennial Circle, Gainesville, GA 30501-3697. (404) 718-0055; Fax: (404) 287-7021.

Clark Atlanta University

School of Business Administration

Atlanta, Georgia

OVERVIEW
Clark Atlanta University is an independent United Methodist coed institution. Founded 1869. Setting: 67-acre urban campus. Total institutional enrollment: 6,000. Program was first offered in 1946. AACSB-accredited.

MBA HIGHLIGHTS
Entrance Difficulty***

Cost $$
Tuition: $328/semester hour
Room & Board: N/R

Enrollment Profile

Full-time: 145	Work Exp: N/R
Part-time: 5	International: 10%
Total: 150	Women: 60%
Average Age: N/R	Minorities: 90%

Average Class Size: 35

ACADEMICS
Length of Program Minimum: 21 months.
Calendar Semesters.
Full-time Classes Main campus; day, summer.
Degree Requirements 60 semester hours.
Curricular Focus Entrepreneurship, problem solving and decision making, teamwork.
Concentrations Finance, management information systems, marketing.
Faculty Full-time: 26, 95% with doctorates; part-time: 6, 66% with doctorates.
Teaching Methodology Case study: 40%, lecture: 40%, simulations: 10%, team projects: 10%.

STUDENT STATISTICS
Geographic Representation State residents 20%. International 10%.

FACILITIES
Information Resources Main library with 750,000 bound volumes, 189,245 titles on microform, 49,481 periodical subscriptions.

ADMISSION
Acceptance 1994-95 220 applied for admission; 55% were accepted.
Entrance Requirements Bachelor's degree, GMAT score.
Application Requirements Written essay, interview, application form, copies of transcript, resume/curriculum vitae, 3 letters of recommendation.
Application Deadlines 4/1 for fall. Applications are processed on a rolling basis.

FINANCIALS
Costs for 1994-95 Tuition: Full-time: $328/semester hour. Fees: Full-time: $150/semester.
Financial Aid In 1994-95, 75% of candidates received some institutionally administered aid in the form of grants, scholarships, loans, assistantships, work-study. Financial aid is not available to part-time students. Application deadline: 3/1 for fall. Applications are processed on a rolling basis. Contact: Ms. Phyllis Riley, Director of Admissions and Financial Aid, School of Business, James P. Branley Drive, Fair Street SW, Atlanta, GA 30314. (404) 880-8479.

INTERNATIONAL STUDENTS
Demographics 10% of students enrolled in the program are international.

Applying TOEFL required, minimum score of 600; proof of health; proof of adequate funds. Financial aid is not available to international students. Admission application deadline: 4/1 for fall. Applications are processed on a rolling basis.

Program Contact: Ms. Phyllis Riley, Director of Admissions and Financial Aid, Clark Atlanta University, School of Business, James P. Branley Drive, Fair Street SW, Atlanta, GA 30314. (404) 880-8479; Fax: (404) 880-8458.

Columbus College

Abbott Turner School of Business

Columbus, Georgia

OVERVIEW
Columbus College is a state-supported comprehensive coed institution. Part of University System of Georgia. Founded 1958. Setting: 132-acre urban campus with easy access to Atlanta. Total institutional enrollment: 6,000. Program was first offered in 1973.

MBA HIGHLIGHTS

Entrance Difficulty**
Mean GMAT: 500
Mean GPA: 3.0

Cost $
Tuition: $551/quarter
(Nonresident: $1,422/quarter)
Room & Board: $3,000 (off-campus)

Enrollment Profile

Full-time: 17	Work Exp: 90%
Part-time: 38	International: 4%
Total: 55	Women: N/R
Average Age: 36	Minorities: 10%

Average Class Size: 14

ACADEMICS
Length of Program Minimum: 24 months. Maximum: 6 years.
Calendar Quarters.
Full-time Classes Main campus; evening, weekends.
Part-time Classes Main campus; evening, weekends.
Degree Requirements 60 quarter hours including 15 elective quarter hours.
Required Courses Advanced managerial finance, communication skills, management information systems, managerial accounting, managerial economics, marketing strategy, operations management, organizational behavior, policy. Courses may be waived through: previous course work.
Curricular Focus General management.
Concentration Management.
Faculty Full-time: 12, 100% with doctorates; part-time: 1, 100% with doctorates.
Teaching Methodology Case study: 60%, lecture: 30%, team projects: 10%.
Special Opportunities International exchange in United Kingdom. Internships include government.

STUDENT STATISTICS
Geographic Representation State residents 86%. By region: South 88%; Midwest 4%; Northeast 3%; West 1%. International 4%.
Undergraduate Majors Business 50%; engineering/technology 30%; humanities 5%; science/mathematics 5%; social sciences 10%.
Other Background Graduate degrees in other disciplines: 10%. Work experience: On average, students have 12 years of work experience on entrance to the program.

FACILITIES
Information Resources Main library with 244,963 bound volumes, 222,494 titles on microform, 1,397 periodical subscriptions, 8,308 records/tapes/CDs.
Housing College housing not available.
Technology Computers are used moderately in course work. 800 computer terminals/PCs, linked by a campus-wide computer network, are available for use by students in program; they are located in the library, the computer center, computer labs. Students in the program are not required to have their own PC. $250 are budgeted per student for computer support.

Computer Resources/On-line Services

Training	Yes	Videoconference Center	Yes
Internet	Yes	CompuServe	Yes
E-Mail	Yes	Dialog	Yes

ADMISSION
Acceptance 1994-95 60 applied for admission; 52% were accepted.
Entrance Requirements Bachelor's degree, GMAT score. Core courses waived through: previous course work.
Application Requirements Application form, copies of transcript.
Application Deadlines 8/15 for fall, 12/1 for winter, 3/1 for spring.

FINANCIALS
Costs for 1994-95 Tuition: Full-time: $551/quarter for state residents, $1,422/quarter for nonresidents; Part-time day: $40/hour for state residents, $120/hour for nonresidents. Fees: Part-time day: $77/quarter for state residents, $77/quarter for nonresidents. Average room and board costs are $3,000 per academic year (off-campus).
Financial Aid In 1994-95, 10% of candidates received some institutionally administered aid in the form of scholarships, loans, fellowships, assistantships. Total awards ranged from $1,000-$6,000. Financial aid is not available to part-time students. Application deadlines: 8/15 for fall, 12/1 for winter, 3/1 for spring. Contact: Mr. Brad Masterson, Director of Financial Aid, 4500 University Avenue, Columbus, GA 31907. (706) 568-2236.

INTERNATIONAL STUDENTS
Demographics 4% of students enrolled in the program are international.
Services and Facilities Language tutoring, special assistance for nonnative speakers of English, counseling/support services.
Applying TOEFL required, minimum score of 500; proof of health; proof of adequate funds. Financial aid is not available to international students. Admission application deadlines: 6/15 for fall, 11/1 for winter, 2/1 for spring. Contact: Mr. James Chappell, Director, Foreign Language Center, 4225 University Avenue, Columbus, GA 31907. (706) 568-2054.

PLACEMENT
Placement services include alumni network, career counseling/planning, job interviews, and resume preparation.

Program Contact: Mr. Ronald D. Klein, Director of the MBA Program, Columbus College, 4225 University Avenue, Columbus, GA 31907. (706) 568-2044; Fax: (706) 568-2184; Internet Address: rklein@uscn.uscn.uga.edu.

Emory University

Roberto C. Goizueta Business School

Atlanta, Georgia

OVERVIEW
Emory University is an independent Methodist coed institution. Founded 1836. Setting: 631-acre suburban campus. Total institutional enrollment: 11,000. Program was first offered in 1954. AACSB-accredited.

MBA HIGHLIGHTS

Entrance Difficulty*****
Mean GMAT: 625
Mean GPA: 3.2

Cost $$$$
Tuition: $18,850
Room & Board: $11,000 (off-campus)

Enrollment Profile

Full-time: 261	Work Exp: 90%
Part-time: 174	International: N/R
Total: 435	Women: N/R
Average Age: 26	Minorities: N/R

Average Class Size: 35

ACADEMICS
Length of Program Minimum: 24 months. Maximum: 2 years.
Calendar Semesters.
Full-time Classes Main campus; day.
Part-time Classes Main campus, Buckhead; evening, summer.

Degree Requirements 58 credits including 24-27 elective credits.

Required Courses Communications workshop, economic analysis for managers, environment of business, financial accounting, international perspectives, introduction to management science, introduction to operations management, managerial accounting and control, managerial finance, managing human resources, marketing management, organization and management, probability and statistical analysis for managers, strategic management. Courses may be waived through examination.

Curricular Focus International business, organizational development and change management, problem solving and decision making.

Concentrations Accounting, consumer business development, Soviet/post-Soviet studies track, Latin American trade, entrepreneurship, finance, human resources management, international business, management, management information systems, marketing, operations management, organizational behavior, quantitative analysis, strategic management.

Faculty Full-time: 54, 100% with doctorates; part-time: 5, 75% with doctorates.

Teaching Methodology Case study: 35%, faculty seminars: 5%, field work, projects, practicum: 10%, lecture: 20%, research: 5%, student presentations: 10%, team projects: 15%.

Special Opportunities International exchange in Austria, Costa Rica, Finland, France, Germany, Italy, Mexico, Spain, United Kingdom, Venezuela. Internships include communications, banking/finance, consumer products, health, and consulting, transportation, manufacturing.

STUDENT STATISTICS
Geographic Representation By region: South 40%; Northeast 21%; Midwest 10%; West 9%.

Other Background Work experience: On average, students have 4 years of work experience on entrance to the program.

FACILITIES
Information Resources Main library with 2.2 million bound volumes, 2.4 million titles on microform, 23,555 periodical subscriptions, 19,755 records/tapes/CDs.

Housing 15% of students in program live in college-owned or -operated housing.

Technology Computers are used heavily in course work. 50 computer terminals/PCs, linked by a campus-wide computer network, are available for use by students in program; they are located in the student center, the library, the computer center, computer labs. Students in the program are not required to have their own PC.

Computer Resources/On-line Services

Training	Yes	CompuServe	No
Internet	Yes	Dun's	No
E-Mail	Yes	Dow Jones	Yes
Multimedia Center	Yes	Dialog	Yes
LEXIS/NEXIS	Yes	Bloomberg	No

Other on-line services: Carl.

ADMISSION
Acceptance 1994-95 730 applied for admission; 36% were accepted.

Entrance Requirements Bachelor's degree, one semester of calculus, GMAT score. Core courses waived through: previous course work.

Application Requirements Written essay, application form, copies of transcript, personal statement.

Application Deadlines 4/15 for fall, 3/1 for evening program. Application discs available.

FINANCIALS
Costs for 1994-95 Tuition: Full-time: $18,850; Part-time evening: $12,570. Fees: Full-time: $190; Part-time evening: $190. Average room and board costs are $11,000 per academic year (off-campus).

Financial Aid In 1994-95, 70% of candidates received some institutionally administered aid in the form of scholarships, loans, assistantships. Total awards ranged from $1,500-$28,122. Financial aid is available to part-time students. Application deadline: 1/9 for fall. Contact: Ms. Harriet Ruskin, Associate Director of Admissions, Goizueta Business School, 1602 Mizell Drive, Atlanta, GA 30322. (404) 727-6644.

INTERNATIONAL STUDENTS
Demographics 17% of students on campus are international; Europe 52%, Asia 33%, Africa 3%, Australia 3%, Central America 3%, South America 3%, Other 3%.

Services and Facilities International student center, visa services, language tutoring, special assistance for nonnative speakers of English, counseling/support services.

Applying TOEFL required, minimum score of 600; proof of health; proof of adequate funds. Financial aid is available to international students.

Assistantships and merit-based scholarships are available to these students. Financial aid application deadline: 3/1 for fall. Admission application deadline: 4/15 for fall. Contact: Ms. Nancy Roth Remington, Director of International Programs, Goizueta Business School, 1602 Mizell Drive, Atlanta, GA 30322. (404) 727-2553.

ALTERNATE MBA PROGRAMS
Executive MBA (EMBA) Length of program: Minimum: 16 months. Degree requirements: 52 credits including 6 elective credits. International trip. Average class size: 50.

One-Year MBA Length of program: Minimum: 11 months. Maximum: 1 year. Degree requirements: 44 credits including 27 elective credits. Undergraduate business degree; minimum one year of full-time work experience. Average class size: 30.

MBA/JD Length of program: Minimum: 45 months. Maximum: 4 years. Degree requirements: 77 credits including 48 elective credits. Separate applications must be submitted to both business and law departments.

MBA/MPH Length of program: Minimum: 28 months. Maximum: 2 years. Degree requirements: 81 credits. Separate applications must be submitted to both business and public health departments.

MBA/M Div Length of program: Minimum: 48 months. Maximum: 4 years. Degree requirements: 115 credits including 27 elective credits. Separate applications must be submitted to both business and theology departments.

MBA/MN Length of program: Minimum: 23 months. Degree requirements: 92 credits. Separate applications must be submitted to both business and nursing departments.

PLACEMENT
In 1993-94, 149 organizations participated in on-campus recruiting; 1,432 on-campus interviews were conducted. Placement services include alumni network, career fairs, career library, career placement, consortia activities, job interviews, mini internships, resume preparation, and resume referral to employers. Of 1994 graduates, 90% were employed within three months of graduation, the average starting salary was $55,000, the range was $37,000-$105,000.

Jobs by Employer Type Manufacturing 2%; service 74%; consulting 24%.

Jobs by Functional Area Marketing/sales 32%; finance 30%; management 8%; consulting 22%; real estate 2%; other 6%.

Program Contact: Admissions Department, Emory University, 1602 Mizell Drive, Atlanta, GA 30322. (404) 727-6036; Fax: (404) 727-0868; Internet Address: admissions@bus.emory.edu.
See full description on page 730.

Georgia College

J. Whitney Bunting School of Business

Milledgeville, Georgia

OVERVIEW
Georgia College is a state-supported comprehensive coed institution. Part of University System of Georgia. Founded 1889. Setting: 696-acre small-town campus. Total institutional enrollment: 5,700. Program was first offered in 1969.

MBA HIGHLIGHTS

Entrance Difficulty**
Mean GMAT: 496
Mean GPA: N/R

Cost $
Tuition: $600/quarter
Room & Board: N/R

Enrollment Profile

Full-time: 100	Work Exp: 75%
Part-time: 273	International: 1%
Total: 373	Women: 45%
Average Age: 30	Minorities: N/R

Average Class Size: 18

ACADEMICS
Length of Program Minimum: 12 months. Maximum: 6 years.

Calendar Quarters.

Full-time Classes Main campus, Dublin, Macon evening, summer, Robins Graduate Center evening, summer; evening, summer.

Part-time Classes Main campus, Dublin, Macon evening, summer, Robins Graduate Center evening, summer; evening, summer.

Degree Requirements 60 credits including 10 elective credits.

Required Courses Accounting, accounting, advanced marketing theory and behavior, business ethics and societal responsibilities, business policy, business statistics, financial policies, international economics, managerial accounting, managerial economics, organizational theory, production and operations management. Courses may be waived through: previous course work.

Curricular Focus Business issues and problems, general management, problem solving and decision making.

Concentrations Accounting, management, management information systems.

Faculty Full-time: 25, 100% with doctorates; part-time: 4.

Teaching Methodology Case study: 30%, lecture: 50%, research: 10%, student presentations: 5%, team projects: 5%.

Special Opportunities International exchange in Brazil, Mexico, People's Republic of China, Spain, United Kingdom. Other: international summer study abroad program: Western Europe, Pacific, Canada and Mexico.

STUDENT STATISTICS
Geographic Representation State residents 98%. By region: South 98%; Northeast 1%. International 1%.

Undergraduate Majors Business 80%; engineering/technology 10%; humanities 4%; science/mathematics 3%; social sciences 3%.

Other Background Graduate degrees in other disciplines: 5%. Work experience: On average, students have 5 years of work experience on entrance to the program.

FACILITIES
Information Resources Main library with 170,834 bound volumes, 257,452 titles on microform, 1,137 periodical subscriptions, 2,206 records/tapes/CDs, 21 CD-ROMs.

Housing 10% of students in program live in college-owned or -operated housing.

Technology Computers are used moderately in course work. Computer terminals/PCs, linked by a campus-wide computer network, are available for use by students in program; they are located in classrooms, the library, the computer center, computer labs. Students in the program are not required to have their own PC.

Computer Resources/On-line Services

Training	No	CompuServe	No
Internet	Yes	Dun's	No
E-Mail	Yes	Dow Jones	No
Videoconference Center	Yes	Dialog	Yes
Multimedia Center	Yes	Bloomberg	No
LEXIS/NEXIS	No		

ADMISSION
Acceptance 1994-95 167 applied for admission; 82% were accepted.

Entrance Requirements Bachelor's degree, GMAT score. Core courses waived through: previous course work.

Application Requirements Application form, copies of transcript.

Application Deadlines 8/28 for fall, 12/16 for winter, 3/10 for spring.

FINANCIALS
Costs for 1994-95 Tuition: Full-time: $600/quarter. Fees: Full-time: $107/quarter.

Financial Aid In 1994-95, candidates received some institutionally administered aid in the form of scholarships, loans, assistantships, work-study. Financial aid is available to part-time students. Application deadline: 4/15 for fall. Contact: Dr. Ken Jones, Dean of Graduate School, 3290 Arkwright Road, Suite 160, Macon, GA 31210. (912) 471-2063.

INTERNATIONAL STUDENTS
Demographics 1% of students enrolled in the program are international; Africa 25%, Asia 25%, Europe 25%, South America 25%.

Services and Facilities International student center, visa services, counseling/support services.

Applying TOEFL required, minimum score of 500; proof of health; proof of adequate funds. Financial aid is available to international students. Financial aid application deadlines: 5/1 for fall, 10/1 for winter, 1/15 for spring. Admission application deadlines: 7/1 for fall, 11/1 for winter, 2/15 for spring. Contact: Ms. Helena Russell, Director, International Programs and Services, Campus Box 049, Milledgeville, GA 31061. (912) 453-4789.

ALTERNATE MBA PROGRAM
MBA/MSN Length of program: Minimum: 18 months. Maximum: 6 years. Degree requirements: 115 credits including 5 elective credits.

PLACEMENT
Placement services include career counseling/planning, career fairs, career library, career placement, resume preparation, and resume referral to employers.

Program Contact: Dr. Kaye Scott, Director, Graduate Programs in Business, Georgia College, Hancock Street, Milledgeville, GA 31061. (912) 453-5115; Fax: (912) 453-5249; Internet Address: scottk@gcnext.gac. peachnet.edu.

Georgia Institute of Technology

School of Management

Atlanta, Georgia

OVERVIEW
Georgia Institute of Technology is a state-supported coed institution. Part of University System of Georgia. Founded 1885. Setting: 330-acre urban campus. Total institutional enrollment: 12,901. Program was first offered in 1945. AACSB-accredited.

PROGRAM HIGHLIGHTS
Entrance Difficulty***
Mean GMAT: 628
Mean GPA: 3.2

Cost $
Tuition: $781/quarter
(Nonresident: $2,311/quarter)
Room & Board: $5,000

Enrollment Profile

Full-time: 225	Work Exp: 87%
Part-time: 0	International: 27%
Total: 225	Women: 30%
Average Age: 27	Minorities: 12%

Average Class Size: 50

ACADEMICS
Calendar Quarters.

Curricular Focus Problem solving and decision making.

Concentrations Accounting, computer integrated manufacturing, technology management, economics, entrepreneurship, finance, human resources management, international business, management, management information systems, marketing, operations management, organizational behavior, public policy, quantitative analysis, strategic management.

Faculty Full-time: 43, 97% with doctorates.

Teaching Methodology Case study: 15%, faculty seminars: 5%, lecture: 50%, seminars by members of the business community: 5%, student presentations: 10%, team projects: 15%.

Special Opportunities International exchange in France, Netherlands, United Kingdom.

STUDENT STATISTICS
Geographic Representation By region: South 31%; Northeast 16%; Midwest 16%; West 9%. International 27%.

Undergraduate Majors Business 40%; engineering/technology 40%; humanities 11%; science/mathematics 2%; social sciences 7%.

Other Background Graduate degrees in other disciplines: 6%. Work experience: On average, students have 4 years of work experience on entrance to the program.

FACILITIES
Information Resources Main library with 1.8 million bound volumes, 3.2 million titles on microform, 11,524 periodical subscriptions, 1,859 records/tapes/CDs.

Housing 15% of students in program live in college-owned or -operated housing.

Technology Computers are used heavily in course work. Computer terminals/PCs, linked by a campus-wide computer network, are available for use by students in program; they are located in the student center, the library, the computer center, computer labs, the research center. Students in the program are not required to have their own PC.

Computer Resources/On-line Services

Training	Yes	Multimedia Center	Yes
Internet	Yes	Dun's	Yes
E-Mail	Yes	Dow Jones	Yes

ADMISSION

Acceptance 1994-95 692 applied for admission; 34% were accepted.

Entrance Requirements Bachelor's degree, GMAT score.

Application Requirements Written essay, application form, copies of transcript, resume/curriculum vitae, 2 letters of recommendation.

Application Deadlines 4/1 for fall. Applications are processed on a rolling basis.

FINANCIALS

Costs for 1994-95 Tuition: Full-time: $781/quarter for state residents, $2,311/quarter for nonresidents. Average room and board costs are $5,000 per academic year (on-campus) and $6,000 per academic year (off-campus).

Financial Aid In 1994-95, 20% of candidates received some institutionally administered aid in the form of fellowships, assistantships. Financial aid is not available to part-time students. Application deadline: 6/1 for fall. Contact: Mr. Jerry McTier, Director of Financial Aid, Student and Financial Planning and Services, Atlanta, GA 30332-0460. (404) 894-0460.

INTERNATIONAL STUDENTS

Demographics 27% of students enrolled in the program are international; North America 73%, Europe 14%, Asia 8%, Africa 2%, South America 1%, Other 2%.

Services and Facilities International student office, visa services, language tutoring, ESL courses, special assistance for nonnative speakers of English, counseling/support services.

Applying TOEFL required, minimum score of 600; proof of health; proof of adequate funds. Financial aid is not available to international students. Admission application deadline: 3/1 for fall. Contact: Mr. Miller Templeton, International Student Programs, Student Services Building, Atlanta, GA 30332-0284. (404) 894-7475.

PROGRAM

MSM Length of program: Minimum: 21 months. Maximum: 2 years. Full-time classes: Main campus; day. Degree requirements: 81 credits including 33 elective credits.

PLACEMENT

In 1993-94, 80 organizations participated in on-campus recruiting; 600 on-campus interviews were conducted. Placement services include alumni network, career counseling/planning, career fairs, career library, career placement, electronic job bank, job interviews, job search course, resume preparation, and resume referral to employers. Of 1994 graduates, 95% were employed within three months of graduation, the average starting salary was $47,000, the range was $31,000-$75,000.

Jobs by Employer Type Manufacturing 15%; service 12%; consulting 31%; telecommunications 12%; accounting 6%; information technology 24%.

Jobs by Functional Area Marketing/sales 9%; finance 16%; operations 29%; technical management 29%; consulting 17%.

Program Contact: Ms. Julie Peterson, Academic Assistant, Georgia Institute of Technology, 212 School of Management, Atlanta, GA 30332-0520. (404) 853-9871, or (800) 869-1014; Fax: (404) 894-6030; Internet Address: julie.peterson@mgt.gatech.edu.

Georgia Southern University

College of Business Administration

Statesboro, Georgia

OVERVIEW

Georgia Southern University is a state-supported comprehensive coed institution. Part of University System of Georgia. Founded 1906. Setting: 601-acre small-town campus with easy access to Savannah. Total institutional enrollment: 14,300. Program was first offered in 1968. AACSB-accredited.

MBA HIGHLIGHTS

Entrance Difficulty*
Mean GMAT: 486
Mean GPA: 3.03

Cost $
Tuition: $370 - $626/quarter
(Nonresident: $1,010 - $1,574/quarter)
Room & Board: $3,600

Enrollment Profile

Full-time: 100		Work Exp: 60%
Part-time: 86		International: 12%
Total: 186		Women: 44%
Average Age: 30		Minorities: 14%

Class Size: 20 - 25

ACADEMICS

Length of Program Minimum: 18 months. Maximum: 7 years.

Calendar Quarters.

Full-time Classes Main campus, Savannah, Brunswick, distance learning option; evening.

Part-time Classes Main campus, Savannah, Brunswick, distance learning option; evening.

Degree Requirements 48 credits including 3 elective credits. Other: Minimum "B" in business policy or terminal oral examination.

Required Courses Accounting for management, business policy, financial problems, international business, managerial economics, managerial quantitative analysis, marketing seminar, organizational behavior and management, production and operations management.

Curricular Focus General management, problem solving and decision making, teamwork.

Concentrations Accounting, economics, finance, management, marketing.

Teaching Methodology Case study: 15%, lecture: 40%, research: 15%, student presentations: 15%, team projects: 15%.

STUDENT STATISTICS

Geographic Representation State residents 88%. By region: South 81%; Midwest 5%; Northeast 1%; West 1%. International 12%.

Other Background Graduate degrees in other disciplines: 6%.

FACILITIES

Information Resources Main library with 451,292 bound volumes, 759,072 titles on microform, 3,511 periodical subscriptions, 4,568 records/tapes/CDs.

Housing College housing available.

Technology Computers are used moderately in course work. 178 computer terminals/PCs, linked by a campus-wide computer network, are available for use by students in program; they are located in learning resource center, the library, computer labs. Students in the program are not required to have their own PC.

Computer Resources/On-line Services

Internet	Yes	LEXIS/NEXIS	Yes
E-Mail	Yes		

ADMISSION

Acceptance 1994-95 219 applied for admission; 68% were accepted.

Entrance Requirements Bachelor's degree, GMAT score, minimum 2.0 GPA. Core courses waived through: previous course work.

Application Requirements Application form, copies of transcript.

Application Deadline Applications are processed on a rolling basis.

FINANCIALS

Costs for 1994-95 Tuition: Full-time: $370-$626/quarter for state residents, $1,010-$1,574/quarter for nonresidents; Part-time day: $185/quarter for state residents, $505/quarter for nonresidents. Average room and board costs are $3,600 per academic year (on-campus) and $4,000 per academic year (off-campus).

Financial Aid In 1994-95, candidates received some institutionally administered aid in the form of grants, scholarships, loans, assistantships, work-study. Application deadline: 4/15 for annual. Contact: Director of Financial Aid, Landrum Box 8065, Statesboro, GA 30460. (912) 681-5431.

INTERNATIONAL STUDENTS

Demographics 12% of students enrolled in the program are international; Asia 45%, Europe 28%, South America 18%, Africa 5%, Australia 4%.

Services and Facilities International student office, language tutoring, ESL courses.

Applying TOEFL required; proof of health; proof of adequate funds. Admission application deadlines: 6/15 for fall, 10/1 for winter, 12/20 for spring. Contact: Dr. James Orr, Associate Dean, Student Affairs, Landrum Box 8063, Statesboro, GA 30460. (912) 681-5185.

Program Contact: Ms. Andrea Sikes, Assistant to the Director, Georgia Southern University, Landrum Box 8033, Statesboro, GA 30460. (912) 681-0290, or (800) 472-3478; Internet Address: apsikes@gsvms2.cc. gasou.edu.

Georgia State University

College of Business Administration

Atlanta, Georgia

OVERVIEW
Georgia State University is a state-supported coed institution. Part of University System of Georgia. Founded 1913. Setting: 24-acre urban campus. Total institutional enrollment: 23,765. Program was first offered in 1958. AACSB-accredited.

MBA HIGHLIGHTS

Entrance Difficulty****
Mean GMAT: 560
Mean GPA: 3.0

Cost $
Tuition: $42/quarter hour
(Nonresident: $144/quarter hour)
Room & Board: N/R

Enrollment Profile

Full-time: 860	Work Exp: 85%
Part-time: 733	International: 12%
Total: 1,593	Women: 37%
Average Age: 27	Minorities: 24%

Average Class Size: 35

ACADEMICS
Length of Program Minimum: 12 months. Maximum: 5 years.
Calendar Quarters.
Full-time Classes Main campus; day, evening, weekends, summer.
Part-time Classes Main campus; day, evening, weekends, summer.
Degree Requirements 60 quarter hours including 4-6 elective quarter hours.
Required Courses Applied decision sciences, corporation finance, economic environment, information technology strategies for management, legal and ethical environment of business, managerial accounting and control, marketing management, microeconomics, operations management, organizational behavior, strategic management. Courses may be waived through: previous course work.
Curricular Focus Problem solving and decision making, teamwork.
Concentrations Accounting, economics, finance, human resources management, international business, management, management information systems, marketing, operations management, organizational behavior, quantitative analysis, real estate, risk management and insurance, strategic management.
Faculty Full-time: 60, 95% with doctorates; part-time: 5, 60% with doctorates.
Teaching Methodology Case study: 30%, faculty seminars: 5%, lecture: 30%, research: 5%, simulations: 5%, student presentations: 10%, team projects: 15%.
Special Opportunities International exchange in France. Internship program available.

STUDENT STATISTICS
Geographic Representation State residents 42%. By region: South 71%; Northeast 9%; Midwest 6%; West 2%. International 12%.
Undergraduate Majors Business 59%; education 1%; engineering/technology 14%; humanities 5%; nursing 1%; science/mathematics 11%; social sciences 6%; other 3%.
Other Background Work experience: On average, students have 5 years of work experience on entrance to the program.

FACILITIES
Information Resources Main library with 1.2 million bound volumes, 25,998 titles on microform, 11,283 periodical subscriptions, 61,808 records/tapes/CDs. Business collection includes 250,000 bound volumes, 2,800 periodical subscriptions, 20 CD-ROMs, 1,000 videos.
Housing College housing not available.
Technology Computers are used heavily in course work. Computer terminals/PCs, linked by a campus-wide computer network, are available for use by students in program; they are located in classrooms, the library, the computer center, computer labs. Students in the program are not required to have their own PC. $317 are budgeted per student for computer support.

Computer Resources/On-line Services

Training	Yes	CompuServe	No
Internet	Yes	Dun's	No
E-Mail	Yes	Dow Jones	No
Multimedia Center	Yes	Dialog	No
LEXIS/NEXIS	Yes	Bloomberg	No

Other on-line services: OCLC, First Search.

ADMISSION
Acceptance 1994-95 2,100 applied for admission; 65% were accepted.
Entrance Requirements Bachelor's degree, GMAT score. Core courses waived through: previous course work.
Application Requirements Written essay, application form, copies of transcript.
Application Deadlines 6/1 for fall, 10/15 for winter, 1/15 for spring, 3/1 for summer.

FINANCIALS
Costs for 1994-95 Tuition: Full-time: $42/quarter hour for state residents, $144/quarter hour for nonresidents. Fees: Full-time: $82/quarter for state residents, $82/quarter for nonresidents.
Financial Aid In 1994-95, candidates received some institutionally administered aid in the form of scholarships, loans, assistantships. Financial aid is available to part-time students. Application deadlines: 5/1 for fall, 9/1 for winter, 12/1 for spring, 3/1 for summer. Contact: Financial Aid Officer, PO Box 4040, University Plaza, Atlanta, GA 30303-3083. (404) 651-2227.

INTERNATIONAL STUDENTS
Demographics 12% of students enrolled in the program are international; Asia 70%, Europe 12%, Africa 6%, South America 5%, Central America 3%, Australia 1%, other 3%.
Services and Facilities Visa services, ESL courses, counseling/support services.
Applying TOEFL required, minimum score of 550; proof of health; proof of adequate funds. Financial aid is not available to international students. Admission application deadlines: 6/1 for fall, 10/15 for winter, 1/15 for spring, 3/1 for summer. Contact: Mr. Dan Paracka, Adviser, International Student Services, University Plaza, Atlanta, GA 30303-3083. (404) 651-2209.

ALTERNATE MBA PROGRAMS
Executive MBA (EMBA) Length of program: Minimum: 18 months. Maximum: 2 years. Degree requirements: 63 credits. Average class size: 50.
MBA/JD Length of program: Minimum: 24 months. Maximum: 6 years. Degree requirements: 50-60 quarter hours for business, 77 semester hours for law. Average class size: 10.
MBA/MHA Length of program: Minimum: 24 months. Maximum: 6 years. Degree requirements: 120 quarter hours including 15-25 elective quarter hours. Average class size: 35.

PLACEMENT
In 1993-94, 40 organizations participated in on-campus recruiting. Placement services include alumni network, career counseling/planning, career fairs, career library, career placement, electronic job bank, job interviews, resume preparation, and resume referral to employers. Of 1994 graduates, 100% were employed within three months of graduation, the average starting salary was $51,000, the range was $32,000-$90,000.
Jobs by Employer Type Manufacturing 9%; service 4%; consulting 16%; other 72%.
Jobs by Functional Area Marketing/sales 19%; finance 24%; operations 7%; management 13%; technical management 20%; other 17%.

Program Contact: Office of Academic Assistance, Georgia State University, University Plaza, Atlanta, GA 30303-3083. (404) 651-1913; Fax: (404) 651-2804.

Kennesaw State College

Michael J. Coles School of Business

Marietta, Georgia

OVERVIEW
Kennesaw State College is a state-supported comprehensive coed institution. Part of University System of Georgia. Founded 1963. Setting: 186-acre suburban campus with easy access to Atlanta. Total institutional enrollment: 12,500. Program was first offered in 1984.

MBA HIGHLIGHTS

Entrance Difficulty***
Mean GMAT: 510
Mean GPA: 3.0

Cost $
Tuition: $474/quarter
(Nonresident: $1,422/quarter)
Room & Board: $5,400 (off-campus)

Enrollment Profile

Full-time: 260	Work Exp: 98%
Part-time: 390	International: 10%
Total: 650	Women: 40%
Average Age: 32	Minorities: 10%

Average Class Size: 35

During the past year, Business Week *and* Entrepreneur Magazine *have heralded the leadership in innovation and entrepreneurship programs developed by the Michael J. Coles School of Business. The M.B.A. program now features the opportunity to major in this most important discipline that is the mainstay of private enterprise systems and economic growth and development worldwide. Course work in entrepreneurship, innovation and creativity, new venture analysis, entrepreneurial finance, the award-winning consulting services class, and family business make this program truly unique and appealing. This expertise combined with what the* Wall Street Journal *has called one of the finest family enterprise programs in the nation makes the Coles School a true leader in the field of small, family, and emerging enterprises. And entrepreneurship is but one of eight formal majors in this American Assembly of Collegiate Schools of Business (AACSB)–accredited program. The Coles School, situated in suburban Atlanta, is committed to supporting the academic and professional needs of the more than 600 students enrolled in graduate business programs. The School combines new, state-of-the-art facilities and 80 committed faculty members for a global educational experience.*

ACADEMICS
Length of Program Minimum: 12 months. Maximum: 10 years.
Calendar Quarters.
Full-time Classes Main campus; day, evening, weekends, summer.
Part-time Classes Main campus; day, evening, weekends, summer.
Degree Requirements 60 credits including 5 elective credits.
Required Courses Financial analysis and decision making, international business, management and organizational behavior, managerial accounting, managerial economics, marketing management, operations management, strategic management.
Curricular Focus Economic and financial theory, entrepreneurship, leadership.
Concentrations Accounting, entrepreneurship, finance, management, management information systems, marketing, organizational behavior.
Faculty Full-time: 40, 100% with doctorates.
Teaching Methodology Case study: 30%, lecture: 30%, seminars by members of the business community: 10%, student presentations: 10%, team projects: 20%.
Special Opportunities International exchange program available. Internships include accounting, human resources, finance, and marketing.

STUDENT STATISTICS
Geographic Representation State residents 90%. International 10%.
Undergraduate Majors Business 50%; education 3%; engineering/technology 25%; humanities 20%; nursing 2%.
Other Background Graduate degrees in other disciplines: 5%. Work experience: On average, students have 8 years of work experience on entrance to the program.

FACILITIES
Information Resources Main library with 474,000 bound volumes, 850,000 titles on microform, 3,300 periodical subscriptions, 7,500 records/tapes/CDs.
Housing College housing not available.
Technology Computers are used heavily in course work. 500 computer terminals/PCs, linked by a campus-wide computer network, are available for use by students in program; they are located in student rooms, classrooms, the library, the computer center, computer labs. Students in the program are not required to have their own PC. $1,000 are budgeted per student for computer support.

Computer Resources/On-line Services

Training	Yes	CompuServe	Yes
Internet	Yes	Dun's	No
E-Mail	Yes	Dow Jones	Yes
Multimedia Center	Yes	Dialog	Yes
LEXIS/NEXIS	Yes	Bloomberg	No

Other on-line services: Carl.

ADMISSION
Acceptance 1994-95 500 applied for admission; 60% were accepted.
Entrance Requirements Bachelor's degree, GMAT score of 450, minimum 2.75 GPA, minimum 2 years of work experience. Core courses waived through: previous course work.
Application Requirements Application form, copies of transcript.
Application Deadlines 8/17 for fall, 11/23 for winter, 2/23 for spring, 5/17 for summer. Applications are processed on a rolling basis.

FINANCIALS
Costs for 1994-95 Tuition: Full-time: $474/quarter for state residents, $1,422/quarter for nonresidents. Fees: Full-time: $46/quarter for state residents, $46/quarter for nonresidents. Average room and board costs are $5,400 per academic year (off-campus).
Financial Aid In 1994-95, 35% of candidates received some institutionally administered aid in the form of grants, scholarships, loans, work-study. Total awards ranged from $5,000-$8,500. Financial aid is available to part-time students. Application deadlines: 8/17 for fall, 11/23 for winter, 2/23 for spring, 5/17 for summer. Applications are processed on a rolling basis. Contact: Dr. Terry Faust, Director of Financial Aid, Michael J. Coles School of Business, Marietta, GA 30061. (404) 423-6525.

INTERNATIONAL STUDENTS
Demographics 10% of students enrolled in the program are international; Africa 30%, North America 30%, Asia 20%, other 20%.
Services and Facilities International student office, international student center, ESL courses, special assistance for nonnative speakers of English.
Applying TOEFL required, minimum score of 550; proof of health; proof of adequate funds. Financial aid is available to international students. Financial aid application deadlines: 8/17 for fall, 11/23 for winter, 2/23 for spring, 5/17 for summer. Applications are processed on a rolling basis. Admission application deadlines: 8/17 for fall, 11/23 for winter, 2/23 for spring, 5/17 for summer. Applications are processed on a rolling basis. Contact: Ms. Julia Griffin, Associate Director of Admissions, Michael J. Coles School of Business, Marietta, GA 30061. (404) 423-6500.

ALTERNATE MBA PROGRAM
Executive MBA (EMBA) Length of program: Minimum: 18 months. Full-time classes: Main campus; weekends, summer. Degree requirements: 60 credits. 5 years professional experience.

PLACEMENT
In 1993-94, 180 organizations participated in on-campus recruiting. Placement services include alumni network, career counseling/planning, career fairs, career library, career placement, electronic job bank, job interviews, resume preparation, and resume referral to employers. Of 1994 graduates, 95% were employed within three months of graduation, the average starting salary was $60,000, the range was $22,500-$80,000.
Jobs by Employer Type Manufacturing 30%; service 50%; government 10%; consulting 10%.
Jobs by Functional Area Marketing/sales 30%; finance 20%; operations 20%; management 30%.

Program Contact: Dr. Tom Miller, Assistant Dean, Graduate Business Programs, Kennesaw State College, Michael J. Coles School of Business, Marietta, GA 30061. (404) 423-6050; Fax: (404) 423-6539; Internet Address: tmiller@kscmail.kennesaw.edu.
See full description on page 772.

LaGrange College

Division of Business and Economics

LaGrange, Georgia

OVERVIEW

LaGrange College is an independent United Methodist comprehensive coed institution. Founded 1831. Setting: 120-acre small-town campus with easy access to Atlanta. Total institutional enrollment: 1,023.

MBA HIGHLIGHTS

Entrance Difficulty
Mean GMAT: 430
Mean GPA: N/R

Cost $
Tuition: $170/quarter hour
Room & Board: $3,630

Enrollment Profile

Full-time: N/R	Work Exp: 90%
Part-time: N/R	International: 6%
Total: 49	Women: 43%
Average Age: N/R	Minorities: 14%

Average Class Size: 14

ACADEMICS

Length of Program Minimum: 24 months. Maximum: 5 years.
Calendar Quarters.
Full-time Classes Main campus; evening.
Part-time Classes Main campus; evening.
Degree Requirements 60 quarter hours including 20 elective quarter hours. Other: Paper; oral exit review.
Required Courses Business strategic policy, international business, management simulation, managerial finance, marketing management, organizational behavior, quantitative methods for management, social and legal environment of business.
Curricular Focus General management, international business, interpersonal relations, managing diversity, teamwork.
Concentration Management.
Teaching Methodology Case study: 25%, faculty seminars: 10%, lecture: 15%, research: 10%, seminars by members of the business community: 5%, student presentations: 20%, team projects: 15%.

STUDENT STATISTICS

Geographic Representation State residents 94%. International 6%.

FACILITIES

Information Resources Main library with 110,000 bound volumes, 150,000 titles on microform, 500 periodical subscriptions, 3,000 records/tapes/CDs.
Housing College housing available.

ADMISSION

Acceptance 1994-95 22 applied for admission; 82% were accepted.
Entrance Requirements Bachelor's degree, GMAT score, minimum 2 years of work experience. Core courses waived through: previous course work.
Application Requirements Written essay, application form, copies of transcript, 3 letters of recommendation.
Application Deadlines 8/15 for fall, 11/15 for winter, 3/1 for spring. Applications are processed on a rolling basis.

FINANCIALS

Costs for 1994-95 Tuition: Full-time: $170/quarter hour. Fees: Full-time: $70/quarter. Average room and board costs are $3,630 per academic year (on-campus).
Financial Aid In 1994-95, 10% of candidates received some institutionally administered aid in the form of loans. Contact: Ms. Sylvia Smith, Director of Student Financial Planning, Office of Financial Planning, LaGrange, GA 30240. (706) 882-7249.

INTERNATIONAL STUDENTS

Demographics 6% of students enrolled in the program are international.
Applying TOEFL required, minimum score of 500; proof of adequate funds. Admission applications are processed on a rolling basis.

Mercer University

Stetson School of Business and Economics

Macon, Georgia

OVERVIEW

Mercer University is an independent Baptist comprehensive coed institution. Founded 1833. Setting: 130-acre suburban campus with easy access to Atlanta. Total institutional enrollment: 8,600. Program was first offered in 1984.

MBA HIGHLIGHTS

Entrance Difficulty*
Mean GMAT: 480
Mean GPA: 3.3

Cost $
Tuition: $130/quarter hour
Room & Board: $4,000

Enrollment Profile

Full-time: 3	Work Exp: 80%
Part-time: 71	International: 2%
Total: 74	Women: 40%
Average Age: 30	Minorities: 10%

Average Class Size: 18

ACADEMICS

Length of Program Minimum: 18 months. Maximum: 7 years.
Calendar Quarters.
Full-time Classes Main campus, Atlanta; evening, weekends, summer.
Part-time Classes Main campus, Atlanta; evening, weekends, summer.
Degree Requirements 65 quarter hours including 15 elective quarter hours. Other: Capstone course.
Required Courses Advanced management, corporation finance, decision theory, ethics and public policy, management information systems, managerial accounting, managerial economics, strategic marketing, the legal environment. Courses may be waived through: previous course work.
Curricular Focus Business issues and problems.
Concentrations Accounting, entrepreneurship, finance, human resources management, management, marketing.
Faculty Full-time: 11, 80% with doctorates; part-time: 1, 50% with doctorates.
Teaching Methodology Case study: 25%, lecture: 50%, team projects: 25%.

STUDENT STATISTICS

Geographic Representation State residents 98%. By region: South 98%. International 2%.
Undergraduate Majors Business 70%; engineering/technology 20%; other 10%.
Other Background Graduate degrees in other disciplines: 10%. Work experience: On average, students have 7 years of work experience on entrance to the program.

FACILITIES

Information Resources Main library with 494,755 bound volumes, 8,687 titles on microform, 5,622 periodical subscriptions, 11,789 records/tapes/CDs, 11 CD-ROMs.
Housing 1% of students in program live in college-owned or -operated housing.
Technology Computers are used moderately in course work. 50 computer terminals/PCs, linked by a campus-wide computer network, are available for use by students in program; they are located in the student center, the library, computer labs. Students in the program are not required to have their own PC.

Computer Resources/On-line Services

Training	No	E-Mail	Yes
Internet	Yes	CompuServe	Yes

ADMISSION
Acceptance 1994-95 Of those applying, 95% were accepted.

Entrance Requirements Bachelor's degree, GMAT score. Core courses waived through: previous course work.

Application Requirements Application form, copies of transcript.

Application Deadline Applications are processed on a rolling basis.

FINANCIALS
Costs for 1994-95 Tuition: Full-time: $130/quarter hour. Average room and board costs are $4,000 per academic year (on-campus).

Financial Aid Financial aid is not available to part-time students. Application deadline: 3/1 for fall. Contact: Financial Aid Office, 1400 Coleman Avenue, Macon, GA 31207-0003. (912) 752-2670.

INTERNATIONAL STUDENTS
Demographics 2% of students enrolled in the program are international.

Applying TOEFL required, minimum score of 550; proof of adequate funds. Financial aid is not available to international students. Admission applications are processed on a rolling basis. Contact: Admissions Office, 1400 Coleman Avenue, Macon, GA 31207-0003. (912) 752-2700.

ALTERNATE MBA PROGRAM
MBA/JD Length of program: Minimum: 48 months. Degree requirements: 200 credits. Separate applications must be submitted to both business and law schools.

PLACEMENT
Placement services include career counseling/planning, career fairs, career library, career placement, job interviews, and resume preparation. Of 1994 graduates, 95% were employed within three months of graduation.

Program Contact: Ms. Shirley Ralph, MBA Coordinator, Mercer University, 1400 Coleman Avenue, Macon, GA 31207-0003. (912) 752-2532, or (800) MERCERU (out-of-state); Fax: (912) 752-2635.

Mercer University, Cecil B. Day Campus

Stetson School of Business and Economics

Atlanta, Georgia

OVERVIEW
Mercer University, Cecil B. Day Campus is an independent Baptist upper-level coed institution. Part of Mercer University. Founded 1968. Setting: 400-acre suburban campus. Total institutional enrollment: 7,000. Program was first offered in 1982.

MBA HIGHLIGHTS

Entrance Difficulty**
Mean GMAT: 450
Mean GPA: 2.9

Cost $
Tuition: $825/course
Room & Board: $12,000 (off-campus)

Enrollment Profile

Full-time: 120	Work Exp: 90%
Part-time: 210	International: 50%
Total: 330	Women: 53%
Average Age: 32	Minorities: 20%

Average Class Size: 25

ACADEMICS
Length of Program Minimum: 18 months. Maximum: 7 years.
Calendar Quarters.
Full-time Classes Main campus; evening, weekends.
Part-time Classes Main campus; evening, weekends, summer.
Degree Requirements 65 quarter hours including 15 elective quarter hours.
Required Courses Corporation finance, decision statistics, ethics, legal environment, management information systems, managerial accounting, managerial economics, marketing, seminar in advanced management. Courses may be waived through: previous course work.

Curricular Focus Entrepreneurship, international business, problem solving and decision making.

Concentrations Accounting, entrepreneurship, finance, international business, management, management information systems, marketing, organizational behavior.

Faculty Full-time: 27, 90% with doctorates; part-time: 15, 60% with doctorates.

Teaching Methodology Case study: 20%, lecture: 50%, research: 5%, student presentations: 10%, team projects: 15%.

Special Opportunities International exchange in Belgium, Russia. Internship program available.

STUDENT STATISTICS
Geographic Representation State residents 15%. By region: South 48%; Northeast 25%; West 8%; Midwest 4%.

Undergraduate Majors Business 35%; engineering/technology 20%; humanities 10%; social sciences 30%; other 5%.

Other Background Graduate degrees in other disciplines: 10%. Work experience: On average, students have 5 years of work experience on entrance to the program.

FACILITIES
Information Resources Main library with 96,600 bound volumes, 24,500 titles on microform, 344 periodical subscriptions, 370 records/tapes/CDs, 30 CD-ROMs.

Housing College housing not available.

Technology Computers are used moderately in course work. 25 computer terminals/PCs, linked by a campus-wide computer network, are available for use by students in program; they are located in the library, the computer center, computer labs, the research center. Students in the program are not required to have their own PC.

Computer Resources/On-line Services

Training	Yes	Multimedia Center	Yes
Internet	Yes	CompuServe	Yes
E-Mail	Yes		

ADMISSION
Acceptance 1994-95 153 applied for admission; 68% were accepted.

Entrance Requirements Bachelor's degree, GMAT score of 400, minimum 2.75 GPA. Core courses waived through: previous course work.

Application Requirements Written essay, application form, copies of transcript.

Application Deadline Applications are processed on a rolling basis.

FINANCIALS
Costs for 1994-95 Tuition: Full-time: $825/course. Average room and board costs are $12,000 per academic year (off-campus).

Financial Aid In 1994-95, 70% of candidates received some institutionally administered aid in the form of grants, scholarships. Financial aid is available to part-time students. Applications are processed on a rolling basis. Contact: Ms. Meg Mc Guiness, Financial Aid Director, 3001 Mercer University Drive, Atlanta, GA 30341. (404) 986-3000.

INTERNATIONAL STUDENTS
Demographics 50% of students enrolled in the program are international; Asia 70%, Africa 10%, Europe 10%, Central America 5%, South America 5%.

Services and Facilities International student center, language tutoring, ESL courses, special assistance for nonnative speakers of English.

Applying TOEFL required, minimum score of 550; proof of health; proof of adequate funds. Financial aid is not available to international students. Admission applications are processed on a rolling basis. Contact: Dr. Tie Lu Yu, International Student Adviser, 3001 Mercer University Drive, Atlanta, CA 30341. (404) 986 3000.

ALTERNATE MBA PROGRAM
Executive MBA (EMBA) Length of program: Minimum: 21 months. Maximum: 7 years. Degree requirements: 65 credits including 15 elective credits. 2 weeks visit to major European or Asian corporations. Average class size: 25.

PLACEMENT
Placement services include career fairs, career library, and career placement. Of 1994 graduates, 90% were employed within three months of graduation.

Jobs by Employer Type Manufacturing 10%; service 50%; government 20%; consulting 10%; nonprofit 10%.

Jobs by Functional Area Marketing/sales 45%; finance 20%; operations 15%; management 20%.

Program Contact: Ms. Kay Anderson, Graduate Admission Coordinator, Mercer University, Cecil B. Day Campus, 3001 Mercer University Drive, Atlanta, GA 30341. (404) 986-3177, or (800) 694-2281; Fax: (404) 986-3337.

Southern College of Technology

School of Management

Marietta, Georgia

OVERVIEW
Southern College of Technology is a state-supported comprehensive coed institution. Part of University System of Georgia. Founded 1948. Setting: 200-acre suburban campus with easy access to Atlanta. Total institutional enrollment: 4,000. Program was first offered in 1986.

PROGRAM HIGHLIGHTS

Entrance Difficulty**
Mean GMAT: 450
Mean GPA: 3.5

Cost
Tuition: N/R
Room & Board: N/R

Enrollment Profile
Full-time: 30	Work Exp: 90%
Part-time: 125	International: 20%
Total: 155	Women: 40%
Average Age: 26	Minorities: 45%

Average Class Size: 20

ACADEMICS
Calendar Quarters.

Curricular Focus Strategic analysis and planning, teamwork, technology management.

Concentration Technology management.

Faculty Full-time: 8, 75% with doctorates; part-time: 1, 100% with doctorates.

Teaching Methodology Case study: 25%, lecture: 35%, student presentations: 25%, team projects: 15%.

Special Opportunities International exchange in Australia, United Kingdom.

STUDENT STATISTICS
Geographic Representation State residents 75%. By region: South 90%; Northeast 5%; Midwest 5%. International 20%.

Undergraduate Majors Business 30%; engineering/technology 50%; science/mathematics 10%; social sciences 10%.

Other Background Graduate degrees in other disciplines: 5%. Work experience: On average, students have 4 years of work experience on entrance to the program.

FACILITIES
Information Resources Main library with 100,000 bound volumes, 40,000 titles on microform, 1,500 periodical subscriptions, 10,000 records/tapes/CDs.

Housing 5% of students in program live in college-owned or -operated housing.

Technology Computers are used heavily in course work. 100 computer terminals/PCs, linked by a campus-wide computer network, are available for use by students in program; they are located in classrooms, computer labs. Students in the program are not required to have their own PC.

Computer Resources/On-line Services
Training	Yes	E-Mail	Yes
Internet	Yes		

ADMISSION
Acceptance 1994-95 50 applied for admission; 80% were accepted.

Entrance Requirements Bachelor's degree, GMAT score. Core courses waived through: previous course work.

Application Requirements Application form, copies of transcript, 3 letters of recommendation.

Application Deadlines 9/1 for fall, 3/1 for spring. Application discs available.

FINANCIALS
Financial Aid In 1994-95, 70% of candidates received some institutionally administered aid in the form of grants, loans, assistantships. Total awards ranged from $1,000-$4,000. Financial aid is not available to part-time students. Application deadlines: 5/5 for fall, 3/5 for spring. Applications are processed on a rolling basis. Contact: Dr. Emerelle McNair, Director of Financial Aid, 1100 South Marietta Parkway, Marietta, GA 30060. (404) 528-7290.

INTERNATIONAL STUDENTS
Demographics 20% of students enrolled in the program are international; North America 65%, Asia 20%, Africa 10%, other 5%.

Services and Facilities International student office.

Applying TOEFL required; proof of health; proof of adequate funds. Financial aid is available to international students. Financial aid application deadlines: 5/15 for fall, 3/15 for spring. Admission application deadlines: 9/1 for fall, 3/1 for spring. Applications are processed on a rolling basis. Contact: Ms. Charlotte Janis, International Student Adviser, 1100 South Marietta Parkway, Marietta, GA 30060. (404) 528-7226.

PROGRAM
MS Length of program: Minimum: 24 months. Maximum: 5 years. Full-time classes: Main campus; evening, weekends, summer. Degree requirements: 82 credits including 10 elective credits.

PLACEMENT
In 1993-94, 50 organizations participated in on-campus recruiting. Placement services include alumni network, career counseling/planning, career fairs, career placement, job interviews, resume preparation, and resume referral to employers. Of 1994 graduates, 90% were employed within three months of graduation, the average starting salary was $45,500.

Jobs by Employer Type Manufacturing 80%; service 15%; government 5%.

Jobs by Functional Area Marketing/sales 35%; operations 35%; management 15%; technical management 15%.

Program Contact: Dr. Robert Yancy, Dean, School of Management, Southern College of Technology, 1100 South Marietta Parkway, Marietta, GA 30060-2896. (404) 528-7440, or (800) 635-3204; Fax: (404) 528-4967; Internet Address: ryancy@sct.edu.

University of Georgia

Terry College of Business

Athens, Georgia

OVERVIEW
The University of Georgia is a state-supported coed institution. Part of University System of Georgia. Founded 1785. Setting: 1,601-acre small-town campus with easy access to Atlanta. Total institutional enrollment: 29,500. AACSB-accredited.

MBA HIGHLIGHTS

Entrance Difficulty*****
Mean GMAT: 630
Mean GPA: 3.2

Cost $
Tuition: $1,899
(Nonresident: $5,197)
Room & Board: $3,255

Enrollment Profile
Full-time: 152	Work Exp: 80%
Part-time: 0	International: 33%
Total: 152	Women: 36%
Average Age: 26	Minorities: 17%

Average Class Size: 50

ACADEMICS
Length of Program Minimum: 21 months. Maximum: 2 years.

Calendar Quarters.

Full-time Classes Main campus; day.

Degree Requirements 99 credits including 48 elective credits.

Required Courses Accounting, business policy, communications, economics, ethics, finance, information systems, legal studies, marketing, negotiation, organizational behavior, production and operations, statistics. Courses may be waived through: previous course work.

Curricular Focus Broad-based specializations, problem solving and decision making, teamwork.

Concentrations Accounting, economics, entrepreneurship, finance, human resources management, international business, management, management information systems, marketing, operations management, organizational behavior, quantitative analysis, real estate, risk management/insurance, pharmacy care administration, strategic management, transportation.

Faculty Full-time: 106, 100% with doctorates.

Teaching Methodology Case study: 25%, faculty seminars: 5%, lecture: 30%, seminars by members of the business community: 5%, student presentations: 10%, team projects: 25%.

Special Opportunities International exchange in Netherlands. Internship program available.

STUDENT STATISTICS

Geographic Representation State residents 19%. By region: South 47%; Northeast 19%; Midwest 8%; West 7%. International 33%.

Undergraduate Majors Business 15%; engineering/technology 25%; humanities 20%; science/mathematics 8%; social sciences 24%; other 8%.

Other Background Graduate degrees in other disciplines: 3%. Work experience: On average, students have 3 years of work experience on entrance to the program.

FACILITIES

Information Resources Main library with 3 million bound volumes, 5.2 million titles on microform, 47,993 periodical subscriptions, 41,202 records/tapes/CDs, 37 CD-ROMs. Business collection includes 342,920 bound volumes, 1,659 periodical subscriptions, 17 CD-ROMs, 10 videos.

Housing 10% of students in program live in college-owned or -operated housing.

Technology Computers are used moderately in course work. 500 computer terminals/PCs, linked by a campus-wide computer network, are available for use by students in program; they are located in dormitories, the student center, classrooms, the library, the computer center, computer labs, the research center. Students in the program are not required to have their own PC.

Computer Resources/On-line Services

Training	No	CompuServe	No
Internet	Yes	Dun's	Yes
E-Mail	Yes	Dow Jones	No
Multimedia Center	Yes	Dialog	Yes $
LEXIS/NEXIS	Yes	Bloomberg	No

ADMISSION

Acceptance 1994-95 Of those applying, 30% were accepted.

Entrance Requirements Bachelor's degree, GMAT score, minimum 2.6 GPA, active in community and school.

Application Requirements Written essay, application form, copies of transcript, resume/curriculum vitae, 3 letters of recommendation.

Application Deadlines 3/15 for fall, 2/15 for summer. Application discs available.

FINANCIALS

Costs for 1994-95 Tuition: Full-time: $1,899 for state residents, $5,197 for nonresidents; Summer: $633/quarter for state residents, $1,899/quarter for nonresidents. Fees: Full-time: $453 for state residents, $453 for nonresidents; Summer: $126/quarter for state residents, $126/quarter for nonresidents. Average room and board costs are $3,255 per academic year (on-campus) and $5,025 per academic year (off-campus).

Financial Aid In 1994-95, 50% of candidates received some institutionally administered aid in the form of scholarships, assistantships. Total awards ranged from $3,500-$8,000. Application deadline: 3/1 for fall. Contact: Office of Student Financial Aid, Academic Building, Athens, GA 30602-6264. (706) 542-6147.

INTERNATIONAL STUDENTS

Demographics 33% of students enrolled in the program are international; Europe 44%, Asia 33%, South America 6%, other 17%.

Services and Facilities Visa services, ESL courses, counseling/support services, community friends and global partners program.

Applying TOEFL required, minimum score of 585; proof of health; proof of adequate funds. Financial aid is available to international students. Financial aid application deadline: 2/15 for fall. Admission application

deadline: 3/15 for fall. Contact: Mr. James Kenaston, Foreign Student Adviser, 310 Memorial Hall, Athens, GA 30602-3108. (706) 542-1557.

ALTERNATE MBA PROGRAMS

One-Year MBA Length of program: 12 months. Degree requirements: 63 credits including 48 elective credits. Participation in MBA P.L.U.S. program activities.

MBA/JD Length of program: Minimum: 38 months. Maximum: 4 years. Degree requirements: Participation in MBA P.L.U.S. activities; 74 quarter hours of law; 78 quarter hours of business including 44 quarter hours of electives in law and 28 quarter hours of electives in business.

PLACEMENT

In 1993-94, 125 organizations participated in on-campus recruiting; 74 on-campus interviews were conducted. Placement services include alumni network, career counseling/planning, career fairs, career library, career placement, job interviews, resume preparation, and resume referral to employers. Of 1994 graduates, 92% were employed within three months of graduation, the average starting salary was $46,121, the range was $32,000-$75,000.

Jobs by Employer Type Manufacturing 19%; service 22%; consulting 21%; real estate 12%; transportation 19%; other 7%.

Jobs by Functional Area Marketing/sales 23%; finance 28%; operations 4%; strategic planning 13%; technical management 13%; real estate 13%; risk management 4%; accounting 2%.

Program Contact: Mr. Donald R. Perry, Director, MBA Admissions, University of Georgia, Athens, GA 30602. (706) 542-5671; Fax: (706) 542-5351.

Valdosta State University

College of Business Administration

Valdosta, Georgia

OVERVIEW

Valdosta State University is a state-supported coed institution. Part of University System of Georgia. Founded 1906. Setting: 168-acre small-town campus. Total institutional enrollment: 9,300. Program was first offered in 1993. AACSB-accredited.

MBA HIGHLIGHTS

Entrance Difficulty*
Mean GMAT: 500
Mean GPA: 3.0

Cost $
Tuition: $521/quarter
(Nonresident: $1,321/quarter)
Room & Board: $930

Enrollment Profile

Full-time: 35	Work Exp: 100%
Part-time: 100	International: N/R
Total: 135	Women: 40%
Average Age: 32	Minorities: 6%

Average Class Size: 28

ACADEMICS

Length of Program Minimum: 18 months. Maximum: 6 years.

Calendar Quarters.

Full-time Classes Evening.

Degree Requirements 60 credits including 20 elective credits.

Required Courses Advanced production technology, business research methods, managerial accounting, managerial economics, managerial finance, organizational behavior and theory, strategic management, strategic marketing.

Curricular Focus International business, leadership, teamwork.

Concentration Management.

Faculty Full-time: 20, 100% with doctorates.

Teaching Methodology Case study: 15%, lecture: 35%, research: 15%, seminars by members of the business community: 5%, student presentations: 10%, team projects: 20%.

STUDENT STATISTICS

Geographic Representation By region: South 100%.

Undergraduate Majors Business 87%; engineering/technology 12%; other 1%.

Other Background Work experience: On average, students have 12 years of work experience on entrance to the program.

FACILITIES

Information Resources Main library with 372,960 bound volumes, 854,468 titles on microform, 3,000 periodical subscriptions, 10,158 records/tapes/CDs, 50 CD-ROMs. Business collection includes 25,000 bound volumes, 225 periodical subscriptions.

Housing College housing available.

Technology Computers are used moderately in course work. 200 computer terminals/PCs are available for use by students in program; they are located in the computer center, computer labs. Students in the program are not required to have their own PC.

Computer Resources/On-line Services

Internet	Yes	E-Mail	Yes

Other on-line services: OCLC.

ADMISSION

Acceptance 1994-95 92 applied for admission; 38% were accepted.

Entrance Requirements Bachelor's degree, prerequisite courses required for applicants with non-business degree, GMAT score of 450, minimum 3.0 GPA.

Application Requirements Written essay, interview, application form, copies of transcript, resume/curriculum vitae.

Application Deadline 3/1 for fall.

FINANCIALS

Costs for 1994-95 Tuition: Full-time: $521/quarter for state residents, $1,321/quarter for nonresidents. Average room and board costs are $930 per academic year (on-campus).

Financial Aid In 1994-95, 33% of candidates received some institutionally administered aid in the form of grants, scholarships, loans, assistantships. Financial aid is not available to part-time students. Application deadlines: 7/1 for fall, 10/1 for winter, 1/1 for spring. Applications are processed on a rolling basis. Contact: Mr. Tommy Moore, Director, Financial Aid, Powell Hall East, Valdosta, GA 31698. (912) 333-5935.

INTERNATIONAL STUDENTS

Services and Facilities International student office, ESL courses.

Applying TOEFL required, minimum score of 550; proof of health; proof of adequate funds. Financial aid is not available to international students. Admission application deadlines: 7/1 for fall, 11/1 for winter, 2/1 for spring, 5/1 for summer. Applications are processed on a rolling basis. Contact: Dr. Tracy Harrington, Director, International Programs, Carswell Hall, Valdosta, GA 31698. (912) 333-7410.

PLACEMENT

Placement services include career counseling/planning, career fairs, career library, career placement, job interviews, resume preparation, and resume referral to employers.

Program Contact: Ms. Juanita Faircloth, Student Advising Center, Valdosta State University, Thaxton Hall, College of Business Administration, Valdosta, GA 31698. (912) 249-2623; Fax: (912) 245-6498.

West Georgia College

School of Business

Carrollton, Georgia

OVERVIEW

West Georgia College is a state-supported comprehensive coed institution. Part of University System of Georgia. Founded 1933. Setting: 400-acre small-town campus with easy access to Atlanta. Total institutional enrollment: 8,327. Program was first offered in 1967. AACSB-accredited.

MBA HIGHLIGHTS

Entrance Difficulty***
Mean GMAT: 515
Mean GPA: 3.13

Cost $
Tuition: $474/quarter
(Nonresident: $1,422/quarter)
Room & Board: $4,684

Enrollment Profile

Full-time: 17		Work Exp: 75%
Part-time: 31		International: 31%
Total: 48		Women: 48%
Average Age: 27		Minorities: 8%

Average Class Size: 15

ACADEMICS

Length of Program Minimum: 12 months. Maximum: 6 years.

Calendar Quarters.

Full-time Classes Main campus; evening, summer.

Part-time Classes Main campus; evening, summer.

Degree Requirements 50 credits including 15 elective credits.

Required Courses Advanced financial management, advanced managerial accounting, managerial economics, marketing strategy, organizational theory, production and operations management, strategic management.

Curricular Focus General management, problem solving and decision making, strategic analysis and planning.

Concentrations Accounting, economics, finance, management, marketing.

Faculty Full-time: 25, 100% with doctorates.

Teaching Methodology Case study: 20%, lecture: 30%, research: 20%, student presentations: 20%, team projects: 10%.

STUDENT STATISTICS

Geographic Representation State residents 65%. By region: South 69%. International 31%.

Undergraduate Majors Business 50%; education 5%; engineering/technology 25%; humanities 5%; science/mathematics 5%; social sciences 10%.

Other Background Graduate degrees in other disciplines: 3%. Work experience: On average, students have 3 years of work experience on entrance to the program.

FACILITIES

Information Resources Main library with 308,051 bound volumes, 871,000 titles on microform, 1,511 periodical subscriptions, 117,000 records/tapes/CDs, 41 CD-ROMs.

Housing 20% of students in program live in college-owned or -operated housing.

Technology Computers are used moderately in course work. 125 computer terminals/PCs, linked by a campus-wide computer network, are available for use by students in program; they are located in classrooms, the library, computer labs. Students in the program are not required to have their own PC.

Computer Resources/On-line Services

Training	No	LEXIS/NEXIS	Yes
Internet	Yes	CompuServe	Yes
E-Mail	Yes		

ADMISSION

Acceptance 1994-95 54 applied for admission; 87% were accepted.

Entrance Requirements Bachelor's degree, GMAT score of 450, minimum 2.5 GPA.

Application Requirements Application form, copies of transcript.

Application Deadlines 8/15 for fall, 3/15 for spring.

FINANCIALS

Costs for 1994-95 Tuition: Full-time: $474/quarter for state residents, $1,422/quarter for nonresidents; Part-time day: $40/quarter hour for state residents, $120/quarter hour for nonresidents. Fees: Full-time: $128/quarter for state residents, $128/quarter for nonresidents; Part-time day:-$128/quarter for state residents, $128/quarter for nonresidents. Average room and board costs are $4,684 per academic year (on-campus).

Financial Aid In 1994-95, 30% of candidates received some institutionally administered aid in the form of assistantships. Total awards ranged from $2,000-$5,000. Financial aid is not available to part-time students. Application deadlines: 8/15 for fall, 3/15 for spring. Contact: Mr. John R. Wells, MBA Director, 1600 Maple Street, Carrollton, GA 30118. (404) 836-6467.

INTERNATIONAL STUDENTS

Demographics 31% of students enrolled in the program are international; Europe 67%, Asia 20%, South America 13%.

Services and Facilities International student office, ESL courses, counseling/ support services.

Applying TOEFL required, minimum score of 550; proof of health; proof of adequate funds. Financial aid is available to international students. Financial aid application deadlines: 8/15 for fall, 3/15 for spring. Admission application deadlines: 8/15 for fall, 3/15 for spring. Contact: Ms. Sylvia Shortt, Student Affairs Counselor, Student Development, 1600 Maple Street, Carrollton, GA 30118. (404) 836-6428.

PLACEMENT

Placement services include career fairs, electronic job bank, job interviews, and resume preparation.

Program Contact: Mr. John R. Wells, MBA Director, West Georgia College, 1600 Maple Street, Carrollton, GA 30118. (404) 836-6467; Fax: (404) 836-6774; Internet Address: jwells@sbf.bus.westga.edu.

HAWAII

Chaminade University of Honolulu

School of Business

Honolulu, Hawaii

OVERVIEW

Chaminade University of Honolulu is an independent Roman Catholic comprehensive coed institution. Founded 1955. Setting: 62-acre urban campus. Total institutional enrollment: 2,513. Program was first offered in 1976.

MBA HIGHLIGHTS

Entrance Difficulty***
Mean GMAT: 520
Mean GPA: 3.2

Cost $$
Tuition: $240/credit hour
Room & Board: N/R

Enrollment Profile

Full-time: 116	Work Exp: 80%
Part-time: 88	International: 20%
Total: 204	Women: 46%
Average Age: 29	Minorities: 45%

Average Class Size: 20

ACADEMICS

Length of Program Minimum: 12 months. Maximum: 5 years.

Calendar Terms.

Full-time Classes Main campus, Pearl Harbor; evening, weekends, summer.

Degree Requirements 36 credit hours including 12 elective credit hours.

Required Courses Applied quantitative methods for business decisions, business ethics, business policy and strategy, financial management, management of business systems, managerial accounting, managerial economics, marketing management and strategy. Courses may be waived through: previous course work.

Curricular Focus General management, international business, leadership.

Concentrations Accounting, entrepreneurship, finance, human resources management, international business, management, management information systems, marketing, quantitative analysis, taxation, contract administration, Japanese business, small business management.

Faculty Full-time: 9, 56% with doctorates; part-time: 12.

Teaching Methodology Case study: 30%, lecture: 30%, student presentations: 10%, team projects: 20%, video presentations: 10%.

Special Opportunities Internship program available.

STUDENT STATISTICS

Geographic Representation State residents 35%. By region: West 77%; Northeast 1%; South 1%; Midwest 1%. International 20%.

Other Background Graduate degrees in other disciplines: 10%.

FACILITIES

Information Resources Main library with 60,000 bound volumes, 10,000 titles on microform, 500 periodical subscriptions, 985 records/tapes/ CDs.

Housing 1% of students in program live in college-owned or -operated housing.

Technology Computers are used moderately in course work. Computer terminals/PCs are available for use by students in program; they are located in the library, the computer center, computer labs. Students in the program are not required to have their own PC.

Computer Resources/On-line Services

Training	Yes	Dialog	Yes
E-Mail	No		

Other on-line services: OCLC.

ADMISSION

Acceptance 1994-95 225 applied for admission; 90% were accepted.

Entrance Requirements Bachelor's degree, prerequisite courses required for applicants with non-business degree, GMAT score, minimum 3.0 GPA, minimum GMAT score of 25% in verbal and quantitative portions. Core courses waived through: previous course work.

Application Requirements Application form, copies of transcript.

Application Deadlines 8/15 for fall, 12/1 for winter, 2/15 for spring, 6/15 for summer.

FINANCIALS

Costs for 1995-96 Tuition: Full-time: $240/credit hour.

Financial Aid In 1994-95, 10% of candidates received some institutionally administered aid in the form of loans. Financial aid is not available to part-time students. Contact: Mr. Eric Nemoto, Financial Aid Director, 3140 Waialae Avenue, Honolulu, HI 96816. (808) 735-4707.

INTERNATIONAL STUDENTS

Demographics 20% of students enrolled in the program are international; Asia 60%, Europe 20%, other 20%.

Services and Facilities Visa services, ESL courses.

Applying TOEFL required, minimum score of 550; proof of health; proof of adequate funds. Financial aid is not available to international students. Admission application deadlines: 8/1 for fall, 11/15 for winter, 2/28 for spring, 6/1 for summer. Contact: Ms. Laurie Cox, International Student Adviser, Campus Life, 3140 Waialae Avenue, Honolulu, HI 96821. (808) 735-4760.

PLACEMENT

Placement services include career counseling/planning, career placement, job interviews, resume preparation, and resume referral to employers.

Program Contact: Mr. James Moses, Assistant Director, Chaminade University of Honolulu, 3140 Waialae Avenue, Honolulu, HI 96816-1578. (808) 739-4612; Fax: (808) 739-4734.

Hawaii Pacific University

Center for Graduate Studies

Honolulu, Hawaii

OVERVIEW

Hawaii Pacific University is an independent nonprofit comprehensive coed institution. Founded 1965. Setting: 135-acre urban campus. Total institutional enrollment: 7,910. Program was first offered in 1987.

MBA HIGHLIGHTS

Entrance Difficulty***
Mean GMAT: N/R
Mean GPA: 3.0

Cost $$
Tuition: $6,300
Room & Board: $6,500

Enrollment Profile

Full-time: N/R	Work Exp: 60%
Part-time: N/R	International: 30%
Total: 548	Women: 42%
Average Age: 30	Minorities: 62%

Average Class Size: 18

ACADEMICS

Length of Program Minimum: 15 months.

Calendar 4-1-4.

Full-time Classes Main campus, distance learning option; day, evening, weekends, early morning, summer.

Part-time Classes Main campus, distance learning option; day, evening, weekends, summer.

Degree Requirements 45 credits including 9 elective credits.

Required Courses Accounting for managers, economic analysis and forecasting, financial management and strategy, human resources management, international business management, law for managers, management information systems, management policy and strategy foundation, marketing strategy for managers, professional paper, quantitative methods. Courses may be waived through: previous course work.

Curricular Focus International business, organizational development and change management, strategic analysis and planning.

Concentrations Accounting, finance, human resources management, international business, management information systems, marketing, travel industry management, nonprofit management.

Faculty Full-time: 28, 80% with doctorates; part-time: 18, 75% with doctorates.

Teaching Methodology Case study: 5%, lecture: 50%, research: 20%, seminars by members of the business community: 5%, student presentations: 10%, team projects: 10%.

Special Opportunities Internships include government and travel.

STUDENT STATISTICS

Geographic Representation State residents 40%. By region: West 50%; Northeast 10%; South 5%; Midwest 5%. International 30%.

Other Background Graduate degrees in other disciplines: 7%. Work experience: On average, students have 2-5 years of work experience on entrance to the program.

FACILITIES

Information Resources Main library with 122,000 bound volumes, 1,000 titles on microform, 1,750 periodical subscriptions, 4,000 records/tapes/CDs, 132 CD-ROMs. Business collection includes 25,000 bound volumes, 500 periodical subscriptions, 9 CD-ROMs, 100 videos.

Housing 10% of students in program live in college-owned or -operated housing.

Technology Computers are used moderately in course work. 225 computer terminals/PCs are available for use by students in program; they are located in learning resource center, the computer center, computer labs. Students in the program are not required to have their own PC.

Computer Resources/On-line Services

Training	Yes	Dun's	No
Internet	No	Dow Jones	No
E-Mail	Yes	Dialog	Yes $
LEXIS/NEXIS	No	Bloomberg	No
CompuServe	No		

ADMISSION

Acceptance 1994-95 Of those applying, 78% were accepted.

Entrance Requirements Bachelor's degree. Core courses waived through: previous course work.

Application Requirements Application form, copies of transcript, 2 letters of recommendation.

Application Deadline Applications are processed on a rolling basis.

FINANCIALS

Estimated Costs for 1995-96 Tuition: Full-time: $6,300. Average room and board costs are $6,500 per academic year (on-campus) and $6,900 per academic year (off-campus).

Financial Aid In 1994-95, 12% of candidates received some institutionally administered aid in the form of scholarships, loans, work-study. Total awards ranged from $3,150-$11,500. Financial aid is available to part-time students. Applications are processed on a rolling basis. Contact: Ms. Donna Lubong, Director of Financial Aid, 1164 Bishop Street, Honolulu, HI 96813. (808) 544-0253.

INTERNATIONAL STUDENTS

Demographics 30% of students enrolled in the program are international; Asia 75%, Europe 11%, Africa 1%, Central America 1%, South America 1%, other 12%.

Services and Facilities International student office, international student center, visa services, language tutoring, ESL courses, special assistance for nonnative speakers of English.

Applying Applicants without minimum 550 TOEFL score must take university's in-house English placement test. Financial aid is not available to international students. Admission applications are processed on a rolling basis. Contact: Ms. Ann Newton, International Student Adviser, 1188 Fort Street, Honolulu, HI 96813. (808) 544-0265.

ALTERNATE MBA PROGRAMS
MBA/MRM
MBA/MSIS

PLACEMENT

In 1993-94, 86 organizations participated in on-campus recruiting; 102 on-campus interviews were conducted. Placement services include alumni network, career counseling/planning, career fairs, career library, career placement, electronic job bank, job interviews, resume preparation, and resume referral to employers. Of 1994 graduates, 75% were employed within three months of graduation, the average starting salary was $49,000, the range was $39,000-$65,000.

Program Contact: Mr. Scott Stensrud, Director of Admissions, Hawaii Pacific University, 1164 Bishop Street, Honolulu, HI 96813. (808) 544-0238, or (800) 669-4724 (out-of-state); Fax: (808) 544-1136.
See full description on page 750.

University of Hawaii at Manoa

College of Business Administration

Honolulu, Hawaii

OVERVIEW

The University of Hawaii at Manoa is a state-supported coed institution. Part of University of Hawaii System. Founded 1907. Setting: 300-acre urban campus. Total institutional enrollment: 19,983. AACSB-accredited.

MBA HIGHLIGHTS

Entrance Difficulty**
Mean GMAT: 584
Mean GPA: N/R

Cost $
Tuition: $83/credit hour
(Nonresident: $254/credit hour)
Room & Board: $9,777 (off-campus)

Enrollment Profile

Full-time: 110	Work Exp: N/R
Part-time: 240	International: 6%
Total: 350	Women: 36%
Average Age: N/R	Minorities: 2%

Average Class Size: 23

ACADEMICS

Length of Program Minimum: 24 months. Maximum: 7 years.

Calendar Semesters.

Full-time Classes Main campus; day, summer.

Part-time Classes Main campus, Maui, distance learning option; evening, summer.

Degree Requirements 36 credits including 15 elective credits.

Required Courses Field studies, financial accounting, integrated functional core, managerial economics, organizational behavior, statistics. Courses may be waived through: previous course work.

Curricular Focus International business, strategic analysis and planning, technology management.

Concentrations Accounting, finance, human resources management, international business, management, management information systems, public administration, real estate.

Teaching Methodology Lecture: 30%, seminars by members of the business community: 10%, student presentations: 30%, team projects: 30%.

Special Opportunities International exchange in Denmark, Japan. Internship program available.

STUDENT STATISTICS

Geographic Representation State residents 80%. International 6%.

FACILITIES

Information Resources Main library with 2.7 million bound volumes, 520,000 titles on microform, 37,601 periodical subscriptions, 27,253 records/tapes/CDs, 32 CD-ROMs. Business collection includes 175,000 bound volumes, 5,000 periodical subscriptions, 25 CD-ROMs.

Housing College housing not available.

Technology Computers are used moderately in course work. 75 computer terminals/PCs are available for use by students in program; they are located in classrooms, computer labs. Students in the program are not required to have their own PC.

Computer Resources/On-line Services

Training	Yes	Videoconference Center	Yes
Internet	Yes	Dialog	Yes
E-Mail	Yes		

Other on-line services: OCLC.

ADMISSION

Acceptance 1994-95 187 applied for admission; 31% were accepted.

Entrance Requirements Bachelor's degree, GMAT score, minimum 2.7 GPA. Core courses waived through: previous course work.

Application Requirements Written essay, application form, copies of transcript, resume/curriculum vitae.

Application Deadlines 3/1 for fall, 9/1 for spring.

FINANCIALS

Costs for 1994-95 Tuition: Full-time: $83/credit hour for state residents, $254/credit hour for nonresidents. Fees: Full-time: $42/semester for state residents, $49/semester for nonresidents. Average room and board costs are $9,777 per academic year (off-campus).

Financial Aid In 1994-95, 17% of candidates received some institutionally administered aid in the form of scholarships, loans, assistantships, East-West Center Scholarship Program. Total awards ranged from $800-$15,699. Financial aid is available to part-time students. Application deadlines: 4/1 for fall, 11/1 for spring. Applications are processed on a rolling basis. Contact: Mrs. Annabelle Fong, Director of Office of Financial Aid, Student Services Center, Room 12, 2600 Campus Road, Honolulu, HI 96822. (808) 956-7251.

INTERNATIONAL STUDENTS

Demographics 6% of students enrolled in the program are international; Asia 90%, North America 10%.

Services and Facilities International student office, international student center, visa services, language tutoring, ESL courses, special assistance for nonnative speakers of English, counseling/support services.

Applying TOEFL required, minimum score of 500; proof of health; proof of adequate funds. Financial aid is not available to international students. Admission application deadlines: 1/15 for fall, 8/1 for spring. Contact: Ms. June Naughton, Director, International Student Office, 2600 Campus Road, Honolulu, HI 96822. (808) 956-8013.

PLACEMENT

In 1993-94, 69 organizations participated in on-campus recruiting; 22 on-campus interviews were conducted. Placement services include career counseling/planning, career library, career placement, electronic job bank, and resume preparation. Of 1994 graduates, 75% were employed within three months of graduation.

Jobs by Employer Type Service 10%; government 20%; consulting 10%; banking 30%; computer-related 30%.

Jobs by Functional Area Marketing/sales 20%; finance 30%; management 20%; technical management 30%.

Program Contact: Dr. Patricia Cleveland, Assistant Dean, Office of Student Academic Services, University of Hawaii at Manoa, College of Business Administration, 2404 Malle Way, Honolulu, HI 96822. (808) 956-8266; Fax: (808) 956-9890.

IDAHO

Boise State University

College of Business

Boise, Idaho

OVERVIEW

Boise State University is a state-supported comprehensive coed institution. Part of Idaho System of Higher Education. Founded 1932. Setting: 130-acre urban campus. Total institutional enrollment: 15,500. Program was first offered in 1970. AACSB-accredited.

MBA HIGHLIGHTS

Entrance Difficulty***
Mean GMAT: 549
Mean GPA: 3.15

Cost $
Tuition: $1,155/semester
(Nonresident: $3,248/semester)
Room & Board: $4,200

Enrollment Profile

Full-time: 26	Work Exp: 100%
Part-time: 151	International: 6%
Total: 177	Women: 41%
Average Age: 32	Minorities: 2%

Average Class Size: 19

ACADEMICS

Length of Program Minimum: 30 months. Maximum: 7 years.

Calendar Semesters.

Full-time Classes Main campus; evening.

Part-time Classes Main campus; evening.

Degree Requirements 33 credits including 9 elective credits.

Required Courses Accounting, decision analysis, finance, global society, management, marketing, strategic planning. Courses may be waived through: previous course work, work experience.

Curricular Focus Business issues and problems, problem solving and decision making, teamwork.

Concentration Management.

Faculty Full-time: 20, 100% with doctorates; part-time: 4, 75% with doctorates.

Teaching Methodology Case study: 17%, computer analysis: 4%, faculty seminars: 13%, lecture: 42%, seminars by members of the business community: 2%, student presentations: 8%, team projects: 14%.

Special Opportunities Internships include government, banking, and computer manufacturing.

STUDENT STATISTICS

Geographic Representation State residents 90%. By region: West 57%; Northeast 22%; Midwest 10%; South 5%. International 6%.

Undergraduate Majors Business 52%; education 1%; engineering/technology 14%; humanities 2%; nursing 3%; science/mathematics 11%; social sciences 9%; other 8%.

Other Background Graduate degrees in other disciplines: 2%. Work experience: On average, students have 6 years of work experience on entrance to the program.

FACILITIES

Information Resources Main library with 403,393 bound volumes, 988,137 titles on microform, 4,709 periodical subscriptions, 55,240 records/tapes/CDs, 14 CD-ROMs. Business collection includes 38,092 bound volumes, 720 periodical subscriptions, 24 videos.

Housing 5% of students in program live in college-owned or -operated housing.

Technology Computers are used heavily in course work. 60 computer terminals/PCs are available for use by students in program; they are located in learning resource center, the library, the computer center, computer labs. Students in the program are not required to have their own PC.

Computer Resources/On-line Services

Training	No	Dun's	Yes
Internet	Yes	Dow Jones	Yes
E-Mail	Yes	Dialog	No
LEXIS/NEXIS	Yes	Bloomberg	No
CompuServe	Yes		

ADMISSION
Acceptance 1994-95 Of those applying, 73% were accepted.

Entrance Requirements Bachelor's degree, prerequisite courses required for applicants with non-business degree, GMAT score of 475, minimum 2.9 GPA, minimum 2 years of work experience, GMAT of 600 without work experience. Core courses waived through: previous course work, work experience.

Application Requirements Written essay, application form, copies of transcript, resume/curriculum vitae, personal statement, 2 letters of recommendation.

Application Deadlines 4/30 for fall, 10/31 for spring, 4/30 for summer.

FINANCIALS
Costs for 1994-95 Tuition: Full-time: $1,155/semester for state residents, $3,248/semester for nonresidents. Average room and board costs are $4,200 per academic year (on-campus) and $5,000 per academic year (off-campus).

Financial Aid In 1994-95, 5% of candidates received some institutionally administered aid in the form of scholarships, assistantships. Total awards ranged from $860-$3,300. Financial aid is not available to part-time students. Application deadlines: 3/1 for fall, 11/1 for spring. Contact: Ms. Renee Anchustegui, Administrative Assistant, Graduate Business College, Boise, ID 83725. (208) 385-1126.

INTERNATIONAL STUDENTS
Demographics 6% of students enrolled in the program are international; Asia 78%, South America 22%.

Services and Facilities Visa services, language tutoring, ESL courses.

Applying TOEFL required, minimum score of 550; proof of adequate funds; English translation of transcripts. Financial aid is available to international students. Financial aid application deadlines: 3/1 for fall, 11/1 for spring. Admission application deadlines: 4/30 for fall, 10/31 for spring, 4/30 for summer. Contact: Ms. Brenda Ross, Foreign Adviser, Foreign Admissions, 1910 University Drive, Boise, ID 83725. (208) 385-1757.

PLACEMENT
In 1993-94, 5 organizations participated in on-campus recruiting; 4 on-campus interviews were conducted. Placement services include alumni network, career counseling/planning, career fairs, career library, career placement, resume preparation, and resume referral to employers.

Jobs by Employer Type Manufacturing 34%; service 59%; government 5%; consulting 2%.

Jobs by Functional Area Marketing/sales 22%; finance 43%; operations 4%; management 7%; strategic planning 22%; technical management 2%.

Program Contact: Ms. Renee Anchustegui, Administrative Assistant, Boise State University, 1910 University Drive, Boise, ID 83725. (208) 385-1126, or (800) 632-6586 (ID only), or (800) 824-7017 (out-of-state); Fax: (208) 385-3637; Internet Address: abuanchu@cabfac.idbsu.edu.

See full description on page 678.

Idaho State University

College of Business

Pocatello, Idaho

OVERVIEW
Idaho State University is a state-supported coed institution. Founded 1901. Setting: 274-acre small-town campus. Total institutional enrollment: 12,500. Program was first offered in 1963. AACSB-accredited.

MBA HIGHLIGHTS
Entrance Difficulty*
Mean GMAT: 525
Mean GPA: 3.25

Cost $
Tuition: $1,015/semester
(Nonresident: $2,822/semester)
Room & Board: $3,000

Enrollment Profile

Full-time: 92	Work Exp: 90%
Part-time: 31	International: 10%
Total: 123	Women: 35%
Average Age: 30	Minorities: 3%

Class Size: 20 - 30

ACADEMICS
Length of Program Minimum: 21 months.

Calendar Semesters.

Full-time Classes Main campus; evening, summer.

Part-time Classes Idaho Falls; evening, summer.

Degree Requirements 30 credits including 12 elective credits.

Curricular Focus Problem solving and decision making, strategic analysis and planning.

Concentrations Accounting, management.

Faculty Full-time: 30, 100% with doctorates.

Teaching Methodology Case study: 65%, lecture: 20%, student presentations: 5%, team projects: 10%.

STUDENT STATISTICS
Geographic Representation State residents 70%. International 10%.

Undergraduate Majors Business 50%; education 5%; engineering/technology 20%; humanities 10%; nursing 5%; social sciences 10%.

Other Background Graduate degrees in other disciplines: 5%. Work experience: On average, students have 8 years of work experience on entrance to the program.

FACILITIES
Information Resources Main library with 511,579 bound volumes, 1.7 million titles on microform, 3,350 periodical subscriptions, 1,378 records/tapes/CDs.

Housing 5% of students in program live in college-owned or -operated housing.

Technology Computers are used moderately in course work. 500 computer terminals/PCs, linked by a campus-wide computer network, are available for use by students in program; they are located in dormitories, the student center, the library, computer labs. Students in the program are not required to have their own PC.

Computer Resources/On-line Services

E-Mail	Yes

ADMISSION
Entrance Requirements Bachelor's degree, GMAT score of 440, minimum 2.75 GPA. Core courses waived through: previous course work.

Application Requirements Application form, copies of transcript, resume/curriculum vitae, 3 letters of recommendation.

Application Deadlines 7/1 for fall, 12/1 for spring, 5/1 for summer.

FINANCIALS
Costs for 1994-95 Tuition: Full-time: $1,015/semester for state residents, $2,822/semester for nonresidents. Average room and board costs are $3,000 per academic year (on-campus).

Financial Aid In 1994-95, candidates received some institutionally administered aid in the form of scholarships, loans, assistantships. Application deadline: 3/1 for fall. Applications are processed on a rolling basis. Contact: Mr. Douglas Severs, Coordinator of Financial Aid, 741 South 7th Avenue, Pocatello, ID 83209. (208) 236-2756.

INTERNATIONAL STUDENTS
Demographics 10% of students enrolled in the program are international.

Applying TOEFL required, minimum score of 550; proof of adequate funds. Financial aid is available to international students. Assistantships are available for these students. Financial aid application deadline: 2/15 for fall. Applications are processed on a rolling basis. Admission application deadlines: 6/1 for fall, 11/1 for spring, 3/1 for summer. Contact: Dr. Ray Wallace, International Student Adviser, Box 8723, 741 South 7th Avenue, Pocatello, ID 83209. (208) 236-2941.

PLACEMENT

Placement services include career counseling/planning, career placement, job interviews, and resume preparation.

Program Contact: Mr. George Johnson, MBA Program Director, Idaho State University, 741 South 7th Avenue, Pocatello, ID 83209. (208) 236-2504, or (800) 888-4781; Fax: (208) 236-4367.

ILLINOIS

Aurora University

School of Business and Professional Studies

Aurora, Illinois

OVERVIEW

Aurora University is an independent nonprofit comprehensive coed institution. Founded 1893. Setting: 26-acre suburban campus with easy access to Chicago. Total institutional enrollment: 2,000. Program was first offered in 1980.

MBA HIGHLIGHTS

Entrance Difficulty*
Mean GMAT: N/R
Mean GPA: 3.1

Cost $$
Tuition: $1,025/course
Room & Board: $3,850

Enrollment Profile

Full-time: 43	Work Exp: 100%
Part-time: 100	International: 2%
Total: 143	Women: 40%
Average Age: 35	Minorities: 8%

Average Class Size: 15

ACADEMICS

Length of Program Minimum: 24 months. Maximum: 6 years.
Calendar Trimesters.
Full-time Classes Main campus; evening, weekends, summer.
Part-time Classes Main campus; evening, weekends, summer.
Degree Requirements 50 credits including 9 elective credits.
Required Courses Advanced managerial implementation, advanced managerial planning, basic managerial implementation, basic managerial planning, competitive management strategy, competitive marketing strategy, environmental influences on management, foundations of business management, foundations of strategic management, fundamentals of management and leadership, fundamentals of team building, seminar in international management, strategic management/leadership/vision.
Curricular Focus Leadership, strategic analysis and planning, teamwork.
Concentration Management.
Faculty Full-time: 9, 55% with doctorates.
Teaching Methodology Case study: 30%, lecture: 5%, research: 5%, seminars by members of the business community: 5%, student presentations: 25%, team projects: 30%.

STUDENT STATISTICS

Geographic Representation State residents 100%. By region: Midwest 98%. International 2%.
Undergraduate Majors Business 70%; engineering/technology 10%; humanities 3%; nursing 5%; science/mathematics 10%; social sciences 2%.
Other Background Graduate degrees in other disciplines: 10%. Work experience: On average, students have 13 years of work experience on entrance to the program.

FACILITIES

Information Resources Main library with 130,000 bound volumes, 72,707 titles on microform, 722 periodical subscriptions, 4,979 records/tapes/CDs, 12 CD-ROMs. Business collection includes 12,000 bound volumes, 91 periodical subscriptions, 2 CD-ROMs, 130 videos.

Housing 2% of students in program live in college-owned or -operated housing.

Technology Computers are used moderately in course work. 80 computer terminals/PCs, linked by a campus-wide computer network, are available for use by students in program; they are located in student rooms, classrooms, learning resource center, the library, the computer center, computer labs. Students in the program are not required to have their own PC.

Computer Resources/On-line Services

Training	Yes	CompuServe	No
Internet	Yes	Dun's	No
E-Mail	Yes	Dow Jones	No
Multimedia Center	Yes	Dialog	No
LEXIS/NEXIS	No	Bloomberg	No

ADMISSION

Acceptance 1994-95 Of those applying, 80% were accepted.
Entrance Requirements Bachelor's degree, prerequisite courses required for applicants with non-business degree, minimum 2.75 GPA, minimum 3 years of work experience.
Application Requirements Interview, application form, copies of transcript, 2 letters of recommendation.
Application Deadlines 8/1 for fall, 12/1 for spring.

FINANCIALS

Costs for 1994-95 Tuition: Full-time: $1,025/course. Average room and board costs are $3,850 per academic year (on-campus).
Financial Aid In 1994-95, 2% of candidates received some institutionally administered aid in the form of loans. Financial aid is not available to part-time students. Application deadlines: 8/1 for fall, 12/1 for spring. Contact: Ms. Heather Gutierrez, Director of Financial Aid, 347 South Gladstone Avenue, Aurora, IL 60506-4892. (708) 844-5448.

INTERNATIONAL STUDENTS

Demographics 2% of students enrolled in the program are international; Asia 100%.
Applying TOEFL required, minimum score of 550; proof of health; proof of adequate funds. Financial aid is not available to international students. Admission application deadlines: 8/1 for fall, 12/1 for spring.

PLACEMENT

Placement services include alumni network, career counseling/planning, career library, career placement, and resume preparation.

Program Contact: Dr. Leo Loughead, MBA Program Manager, Aurora University, 347 South Gladstone Avenue, Aurora, IL 60506-4892. (708) 851-4786; Fax: (708) 851-4877.

Bradley University

Foster College of Business Administration

Peoria, Illinois

OVERVIEW

Bradley University is an independent nonprofit comprehensive coed institution. Founded 1897. Setting: 50-acre urban campus. Total institutional enrollment: 6,100. Program was first offered in 1940. AACSB-accredited.

MBA HIGHLIGHTS

Entrance Difficulty**
Mean GMAT: 545
Mean GPA: 3.2

Cost $$
Tuition: $295/hour
Room & Board: N/R

Enrollment Profile

Full-time: 20	Work Exp: 86%
Part-time: 155	International: 8%
Total: 175	Women: 33%
Average Age: 28	Minorities: 14%

Average Class Size: 30

ACADEMICS
Length of Program Minimum: 12 months. Maximum: 5 years.
Calendar Semesters.
Full-time Classes Main campus; evening, weekends, summer.
Part-time Classes Main campus; evening, weekends, summer.
Degree Requirements 36 credits including 6 elective credits.
Required Courses Accounting, economics, finance, management theory, marketing, operations, policy and strategy, social and legal policy and strategy. Courses may be waived through: previous course work.
Curricular Focus General management.
Concentrations Accounting, economics, finance, management, marketing, operations management, organizational behavior.
Faculty Full-time: 28, 100% with doctorates; part-time: 2, 50% with doctorates.
Teaching Methodology Case study: 25%, faculty seminars: 5%, lecture: 40%, seminars by members of the business community: 5%, student presentations: 10%, team projects: 15%.

STUDENT STATISTICS
Geographic Representation International 8%.
Other Background Work experience: On average, students have 6 years of work experience on entrance to the program.

FACILITIES
Information Resources Main library with 531,744 bound volumes, 26,268 titles on microform, 1,833 periodical subscriptions, 9,775 records/tapes/CDs, 338 CD-ROMs.
Housing 2% of students in program live in college-owned or -operated housing.
Technology Computers are used moderately in course work. 194 computer terminals/PCs, linked by a campus-wide computer network, are available for use by students in program; they are located in student rooms, learning resource center, the library, the computer center, computer labs. Students in the program are not required to have their own PC.
Computer Resources/On-line Services

Training	Yes	CompuServe	Yes
Internet	Yes	Dun's	No
E-Mail	Yes	Dow Jones	Yes
Multimedia Center	Yes	Bloomberg	No
LEXIS/NEXIS	No		

Other on-line services: Carl.

ADMISSION
Acceptance 1994-95 Of those applying, 61% were accepted.
Entrance Requirements Bachelor's degree, GMAT score of 500, minimum 2.5 GPA.
Application Requirements Application form, copies of transcript, resume/curriculum vitae, personal statement, 2 letters of recommendation.
Application Deadline Applications are processed on a rolling basis.

FINANCIALS
Costs for 1994-95 Tuition: Full-time: $295/hour. Fees: Full-time: $48.
Financial Aid In 1994-95, 14% of candidates received some institutionally administered aid in the form of assistantships. Total awards ranged from $5,400-$10,500. Financial aid is available to part-time students. Application deadlines: 3/1 for fall, 10/1 for spring. Contact: Ms. Judith Cole, Director of Graduate Admissions, 1501 West Bradley Avenue, Peoria, IL 61625. (309) 677-2371.

INTERNATIONAL STUDENTS
Demographics 8% of students enrolled in the program are international.
Services and Facilities International student center, ESL courses, counseling/support services.
Applying TOEFL required, minimum score of 525; proof of health; proof of adequate funds. Financial aid is available to international students. Financial aid application deadlines: 3/1 for fall, 10/1 for spring. Admission application deadlines: 3/1 for fall, 10/1 for spring.

PLACEMENT
Placement services include alumni network, career fairs, career library, job interviews, resume preparation, and resume referral to employers.

Program Contact: Graduate School Office, Bradley University, 118 Bradley Hall, Peoria, IL 61625. (309) 677-3215; Fax: (309) 677-3374.

College of St. Francis

Joliet, Illinois

OVERVIEW
College of St. Francis is an independent Roman Catholic comprehensive coed institution. Founded 1920. Setting: 16-acre suburban campus with easy access to Chicago. Total institutional enrollment: 3,379. Program was first offered in 1993.

MBA HIGHLIGHTS

Entrance Difficulty***
Mean GMAT: N/R
Mean GPA: 3.0

Cost $
Tuition: $285/semester hour
Room & Board: N/R

Enrollment Profile

Full-time: 0		Work Exp: 100%
Part-time: 48		International: N/R
Total: 48		Women: 50%
Average Age: 30		Minorities: 3%

Average Class Size: 15

ACADEMICS
Length of Program Minimum: 36 months. Maximum: 8 years.
Calendar Trimesters.
Part-time Classes Main campus; evening, weekends, summer.
Degree Requirements 36 semester hours including 12 elective semester hours.
Required Courses Business research, management theory, managerial accounting, managerial economics, managerial financing, marketing management. Courses may be waived through: previous course work, work experience.
Curricular Focus Business issues and problems, general management, leadership.
Concentration Management.
Faculty Full-time: 3, 100% with doctorates; part-time: 3, 66% with doctorates.
Teaching Methodology Case study: 20%, faculty seminars: 10%, lecture: 20%, research: 20%, student presentations: 20%, team projects: 10%.

STUDENT STATISTICS
Geographic Representation State residents 3%. By region: Midwest 100%.
Undergraduate Majors Business 95%; engineering/technology 5%.

FACILITIES
Information Resources Main library with 192,000 bound volumes, 185,384 titles on microform, 525 periodical subscriptions, 6,851 records/tapes/CDs, 40 CD-ROMs. Business collection includes 50,000 bound volumes, 52 periodical subscriptions, 2 CD-ROMs, 203 videos.
Housing College housing available.
Technology Computers are used heavily in course work. 120 computer terminals/PCs, linked by a campus-wide computer network, are available for use by students in program; they are located in dormitories, classrooms, the library, the computer center, computer labs. Students in the program are not required to have their own PC.
Computer Resources/On-line Services

Training	Yes	Videoconference Center	Yes
Internet	Yes	Multimedia Center	Yes
E-Mail	Yes	CompuServe	Yes

ADMISSION
Acceptance 1994-95 Of those applying, 80% were accepted.
Entrance Requirements Bachelor's degree, GMAT score, minimum 2.75 GPA, minimum 2 years of work experience. Core courses waived through: previous course work, work experience.
Application Requirements Written essay, interview, application form, copies of transcript, personal statement, 2 letters of recommendation.
Application Deadlines 8/30 for fall, 12/15 for spring, 4/10 for summer.

FINANCIALS
Costs for 1994-95 Tuition: Part-time evening: $285/semester hour.
Financial Aid Contact: Mr. Bruce Foote, Director, 500 North Wilcox Street, Joliet, IL 60435-6188. (815) 740-3403.

INTERNATIONAL STUDENTS
Applying TOEFL required; proof of health; proof of adequate funds.

PLACEMENT
Placement services include alumni network, career counseling/planning, career placement, and resume preparation.

Program Contact: Dr. Michael V. LaRocco, Coordinator of Graduate Business Programs, College of St. Francis, 500 North Wilcox Street, Joliet, IL 60435-6188. (815) 740-3478, or (800) 735-4723; Fax: (815) 740-3537.

DePaul University

Kellstadt Graduate School of Business

Chicago, Illinois

OVERVIEW
DePaul University is an independent Roman Catholic coed institution. Founded 1898. Setting: 36-acre urban campus. Total institutional enrollment: 16,747. Program was first offered in 1948. AACSB-accredited.

MBA HIGHLIGHTS

Entrance Difficulty***
Mean GMAT: 540
Mean GPA: 3.15

Cost $$
Tuition: $1,540/course
Room & Board: N/R

Enrollment Profile
Full-time: 0
Part-time: 2,574
Total: 2,574
Average Age: 29

Work Exp: 87%
International: 2%
Women: 43%
Minorities: 9%

Average Class Size: 29

DePaul University's Kellstadt Graduate School of Business enjoys a worldwide reputation for excellence and innovation. The eighteen-month M.B.A. in International Marketing & Finance (M.B.A./IMF) is the prime example of Kellstadt's leading-edge approach to graduate business education. This one-of-a-kind program utilizes an elite network of business partners worldwide along with an international business practicum to give students a competitive advantage.

DePaul Center, right in the heart of Chicago's dynamic financial center, is a state-of-the-art learning environment. DePaul's relationship with Chicago is extraordinary, which is why it has been called "Chicago's University." The University's networks and partnerships in every aspect of the city are unmatched in number and importance. Of course, Chicago itself is reason enough to consider Kellstadt. As the nation's third-largest city, it is a commercial and cultural hub, more affordable and more manageable than most large cities.

The bottom line, the fundamental reason for choosing Kellstadt is its powerful faculty. The 114 full-time faculty members are consistently cited regionally and nationally for their views on current business issues. Over 200 adjunct faculty members, recognized as experts in virtually every aspect of business, create an unparalleled practical advantage in the classroom.

ACADEMICS
Length of Program Minimum: 24 months.
Calendar Quarters.
Degree Requirements 60 credits. Other: Competency in one foreign language for concentration in international marketing and finance.
Required Courses Business conditions analysis, decisions in marketing management, economics for decision making, effective communication, financial accounting, financial institutions and markets, financial management, global economy, legal and ethical environment, management accounting and decision making, management of information technology, managing people, money and banking, operations management.
Concentrations Accounting, economics, entrepreneurship, finance, human resources management, international business, management information systems, marketing, operations management.
Faculty Full-time: 107; part-time: 70.

STUDENT STATISTICS
Geographic Representation State residents 89%. By region: Midwest 99%.
Undergraduate Majors Business 60%; engineering/technology 6%; humanities 5%; science/mathematics 6%; social sciences 2%; other 21%.

FACILITIES
Information Resources Main library with 659,605 bound volumes, 298,899 titles on microform, 16,804 periodical subscriptions, 13,000 records/tapes/CDs, 60 CD-ROMs.
Housing College housing not available.
Technology Computers are used moderately in course work. Computer terminals/PCs, linked by a campus-wide computer network, are available for use by students in program; they are located in classrooms, the library, the computer center, computer labs. Students in the program are not required to have their own PC.
Computer Resources/On-line Services
Videoconference Center   Yes

ADMISSION
Acceptance 1994-95 759 applied for admission; 68% were accepted.
Entrance Requirements Bachelor's degree, GMAT score. Core courses waived through: previous course work.
Application Requirements Application form, copies of transcript, resume/curriculum vitae.
Application Deadlines 8/1 for fall, 11/1 for winter, 3/1 for spring, 5/1 for summer.

FINANCIALS
Costs for 1994-95 Tuition: Part-time evening: $1,540/course.
Financial Aid In 1994-95, candidates received some institutionally administered aid in the form of loans, assistantships. Financial aid is available to part-time students. Applications are processed on a rolling basis. Contact: Office of Financial Aid, Ninth Floor, DePaul Center, Chicago, IL 60604. (312) 362-8091.

INTERNATIONAL STUDENTS
Demographics 2% of students enrolled in the program are international.
Applying TOEFL required; proof of adequate funds. Financial aid is available to international students. Applications are processed on a rolling basis. Contact: International Adviser, Room 9100, 1 East Jackson Boulevard, Chicago, IL 60404. (312) 362-8300.

PLACEMENT
Placement services include career counseling/planning, career fairs, career library, career placement, and resume preparation.

Program Contact: Ms. Christine Munoz, Director of Admissions, DePaul University, 1 East Jackson Boulevard, Chicago, IL 60604. (312) 362-8810; Fax: (312) 362-6677.
See full description on page 718.

Eastern Illinois University

Lumpkin College of Business and Applied Sciences

Charleston, Illinois

OVERVIEW
Eastern Illinois University is a state-supported comprehensive coed institution. Part of Board of Governors Universities. Founded 1895. Setting: 320-acre small-town campus. Total institutional enrollment: 10,000.

MBA HIGHLIGHTS

Entrance Difficulty**
Mean GMAT: 495
Mean GPA: 3.2

Cost $
Tuition: $2,004
(Nonresident: $6,012)
Room & Board: $5,200

Enrollment Profile
Full-time: 33
Part-time: 83
Total: 138
Average Age: 26

Work Exp: 20%
International: 16%
Women: 38%
Minorities: 2%

Average Class Size: 25

ACADEMICS
Length of Program Minimum: 12 months. Maximum: 6 years.
Calendar Semesters.
Full-time Classes Main campus; evening, summer.
Part-time Classes Main campus, Parkland College; evening, summer.
Degree Requirements 33 credits.
Curricular Focus General management.
Concentration Management.
Faculty Full-time: 33, 100% with doctorates.
Teaching Methodology Case study: 30%, lecture: 40%, team projects: 30%.
Special Opportunities Internship program available.

STUDENT STATISTICS
Geographic Representation State residents 84%. By region: Midwest 84%. International 16%.
Other Background Graduate degrees in other disciplines: 5%. Work experience: On average, students have 2 years of work experience on entrance to the program.

FACILITIES
Information Resources Main library with 959,251 bound volumes, 15,500 titles on microform, 2,758 periodical subscriptions, 18,736 records/tapes/CDs, 16 CD-ROMs.
Housing 15% of students in program live in college-owned or -operated housing.
Technology Computers are used heavily in course work. Computer terminals/PCs, linked by a campus-wide computer network, are available for use by students in program; they are located in classrooms, learning resource center, the library, the computer center, computer labs. Students in the program are not required to have their own PC.

Computer Resources/On-line Services

Training	Yes	E-Mail	Yes
Internet	Yes		

ADMISSION
Acceptance 1994-95 Of those applying, 85% were accepted.
Entrance Requirements Bachelor's degree, GMAT score.
Application Requirements Application form, copies of transcript, resume/curriculum vitae, personal statement, 2 letters of recommendation.
Application Deadlines 7/1 for fall, 12/1 for spring, 4/15 for summer.

FINANCIALS
Costs for 1994-95 Tuition: Full-time: $2,004 for state residents, $6,012 for nonresidents. Fees: Full-time: $782 for state residents, $782 for nonresidents. Average room and board costs are $5,200 per academic year (on-campus).
Financial Aid In 1994-95, candidates received some institutionally administered aid in the form of assistantships. Application deadlines: 7/1 for fall, 11/1 for spring. Contact: Mr. John Flynn, Director of Financial Aid, 600 Lincoln Avenue, Charleston, IL 61920-3099. (217) 581-3713.

INTERNATIONAL STUDENTS
Demographics 16% of students enrolled in the program are international; Europe 54%, Asia 38%, Africa 8%.
Services and Facilities International student housing; international student center, language tutoring, counseling/support services.
Applying TOEFL required, minimum score of 550; proof of health; proof of adequate funds. Financial aid is available to international students. Financial aid application deadline: 3/1 for fall. Admission application deadlines: 6/15 for fall, 10/15 for spring, 4/1 for summer. Contact: Ms. Brigette Chen, International Student Adviser, 600 Lincoln Avenue, Charleston, IL 61920-3099. (217) 581-2321.

Program Contact: Mr. Michael Wilson, Coordinator of Graduate Business Studies, Eastern Illinois University, 600 Lincoln Avenue, Charleston, IL 61920-3099. (217) 581-3028; Fax: (217) 581-6642; Internet Address: cfmdwl@eiu.edu.

Governors State University

College of Business and Public Administration

University Park, Illinois

OVERVIEW
Governors State University is a state-supported upper-level coed institution. Part of Board of Governors Universities. Founded 1969. Setting: 750-acre urban campus with easy access to Chicago. Total institutional enrollment: 5,553. Program was first offered in 1971.

MBA HIGHLIGHTS

Entrance Difficulty**
Mean GMAT: 450
Mean GPA: 3.25

Cost $
Tuition: $1,038/trimester
(Nonresident: $3,114/trimester)
Room & Board: $5,000 (off-campus)

Enrollment Profile
Full-time: 11
Part-time: 139
Total: 150
Average Age: 33

Work Exp: 90%
International: 6%
Women: 38%
Minorities: 29%

Average Class Size: 12

ACADEMICS
Length of Program Minimum: 12 months. Maximum: 7 years.
Calendar Trimesters.
Full-time Classes Main campus, Orland Park; day, evening, weekends, summer.
Part-time Classes Main campus, Orland Park; day, evening, weekends, summer.
Degree Requirements 33 credits including 9 elective credits. Other: Minimum 3.0 GPA; written communication and intermediate algebra proficiency requirements.
Required Courses Accounting for administrative control, business policy and strategy, issues in public and private management, problems in financial management, problems in managerial economics, problems in marketing management, problems in organizational behavior, problems in production management.
Curricular Focus General management, problem solving and decision making, teamwork.
Concentrations Accounting, finance, human resources management, international business, management, management information systems, marketing, production management, public administration.
Faculty Full-time: 12, 83% with doctorates; part-time: 1, 100% with doctorates.
Teaching Methodology Case study: 10%, field experience/practical application: 10%, lecture: 35%, research: 10%, seminars by members of the business community: 10%, student presentations: 10%, team projects: 15%.
Special Opportunities International exchange in Egypt, Germany. Internships include business management, accounting, finance, marketing, management information systems, and public administration.

STUDENT STATISTICS
Geographic Representation State residents 94%. By region: Midwest 94%. International 6%.

FACILITIES
Information Resources Main library with 237,000 bound volumes, 630,800 titles on microform, 2,200 periodical subscriptions, 9,000 records/tapes/CDs.
Housing College housing not available.
Technology Computers are used moderately in course work. 69 computer terminals/PCs, linked by a campus-wide computer network, are available for use by students in program; they are located in the computer center, computer labs. Students in the program are not required to have their own PC.

Computer Resources/On-line Services

Training	Yes	Videoconference Center	Yes
Internet	Yes	Multimedia Center	Yes
E-Mail	Yes	Dialog	Yes

Other on-line services: Datastar, Westlaw, Carl.

ADMISSION

Acceptance 1994-95 60 applied for admission; 43% were accepted.

Entrance Requirements Bachelor's degree, prerequisite courses required for applicants with non-business degree, GMAT score. Core courses waived through: previous course work.

Application Requirements Application form, copies of transcript.

Application Deadlines 7/10 for fall, 11/15 for spring. Applications are processed on a rolling basis.

FINANCIALS

Costs for 1995-96 Tuition: Full-time: $1,038/trimester for state residents, $3,114/trimester for nonresidents. Fees: Full-time: $65-$100/trimester for nonresidents. Average room and board costs are $5,000 per academic year (off-campus).

Financial Aid In 1994-95, 50% of candidates received some institutionally administered aid in the form of grants, scholarships, assistantships, work-study, tuition waivers. Total awards ranged from $3,742-$7,484. Financial aid is available to part-time students. Application deadlines: 5/1 for fall, 10/1 for spring, 2/13 for summer. Applications are processed on a rolling basis. Contact: Mr. David Weinberger, Financial Aid Adviser, University Parkway, University Park, IL 60466. (708) 534-4480.

INTERNATIONAL STUDENTS

Demographics 6% of students enrolled in the program are international; Asia 45%, Africa 22%, Central America 11%, Europe 11%, North America 11%.

Services and Facilities International student office, visa services, language tutoring, ESL courses, counseling/support services, housing/transportation assistance.

Applying TOEFL required, minimum score of 550; proof of health; proof of adequate funds; F-1 visa. Financial aid is available to international students. Financial aid application deadlines: 6/30 for fall, 11/15 for spring. Applications are processed on a rolling basis. Admission application deadlines: 6/30 for fall, 11/15 for spring. Contact: Dr. Patricia Carter, Dean of Student Affairs, University Parkway, University Park, IL 60466. (708) 534-4045.

PLACEMENT

In 1993-94, 18 organizations participated in on-campus recruiting; 12 on-campus interviews were conducted. Placement services include career counseling/planning, career fairs, career library, career placement, electronic job bank, job interviews, job search course, resume preparation, and resume referral to employers.

Jobs by Employer Type Manufacturing 30%; service 45%; government 20%; nonprofit 5%.

Jobs by Functional Area Marketing/sales 35%; finance 25%; operations 20%; management 20%.

Program Contact: Ms. Judith Gustawson, Coordinator of Academic Advising, Governors State University, University Parkway, University Park, IL 60466. (708) 534-4390; Fax: (708) 534-8457; Internet Address: j-gustaw@acs.gsu.bgu.edu.

Illinois Benedictine College

Lisle, Illinois

OVERVIEW

Illinois Benedictine College is an independent Roman Catholic comprehensive coed institution. Founded 1887. Setting: 108-acre suburban campus with easy access to Chicago. Total institutional enrollment: 2,600. Program was first offered in 1976.

MBA HIGHLIGHTS

Entrance Difficulty**
Mean GMAT: 475
Mean GPA: 2.8

Cost $$
Tuition: $245/credit hour
Room & Board: N/R

Enrollment Profile

Full-time: 50		Work Exp: 99%
Part-time: 330		International: 5%
Total: 380		Women: 40%
Average Age: 35		Minorities: 5%

Average Class Size: 20

ACADEMICS

Length of Program Minimum: 24 months. Maximum: 6 years.

Calendar Quarters.

Full-time Classes Main campus; evening, weekends.

Part-time Classes Main campus; evening, weekends.

Degree Requirements 64 credit hours including 16 elective credit hours.

Required Courses Business statistics, economics, ethical and legal issues, financial accounting, financial management, information technology management, managerial accounting, managerial economics, marketing management, operations management, organizational behavior, strategic management. Courses may be waived through: previous course work, work experience.

Curricular Focus General management, organizational development and change management, problem solving and decision making.

Concentrations Finance, health services, human resources management, international business, management, management information systems, marketing, operations management, organizational behavior, organizational development, management in a technical environment, public administration.

Faculty Full-time: 5, 80% with doctorates; part-time: 20, 50% with doctorates.

Teaching Methodology Case study: 40%, lecture: 10%, student presentations: 10%, team projects: 40%.

STUDENT STATISTICS

Geographic Representation State residents 100%. By region: Midwest 100%. International 5%.

Undergraduate Majors Business 40%; engineering/technology 10%; humanities 15%; science/mathematics 20%; social sciences 15%.

Other Background Graduate degrees in other disciplines: 10%. Work experience: On average, students have 8 years of work experience on entrance to the program.

FACILITIES

Information Resources Main library with 164,079 bound volumes, 114,183 titles on microform, 700 periodical subscriptions, 10,984 records/tapes/CDs, 150 CD-ROMs.

Housing College housing not available.

Technology Computers are used moderately in course work. 35 computer terminals/PCs, linked by a campus-wide computer network, are available for use by students in program; they are located in computer labs. Students in the program are not required to have their own PC.

Computer Resources/On-line Services

Training	Yes	CompuServe	No
Internet	Yes	Dun's	No
E-Mail	No	Dow Jones	No
Videoconference Center	Yes	Dialog	No
LEXIS/NEXIS	No	Bloomberg	No

ADMISSION

Acceptance 1994-95 Of those applying, 90% were accepted.

Entrance Requirements Bachelor's degree, GMAT score of 400, minimum 2.0 GPA. Core courses waived through: previous course work, work experience.

Application Requirements Written essay, application form, copies of transcript, 2 letters of recommendation.

Application Deadline Applications are processed on a rolling basis.

FINANCIALS

Costs for 1994-95 Tuition: Full-time: $245/credit hour.

Financial Aid In 1994-95, candidates received some institutionally administered aid in the form of loans. Financial aid is available to part-time students. Applications are processed on a rolling basis. Contact: Ms. Laura Day, Director of Financial Aid, 5700 College Road, Lisle, IL 60532-0900. (708) 960-1500.

INTERNATIONAL STUDENTS

Demographics 5% of students enrolled in the program are international.

Applying TOEFL required, minimum score of 600; proof of adequate funds. Financial aid is not available to international students. Admission applications are processed on a rolling basis.

ALTERNATE MBA PROGRAMS

MBA/MS Length of program: Minimum: 48 months. Degree requirements: 96 credits. MS is in management and organizational behavior, counseling psychology, or management information systems.

MBA/MPH Length of program: Minimum: 48 months. Degree requirements: 96 credits.

PLACEMENT

Placement services include alumni network, career counseling/planning, career fairs, career library, job interviews, resume preparation, and resume referral to employers.

Program Contact: Ms. Karen Swenson, Graduate Director, Admissions, Illinois Benedictine College, 5700 College Road, Lisle, IL 60532-0900. (708) 960-1500; Fax: (708) 960-1126.

Illinois Institute of Technology

Stuart School of Business

Chicago, Illinois

OVERVIEW

Illinois Institute of Technology is an independent nonprofit coed institution. Founded 1890. Setting: 120-acre urban campus. Total institutional enrollment: 7,027. Program was first offered in 1969.

MBA HIGHLIGHTS

Entrance Difficulty**
Mean GMAT: 500
Mean GPA: 2.87

Cost $$$
Tuition: $1,260/course
Room & Board: $6,000

Enrollment Profile

Full-time: 71	Work Exp: 75%
Part-time: 297	International: 17%
Total: 368	Women: 23%
Average Age: 30	Minorities: 18%

Class Size: 15 - 20

ACADEMICS

Length of Program Minimum: 24 months. Maximum: 6 years.

Calendar Quarters.

Full-time Classes Main campus, Schaumburg, Wheaton; evening, weekends, summer.

Part-time Classes Main campus, Schaumburg, Wheaton; evening, weekends, summer.

Degree Requirements 72 credits including 40 elective credits. Other: Minimum 2.0 GPA; Capstone course in business policy.

Required Courses Finance, financial accounting, international business, managerial economics, marketing, operations and technology management, organizational behavior, statistical methods. Courses may be waived through: previous course work.

Curricular Focus Organizational development and change management, problem solving and decision making, strategic analysis and planning.

Concentrations Finance, international business, management, management information systems, management science, technology management, quality management, marketing, operations management.

Faculty Full-time: 17, 90% with doctorates; part-time: 10, 40% with doctorates.

Teaching Methodology Case study: 30%, lecture: 50%, team projects: 20%.

STUDENT STATISTICS

Geographic Representation International 17%.

Other Background Graduate degrees in other disciplines: 5%. Work experience: On average, students have 5 years of work experience on entrance to the program.

FACILITIES

Information Resources Main library with 400,000 bound volumes, 175,500 titles on microform, 750 periodical subscriptions, 18 CD-ROMs. Business collection in Stuart School of Business Library includes 3,500 bound volumes, 600 periodical subscriptions, 11 CD-ROMs.

Housing College housing available.

Technology Computers are used moderately in course work. 120 computer terminals/PCs, linked by a campus-wide computer network, are available for use by students in program; they are located in the library, the computer center, computer labs. Students in the program are not required to have their own PC.

Computer Resources/On-line Services

Training	Yes	Dun's	No
Internet	Yes	Dow Jones	No
E-Mail	Yes	Dialog	Yes $
LEXIS/NEXIS	Yes $	Bloomberg	No
CompuServe	No		

ADMISSION

Acceptance 1994-95 Of those applying, 87% were accepted.

Entrance Requirements Bachelor's degree, GMAT score. Core courses waived through: previous course work.

Application Requirements Application form, copies of transcript, personal statement, 3 letters of recommendation.

Application Deadlines 7/1 for fall, 10/1 for winter, 1/1 for spring.

FINANCIALS

Costs for 1994-95 Tuition: Full-time: $1,260/course. Fees: Full-time: $20. Average room and board costs are $6,000 per academic year (on-campus) and $8,000 per academic year (off-campus).

Financial Aid In 1994-95, 10% of candidates received some institutionally administered aid in the form of scholarships. Total awards ranged from $3,000-$5,100. Financial aid is not available to part-time students. Application deadline: 3/1 for fall. Contact: Student Finance Center, 3300 South Federal Street, Chicago, IL 60616. (312) 567-3303.

INTERNATIONAL STUDENTS

Demographics 17% of students enrolled in the program are international.

Services and Facilities International student housing; international student center, counseling/support services.

Applying TOEFL required, minimum score of 500; proof of health; proof of adequate funds. Financial aid is not available to international students. Admission application deadlines: 6/30 for fall, 10/1 for winter, 12/1 for spring. Contact: Ms. Vanita Misquita, Director, International Office, 3300 South Michigan Avenue, Room 402, Chicago, IL 60616. (312) 808-7104.

ALTERNATE MBA PROGRAMS

MBA/JD Length of program: Minimum: 48 months. Maximum: 6 years. Degree requirements: 132 credits.

MBA/MS Length of program: Minimum: 36 months. Maximum: 6 years. Degree requirements: 112 quarter hours including 47 elective quarter hours. Minimum 2.0 GPA. MS is in financial markets and trading.

MBA/MPA Length of program: Minimum: 36 months. Maximum: 6 years. Degree requirements: 66 semester hours including 7.20 elective quarter hours.

PLACEMENT

In 1993-94, 45 organizations participated in on-campus recruiting; 50 on-campus interviews were conducted. Placement services include alumni network, career counseling/planning, career fairs, career library, career placement, electronic job bank, job interviews, resume preparation, and resume referral to employers. Of 1994 graduates, 95% were employed within three months of graduation.

Program Contact: Ms. Lynn Miller, Director, MBA Marketing and Admission, Illinois Institute of Technology, IIT Center, Chicago, IL 60616. (312) 906-6544, or (800) MBA-NEXT (out-of-state); Fax: (312) 906-6549.
See full description on page 758.

Illinois State University

Normal, Illinois

OVERVIEW
Illinois State University is a state-supported coed institution. Founded 1857. Setting: 850-acre urban campus. Total institutional enrollment: 20,000. Program was first offered in 1977. AACSB-accredited.

MBA HIGHLIGHTS

Entrance Difficulty*
Mean GMAT: 545
Mean GPA: 3.26

Cost $
Tuition: $1,113 - $1,459/semester
(Nonresident: $2,690 - $3,563/semester)
Room & Board: $3,600

Enrollment Profile

Full-time: 61	Work Exp: 65%
Part-time: 138	International: 15%
Total: 199	Women: 26%
Average Age: 30	Minorities: 9%

Average Class Size: 22

ACADEMICS
Length of Program Minimum: 15 months. Maximum: 6 years.
Calendar Semesters.
Full-time Classes Main campus; day, evening, summer.
Part-time Classes Main campus, Clinton; day, evening, weekends, summer.
Degree Requirements 39 credits including 9 elective credits.
Required Courses Advanced marketing management, advanced quantitative methods, analysis of organizational behavior, business problems and policy, economic analysis for business decisions, financial management, legal aspects of business decisions, management accounting, management information systems, research methodology.
Curricular Focus Business issues and problems, general management, problem solving and decision making.
Concentrations Accounting, finance, insurance, agribusiness, international business, management, marketing, organizational behavior.
Faculty Full-time: 62, 100% with doctorates.
Teaching Methodology Case study: 20%, lecture: 20%, research: 20%, student presentations: 20%, team projects: 20%.
Special Opportunities Internships include human resources, finance, marketing, and management information systems. Other: summer study abroad.

STUDENT STATISTICS
Geographic Representation State residents 71%. International 15%.

FACILITIES
Information Resources Main library with 1.3 million bound volumes, 1.8 million titles on microform, 9,589 periodical subscriptions, 30,024 records/tapes/CDs.
Housing College housing available.
Technology Computers are used moderately in course work. Computer terminals/PCs, linked by a campus-wide computer network, are available for use by students in program; they are located in dormitories, classrooms, the library, the computer center, computer labs. Students in the program are not required to have their own PC.

Computer Resources/On-line Services

Training	Yes	E-Mail	Yes

ADMISSION
Entrance Requirements Bachelor's degree, prerequisite courses required for applicants with non-business degree, GMAT score, minimum 2.75 GPA. Core courses waived through: previous course work.
Application Requirements Written essay, application form, copies of transcript, resume/curriculum vitae, personal statement, 2 letters of recommendation.
Application Deadlines 3/15 for fall, 11/15 for spring. Applications are processed on a rolling basis.

FINANCIALS
Costs for 1994-95 Tuition: Full-time: $789-$1,051/semester for state residents, $2,366-$3,155/semester for nonresidents; Part-time day: $263-$526/semester for state residents, $789-$1,577/semester for nonresidents. Fees: Full-time: $324-$408/semester for state residents, $324-$408/semester for nonresidents; Part-time day: $83-$167/semester for state residents, $83-$167/semester for nonresidents. Average room and board costs are $3,600 per academic year (on-campus) and $3,000 per academic year (off-campus).
Financial Aid Total awards ranged from $256-$9,323. Financial aid is available to part-time students. Application deadlines: 3/15 for fall, 11/15 for spring. Applications are processed on a rolling basis. Contact: Ms. Linda L. Maxwell, Director of Financial Aid, Normal, IL 61761. (309) 438-2231.

INTERNATIONAL STUDENTS
Demographics 15% of students enrolled in the program are international.
Services and Facilities International student office, international student center, ESL courses, counseling/support services.
Applying TOEFL required, minimum score of 600; proof of health; proof of adequate funds. Financial aid is available to international students. Financial aid application deadlines: 5/15 for fall, 10/15 for spring, 4/1 for summer. Applications are processed on a rolling basis. Admission application deadlines: 5/15 for fall, 10/15 for spring, 4/1 for summer. Applications are processed on a rolling basis. Contact: Ms. Sara Jome, Coordinator, Foreign Student and Scholar Services, International Studies, Campus Box 6120, Normal, IL 61790-6120. (309) 438-5365.

PLACEMENT
Placement services include alumni network, career counseling/planning, career fairs, career library, career placement, job interviews, resume preparation, and resume referral to employers.

Program Contact: Dr. Dixie Mills, Director of MBA Program and Research, Illinois State University, Campus Box 5500, Normal, IL 61790-5500. (309) 438-8388; Fax: (309) 438-5510.

Keller Graduate School of Management

Oak Brook Terrace, Illinois

OVERVIEW
Keller Graduate School of Management is graduate-only institution. Total institutional enrollment: 2,495.

ACADEMICS
Degree Requirements 64 credits.
Concentrations Accounting, finance, human resources management, management, management information systems, marketing, project management.

ADMISSION
Entrance Requirements Bachelor's degree.
Application Requirements Interview, application form, copies of transcript.

FINANCIALS
Financial Aid Contact: Mr. Miguel Sopena, Financial Aid Specialist, 1 Tower Lane, Oak Brook Terrace, IL 60181. (708) 571-7700 Ext. 1985.

Program Contact: Dr. Patrick Mayers, Vice President of Academic Affairs, Keller Graduate School of Management, 1 Tower Lane, Oak Brook Terrace, IL 60181. (708) 571-7700 Ext. 1961.

Lake Forest Graduate School of Management

Lake Forest, Illinois

OVERVIEW
Lake Forest Graduate School of Management is graduate-only institution. Total institutional enrollment: 660.

MBA HIGHLIGHTS

Entrance Difficulty N/R

Cost $$
Tuition: $1,400/course
Room & Board: N/R

Enrollment Profile

Full-time: N/R	Work Exp: N/R
Part-time: N/R	International: N/R
Total: 660	Women: 35%
Average Age: N/R	Minorities: N/R

Average Class Size: N/R

ACADEMICS

Degree Requirements 16 courses.

Concentrations Finance, international business, management information systems, marketing, organizational development, strategic management.

FACILITIES

Information Resources Main library with 250,000 bound volumes.

ADMISSION

Entrance Requirements GMAT score, minimum 4 years of work experience.

Application Requirements Interview, application form, copies of transcript, 1 letter of recommendation.

Application Deadline Applications are processed on a rolling basis.

FINANCIALS

Costs for 1994-95 Tuition: Part-time day: $1,400/course.

Program Contact: Ms. Carolyn Brune, Director of Admissions, Lake Forest Graduate School of Management, 280 North Sheridan Road, Lake Forest, IL 60045. (708) 234-5080; Fax: (708) 295-3656.

Lewis University

Graduate School of Management

Romeoville, Illinois

OVERVIEW

Lewis University is an independent comprehensive coed institution, affiliated with Roman Catholic Church. Founded 1932. Setting: 600-acre suburban campus with easy access to Chicago. Total institutional enrollment: 4,400. Program was first offered in 1979.

MBA HIGHLIGHTS

Entrance Difficulty**
Mean GMAT: 480
Mean GPA: 2.97

Cost $$
Tuition: $348/hour
Room & Board: $7,290

Enrollment Profile

Full-time: 31	Work Exp: 97%
Part-time: 593	International: 7%
Total: 624	Women: 33%
Average Age: 34	Minorities: 35%

Average Class Size: 28

ACADEMICS

Length of Program Minimum: 24 months. Maximum: 5 years.

Calendar Semesters.

Full-time Classes Main campus, Oak Brook, Schaumburg, Naperville, Orland Park; evening, weekends, summer.

Part-time Classes Main campus, Oak Brook, Schaumburg, Naperville, Orland Park; evening, weekends, summer.

Degree Requirements 36 credits including 6 elective credits.

Required Courses Legal and social foundation for business, managerial accounting, managerial communication, managerial economics, managerial finance, marketing management, strategic management. Courses may be waived through: previous course work.

Curricular Focus Business issues and problems, problem solving and decision making, strategic analysis and planning.

Concentrations Finance, healthcare management, human resources management, management information systems, marketing, operations management.

Faculty Full-time: 20, 60% with doctorates; part-time: 32, 5% with doctorates.

Teaching Methodology Case study: 20%, faculty seminars: 5%, lecture: 30%, research: 5%, seminars by members of the business community: 10%, student presentations: 10%, team projects: 20%.

STUDENT STATISTICS

Geographic Representation State residents 93%. By region: Midwest 93%. International 7%.

Undergraduate Majors Business 54%; education 1%; engineering/technology 14%; humanities 4%; nursing 3%; science/mathematics 12%; social sciences 9%; other 3%.

Other Background Graduate degrees in other disciplines: 2%. Work experience: On average, students have 6 years of work experience on entrance to the program.

FACILITIES

Information Resources Main library with 163,040 bound volumes, 23,998 titles on microform, 593 periodical subscriptions, 1,164 records/tapes/CDs.

Housing 7% of students in program live in college-owned or -operated housing.

Technology Computers are used heavily in course work. 35 computer terminals/PCs are available for use by students in program; they are located in the library, the computer center, computer labs. Students in the program are not required to have their own PC. $125 are budgeted per student for computer support.

Computer Resources/On-line Services

Training	Yes	E-Mail	No
Internet	Yes	Multimedia Center	Yes

ADMISSION

Acceptance 1994-95 Of those applying, 88% were accepted.

Entrance Requirements Bachelor's degree, GMAT score. Core courses waived through: previous course work.

Application Requirements Application form, copies of transcript, personal statement.

Application Deadline Applications are processed on a rolling basis.

FINANCIALS

Costs for 1994-95 Tuition: Full-time: $348/hour. Average room and board costs are $7,290 per academic year (on-campus).

Financial Aid In 1994-95, 6% of candidates received some institutionally administered aid in the form of grants, loans. Financial aid is available to part-time students. Applications are processed on a rolling basis. Contact: Ms. Sally Floyd, Director, Route 53, Romeoville, IL 60441-2298. (815) 838-0500 Ext. 263.

INTERNATIONAL STUDENTS

Demographics 7% of students enrolled in the program are international; Asia 57%, South America 43%.

Services and Facilities International student center, visa services, language tutoring, ESL courses, special assistance for nonnative speakers of English, counseling/support services.

Applying TOEFL required. Financial aid is not available to international students. Admission applications are processed on a rolling basis. Contact: Mr. Monty Salyer, Director, Route 53, Romeoville, IL 60441-2298. (815) 838-0500 Ext. 635.

PLACEMENT

In 1993-94, 63 organizations participated in on-campus recruiting. Placement services include alumni network, career counseling/planning, career fairs, career library, career placement, electronic job bank, job interviews, resume preparation, and resume referral to employers. Of 1994 graduates, 96% were employed within three months of graduation, the average starting salary was $26,500, the range was $24,900-$58,500.

Jobs by Employer Type Manufacturing 53%; service 37%; government 6%; consulting 2%; nonprofit 2%.

Jobs by Functional Area Marketing/sales 25%; finance 10%; operations 10%; management 52%; technical management 3%.

Program Contact: Mr. Brad Pearson, Assistant Director, Lewis University, Route 53, Romeoville, IL 60441. (815) 838-0500 Ext. 348; Fax: (815) 838-3330.

Loyola University Chicago

Graduate School of Business

Chicago, Illinois

OVERVIEW
Loyola University Chicago is an independent Roman Catholic (Jesuit) coed institution. Founded 1870. Setting: 105-acre urban campus. Total institutional enrollment: 14,000. Program was first offered in 1965. AACSB-accredited.

MBA HIGHLIGHTS

Entrance Difficulty***
Mean GMAT: 550
Mean GPA: 3.2

Cost $$$$
Tuition: $1,505/course
Room & Board: $5,600

Enrollment Profile
Full-time: 126
Part-time: 767
Total: 893
Average Age: 26

Work Exp: 97%
International: 8%
Women: 36%
Minorities: 9%

Average Class Size: 29

ACADEMICS
Length of Program Minimum: 12 months. Maximum: 5 years.
Calendar Quarters.
Full-time Classes Main campus; evening.
Part-time Classes Main campus; evening.
Degree Requirements 54 semester hours including 24-27 elective semester hours.
Required Courses Business ethics, financial accounting, financial management, foundation of business modeling, international elective, management, managerial economics, managerial statistics, marketing management, operations management, strategy and organization. Courses may be waived through: previous course work.
Curricular Focus Economic and financial theory, minorities in business, problem solving and decision making, strategic analysis and planning.
Concentrations Accounting, economics, finance, health services, international business, management, management information systems, marketing, operations management.
Faculty Full-time: 98, 97% with doctorates; part-time: 3, 67% with doctorates.
Teaching Methodology Case study: 30%, lecture: 45%, seminars by members of the business community: 2%, student presentations: 3%, team projects: 20%.
Special Opportunities International exchange in Italy. Internships include state and federal government.

STUDENT STATISTICS
Geographic Representation State residents 75%. International 8%.
Undergraduate Majors Business 50%; education 3%; engineering/technology 7%; humanities 20%; nursing 3%; science/mathematics 5%; social sciences 12%.
Other Background Graduate degrees in other disciplines: 1%. Work experience: On average, students have 3 years of work experience on entrance to the program.

FACILITIES
Information Resources Main library with 1.3 million bound volumes, 1.2 million titles on microform, 11,545 periodical subscriptions. Business collection includes 43,000 bound volumes, 700 periodical subscriptions, 8 CD-ROMs, 244 videos.
Housing 1% of students in program live in college-owned or -operated housing.
Technology Computers are used moderately in course work. 95 computer terminals/PCs, linked by a campus-wide computer network, are available for use by students in program; they are located in the library, the computer center, computer labs. Students in the program are not required to have their own PC.

Computer Resources/On-line Services

Training	Yes	LEXIS/NEXIS	Yes
Internet	Yes	Dialog	Yes
E-Mail	Yes		

Other on-line services: First Search, OCLC, Carl.

ADMISSION
Acceptance 1994-95 489 applied for admission; 61% were accepted.
Entrance Requirements Bachelor's degree, GMAT score. Core courses waived through: previous course work.
Application Requirements Application form, copies of transcript, resume/curriculum vitae, 3 letters of recommendation.
Application Deadlines 8/1 for fall, 10/1 for winter, 1/1 for spring.

FINANCIALS
Costs for 1995-96 Tuition: Full-time: $1,505/course. Fees: Full-time: $20/quarter. Average room and board costs are $5,600 per academic year (on-campus) and $6,000 per academic year (off-campus).
Financial Aid In 1994-95, 40% of candidates received some institutionally administered aid in the form of loans, assistantships. Financial aid is available to part-time students. Application deadlines: 6/1 for fall, 8/1 for winter, 10/1 for spring. Contact: Ms. Anne McBride, Assistant Director, 820 North Michigan Avenue, Chicago, IL 60611-2196. (312) 915-6639.

INTERNATIONAL STUDENTS
Demographics 8% of students enrolled in the program are international; Asia 18%, Europe 14%, Africa 8%, Central America 6%, South America 6%, Australia 2%, other 46%.
Services and Facilities International student center, visa services, ESL courses.
Applying TOEFL required, minimum score of 550; proof of health; proof of adequate funds. Financial aid is not available to international students. Admission application deadlines: 6/15 for fall, 9/1 for winter, 10/15 for spring. Contact: Ms. Camille Steber, Assistant Director, International Services and Programs, 6455 North Sheridan Road, Chicago, IL 60626. (312) 508-3950.

ALTERNATE MBA PROGRAMS
MBA/JD Length of program: Minimum: 48 months. Maximum: 5 years. Degree requirements: 122 quarter hours including 67 elective quarter hours.
MBA/MSN Length of program: Minimum: 30 months. Maximum: 5 years. Degree requirements: 76 semester hours including 24 elective semester hours.

PLACEMENT
In 1993-94, 23 organizations participated in on-campus recruiting; 141 on-campus interviews were conducted. Placement services include alumni network, career counseling/planning, career fairs, career library, career placement, electronic job bank, resume preparation, and resume referral to employers. Of 1994 graduates, 60% were employed within three months of graduation, the average starting salary was $41,791, the range was $23,000-$90,000.
Jobs by Employer Type Manufacturing 6%; service 69%; government 4%; consulting 9%; nonprofit 5%; real estate 7%.
Jobs by Functional Area Marketing/sales 24%; finance 44%; operations 5%; management 12%; strategic planning 3%; other 12%.

Program Contact: Ms. Carmen Santiago, Admissions Coordinator, Loyola University Chicago, 820 North Michigan Avenue, Chicago, IL 60611-2196. (312) 915-6120; Fax: (312) 915-7207.
See full description on page 778.

North Central College

Department of Business Administration

Naperville, Illinois

OVERVIEW
North Central College is an independent United Methodist comprehensive coed institution. Founded 1861. Setting: 56-acre suburban campus with easy access to Chicago. Total institutional enrollment: 2,500. Program was first offered in 1988.

MBA HIGHLIGHTS

Entrance Difficulty***
Mean GMAT: 450
Mean GPA: 2.8

Cost $$
Tuition: $1,189/course
Room & Board: N/R

Enrollment Profile
Full-time: 3
Part-time: 225
Total: 228
Average Age: 34

Work Exp: 100%
International: 3%
Women: 35%
Minorities: 5%

Average Class Size: 14

ACADEMICS

Length of Program Minimum: 18 months. Maximum: 5 years.
Calendar Quarters.
Full-time Classes Main campus; evening, weekends, summer.
Part-time Classes Main campus, Saint Charles; evening, summer.
Degree Requirements 16 courses including 4 elective courses.
Required Courses Financial accounting, financial management, information management, legal environment of business, managerial accounting, managerial economics, marketing management, operations research, principles of economics, social and ethical responsibilities of business, statistics, strategic management. Courses may be waived through: previous course work, work experience.
Curricular Focus Leadership, problem solving and decision making, strategic analysis and planning.
Concentrations Finance, human resources management, leadership and change management, management, management information systems, marketing.
Faculty Full-time: 16, 70% with doctorates; part-time: 9, 10% with doctorates.
Teaching Methodology Case study: 20%, discussion: 10%, lecture: 50%, research: 5%, seminars by members of the business community: 1%, student presentations: 10%, team projects: 4%.

STUDENT STATISTICS

Geographic Representation State residents 97%. By region: Midwest 97%. International 3%.
Other Background Graduate degrees in other disciplines: 1%. Work experience: On average, students have 5 years of work experience on entrance to the program.

FACILITIES

Information Resources Main library with 113,647 bound volumes, 425 titles on microform, 587 periodical subscriptions, 1,649 records/tapes/CDs, 10 CD-ROMs.
Housing College housing not available.
Technology Computers are used moderately in course work. 36 computer terminals/PCs are available for use by students in program; they are located in the library, computer labs. Students in the program are not required to have their own PC. $100 are budgeted per student for computer support.

Computer Resources/On-line Services

Training	No	Multimedia Center	Yes
Internet	Yes $	CompuServe	Yes $
E-Mail	No		

ADMISSION

Acceptance 1994-95 Of those applying, 85% were accepted.
Entrance Requirements Bachelor's degree, GMAT score, minimum 2.75 GPA, minimum 2 years of work experience. Core courses waived through: previous course work, work experience.
Application Requirements Interview, application form, copies of transcript, personal statement, 2 letters of recommendation.
Application Deadlines 7/1 for fall, 11/1 for winter, 2/1 for spring.

FINANCIALS

Costs for 1994-95 Tuition: Full-time: $1,189/course.
Financial Aid In 1994-95, 5% of candidates received some institutionally administered aid in the form of scholarships. Total awards ranged from $100-$300. Financial aid is available to part-time students. Application deadlines: 7/1 for fall, 11/1 for winter, 2/1 for spring. Contact: Dr. Thomas R. McFaul, Director of Graduate Programs, 30 North Brainerd Street, PO Box 3063, Naperville, IL 60566-7063. (708) 420-3313.

INTERNATIONAL STUDENTS

Demographics 3% of students enrolled in the program are international; Asia 67%, South America 33%.
Services and Facilities Special assistance for nonnative speakers of English.
Applying TOEFL required; proof of adequate funds; foreign transcript evaluation. Financial aid is not available to international students. Admission application deadlines: 6/1 for fall, 10/1 for winter, 1/1 for spring.

PLACEMENT

Placement services include alumni network, career counseling/planning, career placement, and resume preparation. Of 1994 graduates, 98% were employed within three months of graduation.
Jobs by Employer Type Manufacturing 40%; service 50%; government 2%; nonprofit 8%.
Jobs by Functional Area Marketing/sales 40%; finance 15%; management 30%; technical management 15%.

Program Contact: Dr. Thomas R. McFaul, Director of Graduate Programs, North Central College, 30 North Brainerd Street, PO Box 3063, Naperville, IL 60566-7063. (708) 420-3313; Fax: (708) 416-8438.

Northeastern Illinois University

College of Business and Management

Chicago, Illinois

OVERVIEW

Northeastern Illinois University is a state-supported comprehensive coed institution. Part of Board of Governors Universities. Founded 1961. Setting: 67-acre urban campus. Total institutional enrollment: 10,300. Program was first offered in 1990.

MBA HIGHLIGHTS

Entrance Difficulty***
Mean GMAT: 510
Mean GPA: 3.03

Cost $
Tuition: $1,002/semester
(Nonresident: $3,006/semester)
Room & Board: N/R

Enrollment Profile
Full-time: 5
Part-time: 61
Total: 66
Average Age: 32

Work Exp: 95%
International: 8%
Women: 33%
Minorities: 36%

Average Class Size: 14

ACADEMICS

Length of Program Minimum: 24 months.
Calendar Semesters.
Full-time Classes Main campus; evening, weekends, summer.
Degree Requirements 36 credits including 6 elective credits. Other: 9 hours in concentration.
Required Courses Accounting, business law, finance, management, marketing. Courses may be waived through: previous course work, work experience.
Curricular Focus Business issues and problems, managing diversity, teamwork.
Concentrations Accounting, finance, management, marketing.
Faculty Full-time: 17, 100% with doctorates.
Teaching Methodology Case study: 15%, lecture: 50%, research: 10%, student presentations: 10%, team projects: 15%.
Special Opportunities Internships include manufacturing, pharmaceutical, and banking.

STUDENT STATISTICS

Geographic Representation State residents 92%. By region: Midwest 92%. International 8%.
Undergraduate Majors Business 50%; education 4%; engineering/technology 8%; humanities 4%; nursing 2%; science/mathematics 15%; social sciences 2%; other 15%.
Other Background Graduate degrees in other disciplines: 10%.

FACILITIES
Information Resources Main library with 461,120 bound volumes, 722,496 titles on microform, 3,786 periodical subscriptions, 1,016 records/tapes/CDs.

Housing College housing not available.

Technology Computers are used moderately in course work. Computer terminals/PCs are available for use by students in program; they are located in the library, the computer center, computer labs. Students in the program are not required to have their own PC.

Computer Resources/On-line Services

Training	No	E-Mail	Yes
Internet	Yes	Dialog	Yes

Other on-line services: First Search.

ADMISSION
Acceptance 1994-95 Of those applying, 40% were accepted.

Entrance Requirements Bachelor's degree, business calculus, GMAT score of 450, minimum 2.75 GPA. Core courses waived through: previous course work, work experience.

Application Requirements Written essay, application form, copies of transcript, personal statement, 2 letters of recommendation.

Application Deadlines 7/15 for fall, 11/15 for spring.

FINANCIALS
Costs for 1994-95 Tuition: Full-time: $1,002/semester for state residents, $3,006/semester for nonresidents; Part-time day: $84/credit hour for state residents, $251/credit hour for nonresidents. Fees: Full-time: $96/semester for state residents, $96/semester for nonresidents; Part-time day: $64/semester for state residents.

Financial Aid In 1994-95, 32% of candidates received some institutionally administered aid in the form of scholarships, assistantships. Total awards ranged from $3,000-$12,000. Financial aid is available to part-time students. Applications are processed on a rolling basis. Contact: Ms. Kathleen Carlson, Associate Dean, 5500 North St. Louis Avenue, Chicago, IL 60625-4699. (312) 794-2655.

INTERNATIONAL STUDENTS
Demographics 8% of students enrolled in the program are international; Asia 90%, Other 10%.

Applying TOEFL required, minimum score of 550; proof of adequate funds. Financial aid is available to international students. Financial aid application deadlines: 7/15 for fall, 11/15 for spring. Admission application deadlines: 7/15 for fall, 11/15 for spring.

Program Contact: Ms. Kathleen Carlson, Associate Dean and MBA Coordinator, Northeastern Illinois University, 5500 North St. Louis Avenue, Chicago, IL 60625-4699. (312) 794-2647; Fax: (312) 794-6288; Internet Address: k-carlson@bgu.edu.

Northern Illinois University

College of Business

De Kalb, Illinois

OVERVIEW
Northern Illinois University is a state-supported coed institution. Founded 1895. Setting: 589-acre small-town campus with easy access to Chicago. Total institutional enrollment: 22,881. AACSB-accredited.

MBA HIGHLIGHTS
Entrance Difficulty****

Cost $$
Tuition: $113 - $225/credit hour
Room & Board: N/R

Enrollment Profile

Full-time: 564	Work Exp: N/R
Part-time: 0	International: 2%
Total: 564	Women: 40%
Average Age: N/R	Minorities: 6%

Average Class Size: 25

ACADEMICS
Length of Program Minimum: 12 months.
Calendar Semesters.

Part-time Classes Main campus, Hoffmann Estates, Naperville, Rockford; evening, summer.

Degree Requirements 30 credit hours.

Curricular Focus Corporate finance, general management, investments and financial markets, problem solving and decision making.

Concentration Management.

Teaching Methodology Case study: 15%, lecture: 50%, research: 5%, student presentations: 10%, team projects: 20%.

STUDENT STATISTICS
Geographic Representation State residents 95%. International 2%.

FACILITIES
Information Resources Main library with 1.4 million bound volumes, 2.5 million titles on microform, 15,995 periodical subscriptions, 8,684 records/tapes/CDs, 42 CD-ROMs.

ADMISSION
Entrance Requirements Bachelor's degree, GMAT score of 450, minimum 2.75 GPA, minimum 1 year of work experience.

Application Requirements Application form, copies of transcript, resume/curriculum vitae, personal statement, 2 letters of recommendation.

Application Deadlines 6/1 for fall, 11/1 for spring, 4/1 for summer. Applications are processed on a rolling basis.

FINANCIALS
Costs for 1994-95 Tuition: Part-time day: $113-$225/credit hour.

Financial Aid Application deadline: 3/1 for fall. Contact: Dr. Jerry Augsberger, Director of Student Financial Aid, Swen Parsons 245, De Kalb, IL 60115-2872. (815) 753-1395.

INTERNATIONAL STUDENTS
Demographics 2% of students enrolled in the program are international.

Applying TOEFL required, minimum score of 550; proof of health; proof of adequate funds. Financial aid is available to international students. Admission application deadlines: 5/1 for fall, 10/1 for spring. Applications are processed on a rolling basis.

Program Contact: Ms. Sally Wakefield, Director, Northern Illinois University, Wirtz Hall 323, De Kalb, IL 60115. (815) 753-1245, or (800) 323-8714 (IL only); Fax: (815) 753-3300.

Northwestern University

J. L. Kellogg Graduate School of Management

Evanston, Illinois

OVERVIEW
Northwestern University is an independent nonprofit coed institution. Founded 1851. Setting: 231-acre suburban campus with easy access to Chicago. Total institutional enrollment: 12,000. Program was first offered in 1908. AACSB-accredited.

PROGRAM HIGHLIGHTS
Entrance Difficulty*****
Mean GMAT: 630
Mean GPA: 3.3

Cost $$$$$
Tuition: $20,634 - $27,200
Room & Board: N/R

Enrollment Profile

Full-time: 1,128	Work Exp: 99%
Part-time: 1,300	International: 24%
Total: 2,428	Women: 30%
Average Age: 28	Minorities: 18%

Average Class Size: 30

ACADEMICS
Calendar Quarters.

Curricular Focus General management, international business, teamwork.

Concentrations Accounting, arts administration, economics, entrepreneurship, finance, health services, human resources management, international business, management, management information systems, marketing, operations management, organizational behavior, profit management, quantitative analysis, real estate, strategic management, transportation.

Teaching Methodology Case study: 35%, lecture: 20%, team projects: 45%.

Special Opportunities International exchange in Australia, Austria, Chile, Denmark, France, Germany, Italy, Netherlands, Norway, Spain, Thailand, United Kingdom.

STUDENT STATISTICS
Geographic Representation State residents 58%. International 24%.

Undergraduate Majors Business 16%; engineering/technology 21%; humanities 39%; other 24%.

Other Background Work experience: On average, students have 4 years of work experience on entrance to the program.

FACILITIES
Information Resources Main library with 3.7 million bound volumes, 2.9 million titles on microform, 36,626 periodical subscriptions.

Housing 25% of students in program live in college-owned or -operated housing.

Technology Computers are used heavily in course work. Computer terminals/PCs, linked by a campus-wide computer network, are available for use by students in program; they are located in dormitories, the library, the computer center, computer labs. Students in the program are not required to have their own PC.

Computer Resources/On-line Services

Internet	Yes	Dun's	No
E-Mail	Yes	Dow Jones	No
LEXIS/NEXIS	Yes	Dialog	Yes
CompuServe	No	Bloomberg	No

ADMISSION
Acceptance 1994-95 4,842 applied for admission; 21% were accepted.

Entrance Requirements Bachelor's degree, GMAT score. Core courses waived through: previous course work, work experience.

Application Requirements Written essay, interview, application form, copies of transcript, resume/curriculum vitae, personal statement, 1 letter of recommendation.

Application Deadline 3/29 for fall. Application discs available.

FINANCIALS
Costs for 1994-95 Tuition: Full-time: $20,634-$27,200; Part-time day: $1,994/course.

Financial Aid In 1994-95, 68% of candidates received some institutionally administered aid in the form of grants, scholarships, loans, fellowships. Financial aid is available to part-time students. Application deadline: 4/1 for fall. Applications are processed on a rolling basis. Contact: Ms. Effie Barnett, Associate Director of Financial Aid, 2001 North Sheridan Road, Evanston, IL 60208. (708) 491-7400.

INTERNATIONAL STUDENTS
Demographics 24% of students enrolled in the program are international.

Services and Facilities International student office, visa services, counseling/support services.

Applying TOEFL required; proof of adequate funds. Financial aid is available to international students. Applications are processed on a rolling basis. Contact: Ms. Eileen Flanders, Director, Office of International Programs, 2001 North Sheridan Road, Evanston, IL 60208. (708) 491-5613.

PROGRAMS
MM Length of program: Minimum: 21 months. Maximum: 2 years. Full-time classes: Main campus, Chicago; day, evening. Part-time classes: Main campus, Chicago; evening, weekends. Degree requirements: 23 courses including 14 elective courses.

MM/JD Length of program: Maximum: 4 years. Full-time classes: Main campus, Chicago; day, evening, summer. Degree requirements: 86 semester hours in law; 18 courses in management, including 9 elective courses.

MM/MD Length of program: Maximum: 5 years. Full-time classes: Main campus, Chicago; day, evening, summer. Degree requirements: 18 courses in management, 48 courses in medicine.

MM/MSN Length of program: Maximum: 2 years. Full-time classes: Main campus, Chicago; day, evening, summer. Degree requirements: 18 courses in management, 12 courses in nursing.

MMM Length of program: Minimum: 22 months. Maximum: 2 years. Full-time classes: Main campus; day, evening. Degree requirements: 23 courses.

One-year MM Length of program: 12 months. Full-time classes: Main campus; day, evening. Degree requirements: 15 courses. Undergraduate degree in business.

PLACEMENT
In 1993-94, 309 organizations participated in on-campus recruiting. Placement services include alumni network, career counseling/planning, career fairs, career library, career placement, electronic job bank, job interviews, job search course, resume preparation, and resume referral to employers. Of 1994 graduates, 95% were employed within three months of graduation.

Jobs by Employer Type Manufacturing 28%; service 42%; consulting 26%; nonprofit 4%.

Jobs by Functional Area Marketing/sales 22%; finance 31%; operations 2%; management 5%; strategic planning 2%; consulting 35%; real estate 2%; human resources 1%.

Program Contact: Office of Admissions, Northwestern University, 2001 North Sheridan Road, Evanston, IL 60208. (708) 491-3308; Fax: (708) 491-4960.

Olivet Nazarene University

Division of Business

Kankakee, Illinois

OVERVIEW
Olivet Nazarene University is an independent comprehensive coed institution, affiliated with Church of the Nazarene. Founded 1907. Setting: 168-acre suburban campus with easy access to Chicago. Total institutional enrollment: 2,200.

MBA HIGHLIGHTS

Entrance Difficulty**

Cost $
Tuition: $295/credit
Room & Board: N/R

Enrollment Profile

Full-time: N/R	Work Exp: N/R
Part-time: N/R	International: 5%
Total: 725	Women: 50%
Average Age: N/R	Minorities: 30%

Average Class Size: 15

ACADEMICS
Length of Program Minimum: 24 months.

Calendar Semesters.

Part-time Classes Main campus; evening.

Degree Requirements 35 credits.

Curricular Focus Business issues and problems, ethics.

Concentration Management.

Teaching Methodology Case study: 25%, faculty seminars: 15%, lecture: 25%, seminars by members of the business community: 10%, student presentations: 10%, team projects: 15%.

STUDENT STATISTICS
Geographic Representation State residents 95%. International 5%.

FACILITIES
Information Resources Main library with 153,000 bound volumes, 42,000 titles on microform, 900 periodical subscriptions, 6,000 records/tapes/CDs.

ADMISSION
Entrance Requirements Bachelor's degree, minimum 2.5 GPA, minimum 3 years of work experience.

Application Requirements Interview, application form, copies of transcript, resume/curriculum vitae, personal statement, 2 letters of recommendation.

Application Deadline Applications are processed on a rolling basis.

FINANCIALS
Costs for 1994-95 Tuition: Part-time evening: $295/credit.

Financial Aid Applications are processed on a rolling basis. Contact: Ms. Kathleen Moriarity, Adult Studies Counselor, PO Box 592, Kankakee, IL 60901-0592. (815) 939-5162.

INTERNATIONAL STUDENTS
Demographics 5% of students enrolled in the program are international.

Applying TOEFL required, minimum score of 550; proof of adequate funds. Financial aid is available to international students. Applications are processed on a rolling basis. Admission applications are processed on a rolling basis.

Program Contact: Ms. Robin Pierson, Olivet Nazarene University, PO Box 592, Kankakee, IL 60901-0592. (815) 939-9004; Fax: (815) 939-0416.

Quincy University

Division of Business and Computer Science

Quincy, Illinois

OVERVIEW
Quincy University is an independent Roman Catholic comprehensive coed institution. Founded 1860. Setting: 75-acre small-town campus. Total institutional enrollment: 1,665. Program was first offered in 1984.

MBA HIGHLIGHTS

Entrance Difficulty**
Mean GMAT: 535
Mean GPA: N/R

Cost $
Tuition: $915/course
Room & Board: N/R

Enrollment Profile
Full-time: 0	Work Exp: 100%
Part-time: 90	International: 0%
Total: 90	Women: 45%
Average Age: 32	Minorities: 2%

Average Class Size: 25

ACADEMICS
Length of Program Minimum: 24 months. Maximum: 5 years.
Calendar Semesters.
Part-time Classes Main campus; evening, summer.
Degree Requirements 30 credits.
Required Courses Financial management, financial managerment, group dynamics and leadership, international business management, management information systems, managerial accounting, managerial economics, marketing strategies and planning, production and operations management, strategic management, topics in business government and society.
Curricular Focus General management, problem solving and decision making, strategic analysis and planning.
Concentration Management.
Faculty Full-time: 7, 100% with doctorates.
Teaching Methodology Case study: 20%, lecture: 60%, student presentations: 10%, team projects: 10%.

STUDENT STATISTICS
Geographic Representation State residents 85%. By region: Midwest 100%.
Undergraduate Majors Business 30%; education 1%; engineering/technology 40%; humanities 2%; nursing 10%; science/mathematics 12%; other 5%.
Other Background Graduate degrees in other disciplines: 2%. Work experience: On average, students have 9 years of work experience on entrance to the program.

FACILITIES
Information Resources Main library with 229,742 bound volumes, 147,395 titles on microform, 645 periodical subscriptions, 2,841 records/tapes/CDs, 4 CD-ROMs.
Housing College housing not available.
Technology Computers are used moderately in course work. 106 computer terminals/PCs are available for use by students in program; they are located in learning resource center, the library, computer labs. Students in the program are not required to have their own PC.

Computer Resources/On-line Services
Training	No	E-Mail	No
Internet	Yes	CompuServe	Yes

ADMISSION
Acceptance 1994-95 24 applied for admission; 88% were accepted.
Entrance Requirements Bachelor's degree, GMAT score. Core courses waived through: previous course work.
Application Requirements Application form, copies of transcript, 2 letters of recommendation.
Application Deadline Applications are processed on a rolling basis.

FINANCIALS
Costs for 1994-95 Tuition: Part-time evening: $915/course.
Financial Aid Financial aid is not available to part-time students.

INTERNATIONAL STUDENTS
Applying TOEFL required, minimum score of 600. Financial aid is not available to international students.

PLACEMENT
In 1993-94, 25 organizations participated in on-campus recruiting. Placement services include career placement. Of 1994 graduates, 100% were employed within three months of graduation.

Program Contact: Dr. J. K. Breyley Jr., MBA Director, Quincy University, 1800 College Avenue, Quincy, IL 62301. (217) 228-5433; Fax: (217) 228-5354.

Rockford College

Department of Economics, Business and Accounting

Rockford, Illinois

OVERVIEW
Rockford College is an independent nonprofit comprehensive coed institution. Founded 1847. Setting: 130-acre suburban campus with easy access to Chicago. Total institutional enrollment: 1,600. Program was first offered in 1983.

MBA HIGHLIGHTS

Entrance Difficulty***
Mean GMAT: 490
Mean GPA: 3.45

Cost $$$
Tuition: $6,200/semester
Room & Board: $4,100

Enrollment Profile
Full-time: 20	Work Exp: 90%
Part-time: 190	International: 15%
Total: 210	Women: 35%
Average Age: 32	Minorities: 10%

Average Class Size: 20

ACADEMICS
Length of Program Minimum: 24 months. Maximum: 5 years.
Calendar Semesters.
Full-time Classes Main campus; evening, summer.
Part-time Classes Main campus; evening, summer.
Degree Requirements 36 credits including 6 elective credits.
Required Courses Accounting, business and national economy, business communications, business policy and strategy, business research, finance, legal environment of business, management, managerial economics, marketing. Courses may be waived through: previous course work.
Curricular Focus Organizational development and change management, problem solving and decision making, teamwork.
Concentrations Accounting, criminal justice.
Faculty Full-time: 8, 62% with doctorates; part-time: 2.
Teaching Methodology Case study: 40%, lecture: 20%, student presentations: 15%, team projects: 25%.
Special Opportunities International exchange in Ecuador, United Kingdom. Internship program available.

STUDENT STATISTICS

Geographic Representation State residents 75%. By region: Midwest 85%. International 15%.

Undergraduate Majors Business 40%; engineering/technology 40%; humanities 5%; nursing 5%; social sciences 10%.

Other Background Graduate degrees in other disciplines: 10%. Work experience: On average, students have 7 years of work experience on entrance to the program.

FACILITIES

Information Resources Main library with 166,000 bound volumes, 155 titles on microform, 826 periodical subscriptions, 9,541 records/tapes/CDs, 14 CD-ROMs.

Housing 2% of students in program live in college-owned or -operated housing.

Technology Computers are used moderately in course work. 25 computer terminals/PCs are available for use by students in program; they are located in computer labs. Students in the program are not required to have their own PC.

Computer Resources/On-line Services

Training	No	E-Mail	Yes
Internet	Yes		

ADMISSION

Acceptance 1994-95 Of those applying, 80% were accepted.

Entrance Requirements Bachelor's degree, GMAT score. Core courses waived through: previous course work.

Application Requirements Application form, copies of transcript, 3 letters of recommendation.

Application Deadlines 8/1 for fall, 12/1 for spring.

FINANCIALS

Costs for 1994-95 Tuition: Full-time: $6,200/semester; Part-time evening: $320/credit hour. Average room and board costs are $4,100 per academic year (on-campus) and $5,000 per academic year (off-campus).

Financial Aid In 1994-95, 10% of candidates received institutionally administered aid in the form of scholarships. Financial aid is available to part-time students. Application deadlines: 8/1 for fall, 12/1 for spring. Contact: Ms. Miriam King, Director of Admissions, 5050 East State Street, Rockford, IL 61108-2393. (815) 226-4050.

INTERNATIONAL STUDENTS

Demographics 15% of students enrolled in the program are international; Europe 70%, Asia 15%, South America 15%.

Services and Facilities ESL courses.

Applying TOEFL required, minimum score of 550; proof of health; proof of adequate funds. Financial aid is available to international students. Financial aid application deadlines: 8/1 for fall, 12/1 for spring. Admission application deadlines: 8/1 for fall, 12/1 for spring. Contact: Ms. Nancy Rostowsky, Director of International Students, 5050 East State Street, Rockford, IL 61108-2393. (815) 226-3390.

PLACEMENT

In 1993-94, 2 organizations participated in on-campus recruiting. Placement services include career fairs and career placement. Of 1994 graduates, 95% were employed within three months of graduation.

Jobs by Employer Type Manufacturing 60%; service 20%; government 10%; nonprofit 10%.

Jobs by Functional Area Marketing/sales 10%; finance 10%; operations 40%; management 20%; technical management 20%.

Program Contact: Mr. Mick McKean, Dean, Graduate and Continuing Education, Rockford College, 5050 East State Street, Rockford, IL 61108-2393. (815) 226-4013; Fax: (815) 226-4119.

Roosevelt University

Walter E. Heller College of Business Administration

Chicago, Illinois

OVERVIEW

Roosevelt University is an independent nonprofit comprehensive coed institution. Founded 1945. Setting: urban campus. Total institutional enrollment: 6,500. Program was first offered in 1975.

MBA HIGHLIGHTS

Entrance Difficulty***
Mean GMAT: 446
Mean GPA: N/R

Cost $$
Tuition: $350/credit hour
Room & Board: $4,950

Enrollment Profile

Full-time: 100	Work Exp: 90%
Part-time: 325	International: 90%
Total: 425	Women: 60%
Average Age: 28	Minorities: 30%

Average Class Size: 17

The mission of the Walter E. Heller College of Business Administration is to give students a career-oriented business education that emphasizes personal and professional integrity and stresses the social responsibility of business. In the M.B.A. program, special consideration is given to the integration of basic competencies in communications, computers, critical and creative thinking, and quantitative analysis with specialized education in a specific functional area of business to create genuine expertise in one's chosen field.

With over 70 full- and part-time faculty members, many of whom are actively involved in some of the most prestigious businesses in the Chicago area, the Heller College offers an optimum blend of theoretical and practical business knowledge for success in today's global environment. At the same time, the recurring themes of integrity and socially responsible business practices are interwoven into the curriculum, thus reflecting the progressive principles exemplified in the lives of the University's namesakes, Franklin and Eleanor Roosevelt.

Of the more than 400 students currently in the M.B.A. program, about 15 percent are international. Roosevelt University is located in the heart of Chicago's world-famous financial district.

ACADEMICS

Length of Program Minimum: 9 months. Maximum: 5 years.

Calendar Semesters.

Part-time Classes Main campus; evening, weekends, summer.

Degree Requirements 36 credits.

Required Courses Behavioral science systems for management, international business, introduction to information systems, managerial accounting, managerial economics, marketing strategy and policy determination, operations management, statistical inference, theory and cases in financial management. Courses may be waived through: previous course work.

Curricular Focus Leadership, problem solving and decision making, social responsibility.

Concentrations Accounting, economics, finance, international business, management, management information systems, marketing, organizational behavior, quantitative analysis.

Faculty Full-time: 26, 62% with doctorates; part-time: 8, 25% with doctorates.

Teaching Methodology Case study: 20%, lecture: 50%, research: 10%, student presentations: 10%, team projects: 10%.

Special Opportunities International exchange in France.

STUDENT STATISTICS

Geographic Representation State residents 10%. By region: Midwest 90%. International 90%.

Undergraduate Majors Business 40%; education 5%; engineering/technology 10%; humanities 10%; science/mathematics 10%; social sciences 10%; other 15%.

FACILITIES

Information Resources Main library with 410,000 bound volumes, 134,000 titles on microform, 1,611 periodical subscriptions, 18,200 records/tapes/CDs, 6 CD-ROMs.

Housing College housing available.

Technology Computers are used moderately in course work. 90 computer terminals/PCs are available for use by students in program; they are located in learning resource center, computer labs. Students in the program are not required to have their own PC.

Computer Resources/On-line Services

E-Mail	No	Dialog	Yes

Other on-line services: OCLC, Carl.

ADMISSION

Entrance Requirements Bachelor's degree, prerequisite courses required for applicants with non-business degree, GMAT score of 460, minimum 2.7 GPA. Core courses waived through: previous course work.

Application Requirements Application form, copies of transcript.

Application Deadline Applications are processed on a rolling basis.

FINANCIALS

Costs for 1994-95 Tuition: Full-time: $350/credit hour. Fees: Full-time: $60/semester. Average room and board costs are $4,950 per academic year (on-campus) and $4,950 per academic year (off-campus).

Financial Aid In 1994-95, 35% of candidates received some institutionally administered aid in the form of grants, scholarships, loans, assistantships. Total awards ranged from $1,000-$3,500. Financial aid is available to part-time students. Application deadlines: 6/15 for fall, 10/15 for spring, 2/15 for summer. Contact: Ms. Sharon Sweeny, Director of Financial Aid, 430 South Michigan Avenue, Chicago, IL 60605. (312) 341-3612.

INTERNATIONAL STUDENTS

Demographics 90% of students enrolled in the program are international.

Services and Facilities International student center, visa services, language tutoring, ESL courses, special assistance for nonnative speakers of English, counseling/support services.

Applying Proof of adequate funds; English language test, health insurance. Admission application deadlines: 6/1 for fall, 10/1 for spring, 3/1 for summer. Contact: Ms. Jackie Stecki, International Student Adviser, 430 South Michigan Avenue, Chicago, IL 60605. (312) 341-3531.

PLACEMENT

In 1993-94, 25 organizations participated in on-campus recruiting; 15 on-campus interviews were conducted. Placement services include alumni network, career counseling/planning, career fairs, career library, career placement, electronic job bank, job interviews, resume preparation, and resume referral to employers. Of 1994 graduates, 90% were employed within three months of graduation, the average starting salary was $30,000, the range was $25,000-$35,000.

Jobs by Employer Type Manufacturing 10%; service 66%; government 10%; consulting 5%; nonprofit 5%; other 4%.

Jobs by Functional Area Marketing/sales 25%; finance 50%; management 25%.

Program Contact: Associate Dean, Roosevelt University, 430 South Michigan Avenue, Chicago, IL 60605-1394. (312) 341-3822; Fax: (312) 341-3827.

Saint Xavier University

Graham School of Management

Chicago, Illinois

OVERVIEW

Saint Xavier University is an independent Roman Catholic comprehensive coed institution. Founded 1847. Setting: 40-acre urban campus. Total institutional enrollment: 4,060. Program was first offered in 1985.

MBA HIGHLIGHTS

Entrance Difficulty**
Mean GMAT: 550
Mean GPA: 3.0

Cost $$
Tuition: $393/credit hour
Room & Board: N/R

Enrollment Profile

Full-time: 39		Work Exp: 99%	
Part-time: 261		International: 30%	
Total: 300		Women: 45%	
Average Age: 33		Minorities: 10%	

Average Class Size: 13

ACADEMICS

Length of Program Minimum: 12 months. Maximum: 5 years.

Calendar 4-1-4.

Full-time Classes Main campus, Paris (France), Milan (Italy); evening, weekends, summer.

Part-time Classes Main campus, Orland Park, Paris (France), Milan (Italy); evening, weekends, summer.

Degree Requirements 36 credit hours including 12 elective credit hours.

Required Courses Accounting, business and society, business policy, economics, finance, government, management, management information systems, statistics. Courses may be waived through: previous course work.

Curricular Focus International business, organizational development and change management, problem solving and decision making.

Concentrations Accounting, finance, healthcare management, human resources management, international business, management, management information systems, marketing.

Faculty Full-time: 16, 80% with doctorates.

Teaching Methodology Case study: 20%, faculty seminars: 5%, lecture: 40%, research: 10%, seminars by members of the business community: 5%, student presentations: 10%, team projects: 10%.

Special Opportunities International exchange in France, Italy. Internship program available.

STUDENT STATISTICS

Geographic Representation State residents 70%. By region: Midwest 70%. International 30%.

Undergraduate Majors Business 50%; engineering/technology 10%; humanities 10%; science/mathematics 10%; social sciences 20%.

Other Background Graduate degrees in other disciplines: 5%. Work experience: On average, students have 8 years of work experience on entrance to the program.

FACILITIES

Information Resources Main library with 152,000 bound volumes, 25,568 titles on microform, 911 periodical subscriptions. Business collection includes 10,000 bound volumes, 100 periodical subscriptions.

Housing 1% of students in program live in college-owned or -operated housing.

Technology Computers are used moderately in course work. 45 computer terminals/PCs, linked by a campus-wide computer network, are available for use by students in program; they are located in the student center, learning resource center, the library, the computer center, computer labs, the research center. Students in the program are not required to have their own PC.

Computer Resources/On-line Services

Training	Yes	E-Mail	Yes
Internet	Yes	Multimedia Center	Yes

ADMISSION

Acceptance 1994-95 180 applied for admission; 90% were accepted.

Entrance Requirements Bachelor's degree, GMAT score, minimum 2 years of work experience. Core courses waived through: previous course work.

Application Requirements Application form, copies of transcript, personal statement, 2 letters of recommendation.

Application Deadline Applications are processed on a rolling basis.

FINANCIALS

Costs for 1994-95 Tuition: Full-time: $393/credit hour; Summer: $354/credit hour. Fees: Full-time: $110/semester; Summer: $25/semester.

Financial Aid In 1994-95, candidates received some institutionally administered aid in the form of loans, assistantships, work-study. Financial aid is available to part-time students. Applications are processed on a rolling basis. Contact: Ms. Susan Swisher, Director of Financial Aid, 3700 West 103rd Street, Chicago, IL 60655. (312) 298-3070.

INTERNATIONAL STUDENTS

Demographics 30% of students enrolled in the program are international; Europe 60%, Africa 10%, Asia 10%, Central America 5%, South America 5%, Other 10%.

Services and Facilities Visa services, language tutoring, ESL courses, special assistance for nonnative speakers of English, counseling/support services.

Applying TOEFL required, minimum score of 550; proof of adequate funds. Financial aid is available to international students. Applications are processed on a rolling basis. Admission applications are processed on a rolling basis. Contact: Ms. Maggie Eaheart, Admissions Officer, 3700 West 103rd Street, Chicago, IL 60655. (312) 298-3061.

ALTERNATE MBA PROGRAMS

One-Year MBA Length of program: Minimum: 12 months. Full-time classes: Main campus, Orland Park; evening, weekends. Degree requirements: 36 credit hours.

MBA/MSN Length of program: Minimum: 36 months. Maximum: 8 years. Degree requirements: 60 credit hours.

PLACEMENT

Placement services include alumni network, career counseling/planning, career fairs, career library, career placement, electronic job bank, job interviews, resume preparation, and resume referral to employers. Of 1994 graduates, 99% were employed within three months of graduation.

Jobs by Employer Type Manufacturing 25%; service 50%; government 10%; consulting 5%; nonprofit 10%.

Jobs by Functional Area Marketing/sales 15%; finance 25%; management 50%; technical management 10%.

Program Contact: Dr. Charles Shanabruch, Dean, Saint Xavier University, 3825 West 103rd Street, Chicago, IL 60655-3105. (312) 298-3601; Fax: (312) 298-3610.

Sangamon State University

Department of Business Administration

Springfield, Illinois

OVERVIEW

Sangamon State University is a state-supported upper-level coed institution. Founded 1969. Setting: 746-acre urban campus. Total institutional enrollment: 4,384. Program was first offered in 1985.

MBA HIGHLIGHTS

Entrance Difficulty**
Mean GMAT: 500
Mean GPA: 2.8

Cost $
Tuition: $80/semester hour
(Nonresident: $240/semester hour)
Room & Board: $1,800

Enrollment Profile

Full-time: 18	Work Exp: 90%
Part-time: 200	International: 3%
Total: 218	Women: 52%
Average Age: 30	Minorities: 6%

Average Class Size: 21

ACADEMICS

Length of Program Minimum: 18 months. Maximum: 6 years.

Calendar Semesters.

Full-time Classes Main campus; evening, weekends, summer.

Degree Requirements 48 credits including 8-12 elective credits. Other: Minimum 3.0 GPA; no more than 8 hours of "C" grade toward MBA; "B" grade or better in business strategy.

Required Courses Business and government, business strategy, managerial finance, marketing management, organizational behavior, production and operations management, research analysis. Courses may be waived through: previous course work, work experience.

Curricular Focus Business issues and problems, problem solving and decision making, strategic analysis and planning.

Concentrations Finance, human resources management, marketing, operations management, organizational behavior, public policy, quantitative analysis.

Faculty Full-time: 11, 91% with doctorates.

Teaching Methodology Case study: 15%, lecture: 30%, research: 15%, student presentations: 20%, team projects: 20%.

Special Opportunities Internships include public service in government.

STUDENT STATISTICS

Geographic Representation State residents 90%. By region: Midwest 97%. International 3%.

Undergraduate Majors Business 60%; engineering/technology 5%; humanities 10%; science/mathematics 5%; social sciences 10%; other 10%.

Other Background Graduate degrees in other disciplines: 5%. Work experience: On average, students have 3 years of work experience on entrance to the program.

FACILITIES

Information Resources Main library with 503,253 bound volumes, 9,567 titles on microform, 2,915 periodical subscriptions, 9,296 records/tapes/CDs, 196 CD-ROMs. Business collection includes 47,516 bound volumes, 251 periodical subscriptions, 10 CD-ROMs, 75 videos.

Housing 5% of students in program live in college-owned or -operated housing.

Technology Computers are used moderately in course work. 96 computer terminals/PCs are available for use by students in program; they are located in classrooms, learning resource center, the library, computer labs. Students in the program are not required to have their own PC.

Computer Resources/On-line Services

Training	Yes	Multimedia Center	Yes
Internet	Yes	Dialog	Yes
E-Mail	No		

Other on-line services: First Search, Carl.

ADMISSION

Acceptance 1994-95 Of those applying, 40% were accepted.

Entrance Requirements Bachelor's degree, GMAT score of 400, minimum 2.5 GPA. Core courses waived through: previous course work.

Application Requirements Application form, copies of transcript, personal statement.

Application Deadline Applications are processed on a rolling basis.

FINANCIALS

Costs for 1994-95 Tuition: Full-time: $80/semester hour for state residents, $240/semester hour for nonresidents. Fees: Full-time: $88/semester for state residents, $88/semester for nonresidents. Average room and board costs are $1,800 per academic year (on-campus) and $4,200 per academic year (off-campus).

Financial Aid In 1994-95, candidates received some institutionally administered aid in the form of scholarships, loans, assistantships, work-study. Total awards ranged from $300-$8,850. Financial aid is available to part-time students. Application deadlines: 3/1 for fall, 10/1 for spring. Contact: Ms. Yula Jones, Financial Aid Adviser, E-16, Springfield, IL 62794-9243. (217) 786-6724.

INTERNATIONAL STUDENTS

Demographics 3% of students enrolled in the program are international; Asia 50%, Europe 50%.

Services and Facilities International student center, visa services, language tutoring, ESL courses, special assistance for nonnative speakers of English, counseling/support services, host family program.

Applying TOEFL required, minimum score of 550; proof of health; proof of adequate funds; satisfactory completion of English proficiency test. Financial aid is available to international students. Assistantships and internships are available to these students after one year; deadline is 3/1. Admission application deadlines: 6/1 for fall, 11/1 for spring, 4/1 for summer. Contact: Ms. Gerlinde B. Coates, International Student Adviser, Springfield, IL 62794-9243. (217) 786-6678.

PLACEMENT

In 1993-94, 10 organizations participated in on-campus recruiting. Placement services include career counseling/planning, career fairs, career library, career placement, job interviews, and resume preparation.

Jobs by Employer Type Manufacturing 10%; service 30%; government 40%; nonprofit 20%.

Jobs by Functional Area Marketing/sales 30%; finance 30%; operations 10%; management 5%; strategic planning 5%; technical management 20%.

Program Contact: Mr. Lawrence W. Swartz, Admissions Officer, Sangamon State University, Office of Admissions and Records, Springfield, IL 62794-9243. (217) 786-6626, or (800) 252-8533 (IL only), or (800) 722-2534 (out-of-state).

Southern Illinois University at Carbondale

College of Business and Administration

Carbondale, Illinois

OVERVIEW

Southern Illinois University at Carbondale is a state-supported coed institution. Part of Southern Illinois University. Founded 1869. Setting: 1,128-acre small-town campus. Total institutional enrollment: 25,000. Program was first offered in 1965. AACSB-accredited.

MBA HIGHLIGHTS

Entrance Difficulty*
Mean GMAT: 513
Mean GPA: 3.3

Cost $
Tuition: $77/semester hour
(Nonresident: $232/semester hour)
Room & Board: N/R

Enrollment Profile

Full-time: 80	Work Exp: 78%
Part-time: 50	International: 45%
Total: 130	Women: 40%
Average Age: 27	Minorities: 8%

Class Size: 20 - 25

The M.B.A. Program at Southern Illinois University at Carbondale emphasizes the practical aspects of business and executive performance with a particular focus on the international perspective. The 30-credit-hour core curriculum includes 9 credits of electives, with great flexibility given to students in choosing areas of emphasis. Enrollment is limited to ensure small class sizes and encourage in-depth discussion of cases and issues.

SIUC's College of Business and Administration also offers Master of Accountancy (M.Acc.) and Doctorate in Business Administration (D.B.A.) programs.

SIUC has one of the largest international student populations in the United States. International enrollment in the M.B.A. program is approximately 40 percent, with over twenty countries represented.

ACADEMICS

Length of Program Minimum: 16 months. Maximum: 6 years.

Calendar Semesters.

Full-time Classes Main campus; day, evening, weekends, summer.

Degree Requirements 30 credits including 9 elective credits.

Curricular Focus General management, problem solving and decision making, teamwork.

Concentrations Accounting, finance, international business, management, management information systems, marketing, operations management, organizational behavior, strategic management.

Faculty Full-time: 22, 100% with doctorates.

Teaching Methodology Case study: 20%, faculty seminars: 5%, lecture: 30%, research: 10%, seminars by members of the business community: 5%, student presentations: 10%, team projects: 20%.

Special Opportunities International exchange and internship programs available.

STUDENT STATISTICS

Geographic Representation State residents 51%. By region: Midwest 35%; South 15%; Northeast 2%; West 2%. International 45%.

Undergraduate Majors Business 53%; education 5%; engineering/technology 13%; humanities 5%; science/mathematics 9%; social sciences 10%; other 5%.

Other Background Graduate degrees in other disciplines: 6%. Work experience: On average, students have 4 years of work experience on entrance to the program.

FACILITIES

Information Resources Main library with 2.2 million bound volumes, 3.5 million titles on microform, 17,047 periodical subscriptions, 23,301 records/tapes/CDs, 39 CD-ROMs.

Housing 30% of students in program live in college-owned or -operated housing.

Technology Computers are used heavily in course work. 200 computer terminals/PCs, linked by a campus-wide computer network, are available for use by students in program; they are located in the library, the computer center, computer labs. Students in the program are not required to have their own PC. $1,000 are budgeted per student for computer support.

Computer Resources/On-line Services

Training	Yes	LEXIS/NEXIS	Yes
Internet	Yes	Dun's	No
E-Mail	Yes	Dow Jones	No
Videoconference Center	Yes	Dialog	Yes
Multimedia Center	Yes	Bloomberg	No

Other on-line services: OCLC.

ADMISSION

Acceptance 1994-95 Of those applying, 55% were accepted.

Entrance Requirements Bachelor's degree, GMAT score of 500, minimum 2.7 GPA. Core courses waived through: previous course work.

Application Requirements Written essay, application form, copies of transcript, personal statement, 3 letters of recommendation.

Application Deadlines 6/15 for fall, 11/15 for spring, 4/15 for summer.

FINANCIALS

Costs for 1994-95 Tuition: Full-time: $77/semester hour for state residents, $232/semester hour for nonresidents. Fees: Full-time: $18/semester hour for state residents, $18/semester hour for nonresidents.

Financial Aid In 1994-95, 75% of candidates received some institutionally administered aid in the form of scholarships, loans, fellowships, assistantships. Total awards ranged from $5,850-$9,000. Financial aid is available to part-time students. Application deadlines: 3/15 for fall, 9/15 for spring. Contact: Ms. Barbara Humphrey, Administrative Aid, Rehn 133, College of Business and Administration, Carbondale, IL 62901. (618) 453-3030.

INTERNATIONAL STUDENTS

Demographics 45% of students enrolled in the program are international; Asia 67%, Europe 21%, Africa 9%, Central America 2%, other 1%.

Services and Facilities International student center, visa services, language tutoring, ESL courses, special assistance for nonnative speakers of English, counseling/support services.

Applying TOEFL required, minimum score of 550; proof of health; proof of adequate funds. Financial aid is available to international students. Financial aid application deadlines: 3/15 for fall, 9/15 for spring, 2/15 for summer. Admission application deadlines: 4/15 for fall, 9/15 for spring, 2/15 for summer. Contact: Ms. Carla E. Coppi, Assistant Director, International Programs and Services, 910 South Forest Street, Carbondale, IL 62901. (618) 453-5774.

ALTERNATE MBA PROGRAM

MBA/JD Length of program: Minimum: 36 months. Maximum: 6 years. Degree requirements: 102 credits.

PLACEMENT

In 1993-94, 10 organizations participated in on-campus recruiting. Placement services include alumni networks, career counseling/planning, career fairs, career library, career placement, and job interviews.

Jobs by Employer Type Manufacturing 40%; service 40%; consulting 20%.

Jobs by Functional Area Marketing/sales 30%; finance 40%; operations 20%; management 5%; strategic planning 5%.

Program Contact: Mr. Joseph Pineau, MBA Coordinator, Southern Illinois University at Carbondale, Carbondale, IL 62901. (618) 453-3030; Fax: (618) 453-7961.

Southern Illinois University at Edwardsville

School of Business

Edwardsville, Illinois

OVERVIEW

Southern Illinois University at Edwardsville is a state-supported comprehensive coed institution. Part of Southern Illinois University. Founded 1957. Setting: 2,600-acre suburban campus with easy access to St. Louis. Total institutional enrollment: 11,000. Program was first offered in 1965. AACSB-accredited.

MBA HIGHLIGHTS

Entrance Difficulty***
Mean GMAT: 510
Mean GPA: N/R

Cost $
Tuition: $1,112 - $1,368/semester
(Nonresident: $2,267 - $2,964/semester)
Room & Board: N/R

Enrollment Profile

Full-time: 415	Work Exp: 95%
Part-time: 45	International: N/R
Total: 460	Women: 31%
Average Age: 28	Minorities: 8%

Average Class Size: 30

ACADEMICS

Length of Program Minimum: 18 months. Maximum: 6 years.
Calendar Semesters.
Full-time Classes Main campus, St. Louis, Belleville; evening, weekends, summer.
Part-time Classes Main campus, St. Louis, Belleville, Rend Lake, distance learning option; evening, weekends.
Degree Requirements 33 credits including 9 elective credits.
Required Courses External environment of business, finance, international business environment, leadership, influence, and management effectiveness, management information systems, marketing, strategic management.
Curricular Focus International business, managing diversity, strategic analysis and planning.
Concentrations Economics, entrepreneurship, finance, human resources management, international business, management, management information systems, marketing, operations management, organizational behavior, quantitative analysis.
Faculty Full-time: 30, 99% with doctorates; part-time: 3.
Teaching Methodology Case study: 20%, lecture: 20%, research: 10%, student presentations: 10%, team projects: 40%.
Special Opportunities International exchange in France, Germany, Mexico, Netherlands, United Kingdom. Internships include marketing in banking, finance, management information systems, and research.

STUDENT STATISTICS

Geographic Representation By region: Midwest 95%.
Undergraduate Majors Business 60%; education 5%; engineering/technology 10%; humanities 5%; science/mathematics 9%; social sciences 5%; other 6%.
Other Background Graduate degrees in other disciplines: 5%. Work experience: On average, students have 4 years of work experience on entrance to the program.

FACILITIES

Information Resources Main library with 752,108 bound volumes, 1.2 million titles on microform, 6,088 periodical subscriptions, 36,620 records/tapes/CDs.
Housing 10% of students in program live in college-owned or -operated housing. Assistance with housing search provided.
Technology Computers are used heavily in course work. 140 computer terminals/PCs are available for use by students in program; they are located in dormitories, the computer center, computer labs. Students in the program are not required to have their own PC.

Computer Resources/On-line Services

Training	Yes	E-Mail	Yes
Internet	Yes		

ADMISSION

Acceptance 1994-95 110 applied for admission; 82% were accepted.
Entrance Requirements Bachelor's degree, GMAT score of 400. Core courses waived through: previous course work.
Application Requirements Application form, copies of transcript.
Application Deadline Applications are processed on a rolling basis. Application discs available.

FINANCIALS

Costs for 1994-95 Tuition: Full-time: $925-$1,178/semester for state residents, $2,080-$2,774/semester for nonresidents; Part-time evening: $379-$693/semester for state residents, $693-$1,387/semester for nonresidents. Fees: Full-time: $187-$190/semester for state residents, $187-$190/semester for nonresidents; Part-time evening: $119-$131/semester for state residents, $119-$131/semester for nonresidents.

Financial Aid In 1994-95, 5% of candidates received some institutionally administered aid in the form of assistantships. Total awards ranged from $5,400-$6,300. Financial aid is not available to part-time students. Application deadlines: 7/20 for fall, 12/9 for spring. Applications are processed on a rolling basis. Contact: Dr. David Ault, Dean, Box 1051, Edwardsville, IL 62026. (618) 692-3823.

INTERNATIONAL STUDENTS

Services and Facilities International student center, visa services, special assistance for nonnative speakers of English, counseling/support services.
Applying TOEFL required, minimum score of 550; proof of health; proof of adequate funds. Financial aid is not available to international students. Admission applications are processed on a rolling basis. Contact: Dr. Robert Schutzius, Assistant to the Dean, Box 1086, Edwardsville, IL 62026. (618) 692-3851.

PLACEMENT

In 1993-94, 10 organizations participated in on-campus recruiting; 150 on-campus interviews were conducted. Placement services include career fairs, career library, career placement, electronic job bank, job interviews, and resume preparation. Of 1994 graduates, 95% were employed within three months of graduation, the average starting salary was $27,000, the range was $19,000-$35,000.

Jobs by Employer Type Manufacturing 10%; service 60%; government 10%; consulting 10%; nonprofit 5%; other 5%.

Jobs by Functional Area Marketing/sales 30%; finance 10%; operations 5%; management 50%; strategic planning 1%; technical management 4%.

Program Contact: Mr. Robert Schutzius, Assistant to the Dean, Southern Illinois University at Edwardsville, Box 1086, Edwardsville, IL 62026. (618) 692-3851; Fax: (618) 692-3979; Internet Address: rschutz@siue.edu.

See full description on page 832.

University of Chicago

Graduate School of Business

Chicago, Illinois

OVERVIEW

The University of Chicago is an independent nonprofit coed institution. Founded 1891. Setting: 190-acre urban campus. Total institutional enrollment: 11,441. AACSB-accredited.

MBA HIGHLIGHTS

Entrance Difficulty*****
Mean GMAT: 650
Mean GPA: 3.4

Cost $$$$
Tuition: $21,350
Room & Board: $9,054

Enrollment Profile

Full-time: 1,231	Work Exp: 95%
Part-time: 1,472	International: N/R
Total: 2,703	Women: 26%
Average Age: 27	Minorities: 16%

Average Class Size: 45

ACADEMICS

Length of Program Minimum: 18 months. Maximum: 5 years.
Calendar Quarters.
Full-time Classes Main campus; day, early morning, summer.
Part-time Classes Main campus, Chicago; evening, weekends, summer.
Degree Requirements 105 credits including 55 elective credits.
Required Courses Business policy, financial accounting, leadership exploration and development, managing in organizations, microeconomics, statistics.
Curricular Focus General management, international business, leadership.
Concentrations Accounting, economics, finance, human resources management, international business, management, management information systems, marketing, operations management, quality management, quantitative analysis, strategic management.

Faculty Full-time: 121, 100% with doctorates; part-time: 34, 41% with doctorates.

Special Opportunities International exchange in Australia, Austria, Belgium, Chile, France, Hong Kong, Italy, Japan, Netherlands, Republic of Korea, Spain, Sweden, Switzerland, United Kingdom. Internships include finance, operations, and marketing.

STUDENT STATISTICS

Geographic Representation State residents 10%. By region: Northeast 26%; Midwest 22%; West 17%; South 15%.

Undergraduate Majors Business 31%; engineering/technology 20%; humanities 5%; science/mathematics 7%; social sciences 35%; other 1%.

Other Background Graduate degrees in other disciplines: 14%. Work experience: On average, students have 4 years of work experience on entrance to the program.

FACILITIES

Information Resources Main library with 5.7 million bound volumes, 2 million titles on microform, 47,000 periodical subscriptions, 17,500 records/tapes/CDs.

Housing College housing available.

Technology Computers are used heavily in course work. 75 computer terminals/PCs, linked by a campus-wide computer network, are available for use by students in program; they are located in the library, computer labs. Students in the program are not required to have their own PC.

Computer Resources/On-line Services

Training	Yes	LEXIS/NEXIS	Yes
Internet	Yes	Dow Jones	Yes
E-Mail	Yes	Bloomberg	Yes

ADMISSION

Acceptance 1994-95 3,255 applied for admission.

Entrance Requirements Bachelor's degree, GMAT score.

Application Requirements Written essay, application form, copies of transcript, 2 letters of recommendation.

Application Deadline 2/15 for fall. Application discs available.

FINANCIALS

Costs for 1994-95 Tuition: Full-time: $21,350. Fees: Full-time: $306. Average room and board costs are $9,054 per academic year (on-campus) and $9,054 per academic year (off-campus).

Financial Aid In 1994-95, 18% of candidates received some institutionally administered aid in the form of scholarships. Total awards ranged from $5,000-$20,200. Financial aid is not available to part-time students. Application deadline: 2/1 for fall. Contact: Ms. Cori McManus, Associate Director of Financial Aid, 1101 East 58th Street, Chicago, IL 60637-1513. (312) 702-3964.

INTERNATIONAL STUDENTS

Services and Facilities International student center, visa services, language tutoring, counseling/support services.

Applying TOEFL required, minimum score of 550; proof of adequate funds. Financial aid is not available to international students. Admission application deadline: 2/1 for fall. Contact: Ms. Dorothy White, Associate Director, Admissions and Financial School of Business, 1101 East 58th Street, Chicago, IL 60637-1513. (312) 702-7439.

ALTERNATE MBA PROGRAMS

Executive MBA (EMBA) Length of program: Minimum: 30 months. Maximum: 5 years. Degree requirements: 100 credits. International option allows students to complete course work in 1 1/2 years by taking 4 weeks of intensive study, 2 in Chicago and 2 in Barcelona, Spain. Average class size: 80.

MBA/JD Length of program: Minimum: 36 months. Maximum: 5 years. Degree requirements: 195 credits including 20 elective credits.

MBA/MA Length of program: Minimum: 24 months. Maximum: 5 years. Degree requirements: 140 credits including 20 elective credits.

PLACEMENT

In 1993-94, 248 organizations participated in on-campus recruiting. Placement services include alumni network, career counseling/planning, career fairs, career library, career placement, electronic job bank, job interviews, resume preparation, and resume referral to employers. Of 1994 graduates, 95% were employed within three months of graduation, the average starting salary was $68,000, the range was $30,000-$130,000.

Jobs by Functional Area Marketing/sales 6%; finance 49%; operations 1%; management 6%; technical management 2%; strategic planning 1%; other 33%.

Program Contact: Mr. Donald Martin, Director of Admissions, University of Chicago, 5801 Ellis Avenue, Chicago, IL 60637-1513. (312) 702-7369; Fax: (312) 702-9085.

University of Illinois at Chicago

College of Business Administration

Chicago, Illinois

OVERVIEW

The University of Illinois at Chicago is a state-supported coed institution. Part of University of Illinois System. Founded 1946. Setting: 183-acre urban campus. Total institutional enrollment: 25,000. Program was first offered in 1976. AACSB-accredited.

MBA HIGHLIGHTS

Entrance Difficulty**
Mean GMAT: 560
Mean GPA: 3.2

Cost $$
Tuition: $3,300
(Nonresident: $9,900)
Room & Board: N/R

Enrollment Profile

Full-time: 198	Work Exp: 90%
Part-time: 276	International: 36%
Total: 474	Women: 32%
Average Age: 26	Minorities: 9%

Average Class Size: 25

ACADEMICS

Length of Program Minimum: 24 months. Maximum: 6 years.

Calendar Semesters.

Full-time Classes Main campus; day, summer.

Part-time Classes Main campus; evening, summer.

Degree Requirements 54 credits. Other: Professional topics sequence.

Required Courses Accounting, entrepreneurship, finance, international business, management information systems, marketing, microeconomics, operations management, organizational behavior, statistics.

Curricular Focus Entrepreneurship, international business, teamwork.

Concentrations Accounting, economics, entrepreneurship, finance, health information management, statistics for business, nursing, pharmacy administration, gerontology administration, health services, human resources management, international business, management, management information systems, marketing, operations management, organizational behavior, strategic management.

Faculty Full-time: 94, 100% with doctorates.

Teaching Methodology Case study: 10%, faculty seminars: 5%, lecture: 20%, research: 5%, seminars by members of the business community: 15%, student presentations: 10%, team projects: 35%.

Special Opportunities International exchange in Austria, France, United Kingdom. Internship program available.

STUDENT STATISTICS

Geographic Representation International 36%.

Undergraduate Majors Business 30%; engineering/technology 30%; social sciences 20%; other 20%.

Other Background Work experience: On average, students have 4 years of work experience on entrance to the program.

FACILITIES

Information Resources Main library with 1.8 million bound volumes, 15,989 periodical subscriptions, 20,822 records/tapes/CDs, 65 CD-ROMs.

Housing College housing available.

Technology Computers are used heavily in course work. Computer terminals/PCs, linked by a campus-wide computer network, are available for use by students in program; they are located in the library, the computer center, computer labs, the research center. Students in the program are not required to have their own PC.

Computer Resources/On-line Services

Training	Yes	Multimedia Center	Yes
Internet	Yes	LEXIS/NEXIS	Yes
E-Mail	Yes	CompuServe	No

ADMISSION

Acceptance 1994-95 385 applied for admission; 45% were accepted.

Entrance Requirements Bachelor's degree, GMAT score.

Application Requirements Written essay, application form, copies of transcript, resume/curriculum vitae, personal statement, 2 letters of recommendation.

Application Deadlines 5/15 for fall, 11/1 for spring. Applications are processed on a rolling basis.

FINANCIALS

Estimated Costs for 1995-96 Tuition: Full-time: $3,300 for state residents, $9,900 for nonresidents. Fees: Full-time: $5,203 for state residents, $5,203 for nonresidents.

Financial Aid In 1994-95, 16% of candidates received some institutionally administered aid in the form of grants, scholarships, loans, fellowships, assistantships. Total awards ranged from $500-$12,000. Financial aid is not available to part-time students. Application deadline: 1/15 for fall. Contact: Ms. Marsha S. Weiss, Director, Chicago, IL 60680. (312) 996-5563.

INTERNATIONAL STUDENTS

Demographics 36% of students enrolled in the program are international; Europe 48%, Asia 37%, South America 15%.

Applying TOEFL required, minimum score of 570; proof of adequate funds. Financial aid is available to international students. Financial aid application deadline: 2/1 for fall. Applications are processed on a rolling basis. Admission application deadline: 3/31 for fall. Applications are processed on a rolling basis. Contact: Director of Foreign Student Affairs, Chicago, IL 60680. (312) 996-3121.

ALTERNATE MBA PROGRAMS

MBA/MA Length of program: Minimum: 30 months. Full-time classes: Main campus; day, evening, summer. Degree requirements: 66 credits.

MBA/MS Length of program: Minimum: 30 months. Full-time classes: Main campus; day, evening, summer. Part-time classes: Main campus; day, evening, summer. Degree requirements: 66 credits.

MBA/MSN Length of program: Minimum: 36 months. Part-time classes: Main campus; evening. Degree requirements: 66 credits.

MBA/MPH Length of program: Minimum: 30 months. Full-time classes: Main campus; day, evening, summer. Degree requirements: 72 credits.

PLACEMENT

In 1993-94, 100 organizations participated in on-campus recruiting; 500 on-campus interviews were conducted. Placement services include alumni network, career counseling/planning, career fairs, career library, career placement, job interviews, resume preparation, and resume referral to employers. Of 1994 graduates, 74% were employed within three months of graduation.

Jobs by Employer Type Manufacturing 17%; service 47%; government 6%; healthcare 17%; consumer products 13%.

Jobs by Functional Area Marketing/sales 13%; finance 33%; management 30%; technical management 20%; other 4%.

Program Contact: Ms. Shari Holmer Lewis, Assistant Dean and Director, Graduate Professional Business Programs, University of Illinois at Chicago, Chicago, IL 60680. (312) 996-4573; Fax: (312) 413-0338; Internet Address: mba@uic.edu.

See full description on page 878.

University of Illinois at Urbana-Champaign

Champaign, Illinois

OVERVIEW

The University of Illinois at Urbana-Champaign is a state-supported coed institution. Part of University of Illinois System. Founded 1867. Setting: 1,338-acre urban campus. Total institutional enrollment: 36,000. Program was first offered in 1962. AACSB-accredited.

MBA HIGHLIGHTS

Entrance Difficulty**
Mean GMAT: 618
Mean GPA: 4.22 (5.0 scale)

Cost $$
Tuition: $2,400/semester
(Nonresident: $6,314/semester)
Room & Board: $4,500

Enrollment Profile

Full-time: 562	Work Exp: 69%
Part-time: 0	International: 39%
Total: 562	Women: 28%
Average Age: 25	Minorities: 13%

Class Size: 40 - 70

The Illinois M.B.A. is adapting its curriculum to meet the needs of students who will be leaders in a global business environment characterized by vigorous competition and continuous change. Teamwork has long been a part of the Illinois M.B.A. student experience. Now, the faculty has adopted a team approach designed to give students an integrated learning experience that teaches from a real-world point of view. In business, there are not simply accounting problems, marketing problems, or operations problems. There are business problems that have implications for all these functional areas. The new Illinois M.B.A. curriculum leads students to view managerial problems (and opportunities) from a more general point of view. As a result, students gain a more realistic perspective than can be taught in a curriculum that is separated into functional components.

The focus of the new Illinois M.B.A. is on developing managers rather than on teaching management. One outcome of this philosophy is an innovative program of M.B.A. Student Management Leadership Grants. Through this program, the Illinois M.B.A. is largely student-managed. The merit-based grants are awarded to both international and domestic students. By completing work assignments, grant recipients make valuable contributions to the M.B.A. program.

ACADEMICS

Length of Program Minimum: 22 months. Maximum: 5 years.

Calendar Semesters.

Full-time Classes Main campus; day.

Degree Requirements 20 units. Other: Communication workshops.

Required Courses Accounting, capstone, economics, finance, marketing, operations, organizational behavior, quantitative analysis.

Curricular Focus Managing diversity, problem solving and decision making, teamwork.

Concentrations Accounting, economics, entrepreneurship, finance, food and agribusiness management, risk management and insurance, health services, human resources management, international business, management, management information systems, marketing, operations management, organizational behavior, quantitative analysis, real estate, strategic management.

Faculty Full-time: 50, 100% with doctorates; part-time: 2.

Teaching Methodology Case study: 25%, experiential learning: 15%, lecture: 30%, research: 3%, seminars by members of the business community: 2%, team projects: 25%.

Special Opportunities International exchange in Australia, Austria, Canada, Denmark, France, Germany, Japan, Spain, United Kingdom. Internship program available. Other: summer consulting, applied management.

STUDENT STATISTICS

Geographic Representation State residents 38%. By region: Midwest 48%; South 5%; Northeast 4%; West 4%. International 39%.

Undergraduate Majors Business 48%; education 1%; engineering/technology 22%; humanities 8%; science/mathematics 4%; social sciences 9%; other 8%.

Other Background Graduate degrees in other disciplines: 11%. Work experience: On average, students have 2 years of work experience on entrance to the program.

FACILITIES

Information Resources Main library with 8.5 million bound volumes, 91,000 periodical subscriptions, 135,000 records/tapes/CDs, 102 CD-ROMs. Business collection in Commerce Library includes 70,000 bound volumes, 1,650 periodical subscriptions.

Housing 15% of students in program live in college-owned or -operated housing.

Technology Computers are used heavily in course work. 3,000 computer terminals/PCs, linked by a campus-wide computer network, are available for use by students in program; they are located in dormitories, the student center, classrooms, learning resource center, the library, the computer center, computer labs, the research center. Students in the program are not required to have their own PC. $250 are budgeted per student for computer support.

Computer Resources/On-line Services

Training	Yes	Multimedia Center	Yes
Internet	Yes	LEXIS/NEXIS	Yes
E-Mail	Yes	Dialog	Yes $

ADMISSION

Acceptance 1994-95 948 applied for admission; 64% were accepted.

Entrance Requirements Bachelor's degree, college level calculus, GMAT score, minimum 3.0 GPA.

Application Requirements Written essay, application form, copies of transcript, resume/curriculum vitae, 3 letters of recommendation.

Application Deadline 4/1 for fall.

FINANCIALS

Costs for 1994-95 Tuition: Full-time: $2,400/semester for state residents, $6,314/semester for nonresidents. Fees: Full-time: $974/semester for state residents, $974/semester for nonresidents. Average room and board costs are $4,500 per academic year (on-campus) and $6,000 per academic year (off-campus).

Financial Aid In 1994-95, 75% of candidates received some institutionally administered aid in the form of grants, scholarships, loans, fellowships, assistantships. Total awards ranged from $1,000-$18,500. Application deadline: 4/1 for fall. Contact: Ms. Leela Cheryan, Financial Aid Administrator, 610 East John Street, Champaign, IL 61820. (217) 333-0100.

INTERNATIONAL STUDENTS

Demographics 39% of students enrolled in the program are international; Asia 82%, Europe 8%, Africa 3%, Central America 3%, South America 3%.

Services and Facilities International student center, visa services, language tutoring, ESL courses, counseling/support services.

Applying TOEFL required, minimum score of 550; proof of health; proof of adequate funds; Test of Spoken English. Financial aid is available to international students. Student Management Leadership Grants are available to these students. Financial aid application deadline: 4/1 for fall. Admission application deadline: 4/1 for fall. Contact: Mr. Ivor Emmanuel, Director, International Student Affairs, 510 East Daniel, Champaign, IL 61820. (217) 333-1303.

ALTERNATE MBA PROGRAMS

Executive MBA (EMBA) Length of program: Minimum: 18 months. Degree requirements: 16 units. Average class size: 40.

MBA/JD Length of program: Minimum: 48 months. Maximum: 5 years. Degree requirements: GMAT and LSAT; 12 units for business, 74 hours for law.

MBA/MS Length of program: Minimum: 28 months. Maximum: 5 years. Degree requirements: GMAT and GRE; 14 units for business, 6 or 7 units for civil engineering. MS is in civil engineering.

MBA/M Arch Length of program: Minimum: 30 months. Maximum: 5 years. Degree requirements: GMAT and GRE; 12 units for business, 9.5 units for architecture.

MBA/M Ed Length of program: Minimum: 24 months. Maximum: 3 years. Degree requirements: GMAT and GRE; 12 units for business, 8 units for education.

MBA/MCS Length of program: Minimum: 28 months. Maximum: 5 years. Degree requirements: GMAT and GRE; 12 units for business, 9 units for computer science.

MBA/MD Length of program: Minimum: 60 months. Maximum: 5 years. Degree requirements: GMAT and MCAT; 12 units for business, 1376 instruction hours of medicine during first two years, 64 weeks of clinical training during last two years of medicine.

MBA/MS Length of program: Minimum: 28 months. Maximum: 5 years. Degree requirements: GMAT and GRE; 12 units for business, 8 or 9 units for engineering. MS is in mechanical engineering.

MBA/MS Length of program: Minimum: 28 months. Maximum: 5 years. Degree requirements: GMAT and GRE; 14 units for business, 5 units for electrical engineering. MS is in electrical engineering.

MBA/MS Length of program: Minimum: 28 months. Maximum: 5 years. Degree requirements: GMAT and GRE; 12 units for business, 8 or 9 units for industrial engineering. MS is in industrial engineering.

MBA/MS Length of program: Minimum: 28 months. Maximum: 5 years. Degree requirements: GMAT and GRE; 12 units for business, 6 units for general engineering. MS is in general engineering.

MBA/MSJ Length of program: Minimum: 24 months. Maximum: 5 years. Degree requirements: GMAT and GRE; 12 units for business, 8 units for journalism.

PLACEMENT

In 1993-94, 82 organizations participated in on-campus recruiting; 988 on-campus interviews were conducted. Placement services include alumni network, career counseling/planning, career fairs, career library, career placement, electronic job bank, job interviews, resume preparation, and resume referral to employers. Of 1994 graduates, 93% were employed within three months of graduation, the average starting salary was $42,150, the range was $25,000-$118,000.

Jobs by Employer Type Manufacturing 30%; service 70%.

Jobs by Functional Area Marketing/sales 16%; finance 39%; operations 9%; management 7%; technical management 5%; consulting 16%; other 8%.

Program Contact: Ms. Jane G. White, Director, Recruitment and Admissions, University of Illinois at Urbana-Champaign, 601 East John Street, Champaign, IL 61820. (217) 244-2953, or (800) MBA-UIUC; Fax: (217) 333-1156; Internet Address: jwhite@commerce.cba.uiuc.edu.

See full description on page 880.

Western Illinois University

College of Business and Technology

Macomb, Illinois

OVERVIEW

Western Illinois University is a state-supported comprehensive coed institution. Part of Board of Governors Universities. Founded 1899. Setting: 1,050-acre rural campus. Total institutional enrollment: 12,600. Program was first offered in 1968. AACSB-accredited.

MBA HIGHLIGHTS

Entrance Difficulty*

Cost $
Tuition: $972/semester
(Nonresident: $2,916/semester)
Room & Board: $3,193

Enrollment Profile

Full-time: 90	Work Exp: N/R
Part-time: 20	International: 55%
Total: 110	Women: 26%
Average Age: N/R	Minorities: 1%

Average Class Size: 19

ACADEMICS

Length of Program Minimum: 12 months. Maximum: 6 years.

Calendar Semesters.

Full-time Classes Main campus; day, evening, early morning, summer.

Degree Requirements 33 credits including 9 elective credits.

Required Courses Accounting, economics, finance, marketing, operations management, operations research, policy, research methodology. Courses may be waived through: previous course work.

Curricular Focus Business issues and problems, entrepreneurship, general management.

Concentrations Accounting, economics, entrepreneurship, finance, human resources management, international business, management, management information systems, marketing, organizational behavior, quantitative analysis.

Faculty Full-time: 10, 100% with doctorates.

Teaching Methodology Case study: 35%, lecture: 50%, research: 5%, student presentations: 10%.

STUDENT STATISTICS

Geographic Representation State residents 40%. By region: West 55%; South 45%. International 55%.

Undergraduate Majors Business 54%; engineering/technology 8%; science/mathematics 11%, social sciences 12%; other 14%.

FACILITIES
Information Resources Main library with 709,067 bound volumes, 437,586 titles on microform, 3,040 periodical subscriptions, 1,500 records/tapes/CDs, 25 CD-ROMs.
Housing 65% of students in program live in college-owned or -operated housing.
Technology Computers are used moderately in course work. 250 computer terminals/PCs, linked by a campus-wide computer network, are available for use by students in program; they are located in dormitories, the library, the computer center, computer labs. Students in the program are not required to have their own PC.

Computer Resources/On-line Services

Internet	Yes	E-Mail	Yes

ADMISSION
Acceptance 1994-95 Of those applying, 85% were accepted.
Entrance Requirements Bachelor's degree, GMAT score of 450, minimum 2.5 GPA. Core courses waived through: previous course work.
Application Requirements Application form, copies of transcript.
Application Deadlines 8/1 for fall, 12/15 for spring, 5/1 for summer.

FINANCIALS
Costs for 1994-95 Tuition: Full-time: $972/semester for state residents, $2,916/semester for nonresidents. Fees: Full-time: $350/semester for state residents, $350/semester for nonresidents. Average room and board costs are $3,193 per academic year (on-campus).
Financial Aid In 1994-95, candidates received some institutionally administered aid in the form of scholarships, assistantships. Financial aid is not available to part-time students. Applications are processed on a rolling basis. Contact: Mr. William Bushaw, Director of Financial Aid, 1 University Circle, Macomb, IL 61455-1396. (309) 298-2446.

INTERNATIONAL STUDENTS
Demographics 55% of students enrolled in the program are international; Asia 85%, Europe 6%, South America 1%, other 6%.
Services and Facilities Visa services, ESL courses, special assistance for nonnative speakers of English.
Applying TOEFL required, minimum score of 550; proof of health; proof of adequate funds. Financial aid is available to international students. Financial aid application deadlines: 7/1 for fall, 11/15 for spring, 4/1 for summer. Admission application deadlines: 7/1 for fall, 11/15 for spring, 4/1 for summer. Contact: Ms. Julie Rose, Director of International Student Admissions, 1 University Circle, Macomb, IL 61455-1396. (309) 298-2424.

PLACEMENT
Placement services include career counseling/planning, career fairs, career library, career placement, job interviews, resume preparation, and resume referral to employers.

Program Contact: Dr. Larry Wall, Associate Dean, Western Illinois University, 1 University Circle, Macomb, IL 61455-1396. (309) 298-2442; Fax: (309) 298-1039; Internet Address: ccmail@walll.wiu.bgu.edu.

INDIANA

Ball State University

College of Business

Muncie, Indiana

OVERVIEW
Ball State University is a state-supported coed institution. Founded 1918. Setting: 955-acre suburban campus with easy access to Indianapolis. Total institutional enrollment: 20,000. Program was first offered in 1983. AACSB-accredited.

MBA HIGHLIGHTS

Entrance Difficulty***
Mean GMAT: 530
Mean GPA: 3.02

Cost $
Tuition: $1,504/semester
(Nonresident: $3,764/semester)
Room & Board: $4,136

Enrollment Profile

Full-time: 100	Work Exp: 61%
Part-time: 225	International: 11%
Total: 325	Women: 26%
Average Age: 28	Minorities: 8%

Average Class Size: 30

ACADEMICS
Length of Program Minimum: 12 months. Maximum: 6 years.
Calendar Semesters.
Full-time Classes Main campus; day, evening, weekends, early morning, summer.
Part-time Classes Main campus, distance learning option; evening, weekends, early morning, summer.
Degree Requirements 36 credits including 9 elective credits. Other: Minimum 9 hours in entrepreneurship, finance or operations management.
Required Courses Human resource development, international business strategy, macroeconomics, managerial accounting, managerial communications, managerial economics, managerial finance, marketing strategy, production operations, quantitative business decisions, statistics for business, strategic management and business policy.
Curricular Focus Entrepreneurship, problem solving and decision making, teamwork.
Concentrations Economics, entrepreneurship, finance, human resources management, management information systems, operations management.
Faculty Full-time: 25, 100% with doctorates.
Teaching Methodology Case study: 20%, lecture: 40%, research: 10%, student presentations: 10%, team projects: 20%.
Special Opportunities Internship program available.

STUDENT STATISTICS
Geographic Representation State residents 92%. By region: Midwest 80%; Northeast 10%. International 11%.
Undergraduate Majors Business 45%; engineering/technology 38%; humanities 5%; social sciences 7%; other 5%.
Other Background Graduate degrees in other disciplines: 5%. Work experience: On average, students have 2 years of work experience on entrance to the program.

FACILITIES
Information Resources Main library with 1.1 million bound volumes, 288,583 titles on microform, 3,525 periodical subscriptions, 551,157 records/tapes/CDs.
Housing 15% of students in program live in college-owned or -operated housing.
Technology Computers are used heavily in course work. 3,000 computer terminals/PCs, linked by a campus-wide computer network, are available for use by students in program; they are located in dormitories, the student center, learning resource center, the library, computer labs. Students in the program are not required to have their own PC.

Computer Resources/On-line Services

Training	Yes	CompuServe	No
Internet	Yes	Dun's	No
E-Mail	Yes	Dow Jones	No
Videoconference Center	Yes	Dialog	No
Multimedia Center	Yes	Bloomberg	No
LEXIS/NEXIS	No		

ADMISSION
Acceptance 1994-95 212 applied for admission; 82% were accepted.
Entrance Requirements Bachelor's degree, GMAT score of 400, minimum 2.5 GPA. Core courses waived through: previous course work.
Application Requirements Application form, copies of transcript.
Application Deadlines 7/25 for fall, 12/15 for spring. Applications are processed on a rolling basis.

FINANCIALS

Estimated Costs for 1995-96 Tuition: Full-time: $1,504/semester for state residents, $3,764/semester for nonresidents. Average room and board costs are $4,136 per academic year (on-campus) and $4,800 per academic year (off-campus).

Financial Aid In 1994-95, 35% of candidates received some institutionally administered aid in the form of scholarships, loans, assistantships. Total awards ranged from $350-$5,225. Financial aid is not available to part-time students. Application deadline: 1/25 for fall. Applications are processed on a rolling basis. Contact: Mr. Clarence Casazza, Director of Scholarships and Financial Aid, Lucina 245, Muncie, IN 47306. (317) 285-5600.

INTERNATIONAL STUDENTS

Demographics 11% of students enrolled in the program are international; Europe 50%, Asia 25%, Africa 15%, other 10%.

Services and Facilities International student center, visa services, language tutoring, ESL courses, counseling/support services.

Applying TOEFL required, minimum score of 550; proof of health; proof of adequate funds. Financial aid is not available to international students. Admission application deadline: 1/20 for fall. Contact: Mr. Kirk Robey, Associate Director of International Administration, 708 North Calvert, Muncie, IN 47306. (317) 285-5422.

PLACEMENT

Placement services include alumni network, career counseling/planning, career fairs, career placement, electronic job bank, job interviews, and resume referral to employers. Of 1994 graduates, 70% were employed within three months of graduation, the average starting salary was $30,000, the range was $25,000-$35,000.

Jobs by Employer Type Manufacturing 40%; service 30%; government 5%; consulting 15%; nonprofit 10%.

Program Contact: Ms. Tamara Estep, Director of Graduate Business Programs, Ball State University, Whitinger Building, Room 146, Muncie, IN 47306. (317) 285-1931; Fax: (317) 285-8818.

Butler University

College of Business Administration

Indianapolis, Indiana

OVERVIEW

Butler University is an independent nonprofit comprehensive coed institution. Founded 1855. Setting: 290-acre urban campus. Total institutional enrollment: 3,348.

MBA HIGHLIGHTS

Entrance Difficulty***

Cost $
Tuition: $185 - $250/credit hour
Room & Board: N/R

Enrollment Profile

Full-time: N/R	Work Exp: N/R
Part-time: N/R	International: 5%
Total: 425	Women: 30%
Average Age: N/R	Minorities: 5%

Average Class Size: 28

ACADEMICS

Length of Program Minimum: 36 months.

Calendar Semesters.

Part-time Classes Main campus; evening, weekends.

Degree Requirements 39 credits.

Curricular Focus Business issues and problems, international business, organizational development and change management.

Concentration Management.

Teaching Methodology Case study: 10%, faculty seminars: 5%, lecture: 50%, research: 10%, seminars by members of the business community: 5%, student presentations: 10%, team projects: 10%.

STUDENT STATISTICS

Geographic Representation State residents 95%. International 5%.

FACILITIES

Information Resources Main library with 286,112 bound volumes, 235,280 titles on microform, 2,903 periodical subscriptions, 15,722 records/tapes/CDs.

ADMISSION

Entrance Requirements Bachelor's degree, GMAT score.

Application Requirements Application form, copies of transcript, resume/curriculum vitae, 2 letters of recommendation.

Application Deadlines 8/1 for fall, 12/1 for spring, 5/1 for summer.

FINANCIALS

Costs for 1994-95 Tuition: Part-time evening: $185-$250/credit hour.

Financial Aid Applications are processed on a rolling basis. Contact: Mr. Richard M. Bellows, Director of Financial Aid, Financial Aid Office, Indianapolis, IN 46208-3485. (317) 283-9278.

INTERNATIONAL STUDENTS

Demographics 5% of students enrolled in the program are international.

Applying TOEFL required, minimum score of 550; proof of health; proof of adequate funds. Financial aid is available to international students.

Program Contact: Dr. William Reiber, Director of Graduate Studies, Butler University, College of Business Administration, Indianapolis, IN 46208-3485. (317) 283-9221; Fax: (317) 283-9455.

Indiana State University

School of Business

Terre Haute, Indiana

OVERVIEW

Indiana State University is a state-supported coed institution. Founded 1865. Setting: 91-acre urban campus with easy access to Indianapolis. Total institutional enrollment: 11,641. Program was first offered in 1967. AACSB-accredited.

MBA HIGHLIGHTS

Entrance Difficulty***
Mean GMAT: 554
Mean GPA: 3.13

Cost $
Tuition: $120/semester hour
(Nonresident: $271/semester hour)
Room & Board: $3,840

Enrollment Profile

Full-time: 55	Work Exp: 87%
Part-time: 43	International: 45%
Total: 98	Women: 19%
Average Age: 31	Minorities: 0%

Average Class Size: 15

ACADEMICS

Length of Program Minimum: 24 months. Maximum: 5 years.

Calendar Semesters.

Full-time Classes Main campus; evening, summer.

Part-time Classes Main campus; evening, summer.

Degree Requirements 36 credits including 9 elective credits.

Required Courses Accounting, business law, finance, management information systems, marketing, organizational behavior, production, statistics, strategy.

Curricular Focus General management, problem solving and decision making, strategic analysis and planning.

Concentrations Accounting, decision sciences, economics, entrepreneurship, finance, human resources management, management, management information systems, marketing, operations management, organizational behavior, quantitative analysis, strategic management.

Faculty Full-time: 28, 96% with doctorates.

Teaching Methodology Case study: 10%, lecture: 65%, research: 3%, student presentations: 10%, team projects: 10%, tours: 2%.

STUDENT STATISTICS

Geographic Representation State residents 55%. International 45%.

Undergraduate Majors Business 46%; education 1%; engineering/technology 19%; humanities 6%; nursing 1%; science/mathematics 19%; social sciences 7%; other 1%.

Other Background Work experience: On average, students have 5 years of work experience on entrance to the program.

FACILITIES

Information Resources Main library with 1.2 million bound volumes, 853,470 titles on microform, 5,663 periodical subscriptions, 24,616 records/tapes/CDs. Business collection includes 60,000 bound volumes, 200 periodical subscriptions, 40 CD-ROMs, 50 videos.

Housing 35% of students in program live in college-owned or -operated housing.

Technology Computers are used moderately in course work. 245 computer terminals/PCs, linked by a campus-wide computer network, are available for use by students in program; they are located in the library, the computer center, computer labs. Students in the program are not required to have their own PC.

Computer Resources/On-line Services

Training	Yes	CompuServe	No
Internet	Yes $	Dun's	No
E-Mail	Yes	Dow Jones	No
Multimedia Center	Yes	Dialog	Yes $
LEXIS/NEXIS	No	Bloomberg	No

ADMISSION

Acceptance 1994-95 57 applied for admission; 57% were accepted.

Entrance Requirements Bachelor's degree, GMAT score of 470, minimum 2.7 GPA. Core courses waived through: previous course work.

Application Requirements Application form, copies of transcript, personal statement, international students must supply 3 letters of recommendation.

Application Deadline Applications are processed on a rolling basis.

FINANCIALS

Costs for 1994-95 Tuition: Full-time: $120/semester hour for state residents, $271/semester hour for nonresidents. Average room and board costs are $3,840 per academic year (on-campus).

Financial Aid In 1994-95, 21% of candidates received some institutionally administered aid in the form of scholarships, assistantships. Total awards ranged from $6,701-$9,872. Financial aid is not available to part-time students. Application deadlines: 3/1 for fall, 3/1 for spring. Contact: Dr. Herschel N. Chait, MBA Director and Acting Associate Dean, School of Business, MBA Program, Statesman Tower East, Room 1109, Terre Haute, IN 47809-5402. (812) 237-2000.

INTERNATIONAL STUDENTS

Demographics 45% of students enrolled in the program are international; Asia 96%, Europe 3%, Australia 1%.

Services and Facilities ESL courses, special assistance for nonnative speakers of English, counseling/support services.

Applying TOEFL required, minimum score of 550; proof of adequate funds. Financial aid is available to international students. Financial aid application deadlines: 3/1 for fall, 3/1 for spring. Applications are processed on a rolling basis. Admission applications are processed on a rolling basis. Contact: Mr. Roger Lehr, Director, International Student Services, Terre Haute, IN 47809. (812) 237-2440.

PLACEMENT

Placement services include career counseling/planning, career fairs, career library, job interviews, and resume preparation.

Program Contact: Dr. Herschel N. Chait, MBA Director and Acting Associate Dean, Indiana State University, Terre Haute, IN 47809. (812) 237-2000, or (800) 444-4723; Fax: (812) 237-7631.

Indiana University Bloomington

Graduate School of Business

Bloomington, Indiana

OVERVIEW

Indiana University Bloomington is a state-supported coed institution. Part of Indiana University System. Founded 1820. Setting: 1,800-acre small-town campus with easy access to Indianapolis. Total institutional enrollment: 35,594. AACSB-accredited.

MBA HIGHLIGHTS

Entrance Difficulty***
Mean GMAT: 600
Mean GPA: 3.2

Cost $$
Tuition: $3,420/semester
(Nonresident: $6,840/semester)
Room & Board: $4,484

Enrollment Profile

Full-time: 556	Work Exp: 94%
Part-time: 0	International: 14%
Total: 556	Women: 30%
Average Age: 27	Minorities: 11%

Average Class Size: 35

Many M.B.A. programs give the impression that business is tidy, that it is neatly divided up into functional categories, that business decisions come with ample time frames built in, and that management problems lend themselves easily to textbook solutions. The Indiana M.B.A. is different. Business is not about theory and abstractions. It is about fast-paced life in the marketplace. The Indiana M.B.A. program takes the focus out of the classroom and puts it in the boardroom, or on the trading floor, or in the corridor after a high-powered meeting, or in the quiet of an office at 11 p.m. as solutions are finally discovered. That is business, and Indiana M.B.A. graduates are prepared to deal with it.

M.B.A. students at Indiana participate in a breakthrough M.B.A. curriculum. There are no academic barriers. Students maneuver within an M.B.A. structure that is based on integration, not fragmentation. Practically and philosophically, the program is about synthesis: gathering information, linking it together, and finding the connections. Teamwork—a common way of working in corporations these days—is a major focus among both the faculty and students.

The Indiana M.B.A. program is a leader in graduate management education—an innovator preparing for the twenty-first century of business.

ACADEMICS

Length of Program Minimum: 20 months. Maximum: 7 years.

Calendar Semesters.

Full-time Classes Main campus; day.

Part-time Classes Main campus, Indianapolis; evening, summer.

Degree Requirements 54 credits including 16.5 elective credits. Other: Minimum 2.75 GPA.

Required Courses Analysis of business conditions, business law, foundations core, functional core, legal concepts and trends affecting business, professional core, strategy.

Curricular Focus General management, leadership, teamwork.

Concentrations Entrepreneurship, human resources management, international business, management, management information systems, marketing, operations management.

Faculty Full-time: 136, 88% with doctorates.

Teaching Methodology Case study: 40%, lecture: 40%, seminars by members of the business community: 10%, student presentations: 10%.

Special Opportunities International exchange in Australia, Finland, France, Germany, Norway, Spain, United Kingdom. Internship program available.

STUDENT STATISTICS

Geographic Representation State residents 18%. By region: Midwest 40%; Northeast 17%; South 13%; West 13%. International 14%.

Undergraduate Majors Business 40%; education 1%; engineering/technology 15%; humanities 6%; science/mathematics 10%; social sciences 27%; other 1%.

Other Background Graduate degrees in other disciplines: 5%. Work experience: On average, students have 4 years of work experience on entrance to the program.

FACILITIES

Information Resources Main library with 5.6 million bound volumes, 3.4 million titles on microform, 40,548 periodical subscriptions, 122,422 records/tapes/CDs, 400 CD-ROMs. Business collection in School of Business/School of Public and Environmental Affairs Library includes 175,000 bound volumes, 1,000 periodical subscriptions, 25 CD-ROMs, 250 videos.

Housing College housing available.

Technology Computers are used heavily in course work. 250 computer terminals/PCs, linked by a campus-wide computer network, are available for use by students in program; they are located in student rooms, classrooms, the library, the computer center, computer labs, private lab. Students in the program are required to have their own PC.

Computer Resources/On-line Services

Training	Yes	LEXIS/NEXIS	Yes $
Internet	Yes $	CompuServe	Yes $
E-Mail	Yes	Dow Jones	Yes $
Videoconference Center	Yes		

ADMISSION

Acceptance 1994-95 1,334 applied for admission; 48% were accepted.

Entrance Requirements Bachelor's degree, GMAT score of 580.

Application Requirements Written essay, application form, copies of transcript, resume/curriculum vitae, 2 letters of recommendation.

Application Deadline 3/1 for fall.

FINANCIALS

Costs for 1994-95 Tuition: Full-time: $3,420/semester for state residents, $6,840/semester for nonresidents. Fees: Full-time: $190/semester for state residents, $190/semester for nonresidents. Average room and board costs are $4,484 per academic year (on-campus) and $5,094 per academic year (off-campus).

Financial Aid In 1994-95, 39% of candidates received some institutionally administered aid in the form of scholarships, fellowships, assistantships. Total awards ranged from $1,000-$16,000. Financial aid is not available to part-time students. Application deadline: 3/1 for fall. Contact: Ms. Kathi Casey Graves, Assistant Director of Financial Aid, MBA Program, Franklin Hall 208, Bloomington, IN 47405. (812) 855-4416.

INTERNATIONAL STUDENTS

Demographics 14% of students enrolled in the program are international; Asia 53%, Europe 33%, Australia 6%, South America 3%, Africa 1%, other 4%.

Services and Facilities International student center, visa services, language tutoring, ESL courses, special assistance for nonnative speakers of English, counseling/support services.

Applying TOEFL required, minimum score of 580; proof of adequate funds. Financial aid is not available to international students. Admission application deadline: 2/1 for fall.

PLACEMENT

In 1993-94, 223 organizations participated in on-campus recruiting; 3,045 on-campus interviews were conducted. Placement services include alumni network, career counseling/planning, career library, career placement, job interviews, job search course, resume preparation, and resume referral to employers. Of 1994 graduates, 93% were employed within three months of graduation, the average starting salary was $53,620, the range was $35,000-$75,000.

Jobs by Functional Area Marketing/sales 19%; finance 30%; operations 3%; management 17%; technical management 3%; other 28%.

Program Contact: Ms. Becky Vadas, Admissions Coordinator, Indiana University Bloomington, MBA Office 254, Tenth and Fee Lane, Bloomington, IN 47405. (800) 994-8622, or (800) 99-IUMBA; Fax: (812) 855-9039.

See full description on page 760.

Indiana University Kokomo

Division of Business and Economics

Kokomo, Indiana

OVERVIEW

Indiana University Kokomo is a state-supported comprehensive coed institution. Part of Indiana University System. Founded 1945. Setting: 51-acre small-town campus with easy access to Indianapolis. Total institutional enrollment: 3,257. Program was first offered in 1991.

MBA HIGHLIGHTS

Entrance Difficulty*
Mean GMAT: 557
Mean GPA: 3.07

Cost $

Tuition: $127/credit hour
(Nonresident: $286/credit hour)
Room & Board: N/R

Enrollment Profile

Full-time: 5	Work Exp: 90%
Part-time: 59	International: 14%
Total: 64	Women: 25%
Average Age: 32	Minorities: 7%

Average Class Size: 20

ACADEMICS

Length of Program Minimum: 12 months. Maximum: 7 years.

Calendar Semesters.

Full-time Classes Main campus; evening, summer.

Degree Requirements 36 credits including 6-9 elective credits.

Required Courses Advanced financial management, advanced managerial accounting, advanced marketing management, advanced operations management, human resources management, management of international operations, managerial values, ethics, and social responsibility, managing professionals, microeconomic analysis and decision making, organization communication/development/change, organizational strategy, policy, and innovation. Courses may be waived through: previous course work.

Curricular Focus International business, managing diversity, teamwork.

Concentrations Accounting, entrepreneurship, finance, human resources management, international business, management, marketing, operations management, organizational behavior, quantitative analysis, strategic management.

Faculty Full-time: 14, 100% with doctorates; part-time: 1.

Teaching Methodology Case study: 20%, faculty seminars: 5%, lecture: 35%, research: 5%, seminars by members of the business community: 5%, student presentations: 10%, team projects: 20%.

Special Opportunities Corporate policy projects.

STUDENT STATISTICS

Geographic Representation State residents 90%. By region: Midwest 93%. International 14%.

Undergraduate Majors Business 31%; education 5%; engineering/technology 30%; humanities 5%; science/mathematics 5%; social sciences 19%; other 5%.

Other Background Graduate degrees in other disciplines: 12%. Work experience: On average, students have 6 years of work experience on entrance to the program.

FACILITIES

Information Resources Main library with 119,000 bound volumes, 86,000 titles on microform, 938 periodical subscriptions, 4,926 records/tapes/CDs. Business collection includes 11,223 bound volumes, 186 periodical subscriptions, 22 CD-ROMs, 271 videos.

Housing College housing not available.

Technology Computers are used moderately in course work. 106 computer terminals/PCs, linked by a campus-wide computer network, are available for use by students in program; they are located in classrooms, the library, the computer center, computer labs. Students in the program are not required to have their own PC. $840 are budgeted per student for computer support.

Computer Resources/On-line Services

Training	Yes	CompuServe	No
Internet	Yes	Dun's	No
E-Mail	Yes	Dow Jones	Yes
Videoconference Center	Yes	Dialog	No
Multimedia Center	Yes	Bloomberg	No
LEXIS/NEXIS	No		

Other on-line services: Carl, SEC.

ADMISSION

Acceptance 1994-95 61 applied for admission; 83% were accepted.

Entrance Requirements Bachelor's degree, calculus course, GMAT score of 480. Core courses waived through: work experience.

Application Requirements Written essay, application form, copies of transcript, personal statement.

Application Deadlines 7/1 for fall, 12/1 for spring, 3/1 for summer.

FINANCIALS

Costs for 1994-95 Tuition: Full-time: $127/credit hour for state residents, $286/credit hour for nonresidents. Fees: Full-time: $15 for state residents, $15 for nonresidents.

Financial Aid In 1994-95, 5% of candidates received some institutionally administered aid in the form of loans. Financial aid is not available to part-time students. Application deadlines: 3/1 for fall, 3/1 for spring. Contact: Ms. Janet Bates, Director of Financial Aid, Kelley Center Room 201H, Kokomo, IN 46904-9003. (317) 455-9216.

INTERNATIONAL STUDENTS

Demographics 14% of students enrolled in the program are international; Asia 44%, Africa 34%, other 22%.

Services and Facilities International student center, visa services, language tutoring, ESL courses.

Applying TOEFL required, minimum score of 550; 3 letters of recommendation; proof of adequate funds; calculus course. Financial aid is not available to international students. Admission application deadlines: 2/1 for fall, 10/1 for spring, 2/1 for summer. Contact: Mr. Kenneth Rogers, Associate Dean and Director, International Services, 306 Franklin, Bloomington, IN 47405. (812) 855-5099.

PLACEMENT

Placement services include career counseling/planning, career fairs, career library, career placement, and resume preparation. Of 1994 graduates, 10% were employed within three months of graduation.

Jobs by Employer Type Manufacturing 50%; service 25%; other 25%.

Jobs by Functional Area Finance 25%; operations 50%; other 25%.

Program Contact: Dr. Wayne A. Johnson, MBA Director, Indiana University Kokomo, PO Box 9003, Kokomo, IN 46904-9003. (317) 455-9471; Fax: (317) 455-9475; Internet Address: wjohnson@iukfs1. iuk.indiana.edu.

Indiana University Northwest

Division of Business and Economics

Gary, Indiana

OVERVIEW

Indiana University Northwest is a state-supported comprehensive coed institution. Part of Indiana University System. Founded 1959. Setting: 27-acre urban campus with easy access to Chicago. Total institutional enrollment: 5,900. Program was first offered in 1988. AACSB-accredited.

MBA HIGHLIGHTS

Entrance Difficulty**
Mean GMAT: 500
Mean GPA: 3.1

Cost $
Tuition: $116/credit hour
(Nonresident: $265/credit hour)
Room & Board: N/R

Enrollment Profile

Full-time: 7	Work Exp: 98%
Part-time: 273	International: 1%
Total: 280	Women: 37%
Average Age: 30	Minorities: 8%

Average Class Size: 26

ACADEMICS

Length of Program Minimum: 24 months. Maximum: 6 years.

Calendar Semesters.

Part-time Classes Main campus; evening, summer.

Degree Requirements 42-54 credits including 9 elective credits.

Required Courses Accounting function, administrative policy, applied statistical analysis, business conditions analysis, business society and administration, financial management, introduction to international business, legal aspects of business, management accounting, management and organization behavior, management information systems, managerial economics, marketing management, production management, quantitative business analysis.

Curricular Focus Business issues and problems, general management, problem solving and decision making.

Concentrations Finance, human resources management, management, marketing, organizational behavior.

Faculty Full-time: 19, 95% with doctorates; part-time: 2.

Teaching Methodology Case study: 15%, lecture: 45%, seminars by members of the business community: 5%, student presentations: 15%, team projects: 20%.

STUDENT STATISTICS

Geographic Representation State residents 99%. By region: Midwest 100%. International 1%.

Undergraduate Majors Business 45%; education 2%; engineering/technology 28%; humanities 5%; nursing 5%; science/mathematics 5%; social sciences 10%.

Other Background Graduate degrees in other disciplines: 1%. Work experience: On average, students have 6 years of work experience on entrance to the program.

FACILITIES

Information Resources Main library with 206,600 bound volumes, 190,222 titles on microform, 1,100 periodical subscriptions, 40 records/tapes/CDs. Business collection includes 16,000 bound volumes, 150 periodical subscriptions, 10 CD-ROMs, 25 videos.

Housing College housing not available.

Technology Computers are used moderately in course work. 125 computer terminals/PCs, linked by a campus-wide computer network, are available for use by students in program; they are located in learning resource center, the library, the computer center, computer labs. Students in the program are not required to have their own PC.

Computer Resources/On-line Services

Training	No	Dun's	No
Internet	Yes	Dow Jones	No
E-Mail	Yes	Dialog	Yes
LEXIS/NEXIS	No	Bloomberg	No
CompuServe	No		

Other on-line services: OCLC, Carl.

ADMISSION

Acceptance 1994-95 72 applied for admission; 88% were accepted.

Entrance Requirements Bachelor's degree, prerequisite math course which can be taken after admission, GMAT score, minimum 2.0 GPA. Core courses waived through: previous course work.

Application Requirements Application form, copies of transcript, 1 letter of recommendation.

Application Deadlines 7/15 for fall, 11/15 for spring, 4/15 for summer. Applications are processed on a rolling basis.

FINANCIALS

Costs for 1994-95 Tuition: Full-time: $116/credit hour for state residents, $265/credit hour for nonresidents.

Financial Aid In 1994-95, candidates received some institutionally administered aid in the form of loans, assistantships, work-study. Financial aid is available to part-time students. Application deadlines: 3/15 for fall, 3/15 for spring. Applications are processed on a rolling basis. Contact: Mr. William Lee, Director of Financial Aid and Scholarships, 3400 Broadway, Gary, IN 46408-1197. (219) 980-6767.

INTERNATIONAL STUDENTS

Demographics 1% of students enrolled in the program are international; Asia 50%, Europe 50%.

Applying TOEFL required, minimum score of 550; proof of adequate funds. Financial aid is not available to international students. Admission application deadlines: 2/1 for fall, 9/1 for spring. Applications are processed on a rolling basis.

PLACEMENT

Placement services include career counseling/planning, career library, career placement, and resume preparation. Of 1994 graduates, 98% were employed within three months of graduation.

Program Contact: Ms. Kathryn Lantz, Director, Graduate Business Programs, Indiana University Northwest, 3400 Broadway, Gary, IN 46408-1197. (219) 980-6635, or (800) 437-5409 (IN only); Fax: (219) 980-6579; Internet Address: kathryn@iunbus1.iun.indiana.edu.

Indiana University–Purdue University Fort Wayne

School of Business and Management Science

Fort Wayne, Indiana

OVERVIEW
Indiana University–Purdue University Fort Wayne is a state-supported comprehensive coed institution. Part of Indiana and Purdue University Systems. Founded 1917. Setting: 412-acre suburban campus. Total institutional enrollment: 11,071. Program was first offered in 1987. AACSB-accredited.

MBA HIGHLIGHTS

Entrance Difficulty**
Mean GMAT: 550
Mean GPA: 3.2

Cost $
Tuition: $105/credit
(Nonresident: $236/credit)
Room & Board: N/R

Enrollment Profile

Full time: 10	Work Exp: 100%
Part-time: 217	International: 2%
Total: 227	Women: 27%
Average Age: 29	Minorities: 3%

Average Class Size: 35

ACADEMICS
Length of Program Minimum: 36 months. Maximum: 5 years.
Calendar Semesters.
Full-time Classes Main campus; evening, weekends, summer.
Part-time Classes Main campus; evening, weekends, summer.
Degree Requirements 33 credits including 6 elective credits.
Required Courses Administrative policy, advanced financial management, advanced managerial accounting, advanced marketing management, advanced operations management, business, government, and society, management of international operations, microeconomics analysis and decision making, organizational theory and development, quantitative business analysis. Courses may be waived through: previous course work.
Curricular Focus Business issues and problems, general management, strategic analysis and planning.
Concentration Management.
Faculty Full-time: 20, 100% with doctorates; part-time: 3.
Teaching Methodology Case study: 20%, lecture: 35%, research: 15%, student presentations: 10%, team projects: 20%.

STUDENT STATISTICS
Geographic Representation State residents 75%. By region: Midwest 95%; South 2%. International 2%.
Undergraduate Majors Business 40%; engineering/technology 40%; social sciences 10%; other 10%.
Other Background Graduate degrees in other disciplines: 7%. Work experience: On average, students have 5 years of work experience on entrance to the program.

FACILITIES
Information Resources Main library with 208,630 bound volumes, 405,039 titles on microform, 1,694 periodical subscriptions, 2,700 records/tapes/CDs.
Housing College housing not available.
Technology Computers are used heavily in course work. 100 computer terminals/PCs, linked by a campus-wide computer network, are available for use by students in program; they are located in learning resource center, the library, the computer center, computer labs. Students in the program are not required to have their own PC.

Computer Resources/On-line Services

Training	Yes	E-Mail	No

ADMISSION
Acceptance 1994-95 110 applied for admission; 90% were accepted.
Entrance Requirements Bachelor's degree, GMAT score of 430, minimum 2.5 GPA. Core courses waived through: previous course work.
Application Requirements Application form, copies of transcript, personal statement, 3 letters of recommendation.
Application Deadlines 7/1 for fall, 11/1 for spring, 4/1 for summer.

FINANCIALS
Costs for 1994-95 Tuition: Full-time: $105/credit for state residents, $236/credit for nonresidents.
Financial Aid In 1994-95, 5% of candidates received some institutionally administered aid in the form of assistantships. Total awards ranged from $2,800-$5,600. Financial aid is not available to part-time students. Application deadlines: 7/1 for fall, 11/1 for spring. Contact: Mr. Ali Rassuli, Director of Graduate Business, 2101 Coliseum Boulevard East, Fort Wayne, IN 46805-1499. (219) 481-6820.

INTERNATIONAL STUDENTS
Demographics 2% of students enrolled in the program are international.
Services and Facilities Visa services, ESL courses, counseling/support services.
Applying TOEFL required, minimum score of 550; proof of adequate funds. Financial aid is not available to international students. Admission application deadlines: 7/1 for fall, 11/1 for spring, 4/1 for summer. Contact: Mr. Ali Rassuli, Director of Graduate Business, 2101 Coliseum Boulevard East, Fort Wayne, IN 46805-1499. (219) 481-6820.

PLACEMENT
Placement services include alumni network and career placement. Of 1994 graduates, the average starting salary range was $25,000-$50,000.

Program Contact: Mr. Ali Rassuli, Director of Graduate Business, Indiana University–Purdue University Fort Wayne, 2101 Coliseum Boulevard East, Fort Wayne, IN 46805-1499. (219) 481-6820; Fax: (219) 481-6083.

Indiana University–Purdue University Indianapolis

Indiana University School of Business at Indianapolis

Indianapolis, Indiana

OVERVIEW
Indiana University–Purdue University Indianapolis is a state-supported coed institution. Part of Indiana and Purdue University Systems. Founded 1969. Setting: 370-acre urban campus. Total institutional enrollment: 27,000.

MBA HIGHLIGHTS

Entrance Difficulty***
Mean GMAT: 570
Mean GPA: N/R

Cost $
Tuition: $200/credit hour
(Nonresident: $400/credit hour)
Room & Board: N/R

Enrollment Profile

Full-time: 0	Work Exp: 100%
Part-time: 390	International: 5%
Total: 390	Women: 25%
Average Age: N/R	Minorities: 8%

Average Class Size: 55

ACADEMICS
Length of Program Minimum: 32 months.
Calendar Semesters.
Part-time Classes Main campus; evening, summer.
Degree Requirements 50 credit hours including 7.5 elective credit hours.
Curricular Focus General management, problem solving and decision making, teamwork.

Concentration Management.

Teaching Methodology Case study: 20%, lecture: 40%, student presentations: 20%, team projects: 20%.

Special Opportunities International exchange program available.

STUDENT STATISTICS

Geographic Representation State residents 95%. By region: Midwest 95%. International 5%.

Other Background Work experience: On average, students have 5 years of work experience on entrance to the program.

FACILITIES

Information Resources Main library with 700,000 bound volumes, 970,000 titles on microform, 7,000 periodical subscriptions, 100 CD-ROMs.

Housing College housing not available.

Technology Computers are used heavily in course work. Computer terminals/PCs, linked by a campus-wide computer network, are available for use by students in program; they are located in computer labs. Students in the program are required to have their own PC.

Computer Resources/On-line Services

Training	Yes	Multimedia Center	Yes
Internet	Yes	Dow Jones	Yes
E-Mail	Yes		

ADMISSION

Entrance Requirements Bachelor's degree, GMAT score, minimum 2 years of work experience.

Application Requirements Written essay, application form, copies of transcript, resume/curriculum vitae, personal statement, 2 letters of recommendation.

Application Deadlines 5/1 for fall, 11/1 for spring.

FINANCIALS

Costs for 1994-95 Tuition: Part-time day: $200/credit hour for state residents; Part-time evening: $400/credit hour for nonresidents. Fees: Part-time day: $25/semester for state residents; Part-time evening: $25/semester for nonresidents.

Financial Aid Application deadline: 3/1 for fall. Contact: Ms. Natala Hart, Director of Scholarships and Financial Aid, 801 West Michigan Street, Indianapolis, IN 46202-5151. (317) 274-4162.

INTERNATIONAL STUDENTS

Demographics 5% of students enrolled in the program are international.

Applying TOEFL required, minimum score of 550; proof of adequate funds. Financial aid is not available to international students. Admission application deadlines: 3/1 for fall, 9/1 for spring.

ALTERNATE MBA PROGRAM

MBA/JD Length of program: Minimum: 48 months. Full-time classes: Main campus; day, evening, summer. Part-time classes: Main campus; evening, summer. Degree requirements: 120 credit hours.

Program Contact: Mr. Victor Childers, Director of Academic Programs, Indiana University–Purdue University Indianapolis, 801 West Michigan Street, Indianapolis, IN 46202-5151. (317) 274-4895; Fax: (317) 274-2483.

Indiana University South Bend

Division of Business and Economics

South Bend, Indiana

OVERVIEW

Indiana University South Bend is a state-supported comprehensive coed institution. Part of Indiana University System. Founded 1922. Setting: 40-acre urban campus with easy access to Chicago. Total institutional enrollment: 7,582. Program was first offered in 1969. AACSB-accredited.

MBA HIGHLIGHTS

Entrance Difficulty***
Mean GMAT: 521
Mean GPA: 3.47

Cost $
Tuition: $121/credit hour
(Nonresident: $290/credit hour)
Room & Board: N/R

Enrollment Profile

Full-time: 23		Work Exp: 91%
Part-time: 247		International: 9%
Total: 270		Women: 26%
Average Age: 31		Minorities: 2%

Average Class Size: N/R

ACADEMICS

Length of Program Minimum: 24 months. Maximum: 5 years.

Calendar Semesters.

Full-time Classes Main campus, Elkhart; evening, summer.

Part-time Classes Main campus, Elkhart; evening, summer.

Degree Requirements 45 credits including 12 elective credits.

Required Courses Applied organizational behavior, business law, business policy, economic forecasting, financial accounting, financial management, management information systems, managerial accounting, marketing management, price theory, production management, statistics.

Curricular Focus Economic and financial theory, general management, problem solving and decision making.

Concentration Management.

Faculty Full-time: 31, 100% with doctorates; part-time: 4, 25% with doctorates.

Teaching Methodology Case study: 20%, lecture: 30%, research: 5%, seminars by members of the business community: 5%, student presentations: 20%, team projects: 20%.

STUDENT STATISTICS

Geographic Representation State residents 87%. By region: Midwest 85%; West 5%. International 9%.

Other Background Graduate degrees in other disciplines: 3%. Work experience: On average, students have 5 years of work experience on entrance to the program.

FACILITIES

Information Resources Main library with 250,000 bound volumes, 277,455 titles on microform, 1,843 periodical subscriptions, 9,710 records/tapes/CDs.

Housing 10% of students in program live in college-owned or -operated housing.

Technology Computers are used moderately in course work. 70 computer terminals/PCs, linked by a campus-wide computer network, are available for use by students in program; they are located in the library, the computer center, computer labs. Students in the program are not required to have their own PC. $1,000 are budgeted per student for computer support.

Computer Resources/On-line Services

Internet	Yes	Dun's	No
E-Mail	Yes	Dow Jones	No
LEXIS/NEXIS	No	Dialog	Yes
CompuServe	Yes	Bloomberg	No

ADMISSION

Acceptance 1994-95 74 applied for admission; 97% were accepted.

Entrance Requirements Bachelor's degree, GMAT score of 450, minimum 2.5 GPA.

Application Requirements Application form, copies of transcript, personal statement, 3 letters of recommendation.

Application Deadlines 7/1 for fall, 11/1 for spring, 4/1 for summer.

FINANCIALS

Costs for 1995-96 Tuition: Full-time: $121/credit hour for state residents, $290/credit hour for nonresidents.

Financial Aid In 1994-95, candidates received some institutionally administered aid in the form of loans. Financial aid is available to part-time students. Application deadline: 3/1 for fall. Contact: Financial Aid Office, 929 Greenlawn, Box 7111, South Bend, IN 46634-7111. (219) 237-4358.

INTERNATIONAL STUDENTS
Demographics 9% of students enrolled in the program are international.

Services and Facilities International student office, ESL courses, special assistance for nonnative speakers of English, counseling/support services.

Applying TOEFL required, minimum score of 550; proof of adequate funds. Admission application deadlines: 7/1 for fall, 11/1 for spring, 4/1 for summer. Contact: Ms. Julie Williams, Coordinator, 929 Greenlawn, Box 7111, South Bend, IN 46634-7111. (219) 237-4419.

PLACEMENT
Placement services include career placement.

Program Contact: Ms. Sharon Peterson, Indiana University South Bend, 929 Greenlawn, Box 7111, South Bend, IN 46634-7111. (219) 237-4138; Fax: (219) 237-4866.

Indiana Wesleyan University

Division of Adult and Professional Studies

Marion, Indiana

OVERVIEW
Indiana Wesleyan University is an independent Wesleyan comprehensive coed institution. Founded 1920. Setting: 75-acre small-town campus with easy access to Indianapolis. Total institutional enrollment: 4,182.

ACADEMICS
Length of Program Minimum: 26 months.

Calendar 4-4-1.

Full-time Classes Main campus; evening.

Degree Requirements 41 credit hours.

Required Courses Advanced managerial accounting, advanced managerial economics, advanced managerial finance, advanced marketing management, analysis and decision making, applied management project, computer workshop, economics, fundamentals of executive management, management of the total enterprise, managerial accounting, managerial ethics, managerial finance, managing business information systems, organizational development, principles of executive self-management, statistical analysis.

Curricular Focus General management, problem solving and decision making, teamwork.

Concentration Management.

Teaching Methodology Case study: 15%, lecture: 35%, student presentations: 10%, team projects: 40%.

FACILITIES
Information Resources Main library with 119,808 bound volumes, 7,592 titles on microform, 750 periodical subscriptions, 18,604 records/tapes/CDs.

ADMISSION
Entrance Requirements Bachelor's degree, minimum 2.5 GPA, minimum 3 years of work experience.

Application Requirements Written essay, copies of transcript, personal statement, 2 letters of recommendation.

Application Deadline Applications are processed on a rolling basis.

FINANCIALS
Costs for 1994-95 Tuition: Full-time: $225/credit hour.

Financial Aid In 1994-95, 40% of candidates received some institutionally administered aid in the form of loans. Total awards ranged from $500-$8,500. Financial aid is not available to part-time students. Application deadline: 5/1 for fall. Applications are processed on a rolling basis. Contact: Ms. Melinda Troyer, Financial Aid Counselor, 4201 South Washington Street, Marion, IN 46953. (317) 677-2699.

INTERNATIONAL STUDENTS
Applying TOEFL required, minimum score of 550; proof of health; proof of adequate funds. Financial aid is not available to international students. Admission applications are processed on a rolling basis. Contact: Mr. Mario Phillips, 4201 South Washington Street, Marion, IN 46953. (317) 677-2350 Ext. 2725.

Program Contact: Mr. Jerry Shepherd, Director of Student Recruitment, Indiana Wesleyan University, 211 East 45th Street, Marion, IN 46953. (800) 234-5327, or (800) 621-8667 (IN only); Fax: (317) 674-8028.

Purdue University

Krannert Graduate School of Management

West Lafayette, Indiana

OVERVIEW
Purdue University is a state-supported coed institution. Part of Purdue University System. Founded 1869. Setting: 1,579-acre small-town campus with easy access to Indianapolis. Total institutional enrollment: 36,000. Program was first offered in 1956. AACSB-accredited.

PROGRAM HIGHLIGHTS
Entrance Difficulty***
Mean GMAT: 607
Mean GPA: 3.3

Cost $
Tuition: $2,025/semester
(Nonresident: $5,520/semester)
Room & Board: $5,000

Enrollment Profile

Full-time: 131	Work Exp: 86%
Part-time: 0	International: 20%
Total: 131	Women: 36%
Average Age: 26	Minorities: 10%

Average Class Size: 55

ACADEMICS
Calendar Semesters.

Curricular Focus Information technologies, leadership, technology management.

Concentrations Accounting, finance, human resources management, international business, management, management information systems, manufacturing management, marketing, operations management, organizational behavior, strategic management.

Faculty Full-time: 45, 99% with doctorates.

Teaching Methodology Case study: 45%, faculty seminars: 5%, lecture: 25%, research: 5%, seminars by members of the business community: 5%, student presentations: 5%, team projects: 10%.

Special Opportunities Internship program available. Other: Washington campus program.

STUDENT STATISTICS
Geographic Representation By region: Midwest 45%; Northeast 18%; West 9%; South 8%. International 20%.

Undergraduate Majors Business 23%; education 2%; engineering/technology 35%; humanities 13%; nursing 1%; science/mathematics 13%; social sciences 13%.

Other Background Graduate degrees in other disciplines: 10%. Work experience: On average, students have 2 years of work experience on entrance to the program.

FACILITIES
Information Resources Main library with 2.1 million bound volumes, 2.1 million titles on microform, 14,331 periodical subscriptions, 10,664 records/tapes/CDs, 141 CD-ROMs. Business collection in Krannert Library includes 151,538 bound volumes, 1,128 periodical subscriptions, 23 CD-ROMs.

Housing 60% of students in program live in college-owned or -operated housing.

Technology Computers are used heavily in course work. 150 computer terminals/PCs, linked by a campus-wide computer network, are available for use by students in program; they are located in classrooms, the library, the computer center, computer labs. Students in the program are not required to have their own PC. $300 are budgeted per student for computer support.

Computer Resources/On-line Services

Training	Yes	CompuServe	Yes
Internet	Yes	Dun's	Yes
E-Mail	Yes	Dow Jones	Yes
Videoconference Center	Yes	Dialog	Yes
Multimedia Center	Yes		

Other on-line services: Westlaw, OCLC.

ADMISSION

Acceptance 1994-95 Of those applying, 29% were accepted.

Entrance Requirements Bachelor's degree, GMAT score of 550, minimum 3.0 GPA.

Application Requirements Written essay, application form, copies of transcript, resume/curriculum vitae, personal statement.

Application Deadline 4/15 for fall.

FINANCIALS

Estimated Costs for 1995-96 Tuition: Full-time: $2,025/semester for state residents, $5,520/semester for nonresidents; Summer: $860/semester for state residents, $3,075/semester for nonresidents. Average room and board costs are $5,000 per academic year (on-campus) and $6,000 per academic year (off-campus).

Financial Aid In 1994-95, 55% of candidates received some institutionally administered aid in the form of grants, scholarships, fellowships, assistantships, residence hall counselorships. Total awards ranged from $1,000-$14,000. Application deadline: 4/15 for fall. Contact: Ms. Joyce Hall, Director, 1102 Scheleman Hall, West Lafayette, IN 47907. (317) 494-5050.

INTERNATIONAL STUDENTS

Demographics 20% of students enrolled in the program are international; Asia 34%, South America 23%, Europe 22%, Central America 12%, other 9%.

Services and Facilities International student center, language tutoring, ESL courses, special assistance for nonnative speakers of English, counseling/support services.

Applying TOEFL required, minimum score of 575; proof of health; proof of adequate funds. Financial aid is available to international students. Residence hall counselorships are available to these students. Admission application deadline: 4/15 for fall. Contact: Dr. Michael Brzezinski, Director, 1101 Scheleman Hall, Room 136, West Lafayette, IN 47907-1101. (317) 494-5770.

PROGRAMS

MSM Length of program: Minimum: 20 months. Maximum: 2 years. Full-time classes: Main campus; day. Part-time classes: Main campus; weekends. Degree requirements: 60 credits including 18 elective credits.

Executive MBA (EMBA) Length of program: Minimum: 22 months. Maximum: 4 years. Degree requirements: 48 credits. 2 week international seminar in 3rd semester. Average class size: 50.

MSIA Length of program: Minimum: 11 months. Maximum: 1 year. Degree requirements: 48 credits including 9 elective credits. Class size: 30-40.

PLACEMENT

In 1993-94, 75 organizations participated in on-campus recruiting; 1,421 on-campus interviews were conducted. Placement services include career counseling/planning, career placement, job interviews, and resume referral to employers. Of 1994 graduates, 92% were employed within three months of graduation, the average starting salary was $51,327, the range was $31,500-$94,150.

Jobs by Employer Type Manufacturing 54%; service 22%; government 2%; consulting 21%; nonprofit 1%.

Jobs by Functional Area Marketing/sales 15%; finance 35%; operations 40%; management 6%; strategic planning 2%; technical management 2%.

Program Contact: Mr. Ward Snearly, Director of Admissions, Purdue University, West Lafayette, IN 47907. (317) 494-4365; Fax: (317) 494-9841; Internet Address: patz@mgmt.purdue.edu.

See full description on page 810.

Saint Francis College

Department of Business Administration

Fort Wayne, Indiana

OVERVIEW

Saint Francis College is an independent Roman Catholic comprehensive coed institution. Founded 1890. Setting: 73-acre urban campus. Total institutional enrollment: 962. Program was first offered in 1977.

MBA HIGHLIGHTS

Entrance Difficulty**
Mean GMAT: 491
Mean GPA: 2.96

Cost $
Tuition: $279/hour
Room & Board: $4,580

Enrollment Profile

Full-time: 7	Work Exp: 95%
Part-time: 47	International: 16%
Total: 54	Women: 29%
Average Age: 35	Minorities: 5%

Average Class Size: 10

ACADEMICS

Length of Program Minimum: 24 months. Maximum: 5 years.

Calendar Semesters.

Full-time Classes Main campus, Warsaw; evening, weekends, summer.

Part-time Classes Main campus; evening, weekends, summer.

Degree Requirements 33 hours including 9 elective hours. Other: 9 hours of emphasis/concentration.

Required Courses External business environment, field project and internship, financial management, marketing management, operations management, organizational behavior. Courses may be waived through: previous course work, work experience.

Curricular Focus General management, problem solving and decision making, teamwork.

Concentrations Accounting, finance, international business, management, marketing.

Faculty Full-time: 4, 25% with doctorates; part-time: 6, 17% with doctorates.

Teaching Methodology Case study: 15%, lecture: 60%, research: 5%, student presentations: 10%, team projects: 10%.

STUDENT STATISTICS

Geographic Representation State residents 83%. By region: Midwest 84%. International 16%.

Undergraduate Majors Business 50%; education 6%; engineering/technology 26%; humanities 2%; nursing 6%; science/mathematics 2%; social sciences 8%.

FACILITIES

Information Resources Main library with 85,000 bound volumes, 350,000 titles on microform, 485 periodical subscriptions, 5 CD-ROMs. Business collection includes 4,000 bound volumes, 50 periodical subscriptions, 1 CD-ROM.

Housing 1% of students in program live in college-owned or -operated housing.

Technology Computers are used moderately in course work. 19 computer terminals/PCs, linked by a campus-wide computer network, are available for use by students in program; they are located in the library, computer labs. Students in the program are not required to have their own PC.

Computer Resources/On-line Services

Training	Yes	CompuServe	No
Internet	No	Dun's	No
E-Mail	No	Dow Jones	No
Multimedia Center	Yes	Dialog	No
LEXIS/NEXIS	No	Bloomberg	No

ADMISSION

Acceptance 1994-95 32 applied for admission; 95% were accepted.

Entrance Requirements Bachelor's degree, GMAT score of 400, minimum 2.5 GPA. Core courses waived through: previous course work, work experience.

Application Requirements Application form, copies of transcript.

Application Deadline Applications are processed on a rolling basis.

FINANCIALS

Costs for 1994-95 Tuition: Full-time: $279/hour. Fees: Full-time: $80/semester. Average room and board costs are $4,580 per academic year (on-campus) and $5,000 per academic year (off-campus).

Financial Aid In 1994-95, 2% of candidates received some institutionally administered aid in the form of grants, scholarships, assistantships. Total awards ranged from $403-$3,908. Financial aid is available to part-time students. Applications are processed on a rolling basis. Contact: Mr. Troy A. Davis, Assistant Director of Financial Aid, 2701 Spring Street, Fort Wayne, IN 46808-3994. (219) 434-3184.

INTERNATIONAL STUDENTS

Demographics 16% of students enrolled in the program are international; Asia 99%, Africa 1%.

Services and Facilities Visa services, language tutoring, ESL courses.

Applying TOEFL required; proof of adequate funds. Financial aid is not available to international students. Admission application deadlines: 5/1 for fall, 9/15 for spring. Contact: Mr. Eric Murzyn, International Student Adviser, 2701 Spring Street, Fort Wayne, IN 46808-3994. (219) 434-7416.

PLACEMENT

Placement services include alumni network and resume preparation.

Program Contact: Dr. Ruth R. Michael, Dean of Graduate Studies, Saint Francis College, 2701 Spring Street, Fort Wayne, IN 46808-3994. (219) 434-3270, or (800) 729-4732; Fax: (219) 434-3194.

University of Indianapolis

School of Business

Indianapolis, Indiana

OVERVIEW

The University of Indianapolis is an independent comprehensive coed institution, affiliated with United Methodist Church. Founded 1902. Setting: 60-acre suburban campus. Total institutional enrollment: 4,000. Program was first offered in 1974.

MBA HIGHLIGHTS

Entrance Difficulty**
Mean GMAT: 500
Mean GPA: 2.9

Cost $
Tuition: $198/semester hour
Room & Board: N/R

Enrollment Profile

Full-time: 21	Work Exp: 95%
Part-time: 502	International: 10%
Total: 523	Women: 48%
Average Age: N/R	Minorities: 10%

Average Class Size: 30

ACADEMICS

Length of Program May range up to 5 years.

Calendar Semesters.

Full-time Classes Main campus.

Part-time Classes Main campus; evening.

Degree Requirements 42 credits including 6 elective credits.

Required Courses Advanced organizational behavior, business conditions analysis, effective communication, ethical values in business, financial management, managerial application of accounting data, marketing management, math for business and economics, operations management, simulated financial management, statistical inference, strategic management.

Curricular Focus Problem solving and decision making.

Concentration Management.

Faculty Full-time: 9, 89% with doctorates; part-time: 9, 56% with doctorates.

Teaching Methodology Case study: 30%, lecture: 40%, team projects: 30%.

STUDENT STATISTICS

Geographic Representation By region: Midwest 90%. International 10%.

Undergraduate Majors Business 74%; engineering/technology 16%; humanities 5%; nursing 2%; social sciences 1%; other 2%.

Other Background Graduate degrees in other disciplines: 3%. Work experience: On average, students have 3-5 years of work experience on entrance to the program.

FACILITIES

Information Resources Main library with 144,218 bound volumes, 9,475 titles on microform, 1,141 periodical subscriptions, 925 records/tapes/CDs, 14 CD-ROMs. Business collection includes 143,928 bound volumes, 599 periodical subscriptions, 2 CD-ROMs, 35 videos.

Housing 1% of students in program live in college-owned or -operated housing. Assistance with housing search provided.

Technology Computers are used moderately in course work. Computer terminals/PCs, linked by a campus-wide computer network, are available for use by students in program; they are located in classrooms, the computer center, computer labs, the research center. Students in the program are not required to have their own PC.

Computer Resources/On-line Services

Training	No	Dialog	Yes
E-Mail	Yes		

ADMISSION

Acceptance 1994-95 137 applied for admission; 94% were accepted.

Entrance Requirements Bachelor's degree, GMAT score. Core courses waived through: previous course work.

Application Requirements Interview, application form, copies of transcript, personal statement, 2 letters of recommendation.

Application Deadlines 8/1 for fall, 1/1 for spring, 6/1 for summer.

FINANCIALS

Estimated Costs for 1995-96 Tuition: Full-time: $198/semester hour.

Financial Aid In 1994-95, 10% of candidates received some institutionally administered aid in the form of grants, loans. Total awards ranged from $294-$12,140. Financial aid is available to part-time students. Applications are processed on a rolling basis. Contact: Ms. Sandy Osborn, Assistant Director of Financial Aid, 1400 East Hanna Avenue, Indianapolis, IN 46227-3697. (317) 788-3217.

INTERNATIONAL STUDENTS

Demographics 10% of students enrolled in the program are international; Asia 80%, Europe 20%.

Services and Facilities International student office, language tutoring, counseling/support services.

Applying TOEFL required, minimum score of 550; proof of adequate funds. Financial aid is not available to international students. Admission application deadlines: 8/1 for fall, 1/1 for spring, 4/1 for summer, 6/1 for second summer session. Contact: Ms. Mimi Chase, International Student Adviser, 1400 East Hanna Avenue, Indianapolis, IN 46227-3697. (317) 788-3335.

ALTERNATE MBA PROGRAM

Executive MBA (EMBA) Length of program: Minimum: 20 months. Part-time classes: Main campus, USA Group Corporation, Athens, Greece; weekends. Degree requirements: 40 credits.

PLACEMENT

Placement services include alumni network, career counseling/planning, career library, career placement, and resume preparation.

Program Contact: Dr. Gerald Speth, Director, Graduate Business Programs, University of Indianapolis, 1400 East Hanna Avenue, Indianapolis, IN 46227-3697. (317) 788-3340; Fax: (317) 788-3300.

University of Notre Dame

College of Business Administration

Notre Dame, Indiana

OVERVIEW

The University of Notre Dame is an independent Roman Catholic coed institution. Founded 1842. Setting: 1,250-acre suburban campus. Total institutional enrollment: 10,142. Program was first offered in 1967. AACSB-accredited.

MBA HIGHLIGHTS

Entrance Difficulty***
Mean GMAT: 420 - 730
Mean GPA: 2.15 - 3.95

Cost $$$
Tuition: $17,400
Room & Board: $5,000

Enrollment Profile
Full-time: 280
Part-time: 0
Total: 280
Average Age: 25

Work Exp: 67%
International: 24%
Women: 26%
Minorities: 7%

Average Class Size: 45

ACADEMICS

Length of Program Minimum: 24 months. Maximum: 2 years.

Calendar Semesters.

Full-time Classes Main campus; day.

Degree Requirements 62 credits including 27 elective credits.

Required Courses Accounting and decision making, corporate strategy, financial management, global macroeconomics, government, business, and society, international business, management communications, marketing management, microeconomics, operations management, organizational behavior, statistics. Courses may be waived through: previous course work.

Curricular Focus Business issues and problems, international business, teamwork.

Concentrations Accounting, finance, human resources management, international business, management, management information systems, marketing.

Faculty Full-time: 82, 3% with doctorates; part-time: 5, 25% with doctorates.

Teaching Methodology Case study: 40%, lecture: 40%, student presentations: 10%, team projects: 10%.

Special Opportunities International exchange in Austria, Chile, France, United Kingdom. Internship program available.

STUDENT STATISTICS

Geographic Representation State residents 75%. By region: Midwest 35%; Northeast 18%; South 13%; West 13%. International 24%.

Undergraduate Majors Business 28%; engineering/technology 23%; humanities 24%; science/mathematics 1%; social sciences 18%; other 3%.

Other Background Graduate degrees in other disciplines: 1%. Work experience: On average, students have 3 years of work experience on entrance to the program.

FACILITIES

Information Resources Main library with 2.1 million bound volumes, 2.5 million titles on microform, 20,500 periodical subscriptions, 12,000 records/tapes/CDs, 300 CD-ROMs.

Housing 35% of students in program live in college-owned or -operated housing.

Technology Computers are used heavily in course work. Computer terminals/PCs, linked by a campus-wide computer network, are available for use by students in program; they are located in computer labs. Students in the program are not required to have their own PC.

Computer Resources/On-line Services

Training	Yes	Multimedia Center	Yes
Internet	Yes	LEXIS/NEXIS	Yes
E-Mail	Yes		

ADMISSION

Acceptance 1994-95 Of those applying, 52% were accepted.

Entrance Requirements Bachelor's degree, GMAT score. Core courses waived through: previous course work.

Application Requirements Written essay, application form, copies of transcript, resume/curriculum vitae, 2 letters of recommendation.

Application Deadlines 5/12 for fall, 3/1 for summer.

FINANCIALS

Costs for 1994-95 Tuition: Full-time: $17,400. Average room and board costs are $5,000 per academic year (on-campus) and $5,000 per academic year (off-campus).

Financial Aid In 1994-95, 55% of candidates received some institutionally administered aid in the form of scholarships, loans, assistantships, work-study. Total awards ranged from $3,000-$17,430. Application deadline: 2/24 for fall. Contact: Ms. Lee Cunningham, Director of MBA Admissions, 109 Hurley Building, Notre Dame, IN 46556. (219) 631-8488.

INTERNATIONAL STUDENTS

Demographics 24% of students enrolled in the program are international.

Services and Facilities International student center, special assistance for nonnative speakers of English, counseling/support services.

Applying TOEFL required, minimum score of 600; proof of health; proof of adequate funds. Financial aid is available to international students. Financial aid application deadline: 2/24 for fall. Admission application deadline: 5/12 for fall. Contact: Mr. Arthur Grubert, Director, International Student Affairs, 205 Lafortune, Notre Dame, IN 46556. (219) 631-5243.

ALTERNATE MBA PROGRAMS

One-Year MBA Length of program: 12 months. Degree requirements: 44 credits including 27 elective credits. Undergraduate degree in business.

MBA/JD Length of program: Minimum: 48 months. Maximum: 4 years. Degree requirements: 122 credits including 27 elective credits.

PLACEMENT

In 1993-94, 86 organizations participated in on-campus recruiting; 676 on-campus interviews were conducted. Placement services include alumni network, career counseling/planning, career fairs, career library, career placement, job interviews, resume preparation, and resume referral to employers. Of 1994 graduates, 90% were employed within three months of graduation, the average starting salary was $48,000, the range was $30,000-$75,000.

Jobs by Employer Type Manufacturing 43%; service 43%; consulting 13%; nonprofit 1%.

Jobs by Functional Area Marketing/sales 18%; finance 51%; operations 1%; management 9%; consulting 14%; other 7%.

Program Contact: Mr. Lee Cunningham, Director of Admissions, University of Notre Dame, Notre Dame, IN 46556. (219) 631-8671, or (800) 631-8488; Fax: (219) 631-8800.
See full description on page 904.

University of Southern Indiana

School of Business

Evansville, Indiana

OVERVIEW

The University of Southern Indiana is a state-supported comprehensive coed institution. Founded 1965. Setting: 300-acre suburban campus. Total institutional enrollment: 7,443.

MBA HIGHLIGHTS

Entrance Difficulty**
Mean GMAT: 510
Mean GPA: N/R

Cost $
Tuition: $106/credit hour
(Nonresident: $212/credit hour)
Room & Board: N/R

Enrollment Profile
Full-time: N/R
Part-time: N/R
Total: 250
Average Age: N/R

Work Exp: N/R
International: N/R
Women: 33%
Minorities: N/R

Average Class Size: 20

ACADEMICS

Length of Program Minimum: 20 months.

Calendar Semesters plus 3 five-week summer terms.

Full-time Classes Main campus; evening, summer.

Part-time Classes Main campus; evening, summer.

Degree Requirements 36 credit hours.

Curricular Focus General management.

Teaching Methodology Lecture: 70%, student presentations: 30%.

FACILITIES

Information Resources Main library with 200,000 bound volumes, 232,716 titles on microform, 900 periodical subscriptions, 4,500 records/tapes/CDs.

ADMISSION
Entrance Requirements Bachelor's degree, GMAT score of 450, minimum 2.5 GPA.

Application Requirements Application form, copies of transcript, resume/curriculum vitae.

Application Deadline Applications are processed on a rolling basis.

FINANCIALS
Costs for 1994-95 Tuition: Full-time: $106/credit hour for state residents, $212/credit hour for nonresidents.

Financial Aid Application deadlines: 3/1 for fall, 5/31 for spring. Contact: Mr. James Patton, Director of Financial Aid, 8600 University Boulevard, Evansville, IN 47712-3590. (812) 464-1767.

INTERNATIONAL STUDENTS
Applying TOEFL required, minimum score of 550; proof of adequate funds. Financial aid is not available to international students.

Program Contact: Office of Graduate Studies, University of Southern Indiana, 8600 University Boulevard, Evansville, IN 47712-3590. (812) 465-7015, or (800) 467-1965; Fax: (812) 464-1960.

IOWA

Drake University

College of Business and Public Administration

Des Moines, Iowa

OVERVIEW
Drake University is an independent nonprofit coed institution. Founded 1881. Setting: 120-acre urban campus. Total institutional enrollment: 7,900. Program was first offered in 1969. AACSB-accredited.

MBA HIGHLIGHTS

Entrance Difficulty***
Mean GMAT: 519
Mean GPA: 3.15

Cost $$$
Tuition: $7,015/semester
Room & Board: $9,000

Enrollment Profile

Full-time: 3	Work Exp: 97%
Part-time: 394	International: 4%
Total: 397	Women: 38%
Average Age: 29	Minorities: 1%

Average Class Size: 32

ACADEMICS
Length of Program Minimum: 16 months. Maximum: 5 years.

Calendar Semesters.

Full-time Classes Main campus; evening, weekends, summer.

Part-time Classes Main campus, Mason City, Fort Dodge, Spencer.

Degree Requirements 36 hours including 9 elective hours.

Required Courses Accounting, business policy, capital management, information systems, marketing, organization and management, public law and business regulation, quantitative methods, statistics. Courses may be waived through: previous course work.

Curricular Focus Business issues and problems, general management, problem solving and decision making.

Concentration Management.

Faculty Full-time: 25, 100% with doctorates.

Teaching Methodology Case study: 30%, lecture: 20%, student presentations: 20%, team projects: 30%.

Special Opportunities Internship program available.

STUDENT STATISTICS
Geographic Representation State residents 96%. By region: Midwest 96%. International 4%.

Undergraduate Majors Business 62%; engineering/technology 8%; science/mathematics 8%; other 22%.

Other Background Graduate degrees in other disciplines: 1%. Work experience: On average, students have 8 years of work experience on entrance to the program.

FACILITIES
Information Resources Main library with 580,000 bound volumes, 1.1 million titles on microform, 2,400 periodical subscriptions, 6,000 records/tapes/CDs, 30 CD-ROMs.

Housing 5% of students in program live in college-owned or -operated housing.

Technology Computers are used moderately in course work. 110 computer terminals/PCs, linked by a campus-wide computer network, are available for use by students in program; they are located in classrooms, the library, the computer center, computer labs. Students in the program are not required to have their own PC.

Computer Resources/On-line Services

Training	Yes	CompuServe	No
Internet	Yes	Dun's	No
E-Mail	Yes	Dow Jones	No
Multimedia Center	Yes	Dialog	No
LEXIS/NEXIS	No	Bloomberg	No

Other on-line services: First Search.

ADMISSION
Acceptance 1994-95 187 applied for admission; 89% were accepted.

Entrance Requirements Bachelor's degree, GMAT score. Core courses waived through: previous course work.

Application Requirements Application form, copies of transcript.

Application Deadlines 7/15 for fall, 12/1 for spring.

FINANCIALS
Costs for 1994-95 Tuition: Full-time: $7,015/semester. Average room and board costs are $9,000 per academic year (on-campus).

Financial Aid In 1994-95, candidates received some institutionally administered aid in the form of loans, assistantships. Financial aid is available to part-time students. Application deadline: 3/1 for fall. Contact: Mr. John C. Parker, Director of Student Financial Planning, 2507 University Avenue, Des Moines, IA 50311. (515) 271-2905.

INTERNATIONAL STUDENTS
Demographics 4% of students enrolled in the program are international; Asia 94%, Africa 6%.

Services and Facilities International student center, ESL courses.

Applying TOEFL required, minimum score of 550; proof of health; proof of adequate funds. Financial aid is not available to international students. Admission application deadlines: 5/15 for fall, 10/15 for spring, 2/15 for summer. Contact: Dr. Thomas M. Pursel, Director of Graduate Programs, 2507 University Avenue, Des Moines, IA 50311-4505. (515) 271-2188.

ALTERNATE MBA PROGRAMS
MBA/JD Length of program: Minimum: 48 months. Maximum: 5 years. Degree requirements: 108 credits including 3 elective credits.

MBA/Pharm D Length of program: Minimum: 60 months. Maximum: 5 years. Degree requirements: 190 credits including 9 elective credits.

PLACEMENT
Placement services include career counseling/planning, career fairs, career library, career placement, job interviews, resume preparation, and resume referral to employers.

Program Contact: Ms. Ann J. Martin, Graduate Coordinator, Drake University, 2507 University Avenue, Des Moines, IA 50311. (515) 271-3891, or (800) 44-DRAKE; Fax: (515) 271-2831.

Iowa State University of Science and Technology

College of Business

Ames, Iowa

OVERVIEW
Iowa State University of Science and Technology is a state-supported coed institution. Founded 1858. Setting: 1,736-acre small-town campus. Total

institutional enrollment: 24,728. Program was first offered in 1985.

MBA HIGHLIGHTS

Entrance Difficulty**
Mean GMAT: 565
Mean GPA: 3.34

Cost $
Tuition: $2,721
(Nonresident: $7,873)
Room & Board: $3,396

Enrollment Profile
Full-time: 100
Part-time: 85
Total: 185
Average Age: 30

Work Exp: 75%
International: 23%
Women: 38%
Minorities: 6%

Average Class Size: 28

ACADEMICS
Length of Program Minimum: 24 months. Maximum: 5 years.
Calendar Semesters.
Full-time Classes Main campus; day.
Part-time Classes Main campus; weekends.
Degree Requirements 48 credits including 24 elective credits.
Required Courses Applied business statistics, business economics, business policy and strategy, corporate financial decisions, ethics and social responsibility, financial markets and evaluation, human behavior in organizations, international business environment, legal, social, and political environments of business, managerial issues in global business, managing information system technology, managing organizational behavior, marketing mix decisions and strategy, marketing opportunities analysis, operations management for planning and control, operations strategy, product costing and accounting data for planning and control, strategic planning and analysis, survey of financial and managerial accounting, survey of information systems concepts.
Curricular Focus Problem solving and decision making, strategic analysis and planning, teamwork.
Concentrations Accounting, agribusiness, finance, human resources management, management, management information systems, marketing, operations management, transportation.
Faculty Full-time: 47, 100% with doctorates.
Teaching Methodology Case study: 20%, lecture: 50%, student presentations: 10%, team projects: 20%.
Special Opportunities International exchange and internship programs available.

STUDENT STATISTICS
Geographic Representation State residents 71%. By region: Midwest 75%; South 2%. International 23%.
Undergraduate Majors Business 35%; education 2%; engineering/technology 18%; humanities 11%; nursing 1%; science/mathematics 20%; social sciences 13%.
Other Background Graduate degrees in other disciplines: 6%. Work experience: On average, students have 8 years of work experience on entrance to the program.

FACILITIES
Information Resources Main library with 2.1 million bound volumes, 2.6 million titles on microform, 22,000 periodical subscriptions, 14,000 records/tapes/CDs. Business collection includes 160,000 bound volumes, 400 periodical subscriptions, 15 CD-ROMs, 30 videos.
Housing College housing available.
Technology Computers are used heavily in course work. 380 computer terminals/PCs, linked by a campus-wide computer network, are available for use by students in program; they are located in the library, the computer center, computer labs. Students in the program are not required to have their own PC.

Computer Resources/On-line Services

Training	Yes	Multimedia Center	Yes
Internet	Yes	Dialog	Yes
E-Mail	Yes		

Other on-line services: First Search.

ADMISSION
Acceptance 1994-95 236 applied for admission; 54% were accepted.
Entrance Requirements Bachelor's degree, GMAT score.

Application Requirements Written essay, application form, copies of transcript, resume/curriculum vitae, 3 letters of recommendation.
Application Deadline 5/1 for fall.

FINANCIALS
Costs for 1994-95 Tuition: Full-time: $2,721 for state residents, $7,873 for nonresidents; Part-time day: $152/credit for state residents, $438/credit for nonresidents; Part-time evening: $182/credit for state residents, $468/credit for nonresidents. Fees: Full-time: $180/semester for state residents, $180/semester for nonresidents; Part-time evening: $100/semester for state residents, $100/semester for nonresidents. Average room and board costs are $3,396 per academic year (on-campus).
Financial Aid In 1994-95, candidates received some institutionally administered aid in the form of scholarships, loans, fellowships, assistantships, work-study. Financial aid is available to part-time students. Application deadline: 3/1 for fall. Contact: Mr. Earl E. Dowling, Director of Financial Aid, 12 Beardshear Hall, Ames, IA 50011. (515) 294-2223.

INTERNATIONAL STUDENTS
Demographics 23% of students enrolled in the program are international; Asia 74%, Africa 6%, Central America 6%, Europe 6%, other 8%.
Services and Facilities Language tutoring, ESL courses, counseling/support services.
Applying TOEFL required, minimum score of 570; proof of adequate funds. Financial aid is available to international students. Financial aid application deadline: 3/1 for fall. Admission application deadline: 3/1 for fall. Contact: Mr. Dennis Peterson, Director, Office of International Students and Scholars, 4 Hamilton Hall, Ames, IA 50011-2010. (515) 294-1120.

PLACEMENT
In 1993-94, 23 organizations participated in on-campus recruiting. Placement services include alumni network, career counseling/planning, career fairs, career library, career placement, electronic job bank, job interviews, resume preparation, and resume referral to employers. Of 1994 graduates, 93% were employed within three months of graduation, the average starting salary was $42,800, the range was $35,000-$58,000.

Program Contact: Mr. Ronald J. Ackerman, Coordinator of Graduate Programs, Iowa State University of Science and Technology, Graduate Programs Office, 9 E.O. Building, Ames, IA 50011-2081. (515) 294-8118, or (800) 433-3452; Fax: (515) 294-6060; Internet Address: busgrad@iastate.edu.
See full description on page 768.

Maharishi International University

School of Management

Fairfield, Iowa

OVERVIEW
Maharishi International University is an independent nonprofit coed institution. Founded 1971. Setting: 262-acre small-town campus. Total institutional enrollment: 628. Program was first offered in 1984.

MBA HIGHLIGHTS
Entrance Difficulty*

Cost $$$
Tuition: $375/credit
Room & Board: $4,800

Enrollment Profile
Full-time: 20
Part-time: 0
Total: 20
Average Age: N/R

Work Exp: N/R
International: 60%
Women: 40%
Minorities: 20%

Average Class Size: 15

ACADEMICS
Length of Program Minimum: 23 months. Maximum: 5 years.
Calendar Semesters.
Full-time Classes Main campus; day.
Degree Requirements 72 credits including 20 elective credits.
Curricular Focus Leadership, organizational development and change management, teamwork.

Concentrations Accounting, finance, health services, hotel management, human resources management, international business, management, management information systems, marketing, organizational behavior, public administration.

Teaching Methodology Case study: 10%, lecture: 35%, seminars by members of the business community: 5%, small group exercises: 25%, student presentations: 5%, team projects: 20%.

Special Opportunities International exchange in India. Internships include telecommunications, financial services, and entrepreneurship.

STUDENT STATISTICS
Geographic Representation By region: West 15%; South 10%; Midwest 10%; Northeast 5%. International 60%.

FACILITIES
Information Resources Main library with 147,400 bound volumes, 49,510 titles on microform, 1,336 periodical subscriptions, 4,114 records/tapes/CDs, 12 CD-ROMs.

Housing 80% of students in program live in college-owned or -operated housing.

Technology Computers are used moderately in course work. 40 computer terminals/PCs, linked by a campus-wide computer network, are available for use by students in program; they are located in the library, the computer center, computer labs. Students in the program are not required to have their own PC.

Computer Resources/On-line Services

Training	Yes	E-Mail	Yes

Other on-line services: OCLC, First Search, Carl.

ADMISSION
Entrance Requirements Bachelor's degree, GMAT score of 400. Core courses waived through: previous course work.

Application Requirements Written essay, application form, copies of transcript, 2 letters of recommendation.

Application Deadline Applications are processed on a rolling basis.

FINANCIALS
Costs for 1995-96 Tuition: Full-time: $375/credit. Fees: Full-time: $216. Average room and board costs are $4,800 per academic year (on-campus) and $2,288 per academic year (off-campus).

Financial Aid In 1994-95, 95% of candidates received some institutionally administered aid in the form of scholarships, loans, work-study. Financial aid is available to part-time students. Applications are processed on a rolling basis. Contact: Ms. Christine Loyacano, International Financial Aid Officer, 1000 North 4th Street, Fairfield, IA 52557. (515) 472-1166.

INTERNATIONAL STUDENTS
Demographics 60% of students enrolled in the program are international; South America 33%, Africa 16%, Europe 16%, North America 16%, Asia 8%, Central America 8%.

Services and Facilities ESL courses, special assistance for nonnative speakers of English.

Applying TOEFL required, minimum score of 580; proof of adequate funds. Financial aid is available to international students. Applications are processed on a rolling basis. Admission application deadlines: 6/1 for fall, 12/1 for spring. Contact: Ms. Christine Loyacano, International Financial Aid Officer, 1000 North 4th Street, Fairfield, IA 52557. (515) 472-1166.

Program Contact: Mr. Paul Handelman, MBA Admissions Officer, Maharishi International University, 1000 North 4th Street, DB 1155, Fairfield, IA 52557-1155. (515) 472-1166; Fax: (515) 472-1179.

St. Ambrose University

College of Business

Davenport, Iowa

OVERVIEW
St. Ambrose University is an independent Roman Catholic comprehensive coed institution. Founded 1882. Setting: 11-acre urban campus. Total institutional enrollment: 2,518. Program was first offered in 1977.

MBA HIGHLIGHTS

Entrance Difficulty**
Mean GMAT: 550
Mean GPA: 3.2

Cost $
Tuition: $325/credit hour
Room & Board: N/R

Enrollment Profile

Full-time: 58	Work Exp: 98%
Part-time: 590	International: 1%
Total: 648	Women: 38%
Average Age: 32	Minorities: 5%

Average Class Size: 15

ACADEMICS
Length of Program Minimum: 24 months. Maximum: 5 years.
Calendar Semesters.

Part-time Classes Main campus; evening, weekends, summer.

Degree Requirements 45 credit hours including 6 elective credit hours.

Required Courses Financial accounting, human resources management, leadership through people skills, legal and social environment of business, managerial accounting, managerial economics, marketing management, operations management, organization theory, statistical methods.

Curricular Focus General management, leadership, organizational development and change management.

Concentrations Finance, human resources management, management information systems, marketing.

Faculty Full-time: 36, 50% with doctorates; part-time: 37, 38% with doctorates.

Teaching Methodology Case study: 30%, faculty seminars: 5%, lecture: 30%, research: 5%, seminars by members of the business community: 5%, student presentations: 10%, team projects: 15%.

STUDENT STATISTICS
Geographic Representation State residents 80%. By region: Midwest 99%. International 1%.

Other Background Graduate degrees in other disciplines: 5%. Work experience: On average, students have 10 years of work experience on entrance to the program.

FACILITIES
Information Resources Main library with 135,000 bound volumes, 150 titles on microform, 819 periodical subscriptions, 2,877 records/tapes/CDs.

Housing College housing not available.

Technology Computers are used moderately in course work. 50 computer terminals/PCs, linked by a campus-wide computer network, are available for use by students in program; they are located in the library, the computer center, computer labs. Students in the program are not required to have their own PC.

Computer Resources/On-line Services

Training	Yes	CompuServe	No
Internet	Yes	Dun's	No
E-Mail	Yes	Dow Jones	No
Multimedia Center	Yes	Dialog	No
LEXIS/NEXIS	No	Bloomberg	No

ADMISSION
Entrance Requirements Bachelor's degree, GMAT score of 400.

Application Requirements Application form, copies of transcript, personal statement.

Application Deadline Applications are processed on a rolling basis.

FINANCIALS
Costs for 1994-95 Tuition: Full-time: $325/credit hour.

Financial Aid Application deadline: 3/15 for fall. Contact: Ms. Rita O'Connor, Director of Financial Aid, 518 West Locust Street, Davenport, IA 52803-2898. (319) 383-8885.

INTERNATIONAL STUDENTS
Demographics 1% of students enrolled in the program are international.

Applying TOEFL required, minimum score of 550; proof of adequate funds. Financial aid is not available to international students. Admission applications are processed on a rolling basis.

PLACEMENT

Placement services include alumni network, career counseling/planning, career fairs, career library, career placement, resume preparation, and resume referral to employers.

Program Contact: Dr. John Collis, Director, MBA Programs, St. Ambrose University, 518 West Locust Street, Davenport, IA 52803-2898. (319) 383-8899; Fax: (319) 383-8942; Internet Address: jcollis@saunix.sau. edu.

University of Dubuque

School of Business

Dubuque, Iowa

OVERVIEW

The University of Dubuque is an independent Presbyterian comprehensive coed institution. Founded 1852. Setting: 56-acre urban campus. Total institutional enrollment: 1,200. Program was first offered in 1983.

MBA HIGHLIGHTS

Entrance Difficulty***
Mean GMAT: 550
Mean GPA: 3.5

Cost $$
Tuition: $310/semester hour
Room & Board: $4,000

Enrollment Profile

Full-time: 5	Work Exp: 95%
Part-time: 295	International: N/R
Total: 300	Women: 40%
Average Age: 33	Minorities: N/R

Average Class Size: 20

ACADEMICS

Length of Program Minimum: 18 months.

Calendar Semesters.

Full-time Classes Main campus; evening, weekends, summer.

Part-time Classes Main campus, Hong Kong, Petaling Jaya (Malaysia), Penang (Malaysia); evening, weekends, summer.

Degree Requirements 36 credits including 6 elective credits.

Required Courses Business ethics, business policy and strategy, economic analysis for managers, financial decision making, international business, managerial accounting, marketing strategy and planning, operations management, organizational theory and behavior, total quality management: quality control.

Curricular Focus Business issues and problems, general management, problem solving and decision making.

Concentration Management.

Faculty Full-time: 9, 44% with doctorates; part-time: 12, 50% with doctorates.

Teaching Methodology Case study: 40%, faculty seminars: 5%, lecture: 35%, research: 5%, seminars by members of the business community: 5%, student presentations: 5%, team projects: 5%.

Special Opportunities Internship program available. Other: Small Business Institute.

STUDENT STATISTICS

Geographic Representation By region: Midwest 25%.

Undergraduate Majors Business 60%; engineering/technology 10%; humanities 5%; science/mathematics 20%; social sciences 5%.

Other Background Graduate degrees in other disciplines: 5%. Work experience: On average, students have 5 years of work experience on entrance to the program.

FACILITIES

Information Resources Main library with 164,859 bound volumes, 20,739 titles on microform, 801 periodical subscriptions, 2,180 records/tapes/CDs, 3 CD-ROMs.

Housing 5% of students in program live in college-owned or -operated housing.

Technology Computers are used moderately in course work. 46 computer terminals/PCs are available for use by students in program; they are located in computer labs. Students in the program are not required to have their own PC.

Computer Resources/On-line Services

Training	Yes	Dun's	No
Internet	Yes	Dow Jones	No
E-Mail	Yes	Dialog	No
LEXIS/NEXIS	No	Bloomberg	No
CompuServe	No		

ADMISSION

Acceptance 1994-95 Of those applying, 77% were accepted.

Entrance Requirements Bachelor's degree, GMAT score of 400. Core courses waived through: previous course work.

Application Requirements Application form, copies of transcript, 3 letters of recommendation.

Application Deadline Applications are processed on a rolling basis.

FINANCIALS

Costs for 1994-95 Tuition: Full-time: $310/semester hour. Average room and board costs are $4,000 per academic year (on-campus) and $4,000 per academic year (off-campus).

Financial Aid In 1994-95, candidates received some institutionally administered aid in the form of loans. Financial aid is available to part-time students. Contact: Ms. Shari Smith, Assistant Director of Financial Aid, 2000 University Avenue, Dubuque, IA 52001-5099. (319) 589-3169.

INTERNATIONAL STUDENTS

Demographics 17% of students on campus are international.

Services and Facilities International student office.

Applying TOEFL required, minimum score of 500; proof of adequate funds. Financial aid is not available to international students. Admission application deadlines: 7/1 for fall, 11/1 for spring. Applications are processed on a rolling basis. Contact: Mr. Peter Li, Coordinator of International Business Programs, 2000 University Avenue, Dubuque, IA 52001-5099. (319) 589-3191.

PLACEMENT

Placement services include career counseling/planning, career fairs, career library, resume preparation, and resume referral to employers.

Program Contact: Ms. Carol Knockle, Program Coordinator, University of Dubuque, 2000 University Avenue, Dubuque, IA 52001-5099. (319) 589-3300; Fax: (319) 589-3184.

The University of Iowa

School of Management

Iowa City, Iowa

OVERVIEW

The University of Iowa is a state-supported coed institution. Founded 1847. Setting: 1,880-acre small-town campus. Total institutional enrollment: 25,510. Program was first offered in 1959. AACSB-accredited.

MBA HIGHLIGHTS

Entrance Difficulty****
Mean GMAT: 590
Mean GPA: 3.2

Cost $
Tuition: $1,775/semester
(Nonresident: $4,681/semester)
Room & Board: $4,536

Enrollment Profile

Full-time: 219	Work Exp: 80%
Part-time: 240	International: 26%
Total: 459	Women: 30%
Average Age: 26	Minorities: 5%

Class Size: 30 - 60

ACADEMICS

Length of Program Minimum: 21 months. Maximum: 10 years.

Calendar Semesters.

Full-time Classes Main campus; day, summer.

Part-time Classes Main campus, Cedar Rapids, Quad Cities, Newton; evening, summer.

Degree Requirements 60 credits including 24 elective credits.

Required Courses Accounting for managers, business policy, economic environment of the firm, managerial economics, managerial finance, marketing management, models for decision support, operations management, organizational behavior, statistics, strategic management.

Curricular Focus Business issues and problems, economic and financial theory, teamwork.

Concentrations Accounting, entrepreneurship, finance, human resources management, management, management information systems, marketing, operations management, organizational behavior.

Faculty Full-time: 60, 100% with doctorates.

Teaching Methodology Case study: 20%, faculty seminars: 10%, lecture: 25%, research: 5%, seminars by members of the business community: 10%, student presentations: 15%, team projects: 15%.

Special Opportunities International exchange in Austria, Germany, Mexico, United Kingdom. Internship program available.

STUDENT STATISTICS

Geographic Representation State residents 49%. By region: Midwest 57%; West 7%; Northeast 6%; South 5%. International 26%.

Undergraduate Majors Business 41%; education 1%; engineering/technology 14%; humanities 6%; nursing 2%; science/mathematics 10%; social sciences 17%; other 9%.

Other Background Graduate degrees in other disciplines: 5%. Work experience: On average, students have 3 years of work experience on entrance to the program.

FACILITIES

Information Resources Main library with 3.5 million bound volumes, 40,009 periodical subscriptions, 20,837 records/tapes/CDs. Business collection in College of Business Administration Library includes 26,000 bound volumes, 480 periodical subscriptions, 6 CD-ROMs, 8 videos.

Housing 5% of students in program live in college-owned or -operated housing.

Technology Computers are used moderately in course work. 1,500 computer terminals/PCs, linked by a campus-wide computer network, are available for use by students in program; they are located in dormitories, the student center, classrooms, learning resource center, the library, the computer center, computer labs, the research center. Students in the program are not required to have their own PC.

Computer Resources/On-line Services

Training	Yes	CompuServe	Yes
Internet	Yes	Dun's	Yes
E-Mail	Yes	Dow Jones	Yes
Videoconference Center	Yes	Dialog	Yes
Multimedia Center	Yes	Bloomberg	Yes
LEXIS/NEXIS	Yes		

Other on-line services: OCLC, RLIN.

ADMISSION

Acceptance 1994-95 617 applied for admission; 38% were accepted.

Entrance Requirements Bachelor's degree, GMAT score, minimum 2.5 GPA.

Application Requirements Written essay, application form, copies of transcript, resume/curriculum vitae, personal statement, 3 letters of recommendation.

Application Deadlines 4/15 for fall, 11/15 for spring. Application discs available.

FINANCIALS

Costs for 1994-95 Tuition: Full-time: $1,775/semester for state residents, $4,681/semester for nonresidents. Average room and board costs are $4,536 per academic year (on-campus) and $4,536 per academic year (off-campus).

Financial Aid In 1994-95, candidates received some institutionally administered aid in the form of grants, scholarships, loans, assistantships, work-study. Total awards ranged from $1,000-$10,000. Financial aid is available to part-time students. Application deadline: 4/15 for fall. Contact: Mr. Jeffrey L. Emrich, Director of MBA Admission and Financial Aid, School of Management, Suite C140, 108 Pappajohn, Iowa City, IA 52242. (319) 335-1039.

INTERNATIONAL STUDENTS

Demographics 26% of students enrolled in the program are international; Asia 46%, Europe 27%, Central America 4%, other 23%.

Services and Facilities International student center, visa services, language tutoring, ESL courses, special assistance for nonnative speakers of English, counseling/support services.

Applying TOEFL required, minimum score of 600; proof of health; proof of adequate funds. Financial aid is available to international students. Financial aid application deadline: 4/15 for fall. Admission application deadline: 4/15 for fall. Contact: Mr. Jeffrey L. Emrich, Director, MBA Admission and Financial Aid, Business Administration Building, Suite C140, 108 Pappajohn, Iowa City, IA 52242. (319) 335-1039.

ALTERNATE MBA PROGRAMS

Executive MBA (EMBA) Length of program: Minimum: 21 months. Maximum: 2 years. Degree requirements: 48 credits including 12 elective credits.

MBA/JD

MBA/MA Length of program: Minimum: 30 months. Degree requirements: 72 credits including 15 elective credits. 3 courses of business electives and 2 courses of hospital and health administration electives. MA is in hospital and health administration.

MBA/MSN Length of program: Minimum: 36 months. Maximum: 10 years. Degree requirements: 69 credits.

PLACEMENT

In 1993-94, 89 organizations participated in on-campus recruiting; 441 on-campus interviews were conducted. Placement services include alumni network, career counseling/planning, career fairs, career library, job interviews, resume preparation, and resume referral to employers. Of 1994 graduates, 80% were employed within three months of graduation, the average starting salary was $39,700, the range was $28,500-$61,000.

Jobs by Employer Type Manufacturing 28%; service 39%; consulting 22%; nonprofit 5%; utilities 6%.

Jobs by Functional Area Marketing/sales 24%; finance 15%; operations 6%; management 24%; strategic planning 18%; other 13%.

Program Contact: Mr. Arthur Khaw, Director, MBA Admission, The University of Iowa, 108 Pappajohn, Iowa City, IA 52242. (319) 335-1039, or (800) 622-4692; Fax: (319) 335-3604; Internet Address: iowamba@uiowa.edu.

See full description on page 882.

University of Northern Iowa

College of Business Administration

Cedar Falls, Iowa

OVERVIEW

The University of Northern Iowa is a state-supported comprehensive coed institution. Founded 1876. Setting: 865-acre small-town campus. Total institutional enrollment: 12,717.

MBA HIGHLIGHTS

Entrance Difficulty*
Mean GMAT: 550
Mean GPA: N/R

Cost $
Tuition: $1,328/semester
(Nonresident: $3,296/semester)
Room & Board: $2,979

Enrollment Profile

Full-time: 54	Work Exp: N/R
Part-time: 126	International: 10%
Total: 180	Women: 30%
Average Age: N/R	Minorities: 2%

Class Size: 20 - 29

ACADEMICS

Length of Program Minimum: 18 months. Maximum: 7 years.

Calendar Semesters.

Full-time Classes Main campus; evening.

Part-time Classes Main campus; evening.

Degree Requirements 33 hours.
Curricular Focus General management, leadership, problem solving and decision making.
Concentration Management.
Teaching Methodology Case study: 25%, faculty seminars: 10%, lecture: 40%, research: 5%, seminars by members of the business community: 5%, student presentations: 10%, team projects: 5%.

STUDENT STATISTICS
Geographic Representation State residents 90%. International 10%.

FACILITIES
Information Resources Main library with 754,934 bound volumes, 690,512 titles on microform, 3,087 periodical subscriptions, 11,655 records/tapes/CDs, 73 CD-ROMs.
Housing College housing available.

ADMISSION
Entrance Requirements Bachelor's degree, prerequisite courses required for applicants with non-business degree, GMAT score of 500.
Application Requirements Application form, copies of transcript, personal statement.
Application Deadlines 7/20 for fall, 12/15 for spring. Applications are processed on a rolling basis.

FINANCIALS
Costs for 1994-95 Tuition: Full-time: $1,328/semester for state residents, $3,296/semester for nonresidents. Fees: Full-time: $378/semester for state residents, $378/semester for nonresidents. Average room and board costs are $2,979 per academic year (on-campus).
Financial Aid In 1994-95, candidates received some institutionally administered aid in the form of grants, scholarships, loans, fellowships, assistantships. Application deadline: 2/15 for fall. Applications are processed on a rolling basis. Contact: Financial Aid Office, 116 Gilchrist, Cedar Falls, IA 50614-0123. (319) 273-2700.

INTERNATIONAL STUDENTS
Demographics 10% of students enrolled in the program are international.
Applying TOEFL required, minimum score of 500; proof of health; proof of adequate funds. Financial aid is available to international students. Financial aid application deadlines: 4/1 for fall, 10/1 for spring. Applications are processed on a rolling basis. Admission application deadlines: 5/1 for fall, 11/1 for spring. Applications are processed on a rolling basis. Contact: International Services, Baker Room 501, Cedar Falls, IA 50614-0123. (319) 273-6421.

Program Contact: Dr. Geofrey T. Mills, Assistant Dean, University of Northern Iowa, College of Business, Suite 325, Cedar Falls, IA 50614-0123. (319) 273-6240, or (800) 772-2037; Fax: (319) 273-2922; Internet Address: mills@uni.edu.

KANSAS

Emporia State University

School of Business

Emporia, Kansas

OVERVIEW
Emporia State University is a state-supported comprehensive coed institution. Founded 1863. Setting: 207-acre suburban campus. Total institutional enrollment: 6,000. Program was first offered in 1941.

MBA HIGHLIGHTS

Entrance Difficulty**
Mean GMAT: 475
Mean GPA: 3.3

Cost $
Tuition: $1,009/semester
(Nonresident: $2,561/semester)
Room & Board: N/R

Enrollment Profile

Full-time: 55		Work Exp: 85%	
Part-time: 45		International: 35%	
Total: 100		Women: 40%	
Average Age: 26		Minorities: 5%	

Average Class Size: 25

ACADEMICS
Length of Program Minimum: 12 months. Maximum: 10 years.
Calendar Semesters.
Full-time Classes Main campus; day, evening, summer.
Part-time Classes Main campus; day, evening, summer.
Degree Requirements 36 credits including 9 elective credits.
Required Courses Accounting information for managers, behavior aspects of management, business policy and strategic management, management and organization theory, management information systems, managerial economics, marketing management, quantitative analysis, seminar in financial management.
Curricular Focus General management.
Concentration Accounting.
Faculty Full-time: 9, 89% with doctorates.
Teaching Methodology Case study: 25%, lecture: 30%, research: 10%, seminars by members of the business community: 5%, student presentations: 10%, team projects: 20%.
Special Opportunities Internships include finance, marketing, manufacturing, and management.

STUDENT STATISTICS
Geographic Representation State residents 60%. By region: Midwest 65%. International 35%.
Undergraduate Majors Business 80%; education 10%; other 10%.
Other Background Graduate degrees in other disciplines: 5%. Work experience: On average, students have 6 years of work experience on entrance to the program.

FACILITIES
Information Resources Main library with 726,966 bound volumes, 347,300 titles on microform, 1,536 periodical subscriptions, 4,226 records/tapes/CDs, 526 CD-ROMs.
Housing 30% of students in program live in college-owned or -operated housing. Assistance with housing search provided.
Technology Computers are used heavily in course work. 90 computer terminals/PCs, linked by a campus-wide computer network, are available for use by students in program; they are located in the computer center, computer labs. Students in the program are not required to have their own PC.

Computer Resources/On-line Services

Training	Yes	CompuServe	No
Internet	Yes	Dun's	No
E-Mail	Yes	Dow Jones	No
Multimedia Center	Yes	Dialog	Yes
LEXIS/NEXIS	No	Bloomberg	No

Other on-line services: First Search, SEC.

ADMISSION
Acceptance 1994-95 200 applied for admission; 75% were accepted.
Entrance Requirements Bachelor's degree, GMAT score. Core courses waived through: previous course work.
Application Requirements Application form, copies of transcript.
Application Deadlines 6/1 for fall. Applications are processed on a rolling basis.

FINANCIALS
Estimated Costs for 1995-96 Tuition: Full-time: $1,009/semester for state residents, $2,561/semester for nonresidents; Part-time day: $86/credit hour for state residents, $215/credit hour for nonresidents.
Financial Aid In 1994-95, 60% of candidates received some institutionally administered aid in the form of loans, assistantships. Total awards ranged from $500-$5,000. Financial aid is available to part-time students. Application deadlines: 6/1 for fall, 11/1 for spring. Applications are processed on a rolling basis. Contact: Ms. Wilma Kosnic, Director of Financial Aid, 1200 Commercial Street, Emporia, KS 66801. (316) 341-5457.

INTERNATIONAL STUDENTS
Demographics 35% of students enrolled in the program are international; Asia 45%, Africa 30%, South America 10%, North America 10%, Central America 5%.

Services and Facilities International student office, international student center, visa services, language tutoring, ESL courses, special assistance for nonnative speakers of English, counseling/support services.

Applying TOEFL required, minimum score of 550; proof of health; proof of adequate funds. Financial aid is not available to international students. Admission application deadlines: 6/1 for fall, 11/1 for spring. Applications are processed on a rolling basis. Contact: Dr. James Harter, Vice President for International Affairs, 1200 Commercial Street, Emporia, KS 66801. (316) 341-5374.

PLACEMENT
In 1993-94, 50 organizations participated in on-campus recruiting; 50 on-campus interviews were conducted. Placement services include alumni network, career counseling/planning, career fairs, career library, career placement, job interviews, and resume preparation. Of 1994 graduates, 80% were employed within three months of graduation.

Jobs by Employer Type Manufacturing 30%; service 40%; government 20%; nonprofit 10%.

Jobs by Functional Area Marketing/sales 20%; finance 10%; operations 10%; management 60%.

Program Contact: Mr. Donald Miller, MBA Director, Emporia State University, 1200 Commercial Street, Emporia, KA 66801. (316) 341-5456; Fax: (316) 341-5418; Internet Address: millerdn@esuvm.bitnet. See full description on page 732.

Fort Hays State University

College of Business

Hays, Kansas

OVERVIEW
Fort Hays State University is a state-supported comprehensive coed institution. Part of Kansas Regents System. Founded 1902. Setting: 200-acre small-town campus. Total institutional enrollment: 4,523.

MBA HIGHLIGHTS
Entrance Difficulty***
Mean GMAT: 450
Mean GPA: N/R

Cost $
Tuition: $83/credit hour
(Nonresident: $212/credit hour)
Room & Board: N/R

Enrollment Profile
Full-time: N/R
Part-time: N/R
Total: 75
Average Age: N/R
Work Exp: N/R
International: 50%
Women: 40%
Minorities: 5%

Average Class Size: 25

ACADEMICS
Length of Program Minimum: 18 months.
Calendar Semesters.
Full-time Classes Main campus; day, evening, summer.
Part-time Classes Main campus; day, evening, summer.
Degree Requirements 30 credit hours.
Curricular Focus General management.
Teaching Methodology Case study: 10%, discussion: 20%, lecture: 50%, research: 10%, student presentations: 10%.

STUDENT STATISTICS
Geographic Representation State residents 50%. International 50%.

FACILITIES
Information Resources Main library with 605,274 bound volumes, 910,880 titles on microform, 1,181 periodical subscriptions, 412 records/tapes/CDs.

ADMISSION
Entrance Requirements Bachelor's degree, algebra, calculus, statistics, quantitative methods, GMAT score.

Application Requirements Application form, copies of transcript, personal statement.

Application Deadlines 4/1 for fall, 10/1 for spring. Applications are processed on a rolling basis.

FINANCIALS
Costs for 1994-95 Tuition: Full-time: $83/credit hour for state residents, $212/credit hour for nonresidents.

Financial Aid Applications are processed on a rolling basis. Contact: Dean, Graduate School, 600 Park Street, Hays, KS 67601-4009. (913) 628-4236.

INTERNATIONAL STUDENTS
Demographics 50% of students enrolled in the program are international.

Applying TOEFL required, minimum score of 550; proof of health; proof of adequate funds; minimum GMAT score of 450. Financial aid is available to international students. Assistantships are available for these students. Applications are processed on a rolling basis. Admission application deadline: 4/1 for fall. Applications are processed on a rolling basis.

Program Contact: Dr. Bob Masters, MBA Director, Fort Hays State University, 600 Park Street, Hays, KS 67601-4009. (913) 628-4201.

Kansas State University

College of Business Administration

Manhattan, Kansas

OVERVIEW
Kansas State University is a state-supported coed institution. Founded 1863. Setting: 668-acre small-town campus. Total institutional enrollment: 22,000. Program was first offered in 1967. AACSB-accredited.

MBA HIGHLIGHTS
Entrance Difficulty***
Mean GMAT: 524
Mean GPA: 3.32

Cost $
Tuition: $990/semester
(Nonresident: $3,269/semester)
Room & Board: N/R

Enrollment Profile
Full-time: 70
Part-time: 18
Total: 88
Average Age: 28
Work Exp: 40%
International: 44%
Women: 43%
Minorities: 0%

Average Class Size: 32

ACADEMICS
Length of Program Minimum: 24 months. Maximum: 6 years.
Calendar Semesters.
Full-time Classes Main campus; day, evening, early morning, summer.
Degree Requirements 51 credits including 12 elective credits.
Required Courses Accounting, advanced managerial economics, behavior, finance, international business, legal and social environment, management information systems, management science, marketing, operations, strategy.
Curricular Focus Business issues and problems, general management, teamwork.
Concentrations Agribusiness, finance, international business, management, marketing.
Faculty Full-time: 17, 100% with doctorates.
Teaching Methodology Case study: 30%, lecture: 15%, seminars by members of the business community: 5%, student presentations: 30%, team projects: 20%.
Special Opportunities International exchange in Mexico, Paraguay. Internship program available.

STUDENT STATISTICS

Geographic Representation State residents 48%. By region: Midwest 54%; South 1%; West 1%. International 44%.

Undergraduate Majors Business 50%; engineering/technology 23%; humanities 7%; science/mathematics 6%; social sciences 14%.

Other Background Graduate degrees in other disciplines: 3%. Work experience: On average, students have 5 years of work experience on entrance to the program.

FACILITIES

Information Resources Main library with 1.3 million bound volumes, 3.7 million titles on microform, 8,499 periodical subscriptions, 17,717 records/tapes/CDs, 23 CD-ROMs. Business collection includes 10,627 bound volumes, 200 periodical subscriptions, 8 CD-ROMs, 69 videos.

Housing 30% of students in program live in college-owned or -operated housing.

Technology Computers are used moderately in course work. 168 computer terminals/PCs, linked by a campus-wide computer network, are available for use by students in program; they are located in student rooms, the library, the computer center, computer labs. Students in the program are not required to have their own PC.

Computer Resources/On-line Services

Training	Yes	E-Mail	Yes
Internet	Yes	LEXIS/NEXIS	Yes

Other on-line services: OCLC.

ADMISSION

Acceptance 1994-95 352 applied for admission.

Entrance Requirements Bachelor's degree, GMAT score, minimum 3.0 GPA. Core courses waived through: previous course work.

Application Requirements Written essay, application form, copies of transcript, personal statement, 3 letters of recommendation.

Application Deadlines 8/1 for fall, 1/1 for spring, 6/1 for summer.

FINANCIALS

Costs for 1994-95 Tuition: Full-time: $990/semester for state residents, $3,269/semester for nonresidents. Fees: Full-time: $218/semester for state residents, $218/semester for nonresidents.

Financial Aid In 1994-95, 40% of candidates received some institutionally administered aid in the form of scholarships, loans, assistantships. Total awards ranged from $1,000-$8,700. Financial aid is available to part-time students. Application deadlines: 3/1 for fall, 3/1 for spring, 2/1 for scholarships. Contact: Mr. Lawrence Moeder, Director, 104 Fairchild Hall, Manhattan, KS 66506. (913) 532-6420.

INTERNATIONAL STUDENTS

Demographics 44% of students enrolled in the program are international; Asia 60%, Europe 31%, Central America 5%, South America 3%, Africa 1%.

Services and Facilities International student center, language tutoring, ESL courses, special assistance for nonnative speakers of English, counseling/support services.

Applying TOEFL required, minimum score of 590; proof of health; proof of adequate funds. Financial aid is available to international students. Financial aid application deadlines: 6/1 for fall, 11/1 for spring, 4/1 for summer. Admission application deadlines: 6/1 for fall, 11/1 for spring, 4/1 for summer. Contact: Ms. Donna Davis, Director, International Student Center, Manhattan, KS 66506. (913) 532-6448.

PLACEMENT

In 1993-94, 37 organizations participated in on-campus recruiting. Placement services include alumni network, career counseling/planning, career fairs, career library, career placement, electronic job bank, job interviews, resume preparation, and resume referral to employers. Of 1994 graduates, 85% were employed within three months of graduation, the average starting salary was $32,000, the range was $18,000-$42,000.

Jobs by Employer Type Manufacturing 30%; service 23%; government 15%; consulting 25%; nonprofit 7%.

Jobs by Functional Area Marketing/sales 5%; finance 5%; operations 30%; management 40%; strategic planning 15%; technical management 5%.

Program Contact: Ms. Donna Ronde, Director of Graduate Studies, Kansas State University, Anderson Hall, Room 1, Manhattan, KS 66506. (913) 532-7190; Fax: (913) 532-7024.

MidAmerica Nazarene College

Olathe, Kansas

OVERVIEW

MidAmerica Nazarene College is an independent comprehensive coed institution, affiliated with Church of the Nazarene. Founded 1966. Setting: 112-acre suburban campus with easy access to Kansas City. Total institutional enrollment: 1,445. Program was first offered in 1991.

MBA HIGHLIGHTS

Entrance Difficulty*
Mean GMAT: N/R
Mean GPA: 3.14

Cost $
Tuition: $2,684/semester
Room & Board: N/R

Enrollment Profile

Full-time: 95	Work Exp: 100%
Part-time: 0	International: 3%
Total: 95	Women: 34%
Average Age: 36	Minorities: 6%

Average Class Size: 25

ACADEMICS

Length of Program Minimum: 22 months. Maximum: 6 years.

Calendar Semesters.

Full-time Classes Main campus; evening, weekends, summer.

Degree Requirements 43 credits.

Required Courses Advanced statistical process control, computer applications, entrepreneurship, ethical values models for decision making, financial management and planning, leadership for total quality management, legal environment of business, management information systems, marketing management, organizational development and change, quantitative methods, the U.S. in a world economy, total quality management.

Curricular Focus Leadership, organizational development and change management, problem solving and decision making, teamwork.

Concentrations Accounting, economics, entrepreneurship, finance, international business, management, management information systems, marketing, operations management, organizational behavior, quantitative analysis, strategic management.

Faculty Full-time: 2, 100% with doctorates; part-time: 5, 40% with doctorates.

Teaching Methodology Case study: 25%, lecture: 50%, research: 5%, student presentations: 10%, team projects: 10%.

STUDENT STATISTICS

Geographic Representation State residents 74%. By region: Midwest 97%. International 3%.

Undergraduate Majors Business 70%; engineering/technology 4%; humanities 7%; nursing 2%; science/mathematics 14%; social sciences 3%.

Other Background Work experience: On average, students have 15 years of work experience on entrance to the program.

FACILITIES

Information Resources Main library with 79,237 bound volumes, 137,797 titles on microform, 1,000 periodical subscriptions, 3,156 records/tapes/CDs. Business collection includes 7,059 bound volumes, 805 periodical subscriptions, 482 CD-ROMs, 9 videos.

Housing College housing not available.

Technology Computers are used moderately in course work. 40 computer terminals/PCs are available for use by students in program; they are located in the library, computer labs. Students in the program are not required to have their own PC.

Computer Resources/On-line Services

Training	Yes	Dun's	No
Internet	No	Dow Jones	No
E-Mail	No	Dialog	No
LEXIS/NEXIS	No	Bloomberg	No
CompuServe	No		

ADMISSION

Acceptance 1994-95 120 applied for admission; 100% were accepted.

Entrance Requirements Bachelor's degree, minimum 3.0 GPA, minimum 2 years of work experience.

Application Requirements Application form, copies of transcript, 2 letters of recommendation.

Application Deadlines 9/1 for fall, 1/1 for spring.

FINANCIALS
Costs for 1994-95 Tuition: Full-time: $2,684/semester.

Financial Aid Financial aid is not available to part-time students. Applications are processed on a rolling basis. Contact: Mr. Perry Diehm, Assistant Director, Student Financial Services, 2030 East College Way, Olathe, KS 66062-1899. (913) 791-3298.

INTERNATIONAL STUDENTS
Demographics 3% of students enrolled in the program are international; Africa 34%, Asia 33%, other 33%.

Applying TOEFL required, minimum score of 600; proof of adequate funds. Admission applications are processed on a rolling basis. Contact: Dr. James Main, Registrar, 2030 East College Way, Olathe, KS 66062-1899. (913) 782-3750.

PLACEMENT
Placement services include alumni network, career counseling/planning, career fairs, career library, and career placement.

Program Contact: Ms. Karen Bevis, Administrative Assistant, MidAmerica Nazarene College, 2030 East College Way, Olathe, KS 66062-1899. (913) 791-3276; Fax: (913) 791-3409.

Pittsburg State University

Gladys A. Kelce School of Business

Pittsburg, Kansas

OVERVIEW
Pittsburg State University is a state-supported comprehensive coed institution. Founded 1903. Setting: 140-acre small-town campus. Total institutional enrollment: 6,600. Program was first offered in 1975.

MBA HIGHLIGHTS

Entrance Difficulty**
Mean GMAT: 475
Mean GPA: 3.2

Cost $
Tuition: $1,021/semester
(Nonresident: $2,573/semester)
Room & Board: $2,647

Enrollment Profile

Full-time: 85	Work Exp: 20%
Part-time: 40	International: 30%
Total: 125	Women: 50%
Average Age: 28	Minorities: 5%

Average Class Size: 20

ACADEMICS
Length of Program Minimum: 12 months. Maximum: 6 years.
Calendar Semesters.
Full-time Classes Main campus; day, evening, summer.
Degree Requirements 33 credits including 12 elective credits.
Required Courses Administrative control and decision, business, government, and society, management strategy and administration, managerial forecasting and resource allocation, operating in the international environment.
Curricular Focus Business issues and problems, general management, strategic analysis and planning.
Concentrations Accounting, management.
Teaching Methodology Case study: 25%, lecture: 25%, student presentations: 25%, team projects: 25%.

STUDENT STATISTICS
Geographic Representation State residents 50%. By region: Midwest 60%; Northeast 3%; South 3%; West 3%. International 30%.
Undergraduate Majors Business 60%; education 2%; engineering/technology 10%; humanities 3%; nursing 2%; science/mathematics 10%; social sciences 3%; other 10%.

Other Background Graduate degrees in other disciplines: 5%. Work experience: On average, students have 2 years of work experience on entrance to the program.

FACILITIES
Information Resources Main library with 290,798 bound volumes, 516,718 titles on microform, 1,368 periodical subscriptions, 386 records/tapes/CDs.

Housing College housing available.

Technology Computers are used moderately in course work. 182 computer terminals/PCs, linked by a campus-wide computer network, are available for use by students in program; they are located in the library, computer labs. Students in the program are not required to have their own PC.

Computer Resources/On-line Services

Training	Yes	Dun's	No
Internet	Yes	Dow Jones	No
E-Mail	Yes	Dialog	Yes
LEXIS/NEXIS	No	Bloomberg	No
CompuServe	No		

Other on-line services: OCLC, First Search.

ADMISSION
Acceptance 1994-95 300 applied for admission; 80% were accepted.
Entrance Requirements GMAT score. Core courses waived through: previous course work.
Application Requirements Application form, copies of transcript.
Application Deadlines 7/15 for fall, 12/15 for spring, 5/1 for summer. Applications are processed on a rolling basis. Application discs available.

FINANCIALS
Costs for 1994-95 Tuition: Full-time: $1,021/semester for state residents, $2,573/semester for nonresidents; Part-time day: $86/credit hour for state residents, $215/credit hour for nonresidents. Fees: Full-time: $648/semester for state residents, $2,459/semester for nonresidents; Part-time day: $48/credit hour for state residents, $168/credit hour for nonresidents. Average room and board costs are $2,647 per academic year (on-campus).

Financial Aid In 1994-95, candidates received some institutionally administered aid in the form of scholarships, loans, assistantships. Financial aid is not available to part-time students. Applications are processed on a rolling basis. Contact: Mr. Ron Hopkins, Director of Financial Aid, 115 Russ Hall, Pittsburg, KS 66762. (316) 235-4237.

INTERNATIONAL STUDENTS
Demographics 30% of students enrolled in the program are international; Asia 90%, Europe 4%, Africa 2%, South America 2%, other 2%.

Services and Facilities International student office, international student center, visa services, language tutoring, ESL courses, counseling/support services.

Applying TOEFL required, minimum score of 550. Financial aid is available to international students. Applications are processed on a rolling basis. Admission application deadlines: 7/15 for fall, 12/15 for spring, 5/1 for summer. Applications are processed on a rolling basis. Contact: Dr. David Ayers, Director of International Student Services, Mitchell Hall, Pittsburg, KS 66762. (316) 235-4681.

PLACEMENT
Placement services include alumni network, career counseling/planning, career fairs, career library, job interviews, and resume preparation.

Program Contact: Mr. Ronald Wood, MBA Program Director, Pittsburg State University, 101 Kelce Center, Pittsburg, KS 66762. (316) 235-4598; Fax: (316) 232-7515.

University of Kansas

School of Business

Lawrence, Kansas

OVERVIEW
The University of Kansas is a state-supported coed institution. Founded 1866. Setting: 1,000-acre suburban campus with easy access to Kansas City. Total institutional enrollment: 28,600. Program was first offered in 1961. AACSB-accredited.

MBA HIGHLIGHTS

Entrance Difficulty**
Mean GMAT: 584
Mean GPA: 3.3

Cost $
Tuition: $111/credit hour
(Nonresident: $300/credit hour)
Room & Board: $3,236

Enrollment Profile

Full-time: 167	Work Exp: 60%
Part-time: 233	International: 10%
Total: 400	Women: 37%
Average Age: 30	Minorities: 3%

Average Class Size: 25

ACADEMICS

Length of Program Minimum: 24 months. Maximum: 7 years.
Calendar Semesters.
Full-time Classes Main campus; day, summer.
Part-time Classes Main campus, Overland Park; evening, summer.
Degree Requirements 56 credits including 12 elective credits.
Required Courses Business policy, economic environment, financial accounting information, financial management, human resources management, legal and social environment of business, managerial accounting information, managerial economics, managerial information systems, marketing management, operations analysis, organizational behavior, statistical decision making.
Curricular Focus Total quality management, international business, teamwork.
Concentrations Accounting, finance, human resources management, international business, management, marketing, operations management, organizational behavior, strategic management.
Faculty Full-time: 50, 98% with doctorates.
Special Opportunities International exchange in France, Japan, United Kingdom. Internship program available.

STUDENT STATISTICS

Geographic Representation State residents 45%. By region: Midwest 65%; South 6%; Northeast 5%; West 2%. International 10%.
Undergraduate Majors Business 42%; engineering/technology 20%; humanities 28%; other 10%.
Other Background Graduate degrees in other disciplines: 8%. Work experience: On average, students have 4 years of work experience on entrance to the program.

FACILITIES

Information Resources Main library with 3.3 million bound volumes, 2.8 million titles on microform, 33,051 periodical subscriptions, 35,805 records/tapes/CDs, 1,163 CD-ROMs.
Housing 5% of students in program live in college-owned or -operated housing.
Technology Computers are used heavily in course work. 200 computer terminals/PCs, linked by a campus-wide computer network, are available for use by students in program; they are located in learning resource center, the library, the computer center. Students in the program are not required to have their own PC.

Computer Resources/On-line Services

Training	Yes	Dun's	No
Internet	Yes	Dow Jones	No
E-Mail	Yes	Dialog	Yes $
LEXIS/NEXIS	Yes	Bloomberg	No
CompuServe	No		

ADMISSION

Acceptance 1994-95 470 applied for admission; 43% were accepted.
Entrance Requirements GMAT score, 2 years of work experience for part-time MBA. Core courses waived through: previous course work.
Application Requirements Application form, copies of transcript, personal statement, 2 letters of recommendation.
Application Deadline 5/1 for fall.

FINANCIALS

Costs for 1994-95 Tuition: Full-time: $111/credit hour for state residents, $300/credit hour for nonresidents. Fees: Full-time: $193/semester for state residents, $193/semester for nonresidents. Average room and board costs are $3,236 per academic year (on-campus) and $4,000 per academic year (off-campus).

Financial Aid In 1994-95, candidates received some institutionally administered aid in the form of scholarships, loans, assistantships. Financial aid is not available to part-time students. Application deadline: 2/1 for fall. Contact: Office of Student Financial Aid, Lawrence, KS 66045. (913) 864-4700.

INTERNATIONAL STUDENTS

Demographics 10% of students enrolled in the program are international.
Services and Facilities International student housing; international student center, visa services, language tutoring, ESL courses, special assistance for nonnative speakers of English, counseling/support services.
Applying TOEFL required, minimum score of 600; proof of health; proof of adequate funds. Financial aid is not available to international students. Admission application deadline: 5/1 for fall. Contact: Mr. Gerald Harris, Director, International Student Services, 2 Strong Hall, Lawrence, KS 66045. (913) 864-3617.

ALTERNATE MBA PROGRAMS

One-Year MBA Length of program: Minimum: 12 months. Maximum: 7 years. Degree Requirements: undergraduate degree in business or accounting.
MBA/JD Length of program: Minimum: 48 months. Maximum: 7 years. Degree requirements: 72 credits including 2 elective credits. LSAT score acceptable in lieu of GMAT; must apply separately to law and business schools.

PLACEMENT

Placement services include alumni network, career fairs, job interviews, resume preparation, and resume referral to employers.

Program Contact: Mr. David O. Collins, Associate Director of Master's Programs, University of Kansas, Lawrence, KS 66045. (913) 864-4254; Fax: (913) 864-5328.

Washburn University of Topeka

School of Business

Topeka, Kansas

OVERVIEW

Washburn University of Topeka is a city-supported comprehensive coed institution. Founded 1865. Setting: 160-acre urban campus with easy access to Kansas City. Total institutional enrollment: 6,574. Program was first offered in 1972.

MBA HIGHLIGHTS

Entrance Difficulty**
Mean GMAT: 490
Mean GPA: 3.0

Cost $
Tuition: $114/semester hour
(Nonresident: $197/semester hour)
Room & Board: N/R

Enrollment Profile

Full-time: 49	Work Exp: 80%
Part-time: 125	International: 16%
Total: 174	Women: 40%
Average Age: 39	Minorities: 15%

Average Class Size: 25

ACADEMICS

Length of Program Minimum: 12 months. Maximum: 6 years.
Calendar Semesters.
Full-time Classes Main campus; evening, summer.
Part-time Classes Main campus; evening, summer.
Degree Requirements 30 credits including 9 elective credits.
Required Courses Accounting analysis, business policy, computer-based information systems, finance, human resources, legal and ethical issues, management, product systems.
Curricular Focus Business issues and problems, general management, international business.
Concentrations Accounting, international business.
Faculty Full-time: 82, 82% with doctorates; part-time: 5, 1% with doctorates.

Teaching Methodology Case study: 25%, lecture: 25%, student presentations: 25%, team projects: 25%.

STUDENT STATISTICS
Geographic Representation State residents 80%. By region: Midwest 80%; South 2%; West 2%. International 16%.

Undergraduate Majors Business 70%; education 1%; engineering/technology 10%; humanities 1%; nursing 5%; science/mathematics 1%; social sciences 10%; other 2%.

Other Background Graduate degrees in other disciplines: 5%. Work experience: On average, students have 8 years of work experience on entrance to the program.

FACILITIES
Information Resources Main library with 550,000 bound volumes, 110,000 titles on microform, 5,750 periodical subscriptions.

Housing 3% of students in program live in college-owned or -operated housing.

Technology Computers are used moderately in course work. Computer terminals/PCs are available for use by students in program; they are located in the library, the computer center, computer labs. Students in the program are not required to have their own PC.

Computer Resources/On-line Services
Training	Yes	Multimedia Center	Yes
E-Mail	No		

ADMISSION
Acceptance 1994-95 Of those applying, 80% were accepted.

Entrance Requirements Bachelor's degree, GMAT score. Core courses waived through: previous course work.

Application Requirements Application form, copies of transcript, personal statement, 2 letters of recommendation.

Application Deadlines 7/15 for fall, 11/15 for spring.

FINANCIALS
Costs for 1994-95 Tuition: Full-time: $114/semester hour for state residents, $197/semester hour for nonresidents.

Financial Aid Financial aid is available to part-time students. Application deadline: 3/1 for fall. Contact: Mr. Martin McGreevy, Director of Financial Aid, Topeka, KS 66621. (913) 231-1010 Ext. 1451.

INTERNATIONAL STUDENTS
Demographics 16% of students enrolled in the program are international.

Services and Facilities International student center, language tutoring.

Applying TOEFL required, minimum score of 550; proof of adequate funds. Financial aid is not available to international students. Admission application deadlines: 7/15 for fall, 11/15 for spring. Contact: Dr. William Langdon, International Student Adviser, Topeka, KS 66621. (913) 231-1010 Ext. 1714.

Program Contact: Dr. Novella N. Clevenger, Director of Graduate Programs, Washburn University of Topeka, Topeka, KS 66621. (913) 231-1010 Ext. 1307; Fax: (913) 231-1063.

Wichita State University

W. Frank Barton School of Business

Wichita, Kansas

OVERVIEW
Wichita State University is a state-supported coed institution. Founded 1895. Setting: 335-acre urban campus. Total institutional enrollment: 15,000. Program was first offered in 1958. AACSB-accredited.

MBA HIGHLIGHTS

Entrance Difficulty***
Mean GMAT: 535
Mean GPA: 3.25

Cost $
Tuition: $1,174/semester
(Nonresident: $3,442/semester)
Room & Board: $6,000

Enrollment Profile
Full-time: 73	Work Exp: 77%
Part-time: 417	International: N/R
Total: 490	Women: 45%
Average Age: 37	Minorities: 2%

Average Class Size: 30

ACADEMICS
Length of Program Minimum: 24 months. Maximum: 6 years.

Calendar Semesters.

Full-time Classes Main campus; evening, summer.

Part-time Classes Main campus; evening, summer.

Degree Requirements 30 credits including 9 elective credits.

Required Courses Advanced strategic management, business decision making and analysis, managerial accounting, managerial economics, managerial finance, marketing management, organizational behavior. Courses may be waived through: previous course work.

Curricular Focus Business issues and problems, entrepreneurship, problem solving and decision making.

Concentrations Accounting, economics, entrepreneurship, finance, human resources management, international business, management, management information systems, marketing, organizational behavior, real estate, strategic management.

Faculty Full-time: 52, 97% with doctorates; part-time: 10, 30% with doctorates.

Teaching Methodology Case study: 35%, lecture: 45%, seminars by members of the business community: 5%, student presentations: 5%, team projects: 10%.

Special Opportunities International exchange in France. Internship program available.

STUDENT STATISTICS
Geographic Representation State residents 3%.

Undergraduate Majors Business 50%; education 5%; engineering/technology 25%; humanities 2%; nursing 5%; science/mathematics 1%; social sciences 1%; other 11%.

Other Background Graduate degrees in other disciplines: 25%. Work experience: On average, students have 5 years of work experience on entrance to the program.

FACILITIES
Information Resources Main library with 972,116 bound volumes, 971,413 titles on microform, 4,214 periodical subscriptions, 18,480 records/tapes/CDs. Business collection includes 115,000 bound volumes, 325 periodical subscriptions, 2 CD-ROMs, 5 videos.

Housing College housing available.

Technology Computers are used moderately in course work. 500 computer terminals/PCs, linked by a campus-wide computer network, are available for use by students in program; they are located in student rooms, the student center, learning resource center, the library, the computer center, computer labs, the research center. Students in the program are not required to have their own PC.

Computer Resources/On-line Services
Training	Yes	CompuServe	No
Internet	Yes	Dun's	No
E-Mail	Yes	Dow Jones	No
Multimedia Center	Yes	Dialog	Yes
LEXIS/NEXIS	Yes	Bloomberg	No

Other on-line services: OCLC.

ADMISSION
Acceptance 1994-95 Of those applying, 65% were accepted.

Entrance Requirements Bachelor's degree, GMAT score, minimum 2.75 GPA. Core courses waived through: previous course work.

Application Requirements Application form, copies of transcript.

Application Deadlines 7/30 for fall, 12/15 for spring.

FINANCIALS
Costs for 1994-95 Tuition: Full-time: $1,174/semester for state residents, $3,442/semester for nonresidents. Fees: Full-time: $13/semester for state residents, $13/semester for nonresidents. Average room and board costs are $6,000 per academic year (on-campus) and $12,000 per academic year (off-campus).

Financial Aid In 1994-95, candidates received some institutionally administered aid in the form of loans, assistantships. Financial aid is available to part-time students. Application deadlines: 3/15 for fall, 10/1 for spring. Contact: Mr. Larry Rector, Director, 223 Grace Wilkie Hall, Box 24, Wichita, KS 67260-0024. (316) 689-3878.

INTERNATIONAL STUDENTS

Demographics 14% of students on campus are international; Asia 71%, Europe 8%, Africa 7%, South America 5%, Central America 1%, other 7%.

Services and Facilities International student center, visa services, language tutoring, ESL courses, special assistance for nonnative speakers of English, counseling/support services.

Applying TOEFL required, minimum score of 550; proof of adequate funds; credentials translated into English. Financial aid is not available to international students. Admission application deadlines: 3/31 for fall, 8/31 for spring. Contact: Ms. Clara Hascall, Director, 303 Grace Wilkie Hall, Box 8, Wichita, KS 67260-0008. (316) 689-3730.

PLACEMENT

In 1993-94, 38 organizations participated in on-campus recruiting. Placement services include alumni network, career counseling/planning, career fairs, career library, career placement, electronic job bank, job interviews, resume preparation, and resume referral to employers. Of 1994 graduates, the average starting salary was $37,000, the range was $18,000-$45,000.

Program Contact: Dr. Donald Christensen, Director, Wichita State University, 1845 North Fairmount, Wichita, KS 67260. (316) 689-3230; Fax: (316) 689-3845.

KENTUCKY

Bellarmine College

W. Fielding Rubel School of Business

Louisville, Kentucky

OVERVIEW

Bellarmine College is an independent Roman Catholic comprehensive coed institution. Founded 1950. Setting: 120-acre suburban campus. Total institutional enrollment: 2,339.

MBA HIGHLIGHTS

Entrance Difficulty***
Mean GMAT: 550
Mean GPA: N/R

Cost $
Tuition: $286/credit hour
Room & Board: N/R

Enrollment Profile
Full-time: N/R
Part-time: N/R
Total: 313
Average Age: N/R

Work Exp: N/R
International: 2%
Women: 27%
Minorities: 9%

Average Class Size: 14

ACADEMICS

Length of Program Minimum: 24 months.
Calendar Semesters.
Full-time Classes Main campus, General Electric; evening, weekends, summer.
Part-time Classes Main campus, General Electric; evening, weekends, summer.
Degree Requirements 36 credits.
Curricular Focus General management, global perspective, leadership.
Concentration Management.
Teaching Methodology Case study: 20%, faculty seminars: 8%, lecture: 23%, research: 11%, seminars by members of the business community: 6%, student presentations: 15%, team projects: 17%.

STUDENT STATISTICS

Geographic Representation State residents 100%. International 2%.

FACILITIES

Information Resources Main library with 117,358 bound volumes, 614 periodical subscriptions, 4,837 records/tapes/CDs, 9 CD-ROMs.

ADMISSION

Entrance Requirements Bachelor's degree, GMAT score of 500, minimum 3.0 GPA.

Application Requirements Application form, copies of transcript, resume/curriculum vitae, personal statement, 2 letters of recommendation.

Application Deadline Applications are processed on a rolling basis.

FINANCIALS

Costs for 1994-95 Tuition: Full-time: $286/credit hour.

Financial Aid Applications are processed on a rolling basis. Contact: Mr. Patrick Gillooly, Director of Financial Aid, Office of Financial Aid, 2001 Newburg Road, Louisville, KY 40205-0671. (502) 452-8131.

INTERNATIONAL STUDENTS

Demographics 2% of students enrolled in the program are international.

Applying TOEFL required, minimum score of 500; proof of adequate funds. Financial aid is not available to international students. Admission applications are processed on a rolling basis.

Program Contact: Ms. Judy Trummer, Coordinator, Bellarmine College, 2001 Newburg Road, Louisville, KY 40205-0671. (502) 452-8240; Fax: (502) 452-8004.

Eastern Kentucky University

College of Business

Richmond, Kentucky

OVERVIEW

Eastern Kentucky University is a state-supported comprehensive coed institution. Founded 1906. Setting: 350-acre small-town campus. Total institutional enrollment: 17,000. Program was first offered in 1967.

MBA HIGHLIGHTS

Entrance Difficulty**
Mean GMAT: 481
Mean GPA: 3.08

Cost $
Tuition: $870/semester
(Nonresident: $2,610/semester)
Room & Board: N/R

Enrollment Profile
Full-time: 18
Part-time: 111
Total: 129
Average Age: 29

Work Exp: 80%
International: 7%
Women: 46%
Minorities: 3%

Average Class Size: N/R

ACADEMICS

Length of Program Minimum: 15 months. Maximum: 7 years.
Calendar Semesters.
Full-time Classes Main campus; evening, weekends, summer.
Degree Requirements 33 credits including 6 elective credits.
Required Courses Administrative analysis in organizations, business policy, business research and communication, information systems, legal ethics and social environment of business, managerial accounting, managerial economics, marketing problems, problems in managerial finance. Courses may be waived through: previous course work.
Curricular Focus Business issues and problems, general management, problem solving and decision making.
Concentration Management.
Faculty Full-time: 33, 97% with doctorates; part-time: 2, 100% with doctorates.
Teaching Methodology Case study: 20%, faculty seminars: 5%, lecture: 50%, research: 5%, student presentations: 10%, team projects: 10%.
Special Opportunities Internship program available. Other: consulting projects.

STUDENT STATISTICS
Geographic Representation State residents 93%. By region: South 93%. International 7%.

Other Background Graduate degrees in other disciplines: 4%. Work experience: On average, students have 4 years of work experience on entrance to the program.

FACILITIES
Information Resources Main library with 820,610 bound volumes, 1.2 million titles on microform, 3,986 periodical subscriptions, 32 CD-ROMs.

Housing 10% of students in program live in college-owned or -operated housing.

Technology Computers are used moderately in course work. 150 computer terminals/PCs, linked by a campus-wide computer network, are available for use by students in program; they are located in dormitories, learning resource center, the library, the computer center, computer labs. Students in the program are not required to have their own PC.

Computer Resources/On-line Services

Training	Yes	CompuServe	No
Internet	Yes	Dun's	Yes
E-Mail	Yes	Dow Jones	Yes
Multimedia Center	Yes	Dialog	No
LEXIS/NEXIS	Yes		

Other on-line services: SEC.

ADMISSION
Acceptance 1994-95 52 applied for admission; 83% were accepted.

Entrance Requirements Bachelor's degree, GMAT score of 350, minimum 2.5 GPA. Core courses waived through: previous course work.

Application Requirements Application form, copies of transcript, personal statement.

Application Deadlines 7/20 for fall, 11/20 for spring, 5/20 for summer.

FINANCIALS
Costs for 1994-95 Tuition: Full-time: $870/semester for state residents, $2,610/semester for nonresidents; Part-time day: $109/hour for state residents, $302/hour for nonresidents. Fees: Full-time: $105/semester for state residents, $105/semester for nonresidents.

Financial Aid In 1994-95, 10% of candidates received some institutionally administered aid in the form of fellowships, assistantships, work-study. Total awards ranged from $400-$5,700. Financial aid is available to part-time students. Application deadline: 4/1 for fall. Contact: Ms. Susan Luhman, Director of Student Financial Assistance, Coates 200, Richmond, KY 40475-3101. (606) 622-2361.

INTERNATIONAL STUDENTS
Demographics 7% of students enrolled in the program are international; Asia 33%, Africa 22%, other 45%.

Services and Facilities International student center, counseling/support services.

Applying TOEFL required, minimum score of 550; proof of adequate funds. Financial aid is available to international students. Admission application deadlines: 7/20 for fall, 11/20 for spring, 5/20 for summer. Contact: Dr. Neal H. Wright, Director, Office of International Students, Keith Building, Room 142, Richmond, KY 40475-3119. (606) 622-1478.

PLACEMENT
In 1993-94, 54 organizations participated in on-campus recruiting. Placement services include alumni network, career counseling/planning, career fairs, career library, career placement, electronic job bank, job interviews, job search course, resume preparation, and resume referral to employers.

Program Contact: Dr. Jack L. Dyer, MBA Director, Eastern Kentucky University, Richmond, KY 40475-3102. (606) 622-1775; Fax: (606) 622-1020.

Morehead State University

College of Business

Morehead, Kentucky

OVERVIEW
Morehead State University is a state-supported comprehensive coed institution. Founded 1922. Setting: 809-acre small-town campus. Total institutional enrollment: 4,000. Program was first offered in 1968.

MBA HIGHLIGHTS
Entrance Difficulty**
Mean GMAT: 480
Mean GPA: 3.2

Cost $
Tuition: $1,850/semester
(Nonresident: $5,170/semester)
Room & Board: $1,720

Enrollment Profile

Full-time: 32	Work Exp: 31%
Part-time: 40	International: 22%
Total: 72	Women: 46%
Average Age: 26	Minorities: 12%

Average Class Size: 25

ACADEMICS
Length of Program Minimum: 12 months. Maximum: 10 years.

Calendar Semesters.

Full-time Classes Main campus, Ashland; day, evening, summer.

Part-time Classes Main campus, Ashland; day, evening, summer.

Degree Requirements 30 hours including 9 elective hours.

Curricular Focus Problem solving and decision making, strategic analysis and planning, teamwork.

Concentration Management.

Faculty Full-time: 10, 80% with doctorates; part-time: 10, 80% with doctorates.

Teaching Methodology Case study: 20%, lecture: 60%, student presentations: 10%, team projects: 10%.

STUDENT STATISTICS
Geographic Representation State residents 60%. By region: South 60%; Northeast 18%. International 22%.

Undergraduate Majors Business 60%; education 3%; engineering/technology 15%; humanities 2%; science/mathematics 5%; social sciences 5%; other 10%.

Other Background Graduate degrees in other disciplines: 12%. Work experience: On average, students have 1-3 years of work experience on entrance to the program.

FACILITIES
Information Resources Main library with 385,549 bound volumes, 695,795 titles on microform, 2,843 periodical subscriptions, 10,171 records/tapes/CDs, 50 CD-ROMs. Business collection includes 500 bound volumes, 27 periodical subscriptions, 50 videos.

Housing 48% of students in program live in college-owned or -operated housing.

Technology Computers are used moderately in course work. 100 computer terminals/PCs, linked by a campus-wide computer network, are available for use by students in program; they are located in student rooms, the library, computer labs. Students in the program are not required to have their own PC.

Computer Resources/On-line Services

Training	Yes	Dun's	No
Internet	Yes	Dow Jones	No
E-Mail	Yes	Dialog	No
LEXIS/NEXIS	Yes	Bloomberg	No
CompuServe	No		

ADMISSION
Acceptance 1994-95 Of those applying, 90% were accepted.

Entrance Requirements Bachelor's degree, GMAT score of 400, minimum 2.5 GPA. Core courses waived through: previous course work.

Application Requirements Application form, copies of transcript.

Application Deadlines 7/1 for fall, 12/1 for spring.

FINANCIALS
Costs for 1994-95 Tuition: Full-time: $1,850/semester for state residents, $5,170/semester for nonresidents; Part-time day: $103/credit hour for state residents, $287/credit hour for nonresidents. Average room and board costs are $1,720 per academic year (on-campus) and $4,800 per academic year (off-campus).

Financial Aid In 1994-95, 62% of candidates received some institutionally administered aid in the form of grants, scholarships, loans, assistantships, work-study. Total awards ranged from $100-$4,000. Financial aid is not available to part-time students. Application deadlines: 4/1 for fall, 8/1 for spring. Contact: Mr. Tim Rhodes, Director of Financial Aid, HM 305, Morehead, KY 40351. (606) 783-2011.

INTERNATIONAL STUDENTS

Demographics 22% of students enrolled in the program are international; Asia 67%, Africa 16%, other 16%.

Services and Facilities International student center, language tutoring, counseling/support services.

Applying TOEFL required, minimum score of 540; proof of adequate funds. Financial aid is available to international students. Financial aid application deadlines: 7/1 for fall, 12/1 for spring. Admission application deadlines: 7/1 for fall, 12/1 for spring. Contact: Mr. Clement L. Dufus, International Student Adviser, UPO 330, Morehead, KY 40351. (606) 783-2759.

ALTERNATE MBA PROGRAM

Executive MBA (EMBA) Length of program: Minimum: 30 months. Maximum: 10 years. Degree requirements: 30 credits. 2 years executive management experience. Average class size: 29.

PLACEMENT

In 1993-94, 42 organizations participated in on-campus recruiting; 10 on-campus interviews were conducted. Placement services include alumni network, career counseling/planning, career fairs, career library, career placement, electronic job bank, job interviews, resume preparation, and resume referral to employers. Of 1994 graduates, 90% were employed within three months of graduation, the average starting salary range was $20,000-$25,000.

Jobs by Employer Type Manufacturing 40%; service 30%; government 10%; education 20%.

Jobs by Functional Area Marketing/sales 20%; finance 10%; operations 40%; management 10%; strategic planning 10%; technical management 10%.

Program Contact: Ms. Rhonda L. Mackin, Graduate Admissions Officer, Morehead State University, 701 Ginger Hall, Morehead, KY 40351. (606) 783-2039, or (800) 262-7474 (KY only), or (800) 354-2090 (out-of-state); Fax: (606) 783-2678.

Murray State University

College of Business and Public Affairs

Murray, Kentucky

OVERVIEW

Murray State University is a state-supported comprehensive coed institution. Founded 1922. Setting: 238-acre small-town campus. Total institutional enrollment: 8,000. Program was first offered in 1966. AACSB-accredited.

MBA HIGHLIGHTS

Entrance Difficulty***
Mean GMAT: 505
Mean GPA: 3.2

Cost $
Tuition: $1,010/semester
(Nonresident: $2,750/semester)
Room & Board: $3,010

Enrollment Profile

Full-time: 54	Work Exp: 15%
Part-time: 51	International: 30%
Total: 105	Women: 65%
Average Age: 29	Minorities: 5%

Average Class Size: 25

ACADEMICS

Length of Program Minimum: 12 months. Maximum: 8 years.

Calendar Semesters.

Full-time Classes Main campus, Paducah Community College; day, evening, summer.

Part-time Classes Main campus, Paducah Community College; evening, summer.

Degree Requirements 30 credits including 9 elective credits. Other: Minimum 3.0 GPA; one "C" grade allowed in core courses.

Required Courses Business policy and strategy, financial administration of firm, management theory, managerial economics, marketing planning

and application, operations research for decision making, quantitative financial controls. Courses may be waived through: previous course work.

Curricular Focus Business issues and problems, economic and financial theory, problem solving and decision making.

Concentrations Accounting, economics, finance, human resources management, international business, management, management information systems, marketing, operations management, public administration.

Faculty Full-time: 31, 100% with doctorates.

Teaching Methodology Case study: 20%, lecture: 20%, research: 20%, student presentations: 20%, team projects: 20%.

Special Opportunities International exchange in Germany. Internship program available.

STUDENT STATISTICS

Geographic Representation State residents 64%. By region: South 70%; Midwest 2%; Northeast 1%. International 30%.

Undergraduate Majors Business 72%; education 1%; engineering/technology 10%; humanities 3%; science/mathematics 4%; social sciences 7%; other 3%.

Other Background Graduate degrees in other disciplines: 5%. Work experience: On average, students have 2 years of work experience on entrance to the program.

FACILITIES

Information Resources Main library with 370,000 bound volumes, 165,000 titles on microform, 3,000 periodical subscriptions, 7,000 records/tapes/CDs, 1 CD-ROM. Business collection includes 12,000 bound volumes, 128 periodical subscriptions, 3 CD-ROMs, 100 videos.

Housing 20% of students in program live in college-owned or -operated housing.

Technology Computers are used heavily in course work. 100 computer terminals/PCs are available for use by students in program; they are located in dormitories, the student center, the computer center, computer labs. Students in the program are not required to have their own PC.

Computer Resources/On-line Services

Training	Yes	Dialog	Yes
E-Mail	Yes		

ADMISSION

Acceptance 1994-95 Of those applying, 72% were accepted.

Entrance Requirements Bachelor's degree, GMAT score. Core courses waived through: previous course work.

Application Requirements Application form, copies of transcript.

Application Deadlines 8/1 for fall, 12/1 for spring.

FINANCIALS

Costs for 1994-95 Tuition: Full-time: $1,010/semester for state residents, $2,750/semester for nonresidents; Part-time day: $103/hour for state residents, $295/hour for nonresidents. Average room and board costs are $3,010 per academic year (on-campus).

Financial Aid In 1994-95, 10% of candidates received some institutionally administered aid in the form of scholarships, loans, assistantships, work-study. Total awards ranged from $100-$3,600. Financial aid is available to part-time students. Application deadlines: 4/1 for fall, 10/15 for spring, 3/1 for summer. Contact: Mr. Johnny McDougal, Director of Student Financial Aid, Student Financial Aid Office, Murray, KY 42071-0009. (502) 762-2546.

INTERNATIONAL STUDENTS

Demographics 30% of students enrolled in the program are international; Asia 80%, Europe 19%.

Services and Facilities International student center, language tutoring, ESL courses, counseling/support services.

Applying TOEFL required, minimum score of 510; proof of adequate funds. Financial aid is not available to international students. Admission application deadlines: 7/1 for fall, 11/1 for spring. Contact: Ms. Marcie Johnson, Director of International Programs, Center for International Programs, Murray, KY 42071-0009. (502) 762-4251.

PLACEMENT

In 1993-94, 17 organizations participated in on-campus recruiting; 28 on-campus interviews were conducted. Placement services include alumni network, career counseling/planning, career fairs, career library, career placement, job interviews, resume preparation, and resume referral to employers.

Jobs by Employer Type Manufacturing 40%; service 60%.

Jobs by Functional Area Marketing/sales 4%; finance 22%; management 50%; strategic planning 21%; technical management 3%.

Program Contact: Dr. Dannie E. Harrison, Interim Dean and MBA Director, Murray State University, PO Box 9, Murray, KY 42071-0009. (502) 762-4183, or (800) 272-4678; Fax: (502) 762-3482.

Northern Kentucky University

College of Business

Highland Heights, Kentucky

OVERVIEW

Northern Kentucky University is a state-supported comprehensive coed institution. Founded 1968. Setting: 300-acre suburban campus with easy access to Cincinnati. Total institutional enrollment: 12,001. Program was first offered in 1981.

MBA HIGHLIGHTS

Entrance Difficulty*
Mean GMAT: 525
Mean GPA: 2.9

Cost $
Tuition: $900/semester
(Nonresident: $2,720/semester)
Room & Board: $5,600

Enrollment Profile
Full-time: 10
Part-time: 185
Total: 195
Average Age: 36

Work Exp: N/R
International: 5%
Women: 35%
Minorities: 2%

Average Class Size: 18

ACADEMICS

Length of Program Minimum: 24 months. Maximum: 8 years.
Calendar Semesters.
Full-time Classes Main campus; evening.
Part-time Classes Main campus; evening.
Degree Requirements 39 credits including 9 elective credits.
Required Courses Accounting for management, business communications, business strategy, implementation, and control, financial management, information systems in organizations, management and organization dynamics, managerial economics, marketing management, operations management and decision analysis.
Curricular Focus Business issues and problems, problem solving and decision making, teamwork.
Concentrations Accounting, finance, management, management information systems, marketing.
Faculty Full-time: 15, 100% with doctorates; part-time: 5, 70% with doctorates.
Teaching Methodology Case study: 15%, lecture: 55%, student presentations: 15%, team projects: 15%.
Special Opportunities International exchange program available.

STUDENT STATISTICS

Geographic Representation By region: Midwest 98%.
Undergraduate Majors Business 60%; engineering/technology 15%; other 25%.

FACILITIES

Information Resources Main library with 289,891 bound volumes, 667,524 titles on microform, 1,577 periodical subscriptions, 2,528 records/tapes/CDs, 10 CD-ROMs.
Housing College housing available.
Technology Computers are used moderately in course work. 50 computer terminals/PCs, linked by a campus-wide computer network, are available for use by students in program; they are located in the library, the computer center, computer labs. Students in the program are not required to have their own PC.

Computer Resources/On-line Services

Training	Yes	CompuServe	No
Internet	Yes	Dow Jones	Yes
E-Mail	Yes	Dialog	Yes

ADMISSION

Acceptance 1994-95 50 applied for admission.
Entrance Requirements Bachelor's degree, GMAT score of 450, minimum 2.3.0 GPA. Core courses waived through: previous course work.
Application Requirements Application form, copies of transcript, personal statement.
Application Deadlines 8/1 for fall, 12/1 for spring, 5/1 for summer. Applications are processed on a rolling basis.

FINANCIALS

Costs for 1994-95 Tuition: Full-time: $900/semester for state residents, $2,720/semester for nonresidents, $2,720/semester for international students; Part-time day: $107/credit hour for state residents, $300/credit hour for nonresidents, $300/credit hour for international students. Average room and board costs are $5,600 per academic year (on-campus) and $5,250 per academic year (off-campus).
Financial Aid In 1994-95, 3% of candidates received some institutionally administered aid in the form of assistantships. Total awards ranged from $2,980-$5,960. Financial aid is not available to part-time students. Application deadlines: 8/1 for fall, 1/1 for spring. Applications are processed on a rolling basis. Contact: Ms. Peg Griffin, Director of Graduate Center, Science Building 333, Highland Heights, KY 41099. (606) 572-6364.

INTERNATIONAL STUDENTS

Demographics 5% of students enrolled in the program are international; Europe 33%, Other 67%.
Services and Facilities International student office, international student center, visa services, language tutoring, ESL courses, counseling/support services.
Applying TOEFL required, minimum score of 550; proof of health; proof of adequate funds. Financial aid is not available to international students. Admission application deadlines: 8/1 for fall, 12/1 for spring, 5/1 for summer. Applications are processed on a rolling basis. Contact: Ms. Eileen Thornton, Admissions Coordinator, International, Lucas Administrative Center Room 302, Highland Heights, KY 41099. (606) 572-5223.

PLACEMENT

Placement services include career counseling/planning, career library, career placement, job interviews, and resume referral to employers. Of 1994 graduates, 95% were employed within three months of graduation.

Program Contact: Ms. Nina P. Thomas, MBA Program Director, Northern Kentucky University, Louie B. Nunn Drive, Highland Heights, KY 41099. (606) 572-6940; Fax: (606) 572-6177.

University of Kentucky

College of Business and Economics

Lexington, Kentucky

OVERVIEW

The University of Kentucky is a state-supported coed institution. Part of University of Kentucky System. Founded 1865. Setting: 682-acre urban campus with easy access to Cincinnati and Louisville. Total institutional enrollment: 24,458. Program was first offered in 1952. AACSB-accredited.

MBA HIGHLIGHTS

Entrance Difficulty**
Mean GMAT: 598
Mean GPA: 3.28

Cost $
Tuition: $1,200/semester
(Nonresident: $3,600/semester)
Room & Board: N/R

Enrollment Profile
Full-time: 125	Work Exp: 90%
Part-time: 123	International: 16%
Total: 248	Women: 48%
Average Age: 27	Minorities: 1%

Average Class Size: 32

ACADEMICS
Length of Program Minimum: 15 months. Maximum: 8 years.
Calendar Semesters.
Full-time Classes Main campus; day, evening.
Part-time Classes Main campus; day, evening.
Degree Requirements 36 credit hours including 15 elective credit hours.
Required Courses Business policy and strategy, financial and managerial accounting, global business management, management information systems in decision making, managerial economics, quantitative analysis for decisions, top management leadership in the contemporary business. Courses may be waived through: previous course work.
Curricular Focus Cross functional management, general management, leadership, problem solving and decision making, teamwork.
Concentrations Finance, health services, human resources management, international business, management, management information systems, marketing, operations management, real estate, strategic management.
Faculty Full-time: 35, 100% with doctorates.
Teaching Methodology Case study: 40%, lecture: 40%, student presentations: 10%, team projects: 10%.
Special Opportunities International exchange in Austria, France, United Kingdom. Internships include government and finance.

STUDENT STATISTICS
Geographic Representation State residents 50%. By region: South 67%; Midwest 9%; Northeast 4%; West 4%. International 16%.
Undergraduate Majors Business 56%; engineering/technology 22%; humanities 4%; nursing 4%; science/mathematics 4%; social sciences 5%; other 5%.
Other Background Graduate degrees in other disciplines: 2%. Work experience: On average, students have 1 year of work experience on entrance to the program.

FACILITIES
Information Resources Main library with 2.5 million bound volumes, 5 million titles on microform, 26,889 periodical subscriptions, 27,675 records/tapes/CDs.
Housing 20% of students in program live in college-owned or -operated housing.
Technology Computers are used moderately in course work. Computer terminals/PCs, linked by a campus-wide computer network, are available for use by students in program; they are located in dormitories, the student center, classrooms, the library, the computer center, computer labs, business and economics information center. Students in the program are not required to have their own PC.

Computer Resources/On-line Services
Training	Yes	LEXIS/NEXIS	Yes
E-Mail	Yes	Dun's	Yes
Videoconference Center	Yes	Dow Jones	Yes

ADMISSION
Acceptance 1994-95 Of those applying, 25% were accepted.
Entrance Requirements Bachelor's degree, prerequisite courses required for applicants with non-business degree, GMAT score of 500, minimum 2.5 GPA. Core courses waived through: previous course work.
Application Requirements Copies of transcript, resume/curriculum vitae, personal statement, 3 letters of recommendation, submit both program and graduate school application forms.
Application Deadline 7/15 for fall.

FINANCIALS
Costs for 1994-95 Tuition: Full-time: $1,200/semester for state residents, $3,600/semester for nonresidents. Fees: Full-time: $165/semester for state residents, $165/semester for nonresidents.
Financial Aid In 1994-95, 16% of candidates received some institutionally administered aid in the form of scholarships, fellowships, assistantships, work-study. Total awards ranged from $1,300-$12,000. Financial aid is not available to part-time students. Application deadline: 3/1 for fall. Contact: Ms. Marilyn Underwood, MBA Program Coordinator, MBA Center, College of Business and Economics, Lexington, KY 40506. (606) 257-7722.

INTERNATIONAL STUDENTS
Demographics 16% of students enrolled in the program are international; Asia 85%, Europe 4%, Africa 2%, Central America 1%, South America 1%, other 7%.
Services and Facilities International student housing; international student center, visa services, language tutoring, ESL courses, counseling/support services.
Applying TOEFL required, minimum score of 550; proof of adequate funds; health insurance. Financial aid is available to international students. Limited scholarships are available to these students after one year. Admission application deadline: 2/1 for fall. Contact: Ms. Carolyn Holmes, International Student Adviser, Immigration Specialist, Office of International Affairs, Bradley Hall, Lexington, KY 40506-0058. (606) 257-6601.

ALTERNATE MBA PROGRAM
MBA/JD Length of program: Minimum: 48 months. Degree requirements: 126 credits.

PLACEMENT
In 1993-94, 93 organizations participated in on-campus recruiting; 372 on-campus interviews were conducted. Placement services include alumni network, career counseling/planning, career fairs, career library, career placement, electronic job bank, job interviews, resume preparation, resume referral to employers, and southeastern MBA consortium. Of 1994 graduates, 92% were employed within three months of graduation, the average starting salary was $35,750, the range was $28,000-$65,000.
Jobs by Employer Type Manufacturing 15%; service 65%; consulting 20%.
Jobs by Functional Area Marketing/sales 15%; finance 35%; operations 5%; management 10%; technical management 15%; consulting 20%.

Program Contact: Ms. Marilyn Underwood, MBA Program Coordinator, University of Kentucky, Lexington, KY 40506-0034. (606) 257-7722; Fax: (606) 257-3315.

University of Louisville

College of Business and Public Administration

Louisville, Kentucky

OVERVIEW
The University of Louisville is a state-supported coed institution. Founded 1798. Setting: 169-acre urban campus. Total institutional enrollment: 21,089. Program was first offered in 1950. AACSB-accredited.

MBA HIGHLIGHTS
Entrance Difficulty***
Mean GMAT: 550
Mean GPA: 3.3

Cost $
Tuition: $1,305/semester
(Nonresident: $3,705/semester)
Room & Board: N/R

Enrollment Profile
Full-time: 57	Work Exp: 90%
Part-time: 340	International: 7%
Total: 397	Women: 40%
Average Age: 31	Minorities: 6%

Average Class Size: 30

ACADEMICS
Length of Program Minimum: 18 months. Maximum: 6 years.
Calendar Semesters.
Full-time Classes Main campus; evening, summer.
Part-time Classes Main campus; evening, summer.
Degree Requirements 36 hours including 9 elective hours.
Required Courses Advanced organizational behavior, financial management, management information, managerial accounting, managerial economics, marketing management, operations management systems, strategic management, the business environment.

Curricular Focus Business issues and problems, general management, problem solving and decision making.

Concentration Management.

Faculty Full-time: 38, 95% with doctorates.

Teaching Methodology Case study: 18%, lecture: 23%, research: 18%, student presentations: 18%, team projects: 23%.

Special Opportunities International exchange in Germany.

STUDENT STATISTICS

Geographic Representation State residents 77%. By region: South 90%. International 7%.

Undergraduate Majors Business 65%; engineering/technology 15%; science/mathematics 5%; social sciences 10%; other 5%.

Other Background Graduate degrees in other disciplines: 5%. Work experience: On average, students have 5-7 years of work experience on entrance to the program.

FACILITIES

Information Resources Main library with 1.2 million bound volumes, 1.5 million titles on microform, 12,263 periodical subscriptions, 15,556 records/tapes/CDs.

Housing 3% of students in program live in college-owned or -operated housing.

Technology Computers are used moderately in course work. 275 computer terminals/PCs, linked by a campus-wide computer network, are available for use by students in program; they are located in learning resource center, the library, the computer center, computer labs. Students in the program are not required to have their own PC.

Computer Resources/On-line Services

Training	Yes	CompuServe	No
Internet	Yes	Dun's	Yes
E-Mail	Yes	Dow Jones	No
Videoconference Center	Yes	Dialog	No
LEXIS/NEXIS	Yes	Bloomberg	Yes

ADMISSION

Acceptance 1994-95 Of those applying, 85% were accepted.

Entrance Requirements Bachelor's degree, GMAT score, minimum 2.75 GPA. Core courses waived through: previous course work.

Application Requirements Application form, copies of transcript, 2 letters of recommendation.

Application Deadlines 5/1 for fall, 9/1 for spring, 3/1 for summer.

FINANCIALS

Costs for 1994-95 Tuition: Full-time: $1,305/semester for state residents, $3,705/semester for nonresidents. Fees: Full-time: $15/semester for state residents, $15/semester for nonresidents.

Financial Aid In 1994-95, 5% of candidates received some institutionally administered aid in the form of assistantships. Financial aid is not available to part-time students. Application deadlines: 5/1 for fall, 9/1 for spring. Contact: Ms. Betty C. Brown, Associate Dean, College of Business and Public Administration, Louisville, KY 40292-0001. (502) 852-4889.

INTERNATIONAL STUDENTS

Demographics 7% of students enrolled in the program are international; Asia 50%, Europe 50%.

Services and Facilities International student center, visa services, ESL courses.

Applying TOEFL required, minimum score of 550; proof of adequate funds. Admission application deadlines: 5/1 for fall, 9/1 for spring, 3/1 for summer. Contact: Ms. Michele Bulatovic, International Student Coordinator, 2301 South Third Street, Louisville, KY 40292-0001. (502) 852-6602.

ALTERNATE MBA PROGRAM

MBA/JD Length of program: Minimum: 36 months. Maximum: 5 years. Degree requirements: 115 hours. Separate applications must be submitted to both the law and business administration programs.

PLACEMENT

Placement services include alumni network, career counseling/planning, career fairs, career library, career placement, electronic job bank, resume preparation, and resume referral to employers. Of 1994 graduates, 95% were employed within three months of graduation.

Program Contact: Ms. Dolores Calebs, Graduate Adviser, University of Louisville, College of Business Advising Center, Louisville, KY 40292-0001. (502) 852-7439; Fax: (502) 852-4721.

See full description on page 884.

LOUISIANA

Centenary College of Louisiana

Frost School of Business

Shreveport, Louisiana

OVERVIEW

Centenary College of Louisiana is an independent United Methodist comprehensive coed institution. Founded 1825. Setting: 65-acre small-town campus. Total institutional enrollment: 1,014. Program was first offered in 1986.

MBA HIGHLIGHTS

Entrance Difficulty*
Mean GMAT: 475
Mean GPA: 3.5

Cost
Tuition: N/R
Room & Board: N/R

Enrollment Profile

Full-time: 0	Work Exp: 100%
Part-time: 170	International: 0%
Total: 170	Women: 34%
Average Age: 38	Minorities: 1%

Average Class Size: 16

ACADEMICS

Length of Program Minimum: 18 months. Maximum: 7 years.

Calendar Modules.

Part-time Classes Main campus; evening, summer.

Degree Requirements 45 credits. Other: Written and oral entrepreneurial project.

Required Courses Business economics, business ethics, entrepreneurial project, financial accounting, financial management, human resources management, management accounting, management computing, marketing management, policy and strategy, production management, professional communication, professional management workshop, statistics.

Curricular Focus Entrepreneurship, general management, leadership.

Concentration Management.

Faculty Full-time: 12, 66% with doctorates.

Teaching Methodology Case study: 15%, lecture: 60%, student presentations: 15%, team projects: 10%.

STUDENT STATISTICS

Geographic Representation State residents 98%. By region: South 97%; Northeast 1%; Midwest 1%; West 1%.

Undergraduate Majors Business 40%; education 15%; engineering/technology 5%; humanities 5%; nursing 20%; science/mathematics 5%; social sciences 5%; other 5%.

Other Background Graduate degrees in other disciplines: 100%. Work experience: On average, students have 5 years of work experience on entrance to the program.

FACILITIES

Information Resources Main library with 168,000 bound volumes, 250,000 titles on microform, 923 periodical subscriptions, 10,859 records/tapes/CDs, 8 CD-ROMs. Business collection includes 10,000 bound volumes, 78 periodical subscriptions, 5 CD-ROMs.

Housing College housing not available.

Technology Computers are used moderately in course work. 50 computer terminals/PCs are available for use by students in program; they are located in the library, computer labs. Students in the program are not required to have their own PC.

Computer Resources/On-line Services

Training	Yes	Dun's	No
Internet	No	Dow Jones	No
E-Mail	No	Dialog	No
LEXIS/NEXIS	No	Bloomberg	No
CompuServe	No		

ADMISSION

Acceptance 1994-95 58 applied for admission; 91% were accepted.

Entrance Requirements Bachelor's degree, minimum 5 years of work experience, minimum age 27. Core courses waived through: previous course work, work experience.

Application Requirements Written essay, interview, application form, copies of transcript.

FINANCIALS

Financial Aid In 1994-95, candidates received some institutionally administered aid in the form of loans. Financial aid is available to part-time students. Applications are processed on a rolling basis. Contact: Ms. May Sue Rix, Director of Financial Aid, PO Box 41188, Shreveport, LA 71134-1188. (318) 869-5137.

INTERNATIONAL STUDENTS

Applying TOEFL required, minimum score of 550; proof of health; proof of adequate funds.

PLACEMENT

Placement services include alumni network.

Program Contact: Mrs. Charlotte Turnley, Coordinator, Executive MBA Program, Centenary College of Louisiana, PO Box 41188, Shreveport, LA 71134-1188. (318) 869-5141; Fax: (318) 869-5139; Internet Address: cturnley@beta.centenary.edu.

Grambling State University

College of Business

Grambling, Louisiana

OVERVIEW

Grambling State University is a state-supported comprehensive coed institution. Founded 1901. Setting: 340-acre rural campus. Total institutional enrollment: 7,609. Program was first offered in 1985.

MBA HIGHLIGHTS

Entrance Difficulty*
Mean GMAT: 400
Mean GPA: 2.87

Cost $
Tuition: $919/semester
(Nonresident: $1,894/semester)
Room & Board: $5,248 (off-campus)

Enrollment Profile

Full-time: 50	Work Exp: 18%
Part-time: 15	International: N/R
Total: 65	Women: N/R
Average Age: 26	Minorities: N/R

Average Class Size: 25

ACADEMICS

Length of Program Minimum: 24 months. Maximum: 6 years.

Calendar Semesters.

Full-time Classes Main campus; day, evening.

Degree Requirements 36 credits including 12 elective credits.

Curricular Focus General management, international business, problem solving and decision making.

Concentrations International business, management, management information systems.

Faculty Full-time: 6, 100% with doctorates.

Teaching Methodology Case study: 20%, lecture: 60%, student presentations: 10%, team projects: 10%.

Special Opportunities International exchange in India, Indonesia, Malaysia, Mexico, People's Republic of China.

STUDENT STATISTICS

Geographic Representation By region: South 86%; Northeast 1%; Midwest 1%; West 1%.

Undergraduate Majors Business 91%; engineering/technology 1%; social sciences 7%; other 1%.

Other Background Graduate degrees in other disciplines: 1%. Work experience: On average, students have 2-5 years of work experience on entrance to the program.

FACILITIES

Information Resources Main library with 256,743 bound volumes, 25,266 titles on microform, 1,360 periodical subscriptions.

Housing College housing available.

Technology Computers are used moderately in course work. 45 computer terminals/PCs, linked by a campus-wide computer network, are available for use by students in program; they are located in the computer center, computer labs. Students in the program are not required to have their own PC.

Computer Resources/On-line Services

| Training | Yes | E-Mail | No |
| Internet | Yes | Multimedia Center | Yes |

ADMISSION

Acceptance 1994-95 Of those applying, 50% were accepted.

Entrance Requirements Bachelor's degree, GMAT score of 350, minimum 2.5 GPA. Core courses waived through: previous course work.

Application Requirements Application form, copies of transcript, personal statement, 3 letters of recommendation.

Application Deadlines 6/1 for fall, 10/1 for spring.

FINANCIALS

Costs for 1994-95 Tuition: Full-time: $919/semester for state residents, $1,894/semester for nonresidents. Average room and board costs are $5,248 per academic year (off-campus).

Financial Aid In 1994-95, 21% of candidates received some institutionally administered aid in the form of loans, assistantships, work-study. Total awards ranged from $200-$4,500. Financial aid is not available to part-time students. Application deadlines: 6/1 for fall, 10/1 for spring. Contact: Director of Financial Aid, PO Box 606, Grambling, LA 71245. (318) 274-2342.

INTERNATIONAL STUDENTS

Services and Facilities Counseling/support services.

Applying TOEFL required, minimum score of 450; proof of adequate funds. Financial aid is available to international students. Financial aid application deadlines: 6/1 for fall, 10/1 for spring. Admission application deadlines: 6/1 for fall, 10/1 for spring. Contact: Mrs. Audrey Warren, Adviser, International Students and Special Projects, PO Box 847, Grambling, LA 71245. (318) 274-3139.

PLACEMENT

In 1993-94, 12 organizations participated in on-campus recruiting; 22 on-campus interviews were conducted. Placement services include alumni network, career counseling/planning, career fairs, career library, career placement, job interviews, resume preparation, and resume referral to employers. Of 1994 graduates, 50% were employed within three months of graduation.

Jobs by Employer Type Manufacturing 78%; service 5%; government 11%; other 6%.

Program Contact: Dr. T. M. Yung, Associate Dean and Director, Grambling State University, PO Box 606, Grambling, LA 71245. (318) 274-2301; Fax: (318) 274-2191.

Louisiana State University and Agricultural and Mechanical College

College of Business Administration

Baton Rouge, Louisiana

OVERVIEW

Louisiana State University and Agricultural and Mechanical College is a state-supported coed institution. Part of Louisiana State University System. Founded 1860. Setting: 2,000-acre urban campus with easy access to New Orleans. Total institutional enrollment: 25,000. Program was first offered in 1937. AACSB-accredited.

MBA HIGHLIGHTS

Entrance Difficulty****
Mean GMAT: 550
Mean GPA: 3.01

Cost $
Tuition: $1,314/semester
(Nonresident: $2,964/semester)
Room & Board: N/R

Enrollment Profile
Full-time: 150	Work Exp: 28%
Part-time: 150	International: N/R
Total: 300	Women: 28%
Average Age: 29	Minorities: 5%

Class Size: 25 - 30

ACADEMICS
Length of Program Minimum: 21 months. Maximum: 5 years.
Calendar Semesters.
Full-time Classes Main campus; day, summer.
Part-time Classes Main campus; evening, summer.
Degree Requirements 54 credits including 18 elective credits.
Required Courses Accounting for managerial decisions, administration theory and behavior, financial accounting for management, financial management, legal environment of business, macroeconomic analysis and issues, management information systems, managerial statistics, marketing administration, operations management, seminar in policy formation and administration.
Curricular Focus General management.
Concentrations Entrepreneurship, finance, human resources management, internal auditing, international business, management, management information systems, marketing, operations management, organizational behavior, public administration, public policy, quantitative analysis, real estate, strategic management.
Faculty Full-time: 50, 100% with doctorates; part-time: 1, 100% with doctorates.
Special Opportunities International exchange in France. Internship program available.

STUDENT STATISTICS
Geographic Representation By region: South 80%; West 5%; Northeast 3%; Midwest 3%.
Undergraduate Majors Business 44%; engineering/technology 28%; humanities 5%; science/mathematics 6%; social sciences 5%; other 12%.
Other Background Graduate degrees in other disciplines: 5%. Work experience: On average, students have 6 years of work experience on entrance to the program.

FACILITIES
Information Resources Main library with 2.8 million bound volumes, 3.9 million titles on microform, 14,537 periodical subscriptions, 27,761 records/tapes/CDs, 1,130 CD-ROMs.
Housing College housing available.
Technology 100 computer terminals/PCs, linked by a campus-wide computer network, are available for use by students in program; they are located in dormitories, the library, computer labs, the research center. Students in the program are not required to have their own PC.

Computer Resources/On-line Services
Training	Yes	Dun's	Yes
Internet	Yes	Dow Jones	Yes
E-Mail	No	Dialog	Yes
LEXIS/NEXIS	Yes	Bloomberg	Yes

ADMISSION
Acceptance 1994-95 280 applied for admission; 89% were accepted.
Entrance Requirements Bachelor's degree, GMAT score of 500, minimum 3.0 GPA. Core courses waived through: previous course work.
Application Requirements Written essay, application form, copies of transcript, resume/curriculum vitae, personal statement, 3 letters of recommendation.
Application Deadline 5/15 for fall.

FINANCIALS
Estimated Costs for 1995-96 Tuition: Full-time: $1,314/semester for state residents, $2,964/semester for nonresidents, $2,964/semester for international students; Part-time evening: $495/semester for state residents, $1,195/semester for nonresidents.
Financial Aid In 1994-95, 3% of candidates received some institutionally administered aid in the form of loans, assistantships. Financial aid is available to part-time students. Application deadline: 5/15 for fall. Contact: Office of Student Aid and Scholarships, 202 Himes Hall, Baton Rouge, LA 70803. (504) 388-3103.

INTERNATIONAL STUDENTS
Services and Facilities International student housing.
Applying TOEFL required, minimum score of 550; proof of health; proof of adequate funds. Financial aid is not available to international students. Admission application deadline: 5/15 for fall. Contact: Mr. Erin Schmidt, Director, Office of International Student Affairs, Baton Rouge, LA 70803. (504) 388-3191.

PLACEMENT
In 1993-94, 250 organizations participated in on-campus recruiting. Placement services include career counseling/planning, career fairs, career library, career placement, job interviews, and resume preparation.

Program Contact: Office of Graduate Studies, Louisiana State University and Agricultural and Mechanical College, Baton Rouge, LA 70803. (504) 388-8867; Fax: (504) 388-5256.

Louisiana State University in Shreveport

College of Business Administration

Shreveport, Louisiana

OVERVIEW
Louisiana State University in Shreveport is a state-supported comprehensive coed institution. Part of Louisiana State University System. Founded 1965. Setting: 200-acre suburban campus. Total institutional enrollment: 4,500. Program was first offered in 1979. AACSB-accredited.

MBA HIGHLIGHTS

Entrance Difficulty**
Mean GMAT: 490
Mean GPA: N/R

Cost $
Tuition: $95/credit hour
(Nonresident: $285/credit hour)
Room & Board: N/R

Enrollment Profile
Full-time: N/R	Work Exp: 90%
Part-time: N/R	International: 5%
Total: 120	Women: 20%
Average Age: 31	Minorities: 8%

Average Class Size: 18

ACADEMICS
Length of Program Minimum: 18 months. Maximum: 8 years.
Calendar Semesters.
Full-time Classes Main campus; evening, summer.
Part-time Classes Main campus; evening, summer.
Degree Requirements 33 credit hours including 9 elective credit hours.
Required Courses Accounting for managers, financial theory, managerial communications, managerial economics, marketing concepts, organizational behavior, quantitative analysis, seminar in management.
Curricular Focus Economic and financial theory, general management, problem solving and decision making.
Concentration Management.
Faculty Full-time: 15, 100% with doctorates; part-time: 1, 100% with doctorates.
Teaching Methodology Case study: 30%, lecture: 30%, student presentations: 20%, team projects: 20%.
Special Opportunities Internships include accounting in automotive, banking/financial service in electronics, and manufacturing.

STUDENT STATISTICS

Geographic Representation State residents 90%. By region: South 90%; Northeast 5%; Midwest 3%; West 2%. International 5%.

Undergraduate Majors Business 50%; education 5%; engineering/technology 10%; humanities 5%; nursing 10%; science/mathematics 10%; social sciences 10%.

Other Background Graduate degrees in other disciplines: 5%.

FACILITIES

Information Resources Main library with 239,344 bound volumes, 229,511 titles on microform, 2,250 periodical subscriptions, 1,509 records/tapes/CDs, 297 CD-ROMs.

Housing College housing not available.

Technology Computers are used moderately in course work. 80 computer terminals/PCs are available for use by students in program; they are located in computer labs. Students in the program are not required to have their own PC.

Computer Resources/On-line Services

Training	Yes	Dun's	No
Internet	Yes $	Dow Jones	No
LEXIS/NEXIS	No	Dialog	Yes $
CompuServe	No	Bloomberg	No

ADMISSION

Acceptance 1994-95 40 applied for admission; 80% were accepted.

Entrance Requirements Bachelor's degree, GMAT score of 400, minimum 2.75 GPA. Core courses waived through: previous course work.

Application Requirements Application form, copies of transcript.

Application Deadlines 8/10 for fall, 12/15 for spring. Applications are processed on a rolling basis.

FINANCIALS

Estimated Costs for 1995-96 Tuition: Full-time: $95/credit hour for state residents, $285/credit hour for nonresidents. Fees: Full-time: $65/semester for state residents, $65/semester for nonresidents.

Financial Aid In 1994-95, 5% of candidates received some institutionally administered aid in the form of loans, assistantships. Total awards ranged from $3,500-$5,000. Financial aid is not available to part-time students. Application deadlines: 8/10 for fall, 12/15 for spring. Applications are processed on a rolling basis. Contact: Mr. Ed Chase, Director of Financial Aid, 1 University Place, Shreveport, LA 71115. (318) 797-5000.

INTERNATIONAL STUDENTS

Demographics 5% of students enrolled in the program are international; Asia 100%.

Applying TOEFL required, minimum score of 550; proof of health; proof of adequate funds. Financial aid is not available to international students. Admission application deadlines: 8/10 for fall, 12/15 for spring. Contact: Ms. Sylvia Booras, 1 University Place, Shreveport, LA 71115. (318) 797-5057.

PLACEMENT

Placement services include career fairs, career placement, and electronic job bank. Of 1994 graduates, 95% were employed within three months of graduation.

Program Contact: Dr. Michael Brendler, MBA Director, Louisiana State University in Shreveport, 1 University Place, Shreveport, LA 71115. (318) 797-5276; Fax: (318) 797-5208.

Louisiana Tech University

College of Administration and Business

Ruston, Louisiana

OVERVIEW

Louisiana Tech University is a state-supported coed institution. Founded 1894. Setting: 235-acre small-town campus. Total institutional enrollment: 10,023. Program was first offered in 1963. AACSB-accredited.

MBA HIGHLIGHTS

Entrance Difficulty*
Mean GMAT: 497
Mean GPA: 3.16

Cost $
Tuition: $754/quarter
(Nonresident: $1,319/quarter)
Room & Board: N/R

Enrollment Profile

Full-time: 63	Work Exp: N/R
Part-time: 22	International: 23%
Total: 85	Women: 40%
Average Age: 28	Minorities: 1%

Class Size: 15 - 20

ACADEMICS

Length of Program Minimum: 12 months. Maximum: 6 years.

Calendar Quarters.

Full-time Classes Main campus; day, evening, summer.

Part-time Classes Main campus; day, evening.

Degree Requirements 33 semester hours including 12 elective semester hours.

Required Courses Accounting, administrative policy, financial management, human resources management, management science, managerial economics, marketing management. Courses may be waived through: previous course work.

Curricular Focus Business issues and problems, problem solving and decision making, strategic analysis and planning.

Concentrations Accounting, economics, finance, management, management information systems, marketing, quantitative analysis.

Faculty Full-time: 39, 100% with doctorates.

STUDENT STATISTICS

Geographic Representation State residents 58%. By region: South 76%; Northeast 1%. International 23%.

Undergraduate Majors Business 68%; engineering/technology 13%; humanities 6%; science/mathematics 6%; social sciences 2%; other 5%.

Other Background Graduate degrees in other disciplines: 7%.

FACILITIES

Information Resources Main library with 355,368 bound volumes, 2.3 million titles on microform, 2,634 periodical subscriptions, 14,207 records/tapes/CDs, 15 CD-ROMs. Business collection includes 43,597 bound volumes, 466 periodical subscriptions.

Housing 14% of students in program live in college-owned or -operated housing.

Technology Computers are used moderately in course work. Computer terminals/PCs are available for use by students in program; they are located in computer labs. Students in the program are not required to have their own PC.

Computer Resources/On-line Services

Training	Yes	Internet	Yes $

ADMISSION

Acceptance 1994-95 Of those applying, 85% were accepted.

Entrance Requirements Bachelor's degree, GMAT score, minimum 2.25 GPA. Core courses waived through: previous course work.

Application Requirements Application form, copies of transcript.

Application Deadlines 7/25 for fall, 10/15 for winter, 2/14 for spring, 5/9 for summer.

FINANCIALS

Costs for 1994-95 Tuition: Full-time: $754/quarter for state residents, $1,319/quarter for nonresidents. Fees: Full-time: $40/quarter for state residents, $40/quarter for nonresidents.

Financial Aid In 1994-95, 11% of candidates received some institutionally administered aid in the form of scholarships, loans, work-study. Total awards ranged from $1,200-$8,500. Financial aid is available to part-time students. Application deadlines: 3/15 for fall, 3/15 for winter, 10/15 for spring, 2/15 for summer. Contact: Ms. Glenn Theis, Assistant Director, Keeney Hall, 2nd Floor, PO Box 7925, Ruston, LA 71272. (318) 257-2641.

INTERNATIONAL STUDENTS

Demographics 23% of students enrolled in the program are international.

Services and Facilities ESL courses, counseling/support services.

Applying TOEFL required, minimum score of 550; proof of health; proof of adequate funds. Financial aid is not available to international students. Admission application deadlines: 6/9 for fall, 9/1 for winter, 1/3 for spring, 3/21 for summer. Contact: Mr. Daniel W. Erickson, International Student Adviser, PO Box 3177, Tech Station, Ruston, LA 71272. (318) 257-4321.

PLACEMENT

In 1993-94, 78 organizations participated in on-campus recruiting. Placement services include alumni network, career counseling/planning, career fairs, career library, career placement, electronic job bank, job interviews, and resume preparation. Of 1994 graduates, the average starting salary was $27,500, the range was $20,000-$45,000.

Program Contact: Dr. J. Ralph Byington, Director of the Graduate Division, Louisiana Tech University, PO Box 3186, Tech Station, Ruston, LA 71272. (318) 257-4528; Fax: (318) 257-4253.

Loyola University, New Orleans

The Joseph A. Butt, SJ, College of Business Administration

New Orleans, Louisiana

OVERVIEW

Loyola University, New Orleans is an independent Roman Catholic (Jesuit) comprehensive coed institution. Founded 1912. Setting: 23-acre suburban campus. Total institutional enrollment: 5,859. Program was first offered in 1961. AACSB-accredited.

MBA HIGHLIGHTS

Entrance Difficulty***
Mean GMAT: 490
Mean GPA: 3.07

Cost $$
Tuition: $424/credit hour
Room & Board: $7,000

Enrollment Profile
Full-time: 70	Work Exp: 85%
Part-time: 128	International: 12%
Total: 198	Women: 40%
Average Age: N/R	Minorities: 18%

Average Class Size: 25

ACADEMICS

Length of Program Minimum: 12 months. Maximum: 7 years.
Calendar Semesters.
Full-time Classes Main campus; evening, summer.
Part-time Classes Main campus; evening, summer.
Degree Requirements 30 credit hours including 18 elective credit hours.
Required Courses Business strategy, decision making tools and methods, global competitive environment, leadership and interpersonal relations.
Curricular Focus International business, leadership, problem solving and decision making.
Concentration International business.
Faculty Full-time: 22, 100% with doctorates; part-time: 8, 12% with doctorates.
Teaching Methodology Case study: 30%, faculty seminars: 2%, lecture: 30%, research: 5%, seminars by members of the business community: 3%, student presentations: 10%, team projects: 20%.

STUDENT STATISTICS

Geographic Representation State residents 40%. International 12%.
Undergraduate Majors Business 72%; engineering/technology 3%; humanities 15%; science/mathematics 2%; other 6%.
Other Background Work experience: On average, students have 4 years of work experience on entrance to the program.

FACILITIES

Information Resources Main library with 292,005 bound volumes, 161,690 titles on microform, 1,854 periodical subscriptions.
Housing College housing available.
Technology Computers are used heavily in course work. Computer terminals/PCs, linked by a campus-wide computer network, are avail-

able for use by students in program; they are located in dormitories, computer labs. Students in the program are not required to have their own PC.

Computer Resources/On-line Services
Internet	Yes	Multimedia Center	Yes
E-Mail	Yes		

ADMISSION

Entrance Requirements Bachelor's degree, GMAT score. Core courses waived through: previous course work, work experience.
Application Requirements Written essay, application form, copies of transcript, resume/curriculum vitae, 2 letters of recommendation.
Application Deadlines 6/15 for fall, 11/1 for spring, 3/15 for summer.

FINANCIALS

Costs for 1994-95 Tuition: Full-time: $424/credit hour. Fees: Full-time: $125/semester. Average room and board costs are $7,000 per academic year (on-campus) and $7,000 per academic year (off-campus).
Financial Aid In 1994-95, candidates received some institutionally administered aid in the form of loans, assistantships. Financial aid is available to part-time students. Application deadlines: 7/15 for fall, 12/15 for spring. Contact: Dr. E. P. Seybold Jr., Director of Financial Aid, 6363 Saint Charles Avenue, Box 206, New Orleans, LA 70118. (504) 865-3231.

INTERNATIONAL STUDENTS

Demographics 12% of students enrolled in the program are international; Central America 40%, Asia 13%, Europe 13%, South America 13%, North America 13%, Africa 6%.
Services and Facilities International student office, international student center, visa services, language tutoring, ESL courses, special assistance for nonnative speakers of English, counseling/support services.
Applying TOEFL required, minimum score of 550; proof of health; proof of adequate funds. Financial aid is available to international students. Financial aid application deadlines: 5/15 for fall, 10/15 for spring. Admission application deadlines: 8/1 for fall, 1/5 for spring. Contact: Ms. Debbie Danna, Director, International Student Affairs, 6363 Saint Charles Avenue, Box 205, New Orleans, LA 70118. (504) 865-3526.

PLACEMENT

Placement services include career counseling/planning, career fairs, career library, career placement, job interviews, resume preparation, and resume referral to employers.

Program Contact: Dr. Wing Fok, Director of Graduate Programs, Loyola University, New Orleans, 6363 Saint Charles Avenue, New Orleans, LA 70118. (504) 865-3691; Fax: (504) 865-3496; Internet Address: fok@music.loyno.edu.

McNeese State University

College of Business

Lake Charles, Louisiana

OVERVIEW

McNeese State University is a state-supported comprehensive coed institution. Founded 1939. Setting: 171-acre urban campus. Total institutional enrollment: 8,404. Program was first offered in 1975. AACSB-accredited.

MBA HIGHLIGHTS

Entrance Difficulty***
Mean GMAT: 510
Mean GPA: 3.25

Cost $
Tuition: $980/semester
Room & Board: $10,000

Enrollment Profile
Full-time: 16	Work Exp: 85%
Part-time: 82	International: 0%
Total: 98	Women: 36%
Average Age: 35	Minorities: 13%

Average Class Size: 20

ACADEMICS
Length of Program Minimum: 24 months. Maximum: 6 years.
Calendar Semesters.
Full-time Classes Main campus; evening.
Part-time Classes Main campus; evening.
Degree Requirements 33 credits including 9 elective credits.
Required Courses Accounting information for management, financial management policies, managerial economics, marketing management, organizational behavior, quantitative methods in business decisions, research methods in business, seminar in strategic management and business policy.
Curricular Focus Business issues and problems, general management, managing diversity, organizational development and change management, problem solving and decision making, teamwork.
Concentration Management.
Faculty Full-time: 1, 100% with doctorates; part-time: 15, 100% with doctorates.
Teaching Methodology Case study: 10%, lecture: 65%, research: 5%, student presentations: 10%, team projects: 10%.

STUDENT STATISTICS
Geographic Representation State residents 97%. By region: South 40%; Northeast 20%; Midwest 20%; West 10%.
Undergraduate Majors Business 30%; engineering/technology 30%; humanities 5%; nursing 10%; science/mathematics 15%; social sciences 5%; other 5%.
Other Background Graduate degrees in other disciplines: 5%. Work experience: On average, students have 5 years of work experience on entrance to the program.

FACILITIES
Information Resources Main library with 429,093 bound volumes, 543,962 titles on microform, 1,557 periodical subscriptions, 600 records/tapes/CDs.
Housing 13% of students in program live in college-owned or -operated housing.
Technology Computers are used moderately in course work. 83 computer terminals/PCs are available for use by students in program; they are located in classrooms, learning resource center, computer labs. Students in the program are not required to have their own PC.

Computer Resources/On-line Services

Training	Yes	Multimedia Center	Yes
Internet	Yes	Dow Jones	Yes
E-Mail	No	Dialog	Yes

ADMISSION
Acceptance 1994-95 Of those applying, 69% were accepted.
Entrance Requirements Bachelor's degree, GMAT score, minimum 2.5 GPA.
Application Requirements Application form, copies of transcript.
Application Deadlines 8/1 for fall, 12/1 for spring.

FINANCIALS
Costs for 1994-95 Tuition: Full-time: $980/semester for state residents; Part-time evening: $530/semester for state residents. Fees: Full-time: $1,270/semester for state residents; Part-time evening: $636/semester for state residents. Average room and board costs are $10,000 per academic year (on-campus) and $18,000 per academic year (off-campus).
Financial Aid In 1994-95, candidates received some institutionally administered aid in the form of assistantships. Total awards ranged from $1,000-$3,000. Financial aid is available to part-time students. Application deadlines: 6/1 for fall, 12/1 for spring. Contact: Mrs. Mary K. Eason, Director, PO Box 93260, Lake Charles, LA 70609. (318) 475-5065.

INTERNATIONAL STUDENTS
Applying TOEFL required, minimum score of 525; proof of health; proof of adequate funds. Financial aid is available to international students. Financial aid application deadlines: 5/1 for fall, 8/1 for spring. Admission application deadlines: 5/15 for fall, 10/15 for spring, 3/15 for summer.

PLACEMENT
In 1993-94, 50 organizations participated in on-campus recruiting. Placement services include alumni network, career counseling/planning, career fairs, career placement, job interviews, resume preparation, and resume referral to employers. Of 1994 graduates, 99% were employed within three months of graduation, the average starting salary was $39,000, the range was $33,000-$140,000.

Jobs by Employer Type Manufacturing 50%; service 35%; government 5%; consulting 5%; nonprofit 5%.
Jobs by Functional Area Marketing/sales 10%; finance 10%; operations 50%; management 10%; strategic planning 10%; technical management 10%.

Program Contact: Dr. Shane R. Premeaux, Director of the MBA Program, McNeese State University, Ryan Street, PO Box 91660, Lake Charles, LA 70609. (318) 475-5576, or (800) 622-3352 (LA only); Fax: (318) 475-5010.

Nicholls State University

College of Business Administration

Thibodaux, Louisiana

OVERVIEW
Nicholls State University is a state-supported comprehensive coed institution. Founded 1948. Setting: 210-acre small-town campus with easy access to New Orleans. Total institutional enrollment: 7,000. AACSB-accredited.

MBA HIGHLIGHTS

Entrance Difficulty**
Mean GMAT: 460
Mean GPA: N/R

Cost $
Tuition: $993/semester
(Nonresident: $2,289/semester)
Room & Board: $2,566

Enrollment Profile

Full-time: 44	Work Exp: N/R
Part-time: 80	International: 26%
Total: 124	Women: 43%
Average Age: N/R	Minorities: 11%

Average Class Size: 15

ACADEMICS
Length of Program Minimum: 16 months. Maximum: 6 years.
Calendar Semesters.
Full-time Classes Main campus; day, evening, summer.
Part-time Classes Main campus; day, evening, summer.
Degree Requirements 33 credits.
Curricular Focus Business issues and problems, general management, problem solving and decision making.
Concentrations Accounting, computer information systems, economics, finance, management.
Teaching Methodology Case study: 30%, lecture: 40%, research: 10%, student presentations: 10%, team projects: 10%.

STUDENT STATISTICS
Geographic Representation State residents 74%. International 26%.

FACILITIES
Information Resources Main library with 278,386 bound volumes, 356,299 titles on microform, 1,815 periodical subscriptions, 3,568 records/tapes/CDs.
Housing College housing available.

ADMISSION
Entrance Requirements Bachelor's degree, GMAT score, minimum 2.0 GPA. Core courses waived through: previous course work.
Application Requirements Application form, copies of transcript.
Application Deadline Applications are processed on a rolling basis.

FINANCIALS
Costs for 1994-95 Tuition: Full-time: $993/semester for state residents, $2,289/semester for nonresidents, $2,349/semester for international students. Average room and board costs are $2,566 per academic year (on-campus).
Financial Aid In 1994-95, 15% of candidates received some institutionally administered aid in the form of assistantships. Applications are processed on a rolling basis. Contact: Dr. J.B. Stroud, Director of Graduate Studies, Box 2015, Thibodaux, LA 70310. (504) 449-7014.

INTERNATIONAL STUDENTS

Demographics 26% of students enrolled in the program are international.

Applying TOEFL required, minimum score of 550; proof of health; proof of adequate funds. Financial aid is available to international students. Financial aid application deadlines: 6/1 for fall, 11/1 for spring. Admission applications are processed on a rolling basis.

Program Contact: Dr. J. B. Stroud, Director of Graduate Studies, Nicholls State University, Box 2015, Thibodaux, LA 70310. (504) 449-7014; Fax: (504) 448-4922.

Northeast Louisiana University

College of Business Administration

Monroe, Louisiana

OVERVIEW

Northeast Louisiana University is a state-supported comprehensive coed institution. Founded 1931. Setting: 227-acre urban campus. Total institutional enrollment: 11,571. Program was first offered in 1963. AACSB-accredited.

MBA HIGHLIGHTS

Entrance Difficulty**
Mean GMAT: 492
Mean GPA: 2.9

Cost $
Tuition: $825/semester
(Nonresident: $1,905/semester)
Room & Board: N/R

Enrollment Profile

Full-time: 75	Work Exp: N/R
Part-time: 23	International: 40%
Total: 98	Women: 42%
Average Age: 26	Minorities: 2%

Average Class Size: 19

ACADEMICS

Length of Program Minimum: 12 months. Maximum: 6 years.

Calendar Semesters.

Full-time Classes Main campus; day, evening, summer.

Part-time Classes Main campus; day, evening, summer.

Degree Requirements 33 semester hours including 9 elective semester hours.

Required Courses Business research, managerial accounting, managerial economics, managerial finance, quantitative analysis, seminar in management, seminar in marketing strategy, seminar in strategic management. Courses may be waived through: previous course work.

Curricular Focus General management, leadership, problem solving and decision making.

Concentration Healthcare administration.

Faculty Full-time: 33, 100% with doctorates.

Special Opportunities International exchange in Hong Kong.

STUDENT STATISTICS

Geographic Representation International 40%.

Undergraduate Majors Business 58%; education 2%; engineering/technology 17%; humanities 9%; nursing 1%; science/mathematics 3%; social sciences 7%; other 3%.

Other Background Graduate degrees in other disciplines: 3%.

FACILITIES

Information Resources Main library with 539,437 bound volumes, 403,854 titles on microform, 2,917 periodical subscriptions.

Housing College housing available.

Technology Computers are used heavily in course work. 95 computer terminals/PCs, linked by a campus-wide computer network, are available for use by students in program; they are located in learning resource center, computer labs, the research center. Students in the program are not required to have their own PC.

Computer Resources/On-line Services

Training	Yes	E-Mail	No

ADMISSION

Acceptance 1994-95 Of those applying, 62% were accepted.

Entrance Requirements Bachelor's degree, GMAT score of 400, minimum 2.5 GPA. Core courses waived through: previous course work.

Application Requirements Application form, copies of transcript.

Application Deadlines 7/1 for fall, 11/1 for spring.

FINANCIALS

Costs for 1994-95 Tuition: Full-time: $825/semester for state residents, $1,905/semester for nonresidents; Part-time day: $276-$736/semester for state residents, $276-$1,696/semester for nonresidents. Fees: Full-time: $141/semester for state residents, $141/semester for nonresidents; Part-time day: $141/semester for state residents, $141/semester for nonresidents.

Financial Aid In 1994-95, 60% of candidates received some institutionally administered aid in the form of assistantships. Total awards ranged from $4,400-$4,800. Financial aid is not available to part-time students. Application deadlines: 7/1 for fall, 11/1 for spring. Contact: Mr. Keith Joiner, Acting Director, Financial Aid, 700 University Avenue, Monroe, LA 71209-0001. (318) 342-5320.

INTERNATIONAL STUDENTS

Demographics 40% of students enrolled in the program are international; Asia 92%, Europe 8%.

Services and Facilities International student center, ESL courses.

Applying TOEFL required, minimum score of 600; proof of health; proof of adequate funds. Financial aid is available to international students. Financial aid application deadlines: 7/1 for fall, 11/1 for spring. Admission application deadlines: 7/1 for fall, 11/1 for spring. Contact: Ms. Telitha Doke, International Student Coordinator, 700 University Avenue, Monroe, LA 71209-0001. (318) 342-5223.

PLACEMENT

Placement services include alumni network, career counseling/planning, career fairs, career library, career placement, job interviews, resume preparation, and resume referral to employers.

Program Contact: Dr. R. G. Martin, Director, MBA Program, Northeast Louisiana University, 700 University Avenue, Monroe, LA 71209-0001. (318) 342-1100; Fax: (318) 342-1209.

Northwestern State University of Louisiana

Natchitoches, Louisiana

OVERVIEW

Northwestern State University of Louisiana is a state-supported comprehensive coed institution. Founded 1884. Setting: 1,000-acre small-town campus. Total institutional enrollment: 8,761.

ACADEMICS

Calendar Semesters.

Degree Requirements 36 credits.

Concentration Management.

FACILITIES

Information Resources Main library with 308,904 bound volumes, 683,506 titles on microform, 2,438 periodical subscriptions, 2,348 records/tapes/CDs.

ADMISSION

Entrance Requirements Bachelor's degree, prerequisite courses required for applicants with non-business degree, GMAT score, minimum 3 years of work experience.

Application Requirements Copies of transcript, personal statement.

Application Deadlines 7/25 for fall, 12/1 for spring.

INTERNATIONAL STUDENTS

Applying TOEFL required, minimum score of 550; proof of health; proof of adequate funds. Admission application deadlines: 7/25 for fall, 12/1 for spring.

Program Contact: Ms. Marsha Zulick, Director of Recruiting, Northwestern State University of Louisiana, College Avenue, Natchitoches, LA 71497. (318) 357-4503, or (800) 327-1903 (LA only); Fax: (318) 357-4223.

Southeastern Louisiana University

College of Business

Hammond, Louisiana

OVERVIEW

Southeastern Louisiana University is a state-supported comprehensive coed institution. Founded 1925. Setting: 365-acre small-town campus with easy access to New Orleans. Total institutional enrollment: 14,000. Program was first offered in 1969. AACSB-accredited.

MBA HIGHLIGHTS

Entrance Difficulty*
Mean GMAT: 475
Mean GPA: 3.1

Cost $
Tuition: $950/semester
(Nonresident: $950/semester)
Room & Board: N/R

Enrollment Profile
Full-time: 60
Part-time: 70
Total: 130
Average Age: 27

Work Exp: 60%
International: 15%
Women: 45%
Minorities: 10%

Average Class Size: 20

ACADEMICS

Length of Program Minimum: 18 months. Maximum: 6 years.

Calendar Semesters.

Full-time Classes Main campus; day, evening, weekends, early morning, summer.

Part-time Classes Main campus; day, evening, weekends, early morning, summer.

Degree Requirements 33 credits including 12 elective credits.

Required Courses Accounting, economics, finance, marketing, organizational behavior, statistics, strategy. Courses may be waived through: previous course work.

Curricular Focus Business issues and problems, entrepreneurship, general management.

Concentrations Accounting, economics, entrepreneurship, finance, management, marketing, organizational behavior, strategic management.

Faculty Full-time: 16, 100% with doctorates.

Teaching Methodology Lecture: 70%, seminars by members of the business community: 10%, student presentations: 10%, team projects: 10%.

Special Opportunities International exchange in Austria, France.

STUDENT STATISTICS

Geographic Representation State residents 75%. By region: South 85%. International 15%.

Undergraduate Majors Business 85%; humanities 14%; science/mathematics 1%.

Other Background Graduate degrees in other disciplines: 5%.

FACILITIES

Information Resources Main library with 310,000 bound volumes, 573,364 titles on microform, 2,200 periodical subscriptions, 38,843 records/tapes/CDs. Business collection includes 15,200 bound volumes, 250 periodical subscriptions, 100 CD-ROMs, 700 videos.

Housing College housing available.

Technology Computers are used moderately in course work. 100 computer terminals/PCs, linked by a campus-wide computer network, are available for use by students in program; they are located in dormitories, the student center, learning resource center, the library, the computer center, computer labs. Students in the program are not required to have their own PC.

Computer Resources/On-line Services

Training	Yes	Dun's	No
Internet	Yes	Dow Jones	No
E-Mail	Yes	Dialog	Yes
LEXIS/NEXIS	No	Bloomberg	No
CompuServe	No		

ADMISSION

Acceptance 1994-95 Of those applying, 95% were accepted.

Entrance Requirements Bachelor's degree, 33 undergraduate business credits, GMAT score. Core courses waived through: previous course work.

Application Requirements Application form, copies of transcript, personal statement.

Application Deadlines 6/1 for fall, 10/1 for spring, 3/1 for summer.

FINANCIALS

Costs for 1994-95 Tuition: Full-time: $950/semester for state residents, $950/semester for nonresidents.

Financial Aid In 1994-95, 70% of candidates received some institutionally administered aid in the form of scholarships, loans, assistantships, work-study. Total awards ranged from $1,000-$4,000. Financial aid is available to part-time students. Application deadlines: 5/1 for fall, 10/15 for spring. Contact: Mr. Etienna Winzer, Director of Financial Aid, SLU 703, Hammond, LA 70402. (504) 549-2244.

INTERNATIONAL STUDENTS

Demographics 15% of students enrolled in the program are international; Asia 60%, Europe 40%.

Services and Facilities Counseling/support services.

Applying TOEFL required, minimum score of 500; proof of health; proof of adequate funds. Financial aid is not available to international students. Admission application deadlines: 6/1 for fall, 10/1 for spring, 3/1 for summer. Contact: Dr. Deborah Hebert, Associate Dean, International Students, PO Drawer 752, Hammond, LA 70402. (504) 549-2247.

Program Contact: Dr. Brad O'Hara, MBA Director, Southeastern Louisiana University, PO Drawer 752, University Station, Hammond, LA 70402. (504) 549-2146; Fax: (504) 549-5038.

Tulane University

A. B. Freeman School of Business

New Orleans, Louisiana

OVERVIEW

Tulane University is an independent nonprofit coed institution. Founded 1834. Setting: 110-acre urban campus. Total institutional enrollment: 11,362. Program was first offered in 1940. AACSB-accredited.

MBA HIGHLIGHTS

Entrance Difficulty**
Mean GMAT: 600
Mean GPA: 3.14

Cost $$$$
Tuition: $9,020 - $18,040
Room & Board: $6,050

Enrollment Profile
Full-time: 235
Part-time: 143
Total: 378
Average Age: 26

Work Exp: 92%
International: 33%
Women: 30%
Minorities: 14%

Class Size: 21 - 47

ACADEMICS

Length of Program Minimum: 21 months. Maximum: 7 years.

Calendar Semesters.

Full-time Classes Main campus; day.

Part-time Classes Main campus; evening, summer.

Degree Requirements 63 hours including 30 elective hours.

Required Courses Business statistics, economic environment of global business, financial management, financial reporting, management communication, management policy, managerial economics, marketing management, operations management, organizational behavior. Courses may be waived through: previous course work.

Curricular Focus General management, international business, teamwork.

Concentrations Accounting, economics, entrepreneurship, finance, human resources management, international business, management, management information systems, marketing, operations management, organizational behavior, real estate, strategic management.

Faculty Full-time: 34, 100% with doctorates; part-time: 11.

Teaching Methodology Case study: 38%, lecture: 30%, seminars by members of the business community: 2%, student presentations: 10%, team projects: 20%.

Special Opportunities Internships include investment/banking, energy, construction, telecommunications, and accounting, consulting.

STUDENT STATISTICS
Geographic Representation State residents 10%. By region: South 29%; Northeast 21%; West 10%; Midwest 7%. International 33%.

Undergraduate Majors Business 22%; engineering/technology 24%; humanities 18%; science/mathematics 5%; social sciences 29%; other 2%.

Other Background Graduate degrees in other disciplines: 10%. Work experience: On average, students have 3 years of work experience on entrance to the program.

FACILITIES
Information Resources Main library with 2 million bound volumes, 2.3 million titles on microform, 15,112 periodical subscriptions, 162,113 records/tapes/CDs. Business collection in Turchin Library includes 33,769 bound volumes, 700 periodical subscriptions, 14 CD-ROMs, 219 videos.

Housing 10% of students in program live in college-owned or -operated housing.

Technology Computers are used heavily in course work. 51 computer terminals/PCs, linked by a campus-wide computer network, are available for use by students in program; they are located in classrooms, the library, the computer center, computer labs, study rooms. Students in the program are not required to have their own PC. $1,000 are budgeted per student for computer support.

Computer Resources/On-line Services

Training	Yes	Multimedia Center	Yes
Internet	Yes	LEXIS/NEXIS	Yes
E-Mail	Yes	Dialog	Yes
Videoconference Center	Yes	Bloomberg	Yes

ADMISSION
Acceptance 1994-95 550 applied for admission; 58% were accepted.

Entrance Requirements Bachelor's degree, GMAT score. Core courses waived through: previous course work.

Application Requirements Written essay, application form, copies of transcript, resume/curriculum vitae, 2 letters of recommendation.

Application Deadline 4/1 for fall.

FINANCIALS
Costs for 1994-95 Tuition: Full-time: $9,020-$18,040. Fees: Full-time: $1,510. Average room and board costs are $6,050 per academic year (on-campus) and $6,050 per academic year (off-campus).

Financial Aid In 1994-95, 50% of candidates received some institutionally administered aid in the form of scholarships, fellowships, assistantships. Total awards ranged from $7,000-$22,040. Financial aid is available to part-time students. Applications are processed on a rolling basis. Contact: Mr. John C. Silbernagel, Director of Admissions, A. B. Freeman School of Business, Suite 400, New Orleans, LA 70118-5669. (504) 865-5410.

INTERNATIONAL STUDENTS
Demographics 33% of students enrolled in the program are international; Asia 48%, Europe 24%, Central America 15%, South America 6%, other 6%.

Services and Facilities International student center, visa services, language tutoring, ESL courses, special assistance for nonnative speakers of English, counseling/support services.

Applying TOEFL required; proof of health; proof of adequate funds. Financial aid is available to international students. Financial aid application deadline: 4/1 for fall. Admission application deadline: 4/1 for fall. Applications are processed on a rolling basis. Contact: Mr. William Lennon, Director, International Student Center, 7008 Zimple Street, Tate House, New Orleans, LA 70118-5669. (504) 865-5208.

ALTERNATE MBA PROGRAMS
Executive MBA (EMBA) Length of program: Minimum: 19 months. Maximum: 7 years. Degree requirements: 48 hours.

MBA/JD Length of program: Minimum: 45 months. Maximum: 7 years. Degree requirements: 127 hours including 66 elective hours.

MBA/MA Length of program: Minimum: 28 months. Maximum: 7 years. Degree requirements: 72 hours including 27 elective hours. MA is in Latin American studies.

MBA/MPH Length of program: Minimum: 33 months. Maximum: 7 years. Degree requirements: 91 hours including 28 elective hours.

PLACEMENT
In 1993-94, 105 organizations participated in on-campus recruiting; 341 on-campus interviews were conducted. Placement services include alumni network, career counseling/planning, career fairs, career library, career placement, electronic job bank, job interviews, resume preparation, and resume referral to employers. Of 1994 graduates, 87% were employed within three months of graduation, the average starting salary was $46,740, the range was $33,000-$85,000.

Jobs by Employer Type Manufacturing 20%; service 10%; consulting 8%; accounting 10%; banking 24%; oil and gas industry 8%; other 20%.

Jobs by Functional Area Marketing/sales 14%; finance 42%; operations 6%; management 10%; strategic planning 12%; human resources 6%; other 10%.

Program Contact: Mr. John C. Silbernagel, Director of Admissions, Tulane University, 6823 St. Charles Avenue, New Orleans, LA 70118-5669. (504) 865-5000, or (800) 223-5402; Internet Address: admissions@office.sob.tulane.edu.

University of New Orleans

College of Business Administration

New Orleans, Louisiana

OVERVIEW
The University of New Orleans is a state-supported coed institution. Part of Louisiana State University System. Founded 1958. Setting: 345-acre urban campus. Total institutional enrollment: 16,000. AACSB-accredited.

MBA HIGHLIGHTS
Entrance Difficulty**
Mean GMAT: 507
Mean GPA: 2.96

Cost $
Tuition: $373 - $928/semester
(Nonresident: $903 - $1,888/semester)
Room & Board: $3,000

Enrollment Profile

Full-time: 200	Work Exp: 80%
Part-time: 400	International: 20%
Total: 600	Women: 35%
Average Age: 30	Minorities: 15%

Average Class Size: 25

ACADEMICS
Length of Program Minimum: 12 months. Maximum: 8 years.

Calendar Semesters.

Full-time Classes Main campus, Slidell, Metairie; day, evening, summer.

Part-time Classes Main campus, Slidell, Metairie; day, evening, summer.

Degree Requirements 33 hours.

Required Courses Advanced accounting analysis for decision making, financial administration or financial theory, managerial economics, marketing problem analysis, operations management, operations research, seminar in business policies, seminar in organizational behavior. Courses may be waived through: previous course work.

Curricular Focus International business, problem solving and decision making, strategic analysis and planning.

Concentrations Economics, finance, international business, marketing, real estate.

Faculty Full-time: 80, 100% with doctorates.

Teaching Methodology Case study: 30%, faculty seminars: 20%, lecture: 25%, seminars by members of the business community: 5%, student presentations: 5%, team projects: 15%.

Special Opportunities International exchange in Austria, France.

STUDENT STATISTICS
Geographic Representation State residents 70%. By region: South 70%; Midwest 5%; Northeast 3%; West 2%. International 20%.

Undergraduate Majors Business 55%; education 3%; engineering/technology 10%; humanities 5%; nursing 2%; science/mathematics 10%; social sciences 15%.

Other Background Graduate degrees in other disciplines: 5%. Work experience: On average, students have 7 years of work experience on entrance to the program.

FACILITIES
Information Resources Main library with 600,957 bound volumes, 25,793 titles on microform, 3,009 periodical subscriptions, 18,322 records/tapes/CDs, 10 CD-ROMs. Business collection includes 69,332 bound volumes, 451 periodical subscriptions, 34 videos.

Housing 10% of students in program live in college-owned or -operated housing.

Technology Computers are used heavily in course work. 200 computer terminals/PCs, linked by a campus-wide computer network, are available for use by students in program; they are located in the computer center, computer labs, the research center. Students in the program are not required to have their own PC.

Computer Resources/On-line Services

Training	Yes	CompuServe	No
Internet	Yes	Dun's	No
E-Mail	Yes	Dow Jones	No
Multimedia Center	Yes	Dialog	No
LEXIS/NEXIS	Yes	Bloomberg	No

Other on-line services: OCLC.

ADMISSION
Acceptance 1994-95 Of those applying, 45% were accepted.

Entrance Requirements Bachelor's degree, GMAT score of 400, minimum 2.5 GPA. Core courses waived through: previous course work.

Application Requirements Application form, copies of transcript.

Application Deadlines 7/1 for fall, 11/15 for spring, 5/1 for summer.

FINANCIALS
Costs for 1994-95 Tuition: Part-time day: $373-$928/semester for state residents, $903-$1,888/semester for nonresidents. Average room and board costs are $3,000 per academic year (on-campus) and $3,000 per academic year (off-campus).

Financial Aid In 1994-95, 30% of candidates received some institutionally administered aid in the form of grants, loans, fellowships, assistantships. Total awards ranged from $6,500-$12,000. Financial aid is not available to part-time students. Applications are processed on a rolling basis. Contact: Mr. Wally Boudet, Acting Associate Director, AD1005 Lakefront, New Orleans, LA 70148. (504) 286-7272.

INTERNATIONAL STUDENTS
Demographics 20% of students enrolled in the program are international; Asia 65%, Europe 32%, Africa 1%, South America 1%, other 1%.

Services and Facilities International student center, language tutoring, ESL courses, special assistance for nonnative speakers of English, counseling/support services.

Applying TOEFL required, minimum score of 550; proof of adequate funds. Financial aid is available to international students. Assistantships are available for these students. Admission application deadlines: 6/1 for fall, 10/1 for spring, 3/1 for summer. Contact: Mr. Mark Hallett, Office of International Students and Scholars, University Center, Room 260, New Orleans, LA 70148. (504) 286-6021.

PLACEMENT
In 1993-94, 25 organizations participated in on-campus recruiting; 50 on-campus interviews were conducted. Placement services include career counseling/planning, career fairs, career library, and career placement. Of 1994 graduates, 95% were employed within three months of graduation.

Program Contact: Dr. Paul J. Hensel, Associate Dean for Graduate Studies and Research, University of New Orleans, Lake Front, New Orleans, LA 70148. (504) 286-6391; Fax: (504) 286-6958.

University of Southwestern Louisiana

College of Business Administration

Lafayette, Louisiana

OVERVIEW
The University of Southwestern Louisiana is a state-supported coed institution. Founded 1898. Setting: 1,375-acre urban campus. Total institutional enrollment: 16,789.

ACADEMICS
Calendar Semesters.

Concentration Management.

FACILITIES
Information Resources Main library with 701,598 bound volumes, 284,022 titles on microform, 5,949 periodical subscriptions, 4,481 records/tapes/CDs, 508 CD-ROMs.

ADMISSION
Entrance Requirements Bachelor's degree, GMAT score, minimum 2.75 GPA.

Application Requirements Application form, copies of transcript, 3 letters of recommendation.

FINANCIALS
Financial Aid Contact: Ms. Patricia Cottonham, Director of Student Aid, Student Aid Office, Room 110, Foster Hall, Lafayette, LA 70504-1770. (318) 231-6506.

INTERNATIONAL STUDENTS
Applying TOEFL required, minimum score of 550.

Program Contact: Mr. Leroy Broussard Jr., Director of Admissions, University of Southwestern Louisiana, PO Box 41770, Lafayette, LA 70501-1770. (318) 482-6473; Fax: (318) 482-6195.

MAINE

Thomas College

Graduate School

Waterville, Maine

OVERVIEW
Thomas College is an independent nonprofit comprehensive coed institution. Founded 1894. Setting: 70-acre small-town campus. Total institutional enrollment: 900.

MBA HIGHLIGHTS

Entrance Difficulty*
Mean GMAT: 460
Mean GPA: 3.2

Cost $
Tuition: $140/credit
Room & Board: N/R

Enrollment Profile

Full-time: 0	Work Exp: 98%
Part-time: 170	International: N/R
Total: 170	Women: 50%
Average Age: 35	Minorities: N/R

Average Class Size: 18

ACADEMICS
Length of Program Minimum: 18 months.

Calendar Trimesters.

Part-time Classes Main campus, Jay, Augusta; evening, weekends.

Degree Requirements 36 credits including 15 elective credits.

Required Courses Accounting for management decisions, economics of the firm, financial management, managerial statistics, marketing management, organizational theory and behavior, policy formation and corporate strategy.

Curricular Focus General management.

Concentrations Health services, human resources management, management.

Faculty Full-time: 8, 20% with doctorates; part-time: 12, 20% with doctorates.

Teaching Methodology Case study: 30%, lecture: 30%, student presentations: 20%, team projects: 20%.

STUDENT STATISTICS

Geographic Representation By region: Northeast 100%.

Undergraduate Majors Business 50%; education 2%; engineering/technology 30%; humanities 2%; nursing 10%; science/mathematics 2%; social sciences 2%; other 2%.

Other Background Graduate degrees in other disciplines: 3%. Work experience: On average, students have 7 years of work experience on entrance to the program.

FACILITIES

Information Resources Main library with 22,102 bound volumes, 2 titles on microform, 216 periodical subscriptions, 5 CD-ROMs.

Housing College housing not available.

Technology Computers are used moderately in course work. Computer terminals/PCs, linked by a campus-wide computer network, are available for use by students in program; they are located in computer labs. Students in the program are not required to have their own PC.

Computer Resources/On-line Services

Training	No	E-Mail	Yes
Internet	Yes	CompuServe	Yes

ADMISSION

Acceptance 1994-95 64 applied for admission; 86% were accepted.

Entrance Requirements Bachelor's degree, GMAT required for students with GPA less than 3.0.

Application Requirements Written essay, copies of transcript, 3 letters of recommendation.

Application Deadline Applications are processed on a rolling basis.

FINANCIALS

Costs for 1994-95 Tuition: Part-time evening: $140/credit.

Financial Aid Financial aid is not available to part-time students. Applications are processed on a rolling basis. Contact: Ms. Lisa Vashon, Financial Aid Director, 180 West River Road, Waterville, ME 04901-5097. (207) 873-0771.

INTERNATIONAL STUDENTS

Applying TOEFL required.

PLACEMENT

Placement services include career placement.

Jobs by Employer Type Manufacturing 30%; service 25%; government 20%; consulting 2%; nonprofit 10%; other 13%.

Jobs by Functional Area Marketing/sales 10%; finance 5%; operations 10%; management 60%; strategic planning 2%; technical management 5%; other 8%.

Program Contact: Dr. Nelson Madore, Graduate Adviser, Thomas College, 180 West River Road, Waterville, ME 04901-5097. (207) 877-0102; Fax: (207) 877-0114.

University of Maine

College of Business Administration

Orono, Maine

OVERVIEW

The University of Maine is a state-supported coed institution. Part of University of Maine System. Founded 1865. Setting: 3,298-acre small-town campus. Total institutional enrollment: 11,343. Program was first offered in 1965. AACSB-accredited.

MBA HIGHLIGHTS

Entrance Difficulty***
Mean GMAT: 529
Mean GPA: 3.1

Cost $
Tuition: $1,368/semester
(Nonresident: $3,861/semester)
Room & Board: $4,740

Enrollment Profile

Full-time: 45	Work Exp: 85%
Part-time: 57	International: 13%
Total: 102	Women: 30%
Average Age: 30	Minorities: 2%

Average Class Size: 18

ACADEMICS

Length of Program Minimum: 12 months. Maximum: 6 years.

Calendar Semesters.

Full-time Classes Main campus; day, evening, summer.

Part-time Classes Main campus; evening, summer.

Degree Requirements 30 credit hours including 6-9 elective credit hours.

Required Courses Behavioral analysis, financial management, management policy, managerial accounting, marketing management, production management, quantitative methods. Courses may be waived through: previous course work.

Curricular Focus General management, leadership, problem solving and decision making.

Concentration Management.

Faculty Full-time: 15, 93% with doctorates.

Teaching Methodology Case study: 15%, lecture: 50%, student presentations: 20%, team projects: 15%.

STUDENT STATISTICS

Geographic Representation State residents 59%. By region: Northeast 79%; Midwest 4%; South 3%; West 1%. International 13%.

Undergraduate Majors Business 55%; engineering/technology 13%; humanities 6%; science/mathematics 15%; social sciences 11%.

Other Background Graduate degrees in other disciplines: 4%. Work experience: On average, students have 4 years of work experience on entrance to the program.

FACILITIES

Information Resources Main library with 850,000 bound volumes, 1.3 million titles on microform, 5,400 periodical subscriptions, 4,800 records/tapes/CDs.

Housing 10% of students in program live in college-owned or -operated housing.

Technology Computers are used moderately in course work. 150 computer terminals/PCs, linked by a campus-wide computer network, are available for use by students in program; they are located in the student center, the library, the computer center, computer labs. Students in the program are not required to have their own PC.

Computer Resources/On-line Services

Training	Yes	Dun's	No
Internet	Yes	Dow Jones	Yes $
E-Mail	Yes	Dialog	Yes $
LEXIS/NEXIS	No	Bloomberg	No
CompuServe	No		

Other on-line services: OCLC, First Search.

ADMISSION

Acceptance 1994-95 84 applied for admission; 93% were accepted.

Entrance Requirements Bachelor's degree, GMAT score of 470. Core courses waived through: previous course work.

Application Requirements Written essay, application form, copies of transcript, personal statement, 3 letters of recommendation.

Application Deadlines 12/15 for fall, 11/15 for spring, 4/15 for summer.

FINANCIALS

Costs for 1994-95 Tuition: Full-time: $1,368/semester for state residents, $3,861/semester for nonresidents. Fees: Full-time: $203/semester for state residents, $203/semester for nonresidents. Average room and board costs are $4,740 per academic year (on-campus).

Financial Aid In 1994-95, 20% of candidates received some institutionally administered aid in the form of scholarships, loans, assistantships, work-study. Financial aid is available to part-time students. Application deadlines: 3/1 for fall, 3/1 for spring. Contact: Ms. Peggy Crawford, Director of Student Aid, Wingate Hall, Orono, ME 04469. (207) 581-1324.

INTERNATIONAL STUDENTS
Demographics 13% of students enrolled in the program are international; Asia 59%, Europe 20%, Africa 8%, South America 1%, other 12%.

Services and Facilities Visa services, ESL courses, counseling/support services.

Applying TOEFL required, minimum score of 550; proof of health; proof of adequate funds. Financial aid is available to international students. Financial aid application deadline: 12/15 for fall. Admission application deadlines: 3/15 for fall, 10/15 for spring, 3/15 for summer. Contact: Ms. Ruth C. Bentley, Program Coordinator, Office of International Programs, 100 Winslow Hall, Orono, ME 04469. (207) 581-2905.

PLACEMENT
In 1993-94, 35 organizations participated in on-campus recruiting. Placement services include alumni network, career counseling/planning, career library, career placement, job interviews, resume preparation, and resume referral to employers. Of 1994 graduates, 90% were employed within three months of graduation, the average starting salary was $30,000, the range was $20,000-$38,000.

Program Contact: Dr. Roderick A. Forsgren, Director of the Graduate Program, University of Maine, Orono, ME 04469. (207) 581-1973; Fax: (207) 581-1956.
See full description on page 886.

University of Southern Maine

School of Business, Economics, and Management

Portland, Maine

OVERVIEW
The University of Southern Maine is a state-supported comprehensive coed institution. Part of University of Maine System. Founded 1878. Setting: 120-acre urban campus. Total institutional enrollment: 9,500. Program was first offered in 1964.

MBA HIGHLIGHTS
Entrance Difficulty***
Mean GMAT: 570
Mean GPA: 3.1

Cost $
Tuition: $146/credit hour
(Nonresident: $412/credit hour)
Room & Board: N/R

Enrollment Profile
Full-time: 10	Work Exp: 97%
Part-time: 168	International: 3%
Total: 178	Women: 38%
Average Age: 33	Minorities: 3%

Average Class Size: 20

ACADEMICS
Length of Program Minimum: 24 months. Maximum: 6 years.
Calendar Semesters.
Full-time Classes Main campus; evening, summer.
Part-time Classes Main campus; evening, summer.
Degree Requirements 45 credit hours including 12 elective credit hours.
Required Courses Economic environment and business decisions, financial management, international business, management theory, managerial accounting, managerial behavior, marketing management, operations research, organizational strategy and planning, production operations management, social responsibility.
Curricular Focus General management, organizational development and change management, problem solving and decision making.
Concentration Management.
Faculty Full-time: 21, 95% with doctorates.

Special Opportunities Internship program available.
STUDENT STATISTICS
Geographic Representation State residents 96%. By region: Northeast 97%. International 3%.
Undergraduate Majors Business 40%; education 2%; engineering/technology 10%; humanities 5%; nursing 1%; science/mathematics 6%; social sciences 8%; other 28%.
Other Background Graduate degrees in other disciplines: 7%. Work experience: On average, students have 10 years of work experience on entrance to the program.

FACILITIES
Information Resources Main library with 348,952 bound volumes, 992,746 titles on microform, 3,708 periodical subscriptions, 4,480 records/tapes/CDs.
Housing 2% of students in program live in college-owned or -operated housing.
Technology Computers are used moderately in course work. 100 computer terminals/PCs, linked by a campus-wide computer network, are available for use by students in program; they are located in computer labs. Students in the program are not required to have their own PC.
Computer Resources/On-line Services
Training	No	E-Mail	Yes
Internet	Yes		

ADMISSION
Acceptance 1994-95 Of those applying, 77% were accepted.
Entrance Requirements Bachelor's degree, GMAT score of 500. Core courses waived through: previous course work.
Application Requirements Application form, copies of transcript, resume/curriculum vitae, 3 letters of recommendation.
Application Deadline Applications are processed on a rolling basis.

FINANCIALS
Costs for 1994-95 Tuition: Full-time: $146/credit hour for state residents, $412/credit hour for nonresidents. Fees: Full-time: $5/credit hour for state residents, $5/credit hour for nonresidents.
Financial Aid In 1994-95, 6% of candidates received some institutionally administered aid in the form of scholarships, assistantships. Total awards ranged from $1,000-$7,200. Financial aid is not available to part-time students. Application deadline: 2/15 for fall. Contact: Mr. Keith DuBois, Director, 37 College Avenue, Gorham, ME 04038. (207) 780-5250.

INTERNATIONAL STUDENTS
Demographics 3% of students enrolled in the program are international.
Services and Facilities International student center, ESL courses.
Applying TOEFL required, minimum score of 550; proof of health; proof of adequate funds. Financial aid is available to international students. Financial aid application deadline: 3/15 for fall. Admission applications are processed on a rolling basis. Contact: Ms. Domenica Cipollone, Director, International Programs, 96 Falmouth Street, Portland, ME 04103. (207) 780-4959.

PLACEMENT
Of 1994 graduates, 90% were employed within three months of graduation.

Program Contact: Mr. Raymond P. Neveu, Director, University of Southern Maine, 96 Falmouth Street, Portland, ME 04103. (207) 780-4020, or (800) 800-4USM; Fax: (207) 780-4662.

MARYLAND

Frostburg State University

School of Business

Frostburg, Maryland

OVERVIEW
Frostburg State University is a state-supported comprehensive coed institution. Part of University of Maryland System. Founded 1898. Setting: 260-acre small-town campus. Total institutional enrollment: 5,400. Program was first offered in 1971.

MBA HIGHLIGHTS

Entrance Difficulty*

Cost $
Tuition: $146/credit hour
(Nonresident: $161/credit hour)
Room & Board: $5,000

Enrollment Profile

Full-time: 45	Work Exp: 95%
Part-time: 375	International: 5%
Total: 420	Women: 43%
Average Age: 34	Minorities: 7%

Average Class Size: 13

ACADEMICS

Length of Program Minimum: 16 months. Maximum: 6 years.

Calendar Trimesters.

Full-time Classes Main campus; evening, summer.

Part-time Classes Main campus, Hagerstown, Frederick; evening, summer.

Degree Requirements 45 credits.

Required Courses Field experience in management, financial management, human behavior in organizations, human resources management, implementation of management strategy, legal environment of management, management accounting, management decision analysis, management information sciences, managerial communication, marketing management, operations management, planning in the managerial environment, the managerial process. Courses may be waived through: previous course work.

Curricular Focus General management, problem solving and decision making, teamwork.

Concentration Management.

Faculty Full-time: 13, 61% with doctorates; part-time: 18.

Teaching Methodology Case study: 65%, lecture: 20%, student presentations: 5%, team projects: 10%.

STUDENT STATISTICS

Geographic Representation State residents 73%. By region: South 81%; Northeast 14%. International 5%.

Undergraduate Majors Business 40%; education 5%; humanities 10%; science/mathematics 20%; social sciences 25%.

Other Background Graduate degrees in other disciplines: 3%. Work experience: On average, students have 9 years of work experience on entrance to the program.

FACILITIES

Information Resources Main library with 423,782 bound volumes, 153,785 titles on microform, 1,331 periodical subscriptions, 31,448 records/tapes/CDs.

Housing 2% of students in program live in college-owned or -operated housing.

Technology Computers are used moderately in course work. 65 computer terminals/PCs, linked by a campus-wide computer network, are available for use by students in program; they are located in computer labs. Students in the program are not required to have their own PC.

Computer Resources/On-line Services

Training	Yes	E-Mail	Yes
Internet	Yes		

ADMISSION

Acceptance 1994-95 185 applied for admission; 90% were accepted.

Entrance Requirements Bachelor's degree, minimum 2.5 GPA, minimum 2 years of work experience. Core courses waived through: previous course work.

Application Requirements Application form, copies of transcript.

Application Deadlines 8/25 for fall, 1/15 for spring.

FINANCIALS

Costs for 1994-95 Tuition: Part-time evening: $146/credit hour for state residents, $161/credit hour for nonresidents. Fees: Part-time evening: $12/credit hour for state residents, $12/credit hour for nonresidents. Average room and board costs are $5,000 per academic year (on-campus).

Financial Aid In 1994-95, candidates received some institutionally administered aid in the form of loans, fellowships, assistantships. Total awards ranged from $5,000-$8,000. Financial aid is available to part-time students. Application deadlines: 3/15 for fall, 7/15 for spring. Contact: Ms. Katherine Kutler, Director of Financial Aid, Financial Aid Office, Midlothian Road, Frostburg, MD 21532-2302. (301) 689-4301.

INTERNATIONAL STUDENTS

Demographics 5% of students enrolled in the program are international; Asia 50%, Europe 33%, Africa 17%.

Services and Facilities Visa services, counseling/support services.

Applying TOEFL required, minimum score of 560; proof of health; proof of adequate funds. Financial aid is not available to international students. Admission application deadlines: 6/15 for fall, 9/15 for spring.

PLACEMENT

Placement services include career counseling/planning, career fairs, career library, career placement, job interviews, resume preparation, and resume referral to employers.

Program Contact: Dr. Thomas F. Hawk, Chair, MBA Department, Frostburg State University, Midlothian Road, Frostburg, MD 21532-2302. (301) 689-4375; Fax: (301) 689-4380.

Hood College

Department of Economics and Management

Frederick, Maryland

OVERVIEW

Hood College is an independent comprehensive primarily women institution, affiliated with United Church of Christ. Founded 1893. Setting: 50-acre urban campus with easy access to Baltimore and Washington, DC. Total institutional enrollment: 2,020.

MBA HIGHLIGHTS

Entrance Difficulty**
Mean GMAT: 525
Mean GPA: N/R

Cost $
Tuition: $235/credit hour
Room & Board: N/R

Enrollment Profile

Full-time: N/R	Work Exp: N/R
Part-time: N/R	International: 5%
Total: 200	Women: 40%
Average Age: N/R	Minorities: 10%

Average Class Size: 20

ACADEMICS

Length of Program Minimum: 12 months.

Calendar Semesters.

Part-time Classes Main campus; evening, weekends, summer.

Degree Requirements 36 credits.

Curricular Focus Business issues and problems, general management, problem solving and decision making.

Concentrations Accounting, human resources management, information technology management, management, marketing.

Teaching Methodology Case study: 35%, lecture: 45%, student presentations: 10%, team projects: 10%.

STUDENT STATISTICS

Geographic Representation State residents 90%. International 5%.

FACILITIES

Information Resources Main library with 169,183 bound volumes, 424,637 titles on microform, 914 periodical subscriptions, 2,056 records/tapes/CDs, 30 CD-ROMs.

ADMISSION

Entrance Requirements Bachelor's degree, GMAT score, minimum 2.5 GPA.

Application Requirements Application form.

Application Deadline Applications are processed on a rolling basis.

FINANCIALS

Costs for 1994-95 Tuition: Full-time: $235/credit hour. Fees: Full-time: $30-$60/semester.

Financial Aid Application deadlines: 8/15 for fall, 12/15 for spring. Applications are processed on a rolling basis. Contact: Financial Aid Office, 401 Rosemont Avenue, Frederick, MD 21701. (301) 696-3411.

INTERNATIONAL STUDENTS

Demographics 5% of students enrolled in the program are international.

Applying TOEFL required, minimum score of 530; proof of health; proof of adequate funds. Financial aid is not available to international students. Admission applications are processed on a rolling basis.

Program Contact: Graduate School Office, Hood College, 401 Rosemont Avenue, Frederick, MD 21701. (301) 696-3685; Fax: (301) 694-7653.

Loyola College

Joseph A. Sellinger, SJ, School of Business and Mgmt.

Baltimore, Maryland

OVERVIEW

Loyola College is an independent Roman Catholic (Jesuit) comprehensive coed institution. Founded 1852. Setting: 65-acre suburban campus. Total institutional enrollment: 6,261. Program was first offered in 1967. AACSB-accredited.

MBA HIGHLIGHTS

Entrance Difficulty***
Mean GMAT: 530
Mean GPA: 3.2

Cost $
Tuition: $315/credit
Room & Board: N/R

Enrollment Profile

Full-time: 197	Work Exp: 9%
Part-time: 896	International: 1%
Total: 1,093	Women: 39%
Average Age: 30	Minorities: 5%

Average Class Size: 23

ACADEMICS

Length of Program Minimum: 12 months. Maximum: 7 years.

Calendar Semesters.

Full-time Classes Main campus; day, evening, weekends, summer.

Degree Requirements 30 credits including 15 elective credits.

Required Courses Financial strategy, leadership and responsibility, marketing strategy in a changing environment, operating processes and technologies in the information age, the total enterprise: strategy and policy. Courses may be waived through: previous course work.

Curricular Focus General management, leadership, teamwork.

Concentrations Accounting, economics, finance, healthcare management, international business, management, management information systems, marketing.

Faculty Full-time: 55, 91% with doctorates; part-time: 50.

Teaching Methodology Case study: 25%, lecture: 45%, student presentations: 5%, team projects: 25%.

Special Opportunities International exchange and internships programs are arranged on an individual basis.

STUDENT STATISTICS

Geographic Representation State residents 95%. By region: Northeast 98%; South 1%. International 1%.

Undergraduate Majors Business 43%; education 1%; engineering/technology 14%; humanities 3%; science/mathematics 7%; social sciences 4%; other 28%.

Other Background Graduate degrees in other disciplines: 10%. Work experience: On average, students have 5-6 years of work experience on entrance to the program.

FACILITIES

Information Resources Main library with 307,276 bound volumes, 38 titles on microform, 2,057 periodical subscriptions, 4,199 records/tapes/CDs, 14 CD-ROMs. Business collection includes 27,645 bound volumes, 507 periodical subscriptions, 4 CD-ROMs, 265 videos.

Housing College housing not available.

Technology Computers are used moderately in course work. 197 computer terminals/PCs, linked by a campus-wide computer network, are avail-

able for use by students in program; they are located in dormitories, the computer center, computer labs. Students in the program are required to have their own PC.

Computer Resources/On-line Services

Training	Yes	Dun's	No
Internet	Yes	Dow Jones	Yes
E-Mail	Yes	Dialog	Yes
LEXIS/NEXIS	No	Bloomberg	No
CompuServe	No		

Other on-line services: OCLC.

ADMISSION

Acceptance 1994-95 537 applied for admission; 78% were accepted.

Entrance Requirements Bachelor's degree, GMAT score of 500, minimum 3.0 GPA. Core courses waived through: previous course work.

Application Requirements Written essay, application form, copies of transcript, resume/curriculum vitae.

Application Deadlines 7/20 for fall, 11/20 for spring, 4/20 for summer.

FINANCIALS

Costs for 1994-95 Tuition: Part-time evening: $315/credit. Fees: Part-time evening: $25/semester.

Financial Aid In 1994-95, 6% of candidates received some institutionally administered aid in the form of grants, assistantships. Total awards ranged from $1,150-$7,050. Financial aid is available to part-time students. Application deadlines: 7/15 for fall, 11/15 for spring, 4/15 for summer. Contact: Mr. Mark L. Lindenmeyer, Director of Financial Aid, 4501 North Charles Street, Baltimore, MD 21210-2699. (410) 617-2576.

INTERNATIONAL STUDENTS

Demographics 1% of students enrolled in the program are international.

Services and Facilities Visa services, language tutoring, ESL courses, counseling/support services.

Applying TOEFL required, minimum score of 550; proof of adequate funds; Proof of health insurance, letters of sponsorship and summer plans. Financial aid is not available to international students. Admission application deadlines: 5/15 for fall, 8/15 for spring, 1/15 for summer. Contact: Mr. Joseph Healy, International Programs Adviser, 4501 North Charles Street, Baltimore, MD 21210-2699. (410) 617-2910.

ALTERNATE MBA PROGRAMS

Executive MBA (EMBA) Length of program: Minimum: 18 months. Degree requirements: 51 credits. 8-10 years managerial experience.

MBA Fellows Program Length of program: Minimum: 24 months. Degree requirements: 51 credits. 4-5 years managerial experience.

PLACEMENT

In 1993-94, 26 organizations participated in on-campus recruiting; 134 on-campus interviews were conducted. Placement services include alumni network, career counseling/planning, career fairs, career library, career placement, credential service, job interviews, resume preparation, and resume referral to employers. Of 1994 graduates, 93% were employed within three months of graduation, the average starting salary was $41,920, the range was $35,000-$127,000.

Program Contact: Ms. Manette Frese, Director of Executive and Graduate Programs, Loyola College, 4501 North Charles Street, Baltimore, MD 21210-2699. (410) 617-2836, or (800) 221-9107; Fax: (410) 617-2161.

See full description on page 774.

Morgan State University

School of Business and Management

Baltimore, Maryland

OVERVIEW

Morgan State University is a state-supported comprehensive coed institution. Founded 1867. Setting: 122-acre urban campus with easy access to Washington, DC. Total institutional enrollment: 5,858.

MBA HIGHLIGHTS

Entrance Difficulty***
Mean GMAT: 450
Mean GPA: N/R

Cost $
Tuition: $125/credit hour
(Nonresident: $190/credit hour)
Room & Board: N/R

Enrollment Profile

Full-time: 100	Work Exp: 80%
Part-time: 25	International: 20%
Total: 125	Women: 55%
Average Age: N/R	Minorities: 95%

Average Class Size: 20

ACADEMICS
Length of Program Minimum: 24 months.
Calendar Semesters.
Full-time Classes Main campus; evening, weekends, summer.
Part-time Classes Main campus; evening, weekends, summer.
Degree Requirements 33 credits.
Required Courses Accounting for decision making, administration theory and organizational behavior, advanced marketing management, corporate finance, foundations of multinational operations, management of information technologies, managerial economics, quantitative methods for business, strategic management and policy analysis.
Curricular Focus General management, minorities in business, problem solving and decision making.
Concentration Management.
Teaching Methodology Case study: 20%, lecture: 50%, student presentations: 15%, team projects: 15%.

STUDENT STATISTICS
Geographic Representation International 20%.
Other Background Work experience: On average, students have 4-5 years of work experience on entrance to the program.

FACILITIES
Information Resources Main library with 333,101 bound volumes, 141,733 titles on microform, 2,526 periodical subscriptions, 37,422 records/tapes/CDs.
Housing 10% of students in program live in college-owned or -operated housing.
Computer Resources/On-line Services

Training	Yes	Multimedia Center	Yes

ADMISSION
Entrance Requirements Bachelor's degree, GMAT score. Core courses waived through: previous course work.
Application Requirements Written essay, interview, application form, copies of transcript, personal statement.
Application Deadlines 4/30 for fall, 10/30 for spring. Applications are processed on a rolling basis.

FINANCIALS
Costs for 1994-95 Tuition: Full-time: $125/credit hour for state residents, $190/credit hour for nonresidents. Fees: Full-time: $116/semester for state residents, $116/semester for nonresidents.
Financial Aid In 1994-95, 80% of candidates received some institutionally administered aid in the form of scholarships, loans, fellowships, assistantships. Applications are processed on a rolling basis. Contact: Financial Aid Office of Graduate School, Cold Spring Lane and Hillen Road, Baltimore, MD 21239. (410) 319-3185.

INTERNATIONAL STUDENTS
Demographics 20% of students enrolled in the program are international.
Applying TOEFL required; proof of adequate funds. Financial aid is available to international students. Applications are processed on a rolling basis. Admission application deadlines: 4/30 for fall, 8/30 for spring. Applications are processed on a rolling basis.

ALTERNATE MBA PROGRAM
MBA/MRP Length of program: Minimum: 36 months. Maximum: 5 years. Full-time classes: Main campus; evening, weekends, summer. Part-time classes: Main campus; evening, weekends, summer. Degree requirements: 63 credits.

PLACEMENT
Placement services include career counseling/planning, career placement, and resume preparation.

Program Contact: Mr. Bala Subramanian, Assistant Dean, Morgan State University, Cold Spring Lane and Hillen Road, Baltimore, MD 21239. (410) 319-3160; Fax: (410) 319-3358; Internet Address: subrama@moe.morgan.edu.

Mount Saint Mary's College

Emmitsburg, Maryland

OVERVIEW
Mount Saint Mary's College is an independent Roman Catholic comprehensive coed institution. Founded 1808. Setting: 1,400-acre suburban campus with easy access to Baltimore and Washington, DC. Total institutional enrollment: 1,800. Program was first offered in 1976.

MBA HIGHLIGHTS

Entrance Difficulty***
Mean GMAT: 505
Mean GPA: 3.5

Cost $
Tuition: $210/credit hour
Room & Board: N/R

Enrollment Profile

Full-time: 30	Work Exp: 80%
Part-time: 220	International: 10%
Total: 250	Women: 40%
Average Age: 32	Minorities: 2%

Average Class Size: 17

ACADEMICS
Length of Program Minimum: 24 months. Maximum: 5 years.
Calendar Trimesters.
Full-time Classes Main campus; evening, summer.
Part-time Classes Main campus; evening, summer.
Degree Requirements 37 credits including 9 elective credits.
Required Courses Business legal environment, business policy, financial management, management information systems, management self-assessment skills, management theory and practice, managerial accounting, managerial economics, marketing theory and practice, statistical decision theory.
Curricular Focus General management, problem solving and decision making, strategic analysis and planning.
Concentrations Accounting, economics, finance, human resources management, management, management information systems, marketing.
Faculty Full-time: 10, 90% with doctorates; part-time: 10, 10% with doctorates.
Teaching Methodology Case study: 40%, lecture: 40%, student presentations: 20%.

STUDENT STATISTICS
Geographic Representation By region: Northeast 90%. International 10%.
Undergraduate Majors Business 55%; education 10%; engineering/technology 10%; humanities 10%; social sciences 10%; other 5%.
Other Background Graduate degrees in other disciplines: 10%. Work experience: On average, students have 7 years of work experience on entrance to the program.

FACILITIES
Information Resources Main library with 189,000 bound volumes, 1,522 titles on microform, 921 periodical subscriptions, 685 records/tapes/CDs, 7 CD-ROMs.
Housing 10% of students in program live in college-owned or -operated housing.
Technology Computers are used moderately in course work. 50 computer terminals/PCs, linked by a campus-wide computer network, are available for use by students in program; they are located in the library, computer labs. Students in the program are not required to have their own PC.

Computer Resources/On-line Services

Training	Yes	Dun's	No
Internet	Yes	Dow Jones	No
E-Mail	Yes	Dialog	Yes $
LEXIS/NEXIS	No	Bloomberg	No
CompuServe	No		

ADMISSION

Acceptance 1994-95 Of those applying, 90% were accepted.

Entrance Requirements Bachelor's degree, GMAT score of 400. Core courses waived through: previous course work.

Application Requirements Application form, copies of transcript, resume/curriculum vitae, personal statement.

Application Deadlines 8/1 for fall, 1/1 for spring.

FINANCIALS

Costs for 1995-96 Tuition: Full-time: $210/credit hour.

Financial Aid In 1994-95, 3% of candidates received some institutionally administered aid in the form of assistantships, work-study. Financial aid is not available to part-time students. Application deadline: 4/1 for fall. Contact: Dr. William Forgang, Dean, Graduate Studies, Mount Saint Mary's College, Emmitsburg, MD 21727. (301) 447-5326.

INTERNATIONAL STUDENTS

Demographics 10% of students enrolled in the program are international; Asia 100%.

Services and Facilities International student housing; writing assistance.

Applying TOEFL required, minimum score of 500; proof of adequate funds. Financial aid is available to international students. Financial aid application deadline: 4/1 for fall. Admission applications are processed on a rolling basis. Contact: Mr. John Gill, Associate Registrar, Mount Saint Mary's College, Emmitsburg, MD 21727. (301) 447-5215.

PLACEMENT

In 1993-94, 20 organizations participated in on-campus recruiting. Placement services include alumni network, career counseling/planning, career fairs, career placement, electronic job bank, resume preparation, and resume referral to employers.

Program Contact: Dr. William Forgang, Dean, Graduate Studies, Mount Saint Mary's College, Mount Saint Mary's College, Emmitsburg, MD 21727. (301) 447-5326; Fax: (301) 447-5335; Internet Address: forgang@msmary.edu.

Salisbury State University

Franklin P. Perdue School of Business

Salisbury, Maryland

OVERVIEW

Salisbury State University is a state-supported comprehensive coed institution. Part of University of Maryland System. Founded 1925. Setting: 140-acre suburban campus. Total institutional enrollment: 4,806. Program was first offered in 1982.

MBA HIGHLIGHTS

Entrance Difficulty***
Mean GMAT: 490
Mean GPA: 3.0

Cost $
Tuition: $123/credit hour
(Nonresident: $152/credit hour)
Room & Board: N/R

Enrollment Profile

Full-time: 109	Work Exp: 75%
Part-time: 0	International: 12%
Total: 109	Women: 44%
Average Age: 29	Minorities: 6%

Average Class Size: 20

ACADEMICS

Length of Program Minimum: 12 months. Maximum: 7 years.
Calendar Semesters.
Full-time Classes Main campus; evening.

Degree Requirements 30 credits including 3 elective credits. Other: Minimum 3.0 GPA.

Required Courses Corporate financial management, corporate strategic planning and policy, economic environment of the organization, external environment of the organization, international business seminar, management science models, managerial accounting, marketing strategy, organizational theory. Courses may be waived through: previous course work.

Curricular Focus Problem solving and decision making.

Concentrations Accounting, economics, entrepreneurship, finance, human resources management, international business, management, management information systems, marketing, operations management, organizational behavior, public administration, public policy, quantitative analysis, strategic management.

Faculty Full-time: 20, 87% with doctorates.

Teaching Methodology Case study: 20%, lecture: 30%, student presentations: 20%, team projects: 30%.

Special Opportunities Internship program available.

STUDENT STATISTICS

Geographic Representation State residents 70%. By region: Northeast 82%; South 4%; Midwest 1%; West 1%. International 12%.

Undergraduate Majors Business 66%; education 1%; engineering/technology 4%; humanities 7%; nursing 2%; science/mathematics 10%; social sciences 1%; other 9%.

FACILITIES

Information Resources Main library with 254,000 bound volumes, 600,000 titles on microform, 1,800 periodical subscriptions, 29,543 records/tapes/CDs, 29 CD-ROMs.

Housing 1% of students in program live in college-owned or -operated housing.

Technology Computers are used moderately in course work. 190 computer terminals/PCs, linked by a campus-wide computer network, are available for use by students in program; they are located in the student center, classrooms, the library, the computer center, computer labs. Students in the program are not required to have their own PC.

Computer Resources/On-line Services

Training	Yes	CompuServe	No
Internet	Yes	Dun's	No
E-Mail	Yes	Dow Jones	No
Multimedia Center	Yes	Dialog	No
LEXIS/NEXIS	No	Bloomberg	No

Other on-line services: First Search.

ADMISSION

Acceptance 1994-95 Of those applying, 83% were accepted.

Entrance Requirements Bachelor's degree, GMAT score, minimum 3.0 GPA. Core courses waived through: previous course work.

Application Requirements Application form, copies of transcript, resume/curriculum vitae.

Application Deadlines 7/31 for fall, 11/30 for spring.

FINANCIALS

Costs for 1994-95 Tuition: Full-time: $123/credit hour for state residents, $152/credit hour for nonresidents. Fees: Full-time: $3/credit hour for state residents, $3/credit hour for nonresidents.

Financial Aid In 1994-95, 5% of candidates received some institutionally administered aid in the form of assistantships. Total awards ranged from $3,000-$3,500. Financial aid is not available to part-time students. Application deadlines: 3/31 for fall, 10/31 for spring.

INTERNATIONAL STUDENTS

Demographics 12% of students enrolled in the program are international; Asia 91%, Africa 4%, South America 4%.

Services and Facilities International student housing; international student center, visa services, counseling/support services.

Applying TOEFL required, minimum score of 550; proof of adequate funds. Financial aid is not available to international students. Admission application deadlines: 5/31 for fall, 9/30 for spring. Contact: Mr. Gary Grodzicki, Associate Dean, Admissions Office, Salisbury, MD 21801. (410) 543-6161.

PLACEMENT

In 1993-94, 70 organizations participated in on-campus recruiting. Placement services include alumni network, career counseling/planning, career fairs, career library, career placement, electronic job bank, job interviews, resume preparation, and resume referral to employers.

296

Program Contact: Dr. Pamela Alreck, Director of the Graduate Program, Salisbury State University, 1101 Camden Avenue, Salisbury, MD 21801-6837. (410) 543-6317; Fax: (410) 548-2908; Internet Address: plalreck@sae.ssu.umd.edu.

University of Baltimore

Robert G. Merrick School of Business

Baltimore, Maryland

OVERVIEW

The University of Baltimore is a state-supported upper-level coed institution. Part of University of Maryland System. Founded 1925. Setting: 49-acre urban campus. Total institutional enrollment: 5,204. Program was first offered in 1972. AACSB-accredited.

MBA HIGHLIGHTS

Entrance Difficulty***
Mean GMAT: 500
Mean GPA: 3.0

Cost $
Tuition: $179/credit hour
(Nonresident: $210/credit hour)
Room & Board: $4,200 (off-campus)

Enrollment Profile

Full-time: 82	Work Exp: 85%
Part-time: 494	International: 10%
Total: 576	Women: 38%
Average Age: 30	Minorities: 25%

Average Class Size: 28

ACADEMICS

Length of Program Minimum: 30 months. Maximum: 7 years.

Calendar Semesters.

Part-time Classes Main campus; evening, weekends, summer.

Degree Requirements 30 credits including 12 elective credits.

Required Courses Accounting for managerial decisions, applied management science, global and domestic business environment, information systems and technology, organization creation and growth.

Curricular Focus Organizational development and change management, strategic analysis and planning, teamwork.

Concentrations Decision technology, technology, innovation and operations, entrepreneurship, finance, health services, human resources management, international business, marketing.

Faculty Full-time: 42, 100% with doctorates; part-time: 5.

Teaching Methodology Case study: 5%, lecture: 68%, research: 7%, student presentations: 10%, team projects: 10%.

Special Opportunities Internship program available.

STUDENT STATISTICS

Geographic Representation State residents 87%. By region: Northeast 90%. International 10%.

Other Background Graduate degrees in other disciplines: 10%. Work experience: On average, students have 2 years of work experience on entrance to the program.

FACILITIES

Information Resources Main library with 393,376 bound volumes, 52,968 titles on microform, 1,394 periodical subscriptions, 1,730 records/tapes/CDs, 92 CD-ROMs.

Housing College housing not available.

Technology Computers are used moderately in course work. 200 computer terminals/PCs, linked by a campus-wide computer network, are available for use by students in program; they are located in the library, the computer center. Students in the program are not required to have their own PC.

Computer Resources/On-line Services

Training	Yes	CompuServe	No
Internet	Yes	Dun's	No
E-Mail	Yes	Dow Jones	No
Videoconference Center	Yes	Dialog	No
LEXIS/NEXIS	No	Bloomberg	No

ADMISSION

Entrance Requirements Bachelor's degree, GMAT score of 400. Core courses waived through: previous course work.

Application Requirements Application form, copies of transcript, resume/curriculum vitae, personal statement, 2 letters of recommendation.

Application Deadlines 7/15 for fall, 12/1 for spring, 4/1 for summer. Applications are processed on a rolling basis.

FINANCIALS

Costs for 1994-95 Tuition: Full-time: $179/credit hour for state residents, $210/credit hour for nonresidents. Fees: Full-time: $60-$180/course for state residents, $60-$180/course for nonresidents. Average room and board costs are $4,200 per academic year (off-campus).

Financial Aid In 1994-95, candidates received some institutionally administered aid in the form of grants, scholarships, loans, fellowships, assistantships, work-study. Financial aid is available to part-time students. Application deadlines: 4/1 for fall, 11/1 for spring. Applications are processed on a rolling basis. Contact: Ms. Anna Breland, Director of Financial Aid, 1420 North Charles Street, Baltimore, MD 21201-5779. (410) 837-4763.

INTERNATIONAL STUDENTS

Demographics 10% of students enrolled in the program are international; Asia 50%, Europe 10%, Africa 5%, South America 5%, Central America 4%, North America 1%, other 25%.

Services and Facilities International student office, visa services, counseling/support services.

Applying TOEFL required, minimum score of 550; proof of adequate funds. Financial aid is available to international students. Financial aid application deadline: 4/1 for fall. Admission application deadlines: 6/1 for fall, 12/1 for spring, 4/1 for summer. Applications are processed on a rolling basis. Contact: Ms. Wendy Burgess, International Student Adviser, 1420 North Charles Street, Baltimore, MD 21201-5779. (410) 625-3157.

ALTERNATE MBA PROGRAMS

MBA/JD Length of program: Minimum: 60 months. Maximum: 7 years. Part-time classes: Main campus; evening, weekends, summer. Degree requirements: 81 credits including 12 elective credits. Must meet law school admission requirements.

MBA/MSN Length of program: Minimum: 36 months. Maximum: 7 years. Part-time classes: Main campus, University of Maryland at Baltimore; evening, weekends, summer. Degree requirements: 85 credits. Must meet University of Maryland School of Nursing admission requirements.

PLACEMENT

In 1993-94, 44 organizations participated in on-campus recruiting. Placement services include alumni network, career counseling/planning, career fairs, career library, career placement, electronic job bank, job interviews, resume preparation, resume referral to employers.

Program Contact: Mrs. Tracey Jamison, Assistant Director of Graduate Admissions, University of Baltimore, 1420 North Charles Street, Baltimore, MD 21201-5779. (410) 837-4809; Fax: (410) 837-4820; Internet Address: tjamison@ubalt.edu.

University of Maryland College Park

The Maryland Business School

College Park, Maryland

OVERVIEW

The University of Maryland College Park is a state-supported coed institution. Part of University of Maryland System. Founded 1856. Setting: 1,378-acre suburban campus with easy access to Baltimore and Washington, DC. Total institutional enrollment: 34,000. Program was first offered in 1948. AACSB-accredited.

MBA HIGHLIGHTS

Entrance Difficulty***
Mean GMAT: 625
Mean GPA: 3.25

Cost $$
Tuition: $5,040 - $6,300
(Nonresident: $8,760 - $10,950)
Room & Board: $7,500

Enrollment Profile

Full-time: 271	Work Exp: 90%
Part-time: 424	International: 35%
Total: 695	Women: 35%
Average Age: 27	Minorities: 28%

Average Class Size: 29

ACADEMICS

Length of Program Minimum: 19 months. Maximum: 5 years.

Calendar Semesters.

Full-time Classes Main campus; day, evening, early morning, summer.

Part-time Classes Main campus; evening, summer.

Degree Requirements 54 credits including 21 elective credits.

Required Courses Business communications, decision analysis and modeling, financial cost accounting, financial management, global economic environment, group field project, human resources management, managerial accounting, managerial economics and public policy, managerial statistics, marketing management, organizational behavior, strategic information systems, strategic management.

Curricular Focus Entrepreneurship, information technology, international business.

Concentrations Accounting, entrepreneurship, finance, human resources management, international business, management, management information systems, marketing, operations management, organizational behavior, public policy, quantitative analysis, strategic management, transportation.

Faculty Full-time: 80, 100% with doctorates; part-time: 20, 90% with doctorates.

Teaching Methodology Case study: 55%, lecture: 15%, student presentations: 10%.

Special Opportunities International exchange in Australia, Chile, France, Hong Kong, Mexico, Norway, Venezuela. Internship program available. Other: experiential learning modules.

STUDENT STATISTICS

Geographic Representation State residents 37%. International 35%.

Undergraduate Majors Business 24%; education 2%; engineering/technology 20%; humanities 9%; nursing 2%; science/mathematics 16%; social sciences 11%; other 16%.

Other Background Graduate degrees in other disciplines: 14%. Work experience: On average, students have 4 years of work experience on entrance to the program.

FACILITIES

Information Resources Main library with 2.2 million bound volumes, 4.9 million titles on microform, 19,433 periodical subscriptions, 13,400 records/tapes/CDs.

Housing 10% of students in program live in college-owned or -operated housing. Assistance with housing search provided.

Technology Computers are used heavily in course work. 1,500 computer terminals/PCs, linked by a campus-wide computer network, are available for use by students in program; they are located in classrooms, the library, the computer center, computer labs, MBA lounge. Students in the program are not required to have their own PC.

Computer Resources/On-line Services

Training	Yes	CompuServe	Yes
Internet	Yes	Dun's	Yes
E-Mail	Yes	Dow Jones	Yes
Videoconference Center	Yes	Dialog	Yes
Multimedia Center	Yes	Bloomberg	Yes
LEXIS/NEXIS	Yes		

ADMISSION

Acceptance 1994-95 1,250 applied for admission; 19% were accepted.

Entrance Requirements Bachelor's degree, calculus, GMAT score. Core courses waived through: previous course work.

Application Requirements Written essay, application form, copies of transcript, resume/curriculum vitae, 2 letters of recommendation.

Application Deadlines 5/15 for fall. Applications are processed on a rolling basis.

FINANCIALS

Costs for 1994-95 Tuition: Full-time: $5,040-$6,300 for state residents, $8,760-$10,950 for nonresidents. Fees: Full-time: $807 for state residents, $807 for nonresidents. Average room and board costs are $7,500 per academic year (on-campus) and $8,000 per academic year (off-campus).

Financial Aid In 1994-95, 40% of candidates received some institutionally administered aid in the form of scholarships, fellowships, assistantships. Total awards ranged from $1,000-$21,000. Financial aid is available to part-time students. Application deadline: 2/1 for fall. Applications are processed on a rolling basis. Contact: Ms. Florfina Rivera, Director of Financial Aid, Lee Building, College Park, MD 20742. (301) 314-8315.

INTERNATIONAL STUDENTS

Demographics 35% of students enrolled in the program are international; Asia 55%, Europe 15%, Africa 5%, Central America 5%, South America 5%, other 15%.

Services and Facilities International student office, language tutoring, ESL courses, special assistance for nonnative speakers of English.

Applying TOEFL required, minimum score of 580; proof of health; proof of adequate funds. Financial aid is available to international students. Financial aid application deadline: 2/1 for fall. Applications are processed on a rolling basis. Admission application deadline: 2/1 for fall. Applications are processed on a rolling basis. Contact: Mrs. Barbara Varsa, Assistant Director, International Educational Services, Room 3117, Mitchell Building, College Park, MD 20742. (301) 314-7745.

PLACEMENT

Placement services include alumni network, career counseling/planning, career fairs, career library, career placement, electronic job bank, job interviews, job search course, resume preparation, and resume referral to employers. Of 1994 graduates, 92% were employed within three months of graduation, the average starting salary was $46,000, the range was $31,000-$120,000.

Jobs by Employer Type Manufacturing 2%; service 10%; government 11%; consulting 24%; nonprofit 3%; financial services 21%; high technology 11%; other 15%.

Jobs by Functional Area Marketing/sales 17%; finance 33%; operations 3%; management 11%; strategic planning 9%; technical management 14%; other 10%.

Program Contact: Mr. Hayden Estrada, IV, Director, MBA/MS Admission, University of Maryland College Park, College Park, MD 20742. (301) 405-2278; Fax: (301) 314-9862; Internet Address: hestrada@bmgtmail.umd.edu.

See full description on page 890.

MASSACHUSETTS

American International College

Springfield, Massachusetts

OVERVIEW

American International College is an independent nonprofit comprehensive coed institution. Founded 1885. Setting: 58-acre urban campus. Total institutional enrollment: 1,825.

ACADEMICS

Calendar Semesters.

Concentrations Accounting, finance, management, marketing.

FACILITIES

Information Resources Main library with 118,000 bound volumes, 83,700 titles on microform, 390 periodical subscriptions, 1,140 records/tapes/CDs.

ADMISSION

Entrance Requirements Bachelor's degree.

Application Requirements Application form, copies of transcript, 2 letters of recommendation.

Application Deadline Applications are processed on a rolling basis.

INTERNATIONAL STUDENTS
Applying Admission applications are processed on a rolling basis.

Program Contact: Mr. Peter Miller, Dean of Admissions, American International College, 1000 State Street, Springfield, MA 01109-3189. (413) 737-7000 Ext. 201, or (800) 242-3142 (MA only); Fax: (413) 737-2803.

Anna Maria College

Paxton, Massachusetts

OVERVIEW
Anna Maria College is an independent Roman Catholic comprehensive coed institution. Founded 1946. Setting: 180-acre small-town campus with easy access to Boston. Total institutional enrollment: 1,719. Program was first offered in 1974.

MBA HIGHLIGHTS

Entrance Difficulty N/R
Mean GMAT: 490
Mean GPA: N/R

Cost $
Tuition: $595/course
Room & Board: N/R

Enrollment Profile

Full-time: 0	Work Exp: 85%
Part-time: 250	International: 3%
Total: 250	Women: 40%
Average Age: N/R	Minorities: N/R

Average Class Size: 18

ACADEMICS
Length of Program Minimum: 15 months.
Calendar 4-1-4.
Part-time Classes Main campus; evening, weekends, summer.
Degree Requirements 12 courses including 3 elective courses.
Curricular Focus Business issues and problems, leadership, problem solving and decision making.
Concentrations Health services, management.

STUDENT STATISTICS
Geographic Representation State residents 98%. International 3%.
Undergraduate Majors Business 75%; education 5%; engineering/technology 5%; nursing 15%.

FACILITIES
Information Resources Main library with 82,074 bound volumes, 1,526 titles on microform, 284 periodical subscriptions, 3,500 records/tapes/CDs.
Housing 5% of students in program live in college-owned or -operated housing.
Technology Computers are used moderately in course work. 40 computer terminals/PCs, linked by a campus-wide computer network, are available for use by students in program; they are located in learning resource center, the library, computer labs. Students in the program are not required to have their own PC.
Computer Resources/On-line Services
E-Mail   Yes

ADMISSION
Entrance Requirements Bachelor's degree, prerequisite courses required for applicants with non-business degree, GMAT score of 475, minimum 2.6 GPA. Core courses waived through: previous course work.
Application Requirements Interview, application form, copies of transcript, resume/curriculum vitae, 3 letters of recommendation.
Application Deadline Applications are processed on a rolling basis.

FINANCIALS
Costs for 1994-95 Tuition: Part-time day: $595/course. Fees: Part-time day: $30/semester.

Financial Aid In 1994-95, candidates received some institutionally administered aid in the form of loans. Application deadline: 5/1 for fall. Contact: Financial Aid Office, Sunset Lane, Paxton, MA 01612. (508) 849-3366.

INTERNATIONAL STUDENTS
Demographics 3% of students enrolled in the program are international.
Applying TOEFL required, minimum score of 500; proof of health; proof of adequate funds. Financial aid is available to international students. Applications are processed on a rolling basis. Admission applications are processed on a rolling basis. Contact: Sr. Pauline Madore, Director, ESL, Sunset Lane, Paxton, MA 01612. (508) 849-3357.

Program Contact: Mrs. Betty Campbell, MBA Assistant, Anna Maria College, Sunset Lane, Paxton, MA 01612. (508) 849-3348, or (800) 344-1154 (MA only), or (800) 344-4586 (out-of-state).

Arthur D. Little Management Education Institute

Cambridge, Massachusetts

OVERVIEW
Arthur D. Little Management Education Institute is graduate-only institution. Founded 1973. Setting: suburban campus. Total institutional enrollment: 68.

PROGRAM HIGHLIGHTS

Entrance Difficulty***

Cost $$$$$
Tuition: $27,525
Room & Board: N/R

Enrollment Profile

Full-time: N/R	Work Exp: N/R
Part-time: N/R	International: 93%
Total: 68	Women: 25%
Average Age: N/R	Minorities: N/R

Average Class Size: 65

ACADEMICS
Calendar Phases.
Curricular Focus Managing diversity, problem solving and decision making, teamwork.
Concentration International development management.
Teaching Methodology Case study: 60%, faculty seminars: 5%, lecture: 20%, seminars by members of the business community: 5%, student presentations: 10%.

STUDENT STATISTICS
Geographic Representation International 93%.

FACILITIES
Information Resources Main library with 30,000 bound volumes, 2,500 periodical subscriptions.

ADMISSION
Acceptance 1994-95 140 applied for admission; 71% were accepted.
Entrance Requirements Bachelor's degree, minimum 5 years of work experience.
Application Requirements Written essay, application form, copies of transcript, 3 letters of recommendation.
Application Deadline Applications are processed on a rolling basis.

FINANCIALS
Costs for 1995-96 Tuition: Full-time: $27,525. Fees: Full-time: $1,800.
Financial Aid Application deadline: 6/1 for fall. Applications are processed on a rolling basis. Contact: Ms. Judith H. Francis, Director of Admissions, 35 Acorn Park, Cambridge, MA 02140. (617) 498-6268.

INTERNATIONAL STUDENTS
Demographics 93% of students enrolled in the program are international.
Services and Facilities International student office, visa services, language tutoring, ESL courses, special assistance for nonnative speakers of English, counseling/support services, ESL work shops.
Applying TOEFL required, minimum score of 550; proof of health; proof of adequate funds. Financial aid is not available to international students.

Admission applications are processed on a rolling basis. Contact: Ms. Anne Khudari, Director of Participant Affairs, 35 Acorn Park, Cambridge, MA 02140. (617) 498-6284.

PROGRAM
MSM Length of program: Minimum: 11 months. Full-time classes: Main campus; day, summer. Degree requirements: 53.5 credits. Industry research project.

PLACEMENT
Placement services include alumni network, career counseling/planning, career fairs, career library, career placement, job interviews, resume preparation, and resume referral to employers.

Program Contact: Ms. Judith H. Francis, Director of Admissions, Arthur D. Little Management Education Institute, 35 Acorn Park, Cambridge, MA 02140. (617) 498-6268; Fax: (617) 498-7100.
See full description on page 666.

Assumption College

Department of Business Studies

Worcester, Massachusetts

OVERVIEW
Assumption College is an independent Roman Catholic comprehensive coed institution. Founded 1904. Setting: 150-acre suburban campus with easy access to Boston. Total institutional enrollment: 2,500. Program was first offered in 1984.

MBA HIGHLIGHTS

Entrance Difficulty**
Mean GMAT: 450
Mean GPA: 3.0

Cost $
Tuition: $267/credit hour
Room & Board: N/R

Enrollment Profile
Full-time: 10	Work Exp: 85%
Part-time: 110	International: N/R
Total: 120	Women: 40%
Average Age: 35	Minorities: 15%

Average Class Size: 15

ACADEMICS
Length of Program Minimum: 30 months. Maximum: 7 years.
Calendar Semesters.
Part-time Classes Main campus; evening, summer.
Degree Requirements 36 credits including 18 elective credits.
Required Courses Business ethics, business policy, financial strategy development, human and organizational behavior, marketing strategy development, operations strategy development.
Curricular Focus General management, international business, problem solving and decision making.
Concentrations Accounting, international business, management, marketing.
Faculty Full-time: 14, 36% with doctorates; part-time: 5, 40% with doctorates.
Special Opportunities Internships include management.

STUDENT STATISTICS
Geographic Representation By region: Northeast 100%.
Undergraduate Majors Business 70%; engineering/technology 10%; nursing 5%; science/mathematics 5%; social sciences 10%.
Other Background Graduate degrees in other disciplines: 5%. Work experience: On average, students have 5 years of work experience on entrance to the program.

FACILITIES
Information Resources Main library with 198,000 bound volumes, 8,000 titles on microform, 1,250 periodical subscriptions, 9 CD-ROMs.
Housing College housing not available.
Technology Computers are used moderately in course work. 50 computer terminals/PCs are available for use by students in program; they are

located in the library, computer labs. Students in the program are not required to have their own PC.

Computer Resources/On-line Services
Training	No	Multimedia Center	Yes
Videoconference Center	Yes		

ADMISSION
Acceptance 1994-95 Of those applying, 90% were accepted.
Entrance Requirements Bachelor's degree, GMAT score. Core courses waived through: previous course work.
Application Requirements Written essay, application form, copies of transcript, 2 letters of recommendation.
Application Deadline Applications are processed on a rolling basis.

FINANCIALS
Costs for 1994-95 Tuition: Full-time: $267/credit hour; Part-time day: $801/course.
Financial Aid Financial aid is not available to part-time students. Application deadline: 3/1 for fall. Contact: Ms. Anne Moody, Secretary, Graduate Studies Office, Worcester, MA 01615. (508) 767-7387.

INTERNATIONAL STUDENTS
Applying TOEFL required; proof of health; proof of adequate funds. Financial aid is not available to international students. Admission applications are processed on a rolling basis.

PLACEMENT
Placement services include career counseling/planning, job interviews, resume preparation, and resume referral to employers.

Program Contact: Ms. Anne Moody, Secretary of Graduate Studies, Assumption College, Graduate Studies Office, 500 Salisbury Street, Worcester, MA 01615-0005. (508) 767-7387; Fax: (508) 756-1780.

Babson College

Babson Graduate School of Business

Wellesley, Massachusetts

OVERVIEW
Babson College is an independent nonprofit comprehensive specialized coed institution. Founded 1919. Setting: 450-acre suburban campus with easy access to Boston. Total institutional enrollment: 3,263. Program was first offered in 1951. AACSB-accredited.

MBA HIGHLIGHTS

Entrance Difficulty****
Mean GMAT: 585
Mean GPA: 3.1

Cost $$$$
Tuition: $20,000
Room & Board: $8,913

Enrollment Profile
Full-time: 320	Work Exp: 100%
Part-time: 1,277	International: 33%
Total: 1,597	Women: 33%
Average Age: 28	Minorities: 4%

Average Class Size: 34

G roundbreaking for Babson's new graduate school building is targeted for fall 1995. Designed in response to the requirements of the new two-year M.B.A. curriculum, the facility will include designated rooms for each first-year mentor team where the team members can work on their group assignments and, on occasion, host their business mentor representatives. In addition, there will be six interactive classrooms, one large classroom for 100 students, a lecture hall for 200, and a computer lab. An adjacent area containing temporary offices for faculty members to use while they teach in a module will enhance faculty communication.

Entrepreneurial incubator space, which students can use to start and grow businesses, will be available through a competitive application process. Other rooms are designed for group-study, seminars, and the Graduate Student Association (GSA).

Babson's long tradition of emphasizing the global aspects of business continues today with the international concentration and the thriving

International Management Internship Program (IMIP). The international concentration is available to all M.B.A. program participants. The IMIP has inspired M.B.A. graduates to start their careers overseas, some having accepted jobs directly with their IMIP companies, others through connections made while on an IMIP.

ACADEMICS
Length of Program Minimum: 21 months. Maximum: 8 years.

Calendar Semesters.

Full-time Classes Main campus; day.

Part-time Classes Main campus; evening, summer.

Degree Requirements 62 credits including 27 elective credits.

Required Courses Accounting and financial decision making, data analysis and modeling, global trends, historical perspective of business development, law, macroeconomic reasoning and applications, management of change, management of information technology, management of innovation, managing organizational effectiveness, managing values, marketing management in the emerging organization, microeconomic reasoning and applications, the global mind, total quality management, writing and speaking for managers.

Curricular Focus Entrepreneurship, international business, teamwork.

Concentrations Accounting, entrepreneurship, finance, international business, marketing.

Faculty Full-time: 123, 96% with doctorates; part-time: 52.

Teaching Methodology Case study: 70%, lecture: 15%, team projects: 15%.

Special Opportunities International exchange in France, Japan, Norway, Spain, United Kingdom. Internships include communications, finance, consumer products, and healthcare. Other: management consulting field experience, international electives.

STUDENT STATISTICS
Geographic Representation By region: Northeast 91%. International 33%.

Undergraduate Majors Business 27%; engineering/technology 15%; humanities 15%; science/mathematics 12%; social sciences 15%; other 16%.

Other Background Graduate degrees in other disciplines: 5%.

FACILITIES
Information Resources Main library with 120,942 bound volumes, 345,947 titles on microform, 1,400 periodical subscriptions, 1,944 records/tapes/CDs, 1,219 CD-ROMs.

Housing 33% of students in program live in college-owned or -operated housing.

Technology Computers are used moderately in course work. 160 computer terminals/PCs, linked by a campus-wide computer network, are available for use by students in program; they are located in classrooms, learning resource center, the library, the computer center, computer labs. Students in the program are not required to have their own PC. $445 are budgeted per student for computer support.

Computer Resources/On-line Services
Training	Yes	CompuServe	Yes
Internet	Yes	Dun's	Yes
E-Mail	Yes	Dow Jones	Yes $
Multimedia Center	Yes	Dialog	Yes $
LEXIS/NEXIS	Yes		

Other on-line services: First Search, Datastar, SEC.

ADMISSION
Acceptance 1994-95 853 applied for admission; 60% were accepted.

Entrance Requirements Bachelor's degree, GMAT score, minimum 2 years of work experience. Core courses waived through: previous course work.

Application Requirements Written essay, interview, application form, copies of transcript, personal statement, 2 letters of recommendation.

Application Deadlines 5/1 for fall, 12/1 for spring, 6/15 for summer, 2/15 for one-year MBA.

FINANCIALS
Costs for 1994-95 Tuition: Full-time: $20,000; Part-time evening: $1,810/course. Average room and board costs are $8,913 per academic year (on-campus) and $8,913 per academic year (off-campus).

Financial Aid In 1994-95, 21% of candidates received some institutionally administered aid in the form of scholarships, loans, fellowships, assistantships, work-study. Total awards ranged from $3,450-$17,920. Financial aid is available to part-time students. Application deadlines: 5/1

for fall, 12/1 for spring, 6/15 for summer, 2/15 for one year MBA. Contact: Mr. Keith Conant, Associate Director, Office of Financial Aid, Babson Park, MA 02157-0310. (617) 239-4219.

INTERNATIONAL STUDENTS
Demographics 33% of students enrolled in the program are international; South America 41%, Asia 34%, Europe 22%, Africa 3%.

Services and Facilities Language tutoring.

Applying TOEFL required, minimum score of 580; proof of health; proof of adequate funds. Financial aid is available to international students. Financial aid application deadline: 4/1 for fall. Admission application deadlines: 4/1 for fall, 2/15 for one-year MBA.

ALTERNATE MBA PROGRAM
One-Year MBA Length of program: Minimum: 12 months. Maximum: 8 years. Degree requirements: 45 credits including 18 elective credits.

PLACEMENT
In 1993-94, 67 organizations participated in on-campus recruiting; 161 on-campus interviews were conducted. Placement services include alumni network, career counseling/planning, career fairs, career library, career placement, job interviews, resume preparation, and resume referral to employers. Of 1994 graduates, 82% were employed within three months of graduation, the average starting salary was $44,375, the range was $20,000-$84,000.

Program Contact: Mr. William G. Makris, Associate Dean, Director of Admissions, Babson College, Office of Graduate Admissions, Babson Park, MA 02157-0310. (617) 239-4317, or (800) 488-4512; Fax: (617) 239-4194.

See full description on page 668.

Bentley College

Waltham, Massachusetts

OVERVIEW
Bentley College is an independent nonprofit comprehensive coed institution. Founded 1917. Setting: 110-acre suburban campus with easy access to Boston. Total institutional enrollment: 6,815. Program was first offered in 1980. AACSB-accredited.

MBA HIGHLIGHTS

Entrance Difficulty*
Mean GMAT: 520
Mean GPA: 3.1

Cost $$$
Tuition: $1,650/course
Room & Board: $6,400

Enrollment Profile
Full-time: 142	Work Exp: 80%
Part-time: 1,070	International: 5%
Total: 1,212	Women: 44%
Average Age: 27	Minorities: 4%

Class Size: 30 - 35

Bentley College Graduate School of Business offers the M.B.A. degree with eleven areas of concentration: accountancy, advanced accountancy, business communication, business economics, finance, international business, management, management information systems, marketing, operations management, and taxation. The M.B.A. is designed for both full- and part-time students who want to acquire a broad educational base for enhancing, changing, or launching a career in management as well as for those who already have a specialization in business and wish to broaden their perspective in general management. A full-time student with full advanced standing may complete the M.B.A. program in one year. The College also offers an advanced graduate business certificate and Master of Science programs in accountancy, business economics, computer information systems, finance and taxation.

ACADEMICS
Length of Program Minimum: 12 months. Maximum: 7 years.

Calendar Semesters.

Full-time Classes Main campus; day, evening, weekends, early morning, summer.

Part-time Classes Main campus; day, evening, weekends, early morning, summer.

Degree Requirements 30 credits including 24 elective credits.

Required Courses Accounting for decision making, analytical methods for managerial decisions, competing in a global marketplace: analysis of the business environment, economic environment of the firm, financial statement analysis for decision making, human behavior in the organization, information technology in the business environment, management systems in a changing environment, marketing management, marketplace: strategy and implementation, operations management. Courses may be waived through: previous course work.

Curricular Focus General management, international business, organizational development and change management.

Concentrations Accounting, advanced accounting, business communication, taxation, economics, finance, international business, management, management information systems, marketing, operations management.

Faculty Full-time: 108, 75% with doctorates; part-time: 32, 25% with doctorates.

Teaching Methodology Case study: 40%, lecture: 30%, research: 1%, seminars by members of the business community: 1%, simulations: 8%, student presentations: 10%, team projects: 10%.

Special Opportunities International exchange in Japan. Internships include accounting, banking, health care, government, and advertising.

STUDENT STATISTICS
Geographic Representation State residents 81%. By region: Northeast 91%. International 5%.

Undergraduate Majors Business 68%; engineering/technology 16%; social sciences 16%.

Other Background Graduate degrees in other disciplines: 10%. Work experience: On average, students have 5 years of work experience on entrance to the program.

FACILITIES
Information Resources Main library with 192,566 bound volumes, 219,000 titles on microform, 2,606 periodical subscriptions, 4,400 records/tapes/CDs, 5 CD-ROMs.

Housing College housing available.

Technology Computers are used moderately in course work. 95 computer terminals/PCs, linked by a campus-wide computer network, are available for use by students in program; they are located in classrooms, the computer center, computer labs. Students in the program are not required to have their own PC.

Computer Resources/On-line Services

Training	Yes	CompuServe	No
Internet	Yes	Dun's	Yes
E-Mail	Yes	Dow Jones	Yes
Videoconference Center	Yes	Dialog	Yes
Multimedia Center	Yes	Bloomberg	Yes
LEXIS/NEXIS	Yes		

Other on-line services: OCLC.

ADMISSION
Acceptance 1994-95 1,202 applied for admission; 65% were accepted.

Entrance Requirements Bachelor's degree, GMAT score. Core courses waived through: previous course work.

Application Requirements Written essay, application form, copies of transcript.

Application Deadlines 6/15 for fall, 11/1 for spring.

FINANCIALS
Costs for 1994-95 Tuition: Full-time: $1,650/course; Part-time day: $1,650/course. Fees: Full-time: $50; Part-time day: $20. Average room and board costs are $6,400 per academic year (on-campus) and $8,400 per academic year (off-campus).

Financial Aid In 1994-95, 14% of candidates received some institutionally administered aid in the form of grants, scholarships, loans, assistantships, work-study, stipends. Total awards ranged from $500-$13,200. Financial aid is available to part-time students. Application deadlines: 6/1 for fall, 11/1 for spring. Contact: Ms. Linda Gillett, Assistant Director of Financial Assistance, Rauch 208, Waltham, MA 02154-4705. (617) 891-3168.

INTERNATIONAL STUDENTS
Demographics 5% of students enrolled in the program are international; Asia 50%, Europe 27%, South America 7%, Central America 6%, Africa 3%, Australia 1%, other 8%.

Services and Facilities International student center, visa services, language tutoring, ESL courses, special assistance for nonnative speakers of English, counseling/support services, international friendship program.

Applying TOEFL required, minimum score of 580; proof of health; proof of adequate funds; international student data form. Financial aid is not available to international students. Admission application deadlines: 6/15 for fall, 11/1 for spring. Contact: Ms. Jan Newell, Director of International Student Services, Intercultural Center, LaCava #245, Waltham, MA 02154-4705. (617) 891-2829.

PLACEMENT
In 1993-94, 84 organizations participated in on-campus recruiting; 452 on-campus interviews were conducted. Placement services include alumni network, career counseling/planning, career fairs, career library, career placement, electronic job bank, job interviews, resume preparation, and resume referral to employers. Of 1994 graduates, the average starting salary was $47,333, the range was $12,000-$120,000.

Jobs by Employer Type Manufacturing 51%; service 40%; government 2%; consulting 3%; nonprofit 3%.

Jobs by Functional Area Marketing/sales 11%; finance 55%; operations 6%; management 12%; strategic planning 2%; other 15%.

Program Contact: Ms. Sharon Oliver, Director of Graduate Admissions, Bentley College, 175 Forest Street, Waltham, MA 02154-4705. (617) 891-2108, or (800) 442-4723; Fax: (617) 891-2464.

See full description on page 676.

Boston College

Wallace E. Carroll Graduate School of Management

Chestnut Hill, Massachusetts

OVERVIEW
Boston College is an independent Roman Catholic (Jesuit) coed institution. Founded 1863. Setting: 240-acre suburban campus with easy access to Boston. Total institutional enrollment: 14,500. Program was first offered in 1958. AACSB-accredited.

MBA HIGHLIGHTS

Entrance Difficulty**
Mean GMAT: 565
Mean GPA: 3.1

Cost $$$$
Tuition: $17,794
Room & Board: N/R

Enrollment Profile

Full-time: 200	Work Exp: 93%
Part-time: 450	International: 30%
Total: 650	Women: 35%
Average Age: 27	Minorities: 10%

Average Class Size: 40

ACADEMICS
Length of Program Minimum: 21 months. Maximum: 6 years.

Calendar Semesters.

Full-time Classes Main campus; evening, summer.

Part-time Classes Main campus; evening, summer.

Degree Requirements 55 credits including 18 elective credits.

Required Courses Accounting, computer information systems, economics, financial management, international management, marketing, operations management, organizational behavior, perspectives in management, social issues in management, statistics, strategic management. Courses may be waived through: previous course work.

Curricular Focus Hands-on approach, problem solving and decision making, teamwork.

Concentrations Accounting, consulting, entrepreneurship, finance, international business, management, marketing, operations management, organizational behavior, strategic management.

Faculty Full-time: 70, 84% with doctorates; part-time: 17, 35% with doctorates.

Teaching Methodology Case study: 25%, lecture: 25%, projects with local businesses: 15%, seminars by members of the business community: 10%, student presentations: 5%, team projects: 20%.

Special Opportunities International exchange in France, Ireland, New Zealand, Spain. Internship program available.

STUDENT STATISTICS
Geographic Representation By region: Northeast 59%; South 5%; West 4%; Midwest 2%. International 30%.

Other Background Work experience: On average, students have 4 years of work experience on entrance to the program.

FACILITIES
Information Resources Main library with 1.4 million bound volumes, 2.4 million titles on microform, 15,075 periodical subscriptions, 19,581 records/tapes/CDs.

Housing College housing not available.

Technology Computers are used moderately in course work. 180 computer terminals/PCs, linked by a campus-wide computer network, are available for use by students in program; they are located in the library, the computer center, computer labs. Students in the program are not required to have their own PC.

Computer Resources/On-line Services

Training	Yes	LEXIS/NEXIS	Yes
Internet	Yes	Dow Jones	Yes
E-Mail	Yes		

ADMISSION
Acceptance 1994-95 897 applied for admission, 61% were accepted.

Entrance Requirements Bachelor's degree, GMAT score of 500. Core courses waived through: previous course work.

Application Requirements Written essay, application form, copies of transcript, resume/curriculum vitae, 2 letters of recommendation.

Application Deadlines 4/1 for fall, 11/15 for spring.

FINANCIALS
Costs for 1995-96 Tuition: Full-time: $17,794; Part-time evening: $612/credit hour.

Financial Aid In 1994-95, candidates received some institutionally administered aid in the form of grants, scholarships, loans, assistantships, work-study. Financial aid is available to part-time students. Application deadlines: 3/1 for fall, 11/15 for spring. Contact: Ms. Lindsay Carlisle, Program Director, Graduate and Law Financial Aid, Lyons Hall 120, 140 Commonwealth Avenue, Chestnut Hill, MA 02167. (617) 552-4982.

INTERNATIONAL STUDENTS
Demographics 30% of students enrolled in the program are international; Asia 42%, Europe 28%, South America 10%, Central America 3%, Africa 2%, other 15%.

Services and Facilities International student center, visa services, language tutoring, counseling/support services.

Applying TOEFL required, minimum score of 600; proof of health; proof of adequate funds. Financial aid is available to international students. Financial aid application deadline: 3/1 for fall. Admission application deadline: 3/1 for fall. Contact: Ms. Adrienne J. Nussbaum, Director for International Student Services, Office of the Dean for Student Development, McElroy 114, Chestnut Hill, MA 02167. (617) 552-8005.

ALTERNATE MBA PROGRAMS
MBA/JD Length of program: Minimum: 48 months. Maximum: 6 years. Degree requirements: 116 credits including 52 elective credits.

MBA/MSN Length of program: Minimum: 36 months. Maximum: 6 years. Degree requirements: 80 credits including 30 elective credits.

MBA/MSW Length of program: Minimum: 36 months. Maximum: 6 years. Degree requirements: 80 credits including 30 elective credits.

PLACEMENT
In 1993-94, 70 organizations participated in on-campus recruiting; 138 on-campus interviews were conducted. Placement services include career counseling/planning, career fairs, career library, career placement, job interviews, resume preparation, and resume referral to employers. Of 1994 graduates, 74% were employed within three months of graduation, the average starting salary was $50,616, the range was $32,000-$135,000.

Jobs by Functional Area Marketing/sales 15%; finance 50%; operations 7%; management 15%; consulting 13%.

Program Contact: Ms. Simone Marthers, Director of Admissions, Boston College, 140 Commonwealth Avenue, Chestnut Hill, MA 02167. (617) 552-3920; Fax: (617) 552-8078.
See full description on page 680.

See full description on page 680.

Boston University

School of Management

Boston, Massachusetts

OVERVIEW
Boston University is an independent nonprofit coed institution. Founded 1839. Setting: 126-acre urban campus. Total institutional enrollment: 28,594. Program was first offered in 1913. AACSB-accredited.

MBA HIGHLIGHTS

Entrance Difficulty****
Mean GMAT: 580
Mean GPA: 3.1

Cost $$$$
Tuition: $18,420
Room & Board: $11,560

Enrollment Profile

Full-time: 600	Work Exp. 95%
Part-time: 900	International: 33%
Total: 1,500	Women: 40%
Average Age: 27	Minorities: 9%

Average Class Size: 35

At Boston University's School of Management (SMG), the teaching of management is being uniquely transformed. The School seeks to create a class of managers and leaders equipped with the mind-set, the skills, and the perspectives required in an increasingly global and competitive environment. SMG graduates are trained to deal with the potential and the limitations inherent in management control systems and with the human resource systems required for effective organizational performance. Boston University's School of Management is preeminent for producing broadly educated graduates with inquiring minds whose operating orientation is one of business building and adding value. In addition to their functional specializations, SMG graduates approach management issues with an understanding of the interdependencies within organizational systems. This approach is rooted in a comprehensive grasp of the concepts and skills for total quality management. Students who wish to be challenged and intellectually stimulated are invited to consider Boston University's School of Management.

ACADEMICS
Length of Program Minimum: 24 months. Maximum: 6 years.

Calendar Semesters.

Full-time Classes Main campus; day, evening, summer.

Part-time Classes Main campus, Tyngsboro; day, evening, summer.

Degree Requirements 64 credits including 26 elective credits.

Required Courses Financial accounting, financial management, managerial accounting, managerial data analysis, market research, marketing management, microeconomics, operations management, quantitative decision making, the global environment, the global managers, the global organization.

Curricular Focus General management, international business, teamwork.

Concentrations Accounting, economics, entrepreneurship, finance, health services, human resources management, international business, management, management information systems, marketing, operations management, organizational behavior, public administration, public policy, strategic management.

Faculty Full-time: 96, 92% with doctorates; part-time: 80, 24% with doctorates.

Teaching Methodology Case study: 40%, faculty seminars: 5%, field projects: 10%, lecture: 20%, research: 5%, seminars by members of the business community: 5%, student presentations: 5%, team projects: 10%.

Special Opportunities International exchange in France, Japan, United Kingdom. Internships include product marketing in high technology/

telecommunications, finance in investment banking, marketing/policy/ finance in healthcare, accounting in government, and information systems in consulting.

STUDENT STATISTICS

Geographic Representation By region: Northeast 90%; West 6%; South 2%; Midwest 2%. International 33%.

Undergraduate Majors Business 39%; engineering/technology 17%; humanities 11%; science/mathematics 7%; social sciences 26%.

Other Background Work experience: On average, students have 3-5 years of work experience on entrance to the program.

FACILITIES

Information Resources Main library with 1.9 million bound volumes, 3.2 million titles on microform, 28,795 periodical subscriptions, 71,000 records/tapes/CDs, 350 CD-ROMs.

Housing 15% of students in program live in college-owned or -operated housing. Assistance with housing search provided.

Technology 110 computer terminals/PCs are available for use by students in program; they are located in computer labs. Students in the program are not required to have their own PC.

Computer Resources/On-line Services

Training	Yes	Dun's	No
Internet	Yes	Dow Jones	Yes
E-Mail	Yes	Dialog	No
LEXIS/NEXIS	Yes	Bloomberg	No
CompuServe	No		

ADMISSION

Acceptance 1994-95 2,000 applied for admission; 48% were accepted.

Entrance Requirements Bachelor's degree, GMAT score. Core courses waived through: previous course work, exams.

Application Requirements Written essay, application form, copies of transcript, 3 letters of recommendation.

Application Deadlines 4/1 for fall. Applications are processed on a rolling basis.

FINANCIALS

Costs for 1994-95 Tuition: Full-time: $18,420; Part-time day: $576/ credit. Average room and board costs are $11,560 per academic year (on-campus).

Financial Aid In 1994-95, 45% of candidates received some institutionally administered aid in the form of grants, scholarships, loans, workstudy. Total awards ranged from $2,300-$30,000. Financial aid is available to part-time students. Application deadlines: 3/15 for fall, 12/1 for spring. Contact: Mr. Aaron Moyer, Assistant Director, 685 Commonwealth Avenue, Room 129, Boston, MA 02215. (617) 353-2670.

INTERNATIONAL STUDENTS

Demographics 33% of students enrolled in the program are international; Asia 40%, Europe 25%, Central America 10%, South America 10%, North America 5%, Australia 4%, Africa 2%, other 4%.

Services and Facilities International student housing; international student office, international student center, visa services, language tutoring, ESL courses, special assistance for nonnative speakers of English, counseling/ support services, international student orientation.

Applying TOEFL required, minimum score of 580; proof of health; proof of adequate funds. Financial aid is not available to international students. Admission application deadline: 4/1 for fall. Applications are processed on a rolling basis. Contact: Mr. Norman Wilkinson, Assistant Director of Graduate Admissions, 685 Commonwealth Avenue, Boston, MA 02215. (617) 353-2670.

ALTERNATE MBA PROGRAMS

Executive MBA (EMBA) Length of program: Minimum: 17 months. Fulltime classes: Main campus; day, evening, weekends, summer. Degree requirements: 64 credits.

MBA/JD Length of program: Minimum: 48 months. Maximum: 6 years. Full-time classes: Main campus; day. Degree requirements: 124 credits.

MBA/MA Length of program: Minimum: 30 months. Maximum: 6 years. Full-time classes: Main campus; day. Part-time classes: Main campus; day. Degree requirements: 80 credits. MA is in economics, medical science, or international relations.

MBA/MS Length of program: Minimum: 30 months. Maximum: 6 years. Full-time classes: Main campus; day, evening, summer. Part-time classes: Main campus; day, evening, summer. Degree requirements: 80 credits. MS is in information systems, manufacturing engineering, broadcast administration, or medical sciences.

MBA/MIS Length of program: Minimum: 24 months. Maximum: 6 years. Full-time classes: Main campus; day, evening, summer. Degree requirements: 84 credits.

PLACEMENT

In 1993-94, 207 organizations participated in on-campus recruiting. Placement services include alumni network, career counseling/planning, career fairs, career library, career placement, electronic job bank, job interviews, job search course, resume preparation, and resume referral to employers. Of 1994 graduates, 80% were employed within three months of graduation, the average starting salary was $52,700, the range was $29,018-$91,100.

Program Contact: Ms. Bonnie Galinski Roth, Director of Graduate Admissions, Boston University, 685 Commonwealth Avenue, Boston, MA 02215. (617) 353-2670; Fax: (617) 353-7368; Internet Address: mba@bu.edu.

See full description on page 682.

Clark University

Graduate School of Management

Worcester, Massachusetts

OVERVIEW

Clark University is an independent nonprofit coed institution. Founded 1887. Setting: 50-acre urban campus with easy access to Boston. Total institutional enrollment: 2,655. Program was first offered in 1963. AACSB-accredited.

MBA HIGHLIGHTS

Entrance Difficulty**
Mean GMAT: 570
Mean GPA: 3.0

Cost $$
Tuition: $1,600/course
Room & Board: $5,500

Enrollment Profile

Full-time: 120	Work Exp: 94%
Part-time: 270	International: 15%
Total: 390	Women: 45%
Average Age: 25	Minorities: 2%

Average Class Size: 22

ACADEMICS

Length of Program Minimum: 18 months. Maximum: 6 years.

Calendar Semesters.

Full-time Classes Main campus; day, evening, summer.

Part-time Classes Main campus, Westboro; evening, summer.

Degree Requirements 57 credits including 15 elective credits.

Required Courses Business in society, business law and regulatory policy, business policy, financial management, foundations of accounting, general management, international management and global competition, management economics, management information systems, managerial communication, marketing management, operations management, organization behavior, statistical methods. Courses may be waived through: previous course work.

Curricular Focus General management, international business, leadership.

Concentrations Accounting, entrepreneurship, finance, health services, human resources management, international business, marketing.

Faculty Full-time: 18, 95% with doctorates; part-time: 12, 75% with doctorates.

Teaching Methodology Case study: 30%, lecture: 40%, research: 5%, seminars by members of the business community: 5%, student presentations: 10%, team projects: 10%.

Special Opportunities International exchange and internship programs available.

STUDENT STATISTICS

Geographic Representation State residents 40%. By region: Northeast 64%; South 12%; Midwest 3%; West 1%. International 15%.

Undergraduate Majors Business 27%; engineering/technology 14%; humanities 26%; science/mathematics 18%; social sciences 8%; other 7%.

Other Background Graduate degrees in other disciplines: 15%. Work experience: On average, students have 3 years of work experience on entrance to the program.

FACILITIES
Information Resources Main library with 528,000 bound volumes, 14,400 titles on microform, 1,909 periodical subscriptions, 1,000 records/tapes/CDs, 12 CD-ROMs.

Housing 25% of students in program live in college-owned or -operated housing.

Technology Computers are used moderately in course work. 100 computer terminals/PCs, linked by a campus-wide computer network, are available for use by students in program; they are located in the library, the computer center, computer labs. Students in the program are not required to have their own PC.

Computer Resources/On-line Services

Training	Yes	CompuServe	No
Internet	Yes	Dun's	No
E-Mail	Yes	Dow Jones	No
Multimedia Center	Yes	Dialog	Yes
LEXIS/NEXIS	No	Bloomberg	No

Other on-line services: OCLC.

ADMISSION
Acceptance 1994-95 303 applied for admission; 60% were accepted.

Entrance Requirements Bachelor's degree, GMAT score. Core courses waived through: previous course work.

Application Requirements Written essay, application form, copies of transcript, 2 letters of recommendation.

Application Deadlines 6/1 for fall, 12/1 for spring.

FINANCIALS
Costs for 1994-95 Tuition: Full-time: $1,600/course. Fees: Full-time: $50/trimester. Average room and board costs are $5,500 per academic year (on-campus) and $5,500 per academic year (off-campus).

Financial Aid In 1994-95, 70% of candidates received some institutionally administered aid in the form of grants, scholarships, loans, assistantships. Financial aid is available to part-time students. Application deadlines: 6/1 for fall, 12/1 for spring. Contact: Ms. Lynn Terrell, Director of Admissions, Graduate School of Management, Worcester, MA 01610-1477. (508) 793-7406.

INTERNATIONAL STUDENTS
Demographics 15% of students enrolled in the program are international; Asia 62%, Europe 27%, Australia 3%, Africa 2%, South America 2%, other 4%.

Services and Facilities Visa services, language tutoring, ESL courses, special assistance for nonnative speakers of English, counseling/support services.

Applying TOEFL required, minimum score of 550; proof of health; proof of adequate funds. Financial aid is available to international students. Financial aid application deadlines: 6/1 for fall, 12/1 for spring. Admission application deadlines: 6/1 for fall, 12/1 for spring. Contact: Mr. Jeff Davis, Director, International Students and Scholars Office, 950 Main Street, Worcester, MA 01610-1477. (508) 793-7362.

ALTERNATE MBA PROGRAM
One-Year MBA Length of program: Minimum: 9 months. Maximum: 1 year. Degree requirements: 30 courses including 15 elective courses. BA or BS in business administration.

PLACEMENT
Placement services include alumni network, career counseling/planning, career fairs, career library, career placement, job interviews, resume preparation, and resume referral to employers. Of 1994 graduates, 86% were employed within three months of graduation, the average starting salary was $43,000, the range was $20,000-$60,000.

Jobs by Employer Type Manufacturing 6%; service 55%; consulting 16%; nonprofit 17%; merchandising 6%.

Jobs by Functional Area Marketing/sales 39%; finance 12%; management 19%; strategic planning 12%; technical management 6%; human resources 12%.

Program Contact: Ms. Lynn Terrell, Director of Admissions, Clark University, 950 Main Street, Worcester, MA 01610-1477. (508) 793-7406; Fax: (508) 793-8822.
See full description on page 702.

Harvard University

Graduate School of Business

Cambridge, Massachusetts

OVERVIEW
Harvard University is an independent nonprofit coed institution. Founded 1636. Setting: 380-acre urban campus with easy access to Boston. Total institutional enrollment: 18,556. Program was first offered in 1909. AACSB-accredited.

MBA HIGHLIGHTS

Entrance Difficulty***
Mean GMAT: N/R
Mean GPA: 3.4

Cost $$$$$
Tuition: $21,000
Room & Board: $13,506

Enrollment Profile

Full-time: 806	Work Exp: 100%
Part-time: 0	International: 26%
Total: 806	Women: 29%
Average Age: N/R	Minorities: 18%

Average Class Size: N/R

ACADEMICS
Length of Program Minimum: 18 months.

Calendar Semesters.

Full-time Classes Main campus; day, summer.

Required Courses Business government and international economy, competition and strategy, data decisions and negotiations, decision making and ethical values, financial reporting and management accounting, general management, leadership and organizational behavior, marketing, technology and operations management.

Curricular Focus General management, leadership.

Concentration Management.

Faculty Full-time: 187.

Teaching Methodology Case study: 100%.

Special Opportunities Internship program available.

STUDENT STATISTICS
Geographic Representation State residents 74%. International 26%.

Undergraduate Majors Business 24%; engineering/technology 21%; humanities 49%; science/mathematics 4%; other 2%.

Other Background Graduate degrees in other disciplines: 8%. Work experience: On average, students have 4 years of work experience on entrance to the program.

FACILITIES
Information Resources Main library with 12.6 million bound volumes, 6.8 million titles on microform, 96,357 periodical subscriptions. Business collection in Baker Library includes 581,677 bound volumes, 6,906 periodical subscriptions, 143 videos.

Housing 27% of students in program live in college-owned or -operated housing.

Technology Computers are used moderately in course work. Students in the program are required to have their own PC.

Computer Resources/On-line Services

Internet	Yes	CompuServe	No
E-Mail	Yes	Dow Jones	Yes $
Videoconference Center	Yes	Dialog	Yes $
LEXIS/NEXIS	Yes $	Bloomberg	Yes

ADMISSION
Application Requirements Written essay, application form, copies of transcript, 3 letters of recommendation.

Application Deadline Applications are processed on a rolling basis.

FINANCIALS
Costs for 1994-95 Tuition: Full-time: $21,000. Fees: Full-time: $3,584-$7,000. Average room and board costs are $13,506 per academic year (on-campus) and $12,506 per academic year (off-campus).

Financial Aid In 1994-95, 70% of candidates received some institutionally administered aid in the form of loans, fellowships. Applications are processed on a rolling basis. Contact: Financial Aid Office, Baker Library 6, Boston, MA 02163. (617) 495-6640.

INTERNATIONAL STUDENTS

Demographics 26% of students enrolled in the program are international.

Applying TOEFL required; proof of health. Financial aid is available to international students. Applications are processed on a rolling basis. Admission applications are processed on a rolling basis.

ALTERNATE MBA PROGRAM

MBA/JD Length of program: Minimum: 48 months. Full-time classes: Main campus; day.

PLACEMENT

Placement services include alumni network, career counseling/planning, career fairs, career library, career placement, job interviews, resume preparation, and resume referral to employers.

Program Contact: MBA Admissions, Harvard University, Soldiers Field Road, Boston, MA 02163. (617) 495-6127; Internet Address: mba_admissions@nbsqm1.hbs.harvard.edu.

Massachusetts Institute of Technology

Sloan School of Management

Cambridge, Massachusetts

OVERVIEW

Massachusetts Institute of Technology is an independent nonprofit coed institution. Founded 1861. Setting: 146-acre urban campus with easy access to Boston. Total institutional enrollment: 9,774. Program was first offered in 1952. AACSB-accredited.

MBA HIGHLIGHTS

Entrance Difficulty*****
Mean GMAT: 650
Mean GPA: 3.5

Cost $$$$
Tuition: $21,690
Room & Board: $14,000

Enrollment Profile

Full-time: 513	Work Exp: 98%
Part-time: 0	International: 36%
Total: 513	Women: 25%
Average Age: 28	Minorities: 13%

Class Size: 33 - 65

ACADEMICS

Length of Program Minimum: 18 months.

Calendar Semesters.

Full-time Classes Main campus; day.

Degree Requirements 204 credits including 144 elective credits.

Required Courses Applied macro and international economics, communication for managers, data, models, and decisions, financial and managerial accounting, financial management or finance theory, industrial relations and human resources management, information systems, introduction to marketing, introduction to operations management, organizational processes, orientation, strategic management.

Curricular Focus Economic and financial theory, strategic analysis and planning, technology in business.

Concentrations Accounting, economics, entrepreneurship, finance, human resources management, international business, management, management information systems, marketing, operations management, organizational behavior, product/venture development, system dynamics, financial engineering, quantitative analysis, real estate, strategic management.

Faculty Full-time: 86, 100% with doctorates; part-time: 19, 75% with doctorates.

Teaching Methodology Case study: 33%, lecture: 34%, project-based courses and experiential learning: 33%.

Special Opportunities International exchange in Netherlands, United Kingdom. Internship program available.

STUDENT STATISTICS

Geographic Representation By region: Northeast 37%; Midwest 10%; West 10%; South 7%. International 36%.

Other Background Graduate degrees in other disciplines: 26%. Work experience: On average, students have 4 years of work experience on entrance to the program.

FACILITIES

Information Resources Main library with 2.3 million bound volumes, 2 million titles on microform, 21,259 periodical subscriptions, 18,870 records/tapes/CDs, 60 CD-ROMs. Business collection in Dewey Library includes 556,881 bound volumes, 6,788 periodical subscriptions, 24 CD-ROMs, 75 videos.

Housing 40% of students in program live in college-owned or -operated housing. Assistance with housing search provided.

Technology Computers are used heavily in course work. 3,000 computer terminals/PCs, linked by a campus-wide computer network, are available for use by students in program; they are located in the student center, classrooms, the library, the computer center, computer labs, student lounges. Students in the program are not required to have their own PC. $600 are budgeted per student for computer support.

Computer Resources/On-line Services

Training	Yes	CompuServe	No
Internet	Yes	Dun's	Yes $
E-Mail	Yes	Dow Jones	Yes $
Videoconference Center	Yes	Dialog	Yes $
LEXIS/NEXIS	Yes	Bloomberg	Yes

Other on-line services: First Search.

ADMISSION

Acceptance 1994-95 1,671 applied for admission; 23% were accepted.

Entrance Requirements Bachelor's degree, 1 year of college-level calculus and economics, GMAT score.

Application Requirements Written essay, application form, copies of transcript, resume/curriculum vitae, personal statement, 2 letters of recommendation.

Application Deadline 2/3 for fall. Application discs available.

FINANCIALS

Costs for 1995-96 Tuition: Full-time: $21,690. Average room and board costs are $14,000 per academic year (on-campus) and $14,000 per academic year (off-campus).

Financial Aid In 1994-95, 72% of candidates received some institutionally administered aid in the form of grants, scholarships, loans, assistantships. Total awards ranged from $1,000-$21,000. Applications are processed on a rolling basis. Contact: Ms. Donna Kendall, Associate Director, Student Financial Aid Office, 77 Massachusetts Avenue, Room 5-119, Cambridge, MA 02139. (617) 253-4971.

INTERNATIONAL STUDENTS

Demographics 36% of students enrolled in the program are international.

Services and Facilities International student office, international student center, visa services, language tutoring, ESL courses, special assistance for nonnative speakers of English, counseling/support services, summer workshop.

Applying TOEFL required, minimum score of 580; proof of health; proof of adequate funds. Financial aid is available to international students. Applications are processed on a rolling basis. Admission application deadline: 2/3 for fall. Contact: Ms. Milena Levak, Associate Dean, 77 Massachusetts Avenue, Room 5-106, Cambridge, MA 02139. (617) 253-3795.

ALTERNATE MBA PROGRAM

MBA/SM Length of program: Minimum: 24 months. Full-time classes: Main campus; day. Degree requirements: 225 credits including 72 elective credits. Internship; SM is in engineering and management.

PLACEMENT

In 1993-94, 184 organizations participated in on-campus recruiting; 2,800 on-campus interviews were conducted. Placement services include alumni network, career counseling/planning, career fairs, career library, career placement, job interviews, resume preparation, and resume referral to employers. Of 1994 graduates, 98% were employed within three months of graduation, the average starting salary was $68,000, the range was $30,000-$120,000.

Jobs by Employer Type Manufacturing 16%; service 28%; consulting 32%; financial services 24%.

Jobs by Functional Area Marketing/sales 7%; finance 27%; operations 18%; management 5%; strategic planning 4%; technical management 4%; consulting 35%.

Program Contact: Mr. Rod Garcia, Associate Director of Admissions, Massachusetts Institute of Technology, 50 Memorial Drive, Room E52-112, Cambridge, MA 02142-1347. (617) 253-3730; Fax: (617) 253-6405; Internet Address: masters@sloan.mit.edu.

Nichols College

Dudley, Massachusetts

OVERVIEW
Nichols College is an independent nonprofit comprehensive coed institution. Founded 1815. Setting: 210-acre suburban campus with easy access to Boston. Total institutional enrollment: 1,700. Program was first offered in 1974.

MBA HIGHLIGHTS

Entrance Difficulty***
Mean GMAT: 480
Mean GPA: 3.1

Cost $
Tuition: $770/course
Room & Board: $4,800 (off-campus)

Enrollment Profile

Full-time: 0	Work Exp: 95%
Part-time: 398	International: 2%
Total: 398	Women: 46%
Average Age: 32	Minorities: 7%

Average Class Size: 16

ACADEMICS
Length of Program Minimum: 30 months. Maximum: 5 years.
Calendar Semesters.
Part-time Classes Main campus, Southborough, Auburn, Leominster; evening, summer.
Degree Requirements 30 credits including 6-9 elective credits.
Required Courses Administrative theory and practice, financial decision making, management accounting and control, managerial economics, marketing management, operations management, policy formulation, statistical analysis.
Curricular Focus Leadership, problem solving and decision making, strategic analysis and planning.
Concentrations Finance, international business, management, marketing, operations management.
Faculty Full-time: 19, 75% with doctorates; part-time: 6, 33% with doctorates.
Teaching Methodology Case study: 20%, lecture: 30%, research: 10%, student presentations: 20%, team projects: 20%.

STUDENT STATISTICS
Geographic Representation State residents 90%. By region: Northeast 98%. International 2%.
Other Background Graduate degrees in other disciplines: 5%. Work experience: On average, students have 2-5 years of work experience on entrance to the program.

FACILITIES
Information Resources Main library with 65,000 bound volumes, 8,000 titles on microform, 450 periodical subscriptions, 544 records/tapes/CDs.
Housing College housing not available.
Technology 20 computer terminals/PCs, linked by a campus-wide computer network, are available for use by students in program; they are located in the computer center, computer labs. Students in the program are not required to have their own PC.
Computer Resources/On-line Services

Training	Yes	E-Mail	Yes
Internet	Yes	LEXIS/NEXIS	Yes

ADMISSION
Acceptance 1994-95 Of those applying, 95% were accepted.
Entrance Requirements Bachelor's degree, GMAT score. Core courses waived through: previous course work.
Application Requirements Written essay, application form, copies of transcript, personal statement.

Application Deadline Applications are processed on a rolling basis.
FINANCIALS
Costs for 1994-95 Tuition: Part-time evening: $770/course. Average room and board costs are $4,800 per academic year (off-campus).
Financial Aid Financial aid is available to part-time students. Application deadlines: 8/30 for fall, 1/5 for spring. Contact: Ms. Judy Bollens, Financial Aid Manager, Dudley, MA 01571. (508) 943-1560.
INTERNATIONAL STUDENTS
Demographics 2% of students enrolled in the program are international; Asia 80%, South America 15%, Africa 5%.
Services and Facilities Language tutoring, counseling/support services.
Applying TOEFL required, minimum score of 550; proof of adequate funds. Financial aid is not available to international students. Admission application deadlines: 8/1 for fall, 12/1 for spring. Contact: Mr. William Keith, Director, MBA Program, Dudley Road, Dudley, MA 01571. (508) 943-0099.

PLACEMENT
Placement services include alumni network, career fairs, career placement, electronic job bank, job interviews, and resume preparation.

Program Contact: Mr. William F. Keith, Director, MBA Program, Nichols College, Dudley, MA 01571. (508) 943-0099, or (800) 943-4893 (MA only); Fax: (508) 943-1560 Ext. 102.

Northeastern University

Graduate School of Business Administration

Boston, Massachusetts

OVERVIEW
Northeastern University is an independent nonprofit coed institution. Founded 1898. Setting: 55-acre urban campus. Total institutional enrollment: 26,552. Program was first offered in 1952. AACSB-accredited.

MBA HIGHLIGHTS

Entrance Difficulty***
GMAT: 440 - 690
Mean GPA: N/R

Cost $$$
Tuition: $400/credit
(Nonresident: $400/credit)
Room & Board: N/R

Enrollment Profile

Full-time: 156	Work Exp: N/R
Part-time: 113	International: 50%
Total: 269	Women: 32%
Average Age: N/R	Minorities: 13%

Class Size: 25 - 30

ACADEMICS
Length of Program Minimum: 21 months.
Calendar Quarters.
Full-time Classes Main campus; day, evening, summer.
Part-time Classes Main campus, Burlington, Dedham; evening, weekends, summer.
Degree Requirements 84 credits including 27 elective credits.
Required Courses Business enterprise: a total organizational perspective, business in a social context, financial accounting, global management, industry analysis, information management, managerial accounting, managerial economics, managerial finance, marketing management, operations management, organizational behavior, organizational diagnosis, presentation of findings, quantitative analysis, strategic management.
Curricular Focus Economic and financial theory, general management, teamwork.
Concentrations High technology, international business, management.
Faculty Full-time: 100; part-time: 130.
Special Opportunities International exchange in Czech Republic, France, Hungary, Indonesia, Singapore, United Kingdom.
STUDENT STATISTICS
Geographic Representation International 50%.

Other Background Work experience: On average, students have 3 years of work experience on entrance to the program.

FACILITIES
Information Resources Main library with 777,252 bound volumes, 1.8 million titles on microform, 8,831 periodical subscriptions, 14,341 records/tapes/CDs, 58 CD-ROMs.

Housing College housing available.

Technology Computer terminals/PCs are available for use by students in program; they are located in classrooms, learning resource center, the library, the computer center, computer labs, the research center. Students in the program are not required to have their own PC.

Computer Resources/On-line Services

Training	Yes

ADMISSION
Acceptance 1994-95 801 applied for admission; 60% were accepted.

Entrance Requirements Bachelor's degree, GMAT score. Core courses waived through: previous course work.

Application Requirements Written essay, application form, copies of transcript, 2 letters of recommendation.

Application Deadline Applications are processed on a rolling basis.

FINANCIALS
Costs for 1994-95 Tuition: Full-time: $400/credit, $400/credit for international students.

Financial Aid In 1994-95, candidates received some institutionally administered aid in the form of loans, fellowships, work-study. Financial aid is available to part-time students. Application deadline: 3/1 for fall. Applications are processed on a rolling basis. Contact: Ms. Mary Lee Bolan, Dean and Director of Student Financial Services, 360 Huntington Avenue, Boston, MA 02115-5096. (617) 373-5899.

INTERNATIONAL STUDENTS
Demographics 50% of students enrolled in the program are international.

Services and Facilities International student housing; international student office, international student center, visa services, language tutoring, ESL courses, counseling/support services, international cooperative education office.

Applying TOEFL required; proof of health; proof of adequate funds. Financial aid is not available to international students. Admission application deadline: 5/1 for fall. Applications are processed on a rolling basis.

ALTERNATE MBA PROGRAM
Executive MBA (EMBA) Length of program: Minimum: 18 months. Part-time classes: Main campus; evening, weekends. Degree requirements: 84 credits.

PLACEMENT
In 1993-94, 40 organizations participated in on-campus recruiting. Placement services include alumni network, career counseling/planning, career fairs, career library, career placement, job interviews, job search course, resume preparation, and resume referral to employers. Of 1994 graduates, 81% were employed within three months of graduation, the average starting salary was $37,990, the range was $25,000-$77,000.

Jobs by Employer Type Manufacturing 26%; service 73%.

Program Contact: Market Center, Northeastern University, 360 Huntington Avenue, Boston, MA 02115-5096. (617) 373-2714; Fax: (617) 373-8564.

See full description on page 792.

Salem State College

Graduate School

Salem, Massachusetts

OVERVIEW
Salem State College is a state-supported comprehensive coed institution. Part of Massachusetts Public Higher Education System. Founded 1854. Setting: 62-acre suburban campus with easy access to Boston. Total institutional enrollment: 9,719. Program was first offered in 1982.

MBA HIGHLIGHTS
Entrance Difficulty N/R
Mean GMAT: 423
Mean GPA: 2.79

Cost $
Tuition: $140/credit hour
(Nonresident: $230/credit hour)
Room & Board: N/R

Enrollment Profile

Full-time: 8	Work Exp: 90%
Part-time: 189	International: 4%
Total: 197	Women: 42%
Average Age: 30	Minorities: 5%

Average Class Size: 23

ACADEMICS
Length of Program Minimum: 24 months. Maximum: 6 years.

Calendar Semesters.

Part-time Classes Main campus, South Campus; evening, weekends, summer.

Degree Requirements 54 credit hours including 12 elective credit hours.

Required Courses Analysis and policy, applications in financial management, applied operations research, behavior in organization, business policy and strategy, computers in business management, financial and managerial accounting, international business, legal and ethical environment, macroeconomics, management theory and application.

Curricular Focus General management.

Concentration Management.

Faculty Full-time: 12, 50% with doctorates; part-time: 10, 50% with doctorates.

STUDENT STATISTICS
Geographic Representation International 4%.

Other Background Graduate degrees in other disciplines: 3%. Work experience: On average, students have 8 years of work experience on entrance to the program.

FACILITIES
Information Resources Main library with 236,337 bound volumes, 315,979 titles on microform, 1,360 periodical subscriptions, 400 records/tapes/CDs, 2 CD-ROMs.

Housing College housing not available.

Technology Computers are used moderately in course work. 150 computer terminals/PCs are available for use by students in program; they are located in computer labs. Students in the program are not required to have their own PC.

Computer Resources/On-line Services

Training	Yes	CompuServe	No
Internet	Yes	Dun's	No
E-Mail	Yes	Dow Jones	No
Videoconference Center	Yes	Dialog	Yes $
LEXIS/NEXIS	No	Bloomberg	No

Other on-line services: First Search, SEC.

ADMISSION
Acceptance 1994-95 Of those applying, 67% were accepted.

Entrance Requirements Bachelor's degree, GMAT score, minimum 2.5 GPA. Core courses waived through: previous course work.

Application Requirements Interview, application form, copies of transcript, resume/curriculum vitae, personal statement, 3 letters of recommendation.

Application Deadlines 7/1 for fall, 11/1 for spring.

FINANCIALS
Costs for 1994-95 Tuition: Full-time: $140/credit hour for state residents, $230/credit hour for nonresidents. Fees: Full-time: $20/credit hour for state residents, $20/credit hour for nonresidents.

Financial Aid In 1994-95, 5% of candidates received some institutionally administered aid in the form of loans, assistantships, work-study. Financial aid is available to part-time students. Application deadlines: 4/15 for fall, 11/15 for spring. Contact: Ms. Mary Benda, Associate Director, Financial Aid, 352 Lafayette Street, Salem, MA 01970-5353. (508) 741-6113.

INTERNATIONAL STUDENTS
Demographics 4% of students enrolled in the program are international; Asia 62%, Europe 25%, Africa 12%.

Services and Facilities International student office, international student center, visa services, language tutoring, ESL courses, special assistance for nonnative speakers of English, counseling/support services.

Applying TOEFL required, minimum score of 500; proof of adequate funds. Admission application deadlines: 11/1 for fall, 7/1 for spring. Contact: Ms. Nelly M. Wadsworth, International Student Coordinator, 352 Lafayette Street, Salem, MA 01970-5353. (508) 741-6351.

ALTERNATE MBA PROGRAM
MBA/MSN Length of program: Minimum: 42 months. Maximum: 6 years. Degree requirements: 60 credits including 6 elective credits. Average class size: 20.

PLACEMENT
Placement services include alumni network, career counseling/planning, career fairs, career library, career placement, electronic job bank, job interviews, resume preparation, and resume referral to employers.

Program Contact: Mr. A. Richard Anderson, Coordinator, MBA Program, Salem State College, 352 Lafayette Street, Salem, MA 01970-5353. (508) 741-6320; Fax: (508) 741-6336.

Simmons College

Graduate School of Management

Boston, Massachusetts

OVERVIEW
Simmons College is an independent nonprofit comprehensive women only institution. Founded 1899. Setting: 12-acre urban campus. Total institutional enrollment: 3,456. Program was first offered in 1974.

MBA HIGHLIGHTS
Entrance Difficulty**

Cost $$$$$
Tuition: $25,380
Room & Board: N/R

Enrollment Profile

Full-time: 39	Work Exp: 100%
Part-time: 214	International: 8%
Total: 253	Women: 100%
Average Age: 35	Minorities: 12%

Average Class Size: 45

ACADEMICS
Length of Program Minimum: 11 months. Maximum: 5 years.

Calendar Semesters.

Full-time Classes Main campus; day, summer.

Part-time Classes Main campus; day, evening, summer.

Degree Requirements 45 credits including 2 elective credits. Other: Internship.

Required Courses Business government and global economy, career planning and development, economics, finance, financial accounting, human resources management, management and behavior, management communication, managerial accounting, managing, market research, marketing, operations management, organizational structure, quantitative analysis, strategy.

Curricular Focus General management, organizational development and change management, women in business.

Concentration Management.

Faculty Full-time: 12, 66% with doctorates; part-time: 4, 25% with doctorates.

Teaching Methodology Case study: 65%, lecture: 20%, student presentations: 5%, team projects: 10%.

Special Opportunities Internship program available.

STUDENT STATISTICS
Geographic Representation By region: Northeast 91%; West 2%; South 1%; Midwest 1%. International 8%.

Undergraduate Majors Business 13%; education 3%; engineering/technology 2%; humanities 31%; nursing 2%; science/mathematics 6%; social sciences 20%; other 23%.

Other Background Graduate degrees in other disciplines: 10%. Work experience: On average, students have 12 years of work experience on entrance to the program.

FACILITIES
Information Resources Main library with 266,417 bound volumes, 1,400 titles on microform, 2,027 periodical subscriptions, 1,783 records/tapes/CDs, 22 CD-ROMs. Business collection in Graduate School of Management Library includes 5,000 bound volumes, 136 periodical subscriptions, 6 CD-ROMs, 85 videos.

Housing 1% of students in program live in college-owned or -operated housing. Assistance with housing search provided.

Technology Computers are used moderately in course work. 61 computer terminals/PCs are available for use by students in program; they are located in the library, the computer center, computer labs. Students in the program are not required to have their own PC.

Computer Resources/On-line Services

Training	Yes	CompuServe	No
Internet	Yes	Dun's	Yes
E-Mail	Yes	Dow Jones	Yes
Videoconference Center	Yes	Dialog	Yes $
Multimedia Center	Yes	Bloomberg	No
LEXIS/NEXIS	No		

Other on-line services: First Search.

ADMISSION
Acceptance 1994-95 251 applied for admission; 64% were accepted.

Entrance Requirements GMAT score, minimum 2 years of work experience.

Application Requirements Written essay, application form, copies of transcript, personal statement, 3 letters of recommendation.

Application Deadline Applications are processed on a rolling basis.

FINANCIALS
Costs for 1994-95 Tuition: Full-time: $25,380; Part-time day: $564/credit. Fees: Full-time: $125.

Financial Aid In 1994-95, 8% of candidates received some institutionally administered aid in the form of grants, scholarships, loans, work-study. Financial aid is available to part-time students. Application deadline: 3/1 for fall. Applications are processed on a rolling basis. Contact: Ms. Jennifer Rylesworth, Associate Director of Financial Aid, 300 The Fenway, Boston, MA 02115. (617) 521-2031.

INTERNATIONAL STUDENTS
Demographics 8% of students enrolled in the program are international; Asia 50%, Europe 37%, Africa 12%.

Services and Facilities International student office, language tutoring, ESL courses, special assistance for nonnative speakers of English, counseling/support services, audiotaped classes.

Applying TOEFL required, minimum score of 550; proof of health; proof of adequate funds. Financial aid is not available to international students. Admission application deadline: 7/1 for fall. Applications are processed on a rolling basis. Contact: Admissions Office, 300 The Fenway, Boston, MA 02115. (617) 521-3840.

PLACEMENT
In 1993-94, 12 organizations participated in on-campus recruiting; 50 on-campus interviews were conducted. Placement services include alumni network, career counseling/planning, career fairs, career library, career placement, job interviews, job search course, resume preparation, and resume referral to employers. Of 1994 graduates, 68% were employed within three months of graduation, the average starting salary was $54,800, the range was $35,000-$120,000.

Jobs by Employer Type Manufacturing 14%; service 30%; government 2%; consulting 8%; nonprofit 10%; media 6%; computer-related 10%; telecommunications 10%; banking 10%.

Jobs by Functional Area Marketing/sales 20%; finance 25%; operations 15%; management 30%; strategic planning 5%; technical management 5%.

Program Contact: Ms. Caron Hobin, Assistant Director of Admission, Simmons College, 300 The Fenway, Boston, MA 02115. (617) 521-2049.
See full description on page 830.

Suffolk University

School of Management

Boston, Massachusetts

OVERVIEW
Suffolk University is an independent nonprofit comprehensive coed institution. Founded 1906. Setting: 2-acre urban campus. Total institutional enrollment: 6,300. Program was first offered in 1970. AACSB-accredited.

MBA HIGHLIGHTS

Entrance Difficulty***
Mean GMAT: 510
Mean GPA: 3.1

Cost $$$
Tuition: $14,124
Room & Board: $5,000 (off-campus)

Enrollment Profile
Full-time: 65	Work Exp: 80%
Part-time: 585	International: 12%
Total: 650	Women: 40%
Average Age: 27	Minorities: 8%

Average Class Size: 27

ACADEMICS
Length of Program Minimum: 12 months. Maximum: 5 years.
Calendar Semesters.
Full-time Classes Main campus; day, evening, summer.
Part-time Classes Main campus; day, evening, summer.
Degree Requirements 57 credits including 24 elective credits.
Required Courses Human behavior and organization theory, introductory accounting, legal and social environment of business, managerial economics, managerial finance, marketing management, operating management, statistics and quantitative methods, strategy management.
Curricular Focus Economic and financial theory, international business, organizational development and change management.
Concentrations Accounting, entrepreneurship, finance, human resources management, international business, management, management information systems, marketing, organizational behavior, public administration, public policy, strategic management.
Teaching Methodology Case study: 15%, lecture: 50%, seminars by members of the business community: 10%, student presentations: 10%, team projects: 15%.
Special Opportunities International exchange in France. Internship program available.

STUDENT STATISTICS
Geographic Representation State residents 75%. International 12%.
Other Background Work experience: On average, students have 3-5 years of work experience on entrance to the program.

FACILITIES
Information Resources Main library with 386,700 bound volumes, 213,000 titles on microform, 6,965 periodical subscriptions, 213 records/tapes/CDs, 26 CD-ROMs.
Housing College housing not available.
Technology Students in the program are not required to have their own PC.
Computer Resources/On-line Services
E-Mail   Yes

ADMISSION
Acceptance 1994-95 342 applied for admission; 82% were accepted.
Entrance Requirements Bachelor's degree, GMAT score of 450, minimum 2.7 GPA. Core courses waived through: previous course work.
Application Requirements Written essay, application form, copies of transcript, resume/curriculum vitae, personal statement, 2 letters of recommendation.
Application Deadlines 6/15 for fall, 11/15 for spring, 4/15 for summer. Applications are processed on a rolling basis.

FINANCIALS
Costs for 1994-95 Tuition: Full-time: $14,124; Part-time day: $1,413/course; Weekends: $1,737/course. Fees: Full-time: $100; Part-time day: $50. Average room and board costs are $5,000 per academic year (off-campus).
Financial Aid In 1994-95, 48% of candidates received some form of institutionally administered aid. Financial aid is available to part-time students. Application deadlines: 4/1 for fall, 11/1 for spring. Contact: Ms. Christine Perry, Director of Financial Aid, 8 Ashburton Place, Boston, MA 02108-2770. (617) 573-8470.

INTERNATIONAL STUDENTS
Demographics 12% of students enrolled in the program are international.
Services and Facilities International student office, visa services, ESL courses.
Applying TOEFL required, minimum score of 550; proof of adequate funds. Financial aid is available to international students. Financial aid application deadlines: 3/15 for fall, 11/1 for spring. Admission application deadlines: 6/15 for fall, 11/15 for spring. Applications are processed on a rolling basis. Contact: Ms. Margaret Loret, International Student Adviser, 8 Ashburton Place, Boston, MA 02108-2770. (617) 573-8072.

ALTERNATE MBA PROGRAMS
Executive MBA (EMBA) Length of program: Minimum: 22 months. Full-time classes: Main campus; weekends, summer. Part-time classes: Main campus; weekends, summer. Degree requirements: 57 credits.
MBA/JD Length of program: Minimum: 48 months. Full-time classes: Main campus; day, evening, summer. Part-time classes: Main campus; day, evening, summer. Degree requirements: 117 credits.

PLACEMENT
Placement services include alumni network, career counseling/planning, career fairs, career library, career placement, resume preparation, and resume referral to employers.

Program Contact: Ms. Marsha Ginn, Director of Graduate Admissions, Suffolk University, 8 Ashburton Place, Boston, MA 02108-2770. (617) 573-8302; Fax: (617) 523-0116.
See full description on page 836.

University of Massachusetts Amherst

School of Management

Amherst, Massachusetts

OVERVIEW
The University of Massachusetts Amherst is a state-supported coed institution. Part of University of Massachusetts. Founded 1863. Setting: 1,405-acre small-town campus. Total institutional enrollment: 22,000. Program was first offered in 1963. AACSB-accredited.

MBA HIGHLIGHTS

Entrance Difficulty****
Mean GMAT: 575
Mean GPA: 3.2

Cost $
Tuition: $2,780
(Nonresident: $8,570)
Room & Board: $3,500

Enrollment Profile
Full-time: 70	Work Exp: 85%
Part-time: 210	International: 29%
Total: 280	Women: 43%
Average Age: 28	Minorities: 6%

Average Class Size: 30

ACADEMICS
Length of Program Minimum: 21 months. Maximum: 4 years.
Calendar Semesters.
Full-time Classes Main campus; day.
Part-time Classes Main campus, Holyoke Campus; evening, summer.
Degree Requirements 55 credits including 18 elective credits.

Required Courses Accounting for decision making, business and its environment, business data analysis, computer and information systems, financial analysis and decisions, financial management, managerial accounting and control, managerial economics, marketing management, organizational behavior and theory, organizational planning and strategy, production operations management. Courses may be waived through: previous course work, work experience.

Curricular Focus Business issues and problems, problem solving and decision making, teamwork.

Concentrations Accounting, finance, management, marketing, operations management, organizational behavior.

Faculty Full-time: 25, 95% with doctorates.

Teaching Methodology Case study: 20%, lecture: 50%, seminars by members of the business community: 5%, student presentations: 5%, team projects: 20%.

Special Opportunities International exchange in France, Sweden. Internship program available.

STUDENT STATISTICS
Geographic Representation State residents 60%. By region: Northeast 71%. International 29%.

Undergraduate Majors Business 22%; engineering/technology 25%; humanities 11%; science/mathematics 5%; social sciences 30%; other 7%.

Other Background Graduate degrees in other disciplines: 5%. Work experience: On average, students have 5 years of work experience on entrance to the program.

FACILITIES
Information Resources Main library with 2.6 million bound volumes, 2.1 million titles on microform, 15,312 periodical subscriptions, 12,997 records/tapes/CDs, 88 CD-ROMs.

Housing 5% of students in program live in college-owned or -operated housing.

Technology Computers are used moderately in course work. Computer terminals/PCs, linked by a campus-wide computer network, are available for use by students in program; they are located in the library, the computer center, computer labs, the research center. Students in the program are not required to have their own PC.

Computer Resources/On-line Services

Training	Yes	CompuServe	Yes
Internet	Yes	Dun's	No
E-Mail	Yes	Dow Jones	No
Videoconference Center	Yes	Dialog	No
LEXIS/NEXIS	Yes $	Bloomberg	No

ADMISSION
Acceptance 1994-95 260 applied for admission; 27% were accepted.

Entrance Requirements Bachelor's degree, GMAT score, minimum 2.75 GPA, minimum 4 years of work experience. Core courses waived through: previous course work, work experience.

Application Requirements Written essay, application form, copies of transcript, resume/curriculum vitae, 2 letters of recommendation.

Application Deadline 3/1 for fall.

FINANCIALS
Costs for 1994-95 Tuition: Full-time: $2,780 for state residents, $8,570 for nonresidents. Fees: Full-time: $2,820 for state residents, $2,820 for nonresidents. Average room and board costs are $3,500 per academic year (on-campus) and $4,000 per academic year (off-campus).

Financial Aid In 1994-95, 90% of candidates received some institutionally administered aid in the form of assistantships, tuition/fee waivers. Total awards ranged from $3,250-$3,850. Financial aid is not available to part-time students. Application deadline: 3/1 for fall. Contact: Graduate Program Office, Amherst, MA 01003-0001. (413) 545-5608.

INTERNATIONAL STUDENTS
Demographics 29% of students enrolled in the program are international; Asia 40%, Europe 40%, Africa 10%, South America 10%.

Services and Facilities International student center, visa services.

Applying TOEFL required, minimum score of 575; proof of health; proof of adequate funds. Financial aid is available to international students. Financial aid application deadline: 3/1 for fall. Admission application deadline: 3/1 for fall.

PLACEMENT
Placement services include alumni network, career counseling/planning, career library, career placement, electronic job bank, job interviews, resume preparation, and resume referral to employers. Of 1994 graduates, 90% were employed within three months of graduation.

Program Contact: Graduate Program Office, University of Massachusetts Amherst, Amherst, MA 01003-0001. (413) 545-5608; Fax: (413) 545-3858.

University of Massachusetts Boston

College of Management

Boston, Massachusetts

OVERVIEW
The University of Massachusetts Boston is a state-supported coed institution. Part of University of Massachusetts. Founded 1964. Setting: 177-acre urban campus. Total institutional enrollment: 10,456.

MBA HIGHLIGHTS

Entrance Difficulty***
Mean GMAT: 534
Mean GPA: N/R

Cost $
Tuition: $116/credit hour
(Nonresident: $357/credit hour)
Room & Board: N/R

Enrollment Profile

Full-time: N/R	Work Exp: N/R
Part-time: N/R	International: 10%
Total: 400	Women: 40%
Average Age: N/R	Minorities: 20%

Average Class Size: 35

ACADEMICS
Length of Program Minimum: 36 months.

Calendar Semesters.

Full-time Classes Main campus; evening.

Part-time Classes Main campus; evening.

Degree Requirements 57 credit hours.

Curricular Focus General management, international business, strategic analysis and planning.

Concentrations Accounting, finance, management, management information systems, marketing, operations management.

Teaching Methodology Case study: 20%, faculty seminars: 5%, lecture: 20%, research: 20%, seminars by members of the business community: 5%, student presentations: 10%, team projects: 20%.

STUDENT STATISTICS
Geographic Representation International 10%.

FACILITIES
Information Resources Main library with 547,846 bound volumes, 701,529 titles on microform, 3,049 periodical subscriptions, 1,939 records/tapes/CDs, 49 CD-ROMs.

Housing College housing not available.

ADMISSION
Entrance Requirements Bachelor's degree, prerequisite courses required for applicants with non-business degree, GMAT score, minimum 3.0 GPA.

Application Requirements Written essay, application form, copies of transcript, resume/curriculum vitae, personal statement, 3 letters of recommendation.

Application Deadlines 6/1 for fall. Applications are processed on a rolling basis.

FINANCIALS
Costs for 1994-95 Tuition: Part-time day: $357/credit hour for nonresidents; Part-time evening: $116/credit hour for state residents.

Financial Aid Application deadline: 3/1 for fall. Contact: Mr. Frank Casey, Director, 100 Morrissey Boulevard, Boston, MA 02125-3393. (617) 287-6300.

INTERNATIONAL STUDENTS
Demographics 10% of students enrolled in the program are international.

Applying TOEFL required, minimum score of 550; proof of health; proof of adequate funds. Financial aid is not available to international students. Admission application deadline: 5/1 for fall. Applications are processed on a rolling basis.

Program Contact: Ms. Marnee Ennis, Program Coordinator, University of Massachusetts Boston, 100 Morrissey Boulevard, Boston, MA 02125-3393. (617) 287-7720.

University of Massachusetts Dartmouth

College of Business and Industry

North Dartmouth, Massachusetts

OVERVIEW
The University of Massachusetts Dartmouth is a state-supported comprehensive coed institution. Part of University of Massachusetts. Founded 1895. Setting: 710-acre suburban campus with easy access to Boston. Total institutional enrollment: 6,744. Program was first offered in 1976.

MBA HIGHLIGHTS

Entrance Difficulty***
Mean GMAT: 510
Mean GPA: 3.0

Cost $
Tuition: $3,552
(Nonresident: $7,613)
Room & Board: $4,850

Enrollment Profile

Full-time: 12	Work Exp: 80%
Part-time: 78	International: 27%
Total: 90	Women: 38%
Average Age: 26	Minorities: 1%

Average Class Size: 14

ACADEMICS
Length of Program Minimum: 24 months. Maximum: 5 years.

Calendar Semesters.

Full-time Classes Main campus; evening.

Part-time Classes Main campus; evening.

Degree Requirements 39 credits including 6 elective credits. Other: Capstone course.

Required Courses Business ethics, financial management, information resource management, management science, managerial accounting, marketing management, organization theory, strategic management.

Curricular Focus General management, problem solving and decision making, strategic analysis and planning.

Concentration Management.

Faculty Full-time: 12, 90% with doctorates; part-time: 2, 50% with doctorates.

Teaching Methodology Case study: 20%, lecture: 50%, research: 10%, student presentations: 10%, team projects: 10%.

Special Opportunities International exchange in France, Germany, Portugal, Spain.

STUDENT STATISTICS
Geographic Representation State residents 70%. By region: Northeast 70%; South 3%. International 27%.

Undergraduate Majors Business 30%; engineering/technology 22%; humanities 5%; science/mathematics 5%; social sciences 23%; other 15%.

Other Background Graduate degrees in other disciplines: 3%. Work experience: On average, students have 3 years of work experience on entrance to the program.

FACILITIES
Information Resources Main library with 415,658 bound volumes, 43,505 titles on microform, 2,755 periodical subscriptions, 8,991 records/tapes/CDs, 26 CD-ROMs.

Housing 10% of students in program live in college-owned or -operated housing.

Technology Computers are used moderately in course work. 400 computer terminals/PCs, linked by a campus-wide computer network, are available for use by students in program; they are located in the library, computer labs. Students in the program are not required to have their own PC.

Computer Resources/On-line Services

Training	Yes	Dun's	Yes
Internet	Yes	Dow Jones	Yes
E-Mail	Yes	Dialog	Yes
LEXIS/NEXIS	No	Bloomberg	No
CompuServe	Yes		

ADMISSION
Acceptance 1994-95 85 applied for admission; 85% were accepted.

Entrance Requirements Bachelor's degree, prerequisite courses required for applicants with non-business degree, GMAT score. Core courses waived through: previous course work.

Application Requirements Written essay, application form, copies of transcript, personal statement, 2 letters of recommendation.

Application Deadlines 3/20 for fall, 11/15 for spring. Applications are processed on a rolling basis.

FINANCIALS
Costs for 1994-95 Tuition: Full-time: $3,552 for state residents, $7,613 for nonresidents. Average room and board costs are $4,850 per academic year (on-campus).

Financial Aid Financial aid is available to part-time students. Application deadlines: 3/1 for fall, 11/1 for spring. Contact: Ms. Stephanie Pina, Assistant Director, Financial Aid, 285 Old Westport Road, North Dartmouth, MA 02747. (508) 999-8632.

INTERNATIONAL STUDENTS
Demographics 27% of students enrolled in the program are international; Asia 80%, Europe 20%.

Services and Facilities Visa services, language tutoring, counseling/support services.

Applying TOEFL required, minimum score of 500; proof of adequate funds; health insurance. Financial aid is available to international students. Financial aid application deadline: 2/20 for fall. Admission application deadlines: 2/20 for fall, 9/15 for spring. Applications are processed on a rolling basis.

PLACEMENT
Placement services include alumni network, career counseling/planning, career fairs, career library, career placement, electronic job bank, job interviews, and resume preparation.

Program Contact: Ms. Carol Novo, Administrative Assistant, University of Massachusetts Dartmouth, Graduate School, North Dartmouth, MA 02747. (508) 999-8024; Fax: (508) 999-8375; Internet Address: cnovo@umassd.edu.

University of Massachusetts Lowell

College of Management

Lowell, Massachusetts

OVERVIEW
The University of Massachusetts Lowell is a state-supported coed institution. Part of University of Massachusetts. Founded 1894. Setting: 100-acre urban campus with easy access to Boston. Total institutional enrollment: 13,618. Program was first offered in 1980. AACSB-accredited.

MBA HIGHLIGHTS

Entrance Difficulty***
Mean GMAT: 540
Mean GPA: N/R

Cost $
Tuition: $1,130/semester
(Nonresident: $1,695 - $3,514/semester)
Room & Board: N/R

Enrollment Profile
Full-time: 30
Part-time: 150
Total: 180
Average Age: N/R

Work Exp: N/R
International: 25%
Women: 45%
Minorities: 30%

Average Class Size: 25

ACADEMICS
Length of Program Minimum: 24 months. Maximum: 5 years.
Calendar Semesters.
Full-time Classes Main campus; evening, summer.
Part-time Classes Main campus; evening, summer.
Degree Requirements 33 credits including 9 elective credits.
Required Courses Analysis of customers and markets, decision methods and techniques, dynamics of competition and cooperation, enterprise and management dynamics, financial policy and strategy, strategy formulation, implementation, and control, world class operations.
Curricular Focus General management, manufacturing, strategic analysis and planning.
Concentration Management.
Faculty Full-time: 20, 95% with doctorates; part-time: 2, 100% with doctorates.
Teaching Methodology Case study: 30%, lecture: 30%, seminars by members of the business community: 10%, student presentations: 10%, team projects: 20%.

STUDENT STATISTICS
Geographic Representation State residents 75%. By region: Northeast 60%; West 8%; Midwest 7%. International 25%.

FACILITIES
Information Resources Main library with 322,755 bound volumes, 611,799 titles on microform, 4,000 periodical subscriptions, 11,000 records/tapes/CDs.

ADMISSION
Entrance Requirements Bachelor's degree, GMAT score. Core courses waived through: previous course work.
Application Requirements Written essay, application form, copies of transcript, personal statement, 3 letters of recommendation.
Application Deadlines 8/15 for fall, 12/15 for spring. Applications are processed on a rolling basis.

FINANCIALS
Costs for 1994-95 Tuition: Full-time: $1,130/semester for state residents, $1,695-$3,514/semester for nonresidents; Part-time day: $94/credit hour for state residents, $141-$293/credit hour for nonresidents. Fees: Full-time: $1,360/semester for state residents, $1,360/semester for nonresidents; Part-time day: $125-$1,360/semester for state residents, $125-$1,360/semester for nonresidents.
Financial Aid In 1994-95, candidates received some institutionally administered aid in the form of assistantships. Financial aid is not available to part-time students. Application deadlines: 7/15 for fall, 12/1 for spring. Applications are processed on a rolling basis. Contact: Financial Aid Office, 1 University Avenue, Lowell, MA 01854-2881. (508) 934-4000.

INTERNATIONAL STUDENTS
Demographics 25% of students enrolled in the program are international.
Applying TOEFL required, minimum score of 500; proof of health; proof of adequate funds. Financial aid is available to international students. Financial aid application deadlines: 4/1 for fall, 11/1 for spring. Admission application deadlines: 4/1 for fall, 11/1 for spring. Applications are processed on a rolling basis. Contact: Mrs. Anne Dean, Staff Assistant, Graduate School International Office, 1 University Avenue, Lowell, MA 01854-2881. (508) 934-2386.

PLACEMENT
Placement services include alumni network and career fairs.

Program Contact: MBA Program Director, University of Massachusetts Lowell, 1 University Avenue, Lowell, MA 01854-2881. (508) 934-4000.

Western New England College

School of Business

Springfield, Massachusetts

OVERVIEW
Western New England College is an independent nonprofit comprehensive coed institution. Founded 1919. Setting: 131-acre suburban campus. Total institutional enrollment: 4,291.

MBA HIGHLIGHTS
Entrance Difficulty*

Cost $
Tuition: $286/credit hour
Room & Board: N/R

Enrollment Profile
Full-time: 0
Part-time: 585
Total: 585
Average Age: N/R

Work Exp: 95%
International: N/R
Women: 49%
Minorities: 5%

Average Class Size: 20

ACADEMICS
Length of Program Minimum: 36 months. Maximum: 8 years.
Calendar Semesters.
Part-time Classes Main campus, Cape Cod; evening, summer.
Degree Requirements 48 credit hours including 9-12 elective credit hours.
Required Courses Business policy, economics, financial accounting, financial management, information systems, management, managerial accounting, managerial economics, marketing, marketing management, organizational behavior, quantitative methods, statistics. Courses may be waived through: previous course work.
Curricular Focus Economic and financial theory, problem solving and decision making, teamwork.
Concentrations Accounting, finance, health services, management, management information systems, marketing.
Teaching Methodology Case study: 20%, lecture: 40%, research: 10%, student presentations: 10%, team projects: 20%.

STUDENT STATISTICS
Geographic Representation State residents 100%. By region: Northeast 100%.
Undergraduate Majors Business 42%; other 58%.
Other Background Work experience: On average, students have 2-5 years of work experience on entrance to the program.

FACILITIES
Information Resources Main library with 290,865 bound volumes, 1,405 titles on microform, 4,506 periodical subscriptions, 3,427 records/tapes/CDs, 9 CD-ROMs. Business collection includes 13,700 bound volumes, 116 periodical subscriptions, 2 CD-ROMs, 180 videos.
Housing College housing not available.
Technology Computers are used moderately in course work. 50 computer terminals/PCs, linked by a campus-wide computer network, are available for use by students in program; they are located in classrooms, the library, computer labs. Students in the program are not required to have their own PC. $100 are budgeted per student for computer support.
Computer Resources/On-line Services

Training	No	E-Mail	Yes
Internet	Yes		

Other on-line services: OCLC, First Search.

ADMISSION
Entrance Requirements Bachelor's degree, GMAT score. Core courses waived through: previous course work.
Application Requirements Application form, copies of transcript, personal statement.
Application Deadline Applications are processed on a rolling basis.

FINANCIALS
Costs for 1994-95 Tuition: Part-time evening: $286/credit hour.

Financial Aid Financial aid is available to part-time students. Applications are processed on a rolling basis. Contact: Ms. Kathy M. Chambers, Director of Financial Aid, 1215 Wilbraham Road, Springfield, MA 01119-2654. (413) 782-1258.

INTERNATIONAL STUDENTS

Services and Facilities Language tutoring, ESL courses, special assistance for nonnative speakers of English, counseling/support services.

Applying Proof of health; proof of adequate funds. Financial aid is not available to international students. Admission applications are processed on a rolling basis.

ALTERNATE MBA PROGRAM

Executive MBA (EMBA) Length of program: Minimum: 12 months. Part-time classes: Main campus; weekends. Degree requirements: 30 credits. Foundation knowledge of business.

PLACEMENT

Placement services include alumni network, career counseling/planning, career fairs, career library, career placement, job interviews, resume preparation, and resume referral to employers. Of 1994 graduates, 100% were employed within three months of graduation.

Program Contact: Mr. Dave Bowman, Assistant Dean, School of Business, Western New England College, 1215 Wilbraham Road, Springfield, MA 01119-2654. (413) 782-1305; Fax: (413) 796-2068.

Worcester Polytechnic Institute

Worcester, Massachusetts

OVERVIEW

Worcester Polytechnic Institute is an independent nonprofit coed institution. Founded 1865. Setting: 80-acre rural campus with easy access to Boston. Total institutional enrollment: 3,666. Program was first offered in 1980.

MBA HIGHLIGHTS

Entrance Difficulty***
Mean GMAT: 554
Mean GPA: 3.1

Cost $$
Tuition: $532/credit
Room & Board: $5,625 (off-campus)

Enrollment Profile

Full-time: 27	Work Exp: 80%
Part-time: 189	International: 13%
Total: 216	Women: 22%
Average Age: 32	Minorities: N/R

Average Class Size: 23

ACADEMICS

Length of Program Minimum: 24 months. Maximum: 8 years.

Calendar Semesters.

Full-time Classes Main campus, Massachusetts Technology Park Corporation, Nypro Institute, Massachusetts Corporation for Education Telecommunications; evening.

Degree Requirements 45 credits including 15 elective credits.

Required Courses Business law and ethics, business policy, economic theory, financial management, management accounting, management information systems, marketing management, operations management, organizational science, statistical methods in management.

Curricular Focus Technology management.

Concentrations Engineering management, manufacturing, management, management information systems, operations management.

Faculty Full-time: 12, 92% with doctorates; part-time: 7, 57% with doctorates.

Teaching Methodology Case study: 20%, faculty seminars: 5%, lecture: 25%, research: 10%, seminars by members of the business community: 5%, student presentations: 15%, team projects: 20%.

Special Opportunities Internship program available.

STUDENT STATISTICS

Geographic Representation International 13%.

Undergraduate Majors Business 18%; engineering/technology 67%; science/mathematics 15%.

Other Background Graduate degrees in other disciplines: 16%. Work experience: On average, students have 6 years of work experience on entrance to the program.

FACILITIES

Information Resources Main library with 300,000 bound volumes, 785,000 titles on microform, 1,400 periodical subscriptions, 3,342 records/tapes/CDs. Business collection includes 17,183 bound volumes, 65 periodical subscriptions, 3 CD-ROMs, 16 videos.

Housing College housing not available.

Technology Computers are used heavily in course work. 200 computer terminals/PCs, linked by a campus-wide computer network, are available for use by students in program; they are located in the library, the computer center, computer labs. Students in the program are not required to have their own PC.

Computer Resources/On-line Services

Training	No	CompuServe	Yes
Internet	Yes	Dun's	No
E-Mail	Yes	Dow Jones	No
Videoconference Center	Yes	Dialog	Yes
Multimedia Center	Yes	Bloomberg	No
LEXIS/NEXIS	No		

Other on-line services: OCLC, Carl.

ADMISSION

Acceptance 1994-95 Of those applying, 86% were accepted.

Entrance Requirements Bachelor's degree, 2 college level calculus or 3 college level math courses, GMAT score.

Application Requirements Written essay, application form, copies of transcript, personal statement, 3 letters of recommendation.

Application Deadlines 6/1 for fall, 12/1 for spring.

FINANCIALS

Costs for 1994-95 Tuition: Full-time: $532/credit. Fees: Full-time: $20/semester. Average room and board costs are $5,625 per academic year (off-campus).

Financial Aid In 1994-95, candidates received some institutionally administered aid in the form of grants, loans, fellowships, assistantships. Financial aid is not available to part-time students. Application deadlines: 10/1 for fall, 3/1 for spring. Contact: Mr. Michael Curley, Director of Financial Aid, Financial Aid Office, 100 Institute Road, Worcester, MA 01609. (508) 831-5469.

INTERNATIONAL STUDENTS

Demographics 13% of students enrolled in the program are international.

Services and Facilities International student center, visa services, language tutoring, ESL courses, counseling/support services.

Applying TOEFL required, minimum score of 550; proof of adequate funds. Financial aid is not available to international students. Admission application deadlines: 3/1 for fall, 10/1 for spring. Contact: Mr. Tom Thomsen, Associate Dean of Student Life, Student Life Office, 100 Institute Road, Worcester, MA 01609. (508) 831-5201.

PLACEMENT

Placement services include alumni network, career counseling/planning, career fairs, career library, career placement, electronic job bank, job interviews, resume preparation, and resume referral to employers.

Program Contact: Ms. Lisa M. Jernberg, Director, Graduate Management Programs, Worcester Polytechnic Institute, 100 Institute Road, Worcester, MA 01609. (508) 831-5218; Fax: (508) 831-5720; Internet Address: jernberg@wpi.wpi.edu.

See full description on page 940.

MICHIGAN

Andrews University

School of Business

Berrien Springs, Michigan

OVERVIEW

Andrews University is an independent Seventh-day Adventist coed institution. Founded 1874. Setting: 1,650-acre small-town campus. Total institutional enrollment: 2,947. Program was first offered in 1964.

MBA HIGHLIGHTS

Entrance Difficulty**
Mean GMAT: 486
Mean GPA: 3.06

Cost $$
Tuition: $233/credit
Room & Board: N/R

Enrollment Profile

Full-time: 21	Work Exp: 70%
Part-time: 5	International: 54%
Total: 26	Women: 54%
Average Age: 29	Minorities: 73%

Average Class Size: 15

ACADEMICS

Length of Program Minimum: 12 months. Maximum: 7 years.
Calendar Quarters.
Part-time Classes Main campus; evening.
Degree Requirements 48 credits including 16 elective credits.
Required Courses Business research methods, financial management, macroeconomic analysis, managerial accounting, managerial economics and decision models, marketing management, organizational behavior. Courses may be waived through: previous course work.
Curricular Focus Business issues and problems, general management, strategic analysis and planning.
Concentrations Accounting, economics, finance, health services, human resources management, international business, management, management information systems, marketing.
Faculty Full-time: 11, 100% with doctorates; part-time: 4, 25% with doctorates.
Teaching Methodology Case study: 5%, lecture: 75%, research: 3%, student presentations: 3%, team projects: 15%.
Special Opportunities Extension programs in Hong Kong, Taiwan and Trinidad.

STUDENT STATISTICS

Geographic Representation State residents 19%. By region: Midwest 23%; Northeast 16%; South 4%. International 54%.
Undergraduate Majors Business 81%; engineering/technology 8%; humanities 8%; social sciences 4%.
Other Background Graduate degrees in other disciplines: 4%. Work experience: On average, students have 8 years of work experience on entrance to the program.

FACILITIES

Information Resources Main library with 438,154 bound volumes, 390,998 titles on microform, 2,951 periodical subscriptions, 5,563 records/tapes/CDs, 38 CD-ROMs. Business collection includes 30,000 bound volumes, 178 periodical subscriptions, 4 CD-ROMs, 107 videos.
Housing 50% of students in program live in college-owned or -operated housing.
Technology Computers are used moderately in course work. 116 computer terminals/PCs are available for use by students in program; they are located in computer labs. Students in the program are not required to have their own PC.

Computer Resources/On-line Services

Training	No	E-Mail	Yes
Internet	Yes		

Other on-line services: OCLC.

ADMISSION

Entrance Requirements Bachelor's degree, GMAT score of 400. Core courses waived through: previous course work.
Application Requirements Written essay, application form, copies of transcript, personal statement, 2 letters of recommendation.
Application Deadline Applications are processed on a rolling basis.

FINANCIALS

Costs for 1994-95 Tuition: Full-time: $233/credit. Fees: Full-time: $28/quarter.
Financial Aid In 1994-95, 96% of candidates received some institutionally administered aid in the form of scholarships, work-study. Total awards ranged from $50-$2,400. Financial aid is not available to part-time students. Applications are processed on a rolling basis. Contact: Mr. Allen F. Stembridge, Graduate Adviser, Berrien Springs, MI 49103-0022. (616) 471-3584.

INTERNATIONAL STUDENTS

Demographics 54% of students enrolled in the program are international; Asia 43%, Africa 29%, Europe 14%, Central America 7%, other 7%.
Services and Facilities Language tutoring, counseling/support services.
Applying TOEFL required, minimum score of 550; proof of health; proof of adequate funds. Financial aid is available to international students. Applications are processed on a rolling basis. Admission applications are processed on a rolling basis. Contact: Ms. Denise Holder, International Financial Student Adviser, Berrien Springs, MI 49103-0300. (616) 471-6688.

PLACEMENT

In 1993-94, 11 organizations participated in on-campus recruiting. Placement services include career fairs, career placement, job interviews, and resume preparation. Of 1994 graduates, 100% were employed within three months of graduation.

Jobs by Employer Type Service 30%; nonprofit 50%; other 20%.
Jobs by Functional Area Marketing/sales 10%; finance 10%; management 80%.

Program Contact: Mr. Allen F. Stembridge, Graduate Adviser, Andrews University, Berrien Springs, MI 49104. (616) 471-3584, or (800) 253-2874; Fax: (616) 471-6158.

Aquinas College

Grand Rapids, Michigan

OVERVIEW

Aquinas College is an independent Roman Catholic comprehensive coed institution. Founded 1886. Setting: 107-acre suburban campus with easy access to Detroit and Chicago. Total institutional enrollment: 2,443. Program was first offered in 1977.

PROGRAM HIGHLIGHTS

Entrance Difficulty*
Mean GMAT: 475
Mean GPA: N/R

Cost $
Tuition: $281/credit hour
Room & Board: N/R

Enrollment Profile

Full-time: 11	Work Exp: N/R
Part-time: 340	International: N/R
Total: 351	Women: 46%
Average Age: 37	Minorities: 5%

Average Class Size: 25

ACADEMICS

Calendar Semesters.
Curricular Focus General management, managerial skills development, teamwork.

Concentrations Human resources management, international business, marketing.

Faculty Full-time: 13; part-time: 13.

Teaching Methodology Case study: 20%, faculty seminars: 10%, lecture: 20%, research: 5%, student presentations: 15%, team projects: 30%.

STUDENT STATISTICS

Geographic Representation By region: Midwest 100%.

FACILITIES

Information Resources Main library with 104,496 bound volumes, 95,763 titles on microform, 930 periodical subscriptions, 4,150 records/tapes/CDs, 7 CD-ROMs.

Housing College housing not available.

Technology 126 computer terminals/PCs, linked by a campus-wide computer network, are available for use by students in program; they are located in computer labs.

Computer Resources/On-line Services
E-Mail   No

ADMISSION

Acceptance 1994-95 88 applied for admission; 95% were accepted.

Entrance Requirements Bachelor's degree, GMAT score, minimum 2.75 GPA, minimum 2 years of work experience. Core courses waived through: previous course work.

Application Requirements Interview, application form, copies of transcript, personal statement, 3 letters of recommendation.

Application Deadline Applications are processed on a rolling basis.

FINANCIALS

Costs for 1994-95 Tuition: Full-time: $281/credit hour.

Financial Aid In 1994-95, 19% of candidates received some institutionally administered aid in the form of grants, scholarships, loans. Total awards ranged from $100-$8,500. Financial aid is available to part-time students. Applications are processed on a rolling basis. Contact: Mr. David Steffee, Director of Financial Aid, 1607 Robinson Road, SE, Grand Rapids, MI 49506-1799. (616) 459-8281 Ext. 5127.

INTERNATIONAL STUDENTS

Applying Financial aid is not available to international students. Admission applications are processed on a rolling basis. Contact: Mr. Michael Gantt, Coordinator of Transfer and International Student Admissions, 1607 Robinson Road, SE, Grand Rapids, MI 49506-1799. (616) 459-8281.

PROGRAM

M Mgmt Length of program: Minimum: 48 months. Maximum: 7 years. Part-time classes: Main campus; evening, weekends, summer. Degree requirements: 39 credit hours including 12 elective credit hours.

PLACEMENT

Placement services include alumni network, career counseling/planning, career fairs, career library, career placement, electronic job bank, job interviews, resume preparation, and resume referral to employers.

Program Contact: Dr. Joyce McNally, Interim Dean of Graduate Studies, Aquinas College, 1607 Robinson Road, SE, Grand Rapids, MI 49506-1799. (616) 732-4464 Ext. 5441, or (800) 748-0350.

Central Michigan University

College of Business Administration

Mount Pleasant, Michigan

OVERVIEW

Central Michigan University is a state-supported coed institution. Founded 1892. Setting: 854-acre small-town campus. Total institutional enrollment: 16,500. Program was first offered in 1960. AACSB-accredited.

MBA HIGHLIGHTS

Entrance Difficulty*
Mean GMAT: 511
Mean GPA: 3.18

Cost $
Tuition: $122/credit hour
(Nonresident: $243/credit hour)
Room & Board: $4,000

Enrollment Profile

Full-time: 160	Work Exp: 86%
Part-time: 400	International: 7%
Total: 560	Women: 32%
Average Age: 27	Minorities: 21%

Average Class Size: 25

ACADEMICS

Length of Program Minimum: 15 months. Maximum: 7 years.

Calendar Semesters.

Full-time Classes Main campus, Midland; evening, summer.

Part-time Classes Main campus, Midland; evening, summer.

Degree Requirements 36 credit hours including 6 elective credit hours.

Required Courses Business policy and strategy, financial management, managerial accounting, managerial economics, marketing strategy, methods of business research, organizational behavior and change, production and operations management, public policy international law and American enterprise, quantitative decision making. Courses may be waived through: previous course work, work experience.

Curricular Focus Leadership, problem solving and decision making, teamwork.

Concentration Management.

Faculty Full-time: 15, 100% with doctorates.

Teaching Methodology Case study: 30%, lecture: 30%, research: 10%, student presentations: 20%, team projects: 10%.

Special Opportunities International exchange in France. Internship program available.

STUDENT STATISTICS

Geographic Representation State residents 90%. By region: Midwest 90%. International 7%.

Undergraduate Majors Business 50%; education 3%; engineering/technology 31%; humanities 4%; science/mathematics 5%; social sciences 5%; other 2%.

Other Background Graduate degrees in other disciplines: 15%. Work experience: On average, students have 4 years of work experience on entrance to the program.

FACILITIES

Information Resources Main library with 847,899 bound volumes, 1.1 million titles on microform, 5,406 periodical subscriptions, 267,408 records/tapes/CDs.

Housing 5% of students in program live in college-owned or -operated housing.

Technology Computers are used moderately in course work. 200 computer terminals/PCs are available for use by students in program; they are located in student rooms, classrooms, the computer center, computer labs. Students in the program are not required to have their own PC.

Computer Resources/On-line Services

Internet	Yes	Dialog	Yes
E-Mail	Yes		

ADMISSION

Acceptance 1994-95 Of those applying, 71% were accepted.

Entrance Requirements Bachelor's degree, GMAT score of 400, minimum 2.5 GPA. Core courses waived through: previous course work.

Application Requirements Written essay, application form, copies of transcript.

Application Deadline Applications are processed on a rolling basis.

FINANCIALS

Costs for 1994-95 Tuition: Part-time evening: $122/credit hour for state residents, $243/credit hour for nonresidents. Fees: Part-time evening: $130/semester for state residents, $130/semester for nonresidents. Average room and board costs are $4,000 per academic year (on-campus).

Financial Aid In 1994-95, 5% of candidates received some institutionally administered aid in the form of assistantships. Total awards ranged from $800-$6,600. Financial aid is not available to part-time students. Application deadline: 2/6 for fall. Contact: Office of Scholarships and Financial Aid, 204 Warriner Hall, Mount Pleasant, MI 48859. (517) 774-3674.

INTERNATIONAL STUDENTS

Demographics 7% of students enrolled in the program are international; Asia 54%, Europe 41%, other 5%.

Services and Facilities Language tutoring, ESL courses, special assistance for nonnative speakers of English, counseling/support services.

Applying TOEFL required, minimum score of 550; proof of health; proof of adequate funds. Financial aid is not available to international students. Admission application deadlines: 5/1 for fall, 8/1 for spring. Contact: Dr. Edward Grant, Director, Graduate Business Studies, Mount Pleasant, MI 48859. (517) 774-3150.

PLACEMENT
Placement services include career counseling/planning, career library, career placement, electronic job bank, job interviews, resume preparation, and resume referral to employers.

Program Contact: Dr. Edward Grant, Director, Graduate Business Studies, Central Michigan University, Mount Pleasant, MI 48859. (517) 774-3150; Fax: (517) 774-2372.

Eastern Michigan University

College of Business

Ypsilanti, Michigan

OVERVIEW
Eastern Michigan University is a state-supported comprehensive coed institution. Founded 1849. Setting: 460-acre urban campus with easy access to Detroit and Toledo. Total institutional enrollment: 24,000. Program was first offered in 1964. AACSB-accredited.

MBA HIGHLIGHTS

Entrance Difficulty**
Mean GMAT: 525
Mean GPA: 3.01

Cost $
Tuition: $130/credit hour
(Nonresident: $300/credit hour)
Room & Board: $4,800

Enrollment Profile

Full-time: 100	Work Exp: 90%
Part-time: 500	International: 25%
Total: 600	Women: 40%
Average Age: 30	Minorities: 3%

Average Class Size: 24

ACADEMICS
Length of Program Minimum: 12 months. Maximum: 6 years.
Calendar Trimesters.
Full-time Classes Main campus; evening, weekends, summer.
Part-time Classes Main campus; evening, weekends, summer.
Degree Requirements 33 credit hours including 9 elective credit hours.
Required Courses Administrative controls, financial administration policies, management communication theory and practice, managerial economics and decision analysis, marketing policies and problems, organizational theory and behavior, seminar in management strategy and policy, techniques in business research. Courses may be waived through: previous course work.
Curricular Focus General management, problem solving and decision making, strategic analysis and planning.
Concentrations Accounting, finance, human resources management, international business, management, management information systems, marketing, operations management, organizational behavior, strategic management, strategic quality management.
Faculty Full-time: 50, 96% with doctorates; part-time: 1.
Teaching Methodology Case study: 20%, faculty seminars: 5%, lecture: 30%, research: 5%, seminars by members of the business community: 10%, student presentations: 15%, team projects: 15%.
Special Opportunities International exchange in Canada, Germany, Mexico. Internship program available. Other: cooperative education.

STUDENT STATISTICS
Geographic Representation State residents 73%. By region: Midwest 75%. International 25%.

Undergraduate Majors Business 50%; education 3%; engineering/technology 18%; humanities 5%; nursing 2%; science/mathematics 11%; social sciences 9%; other 2%.
Other Background Graduate degrees in other disciplines: 10%. Work experience: On average, students have 6 years of work experience on entrance to the program.

FACILITIES
Information Resources Main library with 828,097 bound volumes, 6,638 titles on microform, 5,172 periodical subscriptions, 12,052 records/tapes/CDs, 51 CD-ROMs. Business collection includes 113,385 bound volumes, 345 periodical subscriptions, 3 CD-ROMs, 85 videos.
Housing 15% of students in program live in college-owned or -operated housing.
Technology Computers are used heavily in course work. 250 computer terminals/PCs, linked by a campus-wide computer network, are available for use by students in program; they are located in the student center, learning resource center, the library, the computer center, computer labs. Students in the program are not required to have their own PC.

Computer Resources/On-line Services

Training	Yes	CompuServe	Yes
Internet	Yes	Dun's	No
E-Mail	Yes	Dow Jones	Yes $
Multimedia Center	Yes	Dialog	Yes $
LEXIS/NEXIS	Yes	Bloomberg	No

ADMISSION
Acceptance 1994-95 Of those applying, 80% were accepted.
Entrance Requirements Bachelor's degree, GMAT score of 450, minimum 2.5 GPA. Core courses waived through: previous course work.
Application Requirements Written essay, application form, copies of transcript, personal statement.
Application Deadlines 3/15 for fall, 9/15 for winter, 2/15 for spring.

FINANCIALS
Costs for 1994-95 Tuition: Full-time: $130/credit hour for state residents, $300/credit hour for nonresidents. Fees: Full-time: $405 for state residents, $405 for nonresidents. Average room and board costs are $4,800 per academic year (on-campus) and $5,000 per academic year (off-campus).
Financial Aid In 1994-95, 10% of candidates received some institutionally administered aid in the form of loans, fellowships, assistantships. Total awards ranged from $500-$10,600. Financial aid is not available to part-time students. Application deadline: 3/15 for fall. Contact: Financial Aid Office, 403 Pierce Hall, Ypsilanti, MI 48199. (313) 487-0455.

INTERNATIONAL STUDENTS
Demographics 25% of students enrolled in the program are international; Asia 82%, Other 18%.
Services and Facilities International student center, language tutoring, ESL courses, special assistance for nonnative speakers of English, counseling/support services, host hospitality service.
Applying TOEFL required, minimum score of 500; proof of health; proof of adequate funds. Financial aid is not available to international students. Admission application deadlines: 3/15 for fall, 9/15 for winter, 2/15 for spring. Contact: Mr. Paul D. Webb, Coordinator, Foreign Student Affairs, 208 Goodison Hall, Ypsilanti, MI 48197. (313) 487-3116.

PLACEMENT
Placement services include alumni network, career counseling/planning, career fairs, career library, career placement, electronic job bank, job interviews, resume preparation, and resume referral to employers. Of 1994 graduates, 95% were employed within three months of graduation, the average starting salary was $38,000, the range was $25,000-$100,000.

Program Contact: Mr. William E. Whitmore, Director, Graduate Business Programs, Eastern Michigan University, Ypsilanti, MI 48197. (313) 487-4444; Fax: (313) 487-7099.
See full description on page 726.

Grand Valley State University

F. E. Seidman School of Business

Allendale, Michigan

OVERVIEW
Grand Valley State University is a state-supported comprehensive coed institution. Founded 1960. Setting: 900-acre urban campus with easy access to Grand Rapids. Total institutional enrollment: 13,400. Program was first offered in 1973.

MBA HIGHLIGHTS

Entrance Difficulty***
Mean GMAT: 540
Mean GPA: 3.2

Cost $
Tuition: $130/credit
(Nonresident: $275/credit)
Room & Board: $4,200

Enrollment Profile

Full-time: 30	Work Exp: 90%
Part-time: 370	International: 1%
Total: 400	Women: 39%
Average Age: 32	Minorities: 1%

Average Class Size: N/R

ACADEMICS
Length of Program Minimum: 12 months. Maximum: 8 years.
Calendar Semesters.
Full-time Classes Main campus, Grand Rapids; evening, summer.
Part-time Classes Main campus, Grand Rapids; evening, summer.
Degree Requirements 33 credits including 9 elective credits.
Required Courses Accounting, economics, finance, management information systems strategy, marketing, operations management, organizational behavior. Courses may be waived through: previous course work.
Curricular Focus Business issues and problems, manufacturing and production management, problem solving and decision making.
Concentrations Accounting, finance, management, marketing.
Faculty Full-time: 13, 100% with doctorates; part-time: 6, 50% with doctorates.
Teaching Methodology Case study: 15%, lecture: 40%, research: 10%, seminars by members of the business community: 10%, student presentations: 10%, team projects: 15%.
Special Opportunities International exchange in Germany, Poland, United Kingdom.

STUDENT STATISTICS
Geographic Representation State residents 99%. By region: Midwest 99%. International 1%.
Undergraduate Majors Business 45%; engineering/technology 25%; humanities 9%; science/mathematics 15%; social sciences 5%; other 1%.
Other Background Graduate degrees in other disciplines: 3%. Work experience: On average, students have 5 years of work experience on entrance to the program.

FACILITIES
Information Resources Main library with 450,000 bound volumes, 577,780 titles on microform, 2,477 periodical subscriptions, 9,816 records/tapes/CDs, 59 CD-ROMs. Business collection includes 20,700 bound volumes, 262 periodical subscriptions.
Housing 1% of students in program live in college-owned or -operated housing.
Technology Computers are used moderately in course work. Computer terminals/PCs, linked by a campus-wide computer network, are available for use by students in program; they are located in dormitories, classrooms, the library, the computer center, computer labs. Students in the program are not required to have their own PC.

Computer Resources/On-line Services

Training	Yes	LEXIS/NEXIS	Yes
Internet	Yes	Dun's	Yes
E-Mail	Yes	Dow Jones	Yes
Videoconference Center	Yes		

ADMISSION
Acceptance 1994-95 210 applied for admission; 85% were accepted.
Entrance Requirements Bachelor's degree, GMAT score of 450, minimum 2.8 GPA. Core courses waived through: previous course work.
Application Requirements Written essay, application form, copies of transcript.
Application Deadlines 7/15 for fall, 11/15 for spring, 3/15 for summer.

FINANCIALS
Costs for 1994-95 Tuition: Full-time: $130/credit for state residents, $275/credit for nonresidents. Fees: Full-time: $272 for state residents, $272 for nonresidents. Average room and board costs are $4,200 per academic year (on-campus).
Financial Aid In 1994-95, candidates received some institutionally administered aid in the form of scholarships, loans, assistantships. Financial aid is available to part-time students. Application deadline: 4/1 for fall. Contact: Mr. Ken Fridsma, Director of Financial Aid, Seidman House, 1 Campus Drive, Allendale, MI 49401. (616) 895-3234.

INTERNATIONAL STUDENTS
Demographics 1% of students enrolled in the program are international; Europe 50%, Asia 35%, Africa 15%.
Services and Facilities ESL courses, counseling/support services.
Applying TOEFL required, minimum score of 550; proof of health; proof of adequate funds. Financial aid is not available to international students. Admission application deadline: 6/1 for fall.

PLACEMENT
Placement services include career placement. Of 1994 graduates, 95% were employed within three months of graduation.

Program Contact: Ms. Claudia Bajema, MBA Program Director, Grand Valley State University, 1 Campus Drive, Allendale, MI 49401-9403. (616) 771-6675; Fax: (616) 771-6642; Internet Address: bajemac@gvsu.edu.

Lake Superior State University

School of Business

Sault Sainte Marie, Michigan

OVERVIEW
Lake Superior State University is a state-supported comprehensive coed institution. Founded 1946. Setting: 121-acre small-town campus. Total institutional enrollment: 3,301. Program was first offered in 1981.

MBA HIGHLIGHTS

Entrance Difficulty**
Mean GMAT: N/R
Mean GPA: 3.68

Cost
Tuition: N/R
(Nonresident: N/R)
Room & Board: $4,228

Enrollment Profile

Full-time: 7	Work Exp: 100%
Part-time: 137	International: 31%
Total: 144	Women: 51%
Average Age: 35	Minorities: 4%

Average Class Size: 14

ACADEMICS
Calendar Semesters.
Curricular Focus International business, strategic analysis and planning, teamwork.
Concentration Management.
Faculty Full-time: 9, 78% with doctorates; part-time: 27, 44% with doctorates.

Teaching Methodology Case study: 15%, lecture: 35%, research: 12%, seminars by members of the business community: 3%, student presentations: 15%, team projects: 20%.

STUDENT STATISTICS
Geographic Representation State residents 69%. By region: Midwest 69%. International 31%.

FACILITIES
Information Resources Main library with 131,000 bound volumes, 79,000 titles on microform, 1,000 periodical subscriptions.

Housing College housing available.

Technology Computers are used moderately in course work. 180 computer terminals/PCs, linked by a campus-wide computer network, are available for use by students in program; they are located in dormitories, classrooms, learning resource center, the library, computer labs. Students in the program are not required to have their own PC.

Computer Resources/On-line Services

Training	No	CompuServe	No
Internet	Yes	Dun's	No
E-Mail	Yes	Dow Jones	No
Videoconference Center	Yes	Dialog	Yes $
LEXIS/NEXIS	No	Bloomberg	No

Other on-line services: OCLC.

ADMISSION
Acceptance 1994-95 36 applied for admission; 92% were accepted.

Entrance Requirements Bachelor's degree, equivalent of a minimum of 120 semester hours, GMAT score, 1 letter of recommendation from employer. Core courses waived through: previous course work.

Application Requirements Application form, copies of transcript, 2 letters of recommendation.

Application Deadlines 8/1 for fall, 12/1 for spring, 4/1 for summer.

FINANCIALS
Financial Aid In 1994-95, 6% of candidates received some institutionally administered aid in the form of grants. Total awards ranged from $450-$1,818. Financial aid is available to part-time students. Application deadlines: 3/1 for fall, 3/1 for spring. Applications are processed on a rolling basis. Contact: Mr. William Munsell, Financial Aid Director, Sault Sainte Marie, MI 49763. (906) 635-2678.

INTERNATIONAL STUDENTS
Demographics 31% of students enrolled in the program are international.

Services and Facilities Counseling/support services.

Applying TOEFL required, minimum score of 550; proof of adequate funds; health insurance. Financial aid is not available to international students. Admission application deadlines: 8/1 for fall, 12/1 for spring, 4/1 for summer. Applications are processed on a rolling basis. Contact: Mr. William Munsell, Financial Aid Director, Sault Sainte Marie, MI 49763. (906) 635-2678.

PROGRAM
Executive MBA (EMBA) Length of program: Minimum: 12 months. Maximum: 8 years. Part-time classes: Main campus, Traverse City, Escanaba, Alpena, Petoskey, distance learning option; evening, weekends, summer. Degree requirements: 36 credits including 15 elective credits. Average class size: 14.

PLACEMENT
Placement services include career counseling/planning, career fairs, career library, career placement, job interviews, resume preparation, and resume referral to employers.

Program Contact: Ms. Susan Camp, Acting Director of Continuing Education, Community Services and Development, Lake Superior State University, Sault Sainte Marie, MI 49783. (906) 635-2554, or (800) 682-4800 (MI only); Fax: (906) 635-2762.

Lawrence Technological University

College of Management

Southfield, Michigan

OVERVIEW
Lawrence Technological University is an independent nonprofit comprehensive coed institution. Founded 1932. Setting: 100-acre suburban campus with easy access to Detroit. Total institutional enrollment: 4,159.

MBA HIGHLIGHTS
Entrance Difficulty N/R

Cost $
Tuition: $300/credit hour
Room & Board: N/R

Enrollment Profile

Full-time: N/R	Work Exp: N/R
Part-time: N/R	International: 10%
Total: 200	Women: 40%
Average Age: N/R	Minorities: N/R

Average Class Size: 20

ACADEMICS
Length of Program Minimum: 36 months.

Calendar Quarters.

Part-time Classes Main campus; evening, weekends, summer.

Degree Requirements 36 credits.

Curricular Focus Leadership, problem solving and decision making, strategic analysis and planning.

Concentrations Human resources management, operations management, strategic management.

Teaching Methodology Case study: 30%, faculty seminars: 10%, lecture: 20%, student presentations: 20%, team projects: 20%.

STUDENT STATISTICS
Geographic Representation State residents 90%. International 10%.

FACILITIES
Information Resources Main library with 80,000 bound volumes, 8,200 titles on microform, 600 periodical subscriptions, 308 records/tapes/CDs.

ADMISSION
Entrance Requirements Bachelor's degree.

Application Requirements Interview, application form, copies of transcript, resume/curriculum vitae.

Application Deadline Applications are processed on a rolling basis.

FINANCIALS
Costs for 1994-95 Tuition: Part-time evening: $300/credit hour. Fees: Part-time evening: $100/semester.

Financial Aid Contact: Mr. Paul Kinder, Director of Financial Aid, 27000 West Ten Mile Road, Southfield, MI 48075-1058. (810) 204-2120.

INTERNATIONAL STUDENTS
Demographics 10% of students enrolled in the program are international.

Applying TOEFL required. Financial aid is available to international students. Admission applications are processed on a rolling basis.

Program Contact: Ms. Sheri Koeberl, Graduate Admissions Counselor, Lawrence Technological University, 21000 West Ten Mile Road, Southfield, MI 48075-1058. (810) 204-3186; Fax: (810) 204-3099.

Madonna University

School of Business

Livonia, Michigan

OVERVIEW
Madonna University is an independent Roman Catholic comprehensive coed institution. Founded 1947. Setting: 49-acre suburban campus with easy access to Detroit. Total institutional enrollment: 4,400.

PROGRAM HIGHLIGHTS
Entrance Difficulty N/R
Mean GMAT: 450
Mean GPA: N/R

Cost $
Tuition: $220/semester hour
Room & Board: N/R

Enrollment Profile

Full-time: N/R	Work Exp: N/R
Part-time: N/R	International: 1%
Total: 250	Women: 75%
Average Age: N/R	Minorities: 1%

Average Class Size: 35

ACADEMICS
Calendar Semesters.

Curricular Focus International business, leadership, organizational development and change management.

Concentrations International business, operations management.

STUDENT STATISTICS
Geographic Representation State residents 100%. International 1%.

FACILITIES
Information Resources Main library with 118,632 bound volumes, 1,244 titles on microform, 1,679 periodical subscriptions, 5,668 records/tapes/CDs.

ADMISSION
Entrance Requirements Bachelor's degree, GMAT score, minimum 3.0 GPA.

Application Requirements Interview, application form, copies of transcript, 2 letters of recommendation.

Application Deadline Applications are processed on a rolling basis.

FINANCIALS
Estimated Costs for 1995-96 Tuition: Part-time evening: $220/semester hour. Fees: Part-time evening: $15/semester.

Financial Aid Contact: Ms. Alisa Carducci-Bieritz, Assistant Director of Financial Aid, 36600 Schoolcraft Road, Livonia, MI 48150-1173. (313) 591-5193.

INTERNATIONAL STUDENTS
Demographics 1% of students enrolled in the program are international.

Applying TOEFL required; proof of health; proof of adequate funds. Admission applications are processed on a rolling basis.

PROGRAMS
MSA Length of program: Minimum: 24 months. Part-time classes: Main campus; evening, weekends, summer. Degree requirements: 36 credits.

MSA/MSN Length of program: Minimum: 48 months. Part-time classes: Main campus; evening, weekends. Degree requirements: 60 credits.

MSBA Length of program: Minimum: 18 months. Part-time classes: Main campus; evening, weekends. Degree requirements: 30 credits. Applicant must be practicing dentist or physician.

Program Contact: Dr. Ernest Nolan, Dean of Graduate Studies and Humanities, Madonna University, 36600 Schoolcraft Road, Livonia, MI 48150-1173. (313) 591-5084; Fax: (313) 591-0156.

Michigan State University

Eli Broad Graduate School of Management

East Lansing, Michigan

OVERVIEW
Michigan State University is a state-supported coed institution. Founded 1855. Setting: 5,000-acre urban campus with easy access to Detroit. Total institutional enrollment: 40,254. Program was first offered in 1960. AACSB-accredited.

MBA HIGHLIGHTS

Entrance Difficulty**
Mean GMAT: N/R
Mean GPA: 3.25

Cost $$
Tuition: $226/credit
(Nonresident: $517/credit)
Room & Board: $3,436

Enrollment Profile

Full-time: 260	Work Exp: 80%
Part-time: 0	International: 31%
Total: 260	Women: 30%
Average Age: 26	Minorities: 11%

Average Class Size: 35

ACADEMICS
Length of Program Minimum: 21 months. Maximum: 2 years.

Calendar Semesters.

Full-time Classes Main campus; day.

Degree Requirements 54 credits. Other: Calculus, statistics.

Required Courses Business communication, decision support models, financial accounting, legal environment of business, macroeconomics, managerial accounting, managerial economics, managerial finance, marketing management, materials and logistics management, organizational behavior and the management of people, strategic management.

Curricular Focus Leadership, problem solving and decision making, teamwork.

Concentrations Accounting, finance, hotel management, human resources management, management, marketing, operations management, purchasing, transportation.

Faculty Full-time: 71, 100% with doctorates.

Teaching Methodology Case study: 40%, lecture: 30%, seminars by members of the business community: 5%, student presentations: 10%, team projects: 15%.

Special Opportunities International exchange in Norway. Internship program available.

STUDENT STATISTICS
Geographic Representation State residents 56%. By region: Midwest 60%; Northeast 3%; South 3%; West 3%. International 31%.

Undergraduate Majors Business 64%; engineering/technology 14%; humanities 3%; science/mathematics 5%; social sciences 10%; other 4%.

Other Background Graduate degrees in other disciplines: 5%. Work experience: On average, students have 2 years of work experience on entrance to the program.

FACILITIES
Information Resources Main library with 3.9 million bound volumes, 3.3 million titles on microform, 28,000 periodical subscriptions, 30,600 records/tapes/CDs. Business collection includes 55,000 bound volumes, 900 periodical subscriptions, 10 CD-ROMs.

Housing 40% of students in program live in college-owned or -operated housing.

Technology Computers are used moderately in course work. 115 computer terminals/PCs, linked by a campus-wide computer network, are available for use by students in program; they are located in computer labs. Students in the program are not required to have their own PC.

Computer Resources/On-line Services

Training	Yes	Dun's	No
Internet	Yes	Dow Jones	Yes
E-Mail	Yes	Dialog	Yes $
LEXIS/NEXIS	No	Bloomberg	No
CompuServe	No		

ADMISSION
Acceptance 1994-95 608 applied for admission; 34% were accepted.

Entrance Requirements Bachelor's degree, calculus, statistics, GMAT score.

Application Requirements Written essay, application form, copies of transcript, resume/curriculum vitae, 3 letters of recommendation.

Application Deadline 4/1 for fall.

FINANCIALS
Costs for 1994-95 Tuition: Full-time: $226/credit for state residents, $517/credit for nonresidents. Fees: Full-time: $262/semester for state residents, $262/semester for nonresidents. Average room and board costs are $3,436 per academic year (on-campus).

Financial Aid In 1994-95, 60% of candidates received some institutionally administered aid in the form of grants, scholarships, loans, assistantships. Contact: Mr. Evan Montague, Senior Financial Aid Adviser, 252 Student Services Building, East Lansing, MI 48824-1113. (517) 353-5940.

INTERNATIONAL STUDENTS

Demographics 31% of students enrolled in the program are international; Asia 45%, Europe 30%, Africa 5%, South America 5%, other 15%.

Services and Facilities International student center, language tutoring, ESL courses, counseling/support services, immigration services.

Applying TOEFL required; proof of adequate funds. Financial aid is available to international students. Assistantships are available for these students. Applications are processed on a rolling basis. Admission application deadline: 4/1 for fall. Contact: Dr. Ken Ebert, Assistant Director, Office of International Education, Exchange/International Students and Scholars, 103 International Center, East Lansing, MI 48824-1035. (517) 353-1720.

ALTERNATE MBA PROGRAM

Executive MBA (EMBA) Length of program: Minimum: 21 months. Degree requirements: 43 credits. 8-10 years of work experience, 5 years in supervision or upper management; GMAT; nomination by employer. Average class size: 60.

PLACEMENT

In 1993-94, 41 organizations participated in on-campus recruiting. Placement services include alumni network, career counseling/planning, career fairs, career library, career placement, job interviews, resume preparation, and resume referral to employers. Of 1994 graduates, 87% were employed within three months of graduation, the average starting salary was $47,202, the range was $21,000-$145,000.

Jobs by Employer Type Manufacturing 35%; service 48%; government 4%; nonprofit 4%; education 9%.

Jobs by Functional Area Marketing/sales 17%; finance 59%; operations 18%; human resources 6%.

Program Contact: Ms. Jennifer Chizuk, Assistant Director of the MBA Program, Michigan State University, 215 Eppley Center, East Lansing, MI 48824-1121. (517) 355-7604, or (800) 4MSU-MBA; Fax: (517) 353-1649.

Northwood University

Richard DeVos Graduate School of Management

Midland, Michigan

OVERVIEW

Northwood University is an independent nonprofit comprehensive coed institution. Founded 1959. Setting: 268-acre small-town campus. Total institutional enrollment: 1,383. Program was first offered in 1992.

MBA HIGHLIGHTS

Entrance Difficulty***
Mean GMAT: 500
Mean GPA: N/R

Cost
Tuition: N/R
Room & Board: N/R

Enrollment Profile

Full-time: 6	Work Exp: N/R
Part-time: 94	International: 6%
Total: 100	Women: 25%
Average Age: N/R	Minorities: N/R

Average Class Size: 15

ACADEMICS

Calendar Quarters.

Curricular Focus Leadership, problem solving and decision making.

Concentration Management.

Faculty Full-time: 4, 100% with doctorates.

Teaching Methodology Case study: 80%, lecture: 20%.

STUDENT STATISTICS

Geographic Representation State residents 94%. International 6%.

FACILITIES

Information Resources Main library with 47,000 bound volumes, 1,500 titles on microform, 520 periodical subscriptions, 500 records/tapes/CDs.

Computer Resources/On-line Services
Training   No

ADMISSION

Entrance Requirements Bachelor's degree, GMAT score, minimum 3.0 GPA, minimum 5 years of work experience.

Application Requirements Written essay, interview, application form, copies of transcript, resume/curriculum vitae.

Application Deadline Applications are processed on a rolling basis.

FINANCIALS

Financial Aid Financial aid is not available to part-time students.

INTERNATIONAL STUDENTS

Demographics 6% of students enrolled in the program are international.

Applying TOEFL required, minimum score of 550; proof of adequate funds. Financial aid is not available to international students. Admission applications are processed on a rolling basis. Contact: Ms. Vivian Romine, International Student Adviser, 3225 Cook Road, Midland, MI 48640-2398. (517) 837-4124.

PROGRAM

Executive MBA (EMBA) Length of program: Minimum: 18 months. Full-time classes: Main campus, Detroit; evening. Part-time classes: Main campus, Detroit; evening. Degree requirements: 56 credits.

Program Contact: Dr. William T. Busby, Dean, Executive MBA Program, Northwood University, 3225 Cook Road, Midland, MI 48640-2398. (517) 837-4488, or (800) MBA-9000; Fax: (517) 832-7744.

Oakland University

School of Business Administration

Rochester, Michigan

OVERVIEW

Oakland University is a state-supported coed institution. Founded 1957. Setting: 1,444-acre suburban campus with easy access to Detroit. Total institutional enrollment: 13,000. Program was first offered in 1979. AACSB-accredited.

MBA HIGHLIGHTS

Entrance Difficulty***
Mean GMAT: 546
Mean GPA: 3.08

Cost $
Tuition: $188/credit hour
(Nonresident: $395/credit hour)
Room & Board: $3,890

Enrollment Profile

Full-time: 29	Work Exp: 95%
Part-time: 296	International: 6%
Total: 325	Women: 37%
Average Age: 28	Minorities: 15%

Average Class Size: 30

Oakland University is a comprehensive, state-assisted institution of approximately 13,000 students that offers a diverse set of academic programs, from baccalaureate to doctoral levels. Located between the cities of Pontiac and Rochester, Oakland University (at the intersection of I-75 and M-59) is easily accessible to millions of Detroit metropolitan area residents. Programs in the School of Business Administration are accredited by the American Assembly of Collegiate Schools of Business (AACSB). Oakland University is among three universities in Michigan that have also achieved AACSB accreditation for their accounting programs.

The M.B.A. program provides a solid foundation in the functional areas of business, with special emphasis on the management of information resources. Seven concentrations (accounting, business economics, finance, management information systems, human resources management, marketing, and production/operations management) allow students to tailor the program to their career goals. Course work includes real-life cases and applications to assist students with the development of problem-solving skills. Classroom interaction provides students with the opportunity to further share and expand their knowledge. Classes are held in the evening or on Saturday mornings to accommodate the working adult. Oakland University's

M.B.A. program is open to both individuals who hold bachelor's degrees in business and nonbusiness majors. Women and minorities are encouraged to apply.

ACADEMICS

Length of Program Minimum: 24 months. Maximum: 6 years.

Calendar Semesters.

Full-time Classes Main campus; evening, weekends, summer.

Part-time Classes Main campus; evening, weekends, summer.

Degree Requirements 36 credit hours including 12 elective credit hours.

Required Courses Human resources management, macroeconomic analysis, management information systems, management of information resources, managerial accounting systems, managerial finance, marketing, operations management, policy strategy and goals. Courses may be waived through: previous course work.

Curricular Focus Management information systems.

Concentrations Accounting, economics, finance, health services, human resources management, international business, management, management information systems, marketing, operations management.

Faculty Full-time: 47, 95% with doctorates.

Teaching Methodology Case study: 20%, lecture: 40%, research: 13%, seminars by members of the business community: 2%, student presentations: 10%, team projects: 15%.

Special Opportunities Internship program available.

STUDENT STATISTICS

Geographic Representation State residents 94%. By region: Midwest 94%. International 6%.

Undergraduate Majors Business 35%; education 5%; engineering/technology 40%; humanities 3%; nursing 2%; science/mathematics 5%; social sciences 10%.

Other Background Graduate degrees in other disciplines: 3%. Work experience: On average, students have 5 years of work experience on entrance to the program.

FACILITIES

Information Resources Main library with 593,868 bound volumes, 113,800 titles on microform, 2,040 periodical subscriptions, 15,773 records/tapes/CDs, 8 CD-ROMs.

Housing College housing available.

Technology Computers are used heavily in course work. 116 computer terminals/PCs are available for use by students in program; they are located in computer labs. Students in the program are not required to have their own PC.

Computer Resources/On-line Services

Training	Yes	Multimedia Center	Yes
Internet	Yes	Dialog	Yes
E-Mail	Yes		

ADMISSION

Acceptance 1994-95 141 applied for admission; 79% were accepted.

Entrance Requirements Bachelor's degree, one course each in college algebra and micro or macroeronomics, GMAT score of 450, minimum 2.5 GPA. Core courses waived through: previous course work.

Application Requirements Written essay, application form, copies of transcript, supplemental application.

Application Deadlines 7/15 for fall, 11/15 for spring. Application discs available.

FINANCIALS

Costs for 1994-95 Tuition: Full-time: $188/credit hour for state residents, $395/credit hour for nonresidents. Fees: Full-time: $230/term for state residents, $115/term for nonresidents. Average room and board costs are $3,890 per academic year (on-campus).

Financial Aid In 1994-95, 2% of candidates received some institutionally administered aid in the form of scholarships, assistantships. Total awards ranged from $500-$7,544. Financial aid is not available to part-time students. Application deadline: 3/15 for fall. Contact: Ms. Sheryl Lynn Clark, Director of MBA Program, 416 Varner Hall, Rochester, MI 48309-4401. (810) 370-3287.

INTERNATIONAL STUDENTS

Demographics 6% of students enrolled in the program are international; Europe 80%, Asia 20%.

Services and Facilities Visa services, counseling/support services.

Applying TOEFL required, minimum score of 500; proof of adequate funds. Financial aid is available to international students. Assistantships are available for these students; deadline is 4/1. Admission application deadline:

5/1 for fall. Contact: Ms. Lisa McGill, Director, Special Advising, 134 North Foundation Hall, Rochester, MI 48309-4401. (810) 370-3266.

PLACEMENT

Placement services include alumni network, career counseling/planning, career fairs, career library, career placement, job interviews, resume preparation, and resume referral to employers. Of 1994 graduates, 98% were employed within three months of graduation.

Program Contact: Ms. Sheryl Lynn Clark, Director, MBA Program, Oakland University, Rochester, MI 48309-4401. (810) 370-3287; Fax: (810) 370-4275; Internet Address: slclark@argo.acs.oakland.edu.

University of Detroit Mercy

College of Business Administration

Detroit, Michigan

OVERVIEW

The University of Detroit Mercy is an independent Roman Catholic (Jesuit) coed institution. Founded 1877. Setting: 70-acre urban campus. Total institutional enrollment: 7,461. Program was first offered in 1942. AACSB-accredited.

MBA HIGHLIGHTS

Entrance Difficulty*
Mean GMAT: 520
Mean GPA: 3.1

Cost $$
Tuition: $408/credit hour
Room & Board: $2,444

Enrollment Profile

Full-time: 76	Work Exp: 85%
Part-time: 550	International: 10%
Total: 626	Women: 31%
Average Age: 31	Minorities: 21%

Average Class Size: 25

ACADEMICS

Length of Program Minimum: 24 months. Maximum: 5 years.

Calendar Semesters.

Full-time Classes Main campus; evening, weekends, summer.

Part-time Classes Main campus; evening, weekends, summer.

Degree Requirements 36 credit hours including 9 elective credit hours.

Required Courses Accounting for management control, analysis of economic conditions, applications of management science in business decision making, financial planning and administration, management development, management information systems, strategic management, strategic marketing, the manager and social responsibility.

Curricular Focus Business ethics and social responsibility, international business, leadership.

Concentrations Accounting, economics, entrepreneurship, finance, health services, human resources management, international business, management, management information systems, marketing, operations management, public administration, strategic management.

Faculty Full-time: 30, 90% with doctorates; part-time: 5, 80% with doctorates.

Teaching Methodology Case study: 20%, lecture: 30%, research: 10%, seminars by members of the business community: 5%, student presentations: 15%, team projects: 20%.

Special Opportunities International exchange in Brazil, Ireland, Mexico, People's Republic of China, United Kingdom. Internship program available.

STUDENT STATISTICS

Geographic Representation State residents 89%. By region: Midwest 80%; Northeast 4%. International 10%.

Undergraduate Majors Business 40%; education 2%; engineering/technology 30%; humanities 3%; nursing 2%; science/mathematics 3%; social sciences 20%.

Other Background Graduate degrees in other disciplines: 8%. Work experience: On average, students have 6 years of work experience on entrance to the program.

FACILITIES
Information Resources Main library with 645,039 bound volumes, 88,650 titles on microform, 5,505 periodical subscriptions, 12,974 records/tapes/CDs, 6 CD-ROMs. Business collection includes 18,851 bound volumes, 22 periodical subscriptions, 303 videos.

Housing 2% of students in program live in college-owned or -operated housing.

Technology Computers are used heavily in course work. 200 computer terminals/PCs, linked by a campus-wide computer network, are available for use by students in program; they are located in the student center, classrooms, learning resource center, the library, the computer center, computer labs, the research center. Students in the program are not required to have their own PC.

Computer Resources/On-line Services

Training	Yes	CompuServe	No
Internet	Yes	Dun's	No
E-Mail	Yes	Dow Jones	Yes
Multimedia Center	Yes	Dialog	No
LEXIS/NEXIS	Yes	Bloomberg	No

Other on-line services: OCLC.

ADMISSION
Acceptance 1994-95 950 applied for admission; 27% were accepted.

Entrance Requirements Bachelor's degree, GMAT score of 450, minimum 3.0 GPA. Core courses waived through: previous course work.

Application Requirements Application form, copies of transcript.

Application Deadlines 8/15 for fall, 12/15 for spring, 4/15 for summer. Applications are processed on a rolling basis. Application discs available.

FINANCIALS
Costs for 1994-95 Tuition: Full-time: $408/credit hour. Fees: Full-time: $55/semester. Average room and board costs are $2,444 per academic year (on-campus).

Financial Aid In 1994-95, candidates received some institutionally administered aid in the form of scholarships, fellowships, assistantships, work-study. Total awards ranged from $6,000-$10,000. Financial aid is available to part-time students. Application deadlines: 9/1 for fall, 1/1 for spring. Applications are processed on a rolling basis. Contact: Ms. Anne Watson, Director of Financial Aid, PO Box 19900 FAC 200, Detroit, MI 48219-0900. (313) 993-3350.

INTERNATIONAL STUDENTS
Demographics 10% of students enrolled in the program are international; Asia 75%, North America 14%, Africa 3%, Central America 2%, Europe 2%, South America 2%, other 2%.

Services and Facilities International student office, international student center, visa services, language tutoring, ESL courses, counseling/support services.

Applying Proof of health; proof of adequate funds. Financial aid is not available to international students. Admission application deadlines: 6/1 for fall, 10/1 for spring. Applications are processed on a rolling basis. Contact: Dr. Robert Graham, Director of International Services Office, SU 210 PO Box 19900, Detroit, MI 48219. (313) 993-1205.

ALTERNATE MBA PROGRAM
MBA/JD Length of program: Minimum: 48 months. Maximum: 6 years. Degree requirements: 48 credit hours.

PLACEMENT
In 1993-94, 10 organizations participated in on-campus recruiting; 130 on-campus interviews were conducted. Placement services include alumni network, career counseling/planning, career fairs, career placement, job interviews, resume preparation, and resume referral to employers. Of 1994 graduates, 89% were employed within three months of graduation, the average starting salary was $53,000, the range was $35,000-$65,000.

Jobs by Employer Type Manufacturing 50%; service 30%; government 5%; consulting 5%; nonprofit 10%.

Jobs by Functional Area Marketing/sales 15%; finance 40%; operations 25%; management 20%.

Program Contact: Dr. Bahman Mirshab, Director of Graduate Business Programs, University of Detroit Mercy, 4001 West McNichols Road, Detroit, MI 48219-0900. (313) 993-1202; Fax: (313) 993-1052; Internet Address: mirshabb@udmercy.edu.

See full description on page 874.

University of Michigan

Michigan Business School

Ann Arbor, Michigan

OVERVIEW
The University of Michigan is a state-supported coed institution. Founded 1817. Setting: 2,665-acre small-town campus with easy access to Detroit. Total institutional enrollment: 36,845. Program was first offered in 1924. AACSB-accredited.

MBA HIGHLIGHTS
Entrance Difficulty***
Mean GMAT: 630
Mean GPA: 3.24

Cost $$$
Tuition: $14,100
(Nonresident: $20,800)
Room & Board: N/R

Enrollment Profile

Full-time: 853	Work Exp: 95%
Part-time: 1,000	International: 17%
Total: 1,853	Women: 27%
Average Age: 27	Minorities: 29%

Class Size: 40 - 62

ACADEMICS
Length of Program Minimum: 16 months. Maximum: 10 years.

Calendar Semesters.

Full-time Classes Main campus; day.

Part-time Classes Main campus, Detroit; evening, summer.

Degree Requirements 60 credits including 27 elective credits.

Required Courses Applied business statistics, applied microeconomics, corporate strategy, financial accounting, marketing management, principles of finance, world economy. Courses may be waived through: previous course work.

Curricular Focus Action-learning, general management, problem solving and decision making.

Concentrations Accounting, arts administration, economics, entrepreneurship, environmental management, manufacturing management, finance, health services, human resources management, international business, management, management information systems, marketing, operations management, organizational behavior, public policy, quantitative analysis, real estate, strategic management.

Faculty Full-time: 130, 100% with doctorates; part-time: 42, 63% with doctorates.

Teaching Methodology Case study: 30%, computer simulations case study: 10%, faculty seminars: 5%, field projects: 15%, lecture: 30%, research: 5%, seminars by members of the business community: 5%.

Special Opportunities International exchange in Australia, Austria, France, Italy, Netherlands, Singapore, Spain, Sweden, Switzerland, United Kingdom. Internship program available.

STUDENT STATISTICS
Geographic Representation State residents 20%. By region: Midwest 34%; Northeast 23%; West 18%; South 7%. International 17%.

Undergraduate Majors Business 27%; education 2%; engineering/technology 23%; humanities 10%; science/mathematics 10%; social sciences 20%; other 8%.

Other Background Graduate degrees in other disciplines: 10%. Work experience: On average, students have 3 years of work experience on entrance to the program.

FACILITIES
Information Resources Main library with 6.6 million bound volumes, 5.1 million titles on microform, 70,336 periodical subscriptions, 29,974 records/tapes/CDs, 283 CD-ROMs. Business collection in Kresge Business Administration Library includes 130,000 bound volumes, 3,200 periodical subscriptions, 27 CD-ROMs, 311 videos.

Housing 20% of students in program live in college-owned or -operated housing.

Technology Computers are used heavily in course work. 180 computer terminals/PCs, linked by a campus-wide computer network, are available for use by students in program; they are located in the student center, classrooms, learning resource center, the library, the computer center, computer labs. Students in the program are not required to have their own PC. $225 are budgeted per student for computer support.

Computer Resources/On-line Services

Training	Yes	LEXIS/NEXIS	Yes
Internet	Yes	CompuServe	Yes
E-Mail	Yes	Dow Jones	Yes
Videoconference Center	Yes	Dialog	Yes
Multimedia Center	Yes	Bloomberg	Yes

Other computer resources: Computer lab, telecommunications center, on-line CD-ROM databases, classroom video/data projection systems.

ADMISSION
Acceptance 1994-95 Of those applying, 33% were accepted.

Entrance Requirements Bachelor's degree, GMAT score, minimum 2 years of work experience. Core courses waived through: previous course work.

Application Requirements Written essay, application form, copies of transcript, resume/curriculum vitae, personal statement, 2 letters of recommendation.

Application Deadline 3/1 for fall.

FINANCIALS
Costs for 1994-95 Tuition: Full-time: $14,100 for state residents, $20,800 for nonresidents. Fees: Full-time: $175 for state residents, $175 for nonresidents.

Financial Aid In 1994-95, 66% of candidates received some institutionally administered aid in the form of scholarships, loans, fellowships, work-study. Total awards ranged from $500-$23,900. Financial aid is available to part-time students. Application deadlines: 12/31 for fall, 12/31 for spring. Contact: Ms. Lorie M. Jager, Senior Financial Aid Officer, Ann Arbor, MI 48109. (313) 764-5139.

INTERNATIONAL STUDENTS
Demographics 17% of students enrolled in the program are international.

Services and Facilities International student center, visa services, language tutoring, ESL courses, counseling/support services.

Applying TOEFL required, minimum score of 600; proof of adequate funds; one semester of college calculus. Financial aid is available to international students. Financial aid application deadline: 3/1 for fall. Admission application deadline: 3/1 for fall. Contact: Director, International Center, Ann Arbor, MI 48109. (313) 764-9310.

ALTERNATE MBA PROGRAMS
MBA/JD Length of program: Minimum: 48 months. Degree requirements: GMAT and LSAT; 60 credits for business and 52-53 credits for law; separate applications must be submitted to both business and law.

MBA/MA Length of program: Minimum: 30 months. Degree requirements: 75 credits. MA is in Russian and East European studies.

MBA/MS Length of program: Minimum: 30 months. Degree requirements: 65 credits. MS is in industrial and operations engineering.

MBA/MSW Length of program: Minimum: 30 months. Degree requirements: 85 credits.

MBA/MA Length of program: Minimum: 30 months. Degree requirements: 69 credits. MA is in South and Southeast Asian studies.

MBA/MA Length of program: Minimum: 30 months. Degree requirements: 75 credits. MA is in modern Middle Eastern and North African studies.

MBA/MA Length of program: Minimum: 36 months. Degree requirements: 70 credits. MA is in Japanese studies.

MBA/MA Length of program: Minimum: 36 months. Degree requirements: 70 credits. MA is in Chinese studies.

MBA/MHSA Length of program: Minimum: 36 months. Degree requirements: 90 credits.

MBA/MM Length of program: Minimum: 24 months. Degree requirements: 65 credits.

MBA/MPP Length of program: Minimum: 36 months. Degree requirements: 84 credits.

MBA/MS Length of program: Minimum: 30 months. Degree requirements: 70 credits. MS is in nursing administration.

MBA/MS Length of program: Minimum: 24 months. Degree requirements: 63 credits. MS is in naval architecture and marine engineering.

MBA/MSE Length of program: Minimum: 30 months. Degree requirements: 66 credits.

PLACEMENT
In 1993-94, 276 organizations participated in on-campus recruiting; 9,101 on-campus interviews were conducted. Placement services include alumni network, career counseling/planning, career fairs, career library,

career placement, electronic job bank, job interviews, job search course, recruiting forums, resume preparation, and resume referral to employers. Of 1994 graduates, 80% were employed within three months of graduation, the average starting salary was $61,000, the range was $12,400-$125,000.

Jobs by Employer Type Manufacturing 53%; service 27%; government 1%; consulting 19%.

Jobs by Functional Area Marketing/sales 26%; finance 28%; operations 3%; management 15%; strategic planning 2%; technical management 26%.

Program Contact: Admissions and Student Services, University of Michigan, Ann Arbor, MI 48109. (313) 764-5796; Fax: (313) 763-7804.

University of Michigan–Dearborn

School of Management

Dearborn, Michigan

OVERVIEW
The University of Michigan–Dearborn is a state-supported comprehensive coed institution. Part of University of Michigan System. Founded 1959. Setting: 210-acre urban campus with easy access to Detroit. Total institutional enrollment: 8,185. Program was first offered in 1981.

MBA HIGHLIGHTS

Entrance Difficulty**
Mean GMAT: 559
Mean GPA: 3.11

Cost $$
Tuition: $216/credit hour
(Nonresident: $694/credit hour)
Room & Board: N/R

Enrollment Profile

Full-time: 14		Work Exp: 98%
Part-time: 259		International: N/R
Total: 273		Women: 26%
Average Age: 30		Minorities: 11%

Average Class Size: 35

ACADEMICS
Length of Program Minimum: 24 months. Maximum: 10 years.

Calendar Trimesters.

Full-time Classes Main campus; evening, summer.

Part-time Classes Main campus; evening, summer.

Degree Requirements 60 semester hours including 12 elective semester hours.

Required Courses Business and government, computer and information systems, economic analysis, financial accounting, financial management, managerial accounting, managerial planning, decision making, and control, managerial statistics and optimization, marketing management, organization and behavior, organization and behavior 2, personnel administration and industrial relations, production and operations management, strategic planning and policy. Courses may be waived through: previous course work.

Curricular Focus Economic and financial theory, general management.

Concentration Management.

Faculty Full-time: 15, 100% with doctorates; part-time: 5, 60% with doctorates.

Teaching Methodology Case study: 20%, faculty seminars: 5%, lecture: 40%, seminars by members of the business community: 5%, student presentations: 10%, team projects: 20%.

Special Opportunities Internship program available. Other: 4 month paid internships in Detroit area corporations.

STUDENT STATISTICS
Undergraduate Majors Education 1%; engineering/technology 63%; humanities 5%; science/mathematics 7%; social sciences 5%; other 19%.

FACILITIES
Information Resources Main library with 299,792 bound volumes, 432,298 titles on microform, 1,169 periodical subscriptions, 1,964

records/tapes/CDs, 60 CD-ROMs. Business collection includes 33,139 bound volumes, 112 periodical subscriptions, 24 videos.

Housing College housing not available.

Technology Computers are used moderately in course work. 300 computer terminals/PCs, linked by a campus-wide computer network, are available for use by students in program; they are located in learning resource center, the library, the computer center, computer labs. Students in the program are not required to have their own PC.

Computer Resources/On-line Services

Training	No	CompuServe	No
Internet	Yes	Dun's	No
E-Mail	Yes	Dow Jones	No
Multimedia Center	Yes	Dialog	No
LEXIS/NEXIS	Yes	Bloomberg	No

Other on-line services: OCLC.

ADMISSION

Acceptance 1994-95 Of those applying, 74% were accepted.

Entrance Requirements Bachelor's degree, calculus I, GMAT score.

Application Requirements Application form, copies of transcript, personal statement.

Application Deadlines 7/18 for fall, 10/31 for winter, 4/1 for spring.

FINANCIALS

Costs for 1994-95 Tuition: Full-time: $216/credit hour for state residents, $694/credit hour for nonresidents.

Financial Aid In 1994-95, 7% of candidates received some institutionally administered aid in the form of loans. Financial aid is available to part-time students. Application deadlines: 4/15 for fall, 4/15 for spring. Contact: Mr. John A. Mason, Director, 4901 Evergreen Road, Dearborn, MI 48128-1491. (313) 593-5300.

INTERNATIONAL STUDENTS

Services and Facilities Visa services, language tutoring, counseling/support services.

Applying TOEFL required, minimum score of 560; proof of health; proof of adequate funds. Financial aid is not available to international students. Admission application deadline: 4/1 for fall. Contact: Ms. Margaret Flannery, International Services Coordinator, 4901 Evergreen Road, Dearborn, MI 48128-1491. (313) 593-5430.

PLACEMENT

In 1993-94, 10 organizations participated in on-campus recruiting; 2 on-campus interviews were conducted. Placement services include career counseling/planning, career fairs, career library, career placement, job interviews, resume preparation, and resume referral to employers.

Program Contact: School of Management, University of Michigan–Dearborn, 4901 Evergreen Road, Dearborn, MI 48128-1491. (313) 593-5460; Fax: (313) 593-5636.

University of Michigan–Flint

School of Management

Flint, Michigan

OVERVIEW

The University of Michigan–Flint is a state-supported comprehensive coed institution. Part of University of Michigan System. Founded 1956. Setting: 42-acre urban campus with easy access to Detroit. Total institutional enrollment: 6,236. AACSB-accredited.

MBA HIGHLIGHTS ━━━━━━━━━━━━━━━

Entrance Difficulty

Mean GMAT: 527

Mean GPA: N/R

Cost $

Tuition: $269 - $309/credit

Room & Board: N/R

Enrollment Profile

Full-time: N/R	Work Exp: N/R
Part-time: N/R	International: N/R
Total: 234	Women: 32%
Average Age: N/R	Minorities: 1%

Average Class Size: 30

ACADEMICS

Length of Program Minimum: 36 months.

Calendar Semesters.

Part-time Classes Main campus, Lansing; evening.

Degree Requirements 48 credits.

Curricular Focus Leadership, strategic analysis and planning, teamwork.

Concentration Management.

FACILITIES

Information Resources Main library with 143,293 bound volumes, 277,163 titles on microform, 1,030 periodical subscriptions, 2,656 records/tapes/CDs.

ADMISSION

Entrance Requirements Bachelor's degree, math prerequisite, GMAT score, minimum 3 years of work experience.

Application Requirements Application form, copies of transcript, resume/curriculum vitae, personal statement, 3 letters of recommendation.

Application Deadlines 7/1 for fall, 11/1 for spring. Applications are processed on a rolling basis.

FINANCIALS

Costs for 1994-95 Tuition: Part-time evening: $269-$309/credit. Fees: Part-time evening: $40/semester hour.

Financial Aid Application deadline: 3/15 for fall. Contact: Ms. Rita Pikowsky, Director of Financial Aid, Financial Aid Office, Flint, MI 48502-2186. (810) 762-3444.

INTERNATIONAL STUDENTS

Applying TOEFL required, minimum score of 550; proof of health; proof of adequate funds. Admission application deadlines: 6/1 for fall, 10/1 for spring. Applications are processed on a rolling basis.

Program Contact: Ms. Kathy Gasper, Administrative Assistant, University of Michigan–Flint, School of Management/MBA Program, Flint, MI 48502-2186. (810) 762-3160, or (800) 942-5636; Fax: (810) 762-3282.

Wayne State University

School of Business Administration

Detroit, Michigan

OVERVIEW

Wayne State University is a state-supported coed institution. Founded 1868. Setting: 185-acre urban campus. Total institutional enrollment: 32,902. Program was first offered in 1946. AACSB-accredited.

MBA HIGHLIGHTS ━━━━━━━━━━━━━━━

Entrance Difficulty***

Mean GMAT: 520

Mean GPA: 3.2

Cost $

Tuition: $142/credit hour

(Nonresident: $307/credit hour)

Room & Board: N/R

Enrollment Profile

Full-time: 179	Work Exp: 70%
Part-time: 1,603	International: 10%
Total: 1,782	Women: 35%
Average Age: 27	Minorities: 7%

Class Size: 35 - 40

ACADEMICS

Length of Program Minimum: 12 months. Maximum: 6 years.

Calendar Semesters.

Full-time Classes Main campus; evening, weekends, summer.

Part-time Classes Main campus; evening, weekends, summer.

Degree Requirements 36 credit hours including 6 elective credit hours.

Required Courses Business and contemporary society, financial reporting framework, management and the organization, managerial economics, managerial finance, marketing strategy, quantitative methods applied to business decisions, seminar in business policy. Courses may be waived through: previous course work.

Curricular Focus Business issues and problems, problem solving and decision making, strategic analysis and planning.

Concentrations Accounting, finance, human resources management, international business, management, management information systems, marketing, organizational behavior, quality management, taxation.

Faculty Full-time: 60, 93% with doctorates; part-time: 32, 60% with doctorates.

Teaching Methodology Case study: 50%, lecture: 10%, research: 10%, seminars by members of the business community: 5%, student presentations: 10%, team projects: 15%.

Special Opportunities International exchange in Ukraine. Internship program available.

STUDENT STATISTICS

Geographic Representation State residents 90%. International 10%.

Undergraduate Majors Business 60%; education 1%; engineering/technology 20%; humanities 4%; nursing 2%; science/mathematics 5%; social sciences 4%; other 4%.

Other Background Graduate degrees in other disciplines: 5%. Work experience: On average, students have 4 years of work experience on entrance to the program.

FACILITIES

Information Resources Main library with 2.8 million bound volumes, 3.3 million titles on microform, 24,574 periodical subscriptions, 33,163 records/tapes/CDs, 81 CD-ROMs.

Housing 8% of students in program live in college-owned or -operated housing.

Technology Computers are used moderately in course work. 100 computer terminals/PCs, linked by a campus-wide computer network, are available for use by students in program; they are located in the student center, computer labs. Students in the program are not required to have their own PC.

Computer Resources/On-line Services

Training	Yes	Dun's	No
Internet	Yes	Dow Jones	No
E-Mail	Yes	Dialog	No
LEXIS/NEXIS	Yes	Bloomberg	No
CompuServe	No		

Other on-line services: OCLC.

ADMISSION

Acceptance 1994-95 Of those applying, 70% were accepted.

Entrance Requirements Bachelor's degree, GMAT score of 450, minimum 2.5 GPA. Core courses waived through: previous course work.

Application Requirements Application form, copies of transcript.

Application Deadlines 7/1 for fall, 11/1 for winter, 3/15 for spring.

FINANCIALS

Costs for 1994-95 Tuition: Full-time: $142/credit hour for state residents, $307/credit hour for nonresidents. Fees: Full-time: $70/semester for state residents, $70/semester for nonresidents.

Financial Aid Application deadline: 3/1 for fall. Contact: Ms. Judy Florian, Director of Scholarships and Financial Aid, 3 W Joy Students Services, 655 West Kirby, Detroit, MI 48202. (313) 577-3378.

INTERNATIONAL STUDENTS

Demographics 10% of students enrolled in the program are international.

Services and Facilities International student center, ESL courses, counseling/support services.

Applying TOEFL required, minimum score of 550; proof of adequate funds. Financial aid is not available to international students. Admission application deadlines: 5/1 for fall, 9/1 for winter, 1/15 for spring. Contact: Ms. Annette Vitale-Salajanu, Director, International Services Office, 5460 Cass, Detroit, MI 48202. (313) 577-3422.

ALTERNATE MBA PROGRAM

MBA/JD Length of program: Minimum: 72 months. Maximum: 6 years. Degree requirements: 122 credit hours including 6 elective credit hours.

PLACEMENT

Placement services include alumni network, career counseling/planning, career fairs, career library, career placement, electronic job bank, job interviews, resume preparation, and resume referral to employers. Of 1994 graduates, 95% were employed within three months of graduation, the average starting salary was $43,699, the range was $29,600-$70,000.

Program Contact: Ms. Linda Zaddach, Assistant Dean, Wayne State University, Detroit, MI 48202. (313) 577-4510; Fax: (313) 577-5299. See full description on page 930.

Western Michigan University

Haworth College of Business

Kalamazoo, Michigan

OVERVIEW

Western Michigan University is a state-supported coed institution. Founded 1903. Setting: 451-acre urban campus. Total institutional enrollment: 22,715. AACSB-accredited.

ACADEMICS

Calendar Semesters.

Concentrations Economics, finance, management, marketing, paper science.

FACILITIES

Information Resources Main library with 1.7 million bound volumes, 609,529 titles on microform, 5,444 periodical subscriptions, 19,232 records/tapes/CDs, 512 CD-ROMs.

ADMISSION

Entrance Requirements Bachelor's degree.

Application Requirements Copies of transcript.

Application Deadlines 6/1 for fall, 11/1 for spring.

INTERNATIONAL STUDENTS

Applying Admission application deadlines: 6/1 for fall, 11/1 for spring.

Program Contact: Dr. David Vellenga, Dean, Western Michigan University, West Michigan Avenue, Kalamazoo, MI 49008. (616) 387-5050; Fax: (616) 387-5710.

MINNESOTA

Mankato State University

College of Business

Mankato, Minnesota

OVERVIEW

Mankato State University is a state-supported comprehensive coed institution. Part of Minnesota State University System. Founded 1868. Setting: 303-acre small-town campus with easy access to Minneapolis–St. Paul. Total institutional enrollment: 13,200. Program was first offered in 1964.

MBA HIGHLIGHTS

Entrance Difficulty***
Mean GMAT: 513
Mean GPA: 3.2

Cost $
Tuition: $79/quarter hour
(Nonresident: $119/quarter hour)
Room & Board: N/R

Enrollment Profile

Full-time: 89	Work Exp: 62%
Part-time: 20	International: 23%
Total: 109	Women: 42%
Average Age: 26	Minorities: 2%

Average Class Size: 18

ACADEMICS

Length of Program Minimum: 12 months. Maximum: 6 years.

Calendar Quarters.

Full-time Classes Main campus; day, evening, summer.

Part-time Classes Main campus, Edina; evening.

Degree Requirements 52 quarter hours including 16 elective quarter hours.

Required Courses Accounting for planning and control, financial management, global and ethical perspectives in business, human behavior in business, introduction to MBA, managerial communications, managerial economics, marketing analysis, seminar for alternate plan paper and thesis, statistical analysis for business and research, strategic management.

Curricular Focus Business issues and problems, strategic analysis and planning, teamwork.

Concentration Management.

Faculty Full-time: 23, 100% with doctorates.

Teaching Methodology Case study: 15%, faculty seminars: 1%, lecture: 58%, research: 5%, seminars by members of the business community: 1%, student presentations: 5%, team projects: 15%.

STUDENT STATISTICS

Geographic Representation State residents 71%. By region: Midwest 71%; Northeast 2%; South 2%. International 23%.

Undergraduate Majors Business 63%; engineering/technology 21%; humanities 4%; science/mathematics 5%; social sciences 2%; other 1%.

Other Background Graduate degrees in other disciplines: 5%. Work experience: On average, students have 2 years of work experience on entrance to the program.

FACILITIES

Information Resources Main library with 1 million bound volumes, 700,000 titles on microform, 3,200 periodical subscriptions, 20,000 records/tapes/CDs.

ADMISSION

Acceptance 1994-95 89 applied for admission; 74% were accepted.

Entrance Requirements Bachelor's degree, GMAT score of 450, minimum 2.75 GPA. Core courses waived through: previous course work.

Application Requirements Application form, copies of transcript.

Application Deadlines 8/1 for fall, 3/1 for spring. Applications are processed on a rolling basis.

FINANCIALS

Costs for 1994-95 Tuition: Full-time: $79/quarter hour for state residents, $119/quarter hour for nonresidents.

Financial Aid In 1994-95, 30% of candidates received some institutionally administered aid in the form of assistantships. Total awards ranged from $2,500-$5,200. Financial aid is not available to part-time students. Application deadline: 7/1 for fall. Contact: Dr. Gayle Stelter, MBA Director, South Road and Ellis Avenue, Mankato, MN 56002-8400. (507) 389-5426.

INTERNATIONAL STUDENTS

Demographics 23% of students enrolled in the program are international; Asia 72%, Europe 3%, South America 3%, Central America 1%, other 20%.

Services and Facilities International student office, international student center, ESL courses.

Applying TOEFL required, minimum score of 550; proof of health; proof of adequate funds. Financial aid is available to international students. Financial aid application deadline: 6/1 for fall. Admission application deadline: 5/1 for fall. Applications are processed on a rolling basis.

Contact: Dr. Kuhn Lee, Director, MSH 1DD International Student Office, South Road and Ellis Avenue, Mankato, MN 56002-8400. (507) 389-1281.

Program Contact: Dr. Gayle Stelter, MBA Director, Mankato State University, South Road and Ellis Avenue, Mankato, MN 56002-8400. (507) 389-5426; Fax: (507) 389-5497; Internet Address: gayle@vax1. mankato.msus.edu.

Moorhead State University

Department of Business Administration

Moorhead, Minnesota

OVERVIEW

Moorhead State University is a state-supported comprehensive coed institution. Part of Minnesota State University System. Founded 1885. Setting: 104-acre urban campus. Total institutional enrollment: 6,751. Program was first offered in 1975.

MBA HIGHLIGHTS

Entrance Difficulty***
Mean GMAT: 510
Mean GPA: 3.35

Cost $
Tuition: $69/credit
(Nonresident: $110/credit)
Room & Board: N/R

Enrollment Profile

Full-time: 4	Work Exp: 95%
Part-time: 39	International: 5%
Total: 43	Women: 35%
Average Age: 33	Minorities: 5%

Average Class Size: 18

ACADEMICS

Length of Program Minimum: 9 months. Maximum: 7 years.

Calendar Semesters.

Full-time Classes Main campus; evening.

Part-time Classes Main campus; evening.

Degree Requirements 48 credits including 8 elective credits. Other: Oral exam.

Required Courses Accounting, business and society, communications, finance, microeconomics, organizational theory and behavior, policy, quantitative methods, statistics. Courses may be waived through: previous course work.

Curricular Focus Business issues and problems, problem solving and decision making, teamwork.

Concentration Management.

Faculty Part-time: 15, 93% with doctorates.

Teaching Methodology Case study: 30%, lecture: 30%, research: 10%, student presentations: 20%, team projects: 10%.

STUDENT STATISTICS

Geographic Representation State residents 40%. By region: Midwest 95%. International 5%.

Undergraduate Majors Business 40%; education 10%; engineering/technology 10%; humanities 5%; nursing 5%; science/mathematics 10%; social sciences 10%; other 10%.

Other Background Graduate degrees in other disciplines: 10%. Work experience: On average, students have 7 years of work experience on entrance to the program.

FACILITIES

Information Resources Main library with 365,430 bound volumes, 582,247 titles on microform, 1,626 periodical subscriptions, 7,212 records/tapes/CDs. Business collection includes 6,053 bound volumes, 135 periodical subscriptions.

Housing College housing available.

Technology Computers are used heavily in course work. 30 computer terminals/PCs, linked by a campus-wide computer network, are available for use by students in program; they are located in dormitories, the library, the computer center, computer labs, the research center. Students in the program are not required to have their own PC.

Computer Resources/On-line Services

Training	No	Dun's	No
Internet	Yes	Dow Jones	No
E-Mail	Yes	Dialog	Yes
LEXIS/NEXIS	No	Bloomberg	No
CompuServe	No		

Other on-line services: Westlaw.

ADMISSION

Acceptance 1994-95 Of those applying, 85% were accepted.

Entrance Requirements Bachelor's degree, GMAT score. Core courses waived through: previous course work.

Application Requirements Application form, copies of transcript, personal statement, 3 letters of recommendation, curriculum worksheet.

FINANCIALS

Costs for 1994-95 Tuition: Full-time: $69/credit for state residents, $110/credit for nonresidents. Fees: Full-time: $8/credit for state residents, $8/credit for nonresidents.

Financial Aid In 1994-95, candidates received some institutionally administered aid in the form of loans, work-study. Total awards ranged from $2,000-$4,000. Financial aid is available to part-time students. Application deadline: 7/31 for fall. Contact: Ms. Karen Knighton, Acting Director of Financial Aid, Financial Aid Office, Moorhead, MN 56563. (218) 236-2082.

INTERNATIONAL STUDENTS

Demographics 5% of students enrolled in the program are international; Asia 100%.

Applying TOEFL required, minimum score of 550; proof of adequate funds. Financial aid is available to international students. Contact: Ms. Francisca Peterson, International Student Adviser, Comstock Memorial Union 222, Moorhead, MN 56563. (218) 236-3853.

PLACEMENT

Placement services include career counseling/planning, career fairs, career library, on-campus recruiting, resume preparation, resume referral to employers, and workshops, on-campus recruiting.

Jobs by Employer Type Service 37%; government 31%; consulting 6%; nonprofit 6%; banking 12%; other 6%.

Jobs by Functional Area Marketing/sales 8%; finance 12%; operations 10%; management 40%; strategic planning 5%; technical management 5%; education/health 20%.

Program Contact: Ms. Claudia Pehler, Administrative Assistant to the Dean of Business, Moorhead State University, 1104 7th Avenue South, Moorhead, MN 56563. (218) 236-2763, or (800) 593-7246; Fax: (218) 236-2168.

St. Cloud State University

College of Business

St. Cloud, Minnesota

OVERVIEW

St. Cloud State University is a state-supported comprehensive coed institution. Part of Minnesota State University System. Founded 1869. Setting: 82-acre suburban campus with easy access to Minneapolis–St. Paul. Total institutional enrollment: 17,000. AACSB-accredited.

MBA HIGHLIGHTS

Entrance Difficulty***
Mean GMAT: 524
Mean GPA: 3.38

Cost $
Tuition: $77/credit
(Nonresident: $110/credit)
Room & Board: N/R

Enrollment Profile

Full-time: 79		Work Exp: N/R
Part-time: 96		International: 5%
Total: 175		Women: 39%
Average Age: 27		Minorities: 10%

Average Class Size: 25

ACADEMICS

Length of Program Minimum: 15 months. Maximum: 7 years.

Calendar Quarters.

Full-time Classes Main campus; day, evening.

Part-time Classes Main campus; day, evening.

Degree Requirements 48 credits including 12 elective credits.

Required Courses Corporate financial reporting, corporate strategies, decision making techniques, financial management policy, management of human resources, managerial accounting, managerial economics, marketing plans and decision making, production and operations management.

Curricular Focus Problem solving and decision making, strategic analysis and planning, teamwork.

Concentrations Accounting, finance, international business, management, management information systems, marketing, operations management, organizational behavior.

Faculty Full-time: 70, 100% with doctorates.

Teaching Methodology Case study: 30%, lecture: 30%, research: 10%, student presentations: 20%, team projects: 10%.

Special Opportunities Internship program available.

STUDENT STATISTICS

Geographic Representation International 5%.

Other Background Graduate degrees in other disciplines: 1%.

FACILITIES

Information Resources Main library with 768,000 bound volumes, 1.4 million titles on microform, 2,109 periodical subscriptions, 13,200 records/tapes/CDs, 20 CD-ROMs. Business collection includes 553,000 bound volumes, 4,000 periodical subscriptions.

Housing College housing available.

Technology Computers are used heavily in course work. 50 computer terminals/PCs are available for use by students in program; they are located in computer labs. Students in the program are not required to have their own PC.

Computer Resources/On-line Services

Training	No	E-Mail	No

ADMISSION

Acceptance 1994-95 90 applied for admission; 79% were accepted.

Entrance Requirements Bachelor's degree, GMAT score of 470, minimum 2.75 GPA. Core courses waived through: previous course work.

Application Requirements Application form, copies of transcript, personal statement, 3 letters of recommendation.

Application Deadline Applications are processed on a rolling basis.

FINANCIALS

Costs for 1994-95 Tuition: Full-time: $77/credit for state residents, $110/credit for nonresidents. Fees: Full-time: $8/credit for state residents, $8/credit for nonresidents.

Financial Aid In 1994-95, candidates received some institutionally administered aid in the form of loans, assistantships. Financial aid is not available to part-time students. Applications are processed on a rolling basis. Contact: Mr. Frank Loncorich, Director of Financial Aid, College of Business, St. Cloud, MN 56301. (612) 255-2047.

INTERNATIONAL STUDENTS

Demographics 5% of students enrolled in the program are international.

Services and Facilities International student office, international student center, ESL courses.

Applying TOEFL required, minimum score of 550; proof of adequate funds. Financial aid is available to international students. Financial aid application deadlines: 7/15 for fall, 10/15 for winter, 1/15 for spring. Applications are processed on a rolling basis. Admission application deadlines: 7/15 for fall, 10/15 for winter, 1/15 for spring. Applications are processed on a rolling basis. Contact: Mr. Roland Fisher, Director, Center for International Studies, College of Business, St. Cloud, MN 56301. (612) 255-4287.

PLACEMENT

In 1993-94, 100 organizations participated in on-campus recruiting. Placement services include alumni network, career counseling/planning, career fairs, career library, and resume preparation. Of 1994 graduates, 60% were employed within three months of graduation, the average starting salary was $28,000, the range was $24,000-$35,000.

Program Contact: Ms. Karen LeBrun, Administrative Assistant, St. Cloud State University, College of Business, St. Cloud, MN 56301. (612) 255-3212; Fax: (612) 255-3986.

University of Minnesota, Duluth

School of Business and Economics

Duluth, Minnesota

OVERVIEW

The University of Minnesota, Duluth is a state-supported comprehensive coed institution. Part of University of Minnesota System. Founded 1947. Setting: 250-acre suburban campus. Total institutional enrollment: 7,600. Program was first offered in 1974.

MBA HIGHLIGHTS

Entrance Difficulty***
Mean GMAT: 520
Mean GPA: 2.95

Cost $
Tuition: $1,836/quarter
Room & Board: $8,200

Enrollment Profile
Full-time: 2
Part-time: 58
Total: 60
Average Age: 30

Work Exp: 95%
International: 5%
Women: 30%
Minorities: 0%

Average Class Size: 16

ACADEMICS

Length of Program Minimum: 24 months. Maximum: 7 years.

Calendar Quarters.

Part-time Classes Main campus; evening.

Degree Requirements 39 credits including 9 elective credits. Other: Research project.

Required Courses Business, government, and society, financial management, international business environment, management accounting, management of human resources, management research, management science, managerial economics, marketing management, policy formulation and implementation, research methodology. Courses may be waived through: previous course work.

Curricular Focus Business issues and problems, problem solving and decision making, strategic analysis and planning.

Concentrations Accounting, economics, finance, human resources management, management, marketing, operations management.

Faculty Full-time: 11, 100% with doctorates.

Teaching Methodology Case study: 20%, lecture: 55%, research: 10%, student presentations: 5%, team projects: 10%.

Special Opportunities Internship program available.

STUDENT STATISTICS

Geographic Representation State residents 80%. By region: Midwest 98%. International 5%.

Undergraduate Majors Business 45%; engineering/technology 25%; humanities 5%; science/mathematics 10%; social sciences 15%.

Other Background Graduate degrees in other disciplines: 7%. Work experience: On average, students have 6 years of work experience on entrance to the program.

FACILITIES

Information Resources Main library with 456,708 bound volumes, 373,150 titles on microform, 2,698 periodical subscriptions, 7,346 records/tapes/CDs.

Housing College housing available.

Technology Computer terminals/PCs, linked by a campus-wide computer network, are available for use by students in program; they are located in the library, the computer center, computer labs. Students in the program are not required to have their own PC.

Computer Resources/On-line Services

Training	No	Dun's	No
Internet	Yes	Dow Jones	No
E-Mail	Yes	Dialog	No
LEXIS/NEXIS	No	Bloomberg	No
CompuServe	Yes		

ADMISSION

Acceptance 1994-95 80 applied for admission; 80% were accepted.

Entrance Requirements Bachelor's degree, prerequisite courses required for applicants with non-business degree, GMAT score, minimum 2.5 GPA.

Application Requirements Application form, copies of transcript, personal statement.

Application Deadlines 7/15 for fall, 9/15 for winter, 1/15 for spring.

FINANCIALS

Costs for 1994-95 Tuition: Full-time: $1,836/quarter for state residents. Average room and board costs are $8,200 per academic year (on-campus) and $8,200 per academic year (off-campus).

Financial Aid In 1994-95, 15% of candidates received some institutionally administered aid in the form of fellowships. Total awards ranged from $600-$1,500. Financial aid is available to part-time students. Contact: Mr. Thomas Duff, Director of MBA Graduate Studies, 10 University Drive, Duluth, MN 55812-2496. (218) 726-8759.

INTERNATIONAL STUDENTS

Demographics 5% of students enrolled in the program are international.

Applying TOEFL required, minimum score of 550; proof of health; proof of adequate funds. Financial aid is not available to international students. Admission application deadlines: 6/30 for fall, 9/1 for winter, 1/15 for spring. Contact: Mr. Bruce Rutherford, International Student Adviser, 101 Kirby Student Center, 10 University Drive, Duluth, MN 55812-2496. (218) 726-8738.

PLACEMENT

Placement services include career counseling/planning, career library, and career placement. Of 1994 graduates, 100% were employed within three months of graduation.

Program Contact: Mr. Thomas Duff, Director of MBA Graduate Studies, University of Minnesota, Duluth, 10 University Drive, Duluth, MN 55812-2496. (218) 726-8759; Fax: (218) 726-6338.

University of Minnesota, Twin Cities Campus

Carlson School of Management

Minneapolis, Minnesota

OVERVIEW

The University of Minnesota, Twin Cities Campus is a state-supported coed institution. Part of University of Minnesota System. Founded 1851. Setting: 2,000-acre urban campus. Total institutional enrollment: 37,548. Program was first offered in 1959. AACSB-accredited.

MBA HIGHLIGHTS

Entrance Difficulty****
Mean GMAT: 600
Mean GPA: 3.2

Cost $$
Tuition: $8,268
(Nonresident: $12,618)
Room & Board: $5,200

Enrollment Profile
Full-time: 248
Part-time: 1,070
Total: 1,318
Average Age: 27

Work Exp: 81%
International: 20%
Women: 23%
Minorities: 8%

Class Size: 17 - 55

ACADEMICS

Length of Program Minimum: 18 months. Maximum: 7 years.

Calendar Quarters.

Full-time Classes Main campus; day, evening.

Part-time Classes Main campus; evening, summer.

Degree Requirements 90 credits including 36 elective credits. Other: Consulting field project.

Required Courses Data analysis for management, ethical environment, financial accounting, financial management, human resources management, information management, international environment, managerial economics, managing for quality, operations management, organizational management of change, strategic management.

Curricular Focus Functional integration, strategic analysis and planning, teamwork.

Concentrations Accounting, entrepreneurship, finance, international business, management, management information systems, marketing, operations management, organizational behavior, strategic management.

Faculty Full-time: 115, 100% with doctorates; part-time: 28, 90% with doctorates.

Teaching Methodology Case study: 40%, lecture: 30%, student presentations: 10%, team projects: 20%.

Special Opportunities International exchange in Australia, Austria, Belgium, Brazil, France, Italy, Japan, Spain, Switzerland. Internship program available. Other: mentorship program, entrepreneurial field project, seminar series, case study tournaments, volunteer consulting program.

STUDENT STATISTICS

Geographic Representation State residents 39%. By region: Midwest 54%; Northeast 9%; West 9%; South 6%. International 20%.

Undergraduate Majors Business 17%; engineering/technology 21%; humanities 9%; science/mathematics 13%; social sciences 38%; other 2%.

Other Background Graduate degrees in other disciplines: 9%. Work experience: On average, students have 4 years of work experience on entrance to the program.

FACILITIES

Information Resources Main library with 5 million bound volumes, 3.1 million titles on microform, 52,018 periodical subscriptions, 535,944 records/tapes/CDs.

Housing College housing available.

Technology Computers are used heavily in course work. 200 computer terminals/PCs, linked by a campus-wide computer network, are available for use by students in program; they are located in dormitories, classrooms, the computer center, computer labs. Students in the program are not required to have their own PC.

Computer Resources/On-line Services

Training	Yes	LEXIS/NEXIS	Yes
Internet	Yes	Dialog	Yes
E-Mail	Yes		

ADMISSION

Acceptance 1994-95 633 applied for admission; 54% were accepted.

Entrance Requirements Bachelor's degree, GMAT score. Core courses waived through: previous course work.

Application Requirements Written essay, application form, copies of transcript, resume/curriculum vitae, personal statement, 2 letters of recommendation.

Application Deadlines 4/1 for fall, 2/1 for winter. Applications are processed on a rolling basis.

FINANCIALS

Costs for 1994-95 Tuition: Full-time: $8,268 for state residents, $12,618 for nonresidents. Average room and board costs are $5,200 per academic year (on-campus) and $5,200 per academic year (off-campus).

Financial Aid In 1994-95, candidates received some institutionally administered aid in the form of grants, scholarships, loans, fellowships, assistantships, work-study. Financial aid is available to part-time students. Applications are processed on a rolling basis. Contact: Ms. Rose Miskowicz, Executive Student Personnel Worker, Office of Student Financial Aid, 210 Fraser Hall, 106 Pleasant Street SE, Minneapolis, MN 55455-0213. (800) 400-8636.

INTERNATIONAL STUDENTS

Demographics 20% of students enrolled in the program are international; Asia 50%, Europe 42%, South America 6%, Central America 2%.

Services and Facilities International student office, international student center, visa services, ESL courses, special assistance for nonnative speakers of English, counseling/support services.

Applying TOEFL required, minimum score of 580; proof of health; proof of adequate funds. Financial aid is not available to international students. Admission application deadline: 3/15 for fall. Applications are processed on a rolling basis.

ALTERNATE MBA PROGRAMS

Executive MBA (EMBA) Length of program: Minimum: 21 months. Maximum: 2 years. Part-time classes: Main campus; weekends. Degree requirements: 74 credits. Class size: 35-45.

One-Year MBA Length of program: Minimum: 12 months. Maximum: 12 years. Full-time classes: Main campus; day, evening. Degree requirements: 64 credits including 28 elective credits.

PLACEMENT

In 1993-94, 95 organizations participated in on-campus recruiting; 1,995 on-campus interviews were conducted. Placement services include alumni network, career counseling/planning, career fairs, career library, career placement, electronic job bank, job interviews, job search course, resume preparation, and resume referral to employers. Of 1994 graduates, 90% were employed within three months of graduation, the average starting salary was $44,598, the range was $30,000-$82,000.

Jobs by Employer Type Manufacturing 39%; service 47%; consulting 5%; government 1%; nonprofit 1%; other 7%.

Jobs by Functional Area Marketing/sales 12%; finance 38%; operations 2%; management 36%; strategic planning 3%; technical management 8%; human resources 1%.

Program Contact: Ms. Bobbi Haasl Blilie, Recruiting Coordinator, University of Minnesota, Twin Cities Campus, MBA Office, 295 Humphrey Building, 271 19th Avenue South, Minneapolis, MN 55455-0213. (612) 625-5555; Fax: (612) 626-7785; Internet Address: bhaasl-bilie@csom. umn.edu.

University of St. Thomas

Graduate School of Business

St. Paul, Minnesota

OVERVIEW

The University of St. Thomas is an independent Roman Catholic comprehensive coed institution. Founded 1885. Setting: 78-acre urban campus. Total institutional enrollment: 10,000. Program was first offered in 1974.

MBA HIGHLIGHTS

Entrance Difficulty*
Mean GMAT: 535
Mean GPA: 3.0

Cost $
Tuition: $996/course
Room & Board: N/R

Enrollment Profile

Full-time: 40	Work Exp: 100%
Part-time: 2,400	International: 1%
Total: 2,440	Women: 42%
Average Age: 31	Minorities: 3%

Average Class Size: 22

ACADEMICS

Length of Program Minimum: 24 months.

Calendar Semesters.

Full-time Classes Minneapolis; day.

Part-time Classes Minneapolis, St. Paul; evening, weekends, summer.

Degree Requirements 36 credits including 12 elective credits.

Curricular Focus Applied orientation, general management, problem solving and decision making.

Concentrations Accounting, entrepreneurship, finance, health services, human resources management, international business, management, management information systems, manufacturing management, nonprofit management, marketing, operations management, real estate.

Faculty Full-time: 20, 100% with doctorates; part-time: 200, 25% with doctorates.

Teaching Methodology Case study: 20%, lecture: 30%, research: 20%, seminars by members of the business community: 5%, student presentations: 5%, team projects: 20%.

STUDENT STATISTICS

Geographic Representation State residents 97%. By region: Midwest 99%. International 1%.

Undergraduate Majors Business 40%; engineering/technology 20%; humanities 20%; science/mathematics 20%.

Other Background Graduate degrees in other disciplines: 5%. Work experience: On average, students have 5 years of work experience on entrance to the program.

FACILITIES

Information Resources Main library with 399,529 bound volumes, 431,274 titles on microform, 3,328 periodical subscriptions.

Technology Computers are used moderately in course work. 100 computer terminals/PCs, linked by a campus-wide computer network, are available for use by students in program; they are located in learning resource center, the library, the computer center, computer labs. Students in the program are not required to have their own PC.

Computer Resources/On-line Services

Training   Yes

ADMISSION

Acceptance 1994-95 1,161 applied for admission; 75% were accepted.

Entrance Requirements Bachelor's degree, GMAT score of 500, minimum 2.5 GPA, minimum 2 years of work experience. Core courses waived through: previous course work.

Application Requirements Written essay, application form, copies of transcript, resume/curriculum vitae.

Application Deadlines 7/1 for fall, 12/1 for spring. Applications are processed on a rolling basis.

FINANCIALS

Costs for 1994-95 Tuition: Full-time: $996/course. Fees: Full-time:-$40.00.

Financial Aid In 1994-95, 5% of candidates received some institutionally administered aid in the form of grants, loans. Total awards ranged from $500-$15,000. Financial aid is available to part-time students. Application deadlines: 6/1 for fall, 11/1 for spring. Contact: Mr. Wayne Vernon, Financial Aid Office, MPL 201, 1000 LaSalle Avenue, Minneapolis, MN 55403-2005. (612) 962-5000.

INTERNATIONAL STUDENTS

Demographics 1% of students enrolled in the program are international; Asia 30%, South America 30%, Europe 20%, Central America 10%, other 10%.

Applying TOEFL required, minimum score of 500; proof of health; proof of adequate funds. Financial aid is not available to international students. Admission application deadlines: 4/1 for fall, 9/1 for spring. Applications are processed on a rolling basis.

ALTERNATE MBA PROGRAM

Executive MBA (EMBA) Length of program: Minimum: 30 months. Part-time classes: Main campus, Minneapolis; weekends. Degree requirements: 42 credits.

PLACEMENT

Placement services include alumni network, career counseling/planning, career library, electronic job bank, job search course, resume preparation, and resume referral to employers. Of 1994 graduates, 98% were employed within three months of graduation, the average starting salary was $48,000.

Program Contact: Ms. Julie Olson, Prospective Student Services, University of St. Thomas, MPL 251, 1000 LaSalle Avenue, Minneapolis, MN 55803-2005. (612) 962-4200, or (800) 328-6819 (out-of-state); Internet Address: jaolsun@stthomas.edu.

Winona State University

Department of Management and Marketing

Winona, Minnesota

OVERVIEW

Winona State University is a state-supported comprehensive coed institution. Part of Minnesota State University System. Founded 1858. Setting: 40-acre small-town campus. Total institutional enrollment: 7,200. Program was first offered in 1978.

MBA HIGHLIGHTS

Entrance Difficulty***
Mean GMAT: 520
Mean GPA: N/R

Cost $
Tuition: $72/credit
(Nonresident: $103/credit)
Room & Board: N/R

Enrollment Profile

Full-time: N/R	Work Exp: N/R
Part-time: N/R	International: 24%
Total: 72	Women: 40%
Average Age: N/R	Minorities: N/R

Average Class Size: 20

ACADEMICS

Length of Program Minimum: 24 months. Maximum: 7 years.

Calendar Quarters.

Part-time Classes Main campus, Rochester; evening, weekends.

Degree Requirements 45 credits including 15 elective credits.

Curricular Focus General management, leadership, organizational development and change management.

Concentration Management.

Faculty Full-time: 24, 24% with doctorates.

Teaching Methodology Case study: 20%, lecture: 20%, research: 20%, student presentations: 20%, team projects: 20%.

STUDENT STATISTICS

Geographic Representation State residents 90%.

FACILITIES

Information Resources Main library with 215,000 bound volumes, 703,000 titles on microform, 1,400 periodical subscriptions.

Technology Computers are used moderately in course work. Computer terminals/PCs, linked by a campus-wide computer network, are available for use by students in program; they are located in the library, the computer center, computer labs. Students in the program are not required to have their own PC.

Computer Resources/On-line Services

E-Mail   Yes

ADMISSION

Acceptance 1994-95 20 applied for admission; 85% were accepted.

Entrance Requirements Bachelor's degree, GMAT score, minimum 2.5 GPA, minimum 2 years of work experience.

Application Requirements Application form, copies of transcript, personal statement.

Application Deadlines 8/7 for fall, 10/31 for winter, 2/17 for spring. Applications are processed on a rolling basis.

FINANCIALS

Costs for 1994-95 Tuition: Full-time: $72/credit for state residents, $103/credit for nonresidents.

Financial Aid In 1994-95, candidates received some institutionally administered aid in the form of assistantships. Applications are processed on a rolling basis. Contact: Mr. Robert Lietzam, Director of Financial Aid, Somsen Hall 108D, Winona, MN 55987-5838. (507) 457-5090.

INTERNATIONAL STUDENTS

Demographics 24% of students enrolled in the program are international.

Applying TOEFL required, minimum score of 575; proof of health; proof of adequate funds. Financial aid is not available to international students. Admission application deadlines: 7/7 for fall, 10/31 for winter, 1/17 for spring. Applications are processed on a rolling basis.

Program Contact: Ms. Mary Zeise, Graduate Office Manager, Winona State University, 114 Somsen Hall, Winona, MN 55987-5838. (507) 457-5038, or (800) 242-8978 (MN only); Fax: (507) 457-5578.

MISSISSIPPI

Delta State University

School of Business

Cleveland, Mississippi

OVERVIEW
Delta State University is a state-supported comprehensive coed institution. Founded 1925. Setting: 274-acre small-town campus. Total institutional enrollment: 4,000. Program was first offered in 1976.

MBA HIGHLIGHTS

Entrance Difficulty**
Mean GMAT: 510
Mean GPA: 3.0

Cost $
Tuition: $1,147/semester
(Nonresident: $2,264/semester)
Room & Board: $2,500

Enrollment Profile

Full-time: 27	Work Exp: 50%	
Part-time: 67	International: 1%	
Total: 94	Women: 41%	
Average Age: 25	Minorities: 23%	

Average Class Size: 15

ACADEMICS
Length of Program Minimum: 24 months. Maximum: 5 years.
Calendar Semesters.
Full-time Classes Main campus, Clarksdale, Greenville; day, evening, summer.
Part-time Classes Main campus, Clarksdale, Greenville; evening, summer.
Degree Requirements 36 credits including 18 elective credits.
Required Courses Communications, financial management, management problems, marketing seminar, project management, statistical methods.
Curricular Focus Business issues and problems, leadership, problem solving and decision making.
Concentrations Accounting, finance, management, marketing.
Faculty Part-time: 14, 100% with doctorates.
Teaching Methodology Case study: 25%, faculty seminars: 5%, lecture: 50%, research: 10%, student presentations: 5%, team projects: 5%.

STUDENT STATISTICS
Geographic Representation State residents 96%. By region: South 90%; Northeast 5%; Midwest 5%. International 1%.
Undergraduate Majors Business 98%; engineering/technology 1%; science/mathematics 1%.
Other Background Graduate degrees in other disciplines: 5%. Work experience: On average, students have 4-6 years of work experience on entrance to the program.

FACILITIES
Information Resources Main library with 208,855 bound volumes, 717,867 titles on microform, 1,460 periodical subscriptions, 11,422 records/tapes/CDs.
Housing College housing available.
Technology Computers are used moderately in course work. Computer terminals/PCs, linked by a campus-wide computer network, are available for use by students in program; they are located in the library, the computer center, computer labs. Students in the program are not required to have their own PC. $100 are budgeted per student for computer support.

Computer Resources/On-line Services

Training	Yes	CompuServe	No
Internet	Yes	Dun's	No
E-Mail	No	Dow Jones	Yes
Videoconference Center	Yes	Dialog	Yes
Multimedia Center	Yes	Bloomberg	No
LEXIS/NEXIS	Yes		

ADMISSION
Acceptance 1994-95 97 applied for admission; 85% were accepted.
Entrance Requirements Bachelor's degree, GMAT score of 400, minimum 2.75 GPA.
Application Requirements Application form, copies of transcript.
Application Deadlines 8/15 for fall, 1/15 for spring.

FINANCIALS
Costs for 1994-95 Tuition: Full-time: $1,147/semester for state residents, $2,264/semester for nonresidents; Part-time day: $110/hour for state residents, $234/hour for nonresidents. Average room and board costs are $2,500 per academic year (on-campus) and $3,200 per academic year (off-campus).
Financial Aid In 1994-95, 40% of candidates received some institutionally administered aid in the form of loans, assistantships. Total awards ranged from $2,400-$4,000. Financial aid is not available to part-time students. Application deadlines: 5/1 for fall, 10/1 for spring. Contact: Ms. Peggy Sledge, Director of Student Financial Assistance, Cleveland, MS 38733. (601) 846-4670.

INTERNATIONAL STUDENTS
Demographics 1% of students enrolled in the program are international; Asia 100%.
Applying TOEFL required, minimum score of 550; proof of health; proof of adequate funds. Financial aid is not available to international students. Admission application deadlines: 1/15 for fall, 7/1 for spring.

ALTERNATE MBA PROGRAM
Executive MBA (EMBA) Length of program: Minimum: 36 months. Maximum: 5 years. Degree requirements: 33 credits. Minimum 5 years professional or managerial experience or minimum 550 GMAT; minimum 3.0 GPA.

PLACEMENT
In 1993-94, 14 organizations participated in on-campus recruiting. Placement services include alumni network, career counseling/planning, career fairs, career placement, job interviews, resume preparation, and resume referral to employers. Of 1994 graduates, 95% were employed within three months of graduation, the average starting salary was $24,000, the range was $18,000-$30,000.
Jobs by Employer Type Manufacturing 80%; service 5%; accounting 15%.
Jobs by Functional Area Marketing/sales 5%; finance 20%; management 75%.

Program Contact: Dr. Jerry Williams, Director of Graduate Studies, Delta State University, Cleveland, MS 38733. (601) 846-4181, or (800) 468-6378 (MS only); Fax: (601) 846-4643.

Jackson State University

College of Commerce and Business Administration

Jackson, Mississippi

OVERVIEW
Jackson State University is a state-supported coed institution. Part of Mississippi Institutions of Higher Learning. Founded 1877. Setting: 128-acre urban campus. Total institutional enrollment: 6,346.

MBA HIGHLIGHTS

Entrance Difficulty**

Cost $
Tuition: $1,115/semester
Room & Board: N/R

Enrollment Profile
Full-time: N/R
Part-time: N/R
Total: 111
Average Age: N/R

Work Exp: N/R
International: 20%
Women: 65%
Minorities: 70%

Average Class Size: 15

ACADEMICS
Length of Program Minimum: 18 months.
Calendar Semesters.
Full-time Classes Main campus; evening.
Part-time Classes Main campus; evening.
Degree Requirements 36 hours.
Curricular Focus Economic and financial theory, general management, managing diversity.
Concentration Management.
Teaching Methodology Case study: 18%, faculty seminars: 5%, lecture: 35%, research: 10%, seminars by members of the business community: 7%, student presentations: 10%, team projects: 15%.

STUDENT STATISTICS
Geographic Representation International 20%.

FACILITIES
Information Resources Main library with 364,628 bound volumes, 311,685 titles on microform, 4,925 periodical subscriptions, 2,856 records/tapes/CDs.

ADMISSION
Entrance Requirements Bachelor's degree, GMAT score, minimum 2.5 GPA.
Application Requirements Application form, copies of transcript, resume/curriculum vitae, 3 letters of recommendation.
Application Deadline Applications are processed on a rolling basis.

FINANCIALS
Costs for 1994-95 Tuition: Full-time: $1,115/semester; Part-time day: $124/hour.
Financial Aid Application deadline: 4/30 for fall. Contact: Dr. McKinley Alexander, Director of Graduate Business Programs, 3825 Ridgewood Road, Box 23, Jackson, MS 39217. (601) 982-6315.

INTERNATIONAL STUDENTS
Demographics 20% of students enrolled in the program are international.
Applying TOEFL required; proof of health; proof of adequate funds. Financial aid is available to international students.

Program Contact: Dr. McKinley Alexander, Director of Business Graduate Programs, Jackson State University, 3825 Ridgewood Road, Box 23, Jackson, MS 39217. (601) 982-6315; Fax: (601) 982-6124.

Millsaps College

Else School of Management

Jackson, Mississippi

OVERVIEW
Millsaps College is an independent United Methodist comprehensive coed institution. Founded 1890. Setting: 100-acre urban campus. Total institutional enrollment: 1,437. Program was first offered in 1979. AACSB-accredited.

MBA HIGHLIGHTS

Entrance Difficulty*
Mean GMAT: 530
Mean GPA: 3.1

Cost $$
Tuition: $449/hour
Room & Board: $5,200

Enrollment Profile
Full-time: 34
Part-time: 78
Total: 112
Average Age: 26

Work Exp: 80%
International: 2%
Women: 41%
Minorities: 11%

Average Class Size: 12

ACADEMICS
Length of Program Minimum: 12 months. Maximum: 6 years.
Calendar Semesters.
Full-time Classes Main campus; day, evening, summer.
Part-time Classes Main campus; day, evening, summer.
Degree Requirements 30 credits including 24 elective credits.
Required Courses Global policy, managerial analysis and forecasting. Courses may be waived through: previous course work.
Curricular Focus Business issues and problems, problem solving and decision making, strategic analysis and planning.
Concentrations Accounting, finance, management, marketing.
Faculty Full-time: 17, 94% with doctorates; part-time: 4, 25% with doctorates.
Teaching Methodology Case study: 30%, lecture: 35%, seminars by members of the business community: 5%, student presentations: 15%, team projects: 15%.
Special Opportunities Internship program available.

STUDENT STATISTICS
Geographic Representation State residents 64%. By region: South 97%; West 1%. International 2%.
Undergraduate Majors Business 49%; education 1%; engineering/technology 14%; humanities 8%; science/mathematics 17%; social sciences 11%.
Other Background Graduate degrees in other disciplines: 3%. Work experience: On average, students have 3 years of work experience on entrance to the program.

FACILITIES
Information Resources Main library with 278,000 bound volumes, 20,000 titles on microform, 804 periodical subscriptions, 6,800 records/tapes/CDs, 9 CD-ROMs.
Housing 1% of students in program live in college-owned or -operated housing.
Technology Computers are used moderately in course work. 40 computer terminals/PCs, linked by a campus-wide computer network, are available for use by students in program; they are located in computer labs. Students in the program are not required to have their own PC.

Computer Resources/On-line Services

Training	Yes	Dun's	No
Internet	Yes	Dow Jones	No
E-Mail	Yes	Dialog	No
LEXIS/NEXIS	No	Bloomberg	No
CompuServe	No		

ADMISSION
Acceptance 1994-95 103 applied for admission; 70% were accepted.
Entrance Requirements Bachelor's degree, GMAT score of 450, minimum 2.5 GPA. Core courses waived through: previous course work.
Application Requirements Written essay, interview, application form, copies of transcript, personal statement, 2 letters of recommendation.
Application Deadlines 6/30 for fall, 11/1 for spring.

FINANCIALS
Costs for 1994-95 Tuition: Full-time: $449/hour. Fees: Full-time: $9/hour. Average room and board costs are $5,200 per academic year (on-campus) and $5,400 per academic year (off-campus).
Financial Aid In 1994-95, 52% of candidates received some institutionally administered aid in the form of scholarships, loans. Total awards ranged from $300-$10,000. Financial aid is available to part-time students. Application deadlines: 4/30 for fall, 11/1 for spring. Contact: Mr. Kevin Russell, Director of Graduate Admissions, 1701 North State Street, Jackson, MS 39210. (601) 974-1253.

INTERNATIONAL STUDENTS
Demographics 2% of students enrolled in the program are international; Asia 50%, Europe 50%.
Services and Facilities International student center.

Applying TOEFL required, minimum score of 560. Financial aid is available to international students. Financial aid is available for those students after one semester. Admission application deadlines: 5/30 for fall, 10/1 for spring.

PLACEMENT
Placement services include career counseling/planning, career fairs, career library, career placement, electronic job bank, executive in residence, job interviews, resume preparation, and resume referral to employers. Of 1994 graduates, 90% were employed within three months of graduation, the average starting salary was $42,500, the range was $22,500-$60,000.

Jobs by Employer Type Manufacturing 9%; service 64%; government 9%; consulting 9%; nonprofit 9%.

Jobs by Functional Area Marketing/sales 36%; finance 40%; management 20%; strategic planning 2%; technical management 2%.

Program Contact: Mr. Kevin Russell, Director of Graduate Admissions, Millsaps College, 1701 North State Street, Jackson, MS 39210. (601) 974-1253; Fax: (601) 974-1260.

Mississippi College

School of Business

Clinton, Mississippi

OVERVIEW
Mississippi College is an independent Southern Baptist comprehensive coed institution. Founded 1826. Setting: 320-acre suburban campus. Total institutional enrollment: 3,781. Program was first offered in 1968.

MBA HIGHLIGHTS

Entrance Difficulty*
Mean GMAT: 420
Mean GPA: 2.9

Cost $
Tuition: $615/course
Room & Board: $2,830

Enrollment Profile
Full-time: N/R
Part-time: N/R
Total: 180
Average Age: 32

Work Exp: 99%
International: N/R
Women: 40%
Minorities: 10%

Average Class Size: 30

ACADEMICS
Length of Program Minimum: 30 months. Maximum: 5 years.
Calendar Semesters.
Part-time Classes Main campus; evening.
Degree Requirements 30 credits including 6 elective credits.
Required Courses Accounting policies, economics of the firm, financial management, human relations in business, law, business, and society, market analysis, policy formulation and administration, quantitative management.
Curricular Focus General management.
Concentration Management.
Faculty Full-time: 8, 85% with doctorates; part-time: 5.
Teaching Methodology Case study: 10%, lecture: 80%, student presentations: 10%.
Special Opportunities International exchange in Austria, United Kingdom.

STUDENT STATISTICS
Geographic Representation By region: South 100%.
Other Background Graduate degrees in other disciplines: 10%. Work experience: On average, students have 8 years of work experience on entrance to the program.

FACILITIES
Information Resources Main library with 230,000 bound volumes, 14,000 titles on microform, 768 periodical subscriptions, 10,576 records/tapes/CDs. Business collection includes 1,000 bound volumes, 74 periodical subscriptions, 25 CD-ROMs, 100 videos.
Housing College housing available.

Technology Computers are used moderately in course work. 30 computer terminals/PCs, linked by a campus-wide computer network, are available for use by students in program; they are located in computer labs. Students in the program are not required to have their own PC. $100 are budgeted per student for computer support.
Computer Resources/On-line Services

| Training | Yes | E-Mail | Yes |
| Internet | Yes | Videoconference Center | Yes |

ADMISSION
Acceptance 1994-95 117 applied for admission; 92% were accepted.
Entrance Requirements Bachelor's degree, GMAT score of 400, minimum 2.5 GPA. Core courses waived through: previous course work.
Application Requirements Application form, copies of transcript.
Application Deadlines 7/1 for fall, 12/1 for spring. Applications are processed on a rolling basis.

FINANCIALS
Costs for 1994-95 Tuition: Full-time: $615/course. Fees: Full-time: $176/trimester. Average room and board costs are $2,830 per academic year (on-campus).
Financial Aid In 1994-95, 5% of candidates received some institutionally administered aid in the form of grants, loans, assistantships, work-study. Financial aid is not available to part-time students. Application deadline: 4/1 for fall. Contact: Dr. Tom Prather, Financial Aid Office, 200 South Capitol Street, Clinton, MS 39058. (601) 925-3212.

INTERNATIONAL STUDENTS
Applying TOEFL required, minimum score of 500; proof of health; proof of adequate funds. Admission application deadlines: 7/1 for fall, 12/1 for spring.

PLACEMENT
In 1993-94, 3 organizations participated in on-campus recruiting; 3 on-campus interviews were conducted. Placement services include career counseling/planning. Of 1994 graduates, 95% were employed within three months of graduation.

Program Contact: Ms. Jeannie Lane, Assistant to Vice President for Graduate Studies, Mississippi College, PO Box 4185, Clinton, MS 39058. (601) 925-3225; Fax: (601) 925-3804.

Mississippi State University

Graduate Studies in Business

Mississippi State, Mississippi

OVERVIEW
Mississippi State University is a state-supported coed institution. Founded 1878. Setting: 4,200-acre small-town campus. Total institutional enrollment: 14,000. Program was first offered in 1957. AACSB-accredited.

MBA HIGHLIGHTS

Entrance Difficulty**
Mean GMAT: 525
Mean GPA: 3.25

Cost $
Tuition: $111/credit hour
(Nonresident: $216/credit hour)
Room & Board: $1,950

Enrollment Profile
Full-time: 50
Part-time: 15
Total: 65
Average Age: 24

Work Exp: 25%
International: 10%
Women: 30%
Minorities: 5%

Average Class Size: 25

ACADEMICS
Length of Program Minimum: 12 months. Maximum: 6 years.
Calendar Semesters.
Full-time Classes Main campus, Meridian, Columbus Air Force Base; day, evening, summer.
Part-time Classes Main campus, Meridian, Columbus Air Force Base; day, evening, summer.

Degree Requirements 30 credit hours including 6 elective credit hours. Other: Minimum 3.0 GPA.

Required Courses Advanced accounting, financial policies, macroeconomics, management policies, marketing policies, microeconomics or managerial economics, policy strategy, statistical analysis.

Curricular Focus General management, problem solving and decision making, teamwork.

Concentrations Accounting, economics, finance, management, management information systems, marketing, quantitative analysis.

Faculty Full-time: 30, 100% with doctorates.

Teaching Methodology Case study: 10%, faculty seminars: 10%, lecture: 30%, research: 5%, seminars by members of the business community: 5%, student presentations: 20%, team projects: 20%.

Special Opportunities International exchange program available.

STUDENT STATISTICS
Geographic Representation State residents 85%. International 10%.

Undergraduate Majors Business 80%; engineering/technology 10%; other 10%.

Other Background Graduate degrees in other disciplines: 100%. Work experience: On average, students have 2 years of work experience on entrance to the program.

FACILITIES
Information Resources Main library with 850,067 bound volumes, 2.1 million titles on microform, 7,387 periodical subscriptions, 8,457 records/tapes/CDs.

Housing 20% of students in program live in college-owned or -operated housing. Assistance with housing search provided.

Technology Students in the program are not required to have their own PC.

Computer Resources/On-line Services

Training	Yes	CompuServe	No
Internet	No	Dun's	No
Videoconference Center	Yes	Dow Jones	No
Multimedia Center	Yes	Dialog	No
LEXIS/NEXIS	Yes	Bloomberg	No

ADMISSION
Acceptance 1994-95 105 applied for admission; 29% were accepted.

Entrance Requirements Bachelor's degree, prerequisite courses required for applicants with non-business degree, GMAT score of 500, minimum 3.0 GPA. Core courses waived through: previous course work.

Application Requirements Written essay, application form, copies of transcript, resume/curriculum vitae, personal statement.

Application Deadlines 1/1 for fall, 11/1 for spring. Applications are processed on a rolling basis.

FINANCIALS
Costs for 1994-95 Tuition: Full-time: $111/credit hour for state residents, $216/credit hour for nonresidents; Part-time day: $142/credit hour for state residents; Part-time evening: $142/credit hour for state residents. Fees: Full-time: $31/credit hour for state residents, $31/credit hour for nonresidents; Part-time day: $31/credit hour for state residents. Average room and board costs are $1,950 per academic year (on-campus) and $3,600 per academic year (off-campus).

Financial Aid In 1994-95, candidates received some institutionally administered aid in the form of loans, assistantships. Financial aid is available to part-time students. Application deadlines: 7/1 for fall, 11/1 for spring. Contact: Ms. Audrey Lambert, Director of Financial Aid, PO Box 9501, Mississippi State, MS 39762. (601) 325-2450.

INTERNATIONAL STUDENTS
Demographics 10% of students enrolled in the program are international; North America 60%, Asia 10%, Europe 10%, South America 10%, other 10%.

Services and Facilities International student office, ESL courses.

Applying TOEFL required, minimum score of 575; proof of health; proof of adequate funds. Financial aid is available to international students. Financial aid application deadline: 4/1 for fall. Applications are processed on a rolling basis. Admission application deadlines: 7/1 for fall, 11/1 for spring, 4/1 for summer. Applications are processed on a rolling basis. Contact: Mr. Stephen Cottrell, International Student Services, PO Box 9733, Mississippi State, MS 39762. (601) 325-8929.

PLACEMENT
In 1993-94, 8 organizations participated in on-campus recruiting; 8 on-campus interviews were conducted. Placement services include alumni network, career counseling/planning, career fairs, career library, career placement, electronic job bank, job interviews, resume preparation, and resume referral to employers. Of 1994 graduates, 80% were employed within three months of graduation, the average starting salary was $30,000, the range was $25,000-$38,000.

Jobs by Employer Type Manufacturing 40%; service 60%.

Jobs by Functional Area Marketing/sales 20%; finance 10%; management 50%; strategic planning 20%.

Program Contact: Dr. R. H. Gilmer Jr., Director of Graduate Studies in Business, Mississippi State University, PO Box 5268, Mississippi State, MS 39762. (601) 325-1891; Fax: (601) 325-2410.
See full description on page 782.

University of Mississippi

School of Business Administration

Oxford, Mississippi

OVERVIEW
The University of Mississippi is a state-supported coed institution. Founded 1844. Setting: 2,300-acre small-town campus with easy access to Memphis. Total institutional enrollment: 10,060. Program was first offered in 1944. AACSB-accredited.

MBA HIGHLIGHTS

Entrance Difficulty*
Mean GMAT: 510
Mean GPA: 3.3

Cost $
Tuition: $998/semester
(Nonresident: $2,228/semester)
Room & Board: $3,810

Enrollment Profile

Full-time: 103	Work Exp: 30%
Part-time: 28	International: 38%
Total: 131	Women: 36%
Average Age: 26	Minorities: 14%

Class Size: 25 - 30

ACADEMICS
Length of Program Minimum: 12 months. Maximum: 5 years.

Calendar Semesters.

Full-time Classes Main campus; day.

Degree Requirements 36 credits including 6 elective credits.

Required Courses Advanced business conditions analysis, business policy and strategy, financial management, management information systems, managerial accounting, managerial economics, marketing management, organizational behavior, production and operations management, statistical methods for business. Courses may be waived through: previous course work.

Curricular Focus General management.

Concentrations Accounting, banking, economics, finance, international business, management, management information systems, marketing, operations management, organizational behavior, quantitative analysis, real estate.

Faculty Full-time: 20, 100% with doctorates.

Teaching Methodology Case study: 15%, computer applications: 10%, lecture: 50%, seminars by members of the business community: 5%, student presentations: 5%, team projects: 15%.

Special Opportunities International exchange in United Kingdom. Internship program available.

STUDENT STATISTICS
Geographic Representation State residents 42%. By region: South 40%; Midwest 10%; Northeast 7%; West 3%. International 38%.

Undergraduate Majors Business 65%; engineering/technology 15%; humanities 5%; science/mathematics 10%; social sciences 5%.

Other Background Graduate degrees in other disciplines: 5%.

FACILITIES

Information Resources Main library with 917,619 bound volumes, 29,795 titles on microform, 14,160 periodical subscriptions, 15,584 records/tapes/CDs, 481 CD-ROMs.

Housing 60% of students in program live in college-owned or -operated housing.

Technology Computers are used heavily in course work. 200 computer terminals/PCs, linked by a campus-wide computer network, are available for use by students in program; they are located in dormitories, the student center, classrooms, the computer center, computer labs. Students in the program are not required to have their own PC.

Computer Resources/On-line Services

Training	Yes	Multimedia Center	Yes
Internet	Yes	Dialog	Yes $
E-Mail	Yes		

ADMISSION

Acceptance 1994-95 Of those applying, 60% were accepted.

Entrance Requirements Bachelor's degree, GMAT score of 450, minimum 3.0 GPA. Core courses waived through: previous course work.

Application Requirements Application form, copies of transcript.

Application Deadlines 5/15 for fall, 10/1 for spring, 4/1 for summer.

FINANCIALS

Costs for 1994-95 Tuition: Full-time: $998/semester for state residents, $2,228/semester for nonresidents. Fees: Full-time: $230/semester for state residents, $230/semester for nonresidents. Average room and board costs are $3,810 per academic year (on-campus) and $5,310 per academic year (off-campus).

Financial Aid In 1994-95, 90% of candidates received some institutionally administered aid in the form of grants, scholarships, loans, fellowships, assistantships, work-study. Total awards ranged from $4,456-$13,320. Financial aid is available to part-time students. Applications are processed on a rolling basis. Contact: Mr. Thomas G. Hood, Director of Financial Aid, Old Chemistry Building, Room 25, University, MS 38677. (601) 232-5788.

INTERNATIONAL STUDENTS

Demographics 38% of students enrolled in the program are international; Asia 88%, Europe 11%, Africa 1%.

Services and Facilities Visa services, language tutoring, ESL courses, counseling/support services.

Applying TOEFL required, minimum score of 550; proof of health; proof of adequate funds. Financial aid is available to international students. Applications are processed on a rolling basis. Admission application deadlines: 5/15 for fall, 10/11 for spring, 4/1 for summer. Applications are processed on a rolling basis. Contact: Ms. Leslie Banahan, Foreign Student Adviser, Office of International Programs, Room 23, Y-Building, University, MS 38677. (601) 232-7404.

PLACEMENT

In 1993-94, 23 organizations participated in on-campus recruiting; 38 on-campus interviews were conducted. Placement services include alumni network, career counseling/planning, career fairs, career library, career placement, electronic job bank, job interviews, job search course, resume preparation, and resume referral to employers. Of 1994 graduates, 75% were employed within three months of graduation, the average starting salary was $29,000, the range was $22,000-$43,000.

Jobs by Employer Type Manufacturing 35%; service 30%; government 3%; consulting 15%; nonprofit 2%; other 15%.

Jobs by Functional Area Marketing/sales 20%; finance 15%; operations 10%; management 25%; technical management 15%; law 10%; education 5%.

Program Contact: Dr. Delvin D. Hawley, Associate Dean, University of Mississippi, University, MS 38677. (601) 232-5820; Fax: (601) 232-5821.

University of Southern Mississippi

College of Business Administration

Hattiesburg, Mississippi

OVERVIEW

The University of Southern Mississippi is a state-supported coed institution. Founded 1910. Setting: 840-acre small-town campus with easy access

to New Orleans. Total institutional enrollment: 12,500. Program was first offered in 1964. AACSB-accredited.

MBA HIGHLIGHTS

Entrance Difficulty***
Mean GMAT: 510
Mean GPA: 3.15

Cost $
Tuition: $1,214/semester
(Nonresident: $2,444/semester)
Room & Board: $2,600

Enrollment Profile

Full-time: 42	Work Exp: 60%
Part-time: 38	International: 12%
Total: 80	Women: 61%
Average Age: 28	Minorities: 10%

Average Class Size: 24

ACADEMICS

Length of Program Minimum: 24 months.

Calendar Semesters.

Full-time Classes Main campus.

Part-time Classes Main campus, distance learning option; evening.

Degree Requirements 61.5 credit hours including 6 elective credit hours.

Required Courses Business and society, business modeling, communication skills for managers, federal taxes and management decisions, financial accounting, integrative management, legal environment of management, macroeconomic analysis for managers, management information systems, management theory, managerial accounting, managerial economics, managerial finance, managerial strategy and planning, managing in a global environment, marketing foundations, operations management, organizational management, problems in corporate finance, problems in marketing management, statistics for managers.

Curricular Focus Business issues and problems, problem solving and decision making, teamwork.

Concentration Management.

Faculty Full-time: 35, 100% with doctorates.

Teaching Methodology Case study: 50%, lecture: 30%, student presentations: 10%, team projects: 10%.

Special Opportunities International exchange in Austria, Germany, Japan, Mexico, United Kingdom. Other: International Business seminars in England, Japan, Jamaica, and Mexico.

STUDENT STATISTICS

Geographic Representation By region: South 90%. International 12%.

Undergraduate Majors Business 60%; engineering/technology 20%; humanities 20%.

Other Background Graduate degrees in other disciplines: 5%. Work experience: On average, students have 3 years of work experience on entrance to the program.

FACILITIES

Information Resources Main library with 872,011 bound volumes, 2.2 million titles on microform, 4,770 periodical subscriptions, 13,701 records/tapes/CDs, 78 CD-ROMs. Business collection includes 9,051 bound volumes, 260 periodical subscriptions, 7 CD-ROMs, 65 videos.

Housing 5% of students in program live in college-owned or -operated housing.

Technology Computers are used heavily in course work. 50 computer terminals/PCs, linked by a campus-wide computer network, are available for use by students in program; they are located in computer labs. Students in the program are not required to have their own PC.

Computer Resources/On-line Services

Training	Yes	Videoconference Center	Yes
Internet	Yes	Multimedia Center	Yes
E-Mail	Yes		

Other on-line services: OCLC, RLIN, First Search.

ADMISSION

Acceptance 1994-95 92 applied for admission; 92% were accepted.

Entrance Requirements Bachelor's degree, GMAT score. Core courses waived through: previous course work.

Application Requirements Written essay, application form, copies of transcript, 2 letters of recommendation.

Application Deadlines 5/15 for fall. Applications are processed on a rolling basis. Application discs available.

FINANCIALS
Costs for 1994-95 Tuition: Full-time: $1,214/semester for state residents, $2,444/semester for nonresidents. Average room and board costs are $2,600 per academic year (on-campus).

Financial Aid In 1994-95, 40% of candidates received some institutionally administered aid in the form of loans, assistantships, work-study. Total awards ranged from $2,428-$10,928. Financial aid is not available to part-time students. Application deadline: 3/15 for fall. Applications are processed on a rolling basis. Contact: Ms. Valerie Horne, Graduate Counselor, Financial Aid, Box 5101, Hattiesburg, MS 39406-5001. (601) 266-4774.

INTERNATIONAL STUDENTS
Demographics 12% of students enrolled in the program are international; Europe 43%, South America 29%, Asia 14%, Central America 14%.

Services and Facilities International student office, international student center, language tutoring.

Applying TOEFL required, minimum score of 550; proof of health; proof of adequate funds. Financial aid is not available to international students. Admission applications are processed on a rolling basis. Contact: Ms. Cathy Carucci, Director, International Student Affairs, Box 5151, Hattiesburg, MS 39406-5001. (601) 266-4841.

ALTERNATE MBA PROGRAM
One-Year MBA Length of program: Minimum: 12 months. Degree requirements: 34.5 credit hours including 6 elective credit hours. Average class size: 47.

PLACEMENT
Placement services include career fairs, career placement, resume preparation, and resume referral to employers.

Program Contact: Dr. Gus Gordon, Director, Graduate Business Programs, University of Southern Mississippi, Box 5001, Hattiesburg, MS 39406-5001. (601) 266-4664; Fax: (601) 266-4920; Internet Address: gordon@cba.usm.edu.

William Carey College

School of Business

Hattiesburg, Mississippi

OVERVIEW
William Carey College is an independent Southern Baptist comprehensive coed institution. Founded 1906. Setting: 64-acre small-town campus with easy access to New Orleans. Total institutional enrollment: 2,032.

MBA HIGHLIGHTS
Entrance Difficulty**

Cost $
Tuition: $160/hour
Room & Board: N/R

Enrollment Profile
Full-time: N/R	Work Exp: N/R
Part-time: N/R	International: 0%
Total: 93	Women: 40%
Average Age: N/R	Minorities: 20%

Average Class Size: 18

ACADEMICS
Length of Program Minimum: 12 months.
Calendar Trimesters.
Full-time Classes Main campus, Guthport; evening, summer.
Degree Requirements 30 credits.
Curricular Focus Entrepreneurship, leadership, teamwork.
Concentrations Arts administration, entrepreneurship, health services, operations management, public policy.
Teaching Methodology Faculty seminars: 15%, lecture: 15%, research: 25%, seminars by members of the business community: 15%, student presentations: 15%, team projects: 15%.

STUDENT STATISTICS
Geographic Representation State residents 100%.

FACILITIES
Information Resources Main library with 103,191 bound volumes, 30,722 titles on microform, 626 periodical subscriptions, 2,712 records/tapes/CDs.

ADMISSION
Entrance Requirements Bachelor's degree, minimum 3 years of work experience.

Application Requirements Written essay, interview, application form, copies of transcript, resume/curriculum vitae, 3 letters of recommendation.

Application Deadline Applications are processed on a rolling basis.

FINANCIALS
Costs for 1994-95 Tuition: Full-time: $160/hour.

Financial Aid Application deadline: 6/15 for fall. Contact: Mr. Bill Curry, Director of Financial Aid, 498 Tuscan Avenue, Hattiesburg, MS 39401-5499. (601) 582-6153.

INTERNATIONAL STUDENTS
Applying TOEFL required, minimum score of 550; proof of health; proof of adequate funds. Financial aid is available to international students. Admission applications are processed on a rolling basis.

Program Contact: Mr. David Manifold, Director of MBA Program, William Carey College, William Carey College, 1568 Beach Drive, Guthport, MS 39507. (601) 865-1513.

MISSOURI

Avila College

Department of Business and Economics

Kansas City, Missouri

OVERVIEW
Avila College is an independent Roman Catholic comprehensive coed institution. Founded 1916. Setting: 50-acre suburban campus. Total institutional enrollment: 1,389. Program was first offered in 1978.

MBA HIGHLIGHTS
Entrance Difficulty***
Mean GMAT: 505
Mean GPA: 3.32

Cost $$
Tuition: $9,000
Room & Board: $4,645

Enrollment Profile
Full-time: 24	Work Exp: 95%
Part-time: 137	International: 9%
Total: 161	Women: 45%
Average Age: 32	Minorities: 5%

Average Class Size: 20

ACADEMICS
Length of Program Minimum: 24 months. Maximum: 7 years.
Calendar Semesters.
Full-time Classes Main campus; evening, summer.
Part-time Classes Main campus; evening, summer.
Degree Requirements 30 credits including 9-12 elective credits.
Required Courses Aggregate income analysis, business government and society, current issues in management, financial management, managerial accounting, managerial economics, marketing strategy, organizational behavior, organizational policy and strategy.
Curricular Focus Business issues and problems, problem solving and decision making, strategic analysis and planning.
Concentrations Accounting, finance, health services, human resources management, international business, management, management information systems, marketing, operations management.

Faculty Full-time: 9, 55% with doctorates; part-time: 10, 20% with doctorates.

Teaching Methodology Case study: 20%, lecture: 35%, research: 5%, student presentations: 20%, team projects: 20%.

Special Opportunities Internship program available.

STUDENT STATISTICS

Geographic Representation By region: Midwest 91%. International 9%.

Undergraduate Majors Business 50%; education 1%; engineering/technology 10%; humanities 1%; nursing 5%; science/mathematics 6%; social sciences 8%; other 19%.

Other Background Graduate degrees in other disciplines: 5%. Work experience: On average, students have 10 years of work experience on entrance to the program.

FACILITIES

Information Resources Main library with 70,000 bound volumes, 383,881 titles on microform, 545 periodical subscriptions, 4,402 records/tapes/CDs, 9 CD-ROMs.

Housing 5% of students in program live in college-owned or -operated housing.

Technology Computers are used moderately in course work. 50 computer terminals/PCs, linked by a campus-wide computer network, are available for use by students in program; they are located in the library, the computer center, computer labs. Students in the program are not required to have their own PC.

Computer Resources/On-line Services

Training	Yes	E-Mail	No
Internet	Yes		

ADMISSION

Entrance Requirements Bachelor's degree, GMAT score of 450, minimum 3.0 GPA. Core courses waived through: previous course work.

Application Requirements Interview, application form, copies of transcript.

Application Deadline Applications are processed on a rolling basis.

FINANCIALS

Costs for 1994-95 Tuition: Full-time: $9,000; Part-time day: $230/credit hour. Average room and board costs are $4,645 per academic year (on-campus).

Financial Aid In 1994-95, 33% of candidates received some institutionally administered aid in the form of loans, assistantships. Total awards ranged from $2,000-$3,000. Financial aid is available to part-time students. Applications are processed on a rolling basis. Contact: Mr. Jerome Curtis, Financial Aid Specialist, 11901 Wornall Road, Kansas City, MO 64145-1698. (816) 942-8400 Ext. 2347.

INTERNATIONAL STUDENTS

Demographics 9% of students enrolled in the program are international; Asia 90%, Europe 10%.

Services and Facilities International student office, visa services, language tutoring, ESL courses, special assistance for nonnative speakers of English, counseling/support services.

Applying TOEFL required, minimum score of 550; proof of adequate funds. Financial aid is not available to international students. Admission applications are processed on a rolling basis. Contact: Mr. Bruce Inwards, ILCP Coordinator and ESL Lecturer, 11901 Wornall Road, Kansas City, MO 64145-1698. (816) 942-8400 Ext. 2372.

PLACEMENT

Placement services include alumni network, career counseling/planning, career fairs, career library, career placement, resume preparation, and resume referral to employers.

Program Contact: Ms. Wendy L. Acker, MBA Director, Avila College, 11901 Wornall Road, Kansas City, MO 64145-1698. (816) 942-8400 Ext. 2321; Fax: (816) 942-3362.

Central Missouri State University

College of Business and Economics

Warrensburg, Missouri

OVERVIEW

Central Missouri State University is a state-supported comprehensive coed institution. Founded 1871. Setting: 1,053-acre small-town campus with easy access to Kansas City. Total institutional enrollment: 11,780. Program

was first offered in 1963.

MBA HIGHLIGHTS

Entrance Difficulty***
Mean GMAT: 493
Mean GPA: 3.05

Cost $
Tuition: $95/hour
(Nonresident: $187/hour)
Room & Board: N/R

Enrollment Profile

Full-time: 54	Work Exp: 45%
Part-time: 39	International: 23%
Total: 93	Women: 42%
Average Age: 30	Minorities: 7%

Average Class Size: 17

ACADEMICS

Length of Program Minimum: 24 months. Maximum: 8 years.

Calendar Semesters.

Full-time Classes Main campus; day, evening, summer.

Part-time Classes Main campus, Kansas City; evening, summer.

Degree Requirements 33 hours including 3 elective hours. Other: Minimum "B" in strategic management course.

Required Courses Management information systems, managerial accounting information, managerial communication, managerial economics, managerial finance, marketing strategy, operations management seminar, organization theory and behavior, research methods, strategic management.

Curricular Focus Business issues and problems, general management, problem solving and decision making.

Concentrations Accounting, management.

Faculty Full-time: 20, 100% with doctorates.

Teaching Methodology Case study: 25%, lecture: 15%, research: 15%, seminars by members of the business community: 5%, student presentations: 15%, team projects: 25%.

Special Opportunities International exchange in Mexico, Sweden, United Kingdom. Internship program available.

STUDENT STATISTICS

Geographic Representation State residents 54%. By region: Midwest 61%; South 6%; West 6%; Northeast 4%. International 23%.

Undergraduate Majors Business 62%; education 4%; engineering/technology 10%; humanities 8%; science/mathematics 3%; social sciences 8%; other 5%.

Other Background Graduate degrees in other disciplines: 15%. Work experience: On average, students have 4 years of work experience on entrance to the program.

FACILITIES

Information Resources Main library with 805,263 bound volumes, 1.2 million titles on microform, 2,890 periodical subscriptions, 4,467 records/tapes/CDs, 55 CD-ROMs. Business collection includes 35,000 bound volumes, 300 periodical subscriptions, 200 CD-ROMs, 500 videos.

Housing 20% of students in program live in college-owned or -operated housing.

Technology Computers are used moderately in course work. 600 computer terminals/PCs are available for use by students in program; they are located in student rooms, classrooms, learning resource center, the library, the computer center, computer labs, the research center. Students in the program are not required to have their own PC.

Computer Resources/On-line Services

Training	Yes	CompuServe	No
Internet	Yes	Dun's	No
E-Mail	No	Dow Jones	No
Multimedia Center	Yes	Dialog	Yes $
LEXIS/NEXIS	No	Bloomberg	No

ADMISSION

Acceptance 1994-95 204 applied for admission; 58% were accepted.

Entrance Requirements Bachelor's degree, GMAT score of 400, minimum 2.5 GPA.

Application Requirements Application form, copies of transcript, personal statement.

Application Deadline Applications are processed on a rolling basis.

FINANCIALS

Estimated Costs for 1995-96 Tuition: Full-time: $95/hour for state residents, $187/hour for nonresidents.

Financial Aid In 1994-95, 65% of candidates received some institutionally administered aid in the form of grants, scholarships, loans, fellowships, assistantships, work-study. Financial aid is available to part-time students. Application deadline: 3/1 for annual. Applications are processed on a rolling basis. Contact: Mr. Phillip Shreves, Director of Financial Aid, Administration Building 316, Warrensburg, MO 64093. (816) 543-4177.

INTERNATIONAL STUDENTS

Demographics 23% of students enrolled in the program are international.

Services and Facilities International student center, ESL courses.

Applying TOEFL required, minimum score of 550; proof of health; proof of adequate funds. Financial aid is available to international students. Financial aid application deadline: 3/1 for fall. Admission application deadlines: 5/19 for fall, 10/10 for spring, 3/15 for summer. Applications are processed on a rolling basis. Contact: Dr. Joy Stevens, Coordinator of International Student Center, International Student Center, University Union, Room 224, Warrensburg, MO 64093. (816) 543-4753.

PLACEMENT

In 1993-94, 107 organizations participated in on-campus recruiting. Placement services include career counseling/planning, career fairs, career library, career placement, job interviews, resume preparation, and resume referral to employers. Of 1994 graduates, 67% were employed within three months of graduation, the average starting salary was $41,800, the range was $27,000-$90,000.

Program Contact: Mr. Harry Poynter, Director of Graduate Programs, College of Business and Economics, Central Missouri State University, Dockery Hall, Suite 212, Warrensburg, MO 64093. (816) 543-8571; Fax: (816) 543-8885; Internet Address: hpoynter@cmsu.vmb.edu.

Drury College

Breech School of Business Administration

Springfield, Missouri

OVERVIEW

Drury College is an independent nonprofit comprehensive coed institution. Founded 1873. Setting: 60-acre suburban campus. Total institutional enrollment: 3,100. Program was first offered in 1963.

MBA HIGHLIGHTS

Entrance Difficulty***
Mean GMAT: 530
Mean GPA: 3.3

Cost $
Tuition: $205/semester hour
Room & Board: N/R

Enrollment Profile

Full-time: 33	Work Exp: 95%
Part-time: 32	International: 90%
Total: 65	Women: 34%
Average Age: 32	Minorities: 3%

Average Class Size: 24

ACADEMICS

Length of Program Minimum: 12 months. Maximum: 4 years.

Calendar Semesters.

Full-time Classes Main campus; evening, summer.

Part-time Classes Main campus; evening, summer.

Degree Requirements 29 semester hours.

Required Courses Accounting for management, aggregate economics, business policies, chief executive officer seminar, computer course, financial management, leadership and human relations, managerial economics, marketing management, organizational behavior, quantitative analysis for managerial decision problems.

Curricular Focus Business issues and problems, general management, leadership, problem solving and decision making, strategic analysis and planning, teamwork.

Concentration Management.

Faculty Full-time: 9, 100% with doctorates.

Teaching Methodology Case study: 40%, lecture: 10%, research: 10%, seminars by members of the business community: 10%, student presentations: 10%, team projects: 20%.

STUDENT STATISTICS

Geographic Representation State residents 3%. By region: Midwest 80%; South 14%; West 3%.

Undergraduate Majors Business 65%; education 3%; engineering/technology 23%; humanities 3%; science/mathematics 3%; social sciences 3%.

Other Background Graduate degrees in other disciplines: 5%. Work experience: On average, students have 10 years of work experience on entrance to the program.

FACILITIES

Information Resources Main library with 165,000 bound volumes, 212 titles on microform, 953 periodical subscriptions, 81 CD-ROMs.

Housing College housing available.

Technology Computers are used moderately in course work. Computer terminals/PCs, linked by a campus-wide computer network, are available for use by students in program; they are located in the student center, the library, the computer center. Students in the program are not required to have their own PC.

Computer Resources/On-line Services

Training	Yes	CompuServe	No
Internet	Yes	Dun's	No
E-Mail	Yes	Dow Jones	No
Videoconference Center	Yes	Dialog	Yes $
Multimedia Center	Yes	Bloomberg	No
LEXIS/NEXIS	No		

ADMISSION

Entrance Requirements Bachelor's degree, business prerequisites, GMAT score of 500, minimum 3.0 GPA. Core courses waived through: previous course work.

Application Requirements Application form, copies of transcript, 2 letters of recommendation.

Application Deadlines 8/1 for fall, 11/1 for spring.

FINANCIALS

Estimated Costs for 1995-96 Tuition: Full-time: $205/semester hour. Fees: Full-time: $255.

Financial Aid In 1994-95, 10% of candidates received some institutionally administered aid in the form of assistantships. Total awards ranged from $1,600-$5,000. Financial aid is not available to part-time students. Application deadlines: 6/1 for fall, 9/1 for spring. Contact: Dr. Clifton D. Petty, Assistant Director, 900 North Benton Avenue, Springfield, MO 65802. (417) 873-7240.

INTERNATIONAL STUDENTS

Demographics 90% of students enrolled in the program are international.

Applying TOEFL required, minimum score of 550; proof of adequate funds. Financial aid is not available to international students. Admission application deadline: 7/1 for fall. Contact: Mr. Xian Liu, Assistant Professor, 900 North Benton Avenue, Springfield, MO 65802. (417) 873-7879.

PLACEMENT

Placement services include alumni network, career counseling/planning, career library, career placement, job interviews, resume preparation, and resume referral to employers. Of 1994 graduates, 100% were employed within three months of graduation.

Program Contact: Dr. Clifton D. Petty, Assistant Director, Drury College, 900 North Benton Avenue, Springfield, MO 65802. (417) 873-7240; Fax: (417) 873-7537.

Fontbonne College

St. Louis, Missouri

OVERVIEW

Fontbonne College is an independent Roman Catholic comprehensive coed institution. Founded 1917. Setting: 13-acre urban campus. Total institutional enrollment: 1,900. Program was first offered in 1991.

MBA HIGHLIGHTS

Entrance Difficulty**

Cost $$
Tuition: $270/semester hour
Room & Board: N/R

Enrollment Profile

Full-time: N/R	Work Exp: 100%
Part-time: N/R	International: 1%
Total: 200	Women: 45%
Average Age: N/R	Minorities: 10%

Average Class Size: 12

ACADEMICS
Length of Program Minimum: 22 months.
Calendar Semesters.
Full-time Classes Main campus; evening, weekends, summer.
Part-time Classes Main campus, Chrystler campus; evening, weekends, summer.
Degree Requirements 43 semester hours.
Curricular Focus Business issues and problems, problem solving and decision making, teamwork.
Concentrations International business, management information systems, marketing, operations management, organizational behavior, quantitative analysis, strategic management.
Faculty Full-time: 1, 100% with doctorates; part-time: 55, 26% with doctorates.
Teaching Methodology Case study: 20%, lecture: 25%, research: 15%, student presentations: 15%, team projects: 25%.

STUDENT STATISTICS
Geographic Representation State residents 80%. International 1%.

FACILITIES
Information Resources Main library with 90,000 bound volumes, 1,643 titles on microform, 510 periodical subscriptions, 6,238 records/tapes/CDs.
Housing College housing not available.
Technology Students in the program are required to have their own PC. $1,250 are budgeted per student for computer support.

ADMISSION
Entrance Requirements Bachelor's degree, minimum 3.0 GPA, minimum 3 years of work experience.
Application Requirements Interview, application form, copies of transcript, resume/curriculum vitae, 3 letters of recommendation.
Application Deadline Applications are processed on a rolling basis.

FINANCIALS
Costs for 1994-95 Tuition: Full-time: $270/semester hour.
Financial Aid Applications are processed on a rolling basis. Contact: Mr. James Neil, Director of Financial Aid, 6800 Wydown Boulevard, St. Louis, MO 63105-3098. (314) 889-4584.

INTERNATIONAL STUDENTS
Demographics 1% of students enrolled in the program are international.
Applying TOEFL required, minimum score of 525; proof of health; proof of adequate funds. Financial aid is not available to international students. Contact: Mr. Bert Barry, International Student Adviser, 6800 Wydown Boulevard, St. Louis, MO 63105-3098. (314) 889-1509.

Program Contact: Sr. Ethel Marie Biri, Director of Student Services, Fontbonne College, 6800 Wydown Boulevard, St. Louis, MO 63105-3098. (314) 889-2220; Fax: (314) 863-0917.

Lincoln University

College of Business

Jefferson City, Missouri

OVERVIEW
Lincoln University is a state-supported comprehensive coed institution. Founded 1866. Setting: 152-acre small-town campus. Total institutional enrollment: 3,800.

MBA HIGHLIGHTS

Entrance Difficulty**
Mean GMAT: 437
Mean GPA: N/R

Cost $
Tuition: $102/hour
(Nonresident: $204/hour)
Room & Board: $2,676

Enrollment Profile

Full-time: N/R	Work Exp: N/R
Part-time: N/R	International: N/R
Total: 50	Women: 52%
Average Age: N/R	Minorities: 30%

Average Class Size: 19

ACADEMICS
Length of Program Minimum: 24 months.
Calendar Semesters.
Part-time Classes Main campus; evening.
Degree Requirements 36 hours.
Curricular Focus Business issues and problems, problem solving and decision making, teamwork.
Concentration Management.
Teaching Methodology Case study: 25%, faculty seminars: 2%, lecture: 45%, seminars by members of the business community: 8%, student presentations: 10%, team projects: 10%.

FACILITIES
Information Resources Main library with 141,640 bound volumes, 27,109 titles on microform, 2,748 periodical subscriptions, 38 CD-ROMs.
Housing College housing available.

ADMISSION
Entrance Requirements Bachelor's degree, GMAT score, minimum 2.5 GPA, score of 80% on Michigan Test of English Language Proficiency.
Application Requirements Application form, copies of transcript, personal statement, 3 letters of recommendation.
Application Deadline Applications are processed on a rolling basis.

FINANCIALS
Costs for 1994-95 Tuition: Part-time day: $102/hour for state residents, $204/hour for nonresidents. Fees: Part-time day: $10/semester for state residents, $10/semester for nonresidents. Average room and board costs are $2,676 per academic year (on-campus).
Financial Aid Application deadlines: 3/1 for fall, 11/1 for spring. Contact: Financial Aid Officer, 820 Chestnut, Jefferson City, MO 65102. (314) 681-5033.

INTERNATIONAL STUDENTS
Applying TOEFL required, minimum score of 500; proof of health; proof of adequate funds; Michigan Test 80%. Admission applications are processed on a rolling basis.

Program Contact: Mr. Gary K. Scott, Dean of the Graduate Program, Lincoln University, Room 452, MLK, 820 Chestnut, Jefferson City, MO 65102. (314) 681-5207; Fax: (314) 681-5566.

Lindenwood College

Division of Management

St. Charles, Missouri

OVERVIEW
Lindenwood College is an independent Presbyterian comprehensive coed institution. Founded 1827. Setting: 172-acre suburban campus with easy access to St. Louis. Total institutional enrollment: 3,137.

MBA HIGHLIGHTS

Entrance Difficulty***

Cost $$
Tuition: $215 - $220/semester hour
Room & Board: $8,000

Enrollment Profile
Full-time: 200
Part-time: 250
Total: 450
Average Age: N/R

Work Exp: N/R
International: 5%
Women: 45%
Minorities: 18%

Average Class Size: 15

ACADEMICS

Length of Program Minimum: 18 months.

Calendar Semesters.

Degree Requirements 36 semester hours.

Curricular Focus Business issues and problems, entrepreneurship, general management, international business, leadership, managing diversity, organizational development and change management, problem solving and decision making, strategic analysis and planning, teamwork, women in business.

Concentrations Accounting, arts administration, entrepreneurship, finance, health services, human resources management, international business, management, management information systems, marketing, real estate, strategic management.

Teaching Methodology Case study: 25%, lecture: 25%, student presentations: 25%, team projects: 25%.

STUDENT STATISTICS

Geographic Representation State residents 90%. International 5%.

FACILITIES

Information Resources Main library with 132,131 bound volumes, 32,300 titles on microform, 447 periodical subscriptions, 2,698 records/tapes/CDs, 1 CD-ROM.

Housing College housing available.

ADMISSION

Entrance Requirements Bachelor's degree, minimum 3.0 GPA.

Application Requirements Interview, application form, copies of transcript, resume/curriculum vitae, personal statement, 2 letters of recommendation.

Application Deadlines 12/1 for fall, 5/15 for spring. Applications are processed on a rolling basis.

FINANCIALS

Estimated Costs for 1995-96 Tuition: Full-time: $215-$220/semester hour. Average room and board costs are $8,000 per academic year (on-campus) and $10,000 per academic year (off-campus).

Financial Aid In 1994-95, 27% of candidates received some institutionally administered aid in the form of grants, loans, assistantships. Total awards ranged from $1,000-$5,000. Financial aid is available to part-time students. Application deadlines: 5/1 for fall, 11/1 for spring. Applications are processed on a rolling basis. Contact: Ms. Linda Mueller, Financial Aid Director, 209 South Kingshighway, St. Charles, MO 63301. (314) 949-4925.

INTERNATIONAL STUDENTS

Demographics 5% of students enrolled in the program are international.

Applying TOEFL required, minimum score of 550; proof of health; proof of adequate funds; enrollment deposit. Financial aid is available to international students. Financial aid application deadlines: 6/1 for fall, 11/1 for spring. Applications are processed on a rolling basis. Admission application deadlines: 8/1 for fall, 11/1 for spring, 6/1 for summer. Applications are processed on a rolling basis. Contact: Ms. Rachel Driskill, International Student Admissions Counselor, 209 South Kingshighway, St. Charles, MO 63301. (314) 949-4989.

Program Contact: Mr. Jerry Bladdick, Director, Evening and Graduate Admissions, Lindenwood College, 209 South Kingshighway, St. Charles, MO 63301. (314) 949-4933; Fax: (314) 949-4910; Internet Address: ataich@lc.lindenwood.edu.

Maryville University of Saint Louis

John E. Simon School of Business

St. Louis, Missouri

OVERVIEW

Maryville University of Saint Louis is an independent nonprofit comprehensive coed institution. Founded 1872. Setting: 130-acre suburban campus. Total institutional enrollment: 3,425.

ACADEMICS

Calendar Semesters.

Concentration Management.

FACILITIES

Information Resources Main library with 144,680 bound volumes, 330,879 titles on microform, 790 periodical subscriptions, 8,012 records/tapes/CDs, 6 CD-ROMs.

ADMISSION

Entrance Requirements Minimum 3.6 GPA.

Application Requirements Personal statement.

Application Deadlines 8/17 for fall, 1/4 for spring.

FINANCIALS

Costs for 1994-95 Tuition: Full-time: $4,325; Part-time day: $275/credit.

INTERNATIONAL STUDENTS

Applying TOEFL required, minimum score of 550. Admission application deadlines: 8/17 for fall, 1/4 for spring.

Program Contact: Ms. Jerri Beggs, Director of MBA Program, Maryville University of Saint Louis, 13550 Conway Road, St. Louis, MO 63141-7299. (314) 529-9418.

Northwest Missouri State University

College of Business, Government, and Computer Science

Maryville, Missouri

OVERVIEW

Northwest Missouri State University is a state-supported comprehensive coed institution. Founded 1905. Setting: 170-acre small-town campus with easy access to Kansas City. Total institutional enrollment: 6,001. Program was first offered in 1937.

MBA HIGHLIGHTS

Entrance Difficulty***
Mean GMAT: 491
Mean GPA: 3.47

Cost $
Tuition: $1,068/semester
(Nonresident: $1,896/semester)
Room & Board: $3,136

Enrollment Profile
Full-time: 29
Part-time: 50
Total: 79
Average Age: 30

Work Exp: 5%
International: 15%
Women: 57%
Minorities: 1%

Average Class Size: 15

ACADEMICS

Length of Program Minimum: 12 months. Maximum: 8 years.

Calendar Semesters.

Full-time Classes Main campus, Saint Joseph; day, evening, summer.

Part-time Classes Main campus, Saint Joseph; day, evening, summer.

Degree Requirements 33 credits. Other: Comprehensive exam.

Required Courses Advanced management theory, advanced marketing, executive seminar, financial management, international business, macroeconomic analysis and business conditions, management information systems decision support systems, managerial accounting, managerial economics, organizational behavior in administration, quantitative analysis. Courses may be waived through: previous course work.

Curricular Focus Business issues and problems, problem solving and decision making, teamwork.

Concentrations Accounting, management.

Faculty Full-time: 25, 92% with doctorates.

Teaching Methodology Case study: 15%, lecture: 40%, research: 15%, student presentations: 15%, team projects: 15%.

STUDENT STATISTICS

Geographic Representation State residents 77%. By region: Midwest 84%; South 1%. International 15%.

FACILITIES

Information Resources Main library with 252,226 bound volumes, 15,864 titles on microform, 1,336 periodical subscriptions, 2,246 records/tapes/CDs, 54 CD-ROMs. Business collection includes 25,400 bound volumes, 314 periodical subscriptions, 30 CD-ROMs, 111 videos.

Housing 1% of students in program live in college-owned or -operated housing.

Technology Computers are used moderately in course work. 800 computer terminals/PCs, linked by a campus-wide computer network, are available for use by students in program; they are located in student rooms, learning resource center, the library, the computer center, computer labs. Students in the program are not required to have their own PC.

Computer Resources/On-line Services

Training	Yes	CompuServe	Yes
Internet	Yes	Dun's	Yes $
E-Mail	Yes	Dow Jones	Yes $
Videoconference Center	Yes	Dialog	Yes $
Multimedia Center	Yes	Bloomberg	No
LEXIS/NEXIS	Yes $		

ADMISSION

Acceptance 1994-95 Of those applying, 85% were accepted.

Entrance Requirements Bachelor's degree, GMAT score, minimum 2.5 GPA. Core courses waived through: previous course work.

Application Requirements Application form, copies of transcript.

Application Deadlines 7/1 for fall, 12/1 for spring, 5/1 for summer.

FINANCIALS

Costs for 1994-95 Tuition: Full-time: $1,068/semester for state residents, $1,896/semester for nonresidents; Part-time day: $89/credit hour for state residents, $158/credit hour for nonresidents. Average room and board costs are $3,136 per academic year (on-campus).

Financial Aid In 1994-95, 25% of candidates received some institutionally administered aid in the form of grants, loans, assistantships. Total awards ranged from $200–$5,000. Financial aid is available to part-time students. Application deadlines: 10/31 for fall, 3/31 for spring, 6/10 for summer. Contact: Mr. Del Morley, Director of Financial Assistance, 208 Administration Building, Maryville, MO 64468-6001. (816) 562-1138.

INTERNATIONAL STUDENTS

Demographics 15% of students enrolled in the program are international; Asia 60%, Central America 10%, other 30%.

Services and Facilities International student center, visa services, language tutoring, ESL courses, counseling/support services.

Applying TOEFL required, minimum score of 550; proof of health; proof of adequate funds. Financial aid is available to international students. Financial aid application deadlines: 10/31 for fall, 3/31 for spring, 6/10 for summer. Admission application deadlines: 7/1 for fall, 12/1 for spring, 5/1 for summer. Contact: Ms. Patricia A. Foster-Kamara, Director of Multicultural Affairs, Student Affairs Office, J. W. Jones Student Union, Maryville, MO 64468-6001. (816) 562-1367.

PLACEMENT

Placement services include career placement.

Program Contact: Dr. Ron C. DeYoung, Dean, College of Business, Government, and Computer Science, Northwest Missouri State University, 800 University Drive, Maryville, MO 64468-6001. (816) 562-1277, or (800) 633-1175; Fax: (816) 562-1484.

Rockhurst College

School of Management

Kansas City, Missouri

OVERVIEW

Rockhurst College is an independent Roman Catholic (Jesuit) comprehensive coed institution. Founded 1910. Setting: 35-acre urban campus. Total institutional enrollment: 2,750. Program was first offered in 1975.

MBA HIGHLIGHTS

Entrance Difficulty***

Cost $
Tuition: $280/credit hour
Room & Board: $3,970

Enrollment Profile

Full-time: 111	Work Exp: 90%
Part-time: 578	International: 0%
Total: 689	Women: 37%
Average Age: 32	Minorities: 6%

Average Class Size: 25

ACADEMICS

Length of Program Minimum: 48 months. Maximum: 6 years.

Calendar Semesters.

Part-time Classes Main campus; evening, weekends, summer.

Degree Requirements 36 credits including 9 elective credits. Other: Minimum of 3.0 GPA.

Required Courses Business policy, corporate social responsibility, introduction to management science, management and organizational behavior, managerial accounting, marketing management, written business communication financial policy. Courses may be waived through: previous course work.

Curricular Focus Business issues and problems, corporate social responsibility, leadership.

Concentrations Accounting, finance, human resources management, international business, management, marketing.

Faculty Full-time: 24, 88% with doctorates; part-time: 10.

Teaching Methodology Case study: 10%, lecture: 50%, student presentations: 20%, team projects: 20%.

STUDENT STATISTICS

Geographic Representation State residents 51%. By region: Midwest 99%.

Undergraduate Majors Business 57%; humanities 13%; science/mathematics 20%; social sciences 10%.

Other Background Graduate degrees in other disciplines: 2%.

FACILITIES

Information Resources Main library with 103,676 bound volumes, 112,261 titles on microform, 704 periodical subscriptions, 2,446 records/tapes/CDs.

Housing College housing available.

Technology Computers are used moderately in course work. Computer terminals/PCs, linked by a campus-wide computer network, are available for use by students in program; they are located in classrooms, the library, the computer center, computer labs. Students in the program are not required to have their own PC.

Computer Resources/On-line Services

Training	No	Multimedia Center	Yes
Internet	Yes	Dialog	Yes
E-Mail	Yes		

ADMISSION

Entrance Requirements Bachelor's degree, GMAT score of 450, minimum 2.75 GPA. Core courses waived through: previous course work.

Application Requirements Interview, application form, copies of transcript.

Application Deadlines 7/15 for fall, 11/15 for spring, 4/15 for summer.

FINANCIALS

Costs for 1994-95 Tuition: Full-time: $280/credit hour. Average room and board costs are $3,970 per academic year (on-campus) and $5,000 per academic year (off-campus).

Financial Aid In 1994-95, 15% of candidates received some institutionally administered aid in the form of grants, scholarships, loans, fellowships, assistantships. Total awards ranged from $1,000-$8,500. Financial aid is available to part-time students. Application deadlines: 4/1 for fall, 12/1 for spring. Contact: Ms. Robin Stimac, Financial Aid Counselor, 1100 Rockhurst Road, Kansas City, MO 64110. (816) 926-4100.

INTERNATIONAL STUDENTS
Services and Facilities Visa services, counseling/support services.

Applying TOEFL required, minimum score of 550; proof of health; proof of adequate funds. Financial aid is not available to international students. Admission application deadlines: 6/15 for fall, 10/15 for spring.

ALTERNATE MBA PROGRAM
Executive MBA (EMBA) Length of program: Minimum: 18 months. Degree requirements: 36 credits. Minimum 3.0 GPA. Average class size: 30.

PLACEMENT
In 1993-94, 57 organizations participated in on-campus recruiting; 40 on-campus interviews were conducted. Placement services include alumni network, career counseling/planning, career fairs, career library, career placement, job interviews, resume preparation, and resume referral to employers.

Program Contact: Ms. Pamela Kerr, Administrative Assistant, Graduate Studies, Rockhurst College, 1100 Rockhurst Road, Kansas City, MO 64110. (816) 926-4090, or (800) 842-6776; Fax: (816) 926-4650.

Saint Louis University

School of Business and Administration

St. Louis, Missouri

OVERVIEW
Saint Louis University is an independent Roman Catholic (Jesuit) coed institution. Founded 1818. Setting: 250-acre urban campus. Total institutional enrollment: 11,325. Program was first offered in 1955. AACSB-accredited.

MBA HIGHLIGHTS

Entrance Difficulty*
Mean GMAT: 509
Mean GPA: 2.97

Cost $$
Tuition: $10,500
Room & Board: $5,500

Enrollment Profile

Full-time: 298	Work Exp: 80%
Part-time: 485	International: 54%
Total: 783	Women: 44%
Average Age: 27	Minorities: 4%

Average Class Size: 25

ACADEMICS
Length of Program Minimum: 12 months. Maximum: 5 years.
Calendar Semesters.
Full-time Classes Main campus; day, evening, weekends, summer.
Part-time Classes Main campus; day, evening, summer.
Degree Requirements 39 credit hours including 12 elective credit hours.
Required Courses Applied theory in organizations and strategic management, business ethics, economics of the firm, integrated modules, managerial accounting concepts, managerial finance, managing information technology, marketing management. Courses may be waived through: previous course work.
Curricular Focus Business issues and problems, general management, international business.
Concentrations Accounting, economics, finance, human resources management, international business, management, management information systems, marketing, quantitative analysis.
Faculty Full-time: 50, 97% with doctorates; part-time: 50.
Teaching Methodology Case study: 25%, lecture: 50%, student presentations: 15%, team projects: 10%.
Special Opportunities International exchange in Hong Kong, Spain.

STUDENT STATISTICS
Geographic Representation By region: Midwest 65%; South 2%; Northeast 1%; West 1%.

Undergraduate Majors Business 63%; education 2%; engineering/technology 20%; humanities 2%; nursing 3%; science/mathematics 5%; social sciences 5%.

Other Background Graduate degrees in other disciplines: 10%. Work experience: On average, students have 2 years of work experience on entrance to the program.

FACILITIES
Information Resources Main library with 1.4 million bound volumes, 1.1 million titles on microform, 13,578 periodical subscriptions, 6,220 records/tapes/CDs. Business collection includes 32,000 bound volumes, 339 periodical subscriptions, 14 CD-ROMs.

Housing 25% of students in program live in college-owned or -operated housing.

Technology Computers are used moderately in course work. 175 computer terminals/PCs, linked by a campus-wide computer network, are available for use by students in program; they are located in the library, the computer center, computer labs. Students in the program are not required to have their own PC.

Computer Resources/On-line Services

Training	Yes	LEXIS/NEXIS	Yes
Internet	Yes	CompuServe	Yes
E-Mail	Yes	Dialog	Yes

ADMISSION
Acceptance 1994-95 439 applied for admission; 84% were accepted.
Entrance Requirements Bachelor's degree, GMAT score. Core courses waived through. previous course work.
Application Requirements Written essay, application form, personal statement, 2 letters of recommendation.
Application Deadline Applications are processed on a rolling basis.

FINANCIALS
Costs for 1994-95 Tuition: Full-time: $10,500. Fees: Full-time: $40/semester. Average room and board costs are $5,500 per academic year (on-campus).

Financial Aid In 1994-95, candidates received some institutionally administered aid in the form of scholarships, loans. Total awards ranged from $1,000-$10,000. Financial aid is available to part-time students. Applications are processed on a rolling basis. Contact: Mr. Hal Deuser, Director of Financial Aid, 221 North Grand Boulevard, St. Louis, MO 63103-2097. (314) 977-2353.

INTERNATIONAL STUDENTS
Demographics 54% of students enrolled in the program are international; Asia 91%, Europe 7%, Africa 1%.

Services and Facilities Visa services, language tutoring, ESL courses, special assistance for nonnative speakers of English, counseling/support services, international student services office.

Applying TOEFL required, minimum score of 550; proof of adequate funds. Financial aid is not available to international students. Admission applications are processed on a rolling basis. Contact: Dr. Young Kim, Director, International Programs, 221 North Grand Boulevard, St. Louis, MO 63103-2097. (314) 977-2318.

ALTERNATE MBA PROGRAMS
MBA/JD Length of program: Minimum: 42 months. Maximum: 5 years. Degree requirements: 103 credits including 18 elective credits. Separate applications must be submitted to both business and law.

MBA/MHA Length of program: Minimum: 36 months. Maximum: 3 years. Degree requirements: 87 credit hours including 15 elective credit hours. Separate applications must be submitted to both business and health administration.

MBA/MSN Length of program: Minimum: 30 months. Maximum: 5 years. Degree requirements: 72 credits including 12 elective credits. Separate applications must be submitted to both business and nursing.

EMIB Length of program: Minimum: 24 months. Degree requirements: 36 credits.

PLACEMENT
In 1993-94, 10 organizations participated in on-campus recruiting. Placement services include alumni network, career counseling/planning, career fairs, career library, career placement, electronic job bank, job interviews, resume preparation, and resume referral to employers. Of 1994 graduates, 94% were employed within three months of graduation, the average starting salary was $39,837, the range was $12,500-$142,000.

Program Contact: Mr. Alquinston Johnson, Graduate Programs Assistant, Saint Louis University, 221 North Grand Boulevard, St. Louis, MO 63103-2097. (314) 977-3801; Fax: (314) 977-3897; Internet Address: johnsonab@sluvca.slu.edu.

See full description on page 822.

Southwest Missouri State University

College of Business Administration

Springfield, Missouri

OVERVIEW
Southwest Missouri State University is a state-supported comprehensive coed institution. Founded 1905. Setting: 210-acre urban campus. Total institutional enrollment: 18,000. Program was first offered in 1974. AACSB-accredited.

MBA HIGHLIGHTS

Entrance Difficulty**
Mean GMAT: 500
Mean GPA: 3.0

Cost $
Tuition: $89/credit hour
(Nonresident: $178/credit hour)
Room & Board: $2,800

Enrollment Profile

Full-time: 80	Work Exp: 75%
Part-time: 70	International: 30%
Total: 150	Women: 43%
Average Age: 26	Minorities: 5%

Average Class Size: 30

The AACSB-accredited M.B.A. degree at Southwest Missouri State University integrates a variety of courses offered by the five departments of the College of Business Administration. The program is designed specifically for students who hold undergraduate degrees in the arts, the sciences, engineering, and law, as well as business administration. Students with little or no undergraduate work in business normally require five semesters to complete the program. Students with appropriate prior academic preparation in business and economics and a strong work ethic may complete the program in one calendar year.

A strength of the SMSU M.B.A. program is its emphasis on the individual. The case method is only one of a variety of teaching methods used in M.B.A. courses. Simulation exercises, business games, research, role playing, videos, collateral readings, report writing, and lectures are all used where deemed most appropriate and effective. High educational productivity for each student is the criterion followed. M.B.A. faculty members recognize that their major responsibilities are teaching and working with students, and they also are actively involved in their areas of professional expertise.

State-of-the-art David D. Glass Hall, home of the College of Business Administration, includes a variety of special-purpose classrooms as well as six computer laboratories.

ACADEMICS
Length of Program Minimum: 18 months. Maximum: 8 years.
Calendar Semesters.
Full-time Classes Main campus; day, evening, summer.
Part-time Classes Main campus; day, evening.
Degree Requirements 33 credit hours including 12 elective credit hours.
Required Courses Advanced financial management, managerial accounting, marketing theory, micro and macroeconomic analysis, organizational behavior, organizational strategy and policy, quantitative methods for business decision making. Courses may be waived through: previous course work.
Curricular Focus Business issues and problems, general management, problem solving and decision making.
Concentrations Administrative office systems, finance, international business, management, management information systems, marketing.
Faculty Full-time: 48, 100% with doctorates.

Teaching Methodology Case study: 10%, lecture: 50%, research: 20%, student presentations: 10%, team projects: 10%.
Special Opportunities International exchange program available. Other: joint research with area business and in faculty-conducted projects.

STUDENT STATISTICS
Geographic Representation By region: Midwest 60%; South 4%; Northeast 3%; West 3%. International 30%.
Undergraduate Majors Business 59%; engineering/technology 5%; humanities 9%; nursing 1%; science/mathematics 4%; social sciences 7%; other 15%.
Other Background Graduate degrees in other disciplines: 3%. Work experience: On average, students have 3 years of work experience on entrance to the program.

FACILITIES
Information Resources Main library with 584,000 bound volumes, 737,866 titles on microform, 4,868 periodical subscriptions, 22,400 records/tapes/CDs, 241 CD-ROMs.
Housing College housing available.
Technology Computers are used moderately in course work. 180 computer terminals/PCs, linked by a campus-wide computer network, are available for use by students in program; they are located in classrooms, computer labs. Students in the program are not required to have their own PC.

Computer Resources/On-line Services

Training	Yes	CompuServe	No
Internet	Yes	Dun's	No
E-Mail	Yes	Dow Jones	No
Videoconference Center	Yes	Dialog	Yes $
LEXIS/NEXIS	Yes $	Bloomberg	No

ADMISSION
Entrance Requirements Bachelor's degree, prerequisite courses required for applicants with non-business degree, GMAT score of 400, minimum 2.75 GPA. Core courses waived through: previous course work.
Application Requirements Application form, copies of transcript.
Application Deadlines 8/5 for fall, 12/17 for spring, 5/20 for summer.

FINANCIALS
Costs for 1994-95 Tuition: Full-time: $89/credit hour for state residents, $178/credit hour for nonresidents. Fees: Full-time: $88/semester for state residents, $88/semester for nonresidents. Average room and board costs are $2,800 per academic year (on-campus) and $2,800 per academic year (off-campus).
Financial Aid In 1994-95, candidates received some institutionally administered aid in the form of loans. Application deadlines: 8/6 for fall, 1/4 for spring, 5/25 for summer. Contact: Financial Aid Office, 901 South National, Springfield, MO 65804-0094. (417) 836-5262.

INTERNATIONAL STUDENTS
Demographics 30% of students enrolled in the program are international; Asia 83%, Europe 10%, Central America 6%.
Services and Facilities International student center, visa services, language tutoring, ESL courses, special assistance for nonnative speakers of English, counseling/support services.
Applying TOEFL required, minimum score of 550; proof of health; proof of adequate funds; transcript translation. Financial aid is not available to international students. Admission application deadline: 8/15 for fall. Contact: Ms. Jan Swann, Coordinator, International Student Services, 901 South National, Springfield, MO 65804-0094. (417) 836-6618.

PLACEMENT
In 1993-94, 12 organizations participated in on-campus recruiting. Placement services include career counseling/planning, career fairs, career library, career placement, job interviews, and resume preparation.

Program Contact: Dr. James B. Pettijohn, Director of Graduate Studies, Southwest Missouri State University, 901 South National, Springfield, MO 65804-0094. (417) 836-5646, or (800) 492-7900; Fax: (417) 836-4407; Internet Address: jbp225f@vma.smsu.edu.

University of Missouri–Columbia

College of Business and Public Administration

Columbia, Missouri

OVERVIEW
The University of Missouri–Columbia is a state-supported coed institution. Part of University of Missouri System. Founded 1839. Setting: 1,335-acre small-town campus. Total institutional enrollment: 22,434. Program was first offered in 1960. AACSB-accredited.

MBA HIGHLIGHTS

Entrance Difficulty**
Mean GMAT: 598
Mean GPA: 3.29

Cost $
Tuition: $128/credit hour
(Nonresident: $373/credit hour)
Room & Board: $4,170

Enrollment Profile

Full-time: 73	Work Exp: 41%
Part-time: 62	International: 16%
Total: 135	Women: 30%
Average Age: 26	Minorities: 3%

Average Class Size: 20

ACADEMICS
Length of Program Minimum: 15 months. Maximum: 8 years.
Calendar Semesters.
Full-time Classes Main campus; day, summer.
Part-time Classes Main campus; day, summer.
Degree Requirements 39 hours including 6 elective hours. Other: 9 hours in emphasis area.
Required Courses Business environment and policy, consulting project, emphasis area (9 hours), marketing strategy, security markets and investments, seminar. Courses may be waived through: previous course work.
Curricular Focus Problem solving and decision making.
Concentrations Finance, health services, human resources management, management, management information systems, marketing, organizational behavior.
Faculty Full-time: 12, 100% with doctorates; part-time: 2, 100% with doctorates.
Teaching Methodology Case study: 10%, faculty seminars: 5%, lecture: 40%, research: 10%, seminars by members of the business community: 5%, student presentations: 10%, team projects: 20%.
Special Opportunities International exchange in France. Internships include state government in banking.

STUDENT STATISTICS
Geographic Representation State residents 82%. By region: Midwest 82%; Northeast 1%; South 1%. International 16%.
Undergraduate Majors Business 56%; engineering/technology 7%; science/mathematics 7%; social sciences 30%.
Other Background Graduate degrees in other disciplines: 1%. Work experience: On average, students have 2 years of work experience on entrance to the program.

FACILITIES
Information Resources Main library with 2.6 million bound volumes, 5.1 million titles on microform, 22,973 periodical subscriptions, 14,674 records/tapes/CDs, 66 CD-ROMs. Business collection includes 200,000 bound volumes, 2,500 periodical subscriptions, 2 CD-ROMs.
Housing 5% of students in program live in college-owned or -operated housing.
Technology Computers are used heavily in course work. 535 computer terminals/PCs, linked by a campus-wide computer network, are available for use by students in program; they are located in student rooms, the student center, classrooms, learning resource center, the library, the computer center, computer labs, the research center. Students in the program are not required to have their own PC. $130 are budgeted per student for computer support.

Computer Resources/On-line Services

Training	Yes	CompuServe	Yes
Internet	Yes	Dun's	No
E-Mail	Yes	Dow Jones	Yes
Videoconference Center	Yes	Dialog	Yes $
Multimedia Center	Yes	Bloomberg	No
LEXIS/NEXIS	Yes		

ADMISSION
Acceptance 1994-95 Of those applying, 28% were accepted.
Entrance Requirements Bachelor's degree, GMAT score of 500, minimum 3.0 GPA. Core courses waived through: previous course work.
Application Requirements Application form, copies of transcript.
Application Deadlines 7/1 for fall, 11/1 for spring.

FINANCIALS
Costs for 1994-95 Tuition: Full-time: $128/credit hour for state residents, $373/credit hour for nonresidents. Fees: Full-time: $12/credit hour for state residents, $12/credit hour for nonresidents. Average room and board costs are $4,170 per academic year (on-campus) and $6,000 per academic year (off-campus).
Financial Aid In 1994-95, 51% of candidates received some institutionally administered aid in the form of scholarships, assistantships. Total awards ranged from $500-$3,500. Financial aid is not available to part-time students. Application deadlines: 7/1 for fall, 11/1 for spring. Contact: Ms. Marilyn Hasselriis, Senior Academic Advisor, 303 Middlebush Hall, Columbia, MO 65211. (314) 882-2750.

INTERNATIONAL STUDENTS
Demographics 16% of students enrolled in the program are international; Asia 77%, Europe 10%, Central America 5%, South America 5%, Africa 3%.
Services and Facilities International student housing; visa services, ESL courses.
Applying TOEFL required, minimum score of 575; proof of health; proof of adequate funds. Financial aid is available to international students. Financial aid application deadlines: 7/1 for fall, 11/1 for spring. Admission application deadlines: 7/1 for fall, 11/1 for spring. Contact: Ms. Becky Brandt, Assistant Director of Admissions, 123 Jesse Hall, Columbia, MO 65211. (314) 882-3754.

ALTERNATE MBA PROGRAMS
MBA/JD
MBA/MHA Length of program: May range up to 8 years.
MBA/MSIE Length of program: May range up to 8 years.

PLACEMENT
In 1993-94, 152 organizations participated in on-campus recruiting; 42 on-campus interviews were conducted. Placement services include alumni network, career counseling/planning, career fairs, career placement, job interviews, resume preparation, and resume referral to employers. Of 1994 graduates, 87% were employed within three months of graduation, the average starting salary was $28,000, the range was $25,400-$42,000.

Program Contact: Ms. Marilyn Hasselriis, Senior Academic Adviser, University of Missouri–Columbia, 303 Middlebush Hall, Columbia, MO 65211. (314) 882-2750; Fax: (314) 882-0365.
See full description on page 894.

University of Missouri–Kansas City

Henry W. Bloch School of Business and Public Administration

Kansas City, Missouri

OVERVIEW
The University of Missouri–Kansas City is a state-supported coed institution. Part of University of Missouri System. Founded 1929. Setting: 191-acre urban campus. Total institutional enrollment: 10,000. Program was first offered in 1957. AACSB-accredited.

MBA HIGHLIGHTS

Entrance Difficulty***
Mean GMAT: 531
Mean GPA: 3.1

Cost $
Tuition: $128/credit hour
(Nonresident: $373/credit hour)
Room & Board: N/R

Enrollment Profile

Full-time: 89	Work Exp: 80%
Part-time: 296	International: 16%
Total: 385	Women: 40%
Average Age: 27	Minorities: 7%

Average Class Size: 30

ACADEMICS

Length of Program Minimum: 12 months. Maximum: 7 years.

Calendar Semesters.

Part-time Classes Main campus; evening, summer.

Degree Requirements 30 credit hours including 3-18 elective credit hours.

Required Courses Economic analysis for management, international business, strategic management. Courses may be waived through: previous course work.

Curricular Focus International business, leadership, teamwork.

Concentrations Direct marketing, entrepreneurship, finance, human resources management, management, management information systems, marketing, operations management, organizational behavior, quantitative analysis.

Faculty Full-time: 21, 100% with doctorates.

Teaching Methodology Case study: 25%, lecture: 45%, student presentations: 15%, team projects: 15%.

Special Opportunities International exchange in Germany, United Kingdom.

STUDENT STATISTICS

Geographic Representation State residents 50%. By region: Midwest 84%. International 16%.

Undergraduate Majors Business 70%; engineering/technology 5%; humanities 10%; social sciences 10%; other 5%.

Other Background Graduate degrees in other disciplines: 3%. Work experience: On average, students have 5 years of work experience on entrance to the program.

FACILITIES

Information Resources Main library with 942,116 bound volumes, 515,778 titles on microform, 8,764 periodical subscriptions, 241,771 records/tapes/CDs, 82 CD-ROMs. Business collection includes 62,000 bound volumes, 375 periodical subscriptions, 107 CD-ROMs, 40 videos.

Housing College housing not available.

Technology Computers are used moderately in course work. 200 computer terminals/PCs, linked by a campus-wide computer network, are available for use by students in program; they are located in classrooms, the library, the computer center, computer labs. Students in the program are not required to have their own PC. $250 are budgeted per student for computer support.

Computer Resources/On-line Services

Training	No	CompuServe	Yes
Internet	Yes	Dun's	Yes
E-Mail	Yes	Dow Jones	Yes
Videoconference Center	Yes	Dialog	Yes
LEXIS/NEXIS	Yes		

Other on-line services: OCLC, First Search, SEC.

ADMISSION

Acceptance 1994-95 Of those applying, 53% were accepted.

Entrance Requirements Bachelor's degree, GMAT score of 500, minimum 2.75 GPA. Core courses waived through: previous course work.

Application Requirements Application form, copies of transcript, personal statement.

Application Deadlines 5/1 for fall, 10/1 for spring, 3/1 for summer.

FINANCIALS

Costs for 1994-95 Tuition: Full-time: $128/credit hour for state residents, $373/credit hour for nonresidents. Fees: Full-time: $15/credit hour for state residents, $15/credit hour for nonresidents.

Financial Aid In 1994-95, 20% of candidates received some institutionally administered aid in the form of scholarships, loans, fellowships, assistantships, work-study. Total awards ranged from $200-$19,300. Financial aid is available to part-time students. Application deadlines: 3/30 for fall, 8/30 for spring. Contact: Mr. Buford Baber, Director, 5100 Rockhill Road, Kansas City, MO 64110. (816) 235-1154.

INTERNATIONAL STUDENTS

Demographics 16% of students enrolled in the program are international; Asia 90%, Europe 10%.

Services and Facilities International student center, visa services, language tutoring, ESL courses, special assistance for nonnative speakers of English, counseling/support services.

Applying TOEFL required, minimum score of 550; proof of adequate funds. Financial aid is not available to international students. Admission application deadlines: 5/1 for fall, 10/1 for spring, 3/1 for summer. Contact: Mr. Thomas Burns, Director, International Student Affairs, 4825 Troost Avenue, Kansas City, MO 64110. (816) 235-1017.

ALTERNATE MBA PROGRAMS

Executive MBA (EMBA) Length of program: Minimum: 21 months. Maximum: 2 years. Full-time classes: Main campus; weekends, summer. Degree requirements: 48 credit hours. 5 years management experience; employer endorsement.

MBA/JD Length of program: Minimum: 36 months. Degree requirements: 99 credits.

PLACEMENT

In 1993-94, 35 organizations participated in on-campus recruiting. Placement services include alumni network, career counseling/planning, career fairs, career library, career placement, electronic job bank, job interviews, resume preparation, and resume referral to employers. Of 1994 graduates, the average starting salary was $34,000, the range was $21,000-$85,000.

Jobs by Employer Type Manufacturing 23%; service 77%.

Jobs by Functional Area Marketing/sales 20%; finance 17%; operations 23%; management 23%; technical management 17%.

Program Contact: UMKC Admissions Office, University of Missouri–Kansas City, 4825 Troost Avenue, Kansas City, MO 64110. (816) 235-1111; Fax: (816) 235-1717.

University of Missouri–St. Louis

School of Business Administration

St. Louis, Missouri

OVERVIEW

The University of Missouri–St. Louis is a state-supported coed institution. Part of University of Missouri System. Founded 1963. Setting: 202-acre urban campus. Total institutional enrollment: 13,000. Program was first offered in 1972. AACSB-accredited.

MBA HIGHLIGHTS

Entrance Difficulty****
Mean GMAT: 555
Mean GPA: 3.1

Cost $
Tuition: $1,534/semester
(Nonresident: $4,476/semester)
Room & Board: $3,965

Enrollment Profile

Full-time: 80	Work Exp: 80%
Part-time: 220	International: 8%
Total: 300	Women: 40%
Average Age: 27	Minorities: 2%

Average Class Size: 20

ACADEMICS

Length of Program Minimum: 24 months. Maximum: 6 years.

Calendar Semesters.

Full-time Classes Main campus; evening, summer.

Part-time Classes Main campus; evening, summer.

Degree Requirements 39 credits including 18 elective credits. Other: 9 hours in controlled electives.

Required Courses Financial accounting, financial management, management information systems, managerial communications, managerial economics, marketing concepts, operations research, organizational behavior, public policies toward business, statistical analysis, strategy formulation. Courses may be waived through: previous course work.

Curricular Focus Business issues and problems, general management, problem solving and decision making.

Concentrations Accounting, economics, finance, human resources management, international business, management, management information systems, marketing, operations management, organizational behavior, public policy, quantitative analysis, strategic management.

Faculty Full-time: 45, 95% with doctorates; part-time: 3, 100% with doctorates.

Teaching Methodology Case study: 30%, lecture: 38%, research: 10%, seminars by members of the business community: 2%, student presentations: 10%, team projects: 10%.

Special Opportunities International exchange in France, Germany, Netherlands, United Kingdom.

STUDENT STATISTICS
Geographic Representation State residents 95%. By region: Midwest 90%; Northeast 1%; West 1%.

Undergraduate Majors Business 50%; engineering/technology 15%; humanities 10%; science/mathematics 10%; social sciences 10%; other 5%.

Other Background Graduate degrees in other disciplines: 2%. Work experience: On average, students have 4 years of work experience on entrance to the program.

FACILITIES
Information Resources Main library with 598,800 bound volumes, 1.8 million titles on microform, 2,823 periodical subscriptions, 1,095 CD-ROMs.

Housing College housing available.

Technology Computers are used moderately in course work. 300 computer terminals/PCs, linked by a campus-wide computer network, are available for use by students in program; they are located in the computer center, computer labs. Students in the program are not required to have their own PC.

Computer Resources/On-line Services

Training	Yes	CompuServe	No
Internet	Yes	Dun's	No
E-Mail	Yes	Dow Jones	No
Videoconference Center	Yes	Dialog	Yes
LEXIS/NEXIS	Yes	Bloomberg	No

ADMISSION
Acceptance 1994-95 Of those applying, 50% were accepted.

Entrance Requirements Bachelor's degree, GMAT score of 500, minimum 3.0 GPA. Core courses waived through: previous course work.

Application Requirements Application form, copies of transcript, personal statement, 2 letters of recommendation.

Application Deadlines 7/1 for fall, 12/1 for spring, 5/1 for summer.

FINANCIALS
Estimated Costs for 1995-96 Tuition: Full-time: $1,534/semester for state residents, $4,476/semester for nonresidents. Fees: Full-time: $175/semester for state residents, $175/semester for nonresidents. Average room and board costs are $3,965 per academic year (on-campus).

Financial Aid In 1994-95, candidates received some institutionally administered aid in the form of loans, assistantships, work-study. Financial aid is available to part-time students. Application deadline: 4/1 for fall. Contact: Ms. Pamela Fowler, Director of Student Financial Aid, 8001 Natural Bridge Road, St. Louis, MO 63121-4499. (314) 516-5526.

INTERNATIONAL STUDENTS
Demographics 8% of students enrolled in the program are international.

Services and Facilities International student center, ESL courses.

Applying TOEFL required, minimum score of 550; proof of health; proof of adequate funds. Financial aid is available to international students. Assistantships are available for these students. Admission application deadlines: 5/1 for fall, 10/1 for spring, 3/1 for summer.

PLACEMENT
In 1993-94, 12 organizations participated in on-campus recruiting. Placement services include career counseling/planning, career fairs, career library, career placement, job interviews, resume preparation, and resume referral to employers. Of 1994 graduates, the average starting salary was $33,000.

Program Contact: Mr. Karl Kottemann, Associate Director of Graduate Studies in Business, University of Missouri–St. Louis, 8001 Natural Bridge Road, St. Louis, MO 63121-4499. (314) 516-5885; Fax: (314) 516-6420.

Washington University

John M. Olin School of Business

St. Louis, Missouri

OVERVIEW
Washington University is an independent nonprofit coed institution. Founded 1853. Setting: 169-acre suburban campus. Total institutional enrollment: 11,500. Program was first offered in 1950. AACSB-accredited.

MBA HIGHLIGHTS
Entrance Difficulty**
Mean GMAT: 608
Mean GPA: 3.16

Cost $$$$
Tuition: $18,350
Room & Board: $5,784 (off-campus)

Enrollment Profile

Full-time: 290	Work Exp: 82%
Part-time: 335	International: 31%
Total: 625	Women: 23%
Average Age: 26	Minorities: 13%

Average Class Size: 30

ACADEMICS
Length of Program Minimum: 22 months.

Calendar Semesters.

Full-time Classes Main campus; day, evening, early morning, summer.

Part-time Classes Main campus; evening, summer.

Degree Requirements 67 credits including 27 elective credits.

Required Courses Design and management of organizations, financial accounting, financial management, human behavior and management of organizations, macroeconomics for managers, management science, managerial accounting, manufacturing and management, marketing management, microeconomics for managers, operations, probabilities and statistics. Courses may be waived through: previous course work, examination.

Curricular Focus General management, managerial intuition, teamwork.

Concentrations Accounting, economics, finance, health services, human resources management, international business, management, management information systems, marketing, operations management, organizational behavior.

Faculty Full-time: 52, 96% with doctorates; part-time: 23, 56% with doctorates.

Teaching Methodology Lecture: 10%, research: 10%, student presentations: 5%.

Special Opportunities International exchange in United Kingdom. Internship program available. Other: MBA Enterprise Corps.

STUDENT STATISTICS
Geographic Representation State residents 71%. By region: Midwest 48%; Northeast 11%; South 9%; West 6%. International 31%.

Undergraduate Majors Business 24%; engineering/technology 25%; humanities 14%; science/mathematics 5%; social sciences 32%.

Other Background Work experience: On average, students have 3 years of work experience on entrance to the program.

FACILITIES
Information Resources Main library with 3 million bound volumes, 2.6 million titles on microform, 18,590 periodical subscriptions, 35,671 records/tapes/CDs. Business collection in Kopolow Business Library includes 28,000 bound volumes, 400 periodical subscriptions, 9 CD-ROMs.

Housing College housing not available.

Technology Computers are used heavily in course work. 103 computer terminals/PCs, linked by a campus-wide computer network, are available for use by students in program; they are located in the computer center, computer labs. Students in the program are not required to have their own PC.

Computer Resources/On-line Services

Training	Yes	Dun's	Yes $
Internet	Yes	Dow Jones	Yes $
E-Mail	Yes	Dialog	Yes $
LEXIS/NEXIS	Yes	Bloomberg	Yes
CompuServe	No		

ADMISSION
Acceptance 1994-95 Of those applying, 41% were accepted.

Entrance Requirements Bachelor's degree, GMAT score. Core courses waived through: previous course work, exams.

Application Requirements Written essay, interview, application form, copies of transcript, 2 letters of recommendation.

Application Deadlines 3/31 for fall. Applications are processed on a rolling basis.

FINANCIALS
Costs for 1994-95 Tuition: Full-time: $18,350; Part-time evening: $555/credit; Summer: $555/credit. Average room and board costs are $5,784 per academic year (off-campus).

Financial Aid In 1994-95, 65% of candidates received some institutionally administered aid in the form of grants, scholarships, loans, fellowships, assistantships, work-study. Total awards ranged from $4,000-$33,600. Financial aid is available to part-time students. Contact: Ms. Barbara B. Jones, Director, MBA Financial Aid, 1 Brookings Drive, St. Louis, MO 63130. (314) 935-7301.

INTERNATIONAL STUDENTS
Demographics 31% of students enrolled in the program are international; Asia 80%, Europe 11%, Central America 2%, South America 2%, Africa 1%, other 1%.

Services and Facilities International student office, international student center, visa services, language tutoring, ESL courses, special assistance for nonnative speakers of English, counseling/support services.

Applying TOEFL required, minimum score of 550; proof of health; proof of adequate funds. Financial aid is available to international students. Financial aid application deadline: 3/31 for fall. Admission application deadline: 3/31 for fall. Applications are processed on a rolling basis. Contact: Mr. Jim Sidwell, Director of MBA Student Affairs, 1 Brookings Drive, St. Louis, MO 63130. (314) 935-5000.

ALTERNATE MBA PROGRAMS
Executive MBA (EMBA) Length of program: Minimum: 21 months. Maximum: 7 years. Degree requirements: 60 credits including 6 elective credits. Average class size: 50.

MBA/JD Length of program: Minimum: 48 months. Maximum: 5 years. Degree requirements: 129 credits including 56 elective credits.

MBA/MA Length of program: Minimum: 36 months. Degree requirements: 76 credits including 24 elective credits. Field experience in target country; language skills in Japanese or Mandarin Chinese. MA is in East Asian studies.

MBA/MHA Length of program: Minimum: 36 months. Degree requirements: 97 credits including 18 elective credits. Average class size: 30.

PLACEMENT
In 1993-94, 125 organizations participated in on-campus recruiting; 1,500 on-campus interviews were conducted. Placement services include alumni network, career counseling/planning, career fairs, career library, career placement, job interviews, job search course, resume preparation, and resume referral to employers. Of 1994 graduates, 93% were employed within three months of graduation, the average starting salary was $46,600, the range was $29,500-$75,000.

Jobs by Employer Type Manufacturing 45%; service 40%; government 6%; consulting 9%.

Jobs by Functional Area Marketing/sales 27%; finance 38%; operations 7%; strategic planning 20%; other 8%.

Program Contact: Ms. Deborah Booker, Director of MBA Admissions, Washington University, 1 Brookings Drive, Campus Box 1133, St. Louis, MO 63130. (314) 935-7301; Fax: (314) 935-4464; Internet Address: mba@olin.wustl.edu.

Webster University

School of Business and Management

St. Louis, Missouri

OVERVIEW
Webster University is an independent nonprofit comprehensive coed institution. Founded 1915. Setting: 47-acre suburban campus. Total institutional enrollment: 10,834. Program was first offered in 1985.

MBA HIGHLIGHTS
Entrance Difficulty*

Cost $$
Tuition: $220 - $280/credit hour
Room & Board: $3,980

Enrollment Profile

Full-time: 409	Work Exp: N/R
Part-time: 913	International: 5%
Total: 1,322	Women: 34%
Average Age: 35	Minorities: 24%

Average Class Size: N/R

ACADEMICS
Length of Program Minimum: 24 months.

Calendar Semesters.

Full-time Classes Main campus, Geneva, Switzerland, Vienna, Austria, London, United Kingdom, Leiden, Netherlands; evening, weekends, summer.

Part-time Classes Main campus, Geneva, Switzerland, Vienna, Austria, London, United Kingdom, Leiden, Netherlands; evening, weekends, summer.

Degree Requirements 48 credit hours including 27 elective credit hours.

Required Courses Business, business accounting systems, business information systems, business policies, economics of the firm, financial planning, operations and production management, statistical analysis.

Curricular Focus General management, international business, organizational development and change management.

Concentrations Computer resources/information management, education management, European business, procurement and acquisitions management, security management, space systems management, telecommunications management, finance, health services, human resources management, international business, management, marketing, real estate.

Faculty Full-time: 12, 100% with doctorates.

Special Opportunities International exchange in Austria, Netherlands, Switzerland, United Kingdom. Internships include international business in chemicals.

STUDENT STATISTICS
Geographic Representation International 5%.

FACILITIES
Information Resources Main library with 204,421 bound volumes, 50 titles on microform, 1,873 periodical subscriptions, 1,090 records/tapes/CDs, 13 CD-ROMs.

Housing 2% of students in program live in college-owned or -operated housing.

Technology Computers are used moderately in course work. 150 computer terminals/PCs, linked by a campus-wide computer network, are available for use by students in program; they are located in the library, the computer center, computer labs. Students in the program are not required to have their own PC.

Computer Resources/On-line Services

Training	No	Dun's	No
Internet	No	Dow Jones	No
E-Mail	No	Dialog	Yes
LEXIS/NEXIS	Yes	Bloomberg	No
CompuServe	No		

ADMISSION
Entrance Requirements Bachelor's degree. Core courses waived through: previous course work, work experience.

Application Requirements Application form, copies of transcript.

Application Deadlines 6/15 for fall. Applications are processed on a rolling basis.

FINANCIALS
Costs for 1994-95 Tuition: Full-time: $220-$280/credit hour. Fees: Full-time: $50/degree program. Average room and board costs are $3,980 per academic year (on-campus).

Financial Aid In 1994-95, candidates received some institutionally administered aid in the form of grants, scholarships, loans, work-study. Total awards ranged from $500-$8,000. Financial aid is available to part-time students. Application deadline: 4/1 for fall. Applications are processed on a rolling basis. Contact: Ms. Sharen Lowney, Director of Financial Aid, 470 East Lockwood Avenue, St. Louis, MO 63119-3194. (314) 961-2660 Ext. 7640.

INTERNATIONAL STUDENTS
Demographics 5% of students enrolled in the program are international.

Services and Facilities International student housing; international student center, language tutoring, ESL courses, special assistance for nonnative speakers of English, counseling/support services.

Applying TOEFL required, minimum score of 550; proof of adequate funds; minimum 2.5 GPA, 100 word autobiographical statement, proof of medical insurance, 2 letters of recommendation. Financial aid is not available to international students. Admission application deadlines: 6/15 for fall, 10/15 for spring. Applications are processed on a rolling basis. Contact: Ms. Betty Mueller, Director, International Student Center, 470 East Lockwood Avenue, St. Louis, MO 63119-3194. (314) 968-6964.

PLACEMENT
Placement services include alumni network, career counseling/planning, career fairs, career library, career placement, job interviews, resume preparation, and resume referral to employers.

Program Contact: Dr. Joseph Olszewski, Associate Dean, Graduate Studies, Webster University, 470 East Lockwood Avenue, St. Louis, MO 63119-3194. (314) 968-7463; Fax: (314) 968-7115.

William Woods University

College of Graduate and Adult Studies

Fulton, Missouri

OVERVIEW
William Woods University is an independent comprehensive primarily women institution, affiliated with Christian Church (Disciples of Christ). Founded 1870. Setting: 160-acre small-town campus with easy access to St. Louis. Total institutional enrollment: 827.

MBA HIGHLIGHTS
Entrance Difficulty**

Cost $
Tuition: $240/credit
Room & Board: N/R

Enrollment Profile
Full-time: N/R	Work Exp: N/R
Part-time: N/R	International: N/R
Total: 142	Women: 40%
Average Age: N/R	Minorities: 10%

Class Size: 18 - 20

ACADEMICS
Length of Program Minimum: 20 months.
Calendar Semesters.
Full-time Classes Main campus, Columbia, Jefferson City, Moberly; evening, summer.
Degree Requirements 36 credits.
Curricular Focus General management, leadership, problem solving and decision making.
Teaching Methodology Case study: 50%, student presentations: 50%.

STUDENT STATISTICS
Geographic Representation State residents 100%.

FACILITIES
Information Resources Main library with 77,853 bound volumes, 6,760 titles on microform, 422 periodical subscriptions, 18,489 records/tapes/CDs, 6 CD-ROMs.

ADMISSION
Entrance Requirements Bachelor's degree, prerequisite courses required for applicants with non-business degree, minimum 2.5 GPA, minimum 2 years of work experience.

Application Requirements Written essay, interview, application form, copies of transcript, resume/curriculum vitae, 2 letters of recommendation.

Application Deadline Applications are processed on a rolling basis.

FINANCIALS
Estimated Costs for 1995-96 Tuition: Full-time: $240/credit.

Financial Aid Applications are processed on a rolling basis. Contact: Ms. Susan Werbach, Assistant Director of Financial Aid, 200 West Twelfth Street, Fulton, MO 65251-1098. (314) 592-4236.

INTERNATIONAL STUDENTS
Applying TOEFL required, minimum score of 550. Financial aid is not available to international students. Admission applications are processed on a rolling basis.

Program Contact: Ms. Mary Henley, Director of Recruitment, William Woods University, 200 West Twelfth Street, Fulton, MO 65251-1098. (314) 592-1149, or (800) 995-3199 (MO only); Fax: (314) 592-1164.

MONTANA

The University of Montana–Missoula

School of Business Management

Missoula, Montana

OVERVIEW
The University of Montana–Missoula is a state-supported coed institution. Part of Montana University System. Founded 1893. Setting: 220-acre small-town campus. Total institutional enrollment: 11,067. Program was first offered in 1966. AACSB-accredited.

MBA HIGHLIGHTS
Entrance Difficulty****
Mean GMAT: 530
Mean GPA: 3.17

Cost
Tuition: N/R
(Nonresident: N/R)
Room & Board: $3,800

Enrollment Profile
Full-time: 117	Work Exp: 95%
Part-time: 46	International: 30%
Total: 163	Women: 28%
Average Age: 28	Minorities: 5%

Average Class Size: 22

ACADEMICS
Calendar Semesters.
Curricular Focus Entrepreneurship, general management, international business, teamwork.
Concentration Management.
Faculty Full-time: 30, 95% with doctorates; part-time: 1.
Teaching Methodology Case study: 8%, faculty seminars: 10%, lecture: 50%, research: 15%, seminars by members of the business community: 2%, student presentations: 5%, team projects: 10%.
Special Opportunities International exchange program available. Internships include accounting, management, and finance.

STUDENT STATISTICS
Geographic Representation State residents 35%. International 30%.
Undergraduate Majors Business 61%; engineering/technology 7%; humanities 5%; science/mathematics 7%; social sciences 5%; other 14%.

FACILITIES
Information Resources Main library with 750,000 bound volumes, 290,000 titles on microform, 5,000 periodical subscriptions, 13,000 records/tapes/CDs, 52 CD-ROMs.

Housing College housing available.

Technology Computers are used moderately in course work. 155 computer terminals/PCs are available for use by students in program; they are located in the library, the computer center, computer labs. Students in the program are not required to have their own PC.

Computer Resources/On-line Services

Internet	Yes	CompuServe	Yes
E-Mail	Yes		

ADMISSION
Acceptance 1994-95 133 applied for admission; 50% were accepted.

Entrance Requirements Bachelor's degree, GMAT score, minimum 2.5 GPA. Core courses waived through: previous course work.

Application Requirements Application form, copies of transcript, resume/curriculum vitae, personal statement, 3 letters of recommendation.

Application Deadline Applications are processed on a rolling basis.

FINANCIALS
Financial Aid In 1994-95, candidates received some institutionally administered aid in the form of loans, assistantships, work-study. Financial aid is available to part-time students. Application deadline: 3/1 for fall. Contact: Financial Aid Office, Missoula, MT 59812-0002. (406) 243-2278.

INTERNATIONAL STUDENTS
Demographics 30% of students enrolled in the program are international.

Services and Facilities International student office, visa services, language tutoring, ESL courses.

Applying TOEFL required, minimum score of 525; proof of health; proof of adequate funds. Financial aid is available to international students. Financial aid application deadlines: 4/1 for fall, 11/1 for spring. Admission applications are processed on a rolling basis. Contact: Ms. Effie Koehn, Director, Foreign Student Office, Missoula, MT 59812-0002. (406) 243-2226.

PROGRAMS
Executive MBA (EMBA) Length of program: Minimum: 36 months. Part-time classes: Main campus, Billings, Butte, Kalispell; day, evening, weekends. Degree requirements: 30 credits.

One-Year MBA Length of program: Minimum: 12 months. Maximum: 5 years. Full-time classes: Main campus; day, evening, summer. Part-time classes: Main campus. Degree requirements: 30 credits including 9 elective credits. Exit exam or thesis.

PLACEMENT
Placement services include alumni network, career counseling/planning, career fairs, career library, career placement, job interviews, and resume preparation. Of 1994 graduates, 90% were employed within three months of graduation, the average starting salary was $32,000.

Program Contact: Dr. Teresa Beed, Director, Graduate Programs in Business, The University of Montana–Missoula, Missoula, MT 59812-0002. (406) 243-0211.

NEBRASKA

Creighton University

College of Business Administration

Omaha, Nebraska

OVERVIEW
Creighton University is an independent Roman Catholic coed institution. Founded 1878. Setting: 85-acre urban campus. Total institutional enrollment: 6,424. Program was first offered in 1967. AACSB-accredited.

MBA HIGHLIGHTS

Entrance Difficulty
Mean GMAT: 540
Mean GPA: 3.06

Cost $$
Tuition: $332/credit hour
Room & Board: $5,000

Enrollment Profile

Full-time: 50	Work Exp: 85%
Part-time: 160	International: 15%
Total: 210	Women: 37%
Average Age: 28	Minorities: 3%

Average Class Size: 25

Experiential learning is a hallmark of many M.B.A. courses. In addition to the mentor and internship programs, the classroom itself is where many students learn firsthand about the business community.

Dean Reznicek's intensive elective course "Leaders, Leadership, and Motivation" has brought executives, CEOs, and nonprofit directors from several of the most important businesses in the area to describe their strengths, weaknesses, opportunities, and threats. This course is the first of the newly established electives designed to expose students to the most current topics in business and management.

In fall 1994, community service was supported by Dr. Beverly Kracher's Business and Society students. Junior high school students throughout Omaha were invited to visit Creighton and the College of Business. Dr. Kracher's students organized tours, meetings with school officials, and classroom activities that helped students to experience negotiating and teamwork.

Dr. Krogstad's Accounting Seminar students are participating in a comprehensive internal audit of a local private high school. Student groups are led by a graduate research assistant holding a CPA. The students themselves have diverse work experience and are involved in all aspects of the school's operations, from financial management to human resources.

ACADEMICS
Length of Program Minimum: 12 months. Maximum: 6 years.

Calendar Semesters.

Full-time Classes Main campus; evening, summer.

Part-time Classes Main campus; evening, summer.

Degree Requirements 33 credits including 9 elective credits.

Required Courses Accounting applications for managerial decision making, business and society, business policy and managerial action, financial management and business strategy, managerial economics, marketing management, organizational behavior, systems theory, analysis, and design.

Curricular Focus Business issues and problems, problem solving and decision making, teamwork.

Concentrations Accounting, economics, finance, international business, management, management information systems, marketing, operations management, organizational behavior, quantitative analysis.

Faculty Full-time: 42, 95% with doctorates.

Teaching Methodology Case study: 25%, faculty seminars: 10%, lecture: 25%, research: 10%, seminars by members of the business community: 5%, student presentations: 10%, team projects: 15%.

STUDENT STATISTICS
Geographic Representation By region: Midwest 75%; Northeast 5%; West 5%. International 15%.

Undergraduate Majors Business 64%; engineering/technology 6%; humanities 3%; science/mathematics 21%; social sciences 3%; other 3%.

Other Background Graduate degrees in other disciplines: 5%. Work experience: On average, students have 6 years of work experience on entrance to the program.

FACILITIES
Information Resources Main library with 713,250 bound volumes, 287,561 titles on microform, 9,859 periodical subscriptions, 3,965 records/tapes/CDs, 236 CD-ROMs.

Housing 5% of students in program live in college-owned or -operated housing. Assistance with housing search provided.

Technology Computers are used heavily in course work. 77 computer terminals/PCs, linked by a campus-wide computer network, are available for use by students in program; they are located in computer labs. Students in the program are not required to have their own PC. $167 are budgeted per student for computer support.

Computer Resources/On-line Services

Training	No	Dun's	No
Internet	Yes	Dow Jones	No
E-Mail	Yes	Dialog	No
LEXIS/NEXIS	Yes $	Bloomberg	No
CompuServe	No		

ADMISSION

Acceptance 1994-95 134 applied for admission; 73% were accepted.

Entrance Requirements Bachelor's degree, prerequisite courses required for applicants with non-business degree, GMAT score of 450, minimum 2.5 GPA. Core courses waived through: previous course work.

Application Requirements Application form, copies of transcript, personal statement.

Application Deadlines 7/15 for fall, 12/15 for spring. Applications are processed on a rolling basis.

FINANCIALS

Costs for 1994-95 Tuition: Full-time: $332/credit hour. Fees: Full-time: $168/semester. Average room and board costs are $5,000 per academic year (on-campus) and $5,000 per academic year (off-campus).

Financial Aid In 1994-95, 8% of candidates received some institutionally administered aid in the form of assistantships, tuition waivers. Total awards ranged from $996-$2,050. Financial aid is available to part-time students. Application deadline: 3/1 for fall. Applications are processed on a rolling basis. Contact: Mr. Thomas Ramacker, Assistant Director, Financial Aid, 2500 California Plaza, Omaha, NE 68178-0001. (402) 280-2731.

INTERNATIONAL STUDENTS

Demographics 15% of students enrolled in the program are international; Asia 65%, Europe 12%, Africa 4%, Central America 4%, South America 4%, North America 4%, other 7%.

Services and Facilities International student office, visa services, language tutoring, ESL courses, special assistance for nonnative speakers of English, counseling/support services.

Applying TOEFL required, minimum score of 550; proof of health; proof of adequate funds. Financial aid is available to international students. Financial aid application deadlines: 3/15 for fall, 12/15 for spring. Applications are processed on a rolling basis. Admission application deadlines: 7/15 for fall, 12/15 for spring. Applications are processed on a rolling basis. Contact: Dr. David Higginson, Director of International Programs, 2500 California Plaza, Omaha, NE 68178-0001. (402) 280-2221.

ALTERNATE MBA PROGRAM

MBA/JD Length of program: Minimum: 48 months. Maximum: 6 years. Full-time classes: Main campus; evening, summer. Part-time classes: Main campus; evening, summer. Degree requirements: 112 credits.

PLACEMENT

In 1993-94, 109 organizations participated in on-campus recruiting. Placement services include alumni network, career counseling/planning, career fairs, career library, and resume preparation. Of 1994 graduates, 90% were employed within three months of graduation, the average starting salary was $40,000.

Program Contact: Ms. Adrian E. Koesters, Coordinator of Graduate Business Programs, Creighton University, 2500 California Plaza, Omaha, NE 68178-0001. (402) 280-2853; Fax: (402) 280-2172.

See full description on page 714.

University of Nebraska at Kearney

College of Business and Technology

Kearney, Nebraska

OVERVIEW

The University of Nebraska at Kearney is a state-supported comprehensive coed institution. Part of University of Nebraska System. Founded 1903. Setting: 235-acre small-town campus. Total institutional enrollment: 8,000. Program was first offered in 1984.

MBA HIGHLIGHTS

Entrance Difficulty**
Mean GMAT: 500
Mean GPA: 3.3

Cost $
Tuition: $69/hour
(Nonresident: $130/hour)
Room & Board: $1,500

Enrollment Profile

Full-time: 25	Work Exp: 80%
Part-time: 110	International: 23%
Total: 135	Women: 35%
Average Age: 33	Minorities: 25%

Average Class Size: 18

ACADEMICS

Length of Program Minimum: 24 months. Maximum: 7 years.

Calendar Semesters.

Full-time Classes Main campus, Columbus, Grand Island, North Platte; evening, summer.

Part-time Classes Main campus, Columbus, Grand Island, North Platte; evening, summer.

Degree Requirements 36 credits including 12 elective credits.

Required Courses Accounting, communications, decision science, economics, finance, management, marketing, policy.

Curricular Focus Business issues and problems, general management, problem solving and decision making.

Concentration Accounting.

Teaching Methodology Case study: 20%, lecture: 20%, research: 20%, student presentations: 20%, team projects: 20%.

STUDENT STATISTICS

Geographic Representation State residents 75%. By region: Midwest 77%. International 23%.

Undergraduate Majors Business 70%; education 7%; engineering/technology 15%; nursing 2%; social sciences 4%; other 2%.

Other Background Graduate degrees in other disciplines: 5%. Work experience: On average, students have 4 years of work experience on entrance to the program.

FACILITIES

Information Resources Main library with 249,955 bound volumes, 845,997 titles on microform, 1,930 periodical subscriptions, 72,470 records/tapes/CDs, 10 CD-ROMs.

Housing 15% of students in program live in college-owned or -operated housing.

Technology Computers are used moderately in course work. 85 computer terminals/PCs, linked by a campus-wide computer network, are available for use by students in program; they are located in dormitories, the library, the computer center, computer labs. Students in the program are not required to have their own PC.

Computer Resources/On-line Services

Training	No	Multimedia Center	Yes
Internet	Yes	LEXIS/NEXIS	No
E-Mail	Yes		

ADMISSION

Acceptance 1994-95 Of those applying, 68% were accepted.

Entrance Requirements Bachelor's degree, GMAT score of 450, minimum 2.75 GPA.

Application Requirements Application form, copies of transcript, personal statement, 2 letters of recommendation.

Application Deadlines 7/1 for fall, 11/1 for spring.

FINANCIALS

Costs for 1994-95 Tuition: Full-time: $69/hour for state residents, $130/hour for nonresidents. Fees: Full-time: $50/semester for state residents, $50/semester for nonresidents. Average room and board costs are $1,500 per academic year (on-campus) and $2,500 per academic year (off-campus).

Financial Aid In 1994-95, 12% of candidates received some institutionally administered aid in the form of grants, assistantships. Total awards ranged from $750-$4,500. Financial aid is available to part-time students. Application deadline: 3/1 for fall. Contact: Mr. Pat McTee, Director of Financial Aid, Student Services Building, Kearney, NE 68849. (308) 865-8520.

INTERNATIONAL STUDENTS
Demographics 23% of students enrolled in the program are international; Asia 75%, Central America 10%, South America 5%, Africa 3%, Europe 2%, other 5%.
Services and Facilities International student center, language tutoring, ESL courses, counseling/support services.
Applying TOEFL required, minimum score of 550; proof of health; proof of adequate funds. Financial aid is available to international students. Applications are processed on a rolling basis. Admission application deadline: 7/1 for fall. Contact: Mr. Jerry Fox, Director of International Studies, Office of International Studies, Kearney, NE 68849. (308) 865-8246.

PLACEMENT
Placement services include alumni network, career counseling/planning, career fairs, career library, career placement, electronic job bank, job interviews, resume preparation, and resume referral to employers. Of 1994 graduates, 90% were employed within three months of graduation.

Program Contact: Ms. Mary A. Lawson, MBA Administrative Assistant, University of Nebraska at Kearney, 905 West 26th Street, Kearney, NE 68849-0001. (308) 865-8348; Fax: (308) 865-8669; Internet Address: smtp%"lawsonm@platte.unk.edu".

University of Nebraska at Omaha

College of Business Administration

Omaha, Nebraska

OVERVIEW
The University of Nebraska at Omaha is a state-supported comprehensive coed institution. Part of University of Nebraska System. Founded 1908. Setting: 88-acre suburban campus. Total institutional enrollment: 7,000. AACSB-accredited.

MBA HIGHLIGHTS

Entrance Difficulty***
Mean GMAT: 525
Mean GPA: 3.43

Cost $
Tuition: $78/credit hour
(Nonresident: $188/credit hour)
Room & Board: N/R

Enrollment Profile
Full-time: N/R   Work Exp: N/R
Part-time: N/R   International: 5%
Total: 347   Women: 45%
Average Age: N/R   Minorities: 2%

Average Class Size: 22

*T*he University of Nebraska at Omaha is a comprehensive public university located on a beautiful 88.5-acre campus in the heart of Nebraska's largest city. The faculty members have achieved national and international distinction through their writing and research.

The M.B.A. program is designed for individuals who seek positions of leadership and responsibility in business. The program is distinctive, as studies are premised upon the theoretic foundation of business with considerable emphasis given to the application of knowledge. The M.B.A. program received two prestigious Exxon Awards for innovative graduate-level programming and was nationally recognized for excellence in computing resources.

M.B.A. students must complete a minimum of 36 hours of graduate-level courses that provide a strong interdisciplinary foundation in business yet allow students to explore areas of individual interest. Elective courses are available in management information systems, management, accounting, finance, marketing, economics, and quantitative analysis. The curriculum is currently being redesigned to meet the needs of the business community and comply with revised AACSB standards.

Students should refer to the World Wide Web (http://unicron.unomaha.edu) for further information on the program.

ACADEMICS
Length of Program Minimum: 12 months. Maximum: 6 years.
Calendar Semesters.
Part-time Classes Main campus; evening, summer.
Degree Requirements 36 credits including 12 elective credits.
Required Courses Business information systems, financial management, human behavior in organization, legal environment of management, managerial accounting, managerial economics, marketing policies, policy, planning, and strategy.
Curricular Focus Application of knowledge, general management.
Concentration Management.
Faculty Full-time: 44, 100% with doctorates.
Teaching Methodology Case study: 20%, lecture: 25%, problem solving/community business: 15%, research: 10%, student presentations: 15%, team projects: 15%.

STUDENT STATISTICS
Geographic Representation International 5%.

FACILITIES
Information Resources Main library with 660,886 bound volumes, 1.4 million titles on microform, 4,317 periodical subscriptions, 3,661 records/tapes/CDs.
Housing College housing not available.

ADMISSION
Acceptance 1994-95 Of those applying, 70% were accepted.
Entrance Requirements Bachelor's degree, GMAT score of 450, minimum 2.7 GPA.
Application Requirements Application form, copies of transcript.
Application Deadlines 6/30 for fall, 11/30 for spring.

FINANCIALS
Costs for 1994-95 Tuition: Full-time: $78/credit hour for state residents, $188/credit hour for nonresidents.
Financial Aid In 1994-95, candidates received some institutionally administered aid in the form of scholarships, assistantships, work-study. Application deadline: 3/1 for fall. Applications are processed on a rolling basis. Contact: Mr. Randy Sell, Director, 60th and Dodge Streets, Omaha, NE 68182-0048. (402) 554-3408.

INTERNATIONAL STUDENTS
Demographics 5% of students enrolled in the program are international.
Services and Facilities International student office, international student center, ESL courses.
Applying TOEFL required, minimum score of 550; proof of health; proof of adequate funds; financial affadavits. Financial aid is not available to international students. Admission application deadlines: 6/30 for fall, 11/30 for spring. Contact: Ms. Sharon Emery, International Student Adviser, 60th and Dodge Streets, Omaha, NE 68182-0048. (402) 554-2366.

Program Contact: Ms. Lex Kaczmarek, Assistant Director, MBA Program, University of Nebraska at Omaha, 60th and Dodge Streets, Omaha, NE 68182-0048. (402) 554-2303, or (800) 858-8648 (NE only), or (800) 858-3648 (out-of-state); Fax: (402) 554-3747.

University of Nebraska–Lincoln

College of Business Administration

Lincoln, Nebraska

OVERVIEW
The University of Nebraska–Lincoln is a state-supported coed institution. Part of University of Nebraska System. Founded 1869. Setting: 582-acre urban campus with easy access to Omaha. Total institutional enrollment: 24,695. Program was first offered in 1970. AACSB-accredited.

MBA HIGHLIGHTS

Entrance Difficulty****
Mean GMAT: 575
Mean GPA: 3.4

Cost $
Tuition: $91/hour
(Nonresident: $224/hour)
Room & Board: N/R

Enrollment Profile

Full-time: 54	Work Exp: 85%
Part-time: 62	International: 20%
Total: 116	Women: 43%
Average Age: 27	Minorities: 10%

Average Class Size: 25

ACADEMICS

Length of Program Minimum: 24 months. Maximum: 6 years.

Calendar Semesters.

Full-time Classes Main campus, Offutt Air Force Base; evening.

Part-time Classes Main campus, Offutt Air Force Base, Scottsbluff; evening.

Degree Requirements 48 credits including 18 elective credits.

Required Courses Administrative policy, international business, management skills seminar, managerial accounting, managerial decision making, managerial economics, managerial finance, managerial marketing, operations and information systems strategy, organizational behavior.

Curricular Focus General management, organizational development and change management, strategic analysis and planning.

Concentrations Finance, human resources management, international business, management information systems, marketing, operations management, organizational behavior, strategic management.

Teaching Methodology Case study: 30%, lecture: 20%, seminars by members of the business community: 3%, student presentations: 17%, team projects: 30%.

Special Opportunities International exchange in Hungary, India, Japan, People's Republic of China, Turkey, United Kingdom. Internship program available.

STUDENT STATISTICS

Geographic Representation State residents 70%. By region: Midwest 70%; Northeast 5%; West 5%. International 20%.

Undergraduate Majors Business 40%; education 10%; engineering/technology 15%; humanities 10%; science/mathematics 10%; social sciences 15%.

Other Background Graduate degrees in other disciplines: 100%. Work experience: On average, students have 2 years of work experience on entrance to the program.

FACILITIES

Information Resources Main library with 2.3 million bound volumes, 3.8 million titles on microform, 18,387 periodical subscriptions.

Housing 15% of students in program live in college-owned or -operated housing.

Technology Computers are used moderately in course work. 100 computer terminals/PCs, linked by a campus-wide computer network, are available for use by students in program; they are located in dormitories, the student center, the library, the computer center, computer labs. Students in the program are not required to have their own PC.

Computer Resources/On-line Services

Training	No	CompuServe	Yes
Internet	Yes	Dun's	Yes
E-Mail	Yes	Dow Jones	Yes
Multimedia Center	Yes	Dialog	Yes
LEXIS/NEXIS	Yes		

ADMISSION

Acceptance 1994-95 182 applied for admission; 26% were accepted.

Entrance Requirements Bachelor's degree, GMAT score of 450, minimum 2.5 GPA. Core courses waived through: previous course work.

Application Requirements Application form, copies of transcript, 3 letters of recommendation.

Application Deadlines 6/15 for fall, 10/15 for spring. Applications are processed on a rolling basis.

FINANCIALS

Estimated Costs for 1995-96 Tuition: Full-time: $91/hour for state residents, $224/hour for nonresidents. Fees: Full-time: $180/semester for state residents, $180/semester for nonresidents.

Financial Aid In 1994-95, 15% of candidates received some institutionally administered aid in the form of loans, fellowships, assistantships. Total awards ranged from $2,000-$7,500. Financial aid is available to part-time students. Application deadline: 4/15 for fall. Contact: Dr. John E. Beacon, Director of Scholarships and Financial Aid, Administration 16, Lincoln, NE 68588-0411. (402) 472-2030.

INTERNATIONAL STUDENTS

Demographics 20% of students enrolled in the program are international; Asia 50%, Europe 35%, Africa 5%, Central America 5%, South America 5%.

Services and Facilities International student office, international student center, language tutoring, counseling/support services.

Applying TOEFL required, minimum score of 550; proof of health; proof of adequate funds. Financial aid is available to international students. Financial aid is available to these students after one year of study. Admission application deadlines: 5/15 for fall, 9/15 for spring. Applications are processed on a rolling basis. Contact: Dr. Jean S. Aigner, Executive Dean, 1237 R, Room 201, Lincoln, NE 68588-0221. (402) 472-5358.

PLACEMENT

Placement services include alumni network, career counseling/planning, career fairs, career library, career placement, electronic job bank, and resume preparation. Of 1994 graduates, 75% were employed within three months of graduation, the average starting salary was $32,000, the range was $27,000-$48,000.

Jobs by Employer Type Manufacturing 50%; service 10%; government 15%; consulting 20%; nonprofit 5%.

Jobs by Functional Area Marketing/sales 25%; finance 30%; operations 5%; management 30%; strategic planning 10%.

Program Contact: Dr. Gordon Karels, Interim Associate Dean and Director of Graduate Programs, University of Nebraska–Lincoln, 14th and R Streets, Lincoln, NE 68588. (402) 472-3860, or (800) 742-8880 (NE only), or (800) 742-8800 (out-of-state); Fax: (402) 472-5180.

Wayne State College

Division of Business

Wayne, Nebraska

OVERVIEW

Wayne State College is a state-supported comprehensive coed institution. Part of Nebraska State College System. Founded 1910. Setting: 128-acre rural campus. Total institutional enrollment: 4,000. Program was first offered in 1991.

MBA HIGHLIGHTS

Entrance Difficulty**
Mean GMAT: 480
Mean GPA: 3.0

Cost $
Tuition: $188/course
(Nonresident: $337/course)
Room & Board: N/R

Enrollment Profile

Full-time: 3	Work Exp: 100%
Part-time: 107	International: N/R
Total: 110	Women: 50%
Average Age: 27	Minorities: N/R

Average Class Size: 15

ACADEMICS

Length of Program Minimum: 24 months. Maximum: 7 years.

Calendar Semesters.

Full-time Classes Main campus, South Sioux City, Norfolk; evening, summer.

Part-time Classes Main campus; evening, summer.

Degree Requirements 36 credits including 12 elective credits.

Required Courses Administrative policy, decision science, management accounting, managerial communication, managerial economics, marketing administration, organizational behavior.

Curricular Focus General management, leadership, problem solving and decision making.

Concentrations Accounting, management.

Faculty Full-time: 8, 80% with doctorates.

Teaching Methodology Case study: 25%, lecture: 15%, seminars by members of the business community: 10%, student presentations: 25%, team projects: 25%.

STUDENT STATISTICS

Geographic Representation By region: Midwest 100%.

Undergraduate Majors Business 50%; education 10%; engineering/technology 20%; humanities 10%; social sciences 10%.

Other Background Graduate degrees in other disciplines: 10%. Work experience: On average, students have 10 years of work experience on entrance to the program.

FACILITIES

Information Resources Main library with 312,000 bound volumes, 71,000 titles on microform, 1,200 periodical subscriptions, 7,500 records/tapes/CDs.

Housing College housing available.

Technology Computers are used moderately in course work. 52 computer terminals/PCs, linked by a campus-wide computer network, are available for use by students in program; they are located in computer labs. Students in the program are not required to have their own PC.

Computer Resources/On-line Services

Training	No	Dun's	Yes
Internet	Yes	Dow Jones	No
LEXIS/NEXIS	No	Bloomberg	No
CompuServe	No		

ADMISSION

Acceptance 1994-95 100 applied for admission; 80% were accepted.

Entrance Requirements Bachelor's degree, GMAT score.

Application Requirements Application form, copies of transcript, 2 letters of recommendation.

Application Deadline Applications are processed on a rolling basis.

FINANCIALS

Costs for 1994-95 Tuition: Full-time: $188/course for state residents, $337/course for nonresidents. Fees: Full-time: $15/course for state residents, $15/course for nonresidents.

Financial Aid In 1994-95, 15% of candidates received some institutionally administered aid in the form of loans, assistantships. Financial aid is not available to part-time students. Applications are processed on a rolling basis. Contact: Ms. Joan Zanders, Director of Financial Aid, 1111 Main, Hahn Administration, Wayne, NE 68787. (402) 375-7000.

INTERNATIONAL STUDENTS

Applying TOEFL required. Financial aid is available to international students. Admission applications are processed on a rolling basis.

PLACEMENT

Placement services include career counseling/planning, career fairs, career library, career placement, job interviews, resume preparation, and resume referral to employers.

Program Contact: Dr. Jeryl Nelson, MBA Director, Wayne State College, 1111 Main, Gardner Hall, Wayne, NE 68787. (402) 375-7251, or (800) 228-9972; Fax: (402) 375-7434; Internet Address: jnelson@wscgate.wsc.edu.

NEVADA

University of Nevada, Las Vegas

Las Vegas, Nevada

OVERVIEW

The University of Nevada, Las Vegas is a state-supported coed institution. Part of University and Community College System of Nevada. Founded 1957. Setting: 335-acre suburban campus. Total institutional enrollment: 20,000. Program was first offered in 1968. AACSB-accredited.

MBA HIGHLIGHTS

Entrance Difficulty***
Mean GMAT: 555
Mean GPA: N/R

Cost $
Tuition: $87/credit hour
(Nonresident: $87/credit hour)
Room & Board: $5,200

Enrollment Profile

Full-time: 70	Work Exp: 95%
Part-time: 200	International: 12%
Total: 270	Women: 30%
Average Age: 31	Minorities: 10%

Average Class Size: 20

ACADEMICS

Length of Program Minimum: 24 months. Maximum: 6 years.

Calendar 3-3.

Full-time Classes Main campus; day, evening, early morning, summer.

Part-time Classes Main campus; day, evening, early morning, summer.

Degree Requirements 30 credit hours including 9 elective credit hours.

Required Courses Advanced statistical modeling, business strategy formulation, managerial accounting, managerial economics, marketing strategy, organization theory, problems in business finance. Courses may be waived through: previous course work.

Curricular Focus Entrepreneurship, general management, leadership.

Concentrations Accounting, economics, finance, human resources management, international business, management, management information systems, marketing, operations management, organizational behavior, public administration, public policy, quantitative analysis, strategic management.

Faculty Full-time: 40, 100% with doctorates; part-time: 2, 50% with doctorates.

Teaching Methodology Case study: 21%, lecture: 41%, research: 6%, student presentations: 16%, team projects: 16%.

STUDENT STATISTICS

Geographic Representation State residents 60%. By region: West 63%; Northeast 10%; Midwest 10%; South 5%. International 12%.

Undergraduate Majors Business 50%; education 2%; engineering/technology 12%; humanities 12%; nursing 5%; science/mathematics 8%; social sciences 10%; other 1%.

Other Background Graduate degrees in other disciplines: 8%. Work experience: On average, students have 4 years of work experience on entrance to the program.

FACILITIES

Information Resources Main library with 626,000 bound volumes, 1.3 million titles on microform, 6,000 periodical subscriptions, 78,000 records/tapes/CDs.

Housing 2% of students in program live in college-owned or -operated housing.

Technology Computers are used moderately in course work. 50 computer terminals/PCs, linked by a campus-wide computer network, are available for use by students in program; they are located in learning resource center, the library, the computer center, computer labs, the research center. Students in the program are not required to have their own PC.

Computer Resources/On-line Services

Training	Yes	LEXIS/NEXIS	Yes
Internet	Yes		

ADMISSION

Acceptance 1994-95 350 applied for admission; 60% were accepted.

Entrance Requirements Bachelor's degree, GMAT score of 450, minimum 2.75 GPA, minimum 1 year of work experience. Core courses waived through: previous course work.

Application Requirements Written essay, application form, copies of transcript, resume/curriculum vitae, personal statement, 2 letters of recommendation.

Application Deadlines 6/1 for fall, 11/15 for spring.

FINANCIALS

Estimated Costs for 1995-96 Tuition: Full-time: $87/credit hour for state residents, $87/credit hour for nonresidents. Fees: Full-time: $4,800 for nonresidents. Average room and board costs are $5,200 per academic year (on-campus).

Financial Aid In 1994-95, 10% of candidates received some institutionally administered aid in the form of assistantships. Total awards ranged from $9,000-$9,500. Financial aid is available to part-time students. Application deadline: 3/1 for fall. Contact: Student Financial Aid, 4505 Maryland Parkway, Las Vegas, NV 89154-9900. (702) 895-3424.

INTERNATIONAL STUDENTS
Demographics 12% of students enrolled in the program are international; Asia 70%, Europe 10%, South America 10%, Africa 5%, Central America 5%.

Services and Facilities Visa services, language tutoring, ESL courses, special assistance for nonnative speakers of English, counseling/support services, international office.

Applying TOEFL required, minimum score of 550; proof of health; proof of adequate funds. Financial aid is not available to international students. Admission application deadlines: 5/1 for fall, 10/1 for spring. Contact: Ms. Theresa Chang, Director, PO Box 451035, Las Vegas, NV 89154-9900. (702) 895-3221.

PLACEMENT
In 1993-94, 15 organizations participated in on-campus recruiting; 100 on-campus interviews were conducted. Placement services include alumni network, career counseling/planning, career fairs, career library, career placement, electronic job bank, job interviews, resume preparation, and resume referral to employers. Of 1994 graduates, 100% were employed within three months of graduation, the average starting salary was $36,000, the range was $28,000-$75,000.

Jobs by Employer Type Manufacturing 15%; service 65%; government 10%; consulting 5%; nonprofit 5%.

Jobs by Functional Area Marketing/sales 15%; finance 30%; operations 15%; management 35%; technical management 5%.

Program Contact: Dr. Duane Baldwin, Director, University of Nevada, Las Vegas, PO Box 456031, Las Vegas, NV 89154-9900. (702) 895-3176; Fax: (702) 895-4306.
See full description on page 896.

University of Nevada, Reno

College of Business Administration

Reno, Nevada

OVERVIEW
The University of Nevada, Reno is a state-supported coed institution. Part of University and Community College System of Nevada. Founded 1874. Setting: 200-acre urban campus. Total institutional enrollment: 11,746. AACSB-accredited.

MBA HIGHLIGHTS
Entrance Difficulty*
Mean GMAT: 511
Mean GPA: N/R

Cost $
Tuition: $81/credit hour
(Nonresident: $81/credit hour)
Room & Board: N/R

Enrollment Profile

Full-time: N/R	Work Exp: N/R
Part-time: N/R	International: N/R
Total: 150	Women: 41%
Average Age: N/R	Minorities: N/R

Average Class Size: 30

ACADEMICS
Length of Program Minimum: 42 months.
Calendar Semesters.
Part-time Classes Main campus; evening, weekends, summer.
Degree Requirements 51 credit hours.
Curricular Focus General management.
Concentrations Economics, entrepreneurship, finance, gaming management, logistics, health services, human resources management, management, management information systems, marketing, organizational behavior.

STUDENT STATISTICS
Geographic Representation State residents 90%.

FACILITIES
Information Resources Main library with 881,223 bound volumes, 2.7 million titles on microform, 6,881 periodical subscriptions, 21,481 records/tapes/CDs.

ADMISSION
Entrance Requirements Bachelor's degree, GMAT score of 450, minimum 2.75 GPA, minimum 2 years of work experience.

Application Requirements Interview, application form, copies of transcript, resume/curriculum vitae, personal statement, 2 letters of recommendation.

Application Deadlines 3/1 for fall, 11/1 for spring.

FINANCIALS
Costs for 1994-95 Tuition: Part-time evening: $81/credit hour for state residents, $81/credit hour for nonresidents. Fees: Part-time evening: $2,375/semester for nonresidents.

Financial Aid Contact: Financial Aid Officer, Reno, NV 89557. (702) 784-4666.

INTERNATIONAL STUDENTS
Applying TOEFL required, minimum score of 550; proof of health; proof of adequate funds. Financial aid is available to international students. Financial aid application deadlines: 4/1 for fall, 11/1 for spring. Admission application deadlines: 3/1 for fall, 11/1 for spring. Applications are processed on a rolling basis.

Program Contact: Ms. Vicki Krentz, Associate Director of Graduate Programs, University of Nevada, Reno, Reno, NV 89557. (702) 784-4912; Fax: (702) 784-1773.

NEW HAMPSHIRE

Dartmouth College

Amos Tuck School of Business

Hanover, New Hampshire

OVERVIEW
Dartmouth College is an independent nonprofit coed institution. Founded 1769. Setting: 265-acre small-town campus. Total institutional enrollment: 5,475. AACSB-accredited.

MBA HIGHLIGHTS
Entrance Difficulty***
Mean GMAT: 657
Mean GPA: 3.37

Cost $$$$
Tuition: $21,225
Room & Board: $8,375

Enrollment Profile

Full-time: 363	Work Exp: 96%
Part-time: 0	International: 17%
Total: 363	Women: 31%
Average Age: 27	Minorities: 11%

Average Class Size: 58

ACADEMICS
Length of Program Minimum: 18 months. Maximum: 2 years.
Calendar Trimesters.
Full-time Classes Main campus; day, evening.
Degree Requirements 54 credits including 12 elective credits.
Required Courses Applied statistics, business policy, capital markets, corporate finance, decision science, financial accounting, global economic environment, international leadership, management communication, managerial accounting, managerial economics, marketing, operations management, organizational behavior.
Curricular Focus General management, organizational development and change management, teamwork.
Concentrations Entrepreneurship, finance, international business, management, management information systems, marketing, organizational behavior, strategic management, technology management.

Faculty Full-time: 37, 98% with doctorates; part-time: 12, 80% with doctorates.

Teaching Methodology Case study: 40%, experiential learning: 10%, lecture: 40%, student presentations: 5%, team projects: 5%.

Special Opportunities International exchange in Japan, Spain, United Kingdom. Internship program available.

STUDENT STATISTICS

Geographic Representation State residents 81%. By region: Northeast 46%; West 16%; Midwest 11%; South 9%. International 17%.

Undergraduate Majors Business 40%; engineering/technology 15%; humanities 16%; science/mathematics 10%; social sciences 14%; other 5%.

Other Background Graduate degrees in other disciplines: 8%. Work experience: On average, students have 4 years of work experience on entrance to the program.

FACILITIES

Information Resources Main library with 2 million bound volumes, 1.6 million titles on microform, 19,000 periodical subscriptions, 218,500 records/tapes/CDs. Business collection in Feldberg Library includes 110,640 bound volumes, 2,714 periodical subscriptions, 18 CD-ROMs, 602 videos.

Housing 37% of students in program live in college-owned or -operated housing. Assistance with housing search provided.

Technology Computers are used heavily in course work. 75 computer terminals/PCs, linked by a campus-wide computer network, are available for use by students in program; they are located in dormitories, classrooms, the library, the computer center. Students in the program are not required to have their own PC. $500 are budgeted per student for computer support.

Computer Resources/On-line Services

Training	Yes	CompuServe	No
Internet	Yes	Dun's	No
E-Mail	Yes	Dow Jones	Yes
Multimedia Center	Yes	Dialog	Yes
LEXIS/NEXIS	Yes	Bloomberg	Yes

Other on-line services: OCLC, RLIN.

ADMISSION

Acceptance 1994-95 2,230 applied for admission; 17% were accepted.

Entrance Requirements Bachelor's degree, GMAT score of 500.

Application Requirements Written essay, application form, copies of transcript, 3 letters of recommendation.

Application Deadlines 4/18 for spring. Applications are processed on a rolling basis. Application discs available.

FINANCIALS

Costs for 1994-95 Tuition: Full-time: $21,225. Average room and board costs are $8,375 per academic year (on-campus) and $9,875 per academic year (off-campus).

Financial Aid In 1994-95, 65% of candidates received some institutionally administered aid in the form of grants, scholarships, loans, fellowships, work-study. Total awards ranged from $3,000-$35,000. Application deadline: 3/1 for spring. Applications are processed on a rolling basis. Contact: Ms. Mado Macdonald, Director of Financial Aid, Hanover, NH 03755. (603) 646-3504.

INTERNATIONAL STUDENTS

Demographics 17% of students enrolled in the program are international; Asia 46%, Europe 33%, South America 8%, Australia 2%, North America 1%, other 10%.

Services and Facilities International student office, international student center, visa services, language tutoring, ESL courses, special assistance for nonnative speakers of English, counseling/support services.

Applying TOEFL required; proof of health; proof of adequate funds. Financial aid is available to international students. Financial aid application deadline: 3/1 for spring. Applications are processed on a rolling basis. Admission application deadline: 4/18 for spring. Applications are processed on a rolling basis. Contact: Ms. Patricia Palmiotto, Director of Student Affairs, Hanover, NH 03755. (603) 646-3938.

PLACEMENT

In 1993-94, 99 organizations participated in on-campus recruiting. Placement services include alumni network, career counseling/planning, career fairs, career library, career placement, electronic job bank, job interviews, job search course, resume preparation, and resume referral to employers. Of 1994 graduates, 89% were employed within three months of graduation, the average starting salary was $67,200, the range was $40,000-$125,000.

Jobs by Employer Type Manufacturing 21%; service 52%; consulting 27%.

Jobs by Functional Area Marketing/sales 11%; finance 50%; operations 2%; management 2%; strategic planning 2%; technical management 1%; consulting 32%.

Program Contact: Mr. Henry Malin, Director of Admissions, Dartmouth College, Hanover, NH 03755. (603) 646-3162; Fax: (603) 646-1308; Internet Address: tuck.admissions@dartmouth.edu.

See full description on page 716.

New Hampshire College

Graduate School of Business

Manchester, New Hampshire

OVERVIEW

New Hampshire College is an independent nonprofit comprehensive coed institution. Founded 1932. Setting: 200-acre small-town campus with easy access to Boston. Total institutional enrollment: 6,500. Program was first offered in 1974.

MBA HIGHLIGHTS

Entrance Difficulty**
Mean GMAT: N/R
Mean GPA: 3.5

Cost $$$
Tuition: $13,436/degree program
Room & Board: $4,200

Enrollment Profile

Full-time: 250	Work Exp: 70%
Part-time: 1,050	International: 10%
Total: 1,300	Women: 40%
Average Age: 28	Minorities: 15%

Average Class Size: 20

ACADEMICS

Length of Program Minimum: 18 months. Maximum: 8 years.

Calendar Quarters.

Full-time Classes Main campus; day, evening, weekends, summer.

Part-time Classes Main campus; day, evening, weekends, summer.

Degree Requirements 36 credits including 6 elective credits.

Curricular Focus General management, international business, strategic analysis and planning.

Concentrations Accounting, finance, health services, human resources management, international business, management, management information systems, marketing.

Faculty Full-time: 18, 60% with doctorates; part-time: 75, 30% with doctorates.

Teaching Methodology Case study: 30%, lecture: 30%, student presentations: 20%, team projects: 20%.

Special Opportunities Internships include management, CIS, and marketing.

STUDENT STATISTICS

Geographic Representation By region: Northeast 90%; Midwest 2%; West 2%. International 10%.

Undergraduate Majors Business 40%; education 10%; engineering/technology 20%; humanities 5%; science/mathematics 5%; social sciences 10%; other 10%.

Other Background Graduate degrees in other disciplines: 10%. Work experience: On average, students have 7 years of work experience on entrance to the program.

FACILITIES

Information Resources Main library with 85,430 bound volumes, 364 titles on microform, 962 periodical subscriptions, 1,450 records/tapes/CDs, 7 CD-ROMs.

Housing 2% of students in program live in college-owned or -operated housing.

Technology Computers are used moderately in course work. 175 computer terminals/PCs, linked by a campus-wide computer network, are available for use by students in program; they are located in the library, the computer center, computer labs. Students in the program are not required to have their own PC.

Computer Resources/On-line Services

Training	Yes	Dun's	No
Internet	Yes	Dow Jones	No
E-Mail	Yes	Dialog	Yes $
LEXIS/NEXIS	No	Bloomberg	No
CompuServe	No		

Other on-line services: First Search.

ADMISSION
Entrance Requirements Bachelor's degree, minimum 2.5 GPA. Core courses waived through: previous course work, work experience.
Application Requirements Application form, copies of transcript.
Application Deadline Applications are processed on a rolling basis.

FINANCIALS
Costs for 1994-95 Tuition: Full-time: $13,436/degree program; Part-time evening: $750/course. Fees: Full-time: $295/degree program. Average room and board costs are $4,200 per academic year (on-campus).
Financial Aid In 1994-95, candidates received some institutionally administered aid in the form of scholarships, loans, work-study. Financial aid is available to part-time students. Applications are processed on a rolling basis. Contact: Mr. Clint Hanson, Director of Financial Aid, 2500 North River Road, Manchester, NH 03106-1045. (603) 644-3102 Ext. 2178.

INTERNATIONAL STUDENTS
Demographics 10% of students enrolled in the program are international; Asia 65%, South America 10%, North America 10%, Africa 5%, Europe 5%, Central America 2%, other 3%.
Services and Facilities International student office, international student center, language tutoring, ESL courses, counseling/support services.
Applying TOEFL required, minimum score of 550; proof of health; proof of adequate funds. Financial aid is available to international students. Applications are processed on a rolling basis. Admission applications are processed on a rolling basis. Contact: Dr. George Commenator, Director of International Admissions, 2500 North River Road, Manchester, NH 03106-1045. (603) 644-3102 Ext. 2242.

ALTERNATE MBA PROGRAM
MBA/MS Degree requirements: MS is in accounting, business education, community economic development, computer information systems, finance, or international business.

PLACEMENT
In 1993-94, 170 organizations participated in on-campus recruiting. Placement services include alumni network, career counseling/planning, career placement, and resume preparation. Of 1994 graduates, 92% were employed within three months of graduation, the average starting salary range was $27,500-$45,000.

Program Contact: Dr. Steven Painchaud, Associate Dean, New Hampshire College, 2500 North River Road, Manchester, NH 03106-1045. (603) 644-3102; Fax: (603) 644-3150.
See full description on page 788.

Plymouth State College of the University System of New Hampshire

Business Department

Plymouth, New Hampshire

OVERVIEW
Plymouth State College of the University System of New Hampshire is a state-supported comprehensive coed institution. Part of University System of New Hampshire. Founded 1871. Setting: 150-acre small-town campus. Total institutional enrollment: 3,936. Program was first offered in 1974.

MBA HIGHLIGHTS
Entrance Difficulty
Mean GMAT: 471
Mean GPA: 3.17

Cost $$
Tuition: $595/course
(Nonresident: $655/course)
Room & Board: N/R

Enrollment Profile

Full-time: 10	Work Exp: 98%
Part-time: 139	International: 2%
Total: 149	Women: 41%
Average Age: 34	Minorities: 1%

Average Class Size: 17

ACADEMICS
Length of Program Minimum: 9 months. Maximum: 6 years.
Calendar Quarters.
Full-time Classes Main campus, Hanover, Conway, Manchester, Keene; evening, summer.
Part-time Classes Main campus, Hanover, Conway, Manchester, Keene; evening, summer.
Degree Requirements 36 credits including 9 elective credits.
Required Courses Accounting for managers, financial analysis and decision making, legal environment of business, managerial economics, managing organizational behavior, marketing techniques, operations management, quantitative analysis for business decisions, seminar in executive management. Courses may be waived through: previous course work, work experience.
Curricular Focus Economic and financial theory, general management, strategic analysis and planning.
Concentrations Accounting, economics, management, management information systems, marketing, school business administration.
Faculty Full-time: 23, 87% with doctorates.
Teaching Methodology Case study: 30%, lecture: 30%, research: 15%, student presentations: 5%, team projects: 20%.

STUDENT STATISTICS
Geographic Representation State residents 84%. By region: Northeast 98%. International 2%.
Undergraduate Majors Business 50%; education 5%; engineering/technology 8%; humanities 20%; nursing 10%; science/mathematics 5%; other 2%.
Other Background Graduate degrees in other disciplines: 6%. Work experience: On average, students have 8 years of work experience on entrance to the program.

FACILITIES
Information Resources Main library with 750,000 bound volumes, 500,000 titles on microform, 1,200 periodical subscriptions. Business collection includes 17,384 bound volumes, 134 periodical subscriptions, 8 CD-ROMs, 30 videos.
Housing 5% of students in program live in college-owned or -operated housing.
Technology Computers are used moderately in course work. 80 computer terminals/PCs, linked by a campus-wide computer network, are available for use by students in program; they are located in dormitories, learning resource center, the library, computer labs. Students in the program are not required to have their own PC. $300 are budgeted per student for computer support.

Computer Resources/On-line Services

Training	Yes	CompuServe	No
Internet	Yes	Dun's	Yes
E-Mail	Yes	Dow Jones	Yes
Videoconference Center	Yes	Dialog	Yes
LEXIS/NEXIS	No	Bloomberg	No

Other on-line services: OCLC, First Search.

ADMISSION
Acceptance 1994-95 75 applied for admission; 92% were accepted.
Entrance Requirements Bachelor's degree, prerequisite courses required for applicants with non-business degree, GMAT score, minimum 2.5 GPA. Core courses waived through: previous course work, work experience.
Application Requirements Written essay, application form, copies of transcript, resume/curriculum vitae, personal statement, 3 letters of recommendation.

Application Deadline Applications are processed on a rolling basis.

FINANCIALS
Costs for 1994-95 Tuition: Full-time: $595/course for state residents, $655/course for nonresidents.

Financial Aid In 1994-95, 48% of candidates received some institutionally administered aid in the form of loans. Total awards ranged from $586-$8,500. Financial aid is available to part-time students. Application deadlines: 3/1 for fall, 3/1 for spring. Contact: Mr. Robert A. Tuveson, Director of Financial Aid, Plymouth, NH 03264-1600. (603) 535-2338.

INTERNATIONAL STUDENTS
Demographics 2% of students enrolled in the program are international.

Services and Facilities ESL courses, special assistance for nonnative speakers of English, counseling/support services.

Applying TOEFL required, minimum score of 550; proof of health; proof of adequate funds. Financial aid is not available to international students. Admission application deadlines: 5/15 for fall, 10/15 for spring. Contact: Ms. Dana Vanderbeck, Graduate Assistant for International Student Affairs, Plymouth, NH 03264-1600. (603) 535-2932.

PLACEMENT
Placement services include alumni network, career counseling/planning, and career placement. Of 1994 graduates, 85% were employed within three months of graduation.

Jobs by Employer Type Manufacturing 12%; service 60%; government 2%; consulting 5%; nonprofit 15%; other 6%.

Program Contact: Ms. Sylvia Horgan, MBA Program Assistant, Plymouth State College of the University System of New Hampshire, Plymouth, NH 03264-1600. (603) 535-5000, or (800) 367-4723; Fax: (603) 535-2648; Internet Address: sylvia.horgan@plymouth.edu.
See full description on page 804.

Rivier College

Graduate Business Department

Nashua, New Hampshire

OVERVIEW
Rivier College is an independent Roman Catholic comprehensive coed institution. Founded 1933. Setting: 60-acre urban campus with easy access to Boston. Total institutional enrollment: 2,737. Program was first offered in 1974.

MBA HIGHLIGHTS

Entrance Difficulty***
Mean GMAT: 511
Mean GPA: 2.73

Cost $$
Tuition: $762/course
Room & Board: $7,000 (off-campus)

Enrollment Profile

Full-time: 7	Work Exp: 92%
Part-time: 411	International: 7%
Total: 418	Women: 45%
Average Age: 36	Minorities: 9%

Average Class Size: 16

ACADEMICS
Length of Program Minimum: 24 months. Maximum: 6 years.
Calendar Semesters.
Full-time Classes Main campus, Castle College; day, evening, weekends.
Part-time Classes Main campus; day, evening, weekends.
Degree Requirements 36 credits including 21 elective credits. Other: GMAT after completing 4 courses.
Required Courses Accounting, corporate strategy, economics, ethics, finance, management, marketing, organizational behavior. Courses may be waived through: previous course work.
Curricular Focus General management, problem solving and decision making, total quality management.
Concentrations Total quality management, human resources management, management, marketing.

Faculty Full-time: 6, 67% with doctorates; part-time: 28, 7% with doctorates.

Teaching Methodology Case study: 47%, faculty seminars: 5%, lecture: 5%, research: 10%, seminars by members of the business community: 3%, student presentations: 20%, team projects: 10%.

STUDENT STATISTICS
Geographic Representation State residents 64%. By region: Northeast 100%. International 7%.

Undergraduate Majors Business 51%; education 4%; engineering/technology 21%; humanities 8%; nursing 3%; science/mathematics 3%; social sciences 10%.

Other Background Graduate degrees in other disciplines: 4%. Work experience: On average, students have 12 years of work experience on entrance to the program.

FACILITIES
Information Resources Main library with 128,473 bound volumes, 161 titles on microform, 752 periodical subscriptions, 4,218 records/tapes/CDs, 6 CD-ROMs.

Housing College housing not available.

Technology Computers are used moderately in course work. 50 computer terminals/PCs are available for use by students in program; they are located in the computer center, computer labs. Students in the program are not required to have their own PC.

Computer Resources/On-line Services

Training	Yes	Dun's	No
Internet	Yes	Dow Jones	No
E-Mail	No	Dialog	No
LEXIS/NEXIS	No	Bloomberg	No
CompuServe	No		

ADMISSION
Acceptance 1994-95 Of those applying, 98% were accepted.

Entrance Requirements Bachelor's degree. Core courses waived through: previous course work.

Application Requirements Interview, application form, copies of transcript.

Application Deadlines 8/31 for fall, 1/14 for spring, 5/23 for summer.

FINANCIALS
Costs for 1994-95 Tuition: Full-time: $762/course. Fees: Full-time: $50. Average room and board costs are $7,000 per academic year (off-campus).

Financial Aid In 1994-95, candidates received some institutionally administered aid in the form of loans. Application deadlines: 8/1 for fall, 12/1 for spring, 4/15 for summer. Contact: Ms. Jolene Mitchell, Financial Aid Director, 420 South Main Street, Nashua, NH 03060-5086. (603) 888-1311 Ext. 8510.

INTERNATIONAL STUDENTS
Demographics 7% of students enrolled in the program are international.

Services and Facilities ESL courses.

Applying TOEFL required, minimum score of 600; proof of adequate funds. Financial aid is not available to international students. Admission application deadlines: 7/1 for fall, 11/1 for spring, 4/1 for summer.

ALTERNATE MBA PROGRAM
MBA/MLS Length of program: Minimum: 24 months. Full-time classes: Main campus, Castle College; day, evening, weekends. Part-time classes: Main campus, Castle College; day, evening, weekends. Degree requirements: 36 credits including 3 elective credits. GRE or GMAT.

PLACEMENT
Placement services include career counseling/planning and career placement.

Program Contact: Dr. George E. Shagory, Chair, Graduate Business, Rivier College, 420 South Main Street, Nashua, NH 03060-5086. (603) 888-1311 Ext. 8237, or (800) 44-RIVIER; Fax: (603) 888-6447.

University of New Hampshire

The Whittemore School of Business and Economics

Durham, New Hampshire

OVERVIEW
The University of New Hampshire is a state-supported coed institution. Part of University System of New Hampshire. Founded 1866. Setting:

200-acre small-town campus with easy access to Boston. Total institutional enrollment: 13,500. Program was first offered in 1968.

MBA HIGHLIGHTS

Entrance Difficulty*
Mean GMAT: 570
Mean GPA: 3.07

Cost $
Tuition: $3,970
(Nonresident: $12,290)
Room & Board: N/R

Enrollment Profile

Full-time: 55	Work Exp: 90%
Part-time: 0	International: 33%
Total: 55	Women: 35%
Average Age: 27	Minorities: N/R

Average Class Size:　35

ACADEMICS

Length of Program Minimum: 21 months. Maximum: 3 years.
Calendar Semesters.
Full-time Classes Main campus; day.
Degree Requirements 60 credits including 15 elective credits.
Required Courses Advanced organizational theory, business, government, and society, economics, financial accounting, financial management, financial policy, management information systems, managerial accounting, managerial statistics, marketing, operations management, organizational behavior, quantitative methods, strategic management decision making, strategic management of operations, strategic marketing.
Curricular Focus Entrepreneurship, general management, problem solving and decision making.
Concentrations Accounting, finance, hotel management, human resources management, marketing, operations management, organizational behavior.
Faculty Full-time: 35, 100% with doctorates.
Teaching Methodology Case study: 20%, faculty seminars: 5%, lecture: 30%, research: 10%, seminars by members of the business community: 5%, student presentations: 15%, team projects: 15%.
Special Opportunities International exchange in Canada, France, Germany. Internships include financial analysis in high technology, insurance, manufacturing and production control in automotive, and management information systems in software.

STUDENT STATISTICS

Geographic Representation By region: Northeast 60%; South 4%; Midwest 3%. International 33%.
Undergraduate Majors Business 25%; education 10%; engineering/technology 25%; humanities 10%; social sciences 30%.
Other Background Graduate degrees in other disciplines: 10%. Work experience: On average, students have 3 years of work experience on entrance to the program.

FACILITIES

Information Resources Main library with 1 million bound volumes, 714,199 titles on microform, 6,500 periodical subscriptions, 11,348 records/tapes/CDs.
Housing 65% of students in program live in college-owned or -operated housing.
Technology Computers are used moderately in course work. 170 computer terminals/PCs, linked by a campus-wide computer network, are available for use by students in program; they are located in the student center, classrooms, learning resource center, the library, the computer center, computer labs, the research center, graduate student resource room. Students in the program are not required to have their own PC.
Computer Resources/On-line Services

Training	Yes	E-Mail	Yes
Internet	Yes	Multimedia Center	Yes

ADMISSION

Acceptance 1994-95 74 applied for admission; 68% were accepted.
Entrance Requirements Bachelor's degree, GMAT score. Core courses waived through: previous course work.
Application Requirements Written essay, application form, copies of transcript, 3 letters of recommendation.
Application Deadlines 7/1 for fall. Applications are processed on a rolling basis.

FINANCIALS

Costs for 1994-95 Tuition: Full-time: $3,970 for state residents, $12,290 for nonresidents. Fees: Full-time: $455 for state residents, $455 for nonresidents.
Financial Aid In 1994-95, 80% of candidates received some institutionally administered aid in the form of grants, scholarships, loans, fellowships, assistantships, work-study. Total awards ranged from $2,000-$15,000. Financial aid is not available to part-time students. Application deadlines: 2/1 for fall, 5/1 for merit-based aid deadline. Contact: Ms. Julie Colligan, Graduate Financial Aid Coordinator, Financial Aid Office, Stoke Hall, Durham, NH 03824. (603) 862-3600.

INTERNATIONAL STUDENTS

Demographics 33% of students enrolled in the program are international; Asia 48%, Europe 48%, North America 4%.
Services and Facilities International student office, international student center, language tutoring.
Applying TOEFL required, minimum score of 550; proof of health; proof of adequate funds. Financial aid is available to international students. Financial aid application deadline: 4/1 for fall. Applications are processed on a rolling basis. Admission application deadline: 4/1 for fall. Applications are processed on a rolling basis. Contact: Dr. Leila Paja-Manola, Director of International Student Office, Hood House, Durham, NH 03824. (603) 862-1508.

ALTERNATE MBA PROGRAM

Executive MBA (EMBA) Length of program: Minimum: 22 months. Degree requirements: 54 credits including 9 elective credits. Interview, resume, 8-10 years work experience.

PLACEMENT

In 1993-94, 5 organizations participated in on-campus recruiting; 15 on-campus interviews were conducted. Placement services include alumni network, career counseling/planning, career fairs, career library, career placement, job interviews, and resume preparation. Of 1994 graduates, 80% were employed within three months of graduation, the average starting salary was $39,500, the range was $30,000-$53,000.

Program Contact: Mr. George Abraham, Director of Graduate Programs, University of New Hampshire, Durham, NH 03824. (603) 862-1367; Fax: (603) 862-4468.
See full description on page 898.

NEW JERSEY

Fairleigh Dickinson University, Teaneck-Hackensack Campus

Samuel J. Silberman College of Business Administration

Teaneck, New Jersey

OVERVIEW

Fairleigh Dickinson University, Teaneck-Hackensack Campus is an independent nonprofit comprehensive coed institution. Founded 1942. Setting: 125-acre suburban campus with easy access to New York City. Total institutional enrollment: 11,000. Program was first offered in 1957.

MBA HIGHLIGHTS

Entrance Difficulty*
Mean GMAT: 475
Mean GPA: 3.2

Cost $
Tuition: $423/credit
Room & Board: N/R

Enrollment Profile
Full-time: 450
Part-time: 2,078
Total: 2,528
Average Age: N/R

Work Exp: 90%
International: 5%
Women: 45%
Minorities: 7%

Class Size: 25 - 30

ACADEMICS

Length of Program Minimum: 24 months.

Calendar Semesters.

Full-time Classes Main campus; day, evening, weekends, summer.

Part-time Classes Main campus; evening, weekends, summer.

Degree Requirements 36 credits including 9 elective credits.

Required Courses Business policy, economic analysis, financial accounting, financial analysis, management information systems, management theory and practice, quantitative analysis in business, social and legal environment of business, statistical analysis, the marketing process. Courses may be waived through: previous course work.

Curricular Focus Entrepreneurship, international business, strategic analysis and planning.

Concentrations Accounting, economics, entrepreneurship, finance, hotel management, human resources management, international business, management, management information systems, marketing, quantitative analysis.

Teaching Methodology Case study: 15%, computer simulation: 5%, lecture: 60%, student presentations: 10%, team projects: 10%.

Special Opportunities Internship program available.

STUDENT STATISTICS

Geographic Representation State residents 90%. By region: Northeast 95%. International 5%.

Undergraduate Majors Business 50%; engineering/technology 20%; humanities 5%; science/mathematics 20%; social sciences 5%.

Other Background Graduate degrees in other disciplines: 5%. Work experience: On average, students have 5 years of work experience on entrance to the program.

FACILITIES

Information Resources Main library with 432,239 bound volumes, 267,407 titles on microform, 2,536 periodical subscriptions, 8,866 records/tapes/CDs, 48 CD-ROMs.

Housing 5% of students in program live in college-owned or -operated housing.

Technology Computers are used heavily in course work. 50 computer terminals/PCs, linked by a campus-wide computer network, are available for use by students in program; they are located in the library, computer labs. Students in the program are required to have their own PC.

Computer Resources/On-line Services

Training	Yes	LEXIS/NEXIS	Yes
Internet	Yes	Dialog	Yes
E-Mail	Yes		

ADMISSION

Acceptance 1994-95 Of those applying, 60% were accepted.

Entrance Requirements Bachelor's degree, GMAT score. Core courses waived through: previous course work.

Application Requirements Application form, copies of transcript.

Application Deadlines 9/1 for fall, 1/15 for spring.

FINANCIALS

Costs for 1994-95 Tuition: Full-time: $423/credit. Fees: Full-time: $130/semester.

Financial Aid In 1994-95, 2% of candidates received some institutionally administered aid in the form of fellowships. Financial aid is not available to part-time students. Application deadlines: 7/15 for fall, 11/15 for spring. Contact: Graduate Admission, 1000 River Road, Teaneck, NJ 07666. (201) 692-2000.

INTERNATIONAL STUDENTS

Demographics 5% of students enrolled in the program are international; Asia 95%, Other 5%.

Services and Facilities Language tutoring, ESL courses.

Applying TOEFL required; proof of adequate funds. Financial aid is available to international students. Financial aid application deadlines: 4/15 for fall, 10/15 for spring. Admission application deadlines: 7/15 for fall, 11/15 for spring. Contact: Ms. Jane Bush, Director, International Students, 1000 River Road, Teaneck, NJ 07666. (201) 692-2745.

ALTERNATE MBA PROGRAM

Executive MBA (EMBA) Length of program: Minimum: 24 months. Full-time classes: Main campus; weekends. Degree requirements: 48 credits. Interview with EMBA director, sponsorship by employer. Average class size: 20.

PLACEMENT

Placement services include career counseling/planning, career placement, and resume preparation. Of 1994 graduates, 90% were employed within three months of graduation.

Program Contact: Graduate Admissions, Fairleigh Dickinson University, Teaneck-Hackensack Campus, 285 Madison Avenue, Madison, NJ 07940. (201) 593-8890; Fax: (201) 593-8804.

See full description on page 738.

Monmouth University

School of Business

West Long Branch, New Jersey

OVERVIEW

Monmouth University is an independent nonprofit comprehensive coed institution. Founded 1933. Setting: 138-acre suburban campus with easy access to New York City and Philadelphia. Total institutional enrollment: 4,200. Program was first offered in 1974.

MBA HIGHLIGHTS

Entrance Difficulty**
Mean GMAT: 500
Mean GPA: N/R

Cost $$
Tuition: $379/credit
Room & Board: N/R

Enrollment Profile
Full-time: 24
Part-time: 646
Total: 670
Average Age: 32

Work Exp: 90%
International: 1%
Women: 42%
Minorities: 8%

Average Class Size: N/R

ACADEMICS

Length of Program Minimum: 18 months. Maximum: 5 years.

Calendar Semesters.

Part-time Classes Main campus; evening, summer.

Degree Requirements 30 credits including 9 elective credits. Other: Capstone course.

Required Courses Managerial accounting, managerial economics or economic policy in society, marketing research or promotional strategy or consumer behavior, monetary theory and financial markets, organizational development or total quality management or operations research or logistics, social responsibility of business. Courses may be waived through: previous course work, work experience.

Curricular Focus Problem solving and decision making, strategic analysis and planning, teamwork.

Concentrations Accounting, economics, finance, management, marketing.

Faculty Full-time: 26; part-time: 8.

STUDENT STATISTICS

Geographic Representation State residents 97%. By region: Northeast 98%. International 1%.

Other Background Graduate degrees in other disciplines: 10%. Work experience: On average, students have 5-10 years of work experience on entrance to the program.

FACILITIES

Information Resources Main library with 243,522 bound volumes, 305,760 titles on microform, 1,336 periodical subscriptions, 1,850 records/tapes/CDs, 138 CD-ROMs.

Housing 10% of students in program live in college-owned or -operated housing.

Technology 300 computer terminals/PCs, linked by a campus-wide computer network, are available for use by students in program; they are located in the student center, classrooms, the library, computer labs. Students in the program are not required to have their own PC.

Computer Resources/On-line Services

Internet	Yes	E-Mail	Yes

ADMISSION

Acceptance 1994-95 Of those applying, 65% were accepted.

Entrance Requirements Bachelor's degree, GMAT score of 450, minimum 3.0 GPA. Core courses waived through: previous course work.

Application Requirements Application form, copies of transcript.

Application Deadlines 8/1 for fall, 12/1 for spring.

FINANCIALS

Costs for 1994-95 Tuition: Full-time: $379/credit. Fees: Full-time: $245/semester.

Financial Aid In 1994-95, 10% of candidates received some institutionally administered aid in the form of loans, assistantships, work-study, employee waivers. Total awards ranged from $2,000-$6,000. Financial aid is available to part-time students. Application deadline: 5/1 for priority filing. Contact: Mr. Hank Mackiewicz, Dean of Financial Aid, Wilson Hall, Cedar Road, West Long Branch, NJ 07764. (908) 571-3463.

INTERNATIONAL STUDENTS

Demographics 1% of students enrolled in the program are international.

Services and Facilities International student center, visa services, counseling/support services.

Applying TOEFL required, minimum score of 525; proof of health; proof of adequate funds. Financial aid is not available to international students. Admission application deadlines: 8/1 for fall, 12/1 for spring. Contact: Mr. David Nelson, Director of International Student Services, Cedar Road, West Long Branch, NJ 07764. (908) 571-7515.

PLACEMENT

In 1993-94, 15 organizations participated in on-campus recruiting; 50 on-campus interviews were conducted. Placement services include alumni network, career counseling/planning, career fairs, career library, career placement, electronic job bank, job interviews, resume preparation, and resume referral to employers. Of 1994 graduates, 85% were employed within three months of graduation, the average starting salary was $32,000, the range was $28,000-$35,000.

Jobs by Employer Type Manufacturing 20%; service 75%; consulting 5%.

Jobs by Functional Area Marketing/sales 20%; finance 40%; management 40%.

Program Contact: Ms. Elizabeth Martin, Director of Graduate Admissions, Monmouth University, West Long Branch, NJ 07764. (908) 571-3452; Fax: (908) 571-3629.

Montclair State University

School of Business Administration

Upper Montclair, New Jersey

OVERVIEW

Montclair State University is a state-supported comprehensive coed institution. Founded 1908. Setting: 200-acre suburban campus with easy access to New York City. Total institutional enrollment: 12,465.

MBA HIGHLIGHTS

Entrance Difficulty***

Cost $
Tuition: $164/credit hour
(Nonresident: $204/credit hour)
Room & Board: $4,834

Enrollment Profile

Full-time: N/R	Work Exp: N/R
Part-time: N/R	International: 6%
Total: 220	Women: 39%
Average Age: N/R	Minorities: 7%

Average Class Size: 20

ACADEMICS

Length of Program Minimum: 24 months.

Calendar Semesters.

Full-time Classes Main campus; evening, weekends, summer.

Part-time Classes Main campus; evening, weekends, summer.

Degree Requirements 33 credits.

Curricular Focus Business issues and problems, economic and financial theory, international business, leadership, problem solving and decision making, strategic analysis and planning, teamwork.

Concentrations Accounting, economics, finance, marketing, quantitative analysis, strategic management.

Teaching Methodology Faculty seminars: 10%, lecture: 55%, research: 15%, student presentations: 20%.

STUDENT STATISTICS

Geographic Representation State residents 94%. International 6%.

FACILITIES

Information Resources Main library with 378,535 bound volumes, 56,249 titles on microform, 3,811 periodical subscriptions, 12,784 records/tapes/CDs, 60 CD-ROMs.

Housing College housing available.

ADMISSION

Entrance Requirements Bachelor's degree, GMAT score of 500, minimum 3.0 GPA.

Application Requirements Written essay, application form, copies of transcript, 3 letters of recommendation.

Application Deadlines 4/1 for fall, 11/1 for spring.

FINANCIALS

Costs for 1994-95 Tuition: Full-time: $164/credit hour for state residents, $204/credit hour for nonresidents. Average room and board costs are $4,834 per academic year (on-campus).

Financial Aid Applications are processed on a rolling basis. Contact: Dr. Randall Richards, Director of Financial Aid, Valley Road and Normal Avenue, Upper Montclair, NJ 07043-1624. (201) 655-7022.

INTERNATIONAL STUDENTS

Demographics 6% of students enrolled in the program are international.

Applying TOEFL required; proof of health; proof of adequate funds; Diagnostic test from department of linguistics. Financial aid is not available to international students.

Program Contact: Director of Graduate Studies, Montclair State University, Valley Road and Normal Avenue, Upper Montclair, NJ 07043-1624. (201) 655-5349.

Rider University

College of Business Administration

Lawrenceville, New Jersey

OVERVIEW

Rider University is an independent nonprofit comprehensive coed institution. Founded 1865. Setting: 340-acre suburban campus with easy access to Philadelphia and New York City. Total institutional enrollment: 5,452. Program was first offered in 1967. AACSB-accredited.

MBA HIGHLIGHTS

Entrance Difficulty****
Mean GMAT: 514
Mean GPA: 3.2

Cost $$
Tuition: $1,044/course
Room & Board: N/R

Enrollment Profile

Full-time: 32	Work Exp: 85%
Part-time: 431	International: 6%
Total: 463	Women: 47%
Average Age: 27	Minorities: 5%

Average Class Size: 22

ACADEMICS

Length of Program Minimum: 12 months. Maximum: 6 years.

Calendar Semesters.

Full-time Classes Main campus; evening.

Part-time Classes Main campus; evening.

Degree Requirements 57 credits including 12 elective credits.

Required Courses Business and environment, economic analysis, financial management, fundamentals of accounting, fundamentals of statistical analysis, management information systems, management theory and application, managerial accounting, managerial economics, marketing management, math for business decisions, operations management, problems in financial management, problems in marketing management, strategic planning and policy.

Curricular Focus International business, leadership, problem solving and decision making.

Concentrations Accounting, economics, finance, human resources management, international business, management, management information systems, marketing, organizational behavior, quantitative analysis.

Faculty Full-time: 60, 97% with doctorates; part-time: 3, 100% with doctorates.

STUDENT STATISTICS
Geographic Representation State residents 94%. By region: Northeast 80%; Midwest 7%; West 5%; South 2%. International 6%.

Undergraduate Majors Business 52%; engineering/technology 25%; humanities 2%; social sciences 16%; other 4%.

Other Background Work experience: On average, students have 6 years of work experience on entrance to the program.

FACILITIES
Information Resources Main library with 357,000 bound volumes, 400,000 titles on microform, 1,500 periodical subscriptions, 1,286 records/tapes/CDs, 15 CD-ROMs. Business collection includes 40,000 bound volumes, 850 periodical subscriptions, 650 CD-ROMs, 215 videos.

Housing College housing not available.

Technology Computers are used moderately in course work. 110 computer terminals/PCs, linked by a campus-wide computer network, are available for use by students in program; they are located in classrooms, computer labs. Students in the program are not required to have their own PC.

Computer Resources/On-line Services

Training	Yes	Multimedia Center	Yes
Internet	Yes	Dow Jones	Yes
E-Mail	Yes	Dialog	Yes

ADMISSION
Entrance Requirements Bachelor's degree, international students must have three years plus one year in Master's level program, GMAT score. Core courses waived through: previous course work.

Application Requirements Written essay, application form, copies of transcript, resume/curriculum vitae.

Application Deadlines 8/1 for fall, 12/1 for spring, 5/1 for summer. Applications are processed on a rolling basis. Application discs available.

FINANCIALS
Costs for 1994-95 Tuition: Full-time: $1,044/course.

Financial Aid In 1994-95, candidates received some institutionally administered aid in the form of loans, assistantships. Total awards ranged from $500-$9,264. Application deadlines: 3/15 for fall, 11/15 for spring, 4/15 for summer. Applications are processed on a rolling basis. Contact: Mr. Larry Sharp, Associate Director of Financial Aid, 2083 Lawrenceville Road, Lawrenceville, NJ 08648-3001. (609) 896-5178.

INTERNATIONAL STUDENTS
Demographics 6% of students enrolled in the program are international.

Applying TOEFL required; proof of health; proof of adequate funds. Financial aid is not available to international students. Admission application deadlines: 8/1 for fall, 12/1 for spring, 5/1 for summer.

PLACEMENT
Placement services include career counseling/planning, career fairs, career library, career placement, job interviews, resume preparation, and resume referral to employers. Of 1994 graduates, the average starting salary was $40,000.

Program Contact: Dr. Joseph Summers, Associate Dean Office of Graduate Services, Rider University, 2083 Lawrenceville Road, Lawrenceville, NJ 08648-3001. (609) 896-5036.

Rowan College of New Jersey

School of Business Administration

Glassboro, New Jersey

OVERVIEW
Rowan College of New Jersey is a state-supported comprehensive coed institution. Part of New Jersey State College System. Founded 1923. Setting: 200-acre small-town campus with easy access to Philadelphia. Total institutional enrollment: 7,674.

MBA HIGHLIGHTS

Entrance Difficulty***
Mean GMAT: 503
Mean GPA: N/R

Cost $
Tuition: $1,752/semester
(Nonresident: $2,772/semester)
Room & Board: $4,600

Enrollment Profile

Full-time: N/R	Work Exp: N/R
Part-time: N/R	International: 5%
Total: 150	Women: 30%
Average Age: N/R	Minorities: N/R

Average Class Size: 20

ACADEMICS
Length of Program Minimum: 12 months.

Calendar Semesters.

Full-time Classes Main campus; evening, weekends, summer.

Part-time Classes Main campus; evening, weekends, summer.

Degree Requirements 36 semester hours.

Curricular Focus Business issues and problems, problem solving and decision making, strategic analysis and planning.

Concentrations Finance, management, public relations, school administration.

STUDENT STATISTICS
Geographic Representation State residents 95%. International 5%.

FACILITIES
Information Resources Main library with 350,800 bound volumes, 77,000 titles on microform, 1,725 periodical subscriptions, 43,500 records/tapes/CDs.

Housing College housing available.

ADMISSION
Entrance Requirements Bachelor's degree, GMAT score, minimum 2.5 GPA.

Application Requirements Application form, copies of transcript, resume/curriculum vitae, personal statement, 2 letters of recommendation.

Application Deadline Applications are processed on a rolling basis.

FINANCIALS
Costs for 1994-95 Tuition: Full-time: $1,752/semester for state residents, $2,772/semester for nonresidents; Part-time day: $146/semester hour for state residents, $231/semester hour for nonresidents. Fees: Full-time: $214/semester for state residents, $214/semester for nonresidents; Part-time day: $18/semester hour for state residents, $18/semester hour for nonresidents. Average room and board costs are $4,600 per academic year (on-campus).

Financial Aid Application deadlines: 3/15 for fall, 11/1 for spring. Contact: Graduate Admissions Office, Memorial Hall, 201 Mullica Hill Road, Glassboro, NJ 08028-1702. (609) 256-4050.

INTERNATIONAL STUDENTS
Demographics 5% of students enrolled in the program are international.

Applying TOEFL required, minimum score of 550; proof of health; proof of adequate funds; foreign transcripts evaluated by World Education Center. Financial aid is not available to international students.

Program Contact: Dr. Gulser Meric, MBA Program Director, Rowan College of New Jersey, Bunce Hall, 201 Mullica Hill Road, Glassboro, NJ 08028-1702. (609) 256-4024; Fax: (609) 256-4439; Internet Address: meri2847@elan.rowan.edu.

Rutgers, The State University of New Jersey, Camden

School of Business

Camden, New Jersey

OVERVIEW

Rutgers, The State University of New Jersey, Camden is a state-supported coed institution. Founded 1927. Setting: 25-acre urban campus. Total institutional enrollment: 48,000. Program was first offered in 1975.

MBA HIGHLIGHTS

Entrance Difficulty***
Mean GMAT: 574
Mean GPA: 3.1

Cost $$
Tuition: $3,591/semester
(Nonresident: $5,353/semester)
Room & Board: $3,456

Enrollment Profile
Full-time: 20
Part-time: 160
Total: 180
Average Age: 28

Work Exp: 100%
International: 5%
Women: 30%
Minorities: 10%

Average Class Size: 20

ACADEMICS

Length of Program Minimum: 24 months. Maximum: 7 years.

Calendar Semesters.

Full-time Classes Main campus; evening, summer.

Part-time Classes Main campus; evening, summer.

Degree Requirements 42 credits.

Required Courses Accounting 1, accounting 2, finance, management information systems, management science, managerial economics, marketing, organizational behavior, productions and operations management, social responsibility of budget. Courses may be waived through: previous course work.

Curricular Focus Business issues and problems, general management, international business.

Concentrations Accounting, finance, health services, human resources management, international business, management, management information systems, marketing.

Faculty Full-time: 32, 100% with doctorates; part-time: 4, 50% with doctorates.

Teaching Methodology Case study: 20%, lecture: 45%, student presentations: 15%, team projects: 20%.

STUDENT STATISTICS

Geographic Representation State residents 90%. By region: Northeast 95%. International 5%.

Undergraduate Majors Business 40%; engineering/technology 40%; humanities 10%; social sciences 10%.

Other Background Graduate degrees in other disciplines: 2%. Work experience: On average, students have 5 years of work experience on entrance to the program.

FACILITIES

Information Resources Main library with 226,700 bound volumes, 133,000 titles on microform.

Housing 7% of students in program live in college-owned or -operated housing.

Technology Computers are used heavily in course work. 92 computer terminals/PCs, linked by a campus-wide computer network, are available for use by students in program; they are located in the student center, the library, the computer center, computer labs. Students in the program are not required to have their own PC. $100 are budgeted per student for computer support.

Computer Resources/On-line Services

Training	No	CompuServe	No
Internet	Yes	Dun's	No
E-Mail	Yes	Dow Jones	No
Multimedia Center	Yes	Dialog	No
LEXIS/NEXIS	Yes	Bloomberg	No

ADMISSION

Acceptance 1994-95 Of those applying, 70% were accepted.

Entrance Requirements Bachelor's degree, prerequisite courses required for applicants with non-business degree, GMAT score of 500, minimum 2.5 GPA. Core courses waived through: previous course work.

Application Requirements Written essay, application form, copies of transcript, personal statement, 3 letters of recommendation.

Application Deadlines 8/30 for fall, 12/31 for spring.

FINANCIALS

Costs for 1994-95 Tuition: Full-time: $3,591/semester for state residents, $5,353/semester for nonresidents; Part-time day: $297/credit for state residents, $444/credit for nonresidents. Fees: Full-time: $215/semester for state residents, $215/semester for nonresidents; Part-time day: $60/semester for state residents, $60/semester for nonresidents. Average room and board costs are $3,456 per academic year (on-campus).

Financial Aid In 1994-95, 5% of candidates received some institutionally administered aid in the form of scholarships, assistantships, work-study. Total awards ranged from $1,500-$10,000. Financial aid is not available to part-time students. Application deadline: 3/1 for fall. Contact: Mr. Richard Woodland, Director of Financial Aid, 406 Penn, Camden, NJ 08102. (609) 225-6039.

INTERNATIONAL STUDENTS

Demographics 5% of students enrolled in the program are international; Asia 40%, Central America 20%, Europe 20%, South America 20%.

Services and Facilities International student center, visa services, counseling/support services.

Applying TOEFL required, minimum score of 550; proof of health; proof of adequate funds. Financial aid is not available to international students. Admission application deadlines: 5/30 for fall, 9/30 for spring. Contact: Ms. Janice Edwards, Graduate Admissions Associate Director, Graduate Admissions Office, Camden, NJ 08102. (609) 225-6104.

PLACEMENT

In 1993-94, 40 organizations participated in on-campus recruiting; 28 on-campus interviews were conducted. Placement services include alumni network, career counseling/planning, career fairs, career library, career placement, electronic job bank, job interviews, job search course, resume preparation, and resume referral to employers. Of 1994 graduates, 100% were employed within three months of graduation.

Program Contact: Ms. Dorothy Juliani, Administrative Assistant, Rutgers, The State University of New Jersey, Camden, School of Business, Camden, NJ 08102. (609) 225-6452; Fax: (609) 225-6231.

Rutgers, The State University of New Jersey, Newark

Graduate School of Management

Newark, New Jersey

OVERVIEW

Rutgers, The State University of New Jersey, Newark is a state-supported coed institution. Founded 1892. Setting: 33-acre urban campus. Total institutional enrollment: 48,000. Program was first offered in 1964. AACSB-accredited.

MBA HIGHLIGHTS

Entrance Difficulty****
Mean GMAT: 581
Mean GPA: 3.12

Cost $$
Tuition. $3,592/term
(Nonresident: $5,354/term)
Room & Board: $3,456

Enrollment Profile

Full-time: 403	Work Exp: 85%
Part-time: 1,006	International: 8%
Total: 1,409	Women: 35%
Average Age: 28	Minorities: 23%

Average Class Size: 35

ACADEMICS

Length of Program Minimum: 15 months. Maximum: 8 years.

Calendar Trimesters.

Full-time Classes Main campus, New Brunswick, Princeton; day, evening, summer.

Part-time Classes Main campus, New Brunswick, Princeton; day, evening, early morning.

Degree Requirements 60 credits including 24 elective credits. Other: Proficiency examinations in calculus and statistics; Capstone consulting project.

Required Courses Accounting for managers, aggregate economic analysis, deterministic optimization models, financial management, international business environment, legal environment, managerial economic analysis, marketing management, operations management, organizational behavior, statistical models. Courses may be waived through: previous course work.

Curricular Focus Economic and financial theory, entrepreneurship, problem solving and decision making.

Concentrations Accounting, arts administration, economics, entrepreneurship, finance, human resources management, international business, management, management information systems, marketing, operations management, organizational behavior, quantitative analysis, real estate, strategic management.

Faculty Full-time: 60, 100% with doctorates; part-time: 72, 50% with doctorates.

Teaching Methodology Case study: 10%, faculty seminars: 10%, lecture: 60%, student presentations: 10%, team projects: 10%.

Special Opportunities International exchange in France. Internships include accounting, finance, and marketing.

STUDENT STATISTICS

Geographic Representation State residents 88%. By region: Northeast 91%. International 8%.

Undergraduate Majors Business 27%; engineering/technology 13%; humanities 7%; science/mathematics 11%; social sciences 5%; other 37%.

Other Background Graduate degrees in other disciplines: 10%. Work experience: On average, students have 5 years of work experience on entrance to the program.

FACILITIES

Information Resources Main library with 357,000 bound volumes, 517,000 titles on microform. Business collection includes 100,000 bound volumes, 500 periodical subscriptions, 30 CD-ROMs.

Housing 10% of students in program live in college-owned or -operated housing.

Technology Computers are used moderately in course work. 90 computer terminals/PCs, linked by a campus-wide computer network, are available for use by students in program; they are located in classrooms, the computer center, computer labs. Students in the program are not required to have their own PC. $900 are budgeted per student for computer support.

Computer Resources/On-line Services

Training	Yes	E-Mail	No
Internet	Yes	Dow Jones	Yes

Other on-line services: RLIN, OCLC.

ADMISSION

Acceptance 1994-95 Of those applying, 34% were accepted.

Entrance Requirements Bachelor's degree, GMAT score, minimum 2.8 GPA. Core courses waived through: previous course work.

Application Requirements Written essay, application form, copies of transcript, 2 letters of recommendation.

Application Deadlines 5/15 for fall, 11/15 for spring.

FINANCIALS

Costs for 1994-95 Tuition: Full-time: $3,592/term for state residents, $5,354/term for nonresidents; Part-time day: $297/credit for state

residents, $444/credit for nonresidents. Fees: Full-time: $215/term for state residents, $215/term for nonresidents; Part-time day: $60/term for state residents, $60/term for nonresidents. Average room and board costs are $3,456 per academic year (on-campus) and $6,300 per academic year (off-campus).

Financial Aid In 1994-95, 35% of candidates received some institutionally administered aid in the form of grants, scholarships, loans, fellowships, work-study. Financial aid is available to part-time students. Application deadlines: 6/1 for fall, 11/1 for spring. Contact: Ms. Alfreda P. Robinson, Assistant Dean, 92 New Street, Newark, NJ 07102. (201) 648-5651.

INTERNATIONAL STUDENTS

Demographics 8% of students enrolled in the program are international.

Services and Facilities ESL courses, counseling/support services.

Applying TOEFL required, minimum score of 600; proof of adequate funds. Financial aid is not available to international students. Admission application deadline: 3/15 for fall. Contact: Mr. Mark Carnesi, Coordinator, International Student Services, Smith Hall, Room 227, 101 Warren Street, Newark, NJ 07102. (201) 648-1427.

ALTERNATE MBA PROGRAMS

Executive MBA (EMBA) Length of program: Minimum: 24 months. Maximum: 8 years. Degree requirements: 60 credits including 12 elective credits.

MBA/JD Length of program: Minimum: 36 months. Maximum: 6 years. Degree requirements: 150 credits including 24 elective credits.

PLACEMENT

In 1993-94, 42 organizations participated in on-campus recruiting; 432 on-campus interviews were conducted. Placement services include alumni network, career counseling/planning, career fairs, career library, career placement, electronic job bank, job interviews, job search course, resume preparation, and resume referral to employers. Of 1994 graduates, 55% were employed within three months of graduation, the average starting salary was $51,245, the range was $30,000-$62,000.

Jobs by Employer Type Manufacturing 38%; service 40%; consulting 20%.

Jobs by Functional Area Marketing/sales 18%; finance 48%; operations 2%; management 9%; technical management 2%; human resources 4%; consulting 13%.

Program Contact: Ms. Alfreda Robinson, Dean of Admissions, Rutgers, The State University of New Jersey, Newark, 92 New Street, Newark, NJ 07102. (201) 648-5651; Fax: (201) 648-1592.

Saint Peter's College

Jersey City, New Jersey

OVERVIEW

Saint Peter's College is an independent Roman Catholic (Jesuit) comprehensive coed institution. Founded 1872. Setting: 10-acre urban campus with easy access to New York City. Total institutional enrollment: 3,500. Program was first offered in 1986.

MBA HIGHLIGHTS

Entrance Difficulty**
Mean GMAT: 400
Mean GPA: 3.4

Cost $$
Tuition: $376/credit
Room & Board: $1,530

Enrollment Profile

Full-time: 6	Work Exp: 92%
Part-time: 53	International: 10%
Total: 59	Women: 37%
Average Age: N/R	Minorities: 23%

Average Class Size: 25

ACADEMICS

Length of Program Minimum: 36 months. Maximum: 5 years.

Calendar Trimesters.

Full-time Classes Main campus, Englewood Cliffs; evening, summer.

Degree Requirements 48 credits including 12 elective credits. Other: Written or video presentation.

Required Courses Business ethics, computer networks, computer-based information systems, concepts of database and database management systems, effective business communication, human behavior in organizations, managerial control systems, managerial finance, microeconomics, operations research, strategic management planning.

Curricular Focus International business, management information systems, problem solving and decision making.

Concentrations International business, management, management information systems.

Faculty Full-time: 15, 73% with doctorates; part-time: 15, 47% with doctorates.

Teaching Methodology Case study: 10%, lecture: 65%, research: 10%, student presentations: 10%, team projects: 5%.

STUDENT STATISTICS
Geographic Representation International 10%.

Other Background Graduate degrees in other disciplines: 5%. Work experience: On average, students have 4-5 years of work experience on entrance to the program.

FACILITIES
Information Resources Main library with 320,958 bound volumes, 65,276 titles on microform, 1,455 periodical subscriptions, 5,169 records/tapes/CDs, 5 CD-ROMs.

Housing College housing available.

Technology Computers are used heavily in course work. 125 computer terminals/PCs, linked by a campus-wide computer network, are available for use by students in program; they are located in dormitories, classrooms, learning resource center, the library, the computer center, computer labs. Students in the program are not required to have their own PC.

Computer Resources/On-line Services

Training	Yes	CompuServe	No
Internet	Yes	Dun's	No
E-Mail	Yes	Dow Jones	No
Multimedia Center	Yes	Dialog	Yes
LEXIS/NEXIS	No	Bloomberg	No

ADMISSION
Acceptance 1994-95 79 applied for admission; 97% were accepted.

Entrance Requirements Bachelor's degree, prerequisite courses required for applicants with non-business degree, GMAT score.

Application Requirements Written essay, application form, copies of transcript, 3 letters of recommendation.

Application Deadlines 9/1 for fall, 11/17 for winter, 2/17 for spring. Applications are processed on a rolling basis. Application discs available.

FINANCIALS
Costs for 1995-96 Tuition: Full-time: $376/credit. Average room and board costs are $1,530 per academic year (on-campus) and $4,500 per academic year (off-campus).

Financial Aid In 1994-95, candidates received some institutionally administered aid in the form of loans. Financial aid is not available to part-time students. Application deadlines: 8/1 for fall, 1/1 for winter, 2/1 for spring. Contact: Director of Student Financial Aid, 2641 Kennedy Boulevard, Jersey City, NJ 07306. (201) 915-9308.

INTERNATIONAL STUDENTS
Demographics 10% of students enrolled in the program are international; Asia 82%, Africa 12%, Europe 3%, other 3%.

Services and Facilities Counseling/support services.

Applying TOEFL required, minimum score of 500; proof of health; proof of adequate funds. Financial aid is not available to international students. Admission application deadlines: 8/11 for fall, 11/3 for winter, 1/27 for spring. Applications are processed on a rolling basis. Contact: Dr. Alessandro Calianese, Director, MBA Program, 2641 Kennedy Boulevard, Jersey City, NJ 07306. (201) 915-9375.

PLACEMENT
Placement services include alumni network and career placement.

Program Contact: Dr. Alessandro Calianese, Director, MBA Program, Saint Peter's College, 2641 Kennedy Boulevard, Jersey City, NJ 07306. (201) 915-9375; Fax: (201) 435-3662.

Seton Hall University

W. Paul Stillman School of Business

South Orange, New Jersey

OVERVIEW
Seton Hall University is an independent Roman Catholic coed institution. Founded 1856. Setting: 58-acre suburban campus with easy access to New York City. Total institutional enrollment: 8,800. Program was first offered in 1951. AACSB-accredited.

MBA HIGHLIGHTS

Entrance Difficulty****
Mean GMAT: 540
Mean GPA: 3.1

Cost $$$
Tuition: $431/credit
Room & Board: $6,500

Enrollment Profile

Full-time: 88		Work Exp: 95%
Part-time: 734		International: N/R
Total: 822		Women: 37%
Average Age: 29		Minorities: N/R

Average Class Size: 21

The graduate programs of the W. Paul Stillman School of Business have professional accreditation from the American Assembly of Collegiate Schools of Business. Seton Hall was the first private university in the state of New Jersey to have earned this accreditation which recognizes that the programs meet the highest academic and professional standards. The Master of Science in International Business is a 33-credit program innovatively designed around 6-credit course modules. The modules provide integrated knowledge about the global business environment and formulation of global business strategies. The curriculum consists of classes in global business environment, economic forecasting and financial strategies for global enterprise, management and marketing strategies for global enterprise, global business electives, global business strategy (capstone), and a practicum. The practicum provides those students without significant international experience with either graduate course work in business approved by Seton Hall and taken outside the United States or an independent research project or internship in the United States with an approved international agency. A joint M.B.A./M.S.I.B. program is also available with 15 credits to be used as cross-credits between the two programs.

ACADEMICS
Length of Program Minimum: 24 months. Maximum: 5 years.

Calendar Semesters.

Full-time Classes Main campus; evening, summer.

Part-time Classes Main campus; evening, summer.

Degree Requirements 60 credits including 27 elective credits.

Required Courses Business policy, corporate financial management, financial accounting, legal and social environment of business, management and organizational behavior, management information systems, managerial accounting, marketing strategies, operations management, statistical inference in decision making, the national economy.

Curricular Focus International business.

Concentrations Accounting, economics, finance, human resources management, international business, management, management information systems, marketing, quantitative analysis.

Faculty Full-time: 48, 89% with doctorates; part-time: 10, 50% with doctorates.

Teaching Methodology Case study: 10%, lecture: 40%, research: 10%, seminars by members of the business community: 10%, student presentations: 10%, team projects: 20%.

Special Opportunities International exchange in Czech Republic, France, Japan, People's Republic of China, Poland, Russia, United Kingdom. Internships include accounting in telecommunications, finance in pharmaceutical, marketing in banking, management in utilities, and management information systems.

STUDENT STATISTICS
Other Background Graduate degrees in other disciplines: 10%. Work experience: On average, students have 5 years of work experience on entrance to the program.

FACILITIES
Information Resources Main library with 403,350 bound volumes, 24,250 titles on microform, 2,163 periodical subscriptions.

Housing 1% of students in program live in college-owned or -operated housing.

Technology Computers are used moderately in course work. 900 computer terminals/PCs, linked by a campus-wide computer network, are available for use by students in program; they are located in student rooms, the student center, classrooms, learning resource center, the library, the computer center, computer labs. Students in the program are not required to have their own PC. $1,000 are budgeted per student for computer support.

Computer Resources/On-line Services
Training	Yes	CompuServe	No
Internet	Yes	Dun's	Yes
E-Mail	Yes	Dow Jones	Yes
Multimedia Center	Yes	Dialog	No
LEXIS/NEXIS	Yes	Bloomberg	No

Other on-line services: Westlaw.

ADMISSION
Acceptance 1994-95 466 applied for admission; 65% were accepted.

Entrance Requirements Bachelor's degree, GMAT score of 500. Core courses waived through: previous course work.

Application Requirements Written essay, application form, copies of transcript, resume/curriculum vitae, 3 letters of recommendation.

Application Deadlines 4/1 for fall, 10/1 for spring. Applications are processed on a rolling basis.

FINANCIALS
Costs for 1994-95 Tuition: Full-time: $431/credit. Fees: Full-time: $105/semester. Average room and board costs are $6,500 per academic year (on-campus).

Financial Aid In 1994-95, 20% of candidates received some institutionally administered aid in the form of assistantships, work-study. Financial aid is available to part-time students. Application deadlines: 4/1 for fall, 10/1 for spring. Applications are processed on a rolling basis. Contact: Mr. Michael Menendez, Director of Financial Aid, W. Paul Stillman School of Business, South Orange, NJ 07079-2697. (201) 761-9350.

INTERNATIONAL STUDENTS
Services and Facilities International student office, international student center, visa services, ESL courses, special assistance for nonnative speakers of English, counseling/support services.

Applying TOEFL required, minimum score of 600; proof of adequate funds. Financial aid is available to international students. Applications are processed on a rolling basis. Admission applications are processed on a rolling basis. Contact: Ms. Kathleen Reilly, Director, International Programs, W. Paul Stillman School of Business, South Orange, NJ 07079-2697. (201) 761-9081.

ALTERNATE MBA PROGRAM
MBA/MS Length of program: Minimum: 24 months. Maximum: 5 years. Degree requirements: 33 credits including 18 elective credits. MS is in international business.

PLACEMENT
In 1993-94, 675 organizations participated in on-campus recruiting; 50 on-campus interviews were conducted. Placement services include alumni network, career counseling/planning, career fairs, career library, career placement, electronic job bank, job interviews, job search course, resume preparation, and resume referral to employers. Of 1994 graduates, 100% were employed within three months of graduation.

Program Contact: Ms. Carmine Fusco, Graduate Student Adviser, Seton Hall University, W. Paul Stillman School of Business, Room 103, South Orange, NJ 07079-2697. (201) 761-9222, or (800) THE HALL; Fax: (201) 761-9217; Internet Address: gradbus@lanmail.shu.edu.

William Paterson College of New Jersey

School of Humanities, Management, and Social Sciences

Wayne, New Jersey

OVERVIEW
William Paterson College of New Jersey is a state-supported comprehensive coed institution. Part of New Jersey State College System. Founded 1855. Setting: 250-acre suburban campus with easy access to New York City. Total institutional enrollment: 10,000.

MBA HIGHLIGHTS

Entrance Difficulty**
Mean GMAT: 475
Mean GPA: N/R

Cost $
Tuition: $148/credit
(Nonresident: $210/credit)
Room & Board: N/R

Enrollment Profile
Full-time: 0	Work Exp: N/R
Part-time: 130	International: N/R
Total: 130	Women: N/R
Average Age: N/R	Minorities: N/R

Average Class Size: 15

ACADEMICS
Length of Program Minimum: 24 months.

Calendar Semesters.

Full-time Classes Main campus; evening, summer.

Part-time Classes Main campus; evening, summer.

Degree Requirements 42 credits including 6 elective credits.

Required Courses Business policy seminar, computers and applications, economic analysis, financial accounting, financial management, legal environment of business, management information systems, management process and organizational theory, managerial accounting, marketing management, multinational business environment and operations, organizational behavior and communication, production management, statistics for quantitative analysis.

Curricular Focus Business issues and problems, general management, strategic analysis and planning.

Concentrations Accounting, finance, management, marketing.

Teaching Methodology Case study: 25%, lecture: 25%, student presentations: 25%, team projects: 25%.

FACILITIES
Information Resources Main library with 307,000 bound volumes, 102,000 titles on microform, 1,400 periodical subscriptions, 6,858 records/tapes/CDs.

ADMISSION
Acceptance 1994-95 Of those applying, 80% were accepted.

Entrance Requirements Bachelor's degree, GMAT score. Core courses waived through: previous course work.

Application Requirements Application form, copies of transcript, personal statement.

Application Deadlines 8/1 for fall, 11/1 for spring. Applications are processed on a rolling basis.

FINANCIALS
Costs for 1994-95 Tuition: Full-time: $148/credit for state residents, $210/credit for nonresidents. Fees: Full-time: $20/credit for state residents, $20/credit for nonresidents.

Financial Aid Application deadline: 6/1 for fall. Contact: Ms. Diane Ackerman, Director of Financial Aid, 300 Pompton Road, Wayne, NJ 07470-8420. (201) 595-2202.

INTERNATIONAL STUDENTS
Applying TOEFL required, minimum score of 550; proof of adequate funds. Financial aid is available to international students. Applications are processed on a rolling basis. Admission application deadlines: 6/1 for fall, 8/1 for spring. Contact: Ms. Barbara Milne, International Student Adviser, 300 Pompton Road, Wayne, NJ 07470-8420. (201) 595-2000.

Program Contact: Dr. E. J. Knaus, Director, MBA Program, William Paterson College of New Jersey, 300 Pompton Road, Wayne, NJ 07470-8420. (201) 831-7598; Fax: (201) 831-2665.

NEW MEXICO

College of Santa Fe

Business Department

Santa Fe, New Mexico

OVERVIEW
College of Santa Fe is an independent nonprofit comprehensive coed institution. Founded 1947. Setting: 98-acre small-town campus with easy access to Albuquerque. Total institutional enrollment: 1,650. Program was first offered in 1985.

MBA HIGHLIGHTS

Entrance Difficulty**
Mean GMAT: 450
Mean GPA: 3.0

Cost $$
Tuition: $204/credit hour
Room & Board: $6,000 (off-campus)

Enrollment Profile
Full-time: 27	Work Exp: 99%
Part-time: 118	International: 2%
Total: 145	Women: 58%
Average Age: 38	Minorities: 50%

Average Class Size: 12

ACADEMICS
Length of Program Minimum: 12 months. Maximum: 5 years.

Calendar 2 nine-week terms per semester.

Full-time Classes Main campus, Albuquerque; evening, weekends, summer.

Part-time Classes Main campus; evening, weekends, summer.

Degree Requirements 36 credits including 9 elective credits.

Required Courses Global business environment, leadership and motivation, management information systems and software planning tools, managerial communication, managerial economics, managerial finance, managerial statistics, marketing strategy and competitive analysis, strategic thinking in management.

Curricular Focus Business issues and problems, general management, problem solving and decision making.

Concentrations Finance, human resources management, management, management information systems.

Faculty Full-time: 7, 25% with doctorates; part-time: 14.

Teaching Methodology Case study: 25%, lecture: 25%, research: 10%, seminars by members of the business community: 5%, student presentations: 10%, team projects: 25%.

STUDENT STATISTICS
Geographic Representation State residents 95%. By region: West 98%. International 2%.

Undergraduate Majors Business 70%; engineering/technology 5%; humanities 5%; science/mathematics 5%; social sciences 10%; other 5%.

Other Background Graduate degrees in other disciplines: 5%. Work experience: On average, students have 10 years of work experience on entrance to the program.

FACILITIES
Information Resources Main library with 150,000 bound volumes, 314 titles on microform, 398 periodical subscriptions, 7,268 records/tapes/CDs, 25 CD-ROMs. Business collection includes 2,500 bound volumes, 69 periodical subscriptions, 1 CD-ROM, 20 videos.

Housing College housing available.

Technology Computers are used moderately in course work. Computer terminals/PCs are available for use by students in program; they are located in computer labs. Students in the program are not required to have their own PC.

Computer Resources/On-line Services
Internet	Yes	Dialog	Yes
E-Mail	Yes		

ADMISSION
Acceptance 1994-95 Of those applying, 95% were accepted.

Entrance Requirements Bachelor's degree, GMAT score of 450, minimum 3.0 GPA.

Application Requirements Interview, application form, copies of transcript, 2 letters of recommendation.

Application Deadline Applications are processed on a rolling basis.

FINANCIALS
Costs for 1994-95 Tuition: Full-time: $204/credit hour. Average room and board costs are $6,000 per academic year (off-campus).

Financial Aid In 1994-95, candidates received some institutionally administered aid in the form of loans. Financial aid is available to part-time students. Application deadline: 5/1 for fall. Contact: Ms. Marian Ruzicka, Director, 1600 Saint Michael's Drive, Santa Fe, NM 87501. (505) 473-6459.

INTERNATIONAL STUDENTS
Demographics 2% of students enrolled in the program are international.

Services and Facilities Counseling/support services.

Applying TOEFL required, minimum score of 500; proof of health; proof of adequate funds; transcripts must be in English. Financial aid is available to international students. Admission applications are processed on a rolling basis.

PLACEMENT
Placement services include career placement. Of 1994 graduates, 95% were employed within three months of graduation.

Program Contact: Mr. Dan Brehery, Chair, Business Department, College of Santa Fe, 1600 Saint Michael's Drive, Santa Fe, NM 87501. (505) 473-6212, or (800) 456-2673; Fax: (505) 473-6504.

Eastern New Mexico University

College of Business

Portales, New Mexico

OVERVIEW
Eastern New Mexico University is a state-supported comprehensive coed institution. Part of Eastern New Mexico University System. Founded 1934. Setting: 240-acre small-town campus. Total institutional enrollment: 4,000. Program was first offered in 1949.

MBA HIGHLIGHTS

Entrance Difficulty**
Mean GMAT: 550
Mean GPA: 3.18

Cost $
Tuition: $591/semester
(Nonresident: $2,622/semester)
Room & Board: $3,148

Enrollment Profile
Full-time: 19	Work Exp: 65%
Part-time: 79	International: 21%
Total: 98	Women: 36%
Average Age: 31	Minorities: 20%

Average Class Size: 12

ACADEMICS
Length of Program Minimum: 15 months. Maximum: 6 years.

Calendar Semesters.

Full-time Classes Main campus; day, evening, summer.

Part-time Classes Main campus; day, evening, summer.

Degree Requirements 33 credits including 9 elective credits. Other: Comprehensive exam.

Required Courses Advanced business policy, advanced studies of organizational behavior, applications in CIS, managerial accounting, managerial economics, managerial finance, marketing management, survey of management science.

Curricular Focus General management, leadership, problem solving and decision making.

Concentration Management.

Faculty Full-time: 15, 100% with doctorates.

Teaching Methodology Case study: 35%, lecture: 35%, research: 5%, student presentations: 15%, team projects: 10%.

STUDENT STATISTICS

Geographic Representation State residents 79%. International 21%.

Undergraduate Majors Business 70%; engineering/technology 30%.

Other Background Work experience: On average, students have 3 years of work experience on entrance to the program.

FACILITIES

Information Resources Main library with 368,000 bound volumes, 67,230 titles on microform, 1,328 periodical subscriptions, 31,081 records/tapes/CDs.

Housing 30% of students in program live in college-owned or -operated housing.

Technology Computers are used heavily in course work. 50 computer terminals/PCs, linked by a campus-wide computer network, are available for use by students in program; they are located in learning resource center, computer labs, graduate student offices. Students in the program are not required to have their own PC.

Computer Resources/On-line Services

Training	Yes	E-Mail	Yes
Internet	Yes	Videoconference Center	Yes

ADMISSION

Acceptance 1994-95 37 applied for admission; 100% were accepted.

Entrance Requirements Bachelor's degree, GMAT score of 450, minimum 3.0 GPA. Core courses waived through: previous course work.

Application Requirements Application form, copies of transcript.

Application Deadline Applications are processed on a rolling basis. Application discs available.

FINANCIALS

Costs for 1994-95 Tuition: Full-time: $591/semester for state residents, $2,622/semester for nonresidents. Fees: Full-time: $258/semester for state residents, $258/semester for nonresidents. Average room and board costs are $3,148 per academic year (on-campus) and $3,148 per academic year (off-campus).

Financial Aid In 1994-95, candidates received some institutionally administered aid in the form of fellowships, assistantships. Contact: Financial Aid Office, Portales, NM 88130. (505) 562-2194.

INTERNATIONAL STUDENTS

Demographics 21% of students enrolled in the program are international.

Services and Facilities International student office, language tutoring.

Applying TOEFL required, minimum score of 550; proof of health; proof of adequate funds. Financial aid is not available to international students. Admission applications are processed on a rolling basis. Contact: Dr. William Brunsen, Coordinator, Program in Business Administration, Portales, NM 88130. (505) 562-1011.

PLACEMENT

Placement services include career counseling/planning, career fairs, career placement, job interviews, resume preparation, and resume referral to employers. Of 1994 graduates, 100% were employed within three months of graduation.

Program Contact: Dr. William Brunsen, Graduate Coordinator, Eastern New Mexico University, Portales, NM 88130. (505) 562-2744; Fax: (505) 562-4331.

New Mexico Highlands University

School of Business

Las Vegas, New Mexico

OVERVIEW

New Mexico Highlands University is a state-supported comprehensive coed institution. Founded 1893. Setting: 120-acre small-town campus. Total institutional enrollment: 2,900.

MBA HIGHLIGHTS

Entrance Difficulty***

Cost $

Tuition: $696/semester
(Nonresident: $2,600/semester)
Room & Board: $3,900 (off-campus)

Enrollment Profile

Full-time: 51	Work Exp: 98%
Part-time: 6	International: 3%
Total: 57	Women: 51%
Average Age: 28	Minorities: 80%

Average Class Size: 10

ACADEMICS

Length of Program Minimum: 18 months. Maximum: 5 years.

Calendar Semesters.

Full-time Classes Main campus; day, evening, summer.

Part-time Classes Main campus; day, evening, summer.

Degree Requirements 36 credits.

Curricular Focus Leadership, minorities in business, problem solving and decision making.

Concentrations Accounting, management.

Faculty Full-time: 1, 100% with doctorates; part-time: 12, 60% with doctorates.

Teaching Methodology Case study: 20%, faculty seminars: 5%, lecture: 40%, research: 10%, seminars by members of the business community: 5%, student presentations: 10%, team projects: 10%.

Special Opportunities Internship program available.

STUDENT STATISTICS

Geographic Representation State residents 91%. International 3%.

Undergraduate Majors Business 100%.

Other Background Graduate degrees in other disciplines: 100%.

FACILITIES

Information Resources Main library with 216,657 bound volumes, 125,465 titles on microform, 1,238 periodical subscriptions, 30 records/tapes/CDs.

Housing College housing available.

Technology Computers are used moderately in course work. Computer terminals/PCs are available for use by students in program; they are located in computer labs. Students in the program are not required to have their own PC.

Computer Resources/On-line Services

Training	Yes	E-Mail	Yes

ADMISSION

Acceptance 1994-95 17 applied for admission; 94% were accepted.

Entrance Requirements Bachelor's degree, minimum 3.0 GPA, review by committee. Core courses waived through: previous course work.

Application Requirements Application form.

Application Deadline Applications are processed on a rolling basis. Application discs available.

FINANCIALS

Costs for 1994-95 Tuition: Full-time: $696/semester for state residents, $2,600/semester for nonresidents; Part-time day: $58/semester hour for state residents, $58/semester hour for nonresidents. Fees: Full-time: $45/semester for state residents, $45/semester for nonresidents; Part-time day: $45/semester for state residents, $45/semester for nonresidents. Average room and board costs are $3,900 per academic year (off-campus).

Financial Aid In 1994-95, 90% of candidates received some institutionally administered aid in the form of scholarships, loans, fellowships, assistantships, work-study. Financial aid is available to part-time students.

Application deadline: 3/1 for fall. Contact: Ms. Darlene Ortiz, Financial Aid Director, Las Vegas, NM 87701. (505) 454-3318.

INTERNATIONAL STUDENTS

Demographics 3% of students enrolled in the program are international.

Applying TOEFL required; proof of adequate funds. Financial aid is not available to international students. Admission applications are processed on a rolling basis.

PLACEMENT

Placement services include alumni network, career counseling/planning, career fairs, career library, career placement, job interviews, resume preparation, and resume referral to employers.

Program Contact: Dr. Manuel Ferran, MBA Coordinator, New Mexico Highlands University, Las Vegas, NM 87701. (505) 454-3575; Fax: (505) 454-0026.

New Mexico State University

College of Business Administration and Economics

Las Cruces, New Mexico

OVERVIEW

New Mexico State University is a state-supported coed institution. Part of New Mexico State University System. Founded 1888. Setting: 5,800-acre small-town campus with easy access to El Paso. Total institutional enrollment: 17,000. Program was first offered in 1969. AACSB-accredited.

MBA HIGHLIGHTS

Entrance Difficulty***
Mean GMAT: 520
Mean GPA: 3.3

Cost $
Tuition: $1,050/semester
(Nonresident: $3,276/semester)
Room & Board: $2,244

Enrollment Profile

Full-time: 87	Work Exp: 85%
Part-time: 71	International: N/R
Total: 158	Women: 55%
Average Age: 32	Minorities: 32%

Average Class Size: 18

ACADEMICS

Length of Program Minimum: 24 months. Maximum: 7 years.

Calendar Semesters.

Full-time Classes Main campus; day, evening, weekends, summer.

Part-time Classes Main campus; day, evening, weekends, summer.

Degree Requirements 36 credits including 15 elective credits.

Curricular Focus Entrepreneurship, international business, strategic analysis and planning.

Concentrations Economics, entrepreneurship, finance, health services, human resources management, international business, management, management information systems, marketing, operations management, transportation.

Faculty Full-time: 54, 100% with doctorates.

Teaching Methodology Case study: 15%, faculty seminars: 10%, lecture: 30%, research: 15%, student presentations: 10%, team projects: 20%.

Special Opportunities International exchange in Mexico, Pakistan. Internships include power generation.

STUDENT STATISTICS

Geographic Representation State residents 40%. By region: West 50%; Midwest 10%; South 8%.

Undergraduate Majors Business 70%; education 1%; engineering/technology 18%; humanities 2%; nursing 1%; science/mathematics 4%; social sciences 2%; other 2%.

Other Background Graduate degrees in other disciplines: 5%. Work experience: On average, students have 6 years of work experience on entrance to the program.

FACILITIES

Information Resources Main library with 848,838 bound volumes, 402,895 titles on microform, 6,718 periodical subscriptions, 31 records/tapes/CDs, 30 CD-ROMs.

Housing 35% of students in program live in college-owned or -operated housing.

Technology Computers are used heavily in course work. 300 computer terminals/PCs, linked by a campus-wide computer network, are available for use by students in program; they are located in classrooms, learning resource center, the library, the computer center, computer labs, the research center. Students in the program are not required to have their own PC. $400 are budgeted per student for computer support.

Computer Resources/On-line Services

Training	Yes	Multimedia Center	Yes
Internet	Yes	CompuServe	Yes
E-Mail	No		

ADMISSION

Acceptance 1994-95 78 applied for admission; 53% were accepted.

Entrance Requirements Bachelor's degree, GMAT score of 500, minimum 3.0 GPA.

Application Requirements Interview, application form, copies of transcript, resume/curriculum vitae.

Application Deadlines 7/1 for fall, 11/1 for spring. Application discs available.

FINANCIALS

Costs for 1994-95 Tuition: Full-time: $1,050/semester for state residents, $3,276/semester for nonresidents; Part-time day: $88/credit for state residents, $88-$273/credit for nonresidents; Summer: $63-$88/credit for state residents, $63-$88/credit for nonresidents. Average room and board costs are $2,244 per academic year (on-campus) and $4,800 per academic year (off-campus).

Financial Aid In 1994-95, 60% of candidates received some institutionally administered aid in the form of grants, scholarships, loans, fellowships, assistantships, work-study. Total awards ranged from $1,000-$3,600. Financial aid is not available to part-time students. Application deadlines: 8/1 for fall, 11/1 for spring. Contact: Dr. Joe Benson, Director of MBA Program, Box 30001 Department 3GSP, Las Cruces, NM 88003. (505) 646-8003.

INTERNATIONAL STUDENTS

Demographics 30% of students on campus are international; Asia 70%, Africa 10%, Australia 5%, Central America 5%, South America 5%, Europe 3%, Other 2%.

Services and Facilities International student office, international student center, language tutoring, ESL courses, special assistance for nonnative speakers of English.

Applying TOEFL required, minimum score of 550; proof of health; proof of adequate funds. Financial aid is not available to international students. Admission application deadlines: 7/1 for fall, 8/1 for spring. Applications are processed on a rolling basis.

PLACEMENT

In 1993-94, 23 organizations participated in on-campus recruiting. Placement services include alumni network, career fairs, career library, career placement, job interviews, resume preparation, and resume referral to employers. Of 1994 graduates, 81% were employed within three months of graduation, the average starting salary range was $28,000-$29,000.

Jobs by Employer Type Manufacturing 80%; service 12%; government 8%.

Program Contact: Dr. Joe Benson, Director, MBA Program, New Mexico State University, Box 30001 Department 3GSP, Las Cruces, NM 88003. (505) 646-8003 Ext. 5164; Fax: (505) 646-6155.

University of New Mexico

Robert O. Anderson Graduate School of Management

Albuquerque, New Mexico

OVERVIEW

The University of New Mexico is a state-supported coed institution. Founded 1889. Setting: 625-acre urban campus. Total institutional enrollment: 26,000. Program was first offered in 1947. AACSB-accredited.

MBA HIGHLIGHTS

Entrance Difficulty***
Mean GMAT: 550
Mean GPA: 3.3

Cost $
Tuition: $86/credit hour
(Nonresident: $305/credit hour)
Room & Board: $12,000 (off-campus)

Enrollment Profile

Full-time: 284	Work Exp: 85%
Part-time: 198	International: 5%
Total: 482	Women: 40%
Average Age: 30	Minorities: 28%

Average Class Size: 30

ACADEMICS

Length of Program Minimum: 24 months. Maximum: 5 years.

Calendar Semesters.

Full-time Classes Main campus; day, summer.

Part-time Classes Main campus; day, evening, summer.

Degree Requirements 60 credits including 18 elective credits.

Curricular Focus Business issues and problems, general management, international business.

Concentrations Accounting, finance, human resources management, international business, management information systems, marketing, operations management, public policy, tax accounting, international management in Latin America.

Faculty Full-time: 44, 98% with doctorates.

Teaching Methodology Case study: 10%, lecture: 50%, research: 10%, student presentations: 10%, team projects: 20%.

Special Opportunities Internship program available.

STUDENT STATISTICS

Geographic Representation State residents 44%. International 5%.

Undergraduate Majors Business 41%; engineering/technology 26%; social sciences 21%; other 12%.

Other Background Work experience: On average, students have 7 years of work experience on entrance to the program.

FACILITIES

Information Resources Main library with 1.9 million bound volumes, 1.8 million titles on microform, 22,000 periodical subscriptions, 33,700 records/tapes/CDs.

Housing College housing not available.

Technology Computers are used heavily in course work. 280 computer terminals/PCs, linked by a campus-wide computer network, are available for use by students in program; they are located in classrooms, computer labs. Students in the program are not required to have their own PC.

Computer Resources/On-line Services

Training	Yes	E-Mail	Yes
Internet	Yes		

ADMISSION

Acceptance 1994-95 Of those applying, 50% were accepted.

Entrance Requirements Bachelor's degree, GMAT score of 500, minimum 3.0 GPA for last 60 hours of bachelors degree. Core courses waived through: previous course work.

Application Requirements Application form, copies of transcript, resume/curriculum vitae, personal statement.

Application Deadlines 7/1 for fall, 11/15 for spring, 4/15 for summer.

FINANCIALS

Costs for 1994-95 Tuition: Full-time: $86/credit hour for state residents, $305/credit hour for nonresidents. Fees: Full-time: $16/semester for state residents, $16/semester for nonresidents. Average room and board costs are $12,000 per academic year (off-campus).

Financial Aid In 1994-95, candidates received some institutionally administered aid in the form of grants, scholarships, loans, fellowships, assistantships, work-study. Financial aid is available to part-time students. Application deadlines: 1/15 for fall, 8/25 for spring. Contact: Mr. John Whiteside, Director of Financial Aid, Mesa Vista Hall, Room 1030, Albuquerque, NM 87131-2039. (505) 277-2041.

INTERNATIONAL STUDENTS

Demographics 5% of students enrolled in the program are international.

Services and Facilities International student center, visa services, counseling/support services.

Applying TOEFL required, minimum score of 550; proof of health; proof of adequate funds; GPA converted to 4.0 scale. Financial aid is not available to international students. Admission application deadlines: 5/1 for fall, 10/1 for spring. Contact: Mr. Gerald Slavin, Director, International Services and Programs, Mesa Vista Hall 2111, Albuquerque, NM 87131-2039. (505) 277-4032.

ALTERNATE MBA PROGRAMS

Executive MBA (EMBA) Length of program: Minimum: 30 months. Maximum: 5 years. Degree requirements: 48 credits. Previous management position.

MBA/JD Length of program: Minimum: 48 months. Maximum: 5 years. Degree requirements: 128 credits including 9 elective credits.

MBA/MA Length of program: Minimum: 30 months. Maximum: 5 years. Degree requirements: 72 credits. Proficiency in Spanish or Portuguese. MA is in Latin American studies.

PLACEMENT

Placement services include alumni network, career counseling/planning, career fairs, career library, career placement, job interviews, resume preparation, and resume referral to employers.

Program Contact: Ms. Sue Podeyn, MBA Program Director, University of New Mexico, Albuquerque, NM 87131-2039. (505) 277-3147; Fax: (505) 277-9356; Internet Address: podeyn@unm.edu.

Western New Mexico University

Department of Business Administration

Silver City, New Mexico

OVERVIEW

Western New Mexico University is a state-supported comprehensive coed institution. Founded 1893. Setting: 83-acre small-town campus. Total institutional enrollment: 2,500.

MBA HIGHLIGHTS

Entrance Difficulty**
Mean GMAT: 400
Mean GPA: N/R

Cost $
Tuition: $787/semester
(Nonresident: $2,714/semester)
Room & Board: N/R

Total Enrollment: 30

Average Class Size: 10

ACADEMICS

Length of Program Minimum: 12 months. Maximum: 7 years.

Calendar Semesters.

Full-time Classes Main campus, Gallup; evening, weekends, summer.

Part-time Classes Main campus, Gallup; evening, weekends, summer.

Degree Requirements 36 credit hours.

Curricular Focus Business issues and problems, problem solving and decision making, strategic analysis and planning.

Concentration Management.

Teaching Methodology Case study: 25%, lecture: 50%, research: 10%, student presentations: 10%, team projects: 5%.

FACILITIES

Information Resources Main library with 148,500 bound volumes, 500,000 titles on microform, 1,000 periodical subscriptions, 2,500 records/tapes/CDs, 9 CD-ROMs.

ADMISSION

Entrance Requirements Bachelor's degree, GMAT score.

Application Requirements Application form.

Application Deadline Applications are processed on a rolling basis.

FINANCIALS
Costs for 1994-95 Tuition: Full-time: $787/semester for state residents, $2,714/semester for nonresidents; Part-time day: $312-$740/semester for state residents, $312-$2,506/semester for nonresidents.

Financial Aid In 1994-95, candidates received some institutionally administered aid in the form of loans, fellowships, assistantships, work-study. Financial aid is available to part-time students. Application deadline: 5/1 for fall. Applications are processed on a rolling basis. Contact: Ms. Terry Holguin, Assistant Director, Financial Aid, Financial Aid Office, Silver City, NM 88062-0680. (505) 538-6173.

INTERNATIONAL STUDENTS
Applying TOEFL required, minimum score of 550. Financial aid is not available to international students. Admission application deadlines: 6/1 for fall, 10/1 for spring. Applications are processed on a rolling basis.

Program Contact: Ms. Betsy Miller, Admissions Office Manager, Western New Mexico University, Admissions Office, Silver City, NM 88062-0638. (505) 538-6106; Fax: (501) 538-6155.

NEW YORK

Adelphi University

School of Management and Business

Garden City, New York

OVERVIEW
Adelphi University is an independent nonprofit coed institution. Founded 1896. Setting: 75-acre suburban campus with easy access to New York City. Total institutional enrollment: 8,012. Program was first offered in 1965.

MBA HIGHLIGHTS

Entrance Difficulty***
Mean GMAT: 450
Mean GPA: 3.0

Cost $$$
Tuition: $6,750/semester
Room & Board: $3,388

Enrollment Profile
Full-time: 50	Work Exp: 87%
Part-time: 685	International: 4%
Total: 735	Women: 44%
Average Age: 29	Minorities: N/R

Average Class Size: 30

ACADEMICS
Length of Program Minimum: 30 months. Maximum: 6 years.
Calendar Semesters.
Full-time Classes Main campus, Huntington; evening, summer.
Part-time Classes Main campus, Huntington; evening, summer.
Degree Requirements 45 credits including 21 elective credits.
Required Courses Accounting, economics, finance, international business, management, marketing, policy, production, quantitative methods. Courses may be waived through: previous course work.
Curricular Focus Business issues and problems, general management, problem solving and decision making, teamwork.
Concentrations Accounting, banking and financial markets, finance, health services, human resources management, international business, management, marketing.
Faculty Full-time: 23, 61% with doctorates; part-time: 8.
Teaching Methodology Case study: 8%, lecture: 75%, research: 5%, seminars by members of the business community: 2%, student presentations: 5%, team projects: 5%.
Special Opportunities Internships include accounting, marketing, and banking.

STUDENT STATISTICS
Geographic Representation State residents 95%. By region: Northeast 96%. International 4%.

Undergraduate Majors Business 42%; education 1%; engineering/technology 7%; humanities 9%; nursing 1%; science/mathematics 10%; social sciences 21%; other 9%.

Other Background Work experience: On average, students have 10 years of work experience on entrance to the program.

FACILITIES
Information Resources Main library with 478,462 bound volumes, 647,346 titles on microform, 3,475 periodical subscriptions, 19,126 records/tapes/CDs, 15 CD-ROMs. Business collection includes 54,281 bound volumes, 80 periodical subscriptions, 6 CD-ROMs, 45 videos.

Housing 1% of students in program live in college-owned or -operated housing.

Technology Computers are used moderately in course work. 78 computer terminals/PCs, linked by a campus-wide computer network, are available for use by students in program; they are located in the library, the computer center, computer labs. Students in the program are not required to have their own PC.

Computer Resources/On-line Services
Training	Yes	Multimedia Center	Yes
Internet	Yes	LEXIS/NEXIS	Yes
E-Mail	Yes	Dialog	Yes $

Other on-line services: OCLC, First Search, Carl.

ADMISSION
Acceptance 1994-95 Of those applying, 75% were accepted.

Entrance Requirements Bachelor's degree, GMAT score of 450, minimum 2.5 GPA. Core courses waived through: previous course work.

Application Requirements Written essay, application form, copies of transcript, resume/curriculum vitae, 3 letters of recommendation.

Application Deadlines 5/1 for fall, 11/1 for spring, 3/1 for summer.

FINANCIALS
Costs for 1994-95 Tuition: Full-time: $6,750/semester; Part-time evening: $400/credit; Summer: $400/credit. Fees: Part-time evening: $150; Summer: $150. Average room and board costs are $3,388 per academic year (on-campus) and $3,925 per academic year (off-campus).

Financial Aid In 1994-95, 1% of candidates received some institutionally administered aid in the form of loans, assistantships. Financial aid is not available to part-time students. Application deadline: 2/15 for fall. Contact: Mr. Joseph Posillico, Assistant Director, Office of Student Financial Services, Garden City, NY 11530. (516) 877-3080.

INTERNATIONAL STUDENTS
Demographics 4% of students enrolled in the program are international; Asia 33%, Other 67%.

Services and Facilities International student center, counseling/support services.

Applying TOEFL required, minimum score of 550; proof of adequate funds. Financial aid is not available to international students. Admission application deadlines: 5/1 for fall, 11/1 for spring, 3/1 for summer. Contact: Mr. George DeBeir, Director, International Student Services, South Avenue, Garden City, NY 11530. (516) 877-4988.

PLACEMENT
In 1993-94, 105 organizations participated in on-campus recruiting; 242 on-campus interviews were conducted. Placement services include career counseling/planning, career fairs, career library, career placement, job interviews, and resume preparation. Of 1994 graduates, the average starting salary was $39,100, the range was $27,500-$60,000.

Program Contact: Mr. Robert W. Buckner, Assistant Dean, Adelphi University, South Avenue, Garden City, NY 11530. (516) 877-4688; Fax: (516) 877-4607.
See full description on page 656.

Baruch College of the City University of New York

School of Business

New York, New York

OVERVIEW

Baruch College of the City University of New York is a state and locally supported coed institution. Part of City University of New York System. Founded 1919. Setting: urban campus. Total institutional enrollment: 15,105. Program was first offered in 1920. AACSB-accredited.

MBA HIGHLIGHTS

Entrance Difficulty**
Mean GMAT: 550
Mean GPA: 3.1

Cost $
Tuition: $1,675/semester
(Nonresident: $2,925/semester)
Room & Board: $8,910 (off-campus)

Enrollment Profile

Full-time: 550	Work Exp: 95%
Part-time: 1,524	International: 20%
Total: 2,074	Women: 44%
Average Age: 31	Minorities: 40%

Average Class Size: 45

ACADEMICS

Length of Program Minimum: 24 months.
Calendar Semesters.
Full-time Classes Main campus; evening, summer.
Part-time Classes Main campus; evening, summer.
Degree Requirements 54 credits.
Required Courses Business policy, financial and management accounting, financial decision making, information systems for managers, introduction to operations management, management: a behavioral approach, managerial economics, marketing management, psychological processes in organizations, the societal and governmental environment of business.
Curricular Focus Economic and financial theory, international business, strategic analysis and planning.
Concentrations Accounting, economics, entrepreneurship, finance, health services, human resources management, international business, management, management information systems, marketing, operations management, organizational behavior, public administration, public policy, quantitative analysis.
Special Opportunities International exchange in France, Germany.

STUDENT STATISTICS

Geographic Representation By region: Northeast 80%. International 20%.
Undergraduate Majors Business 39%; engineering/technology 21%; humanities 36%; other 4%.
Other Background Work experience: On average, students have 5 years of work experience on entrance to the program.

FACILITIES

Information Resources Main library with 270,000 bound volumes, 1.7 million titles on microform, 2,100 periodical subscriptions, 40 records/tapes/CDs, 27 CD-ROMs. Business collection includes 270,000 bound volumes, 2,100 periodical subscriptions.
Housing College housing not available.
Technology Computers are used moderately in course work. 400 computer terminals/PCs are available for use by students in program; they are located in the library, computer labs, graduate resource center, Media Center. Students in the program are not required to have their own PC.

Computer Resources/On-line Services

Training	Yes	CompuServe	No
Internet	Yes	Dun's	No
E-Mail	No	Dow Jones	Yes
Multimedia Center	Yes	Dialog	Yes
LEXIS/NEXIS	Yes	Bloomberg	No

ADMISSION

Acceptance 1994-95 1,552 applied for admission; 71% were accepted.
Entrance Requirements Bachelor's degree, GMAT score of 510. Core courses waived through: previous course work.
Application Requirements Written essay, application form, copies of transcript, resume/curriculum vitae, personal statement, 2 letters of recommendation.
Application Deadline Applications are processed on a rolling basis.

FINANCIALS

Costs for 1994-95 Tuition: Full-time: $1,675/semester for state residents, $2,925/semester for nonresidents; Part-time evening: $145/credit for state residents, $250/credit for nonresidents. Average room and board costs are $8,910 per academic year (off-campus).
Financial Aid In 1994-95, 12% of candidates received some institutionally administered aid in the form of loans, assistantships, work-study. Total awards ranged from $800-$7,500. Financial aid is available to part-time students. Application deadlines: 5/1 for fall, 12/1 for spring. Applications are processed on a rolling basis. Contact: Mr. James Murphy, Director of Financial Aid, 17 Lexington Avenue, Box H-0820, New York, NY 10010. (212) 802-2240.

INTERNATIONAL STUDENTS

Demographics 20% of students enrolled in the program are international.
Services and Facilities International student office.
Applying TOEFL required, minimum score of 570; proof of health; proof of adequate funds; minimum score of 4.5 on Test of Standard Written English. Financial aid is not available to international students. Admission applications are processed on a rolling basis. Contact: Mr. Stephen Goldberg, Director, International Students Office, 17 Lexington Avenue, Box H-0730, New York, NY 10010. (212) 802-2350.

ALTERNATE MBA PROGRAMS

Executive MBA (EMBA) Length of program: Minimum: 24 months. Full-time classes: Main campus; weekends. Degree requirements: 54 credits.
MBA/JD Length of program: Minimum: 54 months. Full-time classes: Main campus, Brooklyn Law School, New York Law School; day, evening, summer. Part-time classes: Main campus, Brooklyn Law School, New York Law School; day, evening, summer. Degree requirements: 122 credits.

PLACEMENT

In 1993-94, 240 organizations participated in on-campus recruiting; 3,054 on-campus interviews were conducted. Placement services include career counseling/planning, career fairs, career library, career placement, job interviews, resume preparation, and resume referral to employers. Of 1994 graduates, 82% were employed within three months of graduation, the average starting salary was $39,747.

Program Contact: Ms. Ellen Washington, Director of Admissions, Baruch College of the City University of New York, 17 Lexington Avenue, New York, NY 10010. (212) 802-2000; Fax: (212) 802-2340.
See full description on page 672.

Canisius College

Richard J. Wehle School of Business

Buffalo, New York

OVERVIEW

Canisius College is an independent Roman Catholic (Jesuit) comprehensive coed institution. Founded 1870. Setting: 25-acre urban campus. Total institutional enrollment: 4,900. Program was first offered in 1969. AACSB-accredited.

MBA HIGHLIGHTS

Entrance Difficulty***
Mean GMAT: 500
Mean GPA: 3.0

Cost $$
Tuition: $400/credit hour
Room & Board: N/R

Enrollment Profile

Full-time: 0	Work Exp: 90%
Part-time: 470	International: 2%
Total: 470	Women: 40%
Average Age: 32	Minorities: 4%

Average Class Size: 36

ACADEMICS

Length of Program Minimum: 36 months. Maximum: 5 years.

Calendar Semesters.

Full-time Classes Main campus; evening, summer.

Part-time Classes Main campus; evening, summer.

Degree Requirements 48 credits including 6 elective credits.

Required Courses Business policy, computers in business, financial accounting, human resources management, introduction to management science, macroeconomic analysis, managerial accounting, managerial environment, managerial finance, marketing management, microeconomic analysis, operations management, organizational behavior, statistical methods.

Curricular Focus Entrepreneurship, problem solving and decision making, strategic analysis and planning.

Concentrations Accounting, entrepreneurship, finance, health care management, health services, human resources management, management, management information systems, marketing.

Faculty Full-time: 42, 100% with doctorates.

Teaching Methodology Case study: 5%, lecture: 80%, student presentations: 5%, team projects: 10%.

STUDENT STATISTICS

Geographic Representation State residents 98%. By region: Northeast 98%. International 2%.

Undergraduate Majors Business 40%; engineering/technology 30%; humanities 10%; science/mathematics 20%.

Other Background Work experience: On average, students have 8 years of work experience on entrance to the program.

FACILITIES

Information Resources Main library with 288,999 bound volumes, 216,586 titles on microform, 1,183 periodical subscriptions, 3,592 records/tapes/CDs, 20 CD-ROMs. Business collection includes 21,904 bound volumes, 306 periodical subscriptions, 2 CD-ROMs.

Housing College housing available.

Technology Computers are used moderately in course work. 150 computer terminals/PCs, linked by a campus-wide computer network, are available for use by students in program; they are located in learning resource center, the library, the computer center, computer labs, the research center. Students in the program are not required to have their own PC.

Computer Resources/On-line Services

Training	Yes	E-Mail	Yes
Internet	Yes	Dialog	Yes

Other on-line services: First Search, OCLC.

ADMISSION

Acceptance 1994-95 Of those applying, 80% were accepted.

Entrance Requirements Bachelor's degree, calculus, GMAT score of 490, minimum 2.85 GPA. Core courses waived through: previous course work.

Application Requirements Written essay, application form, copies of transcript, personal statement.

Application Deadlines 7/1 for fall, 10/1 for spring, 3/1 for summer.

FINANCIALS

Costs for 1994-95 Tuition: Full-time: $400/credit hour. Fees: Full-time: $8/credit hour.

Financial Aid In 1994-95, candidates received some institutionally administered aid in the form of scholarships, assistantships. Financial aid is available to part-time students. Application deadline: 4/15 for fall. Contact: Mr. Curtis Gaume, Director of Student Financial Aid, 2001 Main Street, Buffalo, NY 14208-1098. (716) 888-2300.

INTERNATIONAL STUDENTS

Demographics 2% of students enrolled in the program are international.

Services and Facilities International student center, counseling/support services.

Applying TOEFL required, minimum score of 550; proof of health; proof of adequate funds. Financial aid is not available to international students. Admission applications are processed on a rolling basis. Contact: Ms. Ester Northman, Director, International Student Programs, 2001 Main Street, Buffalo, NY 14208-1098. (716) 888-2784.

PLACEMENT

Placement services include alumni network, career counseling/planning, career library, career placement, and resume preparation. Of 1994 graduates, 95% were employed within three months of graduation.

Program Contact: Mr. Daniel W. Sullivan, Associate Dean, Canisius College, 2001 Main Street, Buffalo, NY 14208-1098. (716) 888-2140; Fax: (716) 888-3211; Internet Address: dsully@weuce.canisius.edu.

Clarkson University

School of Business

Potsdam, New York

OVERVIEW

Clarkson University is an independent nonprofit coed institution. Founded 1896. Setting: 640-acre small-town campus. Total institutional enrollment: 3,000. Program was first offered in 1960. AACSB-accredited.

MBA HIGHLIGHTS

Entrance Difficulty***
Mean GMAT: 540
Mean GPA: 3.3

Cost $$$
Tuition: $17,200
Room & Board: $5,000

Enrollment Profile

Full-time: 87	Work Exp: 20%
Part-time: 0	International: 11%
Total: 87	Women: 29%
Average Age: 24	Minorities: 2%

Average Class Size: 30

ACADEMICS

Length of Program Minimum: 9 months.

Calendar Semesters.

Full-time Classes Main campus; day, evening.

Degree Requirements 32 credits including 12 elective credits. Other: Integrated 5-week modules; 4 elective courses.

Required Courses Applied economics, decision analysis, financial management, information systems, management accounting, managerial behavior and skills, managerial competence seminar, marketing management, production and operations management, strategic planning.

Curricular Focus General management, leadership, teamwork.

Concentrations Accounting, economics, finance, human resources management, international business, management, management information systems, marketing, operations management, strategic management.

Faculty Full-time: 27, 100% with doctorates.

Teaching Methodology Case study: 40%, lecture: 30%, seminars by members of the business community: 5%, student presentations: 10%, team projects: 15%.

Special Opportunities Internships include consulting.

STUDENT STATISTICS

Geographic Representation State residents 89%. By region: Northeast 82%; South 2%. International 11%.

Undergraduate Majors Business 75%; engineering/technology 10%; science/mathematics 5%; social sciences 5%; other 5%.

Other Background Work experience: On average, students have 1-5 years of work experience on entrance to the program.

FACILITIES

Information Resources Main library with 219,948 bound volumes, 264,777 titles on microform, 2,835 periodical subscriptions, 1,080 records/tapes/CDs.

Housing 25% of students in program live in college-owned or -operated housing. Assistance with housing search provided.

Technology Computers are used heavily in course work. Computer terminals/PCs, linked by a campus-wide computer network, are available for use by students in program; they are located in the student center, learning resource center, the library, the computer center, computer labs. Students in the program are not required to have their own PC.

Computer Resources/On-line Services

Training	Yes	Multimedia Center	Yes
Internet	Yes	CompuServe	Yes
E-Mail	Yes		

ADMISSION

Acceptance 1994-95 240 applied for admission; 40% were accepted.

Entrance Requirements Bachelor's degree, prerequisite courses required for applicants with non-business degree, GMAT score of 500, minimum 2.75 GPA. Core courses waived through: previous course work.

Application Requirements Application form, copies of transcript, resume/curriculum vitae, 3 letters of recommendation.

Application Deadline Applications are processed on a rolling basis.

FINANCIALS

Costs for 1994-95 Tuition: Full-time: $17,200; Part-time day: $532/credit hour. Average room and board costs are $5,000 per academic year (on-campus) and $5,000 per academic year (off-campus).

Financial Aid In 1994-95, 60% of candidates received some institutionally administered aid in the form of assistantships. Total awards ranged from $6,400-$17,000. Financial aid is not available to part-time students. Applications are processed on a rolling basis. Contact: Mr. Mark Cornett, Associate Dean of the Graduate School, Box 5770, Potsdam, NY 13699-5770. (315) 268-6613.

INTERNATIONAL STUDENTS

Demographics 11% of students enrolled in the program are international; North America 45%, Asia 37%, South America 9%, other 9%.

Services and Facilities International student office, international student center, visa services, language tutoring, ESL courses, special assistance for nonnative speakers of English, counseling/support services.

Applying TOEFL required, minimum score of 600; proof of health; proof of adequate funds. Financial aid is available to international students. Financial aid application deadlines: 5/15 for fall, 10/15 for spring. Admission application deadlines: 5/15 for fall, 10/15 for spring. Contact: Ms. Mary Theis, Director, International Student Programs, 227 Price Hall, Box 5645, Potsdam, NY 13699-5645. (315) 268-7970.

PLACEMENT

Placement services include alumni network, career counseling/planning, career fairs, career library, career placement, electronic job bank, job interviews, job search course, resume preparation, and resume referral to employers. Of 1994 graduates, 85% were employed within three months of graduation, the average starting salary was $38,000, the range was $30,000-$45,000.

Jobs by Employer Type Manufacturing 18%; service 60%; consulting 20%; education 2%.

Jobs by Functional Area Marketing/sales 20%; finance 10%; operations 20%; management 20%; strategic planning 10%; technical management 20%.

Program Contact: Mr. Mark Cornett, Associate Dean of the Graduate School, Clarkson University, Box 5770, Potsdam, NY 13699-5770. (315) 268-6613; Fax: (315) 268-7994.
See full description on page 700.

College of Insurance

New York, New York

OVERVIEW

College of Insurance is an independent nonprofit comprehensive coed institution. Founded 1962. Setting: urban campus. Total institutional enrollment: 2,388. Program was first offered in 1966.

MBA HIGHLIGHTS

Entrance Difficulty**
Mean GMAT: 500
Mean GPA: 3.0

Cost $$$
Tuition: $427/credit
Room & Board: $7,231

Enrollment Profile

Full-time: N/R	Work Exp: 85%
Part-time: N/R	International: 24%
Total: 189	Women: 65%
Average Age: N/R	Minorities: N/R

Average Class Size: 12

ACADEMICS

Length of Program Minimum: 20 months. Maximum: 5 years.

Calendar Semesters.

Full-time Classes Main campus; evening, weekends, summer.

Part-time Classes Main campus; evening, weekends, summer.

Degree Requirements 51 credits including 4 elective credits.

Required Courses Business policy, financial management, legal environment, management information systems, management organizational behavior, managerial accounting, managerial economics, marketing policies, quantitative analysis, risk management.

Curricular Focus Business issues and problems, leadership, problem solving and decision making.

Concentrations Finance, insurance, actuarial science.

Faculty Full-time: 9; part-time: 20.

Teaching Methodology Case study: 10%, lecture: 50%, research: 10%, student presentations: 10%, team projects: 20%.

STUDENT STATISTICS

Geographic Representation International 24%.

Undergraduate Majors Business 80%; other 20%.

FACILITIES

Information Resources Main library with 95,426 bound volumes, 10,746 titles on microform, 359 periodical subscriptions, 5 CD-ROMs. Business collection includes 95,426 bound volumes, 359 periodical subscriptions, 5 CD-ROMs, 11 videos.

Housing 25% of students in program live in college-owned or -operated housing.

Technology Computers are used heavily in course work. 10 computer terminals/PCs are available for use by students in program; they are located in computer labs. Students in the program are not required to have their own PC.

Computer Resources/On-line Services

Training	Yes	E-Mail	No

Other on-line services: RLIN.

ADMISSION

Acceptance 1994-95 127 applied for admission; 69% were accepted.

Entrance Requirements Bachelor's degree, GMAT score of 500, minimum 3.0 GPA. Core courses waived through: previous course work.

Application Requirements Interview, application form, copies of transcript, personal statement, 2 letters of recommendation.

Application Deadlines 5/1 for fall, 12/1 for spring. Applications are processed on a rolling basis.

FINANCIALS

Costs for 1994-95 Tuition: Full-time: $427/credit. Fees: Full-time: $18. Average room and board costs are $7,231 per academic year (on-campus).

Financial Aid In 1994-95, 28% of candidates received some institutionally administered aid in the form of loans, assistantships. Total awards ranged from $1,281-$5,124. Financial aid is available to part-time students. Application deadlines: 7/1 for fall, 11/1 for spring. Applications are processed on a rolling basis. Contact: Ms. Marjorie Melikian, Financial Aid Officer, 101 Murray Street, New York, NY 10007-2165. (212) 815-9222.

INTERNATIONAL STUDENTS

Demographics 24% of students enrolled in the program are international; Asia 79%, South America 8%, other 13%.

Services and Facilities International student office.

Applying TOEFL required, minimum score of 550; proof of health; proof of adequate funds. Financial aid is not available to international students.

Admission application deadlines: 5/1 for fall, 12/1 for spring. Applications are processed on a rolling basis. Contact: Ms. Theresa Marro, Director of Admissions, 101 Murray Street, New York, NY 10007-2165. (212) 815-9232.

PLACEMENT

Placement services include alumni network, career counseling/planning, job interviews, resume preparation, and resume referral to employers. Of 1994 graduates, 90% were employed within three months of graduation.

Program Contact: Ms. Theresa C. Marro, Director of Admissions, College of Insurance, 101 Murray Street, New York, NY 10007-2165. (212) 815-9232, or (800) 356-5146; Fax: (212) 732-5669. See full description on page 708.

College of Saint Rose

School of Business

Albany, New York

OVERVIEW

College of Saint Rose is an independent nonprofit comprehensive coed institution. Founded 1920. Setting: 22-acre urban campus. Total institutional enrollment: 3,905. Program was first offered in 1981.

MBA HIGHLIGHTS

Entrance Difficulty*
Mean GMAT: 497
Mean GPA: 3.1

Cost $
Tuition: $292/semester hour
Room & Board: N/R

Enrollment Profile

Full-time: 16	Work Exp: 85%
Part-time: 224	International: 3%
Total: 240	Women: 45%
Average Age: 28	Minorities: 6%

Average Class Size: 25

ACADEMICS

Length of Program Minimum: 24 months. Maximum: 8 years.

Calendar Semesters.

Full-time Classes Glens Falls; evening, weekends, summer.

Part-time Classes Main campus, Glens Falls; evening, weekends, summer.

Degree Requirements 36 credit hours including 6 elective credit hours.

Required Courses Advanced taxation, advanced theory of financial accounting, budgeting and cost analysis, decision making methods, financial accounting, financial auditing, human resources management, management communication and social responsibility, managerial economics, managerial finance, managing technology and innovation, marketing for customer satisfaction, organizational motivation, leadership, and design, production and quality management, strategic management.

Curricular Focus Business issues and problems, entrepreneurship, strategic analysis and planning.

Concentrations Accounting, economics, entrepreneurship, finance, human resources management, management, marketing, strategic management.

Faculty Full-time: 13, 90% with doctorates.

Teaching Methodology Case study: 25%, faculty seminars: 5%, lecture: 25%, seminars by members of the business community: 5%, student presentations: 20%, team projects: 20%.

Special Opportunities Internship program available.

STUDENT STATISTICS

Geographic Representation State residents 85%. International 3%.

Undergraduate Majors Business 40%; education 20%; engineering/technology 20%; humanities 10%; social sciences 10%.

Other Background Graduate degrees in other disciplines: 5%. Work experience: On average, students have 6 years of work experience on entrance to the program.

FACILITIES

Information Resources Main library with 190,000 bound volumes, 160,000 titles on microform, 1,050 periodical subscriptions, 600 records/tapes/CDs, 7 CD-ROMs.

Housing 5% of students in program live in college-owned or -operated housing.

Technology Computers are used heavily in course work. Computer terminals/PCs, linked by a campus-wide computer network, are available for use by students in program; they are located in classrooms, learning resource center, the library, the computer center, computer labs. Students in the program are not required to have their own PC. $150 are budgeted per student for computer support.

Computer Resources/On-line Services

Training	Yes	Multimedia Center	Yes
Internet	Yes	LEXIS/NEXIS	Yes
E-Mail	Yes	Dialog	Yes

ADMISSION

Acceptance 1994-95 90 applied for admission; 44% were accepted.

Entrance Requirements Bachelor's degree, GMAT score, minimum 3.0 GPA.

Application Requirements Application form, copies of transcript, resume/curriculum vitae, personal statement, 2 letters of recommendation.

Application Deadlines 8/1 for fall, 12/1 for spring, 4/1 for summer.

FINANCIALS

Costs for 1994-95 Tuition: Full-time: $292/semester hour. Fees: Full-time: $15/semester.

Financial Aid Application deadlines: 7/1 for fall, 11/1 for spring, 3/1 for summer. Contact: Mr. Ken Clough, Director of Financial Aid, 432 Western Avenue, Albany, NY 12203-1419. (518) 454-5168.

INTERNATIONAL STUDENTS

Demographics 3% of students enrolled in the program are international.

Services and Facilities International student office.

Applying TOEFL required; proof of health; proof of adequate funds; health and accident insurance. Financial aid is not available to international students. Admission application deadlines: 4/1 for fall, 8/1 for spring. Contact: Ms. Taia Thorp, Coordinator, International Student Programs, 432 Western Avenue, Albany, NY 12203-1419. (518) 454-5206.

ALTERNATE MBA PROGRAMS

One-Year MBA Length of program: Minimum: 12 months. Maximum: 8 years. Full-time classes: Main campus; day, early morning. Part-time classes: Main campus, Glens Falls; evening, weekends, summer. Degree requirements: 36 credits.

MBA/JD Length of program: Minimum: 36 months. Maximum: 4 years. Full-time classes: Main campus; day, evening, weekends, summer. Part-time classes: Main campus, Glens Falls; evening, weekends, summer. Degree requirements: 102 credits.

PLACEMENT

Placement services include career fairs, career library, career placement, and resume preparation. Of 1994 graduates, 95% were employed within three months of graduation, the average starting salary was $31,000, the range was $23,000-$52,000.

Program Contact: Dr. Mohammad Ghobadian, Assistant Professor of Business, College of Saint Rose, 432 Western Avenue, Albany, NY 12203-1419. (518) 454-5243; Fax: (518) 458-5449.

Columbia University

Columbia Business School

New York, New York

OVERVIEW

Columbia University is an independent nonprofit coed institution. Founded 1754. Setting: urban campus. Total institutional enrollment: 26,000. Program was first offered in 1916. AACSB-accredited.

MBA HIGHLIGHTS ——————————

Entrance Difficulty***
Mean GMAT: N/R
GPA: 3.3 - 3.85

Cost $$$$
Tuition: $2,140/course
Room & Board: N/R

Enrollment Profile

Full-time: 1,289	Work Exp: 99%
Part-time: 0	International: 27%
Total: 1,289	Women: 32%
Average Age: 26	Minorities: 9%

Average Class Size: 40

ACADEMICS

Length of Program Minimum: 16 months. Maximum: 5 years.

Calendar Semesters.

Full-time Classes Main campus; day, early morning, summer.

Degree Requirements 60 credits including 30 elective credits. Other: Integrated project.

Required Courses Accounting, business finance, decision models, global economic environment, managerial economics, managerial statistics, managing human behavior in organizations, marketing, operations management, strategic management of the enterprise.

Curricular Focus Financial services, general management, international business.

Concentrations Accounting, economics, finance, human resources management, international business, management, management information systems, marketing, operations management, organizational behavior, public policy, real estate, strategic management.

Faculty Full-time: 100, 100% with doctorates; part-time: 58.

Teaching Methodology Case study: 20%, lecture: 40%, team projects: 40%.

Special Opportunities International exchange in Australia, Austria, Belgium, Brazil, Finland, France, Hong Kong, Italy, Netherlands, Philippines, Spain, Sweden, Switzerland, United Kingdom. Internship program available.

STUDENT STATISTICS

Geographic Representation State residents 73%. By region: Northeast 54%; West 8%; South 6%; Midwest 5%. International 27%.

Other Background Graduate degrees in other disciplines: 12%. Work experience: On average, students have 4 years of work experience on entrance to the program.

FACILITIES

Information Resources Main library with 6.3 million bound volumes, 4.5 million titles on microform, 63,403 periodical subscriptions. Business collection in Thomas J. Watson Library includes 389,056 bound volumes, 2,073 periodical subscriptions, 7 CD-ROMs, 201 videos.

Housing 30% of students in program live in college-owned or -operated housing.

Technology Computers are used heavily in course work. Computer terminals/PCs, linked by a campus-wide computer network, are available for use by students in program; they are located in student rooms, the student center, classrooms, learning resource center, the library, the computer center, computer labs, the research center, cafeteria, lobby. Students in the program are required to have their own PC. $400 are budgeted per student for computer support.

Computer Resources/On-line Services

Training	Yes	CompuServe	No
Internet	Yes	Dun's	No
E-Mail	Yes	Dow Jones	Yes
Multimedia Center	Yes	Bloomberg	Yes
LEXIS/NEXIS	Yes		

ADMISSION

Acceptance 1994-95 4,131 applied for admission; 20% were accepted.

Entrance Requirements Bachelor's degree, GMAT score.

Application Requirements Written essay, application form, copies of transcript, resume/curriculum vitae, personal statement, 2 letters of recommendation.

Application Deadlines 4/20 for fall, 11/1 for spring. Applications are processed on a rolling basis. Application discs available.

FINANCIALS

Costs for 1994-95 Tuition: Full-time: $2,140/course.

Financial Aid In 1994-95, 60% of candidates received some institutionally administered aid in the form of grants, scholarships, loans, followships, work-study. Total awards ranged from $1,000-$25,000. Application deadlines: 2/1 for fall, 11/1 for spring. Contact: Office of Financial Aid, 218 Uris Hall, New York, NY 10027. (212) 854-4057.

INTERNATIONAL STUDENTS

Demographics 27% of students enrolled in the program are international; Asia 38%, Europe 27%, North America 9%, Africa 8%, South America 5%, Central America 4%, other 9%.

Services and Facilities International student housing; international student office, international student center, visa services, language tutoring, ESL courses, special assistance for nonnative speakers of English, counseling/support services.

Applying TOEFL required, minimum score of 610; proof of health; proof of adequate funds. Financial aid is not available to international students. Admission application deadlines: 3/1 for fall, 10/1 for spring. Applications are processed on a rolling basis. Contact: Ms. Madge Nimocks, Associate Director, Jerome A. Chazen Institute of International Studies, 213 Uris Hall, New York, NY 10027. (212) 854-1754.

PLACEMENT

In 1993-94, 249 organizations participated in on-campus recruiting; 9,500 on-campus interviews were conducted. Placement services include alumni network, career counseling/planning, career fairs, career library, career placement, electronic job bank, job interviews, resume preparation, and resume referral to employers. Of 1994 graduates, 97% were employed within three months of graduation, the average starting salary was $67,290, the range was $40,000-$133,000.

Jobs by Employer Type Manufacturing 13%; service 10%; government 3%; consulting 16%; financial services 58%.

Jobs by Functional Area Marketing/sales 10%; finance 55%; operations 1%; management 6%; strategic planning 2%; consulting 20%; other 6%.

Program Contact: Mr. Ethan Hanabury, Associate Dean, Columbia University, 105 Uris Hall, New York, NY 10027. (212) 854-5567; Fax: (212) 662-6754.

Cornell University

Johnson Graduate School of Management

Ithaca, New York

OVERVIEW

Cornell University is an independent nonprofit coed institution. Founded 1865. Setting: 745-acre small-town campus with easy access to Syracuse. Total institutional enrollment: 16,000. Program was first offered in 1946. AACSB-accredited.

MBA HIGHLIGHTS ——————————

Entrance Difficulty***
Mean GMAT: 630
Mean GPA: 3.2

Cost $$$$
Tuition: $20,400
Room & Board: $6,980 (off-campus)

Enrollment Profile

Full-time: 490	Work Exp: 94%
Part-time: 0	International: 25%
Total: 490	Women: 22%
Average Age: 27	Minorities: 12%

Average Class Size: 55

ACADEMICS

Length of Program Minimum: 21 months.

Calendar Semesters.

Full-time Classes Main campus; day.

Degree Requirements 60 credits including 37.5 elective credits.

Required Courses Financial accounting, managerial finance, marketing management, microeconomics for management, organizational behavior, production and operations management, quantitative methods for management, strategy.

Curricular Focus General management, strategic analysis and planning, teamwork.

Concentration Management.

Faculty Full-time: 43, 98% with doctorates; part-time: 7, 75% with doctorates.

Teaching Methodology Case study: 15%, faculty seminars: 10%, lecture: 20%, research: 15%, seminars by members of the business community: 10%, student presentations: 10%, team projects: 20%.

Special Opportunities International exchange in Australia, Austria, Belgium, Hong Kong, Switzerland, United Kingdom. Other: semester in manufacturing.

STUDENT STATISTICS
Geographic Representation State residents 75%. By region: Northeast 40%; West 20%; South 8%; Midwest 8%. International 25%.

Other Background Graduate degrees in other disciplines: 6%.

FACILITIES
Information Resources Main library with 5.7 million bound volumes, 6.1 million titles on microform, 62,332 periodical subscriptions, 77,566 records/tapes/CDs.

Housing 30% of students in program live in college-owned or -operated housing. Assistance with housing search provided.

Technology Computers are used moderately in course work. 45 computer terminals/PCs, linked by a campus-wide computer network, are available for use by students in program; they are located in the computer center. Students in the program are not required to have their own PC.

Computer Resources/On-line Services

Training	Yes	CompuServe	No
Internet	Yes	Dun's	Yes
E-Mail	Yes	Dow Jones	Yes
Videoconference Center	Yes	Dialog	Yes
LEXIS/NEXIS	Yes	Bloomberg	Yes

ADMISSION
Acceptance 1994-95 1,832 applied for admission; 37% were accepted.

Entrance Requirements Bachelor's degree, GMAT score. Core courses waived through: previous course work, work experience.

Application Requirements Written essay, application form, copies of transcript, resume/curriculum vitae, personal statement, 2 letters of recommendation.

Application Deadlines 3/2 for fall. Applications are processed on a rolling basis.

FINANCIALS
Costs for 1994-95 Tuition: Full-time: $20,400. Average room and board costs are $6,980 per academic year (off-campus).

Financial Aid In 1994-95, 60% of candidates received some institutionally administered aid in the form of scholarships, loans, fellowships, assistantships, work-study. Application deadline: 3/1 for fall. Applications are processed on a rolling basis. Contact: Ms. Anne Coyle, Director of Admissions, 315 Malott Hall, Ithaca, NY 14853-4201. (607) 255-4526.

INTERNATIONAL STUDENTS
Demographics 25% of students enrolled in the program are international; Asia 40%, South America 20%, Europe 15%, North America 10%, Africa 5%, Australia 5%, Central America 5%.

Services and Facilities International student office, international student center, visa services, ESL courses, counseling/support services.

Applying TOEFL required, minimum score of 600; proof of health; proof of adequate funds. Financial aid is available to international students. Financial aid application deadline: 3/1 for fall. Applications are processed on a rolling basis. Admission application deadline: 3/1 for fall. Applications are processed on a rolling basis.

ALTERNATE MBA PROGRAMS
One-Year MBA Length of program: 12 months. Full-time classes: Main campus; day. Degree requirements: 45 credits including 25.5 elective credits. Graduate degree in a scientific or technical field. Average class size: 25.

MBA/JD Length of program: Minimum: 45 months. Full-time classes: Main campus; day.

MBA/MA Length of program: Minimum: 27 months. Full-time classes: Main campus; day. Degree requirements: 75 credits. MA is in Asian studies. Average class size: 3.

MBA/M Eng Length of program: Minimum: 27 months. Full-time classes: Main campus; day. Degree requirements: 75 credits. Undergraduate degree in engineering or closely related discipline; work experience relevant to business or engineering. Average class size: 5.

MBA/MILR Length of program: Minimum: 27 months. Full-time classes: Main campus; day. Degree requirements: 75 credits including 45 elective credits. Average class size: 3.

PLACEMENT
Placement services include alumni network, career counseling/planning, career fairs, career library, career placement, electronic job bank, job interviews, job search course, resume preparation, and resume referral to employers.

Program Contact: Ms. Anne Coyle, Director of Admissions, Cornell University, 315 Malott Hall, Ithaca, NY 14853-4201. (607) 255-4526, or (800) 847-2082; Fax: (607) 254-8886; Internet Address: mba@johnson.cornell.edu.

See full description on page 712.

Dowling College

School of Business

Oakdale, New York

OVERVIEW
Dowling College is an independent nonprofit comprehensive coed institution. Founded 1955. Setting: 51-acre suburban campus with easy access to New York City. Total institutional enrollment: 5,400. Program was first offered in 1976.

MBA HIGHLIGHTS

Entrance Difficulty**
Mean GMAT: 550
Mean GPA: 3.5

Cost $$
Tuition: $380/credit
Room & Board: $3,000

Enrollment Profile

Full-time: 165	Work Exp: 90%
Part-time: 585	International: N/R
Total: 750	Women: 50%
Average Age: 37	Minorities: 10%

Average Class Size: 25

ACADEMICS
Length of Program Minimum: 16 months. Maximum: 5 years.

Calendar Semesters.

Full-time Classes Main campus; evening, weekends, summer.

Part-time Classes Main campus, Manhattan, Riverhead; evening, weekends, summer.

Degree Requirements 36 credits including 12 elective credits.

Curricular Focus Business issues and problems, general management, international business, leadership, managing diversity, organizational development and change management, problem solving and decision making, strategic analysis and planning, teamwork.

Concentrations Finance, management, public administration, public policy, quality management, aviation management, transportation.

Faculty Full-time: 14, 85% with doctorates; part-time: 10, 75% with doctorates.

Teaching Methodology Case study: 10%, lecture: 20%, seminars by members of the business community: 10%, student presentations: 30%, team projects: 30%.

Special Opportunities Internship program available.

STUDENT STATISTICS
Geographic Representation State residents 100%. By region: Northeast 100%.

Undergraduate Majors Business 60%; engineering/technology 5%; humanities 10%; science/mathematics 10%; social sciences 10%; other 5%.

Other Background Graduate degrees in other disciplines: 10%. Work experience: On average, students have 5 years of work experience on entrance to the program.

FACILITIES

Information Resources Main library with 165,000 bound volumes, 367,531 titles on microform, 1,200 periodical subscriptions, 2,200 records/tapes/CDs, 50 CD-ROMs.

Housing 1% of students in program live in college-owned or -operated housing.

Technology Computers are used moderately in course work. 100 computer terminals/PCs, linked by a campus-wide computer network, are available for use by students in program; they are located in dormitories, the computer center, computer labs, the research center. Students in the program are required to have their own PC.

Computer Resources/On-line Services

Training	Yes	Multimedia Center	Yes
Internet	Yes	LEXIS/NEXIS	Yes
E-Mail	No		

ADMISSION

Entrance Requirements Bachelor's degree, GMAT score of 500, minimum 3.0 GPA, minimum 3- 5 years of work experience. Core courses waived through: previous course work, work experience.

Application Requirements Application form, copies of transcript, resume/curriculum vitae, 2 letters of recommendation.

Application Deadline Applications are processed on a rolling basis.

FINANCIALS

Costs for 1994-95 Tuition: Full-time: $380/credit. Fees: Full-time: $26-$95/credit. Average room and board costs are $3,000 per academic year (on-campus).

Financial Aid In 1994-95, candidates received some institutionally administered aid in the form of grants, scholarships, loans, assistantships. Financial aid is available to part-time students. Applications are processed on a rolling basis. Contact: Enrollment Services, Idle Hour Boulevard, Oakdale, NY 11769. (800) 369-5464.

INTERNATIONAL STUDENTS

Services and Facilities Language tutoring, ESL courses, counseling/support services.

Applying TOEFL required; proof of adequate funds; World Education Services Transcripts. Financial aid is not available to international students. Contact: Ms. Susan Thomson, International Student Adviser, Enrollment Services, Idle Hour Boulevard, Oakdale, NY 11769. (516) 244-3130.

ALTERNATE MBA PROGRAM

Executive MBA (EMBA) Length of program: Minimum: 16 months. Maximum: 2 years. Degree requirements: 36 credits. Average class size: 25.

PLACEMENT

In 1993-94, 50 organizations participated in on-campus recruiting. Placement services include alumni network, career counseling/planning, career fairs, career library, career placement, job interviews, and resume referral to employers.

Program Contact: Enrollment Services, Dowling College, Idle Hour Boulevard, Oakdale, NY 11769. (516) 244-3355, or (800) DOWLING; Fax: (516) 589-6644.
See full description on page 720.

Fordham University

Graduate School of Business Administration

New York, New York

OVERVIEW

Fordham University is an independent Roman Catholic (Jesuit) coed institution. Founded 1841. Setting: 85-acre urban campus. Total institutional enrollment: 14,663. Program was first offered in 1969. AACSB-accredited.

MBA HIGHLIGHTS

Entrance Difficulty***
Mean GMAT: 531
Mean GPA: 2.95

Cost
Tuition: N/R
Room & Board: N/R

Enrollment Profile

Full-time: 410	Work Exp: 91%
Part-time: 1,505	International: N/R
Total: 1,915	Women: 46%
Average Age: 27	Minorities: 6%

Average Class Size: 35

ACADEMICS

Length of Program Minimum: 12 months. Maximum: 6 years.

Calendar Trimesters.

Full-time Classes Main campus, Lincoln Center; day, evening, weekends, summer.

Part-time Classes Main campus, Lincoln Center, Tarrytown; evening, weekends, summer.

Degree Requirements 60 credits including 21 elective credits.

Required Courses Business law, business policy, financial environment, fundamentals of accounting, fundamentals of management, information systems, managerial economics, math methods for business, operations management, statistics. Courses may be waived through: previous course work.

Curricular Focus Business issues and problems, international business, organizational development and change management.

Faculty Full-time: 78, 94% with doctorates; part-time: 88, 40% with doctorates.

Teaching Methodology Case study: 1%, lecture: 70%, research: 4%, seminars by members of the business community: 5%, student presentations: 10%, team projects: 10%.

Special Opportunities International exchange program available.

STUDENT STATISTICS

Geographic Representation By region: Northeast 71%; Midwest 17%; South 6%; West 1%.

Other Background Work experience: On average, students have 6 years of work experience on entrance to the program.

FACILITIES

Information Resources Main library with 1.6 million bound volumes, 1.9 million titles on microform, 9,968 periodical subscriptions, 80 CD-ROMs. Business collection in Quinn Library includes 32,000 bound volumes, 480 periodical subscriptions, 6 CD-ROMs.

Housing 1% of students in program live in college-owned or -operated housing.

Technology Computers are used heavily in course work. 92 computer terminals/PCs, linked by a campus-wide computer network, are available for use by students in program; they are located in the library, the computer center, computer labs. Students in the program are not required to have their own PC. $200 are budgeted per student for computer support.

Computer Resources/On-line Services

Training	Yes	CompuServe	No
Internet	Yes	Dun's	No
E-Mail	Yes	Dow Jones	Yes
Multimedia Center	Yes	Dialog	No
LEXIS/NEXIS	Yes	Bloomberg	Yes

Other on-line services: OCLC.

ADMISSION

Acceptance 1994-95 841 applied for admission; 56% were accepted.

Entrance Requirements Bachelor's degree, GMAT score. Core courses waived through: previous course work.

Application Requirements Application form, copies of transcript, resume/curriculum vitae, personal statement, 2 letters of recommendation.

Application Deadlines 6/1 for fall, 1/1 for winter, 3/1 for spring. Applications are processed on a rolling basis.

FINANCIALS

Financial Aid In 1994-95, candidates received some institutionally administered aid in the form of scholarships, loans, assistantships. Total awards ranged from $2,500-$18,500. Financial aid is available to part-time students. Application deadlines: 5/1 for fall, 5/1 for spring. Applications are processed on a rolling basis. Contact: Ms. Dorothy Szekely, Coordinator of Admissions and Financial Aid Processing, East Fordham Road, New York, NY 10458. (212) 636-6109.

INTERNATIONAL STUDENTS
Demographics 3% of students on campus are international; Asia 41%, Europe 27%, Africa 12%, South America 7%, Central America 4%, North America 4%, Australia 3%, other 3%.

Services and Facilities International student office, counseling/support services.

Applying TOEFL required, minimum score of 600; proof of health; proof of adequate funds. Financial aid is not available to international students. Admission applications are processed on a rolling basis. Contact: Ms. Emilie Eklund, Director, Office of International Students, East Fordham Road, Administration Building, Room 303-B, New York, NY 10458. (718) 817-4135.

ALTERNATE MBA PROGRAMS
MBA/JD Length of program: Minimum: 42 months. Maximum: 7 years. Full-time classes: Main campus; day, evening, summer. Part-time classes: Main campus; evening, summer. Degree requirements: 128 credits.

MBA/MS Degree requirements: 90 credits. MS is in taxation.

PLACEMENT
In 1993-94, 21 organizations participated in on-campus recruiting; 100 on-campus interviews were conducted. Placement services include alumni network, career counseling/planning, career library, career placement, job search course, resume preparation, and resume referral to employers. Of 1994 graduates, 90% were employed within three months of graduation, the average starting salary was $58,000, the range was $36,000-$68,000.

Jobs by Employer Type Manufacturing 10%, service 02%.

Jobs by Functional Area Marketing/sales 10%; finance 40%; operations 15%; management 15%; strategic planning 5%; technical management 5%; consulting 5%; real estate 5%.

Program Contact: Ms. Kathy Pattison, Assistant Dean of Admissions, Fordham University, East Fordham Road, New York, NY 10458. (800) 825-4422, or (800) 825-4422; Fax: (212) 765-5573; Internet Address: gbaadmin@mary.fordham.edu.

See full description on page 740.

Hofstra University

Frank G. Zarb School of Business

Hempstead, New York

OVERVIEW
Hofstra University is an independent nonprofit coed institution. Founded 1935. Setting: 238-acre suburban campus with easy access to New York City. Total institutional enrollment: 11,545. Program was first offered in 1952. AACSB-accredited.

MBA HIGHLIGHTS

Entrance Difficulty**
Mean GMAT: 580
Mean GPA: 3.2

Cost $$
Tuition: $382/credit
Room & Board: N/R

Enrollment Profile

Full-time: 180	Work Exp: 70%
Part-time: 661	International: 19%
Total: 841	Women: 40%
Average Age: 27	Minorities: 6%

Average Class Size: 22

ACADEMICS
Length of Program Minimum: 12 months. Maximum: 5 years.
Calendar Semesters.
Full-time Classes Main campus; day, evening, summer.
Part-time Classes Main campus; day, evening, summer.
Degree Requirements 36 credits including 15 elective credits.

Required Courses Advanced managerial accounting, business policy, information systems for management, macroeconomic theory, management of marketing process, managerial finance, organization theory, quantitative analysis in business.

Curricular Focus Business issues and problems, international business, teamwork.

Concentrations Accounting, finance, international business, management, management information systems, marketing.

Faculty Full-time: 60, 90% with doctorates; part-time: 6, 65% with doctorates.

Teaching Methodology Case study: 28%, faculty seminars: 4%, lecture: 30%, research: 3%, seminars by members of the business community: 5%, student presentations: 15%, team projects: 15%.

Special Opportunities International exchange in Czech Republic, Finland, France, Netherlands, Russia, United Kingdom. Internships include marketing, finance accounting, information systems, and accounting. Other: Student consulting practice.

STUDENT STATISTICS
Geographic Representation By region: Northeast 73%; Midwest 4%; South 2%; West 2%. International 19%.

Undergraduate Majors Business 33%; education 3%; engineering/technology 18%; humanities 5%; science/mathematics 9%; social sciences 24%; other 8%.

Other Background Graduate degrees in other disciplines: 5%. Work experience: On average, students have 3 years of work experience on entrance to the program.

FACILITIES
Information Resources Main library with 1.3 million bound volumes, 30,098 titles on microform, 7,017 periodical subscriptions, 427 records/tapes/CDs.

Housing 30% of students in program live in college-owned or -operated housing. Assistance with housing search provided.

Technology Computers are used heavily in course work. 200 computer terminals/PCs, linked by a campus-wide computer network, are available for use by students in program; they are located in classrooms, the computer center, computer labs. Students in the program are not required to have their own PC.

Computer Resources/On-line Services

Training	Yes	CompuServe	No
Internet	Yes	Dun's	No
E-Mail	Yes	Dow Jones	Yes
Videoconference Center	Yes	Dialog	Yes $
Multimedia Center	Yes	Bloomberg	No
LEXIS/NEXIS	Yes		

ADMISSION
Acceptance 1994-95 1,104 applied for admission; 58% were accepted.

Entrance Requirements Bachelor's degree, GMAT score. Core courses waived through: previous course work.

Application Requirements Written essay, 2 letters of recommendation.

Application Deadlines 5/1 for fall, 10/15 for spring.

FINANCIALS
Costs for 1994-95 Tuition: Full-time: $382/credit; Part-time day: $382/credit. Fees: Full-time: $279/semester; Part-time day: $89-$149/semester.

Financial Aid In 1994-95, 40% of candidates received some institutionally administered aid in the form of grants, scholarships, loans, fellowships, assistantships, work-study. Total awards ranged from $1,000-$7,500. Financial aid is available to part-time students. Application deadlines: 4/1 for fall, 10/15 for spring. Applications are processed on a rolling basis. Contact: Ms. Ava Lampel, Financial Aid Administrator, Hempstead, NY 11550. (516) 463-6680.

INTERNATIONAL STUDENTS
Demographics 19% of students enrolled in the program are international; Asia 32%, Europe 28%, Africa 11%, South America 10%, Central America 5%, Other 14%.

Services and Facilities International student housing; international student office, visa services, language tutoring, ESL courses, counseling/support services.

Applying TOEFL required, minimum score of 580; proof of health; proof of adequate funds. Financial aid is not available to international students. Admission application deadlines: 4/1 for fall, 10/1 for spring. Applications are processed on a rolling basis. Contact: Ms. Heather Fellman, Assistant Dean for International Students, 221 Student Center, 200 Hofstra University, Hempstead, NY 11550. (516) 463-6796.

ALTERNATE MBA PROGRAM

MBA/JD Length of program: Minimum: 48 months. Full time classes: Main campus; day, summer. Degree requirements: 105 credits.

PLACEMENT

In 1993-94, 45 organizations participated in on-campus recruiting; 200 on-campus interviews were conducted. Placement services include alumni network, career counseling/planning, career fairs, career library, career placement, job interviews, resume preparation, and resume referral to employers. Of 1994 graduates, 92% were employed within three months of graduation, the average starting salary was $48,897, the range was $25,000-$97,000.

Jobs by Employer Type Manufacturing 23%; service 37%; government 2%; consulting 8%; nonprofit 5%; accounting 8%; investment banking/brokerage 12%; other 5%.

Jobs by Functional Area Marketing/sales 13%; finance 33%; operations 7%; management 20%; strategic planning 5%; technical management 12%; education 4%; other 6%.

Program Contact: Ms. Susan McTiernan, Senior Assistant Dean and Director of Graduate Programs, Hofstra University, 302 Weller Hall, 134 Hofstra University, Hempstead, NY 11550. (516) 463-5683, or (800) HOFSTRA; Fax: (516) 463-5268; Internet Address: bizsmm@vaxc.hofstra.edu.

See full description on page 754.

Iona College

Graduate School of Business

New Rochelle, New York

OVERVIEW

Iona College is an independent nonprofit comprehensive coed institution. Founded 1940. Setting: 35-acre suburban campus with easy access to New York City. Total institutional enrollment: 6,230. Program was first offered in 1965.

MBA HIGHLIGHTS

Entrance Difficulty**
Mean GMAT: 471
Mean GPA: 3.18

Cost $$$
Tuition: $390/credit
Room & Board: N/R

Enrollment Profile
Full-time: 20
Part-time: 430
Total: 450
Average Age: 29

Work Exp: 100%
International: 2%
Women: 50%
Minorities: 5%

Average Class Size: 20

ACADEMICS

Length of Program Minimum: 18 months. Maximum: 6 years.
Calendar Trimesters.
Full-time Classes Main campus, Rockland; evening, weekends, summer.
Part-time Classes Main campus, Rockland; evening, weekends, summer.
Degree Requirements 61 credits including 18 elective credits.
Required Courses Accounting workshop, business organization and administration, business policy, computer workshop, economics workshop, financial management, fundamentals of mathematical science, legal and social environment of business, macroeconomic analysis, management information systems, managerial accounting, managerial economics, marketing management, mathematical tools for management, mathematics workshop, production and operations management, statistics for management. Courses may be waived through: previous course work.
Curricular Focus Economic and financial theory, general management, international business.
Concentrations Economics, entrepreneurship, finance, human resources management, international business, management, management information systems, management science, marketing, operations management, quantitative analysis, strategic management.

Faculty Full-time: 47, 95% with doctorates; part-time: 4, 100% with doctorates.
Teaching Methodology Case study: 20%, lecture: 50%, student presentations: 20%, team projects: 10%.

STUDENT STATISTICS

Geographic Representation State residents 75%. By region: Northeast 93%; South 2%; Midwest 2%; West 1%. International 2%.
Undergraduate Majors Business 75%; education 3%; engineering/technology 6%; humanities 7%; science/mathematics 6%; social sciences 3%.
Other Background Graduate degrees in other disciplines: 2%. Work experience: On average, students have 3 years of work experience on entrance to the program.

FACILITIES

Information Resources Main library with 317,884 bound volumes, 26,000 titles on microform, 1,247 periodical subscriptions, 8,473 records/tapes/CDs.
Housing College housing not available.
Technology Computers are used moderately in course work. 400 computer terminals/PCs, linked by a campus-wide computer network, are available for use by students in program; they are located in learning resource center, the library, the computer center, computer labs. Students in the program are not required to have their own PC.

Computer Resources/On-line Services

Training	Yes	Dun's	Yes
Internet	Yes	Dow Jones	No
E-Mail	Yes	Dialog	Yes
LEXIS/NEXIS	No	Bloomberg	No
CompuServe	No		

Other on-line services: First Search.

ADMISSION

Acceptance 1994-95 396 applied for admission; 70% were accepted.
Entrance Requirements Bachelor's degree, GMAT score of 425, minimum 3.0 GPA. Core courses waived through: previous course work.
Application Requirements Written essay, application form, personal statement, 2 letters of recommendation.
Application Deadline Applications are processed on a rolling basis.

FINANCIALS

Costs for 1994-95 Tuition: Full-time: $390/credit. Fees: Full-time: $140/trimester.
Financial Aid In 1994-95, 5% of candidates received some institutionally administered aid in the form of loans, assistantships. Financial aid is available to part-time students. Applications are processed on a rolling basis. Contact: Ms. Norma McNerney, Director of Financial Aid, 715 North Avenue, New Rochelle, NY 10801. (914) 633-2497.

INTERNATIONAL STUDENTS

Demographics 2% of students enrolled in the program are international.
Services and Facilities International student center, counseling/support services.
Applying TOEFL required; proof of health; proof of adequate funds. Financial aid is not available to international students. Admission applications are processed on a rolling basis. Contact: Sr. Rita Dougherty, Foreign Student Adviser, 715 North Avenue, New Rochelle, NY 10801. (914) 633-2504.

PLACEMENT

Placement services include career counseling/planning, career library, and resume preparation.
Jobs by Employer Type Manufacturing 30%; service 46%; government 7%; consulting 5%; nonprofit 7%; self-employed 5%.
Jobs by Functional Area Marketing/sales 15%; finance 30%; operations 20%; management 20%; strategic planning 10%; technical management 5%.

Program Contact: Ms. Ann Kinnally, Director of MBA Recruitment, Iona College, 715 North Avenue, New Rochelle, NY 10801. (914) 633-2288, or (800) 231-IONA; Fax: (914) 633-2012.
See full description on page 766.

Long Island University, Brooklyn Campus

School of Business, Public Admin. and Information Science

Brooklyn, New York

OVERVIEW

Long Island University, Brooklyn Campus is an independent nonprofit comprehensive coed institution. Part of Long Island University. Founded 1926. Setting: 10-acre urban campus. Total institutional enrollment: 25,000. Program was first offered in 1930.

MBA HIGHLIGHTS

Entrance Difficulty**
Mean GMAT: 480
Mean GPA: 3.2

Cost $
Tuition: $382/credit
Room & Board: N/R

Enrollment Profile
Full-time: 70
Part-time: 230
Total: 300
Average Age: 29

Work Exp: 80%
International: N/R
Women: 40%
Minorities: 50%

Average Class Size: 20

ACADEMICS

Length of Program Minimum: 24 months. Maximum: 6 years.
Calendar Semesters.
Full-time Classes Main campus; evening, weekends.
Part-time Classes Main campus; evening, weekends.
Degree Requirements 36 credit hours including 15 elective credit hours. Other: Capstone course.
Required Courses Accounting, basic quantitative analysis, business law, business, government, and society, computer science, corporate finance, economic environment of business, finance, financial accounting, fundamentals of computing and computer systems, introduction to quantitative analysis, law, management, management processes, managerial economics, marketing, marketing systems, operations management, organizational behavior, personnel administration, quantitative analysis, quantitative methods in business research, social issues.
Curricular Focus Business issues and problems, international business, problem solving and decision making.
Concentrations Accounting, finance, international business, management, management information systems, marketing, operations management, public administration.
Faculty Full-time: 20, 65% with doctorates; part-time: 40, 50% with doctorates.
Teaching Methodology Case study: 40%, lecture: 40%, team projects: 20%.

STUDENT STATISTICS

Other Background Graduate degrees in other disciplines: 3%. Work experience: On average, students have 2-5 years of work experience on entrance to the program.

FACILITIES

Information Resources Main library with 984,804 bound volumes, 813,544 titles on microform, 8,042 periodical subscriptions, 7,902 records/tapes/CDs.
Housing 5% of students in program live in college-owned or -operated housing.
Technology Computers are used heavily in course work. Computer terminals/PCs are available for use by students in program; they are located in student rooms, the student center, learning resource center, the library, the computer center, computer labs, the research center. Students in the program are not required to have their own PC.

Computer Resources/On-line Services

Training	Yes	CompuServe	Yes
Internet	Yes	Dun's	No
E-Mail	Yes	Dow Jones	No
Multimedia Center	Yes	Dialog	Yes
LEXIS/NEXIS	Yes	Bloomberg	No

ADMISSION

Acceptance 1994-95 800 applied for admission; 50% were accepted.
Entrance Requirements Bachelor's degree, GMAT score of 380.
Application Requirements Application form, 2 letters of recommendation.
Application Deadline Applications are processed on a rolling basis.

FINANCIALS

Costs for 1994-95 Tuition: Full-time: $382/credit. Fees: Full-time: $200/semester.
Financial Aid In 1994-95, 10% of candidates received some institutionally administered aid in the form of scholarships, fellowships, assistantships. Total awards ranged from $1,000-$9,000. Application deadlines: 9/1 for fall, 2/1 for spring. Contact: Ms. Rose Iannicelli, Director of Financial Aid, One University Plaza, Brooklyn, NY 11201. (718) 488-1037.

INTERNATIONAL STUDENTS

Demographics 18% of students on campus are international; Asia 37%, South America 37%, Central America 15%, Africa 10%, other 1%.
Services and Facilities International student office, visa services, language tutoring, ESL courses.
Applying TOEFL required; proof of health; proof of adequate funds. Financial aid is not available to international students. Admission application deadlines: 8/31 for fall, 1/15 for spring. Contact: Mr. Steve Chin, Director International Student Program, One University Plaza, Brooklyn, NY 11201. (718) 488-1216.

PLACEMENT

In 1993-94, 25 organizations participated in on-campus recruiting. Placement services include alumni network, career counseling/planning, career fairs, career placement, job interviews, job search course, resume preparation, and resume referral to employers.

Program Contact: Mr. Alan Chaves, Dean of Admissions, Long Island University, Brooklyn Campus, One University Plaza, Brooklyn, NY 11201. (718) 488-1126, or (800) 548-7526; Fax: (718) 488-1125.

Long Island University, C.W. Post Campus

College of Management

Brookville, New York

OVERVIEW

Long Island University, C.W. Post Campus is an independent nonprofit comprehensive coed institution. Part of Long Island University. Founded 1954. Setting: 305-acre rural campus with easy access to New York City. Total institutional enrollment: 22,865. Program was first offered in 1963.

MBA HIGHLIGHTS

Entrance Difficulty***
GMAT: 475 - 500
Mean GPA: 3.1

Cost $$
Tuition: $365/credit
Room & Board: $4,910

Enrollment Profile
Full-time: 110
Part-time: 294
Total: 404
Average Age: 28

Work Exp: 60%
International: 24%
Women: 48%
Minorities: 1%

Average Class Size: 15

ACADEMICS

Length of Program Minimum: 18 months.
Calendar Semesters.
Full-time Classes Main campus, Brantwood; day, evening, weekends, early morning, summer.

Part-time Classes Main campus, West Point; evening.

Degree Requirements 36-60 credits including 15 elective credits. Other: Comprehensive project.

Required Courses Business and government and society capstone courses, business law, corporate finance, economic environment of business, financial accounting, fundamentals of computer systems, introduction of quantitative analysis, management process, managerial economics, marketing systems, operations management, organizational behavior, quantitative methods in business research. Courses may be waived through: previous course work.

Curricular Focus General management, international business, problem solving and decision making.

Concentrations Accounting, finance, international business, management, management information systems, marketing.

Faculty Full-time: 25, 92% with doctorates; part-time: 36, 40% with doctorates.

Teaching Methodology Case study: 20%, faculty seminars: 15%, lecture: 10%, research: 20%, seminars by members of the business community: 5%, student presentations: 10%, team projects: 20%.

Special Opportunities International exchange in Switzerland. Internship program available. Other: Professional Experience Placement Center.

STUDENT STATISTICS

Geographic Representation State residents 25%. By region: Northeast 70%; South 5%; Midwest 3%; West 2%. International 24%.

Undergraduate Majors Business 55%; education 10%; engineering/technology 25%; science/mathematics 5%; social sciences 5%.

Other Background Graduate degrees in other disciplines: 10%. Work experience: On average, students have 4 years of work experience on entrance to the program.

FACILITIES

Information Resources Main library with 583,307 bound volumes, 701,740 titles on microform, 5,295 periodical subscriptions, 7,409 records/tapes/CDs. Business collection in Center for Business Research includes 8,900 bound volumes, 1,100 periodical subscriptions.

Housing 20% of students in program live in college-owned or -operated housing.

Technology Computers are used moderately in course work. 350 computer terminals/PCs, linked by a campus-wide computer network, are available for use by students in program; they are located in the library, computer labs. Students in the program are not required to have their own PC.

Computer Resources/On-line Services

Training	Yes	Dun's	No
Internet	Yes	Dow Jones	No
E-Mail	Yes	Dialog	No
LEXIS/NEXIS	Yes	Bloomberg	No
CompuServe	No		

ADMISSION

Acceptance 1994-95 550 applied for admission; 75% were accepted.

Entrance Requirements Bachelor's in business, GPA, GMAT, and work experience are considered in the admissions decision. Core courses waived through: previous course work.

Application Requirements Application form, copies of transcript, resume/curriculum vitae.

Application Deadlines 10/1 for fall, 3/1 for spring.

FINANCIALS

Costs for 1994-95 Tuition: Full-time: $365/credit. Fees: Full-time: $225/semester. Average room and board costs are $4,910 per academic year (on-campus).

Financial Aid In 1994-95, 5% of candidates received some institutionally administered aid in the form of scholarships, loans, assistantships. Total awards ranged from $250-$2,000. Financial aid is not available to part-time students. Application deadline: 5/15 for fall. Contact: Ms. Joanne Graziano, Director of Financial Aid, Northern Boulevard, Brookville, NY 11548. (516) 299-2423.

INTERNATIONAL STUDENTS

Demographics 24% of students enrolled in the program are international.

Services and Facilities International student housing; international student center, language tutoring, ESL courses, special assistance for nonnative speakers of English, counseling/support services.

Applying TOEFL required, minimum score of 500; proof of health; proof of adequate funds. Financial aid is not available to international students.

Admission application deadlines: 5/15 for fall, 10/15 for spring. Contact: Ms. Renee Olson, Admissions Counselor for International Students, Northern Boulevard, Brookville, NY 11548. (516) 299-2067.

ALTERNATE MBA PROGRAM

International MBA Length of program: Minimum: 16 months. Degree requirements: 36 credits. 2 semesters study in Switzerland, 1 semester at C.W. Post; must have undergraduate business degree.

PLACEMENT

In 1993-94, 30 organizations participated in on-campus recruiting; 75 on-campus interviews were conducted. Placement services include career counseling/planning, career fairs, career placement, electronic job bank, job interviews, resume preparation, and resume referral to employers. Of 1994 graduates, 85% were employed within three months of graduation, the average starting salary was $53,190, the range was $26,500-$120,000.

Program Contact: Ms. Mary Dillon, MBA Adviser, Long Island University, C.W. Post Campus, Northern Boulevard, Brookville, NY 11548. (516) 299-2722 Ext. 2100; Fax: (516) 299-2786.

Manhattan College

School of Business

Riverdale, New York

OVERVIEW

Manhattan College is an independent comprehensive coed institution, affiliated with Roman Catholic Church. Founded 1853. Setting: 50-acre suburban campus with easy access to New York City. Total institutional enrollment: 3,495. Program was first offered in 1974.

MBA HIGHLIGHTS

Entrance Difficulty**
Mean GMAT: 460
Mean GPA: N/R

Cost $$
Tuition: $390/credit
Room & Board: N/R

Enrollment Profile
Full-time: 0
Part-time: 200
Total: 200
Average Age: N/R

Work Exp: 90%
International: N/R
Women: 43%
Minorities: N/R

Average Class Size: 15

ACADEMICS

Length of Program Minimum: 18 months. Maximum: 5 years.

Calendar Semesters.

Part-time Classes Main campus; evening, weekends, summer.

Degree Requirements 39 credits.

Required Courses Accounting systems, financial control systems, management information systems, marketing management systems, operations and total quality management, organizational theory and design, planning and policy formation, quantitative methods for decision analysis, the global economic environment.

Curricular Focus Business issues and problems, problem solving and decision making, technology management.

Concentrations Accounting, engineering management, finance, management.

Teaching Methodology Case study: 20%, lecture: 40%, research: 10%, seminars by members of the business community: 10%, student presentations: 10%, team projects: 10%.

FACILITIES

Information Resources Main library with 193,100 bound volumes, 383,480 titles on microform, 1,527 periodical subscriptions, 644 records/tapes/CDs, 4 CD-ROMs.

ADMISSION

Entrance Requirements Bachelor's degree, GMAT score, minimum 3.0 GPA. Core courses waived through: previous course work.

Application Requirements Application form, copies of transcript, 1 letter of recommendation.

Application Deadlines 8/10 for fall, 1/1 for spring, 5/1 for summer.

FINANCIALS
Costs for 1994-95 Tuition: Full-time: $390/credit. Fees: Full-time: $50/semester.

Financial Aid Financial aid is not available to part-time students. Contact: Office of Financial Assistance, Manhattan College Parkway, Riverdale, NY 10471. (718) 920-0381.

INTERNATIONAL STUDENTS
Applying TOEFL required, minimum score of 550; proof of adequate funds. Financial aid is not available to international students. Admission application deadlines: 8/10 for fall, 1/7 for spring. Applications are processed on a rolling basis.

Program Contact: Dr. Charles Brunner, Director, MBA Program, Manhattan College, Manhattan College Parkway, Riverdale, NY 10471. (718) 920-0222; Fax: (718) 884-0255; Internet Address: mba@mcs2.dls.mancol.edu.

Marist College

Division of Management Studies

Poughkeepsie, New York

OVERVIEW
Marist College is an independent nonprofit comprehensive coed institution. Founded 1929. Setting: 120-acre suburban campus with easy access to Albany and New York City. Total institutional enrollment: 4,000. Program was first offered in 1972.

MBA HIGHLIGHTS

Entrance Difficulty**
Mean GMAT: 542
Mean GPA: 3.1

Cost $
Tuition: $349/semester credit hour
Room & Board: N/R

Enrollment Profile
Full-time: 10	Work Exp: 95%
Part-time: 131	International: 2%
Total: 141	Women: 36%
Average Age: 32	Minorities: 6%

Average Class Size: 17

ACADEMICS
Length of Program Minimum: 16 months. Maximum: 7 years.
Calendar Semesters.
Full-time Classes Main campus, Goshen, Fishkill; evening, weekends, summer.
Degree Requirements 30 semester credit hours including 6 elective semester credit hours.
Required Courses Corporate financial theory, global environment of business, macroeconomic analysis or managerial economics, management accounting, quality management in operations, strategy marketing planning or industrial international marketing, topics in statistics and management science. Courses may be waived through: previous course work.
Curricular Focus General management, problem solving and decision making, strategic analysis and planning.
Concentrations Accounting, finance, health services, human resources management, management, management information systems.
Faculty Full-time: 25, 80% with doctorates; part-time: 3, 67% with doctorates.
Teaching Methodology Case study: 20%, faculty seminars: 2%, lecture: 50%, research: 5%, seminars by members of the business community: 3%, student presentations: 10%, team projects: 10%.

STUDENT STATISTICS
Geographic Representation State residents 98%. By region: Northeast 98%. International 2%.
Undergraduate Majors Business 30%; education 5%; engineering/technology 25%; humanities 10%; nursing 5%; science/mathematics 15%; social sciences 10%.

Other Background Graduate degrees in other disciplines: 20%. Work experience: On average, students have 5 years of work experience on entrance to the program.

FACILITIES
Information Resources Main library with 151,000 bound volumes, 12,000 titles on microform, 1,588 periodical subscriptions, 12,745 records/tapes/CDs.
Housing College housing not available.
Technology Computers are used moderately in course work. 80 computer terminals/PCs, linked by a campus-wide computer network, are available for use by students in program; they are located in dormitories, the student center, classrooms, the computer center, computer labs. Students in the program are not required to have their own PC.
Computer Resources/On-line Services
Training	Yes	Multimedia Center	Yes
Internet	Yes	Dow Jones	Yes
E-Mail	Yes	Dialog	Yes

Other on-line services: OCLC.

ADMISSION
Acceptance 1994-95 171 applied for admission; 90% were accepted.
Entrance Requirements Bachelor's degree, GMAT score of 450, minimum 2.7 GPA. Core courses waived through: previous course work.
Application Requirements Application form, copies of transcript.
Application Deadlines 8/15 for fall, 1/2 for spring, 5/1 for summer.

FINANCIALS
Costs for 1994-95 Tuition: Full-time: $349/semester credit hour. Fees: Full-time: $25/semester.
Financial Aid In 1994-95, 10% of candidates received some institutionally administered aid in the form of grants, work-study. Total awards ranged from $100-$3,000. Financial aid is available to part-time students. Application deadlines: 8/15 for fall, 1/1 for spring. Contact: Ms. Corinne Schell, Associate Director of Financial Aid, 290 North Road, Poughkeepsie, NY 12603-1387. (914) 575-3230.

INTERNATIONAL STUDENTS
Demographics 2% of students enrolled in the program are international.
Services and Facilities ESL courses, counseling/support services.
Applying TOEFL required, minimum score of 550; proof of adequate funds; minimum 4.0 score on Test of Written English. Financial aid is not available to international students. Admission application deadline: 4/30 for fall.

PLACEMENT
In 1993-94, 40 organizations participated in on-campus recruiting. Placement services include alumni network, career counseling/planning, career fairs, career library, career placement, job interviews, resume preparation, and resume referral to employers. Of 1994 graduates, 98% were employed within three months of graduation.

Program Contact: Ms. Carol Vari, Director, Graduate Admissions, Marist College, 290 North Road, Poughkeepsie, NY 12603-1387. (914) 575-3530; Fax: (914) 575-3640.

Mount Saint Mary College

Division of Business

Newburgh, New York

OVERVIEW
Mount Saint Mary College is an independent nonprofit comprehensive coed institution. Founded 1960. Setting: 63-acre urban campus with easy access to New York City. Total institutional enrollment: 1,800. Program was first offered in 1991.

MBA HIGHLIGHTS

Entrance Difficulty**
Mean GMAT: N/R
Mean GPA: 3.2

Cost $$
Tuition: $286/credit hour
Room & Board: N/R

Enrollment Profile

Full-time: 17	Work Exp: 97%
Part-time: 68	International: 2%
Total: 85	Women: 50%
Average Age: 33	Minorities: 16%

Average Class Size: 11

ACADEMICS
Length of Program Minimum: 30 months.
Calendar Semesters.
Full-time Classes Main campus; evening, summer.
Degree Requirements 34 credits including 9 elective credits.
Required Courses Ethics in management, financial management, marketing management, organizational behavior, production and operations management, seminar in management education, speech communication for management, writing for management. Courses may be waived through: previous course work.
Curricular Focus General management, organizational development and change management.
Concentration Management.
Faculty Full-time: 6, 67% with doctorates; part-time: 10, 70% with doctorates.
Teaching Methodology Case study: 20%, lecture: 25%, research: 20%, student presentations: 20%, team projects: 15%.

STUDENT STATISTICS
Geographic Representation State residents 95%. By region: Northeast 100%. International 2%.
Undergraduate Majors Business 85%; engineering/technology 2%; social sciences 7%; other 6%.
Other Background Graduate degrees in other disciplines: 1%. Work experience: On average, students have 10 years of work experience on entrance to the program.

FACILITIES
Information Resources Main library with 116,113 bound volumes, 269 titles on microform, 1,129 periodical subscriptions, 7,307 records/tapes/CDs. Business collection includes 2,792 bound volumes, 94 periodical subscriptions, 4 CD-ROMs, 71 videos.
Housing College housing not available.
Technology Computers are used moderately in course work. 50 computer terminals/PCs are available for use by students in program; they are located in the computer center, computer labs. Students in the program are required to have their own PC. $200 are budgeted per student for computer support.

Computer Resources/On-line Services

Training	Yes	E-Mail	Yes
Internet	Yes		

Other on-line services: SEC.

ADMISSION
Acceptance 1994-95 Of those applying, 90% were accepted.
Entrance Requirements Bachelor's degree, prerequisite courses required for applicants with non-business degree, GMAT score, minimum 2.5 GPA. Core courses waived through: previous course work.
Application Requirements Interview, application form, copies of transcript, personal statement, 3 letters of recommendation.
Application Deadline Applications are processed on a rolling basis.

FINANCIALS
Costs for 1994-95 Tuition: Full-time: $286/credit hour. Fees: Full-time: $120.
Financial Aid In 1994-95, candidates received some institutionally administered aid in the form of loans. Application deadlines: 3/15 for fall, 11/15 for spring. Contact: Ms. Harlene Mehr, Director of Financial Aid, 330 Powell Avenue, Newburgh, NY 12550-3494. (914) 561-0800.

INTERNATIONAL STUDENTS
Demographics 2% of students enrolled in the program are international; Asia 100%.
Services and Facilities Counseling/support services.

Applying Financial aid is not available to international students. Admission applications are processed on a rolling basis. Contact: Dr. Loretta Butler, Associate Dean for Curriculum, 330 Powell Avenue, Newburgh, NY 12550-3494. (914) 561-0800.

Program Contact: Dr. Jerome Picard, Coordinator, MBA Program, Mount Saint Mary College, 330 Powell Avenue, Newburgh, NY 12550-3494. (914) 569-3119; Fax: (914) 562-6762.

New York Institute of Technology

School of Management

Old Westbury, New York

OVERVIEW
New York Institute of Technology is an independent nonprofit comprehensive coed institution. Founded 1955. Setting: 750-acre suburban campus with easy access to New York City. Total institutional enrollment: 9,500. Program was first offered in 1975.

MBA HIGHLIGHTS

Entrance Difficulty**
Mean GMAT: 500
Mean GPA: 3.1

Cost $
Tuition: $320/credit
Room & Board: $5,840

Enrollment Profile

Full-time: 360	Work Exp: 86%
Part-time: 440	International: 30%
Total: 800	Women: 40%
Average Age: 27	Minorities: 7%

Average Class Size: 26

ACADEMICS
Length of Program Minimum: 12 months. Maximum: 5 years.
Calendar Semesters.
Full-time Classes Main campus, New York City, Islip, Boca Raton; evening, weekends, summer.
Part-time Classes Main campus, New York City, Islip, Boca Raton; evening, weekends, summer.
Degree Requirements 36-54 credits including 9-18 elective credits. Other: Thesis, oral exam, or 6 extra credits.
Curricular Focus Economic and financial theory, general management, international business.
Concentrations Accounting, energy management, finance, human resources management, international business, management, management information systems, marketing, quantitative analysis.
Faculty Full-time: 11, 100% with doctorates; part-time: 12, 50% with doctorates.
Teaching Methodology Case study: 15%, faculty seminars: 3%, lecture: 60%, research: 2%, seminars by members of the business community: 2%, student presentations: 8%, team projects: 10%.

STUDENT STATISTICS
Geographic Representation By region: Northeast 61%; Midwest 3%; West 3%; South 2%. International 30%.
Undergraduate Majors Business 36%; education 3%; engineering/technology 30%; humanities 7%; nursing 1%; science/mathematics 10%; social sciences 10%; other 3%.
Other Background Graduate degrees in other disciplines: 10%. Work experience: On average, students have 4 years of work experience on entrance to the program.

FACILITIES
Information Resources Main library with 190,878 bound volumes, 202,755 titles on microform, 4,303 periodical subscriptions, 1,808 records/tapes/CDs. Business collection includes 31,250 bound volumes, 275 periodical subscriptions, 7 CD-ROMs, 40 videos.
Housing 7% of students in program live in college-owned or -operated housing. Assistance with housing search provided.
Technology Computers are used moderately in course work. Computer terminals/PCs are available for use by students in program; they are

located in classrooms, learning resource center, the computer center, computer labs. Students in the program are not required to have their own PC.

Computer Resources/On-line Services

Training	Yes	E-Mail	Yes
Internet	Yes	Videoconference Center	Yes

Other on-line services: OCLC.

ADMISSION

Acceptance 1994-95 520 applied for admission; 85% were accepted.

Entrance Requirements Bachelor's degree, GMAT score of 400, minimum 2.5 GPA. Core courses waived through: previous course work.

Application Requirements Application form, copies of transcript.

Application Deadline Applications are processed on a rolling basis.

FINANCIALS

Costs for 1994-95 Tuition: Full-time: $320/credit. Average room and board costs are $5,840 per academic year (on-campus).

Financial Aid In 1994-95, candidates received some institutionally administered aid in the form of grants, scholarships, loans, assistantships. Total awards ranged from $320-$5,760. Financial aid is available to part-time students. Applications are processed on a rolling basis. Contact: Mrs. Doreen Meyer, Director of Financial Aid, PO Box 8000, Old Westbury, NY 11568. (516) 686-7680.

INTERNATIONAL STUDENTS

Demographics 30% of students enrolled in the program are international; Asia 61%, Europe 20%, Central America 5%, South America 5%, Africa 4%, North America 2%, Australia 1%, other 2%.

Services and Facilities International student housing; international student office, visa services, language tutoring, ESL courses, special assistance for nonnative speakers of English, counseling/support services.

Applying TOEFL required, minimum score of 500; proof of health; proof of adequate funds. Financial aid is available to international students. Applications are processed on a rolling basis. Admission applications are processed on a rolling basis. Contact: Mr. Dilipkumar Kondiparti, International Student Adviser, PO Box 8000, Old Westbury, NY 11568. (516) 686-7520.

PLACEMENT

Placement services include career counseling/planning, career fairs, and resume preparation. Of 1994 graduates, 90% were employed within three months of graduation.

Program Contact: Mr. Glenn Berman, Director of Graduate Admissions, New York Institute of Technology, PO Box 8000, Old Westbury, NY 11568. (516) 686-7519, or (800) 345-NYIT; Fax: (516) 626-0419.

New York University

Leonard N. Stern School of Business, Graduate Division

New York, New York

OVERVIEW

New York University is an independent nonprofit coed institution. Founded 1831. Setting: 28-acre urban campus. Total institutional enrollment: 49,307. Program was first offered in 1916. AACSB-accredited.

MBA HIGHLIGHTS

Entrance Difficulty***
Mean GMAT: N/R
Mean GPA: 3.2

Cost $$$$
Tuition: $19,500
Room & Board: $10,300

Enrollment Profile

Full-time: 1,023		Work Exp: 97%
Part-time: 2,229		International: 11%
Total: 3,252		Women: 35%
Average Age: 27		Minorities: 16%

Average Class Size: 50

ACADEMICS

Length of Program Minimum: 21 months. Maximum: 6 years.

Calendar Semesters.

Full-time Classes Main campus; day, evening, weekends, early morning, summer.

Part-time Classes Main campus, Manhattanville College; evening, weekends, early morning, summer.

Degree Requirements 60 credits including 30 elective credits.

Required Courses Data analysis, finance, financial accounting, information systems, macroeconomics, managerial accounting, managing organization behavior, market, ethics, and law, marketing, microeconomics, operations management, strategy and policy.

Curricular Focus Economic and financial theory, international business, problem solving and decision making, teamwork.

Concentrations Accounting, arts administration, economics, entrepreneurship, finance, health services, human resources management, international business, management, management information systems, marketing, operations management, organizational behavior, public administration, public policy, quantitative analysis, real estate, strategic management.

Teaching Methodology Case study: 35%, lecture: 35%, student presentations: 15%, team projects: 15%.

Special Opportunities International exchange in Australia, Austria, Belgium, Brazil, Denmark, France, Germany, Hong Kong, Israel, Italy, Japan, Netherlands, Republic of Korea, Spain, Sweden, Switzerland, United Kingdom. Internship program available. Other: Consulting UBAC-providing consulting services to minority and women-owned businesses; new business development/entrepreneurship.

STUDENT STATISTICS

Geographic Representation International 11%.

Undergraduate Majors Business 35%; humanities 7%; science/mathematics 21%; social sciences 30%; other 7%.

Other Background Graduate degrees in other disciplines: 8%. Work experience: On average, students have 4 years of work experience on entrance to the program.

FACILITIES

Information Resources Main library with 3.6 million bound volumes, 3 million titles on microform, 29,244 periodical subscriptions, 39,244 records/tapes/CDs. Business collection includes 150,000 bound volumes, 2,500 periodical subscriptions, 20 CD-ROMs.

Housing 15% of students in program live in college-owned or -operated housing.

Technology Computers are used heavily in course work. 300 computer terminals/PCs, linked by a campus-wide computer network, are available for use by students in program; they are located in student rooms, classrooms, learning resource center, the library, the computer center, computer labs. Students in the program are not required to have their own PC.

Computer Resources/On-line Services

Training	Yes	LEXIS/NEXIS	Yes
Internet	Yes	Dun's	Yes
E-Mail	Yes	Dow Jones	Yes
Videoconference Center	Yes	Dialog	Yes
Multimedia Center	Yes	Bloomberg	Yes

Other on-line services: RLIN.

ADMISSION

Entrance Requirements Bachelor's degree, GMAT score, minimum 2 years of work experience.

Application Requirements Written essay, interview, application form, copies of transcript, resume/curriculum vitae, 2 letters of recommendation.

Application Deadline 3/31 for fall.

FINANCIALS

Costs for 1994-95 Tuition: Full-time: $19,500; Part-time evening: $9,294; Summer: $4,647/term. Fees: Full-time: $991; Part-time evening: $441; Summer: $213/term. Average room and board costs are $10,300 per academic year (on-campus) and $9,655 per academic year (off-campus).

Financial Aid In 1994-95, 35% of candidates received some institutionally administered aid in the form of grants, scholarships, loans, fellowships, assistantships, work-study, tuition/fee waivers. Total awards ranged from $1,000-$20,491. Financial aid is available to part-time students. Application deadline: 1/31 for fall. Contact: Office of Financial Aid, 44 West 4th Street, #10-160, New York, NY 10012-1019. (212) 998-0790.

INTERNATIONAL STUDENTS

Demographics 11% of students enrolled in the program are international; Asia 55%, Europe 23%, South America 9%, Africa 2%, Australia 2%, other 6%.

Services and Facilities International student center, visa services, language tutoring, ESL courses, special assistance for nonnative speakers of English, counseling/support services.

Applying TOEFL required, minimum score of 600; proof of health; proof of adequate funds. Financial aid is available to international students. Assistantships are available for these students after first year. Admission application deadline: 3/31 for fall. Applications are processed on a rolling basis. Contact: Ms. Antoinette Darcy, Associate Director of Academic Advising, 44 West 4th Street, #10-160, New York, NY 10012-1019. (212) 998-0585.

ALTERNATE MBA PROGRAMS

Executive MBA (EMBA) Length of program: Minimum: 24 months. Full-time classes: Main campus; day, weekends, summer. Degree requirements: 72 credits.

MBA/JD Length of program: Minimum: 48 months. Maximum: 6 years. Degree requirements: 122 credits including 45 elective credits. Separate applications must be submitted to both business and law schools.

MBA/MA Length of program: Minimum: 36 months. Maximum: 6 years. Degree requirements: 82 credits including 32 elective credits. Separate applications must be submitted to both business and arts and sciences.

PLACEMENT

In 1993-94, 173 organizations participated in on-campus recruiting; 5,215 on-campus interviews were conducted. Placement services include alumni network, career counseling/planning, career fairs, career library, career placement, corporate presentations, corporate career panels, electronic job bank, job interviews, resume preparation, and resume referral to employers. Of 1994 graduates, 88% were employed within three months of graduation, the average starting salary was $58,831, the range was $22,000-$98,000.

Program Contact: Ms. Mary Miller, Director of Admissions, New York University, 44 West 4th Street, #10-160, New York, NY 10012-1019. (212) 998-0600; Fax: (212) 995-4231.
See full description on page 790.

Niagara University

Graduate Division of Business Administration

Niagara Falls, New York

OVERVIEW

Niagara University is an independent nonprofit comprehensive coed institution. Founded 1856. Setting: 160-acre suburban campus with easy access to Buffalo and Toronto. Total institutional enrollment: 2,850. Program was first offered in 1981.

MBA HIGHLIGHTS

Entrance Difficulty*
Mean GMAT: 490
Mean GPA: 3.1

Cost $$
Tuition: $337/credit hour
Room & Board: N/R

Enrollment Profile

Full-time: 30	Work Exp: 90%
Part-time: 135	International: 30%
Total: 165	Women: 33%
Average Age: 28	Minorities: 7%

Average Class Size: 20

ACADEMICS

Length of Program Minimum: 23 months. Maximum: 5 years.
Calendar Semesters.
Full-time Classes Main campus; evening, summer.
Part-time Classes Main campus; evening, summer.
Degree Requirements 48 credits including 6 elective credits.
Required Courses Advanced quantitative methods of decision making, business research, strategy and planning, communications for executives, economic analysis, economic policy, financial accounting, financial management, management and the behavioral sciences, management information systems, managerial accounting, marketing management, moral and ethical aspects of corporations and society, production and operations management, quantitative methods of decision making. Courses may be waived through: previous course work, work experience.
Curricular Focus General management, organizational development and change management, teamwork.
Concentrations Accounting, hotel management, management.
Faculty Full-time: 12, 75% with doctorates; part-time: 5, 60% with doctorates.
Teaching Methodology Case study: 30%, lecture: 30%, research: 10%, student presentations: 10%, team projects: 20%.
Special Opportunities International exchange in United Kingdom. Internship program available.

STUDENT STATISTICS

Geographic Representation State residents 70%. By region: Northeast 70%. International 30%.
Undergraduate Majors Business 40%; education 5%; engineering/technology 20%; humanities 5%; nursing 5%; science/mathematics 10%; social sciences 15%.
Other Background Graduate degrees in other disciplines: 10%. Work experience: On average, students have 4 years of work experience on entrance to the program.

FACILITIES

Information Resources Main library with 288,986 bound volumes, 12,635 titles on microform, 1,311 periodical subscriptions, 742 records/tapes/CDs.
Housing 2% of students in program live in college-owned or -operated housing.
Technology Computers are used moderately in course work. 60 computer terminals/PCs, linked by a campus-wide computer network, are available for use by students in program; they are located in the computer center, computer labs. Students in the program are not required to have their own PC.

Computer Resources/On-line Services

Training	Yes	Videoconference Center	Yes
Internet	Yes	Dialog	Yes
E-Mail	Yes		

ADMISSION

Acceptance 1994-95 80 applied for admission; 50% were accepted.
Entrance Requirements Bachelor's degree, GMAT score. Core courses waived through: previous course work, work experience.
Application Requirements Interview, application form, copies of transcript, resume/curriculum vitae, 2 letters of recommendation.
Application Deadline Applications are processed on a rolling basis.

FINANCIALS

Costs for 1994-95 Tuition: Full-time: $337/credit hour.
Financial Aid In 1994-95, 6% of candidates received some institutionally administered aid in the form of scholarships, assistantships. Total awards ranged from $6,060-$9,650. Financial aid is not available to part-time students. Applications are processed on a rolling basis. Contact: Dr. Gary D. Praetzel, MBA Director, Niagara University, NY 14109. (716) 286-8182.

INTERNATIONAL STUDENTS

Demographics 30% of students enrolled in the program are international; Europe 3%, Asia 2%, other 95%.
Services and Facilities Visa services, language tutoring, ESL courses, special assistance for nonnative speakers of English, counseling/support services.
Applying TOEFL required, minimum score of 500; proof of health; proof of adequate funds. Financial aid is available to international students. Applications are processed on a rolling basis. Admission applications are processed on a rolling basis. Contact: Ms. Anne Sauvageau, Foreign Student Adviser, Niagara University, NY 14109. (716) 286-8772.

PLACEMENT

In 1993-94, 10 organizations participated in on-campus recruiting. Placement services include alumni network, career counseling/planning, career fairs, career library, career placement, electronic job bank, job interviews, resume preparation, and resume referral to employers. Of 1994 graduates, 95% were employed within three months of graduation.

Program Contact: Dr. Gary D. Praetzel, MBA Director, Niagara University, Niagara University, NY 14109. (716) 286-8182.

Pace University

Lubin School of Business

New York, New York

OVERVIEW

Pace University is an independent nonprofit coed institution. Part of Pace University. Founded 1906. Total institutional enrollment: 14,600. Program was first offered in 1958.

MBA HIGHLIGHTS

Entrance Difficulty***
Mean GMAT: 500
Mean GPA: 3.1

Cost $$$
Tuition: $425/credit
Room & Board: $3,600

Enrollment Profile

Full-time: 247	Work Exp: 95%
Part-time: 1,843	International: 20%
Total: 2,090	Women: 43%
Average Age: 28	Minorities: 22%

Average Class Size: 25

ACADEMICS

Length of Program Minimum: 24 months. Maximum: 5 years.

Calendar Semesters.

Full-time Classes Main campus, White Plains; day, evening, summer.

Part-time Classes Main campus, White Plains; day, evening, summer.

Degree Requirements 36 credits including 6 elective credits.

Required Courses Business in the global environment, financial and managerial accounting, global business policy or entrepreneurial policy, managerial economics, managerial finance, managerial marketing, managerial theory and skills, managerial theory and skills 2, quantitative analysis for business, statistical analysis for business.

Curricular Focus General management, international business, professional skills, strategic analysis and planning.

Concentrations Accounting, economics, finance, health services, human resources management, international business, management, management information systems, organizational behavior, quantitative analysis, strategic management, taxation.

Faculty Full-time: 57, 100% with doctorates; part-time: 36, 75% with doctorates.

Teaching Methodology Case study: 10%, faculty seminars: 5%, lecture: 55%, research: 5%, seminars by members of the business community: 5%, student presentations: 10%, team projects: 10%.

Special Opportunities International exchange in France, Germany. Internship program available.

STUDENT STATISTICS

Geographic Representation State residents 72%. By region: Northeast 75%; South 2%; West 2%; Midwest 1%. International 20%.

Undergraduate Majors Business 38%; education 2%; engineering/technology 27%; humanities 10%; nursing 1%; science/mathematics 8%; social sciences 12%; other 2%.

Other Background Graduate degrees in other disciplines: 2%. Work experience: On average, students have 5 years of work experience on entrance to the program.

FACILITIES

Information Resources Main library with 838,827 bound volumes, 716,348 titles on microform, 3,983 periodical subscriptions, 848 records/tapes/CDs, 52 CD-ROMs.

Housing College housing available.

Technology Computers are used moderately in course work. 700 computer terminals/PCs are available for use by students in program; they are located in classrooms, the computer center, computer labs. Students in the program are not required to have their own PC.

Computer Resources/On-line Services

Training	Yes	Dun's	No
Internet	No	Dow Jones	No
E-Mail	No	Dialog	No
LEXIS/NEXIS	No	Bloomberg	No
CompuServe	No		

ADMISSION

Acceptance 1994-95 1,335 applied for admission; 78% were accepted.

Entrance Requirements Bachelor's degree, GMAT score of 500. Core courses waived through: previous course work.

Application Requirements Written essay, application form, copies of transcript, resume/curriculum vitae, personal statement, 2 letters of recommendation.

Application Deadlines 7/31 for fall, 11/30 for spring, 4/30 for summer. Applications are processed on a rolling basis.

FINANCIALS

Costs for 1994-95 Tuition: Full-time: $425/credit. Fees: Full-time: $40-$150/credit. Average room and board costs are $3,600 per academic year (on-campus).

Financial Aid In 1994-95, 30% of candidates received some institutionally administered aid in the form of grants, scholarships, loans, assistantships, work-study. Financial aid is available to part-time students. Application deadlines: 3/15 for fall, 10/1 for spring. Applications are processed on a rolling basis. Contact: Ms. Jean Belmont, Director of Financial Aid, 1 Pace Plaza, New York, NY 10038. (212) 346-1300.

INTERNATIONAL STUDENTS

Demographics 20% of students enrolled in the program are international.

Services and Facilities International student office, ESL courses, counseling/support services.

Applying TOEFL required, minimum score of 550; proof of health; proof of adequate funds. Financial aid is not available to international students. Admission application deadlines: 6/30 for fall, 10/31 for spring, 3/31 for summer. Contact: Ms. Judith Dauduy, Director of International Education, 1 Pace Plaza, New York, NY 10038. (212) 346-1368.

ALTERNATE MBA PROGRAMS

Executive MBA (EMBA) Length of program: Minimum: 18 months. Degree requirements: 54 credits.

MBA/JD Length of program: Minimum: 48 months. Full-time classes: Main campus; day, evening, summer. Part-time classes: Main campus; day, evening, summer. Degree requirements: 129 credits.

PLACEMENT

In 1993-94, 90 organizations participated in on-campus recruiting; 500 on-campus interviews were conducted. Placement services include alumni network, career counseling/planning, career fairs, career library, career placement, job interviews, job search course, resume preparation, and resume referral to employers. Of 1994 graduates, 75% were employed within three months of graduation, the average starting salary was $43,000, the range was $35,000-$55,000.

Jobs by Employer Type Service 19%; government 2%; consulting 7%; nonprofit 32%; other 37%.

Jobs by Functional Area Marketing/sales 6%; finance 35%; operations 2%; management 7%; strategic planning 5%; technical management 12%; other 31%.

Program Contact: Ms. Joanna Broda, University Director of Graduate Admission, Pace University, Office of Graduate Admission, 1 Pace Plaza, New York, NY 19038. (212) 346-1531; Fax: (212) 346-1040.
See full description on page 798.

Rensselaer Polytechnic Institute

School of Management

Troy, New York

OVERVIEW

Rensselaer Polytechnic Institute is an independent nonprofit coed institution. Founded 1824. Setting: 260-acre urban campus with easy access to Albany. Total institutional enrollment: 6,487. Program was first offered in 1963. AACSB-accredited.

MBA HIGHLIGHTS

Entrance Difficulty****
Mean GMAT: 570
Mean GPA: 3.04

Cost $$$
Tuition: $16,200
Room & Board: $6,507

Enrollment Profile

Full-time: 125	Work Exp: 84%
Part-time: 78	International: 40%
Total: 203	Women: 20%
Average Age: 26	Minorities: 5%

Average Class Size: 35

ACADEMICS

Length of Program Minimum: 18 months. Maximum: 5 years.

Calendar Semesters.

Full-time Classes Main campus; day, evening, summer.

Part-time Classes Main campus; day, evening, summer.

Degree Requirements 60 credits including 18 elective credits. Other: Minimum 3.0 GPA.

Required Courses Design, manufacturing, and marketing, designing, developing, & staffing high performance organizations, ethics and social corporate responsibility, financial and managerial accounting, financial management and valuation of the firm, macroeconomics in international environments, managerial economics, practicum in management, statistics and operations management, strategy, technology, and entrepreneurship, technology and competitive advantage.

Curricular Focus Entrepreneurship, strategic analysis and planning, technology management.

Concentrations Entrepreneurship, environmental management, product development, manufacturing systems, technical sales, finance, management information systems.

Faculty Full-time: 60, 100% with doctorates; part-time: 5, 80% with doctorates.

Teaching Methodology Case study: 25%, faculty seminars: 5%, lecture: 25%, practicum: 5%, research: 10%, seminars by members of the business community: 5%, student presentations: 10%, team projects: 15%.

Special Opportunities International exchange in Australia, Denmark, France, Italy, Japan, Spain, Switzerland.

STUDENT STATISTICS

Geographic Representation By region: Northeast 49%; West 4%; South 3%; Midwest 3%. International 40%.

Undergraduate Majors Business 27%; engineering/technology 36%; humanities 4%; science/mathematics 23%; social sciences 9%; other 1%.

Other Background Graduate degrees in other disciplines: 20%. Work experience: On average, students have 4 years of work experience on entrance to the program.

FACILITIES

Information Resources Main library with 430,000 bound volumes, 3,875 periodical subscriptions, 4,900 records/tapes/CDs, 25 CD-ROMs.

Housing 13% of students in program live in college-owned or -operated housing.

Technology Computers are used moderately in course work. 580 computer terminals/PCs, linked by a campus-wide computer network, are available for use by students in program; they are located in student rooms, classrooms, the library, the computer center, computer labs. Students in the program are not required to have their own PC.

Computer Resources/On-line Services

Training	Yes	Videoconference Center	Yes
Internet	Yes	Multimedia Center	Yes
E-Mail	Yes		

ADMISSION

Acceptance 1994-95 337 applied for admission; 80% were accepted.

Entrance Requirements Bachelor's degree, GMAT score. Core courses waived through: previous course work.

Application Requirements Application form, copies of transcript, personal statement, 2 letters of recommendation.

Application Deadlines 5/1 for fall, 11/1 for spring. Applications are processed on a rolling basis.

FINANCIALS

Costs for 1995-96 Tuition: Full-time: $16,200. Fees: Full-time: $515/trimester. Average room and board costs are $6,507 per academic year (on-campus).

Financial Aid In 1994-95, candidates received some institutionally administered aid in the form of scholarships, loans, assistantships. Financial aid is available to part-time students. Application deadlines: 2/1 for fall, 10/1 for spring. Applications are processed on a rolling basis. Contact: Mr. John H. Cerveny, Director of Management and Technology, 110 8th Street, Troy, NY 12180-3590. (518) 276-6809.

INTERNATIONAL STUDENTS

Demographics 40% of students enrolled in the program are international; Asia 53%, Europe 6%, South America 6%, North America 3%, Africa 1%, other 31%.

Services and Facilities International student office, international student center, language tutoring, special assistance for nonnative speakers of English, counseling/support services, orientation, employment workshops, tax seminars.

Applying TOEFL required, minimum score of 550; proof of health; proof of adequate funds. Financial aid is available to international students. Financial aid application deadlines: 2/1 for fall, 10/1 for spring. Applications are processed on a rolling basis. Admission application deadlines: 5/1 for fall, 11/1 for spring. Applications are processed on a rolling basis. Contact: Ms. Jane Harris, Acting Director, International Student Services, Troy Building Room 200, Troy, NY 12180-3590. (518) 276-6561.

ALTERNATE MBA PROGRAMS

Executive MBA (EMBA) Length of program: Minimum: 18 months. Maximum: 3 years. Full-time classes: Main campus; weekends. Degree requirements: 48 credits. Minimum 3.0 GPA.

MBA/JD Length of program: Minimum: 36 months. Full-time classes: Main campus, Albany Law School; day, evening. Degree requirements: 90 credits. Offered in conjunction with Albany Law School of Union University.

MBA/M Eng Length of program: Minimum: 24 months. Maximum: 5 years. Full-time classes: Main campus; day, evening, summer. Degree requirements: 72 credits.

PLACEMENT

Placement services include alumni network, career counseling/planning, career fairs, career library, career placement, electronic job bank, job interviews, job search course, resume preparation, and resume referral to employers. Of 1994 graduates, 79% were employed within three months of graduation, the average starting salary was $45,500.

Jobs by Employer Type Manufacturing 17%; service 50%; consulting 33%.

Jobs by Functional Area Marketing/sales 10%; finance 13%; operations 7%; management 13%; strategic planning 10%; technical management 47%.

Program Contact: Mr. John H. Cerveny, Director, Management and Technology MBA Program, Rensselaer Polytechnic Institute, 110 8th Street, Troy, NY 12180-3590. (518) 276-4800; Fax: (518) 276-8661; Internet Address: cervej@rpi.edu.

See full description on page 814.

Rochester Institute of Technology

College of Business

Rochester, New York

OVERVIEW
Rochester Institute of Technology is an independent nonprofit comprehensive coed institution. Founded 1829. Setting: 1,300-acre suburban campus with easy access to Buffalo. Total institutional enrollment: 15,000. Program was first offered in 1968. AACSB-accredited.

MBA HIGHLIGHTS

Entrance Difficulty***
Mean GMAT: 510
Mean GPA: 3.12

Cost $$$
Tuition: $15,384 - $20,516
Room & Board: N/R

Enrollment Profile

Full-time: 110	Work Exp: 80%
Part-time: 365	International: 24%
Total: 475	Women: 48%
Average Age: 27	Minorities: 12%

Average Class Size: 25

ACADEMICS
Length of Program Minimum: 15 months. Maximum: 7 years.
Calendar Quarters.
Full-time Classes Main campus, Prague, Czech Republic; day, evening, early morning, summer.
Part-time Classes Main campus; evening, summer.
Degree Requirements 72 credits including 40 elective credits.
Required Courses Competitive strategy, economics for managers, financial accounting systems, financial analysis for managers, human behavior, leadership and diversity, marketing for customer satisfaction, operations management and process improvement, statistical analysis for decision making.
Curricular Focus International business, problem solving and decision making, teamwork.
Concentrations Accounting, entrepreneurship, finance, health services, human resources management, international business, management, management information systems, marketing, organizational behavior, public administration, technology management, manufacturing management.
Faculty Full-time: 40, 90% with doctorates; part-time: 5, 20% with doctorates.
Teaching Methodology Case study: 10%, computer simulation and role playing: 30%, lecture: 20%, student presentations: 20%, team projects: 20%.
Special Opportunities Internship program available. Other: cooperative education.

STUDENT STATISTICS
Geographic Representation International 24%.
Undergraduate Majors Business 30%; engineering/technology 30%; social sciences 30%; other 10%.
Other Background Graduate degrees in other disciplines: 5%. Work experience: On average, students have 2 years of work experience on entrance to the program.

FACILITIES
Information Resources Main library with 355,750 bound volumes, 220,168 titles on microform, 4,768 periodical subscriptions, 2,842 records/tapes/CDs, 166 CD-ROMs.
Housing 20% of students in program live in college-owned or -operated housing.
Technology Computers are used moderately in course work. 2,500 computer terminals/PCs, linked by a campus-wide computer network, are available for use by students in program; they are located in dormitories, the library, the computer center, computer labs, the research center. Students in the program are not required to have their own PC.

Computer Resources/On-line Services

Training	Yes	Multimedia Center	Yes
Internet	Yes	LEXIS/NEXIS	Yes
E-Mail	Yes	Dun's	Yes
Videoconference Center	Yes	Dow Jones	Yes

Other on-line services: Carl.

ADMISSION
Acceptance 1994-95 172 applied for admission; 90% were accepted.
Entrance Requirements Bachelor's degree, GMAT score of 500, minimum 2.75 GPA. Core courses waived through: previous course work.
Application Requirements Written essay, application form, copies of transcript, resume/curriculum vitae, personal statement, 2 letters of recommendation.
Application Deadlines 8/10 for fall, 11/10 for winter, 2/10 for spring, 5/10 for summer. Applications are processed on a rolling basis.

FINANCIALS
Costs for 1994-95 Tuition: Full-time: $15,384-$20,516; Part-time day: $1,725-$3,450/quarter.
Financial Aid In 1994-95, candidates received some institutionally administered aid in the form of scholarships, loans, assistantships. Total awards ranged from $3,000-$11,538. Financial aid is available to part-time students. Applications are processed on a rolling basis. Contact: Dr. Peter Giopulos, Acting Dean of Graduate Studies, One Lomb Memorial Drive, Rochester, NY 14623. (716) 475-6523.

INTERNATIONAL STUDENTS
Demographics 24% of students enrolled in the program are international; Asia 75%, Europe 5%, South America 4%, North America 4%, other 12%.
Services and Facilities International student office, international student center, visa services, language tutoring, ESL courses, counseling/support services.
Applying TOEFL required, minimum score of 550; proof of health; proof of adequate funds. Financial aid is available to international students. Financial aid application deadline: 9/1 for fall. Admission application deadlines: 8/10 for fall, 11/10 for winter, 2/10 for spring, 5/1 for summer. Applications are processed on a rolling basis. Contact: Ms. Mary Ann Campbell, Program Coordinator, Center for Student Transition and Support, 42 Lomb Memorial Drive, Rochester, NY 14623. (716) 475-6876.

ALTERNATE MBA PROGRAM
Executive MBA (EMBA) Length of program: Minimum: 24 months. Degree requirements: 72 credits.

PLACEMENT
Placement services include alumni network, career counseling/planning, career library, career placement, electronic job bank, and resume preparation.

Program Contact: Dr. Stanley Widrick, Associate Dean, Director of Graduate Business Programs, Rochester Institute of Technology, 104 Lomb Memorial Drive, Max Lowenthal Building, Rochester, NY 14623. (716) 475-2365; Fax: (716) 475-7450; Internet Address: smwbbu@rit. edu.
See full description on page 816.

Russell Sage College

Sage Graduate School

Troy, New York

OVERVIEW
Russell Sage College is an independent nonprofit comprehensive women only institution. Part of The Sage Colleges. Founded 1916. Setting: 12-acre suburban campus. Total institutional enrollment: 4,000. Program was first offered in 1981.

MBA HIGHLIGHTS

Entrance Difficulty***
Mean GMAT: 500
Mean GPA: 3.2

Cost $$$
Tuition: $825/course
Room & Board: N/R

Enrollment Profile

Full-time: 25		Work Exp: 98%
Part-time: 225		International: 3%
Total: 250		Women: 48%
Average Age: 29		Minorities: 5%

Average Class Size: 18

ACADEMICS

Length of Program Minimum: 36 months. Maximum: 7 years.

Calendar Semesters.

Part-time Classes Main campus, Rome; evening, weekends, summer.

Degree Requirements 51 credits including 15 elective credits.

Required Courses Business ethics, decision support systems, financial management, legal environment of business, management of operations, managerial economics, marketing systems, policy analysis and formation, statistical reasoning for managers, theory of organizational behavior.

Curricular Focus Leadership, problem solving and decision making, strategic analysis and planning.

Concentrations Finance, management, marketing.

Faculty Full-time: 7, 60% with doctorates; part-time: 7, 20% with doctorates.

Teaching Methodology Case study: 20%, lecture: 40%, research: 10%, student presentations: 10%, team projects: 20%.

Special Opportunities International exchange in France. Internships include marketing, human resources, and finance.

STUDENT STATISTICS

Geographic Representation State residents 95%. By region: Northeast 90%. International 3%.

Undergraduate Majors Business 35%; engineering/technology 10%; humanities 20%; science/mathematics 10%; social sciences 25%.

Other Background Graduate degrees in other disciplines: 10%. Work experience: On average, students have 6 years of work experience on entrance to the program.

FACILITIES

Information Resources Main library with 200,000 bound volumes, 12,000 titles on microform, 1,100 periodical subscriptions, 1,400 records/tapes/CDs.

Housing College housing not available.

Technology Computers are used moderately in course work. 50 computer terminals/PCs, linked by a campus-wide computer network, are available for use by students in program; they are located in computer labs. Students in the program are not required to have their own PC.

Computer Resources/On-line Services

Training	Yes	Dun's	No
Internet	Yes	Dow Jones	No
E-Mail	Yes	Dialog	No
LEXIS/NEXIS	No	Bloomberg	No
CompuServe	No		

ADMISSION

Acceptance 1994-95 Of those applying, 90% were accepted.

Entrance Requirements Bachelor's degree, prerequisite courses required for applicants with non-business degree, GMAT score of 500, minimum 2.75 GPA.

Application Requirements Interview, application form, copies of transcript, resume/curriculum vitae, personal statement, 2 letters of recommendation.

Application Deadline Applications are processed on a rolling basis.

FINANCIALS

Costs for 1994-95 Tuition: Full-time: $825/course.

Financial Aid In 1994-95, candidates received some institutionally administered aid in the form of loans, assistantships. Financial aid is available to part-time students. Application deadline: 3/15 for fall. Contact: Ms. Susan Chase, Assistant Director, Financial Aid, 140 New Scotland Avenue, Albany, NY 12208. (518) 445-1758.

INTERNATIONAL STUDENTS

Demographics 3% of students enrolled in the program are international.

Services and Facilities International student housing.

Applying TOEFL required, minimum score of 560. Financial aid is not available to international students.

ALTERNATE MBA PROGRAM

MBA/MSN Length of program: Minimum: 36 months. Maximum: 7 years. Degree requirements: 75 credits.

PLACEMENT

Placement services include career counseling/planning and resume preparation. Of 1994 graduates, 100% were employed within three months of graduation.

Program Contact: Mr. David Kiner, Director, MBA Program, Russell Sage College, 140 New Scotland Avenue, Albany, NY 12208. (518) 445-1763; Fax: (518) 436-0539.

St. Bonaventure University

School of Business

St. Bonaventure, New York

OVERVIEW

St. Bonaventure University is an independent comprehensive coed institution, affiliated with Roman Catholic Church. Founded 1858. Setting: 600-acre small-town campus. Total institutional enrollment: 2,700. Program was first offered in 1975.

MBA HIGHLIGHTS

Entrance Difficulty**
Mean GMAT: 484
Mean GPA: N/R

Cost $$$
Tuition: $1,020/course
Room & Board: $5,000

Enrollment Profile

Full-time: 141		Work Exp: 80%
Part-time: 144		International: 4%
Total: 285		Women: 33%
Average Age: 34		Minorities: 9%

Average Class Size: 22

ACADEMICS

Length of Program Minimum: 12 months. Maximum: 6 years.

Calendar Semesters.

Part-time Classes Main campus; evening, summer.

Degree Requirements 30 credits.

Required Courses Accounting theory, capstone-business policy, financial management, legal environment, marketing, organizational behavior, quantitative methods. Courses may be waived through: previous course work.

Curricular Focus Problem solving and decision making, teamwork.

Concentrations Accounting, business communications, finance, international business, management, marketing.

Faculty Full-time: 22, 77% with doctorates.

Teaching Methodology Case study: 20%, lecture: 40%, seminars by members of the business community: 10%, student presentations: 10%, team projects: 20%.

Special Opportunities International exchange in People's Republic of China. Internship program available.

STUDENT STATISTICS

Geographic Representation State residents 84%. By region: Northeast 95%; South 1%. International 4%.

Other Background Graduate degrees in other disciplines: 3%. Work experience: On average, students have 5 years of work experience on entrance to the program.

FACILITIES

Information Resources Main library with 253,000 bound volumes, 539,260 titles on microform, 1,405 periodical subscriptions, 7,750 records/tapes/CDs, 7 CD-ROMs. Business collection includes 15,270 bound volumes, 199 periodical subscriptions, 2 CD-ROMs.

Housing 10% of students in program live in college-owned or -operated housing.

Technology Computers are used moderately in course work. 140 computer terminals/PCs, linked by a campus-wide computer network, are available for use by students in program; they are located in learning resource center, the library, the computer center, computer labs. Students in the program are not required to have their own PC.

Computer Resources/On-line Services

Training	Yes	LEXIS/NEXIS	Yes
Internet	Yes	Dialog	Yes
E-Mail	Yes		

Other on-line services: OCLC.

ADMISSION

Entrance Requirements Bachelor's degree, GMAT score of 400, minimum 2.0 GPA. Core courses waived through: previous course work.

Application Requirements Application form, copies of transcript, 2 letters of recommendation.

Application Deadline Applications are processed on a rolling basis.

FINANCIALS

Costs for 1994-95 Tuition: Full-time: $1,020/course. Average room and board costs are $5,000 per academic year (on-campus).

Financial Aid In 1994-95, 2% of candidates received some institutionally administered aid in the form of loans, assistantships. Total awards ranged from $5,490-$9,000. Financial aid is available to part-time students. Applications are processed on a rolling basis. Contact: Ms. Mary Piccioli, Director of Financial Aid, Post Office Box D, St. Bonaventure, NY 14778. (716) 375-2528.

INTERNATIONAL STUDENTS

Demographics 4% of students enrolled in the program are international.

Services and Facilities Visa services, counseling/support services.

Applying TOEFL required, minimum score of 600; proof of health; proof of adequate funds. Financial aid is not available to international students. Admission application deadlines: 7/15 for fall, 11/30 for spring. Contact: Ms. Alice Sayegh, Director of Foreign Studies, RC 221-B, St. Bonaventure, NY 14778-. (716) 375-2574.

ALTERNATE MBA PROGRAM

Executive MBA (EMBA) Length of program: Minimum: 18 months. Maximum: 6 years. Degree requirements: 30 credits including 12 elective credits.

PLACEMENT

Placement services include alumni network, career counseling/planning, career fairs, career library, career placement, job interviews, and resume referral to employers. Of 1994 graduates, 95% were employed within three months of graduation.

Program Contact: Mr. Alex Nazemetz, Director of Admissions, St. Bonaventure University, PO Box D, St. Bonaventure, NY 14778-0108. (716) 375-2400, or (800) 462-5050 (NY only); Fax: (716) 375-2005.

St. John Fisher College

Graduate School of Management

Rochester, New York

OVERVIEW

St. John Fisher College is an independent comprehensive coed institution, affiliated with Roman Catholic Church. Founded 1948. Setting: 125-acre suburban campus. Total institutional enrollment: 4,500. Program was first offered in 1983.

MBA HIGHLIGHTS

Entrance Difficulty**
Mean GMAT: 483
Mean GPA: 3.31

Cost $$$
Tuition: $13,050
(Nonresident: $13,050)
Room & Board: $7,500

Enrollment Profile

Full-time: 5		Work Exp: 98%
Part-time: 245		International: 2%
Total: 250		Women: 51%
Average Age: 31		Minorities: 12%

Average Class Size: 22

St. John Fisher College awards an M.B.A. with a focus in accounting, finance, human resources, international business, marketing, MIS, or total quality management. Full-time, part-time, and evening programs are available. The Graduate School of Management is applying for AACSB accreditation. The faculty has a strong international orientation. The purpose of the program is to educate qualified students from any background for successful careers in management in private or public and domestic or international settings. The curriculum provides an integrated program of studies incorporating liberal learning with various functional areas of management. The objective is not to produce specialists but to give students an opportunity to acquire the mix of advanced skills most useful in dealing with the broadest problems at all levels of managerial responsibility. The School believes that theoretical, quantitative, and technical skills have to be integrated with humanistic values, and the program is designed to help the student develop and refine them and express them effectively and responsibly through the use of skills developed in various courses. Among the key strengths of the program are a well-balanced education; an emphasis on communication, as well as theory, and implementation, as well as diagnosis and decision; a small college, and a small, select, diverse student body which provides a close, people-oriented, friendly atmosphere for learning; and a strong faculty, distinguished for both intellectual rigor and work experience, that is dedicated to teaching excellence and helping students.

ACADEMICS

Length of Program Minimum: 24 months. Maximum: 6 years.

Calendar Semesters.

Full-time Classes Main campus; evening, summer.

Part-time Classes Main campus; evening, summer.

Degree Requirements 60 credits including 15 elective credits.

Required Courses Corporate finance, economic principles for management, human resources management, integrated business analysis, international business, introduction to accounting, introduction to computers, management information systems, marketing, operations management, organization theory, perspectives in management, quantitative methods, speaking and writing for management, statistics.

Curricular Focus Business issues and problems, organizational development and change management, problem solving and decision making.

Concentrations Accounting, finance, human resources management, international business, management, management information systems, marketing.

Faculty Full-time: 17, 94% with doctorates.

Teaching Methodology Case study: 10%, lecture: 25%, research: 15%, seminars by members of the business community: 10%, student presentations: 15%, team projects: 25%.

Special Opportunities Internships include marketing, finance, human resources, management information systems, and international business.

STUDENT STATISTICS

Geographic Representation State residents 98%. By region: Northeast 98%. International 2%.

Undergraduate Majors Business 65%; education 2%; engineering/technology 12%; humanities 3%; nursing 5%; science/mathematics 2%; social sciences 11%.

Other Background Graduate degrees in other disciplines: 5%. Work experience: On average, students have 9 years of work experience on entrance to the program.

FACILITIES

Information Resources Main library with 179,000 bound volumes, 281 titles on microform, 1,382 periodical subscriptions, 25,000 records/tapes/CDs, 6 CD-ROMs.

Housing 2% of students in program live in college-owned or -operated housing. Assistance with housing search provided.

Technology Computers are used moderately in course work. 70 computer terminals/PCs, linked by a campus-wide computer network, are available for use by students in program; they are located in learning resource center, the library, the computer center, computer labs. Students in the program are not required to have their own PC. $400 are budgeted per student for computer support.

Computer Resources/On-line Services

Training	Yes	Dun's	Yes $
Internet	Yes $	Dow Jones	No
E-Mail	Yes	Dialog	No
LEXIS/NEXIS	Yes $	Bloomberg	No
CompuServe	Yes $		

ADMISSION

Acceptance 1994-95 80 applied for admission; 90% were accepted.

Entrance Requirements Bachelor's degree, GMAT score. Core courses waived through: previous course work, work experience.

Application Requirements Written essay, application form, copies of transcript, personal statement, 3 letters of recommendation.

Application Deadlines 8/15 for fall, 12/1 for spring. Applications are processed on a rolling basis.

FINANCIALS

Costs for 1994-95 Tuition: Full-time: $13,050, $13,050 for international students; Part-time evening: $1,305/course, $1,305/course for international students. Average room and board costs are $7,500 per academic year (on-campus) and $6,800 per academic year (off-campus).

Financial Aid In 1994-95, 25% of candidates received some institutionally administered aid in the form of scholarships, loans, work-study. Total awards ranged from $200-$12,000. Financial aid is available to part-time students. Application deadlines: 8/15 for fall, 12/1 for spring. Contact: Ms. Anne Steger, Financial Aid Director, 3690 East Avenue, Rochester, NY 14618. (716) 385-8094.

INTERNATIONAL STUDENTS

Demographics 2% of students enrolled in the program are international; Europe 40%, Africa 20%, Asia 20%, other 20%.

Services and Facilities International student office, language tutoring, special assistance for nonnative speakers of English, counseling/support services.

Applying TOEFL required, minimum score of 500; proof of health; proof of adequate funds. Financial aid is not available to international students. Admission application deadlines: 7/15 for fall, 11/1 for spring. Applications are processed on a rolling basis. Contact: Ms. Jean Landes, International Student Adviser, 3690 East Avenue, Rochester, NY 14618. (716) 385-8040.

PLACEMENT

In 1993-94, 2 organizations participated in on-campus recruiting; 16 on-campus interviews were conducted. Placement services include alumni network, career counseling/planning, career library, career placement, resume preparation, and resume referral to employers. Of 1994 graduates, 98% were employed within three months of graduation, the average starting salary range was $32,500-$47,500.

Jobs by Employer Type Manufacturing 51%; service 17%; government 15%; nonprofit 13%; health service 4%.

Jobs by Functional Area Marketing/sales 34%; finance 28%; operations 3%; management 18%; strategic planning 7%; technical management 10%.

Program Contact: Mr. Steven T. Hoskins, MBA Coordinator, St. John Fisher College, 3690 East Avenue, Rochester, NY 14618. (716) 385-8079; Fax: (716) 385-8094.

St. John's University

College of Business Administration

Jamaica, New York

OVERVIEW

St. John's University is an independent coed institution, affiliated with Roman Catholic Church. Founded 1870. Setting: 96-acre suburban campus with easy access to New York City. Total institutional enrollment: 18,000. Program was first offered in 1959. AACSB-accredited.

MBA HIGHLIGHTS

Entrance Difficulty***
Mean GMAT: 480
Mean GPA: 3.0

Cost $$
Tuition: $450/credit
Room & Board: $8,000 (off-campus)

Enrollment Profile

Full-time: 292	Work Exp: 90%
Part-time: 1,136	International: 12%
Total: 1,428	Women: 37%
Average Age: 24	Minorities: 24%

Average Class Size: 27

ACADEMICS

Length of Program Minimum: 15 months. Maximum: 5 years.

Calendar Semesters.

Full-time Classes Main campus, Staten Island; evening.

Part-time Classes Main campus, Staten Island; evening.

Degree Requirements 39 credits including 15 elective credits.

Required Courses Advanced managerial statistics, business fluctuations and forecasting, seminar in business policy formulation, systems management of operations/production.

Curricular Focus Ethics, problem solving and decision making, strategic analysis and planning.

Concentrations Accounting, economics, finance, international finance, financial services, taxation, marketing management, management, management information systems, marketing, quantitative analysis.

Faculty Full-time: 54, 90% with doctorates; part-time: 2, 50% with doctorates.

Teaching Methodology Case study: 15%, lecture: 60%, seminars by members of the business community: 5%, student presentations: 10%, team projects: 10%.

Special Opportunities Internship program available.

STUDENT STATISTICS

Geographic Representation International 12%.

Undergraduate Majors Business 61%; engineering/technology 9%; humanities 5%; science/mathematics 5%; social sciences 10%; other 7%.

Other Background Graduate degrees in other disciplines: 2%. Work experience: On average, students have 4 years of work experience on entrance to the program.

FACILITIES

Information Resources Main library with 1.2 million bound volumes, 836,115 titles on microform, 15,000 periodical subscriptions, 14,007 records/tapes/CDs. Business collection includes 48,974 bound volumes, 542 periodical subscriptions, 2 CD-ROMs, 79 videos.

Housing College housing available.

Technology Computers are used heavily in course work. 306 computer terminals/PCs, linked by a campus-wide computer network, are available for use by students in program; they are located in classrooms, the computer center, computer labs. Students in the program are not required to have their own PC.

Computer Resources/On-line Services

Training	Yes	Dun's	No
Internet	Yes	Dow Jones	No
E-Mail	Yes	Dialog	Yes
LEXIS/NEXIS	Yes	Bloomberg	No
CompuServe	No		

Other on-line services: OCLC, RLIN.

ADMISSION

Acceptance 1994-95 Of those applying, 65% were accepted.

Entrance Requirements Bachelor's degree, prerequisite courses required for applicants with non-business degree, GMAT score. Core courses waived through: previous course work.

Application Requirements Written essay, application form, copies of transcript, personal statement, 2 letters of recommendation.

Application Deadline Applications are processed on a rolling basis.

FINANCIALS

Costs for 1994-95 Tuition: Full-time: $450/credit. Fees: Full-time: $75/semester. Average room and board costs are $8,000 per academic year (off-campus).

Financial Aid In 1994-95, 34% of candidates received some institutionally administered aid in the form of scholarships, loans, assistantships. Total awards ranged from $200-$17,550. Financial aid is available to part-time students. Application deadline: 4/1 for fall. Contact: Mr. Jorge Rodriguez, Assistant Vice President, Executive Director of Financial Aid, Newman Hall, Room B-28, Jamaica, NY 11439. (718) 990-6403.

INTERNATIONAL STUDENTS

Demographics 12% of students enrolled in the program are international; Asia 67%, Europe 16%, Africa 6%, other 7%.

Services and Facilities Language tutoring, ESL courses, counseling/support services.

Applying TOEFL required, minimum score of 500; proof of health; proof of adequate funds. Financial aid is available to international students. Financial aid application deadline: 4/1 for fall. Admission application deadlines: 6/1 for fall, 11/1 for spring. Contact: Ms. June Sadowski-Devarez, Assistant Dean, International Student Services, St. John's Hall B-11A, Jamaica, NY 11439. (718) 990-6083.

ALTERNATE MBA PROGRAM

MBA/JD Length of program: Minimum: 35 months. Maximum: 3 years. Degree requirements: 115 credits including 9 elective credits.

PLACEMENT

In 1993-94, 42 organizations participated in on-campus recruiting; 125 on-campus interviews were conducted. Placement services include alumni network, career counseling/planning, career fairs, career library, job interviews, resume preparation, and resume referral to employers. Of 1994 graduates, 80% were employed within three months of graduation, the average starting salary was $40,000.

Program Contact: Mr. Shamus J. McGrenna, Assistant Director of Graduate Admissions, St. John's University, 8000 Utopia Parkway, Jamaica, NY 11439. (718) 990-6114, or (800) 232-4SJU; Fax: (718) 380-0339.
See full description on page 818.

St. Thomas Aquinas College

Business Administration Division

Sparkill, New York

OVERVIEW

St. Thomas Aquinas College is an independent nonprofit comprehensive coed institution. Founded 1952. Setting: 46-acre small-town campus with easy access to New York City. Total institutional enrollment: 1,454. Program was first offered in 1994.

MBA HIGHLIGHTS

Entrance Difficulty***
Mean GMAT: 400
Mean GPA: N/R

Cost $
Tuition: $325/credit
Room & Board: N/R

Enrollment Profile
Full-time: 3
Part-time: 23
Total: 26
Average Age: N/R

Work Exp: N/R
International: 0%
Women: 42%
Minorities: 5%

Average Class Size: 6

ACADEMICS

Length of Program Minimum: 12 months.

Calendar 4-1-4.

Full-time Classes Main campus; evening, weekends, summer.

Part-time Classes Main campus; evening, weekends, summer.

Degree Requirements 36 credits.

Curricular Focus Computerization, international business, leadership.

Concentrations Finance, management, marketing.

Teaching Methodology Case study: 30%, lecture: 40%, student presentations: 15%, team projects: 15%.

STUDENT STATISTICS

Geographic Representation State residents 54%. By region: Northeast 100%.

FACILITIES

Information Resources Main library with 109,000 bound volumes, 501 titles on microform, 761 periodical subscriptions, 2,675 records/tapes/CDs.

ADMISSION

Entrance Requirements Bachelor's degree, GMAT score, minimum 2.8 GPA. Core courses waived through: previous course work.

Application Requirements Application form, copies of transcript, 3 letters of recommendation.

Application Deadline Applications are processed on a rolling basis.

FINANCIALS

Costs for 1995-96 Tuition: Weekends: $325/credit.

Financial Aid Applications are processed on a rolling basis. Contact: Mr. Peter Brennan, Director of Financial Aid, 125 Route 340, Sparkill, NY 10976. (914) 398-4098.

INTERNATIONAL STUDENTS

Applying TOEFL required; proof of health. Financial aid is available to international students. Applications are processed on a rolling basis. Admission application deadlines: 9/20 for fall, 3/1 for spring.

Program Contact: Mrs. Barbara Donn, Chairperson, Division of Business Administration, St. Thomas Aquinas College, 125 Route 340, Sparkill, NY 10976. (914) 398-4113; Fax: (914) 359-8136.

State University of New York at Binghamton

School of Management

Binghamton, New York

OVERVIEW

State University of New York at Binghamton is a state-supported coed institution. Part of State University of New York System. Founded 1946. Setting: 606-acre suburban campus. Total institutional enrollment: 12,000. AACSB-accredited.

MBA HIGHLIGHTS

Entrance Difficulty****
Mean GMAT: 545
Mean GPA: 3.26

Cost $
Tuition: $4,000
(Nonresident: $7,316)
Room & Board: N/R

Enrollment Profile
Full-time: 132
Part-time: 88
Total: 220
Average Age: 27

Work Exp: N/R
International: 15%
Women: 43%
Minorities: 9%

Average Class Size: N/R

ACADEMICS

Length of Program Minimum: 24 months. Maximum: 5 years.

Calendar Semesters.

Full-time Classes Main campus; day.

Part-time Classes Main campus; evening.

Degree Requirements 32 hours. Other: Legal environment of business, management policy, management G.A.M.E. or MBA project.

Required Courses Financial accounting, information systems, management, managerial economics, managerial finance, marketing, operations management, organizational behavior, statistics. Courses may be waived through: previous course work.

Curricular Focus Problem solving and decision making, strategic analysis and planning, teamwork.

Concentrations Accounting, arts administration, finance, human resources management, international business, management information systems, marketing, operations management.

Teaching Methodology Case study: 20%, faculty seminars: 5%, lecture: 40%, seminars by members of the business community: 5%, team projects: 30%.

STUDENT STATISTICS

Geographic Representation International 15%.

FACILITIES

Information Resources Main library with 1.5 million bound volumes, 1.4 million titles on microform, 9,358 periodical subscriptions, 83,000 records/tapes/CDs, 150 CD-ROMs.

Housing College housing available.

Technology Computers are used moderately in course work. 250 computer terminals/PCs, linked by a campus-wide computer network, are available for use by students in program; they are located in student rooms, learning resource center, the library, the computer center, computer labs. Students in the program are not required to have their own PC. $500-$600 are budgeted per student for computer support.

Computer Resources/On-line Services

Training	Yes	Dun's	No
Internet	Yes	Dow Jones	No
E-Mail	Yes	Dialog	No
LEXIS/NEXIS	No	Bloomberg	No
CompuServe	No		

Other on-line services: Carl, RLIN, OCLC.

ADMISSION

Acceptance 1994-95 Of those applying, 66% were accepted.

Entrance Requirements Bachelor's degree, GMAT score of 500, minimum 3.0 GPA. Core courses waived through: previous course work.

Application Requirements Application form, copies of transcript, personal statement, 2 letters of recommendation.

Application Deadlines 4/15 for fall, 10/1 for spring.

FINANCIALS

Costs for 1994-95 Tuition: Full-time: $4,000 for state residents, $7,316 for nonresidents; Part-time day: $168/hour for state residents, $308/hour for nonresidents. Fees: Full-time: $219 for state residents, $219 for nonresidents.

Financial Aid In 1994-95, candidates received some institutionally administered aid in the form of fellowships, assistantships, work-study. Total awards ranged from $6,500-$7,800. Financial aid is not available to part-time students. Application deadline: 2/1 for fall. Contact: Ms. Frances Littlefield, Coordinator of Graduate Admissions, School of Management and Advising, Binghamton, NY 13902-6000. (607) 777-2317.

INTERNATIONAL STUDENTS

Demographics 15% of students enrolled in the program are international.

Services and Facilities International student center, language tutoring, ESL courses, counseling/support services.

Applying TOEFL required, minimum score of 550; proof of adequate funds. Financial aid is available to international students. Financial aid application deadline: 2/1 for fall. Admission application deadlines: 4/15 for fall, 10/1 for spring. Contact: Ms. Ellen Badger, International Student Adviser, PO Box 6000, Binghamton, NY 13902-6000. (607) 777-2510.

PLACEMENT

In 1993-94, 36 organizations participated in on-campus recruiting. Placement services include alumni network, career counseling/planning, career fairs, career library, electronic job bank, job interviews, resume preparation, and resume referral to employers.

Program Contact: Graduate Admissions Office, State University of New York at Binghamton, PO Box 6000, Binghamton, NY 13902-6000. (607) 777-2284; Fax: (607) 777-4422.

State University of New York at Buffalo

School of Management

Buffalo, New York

OVERVIEW

State University of New York at Buffalo is a state-supported coed institution. Part of State University of New York System. Founded 1846. Setting: 1,350-acre suburban campus. Total institutional enrollment: 23,470.

Program was first offered in 1972. AACSB-accredited.

MBA HIGHLIGHTS

Entrance Difficulty**
Mean GMAT: 572
Mean GPA: 3.29

Cost $
Tuition: $2,000/semester
(Nonresident: $3,658/semester)
Room & Board: $5,500

Enrollment Profile

Full-time: 361	Work Exp: 43%
Part-time: 396	International: 14%
Total: 757	Women: 34%
Average Age: 24	Minorities: 5%

Class Size: 30 - 43

ACADEMICS

Length of Program Minimum: 16 months. Maximum: 4 years.

Calendar Semesters.

Full-time Classes Main campus; day, summer.

Part-time Classes Main campus; evening, summer.

Degree Requirements 60 credit hours including 24 elective credit hours. Other: Internships required for full-time students with less than one year of relevant work experience.

Required Courses Behavioral and organizational concepts for management, economics for managers, financial management, human resources management, introduction to financial and management accounting, introduction to information systems, introduction to management science models, macroeconomics for managers, managerial planning and control, marketing management, probability and statistics for management, strategic management, the government and the firm. Courses may be waived through: previous course work, work experience.

Curricular Focus Business issues and problems, problem solving and decision making, teamwork.

Concentrations Accounting, finance, financial institutions and markets, health services, human resources management, international business, management information systems, marketing, operations management, quantitative analysis.

Faculty Full-time: 39, 97% with doctorates; part-time: 5, 20% with doctorates.

Teaching Methodology Case study: 30%, lecture: 65%, team projects: 5%.

Special Opportunities International exchange in Finland, France, Germany, Mexico. Internship program available.

STUDENT STATISTICS

Geographic Representation State residents 86%. By region: Northeast 87%; Midwest 2%. International 14%.

Undergraduate Majors Business 61%; engineering/technology 20%; humanities 4%; social sciences 8%; other 7%.

Other Background Work experience: On average, students have 1 year of work experience on entrance to the program.

FACILITIES

Information Resources Main library with 2.9 million bound volumes, 4.3 million titles on microform, 20,051 periodical subscriptions, 116,700 records/tapes/CDs. Business collection includes 96,000 bound volumes, 1,025 periodical subscriptions.

Housing 10% of students in program live in college-owned or -operated housing.

Technology Computers are used moderately in course work. 250 computer terminals/PCs, linked by a campus-wide computer network, are available for use by students in program; they are located in student rooms, classrooms, the library, the computer center, computer labs. Students in the program are not required to have their own PC.

Computer Resources/On-line Services

Training	Yes	CompuServe	No
Internet	Yes	Dow Jones	Yes
E-Mail	Yes	Dialog	No
LEXIS/NEXIS	Yes	Bloomberg	No

ADMISSION

Acceptance 1994-95 Of those applying, 54% were accepted.

Entrance Requirements Bachelor's degree, GMAT score, minimum 1- 3 years of work experience. Core courses waived through: previous course work, work experience.

Application Requirements Application form, copies of transcript, personal statement.

Application Deadline 4/15 for fall. Application discs available.

FINANCIALS

Costs for 1994-95 Tuition: Full-time: $2,000/semester for state residents, $3,658/semester for nonresidents. Average room and board costs are $5,500 per academic year (on-campus).

Financial Aid In 1994-95, 35% of candidates received some institutionally administered aid in the form of scholarships, fellowships, assistantships, work-study. Total awards ranged from $334-$15,962. Financial aid is available to part-time students. Application deadline: 5/1 for fall. Contact: Ms. Linda Glose, Assistant Financial Aid Director, 3435 Main Street, Buffalo, NY 14260. (716) 829-2339.

INTERNATIONAL STUDENTS

Demographics 14% of students enrolled in the program are international; Asia 84%, Europe 9%, South America 2%, Africa 1%, other 2%.

Services and Facilities ESL courses, special assistance for nonnative speakers of English, counseling/support services.

Applying TOEFL required; proof of health; proof of adequate funds. Financial aid is not available to international students. Admission application deadline: 4/15 for fall. Contact: Ms. Lisa Felix, Assistant for Exchange Programs, 212 Talbert Hall, Buffalo, NY 14260. (716) 645-2258.

ALTERNATE MBA PROGRAMS

Executive MBA (EMBA) Length of program: Minimum: 21 months. Maximum: 5 years. Degree requirements: 48 credit hours including 12 elective credit hours.

MBA/JD Length of program: Minimum: 48 months. Degree requirements: 123 credit hours including 12 elective credit hours.

MBA/MA Length of program: Minimum: 30 months. Degree requirements: 78 credit hours including 12 elective credit hours. MA is in geography (international trade and commerce concentration).

MBA/M Arch Length of program: Minimum: 30 months. Degree requirements: 96 credit hours including 12 elective credit hours.

PLACEMENT

In 1993-94, 87 organizations participated in on-campus recruiting; 1,044 on-campus interviews were conducted. Placement services include alumni network, career counseling/planning, career fairs, career library, career placement, electronic job bank, job interviews, resume preparation, and resume referral to employers. Of 1994 graduates, 78% were employed within three months of graduation, the average starting salary was $40,942, the range was $24,000-$60,000.

Jobs by Employer Type Manufacturing 49%; service 31%; government 5%; consulting 7%; other 8%.

Jobs by Functional Area Marketing/sales 14%; finance 43%; operations 5%; management 25%; technical management 4%; human resources 5%; other 4%.

Program Contact: Ms. Arlene Bergwall, Assistant Dean, State University of New York at Buffalo, Capen Hall, Buffalo, NY 14260. (716) 645-3204; Fax: (716) 645-2341.

State University of New York at Oswego

School of Business

Oswego, New York

OVERVIEW

State University of New York at Oswego is a state-supported comprehensive coed institution. Part of State University of New York System. Founded 1861. Setting: 696-acre small-town campus with easy access to Syracuse. Total institutional enrollment: 8,817. Program was first offered in 1985.

PROGRAM HIGHLIGHTS

Entrance Difficulty*
Mean GMAT: 485
Mean GPA: 3.25

Cost $
Tuition: $2,000/semester
(Nonresident: $3,658/semester)
Room & Board: $4,300

Enrollment Profile

Full-time: 40	Work Exp: 80%
Part-time: 120	International: 10%
Total: 160	Women: 50%
Average Age: 28	Minorities: 10%

Average Class Size: 16

ACADEMICS
Calendar Semesters.

Curricular Focus Economic and financial theory, general management, leadership.

Concentrations Accounting, management, management information systems.

Faculty Full-time: 15, 85% with doctorates; part-time: 3.

Teaching Methodology Case study: 10%, faculty seminars: 10%, lecture: 50%, research: 5%, seminars by members of the business community: 5%, student presentations: 10%, team projects: 10%.

STUDENT STATISTICS
Geographic Representation By region: Northeast 75%; South 8%; Midwest 3%; West 3%. International 10%.

Undergraduate Majors Business 50%; education 5%; engineering/technology 15%; humanities 10%; science/mathematics 10%; social sciences 10%.

Other Background Graduate degrees in other disciplines: 5%. Work experience: On average, students have 6 years of work experience on entrance to the program.

FACILITIES
Information Resources Main library with 409,000 bound volumes, 1.7 million titles on microform, 1,726 periodical subscriptions, 8,500 records/tapes/CDs, 28 CD-ROMs. Business collection includes 33,008 bound volumes, 72 periodical subscriptions, 6 CD-ROMs, 73 videos.

Housing 10% of students in program live in college-owned or -operated housing. Assistance with housing search provided.

Technology Computers are used moderately in course work. 300 computer terminals/PCs, linked by a campus-wide computer network, are available for use by students in program; they are located in learning resource center, the library, the computer center, computer labs. Students in the program are not required to have their own PC.

Computer Resources/On-line Services

Training	No	Dun's	No
Internet	Yes	Dow Jones	No
E-Mail	Yes	Dialog	Yes
LEXIS/NEXIS	No	Bloomberg	No
CompuServe	No		

Other on-line services: First Search.

ADMISSION
Acceptance 1994-95 90 applied for admission; 84% were accepted.

Entrance Requirements Bachelor's degree, GMAT score of 350. Core courses waived through: previous course work.

Application Requirements Written essay, application form, copies of transcript, personal statement.

Application Deadline Applications are processed on a rolling basis.

FINANCIALS
Costs for 1994-95 Tuition: Full-time: $2,000/semester for state residents, $3,658/semester for nonresidents; Part-time day: $168/credit hour for state residents, $308/credit hour for nonresidents. Average room and board costs are $4,300 per academic year (on-campus).

Financial Aid In 1994-95, candidates received some institutionally administered aid in the form of scholarships, loans, fellowships. Total awards ranged from $500-$10,000. Financial aid is not available to part-time students. Application deadline: 3/1 for fall. Contact: Ms. Margaret Sternberg, Director of Financial Aid, 206 Culkin Hall, Oswego, NY 13126. (315) 341-2248.

INTERNATIONAL STUDENTS
Demographics 10% of students enrolled in the program are international.

Applying TOEFL required, minimum score of 550; proof of health; proof of adequate funds. Financial aid is not available to international students. Admission applications are processed on a rolling basis.

PROGRAM
MS Mgt Length of program: Minimum: 12 months. Maximum: 6 years. Full-time classes: Main campus; day, evening. Part-time classes: Main campus; evening. Degree requirements: 36 credits including 15 elective credits.

PLACEMENT
Placement services include alumni network, career fairs, career library, and resume preparation.

Program Contact: Mr. Charles Spector, Graduate Coordinator, State University of New York at Oswego, Swetman Hall, Oswego, NY 13126. (315) 341-2613; Fax: (315) 341-5440.

Syracuse University

School of Management

Syracuse, New York

OVERVIEW
Syracuse University is an independent nonprofit coed institution. Founded 1870. Setting: 200-acre urban campus. Total institutional enrollment: 13,000. Program was first offered in 1949. AACSB-accredited.

MBA HIGHLIGHTS

Entrance Difficulty**
Mean GMAT: 530
Mean GPA: 3.0

Cost $$$
Tuition: $456/credit
Room & Board: $12,000

Enrollment Profile

Full-time: 220	Work Exp: 90%
Part-time: 330	International: 33%
Total: 550	Women: 34%
Average Age: 26	Minorities: 17%

Average Class Size: 22

Syracuse University's School of Management Career Center offers M.B.A. students comprehensive and continuing support throughout their career planning and job-search activities. In their first semester, students participate in résumé critiques, career workshops, and one-on-one meetings with the Career Center director. Throughout the program, students are also involved with career panels, corporate presentations, and the M.B.A. Career Workshop series.

Other programs and services of the Career Center include a School of Management alumni network; a job referral system listing full-time, part-time, and summer internship opportunities; résumé books that are distributed to several hundred prospective employers; and mock interviews with corporate recruiters and practicing managers. Also many local, national, and international firms recruit directly on the Syracuse University campus on a regular basis.

All of these efforts have a tangible payoff measured in terms of internships and job offers. Syracuse M.B.A. graduates have been hired by a cross-section of companies representing the Fortune 500, Forbes' 200 Best Small Companies, and exceptional emerging enterprises. The 1994 graduates averaged $48,000 in starting salary. Leading employers were General Motors, Goldman Sachs, United Technologies, Price Waterhouse, and Andersen Consulting.

ACADEMICS
Length of Program Minimum: 21 months. Maximum: 7 years.
Calendar Semesters.
Full-time Classes Main campus; day.
Part-time Classes Main campus; evening.
Degree Requirements 39 credits.
Required Courses Computer proficiency, critical thinking and problem solving, data analysis and decision making, economics for managers, ethics for management, financial accounting, formulating strategy, implementing

strategy, innovation management, management accounting, management information systems, managerial finance, managerial law and public policy, managerial mathematics, managing conflict, managing diversity, managing human resources, managing in a global setting, managing in a natural environment, managing organizations, managing total quality, marketing management, operations management, overview and major paradigms of management, teamwork and groups. Courses may be waived through: previous course work.

Curricular Focus International business, leadership, teamwork.
Concentrations Accounting, finance, human resources management, international business, management, management information systems, marketing, operations management, organizational behavior, quantitative analysis, transportation.
Faculty Full-time: 61, 97% with doctorates; part-time: 3, 97% with doctorates.
Teaching Methodology Case study: 25%, lecture: 40%, student presentations: 10%, team projects: 25%.
Special Opportunities International exchange and internship programs available.

STUDENT STATISTICS
Geographic Representation State residents 41%. By region: Northeast 47%; West 8%; South 6%; Midwest 6%. International 33%.
Undergraduate Majors Business 35%; education 3%; engineering/technology 10%; humanities 10%; nursing 1%; science/mathematics 15%; social sciences 20%; other 6%.
Other Background Graduate degrees in other disciplines: 4%. Work experience: On average, students have 5 years of work experience on entrance to the program.

FACILITIES
Information Resources Main library with 2.8 million bound volumes, 3.3 million titles on microform, 15,650 periodical subscriptions, 341,000 records/tapes/CDs.
Housing 30% of students in program live in college-owned or -operated housing.
Technology Computers are used moderately in course work. Computer terminals/PCs, linked by a campus-wide computer network, are available for use by students in program; they are located in the student center, the library, the computer center, computer labs, the research center. Students in the program are not required to have their own PC.

Computer Resources/On-line Services

Training	Yes	E-Mail	Yes
Internet	Yes		

ADMISSION
Acceptance 1994-95 Of those applying, 55% were accepted.
Entrance Requirements Bachelor's degree, GMAT score of 550. Core courses waived through: previous course work.
Application Requirements Written essay, application form, copies of transcript, personal statement, 1 letter of recommendation.
Application Deadline 3/1 for fall.

FINANCIALS
Costs for 1994-95 Tuition: Full-time: $456/credit. Fees: Full-time: $335. Average room and board costs are $12,000 per academic year (on-campus) and $12,000 per academic year (off-campus).
Financial Aid In 1994-95, 70% of candidates received some institutionally administered aid in the form of grants, scholarships, loans, fellowships, assistantships, work-study. Total awards ranged from $1,000-$22,000. Financial aid is available to part-time students. Application deadline: 4/30 for fall. Contact: Ms. Cynthia Roach, Financial Aid Counselor, 200 Archbold North, Syracuse, NY 13244-0003. (315) 443-1513.

INTERNATIONAL STUDENTS
Demographics 33% of students enrolled in the program are international.
Services and Facilities International student center, visa services, language tutoring, ESL courses, counseling/support services.
Applying TOEFL required, minimum score of 580; proof of health; proof of adequate funds. Admission application deadline: 3/1 for fall. Contact: Mr. Michael Smithee, Associate Director, Office of International Services, 310 Walnut Boulevard, Syracuse, NY 13244-0003. (315) 443-2457.

ALTERNATE MBA PROGRAMS
Executive MBA (EMBA) Length of program: Minimum: 24 months. Degree requirements: 54 credits.
MBA/JD Length of program: Minimum: 48 months. Degree requirements: 115 credits.

MBA/MSN Length of program: Minimum: 36 months. Degree requirements: 78 credits.

PLACEMENT

In 1993-94, 60 organizations participated in on-campus recruiting; 500 on-campus interviews were conducted. Placement services include alumni network, career counseling/planning, career fairs, career library, career placement, electronic job bank, job interviews, resume preparation, and resume referral to employers. Of 1994 graduates, 70% were employed within three months of graduation, the average starting salary was $48,000, the range was $24,000-$71,000.

Jobs by Employer Type Manufacturing 55%; service 25%; government 5%; consulting 10%; nonprofit 5%.

Jobs by Functional Area Marketing/sales 20%; finance 20%; operations 10%; management 30%; strategic planning 10%; technical management 10%.

Program Contact: Mr. Jack Huebach, Assistant Dean, Syracuse University, Syracuse, NY 13244-0003. (315) 443-9214; Fax: (315) 443-9517.
See full description on page 838.

Union College

Graduate Management Institute

Schenectady, New York

OVERVIEW

Union College is an independent nonprofit comprehensive coed institution. Founded 1795. Setting: 100-acre urban campus. Total institutional enrollment: 2,500.

MBA HIGHLIGHTS

Entrance Difficulty*
Mean GMAT: 560
Mean GPA: 3.2

Cost $$
Tuition: $10,620
Room & Board: $7,000 (off-campus)

Enrollment Profile

Full-time: 65	Work Exp: 80%
Part-time: 195	International: 7%
Total: 260	Women: 46%
Average Age: N/R	Minorities: 1%

Average Class Size: 20

ACADEMICS

Length of Program Minimum: 18 months.

Calendar Trimesters.

Full-time Classes Main campus; day, evening, summer.

Part-time Classes Main campus; day, evening, summer.

Degree Requirements 60 credits including 10 elective credits.

Curricular Focus Problem solving and decision making, strategic analysis and planning, teamwork.

Concentrations Accounting, finance, health services, management, operations management, quantitative analysis, strategic management.

Faculty Full-time: 12, 100% with doctorates.

Special Opportunities Internship program available.

STUDENT STATISTICS

Geographic Representation International 7%.

Undergraduate Majors Business 24%; engineering/technology 23%; humanities 7%; science/mathematics 7%; social sciences 23%; other 16%.

Other Background Graduate degrees in other disciplines: 10%. Work experience: On average, students have 3-5 years of work experience on entrance to the program.

FACILITIES

Information Resources Main library with 496,337 bound volumes, 31,171 titles on microform, 1,954 periodical subscriptions, 4,858 records/tapes/CDs, 36 CD-ROMs.

Housing College housing not available.

Technology Computers are used heavily in course work. Computer terminals/PCs, linked by a campus-wide computer network, are available for use by students in program; they are located in the computer center, computer labs. Students in the program are not required to have their own PC.

Computer Resources/On-line Services

Training	Yes	E-Mail	Yes
Internet	Yes		

ADMISSION

Acceptance 1994-95 Of those applying, 85% were accepted.

Entrance Requirements Bachelor's degree, GMAT score, minimum 3.0 GPA. Core courses waived through: previous course work.

Application Requirements Written essay, application form, copies of transcript, 3 letters of recommendation.

Application Deadlines 8/1 for fall, 11/30 for winter, 2/28 for spring.

FINANCIALS

Costs for 1994-95 Tuition: Full-time: $10,620. Average room and board costs are $7,000 per academic year (off-campus).

Financial Aid In 1994-95, 40% of candidates received some institutionally administered aid in the form of scholarships, fellowships, assistantships. Total awards ranged from $1,180-$12,120. Financial aid is not available to part-time students. Application deadline: 3/31 for fall. Contact: Ms. Carolyn J. Micklas, Coordinator for Recruiting and Admissions, Schenectady, NY 12308-2311. (518) 388-6239.

INTERNATIONAL STUDENTS

Demographics 7% of students enrolled in the program are international.

Applying TOEFL required, minimum score of 550; proof of health; proof of adequate funds. Financial aid is available to international students. Financial aid application deadline: 3/31 for fall. Admission application deadline: 3/31 for fall.

ALTERNATE MBA PROGRAM
MBA/JD .

PLACEMENT

Placement services include alumni network, career counseling/planning, career fairs, career library, career placement, electronic job bank, job interviews, resume preparation, and resume referral to employers. Of 1994 graduates, 95% were employed within three months of graduation, the average starting salary range was $30,000-$60,000.

Program Contact: Ms. Carolyn J. Micklas, Coordinator for Recruiting and Admissions, Union College, Schenectady, NY 12308-2311. (518) 388-6239; Fax: (518) 388-6686.
See full description on page 846.

University at Albany, State University of New York

School of Business

Albany, New York

OVERVIEW

The University at Albany, State University of New York is a state-supported coed institution. Part of State University of New York System. Founded 1844. Setting: 560-acre suburban campus. Total institutional enrollment: 16,000. AACSB-accredited.

MBA HIGHLIGHTS

Entrance Difficulty*
Mean GMAT: 540
Mean GPA: 3.2

Cost $
Tuition: $2,000/semester
(Nonresident: $3,658/semester)
Room & Board: $4,000

Enrollment Profile
Full-time: 125
Part-time: 180
Total: 305
Average Age: 25

Work Exp: 50%
International: 15%
Women: 40%
Minorities: 10%

Average Class Size: 30

ACADEMICS
Length of Program Minimum: 24 months. Maximum: 6 years.
Calendar Semesters.
Full-time Classes Main campus; day, evening, early morning.
Part-time Classes Main campus; evening, summer.
Degree Requirements 47 credits including 3 elective credits.
Curricular Focus Business issues and problems, problem solving and decision making, teamwork.
Concentrations Finance, information systems, management information systems, marketing.
Faculty Full-time: 28, 96% with doctorates; part-time: 7, 15% with doctorates.
Teaching Methodology Case study: 25%, faculty seminars: 3%, lecture: 30%, research: 5%, seminars by members of the business community: 2%, student presentations: 10%, team projects: 25%.
Special Opportunities Internship program available.

STUDENT STATISTICS
Geographic Representation State residents 80%. By region: Northeast 82%; South 1%; Midwest 1%; West 1%. International 15%.
Undergraduate Majors Business 45%; education 3%; engineering/technology 15%; humanities 10%; nursing 1%; science/mathematics 10%; social sciences 15%; other 1%.
Other Background Graduate degrees in other disciplines: 3%. Work experience: On average, students have 1-2 years of work experience on entrance to the program.

FACILITIES
Information Resources Main library with 1.8 million bound volumes, 2.6 million titles on microform, 7,000 periodical subscriptions, 5,000 records/tapes/CDs. Business collection includes 345,612 bound volumes, 174 periodical subscriptions, 7 CD-ROMs, 37 videos.
Housing 5% of students in program live in college-owned or -operated housing.
Technology Computers are used heavily in course work. 25 computer terminals/PCs, linked by a campus-wide computer network, are available for use by students in program; they are located in computer labs. Students in the program are not required to have their own PC.

Computer Resources/On-line Services
Training	Yes	Multimedia Center	Yes
Internet	Yes	LEXIS/NEXIS	Yes
E-Mail	Yes		

Other on-line services: First Search.

ADMISSION
Acceptance 1994-95 Of those applying, 60% were accepted.
Entrance Requirements Bachelor's degree, GMAT score. Core courses waived through: previous course work.
Application Requirements Written essay.
Application Deadline 4/15 for fall.

FINANCIALS
Costs for 1994-95 Tuition: Full-time: $2,000/semester for state residents, $3,658/semester for nonresidents. Fees: Full-time: $61/semester for state residents, $61/semester for nonresidents. Average room and board costs are $4,000 per academic year (on-campus) and $3,500 per academic year (off-campus).
Financial Aid In 1994-95, 25% of candidates received some institutionally administered aid in the form of scholarships, loans, fellowships, assistantships. Financial aid is not available to part-time students. Application deadline: 4/1 for fall. Contact: Financial Aid Office, 1400 Washington Avenue, Albany, NY 12222-0001. (518) 442-5757.

INTERNATIONAL STUDENTS
Demographics 15% of students enrolled in the program are international; Asia 80%, Europe 10%, Africa 2%, Central America 1%, South America 1%, other 6%.
Services and Facilities International student center.
Applying TOEFL required, minimum score of 580; proof of health; proof of adequate funds. Financial aid is not available to international students.

Admission application deadline: 4/1 for fall. Contact: Mr. Steven Thomson, Director, International Student Services, 1400 Washington Avenue, Albany, NY 12222-0001. (518) 442-5495.

PLACEMENT
In 1993-94, 20 organizations participated in on-campus recruiting; 35 on-campus interviews were conducted. Placement services include alumni network, career counseling/planning, career fairs, career library, job interviews, resume preparation, and resume referral to employers.

Program Contact: Ms. Susan Maloney, Assistant to the Dean, University at Albany, State University of New York, 1400 Washington Avenue, Albany, NY 12222-0001. (518) 442-4961; Fax: (518) 442-3944.

University of Rochester

William E. Simon Graduate School of Business Administration

Rochester, New York

OVERVIEW
The University of Rochester is an independent nonprofit coed institution. Founded 1850. Setting: 534-acre suburban campus. Total institutional enrollment: 9,740. Program was first offered in 1963. AACSB-accredited.

MBA HIGHLIGHTS

Entrance Difficulty*****
Mean GMAT: 604
Mean GPA: 3.22

Cost $$$$
Tuition: $19,080
Room & Board: $5,000

Enrollment Profile
Full-time: 403
Part-time: 387
Total: 790
Average Age: 27

Work Exp: 90%
International: 40%
Women: 24%
Minorities: 15%

Class Size: 36 - 70

ACADEMICS
Length of Program Minimum: 18 months. Maximum: 7 years.
Calendar Quarters.
Full-time Classes Main campus; day, evening.
Part-time Classes Main campus; evening.
Degree Requirements 67 credits including 30 elective credits. Other: Capstone course.
Required Courses Capital budgeting and corporate objectives, capstone in total quality management, data analysis and forecasting, essentials of accounting, information systems for management, management communication, managerial economics, marketing management, operations management, organization theory, probability and decision analysis.
Curricular Focus Economic and financial theory, problem solving and decision making, teamwork.
Concentrations Accounting, economics, entrepreneurship, finance, international business, management, management information systems, marketing, operations management, public policy.
Faculty Full-time: 47, 87% with doctorates; part-time: 19, 58% with doctorates.
Teaching Methodology Case study: 20%, lecture: 60%, student presentations: 10%, team projects: 10%.
Special Opportunities International exchange in Argentina, Australia, Finland, Germany, Israel, Japan, New Zealand, Norway, Italy. Other: MBA Enterprise Corps offers opportunities in Eastern Europe.

STUDENT STATISTICS
Geographic Representation By region: Northeast 32%; South 14%; West 8%; Midwest 6%. International 40%.
Undergraduate Majors Business 35%; engineering/technology 13%; humanities 4%; science/mathematics 13%; social sciences 35%.
Other Background Graduate degrees in other disciplines: 15%. Work experience: On average, students have 3 years of work experience on entrance to the program.

FACILITIES

Information Resources Main library with 2.8 million bound volumes, 3.6 million titles on microform, 13,309 periodical subscriptions, 59,757 records/tapes/CDs, 93 CD-ROMs. Business collection in Management Library includes 125,000 bound volumes, 750 periodical subscriptions, 9 CD-ROMs.

Housing 35% of students in program live in college-owned or -operated housing.

Technology Computers are used moderately in course work. 60 computer terminals/PCs, linked by a campus-wide computer network, are available for use by students in program; they are located in the computer center, computer labs. Students in the program are not required to have their own PC. $250 are budgeted per student for computer support.

Computer Resources/On-line Services

Training	Yes	Dun's	No
Internet	Yes	Dow Jones	Yes
E-Mail	Yes	Dialog	Yes
LEXIS/NEXIS	Yes	Bloomberg	Yes
CompuServe	No		

ADMISSION

Acceptance 1994-95 1,113 applied for admission; 38% were accepted.

Entrance Requirements Bachelor's degree, GMAT score. Core courses waived through: previous course work.

Application Requirements Written essay, application form, copies of transcript, resume/curriculum vitae, personal statement, 2 letters of recommendation, interviews required for candidates with less than 15 months experience.

Application Deadlines 6/1 for fall, 11/15 for spring. Application discs available.

FINANCIALS

Costs for 1994-95 Tuition: Full-time: $19,080. Fees: Full-time: $150. Average room and board costs are $5,000 per academic year (on-campus) and $5,000 per academic year (off-campus).

Financial Aid In 1994-95, 76% of candidates received some institutionally administered aid in the form of grants, scholarships, loans, fellowships, assistantships, work-study. Financial aid is not available to part-time students. Application deadlines: 3/1 for fall, 11/15 for spring. Contact: Ms. Priscilla E. Gumina, Assistant Dean for MBA Admissions and Administration, Wilson Boulevard, Rochester, NY 14627-0001. (716) 275-3533.

INTERNATIONAL STUDENTS

Demographics 40% of students enrolled in the program are international; Asia 48%, Europe 26%, South America 9%, Central America 6%, Africa 2%, Australia 1%, other 8%.

Services and Facilities International student office, international student center, visa services, language tutoring, ESL courses, special assistance for nonnative speakers of English, counseling/support services.

Applying TOEFL required; proof of health; proof of adequate funds. Financial aid is available to international students. Financial aid application deadlines: 3/1 for fall, 11/15 for spring. Admission application deadlines: 6/1 for fall, 11/15 for spring. Contact: Ms. Barbara Harris Smith, Director of International Student Affairs, 209 Morey Hall, Rochester, NY 14627-0001. (716) 275-2864.

ALTERNATE MBA PROGRAMS

Executive MBA (EMBA) Length of program: Minimum: 22 months. Maximum: 2 years. Degree requirements: 64 credits. Average class size: 50.

MBA/MS Length of program: Minimum: 48 months. Maximum: 7 years. Degree requirements: 80 credits including 24 elective credits. Thesis in microbiology. MS is in biotechnology.

MBA/MSN Length of program: Minimum: 54 months. Maximum: 7 years. Degree requirements: 86 credits including 24 elective credits.

MBA/MPH Length of program: Minimum: 54 months. Maximum: 7 years. Degree requirements: 88 credits including 24 elective credits.

PLACEMENT

In 1993-94, 99 organizations participated in on-campus recruiting; 1,582 on-campus interviews were conducted. Placement services include alumni network, career counseling/planning, career fairs, career library, career placement, job interviews, off-site recruiting, resume preparation, and resume referral to employers. Of 1994 graduates, 92% were employed within three months of graduation, the average starting salary was $51,708, the range was $32,450-$107,500.

Jobs by Employer Type Manufacturing 26%; service 66%; consulting 8%.

Jobs by Functional Area Marketing/sales 12%; finance 53%; operations 13%; management 6%; strategic planning 7%; technical management 1%; consulting 8%.

Program Contact: Ms. Priscilla E. Gumina, Assistant Dean for MBA Admissions and Administration, University of Rochester, Schlagel Hall, Room 395, Rochester, NY 14627-0001. (716) 275-3533; Fax: (716) 271-3907; Internet Address: mbaadm@sub-feestaff.ssb.rochester.edu. **See full description on page 912.**

Wagner College

Department of Economics and Business Administration

Staten Island, New York

OVERVIEW

Wagner College is an independent nonprofit comprehensive coed institution. Founded 1883. Setting: 110-acre urban campus with easy access to New York City. Total institutional enrollment: 1,700. Program was first offered in 1952.

MBA HIGHLIGHTS

Entrance Difficulty***
Mean GMAT: N/R
Mean GPA: N/R

Cost $$$
Tuition: $455/hour
Room & Board: $5,800

Enrollment Profile

Full-time: 20	Work Exp: N/R
Part-time: 60	International: 1%
Total: 80	Women: 40%
Average Age: N/R	Minorities: 10%

Average Class Size: 10

ACADEMICS

Length of Program Minimum: 18 months.

Calendar Semesters.

Full-time Classes Main campus; evening.

Part-time Classes Main campus; evening.

Degree Requirements 42 credits including 9 elective credits.

Curricular Focus General management, international business.

Concentrations Finance, international business, management, marketing.

Faculty Full-time: 7, 43% with doctorates; part-time: 15.

Teaching Methodology Case study: 25%, lecture: 25%, student presentations: 25%, team projects: 25%.

STUDENT STATISTICS

Geographic Representation State residents 75%. International 1%.

FACILITIES

Information Resources Main library with 310,000 bound volumes, 22,500 titles on microform, 1,000 periodical subscriptions, 4,600 records/tapes/CDs.

Housing College housing available.

Technology Computers are used moderately in course work. 70 computer terminals/PCs, linked by a campus-wide computer network, are available for use by students in program; they are located in the computer center. Students in the program are not required to have their own PC.

Computer Resources/On-line Services

Training	Yes	E-Mail	No

ADMISSION

Acceptance 1994-95 Of those applying, 80% were accepted.

Entrance Requirements Bachelor's degree, GMAT score of 550, minimum 2.7 GPA.

Application Requirements Written essay, application form, copies of transcript, personal statement, 2 letters of recommendation.

Application Deadlines 8/1 for fall, 12/15 for spring.

FINANCIALS
Costs for 1994-95 Tuition: Full-time: $455/hour. Average room and board costs are $5,800 per academic year (on-campus) and $9,000 per academic year (off-campus).

Financial Aid In 1994-95, candidates received some institutionally administered aid in the form of scholarships, loans, assistantships. Application deadlines: 3/1 for fall, 4/1 for scholarships. Contact: Ms. Beatrice Snyder, Director of Financial Aid, Staten Island, NY 10301. (718) 390-3183.

INTERNATIONAL STUDENTS
Demographics 1% of students enrolled in the program are international.

Services and Facilities ESL courses, special assistance for nonnative speakers of English, counseling/support services.

Applying TOEFL required, minimum score of 550. Admission application deadlines: 6/1 for fall, 10/1 for spring.

ALTERNATE MBA PROGRAM
Executive MBA (EMBA) Length of program: Minimum: 18 months. Degree requirements: 42 credits.

Program Contact: Admissions Office, Wagner College, Staten Island, NY 10301. (718) 390-3411, or (800) 221-1010 (out-of-state).

NORTH CAROLINA

Appalachian State University

John A. Walker College of Business

Boone, North Carolina

OVERVIEW
Appalachian State University is a state-supported comprehensive coed institution. Part of University of North Carolina System. Founded 1899. Setting: 255-acre small-town campus. Total institutional enrollment: 11,800. Program was first offered in 1977. AACSB-accredited.

MBA HIGHLIGHTS
Entrance Difficulty***
Mean GMAT: 510
Mean GPA: 2.95

Cost $
Tuition: $382/semester
(Nonresident: $3,624/semester)
Room & Board: $8,000 (off-campus)

Enrollment Profile

Full-time: 70	Work Exp: 60%
Part-time: 40	International: 5%
Total: 110	Women: 45%
Average Age: 26	Minorities: 15%

Average Class Size: 25

ACADEMICS
Length of Program Minimum: 24 months.

Calendar Semesters.

Full-time Classes Main campus; day, evening, summer.

Part-time Classes Main campus, Winston-Salem; evening.

Degree Requirements 36 credits including 9 elective credits.

Required Courses Applied organizational theory, business economics, information systems, management science, managerial accounting, managerial finance, marketing strategy, organizational communication, organizational strategy and policy. Courses may be waived through: previous course work.

Curricular Focus General management, leadership.

Concentrations Finance, health services, human resources management, international business, management, management information systems, marketing.

Faculty Full-time: 50, 100% with doctorates.

Teaching Methodology Case study: 20%, faculty seminars: 10%, lecture: 50%, team projects: 20%.

STUDENT STATISTICS
Geographic Representation State residents 85%. By region: South 95%. International 5%.

Undergraduate Majors Business 30%; engineering/technology 10%; humanities 30%; science/mathematics 10%; social sciences 20%.

Other Background Graduate degrees in other disciplines: 5%. Work experience: On average, students have 2 years of work experience on entrance to the program.

FACILITIES
Information Resources Main library with 629,576 bound volumes, 1.1 million titles on microform, 3,789 periodical subscriptions, 10,263 records/tapes/CDs.

Housing 10% of students in program live in college-owned or -operated housing.

Technology Computers are used moderately in course work. 100 computer terminals/PCs, linked by a campus-wide computer network, are available for use by students in program; they are located in computer labs. Students in the program are not required to have their own PC. $250 are budgeted per student for computer support.

Computer Resources/On-line Services

Training	Yes	E-Mail	Yes

ADMISSION
Acceptance 1994-95 105 applied for admission; 65% were accepted.

Entrance Requirements Bachelor's degree, GMAT score of 450, minimum 2.5 GPA. Core courses waived through: previous course work.

Application Requirements Application form, copies of transcript.

Application Deadline 5/31 for fall.

FINANCIALS
Costs for 1994-95 Tuition: Full-time: $382/semester for state residents, $3,624/semester for nonresidents; Part-time day: $203/semester for state residents, $1,013/semester for nonresidents. Fees: Full-time: $319/semester for state residents, $319/semester for nonresidents. Average room and board costs are $8,000 per academic year (off-campus).

Financial Aid In 1994-95, 50% of candidates received some institutionally administered aid in the form of scholarships, assistantships. Total awards ranged from $2,500-$6,000. Financial aid is not available to part-time students. Applications are processed on a rolling basis. Contact: Mr. Robert Feld, Director of Student Financial Aid, Boone, NC 28608. (704) 262-2190.

INTERNATIONAL STUDENTS
Demographics 5% of students enrolled in the program are international.

Services and Facilities Counseling/support services.

Applying TOEFL required, minimum score of 550. Financial aid is available to international students. Applications are processed on a rolling basis. Admission application deadline: 5/31 for fall.

PLACEMENT
In 1993-94, 50 organizations participated in on-campus recruiting. Placement services include career counseling/planning, career placement, job interviews, resume preparation, and resume referral to employers. Of 1994 graduates, 80% were employed within three months of graduation, the average starting salary was $32,000, the range was $22,000-$49,000.

Program Contact: Mr. Robert L. Cherry Jr., Director of Graduate Studies, Appalachian State University, Boone, NC 28608. (704) 262-2000; Fax: (704) 262-2925.

Campbell University

Lundy-Fetterman School of Business

Buies Creek, North Carolina

OVERVIEW
Campbell University is an independent Baptist coed institution. Founded 1887. Setting: 850-acre small-town campus with easy access to Raleigh. Total institutional enrollment: 6,700. Program was first offered in 1978.

MBA HIGHLIGHTS

Entrance Difficulty**
Mean GMAT: 485
Mean GPA: 2.95

Cost $
Tuition: $150/semester hour
Room & Board: N/R

Enrollment Profile

Full-time: 22	Work Exp: 85%
Part-time: 303	International: 15%
Total: 325	Women: 38%
Average Age: 30	Minorities: 6%

Average Class Size: 35

ACADEMICS

Length of Program Minimum: 24 months. Maximum: 5 years.

Calendar Semesters.

Part-time Classes Main campus, Fort Bragg, Raleigh, Goldsboro, Jacksonville, Rocky Mount; evening.

Degree Requirements 30 semester hours including 6 elective semester hours. Other: Oral exam.

Required Courses Advanced management accounting, economic analysis and policy, financial analysis, legal environment, management process, marketing management, quantitative methods.

Curricular Focus Economic and financial theory, entrepreneurship, teamwork.

Concentration Management.

Faculty Full-time: 9, 100% with doctorates; part-time: 3, 100% with doctorates.

Teaching Methodology Case study: 20%, lecture: 35%, seminars by members of the business community: 5%, student presentations: 25%, team projects: 15%.

STUDENT STATISTICS

Geographic Representation State residents 85%. By region: South 85%. International 15%.

Undergraduate Majors Business 80%; engineering/technology 10%; humanities 3%; science/mathematics 2%; social sciences 5%.

Other Background Graduate degrees in other disciplines: 5%. Work experience: On average, students have 4 years of work experience on entrance to the program.

FACILITIES

Information Resources Main library with 181,170 bound volumes, 740,311 titles on microform, 995 periodical subscriptions, 4,300 records/tapes/CDs. Business collection includes 10,000 bound volumes, 85 periodical subscriptions.

Housing 8% of students in program live in college-owned or -operated housing.

Technology Computers are used moderately in course work. 30 computer terminals/PCs are available for use by students in program; they are located in the library, the computer center, computer labs. Students in the program are not required to have their own PC.

Computer Resources/On-line Services

Training	No	E-Mail	No
Internet	Yes $	Dialog	Yes

Other on-line services: First Search.

ADMISSION

Acceptance 1994-95 119 applied for admission; 43% were accepted.

Entrance Requirements Bachelor's degree, GMAT score of 450, minimum 2.7 GPA, provisional admission offered if requirements are not met. Core courses waived through: previous course work.

Application Requirements Application form, copies of transcript, 3 letters of recommendation.

Application Deadlines 8/1 for fall, 12/1 for spring, 4/1 for summer.

FINANCIALS

Costs for 1994-95 Tuition: Part-time evening: $150/semester hour.

Financial Aid Financial aid is not available to part-time students.

INTERNATIONAL STUDENTS

Demographics 15% of students enrolled in the program are international; Asia 80%, Africa 5%, Europe 5%, other 10%.

Services and Facilities International student center, counseling/support services.

Applying TOEFL required; proof of health; proof of adequate funds. Financial aid is not available to international students. Admission applica-

tion deadlines: 8/1 for fall, 12/1 for spring, 4/1 for summer. Contact: Mr. George Blanc, International Admissions Officer, Room 100, Baldwin Hall, Buies Creek, NC 27506. (910) 893-1415.

ALTERNATE MBA PROGRAMS

MBA/JD Length of program: Minimum: 24 months. Maximum: 5 years. Degree requirements: 30 semester hours including 6 elective semester hours. Must receive both degrees from Campbell University.

MBA/Pharm D Length of program: Minimum: 24 months. Maximum: 5 years. Degree requirements: 30 semester hours.

PLACEMENT

Placement services include career counseling/planning, career placement, and job interviews.

Program Contact: Mr. Jim Farthing, Director of Graduate Admissions, Campbell University, PO Box 546, Buies Creek, NC 27506-0546. (910) 893-4111; Fax: (910) 893-1424.

Duke University

Fuqua School of Business

Durham, North Carolina

OVERVIEW

Duke University is an independent coed institution, affiliated with United Methodist Church. Founded 1838. Setting: 8,500-acre suburban campus. Total institutional enrollment: 10,000. Program was first offered in 1970. AACSB-accredited.

MBA HIGHLIGHTS

Entrance Difficulty*****
Mean GMAT: 625
Mean GPA: 3.3

Cost $$$$
Tuition: $20,800
Room & Board: $9,300 (off-campus)

Enrollment Profile

Full-time: 654	Work Exp: 98%
Part-time: 0	International: 15%
Total: 654	Women: 29%
Average Age: 27	Minorities: 17%

Average Class Size: 45

ACADEMICS

Length of Program Minimum: 20 months. Maximum: 2 years.

Calendar 2 seven-week terms per semester.

Full-time Classes Main campus; day.

Degree Requirements 85 credit hours including 37 elective credit hours.

Required Courses Decision models, economic environment of the firm, financial accounting, financial management, individual effectiveness, international environment, managerial accounting, managerial economics, managerial effectiveness, marketing management, operations management, statistical analysis for management. Courses may be waived through: previous course work, examination.

Curricular Focus General management, international business, teamwork.

Concentrations Accounting, economics, entrepreneurship, finance, health services, human resources management, international business, management, marketing, operations management, organizational behavior, public policy, quantitative analysis.

Faculty Full-time: 70, 97% with doctorates; part-time: 10, 60% with doctorates.

Teaching Methodology Case study: 30%, lecture: 30%, seminars by members of the business community: 5%, student presentations: 25%, team projects: 10%.

Special Opportunities International exchange in Australia, France, Italy, Netherlands, Spain. Internship program available.

STUDENT STATISTICS

Geographic Representation By region: Northeast 39%; South 20%; West 14%; Midwest 12%. International 15%.

Undergraduate Majors Business 26%; engineering/technology 22%; social sciences 24%; other 28%.

Other Background Work experience: On average, students have 4 years of work experience on entrance to the program.

FACILITIES

Information Resources Main library with 4.2 million bound volumes, 1.9 million titles on microform, 32,732 periodical subscriptions, 22,600 records/tapes/CDs. Business collection in Fuqua School of Business Library includes 20,000 bound volumes, 1,800 periodical subscriptions, 544 CD-ROMs, 382 videos.

Housing 5% of students in program live in college-owned or -operated housing.

Technology Computers are used heavily in course work. 96 computer terminals/PCs, linked by a campus-wide computer network, are available for use by students in program; they are located in student rooms, classrooms, the library, computer labs. Students in the program are required to have their own PC.

Computer Resources/On-line Services

Training	Yes	LEXIS/NEXIS	Yes
Internet	Yes	Dow Jones	Yes
E-Mail	Yes	Dialog	Yes

Other on-line services: OCLC.

ADMISSION

Acceptance 1994-95 2,207 applied for admission; 26% were accepted.

Entrance Requirements Bachelor's degree, GMAT score, minimum 4 years of work experience. Core courses waived through: previous course work.

Application Requirements Written essay, application form, copies of transcript, resume/curriculum vitae, personal statement, 3 letters of recommendation.

Application Deadline 3/31 for fall. Application discs available.

FINANCIALS

Costs for 1994-95 Tuition: Full-time: $20,800. Fees: Full-time: $2,308. Average room and board costs are $9,300 per academic year (off-campus).

Financial Aid In 1994-95, 42% of candidates received some institutionally administered aid in the form of scholarships. Total awards ranged from $3,000-$19,800. Application deadline: 3/1 for fall. Contact: Mr. Paul West, Director of Financial Aid, Box 90128, Fuqua School of Business, Durham, NC 27708. (919) 660-7803.

INTERNATIONAL STUDENTS

Demographics 15% of students enrolled in the program are international; Asia 54%, Europe 20%, South America 15%, Central America 3%, Africa 2%, Australia 1%, other 5%.

Services and Facilities International student center, visa services, special assistance for nonnative speakers of English, counseling/support services.

Applying TOEFL required; proof of adequate funds. Financial aid is available to international students. Financial aid application deadline: 3/31 for fall. Admission application deadline: 3/1 for fall. Contact: Ms. Judith Green, Director of International Student Affairs, Box 90126, Durham, NC 27708. (919) 660-7807.

ALTERNATE MBA PROGRAMS

Executive MBA (EMBA) Length of program: Minimum: 20 months. Maximum: 2 years. Degree requirements: 45 credit hours including 6 elective credit hours. Work experience.

MBA/JD Length of program: Minimum: 48 months. Maximum: 4 years. Degree requirements: 143 credit hours including 21 elective credit hours.

MBA/MS Length of program: Minimum: 27 months. Maximum: 3 years. Degree requirements: 69-93 credit hours including 21 elective credit hours. MS is in engineering.

MBA/MEM Length of program: Minimum: 33 months. Maximum: 3 years. Degree requirements: 105 credit hours.

MBA/MPP Length of program: Minimum: 33 months. Maximum: 3 years. Degree requirements: 99 credit hours including 21 elective credit hours. Summer internship. MA is in public policy.

PLACEMENT

In 1993-94, 244 organizations participated in on-campus recruiting; 6,120 on-campus interviews were conducted. Placement services include alumni network, career counseling/planning, career fairs, career library, career placement, electronic job bank, hotline for job listing, job interviews, resume preparation, and resume referral to employers. Of 1994 graduates, 95% were employed within three months of graduation, the average starting salary was $61,300, the range was $28,000-$90,000.

Jobs by Functional Area Marketing/sales 28%; finance 42%; operations 5%; management 11%; strategic planning 4%; technical management 10%.

Program Contact: Ms. Melinda Bissett, Director of Admissions, Duke University, Durham, NC 27708. (919) 684-8111; Fax: (919) 681-8026.

East Carolina University

School of Business

Greenville, North Carolina

OVERVIEW

East Carolina University is a state-supported coed institution. Part of University of North Carolina System. Founded 1907. Setting: 465-acre small-town campus. Total institutional enrollment: 17,500. Program was first offered in 1966. AACSB-accredited.

MBA HIGHLIGHTS

Entrance Difficulty*
Mean GMAT: 500
Mean GPA: 3.0

Cost $
Tuition: $382/semester
(Nonresident: $3,624/semester)
Room & Board: $4,800

Enrollment Profile

Full-time: 133	Work Exp: 70%
Part-time: 137	International: 3%
Total: 270	Women: 32%
Average Age: 28	Minorities: 6%

Average Class Size: 19

ACADEMICS

Length of Program Minimum: 20 months. Maximum: 9 years.

Calendar Semesters.

Full-time Classes Main campus; day, evening, summer.

Part-time Classes Main campus; day, evening, summer.

Degree Requirements 60 credits including 9 elective credits.

Required Courses Accounting, business law, business policies, business writing, economics, finance, management, management information systems, management science, marketing, operations, organization behavior, statistics. Courses may be waived through: previous course work.

Curricular Focus General management, problem solving and decision making, strategic analysis and planning.

Concentrations Accounting, economics, entrepreneurship, finance, health care management, health services, human resources management, international business, management, management information systems, marketing, operations management, organizational behavior, quantitative analysis, real estate, strategic management.

Faculty Full-time: 38, 97% with doctorates.

Teaching Methodology Case study: 20%, lecture: 50%, research: 5%, student presentations: 5%, team projects: 20%.

Special Opportunities International exchange in Australia, France. Internships include work study through cooperative education.

STUDENT STATISTICS

Geographic Representation State residents 90%. By region: South 90%; Northeast 5%; Midwest 2%. International 3%.

Undergraduate Majors Business 55%; education 1%; engineering/technology 11%; humanities 6%; nursing 3%; science/mathematics 7%; social sciences 13%; other 4%.

Other Background Graduate degrees in other disciplines: 3%. Work experience: On average, students have 6 years of work experience on entrance to the program.

FACILITIES

Information Resources Main library with 1.1 million bound volumes, 283,369 titles on microform, 7,009 periodical subscriptions.

Housing 2% of students in program live in college-owned or -operated housing.

Technology Computers are used heavily in course work. 100 computer terminals/PCs are available for use by students in program; they are located in classrooms, computer labs. Students in the program are not required to have their own PC.

Computer Resources/On-line Services

Training	Yes	Dun's	No
Internet	No	Dow Jones	No
E-Mail	No	Dialog	No
LEXIS/NEXIS	No	Bloomberg	No
CompuServe	No		

ADMISSION

Acceptance 1994-95 159 applied for admission; 52% were accepted.

Entrance Requirements Bachelor's degree, GMAT score. Core courses waived through: previous course work.

Application Requirements Application form, copies of transcript.

Application Deadlines 6/1 for fall, 10/15 for spring, 3/15 for summer, 5/1 for second summer session.

FINANCIALS

Costs for 1994-95 Tuition: Full-time: $382/semester for state residents, $3,624/semester for nonresidents. Fees: Full-time: $397/semester for state residents, $397/semester for nonresidents. Average room and board costs are $4,800 per academic year (on-campus) and $5,200 per academic year (off-campus).

Financial Aid In 1994-95, 40% of candidates received some institutionally administered aid in the form of loans, assistantships, work-study. Total awards ranged from $2,600-$13,700. Financial aid is available to part-time students. Application deadlines: 6/1 for fall, 10/15 for spring, 3/15 for summer, 5/1 for second summer session. Contact: Mr. Rose Mary Stolma, Director of Student Financial Aid, Old Cafeteria Building, Greenville, NC 27858-4353. (919) 328-6610.

INTERNATIONAL STUDENTS

Demographics 3% of students enrolled in the program are international; Asia 72%, Europe 14%, South America 14%.

Services and Facilities International student office, visa services, language tutoring, ESL courses, special assistance for nonnative speakers of English, counseling/support services, special orientation, host family program.

Applying TOEFL required, minimum score of 550; proof of health; proof of adequate funds. Financial aid is available to international students. Financial aid application deadlines: 6/1 for fall, 10/15 for spring, 3/15 for summer, 5/1 for second summer. Admission application deadlines: 6/1 for fall, 10/15 for spring, 3/15 for summer, 5/1 for second summer session. Contact: Dr. Lucinda W. Wright, International Student Adviser, 211 Wichard Building,, Greenville, NC 27858-4353. (919) 326-6882.

PLACEMENT

In 1993-94, 45 organizations participated in on-campus recruiting; 205 on-campus interviews were conducted. Placement services include career counseling/planning, career fairs, career placement, job interviews, and resume preparation. Of 1994 graduates, 75% were employed within three months of graduation, the average starting salary was $35,000, the range was $18,000-$95,000.

Jobs by Employer Type Manufacturing 35%; service 41%; government 19%; nonprofit 3%; other 2%.

Program Contact: Mr. Donald B. Boldt, Director of Graduates Studies, East Carolina University, 3203 General Classroom Building, Greenville, NC 27858-4353. (919) 328-6970; Fax: (919) 328-6664.

Elon College

The Martha and Spencer Love School of Business

Elon College, North Carolina

OVERVIEW

Elon College is an independent comprehensive coed institution, affiliated with United Church of Christ. Founded 1889. Setting: 330-acre small-town campus. Total institutional enrollment: 3,496. Program was first offered in 1984.

MBA HIGHLIGHTS

Entrance Difficulty**
Mean GMAT: 480
Mean GPA: 3.0

Cost $
Tuition: $195/hour
Room & Board: $4,000

Enrollment Profile

Full-time: 8	Work Exp: 90%
Part-time: 135	International: 6%
Total: 143	Women: 38%
Average Age: 31	Minorities: 6%

Average Class Size: 25

ACADEMICS

Length of Program Minimum: 18 months. Maximum: 6 years.

Calendar 4-1-4.

Part-time Classes Main campus, Saint Andrews College; evening, summer.

Degree Requirements 36 credits including 12 elective credits.

Required Courses Business communications, business policy, financial management, managerial accounting, managerial economics, managerial statistics, marketing management, quantitative decision methods. Courses may be waived through: previous course work.

Curricular Focus Business issues and problems, problem solving and decision making, teamwork.

Concentration Management.

Faculty Full-time: 21, 81% with doctorates; part-time: 3, 67% with doctorates.

Teaching Methodology Case study: 35%, lecture: 35%, student presentations: 10%, team projects: 20%.

Special Opportunities International exchange in Japan.

STUDENT STATISTICS

Geographic Representation State residents 94%. By region: South 94%. International 6%.

Other Background Work experience: On average, students have 3 years of work experience on entrance to the program.

FACILITIES

Information Resources Main library with 185,915 bound volumes, 390 titles on microform, 1,000 periodical subscriptions, 3,873 records/tapes/CDs, 6 CD-ROMs.

Housing 5% of students in program live in college-owned or -operated housing.

Technology Computers are used moderately in course work. 90 computer terminals/PCs, linked by a campus-wide computer network, are available for use by students in program; they are located in learning resource center, computer labs. Students in the program are not required to have their own PC.

Computer Resources/On-line Services

Training	No	E-Mail	Yes
Internet	Yes	Multimedia Center	Yes

Other on-line services: First Search.

ADMISSION

Acceptance 1994-95 100 applied for admission; 85% were accepted.

Entrance Requirements Bachelor's degree, GMAT score of 400, minimum 2.0 GPA. Core courses waived through: previous course work.

Application Requirements Application form, copies of transcript, 3 letters of recommendation.

Application Deadlines 7/1 for fall, 12/1 for spring.

FINANCIALS

Costs for 1994-95 Tuition: Full-time: $195/hour. Average room and board costs are $4,000 per academic year (on-campus) and $4,000 per academic year (off-campus).

Financial Aid In 1994-95, 11% of candidates received some institutionally administered aid in the form of grants, scholarships, loans. Total awards ranged from $600-$9,350. Financial aid is available to part-time students. Application deadlines: 4/1 for fall, 10/1 for spring. Contact: Mr. Joel Speckhard, Associate Dean of Admissions and Financial Planning, 2700 Campus Box, Elon College, NC 27244. (800) 334 8448.

INTERNATIONAL STUDENTS

Demographics 6% of students enrolled in the program are international; Asia 56%, Europe 22%, Africa 11%, Central America 11%.

Services and Facilities Visa services, language tutoring, special assistance for nonnative speakers of English, counseling/support services.

Applying TOEFL required, minimum score of 500; proof of adequate funds. Financial aid is not available to international students. Admission application deadlines: 7/1 for fall, 12/1 for spring. Contact: Mr. Jonathan Walker, Assistant Director of International Programs, 2299 Campus Box, Elon College, NC 27244. (910) 538-2636.

PLACEMENT
Placement services include career counseling/planning, resume preparation, and resume referral to employers.

Program Contact: Ms. Alice N. Essen, Director of Graduate Admissions, Elon College, 2700 Campus Box, Elon College, NC 27244. (910) 584-2370, or (800) 334-8448; Fax: (910) 538-5986.

Fayetteville State University

School of Business and Economics

Fayetteville, North Carolina

OVERVIEW
Fayetteville State University is a state-supported comprehensive coed institution. Part of University of North Carolina System. Founded 1867. Setting: 156-acre suburban campus. Total institutional enrollment: 4,300. Program was first offered in 1984.

MBA HIGHLIGHTS

Entrance Difficulty***
Mean GMAT: 480
Mean GPA: 3.2

Cost $
Tuition: $70/credit hour
(Nonresident: $425/credit hour)
Room & Board: $4,000 (off-campus)

Enrollment Profile
Full-time: 0
Part-time: 91
Total: 91
Average Age: 32

Work Exp: 85%
International: 5%
Women: 45%
Minorities: 50%

Average Class Size: 18

ACADEMICS
Length of Program Minimum: 12 months. Maximum: 6 years.
Calendar Semesters.
Part-time Classes Main campus; evening, weekends, summer.
Degree Requirements 36 credit hours including 9 elective credit hours.
Required Courses Accounting, business and society, economics, finance, management information systems, marketing, organizational behavior, quantitative methods. Courses may be waived through: previous course work.
Curricular Focus General management, international business, minorities in business.
Concentrations Finance, international business, management, marketing.
Faculty Full-time: 16, 100% with doctorates; part-time: 1.
Teaching Methodology Case study: 25%, lecture: 50%, student presentations: 10%, team projects: 15%.

STUDENT STATISTICS
Geographic Representation State residents 95%. By region: South 95%. International 5%.
Undergraduate Majors Business 45%; education 3%; engineering/technology 20%; humanities 5%; nursing 2%; science/mathematics 10%; social sciences 10%; other 5%.
Other Background Graduate degrees in other disciplines: 5%. Work experience: On average, students have 5 years of work experience on entrance to the program.

FACILITIES
Information Resources Main library with 179,643 bound volumes, 469,944 titles on microform, 1,874 periodical subscriptions, 71 CD-ROMs.
Housing College housing available.

Technology Computers are used moderately in course work. 25 computer terminals/PCs, linked by a campus-wide computer network, are available for use by students in program; they are located in computer labs. Students in the program are not required to have their own PC.

Computer Resources/On-line Services

Training	No	Dun's	Yes
E-Mail	No	Dialog	Yes

Other on-line services: OCLC.

ADMISSION
Acceptance 1994-95 114 applied for admission; 80% were accepted.
Entrance Requirements Bachelor's degree, GMAT score. Core courses waived through: previous course work.
Application Requirements Application form, copies of transcript, 2 letters of recommendation.
Application Deadlines 7/30 for fall, 12/15 for spring.

FINANCIALS
Costs for 1994-95 Tuition: Part-time evening: $70/credit hour for state residents, $425/credit hour for nonresidents. Average room and board costs are $4,000 per academic year (off-campus).
Financial Aid In 1994-95, candidates received some institutionally administered aid in the form of assistantships. Total awards ranged from $250-$1,500. Financial aid is not available to part-time students. Applications are processed on a rolling basis. Contact: Ms. Gail Winter, Counselor, Financial Aid Office, Fayetteville, NC 28301. (910) 486-1325.

INTERNATIONAL STUDENTS
Demographics 5% of students enrolled in the program are international; Asia 40%, Central America 40%, Africa 20%.
Services and Facilities Visa services.
Applying TOEFL required, minimum score of 550; proof of adequate funds. Financial aid is not available to international students. Admission application deadlines: 8/15 for fall, 12/15 for spring. Contact: Dr. Assad Tavakoli, MBA Director, Newbold Station, Fayetteville, NC 28301. (910) 486-1197.

PLACEMENT
In 1993-94, 5 organizations participated in on-campus recruiting; 10 on-campus interviews were conducted. Placement services include career counseling/planning, career fairs, career library, career placement, electronic job bank, job interviews, and resume preparation. Of 1994 graduates, 90% were employed within three months of graduation.
Jobs by Employer Type Manufacturing 50%; service 30%; government 20%.

Program Contact: Dr. Assad Tavakoli, MBA Director, Fayetteville State University, Newbold Station, Fayetteville, NC 28301. (910) 486-1197; Fax: (910) 486-1033.

Gardner-Webb University

School of Business

Boiling Springs, North Carolina

OVERVIEW
Gardner-Webb University is an independent Baptist comprehensive coed institution. Founded 1905. Setting: 200-acre rural campus with easy access to Charlotte. Total institutional enrollment: 2,300. Program was first offered in 1993.

MBA HIGHLIGHTS

Entrance Difficulty**
Mean GMAT: 480
Mean GPA: 2.9

Cost $
Tuition: $165/semester hour
Room & Board: N/R

Enrollment Profile

Full-time: 0	Work Exp: 100%
Part-time: 70	International: 0%
Total: 70	Women: 49%
Average Age: 38	Minorities: 0%

Average Class Size: 20

ACADEMICS
Length of Program Minimum: 24 months. Maximum: 6 years.
Calendar Semesters.
Full-time Classes Main campus; evening, summer.
Degree Requirements 36 credits including 6 elective credits. Other: Minimum 3.0 GPA.
Required Courses Business law, international business, managerial accounting, managerial economics, managerial finance, marketing management, organizational behavior, production and operations management, quantitative methods, strategic management.
Curricular Focus Business issues and problems, international business, problem solving and decision making.
Concentrations Accounting, economics, entrepreneurship, finance, human resources management, international business, management, management information systems, marketing, operations management, organizational behavior, quantitative analysis, strategic management.
Faculty Full-time: 8, 70% with doctorates; part-time: 6, 50% with doctorates.
Teaching Methodology Case study: 10%, faculty seminars: 10%, lecture: 40%, research: 10%, student presentations: 20%, team projects: 10%.

STUDENT STATISTICS
Geographic Representation State residents 98%. By region: South 96%.
Other Background Work experience: On average, students have 10 years of work experience on entrance to the program.

FACILITIES
Information Resources Main library with 185,000 bound volumes, 195,323 titles on microform, 937 periodical subscriptions, 6,112 records/tapes/CDs. Business collection includes 4,000 bound volumes, 76 periodical subscriptions, 3 CD-ROMs, 45 videos.
Housing College housing available.
Technology Computers are used moderately in course work. Computer terminals/PCs are available for use by students in program; they are located in classrooms, the library, the computer center, computer labs. Students in the program are not required to have their own PC.
Computer Resources/On-line Services

Internet	Yes	E-Mail	No

ADMISSION
Acceptance 1994-95 75 applied for admission; 85% were accepted.
Entrance Requirements Bachelor's degree, undergraduate prerequisites with "C" or better, GMAT score of 450, minimum 2.5 GPA. Core courses waived through: previous course work.
Application Requirements Interview, application form, copies of transcript, resume/curriculum vitae, 3 letters of recommendation.
Application Deadline 8/1 for fall.

FINANCIALS
Costs for 1994-95 Tuition: Full-time: $165/semester hour.
Financial Aid In 1994-95, 10% of candidates received some institutionally administered aid in the form of loans, assistantships. Financial aid is available to part-time students. Applications are processed on a rolling basis. Contact: Mr. Rex R. Rhyne, Director of Financial Planning, Boiling Springs, NC 28017. (704) 434-4497.

INTERNATIONAL STUDENTS
Services and Facilities International student center, language tutoring, counseling/support services.
Applying TOEFL required, minimum score of 500; proof of adequate funds. Financial aid is not available to international students. Admission applications are processed on a rolling basis. Contact: Mrs. Jean Cabaniss, Director, International Student Programs, Box 203, Boiling Springs, NC 28017. (704) 434-4276.

PLACEMENT
In 1993-94, 2 organizations participated in on-campus recruiting; 70 on-campus interviews were conducted. Placement services include career counseling/planning and career fairs.

Program Contact: Dr. Darlene Gravett, Dean of Graduate Studies, Gardner-Webb University, Box 343, Boiling Springs, NC 28017. (704) 434-4723, or (800) 457-4622; Fax: (704) 434-4329.

Meredith College

John W. Weems Graduate School

Raleigh, North Carolina

OVERVIEW
Meredith College is an independent comprehensive women only institution, affiliated with Baptist Church. Founded 1891. Setting: 225-acre urban campus. Total institutional enrollment: 2,300. Program was first offered in 1983.

MBA HIGHLIGHTS

Entrance Difficulty**

Cost $
Tuition: $190/semester hour
Room & Board: N/R

Enrollment Profile

Full-time: 120	Work Exp: 100%
Part-time: 15	International: 5%
Total: 135	Women: 100%
Average Age: 29	Minorities: 20%

Average Class Size: 25

ACADEMICS
Length of Program Minimum: 24 months. Maximum: 6 years.
Calendar Semesters.
Part-time Classes Main campus; evening, summer.
Degree Requirements 36 semester hours including 3 elective semester hours.
Required Courses Accounting for managerial decisions, legal, regulatory, and ethical issues, macroeconomic environment of the firm, management information systems, management processes and policy, management seminar, managerial economics, managerial finance, marketing strategy, organizational theory and behavior, quantitative analysis for management.
Curricular Focus Women in business.
Concentration Management.
Faculty Full-time: 10, 90% with doctorates.
Teaching Methodology Case study: 10%, lecture: 60%, student presentations: 30%.
Special Opportunities Internship program available.

STUDENT STATISTICS
Geographic Representation By region: South 100%. International 5%.
Undergraduate Majors Business 60%; education 10%; humanities 10%; science/mathematics 10%; social sciences 10%.
Other Background Graduate degrees in other disciplines: 1%. Work experience: On average, students have 4 years of work experience on entrance to the program.

FACILITIES
Information Resources Main library with 153,509 bound volumes, 73,201 titles on microform, 778 periodical subscriptions, 9,739 records/tapes/CDs, 9 CD-ROMs.
Housing College housing not available.
Technology Computers are used moderately in course work. 30 computer terminals/PCs are available for use by students in program; they are located in computer labs. Students in the program are not required to have their own PC.

Computer Resources/On-line Services

Training	Yes	Dun's	No
Internet	No	Dow Jones	No
E-Mail	No	Dialog	No
LEXIS/NEXIS	No	Bloomberg	No
CompuServe	No		

ADMISSION

Acceptance 1994-95 Of those applying, 90% were accepted.

Entrance Requirements Bachelor's degree, GMAT score of 350, minimum 2.5 GPA, minimum 2 years of work experience.

Application Requirements Interview, application form, copies of transcript, resume/curriculum vitae.

Application Deadlines 8/1 for fall, 12/1 for spring, 5/1 for summer.

FINANCIALS

Costs for 1994-95 Tuition: Part-time evening: $190/semester hour.

Financial Aid In 1994-95, 3% of candidates received some institutionally administered aid in the form of scholarships, loans. Total awards ranged from $500-$3,340. Financial aid is not available to part-time students. Application deadlines: 8/1 for fall, 12/1 for spring. Contact: Ms. Elizabeth McDuffie, Director of Scholarships and Financial Aid, 3800 Hillsborough Street, Raleigh, NC 27607-5298. (919) 829-8565.

INTERNATIONAL STUDENTS

Demographics 5% of students enrolled in the program are international.

Services and Facilities International student center, visa services, special assistance for nonnative speakers of English, counseling/support services.

Applying TOEFL required, minimum score of 500; proof of adequate funds. Financial aid is available to international students. Financial aid application deadlines: 8/1 for fall, 12/1 for spring. Admission application deadlines: 8/1 for fall, 12/1 for spring, 5/1 for summer. Contact: Ms. Carol Snodgrass, Administrative Assistant, Graduate Office, 3800 Hillsborough Street, Raleigh, NC 27607-5298. (919) 829-8600.

PLACEMENT

Placement services include alumni network, career counseling/planning, career fairs, career library, and career placement. Of 1994 graduates, 100% were employed within three months of graduation.

Program Contact: Ms. Carol Snodgrass, Administrative Assistant, John E. Weems Graduate School, Meredith College, 3800 Hillsborough Street, Raleigh, NC 27607-5298. (919) 829-8423; Fax: (919) 829-2828.

North Carolina Central University

School of Business

Durham, North Carolina

OVERVIEW

North Carolina Central University is a state-supported comprehensive coed institution. Part of University of North Carolina System. Founded 1910. Setting: 103-acre small-town campus. Total institutional enrollment: 6,000. Program was first offered in 1981.

MBA HIGHLIGHTS

Entrance Difficulty***
Mean GMAT: 464
Mean GPA: 3.0

Cost $
Tuition: $1,338
Room & Board: $3,196

Enrollment Profile

Full-time: 12	Work Exp: 80%
Part-time: 20	International: 20%
Total: 32	Women: 50%
Average Age: 31	Minorities: 75%

Class Size: 8 - 10

ACADEMICS

Length of Program Minimum: 24 months. Maximum: 6 years.

Calendar Semesters.

Full-time Classes Main campus; evening.

Part-time Classes Main campus; evening.

Degree Requirements 33 credits including 9 elective credits.

Curricular Focus Entrepreneurship, minorities in business, problem solving and decision making.

Concentrations Accounting, management, marketing, strategic management.

Faculty Full-time: 14, 100% with doctorates.

Teaching Methodology Case study: 10%, lecture: 50%, research: 10%, seminars by members of the business community: 5%, student presentations: 15%, team projects: 10%.

STUDENT STATISTICS

Geographic Representation State residents 50%. By region: South 65%; Northeast 15%. International 20%.

Undergraduate Majors Business 75%; engineering/technology 10%; humanities 5%; social sciences 10%.

Other Background Graduate degrees in other disciplines: 5%. Work experience: On average, students have 8 years of work experience on entrance to the program.

FACILITIES

Information Resources Main library with 58,485 bound volumes, 70,000 titles on microform, 3,930 periodical subscriptions, 1,662 records/tapes/CDs. Business collection includes 20,000 bound volumes, 1,000 periodical subscriptions.

Housing 5% of students in program live in college-owned or -operated housing.

Technology Computers are used moderately in course work. 35 computer terminals/PCs are available for use by students in program; they are located in computer labs. Students in the program are not required to have their own PC.

Computer Resources/On-line Services

Training	No	Dun's	No
Internet	No	Dow Jones	No
E-Mail	No	Dialog	No
LEXIS/NEXIS	No	Bloomberg	No
CompuServe	No		

ADMISSION

Acceptance 1994-95 Of those applying, 70% were accepted.

Entrance Requirements Bachelor's degree, GMAT score.

Application Requirements Written essay, application form, copies of transcript, 2 letters of recommendation.

Application Deadlines 7/15 for fall, 11/1 for spring.

FINANCIALS

Costs for 1994-95 Tuition: Full-time: $1,338 for state residents, $7,821 for nonresidents. Average room and board costs are $3,196 per academic year (on-campus) and $1,568 per academic year (off-campus).

Financial Aid In 1994-95, 15% of candidates received some institutionally administered aid in the form of assistantships. Total awards ranged from $3,000-$5,000. Financial aid is not available to part-time students. Applications are processed on a rolling basis. Contact: Ms. Lola McKnight, Financial Aid Director, School of Business, PO Box 19686, Durham, NC 27707. (919) 560-6202.

INTERNATIONAL STUDENTS

Demographics 20% of students enrolled in the program are international; Africa 40%, Asia 30%, Central America 20%, Europe 10%.

Applying TOEFL required; proof of health; proof of adequate funds. Financial aid is not available to international students. Admission application deadlines: 7/15 for fall, 11/1 for spring.

PLACEMENT

In 1993-94, 10 organizations participated in on-campus recruiting. Placement services include career counseling/planning, career placement, job interviews, and resume referral to employers. Of 1994 graduates, 5% were employed within three months of graduation, the average starting salary was $30,000.

Program Contact: Mr. Raphael N. Thompson, Associate Dean, North Carolina Central University, School of Business, PO Box 19686, Durham, NC 27707. (919) 560-6120; Fax: (919) 560-6163.

North Carolina State University

College of Management

Raleigh, North Carolina

OVERVIEW

North Carolina State University is a state-supported coed institution. Part of University of North Carolina System. Founded 1887. Setting: 1,623-acre urban campus. Total institutional enrollment: 28,000. Program was first offered in 1976.

PROGRAM HIGHLIGHTS

Entrance Difficulty**
Mean GMAT: 550
Mean GPA: 3.1

Cost $
Tuition: $749/semester
(Nonresident: $4,270/semester)
Room & Board: N/R

Enrollment Profile

Full-time: 112	Work Exp: 80%
Part-time: 148	International: 15%
Total: 260	Women: 35%
Average Age: 30	Minorities: 10%

Average Class Size: 35

ACADEMICS

Calendar Modular.

Curricular Focus Business processes, technology management.

Concentrations Total Quality Management, management information systems, operations management.

Faculty Full-time: 23, 96% with doctorates; part-time: 4.

Teaching Methodology Case study: 19%, lecture: 19%, research: 19%, seminars by members of the business community: 5%, student presentations: 14%, team projects: 24%.

Special Opportunities International exchange in France, Japan, Netherlands.

STUDENT STATISTICS

Geographic Representation By region: South 62%; Midwest 10%; Northeast 6%; West 5%. International 15%.

Undergraduate Majors Business 32%; education 1%; engineering/technology 35%; humanities 4%; science/mathematics 18%; social sciences 10%.

Other Background Graduate degrees in other disciplines: 15%. Work experience: On average, students have 5 years of work experience on entrance to the program.

FACILITIES

Information Resources Main library with 2 million bound volumes, 3.7 million titles on microform, 18,086 periodical subscriptions, 128,000 records/tapes/CDs, 185 CD-ROMs.

Housing 10% of students in program live in college-owned or -operated housing.

Technology Computers are used moderately in course work. 75 computer terminals/PCs, linked by a campus-wide computer network, are available for use by students in program; they are located in the library, computer labs. Students in the program are not required to have their own PC.

Computer Resources/On-line Services

Training	Yes	CompuServe	No
Internet	Yes	Dun's	Yes
E-Mail	Yes	Dow Jones	Yes
LEXIS/NEXIS	No		

ADMISSION

Acceptance 1994-95 208 applied for admission; 72% were accepted.

Entrance Requirements Bachelor's degree, GMAT score. Core courses waived through: previous course work.

Application Requirements Written essay, application form, copies of transcript, resume/curriculum vitae, 3 letters of recommendation.

Application Deadlines 6/1 for fall, 11/1 for spring.

FINANCIALS

Costs for 1994-95 Tuition: Full-time: $749/semester for state residents, $4,270/semester for nonresidents; Part-time day: $215-$535/semester for state residents, $1,095-$3,176/semester for nonresidents.

Financial Aid In 1994-95, 25% of candidates received some institutionally administered aid in the form of grants, loans, fellowships, assistantships. Total awards ranged from $1,250-$9,850. Financial aid is not available to part-time students. Application deadlines: 3/15 for fall, 10/1 for spring. Contact: Ms. Pam Bostic, Assistant Director, MSM Program, 1201 University Center, Raleigh, NC 27695. (919) 515-5584.

INTERNATIONAL STUDENTS

Demographics 15% of students enrolled in the program are international; Asia 61%, South America 14%, Central America 11%, Europe 11%, Australia 3%.

Services and Facilities International student office, international student center, visa services, language tutoring, ESL courses, special assistance for nonnative speakers of English, counseling/support services.

Applying TOEFL required, minimum score of 550; proof of health; proof of adequate funds. Financial aid is not available to international students. Admission application deadlines: 5/1 for fall, 9/25 for spring. Contact: Ms. Elizabeth Craven, Director, International Student Office, 1201 University Center, Box 7306, Raleigh, NC 27695. (919) 515-2961.

PROGRAM

MSM Length of program: Minimum: 18 months. Maximum: 6 years. Full-time classes: Main campus, distance learning option; day, evening, summer. Part-time classes: Main campus, distance learning option; day, evening, summer. Degree requirements: 45 credits including 9 elective credits. Integrative management laboratory.

PLACEMENT

Placement services include career counseling/planning, career fairs, career library, career placement, resume preparation, and resume referral to employers. Of 1994 graduates, 85% were employed within three months of graduation, the average starting salary was $40,000, the range was $24,000-$50,000.

Program Contact: Ms. Pam Bostic, Assistant Director, MSM Program, North Carolina State University, 1201 University Center, Raleigh, NC 27695. (919) 515-5584; Fax: (919) 515-5564; Internet Address: pam_bostic@ncsu.edu.

Pfeiffer College

Misenheimer, North Carolina

OVERVIEW

Pfeiffer College is an independent United Methodist comprehensive coed institution. Founded 1885. Setting: 300-acre urban campus with easy access to Charlotte. Total institutional enrollment: 1,005. Program was first offered in 1985.

MBA HIGHLIGHTS

Entrance Difficulty*
Mean GMAT: 480
Mean GPA: 3.4

Cost $
Tuition: $215/credit hour
Room & Board: N/R

Enrollment Profile

Full-time: 200	Work Exp: 90%
Part-time: 50	International: 10%
Total: 250	Women: 50%
Average Age: 32	Minorities: 20%

Average Class Size: 20

ACADEMICS

Length of Program Minimum: 24 months.

Calendar Semesters.

Full-time Classes Main campus, Hickory, Salisbury; evening, summer.

Part-time Classes Main campus, Hickory, Salisbury; evening, summer.

Degree Requirements 36 credit hours.

Curricular Focus Entrepreneurship, international business, teamwork.

Concentrations Finance, health services.

Faculty Full-time: 6, 100% with doctorates; part-time: 4, 50% with doctorates.

Teaching Methodology Case study: 25%, research: 25%, student presentations: 25%, team projects: 25%.

Special Opportunities International exchange in France, Germany, United Kingdom.

STUDENT STATISTICS

Geographic Representation State residents 80%. By region: South 45%; Northeast 25%; Midwest 20%. International 10%.

Undergraduate Majors Business 100%.

Other Background Graduate degrees in other disciplines: 20%. Work experience: On average, students have 7 years of work experience on entrance to the program.

FACILITIES

Information Resources Main library with 111,500 bound volumes, 18,000 titles on microform, 430 periodical subscriptions, 2,300 records/tapes/CDs.

Housing College housing not available.

Technology Computers are used heavily in course work. 10 computer terminals/PCs, linked by a campus-wide computer network, are available for use by students in program; they are located in computer labs. Students in the program are not required to have their own PC. $100 are budgeted per student for computer support.

Computer Resources/On-line Services

Training	Yes	E-Mail	Yes
Internet	Yes		

ADMISSION

Acceptance 1994-95 240 applied for admission; 50% were accepted.

Entrance Requirements Bachelor's degree, GMAT score of 450, minimum 2.7 GPA. Core courses waived through: previous course work.

Application Requirements Interview, application form, 3 letters of recommendation.

Application Deadline 8/15 for fall.

FINANCIALS

Costs for 1994-95 Tuition: Full-time: $215/credit hour.

Financial Aid Financial aid is not available to part-time students. Application deadlines: 8/15 for fall, 1/15 for spring.

INTERNATIONAL STUDENTS

Demographics 10% of students enrolled in the program are international.

Applying TOEFL required, minimum score of 550; proof of adequate funds. Financial aid is not available to international students. Admission application deadline: 8/15 for fall.

Program Contact: Dr. Louis Stone, MBA Director, Pfeiffer College, PO Box 960, Misenheimer, NC 28109-0960. (704) 521-9116; Fax: (704) 521-8617.

Queens College

Division of Business and Economics

Charlotte, North Carolina

OVERVIEW

Queens College is an independent Presbyterian comprehensive coed institution. Founded 1857. Setting: 25-acre suburban campus. Total institutional enrollment: 1,549.

MBA HIGHLIGHTS

Entrance Difficulty*

Cost $
Tuition: $230/credit hour
Room & Board: N/R

Enrollment Profile
Full-time: 510
Part-time: 0
Total: 510
Average Age: N/R

Work Exp: N/R
International: 1%
Women: 44%
Minorities: 8%

Average Class Size: 30

ACADEMICS

Length of Program Minimum: 24 months.

Calendar Semesters.

Part-time Classes Main campus; evening, summer.

Degree Requirements 30 credit hours.

Curricular Focus Ethics/social responsibility, general management, problem solving and decision making.

Concentration Management.

Teaching Methodology Case study: 75%, lecture: 10%, research: 5%, student presentations: 10%.

STUDENT STATISTICS

Geographic Representation State residents 95%. International 1%.

FACILITIES

Information Resources Main library with 116,000 bound volumes, 500 titles on microform, 590 periodical subscriptions, 400 records/tapes/CDs, 10 CD-ROMs.

ADMISSION

Entrance Requirements Bachelor's degree, GMAT score of 450, minimum 2.5 GPA.

Application Requirements Written essay, application form, copies of transcript, 2 letters of recommendation.

Application Deadline Applications are processed on a rolling basis.

FINANCIALS

Costs for 1994-95 Tuition: Part-time day: $230/credit hour. Fees: Part-time day: $15/semester.

Financial Aid Contact: Ms. Eileen Dills, Director of Financial Aid, 1900 Selwyn Avenue, Charlotte, NC 28274-0002. (704) 337-2230.

INTERNATIONAL STUDENTS

Demographics 1% of students enrolled in the program are international.

Applying TOEFL required, minimum score of 550; proof of adequate funds. Financial aid is not available to international students. Admission applications are processed on a rolling basis.

ALTERNATE MBA PROGRAM

Executive MBA (EMBA) Length of program: Minimum: 24 months. Full-time classes: Main campus; day, weekends. Degree requirements: 60 credit hours.

Program Contact: Ms. Katie Wireman, Director of Admissions of Adult Programs, Queens College, 1900 Selwyn Avenue, Charlotte, NC 28274-0002. (704) 337-2313; Fax: (704) 337-2403.

University of North Carolina at Chapel Hill

The Kenan-Flagler Business School

Chapel Hill, North Carolina

OVERVIEW

The University of North Carolina at Chapel Hill is a state-supported coed institution. Part of University of North Carolina System. Founded 1795. Setting: 740-acre small-town campus. Total institutional enrollment: 24,299. Program was first offered in 1952. AACSB-accredited.

MBA HIGHLIGHTS

Entrance Difficulty N/R
Mean GMAT: 622
Mean GPA: 3.2

Cost $
Tuition: $874
(Nonresident: $8,400)
Room & Board: $2,910

Enrollment Profile
Full-time: 397	Work Exp: 99%
Part-time: 0	International: 12%
Total: 397	Women: 26%
Average Age: 27	Minorities: 12%

Average Class Size: 67

ACADEMICS
Length of Program Minimum: 24 months. Maximum: 2 years.
Calendar Semesters.
Full-time Classes Main campus; day.
Degree Requirements 30 credits including 12 elective credits. Other: Practicum; management simulation.
Required Courses Building and managing a globally competitive firm, ethics, financial accounting, financial management, global external environment, integrative management, management communication, managerial accounting, managerial competencies, managerial economics, marketing management, operations management, quantitative decision making, quantitative decision making 2.
Curricular Focus General management, leadership, teamwork.
Concentrations Accounting, entrepreneurship, finance, health services, international business, management, marketing, operations management, organizational behavior, public administration, real estate, strategic management.
Faculty Full-time: 33, 78% with doctorates.
Teaching Methodology Case study: 75%, lecture: 15%, team projects: 10%.
Special Opportunities International exchange in Belgium, Canada, France, Thailand, United Kingdom, Venezuela. Internship program available. Other: MBA Enterprise Corps, Urban Enterprise Corps.

STUDENT STATISTICS
Geographic Representation State residents 25%. By region: Northeast 36%; South 32%; Midwest 11%; West 9%. International 12%.
Other Background Graduate degrees in other disciplines: 100%. Work experience: On average, students have 4 years of work experience on entrance to the program.

FACILITIES
Information Resources Main library with 3.9 million bound volumes, 3.4 million titles on microform, 39,044 periodical subscriptions, 36,716 records/tapes/CDs. Business collection includes 300,000 bound volumes, 800 periodical subscriptions, 110 CD-ROMs.
Housing College housing available.
Technology 75 computer terminals/PCs, linked by a campus-wide computer network, are available for use by students in program; they are located in the computer center, computer labs. Students in the program are required to have their own PC.

Computer Resources/On-line Services
Internet	Yes	Videoconference Center	Yes
E-Mail	Yes	LEXIS/NEXIS	Yes

ADMISSION
Acceptance 1994-95 1,903 applied for admission; 22% were accepted.
Entrance Requirements Bachelor's degree, GMAT score.
Application Requirements Written essay, interview, application form, personal statement, 3 letters of recommendation.
Application Deadline 3/1 for fall.

FINANCIALS
Costs for 1994-95 Tuition: Full-time: $874 for state residents, $8,400 for nonresidents. Fees: Full-time: $1,736 for state residents, $1,736 for nonresidents. Average room and board costs are $2,910 per academic year (on-campus) and $6,300 per academic year (off-campus).
Financial Aid In 1994-95, 54% of candidates received some institutionally administered aid in the form of grants, scholarships, loans, fellowships. Total awards ranged from $8,809-$16,230. Application deadline: 3/1 for fall. Contact: Ms. Eleanor Morris, Director, Office of Scholarships and Student Aid, CB# 2300 Vance Hall, Chapel Hill, NC 27599-2300. (919) 962-8396.

INTERNATIONAL STUDENTS
Demographics 12% of students enrolled in the program are international.

Services and Facilities International student center, visa services, counseling/support services, conversation partners and writing center.
Applying TOEFL required, minimum score of 600; proof of health; proof of adequate funds. Financial aid is not available to international students. Admission application deadline: 3/1 for fall. Contact: Mr. Michael Bustle, Associate Director of the International Center, CB# 5240, Chapel Hill, NC 27599-2300. (919) 962-5661.

ALTERNATE MBA PROGRAMS
Executive MBA (EMBA) Length of program: Minimum: 24 months. Maximum: 2 years. Average class size: 65.
MBA/JD Length of program: Minimum: 48 months. Degree requirements: 123 credit hours.
MBA/MRP Length of program: Minimum: 36 months. Degree requirements: 88.5 credit hours.
MBA/MHA Degree requirements: 82.5 credit hours.

PLACEMENT
In 1993-94, 110 organizations participated in on-campus recruiting; 2,319 on-campus interviews were conducted. Placement services include alumni network, career counseling/planning, career fairs, career library, career placement, job interviews, and resume referral to employers. Of 1994 graduates, 88% were employed within three months of graduation, the average starting salary was $56,871, the range was $35,000-$85,000.

Jobs by Employer Type Manufacturing 42%; service 37%; consulting 13%; entrepreneurial/nonprofit 8%.

Jobs by Functional Area Marketing/sales 26%; finance 35%; operations 8%; management 8%; strategic planning 5%; consulting 14%; real estate 4%.

Program Contact: Ms. Anne Marie Summers, Director of Admissions, University of North Carolina at Chapel Hill, Chapel Hill, NC 27599-2300. (919) 962-3236; Fax: (919) 962-0898.
See full description on page 902.

University of North Carolina at Charlotte

Belk College of Business Administration

Charlotte, North Carolina

OVERVIEW
The University of North Carolina at Charlotte is a state-supported coed institution. Part of University of North Carolina System. Founded 1946. Setting: 1,000-acre suburban campus. Total institutional enrollment: 15,513. Program was first offered in 1970. AACSB-accredited.

MBA HIGHLIGHTS

Entrance Difficulty***
Mean GMAT: 541
Mean GPA: 3.1

Cost $
Tuition: $61 - $81/hour
(Nonresident: $331 - $441/hour)
Room & Board: N/R

Enrollment Profile
Full-time: 86	Work Exp: 95%
Part-time: 329	International: 86%
Total: 415	Women: 35%
Average Age: 27	Minorities: 14%

Average Class Size: 33

ACADEMICS
Length of Program Minimum: 30 months. Maximum: 6 years.
Calendar Semesters.
Full-time Classes Main campus; day, summer.
Part-time Classes Main campus; day, summer.
Degree Requirements 42 credits including 15 elective credits.
Required Courses Business information systems, economics of business decisions, financial management, management policy, managerial account-

ing, marketing management, operations management, organizational leadership and behavior, professional applications. Courses may be waived through: previous course work.

Curricular Focus Business issues and problems, problem solving and decision making, strategic analysis and planning.

Concentrations Accounting, commercial banking, information and technology management, economics, finance, management, marketing.

Faculty Full-time: 35, 100% with doctorates.

Teaching Methodology Case study: 20%, lecture: 35%, research: 10%, seminars by members of the business community: 5%, student presentations: 10%, team projects: 20%.

Special Opportunities International exchange in France. Internship program available. Other: cooperative education.

STUDENT STATISTICS
Geographic Representation State residents 12%. By region: South 75%; Northeast 5%; Midwest 5%; West 3%. International 86%.

Undergraduate Majors Business 55%; engineering/technology 22%; humanities 4%; nursing 1%; science/mathematics 5%; social sciences 4%; other 5%.

Other Background Graduate degrees in other disciplines: 13%. Work experience: On average, students have 3 years of work experience on entrance to the program.

FACILITIES
Information Resources Main library with 557,386 bound volumes, 344,499 titles on microform, 5,039 periodical subscriptions, 5,987 records/tapes/CDs, 405 CD-ROMs.

Housing 57% of students in program live in college-owned or -operated housing.

Technology Computers are used moderately in course work. Computer terminals/PCs, linked by a campus-wide computer network, are available for use by students in program; they are located in dormitories, learning resource center, computer labs. Students in the program are not required to have their own PC.

Computer Resources/On-line Services

Training	Yes	Dun's	No
Internet	Yes	Dow Jones	Yes
E-Mail	Yes	Dialog	Yes
LEXIS/NEXIS	Yes	Bloomberg	No
CompuServe	No		

Other on-line services: SEC.

ADMISSION
Acceptance 1994-95 Of those applying, 62% were accepted.

Entrance Requirements Bachelor's degree, GMAT score of 450, minimum 2.5 GPA. Core courses waived through: previous course work.

Application Requirements Written essay, application form, copies of transcript, 3 letters of recommendation.

Application Deadlines 7/1 for fall, 12/1 for spring.

FINANCIALS
Costs for 1994-95 Tuition: Full-time: $61-$81/hour for state residents, $331-$441/hour for nonresidents.

Financial Aid In 1994-95, candidates received some institutionally administered aid in the form of loans, assistantships. Financial aid is available to part-time students. Application deadline: 4/1 for fall. Contact: Mr. Curtis Whalen, Director of Financial Aid, 117 King Building, Charlotte, NC 28223. (704) 547-2461.

INTERNATIONAL STUDENTS
Demographics 86% of students enrolled in the program are international; Asia 58%, Africa 10%, Europe 10%, Central America 3%, South America 3%, Australia 1%, other 15%.

Services and Facilities International student office, international student center, visa services, language tutoring, ESL courses, special assistance for nonnative speakers of English, counseling/support services.

Applying TOEFL required, minimum score of 550; proof of adequate funds; transcripts must be in English. Financial aid is not available to international students. Admission application deadlines: 5/1 for fall, 10/1 for spring. Contact: Ms. Marian Beane, International Services Director, International Programs, 114 Denny Building, Charlotte, NC 28223. (704) 547-2410.

PLACEMENT
Placement services include alumni network, career counseling/planning, career fairs, career library, career placement, electronic job bank, job interviews, resume preparation, and resume referral to employers.

Program Contact: Dr. Virginia Geurin, Associate Dean for Graduate Studies and Research, University of North Carolina at Charlotte, University City Boulevard, Charlotte, NC 28223. (704) 547-2569; Fax: (704) 547-3123.

University of North Carolina at Greensboro

Joseph M. Bryan School of Business and Economics

Greensboro, North Carolina

OVERVIEW
The University of North Carolina at Greensboro is a state-supported coed institution. Part of University of North Carolina System. Founded 1891. Setting: 178-acre urban campus. Total institutional enrollment: 12,500. Program was first offered in 1969. AACSB-accredited.

MBA HIGHLIGHTS

Entrance Difficulty***
Mean GMAT: 533
Mean GPA: 3.08

Cost $
Tuition: $859/semester
(Nonresident: $4,379/semester)
Room & Board: $1,810

Enrollment Profile

Full-time: 33	Work Exp: 90%
Part-time: 220	International: 5%
Total: 253	Women: 35%
Average Age: 30	Minorities: 12%

Average Class Size: 26

The Bryan M.B.A. Program accommodates a wide range of domestic and international students in master's degree and post-master's degree certificate programs. For the student interested in graduate study with a focus on organizational strategy and international business, the M.B.A. degree offers a variety of required and elective courses that allow for some specialization of interest—all of which can be completed in two years with full-time study. The curriculum ranges from highly technical course work in management information systems to courses focusing on skills such as communication and the leadership and managerial style and effectiveness that managers need to succeed today. For experienced master's degree holders desiring further educational opportunities, post-master's certificate programs are offered in advanced business studies and international business.

The local and state business communities are highly supportive of the Bryan School and are frequently involved in classes and internships with students.

The faculty members hold degrees from many distinguished universities in the U.S. and other countries and are active researchers, teachers, and mentors of students. The University of North Carolina System emphasizes teaching. Graduating students of the Bryan School cite the faculty's degree of professionalism and student orientation as the School's greatest strengths.

ACADEMICS
Length of Program Minimum: 20 months. Maximum: 5 years.

Calendar Semesters.

Full-time Classes Main campus; evening.

Part-time Classes Main campus; evening.

Degree Requirements 48 credits including 15 elective credits.

Required Courses Accounting, communications, economics, ethics, finance marketing, human resources management, management science, managerial assessment and development, operations management, organization behavior, statistics, strategic analysis, formulation, and implementation. Courses may be waived through: previous course work.

Curricular Focus Problem solving and decision making.

Concentrations Accounting, finance, human resources management, international business, management information systems, marketing, operations management, organizational behavior, strategic management.

Faculty Full-time: 40, 100% with doctorates.

Teaching Methodology Case study: 40%, lecture: 30%, research: 5%, seminars by members of the business community: 5%, student presentations: 10%, team projects: 10%.

Special Opportunities International exchange in Germany, United Kingdom. Internship program available.

STUDENT STATISTICS
Geographic Representation State residents 90%. By region: South 90%; Northeast 3%; Midwest 2%. International 5%.
Undergraduate Majors Business 46%; education 2%; engineering/technology 28%; humanities 11%; nursing 2%; social sciences 11%.
Other Background Graduate degrees in other disciplines: 3%. Work experience: On average, students have 6 years of work experience on entrance to the program.

FACILITIES
Information Resources Main library with 851,521 bound volumes, 869,121 titles on microform, 5,447 periodical subscriptions, 9,357 records/tapes/CDs.
Housing 5% of students in program live in college-owned or -operated housing.
Technology Computers are used moderately in course work. 200 computer terminals/PCs, linked by a campus-wide computer network, are available for use by students in program; they are located in the student center, learning resource center, the library, the computer center, computer labs. Students in the program are required to have their own PC.

Computer Resources/On-line Services

Training	Yes	CompuServe	No
Internet	Yes	Dun's	No
E-Mail	Yes	Dow Jones	No
Multimedia Center	Yes	Dialog	Yes
LEXIS/NEXIS	No	Bloomberg	No

ADMISSION
Acceptance 1994-95 Of those applying, 54% were accepted.
Entrance Requirements Bachelor's degree, GMAT score. Core courses waived through: previous course work.
Application Requirements Written essay, application form, copies of transcript, resume/curriculum vitae, 3 letters of recommendation.
Application Deadlines 7/1 for fall, 11/1 for spring.

FINANCIALS
Costs for 1994-95 Tuition: Full-time: $859/semester for state residents, $4,379/semester for nonresidents. Average room and board costs are $1,810 per academic year (on-campus).
Financial Aid In 1994-95, 6% of candidates received some institutionally administered aid in the form of fellowships, assistantships, tuition waivers. Total awards ranged from $2,250-$14,700. Financial aid is available to part-time students. Application deadlines: 5/1 for fall, 5/1 for spring, 6/1 for summer. Contact: Mr. Eric Locklear, Associate Director of Financial Aid, Financial Aid Office, 723 Kenilworth Street, Greensboro, NC 27412. (910) 334-5702.

INTERNATIONAL STUDENTS
Demographics 5% of students enrolled in the program are international; Asia 50%, Europe 37%, South America 12%.
Services and Facilities Visa services, language tutoring, special assistance for nonnative speakers of English, counseling/support services.
Applying TOEFL required, minimum score of 550; proof of health; proof of adequate funds. Financial aid is not available to international students. Admission application deadlines: 5/1 for fall, 10/1 for spring. Contact: Ms. Martha Trigonis, Director of International Student Services, 155 Elliott University Center, Greensboro, NC 27412. (910) 334-5231.

PLACEMENT
Placement services include career counseling/planning, career placement, electronic job bank, job interviews, and resume referral to employers.

Program Contact: Mr. John Simms, Administrative Director, MBA Program, University of North Carolina at Greensboro, 220 Bryan Building, Greensboro, NC 27412. (910) 334-5390; Fax: (910) 334-5580.

University of North Carolina at Wilmington

Cameron School of Business Administration

Wilmington, North Carolina

OVERVIEW
The University of North Carolina at Wilmington is a state-supported comprehensive coed institution. Part of University of North Carolina System.

Founded 1947. Setting: 650-acre urban campus. Total institutional enrollment: 7,731. Program was first offered in 1982. AACSB-accredited.

MBA HIGHLIGHTS

Entrance Difficulty***
Mean GMAT: 525
Mean GPA: 3.0

Cost $
Tuition: $746/semester
(Nonresident: $3,779/semester)
Room & Board: N/R

Enrollment Profile

Full-time: 15	Work Exp: 100%
Part-time: 72	International: N/R
Total: 87	Women: 43%
Average Age: 27	Minorities: N/R

Average Class Size: 35

ACADEMICS
Length of Program Minimum: 24 months. Maximum: 2 years.
Calendar Semesters.
Full-time Classes Main campus; evening, weekends, summer.
Part-time Classes Main campus; evening, weekends, summer.
Degree Requirements 48 credits.
Curricular Focus Managing diversity, problem solving and decision making, strategic analysis and planning.
Concentration Management.
Teaching Methodology Case study: 30%, faculty seminars: 10%, lecture: 20%, research: 10%, seminars by members of the business community: 10%, student presentations: 10%, team projects: 10%.

STUDENT STATISTICS
Undergraduate Majors Business 37%; engineering/technology 24%; humanities 8%; nursing 3%; science/mathematics 10%; social sciences 9%; other 9%.
Other Background Graduate degrees in other disciplines: 2%. Work experience: On average, students have 7 years of work experience on entrance to the program.

FACILITIES
Information Resources Main library with 389,611 bound volumes, 761,747 titles on microform, 4,998 periodical subscriptions. Business collection includes 46,000 bound volumes.
Housing 2% of students in program live in college-owned or -operated housing.
Technology Computers are used heavily in course work. 34 computer terminals/PCs, linked by a campus-wide computer network, are available for use by students in program; they are located in dormitories, the student center, learning resource center, the library, the computer center, computer labs. Students in the program are not required to have their own PC.

Computer Resources/On-line Services

Training	No	E-Mail	Yes
Internet	Yes	Multimedia Center	Yes

ADMISSION
Acceptance 1994-95 Of those applying, 63% were accepted.
Entrance Requirements Bachelor's degree, GMAT score of 480, minimum 1 year of work experience.
Application Requirements Application form, copies of transcript, resume/curriculum vitae, 3 letters of recommendation.
Application Deadline 3/1 for fall.

FINANCIALS
Costs for 1994-95 Tuition: Full-time: $746/semester for state residents, $3,779/semester for nonresidents.
Financial Aid Financial aid is not available to part-time students. Application deadline: 3/1 for fall. Contact: Office of Financial Aid, James Hall, Wilmington, NC 28403-3201. (910) 395-3177.

INTERNATIONAL STUDENTS
Applying TOEFL required; proof of health. Financial aid is available to international students. Financial aid application deadline: 4/15 for fall. Admission application deadline: 4/15 for fall.

Program Contact: Dr. Rebecca Porterfield, MBA Coordinator, University of North Carolina at Wilmington, 601 South College Road, Wilmington, NC 28403-3201. (910) 395-3544; Fax: (910) 395-3815; Internet Address: porterfield@uncw.edu.

Wake Forest University

Babcock Graduate School of Management

Winston-Salem, North Carolina

OVERVIEW

Wake Forest University is an independent nonprofit coed institution. Founded 1834. Setting: 490-acre suburban campus. Total institutional enrollment: 5,157. Program was first offered in 1971. AACSB-accredited.

MBA HIGHLIGHTS

Entrance Difficulty**
Mean GMAT: 602
Mean GPA: 3.0

Cost $$$
Tuition: $17,000
Room & Board: $2,200

Enrollment Profile

Full-time: 214	Work Exp: 60%
Part-time: 295	International: 13%
Total: 509	Women: 28%
Average Age: 25	Minorities: 2%

Class Size: 20 - 50

ACADEMICS

Length of Program Minimum: 20 months. Maximum: 2 years.

Calendar Semesters.

Full-time Classes Main campus; day.

Part-time Classes Main campus; evening, summer.

Degree Requirements 66 credits including 19.5 elective credits.

Required Courses Accounting, analytical methods, field study project, financial management, international business management, international competitive policy, leadership, the law, and values, macroeconomics, management control, management information systems, management simulation and integrative exercises, marketing management, microeconomics, operations management, organizational behavior, written and oral communications.

Curricular Focus General management, international business, teamwork.

Concentration Management.

Faculty Full-time: 28, 96% with doctorates; part-time: 8, 25% with doctorates.

Teaching Methodology Case study: 50%, faculty seminars: 5%, lecture: 5%, research: 5%, seminars by members of the business community: 5%, simulations: 5%, student presentations: 10%, team projects: 15%.

Special Opportunities Internships include government, nonprofit, and for profit business.

STUDENT STATISTICS

Geographic Representation State residents 34%. By region: South 48%; Northeast 27%; Midwest 7%; West 3%. International 13%.

Undergraduate Majors Business 58%; education 1%; engineering/technology 4%; humanities 7%; science/mathematics 9%; social sciences 20%; other 1%.

Other Background Graduate degrees in other disciplines: 2%. Work experience: On average, students have 3 years of work experience on entrance to the program.

FACILITIES

Information Resources Main library with 1.2 million bound volumes, 334,379 titles on microform, 16,808 periodical subscriptions, 5,375 records/tapes/CDs, 1,070 CD-ROMs. Business collection in Professional Center Library includes 22,000 bound volumes, 350 periodical subscriptions, 10 CD-ROMs, 50 videos.

Housing 5% of students in program live in college-owned or -operated housing.

Technology Computers are used heavily in course work. 40 computer terminals/PCs, linked by a campus-wide computer network, are available for use by students in program; they are located in classrooms, the library, computer labs. Students in the program are required to have their own PC. $500 are budgeted per student for computer support.

Computer Resources/On-line Services

Training	Yes	CompuServe	No
Internet	Yes	Dun's	No
E-Mail	Yes	Dow Jones	Yes
Videoconference Center	Yes	Dialog	Yes
Multimedia Center	Yes	Bloomberg	No
LEXIS/NEXIS	Yes		

ADMISSION

Acceptance 1994-95 438 applied for admission; 56% were accepted.

Entrance Requirements Bachelor's degree, GMAT score of 500, minimum 2.0 GPA.

Application Requirements Written essay, application form, copies of transcript, resume/curriculum vitae, 2 letters of recommendation.

Application Deadline 4/1 for fall.

FINANCIALS

Costs for 1994-95 Tuition: Full-time: $17,000; Part-time evening: $1,700/course; Summer: $1,700/course. Fees: Full-time: $100/semester. Average room and board costs are $2,200 per academic year (on-campus) and $2,700 per academic year (off-campus).

Financial Aid In 1994-95, 84% of candidates received some institutionally administered aid in the form of scholarships, loans. Total awards ranged from $500-$14,500. Financial aid is not available to part-time students. Application deadline: 4/1 for fall. Contact: Mr. Eric K. Storey, Associate Director of Admissions and Financial Aid, P.O. Box 7659, Winston-Salem, NC 27109. (910) 759-5422.

INTERNATIONAL STUDENTS

Demographics 13% of students enrolled in the program are international; Asia 50%, Europe 28%, South America 7%, other 14%.

Services and Facilities International student housing; visa services, counseling/support services.

Applying TOEFL required, minimum score of 500; proof of adequate funds. Financial aid is available to international students. Financial aid application deadline: 4/1 for fall. Admission application deadline: 4/1 for fall. Contact: Mr. Jim Clapper, Reynolda Station, Winston-Salem, NC 27109. (910) 759-5038.

ALTERNATE MBA PROGRAMS

Executive MBA (EMBA) Length of program: Minimum: 17 months. Maximum: 2 years. Degree requirements: 51 credits including 3 elective credits.

MBA/JD Length of program: Minimum: 48 months. Maximum: 4 years.

MBA/MD Length of program: Minimum: 60 months. Maximum: 5 years. Degree requirements: 258 credits including 29.5 elective credits.

PLACEMENT

In 1993-94, 41 organizations participated in on-campus recruiting; 533 on-campus interviews were conducted. Placement services include alumni network, career counseling/planning, career fairs, career library, career placement, job interviews, resume preparation, resume referral to employers. Of 1994 graduates, 90% were employed within three months of graduation, the average starting salary was $44,000, the range was $20,000-$100,000.

Jobs by Employer Type Manufacturing 26%; service 25%; consulting 21%; healthcare 4%; transportation 2%; information systems 2%; hospitality 4%; communications 12%.

Jobs by Functional Area Marketing/sales 20%; finance 29%; operations 12%; management 13%; technical management 4%; consulting 10%; other 9%.

Program Contact: Ms. Mary C. Goss, Director of Admissions and Financial Aid, Wake Forest University, Reynolda Station, Winston-Salem, NC 27109. (910) 759-5422, or (800) 722-1622; Fax: (910) 759-5830.

Western Carolina University

College of Business

Cullowhee, North Carolina

OVERVIEW

Western Carolina University is a state-supported comprehensive coed institution. Part of University of North Carolina System. Founded 1889. Setting: 260-acre rural campus. Total institutional enrollment: 6,619.

Program was first offered in 1970. AACSB-accredited.

MBA HIGHLIGHTS

Entrance Difficulty***
Mean GMAT: 480
Mean GPA: 3.14

Cost $
Tuition: $382/semester
(Nonresident: $3,624/semester)
Room & Board: N/R

Enrollment Profile

Full-time: 53	Work Exp: 93%
Part-time: 61	International: 24%
Total: 114	Women: 39%
Average Age: 30	Minorities: 75%

Average Class Size: 20

ACADEMICS
Length of Program Minimum: 16 months. Maximum: 6 years.
Calendar Semesters.
Full-time Classes Main campus, Asheville; day, evening, early morning, summer.
Part-time Classes Main campus; day, evening, early morning, summer.
Degree Requirements 36 credits including 12 elective credits.
Required Courses Decision support systems, financial management, managerial accounting, managerial economics, marketing management, organizational behavior and analysis, quantitative analysis for business, strategic management.
Curricular Focus Organizational development and change management, problem solving and decision making, strategic analysis and planning.
Concentration Management.
Faculty Full-time: 28, 100% with doctorates.
Teaching Methodology Case study: 15%, lecture: 40%, research: 5%, student presentations: 15%, team projects: 25%.
Special Opportunities International exchange in France, Netherlands, United Kingdom.

STUDENT STATISTICS
Geographic Representation State residents 1%. By region: South 74%. International 24%.
Undergraduate Majors Business 71%; education 1%; engineering/technology 14%; humanities 2%; nursing 2%; science/mathematics 2%; social sciences 1%; other 7%.
Other Background Graduate degrees in other disciplines: 7%. Work experience: On average, students have 7 years of work experience on entrance to the program.

FACILITIES
Information Resources Main library with 436,041 bound volumes, 151,249 titles on microform, 2,144 periodical subscriptions, 856 records/tapes/CDs, 760 CD-ROMs.
Housing 8% of students in program live in college-owned or -operated housing.
Technology Computers are used moderately in course work. 75 computer terminals/PCs are available for use by students in program; they are located in the library, the computer center, computer labs. Students in the program are not required to have their own PC.

Computer Resources/On-line Services

Training	Yes	Dun's	No
Internet	Yes	Dow Jones	No
E-Mail	Yes	Dialog	No
LEXIS/NEXIS	No	Bloomberg	No
CompuServe	No		

ADMISSION
Acceptance 1994-95 107 applied for admission; 70% were accepted.
Entrance Requirements Bachelor's degree, "C" or higher in 8 undergraduate prerequisites, GMAT score of 400, ".
Application Requirements Application form, copies of transcript.
Application Deadline Applications are processed on a rolling basis.

FINANCIALS
Costs for 1994-95 Tuition: Full-time: $382/semester for state residents, $3,624/semester for nonresidents. Fees: Full-time: $339/semester for state residents, $339/semester for nonresidents.

Financial Aid In 1994-95, 25% of candidates received some institutionally administered aid in the form of grants, scholarships, loans, assistantships. Total awards ranged from $4,000-$20,984. Financial aid is available to part-time students. Application deadlines: 3/31 for fall, 10/31 for spring. Applications are processed on a rolling basis. Contact: Ms. Terry Jeffries, Student Services Assistant, Financial Aid Office, Cullowhee, NC 28723. (704) 227-7290.

INTERNATIONAL STUDENTS
Demographics 24% of students enrolled in the program are international; Europe 60%, Asia 37%, South America 3%.
Services and Facilities International student housing; international student office, visa services, language tutoring, special assistance for nonnative speakers of English, counseling/support services.
Applying TOEFL required, minimum score of 550; proof of health; proof of adequate funds. Financial aid is available to international students. Applications are processed on a rolling basis. Admission applications are processed on a rolling basis. Contact: Mr. Richard Cameron, Director of Student Services, 460 H.F. Robinson Building, Cullowhee, ND 28723. (704) 227-7234.

PLACEMENT
Placement services include career counseling/planning, career fairs, career library, career placement, electronic job bank, job interviews, job search course, resume preparation, and resume referral to employers. Of 1994 graduates, 95% were employed within three months of graduation, the average starting salary was $32,600, the range was $27,000-$36,000.
Jobs by Employer Type Manufacturing 45%; service 40%; government 5%; nonprofit 10%.
Jobs by Functional Area Marketing/sales 25%; operations 20%; management 10%; strategic planning 15%.

Program Contact: Ms. Faye Deitz, Secretary, Western Carolina University, Graduate Programs in Business, Forsyth Building, Cullowhee, NC 28723. (704) 227-7401; Fax: (704) 227-7414.

Wingate College

School of Business and Economics

Wingate, North Carolina

OVERVIEW
Wingate College is an independent Baptist comprehensive coed institution. Founded 1896. Setting: 330-acre suburban campus with easy access to Charlotte. Total institutional enrollment: 1,570. Program was first offered in 1991.

MBA HIGHLIGHTS

Entrance Difficulty**
Mean GMAT: 450
Mean GPA: 3.2

Cost $
Tuition: $200/credit hour
Room & Board: N/R

Enrollment Profile

Full-time: 0	Work Exp: 100%
Part-time: 95	International: 1%
Total: 95	Women: 40%
Average Age: 31	Minorities: 10%

Average Class Size: 20

ACADEMICS
Length of Program Minimum: 24 months. Maximum: 6 years.
Calendar Semesters.
Part-time Classes Mathews; evening, summer.
Degree Requirements 33 credit hours.
Required Courses Business communication, business ethics, business strategy, financial management, legal environment of business, managerial accounting, managerial economics, marketing management, operations management, organization management, quantitative decision methods.
Curricular Focus General management.
Concentration Management.

Faculty Full-time: 8, 80% with doctorates.

Teaching Methodology Case study: 20%, lecture: 50%, seminars by members of the business community: 5%, student presentations: 10%, team projects: 15%.

STUDENT STATISTICS

Geographic Representation State residents 99%. By region: South 100%. International 1%.

Undergraduate Majors Business 47%; education 10%; engineering/technology 10%; humanities 10%; nursing 3%; science/mathematics 10%; social sciences 10%.

Other Background Work experience: On average, students have 4 years of work experience on entrance to the program.

FACILITIES

Information Resources Main library with 110,000 bound volumes, 20,000 titles on microform, 650 periodical subscriptions, 5,600 records/tapes/CDs, 8 CD-ROMs. Business collection includes 7,700 bound volumes, 60 periodical subscriptions, 4 CD-ROMs, 50 videos.

Housing College housing not available.

Technology Computers are used moderately in course work. 35 computer terminals/PCs, linked by a campus-wide computer network, are available for use by students in program; they are located in learning resource center, the library, computer labs. Students in the program are required to have their own PC.

Computer Resources/On-line Services

Training	Yes	CompuServe	No
Internet	No	Dun's	No
E-Mail	No	Dow Jones	No
Multimedia Center	Yes	Dialog	Yes
LEXIS/NEXIS	No	Bloomberg	No

ADMISSION

Acceptance 1994-95 50 applied for admission; 90% were accepted.

Entrance Requirements Bachelor's degree, prerequisite courses required for applicants with non-business degree, GMAT score. Core courses waived through: previous course work.

Application Requirements Interview, application form, copies of transcript, resume/curriculum vitae, personal statement, 2 letters of recommendation.

Application Deadlines 8/1 for fall, 12/1 for spring. Applications are processed on a rolling basis.

FINANCIALS

Costs for 1994-95 Tuition: Part-time evening: $200/credit hour.

Financial Aid In 1994-95, 10% of candidates received some institutionally administered aid in the form of loans. Total awards ranged from $500-$1,200. Financial aid is available to part-time students. Application deadlines: 8/15 for fall, 12/15 for spring. Applications are processed on a rolling basis. Contact: Ms. Betty Whalen, Director of Student Financial Planning, Box 3001, Wingate, NC 28174. (704) 233-8010.

INTERNATIONAL STUDENTS

Demographics 1% of students enrolled in the program are international.

Services and Facilities Counseling/support services.

Applying TOEFL required, minimum score of 550; proof of health; proof of adequate funds. Financial aid is available to international students. Applications are processed on a rolling basis. Admission applications are processed on a rolling basis.

PLACEMENT

Placement services include career fairs and career placement. Of 1994 graduates, 100% were employed within three months of graduation.

Program Contact: Mrs. Kathryn Rowe, Administrative Assistant, Wingate College, Wingate, NC 28174. (704) 233-8000, or (800) 755-5550; Fax: (704) 233-8146.

NORTH DAKOTA

North Dakota State University

College of Business Administration

Fargo, North Dakota

OVERVIEW

North Dakota State University is a state-supported coed institution. Part of North Dakota University System. Founded 1890. Setting: 2,100-acre small-town campus. Total institutional enrollment: 9,700. Program was first offered in 1981.

MBA HIGHLIGHTS

Entrance Difficulty***
Mean GMAT: 530
Mean GPA: 3.6

Cost $
Tuition: $1,260/semester
(Nonresident: $1,550 - $3,197/semester)
Room & Board: $2,590

Enrollment Profile

Full-time: 29	Work Exp: 25%
Part-time: 38	International: 3%
Total: 67	Women: 30%
Average Age: 26	Minorities: 0%

Average Class Size: 20

ACADEMICS

Length of Program Minimum: 12 months. Maximum: 7 years.

Calendar Semesters.

Full-time Classes Main campus; day, evening, summer.

Part-time Classes Main campus, Jamestown, distance learning option; evening.

Degree Requirements 30 credits including 6 elective credits. Other: Comprehensive exam.

Required Courses Advanced financial management, advanced managerial accounting, advanced organizational behavior, business conditions analysis, marketing research, quantitative models for business, strategic management, strategic marketing and sales management.

Curricular Focus General management, problem solving and decision making, strategic analysis and planning.

Concentrations Accounting, finance, marketing.

Faculty Full-time: 16, 100% with doctorates.

Teaching Methodology Case study: 24%, lecture: 29%, research: 9%, student presentations: 14%, team projects: 24%.

Special Opportunities International exchange in Australia, Mexico, Netherlands. Internship program available.

STUDENT STATISTICS

Geographic Representation State residents 70%. By region: Midwest 97%. International 3%.

Undergraduate Majors Business 52%; education 4%; engineering/technology 19%; humanities 3%; nursing 1%; science/mathematics 15%; social sciences 3%; other 1%.

Other Background Graduate degrees in other disciplines: 3%. Work experience: On average, students have 4 years of work experience on entrance to the program.

FACILITIES

Information Resources Main library with 445,338 bound volumes, 220,119 titles on microform, 4,265 periodical subscriptions, 1,912 records/tapes/CDs, 10 CD-ROMs.

Housing 6% of students in program live in college-owned or -operated housing.

Technology Computers are used moderately in course work. 224 computer terminals/PCs, linked by a campus-wide computer network, are available for use by students in program; they are located in student rooms, the library, the computer center, computer labs. Students in the program are not required to have their own PC.

Computer Resources/On-line Services

Training	No	CompuServe	No
Internet	Yes	Dun's	No
E-Mail	Yes	Dow Jones	No
Videoconference Center	Yes	Dialog	No
Multimedia Center	Yes	Bloomberg	No
LEXIS/NEXIS	No		

ADMISSION

Acceptance 1994-95 47 applied for admission; 72% were accepted.

Entrance Requirements Bachelor's degree, GMAT score of 420, minimum 2.6 GPA. Core courses waived through: previous course work.

Application Requirements Application form, copies of transcript, personal statement, 3 letters of recommendation.

Application Deadlines 7/15 for fall, 11/15 for spring. Applications are processed on a rolling basis.

FINANCIALS

Costs for 1994-95 Tuition: Full-time: $1,260/semester for state residents, $1,550-$3,197/semester for nonresidents, $3,197/semester for international students; Part-time day: $105/credit hour for state residents, $129-$266/credit hour for nonresidents, $266/credit hour for international students. Fees: Full-time: $100/semester for state residents, $100/semester for nonresidents, $100/semester for international students; Part-time day: $8/credit hour for state residents, $8/credit hour for nonresidents, $8/credit hour for international students. Average room and board costs are $2,590 per academic year (on-campus).

Financial Aid In 1994-95, 18% of candidates received some institutionally administered aid in the form of scholarships, loans, assistantships. Total awards ranged from $5,120-$8,994. Financial aid is available to part-time students. Application deadlines: 3/15 for fall, 9/15 for spring. Applications are processed on a rolling basis. Contact: Ms. Janice Glatt, MBA Director, Box 5137, Putnam Hall, Fargo, ND 58105. (701) 231-8820.

INTERNATIONAL STUDENTS

Demographics 3% of students enrolled in the program are international.

Services and Facilities International student office, visa services, ESL courses.

Applying TOEFL required, minimum score of 550; proof of health; proof of adequate funds. Financial aid is available to international students. Assistantships are open to these students. Admission application deadlines: 4/1 for fall, 8/1 for spring. Applications are processed on a rolling basis. Contact: Dr. Virginia Packwood, Director of International Programs, Ceres Hall, Fargo, ND 58105. (701) 231-7895.

PLACEMENT

Placement services include career counseling/planning, career fairs, career library, career placement, job interviews, resume preparation, and resume referral to employers.

Program Contact: Ms. Janice Glatt, MBA Program Director, North Dakota State University, Box 5137, Putnam Hall, Fargo, ND 58105. (701) 231-8820; Fax: (701) 231-7508; Internet Address: jglatt@ndsuvm1.nodak.edu.

University of North Dakota

College of Business and Public Administration

Grand Forks, North Dakota

OVERVIEW

The University of North Dakota is a state-supported coed institution. Part of North Dakota University System. Founded 1883. Setting: 570-acre small-town campus. Total institutional enrollment: 12,500. Program was first offered in 1976. AACSB-accredited.

MBA HIGHLIGHTS ────────────

Entrance Difficulty*
Mean GMAT: 540
Mean GPA: 3.15

Cost $

Tuition: $1,319/semester
(Nonresident: $1,609 - $3,256/semester)
Room & Board: N/R

Enrollment Profile

Full-time: 20		Work Exp: 80%
Part-time: 62		International: 5%
Total: 82		Women: 30%
Average Age: 30		Minorities: 5%

Average Class Size: 25

ACADEMICS

Length of Program Minimum: 12 months. Maximum: 7 years.

Calendar Semesters.

Full-time Classes Main campus; evening, summer.

Degree Requirements 32 credits including 6 elective credits. Other: Independent study paper.

Required Courses Accounting information for decision and control, advanced risk management, business research methods, independent study, macroeconomic decision making, managerial finance, policy formulation and administration, quantitative analysis for management decisions, strategic market planning.

Curricular Focus General management, problem solving and decision making, strategic analysis and planning.

Concentration Management.

Faculty Full-time: 35, 100% with doctorates.

Teaching Methodology Case study: 25%, lecture: 35%, student presentations: 25%, team projects: 15%.

STUDENT STATISTICS

Geographic Representation State residents 95%. By region: Midwest 93%; South 1%. International 5%.

Undergraduate Majors Business 60%; education 5%; engineering/technology 10%; science/mathematics 5%; social sciences 20%.

Other Background Graduate degrees in other disciplines: 1%. Work experience: On average, students have 5 years of work experience on entrance to the program.

FACILITIES

Information Resources Main library with 1.2 million bound volumes, 2.2 million titles on microform, 8,197 periodical subscriptions, 11,619 records/tapes/CDs, 20 CD-ROMs.

Housing 3% of students in program live in college-owned or -operated housing.

Technology Computers are used moderately in course work. 450 computer terminals/PCs, linked by a campus-wide computer network, are available for use by students in program; they are located in dormitories, the student center, learning resource center, the library, the computer center, computer labs, the research center. Students in the program are not required to have their own PC.

Computer Resources/On-line Services

Training	No	CompuServe	Yes $
Internet	Yes $	Dun's	No
E-Mail	Yes	Dow Jones	Yes $
Videoconference Center	Yes	Dialog	Yes $
Multimedia Center	Yes	Bloomberg	No
LEXIS/NEXIS	No		

ADMISSION

Acceptance 1994-95 35 applied for admission; 86% were accepted.

Entrance Requirements Bachelor's degree, GMAT score of 450, minimum 2.75 GPA.

Application Requirements Written essay, application form, copies of transcript.

Application Deadlines 8/15 for fall, 12/15 for spring. Applications are processed on a rolling basis.

FINANCIALS

Costs for 1994-95 Tuition: Full-time: $1,319/semester for state residents, $1,609-$3,256/semester for nonresidents. Fees: Full-time: $159/semester for state residents, $159/semester for nonresidents.

Financial Aid In 1994-95, candidates received some institutionally administered aid in the form of grants, loans, assistantships. Financial aid is available to part-time students. Application deadline: 4/15 for fall. Applications are processed on a rolling basis. Contact: Mr. Mark Brickson, Director of Financial Aid, PO Box 8371, Grand Forks, ND 58202-8371. (701) 777-3121.

INTERNATIONAL STUDENTS

Demographics 5% of students enrolled in the program are international; Asia 50%, Europe 50%.

Services and Facilities International student office, international student center, counseling/support services.

Applying TOEFL required, minimum score of 550; proof of health; proof of adequate funds. Financial aid is not available to international students. Admission application deadlines: 3/15 for fall, 10/1 for spring. Applications are processed on a rolling basis. Contact: Ms. Sharon Rezac Andersen, Director, International Center, PO Box 7109, Grand Forks, ND 58202-7109. (701) 777-4231.

PLACEMENT

Placement services include career counseling/planning, career fairs, career library, and resume preparation. Of 1994 graduates, 95% were employed within three months of graduation.

Program Contact: Mr. Eric Giltner, MBA Program Administrator, University of North Dakota, Grand Forks, ND 58202. (701) 777-2135; Fax: (701) 777-5099; Internet Address: eric_giltner@mail.und.nodak.edu.

OHIO

Ashland University

School of Business Administration and Economics

Ashland, Ohio

OVERVIEW

Ashland University is an independent comprehensive coed institution, affiliated with Brethren Church. Founded 1878. Setting: 98-acre rural campus with easy access to Cleveland. Total institutional enrollment: 5,500. Program was first offered in 1978.

MBA HIGHLIGHTS

Entrance Difficulty***
Mean GMAT: 472
Mean GPA: 3.0

Cost $
Tuition: $275/credit hour
Room & Board: $5,500

Enrollment Profile

Full-time: 287	Work Exp: 100%
Part-time: 322	International: 10%
Total: 609	Women: 34%
Average Age: 34	Minorities: 5%

Average Class Size: 19

ACADEMICS

Length of Program Minimum: 24 months. Maximum: 5 years.

Calendar Trimesters.

Full-time Classes Main campus, Medina, Lima, Massillion, Columbus, Sandusky, Marion; evening, weekends, summer.

Part-time Classes Main campus, Medina, Lima, Massillion, Columbus, Sandusky, Marion; evening, weekends, summer.

Degree Requirements 36 credits including 3 elective credits.

Required Courses Business and society, business cycles and forecasting, business statistics, financial management, international business management, management information systems, managerial accounting, managerial economics, marketing management, operations management, organization analysis, organizational behavior, strategic planning and policy analysis. Courses may be waived through: previous course work.

Curricular Focus General management.

Concentration Management.

Faculty Full-time: 25, 84% with doctorates; part-time: 5, 80% with doctorates.

Teaching Methodology Case study: 3%, faculty seminars: 3%, lecture: 76%, research: 3%, seminars by members of the business community: 3%, student presentations: 6%, team projects: 6%.

STUDENT STATISTICS

Geographic Representation State residents 40%. By region: Midwest 90%. International 10%.

Undergraduate Majors Business 65%; education 3%; engineering/technology 18%; humanities 1%; nursing 2%; science/mathematics 5%, social sciences 2%; other 4%.

Other Background Graduate degrees in other disciplines: 1%. Work experience: On average, students have 6 years of work experience on entrance to the program.

FACILITIES

Information Resources Main library with 260,682 bound volumes, 250,000 titles on microform, 1,101 periodical subscriptions, 8,682 records/tapes/CDs, 50 CD-ROMs. Business collection includes 9,349 bound volumes, 234 periodical subscriptions, 8 CD-ROMs, 75 videos.

Housing 1% of students in program live in college-owned or -operated housing.

Technology 75 computer terminals/PCs, linked by a campus-wide computer network, are available for use by students in program; they are located in computer labs. Students in the program are not required to have their own PC.

Computer Resources/On-line Services

Training	Yes	CompuServe	No
Internet	Yes	Dun's	No
E-Mail	No	Dow Jones	No
Multimedia Center	Yes	Dialog	No
LEXIS/NEXIS	Yes	Bloomberg	No

Other on-line services: First Search.

ADMISSION

Acceptance 1994-95 130 applied for admission; 86% were accepted.

Entrance Requirements Bachelor's degree, minimum 2.75 GPA, minimum 2 years of work experience. Core courses waived through: previous course work.

Application Requirements Application form, copies of transcript, resume/curriculum vitae, personal statement.

Application Deadlines 7/1 for fall, 11/1 for spring, 3/15 for summer.

FINANCIALS

Costs for 1994-95 Tuition: Full-time: $275/credit hour. Average room and board costs are $5,500 per academic year (on-campus) and $5,000 per academic year (off-campus).

Financial Aid In 1994-95, 1% of candidates received some institutionally administered aid in the form of assistantships, tuition waivers. Total awards ranged from $825-$2,475. Financial aid is available to part-time students. Contact: Mr. Steve Howell, Director of Financial Aid, 310 Founders Hall, Ashland, OH 44805. (419) 289-5001.

INTERNATIONAL STUDENTS

Demographics 10% of students enrolled in the program are international; Asia 74%, Africa 10%, Central America 5%, Europe 3%, South America 3%, other 5%.

Services and Facilities Visa services, ESL courses, counseling/support services.

Applying TOEFL required, minimum score of 550; proof of health; proof of adequate funds. Admission application deadlines: 7/1 for fall, 11/1 for spring, 3/15 for summer. Contact: Mr. Thomas Koop, Director, International Student Services, 218 Andrews, Ashland, OH 44805. (419) 289-5068.

PLACEMENT

Placement services include alumni network, career counseling/planning, career fairs, career library, career placement, job interviews, resume preparation, and resume referral to employers. Of 1994 graduates, 95% were employed within three months of graduation.

Program Contact: Mr. Steve Krispinsky, Executive Director of MBA, Ashland University, 401 College Avenue, Ashland, OH 44805. (419) 289-5236, or (800) 882-1548 (OH only); Fax: (419) 289-5910.

Baldwin-Wallace College

Division of Business Administration

Berea, Ohio

OVERVIEW

Baldwin-Wallace College is an independent Methodist comprehensive coed institution. Founded 1845. Setting: 56-acre suburban campus with easy access to Cleveland. Total institutional enrollment: 4,716. Program was first offered in 1984.

MBA HIGHLIGHTS

Entrance Difficulty***
Mean GMAT: 476
Mean GPA: N/R

Cost $$$
Tuition: $1,330/course
Room & Board: N/R

Enrollment Profile

Full-time: 55	Work Exp: 75%
Part-time: 50	International: 49%
Total: 105	Women: 33%
Average Age: 28	Minorities: N/R

Average Class Size: 18

ACADEMICS

Length of Program Minimum: 24 months. Maximum: 4 years.
Calendar Quarters.
Part-time Classes Main campus, Beachwood, Westlake, Cleveland; evening, weekends, summer.
Degree Requirements 60 quarter hours.
Required Courses Accounting and financial management, financial management, information systems for management, macroeconomics for management, management policy and systems analysis, management science and computer models, marketing and management information systems, multinational corporations and international trade, operations analysis, organizational behavior, power, ethics, and society, systems management and organizational theory.
Curricular Focus International business, managing diversity, teamwork.
Concentration International business.
Faculty Full-time: 10, 90% with doctorates; part-time: 5, 60% with doctorates.
Teaching Methodology Case study: 20%, faculty seminars: 5%, lecture: 25%, research: 10%, seminars by members of the business community: 5%, student presentations: 15%, team projects: 20%.
Special Opportunities Internships include marketing in manufacturing, management in international business, and finance in banking. Other: study tours to Japan and Europe.

STUDENT STATISTICS

Geographic Representation State residents 51%. By region: Midwest 51%. International 49%.
Undergraduate Majors Business 44%; education 2%; engineering/technology 18%; humanities 7%; nursing 1%; science/mathematics 8%; social sciences 15%; other 5%.
Other Background Graduate degrees in other disciplines: 3%. Work experience: On average, students have 3 years of work experience on entrance to the program.

FACILITIES

Information Resources Main library with 230,000 bound volumes, 102,865 titles on microform, 950 periodical subscriptions, 18,300 records/tapes/CDs. Business collection includes 25,000 bound volumes, 200 periodical subscriptions, 10 CD-ROMs.
Housing College housing not available.
Technology Computers are used moderately in course work. 100 computer terminals/PCs, linked by a campus-wide computer network, are available for use by students in program; they are located in classrooms, the library, the computer center, computer labs. Students in the program are not required to have their own PC.

Computer Resources/On-line Services

Training	Yes	Dun's	No
Internet	Yes	Dow Jones	No
E-Mail	Yes	Dialog	Yes $
LEXIS/NEXIS	No	Bloomberg	No
CompuServe	No		

Other on-line services: OCLC.

ADMISSION

Acceptance 1994-95 94 applied for admission; 85% were accepted.
Entrance Requirements Bachelor's degree, GMAT score. Core courses waived through: previous course work.
Application Requirements Application form, copies of transcript, resume/curriculum vitae, 2 letters of recommendation.
Application Deadline Applications are processed on a rolling basis. Application discs available.

FINANCIALS

Costs for 1994-95 Tuition: Full-time: $1,330/course; Part-time day: $266/quarter hour. Fees: Full-time: $62/course; Part-time day: $62/course.
Financial Aid Financial aid is not available to part-time students.

INTERNATIONAL STUDENTS

Demographics 49% of students enrolled in the program are international; Asia 82%, Europe 12%, Central America 2%, South America 2%, North America 2%.
Services and Facilities Visa services, language tutoring, ESL courses, special assistance for nonnative speakers of English.
Applying TOEFL required, minimum score of 500; proof of adequate funds. Financial aid is not available to international students. Admission applications are processed on a rolling basis. Contact: Mr. Stanley Maxwell, Associate Dean of Students, 275 Eastland Road, Berea, OH 44017-2088. (216) 826-2116.

ALTERNATE MBA PROGRAMS

Executive MBA (EMBA) Length of program: Minimum: 24 months. Maximum: 4 years. Degree requirements: 60 credits. Average class size: 23.

International MBA .

PLACEMENT

Placement services include alumni network, career counseling/planning, career fairs, career library, career placement, resume preparation, and resume referral to employers.

Program Contact: Ms. Peggy Shepard, MBA Secretary, Baldwin-Wallace College, 275 Eastland Road, Berea, OH 44017-2088. (216) 826-2196; Fax: (216) 826-3868; Internet Address: pshepard@rs6000.baldwinw.edu.
See full description on page 670.

Bowling Green State University

College of Business Administration

Bowling Green, Ohio

OVERVIEW

Bowling Green State University is a state-supported coed institution. Founded 1910. Setting: 1,176-acre small-town campus with easy access to Toledo. Total institutional enrollment: 17,777. AACSB-accredited.

MBA HIGHLIGHTS

Entrance Difficulty***
Mean GMAT: 541
Mean GPA: N/R

Cost $
Tuition: $2,257/semester
(Nonresident: $4,759/semester)
Room & Board: $3,400

Enrollment Profile
Full-time: N/R
Part-time: N/R
Total: 325
Average Age: N/R

Work Exp: N/R
International: 14%
Women: 31%
Minorities: N/R

Average Class Size: 21

ACADEMICS
Length of Program Minimum: 11 months.
Calendar Semesters.
Full-time Classes Main campus; day, evening, summer.
Part-time Classes Main campus; day, evening, summer.
Degree Requirements 34 credits.
Curricular Focus Manufacturing and industrial services, organizational development and change management, problem solving and decision making.
Concentrations Finance, management, marketing, operations management, operations research.
Teaching Methodology Case study: 30%, faculty seminars: 5%, lecture: 20%, research: 10%, seminars by members of the business community: 10%, student presentations: 15%, team projects: 10%.

STUDENT STATISTICS
Geographic Representation State residents 70%. International 14%.

FACILITIES
Information Resources Main library with 1.9 million bound volumes, 1.7 million titles on microform, 5,427 periodical subscriptions, 617,118 records/tapes/CDs.
Housing College housing available.

ADMISSION
Entrance Requirements Bachelor's degree, GMAT score, minimum 2.7 GPA.
Application Requirements Application form, resume/curriculum vitae, personal statement, 2 letters of recommendation.
Application Deadlines 3/1 for fall, 11/1 for spring. Applications are processed on a rolling basis.

FINANCIALS
Estimated Costs for 1995-96 Tuition: Full-time: $2,257/semester for state residents, $4,759/semester for nonresidents. Average room and board costs are $3,400 per academic year (on-campus) and $4,800 per academic year (off-campus).
Financial Aid Application deadline: 3/1 for fall. Contact: Office of Financial Aid and Student Employment, 450 Student Services Building, Bowling Green, OH 43403. (419) 372-2651.

INTERNATIONAL STUDENTS
Demographics 14% of students enrolled in the program are international.
Applying TOEFL required, minimum score of 570; proof of health; proof of adequate funds. Financial aid is available to international students. Financial aid application deadlines: 3/1 for fall, 10/1 for spring. Admission application deadlines: 3/1 for fall, 10/1 for spring. Applications are processed on a rolling basis.

ALTERNATE MBA PROGRAM
Executive MBA (EMBA) Length of program: Minimum: 31 months. Part-time classes: Main campus; day, summer. Degree requirements: 36 credits.

Program Contact: Mr. Chuck Johnson, Director of Graduate Studies in Business, Office of Graduate Admissions, Bowling Green State University, 120 McFall Center, Bowling Green, OH 43403. (419) 372-2488, or (800) 247-8622 (OH only); Fax: (419) 372-2875.

Capital University

Graduate School of Administration

Columbus, Ohio

OVERVIEW
Capital University is an independent comprehensive coed institution, affiliated with Evangelical Lutheran Church in America. Founded 1830. Setting: 48-acre suburban campus. Total institutional enrollment: 3,453.

MBA HIGHLIGHTS
Entrance Difficulty***
Mean GMAT: 530
Mean GPA: N/R

Cost $
Tuition: $235/semester hour
Room & Board: N/R

Enrollment Profile
Full-time: N/R
Part-time: N/R
Total: 300
Average Age: N/R

Work Exp: N/R
International: 2%
Women: 44%
Minorities: 10%

Average Class Size: 25

ACADEMICS
Length of Program Minimum: 30 months.
Calendar Semesters.
Part-time Classes Main campus; evening, weekends, summer.
Degree Requirements 40 semester hours.
Curricular Focus Business issues and problems, general management, strategic analysis and planning.
Concentration Management.
Teaching Methodology Case study: 20%, faculty seminars: 5%, lecture: 30%, research: 5%, seminars by members of the business community: 5%, student presentations: 20%, team projects: 15%.

STUDENT STATISTICS
Geographic Representation State residents 98%. International 2%.

FACILITIES
Information Resources Main library with 180,000 bound volumes, 116,644 titles on microform, 893 periodical subscriptions, 13,600 records/tapes/CDs, 2 CD-ROMs.

ADMISSION
Entrance Requirements Bachelor's degree, GMAT score of 450, minimum 2.7 GPA, minimum 2 years of work experience.
Application Requirements Application form, copies of transcript, personal statement, 3 business references.
Application Deadline Applications are processed on a rolling basis.

FINANCIALS
Costs for 1994-95 Tuition: Part-time evening: $235/semester hour.
Financial Aid Application deadline: 2/15 for fall. Applications are processed on a rolling basis. Contact: Ms. June Schlabach, Director of Financial Aid, 2199 East Main Street, Columbus, OH 43209-2394. (614) 236-6511.

INTERNATIONAL STUDENTS
Demographics 2% of students enrolled in the program are international.
Applying TOEFL required, minimum score of 550. Financial aid is not available to international students. Admission applications are processed on a rolling basis.

ALTERNATE MBA PROGRAMS
MBA/JD Length of program: Minimum: 72 months. Full-time classes: Main campus; day, evening, summer. Part-time classes: Main campus; day, evening, summer. Degree requirements: 122 semester hours.
MBA/MSN Length of program: Minimum: 72 months. Part-time classes: Main campus; evening, weekends, summer. Degree requirements: 76 semester hours.

Program Contact: Dr. Ronald J. Volpe, Dean of Graduate School of Administration, Capital University, 2199 East Main Street, Columbus, OH 43209-2394. (614) 236-6670; Fax: (614) 236-6540.

Case Western Reserve University

Weatherhead School of Management

Cleveland, Ohio

OVERVIEW
Case Western Reserve University is an independent nonprofit coed institution. Founded 1826. Setting: 128-acre urban campus. Total institutional enrollment: 9,100. Program was first offered in 1930. AACSB-accredited.

MBA HIGHLIGHTS

Entrance Difficulty****
GMAT: 552 - 574
GPA: 3.1 - 3.2

Cost $$$
Tuition: $8,808/semester
Room & Board: $5,000

Enrollment Profile
Full-time: 252	Work Exp: 81% - 99%
Part-time: 641	International: 18%
Total: 893	Women: 40%
Average Age: 27	Minorities: 13%

Average Class Size: 40

ACADEMICS

Length of Program Minimum: 21 months. Maximum: 6 years.

Calendar Semesters.

Full-time Classes Main campus; day, evening, early morning, summer.

Part-time Classes Main campus; evening, summer.

Degree Requirements 60 credits including 18 elective credits. Other: Minimum 2.5 GPA.

Required Courses Economics for management, financial and managerial accountancy, human resource analysis and policies, introduction to management information systems, introductory financial management, management policy, managerial statistics, marketing management, operations management, organizational behavior and analysis, quantitative methods for management. Courses may be waived through: previous course work.

Curricular Focus Assessment and development of management abilities, entrepreneurship, organizational development and change management.

Concentrations Accounting, economics, entrepreneurship, finance, health services, human resources management, international business, management information systems, marketing, operations management, organizational behavior, quantitative analysis, strategic management, technology management, nonprofit management.

Faculty Full-time: 75, 97% with doctorates.

Teaching Methodology Case study: 30%, lecture: 20%, research: 10%, student presentations: 10%, team projects: 30%.

Special Opportunities International exchange in Australia, France, Israel, Mexico, Netherlands, Norway, United Kingdom. Internships include financial analysis in banking, strategic planning in industrial, financial analysis in healthcare, and marketing research in consumer goods.

STUDENT STATISTICS

Geographic Representation By region: Midwest 67%; Northeast 6%; West 6%; South 3%. International 18%.

Undergraduate Majors Business 39%; education 2%; engineering/technology 30%; humanities 6%; nursing 3%; science/mathematics 9%; social sciences 7%; other 4%.

Other Background Graduate degrees in other disciplines: 23%.

FACILITIES

Information Resources Main library with 1.9 million bound volumes, 2.1 million titles on microform, 13,819 periodical subscriptions, 31,720 records/tapes/CDs. Business collection in Sears Library includes 42,000 bound volumes, 564 periodical subscriptions, 7 CD-ROMs, 15 videos.

Housing 15% of students in program live in college-owned or -operated housing.

Technology Computers are used moderately in course work. 76 computer terminals/PCs, linked by a campus-wide computer network, are available for use by students in program; they are located in dormitories, classrooms, the library, computer labs, career planning center, group study rooms. Students in the program are not required to have their own PC. $345 are budgeted per student for computer support.

Computer Resources/On-line Services
Training	Yes	Dun's	Yes
Internet	Yes	Dow Jones	Yes
E-Mail	Yes	Dialog	No
LEXIS/NEXIS	No	Bloomberg	No
CompuServe	No		

ADMISSION

Acceptance 1994-95 853 applied for admission; 60% were accepted.

Entrance Requirements Bachelor's degree, BA/BS in business administration required for accelerated MBA program, GMAT score of 470, minimum 2.5 GPA, minimum 1 year of work experience. Core courses waived through: previous course work.

Application Requirements Written essay, interview, application form, resume/curriculum vitae, personal statement, 2 letters of recommendation.

Application Deadlines 4/15 for fall, 12/1 for spring, 4/1 for accelerated track. Application discs available.

FINANCIALS

Costs for 1994-95 Tuition: Full-time: $8,808/semester; Part-time day: $2,202/course. Average room and board costs are $5,000 per academic year (on-campus) and $7,000 per academic year (off-campus).

Financial Aid In 1994-95, 34% of candidates received some institutionally administered aid in the form of grants, scholarships, loans, fellowships, assistantships. Total awards ranged from $5,000-$18,000. Financial aid is available to part-time students. Application deadlines: 3/15 for fall, 12/1 for spring, 3/1 for summer. Contact: Ms. Tracey Cooper, Associate Director of MBA Admissions, Weatherhead School of Management, 310 Enterprise Hall, Cleveland, OH 44106. (216) 368-2031.

INTERNATIONAL STUDENTS

Demographics 18% of students enrolled in the program are international; Asia 70%, Europe 20%, Africa 8%, South America 2%.

Services and Facilities International student office, international student center, visa services, language tutoring, ESL courses, special assistance for nonnative speakers of English, counseling/support services, orientation.

Applying TOEFL required, minimum score of 570; proof of health; proof of adequate funds. Admission application deadlines: 2/15 for fall, 2/15 for accelerated track. Contact: Ms. Laurie Zelman, Director, International Student Services, Pardee Hall, Cleveland, OH 44106. (216) 368-2517.

ALTERNATE MBA PROGRAMS

Executive MBA (EMBA) Length of program: Minimum: 21 months. Maximum: 6 years. Degree requirements: 45 credits including 6 elective credits.

One-Year MBA Length of program: Minimum: 11 months. Maximum: 6 years. Degree requirements: 42 credits including 18 elective credits.

MBA/JD Length of program: Minimum: 48 months. Maximum: 6 years. Degree requirements: 129 credits including 18 elective credits.

MBA/MS Length of program: Minimum: 30 months. Maximum: 6 years. Degree requirements: 75 credits including 21 elective credits.

MBA/MSN Length of program: Minimum: 30 months. Maximum: 6 years. Degree requirements: 75 credits including 21 elective credits.

PLACEMENT

In 1993-94, 92 organizations participated in on-campus recruiting; 435 on-campus interviews were conducted. Placement services include alumni network, career counseling/planning, career fairs, career library, career placement, electronic job bank, job interviews, resume preparation, and resume referral to employers. Of 1994 graduates, 85% were employed within three months of graduation, the average starting salary was $46,900, the range was $25,000-$80,000.

Jobs by Employer Type Manufacturing 34%; service 39%; consulting 22%; nonprofit 2%; healthcare 3%.

Jobs by Functional Area Marketing/sales 13%; finance 36%; operations 4%; management 31%; strategic planning 3%; technical management 5%; other 8%.

Program Contact: Ms. Linda Gaston, Director of MBA Marketing and Admissions, Case Western Reserve University, 10900 Euclid Avenue, Cleveland, OH 44106. (216) 368-2031, or (800) 723-0203; Fax: (216) 368-5548.

See full description on page 688.

Cleveland State University

James J. Nance College of Business Administration

Cleveland, Ohio

OVERVIEW

Cleveland State University is a state-supported coed institution. Founded 1964. Setting: 70-acre urban campus. Total institutional enrollment: 17,300. Program was first offered in 1972. AACSB-accredited.

MBA HIGHLIGHTS

Entrance Difficulty***
Mean GMAT: 510
Mean GPA: 3.1

Cost $
Tuition: $1,457/quarter
(Nonresident: $2,914/quarter)
Room & Board: $9,000

Enrollment Profile

Full-time: 250	Work Exp: 90%
Part-time: 770	International: 15%
Total: 1,020	Women: 32%
Average Age: 27	Minorities: 6%

Average Class Size: 35

ACADEMICS

Length of Program Minimum: 18 months. Maximum: 6 years.

Calendar Quarters.

Full-time Classes Main campus; day, evening, early morning, summer.

Part-time Classes Main campus, NASA Lewis Research Center; evening, summer.

Degree Requirements 48 credits including 12 elective credits.

Required Courses Accounting, advanced marketing management, business decision methods, financial policies, strategic management, survey of industrial relations.

Curricular Focus International business, problem solving and decision making, strategic analysis and planning.

Concentrations Accounting, economics, finance, health services, human resources management, international business, management, management information systems, marketing, operations management, organizational behavior, quantitative analysis, real estate, strategic management.

Faculty Full-time: 70, 100% with doctorates; part-time: 5.

Teaching Methodology Case study: 35%, faculty seminars: 5%, lecture: 40%, student presentations: 10%, team projects: 10%.

Special Opportunities International exchange in France, United Kingdom. Internship program available. Other: cooperative education.

STUDENT STATISTICS

Geographic Representation State residents 82%. By region: Midwest 75%; Northeast 4%; South 4%; West 2%. International 15%.

Undergraduate Majors Business 50%; education 3%; engineering/technology 12%; humanities 3%; nursing 3%; science/mathematics 12%; social sciences 15%; other 2%.

Other Background Graduate degrees in other disciplines: 5%.

FACILITIES

Information Resources Main library with 879,000 bound volumes, 2,959 titles on microform, 6,548 periodical subscriptions, 11,355 records/tapes/CDs. Business collection includes 51,000 bound volumes, 7 CD-ROMs.

Housing 5% of students in program live in college-owned or -operated housing.

Technology Computers are used moderately in course work. 200 computer terminals/PCs, linked by a campus-wide computer network, are available for use by students in program; they are located in the student center, classrooms, the library, the computer center, computer labs. Students in the program are not required to have their own PC.

Computer Resources/On-line Services

Training	Yes	Multimedia Center	Yes
Internet	Yes	LEXIS/NEXIS	Yes
E-Mail	Yes	Dialog	Yes

ADMISSION

Acceptance 1994-95 Of those applying, 70% were accepted.

Entrance Requirements Bachelor's degree, GMAT score of 350, minimum 2.0 GPA. Core courses waived through: previous course work.

Application Requirements Application form, copies of transcript.

Application Deadlines 8/1 for fall, 11/15 for winter, 2/1 for spring.

FINANCIALS

Costs for 1995-96 Tuition: Full-time: $1,457/quarter for state residents, $2,914/quarter for nonresidents. Average room and board costs are $9,000 per academic year (on-campus) and $9,000 per academic year (off-campus).

Financial Aid In 1994-95, 6% of candidates received some institutionally administered aid in the form of scholarships, assistantships, tuition grants.

Total awards ranged from $8,500-$19,000. Financial aid is not available to part-time students. Application deadlines: 6/30 for fall, 10/31 for winter, 1/31 for spring. Contact: Mr. Kevin Galicki, Assistant Director, Financial Aid, 2400 Euclid Avenue, Cleveland, OH 44115. (216) 687-2058.

INTERNATIONAL STUDENTS

Demographics 15% of students enrolled in the program are international; Asia 85%, Europe 8%, Central America 2%, South America 2%, Africa 1%, other 2%.

Services and Facilities International student center, language tutoring, ESL courses, special assistance for nonnative speakers of English, counseling/support services.

Applying TOEFL required, minimum score of 525; proof of health; proof of adequate funds. Financial aid is available to international students. Financial aid application deadlines: 6/30 for fall, 10/31 for winter, 1/31 for spring. Applications are processed on a rolling basis. Admission application deadlines: 6/30 for fall, 10/31 for winter, 1/31 for spring. Contact: Mr. George Burke, Associate Dean, 2121 Euclid Avenue, UC 102, Cleveland, OH 44115. (216) 687-2048.

ALTERNATE MBA PROGRAMS

One-Year MBA Length of program: 12 months. Degree requirements: 48 credits including 16 elective credits. Research project; previous business courses. Average class size: 20.

MBA/JD Length of program: Minimum: 45 months. Degree requirements: 76 credits including 40 elective credits. Minimun of 36 semester hours in business, 62 semester hours in law.

MBA/MH Length of program: Minimum: 12 months. Maximum: 6 years. Degree requirements: 74 credits. Internship; research project.

PLACEMENT

In 1993-94, 75 organizations participated in on-campus recruiting; 30 on-campus interviews were conducted. Placement services include alumni network, career counseling/planning, career fairs, career library, career placement, electronic job bank, job interviews, resume preparation, and resume referral to employers. Of 1994 graduates, 90% were employed within three months of graduation, the average starting salary was $40,063, the range was $29,000-$50,000.

Program Contact: Dr. S. R. Rao, Associate Dean, Cleveland State University, East 24th and Euclid Avenue, Cleveland, OH 44115. (216) 687-3730; Fax: (216) 687-6888.

See full description on page 706.

Franciscan University of Steubenville

Department of Business Administration

Steubenville, Ohio

OVERVIEW

Franciscan University of Steubenville is an independent Roman Catholic comprehensive coed institution. Founded 1946. Setting: 100-acre suburban campus with easy access to Pittsburgh. Total institutional enrollment: 1,903. Program was first offered in 1979.

MBA HIGHLIGHTS

Entrance Difficulty**
Mean GMAT: 500
Mean GPA: N/R

Cost $
Tuition: $275/credit hour
Room & Board: $3,600 (off-campus)

Enrollment Profile

Full-time: 5	Work Exp: 92%
Part-time: 55	International: 2%
Total: 60	Women: 30%
Average Age: N/R	Minorities: 7%

Average Class Size: 16

ACADEMICS

Length of Program Minimum: 15 months.

Calendar Trimesters.

Full-time Classes Main campus; evening, weekends, summer.

Part-time Classes Main campus; evening, weekends, summer.

Degree Requirements 40 credit hours including 8 elective credit hours.

Curricular Focus General management, leadership, teamwork.

Concentrations Accounting, management.

Faculty Full-time: 5, 40% with doctorates; part-time: 4, 25% with doctorates.

Teaching Methodology Case study: 15%, lecture: 45%, research: 10%, student presentations: 15%, team projects: 15%.

STUDENT STATISTICS

Geographic Representation State residents 90%. By region: Northeast 95%; Midwest 3%. International 2%.

Other Background Work experience: On average, students have 4 years of work experience on entrance to the program.

FACILITIES

Information Resources Main library with 201,000 bound volumes, 8,000 titles on microform, 805 periodical subscriptions, 1,500 records/tapes/CDs.

Housing College housing not available.

Technology Computers are used moderately in course work. 150 computer terminals/PCs are available for use by students in program; they are located in learning resource center, the library, the computer center, computer labs. Students in the program are not required to have their own PC.

Computer Resources/On-line Services

Training	Yes	E-Mail	No

ADMISSION

Acceptance 1994-95 19 applied for admission; 95% were accepted.

Entrance Requirements Bachelor's degree, GMAT score of 460, minimum 2.5 GPA. Core courses waived through: previous course work.

Application Requirements Application form, copies of transcript, resume/curriculum vitae, 3 letters of recommendation.

Application Deadlines 7/1 for fall, 11/1 for spring. Applications are processed on a rolling basis.

FINANCIALS

Costs for 1994-95 Tuition: Part-time evening: $275/credit hour. Average room and board costs are $3,600 per academic year (off-campus).

Financial Aid In 1994-95, 61% of candidates received some institutionally administered aid in the form of loans, work-study. Total awards ranged from $500-$8,500. Financial aid is not available to part-time students. Applications are processed on a rolling basis. Contact: Mrs. Ann Johnston, Director of Financial Aid, University Boulevard, Steubenville, OH 43952. (614) 283-6210.

INTERNATIONAL STUDENTS

Demographics 2% of students enrolled in the program are international; North America 98%, Africa 2%.

Services and Facilities International student housing.

Applying TOEFL required, minimum score of 550; proof of health; proof of adequate funds. Financial aid is available to international students. Financial aid application deadlines: 5/1 for fall, 11/1 for spring. Admission application deadlines: 7/1 for fall, 11/1 for spring. Applications are processed on a rolling basis. Contact: Fr. Angeles Migliore, Director of International Students, University Boulevard, Steubenville, OH 43952. (614) 283-6441.

PLACEMENT

Placement services include career counseling/planning, career fairs, career placement, and resume referral to employers.

Program Contact: Mr. Mark McGuire, Assistant Director of Graduate Admissions, Franciscan University of Steubenville, University Boulevard, Steubenville, OH 43952. (800) 783-6220; Fax: (614) 283-6472.

Franklin University

Graduate School of Business

Columbus, Ohio

OVERVIEW

Franklin University is an independent nonprofit comprehensive coed institution. Founded 1902. Setting: 14-acre urban campus. Total institutional enrollment: 5,000. Program was first offered in 1993.

MBA HIGHLIGHTS

Entrance Difficulty***
Mean GMAT: N/R
Mean GPA: 3.1

Cost $
Tuition: $240/hour
Room & Board: N/R

Enrollment Profile

Full-time: 0	Work Exp: 100%
Part-time: 203	International: 7%
Total: 203	Women: 48%
Average Age: 36	Minorities: 13%

Average Class Size: 32

ACADEMICS

Length of Program Minimum: 24 months. Maximum: 2 years.

Calendar Trimesters.

Part-time Classes Main campus; evening, summer.

Degree Requirements 42 hours.

Curricular Focus Leadership, teamwork.

Concentration Management.

Faculty Full-time: 5, 100% with doctorates; part-time: 4, 50% with doctorates.

Teaching Methodology Case study: 20%, lecture: 20%, research: 10%, student presentations: 20%, team projects: 30%.

STUDENT STATISTICS

Geographic Representation State residents 93%. By region: Midwest 100%. International 7%.

Undergraduate Majors Business 80%; education 2%; engineering/technology 5%; humanities 5%; nursing 1%; science/mathematics 2%; social sciences 5%.

Other Background Graduate degrees in other disciplines: 5%. Work experience: On average, students have 11 years of work experience on entrance to the program.

FACILITIES

Information Resources Main library with 86,795 bound volumes, 146,574 titles on microform, 1,120 periodical subscriptions, 639 records/tapes/CDs, 6 CD-ROMs.

Housing College housing not available.

Technology Computers are used moderately in course work. 115 computer terminals/PCs, linked by a campus-wide computer network, are available for use by students in program; they are located in classrooms, learning resource center, the library, the computer center, computer labs, the research center. Students in the program are not required to have their own PC.

Computer Resources/On-line Services

E-Mail	Yes	Multimedia Center	Yes
Videoconference Center	Yes		

ADMISSION

Acceptance 1994-95 229 applied for admission; 27% were accepted.

Entrance Requirements Bachelor's degree, 5 undergraduate courses in micro and macroeconomics, financial accounting, and statistics, minimum 2.75 GPA, minimum 3 years of work experience. Core courses waived through: previous course work.

Application Requirements Written essay, application form, copies of transcript, personal statement, 2 letters of recommendation.

Application Deadlines 7/15 for fall, 11/15 for winter, 3/15 for spring. Applications are processed on a rolling basis.

FINANCIALS

Costs for 1994-95 Tuition: Part-time evening: $240/hour.

Financial Aid In 1994-95, 30% of candidates received some institutionally administered aid in the form of loans. Application deadlines: 5/30 for fall, 9/30 for winter. Contact: Ms. Kathy Fay, Director of Financial Aid, 201 South Grant Avenue, Columbus, OH 43215. (614) 341-6414.

INTERNATIONAL STUDENTS

Demographics 7% of students enrolled in the program are international.

Applying TOEFL required, minimum score of 550; proof of adequate funds; successfully complete Franklin University English Language Evaluation. Financial aid is available to international students. Financial aid application deadlines: 5/30 for fall, 9/30 for winter. Admission application deadlines: 7/15 for fall, 11/15 for winter, 3/15 for spring. Contact:

Mr. Patrick Schumer, Assistant Director of Student Services, International Student Office, 201 South Grant Avenue, Columbus, OH 43215. (614) 341-6309.

PLACEMENT
Placement services include career counseling/planning.

Program Contact: Mr. Richard Curtis, Director, MBA Program, Franklin University, 201 South Grant Avenue, Columbus, OH 43215-5399. (614) 341-6386; Fax: (614) 221-7723.

John Carroll University

School of Business

University Heights, Ohio

OVERVIEW
John Carroll University is an independent Roman Catholic (Jesuit) comprehensive coed institution. Founded 1886. Setting: 60-acre suburban campus with easy access to Cleveland. Total institutional enrollment: 4,358. Program was first offered in 1974. AACSB-accredited.

MBA HIGHLIGHTS

Entrance Difficulty***
Mean GMAT: 481
Mean GPA: 2.94

Cost $
Tuition: $475/credit hour
Room & Board: $5,550

Enrollment Profile

Full-time: 0	Work Exp: 100%
Part-time: 226	International: 0%
Total: 226	Women: 44%
Average Age: 30	Minorities: 5%

Average Class Size: 25

ACADEMICS
Length of Program Minimum: 24 months. Maximum: 5 years.

Calendar Semesters.

Part-time Classes Main campus; evening, weekends, summer.

Degree Requirements 36 credits including 6 elective credits.

Required Courses Comparative accounting systems, comparative business management, financial management, global marketing, international business finance, international economics, macroeconomics for managers, management skills, managerial accounting, managerial economics, marketing management, quantitative methods.

Curricular Focus Business issues and problems, general management, international business.

Concentrations Accounting, economics, entrepreneurship, finance, health services, human resources management, international business, management, management information systems, marketing, operations management, organizational behavior, strategic management, transportation.

Faculty Full-time: 27, 93% with doctorates; part-time: 5, 60% with doctorates.

STUDENT STATISTICS
Geographic Representation State residents 100%. By region: Northeast 100%.

Undergraduate Majors Business 56%; humanities 15%; science/mathematics 24%; other 5%.

Other Background Graduate degrees in other disciplines: 5%. Work experience: On average, students have 3 years of work experience on entrance to the program.

FACILITIES
Information Resources Main library with 549,618 bound volumes, 169,804 titles on microform, 1,691 periodical subscriptions, 7,966 records/tapes/CDs, 35 CD-ROMs. Business collection includes 28,000 bound volumes, 295 periodical subscriptions, 18 CD-ROMs, 200 videos.

Housing College housing available.

Technology Computers are used moderately in course work. 48 computer terminals/PCs, linked by a campus-wide computer network, are available for use by students in program; they are located in the library, the computer center. Students in the program are not required to have their own PC.

Computer Resources/On-line Services

Training	Yes	LEXIS/NEXIS	Yes
Internet	Yes	Dun's	Yes
E-Mail	No	Dialog	Yes

Other on-line services: RLIN, OCLC, SEC.

ADMISSION
Acceptance 1994-95 67 applied for admission; 70% were accepted.

Entrance Requirements Bachelor's degree, prerequisite courses required for applicants with non-business degree, GMAT score, minimum 2 years of work experience. Core courses waived through: previous course work.

Application Requirements Application form, copies of transcript, 1 letter of recommendation.

Application Deadline Applications are processed on a rolling basis.

FINANCIALS
Costs for 1994-95 Tuition: Part-time evening: $475/credit hour. Average room and board costs are $5,550 per academic year (on-campus).

Financial Aid In 1994-95, candidates received some institutionally administered aid in the form of loans, assistantships. Financial aid is available to part-time students. Applications are processed on a rolling basis. Contact: Financial Aid Counselor, Office of Financial Aid, University Heights, OH 44118. (216) 397-4248.

INTERNATIONAL STUDENTS
Applying TOEFL required, minimum score of 550; proof of health; proof of adequate funds. Financial aid is not available to international students.

PLACEMENT
Placement services include alumni network, career counseling/planning, career fairs, career library, career placement, job interviews, and resume preparation. Of 1994 graduates, 100% were employed within three months of graduation, the average starting salary was $49,053, the range was $20,000-$125,000.

Jobs by Employer Type Manufacturing 19%; service 79%; consulting 2%.

Program Contact: Dr. James Daley, Associate Dean and Director, MBA Program, John Carroll University, 20700 North Park Boulevard, University Heights, OH 44118. (216) 397-4391; Fax: (216) 397-1728.

Kent State University

Graduate School of Management

Kent, Ohio

OVERVIEW
Kent State University is a state-supported coed institution. Part of Kent State University System. Founded 1910. Setting: 1,200-acre small-town campus with easy access to Cleveland. Total institutional enrollment: 21,413. Program was first offered in 1950. AACSB-accredited.

MBA HIGHLIGHTS

Entrance Difficulty***
Mean GMAT: 530
Mean GPA: 3.15

Cost $
Tuition: $2,091/semester
(Nonresident: $4,055/semester)
Room & Board: $5,200

Enrollment Profile

Full-time: 125	Work Exp: 60%
Part-time: 319	International: 24%
Total: 444	Women: 34%
Average Age: 26	Minorities: 6%

Average Class Size: 40

ACADEMICS
Length of Program Minimum: 12 months. Maximum: 6 years.

Calendar Semesters.

Full-time Classes Main campus; day, evening, summer.

Part-time Classes Main campus; evening, summer.

Degree Requirements 39 credits including 18 elective credits.

Required Courses Accounting for managerial action and evaluation, business conditions analysis and public policy, business strategy, financial accounting for managerial action, financial management, fundamentals of accounting for managers, management information systems, management of people, managerial economics, marketing management, operations management, statistics for management, strategic global management or modern entrepreneurial management. Courses may be waived through: previous course work.

Curricular Focus Business issues and problems, international business, problem solving and decision making.

Concentrations Change management, nonprofit management, finance, human resources management, international business, management information systems, marketing.

Faculty Full-time: 65, 95% with doctorates.

Teaching Methodology Case study: 10%, faculty seminars: 5%, lecture: 50%, research: 10%, seminars by members of the business community: 5%, student presentations: 5%, team projects: 15%.

Special Opportunities International exchange in France. Internships include government.

STUDENT STATISTICS

Geographic Representation By region: Midwest 66%; South 5%; Northeast 3%; West 2%. International 24%.

Undergraduate Majors Business 66%; education 2%; engineering/technology 5%; humanities 4%; nursing 2%; science/mathematics 5%; social sciences 9%; other 7%.

Other Background Graduate degrees in other disciplines: 5%. Work experience: On average, students have 2 years of work experience on entrance to the program.

FACILITIES

Information Resources Main library with 2.1 million bound volumes, 1.4 million titles on microform, 10,700 periodical subscriptions, 27,901 records/tapes/CDs, 60 CD-ROMs. Business collection includes 18,000 bound volumes, 625 periodical subscriptions, 6 CD-ROMs, 500 videos.

Housing 35% of students in program live in college-owned or -operated housing.

Technology Computers are used heavily in course work. 100 computer terminals/PCs, linked by a campus-wide computer network, are available for use by students in program; they are located in the student center, the library, the computer center, computer labs. Students in the program are not required to have their own PC.

Computer Resources/On-line Services

Training	Yes	Dun's	No
Internet	Yes	Dow Jones	No
E-Mail	Yes	Dialog	No
LEXIS/NEXIS	Yes $	Bloomberg	No
CompuServe	No		

ADMISSION

Acceptance 1994-95 375 applied for admission; 60% were accepted.

Entrance Requirements Bachelor's degree, GMAT score, minimum 2.75 GPA. Core courses waived through: previous course work.

Application Requirements Written essay, application form, copies of transcript, resume/curriculum vitae, personal statement, 3 letters of recommendation.

Application Deadline 4/1 for fall.

FINANCIALS

Costs for 1994-95 Tuition: Full-time: $2,091/semester for state residents, $4,055/semester for nonresidents; Part-time evening: $190/hour for state residents, $369/hour for nonresidents. Average room and board costs are $5,200 per academic year (on-campus) and $4,500 per academic year (off-campus).

Financial Aid In 1994-95, 35% of candidates received some institutionally administered aid in the form of assistantships. Total awards ranged from $3,000-$6,000. Financial aid is not available to part-time students. Application deadline: 4/1 for fall. Contact: Ms. Louise M. Ditchey, Associate Director, Graduate School of Management, Kent, OH 44242-0001. (216) 672-2282 Ext. 235.

INTERNATIONAL STUDENTS

Demographics 24% of students enrolled in the program are international.

Applying TOEFL required, minimum score of 550; proof of adequate funds. Financial aid is available to international students. Financial aid application deadline: 4/1 for fall. Admission application deadline: 4/1 for fall. Contact: Dr. Giovanna Jackson, Director, International Student Affairs, Room 226 KSC, Kent, OH 44242-0001. (216) 672-2718.

ALTERNATE MBA PROGRAMS

Executive MBA (EMBA) Length of program: Minimum: 26 months. Degree requirements: 45 credits including 4 elective credits. Professional work experience. Class size: 25-30.

MBA/MA Length of program: Minimum: 24 months. Maximum: 6 years. Degree requirements: 40 credits including 15 elective credits. One year or one semester abroad.

MBA/MLS Length of program: Minimum: 36 months. Maximum: 6 years. Degree requirements: 70 credits. GRE or GMAT.

MBA/MSN Length of program: Minimum: 36 months. Maximum: 6 years. Degree requirements: 70 credits. GRE or GMAT.

PLACEMENT

Placement services include alumni network, career counseling/planning, career fairs, career library, career placement, electronic job bank, job interviews, resume preparation, and resume referral to employers.

Program Contact: Ms. Louise M. Ditchey, Associate Director, Kent State University, PO Box 5190, Kent, OH 44242-0001. (216) 672-2282 Ext. 235; Fax: (216) 672-2448.

Lake Erie College

Department of Business Administration

Painesville, Ohio

OVERVIEW

Lake Erie College is an independent nonprofit comprehensive coed institution. Founded 1856. Setting: 57-acre suburban campus with easy access to Cleveland. Total institutional enrollment: 732. Program was first offered in 1981.

MBA HIGHLIGHTS

Entrance Difficulty**

Cost $
Tuition: $352/semester hour
Room & Board: N/R

Enrollment Profile

Full-time: 0	Work Exp: 100%
Part-time: 116	International: 1%
Total: 116	Women: 54%
Average Age: 35	Minorities: 11%

Average Class Size: 17

ACADEMICS

Length of Program Minimum: 24 months. Maximum: 5 years.

Calendar Trimesters.

Part-time Classes Main campus, Wickliffe; evening, summer.

Degree Requirements 36 semester hours including 12 elective semester hours.

Required Courses Financial management, information systems for managerial decision making, managerial accounting, managerial economics, marketing strategies, organizational behavior, policy development, systems management. Courses may be waived through: previous course work, work experience.

Curricular Focus General management, problem solving and decision making, teamwork.

Concentrations Healthcare administration, management.

Faculty Full-time: 9, 78% with doctorates; part-time: 1, 100% with doctorates.

Teaching Methodology Case study: 20%, lecture: 20%, research: 20%, student presentations: 20%, team projects: 20%.

Special Opportunities Internship program available.

STUDENT STATISTICS

Geographic Representation State residents 99%. By region: Midwest 99%. International 1%.

Undergraduate Majors Business 65%; engineering/technology 15%; humanities 5%; nursing 15%.

Other Background Graduate degrees in other disciplines: 5%. Work experience: On average, students have 13 years of work experience on entrance to the program.

FACILITIES

Information Resources Main library with 85,381 bound volumes, 236 titles on microform, 767 periodical subscriptions, 1,470 records/tapes/CDs.

Housing College housing not available.

Technology 18 computer terminals/PCs are available for use by students in program; they are located in the library. Students in the program are not required to have their own PC.

Computer Resources/On-line Services

Training	No	E-Mail	No

ADMISSION

Acceptance 1994-95 Of those applying, 95% were accepted.

Entrance Requirements Bachelor's degree, GMAT score. Core courses waived through: previous course work, work experience.

Application Requirements Written essay, interview, application form, copies of transcript, resume/curriculum vitae.

Application Deadline Applications are processed on a rolling basis.

FINANCIALS

Costs for 1994-95 Tuition: Full-time: $352/semester hour. Fees: Full-time: $10/semester hour.

Financial Aid In 1994-95, 4% of candidates received some institutionally administered aid in the form of loans. Total awards ranged from $1,000-$7,500. Financial aid is available to part-time students. Application deadlines: 3/1 for fall, 3/1 for spring. Contact: Ms. Michiale M. Schneider, Director of Financial Aid, 391 West Washington Street, Painesville, OH 44077. (216) 639-7814.

INTERNATIONAL STUDENTS

Demographics 1% of students enrolled in the program are international.

Applying TOEFL required, minimum score of 590; proof of health; proof of adequate funds; proof of health insurance. Financial aid is not available to international students. Admission application deadlines: 6/1 for fall, 11/1 for spring.

PLACEMENT

Placement services include career counseling/planning, career library, career placement, resume preparation, and resume referral to employers. Of 1994 graduates, 100% were employed within three months of graduation.

Program Contact: Ms. Christine Gill, Graduate Studies Admissions Counselor, Lake Erie College, 391 West Washington Street, Painesville, OH 44077. (216) 639-7879, or (800) 533-4996; Fax: (216) 352-3533.

Miami University

Richard T. Farmer School of Business Administration

Oxford, Ohio

OVERVIEW

Miami University is a state-related coed institution. Part of Miami University System. Founded 1809. Setting: 1,900-acre small-town campus with easy access to Cincinnati. Total institutional enrollment: 15,882. Program was first offered in 1947. AACSB-accredited.

MBA HIGHLIGHTS

Entrance Difficulty***
Mean GMAT: 580
Mean GPA: 3.21

Cost $
Tuition: $2,412/semester
(Nonresident: $4,970/semester)
Room & Board: $8,668

Enrollment Profile

Full-time: 67	Work Exp: 50%
Part-time: 38	International: 46%
Total: 105	Women: 36%
Average Age: 26	Minorities: 4%

Average Class Size: 18

ACADEMICS

Length of Program Minimum: 22 months. Maximum: 5 years.

Calendar Semesters.

Full-time Classes Main campus; day, summer.

Part-time Classes Main campus, Middletown; evening, summer.

Degree Requirements 76 credits including 12 elective credits. Other: Summer field study, focus paper.

Required Courses Accounting and managerial decision making, analysis of business finance investments, field study, human resources management, integrative concepts marketing strategy and managerial skills, macro international economics, management information systems, managerial finance, marketing strategy and interpersonal relationships, marketing strategy and managerial skills, microeconomic analysis for managerial decision making, organizational behavior and theory, production operations management foundations, quantitative models for business decision making, research methodology in business, statistical methods for managerial decision making, strategic theme in business, strategic themes in business 2, studies in operations planning and management.

Curricular Focus Integration, problem solving and decision making, teamwork.

Concentrations Finance, management, management information systems, marketing, quantitative analysis.

Faculty Full-time: 120, 94% with doctorates.

Teaching Methodology Case study: 50%, lecture: 30%, student presentations: 10%, team projects: 10%.

Special Opportunities Summer field study.

STUDENT STATISTICS

Geographic Representation State residents 50%. By region: Midwest 68%; Northeast 4%; South 4%; West 4%. International 46%.

Undergraduate Majors Business 28%; engineering/technology 31%; humanities 11%; science/mathematics 14%; social sciences 8%; other 8%.

Other Background Graduate degrees in other disciplines: 6%. Work experience: On average, students have 2 years of work experience on entrance to the program.

FACILITIES

Information Resources Main library with 1.5 million bound volumes, 924,000 titles on microform, 11,850 periodical subscriptions, 185,000 records/tapes/CDs, 90 CD-ROMs. Business collection includes 61,986 bound volumes, 1,044 periodical subscriptions, 25 CD-ROMs, 65 videos.

Housing 10% of students in program live in college-owned or -operated housing.

Technology Computers are used heavily in course work. 60 computer terminals/PCs, linked by a campus-wide computer network, are available for use by students in program; they are located in classrooms, learning resource center, computer labs. Students in the program are not required to have their own PC.

Computer Resources/On-line Services

Training	Yes	Multimedia Center	Yes
Internet	Yes	LEXIS/NEXIS	Yes
E-Mail	Yes		

ADMISSION

Acceptance 1994-95 114 applied for admission; 66% were accepted.

Entrance Requirements Bachelor's degree, GMAT score of 475, minimum 2.75 GPA, minimum 1- 2 years of work experience.

Application Requirements Written essay, interview, application form, copies of transcript, resume/curriculum vitae.

Application Deadline 7/15 for fall.

FINANCIALS

Costs for 1994-95 Tuition: Full-time: $2,412/semester for state residents, $4,970/semester for nonresidents; Part-time day: $165/credit for state residents, $378/credit for nonresidents; Summer: $1,206/term for state residents. Fees: Part-time day: $36-$43/credit for state residents, $36-$43/credit for nonresidents. Average room and board costs are $8,668 per academic year (on-campus) and $9,200 per academic year (off-campus).

Financial Aid In 1994-95, 7% of candidates received some institutionally administered aid in the form of assistantships. Total awards ranged from $2,840-$4,100. Financial aid is not available to part-time students. Application deadline: 3/1 for fall. Contact: Dr. Herbert Waltzer, Acting Dean and Associate Provost, 102 Roudebush Hall, Oxford, OH 45056. (513) 529-4125.

INTERNATIONAL STUDENTS
Demographics 46% of students enrolled in the program are international.

Services and Facilities International student center, language tutoring, special assistance for nonnative speakers of English.

Applying TOEFL required, minimum score of 550; IELTS required; proof of health; proof of adequate funds. Financial aid is available to international students. Financial aid application deadline: 3/1 for fall. Admission application deadline: 7/15 for fall. Contact: Mr. Donald Nelson, Director of International Education Services, Oxford, OH 45056. (513) 529-2512.

PLACEMENT
In 1993-94, 105 organizations participated in on-campus recruiting; 280 on-campus interviews were conducted. Placement services include career counseling/planning, career fairs, career library, career placement, electronic job bank, job interviews, resume preparation, and resume referral to employers. Of 1994 graduates, 76% were employed within three months of graduation, the average starting salary was $34,000, the range was $25,000-$45,000.

Jobs by Employer Type Manufacturing 17%; service 53%; government 6%; consulting 24%.

Jobs by Functional Area Marketing/sales 23%; finance 25%; operations 22%; management 14%; strategic planning 16%.

Program Contact: Ms. Judy Barille, Director of Graduate Programs, Miami University, Oxford, OH 45056. (513) 529-6643; Fax: (513) 529-6992.

Ohio State University

Max M. Fisher College of Business

Columbus, Ohio

OVERVIEW
Ohio State University is a state-supported coed institution. Founded 1870. Setting: 3,303-acre suburban campus. Total institutional enrollment: 50,000. Program was first offered in 1916. AACSB-accredited.

MBA HIGHLIGHTS

Entrance Difficulty***
Mean GMAT: 608
Mean GPA: 3.2

Cost $
Tuition: $1,614/quarter
(Nonresident: $4,000/quarter)
Room & Board: $9,074 (off-campus)

Enrollment Profile

Full-time: 230	Work Exp: 80%
Part-time: 145	International: 22%
Total: 375	Women: 27%
Average Age: 26	Minorities: 12%

Average Class Size: 52

ACADEMICS
Length of Program Minimum: 21 months. Maximum: 2 years.
Calendar Quarters.
Full-time Classes Main campus; day.
Part-time Classes Main campus; evening, summer.
Degree Requirements 104 credits including 36 elective credits.
Required Courses Accounting for decision making, financial accounting and reporting, financial decision making, financial management, information systems for management decision making, legal and regulatory environment, management and individual behavior, managerial economics, marketing management, modeling for decision making, national business conditions analysis, operations management, statistical analysis for decision making, strategy implementation, teamwork and leadership laboratory.

Curricular Focus Business issues and problems, leadership, teamwork.
Concentrations Accounting, class functional and quality management, finance, health services, human resources management, international business, management information systems, marketing, operations management, organizational behavior, real estate.
Faculty Full-time: 44, 100% with doctorates; part-time: 1.
Teaching Methodology Case study: 30%, lecture: 40%, student presentations: 10%, team projects: 20%.
Special Opportunities International exchange in France, Mexico, Switzerland, Russia. Internship program available.

STUDENT STATISTICS
Geographic Representation State residents 70%. By region: Midwest 52%; Northeast 14%; South 4%; West 4%. International 22%.
Undergraduate Majors Business 37%; engineering/technology 25%; humanities 8%; social sciences 27%; other 3%.
Other Background Work experience: On average, students have 4-8 years of work experience on entrance to the program.

FACILITIES
Information Resources Main library with 4.7 million bound volumes, 3.7 million titles on microform, 33,010 periodical subscriptions, 34,337 records/tapes/CDs, 354 CD-ROMs. Business collection includes 186,947 bound volumes, 2,028 periodical subscriptions, 20 CD-ROMs.
Housing College housing not available.
Technology Computers are used moderately in course work. 900 computer terminals/PCs, linked by a campus-wide computer network, are available for use by students in program; they are located in dormitories, classrooms, the library, the computer center, computer labs. Students in the program are not required to have their own PC. $360 are budgeted per student for computer support.

Computer Resources/On-line Services

Training	Yes	CompuServe	Yes
Internet	Yes	Dun's	No
E-Mail	Yes	Dow Jones	Yes $
Multimedia Center	Yes	Dialog	Yes
LEXIS/NEXIS	Yes	Bloomberg	Yes

ADMISSION
Acceptance 1994-95 Of those applying, 44% were accepted.
Entrance Requirements Bachelor's degree, GMAT score. Core courses waived through: exams.
Application Requirements Written essay, application form, copies of transcript, resume/curriculum vitae, 3 letters of recommendation.
Application Deadline 6/1 for fall.

FINANCIALS
Costs for 1994-95 Tuition: Full-time: $1,614/quarter for state residents, $4,000/quarter for nonresidents; Part-time evening: $1,316/quarter for state residents, $3,225-$4,000/quarter for nonresidents. Average room and board costs are $9,074 per academic year (off-campus).
Financial Aid In 1994-95, 15% of candidates received some institutionally administered aid in the form of fellowships, assistantships. Financial aid is not available to part-time students. Application deadline: 2/1 for fall. Contact: Ms. Michelle Jacobson, Manager of Admissions, Fisher College of Business, Hagerty Hall, 1775 College Road, Columbus, OH 43210. (614) 292-8511.

INTERNATIONAL STUDENTS
Demographics 22% of students enrolled in the program are international; Asia 72%, Europe 21%, Africa 3%, South America 3%.
Services and Facilities International student center, visa services, language tutoring, ESL courses.
Applying TOEFL required, minimum score of 600; proof of adequate funds. Financial aid is not available to international students. Admission application deadline: 6/1 for fall. Contact: Mr. John Greisberger, Director, International Education, Oxley Hall, 1712 Neil Avenue, Columbus, OH 43210. (614) 292-6101.

PLACEMENT
In 1993-94, 104 organizations participated in on-campus recruiting; 592 on-campus interviews were conducted. Placement services include alumni network, career counseling/planning, career fairs, career library, career placement, job interviews, resume preparation, and resume referral to employers. Of 1994 graduates, 90% were employed within three months of graduation, the average starting salary was $44,200, the range was $30,000-$90,000.
Jobs by Employer Type Manufacturing 10%; service 50%; government 10%; consulting 25%; nonprofit 5%.

Jobs by Functional Area Marketing/sales 30%; finance 30%; operations 15%, management 15%; strategic planning 5%; technical management 5%.

Program Contact: Ms. Susie Cinadr, Recruitment Coordinator, Ohio State University, Hagerty Hall, 1775 College Road, Columbus, OH 43210. (614) 292-8530; Fax: (614) 292-1651.

Ohio University

College of Business Administration

Athens, Ohio

OVERVIEW
Ohio University is a state-supported coed institution. Part of Ohio University System. Founded 1804. Setting: 1,300-acre small-town campus. Total institutional enrollment: 18,600. Program was first offered in 1955. AACSB-accredited.

MBA HIGHLIGHTS

Entrance Difficulty**
Mean GMAT: 506
Mean GPA: 3.3

Cost $
Tuition: $1,430/quarter
(Nonresident: $2,789/quarter)
Room & Board: $6,000 (off-campus)

Enrollment Profile
Full-time: 30	Work Exp: 100%
Part-time: 37	International: 36%
Total: 67	Women: 50%
Average Age: 24	Minorities: 23%

Average Class Size: N/R

ACADEMICS
Length of Program Minimum: 13 months.
Calendar Quarters.
Full-time Classes Main campus.
Part-time Classes Main campus, Lancaster; evening, weekends, summer.
Degree Requirements 72 hours including 12 elective hours. Other: Study abroad; 12 hours of independent study.
Required Course Team course work with faculty adviser. Courses may be waived through: previous course work, work experience.
Curricular Focus General management, managing diversity, teamwork.
Concentrations Business law, economics, finance, human resources management, international business, management, management information systems, marketing, operations management.
Faculty Full-time: 50, 80% with doctorates.
Teaching Methodology Team projects: 100%.
Special Opportunities International exchange in Hungary, India, Malaysia, Thailand.

STUDENT STATISTICS
Geographic Representation State residents 50%. By region: Midwest 60%; Northeast 4%. International 36%.
Undergraduate Majors Business 5%; engineering/technology 12%; other 83%.
Other Background Graduate degrees in other disciplines: 16%. Work experience: On average, students have 1-3 years of work experience on entrance to the program.

FACILITIES
Information Resources Main library with 1.7 million bound volumes, 2.2 million titles on microform, 11,414 periodical subscriptions, 311,218 records/tapes/CDs, 82 CD-ROMs.
Housing College housing available.
Technology Computers are used heavily in course work. 100 computer terminals/PCs, linked by a campus-wide computer network, are available for use by students in program; they are located in student rooms, classrooms, the library, the computer center, computer labs. Students in the program are not required to have their own PC.

Computer Resources/On-line Services
Training	Yes	Videoconference Center	Yes
Internet	Yes	LEXIS/NEXIS	Yes
E-Mail	Yes		

ADMISSION
Acceptance 1994-95 94 applied for admission; 20% were accepted.
Entrance Requirements Bachelor's degree, GMAT score of 500, minimum 3.0 GPA. Core courses waived through: previous course work, work experience.
Application Requirements Written essay, interview, application form, copies of transcript, 3 letters of recommendation.
Application Deadline 4/1 for fall.

FINANCIALS
Costs for 1994-95 Tuition: Full-time: $1,430/quarter for state residents, $2,789/quarter for nonresidents; Part-time day: $178/hour for state residents, $347/hour for nonresidents. Average room and board costs are $6,000 per academic year (off-campus).
Financial Aid In 1994-95, 50% of candidates received some institutionally administered aid in the form of scholarships, assistantships. Total awards ranged from $5,720-$11,156. Financial aid is not available to part-time students. Application deadline: 4/1 for fall. Contact: Ms. Carolyn Sabatino, Director of Financial Aid, 20 Chubb Hall, Athens, OH 45701. (614) 593-9118.

INTERNATIONAL STUDENTS
Demographics 36% of students enrolled in the program are international; Asia 50%, Europe 43%, Africa 7%.
Applying TOEFL required, minimum score of 600; proof of health; proof of adequate funds. Financial aid is available to international students. Financial aid application deadline: 4/1 for fall. Admission application deadline: 4/1 for fall.

ALTERNATE MBA PROGRAM
Executive MBA (EMBA) Length of program: Minimum: 21 months. Maximum: 2 years. Degree requirements: 66 hours. 7-10 years business experience.

PLACEMENT
Placement services include alumni network, career counseling/planning, career fairs, career library, career placement, job interviews, resume preparation, and resume referral to employers. Of 1994 graduates, 80% were employed within three months of graduation, the average starting salary was $27,000, the range was $24,000-$39,000.
Jobs by Employer Type Manufacturing 47%; service 47%; government 6%.
Jobs by Functional Area Marketing/sales 10%; finance 22%; operations 24%; management 29%; strategic planning 3%; technical management 12%.

Program Contact: Ms. Mykol Kirksey Lewis, Graduate Student Affairs Officer, Ohio University, Athens, OH 45701. (614) 593-2007; Fax: (614) 593-0319; Internet Address: lewism@ouvaxa.cats.ohiou.edu.
See full description on page 796.

Tiffin University

Tiffin, Ohio

OVERVIEW
Tiffin University is an independent nonprofit comprehensive coed institution. Founded 1888. Setting: 25-acre small-town campus with easy access to Toledo. Total institutional enrollment: 1,220. Program was first offered in 1990.

MBA HIGHLIGHTS

Entrance Difficulty**
Mean GMAT: N/R
Mean GPA: 3.3

Cost $$
Tuition: $1,000/course
Room & Board: N/R

Enrollment Profile
Full-time: 54
Part-time: 19
Total: 73
Average Age: 38

Work Exp: 98%
International: 10%
Women: 34%
Minorities: 20%

Average Class Size: 20

ACADEMICS
Length of Program Minimum: 24 months. Maximum: 6 years.
Calendar Semesters.
Full-time Classes Main campus; evening, weekends, summer.
Part-time Classes Main campus; evening, weekends, summer.
Degree Requirements 36 credits.
Required Courses Accounting for planning and control, financial management, global and transnational management, individual and organization, information systems for managers, legal and ethical issues in management, managerial economics, marketing management, operations management, organizational analysis and design, quantitative methods, strategic management.
Curricular Focus General management, leadership, strategic analysis and planning.
Concentration Management.
Faculty Full-time: 12, 80% with doctorates; part-time: 1.
Teaching Methodology Case study: 25%, lecture: 15%, student presentations: 15%, team projects: 45%.
Special Opportunities Internships include banking and health.

STUDENT STATISTICS
Geographic Representation State residents 95%. By region: Midwest 90%. International 10%.
Undergraduate Majors Business 35%; education 5%; engineering/technology 10%; humanities 3%; nursing 25%; science/mathematics 10%; social sciences 10%; other 2%.
Other Background Graduate degrees in other disciplines: 5%. Work experience: On average, students have 13 years of work experience on entrance to the program.

FACILITIES
Information Resources Main library with 17,191 bound volumes, 27,900 titles on microform, 105 periodical subscriptions, 817 records/tapes/CDs, 26 CD-ROMs. Business collection includes 7,000 bound volumes, 75 periodical subscriptions, 8 CD-ROMs, 100 videos.
Housing 5% of students in program live in college-owned or -operated housing.
Technology Computers are used heavily in course work. 35 computer terminals/PCs, linked by a campus-wide computer network, are available for use by students in program; they are located in computer labs. Students in the program are required to have their own PC.
Computer Resources/On-line Services

Training	Yes	E-Mail	Yes
Internet	Yes $	CompuServe	Yes $

Other on-line services: OCLC.

ADMISSION
Acceptance 1994-95 80 applied for admission; 22% were accepted.
Entrance Requirements Bachelor's degree, minimum 2 years of work experience. Core courses waived through: previous course work.
Application Requirements Written essay, interview, application form, copies of transcript, personal statement.
Application Deadlines 8/15 for fall, 12/7 for spring.

FINANCIALS
Estimated Costs for 1995-96 Tuition: Full-time: $1,000/course.
Financial Aid In 1994-95, 10% of candidates received some institutionally administered aid in the form of loans. Financial aid is available to part-time students. Application deadlines: 9/1 for fall, 12/1 for spring. Contact: Financial Aid Office, Seitz Hall, 155 Miami Street, Tiffin, OH 44883-2161. (419) 447-6442.

INTERNATIONAL STUDENTS
Demographics 10% of students enrolled in the program are international; Asia 3%, Other 97%.
Services and Facilities Counseling/support services.

Applying TOEFL required, minimum score of 550; proof of adequate funds. Admission application deadlines: 8/1 for fall, 10/1 for spring.

PLACEMENT
Placement services include alumni network, career counseling/planning, career fairs, career placement, resume preparation, and resume referral to employers. Of 1994 graduates, 100% were employed within three months of graduation.
Jobs by Employer Type Manufacturing 70%; service 25%; government 3%; consulting 2%.
Jobs by Functional Area Marketing/sales 10%; finance 10%; operations 10%; management 65%; technical management 5%.

Program Contact: Mr. Allen Lowery, Assistant Director, Graduate Studies, Tiffin University, 155 Miami Street, Tiffin, OH 44883-2161. (419) 447-6442, or (800) 968-6446; Fax: (419) 447-9605.

University of Akron

College of Business Administration

Akron, Ohio

OVERVIEW
The University of Akron is a state-supported coed institution. Founded 1870. Setting: 170-acre urban campus with easy access to Cleveland. Total institutional enrollment: 27,671. Program was first offered in 1958. AACSB-accredited.

MBA HIGHLIGHTS
Entrance Difficulty*
Mean GMAT: 525
Mean GPA: 3.03

Cost $
Tuition: $145/credit
(Nonresident: $271/credit)
Room & Board: $2,970 (off-campus)

Enrollment Profile
Full-time: 119
Part-time: 497
Total: 616
Average Age: 31

Work Exp: 80%
International: 6%
Women: 36%
Minorities: 4%

Average Class Size: 25

ACADEMICS
Length of Program Minimum: 16 months. Maximum: 6 years.
Calendar Semesters.
Full-time Classes Main campus; evening, summer.
Part-time Classes Main campus; evening, summer.
Degree Requirements 34 credits including 12 elective credits.
Required Courses Accounting management and control, applied business documentation and contact, business strategy and policy, financial management and policy, international business, operations management, professional responsibility, quantitative tools, special topics in professional development, strategic marketing management. Courses may be waived through: previous course work, examination.
Curricular Focus Business issues and problems, problem solving and decision making, teamwork.
Concentrations Accounting, finance, international business, management, marketing.
Faculty Full-time: 75, 80% with doctorates.
Teaching Methodology Case study: 20%, faculty seminars: 5%, lecture: 20%, research: 20%, seminars by members of the business community: 5%, student presentations: 10%, team projects: 20%.
Special Opportunities International exchange in Belgium. Internship program available.

STUDENT STATISTICS
Geographic Representation State residents 89%. By region: Midwest 75%; Northeast 10%; South 5%; West 5%. International 6%.
Undergraduate Majors Business 55%; education 3%; engineering/technology 17%; humanities 4%; nursing 5%; science/mathematics 10%; social sciences 4%; other 2%.

Other Background Graduate degrees in other disciplines: 10%. Work experience: On average, students have 5 years of work experience on entrance to the program.

FACILITIES
Information Resources Main library with 1.1 million bound volumes, 1.6 million titles on microform, 8,734 periodical subscriptions, 28,845 records/tapes/CDs.

Housing College housing not available.

Technology Computers are used moderately in course work. 251 computer terminals/PCs, linked by a campus-wide computer network, are available for use by students in program; they are located in the library, the computer center, computer labs. Students in the program are not required to have their own PC.

Computer Resources/On-line Services

Training	Yes	Dun's	No
Internet	Yes	Dow Jones	No
E-Mail	Yes	Dialog	Yes
LEXIS/NEXIS	Yes $	Bloomberg	No
CompuServe	No		

ADMISSION
Acceptance 1994-95 481 applied for admission; 75% were accepted.

Entrance Requirements Bachelor's degree, prerequisite courses required for applicants with nonbusiness degree, GMAT score of 450. Core courses waived through: previous course work, exams.

Application Requirements Application form, copies of transcript.

Application Deadlines 8/1 for fall, 12/15 for spring, 5/15 for summer.

FINANCIALS
Costs for 1994-95 Tuition: Full-time: $145/credit for state residents, $271/credit for nonresidents. Fees: Full-time: $5/credit for state residents, $5/credit for nonresidents. Average room and board costs are $2,970 per academic year (off-campus).

Financial Aid In 1994-95, 15% of candidates received some institutionally administered aid in the form of scholarships, loans, assistantships. Total awards ranged from $2,610-$7,760. Financial aid is available to part-time students. Application deadlines: 4/1 for fall, 10/1 for spring. Contact: Ms. Myra Weakland, Assistant Director, Graduate Business Program, CBA 412, Akron, OH 44325-4805. (216) 972-7043.

INTERNATIONAL STUDENTS
Demographics 6% of students enrolled in the program are international; Asia 50%, Europe 16%, South America 16%, Africa 10%, other 8%.

Services and Facilities Language tutoring.

Applying TOEFL required, minimum score of 550; proof of adequate funds; insurance. Financial aid is available to international students. Assistantships are available for these students. Admission application deadlines: 5/15 for fall, 12/15 for spring. Contact: Mr. John Jones, Credential Evaluator, International Programs, Polsky 489D, Akron, OH 44325-3106. (216) 972-6349.

ALTERNATE MBA PROGRAM
MBA/JD Length of program: Minimum: 48 months. Maximum: 8 years. Degree requirements: 105 credits including 12 elective credits. 10 MBA credits transfer to school of law, 6 law credits transfer to MBA.

PLACEMENT
Placement services include career counseling/planning, career fairs, career library, career placement, electronic job bank, job interviews, resume preparation, and resume referral to employers.

Jobs by Employer Type Manufacturing 63%; service 11%; government 3%; consulting 3%; other 20%.

Jobs by Functional Area Marketing/sales 6%; finance 12%; operations 11%; management 11%; other 60%.

Program Contact: Dr. J. Daniel Williams, Assistant Dean and Director, University of Akron, 302 Buchtel Common, Akron, OH 44325-0001. (216) 972-7043; Fax: (216) 972-6588.

University of Cincinnati

College of Business Administration

Cincinnati, Ohio

OVERVIEW
The University of Cincinnati is a state-supported coed institution. Part of University of Cincinnati System. Founded 1819. Setting: 137-acre urban campus. Total institutional enrollment: 35,000. Program was first offered in 1958. AACSB-accredited.

MBA HIGHLIGHTS

Entrance Difficulty***
Mean GMAT: 596
Mean GPA: 3.23

Cost $$
Tuition: $7,500
(Nonresident: $15,400)
Room & Board: $8,700

Enrollment Profile

Full-time: 95	Work Exp: 90%
Part-time: 330	International: 10%
Total: 425	Women: 35%
Average Age: 26	Minorities: 6%

Average Class Size: 35

ACADEMICS
Length of Program Minimum: 12 months. Maximum: 7 years.

Calendar 12 month format; starts in summer.

Part-time Classes Main campus; evening, weekends.

Degree Requirements 66 quarter hours including 18 elective quarter hours.

Required Courses Applied statistics, financial accounting, financial analysis, information systems for managers, macroeconomics, management, marketing management, microeconomics. Courses may be waived through: previous course work.

Curricular Focus Business issues and problems, integrated course work, teamwork.

Concentrations Arts administration, construction management, advanced technology and innovation management, finance, international business, management, management information systems, marketing, operations management, quantitative analysis, real estate.

Faculty Full-time: 25, 100% with doctorates.

Teaching Methodology Case study: 35%, lecture: 35%, student presentations: 10%, team projects: 20%.

Special Opportunities Internship program available.

STUDENT STATISTICS
Geographic Representation State residents 70%. By region: Midwest 75%; Northeast 5%; South 5%; West 5%. International 10%.

Undergraduate Majors Business 40%; education 5%; engineering/technology 20%; humanities 5%; nursing 2%; science/mathematics 10%; social sciences 10%; other 8%.

Other Background Graduate degrees in other disciplines: 10%. Work experience: On average, students have 4 years of work experience on entrance to the program.

FACILITIES
Information Resources Main library with 1.9 million bound volumes, 2.5 million titles on microform, 19,650 periodical subscriptions, 34,517 records/tapes/CDs.

Housing 5% of students in program live in college-owned or -operated housing.

Technology Computers are used moderately in course work. 200 computer terminals/PCs are available for use by students in program; they are located in the library, the computer center, computer labs. Students in the program are not required to have their own PC.

Computer Resources/On-line Services

Training	Yes	E-Mail	Yes

ADMISSION

Acceptance 1994-95 Of those applying, 38% were accepted.

Entrance Requirements Bachelor's degree, GMAT score of 550, minimum 3.0 GPA, minimum 2 years of work experience. Core courses waived through: previous course work.

Application Requirements Written essay, application form, copies of transcript, resume/curriculum vitae, personal statement, 2 letters of recommendation.

Application Deadline 2/15 for summer.

FINANCIALS

Costs for 1994-95 Tuition: Full-time: $7,500 for state residents, $15,400 for nonresidents. Fees: Full-time: $850 for state residents, $850 for nonresidents. Average room and board costs are $8,700 per academic year (on-campus).

Financial Aid In 1994-95, 25% of candidates received some institutionally administered aid in the form of scholarships, loans. Total awards ranged from $1,000-$15,000. Financial aid is not available to part-time students. Application deadline: 2/15 for summer. Contact: Ms. Penny Chapman, Academic Adviser, Cincinnati, OH 45221. (513) 556-7020.

INTERNATIONAL STUDENTS

Demographics 10% of students enrolled in the program are international.

Services and Facilities International student center, visa services, counseling/support services.

Applying TOEFL required, minimum score of 600; proof of health; proof of adequate funds. Financial aid is available to international students. Financial aid application deadline: 1/1 for summer. Admission application deadline: 1/1 for summer. Applications are processed on a rolling basis. Contact: Mr. Ron Cushing, Director, 221 Braustein, Cincinnati, OH 45221. (513) 556-2879.

ALTERNATE MBA PROGRAMS

MBA/JD Length of program: Minimum: 42 months. Degree requirements: 80 semester hours in law, 54 quarter hours in business.

MBA/MA Length of program: Minimum: 24 months. Degree requirements: 80 quarter hours. MA is in arts administration.

PLACEMENT

In 1993-94, 130 organizations participated in on-campus recruiting. Placement services include alumni network, career counseling/planning, career library, career placement, job interviews, resume preparation, and resume referral to employers. Of 1994 graduates, 75% were employed within three months of graduation, the average starting salary was $38,500, the range was $24,000-$48,500.

Jobs by Functional Area Marketing/sales 35%; finance 25%; operations 5%; management 10%; technical management 5%; consulting 20%.

Program Contact: Graduate Programs Office, University of Cincinnati, Cincinnati, OH 45221. (513) 556-7020; Fax: (513) 556-4891.

University of Dayton

School of Business Administration

Dayton, Ohio

OVERVIEW

The University of Dayton is an independent Roman Catholic coed institution. Founded 1850. Setting: 110-acre urban campus with easy access to Cincinnati. Total institutional enrollment: 10,600. Program was first offered in 1963. AACSB-accredited.

MBA HIGHLIGHTS

Entrance Difficulty***
Mean GMAT: 503
Mean GPA: 3.02

Cost $

Tuition: $329/semester hour
Room & Board: $6,500

Enrollment Profile

Full-time: 40		Work Exp: 95%
Part-time: 581		International: 7%
Total: 621		Women: 35%
Average Age: 29		Minorities: 5%

Average Class Size: 30

ACADEMICS

Length of Program Minimum: 12 months. Maximum: 5 years.

Calendar Trimesters.

Full-time Classes Main campus; day, evening, weekends, summer.

Part-time Classes Main campus, Ohio Dominican College; evening, weekends, summer.

Degree Requirements 33 credits including 9 elective credits. Other: 3 required electives.

Required Courses Applications of management science, business policies and administrative management, information systems in organizations, managerial accounting, managerial economics, managerial finance, marketing management, organizational behavior.

Curricular Focus Leadership, problem solving and decision making, teamwork.

Concentrations Management, management information systems, manufacturing management.

Faculty Full-time: 50, 95% with doctorates; part-time: 5, 60% with doctorates.

Teaching Methodology Case study: 15%, lecture: 50%, research: 10%, student presentations: 10%, team projects: 15%.

Special Opportunities International exchange in Germany.

STUDENT STATISTICS

Geographic Representation State residents 95%. By region: Midwest 85%; Northeast 5%; South 1%. International 7%.

Undergraduate Majors Business 50%; education 5%; engineering/technology 20%; humanities 10%; science/mathematics 5%; social sciences 8%; other 1%.

Other Background Graduate degrees in other disciplines: 5%. Work experience: On average, students have 6 years of work experience on entrance to the program.

FACILITIES

Information Resources Main library with 1.3 million bound volumes, 408,078 titles on microform, 3,095 periodical subscriptions, 1,000 records/tapes/CDs.

Housing College housing available.

Technology Computers are used moderately in course work. 70 computer terminals/PCs, linked by a campus-wide computer network, are available for use by students in program; they are located in dormitories, classrooms, the library, the computer center, computer labs, the research center. Students in the program are not required to have their own PC.

Computer Resources/On-line Services

Training	Yes	CompuServe	No
Internet	Yes	Dun's	No
E-Mail	Yes	Dow Jones	No
Videoconference Center	Yes	Dialog	No
Multimedia Center	Yes	Bloomberg	No
LEXIS/NEXIS	Yes		

ADMISSION

Acceptance 1994-95 188 applied for admission; 80% were accepted.

Entrance Requirements Bachelor's degree, GMAT score of 400. Core courses waived through: previous course work.

Application Requirements Application form, copies of transcript, personal statement.

Application Deadlines 8/15 for fall, 12/15 for spring, 4/20 for summer. Applications are processed on a rolling basis.

FINANCIALS

Costs for 1994-95 Tuition: Full-time: $329/semester hour. Fees: Full-time: $25/semester. Average room and board costs are $6,500 per academic year (on-campus).

Financial Aid In 1994-95, candidates received some institutionally administered aid in the form of grants, scholarships, loans, fellowships, assistantships. Financial aid is available to part-time students. Application deadline: 4/15 for fall. Applications are processed on a rolling basis.

Contact: Ms. Joyce Wilkins, Director of Office of Financial Aid, 300 College Park Avenue, Dayton, OH 45469-1621. (513) 229-4311.

INTERNATIONAL STUDENTS

Demographics 7% of students enrolled in the program are international; Asia 70%, Europe 25%, South America 3%, Central America 1%.

Services and Facilities International student housing; international student office, international student center, visa services, language tutoring, ESL courses, counseling/support services.

Applying TOEFL required, minimum score of 550; proof of adequate funds; I-20 form. Financial aid is not available to international students. Admission application deadlines: 7/1 for fall, 11/1 for spring, 1/31 for summer. Applications are processed on a rolling basis. Contact: Ms. Alison Glick, Interim Director and International Student Adviser, 300 College Park Avenue, Dayton, OH 45469-1481. (513) 229-2748.

PLACEMENT

Placement services include alumni network, career counseling/planning, career fairs, career library, career placement, job interviews, job search course, resume preparation, and resume referral to employers. Of 1994 graduates, 98% were employed within three months of graduation, the average starting salary was $46,000, the range was $25,000-$75,000.

Jobs by Employer Type Manufacturing 35%; service 55%; government 5%; consulting 5%.

Program Contact: Dr. E. James Dunne, Associate Dean and Director, MBA Program, University of Dayton, 300 College Park Avenue, Dayton, OH 45469-2226. (513) 229-3733; Fax: (513) 229-3301; Internet Address: dunne@quark.sba.udayton.edu.

University of Toledo

College of Business Administration

Toledo, Ohio

OVERVIEW

The University of Toledo is a state-supported coed institution. Founded 1872. Setting: 305-acre suburban campus with easy access to Detroit. Total institutional enrollment: 23,107. Program was first offered in 1933. AACSB-accredited.

MBA HIGHLIGHTS

Entrance Difficulty*
Mean GMAT: 525
Mean GPA: 3.1

Cost $
Tuition: $1,362/quarter
(Nonresident: $1,362/quarter)
Room & Board: $5,560 (off-campus)

Enrollment Profile

Full-time: 74	Work Exp: 75%
Part-time: 290	International: 25%
Total: 364	Women: 37%
Average Age: N/R	Minorities: 12%

Average Class Size: 25

ACADEMICS

Length of Program Minimum: 12 months. Maximum: 6 years.
Calendar Quarters.
Full-time Classes Main campus; day, evening, summer.
Part-time Classes Main campus; day, evening, summer.
Degree Requirements 48 credits. Other: Background in computers and mathematics.
Required Courses Administration accounting, corporate strategy, individual and the organization, management information systems, managerial economics, managerial finance, managerial marketing, managing operations, organization theory and design.
Curricular Focus Business issues and problems, general management, international business.
Concentrations Finance, management, management information systems, marketing.
Faculty Full-time: 34, 100% with doctorates; part-time: 2, 50% with doctorates.

Teaching Methodology Case study: 25%, faculty seminars: 15%, lecture: 30%, research: 10%, student presentations: 10%, team projects: 10%.
Special Opportunities Internships include accounting, health care, marketing, and management information systems.

STUDENT STATISTICS

Geographic Representation State residents 75%. International 25%.
Undergraduate Majors Business 55%; education 1%; engineering/technology 20%; humanities 4%; nursing 1%; science/mathematics 3%; social sciences 15%; other 1%.
Other Background Work experience: On average, students have 3 years of work experience on entrance to the program.

FACILITIES

Information Resources Main library with 1.5 million bound volumes, 1.5 million titles on microform, 6,356 periodical subscriptions, 8,587 records/tapes/CDs, 12 CD-ROMs.
Housing College housing not available.
Technology Computers are used moderately in course work. 487 computer terminals/PCs, linked by a campus-wide computer network, are available for use by students in program; they are located in the student center, the library, the computer center. Students in the program are not required to have their own PC.

Computer Resources/On-line Services

Training	Yes	Dun's	Yes
Internet	Yes	Dow Jones	Yes
E-Mail	Yes	Dialog	Yes $
Multimedia Center	Yes	Bloomberg	No
LEXIS/NEXIS	Yes $		

ADMISSION

Acceptance 1994-95 434 applied for admission; 46% were accepted.
Entrance Requirements Bachelor's degree, GMAT score of 450, minimum 2.7 GPA. Core courses waived through: previous course work.
Application Requirements Written essay, application form, copies of transcript, personal statement, 3 letters of recommendation.
Application Deadlines 8/15 for fall, 11/15 for winter, 2/15 for spring, 4/15 for summer. Applications are processed on a rolling basis.

FINANCIALS

Costs for 1994-95 Tuition: Full-time: $1,362/quarter for state residents, $1,362/quarter for nonresidents. Fees: Full-time: $235/quarter for state residents, $1,818/quarter for nonresidents. Average room and board costs are $5,560 per academic year (off-campus).
Financial Aid In 1994-95, 17% of candidates received some institutionally administered aid in the form of scholarships, assistantships. Total awards ranged from $908-$8,954. Financial aid is available to part-time students. Application deadline: 4/15 for fall. Applications are processed on a rolling basis. Contact: Dr. David A. Reid, Director of MBA Programs, 2801 West Bancroft, Toledo, OH 43606-3398. (419) 537-2774.

INTERNATIONAL STUDENTS

Demographics 25% of students enrolled in the program are international.
Applying TOEFL required, minimum score of 550; proof of health; proof of adequate funds. Financial aid is available to international students. Financial aid application deadline: 4/15 for fall. Applications are processed on a rolling basis. Admission application deadlines: 8/1 for fall, 2/1 for spring, 4/1 for summer. Applications are processed on a rolling basis. Contact: Dr. Debbie Pierce, Associate Dean of International Services, 2801 West Bancroft, Toledo, OH 43606-3398. (419) 537-3807.

ALTERNATE MBA PROGRAMS

Executive MBA (EMBA) Length of program: Minimum: 15 months.
MBA/JD Length of program: Minimum: 42 months.

PLACEMENT

Placement services include career counseling/planning, career fairs, career library, career placement, electronic job bank, job interviews, job search course, resume preparation, and resume referral to employers.

Program Contact: Dr. David A. Reid, Director, MBA Program, University of Toledo, Graduate Studies in Business, Toledo, OH 43606-3398. (419) 537-2774; Fax: (419) 537-7744; Internet Address: fac2786@uoft01. utoledo.edu.
See full description on page 922.

Walsh University

Graduate Studies

North Canton, Ohio

OVERVIEW
Walsh University is an independent Roman Catholic comprehensive coed institution. Founded 1958. Setting: 58-acre suburban campus with easy access to Cleveland. Total institutional enrollment: 1,550. Program was first offered in 1991.

PROGRAM HIGHLIGHTS

Entrance Difficulty***
Mean GMAT: N/R
Mean GPA: 3.1

Cost $$
Tuition: $289/semester hour
Room & Board: $5,000 (off-campus)

Enrollment Profile
Full-time: 5
Part-time: 65
Total: 70
Average Age: 34

Work Exp: 90%
International: N/R
Women: 50%
Minorities: N/R

Average Class Size: 15

ACADEMICS
Calendar Semesters.

Curricular Focus General management, organizational development and change management, problem solving and decision making.

Concentration Management.

Faculty Full-time: 8, 100% with doctorates; part-time: 1, 100% with doctorates.

Teaching Methodology Case study: 40%, lecture: 40%, student presentations: 10%, team projects: 10%.

STUDENT STATISTICS
Geographic Representation By region: Midwest 100%.

Undergraduate Majors Business 50%; education 20%; engineering/technology 10%; science/mathematics 10%; social sciences 10%.

Other Background Graduate degrees in other disciplines: 25%. Work experience: On average, students have 10 years of work experience on entrance to the program.

FACILITIES
Information Resources Main library with 120,000 bound volumes, 7,866 titles on microform, 780 periodical subscriptions, 700 records/tapes/CDs, 18 CD-ROMs.

Housing College housing not available.

Technology 40 computer terminals/PCs are available for use by students in program; they are located in computer labs. Students in the program are not required to have their own PC.

Computer Resources/On-line Services
E-Mail   No

ADMISSION
Entrance Requirements Bachelor's degree, GMAT score, minimum 2.6 GPA, minimum 1 year of work experience. Core courses waived through: previous course work, work experience.

Application Requirements Interview, application form, copies of transcript, 3 letters of recommendation.

Application Deadline Applications are processed on a rolling basis.

FINANCIALS
Costs for 1994-95 Tuition: Full-time: $289/semester hour. Average room and board costs are $5,000 per academic year (off-campus).

Financial Aid Financial aid is available to part-time students. Application deadlines: 9/1 for fall, 1/1 for spring. Applications are processed on a rolling basis. Contact: Office of Graduate Studies, 2020 Easton Street, NW, North Canton, OH 44720-3396. (216) 490-7211.

INTERNATIONAL STUDENTS
Applying Financial aid is available to international students. Applications are processed on a rolling basis. Admission applications are processed on a rolling basis.

PROGRAM
MA Length of program: Minimum: 20 months. Maximum: 5 years. Full-time classes: Main campus; evening, summer. Part-time classes: Main campus; evening, summer. Degree requirements: 42 semester hours including 3 elective semester hours.

Program Contact: Dr. Paul DuMont, Director of Graduate Management, Walsh University, 2020 Easton Street, NW, North Canton, OH 44720-3396. (216) 499-7090 Ext. 7218.

Wright State University

College of Business and Administration

Dayton, Ohio

OVERVIEW
Wright State University is a state-supported coed institution. Founded 1964. Setting: 557-acre suburban campus with easy access to Cincinnati and Columbus. Total institutional enrollment: 16,823. Program was first offered in 1964. AACSB-accredited.

MBA HIGHLIGHTS

Entrance Difficulty***
Mean GMAT: 532
Mean GPA: 3.1

Cost $
Tuition: $1,363/quarter hour
(Nonresident: $2,441/quarter hour)
Room & Board: N/R

Enrollment Profile
Full-time: 115
Part-time: 358
Total: 473
Average Age: 30

Work Exp: 84%
International: 7%
Women: 33%
Minorities: 8%

Average Class Size: 22

ACADEMICS
Length of Program Minimum: 12 months.

Calendar Quarters.

Full-time Classes Main campus; day, evening, summer.

Part-time Classes Main campus; day, evening, summer.

Degree Requirements 48 quarter hours including 18 elective quarter hours.

Required Courses Applied macroeconomics, applied microeconomics, financial management, managerial accounting, marketing strategy, operations management, organized behavior and theory, quantitative methods for decision making, statistical methods for business decisions, strategic management and organizational policy.

Curricular Focus Problem solving and decision making, strategic analysis and planning, teamwork.

Concentrations Entrepreneurship, health services, international business, logistics management, project management, financial administration, management, management information systems, marketing, operations management.

Teaching Methodology Case study: 15%, lecture: 60%, student presentations: 10%, team projects: 15%.

Special Opportunities International exchange in Brazil, Chile, Japan, People's Republic of China. Internship program available.

STUDENT STATISTICS
Geographic Representation State residents 90%. International 7%.

Undergraduate Majors Business 48%; engineering/technology 23%; humanities 11%; science/mathematics 16%; other 2%.

Other Background Graduate degrees in other disciplines: 6%. Work experience: On average, students have 5 years of work experience on entrance to the program.

FACILITIES
Information Resources Main library with 460,000 bound volumes, 940,000 titles on microform, 4,151 periodical subscriptions.

Housing College housing available.

Technology Computers are used moderately in course work. Computer terminals/PCs are available for use by students in program; they are located in computer labs. Students in the program are not required to have their own PC.

ADMISSION
Acceptance 1994-95 270 applied for admission; 57% were accepted.
Entrance Requirements Bachelor's degree, GMAT score. Core courses waived through: previous course work.
Application Requirements Application form, copies of transcript, personal statement.
Application Deadline Applications are processed on a rolling basis.

FINANCIALS
Costs for 1994-95 Tuition: Full-time: $1,363/quarter hour for state residents, $2,441/quarter hour for nonresidents, $2,493/quarter hour for international students.
Financial Aid In 1994-95, candidates received some institutionally administered aid in the form of scholarships, loans, fellowships, assistantships, work-study. Total awards ranged from $1,500-$3,500. Financial aid is available to part-time students. Application deadlines: 1/8 for fall, 4/1 for spring. Applications are processed on a rolling basis. Contact: Mr. David Darr, Director of Financial Aid, Colonel Glen Highway, Dayton, OH 45435. (513) 873-5721.

INTERNATIONAL STUDENTS
Demographics 7% of students enrolled in the program are international.
Services and Facilities International student housing; international student office, international student center, visa services, language tutoring, ESL courses, special assistance for nonnative speakers of English, counseling/support services, host family program.
Applying TOEFL required, minimum score of 550; proof of adequate funds. Financial aid is available to international students. Applications are processed on a rolling basis. Admission application deadlines: 5/1 for fall, 2/1 for winter, 11/1 for spring. Applications are processed on a rolling basis. Contact: Mr. Steve Lyons, Director, International Student Programs, Colonel Glen Highway, Dayton, OH 45435. (513) 873-5145.

PLACEMENT
In 1993-94, 23 on-campus interviews were conducted. Placement services include career counseling/planning, career fairs, career library, career placement, cooperative programs, electronic job bank, job interviews, job search course, resume preparation, and resume referral to employers. Of 1994 graduates, 93% were employed within three months of graduation.
Jobs by Employer Type Manufacturing 30%; service 20%; government 40%; consulting 10%.
Jobs by Functional Area Marketing/sales 12%; finance 16%; operations 20%; management 48%; education 4%.

Program Contact: Mr. James Crawford, Director of Graduate Programs in Business and Logistics Management, Wright State University, 110 Rike Hall, College of Business and Administration, Dayton, OH 45435. (513) 873-2437; Fax: (513) 873-3545; Internet Address: jcrawford@ desire.wright.edu.
See full description on page 942.

Xavier University

College of Business Administration

Cincinnati, Ohio

OVERVIEW
Xavier University is an independent Roman Catholic comprehensive coed institution. Founded 1831. Setting: 100-acre urban campus. Total institutional enrollment: 6,154. Program was first offered in 1952.

MBA HIGHLIGHTS

Entrance Difficulty*
GMAT: 450 - 500
Mean GPA: N/R

Cost $$
Tuition: $325/credit hour
Room & Board: N/R

Enrollment Profile

Full-time: 40	Work Exp: 75%
Part-time: 948	International: 7%
Total: 988	Women: 35%
Average Age: 28	Minorities: 3%

Average Class Size: 35

ACADEMICS
Length of Program Minimum: 24 months. Maximum: 6 years.
Calendar Semesters.
Full-time Classes Main campus; evening, weekends, summer.
Part-time Classes Main campus; evening, weekends, summer.
Degree Requirements 33 credits including 12 elective credits.
Required Courses Accounting, business communications, cases and techniques in management science, economics, finance marketing, introduction to management science, legal environment, managerial computer applications, organizational behavior, statistics. Courses may be waived through: previous course work, work experience.
Curricular Focus International business, problem solving and decision making, quality management.
Concentrations Economics, finance, human resources management, international business, management, management information systems, marketing, quality improvement, taxation.
Faculty Full-time: 90, 95% with doctorates; part-time: 10, 10% with doctorates.
Teaching Methodology Case study: 20%, lecture: 60%, student presentations: 10%, team projects: 10%.

STUDENT STATISTICS
Geographic Representation International 7%.
Other Background Graduate degrees in other disciplines: 3%. Work experience: On average, students have 4 years of work experience on entrance to the program.

FACILITIES
Information Resources Main library with 350,000 bound volumes, 459,327 titles on microform, 1,557 periodical subscriptions, 5,000 records/tapes/CDs.
Technology Computers are used moderately in course work. 63 computer terminals/PCs, linked by a campus-wide computer network, are available for use by students in program; they are located in the library. Students in the program are not required to have their own PC.
Computer Resources/On-line Services

Training	Yes	LEXIS/NEXIS	Yes
Internet	Yes	CompuServe	Yes
E-Mail	Yes		

Other on-line services: First Search.

ADMISSION
Acceptance 1994-95 423 applied for admission; 85% were accepted.
Entrance Requirements Bachelor's degree, GMAT score.
Application Requirements Written essay, application form, copies of transcript, resume/curriculum vitae, personal statement.
Application Deadline Applications are processed on a rolling basis.

FINANCIALS
Costs for 1994-95 Tuition: Full-time: $325/credit hour.
Financial Aid In 1994-95, 5% of candidates received some institutionally administered aid in the form of grants, scholarships, assistantships. Total awards ranged from $500-$3,000. Financial aid is available to part-time students. Application deadline: 2/15 for fall. Contact: Mr. Paul Calme, Director of Financial Aid, Walker Hall, 3800 Victory Parkway, Cincinnati, OH 45207-5411. (513) 745-3142.

INTERNATIONAL STUDENTS
Demographics 7% of students enrolled in the program are international.
Services and Facilities International student center, ESL courses.
Applying TOEFL required, minimum score of 550. Financial aid is not available to international students. Admission applications are processed on a rolling basis. Contact: Ms. Katherine Hammett, Director, International Student Services, 3800 Victory Parkway, Cincinnati, OH 45207-2511. (513) 745-3712.

ALTERNATE MBA PROGRAM
Executive MBA (EMBA) Length of program: Minimum: 19 months. Degree requirements: 48 credits. Average class size: 40.

PLACEMENT
Placement services include alumni network, career counseling/planning, career fairs, career placement, job interviews, resume preparation, and resume referral to employers. Of 1994 graduates, 81% were employed within three months of graduation, the average starting salary was $33,444, the range was $19,000-$60,000.

Program Contact: Mr. Dallas Lower, Director of Admissions, Xavier University, 3800 Victory Parkway, Cincinnati, OH 45207-5311. (513) 745-3000, or (800) 344-4698; Fax: (513) 745-1954.

Youngstown State University

Williamson College of Business Administration

Youngstown, Ohio

OVERVIEW
Youngstown State University is a state-supported comprehensive coed institution. Founded 1908. Setting: 120-acre urban campus with easy access to Cleveland and Pittsburgh. Total institutional enrollment: 13,979. Program was first offered in 1971.

MBA HIGHLIGHTS

Entrance Difficulty**
Mean GMAT: 475
Mean GPA: 3.03

Cost $
Tuition: $72/credit
(Nonresident: $1,536 - $1,992/quarter)
Room & Board: N/R

Enrollment Profile
Full-time: 26	Work Exp: 85%
Part-time: 145	International: 15%
Total: 171	Women: 35%
Average Age: 28	Minorities: 3%

Average Class Size: 18

The M.B.A. program at Youngstown State University was implemented in 1971 to address the growing need and demand for a local graduate business program. Currently, the Williamson College of Business Administration offers graduate studies leading to the Master of Business Administration (M.B.A.) with an optional concentration in management, marketing, accounting, or finance. An Executive M.B.A. program is also available for the working professional.

The weekday M.B.A. program offers an affordable option for individuals who have no work experience as well as for those who have been in the work force for several years. M.B.A. classes, taught by experienced, full-time graduate faculty members, are held in the evening to accommodate the high percentage of fully employed students. The average student-teacher ratio is 18:1, allowing for interactive discussions and individualized attention. Part-time students generally complete the program in two to three years, while full-time students may complete the program in one year.

The two-year Executive M.B.A. program provides employed professionals with the skills and knowledge to function more effectively as administrators. Classes are conveniently held on Saturdays. This intensive, innovative program includes a four-day orientation residency and a two-week international trip.

ACADEMICS
Length of Program Minimum: 12 months. Maximum: 6 years.
Calendar Quarters.
Full-time Classes Main campus; evening, summer.
Part-time Classes Main campus; evening, summer.
Degree Requirements 54 quarter hours including 14 elective quarter hours.
Required Courses Accounting, business and society, business policy, economics, finance, marketing, operations management, organizational behavior, quantitative analysis, research methods.

Curricular Focus General management, problem solving and decision making, strategic analysis and planning.
Concentrations Accounting, finance, management, marketing.
Faculty Full-time: 27, 96% with doctorates.
Teaching Methodology Case study: 20%, lecture: 50%, student presentations: 10%, team projects: 20%.
Special Opportunities Internships include manufacturing and accounting.

STUDENT STATISTICS
Geographic Representation State residents 75%. By region: Northeast 81%; South 2%; Midwest 2%. International 15%.
Undergraduate Majors Business 56%; education 2%; engineering/technology 12%; humanities 4%; nursing 9%; science/mathematics 8%; social sciences 7%; other 2%.
Other Background Graduate degrees in other disciplines: 3%. Work experience: On average, students have 6 years of work experience on entrance to the program.

FACILITIES
Information Resources Main library with 831,586 bound volumes, 561,867 titles on microform, 3,185 periodical subscriptions, 9,100 records/tapes/CDs, 28 CD-ROMs.
Housing 10% of students in program live in college-owned or -operated housing.
Technology Computers are used moderately in course work. 371 computer terminals/PCs, linked by a campus-wide computer network, are available for use by students in program; they are located in student rooms, the student center, classrooms, the library, the computer center, computer labs. Students in the program are not required to have their own PC.

Computer Resources/On-line Services
Training	Yes	Dun's	No
Internet	Yes	Dow Jones	Yes $
E-Mail	Yes	Dialog	Yes
LEXIS/NEXIS	Yes $	Bloomberg	No
CompuServe	No		

Other on-line services: OCLC.

ADMISSION
Acceptance 1994-95 Of those applying, 83% were accepted.
Entrance Requirements Bachelor's degree, prerequisite courses required for applicants with non-business degree, GMAT score of 450, minimum 2.7 GPA. Core courses waived through: previous course work.
Application Requirements Application form, copies of transcript, personal statement.
Application Deadlines 8/15 for fall, 11/15 for winter, 2/15 for spring.

FINANCIALS
Costs for 1994-95 Tuition: Full-time: $72/credit for state residents, $1,536-$1,992/quarter for nonresidents. Fees: Full-time: $202/quarter for state residents, $202/quarter for nonresidents.
Financial Aid In 1994-95, 20% of candidates received some institutionally administered aid in the form of grants, scholarships, assistantships, work-study. Financial aid is available to part-time students. Application deadlines: 6/25 for fall, 1/10 for spring. Contact: Ms. Norma Jean Carney, Administrative Assistant, School of Graduate Studies, 410 Wick Avenue, Youngstown, OH 44555-0002. (216) 742-3092.

INTERNATIONAL STUDENTS
Demographics 15% of students enrolled in the program are international; Asia 83%, Europe 11%, South America 6%.
Services and Facilities International student center, language tutoring, ESL courses.
Applying TOEFL required, minimum score of 525; proof of health; proof of adequate funds. Financial aid is available to international students. Admission application deadlines: 6/30 for fall, 12/30 for spring. Contact: Ms. Susan Khawaja, Coordinator, International Student Services, Kilcawley Student Center, Youngstown, OH 44555-0002. (216) 742-3006.

ALTERNATE MBA PROGRAM
Executive MBA (EMBA) Length of program: Minimum: 24 months. Maximum: 2 years. Degree requirements: 61 quarter hours. 5 years management experience. Average class size: 20.

PLACEMENT
In 1993-94, 12 organizations participated in on-campus recruiting; 20 on-campus interviews were conducted. Placement services include alumni network, career counseling/planning, career library, career placement, electronic job bank, job interviews, resume preparation, and resume refer-

ral to employers. Of 1994 graduates, 90% were employed within three months of graduation, the average starting salary was $28,000, the range was $25,000-$40,000.

Jobs by Employer Type Manufacturing 60%; service 20%; government 3%; consulting 5%; nonprofit 5%; other 7%.

Jobs by Functional Area Marketing/sales 15%; finance 15%; operations 15%; management 45%; technical management 10%.

Program Contact: Ms. Linda Mohn, MBA/EMBA Program Coordinator, Youngstown State University, 410 Wick Avenue, Youngstown, OH 44555-0002. (216) 742-3069, or (800) 336-9978; Fax: (216) 742-1459.

OKLAHOMA

Cameron University

School of Business

Lawton, Oklahoma

OVERVIEW
Cameron University is a state-supported comprehensive coed institution. Founded 1908. Setting: 160-acre suburban campus. Total institutional enrollment: 6,125. Program was first offered in 1988.

MBA HIGHLIGHTS

Entrance Difficulty
Mean GMAT: 476
Mean GPA: N/R

Cost $
Tuition: $68/credit
(Nonresident: $156/credit)
Room & Board: $2,430

Enrollment Profile
Full-time: 15	Work Exp: N/R
Part-time: 36	International: 10%
Total: 51	Women: 40%
Average Age: N/R	Minorities: N/R

Average Class Size: 15

ACADEMICS
Length of Program Minimum: 18 months.
Calendar Semesters.
Full-time Classes Main campus; day, evening, summer.
Part-time Classes Main campus; day, evening, summer.
Degree Requirements 33 credits including 9 elective credits.
Curricular Focus Business issues and problems, general management, teamwork.
Concentration Management.
Faculty Full-time: 10, 100% with doctorates; part-time: 2.
Teaching Methodology Case study: 10%, faculty seminars: 5%, lecture: 40%, research: 10%, seminars by members of the business community: 5%, student presentations: 10%, team projects: 20%.

STUDENT STATISTICS
Geographic Representation State residents 90%. By region: Midwest 90%. International 10%.

FACILITIES
Information Resources Main library with 228,815 bound volumes, 2,803 titles on microform, 2,021 periodical subscriptions, 5,175 records/tapes/CDs.
Housing College housing available.

ADMISSION
Entrance Requirements Bachelor's degree, GMAT score. Core courses waived through: previous course work.
Application Requirements Application form, copies of transcript.
Application Deadlines 8/18 for fall, 12/15 for spring.

FINANCIALS
Estimated Costs for 1995-96 Tuition: Full time: $68/credit for state residents, $156/credit for nonresidents. Average room and board costs are $2,430 per academic year (on-campus) and $3,000 per academic year (off-campus).
Financial Aid In 1994-95, 45% of candidates received some institutionally administered aid in the form of grants, scholarships, loans, assistantships. Application deadlines: 8/18 for fall, 12/15 for spring. Contact: Ms. Caryn Pacheco, Director of Financial Assistance, 2800 West Gore Boulevard, Lawton, OK 73505. (405) 581-2292.

INTERNATIONAL STUDENTS
Demographics 10% of students enrolled in the program are international.
Applying TOEFL required, minimum score of 550; proof of health; proof of adequate funds. Admission application deadlines: 8/18 for fall, 12/15 for spring. Applications are processed on a rolling basis.

Program Contact: Dr. David Carl, Associate Provost, Cameron University, School of Graduate Studies, 2800 West Gore Boulevard, Lawton, OK 73505. (405) 581-2987; Fax: (405) 581-5514; Internet Address: graduate@cuok.cameron.edu.

Northeastern State University

College of Business and Industry

Tahlequah, Oklahoma

OVERVIEW
Northeastern State University is a state-supported comprehensive coed institution. Founded 1846. Setting: 160-acre small-town campus with easy access to Tulsa. Total institutional enrollment: 9,299.

MBA HIGHLIGHTS

Entrance Difficulty
Mean GMAT: 460
Mean GPA: N/R

Cost $
Tuition: $63/hour
(Nonresident: $153/hour)
Room & Board: $3,600

Enrollment Profile
Full-time: N/R	Work Exp: N/R
Part-time: N/R	International: 20%
Total: 51	Women: 55%
Average Age: N/R	Minorities: 20%

Average Class Size: 25

ACADEMICS
Length of Program Minimum: 12 months.
Calendar Semesters.
Full-time Classes Main campus, Muskogee; evening, summer.
Part-time Classes Main campus, Muskogee; evening, summer.
Degree Requirements 32 hours.
Curricular Focus General management, leadership, strategic analysis and planning.
Concentration Management.
Teaching Methodology Case study: 20%, lecture: 40%, research: 5%, seminars by members of the business community: 5%, student presentations: 10%, team projects: 20%.

STUDENT STATISTICS
Geographic Representation State residents 80%. International 20%.

FACILITIES
Information Resources Main library with 180,567 bound volumes, 535,991 titles on microform, 2,107 periodical subscriptions, 3,691 records/tapes/CDs.
Housing College housing available.

ADMISSION
Entrance Requirements Bachelor's degree, GMAT score of 430, minimum 2.5 GPA.
Application Requirements Application form, copies of transcript.

Application Deadlines 7/1 for fall, 11/1 for spring, 4/1 for summer. Applications are processed on a rolling basis.

FINANCIALS
Costs for 1994-95 Tuition: Full-time: $63/hour for state residents, $153/hour for nonresidents. Fees: Full-time: $5/hour for state residents, $5/hour for nonresidents. Average room and board costs are $3,600 per academic year (on-campus) and $3,600 per academic year (off-campus).

Financial Aid Application deadlines: 3/1 for fall, 9/1 for spring. Applications are processed on a rolling basis. Contact: Ms. Kimbra Scott, Administrative Assistant to President, 600 North Grand, Tahlequah, OK 74464. (918) 458-2000.

INTERNATIONAL STUDENTS
Demographics 20% of students enrolled in the program are international.

Applying TOEFL required, minimum score of 550; proof of health; proof of adequate funds. Financial aid is available to international students. Financial aid application deadlines: 7/1 for fall, 11/1 for spring. Applications are processed on a rolling basis. Admission application deadlines: 7/1 for fall, 11/1 for spring. Applications are processed on a rolling basis.

Program Contact: Ms. Kimbra Scott, Administrative Assistant to President, Northeastern State University, 600 North Grand, Tahlequah, OK 74464. (918) 458-2000; Fax: (918) 458-2015; Internet Address: vanallo@cherokee.nsuok.edu.

Oklahoma City University

Meinders School of Business

Oklahoma City, Oklahoma

OVERVIEW
Oklahoma City University is an independent United Methodist comprehensive coed institution. Founded 1904. Setting: 65-acre suburban campus. Total institutional enrollment: 4,571.

MBA HIGHLIGHTS

Entrance Difficulty**

Cost $$
Tuition: $270/credit
Room & Board: N/R

Enrollment Profile
Full-time: N/R	Work Exp: N/R
Part-time: N/R	International: N/R
Total: 850	Women: 40%
Average Age: N/R	Minorities: N/R

Average Class Size: 30

ACADEMICS
Length of Program Minimum: 24 months.
Calendar Semesters.
Full-time Classes Main campus; day, evening.
Part-time Classes Main campus.
Degree Requirements 36-39 credit hours.
Curricular Focus General management, international business, teamwork.
Concentrations Accounting, finance, health services, international business, management, management information systems, marketing.
Teaching Methodology Case study: 15%, lecture: 60%, student presentations: 5%, team projects: 20%.

STUDENT STATISTICS
Geographic Representation State residents 75%.

FACILITIES
Information Resources Main library with 292,651 bound volumes, 38,548 titles on microform, 4,180 periodical subscriptions, 11,594 records/tapes/CDs, 10 CD-ROMs.

ADMISSION
Entrance Requirements Bachelor's degree, minimum 2.5 GPA.
Application Requirements Application form, copies of transcript, personal statement, 2 letters of recommendation.
Application Deadline Applications are processed on a rolling basis.

FINANCIALS
Costs for 1994-95 Tuition: Full-time: $270/credit. Fees: Full-time: $20/semester.

Financial Aid Contact: Ms. Vicki Hendrickson, Director of Financial Aid, 2501 North Blackwelder, Oklahoma City, OK 73106-1402. (405) 521-5211.

INTERNATIONAL STUDENTS
Applying TOEFL required, minimum score of 550; proof of health. Financial aid is not available to international students. Admission applications are processed on a rolling basis.

ALTERNATE MBA PROGRAM
Executive MBA (EMBA) Length of program: Minimum: 18 months. Full-time classes: Laughton, Tulsa; evening, summer. Degree requirements: 36-39 credit hours.

Program Contact: Ms. Laura Mitchell, Director of Graduate Admissions, Oklahoma City University, Graduate Admissions 2501 North Blackwelder, Oklahoma City, OK 73106-1402. (405) 521-5351, or (800) 633-7242 (OK only).

Oklahoma State University

College of Business Administration

Stillwater, Oklahoma

OVERVIEW
Oklahoma State University is a state-supported coed institution. Part of Oklahoma State University. Founded 1890. Setting: 840-acre small-town campus with easy access to Oklahoma City and Tulsa. Total institutional enrollment: 20,000. Program was first offered in 1960. AACSB-accredited.

MBA HIGHLIGHTS

Entrance Difficulty***
Mean GMAT: 590
Mean GPA: 3.31

Cost $
Tuition: $78/credit
(Nonresident: $227/credit)
Room & Board: $6,100

Enrollment Profile
Full-time: 86	Work Exp: 83%
Part-time: 255	International: 17%
Total: 341	Women: 36%
Average Age: 30	Minorities: 11%

Average Class Size: 24

The essence of the Oklahoma State University (OSU) M.B.A. program is its people, their commitment, and their sense of pride. This dedication has resulted in the program's recognition as the eighth-best value-added M.B.A. degree program in the country. The program combines the best of traditionalism and innovation: a strong business foundation; modular course structure; integrative, crossfunctional courses; opportunities for elective concentration; and professional development activities.

While emphasizing pragmatism and organizational reality, the innovative two-year curriculum balances quantitative and behavioral courses. Analytical abilities and managerial perspectives are developed. Teaching methods include case analysis, quantitative methods applications, simulations, lectures, and field projects. The program is acknowledged for its excellence in accounting, telecommunications management, total quality management, and management of innovation and technology. Specializations are available in traditional and emerging business areas. Classroom learning is applied through an annual case competition, a practicum experience, and numerous field projects.

The program offers a low student-faculty ratio, small classes, and personalized instruction designed to meet students' career goals. A collegial atmosphere of friendly competition characterizes the M.B.A. student body. The degree is fully accredited by AACSB. Admissions offers are extended for fall semester only.

ACADEMICS
Length of Program Minimum: 21 months. Maximum: 6 years.
Calendar Semesters.

Full-time Classes Main campus; day.

Part-time Classes Main campus, Tulsa; evening, summer.

Degree Requirements 45 credits including 6-9 elective credits. Other: Professional development activities; annual case competition a minumum of one time; practicum.

Required Courses Business ethics and social responsibility, economic perspectives for managers, financial decision techniques, global competitive environment, information systems technology for managers, internal and external accounting information for decision making, legal issues in business, managerial communication skills, managing individual and group performance, managing information systems, managing operations: decision processes, marketing decisions for management, public environment of business, quantitative modeling for decision support, research methods for business decision making. Courses may be waived through examination.

Curricular Focus Organizational development and change management, systems analysis, teamwork.

Concentrations Accounting, economics, finance, human resources management, international business, management, management information systems, marketing, operations management, organizational behavior, public administration, technology management.

Faculty Full-time: 44, 100% with doctorates.

Teaching Methodology Case study: 40%, lecture: 20%, simulations: 20%, student presentations: 20%.

Special Opportunities International exchange in Japan, United Kingdom. Internship program available.

STUDENT STATISTICS

Geographic Representation State residents 52%. By region: Midwest 74%; South 4%; Northeast 3%; West 2%. International 17%.

Undergraduate Majors Business 36%; education 1%; engineering/technology 27%; humanities 4%; nursing 1%; science/mathematics 12%; social sciences 16%; other 3%.

Other Background Graduate degrees in other disciplines: 14%. Work experience: On average, students have 6 years of work experience on entrance to the program.

FACILITIES

Information Resources Main library with 1.7 million bound volumes, 2.8 million titles on microform, 16,130 periodical subscriptions, 4,456 records/tapes/CDs, 255 CD-ROMs. Business collection includes 110,000 bound volumes, 1,100 periodical subscriptions, 38 CD-ROMs, 28 videos.

Housing 12% of students in program live in college-owned or -operated housing.

Technology Computers are used heavily in course work. 2,300 computer terminals/PCs, linked by a campus-wide computer network, are available for use by students in program; they are located in dormitories, the student center, classrooms, learning resource center, the library, the computer center, computer labs, the research center. Students in the program are not required to have their own PC. $750 are budgeted per student for computer support.

Computer Resources/On-line Services

Training	Yes	Dun's	Yes
Internet	Yes	Dow Jones	Yes
E-Mail	Yes	Dialog	Yes
LEXIS/NEXIS	Yes	Bloomberg	No
CompuServe	No		

ADMISSION

Acceptance 1994-95 333 applied for admission; 41% were accepted.

Entrance Requirements Bachelor's degree, GMAT score, minimum 3 years of work experience for part-time students. Core courses waived through: exams.

Application Requirements Written essay, application form, copies of transcript, 3 letters of recommendation.

Application Deadlines 6/1 for fall, 11/15 for spring, 7/1 for part-time students.

FINANCIALS

Costs for 1994-95 Tuition: Full-time: $78/credit for state residents, $227/credit for nonresidents. Fees: Full-time: $48/semester for state residents, $48/semester for nonresidents. Average room and board costs are $6,100 per academic year (on-campus) and $7,000 per academic year (off-campus).

Financial Aid In 1994-95, candidates received some institutionally administered aid in the form of grants, scholarships, loans, fellowships, assistantships, work-study. Total awards ranged from $400-$7,900. Financial aid is available to part-time students. Application deadlines: 3/1

for fall, 7/1 for spring. Contact: Mr. Charles W. Bruce, Director of Financial Aid, 107 Hanner Hall, Stillwater, OK 74078 (405) 744-6604.

INTERNATIONAL STUDENTS

Demographics 17% of students enrolled in the program are international; Asia 90%, Europe 3%, other 7%.

Services and Facilities International student center, visa services, language tutoring, ESL courses, special assistance for nonnative speakers of English, counseling/support services, family resource center.

Applying TOEFL required, minimum score of 550; proof of adequate funds. Financial aid is available to international students. Financial aid application deadline: 6/1 for fall. Admission application deadline: 2/1 for fall. Contact: Ms. Elaine Burgess, Coordinator, International Student Services, 316 Student Union, Stillwater, OK 74078. (405) 744-5459.

ALTERNATE MBA PROGRAM

MBA/MPH Length of program: Minimum: 30 months. Maximum: 6 years. Degree requirements: 69 credits including 9 elective credits.

PLACEMENT

In 1993-94, 162 organizations participated in on-campus recruiting. Placement services include alumni network, career counseling/planning, career fairs, career library, career placement, electronic job bank, job interviews, resume preparation, and resume referral to employers. Of 1994 graduates, 94% were employed within three months of graduation, the average starting salary was $41,000, the range was $30,000-$54,000.

Jobs by Employer Type Manufacturing 21%; service 46%; government 8%; consulting 9%; nonprofit 13%; other 3%.

Jobs by Functional Area Marketing/sales 22%; finance 28%; operations 4%; management 18%; strategic planning 4%; technical management 21%; education 3%.

Program Contact: Ms. Cynthia S. Gray, MBA Program Director, Oklahoma State University, Stillwater, OK 74078. (405) 744-2951, or (800) 227-6723 (OK only), or (800) 227-4723 (out-of-state); Fax: (405) 744-5180.

Oral Roberts University

School of Business

Tulsa, Oklahoma

OVERVIEW

Oral Roberts University is an independent interdenominational coed institution. Founded 1963. Setting: 500-acre suburban campus. Total institutional enrollment: 4,300. Program was first offered in 1975.

MBA HIGHLIGHTS

Entrance Difficulty*
Mean GMAT: 490
Mean GPA: 3.29

Cost $
Tuition: $215/hour
Room & Board: $4,270

Enrollment Profile

Full-time: 44	Work Exp: 65%
Part-time: 36	International: 38%
Total: 80	Women: 32%
Average Age: 30	Minorities: 17%

Average Class Size: 20

ACADEMICS

Length of Program Minimum: 18 months. Maximum: 5 years.

Calendar Semesters.

Full-time Classes Main campus; day, evening, summer.

Part-time Classes Main campus; day, evening, summer.

Degree Requirements 39.5 hours including 6 elective hours.

Required Courses Accounting, business communication, communication applications, economic theory, ethics, graduate health fitness, holy spirit, international business, management, marketing, microcomputer applications, policy, research methodology, simulation, swimming. Courses may be waived through: previous course work, work experience.

Curricular Focus Economic and financial theory, problem solving and decision making, strategic analysis and planning.

Concentrations Accounting, finance, international business, management, marketing.

Faculty Full-time: 3, 100% with doctorates; part-time: 10, 40% with doctorates.

Teaching Methodology Case study: 15%, lecture: 60%, seminars by members of the business community: 10%, student presentations: 15%.

Special Opportunities International exchange program available. Internships include accounting.

STUDENT STATISTICS
Geographic Representation State residents 38%. By region: Midwest 49%; Northeast 10%; South 3%; West 3%. International 38%.

Undergraduate Majors Business 65%; education 2%; engineering/technology 10%; science/mathematics 5%; other 18%.

Other Background Graduate degrees in other disciplines: 14%. Work experience: On average, students have 3 years of work experience on entrance to the program.

FACILITIES
Information Resources Main library with 306,005 bound volumes, 22,197 titles on microform, 1,500 periodical subscriptions, 14,146 records/tapes/CDs.

Housing 65% of students in program live in college-owned or -operated housing.

Technology Computers are used moderately in course work. Computer terminals/PCs, linked by a campus-wide computer network, are available for use by students in program; they are located in classrooms, learning resource center, the library, the computer center, computer labs. Students in the program are not required to have their own PC.

Computer Resources/On-line Services

Training	Yes	Dialog	Yes $
E-Mail	No		

ADMISSION
Acceptance 1994-95 Of those applying, 80% were accepted.

Entrance Requirements Bachelor's degree, GMAT score of 400, minimum 3.0 GPA, minimum 2 years of work experience. Core courses waived through: previous course work, work experience.

Application Requirements Interview, application form, copies of transcript, personal statement, 2 letters of recommendation, clergy recommendation, signed.

Application Deadlines 7/31 for fall, 12/31 for spring.

FINANCIALS
Costs for 1994-95 Tuition: Full-time: $215/hour. Average room and board costs are $4,270 per academic year (on-campus).

Financial Aid In 1994-95, 45% of candidates received some institutionally administered aid in the form of scholarships, assistantships, work-study. Total awards ranged from $3,600-$5,800. Financial aid is not available to part-time students. Application deadlines: 5/31 for fall, 10/31 for spring. Contact: Mr. David Seward, Financial Aid- Graduates, Athletics and Music, 7777 South Lewis Avenue, Tulsa, OK 74171-0001. (918) 495-6602.

INTERNATIONAL STUDENTS
Demographics 38% of students enrolled in the program are international; Asia 71%, South America 7%, Africa 5%, Central America 5%, Europe 5%, North America 5%.

Services and Facilities Language tutoring, ESL courses, special assistance for nonnative speakers of English, counseling/support services.

Applying TOEFL required, minimum score of 600; proof of health; proof of adequate funds. Financial aid is available to international students. Financial aid application deadlines: 5/30 for fall, 10/31 for spring. Admission application deadlines: 5/30 for fall, 10/31 for spring. Contact: Mr. Danny Ziriax, International Admissions and Transfers Coordinator, 7777 South Lewis Avenue, Tulsa, OK 74171-0001. (918) 495-6506.

PLACEMENT
In 1993-94, 10 organizations participated in on-campus recruiting; 5 on-campus interviews were conducted. Placement services include alumni network, career counseling/planning, career fairs, career library, career placement, job interviews, resume preparation, and resume referral to employers. Of 1994 graduates, 70% were employed within three months of graduation.

Program Contact: Mr. Robert J. Quintana, Admissions Coordinator, Oral Roberts University, 7777 South Lewis Avenue, Tulsa, OK 74171-0001. (918) 495-6117, or (800) 678-8876; Fax: (918) 495-6033.

Phillips University

Enid, Oklahoma

OVERVIEW
Phillips University is an independent comprehensive coed institution, affiliated with Christian Church (Disciples of Christ). Founded 1906. Setting: 35-acre small-town campus with easy access to Oklahoma City. Total institutional enrollment: 774.

MBA HIGHLIGHTS

Entrance Difficulty***
Mean GMAT: 550
Mean GPA: N/R

Cost $
Tuition: $97/credit hour
(Nonresident: $237/credit hour)
Room & Board: $3,700

Enrollment Profile

Full-time: N/R	Work Exp: N/R
Part-time: N/R	International: 10%
Total: 97	Women: 40%
Average Age: N/R	Minorities: 10%

Average Class Size: 30

ACADEMICS
Length of Program Minimum: 24 months.

Calendar Semesters.

Part-time Classes Main campus; evening, summer.

Degree Requirements 36 credits.

Curricular Focus Business issues and problems, general management, problem solving and decision making.

Concentration Management.

Teaching Methodology Case study: 20%, lecture: 50%, student presentations: 10%, team projects: 20%.

STUDENT STATISTICS
Geographic Representation State residents 90%. International 10%.

FACILITIES
Information Resources Main library with 181,516 bound volumes, 6,382 titles on microform, 823 periodical subscriptions, 15,708 records/tapes/CDs, 29 CD-ROMs.

Housing College housing available.

ADMISSION
Entrance Requirements Bachelor's degree, prerequisite courses required for applicants with non-business degree, GMAT score of 500, minimum 2.75 GPA.

Application Requirements Interview, application form, copies of transcript, 3 letters of recommendation.

Application Deadlines 8/1 for fall, 12/30 for spring. Applications are processed on a rolling basis.

FINANCIALS
Costs for 1994-95 Tuition: Full-time: $237/credit hour for international students; Part-time evening: $97/credit hour. Average room and board costs are $3,700 per academic year (on-campus) and $4,500 per academic year (off-campus).

Financial Aid In 1994-95, candidates received some institutionally administered aid in the form of loans. Applications are processed on a rolling basis. Contact: Mrs. Kay Midkiff, Director of Financial Aid, 100 South University Avenue, Enid, OK 73701. (405) 237-4433 Ext. 280.

INTERNATIONAL STUDENTS
Demographics 10% of students enrolled in the program are international.

Applying TOEFL required, minimum score of 550. Financial aid is not available to international students. Admission application deadlines: 8/1 for fall, 12/1 for spring. Applications are processed on a rolling basis.

Program Contact: Ms. Kris Young, Administrative Assistant, Phillips University, 100 South University Avenue, Enid, OK 73701. (405) 237-4433 Ext. 206; Fax: (405) 237-1607.

Southern Nazarene University

Graduate College, Master of Science in Management Dept.

Bethany, Oklahoma

OVERVIEW

Southern Nazarene University is an independent Nazarene comprehensive coed institution. Founded 1899. Setting: 40-acre suburban campus with easy access to Oklahoma City. Total institutional enrollment: 1,800. Program was first offered in 1979.

PROGRAM HIGHLIGHTS

Entrance Difficulty*
Mean GMAT: 480
Mean GPA: 3.5

Cost
Tuition: N/R
Room & Board: N/R

Enrollment Profile

Full-time: 145	Work Exp: 100%
Part-time: 0	International: 5%
Total: 145	Women: 42%
Average Age: 37	Minorities: 15%

Average Class Size: 16

ACADEMICS

Calendar 4 semesters.

Curricular Focus General management, leadership, teamwork.

Concentration Management.

Faculty Full-time: 3, 100% with doctorates; part-time: 12, 75% with doctorates.

Teaching Methodology Case study: 20%, faculty seminars: 10%, lecture: 20%, research: 10%, seminars by members of the business community: 10%, student presentations: 10%, team projects: 20%.

STUDENT STATISTICS

Geographic Representation State residents 90%. By region: South 90%; Midwest 5%; West 5%. International 5%.

Undergraduate Majors Business 20%; education 20%; nursing 15%; science/mathematics 20%; social sciences 15%; other 10%.

Other Background Graduate degrees in other disciplines: 5%. Work experience: On average, students have 10 years of work experience on entrance to the program.

FACILITIES

Information Resources Main library with 108,200 bound volumes, 163,746 titles on microform, 610 periodical subscriptions, 2,927 records/tapes/CDs.

Housing 5% of students in program live in college-owned or -operated housing.

Technology Computers are used heavily in course work. 40 computer terminals/PCs, linked by a campus-wide computer network, are available for use by students in program; they are located in learning resource center, the library, computer labs. Students in the program are not required to have their own PC. $300 are budgeted per student for computer support.

Computer Resources/On-line Services

Training	Yes	E-Mail	Yes
Internet	Yes		

ADMISSION

Acceptance 1994-95 200 applied for admission; 80% were accepted.

Entrance Requirements Bachelor's degree, GMAT score, minimum 2.5 GPA, minimum age 25.

Application Requirements Written essay, application form, copies of transcript, 3 letters of recommendation.

Application Deadline Applications are processed on a rolling basis.

FINANCIALS

Financial Aid In 1994-95, 35% of candidates received some institutionally administered aid in the form of loans. Total awards ranged from $2,142-$7,616. Applications are processed on a rolling basis. Contact: Ms. Gale Langston, Financial Aid Counselor, 6729 Northwest 39th Expressway, Bethany, OK 77008. (405) 491-6686.

INTERNATIONAL STUDENTS

Demographics 5% of students enrolled in the program are international; Asia 60%, Africa 40%.

Services and Facilities International student office, language tutoring.

Applying TOEFL required, minimum score of 550; proof of health; proof of adequate funds. Financial aid is not available to international students. Admission applications are processed on a rolling basis. Contact: Mr. Gary Lange, Registrar, 6729 Northwest 39th Expressway, Bethany, OK 77008. (405) 491-6386.

PROGRAM

MS Mgt Length of program: Minimum: 15 months. Maximum: 6 years. Full-time classes: Main campus, Tulsa; evening. Degree requirements: 32 semester hours. Professional portfolio; case study. Average class size: 20.

PLACEMENT

Jobs by Employer Type Manufacturing 25%; service 20%; government 40%; consulting 5%; nonprofit 10%.

Jobs by Functional Area Marketing/sales 10%; operations 30%; management 50%; technical management 10%.

Program Contact: Dr. B. R. Sloan, Director, Graduate Studies in Management, Southern Nazarene University, 6729 Northwest 39th Expressway, Bethany, OK 77008. (405) 491-6358; Fax: (405) 491-6384.

Southwestern Oklahoma State University

School of Business

Weatherford, Oklahoma

OVERVIEW

Southwestern Oklahoma State University is a state-supported comprehensive coed institution. Part of Southwestern Oklahoma State University. Founded 1901. Setting: 73-acre small-town campus with easy access to Oklahoma City. Total institutional enrollment: 4,882.

MBA HIGHLIGHTS

Entrance Difficulty***
Mean GMAT: 520
Mean GPA: N/R

Cost $
Tuition: $47 - $60/credit hour
(Nonresident: $123 - $148/credit hour)
Room & Board: $2,376

Enrollment Profile

Full-time: N/R	Work Exp: N/R
Part-time: N/R	International: 5%
Total: 50	Women: 55%
Average Age: N/R	Minorities: 5%

Average Class Size: 14

ACADEMICS

Length of Program Minimum: 12 months.

Calendar Semesters.

Full-time Classes Main campus; day, evening, summer.

Part-time Classes Main campus; day, evening, summer.

Degree Requirements 33 credits.

Curricular Focus Problem solving and decision making, strategic analysis and planning, teamwork.

Concentrations Accounting, economics, finance, management, marketing.

Teaching Methodology Case study: 15%, lecture: 60%, student presentations: 10%, team projects: 15%.

STUDENT STATISTICS

Geographic Representation State residents 90%. International 5%.

FACILITIES

Information Resources Main library with 242,406 bound volumes, 854,067 titles on microform, 1,412 periodical subscriptions, 400 records/tapes/CDs, 116 CD-ROMs.

Housing College housing available.

ADMISSION
Entrance Requirements Bachelor's degree, GMAT score, minimum 2.5 GPA.

Application Requirements Application form, copies of transcript, 2 letters of recommendation.

Application Deadline Applications are processed on a rolling basis.

FINANCIALS
Costs for 1994-95 Tuition: Full-time: $47-$60/credit hour for state residents, $123-$148/credit hour for nonresidents. Average room and board costs are $2,376 per academic year (on-campus).

Financial Aid Application deadlines: 4/15 for fall, 10/15 for spring. Contact: Dr. Jerry Kauffman, Dean of the School of Business, 100 Campus Drive, Weatherford, OK 73096-3098. (405) 774-3282.

INTERNATIONAL STUDENTS
Demographics 5% of students enrolled in the program are international.

Applying TOEFL required, minimum score of 500; proof of health; proof of adequate funds. Financial aid is available to international students. Financial aid application deadlines: 4/15 for fall, 10/15 for spring. Admission applications are processed on a rolling basis.

Program Contact: Dr. Ralph D. May, Director of MBA Program, Southwestern Oklahoma State University, 100 Campus Drive, Weatherford, OK 73096-3098. (405) 774-3279; Fax: (405) 774-3795.

University of Central Oklahoma

College of Business Administration

Edmond, Oklahoma

OVERVIEW
The University of Central Oklahoma is a state-supported comprehensive coed institution. Founded 1890. Setting: 200-acre suburban campus with easy access to Oklahoma City. Total institutional enrollment: 16,031. Program was first offered in 1972.

MBA HIGHLIGHTS

Entrance Difficulty**
Mean GMAT: 440
Mean GPA: 2.8

Cost $
Tuition: $54/semester hour
(Nonresident: $54/semester hour)
Room & Board: $2,500

Enrollment Profile

Full-time: 336	Work Exp: 90%
Part-time: 342	International: 40%
Total: 678	Women: 41%
Average Age: 37	Minorities: 2%

Average Class Size: 20

ACADEMICS
Length of Program Minimum: 15 months. Maximum: 6 years.

Calendar Semesters.

Full-time Classes Main campus, distance learning option; day, evening, early morning, summer.

Part-time Classes Main campus, distance learning option; day, evening, early morning, summer.

Degree Requirements 36 credits including 12 elective credits. Other: Comprehensive exam.

Required Courses Business policy, business research methods, controllership and decision accounting, financial administration and control, integrated functions of the firm, macroeconomics for managers, management science, marketing management.

Curricular Focus Economic and financial theory, problem solving and decision making, strategic analysis and planning.

Concentrations Accounting, economics, finance, international business, management, management information systems, marketing, strategic management.

Faculty Full-time: 57, 100% with doctorates; part-time: 14, 100% with doctorates.

Special Opportunities International exchange in Mexico. Internship program available.

STUDENT STATISTICS
Geographic Representation State residents 60%. International 40%.

Undergraduate Majors Business 85%; education 1%; engineering/technology 10%; humanities 1%; nursing 1%; science/mathematics 1%; social sciences 1%.

Other Background Graduate degrees in other disciplines: 1%. Work experience: On average, students have 5 years of work experience on entrance to the program.

FACILITIES
Information Resources Main library with 466,293 bound volumes, 2,200 titles on microform, 4,327 periodical subscriptions, 14,637 records/tapes/CDs, 567 CD-ROMs. Business collection includes 21,690 bound volumes, 352 periodical subscriptions, 2 CD-ROMs.

Housing 15% of students in program live in college-owned or -operated housing. Assistance with housing search provided.

Technology Computers are used heavily in course work. 260 computer terminals/PCs, linked by a campus-wide computer network, are available for use by students in program; they are located in classrooms, learning resource center, the library, the computer center, computer labs, the research center. Students in the program are not required to have their own PC.

Computer Resources/On-line Services

Training	Yes	Multimedia Center	Yes
Internet	Yes	CompuServe	No
E-Mail	Yes	Dialog	No

Other on-line services: OCLC.

ADMISSION
Acceptance 1994-95 202 applied for admission; 99% were accepted.

Entrance Requirements Bachelor's degree, GMAT score of 375, minimum 2.75 GPA.

Application Requirements Application form, copies of transcript.

Application Deadlines 7/1 for fall, 11/1 for spring, 4/1 for summer. Applications are processed on a rolling basis.

FINANCIALS
Costs for 1994-95 Tuition: Full-time: $54/semester hour for state residents, $54/semester hour for nonresidents. Fees: Full-time: $10/semester hour for state residents, $10/semester hour for nonresidents. Average room and board costs are $2,500 per academic year (on-campus).

Financial Aid In 1994-95, candidates received some institutionally administered aid in the form of scholarships, loans, assistantships, work-study. Financial aid is available to part-time students. Application deadlines: 5/1 for fall, 11/1 for spring, 4/1 for summer. Applications are processed on a rolling basis. Contact: Ms. Sheila Fugett, Director of Financial Aid, 100 North University Drive, Box 162, Edmond, OK 73034-0172. (405) 341-2980 Ext. 3336.

INTERNATIONAL STUDENTS
Demographics 40% of students enrolled in the program are international.

Applying TOEFL required, minimum score of 550; proof of health; proof of adequate funds. Financial aid is not available to international students. Admission application deadlines: 7/1 for fall, 11/1 for spring, 4/1 for summer. Contact: Dr. Ronald P. Addack, Director, International Student Services, 100 North University Drive, Box 163, Edmond, OK 73034-0172. (405) 341-2980 Ext. 2374.

PLACEMENT
In 1993-94, 300 organizations participated in on-campus recruiting. Placement services include alumni network, career counseling/planning, career fairs, career library, career placement, job interviews, job search course, resume preparation, and resume referral to employers.

Program Contact: Ms. Gloria Auth, Director, MBA Program,, University of Central Oklahoma, 100 North University Drive, Box 108, Edmond, OK 73034-0172. (405) 341-2980 Ext. 2422; Fax: (405) 330-3821; Internet Address: gauth@aixi.ucok.edu.

University of Oklahoma

College of Business Administration

Norman, Oklahoma

OVERVIEW
The University of Oklahoma is a state-supported coed institution. Founded 1890. Setting: 3,107-acre suburban campus with easy access to Oklahoma City. Total institutional enrollment: 22,029. Program was first offered in 1927. AACSB-accredited.

MBA HIGHLIGHTS

Entrance Difficulty****
Mean GMAT: 570
Mean GPA: 3.4

Cost $
Tuition: $76/credit hour
(Nonresident: $225/credit hour)
Room & Board: $1,770

Enrollment Profile

Full-time: 149	Work Exp: 63%
Part-time: 107	International: 29%
Total: 256	Women: 34%
Average Age: 26	Minorities: 8%

Average Class Size: 25

ACADEMICS
Length of Program Minimum: 24 months. Maximum: 5 years.
Calendar Semesters.
Full-time Classes Main campus; day, summer.
Part-time Classes Main campus; evening, summer.
Degree Requirements 55 credits including 21 elective credits.
Required Courses Accounting, business economics, business integration, corporate finance, legal and ethical environments of business, management information systems, managerial marketing, organizational behavior, production and operations management, quantitative business analysis. Courses may be waived through: previous course work, work experience.
Curricular Focus Business issues and problems, problem solving and decision making, teamwork.
Concentrations Accounting, economics, finance, health services, human resources management, international business, management, management information systems, marketing, operations management, organizational behavior.
Faculty Full-time: 13, 100% with doctorates; part-time: 4, 10% with doctorates.
Teaching Methodology Case study: 10%, faculty seminars: 5%, lecture: 50%, seminars by members of the business community: 5%, student presentations: 5%, team projects: 25%.
Special Opportunities International exchange in France, Mexico, Sweden. Internships include finance, management information systems, and marketing.

STUDENT STATISTICS
Geographic Representation State residents 43%. By region: Midwest 51%; South 8%; Northeast 7%; West 5%. International 29%.
Undergraduate Majors Business 44%; education 2%; engineering/technology 18%; humanities 8%; nursing 6%; science/mathematics 12%; social sciences 4%; other 6%.
Other Background Graduate degrees in other disciplines: 5%. Work experience: On average, students have 3-4 years of work experience on entrance to the program.

FACILITIES
Information Resources Main library with 2.5 million bound volumes, 3.4 million titles on microform, 17,400 periodical subscriptions, 2,200 records/tapes/CDs, 28 CD-ROMs.
Housing 25% of students in program live in college-owned or -operated housing.
Technology Computers are used heavily in course work. 222 computer terminals/PCs, linked by a campus-wide computer network, are available for use by students in program; they are located in dormitories, the student center, classrooms, the library, computer labs, the research center. Students in the program are not required to have their own PC. $150 are budgeted per student for computer support.

Computer Resources/On-line Services

Training	Yes	CompuServe	Yes
Internet	Yes	Dun's	No
E-Mail	Yes	Dialog	No
LEXIS/NEXIS	Yes	Bloomberg	No

ADMISSION
Acceptance 1994-95 356 applied for admission; 65% were accepted.
Entrance Requirements Bachelor's degree, GMAT score. Core courses waived through: previous course work, work experience.
Application Requirements Written essay, application form, copies of transcript, resume/curriculum vitae, personal statement, 3 letters of recommendation.
Application Deadlines 4/1 for fall, 10/1 for spring. Application discs available.

FINANCIALS
Costs for 1994-95 Tuition: Full-time: $76/credit hour for state residents, $225/credit hour for nonresidents. Fees: Full-time: $106/semester for state residents, $106/semester for nonresidents. Average room and board costs are $1,770 per academic year (on-campus) and $3,240 per academic year (off-campus).
Financial Aid In 1994-95, 35% of candidates received some institutionally administered aid in the form of scholarships, assistantships, tuition waivers. Total awards ranged from $200-$7,000. Financial aid is not available to part-time students.

INTERNATIONAL STUDENTS
Demographics 29% of students enrolled in the program are international; Asia 41%, Europe 19%, Central America 2%, other 38%.
Services and Facilities International student office, international student center, visa services, language tutoring, ESL courses, special assistance for nonnative speakers of English, counseling/support services.
Applying TOEFL required, minimum score of 550; proof of health; proof of adequate funds; 35% verbal on GMAT. Financial aid is not available to international students. Admission application deadlines: 4/1 for fall, 10/1 for spring. Contact: Mr. Lee Savage, Assistant Director of Student Support Services, 7331 Elm Avenue, Hester Hall, Room 200, Norman, OK 73019. (405) 325-4006.

ALTERNATE MBA PROGRAMS
MBA/JD Length of program: Minimum: 48 months. Maximum: 6 years. Degree requirements: 135 hours.
MBA/MA Length of program: Minimum: 36 months. Maximum: 6 years. Degree requirements: 57 hours. MA is in French, German or Spanish.
MBA/MLS Length of program: Minimum: 36 months. Maximum: 6 years. Degree requirements: 54 hours.
MBA/MS Length of program: Minimum: 36 months. Maximum: 6 years. Degree requirements: 57 hours. MS is in mathematics or construction science.

PLACEMENT
In 1993-94, 99 organizations participated in on-campus recruiting; 362 on-campus interviews were conducted. Placement services include career counseling/planning, career fairs, career library, career placement, job interviews, resume preparation, and resume referral to employers. Of 1994 graduates, 51% were employed within three months of graduation, the average starting salary was $36,348, the range was $24,000-$44,000.
Jobs by Employer Type Manufacturing 29%; service 18%; government 7%; consulting 25%; nonprofit 3%; oil and gas industry 14%.
Jobs by Functional Area Marketing/sales 7%; finance 18%; operations 25%; management 18%; strategic planning 18%; technical management 11%.

Program Contact: Dr. Alice Watkins, Associate Director, University of Oklahoma, 660 Parrington Oval, Norman, OK 73019. (405) 325-4107, or (800) 522-0772 (out-of-state); Fax: (405) 325-1957.

University of Tulsa

College of Business Administration

Tulsa, Oklahoma

OVERVIEW
The University of Tulsa is an independent coed institution, affiliated with Presbyterian Church. Founded 1894. Setting: 100-acre urban campus.

Total institutional enrollment: 4,579. Program was first offered in 1947. AACSB-accredited.

MBA HIGHLIGHTS

Entrance Difficulty***
Mean GMAT: 530
Mean GPA: 3.23

Cost $$
Tuition: $440/credit hour
Room & Board: N/R

Enrollment Profile
Full-time: 40
Part-time: 143
Total: 183
Average Age: 28

Work Exp: 80%
International: 9%
Women: 49%
Minorities: 15%

Average Class Size: 20

ACADEMICS
Length of Program Minimum: 12 months. Maximum: 6 years.
Calendar Semesters.
Full-time Classes Main campus; day, summer.
Part-time Classes Main campus; evening, summer.
Degree Requirements 30 credit hours including 9 elective credit hours.
Required Courses Advanced marketing management, behavioral sciences in administration, business policy, financial administration, managerial accounting, managerial economic analysis, operations research.
Curricular Focus General management, international business, teamwork.
Concentrations Accounting, finance, management.
Faculty Full-time: 34, 100% with doctorates; part-time: 2, 100% with doctorates.
Teaching Methodology Case study: 20%, lecture: 50%, research: 10%, student presentations: 10%, team projects: 10%.
Special Opportunities International exchange in Finland, France. Internship program available.

STUDENT STATISTICS
Geographic Representation By region: Midwest 91%. International 9%.
Undergraduate Majors Business 65%; education 1%; engineering/technology 10%; humanities 4%; nursing 2%; science/mathematics 5%; social sciences 12%; other 1%.
Other Background Graduate degrees in other disciplines: 2%. Work experience: On average, students have 4 years of work experience on entrance to the program.

FACILITIES
Information Resources Main library with 1.3 million bound volumes, 2.4 million titles on microform, 3,430 periodical subscriptions, 9,682 records/tapes/CDs, 78 CD-ROMs.
Housing 10% of students in program live in college-owned or -operated housing.
Technology Computers are used moderately in course work. 80 computer terminals/PCs, linked by a campus-wide computer network, are available for use by students in program; they are located in computer labs. Students in the program are not required to have their own PC.
Computer Resources/On-line Services
Training   Yes   E-Mail   Yes
Other on-line services: OCLC, RLIN.

ADMISSION
Acceptance 1994-95 178 applied for admission; 83% were accepted.
Entrance Requirements Bachelor's degree, GMAT score. Core courses waived through: previous course work.
Application Requirements Application form, copies of transcript, personal statement, 3 letters of recommendation.
Application Deadline Applications are processed on a rolling basis.

FINANCIALS
Costs for 1994-95 Tuition: Full-time: $440/credit hour.
Financial Aid In 1994-95, candidates received some institutionally administered aid in the form of scholarships, loans, fellowships, assistantships. Total awards ranged from $1,000-$13,000. Financial aid is not available to part-time students. Applications are processed on a rolling basis. Contact: Mr. David Gruen, Director of Student Financial Services, 600 South College Avenue, Tulsa, OK 74104-3126. (918) 631-2526.

INTERNATIONAL STUDENTS
Demographics 9% of students enrolled in the program are international; Asia 27%, Europe 14%, South America 10%, North America 10%, Central America 5%, Africa 1%, other 33%.
Services and Facilities International student office, ESL courses, counseling/support services.
Applying TOEFL required, minimum score of 575; proof of adequate funds. Financial aid is not available to international students. Admission applications are processed on a rolling basis. Contact: Ms. Pam Smith, Associate Dean of Students, International Student Services, 600 South College Avenue, Tu7sa, OK 74104-3126. (918) 631-2329.

PLACEMENT
In 1993-94, 17 organizations participated in on-campus recruiting. Placement services include career counseling/planning, career fairs, career placement, job interviews, and resume preparation. Of 1994 graduates, 85% were employed within three months of graduation.
Jobs by Employer Type Manufacturing 35%; service 50%; government 10%; consulting 5%.
Jobs by Functional Area Marketing/sales 30%; finance 55%; management 10%; strategic planning 5%.

Program Contact: Ms. Tina Hite, Assistant Director, Graduate Business Studies, University of Tulsa, 600 South College Avenue, Tulsa, OK 74104-3126. (918) 631-2242, or (800) 882-4723; Fax: (918) 631-2142; Internet Address: gbs_th@u.tulsa.edu.

OREGON

George Fox College

Department of Business and Economics

Newberg, Oregon

OVERVIEW
George Fox College is an independent Friends comprehensive coed institution. Founded 1891. Setting: 60-acre urban campus with easy access to Portland. Total institutional enrollment: 1,600. Program was first offered in 1992.

MBA HIGHLIGHTS
Entrance Difficulty***

Cost $$
Tuition: $17,900/degree program
Room & Board: N/R

Enrollment Profile
Full-time: 0
Part-time: 85
Total: 85
Average Age: N/R

Work Exp: 100%
International: N/R
Women: 33%
Minorities: 13%

Average Class Size: 22

ACADEMICS
Length of Program Minimum: 24 months.
Calendar Trimesters.
Part-time Classes Main campus, Portland; evening, weekends, summer.
Degree Requirements 39 credits including 3 elective credits.
Required Courses Creativity and entrepreneurship, decision making and information, directed study project, effective communication, ethical and legal issues, functional competencies, functional competency, global awareness, leadership, managing and organizing, people at work, shaping a better world, strategic thinking.
Curricular Focus Leadership, problem solving and decision making, teamwork.
Concentration Management.
Faculty Full-time: 7, 57% with doctorates; part-time: 3, 100% with doctorates.

Teaching Methodology Case study: 15%, lecture: 20%, research: 20%, seminars by members of the business community: 10%, student presentations: 10%, team projects: 25%.

STUDENT STATISTICS
Geographic Representation By region: West 100%.

FACILITIES
Information Resources Main library with 93,658 bound volumes, 1,852 titles on microform, 870 periodical subscriptions, 2,033 records/tapes/CDs, 29 CD-ROMs. Business collection includes 5,935 bound volumes, 74 periodical subscriptions, 4 CD-ROMs.

Housing College housing not available.

Technology Computers are used heavily in course work. 35 computer terminals/PCs are available for use by students in program; they are located in student rooms, the library, computer labs. Students in the program are required to have their own PC.

Computer Resources/On-line Services

Training	Yes	E-Mail	Yes
Internet	Yes	Dialog	Yes

Other on-line services: OCLC.

ADMISSION
Acceptance 1994-95 119 applied for admission; 82% were accepted.

Entrance Requirements Bachelor's degree, GMAT score, minimum 3.0 GPA, minimum 2 years of work experience.

Application Requirements Written essay, interview, application form, copies of transcript, personal statement, 3 letters of recommendation.

Application Deadlines 7/1 for fall. Applications are processed on a rolling basis.

FINANCIALS
Costs for 1994-95 Tuition: Full-time: $17,900/degree program.

Financial Aid In 1994-95, candidates received some institutionally administered aid in the form of loans. Financial aid is available to part-time students. Application deadline: 7/1 for fall. Applications are processed on a rolling basis. Contact: Mrs. Monika Keller, Financial Aid Counselor, 414 North Meridian, Newberg, OR 97132-2697. (503) 538-8383 Ext. 2233.

INTERNATIONAL STUDENTS
Applying TOEFL required, minimum score of 550; proof of health; proof of adequate funds.

PLACEMENT
Placement services include career counseling/planning. Of 1994 graduates, 97% were employed within three months of graduation.

Jobs by Employer Type Manufacturing 27%; service 39%; government 15%; consulting 7%; nonprofit 7%; retail 5%.

Program Contact: Mr. Jeff Rickey, Director of Graduate Enrollment, George Fox College, 414 North Meridian, Newberg, OR 97132-2697. (503) 538-8383 Ext. 2261, or (800) 631-0921 (OR only); Fax: (503) 537-3834.

Marylhurst College

Department of Business and Management

Marylhurst, Oregon

OVERVIEW
Marylhurst College is an independent Roman Catholic comprehensive coed institution. Founded 1893. Setting: 73-acre suburban campus with easy access to Portland. Total institutional enrollment: 2,700. Program was first offered in 1990.

MBA HIGHLIGHTS

Entrance Difficulty***
Mean GMAT: N/R
Mean GPA: 3.5

Cost $
Tuition: $212/credit hour
(Nonresident: $212/credit hour)
Room & Board: N/R

Enrollment Profile

Full-time: 0	Work Exp: 100%
Part-time: 300	International: 10%
Total: 300	Women: 50%
Average Age: 39	Minorities: N/R

Class Size: 15 - 20

*M*arylhurst College is committed to the education of working adults. Both the M.B.A. and Master of Science in Management (M.S.M.) programs emphasize applied skills in problem solving, critical thinking, and decision making based on individual awareness and alignment of personal values with business goals. In addition to technical business skills, the curriculum emphasizes teamwork, presentation skills, innovation, creativity, cultural development, and holistic thinking. Students are encouraged to adapt course work to personal and professional objectives. Graduates possess a philosophy of management that can be applied to problem solving in any environment.

The M.B.A. and M.S.M. curricula share a core of 42 credits. Each program requires completion of a specialization, totaling a minimum of 18 credit hours, as part of the 60-credit degree requirement. Documentation of 30 hours of community service, chosen according to a student's individual interests but completed during graduate training, is required prior to graduation. Classes are scheduled days, evenings, and weekends to accommodate differing work hours and lifestyles.

Founded in 1893, Marylhurst is located in suburban Lake Oswego, just a 20-minute commute from downtown Portland, Oregon. Shoen Library offers a network of research sources including on-line databases. Animated by its Catholic and liberal arts heritage, Marylhurst emphasizes the uniqueness and dignity of each student.

ACADEMICS
Length of Program Minimum: 24 months. Maximum: 5 years.

Calendar Quarters.

Full-time Classes Main campus; evening, weekends.

Part-time Classes Main campus; evening, weekends.

Degree Requirements 60 credits including 6 elective credits.

Curricular Focus Leadership, organizational development and change management, teamwork.

Concentrations Finance, human resources management, management information systems, marketing, organizational behavior.

Faculty Part-time: 30, 75% with doctorates.

Special Opportunities Internship program available.

STUDENT STATISTICS
Geographic Representation State residents 95%. International 10%.

Undergraduate Majors Business 40%; engineering/technology 10%; science/mathematics 10%; social sciences 10%; other 30%.

Other Background Graduate degrees in other disciplines: 10%. Work experience: On average, students have 10 years of work experience on entrance to the program.

FACILITIES
Information Resources Main library with 77,648 bound volumes, 638 titles on microform, 313 periodical subscriptions, 516 records/tapes/CDs, 1 CD-ROM.

Housing College housing not available.

Technology Computers are used heavily in course work. 20 computer terminals/PCs are available for use by students in program; they are located in computer labs. Students in the program are not required to have their own PC.

Computer Resources/On-line Services

Training	No	E-Mail	No

ADMISSION
Acceptance 1994-95 100 applied for admission; 90% were accepted.

Entrance Requirements Bachelor's degree, minimum 3.0 GPA. Core courses waived through: previous course work.

Application Requirements Application form, copies of transcript, resume/curriculum vitae, personal statement, 3 letters of recommendation.

Application Deadlines 8/31 for fall, 3/15 for spring. Applications are processed on a rolling basis. Application discs available.

FINANCIALS
Costs for 1994-95 Tuition: Full-time: $212/credit hour, $212/credit hour for international students.

Financial Aid In 1994-95, 50% of candidates received some institutionally administered aid in the form of loans, work-study. Financial aid is available to part-time students. Applications are processed on a rolling basis. Contact: Ms. Marlena McKee-Flores, Director, PO Box 261, Marylhurst, OR 97036-0261. (503) 636-8141 Ext. 314.

INTERNATIONAL STUDENTS
Demographics 10% of students enrolled in the program are international.

Applying TOEFL required, minimum score of 550. Financial aid is not available to international students. Admission application deadlines: 8/31 for fall, 3/15 for spring. Applications are processed on a rolling basis.

Program Contact: Ms. Nancy Adams, Dean of Student Services, Marylhurst College, PO Box 261, Marylhurst, OR 97036-0261. (503) 636-8140 Ext. 330, or (800) 634-9982; Fax: (503) 636-9526.

Oregon State University

College of Business

Corvallis, Oregon

OVERVIEW
Oregon State University is a state-supported coed institution. Part of Oregon State System of Higher Education. Founded 1868. Setting: 530-acre small-town campus. Total institutional enrollment: 14,500. Program was first offered in 1965. AACSB-accredited.

MBA HIGHLIGHTS

Entrance Difficulty****
Mean GMAT: 540
Mean GPA: N/R

Cost $
Tuition: $1,575/quarter
(Nonresident: $2,530/quarter)
Room & Board: N/R

Enrollment Profile

Full-time: 100	Work Exp: N/R
Part-time: 25	International: 40%
Total: 125	Women: 34%
Average Age: N/R	Minorities: 5%

Average Class Size: 30

ACADEMICS
Length of Program Minimum: 12 months. Maximum: 7 years.
Calendar Quarters.
Full-time Classes Main campus; day, evening, weekends, summer.
Part-time Classes Main campus; day, evening, weekends, summer.
Degree Requirements 59 credits.
Curricular Focus Business issues and problems, problem solving and decision making, teamwork.
Concentration Management.
Teaching Methodology Case study: 10%, faculty seminars: 10%, lecture: 30%, research: 10%, student presentations: 10%, team projects: 30%.

STUDENT STATISTICS
Geographic Representation State residents 25%. By region: West 60%. International 40%.

FACILITIES
Information Resources Main library with 1.2 million bound volumes, 1.9 million titles on microform, 18,929 periodical subscriptions, 434 records/tapes/CDs.

ADMISSION
Acceptance 1994-95 400 applied for admission; 50% were accepted.
Entrance Requirements Bachelor's degree, GMAT score of 500, minimum 3.0 GPA. Core courses waived through: previous course work.
Application Requirements Application form, copies of transcript, personal statement, 3 letters of recommendation.
Application Deadline 3/15 for fall.

FINANCIALS
Costs for 1994-95 Tuition: Full-time: $1,575/quarter for state residents, $2,530/quarter for nonresidents. Fees: Full-time: $180-$280/quarter for state residents, $180-$430/quarter for nonresidents.

Financial Aid In 1994-95, 50% of candidates received some institutionally administered aid in the form of scholarships, loans, assistantships. Financial aid is available to part-time students. Application deadline: 3/15 for fall. Contact: Mr. Keith McCreight, Director of Financial Aid, Administrative Services Building, Corvallis, OR 97331. (503) 737-2241.

INTERNATIONAL STUDENTS
Demographics 40% of students enrolled in the program are international.

Applying TOEFL required, minimum score of 600; proof of health; proof of adequate funds. Financial aid is available to international students. Financial aid application deadline: 3/15 for fall. Admission application deadline: 3/15 for fall.

Program Contact: Ms. Clara Horne, Head Adviser, Oregon State University, Administrative Services Building, Corvallis, OR 97331. (503) 737-3716; Fax: (503) 737-4890; Internet Address: horne@bus.orst.edu.

Portland State University

School of Business Administration

Portland, Oregon

OVERVIEW
Portland State University is a state-supported coed institution. Part of Oregon State System of Higher Education. Founded 1946. Setting: 36-acre urban campus. Total institutional enrollment: 14,486. Program was first offered in 1969. AACSB-accredited.

MBA HIGHLIGHTS

Entrance Difficulty****
Mean GMAT: 550
Mean GPA: 3.4

Cost $
Tuition: $1,389/quarter
(Nonresident: $2,344/quarter)
Room & Board: $2,700

Enrollment Profile

Full-time: 100	Work Exp: 80%
Part-time: 400	International: 10%
Total: 500	Women: 45%
Average Age: 34	Minorities: 5%

Average Class Size: 40

ACADEMICS
Length of Program Minimum: 18 months. Maximum: 7 years.
Calendar Quarters.
Full-time Classes Main campus; day, evening, summer.
Part-time Classes Main campus; day, evening, summer.
Degree Requirements 60 credits including 17 elective credits.
Required Courses Business policy and strategy, business project, competing on a global environment, economic and financial environment of the firm, executive briefings, financial accounting, financial management, integrated process management, managerial responsibility and public policy, marketing, organizational management, quantitative methods for managers, systems for performance measurement.
Curricular Focus Competitiveness, strategic analysis and planning, teamwork.
Concentrations Accounting, entrepreneurship, finance, human resources management, international business, management, management information systems, marketing, operations management, organizational behavior, strategic management.
Faculty Full-time: 30, 90% with doctorates; part-time: 8, 12% with doctorates.
Teaching Methodology Case study: 20%, faculty seminars: 30%, lecture: 30%, student presentations: 5%, team projects: 15%.

Special Opportunities International exchange in Ecuador, France, Germany. Internships include marketing in high technology, management in manufacturing and product control, information systems, accounting in CPA firms, and finance in securities and CRO offices.

STUDENT STATISTICS
Geographic Representation By region: West 95%. International 10%.
Undergraduate Majors Business 50%; engineering/technology 10%; humanities 10%; social sciences 20%; other 10%.
Other Background Work experience: On average, students have 7 years of work experience on entrance to the program.

FACILITIES
Information Resources Main library with 930,693 bound volumes, 54,922 titles on microform, 11,132 periodical subscriptions, 24,200 records/tapes/CDs, 405 CD-ROMs.
Housing 10% of students in program live in college-owned or -operated housing.
Technology Computers are used moderately in course work. 100 computer terminals/PCs, linked by a campus-wide computer network, are available for use by students in program; they are located in the computer center, computer labs. Students in the program are not required to have their own PC.

Computer Resources/On-line Services

Training	Yes	E-Mail	Yes
Internet	Yes	LEXIS/NEXIS	Yes

ADMISSION
Acceptance 1994-95 250 applied for admission; 32% were accepted.
Entrance Requirements Bachelor's degree, GMAT score of 450, minimum 2.75 GPA. Core courses waived through: previous course work, work experience.
Application Requirements Application form, copies of transcript, resume/curriculum vitae.
Application Deadlines 4/1 for fall, 8/1 for winter.

FINANCIALS
Costs for 1994-95 Tuition: Full-time: $1,389/quarter for state residents, $2,344/quarter for nonresidents; Part-time day: $1,224/quarter for state residents, $2,088/quarter for nonresidents. Fees: Full-time: $193/quarter for state residents, $193/quarter for nonresidents; Part-time day: $178/quarter for state residents, $178/quarter for nonresidents. Average room and board costs are $2,700 per academic year (on-campus) and $4,500 per academic year (off-campus).
Financial Aid In 1994-95, candidates received some institutionally administered aid in the form of scholarships, fellowships, assistantships, work-study. Financial aid is available to part-time students. Application deadline: 6/15 for fall. Applications are processed on a rolling basis. Contact: Dr. John Anderson, Director of Financial Aid, PO Box 751, Portland, OR 97207. (503) 725-5445.

INTERNATIONAL STUDENTS
Demographics 10% of students enrolled in the program are international; Asia 60%, Europe 30%, South America 7%, Africa 1%, Central America 1%, North America 1%.
Services and Facilities International student office, international student center, ESL courses, counseling/support services.
Applying TOEFL required, minimum score of 550; proof of health; proof of adequate funds. Financial aid is not available to international students. Admission application deadlines: 3/1 for fall, 8/1 for spring. Contact: Ms. Anne Bender, Student Abroad Adviser, PO Box 751, Portland, OR 97207. (503) 725-5076.

PLACEMENT
Placement services include alumni network, career counseling/planning, career fairs, career library, and resume preparation.

Program Contact: Dr. Ed Grubb, Associate Dean of Graduate Programs and Research, Portland State University, PO Box 751, Portland, OR 97207. (503) 725-3722, or (800) 547-8887 (out-of-state); Fax: (503) 725-5850; Internet Address: edg@sbamail.sba.pdx.edu.
See full description on page 806.

Southern Oregon State College

School of Business

Ashland, Oregon

OVERVIEW
Southern Oregon State College is a state-supported comprehensive coed institution. Part of Oregon State System of Higher Education. Founded 1926. Setting: 175-acre small-town campus. Total institutional enrollment: 4,500. Program was first offered in 1977.

MBA HIGHLIGHTS

Entrance Difficulty**
Mean GMAT: 500
Mean GPA: 3.32

Cost
Tuition: N/R
Room & Board: N/R

Enrollment Profile

Full-time: 51	Work Exp: 60%
Part-time: 33	International: 10%
Total: 84	Women: 36%
Average Age: 34	Minorities: N/R

Average Class Size: 17

ACADEMICS
Calendar Quarters.
Curricular Focus General management, problem solving and decision making, strategic analysis and planning.
Concentrations Accounting, hotel management, human resources management, management, marketing, operations management.
Faculty Full-time: 12, 90% with doctorates.
Teaching Methodology Case study: 20%, lecture: 50%, research: 7%, student presentations: 10%, team projects: 13%.
Special Opportunities Internships include accounting in CPA firms, marketing in mail order, marketing in discount stores, and marketing. Other: economics computer science.

STUDENT STATISTICS
Geographic Representation State residents 90%. International 10%.
Undergraduate Majors Business 60%; education 1%; engineering/technology 5%; nursing 10%; science/mathematics 10%; other 14%.
Other Background Graduate degrees in other disciplines: 2%. Work experience: On average, students have 2 years of work experience on entrance to the program.

FACILITIES
Information Resources Main library with 270,000 bound volumes, 725,000 titles on microform, 2,200 periodical subscriptions.
Housing 2% of students in program live in college-owned or -operated housing.
Technology Computers are used moderately in course work. 130 computer terminals/PCs, linked by a campus-wide computer network, are available for use by students in program; they are located in computer labs. Students in the program are not required to have their own PC.

Computer Resources/On-line Services

Training	No	E-Mail	Yes
Internet	Yes	Multimedia Center	Yes

ADMISSION
Entrance Requirements Bachelor's degree, prerequisite courses may be required for non-business degree applicants, GMAT score of 450.
Application Requirements Application form, copies of transcript.
Application Deadline Applications are processed on a rolling basis. Application discs available.

FINANCIALS
Financial Aid In 1994-95, 30% of candidates received some institutionally administered aid in the form of scholarships, loans, assistantships, work-study. Total awards ranged from $2,000-$8,000. Financial aid is not available to part-time students. Application deadlines: 6/1 for fall, 1/1 for spring. Applications are processed on a rolling basis. Contact: Ms. Lonnie Alexander, Director of Financial Aid, 1250 Siskiyou Boulevard, Ashland, OR 97520. (503) 552-6161.

INTERNATIONAL STUDENTS
Demographics 10% of students enrolled in the program are international; Asia 80%, Central America 20%.

Services and Facilities International student office, international student center, language tutoring.

Applying TOEFL required, minimum score of 540; proof of health; proof of adequate funds. Financial aid is available to international students. Applications are processed on a rolling basis. Admission applications are processed on a rolling basis. Contact: Dr. Keith Chambers, Director International Programs, 1250 Siskiyou Boulevard, Ashland, OR 97520. (503) 552-6336.

PROGRAM
One-Year MBA Length of program: Minimum: 9 months. Maximum: 7 years. Full-time classes: Main campus, distance learning option; day, evening, summer. Part-time classes: Main campus, distance learning option; day, evening, summer. Degree requirements: 45 credits including 18 elective credits.

PLACEMENT
In 1993-94, 20 organizations participated in on-campus recruiting. Placement services include alumni network, career placement, and job interviews. Of 1994 graduates, 100% were employed within three months of graduation, the average starting salary was $22,500, the range was $17,500-$32,000.

Program Contact: Dr. Dennis Varin, MBA Graduate Coordinator, Southern Oregon State College, 1250 Siskiyou Boulevard, Ashland, OR 97520. (503) 552-6724; Fax: (503) 552-6715; Internet Address: varin@wpo. sosc.osshe.edu.

University of Oregon

Charles H. Lundquist College of Business

Eugene, Oregon

OVERVIEW
The University of Oregon is a state-supported coed institution. Part of Oregon State System of Higher Education. Founded 1872. Setting: 250-acre urban campus. Total institutional enrollment: 16,157. Program was first offered in 1962. AACSB-accredited.

MBA HIGHLIGHTS

Entrance Difficulty**
Mean GMAT: 569
Mean GPA: N/R

Cost $
Tuition: $1,645/quarter
(Nonresident: $2,620/quarter)
Room & Board: $4,700

Enrollment Profile

Full-time: 165	Work Exp: 90%
Part-time: 17	International: 33%
Total: 182	Women: 22%
Average Age: 27	Minorities: 1%

Average Class Size: 30

ACADEMICS
Length of Program Minimum: 18 months. Maximum: 7 years.
Calendar Quarters.
Full-time Classes Main campus; day.
Part-time Classes Main campus; day.
Degree Requirements 73 credits including 33 elective credits.
Required Courses Accounting concepts, business government and society, communication and implementation, computer workshop, economic dynamics and segmentation, financial management, introduction to business statistics, management accounting concepts, managerial economics, managing organizations, market dynamics and segmentation, marketing management, production management, strategy and policy implementation. Courses may be waived through: previous course work.
Curricular Focus Entrepreneurship, problem solving and decision making, teamwork.

Concentrations Accounting, entrepreneurship, finance, human resources management, international business, management, marketing, operations management, organizational behavior, quantitative analysis, strategic management.

Faculty Full-time: 42, 99% with doctorates; part-time: 1, 100% with doctorates.

Teaching Methodology Case study: 30%, faculty seminars: 3%, lecture: 10%, research: 10%, seminars by members of the business community: 2%, student presentations: 20%, team projects: 25%.

Special Opportunities International exchange in Denmark, France, Germany, Japan, Netherlands. Internship program available.

STUDENT STATISTICS
Geographic Representation State residents 38%. By region: West 62%; Midwest 6%; Northeast 5%. International 33%.

Undergraduate Majors Business 54%; education 1%; engineering/technology 9%; humanities 13%; science/mathematics 13%; social sciences 8%; other 2%.

Other Background Graduate degrees in other disciplines: 2%. Work experience: On average, students have 4 years of work experience on entrance to the program.

FACILITIES
Information Resources Main library with 2.5 million bound volumes, 1.7 million titles on microform, 21,000 periodical subscriptions, 20,000 records/tapes/CDs.

Housing 10% of students in program live in college-owned or -operated housing.

Technology Computers are used heavily in course work. 290 computer terminals/PCs, linked by a campus-wide computer network, are available for use by students in program; they are located in the student center, the library, the computer center, computer labs. Students in the program are not required to have their own PC.

Computer Resources/On-line Services

Training	Yes	CompuServe	No
Internet	Yes	Dun's	Yes
E-Mail	Yes	Dow Jones	Yes
Videoconference Center	Yes	Dialog	Yes
Multimedia Center	Yes	Bloomberg	No
LEXIS/NEXIS	Yes		

ADMISSION
Acceptance 1994-95 286 applied for admission; 50% were accepted.

Entrance Requirements Bachelor's degree, GMAT score of 550, minimum 3.0 GPA, minimum 2 years of work experience.

Application Requirements Written essay, application form, copies of transcript, resume/curriculum vitae, 2 letters of recommendation.

Application Deadline 3/1 for fall.

FINANCIALS
Costs for 1994-95 Tuition: Full-time: $1,645/quarter for state residents, $2,620/quarter for nonresidents; Part-time day: $1,150/quarter for state residents, $1,804/quarter for nonresidents. Fees: Full-time: $100/quarter for state residents, $250/quarter for nonresidents; Part-time day: $67/quarter for state residents, $167/quarter for nonresidents. Average room and board costs are $4,700 per academic year (on-campus) and $3,400 per academic year (off-campus).

Financial Aid In 1994-95, 50% of candidates received some institutionally administered aid in the form of scholarships, loans, fellowships. Total awards ranged from $500-$8,500. Financial aid is available to part-time students. Application deadline: 3/1 for fall. Contact: Mr. Edmond Vignoul, Director, Office of Student Financial Aid, 260 Oregon Hall, Eugene, OR 97403. (503) 346-3221.

INTERNATIONAL STUDENTS
Demographics 33% of students enrolled in the program are international; Europe 48%, Asia 33%, Australia 5%, Africa 3%, South America 3%, other 8%.

Services and Facilities International student center, visa services, language tutoring, ESL courses, special assistance for nonnative speakers of English, counseling/support services, orientation, host-family program.

Applying TOEFL required, minimum score of 600; proof of health; proof of adequate funds. Financial aid is available to international students. Financial aid application deadline: 3/15 for fall. Admission application deadline: 3/1 for fall. Contact: Mr. Thomas Mills, Director, Office of International Education and Exchange, Eugene, OR 97403. (503) 346-3206.

ALTERNATE MBA PROGRAMS
Executive MBA (EMBA) Length of program: Minimum: 24 months. Degree requirements: 62 credits. Average class size: 29.

One-Year MBA Length of program: Minimum: 35 months. Degree requirements: 12 courses.

MBA/JD Length of program: Minimum: 48 months. Full-time classes: Main campus. Part-time classes: Main campus. Degree requirements: 124 credits.

MBA/MA Length of program: Minimum: 36 months. Degree requirements: 109 credits.

PLACEMENT

In 1993-94, 34 organizations participated in on-campus recruiting; 100 on-campus interviews were conducted. Placement services include alumni network, career counseling/planning, career fairs, career library, career placement, electronic job bank, job interviews, resume preparation, and resume referral to employers. Of 1994 graduates, 55% were employed within three months of graduation, the average starting salary was $42,359, the range was $15,000-$85,000.

Jobs by Employer Type Manufacturing 3%; government 3%; consulting 8%; other 35%; financial services/investments 20%; computers 20%; healthcare 11%.

Jobs by Functional Area Marketing/sales 25%; finance 28%; operations 11%; management 19%; technical management 3%; other 11%; consulting 3%.

Program Contact: Ms. Sue Sullivan, Management Assistant, University of Oregon, Eugene, OR 97403. (503) 346-3306; Fax: (503) 346-3341.
See full description on page 906.

University of Portland

School of Business Administration

Portland, Oregon

OVERVIEW

The University of Portland is an independent Roman Catholic comprehensive coed institution. Founded 1901. Setting: 92-acre urban campus. Total institutional enrollment: 2,856. Program was first offered in 1960. AACSB-accredited.

MBA HIGHLIGHTS

Entrance Difficulty**
Mean GMAT: 520
Mean GPA: N/R

Cost $$
Tuition: $405/credit hour
Room & Board: $4,880

Enrollment Profile
Full-time: 20
Part-time: 135
Total: 155
Average Age: N/R

Work Exp: 80%
International: 15%
Women: 35%
Minorities: 5%

Average Class Size: 20

ACADEMICS

Length of Program Minimum: 12 months. Maximum: 5 years.
Calendar Semesters.
Full-time Classes Main campus; evening, summer.
Part-time Classes Main campus; evening, summer.
Degree Requirements 30-51 credit hours including 6 elective credit hours.
Required Course Policy.
Curricular Focus General management.
Concentration Management.
Faculty Full-time: 23, 100% with doctorates; part-time: 2, 50% with doctorates.

STUDENT STATISTICS

Geographic Representation By region: West 85%. International 15%.
Undergraduate Majors Business 45%; engineering/technology 30%; humanities 5%; social sciences 15%; other 5%.
Other Background Graduate degrees in other disciplines: 15%.

FACILITIES

Information Resources Main library with 350,000 bound volumes, 500 titles on microform, 1,300 periodical subscriptions, 6,500 records/tapes/CDs, 400 CD-ROMs.
Housing 10% of students in program live in college-owned or -operated housing.
Technology Computers are used moderately in course work. 125 computer terminals/PCs, linked by a campus-wide computer network, are available for use by students in program; they are located in computer labs. Students in the program are not required to have their own PC.
Computer Resources/On-line Services

Training	No	Multimedia Center	Yes
E-Mail	Yes		

ADMISSION

Entrance Requirements Bachelor's degree, GMAT score of 450, minimum 2.75 GPA.
Application Requirements Application form, copies of transcript, personal statement, 2 letters of recommendation.
Application Deadlines 8/1 for fall, 12/1 for spring. Applications are processed on a rolling basis.

FINANCIALS

Costs for 1994-95 Tuition: Full-time: $405/credit hour. Average room and board costs are $4,880 per academic year (on-campus).
Financial Aid In 1994-95, candidates received some institutionally administered aid in the form of loans. Financial aid is not available to part-time students. Contact: Financial Aid Office, 5000 North Willamette Boulevard, Portland, OR 97203-5798. (503) 283-7311.

INTERNATIONAL STUDENTS

Demographics 15% of students enrolled in the program are international; Asia 95%, Other 5%.
Services and Facilities International student office.
Applying TOEFL required, minimum score of 570; proof of adequate funds. Financial aid is not available to international students. Admission application deadlines: 8/1 for fall, 12/1 for spring. Contact: Ms. Barbara Segal, International Student Adviser, University of Portland 5000 North Willamette Boulevard, Portland, OR 97203-5798. (503) 283-7367.

PLACEMENT

Placement services include career counseling/planning, career fairs, career placement, resume preparation, and resume referral to employers.

Program Contact: Mr. Neal Higgins, Assistant Dean, University of Portland, 5000 North Willamette Boulevard, Portland, OR 97203-5798. (503) 283-7224; Fax: (503) 283-7399; Internet Address: higgins@uofpost.edu.

Willamette University

George H. Atkinson Graduate School of Management

Salem, Oregon

OVERVIEW

Willamette University is an independent United Methodist comprehensive coed institution. Founded 1842. Setting: 72-acre urban campus with easy access to Portland. Total institutional enrollment: 2,500. Program was first offered in 1974.

PROGRAM HIGHLIGHTS

Entrance Difficulty***
Mean GMAT: 540
Mean GPA: 3.1

Cost $$$
Tuition: $440/credit
Room & Board: $4,500

Enrollment Profile
Full-time: 152
Part-time: 28
Total: 180
Average Age: 27

Work Exp: 75%
International: 20%
Women: 30%
Minorities: 12%

Class Size: 14 - 70

ACADEMICS
Calendar Semesters.

Curricular Focus General management, problem solving and decision making, teamwork.

Concentrations Accounting, finance, human resources management, international business, management, marketing, organization analysis, public administration.

Faculty Full-time: 11, 100% with doctorates; part-time: 6, 50% with doctorates.

Teaching Methodology Case study: 25%, lecture: 25%, research: 10%, seminars by members of the business community: 5%, student presentations: 15%, team projects: 20%.

Special Opportunities International exchange program available. Internships include finance, consulting, accounting, human resources, and marketing. Other: independent study and research courses.

STUDENT STATISTICS
Geographic Representation State residents 80%. International 20%.

Undergraduate Majors Business 35%; engineering/technology 6%; humanities 14%; science/mathematics 5%; social sciences 35%; other 4%.

Other Background Graduate degrees in other disciplines: 3%. Work experience: On average, students have 3 years of work experience on entrance to the program.

FACILITIES
Information Resources Main library with 241,344 bound volumes, 7,353 titles on microform, 1,433 periodical subscriptions, 5,266 records/tapes/CDs, 18 CD-ROMs. Business collection includes 21,486 bound volumes, 321 periodical subscriptions, 4 CD-ROMs, 40 videos.

Housing 10% of students in program live in college-owned or -operated housing.

Technology Computers are used heavily in course work. 17 computer terminals/PCs, linked by a campus-wide computer network, are available for use by students in program; they are located in computer labs. Students in the program are not required to have their own PC. $1,002 are budgeted per student for computer support.

Computer Resources/On-line Services

Training	Yes	Multimedia Center	Yes
Internet	Yes	Dialog	Yes
E-Mail	Yes		

Other on-line services: Carl.

ADMISSION
Acceptance 1994-95 155 applied for admission; 85% were accepted.

Entrance Requirements Bachelor's degree, GMAT score, minimum 2.0 GPA. Core courses waived through: previous course work.

Application Requirements Written essay, application form, copies of transcript, resume/curriculum vitae, personal statement, 2 letters of recommendation.

Application Deadlines 3/31 for fall. Applications are processed on a rolling basis.

FINANCIALS
Estimated Costs for 1995-96 Tuition: Full-time: $440/credit. Fees: Full-time: $50. Average room and board costs are $4,500 per academic year (on-campus) and $6,500 per academic year (off-campus).

Financial Aid In 1994-95, candidates received some institutionally administered aid in the form of scholarships, loans, assistantships, work-study. Total awards ranged from $2,500-$22,100. Financial aid is available to part-time students. Applications are processed on a rolling basis. Contact: Ms. Zofia Miller, Financial Aid Counselor, 900 State Street, Salem, OR 97301-3931. (503) 370-6273.

INTERNATIONAL STUDENTS
Demographics 20% of students enrolled in the program are international; Asia 73%, Europe 10%, Africa 7%, North America 7%, South America 3%.

Services and Facilities International student office, international student center, visa services, counseling/support services.

Applying TOEFL required, minimum score of 550; proof of health; proof of adequate funds. Financial aid is available to international students. Applications are processed on a rolling basis. Admission application deadline: 3/31 for fall. Applications are processed on a rolling basis. Contact: Ms. Donna McElroy, Director, International Student and Faculty Services, 900 State Street, Salem, OR 97301-3931. (503) 375-5404.

PROGRAMS
MM Length of program: Minimum: 18 months. Maximum: 6 years. Full-time classes: Main campus; day, evening, summer. Part-time classes: Main campus; day, evening, summer. Degree requirements: 63 credits including 30 elective credits. One elective from menu of functionally integrated courses; minimum 3.0 GPA.

MM/JD Length of program: Minimum: 48 months. Maximum: 4 years. Full-time classes: Main campus; day, evening, summer. Degree requirements: 120 credits including 18 elective credits. One elective from menu of functionally integrated courses; minimum 3.0 GPA.

PLACEMENT
In 1993-94, 3 organizations participated in on-campus recruiting; 345 on-campus interviews were conducted. Placement services include alumni network, career counseling/planning, career library, career placement, electronic job bank, job interviews, job search course, resume preparation, resume referral to employers, and west coast MBA consortium. Of 1994 graduates, 68% were employed within three months of graduation, the average starting salary was $35,000, the range was $26,000-$50,000.

Jobs by Employer Type Manufacturing 13%; service 11%; government 11%; consulting 25%; nonprofit 8%; import/export 4%; law 11%; transportation 9%; other 8%.

Jobs by Functional Area Marketing/sales 20%; finance 17%; operations 7%; management 4%; strategic planning 7%; technical management 4%; law 11%; human resources 9%; consulting 21%.

Program Contact: Ms. Judy O'Neill, Assistant Dean and Director of Admission, Willamette University, Atkinson Graduate School of Management, 900 State Street, Salem, OR 97301-3931. (503) 370-6167; Fax: (503) 370-3011; Internet Address: joneill@willamette.edu.
See full description on page 936.

PENNSYLVANIA

Allentown College of St. Francis de Sales

Graduate Division

Center Valley, Pennsylvania

OVERVIEW
Allentown College of St. Francis de Sales is an independent Roman Catholic comprehensive coed institution. Founded 1962. Setting: 300-acre rural campus with easy access to Philadelphia. Total institutional enrollment: 2,166. Program was first offered in 1991.

MBA HIGHLIGHTS

Entrance Difficulty***
Mean GMAT: 480
Mean GPA: 3.2

Cost $$
Tuition: $350/credit hour
Room & Board: N/R

Enrollment Profile
Full-time: 0
Part-time: 284
Total: 284
Average Age: 33

Work Exp: 99%
International: 0%
Women: 40%
Minorities: 1%

Average Class Size: 14

ACADEMICS
Length of Program Minimum: 24 months. Maximum: 7 years.
Calendar Semesters.

Part-time Classes Main campus, Easton, Gwynedd-Mercy College; evening, weekends, summer.

Degree Requirements 36 credit hours including 3 elective credit hours.

Required Courses Business and society, executive skills development, financial and managerial accounting, financial management, marketing management, organization management, policy and strategy, quantitative methods. Courses may be waived through: previous course work.

Curricular Focus Ethics, executive skills development, general management.

Concentrations Accounting, finance, health services, management, marketing.

Faculty Full-time: 9, 60% with doctorates; part-time: 10, 20% with doctorates.

Teaching Methodology Case study: 15%, lecture: 45%, seminars by members of the business community: 10%, student presentations: 15%, team projects: 15%.

STUDENT STATISTICS

Geographic Representation State residents 96%. By region: Northeast 100%.

Undergraduate Majors Business 68%; education 2%; engineering/technology 7%; humanities 4%; nursing 2%; science/mathematics 6%; social sciences 4%; other 7%.

Other Background Graduate degrees in other disciplines: 1%. Work experience: On average, students have 10 years of work experience on entrance to the program.

FACILITIES

Information Resources Main library with 145,000 bound volumes, 159,000 titles on microform, 1,400 periodical subscriptions, 3,616 records/tapes/CDs, 11 CD-ROMs. Business collection includes 2,800 bound volumes, 80 periodical subscriptions, 2 CD-ROMs, 50 videos.

Housing College housing not available.

Technology Computers are used moderately in course work. 35 computer terminals/PCs, linked by a campus-wide computer network, are available for use by students in program; they are located in the library, the computer center. Students in the program are not required to have their own PC. $125 are budgeted per student for computer support.

Computer Resources/On-line Services

Training	Yes	CompuServe	No
Internet	Yes	Dun's	No
E-Mail	Yes	Dow Jones	No
Multimedia Center	Yes	Dialog	Yes
LEXIS/NEXIS	No	Bloomberg	No

Other on-line services: OCLC.

ADMISSION

Acceptance 1994-95 Of those applying, 95% were accepted.

Entrance Requirements Bachelor's degree, GMAT score, minimum 3.0 GPA. Core courses waived through: previous course work.

Application Requirements Interview, application form, copies of transcript, personal statement, 3 letters of recommendation.

Application Deadline Applications are processed on a rolling basis.

FINANCIALS

Costs for 1994-95 Tuition: Full-time: $350/credit hour.

Financial Aid Financial aid is not available to part-time students. Contact: Ms. Catherine McIntyre, Director of Financial Aid, 2755 Station Avenue, Center Valley, PA 18034-9568. (610) 282-1100 Ext. 1287.

INTERNATIONAL STUDENTS

Demographics 1% of students on campus are international; Asia 68%, Africa 8%, Central America 8%, Europe 8%, South America 8%.

Services and Facilities Special assistance for nonnative speakers of English, counseling/support services.

Applying Proof of adequate funds. Financial aid is not available to international students. Admission applications are processed on a rolling basis.

PLACEMENT

Placement services include career counseling/planning, career library, career placement, job interviews, and resume referral to employers. Of 1994 graduates, 99% were employed within three months of graduation.

Program Contact: Dr. Harold E. Dolenga, Director, MBA Program, Allentown College of St. Francis de Sales, 2755 Station Avenue, Center Valley, PA 18034-9568. (610) 282-4625; Fax: (610) 282-2254.

Bloomsburg University of Pennsylvania

College of Business

Bloomsburg, Pennsylvania

OVERVIEW

Bloomsburg University of Pennsylvania is a state-supported comprehensive coed institution. Part of Pennsylvania State System of Higher Education. Founded 1839. Setting: 192-acre small-town campus. Total institutional enrollment: 7,375.

MBA HIGHLIGHTS

Entrance Difficulty N/R

Cost $
Tuition: $1,477/semester
(Nonresident: $2,598/semester)
Room & Board: N/R

Total Enrollment: 100

Average Class Size: N/R

ACADEMICS

Calendar Semesters.

Degree Requirements 36 credits.

Concentration Management.

FACILITIES

Information Resources Main library with 309,688 bound volumes, 1.8 million titles on microform, 1,762 periodical subscriptions, 6,841 records/tapes/CDs.

ADMISSION

Entrance Requirements Bachelor's degree, GMAT score of 450, minimum 2.5 GPA.

Application Requirements Copies of transcript, resume/curriculum vitae, 3 letters of recommendation.

FINANCIALS

Costs for 1994-95 Tuition: Full-time: $1,477/semester for state residents, $2,598/semester for nonresidents; Part-time day: $164/semester hour for state residents, $289/semester hour for nonresidents.

Financial Aid (717) 389-4000.

INTERNATIONAL STUDENTS

Applying TOEFL required, minimum score of 550; Test of Spoken English.

Program Contact: Mr. Kenneth Schnure, Registrar, Bloomsburg University of Pennsylvania, 400 East Second Street, Bloomsburg, PA 17815-1905. (717) 389-4263.

Bucknell University

Department of Management

Lewisburg, Pennsylvania

OVERVIEW

Bucknell University is an independent nonprofit comprehensive coed institution. Founded 1846. Setting: 300-acre small-town campus. Total institutional enrollment: 3,698.

PROGRAM HIGHLIGHTS

Entrance Difficulty N/R

Cost
Tuition: N/R
Room & Board: N/R

Enrollment Profile
Full-time: N/R
Part-time: N/R
Total: N/R
Average Age: N/R

Work Exp: N/R
International: N/R
Women: N/R
Minorities: N/R

Average Class Size: N/R

ACADEMICS
Calendar Semesters.

Concentration Management.

FACILITIES
Information Resources Main library with 563,080 bound volumes, 636,900 titles on microform, 2,400 periodical subscriptions, 4,520 records/tapes/CDs, 20 CD-ROMs.

ADMISSION
Entrance Requirements Bachelor's degree, GMAT score, minimum 2.8 GPA.

Application Requirements Copies of transcript, 2 letters of recommendation.

Application Deadlines 6/1 for fall, 11/15 for spring.

FINANCIALS
Financial Aid Application deadline: 3/1 for fall.

PROGRAM
MSBA.

Program Contact: Mr. Mark Davies, Director of Admissions, Bucknell University, Lewisburg, PA 17837. (717) 524-1101, or (800) 523-1271 (PA only).

California University of Pennsylvania

California, Pennsylvania

OVERVIEW
California University of Pennsylvania is a state-supported comprehensive coed institution. Part of Pennsylvania State System of Higher Education. Founded 1852. Setting: 148-acre small-town campus with easy access to Pittsburgh. Total institutional enrollment: 6,200.

PROGRAM HIGHLIGHTS
Entrance Difficulty***
Mean GMAT: N/R
Mean GPA: N/R

Cost $
Tuition: $171/credit hour
(Nonresident: $308/credit hour)
Room & Board: N/R

Total Enrollment: 84

Average Class Size: 12

ACADEMICS
Calendar Semesters.

Curricular Focus Business issues and problems, economic and financial theory, general management, managing diversity, minorities in business, organizational development and change management, problem solving and decision making, strategic analysis and planning, teamwork.

Concentration Management.

Teaching Methodology Case study: 25%, lecture: 50%, research: 25%.

FACILITIES
Information Resources Main library with 338,863 bound volumes, 1.3 million titles on microform, 1,467 periodical subscriptions, 6,791 records/tapes/CDs.

ADMISSION
Entrance Requirements Bachelor's degree, GMAT score.

Application Requirements Interview, application form, copies of transcript, resume/curriculum vitae.

Application Deadline Applications are processed on a rolling basis.

FINANCIALS
Costs for 1994-95 Tuition: Full-time: $171/credit hour for state residents, $308/credit hour for nonresidents.

Financial Aid Application deadline: 4/1 for fall. Applications are processed on a rolling basis. Contact: Mr. Robert Thorn, Director of Financial Aid, 250 University Avenue, California, PA 15419-1394. (412) 938-4415.

INTERNATIONAL STUDENTS
Applying TOEFL required, minimum score of 550; proof of adequate funds; GMAT, transcripts. Financial aid is available to international students.

PROGRAM
MS Length of program: Minimum: 24 months. Full-time classes: Main campus; day, evening, summer. Part-time classes: Main campus; day, evening, summer. Degree requirements: 39 credits.

Program Contact: Dr. George W. Crane, College of Graduate Studies, California University of Pennsylvania, 250 University Avenue, California, PA 15419-1394. (412) 938-4187; Fax: (412) 938-4373.

Carnegie Mellon University

Graduate School of Industrial Administration

Pittsburgh, Pennsylvania

OVERVIEW
Carnegie Mellon University is an independent nonprofit coed institution. Founded 1900. Setting: 103-acre suburban campus. Total institutional enrollment: 7,141. Program was first offered in 1949. AACSB-accredited.

PROGRAM HIGHLIGHTS
Entrance Difficulty***
Mean GMAT: 640
Mean GPA: 3.2

Cost $$$$
Tuition: $15,480 - $20,500
Room & Board: N/R

Enrollment Profile
Full-time: 420
Part-time: 155
Total: 575
Average Age: 26

Work Exp: 95%
International: 36%
Women: 20%
Minorities: 14%

Average Class Size: 65

ACADEMICS
Calendar Minisemesters.

Curricular Focus General management, problem solving and decision making, strategic analysis and planning.

Concentrations Accounting, economics, entrepreneurship, finance, human resources management, international business, management, management information systems, marketing, operations management, organizational behavior, quantitative analysis, strategic management.

Faculty Full-time: 71, 97% with doctorates; part-time: 11, 45% with doctorates.

Teaching Methodology Case study: 20%, computer-aided instruction: 15%, lecture: 60%, team projects: 5%.

Special Opportunities International exchange in Austria, France, Germany, Japan, Mexico, Spain, United Kingdom. Other: MBA Enterprise Corps, Japan Science and Technology Management Program.

STUDENT STATISTICS
Geographic Representation State residents 64%. By region: Northeast 32%; West 12%; South 10%; Midwest 9%. International 36%.

Undergraduate Majors Business 21%; engineering/technology 55%; humanities 4%; social sciences 5%; other 15%.

Other Background Work experience: On average, students have 4 years of work experience on entrance to the program.

FACILITIES
Information Resources Main library with 852,241 bound volumes, 756,985 titles on microform, 3,889 periodical subscriptions, 21,340 records/tapes/CDs, 16 CD-ROMs.

Housing College housing not available.

Technology Computers are used heavily in course work. 106 computer terminals/PCs, linked by a campus-wide computer network, are available for use by students in program; they are located in classrooms, the library, the computer center, computer labs. Students in the program are not required to have their own PC.

Computer Resources/On-line Services

Training	Yes	CompuServe	No
Internet	Yes	Dun's	No
E-Mail	Yes	Dow Jones	Yes
Videoconference Center	Yes	Dialog	No
Multimedia Center	Yes	Bloomberg	No
LEXIS/NEXIS	No		

ADMISSION

Acceptance 1994-95 1,200 applied for admission; 33% were accepted.

Entrance Requirements Bachelor's degree, 2 semesters of calculus, GMAT score. Core courses waived through: previous course work, work experience.

Application Requirements Written essay, interview, application form, copies of transcript, resume/curriculum vitae, 3 letters of recommendation.

Application Deadlines 3/15 for fall. Applications are processed on a rolling basis. Application discs available.

FINANCIALS

Costs for 1994-95 Tuition: Full-time: $15,480-$20,500. Fees: Full-time: $100.

Financial Aid In 1994-95, 51% of candidates received some institutionally administered aid in the form of grants, scholarships, loans, fellowships, assistantships, work-study. Total awards ranged from $1,100-$20,500. Financial aid is available to part-time students. Application deadline: 4/15 for fall. Applications are processed on a rolling basis. Contact: Ms. Lauren Tracey, Financial Aid Counselor, Graduate School of Industrial Administration, Pittsburgh, PA 15213-3890. (412) 268-7581.

INTERNATIONAL STUDENTS

Demographics 36% of students enrolled in the program are international; Asia 63%, Europe 20%, North America 12%, South America 4%, Australia 1%.

Services and Facilities International student office, visa services, counseling/support services, summer institute for international business students.

Applying TOEFL required; proof of adequate funds. Financial aid is not available to international students. Admission application deadline: 3/15 for fall. Applications are processed on a rolling basis. Contact: Dr. Manjula Shvam, Director of International Programs, Graduate School of Industrial Administration, Pittsburgh, PA 15213-3890. (412) 268-7055.

PROGRAMS

MSIA Length of program: Minimum: 15 months. Maximum: 4 years. Full-time classes: Main campus; day, evening. Part-time classes: Main campus; day, evening. Degree requirements: 68 credits including 34 elective credits.

MSIA/JD Length of program: Minimum: 48 months. Full-time classes: Main campus; day, evening, summer. Degree requirements: 156 credits. Separate applications must be submitted to both industrial administration and law departments.

MSIA/MSCF Length of program: Minimum: 27 months. Full-time classes: Main campus; day, evening, summer. Degree requirements: 96 credits. MS is in computational finance.

MSIA/MSE Length of program: Minimum: 28 months. Full-time classes: Main campus; day, evening, summer. Degree requirements: 117 credits.

PLACEMENT

In 1993-94, 122 organizations participated in on-campus recruiting; 2,200 on-campus interviews were conducted. Placement services include alumni network, career counseling/planning, career fairs, career library, career placement, electronic job bank, job interviews, resume preparation, and resume referral to employers. Of 1994 graduates, 97% were employed within three months of graduation, the average starting salary was $58,718, the range was $32,000-$90,000.

Jobs by Employer Type Manufacturing 39%; service 27%; consulting 34%.

Jobs by Functional Area Marketing/sales 10%; finance 31%; operations 8%; strategic planning 4%; technical management 4%; consulting 32%; other 11%.

Program Contact: Ms. Laurie Stewart, Interim Director of Admissions,, Carnegie Mellon University, Graduate School of Industrial Administration, Pittsburgh, PA 15213-3890. (412) 268-2272; Fax: (412) 268-6837; Internet Address: gsia-admissions+@andrew.cmu.edu.

Clarion University of Pennsylvania

College of Business Administration

Clarion, Pennsylvania

OVERVIEW

Clarion University of Pennsylvania is a state-supported comprehensive coed institution. Part of Pennsylvania State System of Higher Education. Founded 1867. Setting: 100-acre small-town campus. Total institutional enrollment: 5,881. Program was first offered in 1973.

MBA HIGHLIGHTS

Entrance Difficulty*
Mean GMAT: 502
Mean GPA: 3.22

Cost $
Tuition: $1,477/semester
(Nonresident: $2,598/semester)
Room & Board: $2,800

Enrollment Profile

Full-time: 79		Work Exp: 46%
Part-time: 33		International: 24%
Total: 112		Women: 39%
Average Age: 30		Minorities: 4%

Average Class Size: 15

ACADEMICS

Length of Program Minimum: 24 months. Maximum: 6 years.

Calendar Semesters.

Full-time Classes Main campus; evening, summer.

Degree Requirements 33 credits including 9 elective credits.

Required Courses Administration and business policy, advanced managerial economics, financial management, management accounting, marketing decision making, organizational structure and behavior, production management, quantitative analysis. Courses may be waived through: previous course work, work experience.

Curricular Focus Problem solving and decision making, strategic analysis and planning, teamwork.

Concentrations Accounting, economics, finance, management, marketing, operations management, organizational behavior, quantitative analysis.

Faculty Part-time: 33, 100% with doctorates.

Teaching Methodology Case study: 10%, lecture: 70%, student presentations: 10%, team projects: 10%.

STUDENT STATISTICS

Geographic Representation State residents 76%. By region: Northeast 76%. International 24%.

Undergraduate Majors Business 66%; engineering/technology 7%; humanities 9%; science/mathematics 2%; social sciences 2%; other 14%.

Other Background Graduate degrees in other disciplines: 1%. Work experience: On average, students have 6 years of work experience on entrance to the program.

FACILITIES

Information Resources Main library with 362,162 bound volumes, 1.2 million titles on microform, 1,689 periodical subscriptions, 4,350 records/tapes/CDs.

Housing 10% of students in program live in college-owned or -operated housing.

Technology Computers are used moderately in course work. 40 computer terminals/PCs, linked by a campus-wide computer network, are available for use by students in program; they are located in the student center, the library, computer labs. Students in the program are not required to have their own PC.

Computer Resources/On-line Services

Training	No	E-Mail	Yes
Internet	Yes	Dialog	Yes

ADMISSION

Acceptance 1994-95 132 applied for admission; 85% were accepted.

Entrance Requirements Bachelor's degree, GMAT score, minimum 2.75 GPA. Core courses waived through: previous course work, work experience.

Application Requirements Application form, copies of transcript, 3 letters of recommendation.

Application Deadlines 7/1 for fall, 11/1 for spring.

FINANCIALS
Costs for 1994-95 Tuition: Full-time: $1,477/semester for state residents, $2,598/semester for nonresidents. Fees: Full-time: $37.50/semester for state residents, $300/semester for nonresidents. Average room and board costs are $2,800 per academic year (on-campus).

Financial Aid In 1994-95, 45% of candidates received some institutionally administered aid in the form of assistantships. Total awards ranged from $2,300-$4,200. Financial aid is not available to part-time students. Application deadlines: 7/1 for fall, 11/1 for spring. Contact: Mr. Kenneth Grugel, Director, Office of Financial Aid, 104 Egbert Hall, Clarion, PA 16214. (814) 226-2315.

INTERNATIONAL STUDENTS
Demographics 24% of students enrolled in the program are international; Asia 46%, Europe 18%, other 36%.

Services and Facilities International student center, counseling/support services.

Applying TOEFL required, minimum score of 550; proof of adequate funds. Financial aid is available to international students. Assistantships are available for these students. Admission application deadlines: 7/1 for fall, 11/1 for spring. Contact: Ms. Linda Heineman, Foreign Student Adviser, International Programs Office, Clarion, PA 16214. (814) 226-2340.

PLACEMENT
Placement services include career placement, resume preparation, and resume referral to employers.

Program Contact: Ms. LaVieta Lerch, Assistant Coordinator, Clarion University of Pennsylvania, 302 Still Hall, Clarion, PA 16214. (814) 226-2605; Fax: (814) 226-1910.

Drexel University

College of Business and Administration

Philadelphia, Pennsylvania

OVERVIEW
Drexel University is an independent nonprofit coed institution. Founded 1891. Setting: 38-acre urban campus. Total institutional enrollment: 9,782. Program was first offered in 1947. AACSB-accredited.

MBA HIGHLIGHTS

Entrance Difficulty***
Mean GMAT: 547
Mean GPA: 3.15

Cost $$
Tuition: $414/credit
Room & Board: $6,933

Enrollment Profile

Full-time: 243	Work Exp: 75%
Part-time: 550	International: N/R
Total: 793	Women: 32%
Average Age: 26	Minorities: N/R

Average Class Size: 25

ACADEMICS
Length of Program Minimum: 12 months. Maximum: 7 years.
Calendar Quarters.
Full-time Classes Main campus; day, evening, weekends, summer.
Part-time Classes Main campus, Beaver College; evening, weekends, summer.
Degree Requirements 48 credits including 18 elective credits.
Required Courses Business policy, decision science, management and technology.
Curricular Focus Economic and financial theory, organizational development and change management, technology management.
Concentrations Accounting, economics, finance, human resources management, international business, investments, banking, quality service, management, management information systems, marketing, operations management, organizational behavior, quantitative analysis.

Faculty Full-time: 54, 95% with doctorates; part-time: 15, 15% with doctorates.

Teaching Methodology Case study: 10%, faculty seminars: 5%, lecture: 50%, research: 5%, seminars by members of the business community: 5%, student presentations: 10%, team projects: 15%.

Special Opportunities International exchange in France. Internship program available.

STUDENT STATISTICS
Geographic Representation By region: Northeast 70%; South 3%; Midwest 2%; West 2%.

Undergraduate Majors Business 45%; education 10%; engineering/technology 25%; humanities 4%; nursing 5%; science/mathematics 5%; social sciences 5%; other 1%.

Other Background Graduate degrees in other disciplines: 5%. Work experience: On average, students have 3 years of work experience on entrance to the program.

FACILITIES
Information Resources Main library with 500,000 bound volumes, 739,635 titles on microform, 4,800 periodical subscriptions, 1,636 records/tapes/CDs, 75 CD-ROMs. Business collection includes 14,605 bound volumes, 33 periodical subscriptions, 86 videos.

Housing 2% of students in program live in college-owned or -operated housing. Assistance with housing search provided.

Technology Computers are used moderately in course work. 100 computer terminals/PCs, linked by a campus-wide computer network, are available for use by students in program; they are located in the computer center, computer labs. Students in the program are not required to have their own PC.

Computer Resources/On-line Services

Training	Yes	CompuServe	Yes
Internet	Yes	Dow Jones	Yes
E-Mail	Yes	Dialog	Yes
LEXIS/NEXIS	Yes		

ADMISSION
Acceptance 1994-95 2,959 applied for admission; 64% were accepted.

Entrance Requirements Bachelor's degree, prerequisite courses, GMAT score of 500, minimum 3.0 GPA. Core courses waived through: previous course work.

Application Requirements Written essay, application form, copies of transcript, resume/curriculum vitae.

Application Deadlines 8/1 for fall. Applications are processed on a rolling basis.

FINANCIALS
Costs for 1994-95 Tuition: Full-time: $414/credit. Average room and board costs are $6,933 per academic year (on-campus).

INTERNATIONAL STUDENTS
Demographics 11% of students on campus are international; Asia 71%, Europe 7%, Africa 5%, South America 3%, Central America 2%, Australia 1%, Other 11%.

Services and Facilities International student office, visa services, language tutoring, ESL courses, counseling/support services.

Applying TOEFL required; proof of health; proof of adequate funds. Financial aid is available to international students. Assistantships are available for these students for applicants with nonbusiness degree. Admission application deadlines: 6/20 for fall, 9/25 for winter, 1/31 for spring, 3/31 for summer. Contact: Mr. Douglas Gill, Director of International Student Office, 32nd and Chestnut Streets, Philadelphia, PA 19104-2875. (215) 895-2502.

Program Contact: Ms. Veronica Cohen, Acting Director of Graduate Admissions, Drexel University, 32nd and Chestnut Streets, Philadelphia, PA 19104-2875. (215) 895-6700, or (800) 2-DREXEL (PA only); Fax: (215) 895-5939.
See full description on page 722.

Duquesne University

Graduate School of Business

Pittsburgh, Pennsylvania

OVERVIEW
Duquesne University is an independent Roman Catholic coed institution. Founded 1878. Setting: 40-acre urban campus. Total institutional enrollment: 9,000. Program was first offered in 1962. AACSB-accredited.

MBA HIGHLIGHTS

Entrance Difficulty***
Mean GMAT: 518
Mean GPA: 3.04

Cost $$
Tuition: $391/credit
Room & Board: $5,400

Enrollment Profile

Full-time: 115	Work Exp: 82%
Part-time: 456	International: 19%
Total: 571	Women: 37%
Average Age: 26	Minorities: 4%

Average Class Size: 26

Duquesne University's Graduate School of Business Administration challenges students to reach their potential in a dynamic, intellectually exciting environment that is driven by a century-long commitment to professional and personal ethics, teaching excellence, continuous improvement, scholarship, and creative academic-business partnerships. The School prepares leaders who can blend technical competence with a broad-based renaissance education.

A distinctive new curriculum focuses on total quality, ethics, the integration of disciplines, communications, the management of technology, and an increased global perspective. The application of these issues through the use of real business problems responds to employers' strongly expressed need for graduates who can immediately add value in real-world situations. A comprehensive reading program helps students relate specific business disciplines to the world at large, reflecting a renaissance approach to graduate education. Executive faculty, executives-in-residence, and advisory boards of business professionals supplement the academic capabilities of a faculty with a roster of outstanding executives who participate in the classroom experience.

The Graduate School of Business Administration provides professional management education of uncompromised quality through instructional excellence in a dynamic environment of change and continuous improvement that offers students excitement, opportunity, and the chance to grow.

ACADEMICS
Length of Program Minimum: 24 months. Maximum: 6 years.
Calendar Semesters.
Full-time Classes Main campus; evening, weekends, summer.
Part-time Classes Main campus; evening, weekends, summer.
Degree Requirements 56 credits including 21 elective credits. Other: Research project; portfolio.
Required Courses Accounting, business problems courses, communications, computer literacy, economics, environment of business, finance, law, management information systems, marketing, organizational behavior, problem analysis, production and operations management. Courses may be waived through: previous course work, work experience.
Curricular Focus Business issues and problems, general management, teamwork.
Concentrations Accounting, economics, environmental management, taxation, finance, human resources management, international business, management, management information systems, marketing, real estate.
Faculty Full-time: 34, 91% with doctorates; part-time: 9.
Teaching Methodology Case study: 25%, lecture: 35%, student presentations: 15%, team projects: 25%.
Special Opportunities International exchange in France, Germany, Japan, Spain. Internship program available.

STUDENT STATISTICS
Geographic Representation State residents 81%. By region: Northeast 81%. International 19%.

Undergraduate Majors Business 60%; engineering/technology 13%; humanities 15%; other 12%.
Other Background Work experience: On average, students have 3 years of work experience on entrance to the program.

FACILITIES
Information Resources Main library with 732,915 bound volumes, 60,840 titles on microform, 8,746 periodical subscriptions, 5,426 records/tapes/CDs, 41 CD-ROMs. Business collection includes 29,500 bound volumes, 341 periodical subscriptions, 1 CD-ROM.
Housing 15% of students in program live in college-owned or -operated housing.
Technology Computers are used moderately in course work. 200 computer terminals/PCs, linked by a campus-wide computer network, are available for use by students in program; they are located in dormitories, the library, computer labs. Students in the program are not required to have their own PC.

Computer Resources/On-line Services

Training	Yes	Multimedia Center	Yes
Internet	Yes	Dialog	Yes
E-Mail	Yes		

Other on-line services: OCLC, First Search.

ADMISSION
Acceptance 1994-95 456 applied for admission; 73% were accepted.
Entrance Requirements Bachelor's degree, GMAT score, minimum 2.5 GPA, minimum 1 year of work experience. Core courses waived through: previous course work.
Application Requirements Written essay, application form, copies of transcript, personal statement, 2 letters of recommendation.
Application Deadlines 6/1 for fall, 11/1 for spring.

FINANCIALS
Costs for 1994-95 Tuition: Full-time: $391/credit. Fees: Full-time: $26/credit. Average room and board costs are $5,400 per academic year (on-campus).
Financial Aid In 1994-95, 40% of candidates received some institutionally administered aid in the form of loans, assistantships. Total awards ranged from $6,200-$7,000. Financial aid is available to part-time students. Application deadlines: 6/30 for fall, 12/1 for spring. Contact: Mr. Frank Dutkovich, Director of Financial Aid, 600 Forbes Avenue, Pittsburgh, PA 15282. (412) 396-6607.

INTERNATIONAL STUDENTS
Demographics 19% of students enrolled in the program are international; Asia 55%, Europe 24%, Africa 6%, South America 4%, other 13%.
Services and Facilities International student center, language tutoring, ESL courses, counseling/support services.
Applying TOEFL required, minimum score of 550; proof of health; proof of adequate funds. Financial aid is available to international students. Assistantships are available for these students. Financial aid application deadlines: 6/1 for fall, 11/1 for spring. Admission application deadlines: 6/1 for fall, 11/1 for spring. Contact: Ms. Valentina DeSilva, International Student Adviser, 601 Duquesne Union, Pittsburgh, PA 15282-1606. (412) 396-6113.

ALTERNATE MBA PROGRAMS
MBA/JD Length of program: Minimum: 48 months. Degree requirements: 116 credits including 24 elective credits. Average class size: 6.
MBA/MLS Length of program: Minimum: 24 months. Maximum: 6 years. Degree requirements: 68 credits including 21 elective credits.
MBA/MS Length of program: Minimum: 26 months. Maximum: 6 years. Degree requirements: 81 credits including 21 elective credits. MS is in industrial pharmacy.
MBA/MSN Length of program: Minimum: 24 months. Maximum: 6 years. Degree requirements: 74 credits including 21 elective credits.
MBA/MS Length of program: Minimum: 24 months. Maximum: 6 years. Degree requirements: 68 credits including 21 elective credits. Internship in business or government agency. MS is in environmental science and management.
MBA/MS Length of program: Minimum: 24 months. Maximum: 6 years. Degree requirements: 80 credits including 24 elective credits. MS is in management information systems.
MBA/MSHMS Length of program: Minimum: 24 months. Maximum: 6 years. Degree requirements: 65 credits including 9 elective credits. 18 prerequisite credits consisting of 12 credits of business and 6 credits of medical sciences.

PLACEMENT
In 1993-94, 42 organizations participated in on-campus recruiting; 83 on-campus interviews were conducted. Placement services include alumni network, career counseling/planning, career fairs, career library, career placement, electronic job bank, job interviews, resume preparation, and resume referral to employers. Of 1994 graduates, 89% were employed within three months of graduation, the average starting salary was $32,500, the range was $25,000-$40,000.

Program Contact: Ms. Mary K. Cunningham, Graduate Adviser, Duquesne University, 600 Forbes Avenue, Pittsburgh, PA 15282. (412) 396-6276; Fax: (412) 396-5304.

Eastern College

St. Davids, Pennsylvania

OVERVIEW
Eastern College is an independent American Baptist comprehensive coed institution. Founded 1932. Setting: 107-acre suburban campus with easy access to Philadelphia. Total institutional enrollment: 2,092. Program was first offered in 1982.

MBA HIGHLIGHTS

Entrance Difficulty***
Mean GMAT: 610
Mean GPA: N/R

Cost $$
Tuition: $340/credit
Room & Board: $3,300 (off-campus)

Total Enrollment: 457

Average Class Size: 15

ACADEMICS
Length of Program Minimum: 24 months. Maximum: 7 years.
Calendar Semesters.
Full-time Classes Main campus; day, evening, summer.
Part-time Classes Main campus; evening, summer.
Degree Requirements 33 credits.
Curricular Focus Entrepreneurship, ethics.
Concentrations Accounting, economics, entrepreneurship, finance, health services, human resources management, international business, management, marketing, nonprofit management, economic development, organizational behavior, public policy, quantitative analysis, strategic management.
Faculty Full-time: 21, 81% with doctorates; part-time: 22, 41% with doctorates.
Teaching Methodology Case study: 20%, lecture: 10%, student presentations: 35%, team projects: 35%.
Special Opportunities International exchange program available. Internships include business development, nonprofit management, and health care administration.

STUDENT STATISTICS
Geographic Representation By region: Northeast 70%.

FACILITIES
Information Resources Main library with 116,875 bound volumes, 326,833 titles on microform, 1,035 periodical subscriptions, 2,708 records/tapes/CDs, 12 CD-ROMs.
Housing College housing not available.
Technology Computers are used moderately in course work. 35 computer terminals/PCs, linked by a campus-wide computer network, are available for use by students in program; they are located in computer labs. Students in the program are not required to have their own PC.
Computer Resources/On-line Services
Training   Yes   E-Mail   No

ADMISSION
Entrance Requirements Bachelor's degree, GMAT score of 450, minimum 2.5 GPA. Core courses waived through: previous course work.
Application Requirements Written essay, interview, application form, copies of transcript, 2 letters of recommendation.
Application Deadline Applications are processed on a rolling basis.

FINANCIALS
Costs for 1995-96 Tuition: Full-time: $340/credit. Average room and board costs are $3,300 per academic year (off-campus).
Financial Aid In 1994-95, 50% of candidates received some institutionally administered aid in the form of scholarships, assistantships. Financial aid is not available to part-time students. Applications are processed on a rolling basis. Contact: Mr. Bruce Palmer, Director of Financial Aid, 10 Fairview Drive, St. Davids, PA 19087. (610) 341-5842.

INTERNATIONAL STUDENTS
Demographics 10% of students on campus are international.
Services and Facilities International student center, visa services, language tutoring, counseling/support services.
Applying TOEFL required; proof of health; proof of adequate funds. Financial aid is available to international students. Applications are processed on a rolling basis. Admission applications are processed on a rolling basis. Contact: Ms. Lisa Pappas, International Student Adviser, 10 Fairview Drive, St. Davids, PA 19087. (610) 341-1454.

ALTERNATE MBA PROGRAM
MBA/M Div Length of program: Minimum: 48 months. Degree requirements: 116 credits.

PLACEMENT
Placement services include alumni network, career counseling/planning, career placement, and resume preparation.

Program Contact: Mr. B. Scott Camilleri, Assistant Director of Graduate Admissions, Eastern College, 10 Fairview Drive, St. Davids, PA 19087. (610) 341-5972; Fax: (610) 341-1466.
See full description on page 724.

Gannon University

Dahlkemper School of Business

Erie, Pennsylvania

OVERVIEW
Gannon University is an independent Roman Catholic comprehensive coed institution. Founded 1925. Setting: 18-acre small-town campus. Total institutional enrollment: 5,000. Program was first offered in 1970.

MBA HIGHLIGHTS

Entrance Difficulty***
Mean GMAT: 520
Mean GPA: 3.2

Cost $$
Tuition: $350/credit
Room & Board: N/R

Enrollment Profile
Full-time: 51   Work Exp: 78%
Part-time: 299   International: 11%
Total: 350   Women: 36%
Average Age: 28   Minorities: 10%

Average Class Size: 15

ACADEMICS
Length of Program Minimum: 12 months.
Calendar Semesters.
Full-time Classes Main campus; evening, weekends, summer.
Part-time Classes Main campus, Warren; evening, weekends, summer.
Degree Requirements 30 credits including 9 elective credits.
Required Courses Business policy, financial management, managerial accounting, managerial economics, marketing management, operations management, organization. Courses may be waived through: previous course work, work experience.
Curricular Focus Business issues and problems, problem solving and decision making, teamwork.
Concentrations Accounting, entrepreneurship, finance, health services, human resources management, management, marketing, operations management, organizational behavior, public administration, public policy, strategic management.
Faculty Full-time: 28, 78% with doctorates; part-time: 42.

Teaching Methodology Case study: 25%, faculty seminars: 5%, lecture: 25%, research: 10%, student presentations: 10%, team projects: 25%.

Special Opportunities Internship program available.

STUDENT STATISTICS

Geographic Representation State residents 80%. By region: Midwest 52%; Northeast 25%; West 7%; South 5%. International 11%.

Undergraduate Majors Business 44%; engineering/technology 21%; humanities 10%; nursing 8%; science/mathematics 11%; social sciences 5%; other 1%.

Other Background Graduate degrees in other disciplines: 5%. Work experience: On average, students have 5 years of work experience on entrance to the program.

FACILITIES

Information Resources Main library with 219,169 bound volumes, 1,527 titles on microform, 1,268 periodical subscriptions, 925 records/tapes/ CDs, 6 CD-ROMs.

Housing 2% of students in program live in college-owned or -operated housing.

Technology Computers are used moderately in course work. 250 computer terminals/PCs, linked by a campus-wide computer network, are available for use by students in program; they are located in learning resource center, the library, the computer center, computer labs, the research center. Students in the program are not required to have their own PC.

Computer Resources/On-line Services

Training	Yes	Multimedia Center	Yes
E-Mail	No		

ADMISSION

Acceptance 1994-95 Of those applying, 85% were accepted.

Entrance Requirements Bachelor's degree, GMAT score of 450, minimum 2.5 GPA. Core courses waived through: previous course work, work experience.

Application Requirements Application form, copies of transcript, 3 letters of recommendation.

Application Deadlines 7/15 for fall, 11/15 for spring.

FINANCIALS

Costs for 1994-95 Tuition: Full-time: $350/credit.

Financial Aid In 1994-95, 38% of candidates received some institutionally administered aid in the form of grants, scholarships, loans, assistantships. Financial aid is available to part-time students. Application deadlines: 7/15 for fall, 11/15 for spring. Contact: Graduate and Adult Academic Services, University Square, Erie, PA 16541. (800) 426-6668.

INTERNATIONAL STUDENTS

Demographics 11% of students enrolled in the program are international.

Services and Facilities ESL courses, special assistance for nonnative speakers of English, counseling/support services.

Applying TOEFL required. Financial aid is available to international students. Financial aid application deadlines: 7/15 for fall, 11/15 for spring. Admission application deadlines: 7/15 for fall, 11/15 for spring. Contact: Dr. Marjorie Krebs, Director of International Students, University Square, Erie, PA 16544. (814) 871-7721.

ALTERNATE MBA PROGRAM

MBA/MSN Length of program: Minimum: 24 months. Maximum: 7 years. Degree requirements: 54 credits.

PLACEMENT

Placement services include alumni network, career counseling/planning, career fairs, career placement, job interviews, resume preparation, and resume referral to employers. Of 1994 graduates, 90% were employed within three months of graduation.

Program Contact: Dr. David Frew, MBA Director, Gannon University, University Square, Erie, PA 16541. (814) 871-7579, or (800) 426-6668; Fax: (814) 871-7210.

Indiana University of Pennsylvania

College of Business

Indiana, Pennsylvania

OVERVIEW

Indiana University of Pennsylvania is a state-supported coed institution. Part of Pennsylvania State System of Higher Education. Founded 1875. Setting: 200-acre small-town campus with easy access to Pittsburgh. Total institutional enrollment: 14,062. Program was first offered in 1970.

MBA HIGHLIGHTS

Entrance Difficulty***
Mean GMAT: 515
Mean GPA: 3.2

Cost $
Tuition: $1,543/semester
(Nonresident: $2,772/semester)
Room & Board: $3,000

Enrollment Profile

Full-time: 92	Work Exp: 55%
Part-time: 48	International: 35%
Total: 140	Women: 38%
Average Age: 26	Minorities: 6%

Average Class Size: 25

The Indiana University of Pennsylvania M.B.A. program has many advantages. It is a public university with the ambiance of a private college. The School offers a high-quality M.B.A. program at an affordable cost. One-year program completion is available for students with undergraduate business majors. Options for concentration are accounting, finance, management information systems, management, and marketing. There is an average class size of 25, with maximum opportunities for interaction with the instructor and for class discussions. There is a strong international focus, with students from over twenty-three countries. Over forty graduate assistantship awards are made, including a 50 percent tuition waiver, and tuition reduction awards are given to qualified international students. Study-abroad opportunities are offered through the University's International Exchange Programs, as well as practical experience opportunities through the College of Business Management Services Group. There is a well-established internship program at regional and national levels. University Career Services provides a CareerLink job search database, on-campus interviewing, résumé referrals, a career library, workshops, and job fairs.

A new $12-million Eberly College of Business complex with state-of-the-art information and instructional technology opens in 1996.

ACADEMICS

Length of Program Minimum: 12 months. Maximum: 5 years.

Calendar Semesters.

Full-time Classes Main campus; day, evening, summer.

Part-time Classes Main campus; evening.

Degree Requirements 33 credits including 9 elective credits.

Required Courses Business policy, economics of corporate decisions, financial management, management accounting, management information systems, marketing management, organizational analysis, quantitative methods. Courses may be waived through: previous course work.

Curricular Focus General management, international business, problem solving and decision making.

Concentrations Accounting, finance, international business, management, management information systems, marketing.

Faculty Full-time: 31, 94% with doctorates.

Teaching Methodology Case study: 15%, lecture: 40%, research: 15%, seminars by members of the business community: 5%, student presentations: 15%, team projects: 10%.

Special Opportunities International exchange in Finland, France, Germany, Spain, United Kingdom. Internships include government, management information systems, marketing, management, and management of nonprofit organizations. Other: small business incubator, business consulting internship program.

STUDENT STATISTICS

Geographic Representation State residents 52%. By region: Northeast 65%. International 35%.

Undergraduate Majors Business 35%; engineering/technology 10%; humanities 15%; science/mathematics 10%; social sciences 15%; other 15%.

Other Background Graduate degrees in other disciplines: 5%. Work experience: On average, students have 2 years of work experience on entrance to the program.

FACILITIES
Information Resources Main library with 731,871 bound volumes, 578,371 titles on microform, 4,724 periodical subscriptions, 35,000 records/tapes/CDs.

Housing 15% of students in program live in college-owned or -operated housing.

Technology Computers are used moderately in course work. 100 computer terminals/PCs, linked by a campus-wide computer network, are available for use by students in program; they are located in dormitories, the library, the computer center, computer labs. Students in the program are not required to have their own PC.

Computer Resources/On-line Services

Training	Yes	LEXIS/NEXIS	Yes
Internet	Yes	CompuServe	No
E-Mail	Yes	Dialog	Yes $

Other on-line services: OCLC.

ADMISSION
Acceptance 1994-95 200 applied for admission; 65% were accepted.

Entrance Requirements Bachelor's degree, GMAT score, minimum 2.75 GPA. Core courses waived through: previous course work.

Application Requirements Written essay, application form, copies of transcript, 2 letters of recommendation.

Application Deadlines 7/30 for fall, 11/1 for spring.

FINANCIALS
Costs for 1994-95 Tuition: Full-time: $1,543/semester for state residents, $2,772/semester for nonresidents. Fees: Full-time: $267/semester for state residents, $267/semester for nonresidents. Average room and board costs are $3,000 per academic year (on-campus) and $3,700 per academic year (off-campus).

Financial Aid In 1994-95, 40% of candidates received some institutionally administered aid in the form of loans, assistantships, work-study. Total awards ranged from $1,500-$10,000. Financial aid is not available to part-time students. Application deadlines: 5/1 for fall, 11/1 for spring. Contact: Dr. Krish S. Krishnan, Director of MBA Program, Business Graduate Programs, Indiana, PA 15705. (412) 357-2522.

INTERNATIONAL STUDENTS
Demographics 35% of students enrolled in the program are international; Europe 40%, Asia 30%, South America 15%, Africa 11%, other 4%.

Services and Facilities International student center, visa services, language tutoring, ESL courses, counseling/support services.

Applying TOEFL required, minimum score of 520; proof of adequate funds. Financial aid is available to international students. Financial aid application deadline: 4/30 for fall. Admission application deadlines: 7/30 for fall, 10/1 for spring. Contact: Ms. Laila Dahan, Director of Office of International Student Services, Sutton Hall, Indiana, PA 15705. (412) 357-2295.

ALTERNATE MBA PROGRAM
Executive MBA (EMBA) Length of program: Minimum: 24 months. Maximum: 2 years. Degree requirements: 51 credits including 9 elective credits. Average class size: 30.

PLACEMENT
In 1993-94, 40 organizations participated in on-campus recruiting. Placement services include alumni network, career counseling/planning, career fairs, career library, career placement, job interviews, resume preparation, and resume referral to employers. Of 1994 graduates, 50% were employed within three months of graduation, the average starting salary range was $28,000-$45,000.

Program Contact: Dr. Krish S. Krishnan, Director, MBA Program, Indiana University of Pennsylvania, Indiana, PA 15705. (412) 357-2522; Fax: (412) 357-6232.

Kutztown University of Pennsylvania

College of Business

Kutztown, Pennsylvania

OVERVIEW
Kutztown University of Pennsylvania is a state-supported comprehensive coed institution. Part of Pennsylvania State System of Higher Education. Founded 1866. Setting: 325-acre small-town campus with easy access to Philadelphia. Total institutional enrollment: 7,916.

ACADEMICS
Calendar Semesters.

Concentration Management.

FACILITIES
Information Resources Main library with 418,839 bound volumes, 1.1 million titles on microform, 1,986 periodical subscriptions, 5,419 records/tapes/CDs, 31 CD-ROMs.

ADMISSION
Application Deadlines 9/1 for fall, 12/25 for spring.

INTERNATIONAL STUDENTS
Applying Admission application deadlines: 9/1 for fall, 12/25 for spring.

Program Contact: Mr. Theodore Hartz, Dean, College of Business, Kutztown University of Pennsylvania, Kutztown, PA 19530. (610) 683-4575; Fax: (610) 683-4010.

La Salle University

School of Business Administration

Philadelphia, Pennsylvania

OVERVIEW
La Salle University is an independent Roman Catholic comprehensive coed institution. Founded 1863. Setting: 120-acre urban campus. Total institutional enrollment: 6,500. Program was first offered in 1976.

MBA HIGHLIGHTS

Entrance Difficulty*
Mean GMAT: 480
Mean GPA: 3.1

Cost $
Tuition: $407/credit
Room & Board: N/R

Enrollment Profile

Full-time: 90	Work Exp: N/R
Part-time: 860	International: 2%
Total: 950	Women: 41%
Average Age: 31	Minorities: 16%

Average Class Size: 25

ACADEMICS
Length of Program Minimum: 24 months. Maximum: 7 years.

Calendar Trimesters.

Full-time Classes Main campus, Doylestown; evening, weekends, summer.

Part-time Classes Main campus, Doylestown; evening, weekends, summer.

Degree Requirements 36 credits.

Curricular Focus Leadership, organizational development and change management, problem solving and decision making.

Concentrations Accounting, finance, human resources management, international business, management, management information systems, marketing, public policy.

Faculty Full-time: 55, 83% with doctorates.

Teaching Methodology Case study: 10%, faculty seminars: 10%, lecture: 30%, research: 10%, seminars by members of the business community: 10%, student presentations: 20%, team projects: 10%.

Special Opportunities Internship program available.

STUDENT STATISTICS
Geographic Representation State residents 97%. International 2%.

455

FACILITIES

Information Resources Main library with 347,000 bound volumes, 36,470 titles on microform, 1,650 periodical subscriptions, 3,250 records/tapes/CDs, 9 CD-ROMs.

Housing College housing available.

Technology Computers are used heavily in course work. Students in the program are not required to have their own PC.

Computer Resources/On-line Services

Training	Yes	Videoconference Center	Yes
E-Mail	Yes	Multimedia Center	Yes

ADMISSION

Acceptance 1994-95 643 applied for admission; 68% were accepted.

Entrance Requirements Bachelor's degree, GMAT score. Core courses waived through: previous course work, work experience.

Application Requirements Application form, copies of transcript, resume/curriculum vitae.

Application Deadlines 8/1 for fall, 12/1 for spring. Applications are processed on a rolling basis.

FINANCIALS

Costs for 1994-95 Tuition: Part-time evening: $407/credit.

Financial Aid In 1994-95, candidates received some institutionally administered aid in the form of scholarships, loans, assistantships. Total awards ranged from $600-$2,400. Financial aid is not available to part-time students. Application deadlines: 8/1 for fall, 12/1 for spring. Contact: Mr. Brian Niles, School of Business Administration, 20th Street at Olney Avenue, Philadelphia, PA 19141-1199. (215) 951-1057.

INTERNATIONAL STUDENTS

Demographics 2% of students enrolled in the program are international.

Services and Facilities International student office, international student center, language tutoring, ESL courses, counseling/support services.

Applying TOEFL required, minimum score of 550; proof of health; proof of adequate funds. Financial aid is not available to international students. Admission application deadlines: 8/1 for fall, 12/1 for spring. Applications are processed on a rolling basis.

Program Contact: School of Business Administration, La Salle University, 20th Street at Olney Avenue, Philadelphia, PA 19141-1199. (215) 951-1057; Fax: (215) 951-1886.

Lehigh University

College of Business and Economics

Bethlehem, Pennsylvania

OVERVIEW

Lehigh University is an independent nonprofit coed institution. Founded 1865. Setting: 1,600-acre small-town campus with easy access to Philadelphia. Total institutional enrollment: 6,400. Program was first offered in 1952. AACSB-accredited.

MBA HIGHLIGHTS

Entrance Difficulty***
Mean GMAT: 574
Mean GPA: 3.2

Cost $$$
Tuition: $525/credit hour
Room & Board: $5,700

Enrollment Profile

Full-time: 72	Work Exp: 85%
Part-time: 267	International: 7%
Total: 339	Women: 35%
Average Age: 30	Minorities: 3%

Average Class Size: 20

ACADEMICS

Length of Program Minimum: 12 months. Maximum: 6 years.

Calendar Semesters.

Full-time Classes Main campus.

Part-time Classes Main campus, distance learning option; evening, summer.

Degree Requirements 30-48 credit hours including 9 elective credit hours.

Required Courses Business law, finance, financial accounting, information systems, macroeconomics, management, management policy, managerial accounting, marketing, microeconomics, operations management, quantitative methods, statistics. Courses may be waived through: previous course work.

Curricular Focus Business issues and problems, problem solving and decision making, strategic analysis and planning.

Concentration Management.

Faculty Full-time: 57, 97% with doctorates; part-time: 7, 50% with doctorates.

Special Opportunities International exchange in France.

STUDENT STATISTICS

Geographic Representation International 7%.

Undergraduate Majors Business 45%; education 2%; engineering/technology 36%; science/mathematics 7%; social sciences 10%.

Other Background Graduate degrees in other disciplines: 12%. Work experience: On average, students have 4 years of work experience on entrance to the program.

FACILITIES

Information Resources Main library with 1.1 million bound volumes, 1.7 million titles on microform, 10,510 periodical subscriptions, 30,000 records/tapes/CDs, 57 CD-ROMs.

Housing College housing available.

Technology Computers are used moderately in course work. 430 computer terminals/PCs, linked by a campus-wide computer network, are available for use by students in program; they are located in classrooms, the computer center, computer labs. Students in the program are not required to have their own PC.

Computer Resources/On-line Services

Training	Yes	LEXIS/NEXIS	Yes
Internet	Yes	CompuServe	Yes
E-Mail	Yes	Dow Jones	Yes
Multimedia Center	Yes		

ADMISSION

Acceptance 1994-95 Of those applying, 54% were accepted.

Entrance Requirements Bachelor's degree, GMAT score. Core courses waived through: previous course work.

Application Requirements Written essay, application form, copies of transcript, 2 letters of recommendation.

Application Deadlines 7/15 for fall, 12/1 for spring, 5/1 for summer.

FINANCIALS

Costs for 1994-95 Tuition: Full-time: $525/credit hour. Average room and board costs are $5,700 per academic year (on-campus) and $4,800 per academic year (off-campus).

Financial Aid In 1994-95, 46% of candidates received some institutionally administered aid in the form of scholarships, assistantships. Total awards ranged from $1,000-$14,475. Financial aid is available to part-time students. Application deadline: 2/1 for fall. Contact: Ms. Kathleen Trexler, Assistant Dean and Director, MBA Program, 27 Memorial Drive West, Bethlehem, PA 18015-3094. (610) 758-3418.

INTERNATIONAL STUDENTS

Demographics 7% of students enrolled in the program are international; Asia 63%, Europe 25%, South America 6%, other 6%.

Services and Facilities Language tutoring, ESL courses, counseling/support services.

Applying TOEFL required, minimum score of 580; proof of health; proof of adequate funds. Financial aid is not available to international students. Admission application deadlines: 7/15 for fall, 12/1 for spring, 5/1 for summer. Contact: Ms. Anne Thomas, Director, International Education, 5 East Packer Avenue, Bethlehem, PA 18015. (610) 758-4859.

PLACEMENT

Placement services include alumni network, career counseling/planning, career fairs, career library, career placement, job interviews, resume preparation, and resume referral to employers. Of 1994 graduates, the average starting salary was $45,105, the range was $32,000-$60,000.

Program Contact: Ms. Kathleen Trexler, Assistant Dean and Director, MBA Program, Lehigh University, 27 Memorial Drive West, Bethlehem, PA 18015. (610) 758-3418; Fax: (610) 758-4499; Internet Address: kat3@lehigh.edu.

Marywood College

Business and Managerial Science Department

Scranton, Pennsylvania

OVERVIEW

Marywood College is an independent Roman Catholic comprehensive coed institution. Founded 1915. Setting: suburban campus. Total institutional enrollment: 4,500. Program was first offered in 1980.

MBA HIGHLIGHTS

Entrance Difficulty*
Mean GMAT: 501
Mean GPA: 2.9

Cost $$
Tuition: $6,300
Room & Board: $4,500

Enrollment Profile

Full-time: 11	Work Exp: 100%
Part-time: 90	International: 3%
Total: 101	Women: 33%
Average Age: 38	Minorities: 2%

Average Class Size: 15

ACADEMICS

Length of Program Minimum: 24 months. Maximum: 7 years.
Calendar Semesters.
Full-time Classes Main campus; evening, weekends, summer.
Part-time Classes Main campus; evening, weekends, summer.
Degree Requirements 36 credits. Other: Comprehensive exam.
Required Courses Financial planning and management, legal aspects of the administrative process, management information systems, operation analysis and management, organizational behavior, policy formulation and strategy management, research methodology.
Curricular Focus Economic and financial theory, general management, information and telecommunication systems.
Concentrations Finance, health services, industrial management, international business, management information systems.
Faculty Full-time: 7, 100% with doctorates; part-time: 6, 50% with doctorates.
Teaching Methodology Case study: 20%, faculty seminars: 10%, lecture: 40%, research: 5%, student presentations: 5%, team projects: 20%.
Special Opportunities Internships include health services.

STUDENT STATISTICS

Geographic Representation By region: Northeast 97%. International 3%.
Other Background Graduate degrees in other disciplines: 5%. Work experience: On average, students have 5 years of work experience on entrance to the program.

FACILITIES

Information Resources Main library with 202,015 bound volumes, 221,089 titles on microform, 1,192 periodical subscriptions, 41,318 records/tapes/CDs, 9 CD-ROMs.
Housing 3% of students in program live in college-owned or -operated housing.
Technology Computers are used moderately in course work. 130 computer terminals/PCs, linked by a campus-wide computer network, are available for use by students in program; they are located in learning resource center, the library, the computer center, computer labs. Students in the program are not required to have their own PC.

Computer Resources/On-line Services

Training	Yes	Multimedia Center	Yes
Internet	Yes	Dialog	Yes $
E-Mail	Yes		

Other on-line services: OCLC.

ADMISSION

Acceptance 1994-95 52 applied for admission; 73% were accepted.
Entrance Requirements Bachelor's degree, prerequisite courses required for applicants with non-business degree, GMAT score. Core courses waived through: previous course work.

Application Requirements Application form, copies of transcript, 2 letters of recommendation.
Application Deadline Applications are processed on a rolling basis.

FINANCIALS

Costs for 1994-95 Tuition: Full-time: $6,300. Fees: Full-time: $140. Average room and board costs are $4,500 per academic year (on-campus).
Financial Aid In 1994-95, 50% of candidates received some institutionally administered aid in the form of scholarships, loans, assistantships. Total awards ranged from $1,000-$18,500. Financial aid is available to part-time students. Application deadlines: 7/1 for fall, 11/1 for spring. Contact: Mr. Stanley F. Skrutski, Director of Financial Aid, 2300 Adams Avenue, Scranton, PA 18509. (717) 348-6225.

INTERNATIONAL STUDENTS

Demographics 3% of students enrolled in the program are international.
Services and Facilities Visa services, language tutoring, special assistance for nonnative speakers of English, counseling/support services.
Applying TOEFL required, minimum score of 500; affidavit of support and $1,000 deposit. Financial aid is not available to international students. Admission application deadlines: 6/1 for fall, 11/1 for spring. Contact: Sr. Dolores Filicko, Registrar, 2300 Adams Avenue, Scranton, PA 18509. (717) 348-6281.

PLACEMENT

Placement services include alumni network, career counseling/planning, career fairs, career placement, resume preparation, and resume referral to employers. Of 1994 graduates, the average starting salary was $40,000, the range was $35,000-$95,000.
Jobs by Functional Area Finance 64%; management 12%; other 24%.

Program Contact: Graduate Director of Admissions, Marywood College, School of Graduate Studies, 2300 Adams Avenue, Scranton, PA 18509. (717) 348-6274; Fax: (717) 348-1817.

Moravian College

Bethlehem, Pennsylvania

OVERVIEW

Moravian College is an independent comprehensive coed institution, affiliated with Moravian Church. Founded 1742. Setting: 80-acre suburban campus with easy access to Philadelphia. Total institutional enrollment: 1,400. Program was first offered in 1985.

MBA HIGHLIGHTS

Entrance Difficulty**
Mean GMAT: 490
Mean GPA: 3.0

Cost $
Tuition: $1,100/course
Room & Board: N/R

Enrollment Profile

Full-time: 5	Work Exp: 98%
Part-time: 185	International: 1%
Total: 190	Women: 40%
Average Age: 30	Minorities: 4%

Average Class Size: 30

ACADEMICS

Length of Program Minimum: 24 months. Maximum: 7 years.
Calendar Semesters.
Part-time Classes Main campus; evening, summer.
Degree Requirements 30 credits including 6 elective credits.
Required Courses Advanced financial management, advanced human resources management, advanced managerial accounting, advanced production and operations management, business, law, and society, management strategy, marketing strategy, organizational behavior. Courses may be waived through: previous course work.
Curricular Focus Business issues and problems, general management, problem solving and decision making.
Concentration Management.
Faculty Full-time: 11, 80% with doctorates; part-time: 5, 40% with doctorates.

Teaching Methodology Case study: 30%, lecture: 50%, student presentations: 10%, team projects: 10%.

STUDENT STATISTICS

Geographic Representation State residents 75%. By region: Northeast 100%. International 1%.

Undergraduate Majors Business 60%; engineering/technology 20%; humanities 10%; social sciences 10%.

Other Background Graduate degrees in other disciplines: 10%. Work experience: On average, students have 5-8 years of work experience on entrance to the program.

FACILITIES

Information Resources Main library with 225,000 bound volumes, 4,840 titles on microform, 1,354 periodical subscriptions, 5,000 records/tapes/CDs, 12 CD-ROMs.

Housing College housing not available.

Technology Computers are used moderately in course work. 25 computer terminals/PCs, linked by a campus-wide computer network, are available for use by students in program; they are located in the computer center, computer labs. Students in the program are not required to have their own PC.

Computer Resources/On-line Services

Training	No	Dun's	No
Internet	No	Dow Jones	Yes
E-Mail	No	Dialog	No
LEXIS/NEXIS	No	Bloomberg	No
CompuServe	No		

ADMISSION

Acceptance 1994-95 Of those applying, 75% were accepted.

Entrance Requirements Bachelor's degree, GMAT score. Core courses waived through: previous course work.

Application Requirements Application form, copies of transcript, 2 letters of recommendation.

Application Deadline Applications are processed on a rolling basis.

FINANCIALS

Costs for 1994-95 Tuition: Part-time evening: $1,100/course.

Financial Aid In 1994-95, 3% of candidates received some form of institutionally administered aid. Financial aid is not available to part-time students. Contact: Dr. Thomas L. Parkinson, Director of the MBA Program, 1200 Main Street, Bethlehem, PA 18018-6650. (610) 861-1559.

INTERNATIONAL STUDENTS

Demographics 1% of students enrolled in the program are international; Europe 100%.

Applying TOEFL required, minimum score of 480; proof of adequate funds. Financial aid is not available to international students. Admission applications are processed on a rolling basis.

Program Contact: Dr. Thomas L. Parkinson, Director of the MBA Program, Moravian College, 1200 Main Street, Bethlehem, PA 18018-6650. (610) 861-1559; Fax: (610) 861-1466; Internet Address: parkinst@moravian.edu.

Pennsylvania State University at Erie, The Behrend College

School of Business

Erie, Pennsylvania

OVERVIEW

Pennsylvania State University at Erie, The Behrend College is a state-related comprehensive coed institution. Part of Pennsylvania State University. Founded 1948. Setting: 708-acre suburban campus. Total institutional enrollment: 3,133. Program was first offered in 1985.

MBA HIGHLIGHTS

Entrance Difficulty*
Mean GMAT: 523
Mean GPA: 3.2

Cost $
Tuition: $267/credit
(Nonresident: $515/credit)
Room & Board: N/R

Enrollment Profile

Full-time: 7	Work Exp: 92%
Part-time: 131	International: N/R
Total: 138	Women: 40%
Average Age: 30	Minorities: 4%

Average Class Size: 18

ACADEMICS

Length of Program Minimum: 15 months. Maximum: 8 years.

Calendar Semesters.

Full-time Classes Main campus; evening, weekends, summer.

Part-time Classes Main campus; evening, weekends, summer.

Degree Requirements 48 credits including 12 elective credits. Other: Minimum 3.0 GPA.

Required Courses Business communication, financial and managerial accounting, financial management, information systems in organizations, legal/political/social environment of business, managerial economics, marketing: statistics for modern business decision making, operations management, organizations, principles of management, strategic planning and policy. Courses may be waived through: previous course work.

Curricular Focus Business issues and problems, general management, problem solving and decision making.

Concentrations Accounting, economics, entrepreneurship, finance, human resources management, international business, management, management information systems, marketing, quantitative analysis, strategic management.

Faculty Full-time: 22, 91% with doctorates; part-time: 1.

Teaching Methodology Case study: 15%, faculty seminars: 1%, individual projects: 5%, lecture: 54%, research: 3%, seminars by members of the business community: 2%, student presentations: 8%, team projects: 12%.

Special Opportunities International exchange in Australia, Egypt, France, Germany, Greece, Israel, Italy, Japan, Kenya, Mexico, Netherlands, People's Republic of China, Russia, Spain, Sweden, Taiwan, United Kingdom. Internship program available.

STUDENT STATISTICS

Geographic Representation State residents 98%. By region: Northeast 100%.

Undergraduate Majors Business 35%; education 1%; engineering/technology 35%; humanities 9%; science/mathematics 13%; social sciences 4%; other 3%.

Other Background Graduate degrees in other disciplines: 3%. Work experience: On average, students have 4 years of work experience on entrance to the program.

FACILITIES

Information Resources Main library with 79,709 bound volumes, 35,460 titles on microform, 972 periodical subscriptions, 1,672 records/tapes/CDs. Business collection includes 6,900 bound volumes, 266 periodical subscriptions, 4 CD-ROMs.

Housing College housing not available.

Technology Computers are used moderately in course work. 145 computer terminals/PCs, linked by a campus-wide computer network, are available for use by students in program; they are located in the library, the computer center, computer labs. Students in the program are not required to have their own PC.

Computer Resources/On-line Services

Training	Yes	LEXIS/NEXIS	No
Internet	Yes	Dun's	No
E-Mail	Yes	Dow Jones	No
Videoconference Center	Yes	Dialog	Yes
Multimedia Center	Yes	Bloomberg	No

ADMISSION

Acceptance 1994-95 73 applied for admission; 85% were accepted.

Entrance Requirements Bachelor's degree, GMAT score. Core courses waived through: previous course work.

Application Requirements Written essay, application form, copies of transcript, 3 letters of recommendation.

Application Deadlines 8/15 for fall, 12/15 for spring.

FINANCIALS
Costs for 1994-95 Tuition: Full-time: $267/credit for state residents, $515/credit for nonresidents. Fees: Full-time: $35/semester for state residents, $35/semester for nonresidents.

Financial Aid In 1994-95, 9% of candidates received some institutionally administered aid in the form of loans, work-study. Total awards ranged from $800-$12,000. Financial aid is available to part-time students. Application deadlines: 2/15 for fall, 9/15 for spring. Contact: Ms. Kate Delfino, Assistant Director of Admissions and Financial Aid, Station Road, Erie, PA 16563. (814) 898-6162.

INTERNATIONAL STUDENTS
Demographics 1% of students on campus are international; Asia 100%.

Services and Facilities Language tutoring, special assistance for nonnative speakers of English, counseling/support services.

Applying TOEFL required, minimum score of 550; proof of adequate funds. Financial aid is not available to international students. Admission application deadlines: 4/30 for fall, 8/31 for spring.

PLACEMENT
Placement services include alumni network, career counseling/planning, career fairs, career library, career placement, electronic job bank, job interviews, resume preparation, and resume referral to employers. Of 1994 graduates, 80% were employed within three months of graduation.

Jobs by Employer Type Manufacturing 64%; service 29%; nonprofit 7%.

Program Contact: Ms. Melissa Grimm, Admissions Counselor, Pennsylvania State University at Erie, The Behrend College, Office of Admissions, Erie, PA 16563. (814) 898-6100; Fax: (814) 898-6461.

Pennsylvania State University at Harrisburg—The Capital College

School of Business Administration

Middletown, Pennsylvania

OVERVIEW
Pennsylvania State University at Harrisburg—The Capital College is a state-related upper-level coed institution. Part of Pennsylvania State University. Founded 1966. Setting: 218-acre suburban campus. Total institutional enrollment: 3,600. Program was first offered in 1984.

MBA HIGHLIGHTS
Entrance Difficulty*
Mean GMAT: 530
Mean GPA: 3.1

Cost $
Tuition: $267/credit
(Nonresident: $515/credit)
Room & Board: $4,698

Enrollment Profile

Full-time: 10	Work Exp: 99%
Part-time: 170	International: 2%
Total: 180	Women: 33%
Average Age: 32	Minorities: 4%

Average Class Size: 20

ACADEMICS
Length of Program Minimum: 18 months. Maximum: 6 years.

Calendar Semesters.

Full-time Classes Main campus; evening, summer.

Part-time Classes Main campus; evening, summer.

Degree Requirements 48 credits including 12 elective credits.

Required Courses Business in a global society, business policy formulation, business research methods, financial accounting, financial concepts, information systems in management, managerial accounting, managerial

economics, marketing management, operations management, organizational behavior, statistical analysis for business decisions. Courses may be waived through: previous course work.

Curricular Focus Organizational development and change management, problem solving and decision making, strategic analysis and planning.

Concentrations Accounting, economics, finance, human resources management, international business, management, management information systems, marketing, operations management, organizational behavior, strategic management.

Faculty Full-time: 25, 100% with doctorates.

Teaching Methodology Case study: 20%, lecture: 40%, research: 5%, seminars by members of the business community: 3%, student presentations: 12%, team projects: 20%.

STUDENT STATISTICS
Geographic Representation State residents 95%. By region: Northeast 95%; South 1%; Midwest 1%; West 1%. International 2%.

Undergraduate Majors Business 55%; education 3%; engineering/technology 25%; humanities 3%; science/mathematics 10%; social sciences 3%; other 1%.

Other Background Graduate degrees in other disciplines: 2%. Work experience: On average, students have 5 years of work experience on entrance to the program.

FACILITIES
Information Resources Main library with 185,804 bound volumes, 1.1 million titles on microform, 1,563 periodical subscriptions, 1,971 records/tapes/CDs. Business collection includes 35,200 bound volumes, 300 periodical subscriptions, 8 CD-ROMs.

Housing 2% of students in program live in college-owned or -operated housing.

Technology Computers are used moderately in course work. 115 computer terminals/PCs, linked by a campus-wide computer network, are available for use by students in program; they are located in the library, the computer center, computer labs. Students in the program are not required to have their own PC.

Computer Resources/On-line Services

Training	Yes	CompuServe	No
Internet	Yes	Dow Jones	Yes
E-Mail	Yes	Dialog	Yes $
LEXIS/NEXIS	Yes	Bloomberg	No

Other on-line services: First Search, Carl, RLIN.

ADMISSION
Acceptance 1994-95 Of those applying, 85% were accepted.

Entrance Requirements Bachelor's degree, GMAT score. Core courses waived through: previous course work.

Application Requirements Written essay, application form, copies of transcript, personal statement.

Application Deadlines 7/18 for fall, 11/18 for spring, 4/18 for summer.

FINANCIALS
Costs for 1994-95 Tuition: Full-time: $267/credit for state residents, $515/credit for nonresidents. Average room and board costs are $4,698 per academic year (on-campus) and $4,698 per academic year (off-campus).

Financial Aid In 1994-95, candidates received some institutionally administered aid in the form of scholarships, assistantships, work-study. Total awards ranged from $1,000-$12,000. Financial aid is available to part-time students. Application deadline: 2/15 for following year. Contact: Ms. Donna Howard, Administrative Specialist, 777 West Harrisburg Pike, Middletown, PA 17057-4898. (717) 948-6307.

INTERNATIONAL STUDENTS
Demographics 2% of students enrolled in the program are international; Asia 85%, South America 10%, other 5%.

Services and Facilities International student center, visa services, counseling/support services.

Applying TOEFL required, minimum score of 550; proof of adequate funds. Financial aid is not available to international students. Admission application deadlines: 4/18 for fall, 7/18 for spring, 11/18 for summer. Contact: Ms. Joan Swetz, International Student Adviser, 777 West Harrisburg Pike, Middletown, PA 17057-4898. (717) 948-6025.

PLACEMENT
In 1993-94, 18 organizations participated in on-campus recruiting. Placement services include alumni network, career counseling/planning, career fairs, career placement, electronic job bank, job interviews, resume preparation, and resume referral to employers.

Program Contact: Dr. Gayle J. Yaverbaum, Director of Graduate Programs, Pennsylvania State University at Harrisburg—The Capital College, 777 West Harrisburg Pike, Middletown, PA 17057-4898. (717) 948-6140; Fax: (717) 948-6456.

Pennsylvania State University University Park Campus

The Smeal College of Business Administration

State College, Pennsylvania

OVERVIEW
Pennsylvania State University University Park Campus is a state-related coed institution. Part of Pennsylvania State University. Founded 1855. Setting: 5,160-acre small-town campus. Total institutional enrollment: 37,658. Program was first offered in 1959. AACSB-accredited.

MBA HIGHLIGHTS

Entrance Difficulty**
Mean GMAT: N/R
Mean GPA: 3.1

Cost $
Tuition: $2,777/semester
(Nonresident: $5,663/semester)
Room & Board: N/R

Enrollment Profile
Full-time: 247	Work Exp: 81%
Part-time: 14	International: 20%
Total: 261	Women: 27%
Average Age: 26	Minorities: 19%

Average Class Size: 38

ACADEMICS
Length of Program Minimum: 18 months. Maximum: 6 years.
Calendar Semesters.
Full-time Classes Main campus; day.
Degree Requirements 48 credits including 22 elective credits.
Required Courses Accounting, communications, economics, ethics, finance, management, marketing, operations management, quantitative business analysis, statistics, strategy.
Curricular Focus Communications, problem solving and decision making, teamwork.
Concentrations Accounting, entrepreneurship, finance, health services, human resources management, international business, logistics, management, management information systems, marketing, operations management, organizational behavior, quantitative analysis, real estate, transportation.
Faculty Full-time: 20, 100% with doctorates.
Teaching Methodology Case study, lecture, research, seminars by members of the business community, student presentations, team projects.
Special Opportunities International exchange in Australia, Belgium, Denmark, Finland, France, Germany, Hong Kong, Italy, New Zealand, Norway, Singapore, Spain, United Kingdom. Internship program available.

STUDENT STATISTICS
Geographic Representation State residents 44%. By region: Northeast 51%; South 10%; Midwest 8%; West 3%. International 20%.
Undergraduate Majors Business 36%; engineering/technology 24%; science/mathematics 5%; social sciences 25%; other 10%.
Other Background Graduate degrees in other disciplines: 5%. Work experience: On average, students have 3 years of work experience on entrance to the program.

FACILITIES
Information Resources Main library with 2.5 million bound volumes, 1.9 million titles on microform, 27,634 periodical subscriptions, 35,733 records/tapes/CDs. Business collection includes 329,000 bound volumes, 1,600 periodical subscriptions, 16 CD-ROMs.
Housing 15% of students in program live in college-owned or -operated housing.
Technology Computers are used heavily in course work. 894 computer terminals/PCs, linked by a campus-wide computer network, are available for use by students in program; they are located in the library, the computer center, computer labs. Students in the program are not required to have their own PC.

Computer Resources/On-line Services
Training	Yes	CompuServe	Yes
Internet	Yes	Dun's	Yes
E-Mail	Yes	Dow Jones	Yes
LEXIS/NEXIS	Yes	Dialog	Yes

Other on-line services: OCLC, RLIN.

ADMISSION
Acceptance 1994-95 Of those applying, 27% were accepted.
Entrance Requirements Bachelor's degree, GMAT score of 500, minimum 2.2 GPA, minimum 2 years of work experience.
Application Requirements Written essay, interview, application form, copies of transcript, 2 letters of recommendation.
Application Deadline 6/1 for fall.

FINANCIALS
Costs for 1994-95 Tuition: Full-time: $2,777/semester for state residents, $5,663/semester for nonresidents; Part-time day: $234/credit for state residents, $473/credit for nonresidents. Fees: Full-time: $235 for state residents, $235 for nonresidents.
Financial Aid In 1994-95, 55% of candidates received some institutionally administered aid in the form of grants, scholarships, loans, assistantships, work-study. Total awards ranged from $1,000-$7,500. Financial aid is not available to part-time students. Application deadline: 2/15 for fall. Contact: Office of Student Aid, 314 Shields Building, 201 Old Main, University Park, PA 16802-1503. (814) 865-6301.

INTERNATIONAL STUDENTS
Demographics 20% of students enrolled in the program are international; Asia 75%, Europe 10%, South America 10%, Africa 5%.
Services and Facilities International student office, international student center, visa services, language tutoring, ESL courses, special assistance for nonnative speakers of English, counseling/support services.
Applying TOEFL required, minimum score of 550; proof of health; proof of adequate funds. Financial aid is not available to international students. Admission application deadline: 4/30 for fall.

PLACEMENT
In 1993-94, 150 organizations participated in on-campus recruiting; 861 on-campus interviews were conducted. Placement services include alumni network, career counseling/planning, career fairs, career library, career placement, job interviews, national recruitment consortia, resume preparation, and resume referral to employers. Of 1994 graduates, 89% were employed within three months of graduation, the average starting salary was $46,244, the range was $23,700-$75,500.
Jobs by Employer Type Manufacturing 47%; service 38%; government 9%; consulting 6%.
Jobs by Functional Area Marketing/sales 21%; finance 32%; operations 13%; management 9%; strategic planning 15%; consulting 7%; other 3%.

Program Contact: Mr. James Hoy, Admissions Manager, Pennsylvania State University University Park Campus, 201 Old Main, University Park, PA 16802-1503. (814) 865-4700.

Philadelphia College of Textiles and Science

School of Business Administration

Philadelphia, Pennsylvania

OVERVIEW
Philadelphia College of Textiles and Science is an independent nonprofit comprehensive coed institution. Founded 1884. Setting: 100-acre suburban campus. Total institutional enrollment: 3,297. Program was first offered in 1976.

MBA HIGHLIGHTS

Entrance Difficulty***
Mean GMAT: 500
Mean GPA: N/R

Cost $$
Tuition: $359/credit hour
Room & Board: $5,500 (off-campus)

Enrollment Profile

Full-time: 135	Work Exp: N/R
Part-time: 446	International: 16%
Total: 581	Women: 45%
Average Age: N/R	Minorities: N/R

Average Class Size: 15

ACADEMICS

Length of Program Minimum: 24 months.

Calendar Semesters.

Full-time Classes Main campus; evening.

Part-time Classes Main campus; evening.

Degree Requirements 37 credits.

Required Courses Accounting for management decisions, art of negotiation: power, politics, conflict and ethics, financial policy and planning, management communications, management of information through technology, managing in the 21st century, manufacturing and operations management, strategic marketing management, strategic planning in a global environment.

Curricular Focus International business, leadership, strategic analysis and planning.

Concentrations Accounting, finance, health services, international business, management, marketing, taxation.

Faculty Full-time: 12, 80% with doctorates; part-time: 20, 40% with doctorates.

Teaching Methodology Case study: 20%, faculty seminars: 10%, lecture: 30%, research: 10%, student presentations: 10%, team projects: 20%.

STUDENT STATISTICS

Geographic Representation State residents 84%. International 16%.

FACILITIES

Information Resources Main library with 85,000 bound volumes, 5,000 titles on microform, 1,800 periodical subscriptions, 800 records/tapes/CDs, 42 CD-ROMs.

Housing College housing not available.

ADMISSION

Acceptance 1994-95 Of those applying, 42% were accepted.

Entrance Requirements Bachelor's degree, GMAT score. Core courses waived through: previous course work, work experience.

Application Requirements Application form, copies of transcript, personal statement, 2 letters of recommendation.

Application Deadline Applications are processed on a rolling basis.

FINANCIALS

Costs for 1994-95 Tuition: Full-time: $359/credit hour. Average room and board costs are $5,500 per academic year (off-campus).

Financial Aid In 1994-95, 20% of candidates received some institutionally administered aid in the form of loans, assistantships. Financial aid is available to part-time students. Application deadlines: 4/15 for fall, 11/30 for spring. Applications are processed on a rolling basis. Contact: Ms. Lisa Cooper, Director of Financial Aid, School House Lane and Henry Avenue, Philadelphia, PA 19144. (215) 951-2940.

INTERNATIONAL STUDENTS

Demographics 16% of students enrolled in the program are international.

Services and Facilities International student office, international student center, language tutoring, counseling/support services.

Applying TOEFL required, minimum score of 550; proof of health; proof of adequate funds. Financial aid is not available to international students. Admission application deadlines: 6/1 for fall, 10/1 for spring. Applications are processed on a rolling basis.

ALTERNATE MBA PROGRAM
MBA/MS

PLACEMENT

Placement services include career counseling/planning, career fairs, job interviews, resume preparation, and resume referral to employers.

Program Contact: Ms. Beth Vorosmarti, Director of Graduate Admissions, Philadelphia College of Textiles and Science, School House Lane and Henry Avenue, Philadelphia, PA 19144. (215) 951-2943; Fax: (215) 951-2907.
See full description on page 802.

Point Park College

Department of Business, Accounting, and Computer Sciences

Pittsburgh, Pennsylvania

OVERVIEW

Point Park College is an independent nonprofit comprehensive coed institution. Founded 1960. Setting: urban campus with easy access to Pittsburgh. Total institutional enrollment: 2,408. Program was first offered in 1984.

MBA HIGHLIGHTS

Entrance Difficulty***
Mean GMAT: 540
Mean GPA: 2.87

Cost $
Tuition: $313/credit
Room & Board: $6,960

Enrollment Profile

Full-time: 33	Work Exp: 76%
Part-time: 46	International: 38%
Total: 79	Women: 37%
Average Age: 33	Minorities: 13%

Average Class Size: 17

ACADEMICS

Length of Program Minimum: 16 months. Maximum: 6 years.

Calendar Semesters.

Full-time Classes Main campus; evening, weekends, summer.

Part-time Classes Main campus; evening, weekends, summer.

Degree Requirements 39 credits including 12-18 elective credits. Other: Language requirement.

Required Courses East Asian survey, European survey, Latin American survey, Middle East survey, cross-cultural management, international business, international financial management, international legal environments, international managerial economics, international marketing management, international political economy, international relations, international studies, statistics and quantitative methods.

Curricular Focus Business issues and problems, international business, strategic analysis and planning.

Concentration International business.

Faculty Full-time: 4, 3% with doctorates; part-time: 6, 1% with doctorates.

Teaching Methodology Case study: 9%, faculty seminars: 1%, lecture: 76%, research: 1%, seminars by members of the business community: 2%, student presentations: 6%, team projects: 5%.

Special Opportunities International exchange in Mexico. Internships include marketing, commerce, logistics, and corporate law.

STUDENT STATISTICS

Geographic Representation State residents 58%. International 38%.

Undergraduate Majors Business 35%; education 3%; engineering/technology 19%; humanities 5%; science/mathematics 6%; social sciences 14%; other 18%.

Other Background Graduate degrees in other disciplines: 3%. Work experience: On average, students have 9 years of work experience on entrance to the program.

FACILITIES

Information Resources Main library with 124,294 bound volumes, 27,734 titles on microform, 449 periodical subscriptions, 3,126 records/tapes/CDs, 3 CD-ROMs. Business collection includes 6,000 bound volumes, 500 periodical subscriptions, 11 CD-ROMs, 254 videos.

Housing 6% of students in program live in college-owned or -operated housing.

Technology Computers are used heavily in course work. 32 computer terminals/PCs are available for use by students in program; they are

---

located in computer labs. Students in the program are not required to have their own PC.

Computer Resources/On-line Services

Training	Yes	Dun's	No
Internet	Yes	Dow Jones	No
E-Mail	Yes	Dialog	No
LEXIS/NEXIS	No	Bloomberg	No
CompuServe	No		

Other on-line services: OCLC, First Search.

ADMISSION

Acceptance 1994-95 133 applied for admission; 36% were accepted.

Entrance Requirements Bachelor's degree, 22 prerequisite credits are required, GMAT score, minimum 2.75 GPA.

Application Requirements Application form, copies of transcript, personal statement, 2 letters of recommendation.

Application Deadlines 7/15 for fall, 11/30 for spring, 3/15 for summer. Applications are processed on a rolling basis.

FINANCIALS

Costs for 1994-95 Tuition: Full-time: $313/credit. Average room and board costs are $6,960 per academic year (on-campus).

Financial Aid In 1994-95, 52% of candidates received some institutionally administered aid in the form of grants, scholarships, loans, assistantships. Total awards ranged from $450-$2,817. Financial aid is available to part-time students. Application deadlines: 7/1 for fall, 11/15 for spring, 3/1 for summer. Applications are processed on a rolling basis. Contact: Ms. Wendy Dunlap, Financial Aid Supervisor, 201 Wood Street, Pittsburgh, PA 15222-1984. (412) 392-3930.

INTERNATIONAL STUDENTS

Demographics 38% of students enrolled in the program are international; Asia 48%, South America 21%, North America 7%, Europe 6%, Africa 5%, Australia 2%, other 11%.

Services and Facilities International student office, international student center, ESL courses, counseling/support services.

Applying TOEFL required, minimum score of 500; proof of health; proof of adequate funds; minimum score of 5.0 on Test of Standard Written English. Financial aid is available to international students. Financial aid application deadlines: 7/1 for fall, 11/15 for spring, 3/1 for summer. Applications are processed on a rolling basis. Admission application deadlines: 7/1 for fall, 11/15 for spring, 3/1 for summer. Contact: Ms. Julia Shepard, International Student Development Coordinator, 201 Wood Street, Pittsburgh, PA 15222-1984. (412) 392-3901.

PLACEMENT

Placement services include career counseling/planning, career library, and resume preparation. Of 1994 graduates, 78% were employed within three months of graduation.

Jobs by Employer Type Manufacturing 14%; service 71%; consulting 15%.

Jobs by Functional Area Marketing/sales 29%; finance 14%; operations 57%.

Program Contact: Ms. Amy Ruffennach, International Graduate Admissions Coordinator, Point Park College, 201 Wood Street, Pittsburgh, PA 15222-1984. (412) 392-3906, or (800) 321-0129 (PA only); Fax: (412) 391-1980.

Robert Morris College

School of Graduate Studies

Coraopolis, Pennsylvania

OVERVIEW

Robert Morris College is an independent nonprofit comprehensive coed institution. Founded 1921. Setting: 230-acre suburban campus with easy access to Pittsburgh. Total institutional enrollment: 5,347. Program was first offered in 1988.

MBA HIGHLIGHTS

Entrance Difficulty**
Mean GMAT: 450
Mean GPA: 2.89

Cost $$
Tuition: $270/credit
Room & Board: $4,326

Enrollment Profile

Full-time: 0		Work Exp: 95%
Part-time: 725		International: 4%
Total: 725		Women: 35%
Average Age: 31		Minorities: N/R

Average Class Size: 15

ACADEMICS

Length of Program Minimum: 24 months. Maximum: 7 years.

Calendar Semesters.

Full-time Classes Main campus; evening, weekends, summer.

Part-time Classes Main campus; evening, weekends, summer.

Degree Requirements 36 credits including 6 elective credits.

Required Courses Business ethics and society, calculus for business, decision support system, economic analysis, financial controls, introduction to decision support systems, management theory and practices, managerial accounting, managerial computing, managerial economics, marketing management, organizational behavior, quantitative decision making, statistical methods, strategy and policy, the legal environment of business. Courses may be waived through: previous course work.

Curricular Focus General management, leadership, problem solving and decision making.

Concentrations Accounting, management, management information systems, marketing, sport management.

Faculty Full-time: 23, 100% with doctorates; part-time: 19.

Teaching Methodology Case study: 10%, faculty seminars: 5%, lecture: 60%, research: 5%, student presentations: 10%, team projects: 10%.

Special Opportunities Internship program available.

STUDENT STATISTICS

Geographic Representation State residents 91%. By region: Northeast 94%. International 4%.

Other Background Work experience: On average, students have 5 years of work experience on entrance to the program.

FACILITIES

Information Resources Main library with 122,645 bound volumes, 290,763 titles on microform, 874 periodical subscriptions, 10,655 records/tapes/CDs, 73 CD-ROMs.

Housing 1% of students in program live in college-owned or -operated housing.

Technology Computers are used moderately in course work. 350 computer terminals/PCs, linked by a campus-wide computer network, are available for use by students in program; they are located in classrooms, computer labs. Students in the program are not required to have their own PC.

Computer Resources/On-line Services

Training	Yes	CompuServe	No
Internet	No	Dun's	No
E-Mail	No	Dow Jones	No
Multimedia Center	Yes	Dialog	Yes
LEXIS/NEXIS	No	Bloomberg	No

Other on-line services: OCLC.

ADMISSION

Acceptance 1994-95 Of those applying, 87% were accepted.

Entrance Requirements Bachelor's degree, GMAT score of 450, minimum 2.5 GPA. Core courses waived through: previous course work.

Application Requirements Application form, copies of transcript, 2 letters of recommendation.

Application Deadline Applications are processed on a rolling basis.

FINANCIALS

Costs for 1994-95 Tuition: Full-time: $270/credit. Fees: Full-time: $11/credit. Average room and board costs are $4,326 per academic year (on-campus).

Financial Aid In 1994-95, 14% of candidates received some institutionally administered aid in the form of loans, assistantships. Total awards ranged from $300-$7,500. Financial aid is available to part-time students.

Application deadline: 5/1 for fall. Contact: Mr. C. Brad Pendell, Director of Financial Aid, Narrows Run Road, Coraopolis, PA 15108-1189. (412) 262-8584.

INTERNATIONAL STUDENTS
Demographics 4% of students enrolled in the program are international; Asia 60%, Europe 30%, Africa 10%.

Services and Facilities Counseling/support services.

Applying TOEFL required, minimum score of 550. Financial aid is not available to international students. Admission applications are processed on a rolling basis. Contact: Dr. Vana N. Nespor, Associate Dean of Admissions for Special Programs, Narrows Run Road, Coraopolis, PA 15108-1189. (412) 262-8572.

PLACEMENT
Placement services include alumni network, career counseling/planning, career fairs, career library, career placement, electronic job bank, job interviews, resume preparation, and resume referral to employers.

Program Contact: Dr. Joseph M. Correa, Dean of Graduate Studies and Continuing Education, Robert Morris College, Narrows Run Road, Coraopolis, PA 15108-1189. (412) 262-8304, or (800) 762-0097; Fax: (412) 262-4049.

Saint Francis College

Loretto, Pennsylvania

OVERVIEW
Saint Francis College is an independent Roman Catholic comprehensive coed institution. Founded 1847. Setting: 600-acre rural campus. Total institutional enrollment: 2,000. Program was first offered in 1990.

MBA HIGHLIGHTS

Entrance Difficulty**
Mean GMAT: 500
Mean GPA: 3.4

Cost $$
Tuition: $345/credit
Room & Board: N/R

Enrollment Profile

Full-time: 12	Work Exp: 90%
Part-time: 97	International: N/R
Total: 109	Women: 39%
Average Age: N/R	Minorities: N/R

Average Class Size: 25

ACADEMICS
Length of Program Minimum: 18 months. Maximum: 5 years.
Calendar Semesters.
Full-time Classes Main campus; evening, weekends.
Part-time Classes Main campus, Johnstown, Altoona; evening, weekends.
Degree Requirements 36-60 credits including 9 elective credits.
Required Courses Business and society, business law, computer science, economics for managers, financial accounting, financial management, management accounting, management communication, managerial economics, managerial finance, marketing, marketing management, perspective management, production operations management, quantitative business analysis, statistics, strategic management and policy analysis.
Curricular Focus Communications and ethics, general management, problem solving and decision making.
Concentrations Employment law, labor relations, finance, human resources management.
Faculty Full-time: 7; part-time: 6.
Teaching Methodology Case study: 25%, lecture: 40%, student presentations: 15%, team projects: 20%.

STUDENT STATISTICS
Undergraduate Majors Business 40%; engineering/technology 20%; humanities 8%; nursing 18%; science/mathematics 7%; social sciences 7%.

Other Background Graduate degrees in other disciplines: 5%. Work experience: On average, students have 5 years of work experience on entrance to the program.

FACILITIES
Information Resources Main library with 198,956 bound volumes, 135 titles on microform, 582 periodical subscriptions, 967 records/tapes/CDs, 2 CD-ROMs.

Housing College housing not available.

Technology Computers are used moderately in course work. 40 computer terminals/PCs are available for use by students in program; they are located in computer labs. Students in the program are not required to have their own PC.

Computer Resources/On-line Services

Training	Yes	Dun's	No
Internet	No	Dow Jones	No
E-Mail	No	Dialog	No
LEXIS/NEXIS	No	Bloomberg	No
CompuServe	No		

ADMISSION
Entrance Requirements Bachelor's degree, GMAT score, minimum 2.5 GPA. Core courses waived through: previous course work.

Application Requirements Written essay, interview, application form, copies of transcript, resume/curriculum vitae, personal statement.

Application Deadlines 8/1 for fall, 12/12 for spring.

FINANCIALS
Costs for 1994-95 Tuition: Full-time: $345/credit.

Financial Aid In 1994-95, 15% of candidates received some institutionally administered aid in the form of grants, assistantships, work-study. Total awards ranged from $1,000-$6,000. Financial aid is available to part-time students. Contact: Ms. Arletta Mangus, Director of Financial Aid, PO Box 600, Loretto, PA 15940. (814) 472-3000.

INTERNATIONAL STUDENTS
Applying TOEFL required, minimum score of 550; proof of health; proof of adequate funds. Financial aid is not available to international students. Admission application deadlines: 8/1 for fall, 12/12 for spring.

PLACEMENT
Placement services include alumni network, career counseling/planning, career library, career placement, electronic job bank, job interviews, resume preparation, and resume referral to employers.

Program Contact: Mr. Randy Frye, Director, Saint Francis College, PO Box 600, Loretto, PA 15940. (814) 472-3087, or (800) 457-6300 (PA only), or (800) 342-5732 (out-of-state); Fax: (814) 472-3044.

Saint Joseph's University

College of Business and Administration

Philadelphia, Pennsylvania

OVERVIEW
Saint Joseph's University is an independent Roman Catholic (Jesuit) comprehensive coed institution. Founded 1851. Setting: 60-acre urban campus. Total institutional enrollment: 6,700. Program was first offered in 1976.

MBA HIGHLIGHTS

Entrance Difficulty**
Mean GMAT: 526
Mean GPA: 2.99

Cost $$
Tuition: $6,930
Room & Board: $5,900

Enrollment Profile

Full-time: 73	Work Exp: 95%
Part-time: 1,268	International: 7%
Total: 1,341	Women: 38%
Average Age: N/R	Minorities: 5%

Average Class Size: 30

ACADEMICS
Length of Program Minimum: 18 months.
Calendar Semesters.

Full-time Classes Main campus, Albright College; evening, weekends, summer.

Part-time Classes Main campus; evening, weekends, summer.

Degree Requirements 33 credits.

Required Courses Business decision making methods, information systems for managers, managerial accounting, managerial finance, marketing management, organizational behavior, social responsibility in business.

Curricular Focus Problem solving and decision making, strategic analysis and planning, teamwork.

Concentrations Accounting, finance, health services, international business, management, management information systems, marketing.

Faculty Full-time: 36, 88% with doctorates; part-time: 34, 32% with doctorates.

Teaching Methodology Case study: 20%, lecture: 40%, student presentations: 20%, team projects: 20%.

Special Opportunities International exchange in Australia, New Zealand, United Kingdom.

STUDENT STATISTICS

Geographic Representation State residents 88%. By region: Northeast 93%. International 7%.

Undergraduate Majors Business 54%; education 2%; engineering/technology 22%; humanities 6%; nursing 3%; science/mathematics 5%; social sciences 4%; other 4%.

Other Background Graduate degrees in other disciplines: 5%. Work experience: On average, students have 5 years of work experience on entrance to the program.

FACILITIES

Information Resources Main library with 317,000 bound volumes, 711,677 titles on microform, 1,700 periodical subscriptions, 1,800 records/tapes/CDs, 14 CD-ROMs. Business collection in Campbell Library includes 32,000 bound volumes, 400 periodical subscriptions, 11 CD-ROMs, 200 videos.

Housing College housing available.

Technology Computers are used moderately in course work. 100 computer terminals/PCs, linked by a campus-wide computer network, are available for use by students in program; they are located in computer labs. Students in the program are not required to have their own PC.

Computer Resources/On-line Services

Training	Yes	CompuServe	No
Internet	Yes	Dun's	No
E-Mail	Yes	Dow Jones	No
Multimedia Center	Yes	Dialog	Yes
LEXIS/NEXIS	Yes	Bloomberg	No

Other on-line services: First Search, OCLC.

ADMISSION

Entrance Requirements Bachelor's degree, GMAT score of 450, minimum 2.8 GPA.

Application Requirements Written essay, application form, copies of transcript, resume/curriculum vitae, 2 letters of recommendation.

Application Deadlines 7/15 for fall, 11/15 for spring, 4/15 for summer. Applications are processed on a rolling basis.

FINANCIALS

Costs for 1994-95 Tuition: Full-time: $6,930; Part-time day: $385/credit; Part-time evening: $4,620. Average room and board costs are $5,900 per academic year (on-campus) and $4,500 per academic year (off-campus).

Financial Aid In 1994-95, 80% of candidates received some institutionally administered aid in the form of loans, assistantships. Total awards ranged from $8,500-$18,500. Financial aid is not available to part-time students. Applications are processed on a rolling basis. Contact: Ms. Nicole Lightbourne, Financial Aid Counselor, 5600 City Avenue, Philadelphia, PA 19131-1376. (610) 660-1340.

INTERNATIONAL STUDENTS

Demographics 7% of students enrolled in the program are international; Asia 50%, Europe 22%, Africa 6%, South America 6%, Central America 3%, other 13%.

Services and Facilities International student office, visa services, language tutoring, ESL courses, counseling/support services.

Applying TOEFL required, minimum score of 550; proof of adequate funds. Financial aid is not available to international students. Admission application deadlines: 7/15 for fall, 11/15 for spring, 4/15 for summer. Applications are processed on a rolling basis. Contact: Ms. Nancy Sando, Director, International Student Services, 5600 City Avenue, Philadelphia, PA 19131-1376. (610) 660-1040.

PLACEMENT

Placement services include alumni network, career counseling/planning, career library, career placement, electronic job bank, resume preparation, and resume referral to employers.

Program Contact: Ms. Adele Foley, Associate Dean and Director, Saint Joseph's University, 5600 City Avenue, Philadelphia, PA 19131-1376. (610) 660-1690; Fax: (610) 660-1599.
See full description on page 820.

Temple University

School of Business and Management

Philadelphia, Pennsylvania

OVERVIEW

Temple University is a state-related coed institution. Founded 1884. Setting: 76-acre urban campus. Total institutional enrollment: 31,000. Program was first offered in 1943. AACSB-accredited.

MBA HIGHLIGHTS

Entrance Difficulty**
Mean GMAT: 540
Mean GPA: 3.1

Cost $$
Tuition: $258/credit
(Nonresident: $366/credit)
Room & Board: $3,168

Enrollment Profile

Full-time: 277	Work Exp: 90%
Part-time: 787	International: 8%
Total: 1,064	Women: 41%
Average Age: 29	Minorities: 17%

Average Class Size: 25

ACADEMICS

Length of Program Minimum: 12 months. Maximum: 6 years.

Calendar Semesters.

Full-time Classes Main campus; day.

Part-time Classes Main campus; evening, summer.

Degree Requirements 36 credits including 6 elective credits.

Required Courses Accounting, business policies, economics, finance, human resources, management, marketing. Courses may be waived through: previous course work.

Curricular Focus Entrepreneurship, international business, organizational development and change management.

Concentrations Accounting, economics, finance, human resources management, international business, management, management information systems, marketing, operations management, quantitative analysis, real estate, risk management and insurance, actuarial science, health administration, strategic management.

Faculty Full-time: 121, 100% with doctorates; part-time: 19, 38% with doctorates.

Teaching Methodology Case study: 25%, lecture: 30%, seminars by members of the business community: 5%, student presentations: 20%, team projects: 20%.

Special Opportunities International exchange in France, Italy.

STUDENT STATISTICS

Geographic Representation International 8%.

Other Background Work experience: On average, students have 4 years of work experience on entrance to the program.

FACILITIES

Information Resources Main library with 2.1 million bound volumes, 1.6 million titles on microform, 15,600 periodical subscriptions, 20,000 records/tapes/CDs, 70 CD-ROMs.

Housing College housing available.

Technology Computers are used moderately in course work. Computer terminals/PCs are available for use by students in program; they are located in the library, the computer center, computer labs. Students in the program are not required to have their own PC.

Computer Resources/On-line Services

Training	Yes	Dun's	No
Internet	Yes	Dow Jones	No
E-Mail	Yes	Dialog	Yes
LEXIS/NEXIS	No	Bloomberg	No
CompuServe	No		

Other on-line services: SEC.

ADMISSION
Acceptance 1994-95 Of those applying, 50% were accepted.

Entrance Requirements Bachelor's degree, GMAT score. Core courses waived through: previous course work.

Application Requirements Written essay, application form, copies of transcript, 2 letters of recommendation.

Application Deadlines 6/1 for fall, 9/30 for spring, 3/15 for summer. Application discs available.

FINANCIALS
Costs for 1994-95 Tuition: Full-time: $258/credit for state residents, $366/credit for nonresidents. Fees: Full-time: $150 for state residents, $150 for nonresidents. Average room and board costs are $3,168 per academic year (on-campus) and $4,500 per academic year (off-campus).

Financial Aid In 1994-95, candidates received some institutionally administered aid in the form of scholarships, assistantships, work-study. Total awards ranged from $500-$18,000. Financial aid is available to part-time students. Application deadlines: 5/1 for fall, 5/1 for spring. Contact: Ms. Janice Contino, Associate Director of Financial Aid, Broad Street and Montgomery Avenue, Philadelphia, PA 19122. (215) 204-1454.

INTERNATIONAL STUDENTS
Demographics 8% of students enrolled in the program are international; Asia 60%, Europe 15%, other 24%.

Services and Facilities ESL courses, orientation.

Applying TOEFL required, minimum score of 575. Financial aid is available to international students. Assistantships are available for these students. Admission application deadlines: 6/1 for fall, 4/15 for spring, 3/15 for summer.

ALTERNATE MBA PROGRAMS
Executive MBA (EMBA) Length of program: Minimum: 21 months. Maximum: 2 years. Degree requirements: 48 credits. 10 years work experience (5-7 managerial level). Average class size: 20.

MBA/JD Length of program: Minimum: 36 months. Maximum: 6 years. Degree requirements: 92 credits.

MBA/MS Length of program: Minimum: 24 months. Maximum: 6 years. Degree requirements: 69 credits. MS is in health care/financial management or environmental health.

One-Year IMBA Length of program: Minimum: 10 months. Maximum: 5 years. Full-time classes: Main campus, Lyons (France), Paris (France); day, evening, summer. Degree requirements: 30 credits. First semester curriculum taken in Paris or Lyons, France; spring semester completed at Temple University.

PLACEMENT
In 1993-94, 70 organizations participated in on-campus recruiting. Placement services include career counseling/planning, career placement, electronic job bank, job interviews, resume preparation, and resume referral to employers.

Program Contact: Ms. Linda Whelan, Director, MBA/MS Programs, Temple University, Broad Street and Montgomery Avenue, Philadelphia, PA 19122. (215) 204-7000.
See full description on page 840.

University of Pennsylvania

The Wharton School

Philadelphia, Pennsylvania

OVERVIEW
The University of Pennsylvania is an independent nonprofit coed institution. Founded 1740. Setting: 260-acre urban campus. Total institutional enrollment: 22,469. Program was first offered in 1921. AACSB-accredited.

MBA HIGHLIGHTS

Entrance Difficulty***
Mean GMAT: 650
Mean GPA: 3.4

Cost $$$$
Tuition: $19,604
Room & Board: $8,000

Enrollment Profile

Full-time: 1,500		Work Exp: 99%
Part-time: 0		International: 33%
Total: 1,500		Women: 27%
Average Age: 27		Minorities: 15%

Average Class Size: 21

ACADEMICS
Length of Program Minimum: 18 months. Maximum: 2 years.

Calendar First year: quarters; second year: semesters.

Full-time Classes Main campus; day.

Degree Requirements 20 courses including 10 elective courses.

Required Courses Competitive strategy, field application project, financial accounting, financial analysis, foundations of leadership, global strategic management, government and legal environment of business, macroeconomic analysis and public policy, management of people at work, management science, managerial accounting, managerial economics, marketing management strategy, marketing management: program design, operations management, operations management: strategy and technology, organizational design and management, statistical analysis for management.

Curricular Focus Entrepreneurship, problem solving and decision making, teamwork.

Concentrations Accounting, arts administration, entrepreneurship, finance, health services, human resources management, international business, management, management information systems, marketing, operations management, organizational behavior, public administration, public policy, real estate, strategic management, transportation.

Faculty Full-time: 180, 98% with doctorates.

Teaching Methodology Case study: 60%, lecture: 30%, team projects: 10%.

Special Opportunities International exchange program available.

STUDENT STATISTICS
Geographic Representation By region: Northeast 47%; Midwest 23%; West 17%; South 13%. International 33%.

Undergraduate Majors Business 19%; engineering/technology 13%; humanities 35%; social sciences 22%; other 11%.

Other Background Graduate degrees in other disciplines: 15%. Work experience: On average, students have 4 years of work experience on entrance to the program.

FACILITIES
Information Resources Main library with 4.2 million bound volumes, 33,384 periodical subscriptions, 42,510 records/tapes/CDs, 186 CD-ROMs. Business collection in Lippincott Library includes 200,000 bound volumes, 3,500 periodical subscriptions.

Housing 30% of students in program live in college-owned or -operated housing. Assistance with housing search provided.

Technology Computers are used heavily in course work. Computer terminals/PCs, linked by a campus-wide computer network, are available for use by students in program; they are located in student rooms, the student center, classrooms, learning resource center, the library, the computer center, computer labs, the research center. Students in the program are not required to have their own PC.

Computer Resources/On-line Services

Training	Yes	LEXIS/NEXIS	Yes $
Internet	Yes	CompuServe	Yes
E-Mail	Yes		

ADMISSION
Acceptance 1994-95 5,019 applied for admission; 22% were accepted.

Entrance Requirements Bachelor's degree, GMAT score.

Application Requirements Written essay, application form, copies of transcript, personal statement, 2 letters of recommendation.

Application Deadlines 4/10 for fall. Applications are processed on a rolling basis. Application discs available.

FINANCIALS
Costs for 1994-95 Tuition: Full-time: $19,604. Fees: Full-time: $1,446. Average room and board costs are $8,000 per academic year (on-campus).

Financial Aid In 1994-95, 75% of candidates received some institutionally administered aid in the form of grants, scholarships, loans, fellowships, assistantships. Total awards ranged from $1,000-$35,000. Application deadline: 3/1 for fall. Applications are processed on a rolling basis. Contact: Ms. Sydney Fredericksen, Associate Director of Financial Aid, 102 Vance Hall, Philadelphia, PA 19104-6361. (215) 898-9784.

INTERNATIONAL STUDENTS
Demographics 33% of students enrolled in the program are international; North America 67%, Asia 15%, Europe 8%, South America 7%, other 3%.

Services and Facilities International student office, visa services, language tutoring, ESL courses, special assistance for nonnative speakers of English, counseling/support services.

Applying TOEFL required; proof of health; proof of adequate funds. Financial aid is available to international students. Financial aid application deadline: 3/1 for fall. Applications are processed on a rolling basis. Admission application deadline: 4/10 for fall. Applications are processed on a rolling basis. Contact: Ms. Julie Stapleton-Carroll, Assistant Director of Graduate Student Programs, 216 Vance Hall, Philadelphia, PA 19104-6362. (215) 898-5000.

ALTERNATE MBA PROGRAM
MBA/MA Length of program: Minimum: 24 months. Degree requirements: MA is in international studies.

PLACEMENT
In 1993-94, 263 organizations participated in on-campus recruiting. Placement services include alumni network, career counseling/planning, career fairs, career library, career placement, electronic job bank, job interviews, job search course, resume preparation, and resume referral to employers. Of 1994 graduates, 93% were employed within three months of graduation, the average starting salary was $80,077.

Program Contact: Mr. Samuel Lundquist, Director of MBA Admissions, University of Pennsylvania, 102 Vance Hall, Philadelphia, PA 19104-6361. (215) 898-6182; Fax: (215) 898-0120; Internet Address: mba. admissions@wharton.upenn.edu.
See full description on page 910.

University of Pittsburgh

Joseph M. Katz Graduate School of Business

Pittsburgh, Pennsylvania

OVERVIEW
The University of Pittsburgh is a state-related coed institution. Part of University of Pittsburgh System. Founded 1787. Setting: 132-acre urban campus. Total institutional enrollment: 26,328. Program was first offered in 1960. AACSB-accredited.

MBA HIGHLIGHTS

Entrance Difficulty**
Mean GMAT: 603
Mean GPA: 3.2

Cost $$$
Tuition: $13,476
(Nonresident: $22,734)
Room & Board: $11,256 (off-campus)

Enrollment Profile

Full-time: 314	Work Exp: 87%
Part-time: 514	International: 26%
Total: 828	Women: 31%
Average Age: 26	Minorities: 8%

Average Class Size: 45

ACADEMICS
Length of Program Minimum: 11 months. Maximum: 6 years.
Calendar Trimesters.
Full-time Classes Main campus; day, evening, early morning, summer.

Part-time Classes Main campus; evening, weekends, early morning, summer.

Degree Requirements 52.5 credits including 21 elective credits.

Required Courses Accounting: financial reporting and control, business ethics and social performance, competing in a global environment, decision technologies, economic analysis for managerial decisions: firms and markets, financial management, human resources for competitive advantage, marketing management, organizational behavior: leadership and group effectiveness, organizational transformation, prediction and quality improvement, statistical analysis: uncertainty. Courses may be waived through: previous course work.

Curricular Focus Economic and financial theory, international business, managerial skills, ethics, interrelationships across business functions, strategic analysis and planning.

Concentrations Accounting, economics, finance, health services, human resources management, international business, management, management information systems, marketing, operations management, organizational behavior, quantitative analysis, strategic management.

Faculty Full-time: 65, 98% with doctorates; part-time: 20, 67% with doctorates.

Teaching Methodology Case study: 25%, lecture: 40%, seminars by members of the business community: 5%, student presentations: 10%, team projects: 20%.

Special Opportunities International exchange program available. Internships include information systems, finance, communications, and government.

STUDENT STATISTICS
Geographic Representation State residents 44%. By region: Northeast 65%; Midwest 3%; West 3%; South 1%. International 26%.

Undergraduate Majors Business 40%; education 1%; engineering/technology 14%; humanities 11%; science/mathematics 14%; social sciences 2%; other 18%.

Other Background Graduate degrees in other disciplines: 12%. Work experience: On average, students have 4 years of work experience on entrance to the program.

FACILITIES
Information Resources Main library with 3.2 million bound volumes, 3.1 million titles on microform, 23,380 periodical subscriptions, 34,406 records/tapes/CDs. Business collection includes 46,381 bound volumes, 825 periodical subscriptions, 93 CD-ROMs.

Housing College housing not available.

Technology Computers are used heavily in course work. 860 computer terminals/PCs, linked by a campus-wide computer network, are available for use by students in program; they are located in classrooms, the library, the computer center, computer labs. Students in the program are not required to have their own PC. $800 are budgeted per student for computer support.

Computer Resources/On-line Services

Training	Yes	CompuServe	Yes
Internet	Yes	Dun's	Yes
E-Mail	Yes	Dow Jones	Yes
LEXIS/NEXIS	Yes $	Dialog	Yes

Other on-line services: OCLC, First Search, Datastar.

ADMISSION
Acceptance 1994-95 1,400 applied for admission; 51% were accepted.

Entrance Requirements Bachelor's degree, GMAT score. Core courses waived through: previous course work.

Application Requirements Written essay, application form, copies of transcript, 2 letters of recommendation.

Application Deadline Applications are processed on a rolling basis. Application discs available.

FINANCIALS
Costs for 1994-95 Tuition: Full-time: $13,476 for state residents, $22,734 for nonresidents. Fees: Full-time: $579 for state residents, $579 for nonresidents. Average room and board costs are $11,256 per academic year (off-campus).

Financial Aid In 1994-95, 76% of candidates received some institutionally administered aid in the form of scholarships, loans, assistantships, work-study. Total awards ranged from $2,000-$21,400. Financial aid is not available to part-time students. Application deadline: 5/1 for fall. Contact: Ms. Kathy Riehle Valentine, Director of Admissions, 276 Mervis Hall, Pittsburgh, PA 15260. (412) 648-1700.

INTERNATIONAL STUDENTS
Demographics 26% of students enrolled in the program are international; Asia 59%, Europe 13%, South America 11%, Australia 1%, other 16%.

Services and Facilities Visa services, language tutoring, ESL courses, counseling/support services.

Applying TOEFL required, minimum score of 600; proof of adequate funds. Financial aid is not available to international students. Admission application deadline: 3/15 for fall. Contact: Ms. Linda Gentile, Foreign Student Adviser, 708 William Pitt Union, Pittsburgh, PA 15260. (412) 624-7120.

ALTERNATE MBA PROGRAMS

Executive MBA (EMBA) Length of program: Minimum: 24 months. Degree requirements: 51 credits including 3 elective credits. 7 years business experience.

MBA/JD Length of program: Minimum: 28 months. Maximum: 6 years. Degree requirements: 119.5 credits including 55 elective credits. Minimum 3.0 QPA.

MBA/MA Length of program: Minimum: 24 months. Maximum: 6 years. Degree requirements: 76.5 credits including 39 elective credits. Foreign language competency; 6 credit research paper; written comprehensive exam; 3.0 GPA.

MBA/MH Length of program: Minimum: 19 months. Maximum: 6 years. Degree requirements: 74 credits. Minimum 3.0 QPA.

MBA/MS Length of program: Minimum: 20 months. Maximum: 6 years. Degree requirements: 76.5 credits including 12 elective credits. C++ and Cobol; internship; minimum 3.0 GPA. MS is in management of information systems.

MBA/MSN Length of program: Minimum: 20 months. Maximum: 6 years. Degree requirements: 81 credits including 8.5 elective credits. Minimum 3.0 QPA.

MBA/MIB Length of program: Minimum: 24 months. Maximum: 6 years. Degree requirements: 76.5 credits including 36 elective credits. Foreign language competency, 6 credit internship and 6 required MIB courses, minimum 3.0 GPA.

PLACEMENT

In 1993-94, 95 organizations participated in on-campus recruiting; 1,000 on-campus interviews were conducted. Placement services include alumni network, career counseling/planning, career library, career placement, electronic job bank, job interviews, resume preparation, and resume referral to employers. Of 1994 graduates, 90% were employed within three months of graduation, the average starting salary was $47,500, the range was $28,500-$100,000.

Jobs by Employer Type Manufacturing 22%; service 52%; government 2%; consulting 21%; nonprofit 1%; higher education 2%.

Jobs by Functional Area Marketing/sales 19%; finance 42%; operations 5%; management 17%; strategic planning 4%; technical management 12%; human resources 1%.

Program Contact: Ms. Kathy Riehle Valentine, Director of Admissions, University of Pittsburgh, 276 Mervis Hall, Pittsburgh, PA 15260. (412) 648-1700; Fax: (412) 648-1693.

University of Scranton

The Graduate School

Scranton, Pennsylvania

OVERVIEW

The University of Scranton is an independent Roman Catholic (Jesuit) comprehensive coed institution. Founded 1888. Setting: 50-acre urban campus. Total institutional enrollment: 4,946. Program was first offered in 1960.

MBA HIGHLIGHTS

Entrance Difficulty*
Mean GMAT: 505
Mean GPA: 3.2

Cost $$
Tuition: $375/credit
Room & Board: $6,800

Enrollment Profile

Full-time: 49	Work Exp: 80%
Part-time: 125	International: 22%
Total: 174	Women: 40%
Average Age: 28	Minorities: 1%

Average Class Size: 18

ACADEMICS

Length of Program Minimum: 18 months. Maximum: 6 years.

Calendar 4-1-4.

Full-time Classes Main campus; evening, summer.

Part-time Classes Main campus; evening, summer.

Degree Requirements 36 credits including 3-12 elective credits. Other: One international course.

Required Courses Accounting, business policy, financial management, management information systems, managerial economics, marketing management, operations management, organizational behavior. Courses may be waived through: previous course work, work experience.

Curricular Focus International business.

Concentrations Accounting, finance, international business, marketing, operations management.

Faculty Full-time: 40, 87% with doctorates.

Teaching Methodology Case study: 10%, faculty seminars: 2%, lecture: 58%, research: 7%, seminars by members of the business community: 1%, student presentations: 11%, team projects: 10%.

Special Opportunities Internship program available.

STUDENT STATISTICS

Geographic Representation State residents 60%. By region: Northeast 75%. International 22%.

Undergraduate Majors Business 60%; engineering/technology 15%; other 25%.

Other Background Graduate degrees in other disciplines: 3%. Work experience: On average, students have 3 years of work experience on entrance to the program.

FACILITIES

Information Resources Main library with 328,081 bound volumes, 306,095 titles on microform, 2,153 periodical subscriptions, 9,392 records/tapes/CDs, 34 CD-ROMs.

Housing 5% of students in program live in college-owned or -operated housing.

Technology Computers are used heavily in course work. Computer terminals/PCs, linked by a campus-wide computer network, are available for use by students in program; they are located in dormitories, the library, the computer center, computer labs. Students in the program are not required to have their own PC.

Computer Resources/On-line Services

Training	Yes	Dun's	Yes $
Internet	Yes	Dow Jones	Yes $
E-Mail	Yes	Dialog	Yes $
LEXIS/NEXIS	No	Bloomberg	No
CompuServe	Yes		

ADMISSION

Acceptance 1994-95 103 applied for admission; 70% were accepted.

Entrance Requirements Bachelor's degree, prerequisite courses required for applicants with non-business degree, GMAT score.

Application Requirements Application form, copies of transcript, resume/curriculum vitae, personal statement, 3 letters of recommendation.

Application Deadline Applications are processed on a rolling basis.

FINANCIALS

Costs for 1994-95 Tuition: Full-time: $375/credit. Average room and board costs are $6,800 per academic year (on-campus) and $7,700 per academic year (off-campus).

Financial Aid In 1994-95, 20% of candidates received some institutionally administered aid in the form of assistantships, work-study. Total awards ranged from $3,800-$7,000. Financial aid is not available to part-time students. Applications are processed on a rolling basis. Contact: Mr. Robert Burke, Director of Financial Aid, Scranton, PA 18510-4622. (717) 941-7700.

INTERNATIONAL STUDENTS
Demographics 22% of students enrolled in the program are international; Asia 85%, Europe 5%, Africa 1%, Central America 1%, other 8%.

Services and Facilities Language tutoring, ESL courses, counseling/support services.

Applying TOEFL required, minimum score of 500; proof of adequate funds. Financial aid is not available to international students. Admission application deadlines: 6/1 for fall, 11/1 for spring. Contact: Mr. Peter J. Blazes, Director, International Student Affairs, Scranton, PA 18510-4622. (717) 941-7575.

PLACEMENT
In 1993-94, 44 organizations participated in on-campus recruiting. Placement services include alumni network, career counseling/planning, career fairs, career library, career placement, electronic job bank, job interviews, resume preparation, and resume referral to employers.

Program Contact: Mr. James L. Goonan, Director, Graduate Admissions, University of Scranton, Scranton, PA 18510-4622. (717) 941-7600, or (800) 366-4723 (PA only); Fax: (717) 941-4252.

Villanova University

College of Commerce and Finance

Villanova, Pennsylvania

OVERVIEW
Villanova University is an independent Roman Catholic comprehensive coed institution. Founded 1842. Setting: 222-acre suburban campus with easy access to Philadelphia. Total institutional enrollment: 11,039. Program was first offered in 1982. AACSB-accredited.

MBA HIGHLIGHTS

Entrance Difficulty****
Mean GMAT: 580
Mean GPA: 3.2

Cost $
Tuition: $410/credit
Room & Board: N/R

Enrollment Profile

Full-time: 65	Work Exp: 85%
Part-time: 595	International: 1%
Total: 660	Women: 39%
Average Age: 27	Minorities: 1%

Average Class Size: 25

ACADEMICS
Length of Program May range up to 10 years.

Calendar Semesters.

Full-time Classes Main campus; evening, summer.

Part-time Classes Main campus; evening, summer.

Degree Requirements 60 credits including 15 elective credits.

Curricular Focus General management, problem solving and decision making, strategic analysis and planning.

Concentration Management.

Faculty Full-time: 50, 100% with doctorates; part-time: 1.

STUDENT STATISTICS
Geographic Representation International 1%.

Undergraduate Majors Business 60%; engineering/technology 20%; humanities 10%; science/mathematics 2%; other 8%.

Other Background Graduate degrees in other disciplines: 5%. Work experience: On average, students have 5 years of work experience on entrance to the program.

FACILITIES
Information Resources Main library with 642,800 bound volumes, 1,456 titles on microform, 2,826 periodical subscriptions, 3,554 records/tapes/CDs, 34 CD-ROMs.

Housing College housing not available.

Technology Computer terminals/PCs are available for use by students in program; they are located in classrooms, the library, the computer center, computer labs. Students in the program are not required to have their own PC.

Computer Resources/On-line Services
Training   Yes

ADMISSION
Acceptance 1994-95 250 applied for admission; 55% were accepted.

Entrance Requirements Bachelor's degree, GMAT score. Core courses waived through: previous course work.

Application Requirements Written essay, application form, copies of transcript.

Application Deadlines 6/30 for fall, 10/30 for spring.

FINANCIALS
Costs for 1994-95 Tuition: Full-time: $410/credit. Fees: Full-time: $30/semester.

Financial Aid In 1994-95, candidates received some institutionally administered aid in the form of loans, research assistantships. Financial aid is available to part-time students. Applications are processed on a rolling basis. Contact: Mr. George J. Walter, Director of Financial Assistance, 800 Lancaster Avenue, Villanova, PA 19085-1699. (610) 519-4010.

INTERNATIONAL STUDENTS
Demographics 1% of students enrolled in the program are international.

Applying TOEFL required, minimum score of 600. Financial aid is not available to international students. Admission application deadlines: 6/30 for fall, 10/30 for spring. Contact: Dr. Stephen McWilliams, International Student Adviser, 800 Lancaster Avenue, Villanova, PA 19085-1699. (610) 519-4095.

PLACEMENT
Placement services include career library and career placement.

Program Contact: Ms. Kathryn Wuest, Coordinator of the MBA, Villanova University, 800 Lancaster Avenue, Villanova, PA 19085-1699. (610) 519-4299; Fax: (610) 519-7599.

Waynesburg College

Waynesburg, Pennsylvania

OVERVIEW
Waynesburg College is an independent comprehensive coed institution, affiliated with Presbyterian Church (U.S.A.). Founded 1849. Setting: 30-acre small-town campus with easy access to Pittsburgh. Total institutional enrollment: 1,350. Program was first offered in 1983.

MBA HIGHLIGHTS

Entrance Difficulty**
Mean GMAT: 425
Mean GPA: 3.1

Cost $$
Tuition: $270/credit
Room & Board: $4,500

Enrollment Profile

Full-time: 2	Work Exp: 95%
Part-time: 63	International: 7%
Total: 65	Women: 40%
Average Age: 30	Minorities: 0%

Average Class Size: 7

ACADEMICS
Length of Program Minimum: 12 months. Maximum: 7 years.

Calendar Semesters.

Full-time Classes Main campus; evening, summer.

Part-time Classes Main campus; evening, summer.

Degree Requirements 36 credits including 9 elective credits.

Required Courses Financial management, international business, management policy, managerial accounting and control, marketing management, operations management, seminar in applied economics, statistical methods. Courses may be waived through: previous course work.

Curricular Focus Business issues and problems, general management, problem solving and decision making.

Concentrations Accounting, economics, finance, human resources management, international business, management, management information systems, marketing, operations management, organizational behavior, strategic management, transportation.

Faculty Full-time: 7, 70% with doctorates; part-time: 3, 33% with doctorates.

Teaching Methodology Case study: 20%, faculty seminars: 5%, lecture: 30%, research: 5%, student presentations: 20%, team projects: 20%.

Special Opportunities International exchange and internship programs available.

STUDENT STATISTICS

Geographic Representation State residents 75%. By region: Northeast 92%. International 7%.

Undergraduate Majors Business 80%; engineering/technology 10%; nursing 5%; science/mathematics 5%.

Other Background Graduate degrees in other disciplines: 5%. Work experience: On average, students have 7 years of work experience on entrance to the program.

FACILITIES

Information Resources Main library with 90,000 bound volumes, 65 titles on microform, 542 periodical subscriptions, 256 records/tapes/CDs, 9 CD-ROMs. Business collection includes 4,785 bound volumes, 50 periodical subscriptions, 3 CD-ROMs.

Housing 1% of students in program live in college-owned or -operated housing.

Technology Computers are used moderately in course work. 48 computer terminals/PCs are available for use by students in program; they are located in computer labs. Students in the program are not required to have their own PC.

Computer Resources/On-line Services

Training	No	Dialog	Yes
E-Mail	No		

ADMISSION

Acceptance 1994-95 Of those applying, 80% were accepted.

Entrance Requirements Bachelor's degree, prerequisite courses required for applicants with non-business degree, GMAT score. Core courses waived through: previous course work.

Application Requirements Interview, application form, copies of transcript, resume/curriculum vitae, 2 letters of recommendation.

Application Deadline Applications are processed on a rolling basis.

FINANCIALS

Costs for 1994-95 Tuition: Full-time: $270/credit. Average room and board costs are $4,500 per academic year (on-campus).

Financial Aid In 1994-95, 14% of candidates received some institutionally administered aid in the form of loans, tuition reimbursements. Total awards ranged from $765-$4,481. Financial aid is available to part-time students. Application deadlines: 8/1 for fall, 12/1 for spring. Contact: Ms. Karen Pratz, Director of Financial Aid, 51 West College Street, Waynesburg, PA 15370-1222. (412) 852-3208.

INTERNATIONAL STUDENTS

Demographics 7% of students enrolled in the program are international; Asia 50%, Europe 50%.

Services and Facilities Language tutoring, counseling/support services.

Applying TOEFL required; proof of adequate funds. Financial aid is not available to international students. Admission applications are processed on a rolling basis. Contact: Mr. William Hastings, Counselor, Admissions Office, 51 West College Street, Waynesburg, PA 15370-1222. (412) 852-3248.

PLACEMENT

In 1993-94, 55 organizations participated in on-campus recruiting. Placement services include alumni network, career counseling/planning, career fairs, career placement, job interviews, and resume preparation. Of 1994 graduates, 100% were employed within three months of graduation.

Jobs by Employer Type Manufacturing 60%; service 30%; government 2%; consulting 2%; nonprofit 4%; other 2%.

Jobs by Functional Area Marketing/sales 15%; finance 30%; operations 30%; management 20%; technical management 5%.

Program Contact: Dr. David E. Smith, Director, MBA Program, Waynesburg College, 51 West College Street, Waynesburg, PA 15370-1222. (412) 852-3200, or (800) 225-7393; Fax: (412) 627-6416.

West Chester University of Pennsylvania

School of Business and Public Affairs

West Chester, Pennsylvania

OVERVIEW

West Chester University of Pennsylvania is a state-supported comprehensive coed institution. Part of Pennsylvania State System of Higher Education. Founded 1871. Setting: 547-acre suburban campus with easy access to Philadelphia. Total institutional enrollment: 12,000. Program was first offered in 1985.

MBA HIGHLIGHTS

Entrance Difficulty*
Mean GMAT: 500
Mean GPA: 3.5

Cost $
Tuition: $1,543/semester
(Nonresident: $2,772/semester)
Room & Board: N/R

Enrollment Profile

Full-time: 20	Work Exp: 80%
Part-time: 135	International: 7%
Total: 155	Women: 40%
Average Age: 28	Minorities: 10%

Average Class Size: 16

ACADEMICS

Length of Program Minimum: 36 months. Maximum: 6 years.

Calendar Semesters.

Full-time Classes Main campus; evening.

Part-time Classes Main campus; evening.

Degree Requirements 36 credits including 9 elective credits.

Required Courses Business communications, financial management, management information systems, management organizational theory, managerial accounting, managerial economics, marketing management, strategic management.

Curricular Focus Economic and financial theory, general management, strategic analysis and planning.

Concentrations Economics, finance, management.

Faculty Full-time: 11, 90% with doctorates; part-time: 4, 50% with doctorates.

Teaching Methodology Case study: 20%, group discussion: 30%, lecture: 35%, student presentations: 10%, team projects: 5%.

STUDENT STATISTICS

Geographic Representation State residents 88%. By region: Northeast 93%. International 7%.

Undergraduate Majors Business 75%; engineering/technology 15%; nursing 2%; social sciences 5%; other 3%.

Other Background Graduate degrees in other disciplines: 2%. Work experience: On average, students have 5 years of work experience on entrance to the program.

FACILITIES

Information Resources Main library with 510,349 bound volumes, 1 million titles on microform, 3,026 periodical subscriptions, 38,746 records/tapes/CDs, 268 CD-ROMs.

Housing 2% of students in program live in college-owned or -operated housing.

Technology Computers are used moderately in course work. 200 computer terminals/PCs, linked by a campus-wide computer network, are available for use by students in program; they are located in the library. Students in the program are not required to have their own PC.

Computer Resources/On-line Services

Training	No	E-Mail	Yes
Internet	Yes $		

ADMISSION

Acceptance 1994-95 85 applied for admission; 76% were accepted.

Entrance Requirements Bachelor's degree, GMAT score of 450, minimum 2.75 GPA. Core courses waived through: previous course work.

Application Requirements Application form, copies of transcript, resume/curriculum vitae, personal statement.

Application Deadline Applications are processed on a rolling basis.

FINANCIALS
Costs for 1994-95 Tuition: Full-time: $1,543/semester for state residents, $2,772/semester for nonresidents; Part-time day: $171/credit for state residents, $308/credit for nonresidents. Fees: Full-time: $226/semester for state residents, $226/semester for nonresidents; Part-time day: $109/semester for state residents, $109/semester for nonresidents.

Financial Aid In 1994-95, candidates received some institutionally administered aid in the form of grants, scholarships, loans, assistantships. Financial aid is available to part-time students. Applications are processed on a rolling basis. Contact: Office of Financial Aid, 138 Elsie O. Bull Center, West Chester, PA 19383. (610) 436-2627 Ext. 2607.

INTERNATIONAL STUDENTS
Demographics 7% of students enrolled in the program are international; Asia 46%, Europe 38%, other 16%.

Services and Facilities International student office, international student center, visa services, language tutoring, special assistance for nonnative speakers of English.

Applying TOEFL required, minimum score of 575; proof of adequate funds. Financial aid is not available to international students. Admission applications are processed on a rolling basis. Contact: Mr. Barry Degler, International Student Services Coordinator, Old Library, West Chester, PA 19383. (610) 436-3515 Ext. 3515.

ALTERNATE MBA PROGRAM
Executive MBA (EMBA) Length of program: Minimum: 24 months. Maximum: 6 years. Part-time classes: Main campus; day, evening. Degree requirements: 36 credits.

PLACEMENT
Placement services include career counseling/planning, career placement, job interviews, and resume referral to employers.

Program Contact: Mr. James W. Hamilton, Director, MBA Program, West Chester University of Pennsylvania, Anderson Hall, West Chester, PA 19383. (610) 436-2608; Fax: (610) 436-3170; Internet Address: hamilton.james@wcu.

Widener University

School of Management

Chester, Pennsylvania

OVERVIEW
Widener University is an independent nonprofit comprehensive coed institution. Founded 1821. Setting: 115-acre suburban campus with easy access to Philadelphia. Total institutional enrollment: 8,700. Program was first offered in 1967.

MBA HIGHLIGHTS

Entrance Difficulty*
Mean GMAT: 495
Mean GPA: 3.1

Cost $$
Tuition: $375/credit
Room & Board: N/R

Enrollment Profile

Full-time: 50	Work Exp: 90%
Part-time: 500	International: N/R
Total: 550	Women: 38%
Average Age: 31	Minorities: 5%

Average Class Size: 22

ACADEMICS
Length of Program Minimum: 18 months. Maximum: 7 years.
Calendar Semesters.
Full-time Classes Main campus, Wilmington; evening.
Part-time Classes Main campus, Wilmington; evening.
Degree Requirements 36 credits including 12 elective credits.
Required Courses Accounting for decision making, managerial economics, managerial finance, operations and technology, quantitative methods for decision making, strategic management, strategic marketing. Courses may be waived through: previous course work.

Curricular Focus Business issues and problems, problem solving and decision making, teamwork.

Concentrations Accounting, economics, finance, health services, human resources management, international business, management, management information systems, marketing, operations management, organizational behavior.

Faculty Full-time: 30, 80% with doctorates; part-time: 20, 65% with doctorates.

Teaching Methodology Case study: 25%, faculty seminars: 5%, lecture: 30%, research: 10%, seminars by members of the business community: 2%, student presentations: 10%, team projects: 18%.

STUDENT STATISTICS
Geographic Representation State residents 5%. By region: Northeast 92%; South 1%; Midwest 1%; West 1%.

Undergraduate Majors Business 50%; education 2%; engineering/technology 10%; humanities 8%; nursing 2%; science/mathematics 10%; social sciences 10%; other 8%.

Other Background Graduate degrees in other disciplines: 5%. Work experience: On average, students have 5-8 years of work experience on entrance to the program.

FACILITIES
Information Resources Main library with 228,000 bound volumes, 4,500 titles on microform, 1,700 periodical subscriptions, 3,000 records/tapes/CDs.

Housing College housing not available.

Technology Computers are used moderately in course work. 400 computer terminals/PCs are available for use by students in program; they are located in the library, the computer center, computer labs. Students in the program are not required to have their own PC.

Computer Resources/On-line Services

Training	No	LEXIS/NEXIS	Yes
E-Mail	No	CompuServe	Yes
Multimedia Center	Yes	Dow Jones	Yes

ADMISSION
Acceptance 1994-95 Of those applying, 66% were accepted.

Entrance Requirements Bachelor's degree, GMAT score of 450, minimum 2.5 GPA. Core courses waived through: previous course work.

Application Requirements Written essay, application form, copies of transcript, personal statement, 2 letters of recommendation.

Application Deadlines 8/1 for fall, 12/1 for spring, 4/1 for summer.

FINANCIALS
Costs for 1994-95 Tuition: Full-time: $375/credit. Fees: Full-time: $15/course.

Financial Aid In 1994-95, 15% of candidates received some institutionally administered aid in the form of loans, assistantships. Financial aid is available to part-time students. Application deadlines: 7/1 for fall, 10/1 for spring, 4/1 for summer. Contact: Ms. Ethel Desmarais, Director of Financial Aid, One University Place, Chester, PA 19013-5792. (610) 499-4171.

INTERNATIONAL STUDENTS
Demographics 5% of students on campus are international.

Services and Facilities International student center, language tutoring, ESL courses, counseling/support services.

Applying TOEFL required, minimum score of 550; proof of adequate funds. Financial aid is not available to international students. Admission application deadlines: 6/1 for fall, 10/1 for spring, 1/2 for summer. Contact: Ms. Lois Fuller, Director International Student Services, One University Place, Chester, PA 19013-5792. (610) 499-4395.

ALTERNATE MBA PROGRAMS
MBA/JD Length of program: Minimum: 36 months. Maximum: 7 years. Degree requirements: 99 credits.

MBA/M Eng Length of program: Minimum: 36 months. Maximum: 7 years. Degree requirements: 66 credits.

MBA/MD

PLACEMENT
In 1993-94, 6 organizations participated in on-campus recruiting. Placement services include alumni network, career counseling/planning, career fairs, career library, career placement, job interviews, resume preparation, and resume referral to employers.

Program Contact: Mr. Richard L. Thompson, Director, Graduate Programs in Business, Widener University, One University Place, Chester, PA 19013-5792. (610) 499-4305; Fax: (610) 499-4615.
See full description on page 934.

Wilkes University

School of Business, Society, and Public Policy

Wilkes-Barre, Pennsylvania

OVERVIEW

Wilkes University is an independent nonprofit comprehensive coed institution. Founded 1933. Setting: 25-acre urban campus. Total institutional enrollment: 3,700. Program was first offered in 1964.

MBA HIGHLIGHTS

Entrance Difficulty**
Mean GMAT: 450
Mean GPA: 3.3

Cost $$
Tuition: $390/credit hour
Room & Board: $4,000

Enrollment Profile
Full-time: 20
Part-time: 246
Total: 266
Average Age: 28

Work Exp: 90%
International: 4%
Women: 40%
Minorities: 1%

Average Class Size: 15

ACADEMICS

Length of Program Minimum: 12 months. Maximum: 6 years.

Calendar Semesters.

Full-time Classes Main campus; evening, weekends, summer.

Part-time Classes Main campus; evening, weekends, summer.

Degree Requirements 33 credit hours including 15 elective credit hours.

Required Courses Business and society, financial and managerial accounting, management science, managerial economics, managerial statistics, strategic management and business policy. Courses may be waived through: previous course work.

Curricular Focus Organizational development and change management, problem solving and decision making, strategic analysis and planning.

Concentrations Accounting, economics, entrepreneurship, finance, health services, human resources management, international business, management, management information systems, marketing, operations management, organizational behavior, quantitative analysis, strategic management.

Faculty Full-time: 11, 82% with doctorates; part-time: 6, 50% with doctorates.

Teaching Methodology Case study: 15%, faculty seminars: 5%, lecture: 50%, research: 5%, seminars by members of the business community: 5%, student presentations: 10%, team projects: 10%.

STUDENT STATISTICS

Geographic Representation State residents 90%. By region: Northeast 91%; South 2%; Midwest 2%; West 1%. International 4%.

Undergraduate Majors Business 75%; education 2%; engineering/technology 6%; humanities 2%; nursing 1%; science/mathematics 3%; social sciences 10%; other 1%.

Other Background Graduate degrees in other disciplines: 5%. Work experience: On average, students have 5 years of work experience on entrance to the program.

FACILITIES

Information Resources Main library with 200,000 bound volumes, 620,000 titles on microform, 1,150 periodical subscriptions, 2,500 records/tapes/CDs, 12 CD-ROMs. Business collection includes 500 bound volumes, 70 periodical subscriptions, 2 CD-ROMs, 7 videos.

Housing 1% of students in program live in college-owned or -operated housing.

Technology Computers are used moderately in course work. 150 computer terminals/PCs are available for use by students in program; they are located in the library, the computer center, computer labs. Students in the program are not required to have their own PC.

Computer Resources/On-line Services

Training	Yes	Videoconference Center	Yes
Internet	Yes	Dialog	Yes
E-Mail	Yes		

Other on-line services: First Search, SEC.

ADMISSION

Acceptance 1994-95 Of those applying, 95% were accepted.

Entrance Requirements Bachelor's degree, GMAT score of 350, minimum 2.75 GPA. Core courses waived through: previous course work.

Application Requirements Interview, application form, copies of transcript, 2 letters of recommendation.

Application Deadline Applications are processed on a rolling basis.

FINANCIALS

Costs for 1994-95 Tuition: Full-time: $390/credit hour. Fees: Full-time: $6/credit hour. Average room and board costs are $4,000 per academic year (on-campus).

Financial Aid In 1994-95, candidates received some institutionally administered aid in the form of assistantships, work-study. Total awards ranged from $300-$2,800. Financial aid is available to part-time students. Application deadline: 2/1 for fall. Contact: Ms. Rachael Lohman, Director, 2nd Floor Sturdevant Hall, Wilkes-Barre, PA 18766-0002. (717) 831-4346.

INTERNATIONAL STUDENTS

Demographics 4% of students enrolled in the program are international; Asia 50%, Europe 25%, South America 25%.

Services and Facilities Visa services, language tutoring, ESL courses, special assistance for nonnative speakers of English, counseling/support services.

Applying TOEFL required. Financial aid is not available to international students. Admission application deadlines: 6/15 for fall, 11/15 for spring. Contact: Ms. Barbara King, Coordinator, Special Projects, 2nd Floor Conyngham Center, Wilkes-Barre, PA 18766-0002. (717) 831-4107.

PLACEMENT

In 1993-94, 20 organizations participated in on-campus recruiting. Placement services include alumni network, career counseling/planning, career fairs, career library, career placement, electronic job bank, job interviews, and resume referral to employers. Of 1994 graduates, 95% were employed within three months of graduation.

Jobs by Employer Type Manufacturing 30%; service 45%; government 5%; consulting 5%; nonprofit 15%.

Jobs by Functional Area Marketing/sales 20%; finance 25%; operations 10%; management 35%; strategic planning 5%; technical management 5%.

Program Contact: Dr. Robert D. Seeley, Director of Graduate Programs, Wilkes University, 107 South Franklin Street, PO Box 111, Wilkes-Barre, PA 18766-0002. (717) 831-4717, or (800) 945-5378; Fax: (717) 831-4917.

York College of Pennsylvania

Department of Business Administration

York, Pennsylvania

OVERVIEW

York College of Pennsylvania is an independent nonprofit comprehensive coed institution. Founded 1787. Setting: 80-acre suburban campus with easy access to Baltimore. Total institutional enrollment: 5,500. Program was first offered in 1977.

MBA HIGHLIGHTS

Entrance Difficulty**
Mean GMAT: 500
Mean GPA: 2.9

Cost $$
Tuition: $243/credit
Room & Board: N/R

Enrollment Profile
Full-time: 3
Part-time: 131
Total: 134
Average Age: 32

Work Exp: 98%
International: 2%
Women: 34%
Minorities: 3%

Average Class Size: 20

ACADEMICS

Length of Program Minimum: 12 months. Maximum: 7 years.

Calendar Semesters.

Full-time Classes Main campus; day, evening, weekends.

Part-time Classes Main campus; day, evening, weekends.

Degree Requirements 33 credits including 9 elective credits.

Required Courses Business policy, management information systems, managerial accounting, managerial economics, marketing management, operations management, organizational theory and behavior, statistical decision analysis. Courses may be waived through: previous course work.

Curricular Focus Business issues and problems, economic and financial theory, general management.

Concentrations Accounting, finance, human resources management, management, management information systems, marketing.

Faculty Full-time: 15, 6% with doctorates.

Teaching Methodology Case study: 25%, lecture: 28%, research: 10%, seminars by members of the business community: 2%, student presentations: 10%, team projects: 25%.

Special Opportunities International exchange in United Kingdom. Internship program available.

STUDENT STATISTICS

Geographic Representation International 2%.

Other Background Graduate degrees in other disciplines: 1%. Work experience: On average, students have 6 years of work experience on entrance to the program.

FACILITIES

Information Resources Main library with 300,000 bound volumes, 500,000 titles on microform, 1,400 periodical subscriptions, 75,000 records/tapes/CDs.

Housing 1% of students in program live in college-owned or -operated housing.

Technology Computers are used moderately in course work. 128 computer terminals/PCs, linked by a campus-wide computer network, are available for use by students in program; they are located in classrooms, the computer center, computer labs. Students in the program are not required to have their own PC.

Computer Resources/On-line Services

Training	Yes	CompuServe	No
Internet	Yes	Dun's	Yes
E-Mail	Yes	Dow Jones	Yes
Videoconference Center	Yes	Dialog	Yes $
Multimedia Center	Yes	Bloomberg	No
LEXIS/NEXIS	No		

ADMISSION

Acceptance 1994-95 Of those applying, 78% were accepted.

Entrance Requirements Bachelor's degree, GMAT score of 450. Core courses waived through: previous course work.

Application Requirements Application form, copies of transcript.

Application Deadlines 8/15 for fall, 12/15 for spring.

FINANCIALS

Costs for 1994-95 Tuition: Full-time: $243/credit. Fees: Full-time: $83/semester.

Financial Aid In 1994-95, 2% of candidates received some institutionally administered aid in the form of grants, scholarships. Total awards ranged from $500-$2,000. Financial aid is available to part-time students. Application deadlines: 4/15 for fall, 11/15 for spring. Contact: Mr. Calvin Williams, Director of Financial Aid, Country Club Road, York, PA 17405-7199. (717) 846-7788 Ext. 1226.

INTERNATIONAL STUDENTS

Demographics 2% of students enrolled in the program are international.

Applying TOEFL required; proof of health; proof of adequate funds. Financial aid is not available to international students. Admission application deadlines: 4/15 for fall, 11/15 for spring.

PLACEMENT

Placement services include alumni network, career counseling/planning, career library, career placement, resume preparation, and resume referral to employers.

Program Contact: Ms. Mary Meisenhelter, MBA Coordinator, York College of Pennsylvania, Country Club Road, York, PA 17405-7199. (717) 846-7788 Ext. 1277.

RHODE ISLAND

Bryant College

The Graduate School

Smithfield, Rhode Island

OVERVIEW

Bryant College is an independent nonprofit comprehensive coed institution. Founded 1863. Setting: 387-acre suburban campus with easy access to Boston. Total institutional enrollment: 3,739. Program was first offered in 1974.

MBA HIGHLIGHTS

Entrance Difficulty*
Mean GMAT: 500
Mean GPA: 2.75

Cost $$$
Tuition: $12,000
Room & Board: $6,070

Enrollment Profile
Full-time: 60
Part-time: 635
Total: 695
Average Age: 28

Work Exp: 90%
International: 3%
Women: 40%
Minorities: 2%

Average Class Size: 23

B*ryant College provides students the chance to use skills acquired in their courses. Students in the second year of the M.B.A. program work between 10 and 12 hours per week as interns in local organizations. This experience enables students to apply concepts learned in the program to gain knowledge of a specific business organization of interest while they form a connection with the local business community. Students can earn up to 6 credits and, in some cases, a salary.*

Interns meet with a faculty adviser on a regular basis to assess their progress and to address issues that may arise at the work site. The faculty adviser evaluates the intern based upon assigned work. Typically, students complete projects and tasks at the work site, maintain an internship journal, and submit a brief report relating their work experience to concepts studied in the program.

Students may locate their own internship positions. Opportunities are available through the Rhode Island Small Business Development Center (RISBDC) or the Rhode Island Export Assistance Center (RIEAC), both located on campus. These centers provide M.B.A. students the opportunity to serve as consultants to small businesses and companies seeking to enter or expand in international markets.

ACADEMICS

Length of Program Minimum: 24 months. Maximum: 6 years.

Calendar Semesters.

Full-time Classes Main campus; day, evening, summer.

Part-time Classes Main campus; day, evening, summer.

Degree Requirements 60 credits including 15 elective credits.

Required Courses Business and society: the ethical and legal foundations, business policy and strategy, economics for business, finance for business, financial accounting, fundamentals of marketing statistics, management information systems, managerial analysis and control, marketing management, operations management, organizational theory and behavior, quantitative analysis for business decisions, theory of the business firm. Courses may be waived through: previous course work.

Curricular Focus International business, organizational development and change management, teamwork.

Concentrations Accounting, economics, finance, health services, international business, management, management information systems, marketing, operations management.

Faculty Full-time: 88, 85% with doctorates.

Teaching Methodology Case study: 20%, lecture: 20%, research: 20%, student presentations: 20%, team projects: 20%.

Special Opportunities Internships include corporate, government, and health care.

STUDENT STATISTICS

Geographic Representation State residents 65%. By region: Northeast 97%. International 3%.

Other Background Graduate degrees in other disciplines: 10%. Work experience: On average, students have 7 years of work experience on entrance to the program.

FACILITIES

Information Resources Main library with 113,224 bound volumes, 338 titles on microform, 1,695 periodical subscriptions, 492 records/tapes/CDs, 492 CD-ROMs.

Housing 18% of students in program live in college-owned or -operated housing.

Technology Computers are used moderately in course work. 215 computer terminals/PCs are available for use by students in program; they are located in the student center, classrooms, learning resource center, the computer center, computer labs, graduate student lounge. Students in the program are not required to have their own PC.

Computer Resources/On-line Services

Training	Yes	Dun's	No
Internet	Yes	Dow Jones	No
E-Mail	Yes	Dialog	Yes
LEXIS/NEXIS	Yes	Bloomberg	No
CompuServe	No		

Other on-line services: OCLC.

ADMISSION

Entrance Requirements Bachelor's degree, GMAT score, minimum 2.75 GPA. Core courses waived through: previous course work.

Application Requirements Written essay, application form, copies of transcript, 2 letters of recommendation.

Application Deadlines 7/15 for fall, 12/1 for spring.

FINANCIALS

Costs for 1994-95 Tuition: Full-time: $12,000; Part-time evening: $750/course. Average room and board costs are $6,070 per academic year (on-campus) and $4,770 per academic year (off-campus).

Financial Aid In 1994-95, 78% of candidates received some institutionally administered aid in the form of loans, assistantships. Total awards ranged from $1,000-$12,000. Financial aid is available to part-time students. Application deadlines: 2/15 for fall, 8/15 for spring. Contact: Mr. James Dorian, Director of Financial Aid, 1150 Douglas Pike, Smithfield, RI 02917. (800) 248-4036.

INTERNATIONAL STUDENTS

Demographics 3% of students enrolled in the program are international; Europe 61%, Asia 33%, South America 6%.

Services and Facilities ESL courses, counseling/support services.

Applying TOEFL required, minimum score of 550; proof of health; proof of adequate funds. Financial aid is not available to international students. Admission application deadlines: 7/1 for fall, 12/1 for spring. Contact: Ms. Jann Douglas Bell, Director Multicultural Student Services, 1150 Douglas Pike, Smithfield, RI 02917. (401) 232-6046.

ALTERNATE MBA PROGRAM

One-Year MBA Length of program: Minimum: 12 months. Maximum: 6 years. Degree requirements: 33 credits including 15 elective credits. Undergraduate degree in business.

PLACEMENT

Placement services include alumni network, career counseling/planning, career library, career placement, job interviews, resume preparation, and resume referral to employers. Of 1994 graduates, the average starting salary was $44,690, the range was $26,000-$90,000.

Program Contact: Ms. Anne C. Parish, Director of Graduate Programs, Bryant College, 1150 Douglas Pike, Smithfield, RI 02917. (401) 232-6230; Fax: (401) 232-6319.

See full description on page 684.

Johnson & Wales University

Providence, Rhode Island

OVERVIEW

Johnson & Wales University is an independent nonprofit comprehensive coed institution. Founded 1914. Setting: 100-acre urban campus with easy access to Boston. Total institutional enrollment: 8,604. Program was first offered in 1989.

MBA HIGHLIGHTS

Entrance Difficulty***
Mean GMAT: N/R
Mean GPA: 3.2

Cost $$
Tuition: $214/quarter hour
Room & Board: $9,000

Enrollment Profile

Full-time: 60	Work Exp: 72%
Part-time: 180	International: 34%
Total: 240	Women: 38%
Average Age: N/R	Minorities: N/R

Average Class Size: 32

ACADEMICS

Length of Program Minimum: 12 months. Maximum: 5 years.

Calendar Trimesters.

Full-time Classes Main campus; day, evening.

Part-time Classes Main campus; evening.

Degree Requirements 54 credits including 3 elective credits.

Required Courses Economics of multinational corporate operations, international accounting and finance, international banking, international business strategy and policy, international marketing, introduction to international business, legal aspects of international business, multinational communications, research methods and design: international business, seminar in international business, social and cultural geography.

Curricular Focus International business, problem solving and decision making, strategic analysis and planning.

Concentrations Hotel management, international business, management.

Faculty Full-time: 4, 75% with doctorates; part-time: 5, 60% with doctorates.

Teaching Methodology Case study: 15%, faculty seminars: 20%, lecture: 35%, research: 5%, seminars by members of the business community: 5%, student presentations: 5%, team projects: 15%.

Special Opportunities International exchange in France, Netherlands, United Kingdom. Internships include marketing and sales, new product development, importing and exporting, and management.

STUDENT STATISTICS

Geographic Representation International 34%.

Undergraduate Majors Business 64%; education 15%; engineering/technology 8%; other 13%.

Other Background Graduate degrees in other disciplines: 11%. Work experience: On average, students have 4-5 years of work experience on entrance to the program.

FACILITIES

Information Resources Main library with 55,516 bound volumes, 797 titles on microform, 748 periodical subscriptions, 396 records/tapes/CDs, 20 CD-ROMs. Business collection includes 6,450 bound volumes, 217 periodical subscriptions, 3 CD-ROMs, 350 videos.

Housing 6% of students in program live in college-owned or -operated housing. Assistance with housing search provided.

Technology Computers are used moderately in course work. 75 computer terminals/PCs are available for use by students in program; they are located in learning resource center, the library, the computer center, computer labs, the research center. Students in the program are not required to have their own PC.

Computer Resources/On-line Services

Training	Yes	Multimedia Center	Yes
Internet	Yes	Dun's	Yes
E-Mail	Yes	Dialog	Yes $

Other on-line services: SEC.

ADMISSION

Acceptance 1994-95 131 applied for admission; 68% were accepted.

Entrance Requirements Bachelor's degree, minimum 2.75 GPA.

Application Requirements Application form, copies of transcript, resume/curriculum vitae, 3 letters of recommendation.

Application Deadline Applications are processed on a rolling basis.

FINANCIALS

Costs for 1995-96 Tuition: Full-time: $214/quarter hour; Part-time evening: $154/quarter hour. Average room and board costs are $9,000 per academic year (on-campus).

Financial Aid In 1994-95, 41% of candidates received some institutionally administered aid in the form of scholarships, loans, assistantships, student employment. Financial aid is not available to part-time students. Applications are processed on a rolling basis. Contact: Ms. Deborah Machowski, Director of Financial Aid, 8 Abbott Park Place, Providence, RI 02903-2807. (401) 598-4648.

INTERNATIONAL STUDENTS

Demographics 34% of students enrolled in the program are international; Asia 44%, Europe 22%, North America 7%, Africa 3%, South America 3%, other 21%.

Services and Facilities International student housing; international student office, visa services, language tutoring, ESL courses, special assistance for nonnative speakers of English, counseling/support services, host family program, mentor program, ambassador program, orientation.

Applying TOEFL required, minimum score of 550; proof of adequate funds. Financial aid is available to international students. Applications are processed on a rolling basis. Admission applications are processed on a rolling basis. Contact: Office of International Student Affairs, Kinsley Building, 334 Westminster Street, Providence, RI 02903-2807. (401) 598-1074.

PLACEMENT

In 1993-94, 37 organizations participated in on-campus recruiting; 150 on-campus interviews were conducted. Placement services include alumni network, career counseling/planning, career fairs, career library, career placement, electronic job bank, job interviews, job search course, resume preparation, and resume referral to employers. Of 1994 graduates, 81% were employed within three months of graduation, the average starting salary was $28,000, the range was $25,000-$31,000.

Jobs by Functional Area Marketing/sales 27%; finance 16%; operations 12%; management 26%; strategic planning 8%; technical management 4%; education 7%.

Program Contact: Dr. Allan G. Freedman, Director, Graduate Admissions, Johnson & Wales University, 8 Abbott Park Place, Providence, RI 02903-2807. (401) 598-1000, or (800) 343-2565.
See full description on page 770.

Providence College

Department of Business Administration

Providence, Rhode Island

OVERVIEW

Providence College is an independent Roman Catholic comprehensive coed institution. Founded 1917. Setting: 105-acre urban campus with easy access to Boston. Total institutional enrollment: 5,825. Program was first offered in 1972.

MBA HIGHLIGHTS

Entrance Difficulty***
Mean GMAT: 493
Mean GPA: 2.9

Cost $$
Tuition: $210/credit
Room & Board: $12,000 (off-campus)

Enrollment Profile

Full-time: 14	Work Exp: 90%
Part-time: 286	International: N/R
Total: 300	Women: 50%
Average Age: 28	Minorities: N/R

Average Class Size: 19

ACADEMICS

Length of Program Minimum: 12 months. Maximum: 5 years.

Calendar Semesters.

Full-time Classes Main campus; evening, weekends, summer.

Degree Requirements 36 credits including 15 elective credits.

Required Courses Business finance, computer systems, human resources management, management seminar, managerial accounting, marketing management and analysis, operations research. Courses may be waived through: previous course work.

Curricular Focus Business issues and problems, organizational development and change management, problem solving and decision making, teamwork.

Concentrations Accounting, economics, finance, international business, management, marketing, public administration, quantitative analysis.

Faculty Full-time: 20, 50% with doctorates; part-time: 6.

Teaching Methodology Case study: 35%, lecture: 35%, research: 3%, seminars by members of the business community: 2%, student presentations: 20%, team projects: 5%.

Special Opportunities Internship program available.

STUDENT STATISTICS

Geographic Representation State residents 90%. By region: Northeast 98%.

Undergraduate Majors Business 35%; education 10%; engineering/technology 5%; humanities 31%; nursing 2%; science/mathematics 15%; social sciences 2%.

Other Background Graduate degrees in other disciplines: 10%. Work experience: On average, students have 6 years of work experience on entrance to the program.

FACILITIES

Information Resources Main library with 307,655 bound volumes, 25,709 titles on microform, 1,894 periodical subscriptions, 1,113 records/tapes/CDs. Business collection includes 80,000 bound volumes, 65 periodical subscriptions, 1 CD-ROM.

Housing College housing not available.

Technology Computers are used moderately in course work. 100 computer terminals/PCs are available for use by students in program; they are located in the computer center, computer labs, the research center. Students in the program are not required to have their own PC.

Computer Resources/On-line Services

Training	Yes	CompuServe	Yes
E-Mail	No	Dialog	Yes
LEXIS/NEXIS	Yes		

ADMISSION

Acceptance 1994-95 Of those applying, 77% were accepted.

Entrance Requirements Bachelor's degree, GMAT score. Core courses waived through: previous course work.

Application Requirements Interview, application form, copies of transcript, 2 letters of recommendation.

Application Deadline Applications are processed on a rolling basis.

FINANCIALS

Costs for 1994-95 Tuition: Full-time: $210/credit. Average room and board costs are $12,000 per academic year (off-campus).

Financial Aid In 1994-95, 33% of candidates received some institutionally administered aid in the form of loans. Total awards ranged from $5,500-$8,500. Financial aid is not available to part-time students. Applications are processed on a rolling basis. Contact: Mr. Herbert J. D'Arcy Jr., Executive Director, River Avenue and Eaton Street, Providence, RI 02918. (401) 865-2286.

INTERNATIONAL STUDENTS

Demographics 5% of students on campus are international.

Services and Facilities Counseling/support services.

Applying TOEFL required; proof of adequate funds. Financial aid is not available to international students. Admission applications are processed on a rolling basis. Contact: Dr. Giacomo A. Striuli, Associate Professor of Italian, River Avenue and Eaton Street, Providence, RI 02918. (401) 865-2234.

PLACEMENT

Placement services include alumni network, career counseling/planning, career library, and career placement. Of 1994 graduates, 90% were employed within three months of graduation.

Program Contact: Dr. Ronald Cerwonka, MBA Program Director, Providence College, River Avenue and Eaton Street, Providence, RI 02918. (401) 865-2333; Fax: (401) 865-2978.
See full description on page 808.

Salve Regina University

The Business Division of the Graduate School

Newport, Rhode Island

OVERVIEW

Salve Regina University is an independent Roman Catholic comprehensive coed institution. Founded 1934. Setting: 100-acre suburban campus with easy access to Boston. Total institutional enrollment: 2,200. Program was first offered in 1989.

MBA HIGHLIGHTS

Entrance Difficulty***
Mean GMAT: 460
Mean GPA: 3.38

Cost $
Tuition: $250/credit
Room & Board: $5,900 (off-campus)

Enrollment Profile

Full-time: 5	Work Exp: N/R
Part-time: 18	International: 0%
Total: 23	Women: 30%
Average Age: 32	Minorities: 13%

Average Class Size: 15

ACADEMICS

Length of Program Minimum: 24 months. Maximum: 5 years.
Calendar Semesters.
Full-time Classes Main campus; evening, summer.
Part-time Classes Main campus; evening, summer.
Degree Requirements 36 credits including 12 elective credits.
Required Courses Business research methods, ethics for managers, financial accounting, financial management, law and business organizations, organizational theory, principles of economics, strategic management and business policy.
Curricular Focus Economic and financial theory, general management, international business.
Concentrations Accounting, international business, management, management information systems.
Faculty Full-time: 2, 100% with doctorates.
Teaching Methodology Case study: 15%, faculty seminars: 5%, lecture: 30%, research: 5%, seminars by members of the business community: 10%, student presentations: 30%, team projects: 5%.

STUDENT STATISTICS

Geographic Representation State residents 70%. By region: Northeast 96%; West 4%.

FACILITIES

Information Resources Main library with 96,735 bound volumes, 11,643 titles on microform, 1,002 periodical subscriptions, 15,166 records/tapes/CDs. Business collection includes 5,200 bound volumes, 89 periodical subscriptions, 420 CD-ROMs, 100 videos.
Housing College housing not available.
Technology 110 computer terminals/PCs, linked by a campus-wide computer network, are available for use by students in program; they are located in learning resource center, the computer center, computer labs. Students in the program are not required to have their own PC.

Computer Resources/On-line Services

Internet	Yes	Dun's	No
E-Mail	Yes	Dow Jones	No
Multimedia Center	Yes	Dialog	Yes
LEXIS/NEXIS	No	Bloomberg	No
CompuServe	No		

Other on-line services: First Search, OCLC.

ADMISSION

Entrance Requirements Bachelor's degree. Core courses waived through: previous course work.
Application Requirements Application form, copies of transcript, 2 letters of recommendation.
Application Deadline Applications are processed on a rolling basis.

FINANCIALS

Costs for 1994-95 Tuition: Full-time: $250/credit. Average room and board costs are $5,900 per academic year (off-campus).
Financial Aid In 1994-95, candidates received some institutionally administered aid in the form of loans. Application deadline: 3/1 for fall. Applications are processed on a rolling basis. Contact: Mrs. Lucile Flanagan, Director of Financial Aid and Veteran's Affairs, 100 Ochre Point Avenue, Newport, RI 02840-4192. (401) 847-6650 Ext. 2901.

INTERNATIONAL STUDENTS

Applying TOEFL required. Financial aid is not available to international students. Admission application deadlines: 3/15 for fall, 9/15 for spring. Contact: Ms. Linda Lue, Admissions Counselor, 100 Ochre Point Avenue, Newport, RI 02840-4192. (401) 847-6650.

Program Contact: Ms. Laura McPhie, Dean of Enrollment Services, Salve Regina University, 100 Ochre Point Avenue, Newport, RI 02840-4192. (401) 847-6650 Ext. 2908, or (800) 321-7124; Fax: (401) 848-2823.

University of Rhode Island

College of Business Administration

Kingston, Rhode Island

OVERVIEW

The University of Rhode Island is a state-supported coed institution. Part of Rhode Island State System of Higher Education. Founded 1892. Setting: 1,200-acre small-town campus. Total institutional enrollment: 16,254. AACSB-accredited.

ACADEMICS

Calendar Semesters.
Degree Requirements 36-59 credits.
Concentrations Finance, international business, management, marketing.

FACILITIES

Information Resources Main library with 1.1 million bound volumes, 1.4 million titles on microform, 8,600 periodical subscriptions, 12,000 records/tapes/CDs, 50 CD-ROMs.

ADMISSION

Entrance Requirements Bachelor's degree, GMAT score.
Application Requirements Written essay, application form, copies of transcript, resume/curriculum vitae, personal statement.
Application Deadlines 9/3 for fall, 12/14 for spring.

INTERNATIONAL STUDENTS

Applying TOEFL required, minimum score of 575. Admission application deadlines: 9/3 for fall, 12/14 for spring.

Program Contact: Mr. David Taggart, Dean of Admissions and Financial Aid, University of Rhode Island, Kingston, RI 02881. (401) 792-9800.

SOUTH CAROLINA

Charleston Southern University

School of Business

Charleston, South Carolina

OVERVIEW
Charleston Southern University is an independent Baptist comprehensive coed institution. Founded 1964. Setting: 350-acre suburban campus. Total institutional enrollment: 2,500. Program was first offered in 1990.

MBA HIGHLIGHTS

Entrance Difficulty*
Mean GMAT: 480
Mean GPA: N/R

Cost $
Tuition: $164/semester hour
Room & Board: $4,222

Enrollment Profile

Full-time: N/R	Work Exp: 90%
Part-time: N/R	International: 3%
Total: 227	Women: 40%
Average Age: 35	Minorities: 25%

Average Class Size: 20

ACADEMICS
Length of Program Minimum: 24 months. Maximum: 5 years.
Calendar Semesters.
Full-time Classes Main campus.
Part-time Classes Main campus; evening, weekends.
Degree Requirements 30 semester hours including 6 elective semester hours.
Required Courses Advanced management theory, advanced managerial accounting, advanced managerial economics and macropolicy in a global economy, advanced marketing management, business, ethical, legal environments, financial management practices, quantitative methods, strategic planning and analysis.
Curricular Focus International business, organizational development and change management.
Concentrations Accounting, finance, marketing, organizational development.
Faculty Full-time: 7, 100% with doctorates.
Teaching Methodology Case study: 20%, lecture: 20%, research: 20%, student presentations: 20%, team projects: 20%.

STUDENT STATISTICS
Geographic Representation State residents 97%. International 3%.
Other Background Graduate degrees in other disciplines: 4%.

FACILITIES
Information Resources Main library with 120,000 bound volumes, 712 titles on microform, 1,206 periodical subscriptions, 979 records/tapes/CDs.
Housing 5% of students in program live in college-owned or -operated housing.
Technology Computers are used heavily in course work. Computer terminals/PCs are available for use by students in program; they are located in the library, computer labs, MBA students lab. Students in the program are not required to have their own PC.
Computer Resources/On-line Services

Training	No	E-Mail	No

ADMISSION
Entrance Requirements Bachelor's degree, prerequisite courses required for applicants with non-business degree, GMAT score. Core courses waived through: previous course work.
Application Requirements Application form, copies of transcript, 2 letters of recommendation.
Application Deadline Applications are processed on a rolling basis.

FINANCIALS
Costs for 1994-95 Tuition: Full-time: $164/semester hour. Average room and board costs are $4,222 per academic year (on-campus).

Financial Aid In 1994-95, candidates received some institutionally administered aid in the form of loans, assistantships. Applications are processed on a rolling basis. Contact: Ms. Ellen Green, Director of Financial Aid, PO Box 118087, Charleston, SC 29423-8087. (803) 863-8034.

INTERNATIONAL STUDENTS
Demographics 3% of students enrolled in the program are international.
Applying TOEFL required, minimum score of 550; proof of health; proof of adequate funds. Financial aid is not available to international students. Admission applications are processed on a rolling basis. Contact: Ms. Barbara Mead, Assistant Dean of Students, PO Box 118087, Charleston, SC 29423-8087. (803) 863-8009.

PLACEMENT
Placement services include career counseling/planning, career placement, electronic job bank, resume preparation, and resume referral to employers.

Program Contact: Dr. Al Parish Jr., Director, MBA Program, Charleston Southern University, PO Box 118087, Charleston, SC 29423-8087. (803) 863-7955; Fax: (803) 863-7922.

The Citadel, The Military College of South Carolina

Department of Business Administration

Charleston, South Carolina

OVERVIEW
The Citadel, The Military College of South Carolina is a state-supported comprehensive men only institution. Founded 1842. Setting: 130-acre urban campus. Total institutional enrollment: 2,866.

ACADEMICS
Calendar Semesters.
Full-time Classes Evening.
Degree Requirements 30 credits. Other: Minimum 3.0 GPA.
Required Courses Financial management, managerial accounting, managerial economics, marketing administration, organizational theory/design/behavior, quantitative methods, strategic management and business policy.
Concentration Management.

FACILITIES
Information Resources Main library with 197,052 bound volumes, 455,000 titles on microform, 1,662 periodical subscriptions.

ADMISSION
Entrance Requirements Bachelor's degree, prerequisite courses required for applicants with non-business degree, GMAT score.
Application Requirements Interview, 2 letters of recommendation.
Application Deadlines 8/10 for fall, 12/5 for spring, 5/10 for summer.

FINANCIALS
Costs for 1994-95 Tuition: Full-time: $120/credit hour. Fees: Full-time: $30.
Financial Aid Contact: Major Henry Fuller Jr., Director of Student Financial Aid, 171 Moultrie Street, Charleston, SC 29409. (803) 953-5187.

INTERNATIONAL STUDENTS
Applying TOEFL required, minimum score of 550. Admission application deadlines: 8/20 for fall, 12/15 for spring.

Program Contact: Dr. Ronald Zigli, Director of MBA Program, The Citadel, The Military College of South Carolina, 171 Moultrie Street, Charleston, SC 29409-0201. (803) 953-5056; Fax: (803) 953-7084.

Clemson University

College of Commerce and Industry

Clemson, South Carolina

OVERVIEW

Clemson University is a state-supported coed institution. Founded 1889. Setting: 1,400-acre small-town campus. Total institutional enrollment: 15,500. Program was first offered in 1982. AACSB-accredited.

MBA HIGHLIGHTS

Entrance Difficulty***
Mean GMAT: 540
Mean GPA: 3.3

Cost $
Tuition: $116/credit hour
(Nonresident: $232/credit hour)
Room & Board: $3,300

Enrollment Profile
Full-time: 50	Work Exp: 63%
Part-time: 176	International: 33%
Total: 226	Women: 25%
Average Age: 27	Minorities: 7%

Average Class Size: 25

ACADEMICS

Length of Program Minimum: 24 months. Maximum: 6 years.
Calendar Semesters.
Full-time Classes Main campus; day.
Part-time Classes Main campus, Greenville; evening, summer.
Degree Requirements 60 credit hours including 12 elective credit hours.
Required Courses Advanced financial management, advanced marketing strategy, business communications and ethics, financial accounting, foundations of economics, legal and social environment of business, management information systems development, management science applications, managerial accounting, managerial economics, managerial finance, managerial marketing, operations management, organization theory and behavior, statistical analysis for business, strategic management.
Curricular Focus International business, problem solving and decision making, strategic analysis and planning.
Concentrations Accounting, economics, finance, international business, management, management information systems, marketing, operations management, organizational behavior.
Faculty Full-time: 20, 100% with doctorates.
Teaching Methodology Case study: 10%, faculty seminars: 2%, lecture: 50%, research: 5%, seminars by members of the business community: 3%, student presentations: 10%, team projects: 20%.
Special Opportunities International exchange in Germany, Italy. Internship program available.

STUDENT STATISTICS

Geographic Representation By region: South 69%; Northeast 10%; Midwest 5%. International 33%.
Undergraduate Majors Business 52%; engineering/technology 36%; humanities 6%; social sciences 6%; other 1%.
Other Background Graduate degrees in other disciplines: 5%. Work experience: On average, students have 2 years of work experience on entrance to the program.

FACILITIES

Information Resources Main library with 1.4 million bound volumes, 2 million titles on microform, 7,114 periodical subscriptions.
Housing 20% of students in program live in college-owned or -operated housing.
Technology Computers are used heavily in course work. 250 computer terminals/PCs, linked by a campus-wide computer network, are available for use by students in program; they are located in the student center, the library, the computer center, computer labs, the research center. Students in the program are not required to have their own PC.

Computer Resources/On-line Services
Training	Yes	E-Mail	Yes
Internet	Yes	Multimedia Center	Yes

ADMISSION

Acceptance 1994-95 530 applied for admission; 58% were accepted.
Entrance Requirements Bachelor's degree, GMAT score, minimum "C" grade in college level calculus, two years work experience for part-time program. Core courses waived through: previous course work.
Application Requirements Application form, copies of transcript, resume/curriculum vitae, 2 letters of recommendation.
Application Deadline 7/1 for fall.

FINANCIALS

Costs for 1994-95 Tuition: Full-time: $116/credit hour for state residents, $232/credit hour for nonresidents. Fees: Full-time: $126/semester for state residents, $147/semester for nonresidents. Average room and board costs are $3,300 per academic year (on-campus) and $3,600 per academic year (off-campus).
Financial Aid In 1994-95, 40% of candidates received some institutionally administered aid in the form of loans, fellowships, assistantships. Financial aid is not available to part-time students. Application deadline: 5/15 for fall. Contact: Ms. Paula Campbell, Financial Aid Counselor, G01 Sikes Hall, Financial Aid, Clemson, SC 29634. (803) 656-2280.

INTERNATIONAL STUDENTS

Demographics 33% of students enrolled in the program are international; Europe 20%, Asia 5%, South America 2%, other 73%.
Services and Facilities International student center, visa services, counseling/support services.
Applying TOEFL required, minimum score of 550; proof of health; proof of adequate funds. Financial aid is available to international students. Financial aid application deadline: 5/15 for fall. Admission application deadline: 5/15 for fall. Contact: Mr. Louis Bregger, Student Services Program Manager, Office of International Programs and Services, E207 Martin Hall, Clemson, SC 29634. (803) 656-2357.

ALTERNATE MBA PROGRAM

International MBA Length of program: Minimum: 12 months. Maximum: 6 years. Degree requirements: 57 credit hours including 6 elective credit hours. 9 months of study in Italy or Germany; final 4 courses taken at Clemson University.

PLACEMENT

In 1993-94, 75 organizations participated in on-campus recruiting; 135 on-campus interviews were conducted. Placement services include career counseling/planning, career fairs, career library, career placement, job interviews, resume preparation, and resume referral to employers. Of 1994 graduates, 60% were employed within three months of graduation, the average starting salary was $33,000, the range was $30,000-$41,000.
Jobs by Employer Type Manufacturing 35%; service 45%; government 2%; consulting 15%; nonprofit 3%.
Jobs by Functional Area Marketing/sales 30%; finance 25%; operations 10%; management 25%; strategic planning 3%; technical management 7%.

Program Contact: Ms. Dot Skelton, Administrative Assistant, MBA Programs, Clemson University, Clemson, SC 29634. (803) 656-3975; Fax: (803) 656-0947; Internet Address: sdoroth@clemson.edu.
See full description on page 704.

Francis Marion University

School of Business

Florence, South Carolina

OVERVIEW

Francis Marion University is a state-supported comprehensive coed institution. Founded 1970. Setting: 309-acre rural campus. Total institutional enrollment: 4,103.

MBA HIGHLIGHTS

Entrance Difficulty*
Mean GMAT: 485
Mean GPA: N/R

Cost $
Tuition: $450/course
Room & Board: N/R

Enrollment Profile
Full-time: N/R	Work Exp: N/R
Part-time: N/R	International: 3%
Total: 70	Women: 50%
Average Age: N/R	Minorities: 10%

Average Class Size: 12

ACADEMICS
Length of Program Minimum: 30 months.
Calendar Semesters.
Part-time Classes Main campus; evening, summer.
Degree Requirements 36 credits.
Curricular Focus Entrepreneurship, problem solving and decision making, strategic analysis and planning.
Concentration Management.
Teaching Methodology Case study: 20%, lecture: 60%, student presentations: 10%, team projects: 10%.

STUDENT STATISTICS
Geographic Representation State residents 95%. International 3%.

FACILITIES
Information Resources Main library with 251,628 bound volumes, 81,492 titles on microform, 1,747 periodical subscriptions, 34,205 records/tapes/CDs.

ADMISSION
Entrance Requirements Bachelor's degree, prerequisite courses required for applicants with non-business degree, GMAT score.
Application Requirements Application form, copies of transcript, personal statement, 2 letters of recommendation.
Application Deadlines 8/15 for fall, 12/15 for spring.

FINANCIALS
Costs for 1994-95 Tuition: Part-time evening: $450/course.
Financial Aid Application deadlines: 8/15 for fall, 12/15 for spring. Contact: Mr. Scott Brown, Director of Financial Assistance, Box 100547, Florence, SC 29501-0547. (803) 661-1190.

INTERNATIONAL STUDENTS
Demographics 3% of students enrolled in the program are international.
Applying TOEFL required, minimum score of 550; proof of health; proof of adequate funds. Financial aid is available to international students. Assistantships are available for these students. Admission application deadlines: 8/15 for fall, 12/15 for spring.

Program Contact: Dr. Robert T. Barrett, Director, Francis Marion University, School of Business, Florence, SC 29501-0547. (803) 661-1419; Fax: (803) 661-1432.

University of South Carolina

College of Business Administration

Columbia, South Carolina

OVERVIEW
The University of South Carolina is a state-supported coed institution. Part of University of South Carolina System. Founded 1801. Setting: 242-acre urban campus. Total institutional enrollment: 26,434. Program was first offered in 1959. AACSB-accredited.

MBA HIGHLIGHTS

Entrance Difficulty**
Mean GMAT: 579
Mean GPA: 3.15

Cost $$
Tuition: $1,670/semester
(Nonresident: $6,650 - $12,600/semester)
Room & Board: $5,280

Enrollment Profile
Full-time: N/R	Work Exp: 70%
Part-time: N/R	International: 19%
Total: 277	Women: 28%
Average Age: 25	Minorities: 4%

Average Class Size: 30

ACADEMICS
Length of Program Minimum: 21 months. Maximum: 6 years.
Calendar Semesters.
Full-time Classes Main campus; day, evening, summer.
Part-time Classes Main campus, distance learning option; evening, weekends, summer.
Degree Requirements 60 credits including 15 elective credits.
Required Courses Business communications, financial and managerial accounting, financial policies, macroeconomics, management information systems, marketing management, microeconomics, organizational behavior, production and operations management, quantitative methods, strategic management, summer field consulting project. Courses may be waived through: previous course work, work experience.
Curricular Focus Economic and financial theory, problem solving and decision making, teamwork.
Concentrations Entrepreneurship, finance, human resources management, international business, management, management information systems, marketing, operations management, organizational behavior, quantitative analysis, strategic management.
Faculty Full-time: 55, 100% with doctorates.
Teaching Methodology Case study: 17%, discussion, problem solving, field trips: 7%, lecture: 50%, research: 3%, seminars by members of the business community: 3%, student presentations: 9%, team projects: 11%.
Special Opportunities International exchange in Australia, Belgium, Denmark, Finland, France, United Kingdom. Other: summer field consulting project.

STUDENT STATISTICS
Geographic Representation State residents 26%. International 19%.
Undergraduate Majors Business 50%; education 1%; engineering/technology 7%; humanities 8%; science/mathematics 7%; social sciences 19%; other 8%.
Other Background Graduate degrees in other disciplines: 2%. Work experience: On average, students have 1 year of work experience on entrance to the program.

FACILITIES
Information Resources Main library with 2.6 million bound volumes, 4 million titles on microform, 18,405 periodical subscriptions, 22,335 records/tapes/CDs. Business collection in Springs-Elliott Library includes 7,000 bound volumes, 350 periodical subscriptions.
Housing 3% of students in program live in college-owned or -operated housing.
Technology Computers are used moderately in course work. 200 computer terminals/PCs, linked by a campus-wide computer network, are available for use by students in program; they are located in the library, the computer center, computer labs. Students in the program are not required to have their own PC.

Computer Resources/On-line Services

Training	Yes	CompuServe	No
Internet	Yes	Dun's	No
E-Mail	Yes	Dow Jones	No
Multimedia Center	Yes	Dialog	No
LEXIS/NEXIS	No	Bloomberg	No

Other on-line services: OCLC.

ADMISSION
Acceptance 1994-95 Of those applying, 50% were accepted.
Entrance Requirements Bachelor's degree, calculus course, GMAT score of 550, minimum 3.0 GPA. Core courses waived through: previous course work, work experience.

Application Requirements Application form, copies of transcript, resume/curriculum vitae, personal statement, 2 letters of recommendation.
Application Deadlines 7/1 for fall, 2/1 for IMBA.

FINANCIALS
Costs for 1994-95 Tuition: Full-time: $1,670/semester for state residents, $2,650-$4,500/semester for nonresidents; Part-time day: $163/hour for state residents, $55-$163/hour for nonresidents. Fees: Full-time: $3,373/semester for state residents, $4,000-$8,100/semester for nonresidents; Part-time day: $331/hour for state residents, $83-$331/hour for nonresidents. Average room and board costs are $5,280 per academic year (on-campus) and $6,000 per academic year (off-campus).
Financial Aid In 1994-95, 60% of candidates received some institutionally administered aid in the form of scholarships, loans, assistantships, work-study. Total awards ranged from $500-$13,000. Financial aid is available to part-time students. Application deadlines: 2/1 for summer, 4/1 for IMBA. Contact: Mr. Bob Patton, Computer System Manager, Office of Student Financial Aid and Scholarship, Columbia, SC 29208. (803) 777-3205.

INTERNATIONAL STUDENTS
Demographics 19% of students enrolled in the program are international; Asia 48%, Europe 47%, Australia 3%, Africa 1%, other 1%.
Services and Facilities International student office, visa services, language tutoring, ESL courses, special assistance for nonnative speakers of English, counseling/support services, international student orientation.
Applying TOEFL required, minimum score of 600; proof of adequate funds. Financial aid is available to international students. Financial aid application deadline: 2/1 for fall. Admission application deadlines: 7/1 for fall, 2/1 for IMBA. Contact: Ms. Patricia Willer, Director of International Programs for Students, Byrnes Building Suite 123, Columbia, SC 29208. (803) 777-7461.

ALTERNATE MBA PROGRAMS
International MBA Length of program: Minimum: 15 months. Maximum: 6 years. Full-time classes: Main campus, Vienna, Austria; day, early morning, summer. Part-time classes: Main campus, distance learning option; evening, weekends, summer. Degree requirements: 45 credits including 12 elective credits.
MBA/JD Length of program: Minimum: 48 months. Maximum: 6 years. Degree requirements: 130 credits including 6 elective credits. Must be accepted to both business and law programs.

PLACEMENT
In 1993-94, 49 organizations participated in on-campus recruiting; 197 on-campus interviews were conducted. Placement services include career counseling/planning, career fairs, career library, career placement, job interviews, resume preparation, and resume referral to employers. Of 1994 graduates, 79% were employed within three months of graduation, the average starting salary was $35,292, the range was $21,000-$48,000.
Jobs by Employer Type Manufacturing 50%; service 49%; consulting 1%.
Jobs by Functional Area Marketing/sales 20%; finance 40%; operations 13%; management 17%; strategic planning 3%; technical management 7%.

Program Contact: Ms. Carol Williams, Managing Director of Admissions, University of South Carolina, Columbia, SC 29208. (803) 777-4346; Fax: (803) 777-0414.
See full description on page 916.

SOUTH DAKOTA

University of South Dakota

School of Business

Vermillion, South Dakota

OVERVIEW
The University of South Dakota is a state-supported coed institution. Founded 1862. Setting: 216-acre small-town campus. Total institutional enrollment: 7,750. Program was first offered in 1958. AACSB-accredited.

MBA HIGHLIGHTS
Entrance Difficulty*
Mean GMAT: 515
Mean GPA: 3.07

Cost $
Tuition: $71/credit hour
(Nonresident: $164/credit hour)
Room & Board: $3,373

Enrollment Profile

Full-time: 40	Work Exp: 70%
Part-time: 120	International: 6%
Total: 160	Women: 29%
Average Age: 29	Minorities: 2%

Average Class Size: 40

ACADEMICS
Length of Program Minimum: 12 months. Maximum: 7 years.
Calendar Semesters.
Full-time Classes Main campus; day.
Part-time Classes Main campus, Aberdeen, Sioux Falls, Rapid City, Sioux City; evening.
Degree Requirements 33 credit hours including 6 elective credit hours. Other: Thesis.
Required Courses Administrative policy, advanced information systems, business and its environment, financial administration, managerial accounting, managerial economics, marketing administration, organizational theory and behavior, production and operations management, quantitative analysis, research problems in business. Courses may be waived through: previous course work.
Curricular Focus Business issues and problems, general management, problem solving and decision making.
Concentrations Health services, management, management information systems.
Faculty Full-time: 42, 100% with doctorates.
Teaching Methodology Case study: 30%, lecture: 35%, student presentations: 5%, team projects: 30%.
Special Opportunities Internship program available.

STUDENT STATISTICS
Geographic Representation State residents 57%. By region: Midwest 98%. International 6%.
Undergraduate Majors Business 59%; education 2%; engineering/technology 9%; humanities 2%; nursing 1%; science/mathematics 12%; social sciences 4%; other 11%.
Other Background Graduate degrees in other disciplines: 2%. Work experience: On average, students have 4 years of work experience on entrance to the program.

FACILITIES
Information Resources Main library with 707,048 bound volumes, 529,394 titles on microform, 4,280 periodical subscriptions. Business collection includes 23,000 bound volumes, 470 periodical subscriptions, 8 CD-ROMs.
Housing 3% of students in program live in college-owned or -operated housing.
Technology Computers are used moderately in course work. 110 computer terminals/PCs, linked by a campus-wide computer network, are available for use by students in program; they are located in the student center, the library, computer labs. Students in the program are not required to have their own PC.

Computer Resources/On-line Services

Training	No	Dun's	No
Internet	No	Dow Jones	No
E-Mail	No	Dialog	No
LEXIS/NEXIS	Yes	Bloomberg	No
CompuServe	No		

ADMISSION
Acceptance 1994-95 Of those applying, 87% were accepted.
Entrance Requirements Bachelor's degree, GMAT score of 400, minimum 2.7 GPA. Core courses waived through: previous course work.
Application Requirements Application form, copies of transcript, personal statement, 2 letters of recommendation.
Application Deadlines 7/15 for fall, 11/1 for spring, 3/15 for summer.

FINANCIALS

Costs for 1994-95 Tuition: Full-time: $71/credit hour for state residents, $164/credit hour for nonresidents. Fees: Full-time: $39/semester for state residents, $39/semester for nonresidents. Average room and board costs are $3,373 per academic year (on-campus) and $6,000 per academic year (off-campus).

Financial Aid In 1994-95, 8% of candidates received some institutionally administered aid in the form of loans, assistantships. Total awards ranged from $1,500-$3,000. Financial aid is available to part-time students. Application deadlines: 7/15 for fall, 11/1 for spring. Contact: Mr. Clarence Shoemaker Jr., Director, Slagle 30, Vermillion, SD 57069-2390. (605) 677-5446.

INTERNATIONAL STUDENTS

Demographics 6% of students enrolled in the program are international.

Services and Facilities International student center, visa services, language tutoring, ESL courses, special assistance for nonnative speakers of English, counseling/support services.

Applying TOEFL required, minimum score of 550; proof of health; proof of adequate funds. Financial aid is available to international students. Assistantships are available for these students. Financial aid application deadlines: 7/15 for fall, 11/1 for spring. Admission application deadlines: 7/15 for fall, 11/1 for spring, 3/15 for summer. Contact: Ms. Judith Wieseler, International Student Adviser, Slagle 133, Vermillion, SD 57069-2390. (605) 677-6305.

ALTERNATE MBA PROGRAM

MBA/JD Length of program: Minimum: 36 months. Maximum: 7 years. Degree requirements: 105 credit hours.

PLACEMENT

In 1993-94, 35 organizations participated in on-campus recruiting. Placement services include career counseling/planning, career fairs, career library, career placement, electronic job bank, job interviews, resume preparation, and resume referral to employers. Of 1994 graduates, 54% were employed within three months of graduation, the average starting salary was $27,500, the range was $17,000-$42,000.

Jobs by Employer Type Service 61%; government 11%; nonprofit 5%; banking 22%.

Program Contact: Mr. Thomas L. Davies, Coordinator, University of South Dakota, 414 East Clark Street, Vermillion, SD 57069-2390. (604) 677-5232; Fax: (605) 677-5427.

TENNESSEE

Belmont University

Jack C. Massey Graduate School of Business

Nashville, Tennessee

OVERVIEW

Belmont University is an independent Baptist comprehensive coed institution. Founded 1951. Setting: 34-acre urban campus. Total institutional enrollment: 3,000. Program was first offered in 1986.

MBA HIGHLIGHTS

Entrance Difficulty***
Mean GMAT: 520
Mean GPA: 3.05

Cost $$
Tuition: $420 - $470/credit hour
Room & Board: N/R

Enrollment Profile

Full-time: 0	Work Exp: 100%
Part-time: 235	International: N/R
Total: 235	Women: 45%
Average Age: 33	Minorities: 7%

Average Class Size: 22

ACADEMICS

Length of Program Minimum: 24 months. Maximum: 4 years.

Calendar Trimesters.

Full-time Classes Main campus; evening.

Part-time Classes Main campus; evening.

Degree Requirements 42 credits including 3 elective credits.

Curricular Focus Total quality management, entrepreneurship, teamwork.

Concentrations Accounting, management.

Faculty Full-time: 16, 94% with doctorates; part-time: 7, 58% with doctorates.

Teaching Methodology Case study: 10%, faculty seminars: 10%, lecture: 20%, research: 10%, seminars by members of the business community: 10%, student presentations: 10%, team projects: 30%.

Special Opportunities International exchange in France. Internship program available.

STUDENT STATISTICS

Geographic Representation State residents 1%. By region: South 100%.

Undergraduate Majors Business 50%; education 5%; engineering/technology 20%; nursing 10%; science/mathematics 15%.

Other Background Graduate degrees in other disciplines: 10%. Work experience: On average, students have 9 years of work experience on entrance to the program.

FACILITIES

Information Resources Main library with 155,000 bound volumes, 10,000 titles on microform, 1,100 periodical subscriptions, 15,000 records/tapes/CDs, 20 CD-ROMs. Business collection includes 11,000 bound volumes, 224 periodical subscriptions.

Housing College housing available.

Technology Computers are used heavily in course work. 120 computer terminals/PCs are available for use by students in program; they are located in the library, the computer center, computer labs. Students in the program are required to have their own PC.

Computer Resources/On-line Services

Training	Yes	E-Mail	Yes
Internet	Yes		

ADMISSION

Acceptance 1994-95 Of those applying, 70% were accepted.

Entrance Requirements Bachelor's degree, GMAT score of 450, minimum 2 years of work experience. Core courses waived through: previous course work.

Application Requirements Written essay, interview, application form, copies of transcript, resume/curriculum vitae, personal statement, 2 letters of recommendation.

Application Deadlines 7/1 for fall, 11/15 for spring, 4/1 for summer.

FINANCIALS

Costs for 1994-95 Tuition: Full-time: $420-$470/credit hour.

Financial Aid In 1994-95, candidates received some institutionally administered aid in the form of scholarships, loans, assistantships. Financial aid is available to part-time students. Application deadlines: 7/1 for fall, 11/1 for spring, 3/1 for summer. Contact: Ms. Kathy Woodard, Financial Aid Counselor, 1900 Belmont Boulevard, Nashville, TN 37212-3757. (615) 385-6403.

INTERNATIONAL STUDENTS

Demographics 5% of students on campus are international.

Applying TOEFL required, minimum score of 550; proof of adequate funds. Financial aid is not available to international students. Admission applications are processed on a rolling basis. Contact: Ms. Kathy Skinner, Director, Office of International Student Services, 1900 Belmont Boulevard, Nashville, TN 37212-3757. (615) 385-6407.

PLACEMENT

Placement services include alumni network, career counseling/planning, career fairs, career library, resume preparation, and resume referral to employers.

Program Contact: Ms. Sally C. McKay, Recruitment Director, Belmont University, 1900 Belmont Boulevard, Nashville, TN 37212-3757. (615) 385-6480; Fax: (615) 385-6455; Internet Address: mckays@belmont.edu.

Christian Brothers University

School of Business

Memphis, Tennessee

OVERVIEW
Christian Brothers University is an independent Roman Catholic comprehensive coed institution. Founded 1871. Setting: 70-acre urban campus. Total institutional enrollment: 1,654. Program was first offered in 1989.

MBA HIGHLIGHTS

Entrance Difficulty*
Mean GMAT: 554
Mean GPA: 2.95

Cost $
Tuition: $275/credit hour
Room & Board: $4,260

Enrollment Profile
Full-time: 3	Work Exp: 99%
Part-time: 154	International: N/R
Total: 157	Women: 60%
Average Age: 31	Minorities: 95%

Average Class Size: 16

ACADEMICS
Length of Program Minimum: 12 months. Maximum: 5 years.
Calendar Semesters.
Full-time Classes Main campus; evening, weekends.
Part-time Classes Main campus; evening, weekends.
Degree Requirements 30 credits including 9 elective credits.
Required Courses Business policy, ethical, societal, and legal aspects of management, managerial accounting, managerial economics, managerial finance, quantitative methods, strategic marketing.
Curricular Focus Business issues and problems, entrepreneurship, leadership.
Concentrations Accounting, finance, health services, information technology management, management, marketing, strategic management.
Faculty Full-time: 14, 72% with doctorates; part-time: 4, 75% with doctorates.
Teaching Methodology Case study: 25%, lecture: 30%, research: 15%, student presentations: 15%, team projects: 15%.

STUDENT STATISTICS
Geographic Representation By region: South 100%.
Undergraduate Majors Business 59%; education 1%; engineering/technology 15%; humanities 7%; nursing 1%; science/mathematics 10%; social sciences 7%.
Other Background Graduate degrees in other disciplines: 10%. Work experience: On average, students have 9 years of work experience on entrance to the program.

FACILITIES
Information Resources Main library with 91,830 bound volumes, 4,000 titles on microform, 582 periodical subscriptions, 300 records/tapes/CDs.
Housing College housing available.
Technology Computers are used moderately in course work. 130 computer terminals/PCs are available for use by students in program; they are located in classrooms, the computer center, computer labs. Students in the program are not required to have their own PC.
Computer Resources/On-line Services
Training	Yes	CompuServe	No
Internet	Yes	Dun's	No
E-Mail	Yes	Dow Jones	No
Videoconference Center	Yes	Dialog	No
Multimedia Center	Yes	Bloomberg	No
LEXIS/NEXIS	No		

ADMISSION
Acceptance 1994-95 145 applied for admission; 83% were accepted.
Entrance Requirements Bachelor's degree, GMAT score of 450.
Application Requirements Application form, copies of transcript, 2 letters of recommendation.
Application Deadline Applications are processed on a rolling basis.

FINANCIALS
Costs for 1994-95 Tuition: Full-time: $275/credit hour. Average room and board costs are $4,260 per academic year (on-campus).
Financial Aid In 1994-95, 10% of candidates received some institutionally administered aid in the form of loans. Financial aid is available to part-time students. Applications are processed on a rolling basis. Contact: Mr. Jim Shannon, Director of Student Financial Resources, 650 East Parkway South, Memphis, TN 38104-5581. (901) 722-0306.

INTERNATIONAL STUDENTS
Demographics 4% of students on campus are international; Asia 39%, North America 26%, Central America 11%, Africa 8%, Europe 8%, South America 8%.
Applying TOEFL required, minimum score of 600; proof of adequate funds. Financial aid is not available to international students. Admission applications are processed on a rolling basis.

PLACEMENT
In 1993-94, 2 organizations participated in on-campus recruiting. Placement services include alumni network, career counseling/planning, career fairs, career library, career placement, resume preparation, and resume referral to employers. Of 1994 graduates, 100% were employed within three months of graduation.

Program Contact: Mr. Michael Smith, Director, MBA Program, Christian Brothers University, 650 East Parkway South, Memphis, TN 38104-5581. (901) 722-0317; Fax: (901) 722-0566; Internet Address: mtsmith@bucs.cbu.edu.

East Tennessee State University

College of Business

Johnson City, Tennessee

OVERVIEW
East Tennessee State University is a state-supported coed institution. Part of State University and Community College System of Tennessee. Founded 1911. Setting: 366-acre small-town campus. Total institutional enrollment: 11,439. AACSB-accredited.

MBA HIGHLIGHTS

Entrance Difficulty*
Mean GMAT: 530
Mean GPA: N/R

Cost $
Tuition: $1,096/semester
(Nonresident: $3,063/semester)
Room & Board: $3,000

Enrollment Profile
Full-time: N/R	Work Exp: N/R
Part-time: N/R	International: 15%
Total: 180	Women: 50%
Average Age: N/R	Minorities: 5%

Average Class Size: 27

ACADEMICS
Length of Program Minimum: 24 months.
Calendar Semesters.
Full-time Classes Main campus; evening, summer.
Part-time Classes Main campus; evening, summer.
Degree Requirements 39 credits.
Curricular Focus Problem solving and decision making, strategic management, teamwork.
Concentration Management.
Teaching Methodology Case study: 30%, lecture: 35%, research: 20%, student presentations: 15%.

STUDENT STATISTICS
Geographic Representation International 15%.

FACILITIES
Information Resources Main library with 617,847 bound volumes, 1.1 million titles on microform, 4,004 periodical subscriptions.
Housing College housing available.

ADMISSION

Entrance Requirements Bachelor's degree, GMAT score of 450, minimum 2.5 GPA.

Application Requirements Written essay, application form, copies of transcript, resume/curriculum vitae.

Application Deadlines 6/1 for fall, 10/1 for spring. Applications are processed on a rolling basis.

FINANCIALS

Costs for 1994-95 Tuition: Full-time: $1,096/semester for state residents, $3,063/semester for nonresidents. Average room and board costs are $3,000 per academic year (on-campus) and $4,200 per academic year (off-campus).

Financial Aid Application deadlines: 6/1 for fall, 9/1 for spring. Applications are processed on a rolling basis. Contact: Director of Financial Aid, Johnson City, TN 37614-0734. (615) 929-4300.

INTERNATIONAL STUDENTS

Demographics 15% of students enrolled in the program are international.

Applying TOEFL required, minimum score of 550; proof of health; proof of adequate funds. Financial aid is available to international students. Financial aid application deadlines: 6/1 for fall, 9/1 for spring. Applications are processed on a rolling basis. Admission application deadlines: 5/1 for fall, 9/1 for spring. Applications are processed on a rolling basis.

Program Contact: Dr. John Nash, Director of Graduate Business Programs, East Tennessee State University, Johnson City, TN 37614-0734. (615) 929-5314; Fax: (615) 929-5274.

Middle Tennessee State University

College of Business

Murfreesboro, Tennessee

OVERVIEW

Middle Tennessee State University is a state-supported coed institution. Founded 1911. Setting: 500-acre small-town campus with easy access to Nashville. Total institutional enrollment: 17,383. AACSB-accredited.

MBA HIGHLIGHTS

Entrance Difficulty**
Mean GMAT: 490
Mean GPA: 3.2

Cost $
Tuition: $1,063/semester
(Nonresident: $3,030/semester)
Room & Board: N/R

Enrollment Profile

Full-time: 75	Work Exp: 85%
Part-time: 300	International: 7%
Total: 375	Women: 48%
Average Age: 29	Minorities: 5%

Average Class Size: 25

ACADEMICS

Length of Program Minimum: 24 months. Maximum: 6 years.

Calendar Semesters.

Full-time Classes Main campus, Bridgestone, Nissan Motor Manufacturing, Saturn Corporation; evening, summer.

Part-time Classes Main campus, Bridgestone, Nissan Motor Manufacturing, Saturn Corporation; evening, summer.

Degree Requirements 36 hours including 12 elective hours.

Required Courses Accounting and business decisions, advanced financial analysis, business policy, economic analysis, information systems management and applications, marketing management, seminar in operations management, study of organizations.

Curricular Focus General management, problem solving and decision making, strategic analysis and planning.

Concentrations Accounting, economics, finance, management.

Faculty Full-time: 50, 100% with doctorates.

Teaching Methodology Case study: 25%, lecture: 50%, student presentations: 10%, team projects: 15%.

Special Opportunities International exchange in France.

STUDENT STATISTICS

Geographic Representation By region: South 90%; Northeast 1%; Midwest 1%. International 7%.

Undergraduate Majors Business 70%; education 1%; engineering/technology 20%; humanities 3%; nursing 1%; science/mathematics 3%; social sciences 2%.

Other Background Graduate degrees in other disciplines: 1%. Work experience: On average, students have 6 years of work experience on entrance to the program.

FACILITIES

Information Resources Main library with 580,676 bound volumes, 399,960 titles on microform, 3,520 periodical subscriptions, 12,150 records/tapes/CDs, 14 CD-ROMs.

Housing College housing available.

Technology Computers are used moderately in course work. 100 computer terminals/PCs, linked by a campus-wide computer network, are available for use by students in program; they are located in computer labs. Students in the program are not required to have their own PC.

Computer Resources/On-line Services

Training	Yes	Dun's	No
Internet	No	Dow Jones	No
E-Mail	No	Dialog	No
LEXIS/NEXIS	No	Bloomberg	No
CompuServe	No		

ADMISSION

Acceptance 1994-95 200 applied for admission; 75% were accepted.

Entrance Requirements Bachelor's degree, GMAT score of 450, minimum 2.5 GPA.

Application Requirements Application form, copies of transcript.

Application Deadlines 7/1 for fall, 10/31 for spring. Applications are processed on a rolling basis.

FINANCIALS

Costs for 1994-95 Tuition: Full-time: $1,063/semester for state residents, $3,030/semester for nonresidents; Part-time day: $107/hour for state residents, $299/hour for nonresidents. Fees: Full-time: $77/semester for state residents, $77/semester for nonresidents; Part-time day: $7-$30/hour for state residents, $7-$30/hour for nonresidents.

Financial Aid In 1994-95, 20% of candidates received some institutionally administered aid in the form of loans, assistantships. Financial aid is not available to part-time students. Applications are processed on a rolling basis. Contact: Mr. R. Winston Wrenn, Director of Financial Aid, PO Box 290, Murfreesboro, TN 37132. (615) 898-2830.

INTERNATIONAL STUDENTS

Demographics 7% of students enrolled in the program are international.

Services and Facilities International student office.

Applying TOEFL required, minimum score of 525; proof of health; proof of adequate funds. Financial aid is available to international students. Assistantships are available for these students. Admission application deadlines: 5/1 for fall, 9/1 for spring, 2/1 for summer. Contact: Dr. Tech Wubneh, Director of International Programs and Services, Cope Administration Building, Room 202, Murfreesboro, TN 37132. (615) 898-2238.

PLACEMENT

In 1993-94, 160 organizations participated in on-campus recruiting; 50 on-campus interviews were conducted. Placement services include career counseling/planning, career fairs, job interviews, resume preparation, and resume referral to employers.

Program Contact: Dr. Dwight Bullard, Director, Graduate Business Studies, Middle Tennessee State University, PO Box 290, Murfreesboro, TN 37132. (615) 898-2964; Fax: (615) 898-5045.

Tennessee State University

School of Business

Nashville, Tennessee

OVERVIEW

Tennessee State University is a state-supported comprehensive coed institution. Part of State University and Community College System of

Tennessee. Founded 1912. Setting: 450-acre urban campus. Total institutional enrollment: 8,000. Program was first offered in 1972.

MBA HIGHLIGHTS

Entrance Difficulty*
Mean GMAT: 510
Mean GPA: 3.0

Cost
Tuition: N/R
(Nonresident: N/R)
Room & Board: $3,000

Enrollment Profile
Full-time: 25
Part-time: 75
Total: 100
Average Age: 28

Work Exp: 90%
International: 15%
Women: 30%
Minorities: 20%

Average Class Size: 15

ACADEMICS
Calendar Semesters.

Curricular Focus General management, organizational development and change management, problem solving and decision making.

Concentrations Accounting, finance, management, marketing.

Faculty Full-time: 17, 100% with doctorates.

Teaching Methodology Case study: 20%, faculty seminars: 10%, lecture: 45%, research: 5%, student presentations: 10%, team projects: 10%.

STUDENT STATISTICS
Geographic Representation By region: South 58%; Midwest 15%; Northeast 5%; West 5%. International 15%.

Undergraduate Majors Business 50%; education 10%; engineering/technology 10%; nursing 5%; social sciences 20%; other 5%.

Other Background Graduate degrees in other disciplines: 5%. Work experience: On average, students have 3 years of work experience on entrance to the program.

FACILITIES
Information Resources Main library with 420,463 bound volumes, 1,498 titles on microform, 1,775 periodical subscriptions. Business collection in Tennessee State University Williams Campus Library includes 33,475 bound volumes, 208 periodical subscriptions, 346 CD-ROMs.

Housing College housing available.

Technology Computers are used moderately in course work. 40 computer terminals/PCs, linked by a campus-wide computer network, are available for use by students in program; they are located in computer labs. Students in the program are not required to have their own PC. $1,000 are budgeted per student for computer support.

Computer Resources/On-line Services

Training	Yes	CompuServe	No
Internet	Yes	Dun's	No
E-Mail	No	Dow Jones	Yes
LEXIS/NEXIS	No	Dialog	Yes

ADMISSION
Acceptance 1994-95 118 applied for admission; 69% were accepted.

Entrance Requirements Bachelor's degree, prerequisite courses required for applicants with non-business degree, GMAT score. Core courses waived through: previous course work.

Application Requirements Application form, copies of transcript.

Application Deadline Applications are processed on a rolling basis.

FINANCIALS
Financial Aid In 1994-95, candidates received some institutionally administered aid in the form of fellowships, assistantships. Total awards ranged from $7,800. Financial aid is not available to part-time students. Application deadlines: 3/30 for fall, 10/30 for spring. Applications are processed on a rolling basis. Contact: Mr. Wilson Lee, Director of Financial Aid, 3500 John A. Merritt Boulevard, Nashville, TN 37209-1561. (615) 320-3750.

INTERNATIONAL STUDENTS
Demographics 15% of students enrolled in the program are international; Asia 70%, Africa 10%, other 20%.

Services and Facilities International student office.

Applying TOEFL required, minimum score of 500. Financial aid is available to international students. Applications are processed on a rolling basis.

Admission applications are processed on a rolling basis. Contact: Ms. Shirley Wingfield, Foreign Student Adviser, 3500 John A. Merritt Boulevard, Nashville, TN 37209-1561. (615) 963-5639.

PROGRAM
One-Year MBA Length of program: Minimum: 12 months. Maximum: 6 years. Full-time classes: Main campus; evening, summer. Degree requirements: 34 credits including 12 elective credits.

PLACEMENT
In 1993-94, 30 organizations participated in on-campus recruiting. Placement services include alumni network, career counseling/planning, career fairs, career library, career placement, and job interviews. Of 1994 graduates, the average starting salary was $30,000, the range was $25,000-$35,000.

Program Contact: Dr. G. Bruce Hartmann, Coordinator of MBA Program, Tennessee State University, 3500 John A. Merritt Boulevard, Nashville, TN 37209-1561. (615) 963-7146; Fax: (615) 963-7139.

Tennessee Technological University

College of Business Administration, Division of MBA Studies

Cookeville, Tennessee

OVERVIEW
Tennessee Technological University is a state-supported coed institution. Part of State University and Community College System of Tennessee. Founded 1915. Setting: 235-acre small-town campus. Total institutional enrollment: 8,300. Program was first offered in 1976. AACSB-accredited.

MBA HIGHLIGHTS

Entrance Difficulty*
Mean GMAT: 505
Mean GPA: 3.1

Cost $
Tuition: $114/hour
(Nonresident: $286/hour)
Room & Board: $3,700

Enrollment Profile
Full-time: 89
Part-time: 82
Total: 171
Average Age: 27

Work Exp: 44%
International: 13%
Women: 41%
Minorities: 7%

Average Class Size: 30

ACADEMICS
Length of Program Minimum: 12 months. Maximum: 7 years.

Calendar Semesters.

Full-time Classes Main campus; day, evening, summer.

Part-time Classes Main campus; evening, summer.

Degree Requirements 36 credits including 12 elective credits.

Required Courses Accounting for management decisions, business policy, communications and case analysis, financial management, global economics, management information systems, marketing management, operations management, organizational behavior.

Curricular Focus Business issues and problems, problem solving and decision making, teamwork.

Concentrations Accounting, management information systems.

Teaching Methodology Case study: 85%, lecture: 5%, student presentations: 5%, team projects: 5%.

Special Opportunities Internship program available.

STUDENT STATISTICS
Geographic Representation State residents 80%. By region: South 82%; Northeast 2%; Midwest 2%; West 1%. International 13%.

Undergraduate Majors Business 72%; education 4%; engineering/technology 14%; humanities 4%; science/mathematics 3%; social sciences 3%.

Other Background Graduate degrees in other disciplines: 1%. Work experience: On average, students have 3 years of work experience on entrance to the program.

FACILITIES

Information Resources Main library with 390,915 bound volumes, 825,459 titles on microform, 3,828 periodical subscriptions, 18,000 records/tapes/CDs, 14 CD-ROMs.

Housing 20% of students in program live in college-owned or -operated housing.

Technology Computers are used heavily in course work. 160 computer terminals/PCs, linked by a campus-wide computer network, are available for use by students in program; they are located in dormitories, the library, the computer center, computer labs, the research center. Students in the program are not required to have their own PC.

Computer Resources/On-line Services

Training	Yes	Dun's	No
Internet	Yes	Dow Jones	Yes
E-Mail	Yes	Dialog	No
LEXIS/NEXIS	No	Bloomberg	No
CompuServe	No		

ADMISSION

Acceptance 1994-95 172 applied for admission; 81% were accepted.

Entrance Requirements Bachelor's degree, prerequisite courses required for applicants with non-business degree, GMAT score of 350, minimum 2.5 GPA. Core courses waived through: previous course work.

Application Requirements Application form, copies of transcript, 3 letters of recommendation.

Application Deadlines 6/30 for fall, 10/31 for spring, 1/30 for summer. Applications are processed on a rolling basis.

FINANCIALS

Estimated Costs for 1995-96 Tuition: Full-time: $114/hour for state residents, $286/hour for nonresidents. Fees: Full-time: $1,141/semester for state residents, $3,108/semester for nonresidents. Average room and board costs are $3,700 per academic year (on-campus) and $5,200 per academic year (off-campus).

Financial Aid In 1994-95, 80% of candidates received some institutionally administered aid in the form of scholarships, loans, fellowships, assistantships. Total awards ranged from $250-$13,500. Financial aid is not available to part-time students. Application deadlines: 6/30 for fall, 10/31 for spring, 4/30 for summer. Applications are processed on a rolling basis. Contact: Dr. Virginia Moore, Assistant Dean and Director of MBA Studies, North Dixie Avenue, Cookeville, TN 38505. (615) 372-3600.

INTERNATIONAL STUDENTS

Demographics 13% of students enrolled in the program are international; North America 87%, Asia 12%, Europe 1%.

Services and Facilities International student office, international student center, language tutoring, ESL courses, special assistance for nonnative speakers of English, counseling/support services.

Applying TOEFL required, minimum score of 550; proof of health; proof of adequate funds. Financial aid is available to international students. Financial aid application deadlines: 1/31 for fall, 6/30 for spring, 10/31 for summer. Applications are processed on a rolling basis. Admission application deadlines: 1/31 for fall, 6/30 for spring, 10/31 for summer. Applications are processed on a rolling basis. Contact: Dr. Virginia Moore, Assistant Dean and Director of MBA Studies, North Dixie Avenue, Cookeville, TN 38505. (615) 372-3600.

PLACEMENT

Placement services include alumni network, career fairs, career placement, job interviews, resume preparation, and resume referral to employers. Of 1994 graduates, 91% were employed within three months of graduation, the average starting salary was $37,500, the range was $22,500-$60,000.

Jobs by Employer Type Manufacturing 40%; service 49%; government 4%; consulting 6%; nonprofit 1%.

Jobs by Functional Area Marketing/sales 13%; finance 33%; operations 12%; management 32%; strategic planning 4%; technical management 6%.

Program Contact: Dr. Virginia Moore, Assistant Dean and Director of MBA Studies, Tennessee Technological University, North Dixie Avenue, Cookeville, TN 38505. (615) 372-3600; Fax: (615) 372-6249.

Union University

Jackson, Tennessee

OVERVIEW

Union University is an independent Southern Baptist comprehensive coed institution. Founded 1823. Setting: 230-acre small-town campus with easy access to Memphis. Total institutional enrollment: 2,025. Program was first offered in 1994.

MBA HIGHLIGHTS

Entrance Difficulty***
Mean GMAT: 490
Mean GPA: 3.21

Cost $$
Tuition: $250/hour
Room & Board: $2,530

Enrollment Profile

Full-time: 0	Work Exp: 100%
Part-time: 32	International: 6%
Total: 32	Women: 50%
Average Age: 32	Minorities: 6%

Average Class Size: 12

ACADEMICS

Length of Program Minimum: 18 months. Maximum: 8 years.

Calendar Semesters.

Full-time Classes Main campus; evening, summer.

Part-time Classes Main campus; evening, summer.

Degree Requirements 33 hours including 9 elective hours.

Required Courses Business policy, executive communications, management theory, managerial accounting, managerial economics, managerial finance, operations management, strategic marketing. Courses may be waived through: previous course work.

Curricular Focus General management, problem solving and decision making, strategic analysis and planning.

Concentrations Accounting, economics, finance, management, marketing.

Faculty Full-time: 9, 100% with doctorates.

Teaching Methodology Case study: 40%, lecture: 20%, research: 10%, student presentations: 10%, team projects: 20%.

STUDENT STATISTICS

Geographic Representation State residents 100%. By region: South 91%; Midwest 3%; West 3%. International 6%.

Undergraduate Majors Business 72%; engineering/technology 7%; other 21%.

Other Background Graduate degrees in other disciplines: 6%. Work experience: On average, students have 5-10 years of work experience on entrance to the program.

FACILITIES

Information Resources Main library with 115,848 bound volumes, 53,206 titles on microform, 1,112 periodical subscriptions, 5,188 records/tapes/CDs, 14 CD-ROMs.

Housing College housing available.

Technology Computers are used moderately in course work. 90 computer terminals/PCs, linked by a campus-wide computer network, are available for use by students in program; they are located in classrooms, the library, the computer center, computer labs. Students in the program are not required to have their own PC. $500 are budgeted per student for computer support.

Computer Resources/On-line Services

Training	Yes	CompuServe	No
Internet	No	Dun's	No
E-Mail	No	Dow Jones	No
Videoconference Center	Yes	Dialog	Yes
Multimedia Center	Yes	Bloomberg	No
LEXIS/NEXIS	No		

ADMISSION

Acceptance 1994-95 Of those applying, 64% were accepted.

Entrance Requirements Bachelor's degree, GMAT score. Core courses waived through: previous course work.

Application Requirements Application form, copies of transcript.
Application Deadlines 8/1 for fall, 1/1 for spring.

FINANCIALS
Costs for 1994-95 Tuition: Full-time: $250/hour. Average room and board costs are $2,530 per academic year (on-campus).
Financial Aid Financial aid is not available to part-time students. Application deadlines: 5/31 for fall, 10/31 for spring. Contact: Mr. Don Morris, Director of Financial Aid, 2447 Highway 45 Bypass, Jackson, TN 38305. (901) 661-5015.

INTERNATIONAL STUDENTS
Demographics 6% of students enrolled in the program are international; Asia 100%.
Services and Facilities Counseling/support services.
Applying TOEFL required, minimum score of 500; proof of health; proof of adequate funds; health insurance. Financial aid is not available to international students. Admission application deadline: 2/15 for fall. Contact: Mrs. Sandy Rich, Admissions, 2447 Highway 45 Bypass, Jackson, TN 38305. (901) 661-5005.

PLACEMENT
Placement services include alumni network, career counseling/planning, career fairs, career placement, job interviews, resume preparation, and resume referral to employers.

Program Contact: Mr. Brent Cunningham, MBA Director, Union University, 2447 Highway 45 Bypass, Jackson, TN 38305. (901) 661-5364, or (800) 338-6466; Fax: (901) 661-5366.

The University of Memphis

Fogelman College of Business and Economics

Memphis, Tennessee

OVERVIEW
The University of Memphis is a state-supported coed institution. Part of State University and Community College System of Tennessee. Founded 1912. Setting: 205-acre suburban campus. Total institutional enrollment: 21,000. Program was first offered in 1959. AACSB-accredited.

MBA HIGHLIGHTS

Entrance Difficulty*
Mean GMAT: 520
Mean GPA: 3.1

Cost $
Tuition: $1,233/semester
(Nonresident: $1,967/semester)
Room & Board: $2,100

Enrollment Profile

Full-time: 297	Work Exp: 90%
Part-time: 308	International: 20%
Total: 605	Women: 35%
Average Age: 29	Minorities: 11%

Average Class Size: 40

ACADEMICS
Length of Program Minimum: 12 months. Maximum: 6 years.
Calendar Semesters.
Full-time Classes Main campus; day, evening, early morning, summer.
Part-time Classes Main campus, Jackson, distance learning option; evening, early morning, summer.
Degree Requirements 33 credits including 9 elective credits. Other: Comprehensive exam.
Required Courses Business applications of economic theory, cases and problems in decision making, financial management 2, international business, quantitative methods for business decisions, seminar in business policy, seminar in organizations, strategic marketing.
Curricular Focus International business, problem solving and decision making, strategic analysis and planning.

Concentrations Accounting, economics, finance, human resources management, insurance, international business, management, management information systems, marketing, organizational behavior, quantitative analysis, real estate, strategic management.
Faculty Full-time: 85, 100% with doctorates.
Teaching Methodology Case study: 10%, lecture: 40%, research: 5%, seminars by members of the business community: 5%, student presentations: 15%, team projects: 25%.
Special Opportunities International exchange in Belgium, Germany, United Kingdom. Internship program available.

STUDENT STATISTICS
Geographic Representation By region: South 75%; Midwest 5%. International 20%.
Undergraduate Majors Business 40%; engineering/technology 15%; humanities 10%; science/mathematics 15%; social sciences 10%; other 10%.
Other Background Graduate degrees in other disciplines: 5%. Work experience: On average, students have 6 years of work experience on entrance to the program.

FACILITIES
Information Resources Main library with 1.1 million bound volumes, 2.6 million titles on microform, 12,239 periodical subscriptions, 45,137 records/tapes/CDs.
Housing College housing available.
Technology Computers are used heavily in course work. 250 computer terminals/PCs, linked by a campus-wide computer network, are available for use by students in program; they are located in computer labs. Students in the program are not required to have their own PC.

Computer Resources/On-line Services

Training	Yes	CompuServe	No
Internet	Yes	Dun's	No
E-Mail	Yes	Dow Jones	No
Videoconference Center	Yes	Dialog	No
LEXIS/NEXIS	Yes	Bloomberg	No

ADMISSION
Acceptance 1994-95 350 applied for admission; 72% were accepted.
Entrance Requirements Bachelor's degree, GMAT score of 430, minimum 2.0 GPA. Core courses waived through: previous course work.
Application Requirements Application form, copies of transcript.
Application Deadlines 8/1 for fall, 12/1 for spring, 5/1 for summer. Applications are processed on a rolling basis.

FINANCIALS
Costs for 1994-95 Tuition: Full-time: $1,967/semester for nonresidents; Part-time day: $172/hour for nonresidents. Fees: Full-time: $1,233/semester for state residents, $1,233/semester for nonresidents; Part-time day: $118/hour for state residents, $118/hour for nonresidents. Average room and board costs are $2,100 per academic year (on-campus) and $3,500 per academic year (off-campus).
Financial Aid In 1994-95, candidates received some institutionally administered aid in the form of scholarships, loans, fellowships, assistantships. Applications are processed on a rolling basis. Contact: Director of Financial Aid, Scates Hall, Room 312, Memphis, TN 38152. (901) 678-4825.

INTERNATIONAL STUDENTS
Demographics 20% of students enrolled in the program are international; Asia 87%, Europe 4%, South America 4%, Africa 2%, North America 2%.
Services and Facilities International student office, international student center, visa services, language tutoring, ESL courses, special assistance for nonnative speakers of English, counseling/support services.
Applying TOEFL required, minimum score of 550; proof of health; proof of adequate funds. Financial aid is available to international students. Applications are processed on a rolling basis. Admission application deadlines: 5/1 for fall, 9/1 for spring. Applications are processed on a rolling basis.

ALTERNATE MBA PROGRAMS
Executive MBA (EMBA) Length of program: Minimum: 22 months. Maximum: 6 years. Full-time classes: Main campus; weekends, summer. Degree requirements: 45 credits. Class size: 20-30.
International MBA Length of program: Minimum: 22 months. Maximum: 6 years. Full-time classes: Main campus; day, summer. Degree requirements: 56 credits including 9 elective credits. Semester of internship and/or foreign studies; advanced language and geographic area expertise. Average class size: 24.

PLACEMENT

Placement services include career counseling/planning, career placement, job interviews, and resume referral to employers.

Program Contact: Associate Dean For Graduate Studies, The University of Memphis, Office of Graduate Programs, Room A101, Memphis, TN 38152. (901) 678-3721; Fax: (901) 678-3759.
See full description on page 892.

University of Tennessee at Chattanooga

School of Business Administration

Chattanooga, Tennessee

OVERVIEW

The University of Tennessee at Chattanooga is a state-supported comprehensive coed institution. Part of University of Tennessee System. Founded 1886. Setting: 101-acre urban campus with easy access to Atlanta. Total institutional enrollment: 8,325. AACSB-accredited.

MBA HIGHLIGHTS

Entrance Difficulty**
Mean GMAT: 480
Mean GPA: 3.06

Cost $
Tuition: $1,026 - $1,087/semester
(Nonresident: $2,619 - $3,053/semester)
Room & Board: N/R

Enrollment Profile

Full-time: 83	Work Exp: 90%
Part-time: 293	International: 9%
Total: 376	Women: 49%
Average Age: 32	Minorities: 8%

Average Class Size: 30

ACADEMICS

Length of Program Minimum: 24 months. Maximum: 6 years.
Calendar Semesters.
Full-time Classes Main campus; evening.
Part-time Classes Main campus, distance learning option; evening.
Degree Requirements 36 hours including 9 elective hours.
Required Courses Business information systems, business policy, business research methods, concepts in marketing, financial management, macroeconomic analysis, managerial accounting, managerial economics, organizational behavior, organizational theory, problems in operations management, theory and practice.
Curricular Focus Entrepreneurship, general management, problem solving and decision making.
Concentrations Accounting, economics, finance, health services, management, management information systems, marketing, operations management, organizational behavior.
Faculty Full-time: 35, 100% with doctorates; part-time: 10, 2% with doctorates.
Teaching Methodology Case study: 10%, lecture: 50%, seminars by members of the business community: 1%, student presentations: 9%, team projects: 30%.
Special Opportunities International exchange program available.

STUDENT STATISTICS

Geographic Representation State residents 80%. International 9%.
Undergraduate Majors Business 70%; engineering/technology 20%; humanities 2%; science/mathematics 1%; social sciences 3%; other 4%.
Other Background Graduate degrees in other disciplines: 5%.

FACILITIES

Information Resources Main library with 433,651 bound volumes, 1.1 million titles on microform, 3,000 periodical subscriptions, 5,200 records/tapes/CDs.
Housing 5% of students in program live in college-owned or -operated housing. Assistance with housing search provided.
Technology Computers are used moderately in course work. 50 computer terminals/PCs, linked by a campus-wide computer network, are avail-

able for use by students in program; they are located in the library, computer labs. Students in the program are not required to have their own PC.

Computer Resources/On-line Services

Training	No	LEXIS/NEXIS	Yes
Internet	Yes	CompuServe	Yes
E-Mail	Yes		

ADMISSION

Entrance Requirements Bachelor's degree, GMAT score, minimum 2.5 GPA.
Application Requirements Application form, copies of transcript.
Application Deadlines 7/1 for fall, 11/1 for spring. Applications are processed on a rolling basis.

FINANCIALS

Costs for 1994-95 Tuition: Full-time: $1,026-$1,087/semester for state residents, $2,619-$3,053/semester for nonresidents; Part-time day: $114/hour for state residents, $177/hour for nonresidents. Fees: Full-time: $104/semester for state residents, $72/semester for nonresidents; Part-time day: $8/hour for state residents, $8/hour for nonresidents.
Financial Aid In 1994-95, candidates received some institutionally administered aid in the form of grants, loans, assistantships. Financial aid is available to part-time students. Applications are processed on a rolling basis. Contact: Ms. Dena Edge, Financial Aid Counselor, 615 McCallie Avenue, Chattanooga, TN 37403-2504. (615) 755-4677.

INTERNATIONAL STUDENTS

Demographics 9% of students enrolled in the program are international; Asia 95%, Africa 1%, other 4%.
Services and Facilities International student office.
Applying TOEFL required, minimum score of 500; proof of health; proof of adequate funds. Financial aid is not available to international students. Admission application deadlines: 7/1 for fall, 11/1 for spring. Applications are processed on a rolling basis. Contact: Ms. Nancy Auberson, Executive Secretary, Graduate Division, 615 McCallie Avenue, Chattanooga, TN 37403-2504. (615) 755-4478.

PLACEMENT

Placement services include career counseling/planning and career fairs.

Program Contact: Mrs. JoAnna Antczak, Director of Graduate Programs, University of Tennessee at Chattanooga, 615 McCallie Avenue, Chattanooga, TN 37403-2504. (615) 755-4210, or (800) 532-3028; Fax: (615) 755-5255.

University of Tennessee at Martin

School of Business Administration

Martin, Tennessee

OVERVIEW

The University of Tennessee at Martin is a state-supported comprehensive coed institution. Part of University of Tennessee System. Founded 1927. Setting: 250-acre small-town campus. Total institutional enrollment: 5,546. Program was first offered in 1987.

MBA HIGHLIGHTS

Entrance Difficulty**
Mean GMAT: 485
Mean GPA: 3.2

Cost $
Tuition: $1,192/semester
(Nonresident: $3,158/semester)
Room & Board: N/R

Enrollment Profile

Full-time: N/R	Work Exp: 90%
Part-time: N/R	International: 3%
Total: 95	Women: 35%
Average Age: 30	Minorities: 4%

Average Class Size: 15

ACADEMICS

Length of Program Minimum: 12 months. Maximum: 6 years.
Calendar Semesters.

Full-time Classes Main campus, Jackson; evening, summer.

Part-time Classes Main campus, Jackson; evening, summer.

Degree Requirements 30 credits.

Curricular Focus Business issues and problems, general management, problem solving and decision making, strategic analysis and planning.

Concentrations Accounting, management.

Faculty Full-time: 26, 100% with doctorates.

Teaching Methodology Case study: 20%, group discussion: 10%, lecture: 30%, research: 2%, student presentations: 18%, team projects: 20%.

STUDENT STATISTICS

Geographic Representation State residents 95%. By region: South 97%. International 3%.

Undergraduate Majors Business 93%; engineering/technology 4%; humanities 1%; other 2%.

FACILITIES

Information Resources Main library with 420,000 bound volumes, 143,496 titles on microform, 1,626 periodical subscriptions, 5,683 records/tapes/CDs, 172 CD-ROMs.

Housing 2% of students in program live in college-owned or -operated housing.

Technology Computers are used moderately in course work. 200 computer terminals/PCs are available for use by students in program; they are located in computer labs. Students in the program are not required to have their own PC.

Computer Resources/On-line Services

Training	Yes	Dun's	No
Internet	No	Dow Jones	No
E-Mail	No	Dialog	No
LEXIS/NEXIS	No	Bloomberg	No
CompuServe	No		

ADMISSION

Entrance Requirements Bachelor's degree, GMAT score of 400, minimum 2.5 GPA. Core courses waived through: previous course work.

Application Requirements Application form, copies of transcript.

Application Deadline Applications are processed on a rolling basis.

FINANCIALS

Costs for 1994-95 Tuition: Full-time: $1,192/semester for state residents, $3,158/semester for nonresidents.

Financial Aid In 1994-95, candidates received some institutionally administered aid in the form of scholarships, fellowships, assistantships. Applications are processed on a rolling basis. Contact: Dr. K. Paul Jones, Assistant Vice Chancellor, 112 Business Administration, Martin, TN 38238. (901) 587-7854.

INTERNATIONAL STUDENTS

Demographics 3% of students enrolled in the program are international.

Services and Facilities International student office.

Applying TOEFL required, minimum score of 525; proof of adequate funds. Financial aid is not available to international students. Admission applications are processed on a rolling basis.

PLACEMENT

Placement services include career counseling/planning.

Program Contact: Dr. William L. Davis, MBA Program Coordinator, University of Tennessee at Martin, 112 Business Administration, Martin, TN 38238. (901) 587-7228, or (800) 829-8861 (TN only); Fax: (901) 587-7241.

University of Tennessee, Knoxville

College of Business Administration

Knoxville, Tennessee

OVERVIEW

The University of Tennessee, Knoxville is a state-supported coed institution. Part of University of Tennessee System. Founded 1794. Setting: 526-acre urban campus. Total institutional enrollment: 26,000. Program was first offered in 1966. AACSB-accredited.

MBA HIGHLIGHTS

Entrance Difficulty***
Mean GMAT: 601
Mean GPA: 3.29

Cost $
Tuition: $1,139/semester
(Nonresident: $3,106/semester)
Room & Board: $3,500

Enrollment Profile

Full-time: 155	Work Exp: 80%
Part-time: 0	International: 4%
Total: 155	Women: 30%
Average Age: 28	Minorities: 5%

Average Class Size: 30

ACADEMICS

Length of Program Minimum: 21 months. Maximum: 2 years.

Calendar Semesters.

Full-time Classes Main campus; day, evening.

Degree Requirements 54 credits including 24 elective credits. Other: Summer internship.

Required Courses Business administration, business administration 2.

Curricular Focus Leadership, strategic analysis and planning, teamwork.

Concentrations Economics, entrepreneurship, environmental management, statistics, finance, human resources management, international business, management, marketing, operations management, strategic management, transportation.

Faculty Full-time: 106, 100% with doctorates; part-time: 12.

Teaching Methodology Case study: 15%, faculty seminars: 5%, lecture: 40%, research: 5%, seminars by members of the business community: 5%, student presentations: 10%, team projects: 20%.

Special Opportunities International exchange in France. Other: case competition team.

STUDENT STATISTICS

Geographic Representation State residents 46%. By region: South 77%; Northeast 8%; Midwest 8%; West 5%. International 4%.

Undergraduate Majors Business 38%; education 2%; engineering/technology 15%; humanities 30%; science/mathematics 10%; social sciences 5%.

Other Background Graduate degrees in other disciplines: 5%. Work experience: On average, students have 4 years of work experience on entrance to the program.

FACILITIES

Information Resources Main library with 2.1 million bound volumes, 1.9 million titles on microform, 14,406 periodical subscriptions, 30,553 records/tapes/CDs, 17 CD-ROMs.

Housing 8% of students in program live in college-owned or -operated housing. Assistance with housing search provided.

Technology Computers are used heavily in course work. 60 computer terminals/PCs, linked by a campus-wide computer network, are available for use by students in program; they are located in the library, computer labs. Students in the program are required to have their own PC.

Computer Resources/On-line Services

Training	Yes	CompuServe	No
Internet	Yes	Dun's	No
E-Mail	Yes	Dow Jones	Yes
Multimedia Center	Yes	Dialog	Yes
LEXIS/NEXIS	No	Bloomberg	No

Other on-line services: First Search, OCLC, RLIN.

ADMISSION

Acceptance 1994-95 540 applied for admission; 29% were accepted.

Entrance Requirements Bachelor's degree, GMAT score.

Application Requirements Written essay, application form, copies of transcript, 2 letters of recommendation.

Application Deadlines 4/1 for fall. Applications are processed on a rolling basis.

FINANCIALS

Costs for 1994-95 Tuition: Full-time: $1,139/semester for state residents, $3,106/semester for nonresidents. Fees: Full-time: $111/semester for state residents, $111/semester for nonresidents. Average room and board costs are $3,500 per academic year (on-campus) and $4,000 per academic year (off-campus).

Financial Aid In 1994-95, candidates received some institutionally administered aid in the form of scholarships, loans, fellowships, assistantships, work-study. Financial aid is not available to part-time students. Application deadline: 4/1 for fall. Applications are processed on a rolling basis. Contact: Mr. John Mays, Director of Financial Aid, 115 Student Services Building, Knoxville, TN 37996. (615) 974-3131.

INTERNATIONAL STUDENTS
Demographics 4% of students enrolled in the program are international.

Services and Facilities International student office, international student center, visa services, language tutoring, ESL courses, special assistance for nonnative speakers of English, counseling/support services.

Applying TOEFL required, minimum score of 550; proof of adequate funds. Financial aid is available to international students. Financial aid application deadline: 3/1 for fall. Admission application deadline: 3/1 for fall. Contact: Mr. David Lawson, Coordinator of International Student Services, 1620 Melrose Avenue, Knoxville, TN 37996-3531. (615) 974-3177.

ALTERNATE MBA PROGRAMS
Executive MBA (EMBA) Length of program: 12 months. Full-time classes: Main campus; day, evening, weekends, summer. Degree requirements: 45 credits. Comprehensive project. Average class size: 25.

MBA/JD Length of program: Minimum: 48 months. Degree requirements: 134 credits.

PLACEMENT
In 1993-94, 100 organizations participated in on-campus recruiting; 450 on-campus interviews were conducted. Placement services include career counseling/planning, career fairs, career library, career placement, electronic job bank, job interviews, job search course, resume preparation, and resume referral to employers. Of 1994 graduates, 90% were employed within three months of graduation, the average starting salary was $42,500, the range was $30,000-$65,000.

Jobs by Employer Type Manufacturing 42%; service 41%; consulting 17%.

Jobs by Functional Area Marketing/sales 21%; finance 35%; operations 6%; management 10%; strategic planning 7%; technical management 4%; consulting 17%.

Program Contact: Ms. Donna Potts, Director of Graduate Admissions, University of Tennessee, Knoxville, Knoxville, TN 37996. (615) 974-5033; Fax: (615) 974-3826.

Vanderbilt University

Owen Graduate School of Management

Nashville, Tennessee

OVERVIEW
Vanderbilt University is an independent nonprofit coed institution. Founded 1873. Setting: 330-acre urban campus. Total institutional enrollment: 10,088. Program was first offered in 1969. AACSB-accredited.

MBA HIGHLIGHTS
Entrance Difficulty**
Mean GMAT: 610
Mean GPA: 3.1

Cost $$$$
Tuition: $19,650
Room & Board: $6,950

Enrollment Profile

Full-time: 393	Work Exp: 85%
Part-time: 0	International: 21%
Total: 393	Women: 26%
Average Age: 25	Minorities: 6%

Average Class Size: 35

ACADEMICS
Length of Program Minimum: 20 months. Maximum: 2 years.
Calendar Semesters.
Full-time Classes Main campus; day.
Degree Requirements 63 credits including 15 elective credits. Other: One law-related course; 12 hours outside of concentration.
Required Courses Economics of businesses and markets, introduction to accounting, macroeconomics, management information systems, manage-

rial finance, managerial problem solving and communication, managerial statistics, marketing management, operations management, organization management and human resources, strategic management. Courses may be waived through: previous course work, work experience.

Curricular Focus Cross functional management, problem solving and decision making, teamwork.

Concentrations Accounting, finance, human resources management, management information systems, marketing, operations management, organizational behavior.

Faculty Full-time: 43, 98% with doctorates; part-time: 13, 54% with doctorates.

Teaching Methodology Case study: 35%, lecture: 60%, team projects: 5%.

Special Opportunities International exchange in Australia, Brazil, France, Germany, Mexico, Norway, United Kingdom. Internship program available.

STUDENT STATISTICS
Geographic Representation By region: South 30%; Northeast 24%; West 15%; Midwest 9%. International 21%.

Undergraduate Majors Business 33%; engineering/technology 10%; humanities 33%; science/mathematics 7%; social sciences 13%.

Other Background Graduate degrees in other disciplines: 2%. Work experience: On average, students have 3 years of work experience on entrance to the program.

FACILITIES
Information Resources Main library with 2.1 million bound volumes, 155,145 titles on microform, 16,009 periodical subscriptions, 21,217 records/tapes/CDs, 1,726 CD-ROMs. Business collection in Walker Management Library includes 26,000 bound volumes, 1,300 periodical subscriptions.

Housing 10% of students in program live in college-owned or -operated housing.

Technology Computers are used heavily in course work. 45 computer terminals/PCs, linked by a campus-wide computer network, are available for use by students in program; they are located in the library, the computer center, computer labs. Students in the program are not required to have their own PC. $225 are budgeted per student for computer support.

Computer Resources/On-line Services

Training	Yes	LEXIS/NEXIS	Yes
Internet	Yes	Dow Jones	Yes
E-Mail	Yes	Bloomberg	Yes

ADMISSION
Acceptance 1994-95 928 applied for admission; 48% were accepted.

Entrance Requirements Bachelor's degree, GMAT score. Core courses waived through: previous course work, work experience.

Application Requirements Written essay, interview, application form, copies of transcript, resume/curriculum vitae, personal statement, 2 letters of recommendation.

Application Deadline 5/31 for fall.

FINANCIALS
Costs for 1994-95 Tuition: Full-time: $19,650. Fees: Full-time: $897. Average room and board costs are $6,950 per academic year (on-campus) and $6,950 per academic year (off-campus).

Financial Aid In 1994-95, 74% of candidates received some institutionally administered aid in the form of grants, scholarships, loans, fellowships, work-study. Total awards ranged from $1,500-$19,650. Application deadline: 3/31 for fall. Contact: Ms. Michelle B. Hartle, Interim Director of Admissions, Nashville, TN 37240-1001. (615) 322-4095.

INTERNATIONAL STUDENTS
Demographics 21% of students enrolled in the program are international; Asia 60%, Europe 15%, South America 9%, Africa 8%, Central America 3%, other 2%.

Services and Facilities International student center, visa services, ESL courses, special assistance for nonnative speakers of English, counseling/support services.

Applying TOEFL required; proof of adequate funds; health insurance. Financial aid is available to international students. Financial aid application deadline: 3/31 for fall. Admission application deadline: 5/31 for fall. Contact: Ms. Lorraine Sciadini, Coordinator of International Programs, Nashville, TN 37240-1001. (615) 343-4087.

ALTERNATE MBA PROGRAMS
Executive MBA (EMBA) Length of program: Minimum: 20 months. Maximum: 2 years. Degree requirements: 60 credits. Minimum 5 years full-time work experience; approval of employer. Average class size: 45.

MBA/JD Length of program: Minimum: 45 months. Maximum: 4 years. Degree requirements: 124 credits. Separate applications must be submitted to both business and law.

MBA/MSN Length of program: Minimum: 30 months. Degree requirements: 69 credits. 2 years experience as a registered nurse.

PLACEMENT

In 1993-94, 144 organizations participated in on-campus recruiting; 2,350 on-campus interviews were conducted. Placement services include alumni network, career counseling/planning, career fairs, career library, electronic job bank, networking trips, resume preparation, resume referral to employers, and Of 1994 graduates, 80% were employed within three months of graduation, the average starting salary was $50,100, the range was $26,000-$95,000.

Program Contact: Ms. Susan M. Motz, Director of the MBA Program, Vanderbilt University, Nashville, TN 37240-1001. (615) 322-6469, or (800) 288-6936; Fax: (615) 343-1175.

TEXAS

Abilene Christian University

Abilene, Texas

OVERVIEW

Abilene Christian University is an independent comprehensive coed institution, affiliated with Church of Christ. Founded 1906. Setting: 208-acre suburban campus. Total institutional enrollment: 4,200. Program was first offered in 1960.

MBA HIGHLIGHTS

Entrance Difficulty***
Mean GMAT: 480
Mean GPA: 3.0

Cost $
Tuition: $248/hour
Room & Board: $1,100

Enrollment Profile

Full-time: 13	Work Exp: 90%
Part-time: 24	International: 15%
Total: 37	Women: 30%
Average Age: 28	Minorities: N/R

Average Class Size: 18

ACADEMICS

Length of Program Minimum: 12 months. Maximum: 5 years.
Calendar Semesters.
Full-time Classes Main campus; evening, summer.
Part-time Classes Main campus; evening, summer.
Degree Requirements 33 hours including 18 elective hours.
Required Courses Current topics in organizational behavior, management of technology, marketing seminar, seminar in finance, strategic management. Courses may be waived through: previous course work, work experience.
Curricular Focus Business issues and problems, leadership, strategic analysis and planning.
Concentration Management.
Faculty Full-time: 9, 89% with doctorates; part-time: 1.
Teaching Methodology Case study: 20%, lecture: 40%, research: 10%, student presentations: 10%, team projects: 20%.
Special Opportunities Internship program available.

STUDENT STATISTICS

Geographic Representation State residents 75%. By region: South 79%; Northeast 2%; Midwest 2%; West 2%. International 15%.
Undergraduate Majors Business 60%; engineering/technology 30%; science/mathematics 5%; social sciences 5%.

Other Background Graduate degrees in other disciplines: 5%. Work experience: On average, students have 5 years of work experience on entrance to the program.

FACILITIES

Information Resources Main library with 420,662 bound volumes, 827,593 titles on microform, 2,130 periodical subscriptions, 35,552 records/tapes/CDs.
Housing 5% of students in program live in college-owned or -operated housing.
Technology Computers are used heavily in course work. 50 computer terminals/PCs, linked by a campus-wide computer network, are available for use by students in program; they are located in student rooms, the library, computer labs. Students in the program are not required to have their own PC.

Computer Resources/On-line Services

Training	No	Multimedia Center	Yes
Internet	Yes	LEXIS/NEXIS	Yes
E-Mail	Yes		

ADMISSION

Acceptance 1994-95 Of those applying, 70% were accepted.
Entrance Requirements Bachelor's degree, GMAT score. Core courses waived through: previous course work.
Application Requirements Application form, copies of transcript, personal statement.
Application Deadline Applications are processed on a rolling basis.

FINANCIALS

Estimated Costs for 1995-96 Tuition: Full-time: $248/hour. Average room and board costs are $1,100 per academic year (on-campus) and $800 per academic year (off-campus).
Financial Aid In 1994-95, 69% of candidates received some institutionally administered aid in the form of scholarships, loans, assistantships. Total awards ranged from $125-$1,674. Financial aid is available to part-time students. Application deadlines: 7/1 for fall, 11/1 for spring. Contact: Mr. Stan Lambert, Director of Student Financial Services, ACU Station, Box 8483, Abilene, TX 79699. (915) 674-2643.

INTERNATIONAL STUDENTS

Demographics 15% of students enrolled in the program are international; Asia 62%, Africa 25%, South America 13%.
Services and Facilities International student center, language tutoring, ESL courses, special assistance for nonnative speakers of English, counseling/support services.
Applying TOEFL required, minimum score of 550; proof of adequate funds. Financial aid is available to international students. Applications are processed on a rolling basis. Admission applications are processed on a rolling basis. Contact: Mr. Ted Presley, Director of International Division, ACU Station, Box 8197, Abilene, TX 79699. (915) 674-2258.

PLACEMENT

Placement services include career counseling/planning, career fairs, career library, career placement, electronic job bank, and resume preparation. Of 1994 graduates, 90% were employed within three months of graduation.

Program Contact: Dr. Monty Lynn, Graduate Adviser, Abilene Christian University, ACU Station, Box 8325, Abilene, TX 79699. (915) 674-2593; Fax: (915) 674-2507; Internet Address: lynn@acuvax.acu.edu.

Amber University

Garland, Texas

OVERVIEW

Amber University is an independent nondenominational upper-level coed institution. Founded 1971. Setting: 5-acre suburban campus with easy access to Dallas–Fort Worth. Total institutional enrollment: 1,500. Program was first offered in 1975.

MBA HIGHLIGHTS

Entrance Difficulty*
Mean GMAT: N/R
Mean GPA: 3.0

Cost $
Tuition: $400/course
Room & Board: N/R

Enrollment Profile

Full-time: 125	Work Exp: 100%
Part-time: 375	International: 0%
Total: 500	Women: 50%
Average Age: 37	Minorities: 35%

Average Class Size: 25

ACADEMICS

Length of Program Minimum: 24 months. Maximum: 7 years.

Calendar 4 ten-week terms.

Full-time Classes Main campus, distance learning option; evening, weekends, summer.

Part-time Classes Main campus, distance learning option; evening, weekends, summer.

Degree Requirements 36 hours including 15 elective hours.

Required Courses Ethics for decision making, human resources management, managerial economics, managerial finance, marketing management, strategic management, theory and application of research methods.

Curricular Focus Entrepreneurship, general management, problem solving and decision making.

Concentrations Accounting, human resources management, management.

Faculty Full-time: 5, 95% with doctorates; part-time: 25, 95% with doctorates.

Teaching Methodology Case study: 20%, lecture: 20%, research: 20%, student presentations: 20%, team projects: 20%.

STUDENT STATISTICS

Geographic Representation State residents 100%. By region: South 100%.

Undergraduate Majors Business 33%; social sciences 33%; other 34%.

Other Background Graduate degrees in other disciplines: 2%. Work experience: On average, students have 5 years of work experience on entrance to the program.

FACILITIES

Information Resources Main library with 21,000 bound volumes, 1,200 titles on microform, 120 periodical subscriptions.

Housing College housing not available.

Technology Computers are used heavily in course work. 20 computer terminals/PCs are available for use by students in program; they are located in the library. Students in the program are not required to have their own PC.

Computer Resources/On-line Services

Training	No	Dun's	Yes $
Internet	No	Dow Jones	Yes $
E-Mail	Yes	Dialog	Yes $
LEXIS/NEXIS	No	Bloomberg	No
CompuServe	No		

Other on-line services: First Search.

ADMISSION

Acceptance 1994-95 200 applied for admission; 98% were accepted.

Entrance Requirements Bachelor's degree, minimum 3.0 GPA.

Application Requirements Application form, copies of transcript.

Application Deadlines 9/1 for fall, 3/1 for spring.

FINANCIALS

Costs for 1994-95 Tuition: Full-time: $400/course.

Financial Aid Financial aid is not available to part-time students.

INTERNATIONAL STUDENTS

Applying Financial aid is not available to international students.

Program Contact: Dr. Algia Allen, Vice President, Academic Services, Amber University, 1700 Eastgate Drive, Garland, TX 75041-5595. (214) 279-6511 Ext. 35; Fax: (214) 279-9773.

Angelo State University

Department of Business Administration

San Angelo, Texas

OVERVIEW

Angelo State University is a state-supported comprehensive coed institution. Part of Texas State University System. Founded 1928. Setting: 268-acre small-town campus. Total institutional enrollment: 6,200.

MBA HIGHLIGHTS

Entrance Difficulty*

Cost $
Tuition: $55 - $67/semester credit hour
(Nonresident: $196 - $208/semester credit hour)
Room & Board: N/R

Enrollment Profile

Full-time: 11	Work Exp: N/R
Part-time: 53	International: 8%
Total: 64	Women: 47%
Average Age: N/R	Minorities: 20%

Average Class Size: 22

ACADEMICS

Length of Program Minimum: 27 months.

Calendar Semesters.

Full-time Classes Main campus; evening, summer.

Part-time Classes Main campus; evening, summer.

Degree Requirements 39 credits including 6 elective credits.

Required Courses Accounting, accounting information systems, advanced management, corporate strategies and policies, decision analysis, economic analysis, financial management, legal and social environment of business, marketing management, operations management, organizational behavior, research methods.

Curricular Focus General management, problem solving and decision making, strategic analysis and planning.

Concentrations Accounting, computer science, management.

Faculty Full-time: 12, 100% with doctorates.

Teaching Methodology Case study: 15%, faculty seminars: 1%, lecture: 50%, research: 10%, seminars by members of the business community: 1%, student presentations: 5%, team projects: 18%.

STUDENT STATISTICS

Geographic Representation State residents 88%. By region: West 88%; Northeast 2%; South 2%; Midwest 2%. International 8%.

FACILITIES

Information Resources Main library with 236,352 bound volumes, 551,967 titles on microform, 2,007 periodical subscriptions, 8,126 records/tapes/CDs.

Housing 10% of students in program live in college-owned or -operated housing.

Technology Computers are used moderately in course work. 150 computer terminals/PCs are available for use by students in program; they are located in the library, computer labs. Students in the program are not required to have their own PC.

Computer Resources/On-line Services

E-Mail	No

ADMISSION

Acceptance 1994-95 56 applied for admission; 73% were accepted.

Entrance Requirements Bachelor's degree, GMAT score, minimum 2.5 GPA. Core courses waived through: previous course work.

Application Deadlines 8/1 for fall, 12/1 for spring. Applications are processed on a rolling basis.

FINANCIALS

Estimated Costs for 1995-96 Tuition: Full-time: $55-$67/semester credit hour for state residents, $196-$208/semester credit hour for nonresidents.

Financial Aid In 1994-95, candidates received some institutionally administered aid in the form of scholarships. Financial aid is available to part-time students. Application deadline: 3/1 for fall. Contact: Dr. Peggy Skaggs, Dean of the Graduate School, 2601 West Avenue N, San Angelo, TX 76909. (915) 942-2169.

INTERNATIONAL STUDENTS
Demographics 8% of students enrolled in the program are international.

Applying TOEFL required, minimum score of 550; proof of adequate funds; $3000 deposit. Financial aid is available to international students. Scholarship is open to these students; deadline is 7/1. Admission application deadline: 6/10 for fall.

PLACEMENT
Placement services include career placement.

Program Contact: Dr. Peggy Skaggs, Dean of the Graduate Program, Department of Business Administration, Angelo State University, 2601 West Avenue N, San Angelo, TX 76909. (915) 942-2169.

Baylor University

Hankamer School of Business

Waco, Texas

OVERVIEW
Baylor University is an independent Baptist coed institution. Founded 1845. Setting: 428-acre suburban campus with easy access to Dallas–Fort Worth. Total institutional enrollment: 12,185. Program was first offered in 1960. AACSB-accredited.

MBA HIGHLIGHTS

Entrance Difficulty*
Mean GMAT: 564
Mean GPA: 3.31

Cost
Tuition: $232/hour
Room & Board: N/R

Enrollment Profile

Full-time: N/R	Work Exp: 60%
Part-time: N/R	International: 11%
Total: 215	Women: 30%
Average Age: 25	Minorities: 16%

Average Class Size: 15

ACADEMICS
Length of Program Minimum: 12 months. Maximum: 5 years.
Calendar Semesters.
Full-time Classes Main campus; day, early morning, summer.
Part-time Classes Main campus.
Degree Requirements 36 hours including 15 elective hours.
Required Courses Corporate finance, financial control, information systems, marketing strategy, microeconomics, organizational behavior, strategic management. Courses may be waived through: previous course work.
Curricular Focus International business, problem solving and decision making, teamwork.
Concentrations Accounting, economics, entrepreneurship, finance, international business, management, management information systems, marketing.
Faculty Full-time: 81, 94% with doctorates.
Teaching Methodology Case study: 20%, lecture: 35%, research: 10%, seminars by members of the business community: 5%, student presentations: 10%, team projects: 20%.
Special Opportunities International exchange in Australia, Canada, France, Mexico, Russia. Internship program available.

STUDENT STATISTICS
Geographic Representation By region: South 57%; Midwest 19%; West 11%; Northeast 2%. International 11%.
Undergraduate Majors Business 67%; engineering/technology 11%; humanities 6%; science/mathematics 6%; social sciences 8%; other 2%.
Other Background Graduate degrees in other disciplines: 7%. Work experience: On average, students have 1 year of work experience on entrance to the program.

FACILITIES
Information Resources Main library with 1.5 million bound volumes, 12,466 titles on microform, 10,561 periodical subscriptions, 40,630 records/tapes/CDs.

Housing 6% of students in program live in college-owned or -operated housing.

Technology Computers are used heavily in course work. 100 computer terminals/PCs, linked by a campus-wide computer network, are available for use by students in program; they are located in classrooms, the library, the computer center, computer labs. Students in the program are not required to have their own PC.

Computer Resources/On-line Services

Training	Yes	Dun's	No
Internet	Yes	Dow Jones	Yes
E-Mail	Yes	Dialog	No
LEXIS/NEXIS	Yes	Bloomberg	No
CompuServe	No		

ADMISSION
Acceptance 1994-95 Of those applying, 75% were accepted.

Entrance Requirements Bachelor's degree, GMAT score of 500, minimum 2.7 GPA.

Application Requirements Written essay, application form, copies of transcript, resume/curriculum vitae, personal statement, 3 letters of recommendation.

Application Deadlines 7/31 for fall, 11/30 for spring, 5/1 for summer.

FINANCIALS
Costs for 1994-95 Tuition: Full-time: $232/hour. Fees: Full-time: $325/semester.

Financial Aid In 1994-95, 37% of candidates received some institutionally administered aid in the form of scholarships, assistantships, work-study. Total awards ranged from $1,000-$6,500. Financial aid is available to part-time students. Application deadlines: 5/1 for fall, 11/1 for spring. Contact: Ms. Jeannette Armour, Director of Financial Aid, PO Box 97028, Waco, TX 76798. (817) 755-2611.

INTERNATIONAL STUDENTS
Demographics 11% of students enrolled in the program are international; Asia 70%, Europe 10%, other 20%.

Services and Facilities Visa services, language tutoring, ESL courses, host family friend program.

Applying TOEFL required, minimum score of 550; proof of health; proof of adequate funds. Financial aid is not available to international students. Admission application deadlines: 8/1 for fall, 12/1 for spring. Contact: Ms. Edna Dietrich, Coordinator, International Programs, PO Box 97381, Waco, TX 76798. (817) 755-1451.

ALTERNATE MBA PROGRAMS
Executive MBA (EMBA) Length of program: Minimum: 24 months. Degree requirements: 47 hours. Minimum 5 years professional work experience. Average class size: 25.

International MBA

MBA/JD Length of program: Minimum: 36 months. Degree requirements: 24 hours including 3 elective hours. 108 quarter hours for law, 24 semester hours for business.

MBA-IM

PLACEMENT
In 1993-94, 102 organizations participated in on-campus recruiting. Placement services include career counseling/planning, career fairs, career library, career placement, job interviews, resume preparation, and resume referral to employers. Of 1994 graduates, 90% were employed within three months of graduation, the average starting salary was $33,403.

Program Contact: Ms. Erin Raymond, Director of Admissions, Baylor University, Waco, TX 76798. (817) 755-1011, or (800) 583-0622.
See full description on page 674.

Dallas Baptist University

College of Business

Dallas, Texas

OVERVIEW
Dallas Baptist University is an independent Southern Baptist comprehensive coed institution. Founded 1965. Setting: 200-acre suburban campus. Total institutional enrollment: 2,989. Program was first offered in 1981.

MBA HIGHLIGHTS

Entrance Difficulty***
Mean GMAT: 450
Mean GPA: 2.9

Cost $
Tuition: $235/credit hour
Room & Board: $3,270

Enrollment Profile
Full-time: 63	Work Exp: 99%
Part-time: 240	International: 14%
Total: 303	Women: 37%
Average Age: 33	Minorities: 29%

Average Class Size: 16

*D*allas Baptist University's Master of Business Administration program exists to serve the educational needs of professionals who desire to enhance their management skills and acquire new ones for more effective service in their organizations. The mission of the College of Business is to graduate individuals capable of assuming impact positions upon graduation by providing leadership, direction, and support and by using learning processes focusing upon competence-building activities.

The University's program is unique among most M.B.A. programs. DBU holds the belief that education is best served when it is taught in a Christian context that stresses the fundamental aspects of the free enterprise system. The University also recognizes that all students, regardless of race, sex, or age, have differing needs in their pursuit of a graduate education. Therefore, the focus of meeting those needs is on quality and convenience.

The majority of M.B.A. students hold full-time positions of employment. Consequently, most classes are conducted once per week in the evenings and on Saturdays. In addition, classes are held on the main campus, which is located near the center of the metroplex, and at various locations throughout the Dallas/Ft. Worth area.

ACADEMICS
Length of Program Minimum: 24 months. Maximum: 5 years.
Calendar 4-1-4.
Full-time Classes Main campus; evening, weekends, summer.
Part-time Classes Main campus, Dallas; day, evening, weekends, summer.
Degree Requirements 36 credit hours including 3-12 elective credit hours.
Required Courses Basic computer skills, business legal environment, financial accounting, leadership and ethical management, management information systems, management theory, managerial economics, managerial finance, marketing concepts, quantitative methods in management, strategic management decision. Courses may be waived through: previous course work.
Curricular Focus Total quality management, general management, problem solving and decision making.
Concentrations Finance, international business, management, management information systems, marketing.
Faculty Full-time: 12, 75% with doctorates; part-time: 15, 67% with doctorates.
Teaching Methodology Case study: 10%, faculty seminars: 5%, lecture: 50%, research: 10%, seminars by members of the business community: 5%, student presentations: 10%, team projects: 10%.
Special Opportunities Internships include government.

STUDENT STATISTICS
Geographic Representation State residents 84%. By region: South 84%; Midwest 1%; West 1%. International 14%.
Undergraduate Majors Business 57%; education 7%; engineering/technology 7%; humanities 9%; science/mathematics 13%; social sciences 7%.
Other Background Work experience: On average, students have 11 years of work experience on entrance to the program.

FACILITIES
Information Resources Main library with 544,781 bound volumes, 537,696 titles on microform, 682 periodical subscriptions, 4,393 records/tapes/CDs.
Housing 1% of students in program live in college-owned or -operated housing.
Technology Computers are used moderately in course work. 80 computer terminals/PCs are available for use by students in program; they are located in computer labs. Students in the program are not required to have their own PC.

Computer Resources/On-line Services
E-Mail	Yes

Other on-line services: First Search.

ADMISSION
Acceptance 1994-95 Of those applying, 79% were accepted.
Entrance Requirements Bachelor's degree, GMAT score of 400, minimum 3.0 GPA. Core courses waived through: previous course work.
Application Requirements Application form, copies of transcript, personal statement, 2 letters of recommendation.
Application Deadline Applications are processed on a rolling basis.

FINANCIALS
Costs for 1994-95 Tuition: Full-time: $235/credit hour. Average room and board costs are $3,270 per academic year (on-campus).
Financial Aid In 1994-95, 3% of candidates received some institutionally administered aid in the form of scholarships. Total awards ranged from $1,215-$3,240. Financial aid is not available to part-time students. Application deadline: 5/1 for fall. Contact: Director of Financial Aid, 3000 Mountain Creek Parkway, Dallas, TX 75211-9299. (214) 333-5363.

INTERNATIONAL STUDENTS
Demographics 14% of students enrolled in the program are international.
Services and Facilities International student center, visa services, language tutoring, ESL courses, special assistance for nonnative speakers of English, counseling/support services, host family program, conversational partners, community liaison program.
Applying TOEFL required, minimum score of 550; proof of health; proof of adequate funds. Financial aid is not available to international students. Admission applications are processed on a rolling basis. Contact: Ms. Rebecca Brown, International Director of Student Services, 3000 Mountain Creek Parkway, Dallas, TX 75211-9299. (214) 333-5426.

PLACEMENT
Placement services include career counseling/planning, career fairs, career library, career placement, electronic job bank, job interviews, and resume referral to employers. Of 1994 graduates, 92% were employed within three months of graduation, the average starting salary was $49,220, the range was $28,000-$90,000.
Jobs by Employer Type Manufacturing 36%; service 51%; government 9%; healthcare 4%.

Program Contact: Mr. David L. Watson, Director of Graduate Programs, Dallas Baptist University, 3000 Mountain Creek Parkway, Dallas, TX 75211-9299. (214) 333-5242; Fax: (214) 333-5579.

East Texas State University

College of Business and Technology

Commerce, Texas

OVERVIEW
East Texas State University is a state-supported coed institution. Part of East Texas State University Complex. Founded 1889. Setting: 140-acre small-town campus with easy access to Dallas-Fort Worth. Total institutional enrollment: 8,800. Program was first offered in 1955. AACSB-accredited.

MBA HIGHLIGHTS

Entrance Difficulty***
Mean GMAT: 510
Mean GPA: 3.3

Cost
Tuition: N/R
(Nonresident: N/R)
Room & Board: $3,400

Enrollment Profile
Full-time: 30
Part-time: 65
Total: 95
Average Age: 32

Work Exp: 95%
International: 35%
Women: 30%
Minorities: 40%

Average Class Size: 19

ACADEMICS
Calendar Semesters.

Curricular Focus International business, leadership, strategic analysis and planning.

Concentrations Accounting, economics, finance, human resources management, international business, management, marketing.

Faculty Full-time: 25, 100% with doctorates.

Teaching Methodology Case study: 20%, lecture: 30%, research: 20%, student presentations: 20%, team projects: 10%.

Special Opportunities International exchange in United Kingdom.

STUDENT STATISTICS
Geographic Representation State residents 65%. By region: South 65%. International 35%.

Undergraduate Majors Business 55%; education 4%; engineering/technology 15%; humanities 10%; nursing 1%; science/mathematics 5%; social sciences 5%; other 5%.

Other Background Graduate degrees in other disciplines: 15%. Work experience: On average, students have 8 years of work experience on entrance to the program.

FACILITIES
Information Resources Main library with 602,122 bound volumes, 110,694 titles on microform, 1,901 periodical subscriptions, 5,261 records/tapes/CDs, 27 CD-ROMs.

Housing College housing available.

Technology Computers are used heavily in course work. 60 computer terminals/PCs are available for use by students in program; they are located in computer labs. Students in the program are not required to have their own PC.

Computer Resources/On-line Services

Training	No	E-Mail	Yes
Internet	Yes	Videoconference Center	Yes

ADMISSION
Acceptance 1994-95 500 applied for admission; 40% were accepted.

Entrance Requirements Bachelor's degree, GMAT score of 375, minimum 2.75 GPA. Core courses waived through: previous course work.

Application Requirements Application form, copies of transcript, resume/curriculum vitae.

Application Deadlines 9/1 for fall, 1/5 for spring. Applications are processed on a rolling basis.

FINANCIALS
Financial Aid In 1994-95, 10% of candidates received some institutionally administered aid in the form of scholarships, assistantships, tuition adjustments. Total awards ranged from $3,000-$14,300. Financial aid is not available to part-time students. Application deadline: 5/1 for fall. Applications are processed on a rolling basis. Contact: Mr. John Patton, Director of Financial Aid, East Texas Station, Commerce, TX 75429-3011. (903) 886-5096.

INTERNATIONAL STUDENTS
Demographics 35% of students enrolled in the program are international; Asia 90%, Africa 5%, Europe 5%.

Services and Facilities International student office, ESL courses, counseling/support services.

Applying TOEFL required, minimum score of 500; proof of health; proof of adequate funds. Financial aid is available to international students. Assistantships are available for these students. Applications are processed on a rolling basis. Admission application deadlines: 7/1 for fall, 11/15 for spring. Applications are processed on a rolling basis. Contact: Ms. Elke Brinker-Cooper, International Student Adviser, East Texas Station, Commerce, TX 75429-3011. (903) 886-5097.

PROGRAM
One-Year MBA Length of program: Minimum: 12 months. Maximum: 6 years. Full-time classes: Main campus, Dallas, distance learning option; evening, summer. Part-time classes: Main campus, Dallas, distance learning option; evening, summer. Degree requirements: 36 credits including 12 elective credits.

PLACEMENT
Placement services include career counseling/planning, career fairs, career placement, and resume referral to employers. Of 1994 graduates, 85% were employed within three months of graduation, the average starting salary was $32,000, the range was $24,000-$42,000.

Jobs by Employer Type Manufacturing 30%; service 60%; government 5%; nonprofit 5%.

Jobs by Functional Area Marketing/sales 25%; finance 40%; operations 35%.

Program Contact: Dr. Robert M. Seay, Assistant Dean, East Texas State University, East Texas Station, Commerce, TX 75429-3011. (903) 886-5190; Fax: (903) 886-5650.

East Texas State University at Texarkana

Division of Business Administration

Texarkana, Texas

OVERVIEW
East Texas State University at Texarkana is a state-supported upper-level coed institution. Part of East Texas State University Complex. Founded 1971. Setting: 1-acre urban campus. Total institutional enrollment: 1,300. Program was first offered in 1972.

MBA HIGHLIGHTS

Entrance Difficulty*

Cost $
Tuition: $70 - $144/hour
(Nonresident: $213 - $215/hour)
Room & Board: N/R

Enrollment Profile
Full-time: 22
Part-time: 90
Total: 112
Average Age: N/R

Work Exp: N/R
International: 5%
Women: 60%
Minorities: 7%

Average Class Size: 20

ACADEMICS
Length of Program Minimum: 12 months.

Calendar Semesters.

Full-time Classes Main campus; evening, summer.

Part-time Classes Main campus; evening, summer.

Degree Requirements 36 hours including 12 elective hours.

Required Courses Administrative controls, data systems management, field experience in business, financial management, macroeconomics, managerial policy, marketing management, research literature and techniques.

Curricular Focus Leadership, problem solving and decision making, teamwork.

Concentration Management.

Faculty Full-time: 8, 75% with doctorates.

Teaching Methodology Case study: 10%, lecture: 50%, research: 10%, student presentations: 10%, team projects: 20%.

STUDENT STATISTICS
Geographic Representation State residents 90%. International 5%.

FACILITIES
Information Resources Main library with 176,258 bound volumes, 307,619 titles on microform, 1,072 periodical subscriptions, 850 records/tapes/CDs, 8 CD-ROMs.

Housing College housing not available.

Technology Computers are used moderately in course work. 46 computer terminals/PCs are available for use by students in program; they are located in computer labs. Students in the program are not required to have their own PC.

Computer Resources/On-line Services

Training	Yes	Multimedia Center	Yes
E-Mail	Yes		

ADMISSION
Entrance Requirements Bachelor's degree, prerequisite courses required for applicants with non-business degree, GMAT score of 375.

Application Requirements Application form, copies of transcript.

Application Deadline Applications are processed on a rolling basis.

FINANCIALS
Costs for 1994-95 Tuition: Full-time: $70-$144/hour for state residents, $213-$215/hour for nonresidents.

Financial Aid In 1994-95, candidates received some institutionally administered aid in the form of grants, scholarships, loans. Financial aid is available to part-time students. Application deadline: 5/1 for fall. Applications are processed on a rolling basis. Contact: Ms. Marilyn Raney, Coordinator for Financial Assistance, 2600 North Robison Road, Texarkana, TX 75501. (903) 838-6514 Ext. 221.

INTERNATIONAL STUDENTS
Demographics 5% of students enrolled in the program are international.

Applying TOEFL required, minimum score of 550; proof of health; proof of adequate funds. Financial aid is available to international students. Financial aid application deadlines: 5/1 for fall, 3/1 for summer.

PLACEMENT
Placement services include career counseling/planning and career placement.

Program Contact: Dr. Larry Davis, Division Head, Business Administration, East Texas State University at Texarkana, PO Box 5518, Texarkana, TX 75505. (903) 838-6514; Fax: (903) 832-8890.

Hardin-Simmons University

School of Business

Abilene, Texas

OVERVIEW
Hardin-Simmons University is an independent Baptist comprehensive coed institution. Founded 1891. Setting: 40-acre small-town campus. Total institutional enrollment: 2,133.

MBA HIGHLIGHTS

Entrance Difficulty**
Mean GMAT: 500
Mean GPA: 3.25

Cost $
Tuition: $220/hour
Room & Board: N/R

Enrollment Profile

Full-time: 20	Work Exp: 95%
Part-time: 10	International: 5%
Total: 30	Women: 45%
Average Age: 28	Minorities: 15%

Average Class Size: 12

ACADEMICS
Length of Program Minimum: 18 months. Maximum: 5 years.

Calendar Semesters.

Full-time Classes Main campus; evening.

Degree Requirements 36 hours including 12 elective hours.

Required Courses Computer information systems, financial management, management strategy, managerial accounting, managerial economics, marketing strategy, quantitative management science, quantitative research methods. Courses may be waived through: previous course work.

Curricular Focus Business issues and problems, leadership, problem solving and decision making.

Concentrations Accounting, economics, finance, management, marketing.

Faculty Full-time: 12, 92% with doctorates.

Teaching Methodology Case study: 15%, faculty seminars: 5%, lecture: 55%, research: 10%, seminars by members of the business community: 1%, student presentations: 9%, team projects: 5%.

STUDENT STATISTICS
Geographic Representation State residents 85%. International 5%.

Undergraduate Majors Business 50%; engineering/technology 40%; science/mathematics 5%; social sciences 5%.

Other Background Graduate degrees in other disciplines: 10%. Work experience: On average, students have 5 years of work experience on entrance to the program.

FACILITIES
Information Resources Main library with 415,752 bound volumes, 18,413 titles on microform, 999 periodical subscriptions, 7,644 records/tapes/CDs.

Housing College housing available.

Technology Computers are used moderately in course work. Computer terminals/PCs are available for use by students in program; they are located in the library, computer labs, the research center. Students in the program are not required to have their own PC.

Computer Resources/On-line Services

Training	Yes	Dun's	No
Internet	Yes	Dow Jones	No
LEXIS/NEXIS	No	Dialog	Yes $
CompuServe	No	Bloomberg	No

Other on-line services: First Search.

ADMISSION
Acceptance 1994-95 Of those applying, 75% were accepted.

Entrance Requirements Bachelor's degree, GMAT score of 450. Core courses waived through: previous course work.

Application Requirements Application form, copies of transcript.

Application Deadline Applications are processed on a rolling basis.

FINANCIALS
Costs for 1994-95 Tuition: Full-time: $220/hour. Fees: Full-time: $240/trimester.

Financial Aid In 1994-95, 10% of candidates received some institutionally administered aid in the form of grants, scholarships, loans, fellowships, assistantships. Application deadlines: 7/15 for fall, 12/1 for spring, 4/15 for summer. Contact: Ms. Fran Strange, Director of Financial Aid, HSU Station, Drawer R, Abilene, TX 79698. (915) 670-1331.

INTERNATIONAL STUDENTS
Demographics 5% of students enrolled in the program are international; Europe 50%, South America 50%.

Applying TOEFL required; proof of adequate funds. Financial aid is available to international students. Financial aid application deadlines: 7/15 for fall, 12/1 for spring, 4/15 for summer. Admission applications are processed on a rolling basis.

PLACEMENT
Placement services include career counseling/planning, career placement, and resume preparation.

Program Contact: Dr. Paul Sorrels, Dean of Graduate Studies, Hardin-Simmons University, HSU Station, Box 984, Abilene, TX 79698. (915) 670-1298; Fax: (915) 670-1527.

Incarnate Word College

Department of Professional Studies

San Antonio, Texas

OVERVIEW
Incarnate Word College is an independent Roman Catholic comprehensive coed institution. Founded 1881. Setting: 54-acre urban campus. Total institutional enrollment: 2,807.

MBA HIGHLIGHTS

Entrance Difficulty**

Cost $
Tuition: $290/hour
Room & Board: N/R

Enrollment Profile
Full-time: N/R
Part-time: N/R
Total: 190
Average Age: N/R

Work Exp: N/R
International: 5%
Women: 50%
Minorities: 55%

Average Class Size: 20

ACADEMICS
Length of Program Minimum: 30 months.
Calendar 4-4-1.
Full-time Classes Main campus, Randolph Air Force Base, Kelly Air Force Base; evening.
Part-time Classes Main campus, Randolph Air Force Base, Kelly Air Force Base; evening.
Degree Requirements 36 hours.
Curricular Focus Business issues and problems, general management, problem solving and decision making.
Concentrations Accounting, economics, finance, human resources management, international business, management, management information systems, marketing, quantitative analysis.
Teaching Methodology Case study: 25%, lecture: 50%, team projects: 25%.

STUDENT STATISTICS
Geographic Representation State residents 60%. International 5%.

FACILITIES
Information Resources Main library with 166,744 bound volumes, 19,100 titles on microform, 1,145 periodical subscriptions, 33,193 records/tapes/CDs.

ADMISSION
Entrance Requirements Bachelor's degree, minimum 2.5 GPA.
Application Requirements Application form, copies of transcript.
Application Deadline Applications are processed on a rolling basis.

FINANCIALS
Costs for 1994-95 Tuition: Full-time: $290/hour. Fees: Full-time: $95/semester.
Financial Aid Financial aid is available to part-time students. Application deadline: 4/1 for fall. Applications are processed on a rolling basis. Contact: Ms. Sandra Holt, Director of Financial Aid, 4301 Broadway, San Antonio, TX 78209-6397. (210) 829-6008.

INTERNATIONAL STUDENTS
Demographics 5% of students enrolled in the program are international.
Applying TOEFL required, minimum score of 560; proof of adequate funds. Financial aid is not available to international students. Admission applications are processed on a rolling basis.

ALTERNATE MBA PROGRAM
MBA/MSN Length of program: Minimum: 24 months. Full-time classes: Main campus, Randolph Air Force Base, Kelly Air Force Base; day, evening, summer. Part-time classes: Main campus, Randolph Air Force Base, Kelly Air Force Base; day, evening, summer. Degree requirements: 66 credits.

Program Contact: Ms. Wynette Hadnott, Director of Graduate Admissions, Incarnate Word College, 4301 Broadway, San Antonio, TX 78209-6397. (210) 829-6005; Fax: (210) 839-3921.

Lamar University–Beaumont

College of Business

Beaumont, Texas

OVERVIEW
Lamar University–Beaumont is a state-supported coed institution. Part of Lamar University System. Founded 1923. Setting: 200-acre urban campus with easy access to Houston. Total institutional enrollment: 9,000. Program was first offered in 1966. AACSB-accredited.

MBA HIGHLIGHTS

Entrance Difficulty***
Mean GMAT: 525
Mean GPA: 3.1

Cost $
Tuition: $336/semester
(Nonresident: $1,944/semester)
Room & Board: $1,800

Enrollment Profile
Full-time: 35
Part-time: 65
Total: 100
Average Age: 32

Work Exp: 80%
International: 20%
Women: 30%
Minorities: 25%

Average Class Size: 20

ACADEMICS
Length of Program Minimum: 12 months. Maximum: 6 years.
Calendar Semesters.
Full-time Classes Main campus; evening, summer.
Part-time Classes Main campus; evening, summer.
Degree Requirements 36 hours including 3-12 elective hours.
Required Courses Advanced statistical theory and analysis for business, business research, environment of business, financial management, managerial accounting, managerial economics, seminar in management, seminar in marketing.
Curricular Focus General management, problem solving and decision making, strategic analysis and planning.
Concentrations Accounting, management.
Faculty Full-time: 18, 100% with doctorates.
Teaching Methodology Case study: 20%, lecture: 50%, research: 10%, student presentations: 10%, team projects: 10%.
Special Opportunities International exchange in Nigeria, People's Republic of China, Poland. Internship program available.

STUDENT STATISTICS
Geographic Representation State residents 70%. By region: West 75%; Northeast 3%; Midwest 2%. International 20%.
Undergraduate Majors Business 30%; engineering/technology 40%; humanities 5%; nursing 10%; science/mathematics 5%; social sciences 10%.
Other Background Graduate degrees in other disciplines: 15%. Work experience: On average, students have 8 years of work experience on entrance to the program.

FACILITIES
Information Resources Main library with 519,111 bound volumes, 299,395 titles on microform, 2,955 periodical subscriptions, 1,297 records/tapes/CDs. Business collection includes 9,971 bound volumes, 176 periodical subscriptions, 1 CD-ROM, 20 videos.
Housing 50% of students in program live in college-owned or -operated housing. Assistance with housing search provided.
Technology Computers are used moderately in course work. 300 computer terminals/PCs, linked by a campus-wide computer network, are available for use by students in program; they are located in classrooms, the library, the computer center, computer labs. Students in the program are not required to have their own PC.

Computer Resources/On-line Services

Training	Yes	CompuServe	Yes
Internet	Yes	Dun's	Yes
E-Mail	Yes	Dow Jones	Yes
Multimedia Center	Yes	Bloomberg	No
LEXIS/NEXIS	Yes		

ADMISSION
Acceptance 1994-95 150 applied for admission; 50% were accepted.
Entrance Requirements Bachelor's degree, GMAT score, minimum 2.75 GPA. Core courses waived through: previous course work.
Application Requirements Application form, copies of transcript, resume/curriculum vitae, personal statement, 3 letters of recommendation.
Application Deadlines 5/15 for fall, 10/1 for spring, 2/15 for summer. Applications are processed on a rolling basis. Application discs available.

FINANCIALS
Costs for 1994-95 Tuition: Full-time: $336/semester for state residents, $1,944/semester for nonresidents. Fees: Full-time: $340/semester for state residents, $340/semester for nonresidents. Average room and board costs are $1,800 per academic year (on-campus).

Financial Aid In 1994-95, 25% of candidates received some institutionally administered aid in the form of scholarships, loans, fellowships, assistantships, work-study. Total awards ranged from $600-$6,500. Financial aid is not available to part-time students. Application deadlines: 3/1 for fall, 9/1 for spring. Applications are processed on a rolling basis. Contact: Ms. Ralynn Castette, Financial Aid Director, PO Box 10042, Beaumont, TX 77710. (409) 880-8450.

INTERNATIONAL STUDENTS

Demographics 20% of students enrolled in the program are international; Asia 40%, Central America 10%, Europe 10%, South America 10%, North America 7%, Africa 5%, Australia 3%, other 15%.

Services and Facilities International student office, visa services, language tutoring, ESL courses, special assistance for nonnative speakers of English, counseling/support services.

Applying TOEFL required, minimum score of 525; proof of adequate funds. Financial aid is available to international students. Financial aid application deadlines: 3/1 for fall, 9/1 for spring. Applications are processed on a rolling basis. Admission application deadlines: 5/15 for fall, 8/1 for spring, 2/15 for summer. Applications are processed on a rolling basis. Contact: Ms. Sandy Drane, International Student Adviser, PO Box 10009, Beaumont, TX 77710. (409) 880-8349.

PLACEMENT

In 1993-94, 20 organizations participated in on-campus recruiting. Placement services include alumni network, career counseling/planning, career fairs, career library, career placement, job interviews, resume preparation, and resume referral to employers. Of 1994 graduates, 75% were employed within three months of graduation, the average starting salary was $42,000, the range was $25,000-$50,000.

Program Contact: Dr. Robert Swerdlow, Interim Dean, Lamar University–Beaumont, PO Box 10059, Beaumont, TX 77710. (409) 880-8604, or (800) 443-5638; Fax: (409) 880-8088; Internet Address: swerdlowra@lub001.lamar.edu.

LeTourneau University

Business Division

Longview, Texas

OVERVIEW

LeTourneau University is an independent nondenominational comprehensive coed institution. Founded 1946. Setting: 162-acre suburban campus. Total institutional enrollment: 2,047. Program was first offered in 1992.

MBA HIGHLIGHTS

Entrance Difficulty*

Cost $$
Tuition: $267/credit
Room & Board: N/R

Enrollment Profile

Full-time: 174	Work Exp: 100%
Part-time: 0	International: 1%
Total: 174	Women: 28%
Average Age: 38	Minorities: 18%

Average Class Size: 15

ACADEMICS

Length of Program Minimum: 20 months. Maximum: 5 years.

Calendar Quarters.

Full-time Classes Main campus, Dallas, Houston; evening, summer.

Degree Requirements 39 credit hours.

Required Courses Business ethics and decision making, business policy and strategy, fundamentals of executive management, human dynamics of business management, international business environment, leadership strategy, legal problems in business management, managerial accounting, managerial economics, managerial finance, marketing management and strategy, organizational behavior, quantitative decision analysis.

Curricular Focus Computer integration, general management, strategic analysis and planning.

Concentration Management.

Faculty Full-time: 6, 100% with doctorates; part-time: 30, 100% with doctorates.

Teaching Methodology Case study: 30%, lecture: 30%, student presentations: 30%, team projects: 10%.

STUDENT STATISTICS

Geographic Representation By region: South 100%. International 1%.

Other Background Work experience: On average, students have 3 years of work experience on entrance to the program.

FACILITIES

Information Resources Main library with 83,577 bound volumes, 39,946 titles on microform, 1,156 periodical subscriptions, 10,658 records/tapes/CDs, 20 CD-ROMs.

Housing College housing not available.

Technology Computers are used heavily in course work. Students in the program are not required to have their own PC.

Computer Resources/On-line Services

Training	Yes	E-Mail	No

ADMISSION

Acceptance 1994-95 205 applied for admission; 70% were accepted.

Entrance Requirements Bachelor's degree, minimum 2.8 GPA, minimum 3 years of work experience. Core courses waived through: previous course work.

Application Requirements Written essay, application form, copies of transcript, resume/curriculum vitae, 3 letters of recommendation.

Application Deadline Applications are processed on a rolling basis.

FINANCIALS

Costs for 1994-95 Tuition: Full-time: $267/credit.

Financial Aid In 1994-95, 70% of candidates received some institutionally administered aid in the form of loans. Financial aid is not available to part-time students. Applications are processed on a rolling basis. Contact: Mr. Bill Rusk, Director of Financial Aid, PO Box 7001, Longview, TX 75607. (903) 753-0231.

INTERNATIONAL STUDENTS

Demographics 1% of students enrolled in the program are international.

Applying TOEFL required, minimum score of 600; proof of health; proof of adequate funds. Financial aid is not available to international students. Admission applications are processed on a rolling basis.

PLACEMENT

Placement services include career counseling/planning and resume preparation.

Program Contact: Ms. Linda Fitzhugh, Associate Dean, LeTourneau University, PO Box 7668, Longview, TX 75607. (903) 237-2780, or (800) 388-5327; Fax: (903) 237-2787.

Midwestern State University

Division of Business Administration

Wichita Falls, Texas

OVERVIEW

Midwestern State University is a state-supported comprehensive coed institution. Founded 1922. Setting: 172-acre suburban campus. Total institutional enrollment: 5,800. Program was first offered in 1968.

MBA HIGHLIGHTS

Entrance Difficulty*
Mean GMAT: 430
Mean GPA: 3.2

Cost $
Tuition: $793/semester
(Nonresident: $2,938/semester)
Room & Board: $3,200

Enrollment Profile

Full-time: 7
Part-time: 83
Total: 90
Average Age: 26

Work Exp: 70%
International: 5%
Women: 40%
Minorities: 10%

Average Class Size: 20

ACADEMICS

Length of Program Minimum: 12 months. Maximum: 6 years.

Calendar Semesters.

Full-time Classes Main campus; day, evening, summer.

Part-time Classes Main campus; day, evening, summer.

Degree Requirements 33 credits including 12 elective credits. Other: Research paper; final oral exam.

Required Courses Advanced applied business statistics, cost analysis and control, current issues in organizational behavior, financial administration, managerial economics or macroeconomics, research methods, seminar in business policy, seminar in marketing.

Curricular Focus General management, problem solving and decision making, strategic analysis and planning.

Concentration Management.

Faculty Full-time: 19, 85% with doctorates.

Teaching Methodology Case study: 20%, lecture: 30%, research: 10%, student presentations: 30%, team projects: 10%.

STUDENT STATISTICS

Geographic Representation State residents 95%. By region: South 98%. International 5%.

Undergraduate Majors Business 55%; education 3%; engineering/technology 35%; humanities 2%; science/mathematics 2%; social sciences 2%; other 1%.

Other Background Graduate degrees in other disciplines: 10%. Work experience: On average, students have 2 years of work experience on entrance to the program.

FACILITIES

Information Resources Main library with 383,120 bound volumes, 15,826 titles on microform, 1,300 periodical subscriptions, 6,451 records/tapes/CDs.

Housing 2% of students in program live in college-owned or -operated housing.

Technology Computers are used moderately in course work. 60 computer terminals/PCs are available for use by students in program; they are located in the library, the computer center, computer labs. Students in the program are not required to have their own PC.

Computer Resources/On-line Services

Training	Yes	Dun's	No
Internet	No	Dow Jones	No
E-Mail	No	Dialog	Yes $
LEXIS/NEXIS	No	Bloomberg	No
CompuServe	No		

ADMISSION

Acceptance 1994-95 50 applied for admission; 80% were accepted.

Entrance Requirements Bachelor's degree, GMAT score of 400, minimum 3.0 GPA. Core courses waived through: previous course work.

Application Requirements Application form, copies of transcript.

Application Deadline 4/1 for fall.

FINANCIALS

Estimated Costs for 1995-96 Tuition: Full-time: $793/semester for state residents, $2,938/semester for nonresidents; Part-time day: $55-$164/credit hour for state residents, $198-$235/credit hour for nonresidents. Fees: Full-time: $100/semester for state residents, $100/semester for nonresidents; Part-time day: $5/credit hour for state residents, $5/credit hour for nonresidents. Average room and board costs are $3,200 per academic year (on-campus).

Financial Aid In 1994-95, 8% of candidates received some institutionally administered aid in the form of scholarships, assistantships. Total awards ranged from $200-$4,200. Financial aid is available to part-time students. Application deadlines: 3/15 for fall, 9/1 for spring. Contact: Mr. Henry VanGeem Jr., MBA Coordinator, 3410 Taft Boulevard, Wichita Falls, TX 76308. (817) 689-4248.

INTERNATIONAL STUDENTS

Demographics 5% of students enrolled in the program are international; Asia 40%, Africa 20%, Europe 20%, other 20%.

Services and Facilities International student center, ESL courses.

Applying TOEFL required, minimum score of 550; proof of health; proof of adequate funds. Financial aid is available to international students. Financial aid application deadline: 4/1 for fall. Admission application deadline: 4/1 for fall. Contact: Mr. David Brinkley, Associate Director of Intensive English Language Institute, 3410 Taft Boulevard, Wichita Falls, TX 76308. (817) 689-4208.

PLACEMENT

Placement services include career counseling/planning, career fairs, and resume preparation.

Jobs by Employer Type Manufacturing 55%; service 10%; government 35%.

Jobs by Functional Area Marketing/sales 30%; finance 10%; operations 30%; management 30%.

Program Contact: Mr. Henry VanGeem Jr., MBA Coordinator, Midwestern State University, 3410 Taft Boulevard, Wichita Falls, TX 76308. (817) 689-4248; Fax: (817) 689-4280.

Our Lady of the Lake University of San Antonio

School of Business and Public Administration

San Antonio, Texas

OVERVIEW

Our Lady of the Lake University of San Antonio is an independent Roman Catholic comprehensive coed institution. Founded 1895. Setting: 75-acre urban campus. Total institutional enrollment: 3,103. Program was first offered in 1983.

MBA HIGHLIGHTS

Entrance Difficulty***
Mean GMAT: 450
Mean GPA: 3.4

Cost $
Tuition: $298/semester hour
Room & Board: N/R

Enrollment Profile

Full-time: 0
Part-time: 221
Total: 221
Average Age: 33

Work Exp: 100%
International: 0%
Women: 54%
Minorities: 36%

Average Class Size: 20

ACADEMICS

Length of Program Minimum: 24 months. Maximum: 6 years.

Calendar Trimesters.

Part-time Classes Main campus; weekends.

Degree Requirements 36 semester hours.

Curricular Focus Leadership, problem solving and decision making, strategic analysis and planning.

Concentrations Finance, healthcare management, international business, management.

Faculty Full-time: 14, 78% with doctorates; part-time: 13, 31% with doctorates.

Teaching Methodology Case study: 40%, lecture: 10%, research: 10%, student presentations: 15%, team projects: 25%.

STUDENT STATISTICS

Geographic Representation State residents 100%. By region: South 100%.

Undergraduate Majors Business 50%; education 2%; engineering/technology 5%; humanities 5%; nursing 10%; science/mathematics 10%; social sciences 5%; other 13%.

Other Background Graduate degrees in other disciplines: 15%. Work experience: On average, students have 10 years of work experience on entrance to the program.

FACILITIES

Information Resources Main library with 255,000 bound volumes, 143 titles on microform, 27,536 periodical subscriptions, 5,069 records/tapes/CDs, 10 CD-ROMs.

Housing College housing not available.

Technology Computers are used moderately in course work. 120 computer terminals/PCs, linked by a campus-wide computer network, are available for use by students in program; they are located in computer labs. Students in the program are not required to have their own PC.

Computer Resources/On-line Services

Training	Yes	Videoconference Center	Yes
Internet	Yes	LEXIS/NEXIS	Yes $
E-Mail	Yes		

ADMISSION

Acceptance 1994-95 65 applied for admission; 91% were accepted.

Entrance Requirements Bachelor's degree, GMAT score of 550, minimum 2.5 GPA, minimum 3 years of work experience.

Application Requirements Application form, copies of transcript, resume/curriculum vitae, 2 letters of recommendation.

Application Deadlines 9/1 for fall, 1/1 for winter, 4/15 for spring.

FINANCIALS

Costs for 1994-95 Tuition: Weekends: $298/semester hour. Fees: Weekends: $46/trimester.

Financial Aid In 1994-95, candidates received some institutionally administered aid in the form of loans, assistantships. Financial aid is available to part-time students. Application deadlines: 9/1 for fall, 1/1 for winter, 4/15 for spring. Contact: Mr. Jeff Scofield, Acting Financial Aid Officer, 411 Southwest 24th Street, San Antonio, TX 78207-4689. (210) 434-6711.

INTERNATIONAL STUDENTS

Applying TOEFL required, minimum score of 550. Financial aid is not available to international students. Admission application deadlines: 9/1 for fall, 1/1 for winter, 4/15 for spring. Applications are processed on a rolling basis.

Program Contact: Mr. Quentin W. Korte, Graduate Adviser, Our Lady of the Lake University of San Antonio, 411 Southwest 24th Street, San Antonio, TX 78207-4689. (210) 434-6711; Fax: (210) 434-0821.

Prairie View A&M University

College of Business

Prairie View, Texas

OVERVIEW

Prairie View A&M University is a state-supported comprehensive coed institution. Part of Texas A&M University System. Founded 1878. Setting: 1,440-acre rural campus with easy access to Houston. Total institutional enrollment: 5,000. Program was first offered in 1972.

MBA HIGHLIGHTS

Entrance Difficulty**
Mean GMAT: 480
Mean GPA: 2.95

Cost $
Tuition: $568 - $1,231/semester
(Nonresident: $1,819 - $4,289/semester)
Room & Board: $4,000 (off-campus)

Enrollment Profile

Full-time: 10	Work Exp: 20%
Part-time: 40	International: 10%
Total: 50	Women: 30%
Average Age: 25	Minorities: 98%

Average Class Size: 15

ACADEMICS

Length of Program Minimum: 24 months. Maximum: 6 years.

Calendar Semesters.

Full-time Classes Main campus; evening.

Part-time Classes Main campus; evening.

Degree Requirements 36-57 credits including 6 elective credits.

Required Courses Management information systems, managerial accounting, managerial communications, managerial economics, marketing

management, organizational behavior, productions and operations management, quantitative analysis, statistics, strategy and policy, theory of financial management.

Curricular Focus General management.

Concentration Management.

Faculty Full-time: 12, 83% with doctorates; part-time: 2.

Teaching Methodology Case study: 10%, lecture: 80%, student presentations: 10%.

STUDENT STATISTICS

Geographic Representation By region: South 100%. International 10%.

Undergraduate Majors Business 95%; engineering/technology 5%.

Other Background Work experience: On average, students have 2 years of work experience on entrance to the program.

FACILITIES

Information Resources Main library with 243,860 bound volumes, 333,788 titles on microform, 1,655 periodical subscriptions, 2,078 records/tapes/CDs. Business collection includes 16,000 bound volumes, 100 periodical subscriptions.

Housing College housing not available.

Technology Computers are used moderately in course work. 20 computer terminals/PCs are available for use by students in program; they are located in computer labs. Students in the program are not required to have their own PC.

Computer Resources/On-line Services

Training	Yes	Dun's	No
Internet	No	Dow Jones	No
E-Mail	No	Dialog	No
LEXIS/NEXIS	No	Bloomberg	No
CompuServe	No		

ADMISSION

Acceptance 1994-95 30 applied for admission; 73% were accepted.

Entrance Requirements Bachelor's degree, GMAT score of 350, minimum 2.75 GPA. Core courses waived through: previous course work.

Application Requirements Application form, copies of transcript, 2 letters of recommendation.

Application Deadline Applications are processed on a rolling basis.

FINANCIALS

Costs for 1994-95 Tuition: Full-time: $288-$704/semester for state residents, $1,539-$3,762/semester for nonresidents; Part-time day: $100-$256/semester for state residents, $171-$1,368/semester for nonresidents. Fees: Full-time: $280-$527/semester for state residents, $280-$527/semester for nonresidents; Part-time day: $73-$254/semester for state residents, $73-$254/semester for nonresidents. Average room and board costs are $4,000 per academic year (off-campus).

Financial Aid In 1994-95, 10% of candidates received some institutionally administered aid in the form of work-study. Financial aid is not available to part-time students. Application deadline: 4/1 for fall. Applications are processed on a rolling basis. Contact: Mr. Advergus D. James, Director of Financial Aid, PO Box 2610, University Drive, FM 1098, Prairie View, TX 77446. (409) 857-2423.

INTERNATIONAL STUDENTS

Demographics 10% of students enrolled in the program are international; Africa 90%, Asia 10%.

Applying TOEFL required, minimum score of 550. Financial aid is not available to international students. Admission applications are processed on a rolling basis. Contact: Ms. Farquema Sirleaf, International Student Adviser, PO Box 2610, University Drive, FM 1098, Prairie View, TX 77446. (409) 857-2423.

PLACEMENT

In 1993-94, 10 organizations participated in on-campus recruiting; 20 on-campus interviews were conducted. Placement services include career fairs.

Program Contact: Dr. Willie Trotty, Dean of the Graduate School, Prairie View A&M University, PO Box 2610, University Drive, FM 1098, Prairie View, TX 77446. (409) 857-2315.

Rice University

Jesse H. Jones Graduate School of Administration

Houston, Texas

OVERVIEW

Rice University is an independent nonprofit coed institution. Founded 1912. Setting: 300-acre urban campus. Total institutional enrollment: 4,000. Program was first offered in 1976.

MBA HIGHLIGHTS

Entrance Difficulty***
Mean GMAT: 623
Mean GPA: 3.23

Cost $$$
Tuition: $12,300
Room & Board: $11,200

Enrollment Profile

Full-time: 216	Work Exp: 78%
Part-time: 0	International: 20%
Total: 216	Women: 25%
Average Age: 27	Minorities: 16%

Average Class Size: 17

ACADEMICS

Length of Program Minimum: 18 months. Maximum: 2 years.

Calendar Semesters.

Full-time Classes Main campus; day.

Degree Requirements 64 credits including 24 elective credits.

Required Courses Dean's seminar, financial accounting, introduction to management information systems, legal and governmental processes, macro and international economics, management accounting, management accounting and finance, managerial communication, managerial economics, marketing management, organizational behavior, quantitative methods.

Curricular Focus Leadership, strategic analysis and planning, teamwork.

Concentrations Accounting, entrepreneurship, finance, human resources management, international business, management, management information systems, marketing, operations management, public administration, strategic management.

Faculty Full-time: 28, 98% with doctorates; part-time: 30, 20% with doctorates.

Teaching Methodology Case study: 30%, lecture: 30%, seminars by members of the business community: 10%, student presentations: 15%, team projects: 15%.

Special Opportunities Internship program available.

STUDENT STATISTICS

Geographic Representation State residents 50%. By region: South 61%; Midwest 10%; West 7%; Northeast 2%. International 20%.

Undergraduate Majors Business 40%; engineering/technology 35%; humanities 7%; science/mathematics 5%; social sciences 7%; other 6%.

Other Background Graduate degrees in other disciplines: 8%. Work experience: On average, students have 4 years of work experience on entrance to the program.

FACILITIES

Information Resources Main library with 1.8 million bound volumes, 1.8 million titles on microform, 13,100 periodical subscriptions, 16,000 records/tapes/CDs. Business collection in Business Information Center includes 9,000 bound volumes, 138 periodical subscriptions, 7 CD-ROMs, 60 videos.

Housing 20% of students in program live in college-owned or -operated housing.

Technology Computers are used heavily in course work. 35 computer terminals/PCs, linked by a campus-wide computer network, are available for use by students in program; they are located in the computer center. Students in the program are required to have their own PC.

Computer Resources/On-line Services

Training	Yes	LEXIS/NEXIS	Yes
Internet	Yes	Dialog	Yes
E-Mail	Yes	Bloomberg	Yes

ADMISSION

Acceptance 1994-95 Of those applying, 34% were accepted.

Entrance Requirements Bachelor's degree, GMAT score.

Application Requirements Written essay, application form, copies of transcript, resume/curriculum vitae, personal statement, 3 letters of recommendation.

Application Deadline 3/1 for fall.

FINANCIALS

Estimated Costs for 1995-96 Tuition: Full-time: $12,300. Fees: Full-time: $250. Average room and board costs are $11,200 per academic year (on-campus) and $13,000 per academic year (off-campus).

Financial Aid In 1994-95, 60% of candidates received some institutionally administered aid in the form of scholarships, loans. Total awards ranged from $1,500-$18,500. Application deadline: 4/1 for fall. Contact: Mr. David Hunt, Director of Financial Aid, Financial Aid Office, MS 12, 6100 Main Street, Houston, TX 77005. (713) 527-4958.

INTERNATIONAL STUDENTS

Demographics 20% of students enrolled in the program are international; Asia 13%, Europe 4%, South America 2%, other 81%.

Services and Facilities International student center, visa services, language tutoring, ESL courses.

Applying TOEFL required; proof of health; proof of adequate funds. Financial aid is not available to international students. Admission application deadline: 3/1 for fall. Contact: Ms. Jane Dunham, International Services Director, Ley Student Center-MS 529, 6100 Main Street, Houston, TX 77005. (713) 527-6095.

PLACEMENT

In 1993-94, 110 organizations participated in on-campus recruiting; 920 on-campus interviews were conducted. Placement services include alumni network, career counseling/planning, career fairs, career library, career placement, electronic job bank, job interviews, resume preparation, and resume referral to employers. Of 1994 graduates, 97% were employed within three months of graduation, the average starting salary was $47,000, the range was $33,000-$102,000.

Jobs by Employer Type Manufacturing 4%; service 53%; consulting 32%; energy/petrochemicals 11%.

Jobs by Functional Area Marketing/sales 11%; finance 25%; operations 14%; management 11%; strategic planning 39%.

Program Contact: Mr. D. Richard Trask, Director of Admissions, Rice University, PO Box 1892, Houston, TX 77005. (713) 527-4918; Fax: (713) 285-5251.

St. Edward's University

School of Business and Public Administration

Austin, Texas

OVERVIEW

St. Edward's University is an independent Roman Catholic comprehensive coed institution. Founded 1885. Setting: 180-acre urban campus. Total institutional enrollment: 3,129. Program was first offered in 1970.

MBA HIGHLIGHTS

Entrance Difficulty*
Mean GMAT: 520
Mean GPA: 3.0

Cost $
Tuition: $333/credit hour
Room & Board: N/R

Enrollment Profile
Full-time: 58
Part-time: 282
Total: 340
Average Age: 32

Work Exp: 95%
International: 12%
Women: 34%
Minorities: 9%

Average Class Size: 24

ACADEMICS
Length of Program Minimum: 12 months. Maximum: 6 years.
Calendar Trimesters.
Full-time Classes Main campus; evening, weekends, summer.
Part-time Classes Main campus; evening, weekends, summer.
Degree Requirements 36 credits including 9 elective credits.
Curricular Focus Business issues and problems, problem solving and decision making, strategic analysis and planning.
Concentrations Accounting, economics, finance, human resources management, international business, management, management information systems, marketing, operations management, organizational behavior, public administration, public policy, quantitative analysis, strategic management, telecommunications management.
Faculty Full-time: 11, 10% with doctorates; part-time: 6, 4% with doctorates.
Teaching Methodology Case study: 20%, lecture: 20%, research: 20%, student presentations: 20%, team projects: 20%.

STUDENT STATISTICS
Geographic Representation State residents 88%. By region: South 87%. International 12%.
Undergraduate Majors Business 33%; engineering/technology 33%; science/mathematics 14%; social sciences 20%.
Other Background Graduate degrees in other disciplines: 10%. Work experience: On average, students have 3-12 years of work experience on entrance to the program.

FACILITIES
Information Resources Main library with 140,000 bound volumes, 500 titles on microform, 1,180 periodical subscriptions, 1,000 records/tapes/CDs, 9 CD-ROMs.
Housing College housing available.
Technology Computer terminals/PCs are available for use by students in program; they are located in dormitories, classrooms, the library, computer labs. Students in the program are not required to have their own PC.
Computer Resources/On-line Services
E-Mail   Yes   Multimedia Center   Yes

ADMISSION
Acceptance 1994-95 142 applied for admission; 90% were accepted.
Entrance Requirements Bachelor's degree, GMAT score of 500, minimum 2.75 GPA, GRE can be substituted for GMAT. Core courses waived through: previous course work.
Application Requirements Written essay, application form, copies of transcript, personal statement.
Application Deadlines 7/1 for fall, 11/1 for spring, 4/1 for summer.

FINANCIALS
Costs for 1994-95 Tuition: Part-time evening: $333/credit hour.
Financial Aid In 1994-95, 3% of candidates received some institutionally administered aid in the form of scholarships, loans. Financial aid is available to part-time students. Applications are processed on a rolling basis. Contact: Ms. Doris Constantine, Director of Financial Aid, 3001 South Congress Avenue, Austin, TX 78704. (512) 448-8525.

INTERNATIONAL STUDENTS
Demographics 12% of students enrolled in the program are international; Asia 7%, Central America 1%, Europe 1%, South America 1%, other 88%.
Services and Facilities International student center, counseling/support services.
Applying TOEFL required, minimum score of 500; proof of adequate funds. Financial aid is not available to international students. Admission application deadlines: 7/1 for fall, 11/1 for spring, 4/1 for summer. Contact: Mr. Victor Betancourt, International Student Adviser, 3001 South Congress Avenue, Austin, TX 78704. (512) 448-8531.

PLACEMENT
Placement services include alumni network, career counseling/planning, career fairs, career library, career placement, and resume preparation.

Program Contact: Mr. Cole Holmes, Graduate Recruiter, St. Edward's University, 3001 South Congress Avenue, Austin, TX 78704. (512) 448-8600; Fax: (512) 448-8492.

St. Mary's University of San Antonio

School of Business and Administration

San Antonio, Texas

OVERVIEW
St. Mary's University of San Antonio is an independent Roman Catholic comprehensive coed institution. Founded 1852. Setting: 135-acre urban campus. Total institutional enrollment: 4,000.

MBA HIGHLIGHTS
Entrance Difficulty***
Mean GMAT: 500
Mean GPA: 3.2

Cost $
Tuition: $303/hour
Room & Board: N/R

Enrollment Profile
Full-time: 10
Part-time: 220
Total: 230
Average Age: N/R

Work Exp: 90%
International: N/R
Women: 50%
Minorities: 15%

Average Class Size: 25

ACADEMICS
Length of Program Minimum: 24 months. Maximum: 5 years.
Calendar Semesters.
Full-time Classes Main campus, U.S. Air Force Academy, Randolph Air Force Base, Kelly Air Force Base; evening, summer.
Part-time Classes Main campus, U.S. Air Force Academy, Randolph Air Force Base, Kelly Air Force Base; evening, summer.
Degree Requirements 33-39 hours including 3-9 elective hours.
Required Courses Accounting for decision making, economics, markets, and public policy, financial management, human resources management, international non-management, management of information and technology, marketing management, operations management, organizational ethics and legal issues, strategic management.
Curricular Focus Business issues and problems, organizational development and change management, problem solving and decision making.
Concentrations Finance, international business, management.
Faculty Full-time: 24, 90% with doctorates; part-time: 4, 25% with doctorates.

STUDENT STATISTICS
Geographic Representation By region: South 95%.
Other Background Graduate degrees in other disciplines: 5%. Work experience: On average, students have 5 years of work experience on entrance to the program.

FACILITIES
Information Resources Main library with 335,000 bound volumes, 68,000 titles on microform, 1,150 periodical subscriptions, 6,000 records/tapes/CDs, 10 CD-ROMs.
Housing 1% of students in program live in college-owned or -operated housing.
Technology Computers are used moderately in course work. 30 computer terminals/PCs are available for use by students in program; they are located in the library, the computer center, computer labs. Students in the program are not required to have their own PC.
Computer Resources/On-line Services
Training   Yes   Multimedia Center   Yes
E-Mail   Yes

ADMISSION
Acceptance 1994-95 94 applied for admission; 80% were accepted.
Entrance Requirements Bachelor's degree, prerequisite courses required for applicants with non-business degree, GMAT score. Core courses waived through: previous course work.
Application Requirements Application form, copies of transcript, resume/curriculum vitae, personal statement, 2 letters of recommendation.
Application Deadline Applications are processed on a rolling basis. Application discs available.

FINANCIALS
Costs for 1994-95 Tuition: Full-time: $303/hour.

Financial Aid In 1994-95, 10% of candidates received some institutionally administered aid in the form of loans, assistantships. Financial aid is available to part-time students. Applications are processed on a rolling basis. Contact: Mr. David Krause, Director of Financial Assistance, 1 Camino Santa Maria, San Antonio, TX 78228-8507. (210) 436-3141.

INTERNATIONAL STUDENTS
Demographics 10% of students on campus are international; Asia 80%, Central America 20%.

Applying TOEFL required, minimum score of 550; proof of health; proof of adequate funds. Financial aid is not available to international students. Admission applications are processed on a rolling basis. Contact: Dr. Suzanne Cory, MBA Program Director, 1 Camino Santa Maria, San Antonio, TX 78228-8507. (210) 436-3708.

ALTERNATE MBA PROGRAM
MBA/JD Length of program: Minimum: 36 months. Maximum: 5 years. Full-time classes: Main campus; evening. Part-time classes: Main campus; evening. Degree requirements: 108 credits.

PLACEMENT
Placement services include career fairs and career placement.

Program Contact: Dr. Suzanne Cory, MBA Program Director, St. Mary's University of San Antonio, 1 Camino Santa Maria, San Antonio, TX 78228-8507. (210) 436-3708; Fax: (210) 431-2115; Internet Address: buscory@vax.stmarytx.edu.

Sam Houston State University

College of Business Administration

Huntsville, Texas

OVERVIEW
Sam Houston State University is a state-supported comprehensive coed institution. Part of Texas State University System. Founded 1879. Setting: 211-acre small-town campus with easy access to Houston. Total institutional enrollment: 12,900. Program was first offered in 1964.

MBA HIGHLIGHTS
Entrance Difficulty**
Mean GMAT: 495
Mean GPA: 3.1

Cost $
Tuition: $28/semester hour
(Nonresident: $162/semester hour)
Room & Board: $8,000

Enrollment Profile
Full-time: 50
Part-time: 51
Total: 101
Average Age: 28

Work Exp: 80%
International: 10%
Women: 35%
Minorities: 10%

Average Class Size: 12

ACADEMICS
Length of Program Minimum: 24 months. Maximum: 7 years.
Calendar Semesters.
Full-time Classes Main campus; evening.
Part-time Classes Main campus; evening.
Degree Requirements 36 hours including 15 elective hours.
Required Courses Accounting for management, marketing seminar, problems in administrative finance, research writing in business, seminar in strategic management and policy, techniques of statistical analysis.
Curricular Focus General management, problem solving and decision making, strategic analysis and planning.
Concentrations Accounting, economics, finance, management, marketing.
Faculty Full-time: 45, 100% with doctorates; part-time: 1, 100% with doctorates.
Teaching Methodology Case study: 15%, lecture: 40%, research: 15%, seminars by members of the business community: 5%, student presentations: 10%, team projects: 15%.

STUDENT STATISTICS
Geographic Representation State residents 80%. By region: South 85%; Midwest 3%; Northeast 1%; West 1%. International 10%.
Undergraduate Majors Business 85%; education 5%; engineering/technology 2%; humanities 5%; nursing 1%; science/mathematics 1%; social sciences 1%.
Other Background Work experience: On average, students have 3 years of work experience on entrance to the program.

FACILITIES
Information Resources Main library with 775,642 bound volumes, 539,363 titles on microform, 3,028 periodical subscriptions, 9,083 records/tapes/CDs.
Housing 10% of students in program live in college-owned or -operated housing.
Technology Computers are used moderately in course work. 250 computer terminals/PCs, linked by a campus-wide computer network, are available for use by students in program; they are located in student rooms, the library, the computer center, computer labs. Students in the program are not required to have their own PC.

Computer Resources/On-line Services

Training	Yes	E-Mail	Yes
Internet	Yes		

Other on-line services: OCLC.

ADMISSION
Acceptance 1994-95 Of those applying, 65% were accepted.
Entrance Requirements Bachelor's in business, GMAT score of 450.
Application Requirements Copies of transcript.
Application Deadlines 5/1 for fall, 10/1 for spring, 3/1 for summer.

FINANCIALS
Costs for 1994-95 Tuition: Full-time: $28/semester hour for state residents, $162/semester hour for nonresidents. Fees: Full-time: $22/semester hour for state residents, $22/semester hour for nonresidents. Average room and board costs are $8,000 per academic year (on-campus) and $8,000 per academic year (off-campus).
Financial Aid In 1994-95, 20% of candidates received some institutionally administered aid in the form of loans, assistantships, work-study. Total awards ranged from $10,000-$15,000. Financial aid is not available to part-time students. Application deadlines: 3/31 for fall, 9/1 for spring, 2/1 for summer. Contact: Mr. Jess Davis, Financial Aid Director, PO Box 2448, Huntsville, TX 77341-2448. (409) 294-1724.

INTERNATIONAL STUDENTS
Demographics 10% of students enrolled in the program are international.
Applying TOEFL required, minimum score of 550; proof of adequate funds. Financial aid is not available to international students. Admission application deadlines: 5/1 for fall, 10/1 for spring, 3/1 for summer.

PLACEMENT
In 1993-94, 25 organizations participated in on-campus recruiting; 150 on-campus interviews were conducted. Placement services include alumni network, career counseling/planning, career fairs, career library, career placement, electronic job bank, job interviews, resume preparation, and resume referral to employers. Of 1994 graduates, 50% were employed within three months of graduation, the average starting salary was $28,000, the range was $25,000-$35,000.
Jobs by Employer Type Manufacturing 20%; service 20%; government 20%; nonprofit 20%; retail 20%.
Jobs by Functional Area Marketing/sales 25%; finance 20%; operations 5%; management 25%; strategic planning 10%; technical management 15%.

Program Contact: Dr. R. Dean Lewis, Associate Dean and Graduate Coordinator, Sam Houston State University, PO Box 2448, Huntsville, TX 77341-2448. (409) 294-1246; Fax: (409) 294-3612.

Southern Methodist University

The Edwin L. Cox School of Business

Dallas, Texas

OVERVIEW

Southern Methodist University is an independent coed institution, affiliated with United Methodist Church. Founded 1911. Setting: 163-acre suburban campus. Total institutional enrollment: 9,500. Program was first offered in 1949. AACSB-accredited.

MBA HIGHLIGHTS

Entrance Difficulty***
Mean GMAT: 612
Mean GPA: 3.05

Cost $$$$
Tuition: $547/hour
Room & Board: $7,000

Enrollment Profile
Full-time: 230
Part-time: 350
Total: 580
Average Age: 26

Work Exp: 85%
International: N/R
Women: 33%
Minorities: 3%

Average Class Size: 42

ACADEMICS

Length of Program Minimum: 21 months.

Calendar Semesters.

Full-time Classes Main campus; day, evening, weekends, early morning, summer.

Part-time Classes Main campus; evening, weekends, summer.

Degree Requirements 60 credits including 27 elective credits.

Required Courses Economics for business decisions, financial accounting, financial management, global business environments, managerial accounting, managerial statistics and forecasting, managing information technology, managing operations in manufacturing and service, marketing management, organizational behavior and diversity, strategic analysis in a global era. Courses may be waived through: previous course work.

Curricular Focus Leadership, problem solving and decision making, teamwork.

Concentrations Accounting, arts administration, entrepreneurship, finance, management, management information systems, marketing, operations management, organizational behavior, quantitative analysis, real estate.

Faculty Full-time: 38, 99% with doctorates; part-time: 8, 50% with doctorates.

Teaching Methodology Case study: 30%, lecture: 50%, seminars by members of the business community: 3%, student presentations: 5%, team projects: 12%.

Special Opportunities International exchange in Australia, Belgium, France, Japan, Mexico, Singapore, Spain, United Kingdom, Venezuela. Internship program available.

STUDENT STATISTICS

Geographic Representation State residents 16%. By region: South 59%; Northeast 10%; Midwest 9%; West 5%.

Undergraduate Majors Business 40%; engineering/technology 20%; humanities 10%; science/mathematics 7%; social sciences 23%.

Other Background Work experience: On average, students have 3 years of work experience on entrance to the program.

FACILITIES

Information Resources Main library with 2.9 million bound volumes, 1.5 million titles on microform, 5,647 periodical subscriptions, 27,775 records/tapes/CDs. Business collection in Business Information Center includes 40,000 bound volumes, 60 periodical subscriptions, 15 CD-ROMs.

Housing 5% of students in program live in college-owned or -operated housing.

Technology Computers are used heavily in course work. Computer terminals/PCs, linked by a campus-wide computer network, are available for use by students in program; they are located in dormitories, classrooms, the library, the computer center, computer labs, the research center. Students in the program are not required to have their own PC. $100 are budgeted per student for computer support.

Computer Resources/On-line Services

Training	Yes	LEXIS/NEXIS	Yes
Internet	Yes	Dun's	Yes
E-Mail	Yes	Dow Jones	Yes
Multimedia Center	Yes	Dialog	Yes

ADMISSION

Acceptance 1994-95 Of those applying, 63% were accepted.

Entrance Requirements Bachelor's degree, GMAT score. Core courses waived through: previous course work.

Application Requirements Interview, application form, copies of transcript, resume/curriculum vitae, 2 letters of recommendation.

Application Deadline Applications are processed on a rolling basis.

FINANCIALS

Costs for 1994-95 Tuition: Full-time: $547/hour. Fees: Full-time: $812/semester. Average room and board costs are $7,000 per academic year (on-campus) and $9,000 per academic year (off-campus).

Financial Aid In 1994-95, 65% of candidates received some institutionally administered aid in the form of grants, scholarships, loans, assistantships, work-study. Total awards ranged from $4,500-$18,000. Financial aid is available to part-time students. Application deadline: 2/1 for fall. Contact: Mr. Mike Novak, Director of Financial Aid, Perkins Administration Building, Dallas, TX 75275. (214) 768-3417.

INTERNATIONAL STUDENTS

Demographics 6% of students on campus are international.

Services and Facilities Visa services, counseling/support services.

Applying TOEFL required; proof of health; proof of adequate funds. Financial aid is available to international students. Financial aid application deadline: 3/1 for fall. Admission application deadline: 5/1 for fall. Contact: Ms. Therese Bishara, International Adviser, Box 381, Dallas, TX 75275. (214) 768-4476.

ALTERNATE MBA PROGRAMS

MBA/JD Length of program: Minimum: 54 months. Maximum: 4 years. Degree requirements: 137 credits. LSAT.

MBA/MA Length of program: Minimum: 30 months. Maximum: 2 years. Degree requirements: 75 credits. Arts experience. MA is in arts administration.

PLACEMENT

In 1993-94, 66 organizations participated in on-campus recruiting; 503 on-campus interviews were conducted. Placement services include alumni network, career counseling/planning, career fairs, career library, career placement, job interviews, resume preparation, resume referral to employers, and Of 1994 graduates, 77% were employed within three months of graduation, the average starting salary was $49,157, the range was $25,000-$145,000.

Jobs by Employer Type Manufacturing 4%; service 41%; consulting 25%; nonprofit 5%; high technology 10%; energy 7%; other 5%.

Jobs by Functional Area Marketing/sales 30%; finance 27%; management 14%; consulting 27%; law 1%.

Program Contact: Mr. R. Keith Pendergrass, Director of MBA Programs, Southern Methodist University, Dallas, TX 75275. (214) 768-2630, or (800) 472-3622; Fax: (214) 768-4099; Internet Address: mbainfo@ mail.cox.smu.edu.

See full description on page 834.

Southwest Texas State University

School of Business

San Marcos, Texas

OVERVIEW

Southwest Texas State University is a state-supported comprehensive coed institution. Part of Texas State University System. Founded 1899. Setting: 332-acre urban campus with easy access to San Antonio and Austin. Total institutional enrollment: 21,000. Program was first offered in 1968.

MBA HIGHLIGHTS

Entrance Difficulty*
Mean GMAT: 530
Mean GPA: 2.8

Cost $
Tuition: $336/semester
(Nonresident: $2,052/semester)
Room & Board: N/R

Enrollment Profile

Full-time: 100	Work Exp: 80%
Part-time: 225	International: 5%
Total: 325	Women: 40%
Average Age: 33	Minorities: 15%

Average Class Size: 25

ACADEMICS

Length of Program Minimum: 12 months. Maximum: 6 years.

Calendar Semesters.

Full-time Classes Main campus; evening, summer.

Part-time Classes Main campus; evening, summer.

Degree Requirements 36 hours including 9 elective hours. Other: Comprehensive written exam.

Required Courses Accounting, advanced statistics, economics, finance, management, marketing, policy, quantitative methods, research.

Curricular Focus General management, problem solving and decision making, teamwork.

Concentrations Accounting, management.

Faculty Full-time: 51, 100% with doctorates.

Teaching Methodology Case study: 5%, lecture: 50%, research: 15%, seminars by members of the business community: 5%, student presentations: 5%, team projects: 20%.

STUDENT STATISTICS

Geographic Representation State residents 80%. International 5%.

Undergraduate Majors Business 60%; engineering/technology 10%; humanities 10%; science/mathematics 10%; social sciences 10%.

Other Background Graduate degrees in other disciplines: 5%. Work experience: On average, students have 5 years of work experience on entrance to the program.

FACILITIES

Information Resources Main library with 966,191 bound volumes, 389,218 titles on microform, 5,496 periodical subscriptions, 18,045 records/tapes/CDs, 126 CD-ROMs.

Housing 5% of students in program live in college-owned or -operated housing.

Technology Computers are used moderately in course work. 400 computer terminals/PCs, linked by a campus-wide computer network, are available for use by students in program; they are located in learning resource center, the library, the computer center, computer labs. Students in the program are not required to have their own PC.

Computer Resources/On-line Services

Training	Yes	CompuServe	No
Internet	Yes	Dun's	No
E-Mail	Yes	Dow Jones	No
Multimedia Center	Yes	Dialog	Yes
LEXIS/NEXIS	No	Bloomberg	No

ADMISSION

Acceptance 1994-95 400 applied for admission; 85% were accepted.

Entrance Requirements Bachelor's degree, GMAT score of 450, minimum 2.75 GPA. Core courses waived through: previous course work.

Application Requirements Application form, copies of transcript.

Application Deadlines 7/15 for fall, 11/15 for spring, 4/15 for summer.

FINANCIALS

Costs for 1994-95 Tuition: Full-time: $336/semester for state residents, $2,052/semester for nonresidents; Part-time evening: $168/semester for state residents, $1,026/semester for nonresidents. Fees: Full-time: $397/semester for state residents, $397/semester for nonresidents; Part-time evening: $367/semester for state residents, $367/semester for nonresidents.

Financial Aid In 1994-95, candidates received some institutionally administered aid in the form of grants, scholarships, loans, work-study. Financial aid is available to part-time students. Application deadlines: 5/1 for fall, 10/15 for spring, 3/15 for summer. Contact: Office of Student Financial Assistance, 240 J.C. Kellam, San Marcos, TX 78666. (512) 245-2315.

INTERNATIONAL STUDENTS

Demographics 5% of students enrolled in the program are international; Asia 70%, Central America 10%, South America 5%, Africa 2%, Europe 1%, other 12%.

Services and Facilities Visa services, counseling/support services.

Applying TOEFL required, minimum score of 550; proof of health; proof of adequate funds; minimum score of 220 on Test of spoken English. Financial aid is available to international students. Financial aid application deadlines: 5/1 for fall, 10/15 for spring, 3/15 for summer. Admission application deadlines: 6/15 for fall, 10/15 for spring, 3/15 for summer. Contact: Ms. Peggy Stansberry, Admissions Specialist, 106 Admissions Building, San Marcos, TX 78666. (512) 245-2364.

PLACEMENT

Placement services include career counseling/planning, career fairs, career library, career placement, job interviews, and resume preparation. Of 1994 graduates, 95% were employed within three months of graduation.

Program Contact: Dr. Robert J. Olney, Associate Dean, Southwest Texas State University, 601 University Drive, San Marcos, TX 78666. (512) 245-3591; Fax: (512) 245-8375; Internet Address: ro02@academia. swt.edu.

Stephen F. Austin State University

College of Business

Nacogdoches, Texas

OVERVIEW

Stephen F. Austin State University is a state-supported comprehensive coed institution. Founded 1923. Setting: 400-acre small-town campus. Total institutional enrollment: 12,500. Program was first offered in 1970. AACSB-accredited.

MBA HIGHLIGHTS

Entrance Difficulty*
Mean GMAT: 505
Mean GPA: 3.4

Cost $
Tuition: $26/hour
(Nonresident: $162/hour)
Room & Board: $4,027

Enrollment Profile

Full-time: N/R	Work Exp: 90%
Part-time: N/R	International: 1%
Total: 109	Women: 33%
Average Age: 28	Minorities: 2%

Average Class Size: 12

ACADEMICS

Length of Program Minimum: 18 months.

Calendar Semesters.

Full-time Classes Main campus; evening, summer.

Part-time Classes Main campus; evening, summer.

Degree Requirements 36-57 credits including 9 elective credits.

Required Courses Accounting for management, administrative policy, advanced financial management, information systems organization, legal and social environment of business, management, managerial economics, marketing management, productions and operations management.

Curricular Focus Problem solving and decision making, strategic analysis and planning, teamwork.

Concentration Management.

Faculty Full-time: 24, 100% with doctorates.

Teaching Methodology Case study: 30%, lecture: 20%, research: 10%, student presentations: 10%, team projects: 30%.

STUDENT STATISTICS

Geographic Representation State residents 90%. By region: West 90%; South 5%; Midwest 4%. International 1%.

Undergraduate Majors Business 56%; engineering/technology 11%; humanities 13%; science/mathematics 10%; social sciences 10%.

Other Background Graduate degrees in other disciplines: 2%. Work experience: On average, students have 5 years of work experience on entrance to the program.

FACILITIES

Information Resources Main library with 1.6 million bound volumes, 669,791 titles on microform, 4,051 periodical subscriptions, 11,859 records/tapes/CDs, 620 CD-ROMs.

Housing 2% of students in program live in college-owned or -operated housing.

Technology Computers are used moderately in course work. 850 computer terminals/PCs are available for use by students in program; they are located in classrooms, the library, the computer center, computer labs, the research center. Students in the program are not required to have their own PC.

Computer Resources/On-line Services

Training	Yes	CompuServe	Yes
Internet	Yes	Dun's	Yes
E-Mail	Yes	Dow Jones	Yes
LEXIS/NEXIS	Yes	Dialog	Yes

ADMISSION

Acceptance 1994-95 40 applied for admission; 90% were accepted.

Entrance Requirements Bachelor's degree, GMAT score. Core courses waived through: previous course work.

Application Requirements Application form, copies of transcript.

Application Deadline Applications are processed on a rolling basis.

FINANCIALS

Costs for 1994-95 Tuition: Full-time: $26/hour for state residents, $162/hour for nonresidents. Fees: Full-time: $30-$347/semester for state residents, $30-$347/semester for nonresidents. Average room and board costs are $4,027 per academic year (on-campus).

Financial Aid In 1994-95, candidates received some institutionally administered aid in the form of loans, assistantships, work-study. Financial aid is not available to part-time students. Application deadline: 6/1 for fall. Contact: Director of Financial Aid, Financial Aid Office, Nacogdoches, TX 75962. (409) 468-2403.

INTERNATIONAL STUDENTS

Demographics 1% of students enrolled in the program are international.

Applying TOEFL required, minimum score of 550; proof of health; proof of adequate funds. Financial aid is available to international students. Assistantships are available for these students. Admission applications are processed on a rolling basis.

PLACEMENT

Placement services include alumni network, career counseling/planning, career fairs, career placement, and job interviews.

Jobs by Employer Type Manufacturing 50%; service 50%.

Jobs by Functional Area Finance 50%; operations 30%; technical management 20%.

Program Contact: Dr. Larry R. Watts, Associate Dean, Stephen F. Austin State University, PO Box 13004 SFA Station, Nacogdoches, TX 75962. (409) 468-3101; Fax: (409) 468-1560.

Sul Ross State University

Department of Business Administration

Alpine, Texas

OVERVIEW

Sul Ross State University is a state-supported comprehensive coed institution. Part of Texas State University System. Founded 1920. Setting: 640-acre small-town campus. Total institutional enrollment: 2,418.

MBA HIGHLIGHTS

Entrance Difficulty**
Mean GMAT: 390
Mean GPA: N/R

Cost $
Tuition. $28 - $100/semester hour
(Nonresident: $171/semester hour)
Room & Board: N/R

Enrollment Profile

Full-time: 22	Work Exp: 60%
Part-time: 9	International: 55%
Total: 31	Women: 36%
Average Age: 30	Minorities: 23%

Average Class Size: 20

ACADEMICS

Length of Program Minimum: 12 months. Maximum: 5 years.

Calendar Semesters.

Full-time Classes Main campus; day, evening, weekends, early morning, summer.

Degree Requirements 36 hours including 12 elective hours.

Required Courses Accounting for management, business research and reporting, management information systems, managerial economics, quantitative analysis and decision theory, seminar in financial management, seminar in management, seminar in marketing.

Curricular Focus Business issues and problems, international business, managing diversity.

Concentrations International business, management.

Faculty Full-time: 4, 75% with doctorates; part-time: 2, 100% with doctorates.

Teaching Methodology Case study: 10%, lecture: 50%, student presentations: 20%, team projects: 20%.

STUDENT STATISTICS

Geographic Representation State residents 39%. By region: West 39%; Northeast 3%. International 55%.

Undergraduate Majors Business 12%; education 11%; humanities 8%; science/mathematics 3%; social sciences 16%; other 47%.

Other Background Graduate degrees in other disciplines: 10%. Work experience: On average, students have 2 years of work experience on entrance to the program.

FACILITIES

Information Resources Main library with 250,266 bound volumes, 351,831 titles on microform, 1,951 periodical subscriptions, 13,266 records/tapes/CDs, 25 CD-ROMs.

Housing 70% of students in program live in college-owned or -operated housing.

Technology Computers are used moderately in course work. 40 computer terminals/PCs are available for use by students in program; they are located in the library, the computer center, computer labs. Students in the program are not required to have their own PC.

Computer Resources/On-line Services

Training	Yes	Dialog	Yes $
E-Mail	No		

ADMISSION

Entrance Requirements Bachelor's degree, prerequisite courses required for applicants with non-business degree, GMAT score of 400, minimum 2.5 for last 60 hours of undergraduate degree. Core courses waived through: previous course work.

Application Requirements Application form, copies of transcript.

Application Deadline Applications are processed on a rolling basis. Application discs available.

FINANCIALS

Costs for 1994-95 Tuition: Full-time: $28-$100/semester hour for state residents, $171/semester hour for nonresidents. Fees: Full-time: $29-$432/semester for state residents, $29-$432/semester for nonresidents.

Financial Aid In 1994-95, 10% of candidates received some institutionally administered aid in the form of scholarships, assistantships. Total awards ranged from $200-$4,995. Financial aid is available to part-time students. Contact: Mr. Robert C. Matthews, Chair, Alpine, TX 79832. (915) 837-8067.

INTERNATIONAL STUDENTS

Demographics 55% of students enrolled in the program are international; Asia 82%, North America 12%, Africa 6%.

Services and Facilities Visa services.

Applying TOEFL required, minimum score of 520; proof of health; proof of adequate funds. Financial aid is available to international students.

Applications are processed on a rolling basis. Admission applications are processed on a rolling basis. Contact: Dr. Jim Case, Chair, Political Science, Alpine, TX 79832. (915) 837-8161.

PLACEMENT

In 1993-94, 30 organizations participated in on-campus recruiting; 15 on-campus interviews were conducted. Placement services include career counseling/planning, career fairs, career placement, resume preparation, and resume referral to employers.

Program Contact: Mr. Robert C. Matthew, Chair, Sul Ross State University, Alpine, TX 79832. (915) 837-8067; Fax: (915) 837-8046; Internet Address: rmatthews@sul-ross-1.sulross.edu.

Tarleton State University

College of Business Administration

Stephenville, Texas

OVERVIEW

Tarleton State University is a state-supported comprehensive coed institution. Part of Texas A&M University System. Founded 1899. Setting: 120-acre small-town campus with easy access to Dallas–Fort Worth. Total institutional enrollment: 6,460.

MBA HIGHLIGHTS

Entrance Difficulty**
Mean GMAT: 480
Mean GPA: N/R

Cost $
Tuition: $168/semester
(Nonresident: $1,026/semester)
Room & Board: $2,698

Enrollment Profile
Full-time: N/R
Part-time: N/R
Total: 130
Average Age: N/R

Work Exp: N/R
International: 2%
Women: 45%
Minorities: 5%

Average Class Size: 20

ACADEMICS

Length of Program Minimum: 12 months.

Calendar Semesters.

Full-time Classes Main campus, Fort Hood, distance learning option; evening, weekends.

Part-time Classes Main campus, Fort Hood, distance learning option; evening, weekends.

Degree Requirements 36 credits.

Curricular Focus Business issues and problems, problem solving and decision making, teamwork.

Concentrations Accounting, finance, management, management information systems, marketing.

Teaching Methodology Case study: 20%, lecture: 30%, student presentations: 25%, team projects: 25%.

STUDENT STATISTICS

Geographic Representation State residents 95%. International 2%.

FACILITIES

Information Resources Main library with 269,000 bound volumes, 750,000 titles on microform, 2,000 periodical subscriptions, 15,000 records/tapes/CDs, 15 CD-ROMs.

Housing College housing available.

ADMISSION

Entrance Requirements Bachelor's degree, minimum 2.5 GPA.

Application Requirements Application form, copies of transcript.

Application Deadline Applications are processed on a rolling basis.

FINANCIALS

Costs for 1994-95 Tuition: Full-time: $168/semester for state residents, $1,026/semester for nonresidents. Fees: Full-time: $169/semester for state residents, $169/semester for nonresidents. Average room and board costs are $2,698 per academic year (on-campus).

Financial Aid Application deadlines: 5/1 for fall, 11/1 for spring. Contact: Dr. Skip Landis, Director of Financial Aid, Tarleton Station, Stephenville, TX 76402. (817) 968-9070.

INTERNATIONAL STUDENTS

Demographics 2% of students enrolled in the program are international.

Applying TOEFL required, minimum score of 550; proof of adequate funds. Financial aid is not available to international students. Admission application deadlines: 4/1 for fall, 10/1 for spring.

Program Contact: Dr. LaVelle Mills, Associate Dean, College of Business Administration, Tarleton State University, Box T-0200 Tarleton Station, Stephenville, TX 76402. (817) 968-9050; Fax: (817) 968-9328.

Texas A&M International University

Graduate School of Int'l Trade and Business Admin.

Laredo, Texas

OVERVIEW

Texas A&M International University is a state-supported upper-level coed institution. Part of Texas A&M University System. Founded 1969. Setting: 196-acre urban campus. Total institutional enrollment: 3,200. Program was first offered in 1978.

MBA HIGHLIGHTS

Entrance Difficulty**

Cost $
Tuition: $539/semester
(Nonresident: $2,255/semester)
Room & Board: N/R

Enrollment Profile
Full-time: 103
Part-time: 149
Total: 252
Average Age: 28

Work Exp: N/R
International: N/R
Women: N/R
Minorities: N/R

Average Class Size: 20

ACADEMICS

Length of Program Minimum: 18 months.

Calendar Semesters.

Full-time Classes Main campus; day, evening, summer.

Part-time Classes Main campus; day, evening, summer.

Degree Requirements 36 credits including 3 elective credits.

Required Courses Global environment of business, information systems concepts, research methodology, strategic management.

Curricular Focus International trade, banking, and logistics.

Concentrations Accounting, international business, international trade management, international banking, international logistics, management, management information systems.

Faculty Full-time: 24, 96% with doctorates; part-time: 1, 100% with doctorates.

Teaching Methodology Case study: 10%, lecture: 60%, research: 15%, seminars by members of the business community: 5%, student presentations: 10%.

Special Opportunities International exchange in Costa Rica, France, Germany.

STUDENT STATISTICS

Undergraduate Majors Business 55%; other 45%.

FACILITIES

Information Resources Main library with 188,653 bound volumes, 416,879 titles on microform, 1,150 periodical subscriptions, 2,146 records/tapes/CDs, 12 CD-ROMs.

Technology Computers are used moderately in course work. Computer terminals/PCs are available for use by students in program; they are located in learning resource center, computer labs. Students in the program are not required to have their own PC.

Computer Resources/On-line Services

Training   No

ADMISSION
Entrance Requirements Bachelor's degree.
Application Requirements Application form, copies of transcript.
Application Deadline Applications are processed on a rolling basis.

FINANCIALS
Costs for 1994-95 Tuition: Full-time: $539/semester for state residents, $2,255/semester for nonresidents; Part-time day: $159-$275/course for state residents, $572-$1,133/semester for nonresidents.

Financial Aid In 1994-95, candidates received some institutionally administered aid in the form of loans, fellowships, assistantships, work-study. Financial aid is available to part-time students. Applications are processed on a rolling basis. Contact: Ms. Araceli Rangel, Director of Financial Aid, 1 West End Washington Street, Laredo, TX 78040. (210) 722-8001 Ext. 435.

INTERNATIONAL STUDENTS
Services and Facilities Language tutoring, ESL courses, counseling/support services.

Applying TOEFL required, minimum score of 550; proof of adequate funds; official transcripts in English from the student's former university. Admission applications are processed on a rolling basis. Contact: Mr. David Ver Milyea, Director, Student Development, 1 West End Washington Street, Laredo, TX 78040. (210) 722-8001.

ALTERNATE MBA PROGRAM
MBA/MS Length of program: Minimum: 18 months. Full-time classes: Main campus; day, evening, summer. Part-time classes: Main campus; day, evening, summer. Degree requirements: 60 credits. MS is in international banking, international logistics, or information systems.

Program Contact: Ms. Betty Lewis Momaye, Director, Enrollment Management and School Relations, Texas A&M International University, 1 West End Washington Street, Laredo, TX 78040. (210) 722-8001.
See full description on page 842.

Texas A&M University

College of Business Admin. and Graduate School of Business

College Station, Texas

OVERVIEW
Texas A&M University is a state-supported coed institution. Part of Texas A&M University System. Founded 1876. Setting: 5,142-acre small-town campus. Total institutional enrollment: 42,018. Program was first offered in 1950. AACSB-accredited.

MBA HIGHLIGHTS

Entrance Difficulty**
Mean GMAT: 602
Mean GPA: 3.25

Cost $
Tuition: $944/semester
(Nonresident: $2,768/semester)
Room & Board: $3,150 (off-campus)

Enrollment Profile
Full-time: 283   Work Exp: 55%
Part-time: 0   International: 27%
Total: 283   Women: 36%
Average Age: 24   Minorities: 10%

Average Class Size: 35

ACADEMICS
Length of Program Minimum: 21 months. Maximum: 7 years.
Calendar Semesters.
Full-time Classes Main campus; day.
Degree Requirements 53 credits including 18 elective credits.
Required Courses Executive leadership workshops, finance, financial accounting, international business corporate strategy, management in accounting, management information systems, managing people in

organizations, marketing management, markets and corporate strategy, operations management, political environment of business, quantitative analysis.
Curricular Focus International business, problem solving and decision making, strategic analysis and planning, teamwork.
Concentrations Accounting, economics, entrepreneurship, finance, human resources management, international business, management, management information systems, marketing, operations management, organizational behavior, public administration, public policy, quantitative analysis, real estate, strategic management, transportation.
Faculty Full-time: 12, 100% with doctorates.
Teaching Methodology Case study: 35%, lecture: 35%, seminars by members of the business community: 5%, student presentations: 10%, team projects: 15%.
Special Opportunities International exchange in Austria, France, Germany. Internship program available.

STUDENT STATISTICS
Geographic Representation State residents 53%. By region: South 61%; Northeast 5%; West 5%; Midwest 3%. International 27%.
Undergraduate Majors Business 41%; education 1%; engineering/technology 18%; humanities 22%; science/mathematics 5%; social sciences 4%; other 9%.
Other Background Graduate degrees in other disciplines: 1%. Work experience: On average, students have 2 years of work experience on entrance to the program.

FACILITIES
Information Resources Main library with 2.1 million bound volumes, 4.3 million titles on microform, 13,000 periodical subscriptions, 9,500 records/tapes/CDs, 60 CD-ROMs. Business collection in West Campus Library includes 150,000 bound volumes, 600 periodical subscriptions, 60 CD-ROMs.
Housing College housing not available.
Technology Computers are used heavily in course work. 500 computer terminals/PCs, linked by a campus-wide computer network, are available for use by students in program; they are located in dormitories, learning resource center, the library, the computer center, computer labs, the research center. Students in the program are not required to have their own PC.

Computer Resources/On-line Services

Training	Yes	CompuServe	No
Internet	Yes $	Dun's	No
E-Mail	Yes	Dow Jones	No
Multimedia Center	Yes	Dialog	No
LEXIS/NEXIS	Yes $	Bloomberg	No

ADMISSION
Acceptance 1994-95 Of those applying, 54% were accepted.
Entrance Requirements Bachelor's degree, GMAT score.
Application Requirements Written essay, interview, application form, copies of transcript, resume/curriculum vitae, personal statement, 3 letters of recommendation, student information sheet.
Application Deadline 2/1 for fall.

FINANCIALS
Costs for 1994-95 Tuition: Full-time: $944/semester for state residents, $2,768/semester for nonresidents, $2,792/semester for international students. Average room and board costs are $3,150 per academic year (off-campus).

Financial Aid In 1994-95, 30% of candidates received some institutionally administered aid in the form of grants, scholarships, loans, fellowships, assistantships. Total awards ranged from $500-$9,000. Financial aid is available to part-time students. Application deadlines: 4/15 for fall, 9/15 for spring. Contact: Ms. Mona Osborne, Financial Aid Administrator, Financial Aid Pavilion, College Station, TX 77843-1252. (409) 845-3211.

INTERNATIONAL STUDENTS
Demographics 27% of students enrolled in the program are international; Asia 60%, Europe 22%, Central America 7%, South America 3%, Africa 1%, other 7%.

Services and Facilities International student office, international student center, visa services, language tutoring, ESL courses, special assistance for nonnative speakers of English, counseling/support services.

Applying TOEFL required; proof of health; proof of adequate funds. Financial aid is available to international students. Assistantships are available for these students; deadline is 2/1. Admission application deadline: 2/1 for fall. Contact: International Student Services, 355 Bizzell Hall West, College Station, TX 77843-1226. (409) 845-1824.

PLACEMENT

In 1993-94, 10 organizations participated in on-campus recruiting. Placement services include alumni network, career counseling/planning, career fairs, career library, career placement, electronic job bank, job interviews, resume preparation, and resume referral to employers. Of 1994 graduates, 95% were employed within three months of graduation, the average starting salary was $36,000, the range was $22,000-$51,000.

Jobs by Employer Type Manufacturing 17%; service 50%; government 6%; consulting 22%; nonprofit 1%; other 1%.

Jobs by Functional Area Marketing/sales 12%; finance 57%; operations 7%; management 5%; strategic planning 7%; other 11%.

Program Contact: Ms. Wendy Boggs, Academic Adviser, Texas A&M University, Room 212 Wehner Building, College Station, TX 77843-4117. (409) 845-4714; Fax: (409) 862-2393.

Texas A&M University–Corpus Christi

College of Business Administration

Corpus Christi, Texas

OVERVIEW

Texas A&M University–Corpus Christi is a state-supported comprehensive coed institution. Part of Texas A&M University System. Founded 1947. Setting: 240-acre urban campus. Total institutional enrollment: 5,152. Program was first offered in 1975.

MBA HIGHLIGHTS

Entrance Difficulty**
Mean GMAT: 497
Mean GPA: 3.45

Cost $
Tuition: $473 - $1,028/semester
(Nonresident: $1,679 - $2,119/semester)
Room & Board: N/R

Enrollment Profile
Full-time: 49
Part-time: 196
Total: 245
Average Age: 33

Work Exp: N/R
International: 2%
Women: 43%
Minorities: 29%

Average Class Size: 22

ACADEMICS

Length of Program Minimum: 12 months. Maximum: 7 years.

Calendar Semesters.

Full-time Classes Main campus; evening, summer.

Part-time Classes Main campus; evening, summer.

Degree Requirements 36 credits including 12 elective credits.

Required Courses Accounting topics, administrative strategy and policy, business research and communications, economic analysis, managerial finance, marketing management, operations research, theory of organizational behavior. Courses may be waived through: previous course work.

Curricular Focus General management, international business.

Concentrations Accounting, health care administration, international business, management, marketing.

Faculty Full-time: 23, 100% with doctorates.

STUDENT STATISTICS

Geographic Representation International 2%.

FACILITIES

Information Resources Main library with 340,000 bound volumes, 505,817 titles on microform, 1,900 periodical subscriptions, 5,417 records/tapes/CDs, 22 CD-ROMs.

Housing College housing available.

Technology Computers are used moderately in course work. 230 computer terminals/PCs, linked by a campus-wide computer network, are available for use by students in program; they are located in computer labs. Students in the program are not required to have their own PC.

Computer Resources/On-line Services

Training	Yes	Videoconference Center	Yes
Internet	Yes	Multimedia Center	Yes
E-Mail	Yes	Dialog	Yes

Other on-line services: OCLC.

ADMISSION

Acceptance 1994-95 51 applied for admission; 77% were accepted.

Entrance Requirements Bachelor's degree, GMAT score of 400. Core courses waived through: previous course work.

Application Requirements Interview, application form, personal statement, 2 letters of recommendation.

Application Deadlines 8/1 for fall, 12/1 for spring, 5/1 for summer.

FINANCIALS

Costs for 1994-95 Tuition: Full-time: $252-$588/semester for state residents, $1,458-$1,679/semester for nonresidents; Part-time day: $100-$224/semester for state residents, $162-$1,296/semester for nonresidents; Summer: $28-$50/credit for state residents, $162/credit for nonresidents. Fees: Full-time: $221-$440/semester for state residents, $221-$440/semester for nonresidents; Part-time day: $29-$197/semester for state residents, $29-$197/semester for nonresidents; Summer: $20-$27/credit for state residents, $20-$27/credit for nonresidents.

Financial Aid In 1994-95, 18% of candidates received some institutionally administered aid in the form of grants, scholarships, loans, assistantships. Financial aid is available to part-time students. Application deadlines: 6/15 for fall, 10/15 for spring, 3/15 for summer. Contact: Office of Student Finance Assistance, 6300 Ocean Drive, Corpus Christi, TX 78412-5503. (512) 994-2338.

INTERNATIONAL STUDENTS

Demographics 2% of students enrolled in the program are international; Europe 50%, Central America 25%, South America 25%.

Applying TOEFL required, minimum score of 550; proof of adequate funds; copy of visa status documentation. Financial aid is available to international students. Financial aid application deadlines: 6/15 for fall, 10/15 for spring, 3/15 for summer. Admission application deadlines: 6/1 for fall, 10/1 for spring, 3/1 for summer.

PLACEMENT

Placement services include career counseling/planning, career fairs, career library, electronic job bank, job interviews, resume preparation, and resume referral to employers.

Program Contact: Director of Graduate Program in Business, Texas A&M University–Corpus Christi, 6300 Ocean Drive, Corpus Christi, TX 78412-5503. (512) 994-2655, or (800) 482-6822; Fax: (512) 994-2725.

Texas A&M University–Kingsville

College of Business Administration

Kingsville, Texas

OVERVIEW

Texas A&M University–Kingsville is a state-supported comprehensive coed institution. Part of Texas A&M University System. Founded 1925. Setting: 255-acre small-town campus. Total institutional enrollment: 6,500.

MBA HIGHLIGHTS

Entrance Difficulty**
Mean GMAT: 450
Mean GPA: N/R

Cost $
Tuition: $501 - $963/semester
(Nonresident: $1,689 - $3,603/semester)
Room & Board: $3,090

Enrollment Profile

Full-time: N/R	Work Exp: N/R
Part-time: N/R	International: 10%
Total: 100	Women: 40%
Average Age: N/R	Minorities: 55%

Average Class Size: 10

ACADEMICS

Length of Program Minimum: 18 months. Maximum: 5 years.

Calendar Semesters.

Full-time Classes Main campus; day, evening, summer.

Part-time Classes Main campus; evening, weekends, summer.

Degree Requirements 36 credits including 12 elective credits.

Required Courses Accounting seminar, advanced production management, advanced statistics, financial seminar, management policy and decision making, management seminar, managerial economics, marketing seminar.

Curricular Focus General management, problem solving and decision making, strategic analysis and planning.

Concentration Management.

Teaching Methodology Case study: 10%, lecture: 50%, research: 20%, team projects: 20%.

STUDENT STATISTICS

Geographic Representation State residents 80%. International 10%.

FACILITIES

Information Resources Main library with 450,000 bound volumes, 15,807 titles on microform, 2,000 periodical subscriptions, 6,000 records/tapes/CDs.

Housing 10% of students in program live in college-owned or -operated housing.

ADMISSION

Entrance Requirements Bachelor's degree, minimum 2.5 GPA. Core courses waived through: previous course work.

Application Requirements Application form, copies of transcript, 3 letters of recommendation.

Application Deadline Applications are processed on a rolling basis.

FINANCIALS

Estimated Costs for 1995-96 Tuition: Full-time: $270-$600/semester for state residents, $1,458-$3,240/semester for nonresidents; Part-time day: $100-$240/semester for state residents. Fees: Full-time: $231-$363/semester for state residents, $231-$363/semester for nonresidents; Part-time day: $31-$206/semester for state residents. Average room and board costs are $3,090 per academic year (on-campus) and $1,500 per academic year (off-campus).

Financial Aid Application deadlines: 5/1 for fall, 3/1 for summer. Contact: Mr. Arturo Pecos, Director of Student Financial Aid, West Santa Gertrudis, Kingsville, TX 78363. (512) 595-3911.

INTERNATIONAL STUDENTS

Demographics 10% of students enrolled in the program are international.

Applying TOEFL required, minimum score of 550; proof of adequate funds. Financial aid is available to international students. Loans are available for these students. Financial aid application deadlines: 5/1 for fall, 3/1 for summer. Admission applications are processed on a rolling basis.

Program Contact: Dr. Darvin Hoffman, Coordinator of Graduate Programs, Texas A&M University–Kingsville, West Santa Gertrudis, Kingsville, TX 78363. (512) 595-2111.

Texas Christian University

M. J. Neeley School of Business

Fort Worth, Texas

OVERVIEW

Texas Christian University is an independent coed institution, affiliated with Christian Church (Disciples of Christ). Founded 1873. Setting: 237-acre suburban campus. Total institutional enrollment: 7,000. Program was first offered in 1939. AACSB-accredited.

MBA HIGHLIGHTS

Entrance Difficulty**
Mean GMAT: N/R
Mean GPA: 3.1

Cost $$
Tuition: $288/semester hour
Room & Board: N/R

Enrollment Profile

Full-time: 150	Work Exp: 65%
Part-time: 120	International: N/R
Total: 270	Women: 32%
Average Age: 26	Minorities: 10%

Class Size: 30 - 35

ACADEMICS

Length of Program Minimum: 24 months. Maximum: 2 years.

Calendar Semesters.

Full-time Classes Main campus; day.

Part-time Classes Main campus; evening.

Degree Requirements 48 semester hours including 15 elective semester hours. Other: Integrative team projects; industry perspective seminar series.

Required Courses Business strategy, data analysis, financial management, financial reporting, legal and social environment of business, managerial accounting, managing information technology, managing people, manufacturing and services operating management, strategic management in a global environment.

Curricular Focus Business communications, general management, international business.

Concentrations Accounting, finance, human resources management, international business, management, management information systems, marketing, operations management, organizational behavior, quantitative analysis, strategic management.

Faculty Full-time: 30, 100% with doctorates.

Teaching Methodology Case study: 25%, lecture: 35%, research: 10%, seminars by members of the business community: 5%, student presentations: 10%, team projects: 15%.

Special Opportunities International exchange in France, Germany, Mexico. Internship program available.

STUDENT STATISTICS

Geographic Representation State residents 22%. By region: South 69%; Northeast 6%; West 4%; Midwest 1%.

Undergraduate Majors Business 47%; engineering/technology 9%; humanities 13%; nursing 1%; science/mathematics 17%; social sciences 12%; other 1%.

Other Background Graduate degrees in other disciplines: 2%. Work experience: On average, students have 2 years of work experience on entrance to the program.

FACILITIES

Information Resources Main library with 760,732 bound volumes, 442,295 titles on microform, 3,765 periodical subscriptions, 16,063 records/tapes/CDs. Business collection includes 29,000 bound volumes, 320 periodical subscriptions, 12 CD-ROMs, 110 videos.

Housing College housing not available.

Technology Computers are used moderately in course work. 73 computer terminals/PCs, linked by a campus-wide computer network, are available for use by students in program; they are located in classrooms, learning resource center, the library, the computer center, computer labs. Students in the program are not required to have their own PC. $600 are budgeted per student for computer support.

Computer Resources/On-line Services

Training	Yes	CompuServe	Yes
Internet	Yes	Dun's	No
E-Mail	Yes	Dow Jones	Yes
Videoconference Center	Yes	Dialog	Yes $
LEXIS/NEXIS	No	Bloomberg	No

Other on-line services: OCLC, RLIN, Carl.

ADMISSION

Acceptance 1994-95 310 applied for admission; 64% were accepted.

Entrance Requirements Bachelor's degree, GMAT score. Core courses waived through: previous course work.

Application Requirements Written essay, application form, copies of transcript, 3 letters of recommendation.

Application Deadline 5/31 for fall.

FINANCIALS

Costs for 1994-95 Tuition: Full-time: $288/semester hour. Fees: Full-time: $22/semester hour.

Financial Aid In 1994-95, 65% of candidates received some institutionally administered aid in the form of grants, scholarships, loans, assistantships, work-study. Total awards ranged from $8,024-$34,824. Financial aid is available to part-time students. Application deadline: 4/15 for fall. Contact: Ms. Peggy Conway, Director of MBA Admissions, P.O. Box 32868, Fort Worth, TX 76129-0002. (817) 921-7531.

INTERNATIONAL STUDENTS

Demographics 5% of students on campus are international; Asia 49%, Europe 23%, Central America 8%, South America 5%, Africa 4%, Australia 1%, Other 10%.

Services and Facilities International student center, visa services, ESL courses, counseling/support services.

Applying TOEFL required, minimum score of 550; proof of health; proof of adequate funds; a special three year program for international students who do not hold a bachelors degree. Financial aid is available to international students. Financial aid application deadline: 4/15 for fall. Admission application deadline: 5/31 for fall. Contact: Mr. Al Mladenka, Director of International Student Affairs, P.O. Box 32926, Fort Worth, TX 76129-0002. (817) 921-7292.

PLACEMENT

Placement services include alumni network, career counseling/planning, career fairs, career library, career placement, electronic job bank, job interviews, resume preparation, and resume referral to employers. Of 1994 graduates, 70% were employed within three months of graduation, the average starting salary was $31,500, the range was $25,000-$50,000.

Jobs by Employer Type Manufacturing 23%; service 66%; government 3%; consulting 8%.

Jobs by Functional Area Marketing/sales 20%; finance 25%; operations 12%; management 25%; strategic planning 12%; technical management 6%.

Program Contact: Ms. Peggy Conway, Director of MBA Admissions, Texas Christian University, P.O. Box 32868, Fort Worth, TX 76129-0002. (817) 921-7531, or (800) 828-3764; Fax: (817) 921-7227; Internet Address: conway@zeta.is.tcu.edu.

See full description on page 844.

Texas Southern University

Jesse H. Jones School of Business

Houston, Texas

OVERVIEW

Texas Southern University is a state-supported coed institution. Founded 1947. Setting: 147-acre urban campus. Total institutional enrollment: 10,800.

MBA HIGHLIGHTS

Entrance Difficulty**
Mean GMAT: 423
Mean GPA: 2.86

Cost $
Tuition: $432/semester
(Nonresident: $2,100/semester)
Room & Board: N/R

Enrollment Profile

Full-time: N/R	Work Exp: 60%
Part-time: N/R	International: N/R
Total: 92	Women: 40%
Average Age: 26	Minorities: N/R

Average Class Size: 20

ACADEMICS

Length of Program Minimum: 12 months. Maximum: 6 years.
Calendar Semesters.
Full-time Classes Main campus; evening, summer.
Part-time Classes Main campus; evening, summer.
Degree Requirements 30 credits including 1 elective credit.

Required Courses Administrative theory, analysis of business conditions, business policy and environment, cost accounting, economics of management, effective business management, financial decision making, marketing problems, statistical methods. Courses may be waived through: previous course work.

Curricular Focus Business issues and problems, economic and financial theory, problem solving and decision making.

Concentration Management.

Faculty Full-time: 12, 100% with doctorates.

Teaching Methodology Case study: 10%, lecture: 40%, research: 10%, student presentations: 15%, team projects: 25%.

STUDENT STATISTICS

Undergraduate Majors Business 70%; engineering/technology 10%; humanities 12%; social sciences 8%.

Other Background Graduate degrees in other disciplines: 1%.

FACILITIES

Information Resources Main library with 457,393 bound volumes, 363,519 titles on microform, 1,950 periodical subscriptions, 25 records/tapes/CDs, 10 CD-ROMs. Business collection includes 50,000 bound volumes, 500 periodical subscriptions, 10 CD-ROMs.

Housing 20% of students in program live in college-owned or -operated housing.

Technology Computers are used moderately in course work. 110 computer terminals/PCs are available for use by students in program; they are located in the library, computer labs. Students in the program are not required to have their own PC.

Computer Resources/On-line Services

Training	No	Dun's	No
Internet	Yes	Dow Jones	No
E-Mail	No	Dialog	Yes $
LEXIS/NEXIS	Yes	Bloomberg	No
CompuServe	No		

Other on-line services: Westlaw.

ADMISSION

Acceptance 1994-95 Of those applying, 30% were accepted.

Entrance Requirements Bachelor's degree, GMAT score, minimum 2.5 GPA. Core courses waived through: previous course work.

Application Requirements Application form, copies of transcript.

Application Deadlines 8/1 for fall, 12/1 for spring, 5/1 for summer.

FINANCIALS

Costs for 1994-95 Tuition: Full-time: $432/semester for state residents, $2,100/semester for nonresidents. Fees: Full-time: $222/semester for state residents, $222/semester for nonresidents.

Financial Aid In 1994-95, candidates received some institutionally administered aid in the form of loans, assistantships. Financial aid is available to part-time students. Contact: Mr. Melvin Plummer, Interim Director, 3100 Cleburne Avenue, Houston, TX 77004-4584. (713) 527-7124.

INTERNATIONAL STUDENTS

Demographics 17% of students on campus are international.

Services and Facilities Visa services, ESL courses, counseling/support services.

Applying TOEFL required, minimum score of 550; proof of health; proof of adequate funds. Financial aid is available to international students. Assistantships are available for these students. Admission application deadlines: 7/15 for fall, 11/15 for spring, 4/1 for summer. Contact: Dr. Iris Perkins, Director, International Student Affairs, 3100 Cleburne Avenue, Houston, TX 77004-4584. (713) 527-7896.

PLACEMENT

Placement services include career fairs, career placement, and resume referral to employers.

Program Contact: Mrs. Clara A. Wiley, Assistant Dean for Business Students Services, Texas Southern University, 3100 Cleburne Avenue, Houston, TX 77004-4584. (713) 527-7590; Fax: (713) 527-7011.

Texas Tech University

College of Business Administration

Lubbock, Texas

OVERVIEW
Texas Tech University is a state-supported coed institution. Founded 1923. Setting: 1,839-acre urban campus. Total institutional enrollment: 33,004. AACSB-accredited.

MBA HIGHLIGHTS

Entrance Difficulty***
Mean GMAT: 560
Mean GPA: 3.25

Cost $
Tuition: $56/credit
(Nonresident: $162/credit)
Room & Board: $2,700 (off-campus)

Enrollment Profile

Full-time: 272	Work Exp: 65%
Part-time: 68	International: 24%
Total: 340	Women: 40%
Average Age: 28	Minorities: 12%

Average Class Size: 25

ACADEMICS
Length of Program Minimum: 12 months. Maximum: 6 years.
Calendar Semesters.
Full-time Classes Main campus; day, evening, summer.
Part-time Classes Main campus; day, evening, summer.
Degree Requirements 36 credits including 9-12 elective credits.
Curricular Focus Leadership, managing diversity, teamwork.
Concentrations Accounting, entrepreneurship, finance, health services, international business, management, management information systems, marketing, operations management, quantitative analysis.
Faculty Full-time: 54, 100% with doctorates.
Teaching Methodology Case study: 10%, lecture: 60%, research: 5%, student presentations: 5%, team projects: 20%.
Special Opportunities International exchange in Finland, Italy. Internship program available.

STUDENT STATISTICS
Geographic Representation State residents 57%. By region: South 57%; Northeast 9%; Midwest 6%; West 4%. International 24%.
Undergraduate Majors Business 65%; education 4%; engineering/technology 4%; humanities 5%; nursing 1%; science/mathematics 2%; social sciences 10%; other 9%.
Other Background Graduate degrees in other disciplines: 14%. Work experience: On average, students have 4 years of work experience on entrance to the program.

FACILITIES
Information Resources Main library with 2.8 million bound volumes, 1.1 million titles on microform, 8,000 periodical subscriptions.
Housing College housing not available.
Technology Computers are used heavily in course work. 35 computer terminals/PCs, linked by a campus-wide computer network, are available for use by students in program; they are located in the student center, learning resource center, the library, computer labs. Students in the program are not required to have their own PC. $200 are budgeted per student for computer support.

Computer Resources/On-line Services

Training	Yes	CompuServe	Yes
Internet	Yes	Dun's	No
E-Mail	Yes	Dow Jones	Yes $
Multimedia Center	Yes	Dialog	Yes
LEXIS/NEXIS	No		

ADMISSION
Acceptance 1994-95 277 applied for admission; 62% were accepted.
Entrance Requirements Bachelor's degree, GMAT score of 500, minimum 3.0 GPA. Core courses waived through: previous course work.
Application Requirements Application form, resume/curriculum vitae, 3 letters of recommendation.

Application Deadlines 4/4 for fall, 11/1 for spring.

FINANCIALS
Costs for 1994-95 Tuition: Full-time: $56/credit for state residents, $162/credit for nonresidents. Fees: Full-time: $225/semester for state residents, $225/semester for nonresidents. Average room and board costs are $2,700 per academic year (off-campus).
Financial Aid In 1994-95, 25% of candidates received some institutionally administered aid in the form of grants, scholarships, loans, assistantships, work-study. Total awards ranged from $200-$5,000. Financial aid is not available to part-time students. Application deadlines: 7/1 for fall, 11/1 for spring. Contact: Mr. Ronny Barnes, Director of Financial Aid, Lubbock, TX 79409. (806) 742-3681.

INTERNATIONAL STUDENTS
Demographics 24% of students enrolled in the program are international; Asia 79%, Europe 11%, South America 3%, Africa 1%, Central America 1%, other 4%.
Services and Facilities International student center, ESL courses, counseling/support services.
Applying TOEFL required, minimum score of 550; proof of adequate funds. Financial aid is not available to international students. Admission application deadlines: 4/30 for fall, 9/30 for spring, 2/15 for summer. Contact: Ms. Banu Altunbas, Academic Adviser, Lubbock, TX 79409. (806) 742-3184.

ALTERNATE MBA PROGRAMS
MBA/JD Length of program: Minimum: 42 months. Maximum: 6 years. Degree requirements: 102 credits.
MBA/MSN Length of program: Minimum: 24 months. Maximum: 6 years. Degree requirements: 69 credits.

PLACEMENT
In 1993-94, 15 organizations participated in on-campus recruiting; 175 on-campus interviews were conducted. Placement services include alumni network, career counseling/planning, career fairs, career library, electronic job bank, job interviews, resume preparation, and resume referral to employers. Of 1994 graduates, the average starting salary was $36,500, the range was $25,000-$90,000.
Jobs by Employer Type Manufacturing 4%; service 41%; government 4%; consulting 41%; health industry 10%.
Jobs by Functional Area Marketing/sales 3%; finance 52%; operations 3%; management 17%; technical management 18%; other 7%.

Program Contact: Dr. Madelaine Lowe, Director of BA Graduate Services, Texas Tech University, Lubbock, TX 79409. (806) 742-3184; Fax: (806) 742-3958.

Texas Woman's University

Department of Business and Economics

Denton, Texas

OVERVIEW
Texas Woman's University is a state-supported primarily women institution. Founded 1901. Setting: 270-acre urban campus with easy access to Dallas–Fort Worth. Total institutional enrollment: 10,000. Program was first offered in 1975.

MBA HIGHLIGHTS

Entrance Difficulty**
Mean GMAT: 450
Mean GPA: 3.25

Cost $
Tuition: $50/semester hour
(Nonresident: $191/semester hour)
Room & Board: N/R

Enrollment Profile

Full-time: 10	Work Exp: 95%
Part-time: 90	International: 15%
Total: 100	Women: 90%
Average Age: 32	Minorities: 15%

Class Size: 15 - 20

ACADEMICS

Length of Program Minimum: 18 months. Maximum: 6 years.

Calendar Semesters.

Part-time Classes Main campus; day, evening, summer.

Degree Requirements 30-36 credits including 6 elective credits.

Required Courses Administrative managerial finance, advanced business policy, advanced macroeconomic theory, advanced management information systems, advanced price theory, management and organization, managerial accounting, marketing management.

Curricular Focus Business issues and problems, problem solving and decision making, strategic analysis and planning.

Concentration Management.

Faculty Full-time: 6, 100% with doctorates; part-time: 4, 75% with doctorates.

Teaching Methodology Case study: 21%, lecture: 21%, research: 21%, student presentations: 16%, team projects: 21%.

Special Opportunities Internship program available.

STUDENT STATISTICS

Geographic Representation State residents 80%. By region: South 85%. International 15%.

Undergraduate Majors Business 90%; engineering/technology 2%; humanities 3%; nursing 1%; social sciences 2%; other 2%.

Other Background Graduate degrees in other disciplines: 8%. Work experience: On average, students have 3 years of work experience on entrance to the program.

FACILITIES

Information Resources Main library with 788,271 bound volumes, 652,861 titles on microform, 2,899 periodical subscriptions, 12,943 records/tapes/CDs, 26 CD-ROMs.

Housing 10% of students in program live in college-owned or -operated housing.

Technology Computers are used heavily in course work. 90 computer terminals/PCs, linked by a campus-wide computer network, are available for use by students in program; they are located in classrooms, learning resource center, the library, the computer center, computer labs, the research center. Students in the program are not required to have their own PC.

Computer Resources/On-line Services

Training	No	Videoconference Center	Yes
E-Mail	Yes	Multimedia Center	Yes

ADMISSION

Acceptance 1994-95 40 applied for admission; 75% were accepted.

Entrance Requirements Bachelor's degree, GMAT score of 400.

Application Requirements Interview, application form, copies of transcript, resume/curriculum vitae.

Application Deadline Applications are processed on a rolling basis.

FINANCIALS

Costs for 1995-96 Tuition: Full-time: $50/semester hour for state residents, $191/semester hour for nonresidents. Fees: Full-time: $40-$45/semester hour for state residents, $40-$45/semester hour for nonresidents.

Financial Aid In 1994-95, 5% of candidates received some institutionally administered aid in the form of scholarships, assistantships, work-study. Total awards ranged from $100-$5,200. Financial aid is available to part-time students. Application deadlines: 4/1 for fall, 9/1 for spring. Applications are processed on a rolling basis. Contact: Mr. Governor Jackson, Director, Denton, TX 76204. (817) 898-3050.

INTERNATIONAL STUDENTS

Demographics 15% of students enrolled in the program are international; Asia 50%, Africa 30%, Europe 10%, South America 10%.

Services and Facilities International student office, visa services, language tutoring, counseling/support services.

Applying TOEFL required, minimum score of 550. Financial aid is available to international students. Financial aid application deadlines: 4/1 for fall, 9/1 for spring. Applications are processed on a rolling basis. Admission applications are processed on a rolling basis. Contact: Ms. Doris Key, Coordinator, Denton, TX 76204. (817) 898-3048.

PLACEMENT

In 1993-94, 20 organizations participated in on-campus recruiting; 15 on-campus interviews were conducted. Placement services include alumni network, career counseling/planning, career fairs, career library, career placement, electronic job bank, job interviews, resume preparation, and resume referral to employers. Of 1994 graduates, 90% were employed within three months of graduation.

Jobs by Employer Type Service 90%; government 10%.

Jobs by Functional Area Marketing/sales 45%; finance 5%; management 45%; strategic planning 5%.

Program Contact: Dr. Derrell Bulls, Chair, Texas Woman's University, Department of Business and Economics, Box 23805, Denton, TX 76204. (817) 898-2111; Fax: (817) 898-2120; Internet Address: d-bulls@twu. edu.

University of Dallas

Graduate School of Management

Irving, Texas

OVERVIEW

The University of Dallas is an independent Roman Catholic coed institution. Founded 1956. Setting: 750-acre urban campus with easy access to Dallas–Fort Worth. Total institutional enrollment: 3,000. Program was first offered in 1966.

MBA HIGHLIGHTS

Entrance Difficulty*

Mean GMAT: 480

Mean GPA: 3.0

Cost $$

Tuition: $316/credit hour

Room & Board: $5,200

Enrollment Profile

Full-time: 402	Work Exp: 59%
Part-time: 880	International: 23%
Total: 1,282	Women: 38%
Average Age: N/R	Minorities: 14%

Average Class Size: 20

ACADEMICS

Length of Program Minimum: 12 months. Maximum: 6 years.

Calendar Trimesters.

Full-time Classes Main campus, Dallas; day, evening, weekends, summer.

Part-time Classes Main campus, Dallas; day, evening, weekends, summer.

Degree Requirements 37 credit hours.

Required Courses Computers for managers, ethics and management, financial accounting, financial management, legal environment, management theory and practice, managerial accounting, managerial economics, marketing management, organizational analysis, statistics.

Curricular Focus Economic and financial theory, organizational development and change management, strategic analysis and planning.

Concentrations Accounting, finance, health services, human resources management, international business, management, management information systems, marketing, telecommunications management, engineering management.

Faculty Full-time: 21, 80% with doctorates; part-time: 84, 28% with doctorates.

Teaching Methodology Case study: 8%, lecture: 50%, research: 5%, seminars by members of the business community: 2%, student presentations: 15%, team projects: 20%.

Special Opportunities International exchange in France, Mexico, Spain. Internship program available.

STUDENT STATISTICS

Geographic Representation State residents 76%. International 23%.

Undergraduate Majors Business 40%; education 2%; engineering/technology 19%; humanities 10%; nursing 5%; science/mathematics 16%; social sciences 8%.

Other Background Graduate degrees in other disciplines: 14%.

FACILITIES

Information Resources Main library with 288,566 bound volumes, 75,416 titles on microform, 1,022 periodical subscriptions, 1,100 records/tapes/CDs, 2 CD-ROMs. Business collection includes 2,000 bound volumes, 538 periodical subscriptions, 8 CD-ROMs, 20 videos.

Housing College housing available.

Technology Computers are used heavily in course work. 75 computer terminals/PCs are available for use by students in program; they are located in classrooms, the computer center, computer labs. Students in the program are not required to have their own PC.

Computer Resources/On-line Services

Training	Yes	Dun's	No
Internet	Yes	Dow Jones	No
E-Mail	Yes	Dialog	Yes
LEXIS/NEXIS	No	Bloomberg	No
CompuServe	No		

Other on-line services: OCLC, First Search.

ADMISSION

Entrance Requirements Bachelor's degree, GMAT score of 400, minimum 3.0 GPA, minimum 5 years of work experience. Core courses waived through: previous course work.

Application Requirements Application form, copies of transcript, resume/curriculum vitae, 2 letters of recommendation.

Application Deadlines 7/14 for fall, 3/15 for winter, 11/14 for spring. Applications are processed on a rolling basis.

FINANCIALS

Costs for 1994-95 Tuition: Full-time: $316/credit hour. Fees: Full-time: $10-$45/trimester. Average room and board costs are $5,200 per academic year (on-campus) and $4,800 per academic year (off-campus).

Financial Aid In 1994-95, 17% of candidates received some institutionally administered aid in the form of grants, scholarships, loans, fellowships. Total awards ranged from $1,500-$18,500. Financial aid is available to part-time students. Application deadlines: 4/1 for fall, 11/1 for spring. Contact: Mr. Kenneth Covington, Director of Financial Aid, Carpender Hall, 1845 East Northgate Drive, Irving, TX 75062-4799. (214) 721-5266.

INTERNATIONAL STUDENTS

Demographics 23% of students enrolled in the program are international; Asia 73%, Europe 14%, Africa 4%, South America 4%, Central America 2%.

Services and Facilities International student office, international student center, visa services, ESL courses, counseling/support services.

Applying TOEFL required; proof of adequate funds; minimum TOEFL score of 520 with a score of 52 or better in each section of the test. Financial aid is available to international students. Assistantships are open to these students. Admission application deadlines: 7/14 for fall, 11/14 for spring, 3/15 for summer. Applications are processed on a rolling basis. Contact: Ms. Deborah Garrison, Director of International Student Services, 1845 East Northgate Drive, Irving, TX 75062-4799. (214) 721-5059.

PLACEMENT

In 1993-94, 35 organizations participated in on-campus recruiting. Placement services include alumni network, career counseling/planning, career fairs, career placement, resume preparation, and resume referral to employers.

Program Contact: Ms. Stephanie DuPaul, Assistant Director of Admissions, University of Dallas, 1845 East Northgate Drive, Irving, TX 75062-4799. (214) 721-5356, or (800) 832-5622; Fax: (214) 721-4009.

See full description on page 870.

University of Houston

College of Business Administration

Houston, Texas

OVERVIEW

The University of Houston is a state-supported coed institution. Part of University of Houston System. Founded 1927. Setting: 557-acre urban campus. Total institutional enrollment: 32,129. Program was first offered in 1939. AACSB-accredited.

MBA HIGHLIGHTS

Entrance Difficulty**
Mean GMAT: 584
Mean GPA: 3.29

Cost $
Tuition: $812 - $1,696/semester
(Nonresident: $1,847 - $4,226/semester)
Room & Board: N/R

Enrollment Profile

Full-time: 361	Work Exp: 80%
Part-time: 646	International: 5%
Total: 1,007	Women: 25%
Average Age: 28	Minorities: 6%

Average Class Size: 35

ACADEMICS

Length of Program Minimum: 24 months. Maximum: 7 years.

Calendar Semesters.

Full-time Classes Main campus; day, evening, summer.

Part-time Classes Main campus; day, evening, summer.

Degree Requirements 54 credits including 12 elective credits.

Required Courses Administrative accounting, corporate strategy and policy, information systems, international environment of business, macroeconomic analysis, managerial finance, marketing administration, microeconomic analysis, organizational behavior and management, production and logistics management, statistical methods for business.

Curricular Focus Business issues and problems, international business, strategic analysis and planning.

Concentrations Accounting, finance, international business, management, management information systems, marketing, operations management, statistics and operations research, taxation.

Faculty Full-time: 85, 98% with doctorates; part-time: 22, 60% with doctorates.

Teaching Methodology Case study: 15%, faculty seminars: 10%, lecture: 40%, research: 5%, seminars by members of the business community: 10%, student presentations: 10%, team projects: 10%.

Special Opportunities International exchange in Canada, France, Germany, Japan, Mexico.

STUDENT STATISTICS

Geographic Representation International 5%.

Undergraduate Majors Business 25%; education 2%; engineering/technology 20%; humanities 10%; nursing 2%; science/mathematics 6%; social sciences 10%; other 25%.

Other Background Graduate degrees in other disciplines: 3%. Work experience: On average, students have 4 years of work experience on entrance to the program.

FACILITIES

Information Resources Main library with 1.8 million bound volumes, 3.5 million titles on microform, 14,198 periodical subscriptions, 343 records/tapes/CDs, 218 CD-ROMs. Business collection includes 85,250 bound volumes, 600 periodical subscriptions, 11 CD-ROMs.

Housing College housing available.

Technology Computers are used moderately in course work. 175 computer terminals/PCs, linked by a campus-wide computer network, are available for use by students in program; they are located in the computer center, computer labs. Students in the program are not required to have their own PC.

Computer Resources/On-line Services

Training	Yes	Dun's	No
Internet	Yes	Dow Jones	No
E-Mail	Yes	Dialog	Yes
LEXIS/NEXIS	No	Bloomberg	No
CompuServe	No		

Other on-line services: OCLC, Carl.

ADMISSION

Acceptance 1994-95 854 applied for admission; 46% were accepted.

Entrance Requirements Bachelor's degree, GMAT score. Core courses waived through: previous course work.

Application Requirements Application form, copies of transcript, resume/curriculum vitae.

Application Deadlines 5/1 for fall, 10/1 for spring. Applications are processed on a rolling basis.

FINANCIALS

Costs for 1994-95 Tuition: Full-time: $504-$1,232/semester for state residents, $1,539-$3,762/semester for nonresidents; Part-time day: $100-$448/semester for state residents, $171-$1,368/semester for nonresidents. Fees: Full-time: $308-$464/semester for state residents, $308-$464/semester for nonresidents; Part-time day: $92-$291/semester for state residents, $92-$291/semester for nonresidents.

Financial Aid In 1994-95, candidates received some institutionally administered aid in the form of scholarships, fellowships, assistantships. Total awards ranged from $200-$3,000. Financial aid is available to part-time students. Application deadline: 4/1 for fall. Contact: Ms. Linda Vincent, Director of Scholarships and Special Programs, 4800 Calhoun, Houston, TX 77204-6283. (713) 743-4620.

INTERNATIONAL STUDENTS

Demographics 5% of students enrolled in the program are international; Asia 57%, Europe 34%, Central America 6%.

Services and Facilities International student office, visa services, language tutoring, ESL courses, counseling/support services, language and cultural center.

Applying TOEFL required; proof of adequate funds. Financial aid is available to international students. Financial aid application deadlines: 5/1 for fall, 10/1 for spring. Admission application deadlines: 5/1 for fall, 10/1 for spring.

ALTERNATE MBA PROGRAMS

Executive MBA (EMBA) Length of program: Minimum: 22 months. Maximum: 2 years. Degree requirements: 54 credits. Minimum 5 years professional work experience; team participation. Average class size: 53.

MBA/JD Length of program: Minimum: 72 months. Maximum: 7 years. Degree requirements: 127 credits including 63 elective credits. Average class size: 35.

MBA/MA Length of program: Minimum: 72 months. Maximum: 7 years. Full-time classes: Main campus; day, evening, summer. Part-time classes: Main campus; day, evening, summer. Degree requirements: 70 credits including 21 elective credits. 21 hours of advanced work in Spanish. MA is in Spanish. Languages: Spanish. Average class size: 35.

MBA/MIM Length of program: Minimum: 36 months. Maximum: 7 years. Degree requirements: 72 credits including 21 elective credits. Foreign language proficiency, international residence. Average class size: 35.

MBA/MSW Length of program: Minimum: 72 months. Maximum: 7 years. Degree requirements: 105 credits including 41 elective credits. Average class size: 35.

MBA/MIE Length of program: Minimum: 36 months. Maximum: 7 years. Degree requirements: 66 credits. Average class size: 35.

Professional MBA Length of program: Minimum: 33 months. Maximum: 3 years. Degree requirements: 54 credits including 6-9 elective credits. Two to five years professional experience and team participation required. Class size: 30-35.

PLACEMENT

In 1993-94, 186 organizations participated in on-campus recruiting; 119 on-campus interviews were conducted. Placement services include career counseling/planning, career fairs, career library, career placement, electronic job bank, job interviews, job search course, resume preparation, and resume referral to employers. Of 1994 graduates, 85% were employed within three months of graduation, the average starting salary was $39,160.

Jobs by Employer Type Manufacturing 40%; service 50%; government 10%.

Program Contact: Mr. Frank Kelley, Director of Academic Advising, University of Houston, Office of Student Services, Houston, TX 77204-6283. (713) 743-4912; Fax: (713) 743-4622; Internet Address: frank@oss.uh.edu.

See full description on page 876.

University of Houston–Clear Lake

College of Business and Public Administration

Houston, Texas

OVERVIEW

The University of Houston–Clear Lake is a state-supported upper-level coed institution. Part of University of Houston System. Founded 1974. Setting: 487-acre suburban campus. Total institutional enrollment: 7,136. AACSB-accredited.

ACADEMICS

Calendar Semesters.

Concentration Management.

FACILITIES

Information Resources Main library with 339,254 bound volumes, 2,455 periodical subscriptions, 4,584 records/tapes/CDs, 22 CD-ROMs.

Program Contact: Dr. Bob Finley, Dean, University of Houston–Clear Lake, 2700 Bay Area Boulevard, Houston, TX 77058-3102. (713) 283-3102.

University of Houston–Victoria

Division of Business Administration

Victoria, Texas

OVERVIEW

The University of Houston–Victoria is a state-supported upper-level coed institution. Founded 1973. Setting: small-town campus. Total institutional enrollment: 1,616. Program was first offered in 1973.

MBA HIGHLIGHTS

Entrance Difficulty**
Mean GMAT: 450
Mean GPA: 2.8

Cost $
Tuition: $456 - $836/semester
(Nonresident: $2,052 - $3,762/semester)
Room & Board: $9,500 (off-campus)

Enrollment Profile

Full-time: 74	Work Exp: 60%
Part-time: 61	International: 11%
Total: 135	Women: 40%
Average Age: 25	Minorities: 10%

Average Class Size: 15

ACADEMICS

Length of Program Minimum: 12 months. Maximum: 7 years.

Calendar Semesters.

Full-time Classes Main campus; day, evening, summer.

Part-time Classes Main campus; day, evening, summer.

Degree Requirements 36 credits including 12 elective credits.

Required Courses Business strategy and policy, management information systems, managerial accounting, managerial economics, organizational development, problems in marketing, problems of financial management, production and logistics management.

Curricular Focus General management, international business, strategic analysis and planning.

Concentration Management.

Faculty Full-time: 8, 100% with doctorates; part-time: 2, 100% with doctorates.

Teaching Methodology Case study: 15%, lecture: 50%, research: 10%, seminars by members of the business community: 5%, student presentations: 10%, team projects: 10%.

STUDENT STATISTICS

Geographic Representation By region: South 89%. International 11%.

Undergraduate Majors Business 40%; education 35%; humanities 25%.

Other Background Graduate degrees in other disciplines: 2%. Work experience: On average, students have 3 years of work experience on entrance to the program.

FACILITIES

Information Resources Main library with 194,000 bound volumes, 690,700 titles on microform, 1,950 periodical subscriptions.

Housing College housing not available.

Technology Computers are used moderately in course work. 50 computer terminals/PCs, linked by a campus-wide computer network, are available for use by students in program; they are located in computer labs. Students in the program are not required to have their own PC.

Computer Resources/On-line Services

Training	Yes	Dun's	Yes
Internet	Yes	Dow Jones	Yes
E-Mail	Yes	Dialog	Yes
LEXIS/NEXIS	Yes	Bloomberg	No
CompuServe	Yes		

ADMISSION

Acceptance 1994-95 68 applied for admission; 76% were accepted.

Entrance Requirements Bachelor's degree, prerequisite courses required for applicants with non-business degree, GMAT score of 450, minimum 2.5 GPA. Core courses waived through: previous course work.

Application Requirements Application form, copies of transcript, personal statement.

Application Deadlines 5/30 for fall, 9/30 for spring.

FINANCIALS

Estimated Costs for 1995-96 Tuition: Full-time: $456-$836/semester for state residents, $2,052-$3,762/semester for nonresidents. Fees: Full-time: $348/semester for state residents, $348/semester for nonresidents. Average room and board costs are $9,500 per academic year (off-campus).

Financial Aid In 1994-95, 20% of candidates received some institutionally administered aid in the form of scholarships, loans, assistantships, work-study. Total awards ranged from $500-$1,000. Financial aid is available to part-time students. Application deadline: 3/15 for fall. Contact: Mr. Richard Phillips, Director of Enrollment Management, 2506 East Red River, Victoria, TX 77901-4450. (512) 788-6615.

INTERNATIONAL STUDENTS

Demographics 11% of students enrolled in the program are international.

Applying TOEFL required; proof of adequate funds. Financial aid is not available to international students. Admission application deadlines: 5/30 for fall, 9/30 for spring. Applications are processed on a rolling basis. Contact: Mr. Richard Phillips, Director of Enrollment Management, 2506 East Red River, Victoria, TX 77901-4450. (512) 788-6615.

PLACEMENT

Placement services include career fairs, career placement, job interviews, resume preparation, and resume referral to employers.

Program Contact: Dr. Ron M. Sardessai, Chair, Division of Business Administration, University of Houston–Victoria, 2506 East Red River, Victoria, TX 77058-1098. (512) 788-6270 Ext. 271; Fax: (512) 572-8463.

University of Mary Hardin-Baylor

School of Business

Belton, Texas

OVERVIEW

The University of Mary Hardin-Baylor is an independent Southern Baptist comprehensive coed institution. Founded 1845. Setting: 100-acre small-town campus with easy access to Austin. Total institutional enrollment: 2,242. Program was first offered in 1988.

MBA HIGHLIGHTS

Entrance Difficulty**
Mean GMAT: 498
Mean GPA: 3.1

Cost $
Tuition: $217/semester hour
Room & Board: $1,500

Enrollment Profile

Full-time: 0		Work Exp: 100%
Part-time: 21		International: N/R
Total: 21		Women: 52%
Average Age: 31		Minorities: 5%

Average Class Size: 12

ACADEMICS

Length of Program Minimum: 12 months. Maximum: 5 years.

Calendar Trimesters.

Full-time Classes Main campus; evening, summer.

Part-time Classes Main campus; evening, summer.

Degree Requirements 36 credits. Other: Comprehensive exam.

Required Courses Advanced statistics and quantitative methods, business law, ethics and leadership, financial management, global competition, international business, management and organizational behavior, management of information systems, managerial accounting, managerial economics and planning, marketing management, operations management and research, strategic management and business policy. Courses may be waived through: previous course work.

Curricular Focus General management.

Concentration Management.

Faculty Full-time: 9, 100% with doctorates; part-time: 1, 100% with doctorates.

Teaching Methodology Case study: 5%, lecture: 75%, research: 5%, student presentations: 10%, team projects: 5%.

STUDENT STATISTICS

Geographic Representation State residents 100%. By region: South 100%.

Undergraduate Majors Business 68%; engineering/technology 12%; humanities 8%; science/mathematics 4%; other 8%.

Other Background Graduate degrees in other disciplines: 5%. Work experience: On average, students have 7 years of work experience on entrance to the program.

FACILITIES

Information Resources Main library with 125,000 bound volumes, 27,749 titles on microform, 830 periodical subscriptions.

Housing College housing available.

Technology Computers are used moderately in course work. 40 computer terminals/PCs are available for use by students in program; they are located in dormitories, classrooms, computer labs. Students in the program are not required to have their own PC.

Computer Resources/On-line Services

Training	No	Dun's	No
Internet	No	Dow Jones	No
E-Mail	No	Dialog	Yes
LEXIS/NEXIS	No	Bloomberg	No
CompuServe	No		

ADMISSION

Acceptance 1994-95 Of those applying, 95% were accepted.

Entrance Requirements Bachelor's degree, GMAT score, minimum 2.5 GPA. Core courses waived through: previous course work.

Application Requirements Interview, application form, copies of transcript.

Application Deadline Applications are processed on a rolling basis.

FINANCIALS

Costs for 1994-95 Tuition: Full-time: $217/semester hour. Average room and board costs are $1,500 per academic year (on-campus).

Financial Aid Financial aid is available to part-time students. Contact: Mr. Ron Brown, Director of Financial Aid, UMHB Box 8004, Belton, TX 76513. (817) 939-4517.

INTERNATIONAL STUDENTS

Services and Facilities International student center, visa services, language tutoring, ESL courses, counseling/support services.

Applying TOEFL required; proof of adequate funds. Financial aid is not available to international students. Contact: Mr. Reed Harris, Director of International Student Services, UMHB Box 8421, Belton, TX 76513. (817) 939-4949.

PLACEMENT
Placement services include career placement. Of 1994 graduates, 100% were employed within three months of graduation.

Program Contact: Dr. Lee Baldwin, Dean, School of Business, University of Mary Hardin-Baylor, UMHB Box 8018, Belton, TX 76513. (817) 939-4644, or (800) 727-8642 (TX only); Fax: (817) 939-4535.

University of North Texas

College of Business Administration

Denton, Texas

OVERVIEW
The University of North Texas is a state-supported coed institution. Founded 1890. Setting: 425-acre urban campus with easy access to Dallas–Fort Worth. Total institutional enrollment: 25,759. AACSB-accredited.

ACADEMICS
Calendar Semesters.

Concentration Management.

FACILITIES
Information Resources Main library with 1 million bound volumes, 2.7 million titles on microform, 8,775 periodical subscriptions, 49,357 records/ tapes/CDs, 95 CD-ROMs.

Program Contact: Dr. Marsha Staf, Associate Dean for Academic and Public Affairs, University of North Texas, PO Box 13737, Denton, TX 76203-6737. (817) 565-3058; Fax: (817) 565-4998.

University of St. Thomas

Cameron School of Business

Houston, Texas

OVERVIEW
The University of St. Thomas is an independent Roman Catholic comprehensive coed institution. Founded 1947. Setting: 20-acre urban campus. Total institutional enrollment: 2,298. Program was first offered in 1980.

MBA HIGHLIGHTS

Entrance Difficulty**
Mean GMAT: 470
Mean GPA: 2.8

Cost $
Tuition: $315/semester hour
Room & Board: N/R

Enrollment Profile

Full-time: 143	Work Exp: 77%
Part-time: 328	International: N/R
Total: 471	Women: 41%
Average Age: 28	Minorities: N/R

Average Class Size: 35

ACADEMICS
Length of Program Minimum: 24 months. Maximum: 6 years.
Calendar Semesters.
Full-time Classes Main campus; evening, summer.
Part-time Classes Main campus; evening, summer.
Degree Requirements 36 credits including 9 elective credits.
Required Courses Behavioral theory, financial management, macroeconomic theory, management and social environment or moral decision making in business, managerial accounting, marketing management and theory,

seminar in management, statistical methods for management decisions, theory of the firm. Courses may be waived through: previous course work.
Curricular Focus Economic and financial theory, general management, problem solving and decision making.
Concentrations Finance, international business, marketing.
Faculty Full-time: 12, 83% with doctorates; part-time: 10, 60% with doctorates.
Teaching Methodology Case study: 12%, lecture: 80%, research: 5%, student presentations: 2%, team projects: 1%.
Special Opportunities International exchange in Singapore, United Kingdom. Internship program available.

STUDENT STATISTICS
Geographic Representation State residents 25%. By region: South 75%.
Undergraduate Majors Business 14%; engineering/technology 13%; humanities 4%; nursing 3%; science/mathematics 8%; social sciences 54%; other 3%.
Other Background Graduate degrees in other disciplines: 4%. Work experience: On average, students have 5 years of work experience on entrance to the program.

FACILITIES
Information Resources Main library with 181,570 bound volumes, 47,609 titles on microform, 792 periodical subscriptions, 3,279 records/ tapes/CDs, 9 CD-ROMs.
Housing College housing not available.
Technology Computers are used moderately in course work. 175 computer terminals/PCs, linked by a campuswide computer network, are available for use by students in program; they are located in student rooms, classrooms, learning resource center, the library, the computer center, computer labs. Students in the program are not required to have their own PC.

Computer Resources/On-line Services

Training	Yes	E-Mail	No
Internet	Yes	Dialog	Yes

Other on-line services: OCLC, Westlaw.

ADMISSION
Entrance Requirements Bachelor's degree, GMAT score of 400, minimum 2.5 GPA. Core courses waived through: previous course work.
Application Requirements Application form, copies of transcript, 3 letters of recommendation.
Application Deadlines 6/30 for fall, 10/31 for spring, 4/30 for summer.

FINANCIALS
Costs for 1994-95 Tuition: Full-time: $315/semester hour. Fees: Full-time: $13/semester.
Financial Aid In 1994-95, 10% of candidates received some institutionally administered aid in the form of grants, loans, assistantships. Total awards ranged from $2,090-$18,500. Financial aid is available to part-time students. Application deadlines: 6/30 for fall, 10/31 for spring, 4/30 for summer. Contact: Ms. Maria Landrau, Assistant Director, 3800 Montrose Boulevard, Houston, TX 77006-4694. (713) 525-2170.

INTERNATIONAL STUDENTS
Demographics 8% of students on campus are international; Central America 30%, Europe 29%, Asia 25%, South America 9%, Africa 2%, other 4%.
Services and Facilities ESL courses, counseling/support services.
Applying TOEFL required, minimum score of 550; proof of adequate funds. Financial aid is not available to international students. Admission application deadlines: 6/30 for fall, 10/31 for spring, 4/30 for summer. Contact: Mr. Richard Glor, Registrar, International Student Adviser, 3800 Montrose Boulevard, Houston, TX 77006-4694. (713) 525-2153.

PLACEMENT
Placement services include career counseling/planning, career fairs, resume preparation, and resume referral to employers.

Program Contact: Ms. Lyn Alaras, Admissions Secretary, University of St. Thomas, 3800 Montrose Boulevard, Houston, TX 77006-4694. (713) 525-2100; Fax: (713) 525-2110.

University of Texas at Arlington

College of Business Administration

Arlington, Texas

OVERVIEW
The University of Texas at Arlington is a state-supported coed institution. Part of University of Texas System. Founded 1895. Setting: 386-acre suburban campus with easy access to Dallas–Fort Worth. Total institutional enrollment: 23,280. Program was first offered in 1968. AACSB-accredited.

MBA HIGHLIGHTS

Entrance Difficulty**
Mean GMAT: 540
Mean GPA: 3.21

Cost $
Tuition: $73 - $78/semester hour
(Nonresident: $217 - $220/semester hour)
Room & Board: N/R

Enrollment Profile

Full-time: 152	Work Exp: 90%
Part-time: 382	International: 18%
Total: 534	Women: 33%
Average Age: 30	Minorities: 29%

Average Class Size: 23

ACADEMICS
Length of Program Minimum: 12 months. Maximum: 6 years.
Calendar Semesters.
Full-time Classes Main campus; day, evening, summer.
Part-time Classes Main campus; day, evening, summer.
Degree Requirements 30 semester hours including 27 elective semester hours.
Required Courses Accounting analysis, advanced statistics, behavioral science, business finance, business policy, introduction to computers, legal environment of business, macroeconomics, management, marketing, microeconomics, quantitative analysis. Courses may be waived through: previous course work.
Curricular Focus General management, international business.
Concentrations Accounting, economics, entrepreneurship, finance, human resources management, international business, management, management information systems, marketing, operations management, organizational behavior, quantitative analysis, real estate.
Faculty Full-time: 107, 76% with doctorates; part-time: 40, 27% with doctorates.
Teaching Methodology Case study: 10%, faculty seminars: 10%, lecture: 50%, research: 5%, seminars by members of the business community: 5%, student presentations: 10%, team projects: 10%.
Special Opportunities International exchange in France, Germany, Mexico, Norway, Switzerland, United Kingdom.

STUDENT STATISTICS
Geographic Representation By region: South 47%; Northeast 23%; West 12%. International 18%.
Undergraduate Majors Business 56%; engineering/technology 18%; humanities 7%; social sciences 11%; other 8%.
Other Background Graduate degrees in other disciplines: 6%. Work experience: On average, students have 6-7 years of work experience on entrance to the program.

FACILITIES
Information Resources Main library with 930,000 bound volumes, 1.3 million titles on microform, 7,686 periodical subscriptions, 410 CD-ROMs. Business collection includes 5,000 bound volumes, 750 periodical subscriptions, 200 CD-ROMs, 175 videos.
Housing 1% of students in program live in college-owned or -operated housing.
Technology Computers are used moderately in course work. Computer terminals/PCs, linked by a campus-wide computer network, are available for use by students in program; they are located in classrooms, learning resource center, the library, the computer center, computer labs. Students in the program are not required to have their own PC.

Computer Resources/On-line Services

Training	Yes	CompuServe	No
Internet	Yes	Dun's	No
E-Mail	Yes	Dow Jones	Yes
LEXIS/NEXIS	Yes	Dialog	Yes

Other on-line services: First Search, Carl, SEC.

ADMISSION
Acceptance 1994-95 Of those applying, 60% were accepted.
Entrance Requirements Bachelor's degree, GMAT score of 480, minimum 3.0 GPA. Core courses waived through: previous course work.
Application Requirements Written essay, application form, copies of transcript, 3 letters of recommendation.
Application Deadlines 6/23 for fall, 10/20 for spring, 3/29 for summer.

FINANCIALS
Costs for 1994-95 Tuition: Full-time: $73-$78/semester hour for state residents, $217-$220/semester hour for nonresidents.
Financial Aid In 1994-95, 21% of candidates received some institutionally administered aid in the form of scholarships, loans, assistantships. Total awards ranged from $100-$4,500. Financial aid is available to part-time students. Application deadlines: 6/1 for fall, 11/15 for spring, 4/15 for summer. Contact: Ms. Judy Schneider, Director of Financial Aid, Box 19199, Arlington, TX 76019. (817) 273-3561.

INTERNATIONAL STUDENTS
Demographics 18% of students enrolled in the program are international.
Services and Facilities Visa services, language tutoring, ESL courses, counseling/support services, intensive English program.
Applying TOEFL required, minimum score of 550; proof of health; proof of adequate funds. Financial aid is available to international students. Financial aid application deadline: 6/30 for fall. Admission application deadlines: 4/14 for fall, 9/1 for spring, 1/19 for summer. Contact: Mr. Marco Rodriguez, International Student Adviser, Box 19028, Arlington, TX 76019. (817) 273-2355.

PLACEMENT
Placement services include alumni network, career counseling/planning, career fairs, career library, career placement, electronic job bank, job interviews, resume preparation, and resume referral to employers.

Program Contact: Mr. James E. Walther, Director of Graduate Advising, University of Texas at Arlington, Arlington, TX 76019. (817) 273-3004; Fax: (817) 794-5799; Internet Address: walther@utarlg.uta.edu.

University of Texas at Austin

Graduate School of Business

Austin, Texas

OVERVIEW
The University of Texas at Austin is a state-supported coed institution. Part of University of Texas System. Founded 1883. Setting: 350-acre small-town campus with easy access to San Antonio. Total institutional enrollment: 47,957. Program was first offered in 1922. AACSB-accredited.

MBA HIGHLIGHTS

Entrance Difficulty***
Mean GMAT: 625
Mean GPA: 3.26

Cost $
Tuition: $56/credit
(Nonresident: $221/credit)
Room & Board: $8,610

Enrollment Profile

Full-time: 846	Work Exp: 95%
Part-time: 0	International: 17%
Total: 846	Women: 30%
Average Age: 27	Minorities: 19%

Class Size: 19 - 61

ACADEMICS

Length of Program Minimum: 24 months. Maximum: 2 years.

Calendar Semesters.

Full-time Classes Main campus; day, summer.

Degree Requirements 60 credits including 33 elective credits.

Required Courses Financial accounting, financial management, information management, legal environment of business, managerial economics, managing people and organizations, marketing management, operations management, statistics and research methods, strategic management.

Curricular Focus Leadership, market-driven curriculum, teamwork.

Concentrations Accounting, entrepreneurship, environmental management, information management, finance, human resources management, management information systems, marketing, operations management, organizational behavior.

Faculty Full-time: 110, 99% with doctorates; part-time: 20, 50% with doctorates.

Teaching Methodology Case study: 40%, lecture: 30%, research: 5%, seminars by members of the business community: 5%, student presentations: 10%, team projects: 10%.

Special Opportunities International exchange in France, Germany, Mexico. Internship program available. Other: 12 one-semester foreign exchange programs.

STUDENT STATISTICS

Geographic Representation By region: South 50%; West 12%; Northeast 10%; Midwest 9%. International 17%.

Undergraduate Majors Business 23%; engineering/technology 24%; humanities 10%; science/mathematics 5%; social sciences 24%; other 14%.

Other Background Graduate degrees in other disciplines: 10%. Work experience: On average, students have 4 years of work experience on entrance to the program.

FACILITIES

Information Resources Main library with 6.8 million bound volumes, 4.2 million titles on microform, 51,338 periodical subscriptions, 91,167 records/tapes/CDs, 284 CD-ROMs. Business collection includes 180,000 bound volumes, 110 periodical subscriptions, 800 videos.

Housing College housing available.

Technology Computers are used moderately in course work. Computer terminals/PCs, linked by a campus-wide computer network, are available for use by students in program; they are located in classrooms, the computer center, computer labs. Students in the program are not required to have their own PC. $125 are budgeted per student for computer support.

Computer Resources/On-line Services

Training	Yes	Dun's	Yes
Internet	Yes	Dow Jones	No
E-Mail	Yes	Dialog	No
LEXIS/NEXIS	Yes	Bloomberg	No
CompuServe	Yes		

ADMISSION

Acceptance 1994-95 2,679 applied for admission; 35% were accepted.

Entrance Requirements Bachelor's degree, GMAT score.

Application Requirements Written essay, application form, copies of transcript, resume/curriculum vitae, 2 letters of recommendation.

Application Deadlines 4/15 for fall. Applications are processed on a rolling basis.

FINANCIALS

Costs for 1994-95 Tuition: Full-time: $56/credit for state residents, $221/credit for nonresidents, $221/credit for international students. Fees: Full-time: $878/semester for state residents, $878/semester for nonresidents, $898/semester for international students. Average room and board costs are $8,610 per academic year (on-campus) and $8,610 per academic year (off-campus).

Financial Aid In 1994-95, candidates received some institutionally administered aid in the form of grants, scholarships, loans, fellowships, assistantships. Total awards ranged from $200-$7,500. Application deadlines: 3/31 for fall, 10/1 for spring, 2/15 for summer. Applications are processed on a rolling basis. Contact: Ms. Laura Caballero, Student Financial Aid Officer, Austin, TX 78712. (512) 471-7612.

INTERNATIONAL STUDENTS

Demographics 17% of students enrolled in the program are international; North America 82%, Asia 6%, Europe 4%, Central America 3%, Australia 2%, South America 2%, Africa 1%.

Services and Facilities International student office, international student center, visa services, language tutoring, ESL courses, special assistance for nonnative speakers of English, counseling/support services.

Applying TOEFL required, minimum score of 550; proof of health; proof of adequate funds. Financial aid is not available to international students. Admission application deadline: 2/1 for fall. Applications are processed on a rolling basis. Contact: Mrs. Darlene Gavenda, Assistant Director, International Office, Austin, TX 78712. (512) 471-1211.

PLACEMENT

In 1993-94, 263 organizations participated in on-campus recruiting; 2,100 on-campus interviews were conducted. Placement services include alumni network, career counseling/planning, career fairs, career library, career placement, electronic job bank, job interviews, job search course, resume preparation, and resume referral to employers. Of 1994 graduates, 93% were employed within three months of graduation, the average starting salary was $54,000.

Jobs by Employer Type Manufacturing 36%; service 43%; consulting 21%.

Jobs by Functional Area Marketing/sales 21%; finance 36%; management 12%; technical management 6%; consulting 25%.

Program Contact: Ms. Fran Forbes, Director of Admissions, University of Texas at Austin, Austin, TX 78712. (512) 471-3434; Internet Address: texasmba@mailbox.bus.utexas.edu.

University of Texas at Dallas

School of Management

Richardson, Texas

OVERVIEW

The University of Texas at Dallas is a state-supported coed institution. Part of University of Texas System. Founded 1969. Setting: 455-acre suburban campus with easy access to Dallas. Total institutional enrollment: 9,000. Program was first offered in 1975.

MBA HIGHLIGHTS

Entrance Difficulty***
Mean GMAT: 524
Mean GPA: N/R

Cost $
Tuition: $82 - $91/semester hour
(Nonresident: $227 - $236/semester hour)
Room & Board: N/R

Enrollment Profile

Full-time: N/R	Work Exp: 98%
Part-time: N/R	International: 25%
Total: 751	Women: 50%
Average Age: 31	Minorities: N/R

Average Class Size: 40

ACADEMICS

Length of Program Minimum: 24 months. Maximum: 6 years.

Calendar Semesters.

Full-time Classes Main campus; day, evening, summer.

Part-time Classes Main campus; day, evening, summer.

Degree Requirements 48 semester hours including 9-12 elective semester hours.

Required Courses Accounting for managers, business strategy, finance, global economy, introduction to operations research, marketing management, operations management, organizational behavior, social and political environment of business, statistics.

Curricular Focus International business, organizational development and change management, problem solving and decision making.

Concentrations Arts administration, entrepreneurship, finance, health services, hotel management, human resources management, management information systems, marketing, operations management, organizational behavior, public administration, public policy, real estate, strategic management, transportation.

Faculty Full-time: 38, 99% with doctorates; part-time: 8, 10% with doctorates.

Teaching Methodology Case study: 30%, faculty seminars: 5%, lecture: 35%, research: 10%, seminars by members of the business community: 5%, student presentations: 10%, team projects: 5%.

Special Opportunities International exchange in Mexico, Russia, Sweden. Internship program available.

STUDENT STATISTICS
Geographic Representation State residents 90%. International 25%.

Undergraduate Majors Business 65%; engineering/technology 10%; humanities 5%; science/mathematics 5%; social sciences 10%; other 5%.

Other Background Graduate degrees in other disciplines: 20%. Work experience: On average, students have 8-10 years of work experience on entrance to the program.

FACILITIES
Information Resources Main library with 474,576 bound volumes, 1.5 million titles on microform, 2,630 periodical subscriptions, 3,314 records/tapes/CDs, 27 CD-ROMs.

Housing College housing available.

Technology Computers are used moderately in course work. 50 computer terminals/PCs, linked by a campus-wide computer network, are available for use by students in program; they are located in the library, the computer center, computer labs. Students in the program are not required to have their own PC.

Computer Resources/On-line Services

Training	Yes	Videoconference Center	Yes
E-Mail	No		

ADMISSION
Acceptance 1994-95 336 applied for admission; 89% were accepted.

Entrance Requirements Bachelor's degree, prerequisite courses required for applicants with non-business degree, GMAT score of 450, minimum 3.0 GPA. Core courses waived through: previous course work.

Application Requirements Application form, copies of transcript, personal statement, 3 letters of recommendation.

Application Deadlines 8/1 for fall, 12/1 for spring. Applications are processed on a rolling basis. Application discs available.

FINANCIALS
Costs for 1994-95 Tuition: Full-time: $82-$91/semester hour for state residents, $227-$236/semester hour for nonresidents; Part-time day: $92-$236/semester hour for state residents, $237-$317/semester hour for nonresidents. Fees: Full-time: $353/semester for state residents, $353/semester for nonresidents; Part-time day: $116-$191/semester for state residents, $116-$191/semester for nonresidents.

Financial Aid In 1994-95, candidates received some institutionally administered aid in the form of scholarships, loans, assistantships, work-study. Total awards ranged from $200-$5,000. Financial aid is available to part-time students. Application deadlines: 8/1 for fall, 12/1 for spring. Contact: Mr. Joe Strickland, Financial Aid Officer, PO Box 830688, MC.12, Richardson, TX 75080-0688. (214) 883-2941 Ext. 2941.

INTERNATIONAL STUDENTS
Demographics 25% of students enrolled in the program are international.

Services and Facilities International student office, special assistance for nonnative speakers of English, counseling/support services.

Applying TOEFL required, minimum score of 550. Financial aid is available to international students. Admission application deadlines: 8/1 for fall, 12/1 for spring. Contact: Ms. Samanthia Spence, PO Box 830688, MC.18, Richardson, TX 75080-0688. (214) 883-2111.

ALTERNATE MBA PROGRAM
Executive MBA (EMBA) Length of program: Minimum: 24 months. Maximum: 2 years. Part-time classes: Main campus; weekends. Degree requirements: 48 semester hours.

PLACEMENT
In 1993-94, 50 organizations participated in on-campus recruiting. Placement services include alumni network, career counseling/planning, career fairs, career placement, job interviews, resume preparation, and resume referral to employers. Of 1994 graduates, 33% were employed within three months of graduation, the average starting salary was $35,000, the range was $28,000-$55,000.

Program Contact: Dr. Gary Horton, Director of Graduate Programs, University of Texas at Dallas, PO Box 830688 GR29, Richardson, TX 75080-0688. (214) 883-2701; Fax: (214) 883-6425.

University of Texas at El Paso

College of Business Administration

El Paso, Texas

OVERVIEW
The University of Texas at El Paso is a state-supported coed institution. Part of University of Texas System. Founded 1913. Setting: 360-acre urban campus. Total institutional enrollment: 17,188. Program was first offered in 1971. AACSB-accredited.

MBA HIGHLIGHTS

Entrance Difficulty***
Mean GMAT: 450
Mean GPA: N/R

Cost $
Tuition: $56/credit hour
(Nonresident: $191/credit hour)
Room & Board: $1,005

Enrollment Profile

Full-time: 33	Work Exp: N/R
Part-time: 115	International: 21%
Total: 148	Women: 35%
Average Age: 34	Minorities: 43%

Average Class Size: 40

ACADEMICS
Length of Program Minimum: 27 months.

Calendar Semesters.

Full-time Classes Main campus; evening, weekends, summer.

Part-time Classes Main campus; evening, weekends, summer.

Degree Requirements 36 credits.

Curricular Focus General management.

Concentration Management.

Faculty Full-time: 25, 100% with doctorates.

Teaching Methodology Case study: 20%, lecture: 60%, student presentations: 10%, team projects: 10%.

Special Opportunities International exchange and internship programs available.

STUDENT STATISTICS
Geographic Representation By region: West 85%.

FACILITIES
Information Resources Main library with 773,553 bound volumes, 4,000 titles on microform, 3,270 periodical subscriptions, 2,122 records/tapes/CDs.

Housing 1% of students in program live in college-owned or -operated housing.

Technology Computers are used moderately in course work. 200 computer terminals/PCs, linked by a campus-wide computer network, are available for use by students in program; they are located in the library, the computer center, computer labs. Students in the program are not required to have their own PC.

Computer Resources/On-line Services

Training	No	E-Mail	Yes
Internet	Yes	Multimedia Center	Yes

Other on-line services: OCLC.

ADMISSION
Acceptance 1994-95 131 applied for admission; 44% were accepted.

Entrance Requirements Bachelor's degree, GMAT score of 500, minimum 2.75 GPA. Core courses waived through: previous course work, work experience.

Application Requirements Application form, copies of transcript.

Application Deadlines 7/1 for fall, 11/15 for spring, 4/1 for summer.

FINANCIALS
Costs for 1994-95 Tuition: Part-time evening: $56/credit hour for state residents, $191/credit hour for nonresidents. Fees: Part-time evening: $328/semester for state residents, $328/semester for nonresidents. Average room and board costs are $1,005 per academic year (on-campus).

Financial Aid Financial aid is available to part-time students. Application deadlines: 7/1 for fall, 11/15 for spring, 4/1 for summer. Contact: Ms. Linda Gonzalez-Hensgen, Director of Financial Aid, West Union 202, El Paso, TX 79968. (915) 747-5204.

INTERNATIONAL STUDENTS

Demographics 21% of students enrolled in the program are international; Central America 65%, Asia 16%, Africa 6%, Europe 6%, other 7%.

Services and Facilities International student office, visa services, ESL courses, special assistance for nonnative speakers of English, counseling/support services.

Applying TOEFL required, minimum score of 600; proof of health; proof of adequate funds. Financial aid is available to international students. Financial aid application deadlines: 7/1 for fall, 11/15 for spring, 4/1 for summer. Admission application deadlines: 7/1 for fall, 11/15 for spring, 4/1 for summer. Contact: Ms. Debbie Agthe, Director, International Student Office, West Union 211, El Paso, TX 79968. (915) 747-5664.

PLACEMENT

Placement services include career counseling/planning, career fairs, career placement, and job interviews.

Program Contact: Mr. Michael Robertson, Graduate Adviser, University of Texas at El Paso, College of Business, El Paso, TX 79968. (915) 747-5241; Fax: (915) 747-5147.

University of Texas at San Antonio

San Antonio, Texas

OVERVIEW

The University of Texas at San Antonio is a state-supported comprehensive coed institution. Part of University of Texas System. Founded 1969. Setting: 600-acre suburban campus. Total institutional enrollment: 17,097. AACSB-accredited.

MBA HIGHLIGHTS

Entrance Difficulty*
Mean GMAT: 525
Mean GPA: N/R

Cost $
Tuition: $144/course
(Nonresident: $516/course)
Room & Board: $4,000

Enrollment Profile
Full-time: N/R
Part-time: N/R
Total: 600
Average Age: N/R

Work Exp: N/R
International: 15%
Women: 52%
Minorities: 22%

Average Class Size: 22

ACADEMICS

Length of Program Minimum: 15 months.

Calendar Semesters.

Full-time Classes Main campus; evening, summer.

Part-time Classes Main campus.

Degree Requirements 33 hours.

Curricular Focus General management, international business, problem solving and decision making.

Concentrations Accounting, economics, finance, human resources management, international business, management information systems, technology management, management science taxation.

Teaching Methodology Case study: 5%, faculty seminars: 5%, lecture: 50%, research: 10%, seminars by members of the business community: 10%, student presentations: 10%, team projects: 10%.

STUDENT STATISTICS

Geographic Representation State residents 78%. International 15%.

FACILITIES

Information Resources Main library with 464,148 bound volumes, 2.1 million titles on microform, 2,148 periodical subscriptions, 7,108 records/tapes/CDs, 77 CD-ROMs.

Housing College housing available.

ADMISSION

Entrance Requirements Bachelor's degree, GMAT score of 500, minimum 3.0 GPA.

Application Requirements Application form, copies of transcript.

Application Deadlines 7/1 for fall, 12/1 for spring, 5/1 for summer. Applications are processed on a rolling basis.

FINANCIALS

Costs for 1994-95 Tuition: Part-time day: $144/course for state residents, $516/course for nonresidents. Fees: Part-time day: $120/semester for state residents, $120/semester for nonresidents. Average room and board costs are $4,000 per academic year (on-campus) and $4,000 per academic year (off-campus).

Financial Aid Contact: Ms. Cynthia Smith, Assistant Vice President for Financial Aid, 6900 North Loop 1604 West, San Antonio, TX 78249-1130. (210) 691-4313.

INTERNATIONAL STUDENTS

Demographics 15% of students enrolled in the program are international.

Applying TOEFL required, minimum score of 550. Admission application deadlines: 6/1 for fall, 10/15 for spring, 3/1 for summer. Applications are processed on a rolling basis.

Program Contact: Dr. Lynda De La Vina, Associate Dean for Graduate Programs, University of Texas at San Antonio, 6900 North Loop 1604 West, San Antonio, TX 78249-1130. (210) 691-4313; Fax: (210) 691-4308.

University of Texas at Tyler

School of Business Administration

Tyler, Texas

OVERVIEW

The University of Texas at Tyler is a state-supported upper-level coed institution. Part of University of Texas System. Founded 1971. Setting: 200-acre small-town campus. Total institutional enrollment: 3,972. Program was first offered in 1975.

MBA HIGHLIGHTS

Entrance Difficulty**
Mean GMAT: 500
Mean GPA: 3.1

Cost $
Tuition: $30/credit hour
(Nonresident: $171/credit hour)
Room & Board: $2,700 (off-campus)

Enrollment Profile
Full-time: 5
Part-time: 121
Total: 126
Average Age: 32

Work Exp: 100%
International: 5%
Women: 40%
Minorities: 5%

Average Class Size: 15

ACADEMICS

Length of Program Minimum: 24 months. Maximum: 6 years.

Calendar Semesters.

Full-time Classes Main campus; evening.

Part-time Classes Main campus; evening.

Degree Requirements 36 credit hours including 9 elective credit hours.

Curricular Focus Business issues and problems, managing diversity, problem solving and decision making.

Concentrations Accounting, finance, health services, human resources management, management, marketing, organizational behavior.

Faculty Full-time: 10, 100% with doctorates.

Teaching Methodology Case study: 10%, lecture: 50%, research: 10%, seminars by members of the business community: 10%, student presentations: 10%, team projects: 10%.

STUDENT STATISTICS

Geographic Representation State residents 93%. By region: South 95%. International 5%.

Undergraduate Majors Business 70%; engineering/technology 20%; nursing 10%.

Other Background Graduate degrees in other disciplines: 1%. Work experience: On average, students have 2-5 years of work experience on entrance to the program.

FACILITIES
Information Resources Main library with 180,226 bound volumes, 446,466 titles on microform, 1,521 periodical subscriptions.

Housing College housing not available.

Technology Computers are used moderately in course work. 60 computer terminals/PCs, linked by a campus-wide computer network, are available for use by students in program; they are located in learning resource center, the library, the computer center, computer labs. Students in the program are not required to have their own PC.

Computer Resources/On-line Services

Training	Yes	Dialog	Yes
Internet	Yes		

ADMISSION
Entrance Requirements Bachelor's degree, GMAT score, index score comprised of GMAT and last 60 hours of bachelors degree. Core courses waived through: previous course work.

Application Requirements Application form, copies of transcript.

Application Deadlines 11/1 for fall, 4/1 for spring.

FINANCIALS
Estimated Costs for 1995-96 Tuition: Part-time evening: $30/credit hour for state residents, $171/credit hour for nonresidents. Fees: Part-time evening: $22/credit hour for state residents, $22/credit hour for nonresidents. Average room and board costs are $2,700 per academic year (off-campus).

Financial Aid In 1994-95, 7% of candidates received some institutionally administered aid in the form of grants, loans. Total awards ranged from $500-$2,500. Financial aid is available to part-time students. Application deadlines: 11/1 for fall, 4/1 for spring. Contact: Ms. Veronica Torrez, Director, 3900 University Boulevard, Tyler, TX 75799-0001. (903) 566-7180.

INTERNATIONAL STUDENTS
Demographics 5% of students enrolled in the program are international; Asia 50%, Europe 50%.

Applying TOEFL required, minimum score of 550. Financial aid is available to international students. Financial aid application deadlines: 11/1 for fall, 4/1 for spring. Admission application deadlines: 6/1 for fall, 12/1 for spring.

ALTERNATE MBA PROGRAM
MBA/MSN Length of program: Minimum: 36 months. Maximum: 6 years. Degree requirements: 75 credit hours including 36 elective credit hours.

PLACEMENT
Placement services include career counseling/planning, career fairs, and career placement.

Program Contact: Dr. Mary Fischer, Coordinator, Graduate Programs, University of Texas at Tyler, 3900 University Boulevard, Tyler, TX 75799-0001. (903) 566-7433; Fax: (903) 566-7211.

University of Texas of the Permian Basin

Division of Business

Odessa, Texas

OVERVIEW
The University of Texas of the Permian Basin is a state-supported comprehensive coed institution. Part of University of Texas System. Founded 1969. Setting: 600-acre urban campus. Total institutional enrollment: 1,989.

MBA HIGHLIGHTS
Entrance Difficulty***

Cost $
Tuition: $336/semester
(Nonresident: $2,052/semester)
Room & Board: N/R

Enrollment Profile

Full-time: N/R	Work Exp: N/R
Part-time: N/R	International: 2%
Total: 65	Women: 60%
Average Age: N/R	Minorities: 10%

Average Class Size: 12

ACADEMICS
Calendar Semesters.

Full-time Classes Main campus; evening, summer.

Degree Requirements 30 credits.

Curricular Focus Economic and financial theory, general management, strategic analysis and planning.

Concentrations Accounting, finance, management, marketing.

Teaching Methodology Case study: 30%, lecture: 30%, student presentations: 25%, team projects: 15%.

STUDENT STATISTICS
Geographic Representation State residents 95%. International 2%.

FACILITIES
Information Resources Main library with 267,531 bound volumes, 827,311 titles on microform, 723 periodical subscriptions, 6,322 records/tapes/CDs, 1 CD-ROM.

ADMISSION
Entrance Requirements Bachelor's degree, GMAT score.

Application Requirements Application form, copies of transcript, resume/curriculum vitae.

Application Deadline Applications are processed on a rolling basis.

FINANCIALS
Costs for 1994-95 Tuition: Full-time: $336/semester for state residents, $2,052/semester for nonresidents. Fees: Full-time: $302/semester for state residents, $307/semester for nonresidents.

Financial Aid Contact: Mr. Rick Renshaw, Director of Financial Aid, 4901 East University, Odessa, TX 79762-0001. (915) 552-2620.

INTERNATIONAL STUDENTS
Demographics 2% of students enrolled in the program are international.

Applying TOEFL required; proof of health; proof of adequate funds. Financial aid is not available to international students.

Program Contact: Admissions Office, University of Texas of the Permian Basin, 4901 East University, Odessa, TX 79762-0001. (915) 552-2608.

University of Texas–Pan American

School of Business Administration

Edinburg, Texas

OVERVIEW
The University of Texas–Pan American is a state-supported comprehensive coed institution. Part of University of Texas System. Founded 1927. Setting: 200-acre rural campus. Total institutional enrollment: 13,468. Program was first offered in 1975. AACSB-accredited.

MBA HIGHLIGHTS
Entrance Difficulty***
Mean GMAT: 515
Mean GPA: N/R

Cost $
Tuition: $465/semester
(Nonresident: $1,671/semester)
Room & Board: N/R

Enrollment Profile
Full-time: 27
Part-time: 46
Total: 73
Average Age: N/R

Work Exp: 80%
International: 37%
Women: 23%
Minorities: N/R

Average Class Size: 25

ACADEMICS
Length of Program Minimum: 24 months.
Calendar Semesters.
Full-time Classes Main campus; evening, weekends, summer.
Part-time Classes Main campus; evening, weekends, summer.
Degree Requirements 33 credits.
Curricular Focus General management, international business, leadership, minorities in business, teamwork.
Concentration Management.
Faculty Full-time: 18, 100% with doctorates.
Teaching Methodology Case study: 20%, lecture: 50%, research: 10%, student presentations: 10%, team projects: 10%.

STUDENT STATISTICS
Geographic Representation State residents 44%. International 37%.
Other Background Graduate degrees in other disciplines: 10%. Work experience: On average, students have 3 years of work experience on entrance to the program.

FACILITIES
Information Resources Main library with 224,012 bound volumes, 12,673 titles on microform, 2,454 periodical subscriptions, 3,943 records/tapes/CDs.

ADMISSION
Acceptance 1994-95 313 applied for admission; 21% were accepted.
Entrance Requirements Bachelor's degree, GMAT score, minimum 2.5 GPA. Core courses waived through: previous course work.
Application Requirements Application form, copies of transcript, 3 letters of recommendation.
Application Deadlines 6/15 for fall, 11/10 for spring. Applications are processed on a rolling basis.

FINANCIALS
Costs for 1994-95 Tuition: Full-time: $465/semester for state residents, $1,671/semester for nonresidents.
Financial Aid In 1994-95, candidates received some institutionally administered aid in the form of scholarships, assistantships. Application deadlines: 4/15 for fall, 9/16 for spring. Contact: Mr. Arnold Trejo, Director of Financial Aid, 1201 West University Drive, Edinburg, TX 78539. (210) 381-2501.

INTERNATIONAL STUDENTS
Demographics 37% of students enrolled in the program are international; Asia 60%, Central America 20%, Africa 10%, Europe 10%.
Applying TOEFL required, minimum score of 600; proof of adequate funds. Financial aid is available to international students. Financial aid application deadlines: 6/1 for fall, 10/1 for spring. Applications are processed on a rolling basis. Admission application deadlines: 6/13 for fall, 11/10 for spring. Applications are processed on a rolling basis.

Program Contact: Dr. Vern Vincent, Director of Graduate Studies, University of Texas–Pan American, 1201 West University Drive, Edinburg, TX 78539. (210) 381-3311 Ext. 2317; Fax: (210) 381-3712.

Wayland Baptist University

Division of Business

Plainview, Texas

OVERVIEW
Wayland Baptist University is an independent Baptist comprehensive coed institution. Founded 1908. Setting: 80-acre small-town campus. Total institutional enrollment: 3,500. Program was first offered in 1983.

MBA HIGHLIGHTS
Entrance Difficulty***
Mean GMAT: 500
Mean GPA: 3.0

Cost $$
Tuition: $180/semester hour
Room & Board: N/R

Enrollment Profile
Full-time: 65
Part-time: 61
Total: 126
Average Age: 35

Work Exp: 95%
International: 0%
Women: 36%
Minorities: 30%

Average Class Size: 14

ACADEMICS
Length of Program Minimum: 12 months. Maximum: 6 years.
Calendar Semesters on main campus, quarters at off-campus locations.
Full-time Classes Main campus, Amarillo, Lubbock, Wichita Falls; day, evening, weekends.
Part-time Classes Main campus, Amarillo, Lubbock, Wichita Falls; day, evening, weekends.
Degree Requirements 36 credits including 3 elective credits.
Required Courses Business ethics, management information systems, managerial accounting, managerial finance, marketing analysis, organization theory. Courses may be waived through: previous course work.
Curricular Focus Business issues and problems, general management, problem solving and decision making.
Concentrations Accounting, computer information systems, health services, management.
Faculty Full-time: 4, 75% with doctorates; part-time: 4, 75% with doctorates.
Teaching Methodology Case study: 1%, faculty seminars: 1%, lecture: 80%, research: 1%, seminars by members of the business community: 2%, student presentations: 10%, team projects: 5%.
Special Opportunities Internships include banking, accounting, and healthcare.

STUDENT STATISTICS
Geographic Representation State residents 90%.
Undergraduate Majors Business 92%; engineering/technology 1%; humanities 2%; nursing 2%; social sciences 2%; other 1%.
Other Background Graduate degrees in other disciplines: 1%. Work experience: On average, students have 8 years of work experience on entrance to the program.

FACILITIES
Information Resources Main library with 128,432 bound volumes, 75,275 titles on microform, 760 periodical subscriptions, 22,597 records/tapes/CDs. Business collection includes 4,880 bound volumes, 47 periodical subscriptions, 35 videos.
Housing 1% of students in program live in college-owned or -operated housing.
Technology Computers are used moderately in course work. 32 computer terminals/PCs are available for use by students in program; they are located in the library, computer labs. Students in the program are not required to have their own PC.

Computer Resources/On-line Services

Training	Yes	LEXIS/NEXIS	Yes
E-Mail	No		

ADMISSION
Acceptance 1994-95 Of those applying, 98% were accepted.
Entrance Requirements Bachelor's degree, prerequisite courses required for applicants with non-business degree, GMAT score of 500, minimum 2.7 GPA. Core courses waived through: previous course work.
Application Requirements Application form.
Application Deadline Applications are processed on a rolling basis.

FINANCIALS
Costs for 1994-95 Tuition: Full-time: $180/semester hour. Fees: Full-time: $175/semester.
Financial Aid In 1994-95, 37% of candidates received some institutionally administered aid in the form of scholarships, assistantships. Financial aid is available to part-time students. Application deadlines: 7/15 for

fall, 11/15 for spring. Contact: Mr. Harold Whitis, Director of Financial Aid, 1900 West Seventh Street, Plainview, TX 79072-6998. (806) 296-4713.

INTERNATIONAL STUDENTS
Services and Facilities Language tutoring, counseling/support services.

Applying TOEFL required, minimum score of 500; proof of health; proof of adequate funds. Financial aid is available to international students. Financial aid application deadlines: 7/1 for fall, 11/1 for spring. Admission application deadlines: 7/1 for fall, 11/1 for spring.

PLACEMENT
In 1993-94, 1 organization participated in on-campus recruiting; 10 on-campus interviews were conducted. Placement services include career counseling/planning, career fairs, career placement, resume preparation, and resume referral to employers. Of 1994 graduates, 99% were employed within three months of graduation.

Program Contact: Dr. Wallace L. Duvall, Director of Graduate Studies, Wayland Baptist University, 1900 West Seventh Street, Plainview, TX 79072-6998. (806) 296-4727, or (800) 588-1928; Fax: (806) 296-4580.

West Texas A&M University

T. Boone Pickens College of Business

Canyon, Texas

OVERVIEW
West Texas A&M University is a state-supported comprehensive coed institution. Part of Texas A&M University System. Founded 1909. Setting: 128-acre small-town campus. Total institutional enrollment: 6,638.

MBA HIGHLIGHTS

Entrance Difficulty***
Mean GMAT: 520
Mean GPA: N/R

Cost $
Tuition: $342/semester
(Nonresident: $1,629/semester)
Room & Board: $1,990

Enrollment Profile

Full-time: N/R	Work Exp: N/R
Part-time: N/R	International: 12%
Total: 190	Women: 40%
Average Age: N/R	Minorities: 15%

Average Class Size: 25

ACADEMICS
Length of Program Minimum: 24 months.

Calendar Semesters.

Full-time Classes Main campus; day, evening, weekends, summer.

Degree Requirements 36 credits.

Curricular Focus Economic and financial theory, general management, international business.

Concentrations Accounting, economics, finance, international business, management, marketing.

Teaching Methodology Case study: 5%, lecture: 50%, research: 5%, seminars by members of the business community: 5%, student presentations: 15%, team projects: 20%.

STUDENT STATISTICS
Geographic Representation State residents 80%. International 12%.

FACILITIES
Information Resources Main library with 270,610 bound volumes, 26,800 titles on microform, 244 periodical subscriptions, 550 records/tapes/CDs, 3 CD-ROMs.

Housing College housing available.

ADMISSION
Entrance Requirements Bachelor's degree.

Application Requirements Application form, copies of transcript.

Application Deadline Applications are processed on a rolling basis.

FINANCIALS
Costs for 1994-95 Tuition: Full-time: $342/semester for state residents, $1,629/semester for nonresidents. Fees: Full-time: $267/semester for state residents, $267/semester for nonresidents. Average room and board costs are $1,990 per academic year (on-campus) and $1,468 per academic year (off-campus).

Financial Aid Application deadlines: 3/1 for fall, 11/1 for spring. Contact: Ms. Lynda Tinsley, Director of Financial Aid, WTAMU Box 748, Canyon, TX 79016-0001. (866) 656-2055.

INTERNATIONAL STUDENTS
Demographics 12% of students enrolled in the program are international.

Applying TOEFL required, minimum score of 500; proof of health; proof of adequate funds. Financial aid is available to international students. Financial aid application deadline: 3/1 for fall.

Program Contact: Dr. Ron R. Hinen, Graduate Coordinator, College of Business, West Texas A&M University, WTAMU Box 748, Canyon, TX 79016-0001. (806) 656-2525; Fax: (806) 656-2927.

UTAH

Brigham Young University

Marriott School of Management

Provo, Utah

OVERVIEW
Brigham Young University is an independent coed institution, affiliated with Church of Jesus Christ of Latter-day Saints. Founded 1875. Setting: 633-acre suburban campus. Total institutional enrollment: 27,000. Program was first offered in 1964. AACSB-accredited.

MBA HIGHLIGHTS

Entrance Difficulty****
Mean GMAT: 598
Mean GPA: 3.49

Cost $$
Tuition: $2,300 - $3,450/semester
Room & Board: $800

Enrollment Profile

Full-time: N/R	Work Exp: 45%
Part-time: N/R	International: 20%
Total: 372	Women: 18%
Average Age: 26	Minorities: 2%

Average Class Size: N/R

ACADEMICS
Length of Program Minimum: 16 months. Maximum: 5 years.

Calendar Semesters.

Full-time Classes Main campus; day.

Degree Requirements 60 credits including 15 elective credits.

Required Courses Business finance, business government and international economy, business policy, data analysis, data exploration, ethics business and society, integrative exercise, introduction to strategy, macro economics and business environment, management and technology, management seminar, marketing management, operations management, organizational behavior, written and oral communication.

Curricular Focus Leadership, problem solving and decision making, teamwork.

Concentrations Accounting, finance, international business, marketing, operations management, organizational behavior.

Faculty Full-time: 50, 100% with doctorates.

Teaching Methodology Case study: 60%, lecture: 20%, student presentations: 10%, team projects: 10%.

STUDENT STATISTICS
Geographic Representation State residents 80%. International 20%.

Undergraduate Majors Business 29%; engineering/technology 9%; humanities 27%; science/mathematics 9%; social sciences 16%; other 10%.

Other Background Graduate degrees in other disciplines: 5%.

FACILITIES
Information Resources Main library with 2.3 million bound volumes, 2.2 million titles on microform, 18,067 periodical subscriptions, 49,291 records/tapes/CDs.

Housing College housing available.

Technology Computers are used heavily in course work. 130 computer terminals/PCs, linked by a campus-wide computer network, are available for use by students in program; they are located in computer labs, graduate computer room.

Computer Resources/On-line Services

Training	Yes	CompuServe	No
Internet	Yes	Dun's	No
E-Mail	Yes	Dow Jones	No
Multimedia Center	Yes	Dialog	No
LEXIS/NEXIS	Yes	Bloomberg	Yes

ADMISSION
Acceptance 1994-95 349 applied for admission; 51% were accepted.

Entrance Requirements Bachelor's degree, prefer applicants with non-business degree, GMAT score of 520, minimum 3.0 GPA.

Application Requirements Written essay, application form, copies of transcript, personal statement, 3 letters of recommendation.

Application Deadlines 3/1 for fall. Applications are processed on a rolling basis.

FINANCIALS
Estimated Costs for 1995-96 Tuition: Full-time: $2,300-$3,450/semester. Average room and board costs are $800 per academic year (on-campus) and $800 per academic year (off-campus).

Financial Aid In 1994-95, 33% of candidates received some institutionally administered aid in the form of scholarships, assistantships, internships. Total awards ranged from $200-$6,900. Financial aid is not available to part-time students. Application deadline: 3/1 for fall. Contact: Ms. Delora Bertelson, Assistant to the Dean, Provo, UT 84602-1001. (801) 378-6824.

INTERNATIONAL STUDENTS
Demographics 20% of students enrolled in the program are international.

Services and Facilities International student center, ESL courses, counseling/support services.

Applying TOEFL required, minimum score of 570; proof of health; proof of adequate funds. Financial aid is available to international students. Financial aid application deadline: 3/1 for fall. Admission application deadline: 3/1 for fall.

ALTERNATE MBA PROGRAM
Executive MBA (EMBA) Length of program: Minimum: 24 months. Maximum: 5 years. Full-time classes: Main campus, Salt Lake City; evening, weekends, summer.

PLACEMENT
In 1993-94, 176 organizations participated in on-campus recruiting; 1,384 on-campus interviews were conducted. Placement services include alumni network, career counseling/planning, career placement, electronic job bank, job interviews, resume preparation, and resume referral to employers. Of 1994 graduates, 93% were employed within three months of graduation, the average starting salary was $49,000, the range was $30,000-$118,000.

Jobs by Employer Type Manufacturing 33%; service 51%; consulting 11%; nonprofit 5%.

Jobs by Functional Area Marketing/sales 22%; finance 34%; operations 16%; management 5%; other 12%; consulting 11%.

Program Contact: Dr. Gary McKinnon, Director, MBA Program, Brigham Young University, 640 Tanner Building, Provo, UT 84602-1001. (801) 378-3500; Fax: (801) 378-4808.

University of Utah

David Eccles School of Business

Salt Lake City, Utah

OVERVIEW
The University of Utah is a state-supported coed institution. Part of Utah System of Higher Education. Founded 1850. Setting: 1,500-acre urban campus. Total institutional enrollment: 27,000. Program was first offered in 1955. AACSB-accredited.

MBA HIGHLIGHTS
Entrance Difficulty****
Mean GMAT: 581
Mean GPA: 3.53

Cost $
Tuition: $748/quarter
(Nonresident: $2,638/quarter)
Room & Board: $7,368

Enrollment Profile

Full-time: 86	Work Exp: 88%
Part-time: 115	International: 7%
Total: 201	Women: 27%
Average Age: 27	Minorities: 4%

Average Class Size: 35

ACADEMICS
Length of Program Minimum: 11 months. Maximum: 6 years.

Calendar Quarters.

Full-time Classes Main campus; day, evening.

Part-time Classes Main campus; day, evening.

Degree Requirements 64 credits including 5-7 elective credits.

Required Courses Business statistics, financial accounting, financial management, introduction to business strategy, leadership, team effectiveness, and communication, management of information systems, managerial accounting, managerial economics, marketing analysis, marketing management, planning and strategy, production and operations management. Courses may be waived through: previous course work.

Curricular Focus General management, international business, teamwork.

Concentrations Entrepreneurship, finance, health services, international business, management, marketing, operations management.

Faculty Full-time: 64, 97% with doctorates; part-time: 17, 59% with doctorates.

Teaching Methodology Case study: 40%, lecture: 20%, seminars by members of the business community: 5%, student presentations: 15%, team projects: 20%.

Special Opportunities International exchange in France, Germany, Japan, Mexico. Internship program available.

STUDENT STATISTICS
Geographic Representation State residents 81%. By region: West 87%; Northeast 3%; Midwest 3%; South 2%. International 7%.

Undergraduate Majors Business 43%; education 2%; engineering/technology 16%; humanities 15%; science/mathematics 7%; social sciences 14%; other 3%.

Other Background Graduate degrees in other disciplines: 6%. Work experience: On average, students have 4 years of work experience on entrance to the program.

FACILITIES
Information Resources Main library with 2.3 million bound volumes, 3.1 million titles on microform, 21,807 periodical subscriptions, 35,538 records/tapes/CDs. Business collection includes 92,758 bound volumes, 1,622 periodical subscriptions, 25 CD-ROMs, 95 videos.

Housing 2% of students in program live in college-owned or -operated housing.

Technology Computers are used heavily in course work. 1,000 computer terminals/PCs, linked by a campus-wide computer network, are available for use by students in program; they are located in the student center, classrooms, learning resource center, the library, the computer center, computer labs. Students in the program are not required to have their own PC. $150 are budgeted per student for computer support.

Computer Resources/On-line Services

Training	Yes	CompuServe	No
Internet	Yes	Dun's	No
E-Mail	Yes	Dow Jones	No
Multimedia Center	Yes	Dialog	No
LEXIS/NEXIS	Yes	Bloomberg	Yes

Other on-line services: OCLC.

ADMISSION
Acceptance 1994-95 Of those applying, 75% were accepted.

Entrance Requirements Bachelor's degree, GMAT score, minimum 3.0 GPA. Core courses waived through: previous course work.

Application Requirements Written essay, application form, copies of transcript, resume/curriculum vitae, 2 letters of recommendation.

Application Deadlines 2/15 for fall, 2/15 for summer.

FINANCIALS
Costs for 1994-95 Tuition: Full-time: $748/quarter for state residents, $2,638/quarter for nonresidents. Fees: Full-time: $144/quarter for state residents, $144/quarter for nonresidents. Average room and board costs are $7,368 per academic year (on-campus) and $7,368 per academic year (off-campus).

Financial Aid Financial aid is available to part-time students. Application deadlines: 2/15 for fall, 2/15 for summer. Contact: Mr. Harold Weight, Director of Financial Aid, 105 SSB, Salt Lake City, UT 84112. (801) 581-6211.

INTERNATIONAL STUDENTS
Demographics 7% of students enrolled in the program are international; Asia 72%, Europe 14%, other 14%.

Services and Facilities International student office, international student center, visa services, language tutoring, ESL courses, special assistance for nonnative speakers of English.

Applying TOEFL required, minimum score of 560; proof of health; proof of adequate funds; minimum score of 250 on Test of Spoken English. Financial aid is available to international students. Financial aid application deadline: 2/15 for fall. Admission application deadline: 2/15 for fall. Contact: Ms. Marilyn L. Owen, Foreign Student Adviser, International Center, 159 Union, Salt Lake City, UT 84112. (801) 581-8876.

ALTERNATE MBA PROGRAMS
Executive MBA (EMBA) Length of program: Minimum: 21 months. Maximum: 6 years. Degree requirements: 72 credits. Minimum 5 years work experience. Average class size: 35.

One-Year MBA Length of program: Minimum: 12 months. Maximum: 6 years. Degree requirements: 64 credits including 6-7 elective credits. Undergraduate degree in business. Average class size: 40.

MBA/JD Length of program: Minimum: 36 months. Maximum: 6 years. Degree requirements: Separate applications must be submitted to both law and business prior to second year; 48 credits in business, 64.5 hours in law. Average class size: 60.

MBA/M Arch Length of program: Minimum: 36 months. Maximum: 6 years. Degree requirements: 136 credits. Separate applications must be submitted to both business and architecture. Average class size: 20.

PLACEMENT
In 1993-94, 106 organizations participated in on-campus recruiting. Placement services include alumni network, career counseling/planning, career fairs, career library, career placement, electronic job bank, job interviews, job search course, resume preparation, and resume referral to employers. Of 1994 graduates, 92% were employed within three months of graduation, the average starting salary was $38,042, the range was $22,500-$100,000.

Jobs by Employer Type Manufacturing 28%; service 41%; government 14%; consulting 5%; nonprofit 4%; other 8%.

Jobs by Functional Area Marketing/sales 12%; finance 53%; management 8%; technical management 17%; other 10%.

Program Contact: Ms. Carrie Radmall, Admissions Specialist, University of Utah, 460 BuC, Salt Lake City, UT 84112. (801) 581-7785; Fax: (801) 581-7214.

Utah State University

College of Business

Logan, Utah

OVERVIEW
Utah State University is a state-supported coed institution. Part of Utah System of Higher Education. Founded 1888. Setting: 456-acre urban campus. Total institutional enrollment: 17,555. Program was first offered in 1961. AACSB-accredited.

MBA HIGHLIGHTS

Entrance Difficulty**
Mean GMAT: 560
Mean GPA: 3.4

Cost $
Tuition: $622/quarter
(Nonresident: $1,869/quarter)
Room & Board: N/R

Enrollment Profile

Full-time: 85	Work Exp: 80%
Part-time: 75	International: 15%
Total: 160	Women: 15%
Average Age: 27	Minorities: 3%

Class Size: 30 - 35

ACADEMICS
Length of Program Minimum: 9 months. Maximum: 6 years.

Calendar Quarters.

Full-time Classes Main campus; day, evening, early morning, summer.

Part-time Classes Main campus, Ogden; evening, summer.

Degree Requirements 45 credits including 9 elective credits.

Required Courses Accounting, finance, information systems, leadership management, marketing, operations management, organizational behavior, statistics, strategic planning. Courses may be waived through: previous course work.

Curricular Focus Organizational development and change management, strategic analysis and planning, teamwork.

Concentrations Accounting, economics, finance, human resources management, management, management information systems, marketing, organizational behavior.

Faculty Full-time: 25, 100% with doctorates.

Teaching Methodology Case study: 20%, lecture: 35%, seminars by members of the business community: 5%, student presentations: 15%, team projects: 25%.

Special Opportunities International exchange in Mexico, United Kingdom. Internship program available.

STUDENT STATISTICS
Geographic Representation State residents 70%. By region: West 80%; Northeast 3%; Midwest 2%. International 15%.

Undergraduate Majors Business 65%; engineering/technology 20%; humanities 5%; science/mathematics 2%; social sciences 7%; other 1%.

Other Background Graduate degrees in other disciplines: 3%. Work experience: On average, students have 4 years of work experience on entrance to the program.

FACILITIES
Information Resources Main library with 1.1 million bound volumes, 1.1 million titles on microform, 14,035 periodical subscriptions, 17,101 records/tapes/CDs, 2,477 CD-ROMs.

Housing 20% of students in program live in college-owned or -operated housing.

Technology Computers are used moderately in course work. 1,200 computer terminals/PCs, linked by a campus-wide computer network, are available for use by students in program; they are located in the student center, learning resource center, the library, the computer center, computer labs. Students in the program are not required to have their own PC.

Computer Resources/On-line Services

Training	Yes	Multimedia Center	Yes
Internet	Yes	LEXIS/NEXIS	Yes
E-Mail	Yes		

ADMISSION

Acceptance 1994-95 Of those applying, 55% were accepted.

Entrance Requirements Bachelor's degree, GMAT score, minimum 3.0 GPA. Core courses waived through: previous course work.

Application Requirements Application form, copies of transcript, personal statement, 3 letters of recommendation.

Application Deadlines 4/15 for fall, 1/1 for spring.

FINANCIALS

Costs for 1994-95 Tuition: Full-time: $622/quarter for state residents, $1,869/quarter for nonresidents.

Financial Aid In 1994-95, 15% of candidates received some institutionally administered aid in the form of scholarships, fellowships, assistantships. Total awards ranged from $1,000-$5,000. Financial aid is not available to part-time students. Application deadlines: 4/15 for fall, 4/15 for spring. Contact: Business Graduate Studies Office, University Hill, Logan, UT 84322. (801) 797-2360.

INTERNATIONAL STUDENTS

Demographics 15% of students enrolled in the program are international; Asia 100%.

Services and Facilities International student center, language tutoring, ESL courses, counseling/support services.

Applying TOEFL required, minimum score of 550; proof of adequate funds. Financial aid is available to international students. Financial aid application deadlines: 4/1 for fall, 4/1 for spring. Admission application deadlines: 4/15 for fall, 1/1 for spring. Contact: Ms. Afton Tew, Director, International Student Services, University Hill, Logan, UT 84322. (801) 797-1124.

PLACEMENT

In 1993-94, 20 organizations participated in on-campus recruiting. Placement services include alumni network, career counseling/planning, career fairs, career library, career placement, job interviews, resume preparation, and resume referral to employers. Of 1994 graduates, 60% were employed within three months of graduation, the average starting salary was $35,000.

Program Contact: Business Graduate Studies Office, Utah State University, University Hill, Logan, UT 84322. (801) 797-2360; Fax: (801) 797-3995.

Westminster College of Salt Lake City

Gore School of Business

Salt Lake City, Utah

OVERVIEW

Westminster College of Salt Lake City is an independent nonprofit comprehensive coed institution. Founded 1875. Setting: 27-acre suburban campus. Total institutional enrollment: 2,190. Program was first offered in 1986.

MBA HIGHLIGHTS

Entrance Difficulty***
Mean GMAT: 530
Mean GPA: N/R

Cost $
Tuition: $2,526/semester
Room & Board: N/R

Enrollment Profile

Full-time: N/R		Work Exp: N/R
Part-time: N/R		International: N/R
Total: 72		Women: 35%
Average Age: N/R		Minorities: N/R

Average Class Size: 19

ACADEMICS

Length of Program Minimum: 24 months.

Calendar Semesters.

Full-time Classes Main campus; evening, weekends, summer.

Part-time Classes Main campus; evening, weekends, summer.

Degree Requirements 43 semester hours.

Curricular Focus Entrepreneurship, general management, teamwork.

Concentrations Accounting, business economics, communication, human and organization development, entrepreneurship, finance, health services, international business, management information systems, marketing.

FACILITIES

Information Resources Main library with 74,500 bound volumes, 3,500 titles on microform, 400 periodical subscriptions, 2,700 records/tapes/CDs.

ADMISSION

Entrance Requirements Bachelor's degree, GMAT score of 500, minimum 3.0 GPA, minimum 3 years of work experience.

Application Requirements Application form, copies of transcript, resume/curriculum vitae.

Application Deadline Applications are processed on a rolling basis.

FINANCIALS

Costs for 1995-96 Tuition: Full-time: $2,526/semester; Part-time day: $358/credit hour. Fees: Full-time: $20/semester; Part-time day: $10/semester.

Financial Aid Application deadline: 4/1 for fall. Applications are processed on a rolling basis. Contact: Mr. Mark Reese, Assistant Director of Admissions, International Student Adviser, 1840 South 1300 East, Salt Lake City, UT 84105-3697. (801) 488-4200.

INTERNATIONAL STUDENTS

Applying TOEFL required, minimum score of 550; proof of adequate funds. Admission applications are processed on a rolling basis.

Program Contact: Ms. Beverly Levy, Associate Director of Admissions, Westminster College of Salt Lake City, 1840 South 1300 East, Salt Lake City, UT 84105-3697. (801) 488-4200, or (800) 798-4753 (UT only).

VERMONT

University of Vermont

School of Business Administration

Burlington, Vermont

OVERVIEW

The University of Vermont is a state-supported coed institution. Founded 1791. Setting: 425-acre suburban campus. Total institutional enrollment: 9,341. AACSB-accredited.

MBA HIGHLIGHTS

Entrance Difficulty****
Mean GMAT: 599
Mean GPA: 3.25

Cost $$
Tuition: $3,105/semester
(Nonresident: $7,758/semester)
Room & Board: N/R

Enrollment Profile

Full-time: 15		Work Exp: 95%
Part-time: 50		International: 16%
Total: 65		Women: 43%
Average Age: 27		Minorities: 3%

Average Class Size: 17

ACADEMICS

Length of Program Minimum: 24 months. Maximum: 5 years.

Calendar Semesters.

Full-time Classes Main campus; evening, summer.

Part-time Classes Main campus; evening, summer.

Degree Requirements 48 credits including 9 elective credits.

Required Courses Business policy, computer programming, corporation finance, oconomics, fundamentals of accounting, fundamentals of legal environment of business, fundamentals of marketing management, management information systems, managerial economics, organization and management studies, organizational theory, production and operations management, statistical analysis for management.

Curricular Focus General management.

Concentration Management.

Faculty Full-time: 13, 92% with doctorates.

Teaching Methodology Case study: 15%, faculty seminars: 4%, lecture: 38%, research: 9%, seminars by members of the business community: 4%, student presentations: 15%, team projects: 15%.

Special Opportunities International exchange in Germany, Russia.

STUDENT STATISTICS

Geographic Representation International 16%.

Undergraduate Majors Business 52%; engineering/technology 11%; humanities 17%; other 17%.

Other Background Work experience: On average, students have 4 years of work experience on entrance to the program.

FACILITIES

Information Resources Main library with 2.2 million bound volumes, 212,000 titles on microform, 17,300 periodical subscriptions.

Housing College housing available.

Technology Computers are used moderately in course work. 200 computer terminals/PCs, linked by a campus-wide computer network, are available for use by students in program; they are located in the library, the computer center, computer labs, graduate student offices, graduate project room. Students in the program are not required to have their own PC. $500 are budgeted per student for computer support.

Computer Resources/On-line Services

Training	No	CompuServe	No
Internet	Yes	Dun's	No
E-Mail	Yes	Dow Jones	Yes
Multimedia Center	Yes	Dialog	No
LEXIS/NEXIS	Yes	Bloomberg	No

ADMISSION

Acceptance 1994-95 65 applied for admission; 63% were accepted.

Entrance Requirements Bachelor's degree, GMAT score, minimum 2 years of work experience. Core courses waived through: previous course work.

Application Requirements Written essay, application form, copies of transcript, 3 letters of recommendation.

Application Deadlines 4/1 for fall, 11/15 for spring.

FINANCIALS

Costs for 1994-95 Tuition: Full-time: $3,105/semester for state residents, $7,758/semester for nonresidents. Fees: Full-time: $112/semester for state residents, $112/semester for nonresidents.

Financial Aid In 1994-95, candidates received some institutionally administered aid in the form of grants, loans, fellowships, assistantships, work-study. Financial aid is available to part-time students. Application deadline: 3/1 for fall. Contact: Ms. Barbara Kleh, Coordinator, MBA Graduate Admissions, Kalkin Hall, Burlington, VT 05405. (802) 656-8369.

INTERNATIONAL STUDENTS

Demographics 16% of students enrolled in the program are international; Asia 50%, Europe 40%, North America 10%.

Services and Facilities International student office, visa services, language tutoring, ESL courses, special assistance for nonnative speakers of English, counseling/support services, orientation, academic advising.

Applying TOEFL required, minimum score of 550; proof of health; proof of adequate funds. Financial aid is available to international students. Applications are processed on a rolling basis. Admission application deadlines: 3/1 for fall, 11/15 for spring. Applications are processed on a rolling basis. Contact: Ms. Jackie Seibert, International Student Adviser, L/L Center Faculty, Box 8, International Educational Services, Burlington, VT 05401. (802) 656-4296.

PLACEMENT

Placement services include alumni network, career counseling/planning, career library, career placement, job interviews, job search course, resume preparation, and resume referral to employers.

Program Contact: Ms. Barbara Kleh, Coordinator, MBA Graduate Admissions, University of Vermont, Kalkin Hall, Burlington, VT 05405. (802) 656-8369, or (800) 886-4992; Fax: (802) 656-8279; Internet Address: kleh@bsadpo.emba.uvm.edu.

VIRGINIA

Averett College

Danville, Virginia

OVERVIEW

Averett College is an independent Baptist comprehensive coed institution. Founded 1859. Setting: 25-acre urban campus. Total institutional enrollment: 2,300. Program was first offered in 1986.

MBA HIGHLIGHTS

Entrance Difficulty*
Mean GMAT: N/R
Mean GPA: 3.0

Cost $$
Tuition: $9,000/degree program
Room & Board: N/R

Enrollment Profile

Full-time: 650	Work Exp: 100%
Part-time: 0	International: 5%
Total: 650	Women: 35%
Average Age: 32	Minorities: 30%

Class Size: 18 - 20

ACADEMICS

Length of Program Minimum: 21 months. Maximum: 6 years.

Calendar Trimesters.

Full-time Classes Main campus, Washington, DC, Richmond, Roanoke, Lynchburg; evening, summer.

Degree Requirements 36 credits.

Required Courses Business legal environment, business policy and strategy, ethical issues in business, financial administration and management, introduction to graduate studies in business, management theory and analysis, managerial accounting, managerial economics, marketing management, quantitative methods and management, research project, research project 3, research projects, seminar in organizational behavior. Courses may be waived through: previous course work.

Curricular Focus General management, international business, teamwork.

Concentration Management.

Faculty Full-time: 7, 50% with doctorates; part-time: 125, 75% with doctorates.

Teaching Methodology Case study: 10%, faculty seminars: 30%, lecture: 20%, research: 5%, seminars by members of the business community: 5%, student presentations: 10%, study groups: 5%, team projects: 15%.

STUDENT STATISTICS

Geographic Representation State residents 95%. By region: South 100%. International 5%.

Undergraduate Majors Business 50%; education 3%; engineering/technology 20%; humanities 5%; science/mathematics 10%; social sciences 10%; other 2%.

Other Background Graduate degrees in other disciplines: 5%. Work experience: On average, students have 3-10 years of work experience on entrance to the program.

FACILITIES

Information Resources Main library with 127,500 bound volumes, 11,500 titles on microform, 452 periodical subscriptions, 450 records/tapes/CDs.

Housing College housing not available.

Technology Computers are used heavily in course work. 40 computer terminals/PCs are available for use by students in program; they are located in the computer center. Students in the program are required to have their own PC. $1,850 are budgeted per student for computer support.

Computer Resources/On-line Services

Training	Yes	Dow Jones	Yes
E-Mail	No	Dialog	Yes
CompuServe	Yes		

Other on-line services: OCLC.

ADMISSION

Acceptance 1994-95 910 applied for admission; 70% were accepted.

Entrance Requirements Bachelor's degree, prerequisite courses required for applicants with non-business degree, minimum 3.0 GPA, minimum 3 years of work experience. Core courses waived through: previous course work.

Application Requirements Interview, application form, copies of transcript, resume/curriculum vitae, personal statement, 3 letters of recommendation.

Application Deadline Applications are processed on a rolling basis.

FINANCIALS

Costs for 1994-95 Tuition: Full-time: $9,000/degree program.

Financial Aid Financial aid is not available to part-time students. Contact: Mrs. Pam Harris, Financial Aid Coordinator, 420 West Main Street, Danville, VA 24541-3692. (804) 791-5600.

INTERNATIONAL STUDENTS

Demographics 5% of students enrolled in the program are international.

Applying TOEFL required. Financial aid is not available to international students.

PLACEMENT

Placement services include career counseling/planning, career placement, resume preparation, and resume referral to employers. Of 1994 graduates, 100% were employed within three months of graduation.

Jobs by Employer Type Manufacturing 60%; service 20%; government 20%.

Jobs by Functional Area Marketing/sales 20%; finance 10%; operations 10%; management 50%; strategic planning 10%.

Program Contact: Ms. Katherine Pappas Smith, Admissions Counselor, Averett College, 420 West Main Street, Danville, VA 24541-3692. (804) 791-5844; Fax: (804) 791-5850.

College of William and Mary

Graduate School of Business

Williamsburg, Virginia

OVERVIEW

College of William and Mary is a state-supported coed institution. Founded 1693. Setting: 1,200-acre small-town campus with easy access to Richmond. Total institutional enrollment: 7,549. Program was first offered in 1966. AACSB-accredited.

MBA HIGHLIGHTS

Entrance Difficulty**
Mean GMAT: 580
Mean GPA: 3.15

Cost $
Tuition: $175/hour
(Nonresident: $456/hour)
Room & Board: $3,000

Enrollment Profile

Full-time: 183	Work Exp: 90%
Part-time: 135	International: 12%
Total: 318	Women: 29%
Average Age: 27	Minorities: 9%

Average Class Size: 45

ACADEMICS

Length of Program Minimum: 24 months. Maximum: 4 years.

Calendar Semesters.

Full-time Classes Main campus; day, early morning.

Part-time Classes Main campus, Newport News; evening, summer.

Degree Requirements 65 hours including 20 elective hours.

Required Courses Accounting, business policy, communications, finance, information systems, macroeconomics, marketing, microeconomics, operations management, organizational behavior, quantitative methods. Courses may be waived through: previous course work.

Curricular Focus Business issues and problems, problem solving and decision making, teamwork.

Concentrations Accounting, entrepreneurship, finance, human resources management, international business, management, management information systems, marketing, operations management, organizational behavior, quantitative analysis, real estate, strategic management.

Faculty Full-time: 50, 100% with doctorates; part-time: 8, 50% with doctorates.

Teaching Methodology Case study: 40%, lecture: 35%, seminars by members of the business community: 5%, student presentations: 10%, team projects: 10%.

Special Opportunities International exchange and internship programs available.

STUDENT STATISTICS

Geographic Representation State residents 60%. By region: Northeast 75%; Midwest 5%; West 5%; South 3%. International 12%.

Undergraduate Majors Business 35%; education 5%; engineering/technology 25%; humanities 10%; science/mathematics 10%; social sciences 10%; other 5%.

Other Background Graduate degrees in other disciplines: 2%. Work experience: On average, students have 3 years of work experience on entrance to the program.

FACILITIES

Information Resources Main library with 1.2 million bound volumes, 1.8 million titles on microform, 10,414 periodical subscriptions, 10,000 records/tapes/CDs, 15 CD-ROMs.

Housing 20% of students in program live in college-owned or -operated housing.

Technology Computers are used heavily in course work. 228 computer terminals/PCs, linked by a campus-wide computer network, are available for use by students in program; they are located in dormitories, classrooms, learning resource center, the computer center, computer labs, the research center. Students in the program are not required to have their own PC.

Computer Resources/On-line Services

Training	Yes	Videoconference Center	Yes
Internet	Yes	Dow Jones	Yes
E-Mail	Yes	Dialog	Yes

Other on-line services: First Search, RLIN, SEC.

ADMISSION

Acceptance 1994-95 395 applied for admission; 65% were accepted.

Entrance Requirements Bachelor's degree, GMAT score of 570, minimum 3.0 GPA, minimum 2 years of work experience. Core courses waived through: previous course work.

Application Requirements Written essay, interview, application form, copies of transcript, resume/curriculum vitae, personal statement, 2 letters of recommendation.

Application Deadline 4/15 for fall.

FINANCIALS

Costs for 1994-95 Tuition: Full-time: $175/hour for state residents, $456/hour for nonresidents. Fees: Full-time: $800 for state residents, $800 for nonresidents. Average room and board costs are $3,000 per academic year (on-campus) and $3,000 per academic year (off-campus).

Financial Aid In 1994-95, 45% of candidates received some institutionally administered aid in the form of scholarships, loans, assistantships. Total awards ranged from $1,000-$13,860. Financial aid is not available to part-time students. Application deadlines: 4/1 for fall, 11/1 for spring. Contact: Ms. Susan Rivera, Director of MBA Admissions and Student Services, Blow Hall Room 255, Williamsburg, VA 23185. (804) 221-2898.

INTERNATIONAL STUDENTS

Demographics 12% of students enrolled in the program are international; Asia 60%, Europe 30%, Central America 5%, South America 5%.

Services and Facilities International student center, visa services, counseling/support services.

Applying TOEFL required, minimum score of 590; proof of health; proof of adequate funds. Financial aid is available to international students. Financial aid application deadline: 3/1 for fall. Admission application deadline: 4/15 for fall. Contact: Ms. Anne Moore, Director of International Admissions and Exchanges, The Reves Center, Williamsburg, VA 23185. (804) 221-3594.

ALTERNATE MBA PROGRAM

Executive MBA (EMBA) Length of program: Minimum: 20 months. Degree requirements: 47 credits. 8-10 years of management experience. Class size: 35-40.

PLACEMENT

In 1993-94, 52 organizations participated in on-campus recruiting; 398 on-campus interviews were conducted. Placement services include alumni network, career counseling/planning, career fairs, career library, career placement, electronic job bank, job interviews, resume preparation, and resume referral to employers. Of 1994 graduates, 83% were employed within three months of graduation, the average starting salary was $45,700, the range was $27,000-$64,000.

Jobs by Employer Type Manufacturing 27%; service 27%; government 5%; consulting 35%; nonprofit 6%.

Jobs by Functional Area Marketing/sales 10%; finance 28%; operations 10%; management 10%; strategic planning 2%; technical management 5%; consulting 35%.

Program Contact: Ms. Susan Rivera, Director of MBA Admissions, College of William and Mary, PO Box 8795, Williamsburg, VA 23185. (804) 221-2898; Fax: (804) 221-2958.

George Mason University

School of Business Administration

Fairfax, Virginia

OVERVIEW

George Mason University is a state-supported coed institution. Founded 1957. Setting: 677-acre suburban campus with easy access to Washington, DC. Total institutional enrollment: 21,000. Program was first offered in 1972. AACSB-accredited.

MBA HIGHLIGHTS

Entrance Difficulty**
Mean GMAT: 577
Mean GPA: 3.15

Cost $
Tuition: $1,515 - $2,020/semester
(Nonresident: $4,050 - $5,400/semester)
Room & Board: $6,000

Enrollment Profile

Full-time: 160	Work Exp: 93%
Part-time: 402	International: 24%
Total: 562	Women: 39%
Average Age: 30	Minorities: 20%

Average Class Size: 28

ACADEMICS

Length of Program Minimum: 21 months. Maximum: 6 years.

Calendar Semesters.

Full-time Classes Main campus; day, evening.

Part-time Classes Main campus; evening.

Degree Requirements 57 credits including 21 elective credits.

Required Courses Applied macroeconomics, financial accounting, management information systems, managerial accounting, managerial finance, managerial microeconomics, managerial statistics, marketing management, operations management, organizational behavior, regulatory structure and ethics, strategy and policy management.

Curricular Focus Business issues and problems, general management.

Concentrations Accounting, finance, international business, management, management information systems, marketing.

Faculty Full-time: 40, 97% with doctorates; part-time: 12, 50% with doctorates.

Teaching Methodology Case study: 30%, lecture: 40%, research: 10%, student presentations: 10%, team projects: 10%.

Special Opportunities International exchange in Costa Rica, Hungary, Mexico, United Kingdom. Internships include financial analysis in telecommunications, management information systems in banking, strategic planning in consulting, marketing in manufacturing, and accounting in consulting.

STUDENT STATISTICS

Geographic Representation By region: South 58%; Northeast 14%; West 8%. International 24%.

Undergraduate Majors Business 29%; education 3%; engineering/technology 20%; humanities 5%; science/mathematics 11%; social sciences 32%.

Other Background Work experience: On average, students have 5 years of work experience on entrance to the program.

FACILITIES

Information Resources Main library with 635,284 bound volumes, 182,854 titles on microform, 9,191 periodical subscriptions, 11,594 records/tapes/CDs, 593 CD-ROMs. Business collection includes 44,421 bound volumes, 422 periodical subscriptions, 15 CD-ROMs, 20 videos.

Housing 1% of students in program live in college-owned or -operated housing. Assistance with housing search provided.

Technology Computers are used moderately in course work. 240 computer terminals/PCs, linked by a campus-wide computer network, are available for use by students in program; they are located in the library, computer labs. Students in the program are not required to have their own PC.

Computer Resources/On-line Services

Training	Yes	CompuServe	Yes
Internet	Yes	Dun's	Yes
E-Mail	Yes	Dow Jones	Yes
LEXIS/NEXIS	Yes	Dialog	Yes

Other on-line services: First Search.

ADMISSION

Acceptance 1994-95 460 applied for admission; 50% were accepted.

Entrance Requirements Bachelor's degree, one semester of calculus, GMAT score of 500.

Application Requirements Written essay, application form, copies of transcript, resume/curriculum vitae, 2 letters of recommendation.

Application Deadlines 5/1 for fall, 11/1 for spring. Applications are processed on a rolling basis.

FINANCIALS

Costs for 1994-95 Tuition: Full-time: $1,515-$2,020/semester for state residents, $4,050-$5,400/semester for nonresidents. Fees: Full-time: $500 for international students. Average room and board costs are $6,000 per academic year (on-campus) and $8,500 per academic year (off-campus).

Financial Aid In 1994-95, 17% of candidates received some institutionally administered aid in the form of scholarships, loans, fellowships, assistantships. Total awards ranged from $506-$18,500. Financial aid is available to part-time students. Application deadline: 4/1 for fall. Applications are processed on a rolling basis. Contact: Ms. Sandy Mitchell, Director of Graduate Admission, School of Business, Mail Stop 5A2, Fairfax, VA 22030. (703) 993-2136.

INTERNATIONAL STUDENTS

Demographics 24% of students enrolled in the program are international; Asia 49%, Europe 23%, Africa 10%, South America 8%, Central America 6%, other 4%.

Services and Facilities International student office, visa services, ESL courses, special assistance for nonnative speakers of English, counseling/support services.

Applying TOEFL required, minimum score of 575; proof of health; proof of adequate funds. Financial aid is not available to international students. Admission application deadline: 4/1 for fall. Applications are processed on a rolling basis. Contact: Ms. Kathryn Dawson, Director of International Programs and Services, Mail Stop 4C3, Fairfax, VA 22030. (703) 993-2970.

ALTERNATE MBA PROGRAM

Executive MBA (EMBA) Length of program: Minimum: 21 months. Part-time classes: Main campus. Degree requirements: 57 credits. 10 years professional work experience.

PLACEMENT

In 1993-94, 25 organizations participated in on-campus recruiting; 125 on-campus interviews were conducted. Placement services include alumni network, career counseling/planning, career fairs, career library, career placement, electronic job bank, job interviews, job search course, mentor program, resume preparation, and resume referral to employers. Of 1994 graduates, 73% were employed within three months of graduation, the average starting salary was $43,500, the range was $27,000-$70,000.

Jobs by Employer Type Service 28%; government 15%; consulting 25%; nonprofit 6%; banking/finance 26%.

Jobs by Functional Area Marketing/sales 19%; finance 21%; operations 7%; management 14%; strategic planning 3%; technical management 14%; consulting 15%; human resources 7%.

Program Contact: Ms. Sandy Mitchell, Director of Graduate Admissions, George Mason University, School of Business, Mail Stop 5A2, Fairfax, VA 22030. (703) 993-2136; Fax: (703) 993-2145; Internet Address: gradadms@sba01.gmu.edu.
See full description on page 742.

Hampton University

School of Business

Hampton, Virginia

OVERVIEW
Hampton University is an independent nonprofit comprehensive coed institution. Founded 1868. Setting: 210-acre suburban campus with easy access to Norfolk. Total institutional enrollment: 5,700. Program was first offered in 1982.

MBA HIGHLIGHTS

Entrance Difficulty**
Mean GMAT: 410
Mean GPA: 3.5

Cost $
Tuition: $185/credit hour
Room & Board: $6,000

Enrollment Profile
Full-time: 0	Work Exp: 75%
Part-time: 50	International: 20%
Total: 50	Women: 60%
Average Age: 28	Minorities: 75%

Average Class Size: 15

ACADEMICS
Length of Program Minimum: 24 months. Maximum: 7 years.
Calendar Semesters.
Full-time Classes Main campus; evening, summer.
Degree Requirements 36 credits including 6 elective credits.
Required Courses Business policy, human resources administration, information systems development, international business, legal environment of business, macro environment of business, managerial accounting, managerial economics, managerial finance, marketing management, organizational theory and practice, quantitative decision making. Courses may be waived through: previous course work.
Curricular Focus General management, managing diversity, minorities in business.
Concentration Management.
Faculty Full-time: 10, 96% with doctorates.
Teaching Methodology Case study: 10%, lecture: 70%, research: 10%, team projects: 10%.
Special Opportunities Internship program available.

STUDENT STATISTICS
Geographic Representation State residents 80%. By region: South 60%; Northeast 14%; Midwest 5%; West 1%. International 20%.
Undergraduate Majors Business 50%; humanities 20%; science/mathematics 10%; social sciences 10%; other 10%.
Other Background Graduate degrees in other disciplines: 3%. Work experience: On average, students have 5 years of work experience on entrance to the program.

FACILITIES
Information Resources Main library with 235,000 bound volumes, 35,000 titles on microform, 1,200 periodical subscriptions, 2 million records/tapes/CDs.

Housing 1% of students in program live in college-owned or -operated housing.
Technology Computers are used moderately in course work. 18 computer terminals/PCs are available for use by students in program; they are located in computer labs. Students in the program are not required to have their own PC.

Computer Resources/On-line Services
Training	No	E-Mail	No
Internet	Yes $	Dialog	Yes

ADMISSION
Acceptance 1994-95 65 applied for admission; 80% were accepted.
Entrance Requirements Bachelor's degree, GMAT score, minimum 2.6 GPA. Core courses waived through: previous course work.
Application Requirements Application form, copies of transcript, 2 letters of recommendation.
Application Deadlines 6/30 for fall, 11/1 for spring.

FINANCIALS
Costs for 1994-95 Tuition: Part-time evening: $185/credit hour. Average room and board costs are $6,000 per academic year (on-campus).
Financial Aid In 1994-95, 2% of candidates received some institutionally administered aid in the form of assistantships, work-study. Total awards ranged from $6,400-$11,000. Financial aid is not available to part-time students. Application deadlines: 6/30 for fall, 11/1 for spring. Contact: Financial Aid Office, Hampton, VA 23668. (804) 727-5332.

INTERNATIONAL STUDENTS
Demographics 20% of students enrolled in the program are international; Africa 60%, Asia 35%, South America 5%.
Services and Facilities ESL courses.
Applying Proof of health; proof of adequate funds. Financial aid is not available to international students. Admission application deadlines: 6/30 for fall, 11/1 for spring.

PLACEMENT
In 1993-94, 50 organizations participated in on-campus recruiting. Placement services include career counseling/planning, career fairs, and career placement. Of 1994 graduates, 96% were employed within three months of graduation.

Program Contact: Director, MBA Program, Hampton University, Hampton, VA 23668. (804) 727-5762; Fax: (804) 727-5048.

James Madison University

College of Business

Harrisonburg, Virginia

OVERVIEW
James Madison University is a state-supported comprehensive coed institution. Founded 1908. Setting: 472-acre small-town campus. Total institutional enrollment: 12,000. Program was first offered in 1970. AACSB-accredited.

MBA HIGHLIGHTS

Entrance Difficulty***
Mean GMAT: 520
Mean GPA: N/R

Cost $
Tuition: $126/credit hour
(Nonresident: $351/credit hour)
Room & Board: $5,000 (off-campus)

Enrollment Profile
Full-time: 15	Work Exp: 95%
Part-time: 172	International: 3%
Total: 187	Women: 40%
Average Age: 30	Minorities: 5%

Average Class Size: 15

ACADEMICS
Length of Program Minimum: 18 months.
Calendar Semesters.
Full-time Classes Main campus, Charlottesville; evening, summer.

Part-time Classes Main campus, Charlottesville; evening, summer.

Degree Requirements 33 credit hours.

Curricular Focus Business issues and problems, economic and financial theory, entrepreneurship.

Concentrations Entrepreneurship, healthcare administration, technology management.

Faculty Full-time: 44, 100% with doctorates.

Teaching Methodology Case study: 50%, lecture: 50%.

Special Opportunities International exchange in Germany, Hong Kong, Japan, Switzerland.

STUDENT STATISTICS
Geographic Representation State residents 80%. International 3%.

Undergraduate Majors Business 50%; engineering/technology 20%; nursing 10%; social sciences 20%.

Other Background Graduate degrees in other disciplines: 5%. Work experience: On average, students have 4 years of work experience on entrance to the program.

FACILITIES
Information Resources Main library with 352,160 bound volumes, 1.3 million titles on microform, 2,312 periodical subscriptions, 12,269 records/tapes/CDs, 33 CD-ROMs.

Housing College housing not available.

Technology Computers are used heavily in course work. Students in the program are not required to have their own PC.

Computer Resources/On-line Services

Training	Yes	Multimedia Center	Yes
Internet	Yes	LEXIS/NEXIS	Yes
E-Mail	No	Dialog	Yes
Videoconference Center	Yes		

ADMISSION
Acceptance 1994-95 250 applied for admission; 75% were accepted.

Entrance Requirements Bachelor's degree, GMAT score of 500, minimum 2.7 GPA. Core courses waived through: previous course work.

Application Requirements Written essay, application form, copies of transcript, resume/curriculum vitae, 2 letters of recommendation.

Application Deadline Applications are processed on a rolling basis.

FINANCIALS
Costs for 1994-95 Tuition: Full-time: $126/credit hour for state residents, $351/credit hour for nonresidents. Average room and board costs are $5,000 per academic year (off-campus).

Financial Aid Total awards ranged from $5,500-$6,500. Financial aid is available to part-time students. Applications are processed on a rolling basis. Contact: Financial Aid Office, Harrisonburg, VA 22807. (703) 568-6644.

INTERNATIONAL STUDENTS
Demographics 3% of students enrolled in the program are international.

Services and Facilities International student office, international student center, counseling/support services.

Applying TOEFL required, minimum score of 500; proof of adequate funds. Financial aid is available to international students. Financial aid application deadline: 3/31 for fall. Applications are processed on a rolling basis. Admission applications are processed on a rolling basis.

PLACEMENT
Placement services include alumni network, career counseling/planning, career placement, electronic job bank, job interviews, and resume referral to employers.

Program Contact: Admissions Office, James Madison University, Harrisonburg, VA 22807. (703) 568-3253; Fax: (703) 568-3275.

Lynchburg College

School of Business

Lynchburg, Virginia

OVERVIEW
Lynchburg College is an independent comprehensive coed institution, affiliated with Christian Church (Disciples of Christ). Founded 1903. Setting: 214-acre urban campus. Total institutional enrollment: 2,067. Program

was first offered in 1967.

MBA HIGHLIGHTS

Entrance Difficulty**
Mean GMAT: 490
Mean GPA: N/R

Cost $
Tuition: $210/credit hour
Room & Board: $5,400

Enrollment Profile

Full-time: 5	Work Exp: 98%
Part-time: 75	International: 3%
Total: 80	Women: 30%
Average Age: 30	Minorities: 4%

Average Class Size: 15

ACADEMICS
Length of Program Minimum: 12 months.

Calendar Semesters.

Full-time Classes Main campus; evening.

Part-time Classes Main campus; evening.

Degree Requirements 31 credits including 16 elective credits. Other: Summer orientation in selected fields of study.

Required Courses Business policy, career development, international business, leadership and ethics, managerial communications, technology for managers. Courses may be waived through: previous course work, work experience.

Curricular Focus General management, leadership, problem solving and decision making.

Concentrations Accounting, human resources management, management, marketing.

Faculty Full-time: 12, 25% with doctorates.

Teaching Methodology Case study: 25%, lecture: 40%, seminars by members of the business community: 10%, student presentations: 10%, team projects: 15%.

Special Opportunities Internship program available.

STUDENT STATISTICS
Geographic Representation State residents 96%. By region: South 97%. International 3%.

Undergraduate Majors Business 38%; education 5%; engineering/technology 20%; humanities 7%; science/mathematics 14%; social sciences 15%; other 1%.

Other Background Work experience: On average, students have 6-8 years of work experience on entrance to the program.

FACILITIES
Information Resources Main library with 178,490 bound volumes, 367,676 titles on microform, 771 periodical subscriptions, 7,554 records/tapes/CDs, 10 CD-ROMs. Business collection includes 8,258 bound volumes, 68 periodical subscriptions, 2 CD-ROMs, 55 videos.

Housing College housing available.

Technology Computers are used moderately in course work. 170 computer terminals/PCs, linked by a campus-wide computer network, are available for use by students in program; they are located in classrooms, learning resource center, the library, the computer center, computer labs. Students in the program are not required to have their own PC.

Computer Resources/On-line Services

Training	Yes	E-Mail	Yes
Internet	Yes	Dialog	Yes

ADMISSION
Acceptance 1994-95 55 applied for admission; 99% were accepted.

Entrance Requirements Bachelor's degree, GMAT score of 450, minimum 2.7 GPA. Core courses waived through: previous course work, work experience.

Application Requirements Written essay, application form, copies of transcript, 2 letters of recommendation.

Application Deadlines 3/15 for fall, 5/15 for part-time students.

FINANCIALS
Costs for 1994-95 Tuition: Full-time: $210/credit hour. Average room and board costs are $5,400 per academic year (on-campus).

Financial Aid In 1994-95, candidates received some institutionally administered aid in the form of assistantships. Financial aid is not available to part-time students. Application deadline: 4/1 for fall. Contact: Ms. Linda Renschler, Director of Financial Aid, 1501 Lakeside Drive, Lynchburg, VA 24501. (804) 522-8228.

INTERNATIONAL STUDENTS
Demographics 3% of students enrolled in the program are international.

Services and Facilities Visa services, ESL courses, counseling/support services.

Applying TOEFL required, minimum score of 550; proof of health; proof of adequate funds. Financial aid is available to international students. Scholarships are available for these students. Admission application deadlines: 3/15 for fall, 3/15 for summer. Contact: Dr. Bruce Mayer, Director of Focus International, 1501 Lakeside Drive, Lynchburg, VA 24501. (804) 522-8447.

PLACEMENT
Placement services include alumni network, career counseling/planning, career fairs, career library, career placement, electronic job bank, job interviews, resume preparation, and resume referral to employers.

Program Contact: Ms. Ann M. Harper, Administrative Assistant, Lynchburg College, 1501 Lakeside Drive, Lynchburg, VA 24501. (804) 522-8417, or (800) 426-8101; Fax: (804) 522-0639.

Marymount University

School of Business Administration

Arlington, Virginia

OVERVIEW
Marymount University is an independent comprehensive coed institution, affiliated with Roman Catholic Church. Founded 1950. Setting: 21-acre suburban campus with easy access to Washington, DC. Total institutional enrollment: 4,000. Program was first offered in 1982.

MBA HIGHLIGHTS

Entrance Difficulty***
Mean GMAT: 490
Mean GPA: 3.0

Cost $$$
Tuition: $340/credit hour
Room & Board: N/R

Enrollment Profile

Full-time: 45	Work Exp: 90%
Part-time: 655	International: 8%
Total: 700	Women: 49%
Average Age: 30	Minorities: 11%

Average Class Size: 20

ACADEMICS
Length of Program Minimum: 18 months. Maximum: 7 years.

Calendar Semesters.

Full-time Classes Ballston; evening, weekends, summer.

Part-time Classes Ballston; evening, weekends, summer.

Degree Requirements 36 credits including 6 elective credits.

Required Courses Accounting theory and practice, applied organizational behavior, business in society, business statistics, conceptual foundations of information management, financial management, history and philosophy of management, law and the business environment, macroeconomics, management decision making using computers, managerial economics, marketing analysis, organizational policy and strategy, production and operations management, writing for decision making. Courses may be waived through: previous course work.

Curricular Focus Business issues and problems, economic and financial theory, problem solving and decision making.

Concentrations Economics, finance, human resources management, international business, management, management information systems, marketing, operations management, organizational behavior, public policy, quantitative analysis.

Faculty Full-time: 28, 80% with doctorates; part-time: 28, 80% with doctorates.

Teaching Methodology Case study: 25%, faculty seminars: 5%, lecture: 60%, research: 5%, team projects: 5%.

Special Opportunities International exchange in United Kingdom. Internships include corporate and government.

STUDENT STATISTICS
Geographic Representation By region: Northeast 92%. International 8%.

Undergraduate Majors Business 60%; education 5%; engineering/technology 10%; humanities 5%; science/mathematics 10%; social sciences 5%; other 5%.

Other Background Graduate degrees in other disciplines: 20%. Work experience: On average, students have 5-10 years of work experience on entrance to the program.

FACILITIES
Information Resources Main library with 134,458 bound volumes, 207,313 titles on microform, 1,248 periodical subscriptions, 3,488 records/tapes/CDs, 569 CD-ROMs.

Housing 6% of students in program live in college-owned or -operated housing.

Technology Computers are used moderately in course work. 250 computer terminals/PCs, linked by a campus-wide computer network, are available for use by students in program; they are located in classrooms, the library, the computer center, computer labs, the research center. Students in the program are not required to have their own PC.

Computer Resources/On-line Services

Training	Yes	LEXIS/NEXIS	Yes
Internet	Yes	CompuServe	Yes
E-Mail	Yes	Dialog	Yes
Multimedia Center	Yes		

ADMISSION
Acceptance 1994-95 Of those applying, 60% were accepted.

Entrance Requirements Bachelor's degree, GMAT score of 400, minimum 2.0 GPA. Core courses waived through: previous course work.

Application Requirements Written essay, interview, application form, copies of transcript, resume/curriculum vitae, personal statement, 2 letters of recommendation.

Application Deadline Applications are processed on a rolling basis.

FINANCIALS
Costs for 1994-95 Tuition: Full-time: $340/credit hour.

Financial Aid In 1994-95, candidates received some institutionally administered aid in the form of grants, assistantships. Financial aid is not available to part-time students. Application deadline: 3/1 for fall. Contact: Ms. Debby Raines, Director of Financial Aid, 2807 North Glebe Road, Arlington, VA 22201. (703) 284-1480.

INTERNATIONAL STUDENTS
Demographics 8% of students enrolled in the program are international; Asia 50%, Africa 12%, Central America 12%, Europe 12%, South America 12%.

Services and Facilities Language tutoring, ESL courses, special assistance for nonnative speakers of English, counseling/support services.

Applying TOEFL required, minimum score of 600; proof of health; proof of adequate funds. Financial aid is not available to international students.

PLACEMENT
In 1993-94, 90 organizations participated in on-campus recruiting; 78 on-campus interviews were conducted. Placement services include alumni network, career counseling/planning, career fairs, career library, career placement, electronic job bank, job interviews, resume preparation, and resume referral to employers. Of 1994 graduates, 100% were employed within three months of graduation, the average starting salary was $48,500, the range was $31,500-$96,900.

Program Contact: Dr. David G. Behrs, Assistant Dean, Marymount University, 2807 North Glebe Road, Arlington, VA 22201. (703) 284-5901; Fax: (703) 527-3815.

Old Dominion University

Graduate School of Business and Public Administration

Norfolk, Virginia

OVERVIEW
Old Dominion University is a state-supported coed institution. Founded 1930. Setting: 172-acre urban campus with easy access to Virginia Beach. Total institutional enrollment: 17,000. Program was first offered in

1964. AACSB-accredited.

MBA HIGHLIGHTS

Entrance Difficulty*
Mean GMAT: 510
Mean GPA: 3.0

Cost $
Tuition: $154 - $166/hour
(Nonresident: $221 - $434/hour)
Room & Board: $5,000

Enrollment Profile

Full-time: 111	Work Exp: 70%
Part-time: 259	International: 20%
Total: 370	Women: 42%
Average Age: 29	Minorities: 11%

Average Class Size: 24

ACADEMICS

Length of Program Minimum: 20 months. Maximum: 6 years.

Calendar Semesters.

Full-time Classes Main campus, Virginia Beach, Portsmouth, Hampton; evening, summer.

Part-time Classes Main campus, Virginia Beach, Portsmouth, Hampton; day, evening, summer.

Degree Requirements 49 hours including 12 elective hours. Other: Writing proficiency exam.

Required Courses Applied financial decision making, business condition analysis, managerial accounting, managerial problems in marketing, organizational behavior, operational management. Courses may be waived through: previous course work, work experience.

Curricular Focus Entrepreneurship, international business.

Concentrations Accounting, economics, entrepreneurship, finance, international business, international maritime transportation and port administration, management, management information systems, marketing, public administration.

Faculty Full-time: 69, 99% with doctorates; part-time: 2.

Teaching Methodology Case study: 30%, lecture: 50%, research: 5%, student presentations: 5%, team projects: 10%.

Special Opportunities Internship program available.

STUDENT STATISTICS

Geographic Representation State residents 80%. By region: South 80%. International 20%.

Undergraduate Majors Business 55%; education 2%; engineering/technology 18%; science/mathematics 12%; social sciences 2%; other 11%.

Other Background Work experience: On average, students have 5 years of work experience on entrance to the program.

FACILITIES

Information Resources Main library with 842,349 bound volumes, 1.1 million titles on microform, 6,835 periodical subscriptions, 50,786 records/tapes/CDs.

Housing 1% of students in program live in college-owned or -operated housing.

Technology Computers are used heavily in course work. Computer terminals/PCs, linked by a campus-wide computer network, are available for use by students in program; they are located in the student center, the library, computer labs. Students in the program are not required to have their own PC.

Computer Resources/On-line Services

Training	No	Videoconference Center	Yes
Internet	Yes	CompuServe	Yes
E-Mail	Yes		

ADMISSION

Acceptance 1994-95 228 applied for admission; 79% were accepted.

Entrance Requirements Bachelor's degree, GMAT score. Core courses waived through: previous course work, work experience.

Application Requirements Written essay, application form, copies of transcript, 1 letter of recommendation.

Application Deadlines 7/1 for fall, 11/1 for spring, 4/1 for summer.

FINANCIALS

Costs for 1994-95 Tuition: Full-time: $154-$166/hour for state residents, $221-$434/hour for nonresidents. Fees: Full-time: $47/semester for state

residents, $47/semester for nonresidents. Average room and board costs are $5,000 per academic year (on-campus) and $5,000 per academic year (off-campus).

Financial Aid In 1994-95, 4% of candidates received some institutionally administered aid in the form of grants, scholarships, loans, fellowships, assistantships. Financial aid is available to part-time students. Application deadline: 3/31 for fall. Contact: Office of Financial Aid, 126 Old Administration Building, Norfolk, VA 23529. (804) 683-3683.

INTERNATIONAL STUDENTS

Demographics 20% of students enrolled in the program are international; Europe 50%, Asia 33%, Africa 8%, Central America 6%, South America 3%.

Services and Facilities International student center, language tutoring, special assistance for nonnative speakers of English, counseling/support services.

Applying TOEFL required, minimum score of 550; proof of health; proof of adequate funds. Financial aid is available to international students. Financial aid application deadline: 3/31 for fall. Admission application deadlines: 4/15 for fall, 10/1 for spring, 2/15 for summer. Contact: Mr. Scott E. King, Director, International Student Service, 5215 Hampton Boulevard, Norfolk, VA 23529. (804) 683-3701.

PLACEMENT

Placement services include alumni network, career counseling/planning, career fairs, career library, career placement, electronic job bank, job interviews, resume preparation, and resume referral to employers.

Program Contact: Ms. Jean Turpin, MBA Program Manager, Old Dominion University, MBA Program Office, Norfolk, VA 23529. (804) 683-3585, or (800) 348-7926 (VA only), or (800) 683-7926 (out-of-state); Fax: (804) 683-6082.

Radford University

College of Business and Economics

Radford, Virginia

OVERVIEW

Radford University is a state-supported comprehensive coed institution. Founded 1910. Setting: 177-acre small-town campus. Total institutional enrollment: 9,000. Program was first offered in 1982. AACSB-accredited.

MBA HIGHLIGHTS

Entrance Difficulty*
Mean GMAT: 500
Mean GPA: 3.0

Cost $
Tuition: $1,593/semester
(Nonresident: $3,030/semester)
Room & Board: $5,800 (off-campus)

Enrollment Profile

Full-time: 32	Work Exp: 60%
Part-time: 38	International: 80%
Total: 70	Women: 32%
Average Age: 28	Minorities: 10%

Average Class Size: 22

ACADEMICS

Length of Program Minimum: 24 months. Maximum: 6 years.

Calendar Semesters.

Full-time Classes Main campus, Roanoke Valley Graduate Center; evening, summer.

Part-time Classes Main campus, Roanoke Valley Graduate Center; evening, summer.

Degree Requirements 36 credits including 6 elective credits. Other: 2 elective courses or thesis.

Required Courses Administrative policy, business research and reporting, financial management, international business, management information systems, managerial accounting, managerial economics, marketing management, operations and production management, organizational behavior.

Curricular Focus International business, problem solving and decision making, strategic analysis and planning.

Concentrations Accounting, economics, finance, international business, management, marketing.

Faculty Full-time: 12, 100% with doctorates.

Teaching Methodology Case study: 10%, lecture: 50%, research: 10%, student presentations: 20%, team projects: 10%.

Special Opportunities International exchange in Belgium. Internships include telecommunications, insurance, banking, and government.

STUDENT STATISTICS

Geographic Representation State residents 8%. By region: South 72%; Northeast 10%; Midwest 10%. International 80%.

Undergraduate Majors Business 80%; education 4%; engineering/technology 7%; nursing 3%; social sciences 6%.

Other Background Graduate degrees in other disciplines: 5%. Work experience: On average, students have 5 years of work experience on entrance to the program.

FACILITIES

Information Resources Main library with 303,654 bound volumes, 2,000 titles on microform, 2,524 periodical subscriptions, 25,000 records/tapes/CDs, 25 CD-ROMs.

Housing College housing not available.

Technology 20 computer terminals/PCs, linked by a campus-wide computer network, are available for use by students in program; they are located in the student center, computer labs. Students in the program are not required to have their own PC. $300 are budgeted per student for computer support.

Computer Resources/On-line Services

Training	No	Dun's	No
Internet	Yes	Dow Jones	No
E-Mail	Yes	Dialog	No
LEXIS/NEXIS	No	Bloomberg	No
CompuServe	No		

ADMISSION

Acceptance 1994-95 Of those applying, 65% were accepted.

Entrance Requirements Bachelor's degree, GMAT score of 450, minimum 2.75 GPA.

Application Requirements Application form, copies of transcript, 2 letters of recommendation.

Application Deadlines 6/20 for fall, 11/1 for spring.

FINANCIALS

Costs for 1994-95 Tuition: Full-time: $1,593/semester for state residents, $3,030/semester for nonresidents; Part-time evening: $133/credit hour for state residents, $253/credit hour for nonresidents. Average room and board costs are $5,800 per academic year (off-campus).

Financial Aid In 1994-95, 50% of candidates received some institutionally administered aid in the form of grants, scholarships, loans, fellowships, assistantships, work-study. Total awards ranged from $1,200-$10,800. Financial aid is not available to part-time students. Application deadline: 3/1 for fall. Contact: Ms. Barbara Porter, Associate Director of Financial Aid, PO Box 6905, Radford, VA 24142. (703) 831-5408.

INTERNATIONAL STUDENTS

Demographics 80% of students enrolled in the program are international; Asia 55%, Europe 30%, Africa 5%, Central America 5%, South America 5%.

Services and Facilities Counseling/support services, English language institute.

Applying TOEFL required, minimum score of 550; proof of adequate funds. Financial aid is available to international students. Financial aid application deadline: 3/1 for annual. Admission application deadlines: 6/20 for fall, 11/9 for spring. Contact: Ms. Teresa Underwood, Coordinator of International Services, PO Box 6978, Radford, VA 24142. (703) 831-5939.

PLACEMENT

Placement services include alumni network, career counseling/planning, career fairs, career library, career placement, and job interviews. Of 1994 graduates, 94% were employed within three months of graduation, the average starting salary was $32,000, the range was $16,500-$59,000.

Jobs by Employer Type Manufacturing 40%; service 30%; government 15%; consulting 10%; nonprofit 5%.

Jobs by Functional Area Marketing/sales 25%; finance 15%; operations 15%; management 30%; strategic planning 10%; technical management 5%.

Program Contact: Dr. Clarence C. Rose, Director, MBA Program, Radford University, Radford, VA 24142. (703) 831-5258; Fax: (703) 831-6103.

Regent University

School of Business

Virginia Beach, Virginia

OVERVIEW

Regent University is an independent nonprofit graduate-only coed institution. Founded 1977. Setting: suburban campus. Total institutional enrollment: 1,316.

MBA HIGHLIGHTS

Entrance Difficulty**
Mean GMAT: 340
Mean GPA: 3.75

Cost $$
Tuition: $295/semester credit hour
Room & Board: N/R

Enrollment Profile

Full-time: 77	Work Exp: N/R
Part-time: 76	International: N/R
Total: 153	Women: 30%
Average Age: 34	Minorities: 21%

Average Class Size: 25

ACADEMICS

Length of Program Minimum: 24 months.

Calendar Trimesters.

Full-time Classes Main campus, distance learning option; day, evening, summer.

Part-time Classes Main campus, distance learning option; day, evening, summer.

Degree Requirements 57 credits including 12 elective credits.

Required Courses Business research, business speaking, business writing, organizational behavior, people skills, servant management, strategic management, successful executive life, total quality management.

Curricular Focus Entrepreneurship, general management, leadership.

Concentrations Accounting, entrepreneurship, international business, management, marketing.

Faculty Full-time: 6; part-time: 3.

Teaching Methodology Case study: 30%, lecture: 50%, student presentations: 10%, team projects: 10%.

STUDENT STATISTICS

Geographic Representation State residents 78%. By region: South 49%; Midwest 20%; Northeast 15%; West 10%.

Other Background Graduate degrees in other disciplines: 6%.

FACILITIES

Information Resources Main library with 269,491 bound volumes, 1.3 million titles on microform, 3,900 periodical subscriptions. Business collection includes 160,000 bound volumes, 1,425 periodical subscriptions, 20 CD-ROMs, 200 videos.

Housing College housing available.

Technology 45 computer terminals/PCs, linked by a campus-wide computer network, are available for use by students in program; they are located in classrooms, the library. Students in the program are not required to have their own PC.

Computer Resources/On-line Services

Training	Yes	Dun's	Yes
Internet	Yes	Dow Jones	No
LEXIS/NEXIS	Yes	Dialog	No
CompuServe	No	Bloomberg	No

ADMISSION

Acceptance 1994-95 71 applied for admission; 96% were accepted.

Entrance Requirements Core courses waived through: previous course work.

Application Requirements Interview, application form, copies of transcript, personal statement.

Application Deadline Applications are processed on a rolling basis. Application discs available.

FINANCIALS

Costs for 1994-95 Tuition: Full-time: $295/semester credit hour. Fees: Full-time: $18/semester.

Financial Aid In 1994-95, 50% of candidates received some institutionally administered aid in the form of grants, scholarships. Total awards ranged from $1,000-$9,000. Financial aid is not available to part-time students. Applications are processed on a rolling basis. Contact: Mr. Robert Black, Director of Financial Aid, Robertson Hall, 1000 Regent University Drive, Virginia Beach, VA 23464-9851. (804) 579-4114.

INTERNATIONAL STUDENTS

Demographics 15% of students on campus are international.

Services and Facilities International student office, ESL courses.

Applying TOEFL required; proof of adequate funds. Financial aid is available to international students. Applications are processed on a rolling basis. Admission applications are processed on a rolling basis.

PLACEMENT

Placement services include alumni network, career counseling/planning, and electronic job bank.

Program Contact: Mr. Michael Gray, Enrollment Manager, Regent University, 1000 Regent University Drive CRB122, Virginia Beach, VA 23464-9851. (804) 579-4096, or (800) 477-2617 (VA only), or (800) 477-3617 (out-of-state); Fax: (804) 579-4369.

Shenandoah University

Byrd School of Business

Winchester, Virginia

OVERVIEW

Shenandoah University is an independent United Methodist comprehensive coed institution. Founded 1875. Setting: 70-acre small-town campus with easy access to Baltimore and Washington, DC. Total institutional enrollment: 1,652.

MBA HIGHLIGHTS

Entrance Difficulty**
Mean GMAT: 525
Mean GPA: N/R

Cost $
Tuition: $350/semester credit hour
Room & Board: $4,800

Enrollment Profile

Full-time: N/R	Work Exp: N/R
Part-time: N/R	International: 33%
Total: 125	Women: 25%
Average Age: N/R	Minorities: N/R

Average Class Size: 15

ACADEMICS

Length of Program Minimum: 15 months.

Calendar Semesters.

Full-time Classes Main campus; evening, weekends, summer.

Part-time Classes Main campus; evening, weekends, summer.

Degree Requirements 36 semester credit hours.

Curricular Focus Problem solving and decision making, strategic analysis and planning, teamwork.

Concentrations Accounting, finance, international business, management, management information systems, marketing.

Teaching Methodology Case study: 25%, lecture: 40%, research: 20%, team projects: 15%.

STUDENT STATISTICS

Geographic Representation State residents 67%. International 33%.

FACILITIES

Information Resources Main library with 105,092 bound volumes, 59,744 titles on microform, 665 periodical subscriptions, 14,507 records/tapes/CDs, 6 CD-ROMs.

Housing College housing available.

ADMISSION

Entrance Requirements Bachelor's degree, prerequisite courses required for applicants with non-business degree, GMAT score.

Application Requirements Interview, application form, copies of transcript, resume/curriculum vitae, personal statement, 2 letters of recommendation.

Application Deadline Applications are processed on a rolling basis.

FINANCIALS

Costs for 1994-95 Tuition: Full-time: $350/semester credit hour. Average room and board costs are $4,800 per academic year (on-campus) and $4,500 per academic year (off-campus).

Financial Aid Application deadline: 4/15 for fall. Applications are processed on a rolling basis. Contact: Mr. Jim Begany, Director of Financial Aid, 1460 University Drive, Winchester, VA 22601-5195. (703) 665-4538.

INTERNATIONAL STUDENTS

Demographics 33% of students enrolled in the program are international.

Applying TOEFL required, minimum score of 450; proof of adequate funds; on-campus English language proficiency assessment. Financial aid is available to international students. Assistantships are available for these students. Admission applications are processed on a rolling basis.

Program Contact: Dr. Daniel Pavsek, Dean, Henry F. Byrd, Jr. School of Business, Shenandoah University, 1460 University Drive, Winchester, VA 22601-5195. (703) 665-4572; Fax: (703) 665-5437; Internet Address: dpavsek@su.edu.

University of Richmond

E. Claiborne Robins School of Business

Richmond, Virginia

OVERVIEW

The University of Richmond is an independent comprehensive coed institution, affiliated with Baptist General Association of Virginia. Founded 1830. Setting: 350-acre suburban campus. Total institutional enrollment: 4,300. Program was first offered in 1976. AACSB-accredited.

MBA HIGHLIGHTS

Entrance Difficulty**
Mean GMAT: 563
Mean GPA: 3.0

Cost $$$
Tuition: $7,300/semester
Room & Board: $10,800 (off-campus)

Enrollment Profile

Full-time: 11	Work Exp: 98%
Part-time: 255	International: 3%
Total: 266	Women: 42%
Average Age: 29	Minorities: 5%

Average Class Size: 20

ACADEMICS

Length of Program Minimum: 20 months. Maximum: 5 years.

Calendar Semesters.

Part-time Classes Main campus; evening, summer.

Degree Requirements 30 semester hours including 6 elective semester hours.

Required Courses Advanced marketing management, business policy and strategy, financial management; strategy and policy, management information systems, managerial accounting and control, managerial economics, operations research, organizational behavior.

Curricular Focus Business issues and problems, problem solving and decision making, strategic analysis and planning.

Concentration Management.

Teaching Methodology Case study: 25%, lecture: 25%, student presentations: 25%, team projects: 25%.

STUDENT STATISTICS
Geographic Representation State residents 97%. By region: South 95%; Northeast 1%. International 3%.

Undergraduate Majors Business 50%; engineering/technology 18%; humanities 12%; science/mathematics 9%; social sciences 7%; other 3%.

Other Background Graduate degrees in other disciplines: 8%. Work experience: On average, students have 2 years of work experience on entrance to the program.

FACILITIES
Information Resources Main library with 559,291 bound volumes, 54,811 titles on microform, 6,827 periodical subscriptions, 18,446 records/tapes/CDs, 38 CD-ROMs. Business collection includes 326,486 bound volumes, 3,362 periodical subscriptions.

Housing College housing not available.

Technology Computers are used moderately in course work. 25 computer terminals/PCs are available for use by students in program; they are located in computer labs. Students in the program are not required to have their own PC.

Computer Resources/On-line Services
Training	No	LEXIS/NEXIS	Yes
Internet	Yes	Dun's	Yes
E-Mail	No	Dow Jones	Yes

ADMISSION
Acceptance 1994-95 159 applied for admission; 72% were accepted.

Entrance Requirements Bachelor's degree, GMAT score of 500, minimum 2 years of work experience. Core courses waived through: previous course work.

Application Requirements Application form, copies of transcript.

Application Deadlines 7/1 for fall, 11/1 for spring, 3/1 for summer.

FINANCIALS
Costs for 1994-95 Tuition: Full-time: $7,300/semester. Average room and board costs are $10,800 per academic year (off-campus).

Financial Aid In 1994-95, 7% of candidates received some institutionally administered aid in the form of grants, loans, assistantships. Total awards ranged from $3,000-$6,000. Financial aid is available to part-time students. Application deadlines: 7/1 for fall, 11/1 for spring, 3/1 for summer. Contact: Mr. James Nolan, Director of Student Financial Aid, Richmond, VA 23173. (804) 289-8438.

INTERNATIONAL STUDENTS
Demographics 3% of students enrolled in the program are international; Europe 87%, Asia 13%.

Services and Facilities International student office, international student center, visa services, language tutoring, special assistance for nonnative speakers of English.

Applying TOEFL required, minimum score of 550; proof of health; proof of adequate funds; financial statement. Financial aid is available to international students. Financial aid application deadlines: 5/1 for fall, 9/1 for spring. Admission application deadlines: 5/1 for fall, 9/1 for spring, 11/1 for summer. Contact: Ms. Michele Cox, Assistant to the Director, International Education, Richmond, VA 23173. (804) 289-8838.

ALTERNATE MBA PROGRAM
MBA/JD Length of program: Minimum: 36 months. Degree requirements: 116 semester hours, completion of MBA within one year after receipt of JD degree.

PLACEMENT
Placement services include alumni network, career counseling/planning, career fairs, career library, career placement, electronic job bank, job interviews, job search course, resume preparation, and resume referral to employers.

Program Contact: Dr. Thomas Giese, Associate Dean and Director, The Richard S. Reynolds Graduate School, University of Richmond, E. Claiborne Robins School of Business, Richmond, VA 23173. (804) 289-8553; Fax: (804) 287-6544.

University of Virginia

Darden Graduate School of Business Administration

Charlottesville, Virginia

OVERVIEW
The University of Virginia is a state-supported coed institution. Founded 1819. Setting: 1,094-acre small-town campus with easy access to Richmond. Total institutional enrollment: 17,708. Program was first offered in 1955. AACSB-accredited.

MBA HIGHLIGHTS

Entrance Difficulty***
Mean GMAT: 643
Mean GPA: 3.2

Cost $$
Tuition: $9,385
(Nonresident: $17,839)
Room & Board: $6,625 (off-campus)

Enrollment Profile
Full-time: 0	Work Exp: 99%
Part-time: 487	International: 13%
Total: 487	Women: 31%
Average Age: 27	Minorities: 17%

Class Size: 45 - 60

ACADEMICS
Length of Program Minimum: 24 months.

Calendar Semesters.

Full-time Classes Main campus; day.

Degree Requirements 78 credits including 24 elective credits.

Required Courses Accounting, analysis and communication, business and the political economy, ethics, finance, marketing, operations, organizational behavior, quantitative analysis.

Curricular Focus Entrepreneurship, general management, leadership.

Concentration Management.

Faculty Full-time: 47, 94% with doctorates; part-time: 23, 48% with doctorates.

Teaching Methodology Case study: 70%, lecture: 5%.

Special Opportunities International exchange in Australia, Sweden. Other: International Field Projects.

STUDENT STATISTICS
Geographic Representation State residents 38%. By region: South 53%; Northeast 16%; West 11%; Midwest 6%. International 13%.

Undergraduate Majors Business 25%; engineering/technology 26%; humanities 30%; other 18%.

Other Background Graduate degrees in other disciplines: 10%. Work experience: On average, students have 4 years of work experience on entrance to the program.

FACILITIES
Information Resources Main library with 4 million bound volumes, 4.1 million titles on microform, 38,192 periodical subscriptions, 61,444 records/tapes/CDs. Business collection in Darden School Camp Library includes 100,000 bound volumes, 1,000 periodical subscriptions, 10 CD-ROMs.

Housing College housing available.

Technology Computers are used heavily in course work. 90 computer terminals/PCs, linked by a campus-wide computer network, are available for use by students in program; they are located in classrooms, the library, computer labs. Students in the program are required to have their own PC. $700 are budgeted per student for computer support.

Computer Resources/On-line Services
Training	Yes	LEXIS/NEXIS	Yes
Internet	Yes	Dow Jones	Yes
E-Mail	Yes	Dialog	Yes
Videoconference Center	Yes	Bloomberg	Yes

ADMISSION
Acceptance 1994-95 2,086 applied for admission; 28% were accepted.

Entrance Requirements GMAT score.

Application Requirements Written essay, application form, copies of transcript, 2 letters of recommendation.

Application Deadlines 3/15 for fall. Applications are processed on a rolling basis.

FINANCIALS

Costs for 1994-95 Tuition: Full-time: $9,385 for state residents, $17,839 for nonresidents. Average room and board costs are $6,625 per academic year (off-campus).

Financial Aid In 1994-95, 65% of candidates received some institutionally administered aid in the form of scholarships, loans. Total awards ranged from $1,000-$17,839. Financial aid is not available to part-time students. Application deadline: 3/31 for fall. Applications are processed on a rolling basis. Contact: Director of Financial Aid, Charlottesville, VA 22906. (804) 924-7281.

INTERNATIONAL STUDENTS

Demographics 13% of students enrolled in the program are international; Asia 50%, Europe 35%, South America 7%, Africa 3%, Australia 3%.

Services and Facilities International student office, international student center, language tutoring, counseling/support services.

Applying TOEFL required; proof of adequate funds; Test of Spoken English. Financial aid is not available to international students. Admission application deadline: 3/15 for fall. Applications are processed on a rolling basis. Contact: Ms. Suzanne Louis, Associate Director, ISSP, 918 Emmet Street, Suite 120, Charlottesville, VA 22903. (804) 982-5548.

ALTERNATE MBA PROGRAMS

MBA/JD Length of program: Minimum: 48 months. Degree requirements: 156 credits including 15 elective credits.

MBA/MA Length of program: Minimum: 36 months. Degree requirements: 105 credits including 15 elective credits. MA is in Asian studies, government, foreign affairs.

MBA/MSN Length of program: Minimum: 30 months. Degree requirements: 93 credits including 15 elective credits.

MBA/M Eng Length of program: Minimum: 36 months. Degree requirements: 93 credits including 15 elective credits.

PLACEMENT

In 1993-94, 173 organizations participated in on-campus recruiting; 3,516 on-campus interviews were conducted. Placement services include alumni network, career counseling/planning, career fairs, career library, career placement, electronic job bank, job interviews, job search course, resume preparation, and resume referral to employers. Of 1994 graduates, 98% were employed within three months of graduation, the average starting salary was $61,000, the range was $32,000-$120,000.

Jobs by Employer Type Manufacturing 26%; government 1%; consulting 21%; nonprofit 6%; banking/financial services 33%; marketing services 3%; telecommunications 3%; other 7%.

Jobs by Functional Area Marketing/sales 18%; finance 38%; operations 4%; management 9%; strategic planning 3%; consulting 23%; other 5%.

Program Contact: Mr. A. Jon Megibow, Director of Admissions, University of Virginia, P.O. Box 6550, Charlottesville, VA 22906. (804) 924-7281, or (800) UVA-MBA1 (VA only); Fax: (804) 924-4859; Internet Address: darden@virginia.edu.

Virginia Commonwealth University

School of Business

Richmond, Virginia

OVERVIEW

Virginia Commonwealth University is a state-supported coed institution. Founded 1838. Setting: 99-acre urban campus. Total institutional enrollment: 22,000. Program was first offered in 1972. AACSB-accredited.

MBA HIGHLIGHTS

Entrance Difficulty**
Mean GMAT: 560
Mean GPA: 3.1

Cost $
Tuition: $1,796/semester
(Nonresident: $5,109/semester)
Room & Board: $4,200

Enrollment Profile

Full-time: 74	Work Exp: 90%
Part-time: 214	International: 5%
Total: 288	Women: 40%
Average Age: 29	Minorities: 10%

Average Class Size: 25

ACADEMICS

Length of Program Minimum: 24 months. Maximum: 7 years.

Calendar Semesters.

Full-time Classes Main campus; evening, summer.

Part-time Classes Main campus; evening, summer.

Degree Requirements 30 credits including 6 elective credits.

Required Courses Business policy, financial management, management information systems, managerial accounting, managerial economics, marketing management, operations research, organizational behavior.

Curricular Focus Entrepreneurship, general management, problem solving and decision making.

Concentrations Accounting, economics, entrepreneurship, finance, human resources management, international business, management, management information systems, marketing, operations management, organizational behavior, quantitative analysis, real estate, strategic management.

Faculty Full-time: 90, 95% with doctorates; part-time: 10, 100% with doctorates.

Teaching Methodology Case study: 20%, lecture: 40%, research: 5%, seminars by members of the business community: 5%, student presentations: 15%, team projects: 15%.

Special Opportunities International exchange in Indonesia, People's Republic of China. Internship program available. Other: cooperative education.

STUDENT STATISTICS

Geographic Representation State residents 85%. By region: South 80%; Northeast 10%; Midwest 3%; West 2%. International 5%.

Undergraduate Majors Business 50%; engineering/technology 15%; humanities 20%; science/mathematics 15%.

Other Background Graduate degrees in other disciplines: 10%. Work experience: On average, students have 3 years of work experience on entrance to the program.

FACILITIES

Information Resources Main library with 1.1 million bound volumes, 10,282 periodical subscriptions, 18,888 records/tapes/CDs. Business collection includes 10,000 bound volumes, 723 periodical subscriptions, 10 CD-ROMs, 45 videos.

Housing 5% of students in program live in college-owned or -operated housing.

Technology Computers are used moderately in course work. 180 computer terminals/PCs are available for use by students in program; they are located in student rooms, classrooms, the library, the computer center, computer labs. Students in the program are not required to have their own PC.

Computer Resources/On-line Services

Training	Yes	CompuServe	No
Internet	Yes	Dun's	Yes
E-Mail	Yes	Dow Jones	No
Multimedia Center	Yes	Dialog	Yes $
LEXIS/NEXIS	Yes	Bloomberg	No

ADMISSION

Acceptance 1994-95 Of those applying, 40% were accepted.

Entrance Requirements Bachelor's degree, GMAT score of 550, minimum 2.7 GPA, minimum 3 years of work experience.

Application Requirements Application form, copies of transcript, personal statement, 3 letters of recommendation.

Application Deadlines 6/1 for fall, 11/1 for spring.

FINANCIALS

Costs for 1994-95 Tuition: Full-time: $1,796/semester for state residents, $5,109/semester for nonresidents. Fees: Full-time: $433/semester for state residents, $433/semester for nonresidents. Average room and board costs are $4,200 per academic year (on-campus) and $6,000 per academic year (off-campus).

Financial Aid In 1994-95, 20% of candidates received some institutionally administered aid in the form of scholarships, loans, fellowships, assistantships, work-study. Total awards ranged from $6,350-$15,000. Financial aid is not available to part-time students. Application deadlines: 4/15 for fall, 11/1 for spring. Contact: Mr. Charles Kinder, Director, 901 West Franklin Street, Richmond, VA 23284-9005. (804) 828-6669.

INTERNATIONAL STUDENTS
Demographics 5% of students enrolled in the program are international; Asia 60%, Other 40%.

Services and Facilities Visa services, language tutoring, ESL courses, counseling/support services.

Applying TOEFL required, minimum score of 550; proof of adequate funds. Financial aid is available to international students. Financial aid application deadlines: 4/1 for fall, 10/1 for spring. Admission application deadlines: 4/1 for fall, 10/1 for spring. Contact: Mr. Bassam Khoury, International Student Adviser, 916 West Franklin Street, Richmond, VA 23284-9005. (804) 828-0595.

PLACEMENT
Placement services include alumni network, career counseling/planning, career fairs, career library, career placement, electronic job bank, job interviews, resume preparation, and resume referral to employers. Of 1994 graduates, 95% were employed within three months of graduation, the average starting salary was $40,000, the range was $30,000-$70,000.

Jobs by Employer Type Manufacturing 25%; service 45%; government 25%; consulting 5%.

Jobs by Functional Area Marketing/sales 13%; finance 11%; operations 9%; management 21%; strategic planning 3%; technical management 24%; other 19%.

Program Contact: Mr. Edward L. Millner, Associate Dean, Virginia Commonwealth University, 901 West Franklin Street, Richmond, VA 23284-9005. (804) 828-1741; Fax: (804) 828-8884.

Virginia Polytechnic Institute and State University

Pamplin College of Business

Blacksburg, Virginia

OVERVIEW
Virginia Polytechnic Institute and State University is a state-supported coed institution. Founded 1872. Setting: 2,600-acre small-town campus. Total institutional enrollment: 23,873. Program was first offered in 1971. AACSB-accredited.

MBA HIGHLIGHTS

Entrance Difficulty**
Mean GMAT: 574
Mean GPA: 3.16

Cost $
Tuition: $2,278/semester
(Nonresident: $3,363/semester)
Room & Board: $4,000

Enrollment Profile

Full-time: 203	Work Exp: 68%
Part-time: 352	International: 24%
Total: 555	Women: 30%
Average Age: 25	Minorities: N/R

Average Class Size: 40

ACADEMICS
Length of Program Minimum: 24 months. Maximum: 5 years.

Calendar Semesters.

Full-time Classes Main campus; day.

Part-time Classes Main campus, distance learning option; evening.

Degree Requirements 48 credits including 12 elective credits.

Required Courses Complex-based decision support systems, dynamics of organizational behavior, economics of business decisions, financial statement analysis of management, fundamentals of accounting, management

science, managerial statistics, marketing policy and strategy, principles of finance, production operations management in a global environment, social, legal, and ethical environment of business, strategic management.

Curricular Focus General management, problem solving and decision making, teamwork.

Concentrations Finance, international business, management, management information systems, marketing.

Faculty Full-time: 91, 100% with doctorates.

Special Opportunities International exchange in Japan, People's Republic of China. Internship program available.

STUDENT STATISTICS
Geographic Representation State residents 75%. International 24%.

Undergraduate Majors Business 53%; education 1%; engineering/technology 25%; humanities 11%; social sciences 5%; other 1%.

Other Background Work experience: On average, students have 3 years of work experience on entrance to the program.

FACILITIES
Information Resources Main library with 1.8 million bound volumes, 5.7 million titles on microform, 20,380 periodical subscriptions, 7,653 records/tapes/CDs.

Housing College housing available.

Technology Computers are used moderately in course work. Computer terminals/PCs, linked by a campus-wide computer network, are available for use by students in program; they are located in dormitories, the library, computer labs. Students in the program are not required to have their own PC.

Computer Resources/On-line Services

Internet	Yes	Dow Jones	Yes
E-Mail	Yes	Dialog	Yes

Other on-line services: SEC, Westlaw.

ADMISSION
Acceptance 1994-95 300 applied for admission; 87% were accepted.

Entrance Requirements Bachelor's degree, GMAT score.

Application Requirements Application form, copies of transcript, resume/curriculum vitae, 3 letters of recommendation.

Application Deadlines 4/15 for fall, 10/15 for spring.

FINANCIALS
Costs for 1994-95 Tuition: Full-time: $2,278/semester for state residents, $3,363/semester for nonresidents. Average room and board costs are $4,000 per academic year (on-campus).

Financial Aid In 1994-95, 50% of candidates received some institutionally administered aid in the form of scholarships, loans, fellowships, assistantships. Total awards ranged from $2,000-$5,780. Financial aid is available to part-time students. Application deadlines: 4/15 for fall, 10/15 for spring. Contact: Dr. Ronald Johnson, Associate Dean for Graduate and International Programs, 1044 Pamplin Hall, Blacksburg, VA 24061-0209. (703) 231-6152.

INTERNATIONAL STUDENTS
Demographics 24% of students enrolled in the program are international.

Services and Facilities International student office, international student center, language tutoring, counseling/support services.

Applying TOEFL required, minimum score of 550; proof of health; proof of adequate funds. Financial aid is not available to international students. Admission application deadlines: 4/15 for fall, 10/15 for spring. Applications are processed on a rolling basis. Contact: Mr. Bernard E. LaBerge, Assistant Dean, Foreign Students, 1044 Pamplin Hall, Blacksburg, VA 24061-0209. (703) 231-6271.

PLACEMENT
Placement services include alumni network, career counseling/planning, career fairs, career library, career placement, electronic job bank, job interviews, job search course, resume preparation, resume referral to employers, and Of 1994 graduates, 82% were employed within three months of graduation, the average starting salary was $37,900, the range was $21,600-$56,400.

Jobs by Employer Type Manufacturing 21%; service 30%; consulting 41%; other 6%.

Jobs by Functional Area Marketing/sales 13%; finance 4%; operations 9%; management 26%; strategic planning 39%; technical management 9%.

Program Contact: Dr. Ronald Johnson, Association Dean for Graduate and International Programs, Virginia Polytechnic Institute and State

University, 1044 Pamplin Hall, Blacksburg, VA 24061-0209. (703) 231-6152, Fax. (703) 231-4407; Internet Address: rdjmba@vtvml.cc.vt.edu.
See full description on page 928.

WASHINGTON

City University

Graduate School of Business and Management Professions

Bellevue, Washington

OVERVIEW
City University is an independent nonprofit comprehensive coed institution. Founded 1973. Setting: suburban campus with easy access to Seattle. Total institutional enrollment: 5,437. Program was first offered in 1977.

MBA HIGHLIGHTS

Entrance Difficulty*

Cost $
Tuition: $232/credit
Room & Board: N/R

Enrollment Profile
Full-time: 382
Part-time: 2,518
Total: 2,900
Average Age: 38

Work Exp: N/R
International: 12%
Women: 34%
Minorities: 34%

Average Class Size: 18

ACADEMICS
Length of Program Minimum: 18 months.
Calendar Quarters.
Full-time Classes Main campus; day, evening, weekends, early morning, summer.
Part-time Classes Main campus; day, evening, weekends, early morning, summer.
Degree Requirements 45 credits including 12 elective credits.
Required Courses Effective managerial behavior, human resources management, introduction to quality management theory, legal systems in a global economy, management information systems, managerial accounting, managerial communications and research methods, marketing management, organization and management. Courses may be waived through: previous course work, work experience.
Curricular Focus General management, leadership, organizational development and change management.
Concentrations Entrepreneurship, finance, management, management information systems, marketing, public administration, quality management, Asia-Pacific management, telecommunications management.
Faculty Full-time: 14; part-time: 391.
Teaching Methodology Case study: 5%, lecture: 45%, research: 35%, student presentations: 10%, team projects: 5%.

STUDENT STATISTICS
Geographic Representation State residents 88%. By region: West 64%; South 6%; Northeast 3%; Midwest 3%. International 12%.

FACILITIES
Information Resources Main library with 18,200 bound volumes, 560 periodical subscriptions, 4 CD-ROMs.
Housing College housing not available.
Technology Computers are used moderately in course work. 100 computer terminals/PCs, linked by a campus-wide computer network, are available for use by students in program; they are located in the library, computer labs. Students in the program are not required to have their own PC.

Computer Resources/On-line Services
E Mail   Yes

Other on-line services: OCLC.

ADMISSION
Acceptance 1994-95 1,348 applied for admission; 100% were accepted.
Entrance Requirements Bachelor's degree. Core courses waived through: previous course work, work experience.
Application Requirements Application form, copies of transcript.
Application Deadline Applications are processed on a rolling basis.

FINANCIALS
Costs for 1994-95 Tuition: Full-time: $232/credit.
Financial Aid In 1994-95, candidates received some institutionally administered aid in the form of scholarships. Total awards ranged from $500-$18,500. Financial aid is available to part-time students. Applications are processed on a rolling basis. Contact: Mr. Caroline Caldwell, Director of Financial Aid, 335 116th Avenue, SE, Bellevue, WA 98004. (800) 426-5596 Ext. 4040.

INTERNATIONAL STUDENTS
Demographics 12% of students enrolled in the program are international.
Services and Facilities ESL courses, special assistance for nonnative speakers of English.
Applying TOEFL required. Admission application deadlines: 9/1 for fall, 2/1 for winter, 3/1 for spring, 6/1 for summer. Contact: Ms. Mei Yang, Adviser, International Students, 919 Southeast Grady Way, Renton, WA 98055. (800) 426-5596 Ext. 3819.

ALTERNATE MBA PROGRAM
MBA/MPA.

Program Contact: Office Admissions, City University, 335 116th Avenue SE, Bellevue, WA 98004. (206) 637-1010, or (800) 426-5596; Fax: (206) 277-2437.
See full description on page 696.

Eastern Washington University

College of Business Administration

Cheney, Washington

OVERVIEW
Eastern Washington University is a state-supported comprehensive coed institution. Founded 1882. Setting: 335-acre urban campus. Total institutional enrollment: 8,065. Program was first offered in 1975. AACSB-accredited.

MBA HIGHLIGHTS

Entrance Difficulty***
Mean GMAT: 534
Mean GPA: 3.37

Cost $
Tuition: $1,200/quarter
(Nonresident: $3,645/quarter)
Room & Board: $3,810

Enrollment Profile
Full-time: 20
Part-time: 70
Total: 90
Average Age: 32

Work Exp: 75%
International: 7%
Women: 31%
Minorities: 1%

Average Class Size: 16

ACADEMICS
Length of Program Minimum: 12 months. Maximum: 6 years.
Calendar Quarters.
Full-time Classes Main campus, Spokane Center; evening.
Part-time Classes Main campus, Spokane Center; evening.
Degree Requirements 48 credits including 8 elective credits. Other: Oral final exam.

Required Courses Administrative controls, administrative policies, business decision analysis, corporate finance, environment of business, management information systems, marketing management, methods of business research, organization theory and management.

Curricular Focus Organizational development and change management, problem solving and decision making, strategic analysis and planning.

Concentrations Health services, management.

Faculty Full-time: 28, 98% with doctorates.

Teaching Methodology Case study: 20%, lecture: 15%, research: 20%, seminars by members of the business community: 5%, student presentations: 20%, team projects: 20%.

Special Opportunities Internships include nonprofit organizations/government agencies.

STUDENT STATISTICS
Geographic Representation International 7%.

Undergraduate Majors Business 62%; engineering/technology 13%; humanities 8%; nursing 3%; science/mathematics 4%; social sciences 6%; other 4%.

Other Background Graduate degrees in other disciplines: 2%.

FACILITIES
Information Resources Main library with 469,727 bound volumes, 1.1 million titles on microform, 3,569 periodical subscriptions, 29,302 records/tapes/CDs, 180 CD-ROMs.

Housing 7% of students in program live in college-owned or -operated housing.

Technology Computers are used moderately in course work. 91 computer terminals/PCs, linked by a campus-wide computer network, are available for use by students in program; they are located in computer labs. Students in the program are not required to have their own PC.

Computer Resources/On-line Services

Training	Yes	E-Mail	Yes
Internet	Yes	LEXIS/NEXIS	Yes

Other on-line services: OCLC, First Search.

ADMISSION
Acceptance 1994-95 Of those applying, 60% were accepted.

Entrance Requirements Bachelor's degree, GMAT score of 500, minimum 3.0 GPA. Core courses waived through: previous course work.

Application Requirements Application form.

FINANCIALS
Costs for 1994-95 Tuition: Full-time: $1,200/quarter for state residents, $3,645/quarter for nonresidents. Fees: Full-time: $40/quarter for state residents, $40/quarter for nonresidents. Average room and board costs are $3,810 per academic year (on-campus).

Financial Aid In 1994-95, candidates received some institutionally administered aid in the form of assistantships. Financial aid is available to part-time students. Application deadline: 2/15 for fall. Contact: Ms. Susan Shackette Howe, Director of Financial Aid, 526 5th Street, Cheney, WA 99004. (509) 359-2314.

INTERNATIONAL STUDENTS
Demographics 7% of students enrolled in the program are international; Asia 80%, Europe 20%.

Services and Facilities International student center, ESL courses, counseling/support services.

Applying TOEFL required, minimum score of 580; proof of adequate funds. Financial aid is not available to international students. Admission application deadlines: 6/30 for fall, 1/30 for spring. Contact: Dr. H. T. Wong, Director, International Student Program, 526 5th Street, Cheney, WA 99004. (509) 359-2331.

ALTERNATE MBA PROGRAM
MBA/MPA Length of program: Minimum: 24 months. Maximum: 6 years. Degree requirements: 75 credits including 18 elective credits. Written research report; oral final.

PLACEMENT
Placement services include career counseling/planning, career library, career placement, resume preparation, and resume referral to employers. Of 1994 graduates, 95% were employed within three months of graduation.

Program Contact: Mr. Bruce Kellam, MBA Director, Eastern Washington University, 705 West First Avenue, Spokane, WA 99204. (509) 458-6413, or (800) 707-6674; Fax: (509) 458-6393.

Gonzaga University

School of Business Administration

Spokane, Washington

OVERVIEW
Gonzaga University is an independent Roman Catholic comprehensive coed institution. Founded 1887. Setting: 83-acre urban campus. Total institutional enrollment: 5,200. Program was first offered in 1961. AACSB-accredited.

MBA HIGHLIGHTS

Entrance Difficulty***
Mean GMAT: 570
Mean GPA: 3.2

Cost $$
Tuition: $340/credit hour
Room & Board: $3,700

Enrollment Profile

Full-time: 40	Work Exp: 70%
Part-time: 77	International: 20%
Total: 117	Women: 25%
Average Age: 27	Minorities: 10%

Average Class Size: 15

ACADEMICS
Length of Program Minimum: 12 months. Maximum: 5 years.

Calendar Semesters.

Full-time Classes Main campus; evening, summer.

Part-time Classes Main campus; evening, summer.

Degree Requirements 33 credits including 12 elective credits.

Required Courses Accounting theory and practice, business ethics, economic environment of business, finance theory and practice, information systems theory and practice, management development, marketing theory and practice, operations theory and practice, research design and analysis, strategic management. Courses may be waived through: previous course work.

Curricular Focus Business issues and problems, entrepreneurship, strategic analysis and planning.

Concentrations Accounting, management.

Faculty Full-time: 27, 100% with doctorates.

Teaching Methodology Case study: 30%, lecture: 40%, research: 10%, student presentations: 10%, team projects: 10%.

Special Opportunities Internships include manufacturing, merchandising, and service.

STUDENT STATISTICS
Geographic Representation State residents 60%. By region: West 65%; Midwest 10%; Northeast 5%. International 20%.

Undergraduate Majors Business 40%; engineering/technology 20%; humanities 10%; science/mathematics 10%; social sciences 20%.

Other Background Graduate degrees in other disciplines: 10%. Work experience: On average, students have 2 years of work experience on entrance to the program.

FACILITIES
Information Resources Main library with 723,994 bound volumes, 801,384 titles on microform, 3,849 periodical subscriptions, 782 records/tapes/CDs, 33 CD-ROMs.

Housing 20% of students in program live in college-owned or -operated housing.

Technology Computers are used moderately in course work. 115 computer terminals/PCs, linked by a campus-wide computer network, are available for use by students in program; they are located in classrooms, the library, computer labs. Students in the program are not required to have their own PC.

Computer Resources/On-line Services

Training	Yes	Videoconference Center	Yes
Internet	Yes	Multimedia Center	Yes
E-Mail	Yes		

ADMISSION

Acceptance 1994-95 70 applied for admission; 80% were accepted.

Entrance Requirements Bachelor's degree, GMAT score of 500. Core courses waived through: previous course work.

Application Requirements Application form, copies of transcript, 2 letters of recommendation.

Application Deadline Applications are processed on a rolling basis.

FINANCIALS

Costs for 1994-95 Tuition: Full-time: $340/credit hour. Fees: Full-time: $50/semester. Average room and board costs are $3,700 per academic year (on-campus).

Financial Aid In 1994-95, 18% of candidates received some institutionally administered aid in the form of scholarships, assistantships. Total awards ranged from $320-$3,840. Financial aid is available to part-time students. Applications are processed on a rolling basis. Contact: Financial Aid Office, Spokane, WA 99258. (509) 328-4220 Ext. 3182.

INTERNATIONAL STUDENTS

Demographics 20% of students enrolled in the program are international; Asia 56%, Africa 16%, South America 12%, other 16%.

Services and Facilities International student center, language tutoring, ESL courses.

Applying TOEFL required; proof of adequate funds. Financial aid is available to international students. Applications are processed on a rolling basis. Admission applications are processed on a rolling basis. Contact: Ms. Elaine Ike, Assistant Director, International Student Programs, International Student Programs, Spokane, WA 99258. (509) 328-4220.

ALTERNATE MBA PROGRAM

MBA/JD Length of program: Minimum: 36 months. Degree requirements: 114 credits.

PLACEMENT

Placement services include alumni network, career counseling/planning, career fairs, career library, career placement, job interviews, resume preparation, and resume referral to employers.

Program Contact: Mr. Lawrence Lewis, Assistant Dean, Gonzaga University, Spokane, WA 99258. (509) 328-4220 Ext. 3430, or (800) 572-9658 (WA only), or (800) 523-9712 (out-of-state); Internet Address: lewis@jepson.gonzaga.edu.

Pacific Lutheran University

School of Business

Tacoma, Washington

OVERVIEW

Pacific Lutheran University is an independent comprehensive coed institution, affiliated with Evangelical Lutheran Church in America. Founded 1890. Setting: 133-acre suburban campus with easy access to Seattle. Total institutional enrollment: 3,400. Program was first offered in 1965. AACSB-accredited.

MBA HIGHLIGHTS

Entrance Difficulty*
Mean GMAT: 520
Mean GPA: N/R

Cost $$
Tuition: $416/semester hour
(Nonresident: $416/semester hour)
Room & Board: $4,488

Enrollment Profile

Full-time: 72	Work Exp: 93%
Part-time: 108	International: 10%
Total: 180	Women: 32%
Average Age: 29	Minorities: 8%

Average Class Size: 16

ACADEMICS

Length of Program Minimum: 16 months. Maximum: 7 years.

Calendar 4-1-4.

Full-time Classes Main campus; evening, summer.

Part-time Classes Main campus; evening, summer.

Degree Requirements 48 semester hours including 16 elective semester hours.

Curricular Focus General management, problem solving and decision making, teamwork.

Concentrations Entrepreneurship, finance, human resources management, international business, management, marketing.

Faculty Full-time: 10, 100% with doctorates; part-time: 1.

Teaching Methodology Case study: 10%, lecture: 50%, research: 10%, student presentations: 10%, team projects: 20%.

Special Opportunities International exchange and internship programs available.

STUDENT STATISTICS

Geographic Representation State residents 90%. By region: West 90%. International 10%.

Undergraduate Majors Business 41%; education 2%; engineering/technology 13%; humanities 2%; nursing 1%; science/mathematics 16%; social sciences 12%; other 13%.

Other Background Work experience: On average, students have 5 years of work experience on entrance to the program.

FACILITIES

Information Resources Main library with 320,382 bound volumes, 72,555 titles on microform, 1,989 periodical subscriptions, 8,739 records/tapes/CDs, 9 CD-ROMs.

Housing 1% of students in program live in college-owned or -operated housing.

Technology Computers are used moderately in course work. 40 computer terminals/PCs are available for use by students in program; they are located in computer labs. Students in the program are not required to have their own PC.

Computer Resources/On-line Services

Training	Yes	CompuServe	No
Internet	Yes	Dun's	No
E-Mail	Yes	Dow Jones	No
Multimedia Center	Yes	Dialog	No
LEXIS/NEXIS	No	Bloomberg	No

ADMISSION

Entrance Requirements Bachelor's degree, GMAT score of 470, minimum 2.75 GPA.

Application Requirements Written essay, application form, copies of transcript, resume/curriculum vitae.

Application Deadlines 8/1 for fall, 1/1 for spring. Applications are processed on a rolling basis.

FINANCIALS

Costs for 1994-95 Tuition: Full-time: $416/semester hour, $416/semester hour for international students. Average room and board costs are $4,488 per academic year (on-campus).

Financial Aid In 1994-95, candidates received some institutionally administered aid in the form of scholarships, loans, assistantships, work-study. Financial aid is available to part-time students. Contact: Ms. Kay Soltis, Director of Financial Aid, Pacific Lutheran University, Tacoma, WA 98447. (206) 535-7161.

INTERNATIONAL STUDENTS

Demographics 10% of students enrolled in the program are international; Europe 53%, Asia 40%, other 7%.

Services and Facilities International student office, international student center, visa services, language tutoring, ESL courses, special assistance for nonnative speakers of English, counseling/support services.

Applying TOEFL required, minimum score of 550; proof of health; proof of adequate funds. Financial aid is not available to international students. Admission application deadlines: 6/1 for fall, 11/1 for spring. Applications are processed on a rolling basis. Contact: Mr. David Gerry, Coordinator of International Student Services, Pacific Lutheran University, Tacoma, WA 98447. (206) 535-7194.

PLACEMENT

Placement services include alumni network, career library, career placement, electronic job bank, resume preparation, and resume referral to employers.

Program Contact: Dr. Laura Polcyn, Associate Dean and Director, MBA Program, Pacific Lutheran University, School of Business, Tacoma, WA 98447. (206) 535-7250, or (800) 274-6758 (WA only); Fax: (206) 535-8723; Internet Address: polcynlj@plu.edu.

Saint Martin's College

Department of Economics and Business Administration

Lacey, Washington

OVERVIEW

Saint Martin's College is an independent Roman Catholic comprehensive coed institution. Founded 1895. Setting: 480-acre suburban campus with easy access to Tacoma. Total institutional enrollment: 1,000.

MBA HIGHLIGHTS

Entrance Difficulty***
Mean GMAT: 550
Mean GPA: N/R

Cost $$
Tuition: $385/semester hour
Room & Board: $4,270

Enrollment Profile
Full-time: 10
Part-time: 145
Total: 155
Average Age: 29

Work Exp: 95%
International: 10%
Women: 35%
Minorities: 20%

Average Class Size: 14

ACADEMICS

Length of Program Minimum: 18 months. Maximum: 7 years.

Calendar 5 terms per year.

Full-time Classes Main campus, Fort Lewis, McChord Air Force Base; evening, summer.

Part-time Classes Main campus, Fort Lewis, McChord Air Force Base; evening, summer.

Degree Requirements 33 credits including 6-9 elective credits. Other: Research projects or thesis.

Required Courses Accounting for managing decision making, advanced quantitative methods, financial planning and control, marketing concepts and theory, organizational behavior and theory, seminar: research methods, strategy and policy.

Curricular Focus General management, problem solving and decision making, teamwork.

Concentration Management.

Faculty Full-time: 6, 20% with doctorates; part-time: 10, 30% with doctorates.

Teaching Methodology Case study: 20%, faculty seminars: 5%, lecture: 30%, research: 10%, seminars by members of the business community: 5%, student presentations: 10%, team projects: 20%.

STUDENT STATISTICS

Geographic Representation By region: West 100%. International 10%.

Undergraduate Majors Business 25%; education 10%; engineering/technology 20%; humanities 20%; science/mathematics 15%; social sciences 10%.

Other Background Graduate degrees in other disciplines: 5%. Work experience: On average, students have 7 years of work experience on entrance to the program.

FACILITIES

Information Resources Main library with 84,019 bound volumes, 362 titles on microform, 528 periodical subscriptions, 734 records/tapes/CDs, 8 CD-ROMs.

Housing 1% of students in program live in college-owned or -operated housing.

Technology Computers are used heavily in course work. 15 computer terminals/PCs, linked by a campus-wide computer network, are available for use by students in program; they are located in the computer center, computer labs. Students in the program are not required to have their own PC.

Computer Resources/On-line Services
Training   No   LEXIS/NEXIS   Yes
Internet   Yes   CompuServe   Yes
E-Mail   Yes

ADMISSION

Entrance Requirements Bachelor's degree, GMAT score. Core courses waived through: previous course work.

Application Requirements Application form, copies of transcript.

Application Deadline Applications are processed on a rolling basis.

FINANCIALS

Costs for 1994-95 Tuition: Part-time day: $385/semester hour. Average room and board costs are $4,270 per academic year (on-campus).

Financial Aid In 1994-95, 30% of candidates received some institutionally administered aid in the form of scholarships, loans. Total awards ranged from $1,000-$4,000. Financial aid is available to part-time students. Applications are processed on a rolling basis. Contact: Ms. Marianna Deeken, Director of Financial Aid, 5300 Pacific Avenue, SE, Lacey, WA 98503. (360) 438-4397.

INTERNATIONAL STUDENTS

Demographics 10% of students enrolled in the program are international; Asia 50%, Other 50%.

Applying TOEFL required, minimum score of 525. Financial aid is available to international students. Financial aid and admissions applications are processed on a rolling basis.

PLACEMENT

In 1993-94, 35 organizations participated in on-campus recruiting. Placement services include career counseling/planning, career fairs, and resume preparation. Of 1994 graduates, 85% were employed within three months of graduation.

Program Contact: Mr. Haldon D. Wilson Jr., Director of Graduate Studies in Business, Saint Martin's College, 5300 Pacific Avenue, SE, Lacey, WA 98503. (360) 438-4512; Fax: (360) 459-4124.

Seattle Pacific University

School of Business and Economics

Seattle, Washington

OVERVIEW

Seattle Pacific University is an independent Free Methodist comprehensive coed institution. Founded 1891. Setting: 35-acre urban campus. Total institutional enrollment: 3,500. Program was first offered in 1983.

MBA HIGHLIGHTS

Entrance Difficulty***
Mean GMAT: 516
Mean GPA: 3.2

Cost $$
Tuition: $355/credit
Room & Board: $6,716

Enrollment Profile
Full-time: 63
Part-time: 147
Total: 210
Average Age: 32

Work Exp: 75%
International: 27%
Women: 40%
Minorities: 30%

Average Class Size: 17

ACADEMICS

Length of Program Minimum: 24 months. Maximum: 6 years.

Calendar Quarters.

Full-time Classes Main campus, Renton; evening, summer.

Part-time Classes Main campus, Renton; evening, summer.

Degree Requirements 45 credits including 15 elective credits.

Required Courses Financial accounting, information systems management, legal environment of business, macroeconomics for managers, managerial finance, managerial marketing, operations management, organizational theory and behavior, quantitative methods. Courses may be waived through: previous course work.

Curricular Focus Entrepreneurship, general management, problem solving and decision making.

Concentrations Entrepreneurship, human resources management, information systems management, management, management information systems.

Faculty Full-time: 17, 94% with doctorates; part-time: 6, 66% with doctorates.

Teaching Methodology Case study: 25%, faculty seminars: 5%, lecture: 40%, research: 5%, seminars by members of the business community: 5%, student presentations: 5%, team projects: 15%.

Special Opportunities Internship program available.

STUDENT STATISTICS

Geographic Representation State residents 73%. By region: West 70%; Northeast 1%; South 1%; Midwest 1%. International 27%.

Undergraduate Majors Business 50%; education 2%; engineering/technology 25%; humanities 2%; nursing 2%; science/mathematics 10%; social sciences 5%; other 4%.

Other Background Graduate degrees in other disciplines: 5%. Work experience: On average, students have 3 years of work experience on entrance to the program.

FACILITIES

Information Resources Main library with 176,500 bound volumes, 417,800 titles on microform, 1,600 periodical subscriptions, 4,300 records/tapes/CDs, 21 CD-ROMs.

Housing 3% of students in program live in college-owned or -operated housing.

Technology Computers are used moderately in course work. 25 computer terminals/PCs, linked by a campus-wide computer network, are available for use by students in program; they are located in learning resource center, the library, computer labs. Students in the program are not required to have their own PC.

Computer Resources/On-line Services

| Training | No | E-Mail | Yes |
| Internet | Yes | Multimedia Center | Yes |

ADMISSION

Acceptance 1994-95 169 applied for admission; 69% were accepted.

Entrance Requirements Bachelor's degree, GMAT score of 450, minimum 3.0 GPA, minimum 2 years of work experience. Core courses waived through: previous course work.

Application Requirements Written essay, application form, copies of transcript, personal statement.

Application Deadlines 8/15 for fall, 11/15 for winter, 2/15 for spring, 5/15 for summer.

FINANCIALS

Costs for 1994-95 Tuition: Full-time: $355/credit. Average room and board costs are $6,716 per academic year (on-campus) and $9,600 per academic year (off-campus).

Financial Aid In 1994-95, 2% of candidates received some institutionally administered aid in the form of grants, scholarships, assistantships. Total awards ranged from $4,000-$9,000. Financial aid is not available to part-time students. Applications are processed on a rolling basis. Contact: Ms. Jeanne Rich, Director of Student Employment and Financial Aid, 3307 Third Avenue West, Seattle, WA 98119-1997. (206) 281-2046.

INTERNATIONAL STUDENTS

Demographics 27% of students enrolled in the program are international.

Applying TOEFL required, minimum score of 560; proof of adequate funds. Financial aid is available to international students. Admission application deadlines: 8/15 for fall, 11/15 for winter, 2/15 for spring, 5/15 for summer. Applications are processed on a rolling basis. Contact: Mr. Brian Bosse, Associate Director, Center for Special Populations, 3307 Third Avenue West, Seattle, WA 98119-1997. (206) 281-2486.

ALTERNATE MBA PROGRAM

MSISM Length of program: Minimum: 24 months. Maximum: 6 years. Degree requirements: 42 credits including 15 elective credits. Project. Average class size: 17.

PLACEMENT

Placement services include career counseling/planning, career library, resume preparation, and resume referral to employers. Of 1994 graduates, 90% were employed within three months of graduation.

Jobs by Employer Type Manufacturing 36%; service 44%; government 1%; consulting 5%; nonprofit 6%; healthcare 8%.

Jobs by Functional Area Marketing/sales 13%; finance 13%; operations 15%; management 22%; strategic planning 13%; technical management 18%; human resources 6%.

Program Contact: MBA Admissions Coordinator, Seattle Pacific University, 3307 Third Avenue West, Seattle, WA 98119-1997. (206) 281-2054; Fax: (206) 281-2733; Internet Address: mba@spu.edu.

See full description on page 828.

Seattle University

Albers School of Business and Economics

Seattle, Washington

OVERVIEW

Seattle University is an independent Roman Catholic comprehensive coed institution. Founded 1891. Setting: 46-acre urban campus. Total institutional enrollment: 6,091. Program was first offered in 1967. AACSB-accredited.

MBA HIGHLIGHTS

Entrance Difficulty****
Mean GMAT: 555
Mean GPA: 3.21

Cost $$$
Tuition: $4,440/quarter
Room & Board: $5,979

Enrollment Profile

Full-time: 95	Work Exp: 98%
Part-time: 600	International: 8%
Total: 695	Women: 39%
Average Age: 32	Minorities: 8%

Average Class Size: 28

ACADEMICS

Length of Program Minimum: 12 months. Maximum: 6 years.

Calendar Quarters.

Full-time Classes Main campus, Bellevue, Everett; day, evening, weekends, summer.

Part-time Classes Main campus, Bellevue, Everett; day, evening, weekends, summer.

Degree Requirements 48 credits including 18 elective credits.

Required Courses Advanced organizational behavior, business policy, ethics, international business, macroeconomics, management science, managerial accounting, managerial finance, marketing management, microeconomics. Courses may be waived through: previous course work.

Curricular Focus Economic and financial theory, general management, international business.

Concentrations Accounting, economics, entrepreneurship, finance, human resources management, international business, management, management information systems, marketing, operations management, organizational behavior, quantitative analysis, real estate, strategic management.

Faculty Full-time: 48, 92% with doctorates; part-time: 4, 50% with doctorates.

Teaching Methodology Case study: 25%, lecture: 40%, research: 5%, student presentations: 10%, team projects: 20%.

Special Opportunities Internship program available. Other: executive mentor program.

STUDENT STATISTICS

Geographic Representation International 8%.

Undergraduate Majors Business 36%; engineering/technology 37%; humanities 20%; other 7%.

Other Background Graduate degrees in other disciplines: 1%. Work experience: On average, students have 4 years of work experience on entrance to the program.

FACILITIES

Information Resources Main library with 199,685 bound volumes, 1,874 titles on microform, 1,430 periodical subscriptions, 283 records/tapes/CDs, 9 CD-ROMs.

Housing 1% of students in program live in college-owned or -operated housing.

Technology Computers are used moderately in course work. 153 computer terminals/PCs, linked by a campus-wide computer network, are available for use by students in program; they are located in dormitories, classrooms, computer labs. Students in the program are not required to have their own PC.

Computer Resources/On-line Services

Training	Yes	Dun's	No
Internet	Yes	Dow Jones	No
E-Mail	Yes	Dialog	Yes
LEXIS/NEXIS	No	Bloomberg	No
CompuServe	No		

Other on-line services: OCLC.

ADMISSION

Acceptance 1994-95 1,103 applied for admission; 63% were accepted.

Entrance Requirements Bachelor's degree, GMAT score of 500, minimum 3.0 GPA, minimum 1 year of work experience. Core courses waived through: previous course work.

Application Requirements Application form, copies of transcript.

Application Deadlines 8/20 for fall, 11/20 for winter, 2/20 for spring, 5/20 for summer.

FINANCIALS

Costs for 1994-95 Tuition: Full-time: $4,440/quarter; Part-time evening: $2,220/quarter. Average room and board costs are $5,979 per academic year (on-campus) and $9,600 per academic year (off-campus).

Financial Aid In 1994-95, 40% of candidates received some institutionally administered aid in the form of scholarships, loans, assistantships. Total awards ranged from $500-$18,500. Financial aid is available to part-time students. Application deadlines: 5/1 for fall, 11/1 for winter, 11/1 for spring, 5/1 for summer. Contact: Mr. Jim White, Director of Financial Aid, Broadway and Madison, Seattle, WA 98122-4460. (206) 296-5840.

INTERNATIONAL STUDENTS

Demographics 8% of students enrolled in the program are international.

Services and Facilities International student center, language tutoring, ESL courses, cultural bridge classes.

Applying TOEFL required, minimum score of 560; proof of adequate funds. Financial aid is not available to international students. Admission application deadlines: 6/1 for fall, 11/1 for winter, 2/1 for spring, 5/1 for summer. Contact: Mr. Faisi Ghodsi, Director, International Student Center, Broadway and Madison, Seattle, WA 98122-4460. (206) 296-6260.

ALTERNATE MBA PROGRAM

One-Year MBA Length of program: Minimum: 12 months. Maximum: 6 years. Degree requirements: 48 credits including 18 elective credits. Undergraduate degree in business.

PLACEMENT

Placement services include career counseling/planning, career fairs, career library, career placement, job interviews, networking programs, and resume referral to employers.

Program Contact: Ms. Deborah Rohovit, Director, Graduate Admissions, Seattle University, Broadway and Madison, Seattle, WA 98122. (206) 296-5900, or (800) 542-0833 (WA only), or (800) 426-7123 (out-of-state); Fax: (206) 296-5656.

University of Washington

Graduate School of Business Administration

Seattle, Washington

OVERVIEW

The University of Washington is a state-supported coed institution. Founded 1861. Setting: 703-acre urban campus. Total institutional enrollment: 35,000. Program was first offered in 1917. AACSB-accredited.

MBA HIGHLIGHTS

Entrance Difficulty***
Mean GMAT: 619
Mean GPA: 3.24

Cost $
Tuition: $4,566
(Nonresident: $11,436)
Room & Board: $6,800

Enrollment Profile

Full-time: N/R	Work Exp: 97%
Part-time: N/R	International: 17%
Total: 320	Women: 34%
Average Age: 29	Minorities: 13%

Average Class Size: 30

ACADEMICS

Length of Program Minimum: 18 months. Maximum: 6 years.

Calendar Quarters.

Full-time Classes Main campus; day.

Degree Requirements 96 credits including 12 elective credits.

Required Courses Business policy and planning, decision support models, financial accounting, financial management, information systems, macroeconomics, managerial and cost accounting, marketing management, operations management, organizational management, statistical data analysis, the corporation in society.

Curricular Focus Environmental management, international business, teamwork.

Concentrations Accounting, economics, entrepreneurship, environmental management, manufacturing management, finance, health services, human resources management, international business, management, management information systems, marketing, operations management, organizational behavior, public administration, public policy, quantitative analysis, real estate, strategic management.

Faculty Full-time: 80, 90% with doctorates.

Teaching Methodology Case study: 24%, faculty seminars: 23%, lecture: 10%, research: 10%, seminars by members of the business community: 5%, student presentations: 5%, team projects: 23%.

Special Opportunities International exchange in Chile, Denmark, Finland, France, Germany, Hong Kong, Japan, Mexico, People's Republic of China, Spain, Taiwan, United Kingdom. Internship program available.

STUDENT STATISTICS

Geographic Representation State residents 65%. By region: West 60%; Northeast 13%; South 5%; Midwest 5%. International 17%.

Undergraduate Majors Business 24%; engineering/technology 28%; humanities 17%; social sciences 30%; other 1%.

Other Background Graduate degrees in other disciplines: 7%. Work experience: On average, students have 4 years of work experience on entrance to the program.

FACILITIES

Information Resources Main library with 5.3 million bound volumes, 5.9 million titles on microform, 54,517 periodical subscriptions. Business collection in Business Administration Library includes 56,113 bound volumes, 800 periodical subscriptions, 10 CD-ROMs.

Housing 20% of students in program live in college-owned or -operated housing.

Technology Computers are used moderately in course work. Computer terminals/PCs, linked by a campus-wide computer network, are available for use by students in program; they are located in computer labs. Students in the program are required to have their own PC.

Computer Resources/On-line Services

Training	Yes	LEXIS/NEXIS	Yes
Internet	Yes	Dun's	Yes
E-Mail	Yes	Dow Jones	Yes

ADMISSION

Acceptance 1994-95 Of those applying, 40% were accepted.

Entrance Requirements Bachelor's degree, GMAT score, minimum 2 years of work experience.

Application Requirements Written essay, application form, copies of transcript, resume/curriculum vitae, personal statement.

Application Deadline 3/1 for fall.

FINANCIALS

Costs for 1994-95 Tuition: Full-time: $4,566 for state residents, $11,436 for nonresidents. Average room and board costs are $6,800 per academic year (on-campus) and $6,800 per academic year (off-campus).

Financial Aid In 1994-95, candidates received some institutionally administered aid in the form of scholarships, assistantships, work-study. Total awards ranged from $600-$5,000. Financial aid is not available to part-time students. Application deadline: 2/1 for fall. Contact: Ms. Barbara Pearson, Assistant to the Dean, Seattle, WA 98195. (206) 685-8916.

INTERNATIONAL STUDENTS

Demographics 17% of students enrolled in the program are international.

Services and Facilities International student center, visa services, ESL courses, counseling/support services.

Applying TOEFL required, minimum score of 580; proof of adequate funds. Financial aid is not available to international students. Admission application deadline: 2/1 for fall.

ALTERNATE MBA PROGRAMS

MBA/JD Length of program: Minimum: 48 months. Degree requirements: 216 credits.

MBA/MA Length of program: Minimum: 36 months. Degree requirements: 132 credits. MA is in international studies.

MBA/MS Length of program: Minimum: 24 months. Degree requirements: 135 credits. MS is in engineering.

MBA/MHA Length of program: Minimum: 36 months. Degree requirements: 132 credits.

PLACEMENT

In 1993-94, 60 organizations participated in on-campus recruiting; 400 on-campus interviews were conducted. Placement services include alumni network, career counseling/planning, career fairs, career library, career placement, electronic job bank, job interviews, resume preparation, and resume referral to employers. Of 1994 graduates, 75% were employed within three months of graduation, the average starting salary was $44,000, the range was $27,600-$80,000.

Program Contact: Dr. Leighanne Harris, Director, MBA Program, University of Washington, Seattle, WA 98195. (206) 543-4661; Fax: (206) 685-9392.

Washington State University

College of Business and Economics

Pullman, Washington

OVERVIEW

Washington State University is a state-supported coed institution. Founded 1890. Setting: 656-acre small-town campus. Total institutional enrollment: 17,000. Program was first offered in 1957. AACSB-accredited.

MBA HIGHLIGHTS

Entrance Difficulty**
Mean GMAT: 550
Mean GPA: 3.4

Cost $
Tuition: $2,283/semester
(Nonresident: $5,718/semester)
Room & Board: N/R

Enrollment Profile

Full-time: 140	Work Exp: 70%
Part-time: 0	International: N/R
Total: 140	Women: 34%
Average Age: 24	Minorities: 17%

Average Class Size: 25

ACADEMICS

Length of Program Minimum: 12 months. Maximum: 6 years.
Calendar Semesters.
Full-time Classes Main campus; day, summer.
Part-time Classes Main campus, Richland, Vancouver; evening.
Degree Requirements 32 credits including 12 elective credits.

Required Courses Accounting control systems, marketing management, organizational behavior, problems in finance, statistical analysis, strategic management. Courses may be waived through: previous course work.

Curricular Focus Economic and financial theory, leadership, problem solving and decision making, teamwork.

Concentrations Accounting, finance, hotel management, human resources management, international business, management, management information systems, marketing, quality control and operations, real estate, strategic management.

Faculty Full-time: 51, 95% with doctorates.

Teaching Methodology Case study: 25%, lecture: 25%, student presentations: 25%, team projects: 25%.

Special Opportunities International exchange in Austria, Denmark. Internships include education.

STUDENT STATISTICS

Geographic Representation State residents 34%.

Other Background Work experience: On average, students have 2 years of work experience on entrance to the program.

FACILITIES

Information Resources Main library with 1.7 million bound volumes, 2.9 million titles on microform, 24,356 periodical subscriptions, 25,986 records/tapes/CDs.

Housing College housing available.

Technology Computers are used heavily in course work. Computer terminals/PCs, linked by a campus-wide computer network, are available for use by students in program; they are located in the computer center, computer labs. Students in the program are not required to have their own PC.

Computer Resources/On-line Services

Training	Yes	Videoconference Center	Yes
E-Mail	Yes		

ADMISSION

Entrance Requirements Bachelor's degree, GMAT score of 500, minimum 3.0 GPA. Core courses waived through: previous course work.

Application Requirements Application form, copies of transcript, 3 letters of recommendation.

FINANCIALS

Costs for 1994-95 Tuition: Full-time: $2,283/semester for state residents, $5,718/semester for nonresidents.

Financial Aid In 1994-95, 35% of candidates received some institutionally administered aid in the form of scholarships, assistantships, work-study. Applications are processed on a rolling basis. Contact: Ms. Lola J. Finch, Interim Director, French 332, Pullman, WA 99164. (509) 335-9711.

INTERNATIONAL STUDENTS

Demographics 7% of students on campus are international; Asia 65%, Europe 11%, Africa 3%, Australia 1%, South America 1%, other 18%.

Services and Facilities International student housing; international student center, visa services, language tutoring, ESL courses.

Applying TOEFL required, minimum score of 580; proof of adequate funds. Financial aid is not available to international students. Admission application deadlines: 4/1 for fall, 9/1 for spring. Contact: Ms. Susan E. Wohld, Associate Director, International Education, Pullman, WA 99164. (509) 335-4508.

PLACEMENT

Placement services include alumni network, career counseling/planning, career fairs, career library, career placement, job interviews, resume preparation, and resume referral to employers. Of 1994 graduates, 75% were employed within three months of graduation, the average starting salary was $37,500, the range was $22,000-$70,000.

Program Contact: Ms. Janet McGough, Program Coordinator, Washington State University, Pullman, WA 99164. (509) 335-3564.

Western Washington University

College of Business and Economics

Bellingham, Washington

OVERVIEW

Western Washington University is a state-supported comprehensive coed institution. Founded 1893. Setting: 223-acre small-town campus with easy access to Seattle. Total institutional enrollment: 10,500. Program was first offered in 1979. AACSB-accredited.

MBA HIGHLIGHTS

Entrance Difficulty*
Mean GMAT: 545
Mean GPA: 3.3

Cost $
Tuition: $1,200/quarter
(Nonresident: $3,645/quarter)
Room & Board: N/R

Enrollment Profile

Full-time: 25	Work Exp: N/R
Part-time: 45	International: 4%
Total: 70	Women: 43%
Average Age: 29	Minorities: 6%

Average Class Size: 25

ACADEMICS

Length of Program Minimum: 18 months. Maximum: 5 years.

Calendar Quarters.

Full-time Classes Main campus; evening.

Part-time Classes Main campus; evening.

Degree Requirements 60 credits including 24 elective credits.

Required Courses Business environment, business policy, managerial accounting, managerial economics.

Curricular Focus General management, international business, teamwork.

Concentration Management.

Faculty Full-time: 43, 86% with doctorates.

Teaching Methodology Case study: 33%, lecture: 67%.

STUDENT STATISTICS

Geographic Representation State residents 96%. By region: West 95%. International 4%.

Undergraduate Majors Business 48%; engineering/technology 15%; humanities 9%; science/mathematics 9%; social sciences 11%; other 8%.

FACILITIES

Information Resources Main library with 558,692 bound volumes, 1.8 million titles on microform, 5,644 periodical subscriptions, 16,331 records/tapes/CDs, 15 CD-ROMs.

Housing 1% of students in program live in college-owned or -operated housing.

Technology Computers are used moderately in course work. 48 computer terminals/PCs are available for use by students in program; they are located in computer labs. Students in the program are not required to have their own PC.

Computer Resources/On-line Services

Training	No	Dun's	No
Internet	Yes	Dow Jones	No
E-Mail	Yes	Dialog	No
LEXIS/NEXIS	No	Bloomberg	No
CompuServe	No		

ADMISSION

Acceptance 1994-95 62 applied for admission; 74% were accepted.

Entrance Requirements Bachelor's degree, GMAT score of 460, minimum 3.0 GPA.

Application Requirements Application form, copies of transcript, resume/curriculum vitae.

Application Deadlines 5/1 for summer. Applications are processed on a rolling basis.

FINANCIALS

Costs for 1994-95 Tuition: Full-time: $1,200/quarter for state residents, $3,645/quarter for nonresidents.

Financial Aid In 1994-95, 17% of candidates received some institutionally administered aid in the form of scholarships, assistantships, work-study. Total awards ranged from $300-$7,000. Financial aid is not available to part-time students. Application deadline: 5/1 for summer. Contact: Student Financial Resource Office, 516 High Street, Bellingham, WA 98225-9006. (360) 650-3470.

INTERNATIONAL STUDENTS

Demographics 4% of students enrolled in the program are international.

Services and Facilities International student center, visa services, language tutoring, counseling/support services.

Applying TOEFL required, minimum score of 565; proof of health; proof of adequate funds. Financial aid is not available to international students. Admission application deadline: 1/1 for summer. Contact: Dr. Arthur Kimmel, Director, International Programs and Exchanges, Bellingham, WA 98225-9046. (360) 650-3298.

PLACEMENT

Placement services include career counseling/planning, career library, and resume preparation.

Program Contact: Dr. Stephen V. Senge, MBA Program Director, Western Washington University, College of Business and Economics, Bellingham, WA 98225-9072. (360) 650-3898; Fax: (360) 650-4844.

WEST VIRGINIA

Marshall University

College of Business

Huntington, West Virginia

OVERVIEW

Marshall University is a state-supported comprehensive coed institution. Part of University System of West Virginia. Founded 1837. Setting: 65-acre small-town campus. Total institutional enrollment: 12,700. Program was first offered in 1967.

MBA HIGHLIGHTS

Entrance Difficulty*
Mean GMAT: 525
Mean GPA: 3.1

Cost $
Tuition: $130/credit hour
(Nonresident: $351/credit hour)
Room & Board: $4,280

Enrollment Profile

Full-time: 40	Work Exp: 70%
Part-time: 93	International: 1%
Total: 133	Women: 37%
Average Age: 41	Minorities: 7%

Average Class Size: 25

ACADEMICS

Length of Program Minimum: 12 months. Maximum: 5 years.

Calendar Semesters.

Full-time Classes Main campus; evening, summer.

Part-time Classes Main campus; evening, weekends, summer.

Degree Requirements 36 credit hours including 6 elective credit hours. Other: One economics course; 2 electiives or thesis.

Required Courses Business law and government relations, business policy, financial management, managerial economics, marketing for management, operations management, organizational behavior, profit planning and controls, quality controls in business. Courses may be waived through previous course work.

Curricular Focus Business issues and problems, general management, problem solving and decision making.

Concentrations Accounting, economics, finance, management, management information systems, marketing, operations management, quantitative analysis, strategic management, transportation.

Faculty Full-time: 28, 100% with doctorates; part-time: 1, 100% with doctorates.

Teaching Methodology Case study: 10%, faculty seminars: 5%, lecture: 50%, research: 10%, seminars by members of the business community: 5%, student presentations: 10%, team projects: 10%.

Special Opportunities International exchange program available. Internships include international trade, research, economic development, and government.

STUDENT STATISTICS

Geographic Representation State residents 79%. By region: Northeast 89%; South 7%; Midwest 2%; West 1%. International 1%.

Undergraduate Majors Business 67%; education 2%; engineering/technology 14%; nursing 1%; science/mathematics 6%; social sciences 2%; other 8%.

Other Background Graduate degrees in other disciplines: 2%.

FACILITIES

Information Resources Main library with 422,025 bound volumes, 186,065 titles on microform, 2,748 periodical subscriptions, 18,166 records/tapes/CDs, 7 CD-ROMs.

Housing 5% of students in program live in college-owned or -operated housing.

Technology Computers are used heavily in course work. Computer terminals/PCs, linked by a campus-wide computer network, are available for use by students in program; they are located in the library, the computer center, computer labs. Students in the program are not required to have their own PC.

Computer Resources/On-line Services

Training	Yes	E-Mail	Yes
Internet	Yes	Dialog	Yes

Other on-line services: OCLC.

ADMISSION

Acceptance 1994-95 172 applied for admission; 79% were accepted.

Entrance Requirements Bachelor's degree, GMAT score of 450, minimum 2.5 GPA. Core courses waived through: previous course work.

Application Requirements Interview, application form, copies of transcript, 3 letters of recommendation.

Application Deadlines 7/22 for fall, 12/3 for spring, 5/1 for summer.

FINANCIALS

Costs for 1994-95 Tuition: Full-time: $130/credit hour for state residents, $351/credit hour for nonresidents. Average room and board costs are $4,280 per academic year (on-campus).

Financial Aid In 1994-95, 25% of candidates received some institutionally administered aid in the form of grants, scholarships, loans, assistantships. Total awards ranged from $3,750-$7,500. Financial aid is available to part-time students. Applications are processed on a rolling basis. Contact: Financial Aid Counselor, 400 Hal Greer Boulevard, Corbly Hall, Room 216, Huntington, WV 25755-2300. (304) 696-3162.

INTERNATIONAL STUDENTS

Demographics 1% of students enrolled in the program are international; Asia 90%, Other 10%.

Services and Facilities International student center, language tutoring, ESL courses.

Applying TOEFL required, minimum score of 525; proof of adequate funds. Financial aid is not available to international students. Admission application deadlines: 5/22 for fall, 10/3 for spring, 3/3 for summer. Contact: Ms. Lena Ji, Coordinator for International Studies, 400 Hal Greer Boulevard, Corbly Hall, Room 216, Huntington, WV 25755-2300. (304) 696-2379.

PLACEMENT

Placement services include alumni network, career counseling/planning, career fairs, career library, career placement, resume preparation, and resume referral to employers.

Program Contact: Dr. Chandra Akkihal, Director, Graduate Studies, Marshall University, 400 Hal Greer Boulevard, Corbly Hall, Room 216, Huntington, WV 25755-2300. (304) 696-2315; Fax: (304) 696-4344.

University of Charleston

Jones-Benedum Division of Business

Charleston, West Virginia

OVERVIEW

The University of Charleston is an independent nonprofit comprehensive coed institution. Founded 1888. Setting: 40-acre urban campus. Total institutional enrollment: 1,434.

MBA HIGHLIGHTS

Entrance Difficulty**

Cost
Tuition: N/R
Room & Board: $3,900 (off-campus)

Enrollment Profile

Full-time: N/R	Work Exp: N/R
Part-time: N/R	International: 5%
Total: 40	Women: 45%
Average Age: N/R	Minorities: 10%

Average Class Size: 20

ACADEMICS

Calendar Semesters.

Curricular Focus General management, problem solving and decision making, strategic analysis and planning.

Concentration Management.

Teaching Methodology Case study: 30%, lecture: 35%, research: 10%, seminars by members of the business community: 5%, student presentations: 10%, team projects: 10%.

STUDENT STATISTICS

Geographic Representation International 5%.

FACILITIES

Information Resources Main library with 75,166 bound volumes, 78,739 titles on microform, 580 periodical subscriptions, 664 records/tapes/CDs, 6 CD-ROMs.

Housing College housing not available.

ADMISSION

Entrance Requirements Bachelor's degree, GMAT score, minimum 2.75 GPA, minimum 4 years of work experience. Core courses waived through: previous course work.

Application Requirements Written essay, application form, copies of transcript, personal statement, 3 letters of recommendation.

Application Deadline Applications are processed on a rolling basis.

FINANCIALS

Financial Aid In 1994-95, candidates received some institutionally administered aid in the form of loans. Application deadline: 7/1 for fall. Applications are processed on a rolling basis. Contact: Ms. Jan Ruge, Director of Financial Aid, 2300 MacCorkle Avenue, SE, Charleston, WV 25304-1099. (304) 357-4760.

INTERNATIONAL STUDENTS

Demographics 5% of students enrolled in the program are international.

Applying TOEFL required, minimum score of 500; proof of adequate funds. Financial aid is available to international students. Applications are processed on a rolling basis. Admission application deadline: 6/1 for fall.

PROGRAM

Executive MBA (EMBA) Length of program: Minimum: 22 months. Part-time classes: Main campus; evening. Degree requirements: 40 hours including 10 elective hours.

PLACEMENT

Placement services include career counseling/planning, career library, career placement, and electronic job bank.

Program Contact: Mr. Dennis McMillen, Division Chair for Business, University of Charleston, 2300 MacCorkle Avenue, SE, Charleston, WV 25304-1099. (304) 357-4870; Fax: (304) 357-4872.

West Virginia Graduate College

School of Business

Institute, West Virginia

OVERVIEW
West Virginia Graduate College is graduate-only institution. Total institutional enrollment: 1,890.

ACADEMICS
Degree Requirements 36 credits.

Concentration Management.

FACILITIES
Information Resources Main library with 47,027 bound volumes, 476,041 titles on microform, 490 periodical subscriptions.

ADMISSION
Entrance Requirements Bachelor's degree.

Application Requirements Application form, copies of transcript.

Application Deadlines 8/4 for fall, 12/10 for spring.

INTERNATIONAL STUDENTS
Applying TOEFL required. Admission application deadlines: 8/4 for fall, 12/10 for spring.

Program Contact: Mr. Kenneth O'Neal, Director of Admissions and Records, West Virginia Graduate College, PO Box 1003, Institute, WV 25112-1003. (304) 766-1907, or (800) 642-9842 (WV only).

West Virginia University

College of Business and Economics

Morgantown, West Virginia

OVERVIEW
West Virginia University is a state-supported coed institution. Part of University of West Virginia System. Founded 1867. Setting: 541-acre small-town campus with easy access to Pittsburgh. Total institutional enrollment: 22,500. Program was first offered in 1954. AACSB-accredited.

MBA HIGHLIGHTS

Entrance Difficulty**
Mean GMAT: 570
Mean GPA: 3.41

Cost $
Tuition: $1,068/semester
(Nonresident: $3,078/semester)
Room & Board: $5,000 (off-campus)

Enrollment Profile

Full-time: 60	Work Exp: 71%
Part-time: 88	International: 9%
Total: 148	Women: 38%
Average Age: 27	Minorities: 5%

Average Class Size: 30

ACADEMICS
Length of Program Minimum: 13 months. Maximum: 8 years.

Calendar Semesters.

Full-time Classes Main campus; day.

Part-time Classes Main campus, Parkersburg, Wheeling, Shepherdstown, distance learning option; weekends.

Degree Requirements 48 credits including 6 elective credits.

Required Courses Applied business statistics, corporate finance, economic decision making, economic policy, financial accounting, legal environment, management information systems, management science, managerial control, managerial finance, marketing management, marketing strategy, operations management, organizational behavior and ethics, organizational processes, policy and strategy.

Curricular Focus General management, problem solving and decision making, teamwork.

Concentration Management.

Faculty Full-time: 32, 100% with doctorates.

Teaching Methodology Case study: 20%, faculty seminars: 10%, lecture: 30%, research: 5%, seminars by members of the business community: 5%, student presentations: 10%, team projects: 20%.

Special Opportunities International exchange in Germany. Internships include human resources, finance, small business strategy, marketing, and policy and strategy.

STUDENT STATISTICS
Geographic Representation State residents 62%. By region: South 66%; Northeast 14%; Midwest 10%; West 1%. International 9%.

Undergraduate Majors Business 42%; engineering/technology 32%; humanities 6%; science/mathematics 9%; social sciences 11%.

Other Background Graduate degrees in other disciplines: 8%. Work experience: On average, students have 4 years of work experience on entrance to the program.

FACILITIES
Information Resources Main library with 1.7 million bound volumes, 2.4 million titles on microform, 11,099 periodical subscriptions.

Housing 4% of students in program live in college-owned or -operated housing. Assistance with housing search provided.

Technology Computers are used heavily in course work. 250 computer terminals/PCs, linked by a campus-wide computer network, are available for use by students in program; they are located in dormitories, the student center, classrooms, learning resource center, the library, the computer center, computer labs, the research center. Students in the program are not required to have their own PC.

Computer Resources/On-line Services

Training	Yes	E-Mail	Yes
Internet	Yes	Dow Jones	Yes

ADMISSION
Acceptance 1994-95 249 applied for admission; 43% were accepted.

Entrance Requirements Bachelor's degree, GMAT score. Core courses waived through: previous course work, work experience.

Application Requirements Copies of transcript, resume/curriculum vitae.

Application Deadline 3/1 for fall.

FINANCIALS
Costs for 1994-95 Tuition: Full-time: $1,068/semester for state residents, $3,078/semester for nonresidents. Average room and board costs are $5,000 per academic year (off-campus).

Financial Aid In 1994-95, 20% of candidates received some institutionally administered aid in the form of assistantships. Total awards ranged from $8,500-$13,800. Financial aid is not available to part-time students. Application deadline: 3/1 for fall. Contact: Dr. Paul J. Speaker, Director of Graduate Programs, PO Box 6025, Morgantown, WV 26506-6025. (304) 293-5408.

INTERNATIONAL STUDENTS
Demographics 9% of students enrolled in the program are international; Asia 72%, North America 14%, Central America 7%, Europe 7%.

Services and Facilities International student office, international student center, visa services, language tutoring, ESL courses, special assistance for nonnative speakers of English, counseling/support services.

Applying TOEFL required, minimum score of 580; proof of health; proof of adequate funds. Financial aid is available to international students. Financial aid application deadline: 3/1 for fall. Admission application deadline: 3/1 for fall. Contact: Dr. Paul J. Speaker, Director of Graduate Programs, PO Box 6025, Morgantown, WV 26506-6025. (304) 293-5408.

PLACEMENT
In 1993-94, 212 organizations participated in on-campus recruiting. Placement services include alumni network, career counseling/planning, career fairs, career library, career placement, electronic job bank, job interviews, resume preparation, and resume referral to employers. Of 1994 graduates, 84% were employed within three months of graduation, the average starting salary was $37,800, the range was $23,400-$56,500.

Jobs by Employer Type Manufacturing 28%; service 47%; government 10%; consulting 12%; nonprofit 3%.

Jobs by Functional Area Marketing/sales 25%; finance 12%; operations 16%; management 36%; technical management 11%.

Program Contact: Dr. Paul J. Speaker, Director of Graduate Programs, West Virginia University, PO Box 6025, Morgantown, WV 26506-6025. (304) 293-5408; Fax: (304) 293-7323; Internet Address: speaker@wvube1.be.wvu.edu.

West Virginia Wesleyan College

Faculty of Business

Buckhannon, West Virginia

OVERVIEW

West Virginia Wesleyan College is an independent comprehensive coed institution, affiliated with United Methodist Church. Founded 1890. Setting: 80-acre small-town campus. Total institutional enrollment: 1,600.

MBA HIGHLIGHTS

Entrance Difficulty N/R

Cost
Tuition: $275/credit hour
Room & Board: N/R

Enrollment Profile

Full-time: N/R	Work Exp: N/R
Part-time: N/R	International: N/R
Total: N/R	Women: N/R
Average Age: N/R	Minorities: N/R

Average Class Size: N/R

ACADEMICS

Calendar 4-1-4.
Part-time Classes Evening, weekends.
Degree Requirements 36 credit hours.
Concentrations Accounting, economics, finance, management, marketing.

FACILITIES

Information Resources Main library with 145,000 bound volumes, 46 titles on microform, 655 periodical subscriptions, 1,446 records/tapes/CDs, 6 CD-ROMs.

ADMISSION

Entrance Requirements Bachelor's degree, GMAT score.
Application Deadlines 9/6 for fall, 12/31 for spring.

FINANCIALS

Costs for 1994-95 Tuition: Part-time day: $275/credit hour.
Financial Aid Contact: Ms. Lana Golden, Director of Student Aid, College Avenue, Buckhannon, WV 26201. (304) 473-8080.

INTERNATIONAL STUDENTS

Applying Admission application deadlines: 9/6 for fall, 12/31 for spring.

Program Contact: Mr. David W. McCauley, Director, MBA Program, West Virginia Wesleyan College, College Avenue, Buckhannon, WV 26201. (304) 473-8479.

Wheeling Jesuit College

Wheeling, West Virginia

OVERVIEW

Wheeling Jesuit College is an independent Roman Catholic (Jesuit) comprehensive coed institution. Founded 1954. Setting: 70-acre small-town campus with easy access to Pittsburgh. Total institutional enrollment: 1,482. Program was first offered in 1978.

MBA HIGHLIGHTS

Entrance Difficulty**
Mean GMAT: 485
Mean GPA: 3.3

Cost $
Tuition: $300/credit hour
Room & Board: $4,370

Enrollment Profile

Full-time: 14	Work Exp: 80%
Part-time: 136	International: 2%
Total: 150	Women: 37%
Average Age: 30	Minorities: 3%

Average Class Size: 20

ACADEMICS

Length of Program Minimum: 15 months. Maximum: 7 years.
Calendar Semesters.
Full-time Classes Main campus; evening, summer.
Part-time Classes Main campus; evening, summer.
Degree Requirements 36 credits including 9 elective credits.
Required Courses Accounting for management control, management of financial resources, managerial economics, managerial policy and strategy, marketing management, operations management, organizational behavior, quantitative business analysis, the ethical environment of business. Courses may be waived through: previous course work, work experience.
Curricular Focus Leadership, problem solving and decision making, strategic analysis and planning.
Concentration Accounting.
Faculty Full-time: 8, 64% with doctorates; part-time: 12, 50% with doctorates.
Teaching Methodology Case study: 20%, faculty seminars: 10%, lecture: 30%, research: 10%, student presentations: 10%, team projects: 20%.
Special Opportunities Internship program available.

STUDENT STATISTICS

Geographic Representation State residents 60%. By region: Midwest 83%; Northeast 15%. International 2%.
Undergraduate Majors Business 40%; education 2%; engineering/technology 28%; humanities 10%; nursing 1%; science/mathematics 3%; social sciences 15%; other 1%.
Other Background Graduate degrees in other disciplines: 8%. Work experience: On average, students have 6 years of work experience on entrance to the program.

FACILITIES

Information Resources Main library with 126,000 bound volumes, 84,000 titles on microform, 549 periodical subscriptions, 1,255 records/tapes/CDs.
Housing 1% of students in program live in college-owned or -operated housing.
Technology Computers are used moderately in course work. 40 computer terminals/PCs, linked by a campus-wide computer network, are available for use by students in program; they are located in the computer center. Students in the program are not required to have their own PC.

Computer Resources/On-line Services

Training	Yes	Dun's	No
Internet	Yes	Dow Jones	No
E-Mail	Yes	Dialog	No
LEXIS/NEXIS	No	Bloomberg	No
CompuServe	No		

ADMISSION

Acceptance 1994-95 Of those applying, 85% were accepted.
Entrance Requirements Bachelor's degree, GMAT score of 470, minimum 2.75 GPA. Core courses waived through: previous course work.
Application Requirements Application form, copies of transcript.
Application Deadlines 8/15 for fall, 1/10 for spring, 5/1 for summer.

FINANCIALS

Costs for 1994-95 Tuition: Full-time: $300/credit hour. Average room and board costs are $4,370 per academic year (on-campus).
Financial Aid In 1994-95, 13% of candidates received some institutionally administered aid in the form of assistantships. Total awards ranged from $7,600-$14,100. Financial aid is available to part-time students. Applications are processed on a rolling basis. Contact: Ms. Su Saunders, Director of Student Financial Planning, 316 Washington Avenue, Wheeling, WV 26003-6295. (304) 243-2304.

INTERNATIONAL STUDENTS

Demographics 2% of students enrolled in the program are international.
Services and Facilities ESL courses, counseling/support services.
Applying TOEFL required, minimum score of 550; proof of adequate funds. Financial aid is available to international students. Assistantships are available for these students. Admission application deadlines: 6/1 for fall,

11/1 for spring, 3/1 for summer. Contact: Ms. Eileen Viglietta, International Student Adviser, Swint Hall, 316 Washington Avenue, Wheeling, WV 26003-6295. (304) 243-2346.

PLACEMENT

In 1993-94, 6 organizations participated in on-campus recruiting. Placement services include alumni network, career counseling/planning, career fairs, career library, career placement, electronic job bank, job interviews, resume preparation, and resume referral to employers. Of 1994 graduates, 90% were employed within three months of graduation.

Jobs by Employer Type Manufacturing 40%; service 40%; government 10%; consulting 5%; nonprofit 5%.

Jobs by Functional Area Marketing/sales 10%; finance 10%; operations 10%; management 40%; strategic planning 10%; technical management 20%.

Program Contact: Mr. Edward W. Younkins, MBA Director, Wheeling Jesuit College, 316 Washington Avenue, Wheeling, WV 26003-6295. (304) 243-2344, or (800) 624-6992; Fax: (304) 243-2243.

WISCONSIN

Cardinal Stritch College

Business and Management Division

Milwaukee, Wisconsin

OVERVIEW

Cardinal Stritch College is an independent Roman Catholic comprehensive coed institution. Founded 1937. Setting: 40-acre suburban campus. Total institutional enrollment: 5,610. Program was first offered in 1988.

MBA HIGHLIGHTS

Entrance Difficulty**

Cost $$$
Tuition: $4,200/term
Room & Board: N/R

Enrollment Profile

Full-time: 366	Work Exp: 100%
Part-time: 0	International: 1%
Total: 366	Women: 47%
Average Age: 36	Minorities: 10%

Average Class Size: 16

ACADEMICS

Length of Program Minimum: 23 months. Maximum: 7 years.
Calendar Semesters.
Full-time Classes Madison, Edina; evening, summer.
Degree Requirements 36 credits. Other: Minimum 3.0 GPA.
Required Courses Advanced managerial accounting, advanced managerial economics, advanced managerial finance, advanced marketing management, applied management decision report, business policy and strategy, business statistics, computer proficiency workshop, fundamentals of executive management, human relations and organizational behavior, legal and ethical issues for managers, management information systems, orientation to graduate education, quantitative analysis. Courses may be waived through: previous course work.
Curricular Focus General management, problem solving and decision making, teamwork.
Concentrations International business, strategic management.
Faculty Full-time: 4, 25% with doctorates; part-time: 382, 20% with doctorates.
Teaching Methodology Case study: 20%, lecture: 10%, research: 20%, student presentations: 10%, team projects: 40%.

STUDENT STATISTICS

Geographic Representation State residents 80%. By region: Midwest 100%. International 1%.

Other Background Work experience: On average, students have 14 years of work experience on entrance to the program.

FACILITIES

Information Resources Main library with 113,355 bound volumes, 108,278 titles on microform, 1,223 periodical subscriptions, 9 CD-ROMs. Business collection includes 3,750 bound volumes, 67 periodical subscriptions, 5 CD-ROMs, 40 videos.
Housing College housing available.
Technology Computers are used heavily in course work. 15 computer terminals/PCs, linked by a campus-wide computer network, are available for use by students in program; they are located in computer labs. Students in the program are required to have their own PC. $2,000 are budgeted per student for computer support.

Computer Resources/On-line Services

Training	Yes	CompuServe	No
Internet	Yes	Dun's	No
E-Mail	Yes	Dow Jones	No
Multimedia Center	Yes	Dialog	No
LEXIS/NEXIS	No	Bloomberg	No

ADMISSION

Acceptance 1994-95 305 applied for admission; 75% were accepted.
Entrance Requirements Bachelor's degree, minimum 2.5 GPA, minimum 3 years of work experience. Core courses waived through: previous course work.
Application Requirements Interview, application form, copies of transcript.
Application Deadline Applications are processed on a rolling basis.

FINANCIALS

Costs for 1994-95 Tuition: Full-time: $4,200/term. Fees: Full-time: $1,270.
Financial Aid In 1994-95, 40% of candidates received some institutionally administered aid in the form of grants, loans. Total awards ranged from $1,000-$18,000. Financial aid is available to part-time students. Applications are processed on a rolling basis. Contact: Mr. Mark Levine, Financial Aid Director, 6801 North Yates Road, Milwaukee, WI 53217-3985. (414) 352-5400.

INTERNATIONAL STUDENTS

Demographics 1% of students enrolled in the program are international.
Services and Facilities Language tutoring, counseling/support services.
Applying TOEFL required, minimum score of 600; proof of health; proof of adequate funds; proof of insurance. Financial aid is not available to international students. Admission applications are processed on a rolling basis.

PLACEMENT

Placement services include alumni network, career counseling/planning, career fairs, career library, and career placement.

Program Contact: Ms. Marlene Lauwasser, Director of Recruiting, Cardinal Stritch College, 6801 North Yates Road, Milwaukee, WI 53217-3985. (414) 352-5400, or (800) 347-8822; Fax: (414) 351-0257.

Marquette University

College of Business Administration

Milwaukee, Wisconsin

OVERVIEW

Marquette University is an independent Roman Catholic (Jesuit) coed institution. Founded 1881. Setting: 80-acre urban campus. Total institutional enrollment: 10,500. Program was first offered in 1953. AACSB-accredited.

MBA HIGHLIGHTS

Entrance Difficulty****
Mean GMAT: 565
Mean GPA: 3.22

Cost $$$
Tuition: $434/credit hour
Room & Board: N/R

Enrollment Profile
Full-time: 55	Work Exp: 96%
Part-time: 472	International: 5%
Total: 527	Women: 36%
Average Age: 28	Minorities: N/R

Average Class Size: 26

ACADEMICS
Length of Program Minimum: 12 months. Maximum: 6 years.
Calendar Semesters.
Full-time Classes Main campus; evening, weekends, summer.
Part-time Classes Main campus; evening, weekends, summer.
Degree Requirements 33 credit hours including 9-12 elective credit hours.
Required Courses Administration policy, environmental influences, financial applications, management accounting, managerial economics, marketing management, organization and behavior, quantitative business analysis.
Curricular Focus Business issues and problems, general management, problem solving and decision making.
Concentrations Economics, finance, human resources management, leadership studies and total quality management, management information systems, marketing.
Faculty Full-time: 62, 96% with doctorates; part-time: 4, 50% with doctorates.
Teaching Methodology Case study: 40%, lecture: 40%, student presentations: 10%, team projects: 10%.
Special Opportunities International exchange in Austria, Belgium, Denmark, Italy, Spain.

STUDENT STATISTICS
Geographic Representation State residents 95%. By region: Midwest 84%; Northeast 7%; South 2%; West 2%. International 5%.
Undergraduate Majors Business 50%; engineering/technology 27%; humanities 4%; nursing 1%; science/mathematics 4%; social sciences 10%; other 4%.
Other Background Graduate degrees in other disciplines: 8%. Work experience: On average, students have 5 years of work experience on entrance to the program.

FACILITIES
Information Resources Main library with 1 million bound volumes, 362,178 titles on microform, 8,964 periodical subscriptions.
Housing 5% of students in program live in college-owned or -operated housing.
Technology Computers are used moderately in course work. 250 computer terminals/PCs, linked by a campus-wide computer network, are available for use by students in program; they are located in dormitories, classrooms, learning resource center, the library, the computer center, computer labs, the research center. Students in the program are not required to have their own PC.

Computer Resources/On-line Services
Training	No	Dun's	No
Internet	Yes	Dow Jones	No
E-Mail	Yes	Dialog	No
LEXIS/NEXIS	Yes	Bloomberg	No
CompuServe	No		

ADMISSION
Acceptance 1994-95 280 applied for admission; 66% were accepted.
Entrance Requirements Bachelor's degree, GMAT score. Core courses waived through: previous course work.
Application Requirements Written essay, application form, copies of transcript, resume/curriculum vitae, personal statement, 3 letters of recommendation.
Application Deadlines 7/15 for fall, 12/1 for spring, 1/1 for summer. Applications are processed on a rolling basis.

FINANCIALS
Costs for 1994-95 Tuition: Full-time: $434/credit hour.
Financial Aid In 1994-95, candidates received some institutionally administered aid in the form of scholarships, loans, fellowships, assistantships, work-study. Total awards ranged from $434-$16,500. Financial aid is available to part-time students. Application deadlines: 2/15 for fall, 11/15 for spring, 2/15 for summer. Contact: Mr. Thomas Marek,

Financial Aid Coordinator, Graduate School, 1217 West Wisconsin Avenue, Milwaukee, WI 53201-1881. (414) 288-7137.

INTERNATIONAL STUDENTS
Demographics 5% of students enrolled in the program are international; Asia 50%, Africa 10%, Europe 10%, South America 10%, Australia 5%, other 15%.
Services and Facilities International student office, international student center, visa services, language tutoring, ESL courses, special assistance for nonnative speakers of English, counseling/support services.
Applying TOEFL required; proof of health; proof of adequate funds. Financial aid is available to international students. Financial aid application deadlines: 2/15 for fall, 11/15 for spring, 2/15 for summer. Applications are processed on a rolling basis. Admission application deadlines: 7/1 for fall, 11/15 for spring, 3/15 for summer. Applications are processed on a rolling basis. Contact: Mr. Robert Brzozowski, Assistant Director of Campus International Programs, 1217 West Wisconsin Avenue, Milwaukee, WI 53201-1881. (414) 288-7700.

PLACEMENT
Placement services include alumni network, career counseling/planning, career fairs, career library, career placement, electronic job bank, job interviews, resume preparation, and resume referral to employers.

Program Contact: Mr. Joseph P. Fox, Director of Graduate Programs, Marquette University, 1217 West Wisconsin Avenue, Milwaukee, WI 53201-1881. (414) 288-7145; Fax: (414) 288-1660; Internet Address: faxjevms.csd.mu.edu.

University of Wisconsin–Eau Claire

School of Business

Eau Claire, Wisconsin

OVERVIEW
The University of Wisconsin–Eau Claire is a state-supported comprehensive coed institution. Part of University of Wisconsin System. Founded 1916. Setting: 333-acre small-town campus. Total institutional enrollment: 10,300. Program was first offered in 1995. AACSB-accredited.

MBA HIGHLIGHTS
Entrance Difficulty***
Mean GMAT: 520
Mean GPA: 3.1

Cost $
Tuition: $117 - $156/credit
(Nonresident: $356 - $475/credit)
Room & Board: $6,000 (off-campus)

Enrollment Profile
Full-time: 4	Work Exp: 80%
Part-time: 16	International: 0%
Total: 20	Women: 55%
Average Age: 30	Minorities: 5%

Class Size: 20 - 25

ACADEMICS
Length of Program Minimum: 18 months.
Calendar Semesters.
Full-time Classes Main campus; evening.
Part-time Classes Main campus; evening.
Degree Requirements 30 credits including 6 elective credits. Other: Minimum 2.2 GPA for foundation courses.
Required Courses Applied field project, communications, communications 2, developing long-term competitive advantages, diversity, management information systems, organizational entrepreneurship, organizational operations.
Curricular Focus General management, integrated business environment, teamwork.
Concentration Management.
Faculty Full-time: 13, 100% with doctorates.
Teaching Methodology Case study: 20%, lecture: 30%, research: 5%, seminars by members of the business community: 5%, student presentations: 20%, team projects: 20%.

STUDENT STATISTICS
Geographic Representation By region: Midwest 100%.
Undergraduate Majors Business 80%; engineering/technology 10%; social sciences 5%; other 5%.
Other Background Graduate degrees in other disciplines: 5%. Work experience: On average, students have 5 years of work experience on entrance to the program.

FACILITIES
Information Resources Main library with 514,650 bound volumes, 1.3 million titles on microform, 1,998 periodical subscriptions, 55,162 records/tapes/CDs, 461 CD-ROMs. Business collection includes 41,950 bound volumes, 151 periodical subscriptions, 5 CD-ROMs, 160 videos.
Housing College housing not available.
Technology Computers are used moderately in course work. 500 computer terminals/PCs, linked by a campus-wide computer network, are available for use by students in program; they are located in classrooms, learning resource center, computer labs. Students in the program are not required to have their own PC.

Computer Resources/On-line Services
Training	Yes	Dun's		No
Internet	Yes	Dow Jones		No
E-Mail	Yes	Dialog		Yes
LEXIS/NEXIS	No	Bloomberg		No
CompuServe	No			

Other on-line services: OCLC, First Search.

ADMISSION
Acceptance 1994-95 50 applied for admission; 50% were accepted.
Entrance Requirements Bachelor's degree, prerequisite courses required for applicants with non-business degree, GMAT score, minimum 2.75 GPA. Core courses waived through: previous course work.
Application Requirements Application form, copies of transcript.
Application Deadlines 12/1 for spring. Applications are processed on a rolling basis.

FINANCIALS
Costs for 1994-95 Tuition: Full-time: $117-$156/credit for state residents, $356-$475/credit for nonresidents. Fees: Full-time: $160/semester for state residents, $160/semester for nonresidents. Average room and board costs are $6,000 per academic year (off-campus).
Financial Aid In 1994-95, 20% of candidates received some institutionally administered aid in the form of fellowships, assistantships. Financial aid is not available to part-time students. Application deadline: 12/1 for spring. Contact: Dr. Ronald Satz, Dean of Graduate School, Human Resources Building, Eau Claire, WI 54702-4004. (715) 836-3400.

INTERNATIONAL STUDENTS
Demographics 1% of students on campus are international; Asia 47%, Europe 29%, Central America 6%, Africa 3%, South America 3%, other 12%.
Services and Facilities International student office, visa services, language tutoring, ESL courses, special assistance for nonnative speakers of English, counseling/support services.
Applying TOEFL required, minimum score of 550; proof of health; proof of adequate funds. Financial aid is available to international students. Financial aid application deadline: 12/1 for spring. Admission application deadlines: 5/1 for fall, 10/15 for spring. Applications are processed on a rolling basis. Contact: Dr. C. Robert Frost, Director of International Students, PO Box 4004, Eau Claire, WI 54702-4004. (715) 836-4411.

PLACEMENT
Placement services include alumni network, career counseling/planning, career fairs, career placement, job interviews, resume preparation, and resume referral to employers.

Program Contact: Dr. Thomas J. Bergmann, MBA Director, University of Wisconsin–Eau Claire, 117 Schneider Hall, Eau Claire, WI 54702-4004. (715) 836-5473; Fax: (715) 836-2380; Internet Address: uwecmba@uwec.edu.

University of Wisconsin–La Crosse

College of Business Administration

La Crosse, Wisconsin

OVERVIEW
The University of Wisconsin–La Crosse is a state-supported comprehensive coed institution. Part of University of Wisconsin System. Founded 1909. Setting: 119-acre small-town campus. Total institutional enrollment: 8,400. Program was first offered in 1977. AACSB-accredited.

MBA HIGHLIGHTS

Entrance Difficulty***
Mean GMAT: 500
Mean GPA: 3.2

Cost $
Tuition: $186/credit
(Nonresident: $467/credit)
Room & Board: $2,500

Enrollment Profile
Full-time: 36	Work Exp: 90%
Part-time: 84	International: 15%
Total: 120	Women: 40%
Average Age: 30	Minorities: N/R

Average Class Size: 25

ACADEMICS
Length of Program Minimum: 18 months. Maximum: 7 years.
Calendar Semesters.
Full-time Classes Main campus; evening.
Part-time Classes Main campus; evening.
Degree Requirements 30 credits including 9 elective credits.
Required Courses Accounting and management control, managerial economics, managerial finance, marketing analysis, operations research and decision making, organizational behavior and theory, strategic management. Courses may be waived through: previous course work.
Curricular Focus General management, international business, problem solving and decision making.
Concentration Management.
Faculty Full-time: 15, 100% with doctorates.
Teaching Methodology Case study: 25%, lecture: 50%, student presentations: 10%, team projects: 15%.

STUDENT STATISTICS
Geographic Representation State residents 80%. By region: Midwest 79%; Northeast 2%; South 2%; West 2%. International 15%.
Other Background Graduate degrees in other disciplines: 1%. Work experience: On average, students have 5-6 years of work experience on entrance to the program.

FACILITIES
Information Resources Main library with 573,258 bound volumes, 990,244 titles on microform, 2,176 periodical subscriptions, 22 CD-ROMs.
Housing 1% of students in program live in college-owned or -operated housing.
Technology Computers are used heavily in course work. 100 computer terminals/PCs, linked by a campus-wide computer network, are available for use by students in program; they are located in the student center, the library, the computer center, computer labs, the research center. Students in the program are not required to have their own PC.

Computer Resources/On-line Services
Training	No	Dow Jones		Yes
Internet	Yes	Bloomberg		No
E-Mail	Yes			

ADMISSION
Acceptance 1994-95 Of those applying, 90% were accepted.
Entrance Requirements Bachelor's degree, GMAT score of 450, minimum 2.85 GPA. Core courses waived through: previous course work.
Application Requirements Application form, copies of transcript.
Application Deadlines 5/30 for fall, 9/30 for spring.

FINANCIALS

Costs for 1994-95 Tuition: Full-time: $186/credit for state residents, $467/credit for nonresidents. Average room and board costs are $2,500 per academic year (on-campus) and $4,500 per academic year (off-campus).

Financial Aid In 1994-95, 5% of candidates received some institutionally administered aid in the form of loans, assistantships. Total awards ranged from $6,000-$8,800. Financial aid is available to part-time students. Application deadlines: 5/30 for fall, 9/30 for spring.

INTERNATIONAL STUDENTS

Demographics 15% of students enrolled in the program are international.

Services and Facilities International student center, ESL courses, counseling/support services.

Applying TOEFL required, minimum score of 550; proof of health; proof of adequate funds. Financial aid is not available to international students. Admission application deadlines: 5/1 for fall, 9/30 for spring. Contact: Ms. Nadine Beezley, 1725 State Street, La Crosse, WI 54601-3742. (608) 785-8016.

PLACEMENT

Placement services include alumni network, career counseling/planning, career fairs, career library, career placement, and resume preparation.

Program Contact: Dr. Bill Colclough, Associate Dean and MBA Director, University of Wisconsin–La Crosse, 1725 State Street, La Crosse, WI 54601-3742. (608) 785-8905; Internet Address: colcloug@uwlax.edu.

University of Wisconsin–Madison

School of Business

Madison, Wisconsin

OVERVIEW

The University of Wisconsin–Madison is a state-supported coed institution. Part of University of Wisconsin System. Founded 1848. Setting: 1,050-acre suburban campus. Total institutional enrollment: 41,000. Program was first offered in 1944. AACSB-accredited.

MBA HIGHLIGHTS

Entrance Difficulty***
Mean GMAT: 604
Mean GPA: 3.42

Cost $$
Tuition: $2,329/semester
(Nonresident: $6,252/semester)
Room & Board: N/R

Enrollment Profile

Full-time: 215	Work Exp: 75% - 80%
Part-time: 0	International: 30%
Total: 215	Women: 42%
Average Age: 25	Minorities: 17%

Average Class Size: 39

ACADEMICS

Length of Program Minimum: 24 months.

Calendar Semesters.

Full-time Classes Main campus; day, summer.

Part-time Classes Main campus; day, weekends.

Degree Requirements 54 credits including 15 elective credits.

Required Courses Corporate finance, decision information systems, financial accounting, international perspectives, managerial accounting, managerial economics, marketing, operations management, organizational behavior, statistics. Courses may be waived through: previous course work.

Curricular Focus Business issues and problems, problem solving and decision making, teamwork.

Concentrations Accounting, finance, human resources management, international business, management, management information systems, marketing, operations management, real estate, transportation.

Faculty Full-time: 90, 100% with doctorates.

Teaching Methodology Case study: 30%, experiential learning: 5%, lecture: 65%.

Special Opportunities International exchange in France, Germany. Internship program available.

STUDENT STATISTICS

Geographic Representation State residents 30%. International 30%.

Undergraduate Majors Business 38%; humanities 12%; science/mathematics 27%; social sciences 23%.

Other Background Graduate degrees in other disciplines: 10%. Work experience: On average, students have 2 years of work experience on entrance to the program.

FACILITIES

Information Resources Main library with 5.3 million bound volumes, 2 million titles on microform, 55,300 periodical subscriptions.

Housing College housing available.

Technology Computers are used heavily in course work. 160 computer terminals/PCs, linked by a campus-wide computer network, are available for use by students in program; they are located in dormitories, classrooms, learning resource center, the library, the computer center, computer labs. Students in the program are not required to have their own PC.

Computer Resources/On-line Services

Training	Yes	LEXIS/NEXIS	Yes
Internet	Yes	Dun's	Yes
E-Mail	Yes	Dow Jones	Yes
Videoconference Center	Yes		

ADMISSION

Acceptance 1994-95 643 applied for admission; 35% were accepted.

Entrance Requirements Bachelor's degree, prerequisite courses required for applicants with non-business degree, GMAT score, minimum 3.0 GPA, minimum 2 years of work experience. Core courses waived through: previous course work.

Application Requirements Written essay, application form, copies of transcript, resume/curriculum vitae, 3 letters of recommendation.

Application Deadlines 6/1 for fall, 10/1 for spring.

FINANCIALS

Costs for 1994-95 Tuition: Full-time: $2,329/semester for state residents, $6,252/semester for nonresidents.

Financial Aid In 1994-95, 18% of candidates received some institutionally administered aid in the form of scholarships, loans, fellowships, assistantships. Total awards ranged from $500-$12,000. Financial aid is not available to part-time students. Application deadline: 1/2 for fall. Contact: Graduate Adviser, Student Financial Services, 432 North Murray Street, Madison, WI 53706-1372. (608) 262-3060.

INTERNATIONAL STUDENTS

Demographics 30% of students enrolled in the program are international.

Services and Facilities Visa services, language tutoring, ESL courses, counseling/support services.

Applying TOEFL required, minimum score of 600; proof of health; proof of adequate funds. Financial aid is not available to international students. Admission application deadlines: 6/1 for fall, 10/1 for spring. Contact: International Students and Scholars Services, 115 Science Hall, Madison, WI 53706-1372. (608) 262-2044.

ALTERNATE MBA PROGRAM

Executive MBA (EMBA) Length of program: Minimum: 18 months. Maximum: 2 years. Degree requirements: 48 credits. 8-10 years of management experience. Average class size: 30.

PLACEMENT

Placement services include alumni network, career counseling/planning, career fairs, career library, career placement, electronic job bank, job interviews, job search course, resume preparation, and resume referral to employers. Of 1994 graduates, the average starting salary was $44,354, the range was $19,500-$72,000.

Program Contact: Graduate Programs Office, University of Wisconsin–Madison, 2266 Grainger Hall, 975 University Avenue, Madison, WI 53706-1323. (608) 262-1555; Fax: (608) 265-4192.

See full description on page 926.

University of Wisconsin–Milwaukee

School of Business Administration

Milwaukee, Wisconsin

OVERVIEW

The University of Wisconsin–Milwaukee is a state-supported coed institution. Part of University of Wisconsin System. Founded 1956. Setting: 90-acre urban campus. Total institutional enrollment: 22,984. AACSB-accredited.

ACADEMICS

Calendar Semesters.

Concentrations Management, strategic management.

FACILITIES

Information Resources Main library with 3.7 million bound volumes, 1.3 million titles on microform, 9,500 periodical subscriptions, 21,000 records/tapes/CDs.

ADMISSION

Entrance Requirements Bachelor's degree, GMAT score, minimum 8 years of work experience.

Application Requirements Application form, copies of transcript.

Application Deadlines 9/13 for fall, 12/24 for spring.

INTERNATIONAL STUDENTS

Applying TOEFL required, minimum score of 550. Admission application deadlines: 9/13 for fall, 12/24 for spring.

Program Contact: Ms. Beth Weckmueller, Director of Admissions, University of Wisconsin–Milwaukee, PO Box 413, Milwaukee, WI 53201-0413. (414) 229-6164.

University of Wisconsin–Oshkosh

College of Business Administration

Oshkosh, Wisconsin

OVERVIEW

The University of Wisconsin–Oshkosh is a state-supported comprehensive coed institution. Part of University of Wisconsin System. Founded 1871. Setting: 192-acre small-town campus. Total institutional enrollment: 11,500. Program was first offered in 1970. AACSB-accredited.

MBA HIGHLIGHTS

Entrance Difficulty*
Mean GMAT: 540
Mean GPA: 3.1

Cost $
Tuition: $170/credit
(Nonresident: $480/credit)
Room & Board: $3,500

Enrollment Profile
Full-time: 35
Part-time: 465
Total: 500
Average Age: 28

Work Exp: 95%
International: 5%
Women: 40%
Minorities: 3%

Class Size: 25 - 30

ACADEMICS

Length of Program Minimum: 18 months.

Calendar Semesters.

Full-time Classes Main campus, Green Bay, Stevens Point; evening, weekends.

Part-time Classes Main campus; evening, weekends.

Degree Requirements 30 credits including 9 elective credits.

Required Courses Corporate strategy, financial management, information systems, managerial accounting, marketing management, organization and environments, quantitative methods. Courses may be waived through: previous course work.

Curricular Focus Business issues and problems, general management, organizational development and change management.

Concentration Management.

Faculty Full-time: 40, 100% with doctorates; part-time: 2.

Teaching Methodology Case study: 20%, discussion: 20%, lecture: 20%, student presentations: 20%, team projects: 20%.

Special Opportunities Internship program available. Other: study abroad in Paris, London and Brussels.

STUDENT STATISTICS

Geographic Representation State residents 90%. By region: Midwest 80%; Northeast 5%; South 5%; West 5%. International 5%.

Undergraduate Majors Business 50%; education 1%; engineering/technology 15%; humanities 5%; nursing 1%; science/mathematics 5%; social sciences 15%; other 8%.

Other Background Graduate degrees in other disciplines: 3%. Work experience: On average, students have 5 years of work experience on entrance to the program.

FACILITIES

Information Resources Main library with 460,988 bound volumes, 127,305 titles on microform, 1,982 periodical subscriptions, 6,110 records/tapes/CDs, 112 CD-ROMs.

Housing 1% of students in program live in college-owned or -operated housing.

Technology Computers are used moderately in course work. 200 computer terminals/PCs, linked by a campus-wide computer network, are available for use by students in program; they are located in computer labs. Students in the program are not required to have their own PC.

Computer Resources/On-line Services

Training	No	Dun's		No
Internet	Yes	Dow Jones		No
E-Mail	Yes	Dialog		No
LEXIS/NEXIS	No	Bloomberg		No
CompuServe	No			

Other on-line services: OCLC.

ADMISSION

Acceptance 1994-95 Of those applying, 85% were accepted.

Entrance Requirements Bachelor's degree, GMAT score of 450, minimum 2.75 GPA, minimum 2 years of work experience. Core courses waived through: previous course work.

Application Requirements Application form, copies of transcript, resume/curriculum vitae.

Application Deadlines 7/1 for fall, 12/1 for spring, 5/1 for summer.

FINANCIALS

Costs for 1994-95 Tuition: Full-time: $170/credit for state residents, $480/credit for nonresidents. Average room and board costs are $3,500 per academic year (on-campus) and $3,500 per academic year (off-campus).

Financial Aid In 1994-95, 5% of candidates received some institutionally administered aid in the form of loans, assistantships. Total awards ranged from $500-$6,700. Financial aid is available to part-time students. Application deadlines: 5/31 for fall, 5/31 for spring. Contact: Mr. Ken Cook, Director of Financial Aid, 800 Algoma Boulevard, Oshkosh, WI 54901-3551. (414) 424-3377.

INTERNATIONAL STUDENTS

Demographics 5% of students enrolled in the program are international; Asia 60%, Europe 40%.

Services and Facilities International student center, counseling/support services.

Applying TOEFL required, minimum score of 550; proof of adequate funds. Financial aid is available to international students. Financial aid application deadlines: 3/15 for fall, 3/15 for spring. Admission application deadlines: 7/1 for fall, 12/1 for spring, 5/1 for summer. Contact: Ms. Judy Jaeger, International Student Adviser, Dean of Students Office, 800 Algoma Boulevard, Oshkosh, WI 54901-3551. (414) 424-3100.

PLACEMENT

Placement services include alumni network, career counseling/planning, career library, resume preparation, and resume referral to employers.

Program Contact: Ms. Lynn Grancorbitz, MBA Program Adviser, University of Wisconsin–Oshkosh, 800 Algoma Boulevard, Oshkosh, WI 54901-3551. (800) 633-1430, or (800) 633-1430; Fax: (414) 424-7413; Internet Address: simons@vaxa.cis.uwosh.edu.

University of Wisconsin–Parkside

School of Business and Administrative Science

Kenosha, Wisconsin

OVERVIEW
The University of Wisconsin–Parkside is a state-supported comprehensive coed institution. Part of University of Wisconsin System. Founded 1968. Setting: 700-acre suburban campus with easy access to Chicago and Milwaukee. Total institutional enrollment: 5,027.

MBA HIGHLIGHTS

Entrance Difficulty***

Cost $
Tuition: $333 - $486/course
(Nonresident: $970 - $1,442/course)
Room & Board: N/R

Enrollment Profile

Full-time: 504	Work Exp: N/R
Part-time: 0	International: 2%
Total: 504	Women: 48%
Average Age: N/R	Minorities: 4%

Class Size: 15 - 20

ACADEMICS
Length of Program Minimum: 30 months.
Calendar Semesters.
Part-time Classes Main campus; evening, summer.
Degree Requirements 33 credits.
Curricular Focus Business issues and problems, economic and financial theory, general management, leadership, managing diversity, organizational development and change management, problem solving and decision making, strategic analysis and planning.
Concentration Management.
Teaching Methodology Case study: 40%, lecture: 20%, team projects: 40%.

STUDENT STATISTICS
Geographic Representation State residents 98%. International 2%.

FACILITIES
Information Resources Main library with 358,000 bound volumes, 155,000 titles on microform, 1,500 periodical subscriptions, 10,300 records/tapes/CDs.

ADMISSION
Entrance Requirements Bachelor's degree, required competency courses, prerequisite courses required for applicants with non-business degree, GMAT score.
Application Requirements Application form, copies of transcript, resume/curriculum vitae, personal statement, 2 letters of recommendation.
Application Deadlines 8/1 for fall, 12/15 for spring, 4/15 for summer. Applications are processed on a rolling basis.

FINANCIALS
Costs for 1994-95 Tuition: Full-time: $333-$486/course for state residents, $970-$1,442/course for nonresidents.
Financial Aid Application deadline: 4/1 for fall. Contact: Mr. Jan K. Ocker, Director, 900 Wood Road, Box 2000, Kenosha, WI 53141-2000. (414) 595-2577.

INTERNATIONAL STUDENTS
Demographics 2% of students enrolled in the program are international.
Applying TOEFL required, minimum score of 550; proof of health. Financial aid is available to international students. Financial aid application deadline: 4/1 for fall.

Program Contact: Ms. Joanne Canyon-Heller, Assistant to the Dean, University of Wisconsin–Parkside, 900 Wood Road, Box 2000, Kenosha, WI 53141-2000. (414) 595-2046; Fax: (414) 595-2680.

University of Wisconsin–Whitewater

College of Business and Economics

Whitewater, Wisconsin

OVERVIEW
The University of Wisconsin–Whitewater is a state-supported comprehensive coed institution. Part of University of Wisconsin System. Founded 1868. Setting: 385-acre small-town campus with easy access to Milwaukee. Total institutional enrollment: 10,438. Program was first offered in 1968. AACSB-accredited.

MBA HIGHLIGHTS

Entrance Difficulty***
Mean GMAT: 495
Mean GPA: 3.25

Cost $
Tuition: $1,588/semester
(Nonresident: $4,457/semester)
Room & Board: $2,200

Enrollment Profile

Full-time: 135	Work Exp: 70%
Part-time: 233	International: 19%
Total: 368	Women: 39%
Average Age: 29	Minorities: 5%

Average Class Size: 20

ACADEMICS
Length of Program Minimum: 18 months. Maximum: 7 years.
Calendar Semesters.
Full-time Classes Main campus; day, evening, early morning, summer.
Part-time Classes Main campus, Waukesha; evening, summer.
Degree Requirements 36 credits including 12 elective credits.
Required Courses Advanced statistical methods, business conditions analysis or managerial economics, business policy and environment, managerial and organizational behavior, operations research, seminar in business communication.
Curricular Focus Business issues and problems, international business, problem solving and decision making.
Concentrations Accounting, finance, hotel management, human resources management, management, marketing, operations management.
Faculty Full-time: 40, 100% with doctorates.
Teaching Methodology Case study: 30%, lecture: 40%, research: 10%, student presentations: 20%.
Special Opportunities International exchange in France, India.

STUDENT STATISTICS
Geographic Representation State residents 70%. By region: Midwest 79%; Northeast 2%; West 1%. International 19%.
Undergraduate Majors Business 60%; education 2%; engineering/technology 20%; humanities 10%; science/mathematics 5%; social sciences 2%.
Other Background Graduate degrees in other disciplines: 1%. Work experience: On average, students have 2 years of work experience on entrance to the program.

FACILITIES
Information Resources Main library with 352,656 bound volumes, 13,734 titles on microform, 2,496 periodical subscriptions, 10,467 records/tapes/CDs, 170 CD-ROMs.
Housing 2% of students in program live in college-owned or -operated housing.
Technology Computers are used heavily in course work. Computer terminals/PCs are available for use by students in program; they are located in dormitories, classrooms, learning resource center, the library, the computer center, computer labs. Students in the program are not required to have their own PC.

Computer Resources/On-line Services

Training	Yes	Videoconference Center	Yes
E-Mail	Yes	Multimedia Center	Yes

ADMISSION

Acceptance 1994-95 180 applied for admission; 84% were accepted.

Entrance Requirements Bachelor's degree, GMAT score of 450, minimum 2.75 GPA. Core courses waived through: previous course work.

Application Requirements Application form, copies of transcript.

Application Deadlines 7/1 for fall, 11/1 for spring, 4/1 for summer.

FINANCIALS

Costs for 1994-95 Tuition: Full-time: $1,588/semester for state residents, $4,457/semester for nonresidents; Part-time day: $176/credit for state residents, $495/credit for nonresidents. Average room and board costs are $2,200 per academic year (on-campus).

Financial Aid In 1994-95, 25% of candidates received some institutionally administered aid in the form of grants, scholarships, loans, assistantships. Application deadlines: 5/1 for fall, 12/1 for spring, 4/1 for summer. Contact: Mr. Tillman Terry Jr., Director of Financial Aid, Financial Aid, Whitewater, WI 53190. (414) 472-1130.

INTERNATIONAL STUDENTS

Demographics 19% of students enrolled in the program are international; Asia 82%, Europe 3%, South America 3%, Africa 2%, other 10%.

Services and Facilities International student office, international student center, visa services, language tutoring, counseling/support services.

Applying TOEFL required, minimum score of 550; proof of adequate funds. Financial aid is available to international students. Financial aid application deadline: 4/1 for fall. Admission application deadlines: 4/1 for fall, 10/1 for spring. Applications are processed on a rolling basis. Contact: Dr. Rama Bharadwat, Director, International Program, Whitewater, WI 53190. (414) 472-5178.

PLACEMENT

Placement services include alumni network, career counseling/planning, career placement, and job interviews. Of 1994 graduates, the average starting salary was $35,000, the range was $27,500-$40,000.

Program Contact: Dr. Harish Batra, Associate Dean, University of Wisconsin–Whitewater, College of Business and Economics, Whitewater, WI 53190. (414) 472-1945; Fax: (414) 472-4863.

University of Wyoming

College of Business

Laramie, Wyoming

OVERVIEW

The University of Wyoming is a state-supported coed institution. Founded 1886. Setting: 785-acre small-town campus. Total institutional enrollment: 12,500. Program was first offered in 1994. AACSB-accredited.

MBA HIGHLIGHTS

Entrance Difficulty***
Mean GMAT: 568
Mean GPA: 3.24

Cost $
Tuition: $1,008/semester
(Nonresident: $3,042/semester)
Room & Board: N/R

Enrollment Profile

Full-time: 40	Work Exp: 80%
Part-time: 65	International: 12%
Total: 105	Women: 40%
Average Age: 27	Minorities: 52%

Average Class Size: 15

ACADEMICS

Length of Program Minimum: 12 months. Maximum: 6 years.

Calendar Semesters.

Full-time Classes Main campus, Laramie; day, evening, summer.

Part-time Classes Casper, Riverton, Rock Springs, Powell, Gillette; evening, weekends, summer.

Degree Requirements 30 hours. Other: Thesis or paper.

Required Courses Business ventures, human resources management, international business, managerial finance, marketing management, production planning, professional skills, seminar in accounting.

Curricular Focus General management, managing diversity, problem solving and decision making.

Concentration Management.

Faculty Full-time: 25.

Teaching Methodology Case study: 20%, lecture: 60%, research: 5%, student presentations: 10%, team projects: 5%.

STUDENT STATISTICS

Geographic Representation International 12%.

Undergraduate Majors Business 60%; engineering/technology 30%; science/mathematics 10%.

Other Background Graduate degrees in other disciplines: 30%.

FACILITIES

Information Resources Main library with 1.2 million bound volumes, 2.4 million titles on microform, 14,467 periodical subscriptions.

Technology Computers are used moderately in course work. Computer terminals/PCs, linked by a campus-wide computer network, are available for use by students in program; they are located in student rooms, the student center, the library, the computer center, computer labs. Students in the program are not required to have their own PC.

Computer Resources/On-line Services

E-Mail	Yes

ADMISSION

Acceptance 1994-95 Of those applying, 80% were accepted.

Entrance Requirements Bachelor's degree, GMAT score of 500, minimum 3.0 GPA. Core courses waived through: previous course work, work experience.

Application Requirements Written essay, application form, copies of transcript, personal statement, 3 letters of recommendation.

Application Deadline Applications are processed on a rolling basis. Application discs available.

FINANCIALS

Costs for 1994-95 Tuition: Full-time: $1,008/semester for state residents, $3,042/semester for nonresidents; Part-time day: $112/credit hour for state residents, $338/credit hour for nonresidents. Fees: Full-time: $150/semester for state residents, $150/semester for nonresidents; Part-time day: $4/credit hour for state residents, $4/credit hour for nonresidents.

Financial Aid Application deadline: 3/1 for fall. Applications are processed on a rolling basis. Contact: Mr. John Nutter, Director of Financial Aid, Box 3335, Laramie, WY 82070. (307) 766-2116.

INTERNATIONAL STUDENTS

Demographics 12% of students enrolled in the program are international.

Applying TOEFL required, minimum score of 550; proof of health; proof of adequate funds. Financial aid is available to international students. Assistantships are available for these students. Financial aid application deadline: 3/31 for fall. Financial aid and admission applications are processed on a rolling basis.

Program Contact: Dr. Del Wells, Director, Graduate Business Programs, University of Wyoming, Laramie, WY 82071. (307) 766-2449; Fax: (307) 766-4028; Internet Address: delwells@uwyo.edu.

GUAM

University of Guam

College of Business and Public Administration

Mangilao, Guam

OVERVIEW

The University of Guam is a territory-supported comprehensive coed institution. Founded 1952. Setting: 100-acre rural campus. Total institutional enrollment: 2,557.

ACADEMICS
Calendar Semesters.

Degree Requirements 36 credits.

FACILITIES
Information Resources Main library with 327,925 bound volumes, 2,901 titles on microform, 3,060 periodical subscriptions, 2,026 records/tapes/CDs.

ADMISSION
Entrance Requirements Bachelor's degree, GMAT score of 400, minimum 3.0 GPA.

Application Requirements Application form, copies of transcript, personal statement, 2 letters of recommendation.

FINANCIALS
Costs for 1994-95 Tuition: Full-time: $63/credit for territory residents, $140/credit for nonresidents. Fees: Full-time: $84/semester hour for territory residents, $84/semester hour for nonresidents.

INTERNATIONAL STUDENTS
Applying TOEFL required, minimum score of 550.

Program Contact: University of Guam, UOG Station, Mangilao, GU 96923. (671) 734-2177.

PUERTO RICO

Inter American University of Puerto Rico, San Germán Campus

Department of Business Administration

San Germán, Puerto Rico

OVERVIEW
Inter American University of Puerto Rico, San Germán Campus is an independent nonprofit comprehensive coed institution. Part of Inter American University of Puerto Rico. Founded 1912. Setting: 260-acre small-town campus. Total institutional enrollment: 5,852.

MBA HIGHLIGHTS
Entrance Difficulty**

Cost $
Tuition: $130/credit
Room & Board: $760

Enrollment Profile

Full-time: N/R	Work Exp: N/R
Part-time: N/R	International: N/R
Total: 400	Women: 52%
Average Age: N/R	Minorities: N/R

Average Class Size: 20

ACADEMICS
Length of Program Minimum: 30 months. Maximum: 7 years.

Calendar Semesters.

Full-time Classes Main campus; evening, weekends.

Part-time Classes Main campus; evening, weekends.

Degree Requirements 42 credits. Other: Comprehensive exam.

Curricular Focus Business issues and problems, leadership, problem solving and decision making, teamwork.

Concentrations Accounting, finance, human resources management, industrial management, marketing.

Faculty Full-time: 12, 67% with doctorates; part-time: 6, 67% with doctorates.

Teaching Methodology Case study: 20%, lecture: 40%, research: 5%, student presentations: 20%, team projects: 15%.

FACILITIES
Information Resources Main library with 136,958 bound volumes, 761 titles on microform, 2,447 periodical subscriptions, 28,184 records/tapes/CDs, 21 CD-ROMs.

Housing College housing available.

ADMISSION
Entrance Requirements Bachelor's degree, GMAT score, minimum 2.5 GPA. Core courses waived through: previous course work.

Application Requirements Application form, copies of transcript, 2 letters of recommendation.

Application Deadlines 5/15 for fall, 11/15 for spring.

FINANCIALS
Costs for 1994-95 Tuition: Full-time: $130/credit. Fees: Full-time: $140/semester. Average room and board costs are $760 per academic year (on-campus).

Financial Aid In 1994-95, candidates received some institutionally administered aid in the form of loans, assistantships, work-study. Application deadlines: 4/30 for fall, 11/15 for spring. Contact: Ms. Maria I. Lugo, Director of Financial Aid, Call Box 5100, San Germán, PR 00683. (809) 264-1912 Ext. 227.

INTERNATIONAL STUDENTS
Services and Facilities International student office, language tutoring, ESL courses.

Applying Financial aid is available to international students. Financial aid application deadlines: 4/30 for fall, 11/15 for spring. Admission application deadlines: 5/15 for fall, 11/15 for spring. Contact: Mr. Diana Jimenez, International Student Program Director, Call Box 5100, San Germán, PR 00683. (809) 264-1912 Ext. 317.

Program Contact: Ms. Mildred Camacho, Admissions Director, Inter American University of Puerto Rico, San Germán Campus, Call Box 5100, San Germán, PR 00683. (809) 892-3090; Fax: (809) 892-6350.

Pontifical Catholic University of Puerto Rico

Ponce, Puerto Rico

OVERVIEW
Pontifical Catholic University of Puerto Rico is an independent Roman Catholic comprehensive coed institution. Founded 1948. Setting: 120-acre urban campus with easy access to San Juan. Total institutional enrollment: 12,250. Program was first offered in 1968.

MBA HIGHLIGHTS
Entrance Difficulty**
Mean GMAT: 500
Mean GPA: N/R

Cost $
Tuition: $120/credit
Room & Board: N/R

Enrollment Profile

Full-time: 50	Work Exp: 80%
Part-time: 215	International: N/R
Total: 265	Women: 51%
Average Age: 25	Minorities: N/R

Average Class Size: 15

ACADEMICS
Length of Program Minimum: 30 months. Maximum: 7 years.

Calendar Semesters.

Full-time Classes Main campus; evening, weekends.

Part-time Classes Main campus; evening, weekends.

Degree Requirements 43 credits including 12 elective credits. Other: 2 courses in theology.

Required Courses Administrative human resources, business policy, financial management, international business, managerial accounting, managerial economics, managerial marketing, research methods.

Curricular Focus Entrepreneurship, general management, international business.

Concentrations Accounting, human resources management, management.

Faculty Full-time: 4, 75% with doctorates; part-time: 12, 50% with doctorates.

Teaching Methodology Case study: 10%, lecture: 30%, research: 25%, student presentations: 25%, team projects: 10%.

STUDENT STATISTICS
Undergraduate Majors Business 88%; engineering/technology 10%; science/mathematics 2%.

Other Background Graduate degrees in other disciplines: 3%. Work experience: On average, students have 2 years of work experience on entrance to the program.

FACILITIES
Information Resources Main library with 236,887 bound volumes, 336,282 titles on microform, 37,113 periodical subscriptions, 7,342 records/tapes/CDs.

Housing College housing not available.

Technology Computers are used moderately in course work. 60 computer terminals/PCs are available for use by students in program; they are located in learning resource center, the computer center. Students in the program are not required to have their own PC. $100 are budgeted per student for computer support.

Computer Resources/On-line Services
Training	Yes	Multimedia Center	Yes
E-Mail	No	Dialog	Yes $
Videoconference Center	Yes		

ADMISSION
Acceptance 1994-95 100 applied for admission; 70% were accepted.

Entrance Requirements Bachelor's degree, minimum 2.5 GPA.

Application Requirements Interview, application form, copies of transcript, 2 letters of recommendation.

Application Deadlines 6/15 for fall, 11/15 for spring, 4/15 for summer. Applications are processed on a rolling basis.

FINANCIALS
Costs for 1994-95 Tuition: Full-time: $120/credit; Part-time evening: $120/credit. Fees: Full-time: $60/semester; Part-time evening: $60/semester.

Financial Aid In 1994-95, 60% of candidates received some institutionally administered aid in the form of loans. Total awards ranged from $1,000-$2,500. Financial aid is available to part-time students. Application deadlines: 4/1 for fall, 10/1 for spring. Applications are processed on a rolling basis. Contact: Ms. Maria Izquierdo, Director of Student Aid, Las Americas Avenue, Ponce, PR 00731. (809) 841-2000 Ext. 441.

INTERNATIONAL STUDENTS
Applying Proof of adequate funds. Financial aid is not available to international students. Admission applications are processed on a rolling basis.

ALTERNATE MBA PROGRAM
MBA/JD Length of program: Minimum: 60 months. Full-time classes: Main campus; day, evening. Degree requirements: 139 credits. Languages: English, Spanish.

PLACEMENT
Placement services include career counseling/planning.

Program Contact: Mrs. Carilin Frau, Director of Admissions, Pontifical Catholic University of Puerto Rico, Las Americas Avenue, Suite 584, Ponce, PR 00731. (809) 841-2000 Ext. 427; Fax: (809) 840-4295.

Universidad del Turabo

Gurabo, Puerto Rico

OVERVIEW
The Universidad del Turabo is an independent nonprofit comprehensive coed institution. Part of Fundación Educativa Ana G. Méndez. Founded 1972. Setting: 113-acre urban campus with easy access to San Juan. Total institutional enrollment: 7,796.

MBA HIGHLIGHTS
Entrance Difficulty**

Cost $
Tuition: $720 - $1,440/semester
Room & Board: $2,400 (off-campus)

Enrollment Profile
Full-time: N/R	Work Exp: N/R
Part-time: N/R	International: 1%
Total: 482	Women: 48%
Average Age: N/R	Minorities: N/R

Average Class Size: 15

T he University of Turabo is a private educational institution and a member of the nonprofit Ana G. Méndez University System. It is located 15 miles southeast of San Juan within easy reach of the entire east-central part of the island.

The Graduate Program in Business Administration at the University of Turabo is housed in the recently built Graduate Programs facilities surrounded by hills and mountains. Courses are taught in comfortable, air-conditioned classrooms.

The graduate student body is a mosaic formed by a broad range of academic and professional backgrounds, which creates a rich learning environment. Over half of the graduate students had their undergraduate training in engineering, chemistry, or biology. They hold managerial positions in manufacturing plants located in the surrounding municipalities. The rest of the student body includes people from different areas of business administration and liberal arts. Graduate student, professional, and social activities are an important part of student life at the University of Turabo. Student organizations include student chapters of American Production and Inventory Control Society, American Marketing Association, and the National Society for Hispanic M.B.A.'s (in process).

The faculty members also have a rich variety of academic backgrounds, gained in the U.S., Puerto Rico, and in Europe. Their professional experience includes positions held in the private as well as the public sectors.

ACADEMICS
Length of Program Minimum: 30 months.

Calendar Semesters.

Full-time Classes Main campus; evening, weekends, summer.

Part-time Classes Main campus; evening, weekends, summer.

Degree Requirements 39 credits.

Curricular Focus Business issues and problems, general management, organizational development and change management.

Concentrations Accounting, human resources management, logistics and materials management, management, marketing.

Teaching Methodology Case study: 10%, lecture: 50%, research: 10%, seminars by members of the business community: 5%, student presentations: 15%, team projects: 10%.

STUDENT STATISTICS
Geographic Representation commonwealth residents 98%. International 1%.

FACILITIES
Information Resources Main library with 66,342 bound volumes, 364 titles on microform, 764 periodical subscriptions, 1,699 records/tapes/CDs.

Housing College housing not available.

ADMISSION
Entrance Requirements Bachelor's degree, minimum 2.75 GPA, Prueba de Admisiones para Estudios Graduados or GRE.

Application Requirements Interview, application form, copies of transcript, 3 letters of recommendation.

Application Deadlines 8/5 for fall. Applications are processed on a rolling basis.

FINANCIALS
Costs for 1994-95 Tuition: Full-time: $720-$1,440/semester. Fees: Full-time: $110/semester. Average room and board costs are $2,400 per academic year (off-campus).

Financial Aid Application deadline: 6/30 for fall. Applications are processed on a rolling basis. Contact: Ms. Ana M. Ortega, Director, PO Box 3030, Gurabo, PR 00778-7001. (809) 743-7979 Ext. 4450.

INTERNATIONAL STUDENTS
Demographics 1% of students enrolled in the program are international.

Applying Proof of health; proof of adequate funds. Financial aid is not available to international students. Admission application deadlines: 6/30 for fall, 11/15 for spring. Applications are processed on a rolling basis.

Program Contact: Ms. Virginia González, Admissions Officer, Universidad del Turabo, PO Box 3030, Gurabo, PR 00778-7001. (809) 743-7979 Ext. 4352; Fax: (809) 744-5427.

University of Puerto Rico, Río Piedras

Graduate School of Business

Río Piedras, Puerto Rico

OVERVIEW

The University of Puerto Rico, Río Piedras is a commonwealth-supported coed institution. Part of University of Puerto Rico System. Founded 1903. Setting: 281-acre urban campus with easy access to San Juan. Total institutional enrollment: 18,690. Program was first offered in 1970.

MBA HIGHLIGHTS

Entrance Difficulty**
Mean GMAT: N/R
Mean GPA: 3.0

Cost $
Tuition: $75/credit
(Nonresident: $75/credit)
Room & Board: N/R

Enrollment Profile
Full-time: 52
Part-time: 299
Total: 351
Average Age: 25

Work Exp: 78%
International: N/R
Women: 57%
Minorities: 100%

Average Class Size: 25

ACADEMICS

Length of Program Minimum: 30 months. Maximum: 6 years.
Calendar Semesters.
Full-time Classes Main campus; day, evening, early morning, summer.
Degree Requirements 36 credits including 9 elective credits. Other: Minimum 3.0 GPA; research project; defense of research findings before proposal committee; final comprehensive exam.
Required Courses Accounting for analysis and control, economics for managers, finance for managers, fundamental aspects of statistics, fundamental factors in managerial activity, managerial production, marketing management, organizational behavior, philosophy of business.
Curricular Focus Business issues and problems, entrepreneurship, problem solving and decision making.
Concentrations Accounting, economics, finance, management, marketing, operations management.
Faculty Full-time: 10, 90% with doctorates; part-time: 6, 90% with doctorates.
Teaching Methodology Case study: 30%, lecture: 30%, research: 20%, student presentations: 20%.

STUDENT STATISTICS

Undergraduate Majors Business 76%; engineering/technology 15%; humanities 1%; science/mathematics 2%; social sciences 4%; other 2%.

FACILITIES

Information Resources Main library with 4 million bound volumes, 1.2 million titles on microform, 4,035 periodical subscriptions, 25,449 records/tapes/CDs. Business collection in Business Administration Library includes 15,819 bound volumes, 523 periodical subscriptions, 481 CD-ROMs, 52 videos.
Housing College housing available.
Technology Computers are used moderately in course work. 54 computer terminals/PCs are available for use by students in program; they are located in the computer center, computer labs. Students in the program are not required to have their own PC.

Computer Resources/On-line Services
Internet   Yes   E-Mail   No

ADMISSION

Acceptance 1994-95 Of those applying, 45% were accepted.
Entrance Requirements Bachelor's degree, math concepts that include a course in differential and integral calculus with a minimum grade of C, minimum 3.0 GPA, Prueba de Admisiones para Estudios Graduados: minimum 550 score; verbal and written mastery of Spanish.
Application Requirements Written essay, application form, copies of transcript, 2 letters of recommendation.
Application Deadline 2/1 for fall.

FINANCIALS

Costs for 1994-95 Tuition: Full-time: $75/credit for commonwealth resident, $75/credit for nonresidents, $1,750/semester for international students. Fees: Full-time: $226-$286 for commonwealth resident, $300-$1,775 for nonresidents, $35/semester for international students.
Financial Aid Contact: Ms. Luz Santiago, Director, P.O. Box 23336, Río Piedras, PR 00931. (809) 764-0000 Ext. 3148.

INTERNATIONAL STUDENTS

Demographics 3% of students on campus are international.
Services and Facilities Visa services, language tutoring, special assistance for nonnative speakers of English, counseling/support services.
Applying Proof of health; proof of adequate funds. Financial aid is not available to international students. Admission application deadline: 2/1 for fall. Contact: Ms. Luz M. Diaz, Director, OSOEI, P.O. Box 23336, San Juan, PR 00931-3336. (809) 764-0000 Ext. 3055.

PLACEMENT

Placement services include career fairs and career placement.

Program Contact: Dr. Eusebio D. Diaz, Director, University of Puerto Rico, Río Piedras, Ponce De Leon Avenue, Río Piedras, PR 00931. (809) 763-5950; Fax: (809) 763-6944.

University of the Sacred Heart

Business School

Santurce, Puerto Rico

OVERVIEW

The University of the Sacred Heart is an independent Roman Catholic comprehensive coed institution. Founded 1935. Setting: 33-acre urban campus. Total institutional enrollment: 4,920. Program was first offered in 1985.

MBA HIGHLIGHTS

Entrance Difficulty*
Mean GMAT: 535
Mean GPA: 3.2

Cost
Tuition: N/R
Room & Board: N/R

Enrollment Profile
Full-time: 5
Part-time: 95
Total: 100
Average Age: 25

Work Exp: 85%
International: 1%
Women: 40%
Minorities: N/R

Average Class Size: 12

ACADEMICS

Length of Program May range up to 7 years.
Calendar Semesters.
Full-time Classes Main campus; evening.
Part-time Classes Main campus; evening.
Degree Requirements 48 credits including 6 elective credits. Other: Thesis.
Curricular Focus Information technology, leadership, organizational development and change management.
Concentrations Management, management information systems.
Faculty Full-time: 2, 50% with doctorates; part-time: 9, 60% with doctorates.
Special Opportunities International exchange program available.

STUDENT STATISTICS
Geographic Representation International 1%.

Undergraduate Majors Business 40%; education 10%; engineering/technology 35%; humanities 5%; science/mathematics 5%; other 5%.

Other Background Graduate degrees in other disciplines: 15%. Work experience: On average, students have 3 years of work experience on entrance to the program.

FACILITIES
Information Resources Main library with 129,549 bound volumes, 15 titles on microform, 1,500 periodical subscriptions, 2,927 records/tapes/CDs.

Housing College housing not available.

Technology Computers are used moderately in course work. 100 computer terminals/PCs, linked by a campus-wide computer network, are available for use by students in program; they are located in classrooms, learning resource center, the library, the computer center, computer labs. Students in the program are not required to have their own PC.

Computer Resources/On-line Services

Internet	Yes	CompuServe	Yes
E-Mail	No	Dow Jones	Yes $
Videoconference Center	Yes	Dialog	Yes $
LEXIS/NEXIS	Yes $		

ADMISSION
Entrance Requirements Bachelor's degree, prerequisite courses required for applicants with non-business degree, GMAT score of 500, minimum 2.8 GPA, minimum 2 years of work experience. Core courses waived through: previous course work.

Application Requirements Written essay, interview, application form, copies of transcript, resume/curriculum vitae, 2 letters of recommendation.

Application Deadlines 11/1 for fall, 4/1 for spring. Applications are processed on a rolling basis.

FINANCIALS
Financial Aid In 1994-95, candidates received some institutionally administered aid in the form of scholarships, loans, work-study. Financial aid is available to part-time students.

INTERNATIONAL STUDENTS
Demographics 1% of students enrolled in the program are international.

Applying Proof of health; proof of adequate funds. Financial aid is not available to international students.

PLACEMENT
Of 1994 graduates, 95% were employed within three months of graduation.

Jobs by Employer Type Manufacturing 30%; service 30%; government 20%; consulting 5%; education 15%.

Program Contact: Admissions Office, University of the Sacred Heart, Box 12383, Loiza Station, Santurce, PR 00914. (809) 728-1515 Ext. 3595; Fax: (809) 727-1250.

VIRGIN ISLANDS

University of the Virgin Islands

Division of Business Administration

Charlotte Amalie, St. Thomas, Virgin Islands

OVERVIEW
The University of the Virgin Islands is a territory-supported comprehensive coed institution. Founded 1962. Setting: 175-acre small-town campus. Total institutional enrollment: 3,206.

MBA HIGHLIGHTS

Entrance Difficulty**
Mean GMAT: 430
Mean GPA: N/R

Cost $
Tuition: $138/credit
(Nonresident: $276/credit)
Room & Board: N/R

Enrollment Profile

Full-time: 299	Work Exp: 90%
Part-time: 0	International: N/R
Total: 299	Women: 67%
Average Age: 25	Minorities: N/R

Average Class Size: 14

ACADEMICS
Length of Program Minimum: 36 months. Maximum: 5 years.

Calendar Semesters.

Part-time Classes Main campus, Saint Croix, distance learning option; evening, summer.

Degree Requirements 36 credits including 9 elective credits.

Curricular Focus Business issues and problems, international business, strategic analysis and planning.

Concentration Management.

Faculty Full-time: 5, 80% with doctorates; part-time: 5.

STUDENT STATISTICS
Other Background Graduate degrees in other disciplines: 5%. Work experience: On average, students have 4 years of work experience on entrance to the program.

FACILITIES
Information Resources Main library with 103,131 bound volumes, 79,069 titles on microform, 1,020 periodical subscriptions, 212 records/tapes/CDs.

Housing College housing not available.

Technology Computers are used moderately in course work. Computer terminals/PCs, linked by a campus-wide computer network, are available for use by students in program; they are located in computer labs. Students in the program are not required to have their own PC.

Computer Resources/On-line Services

Training	Yes	E-Mail	No

ADMISSION
Entrance Requirements Bachelor's degree, GMAT score, minimum 2.5 GPA. Core courses waived through: previous course work.

Application Requirements Application form, copies of transcript.

Application Deadlines 4/15 for fall, 11/15 for spring.

FINANCIALS
Costs for 1994-95 Tuition: Full-time: $138/credit for territory residents, $276/credit for nonresidents.

Financial Aid In 1994-95, candidates received some institutionally administered aid in the form of scholarships, loans. Applications are processed on a rolling basis. Contact: Dr. Lynn McConnell, Financial Aid Director, Charlotte Amalie, St. Thomas, VI 00802-9999. (809) 693-1096.

INTERNATIONAL STUDENTS
Applying TOEFL required, minimum score of 550; proof of health. Financial aid is not available to international students. Admission application deadlines: 4/15 for fall, 11/15 for spring.

Program Contact: Dr. Solomon Kabuka, Coordinator, Graduate Business Studies, University of the Virgin Islands, Charlotte Amalie, St. Thomas, VI 00802-9999. (809) 693-1309; Fax: (809) 693-1311.

AUSTRALIA

Australian National University

Canberra, Australia

OVERVIEW

Australian National University is a government-supported coed institution. Founded 1946. Setting: suburban campus. Program was first offered in 1994.

MBA HIGHLIGHTS

Entrance Difficulty**

Cost
(Nonresident: 25,000 Australian dollars/degree program)
Room & Board: 10,000 Australian dollars

Enrollment Profile

Full-time: 21	Work Exp: 100%
Part-time: 0	Women: 20%
Total: 21	
Average Age: 30	

Average Class Size: 21

ACADEMICS

Length of Program Minimum: 14 months.

Calendar Semesters.

Full-time Classes Main campus; day.

Degree Requirements 24 credits. Other: 3 month work placement in other than candidate's country of origin.

Required Courses Asian Pacific economy, approaches to corporate strategy, business economics, comparative business-government relations, corporate finance, cross-cultural management, dynamics of the international economic system, human resources management, industrial and corporate organization, international business strategy, international finance, legal framework of business in the Asia-Pacific region, managerial accounting, marketing in the Asia- Pacific region, marketing management, operations and project management, organization strategy: managing change, organizational behavior, performance measurement and strategic choices, planning under risk and uncertainty, strategic use of information technology, technology and innovation management and strategy.

Curricular Focus General management, international business, strategic analysis and planning.

Concentration Management.

Faculty Full-time: 3, 100% with doctorates; part-time: 21, 81% with doctorates.

Teaching Methodology Case study: 25%, faculty seminars: 5%, lecture: 50%, student presentations: 10%, team projects: 10%.

Special Opportunities International exchange in Indonesia, Japan, Malaysia, People's Republic of China, Philippines, Republic of Korea, Sri Lanka, Taiwan, Thailand. Internship program available. Other: language training for international internship.

STUDENT STATISTICS

Geographic Representation Asia 60%; Australia 30%; Europe 5%; United States of America 5%.

Undergraduate Majors Business 15%; engineering/technology 20%; humanities 15%; science/mathematics 20%; social sciences 25%; other 5%.

Other Background Graduate degrees in other disciplines: 30%. Work experience: On average, students have 8 years of work experience on entrance to the program.

FACILITIES

Housing 80% of students in program live in college-owned or -operated housing.

Technology Computers are used moderately in course work. Computer terminals/PCs, linked by a campus-wide computer network, are available for use by students in program; they are located in learning resource center. Students in the program are not required to have their own PC.

Computer Resources/On-line Services

Training	Yes	CompuServe	No
Internet	No	Dun's	No
E-Mail	No	Dow Jones	No
Multimedia Center	Yes	Dialog	No
LEXIS/NEXIS	No	Bloomberg	No

ADMISSION

Entrance Requirements First degree, minimum 3 years of work experience. Core courses waived through: previous course work.

Application Requirements Application form, copies of transcript, resume/curriculum vitae, personal statement, 2 letters of recommendation.

Application Deadlines 3/31 for annual. Applications are processed on a rolling basis.

FINANCIALS

Costs for 1994-95 Tuition: Full-time: 25,000 Australian dollars/degree program for international students. Average room and board costs are 10,000 Australian dollars per academic year (on-campus) and 10,000 Australian dollars per academic year (off-campus).

Financial Aid In 1994-95, 10% of candidates received some institutionally administered aid in the form of partial fee waivers. Contact: Mr. Bruce Stening, Director of MBA Program, 0200 Canberra, ACT, Australia. 6-249-4890.

INTERNATIONAL STUDENTS

Demographics 10% of students on campus are international; Asia 82%, Europe 9%, North America 8%, South America 1%.

Services and Facilities International student housing; international student office, international student center, language tutoring, ESL courses, special assistance for nonnative speakers of English, counseling/support services.

Applying TOEFL required, minimum score of 570; IELTS required, minimum score of 6; minimum score of 4.5 on Test of Standard Written English. Financial aid is available to international students. Financial aid application deadline: 2/28 for annual. Applications are processed on a rolling basis. Admission application deadline: 2/28 for annual admissions. Applications are processed on a rolling basis. Contact: Ms. Lynn Sealie, International Student Adviser, 0200 Canberra, ACT, Australia. 6-249-4890.

PLACEMENT

Placement services include career placement.

Program Contact: Ms. Xiao Hua Yang, Australian National University, 0200 Canberra, ACT, Australia. 6-249-4890; Fax: 6-249-4895.

Bond University

School of Business

Gold Coast, Australia

OVERVIEW

Bond University is an independent nonprofit coed institution. Setting: suburban campus. Total institutional enrollment: 1,764. Program was first offered in 1989. Accredited by Australian Vice Chancellor's Committee, Commonwealth Universities.

MBA HIGHLIGHTS

Entrance Difficulty*

Cost
Tuition: 1,980 Australian dollars/unit
Room & Board: 8,400 Australian dollars

Enrollment Profile

Full-time: 40	Work Exp: 100%
Part-time: 5	Women: 20%
Total: 45	
Average Age: 32	

Average Class Size: 25

T he M.B.A. program prepares candidates for top-level management positions through a balanced blend of academic rigour coupled with extensive practical applications. As Australia's leading private university, Bond University has an M.B.A. curriculum tailored to meet current industry requirements, a program that is competitive with the best M.B.A. courses available in Australia and overseas.

The diverse backgrounds of the candidates and the small classes provide a rich environment for animated debate and the development of extensive networking to build contacts and relationships that will last far beyond the formal period of the M.B.A.

The Bond M.B.A. program may be completed on a full-time basis within one calendar year. Entry to the program is in the January semester each year.

The International Entrepreneurial Challenge of MOOT CORP is a New Venture Planning competition, by invitation only, for teams of M.B.A. candidates from the world's best business schools, held annually in Austin, Texas.

Bond University is the only Australian university invited each year to compete in this prestigious international competition. Other invitees include Harvard, Chicago, Wharton, Carnegie-Mellon, Northwestern, North Carolina, Babson, New York, Arizona, Michigan, Chicago, and the University of Texas and selected foreign universities.

Bond's program strengthens its performance each year: 1992—fourth overall; 1993—first runner-up; 1994—international champions. The program has proved its ability to compete successfully in the big league of the world's best business schools. This is the result of combining better candidates with better instructors in a better educational process.

ACADEMICS
Length of Program Minimum: 12 months. Maximum: 6 years.
Calendar Trimesters.
Full-time Classes Main campus; day, evening, weekends, early morning.
Part-time Classes Main campus; day, evening, weekends, early morning.
Degree Requirements 12 full-unit subjects including 4 full-unit electives; MBA project.
Required Courses Accounting, business analysis methods, controllership, economics, financial management, industrial relations, management information systems, managerial role in organizations, marketing, strategic human resources management, strategic management.
Curricular Focus Entrepreneurship, international business, leadership.
Concentrations Accounting, entrepreneurship, finance, human resources management, international business, management, management information systems, marketing, operations management, organizational behavior, real estate, strategic management.
Teaching Methodology Case study: 25%, lecture: 50%, seminars by members of the business community: 5%, student presentations: 20%.
Special Opportunities International exchange in Canada.

STUDENT STATISTICS
Undergraduate Majors Business 32%; engineering/technology 25%; social sciences 23%; other 20%.
Other Background Graduate degrees in other disciplines: 95%. Work experience: On average, students have 10 years of work experience on entrance to the program.

FACILITIES
Housing 8% of students in program live in college-owned or -operated housing. Assistance with housing search provided.
Technology Computers are used heavily in course work. 152 computer terminals/PCs, linked by a campus-wide computer network, are available for use by students in program; they are located in the computer center, computer labs. Students in the program are required to have their own PC.

Computer Resources/On-line Services
Training	Yes	Dun's	No
Internet	Yes	Dow Jones	No
E-Mail	Yes	Dialog	Yes
LEXIS/NEXIS	Yes	Bloomberg	No
CompuServe	Yes		

ADMISSION
Acceptance 1994-95 58 applied for admission; 78% were accepted.
Entrance Requirements First degree, minimum 2 years of work experience. Core courses waived through: previous course work.
Application Requirements Application form, copies of transcript, resume/curriculum vitae, personal statement, 2 letters of recommendation.
Application Deadline Applications are processed on a rolling basis.

FINANCIALS
Costs for 1995-96 Tuition: Full-time: 1,980 Australian dollars/unit. Fees: Full-time: 50 Australian dollars. Average room and board costs are 8,400 Australian dollars per academic year (on-campus) and 7,000 Australian dollars per academic year (off-campus).
Financial Aid In 1994-95, 15% of candidates received some institutionally administered aid in the form of scholarships, loans. Total awards ranged from 7,900-11,850 Australian dollars. Financial aid is not available to part-time students. Applications are processed on a rolling basis. Contact: Mrs. Lyn Cox, Manager of Admissions, University Drive, Robina, 4229 Gold Coast, Queensland, Australia. 75-951036.

INTERNATIONAL STUDENTS
Demographics 28% of students on campus are international; Australia 68%, Asia 22%, North America 6%, Europe 3%, Africa 1%.
Services and Facilities International student office, international student center, visa services, language tutoring, ESL courses, special assistance for nonnative speakers of English, counseling/support services.
Applying TOEFL required, minimum score of 600; IELTS required, minimum score of 6; proof of health; proof of adequate funds. Financial aid is available to international students. Applications are processed on a rolling basis. Admission applications are processed on a rolling basis. Contact: Ms. Jodie Maguire, Liaison Officer, Overseas Students, University Drive, Robina, 4229 Gold Coast, Queensland, Australia. 75-54001.

ALTERNATE MBA PROGRAM
Executive MBA (EMBA) Length of program: Minimum: 13 months. Maximum: 2 years. Full-time classes: Main campus; day, evening, weekends, early morning. Degree requirements: 12 full-unit subjects including 4 full-unit electives; overseas study tour; MBA project. Languages: English. Class size: 12-15.

PLACEMENT
Placement services include alumni network, career counseling/planning, career fairs, career library, career placement, job search course, resume preparation, and resume referral to employers.

Program Contact: Mrs. Lyn Cox, Manager Admissions, Bond University, University Drive, 4229 Gold Coast, Queensland, Australia. 75-951111.

Curtin University of Technology

Perth, Australia

OVERVIEW
Curtin University of Technology is a government-supported coed institution. Accredited by Australian Graduate Management Association.

MBA HIGHLIGHTS
Entrance Difficulty***
Mean GMAT: 550
Mean GPA: N/R

Cost
Tuition: 4,817 Australian dollars
(Nonresident: 24,400 Australian dollars)
Room & Board: 2,160 Australian dollars

Enrollment Profile
Full-time: N/R	Work Exp: N/R
Part-time: N/R	Women: 37%
Total: 171	
Average Age: N/R	

Average Class Size: 40

ACADEMICS
Length of Program Minimum: 18 months.
Full-time Classes Main campus, distance learning option; day, evening, weekends, summer.
Part-time Classes Main campus, distance learning option; evening, weekends, summer.
Degree Requirements 400 credits.
Curricular Focus International business, organizational development and change management, problem solving and decision making.
Concentrations Accounting, economics, engineering management, business law, taxation, finance, health services, human resources management, international business, management, management information systems,

marketing, organizational behavior, public administration, public policy, quantitative analysis, real estate, strategic management.

Teaching Methodology Case study: 1%, faculty seminars: 2%, lecture: 50%, research: 10%, seminars by members of the business community: 8%, student presentations: 10%, team projects: 20%.

FACILITIES
Housing College housing available.

ADMISSION
Entrance Requirements First degree, GMAT score of 520, minimum 3 years of work experience.

Application Requirements Application form, copies of transcript, resume/curriculum vitae, personal statement, 2 letters of recommendation.

Application Deadlines 12/15 for fall, 6/15 for spring. Applications are processed on a rolling basis.

FINANCIALS
Estimated Costs for 1995-96 Tuition: Full-time: 4,817 Australian dollars for residents, 24,400 Australian dollars for nonresidents. Average room and board costs are 2,160 Australian dollars per academic year (on-campus) and 1,800 Australian dollars per academic year (off-campus).

Financial Aid Application deadline: 9/1 for fall. Contact: Ms. Linda Cole, Scholarships Officer, Kent State Bentley, 6102 Perth, Western Australia, Australia. 9-351-2784.

INTERNATIONAL STUDENTS
Applying TOEFL required, minimum score of 550; IELTS required, minimum score of 6; proof of health; proof of adequate funds. Financial aid is not available to international students. Admission application deadlines: 12/15 for fall, 6/15 for spring. Applications are processed on a rolling basis.

Program Contact: Ms. Lee Malone, Enrollments Officer, Curtin University of Technology, Graduate School of Business, QVI, 250 St. Georges Tce, 6000 Perth, Western Australia, Australia. 9-351-6460; Fax: 9-351-3368; Internet Address: malonel@ba1.curtin.edu.au.

Deakin University

Faculty of Management

Geelong, Australia

OVERVIEW
Deakin University is a government-supported coed institution. Founded 1974. Total institutional enrollment: 26,217. Program was first offered in 1981.

MBA HIGHLIGHTS
Entrance Difficulty**

Cost
Tuition: 650 Australian dollars/unit
(Nonresident: 1,300 Australian dollars/unit)
Room & Board: N/R

Enrollment Profile
Full-time: 0
Part-time: 519
Total: 519
Average Age: 35

Work Exp: 100%
Women: 21%

Average Class Size: N/R

ACADEMICS
Length of Program Minimum: 24 months. Maximum: 10 years.
Calendar Semesters.
Part-time Classes distAnce learning option.
Degree Requirements 16 units including 3 elective units.
Required Courses Financial markets and instruments leadership, financial reporting and analysis, human resources management and employee relations, information systems management, leadership, management communication, managerial accounting and control, managerial economics, marketing management, operations management, organizational behavior, quantitative management methods, strategic management.
Curricular Focus Economic and financial theory, general management, leadership.
Concentrations Accounting, management.

Faculty Full-time: 1, 100% with doctorates; part-time: 36, 9% with doctorates.

STUDENT STATISTICS
Geographic Representation Australia/New Zealand 90%; other 10%.
Other Background Work experience: On average, students have 3-5 years of work experience on entrance to the program.

FACILITIES
Technology Computers are used heavily in course work. 120 computer terminals/PCs, linked by a campus-wide computer network, are available for use by students in program; they are located in computer labs. Students in the program are required to have their own PC.

Computer Resources/On-line Services
Internet   Yes   E-Mail   Yes

ADMISSION
Entrance Requirements First degree, minimum 3 years of work experience. Core courses waived through: previous course work.

Application Requirements Application form, copies of transcript, personal statement, 2 letters of recommendation.

Application Deadlines 5/31 for winter, 10/31 for summer.

FINANCIALS
Costs for 1994-95 Tuition: Part-time day: 650 Australian dollars/unit for residents, 1,300 Australian dollars/unit for nonresidents, 1,300 Australian dollars/unit for international students.

Financial Aid Financial aid is not available to part-time students.

INTERNATIONAL STUDENTS
Services and Facilities Counseling/support services.

Applying TOEFL required. Financial aid is not available to international students. Admission application deadlines: 5/31 for winter, 10/31 for summer.

PLACEMENT
Placement services include alumni network.

Program Contact: Ms. Lorraine Sainsbury, MBA Student Adviser, Deakin University, Student Administration, 3127 Geelong, Victoria, Australia. 52-271192; Fax: 52-272655; Internet Address: mbaeng@deakin.edu.au.

Edith Cowan University

Faculty of Business

Churchlands, Australia

OVERVIEW
Edith Cowan University is a government-supported coed institution. Setting: suburban campus. Total institutional enrollment: 18,000.

MBA HIGHLIGHTS
Entrance Difficulty*

Cost
Tuition: N/R
Room & Board: N/R

Enrollment Profile
Full-time: 50
Part-time: 17
Total: 67
Average Age: 28

Work Exp: 100%
Women: N/R

Average Class Size: 15

ACADEMICS
Length of Program Minimum: 24 months. Maximum: 10 years.
Calendar Semesters.
Full-time Classes Main campus; day, evening.
Part-time Classes Main campus; evening.
Degree Requirements 16 credits including 5 elective credits. Other: 2 semester unit project.
Curricular Focus Managerial decision making.
Concentrations Accounting, arts administration, economics, finance, hotel management, human resources management, international business, management, marketing.

Special Opportunities International exchange in Canada.

STUDENT STATISTICS
Geographic Representation Australia 50%; Asia 50%.

Other Background Work experience: On average, students have 4 years of work experience on entrance to the program.

FACILITIES
Housing College housing available.

Technology Computers are used heavily in course work. 10 computer terminals/PCs, linked by a campus-wide computer network, are available for use by students in program; they are located in the research center. Students in the program are not required to have their own PC.

Computer Resources/On-line Services

Training	Yes	E-Mail	Yes

ADMISSION
Entrance Requirements First degree, minimum 1 year of work experience.

Application Requirements Application form, copies of transcript, resume/curriculum vitae, personal statement, 2 letters of recommendation.

Application Deadline 11/30 for fall.

INTERNATIONAL STUDENTS
Services and Facilities International student office, international student center, visa services, language tutoring, ESL courses, special assistance for nonnative speakers of English, counseling/support services.

Applying TOEFL required; IELTS required, minimum score of 6; proof of health; proof of adequate funds. Financial aid is not available to international students. Admission application deadline: 11/30 for fall. Contact: Mr. Robert R. Brown, Pearson Street, 6018 Churchlands, Australia. 9-383-8333.

PLACEMENT
Placement services include alumni network, career counseling/planning, career placement, job interviews, resume preparation, and resume referral to employers. Of 1994 graduates, 100% were employed within three months of graduation.

Program Contact: Mr. Barry Chaphan, Graduate Studies Coordinator, Edith Cowan University, Pearson Street, 6018 Churchlands, Australia. 9-383-8333; Fax: 9-383-8754.

Monash University

Faculty of Economics and Politics, MBA Division

Clayton, Australia

OVERVIEW
Monash University is a government-supported coed institution. Founded 1960. Setting: suburban campus. Total institutional enrollment: 36,515. Program was first offered in 1968. Approved by the Association of MBA Programs (U.K.).

MBA HIGHLIGHTS

Entrance Difficulty*****

Cost
Tuition: 6,800 Australian dollars
(Nonresident: 13,500 Australian dollars)
Room & Board: 9,000 Australian dollars

Enrollment Profile

Full-time: 170	Work Exp: 100%
Part-time: 331	Women: 27%
Total: 501	
Average Age: 32	

Average Class Size: 30

ACADEMICS
Length of Program Minimum: 21 months. Maximum: 3 years.

Calendar Semesters.

Full-time Classes Main campus; day, summer.

Part-time Classes Main campus; day, summer.

Degree Requirements 16 courses including 7 elective courses.

Required Courses Accounting, business and government, corporate finance, foundations of management, general operations management, international

business, labor relations, macroeconomics, management information systems, microeconomics, organizational behavior, orientation analysis, public management, strategic management.

Curricular Focus International business, managing diversity, strategic analysis and planning.

Concentrations Accounting, economics, finance, health services, human resources management, international business, management, management information systems, marketing, operations management, organizational behavior, public administration, public policy, quantitative analysis, strategic management.

Faculty Full-time: 33, 72% with doctorates; part-time: 7, 71% with doctorates.

Teaching Methodology Case study: 7%, faculty seminars: 1%, lecture: 81%, research: 2%, seminars by members of the business community: 1%, student presentations: 5%, team projects: 3%.

Special Opportunities International exchange in Germany, United States of America.

STUDENT STATISTICS
Geographic Representation Australia 77%; Pacific Rim 18%; Thailand 2%; Germany 2%; France 1%.

Undergraduate Majors Business 30%; education 2%; engineering/technology 20%; humanities 10%; nursing 5%; science/mathematics 20%; social sciences 10%; other 3%.

Other Background Graduate degrees in other disciplines: 88%. Work experience: On average, students have 6 years of work experience on entrance to the program.

FACILITIES
Housing 27% of students in program live in college-owned or -operated housing.

Technology Computers are used moderately in course work. 80 computer terminals/PCs, linked by a campus-wide computer network, are available for use by students in program; they are located in computer labs. Students in the program are not required to have their own PC. 600 Australian dollars are budgeted per student for computer support.

Computer Resources/On-line Services

Training	Yes	Dun's	No
Internet	Yes	Dow Jones	No
E-Mail	No	Dialog	No
LEXIS/NEXIS	Yes	Bloomberg	No
CompuServe	Yes		

ADMISSION
Acceptance 1994-95 716 applied for admission; 14% were accepted.

Entrance Requirements First degree, minimum 2 years of work experience for applicants with first degree, 8 years of work experience for applicants who do not possess first degree. Core courses waived through: previous course work.

Application Requirements Application form, copies of transcript, resume/curriculum vitae, personal statement.

Application Deadline Applications are processed on a rolling basis.

FINANCIALS
Costs for 1994-95 Tuition: Full-time: 6,800 Australian dollars, 13,500 Australian dollars for international students; Part-time day: 850 Australian dollars/course. Fees: Full-time: 330 Australian dollars, 559-788 Australian dollars for international students; Part-time day: 207 Australian dollars. Average room and board costs are 9,000 Australian dollars per academic year (on-campus) and 10,000 Australian dollars per academic year (off-campus).

Financial Aid Financial aid is not available to part-time students.

INTERNATIONAL STUDENTS
Demographics 10% of students on campus are international; Asia 88%, Europe 4%, Africa 2%, North America 2%, Central America 1%, South America 1%, Other 2%.

Services and Facilities International student office, international student center, counseling/support services.

Applying TOEFL required, minimum score of 580; IELTS required, minimum score of 6. Financial aid is not available to international students. Admission applications are processed on a rolling basis. Contact: Mrs. Irene Thavarajah, 3168 Clayton, Victoria, Australia. 3-905-5418.

PLACEMENT
Placement services include alumni network, career counseling/planning, career library, career placement, and resume preparation. Of 1994 graduates, the average starting salary was 60,000 Australian dollars, the range was 50,000-80,000 Australian dollars.

Jobs by Employer Type Manufacturing 15%; service 25%; government 35%; consulting 15%; nonprofit 10%.
Jobs by Functional Area Marketing/sales 25%; finance 25%; operations 10%; management 15%; strategic planning 10%; technical management 15%.

Program Contact: Ms. Debra Davidson, Monash University, MBA Programs Division, Faculty of Business and Economics, 3168 Clayton, Victoria, Australia. 3-905-5150; Fax: 3-905-5412.

Murdoch University

School of Economics and Commerce

Perth, Australia

OVERVIEW
Murdoch University is a government-supported primarily male institution. Founded 1975. Setting: suburban campus. Total institutional enrollment: 8,500. Program was first offered in 1990. Accredited by Department of Employment, Education and Training (DEET), Australian Federal Government.

MBA HIGHLIGHTS

Entrance Difficulty*
Mean GMAT: 550
Mean GPA: N/R

Cost
Tuition: $1,010 Australian dollars/semester
(Nonresident: $2,750 Australian dollars/semester)
Room & Board: $11,700

Enrollment Profile
Full-time: 17
Part-time: 33
Total: 50
Average Age: 32
Work Exp: 100%
Women: 20%

Average Class Size: 35

ACADEMICS
Calendar Trimesters.
Curricular Focus General management, international business, teamwork.
Concentrations International business, management.
Faculty Full-time: 16, 57% with doctorates; part-time: 1.
Teaching Methodology Case study: 20%, faculty seminars: 5%, lecture: 20%, research: 10%, seminars by members of the business community: 5%, student presentations: 20%, team projects: 20%.
Special Opportunities International exchange in United States of America.

STUDENT STATISTICS
Geographic Representation Australia 85%; Hong Kong 6%; Europe 5%; Singapore 4%.
Undergraduate Majors Business 45%; education 10%; engineering/technology 10%; humanities 10%; nursing 10%; science/mathematics 5%; social sciences 5%; other 5%.
Other Background Graduate degrees in other disciplines: 10%. Work experience: On average, students have 3 years of work experience on entrance to the program.

FACILITIES
Information Resources Business collection includes 22,000 bound volumes, 549 periodical subscriptions, 13 CD-ROMs, 30 videos.
Housing 10% of students in program live in college-owned or -operated housing.
Technology Computers are used heavily in course work. 35 computer terminals/PCs are available for use by students in program; they are located in computer labs, MBA computer lab. Students in the program are not required to have their own PC. $500 are budgeted per student for computer support.

Computer Resources/On-line Services

Training	Yes	Dun's	No
Internet	Yes	Dow Jones	No
E-Mail	Yes	Dialog	No
LEXIS/NEXIS	No	Bloomberg	No
CompuServe	No		

Other on-line services: OCLC, Datastar.

ADMISSION
Acceptance 1994-95 110 applied for admission; 82% were accepted.
Entrance Requirements GMAT score of 500, minimum 2 years of work experience. Core courses waived through: previous course work, work experience.
Application Requirements Application form, copies of transcript, resume/curriculum vitae, personal statement.
Application Deadline 11/31 for fall. Application discs available.

FINANCIALS
Financial Aid In 1994-95, 15% of candidates received some institutionally administered aid in the form of grants, scholarships. Total awards ranged from 1,000-14,000 Australian dollars. Financial aid is not available to part-time students. Application deadline: 10/31 for fall. Contact: Ms. Ann Randall, Research Officer, School of Economics and Commerce, 6150 Murdoch, Australia. 9-360-2452.

INTERNATIONAL STUDENTS
Services and Facilities International student office, international student center, language tutoring, ESL courses, special assistance for nonnative speakers of English, counseling/support services.
Applying TOEFL required, minimum score of 550. Financial aid is available to international students. Financial aid application deadline: 10/31 for fall. Admission application deadline: 10/31 for fall. Contact: Ms. Anne Boyd, Director of International Office, School of Economics and Commerce, 6150 Murdoch, Australia. 9-360-2756.

PROGRAM
One-Year MBA Length of program: Minimum: 12 months. Maximum: 4 years. Full-time classes: Main campus; day, evening. Part-time classes: Main campus; day, evening. Degree requirements: 12 courses including 2 elective courses. Languages: English.

PLACEMENT
Placement services include alumni network and career counseling/planning.

Program Contact: Mrs. Helen Wiggins, MBA Administrative Assistant, Murdoch University, School of Economics and Commerce, 6150 Murdoch, Australia. 9-360-6046; Fax: 9-310-5004; Internet Address: wiggins@commerce.murdoch.edu.au.

The University of Adelaide

Graduate School of Management

Adelaide, Australia

OVERVIEW
The University of Adelaide is a government-supported coed institution. Founded 1874. Accredited by Consortium of Australian Management Schools.

MBA HIGHLIGHTS

Entrance Difficulty**

Cost
Tuition: 350 Australian dollars/credit
(Nonresident: 650 Australian dollars/credit)
Room & Board: N/R

Enrollment Profile
Full-time: N/R
Part-time: N/R
Total: 347
Average Age: N/R
Work Exp: N/R
Women: 22%

Average Class Size: 25

ACADEMICS

Length of Program Minimum: 17 months.

Full-time Classes Main campus; day, evening, weekends.

Part-time Classes Main campus; evening, weekends.

Degree Requirements 48 credits.

Curricular Focus Business issues and problems, general management, problem solving and decision making.

Concentrations Finance, human resources management, international business, management, marketing, organizational behavior, strategic management.

Teaching Methodology Case study: 20%, lecture: 30%, research: 5%, seminars by members of the business community: 5%, student presentations: 20%, team projects: 20%.

ADMISSION

Entrance Requirements First degree, minimum 2 years of work experience.

Application Requirements Application form, copies of transcript, personal statement, 2 letters of recommendation.

Application Deadlines 11/30 for fall, 6/30 for spring. Applications are processed on a rolling basis.

FINANCIALS

Costs for 1994-95 Tuition: Full-time: 350 Australian dollars/credit for residents, 650 Australian dollars/credit for international students.

Financial Aid Contact: Office of Continuing Education, Graduate School of Management, 5005 Adelaide, Australia. 8-360-5525.

INTERNATIONAL STUDENTS

Applying TOEFL required, minimum score of 550; IELTS required, minimum score of 6; proof of health; proof of adequate funds. Financial aid is not available to international students. Admission applications are processed on a rolling basis.

Program Contact: Ms. Carol McHugh, Executive Officer, The University of Adelaide, Graduate School of Management, 5005 Adelaide, Australia. 8-303-5525; Fax: 8-223-4782; Internet Address: cmchugh@ economics.adelaide.edu.au.

University of Melbourne

Melbourne Business School

Melbourne, Australia

OVERVIEW

The University of Melbourne is an independent nonprofit coed institution. Setting: urban campus. Program was first offered in 1964.

MBA HIGHLIGHTS

Entrance Difficulty***
Mean GMAT: 600
Mean GPA: N/R

Cost $$
Tuition: $7,000
(Nonresident: $12,600)
Room & Board: $8,400

Enrollment Profile

Full-time: 130	Work Exp: 100%
Part-time: 125	Women: 33%
Total: 255	
Average Age: 29	

Average Class Size: 50

ACADEMICS

Length of Program Minimum: 20 months. Maximum: 4 years.

Calendar Semesters.

Full-time Classes Main campus; day.

Part-time Classes Main campus; evening, early morning.

Degree Requirements 20 courses including 8 elective courses.

Required Courses Business law, business strategy, economic policy, employer relations, financial accounting, information systems, management accounting, managerial economics, marketing, organizations, quantitative analysis, valuation and financial analysis.

Curricular Focus Business issues and problems, general management, international business.

Concentrations Accounting, economics, entrepreneurship, finance, international business, management, management information systems, marketing, operations management, organizational behavior, public administration, quantitative analysis, strategic management.

Faculty Full-time: 24, 92% with doctorates; part-time: 18, 78% with doctorates.

Teaching Methodology Case study: 30%, lecture: 50%, seminars by members of the business community: 5%, student presentations: 10%, team projects: 5%.

Special Opportunities International exchange in Austria, Canada, Denmark, France, Italy, Israel, Philippines, Spain, United Kingdom, United States of America.

STUDENT STATISTICS

Geographic Representation Australia 70%; Asia 25%; Europe/North America 5%.

Undergraduate Majors Business 33%; education 2%; engineering/ technology 21%; humanities 8%; nursing 2%; science/mathematics 17%; social sciences 4%; other 13%.

Other Background Graduate degrees in other disciplines: 10%. Work experience: On average, students have 6 years of work experience on entrance to the program.

FACILITIES

Information Resources Business collection in McLennan Library includes 16,000 bound volumes, 500 periodical subscriptions.

Housing 10% of students in program live in college-owned or -operated housing.

Technology Computers are used heavily in course work. 42 computer terminals/PCs, linked by a campus-wide computer network, are available for use by students in program; they are located in computer labs. Students in the program are not required to have their own PC. $300 are budgeted per student for computer support.

Computer Resources/On-line Services

Training	Yes	Dun's	Yes
Internet	Yes	Dow Jones	Yes
E-Mail	Yes	Dialog	Yes
LEXIS/NEXIS	No	Bloomberg	No
CompuServe	Yes		

ADMISSION

Acceptance 1994-95 503 applied for admission; 25% were accepted.

Entrance Requirements First degree, GMAT score, minimum 2 years of work experience. Core courses waived through: previous course work.

Application Requirements Written essay, application form, copies of transcript.

Application Deadlines 11/30 for fall, 5/30 for spring. Applications are processed on a rolling basis.

FINANCIALS

Costs for 1995-96 Tuition: Full-time: $7,000, $12,600 for international students; Part-time day: $700/course. Fees: Full-time: $227; Part-time day: $134. Average room and board costs are $8,400 per academic year (on-campus) and $8,400 per academic year (off-campus).

Financial Aid In 1994-95, 15% of candidates received some institutionally administered aid in the form of scholarships. Total awards ranged from $2,100-$21,000. Financial aid is not available to part-time students. Application deadline: 12/30 for spring. Applications are processed on a rolling basis. Contact: Ms. Anne Sankey, Admissions Officer, 200 Leicester Street, 3052 Melbourne, Victoria, Australia. 3-349-8100.

INTERNATIONAL STUDENTS

Demographics 30% of students on campus are international.

Services and Facilities International student office, visa services, language tutoring, ESL courses.

Applying TOEFL required, minimum score of 620; IELTS required, minimum score of 6; proof of adequate funds. Financial aid is available to international students. Financial aid application deadlines: 11/30 for fall, 5/30 for spring. Applications are processed on a rolling basis. Admission application deadlines: 11/30 for fall, 5/30 for spring. Applications are processed on a rolling basis.

PLACEMENT

In 1993-94, 60 organizations participated in on-campus recruiting; 30 on-campus interviews were conducted. Placement services include alumni network, career counseling/planning, career placement, job interviews, resume preparation, and resume referral to employers. Of 1994 graduates, the average starting salary was $52,500, the range was $28,000-$140,000.

Program Contact: Ms. Anne Sankey, Admissions Officer, University of Melbourne, 200 Leicester Street, 3052 Melbourne, Victoria, Australia. 3-349-8100; Fax: 3-349-8133.

University of Newcastle

Faculty of Economics

Newcastle, Australia

OVERVIEW

The University of Newcastle is a government-supported coed institution. Founded 1968. Setting: suburban campus. Total institutional enrollment: 16,000. Program was first offered in 1975.

MBA HIGHLIGHTS

Entrance Difficulty***
Mean GMAT: 550
Mean GPA: N/R

Cost
Tuition: 10,600 Australian dollars
Room & Board: 6,000 Australian dollars

Enrollment Profile

Full-time: 10	Work Exp: 100%
Part-time: 170	Women: 30%
Total: 180	
Average Age: N/R	

Average Class Size: 25

ACADEMICS

Length of Program Minimum: 26 months. Maximum: 8 years.
Calendar Semesters.
Full-time Classes Main campus; evening.
Part-time Classes Main campus; evening.
Degree Requirements 160 credits including 60 elective credits.
Required Courses Business finance, business policy, computing and information systems, employment relations, financial accounting, legal studies, macroeconomics and policy, management accounting, management issues, marketing concepts and strategy, microeconomics and business decisions, organizational behavior, quantitative methods and data analysis.
Curricular Focus Business issues and problems, economic and financial theory, organizational development and change management, problem solving and decision making, strategic analysis and planning, teamwork.
Faculty Part-time: 20, 50% with doctorates.
Teaching Methodology Case study: 20%, lecture: 60%, research: 5%, student presentations: 5%, team projects: 10%.
Special Opportunities Business mentor system.

STUDENT STATISTICS

Geographic Representation Australia 95%; Asia 4%; United States of America/Europe 1%.
Undergraduate Majors Business 25%; engineering/technology 60%; nursing 10%; other 5%.
Other Background Graduate degrees in other disciplines: 50%. Work experience: On average, students have 8 years of work experience on entrance to the program.

FACILITIES

Housing 5% of students in program live in college-owned or -operated housing.
Technology Computers are used moderately in course work. 200 computer terminals/PCs, linked by a campus-wide computer network, are available for use by students in program; they are located in student rooms, classrooms, the computer center, computer labs. Students in the program are not required to have their own PC. 400 Australian dollars are budgeted per student for computer support.

Computer Resources/On-line Services

Training	Yes	E-Mail	Yes
Internet	Yes	CompuServe	Yes

ADMISSION

Acceptance 1994-95 Of those applying, 70% were accepted.
Entrance Requirements First degree, entry possible without degree depending on GMAT and work experience, minimum 5 years of work experience. Core courses waived through: previous course work.
Application Requirements Application form, copies of transcript, resume/curriculum vitae, personal statement.
Application Deadlines 11/30 for semester 1, 05/30 for semester 2. Applications are processed on a rolling basis.

FINANCIALS

Costs for 1995-96 Tuition: Full-time: 10,600 Australian dollars. Average room and board costs are 6,000 Australian dollars per academic year (on-campus) and 5,500 Australian dollars per academic year (off-campus).
Financial Aid Application deadline: 10/1 for spring. Contact: Ms. Linda Harrigan, Postgraduate Studies, 2308 Newcastle, NSW, Australia. 49-216538.

INTERNATIONAL STUDENTS

Demographics 7% of students on campus are international; Asia 80%, Africa 10%, Europe 5%, North America 5%.
Services and Facilities International student office, international student center, language tutoring, ESL courses, special assistance for nonnative speakers of English, counseling/support services.
Applying TOEFL required, minimum score of 550; IELTS required, minimum score of 6. Financial aid is not available to international students. Admission applications are processed on a rolling basis.

PLACEMENT

Placement services include alumni network, career counseling/planning, career fairs, career library, job interviews, resume preparation, and resume referral to employers.

Program Contact: Ms. Natalie Downing, Administrative Officer, University of Newcastle, Faculty of Economics and Commerce, 2308 Newcastle, NSW, Australia. 49-215981; Fax: 49-216918; Internet Address: ecnjd@ cc.newcastle.edu.au.

University of New South Wales

Australian Graduate School of Management

Kensington, Australia

OVERVIEW

Setting: urban campus. Total institutional enrollment: 30,000. Program was first offered in 1977.

MBA HIGHLIGHTS

Entrance Difficulty****
Mean GMAT: 590
Mean GPA: N/R

Cost
Tuition: 10,000 Australian dollars
(Nonresident: 19,500 Australian dollars)
Room & Board: N/R

Enrollment Profile

Full-time: 240	Work Exp: 100%
Part-time: 0	Women: 24%
Total: 240	
Average Age: 30	

Average Class Size: 45

ACADEMICS

Length of Program Minimum: 24 months.
Calendar Trimesters.
Full-time Classes Main campus; day.
Degree Requirements 21 courses.
Required Course Management foundations and perspectives.
Curricular Focus General management, problem solving and decision making, teamwork.

Concentrations Accounting, economics, finance, human resources management, international business, management, management information systems, marketing, operations management, organizational behavior, public policy, quantitative analysis, strategic management.

Faculty Full-time: 28, 93% with doctorates; part-time: 21, 76% with doctorates.

Teaching Methodology Case study: 15%, lecture: 45%, seminars by members of the business community: 5%, student presentations: 5%, team projects: 30%.

Special Opportunities International exchange in Italy, Japan, Sweden, United Kingdom, United States of America.

STUDENT STATISTICS

Undergraduate Majors Business 23%; engineering/technology 27%; humanities 12%; science/mathematics 18%; other 20%.

Other Background Work experience: On average, students have 6 years of work experience on entrance to the program.

FACILITIES

Information Resources Business collection in Frank Lowy Library includes 28,500 bound volumes, 2,600 periodical subscriptions, 80 CD-ROMs, 70 videos.

Housing 10% of students in program live in college-owned or -operated housing.

Technology Computers are used heavily in course work. 25 computer terminals/PCs, linked by a campus-wide computer network, are available for use by students in program; they are located in computer labs. Students in the program are not required to have their own PC.

Computer Resources/On line Services

Training	No	E-Mail	Yes
Internet	Yes	Bloomberg	Yes

ADMISSION

Entrance Requirements First degree, GMAT score of 500, minimum 2 years of work experience.

Application Requirements Application form, copies of transcript, personal statement, 2 letters of recommendation.

Application Deadline Applications are processed on a rolling basis. Application discs available.

FINANCIALS

Costs for 1994-95 Tuition: Full-time: 10,000 Australian dollars for residents, 19,500 Australian dollars for nonresidents.

Financial Aid In 1994-95, 22% of candidates received some institutionally administered aid in the form of scholarships. Total awards ranged from 1,000-10,000 Australian dollars. Financial aid is available to part-time students. Contact: Ms. Belia Le Tet, 2052 Sydney, New South Wales, Australia. 2-931-9222.

INTERNATIONAL STUDENTS

Services and Facilities International student office, international student center, language tutoring, ESL courses, counseling/support services.

Applying Financial aid is available to international students. Financial aid application deadline: 11/30 for annual. Admission applications are processed on a rolling basis.

PLACEMENT

In 1993-94, 20 organizations participated in on-campus recruiting. Placement services include alumni network, career counseling/planning, career placement, job interviews, and resume referral to employers. Of 1994 graduates, 90% were employed within three months of graduation, the average starting salary was 75,000 Australian dollars, the range was 40,000-120,000 Australian dollars.

Jobs by Employer Type Manufacturing 17%; service 46%; government 3%; consulting 31%; mining 3%.

Jobs by Functional Area Marketing/sales 14%; finance 20%; operations 20%; management 6%; strategic planning 31%; technical management 9%.

Program Contact: Ms. Belia Le Tet, University of New South Wales, 2052 Sydney, New South Wales, Australia. 2-931-9222; Fax: 2-931-9231; Internet Address: belia@agsm.unsw.edu.au.

The University of Sydney

Graduate School of Business

Sydney, Australia

OVERVIEW

The University of Sydney is a government-supported coed institution. Setting: urban campus. Total institutional enrollment: 30,000.

MBA HIGHLIGHTS

Entrance Difficulty***
Mean GMAT: 615
Mean GPA: N/R

Cost
Tuition: 756 Australian dollars/course
(Nonresident: 1,512 Australian dollars/course)
Room & Board: N/R

Enrollment Profile

Full-time: 90		Work Exp: 100%
Part-time: 180		Women: 25%
Total: 270		
Average Age: 31		

Average Class Size: 40

ACADEMICS

Length of Program Minimum: 18 months. Maximum: 3 years.

Calendar Semesters.

Full-time Classes Main campus; day, evening, weekends, summer.

Part-time Classes Main campus; evening, weekends, summer.

Degree Requirements 40 credits including 20 elective credits.

Required Courses Corporate finance, financial reporting, management accounting, marketing theory and applications, microeconomics, organizational behavior, quantitative methods.

Curricular Focus Economic and financial theory, international business, strategic analysis and planning.

Concentrations Accounting, economics, finance, human resources management, international business, management, marketing, organizational behavior, public administration, public policy, quantitative analysis, strategic management, transportation.

Faculty Full-time: 10, 100% with doctorates; part-time: 30, 60% with doctorates.

Teaching Methodology Case study: 5%, lecture: 30%, research: 20%, student presentations: 5%, team projects: 40%.

Special Opportunities International exchange in Canada, Germany, Japan, Republic of Korea, United Kingdom, United States of America.

STUDENT STATISTICS

Geographic Representation Australia 70%; Hong Kong 15%; South East Asia 7%; North America 6%; Europe 2%.

Undergraduate Majors Business 10%; engineering/technology 30%; humanities 5%; science/mathematics 10%; social sciences 40%; other 5%.

Other Background Graduate degrees in other disciplines: 10%. Work experience: On average, students have 9 years of work experience on entrance to the program.

FACILITIES

Information Resources Business collection in Graduate School of Business Library includes 8,000 bound volumes, 120 periodical subscriptions, 200 CD-ROMs, 100 videos.

Housing College housing not available.

Technology Computers are used heavily in course work. 30 computer terminals/PCs are available for use by students in program; they are located in computer labs. Students in the program are not required to have their own PC. $300 are budgeted per student for computer support.

Computer Resources/On-line Services

Training	Yes	CompuServe	No
Internet	No	Dun's	No
E-Mail	No	Dow Jones	No
Multimedia Center	Yes	Dialog	Yes $
LEXIS/NEXIS	Yes $	Bloomberg	No

ADMISSION

Acceptance 1994-95 500 applied for admission; 24% were accepted.

Entrance Requirements First degree, GMAT score, minimum 2 years of work experience. Core courses waived through: previous course work.

Application Requirements Application form, copies of transcript, resume/curriculum vitae, 2 letters of recommendation.

Application Deadlines 4/30 for fall, 10/31 for spring. Applications are processed on a rolling basis.

FINANCIALS

Costs for 1994-95 Tuition: Full-time: 756 Australian dollars/course for residents, 1,512 Australian dollars/course for nonresidents.

Financial Aid In 1994-95, 5% of candidates received some institutionally administered aid in the form of scholarships. Total awards ranged from 2,000-3,000 Australian dollars. Financial aid is not available to part-time students. Applications are processed on a rolling basis. Contact: Ms. Jenny Woodward, Student Liaison Officer, 2006 Sydney, New South Wales, Australia. 2-550-3544.

INTERNATIONAL STUDENTS

Demographics 10% of students on campus are international; Asia 80%, Europe 10%, North America 10%.

Services and Facilities International student office, international student center, ESL courses, counseling/support services.

Applying TOEFL required, minimum score of 580; IELTS required, minimum score of 6; proof of health; proof of adequate funds. Financial aid is not available to international students. Admission application deadlines: 4/30 for fall, 10/31 for spring. Applications are processed on a rolling basis. Contact: Ms. Jenny Woodward, Student Liaison Officer, 2006 Sydney, New South Wales, Australia. 2-550-3544.

PLACEMENT

In 1993-94, 5 organizations participated in on-campus recruiting; 20 on-campus interviews were conducted. Placement services include alumni network, career counseling/planning, resume preparation, and resume referral to employers. Of 1994 graduates, 95% were employed within three months of graduation, the average starting salary range was 30,000-70,000 Australian dollars.

Program Contact: Ms. Jenny Woodward, Student Liaison Officer, The University of Sydney, 2006 Sydney, New South Wales, Australia. 2-550-3544; Fax: 2-550-8603.

The University of Western Australia

The Graduate School of Management

Nedlands, Australia

OVERVIEW

The University of Western Australia is a government-supported coed institution. Part of Commonwealth Higher Education System. MBA program offered jointly with Consortium of Australian Management Schools. Founded 1911. Setting: suburban campus. Total institutional enrollment: 12,000. Program was first offered in 1973. Accredited by Association of MBA Students, Graduate Management Association of Australia.

MBA HIGHLIGHTS

Entrance Difficulty***
Mean GMAT: 590
Mean GPA: N/R

Cost
Tuition: 600 Australian dollars/unit
Room & Board: 9,000 Australian dollars

Enrollment Profile
Full-time: 65		Work Exp: 94%
Part-time: 155		Women: 20%
Total: 220		
Average Age: 30		

Average Class Size: 30

ACADEMICS

Length of Program Minimum: 16 months. Maximum: 5 years.

Calendar Trimesters.

Full-time Classes Main campus, distance learning option; day, evening, weekends, early morning, summer.

Part-time Classes Main campus, distance learning option; day, evening, weekends, early morning, summer.

Degree Requirements 16 units including 8 elective units. Other: Personal development workshop.

Required Courses Accounting, data analysis and decision making, economics for management, human resources management, international management, legal principles for management, management of organizations, managerial finance, marketing management, operations management, organizational behavior, strategic management.

Curricular Focus General management, problem solving and decision making.

Concentrations Accounting, finance, human resources management, international business, management, management information systems, marketing, mining and resources, industrial relations and research, operations management, public administration.

Faculty Full-time: 30, 75% with doctorates; part-time: 10, 50% with doctorates.

Teaching Methodology Case study: 20%, faculty seminars: 5%, lecture: 40%, research: 5%, seminars by members of the business community: 5%, student presentations: 10%, team projects: 15%.

Special Opportunities International exchange in Canada, Denmark, France, Singapore, United States of America. Other: intensive short course language programs.

STUDENT STATISTICS

Geographic Representation Australia 75%; South East Asia 15%; Europe 5%; North America 5%.

Undergraduate Majors Business 23%; engineering/technology 22%; humanities 5%; science/mathematics 34%; social sciences 8%; other 8%.

Other Background Graduate degrees in other disciplines: 15%. Work experience: On average, students have 7 years of work experience on entrance to the program.

FACILITIES

Information Resources Business collection includes 20,000 bound volumes, 500 periodical subscriptions, 12 CD-ROMs, 30 videos.

Housing 3% of students in program live in college-owned or -operated housing.

Technology Computers are used heavily in course work. 80 computer terminals/PCs, linked by a campus-wide computer network, are available for use by students in program; they are located in the student center, learning resource center, the library, computer labs. Students in the program are not required to have their own PC. $300 are budgeted per student for computer support.

Computer Resources/On-line Services

Training	Yes	CompuServe	Yes
Internet	Yes	Dun's	Yes $
E-Mail	Yes	Dow Jones	Yes $
LEXIS/NEXIS	Yes $	Dialog	Yes $

ADMISSION

Acceptance 1994-95 100 applied for admission; 50% were accepted.

Entrance Requirements First degree, GMAT score, minimum 2.75 GPA, minimum 2 years of work experience, if no work experience, an applicant can be considered if he or she has a higher degree. Core courses waived through: previous course work.

Application Requirements Interview, application form, copies of transcript, resume/curriculum vitae, personal statement.

Application Deadlines 12/31 for fall, 7/31 for spring. Applications are processed on a rolling basis. Application discs available.

FINANCIALS

Estimated Costs for 1995-96 Tuition: Full-time: 600 Australian dollars/unit. Average room and board costs are 9,000 Australian dollars per academic year (on-campus) and 8,000 Australian dollars per academic year (off-campus).

Financial Aid In 1994-95, 3% of candidates received some institutionally administered aid in the form of bursaries for full-time students. Total awards ranged from $13,000-$14,000 Australian dollars. Financial aid is not available to part-time students. Application deadlines: 1/31 for fall, 8/31 for spring. Contact: Mr. David Hilditch, GSM Studies Coordinator, Stirling Highway, 6007 Nedlands, Australia. 9 380-2946.

INTERNATIONAL STUDENTS

Demographics 20% of students on campus are international; Asia 90%, Europe 5%, North America 5%.

Services and Facilities International student housing; international student office, international student center, language tutoring, ESL courses, special assistance for nonnative speakers of English, counseling/support services.

Applying TOEFL required, minimum score of 550; IELTS required, minimum score of 6; proof of health; proof of adequate funds. Financial aid is not available to international students. Admission application deadlines: 12/31 for fall, 7/31 for spring. Applications are processed on a rolling basis. Contact: Mr. Andrew Holloway, Executive Director, International Students Center, Stirling Highway, 6007 Nedlands, Australia. 9 380-2477.

PLACEMENT

In 1993-94, 10 organizations participated in on-campus recruiting; 5 on-campus interviews were conducted. Placement services include alumni network, career counseling/planning, career fairs, career library, and resume preparation. Of 1994 graduates, 100% were employed within three months of graduation, the average starting salary was $55,000, the range was $45,000-$65,000.

Jobs by Employer Type Manufacturing 20%; service 35%; government 20%; consulting 20%; nonprofit 5%.

Jobs by Functional Area Marketing/sales 15%; finance 20%; operations 25%; management 20%; strategic planning 10%; technical management 10%.

Program Contact: Mr. David Hilditch, GSM Studies Coordinator, The University of Western Australia, Stirling Highway, 6007 Nedlands, Australia. 9 380-2946; Fax: 9 380-1072; Internet Address: dhildite@ecel.uwa.edu.au.

University of Western Sydney, Macarthur

Faculty of Business and Technology

Campbelltown, Australia

OVERVIEW

Setting: suburban campus. Total institutional enrollment: 15,000. Program was first offered in 1991.

MBA HIGHLIGHTS

Entrance Difficulty***

Cost
Tuition: 16,000 Australian dollars
Room & Board: 10,000 Australian dollars

Enrollment Profile

Full-time: 63	Work Exp: 100%
Part-time: 10	Women: 20%
Total: 73	
Average Age: 27	

Average Class Size: 20

ACADEMICS

Length of Program Minimum: 12 months. Maximum: 4 years.

Calendar Semesters.

Full-time Classes Main campus; day, evening.

Part-time Classes Main campus; day, evening.

Degree Requirements 16 units including 4 elective units. Other: Research project.

Required Courses Asian studies, accounting and finance, comparative human resources management, international business management,

international economics, international finance, international marketing, managerial economics, marketing management, organization and management, organizational behavior.

Curricular Focus International business.

Concentrations Accounting, economics, entrepreneurship, finance, international business, management, marketing, organizational behavior, strategic management.

Faculty Full-time: 30, 80% with doctorates.

Teaching Methodology Case study: 10%, lecture: 30%, research: 10%, seminars by members of the business community: 10%, student presentations: 10%, team projects: 30%.

Special Opportunities International exchange program available.

STUDENT STATISTICS

Undergraduate Majors Business 50%; engineering/technology 30%; humanities 10%; social sciences 10%.

Other Background Graduate degrees in other disciplines: 100%. Work experience: On average, students have 4 years of work experience on entrance to the program.

FACILITIES

Information Resources Business collection includes 8,500 bound volumes, 415 periodical subscriptions, 12 CD-ROMs.

Housing 70% of students in program live in college-owned or -operated housing. Assistance with housing search provided.

Technology Computers are used moderately in course work. 60 computer terminals/PCs are available for use by students in program; they are located in student rooms, the student center, classrooms, the library, the computer center. Students in the program are not required to have their own PC.

Computer Resources/On-line Services

Training	No	CompuServe	Yes
Internet	Yes	Dun's	No
E-Mail	Yes	Dow Jones	No
Videoconference Center	Yes	Dialog	Yes
LEXIS/NEXIS	No		

ADMISSION

Acceptance 1994-95 100 applied for admission; 73% were accepted.

Entrance Requirements First degree.

Application Requirements Application form, copies of transcript, 2 letters of recommendation.

Application Deadlines 12/8 for fall, 6/8 for spring. Applications are processed on a rolling basis.

FINANCIALS

Costs for 1994-95 Tuition: Full-time: 16,000 Australian dollars. Average room and board costs are 10,000 Australian dollars per academic year (on-campus) and 10,000 Australian dollars per academic year (off-campus).

Financial Aid Financial aid is not available to part-time students.

INTERNATIONAL STUDENTS

Services and Facilities International student office, international student center, visa services, language tutoring, counseling/support services.

Applying IELTS required, minimum score of 6; proof of adequate funds. Financial aid is not available to international students. Admission application deadlines: 12/8 for fall, 6/8 for spring. Applications are processed on a rolling basis. Contact: Director of International Programs, PO Box 555, 2560 Campbelltown, New South Wales, Australia. 46-203100.

PLACEMENT

Of 1994 graduates, 100% were employed within three months of graduation, the average starting salary was 30,000 Australian dollars.

Jobs by Employer Type Manufacturing 40%; service 30%; government 10%; consulting 20%.

Jobs by Functional Area Marketing/sales 50%; finance 10%; management 30%; technical management 10%.

Program Contact: Mr. Ross Taylor, Director of International Programs, University of Western Sydney, Macarthur, PO Box 555, 2560 Campbelltown, New South Wales, Australia. 46-203100; Fax: 46-284289; Internet Address: r.taylor@uws.edu.au.

BANGLADESH

International University of Business Agriculture and Technology (IUBAT)

College of Business Administration

Dhaka, Bangladesh

OVERVIEW

International University of Business Agriculture and Technology (IUBAT) is an independent nonprofit coed institution. MBA program offered jointly with Assumption University, Thailand. Setting: urban campus. Total institutional enrollment: 507. Program was first offered in 1992. Accredited by INTERMAN, Graduate Mangement Admission Council (AMDISA).

MBA HIGHLIGHTS

Entrance Difficulty*

Cost $
Tuition: $125/trimester
(Nonresident: $125/trimester)
Room & Board: N/R

Enrollment Profile
Full-time: 10   Work Exp: 25%
Part-time: 2   Women: N/R
Total: 12
Average Age: 24

Average Class Size: 30

ACADEMICS

Length of Program Minimum: 20 months.

Calendar Trimesters.

Full-time Classes Main campus; day, evening, weekends, summer.

Part-time Classes Main campus; evening, weekends, summer.

Degree Requirements 74 credits including 14 elective credits. Other: Internship.

Required Courses Business condition analysis, business government and society, human organization and behavior, human resources management, management of organization, managerial accounting, managerial finance, marketing management, principles of programming, production and operations management, quantitative business analysis and research, strategic management.

Curricular Focus Entrepreneurship, leadership, strategic analysis and planning.

Concentrations Accounting, entrepreneurship, finance, human resources management, management, management information systems, marketing, operations management, organizational behavior, quantitative analysis, strategic management.

Faculty Full-time: 10, 70% with doctorates; part-time: 22, 80% with doctorates.

Teaching Methodology Case study: 10%, faculty seminars: 5%, lecture: 40%, organizational study: 5%, research: 15%, seminars by members of the business community: 5%, student presentations: 10%, team projects: 10%.

Special Opportunities International exchange in Australia, Canada, Thailand, United Kingdom, United States of America. Internships include marketing in manufacturing.

STUDENT STATISTICS

Geographic Representation Bangladesh 100%.

Undergraduate Majors Business 60%; humanities 20%; science/mathematics 10%; social sciences 10%.

Other Background Graduate degrees in other disciplines: 100%. Work experience: On average, students have 2 years of work experience on entrance to the program.

FACILITIES

Information Resources Business collection includes 3,000 bound volumes, 2,000 periodical subscriptions, 70 videos.

Housing College housing not available.

Technology Computers are used moderately in course work. 10 computer terminals/PCs are available for use by students in program; they are located in the library, computer labs. Students in the program are not required to have their own PC. $100 are budgeted per student for computer support.

Computer Resources/On-line Services

Training	Yes	Dun's	No
Internet	No	Dow Jones	No
E-Mail	No	Dialog	No
LEXIS/NEXIS	No	Bloomberg	No
CompuServe	No		

ADMISSION

Acceptance 1994-95 60 applied for admission; 33% were accepted.

Entrance Requirements First degree, GMAT score of 450, admission test.

Application Requirements Written essay, interview, application form, copies of transcript, resume/curriculum vitae, personal statement, 3 letters of recommendation.

Application Deadlines 9/2 for fall, 1/1 for spring, 5/6 for summer.

FINANCIALS

Costs for 1994-95 Tuition: Full-time: $125/trimester for residents, $125/trimester for nonresidents; Part-time day: $48-$50/credit hour for residents, $56-$66/credit hour for nonresidents. Fees: Full-time: $1,250-$2,250 for residents, $2,000-$3,000 for nonresidents.

Financial Aid In 1994-95, candidates received some institutionally administered aid in the form of scholarships, loans, fellowships, assistantships. Financial aid is not available to part-time students. Application deadlines: 9/2 for fall, 1/1 for spring, 5/6 for summer.

INTERNATIONAL STUDENTS

Services and Facilities Visa services, counseling/support services.

Applying TOEFL required, minimum score of 550; proof of health; proof of adequate funds. Financial aid is available to international students. Financial aid application deadlines: 5/6 for fall, 9/2 for spring, 1/1 for summer. Applications are processed on a rolling basis. Admission application deadlines: 5/6 for fall, 9/2 for spring, 1/1 for summer.

PLACEMENT

Placement services include alumni network, career counseling/planning, career placement, job interviews, and resume referral to employers.

Program Contact: Ms. Ferdousi Rahman, Registrial Associate, International University of Business Agriculture and Technology (IUBAT), House 135 Road 9A Dhanmondi R/A, 1209 Dhaka, Bangladesh. 2-816064; Fax: 2-810494.

BELGIUM

European University

International Business School

Antwerp, Belgium

OVERVIEW

European University is an independent proprietary coed institution. Setting: urban campus. Total institutional enrollment: 650. Program was first offered in 1973.

MBA HIGHLIGHTS

Entrance Difficulty***
Mean GMAT: 500
Mean GPA: 3.0

Cost
Tuition: N/R
Room & Board: N/R

Enrollment Profile
Full-time: 240
Part-time: 350
Total: 590
Average Age: 28

Work Exp: 40%
Women: 20%

Average Class Size: 25

ACADEMICS

Calendar Trimesters.

Curricular Focus International business, leadership, problem solving and decision making.

Concentrations Hotel management, management, marketing, strategic management, transportation.

Faculty Full-time: 47, 70% with doctorates; part-time: 38, 69% with doctorates.

Teaching Methodology Case study: 15%, industrial visits: 5%, lecture: 60%, seminars by members of the business community: 5%, student presentations: 5%, team projects: 10%.

Special Opportunities International exchange in Germany, Greece, Indonesia, Netherlands, Peru, Portugal, Spain, Switzerland, United States of America.

STUDENT STATISTICS

Undergraduate Majors Business 45%; engineering/technology 20%; humanities 5%; science/mathematics 15%; social sciences 10%; other 5%.

Other Background Graduate degrees in other disciplines: 20%. Work experience: On average, students have 3-4 years of work experience on entrance to the program.

FACILITIES

Information Resources Business collection includes 25,000 bound volumes, 25 periodical subscriptions, 40 CD-ROMs, 200 videos.

Housing College housing available.

Technology Computers are used moderately in course work. 25 computer terminals/PCs, linked by a campus-wide computer network, are available for use by students in program; they are located in classrooms, the library, the computer center, computer labs. Students in the program are not required to have their own PC.

Computer Resources/On-line Services

Training	Yes	E-Mail	Yes
Internet	Yes $		

ADMISSION

Acceptance 1994-95 1,500 applied for admission; 40% were accepted.

Entrance Requirements First degree, GMAT score of 450, minimum 3.0 GPA.

Application Requirements Written essay, interview, application form, copies of transcript, resume/curriculum vitae, personal statement.

Application Deadlines 6/11 for fall, 2/11 for spring. Applications are processed on a rolling basis.

INTERNATIONAL STUDENTS

Demographics 70% of students on campus are international; Europe 40%, Asia 20%, Africa 12%, North America 9%, South America 8%, Central America 6%, Australia 5%.

Services and Facilities International student center, language tutoring.

Applying TOEFL required, minimum score of 550; proof of health; proof of adequate funds. Financial aid is not available to international students. Admission applications are processed on a rolling basis.

PROGRAM

One-Year MBA Length of program: Minimum: 10 months. Maximum: 3 years. Full-time classes: Evening. Part-time classes: Evening. Degree requirements: 45 credits. Languages: English. Average class size: 25.

PLACEMENT

In 1993-94, 45 organizations participated in on-campus recruiting; 20 on-campus interviews were conducted. Placement services include alumni network, career fairs, career placement, and job search course. Of 1994 graduates, 98% were employed within three months of graduation.

Jobs by Employer Type Manufacturing 57%; service 27%; consulting 16%.

Jobs by Functional Area Marketing/sales 22%; finance 20%; management 38%; strategic planning 20%.

Program Contact: Dr. Xavier Nieberding, President, European University, Amerikalei 131, 2000 Antwerp, Belgium. 3-218-54-31.

Katholieke Universiteit Leuven

Department of Applied Economic Sciences

Leuven, Belgium

OVERVIEW

Katholieke Universiteit Leuven is a government-supported coed institution. Founded 1425. Setting: urban campus. Total institutional enrollment: 23,800. Program was first offered in 1968.

MBA HIGHLIGHTS

Entrance Difficulty**
Mean GMAT: 600
Mean GPA: N/R

Cost
Tuition: 17,600 Belgian francs
Room & Board: N/R

Enrollment Profile
Full-time: 75
Part-time: 45
Total: 120
Average Age: 27

Work Exp: 48%
Women: 12%

Average Class Size: 30

ACADEMICS

Length of Program Minimum: 9 months.

Calendar Semesters.

Full-time Classes Main campus; day, evening, weekends.

Part-time Classes Main campus; day, evening, weekends.

Degree Requirements 12 courses including 5 elective courses.

Required Courses Advanced management accounting and budgeting, advanced marketing, corporate finance, corporate strategy, human resources management, international management, production and inventory management.

Curricular Focus International business, problem solving and decision making, strategic analysis and planning.

Concentrations Accounting, economics, finance, human resources management, international business, management, management information systems, marketing, operations management, organizational behavior, quantitative analysis, strategic management.

Faculty Full-time: 40, 100% with doctorates; part-time: 15, 100% with doctorates.

Teaching Methodology Case study: 25%, lecture: 50%, team projects: 25%.

Special Opportunities International exchange in Spain, United States of America.

STUDENT STATISTICS

Geographic Representation Belgium 50%; South America and Asia 35%; North America 10%; United Kingdom 3%; Russia 2%.

Undergraduate Majors Business 40%; engineering/technology 20%; humanities 8%; science/mathematics 10%; social sciences 8%; other 14%.

Other Background Graduate degrees in other disciplines: 100%. Work experience: On average, students have 3 years of work experience on entrance to the program.

FACILITIES

Housing 20% of students in program live in college-owned or -operated housing.

Technology Computers are used moderately in course work. 55 computer terminals/PCs, linked by a campus-wide computer network, are available for use by students in program; they are located in the library, the computer center. Students in the program are not required to have their own PC.

Computer Resources/On-line Services

Training	Yes	E-Mail	Yes

ADMISSION

Acceptance 1994-95 300 applied for admission; 40% were accepted.

Entrance Requirements First degree, GMAT score of 550.

Application Requirements Application form, copies of transcript, resume/curriculum vitae, personal statement, 2 letters of recommendation.

Application Deadlines 5/31 for fall, 7/15 for European applications. Applications are processed on a rolling basis.

FINANCIALS
Costs for 1994-95 Tuition: Full-time: 17,600 Belgian francs.

Financial Aid Application deadline: 11/30 for fall. Contact: International Center, Naamsestraat 22, B-3000 Leuven, Belgium. 16-284024.

INTERNATIONAL STUDENTS
Demographics 8% of students on campus are international.

Services and Facilities International student housing; international student office, international student center, language tutoring, counseling/support services.

Applying Proof of adequate funds. Financial aid is not available to international students. Admission application deadlines: 5/31 for fall, 7/15 for European applicants. Applications are processed on a rolling basis.

PLACEMENT
In 1993-94, 5 organizations participated in on-campus recruiting; 100 on-campus interviews were conducted. Placement services include career fairs and job interviews. Of 1994 graduates, 85% were employed within three months of graduation.

Jobs by Employer Type Manufacturing 20%; service 3%; government 8%; consulting 8%; chemicals/pharmaceuticals 14%; teaching 11%; information systems 10%; other 27%.

Program Contact: Mrs. Gonda Huybens, MBA Program Coordinator, Katholieke Universiteit Leuven, Dekenstraat 2, B-3000 Leuven, Belgium. 16-326619; Fax: 16-326620; Internet Address: gonda.huybens@econ. kuleuven.ac.be.

St. Ignatius University Faculty of Antwerp (UFSIA)

Center for Business Administration

Antwerp, Belgium

OVERVIEW
Setting: urban campus. Total institutional enrollment: 3,500. Program was first offered in 1983.

MBA HIGHLIGHTS

Entrance Difficulty**
Mean GMAT: 500
Mean GPA: N/R

Cost
Tuition: 17,600 Belgian francs
Room & Board: N/R

Enrollment Profile
Full-time: 42
Part-time: 3
Total: 45
Average Age: 25

Work Exp: 10%
Women: 40%

Average Class Size: 45

ACADEMICS
Length of Program Minimum: 9 months. Maximum: 2 years.

Calendar Trimesters.

Full-time Classes Main campus; day.

Part-time Classes Main campus; day.

Degree Requirements 60 credits including 32 elective credits.

Required Courses Business and society, business policy, data analysis, management and organizational behavior, managerial economics, quantitative decision methods.

Curricular Focus Business issues and problems, entrepreneurship, international business.

Concentrations Accounting, economics, entrepreneurship, finance, human resources management, international business, management, marketing, operations management, organizational behavior, quantitative analysis, strategic management.

Teaching Methodology Case study: 20%, faculty seminars: 10%, lecture: 20%, research: 20%, student presentations: 10%, team projects: 20%.

Special Opportunities International exchange in Canada, Japan, Singapore, United Kingdom, United States of America. Internship program available.

STUDENT STATISTICS
Undergraduate Majors Business 50%; engineering/technology 20%; science/mathematics 10%; social sciences 20%.

Other Background Work experience: On average, students have 2-3 years of work experience on entrance to the program.

FACILITIES
Housing College housing available.

Technology Computers are used moderately in course work. 90 computer terminals/PCs, linked by a campus-wide computer network, are available for use by students in program; they are located in the computer center, computer labs. Students in the program are not required to have their own PC.

Computer Resources/On-line Services

Training	Yes	Videoconference Center	Yes
Internet	Yes	Multimedia Center	Yes
E-Mail	Yes		

ADMISSION
Acceptance 1994-95 80 applied for admission; 56% were accepted.

Entrance Requirements First degree, GMAT score. Core courses waived through: previous course work.

Application Requirements Interview, application form, copies of transcript, resume/curriculum vitae, 2 letters of recommendation.

Application Deadline 9/1 for fall.

FINANCIALS
Costs for 1994-95 Tuition: Full-time: 17,600 Belgian francs.

Financial Aid Financial aid is not available to part-time students.

INTERNATIONAL STUDENTS
Services and Facilities International student housing; international student office.

Applying Proof of adequate funds. Financial aid is not available to international students. Admission application deadlines: 6/1 for fall, 11/1 for spring. Contact: Ms. Marie-Anne Fivez, Prinsstraat 13, B-2000 Antwerp, Belgium. 3-220-44-90.

PLACEMENT
Placement services include alumni network.

Program Contact: Ms. Katrien Dickele, Administrative Coordinator, St. Ignatius University Faculty of Antwerp (UFSIA), Prinsstraat 13, B-2000 Antwerp, Belgium. 3-220-40-35; Fax: 3-220-40-99; Internet Address: cba.dickele.k@alpha.ufsia.ac.be.

CANADA

University of Alberta

Faculty of Business

Edmonton, Alberta, Canada

OVERVIEW
The University of Alberta is a province-supported coed institution. Founded 1906. Setting: 154-acre urban campus. Total institutional enrollment: 30,494. Program was first offered in 1964. AACSB-accredited.

MBA HIGHLIGHTS

Entrance Difficulty***
Mean GMAT: 615
Mean GPA: N/R

Cost
Tuition: 315 Canadian dollars/course
(Nonresident: 630 Canadian dollars/course)
Room & Board: N/R

Enrollment Profile
Full-time: N/R
Part-time: N/R   Work Exp: N/R
Total: 121   Women: 20%
Average Age: N/R   Minorities: N/R

Average Class Size: 40

ACADEMICS
Length of Program Minimum: 18 months.

Calendar standard year.

Full-time Classes Main campus; day, evening, summer.

Part-time Classes Main campus; day, evening, summer.

Degree Requirements 57 credits.

Curricular Focus General management, teamwork.

Concentrations Finance, health services, human resources management, international business, leisure and sport management, educational administration, management, marketing, organizational behavior, public administration.

Faculty Full-time: 40, 100% with doctorates.

Teaching Methodology Case study: 30%, lecture: 30%, student presentations: 20%, team projects: 20%.

FACILITIES
Information Resources Main library with 2.5 million bound volumes, 1.7 million titles on microform, 15,000 periodical subscriptions, 45,000 records/tapes/CDs.

ADMISSION
Acceptance 1994-95 Of those applying, 45% were accepted.

Entrance Requirements Bachelor's degree, GMAT score of 500, minimum 3.0 GPA. Core courses waived through: previous course work, exams.

Application Requirements Application form, copies of transcript, resume/curriculum vitae, personal statement.

Application Deadlines 5/31 for fall. Applications are processed on a rolling basis.

FINANCIALS
Costs for 1994-95 Tuition: Full-time: 315 Canadian dollars/course for Canadian residents, 630 Canadian dollars/course for nonresidents; Part-time day: 315 Canadian dollars/course for Canadian residents, 630 Canadian dollars/course for nonresidents. Fees: Full-time: 259 Canadian dollars/term for Canadian residents, 260 Canadian dollars/term for nonresidents; Part-time day: 65 Canadian dollars/term for Canadian residents, 65 Canadian dollars/term for nonresidents.

Financial Aid In 1994-95, 20% of candidates received some institutionally administered aid in the form of scholarships, assistantships. Total awards ranged from 750-6,500 Canadian dollars. Financial aid is not available to part-time students. Application deadline: 1/31 for fall. Contact: Dr. David Jobson, Associate Dean, MBA Program, Faculty of Business, Edmonton, AB T6G 2R6, Canada. (403) 492-3946.

INTERNATIONAL STUDENTS
Demographics 5% of students on campus are international.

Applying TOEFL required, minimum score of 600. Financial aid is not available to international students. Admission application deadline: 5/31 for fall.

ALTERNATE MBA PROGRAMS
MBA/LL B Length of program: Minimum: 48 months. Full-time classes: Main campus; day, evening, summer. Degree requirements: 120 credits.

MBA/M Eng Length of program: Minimum: 24 months. Full-time classes: Main campus; day, evening, summer. Degree requirements: 60 credits.

MBA/MHSA Length of program: Minimum: 24 months. Full-time classes: Main campus; day, evening, summer. Degree requirements: 60 credits.

Program Contact: Dr. David Jobson, Associate Dean, MBA Program, University of Alberta, Edmonton, AB T6G 2R6, Canada. (403) 492-3946; Fax: (403) 492-3325.

University of Calgary

Faculty of Management

Calgary, Alberta, Canada

OVERVIEW
The University of Calgary is a province-supported coed institution. Founded 1945. Setting: 304-acre urban campus. Total institutional enrollment: 22,311. AACSB-accredited.

MBA HIGHLIGHTS

Entrance Difficulty**
Mean GMAT: 581
Mean GPA: N/R

Cost
Tuition: N/R
(Nonresident: N/R)
Room & Board: $3,500

Enrollment Profile
Full-time: N/R
Part-time: N/R   Work Exp: N/R
Total: 246   Women: 40%
Average Age: N/R   Minorities: N/R

Average Class Size: 50

ACADEMICS
Calendar Semesters.

Curricular Focus Entrepreneurship, general management, teamwork.

Concentrations Accounting, entrepreneurship, finance, human resources management, international business, management information systems, marketing, operations management, organizational behavior, quantitative analysis, tourism, enterprise development.

Teaching Methodology Case study: 20%, lecture: 40%, seminars by members of the business community: 5%, student presentations: 5%, team projects: 30%.

FACILITIES
Information Resources Main library with 1.9 million bound volumes, 3.3 million titles on microform, 12,200 periodical subscriptions, 40,100 records/tapes/CDs, 70 CD-ROMs.

Housing College housing available.

ADMISSION
Entrance Requirements Bachelor's degree, GMAT score of 500, minimum 3.0 GPA, minimum 3 years of work experience.

Application Requirements Application form, copies of transcript, resume/curriculum vitae, personal statement, 3 letters of recommendation.

Application Deadlines 5/1 for fall. Applications are processed on a rolling basis.

FINANCIALS
Financial Aid Application deadline: 5/15 for fall. (403) 220-3808.

INTERNATIONAL STUDENTS
Applying TOEFL required, minimum score of 550; proof of adequate funds. Financial aid is not available to international students. Admission application deadline: 5/1 for fall. Applications are processed on a rolling basis.

PROGRAM
Enterprise Development Length of program: Minimum: 24 months. Full-time classes: Main campus; day, evening, summer. Part-time classes: Main campus; evening, summer. Degree requirements: 20 courses.

Program Contact: Ms. Louise Grunerud, Admissions Officer, University of Calgary, 2500 University Drive, NW, Calgary, AB T2N 1N4, Canada. (403) 220-3808; Fax: (403) 282-0095.

Simon Fraser University

Faculty of Business Administration

Burnaby, British Columbia, Canada

OVERVIEW
Simon Fraser University is a province-supported coed institution. Founded 1965. Setting: 1,200-acre suburban campus with easy access to Vancouver. Total institutional enrollment: 17,102.

MBA HIGHLIGHTS

Entrance Difficulty**
Mean GMAT: 550
Mean GPA: N/R

Cost
Tuition: 823 Canadian dollars/semester
Room & Board: N/R

Enrollment Profile

Full-time: 131	Work Exp: N/R
Part-time: 0	Women: 47%
Total: 131	Minorities: N/R
Average Age: N/R	

Average Class Size: 15

ACADEMICS
Length of Program Minimum: 20 months.
Calendar Semesters.
Full-time Classes Main campus; day.
Degree Requirements 36 credits.
Required Courses Accounting, finance, human resources management, international business, management information systems, management science, marketing, policy.
Curricular Focus Business issues and problems, economic and financial theory, international business, leadership, organizational development and change management, problem solving and decision making, strategic analysis and planning, teamwork.
Concentrations Accounting, finance, human resources management, international business, management information systems, marketing, operations management, organizational behavior, public policy, quantitative analysis, strategic management.
Teaching Methodology Case study: 10%, faculty seminars: 20%, lecture: 30%, research: 10%, student presentations: 20%, team projects: 10%.
Special Opportunities International exchange in United Kingdom. Other: Western Dean's Agreement.

FACILITIES
Information Resources Main library with 1.2 million bound volumes, 902,430 titles on microform, 9,725 periodical subscriptions, 7,278 records/tapes/CDs.

ADMISSION
Entrance Requirements Bachelor's degree, prerequisite courses required for applicants with non-business degree, GMAT score of 550, minimum 3.0 GPA.
Application Requirements Application form, copies of transcript, resume/curriculum vitae, personal statement, 3 letters of recommendation.
Application Deadlines 4/1 for fall, 10/1 for spring, 2/1 for summer.

FINANCIALS
Costs for 1994-95 Tuition: Full-time: 823 Canadian dollars/semester.
Financial Aid Application deadlines: 4/1 for fall, 10/1 for spring, 2/1 for summer. Applications are processed on a rolling basis. Contact: Ms. Charlotte French, Director, Academic Resource Office, Burnaby, BC V5A 1S6, Canada. (604) 291-3892.

INTERNATIONAL STUDENTS
Applying TOEFL required, minimum score of 670; proof of health; minimum score of 5.0 on Test of Standard Written English. Financial aid is not available to international students. Admission application deadlines: 4/1 for fall, 10/1 for spring, 2/1 for summer.

ALTERNATE MBA PROGRAMS
One-Year MBA Length of program: Minimum: 12 months. Full-time classes: Main campus; day. Degree requirements: 36 credits.
MBA/MRM Length of program: Minimum: 24 months. Full-time classes: Main campus; day. Degree requirements: 22 courses.

Program Contact: Ms. Angela Marconi, MBA Program Secretary, Simon Fraser University, Burnaby, BC V5A 1S6, Canada. (604) 291-3047; Fax: (604) 291-3404.

University of British Columbia

Faculty of Commerce and Business Administration

Vancouver, British Columbia, Canada

OVERVIEW
The University of British Columbia is a province-supported coed institution. Founded 1915. Setting: 1,000-acre urban campus. Total institutional enrollment: 31,626. Program was first offered in 1957.

MBA HIGHLIGHTS
Entrance Difficulty**
Mean GMAT: 619
Mean GPA: N/R

Cost
Tuition: 7,350 Canadian dollars/degree program
Room & Board: 6,000 Canadian dollars

Enrollment Profile

Full-time: 300	Work Exp: 80%
Part-time: 125	Women: 36%
Total: 425	Minorities: N/R
Average Age: 26	

Average Class Size: 30

The University of British Columbia (UBC) is launching a new M.B.A. program in September 1995. The program is a challenging, integrated educational experience redesigned to reflect the rapidly changing business climate. The program is completed in fifteen continuous months full-time or in three years part-time. Students are led by experienced faculty members who have a strong commitment to excellence in teaching and research.

The principal components of the program include an integrated core, specializations, and internships and projects. The integrated core component is designed to provide students with a foundation in finance, marketing, human resources, accounting, economics, statistics, and information systems. Following the core, M.B.A. students are required to select a specialization. Students choose among eleven specializations, including international business, entrepreneurship, and finance. Internships and projects are directly related to the area of specialization and are an integral part of the program.

Many exciting opportunities exist to gain a global perspective. Students may select specialized international courses; interact with UBC's multicultural student body, faculty, and visiting scholars; participate in the business consulting program in Hong Kong; and attend one of the faculty's twenty-two exchange programs worldwide.

UBC's M.B.A. program continues to provide students with an innovative approach to management education.

ACADEMICS
Length of Program Minimum: 15 months. Maximum: 5 years.
Calendar 15 continuous months or 3 years.
Full-time Classes Main campus; day, evening, summer.
Part-time Classes Main campus; evening, weekends.
Degree Requirements 51 credits including 9-15 elective credits. Other: Internship or industry related project.
Curricular Focus Economic and financial theory, entrepreneurship, international business.
Concentrations Entrepreneurship, finance, human resources management, international business, management information systems, marketing, operations management, real estate, strategic management, transportation.
Faculty Full-time: 104, 92% with doctorates; part-time: 6, 30% with doctorates.
Teaching Methodology Case study: 25%, lecture: 35%, seminars by members of the business community: 10%, student presentations: 15%, team projects: 15%.
Special Opportunities International exchange in Australia, Austria, Belgium, Brazil, Denmark, France, Germany, Hong Kong, Israel, Italy, Japan, Netherlands, Republic of Korea, Thailand, United Kingdom. Internships

include entrepreneurship, finance, marketing, technology management, and transportation. Other: business consulting program in Hong Kong.

STUDENT STATISTICS

Geographic Representation Canadian residents 80%.

Undergraduate Majors Business 29%; engineering/technology 23%; humanities 9%; science/mathematics 22%; social sciences 17%.

Other Background Graduate degrees in other disciplines: 5%. Work experience: On average, students have 3 years of work experience on entrance to the program.

FACILITIES

Information Resources Main library with 3.3 million bound volumes, 4.2 million titles on microform, 24,440 periodical subscriptions, 182,752 records/tapes/CDs, 537 CD-ROMs. Business collection in David Lane Management Research Library includes 200,000 bound volumes, 700 periodical subscriptions, 30 CD-ROMs, 100 videos.

Housing College housing available.

Technology Computers are used heavily in course work. 90 computer terminals/PCs, linked by a campus-wide computer network, are available for use by students in program; they are located in the library, computer labs. Students in the program are not required to have their own PC.

Computer Resources/On-line Services

Training	Yes	CompuServe	No
Internet	Yes	Dun's	No
E-Mail	Yes	Dow Jones	No
Multimedia Center	Yes	Dialog	Yes
LEXIS/NEXIS	No	Bloomberg	No

Other on-line services: First Search.

ADMISSION

Acceptance 1994-95 700 applied for admission.

Entrance Requirements Bachelor's degree, GMAT score of 550, minimum 3.0 GPA.

Application Requirements Written essay, application form, copies of transcript, resume/curriculum vitae, personal statement.

Application Deadlines 4/30 for fall, 9/30 for part-time students.

FINANCIALS

Estimated Costs for 1995-96 Tuition: Full-time: 7,350 Canadian dollars/ degree program for Canadian residents. Average room and board costs are 6,000 Canadian dollars per academic year (on-campus) and 9,600 Canadian dollars per academic year (off-campus).

Financial Aid In 1994-95, 35% of candidates received some institutionally administered aid in the form of scholarships, loans, fellowships, assistantships, work-study. Total awards ranged from 166-13,500 Canadian dollars. Financial aid is not available to part-time students. Application deadline: 6/30 for fall. (604) 822-8422.

INTERNATIONAL STUDENTS

Services and Facilities International student office, international student center, ESL courses, counseling/support services.

Applying TOEFL required, minimum score of 600. Financial aid is not available to international students. Admission application deadlines: 3/31 for fall, 9/30 for part-time students. Applications are processed on a rolling basis.

ALTERNATE MBA PROGRAM

MBA/LL B Length of program: Minimum: 40 months. Maximum: 5 years. Full-time classes: Main campus; day, summer. Degree requirements: 140 credits including 62 elective credits.

PLACEMENT

In 1993-94, 200 organizations participated in on-campus recruiting. Placement services include alumni network, career counseling/planning, career library, career placement, electronic job bank, job interviews, job search course, resume preparation, and resume referral to employers. Of 1994 graduates, the average starting salary was 42,900 Canadian dollars, the range was 30,000-70,000 Canadian dollars.

Jobs by Functional Area Marketing/sales 11%; finance 30%; operations 8%; management 7%; strategic planning 11%; technical management 10%; real estate 5%; consulting 18%.

Program Contact: Ms. Ethel Davis, Assistant Dean and Director of Masters' Programs, University of British Columbia, Commerce Masters' Programs Office #102, Vancouver, BC V6T 1Z1, Canada. (604) 822-8422; Fax: (604) 822-9030; Internet Address: masters.programs@commerce.uba.ca.

See full description on page 858.

University of Victoria

School of Business

Victoria, British Columbia, Canada

OVERVIEW

The University of Victoria is a province-supported coed institution. Founded 1963. Setting: 380-acre urban campus with easy access to Vancouver. Total institutional enrollment: 15,000. Program was first offered in 1992.

MBA HIGHLIGHTS

Entrance Difficulty***
Mean GMAT:
Mean GPA: 6.0 (9.0 scale)

Cost
Tuition: 908 Canadian dollars/term
Room & Board: 6,000 Canadian dollars (off-campus)

Enrollment Profile

Full-time: 60		Work Exp: 94%
Part-time: 10		Women: 34%
Total: 70		Minorities: 20%
Average Age: 30		

Average Class Size: 20

ACADEMICS

Length of Program Minimum: 17 months. Maximum: 5 years.

Calendar standard year.

Full-time Classes Main campus; day.

Part-time Classes Main campus; evening.

Degree Requirements 26 units including 5 elective units.

Required Courses Accounting, data analysis, economics, finance, international business, law, management consulting, management information systems, marketing, organizational designs, production, research report, strategy.

Curricular Focus Entrepreneurship, international business, teamwork.

Concentrations Entrepreneurship, international business, tourism.

Faculty Full-time: 26, 100% with doctorates; part-time: 6, 50% with doctorates.

Teaching Methodology Case study: 10%, faculty seminars: 10%, lecture: 48%, research: 10%, seminars by members of the business community: 2%, student presentations: 10%, team projects: 10%.

Special Opportunities International exchange in Hong Kong, Indonesia, Malaysia, Singapore, Taiwan. Internship program available.

STUDENT STATISTICS

Geographic Representation Canadian residents 75%.

Other Background Graduate degrees in other disciplines: 15%. Work experience: On average, students have 8 years of work experience on entrance to the program.

FACILITIES

Information Resources Main library with 1.6 million bound volumes, 1.7 million titles on microform, 12,000 periodical subscriptions, 45,000 records/tapes/CDs, 36 CD-ROMs.

Housing College housing available.

Technology Computers are used heavily in course work. Computer terminals/PCs, linked by a campus-wide computer network, are available for use by students in program; they are located in student rooms, the library, computer labs. Students in the program are not required to have their own PC.

Computer Resources/On-line Services

Training	Yes	E-Mail	Yes
Internet	Yes	LEXIS/NEXIS	Yes

ADMISSION

Acceptance 1994-95 165 applied for admission; 27% were accepted.

Entrance Requirements Bachelor's degree, GMAT score, minimum 5.0 GPA (9.0 scale). Core courses waived through: previous course work.

Application Requirements Written essay, interview, application form, copies of transcript, resume/curriculum vitae, 2 letters of recommendation.

Application Deadline Applications are processed on a rolling basis.

FINANCIALS

Costs for 1994-95 Tuition: Full-time: 908 Canadian dollars/term. Fees: Full-time: 4,200 Canadian dollars. Average room and board costs are 6,000 Canadian dollars per academic year (off-campus).

Financial Aid In 1994-95, 10% of candidates received some institutionally administered aid in the form of scholarships. Total awards ranged from 1,500-11,500 Canadian dollars. Financial aid is not available to part-time students. Applications are processed on a rolling basis. Contact: Student Financial Aid Services Office, Box 3025, Victoria, BC V8W 3P2, Canada. (604) 721-7211.

INTERNATIONAL STUDENTS

Services and Facilities International student center.

Applying TOEFL required, minimum score of 575; visa. Financial aid is available to international students. Applications are processed on a rolling basis. Admission applications are processed on a rolling basis.

PLACEMENT

Placement services include career counseling/planning, career placement, resume preparation, and resume referral to employers.

Program Contact: Mr. Nicholas James, MBA Admissions Officer, University of Victoria, PO Box 1700, Victoria, BC V8W 2Y2, Canada. (604) 721-6414; Fax: (604) 721-6067.

University of Manitoba

Faculty of Management

Winnipeg, Manitoba, Canada

OVERVIEW

The University of Manitoba is a province-supported coed institution. Founded 1877. Setting: 685-acre suburban campus. Total institutional enrollment: 25,000. Program was first offered in 1968.

MBA HIGHLIGHTS

Entrance Difficulty**
Mean GMAT: 600
Mean GPA: 3.4

Cost
Tuition: 16,000 Canadian dollars
(Nonresident: 16,000 Canadian dollars)
Room & Board: 6,000 Canadian dollars

Enrollment Profile

Full-time: 50	Work Exp: 95%
Part-time: 125	Women: 35%
Total: 175	Minorities: 15%
Average Age: 30	

Average Class Size: 24

ACADEMICS

Length of Program May range up to 6 years.

Calendar 11 consecutive months.

Part-time Classes Main campus; evening, weekends, early morning, summer.

Degree Requirements 66 credit hours including 6 elective credit hours. Other: Public service project.

Required Courses Accounting data and decision making, accounting data and planning, behavioral skills for effective managers, building the information age organization, business and government relations, business conditions analysis, business research and analysis, country analysis, decision making under certainty, decision making under uncertainty, designing effective organizations, designing fast response operations, entrepreneurship and new venture formation, essential financial concepts for managers, financial techniques for active management, foundations of strategic market advantage, global operations strategy, industry analysis, international business, international study visit and policy project, interpreting and analyzing financial statements, leveraging human resources, management of labor and employee relations, staffing organizations, strategic leadership and managing change, strategy formulation, strategy implementation, sustainable development, understanding financial statements, using information and technology.

Curricular Focus General management, strategic analysis and planning, teamwork.

Concentration Management.

Faculty Full time: 30, 90% with doctorates.

Teaching Methodology Case study: 25%, lecture: 15%, research: 10%, seminars by members of the business community: 10%, student presentations: 15%, team projects: 25%.

Special Opportunities International exchange in India, Mexico. Other: MBA Consulting Program.

STUDENT STATISTICS

Geographic Representation Canadian residents 85%.

Undergraduate Majors Business 10%; education 5%; engineering/technology 20%; humanities 10%; nursing 5%; science/mathematics 10%; social sciences 30%; other 10%.

Other Background Graduate degrees in other disciplines: 20%. Work experience: On average, students have 5 years of work experience on entrance to the program.

FACILITIES

Information Resources Main library with 1.6 million bound volumes, 1.1 million titles on microform, 12,800 periodical subscriptions, 28,000 records/tapes/CDs. Business collection in Albert D. Cohen Library includes 25,000 bound volumes, 500 periodical subscriptions, 3 CD-ROMs, 45 videos.

Housing 5% of students in program live in college-owned or -operated housing. Assistance with housing search provided.

Technology Computers are used heavily in course work. 120 computer terminals/PCs, linked by a campus-wide computer network, are available for use by students in program; they are located in computer labs. Students in the program are not required to have their own PC. 100 Canadian dollars are budgeted per student for computer support.

Computer Resources/On-line Services

Training	No	Dun's	No
Internet	Yes	Dow Jones	No
E-Mail	Yes	Dialog	No
LEXIS/NEXIS	No	Bloomberg	No
CompuServe	No		

ADMISSION

Acceptance 1994-95 300 applied for admission; 25% were accepted.

Entrance Requirements Bachelor's degree, GMAT score of 450, minimum 3.0 GPA, minimum 3 years of work experience.

Application Requirements Interview, application form, copies of transcript, resume/curriculum vitae, personal statement, 3 letters of recommendation.

Application Deadlines 5/1 for fall. Applications are processed on a rolling basis.

FINANCIALS

Costs for 1995-96 Tuition: Full-time: 16,000 Canadian dollars for Canadian residents, 16,000 Canadian dollars for nonresidents. Fees: Full-time: 1,000-3,000 Canadian dollars for Canadian residents, 1,000-3,000 Canadian dollars for nonresidents. Average room and board costs are 6,000 Canadian dollars per academic year (on-campus) and 5,500 Canadian dollars per academic year (off-campus).

Financial Aid In 1994-95, candidates received some institutionally administered aid in the form of scholarships, fellowships. Total awards ranged from 2,000-6,000 Canadian dollars. Financial aid is not available to part-time students. Application deadlines: 2/7 for fall, 5/1 for scholarships.

INTERNATIONAL STUDENTS

Demographics 5% of students on campus are international; Asia 70%, Africa 10%, Europe 6%, Central America 3%, North America 3%, South America 2%, Australia 1%, other 5%.

Services and Facilities International student housing; international student office, international student center, visa services, language tutoring, ESL courses, counseling/support services.

Applying TOEFL required, minimum score of 550; proof of health; proof of adequate funds. Financial aid is not available to international students. Admission application deadline: 1/15 for fall. Applications are processed on a rolling basis.

ALTERNATE MBA PROGRAM

One-Year MBA Length of program: Minimum: 11 months. Maximum: 1 year. Full-time classes: Main campus; day, weekends, summer. Degree requirements: 66 credit hours including 6 elective credit hours. Public service project.

PLACEMENT

In 1993-94, 100 organizations participated in on-campus recruiting; 40 on-campus interviews were conducted. Placement services include alumni network, career counseling/planning, career fairs, career library, career placement, electronic job bank, job interviews, job search course, resume preparation, and resume referral to employers. Of 1994 graduates, 85% were employed within three months of graduation, the average starting salary was 47,000 Canadian dollars, the range was 20,000-150,000 Canadian dollars.

Jobs by Employer Type Manufacturing 14%; service 22%; government 15%; consulting 10%; nonprofit 10%; university administration 10%; financial institutions 7%; healthcare administration 3%; education 6%; law firm 3%.

Jobs by Functional Area Marketing/sales 10%; finance 10%; operations 8%; management 32%; strategic planning 15%; technical management 20%; consulting 5%.

Program Contact: Ms. Susan Eide, MBA Program Manager, University of Manitoba, 268 Drake Centre, Winnipeg, MB R3T 5V4, Canada. (204) 474-8448, or (800) 432-1960 (MB only); Fax: (204) 261-6084; Internet Address: seide@bldgdrake.lan1.umanitoba.ca.
See full description on page 888.

Université de Moncton

Faculté d'Administration

Moncton, New Brunswick, Canada

OVERVIEW
The Université de Moncton is a province-supported comprehensive coed institution. Founded 1963. Setting: 400-acre urban campus. Total institutional enrollment: 4,358.

MBA HIGHLIGHTS

Entrance Difficulty****

Cost $
Tuition: $2,200
(Nonresident: $4,400)
Room & Board: N/R

Enrollment Profile
Full-time: 55
Part-time: 20
Total: 75
Average Age: N/R

Work Exp: N/R
Women: 45%
Minorities: 2%

Average Class Size: 30

ACADEMICS
Length of Program Minimum: 24 months. Maximum: 7 years.
Calendar Semesters.
Full-time Classes Main campus, distance learning option; day, evening.
Part-time Classes Main campus, distance learning option; day, evening.
Degree Requirements 48 credits including 15 elective credits.
Curricular Focus General management, strategic analysis and planning, teamwork.
Concentration Management.
Teaching Methodology Case study: 30%, faculty seminars: 5%, lecture: 15%, research: 10%, student presentations: 25%, team projects: 15%.

FACILITIES
Information Resources Main library with 800,000 bound volumes, 60,000 titles on microform, 2,800 periodical subscriptions, 2,000 records/tapes/CDs, 12 CD-ROMs.

ADMISSION
Entrance Requirements Bachelor's degree, minimum 3.0 GPA, fluency in French and English. Core courses waived through: previous course work.
Application Requirements Interview, application form, copies of transcript, resume/curriculum vitae.
Application Deadlines 3/1 for fall, 12/1 for spring. Applications are processed on a rolling basis.

FINANCIALS
Costs for 1994-95 Tuition: Full-time: $2,200 for Canadian residents, $4,400 for nonresidents.
Financial Aid Application deadlines: 3/15 for fall, 12/1 for spring. Applications are processed on a rolling basis. Contact: Office of Student Services, Moncton, NB E1A 3E9, Canada. (506) 858-4000.

INTERNATIONAL STUDENTS
Applying TOEFL required; proof of health; proof of adequate funds. Financial aid is available to international students. Financial aid application deadlines: 3/1 for fall, 12/1 for spring. Applications are processed on a rolling basis. Admission applications are processed on a rolling basis.

Program Contact: Dr. Georges Wybouw, Director of MBA, Université de Moncton, Moncton, NB E1A 3E9, Canada. (506) 858-4205; Fax: (506) 858-4093.

University of New Brunswick

School of Graduate Studies

Fredericton, New Brunswick, Canada

OVERVIEW
The University of New Brunswick is a province-supported coed institution. Founded 1785. Setting: 7,100-acre urban campus. Total institutional enrollment: 9,562.

ACADEMICS
Calendar standard year.
Degree Requirements 60 credits.
Concentration Management.

FACILITIES
Information Resources Main library with 920,000 bound volumes, 1.6 million titles on microform, 6,700 periodical subscriptions, 2,000 records/tapes/CDs.

ADMISSION
Entrance Requirements Bachelor's degree, GMAT score, minimum 3.0 GPA.
Application Requirements Written essay, application form, copies of transcript.
Application Deadline 9/9 for fall.

INTERNATIONAL STUDENTS
Applying Admission application deadline: 9/9 for fall.

Program Contact: Dr. J. M. Stoppard, Dean, University of New Brunswick, PO Box 4400, Fredericton, NB E3B 5A3, Canada. (506) 453-4672; Fax: (506) 453-3561.

Memorial University of Newfoundland

Faculty of Business Administration

St. John's, Newfoundland, Canada

OVERVIEW
Memorial University of Newfoundland is a province-supported coed institution. Founded 1925. Setting: 220-acre urban campus. Total institutional enrollment: 16,000. Program was first offered in 1978.

MBA HIGHLIGHTS
Entrance Difficulty***
Mean GMAT: 570
Mean GPA: 3.0

Cost
Tuition: 697 Canadian dollars/semester
Room & Board: N/R

Enrollment Profile
Full-time: 35
Part-time: 105
Total: 140
Average Age: 28

Work Exp: 85%
Women: 45%
Minorities: N/R

Average Class Size: 20

ACADEMICS
Length of Program Minimum: 24 months. Maximum: 7 years.
Calendar Semesters.

Full-time Classes Main campus, distance learning option; day, evening, summer.

Part-time Classes Main campus, distance learning option; day, evening, summer.

Degree Requirements 22 credits including 7 elective credits.

Required Courses Economics, finance, financial accounting, human resources management, management information systems, management research, management science, management theory, managerial accounting, marketing, organizational behavior, policy, social responsibility of management, statistics.

Curricular Focus General management, strategic analysis and planning, teamwork.

Concentrations Finance, human resources management, international business, management, marketing.

Faculty Full-time: 15, 80% with doctorates; part-time: 5, 20% with doctorates.

Teaching Methodology Case study: 30%, lecture: 40%, research: 5%, seminars by members of the business community: 5%, student presentations: 10%, team projects: 10%.

Special Opportunities International exchange in France, Ireland, United Kingdom.

STUDENT STATISTICS

Geographic Representation Canadian residents 95%.

Undergraduate Majors Business 39%; education 5%; engineering/technology 20%; humanities 2%; nursing 5%; science/mathematics 16%; social sciences 8%; other 5%.

Other Background Graduate degrees in other disciplines: 5%. Work experience: On average, students have 5 years of work experience on entrance to the program.

FACILITIES

Information Resources Main library with 1.2 million bound volumes, 1.6 million titles on microform, 10,353 periodical subscriptions, 10,488 records/tapes/CDs.

Housing 5% of students in program live in college-owned or -operated housing.

Technology Computers are used moderately in course work. 300 computer terminals/PCs are available for use by students in program; they are located in student rooms, the library, the computer center, computer labs. Students in the program are not required to have their own PC.

Computer Resources/On-line Services

Training	Yes	Dun's	Yes $
Internet	Yes	Dow Jones	No
E-Mail	Yes	Dialog	No
LEXIS/NEXIS	No	Bloomberg	No
CompuServe	No		

ADMISSION

Acceptance 1994-95 100 applied for admission; 49% were accepted.

Entrance Requirements Bachelor's degree, GMAT score of 520, minimum 2.75 GPA. Core courses waived through: previous course work.

Application Requirements Copies of transcript, resume/curriculum vitae, personal statement, 3 letters of recommendation.

Application Deadlines 6/15 for fall. Applications are processed on a rolling basis.

FINANCIALS

Costs for 1994-95 Tuition: Full-time: 697 Canadian dollars/semester; Part-time day: 462 Canadian dollars/semester.

Financial Aid In 1994-95, 10% of candidates received some institutionally administered aid in the form of scholarships, fellowships. Total awards ranged from 3,000-4,000 Canadian dollars. Financial aid is not available to part-time students. Application deadline: 9/8 for fall. Contact: Dr. David Stewart, Associate Dean, Elizabeth Avenue, St. John's, NF A1C 5S7, Canada. (709) 737-8522.

INTERNATIONAL STUDENTS

Applying TOEFL required, minimum score of 590. Financial aid is not available to international students. Admission application deadline: 5/15 for fall. Applications are processed on a rolling basis. Contact: Mr. Blair Winsor, Center for International Business, Elizabeth Avenue, St. John's, NF A1C 5S7, Canada. (709) 737-4504.

Program Contact: Dr. David Stewart, Associate Dean, Memorial University of Newfoundland, Elizabeth Avenue, St. John's, NF A1C 5S7, Canada. (709) 737-8522; Fax: (709) 737-2467; Internet Address: davidb@kean.ucs.mun.ca.

Dalhousie University

School of Business Administration

Halifax, Nova Scotia, Canada

OVERVIEW

Dalhousie University is a province-supported coed institution. Founded 1818. Setting: 67-acre urban campus. Total institutional enrollment: 10,910.

MBA HIGHLIGHTS

Entrance Difficulty**

Cost
Tuition: 3,435 Canadian dollars
Room & Board: N/R

Enrollment Profile

Full-time: N/R	Work Exp: N/R
Part-time: N/R	Women: 37%
Total: 195	Minorities: N/R
Average Age: N/R	

Class Size: 12 - 34

ACADEMICS

Length of Program Minimum: 16 months.

Calendar Semesters.

Full-time Classes Main campus; day, evening.

Part-time Classes Main campus; day, evening.

Degree Requirements 23 courses including 8 elective courses.

Curricular Focus General management.

Concentrations Accounting, finance, international business, management, management information systems, marketing.

FACILITIES

Information Resources Main library with 1.2 million bound volumes, 340,000 titles on microform, 8,182 periodical subscriptions, 13,800 records/tapes/CDs, 45 CD-ROMs.

ADMISSION

Entrance Requirements Bachelor's degree, GMAT score of 500, minimum 3.0 GPA.

Application Requirements Application form, copies of transcript, resume/curriculum vitae, personal statement, 2 letters of recommendation.

Application Deadlines 6/1 for fall. Applications are processed on a rolling basis.

FINANCIALS

Costs for 1994-95 Tuition: Full-time: 3,435 Canadian dollars. Fees: Full-time: 229 Canadian dollars.

INTERNATIONAL STUDENTS

Applying TOEFL required, minimum score of 580; proof of adequate funds. Financial aid is not available to international students. Admission application deadline: 4/1 for fall. Applications are processed on a rolling basis.

Program Contact: Mr. Philip Rees, MBA Coordinator, Dalhousie University, Halifax, NS B3H 3J5, Canada. (902) 494-7080; Fax: (902) 494-1107; Internet Address: prees@sbacoop.sba.dal.ca.

Saint Mary's University

Frank H. Sobey Faculty of Commerce

Halifax, Nova Scotia, Canada

OVERVIEW

Saint Mary's University is a province-supported comprehensive coed institution. Founded 1802. Setting: 30-acre urban campus. Total institutional enrollment: 8,000. Program was first offered in 1974.

MBA HIGHLIGHTS

Entrance Difficulty****
Mean GMAT: 580
Mean GPA: N/R

Cost
Tuition: 2,850 Canadian dollars
(Nonresident: 5,100 Canadian dollars)
Room & Board: 4,710 Canadian dollars

Enrollment Profile
Full-time: 175	Work Exp: N/R
Part-time: 125	Women: 40%
Total: 300	Minorities: N/R
Average Age: N/R	

Average Class Size: 20

ACADEMICS
Length of Program Minimum: 16 months.

Calendar Semesters.

Full-time Classes Main campus; day, evening, summer.

Part-time Classes Main campus; day, evening, summer.

Degree Requirements 11 courses including 4 elective courses. Other: Major research project.

Required Courses Business finance, computers in business, economics of the enterprise, economics of the enterprise environment, financial accounting, introduction to decision analysis, marketing management, organizational behavior, strategic management.

Curricular Focus Economic and financial theory, general management, strategic analysis and planning.

Concentrations Accounting, management.

Faculty Full-time: 60, 90% with doctorates; part-time: 10, 50% with doctorates.

Teaching Methodology Case study: 25%, lecture: 15%, research: 10%, seminars by members of the business community: 10%, student presentations: 25%, team projects: 15%.

FACILITIES
Information Resources Main library with 348,110 bound volumes, 393,400 titles on microform, 1,800 periodical subscriptions.

Housing College housing available.

ADMISSION
Entrance Requirements Bachelor's degree, GMAT score.

Application Requirements Written essay, application form, copies of transcript, resume/curriculum vitae.

Application Deadlines 5/31 for fall. Applications are processed on a rolling basis.

FINANCIALS
Costs for 1994-95 Tuition: Full-time: 2,850 Canadian dollars for Canadian residents, 5,100 Canadian dollars for international students; Part-time day: 530 Canadian dollars/course for Canadian residents, 870 Canadian dollars/course for international students. Average room and board costs are 4,710 Canadian dollars per academic year (on-campus) and 5,000 Canadian dollars per academic year (off-campus).

Financial Aid In 1994-95, candidates received some institutionally administered aid in the form of scholarships, assistantships. Financial aid is available to part-time students. Application deadline: 4/1 for fall. Contact: Mr. G. Ferguson, Director of Admissions, Loyola Building, Robie Street, Halifax, NS B3H 3C3, Canada. (902) 420-5414.

INTERNATIONAL STUDENTS
Applying TOEFL required. Admission application deadline: 4/1 for fall.

ALTERNATE MBA PROGRAM
Executive MBA (EMBA) Length of program: Minimum: 16 months. Degree requirements: 11 courses including 3 elective courses.

Program Contact: Dr. Russel Summers, Director, MBA Program, Saint Mary's University, Loyola Building, Robie Street, Halifax, NS B3H 3C3, Canada. (902) 420-5774; Internet Address: rsummers@shark.stmarys.ca.

Carleton University

School of Business

Ottawa, Ontario, Canada

OVERVIEW
Carleton University is a province-supported coed institution. Founded 1942. Setting: 152-acre urban campus. Total institutional enrollment: 21,908.

MBA HIGHLIGHTS

Entrance Difficulty***

Cost
Tuition: 1,325 Canadian dollars/term
(Nonresident: 5,344 Canadian dollars/term)
Room & Board: N/R

Enrollment Profile
Full-time: N/R	Work Exp: N/R
Part-time: N/R	Women: 36%
Total: 55	Minorities: N/R
Average Age: N/R	

Average Class Size: 6

ACADEMICS
Length of Program Minimum: 14 months.

Calendar standard year.

Full-time Classes Main campus; day, early morning.

Degree Requirements 5 courses. Other: Thesis.

Curricular Focus International business, managing diversity, strategic analysis and planning.

Concentrations Finance, international business, management, marketing, research and development administration, information systems, production and operations.

Teaching Methodology Case study: 10%, faculty seminars: 40%, lecture: 10%, research: 10%, seminars by members of the business community: 10%, student presentations: 10%, team projects: 10%.

FACILITIES
Information Resources Main library with 1.5 million bound volumes, 916,973 titles on microform, 12,903 periodical subscriptions, 19,591 records/tapes/CDs, 30 CD-ROMs.

ADMISSION
Entrance Requirements Bachelor's degree, prerequisite courses, GMAT score of 550, minimum 3.0 GPA.

Application Requirements Application form, copies of transcript, personal statement, 2 letters of recommendation.

Application Deadlines 4/1 for fall, 11/1 for winter.

FINANCIALS
Costs for 1994-95 Tuition: Full-time: 1,325 Canadian dollars/term for Canadian residents, 5,344 Canadian dollars/term for nonresidents.

Financial Aid Application deadline: 2/1 for fall. Contact: Mr. Nicholas Papadopoulos, Director, 1125 Colonel By Drive, Ottawa, ON K1S 5B6, Canada. (613) 788-2388.

INTERNATIONAL STUDENTS
Applying TOEFL required, minimum score of 550; proof of adequate funds. Financial aid is available to international students. Financial aid application deadline: 2/1 for fall. Applications are processed on a rolling basis. Admission application deadlines: 6/1 for fall, 11/1 for winter. Applications are processed on a rolling basis.

Program Contact: Mr. Nicholas Papadopoulos, Director, Carleton University, 1125 Colonel By Drive, Ottawa, ON K1S 5B6, Canada. (613) 788-2388; Fax: (613) 788-4427.

Laurentian University

School of Commerce and Administration

Sudbury, Ontario, Canada

OVERVIEW
Laurentian University is a province-supported comprehensive coed institution. Founded 1960. Setting: 700-acre urban campus. Total institutional enrollment: 7,697. Program was first offered in 1983.

MBA HIGHLIGHTS

Entrance Difficulty**
Mean GMAT: 568
Mean GPA: N/R

Cost
Tuition: 3,174 Canadian dollars
(Nonresident: 15,408 Canadian dollars)
Room & Board: 7,200 Canadian dollars

Enrollment Profile

Full-time: 5	Work Exp: 95%
Part-time: 75	Women: 25%
Total: 80	Minorities: N/R
Average Age: N/R	

Average Class Size: 16

ACADEMICS
Length of Program Minimum: 24 months. Maximum: 8 years.
Calendar standard year.
Full-time Classes Main campus; evening, summer.
Part-time Classes Main campus; evening, summer.
Degree Requirements 60 credits including 15 elective credits.
Curricular Focus General management, problem solving and decision making, strategic analysis and planning.
Concentrations Accounting, finance, human resources management, management, marketing, organizational behavior, strategic management.
Faculty Full-time: 17, 60% with doctorates; part-time: 4.
Teaching Methodology Case study: 90%, lecture: 2%, student presentations: 3%, team projects: 5%.
Special Opportunities International exchange in France, Germany, Italy, Spain, United Kingdom.

FACILITIES
Information Resources Main library with 586,336 bound volumes, 269,524 titles on microform, 2,947 periodical subscriptions.
Housing College housing available.
Technology Computers are used moderately in course work. 40 computer terminals/PCs, linked by a campus-wide computer network, are available for use by students in program; they are located in computer labs. Students in the program are not required to have their own PC.
Computer Resources/On-line Services

Training	No	Multimedia Center	Yes
E-Mail	Yes		

ADMISSION
Acceptance 1994-95 65 applied for admission; 25% were accepted.
Entrance Requirements Bachelor's degree, GMAT score of 500, minimum 3.5 GPA (5.0 scale), minimum 2 years of work experience. Core courses waived through: previous course work.
Application Requirements Written essay, application form, copies of transcript, 2 letters of recommendation.
Application Deadline 5/31 for fall.

FINANCIALS
Costs for 1995-96 Tuition: Full-time: 3,174 Canadian dollars for Canadian residents, 15,408 Canadian dollars for international students. Average room and board costs are 7,200 Canadian dollars per academic year (on-campus) and 8,500 Canadian dollars per academic year (off-campus).
Financial Aid In 1994-95, 5% of candidates received some institutionally administered aid in the form of assistantships. Financial aid is not available to part-time students. Application deadline: 8/15 for fall. Contact: Dr. Ozhand Ganjavi, Chair, MBA Program, Ramsey Lake Road, Sudbury, ON P3E 2C6, Canada. (705) 675-1151 Ext. 2138.

INTERNATIONAL STUDENTS
Applying TOEFL required, minimum score of 500. Financial aid is not available to international students. Admission application deadline: 5/31 for fall. Contact: Dr. Ozhand Ganjavi, Chair, MBA Program, Ramsey Lake Road, Sudbury, ON P3E 2C6, Canada. (705) 675-1151 Ext. 2318.

PLACEMENT
Placement services include alumni network, career placement, and electronic job bank.

Program Contact: Dr. Ozhand Ganjavi, Chair, MBA Program, Laurentian University, Ramsey Lake Road, Sudbury, ON P3E 2C6, Canada. (705) 675-1151 Ext. 2138; Fax: (705) 673-6518.

McMaster University

Michael G. DeGroote School of Business

Hamilton, Ontario, Canada

OVERVIEW
McMaster University is a province-supported coed institution. Founded 1887. Setting: 300-acre urban campus with easy access to Toronto. Total institutional enrollment: 16,000. Program was first offered in 1962.

MBA HIGHLIGHTS

Entrance Difficulty***
Mean GMAT: 611
Mean GPA: 2.77

Cost
Tuition: 3,354 Canadian dollars
(Nonresident: 15,408 Canadian dollars)
Room & Board: N/R

Enrollment Profile

Full-time: 310	Work Exp: N/R
Part-time: 214	Women: 31%
Total: 524	Minorities: N/R
Average Age: 28	

Average Class Size: 28

ACADEMICS
Length of Program Minimum: 20 months.
Calendar Trimesters.
Full-time Classes Main campus; day, evening, summer.
Part-time Classes Main campus; evening, summer.
Degree Requirements 20 half-courses including 9 electives.
Required Courses Business policy, economics, economics for management, finance, financial accounting, human resources and labor relations, managerial accounting, marketing, operations, organizational behavior, quantitative analysis, statistical analysis.
Curricular Focus Cooperative work-study, innovation management.
Concentrations Accounting, finance, health services, human resources management, innovation management, international business, management information systems, marketing, operations management, quantitative analysis.
Faculty Full-time: 51, 86% with doctorates; part-time: 18, 50% with doctorates.
Teaching Methodology Case study: 10%, faculty seminars: 4%, lecture: 60%, research: 4%, seminars by members of the business community: 2%, student presentations: 10%, team projects: 10%.
Special Opportunities International exchange in France, Germany, Italy, Norway, Spain, United Kingdom. Other: Cooperative Program.

STUDENT STATISTICS
Geographic Representation Canadian residents 99%.
Undergraduate Majors Business 18%; engineering/technology 21%; humanities 5%; science/mathematics 25%; social sciences 23%; other 8%.

FACILITIES
Information Resources Main library with 1.6 million bound volumes, 1.4 million titles on microform, 13,859 periodical subscriptions, 38,274

records/tapes/CDs, 136 CD-ROMs. Business collection in Innis Library includes 15,500 bound volumes, 550 periodical subscriptions, 5 CD-ROMs.

Housing 3% of students in program live in college-owned or -operated housing. Assistance with housing search provided.

Technology Computers are used moderately in course work. 80 computer terminals/PCs, linked by a campus-wide computer network, are available for use by students in program; they are located in the library, computer labs. Students in the program are not required to have their own PC. 100 Canadian dollars are budgeted per student for computer support.

Computer Resources/On-line Services

Training	Yes	Dun's	No
Internet	Yes	Dow Jones	No
E-Mail	Yes	Dialog	Yes
LEXIS/NEXIS	No	Bloomberg	No
CompuServe	Yes		

Other on-line services: First Search.

ADMISSION

Acceptance 1994-95 450 applied for admission; 63% were accepted.

Entrance Requirements Bachelor's degree, prerequisites may be waived, GMAT score of 500, minimum 3.0 GPA.

Application Requirements Application form, copies of transcript, 2 letters of recommendation, interview and resume for cooperative only.

Application Deadlines 7/15 for fall. Applications are processed on a rolling basis.

FINANCIALS

Costs for 1994-95 Tuition: Full-time: 3,354 Canadian dollars for Canadian residents, 15,408 Canadian dollars for nonresidents; Part-time day: 1,029 Canadian dollars for Canadian residents, 280 Canadian dollars/course for nonresidents. Fees: Full-time: 190 Canadian dollars for Canadian residents, 190 Canadian dollars for nonresidents; Part-time day: 126 Canadian dollars for Canadian residents, 126 Canadian dollars for nonresidents.

Financial Aid In 1994-95, 40% of candidates received some institutionally administered aid in the form of scholarships, loans, assistantships. Total awards ranged from 1,000-10,000 Canadian dollars. Financial aid is not available to part-time students. Application deadline: 5/1 for fall. Contact: Mr. R. Gary Waterfield, Administrator, MBA Program, 1280 Main Street West, Hamilton, ON L8S 4L8, Canada. (905) 525-9140.

INTERNATIONAL STUDENTS

Demographics 3% of students on campus are international; Asia 50%, Europe 14%, Africa 13%, North America 6%, Central America 5%, South America 4%, Australia 2%, other 6%.

Services and Facilities International student center, visa services, language tutoring, ESL courses, special assistance for nonnative speakers of English, counseling/support services.

Applying Financial aid is not available to international students. Admission application deadlines: 5/1 for fall, 4/1 for spring. Applications are processed on a rolling basis. Contact: Mr. Patrick Fernando, International Student's Adviser, Hamilton Hall, Room 405, Hamilton, ON L8S 4L8, Canada. (905) 525-9140.

PLACEMENT

In 1993-94, 60 organizations participated in on-campus recruiting. Placement services include alumni network, career counseling/planning, career fairs, career library, career placement, electronic job bank, job interviews, job search course, resume preparation, and resume referral to employers. Of 1994 graduates, 75% were employed within three months of graduation, the average starting salary was 42,000 Canadian dollars, the range was $29,000-$61,000.

Jobs by Employer Type Manufacturing 30%; service 30%; government 5%; consulting 5%; nonprofit 15%; other 15%.

Jobs by Functional Area Marketing/sales 20%; finance 25%; operations 5%; management 30%; technical management 5%; other 15%.

Program Contact: Mr. R. Gary Waterfield, Administrator, MBA Program, McMaster University, 1280 Main Street West, Hamilton, ON L8S 4M4, Canada. (905) 525-9140; Fax: (905) 521-8632.

Queen's University at Kingston

School of Business

Kingston, Ontario, Canada

OVERVIEW

Queen's University at Kingston is a province-supported coed institution. Founded 1841. Setting: 160-acre urban campus. Total institutional enrollment: 16,500. Program was first offered in 1962.

MBA HIGHLIGHTS

Entrance Difficulty*****
Mean GMAT: 610
Mean GPA: 3.3

Cost
Tuition: N/R
Room & Board: 4,000 Canadian dollars

Enrollment Profile
Full-time: 170
Part-time: 15
Total: 185
Average Age: 27

Work Exp: 95%
Women: 31%
Minorities: 20%

Average Class Size: 50

ACADEMICS

Calendar 12-month program.

Curricular Focus Leadership, strategic analysis and planning, teamwork.

Concentrations Finance, management information systems, marketing, operations management.

Faculty Full-time: 25, 90% with doctorates.

Teaching Methodology Case study: 20%, lecture: 50%, seminars by members of the business community: 10%, student presentations: 5%, team projects: 15%.

Special Opportunities International exchange program available.

STUDENT STATISTICS

Geographic Representation Canadian residents 94%.

Undergraduate Majors Business 5%; engineering/technology 25%; humanities 10%; nursing 2%; science/mathematics 25%; social sciences 33%.

Other Background Graduate degrees in other disciplines: 12%. Work experience: On average, students have 4 years of work experience on entrance to the program.

FACILITIES

Information Resources Main library with 1.9 million bound volumes, 15,000 periodical subscriptions, 7,000 records/tapes/CDs.

Housing 25% of students in program live in college-owned or -operated housing.

Technology Computers are used moderately in course work. Computer terminals/PCs, linked by a campus-wide computer network, are available for use by students in program; they are located in learning resource center, the computer center, computer labs. Students in the program are not required to have their own PC.

Computer Resources/On-line Services

Training	Yes	CompuServe	No
Internet	Yes	Dun's	Yes $
E-Mail	Yes	Dow Jones	Yes $
Videoconference Center	Yes	Dialog	No
Multimedia Center	Yes	Bloomberg	No
LEXIS/NEXIS	Yes $		

ADMISSION

Acceptance 1994-95 600 applied for admission; 33% were accepted.

Entrance Requirements Bachelor's degree, GMAT score of 550, minimum 3.0 GPA, minimum 2 years of work experience.

Application Requirements Written essay, interview, copies of transcript, resume/curriculum vitae, personal statement, 2 letters of recommendation.

Application Deadlines 12/15 for spring. Applications are processed on a rolling basis.

FINANCIALS

Financial Aid In 1994-95, 25% of candidates received some institutionally administered aid in the form of scholarships, fellowships, assistantships. Total awards ranged from 1,000-5,000 Canadian dollars. Financial aid is not available to part-time students. Application deadline: 12/15 for spring. Applications are processed on a rolling basis. Contact: Mr. Thomas Anger, Assistant Chair, MBA Program, Kingston, ON K7L 3N6, Canada. (613) 545-2311.

INTERNATIONAL STUDENTS
Demographics 15% of students on campus are international.

Services and Facilities International student office, international student center, ESL courses.

Applying TOEFL required, minimum score of 600; proof of health; proof of adequate funds. Financial aid is available to international students. Financial aid application deadline: 12/15 for spring. Applications are processed on a rolling basis. Admission application deadline: 12/15 for spring. Contact: Mr. Thomas Anger, Assistant Chair MBA Program, Kingston, ON K7L 3N6, Canada. (613) 545-2311.

PROGRAM
One-Year MBA Length of program: 12 months. Full-time classes: Main campus; day, early morning, summer. Degree requirements: 23 courses including 9 elective courses.

PLACEMENT
In 1993-94, 70 organizations participated in on-campus recruiting. Placement services include alumni network, career counseling/planning, career fairs, career library, career placement, job interviews, resume preparation, and resume referral to employers. Of 1994 graduates, 92% were employed within three months of graduation, the average starting salary was 48,000 Canadian dollars, the range was 35,000-80,000 Canadian dollars.

Program Contact: Mr. Thomas Anger, Assistant Chair, MBA Program, Queen's University at Kingston, Kingston, ON K7L 3N6, Canada. (613) 545-2311; Fax: (613) 545-2013.
See full description on page 812.

University of Ottawa

Faculty of Administration

Ottawa, Ontario, Canada

OVERVIEW
The University of Ottawa is a province-supported coed institution. Founded 1848. Setting: 70-acre urban campus. Total institutional enrollment: 18,000. Program was first offered in 1969.

MBA HIGHLIGHTS
Entrance Difficulty**
Mean GMAT: 600
Mean GPA: N/R

Cost
Tuition: 1,200 - 1,400 Canadian dollars/semester
(Nonresident: 2,700 - 3,500 Canadian dollars/semester)
Room & Board: 3,500 Canadian dollars

Enrollment Profile

Full-time: 238	Work Exp: N/R
Part-time: 476	Women: 45%
Total: 714	Minorities: 5%
Average Age: N/R	

Average Class Size: 35

ACADEMICS
Length of Program Minimum: 24 months.
Calendar Semesters.
Full-time Classes Main campus, distance learning option; day, evening, summer.
Part-time Classes Main campus; day, evening, summer.
Degree Requirements 60 credits.
Curricular Focus Entrepreneurship, international business, leadership, organizational development and change management, strategic analysis and planning.
Concentrations Entrepreneurship, health services, international business, management information systems, public policy, strategic management.
Faculty Full-time: 93, 98% with doctorates; part-time: 20, 95% with doctorates.

Teaching Methodology Case study: 25%, faculty seminars: 10%, lecture: 25%, research: 20%, student presentations: 10%, team projects: 10%.

STUDENT STATISTICS
Geographic Representation Canadian residents 90%.

FACILITIES
Information Resources Main library with 2.2 million bound volumes, 392,424 titles on microform, 10,563 periodical subscriptions, 10,313 records/tapes/CDs, 45 CD-ROMs.
Housing College housing available.

ADMISSION
Acceptance 1994-95 1,068 applied for admission; 25% were accepted.
Entrance Requirements Bachelor's degree, minimum 3.1 GPA. Core courses waived through: previous course work, exams.
Application Requirements Written essay, application form, copies of transcript, resume/curriculum vitae, personal statement, 2 letters of recommendation.
Application Deadlines 3/1 for fall, 11/30 for spring. Applications are processed on a rolling basis.

FINANCIALS
Costs for 1995-96 Tuition: Full-time: 1,200-1,400 Canadian dollars/semester for Canadian residents, 2,700-3,500 Canadian dollars/semester for nonresidents, 4,600-4,800 Canadian dollars/semester for international students. Fees: Full-time: 50-60 Canadian dollars/semester for international students. Average room and board costs are 3,500 Canadian dollars per academic year (on-campus) and 4,200 Canadian dollars per academic year (off-campus).
Financial Aid In 1994-95, 5% of candidates received some institutionally administered aid in the form of grants, scholarships, loans, fellowships, assistantships. Total awards ranged from 5,000-8,000 Canadian dollars. Financial aid is not available to part-time students. Application deadlines: 3/1 for fall, 10/31 for spring. Contact: Ms. Chantal Gendron, Program Coordinator, Awards Office, School of Graduate Studies, Hagan Hall-115 Seraphin Marion, Ottawa, ON K1N 6N5, Canada. (613) 562-5884.

INTERNATIONAL STUDENTS
Demographics 10% of students on campus are international; Europe 35%, Asia 30%, North America 10%, Africa 8%, Central America 5%, South America 5%, Australia 2%, other 5%.

Services and Facilities International student office, international student center, language tutoring, special assistance for nonnative speakers of English, counseling/support services.

Applying Proof of health. Financial aid is not available to international students. Admission application deadlines: 1/13 for fall, 11/30 for spring. Applications are processed on a rolling basis. Contact: Ms. Sylvia Seguin-Jak, Administrator, PO Box 450, Station A, Ottawa, ON K1N 6N5, Canada. (613) 562-3311.

ALTERNATE MBA PROGRAMS
Executive MBA (EMBA)
International MBA Length of program: Minimum: 24 months. Full-time classes: Main campus, Hong Kong, distance learning option; day. Degree requirements: 60 credits. 8 month internship overseas.
MBA/LL B
MBA/LLL

PLACEMENT
Placement services include alumni network, career counseling/planning, career fairs, career library, career placement, electronic job bank, job interviews, job search course, resume preparation, and resume referral to employers.

Program Contact: Ms. Diane Sarrazin, Administrator, University of Ottawa, PO Box 450, Station A, Ottawa, ON K1N 6N5, Canada. (613) 564-3311.
See full description on page 908.

University of Toronto

Faculty of Management

Toronto, Ontario, Canada

OVERVIEW
The University of Toronto is a province-supported coed institution. Founded 1827. Setting: 900-acre urban campus. Total institutional enrollment: 52,818.

ACADEMICS
Calendar standard year.
Concentration Management.

FACILITIES
Information Resources Main library with 7.4 million bound volumes, 3.4 million titles on microform, 28,000 periodical subscriptions, 392,400 records/tapes/CDs.

Program Contact: Ms. Beverly Nicholson, Executive Assistant to the Director and Admissions Coordinator, University of Toronto, 315 Bloor Street West, Toronto, ON M5S 1A1, Canada. (416) 978-6125.

The University of Western Ontario

Western Business School

London, Ontario, Canada

OVERVIEW
The University of Western Ontario is a province-supported coed institution. Founded 1878. Setting: 402-acre suburban campus. Total institutional enrollment: 26,000. Program was first offered in 1948.

MBA HIGHLIGHTS ─────────────

Entrance Difficulty***
Mean GMAT: 628
Mean GPA: 3.04

Cost
Tuition: 3,300 Canadian dollars
(Nonresident: 11,200 Canadian dollars)
Room & Board: 6,000 Canadian dollars

Enrollment Profile

Full-time: 530	Work Exp: 98%
Part-time: 0	Women: 25%
Total: 530	Minorities: N/R
Average Age: 28	

Average Class Size: 50

ACADEMICS
Length of Program Minimum: 20 months. Maximum: 2 years.
Calendar standard year.
Full-time Classes Main campus; day.
Degree Requirements 18 courses.
Required Courses Accounting, communications, economics, finance, information systems, management science, marketing, operations, organizational behavior, policy.
Curricular Focus General management, problem solving and decision making, strategic analysis and planning.
Concentrations Management, marketing.
Faculty Full-time: 69, 99% with doctorates.
Teaching Methodology Case study: 85%, seminars by members of the business community: 10%, student presentations: 5%.
Special Opportunities International exchange in Australia, Austria, Belgium, Brazil, Finland, France, Germany, Hong Kong, Italy, Japan, Mexico, Netherlands, Philippines, Republic of Korea, Singapore, Spain, Sweden, Switzerland.

STUDENT STATISTICS
Geographic Representation Canadian residents 85%.

Undergraduate Majors Business 22%; engineering/technology 24%; humanities 5%; science/mathematics 14%; social sciences 30%; other 5%.
Other Background Graduate degrees in other disciplines: 97%. Work experience: On average, students have 4 years of work experience on entrance to the program.

FACILITIES
Information Resources Main library with 2.1 million bound volumes, 2.9 million titles on microform, 17,300 periodical subscriptions, 34,876 records/tapes/CDs, 35 CD-ROMs. Business collection in Business Library includes 70,000 bound volumes, 1,800 periodical subscriptions, 18 CD-ROMs.
Housing 2% of students in program live in college-owned or -operated housing. Assistance with housing search provided.
Technology Computers are used heavily in course work. 50 computer terminals/PCs are available for use by students in program; they are located in computer labs. Students in the program are not required to have their own PC.

Computer Resources/On-line Services

Training	Yes	Dow Jones	Yes $
Internet	Yes	Dialog	Yes $
E-Mail	Yes	Bloomberg	Yes
LEXIS/NEXIS	Yes		

Other on-line services: OCLC.

ADMISSION
Acceptance 1994-95 600 applied for admission; 33% were accepted.
Entrance Requirements Bachelor's degree, GMAT score of 560, minimum 2.8 GPA, minimum 2 years of work experience.
Application Requirements Written essay, application form, copies of transcript, resume/curriculum vitae, personal statement.
Application Deadlines 5/15 for fall. Applications are processed on a rolling basis.

FINANCIALS
Costs for 1994-95 Tuition: Full-time: 3,300 Canadian dollars for Canadian residents, 11,200 Canadian dollars for international students. Average room and board costs are 6,000 Canadian dollars per academic year (on-campus) and 6,000 Canadian dollars per academic year (off-campus).
Financial Aid In 1994-95, 5% of candidates received some institutionally administered aid in the form of scholarships, loans. Total awards ranged from 1,000-4,500 Canadian dollars. Applications are processed on a rolling basis. Contact: Mrs. Ella Strong, Programs Manager, Western Business School, London, ON N6A 3K7, Canada. (519) 661-3218.

INTERNATIONAL STUDENTS
Demographics 10% of students on campus are international.
Services and Facilities International student office, international student center, language tutoring, ESL courses, counseling/support services.
Applying TOEFL required, minimum score of 600; proof of adequate funds; Test of Spoken English. Financial aid is available to international students. Applications are processed on a rolling basis. Admission application deadline: 4/1 for fall. Applications are processed on a rolling basis. Contact: Mrs. Ella Strong, Programs Manager, Western Business School, London, ON N6A 3K7, Canada. (519) 661-3218.

ALTERNATE MBA PROGRAMS
Executive MBA (EMBA) Length of program: Minimum: 22 months. Full-time classes: Main campus; weekends. Degree requirements: 18 courses.
MBA/LL B

PLACEMENT
In 1993-94, 141 organizations participated in on-campus recruiting; 3,000 on-campus interviews were conducted. Placement services include alumni network, career counseling/planning, career fairs, career library, career placement, job interviews, job search course, and resume preparation. Of 1994 graduates, 81% were employed within three months of graduation; the average starting salary was 56,353 Canadian dollars, the range was $28,000-$162,500 Canadian dollars.

Program Contact: Ms. Larysa Gamula, Admissions Director, The University of Western Ontario, London, ON N6A 5B8, Canada. (519) 661-3212; Fax: (519) 661-3485; Internet Address: 2lgamula@novell. business.uwo.ca.

See full description on page 924.

University of Windsor

Faculty of Business Administration

Windsor, Ontario, Canada

OVERVIEW
The University of Windsor is a province-supported coed institution. Founded 1857. Setting: 125-acre urban campus with easy access to Detroit. Total institutional enrollment: 15,000. Program was first offered in 1963.

MBA HIGHLIGHTS

Entrance Difficulty**
Mean GMAT: 560
Mean GPA: N/R

Cost
Tuition: 990 - 1,485 Canadian dollars/semester
(Nonresident: 4,190 - 4,201 Canadian dollars/semester)
Room & Board: 9,000 Canadian dollars

Enrollment Profile

Full-time: 110	Work Exp: 70%
Part-time: 53	Women: 24%
Total: 163	Minorities: N/R
Average Age: N/R	

Average Class Size: 18

ACADEMICS
Length of Program Minimum: 18 months.
Calendar standard year.
Full-time Classes Main campus; day, evening, summer.
Part-time Classes Main campus; day, evening, summer.
Degree Requirements 70 credit hours including 24 elective credit hours.
Curricular Focus Environment, general management, international business.
Concentrations Entrepreneurship, finance, human resources management, international business, management, management information systems, marketing, operations management, organizational behavior, quantitative analysis, strategic management.
Faculty Full-time: 20, 100% with doctorates; part-time: 4, 25% with doctorates.
Teaching Methodology Case study: 25%, faculty seminars: 30%, lecture: 20%, seminars by members of the business community: 5%, student presentations: 10%, team projects: 10%.
Special Opportunities International exchange in France, Germany, Italy, Spain, United Kingdom. Internship program available.

STUDENT STATISTICS
Geographic Representation Canadian residents 90%.
Other Background Graduate degrees in other disciplines: 5%. Work experience: On average, students have 3 years of work experience on entrance to the program.

FACILITIES
Information Resources Main library with 1.3 million bound volumes, 711,000 titles on microform, 7,000 periodical subscriptions, 20,000 records/tapes/CDs, 12 CD-ROMs.
Housing 10% of students in program live in college-owned or -operated housing.
Technology Computers are used moderately in course work. 500 computer terminals/PCs, linked by a campus-wide computer network, are available for use by students in program; they are located in the student center, classrooms, the computer center, computer labs. Students in the program are not required to have their own PC.

Computer Resources/On-line Services

Training	Yes	Videoconference Center	Yes
E-Mail	Yes	Multimedia Center	Yes

ADMISSION
Acceptance 1994-95 Of those applying, 50% were accepted.
Entrance Requirements Bachelor's degree, GMAT score of 500, minimum 2.7 GPA. Core courses waived through: previous course work.
Application Requirements Application form, copies of transcript, resume/curriculum vitae, 2 letters of recommendation, interview required for cooperative learning students.
Application Deadlines 7/1 for fall. Applications are processed on a rolling basis.

FINANCIALS
Costs for 1994-95 Tuition: Full-time: 990-1,485 Canadian dollars/semester for Canadian residents, 4,190-4,201 Canadian dollars/semester for nonresidents. Average room and board costs are 9,000 Canadian dollars per academic year (on-campus).
Financial Aid In 1994-95, 70% of candidates received some institutionally administered aid in the form of scholarships, loans, assistantships, work-study. Total awards ranged from 1,500-5,000 Canadian dollars. Financial aid is not available to part-time students. Applications are processed on a rolling basis. Contact: Dr. Eric West, Director of MBA Program, Faculty of Business, Windsor, ON N9B 3P4, Canada. (519) 253-4232 Ext. 3118.

INTERNATIONAL STUDENTS
Demographics 3% of students on campus are international.
Services and Facilities International student office, international student center, ESL courses.
Applying TOEFL required, minimum score of 600. Financial aid is available to international students. Applications are processed on a rolling basis. Admission application deadline: 7/1 for fall. Applications are processed on a rolling basis.

PLACEMENT
In 1993-94, 100 organizations participated in on-campus recruiting. Placement services include alumni network, career counseling/planning, career fairs, career library, career placement, job interviews, job search course, resume preparation, and resume referral to employers. Of 1994 graduates, 95% were employed within three months of graduation.

Program Contact: Mr. Guy Allen, Assistant to the Dean, Faculty of Business Administration, University of Windsor, Odetta Building, Windsor, ON N9B 3P4, Canada. (519) 253-4232 Ext. 3097; Fax: (519) 973-7073.

Wilfrid Laurier University

School of Business and Economics

Waterloo, Ontario, Canada

OVERVIEW
Wilfrid Laurier University is a province-supported comprehensive coed institution. Founded 1911. Setting: 40-acre urban campus with easy access to Toronto. Total institutional enrollment: 6,000. Program was first offered in 1976.

MBA HIGHLIGHTS

Entrance Difficulty***
Mean GMAT: 600
Mean GPA: 3.03

Cost
Tuition: 605 - 1,119 Canadian dollars/term
(Nonresident: 3,790 Canadian dollars/term)
Room & Board: N/R

Enrollment Profile

Full-time: N/R	Work Exp: 100%
Part-time: N/R	Women: 25%
Total: 225	Minorities: 7%
Average Age: 27	

Average Class Size: 30

ACADEMICS
Length of Program Minimum: 12 months.
Calendar Semesters.
Full-time Classes Main campus; day, evening, summer.
Degree Requirements 20 half-term courses.
Curricular Focus Teamwork.
Concentrations Accounting, entrepreneurship, finance, human resources management, international business, management, management information systems, marketing, public policy, quantitative analysis, strategic management.
Faculty Full-time: 15, 100% with doctorates.

Teaching Methodology Case study: 65%, faculty seminars: 2%, lecture: 10%, seminars by members of the business community: 2%, student presentations: 10%, team projects: 10%.

Special Opportunities International exchange in Australia, Chile, France, Germany, Japan, Malaysia, Mexico, United Kingdom. Internship program available.

STUDENT STATISTICS

Undergraduate Majors Business 25%; engineering/technology 40%; humanities 3%; science/mathematics 10%; social sciences 20%; other 1%.

Other Background Graduate degrees in other disciplines: 15%. Work experience: On average, students have 7 years of work experience on entrance to the program.

FACILITIES

Information Resources Main library with 570,000 bound volumes, 425,000 titles on microform, 5,000 periodical subscriptions, 11,100 records/tapes/CDs, 20 CD-ROMs.

Housing 10% of students in program live in college-owned or -operated housing.

Technology Computers are used heavily in course work. 50 computer terminals/PCs, linked by a campus-wide computer network, are available for use by students in program; they are located in learning resource center, the library, computer labs. Students in the program are not required to have their own PC. 200 Canadian dollars are budgeted per student for computer support.

Computer Resources/On-line Services

Training	Yes	E-Mail	Yes
Internet	Yes		

ADMISSION

Acceptance 1994-95 240 applied for admission; 33% were accepted.

Entrance Requirements Bachelor's degree, GMAT score of 550, minimum 3.0 GPA. Core courses waived through: previous course work.

Application Requirements Application form, copies of transcript, resume/curriculum vitae, personal statement, 3 letters of recommendation.

Application Deadline 5/1 for fall.

FINANCIALS

Costs for 1994-95 Tuition: Full-time: 605-1,119 Canadian dollars/term for Canadian residents, 3,790 Canadian dollars/term for nonresidents. Fees: Full-time: 351 Canadian dollars for Canadian residents, 351 Canadian dollars for nonresidents.

Financial Aid In 1994-95, 62% of candidates received some institutionally administered aid in the form of scholarships, assistantships. Total awards ranged from 500-5,000 Canadian dollars. Financial aid is available to part-time students. Application deadline: 9/1 for fall. Contact: Dr. Barry McPherson, Dean, Graduate Studies, 75 University Avenue West, Waterloo, ON N2L 3C5, Canada. (519) 884-1970.

INTERNATIONAL STUDENTS

Services and Facilities International student office, international student center, counseling/support services.

Applying TOEFL required, minimum score of 550. Financial aid is available to international students. Financial aid application deadline: 9/1 for fall. Admission application deadline: 5/1 for fall. Applications are processed on a rolling basis. Contact: Dr. Frank Turner, Dean, Faculty of Social Work, 75 University Avenue West, Waterloo, ON N2L 3C5, Canada. (519) 884-1970 Ext. 2205.

PLACEMENT

Placement services include alumni network, career counseling/planning, career fairs, career library, career placement, electronic job bank, job interviews, job search course, resume preparation, and resume referral to employers. Of 1994 graduates, 90% were employed within three months of graduation.

Program Contact: Coordinator, MBA Program, Wilfrid Laurier University, 75 University Avenue West, Waterloo, ON N2L 3C5, Canada. (519) 884-0710 Ext. 2544; Fax: (519) 884-0201.

York University

Faculty of Admnistrative Studies

North York, Ontario, Canada

OVERVIEW

York University is a province-supported coed institution. Founded 1959. Setting: 650-acre urban campus with easy access to Toronto. Total institutional enrollment: 40,000. Program was first offered in 1966.

MBA HIGHLIGHTS

Entrance Difficulty****
Mean GMAT: 600
Mean GPA: 3.2

Cost
Tuition: 1,349 Canadian dollars/semester
(Nonresident: 5,241 Canadian dollars/semester)
Room & Board: 4,400 Canadian dollars

Enrollment Profile

Full-time: N/R	Work Exp: 65%
Part-time: N/R	Women: 30%
Total: 1,500	Minorities: 15%
Average Age: 29	

Class Size: 37 - 55

ACADEMICS

Length of Program Minimum: 16 months.

Calendar Semesters.

Full-time Classes Main campus; day, evening, early morning, summer.

Part-time Classes Main campus; day, evening, summer.

Degree Requirements 60 credits including 27 elective credits.

Required Courses Economic environment of business, financial accounting, information systems, managerial finance, managing in a contemporary context, marketing management, organizational behavior, strategic management, strategy field study.

Curricular Focus International business, managing diversity, teamwork.

Concentrations Accounting, arts administration, business and the environment, business ethics, economics, entrepreneurship, finance, human resources management, international business, management, management information systems, marketing, operations management, organizational behavior, public administration, public policy, quantitative analysis, real estate, strategic management.

Faculty Full-time: 70, 99% with doctorates; part-time: 35, 50% with doctorates.

Teaching Methodology Case study: 50%, lecture: 25%, research: 5%, seminars by members of the business community: 5%, student presentations: 5%, team projects: 10%.

Special Opportunities International exchange in Argentina, Brazil, Chile, France, Germany, Hong Kong, Italy, Japan, Mexico, Norway, People's Republic of China, Republic of Korea, Spain, Thailand, United Kingdom, Venezuela. Internship program available.

STUDENT STATISTICS

Undergraduate Majors Business 30%; engineering/technology 23%; social sciences 23%; other 24%.

Other Background Graduate degrees in other disciplines: 10-15%. Work experience: On average, students have 3 years of work experience on entrance to the program.

FACILITIES

Information Resources Main library with 2 million bound volumes, 1 million titles on microform, 19,000 periodical subscriptions, 36,000 records/tapes/CDs, 31 CD-ROMs.

Housing 30% of students in program live in college-owned or -operated housing.

Technology Computers are used moderately in course work. 60 computer terminals/PCs are available for use by students in program; they are located in computer labs. Students in the program are not required to have their own PC.

Computer Resources/On-line Services

E-Mail   Yes   Dialog   Yes

Other on-line services: Datastar.

ADMISSION

Acceptance 1994-95 2,000 applied for admission; 50% were accepted.

Entrance Requirements GMAT score of 550, minimum 3.0 GPA, applicants without a college degree must have 8-10 years management experience. Core courses waived through: previous course work.

Application Requirements Application form, copies of transcript, resume/curriculum vitae, personal statement, 2 letters of recommendation.

Application Deadlines 5/15 for fall, 10/15 for winter. Applications are processed on a rolling basis.

FINANCIALS

Costs for 1994-95 Tuition: Full-time: 1,349 Canadian dollars/semester for Canadian residents, 5,241 Canadian dollars/semester for international students. Fees: Full-time: 150-300 Canadian dollars/semester for Canadian residents, 150-300 Canadian dollars/semester for international students. Average room and board costs are 4,400 Canadian dollars per academic year (on-campus) and 4,400 Canadian dollars per academic year (off-campus).

Financial Aid Financial aid is not available to part-time students. Application deadlines: 6/15 for fall, 10/15 for winter. Applications are processed on a rolling basis. Contact: Ms. Charmaine Courtis, Director of Student Affairs and International Relations, Faculty of Administrative Studies, North York, ON M3J 1P3, Canada. (416) 786-5059.

INTERNATIONAL STUDENTS

Demographics 15% of students on campus are international; Asia 67%, Australia 10%, Europe 10%, Africa 8%, Central America 1%, South America 1%.

Services and Facilities International student office, international student center, ESL courses, counseling/support services.

Applying TOEFL required, minimum score of 600; IELTS required; health insurance. Financial aid is not available to international students. Admission application deadlines: 5/15 for fall, 10/15 for winter. Applications are processed on a rolling basis. Contact: Ms. Charmaine Courtis, Director, Student Affairs and International Relations, Faculty of Administrative Studies, North York, ON M3J 1P3, Canada. (416) 786-5059.

ALTERNATE MBA PROGRAM

International MBA .

PLACEMENT

In 1993-94, 145 organizations participated in on-campus recruiting; 1,500 on-campus interviews were conducted. Placement services include alumni network, career counseling/planning, career fairs, career library, career placement, electronic job bank, job interviews, job search course, mentor program, resume preparation, and resume referral to employers. Of 1994 graduates, 80% were employed within three months of graduation, the average starting salary was 45,000 Canadian dollars, the range was 24,000-90,000 Canadian dollars.

Jobs by Employer Type Manufacturing 27%; service 21%; government 2%; consulting 3%; nonprofit 2%; financial services 29%; transportation and communications 16%.

Jobs by Functional Area Marketing/sales 35%; finance 38%; operations 7%; technical management 20%.

Program Contact: Ms. Carol Pattenden, Admissions Office, York University, 4700 Keele Street, North York, ON M3J 1P3, Canada. (416) 736-5060; Fax: (416) 736-5087; Internet Address: as000252@orion. yorku.ca.
See full description on page 944.

Concordia University

Faculty of Commerce and Administration

Montreal, Quebec, Canada

OVERVIEW

Concordia University is a province-supported coed institution. Setting: urban campus. Total institutional enrollment: 23,394.

ACADEMICS

Calendar Trimesters.

Degree Requirements 63 credits.

Concentration Management.

FACILITIES

Information Resources Main library with 1.2 million bound volumes, 387,465 titles on microform, 6,070 periodical subscriptions, 35,000 records/tapes/CDs, 27 CD-ROMs.

ADMISSION

Entrance Requirements Bachelor's degree, GMAT score.

Application Requirements Copies of transcript, personal statement.

INTERNATIONAL STUDENTS

Applying TOEFL required.

Program Contact: Mr. Brian Hawker, MBA Director, Concordia University, 1455 de Maisonneuve Boulevard West, Montreal, PQ H3G 1M8, Canada. (514) 848-2700; Fax: (514) 848-2816.

École des Hautes Études Commerciales

School of Business Administration

Montreal, Quebec, Canada

OVERVIEW

École des Hautes Études Commerciales is a province-supported comprehensive coed institution. Part of Université de Montréal. Founded 1910. Setting: 3-acre urban campus. Total institutional enrollment: 8,801. Program was first offered in 1969.

MBA HIGHLIGHTS

Entrance Difficulty**

Cost
Tuition: 62 Canadian dollars/credit
(Nonresident: 255 Canadian dollars/credit)
Room & Board: N/R

Enrollment Profile

Full-time: 109	Work Exp: 95%
Part-time: 676	Women: 38%
Total: 785	Minorities: N/R
Average Age: 33	

Average Class Size: 26

ACADEMICS

Length of Program Minimum: 16 months. Maximum: 6 years.

Calendar Trimesters.

Full-time Classes Main campus; day, evening, weekends, summer.

Part-time Classes Main campus; day, evening, weekends, summer.

Degree Requirements 60 credits including 27 elective credits.

Required Courses Finance, information systems, management, management service, marketing, microeconomics, organizational behavior, personal administration and labor relations, production and operations management.

Curricular Focus General management, problem solving and decision making, teamwork.

Concentrations Finance, human resources management, international business, management information systems, marketing, operations management, project management.

Faculty Full-time: 79, 60% with doctorates; part-time: 37.

Teaching Methodology Case study: 45%, lecture: 30%, seminars by members of the business community: 5%, student presentations: 10%, team projects: 10%.

Special Opportunities International exchange in Belgium, Finland, France, Mexico, Spain, Switzerland, United Kingdom.

STUDENT STATISTICS

Geographic Representation Canadian residents 98%.

Undergraduate Majors Business 100%.

Other Background Graduate degrees in other disciplines: 15%. Work experience: On average, students have 8 years of work experience on entrance to the program.

FACILITIES

Information Resources Main library with 313,000 bound volumes, 4,100 titles on microform, 7,100 periodical subscriptions, 18 CD-ROMs.

Housing College housing available.

Technology Computers are used heavily in course work. 160 computer terminals/PCs, linked by a campus-wide computer network, are available for use by students in program; they are located in the library, computer labs, the research center. Students in the program are not required to have their own PC.

Computer Resources/On-line Services

Training	No	Dun's	No
Internet	Yes	Dow Jones	No
E-Mail	Yes	Dialog	No
LEXIS/NEXIS	No	Bloomberg	No
CompuServe	No		

ADMISSION

Acceptance 1994-95 359 applied for admission; 55% were accepted.

Entrance Requirements Bachelor's degree, GMAT score of 550, minimum 2.8 GPA, minimum 2 years of work experience. Core courses waived through: previous course work, work experience.

Application Requirements Written essay, application form, copies of transcript, resume/curriculum vitae, 3 letters of recommendation.

Application Deadlines 4/1 for fall, 10/1 for winter.

FINANCIALS

Costs for 1994-95 Tuition: Full-time: 62 Canadian dollars/credit for Canadian residents, 255 Canadian dollars/credit for international students. Fees: Full-time: 36 Canadian dollars/trimester for Canadian residents, 298 Canadian dollars/trimester for international students.

Financial Aid In 1994-95, candidates received some institutionally administered aid in the form of grants, scholarships, loans. Financial aid is not available to part-time students. Application deadlines: 6/30 for fall, 1/31 for winter. Contact: Mr. Robert Bonneau, Director of Student Services, 5255 Avenue Decelles, Montreal, PQ H3T 1V6, Canada. (514) 340-6166.

INTERNATIONAL STUDENTS

Demographics 4% of students on campus are international; Europe 50%, Africa 42%, South America 4%, Asia 2%, Central America 1%, North America 1%, Other 1%.

Services and Facilities International student office, international student center, visa services, language tutoring, special assistance for nonnative speakers of English, counseling/support services.

Applying Proof of health; proof of adequate funds. Financial aid is not available to international students. Admission application deadlines: 4/1 for fall, 10/1 for winter. Contact: Mr. Michel Lemay, International and Exchange Students Adviser, 5255 Avenue Decelles, Montreal, PQ H3T 1V6, Canada. (514) 340-6327.

PLACEMENT

In 1993-94, 150 organizations participated in on-campus recruiting. Placement services include alumni network, career counseling/planning, career fairs, career library, career placement, job interviews, job search course, resume preparation, and resume referral to employers. Of 1994 graduates, 90% were employed within three months of graduation, the average starting salary was 55,000 Canadian dollars.

Jobs by Employer Type Manufacturing 28%; government 3%; consulting 18%; financial services 14%; education/health 11%; communications 9%; other 17%.

Jobs by Functional Area Marketing/sales 20%; finance 14%; operations 3%; management 14%; technical management 16%; other 25%; human resources 8%.

Program Contact: Mrs. Diane St. Pierre, MBA Program Students Adviser, École des Hautes Études Commerciales, 5255 Avenue Decelles, Montreal, PQ H3T 1V6, Canada. (514) 340-6136; Fax: (514) 340-5640.
See full description on page 728.

McGill University

Faculty of Management

Montreal, Quebec, Canada

OVERVIEW

McGill University is a province-supported coed institution. Founded 1821. Setting: 80-acre urban campus. Total institutional enrollment: 31,742. Program was first offered in 1963.

MBA HIGHLIGHTS

Entrance Difficulty****
Mean GMAT: 611
Mean GPA: 3.32

Cost
Tuition: 1,900 - 2,000 Canadian dollars
(Nonresident: 8,250 - 8,500 Canadian dollars)
Room & Board: 6,000 Canadian dollars   (off-campus)

Enrollment Profile

Full-time: 271	Work Exp: 86%
Part-time: 380	Women: 30%
Total: 651	Minorities: N/R
Average Age: 26	

Average Class Size: N/R

ACADEMICS

Length of Program Minimum: 24 months. Maximum: 2 years.

Calendar trimester in first year/two semesters in second year.

Full-time Classes Main campus; day, evening.

Part-time Classes Main campus; evening.

Degree Requirements 60 credits including 30 elective credits.

Required Courses Accounting, finance, human resources management, information systems, international environment, management statistics, managerial economics, marketing, operations management, organizational behavior, organizational strategy, research engineering development, topical course.

Curricular Focus International business, problem solving and decision making, teamwork.

Concentrations Accounting, entrepreneurship, finance, human resources management, international business, management, management information systems, marketing, operations management, organizational behavior, production management, quantitative analysis, strategic management.

Faculty Full-time: 40, 95% with doctorates; part-time: 43, 5% with doctorates.

Teaching Methodology Case study: 25%, independent research: 5%, lecture: 40%, student presentations: 10%, team projects: 20%.

Special Opportunities International exchange in Belgium, Brazil, Denmark, France, Germany, Italy, Mexico, Netherlands, Pakistan, Philippines, Spain, Sweden, Thailand, United Kingdom, United States of America.

STUDENT STATISTICS

Geographic Representation Canadian residents 75%.

Undergraduate Majors Business 32%; engineering/technology 16%; science/mathematics 24%; social sciences 23%; other 5%.

Other Background Graduate degrees in other disciplines: 7%. Work experience: On average, students have 3 years of work experience on entrance to the program.

FACILITIES

Information Resources Main library with 2.7 million bound volumes, 1 million titles on microform, 18,524 periodical subscriptions, 26,564 records/tapes/CDs, 792 CD-ROMs. Business collection in Howard Ross Management Library includes 80,000 bound volumes, 651 periodical subscriptions, 10 CD-ROMs.

Housing College housing not available.

Technology Computers are used moderately in course work. 500 computer terminals/PCs, linked by a campus-wide computer network, are available for use by students in program; they are located in student rooms, the student center, classrooms, the library, the computer center, computer labs. Students in the program are not required to have their own PC. 1,000 Canadian dollars are budgeted per student for computer support.

Computer Resources/On-line Services

Training	Yes	Dun's	No
Internet	Yes	Dow Jones	No
E-Mail	Yes	Dialog	Yes $
LEXIS/NEXIS	No	Bloomberg	No
CompuServe	No		

ADMISSION
Acceptance 1994-95 530 applied for admission; 49% were accepted.

Entrance Requirements Bachelor's degree, GMAT score of 550, minimum 3.0 GPA, minimum 1 year of work experience.

Application Requirements Written essay, application form, copies of transcript, resume/curriculum vitae, 2 letters of recommendation.

Application Deadlines 6/1 for fall. Applications are processed on a rolling basis.

FINANCIALS
Costs for 1994-95 Tuition: Full-time: 1,900-2,000 Canadian dollars for Canadian residents, 8,250-8,500 Canadian dollars for international students; Part-time day: 69-150 Canadian dollars/credit for Canadian residents, 260-343 Canadian dollars/credit for international students. Fees: Full-time: 89 Canadian dollars/term for Canadian residents, 653 Canadian dollars for international students. Average room and board costs are 6,000 Canadian dollars per academic year (off-campus).

Financial Aid In 1994-95, candidates received some institutionally administered aid in the form of grants, scholarships, fellowships, assistantships, term fee waivers. Total awards ranged from 1,000-7,500 Canadian dollars. Financial aid is not available to part-time students. Contact: Ms. Antoinette Molino, Admissions Assistant, 1001 Sherbrooke Street West, Montreal, PQ H3A 2T5, Canada. (514) 398-4066.

INTERNATIONAL STUDENTS
Demographics 12% of students on campus are international; Asia 24%, North America 24%, Europe 21%, Africa 8%, South America 5%, other 18%.

Services and Facilities International student office, international student center.

Applying TOEFL required, minimum score of 600; proof of health; proof of adequate funds. Financial aid is available to international students. Financial aid application deadline: 6/1 for fall. Admission application deadline: 4/15 for fall. Applications are processed on a rolling basis. Contact: Mr. Lawrence Lainey, International Student Adviser, 3637 Peal Street, Montreal, PQ H3A 1X1, Canada. (514) 398-6015.

ALTERNATE MBA PROGRAMS
MBA/Diploma Length of program: Minimum: 24 months. Maximum: 2 years. Full-time classes: Main campus; day. Degree requirements: 84 credits. One level of Chinese or Japanese language. Diploma is in Asian studies.

MBA/LL B Length of program: Minimum: 36 months. Maximum: 4 years. Full-time classes: Main campus; day. Degree requirements: 180 credits including 30 elective credits. Working knowledge of French.

PLACEMENT
In 1993-94, 191 organizations participated in on-campus recruiting; 342 on-campus interviews were conducted. Placement services include alumni network, career counseling/planning, career fairs, career library, career placement, job interviews, job search course, resume preparation, and resume referral to employers. Of 1994 graduates, the average starting salary was 48,500 Canadian dollars, the range was 32,000-125,000 Canadian dollars.

Jobs by Employer Type Manufacturing 40%; service 40%; consulting 10%; other 10%.

Jobs by Functional Area Marketing/sales 25%; finance 30%; management 16%; consulting 10%; other 19%.

Program Contact: Ms. Antoinette Molino, Admissions Assistant, McGill University, 1001 Sherbrooke Street West, Montreal, PQ H3A 2T5, Canada. (514) 398-4066; Fax: (514) 398-2499.
See full description on page 780.

Université de Sherbrooke

Faculty of Administration

Sherbrooke, Quebec, Canada

OVERVIEW
The Université de Sherbrooke is an independent nonprofit coed institution. Founded 1954. Setting: 800-acre urban campus with easy access to Montreal. Total institutional enrollment: 20,864.

ACADEMICS
Calendar standard year.

Concentration Management.

FACILITIES
Information Resources Main library with 1.2 million bound volumes, 237,000 titles on microform, 5,937 periodical subscriptions, 11,800 records/tapes/CDs.

Program Contact: Ms. Chantel Roy, Director of MBA, Université de Sherbrooke, 1150 University Boulevard, Sherbrooke, PQ J1K 2R1, Canada. (819) 821-7333.

Université du Québec à Montréal

École des Sciences de la Gestion

Montreal, Quebec, Canada

OVERVIEW
The Université du Québec à Montréal is a province-supportedcoed institution. Part of Université du Québec. Founded 1969. Setting: urban campus. Total institutional enrollment: 41,057.

MBA HIGHLIGHTS
Entrance Difficulty***

Cost
Tuition: 1,800 Canadian dollars
(Nonresident: 8,000 Canadian dollars)
Room & Board: N/R

Enrollment Profile

Full-time: N/R	Work Exp: N/R
Part-time: N/R	Women: 40%
Total: 250	Minorities: N/R
Average Age: N/R	

Average Class Size: 30

ACADEMICS
Length of Program Minimum: 24 months.

Calendar Trimesters.

Full-time Classes Main campus; day, evening, weekends.

Part-time Classes Main campus; day, evening, weekends.

Degree Requirements 60 credits.

Curricular Focus Problem solving and decision making, strategic analysis and planning, teamwork.

Concentrations Finance, human resources management, international business, management, management information systems, marketing, operations management, organizational behavior, real estate, strategic management.

FACILITIES
Information Resources Main library with 1.4 million bound volumes, 10,296 periodical subscriptions.

ADMISSION
Entrance Requirements Bachelor's degree, minimum 3.2 GPA.

Application Requirements Application form, copies of transcript, 3 letters of recommendation.

Application Deadline 3/1 for fall.

FINANCIALS
Costs for 1994-95 Tuition: Full-time: 1,800 Canadian dollars for Canadian residents, 8,000 Canadian dollars for nonresidents.

Financial Aid Contact: MBA Program Director, CP 8888, Succursale Centre-ville, Montreal, PQ H3C 3P8, Canada. (514) 987-3000.

INTERNATIONAL STUDENTS
Applying Proof of adequate funds; working knowledge of French for visa purposes.

ALTERNATE MBA PROGRAM
Executive MBA (EMBA) Length of program: Minimum: 12 months. Full-time classes: Main campus; day, weekends, summer. Degree requirements: 45 credits. 4-5 years previous work experience. Languages: French.

Program Contact: Ms. Carole Lamoureaux, MBA Director, Université du Québec à Montréal, CP 8888, Succursale Centre-ville, Montreal, PQ H3C 3P8, Canada. (514) 987-4448; Fax: (514) 987-7728.

Université Laval

Faculté des Sciences de l'Administration

Sainte-Foy, Quebec, Canada

OVERVIEW
The Université Laval is an independent nonprofit coed institution. Founded 1852. Setting: 465-acre suburban campus. Total institutional enrollment: 34,000. Program was first offered in 1968.

MBA HIGHLIGHTS

Entrance Difficulty***

Cost
Tuition: 667 Canadian dollars/semester
(Nonresident: 3,728 Canadian dollars/semester)
Room & Board: N/R

Enrollment Profile

Full-time: 360	Work Exp: 60%
Part-time: 327	Women: 35%
Total: 687	Minorities: 5%
Average Age: 25	

Average Class Size: 25

ACADEMICS
Length of Program Minimum: 16 months. Maximum: 4 years.
Calendar Semesters.
Full-time Classes Main campus; day, evening.
Part-time Classes Main campus; day, evening.
Degree Requirements 45 credits.
Curricular Focus Business issues and problems, problem solving and decision making, teamwork.
Concentrations Accounting, economics, finance, health services, international business, management, management information systems, marketing, operations management, quantitative analysis.
Faculty Full-time: 60, 90% with doctorates; part-time: 5, 20% with doctorates.
Teaching Methodology Case study: 20%, lecture: 40%, research: 10%, seminars by members of the business community: 5%, student presentations: 15%, team projects: 10%.
Special Opportunities International exchange in Belgium, France, Sweden, United Kingdom, United States of America.

STUDENT STATISTICS
Undergraduate Majors Business 15%; education 10%; engineering/technology 15%; humanities 15%; nursing 10%; science/mathematics 10%; social sciences 15%; other 10%.
Other Background Work experience: On average, students have 3 years of work experience on entrance to the program.

FACILITIES
Information Resources Main library with 1.9 million bound volumes, 49,400 titles on microform, 16,975 periodical subscriptions, 17,900 records/tapes/CDs, 53 CD-ROMs.
Housing 5% of students in program live in college-owned or -operated housing. Assistance with housing search provided.
Technology 150 computer terminals/PCs, linked by a campus-wide computer network, are available for use by students in program; they are located in computer labs. Students in the program are not required to have their own PC.

Computer Resources/On-line Services

Training	Yes	CompuServe	No
Internet	Yes	Dun's	No
E-Mail	Yes	Dow Jones	No
Multimedia Center	Yes	Dialog	No
LEXIS/NEXIS	No	Bloomberg	No

ADMISSION
Acceptance 1994-95 600 applied for admission; 50% were accepted.
Entrance Requirements Bachelor's degree, minimum 3.2 GPA, minimum 2 years of work experience.
Application Requirements Application form, copies of transcript, resume/curriculum vitae, 3 letters of recommendation.
Application Deadlines 3/1 for fall, 9/1 for spring. Applications are processed on a rolling basis.

FINANCIALS
Costs for 1994-95 Tuition: Full-time: 667 Canadian dollars/semester for Canadian residents, 3,728 Canadian dollars/semester for nonresidents. Fees: Full-time: 131 Canadian dollars for Canadian residents, 131 Canadian dollars for nonresidents.
Financial Aid Financial aid is not available to part-time students. Application deadlines: 3/1 for fall, 9/1 for spring. Contact: Mr. Claude Dufour, Service des Bourses et de L'Aide Financiere, Cité Universitaire, Québec, PQ G1K 7P4, Canada. (418) 656-3332.

INTERNATIONAL STUDENTS
Services and Facilities International student office, language tutoring.
Applying Proof of health; proof of adequate funds. Financial aid is not available to international students. Admission application deadlines: 3/1 for fall, 9/1 for spring. Contact: Mr. Quy Tram Do, Cité Universitaire, Québec, PQ G1K 7P4, Canada. (418) 656-8851.

PLACEMENT
Placement services include career placement.

Program Contact: Mr. Albert Wilhemy, Director of the MBA Program, Université Laval, Cité Universitaire, Québec, PQ G1K 7P4, Canada. (418) 656-2726; Fax: (418) 656-2624.

University of Saskatchewan

College of Commerce

Saskatoon, Saskatchewan, Canada

OVERVIEW
The University of Saskatchewan is a province-supported coed institution. Founded 1907. Setting: 363-acre urban campus. Total institutional enrollment: 17,000. Program was first offered in 1968.

MBA HIGHLIGHTS

Entrance Difficulty***
Mean GMAT: 550
Mean GPA: N/R

Cost
Tuition: 3,038 Canadian dollars
(Nonresident: 3,038 Canadian dollars)
Room & Board: N/R

Enrollment Profile

Full-time: 45	Work Exp: 70%
Part-time: 75	Women: 30%
Total: 120	Minorities: 20%
Average Age: 28	

Average Class Size: 25

ACADEMICS
Length of Program Minimum: 16 months. Maximum: 5 years.
Calendar Semesters.
Full-time Classes Main campus; day, evening, early morning, summer.
Part-time Classes Main campus; day, evening, early morning, summer.
Degree Requirements 51-60 credits including 9-18 elective credits.
Required Courses Business policy and strategy, business policy simulation, economic environment in business, financial accounting, financial management, industrial relations, management accounting, management

information systems, managerial economics, marketing management, organizational behavior, production and operation management, quantitative methods.

Curricular Focus General management.

Concentration Management.

Faculty Full-time: 17, 94% with doctorates; part-time: 5, 20% with doctorates.

Teaching Methodology Case study: 40%, lecture: 35%, research: 8%, seminars by members of the business community: 2%, student presentations: 5%, team projects: 10%.

STUDENT STATISTICS

Undergraduate Majors Business 29%; education 2%; engineering/technology 8%; humanities 14%; nursing 3%; science/mathematics 25%; social sciences 16%; other 3%.

Other Background Graduate degrees in other disciplines: 2%. Work experience: On average, students have 6 years of work experience on entrance to the program.

FACILITIES

Information Resources Main library with 1.5 million bound volumes, 1.7 million titles on microform, 9,395 periodical subscriptions, 28,300 records/tapes/CDs, 42 CD-ROMs.

Technology Computers are used heavily in course work. 100 computer terminals/PCs, linked by a campus-wide computer network, are available for use by students in program; they are located in the library, computer labs, student study carrels. Students in the program are not required to have their own PC.

Computer Resources/On-line Services

Internet	Yes $	E-Mail	Yes

ADMISSION

Acceptance 1994-95 160 applied for admission; 62% were accepted.

Entrance Requirements Bachelor's degree, GMAT score. Core courses waived through: previous course work.

Application Requirements Application form, copies of transcript, 3 letters of recommendation.

Application Deadlines 6/30 for fall, 10/30 for spring. Applications are processed on a rolling basis.

FINANCIALS

Costs for 1994-95 Tuition: Full-time: 3,038 Canadian dollars for Canadian residents, 3,038 Canadian dollars for international students. Fees: Full-time: 214 Canadian dollars for Canadian residents, 314 Canadian dollars for international students.

Financial Aid In 1994-95, 5% of candidates received some institutionally administered aid in the form of scholarships, fellowships. Total awards ranged from 7,900-8,100 Canadian dollars. Financial aid is not available to part-time students. Application deadline: 2/15 for fall. Contact: Mr. Doug Bicknell, Assistant Dean, College of Commerce, 25 Campus Drive, Saskatoon, SK S7N 5A7, Canada. (306) 966-4785.

INTERNATIONAL STUDENTS

Demographics 6% of students on campus are international.

Services and Facilities International student office, international student center, ESL courses.

Applying TOEFL required, minimum score of 550. Financial aid is available to international students. Financial aid application deadline: 2/15 for fall. Admission application deadlines: 6/15 for fall, 11/1 for spring. Applications are processed on a rolling basis. Contact: Mr. Kurt Tichler, International Student Adviser, Room 60, Place Riel Campus Centre, 1 Campus Drive, Saskatoon, SK S7N 5A3, Canada. (306) 966-4923.

PLACEMENT

Placement services include alumni network, career counseling/planning, career fairs, career library, career placement, resume preparation, and resume referral to employers. Of 1994 graduates, 80% were employed within three months of graduation.

Program Contact: Mr. Doug Bicknell, Assistant Dean, University of Saskatchewan, College of Commerce, 25 Campus Drive, Saskatoon, SK S7N 5A2, Canada. (306) 966-4785.

CAYMAN ISLANDS

International College of the Cayman Islands

Newlands, Grand Cayman, Cayman Islands

OVERVIEW

International College of the Cayman Islands is an independent nonprofit comprehensive coed institution. Founded 1970. Setting: 3-acre rural campus. Total institutional enrollment: 519. Program was first offered in 1993.

MBA HIGHLIGHTS

Entrance Difficulty***

Cost $
Tuition: $88/quarter hour
Room & Board: $1,406

Enrollment Profile

Full-time: 9	Work Exp: 100%
Part-time: 7	Women: 50%
Total: 16	
Average Age: N/R	

Average Class Size: 15

ACADEMICS

Length of Program Minimum: 18 months.

Calendar Quarters.

Full-time Classes Main campus, Miami Center; evening, weekends, summer.

Part-time Classes Main campus, Miami Center.

Degree Requirements 60 credits including 5 elective credits. Other: Comprehensive exam.

Required Courses Accounting for executives, computer applications, environment of business, financial management, human resources management, management communications, management policy, managerial economics, marketing management, organization behavior and development, research methodology.

Curricular Focus Business issues and problems, general management, international business.

Faculty Full-time: 3, 100% with doctorates; part-time: 5, 40% with doctorates.

Teaching Methodology Case study: 22%, computer lab: 5%, lecture: 30%, research: 13%, seminars by members of the business community: 5%, student presentations: 17%, team projects: 8%.

Special Opportunities Internships include managerial traineeship.

STUDENT STATISTICS

Other Background Graduate degrees in other disciplines: 13%.

FACILITIES

Information Resources Main library with 30,000 bound volumes, 5,504 titles on microform, 231 periodical subscriptions, 7,000 records/tapes/CDs, 2 CD-ROMs.

Housing 6% of students in program live in college-owned or -operated housing.

Technology Computers are used moderately in course work. 18 computer terminals/PCs are available for use by students in program; they are located in learning resource center, computer labs. Students in the program are not required to have their own PC.

Computer Resources/On-line Services

Training	Yes	Multimedia Center	Yes
E-Mail	No		

ADMISSION

Acceptance 1994-95 Of those applying, 60% were accepted.

Entrance Requirements First degree, prerequisite courses required for applicants with non-business degree. Core courses waived through: previous course work.

Application Requirements Application form, copies of transcript, 3 letters of recommendation.

Application Deadlines 6/5 for fall, 9/9 for winter, 12/3 for spring, 3/2 for summer. Applications are processed on a rolling basis.

FINANCIALS
Costs for 1994-95 Tuition: Full-time: $88/quarter hour. Fees: Full-time: $56-$113/quarter. Average room and board costs are $1,406 per academic year (on-campus).

Financial Aid In 1994-95, 13% of candidates received some institutionally administered aid in the form of grants, loans, work-study. Financial aid is available to part-time students. Application deadlines: 8/5 for fall, 3/3 for spring, 5/25 for summer. Applications are processed on a rolling basis. Contact: Dr. Elsa Cummings, President, PO Box 136, Savannah Post Office, Newlands, Grand Cayman, Cayman Islands. (809) 947-1100.

INTERNATIONAL STUDENTS
Demographics 40% of students on campus are international.

Services and Facilities ESL courses, counseling/support services.

Applying Proof of health; proof of adequate funds. Financial aid is available to international students. Applications are processed on a rolling basis. Admission application deadlines: 6/5 for fall, 9/9 for winter, 12/3 for spring, 3/2 for summer. Applications are processed on a rolling basis.

PLACEMENT
Placement services include alumni network, career counseling/planning, career library, career placement, job interviews, and resume referral to employers.

Program Contact: Dr. Eileen Dounce, Director of Graduate Studies, International College of the Cayman Islands, PO Box 136, Savannah Post Office, Newlands, Grand Cayman, Cayman Islands. (809) 947-1100; Fax: (809) 947-1210.

COSTA RICA

Instituto Centroamericano de Administración de Empresas

La Garita, Alajuela, Costa Rica

OVERVIEW
Instituto Centroamericano de Administración de Empresas is an independent nonprofit graduate-only specialized coed institution. Founded 1964. Setting: suburban campus. Total institutional enrollment: 510. Accredited by American Association of Collegiate Schools of Business (AACSB).

MBA HIGHLIGHTS

Entrance Difficulty***
Mean GMAT: 550
Mean GPA: N/R

Cost $$
Tuition: $8,450
Room & Board: $2,675

Enrollment Profile
Full-time: 380
Part-time: 130
Total: 510
Average Age: 26

Work Exp: 95%
Women: 22%

Average Class Size: N/R

ACADEMICS
Length of Program Minimum: 18 months. Maximum: 2 years.

Calendar Trimesters.

Full-time Classes Main campus; day.

Required Courses Advanced control, advanced marketing, business finance, business strategy, control, decision making and case analysis, finance, human resources management, macro field project, macroeconomics, managerial processes, manufacturing strategy, marketing, microeconomics, organization, political analysis, production, quantitative methods.

Concentrations Economics, management, natural resource management, industry and technology management.

Special Opportunities International exchange in Spain, United States of America.

STUDENT STATISTICS
Geographic Representation South America 50%; Central America 48%; North America 2%.

Undergraduate Majors Business 100%.

Other Background Graduate degrees in other disciplines: 5%. Work experience: On average, students have 4 years of work experience on entrance to the program.

FACILITIES
Housing 98% of students in program live in college-owned or -operated housing. Assistance with housing search provided.

Technology Computers are used heavily in course work. 16 computer terminals/PCs are available for use by students in program; they are located in computer labs. Students in the program are not required to have their own PC.

Computer Resources/On-line Services
Training   Yes   E-Mail   No

ADMISSION
Entrance Requirements First degree, minimum 1 year of work experience, fluency in Spanish.

Application Requirements Written essay, interview, application form, copies of transcript.

Application Deadlines 6/16 for fall. Applications are processed on a rolling basis.

FINANCIALS
Estimated Costs for 1995-96 Tuition: Full-time: $8,450. Fees: Full-time: $1,300. Average room and board costs are $2,675 per academic year (on-campus) and $2,675 per academic year (off-campus).

Financial Aid In 1994-95, 10% of candidates received some institutionally administered aid in the form of scholarships, loans, case writing. Total awards ranged from $4,500-$9,500. Financial aid is not available to part-time students. Application deadline: 6/16 for fall. Contact: Ms. Blanca Ramirez, Administrative Director, Master's Programs, Apartado Postal 960-4050, La Garita, Alajuela, Costa Rica. 443-0506.

INTERNATIONAL STUDENTS
Services and Facilities International student office, visa services, language tutoring, ESL courses.

Applying Proof of health; proof of adequate funds. Financial aid is available to international students. Financial aid application deadline: 6/16 for spring. Admission application deadline: 6/16 for fall. Applications are processed on a rolling basis. Contact: Ms. Blanca Ramirez, Administrative Director, Master's Programs, Apartado Postal 960-4050, La Garita, Alajuela, Costa Rica. 443-0506.

ALTERNATE MBA PROGRAM
Executive MBA (EMBA) Length of program: Minimum: 16 months. Part-time classes: Main campus. Languages: Spanish.

PLACEMENT
In 1993-94, 50 organizations participated in on-campus recruiting; 20 on-campus interviews were conducted. Placement services include alumni network, career library, career placement, electronic job bank, job interviews, job search course, resume preparation, and resume referral to employers. Of 1994 graduates, 100% were employed within three months of graduation.

Program Contact: Dr. Roberto Artavia, Dean of Graduate Programs, Instituto Centroamericano de Administración de Empresas, Apartado Postal 960-4050, La Garita, Alajuela, Costa Rica. 443-0506.

CZECH REPUBLIC

Czechoslovak Management Center

Business School

Celákovice, Czech Republic

OVERVIEW
Czechoslovak Management Center is graduate-only coed institution. MBA programs offered jointly with University of Pittsburgh, Wilfred Laurier University, Tulane University, University of Arizona, Windsor University, Univeristy of Manitoba. Founded 1970. Setting: small-town campus. Total

institutional enrollment: 48. Program was first offered in 1991.

MBA HIGHLIGHTS

Entrance Difficulty**
Mean GMAT: 550
Mean GPA: N/R

Cost
Tuition: 40,000 koruny/term
(Nonresident: 55,000 koruny/term)
Room & Board: N/R

Enrollment Profile

Full-time: 24	Work Exp: 80%
Part-time: 24	Women: 13%
Total: 48	
Average Age: 27	

Average Class Size: 28

The Czechoslovak Management Center (CMC) M.B.A. is a one-year program that offers a variety of completion options. Students may conclude their studies either at CMC with a focus on Central European management issues or complete one or two semesters abroad at one of CMC's American, Canadian, or West European affiliated schools.

CMC's permanent faculty members, who teach in tandem with visiting Western professors, bring their perspectives on management in Central Europe to the classroom. Team teaching, field trips and presentations, team projects, computer simulations, multidisciplinary case studies, and completion options abroad make the CMC M.B.A. degree a unique educational experience. CMC's M.B.A. courses emphasize interpersonal skills, teamwork, and real-world problems.

CMC is situated in a quiet and peaceful location in Ćel kovice, a small town next to the Elbe River, 20 kilometers northeast of Prague. Students are able to concentrate on their studies at CMC, where all resources are available under one roof.

CMC is proud of its recognition in 1993 as a Center of Excellence by the United States government and welcomes applicants to its M.B.A. program who share a commitment to excellence and seek a rewarding career in business management.

ACADEMICS

Length of Program Minimum: 36 months.

Calendar Modular.

Part-time Classes Main campus; weekends.

Degree Requirements 51 credits. Other: Summer project.

Required Courses Economic analysis, financial accounting, financial management, human resources, introduction to global business, management information systems, managerial accounting, marketing, marketing skills development, operations management, organizational behavior, organizational transformation, statistical analysis.

Curricular Focus Economic and financial theory, general management, international business.

Concentrations Accounting, economics, human resources management, international business, management information systems, marketing, operations management, strategic management.

Faculty Full-time: 10, 90% with doctorates; part-time: 1, 100% with doctorates.

Teaching Methodology Case study: 5%, lecture: 60%, seminars by members of the business community: 5%, student presentations: 10%, team projects: 20%.

Special Opportunities International exchange in Canada, United States of America. Internship program available.

STUDENT STATISTICS

Undergraduate Majors Engineering/technology 75%; science/mathematics 20%; social sciences 5%.

Other Background Graduate degrees in other disciplines: 50%. Work experience: On average, students have 3 years of work experience on entrance to the program.

FACILITIES

Information Resources Business collection in Czechoslovak Management Center Business Library includes 4,500 bound volumes, 65 periodical subscriptions, 15 CD-ROMs, 15 videos.

Housing 100% of students in program live in college-owned or -operated housing.

Technology Computers are used heavily in course work. 16 computer terminals/PCs, linked by a campus-wide computer network, are avail-

able for use by students in program; they are located in computer labs. Students in the program are not required to have their own PC.

Computer Resources/On-line Services

Training	No	E-Mail	Yes
Internet	Yes	Videoconference Center	Yes

ADMISSION

Entrance Requirements First degree, GMAT score of 500. Core courses waived through: previous course work.

Application Requirements Written essay, application form, copies of transcript, personal statement, 2 letters of recommendation.

Application Deadline 10/31 for winter.

FINANCIALS

Costs for 1994-95 Tuition: Full-time: 40,000 koruny/term for residents, 55,000 koruny/term for nonresidents, 90,000 koruny/term for international students.

Financial Aid In 1994-95, 42% of candidates received some institutionally administered aid in the form of grants. Total awards ranged from 4,299-7,217 koruny. Financial aid is not available to part-time students. Applications are processed on a rolling basis. Contact: Ms. Suzanne Etcheverry, Director of USAID Programs, Námest&i 5, Kvetna 2, 250 88 Celákovice, Czech Republic. 202-92106.

INTERNATIONAL STUDENTS

Services and Facilities International student office, visa services.

Applying Financial aid is not available to international students. Admission applications are processed on a rolling basis.

ALTERNATE MBA PROGRAM

One-Year MBA Length of program: Minimum: 11 months. Full-time classes: Main campus; day. Degree requirements: 51 credits. Languages: English.

PLACEMENT

In 1993-94, 35 organizations participated in on-campus recruiting; 35 on-campus interviews were conducted. Placement services include alumni network, career counseling/planning, career fairs, career library, career placement, job interviews, resume preparation, resume referral to employers, and videos. Of 1994 graduates, 100% were employed within three months of graduation.

Jobs by Employer Type Manufacturing 20%; service 60%; consulting 20%.

Jobs by Functional Area Marketing/sales 20%; finance 60%; management 20%.

Program Contact: Mr. Patrick Uram, MBA Director, Czechoslovak Management Center, Námestí 5, Kvetna 2, 250 88 Celákovice, Czech Republic. 202-92238; Fax: 202-91997; Internet Address: uram@cmc.cz.

EGYPT

American University in Cairo

Cairo, Egypt

OVERVIEW

American University in Cairo is an independent nonprofit comprehensive coed institution. Founded 1919. Setting: 26-acre urban campus. Total institutional enrollment: 4,268.

ACADEMICS

Calendar Semesters.

Degree Requirements 42 credits.

FACILITIES

Information Resources Main library with 235,000 bound volumes, 7,500 titles on microform, 2,003 periodical subscriptions, 2,000 records/tapes/CDs.

ADMISSION

Entrance Requirements First degree, GMAT score, minimum 2 years of work experience.

Application Deadlines 3/31 for fall, 10/31 for January admission.

INTERNATIONAL STUDENTS

Applying TOEFL required, minimum score of 550; proof of health; Test of Standard Written English. Admission application deadlines: 3/31 for fall, 10/31 for winter, 5/31 for fall admission for North American applicants only.

Program Contact: American University in Cairo, PO Box 2511, Sharia Kasr El Aini St, Cairo, Egypt. In North America, contact: American University in Cairo, 866 United Nations Plaza, New York, NY 10017; (212) 421-6320.

FINLAND

Helsinki School of Economics and Business Administration

International Center

Helsinki, Finland

OVERVIEW

Helsinki School of Economics and Business Administration is a specialized coed institution. Founded 1904. Setting: urban campus. Total institutional enrollment: 4,000. Program was first offered in 1984. Accredited by European Foundation for Management Development.

MBA HIGHLIGHTS

Entrance Difficulty***

Cost
Tuition: 38,000 Finnish markkas/degree program
Room & Board: N/R

Enrollment Profile
Full-time: 130   Work Exp: 100%
Part-time: 30   Women: 35%
Total: 160
Average Age: 32

Average Class Size: 30

ACADEMICS

Length of Program Minimum: 20 months. Maximum: 4 years.

Full-time Classes Main campus; day.

Degree Requirements 98 credits including 56 elective credits. Other: Compulsory foreign study period.

Required Courses Business mathematics, financial accounting, implementation of strategy, introduction to computers, macroeconomics, management accounting, management communication, managerial economics, managerial finance, marketing management, organizational behavior, quantitative methods.

Curricular Focus Business issues and problems, general management, international business.

Concentrations Accounting, economics, entrepreneurship, finance, human resources management, international business, management, management information systems, marketing, operations management, organizational behavior, quantitative analysis, strategic management.

Faculty Part-time: 55, 85% with doctorates.

Teaching Methodology Case study: 20%, faculty seminars: 10%, lecture: 40%, seminars by members of the business community: 10%, student presentations: 10%, team projects: 10%.

Special Opportunities International exchange program available. Other: Consulting projects.

STUDENT STATISTICS

Other Background Graduate degrees in other disciplines: 60%. Work experience: On average, students have 6 years of work experience on entrance to the program.

FACILITIES

Housing College housing not available.

Technology Computers are used heavily in course work. 20 computer terminals/PCs, linked by a campus-wide computer network, are available for use by students in program; they are located in computer labs.

Students in the program are not required to have their own PC.

Computer Resources/On-line Services
Training   Yes   E-Mail   Yes
Internet   Yes

ADMISSION

Acceptance 1994-95 Of those applying, 47% were accepted.

Entrance Requirements First degree, minimum 2 years of work experience. Core courses waived through: previous course work.

Application Requirements Written essay, application form, copies of transcript, resume/curriculum vitae, personal statement.

Application Deadline 9/15 for fall.

FINANCIALS

Costs for 1994-95 Tuition: Full-time: 38,000 Finnish markkas/degree program.

Financial Aid In 1994-95, candidates received some institutionally administered aid in the form of scholarships available for study abroad only. Total awards ranged from 1,000-3,000 Finnish markkas. Financial aid is not available to part-time students. Applications are processed on a rolling basis.

INTERNATIONAL STUDENTS

Services and Facilities International student center, counseling/support services.

Applying TOEFL required; proof of health; proof of adequate funds. Financial aid is not available to international students. Admission applications are processed on a rolling basis. Contact: Ms. Tiina Airila, Foreign Student Adviser, Hietaniemenkatu 7, 00100 Helsinki, Finland. 4313-611.

PLACEMENT

Placement services include alumni network, career fairs, career library, career placement, and electronic job bank.

Program Contact: Ms. Taina Kilpinen, Associate Dean, Helsinki School of Economics and Business Administration, Heitaniemenkatu 7, 00100 Helsinki, Finland. 4313-328; Fax: 4313-613; Internet Address: kilpinen@hkkk.fi.

FRANCE

EAP-European School of Management

Paris, France

OVERVIEW

EAP-European School of Management is a graduate-only specialized coed institution. Administratively affiliated with French Chamber of Commerce and Industry. Founded 1974. Setting: urban campus. Program was first offered in 1987. Approved by the Association of MBA Programs (U.K.).

MBA HIGHLIGHTS

Entrance Difficulty***
Mean GMAT: 600
Mean GPA: N/R

Cost
Tuition: N/R
Room & Board: N/R

Enrollment Profile
Full-time: 33   Work Exp: 100%
Part-time: 0   Women: 25%
Total: 33
Average Age: 32

Class Size: 35 - 40

ACADEMICS

Calendar 7 phases.

Curricular Focus International business, teamwork.

Concentrations Accounting, economics, finance, human resources management, international business, management, management information systems, marketing, operations management, organizational behavior, public policy, sales force dynamics, technology management, strategic management.

Faculty Full-time: 35; part-time: 15, 100% with doctorates.

Teaching Methodology Case study: 30%, faculty seminars: 8%, lecture: 30%, student presentations: 10%.

Special Opportunities Internships include consultancy projects. Other: seminar programs in EAP schools in Madrid and Berlin; European commission in Brussels; integration week.

STUDENT STATISTICS

Undergraduate Majors Business 41%; engineering/technology 43%; humanities 11%; social sciences 2%; other 3%.

Other Background Graduate degrees in other disciplines: 100%. Work experience: On average, students have 5 years of work experience on entrance to the program.

FACILITIES

Information Resources Business collection includes 13,000 bound volumes, 340 periodical subscriptions, 13 CD-ROMs, 200 videos.

Housing College housing not available.

Technology Computers are used heavily in course work. 65 computer terminals/PCs are available for use by students in program; they are located in student rooms, the library, computer labs. Students in the program are required to have their own PC. $800 are budgeted per student for computer support.

Computer Resources/On-line Services

Training	No	CompuServe	No
Internet	Yes	Dun's	No
E-Mail	Yes	Dow Jones	No
Multimedia Center	Yes	Dialog	Yes
LEXIS/NEXIS	No	Bloomberg	No

ADMISSION

Entrance Requirements First degree, GMAT score of 550, minimum 5 years of work experience, fluency in English.

Application Requirements Interview, application form, copies of transcript, resume/curriculum vitae.

Application Deadline Applications are processed on a rolling basis.

FINANCIALS

Financial Aid In 1994-95, candidates received some institutionally administered aid in the form of grants, loans. Contact: Ms. Sylvie Pain, MBA Program Coordinator, 6 Avenue de la Porte de Champerret, 75838 Paris, France. 1-44-09-33-32.

INTERNATIONAL STUDENTS

Services and Facilities Visa services, language tutoring.

Applying TOEFL required. Financial aid is not available to international students. Admission application deadline: 10/30 for fall. Contact: Ms. Sylvie Pain, MBA Program Coordinator, 6 Avenue de la Porte de Champerret, 75838 Paris, France. 1-44-09-33-32.

PROGRAM

Executive MBA (EMBA) Length of program: 12 months. Full-time classes: Main campus, Madrid, Spain, Berlin, Germany; day. Degree requirements: Consulting project. Languages: English.

PLACEMENT

Placement services include alumni network, resume preparation, and resume referral to employers.

Program Contact: Ms. Sylvie Pain, MBA Program Coordinator, EAP-European School of Management, 6 Avenue de la Porte de Champerret, 75838 Paris, France. 1-44-09-33-36; Fax: 1-44-09-33-35.

L'École Nationale des Ponts et Chaussées

Paris, France

OVERVIEW

L'École Nationale des Ponts et Chaussées is an independent nonprofit coed institution. MBA program offered jointly with Belgrano University, Univeristy of California Berkeley, Bristol University, Tufts University, Harvard University, Massachussetts Institute of Technology, Sophia University. Setting: urban campus. Total institutional enrollment: 60. Program was first offered in 1988.

MBA HIGHLIGHTS

Entrance Difficulty***
GMAT: 500 - 600
Mean GPA: N/R

Cost
Tuition: 100,000 French francs/degree program
Room & Board: 80,000 French francs (off-campus)

Enrollment Profile

Full-time: 60	Work Exp: 95%
Part-time: 0	Women: 40%
Total: 60	
Average Age: 28	

Average Class Size: 45

ACADEMICS

Length of Program Minimum: 13 months.

Calendar Trimesters.

Full-time Classes Main campus, Buenos Aires (Argentina), Bristol (United Kingdom), Tokyo (Japan); day, evening, weekends, early morning.

Degree Requirements 19 credits. Other: 4-6 month internship.

Curricular Focus Entrepreneurship, teamwork.

Concentrations Japanese business, entrepreneurship, finance, international business, management, marketing, strategic management.

Faculty Full-time: 6; part-time: 98.

Teaching Methodology Case study: 25%, group discussion: 45%, lecture: 30%.

Special Opportunities International exchange in Argentina, Czech Republic, Japan, United Kingdom, United States of America. Internship program available.

STUDENT STATISTICS

Geographic Representation other 35%; France 28%; Asia 23%; North America 14%.

Undergraduate Majors Business 33%; engineering/technology 47%; other 20%.

FACILITIES

Housing College housing not available.

Technology Computers are used moderately in course work. 30 computer terminals/PCs are available for use by students in program; they are located in the computer center, computer labs. Students in the program are required to have their own PC.

Computer Resources/On-line Services

Training	No	E-Mail	Yes
Internet	Yes		

ADMISSION

Acceptance 1994-95 200 applied for admission; 30% were accepted.

Entrance Requirements First degree, GMAT score of 500.

Application Requirements Written essay, interview, application form, copies of transcript, resume/curriculum vitae, 3 letters of recommendation.

Application Deadlines 8/25 for fall, 3/31 for spring, 5/31 for summer.

FINANCIALS

Estimated Costs for 1995-96 Tuition: Full-time: 100,000 French francs/degree program. Average room and board costs are 80,000 French francs per academic year (off-campus).

INTERNATIONAL STUDENTS

Demographics 72% of students on campus are international.

Applying TOEFL required, minimum score of 500; proof of adequate funds. Financial aid is not available to international students. Admission application deadlines: 8/25 for fall, 3/31 for spring, 5/31 for summer.

PLACEMENT

Placement services include alumni network, career counseling/planning, career fairs, resume preparation, and resume referral to employers.

Program Contact: Mr. Niklas Schlappkohl, Admissions Director, L'École Nationale des Ponts et Chaussées, 28, rue des Saints-Peres, 75007 Paris, France. 1-44-58-28-52; Fax: 1-40-15-93-47; Internet Address: schlappk@paris.enpc.fr.

École Superieur de Commerce de Rouen

Mount Saint Aignan, France

OVERVIEW
École Superieur de Commerce de Rouen is an independent nonprofit specialized primarily male institution. Part of ESC Network, ECRICOME Network. Administratively affiliated with Chamber of Commerce and Industry of Rouen. MBA program offered jointly with Purdue University. Founded 1871. Setting: small-town campus. Total institutional enrollment: 952. Program was first offered in 1991. Accredited by AACSB.

MBA HIGHLIGHTS

Entrance Difficulty**
Mean GMAT: 580
Mean GPA: 3.0

Cost
Tuition: N/R
Room & Board: N/R

Enrollment Profile
Full-time: 0	Work Exp: 100%
Part-time: 17	Women: 6%
Total: 17	
Average Age: 37	

Average Class Size: 30

ACADEMICS
Calendar Semesters.

Curricular Focus International business, problem solving and decision making, strategic analysis and planning.

Concentrations European business law, accounting, economics, finance, human resources management, international business, management, management information systems, marketing, operations management, organizational behavior, public policy, quantitative analysis, strategic management.

Faculty Full-time: 50, 100% with doctorates; part-time: 50, 100% with doctorates.

Teaching Methodology Case study: 40%, faculty seminars: 20%, lecture: 5%, seminars by members of the business community: 5%, student presentations: 15%, team projects: 15%.

STUDENT STATISTICS
Geographic Representation France 36%; Eastern Europe 28%; Nigeria 6%; Canada 6%; Ireland 6%; Italy 6%; Australia 6%; India 6%.

Undergraduate Majors Business 39%; engineering/technology 36%; science/mathematics 13%; social sciences 6%; other 6%.

Other Background Graduate degrees in other disciplines: 100%. Work experience: On average, students have 12 years of work experience on entrance to the program.

FACILITIES
Information Resources Business collection includes 10,000 bound volumes, 370 periodical subscriptions, 3 CD-ROMs.

Housing College housing not available.

Technology Computers are used heavily in course work. 80 computer terminals/PCs, linked by a campus-wide computer network, are available for use by students in program; they are located in classrooms, computer labs. Students in the program are required to have their own PC. 5,000 French francs are budgeted per student for computer support.

Computer Resources/On-line Services
Training	Yes	Videoconference Center	Yes
E-Mail	Yes		

ADMISSION
Acceptance 1994-95 30 applied for admission; 67% were accepted.

Entrance Requirements First degree, GMAT score, minimum 3.0 GPA, minimum 5 years of work experience.

Application Requirements Application form, copies of transcript, personal statement.

Application Deadline Applications are processed on a rolling basis.

FINANCIALS
Financial Aid Financial aid is available to part-time students. Applications are processed on a rolling basis.

INTERNATIONAL STUDENTS
Demographics 12% of students on campus are international; Europe 70%, North America 25%, South America 4%, Asia 1%.

Services and Facilities International student housing; international student office, language tutoring, ESL courses.

Applying TOEFL required, minimum score of 550. Financial aid is available to international students. Financial aid is available to East European students only. Admission applications are processed on a rolling basis. Contact: Ms. Francoise Castel, Responsable Relations International, BP 188, 76136 Mount Saint Aignan Cedex, France. 32-82-74-02.

PROGRAM
Executive MBA (EMBA) Length of program: Minimum: 22 months. Part-time classes: Main campus, Purdue University; day. Degree requirements: 48 credits. Minimum 3.0 GPA. Languages: English.

PLACEMENT
Placement services include alumni network and electronic job bank.

Jobs by Functional Area Marketing/sales 40%; finance 10%; operations 15%; management 20%; strategic planning 10%; technical management 5%.

Program Contact: Ms. Nicole Brinsdon, IMaC Executive MBA Associate Director, École Superieur de Commerce de Rouen, BP 188, 76136 Mount Saint Aignan Cedex, France. 32-82-74-02; Fax: 35-76-06-62.

École Supérieure des Sciences Économiques et Commerciales

Paris, France

OVERVIEW
École Supérieure des Sciences Économiques et Commerciales is an independent nonprofit coed institution. Founded 1907. Setting: urban campus. Total institutional enrollment: 2,000. Program was first offered in 1993. Accredited by Commission D'homologation de Titres et des Diplomes.

MBA HIGHLIGHTS

Entrance Difficulty***
Mean GMAT: 610
Mean GPA: N/R

Cost
Tuition: N/R
Room & Board: N/R

Enrollment Profile
Full-time: 0	Work Exp: 100%
Part-time: 26	Women: 20%
Total: 26	
Average Age: 32	

Average Class Size: 25

ACADEMICS
Calendar Weekends and 6 sessions.

Curricular Focus International business, leadership, teamwork.

Concentrations International business, management.

Faculty Full-time: 18, 90% with doctorates; part-time: 4, 70% with doctorates.

Teaching Methodology Case study: 25%, faculty seminars: 5%, lecture: 30%, research: 5%, seminars by members of the business community: 5%, student presentations: 10%, team projects: 20%.

STUDENT STATISTICS
Geographic Representation France 75%; Italy 10%; Spain 10%; North Africa 5%.

Undergraduate Majors Business 10%; engineering/technology 40%; humanities 20%; science/mathematics 20%; other 10%.

Other Background Graduate degrees in other disciplines: 20%. Work experience: On average, students have 7 years of work experience on entrance to the program.

FACILITIES
Information Resources Business collection includes 100,000 bound volumes, 300 periodical subscriptions, 280 CD-ROMs.

Housing College housing not available.

Technology Computers are used moderately in course work. 20 computer terminals/PCs are available for use by students in program; they are located in classrooms, the library. Students in the program are not required to have their own PC.

Computer Resources/On-line Services

Training	Yes	LEXIS/NEXIS	Yes
Internet	Yes	Dow Jones	Yes
E-Mail	No		

ADMISSION

Acceptance 1994-95 120 applied for admission; 32% were accepted.

Entrance Requirements First degree, GMAT score, minimum 5 years of work experience.

Application Requirements Written essay, interview, application form, copies of transcript, 2 letters of recommendation.

Application Deadline 4/1 for fall.

FINANCIALS

Financial Aid In 1994-95, candidates received some institutionally administered aid in the form of public and company funding.

INTERNATIONAL STUDENTS

Demographics 20% of students on campus are international; Europe 60%, Africa 10%, Asia 10%, South America 5%, North America 5%, other 10%.

Services and Facilities International student housing.

Applying TOEFL required, minimum score of 450. Financial aid is not available to international students. Admission application deadline: 1/30 for fall. Applications are processed on a rolling basis. Contact: Mr. David Manson, Director of Executive Programs, BP 230, 2 Place de la Defense, 92053 Paris, France. 1-46-92-21-00.

PROGRAM

Executive MBA (EMBA) Length of program: Minimum: 18 months. Part-time classes: Main campus; weekends, summer. Languages: English, French.

PLACEMENT

Jobs by Employer Type Manufacturing 40%; service 50%; government 5%; consulting 5%.

Jobs by Functional Area Marketing/sales 35%; finance 15%; operations 15%; management 20%; technical management 15%.

Program Contact: Mr. David Manson, Director of Executive Programs, École Supérieure des Sciences Économiques et Commerciales, BP 230, 2 Place de la Defense, 92053 Paris, France. 1-46-92-21-20; Fax: 1-46-92-21-59.

The European Institute of Business Administration (INSEAD)

Fontainebleau, France

OVERVIEW

The European Institute of Business Administration (INSEAD) is an independent nonprofit specialized coed institution. Setting: small-town campus. Total institutional enrollment: 485. Program was first offered in 1959. Approved by the Association of MBA Programs (U.K.).

MBA HIGHLIGHTS

Entrance Difficulty***
Mean GMAT: 650
Mean GPA: N/R

Cost
Tuition: 145,000 French francs
Room & Board: 40,700 French francs

Enrollment Profile

Full-time: 450	Work Exp: 99%
Part-time: 0	Women: 24%
Total: 450	
Average Age: 28	

Average Class Size: 32

ACADEMICS

Length of Program Minimum: 10 months. Maximum: 2 years.
Calendar 5 eight-week periods.

Full-time Classes Main campus; day, weekends, early morning, summer.

Degree Requirements 21 courses including 5 elective courses. Other: Knowledge of English, French, and 3rd language.

Required Courses Applied statistics, business policy, economic analysis, finance 1, finance 2 or financial management, financial accounting, industrial policy and international competitiveness, international political analysis, management accounting and control, managing organizations, marketing management 1, marketing management 2, people and leadership, prices and markets, production and operations management.

Curricular Focus Entrepreneurship, international business, leadership.

Concentrations Accounting, economics, entrepreneurship, finance, human resources management, international business, management, management information systems, marketing, operations management, organizational behavior, quantitative analysis, strategic management.

Faculty Full-time: 61, 100% with doctorates; part-time: 13, 92% with doctorates.

Teaching Methodology Case study: 15%, lecture: 25%, research: 10%, seminars by members of the business community: 5%, student presentations: 5%, team projects: 40%.

STUDENT STATISTICS

Undergraduate Majors Business 33%; engineering/technology 35%; science/mathematics 18%; social sciences 6%; other 8%.

FACILITIES

Information Resources Business collection includes 35,000 bound volumes, 1,100 periodical subscriptions, 350 CD-ROMs, 500 videos.

Housing 15% of students in program live in college-owned or -operated housing. Assistance with housing search provided.

Technology Computers are used heavily in course work. 58 computer terminals/PCs, linked by a campus-wide computer network, are available for use by students in program; they are located in student rooms, the computer center. Students in the program are not required to have their own PC.

Computer Resources/On-line Services

Training	Yes	E-Mail	Yes
Internet	Yes	Dun's	Yes

ADMISSION

Acceptance 1994-95 Of those applying, 30% were accepted.

Entrance Requirements GMAT score. Core courses waived through: previous course work, work experience.

Application Requirements Written essay, interview, application form, copies of transcript, 2 letters of recommendation.

Application Deadlines 4/3 for fall, 8/7 for spring.

FINANCIALS

Costs for 1994-95 Tuition: Full-time: 145,000 French francs. Average room and board costs are 40,700 French francs per academic year (on-campus) and 37,400 French francs per academic year (off-campus).

Financial Aid In 1994-95, 5% of candidates received some institutionally administered aid in the form of scholarships. Total awards ranged from 36,000-145,000 French francs. Financial aid is not available to part-time students. Contact: Ms. Dominique Nicocia, MBA Admissions Officer, Boulevard de Corstance, F-77305 Fontainebleau Cedex, France. 60-72-42-73.

INTERNATIONAL STUDENTS

Applying TOEFL required, minimum score of 600. Financial aid is available to international students. Funding sources made available to all candidates. Admission application deadlines: 4/3 for fall, 8/7 for spring.

PLACEMENT

In 1993-94, 152 organizations participated in on-campus recruiting; 5,251 on-campus interviews were conducted. Placement services include alumni network, career counseling/planning, career library, career placement, electronic job bank, job interviews, and job search course. Of 1994 graduates, 85% were employed within three months of graduation, the average starting salary was 358,100 French francs, the range was 205,000-500,000 French francs.

Jobs by Employer Type Consulting 30%; financial services 20%; industry 50%.

Program Contact: MBA Admissions Office, The European Institute of Business Administration (INSEAD), Boulevard de Corstance, F-77305 Fontainebleau Cedex, France. 60-72-42-73; Fax: 60-72-42-00; Internet Address: admissions@insead.fr.

See full description on page 734.

Groupe CERAM

Sophia Antipolis, France

OVERVIEW
Groupe CERAM is a specialized primarily male institution. MBA program offered jointly with Institut d'Administration des Enterprise, University of California at Berkeley. Founded 1976. Setting: suburban campus. Total institutional enrollment: 653. Program was first offered in 1991.

MBA HIGHLIGHTS

Entrance Difficulty*

Cost
Tuition: N/R
Room & Board: N/R

Enrollment Profile
Full-time: 0
Part-time: 24
Total: 24
Average Age: 33

Work Exp: 92%
Women: 19%

Average Class Size: N/R

ACADEMICS
Calendar Trimesters.

Curricular Focus General management, international business, problem solving and decision making.

Concentrations Accounting, economics, entrepreneurship, finance, international business, management, management information systems, marketing, operations management, organizational behavior, strategic management.

Faculty Part-time: 17, 50% with doctorates.

Teaching Methodology Case study: 10%, faculty seminars: 30%, lecture: 15%, seminars by members of the business community: 20%, student presentations: 10%, team projects: 15%.

Special Opportunities International exchange in Finland, United Kingdom.

STUDENT STATISTICS
Undergraduate Majors Business 24%; education 6%; engineering/technology 50%; social sciences 12%; other 8%.

Other Background Graduate degrees in other disciplines: 60%. Work experience: On average, students have 6 years of work experience on entrance to the program.

FACILITIES
Information Resources Business collection includes 10,000 bound volumes, 300 periodical subscriptions, 2 CD-ROMs.

Housing College housing not available.

Technology 120 computer terminals/PCs are available for use by students in program; they are located in computer labs. Students in the program are not required to have their own PC.

Computer Resources/On-line Services
Training   No   E-Mail   No

ADMISSION
Acceptance 1994-95 24 applied for admission; 79% were accepted.

Entrance Requirements First degree, minimum 3 years of work experience, fluency in English.

Application Requirements Interview, application form, copies of transcript, resume/curriculum vitae.

Application Deadlines 10/13 for fall. Applications are processed on a rolling basis.

FINANCIALS
Financial Aid Financial aid is not available to part-time students.

INTERNATIONAL STUDENTS
Applying Proof of adequate funds. Admission application deadline: 10/13 for fall. Contact: Ms. Isabelle Guidl, BP 085, 06902 Sophia Antipolis Cedex, France. 93-95-45-85.

PROGRAM
Executive MBA (EMBA) Length of program: Minimum: 18 months. Maximum: 3 years. Part-time classes: Main campus, Univerity of Nice; evening, weekends. Degree requirements: 19 courses. Languages: English.

PLACEMENT
Placement services include career placement and job interviews.

Jobs by Employer Type Service 70%; consulting 30%.

Jobs by Functional Area Marketing/sales 30%; management 40%; technical management 30%.

Program Contact: Ms. Marie Line Gastard, Program Coordinator, Groupe CERAM, BP 085, 06902 Sophia Antipolis Cedex, France. 93-95-45-87; Fax: 93-95-45-40.

Groupe ESC Clermont

Clermont Graduate School of Management

Clermont-Ferrand, France

OVERVIEW
Groupe ESC Clermont is a specialized coed institution. Founded 1919.

MBA HIGHLIGHTS

Entrance Difficulty***

Cost
Tuition: 29,000 French francs
Room & Board: 40,000 French francs

Enrollment Profile
Full-time: N/R
Part-time: N/R
Total: 355
Average Age: N/R

Work Exp: N/R
Women: 50%

Average Class Size: 35

ACADEMICS
Length of Program Minimum: 21 months.

Full-time Classes Main campus; day.

Degree Requirements 60 credits.

Curricular Focus Entrepreneurship, general management, international business.

Concentrations Accounting, entrepreneurship, finance, human resources management, international business, management, management information systems, marketing, strategic management.

Teaching Methodology Case study: 10%, faculty seminars: 5%, lecture: 50%, research: 5%, seminars by members of the business community: 10%, team projects: 20%.

FACILITIES
Housing College housing available.

ADMISSION
Entrance Requirements First degree.

Application Requirements Copies of transcript, resume/curriculum vitae, personal statement, 2 letters of recommendation.

Application Deadlines 5/31 for fall. Applications are processed on a rolling basis.

FINANCIALS
Costs for 1994-95 Tuition: Full-time: 29,000 French francs. Average room and board costs are 40,000 French francs per academic year (on-campus) and 40,000 French francs per academic year (off-campus).

INTERNATIONAL STUDENTS
Applying Financial aid is not available to international students. Admission application deadline: 5/31 for fall. Applications are processed on a rolling basis.

Program Contact: Mr. Gerard Coute, Head of Recruitment, Groupe ESC Clermont, 4 boulevard Trudaine, 63037 Clermont-Ferrand, France. 73-98-24-24; Fax: 73-98-24-49.

Groupe ESC Lyon

Ecully, France

OVERVIEW
Groupe ESC Lyon is an independent nonprofit coed institution. Part of Lyon University. MBA program offered jointly with Cranfield School of Management. Founded 1872. Setting: rural campus. Total institutional enrollment: 1,050. Program was first offered in 1972. Accredited by

AASCB. Approved by the Association of MBA Programs (U.K.).

MBA HIGHLIGHTS

Entrance Difficulty****
Mean GMAT: 590
Mean GPA: N/R

Cost
Tuition: N/R
Room & Board: N/R

Enrollment Profile
Full-time: 70
Part-time: 0
Total: 70
Average Age: 29

Work Exp: 77%
Women: 27%

Average Class Size: 35

ACADEMICS

Calendar Trimesters.

Curricular Focus Entrepreneurship, international business, problem solving and decision making, teamwork.

Concentration Management.

Faculty Full-time: 83, 40% with doctorates; part-time: 300.

Teaching Methodology Case study: 25%, faculty seminars: 15%, lecture: 20%, seminars by members of the business community: 5%, student presentations: 5%, team projects: 30%.

Special Opportunities International exchange in Canada, Spain, United Kingdom, United States of America. Internship program available. Other: Consulting project, company start-up project.

STUDENT STATISTICS

Geographic Representation France 73%; North America 8%; other 7%; Europe 5%; United Kingdom 3%; Germany 2%; Scandinavia 2%; Spain 2%.

Other Background Graduate degrees in other disciplines: 25%. Work experience: On average, students have 6 years of work experience on entrance to the program.

FACILITIES

Information Resources Business collection includes 12,500 bound volumes, 380 periodical subscriptions, 10 CD-ROMs.

Housing 20% of students in program live in college-owned or -operated housing. Assistance with housing search provided.

Technology Computers are used moderately in course work. 70 computer terminals/PCs are available for use by students in program; they are located in the computer center. Students in the program are not required to have their own PC. 1,000-1,800 French francs are budgeted per student for computer support.

Computer Resources/On-line Services

Training	Yes	CompuServe	No
Internet	No	Dun's	No
E-Mail	No	Dow Jones	No
Videoconference Center	Yes	Dialog	No
LEXIS/NEXIS	No	Bloomberg	No

ADMISSION

Acceptance 1994-95 200 applied for admission; 35% were accepted.

Entrance Requirements First degree, GMAT score of 580, minimum 5 years of work experience.

Application Requirements Interview, application form, copies of transcript, resume/curriculum vitae, 1 letter of recommendation.

Application Deadlines 6/15 for fall. Applications are processed on a rolling basis.

FINANCIALS

Financial Aid In 1994-95, candidates received some institutionally administered aid in the form of scholarships, loans. Total awards ranged from 1,800-3,600 French francs. Financial aid is not available to part-time students. Applications are processed on a rolling basis. Contact: Ms. Jacqueline Del Bello, International Relations Assistant, 23, Avenue Guy de Collongue; BP 714, F-69130 Ecully Cedex, France. 78-33-78-65.

INTERNATIONAL STUDENTS

Demographics 20% of students on campus are international; Europe 67%, South America 15%, Asia 5%, Central America 4%, Africa 3%, Australia 2%, North America 1%, other 4%.

Services and Facilities International student office, language tutoring, special assistance for nonnative speakers of French.

Applying TOEFL required, minimum score of 580; French language test. Financial aid is available to international students. Applications are processed on a rolling basis. Admission application deadline: 6/15 for fall. Applications are processed on a rolling basis. Contact: Ms. Jacqueline Del Bello, International Relations Assistant, 23, Avenue Guy de Collongue; BP 714, F-69130 Ecully Cedex, France. 78-33-78-65.

PROGRAM

One-Year MBA Length of program: 12 months. Full-time classes: Main campus; day. Degree requirements: 2 terms of courses; one term of elective courses; final field study or project. Languages: English, French.

PLACEMENT

In 1993-94, 100 organizations participated in on-campus recruiting. Placement services include alumni network, career counseling/planning, career fairs, career library, career placement, job interviews, job search course, resume preparation, and resume referral to employers. Of 1994 graduates, 70% were employed within three months of graduation, the average starting salary was 60,000 French francs, the range was 40,000-75,000 French francs.

Jobs by Employer Type Manufacturing 56%; service 25%; consulting 19%.

Jobs by Functional Area Marketing/sales 45%; finance 11%; operations 3%; management 29%; technical management 5%; other 7%.

Program Contact: Ms. Jacqueline Del Bello, International Relations Assistant, Groupe ESC Lyon, 23, Avenue Guy de Collongue; BP 714, F-69130 Ecully Cedex, France. 78-33-78-65; Fax: 78-33-77-55.

Groupe ESC Nantes Atlantique

Nantes, France

OVERVIEW

Groupe ESC Nantes Atlantique is an independent nonprofit specialized coed institution. Part of French Grandes Ecoles. MBA program offered jointly with Universidad Comercial de Deusto, Bilbao, Spain; University of Bradford Management Center, United Kingdom. Founded 1900. Setting: urban campus. Total institutional enrollment: 1,000. Program was first offered in 1990.

MBA HIGHLIGHTS

Entrance Difficulty****

Cost
Tuition: N/R
Room & Board: N/R

Enrollment Profile
Full-time: 22
Part-time: 0
Total: 22
Average Age: 26

Work Exp: 80%
Women: 40%

Average Class Size: 25

ACADEMICS

Calendar Quarters.

Curricular Focus International business, managing diversity, problem solving and decision making.

Concentrations European management, accounting, economics, finance, human resources management, international business, management, management information systems, marketing, operations management, organizational behavior, quantitative analysis, strategic management.

Faculty Full-time: 25, 75% with doctorates; part-time: 12, 40% with doctorates.

Teaching Methodology Case study: 20%, faculty seminars: 10%, lecture: 25%, research: 25%, student presentations: 5%, team projects: 15%.

Special Opportunities International exchange in Spain, United Kingdom. Internship program available.

STUDENT STATISTICS

Geographic Representation Spain 50%; France 15%; Scandinavia 15%; Belgium/Luxembourg/Netherlands 15%; United Kingdom 5%.

Undergraduate Majors Business 10%; engineering/technology 40%; social sciences 30%; other 20%.

Other Background Work experience: On average, students have 4 years of work experience on entrance to the program.

FACILITIES

Information Resources Business collection includes 9,000 bound volumes, 300 periodical subscriptions, 20 CD-ROMs, 600 videos.

Housing College housing not available.

Technology Computers are used moderately in course work. 100 computer terminals/PCs are available for use by students in program; they are located in the computer center, computer labs. Students in the program are not required to have their own PC.

Computer Resources/On-line Services

Training	Yes	E-Mail	No

ADMISSION

Acceptance 1994-95 Of those applying, 25% were accepted.

Entrance Requirements First degree.

Application Requirements Interview, application form, copies of transcript, resume/curriculum vitae, personal statement.

Application Deadlines 6/15 for fall. Applications are processed on a rolling basis.

INTERNATIONAL STUDENTS

Demographics 20% of students on campus are international; Europe 90%, North America 10%.

Services and Facilities International student office, international student center, language tutoring, counseling/support services.

Applying Financial aid is not available to international students. Admission application deadline: 6/15 for fall. Applications are processed on a rolling basis. Contact: Mr. David Read, Associate Director, International Relations, 8, route de la Joneliére, 44003 Nantes Cedex 01, France. 40-37-34-34.

PROGRAM

One-Year MBA Length of program: Minimum: 13 months. Full-time classes: Main campus; day. Degree requirements: 60 credits. Language credits; internship ternship project. Languages: Spanish, French, English.

PLACEMENT

Placement services include alumni network, career counseling/planning, career fairs, career library, career placement, and job interviews. Of 1994 graduates, 50% were employed within three months of graduation, the average starting salary was 200,000 French francs, the range was 180,000-250,000 French francs.

Jobs by Employer Type Manufacturing 30%; service 40%; consulting 30%.

Jobs by Functional Area Marketing/sales 50%; finance 20%; strategic planning 20%; technical management 10%.

Program Contact: Ms. Martine Froissart, EMP Program Director, Groupe ESC Nantes Atlantique, 8, route de la Joneliére, 44003 Nantes Cedex 01, France. 40-37-34-32; Fax: 40-37-45-30.

HEC Graduate School of Management

Institute Supérieur des Affaires

Jouy-en-Josas, France

OVERVIEW

HEC Graduate School of Management is comprehensive specialized coed institution. Part of Paris Chamber for Commerce and Industry. Founded 1881. Setting: suburban campus. Total institutional enrollment: 1,600. Program was first offered in 1969. Accredited by The Conference of the Grandes Ecoles of France, Educatonal Foundation for Management Developement (EFMD). Approved by the Association of MBA Programs (U.K.).

MBA HIGHLIGHTS

Entrance Difficulty***
Mean GMAT: 610
Mean GPA: 3.2

Cost
Tuition: 12,000 French francs/degree program
Room & Board: 19,500 French francs

Enrollment Profile

Full-time: 240	Work Exp: 95%
Part-time: 0	Women: 23%
Total: 240	
Average Age: 30	

Average Class Size: 120

I SA (Institut Supérieur des Affaires) is the M.B.A. program of HEC School of Management, France's most prestigious management training institution, founded in 1881. ISA was founded in 1969 as a French-speaking M.B.A. program. In 1991, the first fully bilingual class, with 40 percent international representation, started a new era in the institution's development.

At ISA, courses provide a hefty dose of pragmatism through live cases and projects and an opportunity to study comparative management issues. They challenge the analytical and creative skills of the participants. Cross-disciplinary instruction, ethics, art, and an extensive network of student exchange agreements characterize the program. Instruction is in English and French. Much emphasis is placed on teamwork. Cooperation more than competition defines student relationships. Sixty-five percent of the entire class spends several days in a Benedictine monastery debating general and business ethical issues not only with monks but also with business practitioners. Interesting but unusual electives include Geopolitics, Diplomacy, Defense; Cultural Anthropology and the Corporation; The Asiatic Thinking Model as Reflected in "GO"; Ancient Egypt; and Alternative Management.

ACADEMICS

Length of Program Minimum: 16 months.

Calendar Quarters.

Full-time Classes Main campus.

Degree Requirements 1,100 hours including 400 elective hours.

Required Courses Business policy and strategies, comparative law and taxation in Europe, corporate finance, economics and international management, financial accounting, financial dimensions of strategic decisions, financial markets, industrial management, international contracts, management and cost analysis, management of human resources, marketing, organizational behavior, quantitative methods in management.

Curricular Focus Economic and financial theory, entrepreneurship, general management, international business, strategic analysis and planning.

Concentrations Accounting, entrepreneurship, finance, human resources management, international business, management, marketing, operations management, organizational behavior, strategic management.

Faculty Full-time: 102, 70% with doctorates; part-time: 100, 20% with doctorates.

Teaching Methodology Case study: 40%, faculty seminars: 5%, lecture: 20%, seminars by members of the business community: 5%, student presentations: 10%, team projects: 20%.

Special Opportunities International exchange in Brazil, Canada, Hong Kong, Italy, Japan, Mexico, Netherlands, Spain, United Kingdom, United States of America.

STUDENT STATISTICS

Geographic Representation France 58%; Americas 15%; Scandinavia 7%; United Kingdom 7%; other 5%; Germany 4%; other Europe 2%; Russia 1%; Spain 1%.

Undergraduate Majors Business 10%; engineering/technology 37%; humanities 20%; science/mathematics 7%; social sciences 17%; other 9%.

Other Background Graduate degrees in other disciplines: 31%. Work experience: On average, students have 5 years of work experience on entrance to the program.

FACILITIES

Information Resources Business collection in Centre de Documentation Bibliothèque includes 57,000 bound volumes, 612 periodical subscriptions, 12 CD-ROMs, 50 videos.

Housing 100% of students in program live in college-owned or -operated housing.

Technology Computers are used moderately in course work. 100 computer terminals/PCs, linked by a campus-wide computer network, are available for use by students in program; they are located in classrooms, learning resource center, the library, the computer center, computer labs. Students in the program are required to have their own PC. 2,850 French francs are budgeted per student for computer support.

Computer Resources/On-line Services

Training	Yes	CompuServe	Yes $
Internet	Yes $	Dun's	No
E-Mail	Yes	Dialog	Yes $

ADMISSION

Acceptance 1994-95 Of those applying, 30% were accepted.

Entrance Requirements First degree, GMAT score of 450, minimum 2.5 GPA, minimum 2 years of work experience, an oral presentation before a panel of 3, an hour written essay on a topic provided by panel, proficiency in French at level 4 of a 0 to 8 scale.

Application Requirements Written essay, interview, application form, copies of transcript, resume/curriculum vitae, 2 letters of recommendation.

Application Deadline 2/1 for fall.

FINANCIALS

Costs for 1995-96 Tuition: Full-time: 12,000 French francs/degree program. Average room and board costs are 19,500 French francs per academic year (on-campus) and 49,000 French francs per academic year (off-campus).

Financial Aid In 1994-95, 12% of candidates received some institutionally administered aid in the form of grants, scholarships, loans, special loans. Total awards ranged from 10,000-50,000 French francs. Financial aid is not available to part-time students. Application deadline: 2/1 for fall. Contact: Ms. Christine Luckx, Director of Admissions and Financial Aid, 1, rue de la Liberation, F-78350 Jouy-en-Josas, France. 1-39-67-73-83.

INTERNATIONAL STUDENTS

Services and Facilities International student office, visa services, language tutoring, counseling/support services, assistance is provided in the French language.

Applying TOEFL required, minimum score of 600; proof of health; proof of adequate funds; student visa from French Embassy. Financial aid is not available to international students. Admission application deadline: 2/1 for fall. Contact: Ms. Norma Bishop, International Student Counselor, 1, rue de la Liberation, F-78350 Jouy-en-Josas, France. 1-39-67-74-69.

ALTERNATE MBA PROGRAM

MBA/MALD Length of program: Minimum: 24 months.

PLACEMENT

In 1993-94, 120 organizations participated in on-campus recruiting. Placement services include alumni network, career counseling/planning, career fairs, career library, career placement, job search course, resume preparation, and resume referral to employers. Of 1994 graduates, 89% were employed within three months of graduation, the average starting salary was 340,000 French francs, the range was 250,000-400,000French francs.

Jobs by Employer Type Manufacturing 24%; service 28%; government 2%; consulting 22%; health industry 13%; other 11%.

Jobs by Functional Area Marketing/sales 16%; finance 15%; operations 2%; management 9%; strategic planning 4%; technical management 9%; consulting/auditing 21%; other 25%.

Program Contact: Mr. Jason Sedine, International Program Development, HEC Graduate School of Management, 1, rue de la Liberation, F-78350 Jouy-en-Josas, France. 1-39-67-73-76; Fax: 1-39-67-74-65. See full description on page 752.

Institut Superieur de Gestion

Paris, France

MBA HIGHLIGHTS

Entrance Difficulty***
Mean GMAT: 450
Mean GPA: N/R

Cost $$$
Tuition: $15,000
Room & Board: $15,000 (off-campus)

Enrollment Profile

Full-time: N/R	Work Exp: N/R
Part-time: N/R	Women: 40%
Total: 45	
Average Age: N/R	

Average Class Size: 45

ACADEMICS

Length of Program Minimum: 14 months.

Full-time Classes Main campus, Paris, Tokyo, Japan, New York City; day, weekends, summer.

Degree Requirements 60 credits.

Curricular Focus Business issues and problems, international business, strategic analysis and planning.

Concentration Management.

Teaching Methodology Case study: 5%, faculty seminars: 10%, lecture: 40%, seminars by members of the business community: 15%, student presentations: 5%, team projects: 25%.

FACILITIES

Housing College housing not available.

ADMISSION

Entrance Requirements First degree, GMAT score, minimum 2.5 GPA.

Application Requirements Interview, application form, copies of transcript, personal statement, 2 letters of recommendation.

Application Deadline 6/30 for fall.

FINANCIALS

Costs for 1994-95 Tuition: Full-time: $15,000. Average room and board costs are $15,000 per academic year (off-campus).

Financial Aid Application deadline: 6/30 for fall.

INTERNATIONAL STUDENTS

Applying TOEFL required, minimum score of 550. Financial aid is available to international students. Financial aid application deadline: 6/30 for fall. Admission application deadline: 6/30 for fall.

Program Contact: Ms. Nazila Leroy, MBA Program Director, Institut Superieur de Gestion, 75116 Paris, France. 1-53 70 82 22; Fax: 1-47 55 96 31.

Reims Graduate Business School

Reims Business School

Reims Cedex, France

OVERVIEW

Setting: suburban campus. Total institutional enrollment: 1,750. Program was first offered in 1971. Accredited by Ministry of Commerce and Industry.

MBA HIGHLIGHTS

Entrance Difficulty***

Cost
Tuition: N/R
Room & Board: N/R

Enrollment Profile

Full-time: 30	Work Exp: 50%
Part-time: 0	Women: 40%
Total: 30	
Average Age: 28	

Average Class Size: 30

ACADEMICS

Calendar Trimesters.

Curricular Focus Managing diversity, organizational development and change management, teamwork.

Concentrations Finance, international business, law, management, management information systems, marketing, operations management, organizational behavior, quantitative analysis, transportation.

Faculty Full-time: 6, 80% with doctorates; part-time: 4, 60% with doctorates.

Teaching Methodology Case study: 40%, faculty seminars: 20%, research: 15%, seminars by members of the business community: 5%, student presentations: 5%, team projects: 15%.

Special Opportunities International exchange in Czech Republic, Hungary, United Kingdom. Internship program available.

STUDENT STATISTICS

Geographic Representation France 80%; Eastern Europe 10%; Germany 5%; United Kingdom 5%.

Undergraduate Majors Business 25%; engineering/technology 30%; humanities 10%; nursing 5%; science/mathematics 10%; social sciences 10%; other 10%.

Other Background Graduate degrees in other disciplines: 80%. Work experience: On average, students have 7 years of work experience on entrance to the program.

FACILITIES

Information Resources Business collection includes 10,000 bound volumes, 300 periodical subscriptions, 20 CD-ROMs, 150 videos.

Housing 30% of students in program live in college-owned or -operated housing.

Technology Computers are used moderately in course work. 30 computer terminals/PCs are available for use by students in program; they are located in computer labs. Students in the program are not required to have their own PC. $300 are budgeted per student for computer support.

Computer Resources/On-line Services

Training	Yes	Multimedia Center	Yes
E-Mail	No		

ADMISSION

Acceptance 1994-95 120 applied for admission; 25% were accepted.

Entrance Requirements First degree.

Application Requirements Written essay, interview, application form, copies of transcript, resume/curriculum vitae, personal statement, 3 letters of recommendation.

Application Deadline 7/1 for fall.

FINANCIALS

Financial Aid Applications are processed on a rolling basis. Contact: Mr. Alain Bernabe, Financial Aid Director, Agence Societe Generale, 38 rue de Vesle, 51100 Reims Cedex, France. 26-47-94-18.

INTERNATIONAL STUDENTS

Demographics 20% of students on campus are international; Europe 80%, other 20%.

Services and Facilities Language tutoring, counseling/support services.

Applying Financial aid is not available to international students. Admission application deadline: 7/15 for fall. Applications are processed on a rolling basis. Contact: Mr. Paul Crowther, BP 302, 51061 Reims Cedex, France. 26-08-06-04.

PROGRAM

One-Year MBA Length of program: 12 months. Full-time classes: Main campus; day, evening, weekends, summer. Degree requirements: 60 credits including 15 elective credits. 4 field projects. Languages: French, English.

PLACEMENT

In 1993-94, 50 organizations participated in on-campus recruiting. Placement services include alumni network, career counseling/planning, career fairs, career library, career placement, job interviews, job search course, resume preparation, and resume referral to employers. Of 1994 graduates, 70% were employed within three months of graduation, the average starting salary was $40,000, the range was $30,000-$50,000.

Jobs by Employer Type Manufacturing 25%; service 25%; university administration 50%.

Jobs by Functional Area Marketing/sales 30%; finance 10%; operations 40%; technical management 20%.

Program Contact: Mr. Michel Feron, Program Director, Reims Graduate Business School, BP 302, 51061 Reims Cedex, France. 26-08-06-04; Fax: 26-04-69-63.

Schiller International University

Paris, France

OVERVIEW

Schiller International University is an independent nonprofit coed institution. Founded 1964. Setting: urban campus. Total institutional enrollment: 141.

MBA HIGHLIGHTS

Entrance Difficulty**
Mean GMAT: N/R
Mean GPA: 3.0

Cost
Tuition: $5,720/semester
Room & Board: $4,940

Enrollment Profile

Full-time: 48	Work Exp: N/R
Part-time: 7	Women: 37%
Total: 55	
Average Age: 28	

Average Class Size: 15

ACADEMICS

Calendar Semesters.

Curricular Focus International business, problem solving and decision making, teamwork.

Concentrations Hotel management, international business.

Teaching Methodology Case study: 20%, lecture: 40%, research: 20%, student presentations: 10%, team projects: 10%.

Special Opportunities International exchange in Germany, Spain, Switzerland, United Kingdom, United States of America. Internship program available.

STUDENT STATISTICS

Undergraduate Majors Business 87%; engineering/technology 1%; humanities 7%; social sciences 5%.

FACILITIES

Information Resources Main library with 3,797 bound volumes, 3,108 titles on microform, 41 periodical subscriptions.

Housing College housing available.

Technology 15 computer terminals/PCs are available for use by students in program; they are located in the library, computer labs.

Computer Resources/On-line Services

Training	No

ADMISSION

Entrance Requirements First degree, GMAT score, minimum 2.8 GPA. Core courses waived through: previous course work.

Application Requirements Application form, copies of transcript.

Application Deadline Applications are processed on a rolling basis.

FINANCIALS

Financial Aid In 1994-95, candidates received some institutionally administered aid in the form of scholarships, work-study. Application deadline: 4/1 for annual. Contact: Ms. B.J. Slovacek, Financial Aid Officer, Bergstrasse 106, 69121 Heidelberg, Germany, Germany. 6221-45810.

INTERNATIONAL STUDENTS

Demographics 88% of students on campus are international; Europe 40%, Asia 15%, North America 12%, South America 7%, Africa 4%, Central America 2%, Other 20%.

Services and Facilities International student housing; international student office, international student center, visa services, language tutoring, ESL courses, counseling/support services.

Applying TOEFL required, minimum score of 550. Financial aid is available to international students. Financial aid application deadline: 4/1 for annual. Admission applications are processed on a rolling basis. Contact: Ms. Karen Altieri, Director of Information and Alumni Affairs, 453 Edgewater Drive, Dunedin, FL 34698-7532. (813) 736-5082.

PROGRAM

One-Year MBA Length of program: Minimum: 12 months. Full-time classes: Main campus, London, United Kingdom, Heidelberg, Germany, Berlin, Germany, Madrid, Spain, Leysin, Switzerland; day, evening, weekends, summer. Part-time classes: Main campus, London, United Kingdom, Heidelberg, Germany, Berlin, Germany, Madrid, Spain, Leysin, Switzerland;

day, evening, weekends, summer. Degree requirements: 45 credits including 24 elective credits. Final oral comprehensive exam or oral defense of thesis. Languages: English. Average class size: 18.

PLACEMENT
Placement services include alumni network and career counseling/planning.

Program Contact: Ms. Karen Altieri, Director of Information and Alumni Affairs, Schiller International University, 453 Edgewater Drive, Dunedin, FL 34698-7532. (813) 736-5082, or (800) 336-4133; Fax: (813) 736-6263.

Schiller International University

Strasbourg, France

OVERVIEW
Schiller International University is an independent nonprofit coed institution. Founded 1964. Setting: urban campus with easy access to Paris. Total institutional enrollment: 71.

MBA HIGHLIGHTS

Entrance Difficulty**
Mean GMAT: N/R
Mean GPA: 3.0

Cost $$
Tuition: $5,720/semester
Room & Board: $4,940

Enrollment Profile
Full-time: 8　　　　　　　　　Work Exp: N/R
Part-time: 31　　　　　　　　Women: 31%
Total: 39
Average Age: 28

Average Class Size:　15

ACADEMICS
Calendar Semesters.

Curricular Focus International business, problem solving and decision making, teamwork.

Concentrations Hotel management, international business.

Faculty Full-time: 7; part-time: 9.

Teaching Methodology Case study: 20%, lecture: 40%, research: 20%, student presentations: 10%, team projects: 10%.

Special Opportunities International exchange in Germany, Spain, Switzerland, United Kingdom, United States of America. Internship program available.

STUDENT STATISTICS
Undergraduate Majors Business 87%; engineering/technology 1%; humanities 7%; social sciences 5%.

FACILITIES
Information Resources Main library with 3,071 bound volumes, 2,814 titles on microform, 48 periodical subscriptions, 33 records/tapes/CDs.

Housing College housing available.

Technology 15 computer terminals/PCs are available for use by students in the program; they are located in the library, computer labs. Students in the program are not required to have their own PC.

Computer Resources/On-line Services
Training　　　　　　　　　　No

ADMISSION
Entrance Requirements First degree, GMAT score, minimum 2.8 GPA. Core courses waived through: previous course work.

Application Requirements Application form, copies of transcript.

Application Deadline Applications are processed on a rolling basis.

FINANCIALS
Financial Aid In 1994-95, candidates received some institutionally administered aid in the form of scholarships, work-study. Application deadline: 4/1 for annual. Contact: Ms. B.J. Slovacek, Financial Aid Officer, Bergstrasse 106, 69121 Heidelberg, Germany. 6221-45810.

INTERNATIONAL STUDENTS
Services and Facilities International student housing; international student office, international student center, visa services, language tutoring, ESL courses, counseling/support services.

Applying TOEFL required, minimum score of 550. Financial aid is available to international students. Financial aid application deadline: 4/1 for annual. Admission applications are processed on a rolling basis. Contact: Ms. Karen Altieri, Director of Information and Alumni Affairs, 453 Edgewater Drive, Dunedin, FL 34698-7532. (813) 736-5082.

PROGRAM
One-Year MBA Length of program: Minimum: 12 months. Full-time classes: Main campus, Paris (France), Berlin (Germany), Heidelberg (Germany), London (United Kingdom), Madrid (Spain), Leysin (Switzerland); day, evening, weekends, summer. Part-time classes: Main campus, Paris, France, Berlin, Germany, Heidelberg, Germany, London, United Kingdom, Madrid, Spain- Leysin, Switzerland; day, evening, weekends, summer. Degree requirements: 45 credits including 24 elective credits. Final oral comprehensive exam or oral defense of thesis. Languages: English. Average class size: 18.

PLACEMENT
Placement services include alumni network and career placement.

Program Contact: Ms. Karen Altieri, Director of Information and Alumni Affairs, Schiller International University, 453 Edgewater Drive, Dunedin, FL 34698-7532. (813) 736-5082, or (800) 336-4133; Fax: (813) 736-6263.

Theseus Institute

Sophia Antipolis, France

OVERVIEW
Theseus Institute is an independent nonprofit primarily male institution. Part of France Telcom University. Setting: suburban campus. Total institutional enrollment: 20. Program was first offered in 1989. Accredited by The Royal Academy of Engineering (United Kingdom), Fond Indiviuel de Conge de Formation (France), Fondazione Enrio MaHei (Italy).

MBA HIGHLIGHTS

Entrance Difficulty****
Mean GMAT: 570
Mean GPA: N/R

Cost
Tuition: N/R
Room & Board: N/R

Enrollment Profile
Full-time: 20　　　　　　　　Work Exp: 85%
Part-time: 0　　　　　　　　　Women: 20%
Total: 20
Average Age: 30

Average Class Size:　26

ACADEMICS
Calendar September- July.

Curricular Focus Integration of information technology and management, organizational development and change management, strategic analysis and planning.

Concentrations Accounting, economics, entrepreneurship, finance, human resources management, integration of information technology, international business, management, management information systems, marketing, operations management, organizational behavior, public policy, quantitative analysis, strategic management.

Faculty Full-time: 3, 100% with doctorates; part-time: 40, 100% with doctorates.

Teaching Methodology Lecture: 70%, student presentations: 10%, team projects: 20%.

Special Opportunities Internships include innovation/strategy in France Telecom.

STUDENT STATISTICS
Geographic Representation Asia 35%; North America and Mexico 30%; France 20%; Italy 5%; United Kingdom 5%; Algeria 5%.

Undergraduate Majors Business 35%; engineering/technology 40%; humanities 15%; science/mathematics 10%.

Other Background Graduate degrees in other disciplines: 80%. Work experience: On average, students have 7 years of work experience on entrance to the program.

FACILITIES

Information Resources Business collection includes 2,300 bound volumes, 110 periodical subscriptions, 3 CD-ROMs, 10 videos.

Housing College housing not available.

Technology Computers are used heavily in course work. 7 computer terminals/PCs, linked by a campus-wide computer network, are available for use by students in program; they are located in the library, computer labs. Students in the program are not required to have their own PC.

Computer Resources/On-line Services

Training	Yes	CompuServe	No
Internet	Yes	Dun's	Yes
E-Mail	Yes	Dow Jones	No
Videoconference Center	Yes	Dialog	Yes
LEXIS/NEXIS	No	Bloomberg	No

ADMISSION

Acceptance 1994-95 103 applied for admission; 44% were accepted.

Entrance Requirements First degree, GMAT score of 550, minimum 5 years of work experience, minimum age 28.

Application Requirements Written essay, interview, application form, copies of transcript, resume/curriculum vitae, personal statement.

Application Deadlines 4/30 for spring. Applications are processed on a rolling basis.

FINANCIALS

Financial Aid In 1994-95, 80% of candidates received some institutionally administered aid in the form of scholarships, loans, assistantships. Total awards ranged from $10,000-$16,000. Applications are processed on a rolling basis. Contact: Ms. Catherine Harris, Admissions Manager, BP 169, 06903 Sophia Antipolis Cedex, France. 92-96-51-39.

INTERNATIONAL STUDENTS

Demographics 80% of students on campus are international.

Services and Facilities Visa services, language tutoring, ESL courses, counseling/support services.

Applying TOEFL required, minimum score of 600; proof of health; proof of adequate funds. Financial aid is available to international students. Applications are processed on a rolling basis. Admission application deadline: 4/30 for spring.

PROGRAM

One-Year MBA Length of program: Minimum: 10 months. Maximum: 1 year. Full-time classes: Main campus. Degree requirements: Field project. Languages: English, French.

PLACEMENT

Placement services include alumni network, career counseling/planning, career fairs, career placement, electronic job bank, job interviews, job search course, resume preparation, and resume referral to employers. Of 1994 graduates, 76% were employed within three months of graduation.

Jobs by Employer Type Manufacturing 6%; service 42%; consulting 18%; banking/finance 21%; other 13%.

Program Contact: Ms. Catherine Harris, Admissions Manager, Theseus Institute, BP 169, 06903 Sophia Antipolis Cedex, France. 92-96-51-39; Fax: 93-65-38-37; Internet Address: harris@theseus.fr.

GERMANY

Koblenz School of Corporate Management (WHU)

Otto Beisheim Graduate School

Vallendar, Germany

OVERVIEW

Koblenz School of Corporate Management (WHU) is an independent nonprofit coed institution. Setting: suburban campus. Total institutional enrollment: 220. Program was first offered in 1984. Accredited by European Foundation of Management Development (EFMD).

MBA HIGHLIGHTS

Entrance Difficulty****
Mean GMAT: 621
Mean GPA: N/R

Cost
Tuition: 5,500 German marks/semester
Room & Board: N/R

Enrollment Profile
Full-time: 160
Part-time: 0
Total: 160
Average Age: 24

Work Exp: 100%
Women: 15%

Average Class Size: 60

ACADEMICS

Length of Program Minimum: 18 months.

Calendar Semesters.

Full-time Classes Main campus; day.

Degree Requirements 610 hours including 108 elective hours. Other: Project work.

Required Courses Business administration, business policy, computer based management system, dynamic theories of the firm, human resources management, labor relations, managing stress and conflict situations, strategic planning.

Curricular Focus Economic and financial theory, general management, problem solving and decision making.

Concentrations Accounting, economics, entrepreneurship, finance, international business, management information systems, marketing, production management.

Faculty Full-time: 15, 100% with doctorates; part-time: 15, 90% with doctorates.

Teaching Methodology Case study: 10%, faculty seminars: 10%, lecture: 30%, research: 10%, seminars by members of the business community: 5%, student presentations: 20%, team projects: 15%.

Special Opportunities International exchange in Australia, Belgium, Brazil, Canada, Chile, Denmark, Finland, France, Ireland, Italy, Japan, Mexico, Netherlands, Russia, South Africa, Spain, Sweden, United Kingdom, United States of America. Internship program available.

STUDENT STATISTICS

Geographic Representation Germany 71%; France 9%; South America 4%; Russia 3%; Scandinavia 3%; Spain 3%; United Kingdom 3%; Ireland 1%; Italy 1%; Japan 1%; Australia 1%.

Undergraduate Majors Business 30%; engineering/technology 10%; humanities 10%; science/mathematics 25%; social sciences 10%; other 15%.

Other Background Graduate degrees in other disciplines: 5%. Work experience: On average, students have 2-3 years of work experience on entrance to the program.

FACILITIES

Information Resources Business collection includes 22,000 bound volumes, 320 periodical subscriptions, 600 CD-ROMs, 20 videos.

Housing College housing not available.

Technology Computers are used heavily in course work. 60 computer terminals/PCs are available for use by students in program; they are located in the library, computer labs, the research center. Students in the program are not required to have their own PC.

Computer Resources/On-line Services

Training	Yes	CompuServe	No
Internet	Yes	Dun's	No
E-Mail	Yes	Dow Jones	No
LEXIS/NEXIS	Yes	Dialog	No

ADMISSION

Acceptance 1994-95 358 applied for admission; 17% were accepted.

Entrance Requirements First degree, GMAT score of 520, written and oral entrance examination, test in German, English and a third language. Core courses waived through: previous course work.

Application Requirements Application form.

Application Deadline 4/15 for fall.

FINANCIALS

Costs for 1994-95 Tuition: Full-time: 5,500 German marks/semester.

Financial Aid In 1994-95, candidates received some institutionally administered aid in the form of grants, loans, fellowships. Financial aid is not available to part-time students. Application deadline: 4/15 for fall.

Applications are processed on a rolling basis. Contact: Ms. Brigitte Münich, Director of Admissions, Burgplatz, 56179 Vallendar, Germany. 261-65-09.

INTERNATIONAL STUDENTS
Services and Facilities International student office, international student center, language tutoring.

Applying TOEFL required, minimum score of 560; proof of health; proof of adequate funds; basic knowledge of the German language. Admission application deadline: 4/15 for fall. Contact: Mr. Axel Schumacher, Exchange Program Officer, Burgplatz 2, 56179 Vallendar, Germany. 261-65-09 Ext. 142.

PLACEMENT
In 1993-94, 110 organizations participated in on-campus recruiting; 250 on-campus interviews were conducted. Placement services include alumni network, career library, career placement, electronic job bank, job interviews, resume preparation, and resume referral to employers. Of 1994 graduates, 100% were employed within three months of graduation.

Jobs by Employer Type Manufacturing 40%; service 15%; consulting 25%; self-employed 10%; higher education 10%.

Program Contact: Ms. Brigitte Münch, Director of Admissions, Koblenz School of Corporate Management (WHU), Burgplatz 2, 56179 Vallendar, Germany. 261-65-09 Ext. 122; Fax: 261-65-09 Ext. 111.

Schiller International University

Berlin, Germany

OVERVIEW
Schiller International University is an independent nonprofit graduate-only coed institution. Founded 1964. Setting: urban campus. Total institutional enrollment: 25.

MBA HIGHLIGHTS

Entrance Difficulty**
Mean GMAT: N/R
Mean GPA: 3.0

Cost $$
Tuition: $5,720/semester
Room & Board: $5,000 (off-campus)

Enrollment Profile
Full-time: 15   Work Exp: N/R
Part-time: 10   Women: 32%
Total: 25
Average Age: 28

Average Class Size: N/R

ACADEMICS
Calendar Semesters.

Concentration International business.

Faculty Part-time: 8.

Teaching Methodology Case study: 20%, lecture: 40%, research: 20%, student presentations: 10%, team projects: 10%.

Special Opportunities International exchange in France, Spain, Switzerland, United Kingdom, United States of America. Internship program available.

STUDENT STATISTICS
Undergraduate Majors Business 87%; engineering/technology 1%; humanities 7%; social sciences 5%.

FACILITIES
Housing College housing not available.

Technology 15 computer terminals/PCs are available for use by students in program; they are located in computer labs. Students in the program are not required to have their own PC.

Computer Resources/On-line Services
Training   No

ADMISSION
Entrance Requirements First degree, GMAT score, minimum 2.8 GPA. Core courses waived through: previous course work.

Application Requirements Application form, copies of transcript.

Application Deadline Applications are processed on a rolling basis.

FINANCIALS
Financial Aid In 1994-95, candidates received some institutionally administered aid in the form of scholarships, loans, work-study. Financial aid is available to part-time students. Application deadline: 4/1 for annual. Contact: Ms. B.J. Slovacek, Financial Aid Officer, Bergstrasse 106, 69121 Heidelberg, Germany. 6221-45810.

INTERNATIONAL STUDENTS
Demographics 88% of students on campus are international; Europe 40%, Asia 15%, North America 12%, South America 7%, Africa 4%, Central America 2%, Other 20%.

Services and Facilities International student office, international student center, visa services, language tutoring, ESL courses, counseling/support services.

Applying TOEFL required, minimum score of 550. Financial aid is available to international students. Financial aid application deadline: 4/1 for annual. Admission applications are processed on a rolling basis. Contact: Ms. Karen Altieri, Director of Information and Alumni Affairs, 453 Edgewater Drive, Dunedin, FL 34698-7532. (813) 736-5082.

PROGRAM
One-Year MBA Length of program: Minimum: 12 months. Full-time classes: Main campus; day, evening, summer. Part-time classes: Main campus; day, evening, summer. Degree requirements: 45 credits including 24 elective credits. Final oral comprehensive exam or oral defense of thesis. Languages: English.

PLACEMENT
Placement services include alumni network and career placement.

Program Contact: Ms. Karen Altieri, Director of Information and Alumni Affairs, Schiller International University, 453 Edgewater Drive, Dunedin, FL 34698-7532. (813) 736-5082, or (800) 336-4133; Fax: (813) 736-6263.

Schiller International University

Heidelberg, Germany

OVERVIEW
Schiller International University is an independent nonprofit coed institution. Founded 1964. Setting: urban campus with easy access to Frankfurt. Total institutional enrollment: 318.

MBA HIGHLIGHTS

Entrance Difficulty**
Mean GMAT: N/R
Mean GPA: 3.0

Cost $$
Tuition: $5,720/semester
Room & Board: $4,940

Enrollment Profile
Full-time: 66   Work Exp: N/R
Part-time: 20   Women: 37%
Total: 86
Average Age: 28

Average Class Size: 15

ACADEMICS
Calendar Semesters.

Curricular Focus International business, problem solving and decision making, teamwork.

Concentrations Hotel management, international business.

Teaching Methodology Case study: 20%, lecture: 40%, research: 20%, student presentations: 10%, team projects: 10%.

Special Opportunities International exchange in France, Spain, Switzerland, United Kingdom, United States of America. Internship program available.

STUDENT STATISTICS

Undergraduate Majors Business 87%; engineering/technology 1%; humanities 7%; social sciences 5%.

FACILITIES

Information Resources Main library with 8,000 bound volumes, 94 periodical subscriptions.

Housing College housing available.

Technology 15 computer terminals/PCs are available for use by students in program; they are located in computer labs. Students in the program are not required to have their own PC.

ADMISSION

Entrance Requirements First degree, GMAT score, minimum 2.8 GPA. Core courses waived through: previous course work.

Application Requirements Application form, copies of transcript.

Application Deadline Applications are processed on a rolling basis.

FINANCIALS

Financial Aid In 1994-95, candidates received some institutionally administered aid in the form of scholarships, work-study. Application deadline: 4/1 for annual. Contact: Ms. B.J. Slovacek, Financial Aid Officer, Bergstrasse 106, 69121 Heidelberg, Germany. 6221-45810.

INTERNATIONAL STUDENTS

Demographics 88% of students on campus are international; Europe 40%, Asia 15%, North America 12%, South America 7%, Africa 4%, Central America 2%, Other 20%.

Services and Facilities International student office, international student center, visa services, language tutoring, ESL courses, counseling/support services.

Applying TOEFL required, minimum score of 550. Financial aid is available to international students. Financial aid application deadline: 4/1 for annual. Admission applications are processed on a rolling basis. Contact: Ms. Karen Altieri, Director of Information and Alumni Affairs, 453 Edgewater Drive, Dunedin, FL 34698-7532. (813) 736-5082.

PROGRAM

One-Year MBA Length of program: Minimum: 12 months. Full-time classes: Main campus, Berlin (Germany), London (United Kingdom), Strasbourg (France), Paris (France), Madrid (Spain); day, evening, weekends, summer. Part-time classes: Main campus; day, evening, weekends, summer. Degree requirements: 45 credits. Final oral comprehensive exam or oral defense of thesis. Languages: English. Average class size: 18.

PLACEMENT

Placement services include alumni network and career placement.

Program Contact: Ms. Karen Altieri, Director of Information and Alumni Affairs, Schiller International University, 453 Edgewater Drive, Dunedin, FL 34698-7532. (813) 736-5082, or (800) 336-4133; Fax: (813) 736-6263.

HONG KONG

The Chinese University of Hong Kong

Faculty of Business Administration

Shatin, NT, Hong Kong

OVERVIEW

The Chinese University of Hong Kong is a coed institution. Founded 1963. Setting: suburban campus. Total institutional enrollment: 11,600. Program was first offered in 1966. Accredited by Hong Kong Society of Accountants, Program of International Management, AACSB.

MBA HIGHLIGHTS

Entrance Difficulty***
Mean GMAT: 600
Mean GPA: N/R

Cost
Tuition: 12,000 Hong Kong dollars/term
Room & Board: N/R

Enrollment Profile
Full-time: N/R   Work Exp: 60% -100%
Part-time: N/R   Women: 60%
Total: 337
Average Age: 27

Average Class Size: 30

ACADEMICS

Length of Program Minimum: 24 months. Maximum: 5 years.

Calendar Semesters.

Full-time Classes Main campus; day.

Part-time Classes TsimShatsui, Hong Kong; evening.

Degree Requirements 54 credits. Other: Project or thesis.

Required Courses Accounting, business strategy, business systems, economics, financial management, human resources management, international business, legal environment of business, management information systems, marketing management, production and operations management, statistical analysis.

Curricular Focus International business, problem solving and decision making, teamwork.

Concentrations Accounting, economics, finance, international business, management, management information systems, marketing, operations management, quantitative analysis.

Faculty Full-time: 44, 98% with doctorates; part-time: 3, 33% with doctorates.

Teaching Methodology Case study: 30%, lecture: 40%, research: 5%, seminars by members of the business community: 2%, student presentations: 13%, team projects: 10%.

Special Opportunities International exchange in Canada, United Kingdom, United States.

STUDENT STATISTICS

Geographic Representation Hong Kong 90%; People's Republic of China 5%; other 5%.

Other Background Graduate degrees in other disciplines: 95-98%. Work experience: On average, students have 2-6 years of work experience on entrance to the program.

FACILITIES

Information Resources Business collection includes 1,500 bound volumes, 615 periodical subscriptions, 3 CD-ROMs.

Housing 23% of students in program live in college-owned or -operated housing.

Technology Computers are used moderately in course work. 230 computer terminals/PCs, linked by a campus-wide computer network, are available for use by students in program; they are located in student rooms, the computer center, computer labs. Students in the program are not required to have their own PC.

Computer Resources/On-line Services

Training	Yes	Dow Jones	Yes
Internet	Yes	Dialog	Yes
E-Mail	Yes		

Other on-line services: SEC.

ADMISSION

Acceptance 1994-95 546 applied for admission; 27% were accepted.

Entrance Requirements First degree, GMAT score of 550, minimum 3.0 GPA, minimum 3 years of work experience for part time students. Core courses waived through: previous course work.

Application Requirements Interview, copies of transcript.

Application Deadline 2/28 for fall.

FINANCIALS

Costs for 1994-95 Tuition: Full-time: 12,000 Hong Kong dollars/term.

Financial Aid In 1994-95, candidates received some institutionally administered aid in the form of grants, scholarships, loans. Application deadline: 9/1 for fall. Contact: Mr. King H. Chan, Assistant Student Affairs Officer, Office of Student Affairs, Shatin, N.T., Hong Kong. 609-7205.

INTERNATIONAL STUDENTS

Applying Financial aid is not available to international students.

ALTERNATE MBA PROGRAM

Executive MBA (EMBA)

PLACEMENT

In 1993-94, 922 organizations participated in on-campus recruiting. Placement services include alumni network, career library, career placement, job interviews, and resume preparation. Of 1994 graduates, 90% were employed within three months of graduation, the average starting salary was 13,435 Hong Kong dollars, the range was 10,000-35,000 Hong Kong dollars.

Jobs by Employer Type Manufacturing 6%; service 91%; government 3%.

Jobs by Functional Area Marketing/sales 27%; finance 35%; operations 3%; management 32%; technical management 3%.

Program Contact: Ms. Lauren Lee, Admissions Coordinator, The Chinese University of Hong Kong, Shatin, N.T., Hong Kong. 609-7786; Fax: 609-6289; Internet Address: laurenlee@cuhk.hk.

Hong Kong Baptist College

School of Business

Kowloon Tong, Hong Kong

OVERVIEW

Hong Kong Baptist College is a government-supported coed institution. Founded 1956. Setting: urban campus. Total institutional enrollment: 4,800. Program was first offered in 1994.

MBA HIGHLIGHTS

Entrance Difficulty*
Mean GMAT: 500
Mean GPA: N/R

Cost
Tuition: 42,000 Hong Kong dollars
Room & Board: 100,000 Hong Kong dollars (off-campus)

Enrollment Profile

Full-time: 0	Work Exp: 100%
Part-time: 49	Women: 28%
Total: 49	
Average Age: 31	

Average Class Size: 50

ACADEMICS

Length of Program Minimum: 24 months. Maximum: 2 years.

Calendar Trimesters.

Part-time Classes Main campus; evening.

Degree Requirements 36 units including 8 elective units. Other: Project.

Required Courses Dimensions of modern business, information systems in a global environment, international marketing management, legal aspects of international business, management accounting and control, management and organizational behavior, management of international firms, multinational financial management, production, operations, total quality management, quantitative method for decision making.

Curricular Focus Business issues and problems, international business, strategic analysis and planning.

Concentrations Accounting, economics, entrepreneurship, finance, human resources management, international business, management, management information systems, marketing, operations management, organizational behavior, quantitative analysis, strategic management.

Faculty Full-time: 14, 65% with doctorates.

Teaching Methodology Case study: 20%, faculty seminars: 5%, lecture: 30%, research: 5%, seminars by members of the business community: 5%, student presentations: 20%, team projects: 15%.

STUDENT STATISTICS

Geographic Representation Hong Kong 100%.

Undergraduate Majors Business 26%; humanities 21%; science/mathematics 23%; social sciences 19%; other 12%.

Other Background Work experience: On average, students have 7 years of work experience on entrance to the program.

FACILITIES

Housing College housing not available.

Technology Computers are used moderately in course work. 202 computer terminals/PCs, linked by a campus-wide computer network, are available for use by students in program; they are located in the computer

center. Students in the program are not required to have their own PC. $250 are budgeted per student for computer support.

Computer Resources/On-line Services

Training	Yes	CompuServe	No
Internet	Yes	Dun's	No
E-Mail	Yes	Dow Jones	No
Multimedia Center	Yes	Dialog	Yes
LEXIS/NEXIS	No	Bloomberg	No

ADMISSION

Acceptance 1994-95 119 applied for admission; 41% were accepted.

Entrance Requirements First degree, GMAT score of 500, minimum 2 years of work experience.

Application Requirements Interview, application form, copies of transcript, 2 letters of recommendation.

Application Deadline 8/13 for fall.

FINANCIALS

Costs for 1994-95 Tuition: Part-time evening: 42,000 Hong Kong dollars. Average room and board costs are 100,000 Hong Kong dollars per academic year (off-campus).

Financial Aid Financial aid is not available to part-time students. Application deadlines: 9/1 for fall, 6/1 for spring. Contact: Scholarship and Financial Aid Section, Academic Registry, Kowloon, Hong Kong. 339-7400.

INTERNATIONAL STUDENTS

Services and Facilities Visa services, counseling/support services.

Applying Financial aid is not available to international students. Admission application deadline: 6/1 for fall.

Program Contact: Ms. Emily Dan, Assistant Administrative Officer, Hong Kong Baptist College, Admissions Section, Academic Registry, Kowloon, Hong Kong. 339-7937; Fax: 339-7373; Internet Address: edan@ctsc.hkbc.hk.

The Hong Kong University of Science and Technology

The School of Business and Management

Kowloon, Hong Kong

OVERVIEW

The Hong Kong University of Science and Technology is a city-supported coed institution. Administratively affiliated with Anderson Graduate School of Management, University of California, Los Angeles. Setting: suburban campus. Total institutional enrollment: 5,247. Program was first offered in 1991. Accredited by Hong Kong Government.

MBA HIGHLIGHTS

Entrance Difficulty**

Cost $
Tuition: $4,402
Room & Board: $1,321

Enrollment Profile

Full-time: 60	Work Exp: 47%
Part-time: 195	Women: 29%
Total: 255	
Average Age: 25	

Average Class Size: 40

ACADEMICS

Length of Program Minimum: 24 months. Maximum: 2 years.

Calendar Semesters.

Full-time Classes Main campus; day, evening, weekends.

Part-time Classes Main campus; evening, weekends, summer.

Degree Requirements 64 credits including 22 elective credits.

Required Courses Accounting for management, accounting foundation, corporate finance, field study project, financial decisions, international business game, introductory statistics for business, legal environment of business, management communication, management information systems, management of organization, management policy, managerial macroeconomics, managerial microeconomics, managerial problem solving, marketing strategy and policy, operations and technology management.

Curricular Focus Business issues and problems, economic and financial theory, international business.

Concentrations Accounting, economics, entrepreneurship, finance, human resources management, international business, management, management information systems, marketing, operations management, organizational behavior, quantitative analysis, strategic management.

Faculty Full-time: 135, 100% with doctorates.

Teaching Methodology Case study: 20%, lecture: 40%, seminars by members of the business community: 5%, student presentations: 15%, team projects: 20%.

Special Opportunities International exchange in Canada, France, United States of America. Internships include finance. Other: International visiting student program.

STUDENT STATISTICS

Undergraduate Majors Business 19%; engineering/technology 35%; humanities 9%; science/mathematics 18%; social sciences 12%; other 7%.

Other Background Graduate degrees in other disciplines: 100%. Work experience: On average, students have 2 years of work experience on entrance to the program.

FACILITIES

Housing 60% of students in program live in college-owned or -operated housing. Assistance with housing search provided.

Technology Computers are used heavily in course work. 300 computer terminals/PCs, linked by a campus-wide computer network, are available for use by students in program; they are located in classrooms, the library, the computer center, computer labs, the research center, networking lab, workstation lab, behavior lab. Students in the program are not required to have their own PC. $750 are budgeted per student for computer support.

Computer Resources/On-line Services

Training	Yes	Multimedia Center	Yes
Internet	Yes	LEXIS/NEXIS	Yes
E-Mail	Yes		

ADMISSION

Acceptance 1994-95 270 applied for admission; 30% were accepted.

Entrance Requirements First degree, GMAT score, minimum 2.75 GPA. Core courses waived through: previous course work.

Application Requirements Written essay, interview, application form, resume/curriculum vitae, 2 letters of recommendation.

Application Deadline 3/15 for fall.

FINANCIALS

Estimated Costs for 1995-96 Tuition: Full-time: $4,402 for residents; Part-time day: $5,795 for residents. Average room and board costs are $1,321 per academic year (on-campus) and $10,000 per academic year (off-campus).

Financial Aid In 1994-95, 98% of candidates received some institutionally administered aid in the form of part-time demonstrationship. Financial aid is not available to part-time students. Application deadline: 8/1 for fall. Applications are processed on a rolling basis.

INTERNATIONAL STUDENTS

Applying TOEFL required; proof of health; proof of adequate funds. Financial aid is not available to international students. Admission application deadline: 3/15 for fall. Contact: Ms. Doris Chan, Executive Officer, Clear Water Bay, Kowloon, Hong Kong. 358-7534.

PLACEMENT

In 1993-94, 20 organizations participated in on-campus recruiting; 5 on-campus interviews were conducted. Placement services include alumni network, career counseling/planning, career library, career placement, company presentations, electronic job bank, job interviews, recruitment talks, and resume referral to employers. Of 1994 graduates, 93% were employed within three months of graduation, the average starting salary was $20,400, the range was $16,800-$30,000.

Jobs by Employer Type Service 19%; consulting 4%; banking/finance 17%; consumer products 22%; telecommunications 9%; computer market research, oil and chemicals 29%.

Jobs by Functional Area Marketing/sales 53%; finance 26%; management 17%; technical management 4%.

Program Contact: Ms. Stella Y. Ng, Associate Director Postgraduate Program, The Hong Kong University of Science and Technology, Clear Water Bay, Kowloon, Hong Kong. 358-7535; Fax: 358-1467; Internet Address: in%"bmstella@usthk.bitnet".

University of Hong Kong

University of Hong Kong Business School

Hong Kong

OVERVIEW

The University of Hong Kong is a government-supported coed institution. Setting: urban campus. Total institutional enrollment: 13,000. Program was first offered in 1976. Approved by the Association of MBA Programs (U.K.).

MBA HIGHLIGHTS

Entrance Difficulty N/R
Mean GMAT: 585
Mean GPA: N/R

Cost
Tuition: 40,000 Hong Kong dollars
Room & Board: N/R

Enrollment Profile
Full-time: 0	Work Exp: 100%
Part-time: 210	Women: 28%
Total: 210	
Average Age: 28	

Average Class Size: 40

ACADEMICS

Length of Program Minimum: 27 months. Maximum: 5 years.

Calendar Semesters.

Part-time Classes Main campus; evening, weekends.

Curricular Focus Business issues and problems, economic and financial theory, entrepreneurship, general management, international business, leadership, organizational development and change management, problem solving and decision making, strategic analysis and planning, teamwork.

Concentrations Accounting, economics, entrepreneurship, finance, human resources management, international business, management, management information systems, marketing, operations management, organizational behavior, quantitative analysis, strategic management.

Faculty Full-time: 19, 59% with doctorates; part-time: 11, 64% with doctorates.

STUDENT STATISTICS

Undergraduate Majors Business 21%; engineering/technology 31%; humanities 8%; science/mathematics 22%; social sciences 12%; other 6%.

Other Background Graduate degrees in other disciplines: 100%. Work experience: On average, students have 6 years of work experience on entrance to the program.

FACILITIES

Housing College housing not available.

Technology Computers are used moderately in course work. Computer terminals/PCs, linked by a campus-wide computer network, are available for use by students in program; they are located in learning resource center, the computer center, computer labs, the research center. Students in the program are required to have their own PC.

Computer Resources/On-line Services

Training	Yes	E-Mail	Yes

ADMISSION

Acceptance 1994-95 350 applied for admission; 23% were accepted.

Entrance Requirements First degree, GMAT score of 500, minimum 3 years of work experience.

Application Requirements Written essay, interview, application form, copies of transcript, resume/curriculum vitae, personal statement.

Application Deadline 4/15 for fall.

FINANCIALS

Estimated Costs for 1995-96 Tuition: Part-time evening: 40,000 Hong Kong dollars.

Financial Aid Financial aid is not available to part-time students.

INTERNATIONAL STUDENTS

Applying TOEFL required, minimum score of 550. Financial aid is not available to international students. Admission application deadline: 4/15 for fall. Contact: Mr. W. P. J. Brandon, Dean, Office of Student Affairs, Jokfulam Road,, Hong Kong. 859-2305.

Program Contact: Dr. J. Newton, MBA Director, University of Hong Kong, Room 1109, K. K. Leung Building, Pokfulam Road,, Hong Kong. 859-1021; Fax: 858-5614; Internet Address: jnewton@hkucc.bitnet.

INDONESIA

Institut Pengembangan Manajemen Indonesia

Jakarta, Indonesia

OVERVIEW
Institut Pengembangan Manajemen Indonesia is an independent nonprofit specialized primarily male institution. Founded 1982. Setting: urban campus. Total institutional enrollment: 118. Program was first offered in 1984.

MBA HIGHLIGHTS

Entrance Difficulty*
Mean GMAT: 515
Mean GPA: N/R

Cost
Tuition: N/R
Room & Board: N/R

Enrollment Profile
Full-time: 118
Part-time: 0
Total: 118
Average Age: 30

Work Exp: 95%
Women: 10%

Average Class Size: 40

ACADEMICS
Calendar Trimesters.
Curricular Focus General management, international business, problem solving and decision making.
Concentration International business.
Faculty Full-time: 8, 50% with doctorates; part-time: 3, 100% with doctorates.
Teaching Methodology Case study: 60%, lecture: 15%, research: 5%, seminars by members of the business community: 5%, student presentations: 5%, team projects: 10%.
Special Opportunities International exchange in Canada.

STUDENT STATISTICS
Undergraduate Majors Business 20%; engineering/technology 60%; social sciences 20%.
Other Background Graduate degrees in other disciplines: 2%. Work experience: On average, students have 3 years of work experience on entrance to the program.

FACILITIES
Housing College housing not available.
Technology Computers are used heavily in course work. 40 computer terminals/PCs, linked by a campus-wide computer network, are available for use by students in program; they are located in group study rooms. Students in the program are not required to have their own PC. $100 are budgeted per student for computer support.
Computer Resources/On-line Services

Training	Yes	Dun's	No
Internet	No	Dow Jones	No
E-Mail	No	Dialog	No
LEXIS/NEXIS	No	Bloomberg	No
CompuServe	No		

ADMISSION
Acceptance 1994-95 157 applied for admission; 75% were accepted.
Entrance Requirements First degree, GMAT score of 500, minimum 2 years of work experience.
Application Requirements Interview.
Application Deadlines 12/15 for spring, 10/1 for international students. Applications are processed on a rolling basis.

FINANCIALS
Financial Aid Financial aid is not available to part-time students.

INTERNATIONAL STUDENTS
Services and Facilities Visa services.
Applying TOEFL required, minimum score of 500; proof of adequate funds. Financial aid is not available to international students. Admission application deadline: 10/2 for fall. Applications are processed on a rolling basis.

PROGRAM
One-Year MBA Length of program: 12 months. Full-time classes: Main campus; day. Degree requirements: 36 credits. Languages: English. Average class size: 40.

PLACEMENT
In 1993-94, 10 organizations participated in on-campus recruiting; 25 on-campus interviews were conducted. Placement services include alumni network, career counseling/planning, career fairs, career placement, job interviews, and resume referral to employers. Of 1994 graduates, 100% were employed within three months of graduation.
Jobs by Employer Type Manufacturing 40%; service 60%.
Jobs by Functional Area Marketing/sales 25%; finance 30%; operations 20%; management 20%; strategic planning 5%.

Program Contact: Dr. Antarikso Abdulrahman, Program Director, Institut Pengembangan Manajemen Indonesia, JL Rawajati Timur I/1, Kalibata, 12045 Jakarta, Indonesia. 21-797-0419; Fax: 21-797-0374.

IRELAND

University College Cork

Faculty of Commerce

Cork, Ireland

OVERVIEW
The University College Cork is a government-supported coed institution. Founded 1849. Setting: urban campus. Total institutional enrollment: 10,000. Program was first offered in 1991.

MBA HIGHLIGHTS

Entrance Difficulty**
Mean GMAT: 490
Mean GPA: N/R

Cost
Tuition: N/R
Room & Board: N/R

Enrollment Profile
Full-time: 0
Part-time: 13
Total: 13
Average Age: 27

Work Exp: 100%
Women: 15%

Average Class Size: 20

ACADEMICS
Length of Program Minimum: 24 months.
Calendar Semesters.
Part-time Classes Main campus.
Degree Requirements 18 courses including 2 elective courses. Other: Project.
Required Courses Accounting and financial management, business legal environment, corporate finance, data analysis and decision support systems, economics of enterprise, human resources management, industry analysis: the food sector, industry and competition, information systems for executives, international business, international marketing, macroeconomic environment, management accounting and control, management and organization, marketing, strategic management.
Curricular Focus General management, organizational development and change management, teamwork.
Concentration Management.

Faculty Full-time: 20, 50% with doctorates; part-time: 10, 5% with doctorates.

Teaching Methodology Case study: 20%, faculty seminars: 10%, lecture: 20%, research: 10%, seminars by members of the business community: 10%, student presentations: 10%, team projects: 20%.

STUDENT STATISTICS

Geographic Representation Ireland 100%.

Undergraduate Majors Business 20%; engineering/technology 40%; humanities 25%; social sciences 15%.

Other Background Graduate degrees in other disciplines: 10%. Work experience: On average, students have 7 years of work experience on entrance to the program.

FACILITIES

Housing College housing available.

Technology Computers are used heavily in course work. 25 computer terminals/PCs are available for use by students in program; they are located in the computer center, computer labs. Students in the program are not required to have their own PC.

Computer Resources/On-line Services

Training	Yes	E-Mail	Yes
Internet	Yes		

ADMISSION

Acceptance 1994-95 30 applied for admission; 43% were accepted.

Entrance Requirements First degree, GMAT score, minimum 2 years of work experience.

Application Requirements Written essay, interview, application form, copies of transcript, personal statement.

Application Deadline 4/21 for fall.

INTERNATIONAL STUDENTS

Applying TOEFL required.

PLACEMENT

Placement services include career counseling/planning and career library. Of 1994 graduates, 100% were employed within three months of graduation.

Program Contact: Acting MBA Director, University College Cork, Lee House, Cork, Ireland. 21-276871; Fax: 21-273551.

University College Dublin

Graduate School of Business

Blackrock, County Dublin, Ireland

OVERVIEW

The University College Dublin is a government-supported coed institution. Founded 1908. Setting: suburban campus. Total institutional enrollment: 14,000. Program was first offered in 1964.

MBA HIGHLIGHTS

Entrance Difficulty**
Mean GMAT: 550
Mean GPA: N/R

Cost
Tuition: 5,750 Irish pounds
Room & Board: 1,500 Irish pounds

Enrollment Profile

Full-time: 22	Work Exp: 100%
Part-time: 42	Women: 26%
Total: 64	
Average Age: 30	

Class Size: 25 - 30

ACADEMICS

Length of Program Minimum: 12 months. Maximum: 2 years.

Calendar Semesters.

Full-time Classes Main campus; day, evening, weekends, summer.

Part-time Classes Main campus; evening, weekends, summer.

Degree Requirements 21 credits including 3 elective credits.

Required Courses Business economics, business law, business policy, corporate finance, human resources management, international business, major research project, management control systems, management information systems, managerial accounting, marketing management, operations management, organization behavior, principles of finance, principles of strategy, strategic management.

Curricular Focus General management, international business, leadership, problem solving and decision making, strategic analysis and planning, teamwork.

Concentrations Accounting, entrepreneurship, finance, human resources management, international business, management, management information systems, marketing, operations management, organizational behavior, public administration, public policy, strategic management.

Faculty Full-time: 70, 82% with doctorates; part-time: 3, 30% with doctorates.

Teaching Methodology Case study: 15%, faculty seminars: 2%, lecture: 56%, research: 14%, student presentations: 13%.

Special Opportunities International exchange in Denmark, Netherlands, Portugal, United Kingdom.

STUDENT STATISTICS

Geographic Representation Ireland 92%; United Kingdom 5%; Russia 2%; Scandinavia 1%.

Undergraduate Majors Business 32%; education 7%; engineering/technology 37%; humanities 3%; other 21%.

Other Background Graduate degrees in other disciplines: 90%. Work experience: On average, students have 5-7 years of work experience on entrance to the program.

FACILITIES

Information Resources Business collection in Business Information Center includes 4,500 bound volumes, 400 periodical subscriptions, 6 CD-ROMs.

Housing 16% of students in program live in college-owned or -operated housing.

Technology Computers are used heavily in course work. 120 computer terminals/PCs, linked by a campus-wide computer network, are available for use by students in program; they are located in student rooms, classrooms, the library, the computer center, computer labs, the research center. Students in the program are not required to have their own PC.

Computer Resources/On-line Services

Training	Yes	Dun's	No
E-Mail	Yes	Dow Jones	Yes
Videoconference Center	Yes	Dialog	No
LEXIS/NEXIS	No	Bloomberg	Yes
CompuServe	Y es		

ADMISSION

Acceptance 1994-95 Of those applying, 35% were accepted.

Entrance Requirements First degree, GMAT score of 480, minimum 3 years of work experience. Core courses waived through: previous course work.

Application Requirements Application form, copies of transcript, resume/curriculum vitae, 2 letters of recommendation.

Application Deadlines 3/31 for fall. Applications are processed on a rolling basis. Application discs available.

FINANCIALS

Estimated Costs for 1995-96 Tuition: Full-time: 5,750 Irish pounds for residents. Average room and board costs are 1,500 Irish pounds per academic year (on-campus) and 2,500 Irish pounds per academic year (off-campus).

INTERNATIONAL STUDENTS

Demographics 2% of students on campus are international; Europe 42%, Africa 22%, Asia 15%, North America 10%, Central America 3%, Australia 2%, Other 6%.

Services and Facilities International student housing; international student office, international student center, visa services, language tutoring, special assistance for nonnative speakers of English, counseling/support services.

Applying TOEFL required, minimum score of 600. Financial aid is not available to international students. Admission application deadline: 3/31 for fall. Applications are processed on a rolling basis. Contact: Ms. Jean Reddan, International Affairs Officer, Gradute School of Business, Carysfort Avenue, Black Rock, Blackrock, County Dublin, Ireland. 1-906-8969.

ALTERNATE MBA PROGRAM

Executive MBA (EMBA) Length of program: Minimum: 24 months. Maximum: 3 years. Full-time classes: Main campus; day, evening, weekends, summer. Part-time classes: Main campus; evening, weekends, summer. Degree requirements: 21 credits including 3 elective credits. Languages: English. Average class size: 25.

PLACEMENT

Placement services include alumni network, career counseling/planning, career library, and career placement. Of 1994 graduates, 100% were employed within three months of graduation.

Jobs by Employer Type Manufacturing 20%; service 5%; consulting 65%; nonprofit 5%; other 5%.

Jobs by Functional Area Marketing/sales 17%; finance 12%; management 29%; strategic planning 34%; technical management 8%.

Program Contact: Ms. Eleanor Curtis, MBA Program Manager, University College Dublin, Carysfort Avenue, Blackrock, County Dublin, Ireland. 1-706-8355; Fax: 1-283-1911; Internet Address: eleanor@blackrock. lkb.ie.

University College, Galway

School of Economics and Business Studies

Galway, Ireland

OVERVIEW

The University College, Galway is a government-supported coed institution. Part of National University of Ireland. Founded 1845. Setting: urban campus. Total institutional enrollment: 8,000. Program was first offered in 1972.

MBA HIGHLIGHTS

Entrance Difficulty***
Mean GMAT: 500
Mean GPA: N/R

Cost
Tuition: N/R
(Nonresident: N/R)
Room & Board: N/R

Enrollment Profile
Full-time: 0	Work Exp: 100%
Part-time: 26	Women: 25%
Total: 26	
Average Age: 28	

Average Class Size: 27

ACADEMICS

Calendar Terms.

Curricular Focus Entrepreneurship, general management, strategic analysis and planning.

Concentrations Accounting, economics, entrepreneurship, finance, human resources management, management, management information systems, marketing, operations management, organizational behavior, quantitative analysis, strategic management.

Faculty Full-time: 14, 60% with doctorates.

Teaching Methodology Case study: 30%, lecture: 40%, research: 15%, seminars by members of the business community: 5%, student presentations: 10%.

STUDENT STATISTICS

Undergraduate Majors Business 30%; engineering/technology 30%; humanities 20%; science/mathematics 20%.

Other Background Graduate degrees in other disciplines: 100%. Work experience: On average, students have 4 years of work experience on entrance to the program.

FACILITIES

Housing College housing not available.

Technology Computers are used moderately in course work. 40 computer terminals/PCs, linked by a campus-wide computer network, are available for use by students in program; they are located in the computer center, computer labs. Students in the program are required to have their own PC.

Computer Resources/On-line Services
Training	Yes	E-Mail	Yes
Internet	Yes	Dialog	Yes

ADMISSION

Acceptance 1994-95 120 applied for admission; 25% were accepted.

Entrance Requirements First degree, GMAT score of 450, minimum 3 years of work experience.

Application Requirements Interview, application form, copies of transcript.

Application Deadline 3/1 for fall.

FINANCIALS

Financial Aid Financial aid is not available to part-time students.

INTERNATIONAL STUDENTS

Demographics 8% of students on campus are international; Europe 80%, other 20%.

Applying Proof of health; proof of adequate funds. Financial aid is not available to international students.

PROGRAM

Executive MBA (EMBA) Length of program: Minimum: 24 months. Part-time classes: Main campus; weekends. Degree requirements: 15 courses.

Program Contact: Dr. Aidan Daly, Director, Executive MBA Program, University College, Galway, Galway, Ireland. 91-24411 Ext. 2548; Fax: 91-24130; Internet Address: in%"marketing@ucg.ie".

University of Limerick

College of Business

Limerick, Ireland

OVERVIEW

The University of Limerick is a government-supported coed institution. Founded 1972. Accredited by Higher Education Authority.

MBA HIGHLIGHTS

Entrance Difficulty***
Mean GMAT: 500
Mean GPA: N/R

Cost
Tuition: N/R
(Nonresident: N/R)
Room & Board: N/R

Enrollment Profile
Full-time: N/R	Work Exp: N/R
Part-time: N/R	Women: 10%
Total: 40	
Average Age: N/R	

Average Class Size: 20

ACADEMICS

Curricular Focus Business issues and problems, general management, strategic analysis and planning.

Concentrations Entrepreneurship, international business, project management.

Teaching Methodology Case study: 10%, faculty seminars: 10%, lecture: 50%, research: 10%, student presentations: 10%, team projects: 10%.

FACILITIES

Housing College housing available.

ADMISSION

Entrance Requirements First degree, GMAT score of 500, minimum 5 years of work experience.

Application Requirements Application form, copies of transcript, personal statement, 2 letters of recommendation.

Application Deadlines 5/30 for fall. Applications are processed on a rolling basis.

INTERNATIONAL STUDENTS

Applying TOEFL required, minimum score of 550; IELTS required; proof of health; proof of adequate funds. Financial aid is not available to international students. Admission application deadline: 5/30 for fall. Applications are processed on a rolling basis.

PROGRAM
Executive MBA (EMBA) Length of program: Minimum: 24 months. Part-time classes: Main campus; day, evening. Languages: English.

Program Contact: Ms. Ann Lyons, Admissions Office, University of Limerick, National Technological Park, Limerick, Ireland. 61-333644; Fax: 61-338171.

ISRAEL

Tel Aviv University

The Leon Recamaty Graduate School of Administration

Tel Aviv, Israel

OVERVIEW
Tel Aviv University is a coed institution. Setting: urban campus. Total institutional enrollment: 3,500. Program was first offered in 1968.

MBA HIGHLIGHTS

Entrance Difficulty N/R

Cost $
Tuition: $2,400
Room & Board: N/R

Enrollment Profile
Full-time: N/R
Part-time: N/R
Total: 1,250
Average Age: N/R

Work Exp: 60%
Women: 30%

Average Class Size: 45

ACADEMICS
Length of Program Minimum: 24 months. Maximum: 5 years.
Calendar Semesters.
Full-time Classes Main campus; day, evening, early morning, summer.
Part-time Classes Main campus; day, evening, early morning, summer.
Degree Requirements 32 credits including 16 elective credits.
Concentrations Accounting, finance, health services, insurance, international business, management, management information systems, marketing, operations management, organizational behavior.
Faculty Full-time: 65, 100% with doctorates; part-time: 180, 45% with doctorates.
Teaching Methodology Case study: 5%, lecture: 60%, research: 10%, seminars by members of the business community: 5%, student presentations: 10%, team projects: 10%.
Special Opportunities International exchange in Canada, Finland, France, United States of America.

STUDENT STATISTICS
Undergraduate Majors Business 40%; engineering/technology 40%; other 20%.

FACILITIES
Housing College housing not available.
Technology Computers are used moderately in course work. 200 computer terminals/PCs are available for use by students in program; they are located in the library, the computer center, computer labs.
Computer Resources/On-line Services
E-Mail   Yes

ADMISSION
Acceptance 1994-95 946 applied for admission; 43% were accepted.
Entrance Requirements First degree, GMAT score.
Application Requirements Application form, copies of transcript.
Application Deadlines 2/1 for fall, 11/1 for spring.

FINANCIALS
Costs for 1994-95 Tuition: Full-time: $2,400.
Financial Aid In 1994-95, 10% of candidates received some form of institutionally administered aid. Total awards ranged from $600-$2,400. Contact: Financial Aid Office, 69978 Tel Aviv, Israel. 3-640-8067.

INTERNATIONAL STUDENTS
Demographics 1% of students on campus are international.
Services and Facilities Language tutoring.
Applying Financial aid is not available to international students. Admission application deadlines: 5/1 for fall, 11/1 for spring. Contact: Mrs. Rivka Ofir, Faculty of Management, 69978 Tel Aviv, Israel. 3-640-8962.

ALTERNATE MBA PROGRAM
Executive MBA (EMBA) Length of program: Minimum: 16 months. Full-time classes: Main campus; day, evening, early morning, summer. Degree requirements: 32 credits including 4 elective credits. Class size: 40-45.

Program Contact: Mrs. Michal Ras, Secretary, Admission Affairs, Tel Aviv University, Faculty of Management, 69978 Tel Aviv, Israel. 3-640-8096; Fax: 3-640-9560.

ITALY

Bocconi University

Milan, Italy

OVERVIEW
Bocconi University is an independent proprietary coed institution. Founded 1902. Setting: urban campus. Total institutional enrollment: 11,185. Program was first offered in 1975. Approved by the Association of MBA Programs (U.K.).

MBA HIGHLIGHTS

Entrance Difficulty**

Cost
Tuition: N/R
Room & Board: N/R

Enrollment Profile
Full-time: 110
Part-time: 0
Total: 110
Average Age: N/R

Work Exp: 100%
Women: 25%

Average Class Size: 60

ACADEMICS
Length of Program Minimum: 16 months.
Calendar 16-month program (September-December).
Degree Requirements 30 courses including 7 elective courses.
Required Courses Accounting and control, business law, business policy, economics, finance, financial markets and institutions, information systems, management of operation and technology, marketing, organization and personnel, public administration, quantitative methods, strategy, theories and models of the firm.
Curricular Focus Fashion and design, general management, information systems, international business, leadership, problem solving and decision making.
Concentrations Fashion and design, management information systems.
Faculty Full-time: 87; part-time: 52.
Teaching Methodology Case study: 35%, faculty seminars: 11%, lecture: 15%, research: 2%, seminars by members of the business community: 2%, student presentations: 10%, team projects: 25%.
Special Opportunities International exchange in Australia, France, Japan, Netherlands, United Kingdom, United States.

STUDENT STATISTICS
Undergraduate Majors Business 45%; engineering/technology 30%; humanities 7%; science/mathematics 14%; social sciences 4%.
Other Background Work experience: On average, students have 3 years of work experience on entrance to the program.

FACILITIES
Housing College housing not available.
Technology Computers are used heavily in course work. 100 computer terminals/PCs, linked by a campus-wide computer network, are available for use by students in program; they are located in group study rooms. Students in the program are not required to have their own PC.

Computer Resources/On-line Services

Training	Yes	CompuServe	No
Internet	Yes	Dun's	No
E-Mail	Yes	Dow Jones	No
Multimedia Center	Yes	Dialog	No
LEXIS/NEXIS	No	Bloomberg	No

ADMISSION

Acceptance 1994-95 Of those applying, 26% were accepted.

Entrance Requirements First degree, GMAT score, minimum 2 years of work experience.

Application Requirements Written essay, application form, copies of transcript, 2 letters of recommendation.

Application Deadline 4/30 for fall.

FINANCIALS

Financial Aid In 1994-95, candidates received some institutionally administered aid in the form of scholarships, tuition waivers. Application deadline: 4/30 for fall. Contact: Ms. Gabriella Aliatis, Director of Admissions, Via Balilla 16/18, 20136 Milan, Italy. 2-5836-3286.

INTERNATIONAL STUDENTS

Demographics 49% of students on campus are international.

Services and Facilities Language tutoring, ESL courses, counseling/support services, assistance for nonnative speakers of Italian.

Applying TOEFL required, minimum score of 600; proof of health; proof of adequate funds. Financial aid is available to international students. Financial aid application deadline: 4/30 for fall. Admission application deadline: 4/30 for fall.

PLACEMENT

In 1993-94, 115 organizations participated in on-campus recruiting; 741 on-campus interviews were conducted. Placement services include alumni network, career counseling/planning, career fairs, career library, career placement, job interviews, resume preparation, and resume referral to employers.

Jobs by Employer Type Manufacturing 39%; service 17%; consulting 23%; financial services 21%.

Program Contact: Ms. Gabriella Aliatis, Director of Admissions, Bocconi University, Via Balilla 16/18, 20136 Milan, Italy. 2-5836-3286; Fax: 2-5836-3275.

JAPAN

The International University of Japan

Graduate School of International Management

Minami Uonuma-gu, Japan

OVERVIEW

The International University of Japan is an independent nonprofit coed institution. Founded 1982. Setting: rural campus. Program was first offered in 1988. Accredited by Ministry of Education in Japan, AACSB.

MBA HIGHLIGHTS

Entrance Difficulty***
Mean GMAT: 561
Mean GPA: N/R

Cost
Tuition: N/R
Room & Board: N/R

Enrollment Profile

Full-time: 53	Work Exp: 93%
Part-time: 0	Women: 18%
Total: 53	
Average Age: 28	

Average Class Size: 70

---

*I*n July 1994, the International University of Japan (IUJ) welcomed a new president, Dr. George R. Packard, also the director at Reischauer Center, SAIS, Johns Hopkins University. He is a well-established scholar in Japan-U.S. relations; his familiarity and ties with the Japanese government and business community are a perfect fit with IUJ's educational mission.

Under Dr. Packard's new management team, IUJ is focusing its efforts on preparing a new generation of young people to create a better, more prosperous, more peaceful world. What makes IUJ unique is the combination of academic perspectives offered by two schools, one in international relations and a second in international management. These complementary perspectives provide a new breed of professionals with practical skills in international business management and a deeper understanding of the global environment in which business must operate in the twenty-first century.

In accordance with the renewed mission, the IUJ M.B.A. program is expanding its student exchange partners and course offerings to include fair representation from other parts of Asia in its curriculum and student experience. Leading universities such as the Chinese University of Hong Kong, National University of Singapore, and Chulalongkorn University will be involved in these efforts.

ACADEMICS

Length of Program Minimum: 18 months. Maximum: 4 years.

Calendar Quarters.

Full-time Classes Main campus; day.

Degree Requirements 51 credits including 22 elective credits.

Required Courses Advanced seminar, applied statistics, business policy, computing, finance, financial accounting, macroeconomics and policy, management communication, management science, managerial accounting, managerial economics, marketing, operations management, organizational behavior.

Curricular Focus General management, international business, strategic analysis and planning.

Concentrations Finance, international business, management, marketing, strategic management.

Faculty Full-time: 14, 70% with doctorates; part-time: 14, 80% with doctorates.

Teaching Methodology Case study: 50%, lecture: 20%, research: 5%, seminars by members of the business community: 5%, student presentations: 10%, team projects: 10%.

Special Opportunities International exchange in Belgium, Canada, France, Hong Kong, Italy, Netherlands, Singapore, Thailand, United Kingdom, United States of America. Other: Summer Program in the United States of America.

STUDENT STATISTICS

Other Background Graduate degrees in other disciplines: 13%. Work experience: On average, students have 4 years of work experience on entrance to the program.

FACILITIES

Information Resources Business collection includes 2,400 bound volumes, 200 periodical subscriptions, 1 CD-ROM, 120 videos.

Housing 84% of students in program live in college-owned or -operated housing.

Technology Computers are used heavily in course work. 84 computer terminals/PCs, linked by a campus-wide computer network, are available for use by students in program; they are located in dormitories, the library, the computer center, computer labs. Students in the program are not required to have their own PC.

Computer Resources/On-line Services

Training	Yes	Dun's	No
E-Mail	Yes	Dow Jones	No
LEXIS/NEXIS	Yes	Dialog	Yes
CompuServe	No	Bloomberg	No

ADMISSION

Acceptance 1994-95 171 applied for admission; 39% were accepted.

Entrance Requirements First degree, GMAT score of 530. Core courses waived through: previous course work, work experience.

Application Requirements Written essay, interview, application form, copies of transcript, resume/curriculum vitae, personal statement.

Application Deadlines 2/10 for fall, 4/7 for spring.

FINANCIALS

Financial Aid In 1994-95, 47% of candidates received some institutionally administered aid in the form of grants, scholarships, loans, assistantships.

Financial aid is not available to part-time students. Application deadline: 2/10 for fall. Contact: Admissions, MBA Program, Yamato-machi, 949-72 Yamato-machi, Japan. 257-79-1500.

INTERNATIONAL STUDENTS

Demographics 58% of students on campus are international; Asia 73%, Europe 6%, North America 6%, Africa 3%, Central America 3%, South America 3%, Other 6%.

Services and Facilities International student housing; international student office, international student center, visa services, language tutoring, ESL courses.

Applying TOEFL required, minimum score of 530; proof of health; proof of adequate funds. Financial aid is available to international students. Financial aid application deadlines: 2/10 for fall, 4/7 for spring. Admission application deadline: 2/10 for fall.

PLACEMENT

In 1993-94, 1 organization participated in on-campus recruiting; 8 on-campus interviews were conducted. Placement services include alumni network, resume preparation, and resume referral to employers. Of 1994 graduates, 90% were employed within three months of graduation.

Jobs by Employer Type Manufacturing 36%; service 36%; consulting 10%; teaching 3%; other 15%.

Program Contact: Admissions, MBA Program, The International University of Japan, Yamato-machi, 949-72 Yamato-machi, Japan. 257-79-1500; Fax: 257-79-4443; Internet Address: iujadm@jpniujoo.bitnet.
See full description on page 764.

MEXICO

Instituto Tecnológico y de Estudios Superiores de Monterrey, México City Campus

Mexico City, D.F., Mexico

OVERVIEW

Instituto Tecnológico y de Estudios Superiores de Monterrey, México City Campus is an independent nonprofit graduate-only institution. Total institutional enrollment: 2,680.

ACADEMICS

Concentration Management.

FACILITIES

Information Resources Main library with 28,742 bound volumes, 260 titles on microform, 1,210 periodical subscriptions.

Program Contact: Mr. Arturo Soltero Curiel, Campus Principal, Instituto Tecnológico y de Estudios Superiores de Monterrey, México City Campus, Fray Servando Teresa de Meir 99, 06090 Mexico City, Mexico. 5-673-02-43 Ext. 2001; Fax: 5-671-80-35.

MONACO

University of Southern Europe

Monaco Graduate School of Finance and Marketing

Monte Carlo, Monaco

OVERVIEW

The University of Southern Europe is an independent nonprofit coed institution. Founded 1986. Setting: urban campus. Total institutional enrollment: 135. Program was first offered in 1988.

MBA HIGHLIGHTS

Entrance Difficulty***
Mean GMAT: 540
Mean GPA: N/R

Cost
Tuition: N/R
(Nonresident: N/R)
Room & Board: N/R

Enrollment Profile
Full-time: 11   Work Exp: 80%
Part-time: 4   Women: 35%
Total: 15
Average Age: 30

Average Class Size: 20

ACADEMICS

Calendar Trimesters.

Curricular Focus Business issues and problems, international business, problem solving and decision making.

Concentrations Finance, international marketing.

Faculty Full-time: 8, 25% with doctorates; part-time: 191, 20% with doctorates.

Teaching Methodology Case study: 30%, lecture: 40%, research: 5%, seminars by members of the business community: 5%, student presentations: 5%, team projects: 15%.

Special Opportunities International exchange in Canada, Germany, Italy, United States of America.

STUDENT STATISTICS

Undergraduate Majors Business 33%; engineering/technology 6%; social sciences 20%; other 41%.

Other Background Graduate degrees in other disciplines: 13%. Work experience: On average, students have 5 years of work experience on entrance to the program.

FACILITIES

Housing 33% of students in program live in college-owned or -operated housing. Assistance with housing search provided.

Technology Computers are used heavily in course work. 11 computer terminals/PCs are available for use by students in program; they are located in computer labs. Students in the program are not required to have their own PC.

Computer Resources/On-line Services

Training	Yes	Dun's	No
Internet	Yes $	Dow Jones	No
E-Mail	Yes	Dialog	No
LEXIS/NEXIS	No	Bloomberg	No
CompuServe	No		

ADMISSION

Acceptance 1994-95 Of those applying, 68% were accepted.

Entrance Requirements First degree, GMAT score of 500, minimum 1- 2 years of work experience. Core courses waived through: previous course work.

Application Requirements Application form, copies of transcript, 2 letters of recommendation.

Application Deadline 5/31 for fall.

FINANCIALS

Financial Aid In 1994-95, 25% of candidates received some institutionally administered aid in the form of scholarships, loans, assistantships. Financial aid is available to part-time students. Application deadline: 3/31 for fall. Applications are processed on a rolling basis. Contact: Ms. Anne Mickey, Director of Admissions, 2, Avenue Prince Hereditaire Albert, 98000 Monte Carlo, Monaco. 92-057-057.

INTERNATIONAL STUDENTS

Demographics 100% of students on campus are international; Europe 75%, North America 18%, Africa 1%, Asia 1%, Central America 1%, South America 1%, other 3%.

Services and Facilities International student housing; language tutoring, counseling/support services.

Applying Financial aid is available to international students. Financial aid application deadline: 3/31 for fall. Applications are processed on a rolling basis. Admission application deadline: 5/31 for fall. Applications are processed on a rolling basis. Contact: Ms. Anne Mickey, Director of Admissions, 2, Avenue Prince Hereditaire Albert, 98000 Monte Carlo, Monaco. 92-057-057.

PROGRAM
One-Year MBA Length of program: Minimum: 10 months. Maximum: 2 years. Full-time classes: Main campus; day. Degree requirements: 60 credits. Languages: English.

PLACEMENT
Placement services include alumni network, career counseling/planning, job interviews, job search course, resume preparation, and resume referral to employers. Of 1994 graduates, 90% were employed within three months of graduation, the average starting salary was 45,000 French francs, the range was 35,000-110,000 French francs.

Jobs by Employer Type Manufacturing 50%; service 30%; consulting 20%.
Jobs by Functional Area Marketing/sales 10%; finance 75%; management 15%.

Program Contact: Ms. Anne Mickey, Director of Admissions, University of Southern Europe, 2, Avenue Prince Hereditaire Albert, 98000 Monte Carlo, Monaco. 92-057-057; Fax: 92-052-830.

NETHERLANDS

Erasmus University Rotterdam

Rotterdam School of Management

Rotterdam, Netherlands

OVERVIEW
Erasmus University Rotterdam is an independent proprietary coed institution. Founded 1970. Setting: urban campus. Total institutional enrollment: 18,500. Program was first offered in 1985. Accredited by AACSB. Approved by the Association of MBA Programs (U.K.).

MBA HIGHLIGHTS
Entrance Difficulty****
Mean GMAT: 600
Mean GPA: N/R

Cost
Tuition: 39,000 Dutch guilders/degree program
Room & Board: 10,000 Dutch guilders

Enrollment Profile
Full-time: 96	Work Exp: 98%
Part-time: 0	Women: 17%
Total: 96	
Average Age: 28	

Average Class Size: 100

ACADEMICS
Length of Program Minimum: 18 months.
Calendar Semesters.
Full-time Classes Main campus; day.
Degree Requirements 25 credits including 8 elective credits.
Required Courses Business methods, communication skills workshop, financial management, human resources management, management information systems, management science, management technology, managerial accounting, managerial economics, marketing management, operations management, organizational behavior, strategic management.
Curricular Focus General management, international business, teamwork.
Concentrations Information technology management, international business.
Special Opportunities International exchange in Canada, France, Germany, Italy, Japan, South Africa, Spain, United Kingdom, United States of America. Internship program available.

STUDENT STATISTICS
Undergraduate Majors Business 42%; engineering/technology 30%; humanities 9%; science/mathematics 15%; other 4%.
Other Background Graduate degrees in other disciplines: 100%. Work experience: On average, students have 2-4 years of work experience on entrance to the program.

FACILITIES
Housing College housing available.

Technology Computers are used heavily in course work. 200 computer terminals/PCs, linked by a campus-wide computer network, are available for use by students in program; they are located in computer labs. Students in the program are not required to have their own PC.

Computer Resources/On-line Services
Training	Yes	Dun's	Yes
Internet	Yes	Dow Jones	Yes $
E-Mail	Yes	Dialog	Yes $
LEXIS/NEXIS	No	Bloomberg	No
CompuServe	Yes		

ADMISSION
Acceptance 1994-95 500 applied for admission.
Entrance Requirements First degree, GMAT score, minimum 1 year of work experience.
Application Requirements Written essay, interview, application form, copies of transcript, 2 letters of recommendation.
Application Deadlines 6/15 for fall. Applications are processed on a rolling basis.

FINANCIALS
Costs for 1994-95 Tuition: Full-time: 39,000 Dutch guilders/degree program. Average room and board costs are 10,000 Dutch guilders per academic year (on-campus).

INTERNATIONAL STUDENTS
Demographics 84% of students on campus are international; Europe 52%, Asia 17%, North America 11%, Africa 2%, Australia 1%, South America 1%, other 16%.
Services and Facilities International student center, visa services, counseling/support services.
Applying Admission application deadline: 6/15 for fall.

ALTERNATE MBA PROGRAM
MBA/MBI Length of program: Minimum: 18 months. Full-time classes: Main campus; day. Degree requirements: 28 credits including 8 elective credits.

PLACEMENT
In 1993-94, 100 organizations participated in on-campus recruiting; 200 on-campus interviews were conducted. Placement services include alumni network, career counseling/planning, career fairs, career library, career placement, electronic job bank, job interviews, job search course, resume preparation, and resume referral to employers. Of 1994 graduates, 90% were employed within three months of graduation.

Program Contact: Admissions Office, Erasmus University Rotterdam, Room FB61, PO Box 1738, NL-3000 Rotterdam, Netherlands. 10-408-2222; Fax: 10-452-9509.

Nijenrode University, The Netherlands Business School

Breukelen, Netherlands

OVERVIEW
Nijenrode University, The Netherlands Business School is an independent nonprofit coed institution. Founded 1946. Setting: small-town campus. Total institutional enrollment: 600. Program was first offered in 1982. Accredited by AACSB. Approved by the Association of MBA Programs (U.K.).

MBA HIGHLIGHTS
Entrance Difficulty****
Mean GMAT: 600
Mean GPA: N/R

Cost
Tuition: N/R
Room & Board: N/R

Enrollment Profile
Full-time: 60	Work Exp: 100%
Part-time: 0	Women: 32%
Total: 60	
Average Age: 28	

Average Class Size: N/R

Nijenrode Castle provides a thirteenth-century backdrop for one of the most innovative business schools in Europe today. CEOs and chairmen from leading corporations sit on Nijenrode's International Advisory Board, including Citicorp, Deutsche Aerospace, Heineken, Johnson & Son, McKinsey, Microsoft, Mitsubishi, Philips, Qantas, Shell, and Unilever. Nijenrode University has a dedicated international faculty with extensive worldwide teaching, research, and professional business experience.

Nijenrode's thirteen-month International M.B.A. Programme develops "whole" businesspeople, people who can combine business knowledge and analytical capabilities with leadership, teamwork, and communication skills. In essence, the Nijenrode International M.B.A. Programme provides high-potential candidates with the tools required to develop into general managers within corporations that operate across national borders in a continuously changing environment.

Students who are determined to boost their career by obtaining an international M.B.A. degree from one of Europe's leading business schools and who are motivated to develop and learn in a team-oriented, international, and multicultural environment should contact Ms. Renie Vis, Registrar, Nijenrode University, Straatweg 25, 3621 BG Breukelen, Netherlands; Telephone: +31 3462 91607, fax: +31 3462 50595, e-mail: renvis@nijenrode.nl.

ACADEMICS
Calendar 13-month program.

Curricular Focus General management, international business, teamwork.

Concentration International business.

Faculty Full-time: 35, 70% with doctorates; part-time: 10, 70% with doctorates.

Special Opportunities Internship program available.

STUDENT STATISTICS
Geographic Representation Africa, Asia and the Americas 36%; Belgium/Luxembourg/Netherlands 25%; United Kingdom 12%; Eastern Europe 5%; France 3%; Germany 3%; Italy 3%; Scandinavia 3%; Baltic States 2%; Balkan Penninsula 2%; Russia 2%; Spain 2%; Australia 2%.

Undergraduate Majors Business 55%; engineering/technology 15%; humanities 5%; science/mathematics 10%; social sciences 10%; other 5%.

Other Background Graduate degrees in other disciplines: 10%. Work experience: On average, students have 4 years of work experience on entrance to the program.

FACILITIES
Information Resources Business collection includes 25,000 bound volumes, 360 periodical subscriptions, 15 CD-ROMs, 200 videos.

Housing 80% of students in program live in college-owned or -operated housing.

Technology Computers are used heavily in course work. 90 computer terminals/PCs, linked by a campus-wide computer network, are available for use by students in program; they are located in student rooms, classrooms, the library, the computer center, computer labs, the research center. Students in the program are not required to have their own PC.

Computer Resources/On-line Services

Training	Yes	CompuServe	Yes
Internet	Yes	Dun's	Yes
E-Mail	Yes	Dow Jones	Yes
Multimedia Center	Yes	Dialog	No
LEXIS/NEXIS	Yes	Bloomberg	No

ADMISSION
Acceptance 1994-95 350 applied for admission; 24% were accepted.

Entrance Requirements First degree, GMAT score of 550, minimum 2 years of work experience.

Application Requirements Written essay, interview, application form, copies of transcript, resume/curriculum vitae, personal statement, 3 letters of recommendation.

Application Deadlines 4/1 for fall. Applications are processed on a rolling basis.

FINANCIALS
Financial Aid In 1994-95, 15% of candidates received some institutionally administered aid in the form of scholarships, loans. Application deadline: 4/1 for fall. Applications are processed on a rolling basis. Contact: Ms. Renie Vis, Registrar, Straatweg 25, 3621 BG Breukelen, Netherlands. 3462 91607.

INTERNATIONAL STUDENTS
Services and Facilities International student housing; international student office, visa services, language tutoring, ESL courses, special assistance for nonnative speakers of English, counseling/support services.

Applying TOEFL required, minimum score of 600. Financial aid is available to international students. Financial aid application deadline: 4/1 for fall. Applications are processed on a rolling basis. Admission application deadline: 4/1 for fall. Applications are processed on a rolling basis. Contact: Ms. Frouke Gerbens, Assistant Program Director, Straatweg 25, 3621 BG Breukelen, Netherlands. 3462 91607.

PROGRAM
One-Year MBA Length of program: Minimum: 13 months. Full-time classes: Main campus; day. Degree requirements: 99 credits including 17.5 elective credits. 4 month final project/thesis. Languages: English.

PLACEMENT
In 1993-94, 30 organizations participated in on-campus recruiting; 70 on-campus interviews were conducted. Placement services include alumni network, career counseling/planning, career fairs, career library, career placement, electronic job bank, job interviews, job search course, resume preparation, and resume referral to employers. Of 1994 graduates, 90% were employed within three months of graduation, the average starting salary was 85,000 Dutch guilders, the range was 60,000-180,000 Dutch guilders.

Program Contact: Ms. Renie Vis, Registrar, Nijenrode University, The Netherlands Business School, Straatweg 25, 3621 BG Breukelen, Netherlands. 3462 91607; Fax: 3462 50595; Internet Address: renvis@nijenrode.nl.

University of Twente

TSM Business School

Enschede, Netherlands

OVERVIEW
The University of Twente is an independent proprietary primarily male institution. MBA programs offered jointly with University of Twente Groininger, Pepperdine University. Setting: rural campus. Total institutional enrollment: 8,000. Program was first offered in 1987.

MBA HIGHLIGHTS

Entrance Difficulty***
Mean GMAT: 500
Mean GPA: N/R

Cost
Tuition: 79,500 Dutch guilders/degree program
Room & Board: N/R

Enrollment Profile

Full-time: 28	Work Exp: 40%
Part-time: 60	Women: 15%
Total: 88	
Average Age: 28	

Average Class Size: 20

ACADEMICS
Length of Program Minimum: 18 months. Maximum: 2 years.

Calendar Trimesters.

Full-time Classes Main campus; day, evening.

Degree Requirements 17 courses. Other: Practical assignment.

Required Courses Business management in non-western countries, business values and ethics, financial management, high tech marketing project, information technology, international and comparative business law, international management, logistics, marketing for technology-oriented organizations, organization of innovation process, personnel psychology, planning and assessment of research management, project management, social and personnel management, strategic management, technology and new product management, technology and organization.

Curricular Focus Entrepreneurship, technology innovation management.

Concentrations Accounting, economics, entrepreneurship, finance, human resources management, international business, management, management information systems, marketing, operations management, organizational behavior, strategic management, technology management, innovation, high technology marketing.

Faculty Full-time: 80, 40% with doctorates; part-time: 40, 40% with doctorates.

Teaching Methodology Case study: 10%, lecture: 35%, managerial skills: 15%, research: 5%, seminars by members of the business community: 10%, student presentations: 10%, team projects: 15%.
Special Opportunities International exchange in France, Japan, United States of America. Internship program available.

STUDENT STATISTICS
Geographic Representation Netherlands 55%; Eastern Europe 10%; Baltic States 5%; Germany 5%; Russia 5%; Scandinavia 5%; United Kingdom 5%; New Zealand 5%; United States of America 5%.
Undergraduate Majors Engineering/technology 80%; science/mathematics 10%; other 10%.
Other Background Work experience: On average, students have 3 years of work experience on entrance to the program.

FACILITIES
Housing 60% of students in program live in college-owned or -operated housing.
Technology Computers are used moderately in course work. 60 computer terminals/PCs, linked by a campus-wide computer network, are available for use by students in program; they are located in classrooms, the library, the computer center, computer labs, the research center. Students in the program are required to have their own PC.
Computer Resources/On-line Services

Internet	Yes	E-Mail	Yes

ADMISSION
Entrance Requirements First degree, technological background required, GMAT score.
Application Requirements Interview, application form, copies of transcript, resume/curriculum vitae, personal statement.
Application Deadlines 5/31 for fall. Applications are processed on a rolling basis.

FINANCIALS
Costs for 1994-95 Tuition: Full-time: 79,500 Dutch guilders/degree program; Part-time day: 60,000 Dutch guilders/degree program.
Financial Aid Application deadline: 8/1 for fall.

INTERNATIONAL STUDENTS
Demographics 45% of students on campus are international; Europe 80%, Asia 10%, Australia 5%, North America 5%.
Applying TOEFL required; proof of adequate funds. Financial aid is not available to international students. Admission application deadline: 5/31 for fall. Applications are processed on a rolling basis.

ALTERNATE MBA PROGRAM
Executive MBA (EMBA) Length of program: Minimum: 22 months. Maximum: 2 years. Part-time classes: Main campus; day, evening, weekends. Degree requirements: 17 courses. Practical assignment. Languages: English.

PLACEMENT
Placement services include alumni network, career counseling/planning, career fairs, career placement, and job search course. Of 1994 graduates, 80% were employed within three months of graduation, the average starting salary was 60,000 Dutch guilders, the range was 55,000-65,000 Dutch guilders.
Jobs by Employer Type Manufacturing 65%; service 15%; consulting 20%.
Jobs by Functional Area Marketing/sales 35%; operations 25%; technical management 40%.

Program Contact: Ms. Carry Beinker, Operator, University of Twente, PO Box 217, 7500 AE Enschede, Netherlands. 53-898-009; Fax: 53-339-147; Telex: 44200.

NEW ZEALAND

University of Auckland

The Graduate School of Business

Auckland, New Zealand

OVERVIEW
The University of Auckland is a government-supported coed institution. Founded 1883. Setting: urban campus. Total institutional enrollment: 23,500. Program was first offered in 1981. Approved by the Association of MBA Programs (U.K.).

MBA HIGHLIGHTS
Entrance Difficulty***

Cost
Tuition: N/R
Room & Board: N/R

Enrollment Profile

Full-time: 186	Work Exp: N/R
Part-time: 0	Women: 15%
Total: 186	
Average Age: N/R	

Average Class Size: 50

ACADEMICS
Calendar Trimesters.
Curricular Focus Business issues and problems, general management, organizational development and change management.
Concentration Management.
Faculty Full-time: 36, 100% with doctorates.
Teaching Methodology Case study: 10%, lecture: 50%, research: 10%, student presentations: 10%, team projects: 20%.
Special Opportunities International exchange program available. Other: industry studies through post-MBA diploma.

FACILITIES
Housing College housing not available.
Technology 2,700 New Zealand dollars are budgeted per student for computer support.
Computer Resources/On-line Services

Training	Yes	Multimedia Center	Yes

ADMISSION
Acceptance 1994-95 Of those applying, 58% were accepted.
Entrance Requirements GMAT score of 400, minimum 10 years of work experience, test of ability and aptitude.
Application Requirements Interview, application form, copies of transcript, resume/curriculum vitae, personal statement, 3 letters of recommendation.
Application Deadline 10/15 for following year.

FINANCIALS
Financial Aid In 1994-95, 62% of candidates received some institutionally administered aid in the form of loans. Application deadline: 2/23 for fall. Contact: Ms. Marie Wilson, Associate Dean, Graduate School of Business, Private Bag 92019, 1 Auckland, New Zealand. 373-7999.

INTERNATIONAL STUDENTS
Applying TOEFL required. Financial aid is not available to international students. Admission application deadline: 10/15 for following year. Contact: Ms. Carolyn Lynch, Private Bag 92019, 1 Auckland, New Zealand. 373-7999.

PLACEMENT
Placement services include alumni network, career counseling/planning, and resume referral to employers.

Program Contact: Ms. Marie Wilson, Associate Dean, Graduate School of Business, University of Auckland, Private Bag 92019, 1 Auckland, New Zealand. 373-7999; Fax: 373-7477; Internet Address: m.wilson@auckland.ac.nz.
See full description on page 854.

University of Otago

Dunedin, New Zealand

OVERVIEW

The University of Otago is a government-supported coed institution. Founded 1869. Setting: small-town campus. Total institutional enrollment: 14,000. Program was first offered in 1977.

MBA HIGHLIGHTS

Entrance Difficulty***
Mean GMAT: 619
Mean GPA: N/R

Cost
Tuition: N/R
(Nonresident: N/R)
Room & Board: N/R

Enrollment Profile
Full-time: 39
Part-time: 0
Total: 39
Average Age: 32

Work Exp: 100%
Women: 15%

Average Class Size: 40

ACADEMICS

Calendar 4 parts over 16 months.

Curricular Focus General management, strategic analysis and planning, teamwork.

Concentration Management.

Faculty Full-time: 22, 95% with doctorates.

Teaching Methodology Case study: 30%, lecture: 20%, seminars by members of the business community: 10%, student presentations: 20%, team projects: 20%.

STUDENT STATISTICS

Geographic Representation New Zealand 65%; Asia 20%; Europe 10%; United States of America 5%.

Undergraduate Majors Business 35%; engineering/technology 35%; other 30%.

Other Background Graduate degrees in other disciplines: 5%. Work experience: On average, students have 10 years of work experience on entrance to the program.

FACILITIES

Technology Computers are used heavily in course work. 65 computer terminals/PCs, linked by a campus-wide computer network, are available for use by students in program; they are located in student rooms, computer labs. Students in the program are required to have their own PC.

Computer Resources/On-line Services

Internet	Yes $	Dun's	No
E-Mail	Yes	Dow Jones	No
LEXIS/NEXIS	No	Dialog	No
CompuServe	Yes $	Bloomberg	No

ADMISSION

Acceptance 1994-95 Of those applying, 9% were accepted.

Entrance Requirements GMAT score of 550, minimum 5 years of work experience.

Application Requirements Application form, resume/curriculum vitae, 2 letters of recommendation.

Application Deadline Applications are processed on a rolling basis. Application discs available.

INTERNATIONAL STUDENTS

Services and Facilities International student office.

Applying Proof of adequate funds. Financial aid is not available to international students. Admission applications are processed on a rolling basis. Contact: Ms. Anita Wells, Administrative Assistant, PO Box 56, Dunedin, New Zealand. 3-479-8046.

PROGRAM

Executive MBA (EMBA) Length of program: Minimum: 16 months. Full-time classes: Main campus; day. Degree requirements: 100 credits. 4 month consulting project. Languages: English.

PLACEMENT

In 1993-94, 100 organizations participated in on-campus recruiting; 200 on-campus interviews were conducted. Placement services include alumni network, career counseling/planning, career placement, job interviews, resume preparation, and resume referral to employers. Of 1994 graduates, 90% were employed within three months of graduation.

Jobs by Employer Type Manufacturing 20%; service 75%; government 5%.

Jobs by Functional Area Marketing/sales 20%; finance 20%; operations 20%; management 20%; strategic planning 20%.

Program Contact: Mr. David Band, Director, Advanced Business Program, University of Otago, PO Box 56, Dunedin, New Zealand. 3-479-8046; Fax: 3-479-8045; Internet Address: dband@commerce.otago.ac.nz.

Victoria University of Wellington

Graduate School of Business and Government Management

Wellington, New Zealand

OVERVIEW

Victoria University of Wellington is a government-supported coed institution. Founded 1896. Setting: urban campus. Total institutional enrollment: 12,500. Program was first offered in 1984.

MBA HIGHLIGHTS

Entrance Difficulty**
Mean GMAT: 570
Mean GPA: N/R

Cost
Tuition: 17,000 New Zealand dollars/degree program
(Nonresident: 25,000 New Zealand dollars/degree program)
Room & Board: 9,000 New Zealand dollars

Enrollment Profile
Full-time: 30
Part-time: 90
Total: 120
Average Age: 36

Work Exp: 100%
Women: 25%

Average Class Size: 45

ACADEMICS

Length of Program Minimum: 36 months. Maximum: 4 years.

Calendar Semesters.

Full-time Classes Main campus; day, evening, weekends, summer.

Part-time Classes Main campus; day, evening, weekends, summer.

Required Courses Accounting and finance, accounting and financial management, business policy, business policy 2, commercial law, economics, information systems, managing people and organizations, marketing management, operation management and statistics, organizational behavior, problem solving and decision analysis.

Curricular Focus Entrepreneurship, international business, organizational development and change management.

Concentrations Entrepreneurship, international business, management, marketing.

Faculty Full-time: 50, 50% with doctorates; part-time: 3, 100% with doctorates.

Teaching Methodology Case study: 10%, faculty seminars: 5%, lecture: 40%, research: 5%, seminars by members of the business community: 5%, student presentations: 10%, team projects: 25%.

Special Opportunities International exchange in People's Republic of China, Singapore.

STUDENT STATISTICS

Undergraduate Majors Business 12%; education 5%; engineering/technology 13%; humanities 22%; nursing 6%; science/mathematics 22%; social sciences 10%; other 10%.

Other Background Graduate degrees in other disciplines: 20%. Work experience: On average, students have 13 years of work experience on entrance to the program.

FACILITIES

Housing College housing available.

Technology Computers are used heavily in course work. Computer terminals/PCs, linked by a campus-wide computer network, are available for use by students in program; they are located in classrooms, the library, computer labs. Students in the program are required to have their own PC.

Computer Resources/On-line Services

Training	Yes	E-Mail	No

ADMISSION

Entrance Requirements First degree, GMAT score, minimum 5 years of work experience. Core courses waived through: previous course work.

Application Requirements Interview, application form, copies of transcript, resume/curriculum vitae, personal statement, 2 letters of recommendation.

Application Deadline 10/31 for spring.

FINANCIALS

Costs for 1994-95 Tuition: Full-time: 17,000 New Zealand dollars/degree program, 25,000 New Zealand dollars/degree program for international students. Average room and board costs are 9,000 New Zealand dollars per academic year (on-campus) and 10,000 New Zealand dollars per academic year (off-campus).

Financial Aid In 1994-95, candidates received some institutionally administered aid in the form of loans, Student Allowance Scheme. Financial aid is not available to part-time students.

INTERNATIONAL STUDENTS

Services and Facilities International student office, ESL courses.

Applying TOEFL required, minimum score of 580; IELTS required, minimum score of 6; proof of health; proof of adequate funds. Financial aid is not available to international students. Contact: Manager of International Student Office, International Student Office, Wellington, New Zealand. 4-4721000 Ext. 5350.

PLACEMENT

Placement services include alumni network and job search course.

Jobs by Employer Type Manufacturing 25%; service 25%; government 40%; consulting 8%; nonprofit 2%.

Program Contact: Mrs. Angela Dolan, Administrator, Graduate School of Business and Government Management, Victoria University of Wellington, PO Box 600, Wellington, New Zealand. 4-4721000 Ext. 5366; Fax: 4-4965435.

NORWAY

Norwegian School of Management

Graduate School

Sandvika, Norway

OVERVIEW

Norwegian School of Management is an independent nonprofit primarily male institution. Founded 1943. Setting: small-town campus. Total institutional enrollment: 1,700. Program was first offered in 1989. Accredited by United States Department of Education, AACSB.

MBA HIGHLIGHTS

Entrance Difficulty**

Cost
Tuition: N/R
Room & Board: N/R

Enrollment Profile

Full-time: 39	Work Exp: 100%
Part-time: 33	Women: 18%
Total: 72	
Average Age: 33	

Average Class Size: 35

ACADEMICS

Calendar Quarters.

Curricular Focus General management, leadership, problem solving and decision making.

Concentrations Management, strategic management.

Faculty Full-time: 40, 90% with doctorates; part-time: 40, 90% with doctorates.

Teaching Methodology Case study: 20%, lecture: 40%, student presentations: 20%, team projects: 20%.

STUDENT STATISTICS

Geographic Representation Norway 44%; Africa, Western Europe and the Americas 44%; Asia 7%; Eastern Europe 2%.

Undergraduate Majors Business 35%; engineering/technology 35%; social sciences 12%; other 15%.

Other Background Graduate degrees in other disciplines: 39%. Work experience: On average, students have 7 years of work experience on entrance to the program.

FACILITIES

Housing College housing not available.

Technology Computers are used heavily in course work. 200 computer terminals/PCs, linked by a campus-wide computer network, are available for use by students in program; they are located in student rooms, the computer center, computer labs. Students in the program are not required to have their own PC.

Computer Resources/On-line Services

Training	No	E-Mail	Yes
Internet	Yes		

ADMISSION

Acceptance 1994-95 228 applied for admission; 17% were accepted.

Entrance Requirements First degree, GMAT score, minimum 3 years of work experience.

Application Requirements Interview, application form, copies of transcript, personal statement, 3 letters of recommendation.

Application Deadlines 3/15 for fall. Applications are processed on a rolling basis.

FINANCIALS

Financial Aid Application deadline: 8/15 for fall. Applications are processed on a rolling basis.

INTERNATIONAL STUDENTS

Services and Facilities International student office, international student center, language tutoring, counseling/support services.

Applying Proof of adequate funds. Financial aid is not available to international students. Admission application deadline: 3/15 for fall. Applications are processed on a rolling basis. Contact: Ms. Kjersti Engelstad, International Coordinator, PO Box 580, N-1301 Sandvika, Norway. 67-57-50-00.

PROGRAM

One-Year MBA Length of program: Minimum: 11 months. Maximum: 1 year. Full-time classes: Main campus; day, evening, weekends, summer. Part-time classes: Main campus; day, evening, weekends, summer. Degree requirements: 38 credits including 8 elective credits. Strategy project. Languages: English.

PLACEMENT

In 1993-94, 10 organizations participated in on-campus recruiting; 10 on-campus interviews were conducted. Placement services include alumni network, career counseling/planning, career fairs, career placement, job interviews, job search course, resume preparation, and resume referral to employers. Of 1994 graduates, 90% were employed within three months of graduation.

Jobs by Employer Type Manufacturing 30%; service 30%; consulting 20%; other 20%.

Jobs by Functional Area Marketing/sales 20%; finance 20%; management 20%; strategic planning 30%; technical management 10%.

Program Contact: Mr. Oystein Leirtun, Senior Student Adviser MBA, Norwegian School of Management, PO Box 580, N-1301 Sandvika, Norway. 67-57-05-59; Fax: 67-57-05-41; Internet Address: adm93034@bi.no.

PAKISTAN

Lahore University of Management Sciences

Graduate School of Business Administration

Lahore Cantt, Pakistan

OVERVIEW

Lahore University of Management Sciences is an independent nonprofit coed institution. Founded 1984. Setting: suburban campus. Total institutional enrollment: 143. Program was first offered in 1986. Accredited by University Grants Commission, Pakistan.

MBA HIGHLIGHTS

Entrance Difficulty**
Mean GMAT: 550
Mean GPA: N/R

Cost
Tuition: N/R
Room & Board: N/R

Enrollment Profile
Full-time: 89
Part-time: 0
Total: 89
Average Age: 24

Work Exp: 99%
Women: 27%

Average Class Size: 40

ACADEMICS

Length of Program Minimum: 21 months. Maximum: 2 years.

Calendar Quarters.

Full-time Classes Main campus; day.

Degree Requirements 23 courses including 9 elective courses. Other: Internship; group project.

Required Courses Islamic methods in business, business analysis, business policy, financial accounting, financial analysis, management communications, managerial accounting and control systems, managerial economics, marketing management, organizational behavior, production and operations management, quantitative methods, statistical analysis for management.

Curricular Focus General management, problem solving and decision making, strategic analysis and planning.

Concentrations Finance, management, marketing.

Faculty Full-time: 19, 95% with doctorates; part-time: 10, 60% with doctorates.

Teaching Methodology Case study: 85%, seminars by members of the business community: 2%, student presentations: 3%, team projects: 10%.

Special Opportunities International exchange in Canada. Internships include finance and marketing.

STUDENT STATISTICS

Undergraduate Majors Business 14%; engineering/technology 29%; humanities 36%; science/mathematics 19%; other 2%.

Other Background Graduate degrees in other disciplines: 4%. Work experience: On average, students have 1 year of work experience on entrance to the program.

FACILITIES

Housing 37% of students in program live in college-owned or -operated housing.

Technology Computers are used heavily in course work. 64 computer terminals/PCs, linked by a campus-wide computer network, are available for use by students in program; they are located in the computer center, computer labs, discussion rooms. Students in the program are not required to have their own PC.

Computer Resources/On-line Services

Training	Yes	E-Mail	Yes
Internet	Yes $	Multimedia Center	Yes

ADMISSION

Acceptance 1994-95 1,000 applied for admission; 9% were accepted.

Entrance Requirements First degree, GMAT score of 450, in-house math and English tests.

Application Requirements Written essay, interview, application form, copies of transcript, personal statement, 2 letters of recommendation.

Application Deadline 2/9 for fall.

FINANCIALS

Financial Aid In 1994-95, 50% of candidates received some institutionally administered aid in the form of scholarships, loans. Application deadline: 2/9 for fall. Contact: Ms. Shazi Malik, Manager of Student Affairs, Opposite Sector U, Phase II LCCHS, 54792 Lahore Cantt, Punjab, Pakistan. 42-5722140.

INTERNATIONAL STUDENTS

Demographics 3% of students on campus are international; Asia 100%.

Services and Facilities Visa services, language tutoring, counseling/support services.

Applying Proof of adequate funds. Financial aid is not available to international students. Admission application deadline: 2/9 for fall. Contact: Dr. Zafar Qureshi, Associate Dean, BSc Honors Program, Opposite Sector U, Phase II LCCHS, 54792 Lahore Cantt, Punjab, Pakistan. 42-5722141.

PLACEMENT

In 1993-94, 25 organizations participated in on-campus recruiting; 150 on-campus interviews were conducted. Placement services include alumni network, career counseling/planning, career placement, job interviews, resume preparation, and resume referral to employers. Of 1994 graduates, 85% were employed within three months of graduation.

Jobs by Employer Type Service 38%; government 5%; nonprofit 3%; corporate management 35%; other 19%.

Program Contact: Ms. Shazi Malik, Manager, Student Affairs, Lahore University of Management Sciences, Opposite Sector U, Phase II LCCHS, 54792 Lahore Cantt, Punjab, Pakistan. 42-5722440; Internet Address: admissions@lums.edu.pk.

PORTUGAL

Instituto Empresarial Portuense

Matosinhos, Portugal

OVERVIEW

Instituto Empresarial Portuense is an independent nonprofit coed institution. Part of Escuela Superior de Administración y Dirección de Empresas. Setting: suburban campus. Program was first offered in 1992.

MBA HIGHLIGHTS

Entrance Difficulty N/R

Cost
Tuition: N/R
Room & Board: N/R

Enrollment Profile
Full-time: N/R
Part-time: 42
Total: 42
Average Age: N/R

Work Exp: 100%
Women: 14%

Average Class Size: 21

ACADEMICS

Calendar Trimesters.

Curricular Focus Business issues and problems, problem solving and decision making.

Concentrations Finance, international business, management, management information systems, marketing, operations management.

Faculty Full-time: 5, 80% with doctorates; part-time: 37, 40% with doctorates.

Teaching Methodology Case study: 20%, faculty seminars: 5%, lecture: 40%, research: 5%, seminars by members of the business community: 5%, student presentations: 10%, team projects: 15%.

Special Opportunities International exchange in Spain.

STUDENT STATISTICS

Geographic Representation Portugal 98%; Venezuela 2%.

Undergraduate Majors Business 10%; engineering/technology 60%; social sciences 30%.

Other Background Graduate degrees in other disciplines: 100%.

FACILITIES

Housing College housing not available.

Technology 26 computer terminals/PCs, linked by a campus-wide computer network, are available for use by students in program; they are located in classrooms, the library, the computer center. Students in the program are not required to have their own PC.

Computer Resources/On-line Services

Training	No	Multimedia Center	Yes
Videoconference Center	Yes		

ADMISSION

Acceptance 1994-95 Of those applying, 37% were accepted.

Entrance Requirements First degree, GMAT score, minimum 2 years of work experience. Core courses waived through: work experience.

Application Requirements Interview, application form, resume/curriculum vitae, 2 letters of recommendation.

Application Deadline 6/1 for fall.

FINANCIALS

Financial Aid In 1994-95, candidates received some institutionally administered aid in the form of governmental support. Financial aid is available to part-time students. Application deadline: 6/1 for fall.

PROGRAM

Executive MBA (EMBA) Length of program: Minimum: 10 months. Part-time classes: Main campus; day, weekends, early morning. Languages: English, French, Portuguese, Spanish.

PLACEMENT

In 1993-94, 10 organizations participated in on-campus recruiting. Placement services include alumni network and resume referral to employers.

Program Contact: Mr. Jose Pedro Silva, Administrative Officer, Instituto Empresarial Portuense, 4450 Matosinhos, Portugal. 2-995-7274; Fax: 2-995-6984.

Universidade do Porto

Porto, Portugal

OVERVIEW

The Universidade do Porto is government-supported institution.

ACADEMICS

Concentration Management.

Program Contact: Mr. Carlos Barral, Dean, Universidade do Porto, Rua De Salazares, 842, 4100 Porto, Portugal. 2-618-8699; Fax: 2-610-0861.

Universidade Nova de Lisboa

Faculdade de Economia-Gestañao

Lisbon, Portugal

OVERVIEW

The Universidade Nova de Lisboa is a government-supported coed institution. Setting: urban campus. Program was first offered in 1980.

MBA HIGHLIGHTS

Entrance Difficulty**

Cost
Tuition: N/R
Room & Board: N/R

Enrollment Profile

Full-time: 19	Work Exp: 100%
Part-time: 17	Women: N/R
Total: 36	
Average Age: 29	

Average Class Size: 35

ACADEMICS

Calendar Trimesters.

Curricular Focus Business issues and problems, general management, strategic analysis and planning.

Concentrations Finance, management, marketing.

Faculty Full-time: 13, 100% with doctorates; part-time: 11, 55% with doctorates.

Teaching Methodology Case study: 15%, lecture: 70%, seminars by members of the business community: 5%, student presentations: 10%.

Special Opportunities International exchange program available.

STUDENT STATISTICS

Geographic Representation Portugal 100%.

Undergraduate Majors Business 20%; engineering/technology 68%; humanities 6%; science/mathematics 6%.

Other Background Graduate degrees in other disciplines: 100%. Work experience: On average, students have 6 years of work experience on entrance to the program.

FACILITIES

Information Resources Business collection includes 4,000 bound volumes, 350 periodical subscriptions, 7 CD-ROMs, 30 videos.

Housing College housing not available.

Technology Computers are used heavily in course work. 14 computer terminals/PCs, linked by a campus-wide computer network, are available for use by students in program; they are located in the computer center, computer labs. Students in the program are not required to have their own PC.

Computer Resources/On-line Services

Training	No	E-Mail	No

ADMISSION

Acceptance 1994-95 70 applied for admission; 36% were accepted.

Entrance Requirements First degree, GMAT score of 400, minimum 2 years of work experience. Core courses waived through: previous course work, work experience.

Application Requirements Written essay, interview, application form, resume/curriculum vitae, 2 letters of recommendation.

Application Deadline 5/31 for fall.

INTERNATIONAL STUDENTS

Applying Financial aid is not available to international students.

PROGRAM

One-Year MBA Length of program: Minimum: 11 months. Maximum: 2 years. Full-time classes: Main campus; day. Part-time classes: Main campus; day. Degree requirements: 37.5 credits including 5 elective credits. Dissertation. Languages: English, Portuguese.

PLACEMENT

In 1993-94, 15 organizations participated in on-campus recruiting. Placement services include alumni network, job interviews, and resume referral to employers. Of 1994 graduates, 89% were employed within three months of graduation, the average starting salary was $24,000, the range was $17,000-$37,500.

Jobs by Employer Type Manufacturing 3%; service 74%; government 3%; consulting 10%; higher education 10%.

Jobs by Functional Area Marketing/sales 20%; finance 50%; management 20%; strategic planning 10%.

Program Contact: Ms. Odete Fernandes, Universidade Nova de Lisboa, Rua Marquês de Fronteria, 20, 1000 Lisbon, Portugal. 1-387-98-47; Fax: 1-387-39-73.

REPUBLIC OF SINGAPORE

Nanyang Technological University

School of Accountancy and Business

Singapore, Republic of Singapore

OVERVIEW
Nanyang Technological University is a government-supported coed institution. Founded 1981. Setting: suburban campus. Total institutional enrollment: 10,890. Program was first offered in 1991. Accredited by Institute of Certified Public Accountants of Singapore, UK Institute of Chartered Secretaries and Administrators.

MBA HIGHLIGHTS

Entrance Difficulty**
Mean GMAT: 600
Mean GPA: N/R

Cost $$
Tuition: $2,000/trimester
(Nonresident: $2,000/trimester)
Room & Board: N/R

Enrollment Profile
Full-time: 50
Part-time: 350
Total: 400
Average Age: 32

Work Exp: 100%
Women: 35%

Average Class Size: 25

T*he Nanyang M.B.A. Program places emphasis on inculcating in participants a global perspective and industry orientation. A unique feature is the compulsory Business Study Mission to fast-developing economies. Participants learn first hand how such economies function. Industry leaders also participate in class teaching.*

The M.B.A. class has an international mix of participants from some fourteen countries. They come from a diversity of academic backgrounds and careers. M.B.A. participants can choose to specialise in functional areas such as accounting, finance, hospitality and tourism, business law, international business, information technology, and management of technology. This helps them to manage from a position of strength.

Faculty members are highly qualified and have broad industry and international experience.

A "family" atmosphere pervades the learning environment. There is much room for interaction amongst faculty and participants inside and outside the classroom.

ACADEMICS
Length of Program Minimum: 16 months. Maximum: 4 years.
Calendar Trimesters.
Full-time Classes Main campus; day, evening, weekends.
Part-time Classes Main campus; evening, weekends.
Degree Requirements 54 credits including 6 elective credits. Other: Dissertation; business study mission.
Required Courses Accounting, business policy, business study seminar, decision science, economics, financial management, management information systems, organizational behavior, statistical and research methods.
Curricular Focus Business issues and problems, entrepreneurship, international business.
Concentrations Accounting, business law, technology management, finance, hotel management, international business, management information systems.
Faculty Full-time: 74, 59% with doctorates; part-time: 7, 29% with doctorates.
Teaching Methodology Case study: 20%, lecture: 40%, research: 5%, seminars by members of the business community: 5%, student presentations: 20%, team projects: 10%.
Special Opportunities International exchange in Australia, Belgium, Canada, Norway, United Kingdom, United States of America.

STUDENT STATISTICS
Geographic Representation Singapore 90%; Asia 9%; Americas 1%.

Undergraduate Majors Business 20%; engineering/technology 30%; humanities 15%; science/mathematics 20%; social sciences 15%.
Other Background Graduate degrees in other disciplines: 5%. Work experience: On average, students have 7 years of work experience on entrance to the program.

FACILITIES
Information Resources Business collection in Library 2 includes 100,000 bound volumes, 1,350 periodical subscriptions.
Housing 5% of students in program live in college-owned or -operated housing.
Technology Computers are used moderately in course work. 620 computer terminals/PCs, linked by a campus-wide computer network, are available for use by students in program; they are located in the library, the computer center, computer labs. Students in the program are not required to have their own PC.

Computer Resources/On-line Services

Training	Yes	Dow Jones	No
Internet	Yes	Dialog	Yes
E-Mail	Yes	Bloomberg	No
Multimedia Center	Yes		

ADMISSION
Acceptance 1994-95 600 applied for admission; 30% were accepted.
Entrance Requirements First degree, minimum 2 years of work experience. Core courses waived through: previous course work.
Application Requirements Interview, application form, copies of transcript.
Application Deadline 2/28 for July admission. Application discs available.

FINANCIALS
Costs for 1994-95 Tuition: Full-time: $2,000/trimester for residents, $2,000/trimester for nonresidents, $2,000/trimester for international students; Part-time evening: $1,333/trimester for residents, $1,333/trimester for nonresidents, $1,333/trimester for international students.
Financial Aid In 1994-95, 2% of candidates received some institutionally administered aid in the form of scholarships, assistantships. Financial aid is not available to part-time students. Application deadline: 2/28 for July admission. Contact: Mrs. Loo-Hiang Tan-Lee, Administrative Officer, Nanyang Avenue, 0511 Singapore, Republic of Singapore. 799 4722.

INTERNATIONAL STUDENTS
Demographics 5% of students on campus are international; Asia 80%, Australia 5%, Europe 5%, North America 5%, other 5%.
Services and Facilities International student office, counseling/support services.
Applying TOEFL required, minimum score of 550; proof of health; proof of adequate funds. Financial aid is not available to international students. Admission application deadline: 2/28 for July admission. Contact: Ms. Valerie Low, Lecturer, Nanyang Avenue, 0511 Singapore, Republic of Singapore. 799 4763.

PLACEMENT
Placement services include alumni network and resume referral to employers.

Program Contact: Mrs. Loo-Hiang Tan-Lee, Administrative Officer, Nanyang Technological University, Nanyang Avenue, 0511 Singapore, Republic of Singapore. 799 4722; Fax: 791 3561.
See full description on page 786.

National University of Singapore

School of Postgraduate Management Studies

Singapore, Republic of Singapore

Program Contact: Registrar, National University of Singapore, 10, Kent Ridge Crescent, 0511 Singapore, Republic of Singapore. 7756666.

SLOVENIA

International Executive Development Centre

Kranj, Slovenia

OVERVIEW

International Executive Development Centre is a graduate-only institution. Setting: rural campus. Total institutional enrollment: 1,350. Program was first offered in 1991.

MBA HIGHLIGHTS

Entrance Difficulty*
Mean GMAT: 580
Mean GPA: N/R

Cost
Tuition: N/R
Room & Board: N/R

Enrollment Profile
Full-time: 0
Part-time: 26
Total: 26
Average Age: 35

Work Exp: 100%
Women: 35%

Average Class Size: 26

ACADEMICS

Calendar 4 modules.

Curricular Focus International business, strategic analysis and planning, teamwork.

Concentrations Accounting, economics, entrepreneurship, finance, management.

Faculty Part-time: 25, 85% with doctorates.

Teaching Methodology Case study: 30%, lecture: 30%, student presentations: 5%, team projects: 35%.

STUDENT STATISTICS

Geographic Representation Slovenia 76%; Russia 8%; Croatia 8%; Italy 4%; Canada 4%.

Undergraduate Majors Business 25%; engineering/technology 60%; nursing 5%; science/mathematics 5%; social sciences 5%.

Other Background Graduate degrees in other disciplines: 20%. Work experience: On average, students have 10 years of work experience on entrance to the program.

FACILITIES

Housing College housing not available.

Technology Computers are used moderately in course work. 20 computer terminals/PCs, linked by a campus-wide computer network, are available for use by students in program; they are located in classrooms, the library, computer labs. Students in the program are not required to have their own PC.

Computer Resources/On-line Services
Training   No   E-Mail   No

ADMISSION

Acceptance 1994-95 40 applied for admission; 65% were accepted.

Entrance Requirements First degree, minimum 3 years of work experience, English skills assessment.

Application Requirements Interview, application form, 2 letters of recommendation.

Application Deadline 9/15 for fall.

FINANCIALS

Financial Aid In 1994-95, 15% of candidates received some institutionally administered aid in the form of scholarships. Financial aid is available to part-time students. Application deadline: 9/1 for fall. Contact: Mr. Nenod Filipovic, Deputy Director, Brdo pri Kranju, 64000 Kranj, Slovenia. 64-221-761.

INTERNATIONAL STUDENTS

Demographics 25% of students on campus are international; Europe 95%, other 5%.

Applying Financial aid is available to international students. Financial aid application deadline: 9/15 for fall. Admission application deadline: 9/15 for fall. Contact: Mr. Nenod Filipovic, Deputy Director, Brdo pri Kranju, 64000 Kranj, Slovenia. 64-221-761.

PROGRAM

Executive MBA (EMBA) Length of program: May range up to 1 year. Part-time classes: Main campus; day, evening, weekends. Degree requirements: Consulting project; international field trip. Languages: English.

PLACEMENT

Placement services include alumni network, career counseling/planning, and career library.

Program Contact: Mr. Nenod Filipovic, Deputy Director, International Executive Development Centre, Brdo pri Kranju, 64000 Kranj, Slovenia. 64-221-761; Fax: 64-222-070.

SOUTH AFRICA

University of Cape Town

Graduate School of Business

Green Point, South Africa

OVERVIEW

The University of Cape Town is a government-supported coed institution. Setting: urban campus. Program was first offered in 1964.

MBA HIGHLIGHTS

Entrance Difficulty**
Mean GMAT: 570
Mean GPA: N/R

Cost
Tuition: N/R
(Nonresident: N/R)
Room & Board: N/R

Enrollment Profile
Full-time: 70
Part-time: 80
Total: 150
Average Age: 31

Work Exp: 100%
Women: 21%

Average Class Size: 65

ACADEMICS

Curricular Focus Business issues and problems, general management, teamwork.

Concentrations Entrepreneurship, finance, human resources management, management information systems, marketing, operations management, organizational behavior, strategic management.

Faculty Full-time: 14, 70% with doctorates; part-time: 20, 50% with doctorates.

Teaching Methodology Case study: 20%, lecture: 40%, research: 10%, seminars by members of the business community: 10%, student presentations: 10%, team projects: 10%.

Special Opportunities International exchange in United Kingdom, United States of America.

STUDENT STATISTICS

Undergraduate Majors Business 30%; education 10%; engineering/technology 30%; humanities 10%; science/mathematics 10%; social sciences 10%.

Other Background Graduate degrees in other disciplines: 15%. Work experience: On average, students have 6 years of work experience on entrance to the program.

FACILITIES

Information Resources Business collection in Graduate School of Business Library includes 20,000 bound volumes, 300 periodical subscriptions, 20 CD-ROMs, 300 videos.

Housing 20% of students in program live in college-owned or -operated housing. Assistance with housing search provided.

Technology Computers are used heavily in course work. 80 computer terminals/PCs, linked by a campus-wide computer network, are available for use by students in program; they are located in student rooms, the computer center, computer labs. Students in the program are not required to have their own PC.

Computer Resources/On-line Services

Training	No	Dun's	No
Internet	Yes	Dow Jones	No
E-Mail	Yes	Dialog	Yes
LEXIS/NEXIS	No	Bloomberg	No

ADMISSION

Acceptance 1994-95 281 applied for admission; 39% were accepted.

Entrance Requirements First degree, GMAT score of 500, minimum 3 years of work experience, minimum age 25.

Application Requirements Interview, application form, copies of transcript, resume/curriculum vitae, 2 letters of recommendation.

Application Deadlines 10/15 for fall. Applications are processed on a rolling basis.

FINANCIALS

Financial Aid In 1994-95, 5% of candidates received some institutionally administered aid in the form of loans. Total awards ranged from $2,000-$5,000. Financial aid is available to part-time students. Application deadline: 10/15 for fall. Applications are processed on a rolling basis. Contact: Ms. Denny Doyle, MBA Administrator, Portswood Road, 8001 Green Point, West Cape, South Africa. 21-406-1317.

INTERNATIONAL STUDENTS

Demographics 10% of students on campus are international; Africa 90%, Europe 5%, Australia 2%, North America 2%, Asia 1%.

Applying TOEFL required, minimum score of 600; proof of adequate funds; South African study visa. Financial aid is not available to international students. Admission application deadline: 10/15 for fall. Applications are processed on a rolling basis.

PROGRAM

One-Year MBA Length of program: Minimum: 11 months. Maximum: 1 year. Full-time classes: Main campus; day. Part-time classes: Main campus; day, evening, weekends. Degree requirements: 20 credits including 5 elective credits. Research report. Languages: English. Average class size: 45.

PLACEMENT

In 1993-94, 60 organizations participated in on-campus recruiting; 100 on-campus interviews were conducted. Placement services include career placement, job interviews, resume preparation, and resume referral to employers. Of 1994 graduates, 90% were employed within three months of graduation, the average starting salary range was $30,000-$60,000.

Jobs by Employer Type Manufacturing 20%; service 30%; government 10%; consulting 30%; health industry 10%.

Jobs by Functional Area Marketing/sales 20%; finance 30%; operations 20%; management 30%.

Program Contact: Ms. Denny Doyle, MBA Administrator, University of Cape Town, Portswood Road, 8001 Green Point, West Cape, South Africa. 21-406-1317; Fax: 21-21-5693; Internet Address: dendoyle@ gsbz.uct.ac.za.

University of the Witwatersrand

Graduate School of Business Administration

Wits, South Africa

OVERVIEW

The University of the Witwatersrand is a government-supported coed institution. Administratively affiliated with University of the Witwatersrand. Founded 1922. Setting: urban campus. Program was first offered in 1970.

MBA HIGHLIGHTS

Entrance Difficulty***

Cost
Tuition: 21,000 South African rand/degree program
Room & Board: 6,000 South African rand

Enrollment Profile

Full-time: 40		Work Exp: 98%
Part-time: 90		Women: 20%
Total: 130		
Average Age: 31		
Average Class Size:	55	

ACADEMICS

Length of Program Minimum: 18 months. Maximum: 3 years.

Calendar Quarters.

Full-time Classes Main campus; day.

Part-time Classes Main campus; evening.

Required Courses Business law, corporate finance, economics, environment of business, financial accounting, human resource strategy, human resources management, management accounting, management information systems, marketing management, production and operations management, quantitative methods, research methodology, strategy management.

Curricular Focus General management, managing diversity, teamwork.

Concentrations Accounting, economics, finance, human resources management, international business, management, management information systems, marketing, operations management, organizational behavior, public administration, public policy, quantitative analysis, strategic management.

Faculty Full-time: 20, 40% with doctorates; part-time: 40, 10% with doctorates.

Teaching Methodology Case study: 30%, lecture: 50%, student presentations: 5%, team projects: 15%.

STUDENT STATISTICS

Geographic Representation South Africa 95%; other 5%.

Undergraduate Majors Business 10%, education 2%, engineering/technology 50%; humanities 2%; nursing 2%; science/mathematics 6%; social sciences 10%; other 18%.

Other Background Graduate degrees in other disciplines: 30%. Work experience: On average, students have 8 years of work experience on entrance to the program.

FACILITIES

Information Resources Business collection in WITS Library of Management includes 20,000 bound volumes, 350 periodical subscriptions, 2 CD-ROMs.

Housing 1% of students in program live in college-owned or -operated housing.

Technology Computers are used moderately in course work. 35 computer terminals/PCs, linked by a campus-wide computer network, are available for use by students in program; they are located in student rooms, the library, computer labs. Students in the program are not required to have their own PC. 300 South African rand are budgeted per student for computer support.

Computer Resources/On-line Services

Training	Yes	E-Mail	Yes
Internet	Yes	Dialog	Yes

Other on-line services: Datastar.

ADMISSION

Acceptance 1994-95 650 applied for admission; 20% were accepted.

Entrance Requirements First degree, minimum 5 years of work experience.

Application Requirements Application form, copies of transcript, 2 letters of recommendation.

Application Deadline 7/31 for fall.

FINANCIALS

Costs for 1994-95 Tuition: Full-time: 21,000 South African rand/degree program. Average room and board costs are 6,000 South African rand per academic year (on-campus) and 12,000 South African rand per academic year (off-campus).

Financial Aid In 1994-95, 2% of candidates received some institutionally administered aid in the form of scholarships. Financial aid is not available to part-time students. Application deadline: 9/1 for fall. Contact: Financial Aid Office, PO Wits, 2050 Witwatersrand, South Africa. 11-716-1111.

INTERNATIONAL STUDENTS

Services and Facilities International student housing; international student office.

Applying TOEFL required. Financial aid is not available to international students. Admission application deadline: 7/31 for fall. Applications are processed on a rolling basis. Contact: Ms. K. Wendorff, International Student Office, 2050 Witwatersrand, South Africa. 11-716-1111.

PLACEMENT

In 1993-94, 10 organizations participated in on-campus recruiting; 30 on-campus interviews were conducted. Placement services include alumni network, career placement, job interviews, and resume preparation. Of 1994 graduates, 90% were employed within three months of graduation.

Program Contact: Ms. Ann Carthy, Assistant Registrar, University of the Witwatersrand, PO Box 98, 2050 Witwatersrand, South Africa. 11-488-5661; Fax: 11-643-2336.

SPAIN

EAP-European School of Management

Business School

Madrid, Spain

OVERVIEW

EAP-European School of Management is a government-supported primarily male institution. Administratively affiliated with Chamber of Commerce and Industry of Paris, France. Founded 1973. Accredited by Conference de Grandes Ecoles, European Foundation of Management Development, Asociaciòn Española de Escuala de Negicios. Approved by the Association of MBA Programs (U.K.).

MBA HIGHLIGHTS

Entrance Difficulty N/R

Cost
Tuition: N/R
Room & Board: N/R

Enrollment Profile
Full-time: N/R   Work Exp: N/R
Part-time: N/R   Women: 31%
Total: 16
Average Age: N/R
Class Size: 14 - 18

ACADEMICS

Curricular Focus International business, organizational development and change management, strategic analysis and planning.

Concentrations Accounting, economics, entrepreneurship, finance, human resources management, international business, management, management information systems, marketing, operations management, organizational behavior, quantitative analysis, strategic management.

Teaching Methodology Case study: 25%, faculty seminars: 4%, lecture: 35%, research: 6%, seminars by members of the business community: 6%, student presentations: 12%, team projects: 12%.

ADMISSION

Entrance Requirements First degree, minimum 3- 5 years of work experience.

Application Requirements Written essay, interview, application form, copies of transcript, resume/curriculum vitae.

Application Deadlines 9/30 for fall. Applications are processed on a rolling basis.

FINANCIALS

Financial Aid Application deadline: 9/30 for fall. Applications are processed on a rolling basis. Contact: Mr. Ramon Rodriguez, Financial Aid Director, Arroyofresno Street, 1, 28035 Madrid, Spain. 1-386-2511.

INTERNATIONAL STUDENTS

Applying TOEFL required; knowledge of Spanish language. Financial aid is available to international students. Financial aid application deadline: 9/30 for fall. Applications are processed on a rolling basis. Admission application deadline: 9/30 for fall. Applications are processed on a rolling basis.

PROGRAM

Executive MBA (EMBA) Length of program: Minimum: 18 months. Full-time classes: Main campus, Paris, France; day. Part-time classes: Main campus, Oxford, United Kingdom; weekends. Languages: English, French, Spanish.

Program Contact: Ms. Monica Mijangos, European MBA Coordinator, EAP-European School of Management, Arroyofresno Street, 1, 28035 Madrid, Spain. 1-386-2511; Fax: 1-373-9229.

Escola d'Alta Direcció i Administració (EADA)

Barcelona, Spain

OVERVIEW

Escola d'Alta Direcció i Administració (EADA) is an independent proprietary coed institution. Part of Asociacion Espanola de Escuelas de Direccion de Empresos, European Foundation for Management Development. Setting: urban campus. Total institutional enrollment: 2,000. Program was first offered in 1957.

MBA HIGHLIGHTS

Entrance Difficulty N/R

Cost
Tuition: N/R
Room & Board: N/R

Enrollment Profile
Full-time: 50   Work Exp: 100%
Part-time: 40   Women: 20%
Total: 90
Average Age: 30
Average Class Size: 25

ACADEMICS

Length of Program Minimum: 9 months. Maximum: 3 years.
Calendar Trimesters.
Full-time Classes Main campus; day.
Degree Requirements 62 credits.
Curricular Focus Leadership, problem solving and decision making, teamwork.
Concentration Management.
Teaching Methodology Case study: 50%, lecture: 20%, student presentations: 10%, team projects: 20%.
Special Opportunities International exchange in United Kingdom.

STUDENT STATISTICS

Geographic Representation Spain 80%; France 10%; South America 10%.
Undergraduate Majors Business 30%; engineering/technology 30%; humanities 10%; science/mathematics 10%; social sciences 10%; other 10%.
Other Background Graduate degrees in other disciplines: 100%. Work experience: On average, students have 5 years of work experience on entrance to the program.

FACILITIES

Information Resources Business collection includes 10,000 bound volumes.
Technology Computers are used moderately in course work. Computer terminals/PCs, linked by a campus-wide computer network, are available for use by students in program; they are located in student rooms, classrooms, the library, the computer center, computer labs. Students in the program are required to have their own PC.
Computer Resources/On-line Services
Training   Yes   E-Mail   No

ADMISSION

Acceptance 1994-95 45 applied for admission; 56% were accepted.
Entrance Requirements First degree, minimum 3 years of work experience, admission test.
Application Requirements Written essay, interview, application form, copies of transcript, resume/curriculum vitae.
Application Deadlines 7/1 for fall. Applications are processed on a rolling basis.

FINANCIALS
Financial Aid Financial aid is not available to part-time students.

INTERNATIONAL STUDENTS
Applying Financial aid is not available to international students. Admission application deadline: 7/1 for fall.

ALTERNATE MBA PROGRAM
Executive MBA (EMBA) Length of program: Minimum: 20 months. Part-time classes: Main campus; evening, weekends. Degree requirements: 800 hours. Languages: Spanish.

PLACEMENT
Placement services include career counseling/planning, career placement, and job search course.

Program Contact: Ms. Brita Hektoen, MBA Director, Escola d'Alta Direcció i Administració (EADA), 204 Carrer Arago, 08011 Barcelona, Spain. 3-323-12-08; Fax: 3-323-73-17.

Escuela Superior de Administracion y Direccion de Empresas

Barcelona, Spain

OVERVIEW
Escuela Superior de Administracion y Direccion de Empresas is a graduate-only institution. Founded 1958. Setting: urban campus. Total institutional enrollment: 2,758. Program was first offered in 1964.

MBA HIGHLIGHTS
Entrance Difficulty**
Mean GMAT: 550
Mean GPA: N/R

Cost
Tuition: N/R
Room & Board: N/R

Enrollment Profile
Full-time: 245   Work Exp: N/R
Part-time: 298   Women: 25%
Total: 543
Average Age: N/R

Average Class Size: 40

ACADEMICS
Length of Program Minimum: 21 months.
Calendar Trimesters.
Full-time Classes Main campus; day.
Part-time Classes Main campus; evening.
Curricular Focus General management, international business, problem solving and decision making.
Concentrations Corporate taxation, finance, health services, human resources management, international business, marketing, operations management, public administration, public policy.
Faculty Full-time: 99, 40% with doctorates; part-time: 199, 40% with doctorates.
Teaching Methodology Case study: 25%, faculty seminars: 10%, lecture: 40%, seminars by members of the business community: 5%, student presentations: 5%, team projects: 15%.

ADMISSION
Acceptance 1994-95 1,040 applied for admission; 22% were accepted.
Entrance Requirements First degree, GMAT score.
Application Requirements Interview, application form, copies of transcript, resume/curriculum vitae, personal statement.
Application Deadlines 6/26 for fall. Applications are processed on a rolling basis.

INTERNATIONAL STUDENTS
Applying TOEFL required, minimum score of 580. Financial aid is available to international students. Financial aid application deadline: 6/26 for fall. Admission application deadline: 6/26 for fall. Applications are processed on a rolling basis.

Program Contact: Ms. Catalina Pons, Director of Admissions, Escuela Superior de Administracion y Direccion de Empresas, Avenida de Pedralbes 60-62, 08034 Barcelona, Spain. 3-280-6162; Fax: 3-204-8105; Internet Address: info@m.esade.es.

Instituto de Empresa

Madrid, Spain

OVERVIEW
Instituto de Empresa is an independent nonprofit graduate-only coed institution. Founded 1973. Setting: urban campus. Total institutional enrollment: 900. Program was first offered in 1973. Accredited by European Foundation for Management Development. Approved by the Association of MBA Programs (U.K.).

MBA HIGHLIGHTS
Entrance Difficulty**
Mean GMAT: 620
Mean GPA: N/R

Cost $$$$
Tuition: $18,800/degree program
Room & Board: N/R

Enrollment Profile
Full-time: 180   Work Exp: 50%
Part-time: 20   Women: 42%
Total: 200
Average Age: 26

Average Class Size: 50

ACADEMICS
Length of Program Minimum: 15 months.
Calendar Trimesters.
Full-time Classes Main campus; day.
Part-time Classes Main campus; evening.
Degree Requirements Entrepreneurial projects.
Required Courses Advanced control, computer studies, cost systems, economic environment, financial accounting, financial management, human resources management, legal environment, marketing, operations management, organizational behavior, quantitative methods, strategic management, tax environment.
Curricular Focus Entrepreneurship, general management, leadership.
Concentrations Accounting, economics, entrepreneurship, finance, human resources management, international business, management, management information systems, marketing, operations management, organizational behavior, public administration, public policy, quantitative analysis, strategic management.
Faculty Full-time: 53, 50% with doctorates; part-time: 125, 25% with doctorates.
Teaching Methodology Case study: 60%, faculty seminars: 3%, lecture: 5%, research: 5%, seminars by members of the business community: 3%, student presentations: 10%, team projects: 15%.
Special Opportunities International exchange in Mexico, United States of America. Internship program available. Other: global business seminar.

STUDENT STATISTICS
Geographic Representation Spain 80%; South America 10%; Germany 5%; United Kingdom 5%.
Undergraduate Majors Business 45%; engineering/technology 15%; humanities 10%; science/mathematics 5%; social sciences 25%.
Other Background Graduate degrees in other disciplines: 100%. Work experience: On average, students have 2 years of work experience on entrance to the program.

FACILITIES
Housing College housing not available.
Technology Computers are used heavily in course work. 100 computer terminals/PCs are available for use by students in program; they are located in the library, computer labs. Students in the program are not required to have their own PC.

Computer Resources/On-line Services

Training	Yes	E Mail	No

ADMISSION
Acceptance 1994-95 978 applied for admission; 24% were accepted.

Entrance Requirements First degree, GMAT score of 550.

Application Requirements Interview, application form, copies of transcript, 3 letters of recommendation.

Application Deadline Applications are processed on a rolling basis.

FINANCIALS
Estimated Costs for 1995-96 Fees: Full-time: $18,800/degree program.

Financial Aid In 1994-95, 40% of candidates received some institutionally administered aid in the form of scholarships, loans. Financial aid is available to part-time students. Application deadlines: 6/30 for fall, 11/30 for spring. Applications are processed on a rolling basis.

INTERNATIONAL STUDENTS
Demographics 15% of students on campus are international; Europe 40%, South America 20%, North America 15%, Asia 10%, Central America 10%, Africa 5%.

Services and Facilities International student office, counseling/support services.

Applying Financial aid is available to international students. Financial aid application deadlines: 6/30 for fall, 11/30 for spring. Admission applications are processed on a rolling basis. Contact: Mr. Joaquin Uribarri, Admissions and Marketing, c/ Maria de Molina 11, 13 y 15, 28006 Madrid, Spain. 1-562-8100.

PLACEMENT
In 1993-94, 30 organizations participated in on-campus recruiting; 200 on-campus interviews were conducted. Placement services include career placement, job interviews, and job search course. Of 1994 graduates, 50% were employed within three months of graduation.

Jobs by Employer Type Manufacturing 30%; service 30%; government 5%; consulting 30%; nonprofit 5%.

Jobs by Functional Area Marketing/sales 50%; finance 30%; operations 5%; management 10%; strategic planning 5%.

Program Contact: Mr. Jaoquin Uribarri, Admissions and Marketing, Instituto de Empresa, c/ Maria de Molina 11,13 y 15, 28006 Madrid, Spain. 1-562-8100; Fax: 1-411-5503.

Schiller International University

Madrid, Spain

OVERVIEW
Schiller International University is an independent nonprofit coed institution. Founded 1964. Setting: urban campus. Total institutional enrollment: 202.

MBA HIGHLIGHTS

Entrance Difficulty**
Mean GMAT: N/R
Mean GPA: 3.0

Cost $$
Tuition: $5,720/semester
Room & Board: $5,000 (off-campus)

Enrollment Profile

Full-time: 12	Work Exp: N/R
Part-time: 14	Women: 46%
Total: 26	
Average Age: 28	

Average Class Size: 15

ACADEMICS
Calendar Semesters.

Curricular Focus International business, problem solving and decision making, teamwork.

Concentrations Hotel management, international business.

Teaching Methodology Case study: 20%, lecture: 40%, research: 20%, student presentations: 10%, team projects: 10%.

Special Opportunities International exchange in France, Germany, Switzerland, United Kingdom, United States of America. Internship program available.

STUDENT STATISTICS
Undergraduate Majors Business 87%; engineering/technology 1%; humanities 7%; social sciences 5%.

FACILITIES
Information Resources Main library with 4,216 bound volumes, 4,080 titles on microform, 58 periodical subscriptions, 88 records/tapes/CDs.

Housing College housing not available.

Technology 15 computer terminals/PCs are available for use by students in program; they are located in computer labs. Students in the program are not required to have their own PC.

Computer Resources/On-line Services

Training	No

ADMISSION
Entrance Requirements First degree, GMAT score, minimum 2.8 GPA. Core courses waived through: previous course work.

Application Requirements Application form, copies of transcript.

Application Deadline Applications are processed on a rolling basis.

FINANCIALS
Financial Aid In 1994-95, candidates received some institutionally administered aid in the form of scholarships, work-study. Application deadline: 4/1 for annual. Contact: Ms. B.J. Slovacek, Financial Aid Officer, Bergstrasse 106, 69121 Heidelberg, Germany. 6221-45810.

INTERNATIONAL STUDENTS
Demographics 88% of students on campus are international; Europe 40%, Asia 15%, North America 12%, South America 7%, Africa 4%, Central America 2%, Other 20%.

Services and Facilities International student housing; international student office, international student center, visa services, language tutoring, ESL courses, counseling/support services.

Applying TOEFL required, minimum score of 550. Financial aid is available to international students. Financial aid application deadline: 4/1 for annual. Admission applications are processed on a rolling basis. Contact: Ms. Karen Altieri, Director, Information and Alumni Affairs, 453 Edgewater Drive, Dunedin, FL 34698-7532. (813) 736-5082.

PROGRAM
One-Year MBA Length of program: Minimum: 12 months. Full-time classes: Main campus; day, evening, summer. Part-time classes: Main campus; day, evening, summer. Degree requirements: 45 credits including 24 elective credits. Final oral comprehensive exam or oral defense of thesis. Languages: English. Average class size: 18.

PLACEMENT
Placement services include alumni network and career placement.

Program Contact: Ms. Karen Altieri, Director of Information and Alumni Affairs, Schiller International University, 453 Edgewater Drive, Dunedin, FL 34698-7532. (813) 736-5082, or (800) 336-4133; Fax: (813) 736-6263.

University of Navarra

International Graduate School of Management

Barcelona, Spain

OVERVIEW
The University of Navarra is an independent nonprofit coed institution. Founded 1958. Setting: urban campus. Total institutional enrollment: 420. Program was first offered in 1964. Approved by the Association of MBA Programs (U.K.).

MBA HIGHLIGHTS

Entrance Difficulty****
Mean GMAT: 600
Mean GPA: N/R

Cost
Tuition: 1,960,000 Spanish pesetas
Room & Board: 1,572,000 Spanish pesetas (off-campus)

Enrollment Profile
Full-time: 392   Work Exp: 89%
Part-time: 0   Women: 19%
Total: 392
Average Age: 26

Average Class Size: 55

Founded in 1958, IESE International Graduate School of Management, with campuses in Barcelona and Madrid, is one of Europe's leading business schools and highly regarded in Spain. Having established the first bilingual M.B.A. program in the world, IESE not only provides students with a unique and challenging M.B.A. education but also prepares managers in two of the most important languages of commerce in today's increasingly global environment.

Truly international in nature, IESE's faculty and student body represent over thirty-five countries, thus enriching the M.B.A. experience. Students are encouraged to participate in the Exchange Program with thirteen of the top business schools on four continents. The International Advisory Board, composed of chairmen and presidents of some of the world's most important multinational companies, advises IESE's Board of Governors on the state of the international economy and developments in the management profession. In collaboration with the Harvard Business School and the University of Michigan, IESE offers management development courses for senior executives. In additon, IESE has assisted in establishing business schools in Asia, Eastern Europe, Latin America, and Africa and has provided training for professors of business administration from universities in Central and Eastern Europe.

ACADEMICS
Length of Program Minimum: 21 months. Maximum: 4 years.
Calendar Trimesters.
Full-time Classes Main campus; day.
Degree Requirements 30 courses. Other: 3 month internship.
Required Courses Analysis of business programs, business, business ethics, business policy, control systems, corporate finance, decision making under uncertainty, financial accounting, government and the international economy, international financial management, management of uncertainty, marketing management, marketing planning and implementation, operations analysis and design, operations strategy, organizational behavior, organizational design and governance, organizational problems, working capital management.
Curricular Focus Ethics, general management, problem solving and decision making, teamwork.
Concentration Management.
Faculty Full-time: 73, 68% with doctorates; part-time: 36, 39% with doctorates.
Teaching Methodology Case study: 60%, lecture: 10%, student presentations: 10%, team projects: 20%.
Special Opportunities International exchange in Canada, Costa Rica, Japan, Mexico, United Kingdom, United States of America. Internships include general management, finance and marketing, marketing and sales, and accounting/finance/marketing.

STUDENT STATISTICS
Undergraduate Majors Business 42%; engineering/technology 28%; humanities 6%; science/mathematics 8%; social sciences 16%.
Other Background Graduate degrees in other disciplines: 5%. Work experience: On average, students have 2 years of work experience on entrance to the program.

FACILITIES
Information Resources Business collection includes 35,000 bound volumes, 380 periodical subscriptions, 18 CD-ROMs, 295 videos.
Housing College housing not available.
Technology Computers are used moderately in course work. 36 computer terminals/PCs, linked by a campus-wide computer network, are available for use by students in program; they are located in the library, the computer center. Students in the program are not required to have their own PC.

Computer Resources/On-line Services
Training	Yes	Dun's	No
Internet	Yes	Dow Jones	No
E-Mail	Yes	Dialog	Yes
LEXIS/NEXIS	No	Bloomberg	No
CompuServe	No		

Other on-line services: Datastar.

ADMISSION
Acceptance 1994-95 578 applied for admission; 44% were accepted.
Entrance Requirements First degree, GMAT score, minimum 2 years of work experience.
Application Requirements Written essay, interview, application form, copies of transcript, resume/curriculum vitae, personal statement, 2 letters of recommendation, 4 photos.
Application Deadlines 5/15 for fall. Applications are processed on a rolling basis.

FINANCIALS
Financial Aid Contact: Ms. Mary Clark, Marketing Manager, MBA Admissions, Avenida Pearson 21, E-08034 Barcelona, Spain. 3-205-4288.

INTERNATIONAL STUDENTS
Demographics 35% of students on campus are international; Europe 83%, North America 7%, South America 6%, Asia 2%, Africa 1%, Central America 1%.
Services and Facilities Spanish language course.
Applying TOEFL required, minimum score of 600. Financial aid is not available to international students. Admission application deadline: 5/15 for fall. Applications are processed on a rolling basis.

PLACEMENT
In 1993-94, 260 organizations participated in on-campus recruiting; 1,633 on-campus interviews were conducted. Placement services include career counseling/planning, career fairs, career library, career placement, job interviews, job search course, resume preparation, and resume referral to employers. Of 1994 graduates, 80% were employed within three months of graduation.
Jobs by Employer Type Manufacturing 8%; service 23%; consulting 15%; consumer goods 14%; financial services 19%; other 21%.
Jobs by Functional Area Marketing/sales 35%; finance 21%; operations 7%; management 36%; human resources 1%.

Program Contact: MBA Admissions, University of Navarra, Avenida Pearson 21, E-08034 Barcelona, Spain. 3-205-4288; Fax: 3-280-1177; Internet Address: mbainfo@iese.es.

SWITZERLAND

American Graduate School of Business

La Tour-de-Peilz, Switzerland

OVERVIEW
American Graduate School of Business is an independent nonprofit comprehensive specialized coed institution. Setting: small-town campus. Total institutional enrollment: 40. Program was first offered in 1991. Accredited by Commission of Higher Education.

PROGRAM HIGHLIGHTS ━━━━━━━━━━

Entrance Difficulty
Mean GMAT: 520
Mean GPA: N/R

Cost
Tuition: N/R
Room & Board: N/R

Enrollment Profile

Full-time: 18
Part-time: 0
Total: 18
Average Age: 26

Work Fxp: 80%
Women: 45%

Average Class Size: 8

ACADEMICS

Calendar Semesters.

Curricular Focus International business, problem solving and decision making.

Concentration International business.

Faculty Full-time: 4, 60% with doctorates; part-time: 8, 75% with doctorates.

Teaching Methodology Case study: 10%, faculty seminars: 3%, lecture: 60%, research: 6%, seminars by members of the business community: 5%, student presentations: 8%, team projects: 8%.

Special Opportunities Internships include finance in banking, marketing, and management.

STUDENT STATISTICS

Geographic Representation Pacific Rim, Middle East and others 39%; Europe 33%; Americas 28%.

Undergraduate Majors Business 70%; education 6%; engineering/technology 10%; humanities 6%; other 8%.

Other Background Work experience: On average, students have 5 years of work experience on entrance to the program.

FACILITIES

Housing College housing not available.

Technology Computers are used moderately in course work. 8 computer terminals/PCs are available for use by students in program; they are located in the library, computer labs. Students in the program are not required to have their own PC.

Computer Resources/On-line Services

Training	Yes	E-Mail	No

ADMISSION

Acceptance 1994-95 25 applied for admission; 88% were accepted.

Entrance Requirements First degree, prerequisite courses required for applicants with non-business degree, GMAT score. Core courses waived through: previous course work.

Application Requirements Application form, copies of transcript, 2 letters of recommendation.

Application Deadline Applications are processed on a rolling basis.

FINANCIALS

Financial Aid In 1994-95, 17% of candidates received some institutionally administered aid in the form of scholarships, assistantships, work-study. Financial aid is not available to part-time students. Applications are processed on a rolling basis. Contact: Mrs. Cynthia Zoubir, Acting Director of Admissions, Bon-Port 21, 1820 Montreaux, Switzerland. 41-21-963-1454.

INTERNATIONAL STUDENTS

Demographics 92% of students on campus are international; Europe 33%, North America 22%, Asia 15%, Africa 8%, Central America 1%, other 21%.

Services and Facilities Language tutoring, ESL courses, counseling/support services.

Applying TOEFL required; proof of adequate funds. Financial aid is available to international students. Applications are processed on a rolling basis. Admission applications are processed on a rolling basis. Contact: Dr. Yahia Zoubir, MIBA Adviser, Bon-Port 21, 1820 La Tour-de-Peilz, Switzerland. 41-21-963-1454.

PROGRAM

International MBA Length of program: Minimum: 11 months. Full-time classes: Main campus; day, evening, early morning, summer. Degree requirements: 39 credits including 6 elective credits. 3-6 months internship, thesis and defense. Languages: English.

PLACEMENT

Placement services include alumni network, career counseling/planning, and resume preparation. Of 1994 graduates, 100% were employed within three months of graduation.

Program Contact: Mrs. Cynthia Zoubir, Acting Director of Admissions, American Graduate School of Business, Bon-Port 21, 1820 Montreaux, Switzerland. 21-944-9501; Fax: 21-944-9504.
See full description on page 658.

International Institute for Management Development

Lausanne, Switzerland

OVERVIEW

International Institute for Management Development is an independent nonprofit graduate-only specialized primarily male institution. Administratively affiliated with University of Lausanne. Founded 1957. Setting: small-town campus. Total institutional enrollment: 80. Program was first offered in 1972. Accredited by Royal Academy of Engineering. Approved by the Association of MBA Programs (U.K.).

MBA HIGHLIGHTS

Entrance Difficulty*****
Mean GMAT: 620
Mean GPA: N/R

Cost
Tuition: 38,000 Swiss francs/degree program
Room & Board: 35,000 Swiss francs (off-campus)

Enrollment Profile

Full-time: 80
Part-time: 0
Total: 80
Average Age: 30

Work Exp: 100%
Women: 13%

Average Class Size: 80

ACADEMICS

Length of Program 12 months.

Calendar Modular.

Full-time Classes Main campus; day, evening, weekends, early morning, summer.

Degree Requirements 950 hours.

Required Courses Industry analysis and business environment, leading self, management of business functions, management of functions and interfaces, managing a global business, overview of general management, strategic management.

Curricular Focus General management, international business, teamwork.

Concentration Management.

Faculty Full-time: 20, 100% with doctorates.

Teaching Methodology Case study: 75%, lecture: 5%, team projects: 20%.

Special Opportunities International consulting projects.

STUDENT STATISTICS

Geographic Representation North and South America 18%; Germany 17%; Asia 16%; United Kingdom 13%; Scandinavia 11%; France 10%; Italy 8%; Australia 5%; Eastern Europe 2%.

Undergraduate Majors Business 18%; engineering/technology 33%; science/mathematics 9%; social sciences 35%; other 5%.

Other Background Graduate degrees in other disciplines: 45%. Work experience: On average, students have 6 years of work experience on entrance to the program.

FACILITIES

Housing College housing not available.

Technology Computers are used heavily in course work. 30 computer terminals/PCs, linked by a campus-wide computer network, are available for use by students in program; they are located in study rooms. Students in the program are required to have their own PC.

Computer Resources/On-line Services

Training	Yes	CompuServe	Yes $
Internet	Yes $	Dun's	No
E-Mail	Yes	Dow Jones	No
Videoconference Center	Yes	Dialog	No
Multimedia Center	Yes	Bloomberg	No
LEXIS/NEXIS	No		

ADMISSION

Acceptance 1994-95 600 applied for admission; 13% were accepted.

Entrance Requirements First degree, GMAT score of 500, minimum 3 years of work experience.

Application Requirements Written essay, interview, application form, copies of transcript, resume/curriculum vitae, personal statement, 3 letters of recommendation.

Application Deadline Applications are processed on a rolling basis.

FINANCIALS
Costs for 1995-96 Tuition: Full-time: 38,000 Swiss francs/degree program. Average room and board costs are 35,000 Swiss francs per academic year (off-campus).

Financial Aid Financial aid is not available to part-time students.

INTERNATIONAL STUDENTS
Demographics 99% of students on campus are international; Europe 61%, Asia 16%, South America 11%, North America 7%, Australia 5%.

Services and Facilities Visa services.

Applying Proof of adequate funds. Financial aid is not available to international students. Admission applications are processed on a rolling basis.

PLACEMENT
In 1993-94, 49 organizations participated in on-campus recruiting; 700 on-campus interviews were conducted. Placement services include alumni network, career counseling/planning, career library, career placement, job interviews, resume preparation, and resume referral to employers. Of 1994 graduates, 98% were employed within three months of graduation, the average starting salary was 75,000 Swiss francs, the range was 48,000-86,000 Swiss francs.

Jobs by Employer Type Manufacturing 66%; service 17%; consulting 17%.

Jobs by Functional Area Marketing/sales 25%; finance 17%; operations 20%; management 36%; technical management 2%.

Program Contact: Ms. Kal Denzel, Director, MBA Marketing, Admissions and Placement, International Institute for Management Development, Chemin de Bellerive 23, PO Box 915, CH-1001 Lausanne, Switzerland. 21-618-0111; Fax: 21-618-0707; Internet Address: denzel@lmd.ch.

See full description on page 762.

Oekreal Graduate School of Business

Zurich, Switzerland

OVERVIEW
Oekreal Graduate School of Business is an independent nonprofit graduate-only primarily male institution. Founded 1986. Setting: urban campus. Program was first offered in 1986. Accredited by Joint Committee of Management Education.

MBA HIGHLIGHTS
Entrance Difficulty****
Mean GMAT: 540
Mean GPA: N/R

Cost
Tuition: N/R
Room & Board: N/R

Enrollment Profile
Full-time: 0	Work Exp: 100%
Part-time: 250	Women: 10%
Total: 250	
Average Age: 37	

Average Class Size: 27

ACADEMICS
Calendar 2-week block courses.

Curricular Focus General management, leadership, strategic analysis and planning.

Concentrations Economics, entrepreneurship, finance, human resources management, international business, management, management information systems, marketing, operations management, organizational behavior, quantitative analysis, strategic management.

Faculty Part-time: 30, 100% with doctorates.

Teaching Methodology Case study: 20%, faculty seminars: 10%, lecture: 20%, research: 10%, seminars by members of the business community: 10%, student presentations: 10%, team projects: 20%.

Special Opportunities International exchange in United States of America.

STUDENT STATISTICS
Undergraduate Majors Business 30%; engineering/technology 60%; humanities 5%; science/mathematics 5%.

Other Background Graduate degrees in other disciplines: 75%. Work experience: On average, students have 10 years of work experience on entrance to the program.

FACILITIES
Technology Computers are used moderately in course work. Students in the program are required to have their own PC.

ADMISSION
Acceptance 1994-95 Of those applying, 10% were accepted.

Entrance Requirements First degree in business, GMAT score of 500, minimum 5 years of work experience. Core courses waived through: previous course work.

Application Requirements Interview, application form, copies of transcript, resume/curriculum vitae, personal statement.

Application Deadline Applications are processed on a rolling basis.

FINANCIALS
Financial Aid Financial aid is not available to part-time students.

INTERNATIONAL STUDENTS
Demographics 50% of students on campus are international; Europe 95%, South America 2%, North America 2%, other 1%.

Applying TOEFL required, minimum score of 500; proof of adequate funds. Financial aid is not available to international students. Admission applications are processed on a rolling basis.

PROGRAM
Executive MBA (EMBA) Length of program: Minimum: 15 months. Maximum: 4 years. Languages: English, German.

PLACEMENT
Placement services include alumni network. Of 1994 graduates, 100% were employed within three months of graduation.

Program Contact: Admissions Office, Oekreal Graduate School of Business, 8023 Zurich, Switzerland. 1-211-6068; Fax: 1-211-0984.

Schiller International University, American College of Switzerland

Schiller International University

Leysin, Switzerland

OVERVIEW
Schiller International University, American College of Switzerland is an independent nonprofit coed institution. Part of Schiller International University. Founded 1964. Setting: 15-acre urban campus. Total institutional enrollment: 98. Program was first offered in 1994.

MBA HIGHLIGHTS
Entrance Difficulty**
Mean GMAT: N/R
Mean GPA: 3.0

Cost
Tuition: $5,720/semester
Room & Board: $4,940

Enrollment Profile
Full-time: 1	Work Exp: N/R
Part-time: 0	Women: N/R
Total: 1	
Average Age: 28	

Average Class Size: N/R

ACADEMICS
Calendar Semesters.

Curricular Focus International business, problem solving and decision making, teamwork.

Concentrations Hotel management, international business.

Faculty Part-time: 3.

Teaching Methodology Case study: 20%, lecture: 40%, research: 20%, student presentations: 10%, team projects: 10%.

Special Opportunities International exchange in France, Germany, Spain, United Kingdom, United States of America. Internship program available.

STUDENT STATISTICS
Undergraduate Majors Business 87%; engineering/technology 1%; humanities 7%; social sciences 5%.

FACILITIES
Information Resources Main library with 48,355 bound volumes, 16 titles on microform, 200 periodical subscriptions.

Housing College housing available.

Technology 15 computer terminals/PCs are available for use by students in program; they are located in computer labs. Students in the program are not required to have their own PC.

ADMISSION
Acceptance 1994-95 1 applied for admission and was accepted.

Entrance Requirements First degree, GMAT score, minimum 2.8 GPA. Core courses waived through: previous course work.

Application Requirements Application form, copies of transcript.

Application Deadline Applications are processed on a rolling basis.

FINANCIALS
Financial Aid In 1994-95, candidates received some institutionally administered aid in the form of scholarships, work-study. Application deadline: 4/1 for annual. Contact: Ms. B. J. Slovacek, Financial Aid Officer, Bergstrasse 106, 69121 Heidelberg, Germany. 6221-45810.

INTERNATIONAL STUDENTS
Services and Facilities International student office, international student center, visa services, language tutoring, ESL courses, counseling/support services.

Applying TOEFL required, minimum score of 550. Financial aid is available to international students. Financial aid application deadline: 4/1 for annual. Admission applications are processed on a rolling basis. Contact: Ms. Nancy Carrol, Provost, Schiller International University, American College of Switzerland, CH 1854 Leysin, Switzerland. 25-34-22-23.

PROGRAM
One-Year MBA Length of program: Minimum: 12 months. Full-time classes: Main campus; day, evening, summer. Part-time classes: Main campus; day, evening, summer. Degree requirements: 45 credits including 24 elective credits. Final oral comprehensive exam or oral defense of thesis. Languages: English. Average class size: 18.

PLACEMENT
Placement services include alumni network and career placement.

Program Contact: Ms. Nancy Carrol, Provost, Schiller International University, American College of Switzerland, American College of Switzerland, Admissions Office, CH 1854 Leysin, Switzerland. (25) 34-22-23.

Université de Lausanne

École des Hautes Etudes Commerciales

Lausanne, Switzerland

OVERVIEW
The Université de Lausanne is a coed institution. Founded 1918. Setting: suburban campus. Total institutional enrollment: 26. Program was first offered in 1979. Accredited by European Education Ministries.

MBA HIGHLIGHTS

Entrance Difficulty***

Cost
Tuition: N/R
Room & Board: N/R

Enrollment Profile
Full-time: 26
Part-time: 0
Total: 26
Average Age: 31

Work Exp: 100%
Women: 20%

Average Class Size: 25

ACADEMICS
Calendar Trimesters.

Curricular Focus Business issues and problems, managing diversity, problem solving and decision making.

Concentrations Accounting, economics, finance, human resources management, international business, management, management information systems, marketing, operations management, organizational behavior, quantitative analysis, strategic management.

Faculty Full-time: 16, 100% with doctorates.

Teaching Methodology Case study: 20%, faculty seminars: 5%, lecture: 30%, research: 10%, seminars by members of the business community: 5%, student presentations: 10%, team projects: 20%.

STUDENT STATISTICS
Geographic Representation Switzerland 56%; Africa, Asia and others 34%; North and Latin America 10%.

Undergraduate Majors Business 16%; engineering/technology 56%; humanities 6%; science/mathematics 8%; social sciences 6%; other 8%.

Other Background Graduate degrees in other disciplines: 100%. Work experience: On average, students have 5 years of work experience on entrance to the program.

FACILITIES
Housing College housing available.

Technology Computers are used heavily in course work. Computer terminals/PCs, linked by a campus-wide computer network, are available for use by students in program; they are located in classrooms, the computer center, computer labs. Students in the program are not required to have their own PC.

Computer Resources/On-line Services

Training	Yes	E-Mail	Yes
Internet	Yes		

ADMISSION
Acceptance 1994-95 200 applied for admission; 14% were accepted.

Entrance Requirements First degree, minimum 2 years of work experience, fluency in French and English.

Application Requirements Written essay, interview, application form, copies of transcript, resume/curriculum vitae, personal statement, 2 letters of recommendation.

Application Deadlines 2/15 for fall, 5/15 for spring. Applications are processed on a rolling basis.

FINANCIALS
Financial Aid Financial aid is not available to part-time students.

INTERNATIONAL STUDENTS
Services and Facilities International student office, language tutoring, counseling/support services.

Applying Proof of health. Financial aid is not available to international students. Admission application deadlines: 2/15 for fall, 5/15 for spring. Applications are processed on a rolling basis. Contact: Mr. Alexander Bergmann, MBA Director, Ecole Des HEC-BFSH1, CH-1015 Lausannne, Switzerland. 21-692-3452.

PROGRAM
One-Year MBA Length of program: Minimum: 9 months. Maximum: 1 year. Full-time classes: Day, evening, weekends, early morning. Degree requirements: 14 courses. Consulting project, professional report. Languages: English, French. Average class size: 150.

PLACEMENT
Placement services include alumni network, career library, and resume referral to employers. Of 1994 graduates, 60% were employed within three months of graduation.

Program Contact: Ms. Nicole Farcinade, Program Administrator, Université de Lausanne, BFSH1, CH-1015 Lausanne, Switzerland. 21-692-3390.

THAILAND

Bangkok University

Graduate School

Bangkok, Thailand

MBA HIGHLIGHTS

Entrance Difficulty*
Mean GMAT: 450
Mean GPA: N/R

Cost $$
Tuition: $8,000/degree program
Room & Board: N/R

Enrollment Profile
Full-time: N/R   Work Exp: N/R
Part-time: N/R   Women: 50%
Total: 100
Average Age: N/R

Average Class Size: 30

ACADEMICS
Length of Program Minimum: 24 months.
Full-time Classes Main campus; evening, weekends.
Degree Requirements 48 credits.
Curricular Focus Business issues and problems, international business, strategic analysis and planning.
Concentrations Entrepreneurship, finance, human resources management, international business, management, management information systems, marketing, operations management, organizational behavior, quantitative analysis.
Teaching Methodology Faculty seminars: 20%, lecture: 20%, research: 20%, student presentations: 20%, team projects: 20%.

ADMISSION
Entrance Requirements First degree, GMAT score of 450, minimum 2.5 GPA, written examination.
Application Requirements Interview, application form, copies of transcript, 3 letters of recommendation.
Application Deadline 3/1 for fall.

FINANCIALS
Costs for 1994-95 Tuition: Full-time: $8,000/degree program.
Financial Aid Application deadline: 3/1 for fall.

INTERNATIONAL STUDENTS
Applying TOEFL required, minimum score of 550; proof of health; proof of adequate funds. Admission application deadline: 4/7 for fall. Applications are processed on a rolling basis.

Program Contact: Graduate School Office, Bangkok University, 40/4 Rama IV Road, 10110 Bangkok, Thailand. 2-249-6278; Fax: 2-249-6274.

Chulalongkorn University

Sasin Graduate Institute of Business Administration

Bangkok, Thailand

OVERVIEW
Chulalongkorn University is an independent nonprofit coed institution. MBA programs offered jointly with Wharton School, University of Pennsylvania; J. L. Kellogg Graduate School of Management, Northwestern University. Founded 1982. Setting: urban campus. Total institutional enrollment: 309. Program was first offered in 1983. Accredited by Ministry of University Affairs.

MBA HIGHLIGHTS

Entrance Difficulty**
Mean GMAT: 490
Mean GPA: N/R

Cost $$
Tuition: $8,580
Room & Board: $12,000

Enrollment Profile
Full-time: N/R   Work Exp: 100%
Part-time: N/R   Women: 55%
Total: 164
Average Age: 25

Average Class Size: 75

ACADEMICS
Length of Program Minimum: 22 months. Maximum: 4 years.
Calendar Modular.
Full-time Classes Main campus; day.
Degree Requirements 75 credits including 36 elective credits.
Required Courses Accounting for decision making, business communication skills, business law, finance, macroeconomic analysis for management, management of organization, marketing, mathematical methods for management decision, microeconomic analysis, operations management, organization behavior, statistical methods for management decisions, strategy in domestic and international business.
Curricular Focus International business, problem solving and decision making, teamwork.
Concentrations Finance, international business, management, marketing.
Faculty Full-time: 4, 100% with doctorates; part-time: 47, 100% with doctorates.
Teaching Methodology Case study: 30%, lecture: 30%, research: 5%, student presentations: 10%, team projects: 25%.
Special Opportunities International exchange in Canada, France, Japan, United States of America. Internships include marketing in consumer product/service and research in consulting. MBA conference, management forum.

STUDENT STATISTICS
Undergraduate Majors Business 47%; engineering/technology 23%; humanities 7%; science/mathematics 8%; social sciences 5%; other 10%.
Other Background Graduate degrees in other disciplines: 7%.

FACILITIES
Information Resources Business collection in Prajadhipok Rambhai Barni Library includes 8,000 bound volumes, 120 periodical subscriptions, 100 videos.
Housing 10% of students in program live in college-owned or -operated housing.
Technology Computers are used heavily in course work. 60 computer terminals/PCs, linked by a campus-wide computer network, are available for use by students in program; they are located in the library, computer labs. Students in the program are not required to have their own PC.

Computer Resources/On-line Services

Training	Yes	E-Mail	Yes
Internet	Yes $	Dialog	Yes $

ADMISSION
Acceptance 1994-95 210 applied for admission; 46% were accepted.
Entrance Requirements First degree, GMAT score, minimum 2 years of work experience. Core courses waived through: previous course work.
Application Requirements Written essay, interview, application form, copies of transcript, personal statement.
Application Deadline 1/15 for spring.

FINANCIALS
Costs for 1995-96 Tuition: Full-time: $8,580. Average room and board costs are $12,000 per academic year (on-campus) and $12,000 per academic year (off-campus).
Financial Aid Financial aid is not available to part-time students.

INTERNATIONAL STUDENTS
Demographics 5% of students on campus are international; Asia 78%, North America 22%.
Services and Facilities Visa services, counseling/support services.
Applying TOEFL required. Financial aid is not available to international students. Admission application deadline: 1/15 for spring. Contact: Mrs. Oranong Tiradechavataya, Chief, Student Affairs Section, Soi Chulalongkorn 12, Phyathai Road, 10330 Bangkok, Thailand. 2-216-8833 Ext. 3862.

ALTERNATE MBA PROGRAM
Executive MBA (EMBA) Length of program: Minimum: 21 months. Maximum: 4 years. Degree requirements: 72 credits including 36 elective credits. Languages: English. Average class size: 75.

PLACEMENT

In 1993-94, 10 organizations participated in on-campus recruiting; 2 on-campus interviews were conducted. Placement services include alumni network, career counseling/planning, career placement, job interviews, resume preparation, and resume referral to employers. Of 1994 graduates, 95% were employed within three months of graduation.

Jobs by Employer Type Manufacturing 21%; service 14%; consulting 2%; trading 15%; banking/finance 42%; communications 3%; real estate 3%.

Jobs by Functional Area Marketing/sales 23%; finance 29%; operations 2%; management 21%; strategic planning 6%; technical management 7%; accounting 2%; purchasing 2%; research 8%.

Program Contact: Mrs. Lalida Ruangtrakool, Chief, Admissions and Financial Aid Section, Chulalongkorn University, Soi Chulalongkorn 12, Phyathai Road, 10330 Bangkok, Thailand. 2-216-8833 Ext. 3856; Fax: 2-215-3797.

See full description on page 694.

TURKEY

Bilkent University

Faculty of Business

Bilkent, Turkey

OVERVIEW

Bilkent University is an independent nonprofit coed institution. Founded 1984. Setting: suburban campus. Total institutional enrollment: 10,500. Program was first offered in 1986.

MBA HIGHLIGHTS

Entrance Difficulty*
Mean GMAT: 536
Mean GPA: N/R

Cost
Tuition: 90,000,000 Turkish lire
Room & Board: 25,000,000 Turkish lire

Enrollment Profile
Full-time: 123	Work Exp: 14%
Part-time: 0	Women: 34%
Total: 123	
Average Age: N/R	

Average Class Size: 40

ACADEMICS

Length of Program Minimum: 21 months. Maximum: 3 years.

Calendar Semesters.

Full-time Classes Main campus; day.

Degree Requirements 60 credits including 12 elective credits. Other: Summer internship.

Required Courses Business ethics, business law, business policy, corporate finance, decision science, economics, financial and managerial accounting, human behavior in organizations, international business, marketing management, probability and statistics, production and operations management, quality management.

Curricular Focus Economic and financial theory, general management, problem solving and decision making.

Concentrations Finance, management, marketing, organizational behavior, quantitative analysis.

Faculty Full-time: 25, 76% with doctorates; part-time: 2, 50% with doctorates.

Teaching Methodology Case study: 20%, faculty seminars: 5%, lecture: 60%, seminars by members of the business community: 5%, student presentations: 5%, team projects: 5%.

Special Opportunities International exchange in United States.

STUDENT STATISTICS

Geographic Representation Turkey 97%; Middle East 2%; Europe 1%.

Undergraduate Majors Business 10%; engineering/technology 75%; humanities 2%; science/mathematics 1%; social sciences 12%.

Other Background Graduate degrees in other disciplines: 4%.

FACILITIES

Information Resources Business collection includes 1,557 bound volumes, 265 periodical subscriptions.

Housing 5% of students in program live in college-owned or -operated housing.

Technology Computers are used moderately in course work. 150 computer terminals/PCs, linked by a campus-wide computer network, are available for use by students in program; they are located in the computer center, computer labs. Students in the program are not required to have their own PC.

Computer Resources/On-line Services

Training	Yes	Dun's	No
Internet	Yes	Dow Jones	No
E-Mail	Yes	Dialog	No
LEXIS/NEXIS	No	Bloomberg	No
CompuServe	No		

ADMISSION

Acceptance 1994-95 175 applied for admission; 31% were accepted.

Entrance Requirements First degree, GMAT score of 450.

Application Requirements Written essay, interview, application form, copies of transcript, personal statement, 2 letters of recommendation.

Application Deadline 8/1 for fall.

FINANCIALS

Financial Aid In 1994-95, candidates received some institutionally administered aid in the form of scholarships, tuition waivers. Financial aid is not available to part-time students. Application deadline: 5/1 for fall. Contact: Ms. Nihal Sisli, Faculty Secretary, Faculty of Business Administration, 06533 Bilkent, Ankara, Turkey. 312-266-4164.

INTERNATIONAL STUDENTS

Demographics 4% of students on campus are international; Africa 80%, Europe 10%, Australia 5%, North America 5%.

Services and Facilities International student office, international student center, visa services, language tutoring, counseling/support services.

Applying TOEFL required, minimum score of 550; IELTS required, minimum score of 6. Financial aid is available to international students. Financial aid application deadline: 8/1 for fall. Admission application deadline: 9/1 for fall. Applications are processed on a rolling basis. Contact: Mrs. Courtney Lukitsch-Oymen, International Center, Rector's Office, 06533 Bilkent, Ankara, Turkey. 312-266-4000.

PLACEMENT

In 1993-94, 9 organizations participated in on-campus recruiting; 1 on-campus interview was conducted. Placement services include career counseling/planning, career fairs, career library, career placement, job interviews, resume preparation, and resume referral to employers. Of 1994 graduates, 97% were employed within three months of graduation.

Jobs by Employer Type Service 90%; government 10%.

Jobs by Functional Area Marketing/sales 16%; finance 55%; management 19%; other 10%.

Program Contact: Ms. Nihal Sisli, Faculty Secretary, Bilkent University, Faculty of Business Administration, 06533 Bilkent, Ankara, Turkey. 312-266-4164; Fax: 312-266-4958; Internet Address: nihal@bilkent.edu.tr.

UNITED KINGDOM

Ashridge Management College

Berkhamsted, United Kingdom

OVERVIEW

Ashridge Management College is an independent nonprofit graduate-only specialized coed institution. MBA program offered jointly with City University. Founded 1959. Setting: rural campus. Total institutional enrollment: 75. Program was first offered in 1988. Accredited by Association of Business Schools.

MBA HIGHLIGHTS

Entrance Difficulty***
Mean GMAT: 550
Mean GPA: N/R

Cost
Tuition: 6,000 - 14,000 British pounds/degree program
Room & Board: N/R

Enrollment Profile
Full-time: 25   Work Exp: 100%
Part-time: 50   Women: 40%
Total: 75
Average Age: 33

Average Class Size: 25

ACADEMICS

Length of Program Minimum: 12 months. Maximum: 2 years.
Calendar Modular.
Full-time Classes Main campus.
Part-time Classes Main campus.
Degree Requirements 650 hours.
Required Courses Achieving operational effectiveness, analytical processes, business and society, business communications, global business environment, implementing change, improving business processes, integrating strategic resources, interpersonal skills, leadership and team working, personal values and self-managed development.
Curricular Focus General management, leadership, teamwork.
Concentrations Accounting, economics, finance, human resources management, international business, management, management information systems, marketing, operations management, organizational behavior, quantitative analysis, strategic management, transportation.
Faculty Full-time: 1; part-time: 40, 35% with doctorates.
Teaching Methodology Case study: 25%, faculty seminars: 5%, live exercise faculty seminars: 5%, simulations: 15%, student presentations: 40%.
Special Opportunities Internship program available.

STUDENT STATISTICS

Geographic Representation United Kingdom 60%; other 12%; Eastern Europe 10%; Scandinavia 8%; Germany 6%; United States 4%.
Other Background Graduate degrees in other disciplines: 10%. Work experience: On average, students have 10 years of work experience on entrance to the program.

FACILITIES

Information Resources Business collection includes 8,000 bound volumes, 600 periodical subscriptions, 12 CD-ROMs, 400 videos.
Housing 98% of students in program live in college-owned or -operated housing. Assistance with housing search provided.
Technology Computers are used heavily in course work. 75 computer terminals/PCs, linked by a campus-wide computer network, are available for use by students in program; they are located in student rooms, the student center, classrooms, learning resource center, the library, the computer center, computer labs, the research center. Students in the program are required to have their own PC.

Computer Resources/On-line Services

Training	Yes	Dun's	Yes
E-Mail	Yes	Dow Jones	Yes
Multimedia Center	Yes		

ADMISSION

Acceptance 1994-95 Of those applying, 20% were accepted.
Entrance Requirements First degree, GMAT score of 550, minimum 5 years of work experience.
Application Requirements Interview, application form, copies of transcript, resume/curriculum vitae, personal statement, 2 letters of recommendation.
Application Deadlines 8/31 for fall, 12/1 for spring. Applications are processed on a rolling basis.

FINANCIALS

Estimated Costs for 1995-96 Tuition: Full-time: 6,000-14,000 British pounds/degree program.
Financial Aid In 1994-95, 5% of candidates received some institutionally administered aid in the form of grants. Total awards ranged from 13,000-26,000 British pounds. Financial aid is available to part-time students. Applications are processed on a rolling basis. Contact: Mrs. Doris Boyle, Admissions Officer, Ashridge Management College, HP4 1NS Berkhamsted, Hertfordshire, United Kingdom. 442-841143.

INTERNATIONAL STUDENTS

Demographics 60% of students on campus are international.
Services and Facilities Language tutoring.
Applying TOEFL required, minimum score of 570; proof of health. Financial aid is available to international students. Applications are processed on a rolling basis. Admission applications are processed on a rolling basis.

PLACEMENT

Placement services include alumni network, career counseling/planning, electronic job bank, job search course, resume preparation, and resume referral to employers. Of 1994 graduates, 90% were employed within three months of graduation.
Jobs by Employer Type Manufacturing 37%; service 33%; consulting 19%; nonprofit 11%.

Program Contact: Mrs. Doris Boyle, Admissions Officer, Ashridge Management College, Ashridge Management College, HP4 1NS Berkhamsted, Hertfordshire, United Kingdom. 442-841143; Fax: 442-841144.

Aston University

Aston Business School

Birmingham, United Kingdom

OVERVIEW

Aston University is a government-supported coed institution. Founded 1966. Setting: urban campus. Total institutional enrollment: 4,200. Program was first offered in 1970. Approved by the Association of MBA Programs (U.K.).

MBA HIGHLIGHTS

Entrance Difficulty***
Mean GMAT: 580
Mean GPA: N/R

Cost
Tuition: 7,000 British pounds/degree program
(Nonresident: 8,500 British pounds/degree program)
Room & Board: 1,500 British pounds

Enrollment Profile
Full-time: 59   Work Exp: 100%
Part-time: 80   Women: 26%
Total: 139
Average Age: N/R

Average Class Size: 40

ACADEMICS

Length of Program Minimum: 12 months. Maximum: 5 years.
Calendar Trimesters.
Full-time Classes Main campus; day, evening.
Part-time Classes Main campus, distance learning option; day, evening, weekends.
Degree Requirements 12 modules including 4 elective modules.
Required Courses Applied research and project planning, economic environment of business, financial reporting, human resources management, management, management of innovation, marketing management, operations management, strategic management.
Curricular Focus General management, problem solving and decision making, strategic analysis and planning.
Concentrations Total quality management, law industrial relations, accounting, economics, finance, health services, human resources management, international business, management, management information systems, marketing, operations management, organizational behavior, public administration, public policy, quantitative analysis, strategic management.
Faculty Full-time: 20, 95% with doctorates; part-time: 10, 90% with doctorates.
Teaching Methodology Case study: 20%, lecture: 50%, research: 15%, seminars by members of the business community: 5%, student presentations: 2%, team projects: 8%.
Special Opportunities International exchange in France, Netherlands, Spain.

STUDENT STATISTICS

Geographic Representation United Kingdom 75%; Asia 11%; France 5%; other 4%; Ireland 2%; Eastern Europe 1%; Germany 1%; Scandinavia 1%.

Undergraduate Majors Business 60%; education 2%; engineering/technology 17%; nursing 5%; science/mathematics 2%; social sciences 10%; other 4%.

Other Background Graduate degrees in other disciplines: 10%. Work experience: On average, students have 5 years of work experience on entrance to the program.

FACILITIES

Housing 34% of students in program live in college-owned or -operated housing.

Technology Computers are used moderately in course work. Computer terminals/PCs, linked by a campus-wide computer network, are available for use by students in program; they are located in student rooms, the student center, classrooms, the library, the computer center, computer labs. Students in the program are not required to have their own PC.

Computer Resources/On-line Services

Training	Yes	E-Mail	Yes
Internet	Yes	Multimedia Center	Yes

ADMISSION

Acceptance 1994-95 300 applied for admission; 80% were accepted.

Entrance Requirements First degree, GMAT score of 550, minimum 2 years of work experience.

Application Requirements Application form, 2 letters of recommendation.

Application Deadline Applications are processed on a rolling basis.

FINANCIALS

Costs for 1994-95 Tuition: Full-time: 7,000 British pounds/degree program, 8,500 British pounds/degree program for international students. Average room and board costs are 1,500 British pounds per academic year (on-campus) and 2,000 British pounds per academic year (off-campus).

Financial Aid Financial aid is not available to part-time students.

INTERNATIONAL STUDENTS

Services and Facilities International student housing; language tutoring, ESL courses, counseling/support services.

Applying TOEFL required, minimum score of 600; proof of adequate funds. Financial aid is not available to international students. Admission applications are processed on a rolling basis. Contact: Ms. Charlotte Huntly, International Affairs Officer, Aston Triangle, B4 7ET Birmingham, West Midlands, England, United Kingdom. 21-359-3011.

PLACEMENT

In 1993-94, 98 on-campus interviews were conducted. Placement services include alumni network, career counseling/planning, career fairs, career library, job search course, resume preparation, and resume referral to employers. Of 1994 graduates, the average starting salary was 20,000 British pounds, the range was 15,000-48,000 British pounds.

Jobs by Employer Type Manufacturing 37%; service 39%; government 8%; consulting 15%; nonprofit 1%.

Jobs by Functional Area Marketing/sales 19%; finance 16%; operations 7%; management 53%; technical management 5%.

Program Contact: Ms. Jenny Moore, Full Time Course Coordinator, Aston University, Postgraduate Office, B4 7ET Birmingham, West Midlands, England, United Kingdom. 21-359-3011 Ext. 4936; Fax: 21-333-4731.

City University

London, United Kingdom

OVERVIEW

City University is a government-supported comprehensive coed institution. Part of University of London. Founded 1970. Accredited by Higher Education Funding Council. Approved by the Association of MBA Programs (U.K.).

MBA HIGHLIGHTS

Entrance Difficulty*
Mean GMAT: 580
Mean GPA: N/R

Cost
Tuition: 9,000 British pounds
(Nonresident: 9,750 British pounds)
Room & Board: 2,860 British pounds

Enrollment Profile

Full-time: N/R	Work Exp: N/R
Part-time: N/R	Women: 31%
Total: 166	
Average Age: N/R	

Average Class Size: 30

ACADEMICS

Length of Program Minimum: 12 months.

Full-time Classes Main campus; day, summer.

Degree Requirements 7 core courses, 4 integrative modules, 6 points of electives.

Curricular Focus Finance and banking, organizational development and change management, strategic analysis and planning.

Concentrations Finance, human resources management, information technology and management, international business and export management, marketing.

FACILITIES

Housing College housing available.

ADMISSION

Entrance Requirements First degree, GMAT score of 550, minimum 2 years of work experience.

Application Requirements Application form, 2 letters of recommendation.

Application Deadline 5/31 for fall.

FINANCIALS

Costs for 1995-96 Tuition: Full-time: 9,000 British pounds for residents, 9,750 British pounds for nonresidents. Average room and board costs are 2,860 British pounds per academic year (on-campus).

Financial Aid In 1994-95, candidates received some institutionally administered aid in the form of studentships. Applications are processed on a rolling basis. Contact: Ms. Liz Taylor, Post Graduate Admissions Office, Frobisher Crescent, Barbican Center, EC2Y 8HB London, England, United Kingdom. 71-477-8606.

INTERNATIONAL STUDENTS

Applying TOEFL required; proof of adequate funds. Financial aid is available to international students. Applications are processed on a rolling basis. Admission application deadline: 5/31 for fall.

Program Contact: Ms. Liz Taylor, Post Graduate Admissions Office, City University, Frobisher Crescent, Barbican Center, EC2Y 8HB London, England, United Kingdom. 71-477-8606.

Cranfield University

Cranfield School of Management

Cranfield, Bedford, United Kingdom

OVERVIEW

Cranfield University is primarily male institution. Founded 1946. Setting: rural campus. Total institutional enrollment: 1,500. Program was first offered in 1964. Accredited by Higher Education Funding Council for England (HEFCE), Institute of Personnel Development (IPD), Chartered Institute of Marketing. Approved by the Association of MBA Programs (U.K.).

MBA HIGHLIGHTS

Entrance Difficulty**
Mean GMAT: 614
Mean GPA: N/R

Cost
Tuition: 11,000 British pounds/degree program
Room & Board: 6,000 British pounds

Enrollment Profile
Full-time: 160	Work Exp: 100%
Part-time: 70	Women: 24%
Total: 230	
Average Age: 31	

Average Class Size: 45

ACADEMICS
Length of Program 12 months.
Calendar Quarters.
Full-time Classes Main campus; day, early morning, summer.
Degree Requirements 43 credits including 15 elective credits.
Required Courses European business environment, European business law, accounting, business start-up, economics, financial management, human resources management, information management skills, information systems, international and corporate strategy, marketing, operations management, presentation and communication skills, project management, quantitative analysis, strategic management.
Curricular Focus Entrepreneurship, general management, problem solving and decision making.
Concentration Management.
Faculty Full-time: 85, 37% with doctorates.
Teaching Methodology Individual and group preparation, research, and project work team projects: 65%, lecture theaters: 35%.
Special Opportunities International exchange in Australia, France, Singapore, Spain, United States of America.

STUDENT STATISTICS
Geographic Representation United Kingdom 69%; other 14%; Americas 6%; Africa 2%; France 1%; Ireland 1%; Italy 1%; Scandinavia 1%.
Other Background Graduate degrees in other disciplines: 14%. Work experience: On average, students have 8 years of work experience on entrance to the program.

FACILITIES
Information Resources Business collection includes 21,000 bound volumes, 251 periodical subscriptions, 12 CD-ROMs, 170 videos.
Housing 70% of students in program live in college-owned or -operated housing.
Technology Computers are used moderately in course work. 60 computer terminals/PCs, linked by a campus-wide computer network, are available for use by students in program; they are located in dormitories, the library, the computer center, computer labs. Students in the program are not required to have their own PC.

Computer Resources/On-line Services
Training	Yes	Dun's	Yes
Internet	Yes	Dow Jones	No
E-Mail	Yes	Dialog	Yes
LEXIS/NEXIS	No	Bloomberg	No
CompuServe	No		

ADMISSION
Acceptance 1994-95 558 applied for admission; 56% were accepted.
Entrance Requirements First degree, GMAT score of 550, minimum 3 years of work experience.
Application Requirements Written essay, interview, application form, resume/curriculum vitae, 2 letters of recommendation.
Application Deadline Applications are processed on a rolling basis.

FINANCIALS
Costs for 1995-96 Tuition: Full-time: 11,000 British pounds/degree program; Weekends: 16,000 British pounds/degree program. Average room and board costs are 6,000 British pounds per academic year (on-campus).
Financial Aid In 1994-95, candidates received some institutionally administered aid in the form of scholarships, loans. Total awards ranged from 2,000-5,000 British pounds. Financial aid is not available to part-time students. Application deadline: 7/31 for fall.

INTERNATIONAL STUDENTS
Services and Facilities Language tutoring, special assistance for nonnative speakers of English, counseling/support services.

Applying TOEFL required, minimum score of 650; IELTS required, minimum score of 7; proof of adequate funds. Financial aid is not available to international students. Admission applications are processed on a rolling basis.

ALTERNATE MBA PROGRAM
Executive MBA (EMBA) Length of program: Minimum: 24 months. Maximum: 2 years. Part-time classes: Main campus; weekends. Degree requirements: 48 credits including 14 elective credits. Individual project. Languages: English. Average class size: 35.

PLACEMENT
In 1993-94, 103 organizations participated in on-campus recruiting; 858 on-campus interviews were conducted. Placement services include alumni network, career counseling/planning, career library, job interviews, job search course, resume preparation, and resume referral to employers. Of 1994 graduates, 75% were employed within three months of graduation, the average starting salary was 36,400 British pounds, the range was 16,000-250,000 British pounds.
Jobs by Employer Type Manufacturing 24%; service 41%; government 5%; consulting 28%; nonprofit 2%.
Jobs by Functional Area Marketing/sales 24%; finance 18%; operations 10%; management 21%; strategic planning 22%; technical management 5%.

Program Contact: Mrs. Pat Hayes, Admissions Officer, Cranfield University, MK43 0AL Cranfield-Bedford, England, United Kingdom. 1234-754431; Fax: 1234-752439.

De Montfort University

Leicester Business School

Leicester, United Kingdom

OVERVIEW
De Montfort University is a coed institution. Part of British University System. Founded 1989. Setting: urban campus. Total institutional enrollment: 24,000. Program was first offered in 1983. Approved by the Association of MBA Programs (U.K.).

MBA HIGHLIGHTS
Entrance Difficulty***

Cost
Tuition: N/R
Room & Board: N/R

Enrollment Profile
Full-time: 48	Work Exp: 83%
Part-time: 102	Women: 37%
Total: 150	
Average Age: 27	

Average Class Size: 20

ACADEMICS
Calendar Semesters.
Curricular Focus General management, strategic analysis and planning.
Concentrations Accounting, finance, human resources management, international business, management, marketing, operations management, organizational behavior, public policy, strategic management.
Teaching Methodology Case study: 20%, lecture: 25%, research: 10%, seminars by members of the business community: 5%, student presentations: 15%, team projects: 25%.
Special Opportunities International exchange in France.

STUDENT STATISTICS
Other Background Graduate degrees in other disciplines: 5%. Work experience: On average, students have 5-12 years of work experience on entrance to the program.

FACILITIES
Housing College housing available.
Technology Computers are used moderately in course work. Computer terminals/PCs, linked by a campus-wide computer network, are available for use by students in program; they are located in student rooms, the library, the computer center, computer labs. Students in the program are not required to have their own PC.

Computer Resources/On-line Services

| Training | Yes | E-Mail | Yes |

ADMISSION
Acceptance 1994-95 260 applied for admission; 72% were accepted.
Entrance Requirements First degree, minimum 4 years for part time, and 2 years for full time students years of work experience.
Application Requirements Application form, copies of transcript.
Application Deadline Applications are processed on a rolling basis.

FINANCIALS
Financial Aid Financial aid is not available to part-time students.

INTERNATIONAL STUDENTS
Services and Facilities International student housing; international student office, language tutoring.
Applying IELTS required, minimum score of 6; proof of health; proof of adequate funds; 10% of tuition fees as deposit. Financial aid is not available to international students. Admission applications are processed on a rolling basis. Contact: Mr. Barry Weeks, International Liaison Officer, External Relations, Portland Building, LE1 9BH Leicester, England, United Kingdom. 116-255-1551 Ext. 8354.

PROGRAM
One-Year MBA Length of program: Minimum: 12 months. Maximum: 3 years. Full-time classes: Main campus; day, evening. Part-time classes: Main campus, Northamptonshire, United Kingdom; day, evening, weekends. Degree requirements: Dissertation; 16 modules including 8 electives. Languages: English.

PLACEMENT
Placement services include career counseling/planning, career fairs, career library, and resume referral to employers.

Program Contact: Ms. Sue Owen, MBA Programs Administrator, De Montfort University, The Gateway, LE1 9BH Leicester, England, United Kingdom. 116-257-7230; Fax: 116-251-7548.

Henley Management College

Oxfordshire, United Kingdom

OVERVIEW
Henley Management College is an independent nonprofit specialized coed institution. Part of Brunel University. MBA program offered jointly with Brunel University. Founded 1945. Setting: rural campus. Total institutional enrollment: 5,179. Program was first offered in 1979. Approved by the Association of MBA Programs (U.K.).

MBA HIGHLIGHTS
Entrance Difficulty*

Cost
Tuition: 9,790 British pounds
(Nonresident: 12,100 British pounds)
Room & Board: N/R

Enrollment Profile
Full-time: N/R	Work Exp: 100%
Part-time: N/R	Women: 32%
Total: 119	
Average Age: N/R	

Average Class Size: 50

ACADEMICS
Length of Program Minimum: 12 months. Maximum: 2 years.
Calendar Trimesters.
Full-time Classes Main campus, Brunel University; day.
Part-time Classes Main campus, distance learning option; day, weekends.
Degree Requirements 10 courses.
Required Courses International business environment, management information, managing markets, managing operations, managing people, managing resources, managing strategic change, managing strategic information, strategic analysis and choice, strategic management.
Curricular Focus Business issues and problems, economic and financial theory, general management, international business, leadership, organizational development and change management, problem solving and decision making, strategic analysis and planning, teamwork.

Concentrations Accounting, economics, finance, human resources management, international business, management, management information systems, marketing, operations management, organizational behavior, public policy, strategic management.
Faculty Full-time: 27, 30% with doctorates.
Teaching Methodology Case study: 20%, lecture: 30%, research: 10%, student presentations: 20%, team projects: 20%.
Special Opportunities International exchange in Denmark, France, Germany, Netherlands, Russia, Spain, Sweden, United States of America.

FACILITIES
Information Resources Business collection includes 15,000 bound volumes, 375 periodical subscriptions, 11 CD-ROMs, 120 videos.
Housing College housing available.
Technology Computers are used moderately in course work. 35 computer terminals/PCs, linked by a campus-wide computer network, are available for use by students in program; they are located in student rooms, the library, the computer center. Students in the program are not required to have their own PC.

Computer Resources/On-line Services

Training	Yes	E-Mail	Yes
Internet	Yes $	Multimedia Center	Yes

ADMISSION
Entrance Requirements First degree, minimum 2- 5 years of work experience.
Application Requirements Interview, application form, copies of transcript, 2 letters of recommendation.
Application Deadline Applications are processed on a rolling basis.

FINANCIALS
Costs for 1995-96 Tuition: Full-time: 9,790 British pounds for residents, 12,100 British pounds for nonresidents; Part-time day: 6,175 British pounds for residents, 7,888 British pounds for nonresidents.
Financial Aid In 1994-95, candidates received some institutionally administered aid in the form of scholarships, loans. Financial aid is not available to part-time students.

INTERNATIONAL STUDENTS
Applying TOEFL required, minimum score of 550; IELTS required, minimum score of 6. Financial aid is not available to international students. Admission applications are processed on a rolling basis.

PLACEMENT
Placement services include alumni network, career counseling/planning, career fairs, career library, and career placement.

Program Contact: Ms. Beverly Howard, Admissions and Statistics Officer, Henley Management College, Greenlands, Henley-on-Thames, RG9 3AU Oxfordshire, England, United Kingdom. 491 571454; Fax: 491 410184.

Heriot-Watt University

Business School Edinburgh

Edinburgh, United Kingdom

OVERVIEW
Heriot-Watt University is a coed institution. Founded 1966. Setting: rural campus. Total institutional enrollment: 5,500. Program was first offered in 1984. Approved by the Association of MBA Programs (U.K.).

MBA HIGHLIGHTS
Entrance Difficulty N/R
Mean GMAT: 544
Mean GPA: N/R

Cost
Tuition: N/R
Room & Board: N/R

Enrollment Profile
Full-time: 25
Part-time: 41
Total: 66
Average Age: 32

Work Exp: 100%
Women: 25%

Average Class Size: 50

ACADEMICS

Length of Program Minimum: 12 months. Maximum: 4 years.
Calendar Terms.
Full-time Classes Main campus; day.
Part-time Classes Main campus; day.
Degree Requirements Dissertation, research project.
Required Courses Accounting, business economics, human resources management, marketing, quantitative methods, strategic management.
Concentrations Accounting, arts administration, economics, finance, health services, human resources management, management, management information systems, marketing, organizational behavior, quantitative analysis, strategic management.
Special Opportunities International exchange in Hungary.

STUDENT STATISTICS

Undergraduate Majors Business 17%; education 1%; engineering/technology 29%; humanities 8%; nursing 3%; science/mathematics 10%; social sciences 10%; other 22%.
Other Background Graduate degrees in other disciplines: 90%.

FACILITIES

Housing 10% of students in program live in college-owned or -operated housing. Assistance with housing search provided.
Technology Computers are used moderately in course work. 150 computer terminals/PCs, linked by a campus-wide computer network, are available for use by students in program; they are located in the library, computer labs. Students in the program are not required to have their own PC.

Computer Resources/On-line Services

Training	Yes	E-Mail	No

ADMISSION

Acceptance 1994-95 Of those applying, 8% were accepted.
Entrance Requirements GMAT score of 550, minimum 2 years of work experience, minimum age 24. Core courses waived through: previous course work.
Application Requirements Application form, copies of transcript, resume/curriculum vitae, personal statement, 2 letters of recommendation.
Application Deadline 6/1 for fall.

INTERNATIONAL STUDENTS

Applying TOEFL required, minimum score of 600; proof of adequate funds.

PLACEMENT

Placement services include alumni network, career counseling/planning, career library, job search course, and resume preparation.

Program Contact: Ms. Susan Deacon, MBA Director of Programs, Heriot-Watt University, Riccarton Campus, EH14 4AT Edinburgh, Scotland, United Kingdom. 131-449-5111; Fax: 131-451-3190.

Huron University

London Campus

London, United Kingdom

OVERVIEW

Huron University is an independent proprietary comprehensive coed institution. Founded 1883. Setting: urban campus. Total institutional enrollment: 291. Program was first offered in 1986.

MBA HIGHLIGHTS

Entrance Difficulty***
Mean GMAT: 450
Mean GPA: N/R

Cost
Tuition: N/R
(Nonresident: N/R)
Room & Board: N/R

Enrollment Profile
Full-time: 46
Part-time: 9
Total: 55
Average Age: 27

Work Exp: N/R
Women: 40%

Average Class Size: 17

ACADEMICS

Calendar Semesters.
Curricular Focus General management, international business, teamwork.
Concentration Management.
Faculty Full-time: 3; part-time: 8, 25% with doctorates.
Teaching Methodology Case study: 20%, faculty seminars: 10%, lecture: 30%, research: 5%, seminars by members of the business community: 5%, student presentations: 20%, team projects: 10%.
Special Opportunities International exchange in Japan, United States of America. Internship program available.

STUDENT STATISTICS

Undergraduate Majors Business 59%; engineering/technology 17%; humanities 6%; social sciences 13%; other 5%.

FACILITIES

Housing 10% of students in program live in college-owned or -operated housing. Assistance with housing search provided.
Technology Computers are used heavily in course work. 22 computer terminals/PCs are available for use by students in program; they are located in the library, computer labs. Students in the program are not required to have their own PC. $200 are budgeted per student for computer support.

Computer Resources/On-line Services

Training	Yes	CompuServe	No
Internet	Yes $	Dun's	No
E-Mail	Yes	Dow Jones	No
Multimedia Center	Yes	Dialog	No
LEXIS/NEXIS	No	Bloomberg	No

ADMISSION

Entrance Requirements First degree, GMAT score of 450, minimum 2.75 GPA. Core courses waived through: previous course work.
Application Requirements Written essay, application form, copies of transcript, resume/curriculum vitae, 2 letters of recommendation.
Application Deadline Applications are processed on a rolling basis.

FINANCIALS

Financial Aid In 1994-95, candidates received some institutionally administered aid in the form of scholarships, assistantships, work-study. Financial aid is available to part-time students. Application deadlines: 7/15 for fall, 1/1 for spring. Contact: Mrs. Michele Kevill, Director of Student Affairs, 58 Prince's Gate, SW7 2PG London, England, United Kingdom. 71-581-4899.

INTERNATIONAL STUDENTS

Demographics 93% of students on campus are international; Asia 93%.
Services and Facilities Visa services, ESL courses, counseling/support services.
Applying TOEFL required, minimum score of 550; proof of adequate funds. Financial aid is available to international students. Financial aid application deadlines: 9/5 for fall, 1/1 for spring. Admission applications are processed on a rolling basis. Contact: Mrs. Michele Pasqua, Student Affairs Officer, 58 Prince's Gate, SW7 2PG London, England, United Kingdom. 71-581-4899.

PROGRAM

One-Year MBA Length of program: Minimum: 11 months. Full-time classes: Main campus; day, evening, summer. Part-time classes: Main campus; evening, summer. Degree requirements: 36 credits including 3 elective credits. Languages: English.

PLACEMENT

Placement services include alumni network, career counseling/planning, job search course, and resume preparation.

Program Contact: Mr. James Wrightsman, Director of International Admissions, Huron University, 58 Prince's Gate, SW7 2PG London, England, United Kingdom. 71-581-4899; Fax: 71-589-9706.

Imperial College

Management School

London, United Kingdom

ACADEMICS
Calendar Terms.

FACILITIES
Computer Resources/On-line Services
Internet   Yes

ADMISSION
Entrance Requirements First degree, GMAT score.
Application Requirements Interview, application form, 2 letters of recommendation.
Application Deadline 7/31 for fall.

FINANCIALS
Financial Aid In 1994-95, candidates received some institutionally administered aid in the form of grants, scholarships, loans, sponsored by company. Financial aid is not available to part-time students. Contact: Management School, 53 Prince's Gate, Exhibition Road, SW7 2PG London, England, United Kingdom. 071-589-5111.

INTERNATIONAL STUDENTS
Services and Facilities International student housing.
Applying TOEFL required.

PROGRAM
One-Year MBA Length of program: Minimum: 12 months. Full-time classes: Main campus; day, summer. Degree requirements: Project. Languages: English.

PLACEMENT
Placement services include alumni network, career counseling/planning, and resume referral to employers.

Program Contact: Dr. David Norburn, Director, Imperial College, 53 Prince's Gate, Exhibition Road, SW7 2PG London, England, United Kingdom. 071-589-5111; Fax: 071-823-7685.

Kingston University

Kingston Business School

Kingston upon Thames, United Kingdom

ACADEMICS
Length of Program Minimum: 30 months.
Part-time Classes Main campus; evening, weekends.
Curricular Focus General management, problem solving and decision making, teamwork.
Concentration Management.

ADMISSION
Entrance Requirements First degree, GMAT score.
Application Requirements Interview, application form, 2 letters of recommendation.

FINANCIALS
Costs for 1994-95 Tuition: Part-time evening: 3,750 British pounds.

Program Contact: Ms. Martha Mador, MBA Course Director, Kingston University, Kingston Hill, KT2 7LB Kingston upon Thames, Surrey, England, United Kingdom. 81-547-7120; Fax: 81-547-7452.

Lancaster University

The Management School

Lancaster, United Kingdom

OVERVIEW
Lancaster University is a coed institution. Part of British University System. MBA program offered jointly with Koblenz School of Corporate Management. Founded 1964. Setting: small-town campus. Total institutional enrollment: 10,000. Accredited by British Council. Approved by the Association of MBA Programs (U.K.).

MBA HIGHLIGHTS
Entrance Difficulty**
Mean GMAT: 608
Mean GPA: N/R

Cost
Tuition: 7,450 British pounds
(Nonresident: 7,950 British pounds)
Room & Board: N/R

Enrollment Profile

Full-time: 51	Work Exp: 88%
Part-time: 0	Women: 40%
Total: 51	
Average Age: 29	

Average Class Size: N/R

ACADEMICS
Length of Program Minimum: 12 months.
Calendar Trimesters.
Full-time Classes Main campus; day.
Required Courses Accounting, business economics, business planning project, human resources management, managerial roles and capabilities, managing organizational change, marketing, organizational behavior, strategic management.
Curricular Focus General management, international business, organizational development and change management, strategic analysis and planning.
Concentrations Accounting, economics, entrepreneurship, finance, human resources management, international business, management, management information systems, marketing, operations management, organizational behavior, organizational change management, logistics, retail, public policy, quantitative analysis, strategic management.
Special Opportunities International exchange in Austria, Canada, Denmark, France, Germany, Italy, Netherlands, Spain. Internship program available. Other: Study skills program, languages program.

STUDENT STATISTICS
Geographic Representation United Kingdom 44%; Balkan Penninsula 24%; Austria 10%; France 8%; Germany 8%; Italy 6%.
Undergraduate Majors Business 39%; education 2%; engineering/technology 29%; humanities 12%; science/mathematics 8%; social sciences 8%; other 2%.
Other Background Graduate degrees in other disciplines: 12%. Work experience: On average, students have 6 years of work experience on entrance to the program.

FACILITIES
Housing 85% of students in program live in college-owned or -operated housing. Assistance with housing search provided.
Technology 70 computer terminals/PCs, linked by a campus-wide computer network, are available for use by students in program; they are located in the library, the computer center, computer labs. Students in the program are not required to have their own PC.

Computer Resources/On-line Services

Training	Yes	Dun's	No
Internet	Yes $	Dow Jones	Yes $
LEXIS/NEXIS	Yes	Dialog	Yes $
CompuServe	Yes $	Bloomberg	No

ADMISSION
Acceptance 1994-95 595 applied for admission; 25% were accepted.
Entrance Requirements First degree, GMAT score of 580, English language proficiency. Core courses waived through: previous course work.
Application Requirements Application form, copies of transcript, 2 letters of recommendation.

Application Deadline Applications are processed on a rolling basis.

FINANCIALS
Costs for 1995-96 Tuition: Full-time: 7,450 British pounds for residents, 7,950 British pounds for nonresidents, 7,950 British pounds for international students.

Financial Aid In 1994-95, 10% of candidates received some institutionally administered aid in the form of scholarships, bursaries. Total awards ranged from 1,000-10,000 British pounds. Application deadlines: 1/6 for fall, 2/28 for spring. Applications are processed on a rolling basis. Contact: Ms. Catherine Walker, MBA Administrator, MBA Office, The Management School, LA1 4YX Lancaster, England, United Kingdom. 1524-594068.

INTERNATIONAL STUDENTS
Demographics 16% of students on campus are international; Asia 40%, Europe 35%, North America 15%, Africa 5%, Central America 2%, South America 2%, Australia 1%.

Services and Facilities International student office, international student center, language tutoring, ESL courses, special assistance for nonnative speakers of English, counseling/support services, religious facilities.

Applying TOEFL required, minimum score of 580; IELTS required, minimum score of 6; proof of adequate funds. Financial aid is available to international students. Applications are processed on a rolling basis. Admission applications are processed on a rolling basis. Contact: Dr. John Withrington, International Officer, MBA Office, The Management School, LA1 4YX Lancaster, England, United Kingdom. 1524-65201.

PLACEMENT
Placement services include alumni network, career counseling/planning, career library, job search course, and resume preparation.

Program Contact: Ms. Catherine Walker, MBA Administrator, Lancaster University, MBA Office, The Management School, LA1 4YX Lancaster, England, United Kingdom. 1524-594068; Fax: 1524-592417; Internet Address: mba@lancs.ac.uk.

Manchester Metropolitan University

Faculty of Management and Business

Manchester, United Kingdom

ACADEMICS
Length of Program Minimum: 30 months.

Full-time Classes Main campus; evening.

Degree Requirements 12 modules, including 3 elective modules.

Required Courses Accounting for decision making, finance and organizational analysis, human resources management, international business environment, issues in strategy, management and organizations, management science, systems and strategy, marketing and operations, organizational renewal and change.

Curricular Focus General management, problem solving and decision making, teamwork.

Concentrations Accounting, finance, international business, management, operations management, organizational behavior, public administration.

ADMISSION
Entrance Requirements First degree.

Application Requirements Interview, application form, resume/curriculum vitae.

Program Contact: Ms. Kath Hemsworth, MBA Course Administrator, Manchester Metropolitan University, M1 3GH Manchester, England, United Kingdom. 61-247-3717; Fax: 61-247-6319.

Middlesex University

Business School

London, United Kingdom

MBA HIGHLIGHTS
Entrance Difficulty***

Cost
Tuition: N/R
(Nonresident: N/R)
Room & Board: N/R

Enrollment Profile

Full-time: N/R	Work Exp: N/R
Part-time: N/R	Women: 50%
Total: 60	
Average Age: N/R	

Average Class Size: 60

ACADEMICS
Curricular Focus Business issues and problems, general management, international business.

Concentrations Accounting, finance, human resources management, international business, management, marketing, operations management.

Teaching Methodology Case study: 5%, faculty seminars: 5%, lecture: 50%, research: 30%, student presentations: 5%, team projects: 5%.

FACILITIES
Housing College housing available.

ADMISSION
Entrance Requirements First degree, GMAT score of 500, minimum 1 year of work experience.

Application Requirements Application form, copies of transcript, 2 letters of recommendation.

Application Deadlines 7/15 for fall. Applications are processed on a rolling basis.

INTERNATIONAL STUDENTS
Applying TOEFL required, minimum score of 600; IELTS required, minimum score of 6. Financial aid is not available to international students. Admission application deadline: 7/15 for fall.

PROGRAM
One-Year MBA Length of program: Minimum: 12 months. Full-time classes: Hendon Business School; day, evening, summer. Degree requirements: 200 credits. Languages: English.

Program Contact: Ms. Martine Clarke, MBA Admissions Administrator, Middlesex University, The Burroughs, Hendon, NW4 4BT London, England, United Kingdom. 181-362-5832.

Richmond College, The American International University in London

Richmond, Surrey, United Kingdom

OVERVIEW
Richmond College, The American International University in London is an independent nonprofit comprehensive coed institution. Founded 1972. Setting: 5-acre urban campus with easy access to London. Total institutional enrollment: 926. Program was first offered in 1992.

MBA HIGHLIGHTS
Entrance Difficulty***

Cost
Tuition: 4,385 British pounds/semester
(Nonresident: 4,385 British pounds/semester)
Room & Board: N/R

Enrollment Profile

Full-time: 80	Work Exp: 40%
Part-time: 20	Women: 40%
Total: 100	
Average Age: 26	

Average Class Size: 18

ACADEMICS
Length of Program Minimum: 9 months.

Calendar Semesters.

Full-time Classes Kensington; day, evening, summer.

Part-time Classes Kensington; day, evening, summer.

Degree Requirements 30 credits.

Curricular Focus General management, international business, teamwork.

Concentrations International business, international finance, management.

Faculty Full-time: 6, 80% with doctorates; part-time: 10, 50% with doctorates.

Teaching Methodology Case study: 10%, faculty seminars: 5%, lecture: 50%, research: 5%, seminars by members of the business community: 5%, student presentations: 15%, team projects: 10%.

Special Opportunities International exchange in Germany, Japan, United States of America. Internship program available.

STUDENT STATISTICS

Geographic Representation Middle East 20%; Germany 15%; United Kingdom 15%; Asia 15%; France 10%; United States of America 10%; Italy 5%; Russia 5%; Spain 5%.

Undergraduate Majors Business 50%; engineering/technology 35%; other 15%.

Other Background Graduate degrees in other disciplines: 5%. Work experience: On average, students have 2 years of work experience on entrance to the program.

FACILITIES

Information Resources Main library with 80,000 bound volumes, 7 titles on microform, 277 periodical subscriptions, 120 records/tapes/CDs. Business collection includes 15,000 bound volumes, 35 periodical subscriptions, 4 CD-ROMs, 120 videos.

Housing 20% of students in program live in college-owned or -operated housing. Assistance with housing search provided.

Technology Computers are used moderately in course work. 45 computer terminals/PCs, linked by a campus-wide computer network, are available for use by students in program; they are located in learning resource center, computer labs. Students in the program are not required to have their own PC. 800 British pounds are budgeted per student for computer support.

Computer Resources/On-line Services

Training	Yes	E-Mail	No
Internet	Yes	Dialog	Yes

ADMISSION

Acceptance 1994-95 125 applied for admission; 64% were accepted.

Entrance Requirements First degree, minimum 3.0 GPA, minimum 2 years of work experience. Core courses waived through: previous course work, work experience.

Application Requirements Application form, copies of transcript, resume/curriculum vitae, personal statement, 2 letters of recommendation.

Application Deadline Applications are processed on a rolling basis.

FINANCIALS

Costs for 1994-95 Tuition: Full-time: 4,385 British pounds/semester for residents, 4,385 British pounds/semester for nonresidents; Part-time day: 885 British pounds/course for residents, 885 British pounds/course for nonresidents.

Financial Aid In 1994-95, 10% of candidates received some institutionally administered aid in the form of scholarships, fellowships, assistantships, work-study. Total awards ranged from 500-2,000 British pounds. Financial aid is not available to part-time students. Applications are processed on a rolling basis. Contact: MBA Program Director, 16 Young Street, W8 5EH London, England, United Kingdom. 71-938-1761.

INTERNATIONAL STUDENTS

Demographics 80% of students on campus are international; Asia 25%, Europe 20%, North America 18%, Africa 15%, Australia 5%, Central America 5%, South America 5%, other 7%.

Services and Facilities Visa services, language tutoring, ESL courses, special assistance for nonnative speakers of English, counseling/support services.

Applying Financial aid is available to international students. Admission applications are processed on a rolling basis.

PLACEMENT

Placement services include alumni network, career counseling/planning, career library, career placement, electronic job bank, resume preparation, and resume referral to employers. Of 1994 graduates, 85% were employed within three months of graduation, the average starting salary was 25,000 British pounds, the range was 19,000-28,000British pounds.

Jobs by Employer Type Manufacturing 10%; service 75%; government 5%; consulting 5%; nonprofit 5%.

Jobs by Functional Area Marketing/sales 40%; finance 50%; operations 5%; management 5%.

Program Contact: Mr. Clive Bateson, Associate Director of the MBA Program, Richmond College, The American International University in London, Queen's Road, TW10 6JP Richmond, Surrey, England, United Kingdom. 71-938-1761.

Schiller International University

London, United Kingdom

OVERVIEW

Schiller International University is an independent nonprofit coed institution. Founded 1964. Setting: urban campus. Total institutional enrollment: 376. Program was first offered in 1972.

MBA HIGHLIGHTS

Entrance Difficulty N/R
Mean GMAT: N/R
Mean GPA: 3.0

Cost $$
Tuition: $5,720/semester
Room & Board: $4,940

Enrollment Profile

Full-time: 98	Work Exp: N/R
Part-time: 18	Women: 53%
Total: 116	
Average Age: 28	

Average Class Size: 15

S *chiller International University M.B.A. programs aim for the professional development of motivated, globally oriented individuals through intensive interactive learning.*

SIU's graduate school of business administration offers the Master of Business Administration in London, Paris, Heidelberg, Berlin, Madrid, Strasbourg, Leysin, and Florida. The M.B.A. builds upon previous studies in marketing, management, finance, and economics and relates these studies to real-world international management situations via case studies, business games, computer simulations, research projects, and class discussions of current global issues. Program courses involve theoretical and practical applications, strategic decision making, teamwork, and group mobilization. The M.B.A. in international hotel and tourism management is offered in London and Florida. This program is directed at students in the fields of business, hotel/restaurant management, and tourism and related areas who wish to earn an advanced business degree and earn the credentials to enter the industry at management level. Working professionals have the opportunity to undertake the M.B.A. program on a part-time basis by attending between one and four evening courses per semester, plus one or two more during the summer term. Graduate class enrollment is usually between 10 and 25 students per course.

ACADEMICS

Calendar Semesters.

Curricular Focus International business, problem solving and decision making, teamwork.

Concentrations Hotel management, international business.

Faculty Full-time: 12; part-time: 48.

Teaching Methodology Case study: 20%, lecture: 40%, research: 20%, student presentations: 10%, team projects: 10%.

Special Opportunities International exchange in France, Germany, Spain, Switzerland, United States of America. Internship program available.

STUDENT STATISTICS

Undergraduate Majors Business 87%; engineering/technology 1%; humanities 7%; social sciences 5%.

FACILITIES

Information Resources Main library with 21,603 bound volumes, 11,100 titles on microform, 143 periodical subscriptions, 80 records/tapes/CDs.

Housing College housing available.

Technology 15 computer terminals/PCs are available for use by students in program; they are located in computer labs. Students in the program are not required to have their own PC.

ADMISSION

Entrance Requirements First degree, GMAT score, minimum 2.8 GPA. Core courses waived through: previous course work.

Application Requirements Application form, copies of transcript.

Application Deadline Applications are processed on a rolling basis.

FINANCIALS

Financial Aid In 1994-95, candidates received some institutionally administered aid in the form of scholarships, work-study. Financial aid is available to part-time students. Application deadline: 4/1 for annual. Contact: Ms. B.J. Slovacek, Financial Aid Officer, Bergstrasse 106, 69121 Heidelberg, Germany. 6221-45810.

INTERNATIONAL STUDENTS

Demographics 88% of students on campus are international; Europe 40%, Asia 15%, North America 12%, South America 7%, Africa 4%, Central America 2%, Other 20%.

Services and Facilities International student office, international student center, visa services, language tutoring, ESL courses, counseling/support services.

Applying TOEFL required, minimum score of 550. Financial aid is available to international students. Financial aid application deadline: 4/1 for annual. Admission applications are processed on a rolling basis. Contact: Ms. Bella Anand, Associate Director of Admissions, 51-55 Waterloo Road, SE1 8TX London, United Kingdom. 71-928-8484.

PROGRAM

One-Year MBA Length of program: Minimum: 12 months. Full-time classes: Main campus; day, evening, summer. Part-time classes: Main campus; day, evening, summer. Degree requirements: 45 credits including 24 elective credits. Final oral comprehensive exam or oral defense of thesis. Languages: English. Average class size: 18.

PLACEMENT

Placement services include alumni network and career placement.

Program Contact: Dr. Richard Taylor, Campus Director, Schiller International University, 51-55 Waterloo Road, SE1 8TX London, United Kingdom. (071) 928-1372, or (800) 336-4133.

Sheffield Hallam University

Business School

Sheffield, United Kingdom

OVERVIEW

Sheffield Hallam University is a coed institution. Part of United Kingdom University System. Founded 1969. Setting: suburban campus. Total institutional enrollment: 2,500. Program was first offered in 1987. Approved by the Association of MBA Programs (U.K.).

MBA HIGHLIGHTS

Entrance Difficulty*
Mean GMAT: 500
Mean GPA: N/R

Cost
Tuition: N/R
Room & Board: N/R

Enrollment Profile
Full-time: 30
Part-time: 0
Total: 30
Average Age: 29

Work Exp: 90%
Women: 30%

Average Class Size: 30

ACADEMICS

Calendar Semesters.

Curricular Focus International business, organizational development and change management, strategic analysis and planning.

Concentrations Economics, entrepreneurship, finance, human resources management, international business, management, management information systems, marketing, operations management, organizational behavior, public administration, public policy, quantitative analysis, strategic management.

Faculty Full-time: 25, 40% with doctorates; part-time: 2.

Teaching Methodology Case study: 20%, faculty seminars: 15%, lecture: 30%, research: 5%, seminars by members of the business community: 5%, student presentations: 10%, team projects: 15%.

Special Opportunities International exchange in Australia, United States of America.

STUDENT STATISTICS

Geographic Representation United Kingdom 30%; Germany 20%; Hong Kong 20%; Ireland 8%; Scandinavia 8%; Eastern Europe 7%; Italy 4%; India 3%.

Undergraduate Majors Business 53%; engineering/technology 23%; humanities 3%; science/mathematics 13%; social sciences 8%.

Other Background Graduate degrees in other disciplines: 80%. Work experience: On average, students have 5 years of work experience on entrance to the program.

FACILITIES

Housing 60% of students in program live in college-owned or -operated housing.

Technology Computers are used moderately in course work. 40 computer terminals/PCs are available for use by students in program; they are located in the library, the computer center. Students in the program are not required to have their own PC.

Computer Resources/On-line Services

Training	Yes	Dun's	No
Internet	No	Dow Jones	No
E-Mail	Yes	Dialog	No
LEXIS/NEXIS	No	Bloomberg	No
CompuServe	No		

ADMISSION

Acceptance 1994-95 180 applied for admission; 28% were accepted.

Entrance Requirements First degree, minimum 2 years of work experience, minimum age 23.

Application Requirements Interview, application form, 2 letters of recommendation.

Application Deadline Applications are processed on a rolling basis.

FINANCIALS

Financial Aid In 1994-95, candidates received some institutionally administered aid in the form of scholarships. Financial aid is not available to part-time students. Applications are processed on a rolling basis.

INTERNATIONAL STUDENTS

Demographics 10% of students on campus are international.

Services and Facilities International student housing; international student center, visa services, language tutoring, ESL courses, special assistance for nonnative speakers of English, counseling/support services.

Applying TOEFL required, minimum score of 550; IELTS required, minimum score of 6; proof of adequate funds. Financial aid is not available to international students. Admission application deadline: 7/1 for fall. Applications are processed on a rolling basis.

PROGRAM

One-Year MBA Length of program: Minimum: 12 months. Maximum: 7 years. Full-time classes: Totley; day, evening, early morning. Degree requirements: 140 credits including 40 elective credits.

PLACEMENT

Of 1994 graduates, 40% were employed within three months of graduation.

Program Contact: Mr. Ian Boraston, Sheffield Hallam University, Sheffield Business School, Totley Hall Lane, S17 4AB Sheffield, England, United Kingdom. 742-532836; Fax: 742-532980.

University of Bath

School of Management

Bath, United Kingdom

OVERVIEW

The University of Bath is a government-supported coed institution. Founded 1966. Setting: suburban campus. Total institutional enrollment: 6,000. Program was first offered in 1974. Approved by the Association of MBA Programs (U.K.).

MBA HIGHLIGHTS

Entrance Difficulty***
Mean GMAT: 580
Mean GPA: N/R

Cost
Tuition: 8,000 British pounds
Room & Board: 2,184 British pounds

Enrollment Profile

Full-time: 37		Work Exp: 100%
Part-time: 2		Women: 35%
Total: 39		
Average Age: 33		

Average Class Size: 35

ACADEMICS

Length of Program Minimum: 24 months.

Calendar Terms.

Full-time Classes Main campus; day, weekends, summer.

Part-time Classes Main campus; day, weekends.

Degree Requirements Entrepreneurship project.

Required Courses Business policy, finance, managerial economics, marketing, operations management, organizational behavior.

Curricular Focus Entrepreneurship, general management, teamwork.

Concentrations Entrepreneurship, finance, human resources management, marketing, operations management, organizational behavior, strategic management.

Faculty Full-time: 24, 80% with doctorates; part-time: 2.

Teaching Methodology Case study: 25%, lecture: 35%, student presentations: 10%, team projects: 30%.

STUDENT STATISTICS

Undergraduate Majors Business 20%; education 10%; engineering/technology 35%; science/mathematics 20%; social sciences 15%.

Other Background Graduate degrees in other disciplines: 75%. Work experience: On average, students have 4 years of work experience on entrance to the program.

FACILITIES

Housing 40% of students in program live in college-owned or -operated housing.

Technology Computers are used moderately in course work. Computer terminals/PCs, linked by a campus-wide computer network, are available for use by students in program; they are located in student rooms, classrooms, learning resource center, the library, the computer center, computer labs, the research center. Students in the program are not required to have their own PC.

Computer Resources/On-line Services

Training	Yes	E-Mail	No

ADMISSION

Acceptance 1994-95 120 applied for admission; 40% were accepted.

Entrance Requirements Minimum 5 years of work experience.

Application Requirements Application form, resume/curriculum vitae, 2 letters of recommendation.

Application Deadline Applications are processed on a rolling basis.

FINANCIALS

Costs for 1994-95 Tuition: Full-time: 8,000 British pounds. Average room and board costs are 2,184 British pounds per academic year (on-campus) and 4,800 British pounds per academic year (off-campus).

Financial Aid In 1994-95, candidates received some institutionally administered aid in the form of scholarships. Application deadline: 5/31 for fall. Contact: Association of MBAs, Claverton Down, BA2 7AY London, England, United Kingdom. 71-837-3375.

INTERNATIONAL STUDENTS

Services and Facilities International student housing; language tutoring, special assistance for nonnative speakers of English, counseling/support services.

Applying Proof of adequate funds. Financial aid is not available to international students. Admission applications are processed on a rolling basis.

PLACEMENT

Placement services include alumni network, career counseling/planning, career fairs, career library, job interviews, resume preparation, and resume referral to employers. Of 1994 graduates, 90% were employed within three months of graduation.

Program Contact: Mr. John C. Edwards, Director, The Bath MBA, University of Bath, Claverton Down, BN2 4AT Bath, England, United Kingdom. 225-826826.

University of Bradford

Bradford Management Center

Bradford, United Kingdom

OVERVIEW

The University of Bradford is a government-supported coed institution. MBA program offered jointly with Netherlands Institute for MBA Studies. Setting: suburban campus. Total institutional enrollment: 8,000. Program was first offered in 1964. Accredited by ESRC. Approved by the Association of MBA Programs (U.K.).

MBA HIGHLIGHTS

Entrance Difficulty**

Cost
Tuition: N/R
Room & Board: N/R

Enrollment Profile

Full-time: 120		Work Exp: 100%
Part-time: 150		Women: 30%
Total: 270		
Average Age: 29		

Average Class Size: 40

ACADEMICS

Calendar Quarters.

Curricular Focus International business, problem solving and decision making, teamwork.

Concentrations Total Quality Management, accounting, economics, entrepreneurship, finance, human resources management, international business, management information systems, marketing, operations management, organizational behavior, public administration, public policy, quantitative analysis, strategic management.

Faculty Full-time: 60, 80% with doctorates; part-time: 10, 70% with doctorates.

Teaching Methodology Case study: 15%, faculty seminars: 5%, lecture: 50%, research: 9%, seminars by members of the business community: 1%, student presentations: 5%, team projects: 15%.

Special Opportunities International exchange in Germany, Netherlands. Internship program available.

STUDENT STATISTICS

Other Background Graduate degrees in other disciplines: 5%. Work experience: On average, students have 7 years of work experience on entrance to the program.

FACILITIES

Information Resources Business collection in Yvette Jacobson Library includes 35,000 bound volumes, 250 periodical subscriptions, 3 CD-ROMs, 100 videos.

Housing 20% of students in program live in college-owned or -operated housing.

Technology Computers are used moderately in course work. 40 computer terminals/PCs, linked by a campus-wide computer network, are available for use by students in program; they are located in the computer center, computer labs. Students in the program are not required to have their own PC.

Computer Resources/On-line Services

Training	Yes	E-Mail	Yes
Internet	Yes		

ADMISSION

Acceptance 1994-95 1,000 applied for admission; 16% were accepted.

Entrance Requirements First degree, GMAT score of 550, minimum 2 years of work experience.

Application Requirements Interview, application form, copies of transcript, resume/curriculum vitae, 2 letters of recommendation.

Application Deadline Applications are processed on a rolling basis. Application discs available.

FINANCIALS

Financial Aid In 1994-95, 2% of candidates received some institutionally administered aid in the form of grants. Financial aid is not available to part-time students. Application deadline: 6/30 for fall. Contact: Ms. Gail Barbour, MBA Secretary, Emm Lane, BD9 4JL Bradford, West Yorkshire, England, United Kingdom. 1274-383193.

INTERNATIONAL STUDENTS

Demographics 10% of students on campus are international.

Services and Facilities International student housing; international student office, language tutoring, special assistance for nonnative speakers of English, counseling/support services.

Applying TOEFL required, minimum score of 550; IELTS required, minimum score of 6; proof of adequate funds; admission test. Financial aid is not available to international students. Admission application deadline: 7/31 for fall. Applications are processed on a rolling basis.

PROGRAM

One-Year MBA Length of program: 12 months. Full-time classes: Main campus; day, evening, weekends. Part-time classes: Main campus; day, evening, weekends. Degree requirements: 14 courses including 6 elective courses. Venture capital project; management project: dissertation. Languages: English. Average class size: 50.

PLACEMENT

In 1993-94, 70 organizations participated in on-campus recruiting; 210 on-campus interviews were conducted. Placement services include alumni network, career counseling/planning, career fairs, career library, career placement, job interviews, job search course, resume preparation, and resume referral to employers. Of 1994 graduates, 92% were employed within three months of graduation.

Program Contact: Ms. Gail Barbour, MBA Secretary, University of Bradford, Emm Lane, BD9 4JL Bradford, West Yorkshire, England, United Kingdom. 1274-383193; Fax: 1274-385140.

University of Brighton

Business School

Brighton, United Kingdom

OVERVIEW

The University of Brighton is a government-supported coed institution. Part of British University Education System. MBA programs offered jointly with Ecole Supérieure de Commerce (Grenoble, France); IADE Autónome University (Madrid, Spain); Ecole de Amminiucazione de Aziendale University of Turin (Italy). Founded 1900. Setting: small-town campus. Total institutional enrollment: 10,000. Program was first offered in 1991. Accredited by British Goverment.

MBA HIGHLIGHTS

Entrance Difficulty***
Mean GMAT: 500
Mean GPA: N/R

Cost $$
Tuition: $8,000/degree program
(Nonresident: $9,500/degree program)
Room & Board: N/R

Enrollment Profile
Full-time: 250   Work Exp: 100%
Part-time: 212   Women: 40%
Total: 462
Average Age: 25

Average Class Size: 25

ACADEMICS

Length of Program 12 months.

Calendar Semesters.

Full-time Classes Main campus, Grenoble (France), Madrid (Spain), Turin (Italy), Pforzheim (Germany); day, evening.

Part-time Classes Main campus.

Degree Requirements 120 credits including 10 elective credits. Other: Dissertation.

Required Courses European legal context, creating effective organizations, economic context, financial and managerial accounting, financial management, global managerial forum, information systems management, international strategic management, marketing management, operations management.

Curricular Focus General management, international business, teamwork.

Concentrations European business, accounting, economics, finance, hotel management, human resources management, international business, management, management information systems, marketing, operations management, organizational behavior, strategic management, transportation.

Faculty Full-time: 45, 30% with doctorates; part-time: 10.

Teaching Methodology Case study: 10%, lecture: 40%, research: 5%, seminars by members of the business community: 5%, student presentations: 10%, team projects: 30%.

Special Opportunities International exchange in France, Germany, Italy, Spain.

STUDENT STATISTICS

Geographic Representation France 21%; United Kingdom 21%; Asia 19%; United States of American and Latin America 16%; Germany 7%; Greece 7%; Russia 3%; Scandinavia 3%; Spain 3%.

Undergraduate Majors Business 25%; education 3%; engineering/technology 25%; humanities 12%; other 35%.

Other Background Graduate degrees in other disciplines: 97%. Work experience: On average, students have 5 years of work experience on entrance to the program.

FACILITIES

Housing 1% of students in program live in college-owned or -operated housing. Assistance with housing search provided.

Technology Computers are used heavily in course work. 128 computer terminals/PCs, linked by a campus-wide computer network, are available for use by students in program; they are located in student rooms, classrooms, learning resource center, the library, computer labs. Students in the program are not required to have their own PC.

Computer Resources/On-line Services

Training	Yes	E-Mail	Yes

ADMISSION

Acceptance 1994-95 120 applied for admission; 43% were accepted.

Entrance Requirements First degree, GMAT score of 500, minimum 3 years of work experience.

Application Requirements Interview, application form, copies of transcript, resume/curriculum vitae, personal statement.

FINANCIALS

Costs for 1994-95 Tuition: Full-time: $8,000/degree program for residents, $9,500/degree program for international students.

Financial Aid In 1994-95, candidates received some institutionally administered aid in the form of loans. Financial aid is not available to part-time students. Applications are processed on a rolling basis. Contact: European MBA Program Administrator, Mithras House, Lewes Road, BN2 4AT Brighton, Sussex, England, United Kingdom. 273-64-29-58.

INTERNATIONAL STUDENTS

Demographics 7% of students on campus are international.

Services and Facilities International student office, language tutoring, ESL courses, special assistance for nonnative speakers of English, counseling/support services.

Applying TOEFL and IELTS required. Financial aid is available to international students. Admission applications are processed on a rolling basis. Contact: Ms. Jane Kilsby, International Students, Mithras House, Lewes Road, BN2 4AT Brighton, Sussex, England, United Kingdom. 273 642197.

ALTERNATE MBA PROGRAM

Executive MBA (EMBA) Length of program: Minimum: 36 months. Part-time classes: Main campus; evening. Degree requirements: 120 credits. Residential workshops.

PLACEMENT

Placement services include alumni network, career counseling/planning, career library, and resume preparation.

Program Contact: Ms. Judy Barrow, Program Administrator, University of Brighton, European Program Administraton, BN2 4AT Brighton, Sussex, England, United Kingdom. 273-64-21-97; Fax: 276-64-25-45; Internet Address: bls@bton.ac.uk.

University of Bristol

Graduate School of International Business

Bristol, United Kingdom

OVERVIEW

The University of Bristol is a coed institution. Part of Higher Education Funding Council. MBA program offered jointly with Graduate School of International Business, Ecole Nationale del Pointe et Chaussees, Der Rutli Funrung Sicraftesetimare. Founded 1867. Setting: urban campus. Total institutional enrollment: 10,000. Program was first offered in 1991.

MBA HIGHLIGHTS

Entrance Difficulty***
Mean GMAT: 500
Mean GPA: N/R

Cost
Tuition: 11,600 British pounds/degree program
Room & Board: 4,000 British pounds (off-campus)

Enrollment Profile
Full-time: N/R	Work Exp: 90%
Part-time: N/R	Women: 30%
Total: 35	
Average Age: 28	

Average Class Size: 30

ACADEMICS

Length of Program Minimum: 15 months.
Calendar Trimesters.
Full-time Classes Main campus; day.
Part-time Classes Main campus; day.
Degree Requirements 18 modules including 10 elective modules; 4-6 months company placement.
Curricular Focus Entrepreneurship, international business, leadership, managing diversity, strategic analysis and planning.
Concentrations Accounting, economics, entrepreneurship, finance, human resources management, intercultural management, negotiation, ethics, international business, management, marketing, organizational behavior, quantitative analysis, strategic management.
Faculty Full-time: 10.
Teaching Methodology Case study: 15%, faculty seminars: 10%, lecture: 20%, research: 10%, seminars by members of the business community: 10%, student presentations: 15%, team projects: 20%.
Special Opportunities International exchange in Czech Republic, France, Germany, Hong Kong, Slovenia, United States of America. Internship program available.

STUDENT STATISTICS

Undergraduate Majors Business 50%; engineering/technology 15%; humanities 5%; science/mathematics 5%; social sciences 25%.
Other Background Graduate degrees in other disciplines: 20%. Work experience: On average, students have 5 years of work experience on entrance to the program.

FACILITIES

Housing College housing not available.
Technology Computers are used moderately in course work. 100 computer terminals/PCs, linked by a campus-wide computer network, are available for use by students in program; they are located in the library, the computer center, computer labs. Students in the program are not required to have their own PC.

Computer Resources/On-line Services
Training	Yes	E-Mail	Yes
Internet	Yes		

ADMISSION

Acceptance 1994-95 120 applied for admission; 33% were accepted.
Entrance Requirements First degree, GMAT score of 500. Core courses waived through: previous course work.
Application Requirements Written essay, interview, application form, copies of transcript, resume/curriculum vitae, personal statement.
Application Deadlines 7/1 for fall. Applications are processed on a rolling basis. Application discs available.

FINANCIALS

Estimated Costs for 1995-96 Tuition: Full-time: 11,600 British pounds/degree program; Part-time day: 4,000 British pounds. Average room and board costs are 4,000 British pounds per academic year (off-campus).
Financial Aid In 1994-95, 2% of candidates received some institutionally administered aid in the form of scholarships, loans, assistantships. Financial aid is not available to part-time students. Applications are processed on a rolling basis. Contact: Mrs. Lyn Hoffman, MBA Program Manager, Rodney Lodge, Grange Road, BS8 4EA Bristol, England, United Kingdom. 1179 737683.

INTERNATIONAL STUDENTS

Demographics 15% of students on campus are international.
Services and Facilities International student housing; international student office, language tutoring, ESL courses, special assistance for nonnative speakers of English, counseling/support services.
Applying TOEFL and IELTS required; proof of adequate funds. Financial aid is available to international students. Applications are processed on a rolling basis. Admission application deadline: 7/1 for fall. Applications are processed on a rolling basis.

PLACEMENT

In 1993-94, 200 organizations participated in on-campus recruiting. Placement services include alumni network, career counseling/planning, career fairs, career library, career placement, electronic job bank, job interviews, job search course, resume preparation, and resume referral to employers. Of 1994 graduates, 80% were employed within three months of graduation.
Jobs by Employer Type Manufacturing 10%; service 60%; consulting 30%.
Jobs by Functional Area Marketing/sales 20%; finance 60%; management 10%; strategic planning 10%.

Program Contact: Mrs. Lyn Hoffman, MBA Program Manager, University of Bristol, Rodney Lodge, Grange Road, BS8 4EA Bristol, England, United Kingdom. 1179 737683.

University of Durham

Durham, United Kingdom

MBA HIGHLIGHTS

Entrance Difficulty N/R

Cost
Tuition: 7,000 - 9,000 British pounds
Room & Board: 5,000 British pounds

Enrollment Profile
Full-time: N/R	Work Exp: N/R
Part-time: N/R	Women: 30%
Total: N/R	
Average Age: 31	

Average Class Size: N/R

ACADEMICS

Length of Program Minimum: 12 months.
Full-time Classes Main campus, distance learning option.
Part-time Classes Main campus, distance learning option.
Degree Requirements dissertation.
Concentration Management.

STUDENT STATISTICS

Geographic Representation United Kingdom 55%.

ADMISSION

Application Requirements Application form.

FINANCIALS

Costs for 1995-96 Tuition: Full-time: 7,000-9,000 British pounds. Average room and board costs are 5,000 British pounds (on-campus).

INTERNATIONAL STUDENTS

Applying TOEFL or IELTS for nonnative speakers of English.

Program Contact: Dr. David Stoker, MBA Director, University of Durham, DH1 3LB Durham, United Kingdom. 91-374-2233.

University of Edinburgh

Edinburgh University Management School

Edinburgh, United Kingdom

OVERVIEW
The University of Edinburgh is a government-supported coed institution. Founded 1583. Setting: urban campus. Total institutional enrollment: 12,000. Program was first offered in 1980. Accredited by Chartered Institute of Marketing. Approved by the Association of MBA Programs (U.K.).

MBA HIGHLIGHTS
Entrance Difficulty****

Cost
Tuition: 5,950 British pounds
(Nonresident: 7,450 British pounds)
Room & Board: N/R

Enrollment Profile
Full-time: 100	Work Exp: 100%
Part-time: 340	Women: 35%
Total: 440	
Average Age: 30	

Average Class Size: 30

ACADEMICS
Length of Program 12 months
Calendar 3 terms.
Full-time Classes Main campus; day.
Part-time Classes Main campus; evening.
Degree Requirements 13 courses including 4 elective courses. Other: Dissertation.
Required Courses Accounting, business finance, business policy and law, economics, human behavior at work, marketing, operations management, statistics, strategic management.
Curricular Focus Business issues and problems, strategic analysis and planning, teamwork.
Concentrations Accounting, economics, entrepreneurship, finance, international business, management, management information systems, marketing, operations management, organizational behavior, quantitative analysis, strategic management.
Faculty Full-time: 42, 60% with doctorates.
Teaching Methodology Case study: 12%, lecture: 40%, research: 28%, seminars by members of the business community: 5%, student presentations: 3%, team projects: 12%.
Special Opportunities Internship program available.

STUDENT STATISTICS
Undergraduate Majors Business 6%; education 5%; engineering/technology 22%; nursing 1%; science/mathematics 5%; social sciences 38%; other 23%.
Other Background Graduate degrees in other disciplines: 9%. Work experience: On average, students have 7 years of work experience on entrance to the program.

FACILITIES
Housing 24% of students in program live in college-owned or -operated housing. Assistance with housing search provided.
Technology Computers are used heavily in course work. 50 computer terminals/PCs, linked by a campus-wide computer network, are available for use by students in program; they are located in computer labs. Students in the program are not required to have their own PC.

Computer Resources/On-line Services
Training	Yes	Dun's	No
Internet	Yes	Dow Jones	No
E-Mail	Yes	Dialog	Yes
LEXIS/NEXIS	No	Bloomberg	No
CompuServe	No		

ADMISSION
Acceptance 1994-95 535 applied for admission; 41% were accepted.
Entrance Requirements First degree, minimum 2 years of work experience.
Application Requirements Application form, copies of transcript, resume/curriculum vitae, personal statement, 2 letters of recommendation.

Application Deadline Applications are processed on a rolling basis.

FINANCIALS
Costs for 1995-96 Tuition: Full-time: 5,950 British pounds for residents, 7,450 British pounds for nonresidents.
Financial Aid In 1994-95, 22% of candidates received some institutionally administered aid in the form of grants, scholarships. Financial aid is not available to part-time students. Contact: Mrs. Trish Fraser, Administrator, 7 Bristo Square, EH8 9AL Edinburgh, Scotland, United Kingdom. 31 650-3826.

INTERNATIONAL STUDENTS
Demographics 60% of students on campus are international; Europe 59%, Asia 6%, North America 6%, Africa 4%, Australia 2%, Central America 2%, South America 1%, other 20%.
Services and Facilities International student office, international student center, visa services, language tutoring, special assistance for nonnative speakers of English, counseling/support services.
Applying TOEFL required, minimum score of 550; IELTS required, minimum score of 6; proof of adequate funds. Financial aid is not available to international students. Admission applications are processed on a rolling basis. Contact: Mrs. Rona Porteous, International Office, EH8 9AL Edinburgh, Scotland, United Kingdom. 31 650-4296.

PLACEMENT
Placement services include alumni network, career counseling/planning, career fairs, and career library. Of 1994 graduates, 91% were employed within three months of graduation.
Jobs by Employer Type Manufacturing 9%; service 24%; government 7%; consulting 9%; nonprofit 1%; higher education 10%; other 40%.
Jobs by Functional Area Marketing/sales 14%; finance 13%; operations 8%; management 8%; strategic planning 3%; technical management 2%; education 12%; other 40%.

Program Contact: Mrs. Trish Fraser, Administrator, University of Edinburgh, 7 Bristo Square, EH8 9AL Edinburgh, Scotland, United Kingdom. 31 650-8066; Fax: 31 650-8077.

University of Glasgow

Glasgow, United Kingdom

ACADEMICS
Concentration Management.

Program Contact: Dr. Geoff Southern, IMBA Program Director, University of Glasgow, G12 8QQ Glasgow, Scotland, United Kingdom. 41-339-8855; Fax: 41-330-5669.

University of Hull

School of Management

Hull, United Kingdom

MBA HIGHLIGHTS
Entrance Difficulty***

Cost
Tuition: 6,500 British pounds
Room & Board: 2,500 British pounds

Enrollment Profile
Full-time: N/R	Work Exp: N/R
Part-time: N/R	Women: 30%
Total: 170	
Average Age: N/R	

Average Class Size: 50

ACADEMICS
Length of Program Minimum: 12 months.
Full-time Classes Main campus; day, evening, weekends.
Part-time Classes Main campus; day, evening, weekends.
Degree Requirements 12 courses.

Curricular Focus Entrepreneurship, problem solving and decision making, strategic analysis and planning.

Concentrations Finance, management information systems, systems thinking.

Teaching Methodology Case study: 20%, faculty seminars: 10%, lecture: 35%, research: 25%, student presentations: 10%.

FACILITIES
Housing College housing available.

ADMISSION
Entrance Requirements First degree, GMAT score of 500, minimum 3.0 GPA, minimum 2 years of work experience.

Application Requirements Application form, copies of transcript, resume/ curriculum vitae, 2 letters of recommendation.

Application Deadline 8/1 for fall.

FINANCIALS
Costs for 1994-95 Tuition: Full-time: 6,500 British pounds. Average room and board costs are 2,500 British pounds per academic year (on-campus).

Financial Aid Application deadline: 8/1 for fall. Contact: Ms. Marily Howarth, Administrative Assistant, Cottingham Road, HU6 7RX Hull, England, United Kingdom. 482-465-980.

INTERNATIONAL STUDENTS
Applying TOEFL required, minimum score of 550; proof of adequate funds. Financial aid is available to international students. Financial aid application deadline: 8/1 for fall. Admission application deadline: 8/1 for fall. Applications are processed on a rolling basis.

Program Contact: Mr. Louis Fong, Deputy Director, MBA Program, University of Hull, School of Management, Cottingham Road, HU6 7RX Hull, England, United Kingdom. 482-857-493.

University of London

London Business School

London, United Kingdom

OVERVIEW
The University of London is an independent nonprofit coed institution. Setting: urban campus. Program was first offered in 1965.

MBA HIGHLIGHTS
Entrance Difficulty***
Mean GMAT: 620
Mean GPA: N/R

Cost
Tuition: 15,500 British pounds
Room & Board: 9,000 British pounds (off-campus)

Enrollment Profile
Full-time: 323	Work Exp: 100%
Part-time: 210	Women: 23%
Total: 533	
Average Age: 28	

Average Class Size: 60

ACADEMICS
Length of Program Minimum: 21 months. Maximum: 2 years.

Calendar Terms.

Full-time Classes Main campus; day, evening, weekends, summer.

Degree Requirements 25 credits including 12 elective credits. Other: Level III competence in a language other than English; management report.

Required Courses Challenge of management, decision support management, finance, financial analysis, human resources, information management, international macro-economy, leadership skills, managerial economics, marketing, marketing accounting, operations management, organizational behavior, strategic management.

Curricular Focus General management, international business, teamwork.

Concentrations Accounting, economics, entrepreneurship, finance, human resources management, international business, management, management information systems, marketing, operations management, organizational behavior, quantitative analysis, strategic management.

Faculty Full-time: 26, 70% with doctorates.

Teaching Methodology Case study: 45%, lecture: 15%, research: 5%, student presentations: 5%, team projects: 30%.

Special Opportunities International exchange in Australia, Brazil, Canada, France, Germany, Hong Kong, Italy, Japan, Mexico, Republic of Korea, Spain, United States of America, Venezuela. Internship program available.

STUDENT STATISTICS
Undergraduate Majors Business 24%; engineering/technology 29%; humanities 13%; science/mathematics 6%; social sciences 12%; other 16%.

Other Background Work experience: On average, students have 5 years of work experience on entrance to the program.

FACILITIES
Housing 10% of students in program live in college-owned or -operated housing. Assistance with housing search provided.

Technology Computers are used heavily in course work. 65 computer terminals/PCs, linked by a campus-wide computer network, are available for use by students in program; they are located in classrooms, learning resource center, the computer center, computer labs. Students in the program are not required to have their own PC.

Computer Resources/On-line Services

Training	Yes	Dun's	Yes
Internet	Yes	Dow Jones	Yes
E-Mail	Yes	Dialog	Yes
LEXIS/NEXIS	Yes $	Bloomberg	Yes

Other on-line services: Datastar.

ADMISSION
Acceptance 1994-95 562 applied for admission; 42% were accepted.

Entrance Requirements First degree, GMAT score, minimum 3 years of work experience.

Application Requirements Written essay, interview, application form, copies of transcript, personal statement, 2 letters of recommendation.

Application Deadlines 5/1 for fall. Applications are processed on a rolling basis.

FINANCIALS
Costs for 1994-95 Tuition: Full-time: 15,500 British pounds; Part-time day: 13,200 British pounds; Part-time evening: 13,200 British pounds. Average room and board costs are 9,000 British pounds per academic year (off-campus).

Financial Aid In 1994-95, 7% of candidates received some institutionally administered aid in the form of scholarships, assistantships. Financial aid is not available to part-time students. Application deadline: 5/1 for fall. Applications are processed on a rolling basis. Contact: Ms. Fiona Gaffney, Deputy Administrative Director, Sussex Place, Regent's Park, NW1 4SA London, England, United Kingdom. 71-262-5050.

INTERNATIONAL STUDENTS
Demographics 73% of students on campus are international.

Services and Facilities International student housing; international student office, language tutoring, counseling/support services.

Applying TOEFL required. Financial aid is available to international students. Financial aid application deadline: 5/1 for fall. Admission application deadline: 5/1 for fall. Applications are processed on a rolling basis. Contact: Ms. Catherine Gibbs, International Exchange Manager, Sussex Place, Regent's Park, NW1 4SA London, England, United Kingdom. 71-262-5050.

PLACEMENT
In 1993-94, 57 organizations participated in on-campus recruiting; 1,264 on-campus interviews were conducted. Placement services include alumni network, career counseling/planning, career library, career placement, electronic job bank, job interviews, job search course, resume preparation, and resume referral to employers. Of 1994 graduates, 95% were employed within three months of graduation.

Jobs by Employer Type Manufacturing 20%; service 15%; consulting 31%; other 1%; financial services 33%.

Jobs by Functional Area Marketing/sales 9%; finance 29%; operations 4%; management 5%; strategic planning 17%; technical management 9%; consulting 27%.

Program Contact: Ms. Gai LeRoy, Information Officer, University of London, Sussex Place, Regent's Park, NW1 4SA London, England, United Kingdom. 71-262-5050; Fax: 71-724-7875.

University of Newcastle upon Tyne

School of Business Management

New Castle upon Tyne, United Kingdom

OVERVIEW
The University of Newcastle upon Tyne is a government-supported coed institution. Founded 1963. Setting: suburban campus. Total institutional enrollment: 14,000. Program was first offered in 1980. Approved by the Association of MBA Programs (U.K.).

MBA HIGHLIGHTS

Entrance Difficulty***
Mean GMAT: 520
Mean GPA: N/R

Cost
Tuition: N/R
Room & Board: N/R

Enrollment Profile
Full-time: 33
Part-time: 12
Total: 45
Average Age: 27

Work Exp: 98%
Women: 33%

Average Class Size: 30

ACADEMICS
Calendar Semesters.

Curricular Focus Business issues and problems, organizational development and change management, teamwork.

Concentrations Accounting, entrepreneurship, finance, human resources management, international business, management, management information systems, marketing, operations management, organizational behavior, quantitative analysis, strategic management.

Faculty Full-time: 1; part-time: 1.

Teaching Methodology Lecture: 80%, seminars by members of the business community: 20%.

STUDENT STATISTICS
Other Background Graduate degrees in other disciplines: 90%. Work experience: On average, students have 2-3 years of work experience on entrance to the program.

FACILITIES
Housing 25% of students in program live in college-owned or -operated housing. Assistance with housing search provided.

Technology Computers are used moderately in course work. 30 computer terminals/PCs, linked by a campus-wide computer network, are available for use by students in program; they are located in computer labs. Students in the program are not required to have their own PC.

Computer Resources/On-line Services
E-Mail   Yes

ADMISSION
Acceptance 1994-95 200 applied for admission; 20% were accepted.

Entrance Requirements First degree, GMAT score of 500, minimum 2 years of work experience.

Application Requirements Application form, copies of transcript, 2 letters of recommendation.

Application Deadline Applications are processed on a rolling basis.

FINANCIALS
Financial Aid Financial aid is not available to part-time students.

INTERNATIONAL STUDENTS
Applying Financial aid is not available to international students. Admission applications are processed on a rolling basis.

PROGRAM
One-Year MBA Length of program: Minimum: 12 months. Full-time classes: Main campus; day. Part-time classes: Main campus; day. Degree requirements: 12 courses. Languages: English.

PLACEMENT
Placement services include career fairs. Of 1994 graduates, 25% were employed within three months of graduation.

Program Contact: Mrs. Joan Harvey, MBA Program Director, University of Newcastle upon Tyne, NE1 7RU New Castle upon Tyne, England, United Kingdom. 91-222-6188; Fax: 91-222-8131.

University of Nottingham

School of Management and Finance

Nottingham, United Kingdom

OVERVIEW
The University of Nottingham is a government-supported coed institution. Founded 1881. Setting: suburban campus. Total institutional enrollment: 12,000. Program was first offered in 1988. Approved by the Association of MBA Programs (U.K.).

MBA HIGHLIGHTS

Entrance Difficulty****
Mean GMAT: 545
Mean GPA: N/R

Cost
Tuition: 7,100 British pounds/degree program
Room & Board: N/R

Enrollment Profile
Full-time: 80
Part-time: 130
Total: 210
Average Age: 29

Work Exp: 97%
Women: 27%

Average Class Size: 30

ACADEMICS
Length of Program Minimum: 12 months. Maximum: 5 years.

Calendar Semesters.

Full-time Classes Main campus; day, evening.

Part-time Classes Main campus; day, evening.

Degree Requirements 14 units including 7 elective units. Other: Group consultancy project, management dissertation, management skills program.

Required Courses Accounting and finance, managerial economics and business policy, marketing, organizational behavior, quantitative analysis and information technology, strategic management.

Curricular Focus Economic and financial theory, general management, strategic analysis and planning.

Concentrations Accounting, economics, education management, entrepreneurship, finance, health services, human resources management, international business, management, management information systems, marketing, operations management, organizational behavior, public policy, quantitative analysis, strategic management.

Faculty Full-time: 47, 60% with doctorates; part-time: 7, 50% with doctorates.

Teaching Methodology Case study: 21%, faculty seminars: 5%, lecture: 26%, practical consultancy: 5%, research: 11%, student presentations: 11%, team projects: 16%, tutorials team projects: 5%.

Special Opportunities International exchange in France. Other: practical consultancy projects.

STUDENT STATISTICS
Geographic Representation United Kingdom 45%; East Asia 24%; Balkan Penninsula 8%; France 7%; Scandinavia 4%; Middle East 4%; Eastern Europe 2%; Germany 2%; Italy 2%; Spain 2%.

Undergraduate Majors Business 36%; engineering/technology 13%; humanities 6%; science/mathematics 21%; social sciences 14%; other 10%.

Other Background Graduate degrees in other disciplines: 15%. Work experience: On average, students have 5 years of work experience on entrance to the program.

FACILITIES
Housing 50% of students in program live in college-owned or -operated housing. Assistance with housing search provided.

Technology Computers are used heavily in course work. 200 computer terminals/PCs, linked by a campus-wide computer network, are available for use by students in program; they are located in learning resource center, the library, the computer center, computer labs. Students in the program are not required to have their own PC.

Computer Resources/On-line Services

Training	Yes	CompuServe	No
Internet	Yes	Dun's	No
E-Mail	Yes	Dow Jones	No
Multimedia Center	Yes	Dialog	No
LEXIS/NEXIS	No	Bloomberg	No

ADMISSION

Acceptance 1994-95 550 applied for admission; 15% were accepted.

Entrance Requirements First degree, minimum 3 years of work experience.

Application Requirements Application form, copies of transcript, resume/curriculum vitae, personal statement, 2 letters of recommendation.

Application Deadline Applications are processed on a rolling basis. Application discs available.

FINANCIALS

Estimated Costs for 1995-96 Tuition: Full-time: 7,100 British pounds/degree program.

Financial Aid In 1994-95, 30% of candidates received some institutionally administered aid in the form of bursaries. Total awards ranged from 600-12,000 British pounds. Financial aid is available to part-time students. Applications are processed on a rolling basis. Contact: Mr. Scott Goddard, Director of Postgraduate Programs, Portland Building, University Park, NG7 2RD Nottingham, England, United Kingdom. 115-951-5488.

INTERNATIONAL STUDENTS

Demographics 15% of students on campus are international.

Services and Facilities International student office, international student center, language tutoring, special assistance for nonnative speakers of English, counseling/support services.

Applying TOEFL required, minimum score of 600; IELTS required, minimum score of 6; proof of adequate funds. Admission applications are processed on a rolling basis. Contact: Dr. Christine Humphrey, Director, International Office, Portland Building, University Park, NG7 2RD Nottingham, England, United Kingdom. 115-951-5500.

ALTERNATE MBA PROGRAM

Executive MBA (EMBA) Length of program: Minimum: 24 months. Maximum: 5 years. Part-time classes: Main campus; day, evening, summer. Degree requirements: 14 units including 7 elective units. Project. Languages: English.

PLACEMENT

Placement services include alumni network, career counseling/planning, career fairs, career library, career placement, job interviews, job search course, and resume preparation. Of 1994 graduates, 80% were employed within three months of graduation.

Jobs by Functional Area Marketing/sales 27%; finance 27%; operations 8%; management 28%; strategic planning 10%.

Program Contact: Mr. Ron Hodges, Admissions Tutor, University of Nottingham, Portland Building, University Park, NG7 2RD Nottingham, England, United Kingdom. 115-951-5487; Fax: 115-951-5503.

University of Oxford

School of Management

Oxford, United Kingdom

ACADEMICS

Calendar 8-week terms.

Concentration Management.

Teaching Methodology Case study: 25%, lecture: 25%, research: 25%, tutorial essays: 25%.

FACILITIES

Information Resources Business collection in Templeton's Information Center and Library includes 20,000 bound volumes, 550 periodical subscriptions.

Housing College housing available.

ADMISSION

Entrance Requirements First degree, GMAT score.

Application Requirements Written essay, application form, resume/curriculum vitae, 3 letters of recommendation, separate applications to both department and college.

Application Deadline 3/31 for fall.

FINANCIALS

Costs for 1994-95 Tuition: Full-time: 3,750-4,050 British pounds, 7,120-7,420 British pounds for international students. Average room and board costs are 5,500 British pounds per academic year (on-campus) and 5,500 British pounds per academic year (off-campus).

INTERNATIONAL STUDENTS

Applying TOEFL required; Test of Written English. Contact: International Office, University Offices Wellington Square, CX1 2JD Oxford, United Kingdom. 865-27-00-00.

PROGRAM

M Phil in management studies Length of program: Minimum: 24 months. Full-time classes: Main campus. Degree requirements: Thesis, special papers, tutorial essays. Languages: English.

Program Contact: Mr. Richard Hughes, Academic Secretary (Postgraduate), University of Oxford, c/o Templeton College, OX1 5NY Oxford, England, United Kingdom. 865-27-00-00; Fax: 865-27-07-08.

University of Sheffield

Management School

Sheffield, United Kingdom

MBA HIGHLIGHTS

Entrance Difficulty**
Mean GMAT: 570
Mean GPA: N/R

Cost
Tuition: 6,500 British pounds
(Nonresident: 7,700 British pounds)
Room & Board: N/R

Enrollment Profile

Full-time: 65	Work Exp: 60%
Part-time: 1	Women: 25%
Total: 66	
Average Age: 26	

Average Class Size: 65

ACADEMICS

Length of Program Minimum: 18 months. Maximum: 2 years.

Calendar Semesters.

Full-time Classes Main campus; day.

Part-time Classes Main campus; day.

Degree Requirements 15 courses.

Required Courses Accounting, economics, management information systems, marketing, operations management, organizational behavior, statistics, strategic management.

Curricular Focus Business issues and problems, general management, strategic analysis and planning.

Concentrations Accounting, finance, international business, marketing.

Faculty Full-time: 12, 30% with doctorates; part-time: 2, 100% with doctorates.

Teaching Methodology Case study: 10%, lecture: 40%, research: 20%, student presentations: 10%, team projects: 20%.

Special Opportunities International exchange in Denmark, France, Sweden.

STUDENT STATISTICS

Geographic Representation Hong Kong and Taiwan 35%; Malaysia 30%; United Kingdom 25%; Greece 10%.

Undergraduate Majors Business 20%; engineering/technology 20%; humanities 30%; science/mathematics 10%; social sciences 10%; other 10%.

Other Background Graduate degrees in other disciplines: 2%. Work experience: On average, students have 3 years of work experience on entrance to the program.

FACILITIES

Housing 80% of students in program live in college-owned or -operated housing. Assistance with housing search provided.

Technology Computers are used heavily in course work. 100 computer terminals/PCs, linked by a campus-wide computer network, are available for use by students in program; they are located in computer labs.

Students in the program are not required to have their own PC. 400 British pounds are budgeted per student for computer support.

Computer Resources/On-line Services

Training   Yes   E-Mail   Yes
Internet   Yes

ADMISSION

Acceptance 1994-95 400 applied for admission; 16% were accepted.

Entrance Requirements First degree, GMAT score of 550, minimum 3.5 GPA, minimum 2 years of work experience.

Application Requirements Application form, copies of transcript, 2 letters of recommendation.

Application Deadline Applications are processed on a rolling basis.

FINANCIALS

Estimated Costs for 1995-96 Tuition: Full-time: 6,500 British pounds for residents, 7,700 British pounds for nonresidents.

Financial Aid In 1994-95, candidates received some institutionally administered aid in the form of grants, loans. Financial aid is not available to part-time students.

INTERNATIONAL STUDENTS

Services and Facilities International student housing; international student office, international student center, language tutoring, ESL courses, special assistance for nonnative speakers of English, counseling/support services.

Applying TOEFL required, minimum score of 575; IELTS required, minimum score of 6; proof of adequate funds. Financial aid is not available to international students. Admission application deadline: 7/4 for fall. Applications are processed on a rolling basis. Contact: Ms. Debora Green, International Student Officer, Academic Registrar's Office, Firte Court, Western Bank, S10 2TN Sheffield, England, United Kingdom. 114-2824916 Ext. 4916.

PLACEMENT

Placement services include alumni network, career counseling/planning, career fairs, and career library.

Program Contact: Mrs. Elaine Davidson, MBA Program Manager, University of Sheffield, Sheffield University Management School, 9 Mappin Street, S1 4DT Sheffield, England, United Kingdom. 114-2825297; Fax: 114-2725103; Internet Address: e.davidson.@.sheffield.ac.uk.

University of Stirling

School of Management

Stirling, United Kingdom

OVERVIEW

The University of Stirling is a coed institution. Setting: rural campus. Total institutional enrollment: 6,000.

MBA HIGHLIGHTS ──────────────

Entrance Difficulty*

Cost
Tuition: N/R
Room & Board: N/R

Enrollment Profile
Full-time: 43   Work Exp: N/R
Part-time: 0   Women: 35%
Total: 43
Average Age: N/R

Average Class Size: 50

ACADEMICS
Calendar Semesters.

Curricular Focus International business, teamwork.

Concentrations Accounting, economics, finance, human resources management, international business, management, management information systems, marketing, operations management, quantitative analysis, strategic management.

FACILITIES
Technology Computers are used moderately in course work. Computer terminals/PCs, linked by a campus-wide computer network, are avail-

able for use by students in program; they are located in computer labs, student common room. Students in the program are required to have their own PC.

Computer Resources/On-line Services

E-Mail   Yes

ADMISSION

Acceptance 1994-95 328 applied for admission.

Entrance Requirements First degree, minimum 2.7 GPA, minimum 2 years of work experience.

Application Requirements Application form, copies of transcript, personal statement, 2 letters of recommendation.

Application Deadline Applications are processed on a rolling basis.

FINANCIALS

Financial Aid Financial aid is not available to part-time students.

INTERNATIONAL STUDENTS

Applying TOEFL required, minimum score of 550; IELTS required, minimum score of 6; proof of adequate funds. Financial aid is not available to international students. Admission applications are processed on a rolling basis.

PROGRAM

One-Year MBA Length of program: 12 months. Full-time classes: Main campus; day. Degree requirements: 15 courses including 3 elective courses. Dissertation. Languages: English.

Program Contact: Mrs. June Johnston, MBA Administrator, University of Stirling, FK9 4LA Stirling, Scotland, United Kingdom. 1786-467418; Fax: 1786-450776.

University of Strathclyde

Graduate Business School

Glasgow, United Kingdom

OVERVIEW

The University of Strathclyde is a government-supported coed institution. MBA program offered jointly with Strategic Business School, Kuala Lumpur; Groupe ESC Toulouse; Hong Kong Baptist University; Open Learning Resources, Singapore. Setting: urban campus. Program was first offered in 1966. Approved by the Association of MBA Programs (U.K.).

MBA HIGHLIGHTS ──────────────

Entrance Difficulty**

Cost
Tuition: N/R
Room & Board: N/R

Enrollment Profile
Full-time: 108   Work Exp: 100%
Part-time: 300   Women: 25%
Total: 408
Average Age: 32

Average Class Size: 40

ACADEMICS
Calendar Semesters.

Curricular Focus International business, problem solving and decision making, strategic analysis and planning.

Concentrations Management information systems, operations management.

Teaching Methodology Case study: 10%, faculty seminars: 2%, lecture: 60%, research: 10%, seminars by members of the business community: 2%, student presentations: 5%, team projects: 11%.

Special Opportunities International exchange in France.

STUDENT STATISTICS
Other Background Work experience: On average, students have 9 years of work experience on entrance to the program.

FACILITIES
Housing College housing available.

Technology Computers are used moderately in course work. Computer terminals/PCs are available for use by students in program; they are located in computer labs. Students in the program are not required to have their own PC.

Computer Resources/On-line Services
E-Mail   Yes

ADMISSION
Acceptance 1994-95 600 applied for admission; 40% were accepted.
Entrance Requirements First degree, GMAT score of 550, minimum 3 years of work experience.
Application Requirements Application form, copies of transcript, personal statement.
Application Deadlines 7/30 for fall, 3/31 for spring. Applications are processed on a rolling basis.

FINANCIALS
Financial Aid In 1994-95, candidates received some institutionally administered aid in the form of loans. Financial aid is available to part-time students. Contact: Ms. Candace Greensted, Marketing Officer, 199 Cathedral Street, G4 0QU Glasgow, Scotland, United Kingdom. 141-553-6164.

INTERNATIONAL STUDENTS
Services and Facilities International student office, international student center, language tutoring, special assistance for nonnative speakers of English, counseling/support services.
Applying TOEFL required, minimum score of 600; IELTS required; proof of health; proof of adequate funds. Financial aid is not available to international students. Admission applications are processed on a rolling basis.

PROGRAM
One-Year MBA Length of program: Minimum: 12 months. Full-time classes: Main campus, distance learning option; day. Part-time classes: Main campus, distance learning option; evening, weekends. Degree requirements: 60 credits including 8 elective credits. Languages: English.

PLACEMENT
Placement services include alumni network, career library, and resume preparation.

Program Contact: Mrs. Candace Greensted, Admissions Officer, University of Strathclyde, 199 Cathedral Street, G4 0QU Glasgow, Scotland, United Kingdom. 141-553-6164; Fax: 141-552-2501.

University of the West of England, Bristol

Bristol Business School

Bristol, United Kingdom

OVERVIEW
The University of the West of England, Bristol is a government-supported coed institution. Setting: suburban campus. Total institutional enrollment: 18,000. Program was first offered in 1988. Approved by the Association of MBA Programs (U.K.).

MBA HIGHLIGHTS

Entrance Difficulty**

Cost
Tuition: 2,200 British pounds
Room & Board: N/R

Enrollment Profile
Full-time: 0	Work Exp: 100%
Part-time: 120	Women: 30%
Total: 120	
Average Age: 33	

Average Class Size: 20

ACADEMICS
Length of Program Minimum: 30 months. Maximum: 5 years.
Calendar Trimesters.
Part-time Classes Main campus; evening, summer.
Required Courses Business policy, computer-based information systems, decision analysis, economics and political environment, finance, human resources management, information systems, marketing, operations management, organizational behavior, quantitative methods, strategic management, the management of change.

Curricular Focus General management, organizational development and change management, strategic analysis and planning.
Concentrations Accounting, economics, finance, human resources management, management, management information systems, marketing, operations management, organizational behavior, quantitative analysis, strategic management.
Faculty Full-time: 28, 30% with doctorates.
Teaching Methodology Case study: 30%, faculty seminars: 30%, lecture: 25%, seminars by members of the business community: 5%, student presentations: 10%.

STUDENT STATISTICS
Geographic Representation United Kingdom 100%.
Undergraduate Majors Business 10%; engineering/technology 50%; humanities 10%; nursing 10%; science/mathematics 10%; social sciences 10%.
Other Background Graduate degrees in other disciplines: 80%. Work experience: On average, students have 12 years of work experience on entrance to the program.

FACILITIES
Housing College housing available.
Technology Computer terminals/PCs, linked by a campus-wide computer network, are available for use by students in program; they are located in learning resource center, the library, the computer center, computer labs. Students in the program are not required to have their own PC.
Computer Resources/On-line Services
Training   No   E-Mail   Yes

ADMISSION
Acceptance 1994-95 100 applied for admission; 40% were accepted.
Entrance Requirements First degree, minimum 3 years of work experience.
Application Requirements Interview, application form.
Application Deadlines 8/1 for fall. Applications are processed on a rolling basis.

FINANCIALS
Costs for 1994-95 Tuition: Part-time day: 2,200 British pounds.

INTERNATIONAL STUDENTS
Demographics 10% of students on campus are international; Asia 50%, Europe 50%.
Services and Facilities International student center, counseling/support services.
Applying Financial aid is not available to international students.

PLACEMENT
Placement services include career library.

Program Contact: Ms. Rachel Noble, MBA Program Secretary, University of the West of England, Bristol, Cold Harbor Lane, BS16 1QY Bristol, England, United Kingdom. 117-965-6261; Fax: 117-976-3851; Internet Address: r.noble@uwe.ac.uk.

University of Ulster at Jordanstown

Ulster Business School

Newtown Abbey, United Kingdom

OVERVIEW
The University of Ulster at Jordanstown is a government-supported coed institution. Setting: suburban campus.

MBA HIGHLIGHTS

Entrance Difficulty*
Mean GMAT: 500
Mean GPA: N/R

Cost
Tuition: 2,450 British pounds
(Nonresident: 7,000 British pounds)
Room & Board: N/R

Enrollment Profile
Full-time: 42   Work Exp: N/R
Part-time: 460   Women: N/R
Total: 502
Average Age: N/R
Average Class Size: 90

ACADEMICS
Length of Program Minimum: 12 months.
Calendar Semesters.
Full-time Classes Main campus, Londonderry (United Kingdom), Coloraine (United Kingdom); day, summer.
Part-time Classes Main campus, Londonderry (United Kingdom), Coloraine (United Kingdom); evening.
Degree Requirements 23 modules.
Curricular Focus Entrepreneurship, problem solving and decision making, strategic analysis and planning.
Concentrations Accounting, economics, entrepreneurship, finance, information technology management, management, marketing.
Teaching Methodology Lecture: 60%, team projects: 40%.

STUDENT STATISTICS
Geographic Representation United Kingdom 98%; Asia 2%.
Undergraduate Majors Business 30%; engineering/technology 40%; humanities 10%; nursing 10%; social sciences 10%.

FACILITIES
Technology Computers are used moderately in course work. Computer terminals/PCs are available for use by students in program; they are located in computer labs. Students in the program are not required to have their own PC.
Computer Resources/On-line Services
E-Mail   Yes

ADMISSION
Entrance Requirements First degree, GMAT score of 450.
Application Requirements Application form, 2 letters of recommendation.

FINANCIALS
Costs for 1995-96 Tuition: Full-time: 2,450 British pounds for residents, 7,000 British pounds for nonresidents.
Financial Aid Financial aid is not available to part-time students. Application deadline: 5/31 for fall. Contact: Mrs. Conac Lavery, MBA Coordinator, Shore Road, BT37 0QB Newtown Abbey, Northern Ireland, United Kingdom. 232-36-5060.

INTERNATIONAL STUDENTS
Applying TOEFL required, minimum score of 550. Financial aid is not available to international students. Admission application deadline: 5/31 for fall.

Program Contact: Mrs. Conac Lavery, MBA Coordinator, University of Ulster at Jordanstown, Shore Road, BT37 0QB Newtown Abbey, Northern Ireland, United Kingdom. 232-36-5060; Fax: 232-36-6831.

University of Warwick

Warwick Business School

Coventry, United Kingdom

OVERVIEW
The University of Warwick is a government-supported coed institution. Setting: suburban campus. Total institutional enrollment: 2,875. Program was first offered in 1968. Accredited by AACSB. Approved by the Association of MBA Programs (U.K.).

MBA HIGHLIGHTS

Entrance Difficulty***
Mean GMAT: 610
Mean GPA: N/R

Cost
Tuition: 9,300 British pounds
(Nonresident: 11,000 British pounds)
Room & Board: 10,000 British pounds

Enrollment Profile
Full-time: N/R   Work Exp: 100%
Part-time: N/R   Women: 25%
Total: 470
Average Age: 29
Average Class Size: 60

Warwick Business School, based in the heart of England, is internationally renowned for its all-around excellence that attracts students worldwide into its high-quality M.B.A. programme. The School is part of the University of Warwick and has over 130 high-calibre academic teaching and research staff members.

Dual strengths in both research and teaching make the Warwick M.B.A. a programme of distinction, combining academic rigour with practical relevance. The School holds the highest possible rankings for excellence in research and teaching, awarded by the Higher Education Funding Council for England.

Warwick Business School offers four M.B.A. study routes with 1,800 students from every continent, including a one-year full-time M.B.A. and an M.B.A. by distance learning. The Warwick M.B.A. has the breadth and rigour to develop well-rounded managers who can think strategically and operate effectively in an international arena. Warwick M.B.A. graduates can be found in challenging, high-level roles around the world. The programme covers core courses in the key areas of management, a wide choice of electives, a substantial management project, an opportunity to test and apply the knowledge and techniques learned, and personal skills as change agents.

ACADEMICS
Length of Program Minimum: 42 months. Maximum: 8 years.
Calendar Quarters.
Part-time Classes Main campus, distance learning option; summer.
Degree Requirements 12 courses including 3 elective courses.
Required Courses Business policy, financial accounting, information management and strategies, management accounting, management of operations, market analysis, organizational behavior, quantitative methods.
Curricular Focus Business issues and problems, international business, strategic analysis and planning.
Concentrations Accounting, economics, entrepreneurship, finance, human resources management, international business, management, management information systems, marketing, operations management, organizational behavior, quantitative analysis, strategic management.
Faculty Full-time: 75.
Teaching Methodology Faculty seminars: 33%, lecture: 34%, team projects: 33%.
Special Opportunities International exchange in Canada, France.

STUDENT STATISTICS
Undergraduate Majors Business 42%; engineering/technology 36%; social sciences 8%; other 14%.
Other Background Graduate degrees in other disciplines: 85%. Work experience: On average, students have 7-10 years of work experience on entrance to the program.

FACILITIES
Housing 55% of students in program live in college-owned or -operated housing.
Technology Computers are used moderately in course work. 72 computer terminals/PCs, linked by a campus-wide computer network, are available for use by students in program; they are located in classrooms, computer labs. Students in the program are not required to have their own PC.

Computer Resources/On-line Services
E-Mail   Yes

ADMISSION
Acceptance 1994-95 2,146 applied for admission; 58% were accepted.
Entrance Requirements First degree, GMAT score
Application Requirements Interview, application form, copies of transcript, 2 letters of recommendation.
Application Deadlines 10/31 for winter distance learning, 5/31 for summer distance learning. Applications are processed on a rolling basis.

FINANCIALS
Costs for 1995-96 Tuition: Full-time: 9,300 British pounds for residents, 11,000 British pounds for nonresidents. Average room and board costs are 10,000 British pounds per academic year (on-campus) and 12,000 British pounds per academic year (off-campus).
Financial Aid In 1994-95, 5% of candidates received some institutionally administered aid in the form of scholarships. Applications are processed on a rolling basis. Contact: Ms. Victoria Goddard, Admissions Secretary, Full Time MBA Program, CV4 7AL Coventry, England, United Kingdom. 1203 523829.

INTERNATIONAL STUDENTS
Services and Facilities International student office, international student center, language tutoring, counseling/support services.
Applying TOEFL required, minimum score of 600; IELTS required, minimum score of 6; proof of adequate funds. Financial aid is available to international students. Admission application deadline: 10/31 for winter distance learning, 5/31 for summer distance learning. Applications are processed on a rolling basis.

ALTERNATE MBA PROGRAM
One-Year MBA Length of program: 12 months. Full-time classes: Main campus; day. Degree requirements: 17 courses including 1 elective course. Project or dissertation. Languages: English.

PLACEMENT
In 1993-94, 65 organizations participated in on-campus recruiting; 850 on-campus interviews were conducted. Placement services include alumni network, career counseling/planning, career library, career placement, job interviews, job search course, resume preparation, and resume referral to employers. Of 1994 graduates, 80% were employed within three months of graduation.
Jobs by Employer Type Manufacturing 35%; service 18%; consulting 18%; nonprofit 7%; financial services 15%; university administration 2%; other 5%.
Jobs by Functional Area Marketing/sales 20%; finance 8%; operations 5%; management 24%; strategic planning 10%; technical management 8%; consulting 22%; human resources 3%.

Program Contact: Ms. Victoria Goddard, Admissions Secretary, Full Time MBA Program, University of Warwick, Warwick Business School, CV4 7AL Coventry, England, United Kingdom. 1203 523829; Fax: 1203 524643.

University of Westminster

London, United Kingdom

ACADEMICS
Concentration Management.

Program Contact: Mr. Neil Botten, MBA Program Director, University of Westminster, 35 Malibone Road, NW1 5LS London, England, United Kingdom. 71-911-5000 Ext. 3016; Fax: 71-911-5059.

The Victoria University of Manchester

Manchester Business School

Manchester, United Kingdom

OVERVIEW
The Victoria University of Manchester is a coed institution. Setting: urban campus. Total institutional enrollment: 400. Program was first offered in 1965. Accredited by HEFCE, AMBA. Approved by the Association of MBA Programs (U.K.).

MBA HIGHLIGHTS
Entrance Difficulty**
Mean GMAT: 585
Mean GPA: N/R

Cost
Tuition: 15,000 British pounds
(Nonresident: 18,000 British pounds)
Room & Board: 2,500 British pounds (off-campus)

Enrollment Profile
Full-time: 225   Work Exp: 90%
Part-time: 120   Women: 22%
Total: 345
Average Age: 27

Average Class Size: 14

ACADEMICS
Length of Program Minimum: 16 months. Maximum: 2 years.
Calendar Quarters.
Full-time Classes Main campus; day.
Part-time Classes Main campus; evening.
Degree Requirements 1,200 hours.
Required Courses Analysis for decision and control, analysis of the business environment, interdisciplinary project, management of change project, mergers project, operations strategy project, strategies and techniques for change.
Curricular Focus General management, international business, teamwork.
Concentrations Accounting, economics, entrepreneurship, finance, health services, human resources management, international business, management, management information systems, marketing, operations management, organizational behavior, public administration, public policy, strategic management.
Faculty Full-time: 50, 75% with doctorates; part-time: 40, 60% with doctorates.
Teaching Methodology Case study: 20%, faculty seminars: 10%, lecture: 30%, research: 5%, student presentations: 5%, team projects: 30%.
Special Opportunities International exchange in Australia, Canada, Finland, France, Germany, Italy, Japan, Mexico, Netherlands, Norway, Spain, United States of America. Internship program available.

STUDENT STATISTICS
Undergraduate Majors Business 39%; engineering/technology 28%; humanities 12%; science/mathematics 8%; social sciences 4%; other 9%.
Other Background Graduate degrees in other disciplines: 15%. Work experience: On average, students have 4-8 years of work experience on entrance to the program.

FACILITIES
Housing College housing not available.
Technology Computers are used heavily in course work. 50 computer terminals/PCs, linked by a campus-wide computer network, are available for use by students in program; they are located in the library, computer labs. Students in the program are not required to have their own PC.
Computer Resources/On-line Services
Training   Yes   E-Mail   Yes
Internet   Yes

ADMISSION
Acceptance 1994-95 600 applied for admission; 38% were accepted.
Entrance Requirements First degree, GMAT score of 530, minimum 2 years of work experience.
Application Requirements Written essay, application form, copies of transcript.
Application Deadlines 6/30 for fall. Applications are processed on a rolling basis.

FINANCIALS
Estimated Costs for 1995-96 Tuition: Full-time: 15,000 British pounds for residents, 18,000 British pounds for nonresidents. Average room and board costs are 2,500 British pounds per academic year (off-campus).
Financial Aid Applications are processed on a rolling basis. Contact: Admissions Office, Booth Street West, M15 6PB Manchester, England, United Kingdom. 161-275-6311.

INTERNATIONAL STUDENTS
Demographics 70% of students on campus are international.

Services and Facilities International student office, international student center, language tutoring, ESL courses, special assistance for nonnative speakers of English, counseling/support services.

Applying TOEFL required, minimum score of 580; IELTS required, minimum score of 6; proof of adequate funds. Financial aid is not available to international students. Admission application deadline: 6/30 for fall. Applications are processed on a rolling basis. Contact: Ms. Alison Walker, Admissions Officer, Booth Street West, MI5 6PB Manchester, England, United Kingdom. 161 275 6311.

PLACEMENT

In 1993-94, 211 organizations participated in on-campus recruiting; 308 on-campus interviews were conducted. Placement services include alumni network, career counseling/planning, career fairs, career library, career placement, job interviews, job search course, resume preparation, and resume referral to employers. Of 1994 graduates, 92% were employed within three months of graduation, the average starting salary was 34,000 British pounds, the range was 23,000-60,000 British pounds.

Jobs by Employer Type Manufacturing 37%; service 15%; consulting 14%; banking/finance 16%; chemicals 8%; engineering 8%; other 2%.

Jobs by Functional Area Marketing/sales 24%; finance 26%; operations 10%; management 10%; strategic planning 14%; consulting 14%; other 2%.

Program Contact: Ms. Alison Walker, Admissions Officer, The Victoria University of Manchester, Booth Street West, MI5 6PB Manchester, England, United Kingdom. 161-275-6311; Internet Address: a.walker@ mbs.ac.uk.

Full Descriptions of M.B.A. Programs

The following two-page descriptions were prepared for this book by the dean or director of the M.B.A. program or business school. Each description is designed to give the student a sense of the individuality of the school.

An institution's absence from this section does not constitute an editorial decision on the part of Peterson's Guides. Rather, it was offered as an open forum for business schools or departments to expand upon the information provided in the previous 'Profiles' section of this book.

The descriptions are arranged alphabetically by the official name of the institution.

Adelphi University

Garden City, New York

DEVELOPING BUSINESS LEADERS FOR THE TWENTY-FIRST CENTURY

Today, business needs leaders with the analytic sophistication and entrepreneurial judgment who can effectively deal with the forces that are transforming our "global village." Rather than attempting to train individuals for jobs that may not even exist two or three years hence, our progressive interdisciplinary approach to management education is designed to produce broadly educated individuals who have the managerial competence, curiosity, and creativity needed for success in the twenty-first century.

In this era of enormous challenges and radical possibilities, we are guided by a firm commitment to ensuring that our graduates will be thinkers with a broad perspective as well as being proficient in the skills necessary for professional excellence and success.

—Dr. Arnold K. Weinstein, Dean

Programs and Curricular Focus

In keeping with Adelphi University's tradition of a liberal education, all of the School's graduate degree programs provide for a general management orientation along with solid training in all the functional areas of business. This general management orientation is achieved through a highly integrated group of professional foundation core courses. Through the foundation core, students acquire the analytic and quantitative decision-making skills needed for success by learning how to view and resolve management problems from all functional perspectives.

The program's breadth component examines twenty-first-century management issues, such as leadership, future trends, entrepreneurship, technology management, and total quality management on the macro and global levels and is designed to further enrich the students' professional and learning experience.

Topics such as the global perspective, creativity, change and innovation, team building, ethics, and cultural diversity are important components of the programs of study as well. These are not individual courses but unifying themes that are infused into the entire spectrum of the curricula.

Elective and specialization courses are also integral to the programs, affording students the opportunity to tailor their program of study to their own professional interests and career needs.

In addition to the M.B.A. with its eight areas of specialization, the School offers an M.B.A.-CPA degree program; M.S. degrees in accounting and in banking and money management; and graduate certificates in management and human resources management. The number of credits required to earn a degree and the length of time it takes to complete a degree program vary and are dependent upon the student's previous academic background and on whether he or she chooses to study on a full-time or part-time basis.

Students and the M.B.A. Experience

Students come from across the United States and many other countries, bringing with them a wide variety of undergraduate majors and professional backgrounds, and they form a dynamic community whose diversity enriches the educational experience. Professional clubs andorganizations, such as the Accounting Society, Marketing and Finance clubs, Delta Sigma Pi, and the Business Council, bring together students with common interests.

Guest speakers, internship opportunities, and the Distinguished Lecture Series further serve to enhance and enrich the learning environment. Some of those who have recently addressed the student body include the president of *The New Yorker* magazine, the president of Nationwide

Cellular Services, the CEO of Kaplan Educational Centers, and the vice president for planning and development of Pfizer.

There is a Student Board that serves as an advisory council to the dean, and interaction between the faculty, staff, and students is strong, even outside the classroom. Faculty and staff support and participate in events run by students, and students also get the opportunity to network with alumni, advisory board members, and other corporate executives at other special events.

Special Features

Course schedules are designed to accommodate the schedules of men and women engaged in full-time careers. In addition to the main Garden City campus, courses are also offered at the Huntington Center, making graduate business education more accessible to those who reside on eastern Long Island. Courses at both locations are scheduled Monday through Thursday evenings and Saturday mornings. Each course meets once a week.

The Faculty

The School's faculty members have strong academic and professional backgrounds. Many have held top-level positions in business, engage in research and publication activities, and have been educated at many of the best academic institutions around the world.

Excellence in, and equal emphasis on, both teaching and research is the hallmark of the School. The faculty's research is considered to be pioneering and on the cutting edge and consistently wins critical acclaim and praise from both the academic and business worlds. The faculty members' wide range of expertise makes them sought after as consultants to major companies, entrepreneurial firms, and not-for-profit agencies.

The students profit from the faculty's academic and professional backgrounds, as well as from their commitment to the advancement of knowledge in their area of specialization. All of the research and consulting the professors do enriches every course they teach, and this, in combination with their dynamic and superb teaching skills, enables them to effectively communicate the principles and practices of management as it is actually conducted on the firing line.

The Business School Network

Advisory boards help ensure that the programs meet the needs of the corporate community and provide and assist with internships and job placements. Serving on the Management Advisory Board are such corporate notables as the president and CEO of Astoria Federal Savings Bank, the president of Nationwide Cellular Services, the senior vice president of finance of Nabisco Foods, and the senior vice presidents from Computer Associates and NBC News and Sports. The Long Island–based senior or managing partners from KPMG Peat Marwick, Deloitte and Touche, Arthur Andersen, David Berdon and Company, Coopers & Lybrand, and Ernst and Young serve on the School's Accounting Advisory Board.

The College and Environs

Adelphi University is located in Garden City, Long Island, New York, a beautiful suburban community that is approximately 18 miles east of midtown Manhattan. It is the oldest private university on Long Island. Today, a full-time faculty of nearly 300 serves a student body of about 8,000 undergraduate and graduate degree candidates.

The location affords easy access both to the beaches, waters, and quiet living of Long Island and to the commercial and cultural capital of the world, New York City.

Facilities

The average class size in the School of Management and Business is only 24, and many of the classrooms are outfitted with the very latest in multimedia technology.

The library is completely computerized. It houses approximately 625,000 volumes and an ever-growing collection of electronic resources based on CD-ROM technology.

Adelphi boasts one of the largest mainframe computer installations on Long Island, and, in addition, there are more than 450 IBM and Macintosh personal computers that are available for student use. Access to the Internet and a large variety of CD-ROM databases is also available.

Placement

Placement is coordinated through the University's Center for Career Planning and Placement. Many of the top corporations, major banks, and international accounting firms recruit on campus.

Experienced counselors take the time to assess the student's interests and skills and to help the student effectively market himself or herself and make the right career decisions whether he or she is a young graduate student, an experienced professional seeking a career change, or someone returning to the work force.

Admission

Candidates applying for admission must submit a completed application form with essay, official transcripts, three letters of recommendation, and the score on the Graduate Management Admission Test (GMAT) to the Office of Graduate Admissions. The GMAT score for students enrolling at Adelphi has recently averaged between 500 and 550. The average undergraduate GPA has been 3.0.

International applicants must also submit a TOEFL score of at least 550, as well as a declaration and certificate of finances.

Finances

For 1994–95, the comprehensive tuition and fee rate for 12 or more credits was $13,500. The rate for 1-11 credits was $400 per credit plus a $150 nonrefundable University fee. Additional fees and charges may be assessed. Students should consult with the Office of Student Financial Services for the latest tuition rate and fee information, as well as the latest information concerning financial aid.

Students should consult with the Office of Residential Life and Housing for information about the availability and costs for graduate housing.

Application Facts and Dates

Applicants should file their application and supporting credentials by the following dates: fall semester, August 15; spring semester, December 15; and summer sessions, May 15. For more information, applicants should contact:

Ms. Marilyn Nissensohn
Director of Graduate Admissions
Adelphi University
Garden City, New York 11530
Telephone: 516-877-3033
Fax: 516-877-3039

American Graduate School of Business

La Tour-de-Peilz (Montreux), Switzerland

DEVELOPING BUSINESS LEADERS FOR THE TWENTY-FIRST CENTURY

AGSB, the American Graduate School of Business, is a nonprofit private institution of higher education, offering the Master of International Business Administration, the specialized M.B.A. AGSB has the unique ability to claim a dedicated and caring faculty, a small but select student body composed of eighteen nationalities, and a sound academic program designed to prepare students to lead the world and meet the challenges of the future. By providing a basis for competent and responsible leadership in business and politics, AGSB aims to develop in each student a respect and understanding of individuals of different cultures and a desire for continued intellectual growth.
—Carmen Corchon Pernet, President, Steering Committee

Programs and Curricular Focus

The Master of International Business Administration (M.I.B.A.) program offered by AGSB is based on a philosophy that the world's future leaders must operate in a multicultural environment and be able to adapt to changing social, political, legal, and economic conditions. The M.I.B.A. is a one-year intensive program for university graduates who hold a bachelor's degree with a major in business administration. For university graduates who do not hold such a degree, the M.I.B.A. is a two-year program, with the first year consisting of business foundation courses.

To earn the M.I.B.A. degree, the student must successfully complete a program consisting of eight internationally oriented core courses (24 semester credit hours), one two-term seminar course (3 semester credit hours), two advanced foreign language courses (6 semester credit hours), and an internship with project (6 semester credit hours). At least 30 semester credit hours of work (excluding foundation courses) must be completed in residence. For students whose foreign language competence is below the level required for the M.I.B.A. program, AGSB will arrange for special language courses outside the regular curriculum.

Courses for the M.I.B.A. degree include International Business Economics, International Accounting Practices, The International Legal and Ethical Environment, International Management, International Marketing, Decision Theory, Information Systems Concepts, International Finance, the Special Topics

Seminar, Advanced Foreign Language, Business Foreign Language, and the Project Internship.

All of the programs offered by AGSB are authorized by the Department of Education of the Canton of Vaud, Switzerland, and by the Commission of Higher Education of the State of Georgia, United States, under the Nonpublic Postsecondary Educational Institutions Act.

Students and the M.I.B.A. Experience

The student body at AGSB is truly international in scope. While 28 percent of the participants are American, the rest are from Europe (33 percent), the Pacific Rim (17 percent), the Middle East (17 percent), and other regions (5 percent). The average student at AGSB is 26 years old with roughly five years of work experience. Forty-five percent of the student body are women, and most of the students have a previous background in business engineering or related technologies.

Special Features

An integral and distinguishing part of the M.I.B.A. program is the three- to six-month internship, in which the student is involved in the normal business operations of an organization. The nature of the internship is defined prior to a student's placement with a company. This internship must be taken under the sponsorship of the M.I.B.A. program and may be carried out in any country. Over the course of the internship, the student submits periodic reports and a final

internship project, covering an in-depth company and industry analysis relating to the internship. With the directed internship experience and related projects, the substantial language training provided by the M.I.B.A. program, and the international education given through the academic courses, AGSB's M.I.B.A. graduates are well-equipped to enter the international business arena.

The Faculty

The M.I.B.A. program provides a basis for competent and responsible leadership in international business, government, and nonprofit organizations. The language of instruction is English, with courses taught by dedicated, highly-trained, multilingual faculty members with extensive international experience. Methods of teaching include lectures, case analyses, student presentations, seminars with leaders from business and government, and directed internships with national and international organizations. Students benefit from the numerous field trips to such internationally recognized establishments as Nestlé, Caterpillar, and the Zurich Stock Exchange, to name a few.

The Business School Network

All of the AGSB programs are designed to develop an understanding of human behavior, cultural sensitivity, and a global perspective in business and politics. AGSB's location in Switzerland helps accomplish these objectives. The Montreux-Vevey region affords easy access to the culturally rich and internationally active cities of Geneva, Zurich, and Bern. Geneva, with its many international organizations such as the United Nations, GATT, the International Labor Organization, and the World Health Organization, is an ideal setting for students to observe and become involved in the world of international relations. In addition, the university city of Lausanne is only 20 minutes away by car or rail. Switzerland's central location in Europe makes Paris, Milan, Munich, and other business and political centers quickly and easily accessible by rail, air, or private transportation.

"AGSB is more than a valuable education; it is an experience of a lifetime."—student quotation

reference to over 1.2 million volumes, and next-day book delivery service affords quick access within the AGSB facilities.

Placement
All of the programs at AGSB emphasize the importance of oral presentations as a means to enrich interpersonal communication skills. In the end, students are well-prepared for the interview process. Students are assisted in their résumé writing, often into several languages, by experienced professionals. AGSB works directly with M.I.B.A. candidates in their search for an internship that is both stimulating to the student and beneficial to the corporate sponsor. In many cases, the relationship between the intern and the sponsor is so mutually rewarding that the student is requested to remain with the organization following graduation.

Admission
Applicants for the M.I.B.A. program must possess a bachelor's degree from a recognized college or university and demonstrate an academic record indicating potential for success in the M.I.B.A. program. To apply for admission, students must complete application procedures and submit scores for the Graduate Management Admission Test (GMAT) as well as the Test of English as a Foreign Language (TOEFL) for nonnative English speakers.

Finances
For 1994–95, tuition and fees were SwFr 13,300 per semester. Living expenses, including housing, food, and transportation, are estimated at SwFr 1500 per month, depending on the living standard to which the student is accustomed. AGSB is one of the few European business schools whose students are eligible to receive financial assistance through the Graduate Management Admission Council's comprehensive M.B.A. loan program. Scholarships, based on merit and financial need, are available to U.S. and international students.

The College and Environs
Located on the shores of Lac Léman (Lake Geneva) in the heart of the Swiss Riviera, La Tour-de-Peilz offers a relatively mild climate. Long known for its tourist appeal, the Montreux-Vevey region, of which La Tour-de-Peilz is a part, has also built a cultural reputation through events such as the Montreux Jazz Festival. Annual international conferences and symposiums, in communication and direct marketing for example, indicate the region's vibrancy and commitment to the world of business.

Students may take advantage of many extracurricular activities such as cycling, hiking, sailing, and skiing in the internationally known resorts of the Swiss Alps.

The ski areas of Gstaad, Verbier, and Crans-Montana are easily accessible for a day's outing. For an evening's excursion, theaters, museums, and cinemas abound.

Facilities
AGSB is one of the few private schools in Switzerland with modern facilities specially designed to serve the needs of its students. The facilities include modern classrooms, faculty and administrative offices, a computer laboratory, specially-equipped language classrooms, a student lounge, and a library reference room. A special modem link to the University of Lausanne Library complex allows for easy

Application Facts and Dates
AGSB has a policy of rolling admissions, with students admitted on a space-available basis. Notification of acceptance or rejection will be made in writing as soon as possible after an applicant has completed admissions procedures. For more information, applicants should contact:

Director of Admissions
AGSB
The American Graduate School of
    Business
Place des Anciens-Fossés
1814 La Tour-de-Peilz
Switzerland
Telephone: 41-21-994-9501
Fax: 41-21-944-9504

American Graduate School of International Management (Thunderbird)

Master's Program in International Management

Glendale, Arizona

CITIZENS OF THE WORLD

Our students often tell me that Thunderbird is one of the few places where they have found people who think like they do. These students are truly "Citizens of the World," and theirs is a global perspective. Many of them have traveled in several countries and speak several languages. Others, however, may never have owned a passport. Yet for all of them, it is their global viewpoint that sets them apart. If you are seeking a community of internationalists and you thrive on intellectual challenge, I invite you to be a part of the Thunderbird experience. It will change your life.

—Roy A. Herberger Jr., President

Programs and Curricular Focus

Thunderbird's three-part curriculum provides an interrelated program of instruction in three departments—International Studies, Modern Languages, and World Business—leading to the Master of International Management (M.I.M.) degree. This successful educational concept is based on the proven fact that an ability to understand and adapt to the global business environment is a major reason for executive success in international operations.

The curriculum of the Department of International Studies focuses on the international business environment and is designed to acquaint students with foreign areas and their cultural management styles. This curriculum also provides the student with a conceptual framework for informed analysis of a foreign milieu.

The Department of Modern Languages offers courses in ten languages: Arabic, Chinese, French, German, Italian, Japanese, Portuguese, Russian, Spanish, and English as a Second Language. The three-level sequence stresses oral proficiency and heavily emphasizes business vocabulary and usage. In addition, many advanced commercial and issues-oriented courses are also offered.

The Department of World Business offers a far wider range of international courses than traditional graduate schools of business. Courses have a strong international practical orientation. There is heavy reliance on group teamwork and the use of computer simulation games.

The School has long enjoyed a reputation for teaching excellence, featuring an approach that is pragmatic and student-focused.

Thunderbird has developed dual-degree programs with Arizona State University, Arizona State University West, the University of Arizona, Case Western Reserve University, the University of Colorado Denver, Drury College, the University of Florida, the University of Houston, and ESADE in Spain.

Thunderbird also offers a Master of International Health Management (M.I.H.M.) degree, a Master of International Management of Technology (I.M.O.T.) degree, and a post-M.B.A./M.I.M degree for indiviuals who hold an AACSB accredited M.B.A.

Students and the M.B.A. Experience

The School's 1,400 students come from every state in the union. By design, 30 percent are from outside the U.S.; usually sixty to seventy countries are represented. The mean student age is 27 years, and approximately 40 percent are women. Students have an average of 3½ years of full-time postbaccalaureate work experience. Diversity is a Thunderbird student trademark. Over 130 undergraduate college majors are represented, from over 600 undergraduate colleges and universities worldwide.

Thunderbird was established in 1946. More than 28,000 alumni occupy executive offices in multinational enterprises around the world. The bond that unites them is a combination of elements that make up the "Thunderbird Experience." It starts on the Thunderbird campus and extends around the world.

It is a group of alumni living, working, and making business contacts in every state in the United States and nearly 140 countries. It is the "First Tuesday" tradition in New York, Omaha, Paris, Mexico City, Taipei, and 157 other cities around the world where alumni meet to develop social and business relationships. It is strangers who become instant friends when both are T'birds. It is a team spirit that grows from the many challenges of a demanding curriculum. It is the cacophony of students practicing language dialogues in the dining hall. It is an on-campus camaraderie where everyone knows everyone, and lifelong friendships transcend international barriers.

❖ Global Focus

Every year nearly 20 percent of Thunderbird's students study on campuses around the globe in special foreign programs designed to augment their degree program, improve their language skills, and intensify their exposure to other cultures. Semester and/or summer programs are located in Europe, Asia, and Latin America.

The School has established its own campuses in Japan and in France, near Geneva. In addition, a ten-week session is held each summer in Guadalajara, Mexico.

Students may also avail themselves of exchange opportunities in Finland, Norway, Germany, Spain, China, Korea, and Costa Rica.

Special Features

Each January, Thunderbird presents Winterim, a three-week program of seminars that incorporate the newest international business theories along with practical problem-solving tools.

This unique educational opportunity arises from the mutual collaboration of Thunderbird faculty members with distinguished business and government professionals, many of whom are involved in the highest levels of strategic policy planning.

Past Winterim seminars have included Marketing to U.S. Hispanics; International Consumer Marketing Management; Counter Trade/Offset and Barter; International Banking Symposium; Johnson & Higgins International Insurance and Risk Management Conference; The Corporate Executive Officer; Women

Leaders of Today; Competitive Response of U.S. Business; Asia/Pacific Rim Management and Investment; Doing Business in Eastern Europe and Russia; Privatization; Cross-Cultural Communication for International Managers; Opportunity and Risk in the New International Business Order; International Management of Technology; Managing in a Borderless World; and Issues in International Health Care Management.

Winterim courses are also held in numerous international locations, including France, Germany, Austria, Spain/Portugal, Central Europe, Russia, Mexico, Costa Rica/Nicaragua, Chile/Peru, Brazil, Saudi Arabia, Kuwait, United Arab Emirates, Cuba, and Kenya. And for those who want to investigate in detail how U.S. foreign policy affects global business, Thunderbird offers U.S. Foreign Policy and the New Global Environment, which is held in Washington, D.C. Winterim on Wall Street is planned for 1996.

The Faculty

Thunderbird's faculty combines strong academic credentials with significant international and corporate experience. Among the nearly 100 full-time professors are individuals from over two dozen countries—a truly global representation. The Modern Language faculty features native speakers and scholars. Members of the International Studies Department have spent long periods abroad in diplomatic and economic development assignments. World Business faculty members are involved in international consulting. All are hired for their ability to communicate their knowledge to students.

The Business School Network

Thunderbird has an unparalleled network of over 28,000 alumni working internationally in more than 130 countries around the globe. The School also has its own exclusive electronic forum on CompuServe, available only to Thunderbird students, alumni, faculty, and staff. On-line conversations, conferences, and reunions occur regularly, linking alumni around the world. In addition, many of the School's library and career resources are available on the Thunderbird CompuServe Forum.

The College and Environs

Thunderbird is located in the Sun Belt area of the Southwest in a suburb of Phoenix, Arizona, America's eighth-largest city. The Phoenix metropolitan area has numerous cultural resources typical of a major urban center.

Technology Environment

Thunderbird's technology environment and infrastructure are headed by a Director of Global Information Resources. Students have on-campus access to approximately 120 computer terminals through the Lincoln Computer Center and the Merle A. Hinrichs International Business Information Centre (IBIC). CompuServe, Dialog, LEXIS/NEXIS, and the Internet are on-line services available to M.I.M. students. Standard business application software training and software packages are available for student use in the Lincoln Computer Center. Bibliographic services provided to students in the IBIC include NEXIS, Datastar, Dialog, ABI/Inform, Global Vantage, Predicasts F&S, Business Dateline, Datastream, Moody's, Hoovers, Investext, Info South, Emerging Markets, and newspaper abstracts.

Multimedia support through the Multimedia Center is also available to students, and access to worldwide news programming is provided through the SCOLA satellite system. Plans for the near future include distance learning programs.

Placement

Thunderbird's commitment to the success of its graduates extends well beyond the classroom. Over 700 employers recruit Thunderbird graduates for full-time and internship positions in a typical year, including over 250 visits on campus. Each student is assisted in creating a Personal Business Plan that takes full advantage of the skills, experiences, and knowledge that come with a Thunderbird education. Off-campus recruiting events are arranged in major cities in the U.S., and alumni career volunteers are available to help graduates access the 28,000 alumni who are working in global assignments throughout the world. Thunderbird utilizes the latest technology, including an electronic résumé database and the Thunderbird Alumni Forum on CompuServe, to distribute candidate information and link graduates to opportunities in the global market. Several hundred employers around the world are visited each year by Career Services staff to ensure that employers have personalized access to candidates and understand the distinctive capabilities of the Thunderbird graduate.
The Thunderbird Graduate Management Internship program offers credit-bearing full-time and part-time internships to satisfy diverse employer needs and to formally integrate a student's academic study with meaningful, professional experience. Both international and domestic internships are available, based on employer needs and candidate qualifications.

Previous internships have included positions with AT&T, CNN International, Kellogg, Rhone-Poulenc (France), American Business Center (Moscow), Disney Consumer Products, Johnson & Johnson, Merck, Miles, Citibank, U.S. Department of Commerce, U.S. & Foreign Commercial Service, Coca-Cola, General Motors, M&M Mars, Seiko, Sony, Suntory, and Teledyne. Internship assignments have included locations in Europe, Asia, and Latin America as well as in corporate centers through the U.S. and Canada.

Admission

A bachelor's degree from an accredited college or university is required for acceptance into the M.B.A. program. Students must submit a minimum GMAT test score of 500 and must have a minimum 3.0 college GPA. International students must submit a TOEFL score of no less than 500. Two to five years of work experience, international travel or living experience, and proficiency in a foreign language are strongly encouraged.

Finances

Estimated tuition and fees for 1995–96 are approximately $9200 per semester and $6740 for the summer term. Books and instructional supplies run about $500 per semester.

The School estimates that living expenses for a single student living in the residence halls are approximately $1050 for lodging and $1350 for board per semester. Off-campus expenses may be slightly higher. The School requires students to have an IBM or IBM-compatible personal computer. This cost is additional.

Application Facts and Dates

The deadline for summer and fall entrance is January 31; for Winterim and spring entrance, July 31; for summer and fall scholarship applications, March 1; and for Winterim and spring scholarship applications, October 1. For more information, applicants should contact:

Office of Admissions
Thunderbird Campus
American Graduate School of
    International Management
15249 North 59th Avenue
Glendale, Arizona 85306-9903
Telephone: 602-978-7210
            800-848-9084 (toll-free)
            (admissions inquiries only)
Fax: 602-439-5432
Internet: beavers@mhs.t-bird.edu

 # The American University

Washington, D.C.

KOGOD'S ADVANTAGE IN THE GLOBAL ECONOMY

The Kogod M.B.A. Program prepares students to meet the challenges they are sure to encounter as managers in the global marketplace of the twenty-first century. While preserving our 45-year-old tradition of outstanding business education—including small classes, professors who are recognized authorities in their fields, state-of-the-art computer facilities, concern for ethical and social responsibility, and outstanding career placement—we have created dynamic, innovative curricula to give students a competitive edge.

Kogod students train to become complete managers. They learn to see business as a system with interdependent parts, to master at least one functional area of business, and to think creatively, lead, motivate, and inspire. Our location in the nation's capital gives students the unique opportunity to observe the crucial relationship between business and government and the globalization of their field of study.

—Francis D. Tuggle, Dean

Programs and Curricular Focus

Kogod's M.B.A. program is thoroughly integrated with the realities of the global economy. Through its core curriculum, cross-functional teaching approach, teamwork opportunities, internships, and ties with the national and international business community, students gain a broad base of practical skills and a theoretical understanding of the issues in today's global business environment.

The program consists of 54 credit hours: 39 in core courses, 9 in concentration courses, and 6 in electives. Students can choose an area of concentration from one of ten different fields or design their own, with faculty approval, choosing courses from Kogod and AU's other schools and colleges.

The core curriculum, a preset sequence of seven-week modules, includes a leadership practicum and gives students a broad foundation of knowledge in the functional areas of business. Course work in the first year includes subjects such as financial accounting, management information systems, organizational behavior, and managerial decision making.

Through core curriculum, concentration, and elective courses, second-year students gain an in-depth knowledge of a discipline. Course work for the second year includes societal and ethical standards, quality management, and legal and ethical issues confronting the global business manager. For a field practicum, students work in small teams, meeting with company managers to resolve a real-life, real-time problem in a local, national, or international business. Electives can be taken during the seven-week module system or during the semester in one of the University's other colleges or schools.

In both the first and second year of the program, students take part in management skills workshops.

Students entering in the fall can complete the program in twenty-one months; entering in January allows them to graduate in seventeen months. A flexible evening program is also offered.

A joint J.D./M.B.A. degree program, with some courses counting toward both degrees, is an option for students admitted to both Kogod and AU's Washington College of Law. In addition, Kogod offers Master of Science degrees in accounting and in taxation, requiring 30 to 63 credit hours and 30 credit hours, respectively.

Students and the M.B.A. Experience

Students at the University come from all 50 states and 150 countries and represent nearly all age groups and interests. Many business students are already successful executives and bring relevant experience with them into the classroom.

Students in the M.B.A. program have undergraduate degrees from all the disciplines. In a recent entering class, the average age was 26, with five as the average number of years of work experience. Forty percent of the class were women; 20 percent were members of minority groups.

Teamwork shapes a student's studies at Kogod. In the first year, students develop a strong sense of camaraderie as they take all their classes with the same 35 students, or cohort, who are further divided into study teams of about 6 students.

Domestic and international internships give students real-world, hands-on experience.

❖ Global Focus

The Kogod program promotes a global orientation through diversity training, links with international institutions, and international exchange programs. In the M.B.A. program, students can work for one of the many international organizations based in Washington or intern abroad with a multinational organization. They can also choose to become exchange students at a distinguished foreign university.

A global perspective permeates the entire curriculum. More than 40 percent of Kogod graduate students are from one of fifty-five nations. In their classes, students learn to do business with people from Latin America, the Middle East, the Pacific Rim, and Europe by learning about business with them.

The Faculty

Kogod's reputation is distinguished by a faculty of internationally recognized scholars who, like Kogod students, come from every corner of the world. Through their consultancies with all sectors of government and business and their own research, the 59 full-time faculty members have an immense body of knowledge to share with students. Kogod faculty members involve students in developing state-of-the-art solutions to real problems facing industry today.

The Business School Network

Kogod's ties with national and international businesses ensure that students make solid professional contacts and get a thorough grounding in the realities of

the global economy. Executives in residence give students insight into day-to-day problem solving in current business practice. Prominent men and women, high-echelon officials from industry, government, and nonprofit organizations, answer students' queries in a for-credit speaker series. Business leaders, union leaders, and government officials keep students abreast of current trends and strategy at the dean's annual leadership conference. In addition, the Board of Visitors ensures that the program stays in step with the global marketplace.

Field projects and internships with firms in the thriving private sector of Washington (in communications, biotechnology, and software development, to name a few areas) offer outstanding opportunities for making corporate contacts. Through AU's connections to organizations throughout the world, students expand their professional networks abroad.

The College and Environs

The American University is an independent, coeducational university in Washington, D.C., chartered by an Act of Congress in 1893. The Kogod College of Business Administration was the first such college in the nation's capital; its M.B.A. program has been offered since 1949. The University's 76-acre main campus, site of Kogod's offices and classrooms, and an 8-acre satellite campus are located in northwest Washington. In quiet, residential neighborhoods surrounded by embassies and historic buildings, both campuses are minutes from the wealth of historical and cultural resources of the city. Home to political leaders, diplomats, and businesspeople, Washington is vibrant, diverse, and stimulating.

Placement

The University's Career Center and Kogod faculty and advisory staff members assist students in all phases of their job search. AU's ties with more than 1,400 private, public, and nonprofit organizations throughout the world form the basis of its extensive Cooperative Education Program. This program places graduate students in paid professional positions to make professional contacts and to gain both practical experience and academic credit. The International Co-op Education Program sends business graduate students abroad to work with multinational organizations. These co-ops provide students with invaluable contacts and help them gain insight into the cultural, political, and economic forces shaping the international business market today.

Placement coordinators are readily available to discuss employment opportunities and to direct students to appropriate resources. Job search assistance is also provided through an extensive collection of career information.

Admission

To apply to the Kogod graduate business programs, students must have a baccalaureate degree from a regionally accredited institution, a satisfactory score on the Graduate Management Admission Test (GMAT), and a satisfactory grade point average for the last 60 hours of academic work. If English is not an applicant's native language, he or she must present a satisfactory score on the Test of English as a Foreign Language (TOEFL). The M.B.A. program and the M.S. in accounting do not require an undergraduate degree in a particular discipline; the graduate taxation program requires an undergraduate degree in business administration.

The Kogod graduate admissions committee pays close attention to how applicants present themselves in the application's Personal Statements. The committee looks for well-written and carefully crafted statements that indicate an applicant's commitment both to graduate study and to his or her particular field of study. Above all, The American University seeks graduate students who are committed to excellence. Prior work experience is encouraged but not required.

Finances

Tuition for the Kogod M.B.A. Program is $707 per credit hour for part-time students and $9540 per semester for full-time students. This fee also covers the costs for the orientation and all workshops. The cost of both Master of Science degree programs is $605 per credit hour. Additional costs for full-time students include room and board, books, and other miscellaneous fees and expenses.

Financial awards based on merit are available for full-time students, who are automatically considered for this type of aid when they apply for admission. Need-based financial assistance, in the form of federally or commercially sponsored loans, is available for full- and part-time students. To apply, students need to submit the Free Application for Federal Student Aid by March 1. The loan programs have a variety of qualifications and eligibility requirements, which are maintained in the University's collection of information. Only U.S. citizens and permanent residents are eligible for federal need-based aid.

Notification of financial assistance is March 15 through June.

Application Facts and Dates

Applications should be on file by February 1 for fall enrollment and for priority consideration for merit awards but will be considered up to June 1. For spring enrollment, applications should be received by October 1. For more information, students should contact:

Director of Admissions
Kogod College of Business
    Administration
The American University
4400 Massachusetts Avenue, NW
Washington, D.C. 20016
Telephone: 202-885-1913
        800-AN-AU-MBA
Fax: 202-885-1992
E-mail: aumbams@american.edu

Arizona State University

Tempe, Arizona

> The ASU M.B.A. Program is young, dynamic, and rigorous and provides the opportunity for special career options and dual degrees in the second year. It is characterized by two main features. The first is an emphasis on the carefully selected, critical skills of leadership, teamwork, communications, global and multicultural awareness, and realistic knowledge of business practice. The second is a faculty cognizant of the business knowledge and skills necessary to meet the demands of the twenty-first century.
>
> I invite you to visit us and meet the faculty, staff, and students in the M.B.A. Program. See for yourself the campus environment with its semitropical beauty, outstanding computer facilities, nationally ranked research library, and unparalleled recreational facilities.
>
> —Larry Edward Penley, Dean

Programs and Curricular Focus

The objective of the M.B.A. Program at Arizona State University is to provide an enriching educational experience that has lifelong value. The central theme is to build and strengthen students' knowledge, basic skills, and managerial abilities by means of technical, analytical, and case materials associated with the functional areas of business.

There is a strong team emphasis throughout the twelve core courses the first year, and the second year is remarkably flexible. The second-year options build upon the business core and focus on an area of specialization through electives or a dual-degree program. With careful planning, one may complete second-year electives and graduate in less than two years. The dual-degree programs that can be completed in two years are the Master of International Management with Thunderbird (AGSIM), Master of Accountancy, Master of Taxation, Master of Science in economics, Master of Science in decision and information systems, and Master of Health Services Administration. Other master's programs may be considered for concurrent degrees (e.g., M.S. in engineering).

Dual degrees that take more than two years are the M.B.A./J.D. and M.B.A./ M.S. in architecture. Application must be made separately to each program for acceptance. The M.B.A. for Executives program and the Ph.D. degree in business administration and in economics are also available.

Students and the M.B.A. Experience

Students at ASU have diverse academic and geographic backgrounds. In the fall 1994 entering class, the average age was 27, with four years of work experience. Twenty-five percent of the students are ethnic minorities, 12 percent are international students, and 36 percent are women. Sixty percent of the students are from the Southwest and West, but more students are applying from other parts of the country as ASU rises in national prominence. Business and engineering bachelor's degrees are held by the largest percentage of incoming students.

Students automatically become members of the M.B.A. Association and may participate in community service through the Collegiate Volunteer Council, contribute to the M.B.A. Newsletter, work on field projects, do summer internships, or join the Graduate Women in Business organization or the Masters Consulting Group.

Arizona State is one of sixteen universities nationwide that participates in the Washington Campus program. This one-month opportunity is available for credit between the first and second year.

❖ Global Focus

Summer programs are available in Toulouse, France, and Leuven, Belgium, and allow students to graduate in one year. English is the language of instruction in these programs as well as in the exchange program at the Norwegian School of Business in Oslo, Norway. Other exchange programs are under consideration.

The Faculty

The nationally renowned faculty at Arizona State is cognizant of the business knowledge and skills necessary for a changing business environment. All courses are taught by full-time faculty members with established records in business, consulting, leading-edge research, and professional education. The School of Accountancy has one of the largest accounting faculties in the United States. The College has 165 full-time faculty members, 38 of whom teach in the M.B.A. core curriculum.

The Business School Network
Corporate Partnerships

The ASU College of Business, one of the largest comprehensive business schools in the nation, is emerging as a leader in management research and education. Contributing to the College's success is its close relationship with the business community through organizations like the Dean's Council of 100. Faculty members and senior managers recently collaborated in the Business Partners program to develop a challenging vision and responsive strategic plan for the College of Business. A key part of that strategy involves increasing relationships with local and international companies.

The M.B.A. Field Projects Coordinator works with second-year M.B.A. students to set up consulting assignments and research projects with local corporations and nonprofit organizations. These hands-on activities allow students to develop problem-solving skills, enhance communication skills, and gain valuable insight into current issues involving the business community. The teams work with local companies (e.g., Motorola, Intel, Allied Signal, Dial) to define and implement projects with the student's clients. These projects put students in touch with innovations in technology and practical uses of research.

Prominent Alumni

Distinguished alumni include Craig Weatherup, CEO, PepsiCo; Tom Evans, Publisher, *U.S. News & World Report*; John Darragh, President and CEO, Standard Register; Scott Wald, President, ASAP Software Company; Jim Baum, Senior Vice President and Assistant General Manager, Motorola-GSTG; and Steve Evans, Partner, Evans-Withycombe.

The College and Environs

ASU, founded in 1885, is the sixth-largest university in the United States, with more than 45,000 students on its 700-acre main campus. Spacious walkways and modern architecture define the picturesque campus setting. ASU's campus evolved into an arboretum of national status in 1990—one of six in Arizona. The sunny and arid climate contributes to a Southwestern lifestyle with mild winter temperatures that enable students to enjoy the outdoors year-round.

Facilities

The University's Charles Trumbull Hayden Library is one of the largest research libraries in North America. It contains more than 2.7 million volumes, including many in business and economics, and the specialized Arthur C. Young Tax Collection.

The College of Business is housed in two adjacent buildings that contain an auditorium; lecture halls; seminar rooms; faculty, administrative, and graduate offices; and several computer resource centers. The M.B.A. Program Suite includes the M.B.A. student lounge, the Insight Project Room, conference rooms, student organization offices, and classrooms. A media services center and University registration site are also located in the College. The College is home to the L. William Seidman Research Institute, whose affiliated centers and programs conduct specialized research on business topics such as economics, finance, ethics, and quality.

Technology Environment

ASU has one of the largest and most comprehensive computing facilities of all U.S. universities. The Computing Commons provides access to more than 200 computers, split between Macintosh and 486 IBM PCs. All printers are 600 dpi laser printers. A variety of Internet software packages provide students with access to e-mail and Internet news groups and opportunities to browse. There are numerous other computer sites on campus, including three in the College of Business.

Placement

Ninety-one percent of the May 1994 M.B.A. graduating class was placed within three months after graduation, 82 percent within the first month. The M.B.A. Career Management Office assists M.B.A. students to determine their career interest areas and informs potential employers how ASU M.B.A. students will meet their needs. The M.B.A. Director of Career Management works with a wide variety of firms to bring interviewers to ASU.

Admission

Application to ASU's M.B.A. Program is open to individuals holding a bachelor's degree or its equivalent in any discipline from an accredited college or university. During evaluation of M.B.A. candidates, the Admissions Committee looks for well-rounded individuals with strong academic credentials, managerial experience or potential, and the ability to contribute to the diversity of the class. Transcripts, GMAT scores, work history, a personal statement, and letters of recommendation all influence the decision. The entering class of fall 1994 had an average GPA of 3.3 on a 4.0 scale, an average GMAT score of 605, an average TOEFL score of over 600, and average postbaccalaureate work experience of four years. Due to the high volume of applications and the limited size of the entering class, students are strongly encouraged to apply as early as possible.

Finances

Estimated tuition costs for 1995–96 are $1828 for Arizona residents and $7434 for nonresidents. Books and supplies average between $1000 and $1500 per year. Most M.B.A. students live off campus in nearby apartment complexes where the rent ranges from $350 to $600 (one to two bedrooms) per month. On-campus residential facilities are available on a limited basis and cost approximately $7500 (room, board, and personal expenses).

A limited number of tuition scholarships and assistantships are available on a competitive basis. These awards are based strictly on merit. State and federal funds should be pursued through the ASU Financial Assistance Office.

International Students

International diversity is highly valued at ASU, and nearly 12 percent of its M.B.A. students come from outside the U.S., from large countries as well as some of the smallest. During orientation and throughout the year, sponsored activities help international students adjust to the U.S. business and social climate.

Application Facts and Dates

Application deadlines are December 15, March 1, and May 1. Decision letters are usually mailed thirty to forty-five days after each deadline. A file must be complete before it will be evaluated. Annual admission to the full-time and part-time M.B.A. programs is for the fall term only. For more information, students should contact:

Ms. Judy Heilala
Director of M.B.A. Admissions and
   Recruiting
M.B.A. Program
College of Business
Arizona State University
Box 874906
Tempe, Arizona 85287-4906
Telephone: 602-965-3332
Fax: 602-965-8569
Internet: http/www.asu.edu/cwis/
   business/mba.html

Arthur D Little

Arthur D. Little Management Education Institute

Master of Science in Management Program

Cambridge, Massachusetts

▶ We are frequently asked why Arthur D. Little, an international consulting firm, offers a graduate management program. The contemporary response is somewhat different from one we would have given thirty years ago. Today, Arthur D. Little concentrates on helping major economic entities improve their operations, products, and processes, providing pragmatic solutions with visible involvement in the implementation of those solutions.

Similarly, the Master of Science in Management program is designed to provide a practical, experience-based series of courses, with an emphasis on global issues, cross-cultural awareness, and team building among the participants. Courses are taught by practicing Arthur D. Little consultants and university professors who bring their working knowledge to the classroom. Our goal is to engage our participants in an intensive, yearlong dialogue to develop and strengthen their managerial skills, allowing them to become more effective within their organizations.

Visits to the Cambridge headquarters of Arthur D. Little and MEI are encouraged; visitors may attend a class and meet with current participants and members of our faculty and staff.

—Thomas Moore, Dean

Programs and Curricular Focus

The Arthur D. Little Management Education Institute (MEI) offers a Master of Science in Management (M.S.M.) degree designed for early and midcareer professionals moving into positions of increased managerial responsibility. The program is distinguished from most other traditional M.B.A. programs by its practical, experienced-based, problem-solving orientation and by its global learning environment. Many of the professors are Arthur D. Little consultants. The M.S.M. program offers a curriculum similar to that of a two-year M.B.A. program in an intensive eleven-month period. The academic year, which begins in August and ends in July, is carefully organized into three interrelated phases, each lasting from thirteen to seventeen weeks.

The curriculum blends courses in basic managerial skills, including accounting, economics, organizational behavior, and management communication, with the functional areas of management, including finance, marketing, operations management, and information systems. Participants are provided with a comprehensive understanding of international economic growth and change, including national strategies and the global economy. Finally, students are introduced to a strategic framework of the management of business in a globally competitive economy, including industry analysis and strategic planning, policy implementation, and management of technology. Electives include international financial management, marketing research, agribusiness management, and total quality management.

Students and the M.B.A. Experience

Each year, an average of 65 participants from approximately twenty-five countries are enrolled in the M.S.M. program. Courses and projects are designed to incorporate teamwork and team building as an approach to developing managerial skills. Class discussions, study groups, and projects completed in teams provide intense cross-cultural experiences and the opportunity to gain a global perspective in nearly every course.

Enrollment in the M.S.M. program represents the diversity of most work environments, bringing together professionals with different educational backgrounds such as finance, law, and engineering. Although the profile of a typical MEI student varies, most participants have between four and eight years of work experience and are in their early or midthirties. Many are sponsored by their employers or by international agencies and return to their organizations after graduation.

The diversity of the class provides a unique opportunity to learn and practice the skills of international business management by working closely with colleagues from approximately twenty-five countries.

Special Features

Working under the guidance of an Arthur D. Little consultant, participants work in groups of 6 to 8 to carry out major industry research projects. Each group conducts extensive library-based research, culminating in a draft report and plans for the field research portion of the project. Each group then spends time conducting field research by visiting firms in its chosen industry. The groups complete their projects by submitting a final research report and making an oral presentation of their findings.

The Faculty

Professors in the M.S.M. program are Arthur D. Little consultants and visiting faculty from leading Boston-area business schools. The consultants bring their client orientation to the classroom to guarantee a curriculum based more on a practical application than on theory.

The Business School Network

M.S.M. participants learn about Arthur D. Little, as well as the firm's consultants and consulting work, through the Arthur D. Little Connections Program. This program has several components, including one-on-one "matches" between individual participants and consultants, monthly informal meetings with small groups of consultants discussing their work, a guest lecture series that features consultants discussing management topics, and corporate seminars in which consultants lecture on current Arthur D. Little cases.

The College and Environs

The Management Education Institute was founded as a subsidiary of Arthur D.

Verne E. Henderson, B.D., M.S., Consultant. Conflict management, consensus development, ethics, corporate responsibility.

Thomas Moore, M.Ed., Ph.D., M.B.A., Dean; former dean, Graduate School of Business, Babson College; former professor, acting dean, and director, Graduate School of Business, Northeastern University. New product introduction; real estate, hospital, and electronics firm consultation.

Richard J. Morris, Ph.D., Senior Consultant in the Operation Management Section of Arthur D. Little. Transportation and logistics, with a background in industrial engineering; transportation services and infrastructure in operations analysis; supply chain management; feasibility studies; planning.

Ranganath Nayak, Ph.D., Senior Vice President, Arthur D. Little; member, Arthur D. Little Corporate Management Group. Operations improvement, technology and innovation management, product creation process, implementation of quality programs.

Kamal N. Saad, M.A., Vice President of Arthur D. Little; European Director; practice leader in Strategic Management of Technology. Strategic planning assignments in oil and gas, chemical, petrochemical, and pharmaceutical industries in Europe and developing countries.

Little in 1964, was chartered in 1971, and received accreditation by the New England Association of Schools and Colleges in 1976. Participants study with senior management consultants and Boston-area university professors in a professional setting—the corporate headquarters of Arthur D. Little in Cambridge, Massachusetts. Cambridge, located across the Charles River from Boston, is home to other prominent academic institutions. With more than fifty universities, institutes, and colleges, metropolitan Boston is often considered the educational capital of the world.

Boston and Cambridge are easily accessible to MEI students and provide exceptional cultural, social, athletic, and academic resources.

Facilities

Participants in MEI's programs have access to a variety of research resources within the Arthur D. Little headquarters. The Arthur D. Little Information Center manages the MEI Library and provides reference materials, company reports, and case studies. In addition, the library collection includes journal and newspaper subscriptions as well as an on-line database for searching and CD-ROM workstations. A vast interlibrary loan network is available, and students have easy access to the collections at many of the colleges and universities in the Boston area.

Placement

MEI provides career counseling services to M.S.M. participants who do not have a commitment to return to their employers upon graduation. Throughout the year, the Institute offers workshops as well as individual counseling to support a participant's efforts to obtain a challenging professional position. MEI's career services include developing strategies for job searches, identifying opportunities for participants seeking full-time employment in the United States or with multinational organizations abroad, and building skills for interviewing and preparation of résumés and cover letters.

Finances

Tuition for the one-year M.S.M. program is $25,725. The fee covers the cost of all instruction and includes transportation for the travel required for the industry research project. Participants are charged $1800 to cover books and instructional materials. There is an additional fee of $2500 for the Summer Preparatory Program. The estimated annual living expenses, including rent, utilities, food, medical insurance, industry researsh project food and lodging expenses, local transportation, and laptop computer, are $20,500. Participants who are U.S. citizens or permanent residents may be eligible for federally insured Stafford loans, which are available through banks and other lending institutions. Limited partial tuition scholarships are also available.

International Students

Ninety percent of the M.S.M. student body comes from outside the United States. In 1994–95, 37 percent of the class was from Asia; 37 percent, Latin America; 9 percent, Africa and the Middle East; and 6 percent, Europe. There are nearly 3,000 alumni of MEI programs living and working in more than 100 countries throughout Asia, Africa, the Middle East, Europe, and the Americas.

Admission

Applicants for the M.S.M. program are considered on the basis of a qualitative evaluation of the applicant's undergraduate records, the relevance of work experience and career objectives, strength of recommendations, personal motivation, analytical ability, and fluency in English.

Application Facts and Dates

Applicants are reviewed when all documents have been received. Early application is suggested, as enrollment is limited. Correspondence and information should be directed to:

Judith H. Francis
Director of Admissions
Arthur D. Little
Management Education Institute
35 Acorn Park
Cambridge, Massachusetts 02140-2390
Telephone: 617-498-6200
Fax: 617-498-7100

![BABSON logo] **Babson College**

Wellesley, Massachusetts

BABSON'S SPIRIT OF ENTREPRENEURSHIP

Over the last few years, the Babson Graduate School of Business has received increasing attention, especially for its leadership in the field of entrepreneurship. Babson takes a holistic view of business education, encouraging students to look at the big picture and to work effectively in teams. Whether they intend to start their own companies, join a family firm, or enter an established corporation, today's students know that they will need to understand the entrepreneurial process to succeed. And they come to Babson to gain that understanding.
—Henry N. Deneault, Associate Vice President, Academic Affairs

Programs and Curricular Focus

All programs emphasize the global aspects of business and the value of the entrepreneurial spirit.

The Two-Year M.B.A. program is a coordinated curriculum based on the theme of entrepreneurial management in a changing global environment. First-year discussions and course work trace the business development cycle from the invention of a product or service, through assessing the business opportunity, into creating the marketing and delivery systems, and onto further development of products in the cycle. The highlight of the first year is participation in the mentor program, which assigns student teams to year-long projects with local businesses. Students complete two projects for the mentor company: one that analyzes the company's industry externally and another that evaluates an internal system. Teams provide written reports for both projects and present findings to top management. The second year builds on the first-year experience, with two required half-semester courses—The Global Mindset and Global Trends—and a challenging selection of electives.

The One-Year M.B.A. is an accelerated program that allows students with an undergraduate business degree to complete their M.B.A. in three full-time semesters. Beginning each May, students enroll in a series of integrated modules over the first semester and then join the second-year M.B.A. students to complete the equivalent of fifteen courses in one calendar year.

The Evening M.B.A. program begins each fall and spring. Initial steps as part of a larger redesign of the Evening M.B.A. curriculum bring more intensive and integrated course work. Team-taught integrated courses cross at least two subject areas.

Students and the M.B.A. Experience

Students in the Two-Year M.B.A. program are on average 28 years old and have about five years of work experience. GMAT scores range from 500 to 770. Women comprise one third of the class, and almost 60 percent of the student population have undergraduate degrees in business administration or the social sciences and humanities. They come from such diverse industries as banking and investment institutions to advertising, biotechnology, publishing, and telecommunications.

❖ Global Focus

Global business perspectives are not new at Babson. An international concentration is available and requires bilinguality, participation in an International Management Internship Program (IMIP), and completion of two required and one elective international course. The IMIP places students in structured field consulting projects with corporations in Asia, Australia, Europe, and South America. International electives combine intensive classroom experience with industry-based projects in seven international cities. Students may study abroad at one of Babson's partner schools in Norway, France, Spain, Japan, Venezuela, and Ecuador. International internships, electives, and study-abroad opportunities satisfy the Two-Year M.B.A. program cross-cultural requirement and are open to students in all Babson programs.

Special Features

Babson fosters the entrepreneurial spirit through a variety of activities and opportunities, including electives; endowed chairs in entrepreneurship; induction of innovative business people into the Academy of Distinguished Entrepreneurs on Founder's Day; the Douglass Foundation Entrepreneurial Prizes; the Douglass Scholarship for Entrepreneurial Studies; and the Babson Entrepreneurial Exchange, a student-run network of current and future entrepreneurs who exchange information about business development and venture opportunities.

The Faculty

Babson's faculty is an internationally and professionally diverse group, representing nations in Europe, Asia, Australia, and North and South America and with backgrounds in pharmaceutical, banking, high-technology, retailing, and other industries. They are practitioners and scholars, executives and teachers, and researchers and consultants who have lived and worked in international settings.

The Business School Network

Corporate Partnerships

Successful business partnerships have always been a major component of Babson's programs. First-year student teams consult with Boston-area organizations through the year-long mentor program. The Management Consulting Field Experience Office offers about twenty-three second-year consulting projects. In 1994, 53 M.B.A. students went abroad to complete projects for small, local companies and large, multinational corporations.

The Graduate Advisory Board offers feedback on curriculum initiatives and facilitates ongoing relationships with the business community. The International Advisory Board draws its worldwide membership from senior executives with demonstrated expertise in global management.

The College and Environs

Babson College, founded in 1919 by financier and entrepreneur Roger W.

Building on the strength of 75 years of excellence in management education, Babson College embraces new challenges and opportunities and furthers successes.

Babson, is located on a 450-acre wooded site in Wellesley, Massachusetts, just 12 miles from Boston. A commuter train links Wellesley to Boston, and a school shuttle-bus service transports students to public transportation. Boston and the surrounding region offer a pleasing and exciting environment with a rich artistic, historic, and intellectual life.

Facilities

The Horn Library houses 120,000 volumes, 1,400 periodicals, and a collection of business and financial statements from 10,000 corporations. On-line search services provide access to more than 250 databases, covering bibliographical and statistical information, thirty-five newspapers, and 100 magazines. Students and faculty can access the on-line systems of LEXIS/NEXIS, DIALOG, FirstSearch, Prodigy, Bridge, Dow Jones, DataStar, and BRS.

Graduate housing offers 115 living units of various sizes in eleven buildings, with surrounding recreation and picnic areas.

Technology Environment

The Horn Computer Center is equipped with 140 computer workstations, 125 of which are IBM-compatible PCs that run a diversified library of business-oriented programs in a Windows environment. A separate lab houses twenty-five Macintosh SE computers. The center operates a 24-hour computer lab. Fourteen classrooms are equipped with computer projection hardware. Babson expects that entering students are comfortable with basic spreadsheet and word-processing operations.

Placement

Made up of a staff of 4 professionals, M.B.A. Career Services offers a career management curriculum that is integrated into the first-year course work and is required for all full-time students; an on-line professional development survey of work experience and interests, allowing the staff to direct students to internship and employment opportunities; internships offering either stipends or course credit; job fairs; and on-line alumni and employer databases.

Admission

Students are admitted to the program based on a careful evaluation of academic records, professional qualifications, GMAT scores, and personal attributes. Interviews are required. Current class GMAT scores are in the 500 to 770 range, and the average undergraduate GPA is 3.1. International students must submit TOEFL results and official English translations of all academic documents. All candidates should have strong mathematics, computer, economics, and business writing skills.

Finances

Nine-month academic year cost estimates for 1995–96 for the Two-Year M.B.A. program are $20,000 for tuition, $1200 for books and supplies, $6318 for housing, and $2595 for food. Tuition for the One-Year M.B.A. program is $27,945. Per-course tuition is $1810. The pre-M.B.A. for international students costs $1000.

Merit programs that award scholarships include Babson Fellows, Babson Fellowships for Students of Color, Babson Scholars, and the Douglass Scholarship for Entrepreneurial Studies.

International Students

International students representing twenty-nine different countries comprise 32 percent of M.B.A. enrollment. The pre-M.B.A. orientation for international students begins two weeks before Module I classes begin. This intensive program consists of familiarization with the campus, library, computer center, and other services and workshops. Also, Babson faculty members present a basic introduction to economics, marketing, and the case method. Recreational and social events are scheduled. International students may apply for a U.S. internship, as well as being eligible for the International Management Internship Program (IMIP).

Application Facts and Dates

Application deadlines for the Two-Year M.B.A. program are February 15, April 1, and May 1; for the One-Year M.B.A. program, January 15 and February 15; and for the Evening M.B.A. program, November 1 and December 1 for spring admission and May 15 and June 15 for fall admission. Decisions are mailed four to six weeks after each deadline. For more information, applicants should contact:

Office of Graduate Admission
Babson Graduate School of Business
Babson Park, Massachusetts 02157-0310
Telephone: 617-239-4317
    800-488-4512 (toll-free
    within the U.S.)
Fax: 617-239-4194

Baldwin-Wallace College

Berea, Ohio

THE M.B.A. THAT PREPARES INTERNATIONAL MANAGERS FOR SUCCESS

Many of America's most highly respected M.B.A. programs have recently begun to incorporate "new" concepts like teamwork, hands-on experience, and multidisciplinary curricula. At Baldwin-Wallace College, our M.B.A. programs were founded on these fundamental philosophies—in 1972.

Every manager knows that corporations have become increasingly global in their operations and that their work forces have become increasingly diverse. To effectively lead these corporations, the ideal executive of the future needs to be global in outlook, able to capitalize on diversity, and a master of teamwork. The Baldwin-Wallace College M.B.A. in International Management program challenges students to foster these qualities.

—Earl M. Peck, Director, International M.B.A. Programs

Programs and Curricular Focus

The M.B.A. in International Management (I.M.B.A.) is offered through both full-time and part-time programs. The full-time program is designed to meet the needs of individuals seeking significant career advancement or the education necessary to become managers in a global setting. It has a one-year sequential format requiring class attendance 12 hours per week during each of three 14-week terms. Students desiring to complete the program at a slower pace have the option of attending class 9 hours per week during each of four 14-week terms. These students have the opportunity to study with part-time students who, in most cases, are currently employed in international management positions.

The part-time evening program is designed to meet the needs of individuals who are working in such areas as accounting, data processing, engineering, marketing, and management and are seriously seeking significant career advancement as managers in a global corporate setting. The program has a sequential two-year format requiring class attendance 3 hours per evening, two evenings per week. Students have the option of attending class 3 hours per evening, one evening per week, with a corresponding increase in the time required to complete the program.

Students have the opportunity to take prerequisite courses with other graduate students desiring to enter Baldwin-Wallace's M.B.A. programs. These prerequisite courses make it possible for students with little or no undergraduate business education to successfully participate in the program.

Baldwin-Wallace also offers M.B.A and Executive M.B.A. programs through its Division of Business Administration. As in the M.B.A. in International Management, these two-year, part-time programs are based on teamwork, hands-on experience, and multidisciplinary curricula. The M.B.A. program is designed for individuals with at least two years of business experience. Approximately 270 students are currently enrolled in the evening and weekend classes. The Executive M.B.A. program is designed for individuals with at least seven years of managerial experience. Approximately 50 students are currently enrolled in this program, with classes that meet every other weekend for two years.

Students and the M.B.A. Experience

The M.B.A. in International Management welcomes nearly 50 percent of its students from outside the United States. I.M.B.A. students represent six continents and more than nineteen countries including Argentina, China, Germany, Greece, Indonesia, Japan, Korea, Thailand, and Turkey. Of the more than 100 students enrolled in the program, approximately three fourths have prior work experience, one fourth are women, and one half are enrolled full-time.

❖ Global Focus

Students really learn from each other at Baldwin-Wallace. As they are put into mixed groups, they explore differing logic patterns and approaches to solving problems from their various countries. The Internet is used to link students from several countries. Working together and communicating by computer network, this diverse group analyzes all phases of an actual multinational company. Through this project, students gain a better understanding of the business, communication, and organizational skills needed to work with international teams.

Special Features

A series of faculty-led management study tours is available to students in the M.B.A. programs. During the 1994–95 academic year, management study tours to Europe and Nicaragua were conducted. The seventh Japan Management Study Tour is planned for the 1995–96 academic year.

There is an American Language Academy (ALA) program on the Baldwin-Wallace campus. ALA offers English as a foreign language preparation designed specifically for I.M.B.A. applicants and candidates. Many I.M.B.A. students successfully meet the TOEFL requirement while studying at the ALA. In addition, these students receive an orientation to academic life at Baldwin-Wallace as well as to the facilities and resources of the I.M.B.A. program.

The Faculty

Committed to teaching rather than research, the full-time and adjunct faculty share the College's commitment to "Quality Education with a Personal Touch." The faculty members bring a unique combination of educational and professional experiences to their teaching responsibilities. Within the student-centered, teaching-oriented environment, education is the number one priority.

The Business School Network

Through on-site and in-class projects, business partnerships enable students to put their knowledge to work. Field

Gerald Anderson, Ph.D., Indiana; Economist, Federal Reserve Bank of Cleveland. Economics.

Eugene Beem, Ph.D., Pennsylvania. Managerial ethics.

Harry Bury, Ph.D., Case Western Reserve. Management.

Pierre David, Ph.D., Kent State. International marketing.

Thomas Donahue, Murch Professor in Finance; Ph.D., USC.

Robert Ebert, Buckhorn Professor of Economics; Ph.D., Case Western Reserve.

Ronald Ehresman, M.S., Case Tech. Management information systems and finance.

David Krueger, Spahr Professor of Managerial Ethics; Ph.D., Chicago.

Judy Krutky, Ph.D., Columbia. Managerial ethics and political science.

Issac Kofe Kumah, Ph.D., Friendship University (Moscow). International geography and demography.

Albert Machamer, D.B.A., Kent State. Accounting and finance.

Dennis Miller, Ph.D., Colorado. Economics.

Earl Peck, Director, International M.B.A. Programs; Ph.D., Colorado. International finance.

Lee Pickler, D.B.A., Nova. Management.

Timothy Riggle, Ph.D., Ohio State. Mathematics and computer science.

Malcolm Watson, Director, American Language Academy; M.A., Emory. Intercultural communications.

Beverly Winterscheid, Ph.D., Case Western Reserve. Management.

studies, internships, and supervised in-company research projects place students in regional businesses where they work with corporate leaders to identify problems and develop solutions.

The College and Environs

Baldwin-Wallace is a liberal arts college, founded in 1845. The campus features forty buildings on 56 tree-shaded acres. The College serves approximately 4,700 students, of whom 4,100 are undergraduate students and 600 are graduate students.

The campus is located in Berea, a picturesque suburban area 14 miles southwest of Cleveland. It is easily accessible from Cleveland Hopkins International Airport (2 miles) and from interstate highways I-71, I-80, and I-480.

Many cultural and recreational activities are held on the Baldwin-Wallace College campus. Students can attend athletic events, concerts, theater productions, movies, and lectures by speakers who come from throughout the United States to address a variety of topics. For most events, admission is free.

Cleveland is the headquarters city for eighty-three major corporations with annual sales exceeding $100 million, a concentration larger than that of Los Angeles, Boston, or Atlanta. Cleveland is also the twelfth-largest consumer market, the eighth-largest industrial market, and the twelfth-largest retail market in the United States.

The Cleveland area offers a range of cultural, recreational, and entertainment opportunities. Outstanding museums and galleries, professional sports events, exciting nightlife, and a citywide park system are a short distance from campus.

Placement

The College Office of Career Services works aggressively to help students with career placement, career counseling and planning, résumé referral to employers, and résumé preparation. The Office of Career Services also has a career library and sponsors career fairs.

Admission

Required for admission into the I.M.B.A. program are a bachelor's degree from an accredited institution, two letters of recommendation, a résumé, and a satisfactory score on the Graduate Management Admission Test (GMAT). Individuals who have not taken the GMAT are still eligible for acceptance. Students accepted without a GMAT score must take the test during their first term. The average GMAT score for entering students is 476.

For students whose native language is not English, a minimum of 500 is required on the Test of English as a Foreign Language (TOEFL). Applicants who have not taken the TOEFL or those with TOEFL scores of less than 500 are eligible for conditional acceptance. Course work in Business English as a Second Language is required of students with a TOEFL score less than 523. International students must present proof of adequate funds to cover the cost of study.

Finances

Estimated tuition and fees for 1995–96 are $1450 for each of the M.B.A. in International Management program's twelve courses. In addition to the tuition and fees, a book cost of approximately $85 per course is to be expected.

Off-campus housing is available in the immediate area. The Office of Residential Life maintains a list of off-campus rooms, apartments, and houses that may be rented by students. Apartment rents start at $350 per month. An on-campus board plan is offered at approximately $800 per quarter. Even though undergraduate students are given priority, on-campus housing is sometimes available.

Application Facts and Dates

Students may begin the I.M.B.A. program at three times throughout the year: September, January, and late April. Students should apply well ahead of the desired starting date, as it takes approximately three months to complete the process. For more information, students should contact:

Earl M. Peck, Director
International M.B.A. Programs
275 Eastland Road
Berea, Ohio 44017-2088
Telephone: 216-826-2196
Fax: 216-826-3868
E-mail: epeck@rs6000.baldwinw.edu

Baruch College of the City University of New York

New York, New York

AN M.B.A. IN A GLOBAL ENVIRONMENT

> *Baruch College is proud of its place in New York City, the world's most dynamic financial and cultural center. We are uniquely positioned to provide students with an excellent education at a very reasonable cost in a global environment. Our outstanding faculty, flexible full- and part-time programs, and convenient location offer students unequaled access to opportunities for both learning and professional advancement.*
>
> —Sydney Lirtzman, Acting Dean

Programs and Curricular Focus

Baruch has recently completed a two-year revision of its M.B.A. program. The M.B.A. now requires a total of 54 credits: 27 credits of core courses, 9 elective credits, and 18 credits in an area of specialization. One of the strengths of the program lies in its combination of a solid business core with a wide array of specialized courses. The core curriculum is designed to provide students with an understanding of the basic principles of both management and the environment in which managerial decision are made. Courses include economics, finance, behavioral sciences, quantitative methods, information systems, production, and marketing.

Supplementing the core are 9 credits of elective courses, including one international elective, one quantitative elective, and one free elective. Beyond the core, students can specialize in accounting, computer information systems, economics, entrepreneurship, finance and investments, health-care administration, industrial/organizational psychology, international business, management, marketing, operations research, statistics, or taxation.

Those who wish to design their own M.B.A. programs can select unique, cross-disciplinary combinations of courses to fulfill the 18-credit specialization requirement. These combinations are useful for students interested in careers in such fields as marketing in financial institutions or banking operations. A few examples of the many specialization courses available to students are Futures and Forwards Markets, Options Markets, Mergers and Acquisitions, International Trade and Investment Law, International Commodity Trading, International Corporate Finance, Computer

Simulation for Solving Business Problems, Product Planning and Development, and Entrepreneurial Ventures.

Students and the M.B.A. Experience

Baruch's reputation for excellence extends to all parts of the world, attracting students from New York, neighboring states, and abroad. The cohort-style M.B.A. program offers students the option of full-time or part-time study. Full-time students complete the degree program in two years, part-time students in four. The diverse group of men and women doing graduate work at Baruch hold undergraduate degrees from over 200 colleges and universities. There are more than 400 international graduate students, who represent approximately fifty countries.

The average graduate student at Baruch is 31 years old. Although students generally have at least five years of work experience, applicants with little or no work experience are also encouraged to apply. Most M.B.A. students at Baruch have undergraduate degrees in business, but many have majored in engineering, the liberal arts, or the social sciences. Professional experience varies widely, and the majority of Baruch students work full-time while attending school. Forty-four percent of the M.B.A. students at Baruch are women, while members of minority groups represent at least 40 percent of the student body. International students make up 20 percent of the M.B.A. student population.

The Faculty

The faculty at Baruch is top-notch, with strong academic credentials and ties to

New York's business and financial communities. All share a commitment to teaching. Baruch's recently retired Harry Markowitz held the Marvin M. Speiser Professorship when he earned the Nobel Prize in Economics in 1990. Other faculty members recognized for outstanding honors include June O'Neill, the director of the Congressional Budget Office; E. S. Savas, an expert on privatization of public enterprises; and Yoshihiro Tsurumi, an authority on cultural and economic relations between the United States and Japan.

The Business School Network
Prominent Alumni

The Baruch degree is highly valued. Graduates may be found at all levels in business, industry, and public life. Notable graduates include Laura Altschuler, President, New York City League of Women Voters; the Honorable Abraham D. Beame, former Mayor of the City of New York; Dov C. Schlein, President and Chief Operating Officer, Republic Bank of New York; Bert Wasserman, Executive Vice President, Time Warner, Inc.; and Jules L. Winter, Chief Operating Officer, American Stock Exchange.

The College and Environs

Baruch's urban campus is ideally located near the picturesque Gramercy Park area and immediately to the east of the historic Flatiron District. It extends from East 18th Street to East 26th Street and is surrounded by a variety of ethnic restaurants and stores of all kinds. All of New York's museums, theaters, concert halls, clubs, sports arenas, and beaches are easily accessible by public transportation.

Technology Environment

In addition to the seven other buildings comprising Baruch's campus, the first building of the new north campus opened on East 25th Street in 1994. This completely renovated 1890s classic houses The William and Anita Newman Library, the Baruch Computing and Technology Center (which includes 400

One of Baruch College's main buildings, located in the center of activity at 23rd Street and Lexington Avenue in Manhattan.

computer workstations in an open-access lab), student and administrative offices, and a state-of-the-art multimedia center.

More than three times the size of its predecessor, the new 1,450-seat library has local area networks that provide access to a wide variety of electronic information resources. The Dow Jones News/Retrieval, LEXIS/NEXIS, and Dialog services are among the on-line databases available, and students and faculty members can access the Internet, gateway to the libraries and databases of the world. The Newman Library's traditional collections consist of 270,000 volumes, 2,100 current periodical subscriptions, 1.6 million microforms, and 500 audiovisual materials, including films, videos, audio recordings, and CD-ROMs. The Media Resources Lab houses 107 Apple Power PCs, all equipped with CD-ROM for multimedia capability. Twelve of these PCs have interactive videodisc capability and are available for research and information gathering.

Placement

Career counseling is available from the Office of Career Services in person or by telephone. Students can receive advice on résumé writing, job search strategies, interviewing techniques, and individual concerns. Videos that cover such topics as interviewing and career planning are available in the office, as is company literature for students who wish to research prospective employers.

Career fairs are held twice a year and are open to all students. On-campus recruiting takes place twice a year. In addition, graduate roundtables, symposia, and other networking opportunities are held throughout the year. Other services include a job listing service and a résumé book.

Admission

Applicants for any M.B.A. program (with the exception of the M.B.A. program in industrial/organizational psychology) must take the Graduate Management Admission Test (GMAT). Those who apply for the M.B.A. program in industrial/organizational psychology may elect to take either the Graduate Record Examinations (GRE) General Test or the GMAT. Generally, students entering the program have a GMAT score of 550 or better and an undergraduate grade point average of at least 3.0. International students whose native language is not English must take the Test of English as a Foreign Language (TOEFL) and the Test of Written English (TWE). Minimum scores required are 570 and 4.5, respectively. In addition to test scores, applicants must submit an application form, essays, a résumé, official transcripts from every college or university attended, two letters of recommendation, and a nonrefundable application fee of $35.

Finances

Tuition for New York State residents is $1675 per semester for full-time and $145 per credit for part-time study. For out-of-state residents and international students, tuition is $2925 for full-time

and $250 per credit for part-time study. Tuition is subject to change without notice. Average estimated annual costs for books, supplies, transportation, and personal expenses for students living with their parents are about $5000. Students who do not live with their parents should anticipate close to $9000 in expenses per year.

There are a limited number of graduate research assistantships, which are awarded solely on the basis of merit to qualified full-time graduate students. The assistantships carry an annual stipend of $5000 and are renewable for one year. In addition, in the fall the Mitsui USA Foundation awards two annual scholarships of $5000 each to newly admitted full-time students pursuing an M.B.A. degree in international business. Applicants for the Mitsui Scholarships must be United States citizens or permanent residents. Financial aid is also available to graduate students through a wide variety of sources, including various state, federal, and College programs. Other than graduate research assistantships, which do not include tuition waivers, there is no significant financial aid for international students.

Application Facts and Dates

Admission decisions for Baruch's graduate programs are made on a rolling basis. Although there is no set application deadline, applicants are encouraged to submit their applications as early as possible, particularly if they wish to be considered for a graduate research assistantship.

To request application materials or to make an appointment to speak with an admissions counselor, applicants should contact:

Office of Graduate Admissions
17 Lexington Avenue, Box H-0725
New York, New York 10010-5585
Telephone: 212-802-2330

Baylor University

Waco, Texas

BAYLOR AND THE GLOBAL M.B.A.

Baylor emphasizes international study through specifically designated degree programs with international focus, exchange programs, and courses with international emphasis. The M.I.M. and the M.B.A.-I.M. include credit hours for international internships as well as requirements for language competency. These programs are designated to prepare potential managers who can function effectively in the areas of international business and government service. Our exchange relationships focus on universities in Russia, Mexico, Europe, Asia, Canada, and Australia. Through the St. Petersburg University of Economics and Finance, some of our students even have the opportunity to serve as teaching assistants. With Monterey Tech in Mexico, we exchange faculty who serve as guest lecturers, as well as students. These exchange programs enable Baylor students to take abroad courses that will fulfill their respective degree requirements and also learn firsthand the cultural differences in international business. In our popular International Management course, an international corporate executive team-teaches the course and arranges corporate visits with international firms in Dallas and Houston.

—Donald F. Cunningham, Associate Dean, Graduate Business Programs

Programs and Curricular Focus

Baylor University's Hankamer School of Business offers the following graduate degrees: the Master of Business Administration (M.B.A.), the Master of Business Administration in International Management (M.B.A.-I.M.), the Master of International Management (M.I.M.), the Master of Science in Economics (M.S.Eco.), and the Master of Taxation (M.T.).

The M.B.A. is the largest program and is a lockstep program designed to thoroughly educate the participants in the fundamental areas of business as well as the interrelationships between the fundamental areas. The M.I.M. and the M.B.A.-I.M. are specialized degrees in the areas of international management. Both the M.I.M. and the M.B.A.-I.M. are designed to train potential managers in the complexities of the international business world, both on an economic and a political level. Students in this program can choose a geographical area of concentration such as Europe, the Middle East, South America, or the Orient. Students are also required to have a foreign language proficiency. The M.S.Eco. and the M.T. are specialized degrees for students interested in pursuing economic-related or tax-related careers, respectively.

Business background students who meet specific academic criteria can complete their M.B.A. in one calendar year. This is accomplished by satisfactorily completing three consecutive 12-hour semesters, allowing Baylor M.B.A. students to save considerable time and living expense as compared to the traditional two-year M.B.A. program.

Students and the M.B.A. Experience

Students at Baylor are a diverse population in terms of previous work experience, academic background, and geographic origin. This diversity adds dimension to the Baylor M.B.A. by beginning the programs with a broad incoming student knowledge base. The average student has 2½ years of full-time work experience.

The Baylor one-year M.B.A. program accepts only students who have demonstrated a superior grasp of the fundamentals of business concepts in their previous academic training. The Baylor M.B.A. program is a lockstep program designed to deepen and enhance students' grasp of the interrelationships in the fundamental areas of business. Liberal arts or other nonbusiness background students begin their M.B.A. experience with the

Integrated Management Seminar (IMS). The IMS is an intensive 18-hour semester designed to educate nonbusiness background students in the fundamental areas of business. This semester is designed to level the knowledge base of nonbusiness background students with business background students.

The Faculty

Baylor's faculty members are noted not only for their research abilities but also for their teaching ability. All graduate business courses are taught by faculty members holding Ph.D.'s, as Baylor is committed to providing its students with highly trained and dedicated educators. Baylor faculty members have received their training from various prestigious higher education institutions across the nation, including Brown University, Harvard University, the University of Texas, Indiana University, Berkeley, and the University of Minnesota. Baylor's professors are readily available to the student body through posted weekly office hours. Baylor faculty members routinely provide extra review sessions before major exams as well as furnish individual students with extra guidance on problem areas at the students' request.

The Business School Network

The Hankamer School of Business strives to maintain strong relationships with the corporate community. Executives are frequently invited to speak about their global experiences and enjoy entertaining questions from graduate students. Many of the courses involve corporate case studies, and, whenever possible, actual businesses are utilized. Professors also arrange on-site visits with many local firms in an effort to apply principles learned in the classroom to authentic situations.

The College and Environs

Founded in 1845, Baylor University is a private, coeducational institution of higher learning where education may be acquired under the influence of Christian ideals. The University seeks to provide a democratic and Christian atmosphere on

Hankamer School of Business.

campus, so that students and faculty members may work together with inquiring minds in the discovery and propagation of ideas.

Baylor University is located in Waco, Texas, a city of about 110,000. The University has an enrollment of about 13,500 students, of whom approximately 1,200 are graduate students. It is approximately 2 hours from either Austin, the state capital, or the Dallas–Fort Worth area.

Facilities

The main University library houses more than a million volumes as well as substantial periodical holdings and microform collections. The library is a U.S. government document depository, and a full-time documents librarian is available. Other libraries on campus include the law library, the music library, the W. R. Poage Legislative Library Center, the Texas Collection, and the Armstrong Browning Library. The Hankamer School of Business houses six IBM computer labs (housing over 100 computers) and one Macintosh computer lab (with approximately twenty computers). Each lab is equipped with one or more printers and is networked to the University system, with access to the Internet.

Placement

Baylor's students are routinely sought by larger firms in the Southwest region of the United States. Baylor M.B.A. graduates often return to work near their geographic origin; therefore, Baylor has alumni all across the globe. Job opportunities exist wherever Baylor has supportive alumni or wherever the Baylor University name is known and respected. The Graduate Office in Hankamer routinely networks current graduate students with willing alumni to facilitate the job search. A recent sampling of firms that have hired Baylor alumni includes Andersen Consulting; Bank One; Shell Oil; Macy's West; Sprint; EDS, Inc.; The Equitable; NationsBank; and Texas Instruments, Inc.

Admission

Application for admission to graduate study in business is made directly to the Baylor Graduate School Admissions Office. The completed application and required test scores and transcripts are forwarded to the School of Business for evaluation by the Associate Dean for Graduate Studies.

The applicant must meet the following minimum requirements for consideration by the Graduate School—a bachelor's degree from an accredited university or

college and an overall grade point average of 2.7. Only undergraduate or postgraduate (but not graduate) grades are calculated in the GPA. Mere attainment of the mathematical average does not automatically qualify a student for admission. Managerial skills, leadership, and other practical experiences are among the criteria used in evaluating an applicant.

Finances

More than 450 University graduate assistantships are available; these carry stipends of $3000 for the 1995–96 academic year (nine months) or for a twelve-month period, depending on the nature of the service and the amount of time required. Tuition was $232 per semester hour for 1994–95. Baylor University is proud to be one of the most affordable private institutions in the United States. Tuition may be increased in future academic years. At the graduate level, full-time study consists of 9 semester hours.

Application Facts and Dates

Applications for admission and assistantship should be received in the Graduate Office at least three months preceding the semester in which admission is desired. Application material should be mailed to:

Graduate School Admissions
Poage Library
Baylor University
P.O. Box 98001
Waco, Texas 76798

Questions concerning admissions should be addressed to:

Erin Raymond, Director of Graduate Admissions
Telephone: 817-755-3718
Fax: 817-755-2421

▣ BENTLEY Bentley College

Waltham, Massachusetts

BUSINESS SPECIALISTS AT BENTLEY GRADUATE SCHOOL OF BUSINESS

Bentley prepares business specialists through its integrated M.B.A. program with eleven different concentrations and its highly focused Master of Science programs in business. Through extensive curriculum, teaching excellence, and field-based resources, our programs stimulate professionalism, the development of business acumen, and social responsibility. Our programs are flexible and attentive to the needs of individual students. International students are an important part of our student body, making significant contributions to the intellectual and social life. Proximity to Boston enhances the international atmosphere and cultural opportunities available. Our international alumni network spreads across the world, including two newly formed chapters in Istanbul and Bangkok.

—Patricia M. Flynn, Dean

Programs and Curricular Focus

Bentley's M.B.A. program allows students to specialize their broad-based management degree by selecting one of eleven concentrations that include accountancy, advanced accountancy, business communications, business economics, finance, international business, management, management information systems, marketing, operations management, and taxation.

Depth is added to the M.B.A. curriculum by the shared Common Body of Knowledge (CBK) courses and electives available from the Master of Science (M.S.) program in accountancy, business economics, computer information systems, finance, and taxation. Bentley's curriculum, integrated across disciplines, is designed to teach students how to understand, critically evaluate, and contribute to corporate and public policy issues. Bentley's CBK courses cover the functional areas of business, such as accounting, computer information systems, economics, finance, management, marketing, and operations.

The required two-course sequence on Competing in a Global Marketplace provides a broad perspective on how to manage change in a globally interdependent and diverse world. Key themes built into the curriculum include business ethics, diversity, internationalism, and technology.

The M.B.A. program consists of nineteen courses: nine CBK courses, two advanced core courses, four distribution

electives (chosen from at least three business disciplines), and four concentration courses. Students can receive advanced-standing credit (waivers) for up to nine academic business courses taken within the last five years. Full-time students should take at least four courses each fall and spring semester and should be prepared to take a mix of day and evening classes. Many students take summer classes. Full-time students can complete the M.B.A. degree program in one to two years.

Students and the M.B.A. Experience

The Graduate School brings together approximately 2,100 students representing fifty-two countries. This includes 220 full-time and 1,900 part-time students; 44 percent are women. While work experience is preferred, students with no prior work experience are encouraged to apply. Forty percent of the students come from liberal arts or engineering backgrounds, and 60 percent are from business backgrounds.

❖ Global Focus

The global perspective on the new world economy is nurtured by the required two-course sequence, Competing in a Global Marketplace, and by Bentley's solid relationship with twenty-five institutions in fifteen countries for faculty and curricula development through the Office of International Programs. It is

enhanced by the World Business Speaker series and an active International Graduate Association of Business (IGAB).

The Faculty

At Bentley, excellence in teaching is valued and rewarded. Faculty members maintain professional working relationships with business executives to stay in touch with developments in business, both nationally and internationally. The majority of the faculty members publish articles in leading business publications, make professional presentations, conduct applied research, and consult for corporations. Their commitment to scholarly pursuits and professional involvement supports classroom excellence. As one of the largest nationally accredited graduate business schools in the United States, Bentley has a critical mass of faculty in each discipline. Graduate School courses are primarily taught by full-time faculty members, supplemented by working professionals who serve as adjunct professors.

The Business School Network

Prominent executives and international speakers visit Bentley to share their experiences with graduate students, offering students the opportunity to meet and interact with senior executives from a variety of industries and countries.

The Mentor Program pairs graduate students with business professionals in their chosen fields of study. Mentor volunteers are executives in the business world who serve as resources on career-related issues and concerns. Mentors help students understand corporate culture, offer career guidance, and provide feedback. They assist in exploring career paths, encourage ideas, and often introduce students to other business professionals.

Through the Alumni Career Exploration (ACE) network, there are approximately 300 alumni and alumnae employed in business and industry who are available to meet with students to discuss their own career development, share information about work experiences, assist with interviewing skills, and connect students with other resource people. International alumni are available in many countries as resources for those returning to their home country.

The College and Environs

Founded in 1917 by Harry C. Bentley, a pioneer in American business education, the College is an independent, coeducational institution recognized internationally for its excellence in professional business education. In addition to the students at the Graduate School, over 5,000 undergraduates are enrolled in business and liberal arts. Bentley is accredited nationally by the American Assembly of Collegiate Schools of Business (AACSB) and regionally by the New England Association of Schools and Colleges (NEASC).

Located in Waltham, Massachusetts, at the heart of a high-technology region, the 110-acre suburban campus is minutes from Boston's cultural resources, 30 minutes from Logan International Airport in Boston, and a 3-hour drive from New York City.

Facilities

The library houses more than 159,000 volumes, receives more than 1,400 periodicals, and has 155,000 microform titles. It has computer terminals available for students' use, as well as various databases (e.g., Lexis/Nexis, Dow Jones News/Retrieval Service, and Infotrac). The library's media services department provides television facilities, films, and recordings for both instruction and personal enrichment.

On-campus housing provides a limited number of modern, fully furnished one- and two-bedroom apartments and single dormitory rooms that are equipped with a personal computer connection to the campus network. Interested applicants should request a housing application.

The Dana Physical Education Center houses an Olympic-size swimming pool, weight-training rooms, an indoor track, basketball courts, racquetball courts, and a dance studio.

Technology Environment

The computer facilities at the College are state of the art. Bentley has more than 100 microcomputers, a VAX 6410, and a MicroVAX II that enable students and faculty to utilize small computer systems

for a variety of applications, including word processing, spreadsheet analysis, database management, and computer programming. There are twenty-two classrooms equipped with monitors, a Graduate Computer Learning Center, and six other student computer labs. Bentley has a broad-based network to interconnect terminals, microcomputers, and other computer systems, allowing Bentley students to communicate with students in other countries, utilize BITNET, and access e-mail.

Placement

The Office of Career Services assists students with networking plans and provides an impressive array of other career planning resources, from résumé writing seminars to a database with job opportunities. Each year, more than 100 workshops and programs help students obtain information, develop skills, and refine job search strategies. These include seminars on immigration regulations and U.S. employment labor certification. The office also makes available information on international positions. A recent survey shows an overall employment rate of 91 percent for full-time and part-time graduates four months after graduation.

Admission

Students may begin studies in the fall, spring, or summer term. Applicants must submit a completed application form, accompanied by a $45 application fee; official transcripts of all academic work beyond high school; GMAT scores; and two letters of recommendation.

International students must submit their TOEFL scores, complete the International Student Data Form, and document adequate financial resources for one academic year as part of the application process. To complete the International Student Data Form, students must submit a letter of financial support (unless they are financing their own education) and a bank statement indicating sufficient funds for one academic year.

The average GMAT score is 520, and the average GPA is 3.1 on a 4.0 scale. A minimum score of 580 is required for the TOEFL.

Finances

Tuition for the 1994–95 academic year was $13,200 for eight courses (two

semesters: fall and spring). Costs for books and supplies, health insurance, living expenses, and personal expenses for a nine-month academic year were about $9990. Summer tuition for two courses in 1994 was $3300, and summer living expenses were $2200. Costs are subject to change.

Graduate assistantships are available for highly qualified applicants and consist of a tuition waiver and possibly a stipend, in exchange for work as a research assistant.

International Students

Bentley offers international students a noncredit business communication seminar series on the academic, cultural, and social aspects of the U.S. graduate school experience. The instructor is also available for individual tutoring. The Office of International Student Services has programs and events designed to serve the social and academic needs of international students. In addition, the Office of Career Services conducts seminars on immigration regulations and U.S. employment and labor certification and provides information on overseas job postings.

Application Facts and Dates

The preferred application deadline for international applicants and graduate assistantships for fall semester is March 1; candidates with complete applications will be notified by April 1 and can begin classes in May or September. The regular application deadline for fall semester is June 1; candidates with complete applications will be notified by July 1. The preferred application deadline for international applicants and graduate assistantships for spring semester is October 1; candidates with complete applications will be notified by October 30. The regular application deadline for spring semester is November 1; candidates with complete applications will be notified by November 30. For more information, applicants should make inquiries to:

Bentley College
Graduate School of Business
Waltham, Massachusetts 02154-4705
Telephone: 617-891-2108
Fax: 617-891-2464
Internet: gradadm@bentley.edu

৬ Boise State University

Boise, Idaho

> Our program's goal is to equip you, our future leaders, with the skills necessary to manage in the present environment and the learning skills needed to respond to change.
>
> Through the tremendous support of our business advisory council, our program is able to achieve a high level of quality as well as provide excellent opportunities for our students to interact with businesses as part of their educational experience.
>
> Boise State is surrounded by an exciting city that offers a variety of social, educational, cultural, and recreational opportunities. This setting will encourage you to discover more about yourself and the world around you.
>
> When you come to Boise State University, I can promise you a demanding and academic intellectual environment along with an extremely enjoyable social environment. At Boise State University, you will find traditions of pride, determination, and, above all, academic excellence. It will be a road full of challenge, new knowledge, and great change.
>
> —William N. Ruud, Dean

Program and Curricular Focus

The Master of Business Administration degree program at Boise State University is designed to prepare future business leaders to handle the challenges of change in a global economy. Emphasizing the needs of fully employed students, the program strives to provide students with a thorough grounding in each of the functional business areas. Integration of students' knowledge across these functional disciplines is one of the program's key objectives.

The Boise State M.B.A. program provides a general perspective of business management that requires students to consider the social, environmental, and ethical context of managerial actions. It is a high-quality academic program that assists in the development of tomorrow's business leaders. It provides a general management perspective that enables students to target problems, select viable alternatives, and take appropriate action. Boise State makes the international perspective a priority throughout the curriculum.

The Boise State M.B.A. requires a minimum of 33 semester credit hours and a maximum of 54 semester credit hours. The exact number of credits required depends upon the student's prior academic experience. While there is no major available in the M.B.A. program, once students satisfy the functional core

of courses, they emphasize an area of concentration with their elective credits. This specialization can expand beyond business to such areas as public administration or health policy.

Students and the M.B.A. Experience

Students in Boise State University's M.B.A. program bring a wide variety of work experiences and geographic and academic diversity to their M.B.A. experience. Many Boise State M.B.A. students are professional people, continuing their education while working full-time. This mix of backgrounds promotes the beneficial exchange of experience and ideas among peers, a significant factor in the quality and excitement of the program.

A recent student profile shows that the average student is 32 years old, with an average of over six years of full-time work experience. Women comprise 38 percent of the student population, and students who are members of minority groups make up 10 percent of the M.B.A. student body.

Most Boise State M.B.A. students have undergraduate degrees in business, engineering, or science.

Special Features

Boise State University's M.B.A. program is small enough to enable students to

work in groups on classwork and projects. Many projects are required that develop small group, negotiation, and presentation skills—the same skills demanded of successful managers.

The Faculty

The College of Business faculty brings a high standard of excellence to Boise State's M.B.A. program. The M.B.A. faculty members hold doctoral degrees from universities across the nation. Most have extensive experience in business, industry, or consulting. This actual business experience enables the faculty to bring a realistic and pragmatic orientation to the classroom.

Boise State University's faculty members are dedicated to excellence in teaching. The faculty consults with, and researches for, top businesses to constantly update materials and to bring the most practical and current business information and problems/solutions into the classroom. This day-to-day contact allows Boise State's faculty members to gain knowledge of the skills businesses find valuable as well as the tools and information students need to allow insight into tomorrow's business needs. The M.B.A. curriculum incorporates these insights to ensure that the program addresses the demands professional managers confront.

The Business School Network

Corporate Partnerships

Boise is the commercial, financial, health-care, and government center of Idaho, allowing students to reach beyond the classroom for experiences not available elsewhere in the state. Boise State University has the advantage of being situated in a city where major firms are headquartered, including Albertson's, Boise Cascade, Idaho Power, Morrison-Knudsen, Ore-Ida, Simplot, Trus Joist, and the state's leading banks and insurance companies. Major manufacturing locations for Hewlett-Packard and Micron Technology are also located in Boise.

Prominent Alumni

The College of Business counts among its alumni a number of notable business leaders, including William C. Glynn, CEO of Intermountain Gas; George A. Haneke, CFO of Micron Computer; Douglas G. Hansen, Controller, WestOne Bank; Daniel J. Kunz, President and CEO, MK Gold Company; Alan J. Moore, Vice President and CFO, MK Gold Company; Sony M. Perry, Vice President, Telecommunications, NCI Information Systems, Inc.; Lyle R. Price, Bechtel; and Mary J. Schofield, Controller of Hewlett-Packard's Boise Division.

The College and Environs

Boise State University is located in Boise, Idaho's capital and largest city and one of America's most enjoyable places to live and learn, featuring big city opportunities and small town friendliness. Set against a backdrop of mountains where the Boise River flows out of its lava canyons into a fertile valley, Boise is one of the most appealing metropolitan areas in the West. Named for the Boise River, present-day Boise is a green tribute to the magic of irrigation, with its parks, greenbelt, tree-lined neighborhood streets, golf courses, and University campus. Boise has a pleasant four-season climate; it is one of the premier locations in the country for those who like the outdoors.

Founded in 1932 as a private community college, today Boise State University has the largest enrollment in Idaho with about 15,000 students, approximately 200 of whom are in the M.B.A. program. Students come from all parts of the world and from diverse academic and professional backgrounds.

Technology Environment

Through the Center for Data Processing, Boise State University provides student access to the University's computer resources. Many of Boise State's offices and computer labs are connected to the campus fiber-optic network, allowing users to tap into the Campus-Wide Information System or gain access to the Internet, BITNET, and other networks.

The College of Business has its own computing facilities, consisting of two microcomputing laboratories with approximately sixty terminals. Facilities are open seven days a week during convenient hours. The College of Business also houses three electronic classrooms furnished with the latest multimedia systems.

Placement

Boise State University's Career Center provides career guidance and information through computerized career guidance/information systems and from professional staff members. Information and advice on résumé and cover letter writing, application procedures, interviewing, and other job-hunting skills are available. A library of career and employer information is also available. Notification of employment opportunities, participation in on-campus interviews, and optional establishment of a file of professional references are available to M.B.A. students during the academic year in which they complete their degree.

Admission

Applicants must possess a bachelor's degree from an accredited institution. Completed applications must include official transcripts from all institutions previously attended, a GMAT report, two letters of recommendation, a current professional résumé, and an essay. In addition, two years of significant work experience is required but can be waived based on a superior GMAT score. The average GMAT score of enrolling students is 550; the average undergraduate GPA is 3.2.

A score of at least 550 on the TOEFL is required of all students for whom English is not the native language. International students must also present proof of adequate funding and certified English translations of transcripts.

There are no prerequisite courses for admission, but students must have a basic level of proficiency with word processing and spreadsheet programs.

Finances

Estimated tuition and fees for 1995–96 are $2400 for Idaho residents and $7750 for nonresidents. On-campus and off-campus housing is available. Most graduate students choose to live off campus in nearby apartments. Many live within walking distance. On-campus room and board are estimated to cost $5600 for the academic year. Off-campus housing and food costs average $11,000 a year.

A number of graduate assistantships are available. To be eligible, students must be admitted to the M.B.A. program and attend as full-time students during the academic year(s) of the awards. The application deadline is March 1.

Application Facts and Dates

Application deadlines are October 31 and April 30.

For more information, students should contact:

Renee Anchustegui
Business Graduate Studies
College of Business
Boise State University
1910 University Drive
Boise, Idaho 83725
Telephone: 208-385-1126
Fax: 208-385-3637
Internet: abuanchu@cobfac.idbsu.edu

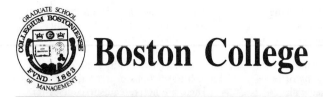

Boston College

Chestnut Hill, Massachusetts

> *These are exciting times for the Carroll School and its M.B.A. programs. We are about to enter a new era built on core values and carried forward by outstanding faculty, new curricula, and a new state-of-the-art educational facility. We are prepared to educate leaders and managers for the twenty-first century.*
>
> *Core values in the M.B.A. program mean our sense of community, our standards, and our scope. Our motto "Through Cooperation and Integrity We Prosper" provides the foundation for emphasis on community and teamwork, the hallmarks of the Carroll M.B.A. experience.*
>
> *The new curriculum features the theme "Management Practice," a set of topics, skills, and projects that spans the entire program. Management Practice, taught by faculty dedicated to learning, educates our students in the art of management. This is in addition to a thorough grounding in the common body of knowledge. The Carroll School M.B.A. can give you the edge you will need to compete successfully in an environment that is both challenging and demanding.*
>
> *—Louis S. Corsini, Graduate Dean*

Programs and Curricular Focus

The Wallace E. Carroll Graduate School of Management M.B.A. program is structured to provide the student with a depth of management knowledge coupled with practical experience in order to develop the management skills required of today's managers. Emphasis is placed on teamwork, business condition analysis, and decision making.

The first-year core program, restructured for the fall 1995 semester, focuses on developing managers whose leadership will enable an organization to reach its full potential. The curriculum enables students to work cooperatively to translate careful reflection into effective management action in an ethical and professional manner. Action learning is afforded first-year students through a semester-long consulting engagement with local businesses and nonprofit organizations.

The first-year course structure is modular, allowing greater flexibility in the allocation of class time to specific topics and enabling a more timely integration of the material covered. A total of twelve first-year courses are taken, including two electives and a five-part "Management Practice" module, which is designed to integrate the material of the first year and provide thematic coherence.

The second-year program calls for six electives and a two-part Management

Practice module. The elective program affords the student the opportunity to concentrate in a selected area of management. The Management Practice module is designed to enhance the student's knowledge and understanding in the areas of information systems and strategic management as well as to raise his or her awareness of the role social issues and global competition play in the successful management of organizations in today's economy.

Other programs at the Carroll Graduate School of Management include dual-degree programs with the Graduate Schools of Nursing, Social Work, Law, and Arts and Sciences (Ph.D. in sociology). Ph.D. programs are also available in finance and organization studies, as is an M.S. degree in finance.

Students and the M.B.A. Experience

The process of selecting students for the M.B.A. program reflects the goal of having the social interaction among students in each class be a contributor to their overall learning experience. The average student admitted to the full-time class of 1996 is 26 years old, with 3.3 years of work experience. Women comprise nearly 45 percent of the class, and international students, representing twenty-two countries, make up 30 percent.

About one quarter of the entering class has an undergraduate major in business, about 40 percent in social sciences or liberal arts, and 20 percent in natural sciences, engineering, or economics. Professional backgrounds are also rich in diversity.

❖ Global Focus

Exposure to international managerial issues is one of the main themes of the M.B.A. program. In addition to the use of case studies of multinational companies discussed in various courses, there are several international courses and opportunities for language studies. One very popular course is the International Experience, which is conducted overseas each year by Boston College faculty members. Students have the opportunity to meet senior-level managers to discuss such issues as trade, competitiveness, strategy, and technology from a non-U.S. perspective.

Approximately one third of the full-time M.B.A. students are international students. Their participation in classroom discussions and student groups brings a richness to the M.B.A. educational experience that cannot be replicated.

Boston College has exchange programs with several excellent business schools around the world. Students are strongly encouraged to study abroad for a semester and in some instances are able to do an internship as well.

Special Features

A new initiative becomes operational in the spring of 1995 with the first session of the new program, Leadership for the Common Good. This is a 12-credit executive program geared to leaders and change agents who want to create new ways to integrate financial and social goals, to develop and demonstrate their leadership skills at work, and to network with other key leaders for the "common good." This program is designed to give leaders the tools to integrate healthy family lives, ethical consciousness, environmental sensitivity, community support, and employer-employee commitment into the corporate fiber while still achieving high productivity, corporate change, and solid profitability.

The Faculty

The M.B.A. faculty includes internationally recognized scholars and professionals whose diversity of training, background, and viewpoint provides a wealth of expertise for students to call upon. Faculty members place a high priority on research, and they are widely published in academic journals, professional journals, textbooks, and scholarly treatises. In addition, the Carroll Graduate School of Management faculty is widely recognized both for its emphasis on the high quality of classroom instruction and for its availability to the students to assist them with issues of concern. The faculty has a strong international representation.

The Business School Network

Corporate Partnerships

As an active member of the Boston business community, the Carroll School of Management sponsors the Boston Citizen's Seminar and the Chief Executive's Club of Boston. The Carroll School is an active member in the International Business Center, the Center for Total Quality Management, and the executive group of the Boston Chamber of Commerce. In addition, Boston College's partnership with a group of Wall Street executives, the Boston College Wall Street Council, provides a foundation for career opportunities on Wall Street.

FACULTY LIST

John J. Neuhauser, Dean and Professor (Computer Science); Ph.D., RPI.

Louis S. Corsini, Dean and Associate Professor (Accounting); Ph.D., LSU.

Richard Keeley, Acting Associate Dean; M.B.A., Boston College.

Chairpersons
Accounting Department: Jeffrey Cohen, Associate Professor; Ph.D., Massachusetts Amherst.

Business Law Department: David Twomey, Professor; J.D., Boston College.

Computer Science Department: Michael McFarland, S.J., Associate Professor; Ph.D., Carnegie Mellon.

Finance Department: Robert Taggart, Professor; Ph.D., MIT.

Marketing Department: Victoria Crittenden, Associate Professor; D.B.A., Harvard.

Operations and Strategic Management Department: Jeffrey Ringuest, Professor; Ph.D., Clemson.

Organization Studies Department: Judith Gordon, Associate Professor; Ph.D., MIT.

The College and Environs

Boston College is a coeducational two-campus university with four undergraduate schools and six graduate and professional schools. The University offers fifteen degree programs and enrolls 14,500 full-time and part-time students. It was originally established in 1863 to educate the sons of Boston's Irish immigrants. It now serves a diverse body of scholars from across the United States and eighty-six other countries.

The quiet walkways and Gothic architecture of Boston College's suburban campus are located in the Chestnut Hill section of Newton, 7 miles west of Boston, a city offering extraordinary cultural and intellectual resources.

Facilities

In a city famous for great libraries, the students of Boston College are served by a university library that is widely recognized for excellence in its collections and its information services. With book collections exceeding 1 million volumes and approximately 10,000 serial titles, the libraries offer a wealth of resources to support teaching and research activities.

The O'Neill Computing Facility is housed in the same building as the main library. This facility contains 180 workstations, providing access to a wide variety of hardware, applications, and peripherals. The computing facility includes Digital Equipment Corporation VAX-type terminals, providing access to a cluster of superminicomputers, and IBM and Macintosh personal computers.

Placement

The Office of Career Services provides graduate management students and alumni with comprehensive services to support all aspects of career planning. These services are tailored to their specific needs and include career advising, skills workshops, career panels, company site visits, and career research resources. The office also manages several placement activities, including a campus recruiting program, a job posting system, first- and second-year résumé books, and two M.B.A. career fairs. In addition, the office maintains a database of several hundred active alumni career advisers who provide students with advice and guidance in their job search.

Admission

The Admissions Committee seeks to predict success in both graduate-level course work and a long-term management career. To this end, the committee reviews undergraduate transcripts, scores from the Graduate Management Admission Test (GMAT), work experience, recommendations, and statements of future career goals. The GMAT score for enrolling M.B.A. students at Boston College averages 570. The average undergraduate GPA is 3.1.

The TOEFL is required of international applicants unless they received an undergraduate degree from an institution accredited by the United States. A score of 600 or higher is required on the TOEFL. International students must document funds to cover two years of tuition and living expenses.

There are no prerequisite courses in business or management required for admission. Students are expected to demonstrate proficiency in mathematics and English language skills. Students in the full-time program average over three years of work experience; however, 15 percent of the class enters the program directly from undergraduate school.

Finances

Tuition for the 1995–96 academic year for a first-year, full-time M.B.A. student is $18,972, based on the per credit hour rate of $612. This per credit hour rate is applicable to both full-time and part-time programs. Room, board, personal expenses, books, supplies, and transportation for the first-year, full-time student are estimated to add an additional $11,605 to the total cost.

Financial aid is available to all M.B.A. students in the form of graduate assistantships and/or scholarships. These awards are based on merit and need.

Application Facts and Dates

Applications to the full-time program are processed on a rolling basis beginning December 1. The deadline for international applicants is March 1. Decisions are mailed approximately six weeks from the date the application is complete. For more information, applicants should contact:

Office of Admissions
Wallace E. Carroll Graduate School of Management
Boston College
140 Commonwealth Avenue
Chestnut Hill, Massachusetts 02167
Telephone: 617-552-3920
Fax: 617-552-8078
E-mail: cgsom@hermes.bc.edu

Boston University

Boston, Massachusetts

THE BOSTON UNIVERSITY M.B.A.: A FOCUS ON THE SYSTEM

The Boston University M.B.A. curriculum is a pioneering program designed to concentrate on management processes instead of functions alone. In this M.B.A. program, you will learn management as a system—a horizontal continuum of interdependent departments or functions. Many graduate schools structure their curriculum to develop general managers. But they tend to take a segmented route, where accounting is isolated from marketing, operations from finance, and so on. In such classes, case studies are usually approached for an accounting (or marketing or operations) solution only. That is not how the real world operates. At Boston University, we develop general managers with a view that extends across multiple departments to encompass the whole organization.

—Louis E. Lataif, Dean

Programs and Curricular Focus

Boston University offers the M.B.A. in general management, M.B.A. in health-care management, M.B.A. in public and not-for-profit management, accelerated M.B.A. with a concentration in accounting, executive M.B.A., M.S. in management information systems, and Doctor of Business Administration.

The M.B.A. program provides graduates with the full range of foundation skills required to be an outstanding and adaptable performer immediately upon graduation, the competencies required for long-term career development, and the perspectives necessary to understand the complex social and ethical dimensions of management. The program provides real-world action learning coupled with a rigorous, research-based conceptual education. Each of the first three semesters of the full-time program is anchored by team-taught courses: The Global Manager, The Global Environment, and The Global Organization. Each offers a cross-disciplinary understanding of organizations and their broader environments.

The optimum way to understand management processes and systems is by pooling the expertise from various disciplines. The faculty members team-teach several courses, interactively dissecting each topic or case study of the day from their own respective viewpoint. Under their guidance, students learn to develop holistic, relevant solutions, rather than one-dimensional, academic ones.

Teamwork is an essential part of today's workplace, and thus it is a major component of the M.B.A. education. In most Boston University M.B.A. courses, students work in consistent cohorts, simulating the way actual organizations work. Students join in study groups, project groups, and consulting groups to outside industry. Each of these experiences helps the student learn how to facilitate the teamwork process in every phase of his or her M.B.A. education and career.

Students and the M.B.A. Experience

Boston University has the most internationally diverse student body in the nation (as reported by the Institute of International Education), and this is reflected in the M.B.A. program. Thirty-three percent of the students are international. The students, who come from six continents, benefit from a rich and varied interchange of views. The M.B.A. curriculum capitalizes on this diversity in its emphasis on the global business environment. The students are highly intelligent, diverse, ambitious, and determined to make a positive difference in society. Their active participation in the evaluations of the programs and activities ensures a continuing vibrancy and responsiveness in the School.

There are approximately 1,500 students enrolled in the M.B.A. programs. Applications are traditionally received from approximately sixty-five countries. The average student is 26 years old, has three to five years of work experience, and entered the program with an average TOEFL score of 601 and GMAT score of 580.

❖ Global Focus

Students can begin their M.B.A. program by joining a ten-week management program in Kobe, Japan. The program draws students from the Pacific Rim and countries around the world for a rich intercultural experience. Courses taught by Boston University professors combine classroom work with field visits and guest lecturers to help students develop an understanding of the social, political, and economic aspects of global business. During their second year, students may live and study abroad through the student exchange programs between Boston University and the University of Manchester, England, or the University of Lyon, France.

Special Features

The School of Management has developed a four-week orientation program to help international students adjust to the dynamic atmosphere of the American M.B.A. classroom and to prepare for the rigorous demands of case discussions. This distinctive program provides both English instruction and an introduction to the M.B.A. curriculum. Attendance may be required for students whose native language is not English and whose prior academic work has not been in English or has not fully prepared them for the case study method.

Students have the opportunity to read, analyze, and discuss actual case studies. The orientation program also introduces students to the American economic system, including the operation of private firms and the role the American government plays in the business environment. Students also receive training in preparation for class presentations and an introduction to the M.B.A. classroom culture. There is a fee for the program.

The Faculty

The faculty is the School of Management's major resource. Committed to advancing management knowledge, through both theoretical and applied research, and to improving the quality of teaching and learning, faculty members bring the benefits of their vast professional experience to the classroom. The faculty members have earned worldwide recognition and respect for their applied research. They bring a refreshing approach to teaching within interdisciplinary frameworks and also bring wide-ranging experience with local, national, and global organizations.

The Business School Network

The Boston University School of Management boasts a wealth of research centers and institutes, each of which addresses issues that extend beyond the boundaries of traditional disciplines. These organizations have become magnets for faculty from disciplines around Boston University and for top-level managers from around the world, who come together and share their understanding of contemporary management challenges.

The research centers and institutes and the School's executive training programs offer significant advantages to students seeking leadership roles in major organizations. Through an industrial network that extends around the globe, faculty members maintain contact and exchange data with colleagues in universities and business firms. This real-world involvement brings exciting results into the classroom—timely and topical material for case studies and a steady stream of high-level managers from a variety of firms.

The College and Environs

The fourth-largest private university in the nation, Boston University is consolidated at the 86-acre Charles River Campus and Boston University's Medical Center in the city's South End. The School of Management was established as the College of Business Administration in 1913 and is located on the Charles River

Campus. Boston offers a wealth of cultural, educational, sports, and social resources. Combining a proud history with a contemporary lifestyle, it is a cosmopolitan center for the financial and insurance industries, the heart of the high-technology industry, an extensive medical and educational center, and the capital of Massachusetts. As the hub of one of the nation's largest metropolitan areas, Boston offers numerous opportunities for strong practical experience in business, government, health, technology, and public management.

Placement

The School of Management's state-of-the-art Career Center assists students in making informed career and life decisions. Through comprehensive career education programming, job development services, and individualized career counseling, the center collaborates with students in developing and managing careers at both the entry and experienced level.

Admission

The requirements for applying are a completed application form with a nonrefundable $45 application fee, official transcripts of the academic record from each college or university attended, three letters of evaluation, and results of the Graduate Management Admission Test (GMAT).

International applicants must also submit English translations of transcripts (the undergraduate degree must be equivalent to a U.S. bachelor's degree), results of the Test of English as a Foreign Language (TOEFL) (if the student's native language is English or if the student received an undergraduate degree from an institution where English is the language of instruction, the TOEFL is not required), and the International Student Data Form and financial documents. Since scholarship funds are not available to international students, applicants must submit a financial declaration showing

adequate funding for both tuition and living expenses for the duration of the M.B.A. program.

Finances

Tuition for the 1994–95 academic year is $18,420, and fees are approximately $215. Single students living off campus should anticipate living costs for nine months of approximately $18,000; the costs for married students are estimated at $22,000. Most students live in apartments in nearby neighborhoods, easily accessible from the School by public transportation. The program offers scholarships, work-study awards, and endowment funding to full-time students who are citizens or permanent residents of the United States. Financial aid is not available to international students. All international students are required to have medical insurance, estimated at $509.

Application Facts and Dates

Students seeking financial aid should apply by March 15. The deadlines for September admission are April 1 for full-time study and May 1 for part-time study. The deadline for January admission is December 1 (part-time study only).

International students are admitted to the M.B.A. program for full-time study in September only. All international applications must be received by the Graduate Admissions Office by April 1.

Applications are reviewed on a rolling basis. Review begins in February for September admission. Students are encouraged to submit applications early to ensure adequate processing time. For more information, applicants should contact:

Boston University School of
  Management
Graduate Admissions Office
685 Commonwealth Avenue
Boston, Massachusetts 02215
Telephone: 617-353-2670
Fax: 617-353-7368
E-mail: mba@bu.edu

Bryant College

Smithfield, Rhode Island

THE M.B.A.: FUTURE TRENDS AND DIRECTIONS

The old ways of preparing individuals for careers in business emphasized acquiring technical knowledge; analytical skills superseded people skills. This approach to business education is no longer sufficient to meet the needs of a highly competitive global economy. To prepare today's men and women for success in this new world of business, Bryant College has reinvented graduate education.

Our graduate programs bridge the gap between theory and practice, course work and experience, tangible skills and all the important intangibles necessary for success in any field at any level. Risk taking is expected; independent study projects are encouraged. And the same rigorous standards applied in teaching finance, management, and marketing are also applied in developing leadership skills and the ability to manage and work in teams and to negotiate.

Students not only learn facts and figures, but finesse as well. Bryant students become students of the art of business.

—Dr. Roger Anderson, Academic Dean

Programs and Curricular Focus

Bryant College's graduate courses are designed to connect to each other and, more importantly, to the real world by developing leadership, communication, and team-building skills. Students pursuing an M.B.A. may choose to concentrate in accounting, computer information systems, finance, health-care management, international business, management, management of operations and technology, or marketing. Bryant's full-time Master of Business Administration degree can be completed in a one- or two-year program. The two-year program is designed to meet the needs of students who hold undergraduate degrees in disciplines other than business. The program is presented through a series of interrelated course modules, professional development workshops, and a corporate live-case study. The academic program is supplemented by a series of specially designed professional development workshops that cover such topics as presentation skills, total quality management, and negotiation skills.

Students with an undergraduate degree in business have the option of completing the M.B.A. in one year of full-time evening study, depending on the number of courses waived. Course work for this program includes the Common Body of Knowledge foundation courses; the Advanced Body of Knowledge that provides in-depth study of key business

disciplines; and the concentration and elective courses that allow students to specialize in an area of particular interest.

The Master of Science in Accounting (M.S.A.) program is designed to meet the needs of students from a variety of academic backgrounds. Students with an undergraduate degree in accounting can complete the M.S.A. program in one year of full-time study. Individuals who possess a bachelor's degree in another academic discipline can generally complete the program in two years, depending on the number of prerequisites that need to be met.

Students and the M.B.A. Experience

Bryant graduate students possess diverse academic and professional backgrounds. Students have completed undergraduate degrees in business, social sciences, and engineering. Entering students are an average age of 28, with five or more years of professional work experience, primarily in service industries or manufacturing. Women represent 40 percent of the total graduate student population, and international students comprise approximately 30 percent of full-time M.B.A. enrollment.

The M.B.A. curriculum is infused with the challenges of professional practice. Courses are designed to connect to each other and to relate to the real

world, adding relevance, coherence, and immediacy to the curriculum. In all classes, the focus is on active, participative learning, using a variety of methods and media, including in-class exercises, role playing, case studies, debates, group projects, and lecture. Bryant's graduate programs provide rigorous immersion into the nuts and bolts of business, in such areas as accounting, finance, marketing, and management. There is also an in-depth examination of the all-important intangibles that can make or break a career. Bryant's programs do not just balance the books; they help students to become balanced professionally by developing skills such as leadership, communication, and team building.

❖ Global Focus

Bryant College created the Center for International Business and Economic Development (CIBED) to strengthen Rhode Island's role in international commerce, to nurture small businesses, and to aid in the conversion of Cold War technologies to peacetime enterprises. Under the CIBED umbrella are five highly successful corporate development programs that provide students with a global perspective in which to serve internships and assistantships: the Center for Management Development (CMD), Rhode Island Small Business Development Center (RISBDC), Rhode Island Export Assistance Center (RIEAC), Institute for Family Enterprise (IFE), and World Trade Center Rhode Island (WTCRI).

The Faculty

Bryant's graduate faculty members are distinguished authors, researchers, consultants, and professional leaders in national and international business, industry, and government. They are full-time professors recognized for their research contributions published in academic and practitioner journals. In addition, faculty members have experience in the areas of public accounting, private accounting, and consulting. They use their practical experience to illustrate and supplement business theories learned in class. Class size averages 23 students, allowing for valuable interaction between the students and professor.

The Business School Network
In the first year of the two-year program, students are provided an opportunity to apply what they are learning in the classroom with the introduction of the Living Case. In this semester-long exercise, students, faculty members, and executives from a corporate partner join in a collaborative effort to address the real-life issues of the sponsoring firm.

Students complete the Top Management Perspectives course during the second year of the program. This course provides students with an opportunity to investigate the depth and complexities of leadership. Through case studies and roundtable discussions with local business leaders, students gain a firsthand appreciation for the varied dimensions of leadership, including strategic vision, risk taking, entrepreneurship, creativity, social responsibility, communications, and relationship building.

Corporate Partnerships
Each year, Bryant College enters into a Living Case agreement with a company, under which the executives agree to allow students access to the company's premises, personnel, and documents. The Living Case modules involve a direct, hands-on encounter with a local company, with the objective of giving students a concrete business context for understanding the concepts presented in their first-year M.B.A. course work.

In module one, the students meet the company's executives, study industry competition, research the company from publicly available documents, and begin to work with specific interest groups, such as manufacturing, finance, marketing, accounting, technology, and international management.

During the second and third modules, students investigate and report on a variety of issues relevant both to their previous course work and to the company itself. Students explore topics of leadership challenges; ethical dilemmas; cross-cultural issues; manufacturing tools and technologies; new management methods, such as business process reengineering; and external issues, including government relations, economic conditions, and international trade agreements.

The College and Environs
Bryant College was founded in 1863. Today it continues in its mission to educate business leaders. In recognition of Bryant's success, it has consistently been rated as one of the best business specialty schools in the country by *U.S. News & World Report*.

The campus is located on 387 beautiful acres. Modern facilities include a comprehensive business library, computer center, language/learning laboratory, student center, classrooms, and a fitness/sports complex. Students interested in living on campus may choose between traditional double rooms and suites or award-winning town houses.

Placement
The Career Services Office offers a variety of services, including counseling and assessment of career decision making. Assistance is also available for résumé writing, interviewing, and job search strategies. Students can access a resource library to research careers or companies. A weekly publication lists current job openings. In their final year of study, students seeking entry-level professional positions can take part in off-campus recruiting and in on-campus recruiting that includes accompanying corporate presentations.

Admission
Because Bryant's program integrates real-world experience with concepts, it is preferred that applicants have a minimum of two years of work experience. Entry requirements include a bachelor's degree from an accredited institution. A strong score on the Graduate Management Admission Test (GMAT) is required. For students for whom English is not their primary language, a satisfactory score on the Test of English as a Foreign Language (TOEFL) is required. Prospective students must also submit an official transcript, two letters of recommendation, and a 500-word statement of objectives.

Finances
Tuition for the 1995–96 academic year is $13,200. The fee for a single room in the town houses during the 1995–96 school year is $4710; for a double, $4620. The cost of a room in the residence halls averages $3820. A $100 deposit is required to reserve a room. A nineteen-meal-per-week plan costs $2750.

Students may compete for graduate assistantships, working with an academic department related to their concentration area or with CIBED. Responsibilities may include faculty support, academic research, or preparation of class materials. Up to 80 percent of tuition cost may be offset with an assistantship, at which a student may work a maximum of 16 hours per week.

Approximately eight research assistantships are offered each academic year. Students support a particular faculty member's research. Income may be used for tuition, books, transportation, or personal expenses.

International Students
Thirty-one percent of the full-time graduate students come from outside of the United States. The Multicultural Student Services Office provides orientation directed to acclimating international students to American classroom conduct and culture. This office provides ongoing support and counsel.

Application Facts and Dates
Application deadlines are June 1 for the fall semester, December 1 for the spring semester, and April 12 for the summer session. There is a $40 application fee that must be submitted with the completed application form. For more information, students should contact:

Dr. Anne Parish
Director of Graduate Programs
Bryant College
1150 Douglas Pike
Smithfield, Rhode Island 02917
Telephone: 401-232-6230

California Institute of Integral Studies

San Francisco, California

"LIVE YOUR VALUES AND STILL PAY THE BILLS."

This quote from Claude Whitmyer, founding director of the MAB (a different kind of M.B.A.) tells what we're about. In the MAB and ODT programs at CIIS, we help students master the art of business, the craft of enterprise, and the way of the entrepreneur in a context of mindfulness of self, community, and planet.

Both our M.A. programs emphasize the concepts and practices of the "new paradigm" in business, including team learning, systems thinking, sustainable development, and accountability to the local community. The goal of the programs and their graduates is to do good while doing well.

Most importantly, in terms of the quality of students' learning, the principles of success in management, business, and organizational development are part of our educational method. Students learn the professional skills through direct practice and immersion. We do our best to function as a learning organization and to walk the talk.

—Dr. James Stuckey, Program Director

Programs and Curricular Focus

CIIS offers M.A. degree programs in business (MAB) and in organizational development and transformation (ODT). Participation in both programs involves total immersion in the language, thought, and reality of the world of business and organizational development. Self-directed study and intensive reflection engage the student in a highly interactive process. This process includes the design, implementation, and evaluation of one's individual learning plan; team learning; and experiential and dialogic exploration of basic business skills.

The MAB program is designed primarily for people interested in creating or re-creating their own businesses, as owners, partners, or managers. The ODT program is designed for people who want to work as independent or internal consultants in businesses or nonprofit organizations. Each serves as background for the other and is aimed at those who want to serve as midwives in the transformation of organizations, helping them meet personal, ethical, social, and ecological goals along with financial ones. The programs share content, method, direction, and faculty.

In the MAB program students work closely in learning teams of 15 to 20 students for most of the two-year program. A six-day intensive series of seminars and workshops inaugurates students into the realities of adult learning and self-evaluation. In the second year, a

strong emphasis is placed on proposal, implementation, and evaluation of the Project Demonstrating Mastery (PDM), which may be a master's thesis.

The basic curriculum is organized around nine monthly seminars, each of which includes a three-day weekend residency. The learning experience begins three weeks prior to the three-day weekend, through a computer-mediated dialogue about the skill being learned, and culminates in the fourth week, during which students write final integration papers.

The ODT curriculum is as forward-looking as the MAB's, but ODT classes are generally held in the evenings on a weekly basis to accommodate the schedules of working professionals. In ODT, the learning teams are formed during the initial retreat, a full weekend of seminars and workshops that develop strong communication patterns among students and between students and faculty members. During their first year, students take classes with others in their learning team, becoming quite efficient at sharing resources and ideas, to accomplish team learning goals as well as to contribute to the individual directions within the group.

Particularly in the second-year, ODT courses are arranged to fit the needs of students who are then more deeply involved in organizational development work, as interns and professionals. Some courses are arranged to meet on week-

ends, and the on-line environment is an option in some courses.

Students and the M.B.A. Experience

Most students in the Institute's MAB and ODT programs are adults, working in the world of business or other organizations. While the need to work is often seen as a problem for graduate students, in this case there are also benefits. The program's method of combining direct experience with theory and disciplined reflection means that a significant portion of students' professional work can be used as fieldwork and as material for case studies.

Students have chosen the Institute's business programs because they want something more than a business-as-usual education. They are seeking integration of personal, social, and spiritual dimensions with the technical knowledge and skills of the business and organizational world.

❖ Global Focus

San Francisco is one of the most international cities in the world, and the student population at CIIS increasingly reflects this, with MAB/ODT students from Canada, China, Japan, Korea, Nepal, and Norway.

In the summer of 1994, a group of 11 students and a faculty member spent one month in a northern province of China operating as a team of consultants to a major wood products factory and learning the skills of cultural synergy. Future projects are being planned for China, Russia, and India.

Special Features

Students in both programs engage in real work as part of the curriculum. That work may be part of their regular job, it may be the real work of starting a new business, or it may be the real work of organizational development within the Institute or within the program. Here, students are invited to participate as on-site consultants.

The Faculty

Faculty members are selected on the basis of their professional knowledge, skill, and

experience and on the basis of their ability to teach in a way that parallels the best of modern management theory. Inviting significant collaboration by "employees," for example, is as important to the teaching/learning process at CIIS as it is in any other organizational or management situation. Along with having academic credentials, MAB/ODT faculty members are successful business-people, managers, and consultants in the Bay Area.

The Business School Network

Alumni in business for themselves or working in local corporate offices, such as Levi-Strauss and Sun Microsystems, bring the real world back to the classroom and also provide contacts for students in that world.

The College and Environs

The Institute's four-story headquarters in San Francisco's Haight-Ashbury district near Golden Gate Park provides a library, bookstore, cafeteria, lounge, and meditation room as well as classrooms and offices. But the Institute is experiencing more growth than its present location can handle. It is expected that during 1995 and 1996 the entire Institute will be moved to much more spacious quarters at the Presidio, a former Army post that has become America's newest national park. This 1,500-acre "campus" of meadows, forests, streams, beaches, and historic buildings, adjacent to the Golden Gate

Bridge, will eventually be the home to dozens of organizations involved in programs of sustainable development and global issues. The Presidio community will share a wide range of intellectual, professional, and athletic facilities. Finally, with San Francisco Bay, the Golden Gate Bridge, and the Pacific Ocean on the north and west borders of the Presidio, and the city on its other doorstep, the Presidio is an ideal location for living and studying at CIIS.

San Francisco is home of the World Business Academy and has the country's greatest concentration of members of Business for Social Responsibility.

Admission

Applicants should have a B.A. from an accredited institution and at least five years of work experience in business, nonprofit, or government settings. A grade point average of 3.0 or higher is required.

Decisions regarding admission are based on consideration of potential for success, maturity, and motivation for educational and personal development and the congruence of the applicant's world view with the Institute's philosophy and purpose.

Finances

The cost of attending CIIS depends on the number of courses and units taken by the student. The MAB is designed as a 72-unit course of study over two years.

The M.A. in ODT requires 60 units, and the Certificate Program in ODT requires 30 units. The per-unit fee was $270 in 1994–95. Books and incidentals are estimated to cost about $1000 per year, and on-line fees for the MAB have averaged $30–$40 per month during the 1994–95 year.

International Students

The Institute welcomes applications from international students. The International Student Office provides newcomers with orientation, special programs, and social and cultural opportunities throughout their stay at the Institute. Other resources include international student advisers, a faculty liaison, process groups, American health insurance information, a student handbook guide, a newsletter, and American Friends of International Students, a volunteer service that supports the International Student Office in its efforts to provide special services and introduce the students to America's cultures.

Application Facts and Dates

All admissions materials must be received by the Admissions Office before a personal interview is offered. These materials must include a completed application form and application fee, a four- to six-page autobiographical statement, a one-page statement of educational and professional goals, and original official transcripts.

The deadlines for application are August 1 for entrance to the MAB program in the fall, July 1 for entrance to the ODT programs in the fall, and October 15 for entrance to the ODT programs in the winter.

For MAB information, students should contact:

Bridget Hughes-Weissmann, Program Coordinator
CIIS
765 Ashbury Street
San Francisco, California 94117
Telephone: 415-753-6100 Ext. 294
Fax: 415-753-1169

For ODT information, students should contact:

Jeff Aitken, Program Coordinator
CIIS
765 Ashbury Street
San Francisco, California 94117
Telephone: 415-753-6100 Ext. 288
Fax: 415-753-1169

Case Western Reserve University

Weatherhead School of Management

Cleveland, Ohio

> ▶ *The Weatherhead School offers an M.B.A. experience unlike other programs. With its focus on creating human, economic, and intellectual value, the Weatherhead M.B.A. program provides the knowledge as well as the skills necessary for effective leadership.*
>
> *Each Weatherhead student receives a personal assessment and designs an individual learning plan. Classes are small, and our faculty are easily accessible. Weatherhead's Mentor Program was the first to provide one-on-one career guidance from executive mentors. Our students gain practical experience through field projects and internships and international perspective through study abroad.*
>
> *We invite you to discover the distinctive Weatherhead M.B.A. experience.*
> —Scott S. Cowen, Dean

Programs and Curricular Focus

The Weatherhead School of Management has developed a unique approach to the M.B.A. degree that has been cited in *Business Week*'s Guide to the Best B-Schools as "one of the world's most innovative M.B.A. programs." The learning objectives of the Weatherhead M.B.A. program are achieved in four stages: management assessment and development, the core courses, perspectives courses, and advanced elective course work.

Management assessment and development begins during the first semester with a course providing the guidance and interpretation needed to plan an effective and relevant M.B.A. experience. Each student develops an individualized learning plan that maximizes the use of resources and course offerings at the Weatherhead School and stimulates a continuing process of self-directed learning.

The core courses form the backbone of the M.B.A. program. The core combines knowledge in each management discipline with the concepts of value creation, global awareness, and management effectiveness. Perspectives courses liberalize the curriculum with an interdisciplinary approach to instruction, decision making, and problem solving.

Students select a sequence of six elective courses in one of eleven concentrations during the final two semesters of the M.B.A. program to develop depth and diversity in their areas of special interest. In selecting concentrations, focus is given to both developing knowledge in the area of interest and accomplishing the objectives of the student's learning plan.

The Weatherhead School offers both a four-semester M.B.A. curriculum and an accelerated program for undergraduate business majors beginning in June and ending in May of the following year. Both programs are available on a full-time and part-time basis. Joint-degree programs with the schools of law, nursing, and engineering are available along with master's programs in accountancy and nonprofit organizations and the Executive Master of Business Administration degree program.

Students and the M.B.A. Experience

The Weatherhead program is composed of highly qualified individuals representing a diversity of academic, professional, and cultural backgrounds and experiences. The average student is 27 years old, with four years of work experience. Women comprise 32 percent of the class. The campus culture is enriched by international students, who represent 25 percent of the class and fifteen countries. A typical class represents twenty-five states and twelve countries.

Weatherhead students have undergraduate degrees in a wide variety of disciplines, including business administration, economics, social sciences, and engineering.

❖ Global Focus

The Weatherhead School of Management is committed to providing its students with the educational and practical experience that will enable them to manage competitively in the global marketplace. M.B.A. students may choose a concentration in international management or complete a joint M.B.A./Master of International Management degree program with the Thunderbird School in Glendale, Arizona. Internship opportunities are available in several countries for M.B.A. students during the summer term. The Weatherhead School participates in third-semester M.B.A. exchange programs with schools of management on four continents. Weatherhead students may participate as Agency for International Development (AID) business advisers in developing countries at the end of their first year in the program and in the M.B.A. Enterprise Corps in one- to two-year post–M.B.A. positions in firms in the former Eastern Bloc nations.

Special Features

During the first year of the program, the Weatherhead Office of Career Planning and Placement matches students with Cleveland-area executives and managers who help to focus students' academic and career interests. Along with the traditional business concentrations, Weatherhead offers concentrations in the areas of health-care management, technology management, nonprofit management, and entrepreneurial studies.

The Faculty

There are 80 full-time faculty members, all of whom have a doctorate in their field. Many of the faculty members have earned international reputations for teaching and research. The faculty is housed in seven different departments: accountancy, banking and finance, economics, MIDS, marketing and policy studies, operations research, and organizational behavior. Students benefit from a student-faculty ratio of 14:1.

The Business School Network

The Weatherhead School has forged a strong network of corporate partners in the northeast Ohio area (headquarters of thirty of the Fortune 500 corporations).

Students engage in a variety of field projects under the guidance of experienced area executives. The curriculum is enhanced by guest lecturers and speakers from the corporate community who represent and communicate excellence, enterprise, and depth of experience in the practice of management.

The Visiting Committee of the Weatherhead School of Management is composed of leaders in the international community who have a continuing concern for the quality of management education. The committee provides counsel and assistance to the School throughout the year.

The College and Environs

The Weatherhead School of Management resides in a parklike campus setting in Cleveland's University Circle. Campus neighbors include Severance Hall, home of the Cleveland Orchestra, and the Cleveland Art and History museums. The Weatherhead campus places students within what is probably the most extensive concentration of educational, scientific, medical, and cultural institutions in the United States.

Technology Environment

The Weatherhead computer laboratory houses both IBM-compatible and Macintosh computers, which are connected via a local area network. The network makes available a wide variety of software, languages, and peripheral equipment. Qualified support personnel are on duty daily, and computer instruction and seminars are available. The laboratory has five computer-supported conference rooms for use by Weatherhead students. The School maintains two computer-supported classrooms used for computer literacy and M.B.A. class instruction. The University computing resources include a unique fiber-optic network linking over eighty-five campus buildings. Users have access to a range of information resources and networks. Other resources include an integrated on-line library system and access to off-campus resources, including the Internet.

Placement

The Weatherhead School's Office of Career Planning and Placement provides a placement program for each student. It assists students in focusing career interests and invites recruiters to campus to participate in information sessions, receptions, career forums, seminars, workshops, and mock interviews. A full schedule of placement interviews for both summer and permanent positions is conducted in the fall and spring semesters. In the CareerNet program, alumni from across the country provide advice and placement assistance to students and graduates. Students can access the entire M.B.A. alumni database through the School computer lab. The Weatherhead School is a founding member of the National M.B.A. Consortium in Chicago, a cooperative corporate interview day for M.B.A. students, with eighty separate corporate schedules.

Admission

Applicants are admitted on the basis of academic and professional accomplishments, performance on the GMAT, individual career goals, written recommendations, and responses to interview and application essay questions. The median GMAT score is 590. The average undergraduate GPA is 3.1. Class size is limited to 140 students.

The Test of English as a Foreign Language is required of all applicants whose native language is not English and who graduated from an educational institution where the language of instruction was not English. Alumnet, a directory of Weatherhead M.B.A. alumni throughout the world, provides prospective students the opportunity to learn more about the School by helping them contact recent graduates.

Finances

The 1995–96 tuition and fees are $9200 per semester. Books and supplies are estimated at $375 per semester. The estimate for room and board is $4400 per semester.

A limited number of merit scholarships are available for individuals with exceptional academic, professional, and life experiences. The School offers an Express Financial Aid Service to expedite determination of the financing options that are available.

International Students

International students represent 25 percent of the student population. The School offers international students a tuition stabilization plan, internships, and multicultural experiences through the multicultural task force and International Business Club.

Application Facts and Dates

The final application deadline for all applicants is usually in early April. For international candidates living outside the United States, the early decision deadline is usually in mid-February. For more information, students should contact:

Ms. Linda Gaston
Director of Admissions
The Weatherhead School of
  Management
Case Western Reserve University
Cleveland, Ohio 44106-7235
Telephone: 800-723-0203
Fax: 216-368-5548
E-mail: lxg10@po.cwru.edu

Central Connecticut State University

New Britain, Connecticut

MEETING TOMORROW'S WORLD TODAY

Our new International M.B.A. is but another indication of CCSU's commitment to international programs and to placing Connecticut firmly in the global community. Keen competition, global environment, changing market conditions, and diverse work forces are a few of the challenges facing business today. Our newly designed program brings together the best new thinking in business administration. The courses are fast-paced, interactive, and intensive. Dialogue provides the forum for our teaching-learning partnership.

The School of Business has sponsored teaching, research, and outreach activities in response to the University's mission to provide international programs and activities that facilitate local participation in the global community. Our faculty has been active in creating The Institute for Business Studies in Wroclaw, Poland, and developing and teaching an accounting program for Moldovan entrepreneurs and students. In the past year, faculty members have been involved in various programs worldwide, including England, Scotland, Moldova, Poland, Hong Kong, the Republic of China, and the People's Republic of China. As a student in this program, you will have the opportunity to work and learn with our distinguished and dedicated faculty.

—Walt Parker, Interim Dean

Programs and Curricular Focus

The program focuses on doing business in the world today. It is not a course of study about managing transnationals; rather, it is a program that teaches the ways the global economy affects competitiveness. The program enables students to develop skill in identifying opportunities and needs, analyzing situations from multiple perspectives, framing arguments for positions in decision making, and building awareness of the downside of decision choices as well as the benefit. The goal is to develop student advocacy in the face of balanced presentation. The program cultivates an active, experiential, interactive learning environment by using cases, computers, presentation, and debate.

An introductory core of courses for students who were nonbusiness undergraduates (24 credit hours) consists of accounting, economics, finance, management, and marketing. Students holding undergraduate degrees in business may begin with the international core of courses (18 credit hours), which includes contemporary issues, international accounting, international marketing, international finance, international management information systems, and international management. The first four courses must be taken in sequence. There

is a choice of elective sets (12 credit hours); this includes a general business set, an international studies set, and an accounting set. A final global strategy capstone course (3 credit hours) is required of all students.

The general business elective set consists of team-taught, integrative courses that feature topics spanning all the functional disciplines, including production/distribution, leadership, performance, and environment. The international studies elective set consists of contemporary world problems, international diversity and integration, global economic development and trade, and cross-cultural communication. The accounting elective set is designed for accountants who would like to meet the 150-hour requirement for CPA certification. It consists of financial theory, advanced auditing, budgeting, and advanced taxation.

Students and the M.B.A. Experience

CCSU has developed a cosmopolitan program in an enriching environment that includes students from different professions, cultures, ages, and experiences. In this new program, students range in age from 24 to 50. Classes include women

and minorities, international students, and students not born in the United States. Currently, students come from the United States and Europe but are sought from all over the world. Students come from the ranks of analysts, managers, teachers, and business owners. Diversity in the I.M.B.A. is part of the special character of the program. Multicultural, multidisciplinary discussion and teamwork are essential thrusts for balanced presentation.

Special Features

The program offers several distinctive features. The international core includes a sequence of intensive courses that fosters the study of competitiveness in the global environment. The general business elective set of team-taught, integrative topics fosters a multidisciplinary view. The diverse student body enhances the discussion of multicultural issues. An intensive, interactive teaching-learning dialogue brings forward the best new thinking in business administration issues.

The Faculty

Faculty members are committed to teaching excellence and are active participants in the international community of teaching and research. The faculty members have had practical business experience in the United States. Eighty percent have had international teaching and research experience. Research ranges from large database studies to survey and directed interviews, as well as from analytic modeling to case research. Many faculty members are currently active in consulting and practical business applications.

The Business School Network

CCSU is ideally located near manufacturing, service, and financial centers. Central Connecticut is the home of United Technology, The Stanley Works, Loctite, Aetna Life and Casualty, and other Fortune 500 companies. The variety of businesses in the central Connecticut area provides knowledgeable guest lecturers and offers students an opportunity to observe global businesses in action. The School of Business Entrepreneurial

CENTRAL CONNECTICUT STATE UNIVERSITY

Support Center offers opportunities for students to assist emerging and small businesses. The University also sponsors high-technology incubators for entrepreneurs.

The College and Environs

CCSU, founded in 1849, is Connecticut's oldest public institution of higher learning. The 314-acre suburban campus is located in central Connecticut, only 15 minutes from the capital city of Hartford, 2 hours from Boston, and 2½ hours from New York City. The ocean lies less than 1 hour south of the campus, and the Berkshires and mountains of Vermont and New Hampshire are not far away.

The thirty-nine-building, coeducational campus enrolls approximately 6,000 full-time and an additional 6,000 part-time students. The School of Business enrolls over 3,000 students in the Departments of Accounting, Finance, International Business, Management and

Organization, Management Information Systems, and Marketing. The School of Business has 48 full-time faculty members, and graduate class size averages 15 students, producing an environment that values teaching excellence and high-quality educational experience.

Placement

CCSU has a placement office that offers career counseling, résumé books, and job listing services. The placement office works to build strong ties with recruiters and business professionals.

Admission

Applicants must meet the general admission requirements of the University. Academic evaluation for M.B.A. admission is based primarily on the applicant's undergraduate record and the score on the GMAT. Applicants are required to submit

evidence of proficiency in microcomputer application software and knowledge of statistics, as well as an essay on how acceptance into the program complements their career goals and aspirations. International students must also submit a satisfactory TOEFL score (not less than 550). Admission is generally for the fall semester. The University adheres to a rolling admission policy for graduate students. Conditional admission is granted to students who need to take all or part of the undergraduate introductory core and meet all other requirements. Applicants are also expected to have a proficiency in a foreign language before program completion. Full- and part-time matriculation is available.

Finances

Tuition and fees are subject to change without notice. In 1995–96, the full-time per semester tuition and required fees are projected to be approximately $1841 for resident students and $4377 for nonresidents. The per credit cost for part-time graduate courses in 1995–96 is projected to be $157 (e.g., a 3-credit course with a $41 per semester registration fee is $512). Limited on-campus housing is available (approximately $1200 per semester). A variety of meal plans are available for on- and off-campus residents (approximately $1000 per semester). Specific information related to financial aid may be obtained from the Financial Aid Office, Davidson Hall, Room 107. A limited number of graduate assistantships are available throughout the campus. These are normally available only to students who have successfully completed a semester of graduate study at Central Connecticut State University. Applicants should contact the Office of the Dean, School of Graduate Studies, regarding assistantships and scholarships. There is at present no financial aid available for non-U.S. students. International students must provide a Declaration of Finance form, which documents financial responsibility. Qualified applicants who cannot demonstrate financial responsibility will not be admitted.

Application Facts and Dates

CCSU has a continuing admission/review process. For more information, contact:

Graduate School Admissions
Central Connecticut State University
1615 Stanley Street
New Britain, Connecticut 06050
Telephone: 203-832-3261
Fax: 203-832-3219

Chapman University

School of Business and Economics

Orange, California

> ### STRONG FACULTY, SMALL PROGRAM = STUDENT SUCCESS
>
> *The Chapman M.B.A. benefits from efforts to build a strong faculty with a commitment to excellent teaching and research, linked to the entrepreneurial heritage of our Orange County location and building on the strong analytical framework of our economics faculty.*
>
> *Combined, this small program offers students good working relationships with a competitive faculty who are committed to student success.*
>
> *The Chapman M.B.A. and our School of Business and Economics represent important resources for competitive U.S. and global learning. We welcome your consideration of our program.*
>
> —Richard McDowell, Dean

Programs and Curricular Focus

The Chapman M.B.A. offers students the concepts, tools, and techniques necessary to solve business problems in a competitive world. The program offers, within a supportive and personalized environment, rigorous training in the analytical skills today's managers and entrepreneurs need. In addition, the Chapman M.B.A. offers its graduates the skills needed to understand the international and strategic dimensions of business decisions. Specifically, the program is designed to provide a solid economic foundation for making business decisions; develop skills in applying financial, marketing, management, and statistical techniques to complex management problems; and improve skills in effectively presenting and implementing solutions to business problems.

The M.B.A. program consists of four segments totaling 51 credit units. The first segment is an 18-credit foundation segment, part or all of which can be waived if the student provides evidence of previous course work or satisfactory scores on a proficiency exam. The second segment consists of 24 credit units, comprising the core courses, which encompass eight functional areas of business: managerial accounting, marketing, organizational behavior, corporate finance, quantitative decision models, international business, business forecasting, and business strategy. Segment three consists of 9 elective units through which the student may customize the M.B.A. program according to interests and career goals. The fourth segment includes the comprehensive examination, which requires the student to integrate the

material covered in the core curriculum across functional lines.

Chapman offers an executive M.B.A. program for working professionals with organizational experience. The two-year program includes two domestic residentials as well as an international trip designed to provide exposure to managerial practices abroad.

Students and the M.B.A. Experience

Chapman's School of Business and Economics has a diverse M.B.A. population totaling 175 full- and part-time students. The average age at entrance to the program is 25, with two and one-half years of work experience. Women comprise 36 percent of the M.B.A. student population, and minority students make up 31 percent. Foreign nationals comprise 20 percent of the student body, with 30 percent coming from Europe, 63 percent from Asia, and the remaining 7 percent from throughout the world.

❖ Global Focus

Chapman's Center for International Business was founded in 1992. Its goal is to establish a high-quality international database and to provide facilities and support for students and faculty engaged in international business and economics research. The center also disseminates results of its research to the business community and consults both U.S. and foreign companies on all data required to make decisions for international trade, including markets, business conditions, and the legal and regulatory environments. Chapman's

School of Business and Economics was recently awarded $1.5 million from the Fletcher Jones Foundation for an endowed Chair in International Business. This greatly widens the work of the faculty and the center.

Special Features

The School of Business and Economics offers the field experience program for M.B.A. students with limited work experience or those seeking to make a major career change. M.B.A. students have the opportunity to gain practical work experience through 6 units of internship. Upon enrollment, students are evaluated based on their

CHAPMAN UNIVERSITY

interests and skills. This assessment is used to assist the students in obtaining career-related internship positions. The program's goal is to produce students who graduate with work experience relevant to their career objectives.

The Faculty

Faculty members at the School of Business and Economics have as their first priority the enhancement of the learning experience. Chapman has a long tradition of emphasizing outstanding teaching. Faculty members have chosen to teach in a small school, with an emphasis on personalized education. They are accessible and approachable. At the same time, the Chapman faculty members are from major universities, are committed to research and scholarly endeavors, and are well-published in major academic journals.

The Business School Network

The Center for Economic Research provides the cornerstone for Chapman's strong relationship with the Southern California business community. The center, with the involvement of students, has developed and continuously improves a complex econometric model used to forecast economic trends for Southern California. Over 900 business leaders participate annually in the School of Business and Economics forecast events. There are numerous additional opportunities for students to interface with business leaders through guest lectures and speaker series. The endowment for the Ralph W. Leatherby Chair in Entrepreneurship sponsors conferences and guest speakers on small business.

The College and Environs

Founded in 1861, Chapman University is situated on a 42-acre parklike campus in Orange, California. The mission of the University is to provide a personalized education of distinction that leads students to inquiring, ethical, and productive lives as global citizens. Chapman is located 35 miles southeast of Los Angeles and 90 miles from San Diego and Mexico. Ocean beaches are less than 10 miles away; mountains and deserts are within an hour's drive.

Facilities

The Thurmond Clark Library contains 184,000 volumes and subscribes to 1,845 periodical titles, 257 of which are business periodicals. Moody's Company Data on CD-ROM provides access to company information on over 10,000 U.S. companies. Business literature can be researched by using the compact disc ABI/INFORM. All items on the business periodical index are available either on the shelves, on disc, or through interlibrary loan.

The use of computer technology is an integral part of the M.B.A. program. The School of Business and Economics has an IBM-based computer lab, with staff available for individual assistance. In addition, workshops are given for those who need to learn or refresh their skills. For those students who prefer to use Macintosh systems, there is a Macintosh lab on campus. The University is part of the Internet system, and each student receives an Internet account number.

Placement

The Career Development Center offers a number of services and programs that

assist students with their professional development. The dual focus includes both assisting students in identifying their career goals and preparing them for an effective job search. On-campus recruiting takes place in the fall (for accounting firms) and spring semesters. National as well as local companies come to campus to recruit students. Networking is encouraged through alumni mentor programs and alumni career days.

Admission

Admission to the M.B.A. program requires a bachelor's degree from an accredited college or university, a completed application for admission, transcripts of all previous course work, an acceptable score on the GMAT, and two letters of recommendation. International students must submit a TOEFL score of 550 or above and a statement of financial resources.

Finances

The 1994–95 tuition for the M.B.A. program was $400 per credit for either part- or full-time study. Tuition for the executive M.B.A. was $32,000 for the two-year program. Financial aid opportunities are offered to graduate students through tuition grants, graduate fellowships, and loans. The loan programs include federally sponsored Stafford subsidized and unsubsidized student loans and privately sponsored loans.

International Students

Twenty percent of Chapman's M.B.A. population comes from outside the United States. The International Students Services office acts as a source of information and assistance, with the goal of making the international experience a comfortable and productive one. The office sponsors an orientation program; counseling on academic, financial and personal matters; assistance in class registration; information on immigration requirements; and information on social and cultural events. Various informational and social events are organized throughout the year.

Application Facts and Dates

Applications for the fall, spring, and summer sessions should be received by June 15, November 15, and April 15, respectively. The deadline for consideration for financial aid is March 2. For information and application materials, students should make inquiries to:

Office of Graduate Admissions
Chapman University
333 N. Glassell Street
Orange, California 92666
Telephone: 714-997-6786

Chulalongkorn University

Bangkok, Thailand

> The Southeast Asian economy is arguably the fastest-growing one in the world, and Thailand is playing a significant role in that expansion. In order to facilitate this dynamism, the Sasin Graduate Institute of Business Administration seeks to meld proven Western business theories and practices with Asian sensibilities by offering a two-year M.B.A. program second to none in this region. A unique academic venture among Chulalongkorn University, the J. L. Kellogg Graduate School of Management of Northwestern University, and the Wharton School of the University of Pennsylvania, Sasin aims at producing graduates comparable in knowledge and skills with those trained at leading business schools abroad.
> —Toemsakdi Krishnamra, Director

Programs and Curricular Focus

The management subjects taught in Sasin's M.B.A. program are of vital importance to Asian countries. Teaching is by case study balanced with lectures, seminars, and group work, with emphasis placed on the relationship between theory and practice. The curriculum stresses the application of the theoretical training to the practical problems managers face today and are likely to face in the future. Student activities, too, address current management issues through direct interaction with the business community in numerous events relevant to Asian needs.

The curriculum is a tightly integrated program, resembling those taught at both Kellogg and Wharton. Some adaptations have been made to suit the Asian environment. The overall program consists of thirteen core and twelve supportive courses. Although intended to emphasize general management education, concentrations in any functional field of management—finance, marketing, operations management, or human resources management—are possible.

By design, M.B.A. classes are small, thus offering students the rare educational experience of personal relationships with faculty and other students. Approximately 110 students are admitted to the program each year.

Sasin also offers a Master of Management degree program for midcareer executives, senior executives, and entrepreneurs. It is a two-year general management program, with classes meeting every Saturday and some Wednesday evenings. The Senior Executive Program, an intensive three-week residential program, is designed for senior executives holding key management positions in business or government who wish to broaden their knowledge in management.

Students and the M.B.A. Experience

It is no cliché to say that enrolling at Sasin gives students the chance to study with Thailand's future leaders. Comprising the crème-de-la-crème of a dynamic middle- to upper-class cross section of the Thai population as well as a strong international representation, the student body is a self-motivating, doggedly loyal web of trust and friendship. The average Sasin student is 25 years old and has two years of work experience; a third of these students already have had considerable experience overseas. The student body is also split evenly along gender lines. Students are diverse in their educational backgrounds and work experiences.

Both inside and outside the classroom, cooperation among students is strongly encouraged. Problems frequently are assigned to groups of students rather than to individuals, thus giving students experience in working as part of a team to achieve a common solution. This teamwork is reinforced in extracurricular activities that enrich the students' academic lives through interactions with the business community in Thailand as well as through organization of charity events centered around traditional Thai celebrations.

❖ Global Focus

Sasin offers the opportunity for second-year students to broaden their international business knowledge by studying abroad. M.B.A. students with superior academic records may participate in the Student Exchange Program by spending a quarter or semester at one of Sasin's cooperating institutions: J. L. Kellogg Graduate School of Management of Northwestern University, The Wharton School of the University of Pennsylvania, The Fuqua School of Business of Duke University, the University of Southern California, Cornell University, York University in Canada, or the International University of Japan. Exchange students may take up to four quarter courses or three semester courses.

Special Features

The first year begins with the four-day orientation program called Conceptual Issues in Management Week. The program is set up to orient students in various fields of management. Prior to the start of the M.B.A. program, Sasin also provides tutorial courses in mathematics, accounting, and economics for students who do not have sufficient background in those areas.

Another feature is the M.B.A. Conference, which is aimed at strengthening the relationships among the students and providing the unique opportunity for them to meet and have informal discussion with Sasin alumni who have succeeded in various fields of business. The conference is a three-day residential seminar held during the break between the first and second modules.

The Faculty

The faculty members for the program are drawn exclusively from Kellogg and Wharton as well as Sasin and its staff of adjunct professors. They offer a rich combination of experience in professional management problems and practices, having often served as consultants in industry, government, health care, education, and transportation throughout the United States. Textbooks and casebooks written by these faculty

Sasin Graduate Institute of Business Administration at Chulalongkorn University.

members are used in management schools both in the United States and in other countries.

The College and Environs

Sasin is located on the campus of Chulalongkorn University, the oldest and best-known university in Thailand. The campus covers an area of 500 acres in the Patumwan District. The University consists of seventeen faculties, three graduate schools, eleven institutes, and other administrative offices. Sasin is situated in downtown Bangkok, within easy reach of an infinite variety of businesses, civil service offices, and shopping centers.

Bangkok, the capital city, has a population of 6 million and is extremely urbanized. It caters to diverse interests. There are temples, museums, and other historic sites for those interested in traditional Thai culture.

Facilities

Sasin students have access to all the University's recreation and sports facilities. Other facilities include a centrally air-conditioned study center, a special business and management library, and access to Chulalongkorn University's highly advanced computer center and international electronic communication networks and microcomputer laboratory.

Placement

Sasin graduates work for most of the best corporations or organizations in Thailand. Major industries often chosen by Sasin graduates are finance and securities, banking, and manufacturing. Many firms hold informal receptions for M.B.A. students to enable them to meet with corporate representatives and to learn about the companies before the interviews. In addition, many employers recruit through the Placement Office, which arranges for formal job interviews on campus. Many employers are familiar with Sasin because they take part in providing internships, corporate scholarships, or otherwise assist the M.B.A. program.

Admission

Sasin looks for students with outstanding potential for leadership as well as the intellectual and interpersonal skills needed to make a meaningful contribution to the academic and extracurricular life of Sasin. Rather than rely on an admissions formula that stipulates a minimum test score, grade point average, or years of work experience, the Admissions Committee prefers to evaluate the combined effect of an applicant's prior academic achievements and personal accomplishments for use as the basis of its decision. In order to make such an evaluation, applicants should take the GMAT, submit official transcripts from all universities previously attended, submit two recommendations, and meet with a Kellogg or Sasin representative for an interview. All nonnative English-speaking applicants must take the TOEFL.

Finances

Estimated expenses for the two-year program are as follows. In the first year, tuition is $8580; in the second year, tuition is $7920. There is an electronic data processing fee of $120. Books and supplies cost $600. Living accommodations are $7200, and meals and personal expenses total $4800; these two figures are estimated for students who live on campus. Miscellaneous expenses are $200. The comprehensive cost comes to $21,500 for the first year and $20,840 for the second.

Application Facts and Dates

The application for May admission must be received by January 15. M.B.A. interviews in Bangkok are normally scheduled for two weeks in February. Notification of the admission decision is normally mailed to the applicants by March 1. For more information, contact:

Admissions Office
Sasin Graduate Institute of Business
  Administration of Chulalongkorn
  University
Sasa Patasala Building
Soi Chulalongkorn 12, Phyathai Road
Bangkok 10330
Thailand
Telephone: 662-216-8833 Ext. 3850-1
  or 3856-7
Fax: 662-215-3797

City University

Bellevue, Washington

DEVELOPING BUSINESS LEADERS FOR THE TWENTY-FIRST CENTURY

Innovation, responsiveness, and commitment to excellence have been City University's standards since our founding in 1973. Our M.B.A. program exemplifies these standards. Well-respected and well-established, the M.B.A. program at City University assists learners in achieving excellence in their chosen field via teaching and learning communities that foster exploration, examination, and extension of professional theory and practice. Students are compelled to reach inward to achieve personal leadership, reach outward to aid their communities, and reach forward to embrace changes and challenges—today, tomorrow, and in the twenty-first century.

—Douglas Arnold, Associate Dean

Programs and Curricular Focus

City University's M.B.A. program is oriented toward adult learners who are self-starters, who seek recognition as leaders among their peers, and whose intellectual curiosity takes them beyond the simple finding of solutions to advanced inquiry and the formulation of new questions.

The M.B.A. program offers a strategic systems approach to leading and managing organizations. Specifically, the M.B.A. focuses on those strategic systems that are critical to transforming the way we work. These systems are approached from a conceptual framework that is
strategy-driven, stakeholder-oriented, and teamwork-based, supported by data-based decision making, guided by vision and a whole systems organizational design, and enhanced by continuous improvement through organizational learning.
Within this framework, students explore established business practices and learn to understand and anticipate future trends as well. They analyze management principles, strategies, and philosophies in regard to the local workplace as well as the global economy.

Students may pursue one of a dozen M.B.A. specializations. The structure of the M.B.A. is simple: a common 33-credit core and (with some exceptions) a 12-credit specialty block.

The common core is a series of eleven courses that build skills essential to the successful completion of a graduate degree program in business. At the same time, they introduce the major sectors of

knowledge whose application is important to each of the respective specializations.

To the greatest extent possible, every core course explores the ethical and philosophical issues underlying the subject, affords an opportunity for oral presentation and analytical research, and relates content to leadership, socially conscious, humanitarian, and environmental dimensions.

The specialty block, effectively the major component, aggregates four courses with content particular to each specialization. Regardless of specialty, all M.B.A. students hone skills in general management, leadership, and organizational development and change management.

City University also offers a combined M.B.A./M.P.A. for those students whose career pursuits place them in the arena of both governmental and profit-oriented organizational management.

Students and the M.B.A. Experience

Of the students enrolled in the M.B.A. program, 34 percent are women, 33 percent represent members of minority groups, and 11 percent are international students. The average age of the students is 38 years. Consequently, students who enter City University's M.B.A. program typically have several years of work experience behind them.

Course work combines textbook theory with current, real-world case studies. Research is a significant component in all courses; it is second in emphasis only to in-class discussion.

Faculty members encourage discussion, rather than sticking to straight lecture; this is facilitated by the fact that City University maintains an average class size of 19 students. Students also engage in team projects and student presentations.

❖ Global Focus

City University's M.B.A. program enjoys a global focus for several reasons. Every core M.B.A. course contains an international business slant, thanks to specially selected texts and readings. Cultural exchange also takes place in the classroom when students from different countries travel to pursue their M.B.A. at the University's various sites in North America, Germany, and Switzerland.

As City University makes its M.B.A. program available on-line, education will become truly global. Students from all around the world will gather in "electronic classrooms" to share learning, ideas, and experience.

Special Features

One of the most innovative features of City University's M.B.A. program is the variety of formats in which it is offered. Students are welcome to take classes in the daytime, evening, or on weekends. They may attend class once a week for ten weeks or twice weekly for five weeks. In addition, the University offers its M.B.A. degree via Distance Learning (DL), which allows students to complete the same course work required for classroom-based courses outside the classroom itself.

City University is especially proud to announce the availability of its M.B.A. program on-line, as of spring 1995. Using the Internet, students are able to register for and complete courses electronically. Through City University's World Wide Web site, students access live forums featuring special guests; post messages to other students and faculty; participate in live, course-specific study groups; and communicate with students, faculty, and advisers via e-mail. Taking advantage of this exciting technology is another example of City University's commitment to maximizing educational opportunities.

The Faculty

Distinguished practitioners in the fields of business, education, government, health care, and human services; civic and research organizations; and the legal community comprise the City University faculty. They unite strong academic preparation and active professional careers in the fields in which they teach. City University employs 15 full-time faculty members and more than 400 adjunct faculty members to deliver its M.B.A. courses. Of these, 30 percent are women, and 9 percent are members of minority groups.

The Business School Network

City University prides itself on the successful relationships it has established with the corporate community. Corporate representatives are an integral part of the community advisory groups that help the University to update course content, relate courses to current trends in the marketplace, and ensure that programs provide students with skills employers are seeking. Every two years, the University gathers additional corporate consultants to review and revise its programs.
In addition, City University is able to offer its M.B.A. program in-house to companies. These have included such industry leaders as Boeing, Weyerhaeuser, and Siemens/Nixdorf Corporation (Germany).

The College and Environs

City University opened its doors in 1973 with one primary purpose: to provide educational opportunities for those segments of the population not being fully served through traditional means. This purpose has guided the University's growth from a single-room facility in Seattle, Washington, to an international leader in education with nearly two dozen locations worldwide. City University's headquarters are located in Bellevue, Washington. It operates instructional sites in other locations in the United States, Canada, Austria, Denmark, Germany, Switzerland, and Slovakia.

City University is accredited by the Northwest Association of Schools and Colleges. It offers over eighty programs at the undergraduate and graduate levels. Students who attend one of the University's North American sites will enjoy the temperate climate of the Pacific Northwest, its beautiful landscape, and its clean and cultured cities.

Facilities

City University's library serves students throughout the Seattle area, providing extensive reference resources, indexes and journals, and on-line databases. The library maintains cooperative arrangements with many other libraries. Furthermore, the library conducts searches for students who call in from outlying areas and arranges to send them annotated bibliographies and other information when possible.

Technology Environment

The University requires students to have access to a computer. Students are expected to use computer technology in the development of research papers; certain M.B.A. courses require computerized data manipulation as well. The University has established two computer labs at sites in the Seattle area and small lab facilities at outlying sites.

Placement

City University's Alumni Association operates a Career Resource Center, which provides assistance to graduates and current students in finding professionally satisfying employment. More than 500 employers currently list position openings with the center. In addition, the Alumni Association publishes a networking directory to help alumni maintain important and useful professional contacts. The University does not provide direct placement services for its students.

Admission

Generally, admission to City University graduate programs requires that students hold a baccalaureate degree or equivalent from an accredited or otherwise recognized institution. No specific undergraduate emphasis or major is required for entrance into a particular graduate program.

If available, reported scores on standardized entrance examinations such as the Graduate Record Examinations (GRE), the Miller Analogies Test (MAT), and the Graduate Management Admission Test (GMAT) should be submitted, although they are not required.

Finances

Standard tuition rates for graduate courses for the 1994–95 academic year were $232 per credit, or $696 per 3-credit class. While the number of required texts and other course materials vary with each course, textbooks typically each cost between $60 and $80.

City University does not provide student housing. In the Seattle area, rental expenses for a one-bedroom apartment are approximately $500.

Financial assistance available includes Federal Stafford Student Loans, scholarships, and Federal Work-Study.

International Students

The University's International Student Affairs Office helps international students to adjust to life and study in the United States and Canada, offering assistance with procedures related to the issuance and maintenance of student visas, counseling in academic matters, and student referral to appropriate agencies for health and other services.

Application Facts and Dates

A rolling admissions policy governs most City University programs. That is, the University accepts applications and announces admissions decisions continuously throughout the year. Most degree programs may be commenced in the fall, winter, spring, or summer quarter or at the monthly start of Fastrack and Weekend programs or Distance Learning courses. For more information, students should contact:

Elaine Asmar, Admissions Coordinator
Office of Admissions
City University
919 Southwest Grady Way
Renton, Washington 98055
Telephone: 206-637-1010 Ext. 3843
Fax: 206-277-2437

The Claremont Graduate School

The Peter F. Drucker Graduate Management Center

Claremont, California

IT ALL BEGINS WITH THE FACULTY

At each level of education, the quality of your experience depends on the ability of the teacher. Drucker Center faculty members are unparalleled in their ability to apply leading-edge theory to the practice of management. Their substantial consulting and managerial experience guarantees the relevance of their instruction, while their accomplished scholarly background ensures its academic rigor. Small class size and ample opportunity for interaction with these superior professors, as well as with your student colleagues, form the basis of the Drucker Center M.B.A. experience.

Please feel free to contact the staff of the M.B.A. program to answer your individual questions.

—Sidney E. Harris, Dean

Programs and Curricular Focus

The M.B.A. program is designed to produce outstanding general managers. Faculty combine theory with practice and place an uncommon amount of emphasis on integrating the functions and processes of an organization. Professors choose the teaching method that best suits the class material and the needs of their students. Teaching methods include case study, lecture/discussion, and field project courses.

Course options include full-time study, part-time study, and a set of options for midcareer executives. Full-time study generally requires two academic years to complete the degree. Part-time and executive courses generally require 2½ to 3½ years, depending on the candidate's rate of progress. Dual-degree programs can be arranged with a variety of other academic programs within the Claremont Graduate School.

The Drucker Center is accredited by the American Assembly of Collegiate Schools of Business (AACSB). The Claremont Graduate School is accredited by the Western Association of Schools and Colleges.

Students and the M.B.A. Experience

Drucker Center students are a highly diverse group who are able to call upon prior and current work experience during classroom discussion. They come from varied professions, educational backgrounds, countries, and ethnic groups.

What unites them is an interest in a rigorous education and the ambition to be superior managers.

Ninety-five percent of M.B.A. students have two or more years of work experience, with the average experience being five years. Approximately 34 percent have business undergraduate majors, 33 percent majored in social sciences, 18 percent in science and engineering disciplines, and 15 percent in the humanities. Twenty percent are international students, with the greatest number being from Asia and Latin America. Another 20 percent are members of American minority groups. Forty-two percent of the class are women. The students represent a large number of industries as well, including pharmaceuticals, utilities, aerospace, health care, financial services, core manufacturing, publishing, and petroleum.

❖ Global Focus

The attributes that make the Drucker Center's approach to the global nature of business extremely strong are the faculty, who are leaders in the United States for their ability to mainstream international issues into the core courses and for whom thinking globally is second nature; a sophisticated group of international students and American students who have operated abroad and share their experiences; a strong concentration in international business for the student who wishes to study international issues as a specialization; and international linkages

that provide exchange opportunities in France, Japan, China, Mexico, and Canada.

Special Features

A unique mentoring program offers students access to senior managers among the Drucker Center's alumni and its Executive Management Program. These are one-on-one relationships designed to facilitate networking and refine career goals, as well as to help the student benefit from the advice of a very experienced executive. Many become lifelong friendships.

Customer service is very high. For the person undertaking a rigorous M.B.A. program, minimizing administrative difficulties is a major issue. Drucker Center staff are unequaled in their ability and desire to deliver this important benefit.

The Faculty

Drucker Center faculty are hired for their ability to add value to the education of experienced people. No junior faculty are appointed to the Center, and classes are only offered by faculty members, not by graduate assistants. Drucker Center faculty have articulated their mission as "advancing the practice of management." In this effort, Peter Drucker, the most senior of the faculty, leads the way.

Twenty-nine percent of the Drucker Center faculty are women, and 14 percent are members of minority groups. All are doctorally qualified.

The Business School Network

The Drucker Center has built a web of productive relationships within the business community. One key group is the center's Board of Visitors—CEOs and other eminent business people who provide guidance and financial resources to further the Drucker Center's programs. Another group are people who give their time to the Dean's Executive Speaker Series, a small-group interaction between M.B.A. students and a senior executive. Still others are corporate partners, such as Deloitte and Touche, which sponsor research, collaborate with Drucker Center faculty, and recruit M.B.A. graduates regularly.

The College and Environs

The Claremont Colleges are a group of small and elite liberal arts colleges that are based on the model of Oxford and are situated on adjoining campuses. They combine resources to provide a university-size library and a strong academic community while keeping the scale and responsiveness of a small college.

The Claremont Graduate School, founded in 1925, was the second member of the Claremont Colleges. It provides graduate-only education in the liberal arts, information technology, and management. The School enrolls approximately 1,900 students, about 200 of them in the M.B.A. program.

Claremont is located 35 miles east of Los Angeles and has easy access to that city. It is a beautiful town, lying in the foothills of the San Gabriel Mountains. Movies are often filmed on location to give the feeling of an Eastern town and Ivy League college environment.

Technology Environment

The Claremont Graduate School has a leading academic computing center reserved for graduate student use. IBM, Apple, and Digital Equipment computers are provided in this area. Most software utilized in instruction is Microsoft products, but many other software packages are available.

The Honnold Library is a leader in electronic access and CD-ROM capability.

Placement

The Claremont Graduate School provides a full-line Office of Career Services. The office provides assistance in three major areas: career development, employer contacts, and databases and directories of potential employers. Career Services staff work in groups and one-on-one to help people refine their résumé, network, and practice their interview techniques. Mechanisms for connecting with employers include on-campus recruiting and the annual recruiting event of the West Coast M.B.A. Consortium.

In 1994, 85 percent of Drucker Center M.B.A. graduates were placed by graduation. The average starting salary was $50,700. These graduates took diverse positions in general management, consulting, marketing, finance, and the management of information systems.

Admission

The M.B.A. program seeks students who are intellectually curious, have strong academic records and work experience, and have the desire to become general managers and leaders. Decisions on admission are made in a rigorous qualitative method, and rigid quantitative indices are not used. The average GMAT score is approximately 550. The average undergraduate GPA is approximately 3.2. The average number of years of professional work experience is five. There are fairly broad ranges to all of these indicators.

Finances

Full-time tuition for the 1994–95 academic year was $16,800. Part-time tuition was $755 per unit. Books and course materials averaged $80 per class. Living expenses were approximately $12,000 for on-campus accommodations and approximately $15,500 for off-campus accommodations for the academic year.

Approximately 21 percent of M.B.A. students received fellowships or other grants, with the average award amounting to $5800 for the year. These programs are based on both academic merit and financial need, with most of the weight placed on academic merit. Loan assistance and work-study programs are also available.

International Students

Over 20 percent of the M.B.A. students are international students. The Claremont Colleges excel in making those students feel welcome and receive maximum benefit from their degrees. In the intimate and collegial environment, international students are encouraged to share their unique experiences. They are never lost in the crowd.

Special services include visa guidance, airport pickup, placement with a host family for the first few days in the country, and assistance with securing living arrangements and bank accounts; there are also specialized courses in advanced college English and extensive one-on-one academic counseling.

Application Facts and Dates

The Drucker Center utilizes a rolling admissions process. June 1 is the deadline for fall admission, and November 1 is the deadline for spring admission. Late applications are sometimes accepted upon consultation with the M.B.A. program office. The deadline for priority decisions on fellowship aid is February 15. Applicants can expect to be notified of the admission decision within four to six weeks of submitting the complete application.

For further information, students should contact:

Felicia Hazelton
Admissions Coordinator
The Claremont Graduate School
925 North Dartmouth Avenue
Claremont, California 91711
Telephone: 909-621-8073
Fax: 909-621-8543

Clarkson University

Potsdam, New York

> Clarkson University's School of Business creates the leaders of today and tomorrow who are energized by the entrepreneurial spirit. At the heart of the curricula are three essential building blocks: technology and information management, personal and leadership development, and cross-functional business thinking. We encourage professional experiences with local, national, and international organizations to develop students' entrepreneurial abilities and to provide pedagogical advantages outside the traditional classroom setting. Our Center for Leadership and Entrepreneurial Development provides resources and opportunities for students to gain valuable experience. With Canada on our doorstep, the opportunity for international business experience is eagerly engaged through our Canadian-U.S. Business Center.
>
> —Victor P. Pease, Dean

Programs and Curricular Focus

Accredited by the American Association of Collegiate Schools of Business, Clarkson University offers M.B.A. and Master of Science in management systems (MSMS) degree programs that prepare students for professional positions within an increasingly global and dynamic environment. The focus of the Clarkson M.B.A. is on developing students' leadership and managerial abilities and in developing their abilities to analyze problems and make effective decisions. The ability to work effectively in teams is critically important in today's business environment. Teamwork, effective communication skills, experiential learning, and leadership development are central to the Clarkson M.B.A. program.

The overwhelming majority of Clarkson M.B.A. students complete the program requirements in nine months (one academic year). As depicted in the illustration below, the fast-paced and highly integrated curriculum includes 10 core modules and 12 academic credits devoted to the development of functional and experiential expertise.

To participate in Clarkson's One-Year M.B.A. Program, students must have completed courses deemed equivalent to first-year foundation requirements—accounting, business law, computer applications, economics, finance, management, marketing, production, and statistics—prior to entering the program. Undergraduate business majors are typically able to complete the M.B.A. in nine months. Non–business majors can also receive transfer credit for foundation courses taken during their un-

dergraduate studies and can complete any remaining foundation requirements at Clarkson, prior to entering the One-Year M.B.A. Program.

The M.S. in management systems (MSMS) program can also be completed in one to two years and allows for the development of highly focused expertise in one of three dynamic areas: information systems, human resources, and manufacturing management. In addition, Clarkson offers a one-year interdisciplinary M.S. in manufacturing systems program specifically designed for engineering and science undergraduate majors.

Students and the M.B.A. Experience

At each year's commencement exercises, students gather to say their good-byes, and, without question, the M.B.A. class produces the loudest cheers and the sincerest tears. This degree of closeness stems from the team emphasis, the

co-experiences, and the intensity of the Clarkson M.B.A. program.

This annual outcome is even more significant when one considers the diversity of each class's membership. Typically one third are women and one fifth represent international students and members of minority groups. Academically, two fifths are from undergraduate programs in engineering, science, or liberal arts. Students returning from industry, who typically account for one quarter of the M.B.A. class, bring an average of nine years of professional experience into the class discussions, team activities, and experiential projects of the program. In addition, Clarkson M.B.A. students are exposed to the daily professional experiences of their part-time classmates.

❖ Global Focus

Modern industries in all countries need managers and business leaders who understand the complexities and opportunities associated with international competition. Clarkson's ties with Canadian industry and its proximity to Montreal and Ottawa allow Clarkson M.B.A. and MSMS students to deal firsthand with international business issues. While Canada is America's largest trading partner, conducting business with Canada still embodies the complexities of foreign trade.

The Center for Canadian-U.S. Business Studies is unique among graduate programs and a major component of the Clarkson M.B.A. and MSMS programs. The Canadian-U.S. Business Consulting Service provides Clarkson students with a unique opportunity to

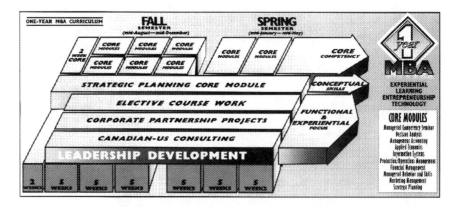

As part of Clarkson's M.B.A. Leadership Development Program, students develop and deliver managerial skill development seminars to local businesses.

gain practical business experience through the study of cross-border trade and economic opportunities. Professionally staffed and managed by Clarkson M.B.A. and MSMS students, the program provides client engagements that can lead to permanent career opportunities after graduation.

Special Features

Clarkson's M.B.A. Leadership Program begins with a two-week Managerial Competency Seminar starting in mid-August. During this core module, students are individually assessed, from which individual developmental plans are created. Individualized feedback is received from a professional assessment organization, Clarkson faculty members, and fellow M.B.A. students. Throughout the remainder of their program, students engage in course work and experiential activities to further develop these skills. In the spring semester, students develop and deliver managerial skill development seminars to local businesses. A follow-up assessment in the spring semester acts as an outcome measure for this central focus of the program.

The Faculty

Over 90 percent of the faculty members possess a doctorate. Faculty members are engaged in a continual process of creativity in the learning process and introduce exciting experiential components into their courses. At the same time, the faculty members conduct research and publish their findings in top scholarly journals.

The Business School Network

Clarkson's graduate business programs reflect the advisory input from an executive council staffed by such firms as Goldman-Sachs, Cigna, Coopers & Lybrand, Digital Equipment, Chase Manhattan Bank, and Imperial Oil.

In addition, the University's Executive-In-Residence program brings corporate executives and other organiza-

tional leaders to campus to share the managerial and leadership philosophies of today's business leaders. Prominent alumni, such as John McLennan, President and CEO of Bell Canada, regularly participate in these activities.

All graduate students have opportunities to participate in projects and intern experiences with corporations such as Alcoa, Corning, Niagara Mohawk, Nynex, and Xerox.

The College and Environs

An intellectual and cultural oasis nestled within a rural setting, Clarkson University enrolls approximately 2,200 undergraduate and 400 graduate students in the disciplines of business, engineering, and science. One-year M.B.A. students typically number 60 to 70. Potsdam, New York (population 10,200), is a short drive from the scenic Adirondack Park; 80 miles from Ottawa, Ontario; and 90 miles from Montreal, Quebec. In addition to Clarkson's 640-acre campus, the region enjoys the presence of three other institutions—Potsdam College of the State University of New York, St. Lawrence University, and SUNY College of Technology at Canton—in a 10-mile radius.

Technology Environment

Clarkson M.B.A. and MSMS students enjoy a robust offering of computer technology: fifty 386/486/RS6000 workstations linked by three Novell servers with access to the Internet. As a Novell Educational Partner, Clarkson offers several Novell Certification Courses to M.B.A. and MSMS students. In addition, students and faculty members regularly utilize the School's fully equipped behavioral sciences lab.

Placement

Placement services include on-line résumé referral, alumni referral networks, and a variety of workshops throughout

the year. In addition, the career center sponsors an industrial fair and participates in the NYS M.B.A. Consortium, an organization focused on placing M.B.A. students. On-campus interviews by over 150 organizations round out Clarkson's placement services.

Admission

Admission decisions are based on upper-division GPA, the highest attained GMAT score, and relevant professional experience. Typical GPA and GMAT averages are 3.3 and 540, respectively. From students for whom English is not the native language, a TOEFL of 600 and TSE of 250 are required. International students must present proof of adequate funds to cover all program costs. All students must have health insurance, either through Clarkson or another provider.

Finances

Tuition and fees for the 1994–95 One-Year M.B.A. Program were $17,200. Books, living expenses, and other costs approximate $7000 per year. Each year, roughly two thirds of incoming M.B.A. students receive merit-based tuition remission awards ranging from 40 to 100 percent. All applicants are considered for these awards, which are based solely on the aforementioned admissions criteria. In addition, candidates can apply for residence life positions that usually include room and board and, in some cases, a stipend.

International Students

Culture nights, diversity festivals, and the International Reading Room are all examples of Clarkson's efforts to enhance the acclimation of international students into Clarkson life. Students needing to improve TOEFL or TSE scores can enroll in intensive English programs at regional institutions with which Clarkson has close working relationships.

Application Facts and Dates

Clarkson accepts applications on a rolling basis. Accepted students, having received credit for all foundation requirements, can begin the One-Year M.B.A. Program in mid-August only. Students enrolling for the MSMS or to fulfill foundation requirements can enter in the fall or spring semester. The cost of applying is free to U.S. and Canadian residents and is $25 (U.S.) for international applicants. For more information, students should contact:

Office of Graduate Professional
  Programs
Clarkson University
P.O. Box 5770
Potsdam, New York 13699
Telephone: 315-268-6613
Fax: 315-268-7994

Clark University

TRAINING MANAGERS FOR THE WORKPLACE OF THE FUTURE

We excel at two things: creating knowledge and developing managers. We involve our students in close working relationships with dedicated teachers. Our classes are small to encourage their active involvement in learning. Our research brings us into contact with the world of practitioners, generates knowledge that cannot be gained through practical experience alone, and results in teaching that is sufficiently based on scientific evidence to provide a foundation for subsequent, lifelong learning.

—Robert A. Ullrich, Dean

Programs and Curricular Focus

As a University offering an M.B.A. degree nationally accredited by the AACSB, Clark has designed a curriculum that reflects the changing needs of business. Consultations with business leaders, alumni, and colleagues at other prestigious universities has lead to the development of a program with an international focus that integrates the various business disciplines while honing teamwork and communication skills.

Clark's M.B.A. program has a single overarching purpose: to develop managers. That is why, regardless of how students tailor their individual programs of studies, they are expected to master the range of skills and knowledge in the functional areas of management. A global thread is woven throughout the curriculum.

The program begins with the fundamental courses in mathematics, statistics, and economics. Next, students engage in studies of the basic functions of management in courses covering the creation and distribution of goods and services; financial reporting, analysis, and markets; and leadership in groups and organizations. Students who are able to demonstrate adequate prior knowledge of a particular area are granted waivers.

The general management course sequence of the curriculum focuses on formulating, analyzing, and implementing strategic and policy decisions for individual business units. Finally, throughout the elective portion of the program, students gain in-depth knowledge and competence in one of seven specific functional areas. Concentrations are offered in accounting, marketing,

finance, management of new ventures, health-care management, global business, and human resource management.

Other curricular features include a one-year M.B.A. for business undergraduates, an ACEHSA-accredited Master of Health Administration degree program offered jointly with the University of Massachusetts Medical School, an expanded accounting concentration that qualifies students to sit for the CPA exam, study-abroad programs, a one-week international management course in Europe, and the opportunity to audit one course per semester in other divisions of the University.

Students and the M.B.A. Experience

Clark's M.B.A. program attracts a diverse student body. Hailing from many states and countries around the world, students come together to form a microcosm of the international business arena. They work together in teams in many courses, notably the Projects in Management course. This course offers students the opportunity to work as a member of a consulting team on actual management problems facing corporations that have contracted with Clark for consulting services.

The average full-time student has one to two years of full-time professional work experience, along with a record of strong undergraduate achievement. Fewer than 30 percent of students have an undergraduate business background. Women comprise 46 percent of the class, and approximately half of the students come from overseas. Because of the

program's small size, students readily form lasting friendships with their classmates and professors; friendships that stand them in good stead as they enter the business world in both the U.S. and abroad.

❖ Global Focus

Recognizing the importance of global studies, all students take required courses in international management and global competition. A new one-week course in Europe is being introduced during the 1995–96 academic year. Through the presence of international students and faculty members, all courses have a strong international component. This perspective is further enhanced through exchange programs offered with several European universities.

Special Features

Clark's Center for the Management of New Ventures offers graduate instruction in the creation and management of new companies or of new ventures in existing firms. M.B.A. students participate in the New Ventures Seminar, a weekly meeting with successful entrepreneurs and executives in venture capital firms.

The Faculty

All managers need a basic tool kit of business skills. Beyond that, they need a full palette of talents to practice the artistry of management. At Clark, the faculty members are also scholars who are constantly redefining their disciplines through research and publications. They bring a wealth of scholarly and practical experience to the classroom. The faculty members enjoy Clark because of the combination of support for their research and the opportunity to teach in small classes and develop relationships with their students.

The Business School Network

Faculty consulting and research activities ensure Clark's link to the business community. Semester after semester, corporations, Fortune 500 firms among them, turn to Clark for assistance in addressing management issues. A visiting

committee, comprising prominent CEOs and other top executives, ensures that the M.B.A. curriculum is continually refined to reflect the dynamic nature of business.

The College and Environs

A teaching and research institution founded in 1887, Clark University is the second-oldest graduate institution in the nation. Clark is one of only three New England universities, with Harvard and Yale, to be a founding member of the Association of American Universities. Clark is the only U.S. institution of its size to have its M.B.A., M.H.A., and undergraduate management program nationally accredited. The University's tree-shaded residential campus is located in Worcester, New England's second-largest city and a center of high technology, biotechnology, and financial services industries. Boston is just a short drive away.

Placement

Because of the program's small size, students have unparalleled access to career-related services for a university of

Clark's quality. From the first day of orientation, career services staff members are ready to help students assess their skills, research career options, develop experience, prepare their résumés, and meet employers. Alumni mentoring, individual advising, mock interviews, and on-campus recruiting are just a few of the many career services offerings. The staff members never forget that students' primary motivating factor in seeking an M.B.A. is to improve employment prospects.

Admission

Clark seeks students who will add to the vitality of the interactions between faculty members and students. Applications from men and women with diverse educational and professional backgrounds are encouraged. The average GMAT for the most recently enrolled class was 570 (80 percent of students scored between 480 and 660). A minimum TOEFL score of 550 is required for international students. In addition to these factors, students' records of undergraduate academic achievement along with letters of

recommendation and a personal statement are considered. Although no formal academic or professional business background is required for admission, a solid preparation in English, mathematics, and economics is beneficial.

Finances

Tuition is calculated on a per course basis, rather than per semester. For the 1995–96 academic year, tuition per course is $1675. Mandatory activity and insurance fees are estimated at $626. Living and personal expenses, including books, are estimated at $7700.

The Graduate School of Management offers scholarship assistance, based exclusively on merit, to both U.S. and international students. Awards range up to 100 percent of tuition. All applicants are considered for these merit-based awards.

International Students

Clark University is an exceptionally hospitable place for international students. With students from over seventy countries and with an M.B.A. class composed of approximately half international students, the University prides itself on the range of support services available to these students. The University maintains a department dedicated to the service of students from overseas, assisting them with the social, cultural, and academic adjustments to life at an American University.

Application Facts and Dates

For the fall semester, the admission deadline is June 1, and, for the spring semester, the admission deadline is December 1. For more information, students should contact:

Ms. Lynn Terrell
Director of Admissions
Graduate School of Management
Clark University
950 Main Street
Worcester, Massachusetts 01610-1477
Telephone: 508-793-7406
Fax: 508-793-8822
E-mail: clarkmba@vax.clarku.edu

Clemson University

Clemson, South Carolina

DISTINCTIVE AND DIVERSE OPPORTUNITIES—A CLEMSON TRADITION

Clemson has a proud history of educating leaders in many fields. Our M.B.A. programs are dedicated to creating leaders in the field of business and preparing them for success in an ever-changing and dynamic global economy. Our unique combination of M.B.A. programs attracts talented, highly motivated young professionals with diverse cultural heritages, academic backgrounds, and business experiences.

Since our clientele have such diverse backgrounds and needs, we offer a variety of M.B.A. programs tailored to address these multiple needs. Whether your requirements are international, needing a multicultural experience and demanding work environment; supplementary, requiring a flexible evening program located in an urban setting; or expanding, looking for a dedicated, intensive but personal program set in a small, scenic collegiate town, Clemson can offer you a challenging and rewarding experience.

—Jerry Trapnell, Dean

Programs and Curricular Focus

Clemson University's M.B.A. programs, which are AACSB accredited, enable individuals to study advanced, integrated concepts of business, industry, and government. Participants include active managers as well as recent graduates interested in expanding their analytical, business, and interpersonal skills.

Full-time participants take a sequence of twenty courses (sixteen predetermined and four elective), including financial accounting, business ethics, quantitative decision making, organizational behavior, managerial competencies, and marketing strategies. The four elective courses, taken in the spring and summer of the second year, allow students to tailor the program for specific interests. Diverse learning environments offer approaches that include role playing, simulations, internships, consulting, and case studies.

Clemson offers a highly concentrated international program in Pordenone, Italy. Participants, selected worldwide, take sixteen courses in Italy during the fall and spring, taught in English, and complete the twelve-month curriculum with four more courses, including two electives, on Clemson's campus. While course content and learning approaches are similar to the full-time program, the faculty members use the students' diverse international and cultural backgrounds to enrich the learning environment. In addition to the full-time program, there

are also weekend executive programs in Pordenone, Italy, and in Ljubljana, Slovenia.

Clemson's part-time, evening program allows business professionals who have at least two years of work experience to pursue a degree in Greenville, South Carolina, on Furman University's campus or in Greenwood, South Carolina, on Lander University's campus. Students with no undergraduate business courses can expect to complete the nine prerequisite, eight core, and two elective courses in approximately 3½ years. Course content and delivery are similar to the full-time program but provide more flexibility for the nontraditional student. Students actively enrich class learning by contributing and integrating business experiences.

Students and the M.B.A. Experience

Clemson's M.B.A. students are drawn worldwide, providing a rich infusion of cultural and business backgrounds. The average student is 26, with two years of work experience. Half have business degrees, 37 percent engineering and pure sciences, and 13 percent social sciences and humanities. A third are women. Thirty-six percent of the students are international, representing over twenty-five countries. The domestic students come from the South (53 percent),

Northeast (35 percent), Midwest (7 percent), and West (5 percent).

❖ Global Focus

Clemson offers students many opportunities to broaden their international perspectives. During the summer between their first and second year, full-time students can take four courses abroad, participate in an internship, or pursue a foreign language on the Clemson campus. Frequent guest lecturers from multinational firms provide a unique international-national perspective. In addition, Clemson's international program in Italy provides visits to and consulting projects for international firms, opportunity for language and cultural immersion, and optional international travel.

The Faculty

Clemson's faculty members all carry a Ph.D. in their teaching discipline. They are highly qualified to bring students outstanding learning opportunities by offering superb teaching skills, applied business research and experience, and high-quality student interaction.

The Business School Network
Corporate Partnerships

As part of a land-grant university with strong traditional ties to the business community, the College of Commerce and Industry maintains dynamic partnerships with area corporate leaders. The 42-member College Advancement Board, composed of prominent business executives from South Carolina industry including IBM, Sonoco, and Price Waterhouse, provides critical business guidance, expertise, and participation for College programs. Field trips, hands-on consulting, and executive guest speakers provide additional real-world exposure for the M.B.A. student.

The College and Environs

Clemson is a state-assisted university located in South Carolina's lake and mountain region. The campus itself consists of more than 1,400 wooded and rolling acres on the former plantation of John C. Calhoun. Founded in 1889, the

Tillman Hall—the first building on campus.

University has a student population of approximately 16,000 and offers over 100 graduate degrees in almost seventy areas.

The town of Clemson is a small college community of 10,000 located on the shores of Lake Hartwell. Large population centers are conveniently located within 30 to 45 minutes of the area.

Technology Environment

The University computing facilities include a large mainframe computer, five VAX machines, network links to the Internet, and microcomputer labs containing almost 400 computers. The computer labs are strategically located throughout the campus. The library's more than 1.5 million items, including books, periodicals, microforms, databases, and government publications, are

accessible for index and catalog search via on-line computer access.

Placement

Clemson's Career Services Center provides assistance to students in identifying and obtaining professional positions through on-campus interviews and student-developed network contacts. The center has resources available for student research and use. In addition, the M.B.A. Career Placement program targets opportunities for students by aggressively researching and identifying potential prospects for students internships, job placement, and professional network building.

Admission

Acceptance is based on careful appraisal of each candidate's academic record,

performance on the Graduate Management Admission Test (GMAT), letters of recommendation, and work experience. The admission process is highly personalized, with emphasis on each applicant's accomplishments. A score of at least 550 on the TOEFL is required for all students whose native language is not English.

Calculus and fundamentals of computers are prerequisites for the full-time program on the Clemson campus. The evening programs require basic prerequisite courses in calculus, statistics, management, marketing, economics, finance, accounting, business law, and management information systems.

Finances

In 1994–95, tuition and fees for the Clemson campus full-time program were $3800 for South Carolina residents and $7350 for nonresidents. Books and supplies cost approximately $600 per year. On-campus housing ranges from $755 per semester for a residence hall to $1190 for a 4-person apartment. Off-campus apartments typically cost around $400 per month. A limited number of graduate assistantships are available. Awards are based on personal interviews and candidates' qualifications.

Tuition for the evening programs in 1994–95 was $160 per semester hour for South Carolina residents and $320 per hour for nonresidents. Tuition for the international M.B.A. program in Italy was $13,400 for the 1994–95 program.

All tuition and fees are subject to change as conditions warrant.

Application Facts and Dates

Application deadlines for the full-time program are April 15 for international students and May 15 for domestic students. For the part-time program, deadlines are April 15, July 15, and November 30. For more information, students should contact:

Director of Admissions
M.B.A. Programs
Clemson University
Box 341315
Clemson, South Carolina 29634-1315
Telephone: 803-656-3975
Fax: 803-656-0947

CSU Cleveland State University

Cleveland, Ohio

NEW CURRICULUM AND FLEXIBLE PROGRAMS

Cleveland State University offers the opportunity to earn an M.B.A. degree in the heart of one of America's most exciting cities. The new M.B.A. curriculum features full integration of the business disciplines, an expanded emphasis on global business practices, new courses in business ethics and management of innovation and technology, and development of personal business skills. Programs are scheduled for full-time or part-time students and meet on weekdays or weekends, daytime or evening, on campus and at business locations outside the downtown area. Flexibility of options enables students to tailor a program to meet their specific needs.

—Edward G. Thomas, Interim Dean

Programs and Curricular Focus

CSU offers a variety of M.B.A. programs. There are full-time and part-time programs, given both in the daytime and evening, where courses normally meet twice a week on weekdays. There is a one-year, accelerated program where classes meet all day Saturday and every other Friday evening, starting in September. The Executive M.B.A. is a twenty-two-month program with classes primarily on Saturdays, featuring international and governmental seminars; the program is limited to experienced businessmen and businesswomen. The M.B.A. in Health Care Administration is a special program that features an internship and course work with a health-care emphasis. The J.D./M.B.A. is a joint program with the Cleveland Marshall College of Law that permits students to work on both degrees at the same time.

The curriculum exposes students to the full range of business disciplines in both skill-building and integrative courses. It consists of three levels of course work: skill development, basic business knowledge (26 quarter credits), and core courses (48 quarter credits).

Skill development courses are offered in spoken and written communications, computer literacy, mathematics, and statistics; these courses may be waived through prior course work or departmental examination.

Basic business knowledge courses are offered in financial accounting, financial management, economics, marketing, management, organizational behavior, and production management; these courses are prerequisite to the M.B.A. core courses and may be waived through prior course work.

Core courses consist of skill-building courses in managerial accounting, finance, marketing, database management, quality management, strategic management, and communications, as well as courses in business environment, ethical analysis, and law; environment of international business; human resource management and labor relations; and management of innovation and technology. There are two integrative capstone seminars, focusing on the interrelationships between the major business disciplines, and three elective courses, one of which may be either a research project or a business internship.

Students and the M.B.A. Experience

CSU has a student population of 17,000, drawn from the city of Cleveland, its suburbs, and many countries of Europe, Central and South America, Africa, and Asia. The 1,100 M.B.A. students are drawn from each of these areas, range in age from their early twenties to sixties, and provide a broad racial and cultural mix. Many have established business careers. The classroom experience gives each student a chance to work alongside persons of different backgrounds and heritages.

❖ Global Focus

International trade is one of Cleveland's and northeastern Ohio's most active business segments. The import-export community has provided CSU with a rich resource of materials for building a global emphasis into the core courses of the M.B.A. program and enables CSU to present the course Environment of International Business as part of the M.B.A. core.

The Faculty

Each member of the graduate faculty of the James J. Nance College of Business Administration has an earned doctorate in his or her academic discipline. The total full-time faculty numbers 69, of whom 10 (14 percent) are women and 18 (26 percent) are foreign-born, representing more than a dozen countries throughout the world.

The Business School Network

CSU's proximity to the central business district affords regular interchange with the rich commercial and industrial activities of the area. Programs emphasize the practical application of business principles, affording students the opportunity to learn from the area's leading practitioners. Members of the College of Business Administration's Visiting Committee represent major corporations in the area, providing students opportunities to interact at the top level of decision making. Frequent guest speakers expose students to a variety of styles and corporate cultures.

The College and Environs

The James J. Nance College of Business Administration is one of seven colleges of Cleveland State University. The campus is located within a short walk of the central business district; Playhouse Square, a major theater and entertainment area; and Gateway, a new major sports complex. Cleveland offers a world-class symphony orchestra, opera and ballet companies, theater companies, three major-league sports teams, and one of the most extensive networks of public parks in the United States. A new building for the College of Business Administration is scheduled to open in 1997.

Facilities

The resources of CSU's main library and Law Library and those of the Cleveland Public Library system are available to M.B.A. students. The Computer Center provides student access to mainframe computing, several personal computer laboratories, on-line interactive processing, and use of the DIALOG information retrieval system.

Placement

CSU's Career Services Center offers advice on career direction and the career development process. It operates a placement service to match student skills with job opportunities from more than 500 companies.

Admission

Applicants for M.B.A. programs must possess a baccalaureate degree from an accredited college or university and must take the Graduate Management Admission Test (GMAT). Admission is based on undergraduate grade point average and GMAT score. International applicants must also take the Test of English as a Foreign Language (TOEFL) and achieve a score of at least 525.

Finances

For 1995–96, graduate tuition is $113 per credit hour, or $1457 per quarter, for Ohio residents; it is $226 per credit hour, or $2914 per quarter, for nonresidents. Books and supplies average $30 to $60 per course. Financial aid in the form of tuition grants is available to a limited number of highly qualified first-year graduate students. Dormitory space ranging from $1331 to $1807 per quarter (including meals) is available on a limited basis. Relatively low-cost rental housing is available in Cleveland and nearby suburbs; monthly rates range from $175 to $350.

International Students

CSU's International Student Services office provides counseling in matters dealing with visas, housing, and academic affairs and conducts an orientation program prior to a student's initial quarter of classes.

Application Facts and Dates

Applicants should submit an application at least two months prior to the quarter of desired entrance. Official copies of transcripts must be forwarded to CSU directly from all institutions previously attended. Test scores (GMAT and TOEFL) must be reported directly by the Educational Testing Service. Copies of program descriptions and application forms may be obtained from:

James J. Nance College of Business Administration
Room 460, University Center
Cleveland State University
2121 Euclid Avenue
Cleveland, Ohio 44115
Telephone: 216-687-3730
Fax: 216-687-6888

The College of Insurance

New York, New York

> ### WHERE LEADERSHIP BEGINS . . . THE M.B.A. WITH AN EDGE
>
> *Graduates of the Master of Business Administration program at the College of Insurance start out on a fast track in the exciting field of finance, insurance, risk management, and actuarial science. Our unique relationship with the industry and our solid curriculum result in exceptional career opportunities...an edge most students are looking for.*
>
> —Jack M. Nelson, Ph.D., Chief Academic Officer

Programs and Curricular Focus

The College of Insurance offers a program leading to the Master of Business Administration (M.B.A.) degree, with concentrations available in finance, insurance, risk management, and actuarial science. The College follows the curriculum guidelines of the American Assembly of Collegiate Schools of Business. A common body of knowledge is incorporated into the core. Elective courses provide breadth to the program. Computers are integrated as tools, and a worldwide dimension is stressed. Although a full-time status exists, the program is primarily designed for professionals who wish to pursue their degree on a part-time basis. Classes are offered in the evening and on Saturdays and meet once a week. The programs of study are designed to prepare students for leadership positions in the financial services industry. The M.B.A. program, with a concentration in actuarial science, allows the student to receive the Master of Business Administration degree while preparing for up to five actuarial examinations. The program is specifically designed for highly motivated individuals who seek a graduate management degree as well as solid credentials in actuarial science.

A large percentage of the students entering the M.B.A. program have undergraduate degrees in areas other than business. The program requires the completion of seventeen courses totaling 51 credit hours. The core courses provide a broad foundation for future managerial assignments; concentration in finance, insurance, and risk management require 27 credits in core courses, and the concentration in actuarial science requires 24 credits. The major area requires 9 credit hours for finance, insurance, and risk management and 15 credit hours for actuarial science. The major area (finance or insurance) comprises 9 credit hours. Electives (12 credits for insurance, finance, and risk management and 9 credits for actuarial science) are chosen from insurance, finance, international business, ethics, personal administration, and other related business topics. Business Policy, the 3-credit capstone course integrating the lessons from early courses, is taken in the last semester of the program. The College may waive courses for students with undergraduate degrees in business administration or with specific courses matching the core. Such students complete the program in less than 51 credit hours.

Students and the M.B.A. Experience

In 1994–95, students enrolled in the Graduate Division for an M.B.A. degree included 123 women and 66 men, of whom 51 were international students. Their average age was 28, about half of them were married, and many were employed in the areas of management and insurance. Most of the students work in the financial services industry during the day and attend classes at night. They find the combination of work and study—with the opportunity to utilize newly acquired classroom knowledge in a genuine work situation—to be beneficial.

The Faculty

The M.B.A. program has an especially well-qualified faculty, whose members are chosen for the knowledge, both theoretical and practical, of all aspects of the insurance and business worlds. The College's faculty members are also active professionally. Many serve as consultants to industry as well as research. The ratio that exists between students and faculty is 12:1. Part-time instructors are drawn directly from the business world, where many occupy high-level positions.

The Business School Network

The College is supported by over 300 of the world's most respected insurance and financial organizations. It is this unique bond with industry that enables students to benefit from hands-on experience, affordable tuition, excellent career opportunities, and extensive academic preparation. Graduates of the M.B.A. program at the College of Insurance start out on a fast track in the exciting field of finance, insurance, risk management, or actuarial science. The College's unique relationship with industry and its solid curriculum result in exceptional career opportunities—an edge most students are looking for. Many alumni have gone on to occupy senior management positions in the industry. The Alumni Organization plays an active role in the career paths of students.

The College and Environs

The College of Insurance traces its beginnings to the founding of its parent organization, the Insurance Society of New York, in 1901. Informal learning sessions developed into classroom situations, and the School of Insurance was founded in 1946. In 1962, it became the College of Insurance—the only undergraduate degree granting institution in the United States established by, and supported by, a particular segment of the business world. In the fall of 1984, the College moved to a new ten-story building, where it enjoys greatly expanded classroom, office, and conference-room space; additional facilities for the College library; and dormitory space. The College of Insurance is located in the heart of New York City's downtown financial and insurance district, within walking distance of the New York Stock Exchange, South Street Seaport, the World Trade Center, the World Financial Center, and the Staten Island Ferry. Conveniently located near public transportation, the College is just a short

ride away from the Broadway and Lincoln Center theaters, Greenwich Village, Chinatown, SoHo, and the uptown department stores, boutiques, restaurants, and museums.

Facilities

The Kathryn and Shelby Cullom Davis Library of the College of Insurance is an outstanding research facility for students, scholars, researchers, and the insurance industry as a whole. Recognized internationally as the largest and the most comprehensive insurance library in the world, it houses more than 95,000 bound volumes, subject files, pamphlets, periodicals, and other pieces of informational material, plus more than 10,750 microform items. The library is divided into the Insurance Society Collection and the Frederick W. Ecker Collection, the latter housing material on liberal arts and business subjects. In addition to the insurance laws and regulations of the fifty states, the library contains information on the insurance laws of many countries and the proceedings and reports of most insurance organizations. The library has historical as well as contemporary collections, with the oldest volume dating back to 1569, and an extensive collection of old insurance policies and documents tracing the development of insurance terminology and contracts since 1665.

Placement

Although the College of Insurance does not have a formal placement service

available, students have the opportunity to attend seminars as well take advantage of individual support in résumé preparation, job search skills, and individual development of employment opportunities. The insurance and financial service industries look to the program to fill their management positions.

Admission

Applicants for the M.B.A. program must be college graduates and have taken the Graduate Management Admission Test (GMAT). As a general guideline, applicants should have a 3.0 QPA or a B average in their undergraduate or graduate programs and a 500 score on the GMAT. Higher scores are sought from the actuarial science students. If English is not a student's native language, he or she must take the TOEFL exam, available from the Educational Testing Service; a minimum score of 550 is required.

Finances

For graduate students, employed by organizations that sponsor the College (by contributing a yearly membership fee), tuition is $445 per credit in 1995–96. For all other students, tuition is $470 per credit. Each term, a registration fee of $15 per credit, not to exceed $180, is charged. The estimated cost of books and supplies is $650 per year.

The College has dormitory rooms available for 120 undergraduate and graduate students. The housing fees per semester in 1995–1996 range between

$3502 and $4692, depending on whether accommodations are for single or double occupancy and on the number of meals eaten on the premises. Some students rent apartments singly or with fellow students. However, a high proportion of M.B.A. degree candidates work in the New York-New Jersey-Connecticut area and already live in the College's vicinity.

International Students

International students may be admitted on a student (F) visa or a (J) visa, provided they present satisfactory academic credentials to qualify for the program and meet immigration and naturalization requirements. In addition, international students must take the TOEFL exam, available from the Educational Testing Service, if English is not their native language. A minimum score of 550 is required. All transcripts listing courses taken and grades received must be officially translated into English. A Certificate of Finances must be completed, indicating the source of financial support. A notarized bank statement or other documentation of finances must accompany this Certificate of Finance. A Supplemental Application for International Students must be submitted, with an application fee of $50.

Application Facts and Dates

Application deadlines are July 15 for the fall term and November 1 for the spring term. The minimum requirements for admission to the program are a bachelor's degree with grades of B or better, a satisfactory score on the Graduate Management Admission Test (GMAT), two recommendations, and a personal statement. There is a one-time $30 application fee for U.S. citizens and permanent residents. Students interested in further information and an application packet should contact:

Theresa C. Marro
Director of Admissions
The College of Insurance
101 Murray Street
New York, New York
Telephone: 212-815-9232
Fax: 212-964-3381

Colorado State University

Fort Collins, Colorado

INNOVATION, EXCELLENCE, AND BALANCED PROGRAMMING WITH A COLORADO STATE M.B.A.

The College of Business at Colorado State University strives for strength from balance. We effectively balance our curriculum, administrative leadership, faculty excellence, and industry-oriented instruction. Our curriculum blends theoretical problem solving with pragmatic real-world experience. We serve a multitude of students by striking a balance between on-campus instruction and educational programs that reach out to students throughout Colorado and around the country. The Colorado State M.B.A. program has a reputation for innovation and excellence. Our newest program combines these two elements in our distance education M.B.A.. Bold new initiatives coupled with a consuming focus on quality in our educational programs give the College of Business at Colorado State University a unique strength.

—Steven F. Bolander, Interim Dean

Programs and Curricular Focus

Diversity is a key word in the College of Business—diversity in programs as well as the student body. The College employs a full range of flexible and adaptable programs to address the needs of the entire spectrum of students: domestic and international, traditional and nontraditional, part-time and full-time, on-campus and off-campus. The College takes pride in offering a variety of programs that meet the needs of each student and address the requirements of individual academic and career goals. Students can obtain a general M.B.A. degree, an M.B.A. degree with a specialization, or an M.S. degree. The College offers a cooperative M.B.A. with the College of Agriculture and another with the College of Engineering. An M.B.A. in technology management is also available. These programs can be accomplished as an on-campus student or (for selected programs) as a distance learner.

The College is very proud to be a nationally recognized leader in distance education. This program, available to residents of the continental United States and military personnel stationed abroad, is part of the College's fully AACSB-accredited program. Except for military personnel, the distance education program is not available to anyone living outside the continental United States. Through the SURGE (State University Resources in Graduate Education) program, the classroom is brought directly to the student via videotape. The "candid

classroom" environment makes the M.B.A. program unique. Each class is videotaped on campus in a specially designed state-of-the-art multimedia classroom. Distance learners view videotapes of the course exactly the way the class progresses on campus, benefiting from the questions asked by the on-campus students. Class material is, therefore, never dated; it is always fresh and current. To integrate the distance education students into the classroom, faculty members may share information, questions, or assignments from the distance learners with the on-campus class. Most distance learners are working professionals and add a valuable dimension to M.B.A. classes. Distance learning students do the same classwork as their on-campus classmates and take their exams with a proctor. Distance education students communicate with their professors and their classmates using voice mail, electronic mail, fax machines, the telephone, regular mail, and even videotape. The degree can be earned without the student ever having to come to the campus. Admissions standards and academic standards are the same as for the on-campus students, and upon completion of the program, students receive their diploma from Colorado State University.

Each graduate student is assigned a faculty adviser to work with him or her to design an individual program to meet the student's career goals. After meeting basic requirements, elective courses are

selected to meet the 33 graduate credits required for a degree. Students may also be required to take additional courses to satisfy background requirements in business.

Colorado State is committed to furthering its reputation for computer-integrated learning. Over 85 percent of graduate business classes, across all academic areas, require computer applications, not including word processing. The on-campus program is fully supported by extensive state-of-the-art computer facilities.

Students and the M.B.A. Experience

Diversity and balance characterize the on-campus graduate student body, resulting in an interactive, stimulating environment in which to learn. In a typical class, students range in age from their early 20s to their 50s. Over half have returned to school after work experience. The College admits a select number of highly qualified international students each year to maintain that enrollment at approximately 30 percent of its graduate population. About fifteen countries are represented in a typical class. The majority of Colorado State business students have undergraduate degrees in business, but a significant number hold degrees in economics, science, and engineering as well as the liberal arts. Over half of the College's U.S. students hold undergraduate degrees from outside Colorado from colleges and universities across the continent.

Students come from diverse backgrounds and invigorate the College with a variety of career objectives, demands, expectations, and perspectives.

The Faculty

Over 90 percent of the regular business faculty members at Colorado State University have doctoral degrees. Their list of graduate programs includes major universities from every part of the United States—from Cornell to the University of Southern California and from the University of Minnesota to Texas A&M. Equally impressive is the applied business depth of the College faculty members.

Over 50 percent have significant business experience in their professional portfolios.

The faculty members' strong academic skills, combined with their years of practical experience, create a learning environment that exemplifies the best in modern management education.

The Business School Network

The College of Business Advisory Council is a vital element in maintaining a productive relationship between the College of Business and the business and professional community. Membership includes upper-level managers from public and private institutions, government, and international firms.

In a typical year, College of Business students have opportunities to interact with over 20 corporate executives from major firms in all areas of business, finance, and manufacturing. In addition, the Graduate Business Council, a student organization, organizes the Graduate Business Forum each year. The participation of industry leaders allows personal interaction between them and the graduate students.

The College and Environs

Founded in Fort Collins in 1862 as the first authorized university in Colorado, Colorado State University is recognized worldwide for its contributions to technology and science, its quality of instruction, and the sharing of discoveries that improve the world's quality of life, health, environment, and economy. A Carnegie Foundation Class I research university, Colorado State represents the best of the land-grant tradition. The College of Business contributes to the University's growth, prestige, and national acclaim through the emphasis on excellence at all levels.

The city of Fort Collins offers a relaxed lifestyle and an abundance of cultural and social activities. Skiing, hiking, backpacking, and water sports areas are all adjacent to Fort Collins. More than 53 miles of bikeways wind along the Cache la Poudre River within the city. Fort Collins has a clear, dry climate with more than 300 days of sunshine and generally pleasant temperatures throughout the year.

Technology Environment

The College of Business supports two computer labs for the exclusive use of business students. They are equipped with one hundred fifty 80486 computers; eighteen laser printers, plotters, and color printers; and over sixty-five software packages. All computers are connected to the Internet and have full Internet capabilities. The College uses a variety of CD-ROM databases, and several UNIX workstations are also accessible from lab computers. Complementing College resources, the University provides an extensive set of UNIX systems with a full range of software support, including a Visualization Laboratory, statistical products, neural networks, and various gopher and web devices. The mission of the College of Business computer labs is to provide College of Business students with the technology they will expect to find in the workplace.

Placement

Placement of graduates is a top priority in the College of Business. The University Career Center and the College of Business career counselor work closely with the faculty to offer a wide range of placement opportunities to master's candidates in business. An amiable recruiting relationship has developed between the College and local and national firms, resulting in a diverse list of companies who hire Colorado State business graduates. For example, Hewlett-Packard considers the College of Business one of their "top 10" recruiting schools, the major accounting firms actively recruit Colorado State business graduates, and major financial, retail, and high-tech firms are well represented among the companies who come to campus.

The College Graduate Office also maintains a Business Alumni Network to assist students and publishes and distributes a student résumé book annually.

Admission

An applicant for admission must have earned a bachelor's degree in any field from an accredited college or university. Admission is dependent primarily on an integrated analysis of an applicant's undergraduate grade point average, score on the Graduate Management Admission Test (GMAT), and letters of recommendation.

If the applicant's native language is not English, the Test of English as a Foreign Language (TOEFL) is also required, with a minimum score of 550. International students are also required to submit proof of adequate funding for support for the length of time necessary to obtain their degree. International students must also have health insurance.

Finances

For 1994–95, tuition and fees per year for full-time students were $3300 for Colorado residents and $9600 for nonresidents. A slight increase is expected for 1995–96. Through 8 credits, part-time Colorado residents paid $102 per credit and nonresidents paid $366 per credit. Fees are prorated for part-time students. Books and supplies typically cost a full-time graduate student $1000 per year.

University-owned furnished apartments are available. For single students, the rates were $360 per month for one-bedroom units and $235 per person per month for two-bedroom units in 1994–95. On-campus meal plan rates for 1994–95 were $1058 per semester for fourteen meals per week and $1117 per semester for twenty-one meals per week. University-owned family housing is also available at rates from $425 per month for a two-bedroom furnished apartment to $650 per month for a three-bedroom unit. Rent for all University-owned housing includes utilities, telephone, and cable TV. Students must submit an application and a deposit to be placed on the waiting list for University housing. Housing rates are subject to change. Married and single students can also find accommodations in numerous privately owned apartment buildings and residences surrounding the campus. Off-campus, monthly rent ranges from $425 for a one-bedroom apartment to $900 for a three-bedroom house. Rentals to share are approximately $265.

The College offers a small number of teaching assistantships each year. These awards are based on prior experience and education. The College also awards approximately twelve Colorado Fellowships each year to students who are United States citizens. All U.S. applicants are eligible for and are considered for these fellowship awards.

Application Facts and Dates

Application for admission to the College of Business at Colorado State University may be made for any term of the year. Applications for the fall, spring, or summer semester are due six months prior to the beginning of the appropriate semester. The College has a rolling admission policy. Approximately two weeks after the application is complete, applicants are notified of the admission decision. The graduate admission application requires a nonrefundable fee. For further information, students should contact:

Dr. Jon Clark, Associate Dean
College of Business
Colorado State University
Fort Collins, Colorado 80523
Telephone: 303-491-6471
Fax: 303-491-0596

Cornell University

Ithaca, New York

SMALL . . . RIGOROUS . . . SELECT . . . INNOVATIVE . . . INTERNATIONAL . . . COLLABORATIVE

. . . and linked to the vast resources of one of the world's top universities. These are the characteristics of the Johnson School M.B.A. experience. Our relatively small size and rural location encourage greater interaction among students than is typically found in larger schools. Our faculty members pride themselves on their accessibility as well as their superior teaching; their office doors—and not infrequently their homes—are open to students. Our diverse, international community ensures that developing a global perspective becomes a personal process rather than an academic exercise. Together, it adds up to a simultaneously challenging and supportive environment conducive to building the ties that will become your business network for years to come.

—Alan G. Merten, Dean

Programs and Curricular Focus

The Johnson School has created one of the most flexible academic programs of any leading business school. Core courses are scheduled so that students may opt to take two (or more) electives by the end of their first year of study, gaining advanced training in areas of interest prior to their summer internship. A new strategy course requirement, expanded managerial-skills offerings, and the faculty's emphasis on teamwork ensure that students also acquire the integrative and interpersonal skills necessary for problem solving, decision making, and leadership in today's complicated organizations.

Whether seeking breadth of perspective or depth in a particular discipline, students are encouraged to make full use of Cornell's other internationally renowned programs—the School of Industrial and Labor Relations, the School of Hotel Administration, and an innovative Asian language program—as well as programs in engineering, law, biotechnology and agricultural science, and advanced computing. One quarter of the M.B.A. program, and sometimes more, may be fulfilled with any graduate-level course at Cornell. The Johnson School is also one of the few business schools that allows academic credit for foreign language study.

Joint-degree programs include the five-semester M.Eng.-M.B.A. in manufacturing management; the six- or seven-semester M.A. in Asian studies-M.B.A.; the five-semester M.I.L.R.-M.B.A.,

combining a general management education with more specialized human resource management; and the four-year J.D.-M.B.A.

A new Twelve-Month Option allows individuals with graduate degrees in scientific or technical fields to complete an accelerated core curriculum during the summer (June to August), join the second-year class in the fall, and graduate the following May.

Students and the M.B.A. Experience

The Johnson School tradition of both working and socializing together combined with the School's relatively small size leads to an unusually strong sense of community. The School's culture of cooperation emphasizes goal-oriented teamwork, and students can expect to learn almost as much from their peers as from the faculty. The average age of the students is 27. Twelve percent hold undergraduate humanities degrees. Four years of work experience is average; however, many successful students have had less. Women and international students each constitute one quarter of the class; minority students make up 11 percent.

❖ Global Focus

Exchange programs with nine overseas universities; intersession study tours to India, Japan, Russia, and Venezuela; and internships through the School's Central and Eastern European Development

(CEED) program allow students to experience international business firsthand. On campus, international business concerns are fully integrated into the curriculum. The joint M.B.A.-M.A. in Asian studies and Cornell's varied offerings in regional and language studies supplement the Johnson School program. The presence of students from more than forty countries ensures the enhancement of students' international business networks.

The Faculty

Johnson School faculty members consistently receive high marks for the quality of their teaching. Many have written books that are staples in management courses throughout the world. Reflecting the School's strong commitment to promoting women in business, one quarter of the faculty members are women.

At the Johnson School, easy access to professors is the norm. Their office doors—and not infrequently their homes—are open to students. Faculty members are also active researchers, and, because of their links with Fortune 500 companies, entrepreneurial firms, and government agencies, they are a good resource for sound career advice.

The Business School Network

Corporate Partnerships

Through the Visiting Executive program, corporate leaders come not only to lecture, but to spend the day (and often longer) interacting informally with students. The innovative Semester in Management was created in partnership with Corning Incorporated and includes twenty other companies as active participants. The Managerial Skills Program draws most of its leaders from the business world, providing well-received training programs offered by General Electric, IBM, McKinsey and Company, and Quaker Oats, among others. The Women's Management Council has established a mentoring program with the President's Council of Cornell Women, a group of Cornell's most successful professional alumnae. A

Cornell University, overlooking Cayuga Lake and the Ithaca Valley, has one of the most beautiful campuses in the world.

number of companies sponsor minority or international scholarships.

Prominent Alumni

CEOs include Lucio Noto of Mobil, Kenneth Derr of Chevron, I. MacAllister Booth of Polaroid, Charles Knight of Emerson Electric, Martin Grass of Rite Aid, and Karel Vinck of Union Miniére.

The College and Environs

Cornell is generally acknowledged as one of the most beautiful campuses in the world. About 19,000 students study at the University, and the campus's international community includes more than 2,500 students, as well as faculty members and visiting scholars, who hail from more than 100 countries. Ithaca, with its combination of cosmopolitan sophistication and small-town accessibility, offers residents the best of both worlds—diverse cultural offerings and recreational activities in a beautiful setting of lakes, waterfalls, forests, and countryside.

Technology Environment

The School maintains both Macintosh and DOS microcomputing laboratories. In addition to the most common on-line business information databases, the School's library offers access to state-of-the-art electronic services such as the Bridge and Bloomberg brokers' information services and First Call (up-to-the-minute financial analysts' reports). The highly sophisticated but user-friendly CareerSearch enables students to quickly identify hard-to-find, small-growth companies that match their specific career interests.

Placement

A strong on-campus recruiting program attracts representatives from more than 100 companies to the Johnson School. The Career Services Office also provides extensive support for a targeted job search. A campuswide electronic résumé database enables Johnson School students to respond to employer inquiries that are di-

rected to any one of Cornell's nine career services offices. Networking programs include the student-organized Week on Wall Street and Consulting Forum. A special fund supplements salaries for summer internships at small entrepreneurial and midsize companies. Through CareerNetwork, 800 alumni in the U.S. and overseas offer information and mock interviews, résumé critiques, job search advice, and correspondence opportunities.

Admission

The Admissions Committee considers applicants' prior academic performance, GMAT scores, range and depth of work experience, demonstrated leadership and interpersonal skills, writing skills, interviewing ability, extracurricular and community involvement, career aspirations, recommendations, and previous achievements. For the class of 1996, the average GMAT score was 630; the average undergraduate GPA, 3.2; and the average TOEFL score, 631. Interviews, while not required, are encouraged. Both staff and alumni interviews are given equal importance.

Finances

In 1994–95, tuition was $20,400, books cost $750, and housing and food cost approximately $7000 (based on the cost of sharing a moderately priced apartment). Personal expenses are estimated at $3600.

The School awards over $1.5 million in merit-based scholarships each year, as well as need-based loans and work-study funds. International applicants receive the same consideration as U.S. citizens for merit-based awards.

Application Facts and Dates

Application deadlines are December 1 for notification of decision by January 31, January 16 for notification by March 15, and March 1 for notification by May 15. For more information, students should contact:

Office of Admissions
315 Malott Hall
Cornell University
Ithaca, New York 14853-4201
Telephone: 607-255-4526
    800-847-2082 (U.S. and
      Canada)
Fax: 607-254-8886
E-mail: mba@johnson.cornell.edu

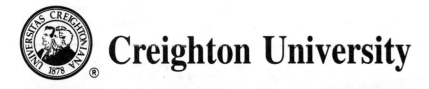

Creighton University

Omaha, Nebraska

CREATING YOUR FUTURE AT CREIGHTON UNIVERSITY

In the College of Business Administration, we believe that to arrive in the future we envision, we must create that future now. Our master's programs are creating a future that will ensure that we remain a leader in education for the next century even as we continue to benefit from the traditions of the past.

Creighton M.B.A. and M.C.S.M. graduates are identified regionally and nationally with an educational tradition of more than 100 years of excellence and values. This reputation attracts students to our programs; they stay with us because of our small size, excellent teaching and research faculty, diverse student population, and unrivaled connection to area business and industry. Another important measure of success is placement upon graduation, and we are more than ever committed to assisting our graduates in finding fulfilling job opportunities.

Through excellence in teaching, tradition, and placement, the Creighton M.B.A. and M.C.S.M. programs prepare successful managerial professionals to meet the complex demands of the present and the future. We welcome you to join us in the creation of that future.

—Bernard W. Reznicek, Dean

Programs and Curricular Focus

Creighton's graduate programs in business administration prepare students to play important roles in the administration of public and private organizations. The College of Business Administration offers two distinct programs in business, the Master of Business Administration and the Master of Computer Systems Management, designed to meet the specific requirements of students with varied interests and professional needs. The Creighton M.B.A. or M.C.S.M. graduate will have had the opportunity to specialize in an area of particular interest while being exposed to a broad-based approach to business. Courses are conducted using a combination of theory, case analysis, and student research to provide an optimal balance of pedagogy and practical application.

The new M.B.A. curriculum, implemented in fall 1994, provides structure and flexibility within the course of study. The core curriculum ensures sufficient breadth of exposure to cover all areas of administration. Consisting of 18 credit hours, the core area includes managerial accounting, finance, marketing, economics, organizational behavior, and information systems. Specialization is possible within the required 9 credit hours of electives; the program is completed with

the integration capstone course, "Business Policy and Managerial Action."

The M.C.S.M. curriculum is structured to combine rigorous study of computer-based systems with course work in the management issues facing computer professionals, including business policy, ethics, technology, and innovation. The student also completes an elective course in business administration, chosen to fulfill the goals of the individual program.

The College also conducts a joint M.B.A./J.D. program, which it is possible to complete within four years. Students who wish to pursue the joint degree make separate application to the Graduate Business Program and the School of Law.

Students and the M.B.A. Experience

Approximately two thirds of graduate business students are fully employed and complete their studies on a part-time basis. They come to the program from virtually all backgrounds and levels of management. The average student is 28 years old, with six years of work experience. About 60 percent of students have undergraduate degrees in business administration. Women comprise one fourth of the student body, and members

of minority groups comprise 10 percent. About 65 percent of graduate business students are natives of the Midwest.

❖ Global Focus

The M.B.A. program offers the intensive elective course International Business, which provides firsthand study of business practices and issues in a selected location abroad. Students have studied in Tokyo and Shizuoka, Japan, and will travel to India in December 1995.

The College has also participated in faculty exchanges with institutions in China, India, Poland, and Australia. Creighton business faculty members have traveled to Germany and Uganda for yearlong visits.

Special Features

Each fall, new students may participate in the Managerial Writing Workshop, which teaches writing and business rhetoric, taught by the University Director of Composition. The annual New Student Orientation provides skills in case analysis, research methodology, and use of library facilities. Each new student is also provided with an orientation to the Wade Computer Center, the College's dedicated technology resource lab.

One option under the new M.B.A. curriculum is to take intensive, 1-credit-hour elective courses, which are designed to address contemporary issues in all areas of business. The first of these courses, titled "Leaders, Leadership, and Motivation," was conducted by Dean Reznicek. The course gave students the opportunity to meet weekly with CEOs and other executives to examine and research business successes, weaknesses, and strategies.

The Faculty

The quality of the faculty in the College of Business Administration is unrivaled in the area. There are many opportunities for interested students to develop rewarding mentoring relationships with their professors. Three faculty members hold endowed research chairs in economics, ethics, and accounting. The College has 41 full-time and 1 part-time faculty member. All full-time faculty members are doctorally qualified; the student-faculty ratio is 19:1.

The Business School Network

Corporate Partnerships

The internship and mentoring programs provide corporate experience in settings as diverse as First Data Corporation, Con Agra Foods, IBM, Union Pacific Railroad, State Farm Insurance, and FirsTier Bank.

Prominent Alumni

Among the many distinguished alumni are those winning the Alumni Merit Award over the past five years: Dean Bernard W. Reznicek, former CEO, Boston Edison and Omaha Public Power District; Robert A. Reed, President and CEO, Physicians Mutual Insurance Company; Warren H. Dunn, President and CEO, Miller Brewing Company; Paul T. Silas, Assistant Coach, New Jersey Nets; and James J. Corboy, Senior Vice President, Finance and Accounting, Dresser Industries, Inc.

The College and Environs

Founded in 1878, Creighton is coeducational and independent and is operated by the Jesuits. The combination of small size (6,340 students and 1,308 faculty members) and unusual diversity is the key to appreciation of Creighton's excellence. Creighton has set as its goal the conduct of higher education in the context of Christian values.

There are fifty-six buildings on Creighton's campus that provide excellent facilities for most of the University's academic and extracurricular activities. Following two decades of expansion and growth, emphasis is now placed on beautification of the central campus.

The University campus is a 15-minute walk from the business district of Omaha. Omaha is a city of 343,385 that serves as a regional center of industry and commerce. The city is the major urban area

between Chicago and Denver and between Minneapolis–St. Paul and Kansas City.

Placement

The Center for Career and Academic Planning (CAP) provides all aspects of placement services, including résumé referral service, employer directories, career fairs, job listings, and on-campus interviews. Strong ties exist between Creighton College of Business and area industry, and Creighton graduates are in demand. About 90 percent of part-time and 75 percent of full-time students have secured employment upon graduation, and graduates have been placed both nationally and internationally.

Admission

Applicants must have completed an undergraduate degree from an accredited institution. The average GPA for incoming students is 3.0. The minimum acceptable score on the GMAT is 450; the average score is 540. The minimum acceptable TOEFL score is 550.

Students who have not completed the nine required foundation-level courses must complete them early in the program. Students may elect to test out of foundation courses for which they feel they have adequate preparation. CLEP and DANTES scores are not acceptable.

Full-time students must purchase or have proof of a health insurance policy. All students born after 1956 must provide proof of immunization against measles, mumps, and rubella before they will be allowed to register for classes.

Finances

Estimated cost per graduate credit hour for the 1995–96 academic year is $339. Registration fees for full-time students are $170 and for part-time students are $17 per semester. Textbook cost per semester for the full-time student is approximately $500.

On-campus housing for graduate students is very limited; an interested student should request a placement from the Director of Housing in the spring preceding fall enrollment. Off-campus housing is available and affordable, with monthly costs ranging from $275 to $400 per month.

The graduate business programs offer ten graduate research assistantships (GRA) each year. The awards comprise 9 credit hours of tuition waiver and a monthly stipend. Partial tuition waivers are also available. GRAs and tuition waivers are merit-based and are the primary avenue of financial aid for the international student.

International Students

Creighton's graduate business programs attract applicants from around the world. Students have come from Germany, China, Thailand, Italy, Canada, India, Malaysia, the Ukraine, and Russia. Students who have not met the TOEFL requirement may apply to enroll in the University's English Language Program. The Office of International Programs provides a strong support system for academic and social success at Creighton.

Application Facts and Dates

Applications are considered year-round. Normally the deadline for the fall semester is July 15 and for the spring semester, December 15. GRA applications are evaluated in the spring semester and are awarded no later than July 15.

For more information, applicants should contact:

Ms. Adrian E. Koesters
Coordinator of Graduate Business
    Programs
Creighton University
2500 California Plaza
Omaha, Nebraska 68178
Telephone: 402-280-2853
Fax: 402-280-2172

Dartmouth College

The Amos Tuck School of Business

Hanover, New Hampshire

► A CHALLENGE YOU FACE TOGETHER

A student once said that when you graduate from Tuck, you've gained your education, your diploma, and friends for life. That statement captures something very special about Tuck that goes beyond statistics. Without a doubt, Tuck is one of the most selective and academically challenging M.B.A. programs. We provide students with an excellent general management education, a true appreciation of effective people skills, and a high level of technical abilities. Although the Tuck experience is rigorous, it is also supportive. Students work closely together, and with faculty, in a small-town, rural New England environment that provides for excellent quality of life. If you are interested in Tuck, I suggest that you contact some of our alumni. They are the best evidence of the value of the Tuck M.B.A..

—Colin Blaydon, Dean

Programs and Curricular Focus

Founded in 1900, Tuck was the first graduate school of management in the world, and it is the only top U.S. business school that offers the M.B.A. degree exclusively.

During the first year of study, all students take a set of fourteen required, equal-credit courses. Integrative, interactive, and international aspects of management weave through the curriculum. During every term of the first year, students participate in an integrative learning exercise. Interactive abilities are enhanced through management communication and organizational behavior courses, frequent team projects, oral presentations, and written assignments. International dimensions of management are emphasized in global economic environment and international leadership courses and in most other courses as well. Over one third of all course content is international. Half of all Tuck faculty members have lived and taught overseas.

Building on their first-year background, second-year students select courses according to their interests and career aspirations. They choose from over fifty elective courses without requiring a specific major. Students may undertake independent study projects that earn credit as second-year electives.

Exchange programs are available with the London Business School; the Instituto de Estudios Superiores de la Empresa in Barcelona, Spain; and the International University of Japan. Joint-degree programs are available in international

affairs (with Tufts University's Fletcher School of Law and Diplomacy), medicine (with Dartmouth Medical School), and engineering (with Dartmouth's Thayer School of Engineering).

Students and the M.B.A. Experience

Tuck's culture encourages students to grow with, rather than at the expense of, their peers. About 20 percent of the students in each class are native to somewhere other than the United States. International and domestic students come from varied ethnic and socioeconomic backgrounds. Minorities represent over 10 percent of the student body. Women constitute about one third of each class and married students represent one quarter of the student population. Nearly all students have worked two years or more before enrollment. The average is 4½ years of work experience. Students average 27 years of age. About half majored in business or economics before coming to Tuck. About 20 percent studied engineering, and many have graduate degrees.

Special Features

Tuck is unique among M.B.A. programs because of its small size of fewer than 400 students. The size allows more intellectual and social involvement between faculty members and students and among students themselves. It allows faculty members to administer more team projects, including a consulting project

for business clients in the first term. In these projects, student teams work with local businesses on predefined problems, presenting solutions to the clients at term's end. Another enriching student project is the TYCOON business simulation game. Devised and implemented by a Tuck graduate, TYCOON is a computerized simulation where teams of students compete with other teams to successfully launch a project.

The Faculty

Tuck faculty members are renowned for their teaching and scholarly excellence. A variety of teaching approaches are used, including lecture/discussions, case studies, team projects, simulation exercises, and independent studies. With a student-faculty ratio of 10:1, each student is assured ample interaction and individual attention.

The Business School Network

Corporate Partnerships

Nearly 100 top executives, many of whom are Tuck alumni, come to Hanover every year to participate in the Visiting Executive Program. Among the visiting executives Tuck has hosted recently are Warren Buffett, Chairman, Berkshire Hathaway Inc.; Michael Eisner, Chairman and CEO, The Walt Disney Company; John E. Pepper, CEO, the Procter & Gamble Company; and John Amerman, Chairman and CEO, Mattel Inc;

Prominent Alumni

Among the best known of Tuck's business graduates are John W. Amerman, Chairman and CEO of Mattel, Incorporated (Class of 1954); Andrew C. Sigler, Chairman of the Board of Champion International (Class of 1956); John H. Foster, Chairman and CEO of NovaCare (Class of 1967); Frank C. Herringer, President of Transamerica Corporation (Class of 1965); Christopher A. Sinclair, President and CEO of PepsiCo Foods and Beverages International (Class of 1973); Paul N. Clark, President of the Pharmaceutical Division and Senior Vice President, Abbott Laboratories (Class of 1971); Lisa A. Conte, President and CEO of Shaman Pharmaceuticals Inc. (Class of

1985); Noreen Doyle, Head of Syndications and Credit, Banking Unit, European Bank for Reconstruction and Development (Class of 1974); Edmond F. Noel Jr., President and CEO of Colorado Sports Council (Class of 1969); Didier R. Pineau-Valencienne, Le President-Directeur Général, Groupe Schneider (Paris) (Class of 1957); and L. William Seidman, Chief Commentator, CNBC (formerly Chairman of FDIC) (Class of 1944).

The College and Environs

Tuck is located on the campus of Dartmouth College in picturesque Hanover, New Hampshire. Students enjoy full use of Dartmouth's academic and cultural facilities. The libraries comprise one of the finest collections in New England. The Hopkins Center for the Performing Arts offers a broad range of locally and internationally produced theater, music, dance, and film. The Hood Museum of Art presents exhibitions from all cultures and periods. Outdoor activities are a favorite of Tuck students and the Dartmouth community at large. Dartmouth's athletic facilities include several gymnasiums, pools, skating rinks, and weight-training equipment. There is also a boat house, golf course, and ski area.

Technology Environment

Students have access to some of the best and most advanced communications technology available on college campuses today. They communicate with each other, with outside businesses, and with the world's research resources at the touch of a finger. State-of-the-art color printers, presentation and layout software, and analytical programs are just a few of the technology resources readily available.

Placement

Beginning early in the fall, first-year students may attend career panels and company briefings. Assistance is offered in résumé writing and interviewing skills. The career resource library contains extensive and frequently updated company information, files on growth industries, and handout materials to help students prepare for their job search. Each year over 100 leading companies send representatives to interview graduating students on campus, and over 50 companies come to select summer interns. In addition, over 300 companies contact Tuck with job listings.

Admission

The application consists of a personal application form, essay questions, official transcripts from every college or university ever attended, at least two letters of recommendation, scores from the GMAT taken since October 1989, and a nonrefundable application fee of $75. Applicants for whom English is not their native language or who have not attended an undergraduate institution in which English is the language of instruction must take the Test of English as a Foreign Language (TOEFL). Interviews are not required for admission but are encouraged. Off-campus interviewing is often available.

Finances

Tuition for the 1994–95 school year was $21,225. This charge covered instruction, instructional facilities, and infirmary care services. For tuition, food, room, books and supplies, and personal expenses, a single student should budget approximately $35,000; a married student, approximately $4000 to $4500 more. The School provides financial assistance to qualified applicants through deferred-payment loans and a limited number of scholarships and fellowships.

International Students

Tuck welcomes international students. In the Class of 1995, there were students from Argentina, Australia, Brazil, China, Denmark, France, Germany, India, Italy, Japan, the Netherlands, Russia, South Korea, Spain, Sweden, Switzerland, Ukraine, and the United Kingdom.

Application Facts and Dates

A rolling decision process is used, so applicants are urged to complete their applications as early as possible. Students whose applications are received by mid-January are notified by mid-February, mid-February by mid-March, and mid-April by mid-May. Applicants may call for exact dates. For more information, students should contact:

Mr. Henry Malin
Director of Admissions
The Amos Tuck School
100 Tuck Hall
Dartmouth College
Hanover, New Hampshire 03755
Telephone: 603-646-3162
Fax: 603-646-1308

DePaul University

Charles H. Kellstadt Graduate School of Business

Chicago, Illinois

CHANGE IS THE ONLY CONSTANT—KELLSTADT PREPARES BUSINESS MANAGERS FOR THE LONG TERM

This much we know about the future of business: Change is the only constant. What this means for people seeking graduate business education is that they must prepare for change. At Kellstadt, we are committed to providing our students with the arsenal of skills needed to be successful managers in today's business climate and throughout their careers.

Our philosophy, our curriculum, and our history reflect that commitment. Our bold and entrepreneurial style, our long-standing relationship with Chicago's most powerful business leaders, our experienced faculty's hard-hitting practical approach to teaching . . . these are the foundation of a Kellstadt education. As a result, our graduates are in demand because they have the knowledge and skills it takes to contribute to the success of their organizations.

Kellstadt has one of the largest graduate business enrollments in the country. Our size supports extraordinary depth among our faculty and the largest number of courses offered anywhere in the Chicago area.

It is, however, our national reputation in which we take the most pride. We are ranked among the top ten part-time M.B.A. programs nationally by U.S. News & World Report and among the top ten according to "Bowman's Accounting Report" for the number of graduates who are currently partners in the "Big Six"; in addition Success magazine has ranked our entrepreneurship program in the top twenty-five; and the Gourman Report ranks us among the top 10 percent of graduate business programs nationally. These rankings reflect the strength of our faculty and the quality of our graduates.

—Ronald J. Patten, Dean

Programs and Curricular Focus

All Kellstadt programs carry the prestigious AACSB accreditation, and Kellstadt is one of the 10 percent of graduate business schools with membership in the General Management Admission Council (GMAC). The M.B.A. program provides a foundation of broad business functions with nine specialized concentrations: business economics, entrepreneurship, finance, human resource management, international business, management accounting, management information systems, marketing management, and operations management. The emphasis of the M.B.A. program is on decision making and the integration of the functional areas of business. With the exception of the intensive M.B.A. in International Marketing & Finance (MBA/IMF) program, all courses are taught in the evening and on weekends, allowing students to pursue careers during the day.

The School's contemporary focus is reflected in the international flavor of its offerings, its expanding ties to the world

business community, and in the scope of course offerings. The curriculum consists of four coordinated components: the internal environment of business, the external environment, managerial decision making, and a functional area of concentration. Mathematics, statistics, and computer literacy are integral components of the curriculum. All students take a course in effective communication, team taught by faculty members in the Departments of Marketing and Management, which is designed to develop the necessary skills to influence the decision-making process.

Students and the M.B.A. Experience

Kellstadt's students are unique in their experience and diversity. Most are working professionals who bring experience from every business area, in large corporations, small firms, and the nonprofit sector. They are known for their work ethic and are interested in real issues and real-world applications.

Kellstadt's students completed their undergraduate studies in institutions throughout the United States and in many other countries. Approximately 60 percent earned undergraduate degrees in business or economics, while the remaining 40 percent have degrees in nonbusiness disciplines.

❖ Global Focus

The intensive eighteen-month M.B.A. in International Marketing & Finance (MBA/IMF) is Kellstadt's most notable example of its global focus. This program evolved in response to extensive discussions with business leaders who expressed the need for managers who have new skills and innovative approaches to what is now a business evolution.

In just eighteen months, this one-of-a-kind program prepares students for rapid changes in the international marketplace. The integration of financial and marketing decision making with a pragmatic international business orientation is the hallmark of the MBA/IMF. Unique features include an international practicum, a network of international contacts that is second to none, and Kellstadt's full-time teaching faculty joined by its business partners and corporate executives.

Special Features

Of particular interest are courses that address current, new, or emerging business issues. A few examples of these special topics courses include Topics in International Money and Banking, Global Environmental Economy, Marketing to the Pacific Rim, and Case Studies in TQM.

The required capstone course, Strategic Analysis for Competing Globally, views the impact of contemporary issues on organizational strategy. Its team interaction, problem solving, and group decision making mirror the way strategic planning occurs in the best of real-world business environments.

The Faculty

One hundred fourteen full-time teaching professionals represent the core of the faculty. All are committed to teaching and scholarship, and many have received na-

DePaul Center, at the Center of Chicago.

tional recognition. Most important, the faculty members illustrate Kellstadt's hard-hitting practical orientation in that many of them are consistently called upon by the business community for their expertise.

Supplementing the full-time faculty is a pool of approximately 200 business professionals currently active in all aspects of business. It is precisely this blend of experts that accounts for the ideal mix of theory and practice that identifies a Kellstadt education.

The Business School Network

A powerful alumni network of over 13,000 Kellstadt graduates provides students with the door opener that can make the difference in career advancement. Leo Burnett, United Airlines, Arthur Andersen, Motorola, Abbott Laboratories, Baxter International, and Amoco are just a few examples of businesses that employ DePaul graduates.

Corporate Partnerships

The 49-member Advisory Council represents a veritable "Who's Who" in American business and keeps the School on the edge of today's business needs. The Senior Executive Lectures Series brings CEOs and senior managers to campus to share their views of current business issues. The Executive-in-Residence program utilizes business leaders as faculty members for one to three years. Cooperative agreements

with countries in Europe, Asia, and Central America have created additional relationships with multinational companies abroad.

The College and Environs

Kellstadt's home in the heart of Chicago's commercial and cultural center and its two suburban campuses in corporate corridors provide abundant career choices and contacts. Chicago indelibly stamps the curriculum and philosophy of the School. The city boasts one of the world's foremost symphony orchestras and art museums and some of the nation's best theater and is home to numerous Fortune 500 companies. Just as Chicago is a resource for the University, so is DePaul a resource for the city.

Technology Environment

DePaul Center, home to the Kellstadt Graduate School of Business, is a twenty-first-century facility. Its features include six U-shaped "case" classrooms; state-of-the-art video, computer simulation, and CD-ROM displays; tiered classrooms wired for PCs at each desk; and a marketing research facility equipped for the most advanced technology necessary to make complex marketing decisions. In short, DePaul Center is one of the most state-of-the-art educational environments in the country.

Placement

DePaul University's Center for Career Development works as a powerful link between the business community and Kellstadt's students and alumni. A computerized database provides a matching service for the most efficient job search. Comprehensive job fairs, workshops, and alumni networking are a few of the services available to students. Last year the center received 1,728 job leads for M.B.A. students, and 122 companies conducted 732 on-campus interviews.

Admission

Applications are considered for entrance in any of four quarters: fall, winter, spring, or summer. Decisions are based on prior academic performance, which must include a bachelor's degree, scores on the General Management Admission Test (GMAT), and work experience.

Admission to the eighteen-month MBA/IMF occurs only for the fall quarter. In addition to the above creden-

tials, students must submit a written statement, and an interview is required. Special consideration is given to students with international backgrounds.

In addition to the above credentials, international students and students educated outside the United States must submit scores on the Test of English as a Foreign Language (TOEFL). For specific information about other requirements for international students, applicants should contact DePaul University's International Student Advisor.

Finances

Evening student tuition for 1994–95 was $1540 per course. Tuition for the eighteen-month MBA/IMF was $1800 per course. On-campus housing is not available. Off-campus room and board are estimated to cost $1500 per month.

In addition to financial aid opportunities that include loans, Federal Work-Study, and part-time employment, the Kellstadt Graduate School of Business offers a number of graduate assistantships that comprise a stipend of $4000 to $4500 and tuition scholarships for a maximum of nine courses per year.

Application Facts and Dates

Application deadlines for the M.B.A. program are August 1 for fall quarter, November 1 for winter quarter, March 1 for spring quarter, and May 1 for summer quarter. The application deadline for the M.B.A. in International Marketing & Finance program is May 1 for fall quarter. The application fee is $40. For information about the M.B.A. program, students should contact:

Ms. Christine Munoz
Director of Admission
Kellstadt Graduate School of Business
DePaul University
1 East Jackson Boulevard
Chicago, Illinois 60604
Telephone: 312-362-8810
Fax: 312-362-6677
Internet: mbainfo@wppost.depaul.edu

For information about the MBA/IMF program, students should contact:

Mr. Paul Roberts
Kellstadt Graduate School of Business
DePaul University
1 East Jackson Boulevard
Chicago, Illinois 60604
Telephone: 312-362-8810
Fax: 312-362-6677
Internet: mba/imf@wppost.depaul.edu

Dowling College

> ## EDUCATING TOMORROW'S BUSINESS LEADERS TODAY
>
> *Dowling's School of Business has been educating business leaders for more than thirty years, and our M.B.A. programs are recognized for addressing issues relative to the global economy.*
>
> *Students enrolled in our M.B.A. programs develop a professional point of view in the science of management with respect to organization, operation, administration, and control of a business enterprise. Key decision-making skills are developed, as well as the ability to practically apply classroom ideology to the professional work world.*
>
> *Dowling is known as The Personal College®, committed to an environment for learning that recognizes and provides for the development of each individual's potential. Classes are small, and our faculty is dedicated. To learn more about Dowling's outstanding M.B.A. programs, I would encourage you to call us.*
>
> *—Michael A. Mogavero, Dean*

Programs and Curricular Focus

Dowling offers students five M.B.A. degree programs from which to choose. These include general management, aviation management, banking and finance, public management, and total quality management.

The degree in general management provides students with a comprehensive foundation in numerous managerial disciplines. It is the ideal degree for students who intend to specialize in one area of business after graduation or for those managers working in small to midsize businesses who must carry out more than one managerial function during the course of a working day.

The M.B.A. in aviation management is designated for professionals already working in the field of aviation management as well as individuals who aspire to positions within the industry. This degree helps managers run their divisions more efficiently and keep pace with the dynamic elements impacting the aviation industry today. This degree is applicable to professionals affiliated with air carriers, airport facilities, aerospace companies, and/or sectors of the industry such as manufacturing, government contractors, or government employees.

Banking and finance are among the most dynamic industries in the global economy. Because of the changing complexity of financial markets worldwide and the greater variety of financial instruments being developed, the knowledge and information needed to thrive in this environment are expanding rapidly.

Acquiring the skills necessary to manage in a not-for-profit or government environment is at the core of Dowling's public management M.B.A. program. Courses such as Quantitative Methods for Public Sector Decision Making, Not-for-Profit Marketing, and Public Sector Finance help focus the 36-credit degree program on the specifics of this diverse field.

The M.B.A. in Total Quality Management (TQM) challenges students to focus their attention on meeting customer needs in addition to the traditional functional operations of business. Students are instructed in theories of TQM by faculty members who are leaders in quality management education.

Dowling also offers busy executives the opportunity to earn their M.B.A. in general management or banking and finance in a distinctive Saturdays-Only program. This three-semester degree program includes an innovative luncheon speakers series; a state-of-the-art notebook computer with word processing, spreadsheet, and presentation software; and all required textbooks and educational software.

Students and the M.B.A. Experience

Dowling's M.B.A. student population is a diverse one, ranging from recent bacca-laureate degree graduates to established business men and women to physicians, Ph.D.'s, and other professionals. The average age is 33, and graduate students comprise 36 percent of the student body. Dowling's international scope continues to grow with the addition of its new National Aviation and Transportation Center, a unique facility dedicated to the study and research of global transportation issues.

Each of Dowling's M.B.A. programs places the student in real-world situations through the management simulation capstone requirement. Students work in teams and must demonstrate the successful start-up of a business venture and direct its capital distribution, purchasing efforts, marketing campaigns, cash flow logistics, and related responsibilities. In addition, students enrolled in Dowling's innovative Saturdays-Only M.B.A. program, which enables students to complete their degrees in only three semesters by attending classes all day on Saturdays, work in assigned groups, facilitating the concept of teamwork, and move in unison throughout the duration of the degree program.

Special Features

The Saturdays-Only M.B.A. program offers students an innovative Luncheon Speakers Series, which features prominent local, national, and international business professionals. Speakers have included George Gallup of Gallup Poll International, Jerry Goodman of Adam Smith's Money World, and Ben Cohen, cofounder of Ben & Jerry's Homemade Ice Cream.

Dowling's Small Business Institute, which is associated with the U.S. Small Business Institute, provides students with the opportunity to work with companies on Long Island, assisting them with problem-solving issues related to accounting, computer information systems, finance, management, and marketing.

The Faculty

The graduate business program at Dowling is conducted within the personalized atmosphere of a small college by a faculty of highly qualified experienced business professionals. Faculty members are noted regularly for their scholarly works, publications, expert testimony, papers and presentations, professional standings, and participation in national conferences.

The Business School Network

Dowling's innovative partnerships with businesses and corporations across Long Island, throughout the nation, and around the globe have spawned numerous benefits for M.B.A. students, including lecture series, internships, and business networking opportunities. Dowling's Board of Trustees and Advisory Council members, whose business acumen and expertise are vital elements in Dowling's

FACULTY LIST

Lawrence Bauer, Ph.D., Assistant Professor. Management.
Reinaldo Blanco, M.S., CPA, Assistant Professor. Accounting.
Glen Brauchle, M.B.A., CPA, Assistant Professor. Accounting.
Gail Butler, J.D., Assistant Professor. Aeronautics.
Cono Casella, Ph.D., Professor. Finance.
Thomas Diamante, Ph.D., Assistant Professor. Management.
Diane Fischer, Ph.D., Associate Professor. Computer information systems.
George Foundotos, M.S., CPA, Professor. Accounting.
Thomas Frye, Ph.D., Assistant Professor. Management.
Leo Giglio, M.S., Instructor. Management.
Bruce Haller, J.D., Assistant Professor. Management.
Allan Hogenauer, Ph.D., Associate Professor. Marketing.
Mitchell Langbert, Ph.D., Assistant Professor. Management.
Nicholas Mauro, Ph.D., Associate Professor. Management.
Joseph Monahan, Ph.D., Associate Professor. Finance.
Carol Okolica, Ph.D., Assistant Professor. Computer information systems.
Allan Oshrin, LL.B., Adjunct Assistant Professor. Management.
Faith Pereira, Ph.D., Assistant Professor. Marketing.
Luis Rivera, Ph.D., Assistant Professor. Finance.
Walter Rosenthal, Ph.D., Associate Professor. Marketing.
Charles Rudiger, Ed.D., Associate Professor. Management.
Walter Schimpf, M.B.A., Assistant Professor. Accounting.
Michael Shapiro, Ph.D., Assistant Professor. Marketing.
Fred Strauss, M.S., Assistant Professor. Computer information systems.

exemplary leadership, serve as successful corporate examples and are often on campus, giving students numerous opportunities to meet with them.

The College and Environs

Originated in 1955 as Suffolk County's first four-year college, Dowling's 51-acre campus is nestled along the picturesque banks of the Connetquot River on the southern shore of Long Island, approximately 50 miles east of midtown Manhattan. It is within easy reach of New York's theaters, museums, sports events, and other cultural attractions. Still, Dowling is just minutes from Long Island's beautiful beaches, parks, and other recreational facilities. At Dowling, students have the best of both worlds: city and country.

Fortunoff Hall is the focal point of the Oakdale campus. Built at the turn of the century by industrial magnate William K. Vanderbilt, this exquisitely preserved mansion houses administrative and faculty offices, as well as ornately designed ceremonial rooms that are used for meeting and lecture purposes.

Facilities

Dowling's library is located in the Nicholas and Constance Racanelli Center for Learning Resources and makes available to students 165,000 volumes, 1,200 current periodicals, 520,000 microforms, and 57,000 government documents.

The Academic Computing Center, which includes three multimedia computing classrooms, three computing laboratories for individual use, and a faculty resource center, is available to students during extended day and evening hours. The College's membership in the New York State Education and Research Network (Nysernet) serves as a gateway to the Internet, a global network providing access to hundreds of computers for research and scholarly communication. Students can also access the collections of thousands of libraries, universities, and research centers worldwide through the Online Computer Library Center.

Placement

The Office of Cooperative Education, Career Counseling and Placement maintains a network of partnerships with businesses on Long Island, in New York, and across the nation. On-campus recruiters from respected companies are regularly scheduled, and Dowling's M.B.A. graduates maintain a high visibility quotient. Students can also

attend special lectures on résumé writing, interviewing skills, and career change strategies. Dowling's alumni organization provides numerous networking activities throughout the year, which current students are encouraged to attend.

Admission

Each candidate's academic record, scores on the required Graduate Management Admission Test (GMAT), and work experience are considered in the admission process. A GMAT score of 475 or more and a minimum 2.8 GPA in undergraduate work are preferred.

Qualified applicants who have limited backgrounds in business administration will be required to complete successfully certain preparatory courses in addition to the minimum 36 credits of graduate work. These areas of study might include accounting, economics, quantitative methods, computer science, and management. For those students who use English as a second language, a TOEFL score of 500 or better is required.

Finances

Tuition is $351 per graduate credit, and certain student fees are applicable. On-campus housing is available in apartment-style suites for $1360 per semester. There are ample off-campus apartments within easy travel distance of the College.

Numerous scholarship programs are available, and optional packages can be explored with a personal financial aid counselor. In addition, the College offers each student an individualized printed guide to the financial aid programs available to him or her, as well as access to CASHE, a computerized search program that can produce a listing of national and international financial aid programs.

International Students

Individualized tutorial programs are available to students who require special assistance with the English language.

Application Facts and Dates

The application deadline for fall is August 15; for spring, it is January 15. For more information, students should contact:

Michael Mogavero, Dean
School of Business
Dowling College
Idle Hour Boulevard
Oakdale, New York 11769-9999
Telephone: 516-244-3355
          800-DOWLING (toll-free)
Fax: 516-589-6644

Drexel University

Philadelphia, Pennsylvania

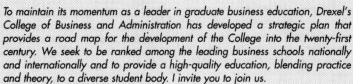

> *To maintain its momentum as a leader in graduate business education, Drexel's College of Business and Administration has developed a strategic plan that provides a road map for the development of the College into the twenty-first century. We seek to be ranked among the leading business schools nationally and internationally and to provide a high-quality education, blending practice and theory, to a diverse student body. I invite you to join us.*
>
> —Arthur H. Baer, Dean

Programs and Curricular Focus

The M.B.A. program at Drexel is designed to meet a wide range of student needs. It can provide a broad, balanced curriculum or one that's more focused. The M.B.A. program offers the conceptual tools to back up previously acquired experience, or it can provide professional experience as part of the M.B.A. studies. In fact, the program can be tailored to match a wide variety of student preferences.

The M.B.A. program has concentrations in fourteen areas and may be pursued on a full-time or part-time basis, day or evening. There is also a general M.B.A. program that is offered on Saturdays. Drexel's academic calendar of four 10-week terms gives students the option to enter most of the College's programs at any time of the year.

The M.B.A. degree program requires completion of 84 credits, consisting of twelve 3-credit foundation courses and sixteen 3-credit advanced courses. It is organized as a two-year program, but the actual time required to complete the degree depends on the number of credits that a student transfers into the program and the number of courses he or she chooses to register for each term.

The foundation courses represent the common body of knowledge required by the American Assembly of Collegiate Schools of Business (AACSB), which has fully accredited the College's M.B.A. program. In general, the foundation courses should be completed before the advanced courses are undertaken. Some or all foundation courses can be waived if a student has completed equivalent courses as an undergraduate.

The advanced level includes five required core courses, five professional electives (one course from each of five business disciplines), four courses in the student's field of concentration, and two business electives.

Students and the M.B.A. Experience

Drexel's M.B.A. program enrolls approximately 1,000 students, one third of whom are enrolled full-time. These students represent widely diverse backgrounds: those entering directly from undergraduate programs and businesspeople with years of experience; those who completed undergraduate degrees at Drexel as well as alumni of universities in Europe and Asia; and those with degrees in business subjects along with engineers, scientists, physicians, liberal arts graduates, and military officers. Not only is Drexel's program flexible enough to accommodate these many individuals, it is also enriched by the variety of their perspectives. Approximately one half of the full-time students are international.

Special Features

The Drexel Career Integrated Education option (CIE) provides a wealth of real-world hands-on career experience. The CIE option allows students to enrich their master's studies in business by earning credit for supervised employment experience related to their academic and career goals. This option provides an outstanding opportunity for recent college graduates to begin building their base of experience as well as their résumés, for international students to gain experience in the American workplace and Americans to gain international experience working abroad, and for established professionals to prepare for a transition from one career field to another. For those students seeking to gain global experience, Drexel's M.B.A. program offers the opportunity to take some courses at L'Ecole Supérieure de Commerce de Paris (ESCP). Drexel students and French students take many of their courses abroad, and both can earn their M.B.A. degrees from Drexel.

The Faculty

Drexel's College of Business and Administration has an outstanding faculty. Over 95 percent hold the doctoral degree, and they have earned distinction for their published research as well as for the many journals and textbooks they have edited or authored. In keeping with the College's practical orientation, faculty members also enjoy strong ties with the business community, dramatically enhancing the educational environment at the College. Drexel faculty members have served as consultants for a range of corporations, government agencies, and other organizations. Corporate and entrepreneurial leaders augment the full-time faculty by coming to campus as guest lecturers or part-time teachers.

The Business School Network

Drexel's College of Business and Administration maintains extensive relationships with the business community through an advisory board consisting of senior executives from major corporations and nonprofit organizations. The advisory board meets with the dean and faculty on a regular basis to provide input for curriculum and program revision and development.

The College's relationship with the local business community is further enhanced by the prestigious Business Leader of the Year Award, which grew out of one student's suggestion that the College cite a business leader as an example of success, service, citizenship, and leadership. The student who made that suggestion, George M. Ross, Class of '55, is now a resident partner with Goldman, Sachs, and Co., chairman of the University's board of trustees, and himself a past Business Leader of the Year Award recipient.

The College and Environs

Philadelphia is an appealing place to earn a graduate degree. As a leading center for commerce, industry, government, and the arts, the city also offers museums, libraries, and other resources that support learning. The metropolitan area provides ample employment opportunities for students and graduates alike, in such growing fields as banking, finance, pharmaceuticals, insurance, and telecommunications.

Philadelphia features countless opportunities for cultural and recreational activi-

ties, as well. Historic sites, such as Independence Hall and the Liberty Bell; major league teams in baseball, basketball, football, and ice hockey; the world-famous Philadelphia Orchestra; and the Philadelphia Museum of Art are only a few of the attractions that students enjoy. Fairmount Park, the nation's largest city park; the Philadelphia Zoo; and Penn's Landing, the city's riverfront development, provide additional options for spare-time activities. Ethnically diverse Philadelphia is often called "the city of neighborhoods," with such colorful communities to visit as Chinatown and South Philadelphia's Italian Market.

Drexel is ideally located for students to take advantage of public transportation. Just two blocks away is 30th Street Station—Philadelphia's major railroad station and a stop for Amtrak trains from New York City and Washington, D.C., local commuter trains, and a shuttle to the airport. New Jersey's beaches and Pennsylvania's Pocono Mountains are each within a 2-hour drive of the city.

Facilities

The College of Business and Administration is housed in two buildings on campus. The buildings contain modern lecture halls, conference rooms, and the Center for Executive Education. University computer facilities include an IBM 3090 VM mainframe, a Prime 6350, an AT&T 3B5, and a Control Data Cyber180/800. The campus is networked, and students have access to the Internet with their own account. In addition, the

University microcomputer support facility contains over 500 Macintosh microcomputers and supports a full range of consulting and training workshop services. Business students also have access to the College of Business and Administration's own IBM PC and Macintosh Power PC computer labs.

Placement

Placement services are provided through the Career Services Center (CSC) free of charge up to one year past date of graduation. Graduates can also obtain job listings and use other resources at any time. For those students who wish to refine their interviewing skills, Drexel offers the General Electric Video Interview Program (GEVIP). This service allows students to practice their interviewing skills on videotape to learn where they can make improvements. Drexel's CSC has its own Career Library. It contains extensive files and videotapes of general career and specific employer information from which students can develop a list of potential employers. Drexel offers an on-campus interview program. Each fall, winter, and spring, employer representatives visit campus to interview the current graduating class for upcoming employment opportunities. Candidates are selected for interviews by the employer organizations.

Admission

All applicants must have received a four-year bachelor's degree from an accredited college or university. Degrees

earned abroad must be deemed equivalent. The College of Business and Administration's admissions committee reviews applicants based on undergraduate accomplishments, performance on the GMAT, previous professional accomplishments, career goals, references, and the personal essay.

Students whose native language is not English and who do not hold degrees from U.S. institutions are required to submit a score on the Test of English as a Second Language (TOEFL). Interviews are not required but can be arranged through the Office of Graduate Admissions.

Finances

Tuition for master's courses is billed by the credit hour. As of the 1994–95 academic year, the cost was $414 per credit hour; all graduate business courses are 3 credits. Tuition is the same for full-time and part-time students.

Graduate assistantships are available to full-time master's business students. An assistantship requires the student to work for 20 hours per week for a department or professor in return for tuition remission for three courses per term plus a monthly stipend. Applications for assistantships are available in the Graduate Business Office. Federal Stafford Student Loans and other loans are available for part-time and full-time students through the University's Financial Aid Office.

International Students

International students are an important component of Drexel's graduate student body and are actively recruited. International students come from all over the world and over forty countries, including Asia, the Pacific Rim, Europe, South America, and Canada. The International Affairs office conducts a weeklong orientation program to assist international students to become acclimated to the American social and educational culture.

Application Facts and Dates

Drexel's College of Business and Administration admits students for each of its four quarters. For the fall quarter, the final application deadline is August 20 for U.S. citizens and June 20 for non–U.S. citizens. For the winter quarter, the deadline is November 2 for U.S. citizens and September 25 for noncitizens. For the spring quarter, it is March 1 for citizens and January 3 for noncitizens, and for the summer, it is May 31 for citizens and March 31 for noncitizens. For more information, students should contact:

Office of Graduate Admissions
Drexel University, Box P
Philadelphia, Pennsylvania 19104
Telephone: 215-895-6700
Internet: admissions-grad@
post.drexel.edu

Eastern College

St. Davids, Pennsylvania

DEVELOPING BUSINESS LEADERS FOR THE TWENTY-FIRST CENTURY

The political landscape of the world has undergone a virtual revolution within the past few years. More than any other time in recent history, the nations of the world have expressed a desire to learn from each other and to cooperate with one another in order to grow culturally, technologically, and economically.

In many respects, globalization is the key concept today in business. Individuals who are conscious of being world citizens and who are at home intellectually and socially in an international business setting have the competitive advantage over the person whose vision is more provincial.

The graduate business programs at Eastern College seek to provide an education with a strong emphasis on having a global perspective within a world Christian perspective.

—Linwood T. Geiger, Dean

Programs and Curricular Focus

The traditional M.B.A. program consists of a general program and five concentrations: finance, human resources management, marketing, general studies, and nonprofit management. The core curriculum for the traditional program consists of courses in accounting, economics, finance, organizational behavior, marketing management, quantitative decision-making, and business ethics. The innovative concentration in nonprofit organizations includes courses in fundraising, legal mandates, public relations, strategic planning, and management of volunteers.

In addition, Eastern College offers an M.B.A. and an M.S. in health administration and an M.B.A. and an M.S. in economic development. In 1994, an M.S. in nonprofit management was added to the business programs.

Courses are organized into three groups: foundation courses, core (required) courses, and specific elective courses for the concentrations. To earn a degree in the traditional M.B.A. or the nonprofit management M.B.A. programs, students must complete 36 semester/credit hours of graduate courses. Students earning a degree in the health administration M.B.A. must complete 39 semester/credit hours of graduate courses. Students may also be required to take foundation courses, contingent on a review of previous course work.

Eastern College offers three dual-degree programs with Eastern Baptist

Theological Seminary. The joint degrees of 116 total credit hours are M.Div./M.S. Economic Development, M.Div./M.B.A. Economic Development and M.Div./ M.B.A. Traditional. Eastern also offers a twenty-two-month intensive M.B.A. program.

Students and the M.B.A. Experience

Students at Eastern College bring diverse résumés as well as culturally varied backgrounds to their M.B.A. experience. The average student is a 32-year-old with nine years of work experience. Women comprise one third of the student population, and minority students make up 16 percent.

The Northeast sends 65 percent of Eastern College M.B.A. students, while 5 percent come from the Midwest. Six percent come from the West Coast, and international students make up the final 24 percent.

Eastern College students not only learn from the professors, they learn from each other. The diverse cultural and business backgrounds of the professors and students offer each student the opportunity to explore other countries and careers without leaving the classroom.

Special Features

The economic development program offers many opportunities to develop a broader understanding of cross-cultural issues. The capstone to this program is a semester in-

ternship project. The internship enables the student to develop professional experience in an urban or international setting. The primary emphasis is placed on the creation and growth of microscale and small-scale enterprises.

The Faculty

The business programs have attracted and employed the talents of an experienced and dynamic faculty. Faculty members have researched, visited, lived, and performed professionally all over the world. They have established and managed businesses and development organizations. They have also served as consultants to international and urban organizations.

The Business School Network

Since the inception of the M.B.A. program, there have been strong partnerships with corporations and organizations in the Philadelphia metro and suburban areas. Students in the nonprofit M.B.A. program have the opportunity to introduce fundraising strategic plans to foundations for professional review and critique. This as well as other networking experiences are available in the business program.

The College and Environs

In 1982, Eastern College launched the first Master of Business Administration program in the western suburbs of Philadelphia. Located in St. Davids on the main line of Philadelphia, Eastern College is a beautiful suburban campus within 3 miles of Interstate 476. Only 20 minutes by train or car from the city, the heart of the campus is the Charles S. Walton estate, built in 1913. Eastern has grown beyond the original estate to include twenty-six buildings and more than 100 acres of woods, ponds, creeks, and lawns. The total population at Eastern College has grown to over 2,040 students.

Technology Environment

Eastern College has its own computing lab facilities, consisting of over fifty terminals. The computer lab is open from 9 a.m. to 11 p.m., Monday through

Friday. It is also open on the weekends. The intensive M.B.A. program (Fast-Track M.B.A.) at Eastern College provides each of the business students with a laptop computer. The Warner Library is an attractive and comfortable facility housing over 13,000 volumes. The library is a part of the OCLC information network, opening 22 million volumes to students as resources.

Placement

The career center at Eastern College enables graduate students the opportunity to develop networks in the Philadelphia area. The career center has contacts with many of the national and international companies based in the eastern Pennsylvania region.

Admission

Admission to an M.B.A. or an M.S. program is open to all qualified college graduates, regardless of field of undergraduate study. Those wishing to apply for admissions to any of the M.B.A. or M.S. programs should submit the following: a complete application form; a nonrefundable application fee of $25; official undergraduate transcripts indicating a GPA of 2.5 or better; two letters of professional recommendation; official results of the GMAT (not required for the M.S. programs), with scores of 450 or better; and for international students, the official results of the TOEFL, with scores of 550 or better. Students who wish to take a limited number of courses at the graduate level may enroll as nondegree, nonmatriculated students.

Finances

Tuition for graduate courses is $325 per semester credit hour, and for foundation courses, the tuition is $270 per semester credit hour. Estimated fees for the 1995–96 year are $550 for all students. Books and miscellaneous expenses are approximately $2500 per year. Estimated living expenses for a single student are approximately $3300 for housing and $1800 for food per year. Married couples typically spend $6000 for housing and $2400 for food.

Assistantships and scholarships are available for certain M.B.A. programs. Students must apply for assistance to be eligible for either an assistantship or for a scholarship.

International Students

Thirty-five percent of the graduate students at Eastern College come from outside the United States. The on-campus international student adviser provides international students assistance in becoming acclimated to their new environment as well as to American culture and practices.

Application Facts and Dates

Once an application is complete, it is evaluated, and a response is given in a timely manner. Eastern's commitment is to keep students well informed through all stages of this process. Admissions are handled on a rolling basis, and there is no application deadline. However, students are urged to apply well in advance of the semester they plan to enter. For more information, students should contact:

Michelle Roush
   Assistant Director of Graduate
   Admissions
B. Scott Camilleri
   Assistant Director of Graduate
   Admissions for Recruiting
Kathleen Hassett
   Administrative Assistant to
   Graduate Admissions

Eastern College
Graduate Admissions
10 Fairview Drive
St. Davids, Pennsylvania 19087
Telephone: 610-341-5972
Fax: 610-341-1466

Eastern Michigan University

Ypsilanti, Michigan

> Eastern Michigan University's College of Business, the third-largest business school in Michigan, combines a progressive curriculum with a diverse student body to create a graduate program that is designed to help transform corporate America. Our graduate programs offer students impressive management tools and practical business experience and develop valuable interpersonal and communication skills. We offer an M.B.A. program and master's programs in accounting, computer-based information systems, and human resource and organizational development.
>
> We are proud of the accomplishments of our graduates. They symbolize the quality of our programs. Our outstanding facilities, experienced faculty, and connections with corporate leaders make Eastern Michigan's College of Business an exceptional learning environment.
>
> —Stewart L. Tubbs, Dean

Programs and Curricular Focus

The M.B.A. program gives students a broad understanding of business functions, including the relationship of business to society as a whole, the impact of legal forces on business, and the internationalization of today's business climate. The program is designed to provide a general M.B.A. or a specialized M.B.A. in financial accounting, tax accounting, finance, international business, strategic quality management, human resource management, organizational development, marketing, or information systems management. This program requires 54 to 63 semester hours of graduate-level courses; however, students with undergraduate business degrees may need as few as 33 semester hours of graduate-level course work to complete the program. The educational emphasis is on a combination of state-of-the-art tools, concepts, and theory for practical application. An international perspective is provided throughout. Courses are offered in the evenings and on weekends. All graduate programs are accredited by the American Assembly of Collegiate Schools of Business.

Students and the M.B.A. Experience

The College of Business has 586 students in the M.B.A. program, representing a wide variety of academic degrees, nationalities, and work experiences. The average student is 30 years old and has

an undergraduate GPA of 3.01, a GMAT score of 520, and seven years of work experience. Forty percent of the students are women, and 3 percent are members of minority groups. International students, representing twenty countries, comprise 28 percent of the student population. Approximately half of the students have undergraduate degrees in business, while the other half have undergraduate degrees in engineering, nursing, education, arts and sciences, and the humanities.

❖ Global Focus

The College of Business offers many opportunities that enhance and strengthen students' perspectives on the global business environment. A double master's degree program with the Export-Akademie Baden-Wuerttemberg in Reutlinger, Germany, affords students the opportunity to earn an M.B.A. in international business from EMU and a master's degree in international marketing from Export-Akademie. Currently, the College of Business is exploring a joint venture E.M.B.A. program in Singapore and joint-degree programs through EMU's World College in France and Spain. EMU is one of six U.S. schools in the nineteen-member Institute of International Education Regional Area Mobility Program. Eastern offers an extensive cooperative education program and was one of nine institutions listed in *International Business* magazine's "Who's Who in International Co-op Programs."

The Faculty

Faculty members of the College of Business are among the finest teachers and researchers in the country. There are 81 full-time tenured faculty members.

The Business School Network

Corporate Partnerships

The College of Business has established a number of strong partnerships with corporations in southeastern Michigan, affording students a variety of opportunities for fieldwork and networking with business leaders. Students interact directly with prominent businesspersons through courses in survey and organizational diagnosis, human resource development, and communication and organizational development and a management practicum. The 28-member College of Business Development Board includes CEOs and high-ranking officers from companies such as Gerber Products Company, Comerica Bank, Chrysler Motor Company, Ford Motor Company, and General Motors.

Prominent Alumni

Graduates of the College of Business include business leaders such as Timothy Adams, Director of New Generation Vehicles at Chrysler Corporation; Dennis Toffolo, President of Hudson's; Marcia Allen, Partner with Coopers and Lybrand; Ron Campbell, Chief Financial Officer for the Detroit Pistons; and Bruce Halle, owner of Discount Tires.

The College and Environs

Eastern Michigan University, founded in 1849, is a coeducational institution located in the heart of the industrial and culturally rich region of southeastern Michigan. The University is a focal point of the historic city of Ypsilanti, located near the Detroit metropolitan area. With a student population of more than 25,000, the University offers instruction through five academic colleges. The University's 200 acres of lawn and wooded areas and 18 miles of walkways and jogging trails make the campus a beautiful learning environment. A 188,000-square-foot recreation/intramural facility, newly renovated student union,

Eastern Michigan's College of Business is one of only 240 business schools in the country accredited by the American Assembly of Collegiate Schools of Business.

University-owned Corporate Education Center, and championship golf course are among the many impressive University facilities.

Facilities
Among the University's 105 campus facilities is the Gary M. Owen College of Business building. Located in downtown Ypsilanti, this new 122,000-square-foot state-of-the-art facility was completed in 1990. It includes classrooms, computer labs, seminar rooms, departmental offices, and behavioral labs that simulate a typical business environment.

Technology Environment
To ensure the success of its graduates, the College of Business has equipped its microcomputer laboratory with fifty microcomputers (386SX's) and ten Macintosh computers connected through an Ethernet interface. The lab also has thirty VAX terminals for accessing the University's mainframe. Computer and video equipment in the behavioral labs allows both presentation of controlled information and accurate recording of subjects' responses.

Placement
EMU's Career Services Office has established strong relationships with on-campus recruiters and offers a number of services, workshops, and programs to aid students in their job searches. Among other strong relationships with Fortune 500 and multinational companies, Eastern Michigan has more than 1,300 graduate business alumni working at Ford Motor Company and is one of the fourteen key universities for Chrysler.

A representative of the Career Services Office works on-site at the College of Business to help students secure job interviews, co-op positions, and internships. Graduates of the M.B.A. program have the highest starting salaries among those who have completed any graduate program in the University, with a reported average salary of $45,000.

Admission
Admission is granted to those graduates of accredited institutions whose undergraduate GPA and GMAT scores indicate a high promise of success in graduate business studies. The average GMAT score for enrolling College of Business graduate students is 520. The average undergraduate GPA is 3.01.

International students must also provide proof of a degree from an accredited college overseas and official transcripts or mark sheets, results of the Test of English as a Foreign Language (TOEFL) or Michigan Test ELI, a statement of financial responsibility, and two letters of recommendation. The I-20 form for the F-1 Visa cannot be issued until the student has been admitted to a degree program.

Finances
Estimated full-time tuition and fees for 1995–96 are $3900 per year for Michigan residents and $9000 per year for nonresidents. Books and supplies cost approximately $1200 per year. Rent for on-campus apartments ranges from $350 to $500 per month; off-campus rents range from $400 to $700 per month.

A limited number of graduate assistantships are available for full-time graduate students. Assistantships require 20 hours of work per week and carry a stipend of $5190 to $5410 for two semesters. Inquiries regarding these programs should be addressed to the head of the department in which the student intends to specialize.

International Students
International students, representing twenty different countries, comprise 28 percent of the total graduate business student population at EMU. The highest percentage of international students come from Taiwan (28 percent), India (22 percent), Thailand (20 percent), and China (9 percent). Programs and services offered through the Foreign Student Affairs office and support from a number of international student organizations help international students acclimate to the University environment.

Application Facts and Dates
Application deadlines are September 15 for winter semester, February 15 for spring and summer terms, and March 15 for fall semester.

For more information, students should contact:

William E. Whitmire
Graduate Business Programs
  Coordinator
401 Gary M. Owen Building
Eastern Michigan University
Ypsilanti, Michigan 48197
Telephone: 313-487-4444
Fax: 313-487-6496

HEC École des Hautes Études Commerciales

Master of Business Administration Program

Montreal, Canada

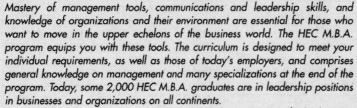

THE HEC M.B.A.: A MASTERING BUSINESS

Mastery of management tools, communications and leadership skills, and knowledge of organizations and their environment are essential for those who want to move in the upper echelons of the business world. The HEC M.B.A. program equips you with these tools. The curriculum is designed to meet your individual requirements, as well as those of today's employers, and comprises general knowledge on management and many specializations at the end of the program. Today, some 2,000 HEC M.B.A. graduates are in leadership positions in businesses and organizations on all continents.

—Jean-Marie Toulouse, Director, École des HEC

Programs and Curricular Focus

In the first two phases of the HEC M.B.A. program, students acquire a global and integrated view of a company and the many facets of a manager's work. They develop a solid understanding of a business environment and how it operates. The focus is put on administration, corporate functions (marketing, finance, human resources management, and production and operations management), accounting, information systems, economics, quantitative methods, and organizational behavior.

During the third phase, students are especially fortunate in that they are offered one of the widest ranges of course options in North America. In fact, the HEC M.B.A. program features no fewer than ten options, including a combined option and an individual option, leading to a great many professional possibilities. Thus, students pursue their own interests and career objectives within the program. The third phase also includes a comprehensive course in corporate strategy.

Stimulating, viable, visionary—the HEC M.B.A. program is the experience of a lifetime, one that leads to significant and determining changes. In this program, students acquire the knowledge and analytical techniques essential to the managerial function, and they develop skills such as determining what is at stake in a management problem; developing and implementing realistic and innovative solutions; working as part of a team—communicating, delegating, and directing; anticipating and taking advantage of business opportunities; and managing change and innovation.

Created more than twenty years ago, the M.B.A. program has been continuously enhanced over the years. New courses are tested every year. Within the past three years, for example, the program has offered students new courses in ethics, technological environment, sustainable development, and free trade.

Students and the M.B.A. Experience

Although all of them have met the same criteria, candidates admitted to the HEC M.B.A. program are nevertheless an extremely diverse group. In nearly 70 percent of cases, they have a bachelor's degree in a field other than business administration. They have acquired their work experience in a wide variety of economic sectors. Their ranks include engineers, lawyers, psychologists, biologists, communications consultants, accountants, information system specialists, and administrators, each of whom brings his or her own wealth of knowledge and experience to the program. One quarter of full-time HEC M.B.A. students come from outside Canada. Thus, students in the HEC M.B.A. program form a veritable mosaic of skills and experience. This collection of human wealth adds greatly to the quality of the discussion and exchanges.

The average student is 30 years old with 6½ years of full-time experience. Women comprise 35 percent of the student population.

❖ Global Focus

"International issues, which have an impact on all corporate functions, are

changing the business game daily for managers. Whether making decisions that have worldwide import or focusing on local or regional issues, executives must think globally."
—Alain Noël, Director, M.B.A. program

HEC has always concentrated on giving its M.B.A. program a distinctly international perspective. Even though an international outlook is an integral part of all teaching, a dozen HEC M.B.A. courses are specifically devoted to it.

The School's M.B.A. program also provides opportunities for students who are eager to broaden their outlook through career training or study trips abroad. In 1991, for example, M.B.A. students and their professors travelled together on a study trip to Poland. Another team went to the Ukraine in 1992, and in 1993, some students travelled to Hong Kong.

Through its exchange program, the School's M.B.A. students have an opportunity to add significant field experience to their classroom learning experience by travelling to another country to study for one term. Possibilities include Belgium, England, Finland, France, Spain, and Switzerland.

The Faculty

École des Hautes Études Commerciales is renowned for its qualified and multidisciplinary teaching staff, the largest business administration faculty in Canada. It comprises 180 career professors, all graduates of major universities in North America and Europe, supported by 225 lecturers who are also full-time managers.

HEC professors are experts in their fields who are much in demand as consultants to companies. A great many of them have backgrounds in management or as corporate executives. Several sit on the boards of large and medium-sized businesses, professional associations, or community organizations.

The Business School Network

Businesspeople are aware that their career advancement—and even the success of some of their projects—depends partly on the quality of their networks. HEC

École des Hautes Études Commerciales.

M.B.A. alumni form just such a network. The close ties they formed with their fellow students during their years of study continue to bear fruit throughout their professional careers. The HEC M.B.A. network includes some 2,000 managers who have graduated from the program since its creation more than twenty years ago.

The M.B.A. program counts among its alumni a number of notable leaders, including François Legault, President, Air Transat; Pauline Marois, Minister, Treasury, Government of Quebec; Serge Bragdon, President and CEO, Uniboard Canada; Wendy Caldwell, Manager, Weyerhaeuser (Denver, Colorado); Daniel Dupont, Vice President, National Bank of Canada (Hong Kong); and Daisy Aubry-Golaz, Vice President of Finance and Administration, New Sulzer Diesel France.

The College and Environs

Montreal's unique blend of intellectual, economic, and cultural characteristics makes it a popular destination for international students.

In Montreal, students find a harmonious blend of North American efficiency and European refinement.

Greater Montreal began assuming a technological vocation several years ago, and today, half of Canada's pharmaceutical companies are clustered there. Nearly one third of Canada's industrial research is conducted in the city. Several Montreal companies are world leaders in high-technology sectors, including telecommunications, aeronautics, aerospace, and biotechnology.

Situated on Mount Royal, an immense park in the heart of Montreal, HEC is just minutes from the downtown core and is served by several bus lines and by a subway station.

Facilities

HEC's Patrick Allen Library is recognized as one of the world's largest business administration libraries. People come from far and wide to consult its unique collection of 300,000 documents, including 7,200 periodicals from a variety of countries, covering all management-related fields. Research is facilitated by the library's computerized reference system.

The library has an imposing collection of annual reports from large and medium-sized businesses, an essential source of information for preparing field studies and corporate projects. Also available are several Canadian, American, and European databanks on compact disc.

The School provides its students with nine laboratories equipped with more than 150 IBM and Apple terminals. About forty of the most widely used software applications and related documentation are also available.

Students who have the necessary equipment at home can also communicate with HEC's mainframe computer via modem.

Placement

The School's Placement Office provides valuable long-term support to HEC M.B.A. graduates, who have free access to this service throughout their careers.

The department provides a wide variety of counselling services to assist students in their search for employment and attainment of their career goals; these services include individual career profile evaluations, proactive job-search techniques, job interview simulations, curriculum vitae writing techniques, descriptions of trends in the job market, and information on companies and career planning.

Admission

Every application for admission to the HEC M.B.A. program is carefully evaluated by a committee composed of professors and members of the program administration. The requirements for admission are a bachelor's degree with a minimum average grade of 70; at least two years of relevant work experience; satisfactory results on the HEC M.B.A. admission tests or in the GMAT (Graduate Management Admission Test), which must be written within prescribed time limits; and a good knowledge of oral and written French (lectures are given in French), as well as sufficient knowledge of written English.

Finances

For the 1994–95 school year, tuition fees for international students were Can$3900 per term for full-time study. However, students from certain countries and those whose status meets certain criteria are exempted from these tuition fees and are required to pay the same amount as Canadian students, which was Can$960 per term for full-time study for the 1994–95 university year.

Application Facts and Dates

Candidates who wish to be admitted for a specific term must submit their applications before the following deadlines: fall term, April 1, and winter term, October 1.

To obtain more information about procedures for applying for residency in Canada, tuition fees, or admission to the HEC M.B.A. program, applicants should contact:

Registrar's Office
École des Hautes Études
    Commerciales
5255 Decelles Avenue
Montreal, Quebec H3T 1V6
Canada
Telephone: 514-340-6151
Fax: 514-340-6411

Emory University

Atlanta, Georgia

ADVANCING OUR MISSION TO BE AN INTERNATIONAL LEADER

Two recent events reflect the value of our M.B.A. program. First, Emory Business School changed its name to Roberto C. Goizueta Business School of Emory University, in honor of the chairman and chief executive officer of The Coca-Cola Company. Second, we reached a milestone in the rankings arena, having been listed twenty-first by U.S. News & World Report among the top twenty-five graduate business schools. Taken together, these two news items are more than milestones in a rich history. They verify the intensity of our drive toward unsurpassed quality and our significant success toward reaching that goal.

—Ronald E. Frank, Dean

Programs and Curricular Focus

The Goizueta Business School (GBS) M.B.A. program offers students the opportunity to pursue an M.B.A. in a flexible, innovative environment. Students are encouraged to work closely with professors, to individualize a course of study, and to customize career goals. The curriculum is contemporary and innovative. Faculty members use teaching methods best suited to the course material, including cases, lectures, class discussions, student presentations, team and field projects, and computer simulations with a balanced emphasis on quantitative and qualitative approaches.

During the first year, students complete a core curriculum that stresses the fundamental building blocks of business and the basic principles in each of the primary functional areas. During the second year, students have the opportunity to develop an area of concentration in finance, marketing, management, accounting, or decision and information analysis.

In addition to the full-time, two-year M.B.A. program, GBS has other programs leading to the M.B.A. degree. Graduates of undergraduate business schools accredited by the American Assembly of Collegiate Schools of Business (AACSB) may start the program in the summer semester and complete the program in one calendar year. GBS also offers a part-time, three-year evening M.B.A. program for working professionals and a sixteen-month Executive M.B.A. program for candidates with significant managerial experience. GBS offers joint-degree programs with the law

school (J.D./M.B.A.—four years), the School of Public Health (M.P.H./ M.B.A.—five semesters), the Candler School of Theology (M.B.A./M.Div.— four years), and the School of Nursing (M.B.A./M.N.—six semesters), as well as certificate programs through an area studies track.

Students and the M.B.A. Experience

GBS consists of 270 full-time and 157 part-time M.B.A. students, who come from a wide variety of academic disciplines, geographic regions, and professions. For the full-time program, the average length of postgraduate work is four years, with 93 percent of the students having over one year of work experience. Thirty-five percent of the students are women, 13 percent are members of minority groups, and 18 percent are international students representing seventeen countries. The range of GMAT scores is 530–710 for the middle 80 percent.

❖ Global Focus

GBS students experience global issues on many levels within the M.B.A. program. The International Perspectives course, taught in the second semester, serves as an introduction using a multidisciplinary, integrated approach. By bringing all the functional disciplines together, the course helps students learn to operate in a global environment and develop political, cultural, ethical, and geographic perspec-

tives. There are also course electives in finance, accounting, management, and marketing.

GBS students have the opportunity to study abroad in exchange programs currently offered with twelve universities in such countries as Austria, Costa Rica, England, Finland, France, Germany, Italy, Mexico, and Venezuela. Specialized programs with Soviet, Post-Soviet, and East European Studies and Latin American Area Studies at Emory University enable students to gain further experience in a geographic area.

Special Features

Students at GBS are very involved in the Atlanta community. A case competition organized by the Emory Marketing Club gives students the opportunity to apply marketing research skills to real business challenges for such companies as the Ritz-Carlton Hotel, the American Red Cross, Georgia-Pacific Corporation, Suntory, and BellSouth. Community involvement also occurs with such projects as volunteer days and fund-raising events for dealing with societal problems of Atlanta's underprivileged residents.

The Faculty

Emory places teaching first among equals with respect to scholarly research and service to the business community. Faculty members have joined GBS from such institutions as Chicago, Harvard, Michigan, MIT, Northwestern, Pennsylvania (Wharton), Stanford, and Yale.

The Business School Network

Corporate Partnerships

The Center for Relationship Marketing (CRM) at Goizueta Business School focuses on the systematic development of ongoing, collaborative business relationships as a key source of sustainable competitive advantage. The center has partnership programs in the form of seminars, executive forums, faculty/ executive residencies, student field projects, and custom programs. The Customer Business Development Track involves such companies as Procter &

Gamble, Coca-Cola, and Chubb in a program that incorporates integration of classroom learning and clinical fieldwork experiences for GBS students. The Center for Leadership and Career Studies, the nation's first and only school for chief executives, has attracted over 3,000 executives to its programs, focusing on themes such as selection, development, and succession of senior executives.

The College and Environs

The city of Atlanta is the business, cultural, and international center of the southeastern United States and, according to *Fortune* magazine, is considered by business leaders to be one of the top five cities in which to do business. It is the sixteenth-largest metropolitan area in the nation and the largest in the Southeast. The moderate climate and reasonable cost of living, in addition to an impressive array of cultural and recreational offerings, attract people from all over the world. Over 450 of the Fortune 500 companies have headquarters or offices in Atlanta. Atlanta is proud to be hosting the 1996 summer Olympic Games.

Emory University is located 6 miles from downtown Atlanta on the northeast side of the city. The campus consists of 550 heavily wooded acres in a nice residential neighborhood. Emory offers students access to the resources of a cosmopolitan university community with over 9,000 students. The diverse learning environment is enhanced by specialized centers and affiliates such as the Carter Center, the Yerkes Primate Center, the Law and Economics Center, Scholars Press, and the Centers for Disease Control and Prevention (CDC).

Facilities

Currently located in the Rich Building, GBS has nine classrooms, computer facilities, faculty and staff offices, and the Career Services Office. Plans are being finalized for the construction of a new, five-story, 108,000-square-foot building to be located on Emory's campus. The state-of-the-art building is scheduled to be completed in 1997.

Technology Environment

Computing at GBS is comprehensive with modern facilities, a professional staff, and extensive documentation. Extensive library resources are available to students with on-line databases such as ABI/Inform business magazine index, LEXIS/NEXIS, and Dow Jones News/Retrieval Service.

Placement

The mission of the Office of Career Services is centered around assisting students in pragmatically focusing particular abilities, experiences, and interests toward a career goal and helping the student develop an individual strategy for marketing himself or herself in order to conduct an effective job search. Workshops, speakers, internships, mentors, and alumni are some of the resources available to GBS students.

Admission

Admission to the M.B.A. program is highly selective. Each candidate is evaluated on the basis of his or her ability to perform in an academically rigorous environment as well as contribute to classroom discussions based on work and/or life experiences. Diversity and international perspectives are valued in the admission process. To apply to Goizueta Business School, a student must submit the results of the Graduate Management Admission Test (GMAT); official transcripts from all previous undergraduate, graduate, and professional work; three letters of recommendation; and the completed application form including statistical data, work history, and essays. Applicants from non-English-speaking countries also must submit scores from the Test of English as a Foreign Language (TOEFL) and a statement of financial resources.

Finances

Tuition for the 1994–95 academic year at Goizueta Business School was $18,850. The estimated annual living expenses and fees for a student living off campus total $12,000. Students who complete an application by March 1 are automatically considered for merit-based scholarships. Need-based aid in the form of loans is available to M.B.A. students. Applicants should file the FAF and FAFSA for loan consideration. To contact Emory University's Financial Aid Office, students should call 404-727-1141 or write to Financial Aid Office, Emory University, Atlanta, Georgia 30322.

International Students

International students are encouraged to apply. Good communication skills are essential to the program. Applicants whose native language is not English must score a minimum of 600 on the TOEFL. A very limited amount of merit-based financial assistance is available for international students.

Application Facts and Dates

The deadline for applying to the two-year, full-time M.B.A. program is April 15. For full scholarship consideration, the application deadline is March 1. Applications for the one-year M.B.A. program are due February 1; for the evening M.B.A. program, March 1. Applications are available on computer disk. Students can obtain applications and admissions information from:

Julie R. Barefoot
Assistant Dean of Admissions and
    Career Services
Goizueta Business School
Emory University
Atlanta, Georgia 30322-2710
Telephone: 404-727-6311
Fax: 404-727-4612

Emporia State University

Emporia, Kansas

PREPARING STUDENTS FOR TOMORROW

ESU's School of Business prepares students to excel in an increasingly global business environment. We are small enough to truly practice a student-oriented philosophy but large enough to provide a quality educational experience.

Our M.B.A. faculty maintains close relations with business practitioners and integrates business experiences into classroom presentations. The School of Business Council of Advisors, comprised of prominent business and government leaders, represents a key link in keeping abreast of current and emerging trends.

We care about students and focus our efforts toward providing a really meaningful educational experience to prepare for tomorrow's business world.

—S. A. Hashmi, Dean

Programs and Curricular Focus

The standard M.B.A. program is a sequence of courses (36 credit hours) designed to assure competency in the functional areas of business and also to enable a student to acquire content breadth by choosing elective courses. Required courses include study in the areas of accounting, management, finance, marketing, quantitative methods, managerial economics, and management information systems. Elective courses may be taken in a wide range of subject-matter areas. Increasingly, many students choose elective courses in international finance, international management, and international marketing.

The School also offers a specialized M.B.A. degree (36 credit hours), with a concentration in accounting. This curriculum, which is designed for persons with undergraduate accounting majors, prepares students for high-level account-ing positions and enables them to meet requirements for admission to the uniform CPA examination. In addition to taking required courses in finance, marketing, and management, students must take three required accounting courses and choose two additional elective courses in accounting.

In both M.B.A. curriculums, comple-tion of a core of undergraduate prerequi-site business courses is necessary before full admission status is granted. These courses may have been taken to fulfill undergraduate degree requirements or may be taken at Emporia State Univer-sity. The reason for requiring prerequisite study is to provide a basic understanding

of business that can be further developed by study at the graduate level.

Students and the M.B.A. Experience

M.B.A. students have diverse academic and experiential backgrounds. While some have a limited amount of work experience, others have extensive experience in various managerial positions. A typical M.B.A. student is 26 years old, has four or five years of work experience, and completes degree requirements primarily for professional career development. Sixty percent of the students are men, and between 30 and 35 percent are students who come to the United States to pursue an M.B.A. degree.

As part of their instructional method-ology, many professors stress teamwork. Also, students have opportunities to complete internships or to work in cooperation with a professor to complete an independent study covering a special-ized topic of mutual interest. Although the majority of students have completed undergraduate business degrees, an undergraduate major in business is not a requirement for admission.

The Faculty

Professors who teach M.B.A. courses are members of the graduate faculty. Approximately one fourth of the faculty are women. In addition to instructional responsibilities, many faculty members work as consultants to businesses, government agencies, and educational

organizations. They conduct research, publish papers, and are leaders in professional organizations. Several faculty members have authored or coauthored textbooks printed by major publishing companies. These different professional activities bring a high level of intellectual excitement and realism to the classroom.

The Business School Network

Corporate Partnerships

The School maintains strong relationships with business and industry. In addition to availability of cooperative study and internship opportunities, some professors work directly with companies to involve students in real-world projects as a component of the classroom educational experience. The business community serves as an important resource to provide valuable expertise and guidance. Each year, the M.B.A. Student Associa-tion sponsors educational programs and hosts business leaders who give lectures and participate in seminars.

Prominent Alumni

Numerous alumni have attained notewor-thy accomplishments during their professional careers. These graduates include Dennis Casarona, president of Graphic Promotions; Kay Gerdes, vice president of operations for Farm Credit Services; Salief Keita, director of agencies for Banque Malienne de Credit et de Depots (Mali); Ken Lerman, a widely known business consultant who formerly served as marketing director for Pizza Hut and Taco Tico; and Yasunori Watanabe, country general manager for TNT Worldwide (Japan).

The College and Environs

"A place where people care about you" is how students describe Emporia State University. With an enrollment of approximately 6,000 students, ESU offers over thirty-seven graduate degree programs. The University is small enough for students to develop friendships, yet large enough to offer a variety of educational programs.

With a population of nearly 30,000, Emporia is an educational, industrial,

The School of Business is housed in Cremer Hall, a modern five-story building.

trade, and medical center serving east-central Kansas. It is situated on the eastern edge of the Bluestem region of the Flint Hills and is surrounded by numerous lakes and recreational facilities. The city is located on the Kansas Turnpike, Interstate 35, and the main line of the Santa Fe Railroad. Three major metropolitan areas of Kansas (Topeka, Kansas City, and Wichita) can easily be reached from Emporia.

Placement

The Office of Career Development, Cooperative Education, and Placement

Services coordinates arrangements for corporate recruiters to visit the campus. Students and alumni have access to weekly listings of position vacancies. Each year, the School sponsors a career fair, which gives students opportunities to become acquainted with potential employers. The M.B.A. Student Association encourages networking with corporate executives and sponsors programs to help develop effective interviewing skills.

Admission

Applicants need a minimum grade point average of 2.5 (A=4.0) for the last 60

credit hours of undergraduate study. In addition, an acceptable score on the Graduate Management Admission Test (GMAT) is required for unconditional admission. The score on the GMAT and the academic transcript are used to determine admission status. Those granted probationary status must submit an acceptable GMAT score before or during their first semester of graduate study.

Finances

For the 1994–95 academic year, fees for a full course load were $2560.75 per semester for nonresidents. During the 1994 summer session, nonresident fees were $170 per credit hour. Fees are established by the Kansas Board of Regents and are subject to change. Estimated cost of housing ranges from $2325 to $3145 per academic year. The University Dining Service provides meal contracts from $1163 to $1572 per academic year. The University Housing Office maintains a list of off-campus rooms, apartments, and houses that may be rented by students. Also, housing is available at the University-owned Emporia State Apartments.

Each year, the School offers a number of graduate assistantships to qualified students. Graduate assistants also may be eligible for reduced fees.

International Students

International students represent approximately one third of the M.B.A. enrollment. The majority of these students come from African, Asian, and South American countries. The University sponsors a number of activities and organizations to accommodate needs of international students. Also, specialized intensive English training is available on the campus.

Application Facts and Dates

Students are admitted for terms beginning in August, January, and June, with corresponding deadlines of June 1, November 1, and April 1. Applications are processed on a continuous basis. For additional information concerning the application process, admission requirements, or graduate assistantships, students should contact:

Dr. Donald S. Miller
Director, M.B.A. Program
School of Business
Campus Box 4059
Emporia State University
Emporia, Kansas 66801-5087
Telephone: 316-341-5456
Fax: 316-341-5418
E-mail: millerdn@esuvm.bitnet

Active interaction between students and professors characterizes classroom sessions.

L'Institut Européen d'Administration des Affaires (INSEAD)

Fontainebleau, France

> ## LEARNING FOR LEADERSHIP
>
> *We live in a world where ideas can increasingly pay off. Translating ideas into action grows more challenging as business becomes ever more complex. An INSEAD M.B.A. stimulates ideas. Faculty members and fellow M.B.A. participants will stretch your mind—and your limits. You will broaden your business perspective and sharpen your economic insight. With a combination of deductive and intuitive understanding, you will learn to set realistic goals and—through action—to achieve them.*
>
> *Management is about getting things done by working with others. A successful international manager not only can work within cultural heterogeneity but thrives on its diversity. INSEAD is indeed a microcosm of the international business environment. The INSEAD experience will enhance your cultural and social skills to enable you to work more effectively in this environment. A year at INSEAD, in the heart of multicultural Europe, is excellent preparation for the challenges of global competition.*
>
> —Herwig Langhor, Associate Dean

Programs and Curricular Focus

INSEAD's M.B.A. programme ensures a solid general management education, while allowing participants to tailor the programme to individual requirements. To achieve this goal, the programme begins with a series of core courses that cover the fundamentals of business. These ensure that participants obtain a common level of knowledge in the fundamentals of business, irrespective of their backgrounds. The second phase of the programme introduces participants to broader management issues and to the wider economic and political environment that influences both corporate strategies and national industrial policies. The programme's final phase allows participants to select courses to match their career needs and interests. Electives allow participants to focus on a field of particular interest or to further investigate general management issues.

INSEAD's pedagogical approach is pragmatic. It seeks to prepare participants by simulating business reality in a low-risk environment. This means that the M.B.A. programme is based on problem solving in small groups, active participation in class, and individual preparation and research.

There are two 10½-month programmes each year. One programme starts in late August and ends in early July; the other runs from January to December, with a six-week summer recess. Although always evolving, the two programmes are virtually identical in structure and content. Both programmes are organised into five periods of eight weeks, each period ending with exams followed by a short break. Each period consists of a minimum number of courses for which a participant must register. In order to qualify for the INSEAD M.B.A. degree, participants must obtain credits in at least twenty-one courses. Courses are taught almost entirely in English.

Students and the M.B.A. Experience

The INSEAD M.B.A. programme is a year of opportunity to make lasting friendships that span the world, to be inspired by professors, and to meet and listen to leading international business figures on campus. Despite the amount of time devoted to studying, INSEAD is a constant hub of varied activities. The level and intensity of the M.B.A. programme demand highly qualified participants. In an atmosphere of camaraderie and competition, participants are pushed to discover their limits, as well as their potential.

The M.B.A. participants represent over forty nationalities. Not only is the group as a whole international, but each individual has an international outlook, with over two thirds of INSEAD's M.B.A. participants speaking three or more languages and over half the class having studied or worked abroad. The average age of participants is 28, and the majority of participants have between three and five years of professional experience.

Special Features

The INSEAD M.B.A. programme is an intensive one that demands that participants commit themselves from day one. A year spent on campus provides a sound generalist management education, broadens horizons, and prepares participants for an international career, without the two-year interruption common to many other programmes. The high quality of faculty and participants, the alumni and corporate network, and a truly international environment have combined to make INSEAD one of the top management schools in the world.

The Faculty

INSEAD prides itself on the many talents of its faculty members and their close ties with both the academic and business communities. The 80 permanent professors, with qualifications from distinguished institutions around the world, represent more than twenty different nationalities. The relevance of their teaching and the innovation in their research are guaranteed by close partnerships with industry, nourished by the constant interaction with more than 3,300 business executives who attend programmes at INSEAD each year. INSEAD's faculty regularly receive international awards for cases, books, and articles and for their contribution to the academic community in management.

The Business School Network

While many of the advantages of an INSEAD M.B.A. degree are obvious during the course of the programme, some become more visible with time. The importance of the International Alumni Association is one. There are over 15,000 INSEAD alumni, of whom 8,300 have graduated from the M.B.A. programme and 6,800 from executive programmes of at least four weeks in length. As corporations push for global integration, the value of international contacts is increasing. The ability to pick up the telephone to question a former classmate is increasingly useful in the context of global competition.

A growing network of leading corporations endorses INSEAD's commitment to education in an international context, expressing confidence in INSEAD's teaching and research through generous and highly valued contributions. Through combined research projects, executive education programmes, and M.B.A. and executive alumni, INSEAD has constructed a unique global network of contacts in influential positions. Over time and across distances, the INSEAD network is proving to be a critical tie in bringing successful people and businesses together.

The College and Environs

Created in 1959, INSEAD is located in Fontainebleau, France, which is 65 kilometers southeast of Paris. The wooded campus is situated on the edge of la Fôret de Fontainebleau, which has an area of roughly 50,000 acres, providing opportunity for hikes, rock-climbing, VTT, and horseback riding. At the same time, Paris is less than an hour away, easily accessible by train or highway.

Technology Environment

Eighty microcomputers, both IBM and Macintosh, are available for student use. Participants have access to the Internet, internal e-mail, and a variety of on-line CD-ROM databases.

Placement

INSEAD's Career Management Service (CMS) is an advisory and information resource for M.B.A. participants preparing for their career after graduation. CMS organises a wide range of activities to assist M.B.A. participants in their job searches and career plans, including career counselling, seminars, workshops, and an extensive company resource centre. Special assistance and information sources are available to facilitate independent job search in parallel with on-campus recruitment.

The CMS acts as the liaison between M.B.A. participants and companies, organising the logistics for all on-campus recruitment. Some 100 companies recruit on INSEAD's campus each recruitment period.

Admission

INSEAD aims to attract talented young professionals from a wide range of cultural, academic, and professional backgrounds with high potential for effective leadership in complex international business environments. Sharp intellectual curiosity, with a desire to learn and stretch oneself in a rigorous academic programme, is expected, as well as personal qualities to contribute meaningfully to the many academic and extracurricular activities at INSEAD.

In addition to completing the application, which includes biographical data, essays, and a job description, applicants must take the GMAT. If preselected, the candidate will be invited to attend at least two evaluative interviews. The TOEFL may also be required for non-native English-speaking candidates.

All candidates must be fluent in English and have a good working level of French before registering in the programme. Upon completion of the programme, all participants must demonstrate knowledge of a third language (besides English and French).

Finances

Tuition for the academic year 1994–95 was Fr145,000, and it was estimated that a single participant should budget a total of Fr240,000.

International Students

The international nature of INSEAD makes it unique. No single nationality typically exceeds 17 percent of the student body; it is the INSEAD culture that dominates. Diversity helps ensure that participants see the world through new perspectives and learn how to benefit from both the conflicts and synergies that arise. Ten months spent studying, working, and living among culturally diverse influences means adapting to new approaches, accepting that listening is also learning, and cooperating to achieve results.

Application Facts and Dates

INSEAD has two intakes, one in September and one in January. Admission is on a rolling basis, but it is strongly recommended that candidates submit their application as soon as it is complete.

A full brochure and application may be obtained by sending a fax request to (33-1) 60.72.42.00, including full name, address, telephone number, date of birth, and nationality. Requests for information may be sent via e-mail to admissions@insead.fr. In the United States, students may contact the INSEAD North American office at:

Telephone: 212-418-6593
E-mail to grayson@insead.fr.
or write:

INSEAD
Boulevard de Constance
77305 Fontainebleau Cedex
France

Fairfield University

Fairfield, Connecticut

THE M.B.A. FOR THE TWENTY-FIRST CENTURY

The Fairfield University M.B.A. is a small, select program focused on the competitiveness of American business as we enter the twenty-first century and on helping better understand the needs of the global village in which we operate. In response to these issues, the School of Business at Fairfield University has adopted a continuous improvement program that has created a new and exciting curriculum, expanded working and educational relationships with business firms around the world, and developed a comprehensive process for supporting faculty in the continuous improvement of teaching, research, and service. This ensures treatment of students as individuals, with programs designed specifically with their needs in mind to help them succeed in the new century of competition.

—Russell P. Boisjoly, Dean

Programs and Curricular Focus

An M.B.A. program is meant to be a generalist degree that covers all the relevant topical areas and gives a student the opportunity to specialize, but not major, in a functional area of business. The M.B.A. program has three components: core courses, breadth courses, and specialization or concentration courses.

The core courses are not required courses; they are designed to provide fundamental tools and functional area competencies for students who either did not major in a business specialty as undergraduates, did not perform well academically as undergraduates, or took only a portion of the functional and tool courses that comprise the M.B.A. core. Therefore, the core courses are prerequisites to the "true" M.B.A. program.

The "true" M.B.A. program comprises the breadth courses and the specialization courses. The new American Assembly of Collegiate Schools of Business (AACSB) accreditation standards require at least 30 semester hours of study beyond the core. Fairfield limits the number of options offered in both the breadth and specialization courses to strengthen the program pedagogically with a strong set of breadth courses that everyone must take and a limited number of specialization electives to provide a focus for each concentration.

Most students admitted to the program are able to waive selected preparatory workshops and/or core courses on the basis of previous course work; upon successful completion of a written qualifying examination; or based on relevant work experience when combined with related course work, qualifying examinations, program of graduate study, and other factors.

All students are expected to demonstrate and/or attain proficiency in the use of microcomputers and the mainframe computer during their program of study. Computer use is integrated throughout the curriculum, and it is expected in each course. The School provides fully equipped microcomputer labs for student use, and each student may obtain a computer account for access to the University's mainframe systems.

The specialization options include courses in accounting, finance, human resource management, information technology, international business, and marketing.

The overall program requirements include 32 credit hours in core courses, 18 credit hours in breadth courses, and 12 credit hours in specialization courses, for a total of 62 credit hours. A minimum of 36 credit hours must be taken at Fairfield.

Students and the M.B.A. Experience

Students in Fairfield's M.B.A. program have a wide variety of academic and work experience. Although some students in the program are recent college graduates, the average age of students is 27 years, with four years of full-time work experience.

❖ Global Focus

Fairfield's M.B.A. program emphasizes the recognition that business is international by nature. One of the key specialization areas for students is in international business. In addition, virtually all courses discuss international implications of their discipline. The student body represents many nations, with connections to many major international corporations. Eventually the program will include a "World M.B.A." component that will provide students with an opportunity to study at universities in Europe, Asia, and Latin America while pursuing their M.B.A. from Fairfield University.

Special Features

For students who need basic strengthening of statistical skills, economics, information systems, and accounting, special intensive analytical skills workshop courses are offered. Courses are offered emphasizing the role of technology in the competitive position of the firm in a global economy.

The Faculty

The Fairfield faculty have always emphasized outstanding teaching. Ninety percent of the 30 full-time graduate faculty members have extensive experience in the business world, and all have their appropriate terminal degrees. There is great diversity among the members of the faculty.

The Business School Network

Corporate Partnerships

The School has been the recipient of several major corporate grants for support of curriculum and faculty development. A close relationship exists with dozens of major corporations in Fairfield County, which is the third-largest center of corporate headquarters in the nation. The School also has an outstanding Advisory Council of business leaders from the nation's largest corporations. Corporate executives participate extensively as guests and lecturers in many courses every semester.

The College and Environs

Fairfield University is a coeducational institution of higher learning founded by the Society of Jesus in 1942 and proudly

Russell P. Boisjoly, Professor of Finance and Dean; D.B.A., Indiana.

Bharat B. Bhalla, Associate Professor of Finance; Ph.D., Cornell.

Bruce Bradford, Assistant Professor of Accounting; Ph.D., Memphis; CPA.

Gerald O. Cavallo, Associate Professor of Marketing; Ph.D., CUNY Graduate Center.

J. Michael Cavanaugh, Assistant Professor of Management; Ph.D., Massachusetts.

Arjun Chaudhuri, Assistant Professor of Marketing; Ph.D., Connecticut.

Elia V. Chepaitis, Associate Professor of Information Systems; Ph.D., Connecticut.

Thomas E. Conine Jr., Professor of Finance; Ph.D., NYU.

Robert L. DeMichiell, Professor of Information Systems; Ph.D., Connecticut.

Sandra J. Ducoffe, Assistant Professor of Marketing; Ph.D., Michigan State.

Walter F. Hlawitschka, Associate Professor of Finance; Ph.D., Virginia.

Brian J. Huffman, Assistant Professor of Operations Management; Ph.D., Minnesota.

Oscar W. Jensen, Professor of Quantitative Analysis; Ph.D., Connecticut.

Lucy V. Katz, Associate Professor of Business Law; J.D., NYU.

Gregory D. Koutmos, Associate Professor of Finance; Ph.D., CUNY Graduate Center.

Philip J. Lane, Associate Professor of Economics; Ph.D., Tufts.

Mark S. LeClair, Assistant Professor of Economics; Ph.D., Rutgers.

Lisa A. Mainiero, Professor of Management; Ph.D., Yale.

R. Keith Martin, Professor of Information Systems; Ph.D., Washington (Seattle).

Sharlene McEvoy, Associate Professor of Business Law; J.D., Connecticut; Ph.D., UCLA.

Krishna Mohan, Associate Professor of Marketing; Ph.D., Wisconsin–Madison.

Milo W. Peck Jr., Assistant Professor of Accounting; J.D., Suffolk; CPA.

Walter G. Ryba Jr., Professor of Business Law and Associate Dean; J.D., Connecticut.

Carl A. Scheraga, Assistant Professor of International Business; Ph.D., Connecticut.

David P. Schmidt, Assistant Professor of Business Ethics; Ph.D., Chicago.

Cheryl L. Tromley, Assistant Professor of Management; Ph.D., Yale.

Michael T. Tucker, Associate Professor of Finance; D.B.A., Boston University.

Michael A. Zigarelli, Assistant Professor of Management; Ph.D., Rutgers.

---

aspires to the Jesuit tradition of developing the whole intellectual potential of its students and creating the true sense of ethical and social responsibility within them.

The 250-acre campus is among the most beautiful in the country. The buildings are modern and well suited to the needs of the students.

U.S. News & World Report in 1994 rated Fairfield one of the top two comprehensive universities in the Northeast in the regional category.

Fairfield University is situated in a suburban area on the Connecticut shore of Long Island Sound about 1 hour from New York City and 3 hours from Boston. The University is in America's "academic corridor," which contains the largest concentration of colleges and universities in the United States along with many cultural, recreational, and intellectual activities.

Facilities

The Nyselius Library contains more than 255,000 volumes, 58,000 volumes in microfilm, and 1,800 journals and newspapers, with extensive business collections. There is access to library facilities throughout the area. Buildings on campus are fiber-optic-equipped. The Computer Center includes a DEC VAX 8600 with terminals throughout the campus; there is also a campuswide network of microcomputers.

Placement

The University offers a placement office with a full-time professional staff to assist students. There are on-campus recruiting visits by representatives of many of the top corporations in the nation. On-site visits also are possible with area corporate headquarters and those in nearby New York City.

Admission

Students who hold a bachelor's degree in any field or major from an accredited college or university and who have demonstrated their ability or potential to do high-quality academic work are encouraged to apply. The criteria for admission to the M.B.A. and the M.S. programs are a strong undergraduate grade point average and an appropriate

score on the Graduate Management Admission Test (GMAT). A formula score of at least 1100, derived by multiplying the grade point average by 200 and adding the GMAT score, is usually required for admission. Complete official transcripts of all undergraduate and graduate work, two letters of recommendation, and a letter of self-evaluation or an enumeration of work experience must all be submitted. Students from non-English-speaking countries are required to submit a Test of English as a Foreign Language (TOEFL) score report. Applicants to the certificate program are not required to submit GMAT scores.

Finances

In 1994–95 tuition was $400 per credit hour for part-time students and $6500 per semester for full-time students. The registration fee was $20 per semester.

The large majority of graduate students live off campus in the surrounding communities. Housing costs in the area vary widely. There is a limited supply of on-campus housing available; single rooms with board are approximately $3500 per semester.

Scholarship aid is available but limited. Most students are employed and receive substantial financial support from their employers. Graduate research assistantships are also available in limited supply. Students may apply to the dean for financial assistance after having been accepted into a program. Assistance is usually limited to U.S. citizens.

Application Facts and Dates

Applications are accepted on a revolving basis and should be completed prior to September 1 for those who wish to begin in the fall semester, prior to December 1 to begin in the spring semester, and prior to May 1 to begin in the summer semester. The application fee is $40.

Students should address all questions or requests for information and application materials to:

Graduate Admissions
School of Business
Fairfield University
Fairfield, Connecticut 06430
Telephone: 203-254-4180
Fax: 203-254-4105

Fairleigh Dickinson University

THE M.B.A. AND THE INDIVIDUAL

The Samuel J. Silberman M.B.A. has been crafted to recognize the new reality of a career in business. Today's business school graduate cannot look to organizations for career security but rather must look to his or her own employability. Whether an individual is employed by a large organization or in his or her own business, he or she must think like an entrepreneur, constantly searching for new opportunities. The Silberman M.B.A. provides students with the skills to identify and capitalize on these opportunities. The work of the faculty in developing a curriculum that meets the needs of the individual who has chosen business as a career received national attention in the September 1994 issue of Success *magazine where the Silberman College was named as being among the twenty-five best business schools in the nation for entrepreneurs.*

The College has a high-quality teaching faculty using an innovative curriculum developed for the contemporary business environment. This combination is designed to give each Silberman M.B.A. graduate the competitive edge necessary to maintain his or her employability and to succeed in a global business community that is characterized by rapid technological and social change.

—Paul Lerman, Dean

Programs and Curricular Focus

The Samuel J. Silberman College of Business Administration has been dedicated to providing high-quality innovative programs for more than thirty years. The College strives to develop graduates who are prepared to compete in a rapidly changing business environment. A completely revised Master of Business Administration curriculum, introduced in January 1995, reflects the integrated, cross-functional manner in which contemporary business operates.

The program is designed to address the complex demands placed on organizations and the individuals who manage them. Global perspectives and ethical concerns of business are integrated into all courses. The development and refinement of student communication skills is an important component of the integrative courses that form the program core. Topics critical to the value creation process, such as entrepreneurship, creativity, and strategic thinking, are introduced early in the program. The influences of politics, the law, the environment, technology, society, and demographic diversity are integrated throughout the program.

Students begin the program by participating in the M.B.A. Preparation Seminar, a modular course that introduces ethical perspectives for business and evaluates student oral communication skills. Program requirements include successful completion of between 34½ and 60 credits, depending on waiver of core courses. Core courses comprise four tiers: The External and Internal Environment of Business, The Manager's Skill Set, Functional Areas and Technical Core, and Capstone. Students major in one of eleven fields of study and complete breadth courses outside of the field of specialization. Students may choose to fulfill their breadth requirements with courses outside of the College in areas such as corporate communication or foreign language and culture.

Other program offerings include an Executive M.B.A. and an M.S. in Taxation.

Students and the M.B.A. Experience

❖ Global Focus

In addition to international business courses offered on the New Jersey campuses, M.B.A. students have the opportunity to attend a two-week summer seminar at the University's historic Wroxton College campus in Oxfordshire, England. During the seminar, students meet with key academic, business, and political leaders and tour major corporate locations. This program immerses students in British culture and invites them to view international business from a different perspective.

Special Features

In addition to traditional majors, the College offers an M.B.A. in pharmaceutical-chemical studies, the only one of its kind in the nation. The program is conducted on the campuses as well as at corporate locations of Bristol-Myers Squibb, Johnson & Johnson, and Miles Pharmaceuticals. CEOs and other top executives of industry companies meet with students on a weekly basis during each semester.

All students participate in at least one course on entrepreneurship offered by the Center for Entrepreneurial Studies. Students may choose to select a sequence of courses in this area. Internship opportunities with new ventures are available.

The Faculty

The 80 faculty members bring a combination of industry experience and academic training to the classroom. The faculty is committed to excellence in teaching. Faculty research interests concentrate on application of theory to business practice and are supported by research centers that include the Center for the New Jersey Economy, the Center for Human Resource Management, the Center for Entrepreneurship, and the Center for Pharmaceutical-Chemical Studies.

The Business School Network

Corporate Partnerships

Each of the academic departments is guided by a corporate advisory board that works with the faculty in developing the curriculum. Members of the advisory boards are often guest lecturers.

Prominent Alumni

The College counts among its alumni a number of leading corporate executives, including Patrick Zenner, President, Roche Laboratories; Steven Sudovar,

Executive Vice-President, Roche Laboratories; Stephen C. Tuminello, President, Philips Electronics North America Corporation; Clark Johnson, CFO, Johnson & Johnson; Arnold Spelker, CFO, Credit Suisse; and Ronald Brill, CFO, Home Depot.

The College and Environs

The 115-acre Teaneck/Hackensack Campus stretches along the east and west banks of the Hackensack River. Robison Hall, the Weiner Library, and Alumni Hall sit on the river's east edge, while the College of Business Administration, located in Dickinson Hall, sits on the west edge. The Florham/Madison Campus is a beautifully landscaped park of 187 acres. Its Georgian-style buildings have been adapted to the educational needs of the University. Both the Teaneck/Hackensack and Florham/Madison campuses are located in attractive residential suburbs close to local theaters, restaurants, and sports arenas. Students can easily reach the business, cultural, and social offerings of New York City by private or public transportation.

Wroxton College, the overseas campus of the University, was originally built as an abbey and later became the home of Lord North in the 1700s. It is centrally located in England between Oxford and Stratford-upon-Avon.

Facilities

The University has recently made a major investment in facilities. Since September 1994, on the Teaneck/Hackensack Campus, the College resides in a building that has undergone a $12-million renovation. College facilities include executive classrooms, three computer laboratories, and an up-to-date business research library. On the Florham/Madison Campus, the College occupies a major part of a 100-room mansion designed by Stanford White. A new recreation center is scheduled for completion by September 1995.

Technology Environment

Graduate students have access to a Prime 5370, VAX 4000/5000, Sun 490, and DEC Alpha Sable 2100 and a wide variety of software for use independent of campus or location. There are several PC laboratories on each campus. All PCs are connected to a central file server through a local area network with access to the University-wide network and the worldwide Internet.

Placement

The Office of Career Development and Placement offers career and placement services to all M.B.A. students and alumni. On-campus recruiting programs and career fairs are augmented by a large network of corporate contacts. Computerized databases and résumé and interviewing workshops are a regular part of the services offered to M.B.A. students.

Admission

The College considers each candidate's academic record, GMAT score, and professional experience in the admission process. International students whose native language is not English are required to submit a TOEFL score. It is recommended that students have a basic knowledge of statistics; computer usage, including spreadsheets and word processing; and mathematics, including calculus.

Finances

Tuition for the 1994–95 academic year was $446 per credit. Books and supplies are approximately $1200 per year. Approximately twenty-five graduate assistantships are available to qualified candidates, offering tuition remission and a stipend.

International Students

International students from twenty-three countries represent 8 percent of the M.B.A. students. Extensive English language preparation and assistance programs are available.

Application Facts and Dates

Application deadlines are August 25 for fall admission and January 12 for spring admission. For additional information, students should contact:

Ms. Dale Herold
University Director of Admissions
Fairleigh Dickinson University
1000 River Road
Teaneck, New Jersey 07666
Telephone: 800-338-8803 (toll-free)

 **Fordham University**

New York, New York

> ### URBI ET ORBI—FOR THE CITY AND THE WORLD
>
> *This headline is one of the first tangible examples of the total redesign of our School. We are committed to making Fordham's Graduate School of Business Administration a leading, world-class business school and are moving toward that goal.*
>
> *Our close ties to New York companies help position us as New York City's business ambassador to the world.*
>
> *As for our students, we know each of them, care about each one's future, and are devoted to doing all we can to insure their success in business, at every level, in any country of the world.*
>
> —Ernest J. Scalberg, Dean

Programs and Curricular Focus

Concern for quality drives Fordham's M.B.A. program. Through the required courses of the program, students acquire the knowledge and basic skills necessary to become leaders in business. In the classroom, faculty members teach fundamental theory and current research tied to pragmatic solutions, so students master both abstract and applied methods of thinking.

Students also develop expertise in a specific field by taking a concentration in one of six areas: accounting, communications and media management, finance, information and communications systems, management systems, and marketing. An International Business Designation is also available as a complement to a student's selected area of concentration. Fordham's course of study is organized on a trimester system (three terms per year) commencing in September, January, and April. Each student can decide how quickly he or she earns the Fordham M.B.A. A full-time student may complete the program in fifteen to eighteen months.

The 60-credit M.B.A. degree program has eight courses (24 credits) in the core business curriculum, including fundamentals of accounting, business law, marketing management, operations management, and business policy. Upper-level courses in a student's selected concentration, together with electives both in and out of that concentration, fill out the M.B.A. program.

Fordham also offers an eighteen-month Deming Scholars M.B.A. Program in Quality Management, a joint J.D./

M.B.A. program with Fordham Law School, and an M.S. in taxation. A 90-credit M.B.A. in taxation and accounting program combines the M.B.A. in professional accounting with the M.S. in taxation to prepare students to be taxation professionals.

The Fordham–Stevens Institute Exchange Program offers GBA students the opportunity to adapt their studies to capitalize on the increasing link between technology and management. GBA students may take selected computer science and engineering courses at the Stevens Institute, located in Hoboken, New Jersey.

Students and the M.B.A. Experience

The total student population of Fordham's graduate business school is approximately 2,000, with 70 percent attending on a part-time/evening basis and 30 percent full-time. The average age is 26; 60 percent are men and 40 percent are women. Seventeen percent of the full-time students come from other countries, with fifty-one nationalities represented.

On average, Fordham business students have had four years of work experience when they commence their M.B.A. studies. As a consequence, many classroom discussions are enriched by students contributing their own on-the-job experiences.

The Faculty

Fordham has 79 full-time faculty members, 96 percent of whom hold a

Ph.D. or similar terminal degree. Women comprise 23 percent of the group. Approximately one third of the faculty members have origins in Western Europe, South America, and Asia. The adjunct faculty pool totals 132, with approximately 50 teaching in a given trimester.

Many members of the faculty serve as consultants to a variety of industries as well as to foreign governments and institutions. The diverse backgrounds of the faculty members provide a multicultural teaching field, with an emphasis on global standards and practices.

The Business School Network

Many of Fordham Graduate School of Business Administration's activities involve relationships with the corporate community. Because of the School's location in New York City, which many consider the business capital of the world, students have easy access to a "who's who" of corporate leaders and Wall Street executives who visit the campus regularly.

Corporate Partnerships

In addition to guest speakers in classes, at seminars, and in panel discussions, students are able to take advantage of several formal programs that provide business contacts: the Mentoring Program, which sponsors one-on-one relationships between individual students and executives; the Field Study Program, in which teams of students solve problems for real corporate assignments; the master's in taxation program, which is funded largely by the accounting and tax industries, which then hire the program's graduates; and student/alumni networking events, held twice a year.

Prominent Alumni

Standard and Poor's most recent Executive/College Survey ranked Fordham in the top forty U.S. colleges and universities and number one in Jesuit institutions with the largest alumni representation in leading executive positions.

The College and Environs

Fordham's Graduate School of Business Administration was established in 1969

Fordham's Lincoln Center campus, looking south to the World Trade Center.

and is founded on the Jesuit tradition of high-quality education. Fordham's business school is located at Lincoln Center on a campus that marks the southern border of the cultural heart of New York City.

Fordham's 7-acre green campus at Lincoln Center consists of the academic building, the residence hall, and the School of Law, all of which are connected by a newly landscaped central plaza that serves as an island of calm in a city of skyscrapers. It is one block from Central Park and Columbus Circle, a major transportation hub in midtown Manhattan.

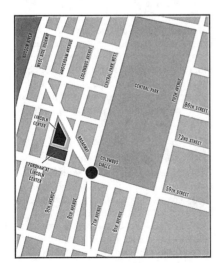

Fordham at Lincoln Center, with Columbus Circle and Central Park.

Placement

Fordham's Career Development Office offers individual counseling, workshops, and mock interview sessions to guide students in the subtleties of networking, information gathering, and interviewing. Eligible candidates also submit résumés for inclusion in the GBA Résumé Book, which is sent to over 500 companies.

Panel discussions by industry representatives provide the chance to learn about career opportunities and trends in particular areas of concentration. In the Mentor Program, students talk to top business executives, one-on-one, to obtain career advice and guidance. Mentors include Fordham alumni and senior executives of Fordham's Visiting Committee.

Admission

The principal elements that define a Fordham student are academic and professional accomplishments, clearly defined career objectives, motivation, and personal integrity. Each candidate must possess the U.S. equivalent of a four-year baccalaureate degree and must have taken the Graduate Management Admission Test (GMAT). The candidate's academic record, GMAT scores, personal statements, professional recommendations, and work experience are considered in the admission process. The average GMAT score in 1994 was 535.

Applicants from non-English-speaking countries must submit the results of the Test of English as a Foreign Language (TOEFL). The minimum TOEFL score accepted is 600.

Finances

The annual tuition for 1994–95 was $20,475 for 45 credit hours of study. The estimated cost of fees, insurance, books, and supplies is $1550 per year. On-campus housing is offered at $6300 to $7400 for shared apartments, and off-campus housing, although greatly varied, is estimated to cost $11,000 per year.

Fordham uses the Free Application for Federal Student Aid (FAFSA) to determine the need of each student for any scholarship, graduate assistantship, or loan, thus the FAFSA should be filed as soon as possible. Deadlines and requirements differ based on the specific aid program.

International Students

Seventeen percent of Fordham's full-time M.B.A. student population comes from other countries; fifty-one nationalities are represented in the School. The International Student Society, which is self-governing, hosts multicultural events and takes advantage of New York City's international character for its many social and business activities.

Application Facts and Dates

Application deadlines are June 1 for the September trimester, November 1 for the January trimester, and March 1 for the April trimester. Decisions are made on a rolling basis. Notification is usually within one month after application is completed.

International students are asked to submit their application one month prior to the regular deadlines, and they must also provide documentation that they have the resources to pay for their studies prior to receiving their visa. For more information, students should contact:

Dean of Admissions
Graduate School of Business
    Administration
Fordham University
113 West 60th Street, Suite 619
New York, New York 10023
Telephone: 01-212-636-6200
Fax: 01-212-765-5573
Internet: gbaadmin@mary.fordham.edu

George Mason University

Fairfax, Virginia

As a relative newcomer to northern Virginia, I am impressed with three unique characteristics of our area that we at GMU are building on with our M.B.A. program: government policy infrastructure, international organizations, and technology firms. First, because we are located within commuting distance of our nation's capital, we are near the center of federal government, where laws and regulations that affect business are created and enforced. Second, we are near embassies representing virtually every country in the world and we have 100 non-U.S. firms with operations in our local area. Third, we are in the center of what some call "the netplex." According to Fortune, there are more high-tech companies in our region than any other area in the United States, with the exception of one. Through our courses, special activities, and mentoring relationships with local businesspeople, we at George Mason expose our students to these unique characteristics of our region and thereby prepare them for successful business careers anywhere in the world.

—William E. Fulmer, Dean

Programs and Curricular Focus

The M.B.A. program at George Mason University is current and comprehensive. Students develop strategic thinking skills to meet the challenges brought forth by high technology in an increasingly global marketplace. They learn to think creatively, to analyze and manage information, to develop their communication skills, and to work as part of a team. Close ties with one of the nation's most dynamic business communities have helped shape a rigorous M.B.A. program that is relevant to today's needs.

The nineteen-course curriculum is oriented toward management in business, government, and high-technology organizations. Students learn to understand business problems, anticipate and manage change, and apply new solutions to enhance productivity and performance. Emphases are on global sensitivity, appreciation of technology, and entrepreneurial enterprise.

The twelve core courses establish solid mastery of finance, accounting, marketing, decision theory, and management. Specializations may be developed through seven elective courses chosen from an extensive selection. Specializations include accounting, decision sciences, management of information systems, finance, marketing, management, and international business.

Full-time students complete the program in two years. Most enhance their educational experience with a professional internship during the summer between the two years. Small classes promote interaction between students and faculty. No single teaching style dominates. Professors use instructional techniques best suited to the subject matter and needs of the class. Typical classes use small groups to develop hands-on activities that support the theoretical learning.

Students and the M.B.A. Experience

Approximately 160 full-time and 400 part-time M.B.A. students bring strong academic and professional credentials to GMU's M.B.A. program. The typical student is 28 years old and has five to six years of work experience. A recent full-time class was made up of 20 percent minority students, 39 percent women, and 24 percent international students. Teamwork, close interaction with faculty, and the M.B.A. student association dominate the atmosphere.

Special Features

Community involvement programs designed to meet the demanding needs of one of the most complex and dynamic communities in the nation include the Small Business Institute, the Small Business Development Center, and the Business Incubator. M.B.A. students often get involved with these programs as they advise and work with developing businesses in Northern Virginia.

Enterprise Hall, a recently opened building housing the business programs, reflects the best of contemporary educational and corporate architecture. The building stands next to the large multifunctional student center, which houses library, retail, and entertainment facilities.

The Faculty

The location and entrepreneurial philosophy of the University have attracted a diverse and accomplished business faculty. These men and women are active researchers and stimulating teachers who are eager to share their research and professional accomplishments with their students. Easy access to professors is standard.

The Business School Network

The School and the business community have forged strong ties and created a number of programs that benefit students as well as area businesses. The Dean's Advisory Council, a group of senior executives representing the area's major corporations, meets regularly with the Dean and acts as a sounding board for the business school's development and activities.

The Century Club builds partnerships between business and education. Students benefit from practical experiences the group provides through its mentor program, which pairs students with local executives. The club also sponsors the summer internship program and provides guest lectures and networking opportunities for M.B.A. students.

The College and Environs

George Mason University's serene, 583-acre, wooded campus is located 16 miles west of Washington, D.C., in the booming high-tech suburbs of northern Virginia. The University benefits from its proximity to the forested Blue Ridge Mountains, the spacious Atlantic beaches, and hundreds of historic and cultural sites.

George Mason University enrolls almost 21,000 students in 108 degree programs. The University has emerged over the past two decades as one of the most

Modern facilities enhance academic experiences at George Mason University.

innovative, visionary universities in the state and in the nation. George Mason focuses not on preserving the past but on welcoming the future through academic excellence, a renowned faculty, a highly diverse student population, and interactive relationships with the business community.

Technology Environment

The University's modern computer facilities are augmented by the business school's LAN, which links students with each other, with faculty, and with databases, networks, and the Internet. Modem access is available.

Placement

The Graduate Career Management Center is a proactive partner in graduate students' career development. The GCMC conducts an intensive three-day job search seminar for first-semester students and provides individual career counseling, a resource room/library, and an array of career workshops. The GCMC also coordinates summer intern, on-campus interview, and mentor programs, as well as an on-campus regional employer symposium. Students may also participate in a fifteen-university M.B.A. Recruiting Consortium.

Admission

The program seeks applicants with diverse ethnic, national, academic, and professional backgrounds. The academic record, GMAT/TOEFL scores, communication skills, and work experience are evaluated. The mean GMAT and TOEFL scores of enrolled M.B.A. students are 575 and 635, respectively. Applicants must hold a degree equivalent to an American bachelor's degree, requiring at least four years of study at the university level. Applicants whose native language is not English must submit a TOEFL score. International applicants must provide proof of financial resources for approximately $20,000 in living and educational expenses. Detailed instructions for international applicants are found in the application.

Finances

Full-time tuition for the 1994–95 academic year was $4044 for Virginia residents and $10,800 for nonresidents. Books and insurance cost approximately $1500 per year. Optional summer-session tuition is additional. A campus apartment (with 2 occupants) and meal plan cost approximately $6000 for two semesters in 1994–95. Off-campus housing, estimated to cost approximately $8000 per year, is abundant and is a popular choice of business students. Assistance in finding housing is provided. Graduate research assistantships, which provide a stipend and partial tuition waiver, are available on a competitive basis.

International Students

George Mason prides itself on the diversity of its student population. Approximately 25 percent of the full-time M.B.A. students are from outside the United States. Typically, more than twenty-five different countries are represented in the M.B.A. population. The University's English Language Institute, Office of International Programs and Services, and International Exchange Programs are valuable resources for all students.

Application Facts and Dates

Because a rolling admission process is used, early applications are encouraged. The application deadline is May 1 for domestic applicants and April 1 for international applicants. For more information, contact:

Sandy Mitchell
Director of M.B.A. Admissions
Mailstop 5A2
George Mason University
Fairfax, Virginia 22030-4444
Phone: 703-993-2136
Fax: 703-993-2145
Internet: gradadms@sba01.gmu.edu

The serene campus is a perfect setting for academic pursuits.

Georgetown University

Washington, D.C.

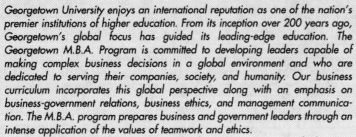

RESPONSIBLE LEADERSHIP FOR A GLOBAL BUSINESS ENVIRONMENT

Georgetown University enjoys an international reputation as one of the nation's premier institutions of higher education. From its inception over 200 years ago, Georgetown's global focus has guided its leading-edge education. The Georgetown M.B.A. Program is committed to developing leaders capable of making complex business decisions in a global environment and who are dedicated to serving their companies, society, and humanity. Our business curriculum incorporates this global perspective along with an emphasis on business-government relations, business ethics, and management communication. The M.B.A. program prepares business and government leaders through an intense application of the values of teamwork and ethics.

I am delighted to invite you to consider the M.B.A. program to further your personal development and professional career.

—Robert S. Parker, Dean

Programs and Curricular Focus

The Georgetown M.B.A. Program is a 60-credit, full-time nonthesis program. Students complete all requirements for the degree in two academic years of four semesters. M.B.A. program requirements fill the curriculum of the first year. Twenty-one hours of elective course work are required in the second year of the program. The primary focus is on courses in the traditional, functional areas of management, finance and economics, marketing, accounting, quantitative methods, and business environment. The curriculum builds on the traditional strengths of Georgetown; a major objective of the program is the integration of the theory and practice of management with the program themes of international business, business-government relations, business ethics, and management communication.

In addition to electives offered by the School of Business, students often enroll in other University courses that focus on international or business issues. To enhance opportunities to pursue regional interests in global business, qualified M.B.A. students are able to receive graduate elective credit for courses offered in various area studies programs or in the International Business Diplomacy Certificate Program. Opportunities to study abroad during the summer or semester are sponsored by the School.

In conjunction with the Georgetown University Law Center and the School of Foreign Service, there are a four-year program leading to the J.D./M.B.A. degree and a three-year program leading to the M.B.A./M.S.F.S. degree, respectively. The International Executive M.B.A. Program is an eighteen-month M.B.A. program for students with a minimum of eight years of work experience. The Georgetown M.B.A. Program is accredited by the American Assembly of Collegiate Schools of Business.

Students and the M.B.A. Experience

Georgetown M.B.A. students bring diverse academic, professional, and personal backgrounds to the program. The fall 1994 entering class numbered 195 and represented every region of the U.S. as well as twenty-eight countries. Twenty-seven percent of the students are international, and 83 percent either have nonnative language proficiency or have lived or studied abroad. Women comprise 36 percent of the class, and minorities represent 14 percent. The average age of the students is 27, and 91 percent of the class has had one year or more of professional, full-time, postbaccalaureate experience, averaging 4.4 years. The diverse backgrounds of Georgetown M.B.A. students contribute greatly to the curricular and cocurricular aspects of the program through class participation, group work, and student activities.

Small class sizes encourage student participation and interaction. Teaching

methodology includes case study and lecture style. Group projects are an integral part of the curriculum.

The Faculty

The School of Business faculty members have strong academic and professional backgrounds. Many have held positions in business or government; lived, worked, or studied abroad; and been educated at many of the best academic institutions around the world. Faculty members concentrate on both research and teaching.

Georgetown University traditionally emphasizes strong student-faculty interaction. School of Business faculty members are available to students, working together with them on research projects and career decision making. Faculty members also serve as advisers to student clubs in the M.B.A. program, where their expertise in functional areas serves as a great resource for students planning events of professional interest.

The Business School Network

The Georgetown School of Business has developed strong ties with local, national, and international business leaders. The School's location in Washington, D.C., is an asset for the M.B.A. program. The program's relationship with business and government provides students with opportunities for on-site projects, internships, and guest speakers.

The School of Business is served by three distinguished boards: the Board of Visitors, the Graduate Advisory Board, and the Parents Council. The boards advise the dean on a broad range of issues related to strategy, program enhancement, faculty, curriculum, resource development, and student career opportunities.

The College and Environs

Georgetown's main campus is located in the heart of the historic Georgetown area of Washington, D.C., alongside the Potomac River. The home of the School of Business, Old North, was constructed in 1795 and is the oldest surviving University building. It is a designated historic landmark. Washington is a world crossroads for political and corporate leaders. As the seat of the federal government, Washington is the headquarters of many international organizations and major corporations. It provides an ideal laboratory for the study of global management issues and business-government relations.

Facilities

The Washington, D.C., area offers excellent research facilities including trade and professional organizations, agencies and departments of the federal government, foreign embassies, and regional, national, and international businesses. The School of Business Technology Center contains the Boland Information Systems Laboratory (BISL), the Decision Support Center (DSC), and personal computer classroom/laboratories for use by the students and faculty members of the business school. Apple Macintosh computers and 80486/80386-class personal computers that are connected to a local area network provide a broad range of application software, access to dot-matrix or laser printers, connections to the University's data network, and software designed to aid in group projects and group decision making. The Center for Business-Government Relations and the Center for International Business Education and Research are research and program arms of the business school.

Placement

M.B.A. career management professionals are available to assist and advise students in developing and attaining their career goals. Through individual and group sessions as well as special programs and events, first- and second-year M.B.A. students develop the skills needed to make sound career decisions and conduct effective job searches. Career management services available to M.B.A. students include consortium events, alumni networking, career advising, career information, workshops, recruiting, résumé referral, résumé books, and summer internships.

While career services are available to all students, international students should be aware that job opportunities in the United States are limited by the type of visa they hold.

Admission

Men and women holding baccalaureate degrees from accredited colleges or universities are eligible for consideration for admission. Georgetown seeks a diverse student body and encourages applications from students with a wide variety of academic backgrounds including the liberal arts and sciences and business.

Academic qualifications are determined by the previous higher education record as indicated by transcripts, letters of recommendation, and results of the Graduate Management Admission Test (GMAT). In addition, international applicants are required to submit results from the TOEFL unless they have obtained an academic degree from a university in a country where English is the native language.

Selection also depends upon an applicant's distinctive achievements, ideas, talents, and motivation for graduate business education. Professional experience, while not required, strengthens an application. International experience, foreign languages, writing ability, interpersonal skills, leadership ability, and entrepreneurship are some favored qualifications. The Admissions Committee seeks to admit students representing various geographic, economic, racial, religious, and minority groups.

Finances

Tuition, fees, books, supplies, transportation, and living expenses for the 1994–95 academic year were approximately $29,810.

The Graduate School and the School of Business award partial- and full-tuition scholarships. Scholarship awards are made on the basis of merit. Recipients of scholarships and stipends are M.B.A. Scholars who provide research assistance to the faculty. All applicants who are offered admission are considered for scholarship awards; no additional application materials are necessary. U.S.

citizens and foreign nationals are considered for scholarships.

The Georgetown University Office of Student Financial Services attempts to assist financially eligible applicants who are U.S. citizens and permanent residents of the U.S. to meet their educational and living costs. Financial eligibility is met by a combination of loans and employment and is awarded on the basis of financial need.

International Students

Services and organizations available to international students include the Office of International Programs, English as a foreign language classes, Off-Campus Housing Office, and the Graduate Business Programs Office. The M.B.A. program office sponsors an Orientation Residency program and preparatory workshops prior to the start of the program.

The fall 1994 M.B.A. entering class included students from the following countries: Argentina, Australia, Bulgaria, Canada, Costa Rica, Egypt, Germany, India, Iran, Italy, Japan, Korea, Mexico, Nigeria, the People's Republic of China, Philippines, Portugal, Russia, Slovenia, South Korea, Spain, Taiwan, Thailand, Turkey, Ukraine, United Kingdom, United States, and Venezuela.

Application Facts and Dates

Admission is for the fall semester only; there are no midyear admissions. Applications are considered on a rolling basis. The final deadline for submission of application materials is April 15. International students and students seeking financial assistance are encouraged to apply before February 1.

For additional information and questions about the Georgetown M.B.A. Program, students should contact:

M.B.A. Admissions Office
School of Business
105 Old North
Georgetown University
Washington, D.C. 20057-1008
Telephone: 202-687-4200
Fax: 202-687-7809

The George Washington University

Washington, D.C.

▶ *It has been aptly referred to as "permanent whitewater"—today's business climate of rapid change, obstacles, and opportunities. With business flowing ever more freely across international boundaries, the times call for a new way of educating leaders. At GW we've responded by redesigning our M.B.A.: strengthening the core curriculum, adding the option of taking all first-year courses with the same group of students, building more flexibility into concentration options, and putting an even greater emphasis on the quality of teaching.*

Fortunately, the strengths we had to build on were formidable. Our diverse and accomplished faculty has far more practical business experience than most, and Washington is the ideal learning laboratory for exploring international business and the interface between the private and public sectors.

Now we have created initiatives that enable our students to have even more enriching experiences. For instance, through the Greater Washington Board of Trade, our international students work with global businesses headquartered here. We are also creating a center for dealing with economic development problems, and to help students develop entrepreneurial skills, we have established the Center for the Advancement of Small Business.

We expect students to be able to find information, analyze it effectively, communicate their ideas convincingly, and work both in teams and independently to find innovative solutions as they become true professionals who can navigate the course of business successfully, with grace and integrity.

—F. David Fowler, Dean

Programs and Curricular Focus

The GW Master of Business Administration degree is a strong general business management degree oriented to international business and the interplay of business and government. The required 60 credit hours of course work are divided into two levels. An integrated core of courses immerses students in the basics, and eleven fields of concentration and many electives offer students the flexibility to create a unique specialization.

The first level, including thirteen core courses, provides a basic foundation in the functions of business, the global environment in which it operates, and the analytical tools needed for intelligent decision making.

The second level consists of four fields of concentration and five elective courses. Students may choose electives from GW's nationally known public administration program—or from any program within the University. Electives must include at least one course with a global focus related to the field of concentration. Fields of concentration

include business economics and public policy; finance and investments; human resources management; information systems management; international business; logistics, operations, and materials management; management decision making; management of science, technology, and innovation; marketing; organizational behavior and development; and real estate and urban development.

Students who find that one of the established fields does not meet their needs may work with advisers to design individualized fields. For instance, a company benefits manager might combine courses in health care, personal finance, and human resources. At GW, students can tailor a program to gain the specific expertise that will enhance their marketability or help them advance in their career.

While M.B.A. core requirements are rigorous, scheduling options are flexible. All degrees may be pursued on either a full- or part-time basis, including optional summer study. Students may choose to participate in the DayOne cohort program, which enhances team-building

skills by developing cohorts and study groups through the core curriculum. If competing professional and personal obligations require full flexibility in scheduling the M.B.A. program, students may choose the Flex M.B.A., which allows them to schedule classes to fit their schedule.

Through a special credit-hour transfer arrangement between the School of Business and Public Management and GW's National Law Center, students can complete both the M.B.A. and J.D. degrees within four years. Also, students may pursue degrees in the School of Business and Public Management and GW's Elliott School of International Affairs simultaneously, thus gaining the M.B.A. and M.A. in two to three years.

The GW Executive M.B.A. program is designed for middle- or senior-level managers looking for an intensive program to enhance career development. The program consists of seven-week courses taught on weekends plus four residencies, including one overseas. It emphasizes management of technology and innovation, management of a culturally diverse work force, and international business.

In addition to the M.B.A. degree, the GW School of Business and Public Management offers the Master of Accountancy, Master of Science in Finance, Master of Science in Information Systems, Master of Taxation, and Master of Science in Tourism Administration. The Ph.D. is offered in accountancy, business administration, health services administration, information and decision systems, management and organization, and public administration.

Students and the M.B.A. Experience

GW M.B.A. students are intellectually mature people who have exhibited a strong potential for management and leadership. The average student is 28 years old. Forty-one percent of M.B.A. students are women, and 11 percent are members of U.S. minority groups. International students comprise 49 percent of the student body.

More than 75 percent of GW M.B.A. students possess substantial business experience before beginning their graduate work. They come from domestic and foreign corporations, family-owned companies, nonprofit organizations, private practices, and the arts. Many work on Capitol Hill or in one of the businesses headquartered in the Washington area.

❖ Global Focus

With students from sixty-five countries, GW offers a culturally diverse environment for learning about life and business around the world. In addition to the core course, The World Economy, students are required to take at least one additional elective that adds international background. For students who choose to study abroad, exchange programs have been established in Europe, Asia, and South America.

The School of Business and Public Management is located within a few blocks of the World Bank, the International Monetary Fund, and embassies from around the world, offering GW M.B.A. students a unique opportunity to gain a global perspective. In addition to internships with international agencies in the Washington area, students may develop opportunities for internships in other countries. For example, a student recently interned at Chase Manhattan Bank in Santiago, Chile, and another in Botswana as a free-market development adviser.

The Faculty

The business faculty members form a diverse group of highly respected experts, many of whom have achieved national and international prominence for their research, writing, and professional accomplishments. These experienced executives, managers, and consultants bring an incisive knowledge of current issues to the classroom. In addition to working closely with students, faculty members work together to address themes that cut across all aspects of business, such as TQM, ethics, and leadership. This collaborative effort makes it easier for students to integrate their knowledge.

The Business School Network

Students of the School of Business and Public Management develop an extraordinary loyalty to their alma mater, as evidenced by more than 30,000 alumni in the fifty states and seventy countries. This extensive network is the key to helping graduating students establish contacts in the area in which they plan to settle. Through the mentor program, alumni

offer guidance in their various areas of expertise, serve on panels to help students make intelligent career decisions, and evaluate students' performance in workshops and case studies.

The Dean's Associates Council includes leaders from both the private and public sector. These partnerships provide direction for the School of Business and Public Management and opportunities for students to meet and learn from today's business leaders.

The College and Environs

Unquestionably one of the most exciting cities in the world, Washington, D.C., is a global center of power and influence. Living in Washington means enjoying the beauty of four glorious seasons and being in the midst of a region filled with historic sites and natural beauty. Attracting interesting people from all over the world, Washington boasts the highest percentage of college graduates of any metropolitan area in the country. In addition to a wide array of Fortune 500 companies and technology-based industries, the area provides a wealth of cultural and recreational attractions that few cities can match.

Located five blocks from the White House in the historic Foggy Bottom area of northwest Washington, The George Washington University is an integral part of the city. Modern and efficient public transportation makes it easy to participate in the exciting life of the capital city.

Placement

Career services are available to GW M.B.A. students from a variety of resources. The GW Career Center offers comprehensive career placement services. The M.B.A. Association and the Alumni Association regularly sponsor networking activities and career panels. Cooperative education opportunities and internships become an excellent network for future career opportunities. M.B.A. students find faculty members ready and willing to provide career advice and networking opportunities. These resources allow each student to develop an aggressive strategy for finding the best opportunities after graduation.

Admission

The School of Business and Public Management seeks candidates who have demonstrated potential for management and who have the intellectual ability, maturity, initiative, and creativity to participate fully in the challenging

interdisciplinary environment. Applicants must have a bachelor's degree from a regionally accredited college or university. Selection is based upon the applicant's academic record, work experience, statement of purpose, recommendations, and scores on the required Graduate Management Admission Test (GMAT).

Applications from international students are welcome. Proficiency in reading, writing, and speaking English must be demonstrated by all students from countries where English is not an official language. International students, in addition to the above listed requirements, must submit certified English translations of all academic records of course work corresponding to a bachelor's degree in the United States; scores for the Test of English as a Foreign Language (TOEFL), with a total score of 550 or higher; and a financial certificate, which is required of any applicant who plans to enter or remain in the United States to study and whose immigration status will be either F-1 (student) or J-1 (exchange visitor).

Finances

Tuition for the academic year 1994–95 was $575 per credit hour plus a University fee of $30 per credit hour. Full-time students normally take 9 to 15 credits per semester. Books and supplies cost approximately $1000 per year. Estimated costs for room, board, and miscellaneous personal expenses total about $9000 per academic year. The majority of graduate students live off campus.

A number of M.B.A. fellowships are available based on academic merit. To be considered, applicants must complete the admissions application process no later than February 1.

Application Facts and Dates

Applications for the fall semester are due no later than April 1. Students who wish to be considered for fellowships must complete the application process no later than February 1. The application deadline for the spring semester is October 1. For more information, students should contact:

The Office of Graduate Enrollment Services
School of Business and Public Management
The George Washington University
710 21st Street, NW
Washington, D.C. 20052
Telephone: 202-994-6584
Fax: 202-994-6382
E-mail: sbpmapp@gwis2.circ.gwu.edu

Golden Gate University

San Francisco, California

> The M.B.A. program at Golden Gate University is designed to help working professionals gain the knowledge, skills, and confidence they need to assume broader corporate responsibilities. Ambitious, professional adult students find a real-world approach to education here and benefit from the experience and knowledge of their classmates as well as from their instructors—full- and part-time scholar-practitioners. We are proud to say that more San Francisco Bay Area business executives have earned their M.B.A. from Golden Gate than from any other university in northern California.
>
> —Hamid Shomali, Dean

Programs and Curricular Focus

The M.B.A. program at Golden Gate University provides a solid grounding in the core areas of business management as well as the opportunity to specialize in one of seventeen separate areas. The program consists of three components: the general business program, or foundation courses; the advanced program, or core courses; and an area of concentration. Eight general business courses provide an essential foundation for the more advanced core and concentration courses. These general business courses may be waived if students have completed comparable courses elsewhere. Seven core courses in areas such as financial management, human resources, managerial analysis and communication, business policy and strategy, marketing, and operations ensure that all M.B.A. program graduates have a comprehensive knowledge of the core areas of business, regardless of their area of concentration. The final five courses are taken in an area of specialization, allowing students to develop expertise in a specific area of business.

An Executive M.B.A. program is offered for managers and professionals who want to integrate a full-time twenty-month M.B.A. program with their current work schedules. A joint M.B.A./J.D. degree program is also available in conjunction with the Golden Gate School of Law.

Students and the M.B.A. Experience

Students in the Golden Gate M.B.A. program bring a wide variety of work experiences and academic diversity to the classroom. About 80 percent of the students attend part-time while working either full- or part-time. Thirty-five percent of M.B.A. students are women.

❖ Global Focus

Among the core courses is The Manager in the International Economy, which provides exposure to the role of multinationals in the global economy; legal, cultural, and financial environments facing multinational corporations; host/home country relationships with multinationals; and policy, strategy, and management challenges faced by multinational corporations. An international perspective also is included throughout the M.B.A. program, as appropriate.

Special Features

One of the special features of the M.B.A. program at Golden Gate is the opportunity to choose one of seventeen areas of concentration, in addition to the foundation and core courses required. Students take five courses to develop expertise in one of the following areas: accounting, arts administration, entrepreneurship, finance, general management, health-care management, hospitality administration, human resource management, information systems, international management, manufacturing management, marketing, organizational behavior and development, operations management, procurement and logistics management, project and systems management, or telecommunications management.

The Faculty

The faculty is composed of scholar-practitioner full- and part-time educators.

Many are career professionals who also have advanced degrees and extensive classroom experience. They bring real-world problems and events to the classroom. The faculty is also specially trained to make sure that classes are relevant, challenging, and meet the needs of adult students.

The Business School Network

Since 1953, feedback from M.B.A. students, alumni, and the business community has been used to continuously improve the M.B.A. program. Advisory boards comprising corporate and industry executives provide valuable input in each management discipline that helps keep the curriculum current.

Prominent Alumni

More San Francisco Bay Area business executives have earned their M.B.A. degrees from Golden Gate University than from any other university in northern California. Some, like Bank of America CEO Richard Rosenberg (M.B.A. class of 1963, J.D. class of 1966), rose to the very pinnacle of their professions. Others, like Eleanor Yu (M.B.A. class of 1986), president and CEO of AdLand Advertising and one of the most powerful Asian women in the American advertising industry, became highly successful entrepreneurs.

The College and Environs

Golden Gate University traces its origins to the founding of the San Francisco YMCA in 1853, the oldest founding date in the city for an institution of higher learning.

A pioneer in the case-study method of instruction, Golden Gate is recognized for applied education for the professions. The University provides instruction for more than 7,000 students at the associate, baccalaureate, master's, and doctoral levels on nine campuses along the West Coast of the United States and abroad.

Classrooms, the general and law libraries, and the principal offices of Golden Gate University are located in San Francisco's financial district. Other University campuses are in San Francisco's East and North Bay, Monterey,

Sacramento, southern California, Silicon Valley, Seattle, and Southeast Asia.

Placement

The skilled staff in the Career Services Center works closely with students and employers. Students benefit from professional career counseling, job-search workshops and programs, computerized skills assessment, placement services, networking opportunities through the STAR (Student Alumni Referral) network, and the annual career fairs that feature on-campus recruiting by major corporations. These free services provide M.B.A. students with the competitive edge in launching and in furthering their careers.

Admission

Applicants to the M.B.A. program must have an earned bachelor's degree from a regionally accredited college or university in the United States or the equivalent from a recognized foreign institution.

Students must also satisfy basic mathematics, writing, and computer proficiencies.

Applicants to the M.B.A. program must submit an official score report from the GMAT (Graduate Management Admission Test), official transcripts from all schools previously attended, a 200- to 300-word statement of purpose, and a completed graduate application form along with the appropriate application fee. (Some applicants are not required to provide a GMAT score.)

Applicants whose native language is not English are required to meet the English language proficiency requirement by having achieved a TOEFL score of at least 550 or by completing (or showing evidence of having completed) courses equivalent to Golden Gate's English 1A and 1B.

Finances

Golden Gate University is one of the most affordable private universities in

northern California. Tuition for 1994–95 was $348 per unit ($362 for telecommunications courses). All M.B.A. classes are 3 units. Each trimester students pay a $40 registration fee and a $30 technology fee.

Application Facts and Dates

The University accepts applications on a rolling admissions basis beginning up to one year prior to enrollment, and applications are reviewed as they become complete. International students should apply by the following dates: July 1 for fall trimester, November 1 for spring trimester, and March 1 for summer trimester. For more information, students should contact:

Pete Johnson, Admissions
    Administrator
Golden Gate University
536 Mission Street
San Francisco, California 94105
Telephone: 415-442-7203
Fax: 415-495-2671

Hawaii Pacific University

Honolulu, Hawaii

MEETING TODAY'S GLOBAL CHALLENGE

Hawaii Pacific's M.B.A. enhances the career development of today's business professional. The HPU student body is culturally diverse, with representatives from Hawaii, the U.S. mainland, and more than eighty countries. HPU offers the skills, knowledge, and training required in today's highly competitive global business environment.

Academic programs combine practice, theory, and the skills needed in modern career fields. Students learn to implement the latest developments in computer technology, business simulations, communications theory, and strategic planning. Our graduates are well prepared for success in today's rapidly changing marketplace.

—Richard T. Ward, Dean of Graduate Studies

Programs and Curricular Focus

The Hawaii Pacific University M.B.A. program requires 45 semester hours of graduate work (fifteen courses). Core requirements (27 semester hours) include accounting, economics, information systems, finance, law, international business management, human resource management, marketing, and quantitative methods. Elective courses (9 semester hours) may be taken in nine different areas. The last area is the capstone series (9 semester hours), which includes Management Policy and Strategy Formulation and completion of the Professional Paper, Parts I and II.

Joint-degree programs (63 semester hours) include the M.B.A./Master of Arts in Human Resource Management and the M.B.A./Master of Science in Information Systems (M.S.I.S.).

Full-time students can complete the program in eighteen months. Part-time students can complete the program in twenty-four months. Students must complete their professional paper within seven years of initial enrollment in graduate courses and within one year from first enrollment in the professional paper (MGMT 720).

Hawaii Pacific University is an independent, not-for-profit, coeducational, nonsectarian, career-oriented postsecondary institution founded in 1965. It is accredited by the Accrediting Commission for Senior Colleges and Universities of the Western Association of Schools and Colleges. The University is a member of the American Assembly of Collegiate Schools of Business. HPU is recognized by the Hawaii Commission of Post-Secondary Education, approved for veteran's benefits, and authorized to issue I-20 documents to international students.

Students and the M.B.A. Experience

The average age of graduate students at Hawaii Pacific University is between 25 and 29 years of age. Students represent over seventy countries. Teamwork is an essential ingredient of the M.B.A. program. In various courses throughout the program, students are formed into teams to solve problems collectively and to achieve a better understanding of group dynamics and challenges while producing specific desired results. Hands-on experience is gained through internships with leading Honolulu corporations. For example, students work in accounting, human resource management, and marketing internships, to name but a few.

The Faculty

The M.B.A. program at Hawaii Pacific University permits students to study with some of the most distinguished professors in the Pacific region. Faculty members have contemporary experience with leading corporations, outstanding academic credentials, and a dedication to teaching. The graduate faculty includes 32 (6 women) full-time and 18 (7 women) part-time teachers. Seventy-five percent of the faculty hold the doctorate or its equivalent. Average class size is 24.

Two full-time academic advisers are available to assist students.

The Business School Network

The Honolulu business community plays an integral role in the Hawaii Pacific University M.B.A. program. Many of Honolulu's leading corporations sponsor students for internships, many of which eventually result in offers of full-time employment. Senior executives of local investment firms, health-care systems, banks, schools, law firms, and trust companies serve on the University Board of Trustees, providing vision and direction for the future. Other HPU M.B.A. graduates serve on the Alumni Board, helping maintain a base of future employment contacts for new graduates as well as supporting the University. HPU also integrates the business community into the curriculum through the use of guest speakers with individual areas of expertise in appropriate academic disciplines, exposing students to current issues and emerging trends.

The College and Environs

Hawaii Pacific combines the excitement of an urban downtown campus with the serenity of a residential campus set in the foothills of the Koolau mountains. The main campus is located in downtown Honolulu, business and financial center of the Pacific. There are also eight satellite campuses located at Pearl Harbor, Barbers Point, Hickam Air Force Base, Schofield Barracks, Fort Shafter, Tripler Army Medical Center, Kaneohe Marine Corps Air Station, and Camp Smith.

Facilities

Meader Library and two additional on-campus libraries are available. Total holdings include 120,000 volumes, 193,058 microforms, and 1,740 current periodical subscriptions. There are thirty-five personal computers in all libraries. CD-ROM players are available for graduate student use. Access is provided to on-line bibliographic retrieval services.

Rooms and/or apartments are available to single students (180 units) at an average cost of $6400, including board; on-campus housing is not available to married students. The typical monthly cost of living in off-campus housing not owned by the University is $600. For further graduate housing information, students should contact Mr. Rick Stepien at 808-233-3184.

Technology Environment

Computer networks run on DOS Novell, UNIX, and Macintosh. Personal computers on campus are linked to the Internet. Computer labs are available from 8 a.m. to 9 p.m. daily and from 8 a.m. to 5 p.m. weekends.

Placement

Hawaii Pacific University's Career Planning and Placement Center provides, free of charge, two sponsored job fairs per year, job search preparation, seminars, on-campus recruiters, employer visits, workshops, job placement, national computerized résumé referral services, a career resource library, internships, and campus employment opportunities. International student advisers are available to provide current information regarding visas, passports, F-1 regulations, work permits, and other concerns critical to international students.

Admission

Admission requirements include a completed application, official transcripts from each postsecondary school attended

(sent directly to HPU), a document showing conferral of the bachelor's degree, and two letters of reference. International students should submit certified copies of "A" level (or similar postsecondary) examinations directly to HPU. The Test of English as a Foreign Language (TOEFL) is recommended unless students have completed a bachelor's degree from an accredited American college or university with a grade point average of 2.7 or above.

Hawaii Pacific University seeks students with academic promise, outstanding career potential, and high motivation.

Finances

For the 1994–95 academic year, graduate tuition was $6300, living expenses were $6500, and other expenses (books and insurance) were $1320; the total cost was $14,120. Part-time cost was $263 per credit hour.

Aid is available to part-time students. The University participates in all federal financial aid programs designated for graduate students. These programs provide aid in the form of subsidized (need-based) and unsubsidized (non-need-based) Federal Stafford Student Loans. Through these loans, funds may be available to cover a student's entire cost of education. To apply for aid, students must submit the Free Application for Federal Student Aid (FAFSA) after January 1. Mailing of student award

letters usually begins in April. For further financial aid information, students should contact Mr. Walter Fleming at 808-544-0253.

International Students

The International Student Office provides a variety of services to international students, including advising on personal, interpersonal, cultural, and academic matters; assisting on immigration matters, especially F-1 requirements, I-20 extensions, and work authorization; advising on money management and housing needs; conducting orientation programs to facilitate academic and social adjustment; and providing medical insurance information. An International Day is held each year to highlight the contributions of HPU's diverse student population. There are fourteen different country-specific organizations on campus.

Application Facts and Dates

Admission decisions for the M.B.A. program are made on a rolling basis, and applicants are notified between one and two weeks after all documents have been submitted. Completed applications should be sent to:

Graduate Admissions
1164 Bishop Street, Suite 1510
Honolulu, Hawaii 96813
Telephone: 808-544-1120
            800-669-4724 (toll-free)
Fax: 808-544-0280

HEC Graduate School of Management

Institut Supérieur des Affaires

Jouy-en-Josas, France

EDUCATING EUROPEAN BUSINESS LEADERS FOR THE TWENTY-FIRST CENTURY

ISA welcomes the challenge of shaping men and women for effective leadership in a competitive, dynamic, and culturally diverse global business setting. Our ambition is not only to train efficient managers or superb analysts, but to educate leaders.

We believe that effective leadership blends practical know-how with a sensitive yet proactive attitude and creative problem-solving strategies. More importantly, we believe that we can impart rigorous know-how, teach creative thinking, and influence attitude within a highly supportive learning environment. Our participants are shareholders whose professional successes, in the long term, will reflect most positively on the educational strategy we have adopted.

—Eric Briys, Dean

Programs and Curricular Focus

Since its founding in 1969, ISA has departed from established practice in three areas: duration, structure, and content. ISA pioneered the sixteen-month generalist M.B.A. This model allows a thorough investigation of the core business issues, without sacrificing the flexibility of the two-year program. Moreover, it ensures a return to employment in a relatively short period. The entire core curriculum, lasting three terms, is offered through interdisciplinary modules taught intensively within two to six weeks. ISA also introduced nongraded personal development and leadership enhancement seminars that cover one to three days. It delayed offering most of its elective courses until the final term to accommodate the participants of the student exchange program. Such a modular structure has recently been adopted by several top institutions in the United States.

Investigating the impact of business decisions from a British, German, Japanese, or American perspective is simply unavoidable at ISA. Teaching materials are often developed in-house, where European and Japanese as much as American corporations are used extensively to provide examples of good or bad management practices. Forty percent of each entering class hails from outside France. In this environment, group work promotes enriching exchanges of ideas and worldviews, tests differing national work habits, and enhances mutual respect, tolerance, and cooperation. Visiting

non-French faculty members constitute 30 to 40 percent of those dedicated to teaching exclusively at ISA. Seventeen distinguished institutions located in North and South America, Europe, and Asia have long-standing student exchange agreements with ISA. This network provides 30 percent of the class with the opportunity to round out its international exposure. As of September 1994, a combined-degree program enables a small number of participants to earn an M.B.A. from ISA and an M.A.L.D. (Master of Arts in Law and Diplomacy) from the Fletcher School at Tufts University in two years.

Yet, the most differentiating characteristic about ISA's curriculum must be its bilingual instruction. All participants should be fluent in either English or French and have a working knowledge of the other language.

Students and the M.B.A. Experience

Students at ISA exhibit strong academic credentials, above-average work experience, and maturity. They represent a large spectrum of educational and geographical backgrounds. The average participant is 30 years old, with 5½ years of full-time professional experience. Women comprise 23 percent of the total population, while international students account for 42 percent. European Union (EU) students, excluding the French, make up 37 percent of the international population. Seventeen percent come from European countries

outside the EU, while North America sends 28 percent. Africa and Asia contribute 9 percent each.

Educational diversity is demonstrated through the following breakdown of undergraduate degrees: 37 percent are engineers, and 20 percent hold B.A. degrees in the humanities, 17 percent in the social sciences, and 7 percent in the physical sciences. Only 10 percent of those enrolled selected business as a discipline. Thirty-one percent of the entire class earned graduate degrees.

Professional backgrounds reflect a similar diversity. Analysts, artists, doctors, government employees, lawyers, naval architects, professors, scientific researchers, and self-made managers bring a wealth of valuable contributions to the program.

Special Features

ISA conforms to the belief in the need for ethics in business behavior. To allow participants the opportunity to debate this issue, the program works hand-in-hand with Benedictine monks from the monastery of Ganagobie in the French Alps. Students spend three to four days in this environment, discussing general and business ethics cases not only with monks but also with business practitioners. The art of "gazing and deciphering" refers to the idea that managers can gain valuable insights by altering their perceptual framework. To encourage and exercise this attitude, ISA developed a course in collaboration with the Louvre museum. A forthcoming initiative based on the same idea will be called Music as an Unexpected Model for Management. It is to be taught by a French conductor who lectures at the Paris School of Philharmony and at well-known American schools of music.

The Faculty

The faculty at HEC School of Management comprises 100 full-time tenured members and approximately 300 adjunct faculty members. All full-time members are required to devote at least 20 percent of their teaching load to consulting. Practical research and a strong commitment to teaching complete the portfolio of faculty obligations. Many of those who teach at ISA do so in the executive program's intracompany and intercompany courses also. Albeit 60 to 70 percent French, most hold Ph.D.'s from distinguished doctoral programs in the United States and Europe. According to the Economist Intelligence Unit (EIU) report, "Most (ISA) students think teaching standards are high."

The Business School Network
Corporate Partnerships
ISA is the M.B.A. program of HEC School of Management, the reputation of which in France is "second to none," writes the EIU. HEC is an affiliate of the Paris Chamber of Commerce and Industry. It enjoys the chamber's financial support, which constitutes 40 percent of its operating budget. Since its founding in 1881, HEC's mission has consistently been to train the managers who lead the top French corporations. This uniquely French relationship between a business school and its corporate patrons continues to be fundamental to the School's success. Internships, hands-on projects, lectures by prominent business practitioners, and visits by national and international political figures have long been expected of this institution.

More recently, the HEC Foundation, which comprises forty major French enterprises, established a special fund to assist the School in its drive to internationalize its curriculum, stimulate research, and draw more international faculty members.

The College and Environs
HEC School of Management is an institution dedicated exclusively to the teaching of business management. It comprises four independently run programs, one of which is ISA. The others include HEC Graduate Program, HEC Doctoral Program, and HEC Management. HEC Graduate Program provides a three-year curriculum for candidates without prior work experience or prior university education. Successful completion of the program leads to the Diplôme HEC, a Master of Science in Management. Holders of a three-year university degree, without work experience, may earn the Diplôme HEC in two years. HEC Management provides short-term executive management training modules. All programs are located in a park close to Versailles and within commuting distance of central Paris. Facilities are excellent and include a fully equipped gym, sports fields, a large fishing lake, and a nearby golf course. Housing on campus is available to all participants.

Technology Environment
There are six microcomputing laboratories equipped with over 100 terminals. Unrestricted access is possible until midnight every day. However, both HEC and ISA students are strongly encouraged to buy their own IBM-compatible microcomputers. Databases and networks available include CompuServe, Dialog, and the Internet. About 1,500 university research centers worldwide may be accessed through the Internet.

Placement
ISA graduates benefit from HEC's strong ties and special relationships established over decades with major corporations. Each April, over 100 multinational firms with either headquarters or affiliates in France visit the campus, where they spend two days providing information and setting up interviews. For ISA exclusively, on-campus company presentations are scheduled throughout September, October, and November. The Careers Development Office also provides individual career counseling, organizes workshops on career management and job search strategies, and prepares and publishes a résumé book that is mailed to over 2,500 potential employers. In addition, it keeps an up-to-date job-listing service and assists in arranging summer internships.

Admission
The goal of the admission process at ISA is to identify academically qualified candidates with significant work experience, not necessarily in management, but coherent with the undergraduate training completed. Motivation for a career in the European Union, working knowledge of French, and a flexible orientation describe other factors important in this process. Quantitative indicators such as the GMAT, TOEFL, and GPA are required. However, the formal panel interview component of the admission process determines the admission decision. This component is made up of a rehearsed oral presentation, followed by an interview, a written essay, and a French proficiency examination.

Finances
Tuition and fees for 1995–96 are Fr120,000. Books and supplies cost approximately Fr8000. On-campus housing costs Fr1950 per month and meals about Fr200 per week. Campus housing and food costs do not reflect market prices in France.

Very few scholarships are awarded based on merit and need. British candidates are eligible for AMBA loans, while Americans should complete a regular financial aid form. Other non-French residents may apply for low-interest bank loans guaranteed by a French national.

Application Facts and Dates

There are two deadlines, February 1 and April 1, for one single annual intake in September. Candidates are invited to interview by the end of February or April. Final decisions are mailed four weeks later. For more information, applicants should write or call:

ISA Admissions
HEC School of Management
1, rue de la Liberation
78351 Jouy-en-Josas Cedex
France
Telephone: 331-3967-7382
Fax: 331-3967-7465

Hofstra University

Hempstead, New York

THE HOFSTRA M.B.A.: TRAINING MANAGERS FOR THE TWENTY-FIRST CENTURY

▶ *The Frank G. Zarb School of Business at Hofstra University is committed to offering to its select student body an excellent integrative business education, combining theory with practice. The School takes full advantage of its beautiful suburban location and proximity to New York City to provide future managers with exposure to a wide variety of internship and employment opportunities and to become personally involved in the dynamism of the New York business community. The M.B.A. program is distinctive in its emphasis on the highest quality of teaching, the global perspective it offers students in classes small enough to allow for meaningful interaction among faculty and with each other, and a faculty and professional staff that cares very much about developing and launching future managers in a world subject to constant change.*
—Ulric S. Haynes Jr., Dean

Programs and Curricular Focus

Individual study programs are designed based on prior education, graduate degree objectives, and a common body of knowledge. The amount of course work needed to obtain the M.B.A. degree depends largely on a student's undergraduate training, although the minimum required course work is 36 semester hours.

The M.B.A. program consists of four components: prerequisite courses for students with nonbusiness degrees who lack specific business course work, core courses that cover the common body of business knowledge, specialization electives that allow a student to master an area of business concentration, and, contingent on the option chosen, either a master's thesis or a graduate research seminar.

Students with appropriate prior course work in business can satisfy degree requirements by completing a 36-credit program that includes a master's thesis or by completing a 39-credit program that includes a seminar on research design in lieu of the thesis. Students who do not have satisfactory prior course work will be required to complete prerequisite survey courses in addition to the 36 or 39 upper-level credits.

Full-time students with bachelor's degrees in business can complete degree requirements in as little as a calendar year by attending both summer sessions and the January session in addition to the fall and spring semesters.

A Juris Doctor/M.B.A. program is also offered jointly with the School of Law.

Students and the M.B.A. Experience

The M.B.A. student body currently includes students from twenty-two countries outside of the United States, including Japan, Ukraine, Venezuela, Greece, Turkey, Hong Kong, China, the Czech Republic, Slovenia, Slovakia, Poland, Hungary, France, Germany, Nigeria, and Canada. Slightly more than one third are women, and approximately 6 percent are members of minority groups. Students range in age from 22 to 55, with an average age of 26. Nearly 75 percent enter the program with full-time work experience.

Team projects are a key part of the M.B.A. experience, as is the application of technology to conducting business in a dynamically changing world. One of the most popular student organizations is the Hofstra University Consulting Group (HUCG). Membership in HUCG is by application and "hire" only, and the organization is run similarly to external consulting practices. In recent years, the group has expanded its client list to include several Fortune 100 companies throughout the Northeast, providing students with hands-on consulting experience as well as remuneration for their services.

Several student exchange programs are offered in the European countries, and

internships are an increasingly important part of the M.B.A. experience. The location of the University provides virtually unlimited opportunity for exposure to any field of business, government, or the not-for-profit sector. International internship opportunities are available through the chapter of the international organization Association of Students in Economics and Commerce (AISEC), which is hosted by the Frank G. Zarb School of Business.

The Faculty

Over 90 faculty members, representing a combination of academicians and business practitioners, teach in the M.B.A. program. It is significant to note that while many institutions of higher education devote senior faculty energies primarily to research, the mission of the faculty of the Frank G. Zarb School has always been to be, above all, excellent teachers. This philosophy results in a faculty that possesses both extensive business experience and excellent academic credentials, allowing for a balanced approach to theory and practice in the curriculum as well as a balance of active scholarship, interaction with students, and involvement in the business community. A complete list of faculty members, showing their credentials and experience, is available from the M.B.A. office.

The Business School Network

The School's primary link to the corporate community is the Dean's Advisory Board, which is composed of business leaders from all over the world. Among them are Joseph L. Dionne, Chairman and CEO, McGraw-Hill, Inc.; Albert R. Dowden, President and CEO, Volvo North America; Daniel T. Napoli, Senior Vice President, Global Risk Management, Merrill Lynch; and Gunnar Riberholdt, Danish Ambassador to the European Community.

Distinguished business practitioners are frequent visitors to the Zarb School, often selected to deliver a "Dean's Lecture" on a timely business topic.

The M.B.A. program also boasts an excellent network of alumni who volunteer to assist students with career exploration and who serve often as panelists for the several alumni career forums held each semester. These forums are designed to provide M.B.A. students with real-world information about various career opportunities. Prominent among the M.B.A. alumni are Frank G. Zarb (for whom the school is named), the current CEO of Alexander & Alexander and former CEO of Smith Barney Shearson; Eugene B. Connolly, Chairman and CEO, USG Corporation; and Patrick Purcell, Publisher of the *Boston Herald*.

Relationships with the corporate community are also fostered through the Retail Management Institute, the Small Business Institute, the Family Business Forum, the Long Island Venture Group, and the Consulting Group, all of which are sponsored by the School of Business.

The College and Environs

The University is located on a parklike 238-acre campus in a suburban, residential area of Long Island, New York. It is within a 40-minute train ride of Manhattan. In addition to the enormous opportunities for cultural, social, and professional development offered through the proximity to New York City, the University hosts over 500 cultural events of its own each year. Athletics facilities include the only indoor Olympic-size pool on Long Island and a fully equipped Physical Fitness Center.

Facilities

The Axinn Library serves the School of Business, and the M.B.A. program in particular, through a fully computerized system featuring LEXICAT, an on-line listing that includes over 500,000 records of books, periodicals, microforms, and media. Other services offered are Business Periodicals on Disc, ABI/Inform database, Newspaper Abstracts on Disc, and the Dow Jones News/Retrieval Service.

Extensive computer lab facilities are also available that support such software applications as Microsoft Windows, WordPerfect, Lotus, Quattro, and over 200 other packages. Hofstra also subscribes to the Standard & Poor's COMPUSTAT database, which contains company reports and market information for over 8,000 companies, as well as PDE, Bank, Full Coverage, and Global Vantage files. The Center for Research in Security Prices (CRSP) database, which includes daily and monthly price and volume information for over 8,000 firms, is also available to M.B.A. students.

The new classroom building, Breslin Hall, contains several rooms equipped for computer demonstration and videoconferencing. On-campus housing is readily available to M.B.A. students in the form of apartments and dormitories.

Placement

A full complement of placement services is available to M.B.A. students under the direction of the M.B.A. Placement Coordinator. These services include on- and off-campus recruiting, general job search information (e.g., interviewing and résumé preparation), a comprehensive interview and placement library, videotaping of interview simulations, computerized job banks, career planning seminars, and internship and part-time employment assistance.

Admission

Admission is selective. Candidates are required to complete the graduate admission application and all supporting forms and to submit two letters of recommendation, a résumé, a statement on professional objectives, official transcripts from every college or university attended, and scores obtained on the Graduate Management Admission Test (GMAT). For the most recently admitted class, the middle 80 percent range of GMAT scores was from 430 to 640; the

average undergraduate grade point average was 3.2 on a 4.0 scale. All credentials submitted in support of the application for admission are carefully considered prior to a decision being made.

Finances

Tuition for 1994–95 was assessed on a per credit basis at $382 for each credit, with most courses carrying 3 credits each. Hofstra is a private institution, so tuition is the same for residents and nonresidents of New York State. Room and board and books and supplies bring the total annual cost of an M.B.A. education to approximately $20,000. Financial aid is available in the form of fellowships that provide partial tuition credit and graduate assistantship positions. Very limited aid is available for international students.

Application Facts and Dates

Hofstra subscribes to a rolling admissions policy, with suggested deadlines of April 1 for fall admission and November 1 for spring admission. Students planning to apply for financial aid should file admission and financial aid application forms no later than March 1 for fall admission. Candidates are generally advised of admission decisions no later than six weeks after an application is completed. Students may obtain additional information and application materials from:

Susan McTiernan
Senior Assistant Dean and Director of
    Graduate Programs
Frank G. Zarb School of Business
    Administration
134 Hofstra University
Hempstead, New York 11550
Telephone: 516-463-5683
Fax: 516-463-5268

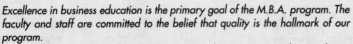

Howard University

Washington, D.C.

> *Excellence in business education is the primary goal of the M.B.A. program. The faculty and staff are committed to the belief that quality is the hallmark of our program.*
>
> *The M.B.A. program draws on its unique characteristics and strengths—a scholarly faculty committed to providing a high-quality educational experience and the School's location in the nation's capital that allows the faculty to utilize the vast resources of the Washington metropolitan area. The M.B.A. program's noteworthiness, coupled with intense motivation from its student body, results in an attractive, distinguished program.*
>
> *Since its founding in 1867, Howard University has offered the finest educational opportunity to all, especially to those who, due to economic or social circumstance, have been unable to pursue an education of the quality provided by the University. The School of Business continues to pursue this tradition as our community builds leaders for the future.*
>
> —Barron H. Harvey, Dean

Programs and Curricular Focus

An internationally renowned institution that serves primarily minority students, Howard University is committed to the highest standards of academic excellence. The M.B.A. program is designed to develop graduates with outstanding leadership potential, offering an educational experience designed to enhance and develop the student's knowledge and skills. The curriculum incorporates a broad view of the management of manufacturing and service organizations. While the curriculum structure is designed around functional areas and disciplines, the goal of the program is to give the student a comprehensive view of the issues and structures that affect the enterprise.

Most students attending on a full-time basis complete the program in two years. The first year of study covers skills such as communications and analysis and develops the fundamental knowledge of the various business disciplines. During this first year, emphasis is placed on developing individual capabilities and knowledge.

The second year expands upon the first year's curriculum and provides more in-depth knowledge of industries and corporations. At this point, students have the opportunity to select from concentrations in general management, finance, or health services administration. During the two years of study, the emphasis is placed on group dynamics and developing

critical-thinking skills. This is accomplished through the use of case studies and team efforts.

Throughout the two-year program, the role of current issues—for example, total quality management and the globalization of the enterprise—are refined with respect to their relationship to the various disciplines in the curriculum.

Students and the M.B.A. Experience

Students in the School of Business of Howard University are an internationally diverse community. One quarter of the students are international; they represent countries from Africa, the Middle East, Asia, and the West Indies. On average, a typical student is 26 years old, with three years of work experience. The population is almost equally divided between women and men, with about three quarters of the students registered on a full-time basis. Typically, 60 percent of the students have undergraduate degrees in business, while most of the remaining 40 percent have degrees in either natural science or social science.

The Faculty

The school's faculty is committed to cultural diversity; Howard University has the highest concentration of black scholars in the world. The international and ethnic mix of the faculty creates an

environment that celebrates diversity and globalism. Faculty members have doctoral degrees from renowned universities; among these are the University of Michigan, UCLA, Indiana University, the University of Wisconsin, the University of Chicago, Ohio State University and the Johns Hopkins University. Thirty percent of the faculty members are women, and 35 percent are international.

The Business School Network

During its twenty-five years, the School of Business has developed strong ties to the business community. The School's Executive Advisory Board acts as a sounding board for innovative ideas and approaches to graduate business education. The board consists of executives from some of the most prestigious corporations in the world. Among these corporations are McDonalds, IBM, AT&T, Walt Disney, Kraft General Foods, and Ford Motor Company.

The College and Environs

The School of Business is located on Howard University's main campus in Washington, D.C. The 89-acre campus is in the northwest section of the nation's capital, 5 minutes from downtown and the federal government's key political institutions. Howard students have easy access to many leading research facilities and libraries, such as the National Archives, the Library of Congress, the Federal Reserve, the Frederick Douglass Home, and the Smithsonian Institution. Washington is also host to an abundance of theaters, concert halls, art galleries, museums, and sports facilities.

Facilities

The School of Business is located in one of the newest buildings on the campus. The School has its own library, with approximately 600,000 microtexts and subscriptions to virtually all of the major periodicals and newspapers. The library maintains modern computer-based search services for the support of research efforts. In addition, the M.B.A. program has its own graduate computer lab. The school also has a Small Business Development Center as

well as centers for banking, insurance, and accounting education.

Placement

The Center for Professional Development has developed strong relationships with major national and international corporations. These corporations recruit at the School of Business in the fall and spring for both permanent and internship positions. In addition, the School receives many requests from companies that do not recruit on campus. Information on these opportunities is made available to students throughout the academic year. The center also supports job fairs and company information sessions.

Admission

Applicants must submit an application with a nonrefundable $25 fee, GMAT scores, two official copies of undergraduate transcripts, an autobiographical sketch, two letters of recommendation, and a one-page résumé. Candidates from non-English-speaking countries must take the Test of English as a Foreign Language (TOEFL) and receive a minimum score of 550.

Finances

The estimated tuition and fees for the 1995–96 academic year are $9250 for a full-time student. Tuition for part-time students is expected to be $500 per credit. For a full-time student, books and supplies are estimated to be $750 for the academic year. Living expenses are estimated to range from $8000 to $10,000 for the year.

Some limited financial aid in the form of graduate assistantships and trustee scholarships is available to students of high academic standing. All new entrants are automatically considered for trustee scholarship awards. The awards are based solely on merit and the availability of funds.

Application Facts and Dates

Application deadlines are February 1 and November 1 for the fall and spring semesters, respectively, and March 15 for the summer semester. For information, applicants should contact:

Dr. Charles M. Ermer
Director of Graduate Studies
School of Business
Howard University
2600 Sixth Street, NW
Washington, D.C. 20059
Telephone: 202-806-1500
Fax: 202-797-6393

Illinois Institute of Technology

Chicago, Illinois

PREPARING FOR SUCCESS IN AN EVOLVING WORLD

Within a university recognized for advanced research, innovative technology, and inventive design, it is not surprising that the Stuart M.B.A. program educates its graduates for a changing business world. The Stuart M.B.A. experience develops graduates with a unique triad of spirit, intellect, and skills: the entrepreneurial spirit to initiate, to persevere, and to lead undertakings to successful completion; the intellect to comprehend the underlying connections among global, national, and corporate organizations, market forces, and new technologies; and the practical skills to manage change.

—M. Zia Hassan, Dean

Programs and Curricular Focus

An evolving global economy, the ferment of multiplying markets, opportunities created by ever-changing technologies, and new entrepreneurial structures are creating a business landscape in which change itself is the dominant characteristic. For this radically changing business world, the Stuart School's M.B.A. program develops managers and leaders with the capabilities to understand the dynamics of change—from the global to the business unit—and to manage it as a process of innovation.

The curriculum is made up of twenty courses. Eight core courses cover the body of knowledge common to the M.B.A. degree: financial accounting, organizational behavior, managerial economics, statistical methods, finance, marketing, operations management, and international business. Students also take eleven electives and may choose to specialize in one or two of nine areas: finance, information management, international business, management science, marketing, operations management, organization and management, quality management, and technology management. All students complete their degree by taking Business Policy, a capstone course that integrates the development and implementation of strategy.

Small, interactive classes stimulate students to develop creative solutions, often using case studies. All classes are conducted in English. Classes, which are held in the evening, follow a schedule of four 11-week quarters a year. Students take from fourteen to twenty courses,

depending on their academic background. Full-time students can complete the program in a year.

The Stuart School offers B.S. degrees in accounting, business administration, financial markets and trading, and management information systems; an M.S. in Financial Markets and Trading (M.S.F.M.T.); an M.S. in operations and technology management; a Master of Environmental Management; and a Ph.D. in operations and technology management. Several joint degrees are available: M.B.A./M.S.F.M.T., M.B.A./M.P.A., J.D./M.B.A., and J.D./M.S.F.M.T.

Students and the M.B.A. Experience

The M.B.A. student body of approximately 400 individuals comprises eighteen nationalities, with 12 percent international students; people with a wide range of academic, cultural, national, and business backgrounds; age ranges from students who have just received their bachelor's degrees to professionals who have spent years in the work force; 20 percent full-time students; and students who hold managerial positions in Chicago corporations. Degree backgrounds include economics (30 percent), science or technology (12 percent), and law (4 percent), with the remainder a mix of other disciplines.

The mix of students and professionals from a wide range of academic, cultural, national, and business backgrounds enriches class interaction. At Stuart, students learn from classmates as well as from professors. Typically, students pool

their strengths and work in teams to solve problems. Most students and professors possess hands-on experience that they share in class discussion. Classmates include students who hold managerial positions in Chicago corporations and students from other countries. This diversity enables the creation of professional networks to prepare for teamwork in the global economy. The Stuart School sponsors several student associations, including the Stuart M.B.A. Association and the Stuart FM&T Association, both for current students, and the Stuart Business Association, for alumni. These groups are active in such areas as continuing education, business networking, and social events.

The Faculty

Faculty members combine distinguished academic credentials and the practical business experience to ensure a practical approach in the classroom. Many members of the faculty have associations with government agencies, financial firms, think tanks, international corporations, international associations, major manufacturers, and telecommunications enterprises.

More than one quarter of the faculty hold undergraduate or graduate degrees from academic institutions outside the United States, giving the Stuart faculty a distinctly international character.

The Business School Network

The Stuart School Overseers/Student Support Program links students with senior-level executives from a range of industries. These executives hold positions at such companies as California Federal Bank; Celtic Life Insurance Company; Eastman Kodak Company; First Chicago Corporation; Kamco Plastics, Inc.; Kelco Industries, Inc.; Motorola, Inc.; and Smith Barney and serve as mentors and career advisers. Students also network with fellow students, many of whom are working professionals, and a network of Stuart alumni and thousands of IIT alumni with contacts in many areas of business, industry, and government. The Stuart M.B.A. Association for current students and the Stuart Business Association for alumni are active in building business networks.

The College and Environs

Founded in 1890, the Illinois Institute of Technology (IIT), a private university with an enrollment of 7,000, is internationally recognized for advanced work in engineering, business, law, architecture, design, and science. IIT offers thirty-three bachelor's, thirty-eight master's, fourteen doctoral, and three law degrees. The Stuart School's main campus is located near the financial district in downtown Chicago. The city offers a wealth of recreational and cultural opportunities, ranging from professional sports teams to avant-garde theater, along with beaches and parks. The area's cosmopolitan population offers an interesting and varied choice of cuisine and activities.

Facilities

The technologically advanced Stuart School Library integrates the traditional business resources of books and journals with modern electronic resources, such as a CD-ROM database with instant access to more than 500 business magazines and journals. Stuart students also have access to IIT's full library system with its extensive holdings. These include the Chicago-Kent College of Law Library, which ranks in the top 15 percent of law libraries across the country in terms of volumes, and materials in the Illinet Online library catalog, which opens the door to hundreds of Illinois libraries.

The Stuart School's First Chicago Corporation Computer Lab is equipped with IBM 486 personal computers linked by a Novell network. The network provides access to IIT minicomputers, the IIT Galvin Library, CD-ROM archives, Illinois library catalogs, and the Internet global network. Each PC supports DOS/Windows business applications. A rich variety of application software is available to support specific course requirements. Classrooms feature state-of-the-art audiovisual and computer capabilities.

Placement

Chicago is a dynamic international center of finance, business, and industry whose economic world includes Fortune 500 companies, many midwestern United States major industries, thriving entrepreneurial ventures, and the world's largest futures and options exchanges. The Stuart Career Planning Center, with strong ties to the business community, offers counseling about career planning, goals, and job search strategies, as well as services in developing students' interviewing and résumé-writing skills. Companies that have recruited Stuart School students include AT&T; Arthur Andersen; Cargill; Chicago Board of Trade; Citicorp; Commonwealth Edison; Ernst & Young; Fuji Securities, Inc.; Morgan Stanley & Company; Reuters; Shell Oil; and Walgreens.

Admission

Admission to the Stuart M.B.A. program requires submission of a completed application form, three letters of recommendation, official transcripts, Graduate Management Admission Test scores, and a summary of work experience. International applicants must have a bachelor's degree or the equivalent, a TOEFL score of 600 (for scores between 500 and 599, IIT's English Proficiency Review is also required), and a financial affidavit, which was $23,920 for the academic year 1994–95.

Finances

Tuition for 1995–96 is $1350 per course. Full-time students must register for at least three courses a quarter. International students attending on a J-1 visa must enroll for $50,000 health insurance coverage; the fee for the basic policy is $57.25 per quarter. Students should anticipate an expense of approximately $100 for books and supplies for each course taken. Room and board on the main campus, 3 miles south of the downtown campus, ranges from $4520 to $7365 for the academic year, depending on occupancy arrangements and meal plans. An hourly shuttle bus connects the two campuses. Discounted apartment rentals are available downtown to currently enrolled Stuart School students.

International Students

The Stuart School student body has a diverse makeup of cultures and nationalities, including 12 percent who are international students. The International Students and Scholars Center at IIT offers a variety of services relating to personal, visa, and immigration concerns; advises students about career planning and internship options; and holds social, cultural, and educational events. IIT also offers counseling and health services, cultural and religious programs, disability resources, and multicultural services.

Application Facts and Dates

Applications are due two months before classes start. Admission decisions typically are sent within three weeks of receipt of all credentials. For more information, students should contact:

Lynn Miller, M.B.A. Director of
  Marketing and Admission
Stuart School of Business
Illinois Institute of Technology
565 West Adams Street
Chicago, Illinois 60661-3691
Telephone: 312-906-6544
Fax: 312-906-6549
E-mail: stumiller@minna.acc.iit.edu

Indiana University Bloomington

Graduate School of Business

Bloomington, Indiana

> ### "BECAUSE BUSINESS SCHOOL AS USUAL ISN'T GOOD ENOUGH ANYMORE."
>
> *The half-life of information is now so short that an M.B.A. student needs a network outside academia. We all need a catalyst, a reminder that business is about progress, that business is change. In this competitive world, a graduate's first four years out of an M.B.A. program must contribute something other than the ability to crunch numbers. I'm not talking about generating technical specialists at Indiana. I'm talking about moving toward an M.B.A. program with an awareness of the major technical and financial trade-offs and trends that will determine where the opportunities are in the next decade.*
>
> —John Rau, Dean

Programs and Curricular Focus

The first year of the M.B.A. curriculum is designed to provide students with basic business principles and management tools. Students complete foundations and functional core sequences that include integrative teaching methods, group work, and consideration of the global economy. Critical issues of cultural diversity, ethics, and communication are integrated across the curriculum. An interdisciplinary professional core is also included in the first-year curriculum. The second year of the program is very flexible. Students usually choose at least one major, but double majors and minors are available, as well as range of electives and a design major option. Marketing, finance, operations, decision and information systems, international business, human resource management, and general management are the primary majors offered.

Students and the M.B.A. Experience

Each year the class size is between 250 and 260 students. International students make up 14 percent, women 30 percent, and minority students 15 percent of the student population. The average age for students is 27 years, with an age range of approximately 20–37. The average number of years of work experience is four, and students come from a broad range of professional backgrounds. Twenty-five percent of students are married. Forty percent of domestic students are from the Midwest, 18 percent from the West and Southwest, 17

percent from the Northeast and Mid-Atlantic, and 11 percent from the South. The program puts heavy emphasis on teamwork, community involvement, and an integrated understanding of business functions and issues.

❖ Global Focus

The Indiana M.B.A. program features several study abroad options, foreign language tutoring and instruction, and integrated exposure to international issues. Students may earn a Certificate of Global Achievement through a combination of course work, cultural exposure, and language accomplishments.

The Faculty

M.B.A. faculty members are some of the most accomplished in the School of Business. Those who volunteer to be part of the core faculty have intensive contact with M.B.A. students in class and outside the classroom, serving as mentors to student teams and participating in orientation activities. Core faculty members work together to prepare an integrated curriculum that eliminates redundancy and emphasizes areas of connection among specific disciplines.

The Business School Network

Corporate Partnerships

Students have access to corporate leaders beginning during orientation, where they meet professionals in a roundtable format to learn about different functions and industries. Case competitions sponsored by corporations such as Deloitte &

Touche and Kraft are a regular feature. Student clubs such as the Finance Guild and Marketing Club regularly sponsor seminars and host speakers from the corporate community.

The College and Environs

Indiana University at Bloomington has 35,000 students on an 18,000-acre campus located in a midwestern "college town" of about 60,000. The town is set among the rolling hills of southern Indiana, and the campus has been rated among the five most beautiful in the U.S. The University boasts one of the finest music schools in the world. Bloomington and the University have efficient, economical public transportation available, and the city and campus are very safe for students and families.

Facilities

On-campus student housing is available for both single and married students. Indiana University maintains an extensive computer network that provides access to mainframe computers, databases, and the Internet. M.B.A. students routinely use the electronic mail system, VAX network, the Dow Jones News/Retrieval Service, and other electronic resources. The School of Business library has more than 150,000 volumes of research materials. The main library, across the street from the School of Business, is internationally recognized as one of the best university libraries.

Technology Environment

All students are required to own personal computers and use them to complete their academic work. Computer clusters in the School of Business and around campus provide access to software, electronic services, and printers. Faculty members regularly use computer technology in the classroom.

Placement

The School's nationally recognized Business Placement Office has comprehensive resources and programs to help students secure internships and full-time employment. More than 300 companies visit the campus each year to recruit M.B.A. students for positions around the country. The Placement Office also produces résumé books and provides students access to an alumni database.

Admission

Indiana University admits M.B.A. students for the fall semester only. A minimum TOEFL score of 580 is required for non-native English speakers. The average GMAT score is approximately 610; 97 percent of admitted students had a GMAT above 500. Applicants who are motivated, interested in working in diverse groups, and have a strong professional focus are usually successful and happy in the program.

Finances

Tuition and fees for the 1994–95 academic year were $7196 for in-state students, $14,036 for out-of-state students. Room and board were approximately $5000, books and supplies $700, personal expenses $3500, and the computer allowance is $3000, for a total budget of around $26,000 for out-of-state students. International students are eligible to apply for merit-based assistantships during their second year of studies only.

International Students

Fourteen percent of Indiana's M.B.A. students are non-U.S. citizens. An active International Business Society within the M.B.A. program provides important professional and personal support. The University has a large graduate student and international student population as well. International students enjoy the supportive atmosphere of the M.B.A. program, and the high level of student services helps them acclimate with a minimum of discomfort.

Application Facts and Dates

The application deadline for students in the U.S. is March 1 of the year in which they plan to enroll, for international students it is February 1. For application materials and information, students should contact:

Graduate School of Business
10th and Fee Lane
Indiana University
Bloomington, Indiana 47405
Telephone: 812-855-8006
          800-994-8622 (toll–free
          within the U.S.)
Fax: 812-855-9039

International Institute for Management Development

M.B.A. Program

Lausanne, Switzerland

IMD—THE LEADER IN INTERNATIONAL MANAGEMENT EDUCATION

The IMD M.B.A. program is designed to enable highly qualified, young professionals, who have demonstrated significant achievement early in their careers, to reach responsible positions in international management. The program aims at the top end of the spectrum in terms of the calibre of the participants and program rigor. The small class size of 80 participants, representing thirty different countries, fosters our belief that world-class business leaders are not mass produced; they are developed with a large degree of personalized attention in a practical, action-oriented environment. This is the only way they can master the craft of leadership in an international arena.

—Kamran Kashani, Director

Programs and Curricular Focus

The IMD M.B.A. program is an intense eleven-month program (January through December) designed to develop in students strong general management skills with an international focus.

The IMD M.B.A. program prepares the student to manage and lead in the increasingly global business environment. In addition to the program content, which is international in its geographic coverage, the multinationality of participants and faculty promotes a truly international perspective. More than thirty nationalities are represented among the 80 participants, and nearly twenty nationalities are represented among the faculty. Learning to manage effectively in an international setting, where no single nationality dominates, is an integral part of the IMD experience.

The eight modules of the M.B.A. program provide the context for integrated learning. In each module, averaging four to five weeks in length, a number of different, yet complementary, fields of management are combined into a unified learning experience. As a result, participants gain a complete understanding of each field, as well as how they work together. Moreover, the learning process is cumulative; skills learned in one module are reinforced and built upon in subsequent modules.

The IMD program is inspired by management practice and not by academic theory. First, the learning material is focused on current and emerging issues in management practice. Second, the M.B.A. faculty also teaches business

leaders in the IMD executive education programs, which allows them to stay in constant touch with management reality. Third, working in teams ensures that the participants tap into the large reservoir of experience among their classmates.

A typical learning activity at IMD is made up of three phases. First, participants study assigned cases individually, identifying issues that require further depth of understanding. They then work in small groups, broadening their outlook by testing their opinions and drawing on the experiences of group members from different cultural and business backgrounds. Participants spend one third of their time working in teams, which develops their skills in problem solving, communication, and leadership in an international environment. Finally, in the classroom, guided by faculty members, participants explore new concepts, share experiences, and are challenged to present their opinions and solutions.

IMD limits the class size to 80 participants, reinforcing the belief that the small class size allows innovation, flexibility, and a personal interplay between students and faculty that few schools can match.

Students and the M.B.A. Experience

IMD strongly believes that each participant is a key source of learning for other participants in the program. Accordingly, every effort is made to ensure that the right balance occurs among the 80 participants, in terms of work experience, nationality, and academic background, to

maximize the learning experience. The students have an average of six years of work experience, with a range of three to eleven years. Fifty percent of the participants have their experience in industry, 20 percent in financial services, 15 percent in consulting, and 15 percent in other areas. All participants have shown fast career progression, and most have international work experience. The program has a standard of requiring significant career accomplishments; therefore, the average age of participants is 30, with a range of 26–35 years.

Women comprise approximately 20 percent of the class. IMD is a truly international environment; no single nationality dominates the classroom. Thirty countries are represented, with 56 percent of the students coming from Europe, 17 percent from North America, 11 percent from Latin America, 11 percent from Asia, 3 percent from Australia, and 2 percent from other areas. The educational background of the M.B.A. participants is also quite varied. For the class of 1995, the breakdown is as follows: economics, accounting, business, and commerce, 45 percent; engineering, 30 percent; science and mathematics, 15 percent; humanities, 6 percent; and law, 4 percent.

Special Features

International Consulting Projects are an integral part of the M.B.A. program. Participants serve as consultants to the top management of client companies and advise them on critical, far-reaching management issues. It is the perfect opportunity to apply their classroom learning to developing creative, results-oriented solutions to real management problems. The projects address issues from strategy formulation to operational problems. The International Consulting Projects follow a systematic four-phase approach: the industry analysis phase, the company analysis phase, the issue analysis phase, and the implementation and feedback phase.

Participants work in teams of 4–6, under the guidance of a faculty adviser. Client companies are located all over the world and include a variety of industries and sectors.

The Team Initiated Enterprise (TIE) projects were developed as a direct response to company comments that M.B.A. graduates are good at analyzing but not very talented at initiating and implementing. The participants are simply told to create an initiative that provides value for someone else and see it through to implementation. The only stipulation is that it be a worthwhile learning experience for the team. The teams are self-selected, and the projects take place across the first half of the program. In the past, participants put a team on top of Mont Blanc; opened a day-care center for students' children; raised SwFr 250,000 for a children's hospital in Budapest, Hungary; and taught business education to entrepreneurs in Eastern Europe.

The Faculty

M.B.A. participants receive a high degree of personal attention at IMD with a student-faculty ratio of 3:1. The faculty also reflects IMD's internationality, with almost twenty different nationalities represented. The M.B.A. faculty members also teach in IMD's executive education programs and, therefore, maintain a close relationship with real-world management issues. The faculty members contribute to the M.B.A. program through teaching and leading discussions in class, as well as serving as advisers for the International Consulting Projects.

The Business School Network

Over 120 companies worldwide have formed a special relationship with IMD through the Partner Program and Business Associate Network. They are IMD's partners in industry and constitute a unique network based on the common goal of improving performance in international management. These companies help ensure that IMD's M.B.A. program addresses the real needs of business via their input on program design and review. In addition, M.B.A. participants have access to hundreds of executives who participate in IMD's executive education program on the same campus.

IMD's partner companies include Andersen Consulting, Astra AB, AT&T, Baxter International, Caterpillar, Citicorp, Exxon, IBM Europe, Mercedes Benz, Nestlé S.A., and Sony Europe. Business associates include Booz Allen & Hamilton, British Steel, Fiat S.p.A., General Motors Corporation, Heineken N.V., Hewlett-Packard S.A., Philip Morris, Pirelli S.p.A., Shell International, Singapore Airlines Ltd., Volkswagen AG, and AB Volvo.

The College and Environs

The history of IMD goes back to 1946 when Alcan created IMI in Geneva, Europe's first business school, and 1957 when Nestlé founded IMEDE, Lausanne, with the active involvement of the Harvard Business School. The merger of the resources and the wide experience of the two institutions gave birth to IMD in 1989.

IMD is located in Lausanne, the heart of French-speaking Switzerland, where there is a strong tradition of international exchange. The campus is just 40 minutes from Geneva, which is home to several international organizations such as the United Nations and the World Health Organization. The IMD community is small and friendly, allowing participants and faculty to mix freely on a first-name basis. The atmosphere strikes the right balance between intensive study and informality. More importantly, IMD's international character brings participants into daily contact with people from many different cultures and traditions.

Placement

IMD M.B.A. graduates are internationally recognized as a select group of professionally trained managers, and they are recruited by leading companies to take on challenging roles in international management. The Career Services Office coordinates activities with experienced professionals for counselling participants on résumés, interviewing, and effective job search. In addition, an IMD M.B.A. Résumé Portfolio, containing participant résumés, is produced and distributed globally. During the second half of the program, companies are invited to interview participants on campus.

For the class of 1994, 94 percent of the participants received at least one job offer by graduation, with an average of two offers per participant. Graduates went around the globe: 75 percent to Europe, 12 percent to Asia and Australia, 7 percent to North America, and 6 percent to Latin America. Forty-nine percent went into industry (in a variety of sectors and functions), 31 percent into consulting, and 20 percent into financial services. The average starting salary was $84,000 (not including bonus), representing a 70 percent increase over pre-M.B.A. salary.

Admission

Admission requirements stress career progression, management potential, and intellectual ability. Only a small number of applicants are selected for admission, and the admissions committee looks for a good balance among the following criteria: career progression, management potential, education, GMAT performance, the interview, and English language ability. Candidates must have a minimum of three years of full-time work experience, during which they have displayed a steady increase in responsibilities. They must demonstrate potential for holding a management position and be motivated toward building a career in international management. Candidates normally possess the equivalent of a bachelor's degree from a university, polytechnic, or a similar institute of higher learning. They must demonstrate strong verbal and quantitative reasoning abilities in their GMAT scores. Candidates whose applications pass the initial assessment of the Admissions Committee are invited to interview at IMD. English is the working language, and candidates must have a full command of spoken and written English. On average, participants speak two languages fluently, including English.

Finances

The fees for a self-sponsored participant are set at a subsidized level of SwFr 38,000. Company-sponsored candidates are charged the full cost of their education, SwFr 58,000. Fees cover tuition, use of the library and computer facilities, lunch at IMD during the week, and hotel accommodations for participants during the first month of the program. An additional fee of SwFr 1000 is assessed to cover course materials and stationery.

Rent and other living expenses vary depending on family situation and lifestyle. IMD estimates the boarding costs for the full year, including travelling to and from Switzerland, to be approximately SwFr 25,000.

Given the broad range of nationalities among participants, it is difficult for IMD to assist in locating sources of financing. However, accepted participants who have difficulty financing their education will be referred to the IMD M.B.A. Alumni Association, which may be able to offer help in the form of loan guarantees.

Application Facts and Dates

Application deadlines are January 15, February 28, March 31, April 30, June 15, July 31, and August 31. Candidates receive notification of the admissions committee's decision approximately six weeks after the deadline date. For more information, applicants should contact:

Ms. Kal Denzel
Director, M.B.A. Admissions
International Institute for Management
    Development
Chemin de Bellerive 23
P.O. Box 915
CH-1001
Lausanne, Switzerland
Telephone: 41-21-618-0111
           41-21-618-0298
Fax: 41-21-618-0707
Internet: denzel@imd.ch

International University of Japan

Yamato-machi, Niigata, Japan

A NEW BREED OF PROFESSIONALS FOR THE TWENTY-FIRST CENTURY

The challenge we face in today's dramatically changing world economy is to effectively and efficiently manage complex webs of linkages of business transactions across different nations. We must be able to understand unfamiliar market and institutional environments, relate to people from different cultural and ethnic backgrounds, and make effective decisions within complex multinational business contexts.

The educational mission of the IUJ M.B.A. program is to develop future managers with the hands-on skills and frame of mind required for international business, including in-depth knowledge of international business management. The program is very rigorous, perhaps much harder than many M.B.A. programs around. However, we firmly believe that the program will likely yield a very high return on the hard work, particularly for those who possess strong motivation, initiative, and an inquisitive mind.

—Yui Kimura, Dean

Programs and Curricular Focus

The program admits about 50 highly qualified students a year from a large number of countries, including Japan, the United States, and Asian and European countries. The faculty, equally as diverse as the students, help highly motivated students acquire the knowledge required in professional management and develop the hands-on skills and the frame of mind needed in international business.

The global orientation is evident throughout the curriculum. A culturally diverse faculty teaching an equally diverse student body brings comparative perspectives to many of the individual courses. This encourages the application of theory and concepts to different national contexts and the recognition of institutional differences among various countries, particularly those of Japan and the United States. The program also offers students an opportunity to learn more about Japanese management and industrial systems and gain a perspective on Japan's international competitiveness in leading-edge, high-technology industries. It also emphasizes development of cross-cultural communication and management skills. It is carefully sequenced to maximize the efficiency of the learning process.

The first year consists of twelve required courses plus appropriate language courses. During the second year, students take one required course and

select at least eleven electives from among the two dozen or so offered each year. In addition, students choose an area of special interest to investigate in depth for their research project.

The curriculum is enhanced by opportunities to meet with visiting executives and scholars, to participate in summer activities (internships with Japanese corporations or attendance at a U.S. summer program), to spend one term on exchange in an M.B.A. program in another country, and to interact daily with people from many different countries and professional backgrounds.

The IUJ M.B.A. program is the only one of its kind accredited by Japan's Ministry of Education.

Students and the M.B.A. Experience

The IUJ M.B.A. program's student body consists of a selected group of experienced managers, of whom roughly 50 percent are Japanese. The others come from North and South America, Europe, Africa, the Indian subcontinent, and other parts of Asia. Only 1 of every 3 to 4 applicants meets the standards set for admission, and each brings a unique perspective and background to the program. As the number of students per graduating class has grown, so has the diversity of students in terms of the number of women and the number of

different national, industrial, educational, and cultural backgrounds represented in the student body.

The entering class of 1996 has an average age of 28, with an average of four years of business management experience. Most of these students obtained their undergraduate degrees in economics, engineering, or social science; most speak two or three languages, some as many as five.

❖ Global Focus

The original mission and purpose of IUJ, as conceived by its founders, is as valid and vital today as it was then. The mission is to train young men and women for professional careers in global business for the twenty-first century. The times call for a new breed of professionals, both in Japan and around the world, who can function successfully anywhere in the world. IUJ strives to develop such new talents.

The Faculty

To teach culturally diverse students with a new management perspective, IUJ has recruited an internationally oriented, multicultural, and highly qualified faculty. The core group of permanent faculty members is augmented by visiting faculty from North America, Europe, and other institutions in Asia. While the vast majority of the faculty have Ph.D. degrees, the research at IUJ focuses on highly relevant international business issues, and the research and consulting activities of the faculty naturally flow back into the classroom and the overall curriculum.

The Business School Network

The International University of Japan is deeply rooted in the Japanese business community; evidence of this is shown in the fact that most of the program's Japanese students are corporate-sponsored. Furthermore, IUJ works cooperatively to actively engage the international business community. Examples of such connections include courses taught by business practitioners from major corporations in Japan, guest executive

speakers in class and through the IUJ Senior Executive Seminars, student course work involving corporate-sponsored projects, faculty research and consulting relationships, and class visits to plant sites.

An impressive array of guest speakers from international business, government, and educational institutions have addressed IUJ's M.B.A. students. In addition to opportunities to meet with these international executives and officials, the IUJ M.B.A. program also provides students with the opportunity to interact with local corporations in the area. The Local Business Community Involvement Program is promoted through regular academic courses throughout the year; students have a chance to work on real-life projects at local corporations and to closely analyze Japanese management approaches from the viewpoint of parts suppliers to major manufacturing companies.

The College and Environs

The International University of Japan, a private graduate-level institution, was founded in 1982, with extensive support from Japan's industrial, financial, and educational circles. The Graduate School of International Management (M.B.A. program) at IUJ was established in 1988, with the support of the Amos Tuck School of Business Administration at Dartmouth College.

Only a 100-minute train ride from central Tokyo, the IUJ campus is located in a beautiful valley surrounded by

magnificent mountains. The IUJ campus houses classrooms and offices and the Matsushita Library and Information Center, which has a constantly expanding collection of books, periodicals, and databases as well as student access to IBM and Macintosh computers with international networking capabilities. Other facilities include dormitories for single and married students, the gymnasium, a school cafeteria, and a campus store.

Placement

A substantial portion of the student body is corporate-sponsored. These students continue as employees while attending the program and form one of the primary connections to Japanese companies. Corporate connections to the IUJ M.B.A. program are enhanced and expanded each year through the graduates who obtain full-time employment with various business organizations. Although, at this time, there is no on-campus recruitment of students, the Student Center and the faculty provide valuable assistance and information to aid graduating students in finding permanent employment.

Admission

Admission requirements include an undergraduate degree, results on the GMAT (the average among native English speakers for the class of 1996 was 610), TOEFL scores (the average among the class of 1996 was 595), two references, and minimum work experi-

ence of two to three years (the average was four years among the class of 1996). Furthermore, applicants are carefully reviewed on the basis of a combination of several criteria, including a well-defined motivation to pursue graduate study in business and the potential to achieve leadership positions in management; the maturity and sense of purpose essential to a demanding educational experience, including a concept of the value of an international M.B.A. program to the applicant's career plans and expectations; and a personal sense of values consistent with the standards and purposes of the IUJ M.B.A. program.

There are no prerequisite courses for admission, but students must have a strong working knowledge of accounting, statistics, and economics.

Finances

There is an admission fee of 300,000 yen. The program tuition fee per academic year is 1,700,000 yen. The cost of the optional summer program in the United States is 1,000,000 yen.

The minimum monthly expenses average about 95,000 yen, broken down as follows: books and supplies, 20,000 yen; a single room with a bath, 30,000 yen; utilities, 5,000 yen; and meals on campus, 40,000 yen.

Scholarships and tuition waivers in varying amounts are available to selected nonsponsored students.

International Students

Approximately one half of the student body is international. Furthermore, exchange students from sixteen prominent business schools impart multifaceted and invaluable perspectives into class discussion. Exchange partners include New York University, Dartmouth College, the University of Washington, the University of Southern California, York University, London Business School, and Erasmus University.

Application Facts and Dates

Application deadlines for overseas applicants for 1995 September enrollment are February 10 and April 7, 1995. For more information, contact:

Admissions, M.B.A. Program Office
International University of Japan
Yamato-machi, Niigata 949-72
Japan
Telephone: 0257-79-1500
Fax: 0257-79-4443 or 79-4441
E-mail: iujadm@jpniuj00.bitnet

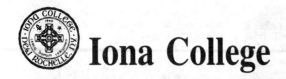

Iona College

New Rochelle, New York

> ▶ *Never before have the demands on today's business leaders been so high. In the face of the swift and complex developments of today's rapidly changing global marketplace, leaders must act quickly and competitively—adding value to their organizations. The most effective leaders will be able to mobilize teams of employees to solve problems creatively. The Hagan M.B.A. aims to give you the skills to be this type of leader. One who understands business and its social responsibilities, who demonstrates awareness of the global character of business, and, finally, the kind of leader who subscribes to high ethical standards.*
>
> *—Nicholas J. Beutell, Dean*

Programs and Curricular Focus

The goal of the Hagan School of Business M.B.A. Program is to produce graduates and future leaders who understand business and its challenges as the twenty-first century approaches. It seeks to graduate women and men who have the skills to work productively in a high-technology society, demonstrate sensitivity to the global and multicultural character of business, provide strategic leadership in a competitive environment, and subscribe to high ethical standards in the practice of their profession.

The M.B.A. curriculum consists of core courses in the functional areas of business, a major concentration allowing for specialized study, advanced electives that provide students an opportunity to custom design the breadth component of the curriculum, and a capstone course. Students without sufficient background in economics, accounting, and mathematics take special courses to prepare them for regular M.B.A. classes.

Computer applications are integrated into the curriculum as are the development of presentation and communication skills. Case studies, team projects, computer simulation games, experiential exercises, and lectures are the commonly used methods of teaching.

The calendar follows a trimester schedule of twelve weeks each, with three summer sessions, allowing students to earn more credits within the year. Classes meet once a week in the evening, Mondays through Thursdays from 6:30 to 9:30, with some Saturday morning classes.

The number of credits required for the degree is 61 before waivers and transfer credits are applied. There is a six-year limit to finish the program. A typical M.B.A. student takes 48 credits and completes the program in four years on a part-time basis or two years full-time.

Students and the M.B.A. Experience

Almost all the students in the program hold full-time jobs at Fortune 500 companies, major brokerage houses, large commercial banks, and insurance companies. Midsize and small companies are also well represented. Many students hold middle-management positions in blue-chip firms such as IBM, NYNEX, Chase Manhattan Bank, Chemical Bank, Kraft-General Foods, and Lederle Laboratories, to cite a few.

The average age of the students is 29. They have, on the average, about seven years of full-time work experience in various industries. It is this maturity, diverse corporate background, and significant work experience that they bring to the program and contribute to the overall quality of the learning process.

The students are about evenly divided between men and women. Most come from the tristate area of New York, New Jersey, and Connecticut. There are a few international students, representing all continents.

❖ Global Focus

The institutional thrust toward global education and the international character of the faculty strengthen the global dimension of the M.B.A. curriculum. An Executive Management Program has brought to campus more than 2,000

Russian and ex-Soviet managers and directors. A special, joint one-year M.B.A. program with the Plekhanov Academy of the Russian Economy in Moscow, one of Russia's most prestigious universities, recently graduated its first class of 26 students from Siberia.

The Faculty

The Hagan School of Business faculty members are dedicated teachers and professionals. As teacher-scholars, they are current in their fields of expertise, doing research, publishing, and giving presentations at academic conferences. As professionals, they blend theory and practice, drawing upon their own and their students' business experience. Among them are internationally recognized experts in such diverse fields as artificial intelligence, case writing, cross-cultural studies, corporate values, and business ethics.

With very few exceptions, those who teach in the M.B.A. program are full-time, with appropriate terminal degrees earned at America's top universities. Students recognize them for their teaching excellence and seek their advice on career matters.

The Business School Network

Corporate Partnerships

Through the Dean's Business Advisory Council, made up of business executives from corporations that send students to the program, the Hagan School has created a partnership venue with business. Through the council, business has a real opportunity to influence the strategic direction of the School. It is mechanisms of this kind that allow the School to be responsive to the needs of the business community and offer a relevant curriculum. The Executive-on-Campus Lecture Series brings successful alumni as well as prominent local business executives to the campus to give lectures on current issues to the student body.

Prominent Alumni

The Hagan School is proud to count among its distinguished alumni senior executives and business leaders from America's largest and best corporations,

Hagan Hall.

such as American Express, Philip Morris, Chemical Bank, Chase Manhattan, and Con Edison Company.

The College and Environs

Iona College was founded in 1940 by the Congregation of Christian Brothers. Its main campus is located in New Rochelle, a small city on the Long Island Sound in Westchester County, about 30 miles north of the heart of Manhattan. The M.B.A. program is also offered in Rockland County, a few miles west of the Hudson River.

With its strategic locations and proximity to New York City, the Hagan School of Business enables students to benefit from a rich, diversified environment that is attuned to the advances and innovations of the global market. The New York metropolitan area is the home of many major national and multinational corporations, such as IBM, Texaco, and Pepsico, to name a few, as well as many of the nation's largest banks, brokerage houses, and insurance firms.

Technology Environment

The academic programs of the Hagan School are strongly supported by state-of-the-art computer equipment and software. More than 500 PCs are available for student use in public facilities, with some of them open around-the-clock seven days a week. The Helen Arrigoni Library and Technology Center houses multimedia systems with access to Internet and other popular on-line databases.

Many course requirements involve the use of computers, and every student is provided with a computer account and access to the system. Advanced computer literacy is among the premier goals of the program.

Placement

The Office of Career Services of Iona College provides students with career counseling and job search assistance. It alerts students to job openings and positions in companies and organizations

that seek the graduates of the College. Résumé referral, mock interviews, and counseling for alumni are among the services available to students.

Admission

Admission is selective and based on an evaluation of the student's academic record, scores on the Graduate Management Admission Test (GMAT), references, and work experience. Applications and credentials should be sent to the Graduate Admissions Office of the Hagan School of Business.

Rolling admissions allow students to begin studies in any trimester: fall, winter, spring, or summer. TOEFL scores are required for all students whose native language is other than English. International students must provide evidence of adequate funds to cover all expenses.

Finances

Tuition per credit in 1994–95 was $390. Books and supplies cost approximately $1500 per year. There are no boarding facilities on campus for graduate students. Living expense estimates range from $10,000 to $12,000 for ten months, not including vacation periods.

A limited number of graduate assistantships are available to full-time students.

Application Facts and Dates

Rolling admissions allow students to submit their application any time. However, completed applications should be received no later than two weeks prior to the start of the trimester for which the student plans to enroll. For more information, students should contact:

Mrs. Ann Kinnally
Director of Admissions and
   Recruitment
Hagan School of Business
Iona College
715 North Avenue
New Rochelle, New York 10801-1890
Telephone: 914-633-2288
Fax: 914-633-2012

Iowa State University

Ames, Iowa

> **EXCELLENCE IN AMERICA'S HEARTLAND**
>
> *The Iowa State University M.B.A. program is staffed with educators who love what they do. We do it well, attracting students from all over the world. Iowa State works to serve you, the education consumer, by providing a flexible and competitive learning environment.*
>
> *Iowa State understands the value you place on your education. Ours is a culture dedicated to excellence in graduate business education and whose faculty is active in research, committed to innovative teaching, and accessible to students.*
>
> *Students are not just numbers here. Iowa State offers a wide array of educational resources in an environment sensitive to individual student needs. We provide an environment where students can stretch and grow as professionals and as people, making Iowa State a warm and inviting place to be.*
> —Dr. Benjamin J. Allen, Interim Dean

Programs and Curricular Focus

The Iowa State University M.B.A. program offers a friendly, personal environment that emphasizes flexibility and teamwork. As our world gets smaller, and its demographics change, the ability to work effectively with a diverse population is vital to the foundation of global success. First-year M.B.A. students are preassigned to small work groups that are chosen to maximize each member's contribution to diversity, personal strengths, and academic and work backgrounds. Students are then challenged with innovative projects and a curriculum that dovetails with global management issues.

M.B.A. candidates may pursue their course work through a resident full-time program or, to accommodate employed students, through the Saturday M.B.A. program. The 48-credit-hour M.B.A. program consists of an integrated core curriculum and 24 credit hours of electives. Within the core is a series of eighteen single-credit modules that emphasize the interdisciplinary nature of graduate management education. Second-year students tailor their course work to meet individual academic and career goals. By placing a premium on flexibility and accessibility, the program guides candidates through interactive projects that recreate a corporate environment.

Students and the M.B.A. Experience

The 225 graduate business students at Iowa State reflect a diversity of educational, cultural, and professional backgrounds. Drawing upon the University's international stature, the Iowa State M.B.A. program attracts students worldwide, today representing over a dozen countries. Thirty-seven percent of the students are women. Thirty-five percent of Iowa State M.B.A. students bring an undergraduate degree in business to their graduate experience, and 26 percent reflect a background in the sciences or medicine. Engineering undergraduates make up 18 percent, and social sciences, humanities, and other degrees illustrate the other varying backgrounds of undergraduates who seek the College of Business for graduate work. Iowa State's Saturday M.B.A. candidates represent industry sectors throughout the state of Iowa, including agriculture, education, financial services, health and human services, manufacturing, and small business.

❖ Global Focus

Iowa State M.B.A. students who wish to study abroad find many programs and countries through which their graduate program could be tailored to add an international dimension. The Study Abroad Center has extensive information on both the ISU Exchange Program and the International Internship Program. The Iowa State College of Business also offers an ongoing exchange program with the University of Glasgow in Scotland to allow M.B.A. students to earn credit toward their graduate management degree by studying abroad.

Special Features

In addition to offering course work in the traditional business disciplines, Iowa State's M.B.A. curriculum offers two distinct specializations. Agribusiness is designed to meet the demands of the agribusiness sector, including nonprofit organizations and governmental agencies. The Transportation and Logistics specialization emphasizes the managerial aspects of transportation and logistics systems. Course work includes the study of the interworkings of air, water, railroad, and pipeline modes. Business logistics is also included, emphasizing materials management and quantitative approaches to the design and operation of a total logistics system. Students interested in transportation and logistics may also be eligible to participate in the Transportation Scholar Program through the Iowa State University Midwest Transportation Center, an organization dedicated to study and research in the transportation field.

The Faculty

The College of Business counts among its faculty members some of the best scholars in the profession, including several Fulbright recipients. Faculty members participate in international faculty exchange programs and have become respected providers of education and research in the international arena. Recent exchanges have involved Portugal, Ireland, and Belgium. In addition, the College of Business has hosted faculty members from Croatia, Egypt, the Czech Republic, and Slovakia. In turn, Iowa State faculty members have also taught in these countries.

The Business School Network
Corporate Partnerships

Iowa State University places immense importance on the exchange of ideas between academic and corporate environments. Speakers from corporations, including Pioneer Hi-Bred International, Texas Instruments, and General Mills, lecture regularly, and students visit local and regional facilities to observe businesses in action. M.B.A. students also have the opportunity to provide consulting services to small businesses through the Iowa Small Business Development Center, housed in the College of Business.

Prominent Alumni

Iowa State University counts among its 14,000 business alumni many business leaders, including Bill Adams, Chairman and CEO, Armstrong World Industries (retired); Lynn Vorbich, President, Iowa Power and Light; Charles S. Johnson, Executive Vice President, Pioneer Hi-Bred International Inc.; Glenn R. Blake, Director, Corporate Personnel, General Mills, Inc.; and Cheryl Gruetzmacher Gordon, Senior Managing Director, Rothschild North America.

The College and Environs

The 1,000-acre campus features a quiet lake and a parklike setting. As part of Ames, a community of 50,000, the University is set in the geographic center of the United States, in an area that offers a pleasing mixture of urban and rural life. Founded in 1858, Iowa State is the first land-grant university to have been established under the Morril Land-Grant Act. The institution was charged with promoting "liberal and practical education . . . in the several pursuits and professions of college life." Today, with close to 25,000 students, Iowa State University is fulfilling that mission: educating students and delivering research discoveries and service to the public.

Facilities

The Parks Library offers a comfortable, friendly environment with over 4 million holdings, including maps, films, government publications, and archival and audiovisual materials. Also, the library's on-line information system, SCHOLAR, provides access to the local on-line catalog. This contains most of the book collection and all cataloged serials as well as important indexing and abstracting databases. SCHOLAR is accessible on campus through the campus network and by dial-up from a personal computer with a modem and communications software.

Technology Environment

The College of Business, with the help of generous corporate support, offers

state-of-the-art technology, including Project Vincent, a UNIX-based operating system modeled after MIT's Project Athena. This network allows access to supercomputing, visualization, and numeric computation both on and off campus, setting Project Vincent apart from other like endeavors and placing Iowa State among the U.S. leaders in networking workstations and computers.

Placement

The College encourages M.B.A. students to meet with the Career Services Office in their first semester to establish placement needs and learn about available services. The office subscribes to the *Nationwide Weekly Job Vacancy Bulletin Exchange,* which includes postings from seventy-eight universities in thirty-eight states. The office also answers requests from companies for M.B.A. students' résumés and arranges on-campus interviews with regional and national recruiters.

Admission

Each applicant is carefully assessed in terms of his or her intellectual potential, academic achievement, work and professional involvement, interpersonal communication skills, career goals, and motivation. Educational records are reviewed from official transcripts, as well as scores from the Graduate Management Admission Test (GMAT). Three letters of recommendation and the candidate's response to the essay portion of the application are also required.

Finances

The College of Business offers a number of graduate assistantships to qualified M.B.A. students. Graduate assistants pay resident fees and receive a monthly stipend. Graduate assistants in good academic standing are also awarded a scholarship covering a portion of the resident fee. M.B.A. students wishing to be considered for a graduate assistantship may indicate so on the ISU Graduate College application form.

Information on scholarships and fellowships is available from the Graduate College, the Office of Minority Student Affairs, and the College of Business. Outstanding students may be qualified to receive a monetary award through the Premium for Academic Excellence (PACE) program in the Graduate College. PACE recipients generally have an undergraduate GPA of 3.5 or better or a GPA of 3.8 in previous graduate work. The Office of Student Financial Aid offers financial assistance through low-interest loans of various types and employment assistance.

International Students

The Office of International Students and Scholars (OISS) provides orientation and advising to new international students. The OISS acts as a route through which international students can utilize local community services. It also serves as a liaison with the U.S. Information Agency and the Immigration and Naturalization Service to bring visiting scholars and students to Iowa State University.

Application Facts and Dates

Admission is granted for the fall semester only in the resident M.B.A. program. Saturday M.B.A. students are admitted in the summer term. Students should submit the Graduate College application form, application fee, official transcripts, and TOEFL scores (if applicable) to the Office of Admissions, 100 Alumni Hall, Iowa State University, Ames, Iowa 50011. Students should submit GMAT scores, letters of reference, and the personal essay to the Graduate Programs Office at the address below. The deadline for submission of all application materials is May 1 (March 1 for international students). For more information, students should contact:

Graduate Programs Office
College of Business
Room 9, E.O. Building
Iowa State University
Ames, Iowa 50011-2081
Telephone: 515-294-8118
　　　　　800-433-3452 (toll-free)
Fax: 515-294-2446
E-mail: busgrad@iastate.edu

Johnson & Wales University

Providence, Rhode Island

CHALLENGES OF THE YEAR 2000 AND BEYOND

The Graduate School is committed to quality. Advanced career education is the central theme of our vision for the twenty-first century at Johnson & Wales University. It is the forefront of our ongoing investment of time and energy in maintaining the highest standards for our faculty and curricula in a students-come-first environment.

—Dr. Louis D'Abrosca, Dean

Programs and Curricular Focus

Reports show that over 25 percent of all business transactions in the world are international in nature. During the last forty years, this percentage has steadily increased, and this trend will continue as the world becomes a smaller place through advanced methods of communication and transportation.

The M.B.A. in international business program is designed for students who are preparing for careers in multinational firms, internationally oriented financial institutions, and national and international agencies dealing with foreign business. Most careers in international business have counterparts in domestic business. These careers require special skills to adapt management methods to foreign environments and to commerce between nations.

Students can apply to the day or evening school. Students entering the day school may be able to complete the graduate courses in one year. The program includes such courses as international banking, international marketing, multinational communications, and a seminar in international business.

The Graduate School also offers the M.S. degree in hospitality administration, accounting, and managerial technology and the M.Ed. degree in educational computing and technology leadership.

Students and the M.B.A. Experience

The graduate students represent diverse cultural, professional, and academic backgrounds. The average student is 27 years old, with four years of work-related experience. The enrollment mix includes students from forty-four countries, with women representing 38 percent of the en-

rollment population. The majority of American students come from the Northeast (52 percent). Another 34 percent of graduate enrollment are international students. Most of the students have undergraduate degrees in business, with many others having backgrounds in education or liberal arts. Employers provide tuition reimbursement for 24 percent of American students, and 71 percent of American students are working while pursuing their graduate studies.

Special Features

There are convenient day and evening classes to accommodate any schedule; accelerated programs that allow a student to graduate in one year; and three terms instead of semesters, allowing the student to complete more courses in less time. There is a diverse student population, representing forty-four countries; a student-focused faculty with esteemed academic and professional experience; creative tuition-payment arrangements; specialized programs with career opportunities; and an outstanding career-placement record.

The Faculty

The Graduate School faculty consists of individuals with excellent teaching skills who focus on professional development and provide a learning environment that encourages student participation. The faculty members are selected based on their academic achievements and professional experiences. They are devoted to preparing students for success in the workplace and go through extensive training on working with a diverse student population and staying informed on the latest technology. The graduate faculty members either hold terminal or

professional degrees or are working toward these degrees.

The Business School Network
Corporate Partnerships

Johnson & Wales University is continuously expanding its relationship with corporate America. Local business leaders take part as University guests to discuss current business trends and developments with the students. Brainstorming and problem-solving skills are sharpened as real-life situations are addressed. As the alumni base grows, many return and discuss how their course work has fit into their daily routine.

Prominent Alumni

Johnson & Wales University prides itself on preparing men and women for leadership roles, often as entrepreneurs in business, industry, and education. Alumni hold top positions in a variety of businesses that range from finance to food. Some prominent alumni are Ira Kaplan, President, Servolift Eastern Corporation; Leonard Pinault, President, Foxboro National Bank; Joseph Damore, President, Food Systems IDBA, Inc.; Tracey Trosko, President, First National Network, Inc.; and William Francis, President, Marbil Enterprises, Inc.

The College and Environs

Johnson & Wales University's main campus is located in Providence, Rhode Island. Providence is New England's second-largest city, but it retains its historic charm in combination with the resources of a cultural, business, and industrial center. An hour from the city of Boston, Massachusetts, and less than 4 hours from New York City, Providence is also within easy reach of such well-known vacation spots as Newport, Rhode Island, and Cape Cod, Massachusetts.

A true city campus, Johnson & Wales's facilities are scattered throughout Providence, a city that provides students with a wide variety of cultural, educational, recreational, and social activities. Students enjoy the local restaurants and shops and are able to take advantage of a myriad of theater, music, and performance opportunities. From museums to

sports events and Broadway shows to shopping, the city offers something for everyone.

Interstate buses and trains are near Johnson & Wales's downtown campus, and the T. F. Green Airport, served by most major U.S. airlines, is adjacent to the J&W's Radisson Airport Hotel in nearby Warwick, Rhode Island.

Technology Environment

The Academic Computer Center in the Xavier Complex features extensive equipment available for student use. Each IBM PS/2 computer features a minimum of 30 megabytes of internal memory. These machines have extensive color graphics capabilities.

The Harborside Computer Lab is made up of two rooms, housing a total of forty-five IBM-compatible machines, fifteen dot-matrix printers, and an NEC Silent Writer 95 laser printer.

Placement

The Career Development Office (CDO) of Johnson & Wales University provides assistance to graduate students as soon as they enroll. The CDO sponsors workshops on résumé writing, company research, and interviewing, as well as

guest speakers. A job hotline also provides postings of full- and part-time jobs on and off campus. Ninety-eight percent of Johnson & Wales students find work after college in their chosen field. Global companies such as Walt Disney; hotel chains such as Four Seasons, Marriott, and Hyatt; resorts such as Canyon Ranch; casinos such as Caesars Palace; and well-known companies such as Abraham & Straus have all hired Johnson & Wales students.

Admission

All applicants must submit a signed application, official college and high school transcripts, and three letters of recommendation to the Graduate Admissions Office. In addition, all international students must submit a TOEFL score (unless they wish to be placed in the University's ESL program), a declaration of financial support, and a financial statement that supports the information given in the declaration of financial support.

Finances

Tuition for the 1995–96 year for day school is $214 per quarter credit hour; for the evening school, it is $154 per quarter credit hour. Foundation courses are $86

per quarter credit hour. All master's programs are 54 quarter credits. Books and supplies cost approximately $800 per year.

Although most graduate students choose to live in independent housing near the campus, room and board are available for graduate students at the University. The University estimates that living expenses for an academic year for a student living off campus are $5500. For more information about room and board, students should contact the Office of Residential Life (telephone: 401-598-1132). For assistance and information regarding independent housing, students should contact the Graduate Admissions Office (telephone: 401-598-1015).

International Students

The uniqueness of Johnson & Wales's Graduate School attracts professionals and students from across the country and around the globe. Thirty-four percent of the students attending the Graduate School are international students, representing forty-four countries. The University offers international students courses in English as a second language, academic counseling, advice on Immigration and Naturalization Service rules, and assistance with off-campus housing. In addition, the University organizes international ambassador and host-family programs and supports international associations.

Application Facts and Dates

Applications are reviewed on a rolling admission basis. Once all application requirements are met, the Graduate Admissions staff takes pride in processing the application materials in a timely manner. Enrollment is very limited, and applicants are encouraged to submit required documents as early as possible for each of the fall, winter, spring, and summer terms. For more information, students should contact:

Allan G. Freedman
Director, Graduate Admissions
8 Abbott Park Place
Providence, Rhode Island 02903
Telephone: 401-598-1015
Fax: 401-598-4773

Kennesaw State College

Michael J. Coles School of Business

Marietta, Georgia

MAXIMIZE THE RETURN ON YOUR INVESTMENT

Obtaining an AACSB-accredited M.B.A. is a challenging, invigorating, and rewarding endeavor. People who invest their time and money to attend such programs are increasingly asking about "bottom-line benefits." "What am I going to gain by attending this program?" Sponsoring companies are asking similar questions. "What are the benefits of sending someone to such a program?" At Kennesaw State we have directed our efforts toward ensuring that associates in the M.B.A. program maximize the return on their investment.

The Coles School M.B.A. is an innovative, interactive, integrated program that incorporates real-life experiences into every component. The program is process-oriented rather than functionally oriented and taught in a team environment that simulates the workplace. Individuals completing the program become complete managers and leaders with new ideas, broad perspectives, technology awareness, and an expanded business network.

We look forward to sharing a learning experience with you and to helping you prepare for an ever-changing, competitive future.

—Timothy S. Mescon, Dean

Programs and Curricular Focus

Participants in the Michael J. Coles School M.B.A. Program don't expect results, they demand them. That's why many have chosen to attend this program. They are looking for fresh new ideas and the opportunity to build skills that can be applied directly to their organizations. Kennesaw State meets these demands by structuring its program to facilitate and encourage the exchange of ideas and problem-solving techniques—real-world, real-business, real-results. Participants leave every class, every meeting, and every function with information, insights, and abilities they can use to make a difference in their own—and their companies'—performance. In this rapidly changing environment, those using old techniques and old ways will be left behind. Only fresh new approaches and ideas can provide the power and leverage needed to meet the challenges facing businesses today.

Teamwork is a vital component of the learning process at the Coles School of Business. Indeed, one challenge that the School accepts is to most closely emulate the challenges and opportunities that students face in the world of work in the private and public sectors. To this end, it has structured a highly concentrated 60-quarter-hour, twelve-course program that enables students to master the core body of graduate business education as

well as to select from one of eight leading-edge program concentrations.

The core competency sequence includes course work in managerial accounting, managerial economics, financial analysis and decision making, operations management, management and organizational behavior, marketing management, and corporate strategy. In addition, all students select at least one international core course from a number that are available.

In the latter half of the program, students select a major concentration from one of eight areas. Students immerse themselves in one of these majors by completing four courses, 20 quarter hours, in a disciplined area of study. M.B.A. major options available to Coles School students include accounting, business administration, business economics, information systems, entrepreneurship, finance, human resources management and development, and marketing. A range of just-in-time course options are available to provide Coles School students with the latest theory and practice in all of the aforementioned optional courses of study.

The Coles School M.B.A. program is offered in the evenings and on weekends; therefore, it particularly appeals to working professionals or full-time students committed to utilizing their days for internships or research and study. All

graduate and undergraduate business programs at the Coles School of Business are fully accredited by the American Assembly of Collegiate Schools of Business (AACSB).

Students and the M.B.A. Experience

The approximately 600 graduate students at the Coles School bring a variety of backgrounds and experiences, and academic and cultural diversity, to the M.B.A. program. The average student is a 30-year-old with six years of full-time professional work experience. Women comprise approximately one half of the graduate student population, and members of minority groups represent about 10 percent. Approximately 60 percent of Coles School M.B.A. students have baccalaureate degrees in business, but a number have completed undergraduate studies in engineering, liberal arts, and the sciences. About 7 percent of Kennesaw State's students are international, coming from more than eighty nations.

❖ Global Focus

The faculty members in the Michael J. Coles School of Business are committed to internationalizing the curriculum through ongoing research, development, and travel. In the past few years alone, faculty members have served as guest lecturers or conducted sophisticated research projects in China, Russia, Rumania, Poland, South Africa, Mexico, Canada, Korea, and India. In addition, students always have the option to complete up to three courses for credit at international universities or term-long exchange programs.

Special Features

The Tetley Distinguished Leader Lecture Series brings 10 or more chief executive officers to campus throughout the academic year. During their visit to the Coles School, these leaders and entrepreneurs formally address students and the faculty and then interact with students in a more casual setting. Endowed by the Tetley (tea) Division of British-based Allied Lyons Corporation, this series has

772

attracted distinguished leaders from business, industry, and the nonprofit sector, including, among others, Bernard Marcus and Arthur Blank, co-founders of The Home Depot; Whit Hawkins, COO of Delta Air Lines; Jerry Dempsey, Chairman, PPG Industries; Thomas Wheeler, President and CEO, Mass Mutual; and A. D. Correll, Chairman, Georgia-Pacific.

The Faculty

The Coles School of Business is proud of the fact that its 80 full-time, tenure-track faculty members are committed to a balance of teaching, scholarship, and service. Across each of the Coles School's five academic departments, the faculty members represent a unique blend of gifted instructors who successfully meld issues in the world of work with leading-edge theory and practice. The School has been cited for its commitment to diversity and has a distinctive number of faculty members across all disciplines who are members of minority groups. Women represent over 30 percent of the faculty in the Coles School of Business.

The College and Environs

Kennesaw State College is nestled on 200 acres in suburban Atlanta, just 25 minutes north of downtown. Because access to the campus is directly off of Interstate 75 north, students have the opportunity to live in a variety of convenient locations throughout the Atlanta area. The College is part of the University System of Georgia and was founded in 1963. With a student population in excess of 12,000, Kennesaw State offers instruction through five schools in more than fifty fields.

The metropolitan Atlanta area is headquarters to a number of Fortune 500 companies and is North American and regional headquarters to a number of other leading multinational organizations.

Facilities

The Coles School is housed in the new 110,000-square-foot state-of-the-art A. L. Burruss Building, with tiered lecture halls, networked computer labs, and all faculty and administrative offices. The College's Sturgis Library is considered by many to be among the finest in the nation for on-line access to periodicals, databases, and network services. A charter member of SOLINET and a member of the Online Computer Library Center, Sturgis Library is part of an international network of libraries. All major on-line systems are available to M.B.A. students both on site and via telephone from remote sites. Sturgis Library houses 550,000 volumes of books and government documents, 3,300 serial publications, and a million pieces of microform.

Technology Environment

The Coles School faculty is committed to leveraging technology. To this end, students find numerous computer applications utilized throughout the curriculum. In addition, networked DOS and Mac labs are available in the School for M.B.A. student use. In collaboration with the Sturgis Library, students have on-line access to LEXIS/NEXIS and NAARS as well as dozens of other on-line services.

Placement

Kennesaw State and the Coles School of Business are proud of the services offered through the CAPS Center (Counseling, Advisement and Placement Services). The CAPS Center works diligently to secure strong linkages with on-campus recruiters and to assist students in developing other professional contacts and resources. CAPS regularly secures interview schedules with leading local, regional, national, and multinational employers. Regular seminars and workshops are offered to students to refine interviewing and presentation skills. The CAPS Center is a national leader in the utilization of technology to assist M.B.A. students in recognizing their career goals. Three technology-based programs available to M.B.A. students are résumé expert; KSC JOBS, a job networking system of positions specifically available to Kennesaw State students; and National Employment Wire Service, NEWS, which lists current job opportunities and positions throughout the United States.

Admission

To be admitted unconditionally to the M.B.A. program, an applicant must satisfy standards involving the following predictors of success: the adjusted GPA, GMAT or GRE scores, and work experience. An applicant is required to have an adjusted undergraduate GPA (UGPA) of at least 2.5 on a 4.0 scale plus a total score of at least 450 on the GMAT or a total score of at least 1350 on the General Test of the GRE. The applicant's admissions index (200 x UGPA + GMAT or GRE) must be at least 1000 for GMAT scores or 1900 for GRE scores. Also, the applicant should have a minimum of two years of work experience for unconditional admission to the M.B.A. program. In reviewing the academic work of applicants, the Admissions Committee evaluates the junior/senior adjusted GPA for all applicants. In cases where the applicant has done additional accredited undergraduate work beyond the bachelor's degree or has done accredited graduate work, the most recent two-year adjusted GPA will be used in the admissions consideration. A score of at least 550 on the TOEFL is required for all students for whom English is not the native language.

Finances

In 1994–95, tuition and fees for students taking fewer than 12 credit hours were $40 per credit hour for Georgia residents and $120 per credit hour for nonresidents. Georgia residents who took more than 12 hours paid $535 in tuition and fees per quarter; nonresidents, $1483 per quarter. There are three quarters during the standard academic year and a fourth, summer quarter.

Loans and scholarships are available on both a merit- and a need-based analysis through the Office of Financial Aid. Various alternatives are available to international students, as well.

Application Facts and Dates

The Coles School of Business admits qualified students to the M.B.A. program for study in the fall, winter, spring, or summer quarters. Approximate application deadlines are May 15, August 20, November 20, and February 20 in any given year. For more information, students should contact:

Michael J. Coles School of Business
Graduate Business Programs
Kennesaw State College
P.O. Box 444
Marietta, Georgia 30061-0444
Telephone: 404-423-6050
Fax: 404-423-6539
E-mail: ralsup@kscmail.kennesaw.edu

Loyola College

The Joseph A. Sellinger, S.J. School of Business and Management

Baltimore, Maryland

DEVELOPING BUSINESS LEADERS FOR THE TWENTY-FIRST CENTURY

Loyola College is first and foremost a Jesuit institution. Our small, caring environment and Jesuit tradition prepare our students for the workplace, where they are integrative thinkers, creative problem solvers, active team players, and, especially, leaders aware of their impact on coworkers, the organization, the community, and the world.

There is a Jesuit philosophy at Loyola that affects every student's experience, and that is personal care—care of the person. We are proud of the way our faculty, staff, and administration make Loyola students their greatest priority, helping them to graduate better businesspeople and individuals.

—Reverend Ronald Anton, S.J., Dean

Programs and Curricular Focus

The Sellinger School M.B.A. program challenges the student to acquire a practical and highly integrated understanding of today's business organizations. Separate functional area courses will be replaced by an advanced, integrated course set called The Value-Added Organization, which reflects the dynamic nature of today's business organizations. Students study the essential components of the modern business enterprise: the operations, marketing, and finance functions that are common to any entity, be it a service provider or manufacturer.

This teaching approach will soon feature an integrated case method. In The Value-Added Organization, for example, a set of cases will be repeated in each course within the set, but from a different functional perspective. The student then gains a cross-functional understanding and an ability to see the impact of decision making at different levels within an organization.

The Sellinger School M.B.A. program totals 51 credits and is open to business and nonbusiness undergraduates. The program includes 21 credits of core courses that are waiveable for recent undergraduates of business and business-related disciplines and 30 credits of advanced course work (or ten courses). Of the ten advanced courses, all students must take five required courses; the remaining five courses are electives. The five required courses feature The Value-Added Organization (three courses), a leadership and social responsi-

bility course, and a final course that serves as a capstone, transforming functional expertise into mission and strategy. The five elective courses may include a concentration—up to three courses in one functional area.

Also available are two Executive M.B.A. programs, a Master of Science in Finance program, and, starting in fall 1996, a full-time day Master of International Business program.

Students and the M.B.A. Experience

Students at the Sellinger School come from a wide variety of professional and academic backgrounds. The average student is 29 years old, works full-time, resides in the state of Maryland, and attends classes part-time in the evening. Full-time students comprise 10 percent of the traditional evening M.B.A. program. Women comprise 40 percent of the student population, and members of minority groups make up 5 percent. There are 18 international students attending the Sellinger School from such countries as France, Germany, Holland, Indonesia, and Thailand.

The majority of Sellinger School M.B.A. candidates have undergraduate degrees in business administration or the social sciences, with 18 percent coming from an engineering or science background.

The Faculty

The Sellinger School faculty numbers 55 full-time teachers, with 91 percent

holding doctoral-level degrees. Only a small portion of an M.B.A. student's experience includes adjunct faculty, due to the Sellinger School's commitment to a professional teaching environment.

A large majority of the faculty worked at high levels within their area of expertise before they became teachers, and many continue to practice in their field through work in corporations, their own companies, or consulting.

Many professors had distinguished careers running business operations in the United States, Europe, and the Orient, adding to their effectiveness in the classroom.

The Business School Network

Corporate Partnerships

The Sellinger School promotes the belief that the M.B.A. student is only one of a program's customers; the other is the student's employer. It is part of the School's mission to train new leaders for today's changing organizations, and there is no better way for a school to impart the knowledge of leadership than by asking its corporate customers what is needed in M.B.A. graduates to make them effective leaders in their respective organizations.

To that end, there are fifteen active advisory boards made up of local and regional business leaders and graduates of Sellinger programs who regularly meet to counsel and advise the faculty on curricular issues and needed skill sets. Some companies with whom Sellinger has particularly close relationships occasionally provide live situations for students to use as case studies in their M.B.A. program, a feature that students find particularly stimulating.

The College and Environs

Loyola College in Maryland is located in a beautiful residential section of northern Baltimore city. The 63-acre campus is known as Evergreen campus, a testament to the many green lawns, evergreen trees, flower-lined walkways, and floral gardens that dot the campus.

Founded in 1852, Loyola College is a small, private, Catholic, Jesuit liberal arts

college that enrolls approximately 3,000 full-time undergraduates in thirty-three majors and 3,000 graduate students studying nine professional disciplines.

The city of Baltimore is located within an hour's drive of Washington, D.C., and within an easy train ride of many East Coast cities, including New York City and Philadelphia.

Facilities

The main campus in Baltimore holds four classroom buildings, a 300,000-volume library, a college center housing state-of-the-art athletic and fine arts facilities, tennis courts, athletic fields, and a beautifully restored Tudor mansion, Evergreen's centerpiece. Undergraduate residence halls and apartments are located on the eastern and western sides of the main campus.

Classes for traditional M.B.A. students are also held at three suburban sites—in Hunt Valley, Columbia, and Aberdeen, Maryland.

Computer labs are located in virtually all buildings on the main and satellite campuses, and students have access 24 hours a day at most sites.

Technology Environment

The College is developing a computer and telephone network to connect classroom facilities, offices, the library, and laboratories to a digital and video network of global and local data and communication systems. The Sellinger School has an excellent MIS laboratory, and the College has IBM, Macintosh, and DEC midframe computing laboratories.

Placement

Loyola College's Career Development and Placement Center provides a variety of services to students seeking employment. Once an applicant to the Sellinger School, a student has immediate access to workshops, testing, and private counseling services designed to assist students in such endeavors as career selection, résumé writing, and interviewing skills.

A year-round, on-campus recruitment program hosts over 200 companies, which interview graduating students for positions. Of those, over 120 companies seek graduating M.B.A. students for jobs. The center also maintains active job referral and alumni advisory networks, which provide leads to graduating students and alumni.

Admission

Admission is based on undergraduate performance (GPA), scores on the Graduate Management Admission Test (GMAT), and career progress. Each program puts a different emphasis on these criteria. International students must also have transcripts evaluated by a recognized service and must submit TOEFL scores if their degree is from a non-English-speaking university. Traditional programs admit students for each term, and the Executive M.B.A. programs admit only for the fall.

The average enrolled M.B.A. student holds a GMAT score of 530, an undergraduate GPA of 3.2, and has been working professionally for four to five years. International students who are required to take the TOEFL are expected to achieve a minimum score of 550.

Finances

M.B.A. program tuition is charged on a per-credit basis and is $330 per credit in 1995–96. Most classes are 3 credits each. There is a $25 registration fee every semester in which a student takes courses, and books are purchased separately. M.B.A. students may attend classes year-round on a full-time (9 credits) or part-time (3–6 credits) basis. Students in the Executive M.B.A. programs pay a flat tuition charge per academic year, with the summers off.

Assistance is available through the Federal Stafford Student Loan programs to qualified students, and limited institutional assistance is available in the form of graduate assistantships.

International Students

The Sellinger School seeks a diverse student population and therefore welcomes applications from students outside the United States. International students should have a command of the English language and some work experience. Due to limited institutional assistance, proof is required of sufficient financial resources to fully meet educational costs while attending Loyola College. An orientation session and assistance in locating housing are provided.

Application Facts and Dates

Application deadlines for the M.B.A. program are July 20 for the fall term (May 15 for international students), November 20 for the spring term (August 15 for international students), and April 20 for the summer term (January 15 for international students). Once an application file is complete with all required and official documents, a student is usually notified in writing within two weeks. For more information, applicants should contact:

Mr. Thomas Bednarsky
Director of Graduate Admissions
Loyola College
4501 North Charles Street
Baltimore, Maryland 21210-2699
Telephone: 410-617-5020

Loyola Marymount University

Los Angeles, California

PREPARING FOR THE TWENTY-FIRST CENTURY

The key word for the last half of the 1990s is transition. These uncertain times create unbelievable opportunities for those who are prepared to make things happen. This is why I call our LMU program M.B.A.+. In addition to functional knowledge, human dynamics skills, global competition, and cultural diversity, our M.B.A. program focuses on the needs of individuals and organizations in transition.

Our faculty is eager to help you reach beyond the demands of the classroom. They are noted for outstanding teaching, widely published research, and experience in a variety of industries.

The M.B.A.+ program stresses the ethical dimensions of decisions. Our annual Business Ethics Week conference helps students learn how business leaders in various fields address ethical issues.

As you prepare for the challenges of the twenty-first century, you will definitely want to put the LMU M.B.A.+ program into your career development equation.

—John T. Wholihan, Dean

Programs and Curricular Focus

The Loyola Marymount M.B.A. Program develops ethical leaders who possess the knowledge and skills to effectively manage organizations in a diverse and global economy. Students are taught how to create value, handle risk, and manage change.

The core curriculum consists of nine courses, some or all of which may be waived by students with recent bachelor's degrees in business. Competence may also be determined by examination.

Upon completion of the core, students select domestic or international electives to gain breadth of knowledge as well as expertise in a particular area. The domestic track requires three courses in an area of emphasis as well as five additional courses from other areas. Students elect either comparative management systems, strategy courses, or an integrative project to complete the program.

Students selecting the international track receive the M.B.A. degree plus a Graduate Certificate in International Business after completing the same number of courses as are required for the domestic track. In addition to international breadth courses, participation in comparative management systems is required. This provides the opportunity to study the area of emphasis within a given industry outside the United States.

Comparative management systems is also available to domestic-track students.

Depending on waivers and the integrative option selected, ten to twenty courses are required. Full-time students with undergraduate degrees in business often complete the M.B.A. program within one year.

Loyola Marymount offers a J.D./M.B.A. program, enabling a student to earn both degrees in four years.

Students and the M.B.A. Experience

Eighty percent of students in the Loyola Marymount M.B.A. Program are fully employed professionals from a wide variety of industries in southern California. Twenty percent of the students attend on a full-time basis. While some students enter the program directly after undergraduate school, most do have work experience. The average student is 28 years old, with four years of work experience. Women account for 44 percent of the student body, and 25 percent are members of minority groups.

Seventeen percent of the population are international students from all over the world. International students often provide alternative analyses of the global dimension of business problems, which are extremely valuable in the classroom.

Half of the students have undergraduate degrees in business, 30 percent in the social sciences, and 20 percent in engineering.

❖ Global Focus

The M.B.A. program offers a wide variety of courses that examine the global nature of business. In addition, students have the opportunity to participate in an exchange program in France.

For fifteen years, the M.B.A. program has sponsored comparative management systems, a two-semester international-strategy sequence. Students form functional-area groups and spend a year analyzing a particular industry and regional area. At the conclusion of the year, students spend three weeks meeting with industry executives in the region selected for study. Most recently, the course examined the computer industry in Asia. Future plans include a study of the management of ports and harbors in a number of European countries, followed by a similar study in Asia the next year.

The Faculty

Loyola Marymount's faculty members are exceptional teachers who actively participate in research in their fields. Approximately 94 percent of all courses are taught by faculty members who have doctoral degrees. Classes are intentionally small, to provide faculty members with opportunities to interact with individual students on a regular basis.

Women comprise 14 percent of the faculty, and 14 percent of the faculty are members of minority groups. Loyola Marymount's strong international emphasis is supported by faculty members from India, Korea, Ghana, Hong Kong, Great Britain, and Russia.

The Business School Network

The Business Advisory Council, comprising corporate leaders from a variety of industries, is actively involved in the M.B.A. program. Some of the members serve as speakers for M.B.A. classes or conferences. Others are involved in the recruiting and placement efforts of the M.B.A. program. One of the members

coordinates a group of students who meet monthly with prominent entrepreneurs.

The College and Environs

Loyola University, a Jesuit institution incorporated in 1928, merged with Marymount College in 1973 to form Loyola Marymount University. The M.B.A. program was instituted in 1974. The Westchester campus has a student population of over 4,500. The Loyola Law School is located in downtown Los Angeles.

Loyola Marymount University is located in a lovely residential neighborhood on a bluff offering magnificent views of Marina del Rey and the Pacific Ocean. Excellent weather plus proximity to local beaches provides the perfect setting for outdoor sports. Los Angeles offers an extraordinary variety of theaters, museums, and professional sports teams, all a short distance from the University.

Technology Environment

M.B.A. students have access via networks to an attractive array of computer and related technologies. Word processing and spreadsheets are available through the campuswide network. Specific applications, such as simulation and statistical packages, are accessible via departmental networks.

With the opening of the Conrad N. Hilton Center for Business in August of 1995, two new hands-on computer classrooms will be added. The Hilton facility is intended to provide access to a new generation of technologies. Traditional videoconferencing will permit students and faculty members to participate in classes from remote locations. Desktop videoconferencing will enable group projects and collaborative research efforts from remote locations.

Placement

Loyola Marymount's Career Development and Placement Office provides a variety of services. Students get advice on résumé preparation and interviewing skills. On-line databases, career fairs, and on-campus interviews are also available. The M.B.A. Office provides additional placement services, including the distribution of résumé books to local employers each semester as well as daily maintenance of a list of jobs and internship opportunities.

Admission

Each applicant's undergraduate record, GMAT scores, and recommendation letters form the basis for evaluation. Although not required, relevant work experience is considered. The minimum GMAT score is 400, with the average score approximately 540. The average undergraduate GPA is 3.2.

International students must achieve a TOEFL score of at least 600 and must present proof of sufficient funds to cover tuition and living expenses for the full period of study.

All entering students are assumed to be proficient in English composition, business mathematics, and computer applications.

Finances

Tuition for 1995–96 is estimated to be $530 per unit. Each course is 3 units. Annual fees for full-time students are estimated to be $421. Fees for part-time students are estimated to be $268. In addition, all students must have health insurance. The cost of books and supplies varies from approximately $60 to $100 per course.

Merit-based research assistantships are available, as are a limited number of need-based grants. In addition, the Financial Aid Office can provide information on loan programs available to M.B.A. students.

Application Facts and Dates

Applications are accepted for the fall, spring, and summer semesters. There are no specific deadlines; the M.B.A. Office has a policy of rolling admissions. Once the University has received all application materials, the application package is reviewed and the applicant notified within two weeks. For more information, students should contact:

Ms. Karen Stevens, Coordinator
M.B.A. Office
Loyola Marymount University
Los Angeles, California 90045
Telephone: 310-338-2848
Fax: 310-338-2899
E-mail: kstevens@lmumail.lmu.edu

Loyola University Chicago

BUILDING SKILLS FOR LIFE

For over 450 years, Jesuits have been educating men and women for positions of leadership in business, government, and the professions. We at Loyola University Chicago are proud to be a part of this tradition. It has provided four main themes that form the foundation of our M.B.A. program: teaching excellence, skills for life, global vision, and socially responsible leadership. These themes are the solid foundation on which you can build an individual program of study tailored to your needs. We invite you to explore how the Loyola University Chicago approach can benefit you as you pursue your career goals.

—Donald G. Meyer, Dean

Programs and Curricular Focus

The Loyola M.B.A. program ranges from fourteen to eighteen courses, depending on the student's undergraduate background. This includes between five and ten required courses and eight to nine electives. Electives can be used to earn a field of specialization in one of eight areas, such as finance and health-care administration, as well as to earn an area of emphasis in financial derivatives or international business.

All classes contain a mix of part-time and full-time students. It is the belief at Loyola that this design is intellectually healthy since it permits all M.B.A. students to interact in the same classroom setting.

The Graduate School of Business offers students the opportunity to pursue an M.B.A. degree, a dual M.B.A./J.D. degree, or a dual M.B.A./M.S.N. degree. Each of the dual-degree programs allows the student to earn the degrees in a shorter period of time than if they were pursued independently.

Students and the M.B.A. Experience

The students have undergraduate degrees from over 200 universities across the globe. The typical Loyola University Chicago M.B.A. student is 26 years old, with 3.5 years of full-time work experience; 36 percent of the students are women, 9.5 percent are members of minority groups, and 8 percent are international. Approximately half of Loyola's students earned their under-graduate degree in business, 30 percent in arts and science, and 10 percent in economics.

❖ Global Focus

Loyola helps prepare students for the international demands of business by routinely including international considerations in all of the courses and by offering courses that focus solely on the international dimensions of a topic. All M.B.A. students must take at least one international course. A student can also earn an international emphasis as part of the overall M.B.A. by building three to four international courses into his or her program.

Students whose career goals demand an intensive grounding in international business can take advantage of the innovative Rome Center program. Under this program, intensive two-week summer courses are offered each year at Loyola's campus in Rome, Italy. Each course focuses on topical international issues and is taught by the best of Loyola's Chicago faculty. Since each session is compressed into a two-week block, both part-time and full-time students have the opportunity to attend. Past courses have focused on such issues as strategic marketing in Europe, international management, and the European Union.

Special Features

Loyola provides Individual Development Seminars for M.B.A. students throughout the year. These seminars are free and address topics such as communication skills, personal quality management, entrepreneurship, negotiating skills, and career strategies. In addition, the Graduate School of Business Distinguished Speaker Series hosts prominent academic, business, and government leaders to speak on current issues. The four research centers embody Loyola University Chicago's philosophy of blending the theoretical with the practical by linking real-world business needs with the University's ongoing research. Research conducted by the centers is incorporated into many classroom programs.

The Faculty

The Loyola University Chicago faculty is strongly committed to teaching as well as research. Because 97 percent of the faculty is full-time, classes are taught by experienced, highly trained leaders in their fields. Part-time faculty members are used on a very selective basis and only when they offer specialized skills. Class size is purposely kept small in order to ensure that the faculty is accessible to students—both inside and outside the classroom.

As leaders in their fields, most faculty members have important industry and community ties in such areas as family business, total quality management, and financial and policy studies. So, in teaching, they offer a scholarly approach gained through research as well as practical business experience.

The faculty's dedication to research invigorates the M.B.A. experience by developing new ideas that can be applied in the classroom. The faculty is involved in an impressive range of research projects in all major areas of business and is also widely published.

The Business School Network

Corporate Partnerships

Seventy-five percent of Loyola's alumni live within the greater Chicago area. Already established and successful in the business world, these alumni provide significant networking opportunities for students. As a result, major businesses in the Chicago area and from around the country are frequently on campus to speak to students and alumni, to advise faculty and administrators on current management education issues, and to recruit Loyola's graduates.

Prominent Alumni

Among Loyola's prominent M.B.A. alumni are Michael Quinlan, Chairman of the Board and CEO, McDonald's Corporation; Brenda Barnes, Chief Operating Officer, Pepsi-Cola Corporation; Gregory LeVert, President, National Accounts, MCI Communications; Joseph Scully, Chairman of the Board and CEO, St. Paul Federal Bank for Savings; and Alfred Wall Jr., President, Louvers International Midwest.

The College and Environs

The Graduate School of Business campus is located adjacent to Chicago's Magnificent Mile. LaSalle Street is home to the Chicago Board of Trade, Chicago Board Options Exchange, and Chicago Mercantile Exchange, making the city one of the largest financial trading centers in the world. Many national and multinational companies in a broad range of industries are headquartered in Chicago. As a result, job opportunities at major firms abound throughout the Chicago area, in fields as diverse as manufacturing, health care, and consulting.

Technology Environment

The Graduate School of Business is housed in the new Graduate Business Center. Loyola's M.B.A. students have state-of-the-art computers and software for instructional and individual use. The Loyola library system offers numerous computerized resources including the Internet, LEXIS/NEXIS, Legal Index, FirstSearch, and LUIS (the Loyola library computerized catalog). Databases on CD-ROM include Business Periodicals on Disc, General Business File, and others.

Placement

The M.B.A. Career Service advisers are available to help students with résumés, cover letters, career counseling and planning, and job search strategies.

Videotaped mock interview sessions, conducted by business professionals who also provide oral and written feedback, are held twice each year. In addition, training workshops on the nuts and bolts of job hunting (such as résumé writing, interviewing techniques, targeting potential employers, salary negotiation, and networking) are scheduled throughout the year.

In addition to the many on-campus recruiting opportunities with an array of employers, Loyola sponsors the Midwest M.B.A. Consortium with four other universities. Opportunities for networking and skill building are also provided through Loyola's Career Consultants Network, the M.B.A. alumni organization dedicated to assisting students in their job search activities. Students can also join alumni in the Chicago area several times each year when they meet on campus for professional and social occasions.

Admission

Students are admitted to the School as candidates for the M.B.A. degree on the bases of interest, aptitude, and capacity for business study as indicated by their previous academic record; achievement scores on the Graduate Management Admission Test (GMAT); recommendations from 3 faculty members or employers; and pertinent information from their applications.

The average student's undergraduate GPA is 3.2, with a range from 2.5 to 4.0. The average GMAT score is 530, with a range from 400 to 720. Average work experience of the entering students is 3.5 years.

Loyola welcomes applications from international students who have completed a four-year bachelor's degree or its equivalent. A minimum TOEFL score of 550 and proof of financial support for one year are required.

Finances

Tuition for 1994–95 was $1332 per course for both full- and part-time students. A wide variety of housing is available both on and off campus. Many

full-time students live in the Gold Coast area of Chicago, which is within walking distance of the Graduate School of Business. Other graduate students choose to live in graduate housing facilities that are located 10 miles north of the Water Tower Campus at Loyola's Lake Shore Campus. The estimated cost of room and board for twelve months is between $9000 and $12,000. The Graduate Business Scholars Program provides over twenty merit-based assistantships per year to full-time students.

International Students

Loyola's M.B.A. program is greatly enhanced by more than 70 international students. Countries represented by 3 or more students include Thailand, China, India, Spain, Canada, Korea, and the Philippines. Loyola's Students of the World chapter provides an immediate link for international students, while the Office of International Services and Programs helps international students adjust to living and studying in the United States. Chicago's ethnic and culinary diversity make this "city of neighborhoods" a comfortable and exciting home for citizens from around the world.

Application Facts and Dates

A student may enter the program at the beginning of any of the four quarters. To ensure admission in the quarter of choice, the student should apply well in advance. Because Loyola functions on a rolling admission basis, however, applications are accepted until these deadlines: for the fall quarter, August 1; the winter quarter, October 1; the spring quarter, January 1; and the summer quarter, April 1. For additional information, students should contact:

Admissions Coordinator
Graduate School of Business
Loyola University Chicago
820 North Michigan Avenue
Chicago, Illinois 60611
Telephone: 312-915-6120
Fax: 312-915-7207

McGill University

CREATING VALUE—A PRACTICAL, INTEGRATIVE APPROACH

To prepare students for truly rewarding careers in a continually changing global business environment, the McGill M.B.A. program provides a unique pedagogical experience. Not only are all the core-year courses fully interconnected, they are team-taught. The rapport that develops between students and professors enhances the flexibility, adaptability, and people-oriented skills the curriculum develops. With an understanding of how to create value for the greatest benefit of an organization as a whole, students get more out of their chosen area of concentration in the second year. As a result, the McGill M.B.A. program produces specialists who can integrate across functional areas—and offer employers a responsible competitive edge.

—Wallace Crowston, Dean

Programs and Curricular Focus

The full-time McGill M.B.A. program is a two-year program designed to provide students with the comprehensive understanding of business, hard and soft skills, specialized knowledge, and international perspective necessary to meet emerging needs as business leaders.

In the core year, all students follow the same sequence of courses in three 10-week modules. The focus is on the value creation process, the collective effort that begins with an idea for a product or service and continues through its development, production, launch, and management in the workplace. Following this integrative approach to functional areas, value creation is placed in its environmental context with the focus on society, ethics, and global change.

The second year is free of required courses. Students may choose or individually tailor one of fifteen concentration options or pursue a joint concentration.

Students who take the program on a part-time basis follow the same course structure and can complete the core year requirements in about two years. At certain points, they may join the full-time program to complete their degree at an accelerated pace.

McGill's joint M.B.A./Diploma in Management (Asian studies) is a Canadian first, combining all mandatory M.B.A. courses and a concentration in international business with graduate level Asian studies courses and language instruction, followed by an optional three-month internship at an Asian institution.

McGill's joint M.B.A./law degree is a four-year program leading to either an M.B.A./LL.B. or an M.B.A./B.C.L. (Bachelor of Civil Law). Applicants must meet the requirements of both faculties. The Faculty of Law requires that applicants demonstrate fluency in English and French.

Students and the M.B.A. Experience

McGill M.B.A. students are proven achievers who bring more than academic excellence and diverse, often international, work experience to the program. Through a personal interest, cause, or commitment, they demonstrate a talent for going beyond what is expected and contributing to society.

This is important because the program's combination of balanced teaching, action learning, team teaching, interaction with the business world, and student and faculty initiatives is as challenging as it is rewarding.

Of the 125 full-time students in the 1994–95 class, the ratio of women to men was 1:3, the average age was 25, and they represented fourteen countries; 40 percent spoke two languages and 42 percent spoke three or more. They came from a cross-section of universities: 12 percent American, 21 percent other international, 41 percent Canadian outside Quebec, and the balance from Quebec; 30 percent held a B.A., 25 percent a B.Sc., 16 percent a B.Eng., and 29 percent a B.Com./B.B.A.

Special Features

McGill is world-renowned as a leader in international management education. All students acquire an inherent understanding of international commerce and an appreciation for other cultures in McGill's multicultural learning environment, and those interested in international business enjoy exceptional opportunities to network and acquire experience.

M.B.A. 1: THE CORE ELEMENTS

MODULE I: INTRODUCTION TO THE VALUE CREATION PROCESS	MODULE II: INTRODUCTION TO THE CRITICAL DOMAINS	MODULE III: THE ORGANIZATION IN CONTEXT
Accounting	Finance	Information Systems
Organizational Behaviour	Marketing	International Environment
Managerial Economics	Operations Management	Organizational Strategy
Management Statistics	Human Resource Management	Topical Courses I & II
Integrative I	Research, Development and Engineering	Integrative III
	Integrative II	

McGill is the founding Canadian member of the Program in International Management (PIM), a consortium of leading business schools in North America, South America, Europe, and Asia. Through this association, McGill offers active exchange programs in Belgium, Brazil, Denmark, England, France, Germany, Holland, Italy, Mexico, Pakistan, the Philippines, Spain, Sweden, Thailand, and the United States.

The Faculty

McGill Management is composed of an eclectic team of faculty members who enjoy the challenges the M.B.A. program affords them, particularly the core year's integrative course, which they jointly plan, teach, and grade.

They represent fifteen nationalities and have all lived, studied, and worked in countries around the world. They bring direct experience of business practices in other countries to the classroom, and many have proven themselves to be in the forefront of research in cross-cultural and multinational business issues. Two interesting faculty-supported initiatives are the McGill Business Consulting Group and its international counterpart, the McGill International Consulting Group (MICG), which offer students professional opportunities.

The Business School Network

Corporate Partnerships

McGill's learning environment includes involvement with businesses of every size in every industry sector, as well as government agencies and departments.

Through various projects, events, and a range of faculty and student initiatives, students interact with CEOs, entrepreneurs, consultants, managers, government officials, conference delegates, and visiting faculty from around the world. They benefit from exceptional opportunities to learn, contribute, network, and explore career directions.

The Faculty continually benefits from valuable counsel from its Faculty of Management International Advisory Board, composed of 11 prominent businesspeople under the chairmanship of Paul Desmarais Jr.

The College and Environs

McGill is recognized around the world for its high standards in teaching and research, and it has achieved international renown for its Faculties of Agriculture, Dentistry, Engineering, Law, Management, and Medicine.

McGill has an undergraduate enrollment of 24,005 and a graduate enrollment of 5,188. Currently, 3,523 international

students and scholars from 129 countries are furthering their education and conducting research.

Founded in 1821, the University now comprises fifty institutional buildings for eleven faculties on 75 acres in downtown Montreal. Montreal, North America's most multicultural business centre and one of its leading centres for high-tech RD&E, is considered to be one of its most cultured and cosmopolitan cities.

Facilities

McGill Management occupies a building specifically designed for its needs, complete with computer-assisted instruction through the Faculty's local area network, an M.B.A. lounge, a computing centre, and an impressive library featuring electronic database searching services and a number of networked databases. Students also have access to over 3 million volumes housed in the University's comprehensive system of libraries and specialized collections.

Students enjoy excellent sports facilities, efficient housing services, a graduate house, and a health service that is also available to part-time students who pay student services fees.

Technology Environment

The large bank of microcomputers located in the management building's computing centre is connected to an extensive network, providing access to network file servers, laser printers, and the campus mainframes.

Systems analysis and design, factor modelling, optimization, statistical, economic, accounting, and financial analysis packages are available through the centre's software library.

Placement

Placement starts in Orientation Week when the M.B.A. Career Centre holds the first of many networking occasions. Students seeking both permanent and summer employment benefit from workshops, videotaped mock interviews, one-on-one career counselling, a resource library, and an alumni reference database.

The centre provides job listings; holds an annual M.B.A. Career Day; publishes a graduating class book, which is distributed to prospective employers in Canada and abroad; and follows up on interviews with both students and employers.

Continual interaction with companies has made McGill's M.B.A. Career Centre a valued resource for employers and students alike.

Admission

Admission is competitive. Decisions are based on many factors: solid academic credentials (minimum 3.0 CGPA, average 3.3); a strong GMAT score (minimum 550, average 611); a TOEFL score of 600 if English was not the language of university education; at least one year of relevant work experience; professional and extracurricular achievements; and letters of reference.

Students should ensure they have a solid grounding in financial accounting, mathematics, and computer/database management prior to starting the program.

Finances

Tuition fees for the 1994–95 academic year were Can$1980 for Canadian citizens and Can$8250 for non-Canadians. They include student services, society fees, and health insurance. Bilateral agreements exist with several nations to obtain an international fee waiver.

Students are eligible for financial aid as well as for a number of scholarships and fellowships.

A minimal figure for living expenses per academic year is Can$6500 for a single student and Can$8000 for a married student.

International Students

International students are warmly received and supported in the Faculty's multicultural environment. In addition, the University runs a combined Student Aid/International Advisor's office to handle all nonacademic matters of concern, such as visa status, immigration procedures, health insurance requirements, and cost estimates for Foreign Exchange boards.

Application Facts and Dates

Applications for the full-time program are accepted for September only. Application deadlines are June 1 for Canadian students and April 15 for international students.

All accepted candidates are automatically considered for financial aid and fellowships. Awards are announced in mid-July. For more information, applicants should contact:

The McGill M.B.A.
Faculty of Management
McGill University
1001 Sherbrooke Street West
Montreal, Quebec H3A 1G5
Canada
Telephone: 514-398-4066
Fax: 514-398-2499
E-mail: mba.management.mcgill.ca

Mississippi State University

Starkville, Mississippi

DRIVEN BY EXCELLENCE

The mission and purpose of the College of Business and Industry is to develop business and professional leaders for the twenty-first century who will positively influence organizations through ethical standards, their management skills, and their ability to manage change in a global society. The College is further dedicated to increasing knowledge through scholarly research and fostering economic development through the application of applied research and services to increase the effectiveness, efficiency, and productivity of business and industry. The M.B.A. program is an integral part, and its graduates a manifestation, of this mission and purpose. The evolutionary nature of business and industry is reflected in the M.B.A. program through the process of continuous improvement. In a phrase, the M.B.A. program is "Driven by Excellence."

—Harvey S. Lewis, Dean

Programs and Curricular Focus

The objective of the M.B.A. program is to provide a broad background for business leadership through an emphasis on practical administrative problems. Candidates for the M.B.A. program must complete 30 hours of course work at the graduate level, including a core of 24 hours in the areas of accounting, economics, finance, management, marketing, and statistics, plus a capstone course in business strategy. The remaining 6 hours of graduate courses are elective and may be selected from either within or outside of business.

For M.B.A. candidates who do not hold undergraduate degrees in business, a set of prerequisite courses must be completed. These include courses in accounting, business information systems, economics, finance, legal environment of business, management, marketing, and statistics.

Full-time students with an undergraduate business degree can complete the M.B.A. program in three semesters or one year, and part-time students with an undergraduate business degree can complete the program in five semesters or slightly less than two years. In the absence of previous academic training in business, full-time students can complete the program within two years, and part-time students can usually complete the program within four. The maximum time frame within which the degree may be completed is six years.

Students and the M.B.A. Experience

While ages may range from early twenties to late forties, the average age of students in the M.B.A. program at Mississippi State University is 27. The average amount of full-time work experience, since receiving their undergraduate degree, is between two and three years. The student body is generally composed of approximately 60 percent men and 40 percent women. African-American students constitute approximately 10 percent and international students approximately 20 percent of the student body. While undergraduate backgrounds vary from animal husbandry to zoology, the majority of the students hold undergraduate degrees in business, with engineering being the second most prevalent undergraduate background.

The Faculty

The graduate faculty in the College of Business and Industry, a subset of the general faculty, consists of approximately 55 members. Members are reviewed every five years for reappointment to the graduate faculty. Members of the graduate faculty all hold advanced degrees in their respective areas of expertise. Approximately 15 percent of the faculty members are women. Foreign nationals compose about 20 percent of the faculty.

The Business School Network

The corporate community cooperates with the University in several ways to provide students with opportunities for hands-on business contact. The annual M.B.A. Welcome and Orientation Program allows students to interact with corporate leaders and ask questions in a casual atmosphere. Brown bag lunches are frequently held, highlighting corporate executives who discuss their company policies and opportunities for employment.

The College and Environs

The College of Business and Industry is located in McCool Hall at the center of MSU's campus. The University forms a part of a cohesive town-university community with the growing agricultural-commercial-industrial town of Starkville. Located in the eastern part of north-central Mississippi, it is 125 miles northeast of Jackson and 23 miles west of Columbus. Away from urban complexities, the community enjoys many intellectual, cultural, and recreational advantages: the MSU-Starkville Civic Symphony and Chorus; the Starkville Community Theater; the University Lyceum series, which presents performances by popular musical groups of regional and national celebrity; frequent intercollegiate athletic events in modern facilities; and a variety of recreational opportunities on playing fields, courts, lakes, and the nearby Tennessee-Tombigbee Waterway.

Technology Environment

The College of Business and Industry has installed and made available for faculty and student use a large-scale local area network. This network contains more than 200 PC stations and is MS-DOS based using Sperry/Novell Netware. Four student labs with state-of-the-art software applications are available for College of Business and Industry student assignments. There is also an electronic classroom that provides interactive instruction opportunities for faculty members and students to deal with more sophisticated data and analytical techniques. Assistance is available to provide students with computer-assisted instruc-

McCool Hall.

tion topics as well as personal problem solving. A Sun 4/280 UNIX system allows access to UNIX software packages as well to the Internet, a worldwide academic computer network.

Placement

Assisting its graduates in finding jobs is a primary concern of Mississippi State University. In order to give its students the best possible opportunities, the University operates the Career Services Center and the Cooperative Education Program.

The Career Services Center brings about eighty-five businesses to campus each semester to interview students for full-time jobs and professional-level summer employment. In preparation for these interviews, the CSC offers résumé critiques and seminars that focus on writing effective résumés, honing interviewing skills, and looking for jobs.

The CSC also maintains an alumni career network and critiques videotaped mock interviews. In addition, the CSC sponsors Career Day, a program that brings over 100 businesses to campus each September to let students make future job contacts and gain more information on potential career paths.

Admission

An applicant for admission to graduate study should hold a bachelor's degree, have an undergraduate GPA of at least 3.0 in the last 60 hours of baccalaureate work, and have a GMAT score of 500 or higher. A student whose GPA or GMAT is insufficient may be considered for admission if he or she exceeds the minimum required in the other criterion and has a well-written statement of purpose and strong reference letters.

An international applicant who does not hold an undergraduate degree from a U.S. institution must submit a TOEFL report reflecting a score of 575 or higher with the application. Students who score below 575 will not be considered for admission into the program.

Finances

For students taking 9 to 13 graduate credit hours in the fall or spring term, estimated tuition and fees are $1237 for Mississippi residents and $2216 for nonresidents. Students enrolling in more than 13 hours must pay according to the rate established per credit hour, which is currently $111 per credit hour, and an activity fee per credit hour, now $31.39. Residence halls cost approximately $600; books and supplies cost approximately $240; meals, $915; and personal expenses, $740. Fees are subject to change without notice.

A number of assistantships are awarded to students working toward their master's degree. These awards, which include a monthly stipend, also include tuition waivers. The awards are based on the student's GMAT score and GPA, with consideration of the student's skills and the needs of the College. Students must be enrolled full-time to be eligible for an assistantship.

Application Facts and Dates

To ensure full consideration for admission to the M.B.A. program, all application materials must be received according to the following deadlines: fall semester, July 1; spring semester, November 1; first summer term, April 1; and second summer term, May 1. For an application and additional information on the M.B.A. program, or on other graduate programs of study in the College of Business and Industry, students should call or write:

Graduate Studies in Business
College of Business and Industry
P.O. Drawer 5288
Mississippi State, Mississippi 39762
Telephone: 601-325-1891
Fax: 601-325-2410
E-mail: gsb@cobilan.msstate.edu

Monterey Institute of International Studies

Monterey, California

GOING INTERNATIONAL WITH THE MONTEREY M.B.A.

The M.B.A. program at the Monterey Institute provides a passport to entrepreneurship in international business. M.B.A. students find they can "meet the world in Monterey." Up to 50 percent of M.B.A. students come from outside the United States. Most students have studied or worked abroad, and all students can communicate in at least one language in addition to English. The emphasis on multicultural teamwork further enhances the atmosphere of a global village.

The Monterey M.B.A. combines this international orientation with an entrepreneurial focus. Our goal is to educate innovative leaders who can function effectively in many cultural environments and in global business. At Monterey, students complement their course work with active learning in real-life business settings. We believe these abilities underlie success in international management. To foster their growth, we have created an intimate, collegial M.B.A. program where students and faculty work together in a supportive learning environment.

—William R. Pendergast, Dean

Programs and Curricular Focus

The Monterey M.B.A. prepares students for leadership in international business by developing competence in basic business disciplines, communication skills in at least one foreign language, and interpersonal skills including problem solving and cross-cultural teamwork. The Monterey Institute offers both a twenty-one-month M.B.A. program and a ten-month advanced-entry M.B.A. program.

The twenty-one-month M.B.A. program enrolls students with prior study in diverse academic fields, work experience, and a minimum of two years of university-level foreign language courses. Students enter this program in September and are encouraged to work with the Career Development Office to obtain a summer internship between their first and second years.

The advanced-entry program enrolls students with previous formal undergraduate business education, significant work experience, and a minimum of three years of university-level foreign language courses. Students enter this program in July and complete their studies the following May.

Concentrations within both M.B.A. programs are offered in international trade management, entrepreneurial management, international marketing, international economics and finance,

regional business environments, international human resources management, and global business.

Students and the M.B.A. Experience

The Monterey M.B.A. emphasizes the development of skills for effective teamwork in multicultural settings, both in individual courses and particularly in the International Business Plan (IBP).

The IBP integrates the functional disciplines of management through the development of a detailed international business plan for a sponsoring company or a start-up venture. It exposes students to the unique aspects of international business environments, hones communication and presentation skills, and develops a strong entrepreneurial orientation. Plans are accomplished in close consultation with a team of experienced faculty members. Students also develop strong relationships with experienced executives at sponsoring companies.

Fifty percent of the M.B.A. students are citizens of countries outside the United States, representing over thirty countries. Forty-five percent of the students are women, and approximately 11 percent of the Americans are members of minority groups.

❖ Global Focus

The Monterey M.B.A. has a distinctive emphasis on cross-cultural communication and effectiveness. During the M.B.A. program, students combine business courses with further advanced language study in Chinese, English, French, German, Japanese, Russian, or Spanish. Although fluency in English is required of all students, one of the Institute's unique opportunities is the availability of professional content courses taught in languages other than English.

Special Features

Students discover numerous extracurricular opportunities, including organizing the annual Export-Import Conference. Internships and participation in international market research and case studies are available through the Business and Economic Development Center, the Small Business Institute, and the International Trade Research Center. The new Center for International Trade provides a context for conferences and other research activities. Internships and advanced language study are also available through the Institute's summer programs in France, Mexico, and China.

The Faculty

Teaching is the paramount mission of the M.B.A. faculty, who are not distracted by the demands of undergraduates or of a research-oriented doctoral program. The small size of the Monterey M.B.A. program creates a sense of intimacy and cohesion between students and faculty members, who encourage lively classroom interaction. The faculty members also maintain an active intellectual and professional agenda and a close involvement with their corporate contacts.

The Business School Network
Corporate Partnerships

Dynamic, innovative companies form partnerships with the Monterey Institute in order to manage expansion, explore foreign markets, and experiment with new business concepts. Corporate partnerships include business plan sponsorship, internships and job placement, and guest speakers. Students, in consultation with faculty, also conduct research through the business assistance centers. These business executives provide feedback that is part of the continuous improvement of the Monterey M.B.A.

Prominent Alumni

Monterey M.B.A. alumni live and work around the world. They provide a network that is available for business and social contacts. Alumni often return to Monterey and maintain supportive relationships with faculty and administration. Access to this alumni network is an enduring asset for Monterey graduates.

The College and Environs

The Monterey Institute of International Studies has been a leader since 1955 in integrating advanced foreign language education into professional graduate programs in international management, international policy studies, and international public administration. The Monterey Institute also offers M.A. degrees in teaching English to speakers of other languages (TESOL), teaching foreign language, and in translation and interpretation. About one third of the 750 students represent over fifty countries outside the United States. Students share a multidisciplinary experience in course work and social activities.

The Monterey Institute is situated in one of the most spectacular natural environments in the world. The Monterey Peninsula is 120 miles south of San Francisco on California's central coast, surrounded by ocean and mountains; it has a population of 100,000. Students benefit from exposure to the nearby high-tech companies of the Silicon Valley, hospitality industries, and a concentration of agribusiness enterprises.

Facilities

The Monterey Institute's specialized international library has a collection of 64,200 carefully selected volumes and 500 periodical titles, about one third in languages other than English. Its state-of-the-art integrated computer system handles all major library functions. In addition, the CD-ROM workstations offer indexing, abstracts, or full text of

periodical articles. On-line database access to a vast array of information is also available through reference services.

Technology Environment

All M.B.A. candidates are expected to achieve literacy in the use of the standard computer software used in today's business environments. DOS-based and Macintosh microcomputer laboratories are available for course-related computing in accounting, finance, quantitative methods, and decision sciences. They also offer workshops and individual assistance. Computer instruction is further integrated in the preparation of the International Business Plans.

Placement

The Career Development Office's programs and counseling facilitate job and internship searches, both in the United States and abroad. It provides career counseling, workshops and videotapes on job search skills, coaching for job and internship searches, and a library of internationally oriented career information. Students have access to databases on internship opportunities and to the Institute's 1,000 M.B.A. alumni, who are available to discuss students' career interests and job hunting in their fields and geographic areas.

Admission

Applicants to the M.B.A. programs must have a bachelor's degree from an approved college or university in the United States or the equivalent, with a minimum grade point average of 3.0 on a 4.0 scale. All M.B.A. applicants must submit the GMAT score report and demonstrate advanced foreign language proficiency, or else extend their program with summer language study. Non-native English speakers must submit a minimum TOEFL score of 550 for the twenty-one-month program and a minimum score of 600 for the ten-month program. Preference is given to applicants with prior business experience.

Finances

The 1995–96 tuition and fees are $15,245 per year for the twenty-one-month M.B.A. program and $22,845 for the

ten-month M.B.A. program. Personal expenses for housing, food, books and supplies, and other incidentals are estimated at an additional $7500 per year.

Competitive half-tuition scholarships are available to students who combine academic merit with international experience. Scholarship applicants must meet eligibility requirements and complete their admission and scholarship application procedures by the date specified on the scholarship application form.

In addition, some forms of need-based financial aid, available only to U.S. citizens and eligible noncitizens, have application deadlines.

International Students

In recent years, the largest numbers of international M.B.A. students have come from Norway, Japan, France, Thailand, Germany, Belgium, Finland, Denmark, and Austria.

Non-native speakers of English must use English as their language of study to fulfill the language component. Students who demonstrate exceptionally high levels of written and oral English may take other elective courses in English or study a third language if they qualify at the appropriate level.

In addition to the required orientation for all new students, there is a supplementary orientation for international students and other workshops during the academic year.

Application Facts and Dates

Application may be made at any time, provided it is received at least one month prior to the applicant's proposed semester of enrollment or three months in advance for international students residing in their home countries. Applicants are notified of their admission status within four weeks after the application file is complete.

To request literature about the Monterey M.B.A. or if there are questions regarding application procedures, students should contact:

Monterey Institute of International
  Studies
Admissions Office
425 Van Buren Street
Monterey, California 93940
Telephone: 408-647-4123
Fax: 408-647-6405

Nanyang Technological University

> ## AN M.B.A. WITH A DIFFERENCE
>
> *The School's M.B.A. programs are characterized by a unique blend of rigorous general management and specialized functional training. The programs capitalize on the strength of the faculty, a highly qualified staff with tried business and professional experience. A global perspective, in terms of structure, curricula, and teaching pedagogy, is emphasized in the programs. Regional and international field trips are an integral feature of the programs. International student exchange programs with reputable universities abroad are also included to inculcate a global outlook in our participants.*
>
> —Teck-Meng Tan, Dean

Programs and Curricular Focus

The objectives of the Nanyang program are to prepare graduates to assume management and leadership roles in business and the professions, to prepare and equip them with general knowledge in management and business issues, and to provide particular knowledge in their selected area of specialization.

In line with the University's continued effort toward academic excellence and to meet the needs of industry for professionally trained managers and entrepreneurs, the University offers a series of M.B.A. programs with specializations. The seven specializations are accountancy, banking and finance, business law, hospitality and tourism management, international business, management of information technology, and management of technology.

The University's collaboration with the MIT Sloan School of Management also makes available to participants in the M.B.A. programs the best in graduate business education.

To complete the M.B.A. program, participants are required to take sixteen subjects, complete a dissertation, undertake a compulsory overseas business mission, and submit a business study report. The sixteen subjects include core subjects, functional subjects in the participant's area of specialization, and electives. Subjects in other functional specializations also serve as electives.

Two of the M.B.A. programs have been accorded professional recognition by professional bodies in Singapore and the United Kingdom. The first is the M.B.A. accountancy program. This degree is recognized by the Institute of Certified Public Accountants of Singapore as a professional qualification, without further examination, subject only to approved practical experience. It is also recognized by the Public Accountants Board (Singapore).

The second is the M.B.A. business law program. Graduates of this program who have completed selected modules will be accorded recognition by the United Kingdom Institute of Chartered Secretaries and Administrators, without further examination, subject to approved practical experience.

A dissertation allows participants to integrate the knowledge acquired during the program with their managerial and business experience. To encourage interaction, teamwork, and cross-fertilization of ideas, participants may elect to complete their dissertation on a group basis.

The student exchange program enables M.B.A. participants to study at another overseas graduate school for one trimester to gain valuable international experience. M.B.A. participants are allowed to transfer credits from approved universities, up to a maximum of four subjects (six subjects for participants in the M.B.A. international business program).

A typical M.B.A. calendar is as follows: trimester 1: July-October (14 weeks, with 1-week recess in October), trimester 2 (first half): October-December (six weeks, with 4-week recess in December), trimester 2 (second half): January-February (eight weeks, with 1-week recess in February), trimester 3: March-June (14 weeks with 4-week recess in June).

Students and the M.B.A. Experience

The enrollment for the entire university as of July 1994 was 13,114, comprising 11,052 undergraduate students and 2,062 graduate students.

Participants in the M.B.A. program come from a broad spectrum of disciplines and bring to the classroom a diversity of experience and backgrounds. An important criterion for selection is the student's potential and aspirations for top management positions and business leadership.

❖ Global Focus

Regional and international business study missions are an integral feature of the programs. Fashioned after the MIT Sloan Fellows program, these missions are designed to expose students to the social, economic, and political environments of countries visited and to facilitate the forging of strategic linkages with business and governmental agencies in those countries.

The Faculty

A distinctive blend of academics and practitioners from industry participate in teaching. Faculty members are selected on the basis of superior and innovative teaching skills, wealth of knowledge, a sound research and publication track record, work experience, and their ability to establish rapport with students.

Special Features

The M.B.A. Business Study Mission is an important and integral part of the program. The mission enables participants to correlate classroom work with fieldwork and to observe management policy in practice as well as to be exposed to international cultural, political, and business environments. The objective is to analyze firsthand the opportunities and challenges arising from managerial, technological, political, and business developments in various countries and regions. Regional and international missions are organized on a regular basis. Apart from extending their perceptions and sharpening their skills in managing in a competitive and dynamic international environment, these missions also enable M.B.A. participants to forge valuable strategic linkages with business leaders and entrepreneurs abroad. All participants are required to undertake a compulsory overseas business study mission and submit a business study report upon completion of the mission.

The College and Environs

Nanyang Technological University (NTU) is one of two universities in Singapore. Established in 1981, the University has acquired a reputation as industry's University. Its research and academic programs are geared toward meeting the needs of business and industry.

The University is situated on a 500-acre campus located in the industrial heartland of Jurong in the southwestern part of Singapore, about 16 miles from the city's center. It is a modern campus with up-to-date teaching and research facilities as well as residential and recreational facilities for staff and students.

Admission

Admission requirements are a bachelor's degree from an accredited college or university; a minimum of two years of management, administrative, professional, or other relevant experience at the time of admission; an acceptable score on the Graduate Management Admissions Test (GMAT); and an acceptable score on the Test of English as a Foreign Language (TOEFL) for those applicants whose medium of instruction at the undergraduate level was not English.

Finances

The estimated cost for a full-time student, including registration, tuition, and exam fees, is $9000; living expenses are $15,000, for a total of $24,000.

International Students

An international student who is successful in gaining admission to the full-time M.B.A. program initially enters Singapore on a social visit pass. Once the candidate has registered as a full-time student of this program, he or she can apply for a student pass. International students may register for the full-time program only.

Application Facts and Dates

The deadline for applications is February 28. Applicants will be notified of the outcome of their application by April 30. There is an application fee of $20. Application inquiries should be made to:

Mrs. Loo Hiang Tan-Lee
M.B.A. Office
School of Accountancy and Business
Nanyang Technological University
Nanyang Avenue
Singapore 2253
Republic of Singapore
Telephone: 65-791-1744 Ext. 4722
Fax: 65-791-3561

New Hampshire College

Manchester, New Hampshire

REAL WORLD MANAGEMENT—THE M.B.A. AT NEW HAMPSHIRE COLLEGE

The M.B.A. degree at New Hampshire College has always been strongly linked to real-world management. From the very beginning we developed a degree with a practical orientation to the business world. And our focus is far more than business in the region or in the United States: we have as well an international orientation to the business world.

Our multinational culture at the Graduate School and our international programs that students may combine with the M.B.A. have long established us as an environment of choice for students directed toward careers in international business.

The response we receive from business leaders, from those who hire and employ our students, is that we are sending them the kind of leader that today's world demands.

—Jacqueline F. Mara, Dean

Programs and Curricular Focus

The New Hampshire College M.B.A. program provides students with a range of learning experiences. The case study method, teamwork, lecture, and practical experience are combined to prepare students for the expectations of complex business environments.

All students are required to take eleven core courses representing such disciplines of business management as financial management, managerial economics, organizational behavior, quantitative analysis, computer information systems, and business environment.

Students thereafter have the option of pursuing a choice of more than seventy electives either as part of their M.B.A. electives or by combining one or more of eleven certificate programs and six M.S. programs.

The certificate programs include the disciplines of accounting, artificial intelligence, computer information systems, finance, health administration, industrial relations, international business, manufacturing and service management, marketing, school business administration, and taxation.

Combined-degree programs are available with the M.S. degree in international business, finance, computer information systems, business education, accounting, or community economic development.

Students and the M.B.A. Experience

The Graduate School's diverse student body creates a dynamic atmosphere for learning. While some of the students enter the program directly out of college, most have two or more years of work experience to share in the classroom. The College realizes the need for students to gain a world view of business and has been successful in recruiting students from more than twenty-five countries.

Students range in age from 21 to 55 and represent a broad spectrum of academic backgrounds and disciplines. Women comprise 40 percent of the graduate enrollment, and international students represent 12 percent.

Forty percent of students have undergraduate degrees in business administration. Other academic backgrounds include engineering, social sciences, education, and the humanities.

❖ Global Focus

New Hampshire College's M.B.A. program includes students from around the world—Japan, Colombia, South Korea, Spain, Turkey, Mexico, South Africa, India, Taiwan, Canada, Russia, and Egypt are among the countries represented in the program.

In small-class settings students are exposed to one another's cultural

backgrounds and business practices, significantly enhancing their M.B.A. experience.

The M.B.A. curriculum is developed to incorporate the program's international perspective. Case studies and practical applications in required course work provide students with a critical understanding of global business issues.

In addition, elective options in such topics as multinational finance, international negotiations, and international trade and competitiveness can be taken with the M.B.A. degree. The Certificate in International Business and the M.S. in International Business may be pursued in combination with the M.B.A. degree.

The Faculty

New Hampshire College's faculty members are strongly oriented toward interactive teaching approaches. The focus is on direct involvement in the realities of business management. In addition to their superior academic credentials, the faculty members have extensive experience in business—many of them in international settings.

The Business School Network

Corporate Partnerships

The Institute for Management Research, Development and Assistance is a program of the Graduate School of Business. Its purpose is to conduct and provide business consulting and assistance services to private and nonprofit companies, both nationally and internationally.

The institute uses graduate students to support its activities in business research, training, and management assistance. Of special interest is its Center for International Business, which focuses on all facets of business in relation to international clients or U.S. clients with international requirements.

In addition, advisory boards composed of corporate leaders consistently assist the Graduate School in developing programs that best match the needs of the business community.

The College and Environs

New Hampshire College offers uncrowded, attractive surroundings and easy access to the cultural and other advantages of metropolitan centers. The campus is an hour's drive from Boston and within easy traveling distance of the state's seacoast, lakes, and mountain areas.

Technology Environment
Graduate students have access to a range of modern computing capabilities through the College laboratories. Personal computers, with applications such as Windows-based Lotus SmartSuite, are provided for instructional and student use at all locations. Access to a Digital MicroVax and an IBM mainframe is also available. All student computing laboratories are linked to the Internet.

Placement
New Hampshire College's Career Development Center provides extensive on-campus recruitment opportunities. In addition, internships for credit are available to full-time degree candidates approved by the faculty. Additional services include career advising and assistance in résumé preparation.

Admission
Students with bachelor's degrees from accredited institutions are invited to apply to New Hampshire College's M.B.A. program. Although many applicants have work experience in business or other professional settings, students who are just completing their undergraduate careers are also encouraged to apply.

Unconditional admission to the M.B.A. program requires that the student have previously completed specific business-related courses. Students lacking the courses may be required to take Graduate School of Business foundation courses.

Finances
Tuition and fees for 1995–96 for full-time students are $14,246, with additional fees of approximately $295. Books and supplies are about $1000 a year.

Application Facts and Dates
Admissions decisions are made on a rolling basis, with a letter normally sent to an applicant within two weeks after the file is complete. International students may obtain applications from the Center for International Education at New Hampshire College (telephone: 603-645-9629, fax: 603-645-9603). For more information, students should contact:

Dean, Graduate School of Business
New Hampshire College
2500 North River Road
Manchester, New Hampshire
  03106-1045
Telephone: 603-644-3102
Fax: 603-644-3144

New York University

New York, New York

THE STERN SCHOOL: A WORLD LEADER IN GLOBAL BUSINESS EDUCATION

The Stern School of Business offers an M.B.A. program that infuses every course with the principles of globalism, teamwork, and communication skills. Stern graduates are leaders in virtually every sector of the world's economy.

Our superb Management Education Center is located at the epicenter of the world's business decision making, a stone's throw away from the corporate suites of Wall Street and midtown Manhattan. We're visited by leaders of industry and finance on a continual basis. And we have a strong sense of community, with over half of our distinguished faculty living within a few blocks of the School.

As a training ground for people equipping themselves to lead business into the next century, Stern is more than the sum of its students, faculty, and curriculum. It's a laboratory where everyday ideas get tested and creative solutions are applied to complex business problems.

George G. Daly, Dean

Programs and Curricular Focus

The Stern M.B.A. program provides an integrated curriculum that establishes a solid foundation for success in business. The excellent faculty, strong global focus, and relationship with the professional community create opportunities for students to gain expertise.

Stern's curriculum is divided into three parts: the core courses, major courses, and electives. The core program, which students take in "blocks" or large cohort groups, provides analytical and conceptual foundations and hones the functional skills required to solve complex business problems. Students specialize in the second semester by taking elective courses that prepare them for summer internships. The program offers numerous electives taught by leading scholars. Independent surveys rank many of Stern's functional areas among the world's best. Most notable are international business, finance, information systems, marketing, and entrepreneurial studies.

Stern's novel Multidisciplinary Teambuilding Exercise (MET) marks the core's second semester. Small teams of students spend five weeks examining a company. The exercise stresses management communication and holistic business insights. The culmination of the MET finds teams presenting their corporate strategy to a Board of Directors composed of faculty members and business executives. Students concentrate on major and elective course work

during the second year, while the "block" structure continues in the required capstone courses.

Students and the M.B.A. Experience

Stern's integrative approach to management education requires teams of teachers to present a holistic view of a common problem. For example, Stern's analysis of General Motors' purchase of Electronic Data Systems incorporated several disciplines. The management professor outlined the strengths and weaknesses of corporate diversification. The information systems faculty member detailed the technological imperatives of the deal. The accounting professor pinpointed a financial concept that caused disputes between parent and subsidiary. Finally, the statistics professor charted the quantitative performance of corporate diversification strategies. This integrative approach brings subjects to life.

Stern students come from all over the world; one third of the students are from more than sixty-two countries. They form a lively community whose diversity enriches Stern. Students have ambitious and unique career goals. Many hope to work on Wall Street; others want to help emerging Eastern European companies, start new businesses, work with nonprofit organizations, and more. They do not limit their talents and capabilities to the classroom.

All students have a minimum of two years of work experience. They come

from many industries, and the majority range in age from 24 to 32. Women comprise 29 percent of the population, and minority students make up 9 percent. As undergraduates, Stern students have studied social sciences (38 percent), business administration (29 percent), mathematics/science (23 percent), and humanities (10 percent).

❖ Global Focus

The Stern School is uniquely qualified to provide one of the world's most internationally oriented M.B.A. programs. Nowhere else can as wide and diverse a range of nationalities, cultures, and backgrounds be found in a business school. Stern's international business department offers many electives and the opportunity to co-major with another functional area.

As a founding member of the International Management Program, the first truly global exchange program, Stern has been providing students the opportunity to gain further education at one of over twenty other top business schools around the world. Stern is one of three U.S. graduate business schools to offer certification in European–North American Studies in Management.

For less formal education, student groups conduct trips to learn about business practices and cultures in other countries. Previous trips have included visits to the Far East, Eastern Europe, South America, Africa, Europe, and the Middle East. Through the M.B.A. Enterprise Corps, Stern graduates have acquired jobs in countries that are transforming from socialist to free market economies.

Special Features

The Entrepreneurs' Exchange, Graduate Finance Association, and Graduate Marketing Association enable students to discuss career options. Student-run professional consulting groups, such as the Urban Business Assistance Corporation (UBAC), help members of minority groups and women start businesses. The European-American Consulting Forum enables students to consult for multinational firms.

The Office of Student Activities is committed to enhancing the lives of

The new Management Education Center at the Stern School of Business.

students and providing close interaction among faculty members, administrators, and students. There are several Dean's Hours, which enable students to meet informally to discuss pressing issues. Faculty members meet with students through activities such as the Take a Faculty Member to Lunch program. Students meet alumni and other corporate executives at special events, such as Stern's Annual Alumni Business Conference, and through speaking engagements like "Meet America's CEO's."

Faculty

The faculty members bring practical business expertise into the classroom. One third hold non-U.S. passports. They were among the first in management education to recognize the need to balance solid research with strong classroom skills. They unanimously agreed to lend equal weight to teaching effectiveness and research skills when considering promotion and tenure.

Stern professors often rank highest for published work. The 200 full-time and 90 adjunct faculty members are regularly sought as consultants by such organizations as the World Bank, General Electric, AT&T, and General Motors.

The Business School Network

Prominent business leaders teach in the classroom and also speak frequently at student-organized events.

Prominent Alumni

Over 70,000 Stern alumni hold positions in every major industry worldwide. Stern counts among its alumni a number of notable business leaders, including Fiona Biggs, President of Dreyfus Strategic

World Investing Fund; Alan Greenspan, Chairman of the Federal Reserve; Sten Gustafsson, Chairman of the Board of Saab Scania; Shigekuni Kawamura, President of Dainippon Ink and Chemicals, Inc.; Jeffrey Koo, Chairman and CEO of Chinatrust Commercial Bank; Ismail Merchant, film producer and President of Merchant Ivory Productions; Marion Sandler, President and CEO of Golden West Financial Corporation; Leonard N. Stern, Chairman and CEO of The Hartz Group, Inc.; and Tatsuro Toyoda, President of Toyota Motor Company.

The College and Environs

New York University, established in 1831, has thirteen schools, colleges, and divisions at five major centers in Manhattan. The graduate business school was opened in 1916.

Stern has over thirty student organizations that enhance extracurricular life at the School. Students have free use of the Coles Sports and Recreation Center, one of NYC's best-equipped fitness facilities. The cultural wealth of New York City enriches students. Numerous off-Broadway theaters, concert halls, jazz clubs, and cafés are within steps of campus.

Facilities

In the 1980s, several internationally renowned research centers were established at the University. They are the Center for Japan-U.S. Business and Economic Studies, the Salomon Center, the Glucksman Institute for Research in Securities Markets, and the Center for Entrepreneurial Studies. In 1992, the Stern School opened the Management Education Center (MEC). The MEC

offers spacious, modern classrooms as well as advanced computing and communications technology.

Placement

Stern's Office of Career Development offers recruiting, counseling, and career development services. First-year students begin with summer internship programs and special workshops. Second-year students utilize extensive recruiting activities, company presentations, and alumni networking opportunities.

Over 200 companies recruit Stern students for full-time employment. The major industries chosen by graduates are investment banking (30 percent), consulting (16 percent), commercial banking (13 percent), other diversified financial industries (9 percent), consumer products (7 percent), and other industries (25 percent).

Admission

The M.B.A. program is open to any qualified person who holds a bachelor's degree from an accredited undergraduate institution. When reviewing applications, the candidate's previous academic work, GMAT score, nature and extent of previous work experience, personal essays, and letters of recommendation are evaluated. All applicants whose native language is not English must take the TOEFL. Interviews are conducted by Admission Committee invitation only.

Finances

Full-time tuition and fees for the 1994–95 academic year were $20,210. Merit-based scholarships are available.

International Students

Over one third of Stern's class comes from outside of the United States. The Management Communication Program offers a seven-day seminar: Communicating in American Business. The workshop offers an opportunity to work with faculty members and businesspeople. Several student groups promote international partnerships throughout Stern.

Application Facts and Dates

The full-time M.B.A. program begins in the fall only (March 31 deadline). For more information, students should contact:

Mary Miller
Director of Graduate Admissions
Leonard N. Stern School of Business
New York University
44 West Fourth Street, Suite 10-160
New York, New York 10012-1126
Telephone: 212-998-0600
Fax: 212-995-4231
E-mail: sternmba@stern.nyu.edu

Northeastern University

Boston, Massachusetts

> *Established in 1952, Northeastern University's Graduate School of Business Administration offers five M.B.A. programs. This text focuses on the full-time M.B.A. programs. Prospective students who intend to continue working full-time should contact the Market Center for information about the Part-Time M.B.A., High Technology M.B.A., or Executive M.B.A. programs. All M.B.A. programs are accredited by the American Assembly of Collegiate Schools of Business (AACSB).*
>
> —Ellen Ober, Director

Programs and Curricular Focus

The Cooperative Education M.B.A. Program grows out of Northeastern's sustained success in combining work and study. After six intensive months of acquiring skills and knowledge, Cooperative Education M.B.A. students join the work force in paid positions appropriate to entry-level M.B.A.'s; six months later, they return to the classroom for another nine months of study. The entire program, including the six months of résumé-building experience, is completed within twenty-one months. Cooperative M.B.A. students are admitted in January and June of each year.

In the two-year full-time M.B.A. Program, students stay connected to the work force through relationships with mentors and through internships, independent study, and special consulting projects. A typical entering class includes students from about twenty-five other countries. Career goals can be equally diverse. Students are admitted to this program each September.

In both programs, students master a general management curriculum and are welcome to tailor their electives to special interests. Electives can be taken within any of Northeastern's nine graduate and professional schools. Independent study projects can be designed for in-depth pursuit of a subject of special interest. Curricula for both programs were revised in 1994. Brochures of the individual M.B.A. programs elaborate the missions, objectives, required courses, and elective offerings of each one.

The Faculty

More than 100 full-time professors, organized in six groups and eighteen functional areas, teach M.B.A. students in the Graduate School of Business Administration. Their credentials, experience, research interests, and publications are profiled in a booklet that will be mailed on request. Many are active as consultants to businesses around the world. All are accustomed to being challenged on the practical applications of their research.

Placement

M.B.A. students at Northeastern have their own dedicated Career Center next to their classrooms and lounges. Recognizing the changing nature of the work force, Northeastern actively trains students in a broad range of skills for job search and career advancement. Workshops are tailored each year to student needs. More than half of the M.B.A. Career Center Director's time is spent creating and renewing relationships with local and national employers. The M.B.A. Career Center serves the employers by matching résumés for employment openings and provides students with advanced technology for targeting job search campaigns. Panels of graduates and mentors provide stimulus and

support. Alumni are welcome to use the M.B.A. Career Center to refresh their skills.

Admission

Successful applicants demonstrate academic competence through their undergraduate records and a GMAT score; motivation and maturity are demonstrated through essays and recommendations. Personal interviews are required for admission to the Cooperative Education M.B.A. Program and are encouraged for the full-time M.B.A. Program. Prospective students are welcomed to campus by current students, who conduct tours and answer questions. When possible, prospective students accompany current students to classes.

Finances

Tuition costs for the full-time and Cooperative M.B.A. programs in 1994–95 totaled $33,600 (twenty-eight courses at $1200 per course, spread over twenty-one

months). Average earnings of about $15,000 during the Cooperative Education employment period help students defray these costs. Tuition rates, fees, rules, regulations, and curricula are subject to revision by the president and the Board of Trustees at any time.

Prospective students comparing costs of various programs are advised to compare the full tuition cost of the M.B.A. program rather than the cost per course or number of courses. Northeastern schedules on the quarter system; other schools schedule on the semester system. A school on the quarter system is likely to require more courses because each course is shorter, but the total cost is not necessarily greater. Comparing costs can be like converting currencies.

International Students

The University's International Student Office helps with the issues associated with living in a foreign country. It offers counseling on immigration regulations, as

well as with academic, financial, and personal concerns. The office also acts as a liaison between the departments, colleges, and agencies concerned with foreign nationals in the academic community.

Application Facts and Dates

The application deadline for the full-time M.B.A. Program is May 1 (for September enrollment). The deadline for the January Cooperative Education class is November 1, and for the June Cooperative Education class, the deadline is April 15. Students are admitted on a rolling basis. Decisions are made within a month after receipt of a complete application.

Graduate School of Business
350 Dodge Hall
360 Huntington Avenue
Northeastern University
Boston, Massachusetts 02115
Telephone: 617-373-2714
Fax: 617-373-8564

Nova Southeastern University

Fort Lauderdale, Florida

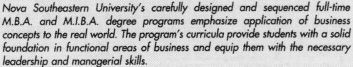

> *Nova Southeastern University's carefully designed and sequenced full-time M.B.A. and M.I.B.A. degree programs emphasize application of business concepts to the real world. The program's curricula provide students with a solid foundation in functional areas of business and equip them with the necessary leadership and managerial skills.*
>
> —Dr. Robert C. Preziosi, Dean

Programs and Curricular Focus

Nova Southeastern University's School of Business and Entrepreneurship offers innovative and highly flexible full-time Master of Business Administration (M.B.A.) and Master of International Business Administration (M.I.B.A.) degree programs designed for students with an undergraduate degree who have little or no work experience. The format and schedule enable students to enroll full-time and complete all degree requirements in one calendar year. The program format consists of four terms or blocks per year, commencing in January, April, July, and October. Students may enter the program in any term and enroll in classes scheduled on Monday through Thursday. Although not recommended, students may also choose to enroll for classes in the weekend program. The weekend classes include adult, postentry professional students who are pursuing graduate degrees on a part-time basis.

The school also offers a joint program leading to a simultaneous awarding of the J.D. and the M.B.A. or M.I.B.A. degrees. Students admitted to the joint program must complete the first-year program at the law center (28 hours). They are not permitted to enroll in courses at the School of Business and Entrepreneurship during that period.

Students and the M.B.A. Experience

The typical student enrolled in the full-time M.B.A. program is 27 years of age, with less than two years of full-time work experience. Fifty-four percent of the students are men, and minority students make up 28 percent of the population. Southeastern states send 53 percent of the School of Business and Entrepreneurship

students, while 31.5 percent of the student body comes from Northeastern states.

Students in the full-time M.I.B.A. program bring a wide variety of geographic and academic diversity to the classroom. The average age is equivalent to that of the M.B.A. student; however, the ethnic distribution is quite broad. Twenty-four percent of M.I.B.A. students are Hispanic, 22 percent are Asian or Pacific Islander, and 13 percent are African American. The majority of M.B.A. and M.I.B.A. students possess undergraduate degrees in business administration; however, such a degree is not a requirement.

Special Features

Full-time M.B.A. and M.I.B.A. students are required to fulfill the internship requirement before graduation. The internship consists of 240 work hours in a private or public institution. The ultimate goal of the internship requirement is to help the student gain further insight into the practical nature of business. Block-Buster Video, the Florida Marlins, Smith-Barney-Shearson, and Holy Cross Hospital are but a few of the high-quality organizations that have trained and supported NSU's M.B.A. and M.I.B.A. students.

The Faculty

All full-time faculty members at the School of Business and Entrepreneurship have earned doctorates in their respective fields and have either owned their own business, worked in business, or engaged in consulting. A national core of adjunct faculty complements NSU's full-time professional staff. The diverse backgrounds and years of experience of the

faculty facilitate in-depth discussion across a broad spectrum. A special effort is made to integrate practical with theoretical points of view.

The College and Environs

Nova Southeastern University is located on 200 acres in the town of Davie, Florida, just southwest of Fort Lauderdale. While the students enjoy a quiet, safe, suburban campus, NSU is easy to reach by public and private transportation. The graduate School of Business and Entrepreneurship is located on a separate 10-acre campus in downtown Fort Lauderdale.

The area is a principal coastal region in South Florida. The climate is subtropical and has an average year-round temperature of 75 degrees. The nearby cities of Fort Lauderdale and Miami offer many activities, including the Fort Lauderdale Museum of Art, the Museum of Science and Discovery, the Center for Performing Arts, the Miami Dolphins training camp, Bayside Marketplace, and Cocowalk.

Facilities

To provide a high-quality educational experience, the School has invested many resources to improve the students' technological and research training. One of the University's major computer resources, the MicroLab, offers hardware and software resources for course work and workshops based on applied microcomputer technology. The lab has the most popular microcomputers—IBM, Zenith, Gateway, and Apple—and on-line facilities are available for access to the UNIX operating system.

Also, the Albert and Birdie Einstein Library houses the University's major collection of books and journals in the humanities and sciences. Its more than 75,000 volumes can be searched through the library's computer catalog. In addition, more than twenty specialized indexes in CD-ROM format are available, as is dial-up access to the on-line catalog.

Placement

The purpose of NSU's Career Resource Center is to assist students in all aspects of the decision-making, planning, and placement process. Its mission is to support students and alumni and enhance their development through a variety of career-related services. The center strongly encourages active participation in students' development throughout their college years and beyond.

Admission

Admission to NSU's full-time M.B.A. and M.I.B.A. programs is competitive and is based on a number of important factors, including a student's undergraduate grade point average, Graduate Management Admission Test scores, letters of recommendation, and a 500- to 1,000-word essay.

Finances

Financial support is usually provided in the form of loans, with eligibility based on financial need. Individuals wishing to apply for financial assistance must fill out the NSU financial aid application and a College Scholarship Service Financial Aid Form (FAF). Financial aid transcripts must be submitted from each institution that the student previously attended, regardless of whether financial aid was received. Estimated costs for the one-year M.B.A. or M.I.B.A. degree, including room and board, range from $24,000 to $26,000. Students who have questions concerning financial assistance are encouraged to contact the office of Student Financial Aid at 800-522-3243 (toll-free).

International Students

International applicants must submit a TOEFL score of 550 or higher, accompanied by a copy of their undergraduate transcripts printed in or translated to English. Transcripts must show specific subjects taken and the grade earned in each. If grades are expressed other than in an American system, a statement from the school must accompany the transcript showing conversion to an American scale. Diplomas, certificates, or general letters indicating attendance at a school do not substitute for transcripts. In addition, all international student applicants must submit transcripts and documents from international institutions to World Education Services, Inc., for a multipurpose evaluation of the undergraduate degree earned and the institution granting it.

To further develop the student, graduate assistantships are available to students who have completed the first level of courses in the M.B.A. or M.I.B.A. program. The assistantships pay the equivalent of the course tuition in exchange for negotiated student services.

Application Facts and Dates

Application deadlines are March 1, May 31, August 30, and November 30. For more information, contact:

Mr. Pablo R. Zayas
Marketing Manager
Nova Southeastern University
3100 SW Ninth Avenue
Fort Lauderdale, Florida 33315
Telephone: 800-672-7223 Ext. 1566
  (toll-free)
Fax: 305-476-4865

Ohio University

Athens, Ohio

> **EXPERIENCE THE DIFFERENCE**
>
> *Our mission in the College of Business at Ohio University is to provide a learning environment that enables individuals to develop the knowledge, skills, and capabilities needed for success in the complex, global business community of the twenty-first century.*
>
> —C. Aaron Kelley, Dean

Programs and Curricular Focus

An intense thirteen-month learning experience, the full-time M.B.A. program uses an action-learning format that places the learner into exactly the type of projects and work situations that he or she will face as a leader of information-age organizations in the twenty-first century. The students learn basic business concepts but learn them in the context of their use, maximizing the students' ability to both recall and apply those concepts as they move back into the work world. The students develop the skills (communication, collaboration, teamwork) and the personal characteristics (initiative, creativity, personal responsibility) that are becoming so necessary to succeed. The understanding of the complexities of international business is enhanced through participation in the Joint Student Study Project Abroad. Comfort with information technology increases dramatically as the students regularly access information through the resources of the Internet, collaborate electronically over time and space, and develop and make professional-level computer-driven presentations.

Classes are lock-stepped beginning August 1 and ending September 1. The central learning core of the program is a series of projects. Students approach and solve the problems, in groups and individually. As students approach the problem, content is presented to them in modules, with each module presented at the time when it is useful to the students for solution of the current learning problem. Modules are delivered by a core faculty team.

Because of the learning environment, students learn to work utilizing the latest information technology, and they learn how to work together collaboratively, managing ill-structured problems with a minimum of direction.

The M.B.A. program is accredited by the American Assembly of Collegiate Schools of Business.

Students and the M.B.A. Experience

There are about 40 students in the full-time M.B.A. program; all parts of the United States and many other countries are represented. About half of the students have liberal arts or technical backgrounds. Diversity of class makeup is a priority. The typical class is about 50 percent women; age ranges from 21 to 45, experience ranges from summer internships to 20 years, minorities range from 5 to 10 percent, and about 40 percent of the student body is international (from such countries as Hungary, Germany, Hong Kong, Belgium, China, Ghana, India, Taiwan, France, Thailand, and Malaysia). There are a number of graduate student associations on campus, including an active M.B.A. student association that sponsors many activities.

❖ Global Focus

In addition to an overall global perspective, there is a mandatory requirement for each student to participate in the Joint Student Study Project Abroad. This project is a two-week experience in which students are placed in teams with students from the host country; each team is assigned to one company, analyzes a problem of the company's choosing, and then presents the results to management.

The Faculty

Program modules are delivered by faculty members who hold doctoral degrees and have relevant experience. For a class of 40 full-time M.B.A. students, 6 faculty members are assigned to the class; as an inte-

grated team they are responsible for the selection of projects and the modules to be delivered. The team relies on other faculty members within the College to deliver modules depending on the expertise needed for the problem at hand. Typically, the core team is composed of men and women faculty members with domestic and international experience and provides expertise in accounting, management, business law, finance, human resource management, management information systems, operations, marketing, and quantitative business analysis.

The Business School Network

Corporate Partnerships

Corporate leaders from Athens and other communities are asked to be part of continuous improvement teams that reside within the College of Business. These continuous improvement teams deal with student development and curriculum development, among other things.

The Executive Advisory Board and the Society of Alumni and Friends are composed of business managers who provide advice and direction to the program. Often members of these organizations become mentors to students; meetings are formally set up in fall and spring quarters to introduce these businesspeople to M.B.A. students.

The College and Environs

Founded in 1804, Ohio University has grown from a single building to 108 principal buildings covering 623 acres. Full-time enrollment was about 18,000 in 1994–95, including about 2,200 in the Graduate College, University-wide. Student facilities include the aquatic center, an indoor ice-skating rink, a golf course, and basketball, tennis, and racquetball courts.

Facilities

Ohio University's Alden Library, a modern seven-story air-conditioned building, has well over a million bound volumes, including more than 50,000 documents on business topics. Alden is a repository for U.S. government documents.

Technology Environment

The College of Business is wired for information technology well into the twenty-first century. The physical and technological environments are designed to support the team-oriented, project-based nature of the learning process.

The College of Business Administration maintains four microcomputer labs containing a mixture of Macintosh and IBM-compatible computers. Numerous word processing, spreadsheet, database, graphics, and statistical software packages are available in these labs. In addition, the College of Business maintains a Digital Equipment Corporation VAX 6210 connected to an instructional terminal lab. All facilities are fully networked together and to the Ohio University wide-area network, which includes IBM mainframes, on-line library systems, electronic mail, and Internet access.

Placement

There are two major recruiting fairs at Ohio University for meeting employers, as well as a constant flow of campus visits by recruiting organizations. A listing of companies who wish to interview is posted weekly on the campuswide electronic network, and students are encouraged to sign up for interviews with companies of their choice.

Admission

Factors considered for admission include undergraduate grade point average, scores on the GMAT (Graduate Management Admission Test), work experience, a personal essay, an interview (in person or by phone), and recommendations. Successful applicants typically have at least a 3.0 undergraduate cumulative average (on a 4.0 scale) and a score of 500 or better on the GMAT. In addition, international applicants typically have a TOEFL score of 600 or better. All applicants for admission must submit two official transcripts of undergraduate work and three letters of recommendation.

Finances

For 1994–95, the comprehensive fee for a normal quarter's load (9–18 hours inclusive) was $1430 for Ohio residents and $2789 for nonresidents. The fee for the Joint Student Study Project Abroad was $1500. In addition, there was a general fee of $243 per quarter and a program activity fee of $150 per quarter. Scholarships of up to $7224 and/or tuition waivers are available to qualified applicants based on merit. A number of scholarships have been designated for members of qualified minority groups. Awards of aid are generally announced in May.

Both University and private housing are available for single and married students. Housing costs vary from $400 to $600 per month, depending upon accommodations and furnishings. Room and board costs in University housing were $1500 per quarter in 1994–95.

International Students

About 40 percent of the candidates are international students who represent such countries as Hungary, Germany, Hong Kong, Belgium, China, Ghana, India, Taiwan, France, Thailand, and Malaysia, among others.

Application Facts and Dates

Applications, with a $25 fee and all supporting credentials, must be received no later than April 1. Students are encouraged to forward application materials well in advance of the April deadline. Students are notified no later than May 1 about acceptance into the program. Prerequisites include successful completion of one course each in accounting, economics, statistics, and critical thinking (e.g., logic, persuasion, rhetoric, cognitive methods, integrated case courses, literary analysis, and econometrics, to name a few) with at least a grade of B. In addition, there needs to be evidence of computer proficiency in word processing and spreadsheets. For additional information, students should contact:

Graduate Student Affairs Officer
Copeland Hall
College of Business Administration
Ohio University
Athens, Ohio 45701
Telephone: 614-593-2007

FACULTY LIST

School of Accountancy
Yining Chen, Ph.D., Assistant Professor.
Ted Compton, Ph.D., Professor.
James Cox, Ph.D., Associate Professor.
Carol Anne Hilton, Ph.D., Assistant Professor.
Joseph N. Hilton, Ph.D., Assistant Professor.
Leon Hoshower, Ph.D., Associate Professor.
Robert Jamison, Ph.D., Professor.
E. James Meddaugh, Ph.D., Professor.
David Senteney, Ph.D., Assistant Professor.
Florence Sharp, Ph.D., O'Bleness Professor of Accounting.
Robert Sharp, Ph.D., Associate Professor and Director.

Department of Finance
Bruce Berlin, Ph.D., Assistant Professor.
Natalie Chieffe, Ph.D. candidate, Assistant Professor.
Jeffrey A. Manzi, Ph.D., Assistant Professor.
Azmi Mikhail, Ph.D., Professor.
Dwight Pugh, Ph.D., Associate Professor.
Ganas K. Rakes, Ph.D., O'Bleness Professor of Banking and Chair.
John Reynolds, M.B.A., Lecturer.

Department of Management Systems
Frank Barone, Ph.D., Associate Professor and Associate Dean.

Thomas W. Bolland, Ph.D., Professor of Quantitative Business Analysis.
Carl Bridges, Ph.D., Associate Professor.
Gerard Carvalho, Ph.D., Associate Professor.
Garth Coombs, Ph.D., Assistant Professor.
Kenneth Cutright, Ph.D., Associate Professor.
Francis Fuller, A.M., Associate Professor.
Stephen Fuller, D.B.A., Professor.
C. Michael Gray, J.D., Lecturer in Law.
Patricia C. Gunn, J.D., Associate Professor of Law.
John Keifer, Ph.D. candidate, Lecturer.
Mary Carter Keifer, J.D., Associate Professor of Law.
C. Aaron Kelley, Ph.D., Dean, College of Business.
Manjulika Koshal, Ph.D., Professor of Business Administration.
Arthur Marinelli, Ph.D., Professor of Law and Chair.
Clarence Martin, Ph.D., Associate Professor.
Peggy Miller, Ph.D., Lecturer.
Richard Milter, Ph.D., Associate Professor.
Valerie Perotti, Ph.D., Professor.
Bonnie Roach, Ph.D., Associate Professor of Human Resource Management.
Jessie C. Roberson Jr., J.D., Associate Professor of Law.
Richard C. Scamehorn, M.B.A., Executive in Residence.

John Schermerhorn, Ph.D., O'Bleness Professor of Management.
Hugh Sherman, Ph.D., Assistant Professor.
Lucian Spataro, Ph.D., Professor.
John E. Stinson, Ph.D., Professor.
Rebecca Thacker, Ph.D., Assistant Professor of Human Resource Management.
Lane Tracy, Ph.D., Professor.
Ed Yost, Ph.D., Associate Professor.

Department of Marketing
Catherine N. Axinn, Ph.D., Associate Professor.
Elizabeth Blair, Ph.D., Assistant Professor.
Barbara Dyer, Ph.D., Assistant Professor.
Ashok Gupta, Ph.D., Professor and Chair.
Timothy P. Hartman, Ph.D., Associate Professor.
Daniel Innis, Ph.D., Assistant Professor.
Kahandas Nandola, Ph.D., Professor.

Department of Management Information Systems
John Day, Ph.D., Professor and Chair.
Ellsworth Holden, M.A., Assistant Professor.
Hao Lou, Ph.D., Assistant Professor.
Thomas G. Luce, Ph.D., Professor.
Anne H. McClanahan, Ph.D., Professor.
James Perotti, Ph.D., Professor.
David Sutherland, Ph.D., Assistant Professor.

Pace University

New York and Westchester, New York

A DYNAMIC M.B.A.—DEVELOPING GLOBAL MANAGERS FOR THE TWENTY-FIRST CENTURY

In a rapidly changing business environment, major corporations depend on Pace University's Lubin School of Business to provide global business managers to lead them into the twenty-first century. Lubin's state-of-the-art M.B.A. program, recently revised and continually being improved, carefully integrates theory and practical applications and offers exciting opportunities for experiential and team learning. Our campus locations, in downtown New York City, minutes away from Wall Street, and at the White Plains Graduate Center, convenient to the headquarters of Fortune 500 companies, provide particularly vibrant environments for professional development. Importantly, Lubin's distinguished faculty members are committed to excellence in teaching and are dedicated to producing successful graduates. Attesting to that success, Lubin alumni are and will continue to be leaders in all fields of business.

—Arthur L. Centonze, Dean

Programs and Curricular Focus

The M.B.A. degree program at the Lubin School of Business is characterized by a new curriculum that stresses professional skills while offering students the opportunity to specialize in accounting, business economics, financial management, information systems, international business, management, management science, marketing, or taxation. M.B.A. courses reflect the integrated, cross-functional way business operates. Global considerations appear in all appropriate courses, as do critical issues such as technology, ethics, work-force diversity, quality management, and entrepreneurship. Depending upon prior academic course work, between 36 and 61 degree credits are required for most specializations. All Lubin students must demonstrate proficiency in computing, business writing, and quantitative methods.

A core of foundation courses covers fundamental managerial and analytical skills. At the next level, the integrative core builds on the foundation courses to provide the managerial breadth of the curriculum. Cohort classes for the managerial skills courses place the same students together during their first year of study, creating a platform for mastering teamwork and setting up opportunities for networking throughout the M.B.A. experience and beyond. The critical business skills developed translate into greater job success and new opportunities long before graduation.

Lubin also offers a number of special programs for students seeking advanced professional business education. The One-Year M.B.A. in Financial Management program offers qualified business professionals and recent college graduates an accelerated M.B.A. program. The eighteen-month Executive M.B.A. program affords middle- and upper-level managers the opportunity to enhance and sharpen their business knowledge and skills. Also available are the J.D./M.B.A. program (in conjunction with the Pace University School of Law); Master of Science degree programs in accounting, economics, investment management, and taxation; post-master's Advanced Professional Certificate programs; and a doctoral program in business.

Students and the M.B.A. Experience

Lubin students are busy, highly motivated individuals who seek graduate business education to advance their careers or to enter the business world. The average M.B.A. student at Pace University has five to seven years of work experience and is 28 years old. Women comprise nearly 45 percent of the current enrollment, minority students 20 percent, and international students 21 percent. Approximately 75 percent of the student population is from the northeast region of the United States.

Students enter the Lubin M.B.A. program with a broad range of academic backgrounds. Thirty-eight percent pursued business at the undergraduate level, 27 percent engineering and technology, and 35 percent humanities, social sciences, physical sciences, mathematics, nursing, and education.

❖ Global Focus

Lubin's strong international focus and reputation for excellence attract many international students to its New York City and Westchester County campuses. These students' diverse cultural perspectives and backgrounds contribute significantly to the global focus and flavor of business education at Lubin. The Lubin School participates in a variety of student and faculty relationships with universities and business schools around the world. Since 1989, the School has been engaged in an exchange of faculty members and students with Tokyo Keizai University, including joint research projects in marketing and advertising. It has had an exchange program with Heidelberg University in Heidelberg and various business schools in Paris and Grenoble, France.

Special Features

New Lubin M.B.A. students participate in a special orientation program that includes a series of workshops and presentations designed to familiarize them with the curriculum, faculty, and student services. Full-time and part-time students take the same courses, taught by the same faculty members, throughout the M.B.A. program. During the first year of study, cohort groups of students participate in a 6-credit managerial theory and skills course. The faculty facilitates classwork through experiential and interactive team exercises, enabling students to increase their cognitive and effective capacity to build constructive relationships with individuals and groups.

The Faculty

Virtually all of the full-time faculty members are doctorally prepared, and 75 percent of the part-time faculty members hold doctoral degrees. The faculty members of the Lubin School are committed to excellence in teaching and the professional growth of students. Classes are small (average class size is 22 students), and professors are firmly committed to being accessible to students. Outside of the classroom, opportunities are provided for students to conduct research with faculty members, publish findings jointly, and take active roles in coordinating conferences and special programs.

The Business School Network
Corporate Partnerships
Top executives from major corporations participate in Lubin's Executive-in-Residence Program every year, providing opportunities for Lubin graduate students to interact with prominent business leaders from around the world. In addition, an advisory board of business executives and the School's extensive corporate network ensure that the curriculum reflects the changing needs of business.

The College and Environs
Founded in 1906, Pace University is a comprehensive, diversified, coeducational institution with campuses in New York City and Westchester County. Degrees are offered through the Dyson College of Arts and Sciences, the School of Computer Science and Information Systems, the Lubin School of Business, the School of Education, the Lienhard School of Nursing, and the School of Law. Pace University is chartered by the Regents of the State of New York and accredited by the Middle States Association of Colleges and Schools. The M.B.A. program may be pursued at the New York City Campus, which is a self-contained educational complex in lower Manhattan serving the adjacent Wall Street financial community, or the Lubin Graduate Center in White Plains, Westchester County, New York. The Graduate Center is located in the heart of the White Plains business district. Both locations provide easy access to the nation's most significant cultural resources, including major theaters, museums, and concert halls.

Facilities
The research facilities accessible to graduate business students include the University library's extensive holdings, the virtually unlimited library resources of the New York City area, and the University Computer Center. In addition to the computing facilities housed in Lubin's Chase Computer Center, there are computing facilities, including PCs, that are available exclusively for the Lubin graduate community. More than 400 IBM personal computers, mostly in student

labs, provide access to a variety of the most popular and useful software packages. The Lubin School of Business's Center for Applied Research, Center for Global Financial Markets, Center for International Business Studies, and Center for Innovation and Entrepreneurship offer students diverse research opportunities.

Placement
The University Career Development and Placement Services help graduate business students make informed choices. Pace's Cooperative Education Program places Lubin graduate students in paid, career-related working experiences while they pursue their degrees. Because of its close ties to business, the Pace Cooperative Education Program is one of the largest in the United States. Career counseling, which includes job search preparation, résumé writing, and interviewing skills, is provided. Leading corporations, banks, accounting firms, insurance companies, retailers, brokerage houses and nonprofit and government organizations regularly recruit Pace M.B.A. students and utilize Pace's Résumé Referral Program. The Alumni Mentor Program gives students an opportunity to speak with Pace alumni about their individual occupations, and the Pace Network offers a medium through which to obtain career information and develop personal contacts with Lubin graduates and other students.

Admission
Admission is open to qualified recipients of bachelor's degrees in any field from accredited undergraduate institutions. All applicants for the M.B.A., M.S., and doctoral programs are required to submit official Graduate Management Admission Test score reports. The Lubin School of Business welcomes applications from graduates of colleges and universities in other countries. International students are expected to have sufficient finances available to cover all expenses for the entire period of graduate study. Applicants whose native language is not English are required to submit official TOEFL scores. The evaluation of applicants is based upon capacity for scholarship as indicated by the undergraduate record, GMAT scores, class rank, previous graduate study (if any), letters of reference, career objectives, and other available information.

Finances
Tuition in 1994–95 was $425 per credit. The registration and library fee was $45 for 1 to 4 credits, $70 for 5 to 7 credits,

$100 for 8 to 11 credits, and $150 for 12 or more credits. Several deferment plans are available.

A number of graduate scholarships and assistantships are available. Scholarships are awarded on the basis of outstanding academic performance as indicated by the applicant's previous college record and standardized test scores. Research and administrative assistantships are available for full-time students. Graduate assistants received stipends of up to $4780 per year for 1994–95 and tuition remission for 24 credits. Students interested in applying for a graduate assistantship are advised to apply early because in-person interviews are required.

Room and board in 1994–95 cost $7200 for the academic year. Books, supplies, health insurance, and personal expenses are estimated to cost an additional $5500. Students planning to pursue summer study should anticipate an additional cost of $2800, excluding tuition and fees.

International Students
International students at the Lubin School make up about 20 percent of the enrollment. Home countries include Canada, China, Columbia, France, Germany, India, Japan, Mexico, Pakistan, Russia, Taiwan, and Turkey.

Pace University and the Lubin School of Business are dedicated to providing a supportive environment for international students. Special services are provided through the International Education Advisement Offices and the English Language Institute.

Application Facts and Dates
The application fee is $50. Application deadlines are July 31 for fall, November 30 for spring, April 30 for summer session I, and May 31 for summer session II. International applicants are requested to submit credentials one month earlier than the aforementioned dates. For more information, students should contact:

New York City Campus:
Office of Graduate Admission
Pace University
1 Pace Plaza
New York, New York 10038
Telephone: 212-346-1531
Fax: 212-346-1040

White Plains Campus:
Office of Graduate Admission
Pace University
1 Martine Avenue
White Plains, New York 10606
Telephone: 914-422-4283
Fax: 914-422-4287

Pepperdine University

Malibu, California

TWENTY-FIRST CENTURY GLOBAL LEADERS

Typical of its "cutting edge" desire in business education, Pepperdine University began "internationalizing" its graduate programs in business many years ago. As other schools are beginning to look at the global economy in business education, Pepperdine continues to offer cross-cultural studies, to utilize professors with extensive foreign experience, to attract top students (one third are international), and to offer foreign study and experience in selected programs.

The international environment at Pepperdine reflects small classes, projects cleverly designed for team effort, and professors with real-world experience and teaching excellence in their respective disciplines.

Pepperdine is not for those desiring only to observe. Pepperdine is for students motivated to boldly explore and participate in new, unfamiliar learning experiences.

—Dr. Stanley K. Mann, Director

Programs and Curricular Focus

Designed to prepare men and women for managerial leadership roles, the Master of Business Administration (M.B.A.) and Master of International Business (M.I.B.) degrees are offered in an environment that fosters an understanding of the behavioral aspects of management. The program organizes faculty and students to interact in a learning community. The curriculum emphasizes international business, ethics, communication, and decision-making skills. International concerns and ethics are specifically addressed in much of the curriculum.

The M.B.A. is offered in one or two years. Students who have prerequisite business courses and a minimum of two years of full-time work experience may be eligible for the eleven-month, 48-unit M.B.A. program. A two-year, twenty-month program is available for students with academic study in disciplines other than business and for those who lack significant work experience. All students in the M.B.A. program choose an emphasis in finance or marketing. A joint J.D./M.B.A. program is offered in conjunction with the School of Law.

The twenty-month M.I.B. program requires the first year of study in Malibu and the second year overseas, where students complete their course work and an internship. Several locations are offered in France and Germany. Language study in French or German is incorporated into the curriculum. While fluency is not required, it is preferred that a student have some knowledge of the language or show fluency in another.

Students and the M.B.A. Experience

The business school students represent a diverse range of professional and educational backgrounds. Such diversity contributes to a culture of collaboration in which experiences are utilized to enhance the practical, hands-on learning process. New students are quickly initiated into the M.B.A. program through the Communications Workshop. The three-day event develops the trust and camaraderie that characterize the entire M.B.A. experience. Teamwork is encouraged and reinforces the necessary competencies for today's business environment.

❖ Global Focus

While the full-time programs offer an international focus in both the M.I.B. and M.B.A. programs, the executive and professional programs address global issues. Of major significance is the Master of Science in Technology Management (M.S.T.M.), which prepares executives to anticipate and effectively compete in the international technology-driven business environment.

Special Features

Pepperdine is distinguished by programs designed to enhance the student's practical learning experience. During the first semester, students participate in the Civic Leadership Program, a nonprofit consulting project. It is an excellent opportunity for students to observe organizations and to recommend change. The project, in return, supports the community and has served nearly 100 organizations.

Ethical and legal issues are also reinforced through the Seminar in Business Ethics at the Nellis Federal Prison Camp outside Las Vegas, Nevada. Students interview a panel of white-collar criminals about the potential impact of business decisions.

The Faculty

Each academic year, about 20 members of the business school's faculty are selected to teach in the Malibu programs; over 90 percent hold Ph.D.'s. Faculty members represent a diverse range of teaching, research, and management experiences. Many remain active in business through consulting relationships and involvement with advisory boards. The small class sizes foster interactive and personal relationships between faculty and students.

The Business School Network

With over 20,000 graduates, Pepperdine University's School of Business and Management has one of the largest business school alumni networks in the United States.

Corporate Partnerships

The business school is active in the community, with close ties to corporations and industry through its professional and executive programs. The full-time M.B.A. and M.I.B. programs in Malibu benefit from the School's vast network of alumni and corporate relationships. Students have the opportunity to complete a practicum with an executive, to perform executive interviews, and to consult with nonprofit organizations.

Prominent Alumni

Pepperdine University's School of Business and Management has many alumni who are top executives of major corporations and leaders in the commu-

The Malibu Graduate Business Programs are located at Pepperdine University's main campus in Malibu, California.

nity. The Presidential/Key Executive M.B.A. program alone boasts a long list of impressive names in the business community, representing such industries as aerospace, manufacturing, health care, biotechnology, and entertainment.

The College and Environs

Founded in 1937, Pepperdine University is a private institution located in Malibu, California, about 35 miles northwest of Los Angeles, where the Santa Monica mountains meet the Pacific Ocean. The moderate climate and quiet city of Malibu provide an excellent location in which to live and learn, while Los Angeles remains accessible.

The School of Business and Management, established in 1969, pioneered the executive M.B.A. and developed its hallmark of practical-based business education. While the full-time programs enroll only about 150 new students each year, Pepperdine's business school is one of the largest in the United States. It offers part-time and executive programs at five educational centers in and around Los Angeles.

The Facilities

A variety of research facilities are also available to students. These include the Payson Library, libraries at the University's educational centers, and the School of Law library. Academic computing facilities are located in the School of Business and Management Center. Students have Internet access, and a telecommunications center has recently

been established at the School of Business and Management headquarters in Culver City.

Athletic facilities include an Olympic-size swimming pool, a track and soccer field, a weight room, tennis courts, and a racquetball court.

Placement

The Career Development Center recognizes the complexity of career planning and the variety of options available to Pepperdine graduates. It provides programs and services to meet the professional development needs of the students. The following services are among those offered: career consultation, professional development seminars, industry forums, internship support, an automated résumé referral system, a resource library, the alumni association, recruiting events, and on-campus interviewing. As a result, graduates from Pepperdine programs are sought by a variety of domestic and international firms seeking to fill leadership positions within their organizations.

Admission

Consideration is based on many factors in the application process. The average GPA is 3.0, and the average GMAT score is 550. While work experience is not required for the two-year M.B.A. program and the M.I.B. program, it is preferred and can greatly enhance an individual's application. Leadership qualities and personal characteristics are considered along with the written essays

and recommendations. The admission committee seeks individuals who display academic strength and show promise to make a positive contribution to the small-group and interactive classroom environment.

Finances

Tuition varies, depending upon length of program. Tuition for the 1994–95 academic year for the full-time programs was $9100 per trimester. Tuition for the part-time program was $570 per unit. Students typically enroll in 8 semester units per term, three times per year.

Merit-based scholarships and graduate assistantships are available to full-time students. The admission packet contains the information necessary to apply for scholarships.

On-campus graduate housing is available for $2165 per trimester. Typically, 4 students share a two-bedroom apartment. Many students choose to live off campus, with costs averaging $600 per month.

International Students

International students represent 31 percent of the enrollment in the full-time business programs. The Office of International Student Services provides credential evaluations, language tutoring, visa services, and ESL courses.

Application Facts and Dates

The application deadline is May 1 for fall entrance only. Admission is on a rolling basis, beginning in January. Decisions are made monthly and applicants notified immediately. For more information, students should contact:

Director of Marketing
School of Business and Management
Pepperdine University
24255 Pacific Coast Highway
Malibu, California 90263-4100
Telephone: 800-726-9283 (toll-free)
310-456-4858 (outside the
United States)
Fax: 310-456-4126
Internet: npapen@pepperdine.edu

Philadelphia College of Textiles & Science

Philadelphia, Pennsylvania

GRADUATE STUDY—AN ECLECTIC APPROACH

The Philadelphia College of Textiles & Science graduate programs include an M.B.A. program with seven major areas of study and an M.S. in Taxation degree program.

Our programs are designed to ensure that our graduate students are provided with an educational experience and the knowledge to be successful leaders in their chosen profession. Both full-time professors and experienced professionals are members of our faculty. The culture of our small, coeducational college is such that significant faculty-student interaction is a virtual certainty. While ongoing research is of the utmost importance, the primary emphasis of our graduate programs is on teaching and student learning of skills needed in modern global commerce. We are very proud of our faculty, students, and alumni, and we invite you to become a member of our team of dedicated professionals.

—Raymond R. Poteau, Dean

Programs and Curricular Focus

The M.B.A. program at Philadelphia College of Textiles & Science (PCT&S), M.B.A.: Leadership for the Year 2010, is designed to provide students with the skills and abilities that employers are looking for to lead corporate America into the twenty-first century—a global perspective, competence in leading-edge technology, and innovative and entrepreneurial thinking. The curriculum responds to global and managerial skills needed to be successful in the years to come as recently reported by the leading business publications such as the *Wall Street Journal, Forbes,* and the *Financial Times.* Students analyze important and challenging issues in an action-learning and team-building environment, while sharpening decision-making, managerial, and entrepreneurial skills. Furthermore, students develop the ability to interact and communicate with diverse groups, so that they can function effectively in a competitive business environment.

The program comprises eight core courses (22 credits), three option area courses (9 credits), a capstone course in strategic planning (3 credits), and one free elective (3 credits) that may be selected from the M.B.A. program or other graduate program. The eight core courses include Management Communications, the Art of Negotiations, and Managing in the 21st Century, along with courses in the functional areas of business. Students may select from one of

the option areas in international business, leadership, accounting, finance, marketing, taxation, or health-care management. It is also possible to construct a custom option based on special interests and goals. All students are required to fulfill foundation requirements that may be waived based on undergraduate curriculum and/or work experience.

Other opportunities at PCT&S include joint-degree programs. The joint degrees offered are an M.B.A./M.S. in Taxation (55 credits), an M.B.A./M.S. in textile marketing (58 credits), and an M.B.A./M.S. in instructional technology (55 credits).

Students and the M.B.A. Experience

Students come from the Northeast region of the country and abroad to study in the M.B.A. program at Philadelphia College of Textiles & Science. The average student is 30 years old and has eight years of work experience. Nearly one half of the students are women, and approximately 11 percent are international students.

❖ Global Focus

International dimensions are incorporated into all courses. In addition, students have the opportunity to participate in an overseas trip that exposes them to a number of foreign cultures and businesses. Over the last two years, the class

has traveled to France, Belgium, and Germany, where students met with business leaders, labor leaders, and academicians.

The Faculty

Philadelphia College of Textiles & Science is truly a teaching institution where the primary focus is the students. Classes are small (average size is 16), which allows for extensive faculty-student interaction. The M.B.A. faculty combines both full-time professors and business leaders from the Philadelphia area. For example, Total Quality Management is taught by a member of the Malcolm Baldridge National Quality Award Team. This unique combination provides an interesting mix of real-world experiences and applied research in the classroom.

The College and Environs

Founded in 1884, the Philadelphia College of Textiles & Science is an independent, career-oriented institution that offers both graduate and undergraduate programs of study. Currently, Philadelphia Textile offers eight professionally oriented graduate programs, each providing a blend of academic theory and real-world applications.

As a small, coeducational college, Philadelphia Textile fosters close relationships between faculty and students and enrolls a student body that is academically and culturally diverse. Philadelphia Textile is primarily a teaching institution that also encourages research as a service to industry and as a vehicle for faculty and student development. The 100-acre campus is situated 15 minutes from Center City Philadelphia, the fifth-largest city in the nation.

Facilities

The new Paul J. Gutman Library is truly a state-of-the-art facility. A fully computerized book catalog allows access via computer both in the library and from remote locations. The main book collection consists of over 80,000 volumes, with special emphasis in the areas of architecture, business, design, and textile arts. Networked electronic databases provide access to over 1,700 journals, publications, and newspapers, including Infotrac, General Business Index, and SEC 10K Filings. The library has over 500 journal titles available in full-text retrieval format.

Placement

Graduates of Philadelphia College of Textiles & Science are guaranteed lifetime assistance with career counseling. Last year, nearly 200 companies visited the campus, well above the national average of 23 recruiters per year. Full-time graduate students may take advantage of the extensive on-campus recruiting schedule. Evening hours are also available twice a week, and workshops in résumé writing, interview skills, and job search tips are scheduled regularly throughout the semester.

Admission

Candidates who seek admission are reviewed based on the merit of their academic record, work experience, and the required Graduate Management Admission Test (GMAT). Depending on the applicant's academic background, foundation courses may be required.

International students may begin in either the spring or fall semester. A minimum TOEFL score of 550 is required for students for whom English is not their native language. International students must provide proof of adequate funds to cover the cost of tuition, room and board, and expenses.

Finances

The estimated cost for full-time enrollment in 1995–96 is $6912 ($384 per credit). Books and supplies cost approximately $500.

International Students

Eleven percent of M.B.A. students at Philadelphia College of Textiles & Science come from outside the United States. International students must take the English language placement exam prior to registering for classes. The International Society is one of the largest groups on campus. It provides students with a network of support for problem solving, social activities, and general advising.

Application Facts and Dates

Applications are accepted for fall and spring semesters and are reviewed on a rolling basis. International applicants should send complete applications by June 1 for fall semester and October 1 for spring semester. For more information, applicants should contact:

Ms. Beth Vorosmarti
Director of Admissions
Philadelphia College of Textiles & Science
School House Lane and Henry Avenue
Philadelphia, Pennsylvania 19144
Telephone: 215-951-2943
Fax: 215-951-2907

Plymouth State College

Plymouth, New Hampshire

LEARN WITH WORKING PROFESSIONALS

The PSC M.B.A. program has students with an average age of 35, most of whom are working professionals. Our courses are delivered in an evening schedule so that both part-time and full-time students learn together, in classes averaging about 17 students. All of our classes are taught by full-time PSC faculty members, most of whom have extensive experience in business or government. Faculty members remain at the leading edge of their fields through continuing studies and publishing in their areas of expertise. A particularly exciting opportunity for M.B.A. students is the Small Business Institute (SBI) program; M.B.A. students team with a professor and conduct a consultation with a New Hampshire business. Since 1976, SBI student teams have earned thirty-one state, regional, and/or national awards from the Small Business Administration. Come to the beautiful Lakes Region at the foothills of the White Mountains of New Hampshire and learn with working professionals.

—William R. Benoit, Director, Graduate Studies in Business

Programs and Curricular Focus

As a regional state college of the University System of New Hampshire, Plymouth State College (PSC) is dedicated to bringing high-quality business education to regional and international students who join the journey to excellence. A major goal is to provide this educational experience at an extremely attractive cost to the student.

Because the students come from the most diverse of academic backgrounds, PSC has adopted a distinctive two-part curriculum. The first part consists of taking undergraduate courses or demonstrating competence in financial accounting, macroeconomics, microeconomics, statistics, psychology, and microcomputers. Students with a bachelor's degree in business would, ordinarily, have fulfilled these undergraduate requirements before beginning their graduate courses at PSC. Those students who have not already taken these undergraduate courses may complete them at any accredited college or university of their choice before coming to PSC or may complete this first part of the curriculum at PSC. Alternatively, the student may satisfy these first-part undergraduate requirements by examination, i.e., the College Level Entrance Proficiency (CLEP) or PSC competency examination(s). The PSC competency examinations are prepared, administered, and evaluated by PSC.

The second part of the curriculum consists of nine core and three elective graduate courses, for a total of twelve courses of 3 credits each (36 graduate credits). As an option, the student may complete a Master's Research Project (MRP) of 6 credits in lieu of two electives. The MRP can vary from traditional research to examination of a contemporary business problem. Also, there is the opportunity for individual enrollments and/or independent studies. The faculty has been quite eager to work with students on such projects. The nine core courses are modeled after the strongest academic curricula. These courses are Legal Environment of Business, Management of Organizational Behavior, Marketing Techniques, Quantitative Analysis for Business Decisions, Accounting for Managers, Financial Analysis and Decision Making, Operations Management, Managerial Economics, and Seminar in Executive Management.

As a benefit of the two-part curriculum approach, students who have completed the program's undergraduate competency requirements before their arrival at PSC can complete the M.B.A. program in nine months by taking four M.B.A. courses in each of three 12-week terms. This scheduling approach has the dual benefit of dramatic reductions in both tuition costs and the time to earn the M.B.A. degree.

The schedule allows for completion in different time periods as well. Many full-time students complete the program in anywhere from twelve to twenty-one months or more, depending on the number of course requirements that must be satisfied at the start of their program. Flexibility is a keynote of the program.

Students and the M.B.A. Experience

Students average 35 years of age, with over ten years of work experience. They come from banking, medical, retailing, manufacturing, government, and educational organizations, to name only a few. About 45 percent are women, 8 percent are members of minority groups, and 92 percent are from New Hampshire, Maine, Massachusetts, and Vermont. Each year, there are between 5 and 12 international students.

Students work in teams, develop joint papers, and make team presentations. The program averages between 15 and 20 full-time students and over 300 part-time working professionals, which enables the full-time students to gain much from the interaction with their working colleagues. As a result, many of the full-time students gain employment in the organizations of their part-time colleagues. This symbiotic relationship has flourished over the twenty-year history of the program.

Special Features

Because international students have diverse interests and come from many different countries, the faculty generously devotes time to individual enrollments and independent studies. These opportunities help the international student explore topics of interest. Typical topics are comparative studies in economics and/or law, marketing issues, and organizational behavior.

For international students desiring postgraduate training, the program has been successful in finding suitable placement. About one third of the international students take advantage of this postgraduate training.

The Faculty

The Department of Business at PSC has 23 full-time faculty members, all of whom teach in both the graduate and undergraduate programs. Four of the faculty members are women, and 3 are members of minority groups. Over half have extensive experience in business or management. Teaching and advising are strong components of the faculty culture and a great source of satisfaction to the faculty.

The Business School Network

The Board of Trustees of the University System includes several prominent business leaders who develop guidance for the M.B.A. program. In addition, the Small Business Institute program places the faculty in continual contact with regional business leaders who give advice and valuable feedback to the program.

Prominent Alumni

Some prominent graduates of the M.B.A. program are Jane Babin, Assistant Professor, PSC; Stanley Arnold, Director of Revenue, State of New Hampshire; Christina Ferris, Associate Professor, Johnson State College, Johnson, VT; Jeffrey Coombs, President, Ossipee Mountain Land Company, Tamworth, NH; Frank Johns, Vice President of Operations, Locktite Luminescent Systems, Lebanon, NH; and Nancy Stewart, President, North Country Management Systems, North Conway, NH.

The College and Environs

Plymouth State College is a unit of the University System of New Hampshire. Founded in 1871, the College has undergone many changes and has shifted its role from that of a normal school, and later (1970) a state teachers college, to that of a multipurpose institution. It offers the Master of Education and the Master of Business Administration, as well as associate and bachelor's degrees.

Plymouth is situated in the Lakes and White Mountain region of New Hampshire. The scenic beauty of the area is breathtaking, and the surrounding countryside is a center for extensive recreational activities, available year-round. Students have access to skiing, boating, fishing opportunities, and lovely camps with a wealth of amenities. The town of Plymouth has a year-round population of 6,000, with a seasonal increase of twice that number. Plymouth is approximately 2 hours from both Boston, Massachusetts, and Portland, Maine. Hartford, Connecticut, is 3½ hours away. The capital city of Concord is only 40 minutes south on Interstate 93. A new jetport is located in Manchester, about 1 hour south on Interstate 93.

Facilities

Classes are taught in Hyde Hall, which also contains the Department of Business

computer cluster with over forty IBM microcomputers. There are several other clusters about the campus shared by all students.

Also available is a teleconferencing studio that is connected to other colleges of the University System. Some M.B.A. courses have used this system.

On-campus apartments are available for full-time students, and there are also apartments available in the town of Plymouth. These apartments are all within walking distance of the academic buildings on campus.

Research in the field of business management is facilitated by the rapidly expanding holdings of the Lamson Library. In addition to 250,000 volumes and 475,000 units of filmed and recorded materials, the library houses a remote-access system for retrieval of appropriate audiovisual programs. Formal library support services are supplemented by a Department of Business collection and by interlibrary agreements with other institutions. Computer resources available allow communication with other institutions throughout the country. In addition, there are microcomputers, which include IBM and Macintosh PCs, available in public clusters.

Technology Environment

PSC uses Digital VAX minicomputers for both administrative and academic computing. There are over 100 terminals distributed throughout the campus and dormitories, as well as over twenty port selectors for students who live off campus and have their own computers. Services include e-mail and access to the Internet. Although students are encouraged to bring a computer to PSC, there are seven microcomputer clusters in addition to the terminals.

Placement

The Career Development Office serves both undergraduate and graduate students. Because most of the graduate students are working professionals, only the few full-time students need these services. The office has been highly successful in helping international students find opportunities for postgraduate training. Internships are also arranged when appropriate.

Admission

Applicants must submit proof of a bachelor's degree (official transcripts), a GPA of 2.5 or higher, three letters of recommendation (on the forms provided), and acceptable GMAT scores. International applicants must also submit acceptable TOEFL scores and notarized certification of financial resources to cover the costs of education and living expenses.

The admissions board considers the total aspect of the application; therefore there are no cut-off scores, except for a minimum TOEFL score of 550 that cannot be waived.

The average GMAT score is about 490, with a range of 400 to 760. The average undergraduate GPA is about 3.1 on a 4.0 scale. The GPA of the student is often more reliable as a predictor than the GMAT score, so more weight is given to the GPA of the applicant. About 70 percent of the students have bachelor's degrees in fields other than business.

Finances

The 1995–96 tuition rate is $208 per credit for state residents and $229 per credit for all others. Therefore, the 36-credit graduate program costs are $7488 for state residents and $8244 for all others. All fees are included in the above rates, including graduation fees.

In addition to tuition, books may cost between $60 and $150 per course, for a total of about $1500. An additional $3500 for other living expenses should be anticipated.

Graduate students may live in single and double rooms in College residence halls, with meal service included. The costs for room and board for the 1995–96 year are $1565 per semester for a single and $1410 per semester per person for a double. Apartments for married and single students are available on campus. Off-campus living arrangements can also be made; these vary greatly in cost.

International Students

International students have a unique opportunity to learn with working professionals in a small regional state college environment. The academic experiences include current practice in real business organizations as learned from fellow students.

Application Facts and Dates

The application deadline for fall or winter admission is May 15; for spring or summer admission the deadline is October 15. For more information, applicants should contact:

Ms. Sylvia Horgan, Program Assistant
Office of Graduate Studies—M.B.A.
  Program
Plymouth State College
Plymouth, New Hampshire 03264
Telephone: 603-535-2736
          800-367-4723 (toll-free in
          the continental U.S.
          (except Florida), Canada,
          and Hawaii)
Fax: 603-535-2648

Portland State University

Portland, Oregon

EXPLORING BUSINESS IN AN URBAN ENVIRONMENT

At Portland State University's School of Business Administration, we are setting a pace for the twenty-first century by moving above and beyond the boundaries of conventional business education. Our graduate programs combine academic integrity with an applied, practical orientation, including involvement with business partners, to produce leaders and professionals to meet the challenges of the global marketplace.

The urban setting of Portland State University provides the best possible learning environment to prepare our graduates for the increasingly competitive world of business. We are committed to providing an outstanding learning experience that prepares our graduates to enter the workplace with needed knowledge, skills, understanding, and drive to be successful for themselves and their employers.

—Dr. Roger S. Ahlbrandt, Dean

Programs and Curricular Focus

In the newly revised M.B.A. curriculum, emphasis is given to an integrated and systemic perspective of how business competitiveness is achieved. The themes of decision making, problem solving, managing innovation and change, quality management practices, and global competitiveness cut across the program. Careful attention is given to communication, leadership, teamwork skills, and close involvement with the business community.

The two-year, 72-quarter-credit M.B.A. program is composed of five distinct elements designed to produce a systematic and integrated understanding of business operations. These elements are business perspective and foundation skills, business disciplines, integrated applications, a business project, and a specialization. Learning is facilitated by use of team and project-based learning, information and information technology, and continued exposure to the thinking and practices of world-class business firms and their leaders.

The Master of International Management (M.I.M.) is an innovative twelve-month (August to August) full-time program that places emphasis on the dynamic and rapidly growing Pacific Rim markets. The M.I.M. is a cohort program that requires 63 hours of course work, Pacific Rim executive seminars, corporate field visits, tutorials, foreign language study, and a culminating field study trip to China and Japan.

The Master of Taxation (M.T.) program provides 45 hours of intense study in the compliance, planning, and policy aspects of taxation. It prepares graduates to work with companies and government agencies and in the professions of public accounting and law.

The School of Business Administration participates in the systems science Ph.D. program, which combines the study of systems with the study of business. Students work closely with faculty to design an individualized program of study that will give the student the needed foundation in systems, research, and two fields of business.

Students and the M.B.A. Experience

Students in the PSU graduate business programs are a major resource for the total learning experience. Over 70 percent are employed at the time of admission, with an average of six years of business experience. The average age is 34, and 45 percent are women. Approximately 15 percent are minority and international students. The classroom environment, which includes teams and active student interaction, is rich in diversity of experience, gender, and culture. Sharing and learning from each other is a hallmark of PSU graduate business education.

❖ Global Focus

In addition to the M.B.A. program's focus on competing in a global environ-

ment, the School of Business, in association with the Oregon Joint Professional Schools of Business, now offers the Master of International Management degree for those who wish to specialize in international business. The M.I.M. is designed to provide talented and highly motivated professionals with the specialized skills and in-depth knowledge to perform successfully and responsibly in competitive global markets.

Special Features

Students in the M.B.A. program are members of a cohort group and complete two 8-hour integrated courses, with each team taught by several faculty members. Students also participate, individually or in teams, in an applied business project. Noncredit activities are available to help in career planning and development of computer skills.

There is a pre–Master of International Management program designed for those with limited academic business preparation in the foundation functional areas of accounting, finance, marketing, and management. In addition, the M.I.M. students study a second language and participate in a field study trip to Japan and China.

The Faculty

The faculty is a significant strength of the School of Business Administration, bringing to the classroom a strong educational foundation, practical business experience, and dedication to student learning. Faculty members have traveled and taught in the Pacific Rim, the Middle East, Europe, Russia, and the Commonwealth of Independent States. In addition, the best talents within the business community are brought to the classroom as lecturers and guest speakers.

A unique feature of the Master of International Management program is that the faculty is drawn from the internationally oriented faculty members at Portland State University, the University of Oregon, Oregon State University, and Southern Oregon State College. Furthermore, the M.I.M. program invites internationally recognized professors and business and governmental leaders from around the world to participate in the program.

Students can enjoy Portland's beautiful waterfront.

The Business School Network

Corporate Partnerships

The School of Business Administration has forged close ties with the business community of the Pacific Northwest and the Pacific Rim. Partnership relationships are used to facilitate applied research, student projects, internships, faculty development, classroom participation by business executives, and networking for employment opportunities for graduates of the School of Business Administration.

The Master of International Management utilizes international business executives in leading the program's executive seminars. Students also travel to corporations to visit with business executives to gain firsthand knowledge about doing business internationally.

The College and Environs

Portland State University is ideally situated only 90 minutes from the ocean beaches and mountain slopes. As Oregon's economic and population center and as a gateway to the Pacific Rim, Portland offers unique opportunities for business, industry, government, and the University to enhance partnerships that promote economic, social, cultural, and international development.

Founded in 1946, the campus of nearly 15,000 students occupies forty buildings in a 36-acre area. Portland State University is built around the Park Blocks, a greenway area reserved for pedestrians and bicyclists.

Facilities

The School of Business is located just a few minutes' walk from the downtown Portland business district. Students have access to the University's main library, which houses nearly 1 million volumes, including approximately 10,000 serial publications, a growing number of CD-ROM and on-line computer data-

bases, and an extensive collection of government documents. Portland State University has numerous housing facilities and options in providing desirable and affordable housing to students of the University.

The Master of International Management program is located about 20 minutes away from the main campus in the midst of the "Silicon Forest." Surrounded by numerous high-technology firms and other graduate programs, students study in a modern facility equipped with the latest teaching technology.

Technology Environment

The School of Business Administration has a special computer lab for graduate students, equipped with high-speed laser printers and over twenty-five workstations. From here, students have access to the University's main computer, the Portland Area Library System (PORTALS), the Internet, and numerous other databases.

The Master of International Management program provides a new, state-of-the-art language/computer lab. Students can do their language study or computer work in one of thirty workstations.

Placement

Career development and networking opportunities, coordinated through Corporate, Student, and Alumni Relations, are provided through seminars, workshops, and information meetings. Other resources include an internship program, the Portland State University Career Center, the PSU Business Association (PSUBA), and the MBA Student Association (MBASA).

Admission

Each candidate's academic record, scores on the required Graduate Management Admission Test (GMAT), and work experience are considered in the M.B.A.

admission process. The averages for recently admitted students are a GMAT score of 530 and an undergraduate GPA of 3.3. Students may elect to participate in the full-time day program (fall admittance only) or in the evening program (fall and winter admittance). The evening program is primarily for part-time students.

The Master of International Management seeks students who have at least three years of professional work experience, a GMAT score of at least 500 or an acceptable GRE score, and outstanding letters of recommendation and personal essay. Students who lack academic preparation in the fundamentals of business are required to take an eight-week summer pre-M.I.M. course.

International students whose native language is not English must score at least 550 on the TOEFL and must present proof of their financial resources.

Finances

Estimated full-time tuition for the M.B.A. and M.T. programs in 1994–95 was $4122 for in-state residents and $6612 for non-residents. A limited number of scholarships and graduate assistantships are available.

Tuition for students enrolling in the Master of International Management program is $15,000 for 1995–96 plus a $3500 travel fee for the field study to China and Japan. Students enrolled in the pre-M.I.M. program pay an additional $2000 fee.

International Students

A number of international students from countries in South America, Asia, and Europe participate in the M.B.A. program at Portland State University. The goal of the Master of International Management program is to enroll 50 percent American students and 50 percent international students.

Application Facts and Dates

Application deadlines for the M.B.A. and Master of Taxation programs for international students are March 1 for fall admission and July 1 for winter admission; for domestic students, the dates are April 1 for fall admission and August 1 for winter admission. The Master of International Management program has no fixed application deadline. The admission process continues until the class of 40 is filled. For more information, applicants should contact:

Barbara Alberty
Director of Student Services
School of Business Administration
Portland State University
P.O. Box 751
Portland, Oregon 97207-0751
Telephone: 503-725-3712
Fax: 503-725-5850

Providence College

Providence, Rhode Island

GRADUATE STUDY AT THE COLLEGE

Providence College is a coeducational, equal opportunity institution and is duly accredited by the New England Association of Schools and Colleges. It is also a member of the American Assembly of Collegiate Schools of Business (AACSB) and, wherever feasible, adheres to its principles.

The Graduate Business Program at Providence College provides opportunity to the qualified student to develop his or her individual aptitudes and skills to achieve personal and occupational goals. By fostering an interdisciplinary approach to problems facing local, national, and international business, students are challenged to promote scientific research as well as to develop as scholars, business leaders, and teachers.

—Ronald Cerwonka, Director

Programs and Curricular Focus

The Graduate Business Program consists of practical courses that are useful in the workplace. Each course is planned so that it will be a meaningful learning experience beneficial to the individual. While M.B.A. programs are often criticized for producing graduates who merely master technique but lack substance, due consideration to the social purpose and responsibilities as well as the technical aspects of business is encouraged. In short, Providence College recognizes the critically important challenge of humanizing the program in business administration.

In fostering an interdisciplinary approach, professors from the business areas as well as sociology, mathematics, psychology, political science, and economics are utilized. Approximately one third of the courses are taught by adjunct faculty members and businessmen-in-residence who bring to their classes a myriad of practical business experiences.

Courses are scheduled Monday through Thursday evenings, with some electives offered on Saturday mornings. A student can elect to take courses in the fall semester, a winter intersession, the spring semester, or two summer semesters per year. Depending upon the student's undergraduate preparation, the total number of courses varies from twelve to eighteen. A thesis, while not required, may, in come cases, substitute for the two elective courses. The College maintains linkages with local businesses and with state government for promotion of research projects and internships.

Students and the M.B.A. Experience

Approximately 90 percent of the 270 M.B.A. students in the program work full-time. Most have several years of work experience upon entering the program. This consists of work in such diverse areas as public and private accounting practice, teaching, hospital administration, military service, bank administration, law practice, law enforcement, and a whole spectrum of positions with local and national corporations. The 1994 graduating class of 76 students averaged 32 years of age and consisted of 38 men and 38 women. While the majority of students are from Rhode Island and nearby Massachusetts, more and more students are being attracted from other regions of the United States. In the past several years, students have been accepted from Canada, Ecuador, England, India, Indonesia, Ireland, Japan, Nigeria, Pakistan, Panama, People's Republic of China, the Philippines, Spain, Sri Lanka, Switzerland, Thailand, and Turkey.

An effort is under way to add to the cultural diversity of the student body by encouraging applications from as many ethnic groups as possible. The use of teams in course assignments enhances knowledge and understanding between the diverse groups represented in the student body.

The Faculty

Diversity in the student composition of the program is matched by diversity in the educational and work experience of the graduate faculty. Fully one quarter of this group consists of women and members of minority groups, some possessing doctoral degrees from leading universities in other nations of the world. International students find the members of the faculty who are of foreign origin themselves to be most helpful in career counseling and course selection.

The Business School Network

Corporate Partnerships

The graduate program maintains a close relationship with several firms in the area. Executives of these firms are invited to lecture on some aspect of the business world in a number of courses. Occasionally, an executive-in-residence teaches a course in the area of his or her expertise. Internships are made available for the student to get hands-on experience in a specialized area.

The College and Environs

Providence College's 105-acre campus is located about a mile from the state capitol and 3 miles from the center of Providence. The College enjoys the advantages of an atmosphere far removed from the traffic and commerce of the metropolitan area, yet it provides easy access to the cultural attractions of a city that is not only the capital of one of the original thirteen states but also the location of a variety of institutions of higher learning.

Facilities

The Phillips Memorial Library holds 280,000 volumes in open stacks and has seating accommodation for 1,000 students. The library is a member of the Consortium of Rhode Island Academic and Research Libraries (which includes the libraries of Brown University, the University of Rhode Island, and the Naval War College), making the resources of most of the libraries of the state available to Providence College students. The library is also a member of the New England Library Network (NELINET) and of the Online Computer Library Center (OCLC), which has 3,800 member libraries and a database containing over 10.6 million records. Through interlibrary loan, resources of these libraries are available to Providence College students.

Technology Environment

M.B.A. students have access to five computer labs strategically located on campus that contain approximately 125 IBM and Apple desktop computers. There are also several small research computer labs for the individual who may be working on an extensive assignment. In some locations there are also wide-screen data projectors primarily for computer instruction.

Students also have access to Brown University's mainframe via computers located on campus. Software for word processing and data manipulation is in the aforementioned labs. Data sets and services such as Lexis/Nexis, Dialog, Compustat, and Internet are also available for class assignments.

Placement

Career opportunities are kept on file for review by graduates. Job newsletters are kept in binders on the placement office library shelves. Graduates are encouraged to register their résumé with the office for referral to employers.

Admission

Application materials may be obtained from the M.B.A. program director. Applications are considered throughout the year, and students may enter the program in any semester. Full semesters start in September and January, and two 5-week semesters start in May and July. Detailed application instructions are contained in the Graduate School catalog.

Students must submit the completed application form, the application fee ($30), two letters of reference (preferably one academic and one professional), and an official undergraduate transcript from a regionally accredited U.S. college or university (or, if a foreign institution, one recognized by the American Council on Education). Applicants are required to take the GMAT prior to formal admission to the M.B.A. program. Applicants whose native language is not English are required to take the TOEFL. International students must present proof of adequate funds to cover two full years of residence.

Finances

In 1994–95, tuition was $630 per 3-credit course. Tuition cost for the M.B.A. program ranged from $7560 (for twelve courses) to $10,680 (for eighteen courses). Book costs average $75 per course. The graduation fee is $110. No college housing is available for M.B.A. students, but there is an adequate supply of rental accommodations in the Providence College area. While prices vary depending upon quality, a two-bedroom apartment in the area rents for approximately $350–$550 per month. M.B.A. scholarships and fellowships are available, and candidates applying for the program are automatically considered. The awards are based strictly on merit.

International Students

The College maintains the Balfour Center for Multicultural Affairs. There is also an International House in the Providence area that provides a number of social events and services for international students.

Application Facts and Dates

The graduate program has a rolling admissions system. Students are considered by the admissions committee immediately after their admission folder is completed. For more information, students should contact:

Director, M.B.A. Program
Providence College
Providence, Rhode Island 02918-0001
Telephone: 401-865-2333
Fax: 401-865-2978

FACULTY LIST

Anwar Ahady, Assistant Professor; Ph.D., Northwestern. International finance.

Helen M. Caldwell, Instructor; M.B.A., Boston College. International advertising.

Frank Capecci, Special Lecturer; M.B.A., Rhode Island. Management strategy.

Ronald P. Cerwonka, Professor; Ph.D., Missouri. Financial analysis.

Edwin W. Chaffee, Special Lecturer; M.S., Minnesota. Policy organization.

Joseph M. D'Adamo, Assistant Professor; M.B.A., Indiana. Managerial accounting.

Clement Demayo, Associate Professor; Ph.D., Clark. Mathematics.

Norman Desmarais, Special Lecturer; M.B.A., Providence. Computer systems.

Roger Deveau, Special Lecturer; Ph.D., Boston University. Production management.

Cemal A. Ekin, Associate Professor; Ph.D., Academy of Economics and Commercial Sciences (Turkey). Marketing.

Richard B. Goldstein, Professor; Ph.D., Brown. Management information systems.

Peter S. Goodrich, Associate Professor; Ph.D., Manchester College (United Kingdom); CMA. International accounting.

Carol A. Hartley, Assistant Professor; M.B.A., Rhode Island; CPA. EDP auditing.

Linda F. Jamieson, Assistant Professor; Ph.D., Texas. Research methodology.

Richard H. Lavoie, Associate Professor; Ph.D., Connecticut. Statistical analysis.

Hugh F. Lena, Professor; Ph.D., Connecticut. Organizational behavior.

MaryJane Lenon, Assistant Professor; Ph.D., Connecticut. Urban economics.

James W. Martin, Special Lecturer; M.S., Northeastern. Quantitative methods.

Stephen G. Misovich, Professor; Ph.D., Connecticut. Human resource management.

Ian Morris, Special Lecturer; M.S., Liverpool (United Kingdom). Artificial intelligence.

Judith Morse, Assistant Professor; M.S.T., Bryant. Taxation.

Francis T. O'Brien, Associate Professor; M.A., Boston College. Labor relations.

Charlotte G. O'Kelly, Professor; Ph.D., Connecticut. International management.

Vivian Okere, Assistant Professor; Ph.D., Rhode Island. Financial modeling.

Charles S. Sadoski, Special Lecturer; J.D., Massachusetts. Law.

George F. Sawdy, Associate Professor; Ph.D., Brown. Economics of the firm.

Daniel Scotti, Special Lecturer; M.S., Lesley. Strategic management.

John J. Shaw, Associate Professor; D.B.A., Oklahoma. Consumer behavior.

Robert C. Stiepock, Special Lecturer; M.B.A., Columbia. Human resource management.

David A. Zalewski, Assistant Professor; Ph.D., Clark. Managerial economics.

Purdue University

Krannert Graduate School of Management

West Lafayette, Indiana

PREPARING LEADERS FOR THE FUTURE

Our mission at the Krannert Graduate School of Management is to prepare you to become a leader in the "new management environment"—one that is characterized by teamwork and alliances, continuous changes in technologies, globalization, and networks that are in instantaneous communication with each other.

You are fortunate to be preparing for a management career at a time when opportunities for new products, markets, processes, and resources have a good chance of becoming tomorrow's realities through the vision, determination, and leadership you will bring to the global marketplace. At Krannert, we believe future managers must be grounded in a rigorous analytical foundation for problem solving, broad and forward-looking perspectives for creating new solutions, skills for taking visions into actions, and values of accountability and citizenship for achieving results in the context of the larger environment.

The Krannert programs and learning environment are products of our vision and our mission, energized by the aspirations of our faculty and staff, and rooted in the legacy of learning, innovation, and academic excellence that are part of Purdue University.

—Dennis J. Weidenaar, Dean

Programs and Curricular Focus

Three distinct programs are available at Krannert. The Master of Science in Administration (M.S.I.A.) is an eleven-month program consisting of core courses in all the functional areas of management. The shorter time-frame of this degree program lends itself to individuals who are seeking a general management orientation and a short period of absence from the workforce.

The Master of Science in Management (M.S.M.) is a two-year program consisting of the same core as the M.S.I.A., and it offers students the opportunity to specialize in one of ten option areas including finance, marketing, strategic management, operations management, management of information systems, human resource management, accounting, and the three interdisciplinary options of international management, manufacturing management, and general management.

The Master of Science in Human Resource Management (M.S.H.R.M.) helps future managers evaluate and adapt to the need for human resource development in contemporary organizations. This two-year plan of study incorporates three components: human resource management, general management, and an analytical core.

The Krannert Graduate School of Management's enhanced programs anticipate and reflect the changes reshaping and revolutionizing the principles and practices of business. All three programs emphasize learning through basic theory, case method, teamwork, and consulting projects. The education of Krannert students is guided by the belief that personal effectiveness and lifelong learning rest on a solid analytical foundation for problem solving, forward-looking perspectives for creating solutions, skills for implementation, and values of accountability and community.

Students develop interpersonal and leadership skills by working in teams when completing a majority of assignments and analyzing case studies. Students also participate in team-building exercises outside of Krannert. In addition to the in-class course work, students attend special lectures and skill development workshops and engage in business simulations and problem-solving scenarios.

Students and the M.B.A. Experience

Students attending Krannert learn alongside an exceptional group of individuals. Eighty-seven percent of the master's students have one or more years of full-time work experience. The majority of the students have a strong educational background in engineering, science, and mathematics.

The average student is 26 years of age at entry. Thirty-six percent of the Krannert students are women, 13 percent are members of minority groups, and 30 percent are international students from over twenty-five countries.

The Faculty

At Krannert, students study with faculty members who are not only admired by their peers at other institutions but sought out by practitioners throughout industry. The topics covered by the faculty are rigorous and contemporary. The faculty members take pride in the School's programs and are dedicated to providing the students with a positive educational experience. To that end, they are responsive to student input concerning everything from course topics and speakers to class administration. Faculty members are also very accessible outside of class and at social events.

The Business School Network

By attending Krannert, students are provided access to a network of alumni and corporate contacts who enrich their professional lives. Because of their experiences, and the culture of the Krannert School, the alumni are extremely loyal. They are active, committed participants in student recruitment and placement, curriculum delivery and review, and School financial support. In addition to the alumni, students meet a large number of corporate friends. Krannert's contacts, with both large and small firms, are extensive and continually grow because of the quality of the programs and graduates.

The College and Environs

Established in 1869, Purdue University has grown to contain more than 145 principal buildings located on 1,579 acres. On-campus facilities include a recreation center, golf courses, and an

Students and faculty and staff members celebrate Krannert's entrance into *Business Week's* rankings of the top twenty business schools.

airport. The University has a full-time faculty of over 3,000 and a total undergraduate enrollment of approximately 35,000 students; there are over 5,800 graduate students enrolled in approximately sixty different programs.

The greater Lafayette area occupies a site on the Wabash River 65 miles northwest of Indianapolis and 125 miles southeast of Chicago. The community offers many cultural and athletic options, including Big Ten athletics, the Purdue Convocation Series, the Black Cultural Center, and a student recreational gymnasium.

Facilities

Krannert offers students access to an exceptional information technology infrastructure. Several computing laboratories, developed in conjunction with corporate partners including AT&T, Hewlett-Packard, IBM, Microsoft, and PictureTel, provide access to information from sources as close as the Krannert Library or from anywhere in the world via the Internet. Videoconferencing is used for classroom presentations and off-site interviews with corporations. The School is investigating new ways to visualize data for managerial problem solving and to bring virtual reality to the classroom.

The Krannert Library offers an extensive traditional library with a large reference collection, a range of periodicals, a storehouse of corporate reports and proxies, and on-line full text databases of periodicals and government data sources.

The Krannert School complex is very convenient for students. All classes are held in the Krannert Building, and break-out rooms are available for group meetings.

Placement

Recruiting at Krannert is a year-round process. The Management Placement Office aggressively recruits companies in a wide variety of industries, such as heavy manufacturing, consumer products manufacturing, consulting, computers and electronics, diversified financial services, and communications. Each year, Krannert develops targeted résumé books that are sent to a large number of companies. High-quality, invitational job fairs are also available to domestic and international students.

The Management Placement Office assists students in maximizing their job search by inviting specialists and employer representatives to address issues such as job search strategies, networking, and other relevant career management topics. One-on-one counseling services are available to every student. Krannert

provides free telephone, fax, and résumé printing services along with on-line resources and a library of corporate information to support placement.

Admission

The Krannert School seeks highly qualified applicants for its graduate programs. Previous academic records, test scores, previous work experience, recommendations, leadership experiences, and other evidence of maturity and motivation are considered in the admission process. The Graduate Management Admission Test (GMAT) is required for the master's programs. Average GMAT scores and GPA are 604 and 3.24, respectively. TOEFL scores are required of applicants from non-English-speaking countries.

Finances

Estimated tuition for the M.S.I.A. program for 1995–96 is $4708 for in-state residents and $13,260 for nonresidents. Estimated tuition for the M.S.M. and M.S.H.R.M. programs is $4025 for in-state residents and $11,200 for nonresidents. Costs for room and board and miscellaneous expenditures are not included in these figures. Per month rentals range from $237 to $420 for on-campus housing.

Cash fellowships and a limited number of graduate assistantships are awarded to qualified students. Minority fellowships and Federal Stafford Student Loans are also available. Single students may be eligible to hold residence hall counselorships.

Application Facts and Dates

Admissions are conducted on a rolling basis, but most applications are received on or before April 15 of the academic year. For additional information, students should contact:

Krannert Graduate School of
    Management
1310 Krannert Building
Purdue University
West Lafayette, Indiana 47907-1310
Telephone: 317-494-4365
Fax: 317-494-9841
E-mail: patz@mgmt.purdue.edu

Purdue University is an Equal Access/Equal Opportunity University.

Queen's University

Kingston, Ontario, Canada

MAKING A DIFFERENCE

The decision to pursue an M.B.A. says a great deal about you. It says you want to achieve career success. It says you want to develop the kinds of knowledge, skills, and perspectives required to be an effective manager. It says you are prepared to make a major investment in your future. Above all, it says you want to make a difference in this world.

The Queen's M.B.A. for Science and Technology will prepare you to make that difference. The program augments traditional M.B.A. programming with a special emphasis on the distinctive challenges facing science- and technology-focused organizations and the professional needs of those who lead them. The result is a one-year, comprehensive program of study and application that embodies a bold new approach to graduate management education.

—Ken Wong, Chair

Programs and Curricular Focus

The Queen's M.B.A. for Science and Technology curriculum provides knowledge, skill, and perspective through a combination of course modules and professional development programs. The curriculum takes full advantage of the educational background of science and technology graduates, leveraging their resident skills and knowledge into sophisticated applications.

Course modules provide the technical know-how and managerial perspectives necessary to chart a course of action. Early modules build a solid foundation of general business knowledge. Later modules expand and deepen that knowledge core while developing expertise in the application of analytical skills and emerging technologies to problem solving and strategy development in an environment of rapid change. The result is graduates who possess both a general management perspective and a specific area of expertise that distinguishes them from others.

Students and the M.B.A. Experience

Students enrolled in the Queen's M.B.A. for Science and Technology have undergraduate degrees in engineering, science, health science, and economics. They bring a wide variety of work experiences and geographic diversity. The average age is 27. Women represent approximately one third of the class.

Lectures, case studies, and individual and group exercises are used in varying proportions depending on the subject matter. Field projects, in particular the mandatory five-week major project, provide a hands-on learning experience in which students apply course materials in real-world, real-time applications.

Students are assigned to a team. Each team is provided with a faculty mentor. Team members operate in an atmosphere of codependency and mutual support that mirrors the kinds of professional relationships encountered in the workplace.

Special Features

One distinctive feature of the Queen's M.B.A. for Science and Technology is its professional development programs. These sessions provide an array of tools to enhance personal and managerial productivity while sensitizing students to major developments in the business environment. Early sessions provide the means for improved personal productivity: they raise students' capacity to obtain the resources they need and to organize and process those resources in an efficient and effective manner. Later sessions enhance managerial productivity: students gain both the people skills necessary to communicate, motivate, and develop those around them and the project management skills needed to implement ideas.

Another feature is the mandatory five-week major project. This project provides a hands-on learning experience in which students apply course materials and knowledge gained in earlier stages to a real-time project under the sponsorship of a participating corporation.

The Faculty

The faculty for the M.B.A. Program for Science and Technology is selected from over 50 full-time faculty members in the School of Business. Criteria include excellence in teaching, research, consulting, a science and technology background, and publication.

The faculty at Queen's has long prided itself in accessibility to students and commitment to teaching excellence. Beyond the classroom, Queen's faculty has a history of widespread involvement in student-initiated programs.

Faculty members from other universities around the world also participate in the M.B.A. for Science and Technology through videoconferencing or satellite communication to add specialized insight. Guest speakers from industry and government actively participate in the professional development programs.

The College and Environs

Since its first day of classes in 1842, Queen's University has embodied a standard of excellence in education that makes it one of Canada's leading universities. Queen's distinctiveness is illustrated in the "Queen's Spirit," which has developed from the combination of a close-knit campus community, educational excellence, and beautiful surroundings.

Queen's University is located in the heart of Kingston, Ontario, Canada. Kingston is set within a labyrinth of lakes and waterways. With a population of 120,000, Kingston offers an outstanding quality of life to both families and singles. Kingston enjoys an abundance of cultural and recreational activities. From its many specialized museums and rich historical heritage to its outstanding fishing and sailing waters, Kingston provides a wide variety of attractions. Kingston also provides easy access to major centers of business, technology development, and government, as it is

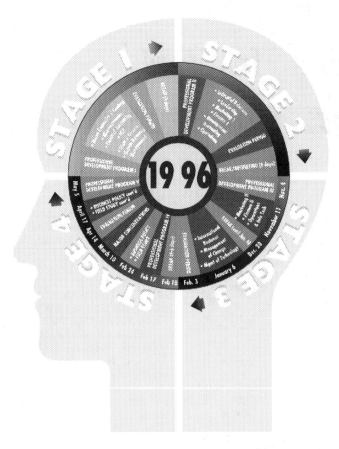

virtually equidistant from Ottawa, Toronto, and Montreal.

Facilities

The M.B.A. Program for Science and Technology has a dedicated facility designed to meet the needs of the program and its participants. The facility contains fully equipped seminar rooms, student offices, and library facilities and features a seventy-seat amphitheatre equipped with state-of-the-art educational technology.

Beyond these dedicated facilities, members of the M.B.A. class have full access to all the athletic, academic, and student service facilities that Queen's University has to offer. These include a new $43-million library and electronic information centre, a $25-million Bioscience Complex, and the $20-million Walter Light Technology Centre. In addition, students electing further instruction in international business have access to programs at Queen's Herstmonceux Castle in England.

Technology Environment

Queen's M.B.A. Program for Science and Technology boasts a state-of-the-art computerized amphitheatre that is equipped with two computerized projec-tion systems, videoconference capability, network ports for students, and a computerized white board.

The student offices are fully net-worked, with access to the Queen's mainframe and worldwide access through the Internet.

Placement

The program serves as an active partner in the career development and placement efforts of students. Students benefit from both a dedicated M.B.A. placement counsellor and an affiliation with the University-wide Career, Planning and Placement Services.

Special workshops focusing on career development skills, résumé writing, and interviewing are held regularly. The M.B.A. Résumé Book for the graduating class is very well regarded by the business community and is circulated to potential employers.

Each year over seventy companies actively recruit business graduates at Queen's, and over thirty companies host on-campus prerecruitment sessions for business students.

Admission

The Queen's M.B.A. for Science and Technology is designed for graduates in the science and engineering fields who have significant professional experience and the potential for continued career growth in management. Engineers, scientists, computer specialists, health-care professionals, and entrepreneurs, among others, represent the professions of candidates chosen to participate.

Candidates for admission are required to have at least two years of work experience, part of which includes management responsibilities; an under-graduate degree in health science, science, engineering, mathematics, or computer science; an acceptable score on the Graduate Management Admission Test (GMAT); two personal evaluations; and a willingness and desire to actively participate in highly intensive interactive classes. After an initial review of all submitted documentation, an interview with an officer of the program is scheduled. A final evaluation is made by the admissions committee on a wide range of criteria, including the candi-date's overall potential, field specializa-tion, experience and performance, and contribution to the group learning experience.

Finances

Fees for the 1996–97 year have been set at Can$22,000. In order to maintain the broadest possible level of accessibility, the University is currently engaged in discussions with financial institutions for the development of an income-contingent loan plan.

Subject to residence requirements, all students accepted into the program automatically qualify for the financing of their tuition and living expenses to a maximum of Can$30,000. Students are not required to make any payments against interest or principal while registered in the program.

Application Facts and Dates

Applicants are encouraged to apply early, as enrollment is limited to a maximum of 50. Applications are reviewed on a rolling basis. The deadline for submitting applications is December 15, 1995, for the session beginning in May 1996.

For more information, students should contact:

M.B.A. for Science and Technology
School of Business
Queen's University
Kingston, Ontario K7L 3N6
Canada
Telephone: 613-545-2302
Fax: 613-545-2013

Rensselaer Polytechnic Institute

Troy, New York

MANAGEMENT AND TECHNOLOGY M.B.A. AT RENSSELAER

The School of Management is focused on the intersection of management and technology, and everything we do begins with the conviction that for all firms in all future markets, sustainable competitive advantage will be built upon a technological foundation. Our mission is to educate a new breed of managers who are prepared to lead their companies in the effective and strategic use of technology.

—Joseph G. Morone, Dean

Programs and Curricular Focus

The Management and Technology M.B.A. program is designed to achieve a dual purpose: the development of technical managers who understand and are able to perform effectively in general management functions and the development of general managers who understand and are able to interact effectively within the technological environment. Course modules are offered in a "stream" format that provides integration across disciplines and between traditional management and technical areas.

The M&T M.B.A. program is a 60-credit, two-year residency program for full-time students. The first year emphasizes breadth and integration, while the second year emphasizes depth and allows students to branch out into their own areas of specialization. A capstone practicum, in which teams of students are assigned field projects with local firms, is a highlight of the second year.

In the first year, courses are composed of modules, which are grouped into different "streams" or clusters of management and technology disciplines. For example, one stream focuses on the new product development process by integrating modules on marketing, design, manufacturing, managerial accounting, pricing and distribution, and performance measurement. Students are organized in teams, and each team develops a new product idea as the members experience each of these modules. Other streams include statistics and operations management and designing, developing, and staffing high-performance organizations as well as accounting, economics, and financial management.

The second year is composed of four required courses and six electives. Two of the required courses form a strategy sequence on trends in science and technology that are likely to lead to new classes of products and businesses in decades ahead. The practicum experience and a course in international macroeconomics fulfill the required courses. The remainder of the program is tailored to the student's interest, and the plan of study may include a concentration. During the second year, students have the option of participating in the School's International Management Exchange Program by spending a semester abroad at one of eight leading universities in Western Europe and Asia.

The standard academic year for the full-time M.B.A. program begins in late August and ends in mid-May of the following year. The schedule for the part-time program is flexible and can be tailored to the student's needs. Matriculation for either program can begin in January as well as in August. A selection of courses is also offered in the summer for students who wish to accelerate or who prefer to take fewer courses during the academic year.

Students and the M.B.A. Experience

The average enrolling M.B.A. student at Rensselaer is 26 years old, with four years of previous work experience. Eighty percent of the students are men; 49 percent are from the northeastern United States.

Nearly one third of the full-time M.B.A. students in the program come from countries other than the United States. This strong international representation helps to create a dynamic and globally aware environment for class discussions, team projects, and the overall M.B.A. community.

Special Features

Entrepreneurship is a mainstream activity of the School, reflecting a deeply held conviction that all technology-driven firms must continuously pursue new business creation for long-term survival and success. Rensselaer has developed a systematic program for preparing students for entrepreneurship, both within established corporations and in new, start-up ventures. The School of Management is not only one of a handful of institutions that offer a curriculum in entrepreneurship, it is also one of the best. *Success* magazine listed Rensselaer among the top twenty-five entrepreneurial schools in the country. In the fall of 1993, *Business Week* produced a special issue entitled *Enterprise* and recognized Rensselaer's Center for Entrepreneurship among the twenty best entrepreneurship programs in the United States.

The School of Management offers a number of entrepreneurship courses, including New Ventures and Technological Entrepreneurship. New Ventures covers the analysis of new ventures, characteristics of people who successfully start new companies, and identification of a market niche. It also covers establishing and building an organization, beginning to produce the first product, marketing the first product, financing the new company, and making the transition from a start-up company to a successful company.

The objective of the course entitled Technological Entrepreneurship is to learn, by practical field work, how successful new technological ventures are created, developed, and financed. Students work in teams to prepare business, marketing, and financial plans for selected companies. Guidance is given by experienced entrepreneurs and consultants. The output of each team is a formal report to the sponsoring company, with specific conclusions and recommendations.

The Faculty

Faculty members at Rensselaer's School of Management are characterized by vigor, dynamism, and a strong commitment to the business application of technology. Their courses provide historical context, classical applications, and current perspectives—but the emphasis is on the future: providing M.B.A. students with the innovative tools needed for success in the high-technology business environment of the twenty-first century.

The faculty includes experts in finance, computer applications, artificial intelligence, manufacturing, statistics, policy and strategy, international business, organizational design, product development, and marketing. Almost all of the full-time faculty members have substantial managerial experience in business or government.

The Business School Network

Rensselaer has always had exceptionally strong ties with business and industry. Many of Rensselaer's graduates have chosen to apply their talents and ingenuity to founding, growing, and leading successful high-tech firms.

The College and Environs

Troy, Albany, and Schenectady form an upstate metro area, New York's Capitol Region, with a population of nearly 750,000. The area is a major center for government, industrial, research, and academic activity. The headquarters and research centers for some of the world's largest technology-based firms are within easy driving distance of the Capitol Region.

Technology Environment

Rensselaer has a technology-rich environment, and the School of Management takes full advantage of this fact. M.B.A. classes make extensive use of PC-based software for course work. Teams of students are assigned the use of a laptop computer for the first year of the program. A wide variety of high-end computing facilities are located throughout the campus, including a network of over 600 UNIX-based workstations and many PC, Macintosh, and multimedia labs.

In addition to computing facilities, Rensselaer M.B.A. students have the opportunity to draw on the abilities, knowledge, and resources of world-class researchers and research centers located on the campus. As one example, when a team of students in the product development course needed to design a plastic housing for their product, they consulted materials experts in the Rensselaer Design and Manufacturing Institute to assist them.

Placement

The School views placement of its students as its ultimate measure of success. To that end, students are provided with assistance in their job search efforts by both the campuswide Career Development Center and the School of Management Placement Office. Companies that have hired Rensselaer M.B.A. graduates over the past five years include Andersen Consulting, American Management Systems, AT&T, Boeing, Ernst & Young, General Electric, IBM, Oracle, Pitney Bowes, Procter & Gamble, Salomon Brothers, and a host of others. Nearly one third of the graduates each year choose positions in the financial services or management consulting fields, another third go to jobs in more traditional manufacturing positions, and the remainder choose to work for myriad small to medium-size enterprises.

Admission

With the focus of the School of Management on the intersection of management and technology, most applicants to the M.B.A. program have undergraduate or master's degrees in engineering and science. However, applicants with degrees in humanities and social sciences who have strong interest and skills in technology are also welcome. Most of the applicants have significant work experience, though each year a small number of recent college graduates from programs in engineering and science are considered for admission.

In addition to official transcripts, applicants must submit test score reports for the Graduate Management Admission Test (GMAT). Applicants whose native language is not English must also take the TOEFL examination.

Finances

Tuition is $540 per credit hour. Full-time students pay tuition and fees of $16,715 per year. Living expenses are estimated at $9145 per year.

Approximately 20 percent of entering full-time M.B.A. students receive partial, merit-based scholarships. These scholarships consist of 6 tuition credits per semester for four semesters, which are currently valued at $12,960 each or 40 percent of overall tuition costs. Other types of scholarships are available for highly qualified students, including full-tuition fellowships for one student per year in manufacturing and for one female entrepreneur.

Graduate assistantships are awarded to M.B.A. students entering their second year of study. These assistantships provide a stipend of $2150 per semester in return for 10 hours of work per week. The work entails such activities as grading and research. Approximately fifteen assistantships are offered on a competitive basis each year.

Application Facts and Dates

The application deadline for the fall semester is May 1; it is December 1 for the spring semester. Early submission of applications is strongly encouraged. Applications are considered on a first-come, first-served basis.

To request an informational brochure and application, students should contact:

John H. Cerveny
Director, M&T M.B.A. Program
RPI School of Management
Troy, New York 12180-3590
Telephone: 518-276-4800
Fax: 518-276-8661
Internet: management@rpi.edu
WWW: http//www.rpi.edu/dept/mgmt/
SOM.pages

R·I·T Rochester Institute of Technology

Rochester, New York

SHARPENING OUR FOCUS

Quality is here to stay. The slogans and catchwords may change, but customers accustomed to dealing with organizations that have successfully adopted the principles of the quality movement are increasingly unwilling to accept less than the best. We have woven the concepts of quality throughout our graduate business programs. Our rapid response has placed the RIT College of Business at the forefront of the quality movement in higher education.

On behalf of the RIT College of Business, I am proud to offer you an opportunity to broaden your perspective and prepare for the larger responsibilities that lie ahead.

—Richard N. Rosett, Dean

Programs and Curricular Focus

The M.B.A. program and M.S. programs blend the expert knowledge of the faculty with a team approach and the technological resources available at RIT. The M.B.A. program provides a broad-based business education. All functions of business (accounting, finance, marketing, production, and management) are covered. The M.B.A. program emphasizes strategic issues and integrated decision making in a high-quality organization.

The new M.B.A. curriculum includes eighteen courses—eight required core courses and ten electives. Students may concentrate in one or two areas. The M.B.A. program may be completed in fifteen months. Students who qualify for course waivers may be able to complete the program in one year. RIT is a cooperative education school that provides students with the opportunity to get hands-on experience in the workplace.

Concentration selections include public and corporate accounting, finance, marketing management, sales management, marketing research, international business, management and leadership, quality and organizational improvement, human resources development and training, service management, information systems, manufacturing management, technology management, and quality and applied statistics.

The College of Business also offers a one-year M.S. in finance, preparing students for courses in corporate finance, investment analysis and portfolio management, financial consulting, and financial institutions.

The M.S. in international business enables students to specialize in a functional area and to improve skills and understanding of global business operations.

Students and the M.B.A. Experience

Students in the College of Business come from diverse backgrounds and have a variety of work experience. The average full-time student is 26 years old, with three years of work experience. Students without work experience are encouraged to participate in the cooperative education program. International students comprise one quarter of the full-time student population, and women make up one third of the M.B.A. population.

Approximately one third of RIT's M.B.A. students have technical undergraduate degrees, and another third have degrees in business administration. Students share their hands-on experience with their team members and classmates, enriching the learning experience.

❖ Global Focus

The International Business Department is headed by Dr. Riad Ajami, who brings new perspectives to current issues in a global competitive environment. Courses in international marketing and international finance complement traditional functional business areas. The international management course strengthens the student's perspective of cultural differences in the global business environment. An international seminar provides the

opportunity for students to meet real-life practitioners. In addition, the international perspective is integrated throughout the M.B.A. curriculum.

The Faculty

The College of Business faculty and staff have enhanced their quality approach to education and student service and have revised the curriculum to reflect changing realities in the business world. Faculty members integrate theory with hands-on application. Ninety percent have earned Ph.D.'s in their fields of study. The ratio of students to faculty is 18:1.

The Business School Network

The College of Business has built strong relationships with corporate leaders in the Rochester area and beyond. Rochester is home to Rank Xerox Corporation, Eastman Kodak Company, and Bausch & Lomb, Inc. Other employers in the Rochester area include ABB Process Automation, Inc.; AC Rochester, Division of General Motors; Harris Corporation; and Mobil Chemical Company.

Students take advantage of the corporate presence in Rochester to gain cooperative education experience. Other co-op employers include PepsiCo, IBM, and the Carrier Corporation. Traditionally, RIT has had close ties with industry through curriculum development, internships, co-ops, and adjunct faculty.

The College and Environs

The Rochester Institute was founded in 1829 in Rochester, New York. The Institute is located on 1,400 acres of beautiful rolling suburban land. RIT enrolls more than 13,000 students in its eight colleges and is ranked among the top colleges and universities in the nation. The western New York area offers cultural centers and sports events. Rochester is a 3-hour trip from Toronto, Canada, and a 6-hour drive from New York City.

Facilities

The 350,000-volume Wallace Library has a collection of over twenty-five CD-ROM elective indexes with access to Internet resources, all available through a menu maintained by the campus computer network (VAX). Article citation and 10,000 journal titles are available on-line through CARL (Colorado Alliance of Research Libraries). Information Systems and Computing (ISC) manages a large VMS cluster (networked Digital VAX computers), a high-speed ULTRIX system, a campuswide network, dial-in access, and 1,400 computer terminals on campus.

Placement

At RIT, preparation for final placement begins a year before graduation. The Office of Cooperative Education and Placement offers an array of services including self-assessment, résumé preparation, interviewing techniques, job-search strategies, and career opportunities in different areas of business. M.B.A. placement staff act as the "point people," providing critical job leads and individual counseling.

Admission

Admission to RIT's M.B.A. program is granted to promising graduates of accredited baccalaureate degree programs. A student's transcript(s), Graduate

Management Admission Test (GMAT) scores, relevant professional experience, personal statement, and recommendations are evaluated by the Graduate Admissions Committee. International applicants must take and submit the results of the Test of English as a Foreign Language (TOEFL) as a part of the application process. The TOEFL requirement is waived for native speakers of English and for those submitting transcripts and diplomas from American undergraduate schools.

Finances

Tuition and fees for 1994–95 were $15,384 plus $150 for student activity fees during an academic year. Books and supplies cost approximately $1500 per year. There is approximately a 5 percent increase expected for 1995–96.

Four apartment complexes and nearly 1,000 apartment and townhouse units on campus are serviced by a shuttle-bus system. Prices vary, depending upon apartment size and complex chosen. Currently, prices start at $515 per month, including utilities.

Scholarships and assistantships are available. The awards are based on academic merit.

International Students

Twenty-four percent of graduate business students at RIT's College of Business come from outside the United States. The International Student Affairs office on campus helps students become acclimated to RIT and the Rochester area. The English as a second language (ESL) department provides support programs that help international students succeed in their academic pursuits.

Application Facts and Dates

International students are strongly encouraged to begin their studies in the fall quarter. RIT maintains rolling admissions. Those students seeking an assistantship should apply before March 1; international students are encouraged to apply before May 1. For more information, students should make inquiries to:

Graduate Business Programs Office
College of Business
Rochester Institute of Technology
104 Lomb Memorial Drive
Rochester, New York 14623-5608
Telephone: 716-475-2256
Fax: 716-475-7450
E-mail: smwbbu@rit.edu

> ### GLOBAL PERSPECTIVE TO BUSINESS: THE ST. JOHN'S M.B.A. ADVANTAGE
>
> *St. John's objective is to produce M.B.A. graduates who will be successful in business. We strive to give our students a long-term advantage by enabling them to acquire a broad base of skills in the major business disciplines to adapt to changing job requirements.*
>
> *The program is fully accredited by the AACSB and emphasizes critical thinking in analytical decision making. Students are prepared for an entrepreneurial future in a global economy, while receiving a strong indoctrination in ethical values. It is these elements of the M.B.A. program that enable our graduates to successfully exercise their leadership skills in business.*
> —Laurence J. Mauer, Associate Vice President and Dean

Programs and Curricular Focus

The College of Business Administration offers programs of study leading to the M.B.A. degree, with concentrations in accounting and taxation, economics, finance, financial services, international finance, management, marketing, marketing management, quantitative analysis, and computer information systems for managers. The program requires the completion of a minimum of 39 credits taken on either a part-time or full-time basis. These credits are divided into three parts: the core (seven courses), the field of specialization (four courses), and the electives (two courses). In addition, a student who has not taken undergraduate business and economics courses may be required to complete additional credits in the prerequisite area, which is determined on an individual basis. The master's thesis option provides the opportunity to plan and execute research study while responding creatively to an intellectual challenge determined by the student's own interests.

The College of Business Administration is accredited by the AACSB, the sole accrediting agency for M.B.A. degree programs.

A joint M.B.A./J.D. degree program is offered. Completion requires three years of full-time study.

Students and the M.B.A. Experience

St. John's student population comprises a large number of individuals with diverse work experience. Most are employed full-time in career-track jobs while pursuing their M.B.A. All candidates are groomed to effectively communicate with executives in all fields.

Students are exposed to the dynamics of group interaction by simulated business situations. They learn negotiation and persuasion skills, how to motivate people, and how to excel in a team environment.

Classes focus on the applications of business theory to real-world situations. Students learn to analyze information and make informed decisions in a variety of realistic business situations.

The M.B.A. program is international in scope to provide the student with knowledge of international operations and corporations. Two study-abroad courses are offered: the London Economics/Finance Seminar and the International Marketing Seminar.

A new center of study is slated to open in September, 1995, in Rome, Italy. Initial areas of concentration for the M.B.A. degree program will be in international finance and executive management. Students can take some or all of their courses in Rome or in New York City.

Special Features

The St. John's Executive-in-Residence Program provides a select group of students with a practical exposure to business as a preparation for entering the business world. Students meet with high-level business executives who candidly discuss the nature of their firms, corporate problems, and possible solutions. Sessions use a case study method, drawing examples from actual business situations, a format that helps students react responsibly to the complexities of upper-level decision making. Strategic plans are also developed by students and evaluated by upper management.

The Advanced Professional Certificate Program (APC) enables M.B.A. students to gain additional knowledge in a new field, providing the competitive edge necessary to move forward in the 1990s. The APC is earned by the satisfactory completion of at least 18 credits with an index of 3.0 in all courses.

The Faculty

St. John's faculty members possess strong academic credentials as well as professional business experience; over 90 percent hold a doctorate. Professors are selected on the basis of their moral and ethical strengths, since they must serve as role models for the next generation of business leaders.

The overriding goal is to have St. John's graduates be considered complete professionals, promoted through the working partnership of a skilled and caring faculty that instills intellectual curiosity in students and helps them grow personally and academically.

The Business School Network

The College forges a strong partnership with corporations and focuses on the issues that are of concern in today's global economy. The annual Business Conference headlines distinguished guest speakers, including CEOs and other senior executives of major corporations. In addition, the Henry George Lecture Series is a semiannual event that features a prominent expert in the field of economics who speaks to the students on current topics.

The Business Research Institute is an integral part of the College. It promotes research in the field of business administration and publishes the *Review of Business,* a refereed publication with a national review board consisting of distinguished business leaders.

Bent Hall.

The College and Environs

The Queens and Staten Island campuses provide easy access to the vast resources of the world's foremost metropolis. The Queens campus has 100 rolling acres in residential Hillcrest, with broad lawns, modern buildings, and a spectacular view of the New York skyline. It is a mere 11 miles from midtown Manhattan, providing easy access to all boroughs of New York City and Long Island.

The Staten Island campus is on 16.5 acres on Grimes Hill, overlooking New York Harbor. It offers the full facilities, activities, and resources of the University in a "small college" setting, while being easily accessible from Brooklyn and New Jersey.

Facilities

University libraries consist of three facilities: the Main University Library and the Law School Library on the Queens campus and the Loretto Memorial Library on the Staten Island campus. In addition to over 1.5 million volumes of books, bound periodicals, and microfilm/microfiche materials, extensive government research reference materials are housed in the main library, a significant repository for U.S. government documents. Specific support for the study of business is provided by a collection of more than 59,220 book titles and 635 business periodical subscriptions. There is also an extensive collection of abstracts and a comprehensive interloan program. The library houses specialized services from Commerce Clearing House, Research Institute of America, Standard and Poor's, Moody's, Dun & Bradstreet, and Value Line.

Technology Environment

Students and the faculty have access to six academic computer labs, four microclassrooms, and five multimedia classrooms to satisfy informational technology requirements. Computers in all facilities are networked to each other and to an IBM 4381 mainframe for easy access to a wide range of applications. The microlabs provide access to over 200 IBM PS/2s and Apple Macintosh computers, which run on the latest versions of software applications used in the business environment. The mainframe also supports campuswide and worldwide electronic communications services, including electronic mail, electronic forums, and full access to the global Internet.

Placement

The Career Center's professional placement programs offer a wide variety of services designed to give each graduate student and alumnus the competitive edge. Services and resources include career advisement, on-campus interviews, full-time and part-time employment opportunities, a career resource library, résumé preparation and interview techniques, a videotape library, and mock interview sessions.

Admission

All applicants must possess a baccalaureate degree from an accredited undergraduate institution. The candidate should submit, in addition to the $40 nonrefundable application fee, official transcripts from all undergraduate, graduate, and professional schools attended and the results of the GMAT. Applicants whose native language is not English must submit the results of the TOEFL. In addition, an English as a second language placement test is administered to all international students holding an F-1 or J-1 visa.

Finances

Tuition in 1995–96 is $500 per credit. An additional $75 general fee per term is due at the time of registration. A limited number of graduate assistantships are awarded, based on academic merit.

Living expenses in the New York metropolitan area vary widely, depending on housing and lifestyle. The University does not provide residences for students. Private rentals in Queens begin at approximately $800 per month.

Application Facts and Dates

Applications are accepted on a rolling basis. For more information, students should contact:

Mr. Gregory D. Pizzigno
Assistant Dean/Director of Graduate Programs
College of Business Administration
St. John's University
8000 Utopia Parkway
Jamaica, New York 11439
Telephone: 718-990-6417
Fax: 718-380-3803

Ms. Donna M. Narducci
Assistant Dean/Director of Business Programs, Staten Island
College of Business Administration
St. John's University
300 Howard Avenue
Staten Island, New York 10301
Telephone: 718-390-4509
Fax: 718-390-4590

Saint Joseph's University

College of Business & Administration

Philadelphia, Pennsylvania

CREATING BREADTH, DEPTH, AND WHOLENESS

We encourage you to explore the Saint Joseph's University of Philadelphia M.B.A. program.

We seek excellence in business education that offers breadth in terms of broad-based coverage of business concepts and skills, depth through focus on specific industries and professions, and wholeness via the education of men and women for others in accordance with the Jesuit tradition.

Our M.B.A. allows you the flexibility to concentrate your studies in the particular field or industry that interests you. We are located at four sites: our main campus in Philadelphia, at Ursinus College in Collegeville, at Albright College in Reading, and at the Great Valley Business Development Training Center in Malvern.

—James L. Bowditch, Dean

Program and Curricular Focus

Saint Joseph's M.B.A., designed for working professionals, is a part-time evening and Saturday program that provides a practical, real-world-based curriculum. It has been developed to give every student the breadth of knowledge necessary in all areas of business as well as the depth of knowledge required to become a specialist in one particular area of study. This winning combination of course offerings provides Saint Joseph's M.B.A. students with the appropriate knowledge to succeed in their chosen fields. The M.B.A. curriculum consists of twenty courses. The first nine foundation core courses introduce students to basic business theories and applications. These nine courses have been developed for students who do not have an undergraduate background in business. Students who have earned an undergraduate degree in business may receive waivers for the foundation core. Students who establish competency through work experience or in-house training may also receive a waiver of a foundation course by passing a challenge examination for the applicable course. The advanced core contains seven courses that provide additional breadth of coverage of the common body of knowledge. Additionally, students are also required to take three courses in an area of specialization. These three courses allow the development of expertise in a specific area of interest. The specialization areas offered at Saint Joseph's University include accounting, finance, health administration, information

systems, international business, management, marketing, and a general M.B.A. Saint Joseph's M.B.A. program culminates in the ultimate team project: the required integrative course, Business Policy, which utilizes all of the knowledge gained in the program to develop a business plan. Integral to success in this course are the skills to work in the "team" framework, developed throughout the program.

Students and the M.B.A. Experience

One of the measures of an effective M.B.A. program is the number of students who choose that particular program because it meets their needs and professional goals. Today, about 1,500 working professionals from 500 corporate and not-for-profit organizations pursue their M.B.A. at Saint Joseph's University. Students are employed as managers, bankers, engineers, programmers, accountants, lawyers, and other professionals who contribute to Saint Joseph's unique M.B.A. environment. The student mix provides a challenging forum where principles are discussed in light of practical applications and real contexts. This setting also furnishes an atmosphere where students can develop leadership qualities and learn dynamics for team presentations.

Students specializing in international business, marketing, or management may participate in the management and marketing study tours. These study tours

allow students to meet with top management and marketing executives while exploring another part of the world.

The Faculty

In Saint Joseph's M.B.A. program, students are taught by well-qualified full- and part-time professors whose combination of academic credentials and business experience provides for dynamic classroom interaction. Program professors hold doctoral degrees from well-known universities. Just as important, they possess hands-on business expertise coupled with a commitment to work with students on creative solutions to tough business problems.

The Business School Network

Corporate Partnerships

Saint Joseph's M.B.A. program strives to establish partnerships with area corporations by affording these corporations the opportunity to develop their employees professionally by supporting their bid for graduate studies in the evening. Working students contribute greatly to dynamic classroom interaction and in return can apply these new business principles to their current workplace.

Prominent Alumni

Saint Joseph's M.B.A. program counts among its alumni a number of business leaders, including Roseanne S. Gatta, Assistant Vice President and Treasurer, Provident Mutual Life Insurance Company; Gary G. Kyle, Director of Marketing and National Sales, Tasty Baking Company; John H. Teaford, President, Aloette Cosmetics; John L. Volpe, Assistant Vice President, CoreStates

DEPARTMENT CHAIRS

Accounting: *Joseph M. Ragan, Assistant Professor; M.B.A.; CPA.*
Finance: *Harold F. Rahmlow, Assistant Professor; Ph.D.*
Management & Information Systems: *Elizabeth B. Davis, Assistant Professor; Ph.D.*
Marketing: *Richard H. Kochersperger, Assistant Professor; M.S.*

Barbelin/Lonergan Building.

Bank; and Ms. Catharine R. Brady, Vice President, Merrill Lynch Asset Management.

The College and Environs

Founded in 1851, Saint Joseph's University is one of twenty-eight Jesuit colleges and universities in the United States. The total University enrollment is 6,700 students, about 1,500 of whom are M.B.A. students. The University is conveniently located on the western boundary of the city of Philadelphia on wooded and landscaped grounds and combines urban accessibility with the traditional charm of the city's well-known Main Line. The environment provides an aura of seclusion, yet the educational, cultural, and entertainment resources of metropolitan Philadelphia are easily accessible.

Off-campus sites at Albright College in Reading, Pennsylvania, at Ursinus College in Collegeville, Pennsylvania, and at the Business Development Training Center located in Malvern, Pennsylvania, are available for Saint Joseph's M.B.A. students residing or employed in the northern part of the Greater Delaware Valley.

Facilities

The Francis A. Drexel Library, located near the center of campus, contains a business collection of approximately 32,000 bound volumes, 400 periodical subscriptions, eleven CD-ROMs, 200 videos, and Fortune 500 annual reports. It also serves as a selective depository for U.S. government documents. The library has an on-line public access catalog for searching its holdings, accessible from remote locations via the University's academic computer. There are 100 computer terminals available to Saint Joseph's students, and the following on-line services are available to M.B.A. students: Dialog, NEXIS/LEXIS, the Internet, FirstSearch, and Uncover. The Instructional Media Center at Saint Joseph's University offers students assistance with presentation materials. The IMC has over 900 videotapes, which can be viewed in the center or signed out if needed as part of a presentation. Other equipment available to M.B.A. students includes video cameras, a slide copying service, and overhead and slide projectors.

Placement

Services at the Career Services Center include individual career counseling, job search advising, access to alumni contact lists, and the career resource library, which contains occupational information, employer literature/directories, and current employment listing. Workshops are offered on résumé writing, interviewing, and job search techniques. Graduating students can also participate in on-campus recruiting. In addition, job search assistance is available in the form of a résumé referral program.

Admission

Applicants for admission must possess a baccalaureate degree from an accredited college or university. The applicant must submit the following documentation: a completed application form accompanied by the application fee and an essay, official transcripts indicating receipt of a baccalaureate degree, official scores on the Graduate Management Admission Test (GMAT), two letters of recommendation, and an updated résumé. International applicants whose native language is not English are required to take the Test of English as a Foreign Language (TOEFL) and submit proof of adequate financial resources. The decision for accepting applicants into the program will be made by the admissions committee after they have reviewed the completed application package.

Finances

Tuition and fees for the 1994–95 academic year were $385 per credit hour or $1155 per course. On-campus housing for graduate students is available, subject to space limitations. Since the majority of the graduate students are fully employed, they live in the local geographic area. Living costs in the greater Delaware Valley area are reasonable when compared to costs in other large urban centers. Additionally, a limited number of graduate assistantships are available for full-time graduate students.

Application Facts and Dates

Students are admitted for enrollment in September, January, or May of each year. Application should be submitted as far in advance as possible for the following deadlines: July 15 for the fall semester; November 15 for the spring semester; and April 15 for the summer semester. For more information, applicants should contact:

Mrs. Adele C. Foley
Associate Dean/Director, M.B.A.
   Programs
Saint Joseph's University
5600 City Avenue
Philadelphia, Pennsylvania 19131-
   1395
Telephone: 610-660-1690
Fax: 610-660-1599
E-mail: sjumba@sju.edu

Saint Louis University

School of Business and Administration

St. Louis, Missouri

THE PARTNERSHIP

Selecting an M.B.A. program binds both the student and the institution to an education partnership. While students devote great energy and time to academic studies, we dedicate ourselves to preparing them not only to meet, but to exceed the challenges of today's dynamic business world. This is accomplished by providing a newly revised M.B.A. program that better responds to the demands of the marketplace.

We look forward to the opportunity to welcome you into an education partnership, to work together toward your professional and personal success. I hope you will contact me or Dr. Paul Boughton, director of graduate and professional programs, to learn more about the M.B.A. at Saint Louis University's School of Business and Administration.

—Neil E. Seitz, Dean

Programs and Curricular Focus

A revised M.B.A. program, developed after extensive research comparing current requirements with business realities and expectations, will begin in the fall of 1995. This revised program will not only furnish the basic business foundation but also advance subject matter into areas indicated as essential by top corporate professionals. The rigors of academic learning are blended with opportunities to increase proficiency in oral and written communications, in leadership and teamwork skills, and in understanding group dynamics and the importance of a global perspective.

The M.B.A. program is 57 credit hours in length. Competency in calculus is required. Students begin with 18 credit hours of core requirements that provide an overview of the key business disciplines. Nine 2-credit-hour courses are completed in accounting, economics, finance, management, business statistics, information technology, marketing, legal environment of business, and managerial communications. Some of these courses are waived for students who have demonstrated sufficient academic background.

The advanced requirements (27 credit hours) consist of seven 3-credit-hour courses that more deeply examine the business fields. Students must also complete a 2-credit-hour business ethics course and two integrated modules. The modules are each 2 credit hours and are team taught case and simulation courses that approach learning from an interdisci-plinary focus, allowing students to employ problem-solving techniques.

Twelve hours of electives are then chosen by the student to build areas of specialization or broaden overall business knowledge.

The M.B.A. can be completed alone or as part of a joint-degree program. The University offers the Juris Doctor/M.B.A., the Master of Science in Nursing Administration/M.B.A., and the Master of Health Administration/M.B.A.

Students and the M.B.A. Experience

During 1994, nearly 800 students were completing graduate business degrees at the School. Approximately 60 percent of those students were men, and 40 percent of the students were studying on a full-time basis.

Students bring a variety of educational and professional backgrounds to the program. While the majority are from undergraduate business disciplines, students often combine an M.B.A. with engineering, nursing, social services, law, and medical careers, to name a few. Many of the students are returning to school—on either a part-time or full-time basis—after years of professional employment, while some enroll directly from an undergraduate program.

❖ Global Focus

To strengthen efforts toward globalizing the M.B.A. experience, the School actively recruits students from abroad.

Domestic M.B.A. students are also encouraged to study abroad by enrolling in courses offered by the School itself or other institutions. The School has sponsored intersession M.B.A. classes in Madrid, Spain, and at the City University in Hong Kong. Ten years ago, the School recognized the growing importance of the globalization of business and created a special Institute of International Business. The first of its kind a decade ago, the institute continues to sponsor a number of conferences throughout the year and has created the executive master's degree in international business.

The Faculty

Faculty members in the School of Business and Administration are key elements in the education partnership. Fifty-three full-time, tenure-track faculty members support the School's six business departments. Within these academic units, 98 percent of the faculty members are doctorally qualified.

As scholars in their fields, faculty members are invited to engage actively in research and professional activities. Nearly 90 percent have published or presented their research in the past five years. Their accomplishments include regional, national, and international efforts with books, journal articles, proceedings, and professional presenta-tions.

In furthering efforts to blend a global focus into all aspects of the M.B.A. program, business faculty members have embraced the challenge to participate in programs abroad, traveling to a number of countries in roles such as visiting scholars, guest lecturers, and conference attendees.

The Business School Network

Corporate Partnerships

St. Louis ranks fifth nationwide as headquarters for Fortune 100 companies, providing a wealth of business opportuni-ties. Strong bonds have already been forged with many companies. For example, the Mercantile Foundation recently funded Business Leadership: The Mercantile Program for Women. This

The School of Business and Administration is housed in Davis-Shaughnessy Hall, which has been renovated to provide modern facilities, including two fully equipped computer labs and a student lounge for relaxing.

innovative program, the first of its kind nationwide, will provide female M.B.A. students with special opportunities and programs. Emerson Electric supports a Center for Business Ethics, and the Jefferson Smurfit Corporation funded a Center for Entrepreneurial Studies.

Prominent Alumni

Many alumni remain in St. Louis, while others return to their homes in the United States and in countries abroad, extending the School's ties throughout the world. Part of the success of the corporate partnerships is the strong contingent of loyal and committed local alumni who hold titles such as president, CEO, chairman of the board, and partner for large local, national, and international firms.

The College and Environs

Saint Louis University, a private, Jesuit institution offering undergraduate, graduate, and professional degrees in more than eighty programs of study, has grown into an academic institution with a reputation for excellence in education and attentiveness to the individual student. Last year enrollment neared 11,500 students from all over the United States and seventy-seven other countries. Located in an urban area, the campus provides a parklike setting with attractive surroundings, including fountains, grassy quads, and a clock-tower. Student housing options include on-campus dormitories or off-campus apartments within walking distance of the School.

As for recreation, the city of St. Louis offers many cultural and recreational activities, while Saint Louis University's nationally ranked Billiken basketball and soccer teams provide sports entertainment. Students can also use the University's recreation center, gym, and sport field.

Technology Environment

The extensive University facilities include a library network equipped with CD-ROM catalog service and electronic databases (ABI/INFORM, LEXIS/NEXIS, and Business Periodicals ONDISC). Technology is ever expanding, with two fully equipped computer labs in the School of Business and Administration.

Placement

The University's Career Center and the School of Business and Administration collaborate to provide a convenient satellite Career Center office in the business school. The site also houses the staff of the School's internship program, who are building a network of opportunities for M.B.A. students.

Admission

Each candidate for admission to the M.B.A. program in the School of Business and Administration is evaluated based on the information submitted during the application process: an application with a nonrefundable $30 fee,

two letters of recommendation, transcripts from prior institutions, and the GMAT score report.

International students are asked to apply at least six months in advance of desired entry. International applicants are also required to take the TOEFL and, if a student visa is desired, to submit certification of financial support for the full period of study.

Finances

In 1995–96, tuition is $500 per credit hour. Housing rates for facilities on campus range from $1000 to $2000 per semester, depending on the dorm selected and the number of occupants per room. A full meal plan (nineteen meals per week) costs $1320.

Off-campus housing close to the campus averages $500 per month (including utilities), with food expenses approximating $75 per week.

Textbooks cost approximately $50 to $100 per class, and, for those students who prefer to park in campus lots, parking permits range from $50 to $90 per semester.

Full-time M.B.A. students beginning in a fall semester who wish to be considered for scholarships and research assistantships must apply by April 1. Federal aid and a special budget plan are also available through the University's Office of Financial Aid.

International Students

Over 30 percent of current M.B.A. students come from outside the United States. Special programs for international students include English courses upon arrival and a progressive orientation throughout the first several weeks of school. International student organizations are also available for socializing and as an added support network.

Application Facts and Dates

Application deadlines are July 15 for fall entry, November 15 for spring entry, and April 15 for summer entry. International students are asked to apply six months in advance. For more information, students should contact:

M.B.A. Admissions
The School of Business and
 Administration
Saint Louis University
3674 Lindell Boulevard
St. Louis, Missouri 63108
Telephone: 314-977-3800
Fax: 314-977-3897
E-mail: johnsonab@sluvca.slu.edu

Saint Mary's College of California

Moraga, California

> We seek to educate mature adults for challenging and productive management careers in the dynamic global marketplace of the 1990s and into the twenty-first century. The programs are designed to prepare students who have a strong knowledge base, analytical skills, intellectual openness and flexibility, and an instinct for inquiry; will operate creatively, with vision and imagination, in a complex domestic and international business environment; can apply theory-based knowledge and analytical approaches to diverse, "real-life" management problems; and understand that business management is a profession and not simply a vocation. The School's highly regarded faculty includes teacher/scholars with earned doctorates from leading universities and substantial professional experience, as well as senior-level business practitioners. An underlying premise of education at Saint Mary's is that integrity is not a nicety but a necessity for a successful and satisfying life. Accordingly, a consideration of the ethical implications of business policies and operations is an integral aspect of our curricula.
>
> —Edwin M. Epstein, Dean

Programs and Curricular Focus

Graduate study in business administration began at Saint Mary's in 1975 with the establishment of the well-respected executive M.B.A. program. It was followed by the evening M.B.A. program in 1984 and the M.B.A. in international business program in 1990. Most graduate business students at Saint Mary's College are working business professionals who have chosen to earn their M.B.A. degrees on a part-time basis. Students of the M.B.A. in international business program have left the workplace for one year to complete their degrees on a full-time basis.

The executive M.B.A. program is offered in two formats, weeknight or Saturday, for twenty-one months. The flexibility of the evening M.B.A. program allows students to enroll in one, two, or three courses per quarter. Most students complete this program in 2½ years. The M.B.A. in international business program is taught in an intensive 13½-month schedule, with four courses per quarter. Courses are held in the afternoons and evenings.

The executive M.B.A. program offers a general management perspective. Classes are scheduled in a lock-step pattern, with two classes per quarter, including three electives. The evening M.B.A. program comprises foundation courses, core courses, and electives in

finance, marketing, and international business. Class times are determined two years in advance, so students may plan their own schedules when they begin the program. The M.B.A. in international business program provides students with core M.B.A. skills while immersing them in the international environment of business. Courses cover business competition in the regional markets, international economics, and political and social differences that affect transnational and multinational businesses.

Students and the M.B.A. Experience

Students in the graduate business programs have earned undergraduate degrees in engineering, science, and the liberal arts, as well as in business and economics. This diversity of backgrounds contributes to the learning that takes place in study groups, an integral part of the curriculum. Students represent virtually all industries, including telecommunications, financial services, engineering, health care, scientific research, consumer product sales, and nonprofit organizations. A strength of the graduate business programs most often cited by students is the professors' emphasis on practical, everyday application of the theory taught in the classroom. Students in the executive M.B.A. program have

worked an average of nine years before beginning their studies, while students in the evening M.B.A. and international business programs have worked approximately four years. The average age of students in the executive M.B.A. program is 36, while in the evening M.B.A. and international business programs, the average age is 28. Students in the evening M.B.A. and the executive M.B.A. programs live and work in counties surrounding San Francisco and Oakland. Students in the M.B.A. in international business program come from a variety of other countries as well as the United States.

Special Features

Short-term study-abroad opportunities are available to M.B.A. students. Saint Mary's offers a two-week study tour to Sheffield University in the United Kingdom and to Prague in the Czech Republic for students of the M.B.A. in international business program. Students in the evening M.B.A. program may spend a semester as an exchange student at the University of Rennes, France. Students from the University of Rennes may study at Saint Mary's.

Management development seminars are offered on a quarterly basis to students in the evening M.B.A. program. These seminars cover practical aspects of business, such as negotiation, time management, and career development. Evening M.B.A. students must participate in four seminars to complete graduation requirements.

The Faculty

The graduate business faculty includes both Ph.D.-trained scholars and experienced business professionals, a combination that reinforces the balance between theory and practice and is a distinguishing characteristic of M.B.A. education at Saint Mary's. Both groups of teachers share a deep commitment to provide academically sound training for professional managers. Because the College places emphasis on teaching rather than research, the primary measure of faculty success is teaching effectiveness, with student evaluation of professors' performance taken very seriously. Professor accessibility is a key element of student satisfaction with the graduate business programs.

The Business School Network

The ties between the San Francisco Bay corporate community and the graduate business programs are varied. Professors invite local business leaders to be guest lecturers. Students interact with local firms, developing strategic business plans that serve as final class projects for the students and as future direction for the companies. Local employers, who believe that a Saint Mary's M.B.A. education adds value to their organizations, sponsor students in the graduate business programs. Members of the alumni association serve as resources as graduate business students seek new professional opportunities.

The College and Environs

Saint Mary's College, established in 1863, is one of the oldest institutions of higher learning in California. It is owned and directed by the Christian Brothers, a Catholic teaching congregation. The student population totals about 3,900. The 450-acre campus in Moraga, 20 miles east of San Francisco, lies in a valley surrounded by the hills of a former ranch, which is now parkland open to recreation. It is considered one of the most beautiful and safest colleges in California. The College possesses a rural serenity yet is located in Contra Costa County, a rapidly developing commercial center specializing in financial services, telecommunications, manufacturing, and retail operations.

Placement

The Career Development Center at Saint Mary's College offers self-assessment and career counseling services to graduate students and alumni. Job search strategies, on-campus interviewing, and placement services are also offered. A career newsletter with job postings is circulated to all M.B.A. students. The Career Placement Coordinator facilitates student and graduate networking with the alumni association.

Admission

Applicants with an undergraduate degree in any area are welcome. For students applying to the evening M.B.A. and the M.B.A. in international business programs, the undergraduate GPA, score on the required Graduate Management Admission Test (GMAT), and two letters of recommendation are considered. Applicants to the executive M.B.A. program must currently be employed and have a minimum of five years of business experience, as well as a baccalaureate degree and two recommendations. These candidates are interviewed once their applications are complete; the extent of management experience is given special consideration. The GMAT is not required of executive M.B.A. applicants. A TOEFL score of 550 is required of all candidates whose undergraduate study was not in English.

Students are admitted to the executive M.B.A. program in October, January, and April; to the evening M.B.A. program in October, January, April, and July; and to the M.B.A. in international business program in October.

International applicants must show proof of sufficient funds to cover tuition, fees, and living expenses for the duration of the entire program to which they are applying.

Finances

Tuition is calculated per quarter unit, estimated at $304 for the 1995–96

academic year. Each M.B.A. course is worth 4 quarter units. In the evening M.B.A. and the M.B.A. in international business programs there are eighteen courses each; the executive M.B.A. program has fourteen courses. Living and personal expenses vary according to where students live in the community; on-campus housing is not available for graduate students. Books and supplies average $200 per quarter. Financial aid for graduate study at Saint Mary's is limited to student loans. No teaching fellowships are available.

International Students

Conditional admission is possible for graduates of Saint Mary's Intensive English Program. These applicants must meet the minimum admission requirements for either the evening M.B.A. or the M.B.A. in international business programs. Students from Asia comprise 70 percent of the international student population; European students make up 13 percent.

Application Facts and Dates

There are no application deadlines; it is recommended that applicants send admission materials eight weeks prior to the quarter in which they wish to begin M.B.A. studies. Admission is made on a rolling basis, and decision letters are mailed within two weeks of the date applicants' files are complete. For more information, applicants should contact:

Director of Admissions
Graduate Business Programs
Saint Mary's College
P.O. Box 4240
Moraga, California 94575-4240
Telephone: 510-631-4500
Fax: 510-376-6521

Santa Clara University

Santa Clara, California

THE SANTA CLARA TRADITION

The M.B.A. program at the Leavey School of Business and Administration combines tradition with innovation, research with teaching, and theory with practice, all within an excellent program designed to develop professional managers for the twenty-first century. The Jesuit tradition of education stresses development of the whole person. In the Leavey School, this emphasis is reflected in a commitment to ethics and leadership.

Our mission is to develop leaders who will guide organizations to positions of competitive strength in today's rapidly changing, technologically advanced global business environment. To paraphrase Thoreau, we know of no more encouraging fact than the unquestionable ability of men and women to elevate their lives through conscious endeavor. In this spirit, we look for applicants who seek the challenge of a dynamic learning community in a distinguished graduate school of management.

—James L. Koch, Dean

Programs and Curricular Focus

Santa Clara's M.B.A. program was among the first group of M.B.A. programs accredited by the AACSB, in 1961, and has consistently met the AACSB's high standards on applicant admissions, curriculum design and content, faculty scholarship, and instructional acumen. The program is ideally suited for people who want to pursue their education while continuing in their current job positions. (Each class meets twice a week in the evenings, for 75 minutes per session.) However, many students attend on a full-time basis, taking advantage of the flexible class scheduling and the opportunity to meet and study with employees from over 500 Silicon Valley companies.

The course of study at Santa Clara University primarily takes a generalist perspective, preparing students to be decision makers across the various functional fields rather than specialists or technocrats. A full range of electives does, however, also allow in-depth concentration in selected areas. Students may choose their own pattern of electives or follow one of the suggested study plans leading to a concentration in finance, information systems, international business, managing technology and innovation, marketing, or quantitative approaches to business problems.

Depending on prior academic background, students take between fifteen and twenty-four courses to obtain their degrees. Two courses bracket the

program: MGMT 501 (Managerial Competencies and Team Effectiveness), taken within the first two quarters of residence, and the capstone course, MGMT 519 (Business Policy), taken within the last two quarters of residence.

The Leavey School of Business also offers a joint J.D./M.B.A. program with the School of Law. This combined-degree program allows students who are interested in obtaining both the J.D. and the M.B.A. degree to do so in less time than if the degrees were earned independently. To participate in the J.D./M.B.A. program, students must first be admitted to the School of Law. During the first year of the J.D. program, students complete the regular admissions process for the M.B.A. program.

The Institute of Agribusiness at Santa Clara University, in conjunction with the Leavey School of Business, offers an M.B.A. in agribusiness. The Institute, founded in 1973, is an internationally recognized center for agribusiness management education. The curriculum incorporates both general management courses and agribusiness management courses, and many students complement their course work by participating in the institute's internship, mentor, and site visit programs.

Students and the M.B.A. Experience

Approximately 82 percent of the 1,100 M.B.A. students at Santa Clara study

part-time as they pursue their careers. Attending part-time, students generally take 3½ years to complete the program, while full-time students complete the program in 2 years. The average student is 27 years old upon entering the program and has more than five years of work experience. Thirty-seven percent of M.B.A. students are women, and 18 percent of the student body is composed of international students representing sixteen different countries.

Current M.B.A. students come from more than 400 undergraduate colleges and universities across the United States, as well as from international institutions. Approximately one third of these students had an undergraduate business major, while one third pursued undergraduate engineering degrees, one sixth pursued humanities and social sciences, and one sixth had other majors. Ten percent of M.B.A. students already have an advanced degree.

Special Features

Santa Clara's emphasis on developing the whole person begins with the M.B.A. orientation program. In this one-day Saturday session, students are introduced to the Santa Clara campus, the M.B.A. curriculum, and their new classmates. Beyond addressing such mundane but potentially frustrating issues as how to obtain a parking permit, the program provides a foundation for MGMT 501, enhancing appreciation for and skills in teamwork and leadership and building a sense of esprit de corps among entering students. Throughout the time that they spend at Santa Clara, students are challenged as individuals and as teams to develop their critical-thinking skills and effectiveness in complex problem-solving environments. This innovative orientation is the gateway to the Santa Clara M.B.A. experience.

The Faculty

The faculty of the Leavey School possesses national stature in each of its six major departments—Economics, Organizational Analysis and Management, Marketing, Finance, Decision and Information Sciences, and Accounting as

well as the Institute of Agribusiness. In each department, faculty members play leading roles in their professional associations and in editorial capacities for the top scholarly journals in their fields. This excellence in scholarship is balanced by a strong commitment to teaching and continuous improvement in service to students. The faculty also represents the global world of business today, representing twelve different countries.

The Business School Network

Alumni of the M.B.A. program at Santa Clara University hold executive positions in more than 800 innovative and rapidly growing businesses. The M.B.A. Alumni Association plays an active role in supporting personal and career development of both fellow alumni and current students. As a vital link between the business school and its alumni, the association sponsors a series of social events and educational programs.

Corporate Partnerships

The Leavey School of Business and Administration Advisory Board consists of 41 distinguished CEOs and business leaders. This active board provides a vehicle for the business community to provide input and communicate concerns directly to top administrators and faculty at Santa Clara. The composition of this board and the willingness of top executives to serve on it reflect and reinforce awareness of the Leavey School and its M.B.A. program at the highest levels in local and national organizations. The high regard for the Santa Clara M.B.A. is also demonstrated by the number of companies that interview on campus and provide tuition reimbursement plans to encourage their employees to continue their professional development at Santa Clara.

Prominent Alumni

SCU alumni hold prominent positions in a wide variety of local and national companies, including Pacific Bell; Fujitsu American, Inc.; IBM; Hewlett-Packard; Intel Corporation; Lockheed Missiles and Space; Wells Fargo Bank; Sun Microsystems; Xerox; and Apple Computer. In addition, many alumni have started successful entrepreneurial ventures.

The College and Environs

Santa Clara University, founded in 1851, was the first institution of higher learning on the West Coast. The University was established on the Mission Santa Clara de Asis, and the Mission remains at the center of the University. Santa Clara University currently enrolls over 7,500 students in its graduate and undergraduate programs.

Santa Clara is located 46 miles south of San Francisco, in Silicon Valley, an area rich in opportunities. The cultural and entertainment center of San Francisco and the magnificent vistas of Marin County are within 1 hour's travel. Also close by are the beaches of Santa Cruz and the Napa Valley wine country, and even closer are the cultural and sports opportunities available in San Jose.

Placement

Career Services offers complete career services for students and alumni, including counseling, on-campus recruiting, seminars, and workshops. Recruiting is ongoing due to Santa Clara's year-round admission and graduation schedule for M.B.A. students. Workshops help students focus on self-assessment, résumé writing, and job-search strategies. Career Services also maintains extensive resource materials on career fields and prospective employers, company directories, and job-search books. They work closely with alumni and students, coordinating networking opportunities.

Admission

Applicants are required to submit their GMAT results, transcripts from all schools previously attended, two essays, two recommendations, and the Santa Clara application form, which discusses work experience and extracurricular activities. All of these factors are taken into account by the Admissions Committee when evaluating an application. The average GMAT score of entering M.B.A. students is 580, and the average GPA is 3.1. Although there is no academic business background required before entering the program, applicants should be proficient in algebra and possess basic computer skills.

For any applicant whose first language is not English, the TOEFL and TWE are also required. The minimum acceptable TOEFL score is 580, and the minimum TWE score is 4.0.

Finances

Tuition for 1994–95 was $357 per quarter unit, and all classes are 3 units. Tuition for the Institute of Agribusiness was $367 per quarter unit. Each quarter, there was a $12 registration fee and a $7 Student Association fee. Books and supplies cost approximately $50 per course.

Financial assistance is generally available to M.B.A. students who have good academic records and can show financial need. Most financial aid covers partial tuition only and is in the form of M.B.A. Project Assistantships, which require working on administrative and/or research tasks for the School. The Institute of Agribusiness offers separate grants and awards for students enrolled in their program. Additional financial aid programs for minority students are also available. The deadlines to apply for financial aid are two weeks after the application deadline for each quarter.

Application Facts and Dates

Application deadlines are June 15 for the fall quarter, September 15 for the winter quarter, December 15 for the spring quarter, and March 15 for the summer quarter. Decision letters are mailed out four to six weeks after the application deadline. For more information, contact:

Ms. Elizabeth Ford
Director, M.B.A. Admissions and
   Recruitment
Leavey School of Business and
   Administration
Kenna Hall, #323
Santa Clara University
Santa Clara, California 95053
Telephone: 408-554-4500
Fax: 408-554-4571

Seattle Pacific University

Seattle, Washington

M.B.A. WITH A CAN-DO ATTITUDE

We work closely with the Pacific Northwest business community to provide a curriculum that deals directly with the competencies desired by today's firms. Our rigorous management curriculum provides experiences that strengthen individual effectiveness. The competencies we seek to develop include analytical thinking, team skills, ethical reasoning, oral and written communication, and the willingness to take initiative and be creative. Because our M.B.A. combines the latest theoretical knowledge with practical applications, we are developing graduates that can get the job done.

—Kenneth E. Knight, Dean

Programs and Curricular Focus

The M.B.A. program at Seattle Pacific University offers the highest quality graduate management education informed by Christian faith and values. Beyond the advanced instruction in management covered by all students, the degree can be tailored by one's choice of electives to provide depth in specific areas. Current areas of emphasis include general management, information systems management, entrepreneurship/small business, and human resource management. A separate Master of Science in Information Systems Management (M.S.I.S.M.) degree is also offered.

The M.B.A. curriculum consists of twenty-five courses divided between ten core, ten advanced, and five elective subjects. The ten core courses are waivable based upon prior college course work. Each course is 3 quarter credits and meets for one 3-hour session each week. A flexible schedule of summer classes is also offered. The related M.S.I.S.M. degree consists of a total of nineteen courses. This more specialized degree may be pursued individually or can be earned by completing 27 credits (nine courses) beyond the M.B.A.

Courses are taught at two Seattle-area locations in a convenient evening format. Some Saturday morning classes are also available. The program may be pursued on either a full-time or part-time basis.

Students and the M.B.A. Experience

With an average age of 31, Seattle Pacific graduate students bring a wealth of experiences with them to the classroom.

Small classes allow dynamic interaction between professors and students, individually or in teams. Students come with diverse employment backgrounds ranging from manufacturing and high-technology industries, for which the Puget Sound region is noted, to service and small-business sectors.

International students comprise 20 percent of the M.B.A. student body; women account for over 40 percent of the students. Three-quarters of the M.B.A. students are employed full-time.

Special Features

The Center for Entrepreneurship matches interested students seeking real-world consulting experience with small business CEOs and not-for-profit organizations in the Management Consulting Practicum course. Other students may choose to develop their own business plans or conduct independent research in Practice of Business. Electives may be chosen across a variety of disciplines. Popular electives have included such courses as Negotiating Skills, Turnaround Management, Pacific-Rim Enterprise, and Telecommunications and Networking.

The Faculty

The faculty is known for its high quality of instruction and broad experience in the marketplace. Additional faculty members in the M.S.I.S.M. program are drawn from SPU's Department of Computer Science and from industry. An executive-in-residence and a small number of effective adjunct instructors complete the teaching faculty. There are currently 18 full-time faculty members teaching in the

M.B.A. program. Of these, 94 percent hold doctoral degrees, 22 percent are women, and many have significant international experience in their academic disciplines.

The Business School Network

Comprised of more than 30 senior executives from Puget Sound-area companies, SPU's Executive Advisory Council (EAC) is a valuable networking resource for the School of Business and Economics. Through example and professional guidance, these executives interact with faculty and students to assist in providing a quality M.B.A. program based on Christian ethical principles. EAC members meet with faculty members at quarterly luncheons to discuss academic programs and needs of the Pacific Northwest business community. Many of these executives also participate in a special breakfast program in which M.B.A. students also participate. A separate Human Resource (HR) Advisory Board brings Seattle-area HR professionals together quarterly with faculty and staff to discuss issues in this field.

The College and Environs

Founded in 1891 as an outreach of the Free Methodist Church of North America, Seattle Pacific University has served the Seattle community through Christian higher education for more than 100 years. On-campus enrollment includes 2,400 undergraduate students and 1,200 graduate students, of whom approximately 250 are pursuing M.B.A. or M.S.I.S.M. degrees. The School of Business and Economics is one of three professional schools which, along with the College of Arts and Sciences, administer the academic programs of the University.

Seattle Pacific University is located on the north side of Queen Anne Hill, just north of downtown Seattle, Washington. The attractive campus borders the Lake Washington Ship Canal, which joins Lake Union with Puget Sound. Seattle is the premier business and trade center of the Pacific Northwest and is the U.S. gateway to the Pacific Rim. Bounded by

Seattle Pacific University has served the Pacific Northwest through Christian higher education for more than 100 years.

the Cascade mountains to the east, by the Olympic mountains and Puget Sound to the west, and by Mount Rainier to the south, the region is a haven for all forms of outdoor recreation. The city and region also boast a wide variety of cultural and sporting attractions.

Facilities

The School of Business and Economics is housed in McKenna Hall, built in 1981. Second-floor faculty and administrative offices and conference rooms, together with first-floor classrooms and a student lounge, provide a convenient, safe, and attractive educational setting.

Graduate business courses are also taught at a South King County classroom location. Students may elect to take classes at either site.

Construction of the new campus library was completed in 1994. This spacious, state-of-the-art facility offers on-line access to a wide range of publications and research materials, as well as traditional periodical and text sources. Two networked computer labs are available for student use.

Placement

Career services and resources are available from the University's Career Development Center. These include job opening notebooks (for full-time jobs); internship opening notebooks; career library (career, job search, and company information); career workshops; and career fairs.

Admission

Admission to the M.B.A. program requires successful completion of the GMAT exam; the GRE test is required for admission to the M.S.I.S.M. program. A minimum TOEFL score of 560 is required of all applicants whose native language is not English. An essay and two recommendations are also required for admission. Significant work experience and clearly expressed career goals are very important factors in the admission decision process. Applications are encouraged from students holding accredited bachelor's degrees from all disciplines. M.S.I.S.M. applicants should also be able to document experience with at least two programming languages.

Finances

A limited number of graduate assistantship positions are offered each year, and student loans are available for U.S. students taking at least two courses each term. Tuition for the 1995–96 academic year is $385 per quarter credit hour ($1155 per course). One-time application ($35) and matriculation ($50) fees and a refundable $100 registration deposit are charged. Typical textbook and miscellaneous costs average $100 per course. Representative room and board costs for three quarters of study range from approximately $4500 in campus residence halls or University-owned, nontraditional housing to $6000 for off-campus residence.

International Students

Seattle Pacific welcomes the enrollment of international students. Special educational and social programs are designed to enhance the student's cross-cultural experiences. Counseling assistance is also provided for academic achievement, cultural adaptations, and financial and legal concerns at the Center for Special Populations.

Application Facts and Dates

Applications are accepted for all quarters, including summer. Admission deadlines generally precede the quarter of admission by two months. Applicants should contact one of the graduate admission coordinators for additional information and an admission packet.

Ms. LaVonne DuBois
Coordinator of M.B.A. Admissions
School of Business and Economics
Seattle Pacific University
3307 Third Avenue West
Seattle, Washington 98119
Telephone: 206-281-2054
Fax: 206-281-2733
E-mail: mba@spu.edu

Ms. Debra Wysomierski
Coordinator of M.S.I.S.M. Admissions
School of Business and Economics
Seattle Pacific University
3307 Third Avenue West
Seattle, Washington 98119
Telephone: 206-281-2753
Fax: 206-281-2733
E-mail: ism@spu.edu

Simmons College

Boston, Massachusetts

> The Simmons M.B.A. degree is an original, yet it is rooted in Simmons College's century-old tradition of educating women to earn their own livelihoods.
>
> With more than 2,000 graduates in twenty years, the Simmons Graduate School of Management has taken on its newest challenge: helping women break through into the highest management positions in organizations of every kind, helping them compete equally, with insight and real understanding in an organizational culture that is more pervasively masculine the more senior it becomes.
>
> We are the first business school to do this. To a rigorous traditional curriculum, we have added courses that provide insight into the motivational differences between men and women. We look at differences in the meaning and exercise of power, in the choice between authority and responsibility, in the pursuit of status, in leading and following, in forming teams and working in groups. We bring organizational reality into our classrooms, and in the clear-sighted understanding of difference we give women the power to assess risk, to choose, and to act.
>
> —Margaret Hennig, Dean
> —Anne Jardim, Dean

Programs and Curricular Focus

In its emphasis on functional knowledge and quantitative skills, the Simmons M.B.A. program is very similar to those offered by other business schools. What sets Simmons apart is its unique behavioral focus. This is available nowhere else, and it is available to full-time and part-time students alike.

Simmons offers three M.B.A. program options. The full-time option provides the content of a traditional two-year, four-semester M.B.A. curriculum in an intensive three-semester program. Women who want to continue to work or to balance career and family concerns can earn their M.B.A. part-time in either a two-year or a three-year sequence.

The M.B.A. curriculum is a structured sequence of courses, carefully integrated to build upon and reinforce one another. Students take courses in economics, quantitative analysis, and computer skills and applications; in accounting, finance, marketing, operations, and strategic planning with a special focus on national and international markets and competition; in the management of organizations—with courses in management and behavior, organizational structure, human resources management, communication, and negotiations; and in individual career development—with an integrated course in career planning, self-assessment, and résumé development that is climaxed by a

six-week internship. There are electives in advanced accounting, finance, product management, and entrepreneurship.

Students and the M.B.A. Experience

With work experience averaging ten years and an average age of 35, students come to Simmons knowing a great deal about themselves and what they want from their education. They include women in the process of career change, women who have reached a career plateau, and women with substantial management experience who want to move up.

In the current class, minority enrollment is 16 percent and international enrollment is 12 percent. Sixty percent of the students with undergraduate degrees majored in the humanities or social sciences, while 40 percent majored in math, economics, or the sciences. Simmons also admits well-qualified, nontraditional students without a baccalaureate degree.

Study groups and structured group projects encourage team development, as leaders and as followers, and the required internship further deepens the impact of classroom learning.

The Faculty

Sixteen faculty members teach in the M.B.A. program; 13 are women. They

are graduates of leading doctoral and M.B.A. programs, and they all believe in women's ability to manage effectively and lead creatively.

The faculty members have an unmatched expertise in teaching women from very varied backgrounds the fundamentals, and the complexities, of business.

The Business School Network

Corporate Partnerships

Simmons students connect with the New England business community through major consulting projects and internships. Corporate leaders are frequent guest lecturers, and the School actively develops corporate partnerships, such as pioneering a move to bring current students into the Gillette Corporation's international management trainee program.

The College and Environs

The School is centrally located on Commonwealth Avenue in Boston's Back Bay, within easy reach of Boston's attractions and just across the Charles River from Cambridge.

Just around the corner from the campus lies the best of Boston shopping, including famed Newbury Street with its specialty boutiques and sidewalk cafés. Within walking distance are the world-renowned Boston Symphony Orchestra and the Museum of Fine Arts.

Relatively compact among major cities, Boston is a walkable city with an old seaport that is now a completely revitalized waterfront with marinas, shops, theaters, island ferries, seafood restaurants, miniparks, and walkways.

Facilities

The School is housed in the Mary Garland Center, a complex of turn-of-the-century town houses. Classrooms, administrative and faculty offices, the computer laboratory, and the library are situated within one city block.

The GSM library contains the latest volumes and periodicals in business and business-related fields as well as a media center with videotaping facilities. Students also have access to the Simmons College main campus library as well as several major libraries in the immediate area, including the famous Kirstein Business Library in Boston's financial district.

All the facilities of Simmons College, including a new sports center, are available to GSM students at the main campus, a short distance away.

Technology Environment

The School is equipped with its own computer lab. There are microcomputing terminals with laser printers available to students from 8 a.m. to 11 p.m. The computer lab also offers terminals exclusively for work on the Internet and e-mail. Additional microcomputing terminals are available in the undergraduate computing facility.

Through the library's on-line computer terminals, students can access over fifty Boston-area university and public library catalogs and forty subject-divided databases, including the Business Periodical Index, Business News Abstracts, Wilson Business Abstracts, and Paperchase (medical information). ABI/Inform, Business Dateline, Morningstar Mutual Funds, SEC/Disclosure, and the National Trade Data Bank are all available on CD-ROM computer workstations. Simmons is a member of the Fenway Library Consortium.

Placement

The Career Planning and Placement Office, dedicated to the M.B.A. program, provides personalized and comprehensive career planning and placement services. Advice on appropriate career directions, résumé writing, interview preparation,

and salary negotiation is integrated with a required Career Planning and Development course. The office provides students with access to job opportunities through its on-campus recruiting program, correspondence recruiting services, job bank, and two job fairs that are attended by a wide range of companies. Approximately 1,000 employers receive the résumés of all graduating students in an annual mailing of the class résumé book.

Admission

Admission is competitive. The committee attempts to measure potential for both academic success in the program and professional success thereafter. The committee looks closely at the candidate's preparation for a highly quantitative course of study. It does not follow a formula in making its decisions; rather it strives to evaluate the candidate's ability, aptitude, and promise by examining the whole as revealed in the application materials. An applicant must have at least two years of full-time work experience.

The following materials are needed to fulfill application requirements: a completed application form, an application fee, three letters of recommendation, official transcripts of all academic study beyond high school, and a score report from the GMAT. International students whose native language is not English must submit a TOEFL score.

Finances

The cost of tuition for the 1994–95 academic year was $564 per credit. Forty-five credits are required for the degree. The estimated cost for fees, books, and supplies is $2400.

Financial assistance consists of scholarships, grants, and federal loans, which may be offered separately or in combination. Deans' Scholarships and International Deans' Scholarships are available, and candidates applying to the program are automatically considered. These awards are based on merit.

To be considered for aid, a student should file the necessary aid forms by March 1, if possible.

International Students

Twelve percent of Simmons M.B.A. students come from outside the United States, with representation this year from Europe, Asia, Africa, and the Caribbean.

An ESL specialist is available to help strengthen students' written and oral communication skills. Alumnae or current students greet international students on their arrival in the United States, and alumnae have often hosted students until they secure permanent housing.

Application Facts and Dates

The School has a rolling admission policy designed to let students choose their admission decision date. Recommended deadlines, related to the dates on which the GMAT is offered, are November 15, February 15, May 1, and July 1. For more information, students should contact:

Admission Office
Simmons Graduate School of
 Management
409 Commonwealth Avenue
Boston, Massachusetts 02215
Telephone: 617-521-3845
Fax: 617-521-3880
E-mail: kashness@
 vmsvax.simmons.edu

Southern Illinois University at Edwardsville

Edwardsville, Illinois

THE SIUE M.B.A.: EDUCATIONAL ENHANCEMENT FOR THE WORKING PROFESSIONAL

The M.B.A. program offers practicing professionals the opportunity to build an educational foundation for career growth while remaining employed. Classes are taught in the evening and on weekends, using full-time faculty at three locations in the St. Louis metropolitan area. Classes are also offered by interactive video to locations on community college campuses in Southern Illinois.

The faculty is noted for teaching that is current, with respect to theory and practice. Instruction emphasizes the application of concepts and principles to business issues and the development of interpersonal and team-building skills.

Students must develop the oral, written, and presentation skills demanded by the business community to complete the M.B.A. successfully. The program promotes the ability to integrate disciplinary concepts.

—David E. Ault, Dean

Programs and Curricular Focus

The M.B.A. curriculum aims at preparing individuals for managerial careers leading to advancement through middle- and upper-level positions in business and not-for-profit organizations.

The M.B.A. degree requires a minimum of 30 hours of graduate level course work consisting of four required courses (12 hours), plus six elective courses (18 hours). The number of hours to be taken in core and pre-entry courses is determined after an analysis of the candidate's previous academic background. Students complete four required courses: MBA 531, External Environment of Business; MBA 532, International Business; MBA 533, Leadership, Influence, and Management Effectiveness; and MBA 534, Strategic Management.

Elective courses provide the opportunity for concentration in one or more of the business disciplines.

Students can earn a specialization in management information systems. The M.B.A./M.I.S. specialization combines management skills with the study of information systems and design.

Students and the M.B.A. Experience

The typical M.B.A. student is employed on a full-time basis while working on the degree. As such, most students have significant business experience. The average student is 31 years old with eight years of full-time work experience. Women represent 35 percent of the student population.

Over two thirds of the students are professionals such as architects, engineers, lawyers, nurses, or doctors or have management positions as accountants, management analysts, education administrators, financial managers, or marketing managers.

❖ Global Focus

The School of Business has developed student and faculty exchange programs with business schools and universities in France, Great Britain, Germany, Mexico, and the Netherlands.

Special Features

In addition to graduate fellowships and department-based graduate assistantships, the program provides students with the possibility of corporate-sponsored assistantships/internships.

The Faculty

The faculty of the School of Business is dedicated to providing high-quality instruction and to the personal and professional development of the students enrolled in the M.B.A. program. The skills and backgrounds of the faculty span nearly the entire range of the research-practical experience continuum.

The Business School Network

Corporate Partnerships

The School's Advisory Board includes business executives from a wide range of fields, and students have several opportunities to meet with these corporate leaders.

Prominent Alumni

Notable business leaders who are alumni of the School of Business include Robert Baer, President and Chief Executive Officer, United Van Lines; Wilton Heylinger, Dean, School of Business, Morris Brown College; Ralph Korte, President, Korte Construction Company; Mitch Meyers, President, Zipatoni Company; and James Milligan, President (retired), Spaulding Sports Centers.

The College and Environs

The Edwardsville campus of Southern Illinois University is located on 2,600 acres of gently rolling hills and timberland near the Mississippi River, 17 miles northeast of St. Louis, Missouri. Current enrollment is approximately 11,000 students, of whom nearly 2,800 are graduate students. Master's level programs are offered in over thirty fields.

Facilities

The Elijah P. Lovejoy Library is a member of ILLNET Online, a statewide automated resource-sharing network. Through it, 20 million items at thirty-five academic libraries as well as 800 other Illinois libraries can be identified and borrowed. The library also belongs to the Online Computer Library Center (OCLC), which provides access to collections at more than 13,000 libraries in the United States and forty-five other countries. Special arrangements also permit graduate students access to many of the academic, special, and public libraries in the metropolitan St. Louis area.

Technology Environment

The School of Business has its own microcomputer laboratory with about forty computers for student use. In addition, there are two computerized classrooms with a total of over sixty microcomputers that are networked to a video-projection system and to the campus backbone fiber optic network.

Placement

Top international companies regularly conduct on-campus interviews at the Placement Office. The Office also presents numerous workshops covering such topics as job search strategies, interviewing, résumé writing, and goal setting. In addition, the office works closely with students to formulate specific career plans.

Admission

The following formula is used by the School of Business to evaluate applicants for the M.B.A. degree program: admission score equals 200 times the undergraduate grade-point average (A=4.0), plus the GMAT score. For unconditional admission, unless otherwise noted, applicants must have a minimum admission score of 950, using the four-year cumulative undergraduate grade-point average, or 1000, using the grade-point average of the last

two years of undergraduate courses. Applicants must earn a minimum total score of 400 on the GMAT, with raw scores of at least 20 on both the verbal and quantitative portions of the test, and an Analytical Writing Score of at least 4.0. International students must also earn a score of 550 on the TOEFL examination and submit a test score on the Test of Spoken English (TSE).

Finances

Tuition and fees in 1995–96 for 9 semester hours (three courses) is $930 for Illinois residents and $2410 for nonresidents. Part-time tuition (6 hours) is $673 for Illinois and St. Louis residents and $1660 for nonresidents. Additional cost of books and supplies varies from $500 to $1000 per year.

Single-student living expenses at the campus Tower Lake Apartments are estimated at $1500 for housing, including utilities and local phone, and $700 per semester for food. Off-campus housing is estimated to be $2000 per semester. Family on-campus housing is approximately $500 per month.

International Students

Special exchange programs are available with schools in Germany, England, and Mexico. The St. Louis area has many opportunities for international business interests, and the M.B.A. program offers an array of international business courses.

Application Facts and Dates

Students should apply for admission no fewer than five weeks prior of the start of the semester in which they want to begin taking classes. Once the university has received official transcripts and GMAT scores, applicants will be notified as to admission within two weeks. For more information, applicants should contact:

Office of Advisement and Counseling
School of Business
Box 1086
Southern Illinois University at Edwardsville
Edwardsville, Illinois 62026-1086
Telephone: 618-692-3840
Fax: 618-692-3979

FACULTY LIST

Accounting

M. Robert Carver, Professor and Associate Dean; Ph.D. Financial accounting, taxation.
Michael Costigan, Associate Professor; Ph.D. Managerial accounting.
Maurice L. Hirsch Jr., Professor; Ph.D. Managerial accounting.
Thomas E. King, Professor and Chairperson; Ph.D. Financial accounting, theory.
Linda Lovata, Associate Professor; Ph.D. Accounting systems, managerial accounting.
Alan K. Ortegren, Associate Professor; Ph.D. Financial accounting, theory.
Marsha Puro, Associate Professor; Ph.D. Financial accounting.

Economics

David E. Ault, Professor and Dean; Ph.D. International economics, labor economics.
Radcliffe G. Edmonds Jr., Associate Professor; Ph.D. Econometrics, international economics.
Donald S. Elliott Jr., Professor and Chairperson; Ph.D. State and local finance.
Rik W. Hafer, Professor; Ph.D. Monetary theory and policy, macroeconomics.
Ali Kutan, Assistant Professor; Ph.D. International economics, macroeconomics.
Stanford L. Levin, Professor; Ph.D. Public utility regulation, industrial organization.
An-Yhi Lin, Professor; Ph.D. Econometrics, mathematical economics, economic development.
John B. Meisel, Professor; Ph.D. Industrial organization, antitrust policy.
John C. Navin, Assistant Professor; Ph.D. Public finance, labor economics.

Gilbert L. Rutman, Professor; Ph.D. Labor economics, African economic development.

Finance

Rakesh Bharati, Assistant Professor; Ph.D. Investment, information economics.
Roy Fletcher, Assistant Professor; Ph.D. Corporate finance and financial markets.
Richard Nyerges, Associate Professor; Ph.D. Corporate finance, portfolio management.
Jacky C. So, Professor and Chairperson; Ph.D. International and corporate finance.

Management

Edward J. Harrick, Professor; Ph.D. Personnel administration, manpower development.
Janice R. Joplin, Assistant Professor; Ph.D. Organizational behavior.
Kathryn Martell, Assistant Professor; Ph.D. Strategy, international.
Joseph F. Michlitsch, Assistant Professor; Ph.D. Organizational theory, strategy, and policy.
Timothy S. Schoenecker, Assistant Professor; Ph.D. Strategy.
Hans H. Steffen, Professor; Ph.D. International business operations and management.
Donald E. Strickland, Professor and Chairperson; Ph.D. Organizational behavior.
George M. Sullivan, Associate Professor; J.D. Regulation, business law, organizational design, business and society.
Laura Swanson, Assistant Professor; Ph.D., candidate. Production and operations management.
John M. Virgo, Professor; Ph.D. Manpower planning, business and society.

Management Information Systems

Douglas Bock, Associate Professor and Chairperson; Ph.D. Management information systems and design.
Robert W. Klepper, Associate Professor; Ph.D. Management information systems.
John F. Schrage, Associate Professor; Ph.D. Management information systems theory and design.
Robert A. Schultheis, Professor; Ph.D. Data processing, information storage and retrieval, word processing.
Mary R. Sumner, Professor; Ed.D. Educational administration, end-user computing, information systems for business-structured systems analysis and design, CASEtools, decision support systems.
David J. Werner, Professor and Provost; Ph.D. Management information systems theory and design, simulation.

Marketing

Ralph W. Giacobbe, Associate Professor; Ph.D. Marketing research, consumer behavior, personal selling, services marketing, product marketing.
Jack Kaikati, Professor and Chairperson; D.B.A. International marketing, marketing management.
Raymond F. LaGarce, Professor; Ph.D. Marketing strategy, management, promotion management.
James M. Lynch, Associate Professor; J.D., Ph.D. Advertising and promotion, marketing research.
Madhav Segal, Professor; Ph.D. Marketing research and information management, product/services marketing management.

Southern Methodist University

Dallas, Texas

BUSINESS LEADERSHIP CENTER AND EXECUTIVE MENTORS ... ADDED BENEFITS FOR YOU

Getting an M.B.A. certainly means increasing your analytical skills. But I believe—and our M.B.A. program is based on the belief—that it should do more.

Through our unique Business Leadership Center, you will be trained in areas that aren't taught in the classroom—personal skills that can make all the difference to your career.

The prominence of our Executive Mentors and the wide-open structure of the mentor/student relationship can create exceptional opportunities, from personal coaching to networking to internships to lifelong business relationships.

We are here not just to launch a career but to enrich a life. Possibly your life. I look forward to your inquiries.

—David H. Blake, Dean

Programs and Curricular Focus

As students become acquainted with the Cox School of Business at SMU, chances are one all-encompassing characteristic will emerge. It is an intensely invigorating workshop that allows students to mold themselves into astute business leaders. It is a holistic educational experience that enriches students personally as well as intellectually. It is a place students expand their outlooks, where doing business globally comes as naturally as doing business across the street. It is a business laboratory situated squarely in the heart of one of the nation's leading business centers—a place where students do not merely absorb theories but test them in the trenches of dynamic corporations. Here, students establish real connections to the business world, supported by several executive mentors. In short, the Cox School is a place to realize potential.

The M.B.A. curriculum comprises 60 credit hours or twenty courses. First-year students take nine core courses and one elective. During the second semester, through a community service requirement, students work on a team as consultants for a not-for-profit organization, refining their consulting skills.

Second-year students have the opportunity to take eight electives from such areas as accounting, business administration, entrepreneurship, finance, real estate, law, MIS, organizational behavior, and business policy.

The J.D./M.B.A. program permits students to earn both degrees in 4½ academic years.

The M.A./M.B.A. program offers individuals the opportunity to develop contemporary management skills, with an in-depth study of today's professional art world.

Students and the M.B.A. Experience

Cox students come from all regions of the United States and the world. The average age is 26, while the average work experience is three years.

Because Cox is highly selective and enrolls the smallest class among the top forty U.S. business schools, a rapport exists among students, who receive personal support not found in larger programs from the faculty.

Students take the initiative to manage various organizations, such as the Finance, Women in Business, and Entrepreneur clubs.

❖ Global Focus

International study programs bring students firsthand knowledge of the challenges and opportunities offered by today's global economy. These programs in Australia, Belgium, Brazil, England, France, Japan, Mexico, Singapore, Spain, and Venezuela allow students to spend one semester in another country. Because

many programs are conducted in English, language proficiency is not a barrier to participation.

Even without participation in an international exchange, students are ably equipped to function in the global marketplace. A location at the gateway to business opportunities afforded by NAFTA makes the Cox School a prime site for sharpening international perspective. Moreover, cross-cultural learning is enhanced by a diverse student population, 25 percent of whom are international.

Special Features

In today's corporations, academic intelligence is a necessary but not sufficient condition for managers. Firms seek individuals equipped with a fundamentally different managerial skill set—one that allows managers to work with diverse employee and customer groups, to effectively communicate ideas, and to be fleet-footed and resourceful in responding to companies' ever-changing needs.

The Cox School created the Business Leadership Center to hone these skills. As an innovative program offered along with the M.B.A. curriculum, the Business Leadership Center workshops and seminars build strategic interpersonal, communication, team-building, and leadership skills—the very skills that are prized in organizations but overlooked in many M.B.A. programs.

The Faculty

It is refreshing to find at Cox a faculty as interested in teaching as in research.

Business Week magazine named Randolph Beatty one of the top 12 "Masters of the Classroom." Rex Thompson, chair of the finance department, enjoys guiding students as they apply investment analysis and portfolio management skills to an actual portfolio of approximately $1 million.

Students benefit from a nationally recognized faculty that is approachable and accessible.

The Business School Network

Executive Mentor Program
One of the important ways the Cox School helps students make real-world connections is through the Executive Mentor Program.

Over 150 top executives serve as mentors to Cox M.B.A. students. The structure of the student/mentor relationship is as diverse as the individuals participating. In addition to being a valuable source of industry-specific business contacts, a relationship with a professional mentor provides students with insightful career advice, an inside track on current business trends, a resource for class assignments, and valuable perspective and coaching from an experienced businessperson.

Prominent Alumni
Prominent Cox alumni include Lodwrick M. Cook, Chairman, Atlantic Richfield; Howard M. Dean, Chairman and CEO, Dean Foods; Richard C. Green Jr., Chairman, President, and CEO, Utilicorp United; Paul B. Loyd Jr., CEO, Reading and Bates; John H. Massey, Chairman and CEO, Life Partners Group; John J. Murphy, Chairman, President, and CEO, Dresser Industries; Eckhard Pfeiffer, CEO, Compaq Computers; Robert J. Paluck, CEO, Convex Computer; and Roy M. Speer, Chairman and CEO, Home Shopping Network.

The College and Environs
Founded in 1911, SMU is a diverse institution, with approximately 9,000 undergraduate students.

Its location in one of the world's major business centers gives students an excellent advantage. Dallas ranks third in the United States as a site of major corporate headquarters and ninth in the world for multinational corporate headquarters.

Technology Environment
Students are invited to learn more about Cox on the World Wide Web (http://www.cox.smu.edu/Welcome.html).

Placement
The approach of the M.B.A. Career Services office is to act like an executive search firm on a student's behalf. Students enrolled in the two-year program take advantage of individual career guidance and year-round recruiting events.

Admission
The goal of the program is to identify applicants who will flourish academically and professionally in an environment that encourages teamwork and collegial support. Cox student body GMAT scores have averaged 612; the G.P.A., approximately 3.1. The school requires a TOEFL score of at least 600 for students whose native language is not English.

Finances
The cost of tuition and fees for 1995–96 is estimated at $19,502; books and supplies are $1200. Living off-campus generally costs between $800 and $1100 per month. Scholarships are available and are awarded strictly on merit.

Application Facts and Dates
Students enter the full-time program in the fall semester only (mid-August). Applications are processed on a continuous basis. After May 15, applications are accepted but are considered on a space-available basis.

Students enter the part-time program in the fall and spring semesters. It is recommended that applications for August admission be submitted before May 15 and for January admission, before November 1.

Mr. R. Keith Pendergrass
Director of Admissions
Edwin L. Cox School of Business
Southern Methodist University
P.O. Box 750333
Dallas, Texas 75275-0333
Telephone: 214-768-2630
         800-472-3622 (toll-free)
Fax: 214-768-4099
Internet: mbainfo@mail.cox.smu.edu

EDWIN L. COX SCHOOL OF BUSINESS

Suffolk University

Boston, Massachusetts

IT ALL COMES DOWN TO TEACHING

At Suffolk University, students are our most important customers. We provide you with an exceptionally qualified faculty, a flexible, carefully crafted curriculum that prepares you to anticipate—not merely respond to—the political, social, and economic transformations of the coming decades. You graduate as a skilled, ethical manager—a leader as well as a team player—who blends theoretical and technical expertise with practical work experience in your field.

But we do not stop there. Every professor we hire must care passionately about teaching. I am proud of the faculty we have built: they are teachers who incorporate considerable scholarly research and professional experience into the classroom. Many are nationally and internationally known for their work and must juggle lecture, consulting, and research demands, but nothing interferes with their teaching and office hour schedules. Students are the highest priority.

Thousands of success stories have emerged from our classrooms. Come join us at Suffolk University School of Management. Let us help you create your own success story.

—John F. Brennan, Dean

Programs and Curricular Focus

The Suffolk University School of Management enrolls 2,300 students, of whom 1,200 are graduate students. All degree programs are offered on a full- or part-time basis so that students can complete their graduate programs while still working in their chosen professions. The School offers fifteen degree programs, which include an executive program, degrees in public policy (M.P.A.), and joint programs with the Law School. Class schedules are flexible, with most courses offered in the late afternoon or evening so that students can keep full- or part-time positions or begin an internship or co-op job as part of a full-time course of study.

Suffolk's full-time faculty members have excellent academic training and credentials. Everything a student learns is grounded in the realities of professional experience. One professor might be a former vice president of Gillette, another a senior executive from a Big Six accounting firm or a consultant to a government or international agency. Students might include a portfolio manager from a brokerage firm or a nurse manager from a local hospital.

M.B.A. students complete a core and required curriculum of eleven courses and then choose eight electives from a field of sixty. Full-time students complete many of the courses together as a cohort.

The core courses cover the major functional areas of management to include accounting, computer systems, marketing, management, finance, economics, statistics, business law, communication, and human behavior. With strong undergraduate preparation in business, a student can utilize the waiver policy and complete the M.B.A. program in as few as ten courses in a year or less of full-time study. Courses are waived through proficiency exams or equivalent academic work that was taken at the undergraduate or graduate level. Students may also choose to specialize in one functional area by taking a core course and three advanced electives.

The School of Management offers graduate degree programs in specialty areas, as well as several joint-degree programs. The Master of Science in Accounting (M.S.A.), Master of Science in Taxation (M.S.T.), and Master of Science in Finance (M.S.F.) are offered. There are also several health-related programs. These include an M.B.A. with a concentration in health administration; an M.P.A. with a concentration in health administration; an M.P.A. with a concentration in disability studies; and a Master of Health Administration for those students already possessing a master's degree in another field. Joint degrees include the M.B.A./J.D., M.P.A./J.D., and a Master of Science in International Economics (M.S.I.E.)/J.D. in the College

of Liberal Arts and Sciences. There are Executive M.B.A. and accelerated M.P.A. programs, with classes taught only on Saturdays.

Students and the M.B.A. Experience

Diversity and flexibility are the keys to the M.B.A. programs at Suffolk University. Students in the M.B.A. degree programs have an average of three to five years of work experience, while students in the Executive M.B.A. program may have ten or more years of experience. Full-time M.B.A. students are not required to have work experience. Last year the average work experience for full-time students was 3.8 years. The average age is 27 in the M.B.A. programs and 34 in the Executive M.B.A. program. Women comprise approximately 40 percent of each program. Approximately 12 percent of the graduate students are international students from over twenty countries. In the full-time M.B.A. program, at least one third of the students are international.

❖ Global Focus

Each year more than 350 international students from sixty-two countries come to Boston to attend Suffolk University. A global perspective is an integral part of the School of Management at every level—curriculum, faculty, student body, and linkages to the international business community. In addition, the School of Management offers a selection of international business courses, including short seminars and site visits to businesses, universities, and government agencies in Spain, England, Italy, Hong Kong, China, and the Czech Republic. Not all sites are visited every year.

The University also maintains the Center for International Education, which supports the English Language for Internationals (ELI) program, sponsors short-term executive programs for internationals, and provides full-time assistance to international students for immigration advising, housing placement, and travel purposes. The center also sponsors orientation and other short-term cultural programs for international students.

The Faculty

The Suffolk faculty members are well known for their expertise in such diverse fields as investment analysis and financial policy, direct marketing, personal selling, buyer behavior, health-care marketing, public accounting, total quality management, and professional ethics. There are more than 60 full-time faculty members, 93 percent of whom hold Ph.D. degrees, giving the School of Management one of the highest faculty-Ph.D. ratios in the country.

The Business School Network

Corporate Partnerships

Suffolk's School of Management maintains close ties with senior managers in both the public and private sectors through active advisory boards that meet regularly with the faculty of each department. Advisory board members include representatives from the Big Six accounting firms, banks, and insurance companies, in addition to executives from large and small businesses, health administrators, government officials, and managers in not-for-profit organizations. Students in the full-time M.B.A. program have an opportunity to complete internships or co-op experiences with such firms as Gillette, Polaroid, Fidelity, and Digital Equipment Company.

Prominent Alumni

Suffolk School of Management is proud of its many accomplished alumni. Among these are Edward McDonnell, President of Seagram International, and Richard Rosenberg, CEO of Bank of America. Both have been actively involved in speaking with the alumni and with current students. Two prominent M.B.A. graduates are John W. Tynan, Executive Vice President of Store 24, and Edward J. Boudreau Jr., Chairman and CEO of John Hancock Mutual Funds Company.

The College and Environs

Located on historic Beacon Hill in the heart of Boston, Suffolk University was founded in 1937 and comprises the School of Management, the College of Liberal Arts and Sciences, and the Law School, with a total enrollment of 6,000 students. The Suffolk School of Management is the only school of management in New England to be accredited by both the American Assembly of Collegiate Schools of Business (AACSB) and the National Association of Schools of Public Affairs and Administration (NASPAA).

The urban location of the University, next door to the Massachusetts State House, is a special advantage. Students are within walking distance of Boston's financial and world trade districts, the center of government, renowned medical centers, and major cultural institutions. The location and reputation of the School of Management make it possible to draw upon the resources and expertise of these institutions to complement and enrich its approach to global business.

Technology Environment

Students have access to the University's PRIME 6350 superminicomputer seven days a week from computer stations on campus or by phone. Electronic access is available to the worldwide Internet system and the LEXIS/NEXIS service. There is a University-wide electronic mail system and user access to on-line library services such as ABI/INFORM. Microcomputer resources are centered in a modern computing facility, which includes a large student computer laboratory and a computerized classroom with systems connected by a Norvell LAN. A separate facility is dedicated to word processing.

Placement

Career services available to graduate students include the Alumni/ae Career Resources Network, which is an active association of more than 275 recent graduates in every area of management. Network members serve as an important source of information and contacts for job search strategies and placement.

Other career services include career assessment and individual career counseling; extensive listings of full- and part-time jobs, co-op opportunities, and internships; workshops on résumés and interview and job search strategies; a comprehensive career library; regularly scheduled career fairs; and on- and off-campus recruitment programs.

Admission

The School of Management seeks qualified, capable applicants with distinguished undergraduate degrees from diverse educational and professional backgrounds. To apply, students must submit an application, transcripts of all academic work, GMAT scores, two letters of recommendation, a current résumé, and a statement of professional goals. The average GMAT score for M.B.A. students is 510. M.P.A. students are not required to submit any test scores.

International applicants must submit a TOEFL score of at least 550 and a statement of financial resources.

Finances

The School of Management offers several innovative financial aid programs. Last year, graduate management students were awarded more than $1.5 million in aid in the form of grants, loans, employment programs, fellowships, and assistantships. Tuition varies by program. For 1994–95, the costs were $14,124 full-time or $1413 per course for the M.B.A. and M.P.A.; $15,730 full-time or $1572 per course for the M.S.F., M.S.A., and M.S.T.; $1737 per course for the Executive M.B.A.; and $15,490 per year for the M.B.A./J.D. and M.P.A./J.D. Additional costs are estimated at $10,000 per year.

Application Facts and Dates

Suffolk University accepts applications for fall (September), spring (January), or summer (May). The M.S.F. and Executive M.B.A. programs admit students in the fall and spring only. Application deadlines are June 15 for fall, November 15 for spring, and April 15 for summer. For the M.S.F. program, application dates are June 15 and November 15. For the Executive M.B.A. program, the deadlines are August 15 and February 15. Students applying for financial aid for the fall semester must submit their admission application by March 15. For more information, students should contact:

Marsha Ginn
Director of Graduate Admission
Suffolk University
8 Ashburton Place
Boston, Massachusetts 02108
Telephone: 617-573-8302
Fax: 617-523-0116

Syracuse University

Syracuse, New York

NEW DIRECTIONS FOR THE M.B.A.

A sleek, new American corporation has emerged from years of stress, self-analysis, and tough decisions. It is smart and responsive—more flexible than at any time in its history. Moreover, it is superbly positioned for leadership in the global economy.

In the borderless corporation, managers will operate in a global context, working in diverse teams, partnering, factoring social and ethical considerations into their decisions—the more creatively, the better. This generalization holds true for midsize and entrepreneurial enterprises as well as the giants.

Graduates of the Syracuse M.B.A. program will acquire a new mindset and special skills, as well as a firm grounding in the traditional disciplines of business. Our program has been recognized as innovative and progressive. Our graduates will thrive in a constantly changing environment.

I urge you to weigh the merits of the Syracuse M.B.A. program, to compare it with others, to hold it to the highest standards. I invite you to consider it as the decisive step in your business career—a bold journey into a new millennium.

—*George R. Burman, Dean*

Programs and Curricular Focus

The newly redesigned M.B.A. program is based on the premise that all managers need broad knowledge and skills, as well as functional expertise. The seven pervasive theme courses are the signature of the new curriculum. The themes—diversity, globalization, quality, ethics, the environment, critical thinking, and paradigms of management—represent the challenges that pervade every function of management today.

The heart of the curriculum is its highly integrated group of professional core courses that introduce the concepts of the functional areas of business and the relationships that exist among them. Seven elective courses are also integral to the program, offering students the opportunity to tailor the program to their own professional and career interests.

Concentrations are offered in ten areas: accounting, finance, human resource management, international business, management information systems, managerial statistics, marketing management, operations management, organizational management, and transportation and distribution management. Elective courses may also be selected from any other graduate program at Syracuse University; engineering, communications, law, computer science, and economics are such examples. Joint-degree programs may also be

designed that combine a master's degree in any other graduate program with an M.B.A.

The M.B.A. program includes a 60-credit curriculum that comprises 39 credits of required courses and 21 credits of electives. During the first year, students follow a prescribed sequence that includes pervasive theme courses, personal skills courses, and most professional core courses. During the second year, students complete their required core courses, as well as seven electives.

Additional graduate degree programs include the Master of Science (M.S.) in accounting; the Juris Doctor (J.D./ M.M.A. and J.D./M.S. in accounting) in cooperation with the College of Law; a Master of Professional Studies (M.P.S.) in media administration, offered jointly with the S.I. Newhouse School of Public Communications; and an independent study program.

Students and the M.B.A. Experience

The Syracuse M.B.A. program has a diverse, talented, and interactive student body. Over one third of the 230 full-time M.B.A. students are women, 17 percent are minorities, and 33 percent are from seventeen other countries. Eighty-five percent of the M.B.A. students have

worked full-time for at least one year prior to enrolling; the average is approximately four years.

Undergraduate majors include such diverse areas as history, engineering, nursing, accounting, and economics. Students are placed in teamwork groups of 4 to 5 individuals of various educational/professional experiences and backgrounds; these groups, in addition to small classes averaging 27 students, help create a feeling of intimacy within a large collegiate environment of 14,000 students and prepare graduates for today's team-oriented organizational environment.

❖ Global Focus

There are both required and elective courses in international business. Summer internship programs are offered in London and Singapore. As a member of the Thunderbird consortium of business schools, students can spend a semester of study at The American Graduate School of International Management in Arizona or at any of their campuses abroad. Another important aspect of the program is that over one third of M.B.A. students are from other countries, contributing to a global classroom experience.

Special Features

New students begin the fall semester with Leadership Week, a five-day orientation period; participants include the faculty and distinguished business leaders. Leadership Week offers new students opportunities for building teams and support groups and an introduction to other personal skills areas, including managing conflict, communication, ethics in management, and teamwork and groups.

Faculty

The members of the faculty of the Syracuse School of Management are distinguished by their accomplishments in research and consulting, their effectiveness in the classroom, and their genuine concern for students. Teaching methods vary from subject to subject, as appropriate. Methods of instruction include lectures, student presentations, class discussions, case studies, small-group projects, computer and management simulations, and other techniques. Instructional methods take full advantage of the program's small group structure and unique experience base represented by the students in the program.

The Business School Network

"In considering new hires," says Peter M. Sturtevant, a vice president of Xerox Corporation, "one of the qualities we look for is the ability to be a quick study—to get a good understanding of the company quickly."

If Syracuse M.B.A. program graduates are quick studies—and Sturtevant believes they are—it is because they can draw on broad exposure to business and business practitioners. Corporate ties are woven throughout the fabric of the program, affording contact with managers in every relevant field and speciality. This explains why graduates find themselves at home in today's complex corporate environment.

The College and Environs

Founded in 1870, Syracuse University—a private, nonsectarian liberal arts institution—is one of the largest and most comprehensive independent universities in the nation. The School of Management, in existence since 1919, has offered graduate programs since 1947.

Syracuse is a moderately sized, friendly city located in upstate New York. New York City, Boston, Philadelphia, Toronto, and Montreal are all less than a one-half-day drive away. Most importantly, being so close to these major metropolitan centers provides ease for graduates to the vast northeastern U.S. M.B.A. job market.

Facilities

The University libraries serve the informational and research needs of the entire Syracuse University community. The library system is one of the largest in the country and ranks in the top 2 percent of university libraries nationally. It contains more than 5 million books, periodicals, and pieces of microform information housed in the main Ernest Stevenson Bird Library and five branch libraries. Also available are six micro-computer clusters of twenty to fifty IBM, Zenith, and Macintosh personal computers, which are found at several campus locations, including the School of Management.

Placement

The placement office provides students with personal help on developing interview skills, résumé preparation, alumni networking, and access to on-campus corporate recruiting. In 1994, graduates averaged $48,000 in starting salary, considerably above the national average for M.B.A. graduates. Employers of the class of 1994 included such diverse organizations as Goldman Sachs, Andersen Consulting, Microsoft, and The Federal Reserve Bank.

Admission

Applicants must submit transcripts of all previous college work, their GMAT and TOEFL scores, a completed application for admission, and letters of recommendation, together with a $40 application fee. Prior work experience is encouraged, and personal interviews are strongly suggested.

Finances

Tuition in 1995–96 is $479 per credit ($14,370 for an academic year of 30

credits). Books and other course materials are estimated at $1100 per academic year.

Almost 20 percent of the M.B.A. students receive merit-based assistance in the form of fellowships, assistantships, or scholarships. For 1995–96, fellowships carry a stipend of $9680 and 30 credits of remitted tuition; scholarships include 24 credits of remitted tuition, and assistantships include a stipend of $6800. Most assistantships also receive a scholarship. All international students are eligible for assistantships in their second year of full-time study.

Application Facts and Dates

Applications for admission to the full-time M.B.A. program from international applicants should be submitted by March 1 for fall admission. For more information, applicants should contact:

For the master's program:
Jack Huebsch
Assistant Dean, M.B.A. Programs
Suite 222 CHM
Syracuse University
Syracuse, New York 13244-2130
Telephone: 315-443-9214
Fax: 315-443-9517
Electronic mail: anderscb@suadmin

For the Ph.D. program:
Associate Dean Raj
Director, Ph.D. Program
Suite 200 CHM
Syracuse University
Syracuse, New York 13244-2130
Telephone: 315-443-1001
Fax: 315-443-5389

T Temple University

Philadelphia, Pennsylvania

NEW DIRECTION—NEW OPPORTUNITIES

In refining and sharpening our M.B.A. program, we listened to our alumni, current students, and employers. Our new program is intense, integrating the various business disciplines throughout, and actively involving the Philadelphia-area business community.

You will meet professors who practice what they teach. You will find that dialogue, case studies, and consultation are an important part of your M.B.A.

Our new daytime program has an international focus and is enriched by Temple's campuses in Japan and Rome as well as our linkages with French business schools. Our evening program has a breadth and flexibility suitable for working students.

Grow professionally with us at Temple.

—Jonathan Scott, Acting Dean

Programs and Curricular Focus

The School of Business and Management (SBM) seeks to improve business practices by graduating students who have the skills to lead and manage profit and not-for-profit organizations into the twenty-first century. Alumni, the local business community, nonprofit organizations, government officials, students, and faculty are actively involved in a continual review of the program's curriculum to ensure the students' needs receive primary consideration in program delivery.

Students receive a results-oriented education linking current management theory with practice. SBM graduates have a firm understanding of the core areas of business and have the ability to respond to organizational problems and opportunities from a total enterprise perspective.

The new M.B.A. curriculum fosters an appreciation for the new team-based, quality-oriented, and lean models of management. An integrative, cross-disciplinary experience is provided to better prepare students for the work environment they are likely to face upon graduation. The new curriculum conveys the sense that managerial knowledge is constantly evolving and that the future manager must be a master learner, capable of assessing situations and developing new, effective responses. The program has a strong real-world focus, with increased attention to the needs of specific industries.

In addition to a full-time day M.B.A. program, Temple University also offers a part-time evening program in center city Philadelphia and at the Ambler campus, a suburb of the city. Approximately 80 percent of the 1,200 M.B.A. students attend part-time in the evening. A twenty-two-month executive M.B.A. program is offered on alternate Fridays and Saturdays at an executive conference center just outside the city.

Joint programs are offered with the Law School, leading to a J.D. and M.B.A. degree; with the School of Dentistry, which awards a D.M.D. and M.B.A. degree; and with the Department of Civil Engineering, which confers an M.S. degree in environmental safety and an M.B.A. degree.

Students and the M.B.A. Experience

The average Temple M.B.A. student is 29 years old. Most of the students are from the Mid-Atlantic region, and approximately 9 percent are international. Students in the program have an average of four years of work experience. The minority enrollment in the program is approximately 10 percent.

To help students reach their greatest potential, a series of noncredit workshops and seminars have been developed. These programs, offered at no additional charge, include the Leadership Development Program, Power Presentations, and a Career Development Workshop.

❖ Global Focus

The School of Business and Management has several opportunities for international educational experiences. A unique experience is the international M.B.A. program where students spend one semester studying international business in France, one semester in Philadelphia, and an optional corporate experience in Japan during the summer. Depending upon the student's undergraduate business preparation, additional foundation course work may be required. All of the courses in the program have been re-engineered and are geared to prepare the student for the world of international business. On each side of the Atlantic, students are assigned mentors from multinational corporations.

In addition, students in the traditional M.B.A. program may spend a summer or fall semester enrolled in graduate business courses at a campus in Rome, Italy, where Temple University has offered courses for over twenty-five years.

All M.B.A. students, whether they have the flexibility to study abroad or not, are exposed to the operations of multinational corporations and the complexities of international business. A 1-credit course in international business is required of all M.B.A. students. A concentration in international business administration, which can be completed in Philadelphia, is available in the day and evening programs.

Special Features

Temple University's large M.B.A. program offers a full-time day program on its main campus for students concentrating in international business administration. The evening M.B.A. program is offered in center city Philadelphia, the heart of the area's business community, and in Ambler, a suburban campus. During the evening, twelve areas of concentration are available, including accounting, business administration, computer information sciences, finance, general and strategic management, health administration, human resource administration, international business administration, management science/operations management, marketing, real estate and urban land studies, and risk management and insurance.

The Faculty

The faculty of the School of Business and Management is actively involved in research and has published in many major business journals, including *Accounting Review, Journal of Accounting and Economics, Journal of Finance, Management Science, Strategic Management Journal, Industrial and Labor Relations Review,* and *Marketing Research.* There are over 150 full-time faculty members, and more than 85 percent of all M.B.A. classes are taught by those faculty members.

The College and Environs

Temple University enrolls over 32,000 students in its sixteen schools and colleges. Students come from over seventy-five countries to study at the University. Founded in 1884, Temple is a senior comprehensive research institution that awards bachelor's degrees in 100 disciplines, master's degrees in 80, and doctorates in 60.

Philadelphia, the fifth-largest city in the United States, is an international center of commerce, culture, and history. Strategically located in the dynamic industrial region between New York and Washington, D.C., the region is home to many major corporations, including Merck and Company, Rhone-Poulenc Rorer, CIGNA, Sun Company Inc.,

Unisys, Campbell Soup, Alco Standard Corporation, Crown Cork & Seal, Rohm and Haas, and Scott Paper.

Students also enjoy the many cultural activities the city has to offer at the ballet, theater, the world-famous orchestra, and art museums. Philadelphia is one of the oldest cities in the United States and is home to Independence National Park, the Liberty Bell, Betsy Ross House, and Elfreth's Alley (the oldest continuously occupied residential street in the nation). The downtown and historic areas of the city are located 2 miles from the University's main campus.

Placement

The Office of Business Relations and Placement is dedicated to developing employment opportunities for M.B.A. students and alumni. Services include on- and off-campus interviews, corporate presentations, a résumé databank, career workshops, and a résumé book. During the 1994–95 academic year, over seventy companies interviewed Temple M.B.A. students for employment.

Admission

Prospective students may apply for admission to begin the M.B.A. program during the September, January, or May semester. The acceptance rate is approxi-

mately 50 percent. The average GMAT score is 540, and the average undergraduate grade point average is 3.1. Applicants are encouraged to have work experience.

Finances

Tuition for the academic year 1994–95 for Pennsylvania residents was $366 per credit and for non-Pennsylvania residents, $258 per credit. Student fees for full-time students were $150 per year. Most full-time students enroll in 12 to 15 credits per semester.

A variety of housing options are available both on and off campus. On-campus housing for graduate students ranged from $352 to $487 a month for the 1994–95 academic year. In addition, Philadelphia has a large student population and can offer a great variety of affordable housing choices.

Application Facts and Dates

The deadlines are June 1 for the September semester, September 30 for the January semester, and March 15 for the May semester. Students should address application inquiries to:

School of Business and Management
Speakman Hall, Room 5
Temple University
Philadelphia, Pennsylvania 19122
Telephone: 215-204-7678
Fax: 215-204-8300

Texas A&M International University

Laredo, Texas

> We take pride in the tradition of providing specialized graduate business education to our small but very dynamic cadre of students. During the last two decades, we have trained over 500 M.B.A.'s with specialization in international trade. Recently we have added the M.S. in international banking and the M.S. in international logistics to the list of pioneering programs.
>
> Students in the Graduate School of International Trade and Business Administration have lived and studied in a microcosm of international business. In addition to having gone through an eminently specialized curriculum, they have benefitted from interaction with a highly diversified faculty and student body. The faculty in the College of Business represents ten countries, and the alumni, fifty-two countries and thirty-two states.
>
> —Dr. Khosrow Fatemi, Dean

Programs and Curricular Focus

In foreseeing the ever-accelerating changes in the global economy and international commerce, the Graduate School of International Trade and Business Administration has pioneered specialized graduate business programs responsive to these changes. The M.B.A. with a concentration in international trade prepares students from a broad spectrum of experiences, cultures, and academic disciplines with the skills necessary to assume leadership roles in the international business community.

Through the use of specialized lectures, attendance at various international trade and international economic-related conferences, guest speakers from the international business community, workshops, and case studies, students are exposed to a wide variety of business experiences. The major strengths are the commitment to the actual application of concepts grounded in sound theoretical underpinnings and the requirement to complete a major portion of the program in international business administration courses.

To ensure students are prepared to pursue the specialized international business curriculum, all entering students are required to complete seven business core courses. Students having completed prior courses may apply for course waivers. Students then proceed to the M.B.A. program and complete a combination of general M.B.A. courses, international trade courses, and business elective courses. This combination

provides the graduate with a solid conceptual and theoretical framework to launch a career in manufacturing, importing, exporting, transportation, warehousing, insurance, custom brokerage, freight forwarding, or marketing.

In addition to the M.B.A., the Graduate School of International Trade and Business Administration offers the M.S. in international banking, the M.S. in international logistics, the M.S. in Information Systems and the Master of Professional Accountancy. Students may also pursue a 57-semester-hour joint M.B.A./M.S.

Students and the M.B.A. Experience

Students at the Graduate School of International Trade and Business Administration bring to the classroom a wide variety of academic backgrounds, such as international relations, area studies, various business disciplines, foreign languages, and other degree fields. They emanate from all regions of the world. Since 1979, fifty-two countries and thirty-two states have been represented in these specialized international business programs. The average age of the graduate business student is approximately 27, and half are full-time working professionals from the community and across the border in Mexico.

❖ Global Focus

The strength of the international business programs offered by the Graduate School

of International Trade and Business Administration is exemplified by a curriculum that consists of forty graduate international business courses; a faculty with extensive practical international business experience; international exposure through study or exchange programs in Germany, France, Costa Rica, Lithuania, and Morocco; research opportunities and activities that include publication of *The International Trade Journal, Border Business Indicators,* and the *NAFTA Digest;* and an internationally diverse student body.

The geographic location of the University is in Laredo, Texas, one of the United States' largest inland ports of trade and the only city on the juncture of Interstate 35 and the Pan American Highway. This provides an ideal "laboratory" to observe international business activities on a daily basis.

The Faculty

The faculty members of the Graduate School of International Trade and Business Administration have a very diverse and international background. Approximately 84 percent of the faculty members have extensive international business experience or are foreign nationals. Faculty members collectively possess functional literacy in twenty different languages and have living and/or working experience in Africa, Europe, the Middle East, South and Central America, and Asia.

The College and Environs

Texas A&M International University is one of the newest "stars" in the Texas A&M University System. Founded in 1969 as Texas A&I at Laredo, the University served upper-level and graduate students and was located on the historic site of old Fort McIntosh. As of its twenty-fifth anniversary, TAMIU is now a comprehensive university offering a wide variety and level of degrees and majors, many of which have an international component. Of additional significance, the University moved to a brand-new, state-of-the-art campus in 1995.

The Radcliffe and Sue Killam Library.

Located in south Texas on the Rio Grande River, the city of Laredo is 150 miles south of historic San Antonio, 150 miles west of the beaches of Corpus Christi, and 150 miles north of cosmopolitan Monterrey, Mexico.

Facilities

All buildings and facilities at Texas A&M International University are new as of 1995. Phases I and II of construction include a joint library and administration building; business administration, science, arts and humanities, and all-purpose classroom buildings; and a kinesiology building. There are also on-campus apartments, featuring security fencing, two- and four-bedroom units, a pool, a clubhouse, sand volleyball courts, and laundry facilities.

Placement

The Office of Career Planning and Placement provides a spectrum of services to students and graduates in the areas of career development and profes-

sional employment. Professional staff members advise students on all aspects of career preparation and the job search.

Recruiters visit the University each March for annual career fairs. Other services include a career resources library, posting of current job vacancies, and a candidate referral service.

Admission

Students from a wide range of academic disciplines are accepted. Full graduate standing is granted to applicants whose undergraduate GPA on all upper-division course work is at least 3.0 (on a 4.0 scale). Applicants who do not meet this requirement must submit GMAT or GRE scores.

International students whose native language is not English must earn a minimum score of 550 on the TOEFL and also must present proof of adequate funds.

Finances

Tuition and fees for 1994–95 were $539 for a 12-semester-hour load for Texas resi-

dents and $2255 for non-Texas residents and international students. Full-time students generally take 12 hours per long term, summer being optional. Books and supplies average $75 per class.

Fellowships are available to students in the International Trade, International Banking, International Logistics, and Information Systems programs. The fellowships are competitive and awarded according to merit criteria. Recipients receive a stipend based on residency, and the stipend permits out-of-state and international students to pay in-state tuition.

International Students

Fifty percent of the full-time students are foreign nationals. In any given semester, 25 percent are from Asia, 25 percent from Latin America, and 20 percent from Europe, Africa, and the Middle East, with the remaining 30 percent emanating from both near and far states. Students needing to strengthen their English may do so at the University's International Language Institute.

Application Facts and Dates

Although applications are accepted for any semester, and admission is granted on a rolling basis, students are encouraged to begin the admission process as far in advance as possible. For more information, applicants should contact:

Betty Lewis Momayezi
Director of Enrollment Management
    and School Relations
Texas A&M International University
7411 E. Loop 20
Laredo, Texas 78041
Telephone: 210-722-8001

FACULTY LIST

Jan Berg-Andereasen, Associate Professor; Ph.D. Project management.

Martin Broin, Assistant Professor of Operations Management; Ph.D. Location theory.

Willie Newton Cargill, Associate Professor of Accounting; Ph.D. Accounting.

Barry Carr, Assistant Professor of Agribusiness; Ph.D. Agricultural economics.

Khosrow Fatemi, Professor of International Trade and Dean of the College of Business Administration; Ph.D.

Carolyn Gardner, Associate Professor of Management.

Alain D. Genestre, Assistant Professor of Marketing; D.B.A., Ph.D. French, marketing.

Jim Giermanski, Professor of International Trade and Chair of the Department of Management and Marketing; D.A.

Pedro S. Hurtado, Associate Professor of Business Administration; Ph.D. Transportation.

Muhammad Mazharul Islam, Associate Professor of International Trade; Ph.D. International finance.

Kurt R. Jesswein, Assistant Professor of International Trade; Ph.D. International banking and finance.

Michael Landeck, Associate Professor of Marketing and International Business; Ph.D. North American Free Trade Agreement.

Jane LeMaster, Assistant Professor of International Business; Ph.D. International management.

Stephen Lunce, Assistant Professor of Computer Information Systems; Ph.D. Systems analysis and design.

Balasundram Maniam, Assistant Professor of Finance; Ph.D. Application of artificial neural networks to finance.

Charles Maxwell, Professor of Finance and Chair of the Department of Economics and Finance, Ph.D. International banking.

Thomas McGhee, Assistant Professor of Accounting; Ph.D. International accounting.

Stephen McNett, Associate Professor of Accounting and Chair for the Department of Accounting and Information Systems; Ph.D. Accounting.

Kamal D. Parhizgar, Professor of Business Administration; Ph.D. Strategic management.

J. Michael Patrick, Assistant Professor of Accounting and Economics and Director of the Institute for International Trade; Ph.D.

Armand E. Picou, Assistant Professor of Finance; Ph.D. International acquisitions.

Jacqueline Lou Power, Assistant Professor of Accounting; Ph.D. International accounting standards.

William Renforth, Professor of Marketing, D.B.A. International marketing.

David Norton Roberts, Assistant Professor of Accounting/Business Law; J.D. Commercial law.

Antonio J. Rodriguez, Associate Professor of Business Administration/Economics; Ph.D. Treasury bills, futures trading.

Henry Smith, Assistant Professor of Accounting; Ph.D. candidate. Managerial accounting.

Stephanie Underhill-Smith, Assistant Professor of Finance; Ph.D. Corporate finance.

Texas Christian University

Fort Worth, Texas

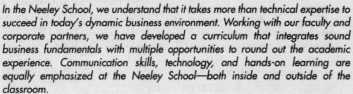

THE NEELEY ADVANTAGE

In the Neeley School, we understand that it takes more than technical expertise to succeed in today's dynamic business environment. Working with our faculty and corporate partners, we have developed a curriculum that integrates sound business fundamentals with multiple opportunities to round out the academic experience. Communication skills, technology, and hands-on learning are equally emphasized at the Neeley School—both inside and outside of the classroom.

Neeley School faculty and staff are committed to providing students with opportunities to achieve their academic as well as professional potential. Knowledgeable. Confident. Prepared. Neeley graduates are ready to face the challenges and contribute to the success of today's organizations.

—H. Kirk Downey, Dean

Programs and Curricular Focus

Because managers seldom face clearly defined problems or opportunities, the Neeley School designed a curriculum to give its graduates a strategic, integrated perspective of business. Eleven required core courses cover a myriad of business principles. Five elective courses allow for more detailed study in one or more areas. The 48-semester-hour program is completed in two academic years by full-time students.

Neeley School faculty members work closely across functional departments to integrate core classes through special case studies and group projects. Classroom instruction is tied to the business world through guest presentations by visiting executives and corporate-based field projects. Faculty members employ a variety of teaching methods in the classroom. The environment is highly interactive and team-oriented.

In addition to a strong conceptual framework, the program emphasizes the development of essential managerial skills, such as effective communication. The innovative Center for Productive Communication provides dedicated professional staff and state-of-the-art facilities as a resource to M.B.A. students.

Students and the M.B.A. Experience

The Neeley School M.B.A. program attracts a diverse group of students. As a private university, TCU does not serve a

defined geographic area. The objective is to bring talented students from many countries and regions to share experiences and learn from each other. Approximately one fourth of the full-time M.B.A. class comes from outside the United States. Of the remaining students, about half are from Texas and half are from other parts of the United States. Neeley School M.B.A. students also come from a broad range of academic and professional backgrounds. About half hold undergraduate degrees in business. The others have majored in liberal arts, science, technology/engineering, and the fine arts. On average, full-time students have completed two years of professional experience after earning their undergraduate degrees.

Although diverse, all Neeley School M.B.A. students do share certain characteristics. They are academically talented individuals with demonstrated leadership skills. They are highly motivated and possess a history of success. A typical entering full-time M.B.A. class at TCU includes about 80 students.

❖ Global Focus

Second-year M.B.A. students may participate in semester-long exchange programs with universities in Dijon, France; Freiburg, Germany; and Chihuahua or Puebla, Mexico. In addition, TCU faculty lead a summer study program in Germany featuring visits to leading business firms, homestays with German

families, and sessions sponsored by German alumni of the Neeley School.

Special Features

Throughout the curriculum and in several innovative programs, Neeley School M.B.A. students put business theory into practice. Students in the Educational Investment Fund (EIF), the largest student-run investment portfolio in the United States, manage over $1 million. Through the Student Enterprise Program, teams of M.B.A. student consultants are hired by companies to solve real business problems. Through the Summer Internship Program, approximately 95 percent of the M.B.A. students secure professional-level positions in a variety of industries.

The Faculty

The Neeley School's graduate faculty includes 30 individuals widely recognized as leaders in their academic fields. The dedicated faculty members are respected researchers and frequent consultants to industry. All M.B.A. faculty members hold a Ph.D. or a terminal degree in their field. All classes are taught by faculty members; there are no teaching assistants.

The Business School Network

Corporate Partnerships

The Neeley School works closely with business leaders in developing the M.B.A. curriculum and special programs. The International Board of Visitors, a corporate advisory board of senior-level executives from the U.S. and abroad, serves as a sounding board for the dean and faculty.

The Neeley School's extensive corporate ties directly impact the M.B.A. student's experience. Through the Executive-in-Residence Program, 15 to 20 executives are brought to campus each year for guest lectures and small group discussions with students. The required Industry Perspectives Series of seminars led by seasoned professionals offers students detailed exploration of important issues, such as diversity in the workplace, managing change and technology, and ethical and global issues. The M.B.A.

Alumni Association's mentor program matches students with alumni from their chosen career field.

Prominent Alumni

Many TCU alumni have established themselves as business leaders, including John Roach, Chairman and CEO, Tandy Corporation; Gordon England, President, Lockheed; Roger King, Senior Vice President of Human Resources, PepsiCo; and Webb Joiner, President, Bell Helicopter-Textron, Inc.

The College and Environs

Founded in 1873, Texas Christian University is a private university located in Fort Worth, Texas. TCU limits its total undergraduate and graduate enrollment to approximately 7,000 students so that all may benefit from personalized programs and services. TCU has a long-standing reputation for excellence in teaching and research and is accredited by all major accreditation associations.

Although founded by a Christian denomination, TCU is today an independent institution attracting students from many different cultures and faiths. Religious instruction is not a component of the M.B.A. curriculum.

TCU's location provides access to the Dallas–Fort Worth metroplex, a thriving metropolitan area of approximately 4 million people and home to a broad range of industries. Because of the area's central U.S. location, pleasant climate, and relatively low cost of living, many major firms have headquarters or branch offices based in Dallas–Fort Worth. The area is also home to world-class museums, major professional sports, and numerous other recreational opportunities.

Technology Environment

M.B.A. students have access to approximately sixty microcomputers in on-site computer labs. The labs are open daily from 8 a.m. to midnight. All computers are linked to a campus network with access to worldwide networks via the Internet and BITNET. Many of TCU's library resources are available through the computer network, including the card catalog, CD-ROM databases, and on-line

information services such as Dow Jones News/Retrieval Service.

Placement

In addition to the full range of programs offered by TCU's Career Planning and Placement Center, the Neeley School dedicates professional staff and developmental resources to career activities. The relatively small program size allows for an individualized approach to career planning and placement. Student career goals and planning skills are evaluated early in the program. Emphasis is placed on helping students build meaningful professional networks during their years as a student.

Admission

The nature of the Neeley School M.B.A. program requires that a holistic approach be used in the admissions process. No single criterion, such as a test score, can determine eligibility for admission. The applicant must demonstrate not only academic ability but also the desire and ability to perform in a highly interactive, team-based environment. The previous academic record, relevant test scores, experience, motivation, maturity, and leadership ability are all considered in the admissions process. Professional work experience is preferred but not required.

Applicants are asked to submit a completed application, personal essays, official transcripts from each university attended, three letters of reference, official GMAT scores, and official TOEFL scores for international applicants (minimum score of 550 required).

Finances

As a private university, TCU does not charge higher tuition for out-of-state or international students. For full-time M.B.A. students at TCU for the 1994–95 academic year, tuition was $6912 ($288 per semester hour), fees were $990, and the estimated cost of books and supplies was $600. The cost of room and board varies depending on the lifestyle of the individual student. The estimated cost for rent, meals, and living expenses for international students is about $5700 per academic year.

Through the Neeley School's aggressive scholarship program, approximately 40 percent of full-time M.B.A. students receive merit-based awards. Financial assistance based on academic merit is available to students of all nationalities. A number of special corporate-sponsored scholarships include a guaranteed summer internship and a generous living stipend.

International Students

Approximately 25 percent of TCU's full-time M.B.A. students come from outside the United States. Typically, international students come to TCU from Europe, Mexico, South America, and Asia. The Neeley School's small class sizes and emphasis on personal attention can be especially important to students from other cultures. Dedicated faculty members are committed to working closely with students, in and out of the classroom.

Application Facts and Dates

Application deadlines are March 15 for scholarship consideration, April 31 as the general deadline, and May 30 for international applications. Following the deadlines, applications are accepted on a space-available basis only. Due to the limited class size, students are encouraged to apply early. Applications are received as early as a year prior to admission.

Admission decisions are made on a rolling basis. Decisions are usually communicated three to four weeks after the completed application is received. For more information, applicants should contact:

Ms. Peggy Conway
Director of M.B.A. Admissions
M. J. Neeley School of Business
Texas Christian University
P.O. Box 32868
Fort Worth, Texas 76129
Telephone: 817-921-7531
        800-828-3764 Ext. 7531
        (toll-free within the U.S.)
Fax: 817-921-7227
E-mail: mbainfo@zeta.is.tcu.edu
Internet: http://www.tcu.edu

Union College

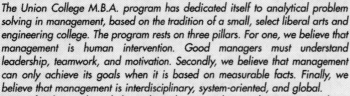

Schenectady, New York

> The Union College M.B.A. program has dedicated itself to analytical problem solving in management, based on the tradition of a small, select liberal arts and engineering college. The program rests on three pillars. For one, we believe that management is human intervention. Good managers must understand leadership, teamwork, and motivation. Secondly, we believe that management can only achieve its goals when it is based on measurable facts. Finally, we believe that management is interdisciplinary, system-oriented, and global.
>
> Our faculty members dedicate themselves to teaching and supporting students. We seek interaction with and among students. We invite our students to collaborate with us on state-of-the-art research. Our overall aim is to challenge students to achieve individual growth, strong analytical skills, and sharpened global perspectives. We seek to reinforce the intellectual tradition taught in a high-quality college.
>
> —Martin A. Strosberg, Director

Programs and Curricular Focus

Union College's Graduate Management Institute offers M.B.A. students an opportunity to study in the attractive environment of a liberal arts campus, where students get to know both the faculty and their peers. Union's M.B.A. curriculum blends theory with practice in a well-balanced approach consisting of lectures, case studies, written reports, computer models, and business games. For curricular development, the Institute benefits from the advice of a distinguished council that includes prominent leaders from business, government, and education. Union management students learn problem-solving techniques directly applicable to a progressive decision-making environment.

Union's M.B.A. programs develop the traditional knowledge of accounting, economics, finance, operations, marketing, and organizational behavior. The programs provide a foundation for effective team building, quantitative decision making, creative problem solving, and total quality management process skills. Students are assigned group projects in a number of core courses. These groups are carefully selected to include students with diverse educational and work experiences.

In addition to the M.B.A. in management, Union offers two other M.B.A. programs. The M.B.A. in accounting program at Union includes an internship at one of the "Big Six" accounting firms.

This program also prepares students to sit for the first section of the CPA examination. The M.B.A. in health systems administration includes a paid residency at a health-care institution during the summer between the two years of the program. This program, fully accredited by the Accrediting Commission on Education for Health Services Administration (ACEHSA), prepares graduates for management positions in health services delivery and related institutions.

Union also offers a combined M.B.A./J.D. program with the Albany Law School of Union University. Students in this program can earn their M.B.A. degree in management, accounting, or health systems along with their J.D. degree in four academic years.

Students and the M.B.A. Experience

The Graduate Management Institute includes both full- and part-time students with very diverse backgrounds and work experiences. Full- and part-time students take the same classes. They are offered the flexibility to transfer between full-time and part-time status as personal and professional circumstances dictate. Women comprise approximately 40 percent of the student population, and international and minority students comprise 10 percent of the full-time students.

Approximately 25 percent of the students have undergraduate degrees in

business or finance. Another 25 percent come from engineering or technical disciplines, with the remaining 50 percent coming from science, social science, humanities, and other disciplines. About 10 percent of the students are pursuing a joint degree in law and business.

The Faculty

Faculty ideas and attitudes make one institution different from another. The composition of GMI's faculty attests to Union's concern with providing a comprehensive education that remains relevant in the future. Every full-time member of the faculty is engaged in research, and all publish regularly in national journals. Research allows faculty members to remain current in their fields, and classroom teaching translates this expertise into an educational experience.

The adjunct faculty members are all either researchers in industry or successful in business in their field. They bring practical experience and diversity to all programs.

The Business School Network

Corporate Partnerships

The Graduate Management Institute has recently begun a Corporate Fellowship Program. This is a joint venture between GMI and various companies that provides opportunities for talented students to receive a scholarship from GMI and the sponsoring company and to work for the sponsoring company for 10 hours per week during the school year and 40 hours per week during the summer. Students are paid by the company for this work. Students in this program increase their work experience during the educational process. Permanent employment opportunities may result from these fellowships.

GMI's Advisory Council consists of business leaders in industry and in the fields of health and accounting as well as alumni and faculty members. This council functions to advise GMI on the changing needs in the corporate, health, and accounting industries. Council members are also encouraged to visit classes and to meet with students informally.

A series of roundtable lectures features prominent business leaders who address Union's graduate students on current business issues. Students attend luncheons with these guests, giving them an opportunity to interact with current business leaders in a less formal setting. In addition to these lectures, each term a colloquium series is featured. The guests for this series generally address specific functional areas of business. Students are encouraged to attend these functions as part of their educational experience.

The College and Environs

In 1795, Union College became the first college chartered by the Regents of the State of New York. Since its beginnings, Union has been committed to innovative education, offering scientific studies in the early nineteenth century. In 1845, Union became the first liberal arts college to offer engineering. In the 1950s, the College established programs that cut across the barriers separating the traditional academic disciplines. It was in this spirit that the Graduate Management Institute evolved as a center that builds on the values of a broad education.

The Graduate Management Institute offers its programs on the Union College grounds, a campus of some 100 acres located on a hill overlooking Schenectady, a city founded by the Dutch in 1661. The campus, designed by the French architect Joseph Jacques Ramée in 1813, is recognized as a historic landmark in the development of the American college campus.

Technology Environment

Housed in the Stanley G. Peschel Center for Computer Science and Information Systems, Union's computer center is the home of a distributed network that provides access to various computer resources, including a cluster of four VAX computers and a DEC system 5000/200 running UNIX. There are more than 700 personal computers (and workstations) and 100 terminals on campus. All students have access to national and international resources of the Internet through the College's membership in the NYSERnet. There is no charge for a student computer account. The on-line catalog in Schaffer Library is accessible from any point on the network.

Schaffer Library houses some 490,000 volumes and 1,600 current periodical subscriptions. It operates on the open stack plan and offers bibliographic instruction, interlibrary loan services, on-line bibliographic retrieval services, document delivery, CD-ROM workstations, and public-use computer terminals connected to the campus computer center. Automated circulation of books and other library materials as well as the on-line catalogs are in place. The library has been a depository for federal government documents since 1901. Professional reference service is offered during nearly all hours that the library is open.

Placement

The Career Development Center offers a variety of services for graduate students, including career planning, résumé writing, and interviewing skills. On-campus recruiting generally takes place during the fall and winter terms. In addition, the Graduate Management Institute has a strong alumni network to help with placement for its graduates.

Admission

The Graduate Management Institute requires all students to submit official transcripts from all undergraduate and graduate schools, GMAT scores, three letters of recommendation, and an essay. The average GMAT score for enrolling M.B.A. students is 580, with a range of 500 to 700. The average undergraduate GPA is 3.2.

TOEFL results are required for all students for whom English is not the native language. A score of 550 to 600 is required. International students must present proof of adequate funds to cover two full years. International students are considered for assistantships based on academic merit.

There are no specific prerequisite courses except for precalculus. Basic skills in writing and computing are expected. Students who have not taken precalculus may take a two-course sequence in precalculus and calculus at the Graduate Management Institute, but only one of these courses may be applied toward the degree.

All students must provide proof of immunization for measles and rubella. This is a New York State Health Law

requirement. Health insurance is available from the College at a very reasonable price.

Finances

Estimated tuition for the 1995–96 academic year is $11,260. Books and fees cost approximately $1000 per year.

There is no on-campus housing provided for graduate students at Union College, but housing is plentiful within walking distance of the campus. The cost of housing, utilities, and living expenses is estimated to be approximately $7000 per year. Students are not required to purchase a computer, but it is strongly encouraged.

A number of M.B.A. assistantships are available, and candidates applying for the program are considered if they request this on their application. The awards are based on academic merit and may be awarded to international students.

International Students

Approximately 15 percent of the full-time student population are international students. They are encouraged to attend the orientation held for international students prior to the beginning of classes in September. Graduate international students are also encouraged to participate in the International Club on Union's campus.

Application Facts and Dates

The Graduate Management Institute has a rolling admission process, and students may begin during any of the trimesters or summer sessions. However, most full-time students begin in the fall. For full-time students who wish to be considered for assistantships or fellowships, completed applications must be received no later than March 31. For more information, students should contact:

Carolyn J. Micklas, Coordinator for
  Recruiting and Admissions
Graduate Management Institute
Union College
Schenectady, New York 12308
Telephone: 518-388-6239
Fax: 518-388-6686
E-mail: micklasc@gar.union.edu

University of Alabama

Tuscaloosa, Alabama

> In selecting a business school and a strong M.B.A. program, you want to not only look at its past history and record but also at the future prospects. Here at the University of Alabama's Manderson Graduate School of Business, we are proud of our past and excited about our future. Part of our future will include the new Mercedes-Benz project, plus neighbors like JVC, Michelin, and others.
>
> We have recently completed a building campaign that includes three campus buildings with state-of-the-art equipment. Our new business library and new computer facility are poised to take us into the exciting technology of the future.
>
> Our faculty is recognized nationally for its excellence. But, as important, they are also recognized by our M.B.A.'s for being available and interested in helping the student to build a foundation for a career in business.
>
> We are celebrating our fiftieth anniversary as an M.B.A. program and our seventy-fifth anniversary as a college. We look back with pride, but we look forward with excitement. We are committed to remaining a national business school and we are committed to working one-on-one with each M.B.A. to help them get ready for their own future.
>
> —J. Barry Mason, Dean College of Commerce and Business Administration

Programs and Curricular Focus

The Alabama M.B.A. program is a two-year, four-semester program that consists of 49 academic hours and includes a focus on teamwork and professional development. The program consists of 34 required core hours, including classes in accounting, economics, management information systems, marketing, and business law. Students develop skills through teamwork by working in groups in and outside of the classroom on projects and assignments. There is also a yearlong professional development course that looks at the social and professional aspects of business. In the second year of study, students select a concentration option, which consists of 12 to 15 hours of electives. Areas of concentration include accounting, finance, human resource management, marketing, international business, and strategy in the business area and engineering, communications, and computer information systems in the nonbusiness area.

In addition to the traditional two-year program, the University of Alabama also offers an Executive M.B.A. degree, which can be completed in seventeen months. The program was designed for those individuals who have at least five years of work experience and wish to complete their M.B.A. while maintaining their professional careers.

The University of Alabama also offers a joint-degree M.B.A./Juris Doctorate program that combines the work for both degrees into a four-year program. Individual applications must be submitted to both the M.B.A. program and the Law School. Both the GMAT and the LSAT are required for admissions purposes.

Students and the M.B.A. Experience

The Alabama M.B.A. program emphasizes a personal approach with its students. The class size is 60 to 65 students, so professors have more time to spend with their students on an individual basis. Students have a wide variety of work experiences and come from throughout the United States. In 1994, the M.B.A. class was 65 percent men, 35 percent women. Ten percent were international students, and 6 percent were minority students.

Special Features

The Alabama M.B.A. program features a one-week M.B.A. orientation, where students get to know each other better before classes begin, work on computer skills, and address teamwork and leadership concepts. During the program, students are required to participate in a program called Marketing You, which helps students prepare their résumés, interviewing skills, and general career services perspective.

Students also participate in a yearlong class called Professional Development; this class looks at the social side of business, such as etiquette and ballroom dancing, as well as more academic business issues, such as ethics. Guest speakers often attend the class to speak about a specific issue.

The Faculty

Manderson's faculty offer a personal approach and excellent teaching ability, along with their applied business research in various areas.

The Business School Network

The city of Tuscaloosa is the proud new home of the first Mercedes-Benz plant in the United States. Tuscaloosa is also the proud home of JVC, Victor Corporation, Gulf States Paper, and Michelin Tires. The University of Alabama and the West Alabama Chamber of Commerce support cooperative programs with these companies.

The College and Environs

The University of Alabama is located in Tuscaloosa, Alabama, which is 60 minutes from Birmingham, Alabama, and is also near Atlanta, Georgia, and New Orleans, Louisiana. With its attractive countryside and location near the Black Warrior River, the town has a historic quality. The University has about 20,000 students, 380 of whom are graduate business students. Tuscaloosa has about 150,000 residents. It is a pleasant, small town that is growing into a thriving business center. The climate is usually comfortable, and favorite pastimes include outdoor activities such as waterskiing, fishing, camping, biking, and jogging, to name a few. Nationally and internationally known performers often come to campus to perform, and the local community is very supportive of the arts.

FACULTY LIST

Brian Gray, Ph.D.: statistics.
Thomas Albright, Ph.D.: accounting.
Giles D'Souza, Ph.D.: marketing.
William Gunther, Ph.D.: economics.
Mickey Petty, Ph.D.: human resources management.
H. K. Wu, Ph.D.: finance.
Daryl Webb, J.D.: legal studies.
Ronald Dulek, Ph.D.: business communications.
Larry Foster, Ph.D.: policy/strategy.
Carl Ferguson, Ph.D.: management information systems.
A. J. Strickland, Ph.D.: professional development.
David Miller, Ph.D.: production management.
Robert McLeod, Ph.D.: finance.

Facilities

The College of Commerce and Business Administration is the proud home of Bidgood Hall, Mary Hewell Alston Hall, and the 65,000-square-foot Angelo Bruno Business Library and Sloan Y. Bashinsky Computer Center. All three buildings house state-of-the-art classrooms and facilities. Alston Hall includes faculty and departmental offices, along with the Insurance Hall of Fame. Bidgood Hall, reopened after a beautiful refurbishing, houses multimedia classrooms and study areas for graduate students, as well as the home offices for the Center of Economic Research, the Alabama Small Business Center, the International Trade Center, and the Manderson Graduate School of Business. The Bruno-Bashinsky Library and Computer Center is a brand-new facility that houses over 100 computer terminals for student use, group-study rooms, and computerized library reference systems.

Technology Environment

Open daily, the Sloan Y. Bashinsky Computer Center is the home of over 100 computer terminals; the center is exclusively for the use of undergraduate and graduate business students in the College of Commerce and Business Administration at the University of Alabama.

Students also experience working with laptop computers offered by the Manderson Graduate School of Business.

Placement

The University of Alabama Career Center offers students and alumni an extensive array of services, including career exploration and guidance, a resource center, mock interviews, employer contacts and literature, and a diverse range of workshops concerning job-search issues. A wide variety of organizations representing business, industry, and government recruit for internship and full-time positions through on-campus interviewing, job listings, résumé referral, and career fairs.

Admissions

The University of Alabama requires GMAT scores for all individuals seeking admission. The TOEFL is required for those applicants who have not received a degree from a four-year program at an accredited United States university. The M.B.A. program considers a minimum of 500 on the GMAT and a minimum GPA of 3.0 as positive scores for admission. Work experience, letters of recommendation, and a statement of purpose are all considered important as well. Applicants must also have taken statistics and calculus as prerequisites and must have basic computer skills.

Finances

The costs for tuition at Alabama have been cited by a leading business publication as a "best bang for your buck." Tuition and fees are approximately $5500 per academic year (two 16-week semesters) or approximately $11,000 for the entire program. Additional fees for living expenses may include an estimated rent for an off-campus apartment, ranging between $300 and $500 per month. Additional bills for water, cable, telephone, and power can vary according to use. University dorms or apartments are also available.

Applicants may obtain more information about University housing by contacting Housing and Residential Life, the University of Alabama, Box 870339, First Floor, Mary Burke East, Tuscaloosa, Alabama 35487-0223.

Individuals who wish to be considered for any fellowships, scholarships, or assistantships offered by the University of Alabama's M.B.A. program must first apply to the program, be unconditionally accepted, and have competitive academic credentials. All students who are accepted unconditionally into Alabama's M.B.A. program are put into consideration for all academic awards. There are no additional forms that must be completed and submitted. It is advisable for those

international students who wish to be considered for financial assistance to apply as early as possible, preferably before April 1 of each year.

International students must show acceptable proof of sufficient financial support before an official letter of acceptance will be sent by the University of Alabama Graduate School office. International students are advised that, in most cases, any financial assistance offered by Alabama's M.B.A. program will not cover all expenses incurred during the duration of the program. Therefore, international students are encouraged to find additional financial support before applying.

Additional questions concerning financial assistance should be addressed to the Coordinator of Graduate Recruiting for the Manderson Graduate School of Business.

International Students

The University of Alabama welcomes diversity in its graduate programs and encourages citizens from all countries to apply. Currently, there are students enrolled from Japan, Canada, Korea, Thailand, the People's Republic of China, and other locations. Some organizations that are available for international students include International Student and Scholar Services and the Japan Culture and Information Center.

Application Facts and Dates

Applicants are encouraged to submit their applications to the University of Alabama as early as possible. The application process begins on October 1 of the year prior to the year applicants wish to start. The process continues until June 1. Students who wish to be considered for scholarships, fellowships, or assistantships should apply by January 15. All University of Alabama offices are open between 8 a.m. and 4:45 p.m. Central Standard Time. Students with any questions regarding international applications should contact:

Mrs. Edwina Crawford
The University of Alabama Graduate
  School
Box 870118, 102 Rose Administration
  Building
Tuscaloosa, Alabama 35487-0223
Telephone: 205-348-5921
800-365-8583 (toll-free in the U.S.)
Students may also contact:

Coordinator of Graduate Recruiting
The University of Alabama
Manderson Graduate School of
  Business
Box 870223, 101 Bidgood Hall
Tuscaloosa, Alabama 35487-0223
Telephone: 205-348-6517
E-mail: mba@alston.cba.ua.edu

The University of Arizona

Tucson, Arizona

INNOVATIVE MANAGEMENT EDUCATION—THE ELLER SCHOOL APPROACH

The goal of the Eller School M.B.A. program is to provide the foundation for a lifetime of development so that each student can maximize his or her potential for success. We accomplish this by providing a curriculum that combines the benefits of education based in the business disciplines with the relevance of dealing with real business problems. When you finish our program, you will be able to identify and formulate business problems, to specify and locate the information needed to solve them, and to develop and implement practical solutions. In short, you will know what questions to ask, where to go for information, and how to use that information to make effective managerial decisions. These are the keys to success in business, and they are the cornerstones of our program. We promise you hard work, a measure of fun, a friendly and supportive learning environment, and the knowledge and skills to be an effective business leader when you graduate. Join us for an unmatched learning experience!

—Christopher P. Puto, Associate Dean and Director of the M.B.A. Program

Programs and Curricular Focus

The Eller School's philosophy is that successful business leaders must have a solid understanding of business concepts and how they are interrelated in the overall business system.

The M.B.A. curriculum is based on two years of full-time study, with an optional internship in industry during the summer between the first and second years. The first year comprises the M.B.A. Core. Nine courses (plus the three communications modules) are designed to introduce students to crucial concepts and skills for professional managers.

The second-year curriculum offers students the opportunity to pursue their professional interests and goals through a wide selection of electives. Individual majors are not required in the Eller School M.B.A. program. By planning elective choices carefully, students can achieve functional depth and interdisciplinary breadth.

This combination of flexibility and structure lets students customize their individual course of study while ensuring that each student leaves the program with the knowledge and skills required to identify, create, and deliver superior customer value in his or her chosen career. Areas of study and concentration include highly ranked MIS and marketing departments, a nationally recognized

entrepreneurship program, and an expanded finance concentration. The final semester of the second year also includes a required business policy course, which serves as the capstone for the program.

Students and the M.B.A. Experience

Communications skills are vital for successful managers. To ensure relevance for business, the Eller School communications component is directly connected to and completely integrated with the first-year core courses. Each oral and written business communications activity has a theoretical and a practical component that relates directly to a corresponding business topic.

Similarly, team building and teamwork are vital aspects of business success. Because these skills are essential to long-term success, M.B.A. students in the Eller School are taught the theoretical underpinnings of good teamwork, and they are coached in the practical methods for achieving it.

The Eller School is deliberately kept small (approximately 100 full-time students are admitted each year) so that students can grow and develop in a friendly, professional environment. A variety of opportunities for interactions with faculty and staff members in both academic and social settings result in a

friendly, supportive atmosphere in which each individual can feel comfortable and confident. Where competition exists, such as in the simulation, it is good-natured and focused on mutual goals of learning and success.

Social life in the M.B.A. program is plentiful and varied. The close-knit, team-oriented nature of the program produces deep and lasting friendships. This past year, students participated in a tour of regional wineries, hiking and camping in the surrounding mountains, intramural sports, and the Eller Cup semiannual golf tournament.

Special Features

Classroom activities alone are not sufficient to prepare students for leadership roles when they finish the program. Dealing with real business situations and having the opportunity to confront issues, make decisions, and see the results is one way to enhance the learning experience for M.B.A. students. At the Eller School, a unique approach has been developed for introducing students to the real world of business and integrating the material of the first-year curriculum. It is called The Management Experience. Beginning in the third week of the first semester, students are organized into teams of 4 to 6 individuals, who compete in an advanced, highly complex computerized business simulation. As the semester progresses, students make weekly decisions regarding market opportunities, product development, marketing strategy, production planning, and strategic positioning. They receive weekly feedback in the form of sales results, market-share data, stock prices, and bottom-line profits. Students have the opportunity to apply their classroom knowledge in a controlled, but highly competitive, environment. They sharpen their analytical, team-building, and communications skills while they learn how the various components of a business system combine to form a successful enterprise. The results of the simulation are then stored until the fourth semester, when they are revisited in the capstone course. Second-year M.B.A. students recruit and form their own

teams, who then bid to take over the management of their former companies. Using the knowledge and skills developed in the first three semesters of their M.B.A. program, these fourth-semester students then have the opportunity to demonstrate their abilities to successfully operate a business. When students complete this activity, they leave the program with a level of maturity, competence, and business savvy that is well beyond what is typically learned in a classroom setting. This activity, and the level of interaction generated among the M.B.A. students, is one of the highlights of the Eller School M.B.A. program. It is the only major M.B.A. program in the country that applies this advanced learning system in this manner.

The Faculty

Faculty members serve as mentors and coaches to students entering a new realm of experience. All are highly credentialed scholars who bring their extensive research, consulting, and business backgrounds to the classroom experience. Representing a full range of management disciplines, Eller School faculty members have received national attention for the quality, originality, and leadership of their work. In addition to advancing the state of knowledge in traditional fields, they are pioneering new areas such as judgment and decision making and group decision support systems.

The Business School Network

M.B.A. students find a ready source of mentoring and helpful support in the M.B.A. Student Association (MBASA). One special aspect of the MBASA is the student consulting group. Student consult-

ants work with area businesses to help them solve real business problems. Recent clients include the Tucson Urban League, which retained the MBASA Consulting Group to instruct minority businesspeople in the business planning process.

The College and Environs

The University of Arizona is located in Tucson, a city of over 500,000 in the southeastern corner of the state. Surrounded by mountains and blessed with an eternally blue sky, the high Sonoran Desert is a delightful place to live and to learn. Housing is readily available and reasonably priced.

Technology Environment

The routine use of the computer is incorporated throughout the curriculum. Students regularly use group collaboration software, electronic mail, statistical analysis, word processing, and presentation software packages. Because information technologies are a pervasive component of the M.B.A. program, students should enter with a reasonable comfort with either a DOS/Windows or Macintosh computing environment and familiarity with a spreadsheet package (such as Microsoft Excel or Lotus 1-2-3) and a word processing package (such as Microsoft Word or WordPerfect). The Business School Information Technology Service (BITS) offers refresher courses in each of these areas throughout the semester for those students who wish to brush up or expand their skills. BITS also offers courses in the popular statistical packages, so it is not necessary for students to know this material prior to the start of school. Access to computers is available throughout the campus, and graduate student labs are available during the hours when McClelland Hall is open. If individual resources permit, it is recommended that students own a personal computer with a modem to facilitate 24-hour access to technology.

Placement

The Eller School Graduate Placement Office assists students in developing career plans and job search strategies and actively markets the School and the students to regional and national employers. In addition to on-campus interviews for full-time positions and summer internships, the Eller School participates in the West Coast M.B.A. Consortium, an annual recruiting event held in Irvine, California, and has recently utilized videoconference technology to enable employers to conduct "video interviews"

with Eller School students. The newly launched EllerNet Alumni Network enables students to make contacts with M.B.A. alumni across the country.

Admission

Applicants for admission to the M.B.A. program must submit transcripts from all undergraduate and graduate institutions attended, essays in response to specific questions, a résumé, GMAT scores, application forms, and a nonrefundable application fee. International students must submit TOEFL scores (minimum of 650). Mathematics prerequisites for admission include finite mathematics and calculus.

The entering class in the fall of 1994 had an average GMAT score of 599, average GPA of 3.2 (on a 4.0 scale), average age of 27, and an average of four years of work experience after the bachelor's degree.

Finances

The 1994–95 registration fee for full-time in-state students was $1894 per year. Tuition and fees for full-time nonresident students totaled $7500 per year. In-state part-time students paid $1210 per year for registration fees; part-time nonresident students, $3778 per year. Room and board cost approximately $5000 per year. Students should budget $1000 for books, software, and photocopying for the first year of study and approximately $800 for the second year. They should also budget $600 for insurance and $2500 for miscellaneous expenses per year.

Merit-based financial aid is available through the Eller School for full-time students only. This includes waivers of nonresident tuition, graduate assistantships, waivers of registration fees, and donor-funded scholarships. Need-based loans are available through the Office of Student Financial Aid.

Application Facts And Dates

Applications for fall admission are processed as they are received. Deadlines are February 1 for financial aid and for international students and March 15 for domestic students. Decision letters are mailed within four to six weeks after receipt of completed applications. For more information, students should contact:

Ms. Diana Vidal
Director of Admissions
Eller Graduate School of Management
210 McClelland Hall
The University of Arizona
Tucson, Arizona 85721
Telephone: 602-621-2169
Fax: 602-621-2606

University of Arkansas

Fayetteville, Arkansas

TOMORROW'S HORIZONS TODAY—THE ARKANSAS M.B.A.

The Arkansas M.B.A. is founded in the concepts of excellence and personalization. M.B.A. candidates work closely with the graduate faculty, leaders of national corporations, and student teams to create real-time solutions to real-world problems for domestic corporations in the Arkansas Partnership in Learning Program. A project-team orientation challenges our students each semester to combine their problem-solving efforts to meet target outcomes.

From their first exposure to the beauty of the Ozark Mountain countryside during new-student orientation to their day of graduation, Arkansas M.B.A. students gain new friendships and experiences that underscore lifelong personal and business successes. The Arkansas M.B.A. degree program provides candidates with experiences and knowledge necessary to manage and lead organizations in an environment of global challenge and cultural diversity.

—Doyle Z. Williams, Dean

Programs and Curricular Focus

The Arkansas M.B.A. program seeks to challenge students to investigate decision-making approaches to those questions that confront corporations and small businesses daily. The program provides conceptual and applied learning in quantitative decision making, human resources management, marketing planning and problem solving, applied managerial economics, accounting controls, financial management, and corporate leadership. The integration of these several disciplines, when coupled with a project-team orientation, provides graduates with knowledge and experiences that prepare them to make sustained contributions to organizations and society in a global, diverse, and dynamic environment. The Arkansas M.B.A. develops an individual's problem-solving skills, interpersonal and communication skills, ability to adapt to changing technology, spirit of entrepreneurial innovation, and ethical and professional values.

Through the selection of elective course work, students are encouraged to concentrate their efforts on more specific material that may be of interest. Students may concentrate in management information systems, marketing, human resources management, finance and investments, business economics, and international business studies. A joint M.B.A./J.D. program is available for those students interested in corporate legal studies. The College also offers the Master of Accountancy and Master of Arts in economics degrees.

Students and the M.B.A. Experience

Diversity describes the composition of the Arkansas M.B.A. student population. Students average 27 years of age and nearly three years of professional experience prior to joining the Arkansas M.B.A. program. Nearly 40 percent are female, and approximately 8 percent are protected-class students. Student enrollment reflects participants from twenty-two different states representing all regions of the United States. The program's global focus is enhanced by the nearly 35 percent of students who represent eastern and western European, Asian, Chinese, Russian, and Central and South American cultures. The opportunity to study abroad in Indonesia is a new feature that will become available in 1996.

Undergraduate degrees of the M.B.A. students include majors in business, education, economics, psychology, and history. Nearly 20 percent of the students possess undergraduate degrees and experience in chemical, civil, industrial, mechanical, and electrical engineering.

Special Features

The Partnership in Learning Program is a feature that enhances the student's ability to integrate course work and experience in a real-time, real-world challenge. A project-team orientation provides the arena for students to work closely with corporate executives in solving real corporate problems. Project teams travel throughout national and regional markets to gather information for major corporate partners, investigate alternative solutions, and formally present major project reports to corporate management. As one graduate remarked, "When you work in a real-life situation like this, you have to complete the assignments; you have to reach your goals. There are no Cs in real life. You either satisfy the customer or you don't."

The Faculty

Arkansas M.B.A. faculty members possess extensive experience in corporate problem solving. Graduate faculty members have received doctoral degrees from major research institutions, including Harvard, Michigan, Indiana, Purdue, North Carolina, Texas, Pennsylvania State, Virginia Tech, Carnegie Mellon, Syracuse, Tennessee, Louisiana State, and Georgia. Faculty members are active in both research and corporate consulting.

The Business School Network

The Dean's Executive Advisory Board provides regular input concerning the challenges and opportunities that face the College. The board consists of 27 corporate leaders, 19 of whom are chairmen, CEOs, or presidents of large regional and national corporations, including Wal-Mart Stores, Dillard Department Stores, J.B. Hunt Transport, Beverly Enterprises, and WITCO Corporation. These industrial leaders provide valuable contacts with corporate America and the international marketplace.

The College and Environs

The University of Arkansas, Fayetteville, serves as the major center of liberal and professional education and as the primary land-grant campus in the state. The University offers graduate education leading to the master's degree in over

Expectations of excellence. Performance to match.

seventy fields and to the doctoral degree in twenty-four carefully selected areas. The University currently enrolls approximately 14,300 students who represent global demographics.

The College of Business Administration is a professional learning community that seeks the discovery of knowledge and to produce graduates who are valued for their contributions to the marketplace and to society. In this way, the College contributes to the well-being of local, regional, national, and global economies. The College currently enrolls approximately 2,950 undergraduate and 250 graduate students.

Fayetteville is a community of 45,000 residents in Washington County. It is situated in the northwestern corner of the state in the heart of the Ozark Mountains at an elevation of 1,400 feet. The surroundings are of great natural beauty, and the climate of the region is pleasant in all seasons.

Facilities

Programs are offered in a modern facility that provides readily available access to contemporary computer technology and excellent library facilities. Four computer labs are currently available in the College of Business Administration. A separate state-of-the-art computer lab is planned for fall 1995, and it will be for the exclusive use of graduate students.

On-campus and off-campus housing is readily available and within walking distance to the campus. A no-cost transit system provides mass transportation for the campus and the surrounding student communities. However, it is advised that if on-campus housing is desired, application should be made at least three months prior to planned enrollment.

Technology Environment

Computing facilities are updated each twelve- to twenty-four-month period. Currently, the College supplies 486-Pentium units for student use in its primary computer labs. A variety of software is available for students, including word processing, spreadsheets, graphics, and analysis. Library support includes LEXIS/NEXIS, ABI Inform, and Wilson Business Abstracts. COMPUSTAT is also accessible to students. Each of these support systems is provided within the framework of normal student fees. Twenty-four-hour access is available.

Placement

The University of Arkansas provides the services of the Career Planning and Placement Office to support student placement needs. Services that are provided include résumé preparation, counseling, internships, cooperative education programs, career workshops, employer information services, and employment search assistance. Beginning in July 1995, the College of Business Administration will introduce its own dedicated placement program. Currently, approximately 90 percent of Arkansas M.B.A. graduates are placed in career positions within three months of graduation.

Admission

Admission to the Master of Business Administration program requires a bachelor's degree from a recognized institution, with a cumulative grade point average (CGPA) of 3.0 or above. Students having a CGPA between 2.7 and 3.0 may be considered for conditional admission. Admission to the M.B.A. program requires acceptance by both the Graduate School and the College of Business Administration of the University of Arkansas, Fayetteville. Admission decisions are based upon acceptable Graduate Management Admission Test (GMAT) scores, an acceptable cumulative grade point average, and letters of recommendation. The average GMAT and CGPA for students entering in the fall of 1994 were 588 and 3.43, respectively.

All admission requirements, including the GMAT, should be completed at least 90 days prior to entering the program.

Finances

Estimated tuition fees for 1995–96 are $1310 per semester for residents of Arkansas and $3000 per semester for nonresidents. Students enrolled in 6 or more hours are assessed an additional $61 to cover health, activity, and recreation facilities fees. International students must show proof of health insurance and are required to pay a Non-Immigrant Student Services Fee of $35 per semester.

Among American cities, Fayetteville, which has been selected for the past five years as one of America's top fifteen cities in which to live, is a relatively low cost-of-living city. The nine-month cost-of-living in Fayetteville is approximately $6000, and the summer-session costs are approximately $2500. These costs include room and board, personal expenses, books and supplies, and equipment and enhancement fees.

International students may apply for graduate assistantships, which currently provide a waiver of tuition and an academic year stipend of $4500. Students who are granted assistantships are required to be available for 20 hours per week to support the instructional or research needs of professors in the College.

Application Facts and Dates

Candidates are admitted for fall, spring, and summer semesters. International student applications should be received by March 15 for summer and fall admission decisions and November 1 for spring admission. Application processing requires approximately one month. Applicants will be notified at least 45 days prior to the requested admission date. For additional information, students should contact:

Dub Ashton, Associate Dean
Graduate Studies Office
CBA Suite 475
College of Business Administration
University of Arkansas
Fayetteville, Arkansas 72701
Telephone: 501-575-2851

The University of Auckland

Auckland, New Zealand

AUSTRALASIAN LEADERSHIP

The Graduate School of Business at the University of Auckland is uniquely positioned at the gateway to the Pacific Rim and within one of the most prestigious universities in Australasia. The School is an innovator in curriculum (amongst the first Australasian M.B.A. programmes), technology (the first remote-access technology programme in Australasia and amongst the first in the world), and linkages (with business and other universities). The programme is consistently increasing the relevance and integration of its offerings, strengthening its management research component, and integrating world-class technology into its development and delivery.

—Marie Wilson, Associate Dean

Programs and Curricular Focus

The M.B.A. programme focuses on developing a balance of strategic and operational thinking through a three-part curriculum of theoretical development (e.g., organisational theory, microeconomics, macroeconomics), specific business operations (e.g., MIS, marketing), and personal skills (e.g., presentation and communication skills, community leadership). The culmination of the programme is a research thesis, which captures a theoretical and operational analysis of strategic import to a given organisation. The course is taught for forty-four weeks of the year on alternating Fridays and Saturdays for two years. This schedule allows for extensive team interaction during the intervening weeks and in-depth focus one day a week to accommodate a fully employed student body, many of whom hold general manager–level positions within the national business community. Key factors in the programme include the emphasis on teamwork, the requirement of technology linkage within teams and with the University and academic staff, and the emphasis on action learning integrated throughout the curriculum.

Students and the M.B.A. Experience

The Auckland M.B.A. programme is structured for a mature, fully employed managerial student. The entering class of 1995 is 17 percent women, and 80 percent of the students were born outside of New Zealand, although most are now permanent residents or citizens. The

students range in age from their late twenties to late fifties, with an average age of 43. Ten years of business experience, with five years in a management position, is the minimum requirement, but the average is over seventeen years of managerial experience. Students work in teams of 6 or 7 to analyse their own and competitor businesses and to audit their own organisation in a number of domains.

Special Features

All M.B.A. students operate an Apple Powerbook, with a remote server that allows 24-hour access to the University, the Internet, and each other. All course material, course work, and routine instructor communication are presented by computer. Students are assigned to teams each year, which form the basis for one third of the assignments, and participate in class exercises and presentations. Each year, the students structure an international study tour of up to two weeks that strengthens their expertise as well as their connections to Australasian business.

The Faculty

The Graduate School of Business is a member of the School of Business and Economics, which, with over 200 academic staff members, represents one of the strongest research and teaching faculties in the Southern Hemisphere. This faculty is further strengthened by ties with the other professional faculties,

particularly Medicine, Engineering, Education, Fine Arts, and Environmental Science.

The Business School Network

Because this is an M.B.A. programme of fully employed senior managers, the primary network is through the 200 participants, as well as through the regional business leaders who join the programme for workshops, class presentations, and weekly class dinners. Recent events have included evenings with the governor of the New Zealand Reserve Bank and the CEOs of New Zealand's largest corporations, as well as the leader of the Opposition and the ministers of major government portfolios.

The College and Environs

The University of Auckland is an urban campus for over 20,000 students, established at the original seat of government in 1883. Gothic and modern architecture are combined in a city campus bordered by large parks and located just above the harbour and central business district. Auckland is a city of over 1 million people, often referred to as the "Commercial Capital of Polynesia," with a well-developed commercial sector, as well as opera, ballet, and theatre of international stature, and a wealth of outdoor recreational opportunities—Auckland is also called the "City of Sails."

Facilities

In late 1995, the Graduate School of Business, including the M.B.A. programme, will move to a new seven-story facility with high-technology interactive classrooms, attractive dining and social facilities, and a business "library" with a state-of-the-art videoconferencing and interactive editing suite, as well as Microsoft advanced computer labs. A business amenities suite will provide printer, fax, and modem interfaces for students, and there will be a boardroom-style meeting space.

Technology Environment

Computing is an integral part of the programme. Instruction, assignments, and communication are maintained on an interactive Powerbook system with standardised software and a remote server for students and alumni. Staff, students, and alumni utilise the Internet and internal software to access local databases as well as international collections.

Admission

Requirements for admission include solid academic performance in an undergraduate degree programme and/or exemplary business experience; a minimum of ten years of business experience, with five of those years in management; superior

assessment on a range of psychometric assessments; and GMAT scores that are balanced across indices and represent median- to upper-quartile performance.

Finances

Tuition and fees for the 1995 academic year for residents are approximately NZ$10,000 per year, plus a one-time expense of NZ$6000–$10,000 for the required hardware and software for programme participation. Books, supplies, and personal expenses are estimated at NZ$3000 per year.

Application Facts and Dates

Applications are accepted from August 15 to October 15, with acceptance decisions communicated by November 15 for February 1 classes. Students should direct enquiries to:

M.B.A. Programme
Graduate School of Business
University of Auckland
Private Bag 92019
Auckland, New Zealand
Telephone: 64+9 3737-999
Fax: 64+9 3737-437

University of Bridgeport

▶ *The School of Business offers a Master of Business Administration degree program in general administration. It features a combination of courses from accounting, finance, international business, management, marketing, and information systems. Degree completion normally requires two years of full-time or three to five years of part-time study. Accelerated study is available for qualified students who have recently completed a business degree from an accredited college. A weekend M.B.A. program also is available at the University's Stamford Center on alternate weekends. The M.B.A. program begins with a focus on analysis and evaluation of the control of an organization and of the environment for leadership. Courses include accounting, decision theory, economics, the Organization and Management of Finance, production and marketing, and the Socio-Cultural Aspects of People in Organizations. Advanced courses expand and integrate topics explored in introductory courses and provide a strong focus on the global perspective necessary for contemporary management. The School also holds membership in the American Assembly of Collegiate Schools of Business (AACSB) and the Association of Collegiate Business Schools and Programs (ACBSP), and its programs are designed to adhere to the standards of these professional accreditation agencies.*
—Frank Moriya, Dean

Programs and Curricular Focus

The M.B.A. program at the University of Bridgeport develops effective and responsible leaders for business, industry, and government. It not only emphasizes traditional management skills but also stresses the technical and cultural preparation necessary to understand the increasingly complex international environment. The M.B.A. addresses a global perspective.

The M.B.A. requires between 30 and 54 semester credit hours of study, depending on the student's academic background and level of academic achievement. The curriculum is designed to recognize substantial diversity in preparation and experience for students entering M.B.A. study, as well as different goals and expectations of students.

Core courses provide the management tools for analysis, decision making and communications; concepts, theory, and current practice in the major functional areas of operation; and the opportunity to study continuing and contemporary problems of management responsibility. The core is central to M.B.A. study, providing a base of knowledge for additional study in electives and a specific professional discipline. The M.B.A. core courses (27 credits) are as follows: Accounting Concepts, Economic Analysis, Financial Management, Organizational Behavior, Operations Management, Marketing Concepts, Management Science and Linear Programming, Management Information Systems, Decision Theory, Business and

Society, and policy (capstone); no waiver is granted for the capstone course.

Listed below are the advanced courses for which the M.B.A. core is only a prerequisite: Accounting for Managers, International Accounting, International Trade and Finance, Advanced Financial Management and Policy, the Financial Management of Financial Institutions, Management Theory, Small Business Entrepreneurship, Advanced Operations Management, Buyer Analysis, Global Market Management and Strategy Planning, Advanced Statistical Decision Theory, Business Simulation, Business and Society, and Business Policy. The Global Management group of electives comprises International Issues and Languages. The Experiential Learning group comprises Leadership and Organizational Change, Business Games, and internships. Teaching methods include a mix of lecture, case study, experiential learning, and an analysis of international social-political issues.

Students and the M.B.A. Experience

M.B.A. program participants represent thirty-five nationalities. Five percent are from Europe, 50 percent are from North America, and 45 percent from other countries. Thirty-five percent of the students have a degree background in sciences/technology, 40 percent in economics, 2 percent in law, and 23 percent in other majors. Student GMAT scores range from 375 to 600; the average is 500. International

student TOEFL scores average 575. Women comprise 45 percent of the student population. Student ages range from 27 to 55. The average age is 27. The average length of student work experience is three to five years.

Special Features

The program features a flexible course of study to meet the convenience of all kinds of students; a strong emphasis on global business to prepare for the twenty-first century business world; experiential learning to facilitate learning by experience in a small group setting; a diverse student body composed of domestic and international students learning how to work in harmony; and a systematic understanding of discipline, value, and an ethical code of behavior in business.

The Faculty

The faculty is as diverse as the student body. It is composed of domestic and international members with superb academic qualifications and industrial experience. They are also highly research-active, authoring books, journals, and conference papers. They pride themselves on excellence in teaching as a primary goal of their profession.

The Business School Network

The University of Bridgeport's 86-acre campus is situated on Long Island Sound. Located in Fairfield County, the area is home to the nation's largest multinational corporate headquarters and provides students with excellent opportunities for jobs, internships, and co-op training. Through the Dean's Advisory Board, the School interfaces with many executives from corporations, who give advice and direction as well as instruction in the classroom.

The University's Stamford Center is conveniently located in Stamford, Connecticut, and is easily accessible to working professionals from southern Fairfield County and Westchester County, New York.

Corporate Partnership

Through the Trefz Center for Venture Management, which is housed in the School of Business, the School sponsors a number of activities that link the School with the business community. Components of Trefz Center of Venture Manage-

ment include The Business Development Institute, which assists potential entrepreneurs and small business persons in start-up, business organization, finance, marketing, staffing and management, and evaluating technology and development planning. The Bridgeport Foreign Trade Institute sponsors monthly international business seminars and conferences; develops networks of international business firms; provides consultation services to those individuals and organizations who attempt to enter international business; and assists local governments in promoting local businesses and products made in the state of Connecticut for foreign markets and investors. The Urban Management Institute studies socioeconomic issues in the region and recommends appropriate policy initiatives. The Special Projects Unit promotes activities especially targeted for small business people in the region through conferences, seminars, and special events.

The College and Environs

Founded in 1927, the University of Bridgeport is a private, nonsectarian, comprehensive, coeducational, urban university located in Bridgeport, Connecticut, just one hour (50 miles) from New York City and three hours (160 miles) from Boston. The University has a long-standing partnership with the local community to provide its employees with excellent educational opportunities that lead to degrees and career advancement. Sixty-five of Connecticut's largest multinational corporations are located in Fairfield County. There are about 1,000 graduate students enrolled at the University, representing a diverse group of interests, professions, nationalities, and ages. The University maintains an international focus, with 19 percent of its students coming from outside the U.S.

Facilities

The Wahlstrom Library contains approximately 270,000 bound volumes, 3,200 records and tapes, and 400,000 microforms and subscribes to 1,000 periodicals and serials. On-line database searching is available on DIALOG; CD-ROM databases include ERIC, ABI/INFORM, and periodicals abstract. The School of Business' Mellen Computer Lab is equipped with IBM-compatible, 486 SX-25 PCs and HP Laser Jet printers. Financial databases and various statistical packages are also available.

Placement

Most of the University's students are already employed and seek M.B.A. study on a part-time basis. However, because of the University's location in Fairfield county, where sixty-five of Connecticut's Fortune 500 companies are located, students have access to a number of employment opportunities.

Admission

As a professional program, the M.B.A. is designed to build upon undergraduate study in the arts, humanities, science, engineering, or other disciplines. No specific undergraduate curriculum is expected or preferred before entry to M.B.A. study. Admission is based on a bachelor's degree or equivalent in any discipline, scores on the Graduate Management Admission Test (GMAT), and two letters of recommendation. Provisional admission may be granted to a limited number of students, pending GMAT scores, provided that the undergraduate records are exceptionally strong and the applicant has at least three years of management experience. If a student is admitted provisionally, the GMAT must

be taken during the first semester of residency. For students whose native language is not English, a TOEFL score of 575 is required.

Finances

For the program, tuition costs $310 per credit (1–12 credits) or $6250 per semester (13 or more credits). Room and board cost $6810 per year, and students should have approximately $1600 allotted for miscellaneous expenses, excluding travel. There is a $35 application fee for domestic students ($50 for international students).

Financial aid is available to U.S. citizens in the form of endowed scholarships, Federal Stafford Student Loans, graduate assistantships, and internships. International students must demonstrate that they have sufficient funds to finance their studies in the United States.

International Students

The focus on internationalism at the University of Bridgeport offers the international student the opportunity to obtain vital training in a specialized field of study, to enrich his or her life by experiencing another culture, and to gain new perspective on the world and to develop contacts, interpersonal skills, and knowledge necessary to those who work in the international community as technicians, scholars, businessmen, politicians, and scientists.

The University's English Language Institute (ELI) is located on the campus of the University of Bridgeport. ELI offers intensive instruction in English as a second language as well as trips and activities designed to introduce the student to America and its people.

The University's Office of International Affairs provides services and assistance to international students with immigration, personal, and other nonacademic concerns.

Application Facts and Dates

Applications must be submitted two months prior to the date of intended entry. Students may enter in the fall, spring, and summer. For more information, applicants should contact:

Office of Admissions
  University of Bridgeport
  126 Park Avenue
  Bridgeport, Connecticut 06601
  Telephone: 203-576-4552
              800-898-8278 (toll-free)
  Fax: 203-576-4941
  E-mail: fred@cse.bridgeport.edu

M.B.A. Program
  School of Business
  University of Bridgeport
  230 Park Avenue
  Bridgeport, Connecticut 06601
  Telephone: 203-576-4363
  Fax: 203-576-4388

The University of British Columbia

Faculty of Commerce and Business Administration

Vancouver, British Columbia, Canada

NEW DIRECTIONS FOR UBC'S M.B.A.

In the complex and competitive business environment of the 90s, the generalist training traditionally associated with an M.B.A. needs to be supported by in-depth specialist knowledge. Not only is competence across the range of key business disciplines, such as finance, accounting, and marketing, essential, but also the interconnections between these disciplines need to be clearly understood.

Our redesigned M.B.A. program commences with a highly integrated core centred on current business situations. Following this, students develop an area of expertise by selecting from a wide range of specializations. Through projects and internships, students analyze existing business problems and are exposed to leading practitioners.

Our approach to management education stresses the development of graduates with broad management skills complemented by expert knowledge in one area of business.

—Michael A. Goldberg, Dean

Programs and Curricular Focus

UBC's M.B.A. program is rigorous and challenging, offering both structure and flexibility. Students complete the integrated core, after which they choose the specialization that meets their career objectives. Both the core and the specializations are supported and strengthened through business applications in internships, projects, and a professional development program. UBC offers small classes and a balance of instructional techniques, including lecture, case discussion, simulations, and group projects. The full-time program starts in September and is fifteen continuous months. The part-time program is three years.

The core provides students with a foundation in finance, marketing, human resources, accounting, statistics, economics, and information systems. Instruction in these functional areas focuses on their interconnections, to more closely emulate the multidimensional problems encountered in business.

Following the core, students select one of the following eleven specializations: international business, entrepreneurship, production/operations management/logistics, strategic management, marketing, human resource management, corporate finance, financial investments, banking and international finance, information technology, and urban land economics. Students may also choose from a range of electives, including transportation, policy, not-for-profit management, law, and technology management.

Additional opportunities at UBC include two combined programs. The M.B.A./LL.B. program combines law and business, and M.Eng./Advanced Technology Management combines engineering and management. Also offered are Master of Science in Business Administration (M.Sc.Bus.Admin.) and Doctor of Philosophy (Ph.D.) in business administration degree programs for students wishing to pursue research in business.

Students and the M.B.A. Experience

Students are one of the Faculty's greatest resources. M.B.A. classmates have diverse professional, cultural, and academic backgrounds, which create a unique and dynamic learning environment. On average, students are 27 years of age with two years of full-time work experience. The class is composed of 39 percent women.

❖ Global Focus

UBC is committed to offering students unique international educational experiences. A global perspective is gained through specialized international courses, interaction with the multicultural student body and faculty, and through UBC's extensive exchange program. Exchanges are available with twenty-two leading universities located in eighteen countries in Asia, Australia, Brazil, Israel, Great Britain, and Europe.

UBC also offers a unique business consulting program in Hong Kong. Faculty-led teams of students travel to Hong Kong for five weeks, to work with Hong Kong–based companies in examining issues or investigating new market opportunities.

Special Features

Internships and projects are a key part of UBC's M.B.A. program. During the specialization component, students have the opportunity to apply their knowledge in either an internship or an industry-related project directly related to their area of specialization.

Throughout the M.B.A. program, several weeks are devoted to developing professional skills in areas such as communications, teamwork, negotiation, and leadership.

Students without adequate general knowledge of economics, statistics, accounting, and computers should attend the Pre-core, held immediately prior to the start of the program.

The Faculty

UBC is committed to excellence in teaching. The M.B.A. program has a large number of outstanding instructors, some of whom have received national and international recognition for their contributions to teaching. UBC's revised program has a strong focus on teaching innovation and course development.

In addition, the Faculty's reputation for research excellence is unmatched by any other Canadian business school. Exceptional work is ongoing in many areas, such as international business and trade policy, entrepreneurship, nonprofit marketing, decision making and creative problem solving, and strategic thinking in negotiating and bargaining.

The Business School Network
Corporate Partnerships

Strong linkages have been developed between UBC and the corporate community. The Dean's Advisory Council, which

assists the Dean in developing and evaluating commerce initiatives, consists of senior representatives from government, labour, and the private sector.

The corporate community provides opportunities for students to apply their business knowledge through projects and internships. In addition, M.B.A. students interact directly with prominent business leaders in UBC's speakers program and by participating in a wide range of professional and social events.

Prominent Alumni

Among the alumni of the Faculty of Commerce and Business Administration are Jim Cleave, former CEO, Hongkong Bank of Canada, currently President and CEO, Marine Midland Bank; George Kosich, President and CEO, Hudson Bay Company; Yong Quek, President, Procter & Gamble Inc.; Janet Smith, Deputy Minister, Western Economic Diversification; and Paul Walter, President and CEO, Zellers Inc.

The College and Environs

The University of British Columbia is located in Vancouver, one of the world's most beautiful cities. UBC is Canada's second-largest university, with over 30,000 academic students.

The campus, a few kilometres from the city centre, is on a 1,000-acre forested peninsula overlooking the Pacific Ocean and the Coastal Mountain range. Students find that the campus offers an exceptional variety of cultural and recreational facilities.

In addition, Vancouver offers a wonderful lifestyle in which people can ski, sail, cycle, and stroll along the beach all year round.

Facilities

At UBC, the Faculty of Commerce and Business Administration is committed to providing the highest quality student services. This is accomplished by the professional staff in the Commerce Masters' Programs Office, Commerce Career Centre, Study Abroad and Exchange office, the David Lam Management Research Library, and the Computer Lab.

Placement

Students' job searches are supported by the Commerce Career Centre, which is instrumental in marketing UBC graduates to major national and international corporations. Each year, on-campus information and recruiting sessions are held for over 200 companies. Career Centre staff also organize seminars in résumé writing, interviewing techniques, and job search strategies, to assist M.B.A. students in the competitive job market.

Admission

The admissions committee assesses undergraduate performance, GMAT scores, full-time work experience, extracurricular involvement, and demonstrated leadership. Specific minimum academic requirements are outlined in the M.B.A. application. A TOEFL score is required from an applicant whose prior degree is from a country other than Canada, the United States, the United Kingdom, Ireland, Australia, New Zealand, Kenya, South Africa, and the English-speaking countries of the West Indies. A minimum TOEFL score of 600 is required.

Applicants are not required to complete prerequisite courses, but a basic level of knowledge in economics, financial accounting, statistics, and computers is required.

Finances

Estimated program fees for 1995–96 are Can$7350 for full-time students for fifteen months and Can$8350 for part-time students over three years. Fees are the same for Canadian and international students. Annual costs for books and materials are approximately Can$1200. The University estimates room and board for a single student living off campus at Can$760 per month.

All applicants are considered for merit-based awards and fellowships at the time of admission.

Application Facts and Dates

Application deadlines are March 31 for international applicants and April 30 for North American applicants. For additional information, students should contact:

Commerce Masters' Programs Office
University of British Columbia
102-2053 Main Mall
Vancouver, British Columbia
Canada V6T 1Z2
Telephone: 604-822-8422
Fax: 604-822-9030
E-mail: masters.programs@
    commerce.ubc.ca
Internet: http://acme.commerce.ubc.ca/
    mbapage/mbahome.html

UCD GSM University of California, Davis

Graduate School of Management

Davis, California

> At the Graduate School of Management at UC Davis, we believe that students learn best in a supportive, cooperative learning environment that encourages them to stretch intellectually. To create this environment, we've developed a rigorous program that features small classes, a faculty committed to teaching excellence, and opportunities to work closely with that faculty and a select group of bright and energetic students. We then guide you to test your new knowledge and creative thinking in real-world business situations. I invite you to take advantage of an outstanding opportunity to fully develop your managerial potential and leadership skills.
>
> —Robert H. Smiley, Dean

Programs and Curricular Focus

The UC Davis Graduate School of Management is accredited by the American Assembly of Collegiate Schools of Business (AACSB). Conceived just over fifteen years ago, each year the program has gained greater stature. It is recognized for the quality of its graduates, its world-class faculty, and the excellence of its overall program.

The UC Davis M.B.A. program cultivates each student's ability to deal successfully with the challenges of a continually changing, increasingly complex business environment. The program's strengths come from a managerial approach to the basic business disciplines; a student/faculty ratio of 10:1; a curriculum that integrates the social, political, economic, and ethical aspects of business; and a variety of teaching methodologies, including case studies, lectures, class discussions, computer simulations, team projects, and real-world applications.

The program is twenty-four classes (72 quarter units). Joint degrees are available in law (M.B.A./J.D.), engineering (M.B.A./M.Eng.), and agricultural management (M.B.A./M.S.). All students spend their first year in core classes, mastering the curriculum, which provides a common foundation of fundamental management knowledge and skill. Elective concentrations are available either in the full-time day program or in the evening M.B.A. Program for Working Professionals, in accounting, agricultural management, environmental and natural resources management, finance, general management, health services management, information systems, management

science, marketing, and science and technology management. Students can also design a customized concentration. The second-year capstone course, Management Policy and Strategy, places students in teams and gives them an opportunity to apply their decision-making and problem-solving skills, developing a strategic plan for a real "client" business.

Students and the M.B.A. Experience

UC Davis M.B.A. students bring to the school a wide variety of academic and work experiences, and the School's personalized focus and hands-on teaching approach is augmented by this diversity. While 25 percent of the student body reflects preparation in business and economics, the school is also traditionally very attractive to students from engineering and the sciences because of the strong emphasis in technology management. Many of the 1996 graduating class came from undergraduate majors in the humanities and social sciences as well. The most recently admitted class represents over thirty-five different undergraduate institutions and seventy-five different employers.

The average full-time student is 27 years old, with 4½ years of full-time work experience. Women make up 30 percent of the student population, and minority students, almost 15 percent. Six percent are international students, and the School sponsors several student exchange programs.

Special Features

To enhance students' preparation for M.B.A. study, summer "boot camps" provide opportunities to brush up on necessary analytical skills. And to enhance preparation for the job market, the school requires that students participate in a videotaped mock interview with one of several volunteer executives from both the public and private sector. This program gives students a unique chance to meet top executives in a one-on-one situation, as well as to improve interviewing skills dramatically. The annual Alumni Day, created to provide current students with the "inside track" on up-to-date industry information and career opportunities, also provides a valuable networking activity.

The Faculty

Faculty members of the UC Davis Graduate School of Management represent doctoral preparation from many of the most prestigious schools in the country and excel both as teachers and researchers. Their current consulting projects keep them in touch with managerial concerns of leading U.S. corporations as well as federal and state agencies. But one of the most distinctive features of this faculty is the close relationships it forges with students. The school recognizes the academic value students receive when given the opportunity to work closely and individually with faculty members and offers many formal and informal chances to do so.

The Business School Network

Business and government leaders are frequent visitors to campus, serving as guest lecturers in classes, resources for career development, or speakers at frequent School-sponsored forums and lectures. Through these important contacts, students can gain a pragmatic viewpoint that balances the academic and theoretical perspective they find in the classroom.

The Executive in Residence program gives students and faculty alike a unique opportunity to work closely with a top business leader during the executive's quarter-long visit to the School. The

Dean's Advisory Council, made up of many of California's top business leaders, provides the School with one of its strongest connections to the business community. The School's Business Partnership program offers companies a special series of benefits when they make an annual contribution to the School, and students have the opportunity to network with representatives from major corporations.

The College and Environs

UC Davis has been rated by *U.S. News & World Report* as one of the top "up and coming" universities in the nation. It is the most academically diverse of the University of California campuses, with scholars of worldwide reputation in more than 100 academic fields.

The campus and the city of Davis, one of California's last remaining "college towns," lie amid some of the richest, most productive farmland in the world. Yet close-by Sacramento, the state capital, offers everything expected from a major metropolitan area, while the city of San Francisco and the rugged Sierra Nevada mountains provide additional diversions.

Facilities

Academic resources include a library of 2.3 million volumes, ranked among the top research libraries in North America. A full-time business reference librarian is available to assist students with the latest information-gathering strategies, including several on-line services. The School's newly-remodeled classrooms feature state-of-the-art multimedia instructional support.

Technology Environment

The School maintains a 24-hour computer lab, with all necessary business software, networking to library services, and access to the Internet. Each student is issued a University computer account, which includes electronic mail.

Placement

The Career Services Center begins offering support and personal guidance to students in the first few weeks of the program. In addition to the availability of several national databases that provide students with job openings and recruiter information, over 425 on-campus interviews were scheduled last year. Summer internships are strongly encouraged, and each year the Career Services Center works aggressively to broaden the number of internship possibilities available. The School also actively participates in the West Coast M.B.A. Consortium recruiting event to give students a special avenue for seeking career employment.

Admission

Admission to the UC Davis Graduate School of Management is highly selective. Applicants are evaluated on the basis of demonstrated academic achievement, performance on the Graduate Management Admission Test (GMAT), and interest in professional management. Full-time business experience is considered an asset. No particular area of undergraduate preparation is required, but the University requires the completion of a bachelor's degree from an accredited college or university. The 1996 graduating class had an average GMAT score of 640, an average undergraduate GPA of 3.2, and an average of 4½ years of work experience at entry.

Finances

In 1995–96, fees for full-time study are $7353 per year for California residents and $15,052 for nonresidents; these fees are subject to change. The M.B.A. Program for Working Professionals is $890 per class in 1995–96. Many reasonably-priced apartments are within biking distance. Monthly rents range from $450 for a studio to $1000 for a three-bedroom apartment. Student-family housing monthly rents range from $366 to $495. Need-based grants, loans, and fee offsets are available, as is the merit-based GSM Scholar's Grant.

International Students

The School encourages applications from International students. The University's nonresident fee surcharge of $7699 does apply. International students must provide a statement of finances showing at least $27,000 for one year and submit a TOEFL score of at least 600 prior to application.

Application Facts and Dates

Application deadlines are: April 1 (full-time program) and May 15 (evening program) for fall quarter admission. Applicants should contact:

Donald A. Blodger
Director of Admissions and Student
  Services
Graduate School of Management
Davis, California 95616
Telephone: 916-752-7399
Fax: 916-752-2924
Electronic Mail: gsm@ucdavis.edu
World Wide Web: http//www-gsm.
  ucdavis.edu

The University of California, Irvine

Graduate School of Management

Irvine, California

ANSWERS FOR THE FUTURE

At the UC Irvine M.B.A. program, we are dedicated to seeking answers for the future. That means a commitment to developing business leaders who will be able to create new business environments, rather than simply recreating old ones, business leaders who will innovate, not just administrate, and who will extend, rather than merely maintain, their capabilities. It means providing a solid management education that imparts fundamental business skills while simultaneously developing a student's ability to use those basic skills in new ways. This quest to find answers—and leaders—for the future has created a sense of excitement that is shared by the faculty, students, and staff of the UCI M.B.A. program. We hope that it is an excitement you will share and help extend by enrolling in our program.

—Dennis J. Aigner, Dean

Programs and Curricular Focus

The Graduate School of Management (GSM) offers three M.B.A. degree options, two of which are designed for the working professional, and a Ph.D. program. The curriculum for the M.B.A. programs is a broad-based, integrative, and comprehensive one that responds to the needs of the high-tech, international, and global economic environment.

The full-time M.B.A. program consists of twenty-three courses and takes eighteen months to two years to complete. The first year of study incorporates eleven of the fourteen core courses; the second year is primarily electives of the students' choosing. Functional areas of study include accounting, marketing, management information systems, strategy, operations and decision technologies, health care, public policy, finance, and organizational behavior.

The Executive M.B.A. is a two-year program designed for managers and working professionals. The Fully Employed M.B.A. Program is a thirty-three-month program intended for working professionals who require a program conducted entirely outside of regular working hours.

The doctoral program prepares individuals for teaching and scholarly positions in academic and other institutions where demonstrated ability to do original research is required. It is neither course- nor unit-based and consists of three separate and distinct phases. It is also a small and highly individualized

program and allows students to pursue their own areas of interest.

Students and the M.B.A. Experience

GSM makes a special effort to admit a diverse group of students each year who represent a wide range and variety of academic, cultural, and professional backgrounds. The average age for the class of 1996 is 28, with about five years of work experience. Women comprise approximately 40 percent of the student population; students who are members of minority groups, around 12 percent; and international students, about 20 percent.

Special Features

As part of their educational experience, GSM students are also offered the opportunity to supplement their course work through the International and Intercampus Exchange Programs.

The Faculty

The faculty members of the Graduate School of Management at UCI are scholars from some of the most esteemed institutions nationally and internationally. They are a diverse group, and their composition is perhaps one of the most international in all business schools. Due to the smaller size and nature of the program, students also have the opportunity to work closely with the faculty throughout the program.

The Business School Network
Corporate Partnerships

The Corporate Partners program actively brings together GSM students, faculty, and professional staff with the business community through activities such as the Corporate Partners/M.B.A. Roundtable series, Day-on-the-Job, Corporate Speakers Series, and Management Practicum. Companies such as IBM, KPMG Peat Marwick, Hewlett-Packard, Taco Bell Corporation, Western Digital, Monex International, Merrill Lynch, American Airlines, and Manufacturers Bank are just a few represented within the ranks of GSM's Corporate Partners.

The College and Environs

The University emerged from what had been a 170,000-acre ranch whose origins lay in a Mexican land grant. James Irvine Jr. inherited the land from his father, and in 1947 the James Irvine Foundation came into control of the Irvine Company. The foundation foresaw the need for housing to replace orange groves, but there was a determination not to replicate the urban sprawl of Los Angeles. One of the foundation's first acts was to deed 1,000 acres of land to the state so it could build a new University of California campus, which many feel is the most beautiful of the nine UC campuses. The UCI campus incorporates significant amounts of open space, and the surrounding environment includes the San Joaquin Freshwater Marsh Reserve.

UCI is located midway between Los Angeles and San Diego and is in the center of Orange County, one the nation's fastest-growing regions. It is also one of the most prolific and dynamic seedbeds for entrepreneurial, high-growth, and high-technology companies. The area provides easy access to professional theater, first-run movies, and dance companies, as well as a rich diversity of international cuisine at world-class restaurants. Other advantages include proximity to the mountains and beaches, which offer a variety of recreational opportunities such as water and snow skiing, hang gliding, bicycling, tennis, hiking, sailing, golf, and surfing on a year-round basis.

Technology Environment

The ability to use and manage electronic resources plays an increasingly significant role in today's information age. Of special note is the GSM Computing Facility, which is dedicated entirely to GSM students and is consistently ranked as one of the top business school computing facilities in the country. All GSM students are connected to electronic mail, and every seat in GSM's largest classrooms has a network connection, enabling the student to maximize productivity within the classroom setting. While not required at the present time, it is likely that the purchase of a notebook computer will be required by fall 1996.

Placement

The Graduate School of Management provides a full range of placement and career services designed to assist M.B.A. students. Along with the placement director, faculty and staff members work collectively to provide graduates with employment opportunities and contacts with major business and governmental units. Services offered include on-campus recruitment visits, career expo events, résumé books, interview skills workshops, and the latest in electronic candidate identification databases. A variety of internship and part-time positions are also available. Graduates receive starting salaries at or above the national average.

Admission

Admission for the M.B.A. and Ph.D. programs is offered each fall and is on a rolling basis. The deadline for the full-time program is May 1; for the Executive and Fully Employed M.B.A. programs, July 1; and for the Ph.D. program, April 1. Admissions decisions for the M.B.A. programs are based on an overall evaluation of undergraduate GPA, GMAT scores (required), letters of recommendation, statement of purpose, and work experience. A personal interview is also strongly encouraged. A minimum TOEFL score of 600 is required for international applicants whose native language is not English, and proof of adequate funds to cover two years of study is necessary. Introductory courses in calculus and statistics with probability are required prior to beginning the M.B.A. program.

Finances

Fees for the M.B.A. program for 1994–95 were $6807 per year for California residents, $14,506 per year for nonresidents; room and board averaged $9831 for on-campus accommodations. Fees were $20,000 per year for the Executive M.B.A. Program and $14,167 per year for the Fully-Employed M.B.A. Program. Fees for the Ph.D. program were $4807 per year for California residents and $12,506 per year for nonresidents. Books and supplies amounted to approximately $1290.

Primary sources of financial aid for the M.B.A. program include loans, grants, and fellowships. The School also has an on-site financial aid director to assist and guide students in this process. Ph.D. applicants may also be considered for Regent's, Chancellor's, and tuition fellowships, in addition to teaching and research assistant positions. To be considered for the full range of financial aid programs, applicants are strongly encouraged to meet the institutional financial aid deadline of March 2. Financial aid is awarded only to citizens or permanent residents of the United States.

Application Facts and Dates

Each program can be contacted directly by telephone: the M.B.A. program (telephone: 714-824-5232; fax: 714-824-2235); the Executive Programs Office (telephone: 714-824-5374); and the Ph.D. program (telephone: 714-824-8318). Or students may write to:

(Name of Program)
Graduate School of Management
University of California, Irvine
Irvine, California 92717-3125

FACULTY LIST

Dennis J. Aigner, Dean of the Graduate School of Management; Ph.D., Berkeley.

Yannis Bakos, Ph.D., MIT. Management information systems.

Richard A. Brahm, Ph.D., Pennsylvania (Wharton). Business strategy.

George W. Brown, Professor Emeritus of Management; Ph.D., Princeton.

Thomas C. Buchmueller, Ph.D., Wisconsin–Madison. Health care/economics.

Nai-fu Chen, Ph.D., Berkeley; Ph.D., UCLA. Finance.

Charles J. Cuny, Ph.D., Stanford. Finance.

Imran S. Currim, Ph.D., Stanford. Marketing.

Christopher Earley, Ph.D., Illinois at Urbana-Champaign. Organizational behavior.

Paul J. Feldstein, FHP Foundation Distinguished Chair in Health Care Management; Ph.D., Chicago. Health care/economics.

Mary Gilly, Ph.D., Houston. Marketing.

Daniel Givoly, Ph.D., NYU. Accounting.

John Graham, Ph.D., Berkeley. Marketing.

Vijay Gurbaxani, Ph.D., Rochester. Management information systems.

Robert A. Haugen, Ph.D., Illinois at Urbana-Champaign. Finance.

Carla Hayn, Ph.D., Michigan. Accounting.

Joanna L. Ho, Ph.D., Texas at Austin. Accounting.

Philippe Jorion, Ph.D., Chicago. Finance.

L. Robin Keller, Ph.D., UCLA. Operations and decision technologies.

John Leslie King, Ph.D., California, Irvine. Management information systems.

Kenneth L. Kraemer, Director, Center for Research on Information and Technology in Organizations (CRITO); Ph.D., USC. Management information systems.

Newton Margulies, Professor Emeritus of Management; Ph.D., UCLA. Organizational behavior.

Joseph W. McGuire, Professor Emeritus of Management; Ph.B., Marquette; Ph.D., Columbia. Business strategy.

Richard B. McKenzie, Walter B. Gerken Distinguished Chair in Enterprise and Society; Ph.D., Virginia Tech. Public policy.

Barrie Nault, Ph.D., British Columbia. Management information systems.

Peter Navarro, Ph.D., Harvard. Public policy.

Paul Olk, Ph.D., Pennsylvania (Wharton). Organizational behavior.

Jone L. Pearce, Associate Dean, Executive Degree Programs; Ph.D., Yale. Organizational behavior.

Cornelia Pechmann, Ph.D., Vanderbilt. Marketing.

Lyman W. Porter, Director, International Programs; Ph.D., Yale. Organizational behavior.

Judy B. Rosener, Senior Lecturer in Management; Ph.D., Claremont. Public policy.

Carlton H. Scott, Ph.D., New South Wales (Australia). Operations and decision technologies.

Kut C. So, Ph.D., Stanford. Operations and decision technologies.

Jing-Sheng Song, Ph.D., Columbia. Operations and decision technologies.

Neal M. Stoughton, Ph.D., Stanford. Finance.

Eli Talmor, Ph.D., North Carolina at Chapel Hill. Finance.

Anne S. Tsui, Director, Doctoral Program; Ph.D., UCLA. Organizational behavior.

Alladi Venkatesh, Ph.D., Syracuse. Marketing.

Margarethe F. Wiersema, Ph.D., Michigan. Business strategy.

William F. Wright, Ph.D., Berkeley. Accounting.

University of California, Los Angeles

Los Angeles, California

WELCOME TO ANDERSON

UCLA's John E. Anderson Graduate School of Management has long been a leader and innovator in management education. Driven by superior research as well as an astute responsiveness to indicators and trends in the ever-expanding business environment, the Anderson School is preparing the management leaders who will define success in the years to come.

These leaders will have a strong fundamental grounding in contemporary management and business theory, they will have a thorough knowledge of the role of technology in business, and they will understand the intricacies of global business relations and be skilled in working with people from widely differing personal and professional backgrounds.

If you aspire to the highest levels of managerial success, we invite you to take your place now among the leaders of the future; we invite you to join the Anderson School M.B.A. Program.

—William P. Pierskalla, Dean

Programs and Curricular Focus

The Anderson School M.B.A. Program is designed for highly motivated, exceptional students and is structured to ensure that each graduate leaves with a leadership-level knowledge of all key management disciplines as well as the conceptual and analytical frameworks underlying those disciplines. Consisting of three components—the management core, advanced electives, and the management field study—the curriculum is regularly updated to address the evolving challenges today's business managers must meet.

The management core is a set of twelve courses of which the student must take eleven. Students are assigned to a section during their first quarter and take all required core courses for that quarter with their assigned section.

Almost half of the M.B.A. curriculum comprises advanced electives, which are chosen from course offerings in nine curriculum areas and several interdisciplinary areas. These areas include accounting, business economics, finance, human resources and human systems development, information systems, management science, marketing, operations and technology management, and policy and organization. Students may tailor an individual M.B.A. program that reflects several interdisciplinary areas of study. These include arts management, entertainment management, entrepreneurial studies, finance and real estate, interna-

tional business and comparative management, and public/not-for-profit management.

Management Field Study is the capstone requirement of the M.B.A. program and is conducted during the second year of the program. In this project, students integrate and apply their knowledge and skills in a professional setting outside the classroom.

The Anderson School provides two M.B.A. programs for individuals whose professional goals require that they remain employed while completing their M.B.A. degree. The Fully Employed M.B.A. Program is targeted toward emerging managers, typically junior-level professionals averaging 29 years of age and 6 years of work experience. The Executive M.B.A. Program is an intensive twenty-four-month program designed for midcareer executives seeking a high-quality advanced management education while continuing in their professional role.

Students and the M.B.A. Experience

The Anderson School at UCLA boasts a vibrant student body whose extraordinary intellectual, cultural, social, and athletic energies spill out of the classroom into a plethora of nonacademic activities. The average full-time student is 27 years old, with just over four years of full-time work experience. Women comprise 29

percent of the student population, members of minority groups make up 19 percent, and international students make up 21 percent.

From day one, the Anderson School teaches students how to work effectively with others to transform ideas into realities. Teamwork is part of everyday life at Anderson. Students work together in study groups or on class assignments or Field Study and other projects.

❖ Global Focus

The Anderson School offers students a wide range of exciting opportunities to increase their international perspectives, from working on group projects with students from among the forty-three countries represented at Anderson to studying abroad and from enrolling in the International Management Fellows Program to touring a factory in Prague.

The Anderson School encourages students to participate in academic exchange programs with universities located abroad. Currently, the School participates in over twenty academic foreign exchange programs.

The Faculty

The renowned Anderson faculty, whose members are widely acclaimed for their expertise and compelling research, teaches advanced management theory and practice in a contemporary and vibrant interactive model of course work and field-based study. The Anderson School has 73 full-time ladder-track faculty members, 17 temporary full-time faculty members, 48 temporary part-time faculty members, and 20 endowed chairs.

The Business School Network
Corporate Partnerships

The Anderson School Board of Visitors plays a vital and active leadership role at the Anderson School. Successful entrepreneurs and business executives in their own right, board members represent a broad range of national and international industries and professions and bring to the School a wealth of leadership, expertise, energy, and commitment. The Anderson Board is actively committed to

helping the School achieve its mission and establish future goals. Members work closely with the faculty, administration, and students to ensure that the School retains its position as one of the nation's premier business schools. In addition, over fifty corporations provide annual support to the School as a demonstration of their commitment to the best in management education.

Prominent Alumni

Anderson School graduates are an eclectic body of talented business leaders and research professionals. Managing enterprises ranging from financial services institutions to arts organizations, Anderson alumni form a valuable management network that spans the globe. This list includes John E. Anderson, President, Topa Equities, Inc.; Howard Davis, President and Chief Executive Officer, Tracy Locke, Inc.; and Laurence D. Fink, Chairman and Chief Executive Officer, BlackRock Financial Management Group.

The College and Environs

Strolling to classes through the serene gardens on UCLA's campus, it is easy to forget that the Anderson School is located in the middle of the second-largest city in the United States. For Anderson students, Los Angeles offers

the best of many worlds. Beach, mountain, and desert recreation areas are plentiful and easily accessible by car. Los Angeles museums and theaters offer the world's most acclaimed entertainment. In addition, Westwood Village, which adjoins the UCLA campus to the south, offers shopping, dining, and a wide range of services.

Facilities

The fall of 1995 will be an exciting and memorable one for the Anderson School as the first full academic year begins in its landmark new building complex. The new seven-building 280,000-square-foot academic village is a testament to the School's vision of the growing importance of superior management education. Continuing its reputation as a national leader in the use of computing in M.B.A. instruction, the eleven specially designed case study rooms will have data ports at each seating station to integrate the instructional program of each faculty member with the School's central computing facility in the Rosenfeld Library.

Placement

Career planning begins before students enter the Anderson School and becomes increasingly focused during the M.B.A. program. Through the Career Manage-

ment Services Office, the School offers sound guidance and multiple resources for career management. Students acquire the connections, tools, and techniques needed to find a position that perfectly fits their career goals.

Throughout their search for the "just right job," students experience extraordinary support from the professional career management staff: counseling and advising sessions, workshops and seminars, career resource library, employer briefings, résumé books (summer and career), vacancy listings, and the campus interview program.

Admission

The Anderson School admission policy emphasizes academic ability, leadership, and work experience. The Admissions Committee evaluates applicants' prospects as effective managers and their projected ability to succeed in and profit from the M.B.A. program. Committee members carefully consider biographical and academic background information, GMAT and TOEFL (for most international applicants) scores, achievements, distinctions, awards and honors, employment history, letters of recommendation, and college and community involvement, especially when candidates have served in a leadership capacity.

Finances

The estimated cost of attending the UCLA M.B.A. program during the 1994–95 academic year was $21,640 for California residents and $29,339 for nonresidents. Students can expect 1995–96 costs to increase from 10 percent to 20 percent over 1994–95 costs. Fellowships and scholarships are available, and, upon admission, students automatically receive a financial aid application packet.

Application Facts and Dates

Applicants may apply for fall 1996 admission from October 9, 1995 through March 29, 1996. The Admissions Committee begins considering applications in December of each year. For more information, students should contact:

Ms. Linda Baldwin
Director of M.B.A. Admissions
The Anderson School at UCLA
Box 951481
Los Angeles, California 90095-1481
Telephone: 310-825-6944
Fax: 310-206-2002

University of California–Riverside

The A. Gary Anderson Graduate School of Management

Riverside, California

BALANCING THE ART AND SCIENCE OF MANAGEMENT

At the A. Gary Anderson Graduate School of Management, our M.B.A. curriculum provides a balance of the art and science of management. This recognition of the dual challenges that face today's manager permeates one's educational experience at AGSM. The Anderson School offers an intimate educational environment where classes are small by typical M.B.A. standards, professors are accessible, and the business community is very supportive and closely involved with the School's myriad activities.

—Michael E. Granfield, Dean

Programs and Curricular Focus

The M.B.A. curriculum balances the art and science of management, with a particular emphasis on managing through information, and recognizes the global context of management. The program stresses the essential interdependencies that exist across functional areas, emphasizing the development of superior management skills as well as theoretical foundations. Great importance is placed on teamwork, relationships, and communication.

The core courses provide the foundation in analytical and managerial skills. The twelve-course core culminates in an integrative case course that synthesizes the various functional area approaches to managerial issues. After a required internship experience, which may be based on current employment, students proceed to study elective topics in greater depth. Most students choose nine elective courses from areas including accounting, finance, general management, human resources management/organizational behavior, international management, management information systems, management science, marketing, and production/operations management. Students conclude the twenty-three-course, 92-unit program with a capstone strategic management course and a case analysis presentation. There is a thesis option for students who wish to do significant research on a special topic.

The program is designed to accommodate the unique requirements of both career professionals and full-time students. Sufficient sections of courses are offered in the evenings to permit career professionals to complete the M.B.A. on a part-time basis. In this way, full-time and part-time students take classes together, enriching the educational experience of both.

Students and the M.B.A Experience

Diverse backgrounds and experiences are characteristic of students in the AGSM M.B.A. program. The average age of students is 27, with an age range from 21 to 49. Approximately 38 percent are women, and 27 percent are minority students. Sixty-five percent of the students have an average of three years' work experience in fields ranging from medicine to manufacturing; 35 percent come directly from undergraduate programs. In recent classes, 45 percent of the student body has come from the Western United States, 15 percent from the Northeast and South, and 10 percent from the Midwest. Approximately 30 percent are international students. Forty percent of AGSM's students have undergraduate degrees in business or economics, 30 percent have degrees in science or engineering, and 30 percent have backgrounds in the humanities or social sciences.

❖ Global Focus

Most AGSM required courses include a global perspective, with recognition of the international issues that affect each functional area. In addition, electives in many of the functional areas provide opportunities for in-depth study of international topics. The campus maintains liaison with most of the networks offering international internships, and overseas study options are available in thirty countries through the University of California Education Abroad Program.

Special Features

The management synthesis course at the end of the first year of study and the required internship are key elements of the AGSM M.B.A. program. The synthesis course is a team-taught, integrative, cross-functional case course that places students in actual managerial decision situations. The required internship enables students to apply their academic background to real-world projects, where they learn to perfect their professional, interpersonal, and communication skills.

The Faculty

The A. Gary Anderson Graduate School of Management has a renowned, multicultural faculty, representing excellence in its respective areas. Faculty members have doctorates from world-class universities and publish research in top journals in their fields. Faculty members also have industry and consulting experience and teach in executive programs and workshops.

The Business School Network

Relationships with the corporate community are an integral part of the AGSM M.B.A. program. The AGSM Advisory Council assists the School with developing and maintaining a relevant curriculum and interacts with M.B.A. students at numerous events. Every year, the School also names two distinguished business leaders as AGSM Fellows. Each Fellow spends one day each quarter speaking to classes and consulting with M.B.A. students. In the spring, a contemporary issues seminar series brings 8–10 corporate executives to the School to discuss emerging issues with M.B.A. students. These and other activities ensure that each M.B.A. student has the opportunity to develop a network of business contacts prior to graduation.

The College and Environs

The 1,200-acre Riverside campus of the University of California is conveniently

located some 50 miles east of Los Angeles, within easy driving distance of most of the major cultural and recreational offerings in southern California. Enrollment at UCR is approximately 8,900, nearly 20 percent of whom are graduate students. The campus, with its modern classroom buildings, its beautiful commons, and its 161-foot Carillon Tower, is designed to support the academic and research programs that are part of its assigned mission as a campus in the University of California system.

A city of 242,000, Riverside has several major shopping malls, a symphony orchestra, an opera association, two community theaters, an art center, and many restaurants in proximity to the campus.

Facilities

The University library is the focal point of research and study at UCR. The collection includes more than 1.6 million bound volumes, 13,621 serial subscriptions, and 1.4 million microforms. The collections are arranged and staffed to support programs of instruction and research for faculty and students.

The M.B.A. program is housed in newly completed Anderson Hall. M.B.A. students have access to the latest computing equipment, a behavioral lab, and a teleconferencing center.

UCR offers graduate students several affordable housing options both on and off campus. Campus housing includes Bannockburn Village, University Plaza Apartments, and Canyon Crest Married Student Housing.

Technology Environment

The AGSM Microcomputer Facility consists of fifty-four state-of-the-art microcomputers, including both 80486-based DOS-compatible machines and Apple Ma-

cintosh Centris 650s. The facility is networked to the campus network and to the Internet. Special-purpose workstation labs are located adjacent to the main facility to provide opportunities for specialized graduate research.

A variety of software packages and databases are available, including SAS, SPSS, BMDP, Minitab, ARC-Info geographic information system, Citibase, and CRSP stock market data.

Placement

A full range of career planning and placement services is offered through the M.B.A. Career Services Center. The center is staffed by professional counselors to address the specific career needs of graduate business students. Services available include on-campus interviews, career seminars and workshops, individual counseling, an alumni career network, a résumé directory, and an extensive career library, including computerized employment databases. The school participates in the West Coast M.B.A. Consortium and also sponsors a career night, which provides M.B.A. candidates the opportunity to meet with local and national corporate representatives.

Admission

Admission is open to eligible students from all undergraduate majors. Admission is based on several criteria, including the quality of previous academic work as measured by GPA for the last two years of undergraduate work, scores on the Graduate Management Admission Test (GMAT), letters of recommendation, and potential for success in the program. In recent years, the average GPA for entering students has been approximately 3.3 and the average GMAT score has been 560–565. Applicants whose first

language is not English are required to score a minimum of 550 on the TOEFL.

Basic accounting and quantitative methods are prerequisites to the program. Students may be admitted without these courses but must meet these requirements during their first two quarters in residence.

Finances

Tuition and fees for 1994–95 for full-time students were $4810 for California residents and $12,509 for nonresidents. An additional $2000 per year professional school fee is also assessed, although in 1994–95, AGSM provided grants to all M.B.A. students to cover 50 percent of this fee. Annual fees for part-time students in 1994–95 ranged from $3023 to $3767 for California residents, including the professional school fee. Approximate costs for books and supplies are $900 per year. Living expenses, including housing and personal expenses, are estimated at $6500 to $7500 per year.

Several kinds of financial assistance are available. These include fellowships, teaching assistantships, and research assistantships. Applicants indicate interest in support on the application form. Loans and work study may be applied for through the UCR Financial Aid Office.

International Students

Approximately 30 percent of AGSM's M.B.A. students are international students. The International Services Center provides special assistance to international students and their dependents. An orientation program is held at the beginning of each quarter to help new students adjust to their new environs and the campus. Throughout the year, workshops, excursions, and individual advising sessions are offered. In addition, language workshops tailored to the needs of the international M.B.A. students are available.

Application Facts and Dates

Application deadlines for domestic students are May 1 for fall quarter, September 1 for winter quarter, and December 1 for spring quarter. Deadlines for international students are February 1 for fall, July 1 for winter, and October 1 for spring. Applications are processed on a rolling basis, and decisions are made when files are complete. For further information, applicants should contact:

Dr. Charlotte Weber
Associate Dean
The A. Gary Anderson Graduate
    School of Management
University of California
Riverside, California 92521-0203
Telephone: 909-787-4551
Fax: 909-787-3970
Internet: agsmmba@ucrac1.ucr.edu

University of Connecticut

Storrs, Connecticut

> You will invest a significant amount of time and money in working toward an M.B.A. degree. The program you select should provide you with a multidimensional and integrated series of challenging learning experiences that prepare you for a business leadership position. Concern for quality is a key consideration in choosing an M.B.A. program. The "Connecticut M.B.A." has a well-established tradition of excellence in four essential areas: the quality and diversity of our students, the quality of our faculty, the quality of the curriculum, and the quality of the support services. Our students' geographic and cultural diversity creates a supportive learning environment for all. The faculty members have a strong commitment to teaching, and they bring relevant research and consulting experience to their classes. The curriculum gives you many choices and provides flexibility in selecting electives for a concentration. Finally, the support services, including the library, computer labs, and counseling and placement services, provide the support you need, when you need it.
>
> —Thomas G. Gutteridge, Dean

Programs and Curricular Focus

The M.B.A. curriculum requires a total of nineteen courses/57 credits to earn the degree, which typically takes two academic years. By taking courses during intersessions or summer, students can complete the entire program in only sixteen months. Students with previous academic course work in core subjects may be able to substitute electives for two or three required courses, which adds to the choices and flexibility in selecting courses. Concentrations are available in international business, accounting, finance, health-care management, human resources, marketing, real estate, and management.

The UConn M.B.A. Program integrates international business into the curriculum and provides several opportunities for students to study and work overseas. M.B.A. students may concentrate in international business or in any of the functional areas or they may complete a double concentration in international business and one of the functional areas. M.B.A. courses taught in English, French, and German are available as part of the study overseas, dual-degree, and exchange programs in France, Germany, and the Netherlands. Students are expected to take advantage of the diversity of backgrounds in their classes to develop perspectives and skills that are critically relevant to managing in this increasingly complex and ever-shrinking world.

Students and the M.B.A. Experience

The class of 114 students who entered the program in the fall of 1994 included 40 international students representing nineteen countries. Many noninternational students have studied foreign languages or traveled extensively abroad. The average age of the entering class was 26, with a range from age 20 to over 40. Most of the students were in their mid-20s, and most of them had between one and six years of work experience. This diversity of geographic, cultural, and work backgrounds is a key ingredient to the success of the UConn M.B.A. Program.

The Graduate Business Association (GBA) is an important and integral part of the learning experience. The GBA is student-run, and it sponsors the Executive Speaker Series, career and interviewing workshops with alumni, and the annual Career Interview Conference. One of the elected officers of the GBA, the Vice President of International Affairs, must be an international student.

Many of the students obtain paid internships during the summer, both to earn money and to obtain work experience that is relevant to their choice of career. Other students extend the length of their M.B.A. studies to take advantage of internship opportunities that occur during the academic year. One M.B.A. student is working on an internship in Morocco, as one of only 16

chosen by the U.S. Agency for International Development for its Free Market Advisers Program. Several M.B.A. students are working as paid interns for Connecticut-based companies. Another M.B.A. student is working as a part-time intern in the area of foreign trade for the U.S. Department of Commerce. When combined with an independent study, internships can also be done for academic credit.

The Faculty

With very few exceptions, all of the faculty members who teach in the full-time M.B.A. program have earned their Ph.D. or the equivalent terminal degree in their field. The faculty members have very diverse academic backgrounds, with alma maters that include Harvard, Yale, and MIT. They also have equally interesting and diverse cultural backgrounds, including professors from Australia and from countries in Africa, South America, and Asia. New electives are introduced almost every semester, and teaching assignments for required core courses are rotated frequently so that students benefit from the latest developments in research and consulting conducted by the faculty. Many faculty members conduct research, consult, teach, or maintain professional contacts in other countries. At UConn, the world is in the classroom.

The Business School Network

Connecticut is the "Insurance Capital of the World," a major center for financial services, a major manufacturing area with a strong involvement in international trade, and the incredible retail market for the highest per capita income population of any state. This very diverse corporate community provides the context and, ultimately, the resources by which the School of Business Administration maintains its preeminence within the state. Essentially all of the major corporations, as well as many small and medium-size companies in the corporate corridor connecting New York City and Boston, employ the School's alumni, which greatly facilitates both placement and maintenance of a state-of-the-art curriculum.

The College and Environs

Centrally located in the "corporate corridor" between New York and Boston, Connecticut is one of the most commercially diverse states in the country. The University of Connecticut is a large, multifaceted institution with nationally recognized professional schools of business, dentistry, engineering, law, and medicine. The University is one of the nation's major public research universities, with 25,000 students, 95,000 alumni, and 120 major buildings on 3,100 acres at the main campus in Storrs. All of the academic, library, computer, social, and cultural opportunities and facilities of a major university are readily available to all M.B.A. students. The immediate area surrounding the main campus is rural, with the bucolic charm of New England. Compared to most major universities, the University campus is a safe and very scenic environment. The cost of living is substantially less than in most metropolitan areas. However, many internship and employment opportunities are available nearby. The capital and metropolitan area of Hartford is a ½-hour, Boston is a 1½-hour, and New York City is a 3-hour drive. One third of the Fortune 500 companies, and hundreds of small and medium-size firms, have their corporate headquarters in this unique corporate corridor.

Placement

For most M.B.A. students, building and developing a challenging and satisfying management career is their primary purpose in attending an M.B.A. program. The University of Connecticut M.B.A. Program provides the education, training, support, and opportunities to advance toward this goal. Activities in career planning begin during orientation and continue throughout the two academic years. Coaching and opportunities to practice specific skills, such as developing effective résumés and cover letters, interview techniques, arranging interviews, and networking, are available to all M.B.A. students. Mock interviews with supportive but tough alumni executives make a significant difference in preparing students for successful interviews. Many M.B.A. students acquire new and relevant work experience through summer internships or semester co-ops. These experiences augment the academic program and develop skills that make effective managers. Internships can also provide a very important source of financial support.

Admission

The minimum requirements for admission include a 3.0 GPA, out of a possible 4.0, or the equivalent and a total GMAT score of at least 500. However, applicants who do not meet all these requirements may be considered for admission based on strengths in other areas of their application. For international students whose native language is not English, a TOEFL score of at least 550 is required.

Finances

Total costs for students attending the University of Connecticut M.B.A. Program are approximately $20,000 per academic year. Financial aid in the form of scholarships and graduate assistantships is available to students who are U.S. citizens; it is also available to international students on a very limited basis. Scholarships and graduate assistantships are more available to international students during their second year in the program.

Application Facts and Dates

Admission decisions are made on a rolling basis as completed applications are received, so there is no rigid deadline for submitting an application. However, the size of the entering class is constrained, and very few applications from international students submitted after April are approved for admission. The earlier an application is submitted, the better. International applicants are encouraged to submit their application prior to taking the GMAT. Admission is available only for the fall semester. For additional information, students should contact:

UConn M.B.A. Program
368 Fairfield Road, U-41MBA
Storrs, Connecticut 06269-2041
Telephone: 203-486-2872
Fax: 203-486-5222

University of Dallas

Irving, Texas

THE GRADUATE SCHOOL OF MANAGEMENT IN THE GLOBAL ARENA

The Graduate School of Management is a real-world and performance-oriented graduate business school. We believe the best education for business leadership is a high-quality, global, applied, action-oriented, and customer-driven academic curriculum tied to the realities of the world in which we live and work. In that regard, we made a commitment to "internationalize" a significant portion of our academic program long before it became fashionable. We plan to do even more in the global arena in order to be totally prepared for the future.
—Charles Edward Perry, Dean

Programs and Curricular Focus

The Master of Business Administration programs of the Graduate School of Management (GSM) provide multiple options to suit a variety of career paths. Students seeking a generalist approach may select the M.B.A. in business management, which provides the broadest management education.

Students who wish to develop more specific skills or focus on a particular business environment may select from the following concentrations or tracks within the M.B.A. program: marketing management, corporate finance, international finance, corporate investment analysis, managerial accounting, treasury management, engineering management, industrial management, operations management, materials management, quality management, logistics management, purchasing and contract management, financial and estate planning, investment management, financial services management, health services management, human resource management, international human resource management, international accounting, international management, inter-Americas trade, information systems management, applications development, and telecommunications management.

The curriculum for each M.B.A. program includes a set of core courses designed to provide a strong business foundation and a set of specialized courses unique to each concentration.

M.B.A. programs require the completion of 49 credit hours (sixteen courses). This may be reduced to a minimum of 37 credit hours (twelve courses) for students who have courses transferred from another graduate institution or waived on

the basis of undergraduate course work. On GSM's thirteen-week trimester system, most full-time M.B.A. students can complete their degree requirements in three or four trimesters.

Students who have already earned an M.B.A. may pursue a second master's degree, the Master of Management. This degree requires the completion of 25 credit hours (eight courses) in the selected area of concentration.

GSM's noncredit pre-M.B.A. and intensive English programs allow international students to prepare for graduate studies in business while becoming acclimated to life in the United States.

The pre-M.B.A. program is an intensive, thirteen-week preparatory program that is designed to enhance communication skills, improve GMAT scores, and teach fundamental business concepts. This program is specifically designed to meet the needs of international students who wish to improve their GMAT score or who may not have an undergraduate degree in business.

The full-time intensive English program utilizes the "focal skills" method of instruction, allowing students to progress at their own pace through classes in listening, reading, writing, and immersion, which focuses on all skill areas. Students continuing to GSM may take a business fluency course designed to prepare them for oral presentations and writing research papers.

Students and the M.B.A. Experience

The Graduate School of Management attracts mature students who have

substantial professional experience. The average GSM student is 32 years old and has seven years of work experience. The student body includes 36 percent women, 15 percent minorities, and 23 percent international students from fifty-seven countries. Nineteen percent of GSM students have engineering degrees, 16 percent were science majors, and 18 percent have various undergraduate degrees, including liberal arts and social sciences. Fourteen percent already hold graduate degrees. This mature, diverse student body is one of the GSM's outstanding educational resources.

❖ Global Focus

The Graduate School of Management has long recognized the importance of global education. The M.B.A. in international management program at GSM is one of the ten largest in the United States and has recently been expanded to include a specialization in inter-Americas trade. Travel courses, which include faculty-guided study in international business capitals, are offered between trimesters. Study abroad and exchange opportunities are also available.

Special Features

The Graduate School of Management was the first business school in the region to assign students to real consulting projects for local, national, and international firms. These strategic planning projects allow students to apply the concepts and methods taught in their previous courses to real business problems.

The Faculty

GSM's faculty provides a rare mix of competence in both the theoretical aspects of management and the applied working knowledge of its practical aspects. The faculty is organized into a relatively small resident group and a larger adjunct group. The resident faculty members are full-time instructors with extensive backgrounds in business, teaching, applied research, and consulting. The adjunct faculty consists of practicing managers, attorneys, accountants, consultants, and other professionals, who

teach part-time. GSM students enjoy the best of both the academic and the practical worlds.

The Business School Network

Over the years, GSM has developed significant alliances and corporate partnerships. Each concentration has an advisory board made up of prominent professionals in related fields who assist the program directors in the development of their programs. Through the Management Lecture Series, world business leaders visit the University to lecture to GSM students. In their capstone courses, all GSM students have the opportunity to work on a real project for a corporation.

The College and Environs

The University of Dallas was founded in 1956 as an independent Catholic university dedicated to the pursuit of excellence in its educational programs. The current total enrollment in undergraduate and graduate programs exceeds 3,000 students.

The Graduate School of Management was founded in 1966 as an evening graduate school for individuals who were already employed in business and the professions. Over the years, the school's educational scope has broadened to serve a diverse student population, while its programs have remained focused on the practical realities of managerial life.

The University of Dallas is located in the suburban community of Irving, Texas, a part of the Dallas–Fort Worth metroplex, and is within 10 miles of downtown Dallas and the Dallas–Fort Worth International Airport. The scenic campus, on over 600 acres of rolling hills, is directly adjacent to Texas Stadium, home of the Dallas Cowboys football team.

The Dallas–Fort Worth metroplex has 3.4 million people and is one of the fastest-growing population centers in the country. Its diversified economy includes important industries in electronics, aerospace, insurance, and banking. The moderate climate and abundance of lakes and parks in the surrounding area offer numerous recreational opportunities. The metroplex also provides rich cultural and entertainment opportunities.

Technology Environment

Faulkner's Communications Infodisk, Computer Select, the National Trade Data Base, Compact Disclosure, and the ABI-Inform full text system are a few of the technical resources available in the University of Dallas Blakley Library. Students also have access to the resources of many other public and university libraries in north Texas.

Computer facilities are available to all students. The on-campus computer center provides access to personal computers and the University's Prime superminicomputer.

Placement

The University of Dallas Career Counseling Center assists M.B.A. students with their job search and offers workshops on résumé preparation and interviewing skills. Students participate in job fairs on- and off-campus, and many corporations come to GSM to select students for professional internships.

Admission

Applicants must have a bachelor's degree from an accredited institution. Other admission criteria include an undergraduate grade point average of at least 3.0, a satisfactory score on the GMAT, and a work history of professional managerial work experience. International students whose native language is not English must submit satisfactory TOEFL scores; for immigration purposes, these students must show the availability of $21,750 for each year of study.

Finances

Tuition for the Graduate School of Management in 1994–95 was $316 per credit hour. Books and supplies cost approximately $100 per class. Living expenses, including housing, meals, utilities, and miscellaneous expenses, average $850 per month. Mandatory health insurance is $192 each trimester. Students should plan to purchase a car for local transportation.

International Students

International students comprise over 23 percent of the GSM student body. International students become members of the International Student Association, and many join a regional or country-specific student organization.

Application Facts and Dates

Applications are accepted for the fall, spring, and summer trimesters. Applications from outside the United States should be sent at least eight weeks before the trimester desired. The nonrefundable application fee for international students is $50.

For more information on the University of Dallas Graduate School of Management, applicants should contact:

The Graduate School of Management
Office of Admissions
1845 East Northgate Drive
Irving, Texas 75062-4799
Telephone: 214-721-5174
Fax: 214-721-4009

The University of Delaware

Newark, Delaware

> *Earning an M.B.A. degree is a significant undertaking that requires considerable dedication, energy, and time. We put powerful resources behind our program to make sure students receive a superlative business education. Consequently, at the University of Delaware, you will find an academically accomplished faculty, a demanding and exciting curriculum, and—because of our commitment to admissions quality—highly accomplished classmates. Because we believe that students develop their critical problem-solving and decision-making skills from each other, as well as from the faculty, you will be in a classroom of no more than 35 students, immersing you in a highly concentrated and learning-supportive environment.*
>
> *—Kenneth R. Biederman, Dean*

Programs and Curricular Focus

The College of Business and Economics offers rigorous programs for superior students leading to the M.B.A. and the M.A./M.B.A. degrees. The special combination of academically accomplished faculty, highly qualified students, and ideal location—a small university town in the midst of the large eastern megalopolis—provides the necessary ingredients for an outstanding experience in graduate business education. The Delaware M.B.A. program is accredited by the American Assembly of Collegiate Schools of Business (AACSB).

The Delaware M.B.A. curriculum has been redesigned in recognition of today's business needs. The new curriculum includes courses that focus on capable leadership, effective team building, group decision making, strategic use of technology, power negotiating, creative problem-solving techniques, international concerns, coordinating an effective total quality management process, and ethical considerations. The new courses complement the traditional courses in accounting, economics, finance, operations, and marketing. Students who wish to pursue more in-depth course work are offered the option of concentrating in accounting, business economics, finance, international business, management, marketing, operations, or technology and innovation management.

The 48-credit M.B.A. program can normally be completed in eighteen to twenty-one months. Up to 12 credits may be waived for students with prior instruction in accounting, business, and/or economics, making it possible for some individuals to complete the program in twelve months. An Executive M.B.A. program allows students with at least five years of professional experience to complete the degree in nineteen months by taking classes Friday evenings and Saturdays. The combination of small class sizes, classroom theory, and students' practical experiences creates a stimulating environment for the analysis of today's business world.

Students and the M.B.A. Experience

For fall 1994, the average length of work experience for entering M.B.A. students was four years, and the average age was 26. In 1994–95, 400 students were enrolled in the M.B.A. program, of whom 37 percent were women, 7 percent were members of minority groups, and 7 percent were international students (20 percent of the full-time student body), including students from Bulgaria, China, France, Iceland, India, and Singapore. The diversity of the student body adds to the interactive learning environment in the classroom.

Special Features

All Delaware M.B.A. students are given an account on the Internet and are introduced to its many tools during the new student orientation program. The M.B.A. program has its own Usenet news group that is used for information sharing. Some M.B.A. classes also use news groups as an additional learning environment. E-mail is the preferred form of communication between students, faculty, and administrators.

The Faculty

The faculty members who teach M.B.A. classes hold doctoral degrees in their disciplines. Through widely respected research and publishing efforts, they have earned national reputations in their fields of study. M.B.A. faculty members have also enhanced their respective skills through consulting positions with major national and international corporations, a good number of which are headquartered a short distance from the University.

The Business School Network

Because of the excellent reputation of the Delaware M.B.A., positive program relations exist with members of the corporate community, including DuPont, MBNA America, Bank of New York, J. P. Morgan Delaware, ICI America, and Zeneca. For example, M.B.A. classes are currently offered on-site at DuPont and MBNA America. These relationships have fostered the development of internship opportunities for Delaware M.B.A. students at these and other firms (e.g., Hewlett-Packard, First USA Bank, Arco, and Cyanamid).

The College's Visiting Board, composed of high-ranking corporate executives from major corporations, serves as an advisory group to the dean of the College on various matters, including those pertaining to the M.B.A. program.

The activities of an M.B.A. alumni network are supported by the regular publication of the M.B.A. Alumni Resource Directory, which is available to all M.B.A. students and alumni. The directory is a main source of M.B.A. career planning and placement.

The College and Environs

The University of Delaware, founded in 1743 as a small liberal arts school, now ranks among the finest of the nation's medium-sized universities, with approximately 14,000 undergraduate and 3,000 graduate students. Included in the College of Business and Economics are four departments: accounting, business administration, economics, and finance.

The University of Delaware is located in Newark, a suburban community of approximately 30,000 residents. Newark is situated in the northwest corner of Delaware within 3 miles of the Pennsylvania and Maryland borders. It is located within easy driving distance of Philadelphia (45 miles), Baltimore (50 miles), Washington, D.C. (100 miles), and New York City (130 miles). Newark is also less than 100 miles from the Delaware and New Jersey beaches. Nearby Wilmington is a major center for credit banking and the chemical industry. Eighty percent of all Fortune 500 companies are incorporated in Delaware, which allows the College to maintain strong ties with the corporate sector.

Facilities

The University library is a modern research facility with over 2 million volumes, is a member of the Association of Research Libraries, and is a depository for U.S. government documents and patents.

Mainframe computer facilities include an extensive array of both hardware and software. Sun Workstations operating under UNIX are used for research, course work, text processing, and communication. The College has a computer laboratory that focuses on business applications, as well as a state-of-the-art local area network.

Placement

In addition to on-campus interviews, the Delaware M.B.A. program participates in two M.B.A./Graduate Business Consortia Talent Finders in Philadelphia and Washington, D.C. Along with graduates from other top schools in the mid-Atlantic

region, Delaware's M.B.A. graduates network and arrange interviews with a number of prospective employers. The average annual salary for 1994 graduates of the full-time M.B.A. program was $40,000.

Admission

A student must submit official copies of all undergraduate and graduate transcripts, GMAT scores, and two letters of recommendation. In some cases, a personal interview is also required to determine an applicant's qualifications. Delaware M.B.A. students are a highly accomplished group. For fall 1994, the mean GMAT score of entering students was 580 and the mean undergraduate GPA was 3.1. A score of 585 is required on the TOEFL for all students for whom English is not the native language. No prior work experience is required, although it is strongly recommended. Although no prerequisite courses are required, applicants are assumed to possess basic skills in written and oral communication, mathematics, and computer use.

Finances

In 1994–95, the yearly tuition for full-time M.B.A. students was $4642 for Delaware residents and $10,220 for nonresidents. Part-time study was $258 per credit hour for Delaware residents and $568 per credit hour for nonresident students. Rental costs for shared occupancy in a graduate student complex were $350 per month. University and privately owned apartments, furnished and unfurnished, are available at costs ranging from $350 to $900 per month.

Numerous financial aid packages are available to superior full-time M.B.A. students. These include assistantships and tuition grants that are awarded on a

competitive basis regardless of nationality or financial need. Preference is given to current students who have excelled in the program. Awards to first-year students are based on prior academic performance. Awards to second-year students are based on academic performance in the program.

A typical aid package may include a $4000 per year stipend and/or a 50 percent waiver of tuition. These awards are administered by the M.B.A. Programs Office. Information on other possible sources of aid can be obtained by writing to the University's Office of Scholarships and Student Financial Aid.

International Students

More than 20 percent of the full-time student body is international. The Cosmopolitan Club provides activities for international students that help them understand the American culture as well as the cultures of other countries. International students are also oriented to the needs placed on them in a highly interactive M.B.A. classroom.

Application Facts and Dates

Applications for the fall semester must be submitted by May 1. Students seeking financial aid should submit their applications by February 15. Applications for the spring semester are due November 1. For more information, students should contact:

Robert B. Barker, Director
M.B.A. Programs
College of Business and Economics
108 Purnell Hall
University of Delaware
Newark, Delaware 19716
Telephone: 302-831-2221
Fax: 302-831-6750
E-mail: mba@chopin.udel.edu
URL: http://www.udel.edu/aamsler/
    mba/mbapage1.html

University of Detroit Mercy

Detroit, Michigan

DEVELOPING VALUE-ORIENTED BUSINESS LEADERS

The College of Business Administration provides professional education in business and related fields, recognizing the importance of a liberalizing education as a foundation for a career of continuing self-education. The College aims to instill in its students, through a personalized educational process, a sense of personal integrity, a high measure of intellectual curiosity, and a deep awareness of personal and social values in contemporary society. One of the hallmarks of the University of Detroit Mercy is the ability to offer individualized education in small classes. Graduate business students are able to tailor their programs to specific needs and interests and build on their current bases of knowledge and work experiences. Students benefit from personal contact with our highly experienced faculty members, many of whom serve as consultants in the private and public sectors. We look forward to helping you achieve your career objectives.

—Dr. Gregory W. Ulferts, Dean

Programs and Curricular Focus

In the program's current format, the number of credit hours required for completion ranges from a minimum of 36 to a maximum of 60. Courses in the curriculum are divided into three groups: pre-core (24 credit hours), core (24 credit hours), and post-core (12 hours). The pre-core consists of eight foundation courses, which may be waived depending on the individual's academic background. The core consists of eight courses that are required for all students. Post-core is composed of a required capstone course and three electives that allow students to individualize their programs in specific areas of management, marketing, finance, accounting, economics, international business, decision analysis, or computer information systems. Depending upon academic background, it is possible to complete the degree requirements in one year on a full-time basis. In addition, a joint M.B.A./J.D. program is offered, which enables students to complete both degrees in approximately four years.

Students and the M.B.A. Experience

Students at the University of Detroit Mercy bring a wide variety of work experiences and academic and cultural diversity to the M.B.A. program. The average age of the student body is about 30; approximately 30 percent are women, 20 percent are members of minority groups, and 10 percent are international students. The average length of work experience is seven to eight years. Ninety-five percent of the students matriculate on a part-time basis.

❖ Global Focus

In response to the importance of globalization in the business world, the College offers students intensive courses during the summer in England, Ireland, China, Brazil, and Mexico for up to 6 hours of credit.

Special Features

Detroit Mercy is one of eleven members of a consortium with other Jesuit institutions across the United States, whereby courses taken at one institution are accepted by the others.

To accommodate students who cannot take classes during the week, Saturday classes are offered. In addition to the fourteen-week fall and winter semesters, two accelerated seven-week summer sessions are offered, which allow students to move more quickly through the program.

The Faculty

The College of Business Administration has highly qualified faculty members with superb academic and professional backgrounds. Many have lived, worked, and studied abroad, bringing global perspectives to the classroom.

A faculty-student ratio of 1:17 keeps classes small and ensures individual attention. Faculty members often act as academic advisers to students and assist with their research projects and career objectives.

The Business School Network

The University has an excellent reputation in the metropolitan Detroit business community. Over 275 business and professional organizations are represented in the graduate business program. An independent study conducted by Dun & Bradstreet revealed that there are more graduates from Detroit Mercy in top management positions with Michigan firms than from any other private college or university in the state. Strong ties between the College and corporate leaders in the area continuously contribute to the success and excellence of the program.

The College and Environs

In December 1990, the University of Detroit consolidated with Mercy College of Detroit and formed the University of Detroit Mercy. The University is an independent Catholic institution of higher education that is sponsored by the Religious Sisters of Mercy and the Society of Jesus.

The University of Detroit Mercy's M.B.A. program is one of the oldest graduate business programs in the United States. Instituted in 1948, it was given full recognition by the American Assembly of Collegiate Schools of Business (AACSB) in 1963. It was among the first sixty universities in the United States to be so accredited. The College is the second-oldest AACSB-accredited M.B.A. program in Michigan. The mission of the College is to offer an integrated, value-oriented, high-quality business education within the Jesuit and Mercy traditions that will enable students to utilize and expand their knowledge and skills to improve and serve the organizations in which they work and the society in which they live.

The University's environment is highly conducive to learning. The Graduate Business Programs Office is located on the attractive 70-acre McNichols campus in the College Park area of northwest Detroit. The city offers a world-famous symphony orchestra, an opera company, numerous theatrical and dance groups, and a host of art, science, and history museums. The city is home to professional baseball, basketball, football, and hockey teams.

Technology Environment

In addition to various computer laboratory locations across the campus, the College has two state-of-the-art computer labs. A rich library of software packages is available to students. Computer integration is an essential feature of the graduate program.

Placement

The Professional Practice and Career Development Office offers full service to graduate students. Opportunities for practical training, seminars, and on-campus recruiting are all available through this office. After completion of the appropriate credit hours, students are eligible for career-related assignments. Students are provided the opportunity to select full-time assignments, alternating semesters of work and study, or part-time assignments with parallel semesters of work and study.

Admission

Admission decisions are based on a combination of the score attained on the required Graduate Management Admission Test (GMAT), undergraduate GPA, work experience, and any other supporting material. The average GMAT score of accepted students is 520; the average GPA is 3.1.

It is not necessary for international students to take the TOEFL because English proficiency will be established on campus. However, a TOEFL score of 600 and a TWE score of 4.0 will exempt an individual from testing. International students must apply through International Services at the University of Detroit Mercy.

Finances

The current tuition rate for graduate business courses is $408 per credit hour. The registration fee each term is $30 for a part-time student and $50 for a full-time student. There is also an activities fee of $5 per term. The University estimates that the average cost per month for on-campus room and board is $700. Off-campus living expenses range from $600 to $1000 per month. Since the University is located in a large metropolitan area, a variety of living arrangements are available.

A limited number of graduate assistantships are available each term. Normally, applications are accepted after the individual has completed one semester of course work. Students should contact the Financial Aid Office for other kinds of assistance that may be available.

International Students

The Detroit area was ranked in the top six "most desirable metropolitan international living areas" by a recent international study reported in *Asia Week*. The University offers many specialized services, such as a weekly international coffee hour, a free American studies class about living in the United States, international housing, student organizations, and a dedicated international service staff. Assistantships are open to international students after one semester of study.

Application Facts and Dates

Application deadlines for international students are Term I, May 1; Term II, September 1; and Summer I and Summer II, January 1. Application deadlines for all others are four weeks prior to the start of each particular term. Deviations from these deadlines are possible through the approval of the Director of Graduate Business Programs. Usually decision letters are mailed within a week of receipt of all required documents. For more information, students should contact:

Bahman Mirshab
Director, Graduate Business Programs
College of Business Administration
University of Detroit Mercy
P.O. Box 19900
Detroit, Michigan 48219-0900
Telephone: 313-993-1202 or 1203
Fax: 313-993-1052
Internet: mirshabb@udmercy.edu

University of Houston

Houston, Texas

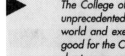

> The College of Business Administration is committed to keeping pace with the unprecedented changes in how business is transacted and negotiated around the world and exerts its resources and energy to stay in the forefront. What was good for the College, the city of Houston, the state of Texas, and the world a few short years ago differs dramatically from the theories, programs, and practices essential to meeting today's challenges. Thus, the College accepts the challenge, looks to the future, and prepares its faculty and students for a dynamic city, state, nation, and world.
>
> —John M. Ivancevich, Dean

Programs and Curricular Focus

The master's programs in the College are designed to enhance work experience and academic accomplishments with a focus on globalization and international exposure. As the business environment changes, the demand increases for managers with the knowledge, skills, courage, and foresight to effectively and proactively manage change. M.B.A. students are given opportunities in an urban environment to develop and implement managerial and leadership skills in analysis, problem solving, quality management, leadership, interpersonal relationships, and communication.

The M.B.A. program offers concentrations in accountancy, finance, international business, management, management information systems, marketing, operations management, statistics and operations research, and taxation. Joint M.B.A. programs offer the advantage of earning two advanced degrees concurrently in less time than if they were pursued separately. Joint programs include an M.B.A./J.D. degree program in conjunction with UH Law Center; M.B.A./M.I.E. program with UH Cullen College of Engineering; M.B.A./M.A. in Spanish with the College of Humanities, Fine Arts, and Communication; and M.B.A./M.S.W. in conjunction with the Graduate School of Social Work. The College has partnered with The American Graduate School of International Management (Thunderbird) in Glendale, Arizona, to offer an M.B.A./M.I.M. degree (Master of International Management). An Executive M.B.A., which includes weekend classes and can be completed in two years, as well as a Professional M.B.A., which accommodates working professionals and entry-level managers, are also offered.

Scheduling for the 54-semester-hour M.B.A. program allows students to attend classes full- or part-time, day or night. The programs are fully accredited by the American Assembly of Collegiate Schools of Business.

Opportunities to study abroad are available, as are scholarships for foreign study. The College has exchange programs with universities in France, Germany, Japan, Mexico, and Canada.

Students and the M.B.A. Experience

Diversity among the students in the M.B.A. programs is a significant part of the M.B.A. experience. More than 10 percent of the M.B.A. students are international. Learning side-by-side with highly motivated international students gives all students a unique perspective as they share business strategies from a variety of cultures. Women make up more than 33 percent of the M.B.A. students and members of minority groups, approximately 10 percent. Total enrollment in the M.B.A. programs is just over 1,000. Of those, one third are full-time students. The average M.B.A. student is 28 years old, with four years of full-time work experience. Students with undergraduate degrees in virtually any area of study, including liberal arts, social sciences, physical sciences, education, engineering, and other fields, have found the M.B.A. degree from the University of Houston beneficial.

Special Features

The College has several programs, centers, and institutes designed to support and promote academic activities in a number of business areas. These include the Southwest Center for International Business, Center for Executive Development, UH Small Business Development Center, Center for Entrepreneurship and Innovation, Institute for Diversity and Cross-Cultural Management, Center for Global Manufacturing, Information Systems Research Center, Institute for Health Care Marketing, Institute for Corporate Environmental Management, and the Institute for Business, Ethics, and Public Issues.

The Faculty

The College's strong academic programs are enhanced by the enthusiasm and dedication of the faculty. There are 85 full-time faculty members, 11 executive professors, 8 visiting professors, and adjunct lecturers. Ninety-eight percent hold doctoral degrees, and many are nationally renowned teachers and scholars. Executive professors, who share their business acumen, come from the top corporations in the Houston business community, providing unequaled opportunities for students to learn firsthand from corporate leaders. Faculty members often act as advisers or consultants to financial institutions, businesses, and government agencies and keep their classrooms current through these experiences.

The Business School Network
Corporate Partnerships

The urban location of the College provides a number of advantages, including the availability of business leaders willing to visit classrooms, teach, work on committees, coordinate special projects, help faculty members and graduate students establish research contacts, and offer advice to the dean and other administrators. Students gain valuable experience as they interact with the diverse management styles within a metropolitan business world. Another opportunity for students is access to real-world work experiences through internships.

Melcher Hall, opened in 1986, houses the College of Business Administration.

Prominent Alumni

The College recognizes a number of prominent alumni, including LeRoy Melcher, Chairman of the Board and CEO (retired), Fairmont Foods; Sam P. Douglas, Chairman, Equus International; Kenneth W. Reese (deceased), Executive Vice President, Tenneco, Inc.; Jack Valenti, President, Motion Picture Association of America; Kathryn J. Whitmire, National Director of Junior Achievement and former Mayor of Houston; Elizabeth Rockwell, Senior Vice President, Oppenheimer & Company; Gene McDavid, President, *Houston Chronicle;* Lane Sloan, Regional Coordinator East and Australasia, Shell Oil; and Thaddeus Smith, President, Brown & Root Service Corporation.

The College and Environs

The University consists of ninety-two modern classroom and laboratory buildings spread over 556 acres of woodlands and open spaces nestled in the heart of the nation's fourth-largest city. This world-class city offers students concerts; nightclubs; major symphony orchestra, opera, and ballet companies; shopping; country and western dance halls; comedy clubs; museums; and professional sports events. Blue skies and sunshine are the rule. The Gulf Coast

beaches at historic Galveston, Freeport, and Bolivar Peninsula lie an hour to the south. Northwest is the beautiful hill country, and to the northeast there are piney woods and lakes to fulfill all recreational needs.

Facilities

The University's M. D. Anderson Library boasts more than 1.4 million volumes, supplemented by professional libraries in art, architecture, law, music, optometry, and pharmacy. The libraries add more than 50,000 volumes and microtexts to their collections annually and subscribe to more than 14,000 periodicals. The business collection holds 85,250 bound volumes, 600 periodicals, and 11 CD-ROMs and offers access to DIALOG, Legislate, ASI Inform, and other business on-line services.

Technology Environment

With access to more than 175 computers within the business school, the College offers M.B.A. students computing resources that rank among the finest anywhere. Internet on-line services are available at no charge. As businesses begin to apply the technology base of the information superhighway, M.B.A. graduates from UH will be prepared.

Placement

The Office of Career Planning and Placement offers career counseling, placement, and job search opportunities. Recruiters are on campus between September and May. Nearly 200 employers from around the country recruited M.B.A. students during the past academic year. More than 85 percent of graduating M.B.A. students were employed within three months of graduation.

Admission

Admission to the College is highly competitive. The admission process involves a comprehensive review of past academic accomplishments, GMAT scores, career goals, and work experience. International applicants whose native language is not English must submit official TOEFL scores with their M.B.A. application.

Finances

Full-time tuition and fees per semester for spring and fall average $1020 for Texas residents and $2400 for nonresidents. In addition, the College offers a variety of scholarships and fellowships, including funds specifically for study abroad. Payment plans and financial aid are available.

International Students

The International Student Services Office works with new students on enrollment, legal status of immigration documents, and orientation. Students who are not U.S. citizens, are nonnative speakers of English, and have a nonimmigrant visa (F-1 or J-1) are classified as international students.

Application Facts and Dates

A résumé or statement of career goals, application, two official transcripts, official GMAT scores, and a nonrefundable application fee are required. Deadlines are May 1 for the fall semester and October 1 for spring.

For more information, students should contact:

Office of Student Services
College of Business Administration
University of Houston
Houston, Texas 77204-6282
Telephone: 713-743-4900

The University of Houston is an Equal Opportunity/Affirmative Action Institution. Minorities, women, veterans, and persons with disabilities are encouraged to apply.

The University of Illinois at Chicago

College of Business Administration

Chicago, Illinois

UIC: A DYNAMIC LEARNING ENVIRONMENT

Synergy is the force that propels the University of Illinois at Chicago (UIC) M.B.A. program. The curriculum and learning environment have been carefully crafted to build upon the expertise of our faculty members and the experience of our students, utilizing the dynamic Chicago community as a learning laboratory. Whether it is in the interdisciplinary projects set at area corporations, in formal presentations or informal discussions with CEOs, in career planning, in meetings of faculty instructional teams, or in get-acquainted conversations among incoming students, the connection between academic study of business disciplines and business operations and decision making is clear.

The integration of functional knowledge; the incorporation of international opportunities to complement business study; the explicit recognition of firms of various sizes; the drive to know, to do, to learn, and to experience; and the desire to be one's best by bringing out the best in one's team—these are the characteristics of the UIC M.B.A. program. This is an environment in which you help to shape the focus of synergy that in turn will propel your career. We welcome your interest.

—Shari Holmer Lewis, Dean

Programs and Curricular Focus

UIC offers both a full-time program and an evening (part-time) program. The full-time program emphasizes the integration of business knowledge needed to meet the challenges presented by the variety of business settings—domestic and international, large, small, and medium-sized enterprises. The development of this knowledge is facilitated by the design of the program, which is divided into four components: the managerial core, first-year options, advanced course work, and the professional topics sequence.

The managerial core consists of three eight-week modules, each based on an integrating theme and taught by an interdisciplinary faculty team. These themes are the business environment and the goal of the firm, business operation, and competition and strategy. The intensive core sequence utilizes 5-member study teams whose composition mirrors the diversity of the student body and that complete all group assignments and presentations.

First-year options concern the last eight weeks of the first year, when students may choose to study abroad at a partner institution, complete an approved thesis project in conjunction with an international internship, or complete an on-campus program of topical electives.

The third component of the program, advanced course work, is designed for the elective nature of the second year; this allows students to devise a tailored set of courses incorporating both formal areas of concentration and individualized study plans as appropriate.

The professional topics sequence (PTS) is a series of workshops, seminars, and lectures that focuses on areas of skill acquisition and managerial practice. PTS runs concurrently with course work throughout all four semesters of the program. The development of team skills is supplemented by PTS sessions on group dynamics, critical thinking, and presentation skills, many of which are facilitated by professional business consultants. A highlight of the PTS is the Business Game, a simulation that helps students integrate business knowledge and refine critical-thinking skills.

UIC's evening M.B.A. program is intended primarily for students who plan to continue full-time employment while earning their degree. Semester courses meet one night per week; summer courses meet two nights per week. The program may be completed in just under three years, but most students take between three and four years to finish. Evening program course work is divided between two components: the managerial core and advanced study courses. The managerial core is composed of nine independent courses that cover essential knowledge in the business disciplines. Students also complete five advanced study courses that enable them to broaden their managerial scope or to add more depth to knowledge of a previously chosen field.

Areas of advanced study for both the full-time and evening programs include accounting, economics, entrepreneurship, finance, health administration, health information management, human resources, international business, management information systems, marketing, operations management, pharmacy administration, business statistics, and strategic management.

Joint-degree programs are offered with accounting, economics, nursing, and public health.

Students and the M.B.A. Experience

Diversity is a hallmark of M.B.A. student life at UIC. The student body is drawn from a variety of backgrounds in terms of previous academic background, professional experience, and geographic origin. Current students come from throughout the United States and over twenty countries. Over 80 percent of full-time students have previous full-time work experience, and 13 percent are members of historically underrepresented populations.

Special Features

International study is available to students with appropriate backgrounds during the spring of the first year and during the second year of study. Overseas study sites include business schools in England, France, and Austria. A summer program in France, offered in conjunction with the Normandy Business School, is also open to all M.B.A. students. In addition to study, the UIC M.B.A. program has offered international internships for over ten years.

The Faculty

The graduate business faculty is a leader in academic productivity and research. Almost all faculty members have Ph.D.

degrees from leading institutions such as Northwestern University, Harvard University, the University of Chicago, and the University of Pennsylvania.

The Business School Network

Through the professional topics sequence, students in the full-time program are able to interact with many corporate executives during the course of the year. These executives range from recent graduates providing insights on current career and employment issues to senior corporate executives. Recent speakers have included the CEOs of TWA and Apple Computer. The UIC College of Business Administration also recently inaugurated an international executive-in-residence program.

The College and Environs

The University of Illinois at Chicago, founded in 1947, has grown into one of the top seventy research institutions in the United States. UIC is one of two constituent campuses of the University of Illinois system and enrolls approximately 26,000 students. The campus is located adjacent to the Loop, Chicago's commercial and social hub. Cultural, recreational, and professional sports facilities are all just minutes from campus. With these resources at the University's doorstep, students enjoy exceptional opportunities to experience the energy of the city's neighborhoods and a range of cultural, intellectual, and recreational activities that few other cities can match.

Facilities

The UIC Library system comprises over 2.1 million books and periodicals, 18,000 current journal and serial subscriptions, and 1.5 million other items. UIC offers an extensive array of recreational and fitness facilities. A comprehensive intramural sports program offers opportunities for organized competition throughout the academic year.

Technology Environment

In addition to a computer lab with use limited to business students, UIC M.B.A. students have full access to the UIC Computer Center, with resources that include mainframe computers, electronic mail (with Internet access), and a network of microcomputer labs on campus; these labs operate both Macintosh and Windows environment personal computers. Within the campus computer system, the M.B.A. Student Association operates an electronic mail network for use by M.B.A. students.

Placement

The UIC M.B.A. program has a strong record of providing career services that assist students in pursuing managerial careers in a wide variety of settings and fields. The College of Business Administration's Corporate Internship Program has a very strong record of developing internship opportunities and maintaining strong ties with corporate employers. All campus placement services available to M.B.A. students have been consolidated into a placement office dedicated solely to the career development and employment needs of M.B.A. students. The M.B.A. placement office will assist M.B.A. students in developing career plans, exploring possible paths, and securing both full-time and internship positions. The M.B.A. program also maintains an international network of alumni who are available to serve as resources for students who wish to explore employment opportunities outside of the United States.

Admission

The UIC M.B.A. program seeks individuals with proven academic ability and strong managerial potential who work well in teams and who are comfortable working with persons from diverse backgrounds. To receive consideration, applicants must have completed an undergraduate program at an accredited U.S. institution or its equivalent in another country and must submit a completed UIC M.B.A. application for admission along with results of the Graduate Management Admissions Test (GMAT).

Finances

Tuition and fees for the full-time program for the 1995–96 academic year are estimated to be $8515 for Illinois residents and $15,115 for nonresidents. These figures include health insurance and services. Full-time students, including international students, are eligible to apply for scholarships during their first year and assistantships in their second year. A Minority Fellowship Program is also offered for qualified African-American, Hispanic, and Native American applicants. Part-time costs are based on the number of courses taken per term. For the 1995–96 academic year, tuition and fees for resident students are approximately $900 for one course per semester and $1500 for two courses per semester.

Application Facts and Dates

For full-time enrollment, the priority deadline for financial aid is February 1. The application deadline is April 1 for international applicants and May 15 for U.S. citizens and permanent residents. For part-time enrollment in the fall semester, the application deadline is July 1; for the spring semester, November 1; and for the summer term, April 1. For further information, students should contact:

The M.B.A. Program
The University of Illinois at Chicago
  (M/C 077)
815 West Van Buren Street, Suite 220
Chicago, Illinois 60607
Telephone: 312-996-4573
Fax: 312-413-0338
Internet: mba@uic.edu

University of Illinois at Urbana-Champaign

Illinois M.B.A.

Urbana, Illinois

THE ILLINOIS M.B.A.—A WORLD-CLASS EDUCATION

At the Illinois M.B.A., we recognize that a quality management education can no longer be defined simply by the traditional, prescribed set of loosely connected business courses. Therefore, in addition to the basic disciplines, we focus on creating highly integrated learning experiences that emphasize flexibility, communication, teamwork, and ethics. By providing broad theoretical foundations, extensive practical experience, specialized professional training, and a clear understanding of the global business environment, we are producing a new breed—M.B.A. graduates skilled at combining analytical and creative approaches to formulate modern business strategies. —Howard Thomas, Dean and James F. Towey Professor of Strategic Management

Programs and Curricular Focus

Fully accredited by the American Assembly of Collegiate Schools of Business, the Illinois M.B.A. is a two-year, full-time program consisting of three primary components—Business Foundations, Business Environments, and the Professional Track.

The first year of the Illinois M.B.A. is devoted to a four-module curriculum of integrated theoretical and practical Business Foundations and Business Environments courses. Faculty teams identify and coordinate topics using case studies and specific industry analyses. Students are introduced to the functional areas of business (finance, economics, marketing, organizational behavior, operations, and accounting), but the unified approach encourages students to apply concepts learned in one area to problems raised in another.

The Managing Change and Choosing Directions module allows students to choose from a set of courses that examine such issues of contemporary society as business and organizational behavior, management of diversity in the workplace, leadership styles, government regulation, environment, and international business.

Halfway through each first-year semester, a weeklong Applying Perspectives Seminar is held. During the seminar, students apply theoretical concepts to the real-world business issues of ethics, regulation, diversity, and globalization.

During the second year, students focus their attention on future career goals. The Professional Track includes specialties in accounting, marketing, finance, human resource management, operations management, management of technology, management of change, strategy, health-care management, environmental management, and food and agribusiness management. Students may design their own professional track to meet individual education objectives.

In addition, joint degree students can earn an M.B.A. along with a second graduate degree, including J.D., M.D., M.Arch. (Master of Architecture), M.C.S. (Master of Computer Science), M.Ed. (Master of Education), and M.S. in civil, electrical, general, industrial, or mechanical engineering or in journalism. Students pursuing a joint degree spend one year in the Illinois M.B.A., and the remaining M.B.A. units are incorporated within their major area of study.

Students and the M.B.A. Experience

The Illinois M.B.A. class of 1996 is 61 percent U.S. citizens and 39 percent international students; 28 percent are women and 72 percent are men. Thirteen percent of the class are members of racial or ethnic minorities. The average student is 26 years old and brings 2½ years of work experience to the program. Of the 550 students in the M.B.A. programs 100 students are pursuing joint degrees.

❖ Global Focus

The Illinois M.B.A.—represented by students from 45 countries, 29 states, and 155 undergraduate institutions—is committed to cultural diversity within the program, and study groups are an integral part of this philosophy. Each student is assigned to an academically and culturally diverse group that works together on projects in all the core courses. Semester exchange programs with prestigious business schools worldwide facilitate overseas study for students desiring an international educational experience.

Special Features

During an intensive weeklong orientation prior to the first semester, students are introduced to the campus and given an opportunity to meet their classmates and faculty members. Students also develop a personal learning plan based on substantial self-assessment. This personal plan allows each student to define a unique and individual set of developmental needs and expectations.

The Faculty

The Illinois M.B.A. is privileged to have an outstanding faculty committed to "faculty-team ownership" of the core curriculum. In order to present a coherent set of topics realistically woven together to portray the complexity of managerial decisions, three of the four first-year modules are team-taught by faculty members. To achieve a high level of curriculum integration, faculty members are of necessity intimately familiar with the structure and content of the entire M.B.A. curriculum.

The Business School Network

One or more of the elective units during the second year of study can be satisfied by a study-research project completed under faculty direction and linked, through the Office for the Study of Business Issues, to a community business sponsor. The Office for the Study of Business Issues also facilitates student internships in corporate settings—internships may be held between the first and second years of study. The office also coordinates faculty-supervised consulting and applied management experiences for teams of M.B.A. students. An Executive-in-Residence program, plant visits, and other outreach activities with the business community are included in the program.

The College and Environs

Located within a 3-hour drive of Chicago, St. Louis, and Indianapolis, the University of Illinois and the twin cities of Urbana and Champaign form a thriving community rich in social, cultural, and recreational opportunities. Each year, the University's nationally renowned Krannert Center for the Performing Arts presents over 350 plays, concerts, ballets, and operas. The University's Krannert Art Museum is second only to Chicago's Art Institute among Illinois public museums. The Division of Campus Recreation administers one of the most comprehensive recreational programs in the world. In addition to an array of intramural athletics, the division operates facilities for year-round basketball, tennis, squash, racquetball, and swimming. As a leader in the Big Ten Athletic Conference, the University of Illinois sponsors men's and women's varsity sports, including football, basketball, and volleyball.

Facilities

Long heralded for its accomplishments in graduate education and research, the University of Illinois is home to national research centers for many disciplines, including supercomputing, engineering, education, and genetics. The Beckman Institute's research brings together the biological and physical sciences to develop a better understanding of human and artificial intelligence. The National Center for Supercomputing Applications established the University of Illinois as a world leader in supercomputer architecture, design, and applications.

Housing more than 15 million items in its collection, the University's library is the nation's third largest among academic libraries. Of particular interest to M.B.A. students is the Commerce Library, which maintains a working collection of 66,000 volumes, 1,600 periodical and serial titles, and an extensive collection of corporate annual reports.

Technology Environment

The University's technology-rich environment provides students throughout the University with over 8,000 computer workstations. Within the Illinois M.B.A., the Office for Information Management offers students a state-of-the-art computer laboratory designed to emulate the technological environment students will encounter after graduation. Students learn popular business software and use computer simulations to develop business strategies and tactics.

Placement

By combining an up-to-date job listing service with an aggressive program of on-campus interviews, Career Services helps M.B.A. students compete for jobs in both the national and international arenas. Career Services works directly with M.B.A. students as they develop career plans, search for internships, and conduct job searches. Throughout the two-year program, students benefit from résumé books sent to corporations, individual consultations, on-line self-assessment testing, and mock interviews. The annual Career Focus Conference provides one of many opportunities for students to network with corporate representatives.

Admission

Admission to the Illinois M.B.A. is based on undergraduate grade point average over the last 60 credit hours, GMAT results, verbal and written communication skills demonstrated in essays and interviews, TOEFL and TSE scores for nonnative speakers of English, demonstrated leadership qualities, professional work experience, analytical ability, and letters of recommendation. The average GMAT score for the class of 1996 was 618, and the average grade point average was 4.3 on a 5.0 scale.

Applicants for admission should hold a bachelor's degree from an accredited U.S. college or university or the equivalent from another country. Prior academic experience in business is not required. Students should have a minimum grade of B in at least one semester of calculus.

Finances

Tuition and fees for Illinois residents enrolling in the fall of 1995 are $8400 for the academic year. Nonresident tuition and fees are $15,000. Students can expect to spend about $1000 for books, $6000 for room and board, and $2000 for personal expenses.

Approximately 200 M.B.A. Student Management Leadership Grants are available to each class of 300 students. Grants are awarded to both domestic and international students on the basis of merit and range from $3000 to $10,000 per year. Each grant recipient will hold an assignment requiring 10 hours of work per week. Decisions on the leadership grants are made by April. The application for admittance to the Illinois M.B.A. is used in choosing recipients.

Application Facts and Dates

The application deadline is April 1, but early application is encouraged because most grants are awarded before that date. Students interested in an application or additional information should contact:

Illinois M.B.A. Admissions
410 David Kinley Hall
University of Illinois at Urbana-
Champaign
1407 West Gregory Drive
Urbana, Illinois 61801
Telephone: 217-244-7602
800-MBA-UIUC (toll-free
in the U.S. only)
Fax: 217-333-1156
E-mail: marketing@commerce.cba.
uiuc.edu

The University of Iowa

Iowa City, Iowa

> *The Iowa M.B.A. program is small enough to encourage a spirit of camaraderie and cooperation among its students, faculty, and staff and small enough so that no student gets lost in the academic shuffle.*
>
> *The home of the Iowa M.B.A. program, the John Pappajohn Business Administration Building, was designed with students in mind. A convenient restaurant (Pat's Diner), a spacious patio overlooking a quiet courtyard where people can eat or study outside during good weather, an ATM machine, small-group study rooms, comfortable seating throughout the building, and individual lockers for M.B.A. students are just a few of the amenities in the Pappajohn Building. But these comfortable and convenient surroundings only complement the excellent learning facilities and technological capabilities that are the building's main focus. The Iowa School of Management has it all.*
>
> *If a student wants to be more than just a number, to study in an environment that provides comfort and an excellent learning environment, and to participate in an M.B.A. program that is first-rate, Iowa is an excellent choice.*
>
> *—Gary Fethke, Dean*

Programs and Curricular Focus

The University of Iowa M.B.A. program provides students with a solid foundation for future growth and flexibility in business management. The curriculum is rigorous, but learning takes place in a collaborative environment that builds teamwork while encouraging independent problem solving.

Students tailor individual course portfolios to combine analytical skills, broad-based knowledge, and professional experiences into a package that will advance their personal career goals.

Concentrations are available in accounting, finance, management and organizations, human resource management, production and operations, management information systems, and marketing. Students may also create their own concentration, incorporating courses from the University's other colleges, or pursue a dual-degree program in hospital and health administration, nursing, law, or library and information science.

Students and the M.B.A. Experience

IMPACT, the first-week orientation program for entering M.B.A. students, links students with one another and with faculty even before course work begins. This collaborative atmosphere is sustained throughout the program through team projects, student organization activities, alumni functions, corporate visits, and daily communication. Dedicated and diverse, Iowa M.B.A. students come from top undergraduate institutions worldwide and hold degrees and honors in disciplines ranging from English to engineering.

The average student is 26 years old and has three years of professional experience. Women comprise one third of the student population, and minority students make up 5 percent.

Fifty-eight percent of students come from the Midwest. Of the remaining 42 percent, half are international students. Currently, the M.B.A. program has representatives from every continent.

❖ Global Focus

The University of Iowa M.B.A. program offers many opportunities for developing a global business perspective. Corporate partners include Fortune 100 companies with multinational operations and middle-market businesses with extensive import/export activities. These companies provide internship and consulting opportunities and willingly share their vast knowledge of global markets and emerging economies.

Iowa M.B.A. students gain international experience in other ways as well. For the past several years, student-faculty consulting groups have traveled to the Czech and Slovak republics and to Russia to work with local business executives.

Special Features

Information technology is dramatically altering the way most business is conducted these days. Managers now have nearly instantaneous access to information about changing financial markets, customer demand, and competitive conditions in international and domestic markets. In addition to a state-of-the-art computer lab, Iowa M.B.A. students and faculty benefit from the program's substantial investment in information technology: real-time electronic links to more than thirty financial markets worldwide; on-line access to major business periodicals, investment analysts' research reports, and consumer demographics databases; and videoconferencing facilities that enable communication with business leaders throughout the world.

The Faculty

Iowa M.B.A. faculty members are accomplished, dynamic, and dedicated to providing a comprehensive business education to students. Holding Ph.D.'s from some of the world's top educational institutions, all can apply practical experiences gained in such places as Tenneco, Inc.; Andersen Consulting; Citicorp; General Motors; and the Commodity Futures Trading Commission to the M.B.A. classroom.

Beyond their impressive credentials, Iowa M.B.A. faculty members are dedicated professionals who share a passion for teaching. They are enthusiastic about challenging students to excel, and they interact with students both inside and outside the classroom. This personal approach to management education is not often available to students in larger M.B.A. programs.

The Business School Network

Corporate Partnerships

The University of Iowa School of Management is fortunate to have excellent ties to and communication with the business community—regionally,

The Pappajohn Building is designed to provide a conducive learning environment.

nationally, and globally. Prominent business leaders often visit campus to talk about issues facing their industries. Internship opportunities are plentiful, and many classes routinely involve students on consulting projects with the University's corporate partners, who span the globe and include companies representing every economic sector.

The College and Environs

Iowa City is a uniquely wonderful community. Here, students, faculty, and townspeople work and play together harmoniously.

The University of Iowa is the very heart of Iowa City, both in fact and spirit. The oldest of Iowa's three state universities, it includes, in addition to the College of Business Administration, the Colleges of Dentistry, Education, Engineering, Law, Liberal Arts, Medicine, Nursing, and Pharmacy. There are approximately 27,000 students, of whom 6,500 are pursuing graduate study.

Chicago, Minneapolis, St. Louis, and Kansas City are almost equidistant from the Iowa campus, providing urban advantages when desired. The Iowa City community itself offers an impressive array of cultural and recreational diversions.

Facilities

The M.B.A. program is housed in the John Pappajohn Business Administration Building, a beautiful, functional, and up-to-date setting that fosters interpersonal and technological interactions. The facility's classrooms, restaurant, and informal spaces encourage one-on-one communication, group discussion, and the impromptu exchange of ideas between

students and faculty. Completed in 1994, the John Pappajohn Building provides an ideal learning environment for M.B.A. study.

Technology Environment

In addition to the global information and videoconferencing capabilities of the Pappajohn Building, the facility houses the largest student computing facility on the University of Iowa campus. Three computing classrooms, available for M.B.A. student use, complement a laboratory of nearly 100 workstations. Technology in the computer laboratory, library, and classrooms provides direct links to the global community, ranging from real-time national and international stock market feeds and information databases to a full spectrum of electronic resources.

Placement

The M.B.A. placement staff provides everything from resources to referrals. Beginning early in a student's program, staff members help develop a résumé, research companies, and explore career options. Utilizing a far-reaching alumni network, brokering services, and videoconferencing capabilities, Iowa M.B.A. placement personnel work with students to find internships and employment opportunities in the students' chosen fields and geographic locations. Interviews are arranged at on-campus locations, employer offices, and national job fairs. Placement staff members also conduct career development workshops that enable Iowa M.B.A. students to sharpen those personal skills so necessary to succeed in the business world.

Admission

Each applicant's entire portfolio is considered. The admissions committee reviews each file individually and in full, looking for candidates who are a good match with the Iowa program. Students are asked to submit a completed application form, transcripts of all undergraduate and graduate work, a résumé, responses to essay questions, GMAT scores, three references, and an application fee. Admission is only available for the fall term (late August), and preference is given to international applications completed by April 15. Application reviews begin in January.

A minimum score of 600 on the TOEFL is required for all students for whom English is not the native language. International students must present proof of adequate funds to cover the full two years of study. All students must have health insurance.

Finances

Estimated tuition and fees for 1995–96 are $3713 for Iowa residents and $9922 for nonresidents. Books and supplies cost approximately $938 per year. Estimates provided by the Office of Student Financial Aid suggest that M.B.A. students budget approximately $470 per month for room and board.

Merit-based scholarships and fellowships are available to M.B.A. students. All applicants are considered for these competitive awards. Awards are based on information found within the application portfolio (including GMAT scores, GPA, and work experience). Students are also encouraged to apply for need-based financial assistance through the University Office of Student Financial Aid. Second-year students are eligible for assistantships in the School of Management.

International Students

International students and issues are integrated into the Iowa M.B.A. program as critical elements of the learning process. Built-in global connections occur within the classroom when discussion takes place between international and domestic students under the direction of knowledgeable faculty members who weave global issues into the fabric of their courses.

Application Facts and Dates

Admission preference for the full-time program (fall entrance) will be given to those applications completed by April 15.

School of Management
The University of Iowa
Iowa City, Iowa 52242
Telephone: 319-335-1039
        800-622-4692 (toll-free)

UofL The University of Louisville

Louisville, Kentucky

THE M.B.A.: FUTURE TRENDS AND DIRECTIONS

Managers and leaders face unprecedented challenges in our rapidly changing world. The global marketplace is creating new structures and processes for business and government. To be competitive, the required skills and attitudes are innovation in solving complex problems, self-knowledge and confidence in making a difference, and a comprehensive understanding of theory and practice.

The University of Louisville M.B.A. program is designed to meet these challenges and your needs. Our faculty have current business experience, state-of-the-art research, and a sincere commitment to teaching excellence. They will help you discover your potential.

We believe that U of L offers you one of the best opportunities to study, learn, and experience the world of organizations—whether they be large industrial firms, small entrepreneurial businesses, or government and not-for-profit agencies. Our goal is to help you succeed.

—Robert L. Taylor, Dean

Programs and Curricular Focus

The mission of the University of Louisville College of Business and Public Administration is to provide high-quality education and professional development in business, public administration, and urban policy that meets the special needs of an urban constituency. Teaching, research, and service reflect innovation and responsiveness to a rapidly changing global environment. Undergraduate and graduate education are complemented with continuing education and training programs, scholarly activity, student involvement, and community outreach. Faculty and staff are committed to programs that reflect continuing intellectual growth, pragmatism, and the importance of human values.

A student's degree program will be 36 semester credit hours, possibly more, depending upon undergraduate preparation and placement test results. The M.B.A. program's 36-hour core curriculum consists of nine requisite 600-level courses and three approved electives. Serving as the academic common body of knowledge for the M.B.A. core requirements, the foundation core of 500-level courses provides those students with less extensive undergraduate business curricula a means toward preparing for the M.B.A. core courses.

All required 600-level courses are offered in the fall and spring semesters, along with a variety of elective courses.

A smaller selection of 600-level courses is offered during the two summer sessions. The foundation core's 500-level course offerings are split between the fall and spring semesters and normally are not part of the summer course schedule. Two-year advanced course schedule planners are available to assist students in planning their curriculum and avoiding unforeseen delays in degree completion.

In order to foster international expertise, the College of Business and Public Administration provides frequent opportunities for M.B.A. students to learn the international aspects of business administration, including cross-cultural perspectives. Such opportunities consist of courses, seminars, exchange programs, and independent study. M.B.A. students are strongly encouraged to take advantage of these opportunities.

Students and the M.B.A. Experience

The M.B.A. students at U of L bring a wide variety of work experiences and academic diversity to the program. With approximately two thirds of the students pursuing their graduate degrees on a part-time basis, classes benefit from a wealth of current and diverse real-world business experiences. In addition, the program is proud of its progress in attracting women and students of diverse ethnic and cultural backgrounds.

The M.B.A. program is primarily an evening program in which an individual can enroll as either a part-time or full-time student. During the fall and spring semesters, courses typically are offered Monday through Thursday, one evening per week, from 5:30 to 8:15 p.m. During the summer session, there are two successive six-week sessions in which classes meet three evenings per week: Monday, Tuesday, and Thursday. Although the majority of the program's student population enrolls on a part-time basis, courses are scheduled so that a student may pursue the program on a full-time basis of 9 hours per semester.

The M.B.A./J.D. program is offered jointly by the College of Business and Public Administration and the School of Law. The program combines the two-year M.B.A. program and the three-year Juris Doctor (J.D.) program into one four-year, full-time program. Upon successful completion of the program, the student is awarded both the M.B.A. and J.D. degrees. Requests for further information regarding this program should be directed to the M.B.A. coordinator.

The Faculty

The College's faculty members offer exceptional teaching ability, applied business research, and individualized, high-quality interactions with students. Diversity, commitment, and professionalism characterize the faculty. Like the curriculum itself, the more than 75 faculty members reflect the changing nature of the workforce.

Ninety-five percent of the M.B.A. course work is taught by doctorally qualified faculty members who enrich the learning experience by providing a balance of theory and application. Faculty members enlist a wide variety of classroom approaches, including lectures, case studies, computer simulation, group projects, and discussions. In addition, the development and demonstration of appropriate oral and written communication skills are integrated throughout M.B.A. course objectives.

The Business School Network

Corporate Partnerships

While preparing individuals to add value to the community, the College of Business and Public Administration recognizes its role as an active partner in the development and growth of organizations in the region. The M.B.A. program is committed to working with the regional business community through applied research, consulting, and training. On a continual basis, M.B.A. students are offered special opportunities to meet and learn from some of the region's most dynamic, successful business leaders.

Prominent Alumni

The College notes among its alumni a number of the region's most distinguished business leaders, including Malcolm Chancey Jr., Chairman, Banc One Kentucky Corporation, Louisville; Dan Ulmer, former chairman of Citizen's Fidelity Bank (now PNC Bank), Louisville; David Jones, Chairman of the Board, Humana, Inc.; Gene Gardner, retired president of a major Louisville company and co-owner of the Louisville Redbirds AAA baseball organization; Charles McCarty, retired president, BATUS Industries; and James Patterson, fast-food executive, Long John Silver's, Chi Chi's, Wendy's, and Rally's.

The College and Environs

The University of Louisville is an urban educational institution that will celebrate its bicentennial in 1998. Consisting of thirteen academic units and spanning three campuses, the University became part of the Kentucky state system of higher education in 1970.

The College of Business and Public Administration is located on the 140-acre Belknap campus in the historic Old Louisville section of the city. Kentucky's largest urban center, Louisville offers some of the region's most diverse, enjoyable cultural surroundings and events. From the Kentucky Derby and its weeklong festival to the Kentucky Center for the Arts, "the river city" offers enough variety in cultural, recreational, and sports opportunities to rival cities three times its size.

Technology Environment

The College of Business and Public Administration provides an outstanding computer and technology environment. A computer classroom and lab, with over fifty networked workstations dedicated for use by business faculty and students, supports the latest software applications. In addition, the building houses the University's North Computing Center, containing seventy additional workstations. Multimedia applications, electronic mail, interactive television, and LANs comprise an integral part of the M.B.A. curriculum.

Placement

The College works aggressively to build strong ties with regional organizations and on-campus recruiters in order to help students construct a network of professional contacts. Regional, national, and international companies visit regularly to recruit for full-time and internship positions.

Admission

Admission into the M.B.A. program is competitive. Entering M.B.A. candidates at the University of Louisville are in the top third of all entering M.B.A. candidates nationwide.

Applicants must submit a completed graduate application, along with a nonrefundable $25 application fee. In addition, applicants must have sent to the University Admissions Office official transcripts, GMAT results, and two letters of recommendation from individuals familiar with the applicant's academic performance.

International applicants are required to take the TOEFL if English is not their native language. Though optional, a written personal statement is highly recommended for applicants with marginal GMAT scores, undergraduate grade point averages, or both.

Finances

Estimated tuition and fees for full-time students in 1994–95 were $1305 for Kentucky residents and $3705 for nonresidents. For part-time residents, courses cost approximately $144 per semester hour, while nonresidents paid $410 per hour. University fees are subject to approval of the Board of Trustees and may be changed without prior notice.

Although many graduate students live off campus, the University provides some graduate dormitory rooms and apartments. The Housing/Resident Administration maintains a referral file of off-campus rooms and apartments. Housing costs in Louisville are lower than in most other metropolitan areas.

A limited number of graduate research assistantships are available to full-time students. These grants require students to work up to 20 hours per week as research aides to departmental faculty members and provide living stipends plus tuition. The University's Financial Aid Office and Student Employment Office also provide four types of assistance: scholarships, grants, educational loans, and part-time employment.

Application Facts and Dates

The College employs a rolling application deadline. For students wishing to begin course work in either the fall or spring semester, all application materials must be received at least 120 days prior to the semester's start. Those students planning to begin in the summer term must have all materials submitted at least eighty days before the start of course work in mid-May. For more information, applicants should address inquiries to:

M.B.A. Coordinator
Advising Center
College of Business and Public
   Administration
University of Louisville
Louisville, Kentucky 40292
Telephone: 502-852-7439

University of Maine

Orono, Maine

LEADERSHIP IN THE GLOBAL ECONOMY

Maine's M.B.A. program specifically meets the needs of graduate students who desire the benefits of small classes and close interaction with the faculty and staff.

Diversity in the student body provides an excellent opportunity for an optimal learning environment. The residential experience on the University campus fosters dialogue with students from a wide range of backgrounds and cultures.

The combination of a committed teaching faculty and high-quality students has resulted in an outstanding M.B.A. program that prepares students for leadership positions in the global economy.

—W. Stanley Devino, Dean

Programs and Curricular Focus

The University of Maine M.B.A. program is designed to equip candidates with the concepts, analytical tools, and executive skills required for competent and responsible management. Built-in course and program flexibility enables the College to meet the needs of the individual student. Students have the opportunity to take up to 40 percent of their graduate course work in a specific business field (finance, management, or marketing) in order to meet their own career goals. Full-time students with an undergraduate degree in business administration can usually complete the 30-hour graduate program in one calendar year. Required core courses include behavioral analysis for administrative decisions, quantitative methods for business decisions, managerial accounting, financial management, marketing management, production management, and management policy. Students with no business course work can complete requirements in two years of full-time study. Prerequisite courses (the equivalent of 30 semester hours) taken during the first year include introduction to accounting, computer-based information systems, quantitative methods (matrices, linear programming, probability, systems of equations and inequalities, analytical geometry, and basic statistics), legal environment of business, principles of management and organization, business finance, marketing, and economics.

Both the undergraduate and graduate programs in business administration are accredited by the American Assembly of Collegiate Schools of Business.

Students and the M.B.A. Experience

The current M.B.A. class comprises a significant heterogeneous group, with representatives from more than fifty undergraduate colleges and universities and more than thirty-five different undergraduate majors. In 1994, fourteen countries were represented. More than 50 percent of the class have undergraduate preparation in fields other than business administration. The average age of entering students is 28. Women comprise 30 percent of the enrollment. Of the 11,000 University students, more than 2,000 are graduate students. Academic rigor, emphasis on teamwork, and esprit de corps among students and faculty are noted by many alumni as key components of their experience at UM.

The Faculty

Faculty are actively engaged in scholarly work and public service activities, offering seminars and workshops for business practitioners and providing consulting services both nationally and internationally, greatly enriching the classroom experience.

The Business School Network

Since 1965, more than 800 M.B.A. alumni have achieved positions of significant authority and responsibility in many organizations locally, nationally, and internationally. Many serve as mentors through the Maine Mentor Program.

The College and Environs

Students at the University of Maine benefit from the advantages of both rural and urban environments. Located just a 1- to 2-hours' drive from Mount Katahdin, state parks, ski slopes, and the Maine coast, the University is a 4-hour drive on Interstate 95 from Boston. Bangor International Airport, located 8 miles from campus, provides service to many major U.S. and international cities. The 1,200-acre campus is the site of a dynamic modern university, encompassing eight colleges, various schools and academic programs, and a graduate school. The College has offered the M.B.A. degree since 1965. In 1993, a $7-million College of Business Administration facility, the Donald P. Corbett Business Building, opened with several high-technology, seminar, and core classrooms. The Maine Center for the Arts provides cultural focus for the University campus, the communities of the region, and all Maine citizens. Musical, dance, and theatrical performances and lectures by distinguished speakers are presented in the 1,628-seat Hutchins Concert Hall. The center also includes the Hudson Museum and Palmer Gallery.

Facilities

The UM M.B.A. program exposes students to state-of-the-art systems for management decision support. Both mainframe and microcomputer facilities on the Orono campus are excellent. The central computing facility for the entire University of Maine System, an IBM 3090, is located on the Orono campus. SAS, SPSSX, and IFPS are supported. The complete SAS library is available using SAS/OR, SAS/Graph, and a wide variety of technical enhancements. Public access microcomputer clusters are available in Fogler Library, the Computing Center, and the Student Union. The Fogler Library houses more than 807,000 volumes, subscribes to more than 5,600 journals, and is a regional depository for publications of the U.S. government and a selective depository for Canadian government documents.

Technology Environment

The College of Business Administration supports sixty networked 386 and 486 microcomputers. The lab provides access to an extensive DOS/Windows software library as well as access to Internet, the library, and the mainframe. Satellite access to Chicago and New York boards of trade is also available.

Placement

The University's Career Center provides a variety of services to assist students in obtaining positions following graduation. Services include individual career counseling, career information for exploring options, the mentor program, résumé/vita critiques, job search workshops, mock interviews, job listings, employer information, and assistance in identifying potential employers.

Admission

All applicants must hold a four-year baccalaureate degree from a regionally accredited college or university. Consideration is given to an applicant's official transcript(s), GMAT scores, three letters of recommendation on forms provided in the application material, and potential for leadership in business. The mean GMAT score of entering students is 529. All applicants whose native language is not English must submit official TOEFL scores. The minimum score required is 550. Although work experience is not required, the majority of students have three or more years of work experience. Students can apply for fall, spring, or summer admission.

Finances

In 1994–95, tuition charges for one semester were $3861 per 9 credit hours for nonresidents or $1368 per 9 credit hours for residents. Part-time resident students paid $152 per credit hour; part-time nonresidents paid $429 per credit hour. Room and board (full meal plan included) cost $2350. A comprehensive fee for 12 credit hours or more was $167.50; for 7–11 credit hours, $83.75; and for 1–6 credit hours, no charge. Other fees included a student activity fee of $17.50, a communications fee of $8, a recreation fee of $10, and a technology fee of $3 per credit hour. In addition, all international students and their dependents must purchase health insurance through the University unless they are sponsored by agencies providing comparable insurance coverage. Financial aid is extremely limited and highly competitive when available.

International Students

International students currently in the M.B.A. program represent thirteen countries; campuswide, sixty-nine countries are represented. More than 75 international students have graduated with an M.B.A. degree since 1980. The relatively small size of graduate classes permits students a one-on-one working relationship with faculty members. The International Programs Office assists with immigration matters and offers intercultural opportunities. The friendliness of fellow students makes the learning experience at UM positive. Classes with both full-time and part-time students add to the international student experience. Classmates are academic resources and constitute a network of professional contacts and allies for the future. For students who have met the prerequisites, the program can be completed within one year.

Application Facts and Dates

For program information, students should call 207-581-1973. It is recommended that all application material be received by December 15 for fall admission. Applications must be submitted no later than six weeks prior to the beginning of the semester. All official transcripts, test scores, letters of recommendation, and the $35 application fee must be on file prior to a review being made. Application fees cannot be waived. Application material should be sent directly to:

Graduate School
5782 Winslow Hall
University of Maine
Orono, Maine 04469-5782
Telephone: 207-581-3218
Fax: 207-581-3232

The University of Manitoba

Winnipeg, Manitoba, Canada

M.B.A. MANITOBA—A FULLY INTEGRATED ONE-YEAR M.B.A. PROGRAM

M.B.A. Manitoba is a newly designed program targeted for individuals with a minimum of three years' full-time managerial experience. In addition to a curriculum designed for today's and tomorrow's managers operating in a global, competitive economy, M.B.A. Manitoba offers a fully complete M.B.A. degree in eleven months of full-time, concentrated study. The new curriculum is the product of in-depth research with alumni and businesspeople to identify the skills and knowledge that are desired in M.B.A. graduates.

M.B.A. Manitoba is an integrated program rather than a collection of courses. This means that the participants experience a managed curriculum with each part complementing the other parts. Courses are offered in a modular format, which gives increased flexibility in the design of course topics.

We believe this new curriculum and format will set the standard for all M.B.A. programs in the future. In today's competitive job market, traditional two-year programs often present insurmountable opportunity costs in lost income and foregone career progression. A complete, fully qualified M.B.A. curriculum offered on an eleven-month basis presents a unique educational opportunity for midcareer individuals.

—William Mackness, Dean

Programs and Curricular Focus

M.B.A. Manitoba is a 66-credit-hour program offered in an eleven-month format. The program has a general management focus, and its purpose is to train leaders for the Canadian economy. The program design consists of three major phases: Foundations, Functions, and Implementation and Strategy. Each phase is divided into three modules of four weeks in duration, and each module develops an integrative theme. Emphasis is also placed on the "soft skills," such as teamwork, communication, leadership, and interpersonal skills. Other program design elements include international study trips, a public service component, professional seminars, and a consulting skills component. The curriculum is managed by a Program Director and a Core Teaching Team. The M.B.A. Manitoba faculty is supplemented by guest faculty members from other universities and from the private sector through videoconferencing technology.

Students and the M.B.A. Experience

Students enter the program with a minimum of three years of full-time managerial experience. Most do not have a previous degree in business or management. The average age of students is 29, with approximately 40 percent women. Students come from most Canadian provinces, and international students typically constitute 10–15 percent of the class. M.B.A. Manitoba students work as a cohesive unit since all students proceed through the program as a cohort. M.B.A. facilities within the Drake Management Centre are designed specifically for M.B.A. students and encourage interaction and group work.

Special Features

M.B.A. Manitoba offers a series of one-week preparatory sessions for individuals needing upgrading in economics, statistics, and quantitative methods. These sessions are offered immediately preceding the start of the program. There is also a one-week orientation program prior to the start of regular classes. The curriculum includes twenty days of professional seminars designed to develop professional skills not normally taught in academic programs. Seminars vary from year to year but usually include topics such as negotiating skills, career management, interviewing skills, and working with the

media. The required public service component is designed to broaden the experiences of students. A course in sustainable development is also offered to integrate the goals of management with those of the environment.

The Faculty

The Faculty of Management consists of 60 full-time faculty members, supplemented by adjunct professors who are brought in for specialized expertise. Ninety percent of the faculty members have Ph.D.'s. The M.B.A. Manitoba teaching faculty members are selected specifically for their experience and skill in developing a learning environment for M.B.A. students. Previous business experience, consulting activities, and/or executive development experience are all prerequisites for teaching in the program. In addition to the regular teaching faculty, the Core Teaching Team monitors the course development and integration of course materials.

The Business School Network

The Associates Program of the Faculty of Management is Canada's largest business school support group. With over 200 members and chapters in Winnipeg, Vancouver, and Toronto, the Associates Program provides financial, administrative, and academic support to the Faculty. The Associates' membership consists of the leading businesspeople across Canada, many of whom are graduates of the Faculty of Management. Interaction between the Associates and M.B.A. students occurs at numerous functions held throughout the year, as well as at the popular "M.B.A. for a Day" program in which members of the Associates Program spend a day on campus taking classes with the M.B.A. students.

In 1982 the Faculty of Management, in cooperation with the Associates Program, initiated the International Distinguished Entrepreneur Award (IDEA), which honours a businessperson who has made world-renowned contributions to the quality of business and community life. The presentation is made annually at the IDEA Dinner held in Winnipeg. Some of the recipients are

H. Ross Perot, Chairman and CEO, The Ross Perot Group; Akio Morita, Chairman and CEO, Sony Corporation; Paul Desmarais, Chairman and CEO, Power Corporation of Canada; and Roberto Goizueta, Chairman and CEO, The Coca-Cola Company.

The Faculty of Management's Executive-in-Residence Program is one of several strategies used to integrate the academic programs with the activities of the business community. The Executive-in-Residence is an individual who joins the Faculty on a full-time basis to serve as a resource to students and faculty. The present Executive-in-Residence is Mr. Kevin Kavanagh, former President and CEO of The Great-West Life Assurance Company of Canada.

The College and Environs

The University of Manitoba, established in 1877, is the oldest university in western Canada. The main campus is located on a 677-acre site in south Winnipeg. The University has over 25,000 students and offers programs in sixty-four disciplines. Over 120,000 students have graduated from the University during its 116-year history.

The Faculty of Management's origins go back to 1937 when a complete business curriculum was first established at the University of Manitoba. Since that time the Faculty has grown to offering bachelor's, master's, Ph.D., and executive programs in a variety of business disciplines.

Winnipeg, Manitoba, is the fifth-largest city in Canada, with a population of over 600,000. Located in the centre of Canada, Winnipeg is an ethnically diverse city and has a broadly diversified economy led by such major industries as aerospace, agriculture, banking, insurance, and tourism. Winnipeg sees more hours of sunshine per year than any other Canadian city and enjoys hot, dry summers and crisp, bright winters. Within an hour's drive from the city are numerous white sand beaches along one of the world's best freshwater lakes. Only 63 miles from the U.S. border, Winnipeg is easily reached by highway, rail, and major airlines. Winnipeg is a clean, safe, comfortable city and was recently named by the *Toronto Globe and Mail Report on Business* as "one of Canada's best cities for business."

Facilities

The Faculty of Management is housed in the Drake Centre for Management Education, one of the most modern business education facilities in Canada. Constructed in 1988 at a cost of $15 million, the building also houses the Centre for Entrepreneurship, the Centre for Accounting Research and Education, the Transport Institute, the Warren Centre for Actuarial Sciences, the Centre for International Business Studies, the Albert D. Cohen Library, and three separate computer facilities for students.

Placement

The Career Development and Placement Centre is a major career resource centre devoted exclusively to the use of students in the Faculty of Management. The Centre organizes visits by corporate recruiters and assists students in preparing for job interviews. Seminars on career planning, résumé writing, and interviewing skills are offered on a regular basis. The Centre annually publishes an M.B.A. résumé book that is sent to over 2,000 employers across Canada.

Admission

The factors considered in the admission decision are undergraduate grades, work and managerial experience, GMAT score, references, leadership potential, entrepreneurial potential, and career goals. A TOEFL score is required of all students for whom English is a second language. The CANTEST must be taken upon arrival at the University. GMAT scores of students typically average 575–600. Occasionally, students without undergraduate degrees are admitted if they show outstanding accomplishments and potential in other areas of qualification.

Finances

Tuition fees for the 1995–96 academic year are Can$16,000. Books, participant fees, living expenses, and the international study trips are not included in the tuition fee. Living costs for students vary with lifestyle, but Winnipeg is noted for having living costs among the lowest of the major Canadian cities. All applicants are automatically considered for financial aid. Decisions are based upon admission qualifications.

Application Facts and Dates

The application deadline for M.B.A. Manitoba is May 1, although applications will be considered after this date if space permits. Admission decisions are made once the applicant's file is complete. Application fees are Can$30 for graduates of the University of Manitoba, Can$45 for graduates of other Canadian universities, and Can$50 for applicants from outside Canada. For more information and application forms, students should contact:

Susan Eide, M.B.A. Manitoba
Faculty of Management
The University of Manitoba
Winnipeg, Manitoba R3T 5V4
Canada
Telephone: 204-474-8448
         800-MBA-6296 (toll-free)
Fax: 204-261-6084
E-mail: seide@bldgdrake.lan1.
   umanitoba.ca

University of Maryland at College Park

Maryland Business School

College Park, Maryland

▶ *The Maryland Business School has put together a unique combination of resources that will provide you with an incomparable educational value. As you learn about our program, you should glean three primary elements that allow us to provide you with a great experience: quality, reasonable cost, and location.*

Our implementation of a cutting-edge curriculum and the use of state-of-the-art information technologies is the keystone to the quality education that we provide. The Maryland Business School is about half the cost of other top thirty M.B.A. programs, and our program is in a prime location that is just 35 minutes from both Baltimore and Washington, D.C.

I urge you to visit us to learn why the Maryland M.B.A. deserves its place among the top 4 percent of all M.B.A. programs in the United States.
—William E. Mayer, Dean

Programs and Curricular Focus

The Maryland Business School has put together an exceptional combination of resources that provides students with an incomparable educational value. Some of the many strengths of the Maryland Business School are the top-quality and cutting-edge master's programs, a location that is minutes from Washington, D.C., financial aid for international students, and an M.B.A. that costs about half the amount of other top M.B.A. programs. Accredited by the American Assembly of Collegiate Schools of Business, and a full member of the Graduate Management Admission Council, the Maryland Business School is a leader in the field of graduate management education.

The Master of Business Administration (M.B.A.) program has a fully integrated experience-based curriculum designed to create the type of graduate that business has long demanded. The first half of the curriculum is spent gaining the fundamental skills and judgment necessary to succeed in a contemporary management team. Experiential Learning Modules (ELMs) and course work ensure that new skills are applied in and out of the classroom.

ELMs are intensive weeklong, experience-based courses that focus on specific topics such as interaction with the federal government in Washington, D.C., an international business simulation, total quality management, and leadership and the management of diversity. These courses provide the student with experi-

ence in areas often ignored by other American M.B.A. programs.

The second year allows the student to specialize in a particular area of business and to participate in a Group Field Project. Group Field Projects assign teams of students to work as consultants to an American company for a semester. The teams address specific concerns within a company and make recommendations regarding those concerns to the management staff of the client companies. This program is required of all second-year students.

The Master of Science (M.S.) program requires a strong quantitative background. There are several areas of concentration available: information systems, operations research, statistics, accounting information systems, logistics and transportation, finance, and human resource management. The M.S. program can be completed in two to five semesters, depending on previously completed course work.

The doctoral (Ph.D.) program is designed to develop outstanding research scholars and teachers in the management-related disciplines. Specializations include accounting, finance, human resource management and labor relations, information systems, management science and statistics, management strategy and policy, marketing, organizational behavior, and transportation and logistics.

Students and the M.B.A. Experience

The student population of the M.B.A. program in composed of about 270

full-time M.B.A. students, 20 M.S. students, and 100 Ph.D. students. Of the 1994 incoming class, 35 percent were international students and about 30 percent were women.

Special Features

The Maryland Business School maintains formal and informal exchange arrangements with graduate business programs in seven countries around the world. Students spend one semester of their second year at their exchange school.

The Faculty

There are 80 full-time faculty members assigned to M.B.A. programs, all of whom hold doctoral-level degrees. The following is a listing of chairpersons and their corresponding department areas of research.

Accounting: Dr. Stephen Loeb, Chair. Department research: Management accounting, accounting for regulated industries, government contract accounting, capital budgeting, decision support systems, financial accounting, accounting information systems, tax, auditing, accounting ethics.

Finance: Dr. Richard Kolodny, Chair. Department research: Corporate finance, financial institutions, investments, futures and options contracts, investment analysis, portfolio management, capital asset pricing theory, international finance, portfolio analysis, capital market theory, commercial banking, financial theory, agency theory.

Information Systems: Maryam Alavi, Chair.
Department research: End-user computing, information systems analysis and design, knowledge-based systems, expert systems, production management systems, parallel computing, database systems.

Management Science and Statistics: Dr. Bruce Golden, Chair.
Department research: Statistical quality control, multivariate process control, applied mathematical programming, network and combinatorial optimization, network optimization, transportation planning, applied operations research,

quality improvement methodology, facilities layout, cellular manufacturing, multivariate symmetric distributions, linear and nonlinear programming.

Management and Organization: Dr. Edwin Locke, Chair.
Department research: Performance appraisal and compensation design, management by objectives systems, executive leadership, strategy implementation, labor relations, goal setting, employee motivation, organizational staffing, teamwork, organizational life cycles, competitive strategy.

Marketing: Dr. Richard Durand, Chair.
Department research: New product development, marketing strategy, international marketing, business-to-business marketing, consumer behavior, advertising.

Transportation, Business and Public Policy: Dr. Thomas Corsi, Chair.
Department research: Deregulation, international aviation, airline pricing and competition, carrier management, government policies toward business, international business regulation, global management strategies, international trade policies, international joint ventures, public utility pricing.

The College and Environs

The University at College Park is the flagship institution of the University of Maryland System. The enrollment of approximately 34,000, of whom about 9,000 are graduate students, supports nearly 100 doctoral and master's programs. The University is a member of the prestigious fifty-eight member Association of American Universities. The University of Maryland is further recognized as having more than a dozen programs rated among the ten best at public universities in the United States by the National Academy of Sciences and other prestigious organizations.

Nine miles from the White House, the Maryland Business School is located on a 1,300-acre campus. This location affords students the benefits of a suburban setting while maintaining the cultural and employment opportunities of Washington, D.C., and Baltimore. In fact, the concert halls, museums, art galleries, and restaurants are a short 15-minute subway ride away in Washington, D.C.

Facilities

Classified as a Research I facility by the Carnegie Foundation (its highest ranking), the research facilities at the University of Maryland are among the best in the world. With the addition of National Archives II, the main repository of information for the government of the United States of America, Maryland offers access to one of the world's most complete collections of research material right in College Park. The University proper offers an outstanding library collection of about 2 million volumes, state-of-the-art laboratories, a network of campus research centers, and excellent microcomputing and mainframe computing facilities. Beyond the facilities at College Park, students have access, within minutes, to other world-class research facilities at sites such as the Library of Congress, the Smithsonian Institution, the Federal Reserve, and the National Libraries of Medicine and Agriculture, to name a few.

Admission

Application to the M.B.A. program is open to individuals holding a bachelor's degree or its equivalent from an accredited college or university. Submission of a GMAT score is required. International students must submit a minimum score of 580 on the TOEFL, provide proof of adequate funds, and provide proof of immunizations.

Finances

Students are eligible for merit-based financial aid that is awarded as fellowships, which provide a waiver of all tuition plus a stipend for living expenses, and as graduate and teaching assistantships, which cover almost all tuition charges.

The low cost of the University of Maryland is a benefit to both domestic and international students. For the 1994-95 academic year, tuition was $210 per credit hour for in-state students and $365 per credit hour for out-of-state students.

Living expenses in the Washington, D.C., area are comparable to those of other metropolitan areas in the United States. Students live both on and off campus, and the average cost for room and board is about $10,000 per academic year.

Application Facts and Dates

The decision to admit an applicant is based on a thorough evaluation of the candidate's managerial and leadership potential, ability to add perspective to the class, and evidence of academic excellence. Admission to the M.B.A. program is for fall only. Applicants should make inquiries to:

Director of M.B.A./M.S. Programs
2308 van Munching Hall
University of Maryland
College Park, Maryland 20742
Telephone: 301-405-2278
Fax: 301-314-9862
E-mail: bmgtgrad@deans.umd.edu

The University of Memphis

Memphis, Tennessee

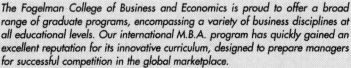

> The Fogelman College of Business and Economics is proud to offer a broad range of graduate programs, encompassing a variety of business disciplines at all educational levels. Our international M.B.A. program has quickly gained an excellent reputation for its innovative curriculum, designed to prepare managers for successful competition in the global marketplace.
>
> M.B.A. courses with a strong international emphasis are combined with graduate training in foreign languages, geographic area studies, and culture, leading to a semester-long business internship abroad.
>
> The I.M.B.A. and other graduate programs of the Fogelman College benefit from our excellent location and from such College resources as the Wang Center for International Business and the Fed Ex Center for Cycle Time Research. We encourage you to explore The University of Memphis.
>
> —O. C. Ferrell, Dean

Programs and Curricular Focus

As one of the 5 percent of American Assembly of Collegiate Schools of Business (AACSB) schools that have achieved all levels of accreditation, the Fogelman College of Business and Economics strives for excellence in all programs. These include programs leading to the Master of Business Administration (M.B.A.), with concentrations in accounting, economics, finance, insurance and real estate, management, management information systems, management science and operations management, and marketing; the Master of Science (M.S.) in accounting; the Master of Science in business administration; and the Master of Arts (M.A.) in economics. A joint M.B.A./J.D. program is offered in conjunction with the School of Law. An Executive M.B.A. program meets over a twenty-two-month period and allows successful managers to obtain the M.B.A. degree without interrupting their careers. The Ph.D. in business administration is also offered with many different concentration areas.

The International M.B.A. program incorporates language, cultural, and geographic area studies with business instruction in a full-time twenty-two-month program. It offers rigorous, intensive, and challenging international business education and five language tracks (German, French, Spanish, Chinese, and English) for highly qualified students. The I.M.B.A. program features a semester-long, University-arranged internship in the country or region of the

student's language track, personalized faculty involvement, and scholarships or assistantships for superior applicants.

Students and the M.B.A. Experience

The student body is international, highly competent, and talented. Students enjoy living in Memphis and bring a unique richness to the University that builds on tradition and history.

The average student has a mean undergraduate GPA of 3.2 and an average GMAT score of 540. The total number of master's students in the Fogelman College of Business and Economics is 850, and there are more than 100 students working toward the Ph.D. degree.

Special Features

The Robert Wang Center for International Business was established in 1988 through the support of Mr. Robert Wang, an alumnus of the University and president of Wang International. The activities of the Wang Center for International Business greatly enrich the learning environment of the I.M.B.A. program.

The Center for International Business Education and Research (CIBER), one of only twenty-five in the U.S., was established in 1990 when the University received a major grant from the U.S. Department of Education. The University received a renewal of the grant in 1993. Housed in the Wang Center, CIBER provides national leadership on international business issues. The combined

efforts of the centers support the innovative International M.B.A. program and the richness of its interdisciplinary and cross-cultural components.

The Faculty

The College catalog lists more than 80 business faculty members with graduate status. The faculty members teaching at Fogelman College hold the highest possible degrees in their areas of expertise.

The Business School Network

Memphis is known nationally as "America's Distribution Center." It is also a primary medical, educational, communication, and transportation center. The University of Memphis enjoys close ties to these local and regional businesses. In addition, faculty members receive national and international recognition from the business and academic communities. Thus, students are able to utilize many resources, including those available to the University as one of only twenty-five CIBERs nationally.

Due to these factors, the University is able to organize excellent internship opportunities, especially for the International M.B.A. students, who intern in other countries such as Brazil, France, Germany, and Mexico. Additional connections with the business community of benefit to M.B.A. students include outstanding speakers from local and regional businesses who regularly address students, a Dean's Executive Advisory Council composed of 75 highly placed executives from the regional and business community, and an active Executive in Residence program.

The College and Environs

The University of Memphis was founded in 1908 and has a student population of 21,000. Instruction is offered in six colleges and one school in more than 100 fields. Fogelman College of Business and Economics has an enrollment of about 4,000 students.

With a population of over 900,000, Memphis is one of the South's largest and most attractive cities. As a primary

medical, communication, and transportation center, Memphis offers a full range of research opportunities and cultural experiences. The city, known for its musical heritage, has many fine restaurants, museums, and theaters. Built on a bluff that towers over the Mississippi River, Memphis is devoted to preserving its heritage while it builds for the future.

Technology Environment

The Fogelman College of Business and Economics has contemporary business research facilities. Six computer laboratories are devoted to microcomputer instruction and research, and several classrooms have integrated video-computer facilities, enabling students and faculty members to develop state-of-the-art case presentations. The College is known for its information systems capability and its market research laboratory.

Placement

University Placement Services are provided to assist graduating students and alumni in locating career employment in business and industry, government, and service organizations. Students are encouraged to register with University Placement three semesters prior to graduation. Services that are offered include state-of-the-art computerized résumé referral and job notification

systems, on-campus interviews, job-seeking skill-development programs, an employer information library, and comprehensive career fairs. In addition, professional staff members are available by appointment to assist students with all aspects of their job search.

Admission

A bachelor's degree from an accredited college or university is required for admission to the M.B.A. program. Students must submit a minimum GMAT score of 430 and have a minimum college GPA of 2.0. International students must have a minimum score of 550 on the Test of English as a Foreign Language (TOEFL), provide proof of adequate funds, and submit proof of immunizations. Up to 6 graduate credit hours from an AACSB accredited program may be transferred.

Finances

The 1995–96 tuition for students who are Tennessee residents is $122 per credit hour; tuition for out-of-state students is $298 per credit hour. All students must pay an activities fee of $34 per semester. Rates for residence halls on campus ranges from $780 to $1190 per semester. The University has 126 apartments for student families on the south campus, with some units constructed specifically

for handicapped students. Rates for these apartments ranges from $320 to $480 per month. Students are responsible for the cost of utilities. Numerous housing facilities are available off campus.

A number of graduate research and teaching assistantships are available each year. These assistantships, which provide a monthly stipend, are granted on the basis of GMAT scores, GPA, and personal interviews. Recipients of assistantships are granted in-state tuition status. A student must be fully admitted to the graduate program by mid-July to be considered for an assistantship. Other sources of aid may be coordinated through the Office of Student Aid at the University.

International Students

All applicants who attend the University of Memphis on a student visa must have received a minimum score of 550 on the TOEFL. Scores must be sent directly from the testing agency to the University of Memphis.

Application Facts and Dates

Applications may be obtained from the Office of Graduate Admissions or from the address below. Completed forms must be returned with a $5 nonrefundable application fee ($30 for international students). Application deadlines are August 1 for the fall semester, December 1 for the spring semester, and May 1 for the summer term (three months earlier for international students). The International M.B.A. and Executive M.B.A. programs accept students only for the fall semester, and applicants are encouraged to submit their materials in the preceding spring to ensure a place in the class. GMAT scores must be submitted for the M.B.A., M.S., and Ph.D. programs; GRE scores are acceptable for the M.A. program. All scores must be sent directly from the testing agency to the University of Memphis. For further information on all graduate programs, applicants should write or call:

Office of Graduate Programs
Fogelman College of Business and
  Economics
Room A101
The University of Memphis
Memphis, Tennessee 38152
Telephone: 901-678-3721
Fax: 901-678-3759

University of Missouri–Columbia

Columbia, Missouri

THE MISSOURI M.B.A.—DESIGNED TO MEET YOUR GOALS

Besides being challenging and contemporary, the Missouri M.B.A. program is flexible and friendly, with small class sizes and individualized attention from faculty and staff. Our format allows you the flexibility to join the program at a time that better fits your schedule and the freedom to tailor your program of study to satisfy your personal interests and career goals. Missouri M.B.A. candidates are top caliber. Our admission standards are high and the curriculum is rigorous; you'll graduate with the knowledge, skills, and values necessary for success in the business world. Our M.B.A. program, with classes taught by the College's award-winning faculty, will provide the foundation you need to realize your professional goals.

—Bruce J. Walker, Dean

Programs and Curricular Focus

Flexibility and individuality are the hallmark of the M.B.A. program at the University of Missouri (MU). The MU M.B.A. provides graduate professional management education to students from diverse backgrounds while allowing them to prepare for specific career paths. A student may enter the program at three times during the year. Foundation courses provide training in basic business functions; however, they may be waived for students having equivalent prior course work. Students may concentrate electives in the business areas of finance, marketing, and management, or they may individualize their programs with outside course work in areas as diverse as law, engineering, journalism, public relations, health-services management, sports administration, or computer science. To complement the foundation and electives, the Missouri M.B.A. offers skill-enhancing experiences in communication, leadership, and teamwork. A professional perspective is infused through small group meetings with executives, summer internships, real-world case experiences, and professional development seminars designed specifically for M.B.A. students.

The Missouri M.B.A. program permits broad flexibility in the second year, enabling students to tailor programs of study to meet their specific needs and interests. Students complete a minimum of 39 and a maximum of 55 semester hours, assuming completion of prerequisite course work in business calculus, basic and intermediate statistics, and microeconomic theory, which must be accomplished prior to or concurrent with entering the program. A typical program is 46 semester hours. Joint-degree programs are also available for students wishing to pursue an M.B.A. degree simultaneously with a J.D., Master of Health Administration, or Master of Science in Industrial Engineering degree.

Students and the M.B.A. Experience

Admission to the Missouri M.B.A. program is selective; students admitted to the program are committed to and capable of academic and professional success. The program is kept relatively small, enrolling between 80 and 120 students a year. MU's M.B.A. students represent more than fifty colleges in twenty states and thirteen countries; they hold undergraduate degrees in thirty different disciplines. Managerial experience is not a prerequisite for admission.

❖ Global Focus

Students can study abroad through MU's formal relationships with various foreign universities and selected exchange programs. Currently, MU's Business and Public Administration (B&PA) faculty members are assisting in the development of a Business Management Program at the University of Sibiu in Romania. Through this program, several MU M.B.A. students have had the opportunity to visit Romania to work in a managerial capacity in an industrial firm or small business consulting center. B&PA recently offered its M.B.A. program at Nanjing University in the People's Republic of China and cooperates in several M.B.A. exchanges. The MU M.B.A. network of alumni stretches to nations all around the globe.

Special Features

Beginning with the orientation, students have the opportunity to know their instructors and actively participate in and out of class. They might attend a reception at the home of a faculty member, have lunch with a visiting executive, help design a business plan for a small local business, and intern with a large company or maybe a start-up firm. By becoming a member of the student-led M.B.A. Association, a student has frequent social opportunities. MU M.B.A. students participate in an MBAs Make a Difference service project and frequently socialize with fellow M.B.A. students after an executive presentation. These opportunities promote personal involvement in the M.B.A. program and provide a personal touch difficult to find in larger, lock-step programs.

The Faculty

Effective teaching is a priority among B&PA faculty members, many of whom have won national and campus awards in recognition of their teaching. Innovative classroom techniques, computer technology, and effective class materials strengthen the learning process. In addition to the high quality of its classroom instruction, the College's faculty, which includes a large number of young, doctorally qualified instructors along with well-known senior professors, is recognized for its research productivity.

The Business School Network

Corporate Partnerships

Interaction between business leaders and M.B.A. students is facilitated through the College's Executive-in-Residence, Professor-for-a-Day, and M.B.A. seminar programs. Held each fall, M.B.A. Institute Week invites business leaders to offer special seminars and presentations centered around a selected theme.

Prominent Alumni

The College's more than 21,000 alumni contribute their expertise to organizations in every state and a multitude of other countries. *Business Week* magazine ranked MU as the number-one producer of corporate CEOs in both the state of Missouri and the Big Eight, while *Fortune* ranked MU in the top fifteen nationally. The College has six advisory boards that bring CEOs, CFOs, and other top officials from Fortune 500 companies back to Mizzou for regular visits and support.

The College and Environs

MU is the oldest state university west of the Mississippi River and the largest of the four campuses of the University of Missouri System. The University, which enrolls approximately 22,300 students, offers many cultural and sports events. Columbia is a warm, friendly, cosmopolitan, and safe college community with a population in excess of 71,000. Columbia's growing economy and low unemployment rate offer job opportunities for student family members. The community includes a large number of both student-oriented and professionally oriented private apartment complexes conveniently located to MU. Sidewalk restaurants, pubs, coffeehouses, and the quaint downtown shopping district are within three blocks of MU and help make the community a very pleasant place to live.

Facilities

Ellis Library houses more than 1.5 million volumes, 4.8 million microforms, and nearly 18,000 serial titles. Friendly, professional staff are available to answer questions, help solve research problems, and support numerous on-line and CD-ROM databases. MU has excellent recreational facilities as well as residence halls for men and women students. Over 300 unfurnished University apartments are available for married student families and single graduate students.

Technology Environment

Middlebush Hall, which houses B&PA, contains a computer lab and classroom with a help desk staffed by user consultants. Networked PCs in Middlebush classrooms and computer labs provide access to the mainframe and the Internet as well as to a variety of up-to-date business software. On-line database access available to students includes the BRIDGE System for real-time stock market data, LEXIS/NEXIS, Dow Jones News/Retrieval Service, ABI/Inform, Compact Disclosure SEC and Worldscope, Extell, and Compustat PC+. The B&PA Research Center also provides computer support services, including COMPUSTAT, Census, CRSP, FDIC, and Citibank files.

Placement

The College's Career Services office brings more than 150 recruiting firms to campus each year. Recent graduates have accepted employment throughout the United States, with annual starting salaries ranging from $28,000 to $70,000. Internships allow many students the opportunity to preview positions and companies prior to accepting employment offers. The Career Services office also sponsors a career fair each fall, coordinates and schedules on-campus interviews, maintains a job listing service for employers, and holds career development workshops and seminars.

Admission

Admission depends primarily upon the quality of the undergraduate work and the score received on the Graduate Management Admission Test (GMAT). The average entering grade point average is 3.3, and the average GMAT score ranges between 580 and 600. The Test of English as a Foreign Language (TOEFL) is required of applicants whose native language is other than English and who do not have a degree from an institution in the United States.

Finances

Missouri residents and out-of-state graduate students enrolled are required to pay educational fees of approximately $140 and $385 per credit hour, respectively. A student health fee of $47.50 per semester is charged to all full-time graduate students. Fees are subject to change without notice. M.B.A. assistantships are widely available to academically qualified students. These assistantships typically involve 10 hours of work per week at a rate of $1750 per semester; educational fees may be waived. Scholarships that may waive out-of-state tuition charges are also available to students with outstanding academic credentials. Scholarships, grants, and loans are also available through the MU Financial Aid Office. International students enrolled at MU can apply for a Curator's Grant-in-Aid that allows them to remit educational fees at the in-state rate.

Application Facts and Dates

Students may enter the M.B.A. program in the fall semester (August), winter semester (January), or summer session (June). Application deadlines are August 1, December 1, and May 1, respectively. Exceptions to deadlines are possible if GMAT scores and transcripts are available. For more information, applicants should contact:

Ms. Marilyn Hasselriis
Senior Academic Advisor
Graduate Studies in Business
College of Business and Public
    Administration
303D Middlebush Hall
University of Missouri
Columbia, Missouri 65211
Telephone: 314-882-2750
Fax: 314-882-0365
E-mail: grad@bpa.missouri.edu

UNLV The University of Nevada, Las Vegas

College of Business and Economics

Las Vegas, Nevada

> ### EDUCATION FOR LIFE'S CAREER
>
> *At the University of Nevada, Las Vegas, we have taken the position that the best education package we can offer to our students is a broad educational experience. Most professional managers are faced with a dynamic business environment that changes frequently. M.B.A. graduates from UNLV are prepared to accept and meet the business challenges that will come to them.*
>
> *We make every effort to challenge all students to magnify their talents in such a way that they will be ready to face the exciting challenges of a global economy.*
> —William Theodore Cummings, Dean

Programs and Curricular Focus

The University of Nevada, Las Vegas, is honored to offer students degree programs in the College of Business that are accredited by the highest accrediting body for business studies in the United States—the American Assembly of Collegiate Schools of Business.

The primary focus of UNLV's M.B.A. program is to provide an educational experience that will prepare a graduate to assume administrative responsibilities in either business or governmental institutions. The M.B.A. curriculum is designed to expose the student to a broad general business education. The program motto is "Preparation for a Career Not for a Specific Job." The candidate is required to finish advanced courses in all the business functional areas.

The length of the M.B.A. program depends on the candidate's previous degrees, academic grades, and business courses already completed. Students from all majors and all geographic areas are encouraged to enter the program. The current student body has undergraduate majors in eighty different disciplines from 140 universities—diversity is one of the College's strongest attributes. Depending on the student's background, the program consists of between 30 and 60 semester units.

Students study topics that are essential for making intelligent management decisions. The topics include international business, ethics and legal issues, quantitative decision making, and financial, accounting, marketing, and managerial competencies. The student can use three elective courses to enhance topics of individual career interest. Every effort is made to awaken and encourage the entrepreneurial spirit so necessary in a dynamic economic society.

The College of Business and Economics also offers master's degrees in accounting, economics, and public administration.

Students and the M.B.A. Experience

Since UNLV has taken the position that an M.B.A. candidate is best served with a broad general education, it follows that students from all academic majors are welcome in the program. The only prerequisites for students with a good academic record are that they come into the program with good computer, math, and English skills and that they have meaningful work experience.

An M.B.A. education is much more meaningful if the student has had pertinent work experience. The student should have been employed for a few years so as to be familiar with the stresses as well as the opportunities common in the business world. An M.B.A. is not an extension of undergraduate education, but rather it is a degree allowing the student to become a scholar with specific career goals in mind.

The average age of students entering UNLV's M.B.A. program is 29 years, with five years of full-time work experience. The age range is 24 to 52 years. Women make up 30 percent of the student body, members of minority groups represent 10 percent, international students make up 12 percent of entering students, and 6 percent of the students already have advanced degrees.

Special Features

Students may attend either part-time or full-time. Some courses are offered during the day, and all courses are offered in the evening. With a more mature student body, many of the students are employed. Students are often able to apply the theories learned in the classroom to their current employment environment. Also, when topics are being evaluated during the class discussion, the students are often able to provide classroom enrichment to the theory being discussed by relating their own work experiences.

Many courses are offered during the summer sessions, permitting a student to shorten the time required to complete the degree.

The Faculty

All faculty members chosen to teach in the M.B.A. program are outstanding in their field of expertise. It is rare for a course to be taught by a faculty member who does not have a doctorate. The faculty members have extensive experience in their chosen areas of instruction. The faculty includes professors with training and experience from many nations. Every M.B.A. candidate is assigned a faculty member to serve as his or her adviser and guide.

UNLV continues to value outstanding classroom instruction. Professors have many additional duties, but there is no excuse for failing to provide a rich learning environment that will motivate young scholars.

The Business School Network

Many of the faculty members consult with businesses in an attempt to find solutions to various problems confronting modern managers. These relationships provide a network that is beneficial to all concerned. The faculty is made aware of current business issues and is provided an opportunity to invite business leaders to visit and/or lecture in their classes. The city of Las Vegas is very proud of UNLV, and many business executives provide support to the University and look at UNLV as their institution.

The College and Environs

While the University is relatively young, it has experienced rapid growth in recent years. The student enrollment is 20,000, with approximately 3,500 graduate students. Las Vegas is one of the fastest-growing cities in the United States and is the primary shopping and business district for more than 1 million people.

The University is located within the city, so students have easy access to all city services. The airport is less than 2 miles from the campus. The airport is one of the busiest in the United States, with easy connection to any location. Las Vegas is only a half-day automobile ride from Los Angeles or Phoenix.

Many international visitors come to Las Vegas, which indirectly provides many opportunities for the students. Students are able to find many ethnic restaurants and grocery stores and will probably have visitors from their home country.

Las Vegas is located on the edge of the desert, where the residents enjoy hot summers and mild winters. There are also large lakes and high mountains nearby, which provide students the opportunity to appreciate the beauties of nature and to enjoy many forms of outdoor recreation.

Facilities

For the single student, there is excellent campus housing available. There are six new dormitories where 2 students share each room. There are a few rooms available for single occupants, but this requires an additional fee. The dormitory room and board cost is $2600 per semester. There are hundreds of apartments available near the University, with prices starting at $400 per month.

There is a fine health facility on campus to provide emergency medical services. All students must purchase the comprehensive student health plan offered by UNLV.

For additional information, students may contact the Office of Residential Life, 4760 Gym Road, Las Vegas, Nevada 89119; telephone: 702-895-3489; fax: 702-895-4332.

Technology Environment

The College of Business has excellent computer facilities available for student use, and for the rare computer expert with expanded computer requirements, UNLV is one of the few universities in the world that has a Cray Supercomputer.

The College also sponsors research centers that make extensive use of modern facilities, such as the Center for Business and Economic Research, the Small Business Development Center, and the Center for Management Programs.

Placement

The University has a very active student placement office on campus, offering numerous services to students. These include career workshops, résumé preparation assistance, placement file services for current or future use, counseling, and information on job expectations and the future employment outlook.

Admission

Admission requirements include a four-year bachelor's degree and a minimum score of 450 on the GMAT. International students must also pass the TOEFL with a minimum score of 550. The average GMAT score of the current student body is 555, and the average undergraduate GPA is 3.15. Admission decisions are made by the faculty on the basis of all documents required in the application packet. All application materials must be complete and received by May 1 for admission to the fall semester and October 1 for admission to the spring semester.

Finances

UNLV is relatively inexpensive because it is a state-supported institution. Estimated fees and living expenses per semester for 1995–96 include $81 per semester credit hour, a nonresident fee of $2375, $2600 for dormitory and meals, $300 for books and supplies, $300 for student health insurance, and $500 for personal expenses. Assuming the student takes 9 credit hours, the total per semester cost is approximately $6800.

Food and housing are relatively inexpensive as compared to many other states, if a student chooses to live off campus.

Students may also apply for graduate assistant positions after being on campus for one semester. These positions are very competitive and are filled on the basis of student merit and University needs.

International Students

All international students are required to register with the Office of International Student Services (OISS). This office exists only to serve the students and to make their adjustment to campus life pleasant and productive. If necessary, an OISS representative will meet new students at the McCarran Airport upon arrival. For additional information regarding the OISS, students may call 702-895-3221.

There are over 600 international students on campus representing over fifty countries. Resident hall, alumni, and student organizations provide important support groups for international students interested in affiliating with social and business organizations.

For students who need to reinforce their language skills, the University provides education through the Center for English Language Studies. Beginning, intermediate, and advanced-level courses are offered.

Application Facts and Dates

For additional information, students should contact:

Duane Baldwin
Director of M.B.A. Program
University of Nevada, Las Vegas
4505 Maryland Parkway
P.O. Box 456031
Las Vegas, Nevada 89154-6031
Telephone: 702-895-3655
Fax: 702-895-4306

University of New Hampshire

Durham, New Hampshire

THE NEW M.B.A. IN THE GLOBAL ECONOMY

The mission of the Whittemore School of Business and Economics is to be a distinguished professional school in which the liberal arts are the basic foundation and the management of change in a global economic community is the major emphasis. In order to achieve this mission, the school is committed to a broad set of goals that preserves our commitment to excellence in critical thought, verbal and written communications, quantitative skills, computer literacy and ethical reasoning.

Our environment fosters collegiality and fairness through continuous interaction with business and other external entities. The promotion of international awareness and cross-cultural understanding is an essential component of the educational student experience at The Whittemore School.

—Lyndon E. Goodridge, Dean of the Whittemore School

Programs and Curricular Focus

The M.B.A. program is intentionally small (approximately 30 to 40 students) to foster a close association between students and faculty. Although each incoming M.B.A. class has its own particular blend of individuals with a wide range of experiences, the small size allows classes to be informal and maximizes student involvement with the program.

A sequence of fifteen required and five elective courses can only be started in September and requires two years of full-time study to complete. During the first year, ten required courses make up a common schedule for the entire entering class. The first-year curriculum is both demanding and highly structured.

During the second year, M.B.A. students complete their last five required courses. The remainder of the year is allocated for electives that can develop and expand areas of individual career interest. Elective classes in the second year of study can take the form of traditional classroom experiences, off-campus consulting opportunities, or team project work. A mixture of experiences is often chosen to allow a gradual transition to the workplace.

Other program opportunities offered at the Whittemore School include joint B.A./M.B.A. programs, which allow highly qualified students to complete both degrees in five years instead of the traditional six years. An M.A. and Ph.D. program in economics is offered both on a full-time and part-time framework to

those students who are interested in research and academic careers. For the corporate managers who wish to mix full-time work with graduate study, the University offers a highly acclaimed twenty-two-month Executive M.B.A. and a residential three-week Executive Development Program.

Students and the M.B.A. Experience

While 4 out of every 10 students in the M.B.A. program are from the local region, the remaining 6 are split almost evenly between other New England regions, the rest of the United States, and other countries. The academic background of each class also varies significantly. Half of the students are prepared in the liberal arts and social science disciplines, while a quarter of each entering class have been prepared in the physical sciences and business and economics. The mix of men to women is two thirds to one third, with the average age of an entering class at 27.

❖ Global Focus

The Whittemore School's M.B.A. program encourages student development in the international arena via a mixture of classroom, study-abroad, and international residential experiences. In the second year of study, elective courses are offered with a purely international orientation, courses such as international business and international finance and international management are regularly part of the

second-year offerings. In addition, courses may include international residence; for example, a recent course in international management had a mandatory residence in Quebec, Canada.

Special Features

The Whittemore School M.B.A. Investment Fund allows students who are interested in a career in the investment field an opportunity to try their hands at managing a real fund portfolio. With funds provided by alumni, two teams of selected students are allowed to actually invest funds over an eighteen-month period.

The Faculty

Unlike many other institutions, all of the faculty members of the Whittemore School are researchers and teachers; they perform both at a high level of excellence. The 53 faculty members in the school support the business management, economics, and hotel management programs. Frequently, practitioners are invited into the classrooms as guest lecturers, and on occasion the University has invited top-notch practitioners to teach a course in their fields of specialty. The Whittemore School does not use graduate assistants to teach in any of its masters or doctoral programs.

The Business School Network

Corporate Partnerships

The Whittemore School Executive Board is made up of 40 senior officers from many of the top businesses in the Northeast and Atlantic regions of the United States. These senior officers interact with the schools' leadership and students to provide an educational experience that is both up-to-date and real-world. Many members of the Executive Board fund corporate fellowships in their companies' name. These fellowships provide M.B.A. students with financial support, as well as summer research opportunities. All M.B.A. students have an opportunity to meet these corporate leaders and compete for the summer work opportunities provided by their companies.

The College and Environs

The University of New Hampshire, founded in 1866, is located in Durham—a small town in a semirural area that retains many traces of its colonial past. The 200-acre campus is surrounded by more than 3,000 acres of fields, farms, and woodlands owned by the University. A stream running through a large wooded area in the middle of the campus enhances a sense of openness and natural beauty. The University enrolls more than 12,000 students in both its undergraduate and graduate programs and as such is the largest academic institution in the state. The accessibility of Boston's cultural opportunities (65 miles south); the skiing, hiking, and scenery of the White Mountains (60 miles north); and the sandy beaches and rocky coast of New Hampshire and Maine (10 miles east) make it an ideal location to live and study.

Placement

The University maintains a comprehensive full-time career planning and placement staff for the benefit of all graduate students. In addition to the on-campus interview system, the office maintains an active alumni file for those students interested in career networking. In cooperation with Career Services, the Whittemore School conducts a number of workshops throughout the year that include résumé writing, interviewing techniques, salary negotiations, and overviews of the current job market.

Admission

The crucial requirement for admission to the M.B.A. program is a history that demonstrates that the applicant has the potential and desire for graduate study in business. All students must have completed a bachelor's degree before beginning the M.B.A. program. The focus of the applicants' undergraduate studies is of less importance than evidence of academic ability and potential for becoming a responsible manager and leader. The GMAT exam is required of all applicants, along with the TOEFL exam for all international applicants. In recent years, the average GMAT score was 570 and the average grade point average was 3.1. The minimum TOEFL score is 550.

Finances

Yearly tuition for the M.B.A. program in 1994–95 was $12,290. Mandatory fees were $455. Babcock House is the graduate student residence for single students, where a single room costs $2620 per school year. Students may remain in Babcock during summer at reduced rates. Limited on-campus housing is available for married students in Forest Park. Prices for efficiencies and one- and two-bedroom apartments range from $309 to $411 per month. Graduate assistantships and tuition scholarships are competitive and awarded to applicants of high academic achievement and promise.

Application Facts and Dates

Application deadlines are July 1 for U. S. nationals and April 1 for international applicants. For information, applicants should contact:

George Abraham
Director of Graduate Programs
The Whittemore School of Business
University of New Hampshire
Box PI, McConnell Hall, 15 College
  Road
Durham, New Hampshire 03824-3593
Telephone: 603-862-1367
Fax: 603-862-4468

University of New Haven

West Haven, Connecticut

AN M.B.A. PROGRAM FOR THE WORKING PROFESSIONAL

The University of New Haven is a private, comprehensive university specializing in providing high-quality education and preparation for self-reliant, productive careers in a technologically advanced, global marketplace. The M.B.A. degree is designed to prepare working professionals for management roles in diverse organizations. The program emphasizes the integration of relevant theory and practical business applications, with an opportunity for students to select a concentration that will make their degree personally and professionally meaningful. Well-qualified, caring faculty take great pains to ensure that our M.B.A. students have the knowledge and analytical and technical skills necessary to lead in the next century.

—Jerry L. Allen, Dean

Programs and Curricular Focus

A primary objective of the M.B.A. program at UNH is the development of a professional management perspective that enables students to see the totality of management rather than the limited focus of the specialist. Equally important is the development of the student's ability to utilize the newest analytic and quantitative techniques employed in corporate decision making. Students are also exposed to an in-depth analysis of various theories of business and managerial behavior, emphasizing the business organization in relation to its internal and external environments.

Another important option in the M.B.A. program is the opportunity for the student to develop special skills by selecting a concentration in a given study area. The M.B.A. curriculum consists of nineteen courses, usually including fourteen required courses and five elective/concentration courses. Some waiver of required courses is possible based on previous academic credits earned at the undergraduate level. Awarding of waivers is part of the admissions process; however, certain specific restrictions apply.

Most concentrations consist of four courses; however, finance concentration students substitute finance department courses for three of the core courses, thus having a total of seven concentration courses. Health-care concentration students substitute a health-care organization management course for the standard management course in the required core courses. Students in the concentrations in

hotel and restaurant management and in travel and tourism administration have the opportunity to acquire practical experience as part of the program if they lack background in the field.

Those students choosing to specialize may select a concentration for the elective portion of the program from accounting, business policy and strategy, computer and information science, finance, health-care management, health-care marketing, human resources management, international business, logistics, long-term health care, management and organization, management science, marketing, operations research, public relations, technology management, and telecommunication.

Applicants to the M.B.A. program who lack adequate preparation in accounting, economics, finance, or quantitative techniques may be required to enroll in a maximum of four graduate-level, noncredit courses or their equivalent to satisfy prerequisite requirements. Students in the M.B.A. program are expected to be familiar with, or become familiar with, the use of computers and computer software for solving problems. In appropriate cases, the M.B.A. student may choose to write a thesis as part of the elective/concentration portion (52 credits) of the program.

Students and the M.B.A. Experience

Nearly 800 students, many holding full-time jobs, are enrolled in the M.B.A. program at the University of New Haven.

Most students are from the Northeastern United States, but the University has made a strong commitment to maintain a diverse student body. Women comprise 40 percent of the student population, and 10 percent are international students, representing approximately fifty countries.

Special Features

Trimester scheduling allows students to accelerate progress toward their degree, and, while a complete curriculum is available to full-time students, there are evening and weekend classes suitable for working adults.

Students can enrich their personal and professional competences by selecting a concentration in a particular discipline, and some departments offer students the opportunity to obtain additional credit and practical experience by participation in an internship program.

The Faculty

The highly qualified faculty represents a combination of full-time academics who hold doctoral degrees in their specialties from a variety of prestigious institutions and part-time faculty members employed in Connecticut businesses, industries, and professions who bring practical insight and experience to the classroom.

Class size within the Graduate School is relatively small, averaging less than 25 students. Classes are kept small to allow for interaction and personal attention. The faculty members at UNH get to know students and act as sounding boards in discussions about career options and plans for personal and professional growth and development. UNH faculty members have international, national, and regional reputations in their fields through outstanding accomplishments in research and writing and as visiting lecturers.

The Business School Network

Most students in the M.B.A program hold full-time positions in regional businesses and nonprofit corporations; that experience allows the classroom to become a mechanism for extending students' learning into varied practical environments. Ongoing interaction with the business community also occurs throughout the Business School Advisory Board, composed of leaders from private and public sectors; the Institute for Business Evolution; the Center for Family Business; and a vast network of alumni. Additional networking occurs through students' participation in the recently chartered chapter of Sigma Beta Delta, the National Honor Society in Business, Management, and Administration.

Each fall and spring, the Bartels' Fellowship Lecture Series brings a successful CEO or entrepreneur to campus to lecture and interact with faculty and students. Some Distinguished Bartels' Fellows have been David Beckerman, President of Starter Corporation; Robert Beavers Jr., Senior Vice President of McDonald's Corporation; Francis Freidman, former CEO of GCI Group, Grey Advertising; Ronald G. Shaw, President and CEO of Pilot Pen; and William J. Weisz, former CEO of Motorola, Inc.

The College and Environs

The University's 73-acre campus is located in south-central Connecticut, on a hillside in West Haven that overlooks Long Island Sound and downtown New Haven. The area is semisuburban and is easily accessible by car, bus, train, or plane. The campus, located near the intersection of interstate highways 95 and 91, is 75 miles northeast of New York City and 135 miles southwest of Boston.

New Haven, just 10 minutes away from campus, is a city where arts and cultural activities flourish and coexist with science and business. Settled in the early 1600s and rich in history and heritage, the New Haven area is proud of its past, prouder of its present, and actively planning for its future. The city, considered by many as the "Gateway to New England," is a manufacturing center, a deep-water harbor, a major art center,

and a college town with seven colleges and universities in the immediate area.

Facilities

The University of New Haven provides facilities for a full complement of student services, including career development and placement services; academic, vocational, and personal counseling; alumni relations; health services; housing; international student services; veterans' affairs; minority affairs; and services for students with disabilities. In addition, there are athletic facilities and a campus store for the students' use and convenience.

Limited on-campus housing is available, but most graduate students find living accommodations off campus.

Technology Environment

The UNH Center for Computing Services provides both administrative and academic computing support. Clusters of terminals and personal computers for student use are spread throughout the campus. Access to the Internet, graphics terminals, printing and plotting devices, laser printing, and a wide variety of data files and software and simulation packages are available.

Placement

The University of New Haven provides career development and placement services as well as academic, vocational, and personal counseling.

Admission

Admission decisions are based primarily on an applicant's undergraduate record. In support of their applications, students may submit scores from the Graduate Record Examinations (GRE) and/or the Graduate Management Admission Test (GMAT).

Students for whom English is not their native language must present a TOEFL score of at least 500. International students must submit official, certified documents showing sufficient financial support from personal or sponsor's funds or a scholarship.

Finances

For the 1995–96 academic year, the tuition rate is $1020 per 3-credit course. There are no other regular fees; however, there is a nonrefundable application fee of $50 and an additional nonrefundable acceptance fee of $200 for international students not on scholarship. Students should calculate additional expenses for books, supplies, and housing.

Financial aid is available for domestic students in a variety of forms, including loans, grants-in-aid, work-study, fellowships, and assistantships. Financial aid is not available for international students.

International Students

Qualified international students are welcome in the M.B.A. program at the University of New Haven. Ten percent of the students currently enrolled are from approximately fifty countries outside the United States. To qualify, a prospective student must have completed an acceptable undergraduate degree program. All transcripts must be submitted in English.

The University has an Office of International Student Services that provides a full range of support services for international students.

Application Facts and Dates

For more information or applications, students should contact:

Joseph F. Spellman
Director of Graduate Admissions
University of New Haven
West Haven, Connecticut 06516-1999
Telephone: 203-932-7135
 800-DIAL-UNH Ext. 7135
 (toll-free)

The University of North Carolina at Chapel Hill

The Kenan-Flagler Business School

Chapel Hill, North Carolina

WORKING TOGETHER—THE KENAN-FLAGLER FORMULA FOR SUCCESS

The Kenan-Flagler M.B.A. Program is small and select, allowing us to create a collegial, team-oriented environment. We treat the M.B.A. student as a customer. Customer satisfaction was one of the most important tenets in my business career, and I believe it is just as important in the business school setting.

We have a culture here that emphasizes superior teaching ability, applied research experiences, and support of students. Those are the kinds of people we hire and who, according to our students, help make our faculty among the best in the business and Kenan-Flagler such a special place.

We are not an M.B.A. factory. Rather, we are a place where students come to grow both professionally and personally among peers and professors who truly understand the value of working together.

—Paul Fulton, Dean

Programs and Curricular Focus

The Kenan-Flagler M.B.A. Program challenges the student to embrace an integrated understanding of all business functions by focusing on issues and problems, not functional areas. This integrated approach underscores today's business realities, in which effective decision making requires cross-functional knowledge and an entrepreneurial spirit.

First-year students develop vital teamwork skills by working in study groups of 5 to 6 participants selected for diversity of experience and background. Study groups meet regularly to discuss cases, collaborate on class projects, solve problems, and brainstorm.

All first-year students take a sequence of thirteen core courses, including financial accounting, quantitative decision making, managerial competencies, and ethics.

Second-year students choose from a range of electives that center on one core course, which incorporates the Kenan-Flagler Management Simulation and the Practicum. The Simulation is a hands-on management experience in which students run companies in a computer-simulated, global business environment. The Practicum challenges small teams, supported by a faculty adviser, to put theory into practice by working on a project addressing a significant business problem.

Other opportunities at Kenan-Flagler include combined-degree programs. The joint M.B.A./J.D. program enables

students to earn both degrees in four academic years. The three-year M.B.A./M.R.P. program combines real estate development and urban planning with the M.B.A. The application deadline for both the School of Law and the City and Regional Planning Department is usually in February.

A three-year joint M.B.A./M.H.A. (Master of Healthcare Administration) is offered in cooperation with the nationally ranked UNC School of Public Health. The application deadline for the School of Public Health is also in February. Also offered are Master of Accounting (M.A.C.), Executive M.B.A., and Ph.D. programs in business.

Students and the M.B.A. Experience

Students at Kenan-Flagler bring a wide variety of work experiences and geographic and academic diversity to their M.B.A. experience. The average student is a 27-year-old with four years of full-time work experience. Women comprise one third of the student population, and minority students make up 12 percent.

The Northeast and Middle Atlantic states send 38 percent of Kenan-Flagler's students, while 31 percent of the student body comes from the South. Twelve percent are international students, 9 percent are Midwestern, and 10 percent are from the West.

Most Kenan-Flagler students have undergraduate degrees in business

administration or social sciences and bring professional backgrounds in either the service industries or manufacturing.

❖ Global Focus

Kenan-Flagler's M.B.A. Program offers many opportunities for qualified second-year students to enhance their international business knowledge by working or studying abroad. In summer 1994, nearly 20 percent of student internships were in countries outside the United States. Occasionally, courses may be taken for credit at international universities in conjunction with summer internships. In special cases, students may participate in semester-long exchange programs in England, France, Belgium, Canada, Venezuela, and Thailand.

Another example of Kenan-Flagler's global focus is the International Economic Seminars in which faculty-led trips take students to such places as Paris and Mexico City to meet with business leaders, tour plants and facilities, and experience local business culture firsthand. In addition, Kenan-Flagler makes the international perspective a priority throughout the curriculum.

Special Features

The first year begins with five days of intensive sessions called A Week in the Life of a General Manager, which serves as an overview of the entire two-year M.B.A. curriculum. The week demonstrates the broad range of human and technical skills, knowledge, and talents necessary to manage effectively in today's global economy.

For students who want to strengthen their statistics, economics, or accounting knowledge, the Analytical Skills Workshop provides a summer brush-up opportunity prior to beginning courses.

The Faculty

Kenan-Flagler's faculty members offer superb teaching ability, applied business research, and high-quality interactions with students. Like the curriculum itself, the more than 80 faculty members reflect the changing nature of the workforce. For example, Kenan-Flagler has the highest

percentage of tenured female faculty members among the nation's top twenty business schools and ranks near the top in percentage of black professors.

The Business School Network

Corporate Partnerships

Strong partnerships between the School and corporate leaders play an increasingly important role in the Kenan-Flagler educational experience. Second-year students interact directly with prominent business executives through the Practicum and Simulation programs, gaining valuable problem-solving skills and further extending their growing business networks.

Kenan-Flagler's Board of Visitors includes business leaders from a broad range of endeavors and a number of alumni. Students have many opportunities to meet with these corporate leaders.

Prominent Alumni

The Kenan-Flagler Business School counts among its alumni a number of notable business leaders, including Hugh L. McColl Jr., chairman and CEO of NationsBank Corporation; William O. McCoy, vice chairman of the board, BellSouth Enterprises Inc.; Julian H. Robertson Jr., president, Tiger Management Corporation; and David S. Van Pelt, senior corporate officer, Citibank, N.A.

The College and Environs

The University of North Carolina at Chapel Hill's Greek Revival architecture, green lawns, and brick walkways make the campus a beautiful educational environment. Founded in 1795, the University, with a student population of more than 23,000, offers instruction through fourteen colleges and schools in more than 100 fields.

The town is a part of the renowned Research Triangle area, which also en-compasses Durham and Raleigh. The Triangle, a population center of almost 1 million, is home to three major universities and several smaller colleges, featuring a wealth of cultural and sports events.

Technology Environment

The School has its own computing facilities, consisting of a microcomputing laboratory with about sixty terminals. Facilities are open daily from 9 a.m. to 11 p.m. Graduate students are required to have their own microcomputers.

Student-accessible databases and networks include Dialog, BRS, and Dow Jones News/Retrieval. The School is a member of the Center for Research Libraries and also features a machine-readable data files center, which includes data from the Department of Commerce.

Placement

Kenan-Flagler's Office of Career Services (OCS) works aggressively to build strong ties with on-campus recruiters and to help students build a network of other professional contacts. Top multinational companies come regularly to Kenan-Flagler to recruit for full-time and summer internship positions. In addition, OCS helps to arrange on-site interviews in New York City and other areas for students. Other services include a Job Listing Service, advisement, an alumni database, and résumé books.

Admission

Each candidate's academic record, scores on the required Graduate Management Admission Test (GMAT), and work experience are considered in the admission process. The GMAT score for enrolling Kenan-Flagler M.B.A. students has averaged between 620 and 625. The average undergraduate GPA has been 3.2.

Interviews are also crucial to each candidate's assessment.

A score of at least 600 on the TOEFL is required for all students for whom English is not the native language. International students must present proof of adequate funds to cover two full years.

There are no prerequisite courses for admission, but students must have a strong working knowledge of accounting, statistics, economics, and basic personal computer spreadsheet programs. All students must have health insurance.

Finances

Estimated tuition and fees for 1994–95 are $2550 for North Carolina residents and $9950 for nonresidents. Books and supplies cost approximately $1500 per year.

The University estimates that living expenses for a single student living at Craige Graduate Center are approximately $2700 for rent and $770 for meals each semester. Off-campus students who are married typically spend about $1000 per month for food and housing, including utilities and telephone, while single students spend about $700 per month. The cost of an IBM or IBM-compatible personal computer must also be considered, as this is a requirement.

A number of M.B.A. fellowships are available, and candidates applying to the program are automatically considered. The awards are based strictly on merit.

International Students

Twelve percent of M.B.A. students at Kenan-Flagler come from outside the United States. The pre–course work International Student Program combines academic and social activities to help international students become acclimated to American business culture and practices and participate fully in the M.B.A. program.

Application Facts and Dates

Application deadlines are usually in November, December, January, and March. Decision letters are mailed in January, February, March, and May. Applicants are encouraged to apply early. For more information, students should contact:

Ms. Anne-Marie Summers
Director of Admissions
Kenan-Flagler Business School
Carroll Hall, CB #3490
University of North Carolina at
 Chapel Hill
Chapel Hill, North Carolina 27599-
 3490
Telephone: 919-962-3236
Fax: 919-962-0898

University of Notre Dame

Notre Dame, Indiana

NEW M.B.A. INITIATIVES

Propelled by a new 153,000-square-foot, state-of-the-art building that houses a distinguished faculty and quality student body, Notre Dame's program is on the move. In addition to a substantial core program, Notre Dame offers our own full semester programs in London, England, and Santiago, Chile, plus new NAFTA-connected visits and internships in Mexico. Our global internship programs include Japan, Hong Kong, and the Netherlands. Financial aid has recently been doubled with the addition of the Hesburgh and O'Hara scholarships, which have been designed to attract superior students. We pride ourselves on our emphasis on values and business ethics, which are addressed in all disciplines and special courses. Lastly, the Dean's M.B.A. Success Forum, Office of Career Development, Business Advisory Council, expanded staff, and the Notre Dame alumni network forge a renewed emphasis on career placement. I invite you to become a part of our vibrant program.

—John Keane, Dean

Programs and Curricular Focus

Notre Dame business education focuses on the foundation, organization, operation, and control of business enterprises. Special attention is paid to the manager's responsibility for diagnosing, isolating, and defining problems; creating and evaluating alternative courses of action; and making practical and ethical decisions. The approach to all subject matter underscores the need for moral, spiritual, aesthetic, and intellectual values in successful managers.

The Notre Dame program has two tracks leading to the M.B.A. degree. The two-year program is designed for students with little or no academic background in business. An alternative three-semester program is available for students with undergraduate degrees in business primarily from U.S. universities.

The traditional two-year program requires limited prerequisites that must be fulfilled prior to enrollment. Applicants must be comfortable with quantitative material; academic preparation in calculus, advanced algebra, or statistics is strongly recommended. The first year of the program is structured to provide the student with an introduction to the functional areas of business. As the students move into their second year, the program becomes more flexible, allowing them to tailor their schedule to fit their specific career needs.

All two-year M.B.A. students, regardless of their undergraduate back-grounds, are expected to complete 62 credit hours of work over four semesters as candidates for the degree of Master of Business Administration. The program is offered on a full-time, daytime, regular academic year basis. Admission is granted for the fall semester only.

The three-semester program is designed for students presumed to be proficient in the foundation areas of business. The program begins with a nine-week summer semester in which students attend seven intensive business review courses. Thus, the three-semester student is expected to complete 44 credit hours of work over eleven months in order to obtain the M.B.A. degree.

Other program opportunities include a joint M.B.A./J.D. degree (completed in four years) as well as a three-semester taxation program.

Students and the M.B.A. Experience

The variety of work experiences as well as geographic and academic diversity is quite prevalent within the Notre Dame M.B.A. student body. Although approximately 40 percent of the student body comes from the Midwest, about 25 percent are international students, 15 percent are from the West, and 14 percent are from the Middle Atlantic.

The traditional two-year students at Notre Dame represent a good mix of undergraduate majors, including business, engineering, economics, math and sciences, and humanities. Their professional backgrounds are primarily in the service industries.

The age range for Notre Dame M.B.A. students is 20–38 years, and they entered the program with approximately three years of professional experience. Twenty-seven percent of the student body are women, and 5 percent are members of minority groups.

❖ Global Focus

Long committed to education with an international perspective, Notre Dame's M.B.A. program offers a number of opportunities to study and work abroad. The London and Santiago programs provide students in the two-year program with a semester during their second year in London, England, or Santiago, Chile, studying international business courses taught by Notre Dame professors and faculty from the British and Chilean higher educational system. Typically some 40 students study abroad, living and learning in other cultures through these two distinct opportunities for international exposure.

Other overseas opportunities include exchange programs with the University of Innsbruck in Austria and with École des Hautes Études Commerciales in either Lille or Nice, France. Summer internships for graduate business students in Japan, Hong Kong, and the Netherlands provide further avenues for international interaction.

Special Features

The Notre Dame M.B.A. program offers Project Lead to both two-year and three-semester students. This minicourse focuses on the teamwork skills and leadership qualities that are so highly sought in the corporate world. Project Lead features both classroom and outdoor exercises designed to foster working together to solve problems.

Two-year M.B.A. students, including international students, are required to attend two-week workshops in accounting and math. These workshops run concurrently two weeks prior to the start of the fall semester. International students are also required to attend a two-week English Review Workshop prior to the math and accounting workshops.

The Faculty

To discharge the mission of the program, there is an outstanding faculty that is dedicated to research and teaching. Notably, the research ranges from theoretical developments at the cutting edge of the disciplines to applications-oriented studies intended to help operating managers and students apply those theoretical breakthroughs to contemporary society.

The Business School Network

Partnerships between corporate leaders and Notre Dame have led to the establishment of scholarship and intern programs to attract top students to the program. Summer internship opportunities now exist in Japan, Hong Kong, the Netherlands, and various countries in Latin America because of the program's corporate partners.

The College of Business Advisory Council, which consists of prominent business leaders, assists the Dean, Director of Career Planning, and student body by presenting lectures, acting as mentors, and providing the program with potential employment opportunities.

The College and Environs

Notre Dame was founded in 1842 by Rev. Edward Frederick Sorin and 6 brothers of the French religious community known as the Congregation of Holy Cross. The University's 1,250-acre campus is situated immediately north of the city of South Bend, Indiana. Its twin lakes and many wooded areas provide a setting of natural beauty for more than ninety University buildings. The total University enrollment is about 9,700 students, of whom approximately 7,400 are enrolled at the undergraduate level. The Law School has 520 students and the Graduate Division of the College of Business Administration has 330, while the Graduate School has an enrollment of 1,300 students. The student body is drawn from every state in the Union and more than fifty countries.

The South Bend–Mishawaka area is an important industrial, trade, service, and professional center in northern Indiana and has a combined population of 150,000. Recreation in the area is served by fifty-nine city parks, sixty-six intersecting-street center parks, six 18-hole golf courses, and county facilities that offer canoeing, skiing, camping, and other recreation. Medical and religious needs are adequately met by three hospitals and over 220 churches and synagogues of all major denominations.

Facilities

The new College of Business complex houses a world-class facility that includes state-of-the-art appointments, such as fiber optics and networked classrooms, a graduate electronic library, and classrooms designed for case study.

Technology Environment

Ten public clusters throughout the campus include 448 workstations and several dedicated terminals. The clusters and most academic buildings are linked in a fiber-optics-based network to campus resources, including the Hesburgh Library's on-line catalog, an all-inclusive electronic mail system, a campuswide information system, and research computing facilities. The Notre Dame Network provides access to national supercomputing and data resource facilities via its regional link to the Internet.

Placement

The goal of the M.B.A. Career Development (MBACD) office is to increase the quality and quantity of employment opportunities and to assist students in making informed career decisions. It provides students with the resources to define job objectives, to explore career options, and to identify potential employers consistent with individual qualifications and career plans. In addition to overseeing on-campus recruiting, the program participates in the National M.B.A. Consortium in Chicago, a nontraditional placement opportunity for students to interview with over thirty-five national and multinational corporations. MBACD works with alumni clubs throughout the United States to organize networking events to bring current students and alumni together. Other services provided include a variety of workshops, a job-posting system that brings full-time and summer intern opportunities to students (over 350 in 1994), a résumé referral service, and résumé books.

Admission

In making its decisions, the admissions committee considers the results of the Graduate Management Admission Test (GMAT), work experience, undergraduate academic record, letters of recommendation, track record of leadership, and answers to the essays. The GMAT scores averaged between 570 and 580 for the enrolled 1994 class, and their average undergraduate GPA was 3.12. International applicants whose native language is not English must take the Test of English as a Foreign Language (TOEFL) and score a minimum of 600.

Admission to the two-year program is granted for the fall semester only, and the three-semester program begins only in the summer. All applicants are strongly encouraged to schedule an evaluative interview.

Finances

The estimated tuition for Notre Dame graduate students for 1995–96 is approximately $18,000. Books and supplies average $2000 per year.

Living expenses, including housing, food, and utilities, total around $6000 per academic year for an average single student living on or off campus. Married students should expect to increase their living expenses by about $150 a month.

Scholarships and fellowships are awarded primarily on merit. Completed applications must be submitted by February 24 to be considered for these awards. All applicants will be considered for scholarship awards if they mark the appropriate box on the application.

International Students

Approximately 25 percent of the M.B.A. student body are international and usually represent about twenty countries. International students have traveled from North and South America, Asia, East and West Europe, and Africa to study graduate business at Notre Dame.

The University's International Student Office (ISO) as well as the M.B.A. Student Association provides advice, information, and avenues for international students to ease their transition into the academic environment and enhance their educational experiences at Notre Dame.

Application Facts and Dates

Admission decisions are made on a rolling basis. Applicants to the two-year program must submit their material on or before May 10, 1996, with a decision being mailed four to six weeks after the application is completed. The deadlines for applicants to the three-semester program are December 1, 1995; January 12, 1996; and March 1, 1996. Decisions will be mailed on or before January 12, 1996; March 1, 1996; and April 12, 1996, respectively. For more information, applicants should contact:

Ms. Lee Cunningham
Director of Admissions
University of Notre Dame M.B.A.
  Program
109 Hurley
Notre Dame, Indiana 46556
Telephone: 219-631-8488
        800-631-8488 (toll-free
          within the U.S.)
Fax: 219-631-8800
E-mail: anthony.n.jowid.2@nd.edu

University of Oregon

Charles H. Lundquist College of Business

Eugene, Oregon

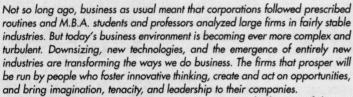

> Not so long ago, business as usual meant that corporations followed prescribed routines and M.B.A. students and professors analyzed large firms in fairly stable industries. But today's business environment is becoming ever more complex and turbulent. Downsizing, new technologies, and the emergence of entirely new industries are transforming the ways we do business. The firms that prosper will be run by people who foster innovative thinking, create and act on opportunities, and bring imagination, tenacity, and leadership to their companies.
>
> The Oregon M.B.A. program prepares managers to make the most of change. As students integrate the functional areas of business—accounting, decision sciences, finance, marketing, and management—they learn to recognize business opportunities and evaluate new ideas. Students gain the skills to scan globally, think creatively, and act quickly and surely to discover and take advantage of the opportunities created by the rapidly changing business environment.
>
> —Timothy W. McGuire, Dean

Programs and Curricular Focus

The M.B.A. program provides a rigorous and challenging exposure to the concepts and techniques of successful management, preparing students for a variety of managerial positions in a wide range of industries and countries. Students gain foundation skills and knowledge in accounting, decision sciences, finance, international business, and marketing while learning how to identify, evaluate, and manage business opportunities. The integrated first-year core requires students to address management decisions through an interactive, cross-disciplined approach. Case analyses, business simulations, group projects, and oral presentations are an integral part of many classes.

The University offers the following degree programs: M.B.A. (regular two-year program, accelerated one-year program for students who were undergraduate business majors); J.D./M.B.A.; M.B.A./M.A. in international studies or Asian studies; M.S. in industrial relations; and Ph.D.

Students and the M.B.A. Experience

A majority of M.B.A. students come to Oregon with some work experience; the average is 4.5 years. Thirty-two percent of the class are women, 60 percent have a nonbusiness bachelor's degree, and the average age is 27 (the range is 21 to 45). Fifty percent of the students come from the West Coast, and 35 percent are international, representing twenty countries.

Oregon M.B.A. students are a diverse group in terms of age, cultural background, and personal and professional experience. They work together in dozens of teams as they analyze cases and consult with businesses in the region, pooling problem-solving skills in a supportive environment. Small class size and an emphasis on group work ensure that students get to know one another well, developing solid working relationships and strong friendships across all boundaries. Students may choose to enhance their international education by studying abroad in Japan, France, the Netherlands, or Denmark.

Special Features

The Lundquist Center for Entrepreneurship promotes entrepreneurship across the curriculum. The center sponsors speakers, a $10,000 New Venture Competition, and student-run clubs and activities. It houses an extensive library of books, cases, and videotapes. The center also sponsors internships whereby students gain invaluable experience in the dynamics of new industries and growth ventures. Courses available include a business design class offered in collaboration with the architecture and journalism schools.

The Lundquist College of Business participates in the BELL program, which integrates environmental issues into the curriculum. Students may augment their M.B.A. with projects and classes offered through environmental studies.

The Warsaw Sports Marketing Center brings guest speakers and internship opportunities to students.

The Faculty

Thirty-nine faculty members—24 percent are women—teach in the M.B.A. program. Most have taught, worked, and traveled extensively overseas; they bring an international perspective, reflecting the global marketplace. Faculty members are readily accessible for academic advising, consulting, and support.

The Business School Network

Many advanced courses are built around student projects that involve firms in the region. Teams may develop a business plan, research a new product, or value assets for such firms as Fax Back, Inc., In Focus Systems, Intel Corporation, Full Sail Brewing Company, Hewlett-Packard, Percon, and Dynamix. Alumni and/or recent speakers include Edwin Artzt, Chairman and CEO, Proctor and Gamble, Inc.; Gun Denhart, CEO, Hanna Andersson; Harry DeBoer, President, Avia Group International, Inc.; Junji Numata, Lexus Division, Toyota Motor Corporation; Julie Lewis, Founder, Deja Shoe, Inc.; Marc Fermont, Vice President, Dow Europe; Mike Coughlin, President, Percon, Inc.; and Jim Warsaw, Founder and former CEO, Sports Specialties.

The College and Environs

The University of Oregon, founded in 1876, is in a parklike setting located on 250 acres. M.B.A. students can draw upon up-to-the-minute business and economic resources through the Northwest's second-largest library. Eugene/Springfield (population 200,000) has excellent schools, low crime, exceptional recreational opportunities, and affordable housing. Woods and open spaces, green lawns and year-round flowers, and a mild, temperate climate create a congenial environment for learning and living. The spectacular Oregon coast and snow-covered Cascade mountains are each an hour's drive from campus. The University and Eugene's Hult Center for the Performing Arts combine to offer events to suit any taste, and Portland, Seattle, and San Francisco offer big-city getaways within easy travel distance.

Technology Environment

The Chiles Business Computing Laboratory serves as the focal point for computing and technology support to students in the M.B.A. program. The Computer Center offers both Windows-based and Macintosh computers housed in laboratories for M.B.A. students that provide settings for individual study, class instruction, and group study. Complementing the suite of software for word processing, spreadsheet analysis, presentation development, and statistical analysis offered in the center, new multimedia capabilities give students the ability to blend live video, sound, and animation.

Placement

The Career Services office provides extensive resources and services dedicated to empowering M.B.A. students to design and implement individual career campaigns. Workshops and counseling services focus on résumé writing, networking, in-

terviewing skills, negotiating, employment strategies, and internships. Special seminars and forums are scheduled by private industry and the public sector.

Admission

Students who are admitted to Oregon's M.B.A. program have demonstrated their ability and potential to become responsible and effective managers. The average GPA in the program is 3.2, the average GMAT score is 570, and the average TOEFL score is 620. Applicants are evaluated by their professional work experience, academic performance, and demonstrated leadership. No arbitrary cut-off scores or single criterion is applied, and all applicants are given the fullest consideration.

Finances

Tuition fees for the 1994–95 academic year were $5385 for the Oregon resident and $8760 for the nonresident. Off-campus housing is approximately $4050 for a year; on-campus housing is approximately $1900. Personal expenses, books, and supplies total $3375. Oregon has no sales tax; UO students ride free on the bus. Various types of financial assistance are available in the form of tuition waivers, scholarships, loan programs, and work-study employment.

International Students

International students comprise 30 percent of each M.B.A. class, coming from several Asian countries, Western and Eastern Europe, Africa, and South America. Extensive academic and social support services are available to international students. A summer pre-M.B.A. program is available for international students to help them meet the linguistic and cultural demands of the M.B.A. program.

Application Facts and Dates

Applications for admission are due March 1. Admission is for the fall term only; however, accelerated M.B.A. students may apply for summer or fall. For more information, students should contact:

Wendy Mitchell, Director of M.B.A. Program
Graduate School of Management
Charles H. Lundquist College of Business
University of Oregon
Eugene, Oregon 97403
Telephone: 503-346-3302
Fax: 503-346-3341

FACULTY LIST

Gerald S. Albaum, Professor of Marketing; Ph.D., Wisconsin–Madison. International marketing, research methodology.

Roger J. Best, Professor of Marketing; Ph.D., Oregon. Marketing strategy and planning, new product analysis, industrial marketing.

David M. Boush, Associate Professor of Marketing; Ph.D., Minnesota. Consumer behavior, brand strategy, deceptive advertising.

Warren B. Brown, Professor of Management; Ph.D., Carnegie Mellon. Management of innovation, corporate policy and strategy.

Roger Chope, Senior Instructor; Ph.D., Oregon. Financial accounting.

Robert T. Clemen, Associate Professor of Decision Sciences; Ph.D., Indiana. Decision theory, Bayesian statistics, negotiation analysis.

Larry Dann, Professor of Finance and Taxation; Ph.D., UCLA. Corporate finance, corporate governance, valuation.

Diane G. Del Guercio, Assistant Professor of Finance; Ph.D., Chicago. Investments, corporate governance.

David Dusseau, Visiting Assistant Professor of Management; Ph.D., Oregon. Organizational theory and behavior.

Neil Fargher, Assistant Professor of Accounting; Ph.D., Arizona. Accounting information systems.

Gregory V. Frazier, Assistant Professor of Decision Sciences; Ph.D., Texas A&M. Production/operations management.

Marian Friestad, Associate Professor of Marketing; Ph.D., Wisconsin–Madison. Marketing communications, advertising.

Paul Frishkoff, Professor of Accounting; Ph.D., Stanford; CPA. Financial reporting, corporate external reporting.

Helen Gernon, Professor of Accounting; Ph.D., Penn State; CPA. International accounting, taxation.

Susan R. Glaser, Professor of Communication; Ph.D., Penn State. Team-building and communication, managing organizational culture.

Del I. Hawkins, Professor of Marketing; Ph.D., Texas at Austin. Corporate strategy, marketing research.

Lynne Kahle, Professor of Marketing; Ph.D., Nebraska. Consumer behavior, communications, applied social psychology.

Raymond D. King, Associate Professor of Accounting; Ph.D., Oregon; CPA. Financial accounting regulation, accounting information, firm values.

Marianne J. Koch, Assistant Professor of Management; Ph.D., Columbia. Human resource management, labor relations.

Sergio Koreisha, Professor of Decision Sciences; D.B.A., Harvard. Forecasting, energy modeling, production planning, strategic planning.

Timothy McGuire, Professor and Dean; Ph.D., Stanford. Individual and group decision making.

Nancy Melone, Associate Professor of Management; Ph.D., Minnesota. Information technologies and organization.

Alan D. Meyer, Professor of Management; Ph.D., Berkeley. Organizational theory and behavior, organization design.

Wayne H. Mikkelson, Professor of Finance; Ph.D., Rochester. Corporate finance, economics of organizations.

Dale Morse, Professor of Accounting; Ph.D., Stanford. Cost accounting, international financial markets, earnings and security returns.

Richard T. Mowday, Professor of Management; Ph.D., California, Irvine. Organizational behavior.

M. Megan Partch, Associate Professor of Finance; Ph.D., Wisconsin–Madison. Determinants of capital structure.

Mark M. Phelps, Senior Instructor; J.D., Oregon. International business law and social responsibility.

George A. Racette, Associate Professor of Finance; Ph.D., Washington (Seattle). Firm valuation, capital structure planning, financial policy.

Kenneth D. Ramsing, Professor of Decision Sciences; Ph.D., Oregon. Operations research, production management.

James E. Reinmuth, Professor of Decision Sciences; Ph.D., Oregon State. Technological forecasting, strategic planning, effective leadership.

Larry E. Richards, Associate Professor of Decision Sciences; Ph.D., UCLA. Analytical modeling, nonparametric techniques.

Michael V. Russo, Assistant Professor of Management; Ph.D., Berkeley. Strategic management, management of regulated firms, technology policy, business-government relations.

Mark Spriggs, Assistant Professor of Marketing; Ph.D., Wisconsin–Madison. Marketing management, industrial marketing.

Nicole A. Steckler, Assistant Professor of Management; Ph.D., Harvard. Human resource management, organizational behavior.

Richard M. Steers, Professor of Management; Ph.D., California, Irvine. Organizational behavior, cross-cultural management.

James R. Terborg, Professor of Management; Ph.D., Purdue. Organizational psychology.

Gerardo R. Ungson, Professor of Management; Ph.D., Penn State. Business policy, international management.

Jennifer A. H. Van Heeckeren, Assistant Professor of Finance; Ph.D., Harvard. Market for corporate control, corporate finance.

University of Ottawa

Ottawa, Ontario, Canada

> ### NEW DIRECTION FOR THE M.B.A.
>
> *It is my firm belief that in order to develop business managers for the twenty-first century, the formula for success is to maintain an M.B.A. program that is sound, pragmatic, challenging, well-integrated, and technologically innovative.*
>
> *Let's face it, the University of Ottawa has been established as a bilingual university since 1848 and has an M.B.A. program that has recently celebrated twenty-five years of renowned success. Our graduates can be found in every corner of the universe as top managers or business leaders.*
>
> *There is no secret. We hire the best professors and search out the best students with promising potential and develop their interpersonal skills to be effective business leaders in a multicultural setting.*
>
> —Jean-Louis Malouin, Dean

Programs and Curricular Focus

The Faculty of Administration has embarked on a more general and all-encompassing approach, offering programs of study leading to the Master of Business Administration, the International M.B.A., the Master of Health Administration, and the Executive M.B.A., which is offered in the business school in both Ottawa and Hong Kong.

The Faculty of Administration offers joint programs with other faculties to include an M.B.A./LL.B. with the Faculty of Law and an M.B.A./L.L.L. in the Master of Science with the Departments of Computer Science, Mathematics, Economics, and Electrical Engineering.

The pedagogical approach is to use the classroom as a laboratory to test the decision-making and communication skills of the student by using live case scenarios in a problem-solving mode. The M.B.A. program is designed to prepare students to assume increasing managerial responsibilities in order to become effective business leaders in a changing business environment.

The structure of the M.B.A. program includes fourteen core courses that are compulsory. All first-year students include in their curriculum financial accounting, quantitative decision making, managerial competencies, and the application of information systems in management.

In the second year, students have the opportunity to choose elective courses in which the case study method is used to simulate and encapsulate a more action-oriented approach. This approach helps students acquire a strategic balance that once acquired is never entirely forgotten.

Students and the M.B.A. Experience

The presence of a significant number of students who work full-time and study part-time brings a certain amount of experience that enriches the teaching and learning process. The average length of work experience for part-time students is 4.89 years, while the minimum for full-time students is 2.65 years.

Because Ottawa is a bilingual university, teaching courses in both French and English, the student population is drawn from around the world, with strong concentration across Canada, the United States, Europe, and Asia. The students all have undergraduate business degrees in business administration or the social sciences and bring with them professional expertise from either the private or public sector.

The number of students in the program averages 650, of whom 200 are full-time and 450 are part-time. The percentage of women is 50 percent and 55 percent, respectively, for part-time and full-time students.

Although students work in teams on research projects, they also have the opportunity to complete a portion of the program abroad or include a thesis in their course work. Overall, the quality of the M.B.A. has been highly endorsed by Ottawa's graduate students and members of the public and private sectors.

❖ Global Focus

The Faculty of Administration International M.B.A. program covers broad international and environmental issues, such as trade policy, international business policy, and cross-cultural management, as well as functional topics, such as international business contracts, marketing, finance, accounting, human resources, industrial relations, information systems, and operations management. There is a required summer internship in an international setting in Canada or abroad. This opportunity provides students with valuable hands-on international management experience.

In addition, the Faculty plays an impressive role in the international field. The professors and students are active in virtually every corner of the world. They are called upon as experts by the United Nations and as advisers to international organizations and foreign governments.

Special Features

The Faculty believes that offering an M.B.A. in both official languages is a strong and innovative feature that exemplifies Canada's linguistic duality. Core courses are offered in both languages at least once every academic year, and sample electives are offered in both languages based upon demand. Individual students are not required to know both languages, as they may take the program entirely in either French or English.

The Faculty

The Faculty of Administration has over 90 full-time faculty members. This critical mass creates a strong academic environment that permits joint research activities and specialized seminars that would not be feasible with a smaller number of professors.

The ready availability of professional expertise from high-tech industry, the federal government, and other outside sources is a prime prerequisite for keeping up with future trends and technological advances. The Faculty's research output is commendable in terms of annual publications in professional journals.

The Business School Network

Corporate Partnerships

M.B.A. students work on co-op programs administered jointly by the University and both public and private enterprise. The program includes the Canadian Institute of Chartered Accountants, the Institute of Canadian Bankers, National Research of Canada, and the high-tech industry. Other corporate partnerships include the federal and provincial governments and a nonprofit unit that provide professional training and consulting as well as contract research activities.

Prominent Alumni

Some of the local alumni business leaders include Paul Desmarais, Chairman, Power Corporation Inc.; Richard Bertrand, Vice Chairman and Managing Director, Burson-Marsteller, Executive Consultants; Jocelyne Côté O'Hara, President and Chief Executive Officer, Stentor Telecom Policy, Inc.; Pierre Gravelle, Deputy Minister, National Revenue, Customs, Excise, and Taxation; and Manon Vennat, Chairman and Managing Director, Spencer Stuart (Montreal).

The College and Environs

The University is located in Canada's capital, which is considered the high-tech capital of the North. This represents a special opportunity for M.B.A. students to capitalize on employment opportunities and gain a significant amount of training in their field of endeavour.

Facilities

M.B.A. students have access to an on-line bibliographic service offered by the University, as well as to the specialized libraries of various government departments, including the National Library of Public Archives. Students also have access to books held in libraries of other universities in Ontario. Approximately 1.5 million books are maintained through circulation and are available to registered Ottawa students through various university libraries. These include the collection of Saint-Paul Library, which is federated with the University of Ottawa.

To facilitate the learning process, the computer facilities are constantly upgraded to maintain the latest in technology, information retrieval services, and programming.

Placement

The Faculty of Administration has a Career Services Office that accommodates students of both the undergraduate and graduate divisions of the University.

Because the Faculty has built strong ties with employers in the community, the office maintains a database of profes-

sional contacts. This has proved to be successful, as the alumni database is well-integrated into the information retrieval system. With institutional pride, the University draws on alumni who are found as top managers and business leaders in virtually every part of the world.

Admission

Students are admitted for September entrance only. Applications must be filed no later than March 1. Because of immigration requirements, students who are not from Canada, the United States, or Europe must apply no later than January 1. In addition to sending the application form and the appropriate application fee, candidates must submit official transcripts of all previous academic work, two letters of reference, an official record of scores on the GMAT, a narrative statement, and a curriculum vitae.

International students whose native language is neither English nor French must obtain a minimum score of 550 on the Test of English as a Foreign Language (TOEFL) or an equivalent result on a test of proficiency in French.

Finances

The program fees for the M.B.A. and M.H.A. programs are approximately Can$1200 per semester, with an application fee of Can$50. For the I.M.B.A. program, the program fees are Can$1200 per semester for Canadian students and Can$4600 for international students. In addition, there are accommodation fees averaging Can$3500 for a period of eight months. All I.M.B.A. students must pay full-time fees for summer internships and Can$50 for the application fee. The

Executive M.B.A. program's fees are Can$33,000 for two years; there is an additional Can$150 for the application fee.

On and off campus lodging is offered through the University Housing Services. Students can expect to pay from Can$2700 to Can$3500 per academic year. Graduate students are eligible for bursaries, loans, scholarships, and teaching assistantships. A limited number of entrance scholarships and differential fee waivers are also available for international students. Additional information is available at the Awards Office of the School of Graduate Sudies.

Application Facts and Dates

In accordance with admission requirements, all correspondence and information must be forwarded to the director of the specific program of interest by the due date. Deadlines are March 1 for fall and November 30 for spring (January 1 for fall and November 30 for spring for international students).

M.B.A., M.H.A., and I.M.B.A.
Faculty of Administration
University of Ottawa
136, Jean-Jacques Lussier
P.O. Box 450, Station A
Ottawa, Ontario K1N 6N5
Canada
Telephone: 613-562-5800
Fax: 613-562-5154

E.M.B.A.
Suite 350
World Exchange Plaza
University of Ottawa
45, O'Connor
Ottawa, Ontario K1P 1A4
Canada
Telephone: 613-564-9500
Fax: 613-564-9927

The Wharton School of the University of Pennsylvania

University of Pennsylvania

The Wharton School

Philadelphia, Pennsylvania

WHAT WILL IT TAKE TO LEAD IN THE TWENTY-FIRST CENTURY?

Modern organizations are undergoing fundamental transformations. As companies become more dynamic, more global, and more entrepreneurial, business leaders will need both broader and deeper skills to succeed.

From its founding in 1881 as the world's first school of management, Wharton has always been the leader in extending the frontiers of management education. Our new M.B.A. curriculum takes that leadership into the next century. The program builds upon Wharton's substantial strengths—our expertise across the widest range of areas, our extensive global initiatives, and our long-standing commitment to innovation and entrepreneurship. It breaks new ground to provide the new skills and perspectives that forward-thinking business leaders have identified as critical to success today and in the future.

The evolving business environment presents great challenges. The Wharton M.B.A. program is equally demanding. But both also offer tremendous opportunities for those with the insights, skills, and drive to succeed.

—Thomas P. Gerrity, Dean

Programs and Curricular Focus

Wharton's new curriculum is designed to generate innovative ideas and creative thinking and to instill an excitement about learning. Students are challenged through their core courses, case studies, and leadership course work to formulate and solve problems.

The first year focuses on Wharton's new business core, providing fundamental skill, knowledge, and perspectives. Traditional semesters are replaced by four tightly focused six-week quarters to expose students to the greatest number of subjects and to allow faculty to coordinate material across courses. Cohorts of 60 students, who take core courses together in the first year, form a strong social and academic group. Clusters of three cohorts form "a class within a class."

The second year allows students to choose electives from one of the largest selections of courses of any business school; this selection allows students to pursue one of two dozen majors or create joint majors or individualized programs. Students work individually and in 5-person learning teams to examine issues of self-awareness, teamwork, ethics, communication, effective negotiation, managing differences, managing careers, and power and authority.

The Lauder Institute offers a twenty-four-month joint-degree program to prepare future leaders to operate effec-

tively and comfortably in a language and culture other than their own. This program leads to an M.B.A. from Wharton and an M.A. in international studies from the University's School of Arts and Sciences.

Wharton also offers joint-degree programs, which generally require one less year of study, in the areas of communication, engineering, law, medical sciences, dental, veterinary, nursing, social work, and Wharton doctoral programs.

The Wharton Executive M.B.A. program enables individuals with full-time job responsibilities in the private and public sectors to gain an M.B.A. degree without interrupting their careers. Experienced executives and highly promising managers nominated by their organizations enroll in the program. Classes meet all day Friday and Saturday on alternate weekends for two years.

Students and the M.B.A. Experience

Wharton students have outstanding records of professional achievement and bring a wide range of experience, insights, and interests to the classroom and to campus. Drawing on their experiences throughout the world, students offer diverse cultural viewpoints on business issues. They bring perspectives from undergraduate majors that range from English to engineering and

work experience that extends from nonprofit management to marketing to corporate finance. Wharton M.B.A. students help shape the intellectual atmosphere of challenge and collaboration that is a central part of a Wharton education.

About 35 percent of incoming students have liberal arts and science degrees, and 17 percent have training in engineering. Almost all have had significant work experience in private, public, or nonprofit enterprises. Of an average class of 750 students entering Wharton each fall, about 27 percent are women, 15 percent are members of minority groups, and 33 percent are foreign nationals from more than sixty countries.

❖ Global Focus

Wharton's curriculum has a strong international perspective, reinforced by a core course on global strategic management and a range of electives that provide insights into global business. In addition, the Wharton Global Immersion Program option offers four weeks of intense, hands-on experience and education abroad, following six weeks of classroom study. Recent groups have traveled to Japan, Germany, Brazil, China, and Russia. Wharton also offers two international joint-degree programs, exchange programs with ten leading international business schools, and opportunities to develop foreign language skills.

Special Features

A four-week preterm program ensures that students from diverse backgrounds begin the M.B.A. program on equal academic footing. The program includes an introduction to accounting, microeconomics, and statistics and optional courses in humanities and business history. The program ends with a two-day team-building retreat.

Beyond cohorts and learning teams, students pursue individual interests through more than 125 professional, social, and academic affairs clubs and task forces. Wharton also offers opportunities to work on service projects with area students and community organizations.

The Faculty

Wharton's 179 standing faculty members bring a diversity of perspectives, both theoretical and practical, to the classroom. They have earned worldwide recognition for excellence in both teaching and research. Their work has extended the frontiers of many fields—from conducting groundbreaking studies in international finance to developing one of the most widely used methods of marketing research to creating the first center for the study of entrepreneurship. Wharton professors have received numerous awards, including the Nobel Prize in Economic Sciences and honors from the White House and the National Science Foundation.

The Business School Network

Corporate Partnerships

An advisory board of executives as well as corporate recruiters and alumni help shape the future development of the curriculum. In addition, more than 200 guest executive lecturers and speakers visit Wharton each year. In addition to contact with senior executives as guest lecturers in the classroom and in presentations and professional clubs, Wharton students have the opportunity to interact in a more intimate and informal context with business leaders through the Zweig Executive Dinner Series.

Prominent Alumni

Prominent alumni include the Hon. Walter H. Annenberg, a former ambassador and publisher; the Hon. William Brennan, a former chief justice; Charles S. Sanford Jr., Chairman, Bankers Trust; Reginald Jones, Chairman Emeritus, General Electric; Lewis Platt, Chairman and CEO, Hewlett-Packard; Yataro Kobayashi, Chairman and CEO, Fuji Xerox; Robert Crandall, CEO, American

Airlines; John Sculley, former CEO, Apple Computer; and Stanley R. Jaffe, COO, Paramount Communications.

The College and Environs

The University of Pennsylvania was founded in 1740 by Benjamin Franklin. The 260-acre Ivy League campus is located in University City, which contains several colleges, business and government offices, and one of the largest urban research parks in the nation. The University includes twelve leading graduate schools and serves more than 22,000 undergraduate, master's, and doctoral students.

Facilities

In addition to a University library with nearly 3.6 million volumes, students use Wharton's Lippincott Library, which contains approximately 200,000 volumes and 3,500 periodical titles specifically related to business, as well as copies of 5,000 corporate annual reports. Wharton's library computing center offers access to a variety of business, news, and information databases on optical disk and on-line.

Technology Environment

Computing facilities available to M.B.A. students include a cluster of Digital VAX 6400 mainframes, more than 125 microcomputers in student labs, and a Schoolwide data communications network accessible by modem. Wharton also offers training courses, user documentation, and consulting services.

Placement

The Wharton Career Development and Placement Office coordinates over thirty-five different programs for students, from identifying potential career areas and developing effective job search

strategies to interviewing, negotiating, and evaluating offers. Programs include career management classes in the first year, alumni career panels, videotaped interview training, and seminars on negotiating offers.

Admission

Prerequisites for admission include completion of an undergraduate program in an accredited U.S. college or its equivalent in another country, results of the Graduate Management Admission Test (GMAT) for which no minimum score is required, and completion of the Wharton application. A TOEFL score is required of all applicants for whom English is not the native language. Applicants are evaluated based on their personal qualities, academic background, and professional experience. Personal interviews are strongly encouraged but not required.

Finances

The 1995–96 educational budget for first-year students is $35,750. This cost includes tuition and fees, room and board, books and supplies, miscellaneous fees, and preterm expenses. Preterm fees apply only in the first year and vary, depending on the program components in which a student enrolls.

International Students

There is a strong international student community at Wharton, with resources and programs to meet social, cultural, and professional interests. International students make up one third of the M.B.A. student body, and they represent over sixty nationalities. Many of the campus club activities are generated by the cultural interests of M.B.A. students.

Application Facts and Dates

Although the final deadline for application is in early April, Wharton begins to evaluate applications and make admissions decisions in the middle of the previous November. Wharton uses a rolling admission process, evaluating applications in order of their receipt and completion. Applicants receive a decision approximately eight weeks after Wharton receives a completed application.

Mr. Samuel T. Lundquist
Director of M.B.A. Admissions
The Wharton School
University of Pennsylvania
3733 Spruce Street
Philadelphia, Pennsylvania 19104-6361
Telephone: 215-898-6182
Fax: 215-898-0120
Internet: mba.admissions@wharton.upenn.edu

University of Rochester

Rochester, New York

A SIMON SCHOOL EDUCATION—PREPARATION FOR A LIFETIME CAREER IN MANAGEMENT

The Simon School's integrated, cross-functional approach to management is enhanced by our small size and significant international composition. The small size promotes communication among faculty and students that is very difficult to achieve in a large, departmentalized school. The international student body, combined with the School's emphasis on student teams, brings the global workplace to life for the Simon School student.

—Charles I. Plosser, Dean

Programs and Curricular Focus

The Simon School's M.B.A. programs are designed to train individuals to solve management problems as team members in a study-team structure. The curriculum emphasizes learning the principles of economics and effective decision making through a mix of lecture, case study, and project courses. The degree program requires 67 hours (twenty quarter courses) and can be completed in six quarters of full-time study. Five core courses are required in the underlying disciplines of economics, applied statistics, accounting, and computers and information systems. One course must be taken in each of the functional areas of finance, marketing, operations management, and organization theory. A 2-credit course in business communications and a Total Quality Management capstone course are required of all full-time students. Ten elective courses are required, of which five or more may form a sequence of concentration, although a concentration is not required for graduation. The twelve areas of concentration offered are corporate accounting, public accounting, accounting and information systems, business environment and public policy, computers and information systems, entrepreneurship, finance, international management, marketing, operations management–manufacturing, operations management–services, and organizations and markets. Students may select an individualized double-concentration to customize their course of study in preparation for specific career objectives. Of the ten elective courses, one must include an integrative course in business policy or corporate strategy near the end of the M.B.A. program.

Students and the M.B.A. Experience

Each September approximately 150 students enter the Simon community as members of four cohorts (class teams). Another 50 students join their classmates in January as cohort number five. Each cohort takes all core classes together. September entrants complete the first-year core courses during the fall, winter, and spring quarters; the majority of January entrants complete core courses during the winter, spring, and summer quarters. Within each cohort, students are assigned to a study team of 4 or 5 members. Due to the large number of students from outside the United States (42 percent), the study-team structure at the Simon School takes on special significance. Each team always includes representatives from at least three countries.

Simon students enter the program with a wide range of educational, professional, and geographic backgrounds. In the class of 1996, 120 undergraduate institutions and twenty-six countries are represented. Undergraduate majors include economics, humanities, social sciences, business and commerce, engineering, and math and science. Prior full-time work experience averages 3.6 years, and the average age is 26. Women comprise 22 percent of the class. Twelve percent of Simon students are members of American minority groups.

❖ Global Focus

Of the leading business schools, the Simon School is one of the most geographically diverse. Over 40 percent of its students come from outside the United States. Approximately one third of

its alumni reside and work outside of the United States, and about one third of its tenure-track faculty members have non-U.S. backgrounds. The Simon School emphasizes the high percentage of international students because the success of its hands-on approach to global management education depends in part on the cultural, geographic, and professional composition of the student management teams. The benefits of such a richly internationalized student and alumni population are obvious. A Simon School education combines rigorous training in the business disciplines and functions with cross-cultural training and lifelong professional contact with an international alumni network.

During the Broaden Your Horizons seminar series, students present lunch hour seminars about their various countries' cultures, economies, political environments, and business protocols. Exchange programs are offered with schools in eight countries, each approved by a faculty committee for compatibility with Simon M.B.A. program objectives. Interested students pursue study abroad during one quarter of their second year of study.

Special Features

VISION: A Partnership for Developing Future Managers is the student-managed portion of the Simon School's M.B.A. program. Designed each year by a committee of second-year M.B.A. students, the VISION program consists of sixteen teaching modules that supplement and enhance the academic curriculum. Student managers use the human resources and expertise of corporate sponsors—in partnership with Simon administrators, faculty members, and other students—to present required (and some optional) modules covering such topics as time management, team building, negotiation skills, leadership training, and ethics. Past corporate partners have included AT&T, IBM, Levi-Strauss, PepsiCo, Wells Fargo Bank, and Xerox Corporation, among others.

To ensure that Simon School graduates possess effective oral and written communication skills, they are required to complete a management-communication sequence comprising two courses, Presentation Skills and Business Writing and Editing.

The Faculty

The Simon School faculty is known internationally for leading scholarship in management education. There is a long tradition at Simon of coordinating teaching and research, as well as integrating knowledge from all of the functional areas into the curriculum. Faculty accessibility is a specific benefit of a Simon education. Teaching awards for the best teachers are presented annually by each M.B.A. class, and teaching is improved continuously through a formal faculty peer-review. Leading-edge research is intrinsic to teaching the basic scientific principles of management. Many research findings used by the Simon faculty in classroom study have served as foundations for corporate practices in use today. Simon faculty members serve as editors on six major academic journals, and six recent studies of research productivity rank them among the top five faculties in the United States.

The Business School Network

Corporate Partnerships

The Frederick Kalmbach Executive Seminar Series, jointly sponsored by the Simon School and the Graduate Business Club, features senior corporate executives who lecture annually on current issues in management. Each year a number of the series' speakers include members or professional associates of Simon's internationally prominent Executive Advisory Committee. Simon students participate in an annual marketing-case competition sponsored by Procter & Gamble, and, through the VISION program described above, students interact directly with the employees of top international corporate partners. Students work directly with local worldwide corporations, such as Bausch & Lomb and Eastman Kodak Company, in project courses offered as part of the regular academic curriculum.

Prominent Alumni

The long list of successful Simon alumni includes Ronald L. Bittner, President and CEO, Frontier Corporation; Richard C. Couch, Principal, Diablo Management Group; Charles A. Dowd Jr., President, Plumbing Product Division, Masco Corporation; Mark B. Grier, Executive Vice President, Global Risk Management, The Chase Manhattan Bank, N.A.; Charles R. Hughes, President and CEO, Land Rover North America, Inc.; Karen Smith-Pilkington, General Manager and Vice President, Cardiology Group,

Eastman Kodak Company; and Joseph T. Willet, Senior Vice President and CFO, Merrill Lynch, Inc.

The College and Environs

The Simon School is part of the ivy-clad University of Rochester, an independent leading research university offering graduate study in approximately fifty fields to about 2,200 of its 6,600 students. Situated near Lake Ontario, one of the Great Lakes, the metropolitan Rochester area (population 1 million) is home to many major international industries and entrepreneurial ventures, including Eastman Kodak Company, Bausch & Lomb, and Xerox Corporation's marketing group. Numerous cultural and recreational opportunities include the Rochester Philharmonic Orchestra and the University's own Eastman School of Music.

Facilities

Schlegel Hall, opened in 1991, is the Simon School's classroom and student services building. It contains case-style classrooms equipped with state-of-the-art technology and rear projection equipment, study rooms, a student lounge, and its own Computing Center. The center supports student-accessible IBM-compatible and Macintosh personal computers linked for data sharing and laser printing via local area networks and access to several external data sources, such as Bloomberg, Business News, and Dow Jones, as well as e-mail services on the Internet. On-campus graduate housing, both high-rise apartments and town houses, is available to Simon students.

Placement

The hallmark of the Career Services Office is personalized support for the internship and full-time M.B.A. job search. Campus interviews are the leading source of offers (27 percent), with off-site recruiting events in New York City and Atlanta, Georgia; résumé referrals; *The Hire Authority* (job listing newsletter for Simon students); and résumé books accounting for another 33 percent annually. The mean accepted offer for 1994 graduates was $51,708, with salary offers ranging from $32,450 to $107,500.

Admission

A Simon School Admissions Committee reads each application individually and evaluates recommendations, teamwork and communication skills, the nature and scope of prior work experience, the undergraduate academic record, GMAT scores, TOEFL scores as an indicator of

English-language skills, evidence of leadership and maturity, and career focus. English language proficiency is critically important for successful interaction in the Simon School's geographically diversified study-team structure. Potential contributions to Simon classmates and to the world's business community are carefully considered. All undergraduate majors are represented in the program.

Finances

In addition to the $75 application fee, tuition was $636 per credit hour or $19,080 per year in 1994–95. The cost of books and supplies averages $750 a year, and living expenses (rent, food supplies, personal expenses, and health insurance) were estimated at under $9900 for the 1994–95 academic year. Both U.S. and international applicants are eligible for merit awards. The deadline for applying for merit-scholarship assistance is March 1 for September applicants and November 15 for January applicants.

International Students

There is an active program of support for international students in Rochester. In addition to Simon International, a graduate business school student organization, the University of Rochester's International Student Affairs Office provides professional guidance to incoming international students. They are assisted by an independent, but University-affiliated, community volunteer group, the Rochester International Friendship Council, which locates host families for interested Simon students and helps students' spouses in language instruction and acculturation. Social outings and employment and cultural adjustment workshops are offered during late August orientation for all University international students. Instruction in English as a second language is also available.

Application Facts and Dates

Application deadlines are March 1 (for merit-scholarship consideration) and June 1 for September enrollment, November 15 for January enrollment. Students are notified of admissions decisions on a rolling basis. For additional information, students should contact:

Priscilla E. Gumina
Assistant Dean for M.B.A. Admissions and Administration
William E. Simon Graduate School of Business Administration
University of Rochester
Rochester, New York 14627-0107
Telephone: 716-275-3533
Fax: 716-271-3907

⳨USF University of San Francisco

San Francisco, California

▶ The Executive M.B.A. program at the University of San Francisco is offered in response to a consistently expressed need in the business community for a high-quality M.B.A. program in an accredited school of business addressing the specific needs of practicing and experienced professionals. This exciting and innovative format is embedded with three essential features. First, participants can earn an M.B.A. in less than two years while continuing full-time employment. Second, each Executive M.B.A. class moves through the program as a unit so that there can be a maximum learning experience both from the faculty and fellow students. Finally, the program reflects the needs of our times with its emphasis on international issues and state-of-the-art management skills.

Program participants work with first-rate faculty members, each of whom has a combination of academic and practical experience to bring to the classroom.

The USF Executive M.B.A. meets a variety of needs and provides professional experience in direct response to the educational priorities of both individuals and companies in the San Francisco Bay Area.

—Gary Williams, Dean

FACULTY LIST

Steven Alter, Ph.D., Professor of Information Systems and Decision Sciences.
Arthur H. Bell, Ph.D., Professor of Business Communication.
Alev Efendioglu, Ph.D., Professor of Management.
Shenzho Fu, Ph.D., Associate Professor of Marketing.
Stephen J. Huxley, Ph.D., Professor of Business Administration.
Nicholas Imparato, Ph.D., Professor of Management and Marketing.
Kathleen Kane, Ph.D., Associate Professor of Management.
Laurie Macpherson, M.B.A., Assistant Professor of Management.
Nanshi P. Matsuura, D.B.A., Professor of International Business.
Robert N. Mefford, Ph.D., Professor of International Business and Operations Management.
Michael Middleton, Ph.D., Professor of Information Systems and Decision Sciences.
L. W. Murray Jr., Ph.D., Professor of Finance.
Denis Neilson, Professor of Accounting, Associate Dean and Director of E.M.B.A. Program, Ph.D.
Joel Lee Oberstone, Ph.D., Professor of Decision Sciences.
Richard Puntillo, M.B.A., Associate Professor of Finance.
William Rodgers, M.B.A., Associate Professor of Management.
Dayle M. Smith, Ph.D., Associate Professor of Management.
Heinz Weihrich, Ph.D., Professor of International Business and Management.
Gary Williams, Ph.D., Professor of Management and Dean.

Program and Curricular Focus

The Executive M.B.A. program comprises a sequence of courses judged to be appropriate to the graduate education of executive-level managers of organizations for the twenty-first century global business environment. Successful completion of the program prepares the individual for career changes and advancement within organizations and also for undertaking entrepreneurial opportunities.

The E.M.B.A. program encompasses a blend of theory and practice in that participants are exposed to current conceptual and theoretical ideas accompanied by demonstrated real-world applications and implementations. Throughout all courses in the program, five major themes are presented: global perspectives, social philosophy and ethics, communication skills, leadership and group dynamics, and creative problem solving.

Students and the E.M.B.A. Experience

The Executive M.B.A. program of the McLaren Graduate School of Management provides the individual seeking personal and professional growth and development with the means to achieve those goals. The various program components—formal lectures, class discussions and debates, group and individual projects and presentations, lab and tutorial workshops, study groups, exams and assignments, and informal and social activities—all contribute to a rich, total learning environment. Add to that the experience, ability, and diversity of both faculty and students, and a dynamic, synergistic setting for education and intellectual growth is created and sustained.

❖ Global Focus

Shifting national competitive advantages, instantaneous global communications, and an emerging multicultural workforce are redefining traditional assumptions about management and markets. Businesses worldwide face enormous challenges, as each strives to expand its market share in fast-growing global markets. National domestic agendas concerning public education, job training, and health care will help determine competitive success or failure as much as international trade laws, the relative strength of currencies, and the availability of natural resources.

Special Features

The program commences with a four-day, intensive learning experience that allows students to be reexposed to basic academic skills that are a fundamental requirement for success in the course work ahead. Workshops, exercises, presentations, discussions, and other learning activities are provided, covering the areas of mathematics and statistics; computer skills; writing, communications, and presentation skills; and group study, learning, and problem-solving skills.

The International Study Tour continues to be a key centerpiece and a distinguishing feature of the program. Faculty and students visit major business enterprises in overseas venues for a two-week period each July.

The Faculty
The faculty of the McLaren School of Business is dedicated to the personal and professional development of its students. Faculty members bring to the classroom an innovative enthusiasm for education and a functional expertise developed over years of experience in their fields.

The Business School Network
Corporate Partnerships
During its first five years of operation, the E.M.B.A. program has attracted and is sustaining the support of many major international (Fortune 500) corporations. Each E.M.B.A. class has included students receiving full or partial financial support of their employers, who include IBM, AT&T, Procter & Gamble, Pacific Bell, Bank of America, and Pacific Gas & Electric.

Graduates have secured in-house promotions or career advancements with new employers on the basis of their academic achievements and experiences in the E.M.B.A. program. Several instances of new entrepreneurial ventures have also occurred.

The practicum component of the program, where new students undertake a major strategic planning assignment with

practical applicability, has been instrumental in assisting students in these regards.

The College and Environs
USF is a 55-acre hilltop refuge, with views of the Pacific Ocean, the San Francisco Bay, and the downtown skyline. The campus is situated in a centrally located residential neighborhood, with excellent public transportation to the rest of the city and beyond. Key campus landmarks are the St. Ignatius Church; the Koret Health and Recreation Center, with its indoor Olympic-size swimming pool; and the historic Lone Mountain campus, all within walking distance of Golden Gate Park.

Facilities
E.M.B.A. classes are conducted in the McLaren Executive Classroom, designed for and dedicated to executive education programs. The room features modern instructional display capabilities; comfortable, flexible seating arrangements; food and beverage facilities; and computer, TV, VCR, and radio access.

Technology Environment
Students have access to a wide range of modern educational technological

resources. Computer facilities explore and promote the use of high-technology systems through basic and applied research areas such as technology-based instructional systems and technology-based business systems. Teleconferencing services are available, along with in-class videotaping and a variety of audiovisual instructional display media.

Admission
Admission to the Executive M.B.A. program is available to individuals who satisfy the following criteria: submission of transcripts of undergraduate college degree (and any advanced degrees); full-time employment experience of at least ten years, with at least five years of significant management experience; completion of an admissions essay; three letters of reference, including one from the applicant's current immediate supervisor; and satisfactory completion of the GMAT examination (prior to graduation).

Finances
The amount of tuition for the E.M.B.A. program is determined each spring by the Board of Trustees of the University. For 1995 admissions, the estimated total program cost is $42,500. This amount is an all-inclusive charge and includes registration and tuition for instruction and payment for textbooks, journals, magazines, and other required reading materials; educational software; meals and refreshments while attending regular class sessions; on-campus parking; membership at USF Koret Recreation facility; basic travel and accommodation while participating in the international study tour; and duplicating services for course-related materials.

Several loan programs are available to E.M.B.A. students. Information on these programs is available from the E.M.B.A. Program Office or from the University's Financial Aid Office.

Application Facts and Dates
One class (cohort) of approximately 30 students is admitted to the E.M.B.A. program in August each year. Applications are accepted year-round until July 15 of the year of admission. For full information, contact:

E.M.B.A. Program Office
McLaren School of Business
University of San Francisco
2130 Fulton Street
San Francisco, California 94117-1080
Telephone: 415-666-2511
Fax: 415-666-2052
Internet: raher@usfca.edu

University of South Carolina

Columbia, South Carolina

> ### INNOVATION—THE KEY TO SUCCESS
>
> *Since 1946, innovation has been the key to the success of the University of South Carolina's College of Business Administration. We have a history of keeping pace with the ever-changing global market through a blend of academic preparation and real-world experience. Through three different degree options and many elective course offerings, we offer students the opportunity to choose their area of specialization. By emphasizing internships, consulting projects, and study-abroad programs, the College has earned international recognition. We continue to believe that such innovation is essential for business students in a world of few boundaries and constant change.*
>
> *—David L. Shrock, Dean*

Programs and Curricular Focus

The College offers a Master of International Business Studies (M.I.B.S.) program, a Master of Business Administration (M.B.A.) program, and an International Master of Business Administration (I.M.B.A.) program.

The M.I.B.S. core curriculum spans all of the traditional disciplines in business administration, but with courses that are fully international in scope. Core courses are taught in four- to eight-week integrated modules, as well as some full-semester core and elective courses. Students start in the summer (June) or fall term, depending on undergraduate degree and foreign language proficiency. The M.I.B.S. program currently offers the following language tracks for U.S. nationals: Chinese, French, German, Italian, Japanese, Portuguese, Russian, and Spanish. Chinese and Japanese are three-year language tracks, and all others are two-year language tracks. All foreign national applicants are carefully screened for English language skills and enter the two-year foreign national (English) track. All M.I.B.S. students are required to learn a foreign language and to develop that language as well as cultural understanding through a six-month internship in a country where that language is spoken (foreign nationals in the United States).

The M.B.A. core curriculum of thirteen courses (39 hours) focuses on the fundamentals of business administration and starts in the fall of each year. In addition, five elective courses (15 hours) enable students to further develop their skills in a variety of areas or to specialize in a particular area of their choice. All

eighteen of these courses are taught in four traditional sixteen-week semesters. The required summer (between first and second year) field consulting project (6 hours) places teams of students in a consulting environment with corporations, nonprofit organizations, or government agencies. Study abroad as a part of the M.B.A. program is also encouraged. The combined 60-hour program prepares students from all educational backgrounds to assume managerial positions.

The International Master of Business Administration (I.M.B.A.) program, the College's most recent innovation in graduate business education, is a joint venture with Austria's most prestigious business school, the Wirtschaftsuniversität Wien (WU-Wien), more commonly known as the Vienna University of Economics and Business Administration. Through this partnership, the College is able to offer a fifteen-month, 45-credit-hour, all English language program of instruction leading to the I.M.B.A. degree. The I.M.B.A. core curriculum is a combination of the traditional M.B.A. and M.I.B.S. programs, with the first seven months of instruction in Vienna and the next eight months at USC. The curriculum includes twelve months of intensive business course work followed by a three-month project in management consulting. The instruction in Vienna is conducted by faculty from both WU-Wien and USC, while the instruction in Columbia is conducted by USC faculty. The program starts at WU-Wien each May, with two terms of highly integrated business course modules. After completing this core curriculum in Vienna, the

students come to USC for a semester of four electives and a capstone course on strategy and policy in a global enterprise. I.M.B.A. students then complete their curriculum with the field consulting project.

Students and the M.B.A. Experience

The students in USC's graduate business programs come from a wide variety of backgrounds, with qualifications varying from program to program. The total enrollment for all three programs for fall 1994 was 560 students. Women represent 34 percent of this student population, while minorities represent 5 percent. Foreign national students make up 24 percent of the student body; this adds greatly to the global perspective in business, as these students bring their experiences to the classroom. The typical entering student is 27 years old and has approximately four years of work experience.

The Faculty

The faculty of USC's College of Business Administration has strong research interests that have won national and international visibility. Publishing nearly 100 articles and over a dozen books in a typical year, the faculty remains on the cutting edge of the various academic disciplines represented in the College.

The Business School Network

The College's ties to the business community are strong, and these ties play several critical roles in the educational process. Relationships with local, national, and international corporations lead to field consulting projects for M.B.A. and I.M.B.A. students, to internships for M.I.B.S. students, and to employment opportunities for all graduates. The USC-Business Partnership Foundation is composed of business and academic leaders who play an active leadership role for the College and are an integral part of the review process for curriculum and other program innovations.

The H. William Close and Francis M. Hipp buildings comprise the College of Business Administration's nine-story complex. The twin towers symbolize the working partnership between the College and the business community in South Carolina.

The College and Environs

Founded in 1801, the University of South Carolina's main campus (and the College of Business Administration) is located in downtown Columbia, the state's capital. The University has a total enrollment of more than 38,000 students, including USC's two other four-year campuses and five regional campuses. USC is a progressive, comprehensive institution committed to excellence in education and public service. On the Columbia campus, eleven colleges offer seventy-nine undergraduate degree programs. The commitment extends to the continued development and support of graduate education, and research is a priority. This commitment has led to growth in the variety and number of graduate programs available. Currently, USC enrolls more than 11,000 graduate students.

The city of Columbia is the seat of state government, is rich in culture and history, and is considered one of the most progressive cities in the Southeast. The current metropolitan population of 453,000 is expected to rise to 510,700 by the year 2000. The state's economy is flourishing, thanks to the tourism industry, foreign and domestic business, and industry giants. Government and industry are working together to provide excellent employment opportunities throughout the state.

South Carolinians appreciate the fine arts and are committed to the cultivation of the arts throughout the state. Columbia is the home of several outstanding museums and the nationally ranked Riverbanks Zoo. Diverse vacation spots are abundant throughout the state, including ocean resorts, historic cities, and the Blue Ridge Mountains.

Facilities

The College of Business Administration is housed in the H. William Close and Francis M. Hipp buildings. The twin towers of the complex symbolize the working partnership between the College and the business community. Within the complex, the College is relatively self-sufficient with its business library, computer center, classrooms, and faculty offices. The library features a circulation collection that includes business and industrial directories and publications, with approximately 100 current subscriptions and back issues of selected magazines and newspapers and nearly 500 journals in microfilm format. Students also have access to the University's main library, which seats 2,500 users at one time and allows access to more than 7 million volumes, microfilm entries, manuscripts, and periodicals. The computer center has 128 interactive workstations accessing a large open-system network comprising multiple Novell and UNIX servers, with 650 clients and more than 32 billion characters of on-line storage. Through the campus network, users also have access to numerous software packages and mainframe processing.

Placement

Most placement services are coordinated by the College's Graduate Placement Office, which acts as a liaison between graduate students and prospective employers. In addition to on-campus interviewing opportunities, students benefit from the following available resources: a résumé book, correspondence recruiting, placement referral network, career development seminars, and the M.I.B.S. alumni job bank.

Admission

Every applicant's complete file, including his or her academic record, résumé, required essays, and GMAT scores, is evaluated through comparison with the current applicant pool for the appropriate program. Average GMAT scores and GPAs vary for the different programs, with M.I.B.S. being the most selective (a 1994 average GMAT score of 611 and an average GPA of 3.37). The College looks for reasons to admit students, not a reason to decline them.

Finances

Tuition for 1995–96 for all M.B.A. and M.I.B.S. students is estimated at $1670 per semester for in-state students and $3373 per semester for out-of-state students. There is a one-time, nonrefundable enrichment fee for the M.B.A. program of $2900 for in-state students and $4400 for out-of-state students. The M.I.B.S. program enrichment fee is estimated at $5000 in-state and $8800 out-of-state. Tuition and fees for the I.M.B.A. program are $22,000 total cost, with no enrichment fees.

A number of graduate assistantships and fellowships are available. Applications for these awards are considered in February, and the awards are based on merit, not need.

Application Facts and Dates

For best consideration, applications for all programs should be submitted by February 1. All applications for assistantships and fellowships must be received by February 1. Applications for all programs will be considered until the program is full or until approximately one month prior to the start of the program. For more information or an application package, students should contact:

Graduate Division, PGG95
College of Business Administration
University of South Carolina
Columbia, South Carolina 29208
Telephone: 803-777-4346
Fax: 803-777-0414

University of Southern California

Los Angeles, California

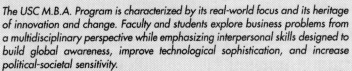

THE USC M.B.A.—A BUSINESS EDUCATION FOR THE REAL WORLD

The USC M.B.A. Program is characterized by its real-world focus and its heritage of innovation and change. Faculty and students explore business problems from a multidisciplinary perspective while emphasizing interpersonal skills designed to build global awareness, improve technological sophistication, and increase political-societal sensitivity.

Working with one of the largest alumni networks of any business school in the world, we have created an environment that fosters innovative ways of understanding and improving business today. Teams of students are often assigned to tackle tough, real-world issues by applying theoretical concepts to real-time business problems in both profit and nonprofit settings.

The USC M.B.A. is a business education for the real world.

—Randolph W. Westerfield, Dean

Programs and Curricular Focus

The USC M.B.A. Program prepares men and women to become leaders at all levels of organizations in all sectors of the economy. Intellectual and practical in nature, the two-year M.B.A. program provides grounding in the functional business disciplines, hones analytic tools required to address management problems, and develops the interpersonal and communication skills necessary to lead. Throughout the program, the responsibilities of leadership are framed in terms of both the organization and society. Along with the program's real-world focus, an emphasis on teamwork and the development of interpersonal skills are key elements of the USC M.B.A. Program.

Year one is structured around a set of required courses designed to establish a basis for assuming the general manager role. In the second year, students design their curriculum individually, choosing to concentrate in a specific area of business or to pursue a general path. The thirteen required courses of the first year are arrayed sequentially in a graduated system in which concepts in one discipline are introduced to correspond with, and build upon, concepts established earlier in others. Courses begin and end at varying points within the academic year, allowing analytical tools to be introduced in a practical order as needed for application in functional business areas. Throughout the first year, faculty members work closely with one another, integrating selected material across

courses and sharing time in the same classroom to illustrate links across disciplinary boundaries. The second year of the M.B.A. program builds on the knowledge of business fundamentals established during the first year and offers students the opportunity to pursue particular interests in depth. The thirteen required courses of year one give way to the single requirement of a field course in year two. The program's flexibility allows students to tailor a course of study to their individual needs and long-term career objectives. The Dean's International Fellows Program, which provides international exchange opportunities with more than thirty leading business schools on six continents, is available in year two.

Joint-degree options are available combining the M.B.A. with the J.D. (Juris Doctor), M.S. in industrial engineering, Master of Planning, Master of Real Estate Development, Doctor of Pharmacy, M.S. in nursing, M.S. in gerontology, and Doctor of Dental Surgery degrees. The School also offers an evening M.B.A. program; the Executive M.B.A. Program; the intensive, twelve-month midcareer M.B.A. program (IBEAR), which emphasizes international business; an M.S. in business administration degree program, designed for those holding an M.B.A. degree who wish to pursue an area of specialization; an M.S. in information and operations management; the Master of Accounting; the

Master of Business Taxation; and a Ph.D. in business degree program.

Students and the M.B.A. Experience

The USC M.B.A. Program enrolls approximately 200 students each year. The class is divided into four "core" sections, composed to reflect the diversity of the overall student body. The average USC M.B.A. student is 28 years of age, with between four and five years of work experience. International students comprise approximately 15 percent of the student population and represent more than twenty countries from around the world. Twenty-eight percent of the students are women. Every geographic region and major ethnic group of the United States is represented, with 15 percent African, Hispanic, and Native Americans as part of the class.

Special Features

At orientation, the entering class, second-year M.B.A. students, and core faculty and staff members engage in a series of intellectual and physical exercises aimed at demonstrating the power of teams to accomplish challenging tasks in high-quality ways. Sustained project teams, established at orientation, return to campus and become responsible for collaborative work in selected first-year classes. Throughout the fall and the early spring semester, these groups are evaluated and receive feedback on not only their completed projects but also their teamwork skills.

The Faculty

There are more than 160 faculty members in the School of Business Administration, with expertise in such areas as accounting, entrepreneurship, real estate, consulting, finance, human resources management, marketing, operations, information systems, business economics, regulation, international business, the management of nonprofit organizations, and health care. They are noted for their cutting-edge research, for a constant drive to apply the business theories they develop to the real world, for teaching excellence in the classroom, and for an open-door policy toward students.

The Business School Network
The more than 40,000 alumni of the USC School of Business form a renowned global network and have achieved remarkable success in the national and international business community. Dedicated alumni encourage their companies to recruit USC M.B.A. students and regularly return to campus to speak about careers, act as mentors, and provide consulting opportunities.

The College and Environs
Located on the University's main campus on 150 park-like acres just south of the downtown Los Angeles business center, the Graduate School of Business Administration (GSBA) is well positioned in a city where the diversity of manufacturing, financial, telecommunications, and trade activities rivals that of many countries. Increasingly dominant as America's gateway to the Pacific Rim, Los Angeles provides an incomparable learning laboratory for developing managers. The opportunity to mesh hands-on business experience with classroom study has long been a mark of distinction of the USC M.B.A. Program.

Technology Environment
Each classroom is equipped as a multimedia instructional environment with full Internet access. More than 225 state-of-the-art microcomputers and numerous laser printers are available within the School for student use. Regularly

conducted workshops provide training on the large array of applications accessible through the School's network software library. In addition, a large collection of instructional videotapes and an inventory of presentation graphics equipment are maintained for student use. The business libraries offer electronic gateways to LEXIS/NEXIS, the major research information repositories of the world, and to a collection of over 150 informational databases. Study carrels are wired into the network for laptop computer use. Five mini-studios provide instructional videotaping for the development of business and presentation skills.

Placement
The Office of Career Services is designed specifically to assist graduate-level students in the career planning and placement process. It provides services such as seminars and workshops, career counseling, job data and resources, résumé books, on-site visits by corporate recruiters, and opportunities to sharpen interviewing and negotiating skills. In addition, events such as Brown Bag Lunches, Industry Nights, and Days-on-the-Job offer students opportunities to meet and exchange information with prospective employers in informal settings.

Admission
The USC M.B.A. Program is academically and culturally diverse. It seeks applicants from all areas of the nation

and the world and from every ethnic group. Successful applicants are those whose profiles include a strong undergraduate record, a competitive GMAT score, significant work experience, effective communication skills, and evidence of leadership potential. International applicants must also submit an official TOEFL score. Full-time students are accepted for the fall semester only.

Finances
Tuition and fees for the 1994–95 academic year totaled approximately $17,620. Books and supplies cost approximately $2000 per year. Living expenses, including housing, transportation, and miscellaneous costs, are estimated at $15,740 per year.

USC is committed to enrolling the best-qualified students and to assisting them in meeting their financial needs. Through the generosity of alumni, corporations, and interested individuals, the School awards substantial funds to M.B.A. students each year. The GSBA awards fellowships and scholarships based on scholastic merit, evidence of leadership, GMAT scores, and full time work experience. Awards are granted for the fall and spring semesters only. Recipients must be U.S. citizens or permanent residents who are enrolled in the full-time program. Awards vary from full tuition to partial tuition; most are half-tuition fellowships. U.S. students may also apply for need-based financial aid through the University's Financial Aid Office.

International Students
USC has one of the largest populations of international students of any private university in the U.S. Within the business school, approximately 15 percent of the full-time M.B.A. class comes from outside the U.S. A six-day, presemester International Institute combines programs and activities to help international students become acclimated to Los Angeles, the University, and the M.B.A. program.

Application Facts and Dates
The School offers an early application deadline of December 1 for those who want to know their admissions decisions by January 31. All applications for full-time study must be received by March 15. Early application is encouraged. For more information, students should contact:

Annette Loschert, Assistant Dean
M.B.A. Admissions
University of Southern California
Los Angeles, California 90089-1421
Telephone: 213-740-7846
Fax: 213-749-8520
E-mail: uscmba@sba.usc.edu

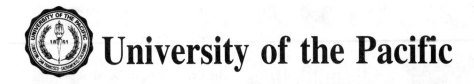

University of the Pacific

School of Business and Public Administration

Stockton, California

EDUCATING INNOVATIVE LEADERS

The University of the Pacific M.B.A. program is committed to cultivating the leadership ability and innovative spirit of our students, in addition to training them in state-of-the-art technical business skills.

Our unique curriculum includes a heavy emphasis on experience in the workplace, which we achieve through class consulting projects, internships, and a mentor program that teams each full-time student with a senior business executive. Our small, highly interactive classes also encourage close working relationships between students and faculty, enabling faculty to challenge students to achieve their full potential.

Whether you are interested in the general M.B.A. or the entrepreneurship track, the University of the Pacific M.B.A. is designed for students who want to make a difference.

—Mark Plovnick, Dean

Programs and Curricular Focus

The focus of the M.B.A. programs at the University of the Pacific is on training future business leaders to be competitive in the twenty-first century. The course work is challenging and provides a firm grounding in various academic disciplines yet goes beyond the traditional business school curriculum to emphasize critical leadership skills and a global perspective. The classes are small to encourage close student-faculty relationships.

There are two M.B.A. programs offered through the School of Business and Public Administration (SBPA): the one-year, full-time day program and the evening program, which can be completed on a full- or part-time basis. The evening program curriculum is divided into two phases, each consisting of 24 semester units. Phase One includes eight courses covering basic business skills; these courses can be waived if similar courses have been successfully completed at the undergraduate or graduate level. Phase Two embodies the heart of the M.B.A. program, with two tracks—the general management M.B.A. and the entrepreneurship M.B.A. In each track, students take two courses that develop leadership and innovation skills, four courses that integrate the foundation course work into a managerial framework, and at least two elective courses that allow students to explore their areas of interest, such as finance, marketing, or accounting.

The one-year M.B.A. program is a full-time program in which a small group of students begins as a cohort, or team,

going through the entire program together. The one-year M.B.A. is a unique, customized program that enables a limited number of students, with sufficient previous course work in business, to complete the M.B.A. program in ten months. The team begins the program in August, taking a three-week class called Leadership and Change that involves off-campus activities, including outdoor adventure challenges, corporate visits, and other experiential assignments. The curriculum for the fall semester includes corporate finance, business and public policy, strategic marketing, and technology and innovation. In January, the entire cohort travels overseas to take the Global Business Competition course. This includes classroom work, corporate visits, and cultural events. The entire experience provides students with the opportunity to actually live the culture and to attain the international perspective that is critical for M.B.A. degree holders today. The spring semester includes Managing Productivity and Quality and Strategic Management, as well as the flexibility to choose a concentration with two elective courses. Students in the full-time day program are also matched with a senior manager from the business community who acts as a mentor and helps guide them through the M.B.A. program. Internships and consulting projects round out the workplace exposure emphasized by the M.B.A. program.

Students and the M.B.A. Experience

The M.B.A. students at the University of the Pacific come from a wide variety of academic institutions, with diverse academic credentials. Geographically, a high percentage of students are from California, although there are students from throughout the United States and ten other countries. Women comprise about 40 percent of the program, and approximately 30 percent of the students identify themselves as minorities. The average age of the students is 27.8, with six years of full-time work experience.

Special Features

The University of the Pacific M.B.A. program is unique in its overall emphasis on integrating the classroom experience with the business world and its focus on the personal as well as academic development of each student. The entrepreneurship M.B.A. program is a specialized course of study that complements the general management M.B.A. program and provides students with an intensified and rigorous exposure to the principles, tools, and ideas needed to succeed in entrepreneurial pursuits. Also available is the one-year M.B.A. program, which provides an unusual opportunity for a small group of students to experience an innovative fast-track M.B.A.

The Faculty

The School of Business and Public Administration (SBPA) is committed to teaching excellence. Teaching is the primary responsibility of the faculty. Research complements the teaching mission and enables faculty to offer instruction that is relevant and current, providing a high-quality learning experience for every student. While the faculty members have earned their academic credentials from the finest universities, most have significant experience in management or consulting; they integrate such experience into their course work.

Michael H. Ballot, Professor; M.B.A., Ph.D.
David K. Banner, Professor; M.B.A., Ph.D.
John W. Blasingame, Associate Professor; M.B.A., Ph.D.
Thomas Brierton, Associate Professor; J.D.
Donald W. Bryan, Associate Professor; Ph.D.
C. Gregory Buntz, Professor; Ph.D.
Elaine Gagne, Visiting Assistant Professor; Ed.D.
James A. Goodrich, Professor and Director of Westgate Center for Management Development; Ph.D.
Joel Herche, Visiting Assistant Professor; Ph.D.
Sue N. Hinrichs, Associate Professor; Ph.D.
Ronald Hoverstad, Associate Professor and Director of M.B.A. Program; M.B.A., Ph.D.
Elizabeth R. Koller, Visiting Assistant Professor; J.D.
W. Anthony Kulisch, Associate Professor; D.B.A./Ph.D.
Unro Lee, Assistant Professor; Ph.D.
H. Chang Moon, Assistant Professor; Ph.D.
JoNel Mundt, Assistant Professor; M.B.A., Ph.D.
Newman Peery Jr., Professor; M.B.A., Ph.D.
Mark S. Plovnick, Professor and Dean; Ph.D.
Willard T. Price, Professor; M.P.W.A., Ph.D.
Ray Sylvester, Professor and Associate Dean of Student Affairs; M.B.A., Ph.D.
Paul Tatsch, Associate Professor; Ph.D.
Richard Vargo, Professor; M.B.A., Ph.D.
Cynthia Wagner, Assistant Professor; Ph.D.
Stephan W. Wheeler, Associate Professor; Ph.D.

The Business School Network

Corporate Partnerships

The University of the Pacific SBPA has built strong relationships with the corporate community and strives to integrate the classroom experience with the business world in a variety of ways, including the Pacific Business Forum, which brings nationally and internationally recognized corporate or government leaders to campus several times a year to talk about current issues in the world today; the Westgate Center for Management Development, which provides management training for the regional business community; the Community Consulting Corps, which brings students together with managers of nonprofit organizations to work in a client-consultant relationship to solve business problems; the Business Advisory Board, which includes 26 executives from local, regional, and national businesses who work closely with the dean and faculty at integrating the business school and the business world; the Mentorship Program, in which every student in the full-time program is matched with an executive to help him or her make decisions regarding

classes, careers, and the job search; and the Internship Program, which provides business exposure for students, either on an individual basis or as part of a consulting team.

The College and Environs

The University of the Pacific, with its red-brick buildings and ivy-covered walls, is now in its 142nd year. California's first chartered university, the University of the Pacific was established one year after California became a state, in 1851. The main campus spreads over 170 acres along the Calaveras River. Stockton is a short drive from San Francisco, Yosemite National Park, Lake Tahoe, the Napa and Sonoma wine country, Sierra skiing, and the state capitol in Sacramento. The University also has a dental school in San Francisco and a law school in Sacramento.

Technology Environment

The University has substantial academic computing resources available for students, with multiple laboratories distributed across the campus and a network linking the labs, personal computers, and the campus mainframe. The computer lab in the SBPA has HP 486/33DX and Macintosh computers available and is networked. All graduate students are expected to take advantage of the University's electronic mail system and the Internet.

Placement

The Office of Career Services facilitates career decision making and job search assistance for all students on an individual basis and in small group sessions. It annually coordinates an on-campus recruiting program and a career fair, in addition to a variety of workshops and special programs. The office also maintains a Career Advisory Network, which links students to alumni of the University to help build their professional connections. In addition to the work of Career Services, the faculty and staff in the School of Business and Public Administration work with alumni and corporations to secure internships and full-time positions for M.B.A. students.

Admission

Qualified candidates are admitted to the part-time evening program on a rolling basis for the fall semester, spring semester, and summer sessions. The one-year full-time day program is limited to 25 students per class, and that class is admitted each year and begins in August as a cohort. Each candidate's file is evaluated on the basis of academic record, scores on the required Graduate

Management Admission Test (GMAT), a personal essay, and letters of recommendation. Although the entire "package" is considered for each applicant, the typical undergraduate GPA considered is 3.0 or higher. GMAT scores are generally 500 and above. A score of 550 or better on the TOEFL is required for all students for whom English is not the native language. International students must present proof of adequate funds to cover expenses for the entire M.B.A. program.

Finances

The annual expenses for an M.B.A. student at the University of the Pacific depend on a variety of factors. The 1994–95 tuition for the one-year program was $15,300. In the part-time program, costs are based on the number of courses students take (at $1530 per course in 1994–95). The cost of living in Stockton is relatively low, and students can find housing for about $380–$500 per month. Room and board on campus are approximately $5330 per year, depending on the housing and meal plan options chosen. Full-time students must also pay a health services fee, which is approximately $225, and a University Center fee of $20. Financial assistance is available through scholarships, assistantships, and loans. Merit-based scholarships and teaching and research assistantships are available directly from the School of Business and Public Administration. These awards are generally determined by June 30, so students should submit applications by March 1 to be considered.

Application Facts and Dates

Application deadlines are July 31 for the fall semester, December 31 for the spring semester, and April 30 for the summer session. Since the one-year M.B.A. program is limited to 25 students per year, applicants to this program are advised to submit their applications by March 1 to guarantee consideration. M.B.A. admission decisions are made on a rolling basis, and applicants are notified immediately when decisions have been made. To ensure a quick response, application packages should be complete. For more information, contact:

Paula S. Tatsch
Director of M.B.A. Recruiting
School of Business and Public Administration
University of the Pacific
3601 Pacific Avenue
Stockton, California 95211
Telephone: 209-946-2629
Fax: 209-946-2586

The University of Toledo

College of Business Administration

Toledo, Ohio

THE UNIVERSITY OF TOLEDO M.B.A. PROGRAM—DEVELOPING BUSINESS LEADERS

At The University of Toledo, we understand what it takes to succeed. After all, we have been educating and developing business leaders since 1933. Our rigorous M.B.A. curriculum skillfully integrates academic theory with real-world application. And like the business community we serve, we are committed to continuous improvement to keep our program in the forefront of business thought and practice. Our commitment to this philosophy is reflected in our faculty's superior records of accomplishment in mentoring, teaching, research, and consulting. The quality of our faculty, combined with our small class size, state-of-the-art facilities, and beautiful suburban setting, makes for a memorable and fulfilling learning experience that provides students with the needed skills and knowledge to succeed in an increasingly competitive environment.

—Robert H. Deans, Dean

Programs and Curricular Focus

The basic disciplines underlying managerial decision making serve as the main focus of the Master of Business Administration program. UT's M.B.A. program helps students master managerial techniques and the fundamentals that are the prerequisites of success.

The graduate program consists of a sequence of integrated building blocks. These building blocks include basic, analytical, and functional fields of knowledge; applied specializations; and a capstone course on corporate strategy, policy, and planning. Students may choose a general program or one with special emphasis on related areas in which they have an interest. Specializations are available in finance, health-care administration, human resource management, international business, information systems, management, marketing, and operations management. Students may attend on either a full-time or part-time basis. An accelerated program is also available to qualifying students.

In addition to the M.B.A. program, The University of Toledo offers many other graduate business programs. The new Executive M.B.A. is an innovative fifteen-month program designed specifically for executives of midsized and growing companies. The program's lockstep weekend format enables executives to complete their degrees without interrupting their careers.

A joint J.D./M.B.A. program provides students with the opportunity to earn the

J.D. and the M.B.A. in just 3½ academic years. Master of Science in Accounting, Master of Taxation, Master of Science, and Ph.D. in manufacturing management degree programs are also offered.

Students and the M.B.A. Experience

Variety best describes The University of Toledo. Students at UT come from around the United States and around the world and bring with them rich and varied backgrounds. The profile of an average student in the program in 1994–95 is a 27-year-old with between three and four years of experience. Approximately 20 percent of the students in the program are full-time. Women account for a little more than a third of the students, while minority students account for 12 percent. International students account for approximately 25 percent.

Special Features

In addition to traditional classwork, M.B.A. students can get hands-on experience through the Office of Professional Experience Programs (OPEP) or the College's Small Business Institute (SBI). Students can opt to do a 4-credit internship as part of their M.B.A. specialization through OPEP. OPEP maintains listings of companies interested in hiring interns. The SBI program creates opportunities for students to interact with owners/managers by assigning students to businesses in need of assistance.

The Faculty

UT's faculty provides students with a dynamic and challenging learning environment. The faculty members in the College of Business Administration hold advanced degrees from a variety of distinguished institutions. Many are nationally and internationally recognized researchers whose articles have appeared in leading business and academic publications.

The Business School Network

Corporate Partnerships

The distinguished members of the College of Business Administration's Business Advisory Council (BAC) serve as a vital link to the corporate world. The BAC provides the College with valuable direction and advice, ensuring that a UT business education addresses current issues in today's business world. In addition, the College's Visiting Executives Program exposes students to executives from a variety of business backgrounds and helps to complement and build on students' classroom experiences. Business leaders in the program share their thoughts with students in designated classes on issues of concern to them and business in general. Several students are also selected to join the visiting executive and the dean of the College for either breakfast or lunch.

Prominent Alumni

The UT-M.B.A. Program provides individuals with the high-quality graduate business education they need to succeed. The results speak for themselves. Many UT-M.B.A. graduates hold leadership positions in the business world. Among the school's prominent alumni are Ora Alleman, Executive Vice President, National City Bank; William Ammann, Vice President, Administration, Trinova Corporation; Michael Durik, Executive Vice President, The Limited Stores Inc.; Marvin Herb, CEO, Coca-Cola Bottling Company, Chicago; Julie Higgins, Executive Vice President, The Trust Company of Toledo; Donald Saunders, Vice Chairman, Toledo Edison; and Mark Tincher, Senior Portfolio Manager, Chase Manhattan Bank.

The beautiful Stranahan Hall, which won an award for its unique architectural design, is the home of the College of Business Administration at The University of Toledo.

The College and Environs

Founded in 1872, The University of Toledo is Ohio's fourth-largest state-assisted university, with more than 23,000 students, and the fastest-growing state university. Through its eight different colleges and schools, UT offers nearly 150 different academic majors. Located in a tree-lined suburban area 6 miles from downtown Toledo, the more than 200-acre main campus combines classic architecture with beautifully landscaped grounds to make learning a truly enjoyable experience. As Ohio's fourth-largest city, Toledo also offers a host of business, industrial, social, and cultural opportunities. Toledo houses the headquarters of several Fortune 500 companies and features the Toledo Symphony, the Toledo Zoo, and the Toledo Museum of Art, one of the world's leading museums.

Facilities

The College of Business Administration's classrooms, computer labs, and faculty and administrative offices are located in Stranahan Hall. The main University library contains over 1.5 million volumes and over 1.4 million microform items. In addition, the library is a U.S. government documents depository library and contains materials from the Census Bureau and the Department of Commerce. An on-line computer system allows students to access the catalog and serial records as well as databases, abstracts, and periodical indexes.

Technology Environment

Students in the College of Business Administration have access to computer facilities at many points on campus. In addition to the 87 PCs located in the three microcomputer labs in the College

of Business Administration, there are approximately 400 more PCs located in various buildings across the campus. All machines on campus are networked. Students have access to the terminal software, the mainframe, VAX, and the campuswide network. This provides for direct access to the library, among other locations, from any terminal on campus.

Placement

The University of Toledo's Office of Career Services offers M.B.A. students a broad support system throughout their program. Advising, workshops, and other programs are offered to enhance students' job-seeking skills and to help students make the contacts necessary to compete effectively for jobs in today's competitive job market. Assistance in assessing career goals and employment objectives is provided through individual counseling, workshops, seminars, and videotapes. The placement and career services also bring organizational representatives from both profit and nonprofit firms and health, education, and government agencies for on-campus interviews. In addition, students have access to computerized employment databases for job referrals in the tristate region and nationwide.

Admission

Admission is granted to individuals showing high promise of success in graduate business study. Applicants are considered for admission based on their undergraduate record; scores on the Graduate Management Admission Test (GMAT); managerial, professional, and leadership potential as exhibited by extracurricular activities, job experience, and community service; and a statement of purpose describing

long-term goals and objectives. The GMAT score for students accepted into the M.B.A. program has averaged between 500 and 525. The average undergraduate GPA is approximately 3.1.

Finances

Tuition and fees for full-time enrollment for 1994–95 were approximately $4790 for Ohio residents and $9540 for nonresidents. Estimated personal expenses for the 1994–95 academic year, including books and room and board based on shared living, transportation, and recreation, were $5560. Graduate students live in off-campus housing.

The College of Business Administration offers graduate assistantships, tuition scholarships, and fellowships based primarily on achievement or merit. Most forms of assistance are awarded to students beginning their program in the fall.

Application Facts and Dates

Application deadlines are August 15 for fall quarter, November 15 for winter quarter, February 15 for spring quarter, and April 15 for summer. Admission decisions typically take one to two weeks once a student's admission file is complete. For more information, students should contact:

The M.B.A. Program
Office of Graduate Studies in Business
College of Business Administration
The University of Toledo
Toledo, Ohio 43606-3390
Telephone: 419-537-2774
            419-537-2775
Fax: 419-537-7744

The University of Western Ontario

London, Ontario, Canada

> The Western M.B.A. has long been regarded as one of the leading M.B.A. programs in the world. The Western program is highly integrated and focuses on the leadership skills and perspectives essential for success in a global marketplace. Our faculty are dedicated to teaching and creating an intense and "real world" learning environment. As the second-largest producer of teaching cases in the world, Western utilizes a variety of interactive and experiential learning methods that capitalize on the rich base of experience in the class.
>
> Our general management focus and global perspective have led Western to be ranked repeatedly the best business school in Canada by Canadian Business, Business Week, The Economist Intelligence Unit, and Asia, Inc.
>
> —A. B. Ryans, Dean

Programs and Curricular Focus

The M.B.A. program is two years in length. The first year is the same for all students, while the second year allows choice from an array of options.

The LL.B./M.B.A. program is a four-year limited-enrollment program offered jointly by the Business School and the Faculty of Law to train students for careers in which business and law overlap.

The executive M.B.A. and videoconferencing executive M.B.A. programs are for managers with exceptional potential and a minimum of eight years of work experience. The Ph.D. program provides advanced training in research and teaching and advanced substantive work in a specialized field.

Students and the M.B.A. Experience

The students in the M.B.A. program are distinguished by the diversity of their educational and professional backgrounds and their history of outstanding achievement. On average, they are 28 years of age, with four years of full-time work experience. They come from over twenty countries worldwide. About 40 percent have substantial work or educational experience outside Canada, and about one third speak at least two languages.

❖ Global Focus

Western helps develop a global perspective—to work in a business environment that increasingly transcends national boundaries. A multinational student body,

faculty members with international experience as consultants and teachers, specialized international courses, and the integration of global issues in all core courses work to foster this perspective. The School also offers several special opportunities.

International exchanges are arranged with top business schools in Sweden, Denmark, the Netherlands, France, Spain, Germany, Italy, Austria, Switzerland, Mexico, Brazil, Japan, Korea, Hong Kong, Singapore, the Philippines, and Australia.

Each year approximately 50 M.B.A. students travel to Eastern Europe and China to teach basic management skills to managers and entrepreneurs as part of the LEADER and China projects.

Western students have won case competitions in the United States and Hong Kong against teams from around the world.

In the second year, courses covering various international topics, such as "Doing Business in Mexico, Japan, or Eastern Europe" and "Managing in Developing Countries," are available.

Special Features

Learning at Western is highly interactive. Although there are some lectures, most of the classes rely heavily on case discussions, computer simulations, and role plays. Western is especially well known for its business cases. A case presents an actual business situation rather than theories about business. Usually it describes a particular manager's problem

that must be resolved. Students first analyze the case individually, trying to reach a decision, and then meet in a small study group to compare approaches. Finally, students meet with the entire class to discuss the case and its implications for management. During this time, students are also interacting frequently with executives and managers from various organizations. The whole process is designed to help students become effective decision makers. An essential part of Western's learning process is the study group. With organizational activity increasingly taking place in teams, this experience is critical for every effective manager.

In the first year, students are also exposed to an intensive workshop in Managing Diversity to help them understand the impact of greater diversity on management and how to harness that diversity to get better organizational performance.

The Faculty

The Western faculty members are renowned as excellent teachers. With degrees from esteemed universities, they welcome the challenge of creating a stimulating learning environment. As a result, they can be found as guest professors in universities around the world, and since their research centers on the practical problems of managers, they consult widely with diverse national and international businesses.

The Business School Network

Corporate Partnerships

The corporate community plays a significant role in the educational experience at Western. Class projects undertaken with corporations allow companies to show future managers how major institutions operate and implement key strategic changes. This interaction with executives and managers results in a strong integration of material in the first year of the program.

A board of advisers, consisting of key players in the Canadian business community, is also actively involved in maintaining the M.B.A. program's relevance in an increasingly demanding global environment.

A program of industry tours, seminars, and guest speakers features prominent business and government leaders, many of whom are Western Business School graduates.

Prominent Alumni

The Western experience does not end when the program is over. Students join a network of more than 11,000 men and women who have gone on to occupations in almost every place imaginable. Some of the prominent Business School alumni include Robert Nourse, voted entrepreneur of the year by *Inc.* magazine and president of the Bombay Company; Laurie Campbell, president of Morgan Stanley; David Thomas, president of Lloyds Bank Brazil; Raymond Verdon, president of Nabisco; and over 1,000 other presidents and chief executive officers in companies around the world.

The College and Environs

Since it was founded in 1878, the University of Western Ontario has established a tradition of excellence in teaching and research. One of Canada's oldest and largest universities, Western consists of seventeen faculties in the sciences, arts, social sciences, and professions, serving a body of over 22,000. The University is particularly well known nationally and internationally for its professional schools, which include Business Administration, Dentistry, Law, and Medicine.

London is called the Forest City in recognition of the many trees that line the streets and add beauty to its parks. With a population of 320,000, London is a university city as well as a center of services, light industry, and commerce.

The city is small enough to have a sense of community but sufficiently large and diverse to have many of the cultural, entertainment, and recreational amenities of a big city. Beyond the city, the beaches and parks of two of the Great Lakes are within an hour's drive. It is just 2 hours by car or train to both Toronto and Detroit.

Facilities

Students have access to all the University's libraries, including a specialized and well-stocked business library. The School operates its own computer facility and two student laboratories with Hewlett-Packard and IBM PCs that are accessible 24 hours a day. The National Centre for Management Research and Development undertakes full-time research on major challenges facing management today.

Placement

The Career Services Department helps students plan their job search, write résumés, and develop interviewing skills. The office organizes on-campus visits by major corporations and helps both those corporations and students "make the match." Each fall, Career Services sends hundreds of employers résumé books containing profiles of all second-year students. These companies may then invite students for an interview. The office also coordinates the activities of over 300 organizations from across Canada and around the world that contact students for employment in a variety of fields.

The records show that Western graduates are highly valued in the job market—companies want the kinds of insights, perspectives, and skills that students develop in the program. Western graduates have achieved success in a wide range of careers. Many have become CEOs of major corporations. Other Western M.B.A. graduates are top civil servants, leading consultants, deans of other business schools, and entrepreneurs. Many decide to spend a few years in the corporate world and then start their own business.

Admission

Students must normally hold an undergraduate degree with high academic standing from an accredited university. The applicant's leadership skills, achievements, undergraduate grades, GMAT score, TOEFL score (600 minimum), TSE score, full-time work experience, and extracurricular involvement are all carefully considered. Western looks for applicants who have thoughtfully analyzed their personal and career goals and have demonstrated the potential to become leaders. Western is interested in individuals whose accomplishments indicate an ability to benefit from and contribute to the Business School. A few applicants without an undergraduate degree, who have at least seven years of challenging work experience, some university courses with high standing, and other strong management qualities, may also gain admission. Western encourages applications from international students and members of minority groups.

Finances

The estimated tuition fee for international students is Can$11,000 and for Canadian citizens, Can$3000. The application fee is Can$100.

Costs of housing, medical insurance, food, transportation, and personal items add from Can$13,000 to Can$18,000 for single students and from Can$20,000 to Can$25,000 for a family of four. The cost of books and supplies ranges from Can$1500 to Can$2000 per year.

Well-qualified students are automatically considered for scholarships and awards.

International Students

With the globalization of trade, there is an increasing need for businesspeople to see beyond their own geographic boundaries. At Western, students will find outstanding people from diverse educational and cultural backgrounds, working in an intense environment.

Students will discover the global economic, political, and technological factors that shape business activity in Canada and around the world. Students will also tap into the powerful network of Canadian business alumni.

Application Facts and Dates

Because the class fills early, students should submit an application as soon as possible. Files are evaluated on a rolling basis starting in November, and this process continues to May. The deadline for applications from outside Canada and the United States is April 1. The deadline for applications from Canada and the United States is May 15. For more information, applicants should contact:

Admissions Office
Western Business School
University of Western Ontario
London, Ontario N6A 3K7
Canada
Telephone: 519-661-3212
Fax: 519-661-3485

University of Wisconsin–Madison

Madison, Wisconsin

A SPECIAL SCHOOL IN A SPECIAL CITY

The University of Wisconsin–Madison School of Business offers a unique package to graduate students—the resources of a large, top-notch public research institution; one of the finest business school facilities in the nation; faculty noted for outstanding teaching and research; and a superb track record in placing our graduates. Best of all, we are located in the heart of Madison, Wisconsin, long recognized as one of America's most livable cities.
—Andrew J. Policano, Dean

Programs and Curricular Focus

The graduate program of the University of Wisconsin–Madison School of Business offers intensive study in small, personalized classes. Students may opt for either a generalized M.B.A. degree or one of several M.S. or M.A. programs in specialized fields, such as marketing research, distribution management, accounting, real estate appraisal and investment, manufacturing and technology management, and international business, among others.

The Wisconsin approach to graduate business education combines a solid foundation in core areas of business management within a two-year curriculum that stresses four basic themes: global perspectives, team building and communication skills, total quality management, and ethics and social responsibility. It also embodies the marriage of analytical skills to pragmatic managerial problems. Manufacturing and technology students, for example, work closely with counterparts in the University's College of Engineering. Real estate students regularly travel to Asia, Latin America, and Eastern Europe for investment and appraisal seminars. The applied security analysis program requires its majors to manage an actual securities portfolio valued at more than $500,000.

Students and the M.B.A. Experience

Students bring a variety of backgrounds and experiences to the graduate program of the UW–Madison School of Business. In a typical graduate class, about 40 percent of the members are women, about 30 percent have international backgrounds, and 15 percent are students of color.

Diversity also marks the academic backgrounds of graduate business students at Wisconsin. Nearly two thirds of entering master's students come from nonbusiness undergraduate majors, including 25 percent from engineering, mathematics, and science, with the remainder from economics and liberal arts. A majority also bring real-world business experience to the program.

Students are encouraged to go beyond the boundaries of the School of Business. The University of Wisconsin–Madison, with nearly 40,000 students, is a world-class center of research and learning. It provides an unparalleled opportunity to enrich a business student's knowledge and understanding in fields such as law, health administration, and engineering.

Special Features

The School of Business offers semester-long study-abroad programs for M.B.A. students majoring in international business. Formal for-credit programs have been established between the School of Business and several foreign universities. In addition, shorter-term international study programs are offered each spring. In 1995, for example, the School of Business is offering a 2½-week program to Germany, Switzerland, France, Hungary, and the Czech Republic.

The Faculty

Close interaction between faculty members and students is a hallmark of the UW–Madison School of Business.

More than 80 professors teach and conduct research. Many are leaders in their academic disciplines. In recent years, School of Business faculty members have been elected presidents of a variety of prestigious professional organizations, including the American Accounting Association, the American Academy of Management, and the American Risk and Insurance Association. Business school faculty members have been recognized for the caliber of their teaching, winning University and national teaching awards.

The Business School Network

Corporate Partnerships

The UW–Madison School of Business is well known for responding to the business community's need for high-quality programs in emerging fields. For example, in the late 1980s, an explosion in marketing data created the need for graduates trained in statistical methods in marketing research. The School responded in 1990 by establishing the A. C. Nielsen Center in Marketing Research, which has earned international attention for its interdisciplinary program in marketing and statistics. Invaluable input from businesses is provided to the School in a variety of ways: advisory boards, mentor programs, internships, and an extensive program to bring top executives into the classroom to share their experience with students.

Prominent Alumni

The UW–Madison School of Business has many nationally recognized business leaders among its more than 26,000 alumni, including Paul J. Collins, Vice Chairman, Citibank, N.A.; John P. Morgridge, Chairman of the Board, Cisco Systems, Inc.; Arthur C. Nielsen Jr., former Chairman and CEO, A. C. Nielsen Company; Thomas F. Pyle Jr., Chairman, President, and CEO, Rayovac Corporation; and Mary Ann West, Vice President, Morgan Stanley.

The College and Environs

The University of Wisconsin–Madison is a university of Nobel Prize winners, recipients of the National Medal of

Grainger Hall is the new home of the University of Wisconsin–Madison School of Business and is one of the most technologically advanced facilities in the nation.

Science, and members of the National Academies of Science, Engineering, and Education. It routinely ranks among the top five universities in the nation in terms of funded research. UW–Madison's 40,000-member student population is one of the most diverse in the nation. It is considered one of the most picturesque college campuses in the country, lying as it does along the shores of Lake Mendota, one of five lakes within the city's borders.

Facilities

The UW–Madison School of Business moved into a new home, Grainger Hall, in 1993. The $40-million facility incorporates leading-edge instructional technology throughout its 260,000 square feet. It is one of the most visually appealing and technically advanced business school facilities in the country.

The two lower levels of the building house thirty modern, spacious classrooms with the latest teaching technology, including an auditorium and two large lecture halls. The upper three levels contain continuing education facilities and offices for research and career services as well as for members of the faculty and administration. The library offers electronic access to specialized databases across campus and around the world.

The School has several instructional computer labs, including a dedicated lab for graduate students, computer classrooms, its own research computer, and a building-wide network of computer outlets to allow students to use laptop computers in almost every corner of the building.

A state-of-the-art videoconferencing room allows School of Business faculty members and students to interact with employers, industry experts, and business leaders, in real time, anywhere in the world.

Grainger Hall was designed from the ground up to be "student friendly," offering student lockers, a graduate student lounge, mailboxes for students, and several other special features that students indicated were important.

Placement

UW–Madison is known for the strength of its career development and placement assistance. Each year more than 115 regional, national, and international corporations interview School of Business graduate students on campus. In addition, more than 700 job listings are received and posted each year. The staff of the Business Career Center includes an adviser dedicated to providing assistance and resources to master's students. A career development center designed specifically for the needs of graduate students offers a telephone, computer, and reference materials. The Business Career Center uses new technology through distribution of electronic résumé books and a Fax-a-Job program. It is one of few business schools that provides employers with the opportunity to interview students via two-way, interactive video links through its own specially equipped video interviewing room.

Admission

An undergraduate degree in any discipline from an approved institution is required for admission. At least two years of full-time, relevant work experience is strongly recommended and strengthens the application for admission. The GMAT is required of all students who apply to the School of Business; the exam must have been taken within five years of applying to the School.

In addition, for international students, the School of Business requires the Test of English as a Foreign Language (TOEFL), taken within two years of applying. The University of Wisconsin–Madison's graduate school requires all international applicants to submit evidence of financial ability along with the application for admission.

Finances

Tuition for the 1994–95 school year was $4658 for residents of Wisconsin and $12,505 for nonresidents.

Students with a superior grade point average and GMAT scores may qualify for all-university scholarships. The School of Business also offers a substantial number of merit-based graduate fellowships, scholarships, and teaching or project/research assistantships. Additional assistance is available for students who are members of minority groups through the Consortium for Graduate Study in Management and the Wisconsin Investment Scholarship Program.

Application Facts and Dates

Application deadlines are June 1 for September enrollment and October 1 for January enrollment.

For more information, students should contact:

Graduate Programs Office
University of Wisconsin–Madison
School of Business
2266 Grainger Hall
975 University Avenue
Madison, Wisconsin 53706-1323
Telephone: 608-262-1555
Fax: 608-265-4192
E-mail: uwmadmba@bus.wisc.edu
WWW: http://www.wisc.edu/bschool

Virginia Polytechnic Institute and State University

Blacksburg, Virginia

WHY THE PAMPLIN COLLEGE OF BUSINESS?

Besides being one of the Southeast's top business schools, we are Virginia's largest business school, accounting for 20 percent of all business degrees awarded from the state's fifteen public senior institutions. Our M.B.A. and other degree programs are all accredited by the American Assembly of Collegiate Schools of Business, which is the nationally recognized accrediting agency for graduate and undergraduate business programs.

We are committed to providing top-quality business education through outstanding teaching by full-time faculty members who are nationally recognized in theoretical and applied research. We are also committed to developing a global perspective in our students so that they may better understand the interdependence of nations in the world economy and how cultural differences can become the basis of strength. We are preparing our students for global business challenges with core courses that include the global context of business, international summer internships, and faculty-led study-abroad programs.

—Richard E. Sorensen, Dean

Programs and Curricular Focus

The Master of Business Administration degree at the Pamplin College of Business requires the completion of 48 semester credit hours. The program consists of a twofold educational process. First, through program prerequisites and a set of required courses, students gain proficiency in the basic disciplines of accounting, finance, management, marketing, and production/operations management. Students also acquire an understanding of the quantitative, economic, behavioral, and statistical tools required of a competent manager and a contributing team member.

Next, students are given an opportunity to strengthen their knowledge in a particular area through the careful selection of elective courses. They may concentrate in finance, management, management science, marketing, or international business. They may also select a broader range of electives and not declare a formal concentration. Students are thus given some flexibility to put together an M.B.A. program that is tailored to their individual professional goals.

The two-year, full-time program has two program prerequisites. These requirements can be fulfilled by completing at least one college-level course in differential calculus and one college-level course each in microeconomics and macroeconomics. Students should also be familiar with matrix algebra.

The program provides a strong theoretical base, vital to the foundation of a future manager. A solid understanding of business functions and a sensitivity to the needs of organizational stakeholders enable managers to better understand and adapt to change. The classroom procedures offer students a blend of case study, lectures, role play, individual and group presentations, and simulation exercises.

Students and the M.B.A. Experience

The M.B.A. program has about 220 full-time students on campus. The students represent a diversity of ages, work experiences, undergraduate studies, nationalities, cultural backgrounds, and career interests. About one quarter of the students obtained their undergraduate degrees from out-of-state institutions, with approximately another quarter having undergraduate degrees from universities outside the United States. The students come from about twenty-five countries. Business undergraduate majors comprise about 55 percent of the students; engineering or technical majors represent just under 20 percent. The average age of the entering students is 26. Students typically have more than two years of work experience. Men account for 67 percent of the students; women, 33 percent.

The College seeks to attract a cross-section of highly qualified individuals from different cultural and career backgrounds. Because diversity is a reality in today's workplace and in the global economy, students are encouraged to be open to and embrace differing views and interpretations of the world.

Special Features

The College also enrolls about 325 part-time students in its off-campus M.B.A. programs, offered in northern Virginia and, by satellite downlink, in other sites around the state.

The Northern Virginia M.B.A. Program has been fully accredited since 1971. The program offers professionals in the Washington, D.C., area an opportunity to earn an M.B.A. without interrupting their careers. Of the approximate 240 students enrolled in this program, more than 95 percent have full-time careers in engineering, computer applications, accounting, finance, human resources, and marketing.

The M.B.A. Program via Satellite Downlink provides courses that are received at sites through live satellite telecast plus a two-way audio connection via telephone lines—permitting students at various locations to interact with the instructor and with students in classrooms at other sites.

The Faculty

The College has about 125 full-time faculty members, many of whom are nationally recognized teachers and scholars with practical business experience. As a result of their dedication to advancing leading-edge business concepts, the faculty members have been involved with instituting nationally recognized research entities, such as the Center for Study of Futures and Options Markets, Center for Wireless Telecommunications, Center for Relationship Development, and the Business/Technology Center.

The Business School Network

The Pamplin Advisory Council is a select group of 65 prominent business and government leaders from across the country who meet with College administrators to provide guidance on College programs, fund-raising, and ties with industry and government.

Alumni volunteers assist students in various capacities, including information interviews, networking referrals, referring résumés in their respective companies, and advising students seeking jobs within the alumni's specific geographic areas.

The alumni return to their alma mater to share their work experiences and to discuss factors for success that go beyond their technical knowledge.

Experienced recruiters conduct panel discussions and practice interviews for first-year students. M.B.A. students receive straightforward feedback on how they performed during the mock interviews, how they were perceived by recruiters, and what they can do to prepare for live interviews during their second year.

The College and Environs

Virginia Polytechnic Institute and State University, commonly known as Virginia Tech, was founded in 1872 as a land-grant college. Its recent history is one of rapid, well-planned growth. Virginia Tech is the largest university in the state in terms of full-time enrollment.

Virginia Tech, ranked in the nation's top fifty in terms of research expenditures, conducts a $121-million-a-year research program supporting over 3,500 research projects. The Virginia Tech Corporate Research Center offers businesses the opportunity to establish close working relationships with the University.

Facilities

The Pamplin M.B.A. Program is housed in Pamplin Hall, a state-of-the-art academic facility. An atrium, combining large skylights with natural foliage, forms a creative yet relaxing environment for both students and faculty to interact.

Virginia Tech's Newman Library currently contains over 1.7 million bound volumes, 5.2 million microforms, 5,000 videos and films, 6,700 cassettes and recordings, and over 13,000 journals and periodicals. Access to the collection is provided through an on-line computer system, VTLS, which is an integrated system used by more than seventy-five other libraries around the world.

Technology Environment

The Computing Center operates the centralized mainframes and server computers. The center's resources include an IBM 3090 300E/VF running VM/CMS, an IBM 3084Q running MVS, an HP3000 960 running VTLS, and a VAXstation 3100 running VMS and Ultrix. Several workstations, including IBM RS/6000s, Sun SPARCstations, HP 9000s, and DECstations, provide high-performance, numerically intensive computing, mail service, and document services for faculty and students 24 hours a day.

Placement

The M.B.A. career service's mission is to help students identify and capitalize on their distinctive talents and focus on how their career objectives fit their personal and professional priorities. Individual counseling focuses on customizing the career planning and marketing process for each student. Students are introduced to a holistic, proactive approach to the job search. Seminars require students to develop an integrated marketing approach so that they become their own personal marketing product managers to plan and manage their career and personal priorities.

Admission

Applicants to the Pamplin M.B.A. Program must take the Graduate Management Admission Test (GMAT) and have the official scores reported to Virginia Tech. In addition, each applicant is required to submit an application for admission, official transcripts of all past course work, two letters of recommendation, and a current résumé.

Undergraduate grades (particularly those from the junior and senior years), GMAT scores, work experience, and letters of recommendation are all important, although each is only one measure of an individual's potential to pursue graduate study. Considered collectively, however, this information helps to determine which applicants are most likely to succeed in the program.

Finances

In-state tuition for the 1994–95 academic year was $4557. The out-of-state student rate was $6726. Estimated living expenses are $6700, and miscellaneous expenses are estimated at $1100 for both in-state and out-of-state students. Travel expenses are not included.

Merit-based financial aid is available for students with outstanding academic background, GMAT scores, work experience, leadership skills, and references. Financial aid is available for graduate students in the form of fellowships, instructional fee waivers, and graduate assistantships.

Need-based financial aid is based primarily on demonstrated financial need. In order to be considered, students must submit a Financial Aid Form (FAF) to the College Scholarship Service for the appropriate year no later than February 15. The University will advise applicants of their financial aid awards by August 1.

International Students

Approximately twenty-five countries are represented in the M.B.A. program, and international students comprise about 25 percent of the program's student body. At the university level, there are thirty-five international student organizations and an international center, the Cranwell International Center, which is a focal point for cultural, social, and educational programs with a global focus. Films, dinners, lectures, parties, orientation programs, and community contacts are facilitated throughout the center.

Application Facts and Dates

Applications for admission are accepted at any time. Admission decisions are made within six to eight weeks after the application file is complete. Although most students enter the program in August, students may also enter in January (spring semester). Application materials should be received at least eight weeks before the beginning of the semester for which enrollment is requested. For more information, students should contact:

Ronald D. Johnson
Associate Dean for Graduate and
  International Programs
1044 Pamplin Hall
Virginia Polytechnic Institute and
  State University
Blacksburg, Virginia 24061-0209
Telephone: 703-231-6152
Fax: 703-231-4487
E-mail: rdjmba@vtvm1.cc.vt.edu

Wayne State University

Detroit, Michigan

THE WAYNE STATE M.B.A.—A PROGRAM FOR YOUR FUTURE

The M.B.A. program at Wayne State University is one of the oldest in the United States and, we believe, one of the finest. The School has assembled graduate faculty members who publish regularly in their discipline's most prestigious journals and who are dedicated to the highest teaching standards. The fine academic credentials and impressive professional backgrounds of the students in the M.B.A. program serve not only to attract and retain our fine faculty but also to enrich the educational experience in the program through the insights they bring to the classroom.

The faculty and staff of the School of Business Administration have worked hard to make the graduate study of business an enjoyable and exciting experience for our M.B.A. students. Thank you for taking a closer look!

—William H. Volz, Dean

Programs and Curricular Focus

Wayne State University's Master of Business Administration emphasizes the dynamic, global nature of modern commerce. It is intended to prepare men and women for leadership and management positions in business, government, and other types of organizations. The core and concentration requirements for the program consist of 36 semester hours of study (twelve courses). Applicants with a baccalaureate degree in business administration usually meet all of the program's foundation requirements. Applicants with baccalaureate degrees in fields other than business administration may have to complete certain foundation requirements in the following areas: accounting, business law, economics, finance, management, management information systems, marketing, mathematics, production management, and statistics. Special accelerated foundation courses have been developed for entering M.B.A. students to meet these requirements.

In addition to taking eight core courses, the M.B.A. student, after consultation with a graduate faculty adviser, may select from an extensive number of concentration and elective courses in accounting, business economics, finance, industrial relations, international business, management and organization behavior, management information systems, marketing, personnel/human resources management, quality management, and taxation. Graduate-level courses in other schools and colleges of

the University may also be elected with special approval of the M.B.A. program director. Students interested in pursuing a J.D./M.B.A. should contact an adviser in the Office of Student Services.

The academic year is divided into two 15-week semesters and a split spring/summer semester; a full schedule of graduate courses is offered each term. Courses are taught in convenient suburban locations as well as on campus.

Students and the M.B.A. Experience

Wayne State M.B.A. students bring a cross-cultural diversity and broad range of employment experience to the program. More than 93 percent of the students are employed full- or part-time, with an average of three years of work experience. Half of the M.B.A. students hold supervisory positions within their corporations.

The average student is 27 years old, with women making up 36 percent of the student base. International students comprise 10 percent of the M.B.A. population, bringing to the program valued input on business in their regions of the world.

Students in the Wayne State M.B.A. program find its strength to be the successful combination of the real-world experience their peers bring to classroom discussions and projects, in conjunction with relevant business theory presented by the faculty. While 55 percent of

current M.B.A. students hold undergraduate degrees in business, the remaining half are made up of engineering, liberal arts, fine arts, and science graduates.

The Faculty

Faculty members of Wayne State's School of Business Administration are recruited from the finest graduate programs both in America and abroad, and the excellent quality of both the graduate and undergraduate students has proven to be a powerful force in retaining this talented group. The business school faculty members publish more than 200 books, journal articles, and scholarly papers each year. They are regular contributors to the finest academic journals in the business disciplines.

In addition, the School is proud of the energetic group of business executives who teach as part-time faculty in the M.B.A. program. These experienced professional managers are consistently well-received by their graduate classes.

The Business School Network

Corporate Partnerships

Among the strong partnerships that have been established between the School of Business Administration and prominent local and international corporations are relationships with Ford Motor Company, Federal Mogul, ANR Pipeline Company, and Kmart Corporation.

Prominent Alumni

The School of Business Administration at Wayne State University counts among its alumni a number of notable business leaders, including Victor J. Fryling, president, CMS Energy Corporation, and vice president, Consumers Power Company; Dennis O. Green, chief auditor, Citicorp and Citibank, N.A.; Eric Mittelstadt, president and CEO, GMFanuc Robotics Corporation; and Anne Regling, executive vice president, operations, Children's Hospital of Michigan.

The College and Environs

Tracing its origins to 1868, Wayne State occupies a 185-acre campus that is graced by open courtyards and malls and whose

105 buildings represent a blend of traditional and ultramodern architecture. The modern University campus is a distinctive element in Detroit's expansive cultural center, which includes the Fisher Theater, Detroit Institute of Arts, Historical Museum, Science Center, Public Library, and four University Theaters. Also near the campus are the Engineering Society of Detroit, the Detroit Medical Center, the Merrill Palmer Institute, and the General Motors World Headquarters. Detroit and southeastern Michigan provide extensive opportunities for study, research, cultural enjoyment, and employment.

Facilities

Wayne State, with three mainframe computers, operates one of the largest computing centers in the Detroit area. Links with MichNet provide users with access to the Internet (NSFNET), SprintNet, AutoNet, and Datapac networks. The University is also linked to the BITNET academic network. The total system is available 24 hours a day.

Currently, 300 terminals and 128 dial-up lines are available for student use. Students use terminals and microcomputers in the School's six microcomputer classrooms and laboratories as an integral part of many graduate courses.

Wayne State University is the host institution for DALNET, Detroit Area Library Network, made up of twelve local libraries. Through computer terminals in the libraries, users can access over 7.8 million volumes, representing the majority of holdings in the area's educational institutions.

Placement

Working together with the School of Business Administration, the WSU Placement Office regularly places M.B.A. students in permanent positions locally, nationally, and internationally. The School of Business Administration annually offers a Career Day, providing students with an opportunity to meet recruiters from dozens of national and international manufacturing and service corporations; "Strategies for Your Future" is an annual conference for students interested in learning where to find the best jobs; and the M.B.A. Student Association publishes a résumé book for annual corporate distribution. The University's Placement Reference Center offers information on major corporations, job searching, interviewing, and résumé writing.

Admission

Admission to the Master of Business Administration program is open to students who have a baccalaureate degree in any discipline from a regionally accredited institution and who demonstrate high promise of success in the graduate study of business. A minimum 2.5 overall undergraduate honor point average or 2.75 honor point average in the last half of the undergraduate program is required. In addition, a minimum Graduate Management Admission Test (GMAT) score of 450 is required regardless of the strength of the undergraduate HPA. No decision regarding a student's admission will be made without the GMAT results.

International students must have completed an appropriate four-year university-level program and, in addition to the above requirements, achieve a minimum score of 550 on the Test of English as a Foreign Language (TOEFL) and a score of at least 95 on the Michigan English Language Assessment Battery (MELAB).

Finances

The Office of Scholarships and Financial Aid provides students with information regarding sources of funds. Graduate teaching and research assistantships are offered through the School's academic departments and its Bureau of Business Research. Stipends for 1994–95 averaged $8200 for nine-month appointments. University graduate and professional scholarships are also available.

Tuition per semester in 1994–95 for Michigan residents was $340–$1015 (part-time) and $1150–$1690 (full-time). Non-Michigan residents paid $654–$2114 (part-time) and $2406–$3574 (full-time).

International Students

International students constitute 10 percent of the M.B.A. student body. The International Services Office offers assistance to all students with their new surroundings. The International Business Association also offers students an opportunity to know their fellow classmates and develop international networks through special events and business functions.

Application Facts and Dates

Application deadlines for graduate admission are August 1 for the fall term, December 1 for the winter term, and April 1 for the spring/summer term. International students must provide required materials four months prior to the beginning of the term. For more information, students should address inquiries to:

Office of Student Services
School of Business Administration
Wayne State University
Detroit, Michigan 48202
Telephone: 313-577-4510
Fax: 313-577-5299

Western International University

Phoenix, Arizona

PREPARING BUSINESS LEADERS TODAY FOR THE WORLD TOMORROW

The commitment to global education is a natural and essential element of the University and is a driving force behind many of the programs and activities. The internationalized curriculum emphasizes the importance of cross-cultural understanding and the global dimension in management. The University is convinced that this strategy is essential to prepare its students to be effective managers and leaders in an interdependent business world.

Programs and Curricular Focus

Western International University (WIU) prepares adults to compete in an ever-changing global marketplace. The University offers distinctive, high-quality programs that emphasize in-depth knowledge of business disciplines built on a foundation of broad liberal learning.

Graduate degree programs and executive development programs are offered at the University's main campus in Phoenix, its European branch campus in London, and at multinational corporate locations throughout the United States and overseas.

WIU specializes in offering high-quality education that addresses the complexities of an interdependent business world. The University offers a traditional program that is packaged in a format that allows rapid progress toward academic goals. In addition to degree programs, WIU offers certificate programs for individuals who are interested in functional knowledge in a particular business area.

Class offerings are designed to provide maximum flexibility in building a curriculum suitable to the lifestyles of today's adults. Students are able to complete programs in time frames convenient to their schedules. Small classes contribute to a dynamic teaching and learning environment.

WIU offers the Master of Science (M.S.) in accounting, health-care information resources management, and information systems; Master of Business Administration (M.B.A.) in finance, health-care management, international business, management, management information systems, and marketing; and Master of Public Administration (M.P.A.).

Students and the M.B.A. Experience

The University takes pride in the international character of its student body. Students come from over fifty nations, including the United States. International and adult students bring a wide breadth of knowledge and experience to the classroom, where the exchange of practical information is dynamic. Classes are relatively small, ranging in size from 10 to 35. The student-teacher ratio is 18:1.

Special Features

Western International University offers a unique Executive M.B.A. program to key business executives from other countries. Through this program, international business leaders are immersed in a comprehensive, integrative curriculum that is relevant to today's global business issues and strategies for the future. They have their time optimized while they are away from their businesses, while preparing their businesses for the future. The business leaders prepare for the challenging global economy that is affecting their business plans today, and they return to their organizations with practical management strategies that can be implemented to help their businesses reach higher levels of success.

These international business leaders actively participate in workshops scheduled prior to each four-week intensive session and in conjunction attend English proficiency sessions at the Phoenix, Arizona, campus. The heart of the Executive M.B.A. program consists of students' attendance at the Phoenix campus for four intensive weeks, taking classes at the Phoenix campus and then returning to their businesses to implement the business processes that they have learned. The fourth week of classes includes presentation of the Business Plan Project, both verbally and in typewritten form. Students also spend one week concentrating on the overall Business Case Study Project for the Executive M.B.A. program between the three months of intensive classes. This capstone course is called Corporate Strategy Formulation and Implementation.

Groups of 10 to 15 international business executives are invited to apply to this excellent and innovative program.

The Faculty

The faculty members of Western International University are scholars and practitioners who bring real-world experience to the University's learning environment. All faculty members hold formal academic credentials from some of the finest universities in the world.

Students benefit from the faculty's scholarly background, teaching effectiveness, and active involvement in the business community.

The Business School Network
Corporate Partnerships

The University has established strong partnerships with multinational corporations that have found WIU to be an innovative institution available to assist with their educational programming needs. WIU offers educational programs on-site at a number of multinational corporations, including Intel Corporation, Motorola Inc., and McDonnell Douglas Helicopter Systems, to name a few. Other dimensions of the partnerships include tuition reimbursement for employees, corporate executives as WIU lecturers, executive training programs, and financial contributions.

An example of WIU's ongoing partnership with the corporate community is the strategic alliance that has been established with AT&T School of Business. WIU was selected by AT&T to offer undergraduate and graduate degrees as well as an advanced certificate program in international business for its employees.

The College and Environs

Western International University's main campus is located in Phoenix, Arizona. Phoenix and the surrounding cities are considered one of the country's most rapidly growing metropolitan areas in terms of population, employment, and income. Year-round sunshine provides opportunities for such sports as swimming, golf, tennis, hiking, camping, and boating. Cultural activities in music, theater, and dance are offered throughout the year. Arizona is also home to one of the natural wonders of the world, the Grand Canyon.

WIU's campus in London is located in the heart of the Docklands development. As the largest redevelopment project in Europe, Docklands offers a unique environment that combines offices, shopping, entertainment, and sports.

Technology Environment

Computer facilities provide resources for instructional and research purposes at the main campus in Phoenix; teaching sites at Fort Huachuca and Douglas, Arizona; and the campus in London. The computer labs provide free and unrestricted access for students and faculty to support educational activities.

Admission

Admission to Western International University is based on a number of factors. Emphasis is placed on previous scholastic attainment and professional experience, as well as personal achievements that demonstrate a student's maturity, leadership capabilities, and motivation.

The Admissions Office receives and processes all applications, evaluates transcripts, and makes decisions regarding acceptance and application of transfer credit to the program of study.

International students wishing to attend Western International University on a student visa must meet academic requirements for admission and provide proof of financial resources. They must also provide proof of their English proficiency or participate in the English as a second language (ESL) program in Phoenix prior to taking academic courses.

Finances

For 1995–96, tuition is $175 per credit hour ($525 per course) for U.S. residents. International student tuition is $225 per credit unit ($675 per course).

The University has no on-campus living accommodations. Students can find suitable apartments located within easy reach of the main campus.

International Students

Western International University offers a year-round course in English as a second language (Intensive ESL) with eleven 4-week sessions. Students may enroll at the beginning of every month except December. The Intensive ESL program prepares students for academic study, with particular emphasis on international business. For the purpose of entering a WIU degree program, no TOEFL score is required with graduation from the Intensive ESL program. The program features six levels of instruction, beginning through advanced. As part of the program, students receive basic instruc-

tion in computer skills, participate in pronunciation workshops, and have access to the campus library and computer lab, as well as to academic advising. They also enjoy parties and class dinners, as well as tours and field trips to places of interest in Arizona. No test is required for admission to the Intensive ESL program. A placement test is administered during orientation to determine at which of the six levels of the program students must begin instruction.

Application Facts and Dates

Application can be made at any time during the year. Because of the two-month semester, students do not have to wait half a year to enroll as they would in a traditional four-year semester-based institution. Students can begin graduate study on the first day of the month subsequent to receiving their letter of acceptance. An international student admission packet is available from the Office of Admissions at the campus where enrollment is desired. For more information, students should contact:

Admissions Office
Western International University
9215 North Black Canyon Highway
Phoenix, Arizona 85021
Telephone: 602-943-2311
Fax: 602-371-8637

Administration Office
Thames Lea College Ltd.
3 Muirfield Crescent
Glengall Bridge West
Millharbour, London E14 9SZ
England
Telephone: 44-71-712-9277
Fax: 44-71-712-9220

Widener University

Chester, Pennsylvania

THE PROGRAM'S PHILOSOPHY

The Graduate Program in Business Administration is designed to provide aspiring and practicing managers with the skills, social sensitivity, and interdisciplinary perspective needed to assume leadership roles in society. By combining a core curriculum with a variety of options for advanced studies in applied fields, the program offers an integrated and reasonably comprehensive exposure to the knowledge believed to be of essential and lasting value to the business or institutional manager.

—Joseph A. DiAngelo Jr., Dean

Programs and Curricular Focus

Widener's School of Management provides graduate and professional programs focusing on the self-paced graduate student and the special needs of the part-time student, so that Widener's commitment to taking the education of students personally is fulfilled. The program is designed to take full advantage of the working status of the majority of its students. Unlike the full-time student, the student/employee is immersed daily in the realities of organizational life. This concurrent relationship provides students with immediate opportunities to test and validate the relevancy of classroom learning. The blending of directed classroom study and daily work-related experience reinforces learning while supplementing it with the fuller understanding of how theoretical principles must be modified and adapted to fit particular environments.

The curriculum consists of a core program comprising key elements of economic and administrative theories that underlie managerial and entrepreneurial activity and advanced courses in specialized fields. The core program includes course work in accounting, economic analysis, finance, marketing, operations of technology, quantitative methods and behavioral aspects of management, and strategic management. Option tracks offer specialization in accounting, economics, environmental management, finance marketing, management information systems, manpower management, and production management.

Graduate transfer credit must be approved by the dean of the School of Management and may be permitted subject to various restrictions.

The specific degree programs that are offered are the Master of Business Administration (M.B.A.) with options in environmental management, financial administration, human resource management, international business, legal studies, management information systems, marketing management, production management, and taxation; the Master of Business Administration, Health and Medical Services Administration (M.B.A./HMSA); Master of Health Administration (M.H.A.); Master of Science in accounting; and Master of Science in taxation. Dual-degree programs offered are the J.D./M.B.A. in conjunction with the School of Law; M.E./M.B.A. with the School of Engineering; B.S./M.B.A. and B.S./M.S. through the School of Management's undergraduate and graduate programs; Psy.D./M.B.A.(HMSA) and Psy.D./M.H.A. with Graduate Clinical Psychology; and M.D./M.H.A. and M.D./M.B.A.(HMSA) in conjunction with Jefferson Medical College of Thomas Jefferson University.

Widener also offers a Master of Public Administration degree program in the College of Arts and Sciences and, through the School of Law, LL.M. programs in corporate law and finance and health law.

Students and the M.B.A. Experience

More than 1,000 students, mostly in their late twenties or early thirties, are currently enrolled in a Widener part-time evening graduate business program. Classes are conveniently held in the evening between 6:30 and 9:30. Some students choose to take as many as three courses, which is considered a full-time

program. While attending Widener, most are fully employed in a cross section of business environments, from small to large in size, encompassing manufacturing, the service industries, government, and nonprofit organizations.

❖ Global Focus

The International Executive in Residence program offers students a chance to meet a senior executive from an international corporation in a small group environment. In addition to attending presentations on business in a global environment, students are able to ask questions about international business trends and career opportunities.

Special Features

Learning by experience is incorporated into the programs in several ways. Some of the programs require clerkships, management and career development seminars, and residency experience. These are designed as vehicles to gain actual on-the-job learning and integration of academic theory with practice.

The Faculty

The unique blend of faculty talents combines state-of-the-art education with doctorally prepared as well as industry- and public administration–experienced professionals. The primary interest of each faculty member is teaching while simultaneously developing his or her own potential through ongoing research. Teaching style focuses not only on theory but also on the practical application of this material in the workplace. Widener is proud of its mandate as a teaching institution, featuring personal attention for each student at both the undergraduate and graduate level.

The Business School Network

Widener M.B.A. students are employed by such companies and organizations as A. I. DuPont Institute; ARCO; Arthur Andersen & Company; Bell of Pennsylvania; Blue Cross/Blue Shield; Campbell Soup; Chase Manhattan Bank; CIGNA; Conrail; CoreStates; Department of Defense; E. F. Hutton; General Electric;

Widener University is located on a 100-acre suburban campus. The eighty-five buildings include a mixture of modern and Victorian architecture.

HMO; Honeywell; KPMG Peat Marwick; McDonald's; McNeil Lab; PECO; PNB; RCA; Reynolds SEPTA; SmithKline Beckman; Springfield School District; State of Delaware; Tasty Baking Company; Texaco; Upjohn; Vanguard and Xerox.

The College and Environs

Widener University is recognized nationally and internationally as a distinguished private educational institution. An accredited university chartered in Pennsylvania and Delaware, Widener is today a three-campus university offering ninety-five programs of study leading to associate, baccalaureate, master's, or doctoral degrees.

Founded in Wilmington, Delaware, in 1821, the University is composed of eight schools and colleges that offer liberal arts and sciences, professional, and preprofessional curricula. The University's schools include the College of Arts and Sciences, School of Engineering, School of Hotel and Restaurant Management, School of Human Service Professions, School of Management, School of Nursing, School of Law, and University College.

Facilities

Graduate business students may take advantage of the variety of facilities and services offered on both the main (Chester, Pennsylvania) campus and the Delaware Campus. Classes average fewer than 20 students each in Kapelski Learning Center or Academic Center North on the main campus and in Polishook Hall on the Delaware Campus.

Libraries are equipped with on-line computer indexing and personal computer labs for class or individual use. Bookstores, accessible parking, and evening advisers are available on both campuses.

Placement

Graduate advisers are present each evening to help merge career goals with programs offered. To assist those who are relocating in the job market, there is a professionally staffed Career Advising and Placement Service (CAPS) on the main campus.

Admission

Admission to any of the graduate business programs involves completing the application and paying the nonrefundable application fee, submitting two letters of recommendation, and possessing a bachelor's degree. In addition, various programs require GMAT, GRE, or MAT scores, and the M.S. degree programs in taxation and accounting require the GMAT or documentation of CPA, CIA, or CMA certification. International students from non-English-speaking countries must take the Test of English as a Foreign Language (TOEFL).

Finances

For the 1995–96 academic year students in the M.B.A. programs will pay $400 per credit.

Graduate assistantships are available for full-time students (up to three courses per semester). Graduate assistants aid the faculty in research projects and work approximately 20 hours per week. Assistantships are awarded to students on campus. Assistantships are compensated by a stipend and tuition remission for up to three courses.

Application Facts and Dates

Applications must be received for fall semester entrance by June 1, spring semester by October 1, and for the summer semester by February 1. Applications from international students must be received two months prior to the dates given.

For more information, students should contact:

Dean
Graduate Programs
School of Management
Widener University
One University Place
Chester, Pennsylvania 19013
Telephone: 610-499-4305
Fax: 610-499-4614

Willamette University

Salem, Oregon

A QUALITY LEARNING EXPERIENCE

The education and professional development of Atkinson students are the top priority of Atkinson faculty and staff.

Our focus on teaching, integration, and the practical application of knowledge builds the perspective, experience, and decision-making skills needed for successful managerial careers, and our collegial atmosphere helps students develop the confidence and team skills of successful managers.

Our learning environment has already earned national recognition for the Atkinson School, and we remain firmly committed to providing a distinctive graduate management education—an education that offers the strategic benefits of professional growth, real-world experience, and confidence to meet the managerial challenges of today and tomorrow.

—G. Dale Weight, Dean

Programs and Curricular Focus

The Master of Management program prepares students for careers in business, government, and not-for-profit organizations. The M.M. enhances understanding of management decision making through an integrated curriculum, global perspective, and emphasis on the practical application of knowledge.

The program is two academic years in length and comprises a 30-credit core curriculum (10 courses), 3 credits of cocurricular courses (2 courses), and 30 credits of elective courses (10 courses). The balance of required and elective courses ensures a broad understanding of the functions of management and the flexibility to pursue career goals. Cocurricular courses enhance teamwork, strategic career management, and communication skills.

The core curriculum is cross-functional and cross-sector in nature and integrates the legal, international, negotiation, and ethical issues of management. The multifaceted integrated curriculum helps students apply their knowledge to changing environments and recognize the internal and external factors that influence managerial decisions.

The elective curriculum provides the opportunity to pursue a generalist perspective or greater knowledge in an area of interest, including accounting, finance, general management, human resource management, international management, marketing, public management, and quantitative analysis/management science.

Teaching methods include lecture, case study, team projects, consulting projects with organizations, group discussions, simulations, student presentations, internships, and independent study/research.

Willamette University also offers a four-year joint degree in law and management (J.D./M.M.).

Students and the M.B.A. Experience

The Atkinson student profile is characterized by a diversity of age and experience common in organizations. The average student is 27 years of age and has three years' work experience. Thirty percent of the student population are women, 24 percent are international students, and 12 percent are minority students. Although generally from the Western United States, students come from fifteen states and fifteen countries. Most Atkinson students have undergraduate degrees in social science, liberal arts, or business. Most enter the program with experience in business, government, or not-for-profit organizations, but some enter directly after their undergraduate education.

The School's size and exclusive focus on the master's level of study facilitates a high degree of accessibility and interaction between faculty and students. The learning environment is collegial and emphasizes teamwork, team projects, and the practical application of knowledge. The program demands approximately 60 hours of academic work per week.

❖ Global Focus

The core curriculum integrates international issues of management, and the elective curriculum supports career interests in international management.

Special Features

Each year begins with Compass Week, a program of teamwork, strategic career management, academic review, and perspectives on new and important issues of management.

A strong relationship with the Pacific Northwest International Trade Association provides opportunities to prepare, present, and publish reports evaluating key international issues facing business, especially those related to government policy.

The Faculty

The Atkinson School faculty members are excellent teachers and nationally and internationally respected scholars. They are recipients of awards for outstanding teaching and research; leaders of professional and community organizations; authors of books, articles, software, and simulations; and consultants to business and government.

One hundred percent of the 11 full-time faculty members have the doctorate. Ninety-one percent have worked, consulted, or completed academic work internationally. Eighteen percent are women.

Three endowed faculty chairs (business, public policy, and international management) provide additional resources for faculty to pursue teaching innovation and scholarly research.

The Business School Network
Corporate Partnerships

Interaction with leaders of business, government, and not-for-profit organizations is frequent and occurs through class projects, faculty/student consulting projects, internships, the visiting executive program, guest speakers, career services seminars, and site visits. The School also has a long-standing commitment to entrepreneurship and provides

research and consulting services for emerging and existing businesses in the Northwest.

Prominent Alumni

The average alumnus is 39 years old and pursuing a career path in small to large business, entrepreneurial ventures, government service, or not-for-profit organizations. Seventy percent of Atkinson alumni live and work in the Pacific Northwest. Thirty percent are located throughout the United States and internationally.

Information regarding titles and employers of Atkinson alumni will be provided on request.

The College and Environs

Willamette University is an independent coeducational university with a total of 2,100 students enrolled in the College of Liberal Arts (1,500), College of Law (400), and Atkinson Graduate School of Management (180). The University was founded in 1842 and is recognized for excellence and innovation in academic and professional education. Willamette University is located in Salem, Oregon. Salem, the state capital of Oregon, is recognized as one of the most livable cities in the United States and has been named an "All America City." Acclaimed for its balance of career opportunities and quality of life, the Pacific Northwest is one of the fastest-growing areas of the United States.

Facilities and Technology Environment

Atkinson students have 24-hour-a-day access to the computer laboratory, which provides Macintosh and IBM-compatible personal computers. A local network provides all standard word processing, spreadsheet, and graphics applications. The Internet provides a national and international network to access worldwide information services and electronic mail. University library resources include books, periodicals, journals, and specialized computerized information databases, such as ABI/INFORM, CD-ROM Compact Disk Disclosure, CD-ROM National Trade Data Bank, and CD-ROM Predicast F&S.

Placement

The Atkinson School works with employers to provide a complete program of services connecting students and alumni with employment opportunities. Career service programs help students develop strategic career management skills, improve job search skills, and obtain internships and employment. Services include workshops, internship programs, on-campus interviews, employment opportunity postings, national employment databases, individual counseling, mentoring programs, and the West Coast MBA Consortium interview program with national employers.

Admission

The Atkinson School welcomes applicants with diverse career objectives and experiences. Admission is based on academic ability and managerial potential. All applicants must submit an application for admission, the application fee, a personal statement of experience and professional goals, two letters of reference, official transcripts of all undergraduate and graduate course work, and official GMAT or GRE scores. International students for whom English is not the first language must also submit a minimum TOEFL score of 550 and provide documentation of funds sufficient to cover two years of educational and living expenses.

The average GMAT score is between 540 and 560. The undergraduate GPA is 3.2. There are no specific prerequisite courses for admission, but students should have a solid understanding of mathematical principles and well-developed writing skills. Previous experience with economics, accounting, and personal computers (word processing and spreadsheet applications) is helpful.

Finances

Tuition and fees for 1995–96 total $13,250. Books and supplies cost approximately $1000. Room and board expenses range from $4500 to $6800 per year, depending on personal choice of accommodations and lifestyle. Approximately 50 percent of full-time students receive merit-based scholarship assistance ranging from 25 percent to 50 percent of tuition. Loans and work-study are available to eligible students.

Application Facts and Dates

Applications completed by March 31 receive priority consideration in admission and scholarship decisions. Applicants are notified by mail when their application materials are received and are notified of the admission decision within three weeks after completion of the application process. For further information, contact:

Director of Admission
Atkinson Graduate School of
    Management
Willamette University
Salem, Oregon 97301
Telephone: 503-370-6167
Fax: 503-370-3011

Woodbury University

Burbank, California

PREPARING BUSINESS LEADERS FOR THE TWENTY-FIRST CENTURY

Higher education has often been described as a safe haven, a sheltered port where minds can retreat to libraries and lecture halls to ready themselves for the battles of the real world. Today, however, those who seek to educate students about the world of business must provide much more. With each passing moment, the business world our graduates must inhabit is being reshaped by technological, political, social, legal, regulatory, and environmental forces. We must educate our students not just for what is, but for what will be.

Woodbury University is committed to preparing M.B.A. candidates for a lifetime of continual learning. We trust that the knowledge we impart will provide the tools, the techniques, and the vision to enable our graduates to create or to seize opportunities as they come into view. Though it builds on a 110-year tradition of excellence in business education, Woodbury does not rest on its laurels. Rather, it is an institution firmly oriented toward the future.

—Marvin Richman, Dean

FACULTY LIST

Frank Benson, Ph.D.; CPA, CIA, CMA, CFP.
David Black, M.B.A.
Joan Branin, M.B.A.
Ray Briant, M.A.
Anthony K. Chan, Ph.D.
John Charnay, J.D.
Richard A. Cross, M.B.A.
Satinder Dhiman, M.B.A.
Thomas E. Duffy, J.D.
Joel Fisher, Ph.D.
Jack L. Fitzgerald, M.A.
John Gleiter, M.B.A.
Robert T. Holland, Ph.D.
Norman Kaderlan, Ph.D.
William Lieberman, Ph.D.
F. Stuart Magie, D.B.S.
Michael McGrath, Ph.D.
Krishnan R. Mohandie, Ph.D.
Vishwa Mudaliar, Ph.D.
Frank Murphy, B.B.A.; CPA.
Jon Myers, M.B.A.
Larry D. Nelson, M.A.
Jesse Overall IV, Ph.D.
Marvin Richman, Ph.D.; Dean.
Alexandra Saba, Ph.D.
Stanley C. Sandell Jr., M.B.A., J.D.
Mohammad A. Sangeladji, Ph.D.
Robert A. Schultz, Ph.D.
Jacqueline A. Shadko, Ph.D.; Cert., Business and Finance.
Kendall L. Simmonds, M.B.A.
Irwin I. Steinberg, M.B.A.
Hamid Taheri, M.B.A.; CPA.
Chidi Ben Uzomah, D.B.A.
Richard K. Yamauchi, M.S.; CPA.

Programs and Curricular Focus

Woodbury University offers the M.B.A. with courses in accounting, computer information systems, finance, international business, management, and marketing. Designed primarily for those in full-time employment, Woodbury's M.B.A. can be pursued evenings only, weekends only, or in a combination of both formats.

The M.B.A. curriculum has a comprehensive management core that provides the basic foundation for understanding the various business disciplines and prepares the student for further study in general or specific interest areas. Areas of emphasis provide the opportunity for students to study more intensively according to their goals. Accounting covers major areas required for the CPA examination. Computer information systems includes systems design and development, communication networks, and artificial intelligence applications. Finance includes financial institutions, corporate finance, mergers and acquisitions, investment analysis, and capital markets. International business includes finance, economics, marketing, world business area studies, and comparative management. Management includes organizational behavior/human relations, policy studies, organizational theory, management systems, strategic planning, entrepreneurship, and strategy formulation. Marketing

includes international marketing, advertising, contemporary marketing problems, and market research.

All Woodbury courses are offered on the quarter system. Candidates for the degree must complete 48 graduate quarter units or a total of sixteen 3-unit courses. Up to 9 graduate quarter units may be transferred from another regionally accredited institution. The program's flexibility allows for many scheduling variations. The typical person in full-time employment takes two courses at a time, anticipating the completion of the degree in twenty-four months. There is no pressure, however, to conform to a particular timetable. Within the statute of a six-year limit from matriculation to the completion of the degree, one may vary enrollment according to need or inclination.

Students and the M.B.A. Experience

Professional men and women are drawn to the Woodbury M.B.A. program from a variety of industries in the United States and abroad. Often sponsored by their home governments or multinational corporations, international students come to Woodbury's program from Brazil, China, Egypt, and Mexico, as well as thirty other nations. Approximately 40 percent have undergraduate business degrees; the remaining 60 percent have

done their undergraduate work in such fields as engineering, humanities, and the social sciences.

The Woodbury M.B.A. program does not lock candidates into one particular peer group. Instead, students get the opportunity to work with a variety of different men and women as they explore each new subject area. In addition to strengthening the key business skill of team building, this structure allows an M.B.A. candidate to acquire the widest possible interaction with fellow students and professors.

The Faculty

The Woodbury M.B.A. program augments its forward-looking orientation with faculty members who are leaders in their respective fields. A combination of full-time academics and seasoned

professionals, professors have excellent academic credentials, which are often complemented with current corporate executive and management experience. These teaching professionals come to Woodbury from the management ranks of major corporations and from entrepreneurial efforts in fields such as artificial intelligence and global management consulting, as well as from the most distinguished academic institutions, including Harvard, Stanford, and the Wharton School.

The Business School Network

Corporate Partnerships

Ties between Woodbury's M.B.A. program and the southern California business community are strengthened by a large number of faculty members who are active participants in the day-to-day world of free enterprise. Teaching professionals come to Woodbury from such firms as The Walt Disney Company, Pacific Bell, and NASA.

Prominent Alumni

Woodbury graduates join a network of professionals who are business leaders in every part of the world—from a regional manager for a multinational oil company in Bangkok, to an international banker from Mexico, to an information systems director in Toronto. In Los Angeles, Woodbury alumni are found in the major accountancy firms and investment houses and in the entertainment industry, as well as in the fields of health care and telecommunications.

Alumni forums and a mentor program provide opportunities to solidify business relationships formed in the classroom.

The College and Environs

Situated in the hills of Burbank, the northernmost suburb of Los Angeles and media capital of the world, Woodbury offers students easy access to beaches, mountains, and deserts; it is within a 20-minute drive of downtown Los Angeles. Art, history, and science museums; professional sports events; and world-class entertainment are activities readily accessible to Woodbury students.

One of the largest cities in the United States, Los Angeles serves as a worldwide business and financial center. The University is linked to the international business, financial, design, and commercial communities, providing networking and career development opportunities for students who choose to take advantage of the wealth of business opportunities in southern California.

Facilities

Housed in a beautiful, cathedral-style building, Woodbury's Los Angeles Times Library provides a valuable resource to the M.B.A. candidate. Particularly strong in historical materials, the library houses a comprehensive collection of books, periodicals, technical reports, and other materials that are carefully selected to

meet fully the curricular needs of students. Access to reference material and information is available via CD-ROM and the Internet.

Woodbury also provides a complete computer resource center, featuring IBM-compatible and Macintosh computers, with a variety of business software programs.

On-campus housing is available in two residence halls, which accommodate up to 189 students. Residential areas surrounding Woodbury provide plenty of options for off-campus housing.

Placement

The Woodbury M.B.A. program receives strong support from the Office of Career Services. In addition to an annual career fair, the office coordinates mentor seminars, internships, job referrals, and career development workshops.

Admission

M.B.A. candidates may begin study during any quarter. A bachelor's degree from a regionally accredited institution and a minimum GPA of 2.5 are required for admission. The completed application should be submitted with a $50 fee, transcripts from all colleges attended, GMAT scores, TOEFL scores, and two letters of recommendation from professors or employers.

Finances

Tuition is based on the total number of courses the student enrolls in each quarter. Costs for the 1995–96 academic year amount to $325 per unit; the average course consists of 3 units. A University services fee of $100 per quarter is also required.

To approximate living and housing costs, the University uses the California Student Aid Commission estimate of at least $8370 for three quarters for food, housing, transportation, and miscellaneous expenses.

Application Facts and Dates

Application forms may be obtained by contacting:

Master of Business Administration
Woodbury University
7500 Glenoaks Boulevard
Burbank, California 91510-7846
Telephone: 818-767-0888
　　　　　800-290-8090 (toll-free)
Fax: 818-768-8628

Worcester Polytechnic Institute

Worcester, Massachusetts

THE MANAGEMENT OF TECHNOLOGY

An exciting opportunity in graduate management education is available through the Department of Management at Worcester Polytechnic Institute, the nation's third-oldest private engineering college. Our mission, "to educate our students to contribute meaningfully to the management of organizations in a global, technical, and competitive environment," clearly prepares students to address key issues facing businesses today.

A New England location, small college environment, dedicated faculty, outstanding facilities, and an excellent record of graduates' successes make WPI one of the nation's most respected names in technology based education.

—Francis Noonan, Department Chair

Programs and Curricular Focus

Worcester Polytechnic Institute offers over fifty graduate programs in engineering, science, mathematics, computer science, and management. The Department of Management offers three graduate degree programs: the Master of Business Administration (M.B.A.), the Master of Science in Management (M.S.M.), and the Master of Science in Manufacturing Management (M.S.M.M.). Each of these programs includes ten core and five elective courses.

In the core curriculum, students develop the analytical and judgmental skills required to make and implement decisions for a broad range of management situations. Students also sharpen their awareness of the external political, social, economic, legal, and ethical issues affecting managerial decisions. The core covers accounting, finance, organizational science, operations management, quantitative methods, marketing, management information systems, economics, law and ethics, and business policy.

The M.B.A., M.S.M., and M.S.M.M. programs differ in the distribution of the five elective courses. M.B.A. students select two breadth electives that expand upon core topics. The final three electives are graduate-level management engineering or science courses offered by WPI's other academic departments or by thesis/independent study.

The department offers concentrations in such areas as the management of technology, engineering management, manufacturing management, production/operations management, risk management, fire protection engineering,

construction project management, environmental management, and management information systems. Overall, programs emphasize quantitative and technical areas and the development and innovation of new technology.

Students and the M.B.A. Experience

More than 215 students are currently enrolled in WPI's M.B.A., M.S.M., and M.S.M.M. programs, with approximately an additional 100 nondegree students taking up to two courses prior to matriculating. Most are professionals working in industry full-time and taking classes part-time in the evening. Most of the students have prior work experience, the average being six years for those just entering the program, many in the high-technology sectors of the Massachusetts economy. Students bring to class their experiences from the computer, electronics, biotechnology, machine tool, chemical, software, and defense industries, to name a few. This diversity facilitates in-class discussion of theories learned in a framework of real-world grounds. Women comprise 23 percent of the student population, 12 percent are students from other nations, and the average age of students upon admission is 33. Students range in age from 21 to 55.

Special Features

WPI's Graduate Management programs were established in 1970 with the Master of Science in Management degree. The Master of Business Administration was

introduced in 1980 and the Master of Science in Manufacturing Management, several years ago.

Graduate programs are ideally suited to the working professional, with classes held evenings at several convenient sites in central and eastern Massachusetts.

Courses are offered at the main campus in Worcester, at the Massachusetts Technology Park Corporation in Westboro, and at the Nypro Institute in Clinton. In addition, classes are delivered to the MCET studios in Cambridge, Massachusetts, via interactive teleconferencing and at selected industrial sites as part of the Advanced Distance Learning Network (ADLN).

The Faculty

The WPI management faculty is dedicated to academic excellence through scholarship and teaching. Faculty members are also involved in sponsored research and consulting to a number of high-technology institutions. Faculty members approach the study of management from both theoretical and applications-oriented perspectives and use the classroom as a forum for relating traditional management principles and practices and current management issues. A sampling of current research includes management information systems, health care and biotechnology management, manufacturing management, total quality management, innovation management, technology management, marketing information management, quality control, and risk management. WPI's interdisciplinary focus leads to research with faculty in the other academic departments, resulting in a breadth of faculty research areas and academic offerings similar to those offered at large research universities.

The Business School Network
Corporate Partnerships
The strong ties between WPI and the business world are evident when reviewing the Department of Management Board of Advisors. This group includes executives and academics from Harvard University, Neles-Jamesbury Inc.,

Intercultural Business Center, Commonwealth Energy Systems, Polaroid Corporation, Alpha Industries, Digital Equipment Corporation, and Shearson Lehman.

Prominent Alumni

Numerous area business leaders are from the ranks of WPI alumni, including Steve Anderson, chief engineer, Neles-Jamesbury; Raymond Baker, vice president of manufacturing, Uvex Safety; Neil Buske, director of division engineering, Niagara Mohawk Power; Thomas Copp, president, Spectrum Wire; Leonard Devanna, vice president, Commonwealth Energy Systems; Robert Flaherty, first vice president for investments, Prudential Securities; Robert Foley, site operations manager, Texas Instruments; Charles Gordon, senior vice president, Swank; Ira Gregorman, vice president information systems, State Street Bank; Eric Gulliksen, vice president marketing, Koehler Manufacturing; David Holt, vice president of engineering, New England Electric; Michael Horgan, area operations manager, NYNEX; James Montagnino, North American operations manager, Data General; David Oberhauser, senior scientist, Polaroid; and David White, president, R.H. White Construction.

The College and Environs

Founded in 1865, Worcester Polytechnic Institute is a highly selective school of engineering, science, and management. Located on an attractive 80-acre campus within a one-hour drive of Boston, WPI is near many national and international businesses. Many faculty members are actively engaged in research and consulting projects for these companies.

WPI's personalized environment makes it a natural choice for students who wish to have considerable interaction with both the faculty and fellow students in small research groups and classes. WPI has about 1,050 full- and part-time graduate students in total.

Facilities

The Management Computer Lab houses fourteen 386 and 486 networked personal computers. Spreadsheet, word processing, and database management packages are accessible from the lab, as well as software for simulation, quality control, and management science analysis.

The College Computer Center provides a wide range of services and access to computer resources for the WPI community and manages an array of powerful UNIX workstations. WPI students can obtain a login ID for academic course work, research, and self-education. CCC facilities are accessible from a many locations on campus, via modem, or from around the world via the Internet.

Placement

The services of WPI's Career Development Center are available to all WPI students and alumni. Typically, recruiters from more than 300 organizations, including large and small industrial firms and government, civic, and professional associations, visit annually. The CDC also maintains a large reference library for WPI students and alumni. The CDC is involved in on-campus recruiting, hot-line job listings, résumé referral, and corporate presentations.

Admission

Applicants should have the analytical aptitude and academic preparation necessary to complete a technically-oriented management program. This includes an understanding of computer systems and either two semesters of calculus or three semesters of college mathematics.

Applicants may be admitted as regular degree candidates or on a provisional basis. Evaluation for admission is based on all information supplied by the applicants. Of recently accepted students, the average GMAT is 562, and the average undergraduate CQPA is 3.11. The minimum TOEFL requirement is 550.

Finances

The estimated tuition and fees for full-time graduate students are $14,000 per academic year. Books and supplies cost approximately $750 per year. Estimates for local apartment rentals are $400 and for food are $250 monthly. Other miscellaneous expenses (supplies, transportation, etc.) are estimated at $200 monthly. The 1994–95 per-course tuition is $1596.

A limited number of assistantships for full-time students are available and are filled as positions become available.

Application Facts and Dates

Applicants are required to submit a formal application, a nonrefundable $40 application fee (waived for WPI alumni), official transcripts of all college work, three recommendations, a GMAT report (GRE may be substituted for M.S.M. or M.S.M.M. applicants), and a TOEFL score if applicable. Applications are accepted on a rolling admissions basis. Applicants should contact:

Lisa M. Jernberg
Director of Graduate Management
  Programs
Worcester Polytechnic Institute
100 Institute Road
Worcester, Massachusetts 01609
Telephone: 508-831-5218
Fax: 508-831-5720
Internet: jernberg@wpi.edu

Wright State University

Dayton, Ohio

> The College of Business and Administration at Wright State University is proud to be part of a major metropolitan university that cherishes and embraces its neighboring communities. Wright State University's mission includes a "... commitment to providing leadership addressing the educational, social, and cultural needs of the Greater Miami Valley and to promoting the economic and technological development of the region through a strong program of basic and applied research and professional service. Wright State desires to create an intellectually exciting community and encourages all students and faculty to strive for excellence." The College of Business and Administration, which is endowed with a rich tradition of academic excellence, is an integral part of this exciting endeavor and is committed to playing a critically important role in meeting the business and educational challenges in our region and beyond.
>
> As the dean of the College of Business and Administration, I am proud to serve as the articulator and facilitator for many new and challenging initiatives as we embark on the twenty-first century. The faculty, students, and staff form a collaborative team that is involved in moving our college into the future. New initiatives focus on quality in education, leadership through teamwork, economic development, globalization, faculty and staff development, new program and new process developments, and developing networking relationships with businesses and other professional organizations.
>
> —Rishi Kumar, Dean

Programs and Curricular Focus

The Wright State M.B.A. program provides a high-quality education that is both broad-based and professionally relevant. The program addresses the diverse needs of students through a three-stage curriculum. The first stage provides preparatory business course work for those individuals who lack such preparation or who need to update their background. The second stage gives the student a broad business base, utilizing quantitative tools and teamwork within the case method approach. Stage three allows students to pursue an area of study of particular interest to them.

Roughly 50 percent of the students entering the Wright State M.B.A. program do not have any undergraduate business courses, and others need to update or upgrade their knowledge. The first stage of the program consists of a series of survey courses. The courses provide the students with the necessary academic background to be successful in the program. The courses entail accountancy, economics, finance, management, management science, and marketing. The focus of the courses is to relate material that the student will need to better understand and master the advanced

M.B.A. course work. Students with a strong undergraduate background in business may not need to take any of these courses.

The second phase of the program, common to all students, entails advanced study of business, including an integration of the business disciplines. There is a significant case study and teamwork component in this stage of the course work. Cases from business in the areas of accountancy, finance, management, operations, and marketing are analyzed by individuals within their team of students and presented to the class. The students thus apply their knowledge of the discipline to real-world situations, while developing their communication skills. Approximately 50 percent of the courses, including economics, management science, and operations management, utilize quantitative methods. This helps students further develop their analytical skills.

The third stage of the students' study has a concentrated focus. Students can choose one or two areas from finance, financial administration, health-care management, international business, logistics management, management, management information systems,

marketing, operations management, and project management. This stage of study is planned with faculty advisers.

Students may choose to complete an additional degree while pursuing the M.B.A. degree. Degrees in social and applied economics, nursing, and logistics management are available.

Students and the M.B.A. Experience

The M.B.A. student body is one of the program's greatest strengths. The diversity of backgrounds enriches the educational experience of all. Upon admission to the program, almost 50 percent of the students have an undergraduate degree in business, another 25 percent studied engineering, around 15 percent were in mathematics and the sciences, and the remaining 10 percent studied the humanities, nursing, education, and other disciplines. Over 5 percent of the students have already earned another advanced degree. Although 57 percent of the students graduated from Midwestern colleges, almost 10 percent attended colleges in the South, another 10 percent in the West, and 5 percent in the Northeast. Nearly 23 percent of the students earned their degree from a non-U.S. institution.

Students bring with them a wealth of work experience, averaging about six years of full-time work experience from a wide array of industries and occupations. About 15 percent of admitted students have no full-time work experience. Women comprise one third of the student body. This diverse student body contributes to lively classroom discussion and enhances the analyzing of cases by student teams.

The Faculty

The 59 graduate faculty members of the College also have very diverse backgrounds. Over 90 percent (54) hold a doctoral degree in their area of teaching responsibilities. Sixty percent of the degrees were earned at Midwestern institutions, over 15 percent from institutions in the West, over 10 percent at schools in the South, and the remainder from universities in the Northeast or overseas. Almost 15 percent (8) are women. Although research is important, the emphasis is on the application of knowledge. A number of the faculty members have been employed outside of academia as full-time employees and consultants. They bring this wealth of experience to the classroom to bring theory to life.

The Business School Network

The College's Board of Advisors are respected leaders from the greater Dayton area. They come from manufacturing, banking, retailing, consulting, and nonprofit and governmental organizations. The board advises the College on a wide range of important issues, such as curricula and faculty development.

The College and Environs

Wright State University, founded in the mid-1960s, is located in suburban Dayton, Ohio. Over 16,000 students (more than 3,000 graduate students) from almost fifty different countries are pursuing studies in approximately 100 undergraduate majors and more than 30 graduate programs. The 557-acre campus has twenty-two major buildings, including a 10,632- to 13,000-seat multipurpose sports and entertainment complex, while also maintaining a 200-acre biological preserve.

The campus in Dayton is 75 minutes from Cincinnati and Columbus. Students can take advantage of cultural, entertainment, sports, and educational events in all three of these cities. The climate in southwestern Ohio allows one to enjoy all four seasons, with the average normal temperature ranging from 80°F in the summer to 20°F in the winter.

Placement

Wright State's placement activities are centralized in the Office of Career Services. This office assists undergraduate and graduate students from all degree programs in finding internship and co-op positions during their education and employment after graduation. Individual and group career counseling and planning are available. The office offers a job search course, résumé preparation assistance, and résumé referral (electronic and paper); it also arranges interviews and conducts successful career fairs. The office has available many publications that can assist students with their job search and career planning.

Admission

The College considers a number of factors in making admission decisions. All applicants must hold a baccalaureate degree from a regionally accredited institution (individuals graduating from a non-U.S. institution must hold the equivalent of a four-year U.S. baccalaureate), submit official transcripts from all postsecondary institutions attended, have official scores on the Graduate Management Admission Test (GMAT) sent, and pay a $25 application fee. International students need to send official scores on the Test of English as a Foreign Language (TOEFL).

Students who have met all standards for admission to the program will be considered for admission on a regular basis and without conditions. Students with an admission index (AI) of 1000 using the overall undergraduate grade point average (UGPA) or an AI of 1050 using the last half UGPA are eligible for regular admission but are not guaranteed this status. The AI is computed by multiplying the UGPA by 200 and adding the total GMAT score. Applicants who have completed graduate-level course work must have a 3.0 graduate GPA to be considered for regular admission. International applicants must meet the 550 minimum acceptable score on the TOEFL. Once these thresholds are met, the College's admission committee reviews the application materials and makes its recommendation to the School of Graduate Studies for a final determination.

Admission is granted for each quarter: fall, winter, spring, and summer. Approximately 580 students were admitted to the M.B.A. program during 1993 and 1994. The average UPGA was 3.1 (90 percent had a 2.6 or above), and the average GMAT score was 527 (90 percent had a score of 450 or above). The average age was 30, the average length of full-time work experience was six years (although about 11 percent had none), over one third were women, over 10 percent were members of minority groups, and 20 percent were international. They held degrees in a wide array of disciplines, with 10 percent having previously earned another graduate degree.

Finances

For 1994–95 the cost of 1 to 10½ credit hours was $129 per credit hour for Ohio residents and $230 for nonresidents. For 11 to 18 credit hours, it was $1363 per quarter for Ohio residents and $2441 per quarter for nonresidents. The graduate application fee was $25, and the international student fee was $52 per quarter. The campus shuttle fee was $5 per quarter. On-campus room and board (double occupancy) averaged $428 per month per person; off-campus room and board (double occupancy) averaged $410 per month per person. The approximate cost of books and supplies was estimated at $75 per course.

Graduate assistantships and fellowships (for both part-time and full-time students) are available to M.B.A. students, including first-year students, in addition to other traditional student loan programs. The Office of Financial Aid, E136 Student Union, administers the campus-based aid and student loan programs; there is an April 1 application deadline. The School of Graduate Studies administers the graduate fellowship program for part-time and full-time programs and has a January 3 deadline. The fellowships are academically based and during 1994–95 ranged from $1500 for part-time students to $4090 for full-time students. The College administers the graduate assistantship (GA) program. GA applications are circulated to the departments for a decision approximately two months prior to the requested starting quarter. Over 40 GAs are employed by the College. A monthly (September through June) stipend of $345 (minimum) plus tuition waiver is paid in exchange for the student working an average of 20 hours per week for the College.

Application Facts and Dates

Admission application decisions are made up to and including the first week of classes for a quarter. The School of Graduate Studies notifies students of the admission decision by mail within a week after the decision is made. To obtain information and application materials for the M.B.A. program, students should contact:

James Crawford
College of Business and
    Administration
110 Rike Hall
Wright State University
Dayton, Ohio 45435
Telephone: 513-873-2437
Fax: 513-873-3545
E-mail: jcrawford@desire.wright.edu

Students should send all admission application materials to:

School of Graduate Studies
106 Oelman Hall
Wright State University
Dayton, Ohio 45435
Telephone: 513-873-2975

For information regarding international student admission, students should contact:

Office of International Student
    Programs
E190 Student Union
Wright State University
Dayton, Ohio 45435
Telephone: 513-873-5745
Fax: 513-873-5795

York University

North York, Ontario, Canada

> Since 1966, York's Faculty of Administrative Studies (FAS) has developed a first-class reputation for excellence, innovation, and flexibility. As Canada's largest graduate management school, we are proud of our many strengths—the motivation of our carefully selected students, the international reputation of our faculty, and the diversity of our many academic and executive programs. In the fall of 1994, after three years of careful analysis, consultation, and development, FAS launched a completely redesigned and restructured M.B.A. degree program. To do this we listened to our stakeholders. We talked with executives and practising managers. We consulted with our corporate advisers, alumni, students, and faculty. The new M.B.A. graduate from York will be ready for a world of change. In 1995 we continue our tradition of innovation and look forward to the many opportunities that lie ahead.
>
> —Dezsö J. Horváth, Dean

Programs and Curricular Focus

York's new M.B.A. program has been designed to create relevance and applied focus and to help students develop critical skills essential to any management situation. The graduate must have excellent communication, team-building, and problem-solving skills. The new M.B.A. program offers students the opportunities to develop these skills while continuing to promote the learning of fundamental theories and techniques required for management.

Students entering the first year are required to participate in the Intensive Skills Week, which leads directly into the core of the new curriculum: Managing in a Contemporary Context and Management Skills Development.

Full-time students are assigned to a cohort of 55 students, with whom they stay throughout the first year of the program. Much of the course work is done in smaller groups of 5 or 6. This practice helps develop the essentials of team-building and leadership skills. Working together also creates an atmosphere that fosters the esprit de coeur for lifelong relationships.

In the second year, students are required to complete the Strategy Field Study. This intensive five-month examination of an actual business site requires the students, working together in small groups, to do an analysis of a company and present this analysis with recommendations to the company leaders. This offers the students a significant opportunity to apply their new knowledge and skills to a real-life situation.

At the master's level, FAS offers three degrees: the M.B.A., the M.P.A. (Master of Public Administration), and the International M.B.A. (I.M.B.A.). The M.B.A. and the M.P.A. can be completed on either a full-time or a part-time basis, with entrance in September or January. The I.M.B.A. is a full-time, six-semester program limited to 60 students entering in September. FAS also offers a Ph.D. program and at the undergraduate level a four-year, full-time bachelor's degree in business administration.

Students and the M.B.A. Experience

FAS's multifaceted M.B.A. program attracts students from a diverse range of academic backgrounds and from all over the world. The average student is 28 years of age, with three years of full-time work experience. Women comprise 30 percent of the enrollment and international students, about 15 percent. As a large, urban university, York is known for its multicultural campus, which provides an experience that is rich and rewarding in its diversity.

❖ Global Focus

FAS infuses a global focus throughout its curriculum—in the design of course content and in opportunities for international experience. In addition to the I.M.B.A. program with its internship abroad, the Faculty has twenty-two different exchange agreements in seventeen countries. FAS continues to expand this network with top-quality

management institutions around the world. This exchange experience has aided many graduates in placements in major international corporations.

Special Features

FAS has always been a leader in new program development. It established the first graduate programs in arts and media administration, entrepreneurial studies, and now the voluntary sector management program. In 1992, FAS launched the first International M.B.A. (I.M.B.A.) degree in Canada. More recently, concentrations in business and the environment and real property development have been introduced.

Two new diploma programs have been established, one in arts and media management and one in real property development. In addition, the Faculty has joint programs such as the M.B.A./LL.B. and a joint York-Laval M.B.A. degree program.

In November 1994, FAS opened the doors of the Downtown Management Centre, which houses many of its executive development programs. These new headquarters are located in the historic Stock Exchange building, at Bay and King streets in the heart of Toronto's financial district.

The Faculty

The FAS has recruited its faculty internationally. There are currently 70 full-time faculty members. They have graduated from the world's top business schools, and research is as fundamental to their mandate as educating tomorrow's corporate leaders. This pursuit of academic excellence is balanced by a belief in the need to bring the boardroom into the classroom.

The Business School Network

FAS has recognized that strong ties with the business community in Canada and abroad are essential. To this end, the dean has an advisory board of distinguished CEOs and senior government representatives to advise him. In addition, the Faculty relies on an additional 150 senior executives from both the private and public sectors for advice and support in individual programs and segments of the program development.

Throughout the school year, prominent executives deliver talks and attend student-sponsored conferences. The York Consulting Group provides consulting services for small and medium-sized businesses and an action-learning opportunity for FAS students. In addition, the FAS Alumni Mentorship Program matches M.B.A. students with FAS alumni for rewarding mentoring relationships that help the students to find windows into their fields of interest.

The College and Environs

York University is the third-largest university in Canada, located in Toronto, Ontario—the country's industrial, commercial, and financial heartland.

York's main campus is situated on a 600-acre block of farmland at the northwest perimeter of the city. With a population of 40,000 students, York has all the necessary amenities and facilities typical of an urban university campus. York is accessible by bus or car. The majority of FAS students commute, although many of the full-time students live in apartment-like housing on campus.

Technology Environment

Computer Services employs state-of-the-art hardware and software. Full-time staff are available to assist students in the PC lab. The PCs are a mix of multimedia 486 IBM machines and standard 486 computers. Student-owned laptops may also be connected to the network at any time. The computers are networked and are linked with a DEC/VMS VAX 4000-300 and with the Internet. Modem accessibility is also possible with the VAX.

Placement

FAS offers placement services geared specifically to the needs of its students. These services are part of students' activities from their first term through graduation and beyond. The services include Career Day, on-campus recruiting, a Company and Career Information Library, an Immediate Opening Service, individual and group counselling, a graduate directory, a summer employment program, and instruction in résumé writing, interviewing, and job search techniques. An effort is made to include in the job search process not only the large multinational companies but also the small to medium-size firms.

Admission

An applicant must possess an undergraduate degree from a recognized university and submit scores for the GMAT (Graduate Management Admission Test). Normally, an applicant will be accepted only if he or she has achieved a B average or better in the last two full years (or equivalent) of academic work and achieved a set of acceptable scores on all three GMAT measurements. In addition, the applicant's work experience, demonstrated leadership qualities, communication skills, and apparent creativity and innovation are considered. In lieu of a degree, a nonbaccalaureate candidate must have at least eight years of high-quality management experience and must have demonstrated a strong upward progression in his or her career.

Finances

At the master's level, students pay fees each semester, according to activity level. The 1994–95 full-time tuition was approximately Can$1400 per semester for Canadian residents and approximately Can$5000 per semester for the non-Canadian resident. The 1994–95 part-time tuition for Canadian students was approximately Can$675 per semester and for the non-Canadian resident, approximately Can$2700 per semester.

Application Facts and Dates

Application deadlines for regular M.B.A. or M.P.A. programs are May 15 for the fall term and October 15 for the winter term. The application deadlines for the M.B.A./LL.B. program (for September only) are February 1 for the law application and April 1 for the M.B.A. application. The application deadline for the I.M.B.A. (for September only) is May 15. Applications must be submitted to:

Office of Student Affairs, Room 106
Administrative Studies Building
Faculty of Administrative Studies
York University
4700 Keele Street
North York, Ontario M3J 1P3
Canada
Telephone: 416-736-5060

FACULTY LIST

Dezsö J. Horváth, Ph.D., Professor of Policy and Dean.

Accounting
Daniel P. Armishaw, Ph.D. candidate, Assistant Professor.
Thomas H. Beechy, D.B.A., Professor.
Jerry D. Dermer, Ph.D., Professor.
John E. Dewhirst, Ph.D., Associate Professor.
John Friedlan, Ph.D., Assistant Professor.
L. S. (Al) Rosen, Ph.D., Professor.
S. Paul Roy, Ph.D., Associate Professor.
Brenda J. Zimmerman, Ph.D., CA, Associate Professor.

Policy
Ellen Auster, Ph.D., Associate Professor.
Wesley Cragg, D.Phil., Professor.
Robert Cuff, Ph.D., Professor.
James L. Darroch, Ph.D., Associate Professor.
Jerry D. Dermer, Ph.D., Professor.
James M. Gillies, Ph.D., Professor.
I. A. (Al) Litvak, Ph.D., Professor.
H. Ian Macdonald, B.Phil., Professor and President Emeritus.
Charles J. McMillan, Ph.D., Professor.
Stephanie Newell, Ph.D., Assistant Professor.
Theodoros Peridis, Ph.D., Associate Professor.
Rein Peterson, Ph.D., Professor.
Phillip Phan, Ph.D., Assistant Professor.

Nigel J. Roome, Ph.D., Professor and Director, Erivan K. Haub Program in Business and the Environment.
Stephen Weiss, Ph.D., Associate Professor.
Tom Wesson, Ph.D., Assistant Professor.
H. Thomas Wilson, Ph.D., Professor.

Organizational Behaviour/International Business
Steven T. Barnett, Ph.D., Assistant Professor.
Patricia Bradshaw, Ph.D., Associate Professor.
Ronald J. Burke, Ph.D., Professor.
David E. Dimick, Ph.D., Associate Professor.
Rekha Karambayya, Ph.D., Assistant Professor.
Robert G. Lucas, Ph.D., Associate Professor.
Graeme H. McKechnie, Ph.D., Associate Professor.
Gareth Morgan, Ph.D., Distinguished Research Professor.
Victor V. Murray, Ph.D., Professor.
Christine Oliver, Ph.D., Associate Professor.
Hazel Rosin, Ph.D., Associate Professor.

Economics
Atipol Bhanich Supapol, Ph.D., Associate Professor.
Irene Henriques, Ph.D., Assistant Professor.
Fred Lazar, Ph.D., Associate Professor.
Perry Sadorsky, Ph.D., Assistant Professor.
John N. Smithin, Ph.D., Associate Professor.
Bernard M. Wolf, Ph.D., Professor.

Management Science
John Buzacott, Ph.D., Professor.

Wade D. Cook, Ph.D., Professor.
Richard H. Irving, Ph.D., Associate Professor.
David Johnston, Ph.D., Associate Professor.
Ronald J. McClean, Ph.D., Assistant Professor.
James McKellar, M.C.P., Professor.
Daniele Thomassin, Ph.D., Assistant Professor.
Peter Tryfos, Ph.D., Professor.
J. Scott Yeomans, Ph.D., Assistant Professor.

Finance
Dawson E. Brewer, Ph.D., Associate Professor.
David J. Fowler, Ph.D., Associate Professor.
Kevin Hebner, Ph.D., Assistant Professor.
Elizabeth M. Maynes, Ph.D., Associate Professor.
Eliezer Prisman, D.Sc., Professor.
Gordon S. Roberts, Ph.D., Professor.
Christopher M. Robinson, Ph.D., CA, Associate Professor.
Savita Verma, Ph.D., Assistant Professor.

Marketing
Alexandra Campbell, Ph.D., Assistant Professor.
Ian D. Fenwick, Ph.D., Professor.
Eileen Fischer, Ph.D., Associate Professor.
Brenda Gainer, Ph.D., Assistant Professor.
Roger M. Heeler, Ph.D., Professor.
Deepika Nath, Ph.D., Assistant Professor.
Marshall D. Rice, Ph.D., Associate Professor.
Ajay K. Sirsi, Ph.D., Assistant Professor.
Donald N. Thompson, Ph.D., LL.M., Professor.

Indexes

There are three indexes in this section. The first, *Program Index,* is an index arranged alphabetically by program type. The second, *School Index,* lists alphabetically and gives page references for all colleges and universities in the guide. The third, *Areas of Concentration Index,* lists schools in alphabetical order under the specific areas of study available within the M.B.A. program.

School Index

In this index the page locations of the profiles are printed in regular type, announcements in italic type, and full-page descriptions in bold type.

Abbott Turner School of Business
See Columbus College
A. B. Freeman School of Business
See Tulane University
Abilene Christian University, College of Business Administration 489
Adelphi University, School of Management and Business 371, **656**
Alabama Agricultural and Mechanical University, Department of Business Administration 116
Alaska Pacific University, Management Department 127
Albany State College, School of Business 215
Albers School of Business and Economics
See Seattle University
Allentown College of St. Francis de Sales, Graduate Division 447
Amber University, Department of Business Administration 489
American Graduate School of Business 627, **658**
American Graduate School of International Management 129, **660**
American International College, School of Business Administration 298
American University, Kogod College of Business Administration 193, **662**
American University in Cairo 592
Amos Tuck School of Business
See Dartmouth College
Ancell School of Business
See Western Connecticut State University
Andreas School of Business
See Barry University
Andrews University, School of Business 315
Angelo State University, Department of Business Administration 490
Anna Maria College 299
Appalachian State University, John A. Walker College of Business 400
Aquinas College (MI) 316
Arizona State University, College of Business 130, **664**
Arizona State University West, School of Management 131
Arkansas State University, College of Business 135
Armstrong University, Graduate School of Business Administration 138
Arthur D. Little Management Education Institute 300, **666**
Ashland University, School of Business Administration and Economics 416
Ashridge Management College 632

Assumption College, Department of Business Studies 300
Aston University, Aston Business School 633
Auburn University, College of Business 116
Auburn University at Montgomery, School of Business 117
Augusta College, School of Business Administration 215
Aurora University, School of Business and Professional Studies 233
Australian Graduate School of Management
See University of New South Wales
Australian National University 560
Averett College 526
Avila College, Department of Business and Economics 337
Azusa Pacific University, School of Business and Management 139
Babcock Graduate School of Management
See Wake Forest University
Babson College, Babson Graduate School of Business 300, *300*, **668**
Baldwin-Wallace College, Division of Business Administration 417, **670**
Ball State University, College of Business 254
Bangkok University, Graduate School 630
Barney School of Business and Public Administration
See University of Hartford
Barry University, Andreas School of Business 197
Baruch College of the City University of New York, School of Business 372, **672**
Baylor University, Hankamer School of Business 491, **674**
Belk College of Business Administration
See University of North Carolina at Charlotte
Bellarmine College, W. Fielding Rubel School of Business 276
Belmont University, Jack C. Massey Graduate School of Business 480
Bentley College, Graduate School of Business 301, *301*, **676**
Berry College, School of Business 216
Bilkent University, Faculty of Business 632
Bloomsburg University of Pennsylvania, College of Business 448
Bocconi University 611
Boise State University, College of Business 231, **678**
Bond University, School of Business 560, *561*
Boston College, Wallace E. Carroll Graduate School of Management 302, **680**
Boston University, School of Management 303, *303*, **682**
Bowling Green State University, College of Business Administration 417
Bradley University, Foster College of Business Administration 233
Breech School of Business Administration
See Drury College

Brenau University, Department of Business 217
Brigham Young University, Marriott School of Management 522
Bristol Business School
See University of the West of England, Bristol
Bryant College, The Graduate School 472, *472*, **684**
Bucknell University, Department of Management 448
Business School Edinburgh
See Heriot-Watt University
Butler University, College of Business Administration 255
Byrd School of Business
See Shenandoah University
California Institute of Integral Studies, School for Transformative Learning 139, **686**
California Lutheran University, School of Business 140
California Polytechnic State University, San Luis Obispo, College of Business 141
California State Polytechnic University, Pomona, College of Business Administration 141
California State University, Bakersfield, School of Business and Public Administration 142
California State University, Chico, College of Business 143
California State University, Dominguez Hills, School of Management 143
California State University, Fresno, Sid Craig School of Business 144
California State University, Fullerton, School of Business Administration and Economics 145
California State University, Hayward, School of Business and Economics 146
California State University, Long Beach, College of Business Administration 146
California State University, Los Angeles, School of Business and Economics 147
California State University, Northridge, School of Business Administration and Economics 148
California State University, Sacramento, School of Business Administration 149
California State University, San Bernardino, School of Business and Public Administration 149
California State University, Stanislaus, School of Business Administration 150
California University of Pennsylvania 449
Cameron School of Business
See University of St. Thomas (TX)
Cameron School of Business Administration
See University of North Carolina at Wilmington
Cameron University, School of Business 434
Campbell University, Lundy-Fetterman School of Business 400
Canisius College, Richard J. Wehle School of Business 372

Programs Index

In this index the page locations of the profiles are printed in regular type, announcements in italic type, and full-page descriptions in bold type.

International MBA Programs

Combined MBA/MSW (Master of Social Work)

Areas of Concentration Index

In this index the page locations of the profiles are printed in regular type, announcements in italic type, and full-page descriptions in bold type.

Accounting/Finance

Adelphi University, School of Management and Business 371, **656**

Alabama Agricultural and Mechanical University, Department of Business Administration 116

Albany State College, School of Business 215

Allentown College of St. Francis de Sales, Graduate Division 447

Amber University, Department of Business Administration 489

American Graduate School of International Management 129, **660**

American International College, School of Business Administration 298

American University, Kogod College of Business Administration 193, **662**

Andrews University, School of Business 315

Angelo State University, Department of Business Administration 490

Appalachian State University, John A. Walker College of Business 400

Arizona State University, College of Business 130, **664**

Arizona State University West, School of Management 131

Armstrong University, Graduate School of Business Administration 138

Ashridge Management College 632

Assumption College, Department of Business Studies 300

Aston University, Aston Business School 633

Auburn University, College of Business 116

Auburn University at Montgomery, School of Business 117

Avila College, Department of Business and Economics 337

Babson College, Babson Graduate School of Business 300, *300,* **668**

Ball State University, College of Business 254

Bangkok University, Graduate School 630

Barry University, Andreas School of Business 197

Baruch College of the City University of New York, School of Business 372, **672**

Baylor University, Hankamer School of Business 491, **674**

Belmont University, Jack C. Massey Graduate School of Business 480

Bentley College, Graduate School of Business 301, *301,* **676**

Bilkent University, Faculty of Business 632

Bond University, School of Business 560, *561*

Boston College, Wallace E. Carroll Graduate School of Management 302, **680**

Boston University, School of Management 303, *303,* **682**

Bowling Green State University, College of Business Administration 417

Bradley University, Foster College of Business Administration 233

Brenau University, Department of Business 217

Brigham Young University, Marriott School of Management 522

Bryant College, The Graduate School 472, *472,* **684**

California Lutheran University, School of Business 140

California State Polytechnic University, Pomona, College of Business Administration 141

California State University, Chico, College of Business 143

California State University, Fresno, Sid Craig School of Business 144

California State University, Fullerton, School of Business Administration and Economics 145

California State University, Hayward, School of Business and Economics 146

California State University, Long Beach, College of Business Administration 146

California State University, Los Angeles, School of Business and Economics 147

California State University, Northridge, School of Business Administration and Economics 148

California State University, Sacramento, School of Business Administration 149

California State University, San Bernardino, School of Business and Public Administration 149

California State University, Stanislaus, School of Business Administration 150

Canisius College, Richard J. Wehle School of Business 372

Carleton University, School of Business 579

Carnegie Mellon University, Graduate School of Industrial Administration 449

Case Western Reserve University, Weatherhead School of Management 418, **688**

Central Missouri State University, College of Business and Economics 338

Chaminade University of Honolulu, School of Business 229

Chapman University, School of Business and Economics 151, **692**

Charleston Southern University, School of Business 476

The Chinese University of Hong Kong, Faculty of Business Administration 605

Christian Brothers University, School of Business 481

Chulalongkorn University, Sasin Graduate Institute of Business Administration 631, **694**

City University, Graduate School of Business and Management Professions 538, **696**

City University 634

Claremont Graduate School, The Peter F. Drucker Graduate Management Center 152, **698**

Clarion University of Pennsylvania, College of Business Administration 450

Clark Atlanta University, School of Business Administration 217

Clarkson University, School of Business 373, **700**

Clark University, Graduate School of Management 304, **702**

Clemson University, College of Commerce and Industry 477, **704**

Cleveland State University, James J. Nance College of Business Administration 419, **706**

College of Insurance 374, **708**

College of Notre Dame, Business Division 152

College of Saint Rose, School of Business 375

College of Santa Fe, Business Department 367

College of William and Mary, Graduate School of Business 527

Colorado State University, College of Business 178, **710**

Columbia University, Columbia Business School 375

Creighton University, College of Business Administration 350, *350,* **714**

Curtin University of Technology 561

Czechoslovak Management Center, Business School 591, *592*

Dalhousie University, School of Business Administration 578

Dallas Baptist University, College of Business 491, *492*

Dartmouth College, Amos Tuck School of Business 355, **716**

Deakin University, Faculty of Management 562

Delta State University, School of Business 332

De Montfort University, Leicester Business School 635

DePaul University, Kellstadt Graduate School of Business 235, *235,* **718**

Dowling College, School of Business 377, **720**

Drexel University, College of Business and Administration 451, **722**

Duke University, Fuqua School of Business 401

Duquesne University, Graduate School of Business 452, *452*

EAP-European School of Management 593

EAP-European School of Management, Business School 624

East Carolina University, School of Business 402

Eastern College 453, **724**

Eastern Michigan University, College of Business 317, **726**

East Texas State University, College of Business and Technology (Commerce) 492

Arts Administration

Economics

Entrepreneurial

Health Care

International Business

Management

Marketing

Organizational Behavior/Development

Public Administration

Public Policy

Quantitative Analysis

Strategic Analysis

Taxation

Transportation

Other Concentrations

Hard Career Choices Made Easier

PETERSON'S GUIDES TO GRADUATE AND PROFESSIONAL PROGRAMS 1996

An Overview 1996 (Book 1)

Provides the most complete look at the vast array of graduate and professional programs offered for 310 fields of study in over 1,500 accredited colleges and universities in the U.S. and Canada.
ISBN 1-56079-501-8, 1,186 pages, 8 1/2 x 11, $25.95 pb

The Humanities, Arts, and Social Sciences 1996 (Book 2)

Lists more than 10,500 programs from anthropology through gerontology, technical writing, and political science.
ISBN 1-56079-502-6, 1,511 pages, 8 1/2 x 11, $34.95 pb

The Biological and Agricultural Sciences 1996 (Book 3)

Includes over 4,500 programs in areas such as cancer biology, forestry, pharmacology, and zoology.
ISBN 1-56079-503-4, 2,608 pages, 8 1/2 x 11, $41.95 pb

The Physical Sciences and Mathematics 1996 (Book 4)

Over 2,300 options for graduate study in chemistry, geology, marine sciences, physics, and statistics.
ISBN 1-56079-504-2, 784 pages, 8 1/2 x 11, $32.95 pb

Engineering and Applied Sciences 1996 (Book 5)

From biomedical engineering and computer science to mechanical engineering and construction management, this volume lists over 3,500 programs.
ISBN 1-56079-505-0, 1,424 pages, 8 1/2 x 11, $35.95 pb

Business, Education, Health, and Law 1996 (Book 6)

Contains listings for the most popular professions, covering over 13,000 programs in allied health, business, education, law, medicine, nursing, pharmacy, and more!
ISBN 1-560679-506-9, 1,632 pages, 8 1/2 x 11, $24.95 pb

How to Write a Winning Personal Statement for Graduate and Professional School

Richard J. Stelzer

Grad school applicants turn to this unique guide for exclusive insider perspectives of admissions officers, over 30 examples of successful personal statements, lists of important questions to ask themselves and others, and tips on what not to include, too!

**ISBN 1-56079-287-6, 151 pages, 6 x 9, $10.95 pb
2nd edition**

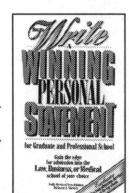

To Order Call
1-800-338-3282
Fax: 1-609-243-9150

New on the Internet!

**Peterson's Education Center
http://www.petersons.com**

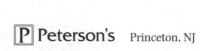

Peterson's   Princeton, NJ